Critical Values of *t*

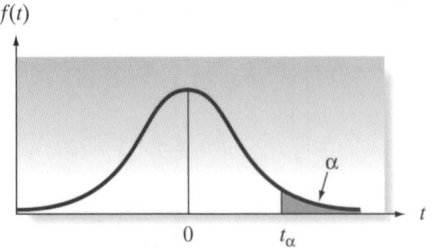

v	$t_{.100}$	$t_{.050}$	$t_{.025}$	$t_{.010}$	$t_{.005}$	$t_{.001}$	$t_{.0005}$
1	3.078	6.314	12.706	31.821	63.657	318.31	636.62
2	1.886	2.920	4.303	6.965	9.925	22.326	31.598
3	1.638	2.353	3.182	4.541	5.841	10.213	12.924
4	1.533	2.132	2.776	3.747	4.604	7.173	8.610
5	1.476	2.015	2.571	3.365	4.032	5.893	6.869
6	1.440	1.943	2.447	3.143	3.707	5.208	5.959
7	1.415	1.895	2.365	2.998	3.499	4.785	5.408
8	1.397	1.860	2.306	2.896	3.355	4.501	5.041
9	1.383	1.833	2.262	2.821	3.250	4.297	4.781
10	1.372	1.812	2.228	2.764	3.169	4.144	4.587
11	1.363	1.796	2.201	2.718	3.106	4.025	4.437
12	1.356	1.782	2.179	2.681	3.055	3.930	4.318
13	1.350	1.771	2.160	2.650	3.012	3.852	4.221
14	1.345	1.761	2.145	2.624	2.977	3.787	4.140
15	1.341	1.753	2.131	2.602	2.947	3.733	4.073
16	1.337	1.746	2.120	2.583	2.921	3.686	4.015
17	1.333	1.740	2.110	2.567	2.898	3.646	3.965
18	1.330	1.734	2.101	2.552	2.878	3.610	3.922
19	1.328	1.729	2.093	2.539	2.861	3.579	3.883
20	1.325	1.725	2.086	2.528	2.845	3.552	3.850
21	1.323	1.721	2.080	2.518	2.831	3.527	3.819
22	1.321	1.717	2.074	2.508	2.819	3.505	3.792
23	1.319	1.714	2.069	2.500	2.807	3.485	3.767
24	1.318	1.711	2.064	2.492	2.797	3.467	3.745
25	1.316	1.708	2.060	2.485	2.787	3.450	3.725
26	1.315	1.706	2.056	2.479	2.779	3.435	3.707
27	1.314	1.703	2.052	2.473	2.771	3.421	3.690
28	1.313	1.701	2.048	2.467	2.763	3.408	3.674
29	1.311	1.699	2.045	2.462	2.756	3.396	3.659
30	1.310	1.697	2.042	2.457	2.750	3.385	3.646
40	1.303	1.684	2.021	2.423	2.704	3.307	3.551
60	1.296	1.671	2.000	2.390	2.660	3.232	3.460
120	1.289	1.658	1.980	2.358	2.617	3.160	3.373
	1.282	1.645	1.960	2.326	2.576	3.090	3.291

Statistics

For Business and Economics

Statistics

For Business and Economics

Ninth Edition

James T. McClave

Info Tech, Inc.
University of Florida

P. George Benson

Terry College of Business
University of Georgia

Terry Sincich

University of South Florida

PEARSON

Prentice
Hall

Upper Saddle River, NJ 07458

Executive Acquisitions Editor: *Petra Recter*
Editor in Chief: *Sally Yagan*
Production Editor: *Jeanne Audino*
Assistant Managing Editor: *Bayani Mendoza DeLeon*
Senior Managing Editor: *Linda Mihatov Behrens*
Executive Managing Editor: *Kathleen Schiaparelli*
Vice President/Director of Production and Manufacturing: *David W. Riccardi*
Media Production Editor: *Zach Hubert*
Assistant Manufacturing Manager/Buyer: *Michael Bell*
Manufacturing Manager: *Trudy Pisciotti*
Marketing Manager: *Krista Bettino*
Marketing Assistant: *Rachel Beckman*
Editorial Assistant/Print Supplements Editor: *Joanne Wendelken*
Art Director: *Maureen Eide*
Interior Designer: *Joseph Sengotta*
Cover Designer/Assistant to the Art Director: *Suzanne Behnke*
Art Editor: *Thomas Benfatti*
Creative Director: *Carole Anson*
Director of Creative Services: *Paul Belfanti*
Photo Researcher: *Sheila Norman*
Image Coordinator: *Carolyn Gauntt*
Cover Photo: *Digital Vision*
Cover Image Specialist: *Karen Sanatar*
Art Studio: *Precision*
Compositor: *Progressive Information Technologies*

 © 2005 Pearson Education, Inc.
Pearson Prentice Hall
Pearson Education, Inc.
Upper Saddle River, New Jersey 07458

ISBN 0-13-046643-3 (instructor's edition)
ISBN 0-13-046641-7 (student edition)

Pearson Education LTD., *London*
Pearson Education Australia PTY, Limited, *Sydney*
Pearson Education Singapore, Pte. Ltd
Pearson Education North Asia Ltd, *Hong Kong*
Pearson Education Canada, Ltd., *Toronto*
Pearson Educacíon de Mexico, S.A. de C.V.
Pearson Education—Japan, *Tokyo*
Pearson Education Malaysia, Pte. Ltd

Contents

Preface xiii

CHAPTER 11   Categorical Data Analysis   642

CHAPTER 12   Simple Linear Regression   690

CHAPTER 13   Multiple Regression and Model Building   766

CHAPTER 14   Methods for Quality Improvement   912

Preface

This Ninth edition of *Statistics for Business and Economics* is an introductory business text emphasizing inference, with extensive coverage of data collection and analysis as needed to evaluate the reported results of statistical studies and make good decisions. As in earlier editions, the text stresses the development of statistical thinking and the assessment of credibility and the value of the inferences made from data, both by those who consume and those who produce them. It assumes a mathematical background of basic algebra.

NEW IN THE NINTH EDITION

General

Over 1400 Exercises, with Revisions and Updates to 50%   Revised to provide a greater variety in level of difficulty. In addition to "Learning the Mechanics" exercises, "Applied Exercises" are categorized into "Basic", "Intermediate", and "Advanced" at the end of each section. Many of these exercises foster and promote critical thinking skills.

Over 150 Examples   All examples now have three components: (1) "problem"; (2) "solution"; (3) "look back". This step-by-step process provides students with a defined structure by which to approach problems and enhances their problem-solving skills. The "look back" feature fosters their critical thinking skills as they are asked to interpret the solution.

Now Work   A "Now Work" exercise follows each example. "Now Work" suggests an end-of- section exercise that is similar in style and concept to the preceding example. This gives students the opportunity to test and confirm their understanding.

9 New Statistics in Action Cases   Each chapter now begins with a description of an actual, engaging, business case ("Statistics in Action") and the accompanying data. We revisit the case throughout the chapter to demonstrate how to analyze the data and interpret the results ("Statistics in Action Revisited"). Our goal is to show students the importance of applying sound statistical techniques to answer critical questions asked in business.

Statistical Software Tutorials   At the end of each chapter, there are "technology tutorials" with point-and-click instructions (with screen shots) for EXCEL, MINITAB, and SPSS. These tutorials are easily located and provide students with useful information on how to best use and maximize their statistical software.

Statistical Software Printouts   These appear at appropriate moments throughout the text and exercises and include EXCEL (with the PHStat add-in), as well as SPSS and MINITAB printouts. Students are exposed to the computer printouts they will encounter in the high-tech business world.

Profiles of Statisticians in History   Side boxes (with photo) of a famous statistician and brief description of his or her achievements. With these profiles, students will develop an appreciation of the statistician's efforts and the discipline of statistics as a whole.

Chapter Summary Notes   Now provided with end-of-chapter material. These notes help the students summarize and reinforce the important points from the chapter, and are useful as study tools.

Student Data CD   The text is accompanied by a CD that contains files for all of the data sets marked with a CD icon in the text. These include data sets for text examples, exercises, "Statistics in Action" cases, and "Real-World" cases. All data files are saved in four different formats: EXCEL, MINITAB, SPSS, and ASCII (for easy importing into other statistical software packages).

Chapter Specific

Chapters Reordered   Several chapters are reordered as a result of significant user feedback. This change reflects the way material is presented in most business statistics courses. Analysis of Variance (Chapter 10) and Categorical Data Analysis (Chapter 11) now follow the chapter on comparing two populations (Chapter 9). However, the chapters are written so that the instructor can cover the material in the order he or she desires.

Chapter 3 (Probability)   An optional section on Bayes's rule has been added (Section 3.8).

Chapter 4 (Discrete Random Variables)   An optional section on the hypergeometric random variable has been added (Section 4.6).

Chapter 10 (Analysis of Variance)   An optional section on randomized block designs has been added (Section 10.4).

Chapter 11 (Categorical Data Analysis)   The introduction to the chapter has been rewritten, with emphasis on whether one or two qualitative variables are analyzed.

Chapter 13 (Multiple Regression and Model Building)   Now includes a more detailed discussion of multicollinearity, with a real-data example and guidelines on detecting and dealing with the problem (Section 13.14).

Chapter 16 (Nonparametric Statistics)   An optional section on the Friedman test for a randomized block design has been added (Section 16.6).

TRADITIONAL STRENGTHS

We have maintained the features of *Statistics for Business and Economics* that we believe make it unique among business statistics texts. These features, which assist the student in achieving an overview of statistics and an understanding of its relevance in the business world and in everyday life, are as follows:

Use of Examples as a Teaching Device   Almost all new ideas are introduced and illustrated by real data-based applications and examples. We believe that students better understand definitions, generalizations, and theoretical concepts after seeing an application.

Real Data Exercises   The text includes more than 1,400 exercises based on applications in a variety of areas of business research. All the applied exercises employ the use of current real data extracted from a wide variety of publications (e.g., newspapers, magazines, journals, and the Internet). Some students have difficulty learning the mechanics of statistical techniques when all problems are couched in terms of realistic applications. For this reason, all exercise section divided into four parts:

Learning the Mechanics. Designed as straightforward applications of new concepts, these exercises allow students to test their ability to comprehend a mathematical concept or a definition.

Applying the Concepts—Basic. Based on applications taken from a wide variety of journals, newspapers, and other sources, these short exercises help students developing the skills necessary to diagnose and analyze real-world problems.

Applying the Concepts—Intermediate. Based on more detailed real-world applications, these exercises require students to apply critical thinking and their knowledge of the technique presented in the section.

Applying the Concepts—Advanced. These more challenging real-data exercises require students to utilize their critical thinking skills.

Real-World Business Cases   Six extensive business problem-solving cases, with real data and assignments for the student. Each case serves as a good capstone and review of the material that has preceded it. Typically, these cases follow a group of two or three chapters and require the student to apply the methods presented in these chapters.

Exploring Data with Statistical Computer Software and the Graphing Calculator   Each statistical analysis method presented is demonstrated using output from three leading Windows-based statistical software packages: EXCEL, MINITAB, and SPSS. In addition, output and keystroke instructions for the TI-83 Graphing Calculator are covered in optional boxes which are easy to locate throughout the text.

End-of-Chapter Materials: Include

- *Quick Review* A list of key terms and formulas, with reference to the page number where they first appear, as well as a brief summary of the concepts covered.
- *Language Lab* Following the Quick Review is a pronunciation guide to Greek letters and other special terms. Usage notes are also provided. This lab gives students a quick reference to the myriad of symbols encountered in statistics.

FLEXIBILITY IN COVERAGE

The text is written to allow the instructor flexibility in coverage of topics through sections marked "optional" in relevant chapters. Suggestions for covering two topics, probability and regression, are as follows.

Probability and Counting Rules   One of the most troublesome aspects of an introductory business statistics course is the study of probability. Probability poses a challenge for instructors because they must decide on the level of presentation, and students find it a difficult subject to comprehend. We believe that one cause for these problems is the mixture of probability and counting rules that occurs in most introductory texts. Consequently, we have included the counting rules (with examples) in an appendix (Appendix A) rather than in Chapter 3 (Probability). Thus, the instructor can control the level of coverage of probability.

Multiple Regression and Model Building   This topic represents one of the most useful statistical tools for the solution of applied problems. Although an entire text could be devoted to regression modeling, we feel that we have presented coverage that is understandable, usable, and much more comprehensive that the presentations in other introductory statistics texts. We devote two full chapters to discussing the major types of inferences that can be derived from a regression analysis, showing how these results appear in the output from statistical software, and, most important, selecting multiple regression models to be used in an analysis. Thus, the instructor has the choice of a one-chapter coverage of simple linear regression (Chapter 12), a two-chapter treatment of simple and multiple regression (excluding the optional sections in Chapter 13 on model building), or complete coverage of regression analysis, including model building and regression diagnostics. This extensive coverage of such useful statistical tools will provide added evidence to the student of the relevance of statistics to real-world business problems.

Footnotes   Although the text is designed for students with a non-calculus background, footnotes explain the role of calculus in various derivations. Footnotes are also used to inform the student about some of the theory underlying certain methods of analysis. These footnotes allow additional flexibility in the mathematical and theoretical level at which the material is presented.

ACKNOWLEDGMENTS

This book reflects the efforts of a great many people over a number of years. First, we would like to thank the following professors, whose reviews and comments on this and prior editions have contributed to the ninth edition:

Reviewers Involved with the Ninth Edition of Statistics for Business and Economics

Paul W. Guy, *California State University, Chico*
Barry P. Cuffe, *Wingate University*
Tim E. McDaniel, *Buena Vista University*
Farhad Saboori, *Albright College*
Grace Esimai, *University of Texas at Arlington*
Jeffrey W. Steagall, *University of North Florida*
Phil Cross, *Georgetown University*

Reviewers of Previous Editions

Atul Agarwal, GMI Engineering and Management Institute; Mohamed Albohali, Indiana University of Pennsylvania; Gordon J. Alexander, University of Minnesota; Richard W. Andrews, University of Michigan; Larry M. Austin, Texas Tech University; Golam Azam, North Carolina Agricultural & Technical University;

Donald W. Bartlett, University of Minnesota; Clarence Bayne, Concordia University; Carl Bedell, Philadelphia College of Textiles and Science; David M. Bergman, University of Minnesota; William H. Beyer, University of Akron; Atul Bhatia, University of Minnesota; Jim Branscome, University of Texas at Arlington; Francis J. Brewerton, Middle Tennessee State University; Daniel G. Brick, University of St. Thomas; Robert W. Brobst, University of Texas at Arlington; Michael Broida, Miami University of Ohio; Glenn J. Browne, University of Maryland, Baltimore; Edward Carlstein, University of North Carolina at Chapel Hill; John M. Charnes, University of Miami; Chih-Hsu Cheng, Ohio State University; Mary C. Christman, University of Maryland; Larry Claypool, Oklahoma State University; Edward R. Clayton, Virginia Polytechnic Institute and State University; Ronald L. Coccari, Cleveland State University; Ken Constantine, University of New Hampshire, Lewis Coopersmith, Rider University; Robert Curley, University of Central Oklahoma; Joyce Curley-Daly, California Polytechnic State University; James Czachor, Fordham-Lincoln Center, AT&T; Jim Daly, California Polytechnic State University; Jim Davis, Golden Gate University; Dileep Dhavale, University of Northern Iowa, Bernard Dickman, Hofstra University; William Duckworth II, Iowa State University; Mark Eakin, University of Texas at Arlington; Rick L. Edgeman, Colorado State University; Carol Eger, Stanford University; Robert Elrod, Georgia State University; Douglas A. Elvers, University of North Carolina at Chapel Hill; Iris Fetta, Clemson University; Susan Flach, General Mills, Inc.; Alan E. Gelfand, University of Connecticut; Joseph Glaz, University of Connecticut; Edit Gombay, University of Alberta; Jose Luis Guerrero-Cusumano, Georgetown University; Paul W. Guy, California State University, Chico; Judd Hammack, California State University-Los Angeles; Michael E. Hanna, University of Texas at Arlington; Don Holbert, East Carolina University; James Holstein, University of Missouri, Columbia; Warren M. Holt, Southeastern Massachusetts University; Steve Hora, University of Hawaii, Hilo; Ann Hussein, Ph.D., Philadelphia University; Petros Ioannatos, GMI Engineering & Management Institute; Marius Janson, University of Missouri, St. Louis; Ross H. Johnson, Madison College; P. Kasliwal, California State University-Los Angeles; Timothy J. Killeen, University of Connecticut, Tim Krehbiel, Miami University of Ohio; David D. Krueger, St. Cloud State University; Richard W. Kulp, Wright-Patterson AFB, Air Force Institute of Technology; Mabel T. Kung, California State University-Fullerton; Martin Labbe, State University of New York College at New Paltz; James Lackritz, California State University at San Diego; Lei Lei, Rutgers University; Leigh Lawton, University of St. Thomas; Peter Lenk, University of Michigan; Benjamin Lev, University of Michigan-Dearborn; Philip Levine, William Patterson College; Eddie M. Lewis, University of Southern Mississippi; Fred Leysieffer, Florida State University; Xuan Li, Rutgers University; Pi-Erh Lin, Florida State University; Robert Ling, Clemson University; Benny Lo; Karen Lundquist, University of Minnesota; G. E. Martin, Clarkson University; Brenda Masters, Oklahoma State University; William Q. Meeker, Iowa State University; Ruth K. Meyer, St. Cloud State University; Edward Minieka, University of Illinois at Chicago; Rebecca Moore, Oklahoma State University; June Morita, University of Washington; Behnam Nakhai, Millersville University; Paul I. Nelson, Kansas State University; Paula M. Oas, General Office Products; Dilek Onkal, Bilkent University, Turkey; Vijay Pisharody, University of Minnesota; Rose Prave, University of Scranton; P. V. Rao, University of Florida; Lawrence D. Ries, University of Missouri-Columbia; Don Robinson, Illinois State University; Beth Rose, University of Southern California; Jan Saraph, St. Cloud State University; Lawrence A. Sherr, University of Kansas; Craig W. Slinkman, University of Texas at Arlington; Robert K. Smidt, California Polytechnic State University; Toni M.

Somers, Wayne State University; Donald N. Steinnes, University of Minnesota at Duluth; Virgil F. Stone, Texas A & M University; Katheryn Szabet, La Salle University; Alireza Tahai, Mississippi State University; Kim Tamura, University of Washington; Zina Taran, Rutgers University; Chipei Tseng, Northern Illinois University; Pankaj Vaish, Arthur Andersen & Company; Robert W. Van Cleave, University of Minnesota; Charles F. Warnock, Colorado State University; Michael P. Wegmann, Keller Graduate School of Management; William J. Weida, United States Air Force Academy; T.J. Wharton, Oakland University; Kathleen M. Whitcomb, University of South Carolina; Edna White, Florida Atlantic University; Steve Wickstrom, University of Minnesota; James Willis, Louisiana State University; Douglas A. Wolfe, Ohio State University; Gary Yoshimoto, St. Cloud State University; Doug Zahn, Florida State University; Fike Zahroom, Moorhead State University; Christopher J. Zappe, Bucknell University.

Other Contributors

Special thanks are due to our ancillary authors, Nancy Shafer Boudreau and Mark Dummeldinger, and to typist Kelly Barber, who have worked with us for many years. Sarah Streett has done an excellent job of accuracy checking the ninth edition and has helped us to ensure a highly accurate, clean text. Finally, the Prentice Hall staff of Petra Recter, Joanne Wendelken, Krista Bettino, Jeanne Audino, Jacquelyn Riotto, Sally Yagan, Bayani DeLeon, Thomas Benfatti, Annett Uebel, Michael Bell, and Linda Behrens helped greatly with all phases of the text development, production, and marketing.

SUPPLEMENTS FOR THE INSTRUCTOR—AVAILABLE VIA YOUR PRENTICE HALL SALES REPRESENTATIVE

Annotated Instructor's Edition (AIE) (ISBN: 0-13-046643-3)

Marginal notes placed next to discussions of essential teaching concepts include

- *Teaching Tips*—suggest alternative presentations or point out common student errors
- *Exercises*—reference specific section and chapter exercises that reinforce the concept
- *Short Answers*—section and chapter exercise answers are provided next to the selection exercises

Instructor's Solutions Manual, by Nancy S. Boudreau (ISBN: 0-13-046644-1)

Solutions to all of the even-numbered exercises are given in this manual. Careful attention has been paid to ensure that all methods of solution and notation are consistent with those used in the core text. Solutions to the odd-numbered exercises are found in the *Students Solutions Manual*.

Test Bank, by Mark Dummeldinger (ISBN: 0-13-046646-8)

The *Test Bank* includes more than 1,000 problems that correlate to problems presented in the text.

Test Gen (ISBN: 0-13-046647-6)

Test Gen is a computerized test bank that allows you to view and edit test bank questions, transfer them to exams, and print in a variety of formats. The program offers many options for organizing and displaying test banks and tests, and a built-in random number and test generator allows instructors to create multiple versions of exams. Quiz Master feature allows for online delivery.

Course Management Systems (Course Compass, Blackboard, and WebCT)

Includes course compatible content, including the *Student Solutions Manual*, technology help, quizzes, and lecture content. These sites also offer Web-based statistical applets (STALETSTM), which encourage students to develop their conceptual understanding of statistics by providing accessible computational and graphing capabilities matched with specific questions to reinforce understanding of key concepts from the text.

SUPPLEMENTS AVAILABLE FOR THE STUDENT

Valuepacks, which provide study resources for the student and provide value because they are offered bundled with the main textbook for free with the purchase of a new textbook, are available. These valuepacks are also available for standalone purchase through the bookstore.

The valuepacks available are:

- *The Student Solutions Manual,* which contains fully worked out solutions to the odd-numbered text exercises and **Tutor Center**, which provides text-specific tutoring for students by trained mathematicians. Students can access tutors by toll free phone, fax and e-mail. For more information, see **www.prenhall.com/tutorcenter**.

- *The Student Solutions Manual, Tutor Center, and TI-83 Technology Manual.* The technology manual contains tutorial instructions and worked out solutions for the TI-83 Calculator.

- *The Student Solutions Manual, Tutor Center, and EXCEL Technology Manual.* The technology manual contains tutorial instructions and worked out solutions for EXCEL.

- *The Student Solutions Manual, Tutor Center, and MINITAB Technology Manual.* The technology manual contains tutorial instructions and worked out solutions for MINITAB.

    There is also a companion website available: www.prenhall.com/mcclave. This is an online, interactive study guide, matched to each chapter of the text, with technology help, quizzes, objectives, Internet destinations, PowerPoint downloads, and the text's data files available for download.

Student Study Pack:

This valuable study package contains the following student resources:

- *Student Solutions Manual:* Contains fully worked out solutions to the odd-numbered text exercises.

- *Technology Manual:* Contains tutorial instruction and worked out examples for the TI-83 calculator, EXCEL, and MINITAB.
- *Tutor Center:* Provides text-specific tutoring for students by trained mathematicians. Students can access tutors by toll free phone, fax, and e-mail. For more information see **www.prenhall.com/tutorcenter**.
- *Companion Web Site—***www.prenhall.com/mcclave**. This is an online, interactive study guide, matched to each chapter of the text, with technology help, quizzes, objectives, Internet destinations, PowerPoint downloads, and the text's data files available for download.

Designed for Your Success...

Over 1000 Interesting and Diverse Applications

- Represent a wide and diverse array of relevant business and decision making applications.

- Feature unique and sourced data that illustrates the role that business statistics play in decision making.

- Using real-world data to emphasize that statistics is important to understanding the world around us.

- Emphasis is placed on the interpretation of real problems and adapting them to standard methods of analysis.

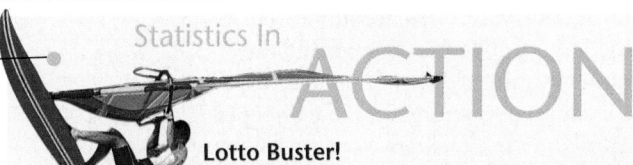

Statistics In ACTION

Lotto Buster!

"Welcome to the Wonderful World of Lottery Bus$ters." So began the premier issue of *Lottery Buster*, a monthly publication for players of the state lottery games. *Lottery Buster* provides interesting facts and figures on the 37 state lotteries currently operating in the United States and, more important, tips on how to increase a player's odds of winning the lottery.

New Hampshire, in 1963, was the first state in modern times to authorize a state lottery as an alternative to increasing taxes. (Prior to this time, beginning in 1895, lotteries were banned in America because of corruption.) Since then, lotteries have become immensely popular for two reasons. First, they lure you with the opportunity to win millions of dollars with a $1 investment, and second, when you lose, at least you believe your money is doing to a good cause. Many state lotteries, like Florida, designate a high percentage of lottery revenues to fund state education.

The popularity of the state lottery has brought with it an avalanche of "experts" and "mathematical wizards" (such as the editors of *Lottery Buster*) who provide advice for a fee, of course! Many ~~f~~ winning through computer ~~e~~ names such as lotto Wizard, ~~...~~ luck. ~~...~~wledgeable lottery players ~~...~~ule" or "first rule" in winning ~~...~~ate lotteries generally offer ~~...~~scratch-off tickets or online)

game, Daily Numbers (Pick-3 or Pick-4), and weekly Pick-6 lotto' game.

One version of the Instant game involves scratching off the thin opaque covering on a ticket with the edge of a coin to determine whether you have won or lost. The cost of a ticket ranges from 50¢ to $5, and the amount won ranges from $1 to $100,000 in most states, and to as much as $1 million in others. *Lottery Buster* advises against playing the Instant game because it is "a pure chance play, and you can win only by dumb luck. No skill can be applied to this game."

The Daily Numbers game permits you to choose either a three-digit (Pick-3) or four-digit (Pick-4) number at a cost of $1 per ticket. Each night, the winning number is drawn. If your number matches the winning number, you win a large sum of money, usually $100,000. You do have some control over the Daily Numbers game (since you pick the numbers that you play) and, consequently, there are strategies available to increase your chances of winning. However, the Daily Numbers game, like the Instant game, is not available for out-of-state play.

To play Pick-6 Lotto, you select six numbers of your choice from a field of numbers ranging from 1 to N, where N depends on which state's game you are playing. For example, Florida's current Lotto game involves picking six numbers ranging from 1 to 53. (See Figure SIA3.1 below.) The cost of a ticket is $1 and the payoff, if your six numbers match the winning numbers drawn, is $7 million or more, depending on the number of tickets purchased. (To date, Florida has had the largest state weekly payoff of over $200 million.) In

Page 145

EXAMPLE 3.5 — APPLYING THE FIVE STEPS

Problem Diversity training of employees is the latest trend in U.S. business. *USA Today* (Aug. 15, 1995) reported on the primary reasons businesses give for making diversity training part of their strategic planning process. The reasons are summarized in Table 3.2. Assume that one business is selected at random from all U.S. businesses that use diversity training and the primary reason is determined.

a. Define the experiment that generated the data in Table 3.2, and list the sample points.

TABLE 3.2 Primary Reasons for Diversity Training

Reason	Percentage
Comply with personnel policies (CPP)	7
Increase productivity (IP)	47
Stay competitive (SC)	38
Social responsibility (SR)	4
Other (O)	4
Total	100%

b. Assign probabilities to the sample points.

c. What is the probability that the primary reason for diversity training is business related; that is, related to competition or productivity?

d. What is the probability that social responsibility is not a primary reason for diversity training?

Solution

a. The experiment is the act of determining the primary reason for diversity training of employees at a U.S. business. The sample points, the simplest outcomes of the experiment, are the five response categories listed in Table 3.2. These sample points are shown in the Venn diagram in Figure 3.5.

b. If, as in Example 3.1, we were to assign equal probabilities in this case, each of the response categories would have a probability of one-fifth ($1/5$), or .20. But, by examining Table 3.2 you can see that equal probabilities are not reasonable here because the response percentages were not even approximately the same in the five classifications. It is more reasonable to assign a probability equal to the response percentage in each class, as shown in Table 3.3.*

c. Let the symbol B represent the event that the primary reason for diversity training is business related. B is not a sample point because it consists of more than one of the response classifications (the sample points). In fact, as shown in Figure 3.5, B consists of two sample points, IP and SC. The probability of B is defined to be the sum of the probabilities of the sample points in B.

$$P(B) = P(\text{IP}) + P(\text{SC}) = .47 + .38 = .85$$

d. Let NSR represent the event that social responsibility is not a primary reason for diversity training. Then NSR consists of all sample points except SR, and the probability is the sum of the corresponding sample point probabilities:

$$P(NSR) = P(\text{CPP}) + P(\text{IP}) + P(\text{SC}) + P(\text{O})$$
$$= .07 + .47 + .38 + .04 = .96$$

Look Back The key to solving this problem is to follow the steps outlined in the box. We defined the experiment (Step 1) and listed the sample points (Step 2) in part a. The assignment of probabilities to the sample points (Step 3) was done in part b. For each probability in parts c and d, we identified the collection of points in the event (Step 4) and summed their probabilities (Step 5).

Now Work *Exercise 3.13*

Figure 3.5
Venn diagram for diversity training survey

- CPP - IP
- SR   - SC
- O B

S

TABLE 3.3 Sample Point Probabilities for Diversity Training Survey

Sample Point	Probability
CPP	.07
IP	.47
SC	.38
SR	.04
O	.04

More than 150 Clear and Interesting Examples with Solutions

- A step-by-step approach to reaching the solution with thorough explanations built into each step. The problem is identified, the solution is presented in a step-by-step manner, then the "Insight" is given which offers a look back at what has just been learned.

- Solutions are carefully explained to better prepare you for the end-of-section exercises.

- "Now Work" appears after each example and directs students to an exercise at the end of section that allows them to practice the skill and concept presented in the example.

Page 153

Thorough and Extensive Exercise Sets—Over 1400 Exercises Total!

- End-of-Section Exercises are numerous and divided into two parts: **Learning the Mechanics** (straightforward applications of new concepts) and **Applying the Concepts**. The *Applying the Concepts* word problems are divided into three levels of difficulty (Basic, Intermediate, Advanced), emphasizing critical thinking skills and requiring you to apply statistical techniques in solving real-world problems.

- Many exercises contain data and information taken from newspaper articles, magazines and journals. Inclusion of this data serves to illustrate the relevancy of this material. Each data set is saved in a file on a CD for the student to analyze using statistical software.

- Includes, where appropriate, computer output screens to give you practice in interpretation of data.

Exercises 2.16–2.32

Learning the Mechanics

2.16 Graph the relative frequency histogram for the 500 measurements summarized in the accompanying relative frequency table.

Measurement Class	Relative Frequency
.5–2.5	.10
2.5–4.5	.15
4.5–6.5	.25
6.5–8.5	.20
8.5–10.5	.05
10.5–12.5	.10
12.5–14.5	.10
14.5–16.5	.05

2.17 Refer to Exercise 2.16. Calculate the number of the 500 measurements falling into each of the measurement classes. Then graph a frequency histogram for these data.

2.18 Consider the stem-and-leaf display shown here.

Stem	Leaf
5	1
4	457
3	00036
2	1134599
1	2248
0	012

   a. How many observations were in the original data set?
   b. In the bottom row of the stem-and-leaf display, identify the stem, the leaves, and the numbers in the orignal data set represented by this stem and its leaves.
   c. Re-create all the numbers in the data set and construct a dot plot.

2.19 MINITAB was used to generate the following histogram:

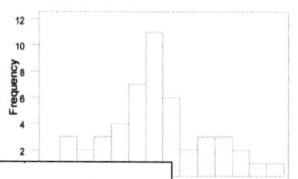

   a. Is this a frequency histogram or a relative frequency histogram? Explain.
   b. How many measurement classes were used in the construction of this histogram?
   c. How many measurements are in the data set described by this histogram?

Applying the Concepts—Basic

2.20 The next graph summarizes the scores obtained by 100 students on a questionnaire designed to measure managerial ability. (Scores are integer values that range from 0 to 20. A high score indicates a high level of ability.)
   a. Which measurement class contains the highest proportion of test scores?
   b. What proportion of the scores lie between 3.5 and 5.5?
   c. What proportion of the scores are higher than 11.5?
   d. How many students scored less than 5.5?

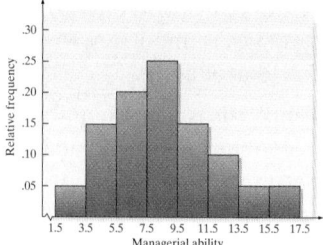

2.21 The United States Golf Association (USGA) Handicap System is designed to allow golfers of differing abilities to enjoy fair competition. The handicap index is a measure of a player's potential scoring ability on an 18-hole golf course of standard difficulty. For example, on a par-72 course, a golfer with a handicap of 7 will typically have a score of 79 (seven strokes over par). Over 4.5 million golfers have an official USGA Handicap index. The handicap indexes for both male and female golfers were obtained from the USGA and are summarized in the following two histograms.
   a. What percentage of male USGA golfers have a handicap greater than 20?
   b. What percentage of female USGA golfers have a handicap greater than 20?

Page 64

Statistics in ACTION.

Super Weapons Development—Optimizing the Hit Ratio

The U.S. Army is working with a major defense contractor to develop a "super" weapon. The weapon is designed to fire a large number of sharp tungsten bullets—called flechettes—with a single shot that will destroy a large number of enemy soldiers. Flechettes are about the size of an average nail, with small fins at one end to stabilize them in flight. Since World War I, when France dropped them in large quantities from aircraft on masses of ground troops, munitions experts have experimented with using flechettes in a variety of guns. The problem with using flechettes as ammunition is accuracy—current weapons that fire large quantities of flechettes have unsatisfactory hit ratios when fired at long distances.

The defense contractor (not named here for confidentiality and security reasons) has developed a prototype gun that fires 1,100 flechettes with a single round. In range tests, three 2-feet-wide targets were set up a distance of 500 meters (approximately 1,500 feet) from the weapon. Using a number line as a reference, the centers of the three targets were at 0, 5, and 10 feet, respectively, as shown in Figure SIA5.1. The prototype gun was aimed at the middle target (center at 5 feet) and fired once. The point where each of the 1,100 flechettes landed at the 500-meter distance was measured using a horizontal and vertical grid. For the purposes of this application, only the horizontal measurements are considered. These 1,100 measurements are saved in the MOAGUN file. (The data are simulated for confidentiality reasons.) For example, a flechette with a value of $x = 5.5$ hit the middle target, but a flechette with a value of $x = 2.0$ did not hit any of the three targets (See Figure SIA5.1).

The defense contractor is interested in the likelihood of any one of the targets being hit by a flechette and, in particular, wants to set the gun specifications to maximize the number of target hits. The weapon is designed to have a mean horizontal value equal to the aim point (e.g., $\mu = 5$ feet when aimed at the center target). By changing specifications, the contractor can vary the standard deviation, σ. The MOAGUN file contains flechette measurements for three different range tests—one with a standard deviation of $\sigma = 1$ foot, one with $\sigma = 2$ feet, and one with $\sigma = 4$ feet.

In this chapter, two Statistics in Action Revisited examples demonstrate how we can use one of the probability models discussed in this chapter—the normal probability distribution—to aid the defense contractor in developing its "super" weapon.

Statistics in the Action Revisited

- Using the Normal Model to Maximize the Probability of a Hit with the Super Weapon (p. 283)
- Assessing whether the Normal Distribution is Appropriate for Modeling the Super Weapon Hit Data (p. 290)

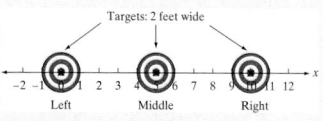

Figure SIA5.1
Target placement on gun range

Statistics in Action

- Each chapter opens with a **Statistics in Action** case study that highlights controversial, contemporary issues that involve statistics. Over 70% of these have been updated for this new edition.

- The themes and issues are revisited and built upon throughout the chapter, by way of easily identifiable boxes labeled **Statistics in Action Revisited**.

Page 261

Real-World Cases

- Six Real-World Case, appearing at the end of every 2-3 chapters, are included. They serve as a good capstone and review of the material that has preceeded it.

- They require the student to apply the methods presented in these chapters.

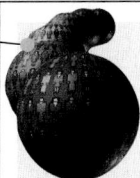

Real-World Case

The Kentucky Milk Case—Part 1

(A Case Covering Chapters 1 and 2)

Many products and services are purchased by governments, cities, states, and businesses on the basis of scaled bids, and contracts are awarded to the lowest bidders. This process works extremely well in competitive markets, but it has the potential to increase the cost of purchasing if the markets are noncompetitive or if collusive practices are present. An investigation that began with a statistical analysis of bids in the Florida school milk market in 1986 led to the recovery of more than $33,000,000 from dairies who had conspired to rig the bids there in the 1980s. The investigation spread quickly to other states, and to date settlements and fines from dairies exceed $100,000,000 for school milk bidrigging in twenty other states. This case concerns a school milk bidrigging investigation in Kentucky.

Each year, the Commonwealth of Kentucky invites bids from dairies to supply half-pint containers of fluid milk products for its school districts. The products include whole white milk, low-fat white milk, and low-fat chocolate milk. In 13 school districts in northern Kentucky, the suppliers (dairies) were accused of "price-fixing," that is, conspiring to allocate the districts, so that the "winner" was predetermined. Since these districts are located in Boone, Campbell, and Kenton counties, the geographic market they represent is designated as the "tri-county"

market. Between 1983 and 1991, two dairies—Meyer Dairy and Trauth Dairy—were the only bidders on the milk contracts in the school districts in the tri-county market. Consequently, these two companies were awarded all the milk contracts in the market. (In contrast, a large number of different dairies won the milk contracts for the school districts in the remainder of the northern Kentucky market—called the "surrounding" market.) The Commonwealth of Kentucky alleged that Meyer and Trauth conspired to allocate the districts in the tri-county market. To date, one of the dairies (Meyer) has admitted guilt, while the other (Trauth) steadfastly maintains its innocence.

The Commonwealth of Kentucky maintains a database on all bids received from the dairies competing for the milk contracts. Some of these data have been made available to you to analyze to determine whether there is empirical evidence of bid collusion in the tri-county market. The data, saved in the **MILK** file, are described in detail below. Some background information on the data and important economic theory regarding bid collusion is also provided. Use this information to guide your analysis. Prepare a professional document which presents the results of your analysis and gives your opinion regarding collusion.

Page 142

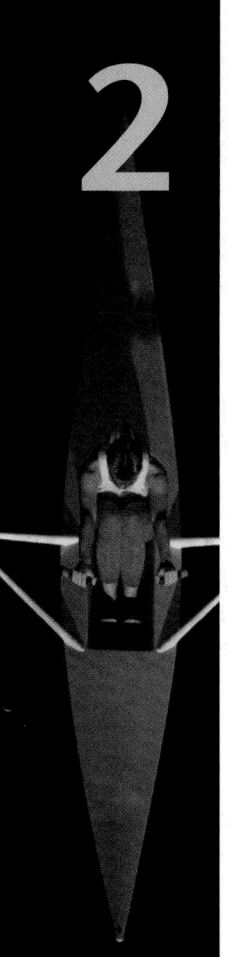

2

Methods for Describing Sets of Data

Contents

Statistics in Action

Characteristics of Physicians Who Use or Refuse Ethics Consultation

Using Technology

Where We've Been

- Examined the difference between inferential and descriptive statistics
- Described the key elements of a statistical problem
- Learned about the two types of data—quantitative and qualitative
- Discussed the role of statistical thinking in managerial decision making

42

Chapter Openers Provide a Valuable Roadmap.

- Chapter Contents provide a navigational study path through the material.

- *Where We've Been* quickly reviews how information learned previously applies to the chapter at hand.

- *Where We're Going* highlights how the chapter topics fit into your growing understanding of statistics.

Technology

Optional technology boxes appear throughout the text, both in the discussion and the exercises facilitating computer-based analysis.

* They include output from EXCEL, MINITAB, and SPSS.

* Includes step-by-step instructions on how to use the TI-83 calculator in a variety of applications.

* Technology Tutorials appear at the end of chapters. They are approximately 10 pages in length and include point & click instructions and screen shots for EXCEL, MINITAB and SPSS.

* The technology instruction helps students better understand what statistical tools to use, how to apply them and how to interpret the results.

One-Variable Descriptive Statistics

Using the TI-83 Graphing Calculator

Step 1 Enter the data
Press STAT and select 1:Edit
Note: If the list already contains data, clear the old data. Use the up arrow to highlight 'L1'. Press CLEAR ENTER.
Use the arrow and ENTER keys to enter the data set into L1.

Step 2 Calculate descriptive statistics
Press STAT
Press the right arrow key to highlight CALC

Press ENTER for 1-Var Stats
Enter the name of the list containing your data.
Press 2nd 1 for L1 (or 2nd 2 for L2 etc.)
Press ENTER

You should see the statistics on your screen. Some of the statistics are off the bottom of the screen. Use the down arrow to scroll through to see the remaining statistics. Use the up arrow to scroll back up.

Example The descriptive statistics for the sample data set

86, 70, 62, 98, 73, 56, 53, 92, 86, 37, 62, 83, 78, 49, 78, 37, 67, 79, 57

The output screens for this example are shown below.

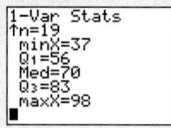

```
1-Var Stats
 x̄=68.57894737
 Σx=1303
 Σx²=94897
 Sx=17.54142966
 σx=17.07357389
↓n=19
```

```
1-Var Stats
↑n=19
 minX=37
 Q₁=56
 Med=70
 Q₃=83
 maxX=98
■
```

End of Chapter Review

Each chapter concludes with information designed to help check your understanding of the material and study for tests. These resources include:

• **Quick Review**, a list of key terms and formulas with page number references for easy look up.

• **Language Lab**, which helps you learn the language of statistics through pronunciation guides, descriptions of symbols, names, etc.

• **Supplementary Exercises,** a review of the important topics introduced in the chapter.

Quick Review

[Note: Items marked with an asterisk (*) are from the optional section in this chapter.]

Key Terms

Additive rule of probability 165
*Bayes's rule 191
*Bayesian statistical methods 190
Combinations rule 156
Combinatorial mathematics 156
Complementary events 164

Compound event 160
Conditional probability 172
Dependent events 178
Event 152
Experiment 147
Independent events 178
Intersection 161
Law of large numbers 149
Multiplicative rule of probability 175
Mutually exclusive events 166
Odds 160

Probability rules (sample points) 150
Random number generator 187
Random number table 188
Random sample 187
Sample point 147
Sample space 148
Tree diagram 177
Two-way table 162
Unconditional probabilities 172
Union 160
Venn diagram 148

Key Formulas

$$\binom{N}{n} = \frac{N!}{n!(N-n)!}$$
where $N! = N(N-1)(N-2)\cdots(2)(1)$
$P(A) + P(A^c) = 1$
$P(A \cup B) = P(A) + P(B) - P(A \cap B)$
$P(A \cap B) = 0$
$P(A \cup B) = P(A) + P(B)$
$P(A|B) = \frac{P(A \cap B)}{P(B)}$

Combinations rule 156
Rule of Complements 164
Additive rule 165
Mutually exclusive events 166
Additive rule for mutually exclusive events 166
Conditional probability 172

Language Lab

Symbol	Pronunciation	Description
S		Sample space
$S: \{1, 2, 3, 4, 5\}$		Set of sample points, 1, 2, 3, 4, 5, in sample space
$A: \{1, 2\}$		Set of sample points, 1, 2, in event A
$P(A)$	Probability of A	Probability that event A occurs
$A \cup B$	A union B	Union of events A and B (either A or B or both occur)
$A \cap B$	A intersect B	Intersection of events A and B (both A and B occur)

Supplementary Exercises 3.82–3.116

[Note: Exercises marked with an asterisk (*) are from the optional section.]

Learning the Mechanics

3.82 A sample space consists of four sample points, where $P(S_1) = .2, P(S_2) = .1, P(S_3) = .3$, and $P(S_4) = .4$.
a. Show that the sample points obey the two probability rules for a sample space.
b. If an event $A = \{S_1, S_4\}$, find $P(A)$.

3.83 A and B are mutually exclusive events, with $P(A) = .2$ and $P(B) = .3$.
a. Find $P(A|B)$.
b. Are A and B independent events?

3.84 For two events A and B, suppose $P(A) = .7, P(B) = .5$, and $P(A \cap B) = .4$. Find $P(A \cup B)$.

3.85 Given that $P(A \cap B) = .4$ and $P(A|B) = .8$, find $P(B)$.

3.86 Which of the following pairs of events are mutually exclusive? Justify your response.
a. [The Dow Jones Industrial Average increases on Monday], {A large New York bank decreases its prime interest rate on Monday]

c. Find $P(A \cup B)$.

3.89 Find the numerical value of
a. 6! **b.** $\binom{10}{9}$ **c.** $\binom{10}{1}$ **d.** $\binom{6}{3}$ **e.** 0!

3.90 A random sample of five graduate students is to be selected from 50 MBA majors for participation in a case competition.
a. In how many different ways can the sample be drawn?
b. Show how the random number table, Table 1 of Appendix B, can be used to select the sample of students.

Applying the Concepts—Basic

3.91 Refer to the National Highway Traffic Safety Administration (NHTSA) crash tests of new car models, Exercise 2.127 (p. 124). Recall that the NHTSA has developed a "star" scoring system, with results ranging from one star (*) to five stars (*****). The more stars in the rating, the better the level of crash protection in a head-on collision. A summary of the driver-side star

Statistics, Data, and Statistical Thinking

Contents

Statistics in Action

A *20/20* View of Survey Results: Fact or Fiction?

Technology Tutorials

Where We're Going

- Introduce the field of statistics.
- Demonstrate how statistics applies to business.
- Establish the link between statistics and data.
- Identify the different types of data and data collection methods.
- Differentiate between population and sample data.
- Differentiate between descriptive and inferential statistics.

Statistics in

ACTION

A *20/20* View of Surveys: Fact or Fiction?

"Did you ever notice that, no matter where you stand on popular issues of the day, you can always find statistics or surveys to back up your point of view—whether to take vitamins, whether day care harms kids, or what foods can hurt you or save you? There is an endless flow of information to help you make decisions, but is this information accurate, unbiased? John Stossel decided to check that out, and you may be surprised to learn if the picture you're getting doesn't seem quite right, maybe it isn't."

Barbara Walters gave this introduction to a March 31, 1995 segment of the popular prime-time ABC television program *20/20*. The story is titled "Facts or Fiction?—Exposés of So-Called Surveys." One of the surveys investigated by ABC correspondent John Stossel compared the discipline problems experienced by teachers in the 1940s and those experienced today. The results: In the 1940s, teachers worried most about students talking in class, chewing gum, and running in the halls. Today, they worry most about being assaulted! This information was highly publicized in the print media—in daily newspapers, weekly magazines, Ann Landers's column, *The Congressional*

Quarterly, and *The Wall Street Journal,* among others—and referenced in speeches by a variety of public figures, including former first lady Barbara Bush and former Education Secretary William Bennett.

"Hearing this made me yearn for the old days when life was so much simpler and gentler, but was life that simple then?" asks Stossel. "Wasn't there juvenile delinquency [in the 1940s]? Is the survey true?" With the help of a Yale School of Management professor, Stossel found the original source of the teacher survey—Texas oilman T. Colin Davis — and discovered it wasn't a survey at all! Davis had simply identified certain disciplinary problems encountered by teachers in a conservative newsletter—a list he admitted was not obtained from a statistical survey, but from Davis's personal knowledge of the problems in the 1940s. ("I was in school then") and his understanding of the problems today ("I read the papers").

Stossel's critical thinking about the teacher "survey" led to the discovery of research that is misleading at best and unethical at worst. Several more misleading (and possibly unethical) surveys were presented on the ABC program. Listed here, most of these were conducted by businesses or special interest groups with specific objectives in mind.

Reported Information (Source)	Actual Study Information
Eating oat bran is a cheap and easy way to achieve a slightly lower cholesterol. (Quaker Oats)	Diet must consist of nothing but oat bran to reduce your cholesterol count.
150,000 women a year die from anorexia. (Feminist group)	Approximately 1,000 women a year die from problems that were likely caused by anorexia.
Domestic violence causes more birth defects than all medical issues combined. (March of Dimes)	No study—false report.
Only 29% of high school girls are happy with themselves, compared to 66% of elementary school girls. (American Association of University Women)	Of 3,000 high school girls, 29% responded "Always true" to the statement, "I am happy the way I am." Most answered, "Sort of true" and "Sometimes true."
One in four American children under age 12 is hungry or at risk of hunger. (Food Research and Action Center)	Based on responses to questions: "Do you ever cut the size of meals?" "Do you ever eat less than you feel you should?" "Did you ever rely on limited numbers of foods to feed your children because you were running out of money to buy food for a meal?"

The *20/20* segment ended with an interview of Cynthia Crossen, author of *Tainted Truth,* an exposé of misleading and biased surveys. Crossen warns, "If everybody is misusing

numbers and scaring us with numbers to get us to do something, however good [that something] is, we've lost the power of numbers. Now, we know certain things from research. For example, we know that smoking cigarettes is hard on your lungs and heart, and because we know that, many people's lives have been extended or saved. We don't want to lose the power of information to help us make decisions, and that's what I worry about."

In the following *Statistics in Action Revisited* sections, we discuss several key statistical concepts covered in this chapter that are relevant to the misleading surveys exposed in the *20/20* program.

Statistics in Action Revisited for Chapter 1

- Identifying the population, sample, and inference (p. 13)
- Identifying the data collection method and data type (p. 21)
- Critically assessing the ethics of a statistical study (p. 24)

1.1 The Science of Statistics

What does statistics mean to you? Does it bring to mind batting averages. Gallup polls, unemployment figures, or numerical distortions of facts (lying with statistics!)? Or is it simply a college requirement you have to complete? We hope to persuade you that statistics is a meaningful, useful science whose broad scope of applications to business, government, and the physical and social sciences is almost limitless. We also want to show that statistics can lie only when they are misapplied. Finally, we wish to demonstrate the key role statistics play in critical thinking— whether in the classroom, on the job, or in everyday life. Our objective is to leave you with the impression that the time you spend studying this subject will repay you in many ways.

The *Random House College Dictionary* defines *statistics* as "the science that deals with the collection, classification, analysis, and interpretation of information or data." Thus, a statistician isn't just someone who calculates batting averages at base-

Biography

FLORENCE NIGHTINGALE (1820–1910) The Passionate Statistician

In Victorian England, the "Lady of the Lamp" had a mission to improve the squalid field hospital conditions of the British army during the Crimean War. Today, most historians consider Florence Nightingale to be the founder of the nursing profession. To convince members of the British Parliament of the need for supplying nursing and medical care to soldiers in the field, Nightingale compiled massive amounts of data from the army files. Through a remarkable series of graphs (which included the first "pie chart"), she demonstrated that most of the deaths in the war were due to illnesses contracted outside the battlefield or long after battle action from wounds that went untreated. Florence Nightingale's compassion and self-sacrificing nature, coupled with her ability to collect, arrange, and present large amounts of data, led some to call her the "Passionate Statistican."

ball games or tabulates the results of a Gallup poll. Professional statisticians are trained in *statistical science*. That is, they are trained in collecting numerical information in the form of **data,** evaluating it, and drawing conclusions from it. Furthermore, statisticians determine what information is relevant in a given problem and whether the conclusions drawn from a study are to be trusted.

> **DEFINITION 1.1**
>
> **Statistics** is the science of data. It involves collecting, classifying, summarizing, organizing, analyzing, and interpreting numerical information.

In the next section, you'll see several real-life examples of statistical applications in business and government that involve making decisions and drawing conclusions.

1.2   Types of Statistical Applications in Business

Statistics means "numerical descriptions" to most people. Monthly unemployment figures, the failure rate of a new business, and the proportion of female executives in a particular industry all represent statistical descriptions of large sets of data collected on some phenomenon. Often the data are selected from some larger set of data whose characteristics we wish to estimate. We call this selection process *sampling*. For example, you might collect the ages of a sample of customers at a video store to estimate the average age of *all* customers of the store. Then you could use your estimate to target the store's advertisements to the appropriate age group. Notice that statistics involves two different processes: (1) describing sets of data and (2) drawing conclusions (making estimates, decisions, predictions, etc.) about the sets of data based on sampling. So, the applications of statistics can be divided into two broad areas: *descriptive statistics* and *inferential statistics*.

Teaching Tip

Descriptive statistics summarizes the data set collected.

> **DEFINITION 1.2**
>
> **Descriptive statistics** utilizes numerical and graphical methods to look for patterns in a data set, to summarize the information revealed in a data set, and to present the information in a convenient form.

Teaching Tip

Inferences make statements about populations (the data that information is desired for).

> **DEFINITION 1.3**
>
> **Inferential statistics** utilizes sample data to make estimates, decisions, predictions, or other generalizations about a larger set of data.

Although we'll discuss both descriptive and inferential statistics in the following chapters, the primary theme of the text is **inference.**

Let's begin by examining some business studies that illustrate applications of statistics.

Study 1 "U.S. Market Share for Credit and Debit Cards" (U.S. Payment Card Information Network, June 6, 2003)

CardWeb.com, Inc. is a leading online publisher of information pertaining to payment cards (e.g., credit, debit, smart, prepaid, and phone cards). The company tracked all credit or debit card purchases in the United States during the first three months of 2003. The amount of each purchase was recorded and classified according to type of card used. The results are shown in Figure 1.1. From the graph, you can clearly see that over half of the purchases were made with a VISA card and 30% with a MasterCard. Since Figure 1.1 *describes* the type of card used in all credit card purchases for first quarter of 2003, the graphic is an example of descriptive statistics.

Teaching Tip

Use Studies 1–3 to point out the difference between descriptive and inferential statistics. Focus on the data that statements are being made about (i.e., the sample or population).

Figure 1.1

U.S. credit card market shares

Source: www.cardweb.com

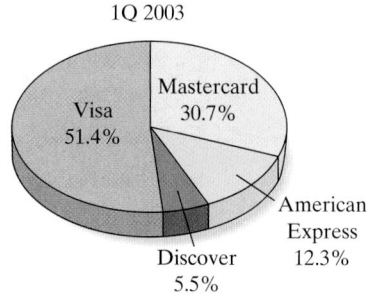

1Q 2003

Mastercard 30.7%

Visa 51.4%

American Express 12.3%

Discover 5.5%

Study 2 "The Executive Compensation Scoreboard" (*Business Week*, Apr. 21, 2003)

TABLE 1.1 Average Return-to-Pay Ratios of CEOs, by Industry

Industry	Average Ratio
Resources	25.20
Financial	24.63
Retailing	18.15
Services	16.13
Consumer Products	15.81
Utilities	14.43
Industrial Low-Tech	12.92
Transportation	9.37
Industrial High-Tech	8.98
Telecommunications	2.87

Source: Analysis of data in "Executive Compensation Scoreboard," Business Week, *April 21, 2003.*

How much are the top corporate executives in the United States being paid and are they worth it? To answer these questions, *Business Week* magazine compiles its "Executive Compensation Scoreboard" each year based on a survey of executives at the highest-ranking companies listed in the *Business Week 1000*. The average* total pay of chief executive officers (CEOs) at 363 companies sampled in the 2003 scoreboard was $7.4 million—a decrease of 33% from the previous year.

To determine which executives are worth their pay, *Business Week* also records the ratio of total shareholder return (measured by the dollar value of a $100 investment in the company made 3 years earlier) to the total pay of the CEO (in million dollars) over the same 3-year period. For example, a $100 investment in the computer systems company, Oracle, in 2000 was worth $39 at the end of 2002. When this shareholder return ($39) is divided by oracle CEO Lawrence Ellison's total 2000–2002 pay of $781.4 million, the result is a return-to-pay ratio of only .049, the lowest among all other chief executives in the survey.

An analysis of the sample data reveals that CEOs in the financial services industry have one of the highest average return-to-pay ratios (24.63) while the CEOs in the telecommunications industry have one of the lowest average ratios (2.87). (See Table 1.1.) Armed with this sample information, *Business Week* might *infer* that, from the shareholders' perspective, typical chief executives in telecommunications are overpaid relative to CEOs in finance. Thus, this study is an example of *inferential statistics*.

*Although we will not formally define the term *average* until Chapter 2, *typical* or *middle* can be substituted here without confusion.

Study 3   "The Consumer Price Index" *(U.S. Department of Labor)*

A data set of interest to virtually all Americans is the set of prices charged for goods and services in the U.S. economy. The general upward movement in this set of prices is referred to as *inflation;* the general downward movement is referred to as *deflation.* In order to *estimate* the change in prices over time, the Bureau of Labor Statistics (BLS) of the U.S. Department of Labor developed the Consumer Price Index (CPI). Each month, the BLS collects price data about a specific collection of goods and services (called a *market basket*) from 85 urban areas around the country. Statistical procedures are used to compute the CPI from this sample price data and other information about consumers' spending habits. By comparing the level of the CPI at different points in time, it is possible to *estimate* (make an inference about) the rate of inflation over particular time intervals and to compare the purchasing power of a dollar at different points in time.

One major use of the CPI as an index of inflation is as an indicator of the success or failure of government economic policies. A second use of the CPI is to escalate income payments. Millions of workers have *escalator clauses* in their collective bargaining contracts; these clauses call for increases in wage rates based on increases in the CPI. In addition, the incomes of Social Security beneficiaries and retired military and federal civil service employees are tied to the CPI. It has been estimated that a 1% increase in the CPI can trigger an increase of over $1 billion in income payments. Thus, it can be said that the very livelihoods of millions of Americans depend on the behavior of a statistical estimator, the CPI.

Like Study 2, this study is an example of *inferential statistics.* Market basket price data from a sample of urban areas (used to compute the CPI) are used to make inferences about the rate of inflation and wage rate increases.

These studies provide three real-life examples of the uses of statistics in business, economics, and government. Notice that each involves an analysis of data, either for the purpose of describing the data set (Study 1) or for making inferences about a data set (Studies 2 and 3).

Teaching Tip

Include examples of other studies and discuss whether descriptive, inferential, or both areas of statistics will be used.

1.3   Fundamental Elements of Statistics

Statistical methods are particularly useful for studying, analyzing, and learning about *populations* of *experimental units.*

DEFINITION 1.4

An **experimental unit** is an object (e.g., person, thing, transaction, or event) upon which we collect data.

DEFINITION 1.5

A **population** is a set of units (usually people, objects, transactions, or events) that we are interested in studying.

Teaching Tip

Emphasize *entire* set of data for which information is desired.

For example, populations may include (1) *all* employed workers in the United States, (2) *all* registered voters in California, (3) *everyone* who has purchased a particular brand of cellular telephone, (4) *all* the cars produced last year by a particular assembly line, (5) the *entire* stock of spare parts at United Airlines' maintenance facility, (6) *all* sales made at the drive-through window of a McDonald's restaurant during a given year, and (7) the set of *all* accidents occurring on a particular stretch of interstate highway during a holiday period. Notice that the first three population examples (1–3) are sets (groups) of people, the next two (4–5) are sets of objects, the next (6) is a set of transactions, and the last (7) is a set of events. Also notice that each set includes all the experimental units in the population of interest.

In studying a population, we focus on one or more characteristics or properties of the experimental units in the population. We call such characteristics *variables*. For example, we may be interested in the variables age, gender, income, and/or the number of years of education of the people currently unemployed in the United States.

Teaching Tip
The values of the variable will change from one unit in the population to the next.

> **DEFINITION 1.6**
>
> A **variable** is a characteristic or property of an individual experimental unit.

The name *variable* is derived from the fact that any particular characteristic may vary among the experimental units in a population.

In studying a particular variable it is helpful to be able to obtain a numerical representation for it. Often, however, numerical representations are not readily available, so the process of measurement plays an important supporting role in statistical studies. **Measurement** is the process we use to assign numbers to variables of individual population units. We might, for instance, measure the preference for a food product by asking a consumer to rate the product's taste on a scale from 1 to 10. Or we might measure workforce age by simply asking each worker how old she is. In other cases, measurement involves the use of instruments such as stopwatches, scales, and calipers.

Teaching Tip
We very rarely collect all the data contained in the population.

If the population we wish to study is small, it is possible to measure a variable for every unit in the population. For example, if you are measuring the starting salary for all University of Michigan MBA graduates last year, it is at least feasible to obtain every salary. When we measure a variable for every experimental unit of a population, the result is called a **census** of the population. Typically, however, the populations of interest in most applications are much larger, involving perhaps many thousands or even an infinite number of units. Examples of large populations include those following Definition 1.5, as well as all invoices produced in the last year by a *Fortune* 500 company, all potential buyers of a new fax machine, and all stockholders of a firm listed on the New York Stock Exchange. For such populations, conducting a census would be prohibitively time-consuming and/or costly. A reasonable alternative would be to select and study a *subset* (or portion) of the units in the population.

Teaching Tip
Emphasize the word *subset*.

> **DEFINITION 1.7**
>
> A **sample** is a subset of the units of a population.

For example, suppose a company is being audited for invoice errors. Instead of examining all 15,472 invoices produced by the company during a given year, an auditor may select and examine a sample of just 100 invoices (see Figure 1.2). If he is interested in the variable "invoice error status," he would record (measure) the status (error or no error) of each sampled invoice.

Teaching Tip
Use examples to illustrate the difference between the population of interest and the sample that has been collected.

After the variable(s) of interest for every experimental unit in the sample (or population) is measured, the data are analyzed, either by descriptive or inferential statistical methods. The auditor, for example, may be interested only in *describing* the

Figure 1.2
A sample of all company invoices

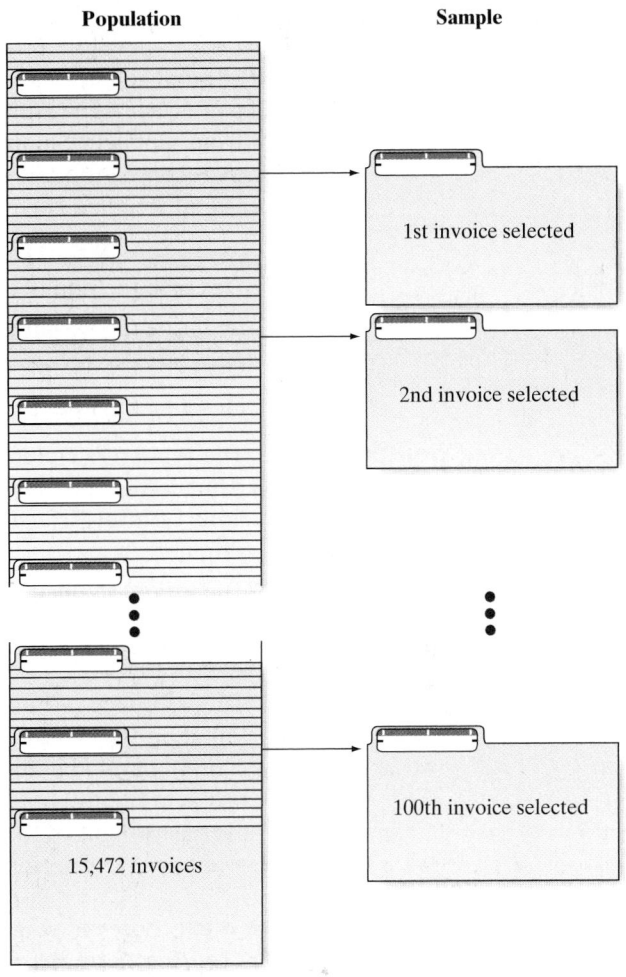

error rate in the sample of 100 invoices. More likely, however, he will want to use the information in the sample to make *inferences* about the population of all 15,472 invoices.

DEFINITION 1.8

A **statistical inference** is an estimate or prediction or some other generalization about a population based on information contained in a sample.

That is, we use the information contained in the sample to learn about the larger population.* Thus, from the sample of 100 invoices, the auditor may estimate the total number of invoices containing errors in the population of 15,472 invoices. The auditor's inference about the quality of the firm's invoices can be used in deciding whether to modify the firm's billing operations.

---

*The terms *population* and *sample* are often used to refer to the sets of measurements themselves, as well as to the units on which the measurements are made. When a single variable of interest is being measured, this usage causes little confusion. But when the terminology is ambiguous, we'll refer to the measurements as *population data sets* and *sample data sets*, respectively.

EXAMPLE 1.1   KEY ELEMENTS OF A STATISTICAL PROBLEM

Problem   A large paint retailer has had numerous complaints from customers about under-filled paint cans. As a result, the retailer has begun inspecting incoming shipments of paint from suppliers. Shipments with underfill problems will be returned to the sup-plier. A recent shipment contained 2,440 gallon-size cans. The retailer sampled 50 cans and weighed each on a scale capable of measuring weight to four decimal places. Properly filled cans weigh 10 pounds.

   a. Describe the population and experimental units.

   b. Describe the variable of interest.

   c. Describe the sample.

   d. Describe the inference.

Solution   **a.** The retailer is collecting data on paint cans; therefore, a 2,440 gallon can of paint is the experimental unit. The population is the set of experimental units of interest to the retailer, which is all the cans of paint in the recent shipment.

Population: All 2,440 cans of paint. Experimental unit: A single can of paint.

   b. The weight of the paint cans is the variable the retailer wishes to evaluate.

Weight of can

   c. The sample is a subset of the population. In this case, it is the 50 cans of paint selected by the retailer.

50 cans of paint

   d. The inference of interest involves the *generalization* of the information con-tained in the weights of the sample of paint cans to the population of paint cans. In particular, the retailer wants to learn about the extent of the underfill problem (if any) in the population. This might be accomplished by finding the average weight of the cans in the sample and using it to estimate the average weight of the cans in the population.

Look Back   A key to diagnosing a statistical problem is to identify the data set col-lected (in this example, the weights of the 50 cans) as a population or sample.

■ ■ ■

EXAMPLE 1.2   KEY ELEMENTS OF A STATISTICAL PROBLEM

Problem   "Cola wars" is the popular term for the intense competition between Coca-Cola and Pepsi displayed in their marketing campaigns. Their campaigns have featured movie and television stars, rock videos, athletic endorsements, and claims of consumer prefer-ence based on taste tests. Suppose, as part of a Pepsi marketing campaign, 1,000 cola consumers are given a blind taste test (i.e., a taste test in which the two brand names are disguised). Each consumer is asked to state a preference for brand A or brand B.

Suggested Exercises 1.28

   a. Describe the population.

All cola consumers

   b. Describe the variable of interest.

Cola preference

   c. Describe the sample.

1,000 cola consumers

   d. Describe the inference.

Solution   **a.** Since we are interested in the responses of cola consumers in a taste test, a cola consumer is the experimental unit. Thus, the population of interest is the collection or set of all cola consumers.

b. The characteristic that Pepsi wants to measure is the consumer's cola preference as revealed under the conditions of a blind taste test, so cola preference is the variable of interest.

c. The sample is the 1,000 cola consumers selected from the population of all cola consumers.

d. The inference of interest is the *generalization* of the cola preferences of the 1,000 sampled consumers to the population of all cola consumers. In particular, the preferences of the consumers in the sample can be used to *estimate* the percentage of all cola consumers who prefer each brand.

Look Back In determining whether the inference is inferential or descriptive, we assess whether Pepsi is interested in the responses of only the 1,000 sampled customers (descriptive statistics) or in the responses for the entire population of consumers (inferential statistics).

| Now Work | *Exercise 1.14b* |

■ ■ ■

The preceding definitions and examples identify four of the five elements of an inferential statistical problem: a population, one or more variables of interest a sample, and an inference. But making the inference is only part of the story. We also need to know its **reliability**—that is, how good the inference is. The only way we can be certain that an inference about a population is correct is to include the entire population in our sample. However, because of *resource constraints* (i.e., insufficient time and/or money), we usually can't work with whole populations, so we base our inferences on just a portion of the population (a sample). Consequently, whenever possible, it is important to determine and report the reliability of each inference made. Reliability, then, is the fifth element of inferential statistical problems.

The measure of reliability that accompanies an inference separates the science of statistics from the art of fortune-telling. A palm reader, like a statistician, may examine a sample (your hand) and make inferences about the population (your life). However, unlike statistical inferences, the palm reader's inferences include no measure of reliability.

Suppose, like the paint retailer in Example 1.1, we are interested in the *error of estimation* (i.e., the difference between the average weight for the population of paint cans and the average weight of a sample of cans). Using statistical methods, we can determine a *bound on the estimation error*. This bound is simply a number that our estimation error (the difference between the average weight of the sample and the average weight of the population of cans) is not likely to exceed. We'll see in later chapters that this bound is a measure of the uncertainty of our inference. The reliability of statistical inferences is discussed throughout this text. For now, we simply want you to realize that an inference is incomplete without a measure of its reliability.

Teaching Tip
Without reliability, the inferences made would be of little value.

Teaching Tip
Later in the text, we express reliability in two manners: confidence in our inferences and error rates associated with our conclusions.

DEFINITION 1.9

A **measure of reliability** is a statement (usually quantified) about the degree of uncertainty associated with a statistical inference.

Let's conclude this section with a summary of the elements of both descriptive and inferential statistical problems and an example to illustrate a measure of reliability.

Four Elements of Descriptive Statistical Problems

Teaching Tip

First part of *Statistics for Business and Economics* textbook.

1. The population or sample of interest
2. One or more variables (characteristics of the population or sample units) that are to be investigated
3. Tables, graphs, or numerical summary tools
4. Identification of patterns in the data

Five Elements of Inferential Statistical Problems

Teaching Tip

Latter part of *Statistics for Business and Economics* textbook.

1. The population of interest
2. One or more variables (characteristics of the population units) that are to be investigated
3. The sample of population units
4. The inference about the population based on information contained in the sample
5. A measure of reliability for the inference

EXAMPLE 1.3   RELIABILITY OF AN INFERENCE

Problem   Refer to Example 1.2, in which the cola preferences of 1,000 consumers were indicated in a taste test. Describe how the reliability of an inference concerning the preferences of all cola consumers in the Pepsi bottler's marketing region could be measured.

Solution   When the preferences of 1,000 consumers are used to estimate the preferences of all consumers in the region, the estimate will not exactly mirror the preferences of the population. For example, if the taste test shows that 56% of the 1,000 consumers chose Pepsi, it does not follow (nor is it likely) that exactly 56% of all cola drinkers in the region prefer Pepsi. Nevertheless, we can use sound statistical reasoning (which is presented later in the text) to ensure that our sampling procedure will generate estimates that are almost certainly within a specified limit of the true percentage of all consumers who prefer Pepsi. For example, such reasoning might assure us that the estimate of the preference for Pepsi from the sample is almost certainly within 5% of the actual population preference. The implication is that the actual preference for Pepsi is between 51% [i.e., $(56 - 5)\%$] and 61% [i.e., $(56 + 5)\%$]—that is, $(56 \pm 5)\%$. This interval represents a measure of reliability for the inference.

Look Back The interval 56 ± 5 is called a *confidence interval*, since we are "confident" that the true percentage of customers that prefer Pepsi in a taste test falls into the range (51, 61). In Chapter 7, we learn how to assess the degree of confidence (e.g., 90% or 95% confidence) in the interval.

■ ■ ■

Statistics in Action Revisited

Identifying the Population, Sample, and Inference

Consider the study by the Food Research and Action Center (FRAC), reported on the *20/20* television program, that found one in four (25%) of American children are at risk of hunger. These results were based on the responses of parents to questions such as "Do you ever rely on limited funds to feed your children because you were running out of money to buy food?" The experimental unit for the study is a parent, and the variable measured is the response ("yes" or "no") to the question. Although the actual number of parents who participated in the study was not mentioned, it is obvious that the FRAC did not interview every parent of a U.S.-born child—a virtually impossible task. Consequently, the responses (for, say, 1,000 parents) represent a sample selected from the much larger population of all parents of American children.

Apparently, 25% of the sampled parents responded affirmatively to the survey question. Thus, the FRAC inferred that 25% of all parents would answer affirmatively. This inference lead to the "one in four" figure that was presented on the *20/20* program.

1.4   Processes (Optional)

Sections 1.2 and 1.3 focused on the use of statistical methods to analyze and learn about populations, which are sets of *existing* units. Statistical methods are equally useful for analyzing and making inferences about *processes*.

> **DEFINITION 1.10**
>
> A **process** is a series of actions or operations that transforms inputs to outputs. A process produces or generates output over time.

Teaching Tip

Think of processes as any procedure that produces outcomes over time.

The most obvious processes that are of interest to businesses are production or manufacturing processes. A manufacturing process uses a series of operation performed by people and machines to convert inputs, such as raw materials and parts, to finished products (the outputs). Examples include the process used to produce the paper on which these words are printed, automobile assembly lines and oil refineries.

Figure 1.3 presents a general description of a process and its inputs and outputs. In the context of manufacturing, the process in the figure (i.e., the transformation process) could be a depiction of the overall production process or it could be

Figure 1.3

Graphical depiction of a manufacturing process

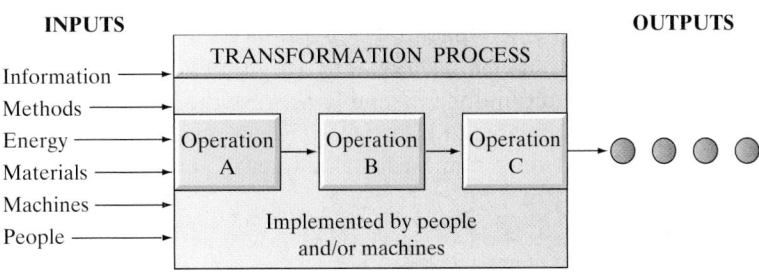

a depiction of one of the many processes (sometimes called subprocesses) that exist within an overall production process. Thus, the output shown could be finished goods that will be shipped to an external customer or merely the output of one of the steps or subprocesses of the overall process. In the latter case, the output becomes input for the next subprocess. For example, Figure 1.3 could represent the overall automobile assembly process, with its output being fully assembled cars ready for shipment to dealers. Or, it could depict the windshield assembly subprocess, with its output of partially assembled cars with windshield ready for "shipment" to the next subprocess in the assembly line.

Besides physical products and services, businesses and other organizations generate streams of numerical data over time that are used to evaluate the performance of the organization. Examples include weekly sales figures, quarterly earnings, and yearly profits. The U.S. economy (a complex organization) can be thought of as generating streams of data that include the Gross Domestic Product (GDP), stock prices, and the Consumer Price Index (see Section 1.2). Statisticians and other analysts conceptualize these data streams as being generated by processes. Typically, however, the series of operations or actions that cause particular data to be realized are either unknown or so complex (or both) that the processes are treated as *black boxes*.

Teaching Tip

The output is the only emphasis in a black box process.

DEFINITION 1.11

A process whose operations or actions are unknown or unspecified is called a **black box.**

Frequently, when a process is treated as a black box, its inputs are not specified either. The entire focus is on the output of the process. A black box process is illustrated in Figure 1.4.

Figure 1.4

A black box process with numerical output

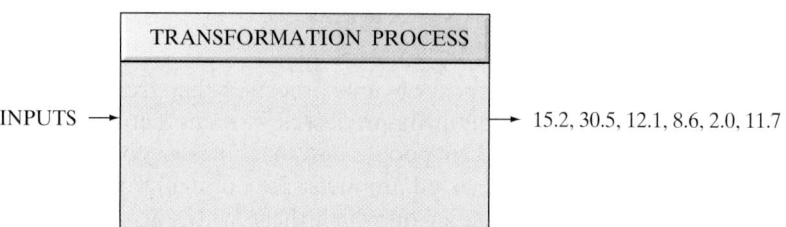

In studying a process, we generally focus on one or more characteristics, or properties, of the output. For example, we may be interested in the weight or the length of the units produced or even the time it takes to produce each unit. As with characteristics of population units, we call these characteristics *variables*. In studying processes whose output is already in numerical form (i.e., a stream of numbers), the characteristic, or property, represented by the numbers (e.g., sales, GDP, or stock prices) is typically the variable of interest. If the output is not numeric, we use *measurement processes* to assign numerical values to variables.* For example, if in the automobile assembly process the weight of the fully assembled automobile is the variable of interest, a measurement process involving a large scale will be used to assign a numerical value to each automobile.

*A process whose output is already in numerical form necessarily includes a measurement process as one of its subprocesses.

As with populations, we use sample data to analyze and make inferences (estimates, predictions, or other generalizations) about processes. But the concept of a sample is defined differently when dealing with processes. Recall that a population is a set of existing units and that a sample is a subset of those units. In the case of processes, however, the concept of a set of existing units is not relevant or appropriate. Processes generate or create their output *over time*—one unit after another. For example, a particular automobile assembly line produces a completed vehicle every four minutes. We define a sample from a process in the box.

DEFINITION 1.12

Any set of output (object or numbers) produced by a process is called a **sample.**

Thus, the next 10 cars turned out by the assembly line constitute a sample from the process, as do the next 100 cars or every fifth car produced today.

EXAMPLE 1.4   KEY ELEMENTS OF A PROCESS

Problem   A particular fast-food restaurant chain has 6,289 outlets with drive-through windows. To attract more customers to its drive-through services, the company is considering offering a 50% discount to customers who wait more than a specified number of minutes to receive their order. To help determine what the time limit should be, the company decided to estimate the average waiting time at a particular drive-through window in Dallas, Texas. For seven consecutive days, the worker taking customers' orders recorded the time that every order was placed. The worker who handed the order to the customer recorded the time of delivery. In both cases, workers used synchronized digital clocks that reported the time to the nearest second. At the end of the 7-day period, 2,109 orders had been timed.

a. Describe the process of interest at the Dallas restaurant.

b. Describe the variable of interest.

c. Describe the sample.

d. Describe the inference of interest.

e. Describe how the reliability of the inference could be measured.

Solution   **a.** The process of interest is the drive-through window at a particular fast-food restaurant in Dallas, Texas. It is a process because it "produces." or "generates," meals over time. That is, it services customers over time.

b. The variable the company monitored is customer waiting time, the length of time a customer waits to receive a meal after placing an order. Since the study is focusing only on the output of the process (the time to produce the output) and not the internal operations of the process (the tasks required to produce a meal for a customer), the process is being treated as a black box.

c. The sampling plan was to monitor every order over a particular 7-day period. The sample is the 2,109 orders that were processed during the 7-day period.

d. The company's immediate interest is in learning about the drive-through window in Dallas. They plan to do this by using the waiting times from the sample to make a statistical inference about the drive-through process. In particular, they might use the average waiting time for the sample to estimate the average waiting time at the Dallas facility.

e. As for inferences about populations, measures of reliability can be developed for inferences about processes. The reliability of the estimate of the average waiting time for the Dallas restaurant could be measured by a bound on the error of estimation. That is, we might find that the average waiting time is 4.2 minutes, with a bound on the error of estimation of .5 minute. The implication would be that we could be reasonably certain that the true average waiting time for the Dallas process is between 3.7 and 4.7 minutes.

Look Back Notice that there is also a population described in this example: the company's 6,289 existing outlets with drive-through facilities. In the final analysis, the company will use what it learns about the process in Dallas and, perhaps, similar studies at other locations to make an inference about the waiting times in its populations of outlets.

Now Work *Exercise 1.30*

━━━━━━ ■ ■ ■ ━━━━━━

Note that output already generated by a process can be viewed as a population. Suppose a soft-drink canning process produced 2,000 twelve-packs yesterday, all of which were stored in a warehouse. If we were interested in learning something about those 2,000 packages—such as the percentage with defective cardboard packaging—we could treat the 2,000 packages as a population. We might draw a sample from the population in the warehouse, measure the variable of interest, and use the sample data to make a statistical inference about the 2,000 packages, as described in Sections 1.2 and 1.3.

In this optional section we have presented a brief introduction to processes and the use of statistical methods to analyze and learn about processes. In Chapters 14 and 15 we present an in-depth treatment of these subjects.

Teaching Tip

Discuss different definitions for a population when each of these definitions might be appropriate. Focus on the data that information is needed about when defining the population.

1.5 Types of Data

You have learned that statistics is the science of data and that data are obtained by measuring the values of one or more variables on the units in the sample (or population). All data (and hence the variables we measure) can be classified as one of two general types: *quantitative data* and *qualitative data*.

Quantitative data are data that are measured on a naturally occurring numerical scale.* The following are examples of quantitative data:

1. The temperature (in degrees Celsius) at which each unit in a sample of 20 pieces of heat-resistant plastic begins to melt

2. The current unemployment rate (measured as a percentage) for each of the 50 states

---

*Quantitative data can be subclassified as either *interval data* or *ratio data*. For ratio data, the origin (i.e., the value 0) is a meaningful number. But the origin has no meaning with interval data. Consequently, we can add and subtract interval data, but we can't multiply and divide them. Of the four quantitative data sets listed, (1) and (3) are interval data, while (2) and (4) are ratio data.

3. The scores of a sample of 150 MBA applicants on the GMAT, a standardized business graduate school entrance exam administered nationwide

4. The number of female executives employed in each of a sample of 75 manufacturing companies

DEFINITION 1.13

Quantitative data are measurements that are recorded on a naturally occurring numerical scale.

In contrast, qualitative data cannot be measured on a natural numerical scale; they can only be classified into categories.* Examples of qualitative data are as follows:

Suggested Exercises 1.23

1. The political party affiliation (Democrat, Republican, or Independent) in a sample of 50 chief executive officers

2. The defective status (defective or not) of each of 100 computer chips manufactured by Intel

3. The size of a car (subcompact, compact, mid-size, or full-size) rented by each of a sample of 30 business travelers

4. A taste tester's ranking (best, worst, etc.) of four brands of barbecue sauce for a panel of 10 testers

Often, we assign arbitrary numerical values to qualitative data for ease of computer entry and analysis. But these assigned numerical values are simply codes: They cannot be meaningfully added, subtracted, multiplied, or divided. For example, we might code Democrat = 1, Republican = 2, and Independent = 3. Similarly, a taste tester might rank the barbecue sauces from 1 (best) to 4 (worst). These are simply arbitrarily selected numerical codes for the categories and have no utility beyond that.

Teaching Tip

Another way of thinking about qualitative data is that they are non-numerical.

DEFINITION 1.14

Qualitative data are measurements that cannot be measured on a natural numerical scale; they can only be classified into one of a group of categories.

EXAMPLE 1.5   DATA TYPES

Problem   Chemical and manufacturing plants sometimes discharge toxic-waste materials such as DDT into nearby rivers and streams. These toxins can adversely affect the plants and animals inhabiting the river and the river bank. The U.S. Army Corps of Engineers conducted a study of fish in the Tennessee River (in Alabama) and its three tributary creeks: Flint Creek, Limestone Creek, and Spring Creek. A total of 144 fish were captured and the following variables measured for each:

Qualitative

Qualitative

1. River/creek where each fish was captured

2. Species (channel catfish, largemouth bass, or smallmouth buffalofish)

---

*Qualitative data can be subclassified as either *nominal data* or *ordinal data*. The categories of an ordinal data set can be ranked or meaningfully ordered, but the categories of a nominal data set can't be ordered. Of the four qualitative data sets listed above, (1) and (2) are nominal and (3) and (4) are ordinal.

Quantitative   **3.** Length (centimeters)

Quantitative   **4.** Weight (grams)

Quantitative   **5.** DDT concentration (parts per million)

Classify each of the five variables measured as quantitative or qualitative.

Solution   The variables length, weight, and DDT are quantitative because each is measured on a numerical scale: length in centimeters, weight in grams, and DDT in parts per million. In contrast, river/creek and species cannot be measured quantitatively: They can only be classified into categories (e.g., channel catfish, largemouth bass, and smallmouth buffalofish for species). Consequently, data on river/creek and species are qualitative.

Look Back It is essential that you understand whether data are quantitative or qualitative in nature, since the statistical method appropriate for describing, reporting, and analyzing the data depends on the data type (quantitative or qualitative).

Now Work   *Exercise 1.16*

■ ■ ■

We demonstrate many useful methods for analyzing quantitative and qualitative data in the remaining chapters of the text. But first, we discuss some important ideas on data collection.

1.6   Collecting Data

Once you decide on the type of data—quantitative or qualitative—appropriate for the problem at hand, you'll need to collect the data. Generally, you can obtain the data in four different ways:

1. Data from a *published source*
2. Data from a *designed experiment*
3. Data from a *survey*
4. Data collected *observationally*

Sometimes, the data set of interest has already been collected for you and is available in a **published source**, such as a book, journal, newspaper or Internet Web site. For example, you may want to examine and summarize the unemployment rates (i.e., percentages of eligible workers who are unemployed) in the 50 states of the United States. You can find this data set (as well as numerous other data sets) at your library in the *Statistical Abstract of the United States*, published annually by the U.S. government. Similarly, someone who is interested in monthly mortgage applications for new home construction would find this data set in the *Survey of Current Business*, another government publication. Other examples of published data sources include *The Wall Street Journal* (financial data) and *The Sporting News* (sports information).*

Teaching Tip
Bring examples from a journal or newspaper to class to illustrate published sources of data.

*With published data, we often make a distinction between the *primary source* and *secondary source*. If the publisher is the original collector of the data, the source is primary. Otherwise, the data are secondary source data.

A second method of collecting data involves conducting a **designed experiment,** in which the researcher exerts strict control over the units (people, objects, or events) in the study. For example, a recent medical study investigated the potential of aspirin in preventing heart attacks. Volunteer physicians were divided into two groups—the *treatment* group and the *control* group. In the treatment group, each physician took one aspirin tablet a day for one year, while each physician in the control group took an aspirin-free placebo (no drug) made to look like an aspirin tablet. The researchers, not the physicians under study, controlled who received the aspirin (the treatment) and who received the placebo. As you will learn in Chapter 10, a properly designed experiment allows you to extract more information from the data than is possible with an uncontrolled study.

Surveys are a third source of data. With a **survey,** the researcher samples a group of people, asks one or more questions, and records the responses. Probably the most familiar type of survey is the political polls conducted by any one of a number of organizations (e.g., Harris, Gallup, Roper, and CNN) and designed to predict the outcome of a political election. Another familiar survey is the Nielsen survey, which provides the major television networks with information on the most watched TV programs. Surveys can be conducted through the mail, with telephone interviews, or with in-person interviews. Although in-person interviews are more expensive than mail or telephone surveys, they may be necessary when complex information must be collected.

Finally, observational studies can be employed to collect data. In an **observational study,** the researcher observes the experimental units in their natural setting and records the variable(s) of interest. For example, a company psychologist might observe and record the level of "Type A" behavior of a sample of assembly line workers. Similarly, a finance researcher may observe and record the closing stock prices of companies that are acquired by other firms on the day prior to the buyout and compare them to the closing prices on the day the acquisition is announced. Unlike a designed experiment, an observational study is one in which the researcher makes no attempt to control any aspect of the experimental units.

Regardless of the data collection method employed, it is likely that the data will be a sample from some population. And if we wish to apply inferential statistics, we must obtain a *representative sample.*

DEFINITION 1.15

A **representative sample** exhibits characteristics typical of those possessed by the population of interest.

For example, consider a political poll conducted during a presidential election year. Assume the pollster wants to estimate the percentage of all 120,000,000 registered voters in the United States who favor the incumbent president. The pollster would be unwise to base the estimate on survey data collected for a sample of voters from the incumbent's own state. Such an estimate would almost certainly be *biased* high.

The most common way to satisfy the representative sample requirement is to select a random sample. A **random sample** ensures that every subset of fixed size in the population has the same chance of being included in the sample. If the pollster samples 1,500 of the 120,000,000 voters in the population so that every subset of 1,500 voters has an equal chance of being selected, he has devised a random sample.

The procedure for selecting a random sample is discussed in Chapter 3. Here, however, let's look at two examples involving actual sampling studies.

Teaching Tip

Random samples are the easiest sampling procedure that will ensure a representative sample.

DEFINITION 1.16

A **random sample** of n experimental units is a sample selected from the population in such a way that every different sample of size n has an equal chance of selection.

EXAMPLE 1.6   METHOD OF DATA COLLECTION

Problem   What percentage of Web users are addicted to the Internet? To find out, a psychologist designed a series of 10 questions based on a widely used set of criteria for gambling addiction and distributed them through the Web site. *ABCNews.com*. (A sample question: "Do you use the Internet to escape problems?") A total of 17,251 Web users responded to the questionnaire. If participants answered "yes" to at least half of the questions, they were viewed as addicted. The findings, released at the 1999 annual meeting of the American Psychological Association, revealed that 990 respondents, or 5.7%, are addicted to the Internet (*Tampa Tribune*, Aug. 23, 1999).

Survey

All Internet users

Unclear

a.   Identify the data collection method.

b.   Identify the target population.

c.   Are the sample data representative of the population?

Solution   **a.**   The data collection method is a survey: 17,251 Internet users responded to the questions posed at the *ABCNews.com* Web site.

b.   Since the Web site can be accessed by anyone surfing the Internet, presumably the target population is *all* Internet users.

c.   Because the 17,251 respondents clearly make up a subset of the target population, they do form a sample. Whether or not the sample is representative is unclear, since we are given no information on the 17,251 respondents. However, a survey like this one in which the respondents are *self-selected* (i.e., each Internet user who saw the survey chose whether or not to respond to it) often suffers from *nonresponse bias*. It is possible that many Internet users who chose not to respond (or who never saw the survey) would have answered the questions differently, leading to a higher (or lower) percentage of affirmative answers.

Look Back   Any inferences based on survey samples that employ self-selection are suspect due to potential nonresponse bias.

■ ■ ■

EXAMPLE 1.7   DATA COLLECTION METHOD; REPRESENTATIVE DATA

Problem   Marketers use wording such as "was $100, now $80" to indicate a price promotion. The promotion is typically compared to the retailer's previous price or to a competitor's price. A study in the *Journal of Consumer Research* (September 1996) investigated whether between-store comparisons result in greater perceptions of value by consumers than within-store comparisons. Suppose 50 consumers were randomly selected from all consumers in a designated market area to participate in the study. The researchers randomly assigned 25 consumers to read a within-store price promotion advertisement ("was $100, now $80") and 25 consumers to read a between-store price promotion ("$100 there, $80 here"). The consumers then gave their opinion on the value of the discount offer on a 10-point scale (where 1 = lowest value and 10 = highest value). The value opinions of the two groups of consumers were compared.

Designed Experiment

Yes

a. Identify the data collection method.

b. Are the sample data representative of the target population?

Solution

a. Here, the experimental units are the consumers. Since the researchers controlled which price promotion ad—"within-store" or "between-store"—the experimental units (consumers) were assigned to, a designed experiment was used to collect the data.

b. The sample of 50 consumers was randomly selected from all consumers in the designated market area. If the target population is all consumers in this market, it is likely that the sample is representative. However, the researchers warn that the sample data should not be used to make inferences about consumer behavior in other, dissimilar markets.

Look Back By using randomization in a designed experiment, the researcher is attempting to eliminate different types of bias, including self-selection bias.

Now Work *Exercise 1.15*

▪ ▪ ▪

Statistics in Action Revisited

Identifying the Data Collection Method and Data Type

In the Food Research and Action Center (FRAC) study, reported on a *20/20* television program, parents of American children were asked to respond to questions concerning the amount of food they prepare for their children's meals. Although details of the study were not broadcast, it is very likely that the data were collected using a survey of parents. A sampling scheme was used to select the parents; then each parent was asked a series of questions on food for meals. Each question (e.g., "Do you ever cut the size of meals?") is phrased to elicit a "yes" or "no" response. Thus, the data produced for each question are categorical in nature—qualitative data.

1.7   The Role of Statistics in Managerial Decision-Making

According to H. G. Wells, author of such science fiction classics as *The War of the Worlds* and *The Time Machine*, "Statistical thinking will one day be as necessary for efficient citizenship as the ability to read and write." Written more than a hundred years ago, Wells's prediction is proving true today.

Biography

**H. G. WELLS
(1866–1946)
Writer and
Novelist**

English-born Herbert George Wells published his first novel, *The Time Machine,* in 1895 as a parody of the English class division and as a satirical warning that human progress is inevitable. Although most famous as a science fiction novelist, Wells was a prolific writer as a journalist, sociologist, historian, and philosopher. Wells's prediction about statistical thinking (see p. 21) is just one of a plethora of observations he made about life on this world. Here are a few more of H.G. Wells's more famous quotes:

"Advertising is legalized lying."

"Crude classification and false generalizations are the curse of organized life."

"The crisis of today is the joke of tomorrow."

"Fools make researchers and wise men exploit them."

"The only true measure of success is the ration between what we might have done and what we might have been on the one hand, and the thing we have made and the things we have made of ourselves on the other."

The growth in data collection associated with scientific phenomena, business operations, and government activities (quality control, statistical auditing, forecasting, etc.) has been remarkable in the past several decades. Every day the media present us with the published results of political, economic, and social surveys. In increasing government emphasis on drug and product testing, for example, we see vivid evidence of the need to be able to evaluate data sets intelligently. Consequently, each of us has to develop a discerning sense—an ability to use rational thought to interpret and understand the meaning of data. This ability can help you make intelligent decisions, inferences, and generalizations; that is, it helps you *think critically* using statistics.

DEFINITION 1.17

Statistical thinking involves applying rational thought and the science of statistics to critically assess data and inferences. Fundamental to the thought process is that variation exists in populations and process data.

To gain some insight into the role statistics plays in critical thinking, let's look at a study evaluated by a group of 27 mathematics and statistics teachers attending an American Statistical Association course called "Chance." Consider the following excerpt from an article describing the problem.

There are few issues in the news that are not in some way statistical. Take one. Should motorcyclists be required by law to wear helmets? . . . In "The Case for No Helmets" (New York Times, June 17, 1995), Dick Teresi, editor of a magazine for Harley-Davidson bikers, argued that helmets may actually kill, since in collisions at speeds greater than 15 miles an hour the heavy helmet may protect the head but snap the spine. [Teresi] citing a "study," said "nine states without helmet laws had a lower fatality rate (3.05 deaths per 10,000 motorcycles) than those that mandated helmets (3.38)," and "in a survey of 2,500 [at a rally], 98% of the respondents opposed such laws."

[The course instructors] asked: After reading this [New York Times] piece, do you think it is safer to ride a motorcycle without a helmet? Do you think 98% might be a valid estimate of bikers who oppose helmet laws? What further statistical information would you like? [From Cohn, V. "Chance in college curriculum," AmStat News, Aug.–Sept. 1995, No. 223, p. 2.]

You can use "statistical thinking" to help you critically evaluate the study. For example, before you can evaluate the validity of the 98% estimate, you would want to know how the data were collected for the study cited by the editor of the biker magazine. If a survey was conducted, it's possible that the 2,500 bikers in the sample were not selected at random from the target population of all bikers, but rather were "self-selected." (Remember, they were all attending a rally—a rally likely for bikers who oppose the law.) If the respondents were likely to have strong opinions regarding the helmet law (e.g., strongly oppose the law), the resulting estimate is probably biased high. Also, if the biased sample was intentional, with the sole purpose to mislead the public, the researchers would be guilty of **unethical statistical practice.**

You'd also want more information about the study comparing the motorcycle fatality rate of the nine states without a helmet law to those states that mandate helmets. Were the data obtained from a published source? Were all 50 states included in the study? That is, are you seeing sample data or population data? Furthermore, do the helmet laws vary among states? If so, can you really compare the fatality rates?

These questions led the Chance group to the discovery of two scientific and statistically sound studies on helmets. The first, a UCLA study of nonfatal injuries, disputed the charge that helmets shift injuries to the spine. The second study reported a dramatic *decline* in motorcycle crash deaths after California passed its helmet law.

As in the motorcycle helmet study, many statistical studies are based on survey data. Most of the problems with these surveys result from the use of *nonrandom samples*. These samples are subject to potential errors, such as *selection bias, nonresponse bias* (recall Example 1.6), and *measurement error*. Researchers who are aware of these problems and continue to use the sample data to make inferences are practicing unethical statistics.

DEFINITION 1.18

Selection bias results when a subset of the experimental units in the population is excluded so that these units have no chance of being selected in the sample.

DEFINITION 1.19

Nonresponse bias results when the researchers conducting a survey or study are unable to obtain data on all experimental units selected for the sample.

DEFINITION 1.20

Measurement error refers to inaccuracies in the values of the data recorded. In surveys, the error may be due to ambiguous or leading questions and the interviewer's effect on the respondent.

Statistics in Action Revisited

Ethics of a Statistical Study

The Food Research and Action Center (FRAC) concluded that one in four American children is hungry or at risk of hunger. The FRAC based their conclusions on the following questions asked to a sample of parents:

Question 1: "Do you ever cut the size of meals?"

Question 2: "Do you ever eat less than you feel you should?"

Question 3: "Did you ever rely on limited numbers of foods to feed your children because you were running out of money to buy food for a meal?"

Several problems lead a critical thinker to cast doubt on the validity of the inference. First, the wording in the questions does not match exactly the inferential statement about hungry children. It is not clear whether a "yes" response implies that a child is hungry or at risk of hunger. Second, FRAC does not explain how many of the questions must be answered "yes" before a parent is classified as having a child at risk of hunger. Do all three questions need to be answered affirmatively, or at least one of the three? These ambiguities will likely result in measurement error in the data.

Finally, we don't know how the sampled parents were selected. Were they randomly selected from all parents in the United States, or (more likely) were they self-selected or selected from a group of parents with an agenda (e.g., on welfare)? Thus, the potential for selection and/or nonresponse bias is extremely high.

Successful managers rely heavily on statistical thinking to help them make decisions. The role statistics can play in managerial decision-making is displayed in the flow diagram in Figure 1.5. Every managerial decision-making problem begins with a real-world problem. This problem is then formulated in managerial terms and framed as a managerial question. The next sequence of steps (proceeding counterclockwise around the flow diagram) identifies the role that statistics can play in this process. The managerial question is translated into a statistical question, the sample data are collected and analyzed, and the statistical question is answered. The next step in the process is using the answer to the statistical question to reach an answer to the managerial question. The answer to the managerial question may suggest a reformulation of the original managerial problem, suggest a new managerial question, or lead to the solution of the managerial problem.

Figure 1.5

Flow diagram showing the role of statistics in managerial decision making

Source: Chervany, Benson, and Iyer (1980)

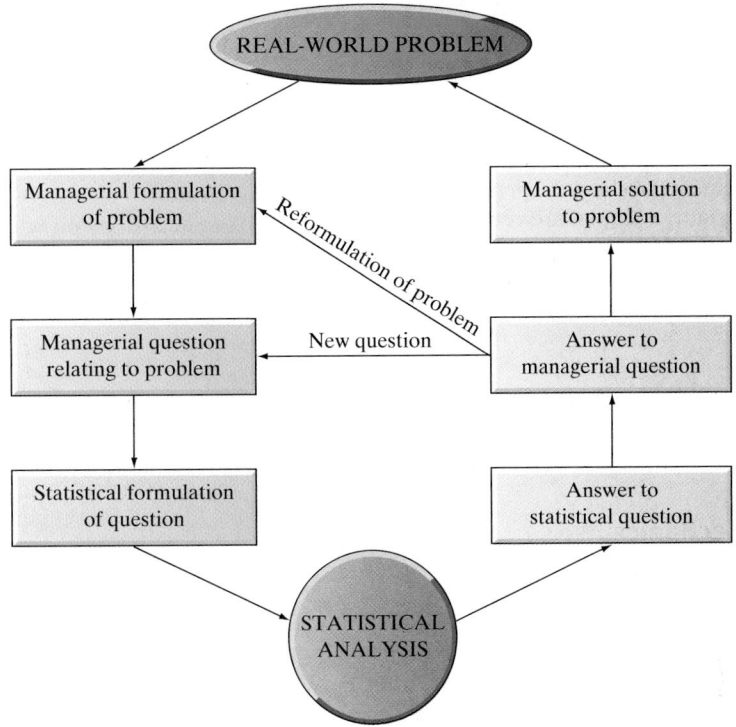

One of the most difficult steps in the decision-making process—one that requires a cooperative effort among managers and statisticians—is the translation of the managerial question into statistical terms (for example, into a question about a population). This statistical question must be formulated so that, when answered, it will provide the key to the answer to the managerial question. Thus, as in the game of chess, you must formulate the statistical question with the end result, the solution to the managerial question, in mind.

In the remaining chapters of the text, you'll become familiar with the tools essential for building a firm foundation in statistics and statistical thinking.

Quick Review

Key Terms

Note: Starred (*) terms are from the optional section in this chapter.

Black box*   14
Census   8
Data   5
Descriptive statistics   5
Designed experiment   19
Experimental unit   7
Inference   5

Inferential statistics   5
Measure of reliability   11
Measurement   8
Nonresponse bias   24
Measurement error   24
Observational study   19
Population   7
Process*   13
Published source   18
Qualitative data   17
Quantitative data   17

Random sample   20
Reliability   11
Representative sample   19
Sample   8, 15
Selection bias   23
Statistical inference   9
Statistical thinking   22
Statistics   5
Survey   19
Unethical statistical practice   23
Variable   8

·Summary

- Two types of statistical applications: descriptive and inferential
- Fundamental elements of statistics: population, experimental units, variable, sample, inference, measure of reliability

- Two types of data: quantitative and qualitative
- Data collection methods: published source, designed experiment, survey, and observationally
- Potential problems with nonrandom samples: selection bias, nonresponse bias, measurement error

Exercises 1.1–1.31

Note: Starred (*) exercises are from the optional section in this chapter.

Learning the Mechanics

1.1 What is statistics?

1.2 Explain the difference between descriptive and inferential statistics.

1.3 List and define the four elements of a descriptive statistics problem.

1.4 List and define the five elements of an inferential statistical analysis.

1.5 List the four major methods of collecting data and explain their differences.

1.6 Explain the difference between quantitative and qualitative data.

1.7 Explain how populations and variables differ.

1.8 Explain how populations and samples differ.

1.9 What is a representative sample? What is its value?

1.10 Why would a statistician consider an inference incomplete without an accompanying measure of its reliability?

*1.11 Explain the difference between a population and a process.

1.12 Define statistical thinking.

1.13 Suppose you're given a data set that classifies each sample unit into one of four categories: A, B, C, or D. You plan to create a computer database consisting of these data, and you decide to code the data as A = 1, B = 2, C = 3, and D = 4. Are the data consisting of the classifications A, B, C, and D qualitative or quantitative? After the data are input as 1, 2, 3, or 4, are they qualitative or quantitative? Explain your answers.

Applying the Concepts—Basic

1.14 Refer to the CardWeb.com, Inc., study of credit card purchases in the United States in Section 1.2 (Study 1, p. 6). Recall that the company tracked all credit card purchases during the first quarter of 2003

and measured two variables: (1) the type of credit card used (VISA, MasterCard, American Express, or Discover), and (2) the amount (in dollars) of each purchase.

a. Identify the type (quantitative or qualitative) of each variable measured.   Qualitative, Quantitative

b. Does the data set collected represent a population or a sample? Explain.   Population

1.15 Pollsters regularly conduct opinion polls to determine the popularity rating of the current president. Suppose a poll is to be conducted tomorrow in which 2,000 individuals will be asked whether the president is doing a good or bad job. The 2,000 individuals will be selected by random-digit telephone dialing and asked the question over the phone.

a. What is the relevant population?

b. What is the variable of interest? Is it quantitative or qualitative?

c. What is the sample?   2,000 individuals

d. What is the inference of interest to the pollster?

e. What method of data collection is employed?

f. How likely is the sample to be representative?

1.16 Colleges and universities are requiring an increasing amount of information about applicants before making acceptance and financial aid decisions. Classify each of the following types of data required on a college application as quantitative or qualitative.

a. High school GPA   Quantitative

b. Honors, awards   Qualitative

c. Applicant's score on the SAT or ACT   Quantitative

d. Gender of applicant   Qualitative

e. Parents' income   Quantitative

f. Age of applicant   Quantitative

1.17 Windows is a computer software product made by Microsoft Corporation. In designing Windows NT, Microsoft telephoned thousands of users of Windows 98 (an older version) and asked them how the product could be improved. Assume customers were asked the following questions:

I. Are you the most frequent user of Windows in your household?   Qualitative

II. What is your age?   Quantitative

III. Are the tutorial instructions that accompany Windows helpful?   Qualitative

IV. When using a printer with Windows, do you most frequently use a laser printer or another type of printer?   Qualitative

V. If the speed of Windows could be changed, which one of the following would you prefer: slower, unchanged, or faster?   Qualitative

VI. How many people in your household have used Windows at least once?   Quantitative

Each of these questions defines a variable of interest to the company. Classify the data generated for each variable as quantitative or qualitative. Justify your classification.

1.18 The Cutter Consortium surveyed 154 U.S. companies to determine the extent of their involvement in electronic commerce (called *e-commerce*). Four of the questions they asked follow. (*Internet Week*, September 6, 1999.)

1. Do you have an overall e-commerce strategy?
2. If you don't already have an e-commerce plan, when will you implement one?
3. Are you delivering products over the internet?
4. What was your company's total revenue in the last fiscal year?

a. For each question, determine the variable of interest and classify it as quantitative or qualitative.   1–3: Qualitative; 4: Quantitative

b. Do the data collected for the 154 companies represent a sample or a population? Explain.   Sample

1.19 Refer to *Business Week* "2003 Executive Compensation Scoreboard" described in Section 1.2 (Study 2, p. 6). Data were collected for a sample of 370 chief executive officers. Several of the many variables measured for each CEO include (1) the industry type of the CEO's company (e.g., banking, consumer products, etc.), (2) the CEO's total compensation (in $ millions) for 2002, (3) the CEO's total compensation (in $ millions) for the 3-year period 2000–2002, and (4) the return (in dollars) on a $100 investment in the CEO's company made in 2000.

a. Describe the population of interest to *Business Week*.   All CEOs

b. Identify the type (quantitative or qualitative) of each variable measured.

c. *Business Week* surveyed only CEOs from the top-ranked companies listed in the *Business Week 1000*. Discuss any biases that may exist in the sample.

1.20 The Computer Security Institute (CSI) conducts an annual survey of computer crime at United States businesses. CSI sends survey questionnaires to computer security personnel at all U.S. corporations and government agencies. In 2001, 538 organizations responded to the CSI survey. Sixty-four percent of the respondents admitted unauthorized use of computer systems at their firms during the year. (*Computer Security Issues & Trends*, Spring 2001)

a. Identify the population of interest to CSI.

b. Identify the data collection method used by CSI. Are there any potential biases in the method used?   Survey

c. Describe the variable measured in the CSI survey. Is it quantitative or qualitative?   Qualitative

d. What inference can be made from the study result?

Applying the Concepts—Intermediate

1.21 To help employers better understand what employees value, Fort Lauderdale–based Interim Services, Inc. surveyed a random sample of 1,000 employees in the United States. One question they asked was, "If your employer provides you with mentoring opportunities are you likely to remain in your job for the next five years?" They found that 620 members of the sample said "yes." (*HRMagazine*, Sept. 1999).

a. Identify the population of interest to Interim Services, Inc.   All employees in the U.S.

b. Based on the question posed by Interim Services, Inc., what is the variable of interest?

c. Is the variable quantitative or qualitative? Explain.

d. Describe the sample.   1,000 employees sampled

e. What inference can be made from the results of the survey?

1.22 According to the American Lung Association, lung cancer accounts for 28% of all cancer deaths in the United States. A new type of screening for lung cancer, computed tomography (CT), has been developed. Medical researchers believe CT scans are more sensitive than regular X-rays in pinpointing small tumors. The H. Lee Moffitt Cancer Center at the University of South Florida is currently conducting a clinical trial of 50,000 smokers nationwide to compare the effectiveness of CT scans with X-rays for detecting lung cancer. (*Todays' Tomorrows*, Fall 2002) Each participating smoker is randomly assigned to one of two screening methods, CT or chest X-ray, and his or her progress is tracked over time. The age at which the scanning method first detects a tumor is the variable of interest.

a. Identify the data collection method used by the cancer researchers.   Designed Experiment

b. Identify the experimental units of the study.   A smoker

c. Identify the type (quantitative or qualitative) of the variable measured.   Quantitative

d. Identify the population and sample.   Population–all smokers; Sample–50,000 smokers

e. What is the inference that will ultimately be drawn from the clinical trial?

1.23 All highway bridges in the United States are inspected periodically for structural deficiency by the Federal

Highway Administration (FHWA). Data from the FHWA inspections are compiled into the National Bridge Inventory (NBI). Several of the nearly 100 variables maintained by the NBI are listed below. Classify each variable as quantitative or qualitative.

a. Length of maximum span (feet)   Quantitative
b. Number of vehicle lanes   Quantitative
c. Toll bridge (yes or no)   Qualitative
d. Average daily traffic   Quantitative
e. Condition of deck (good, fair, or poor)   Qualitative
f. Bypass or detour length (miles)   Quantitative
g. Route type (interstate, U.S., state, county, or city)

1.24 Refer to Exercise 1.23. The most recent NBI data were analyzed and the results published in the *Journal of Infrastructure Systems* (June 1995). Using the FHWA inspection ratings, each of the 470,515 highway bridges in the United States was categorized as structurally deficient, functionally obsolete, or safe. About 26% of the bridges were found to be structurally deficient, while 19% were functionally obsolete.

a. What is the variable of interest to the researchers?   Bridge rating
b. Is the variable of part **a** quantitative or qualitative?   Qualitative
c. Is the data set analyzed a population or a sample? Explain.   Population
d. How did the researchers obtain the data for their study?   Observational Study

*1.25 The Wallace Company of Houston is a distributor of pipes, valves, and fittings to the refining, chemical, and petrochemical industries. The company was a recent winner of the Malcolm Baldrige National Quality Award. According to *Small Business Reports* (May 1991), one of the steps the company takes to monitor the quality of its distribution process is to send out a survey twice a year to a subset of its current customers, asking the customers to rate the speed of deliveries, the accuracy of invoices, and the quality of the packaging of the products they have received from Wallace.

a. Describe the process studied.
b. Describe the variables of interest.
c. Describe the sample.
d. Describe the inferences of interest.
e. What are some of the factors that are likely to affect the reliability of the inferences?

1.26 To assess how extensively accounting firms in New York State use sampling methods in auditing their clients, the New York Society of CPAs mailed a questionnaire to 800 New York accounting firms employing two or more professionals. They received responses from 179 firms of which four responses were unusable and 12 reported they had no audit practice. The questionnaire asked firms whether they use audit sampling methods and, if so, whether or not they use random sampling. (*CPA Journal,* July 1995)

a. Identify the population, the variables, the sample, and the inferences of interest to the New York Society of CPAs.
b. Speculate as to what could have made four of the responses unusable.
c. In later chapters you will learn that the reliability of an inference is related to the size of the sample used. In addition to sample size, what factors might affect the reliability of the inferences drawn in the mail survey described above?

Applying the Concepts—Advanced

1.27 The *Journal of Retailing* (Spring 1988) published a study of the relationship between job satisfaction and the degree of *Machiavellian orientation*. Briefly, the Machiavellian orientation is one in which the executive exerts very strong control, even to the point of deception and cruelty, over the employees he or she supervises. The authors administered a questionnaire to each in a sample of 218 department store executives and obtained both a job satisfaction score and a Machiavellian rating. They concluded that those with higher job satisfaction scores are likely to have a lower "Mach" rating.

a. What is the population from which the sample was selected?   All dept. store executives
b. What variables were measured by the authors?
c. Identify the sample.   218 executives
d. Identify the data collection method used.
e. What inference was made by the authors?

1.28 Media reports suggest that disgruntled shareholders are becoming more willing to put pressure on corporate management. Is this an impression caused by a few recent high-profile cases involving a few large investors, or is shareholder activism widespread? To answer this question the Wirthlin Group, an opinion research organization in McLean. Virginia, sampled and questioned 240 large investors (money managers, mutual fund managers, institutional investors, etc.) in the United States. One question they asked was: Have you written or called a corporate director to express your views? They found that a surprisingly large 40% of the sample had. (*New York Times,* Oct. 31, 1995)

a. Identify the population of interest to the Wirthlin Group.   All U.S. large investors
b. Based on the question the Wirthlin Group asked, what is the variable of interest?
c. Describe the sample.   240 large investors
d. What inference can be made from the results of the survey?

1.29 *Corporate merger* is a means through which one firm (the bidder) acquires control of the assets of another firm (the target). During the late 1990s there was a frenzy of bank mergers in the United States, as the banking industry consolidated into more efficient and more competitive units.

a. Construct a brief questionnaire (two or three questions) that could be used to query a sample of bank presidents concerning their opinions of why the industry is consolidating and whether it will consolidate further.

b. Describe the population about which inferences could be made from the results of the survey.

c. Discuss the pros and cons of sending the questionnaire to all bank presidents versus a sample of 200.

*1.30 Coca-Cola and Schweppes Beverages Limited (CCSB), which was formed in 1987, is 49% owned by the Coca-Cola Company. According to *Industrial Management and Data Systems* (Vol. 92, 1992), CCSB's Wakefield plant can produce 4,000 cans of soft drink per minute. The automated process consists of measuring and dispensing the raw ingredients into storage vessels to create the syrup, and then injecting the syrup, along with carbon dioxide, into the beverage cans. In order to monitor the subprocess that adds carbon dioxide to the cans, five filled cans are pulled off the line every 15 minutes and the amount of carbon dioxide in each of these five is measured to determine whether the amounts are within prescribed limits.

a. Describe the process studied.

b. Describe the variable of interest.

c. Describe the sample.

d. Describe the inference of interest.

e. *Brix* is a unit for measuring sugar concentration. If a technician is assigned the task of estimating the average brix level of all 240,000 cans of beverage stored in a warehouse near Wakefield, will the technician be examining a process or a population? Explain.

1.31 The employment status (employed or unemployed) of each individual in the U.S. workforce is a set of data that is of interest to economists, businesspeople, and sociologists. To obtain information about the employment status of the workforce, the U.S. Bureau of the Census conducts what is known as the *Current Population Survey*. Each month interviewers visit about 59,000 of the 98 million households in the United States and question the occupants over 14 years of age about their employment status. Their responses enable the Bureau of the Census to *estimate* the percentage of people in the labor force who are unemployed (the *unemployment rate*).

a. Define the population of interest to the Census Bureau.   All U.S. people over 14 years old

b. What variable is being measured? Is it quantitative or qualitative?

c. Is the problem of interest to the Census Bureau descriptive or inferential?   Inferential

d. In order to monitor the rate of unemployment, it is essential to have a definition of "unemployed." Different economists and even different countries define it in various ways. Develop your own definition of an "unemployed person." Your definition should answer such questions as: Are students on summer vacation unemployed? Are college professors who do not teach summer school unemployed? At what age are people considered to be eligible for the workforce? Are people who are out of work but not actively seeking a job unemployed?

REFERENCES

Careers in Statistics, American Statistical Association, Biometric Society, Institute of Mathematical Statistics and Statistical Society of Canada, 1995.

Cochran, W. G. *Sampling Techniques,* 3rd ed. New York: Wiley, 1977.

Deming, W. E. *Sample Design in Business Research.* New York: Wiley, 1963.

Ethical Guidelines for Statistical Practice, American Statistical Association, 1995.

Hansen, M. H., Hurwitz, W. N., and Madow, W. G. *Sample Survey Methods and Theory,* Vol. 1. New York: Wiley, 1953.

Kirk, R. E. ed. *Statistical Issues: A Reader for the Behavioral Sciences.* Monterey, Ca.: Brooks/Cole, 1972.

Kish, L. *Survey Sampling.* New York: Wiley, 1965.

Scheaffer, R., Mendenhall, W., and Ott, R. L. *Elementary Survey Sampling,* 2nd ed. Boston: Duxbury, 1979.

Tanur, J. M., Mosteller, F., Kruskal, W. H., Link, R. E., Pieters, R. S., and Rising, G. R. *Statistics: A Guide to the Unknown* (E. L. Lehmann, special editor). San Francisco: Holden-Day, 1989.

What Is a Survey?, Section on Survey Research Methods, American Statistical Association, 1995.

Yamane, T. *Elementary Sampling Theory,* 3rd ed. Englewood Cliffs, N.J.: Prentice Hall, 1967.

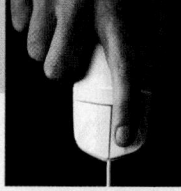

Using Technology

1.1 Creating and Listing Data in SPSS

Upon entering into an SPSS session, you will see a screen similar to Figure 1.S.1. The main portion of the screen is an empty spreadsheet, with columns representing variables and rows representing observations (or cases). The very top of the screen is the SPSS main menu bar, with buttons for the different functions and procedures available in SPSS. Once you have entered data into the spreadsheet, you can analyze the data by clicking the appropriate menu buttons.

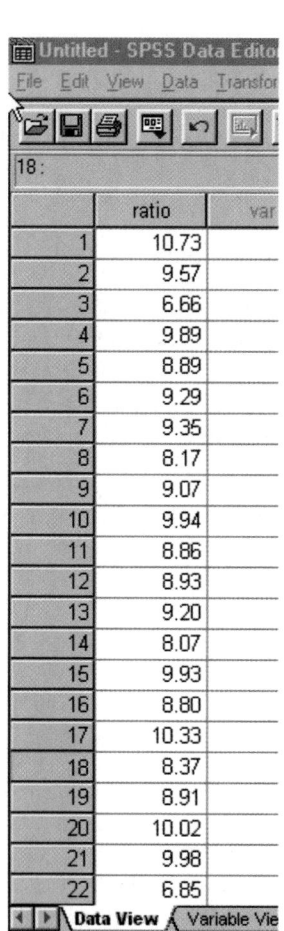

Figure 1.S.2
Data entered into the SPSS spreadsheet

Figure 1.S.1
Initial screen viewed by SPSS user

You can create an SPSS data file by entering data directly into the spreadsheet. Figure 1.S.2 shows data entered on a variable called "Ratio". The variables (columns) can be named by selecting the "Variable View" button at the bottom of the screen and typing in the name of each variable.

If the data are saved in an external data file (e.g., the *Business Week* Executive Compensation Scoreboard data set), you can access the data using the options available in SPSS. Click the "File" button on the menu bar, then click "Read Text Data", as shown in Figure 1.S.3. The dialog box shown in Figure 1.S.4 will appear.

Specify the disk drive and folder that contains the data file, click on the data file, then click "Open", as shown in Figure 1.S.4. This will invoke the SPSS Text Import Wizard. The Text Import Wizard presents a series of six screen menus, the first of which is shown in Figure 1.S.5. Make the appropriate selections on the screen, and click "Next" to go to the next screen. When finished, click "Finish". The SPSS spreadsheet will reappear with the data from the external data file, as shown in Figure 1.S.6.

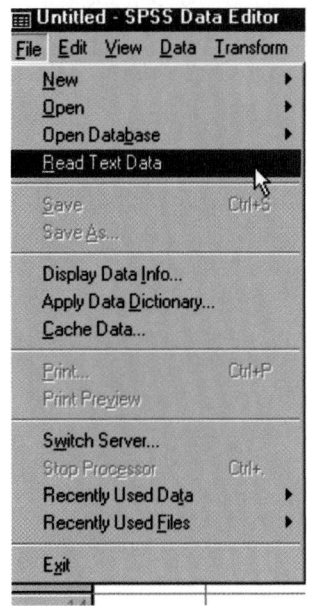

Figure 1.S.3
SPSS options for reading data from an external file

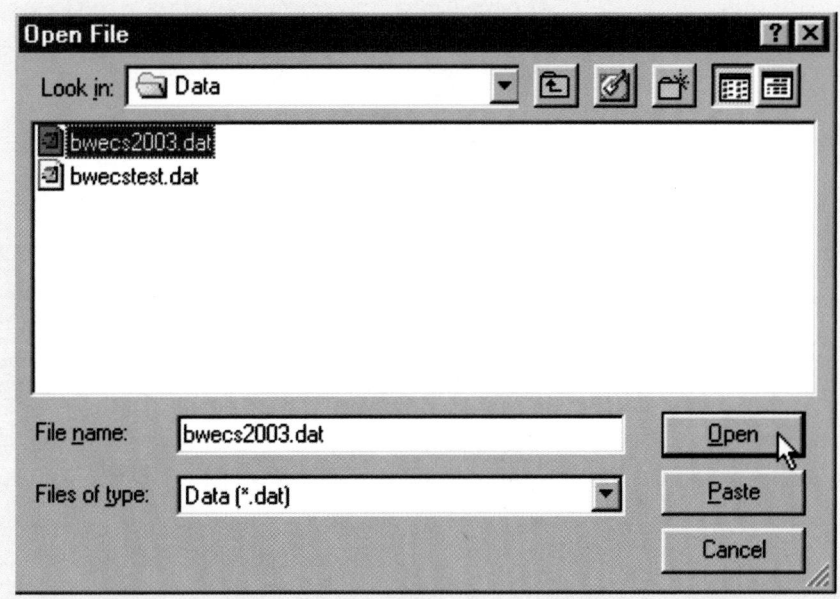

Figure 1.S.4
Selecting the external data file

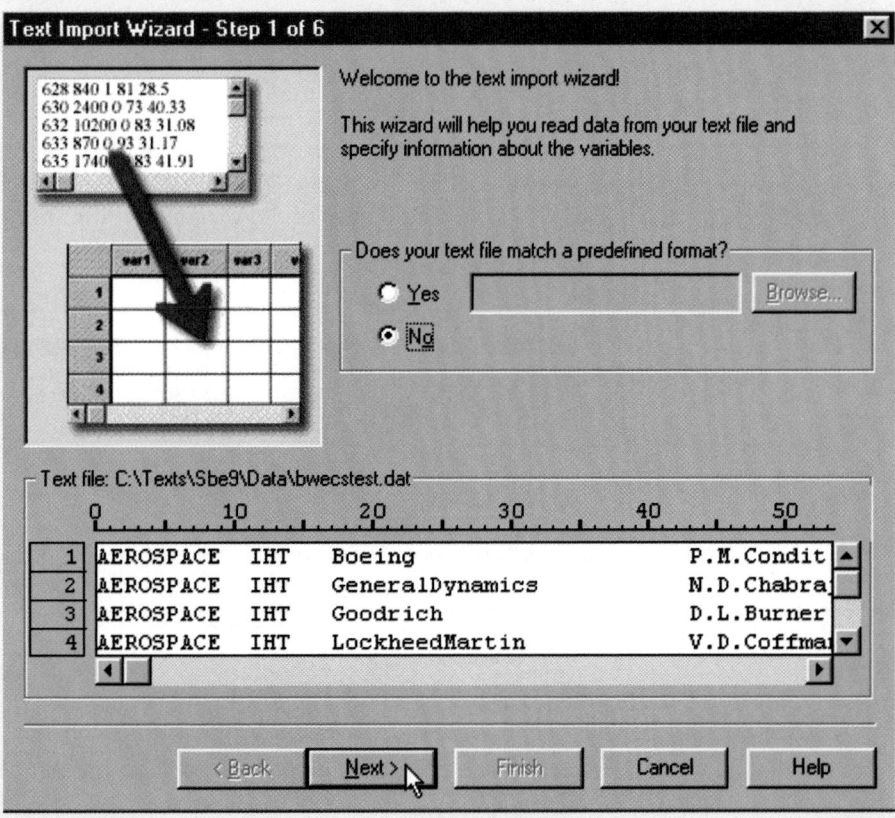

Figure 1.S.5
The SPSS Text Import Wizard, Screen 1

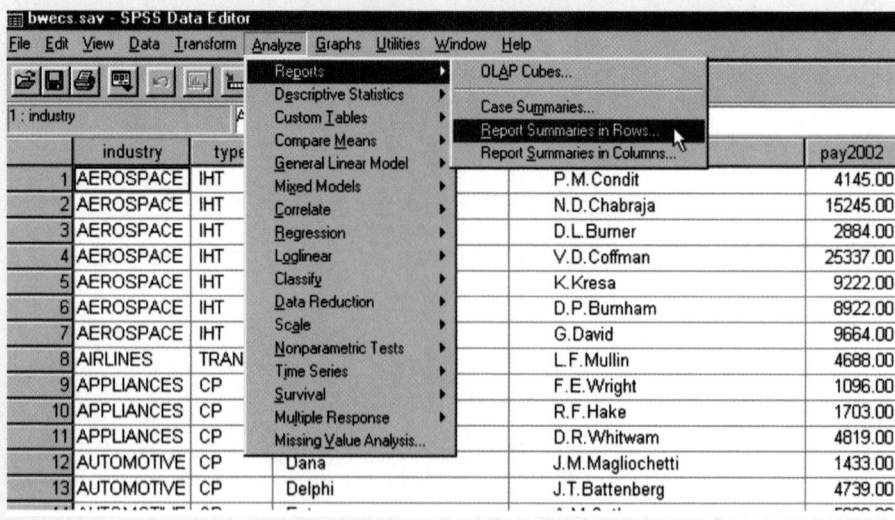

	v1	v2	v3	v4	v5	v6
1	AEROSPACE	IHT	Boeing	P.M.Condit	4145.00	27794.00
2	AEROSPACE	IHT	GeneralDynamics	N.D.Chabraja	15245.00	31367.00
3	AEROSPACE	IHT	Goodrich	D.L.Burner	2884.00	7449.00
4	AEROSPACE	IHT	LockheedMartin	V.D.Coffman	25337.00	47702.00
5	AEROSPACE	IHT	NorthropGrumman	K.Kresa	9222.00	23927.00
6	AEROSPACE	IHT	Raytheon	D.P.Burnham	8922.00	19591.00
7	AEROSPACE	IHT	UnitedTech.	G.David	9664.00	51136.00
8	AIRLINES	TRAN	DeltaAirLines	L.F.Mullin	4688.00	9931.00
9	APPLIANCES	CP	Leggett&Platt	F.E.Wright	1096.00	5017.00
10	APPLIANCES	CP	Maytag	R.F.Hake	1703.00	.
11	APPLIANCES	CP	Whirlpool	D.R.Whitwam	4819.00	11381.00
12	AUTOMOTIVE	CP	Dana	J.M.Magliochetti	1433.00	4416.00
13	AUTOMOTIVE	CP	Delphi	J.T.Battenberg	4739.00	13403.00
14	AUTOMOTIVE	CP	Eaton	A.M.Cutler	5838.00	13045.00
15	AUTOMOTIVE	CP	Paccar	M.C.Pigott	3225.00	7748.00

Figure 1.S.6
The SPSS spreadsheet with the imported data

Reminder: The variables (columns) can be named by selecting the "Variable View" button at the bottom of the spreadsheet screen and typing in the name of each variable.

To obtain a listing (printout) of your data, click on the "Analyze" button on the SPSS main menu bar, then click on "Reports", then on "Report Summaries in Rows" (see Figure 1.S.7). The resulting menu, or dialog box, appears as in Figure 1.S.8. Enter the names of the variables you want to print in the "Data Columns"

Figure 1.S.7
SPSS menu options for obtaining a list of your data

Figure 1.S.8
Report data dialog box

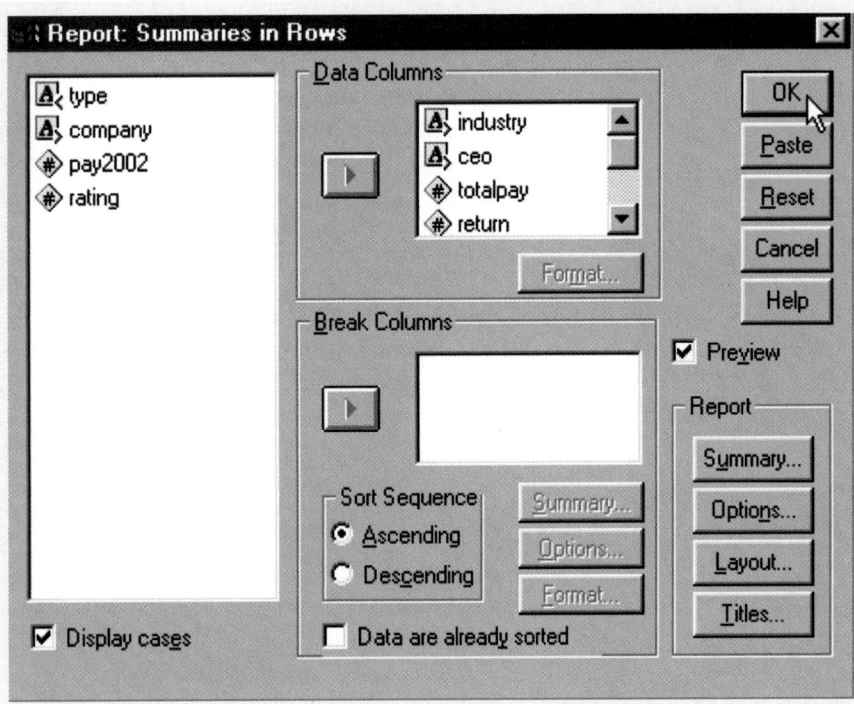

box (you can do this by simply clicking on the variables), check the "Display cases" box at the bottom left, then click "OK". The printout will show up on your screen.

1.2 Creating and Listing Data in MINITAB

Upon entering into a MINITAB session, you will see a screen similar to Figure 1.M.1. The bottom portion of the screen is an empty spreadsheet—called a

Figure 1.M.1
Initial screen viewed by MINITAB user

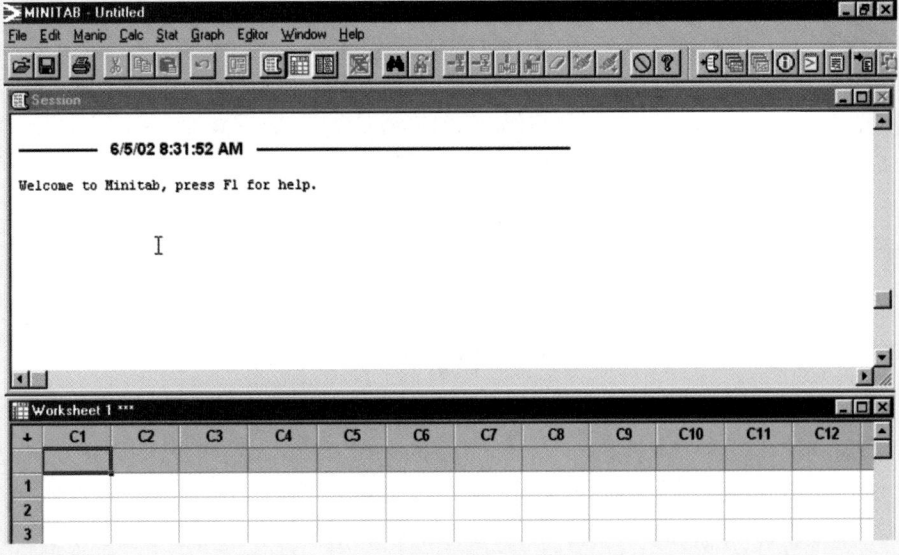

MINITAB worksheet—with columns representing variables and rows representing observations (or cases). The very top of the screen is the MINITAB main menu bar, with buttons for the different functions and procedures available in MINITAB. Once you have entered data into the spreadsheet, you can analyze the data by clicking the appropriate menu buttons. The results will appear in the Session window.

You can create a MINITAB data file by entering data directly into the worksheet. Figure 1.M.2 shows data entered for a variable called "Ratio". The variables (columns) can be named by typing in the name of each variable in the box below the column number.

If the data are saved in an external data file (e.g., the *Business Week* Executive Compensation Scoreboard data set), you can access the data using the options available in MINITAB. Click the "File" button on the menu bar, then click "Open Worksheet", as shown in Figure 1.M.3. The dialog box shown in Figure 1.M.4 will appear.

Specify the disk drive and folder that contains the external data file and the file type, then click on the file name, as shown in Figure 1.M.4. If the data set contains qualitative data or data with special characters, click on the "Options" button as shown in Figure 1.M.4. The Options dialog box, shown in Figure 1.M.5, will appear. Specify the appropriate options for the data set, then click "OK" to

Figure 1.M.2
Data entered into the
MINITAB worksheet

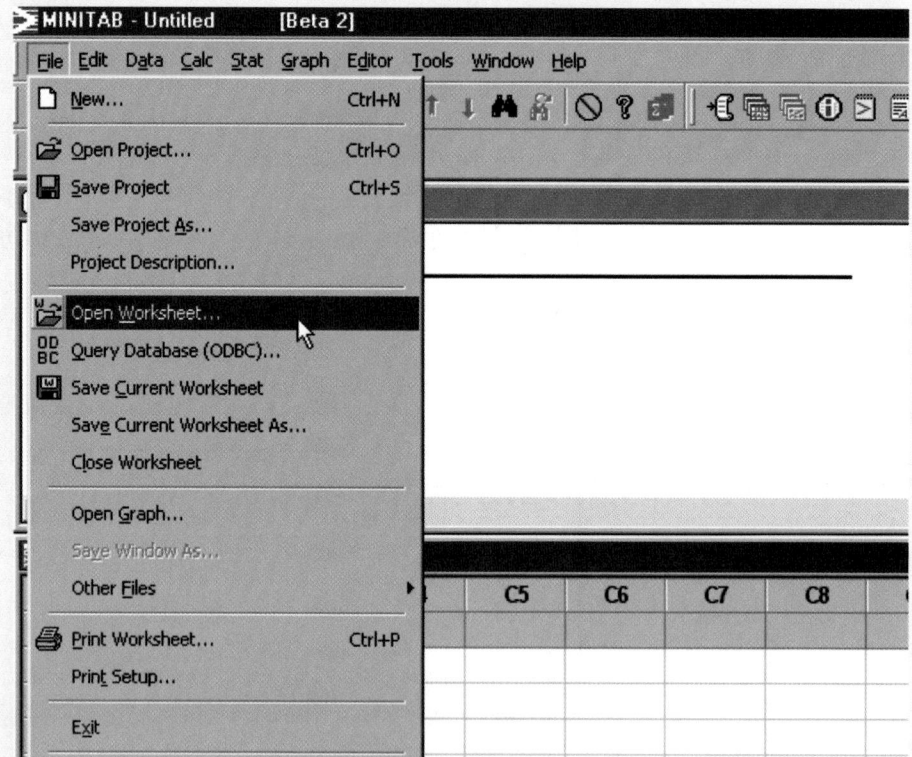

Figure 1.M.3
MINITAB options for reading data from an external file

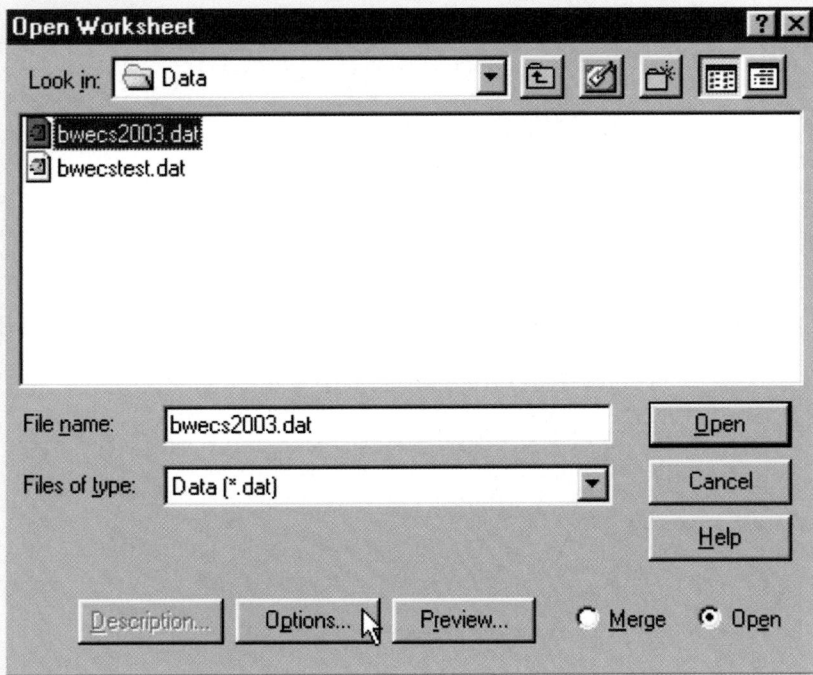

Figure 1.M.4
Selecting the external data file

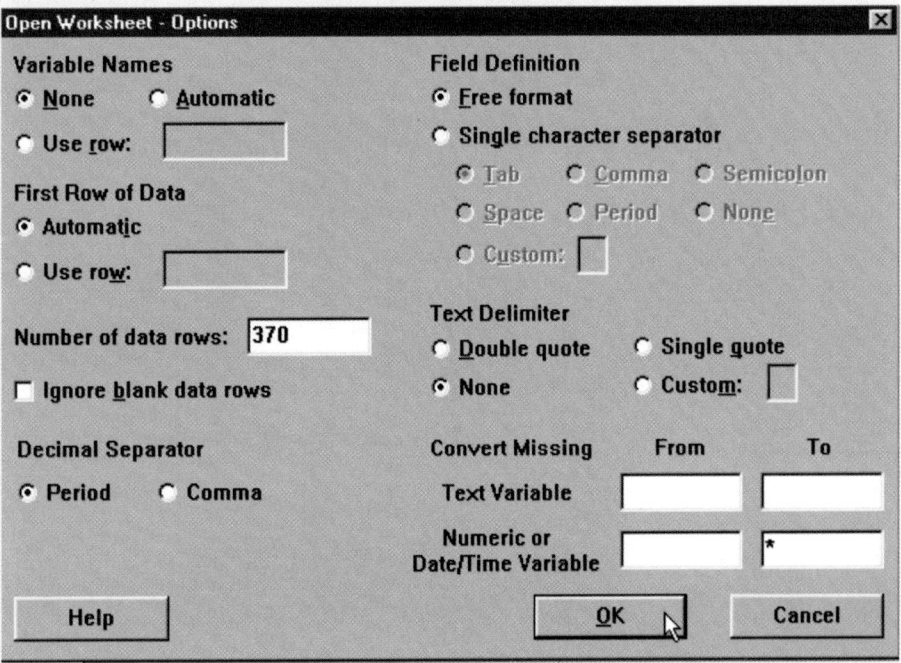

Figure 1.M.5
Selecting the data input options

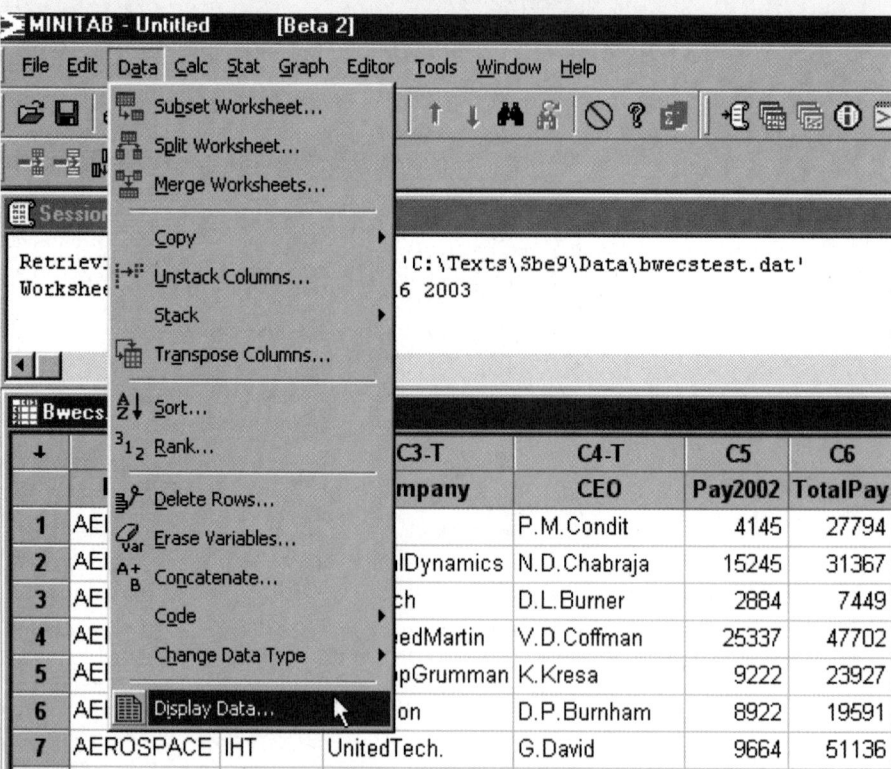

Figure 1.M.6
The MINITAB worksheet with the imported data

Figure 1.M.7
MINITAB menu options for obtaining a list of your data

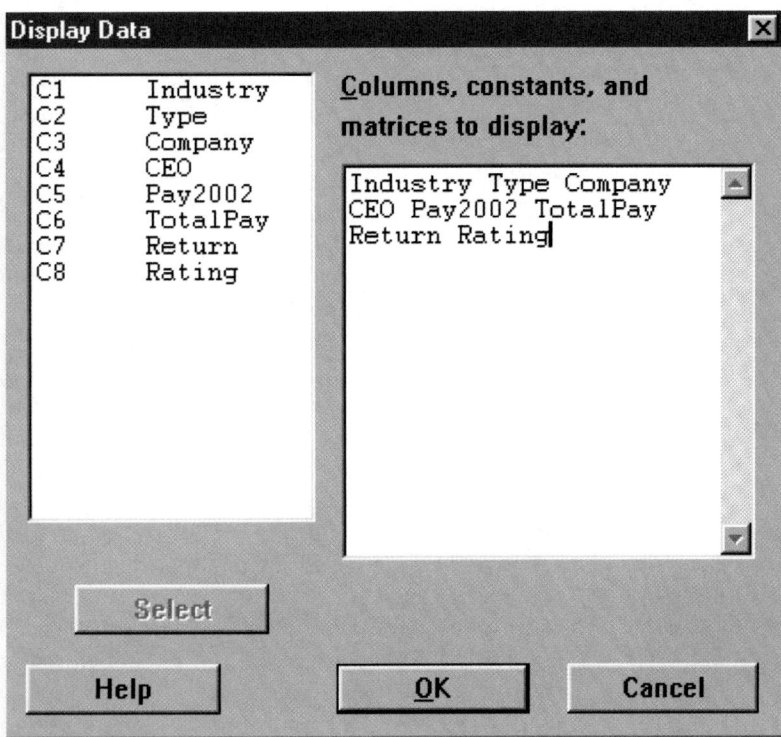

Figure 1.M.8
Display data dialog box

return to the "Open Worksheet" dialog box (Figure 1.M.4). Click "Open" and the MINITAB worksheet will appear with the data from the external data file, as shown in Figure 1.M.6.

Reminder: The variables (columns) can be named by typing in the name of each variable in the box under the column number.

To obtain a listing (printout) of your data, click on the "Data" button on the MINITAB main menu bar, then click on "Display Data" (see Figure 1.M.7). The resulting menu, or dialog box, appears as in Figure 1.M.8. Enter the names of the variables you want to print in the "Columns, constants, and matrices to display" box (you can do this by simply clicking on the variables), then click "OK". The printout will show up on your MINITAB session screen.

1.3 Creating and Listing Data in EXCEL

Upon entering into an EXCEL session, you will see a screen similar to Figure 1.E.1. The majority of the screen window is comprised of a spreadsheet—called an EXCEL workbook—with columns (labeled A, B, C, etc.) representing variables and rows representing observations (or cases). The very top of the screen is the EXCEL main menu bar, with buttons for the different functions and procedures available in EXCEL. Once you have entered data into the spreadsheet, you can analyze the data by clicking the appropriate menu buttons. The results will appear in a new workbook.

You can create an EXCEL workbook by entering data directly into the appropriate row and column of the spreadsheet. Figure 1.E.2 shows data entered in the first (A) column for a variable called "Ratio". Optionally, you can add names for the variables (columns) in the first row of the workbook.

If the data are saved in an external data file (e.g., the *Business Week* Executive Compensation Scoreboard data set), you can access it using the options available in EXCEL. Click the "File" button on the menu bar, then click "Open", as shown in Figure 1.E.3. The dialog box shown in Figure 1.E.4 will appear.

Specify the disk drive and folder that contains the external data file and the file type, then click on the file name, then click on "Open", as shown in Figure 1.E.4. This will invoke the Excel Text Import Wizard. The Text Import Wizard presents a series of three screen menus, the first of which is shown in Figure 1.E.5. Make the appropriate selections on the screen, and click "Next" to go to the next screen. When finished, click "Finish". The Excel workbook will reappear with the data from the external data file, as shown in Figure 1.E.6.

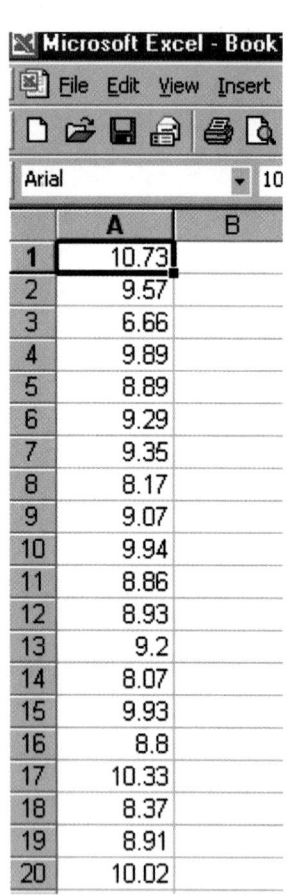

Figure 1.E.2

Data entered into the EXCEL Workbook

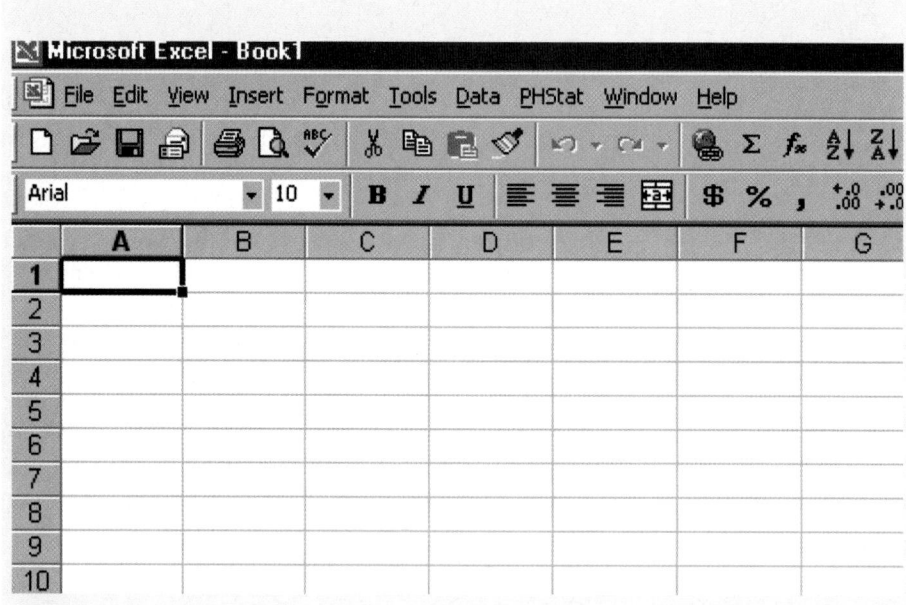

Figure 1.E.1

Initial screen viewed by EXCEL user

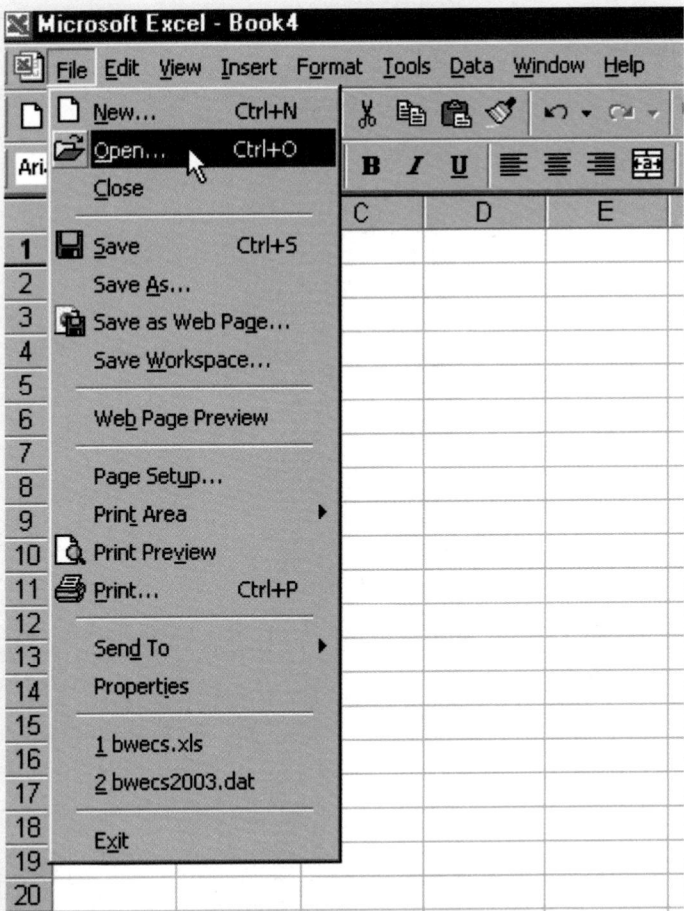

Figure 1.E.3
EXCEL options for reading data from an external file

Note: The variables (columns) can be named as follows: Select "Insert" from the EXCEL main menu, then select "Rows". A blank (empty) row will be added in the first row of the spreadsheet. Type the name of each variable in the first row under the appropriate column.

To obtain a listing (printout) of the data in the EXCEL workbook, click on the "File" button on the EXCEL main menu bar, then click on "Print" (see Figure 1.E.7).

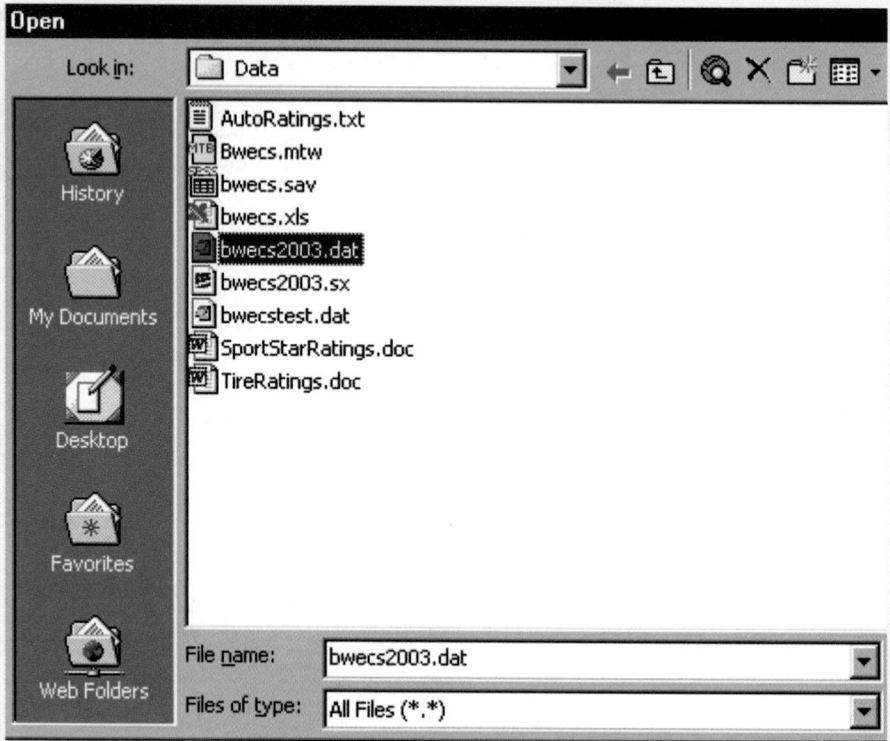

Figure 1.E.4
Selecting the external data file

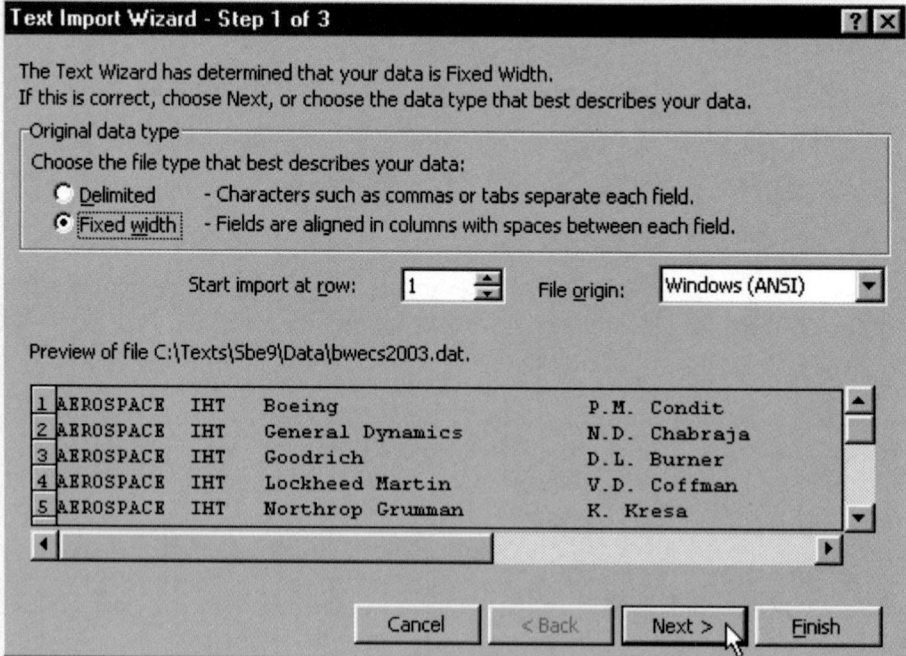

Figure 1.E.5
Excel Text Import Wizard, screen 1

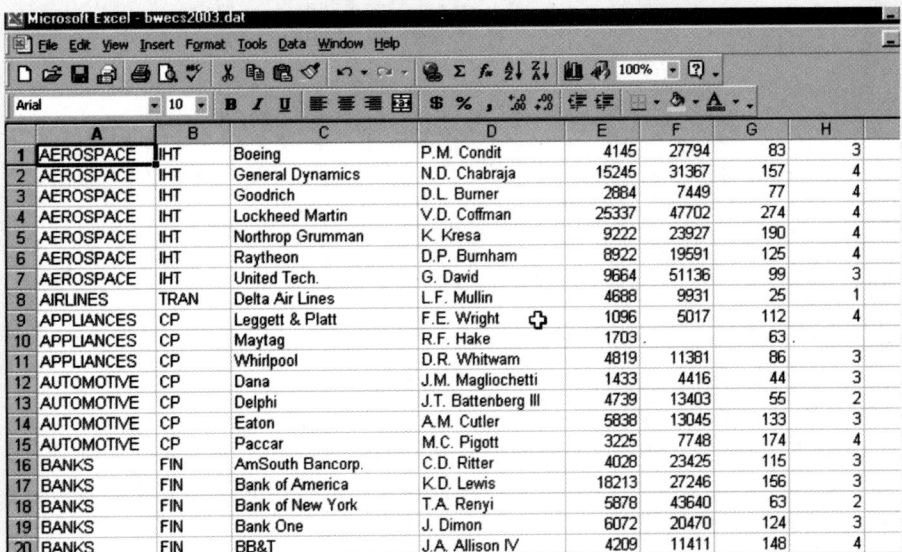

Figure 1.E.6
The EXCEL workbook with the imported data

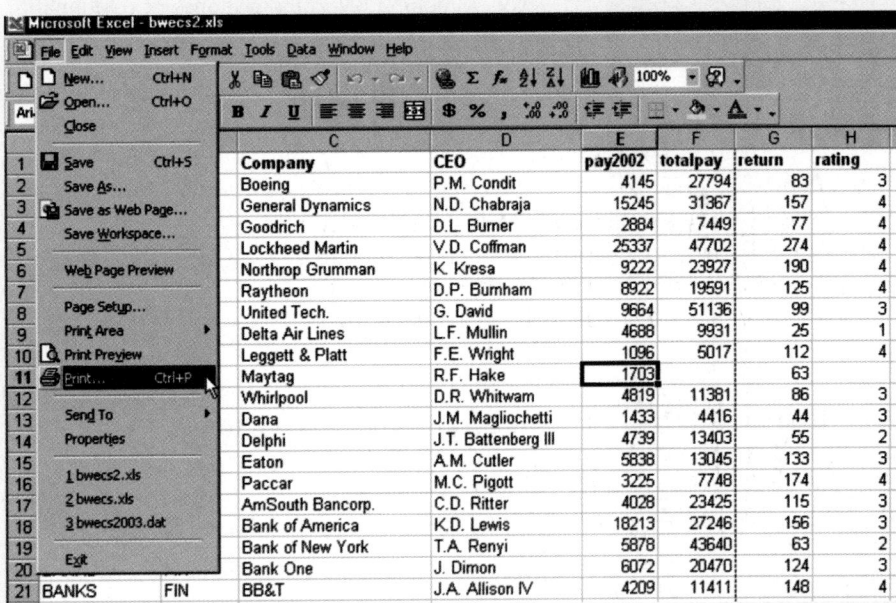

Figure 1.E.7
EXCEL menu options for obtaining a list of your data

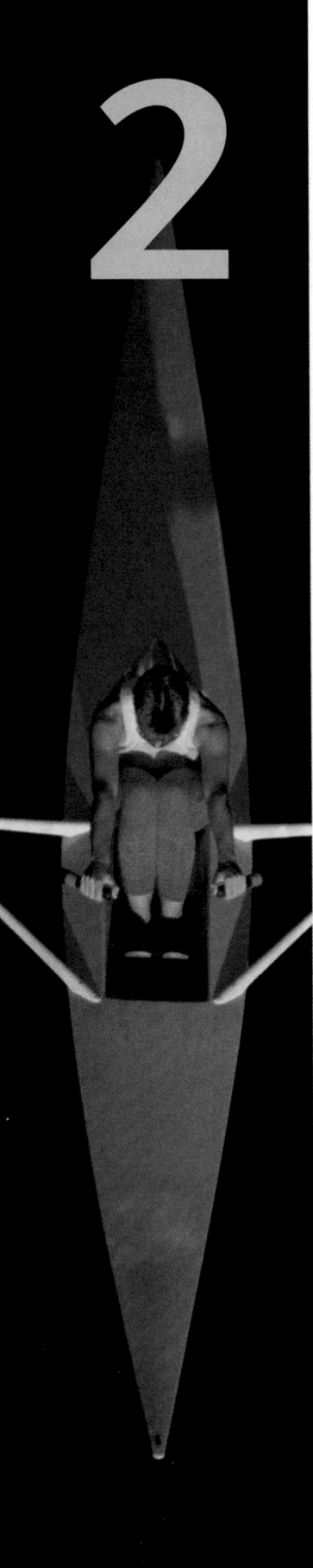

2

Methods for Describing Sets of Data

Contents

Statistics in Action

Characteristics of Physicians Who Use or Refuse
Ethics Consultation

Using Technology

Where We've Been

- Examined the difference between inferential and descriptive statistics
- Described the key elements of a statistical problem
- Learned about the two types of data—quantitative and qualitative
- Discussed the role of statistical thinking in managerial decision making

Where We're Going

- Describe data using graphs.
- Describe data using numerical measures.

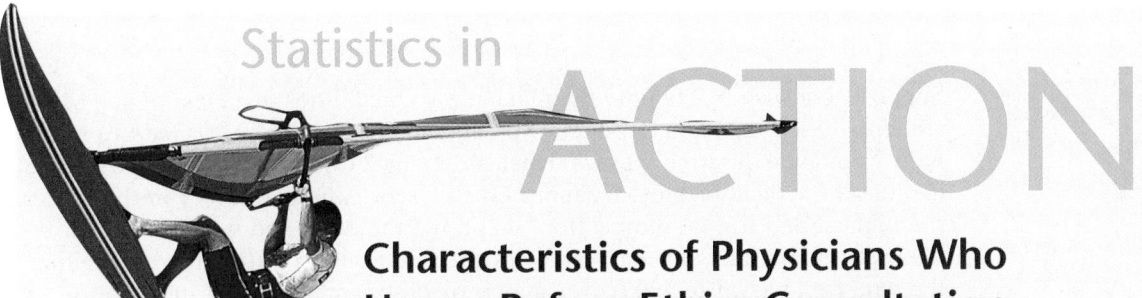

Statistics in ACTION

Characteristics of Physicians Who Use or Refuse Ethics Consultation

Ethical dilemmas commonly arise in the course of a physician's clinical practice. These dilemmas include (but are not limited to) end-of-life issues, treatment of patients without health insurance, providing nonbeneficial treatment at the patient's request, obtaining informed consent, maintaining patient autonomy, truth-telling and confidentiality, involvement of children in research, designing of clinical trials, and termination of subject participation in research protocols. Empirical studies have found that an ethical issue will arise in one of every five clinical encounters.

Over the past ten years ethics consultation has evolved as a means of assisting physicians who are confused about how to best approach an ethical dilemma. About 80% of general hospitals in the United States now provide ethics consultation services to staff physicians. When faced with a difficult ethical decision, the doctor may request advice from a panel of ethics experts, with assurances that all communications will be anonymous and confidential. However, not all physicians take advantage of this service; in fact, some doctors refuse to use ethics consultation.

Medical researchers at University Community Hospital (UCH) in Tampa, Florida undertook a study to determine the factors that might influence a physician's decision request or to refuse ethics consultation.*

Survey questionnaires were distributed to all 746 physicians on staff at UCH; 118 of the questionnaires were returned, yielding a response rate of approximately 16%. The survey was designed to obtain data on the following variables for each physician:

1. *Level of previous ethics consultation use* at UCH ("used at least once" or "never used")

2. *Practitioner specialty* ("medical" or "surgical")

3. *Length of time in practice* (number of years)

4. *Amount of exposure to ethics in medical school* (number of hours)

5. *Would you ever consider using ethics consultation* in the future ("yes" or "no")

The physicians were also asked to elicit opinions on the following statements about ethics consultants. (All responses were measured on a 5-point scale, where 1 = "strongly disagree," 2 = "somewhat disagree," 3 = "neither agree nor disagree," 4 = "somewhat agree," or 5 = "strongly agree.")

6. *Ethics consultants have extensive training in ethics and ethics principles.*

7. *Ethics consultants participate in frequent ethics education.*

8. *Ethics consultants think they are "moral experts."*

9. *Ethics consultants cannot grasp the full picture from the "outside."*

 ## ETHICS

The UCH medical researchers wanted to use the survey results to develop insight into why certain physicians use ethics consultation and others do not. The researchers hypothesized that more experienced doctors and physicians who specialize in surgery would be less likely to use ethics consultation. The data for the study are stored in the file named **ETHICS** in SPSS, MINITAB, and EXCEL.

In the following *Statistics in Action Revisited* sections, we apply the graphical and numerical descriptive techniques of this chapter to the **ETHICS** data to answer some of the researchers' questions.

*Hein, S., Orlowski, J. P., Meinke, R., and Sincich, T. "Why Physicians Do or Do Not Use Ethics Consultation," paper presented at the annual meeting of the American Society for bioethics and Humanities, Nashville, TN, Oct. 2001.

Statistics in Action Revisited for Chapter 2

- Interpreting a pie chart (p. 51)
- Interpreting a histogram (p. 63)

- Interpreting numerical descriptive measures (p. 92)
- Detecting outliers (p. 107)
- Interpreting a scatterplot (p. 112)

Teaching Tip

Explain to the students that descriptive techniques will also be useful in inferential statistics for generating the sample statistics necessary to make inferences and also in generating the graphs necessary to check assumptions that will be made.

Suppose you wish to evaluate the managerial capabilities of a class of 400 MBA, students based on their Graduate Management Aptitude Test (GMAT) scores How would you describe these 400 measurements? Characteristics of the data set include the typical or most frequent GMAT score, the variability in the scores, the highest and lowest scores, the "shape" of the data, and whether or not the data set contains any unusual scores. Extracting this information by "eye-balling" the data isn't easy. The 400 scores may provide too many bits of information for our minds to comprehend. Clearly we need some formal methods for summarizing and characterizing the information in such a data set. Methods for describing data sets are also essential for statistical inference. Most populations are large data sets. Consequently, we need methods for describing a sample data set that let us make descriptive statements (inferences) about the population from which the sample was drawn.

Two methods for describing data are presented in this chapter, one *graphical* and the other *numerical*. Both play an important role in statistics. Section 2.1 presents both graphical and numerical methods for describing qualitative data. Graphical methods for describing quantitative data are presented in Section 2.2 and optional Sections 2.8, 2.9, and 2.10; numerical descriptive methods for quantitative data are presented in Sections 2.3–2.7. We end this chapter with a section on the *misuse* of descriptive techniques.

2.1 Describing Qualitative Data

Teaching Tip

Use data collected in the class to illustrate the techniques for describing qualitative data. Collect data such as year in school, major discipline, state of residency, etc. Use these data to illustrate class frequency and class relative frequency.

Recall the "Executive Compensation Scoreboard" tabulated annually by *Business Week* (see Study 2 in Section 1.2). *Forbes* magazine also conducts a salary survey of chief executive officers each year. In addition to salary information, *Forbes* collects and reports personal data on the CEOs, including level of education. Do most CEOs have advanced degrees, such as masters degrees or doctorates? To answer this question, Table 2.1 gives the highest college degree obtained (bachelors, masters, law, Ph.D., or none) for each of the 25 best-paid CEOs in 2003.

For this study, the variable of interest, highest college degree obtained, is qualitative in nature. Qualitative data are nonnumerical in nature; thus, the value of a qualitative variable can only be classified into categories called *classes*. The possible degree types — bachelors, masters, law, Ph.D., or none — represent the classes for this qualitative variable. We can summarize such data numerically in two ways: (1) by computing the *class frequency* — the number of observations in the data set that fall into each class; or (2) by computing the *class relative frequency* — the proportion of the total number of observations falling into each class.

DEFINITION 2.1

A **class** is one of the categories into which qualitative data can be classified.

 FORBES25

TABLE 2.1   Data on 25 Best-Paid Executives

CEO	Company	Degree	Age
1. Jeffry C. Barbakow	Tenet Healthcare	Masters	59
2. Dwight C. Schar	NVR	Bachelors	61
3. Michael S. Dell	Dell Computer	None	38
4. Irwin M. Jacobs	Qualcomm	Masters	69
5. Barry Diller	USA Interactive	None	61
6. Dan M. Palmer	Concord EFS	Bachelors	60
7. Charles T. Fote	First Data	None	54
8. Orin C. Smith	Starbucks	Masters	60
9. Richard S. Fuld, Jr.	Lehman Bros Holding	Masters	57
10. Maurice R. Greenberg	American Int Group	Law	78
11. Charles M. Cawley	MBNA	Bachelors	62
12. James E. Cayne	Bear Stearns	None	69
13. Scott G. McNealy	Sun Microsystems	Masters	48
14. Philip J. Purcell	Morgan Stanley	Masters	59
15. Vance D. Coffman	Lockheed Martin	PhD	59
16. Lee R. Raymond	ExxonMobil	PhD	64
17. Richard J. Kogan	Schering-Plough	Masters	61
18. Kenneth W. Freeman	Quest Diagnostics	Masters	52
19. Leonard D. Schaeffer	WellPoint Health	Bachelors	57
20. Stuart A. Miller	Lennar	Law	45
21. Robert L. Tillman	Lowe's	Bachelors	59
22. Sumner M. Redstone	Viacom	Law	79
23. Peter Cartwright	Calpine	Masters	73
24. David D. Halbert	Advance PCS	Bachelors	47
25. Craig R. Barrett	Intel	PhD	63

Source: Forbes, April 23, 2003.

DEFINITION 2.2

The **class frequency** is the number of observations in the data set falling into a particular class.

DEFINITION 2.3

The **class relative frequency** is the class frequency divided by the total number of observations in the data set.

Examining Table 2.1, we observe that 4 of the 25 best-paid CEOs did not obtain a college degree, 6 obtained bachelors degrees, 9 masters degrees, 3 Ph.D.s, and 3 law degrees. These numbers — 4, 6, 9, 3, and 3 — represent the class frequencies for the five classes and are shown in the summary table, Figure 2.1, produced using SPSS.

DEFINITION 2.4

The **class percentage** is the class relative frequency multiplied by 100.

Figure 2.1

SPSS summary table for degrees of 25 CEOs

DEGREE

		Frequency	Percent	Valid Percent	Cumulative Percent
Valid	Bachelors	6	24.0	24.0	24.0
	Law	3	12.0	12.0	36.0
	Masters	9	36.0	36.0	72.0
	None	4	16.0	16.0	88.0
	PhD	3	12.0	12.0	100.0
	Total	25	100.0	100.0	

Figure 2.1 also gives the relative frequency of each of the five degree classes. From Definition 2.3, we know that we calculate the relative frequency by dividing the class frequency by the total number of observations in the data set. Thus, the relative frequencies for the five degree types are

$$\text{None: } \frac{4}{25} = .16$$

$$\text{Bachelors: } \frac{6}{25} = .24$$

$$\text{Masters: } \frac{9}{25} = .36$$

$$\text{Law: } \frac{3}{25} = .12$$

$$\text{Ph.D.: } \frac{3}{25} = .12$$

Suggested Exercise 2.4

These values, expressed as a percentage, are shown in the "Percent" column in the SPSS Summary table, Figure 2.1. If we sum the relative frequencies for masters, law, and Ph.D., we obtain $.36 + .12 + .12 = .60$. Therefore, 60% of the 25 best-paid CEOs obtained atleast a masters degree (masters, law, or Ph.D.).

Although the summary table of Figure 2.1 adequately describes the data of Table 2.1, we often want a graphical presentation as well. Figures 2.2 and 2.3 show two of the most widely used graphical methods for describing qualitative data—**bar graphs** and **pie charts.** Figure 2.2 is a bar graph for "highest degree obtained" produced with MINITAB. Note that the height of the rectangle, or "bar," over each class is equal to the class frequency. (Optionally, the bar heights can be proportional to class relative frequencies.) In contrast, Figure 2.3 (also created using MINITAB) shows the relative frequencies (expressed as a percentage) of the five degree types in a *pie chart*. Note that the pie is a circle (spanning 360°) and the size (angle) of the "pie slice" assigned to each class is proportional to the class relative frequency. For example, the slice assigned to masters degree is 36% of 360°, or $(.36)(360°) = 129.6°$.

Before leaving the data set in Table 2.1, consider the bar graph shown in Figure 2.4, produced using EXCEL with the PHStat2 add-in. Note that the bars for the CEO degree categories are arranged in descending order of height from left to

Figure 2.2
MINITAB bar graph for
degrees of 25 CEOs

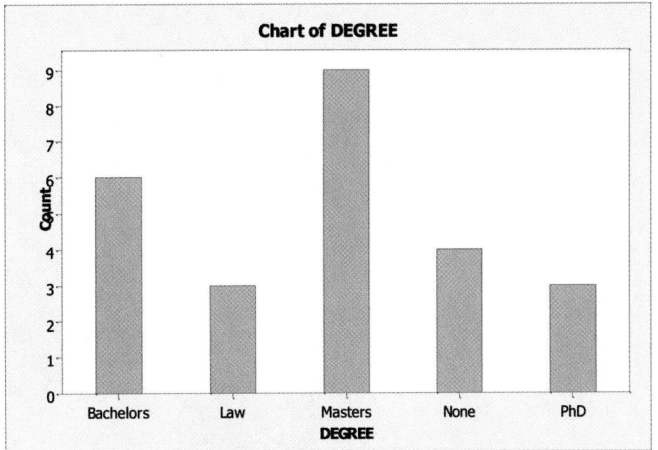

Figure 2.3
MINITAB pie chart for
degrees of 25 CEOs

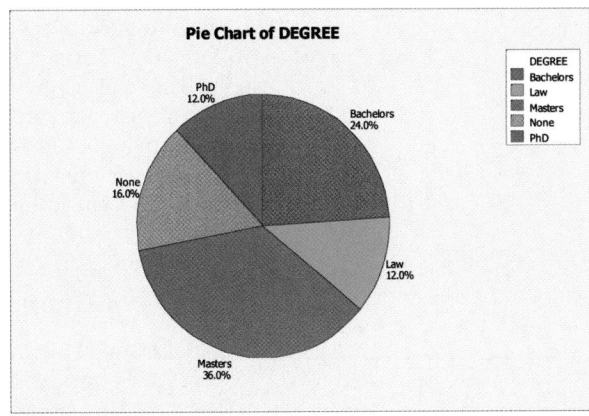

right across the horizontal axis. That is, the tallest bar (Masters) is positioned at the far left and the shortest bars (Law and Ph.D.) are at the far right. This rearrangement of the bars in a bar graph is called a **Pareto diagram.** One goal of a Pareto diagram (named for the Italian economist, Vilfredo Pareto) is to make it easy to locate the "most important" categories — those with the largest frequencies. For the 25

Figure 2.4
EXCEL/PHStat2 Pareto
diagram for degrees
of 25 CEOs

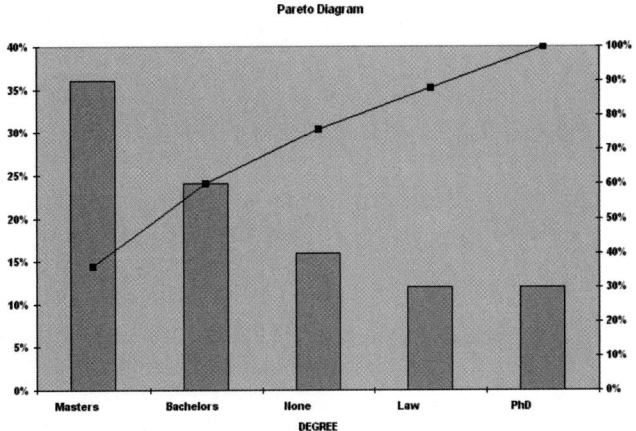

best-paid CEOs in 2003, a masters degree was the highest degree obtained by the most CEOs (36%).

Note: In the Pareto diagram in Figure 2.4, the left vertical axis gives the scale for the relative frequencies (percentages) of the bars and the right vertical axis gives the scale for the cumulative relative frequencies. The actual cumulative percentages are represented by the black squares connected with straight lines.

Biography

VILFREDO PARETO
(1843–1923)
The Pareto Principle

Born in Paris to an Italian aristocratic family, Vilfredo Pareto was educated at the University of Turin, where he studied engineering and mathematics. After the death of his parents, Pareto quit his job as an engineer and began writing and lecturing on the evils of the economic policies of the Italian government. While at the University of Lausanne in Switzerland in 1896, he published his first paper, *Cours d'economie politique*. In the paper, Pareto derived a complicated mathematical formula to prove that the distribution of income and wealth in society is not random, but that a consistent pattern appears throughout history in all societies. Essentially, Pareto showed that approximately 80% of the total wealth in a society lies with only 20% of the families. This famous law about the "vital few and the trivial many" is widely known as the Pareto principle in economics.

Summary of Graphical Descriptive Methods for Qualitative Data

Bar graph: The categories (classes) of the qualitative variable are represented by bars, where the height of each bar is either the class frequency, class relative frequency, or class percentage.

Pie chart: The categories (classes) of the qualitative variable are represented by slices of a pie (circle). The size of each slice is proportional to the class relative frequency.

Pareto diagram: A bar graph with the categories (classes) of the qualitative variable (i.e., the bars) arranged by height in descending order from left to right.

Now Work   *Exercise 2.4*

Let's look at a practical example that requires interpretation of the graphical results.

EXAMPLE 2.1   GRAPHING AND SUMMARIZING QUALITATIVE DATA

Problem   A group of cardiac physicians in southwest Florida have been studying a new drug designed to reduce blood loss in coronary artery bypass operations. Blood loss data for 114 coronary artery bypass patients (some who received a dosage of the drug and others who did not) are saved in the BLOODLOSS file. Although the drug shows promise in reducing blood loss, the physicians are concerned about possible side effects and complications. So their data set includes not only the qualitative variable, DRUG, which indicates whether or not the patient received the drug, but also the qualitative variable, COMP, which specifies the type (if any) of complication experienced by the patient. The four values of COMP recorded by the physicians are: (1) redo surgery, (2) postop infection, (3) both, or (4) none.

BLOODLOSS

a. Figure 2.5, generated using SPSS, shows summary tables for the two qualitative variables, DRUG and COMP. Interpret the results.

b. Interpret the MINITAB output shown in Figure 2.6 and the SPSS output shown in Figure 2.7.

Solution

a. The top table in Figure 2.5 is a summary frequency table for DRUG. Note that exactly half (57) of the 114 coronary artery bypass patients received the drug and half did not. The bottom table in Figure 2.5 is a summary frequency table for COMP. We see that about 69% of the 114 patiens had no complications, leaving about 31% who experienced either a redo surgery, a post-op infection, or both.

Figure 2.5

SPSS summary tables for DRUG and COMP

DRUG

		Frequency	Percent	Valid Percent	Cumulative Percent
Valid	NO	57	50.0	50.0	50.0
	YES	57	50.0	50.0	100.0
	Total	114	100.0	100.0	

COMP

		Frequency	Percent	Valid Percent	Cumulative Percent
Valid	BOTH	6	5.3	5.3	5.3
	INFECT	15	13.2	13.2	18.4
	NONE	79	69.3	69.3	87.7
	REDO	14	12.3	12.3	100.0
	Total	114	100.0	100.0	

Figure 2.6

MINITAB side-by-side bar graphs for COMP by value of DRUG

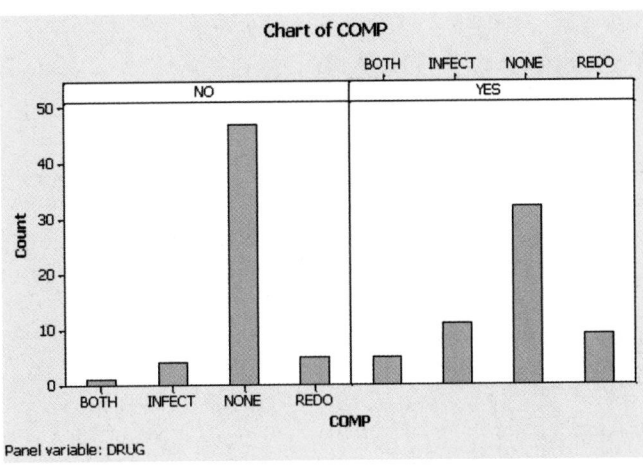

Figure 2.7

SPSS summary tables for COMP by value of DRUG

COMP

DRUG			Frequency	Percent	Valid Percent	Cumulative Percent
NO	Valid	BOTH	1	1.8	1.8	1.8
		INFECT	4	7.0	7.0	8.8
		NONE	47	82.5	82.5	91.2
		REDO	5	8.8	8.8	100.0
		Total	57	100.0	100.0	
YES	Valid	BOTH	5	8.8	8.8	8.8
		INFECT	11	19.3	19.3	28.1
		NONE	32	56.1	56.1	84.2
		REDO	9	15.8	15.8	100.0
		Total	57	100.0	100.0	

Teaching Tip

Use the bar graph to compare the complications of the group who received the drug with the group who did not receive the drug. Discuss other graphical techniques appropriate for the data.

Suggested Exercise 2.3

b. Figure 2.6 is a side-by-side bar graph for the data. The four bars on the left represent the frequencies of COMP for the 57 patients who did not receive the drug; the four bars on the right represent the frequencies of COMP for the 57 patients who did receive a dosage of the drug. The graph clearly shows that patients who did not get the drug suffered fewer complications. The exact percentages are displayed in the summary tables of Figure 2.7. About 56% of the patients who got the drug had no complications, compared to about 83% for the patients who got no drug.

Look Back Although the drug may be effective in reducing blood loss, the results in Figures 2.6 and 2.7 also imply that patients on the drug may have a higher risk of complications. But before using this information to make a decision about the drug, the physicians will need to provide a measure of reliability for the inference. That is, the physicians will want to know whether the difference between the percentages of patients with complications observed in this sample of 114 patients is generalizable to the population of all coronary artery bypass patients.

Now Work *Exercise 2.7*

■ ■ ■

Exercises 2.1–2.15

Learning the Mechanics

2.1 Complete the following table.

Grade on Business Statistics Exam	Frequency	Relative Frequency
A: 90–100	—	.08
B: 80–89	36	—
C: 65–79	90	—
D: 50–64	30	—
F: Below 50	28	—
Total	200	1.00

2.2 A qualitative variable with three classes (X, Y, and Z) is measured for each of 20 units randomly sampled from a target population. The data (observed class for each unit) are listed below.

Y X X Z X Y Y Y X X Z X
Y Y X Z Y Y Y X

a. Compute the frequency for each of the three classes.
b. Compute the relative frequency for each of the three classes.   .4, .45, .15
c. Display the results, part **a,** in a frequency bar graph.
d. Display the results, part **b,** in a pie chart.

Statistics in Action Revisited

Interpreting Pie Charts

In the survey of University Community Hospital physicians, the medical researchers measured three qualitative variables: *Level of previous ethics consultation* use ("never used" or "used"), *Practitioner specialty* ("medical" or "surgical"), *and Future use of ethics consultation* ("yes" or "no"). Pie charts and bar graphs can be used to summarize and describe the physicians' responses to these survey questions. Recall that the data are saved in the **ETHICS** file. These variables are named PREVUSE, SPEC, and FUTUREUSE in the data file. We created pie charts for these variables using MINITAB.

Figure SIA2.1 is a pie chart for the PREVUSE variable. Clearly, a higher percentage of physicians (71.2%) has previously never used ethics consultation at the hospital than have (28.8%). The researchers want to know if this "previous use" pattern differs for the two practitioner specialties. Figure SIA2.2 shows side-by-side pie charts of the PREVUSE variable for each level of the SPEC variable. The left-side chart describes the pattern of previous use by medical specialists and the right-side chart describes the pattern of previous use by surgeons. Figure SIA2.2 shows that slightly fewer surgeons (27.9%) have used ethics consultation in the past than have medical practitioners (29.3%).

We produced a similar set of side-by-side pie charts to describe the qualitative variable FUTUREUSE in Figure SIA2.3. Apparently, the gap between surgeons and medical specialists has widened. These charts again show that fewer surgeons (76.7%) would consider using ethics consultation in the future than medical specialists (82.7%), but the difference in the percentages is greater than for previous use. The researchers' theory that surgical specialists at UCH are less likely to use ethics consultation than medical specialists is supported by the pie charts.

Figure SIA2.1

MINITAB pie chart for previous use of ethics consultation

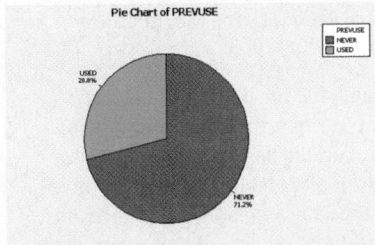

Figure SIA2.2

MINITAB pie charts for previous use of ethics consultation — medical versus surgical specialty

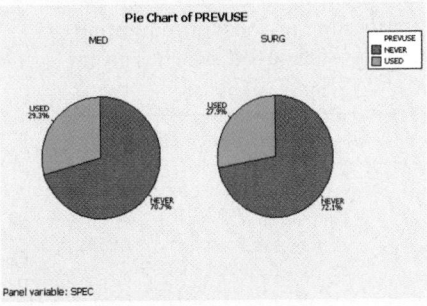

Figure SIA2.3

MINITAB pie charts for future use of ethics consultation — medical versus surgical specialty

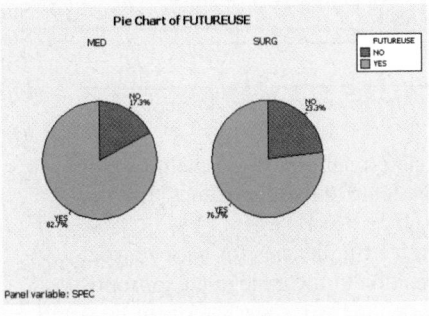

Applying the Concepts—Basic

2.3 The Moffitt Cancer Center at the University of South Florida treats over 25,000 patients a year. The graphic below describes the types of cancer treated in Moffitt's patients during fiscal year 2002.
  a. What type of graph is portrayed?   Pie chart
  b. Which type of cancer is treated most often at Moffitt?   Breast cancer
  c. What percentage of Moffitt's patients are treated for melanoma, lymphoma, or leukemia?   19%

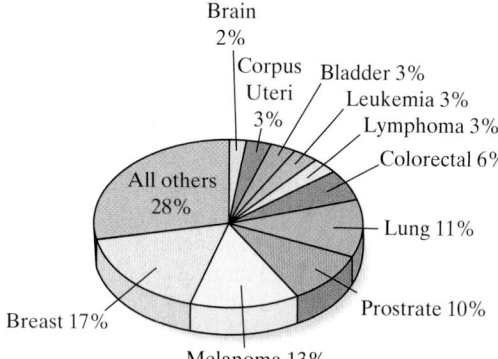

Source: Today's Tomorrows, Annual Report, H. Lee Moffitt Cancer Center & research Institute, Winter 2002–2003.

2.4 Driver-side and passenger-side air bags are installed in all new cars to prevent serious or fatal injury in an automobile crash. However, air bags have been found to cause deaths in children and small people or people with handicaps in low-speed crashes. Consequently, in 1998 the federal government began allowing vehicle owners to request installation of an on–off switch for air bags. The table describes the reasons for requesting the installation of passenger-side on–off switches given by car owners in 1998 and 1999.

Reason	Number of requests
Infant	1,852
Child	17,148
Medical	8,377
Infant & medical	44
Child & medical	903
Infant & child	1,878
Infant & child & medical	135
Total	30,337

Source: National Highway Transportation Safety Administration, September 2000.

  a. What type of variable, quantitative or qualitative, is summarized in the table? Give the values that the variable could assume.   Qualitative
  b. Calculate the relative frequencies for each reason.
  c. Display the information in the table in an appropriate graph.

  d. What proportion of the car owners who requested on–off air bag switches gave medical as one of the reasons?   .312

2.5 Consider the following data from the automobile industry (adapted from Kane, 1989). All cars produced on a particular day were inspected for defects. The 145 defects found were categorized by type as shown in the accompanying table.

Defect Type	Number
Accessories	50
Body	70
Electrical	10
Engine	5
Transmission	10

  a. Construct a Pareto diagram for the data. Use the graph to identify the most frequently observed type of defect.
  b. All 70 car body defects were further classified as to type. The frequencies are provided in the following table. Form a Pareto diagram for type of body defect. (Adding this graph to the original Pareto diagram of part **a** is called *exploding the Pareto diagram.*) Interpret the result. What type of body defect should be targeted for special attention?   Paint and dents

Body Defect	Number
Chrome	2
Dents	25
Paint	30
Upholstery	10
Windshield	3

2.6 Port Canaveral (Florida) handles over 1.5 million cruise passengers per year. The number of passengers handled by each of the cruise ships that sail out of Port Canaveral in a recent year is listed in the table.

Cruise Line (Ship)	Number of Passengers
Canaveral (Dolphin)	152,240
Carnival (Fantasy)	480,924
Disney (Magic)	73,504
Premier (Oceanic)	270,361
Royal Caribbean (Nordic Empress)	106,161
Sun Cruz Casinos	453,806
Sterling Cruises (New Yorker)	15,782
Topaz Int'l. Shipping (Topaz)	28,280
Other	10,502
Total	1,591,560

Source: Florida Trend, Vol. 41, No. 9, January 1999.

  a. Find the relative frequency of the number of passengers for each cruise ship.
  b. Identify the cruise ship with the highest relative frequency. Interpret this number.   Carnival

c. Construct a bar graph to describe the popularity of cruise ships that sail from Port Canaveral.

2.7 Customer satisfaction and loyalty are valued and monitored by all world-class organizations. But are satisfied customers necessarily loyal customers? Harte-Hanks Market Research surveyed customers of department stores and banks and published the following results in *American Demographics* (Aug. 1999).

	Banks	Department Stores
Totally satisfied and very loyal	27%	4%
Totally satisfied and not very loyal	18%	25%
Not totally satisfied and very loyal	13%	2%
Not totally satisfied and not very loyal	42%	69%
	100%	100%

Source: American Demographics, Aug. 1999.

a. Construct side-by-side relative frequency bar charts for banks and department stores.

b. Could these data have been described using pie charts? Explain.   Yes

c. Do the data indicate that customers who are totally satisfied are very loyal? Explain.

Applying the Concepts—Intermediate

2.8 "Made in the USA" is a claim stated in many product advertisements or on product labels. Advertisers want consumers to believe that the product is manufactured with 100% U.S. labor and materials — which is often not the case. What does "Made in the USA" mean to the typical consumer? To answer this question, a group of marketing professors conducted an experiment at a shopping mall in Muncie, Indiana (*Journal of Global Business*, Spring 2002). They asked every fourth adult entrant to the mall to participate in the study. A total of 106 shoppers agreed to answer the question, "'Made in the USA' means what percentage of U.S. labor and materials?" The responses of the 106 shoppers are summarized in the following table.

Response to "Made in the USA"	Number of shoppers
100%	64
75 to 99%	20
50 to 74%	18
Less than 50%	4

Source: "'Made in the USA': Consumer Perceptions, Deception and Policy Alternatives," *Journal of Global Business*, Vol. 13, No. 24, Spring 2002 (Table 3).

a. What type of data collection method was used?
  Survey

b. What type of variable, quantitative or qualitative, is measured?   Quantitative

c. Present the data in the table in graphical form. Use the graph to make a statement about the percentage of consumers who believe "Made in the USA" means 100% U.S. labor and materials.

DDT

2.9 Refer to Example 1.5 (p. 17) and the U.S. Army Corps of Engineers data on fish contaminated from the toxic discharges of a chemical plant located on the banks of the Tennessee River in Alabama. The engineers determined the species (channel catfish, largemouth bass, or smallmouth buffalofish) for each of the 144 captured fish. The data on species are saved in the **DDT** file. Use a graphical method to describe the frequency of occurrence of the three fish species in the 144 captured fish.

BWECS

2.10 Refer to the *Business Week* "Executive Compensation Scoreboard" for 2003, first discussed in Chapter 1 (p. 6). One of the variables recorded in the survey of 363 chief executive officers is Industry type of each CEO's company. *Business Week* classified the companies into one of nine industry types: Financial, Retailing, Services, Consumer Products, Utilities, Industrial Low-Tech, Transportation, Industrial High-Tech, and Telecommunications. The "Executive Compensation Scoreboard" data are saved in the **BWECS** file. Use a graphical method to describe the frequency of occurrence of the nine industry types.

DIAMONDS

2.11 Diamonds are categorized according to the "four C's": carats, clarity, color, and cut. Each diamond stone that is sold on the open market is provided a certificate by an independent diamond assessor that lists these characteristics. Data for 308 diamonds were extracted from Singapore's *Business Times* and are saved in the **DIAMONDS** file (*Journal of Statistics Education*, Vol. 9, No. 1, 2001). Color is classified as D, E, F, G, H, or I, while clarity is classified as IF, VVS1, VVS2, VS1, or VS2. Use a graphical technique to summarize the color and clarity of the 308 diamond stones. What is the color and clarity that occurs most often? Least often?   Most: F, VS1; Least: D, IF

2.12 Refer to the Computer Security Institute (CSI) annual survey of computer crime at United States businesses, Exercise 1.20 (p. 27). One question asked, "If your business Web site suffered unauthorized use, where did the attack come from, inside or outside the company?" The responses for those business Web sites that did, in fact, experience unauthorized use are summarized in the next table for two survey years, 1999 (125 reported attacks) and 2001 (163 reported attacks). Compare the responses for the two years using side-by-side bar charts. What inference can be made from the charts?

WWW Site Attack	Percentage in 1999	Percentage in 2001
Inside	7	4
Outside	38	47
Both	41	22
Don't know	14	27
Totals	100	100

Source: "2001 CSI/FBI Computer Crime and Security Survey," *Computer Security Issues & Trends,* Vol. 7, No. 1, Spring 2001.

Applying the Concepts—Advanced

2.13 "Reader-response cards" are used by marketers to advertise their product and obtain sales leads. These cards are placed in magazines and trade publications. Readers detach and mail in the cards to indicate their interest in the product, expecting literature or a phone call in return. How effective are these cards (called "bingo cards" in the industry) as a marketing tool? Performark, a Minneapolis business that helps companies close on sales leads, attempted to answer this question by responding to 17,000 card-advertisements placed by industrial marketers in a wide variety of trade publications over a 6-year period. Performark kept track of how long it took for each advertiser to respond. A summary of the response times, reported in *Inc.* magazine (July 1995), is given in the table.

Advertiser's Response Time	Percentage
Never responded	21
13–59 days	33
60–120 days	34
More than 120 days	12
Total	100

a. Describe the variable measured by Performark.
b. *Inc.* displayed the results in the form of a pie chart. Reconstruct the pie chart from the information given in the table.
c. How many of the 17,000 advertisers never responded to the sales lead?   3,570
d. Advertisers typically spend at least a million dollars on a reader-response card marketing campaign. Many industrial marketers feel these "bingo cards" are not worth their expense. Does the information in the pie chart, part **b**, support this contention? Explain why or why not. If not, what information can be gleaned from the pie chart to help potential "bingo card" campaigns?   No

OILSPILL

2.14 Owing to several major ocean oil spills by tank vessels Congress passed the 1990 Oil Pollution Act, which requires all tankers to be designed with thicker hulls. Further improvements in the structural design of a tank vessel have been implemented since then, each with the objective of reducing the likelihood of an oil spill and decreasing the amount of outflow in the event of hull puncture. To aid in this development, the spillage amount and cause of puncture for 50 recent major oil spills from tankers and carriers was reported in (*Marine Technology*, Jan, 1995). The data are saved in the **OILSPILL** file.
a. Use a graphical method to describe the cause of spillage for the 50 tankers. [*Note*: Cause is classified as collision (C), fire/explosion (FE), hull failure (HF), grounding (G), or unknown (U).]
b. Does the graph, part **a**, suggest that any one cause is more likely to occur than any other? How is this information of value to the design engineers?   No

2.15 Since opening its doors to Western investors in 1979, the People's Republic of China has been steadily moving toward a market economy. However, because of the considerable political and economic uncertainties in China, Western investors remain uneasy about the investments in China. In 1995 an agency of the Chinese government surveyed 402 foreign investors to ascertain their concerns with the investment environment. Each was asked to indicate their most serious concern. The results appear below.
a. Construct a Pareto diagram for the 10 categories.

CHINA

Investor's Concern	Frequency
Communication infrastructure	8
Environmental protection	13
Financial services	14
Government efficiency	30
Inflation rate	233
Labor supply	11
Personal safety	2
Real estate prices	82
Security of personal property	4
Water supply	5

Source: Adapted from China Marketing News, No. 26, November 1995.

b. According to your Pareto diagram, which environmental factors most concern investors?
c. In this case, are 80% of the investors concerned with 20% of the environmental factors as the Pareto principle would suggest? Justify your answer.   Yes

2.2 Graphical Methods for Describing Quantitative Data

Recall from Section 1.5 that quantitative data sets consist of data that are recorded on a meaningful numerical scale. For describing, summarizing, and detecting patterns in such data, we can use three graphical methods: **dot plots, stem-and-leaf displays,** and **histograms.** Since almost all statistical software packages can produce these graphs, well focus here on their interpretations rather than their construction.

For example, suppose a financial analyst is interested in the amount of resources spent by computer hardware and software companies on research and development (R&D). She samples 50 of these high-technology firms and calculate the amount each spent last year on R&D as a percentage of their total revenue. The results are given in Table 2.2. As numerical measurements made on the sample of 50 units (the firms), these percentages represent quantitative data. The analyst's initial objective is to summarize and describe these data in order to extract relevant information.

Teaching Tip

Explain that quantitative data must be condensed in some manner to generate any kind of meaningful graphical summary of the data.

 R&D

TABLE 2.2   Percentage of Revenues Spent on Research and Development

Company	Percentage	Company	Percentage	Company	Percentage	Company	Percentage
1	13.5	14	9.5	27	8.2	39	6.5
2	8.4	15	8.1	28	6.9	40	7.5
3	10.5	16	13.5	29	7.2	41	7.1
4	9.0	17	9.9	30	8.2	42	13.2
5	9.2	18	6.9	31	9.6	43	7.7
6	9.7	19	7.5	32	7.2	44	5.9
7	6.6	20	11.1	33	8.8	45	5.2
8	10.6	21	8.2	34	11.3	46	5.6
9	10.1	22	8.0	35	8.5	47	11.7
10	7.1	23	7.7	36	9.4	48	6.0
11	8.0	24	7.4	37	10.5	49	7.8
12	7.9	25	6.5	38	6.9	50	6.5
13	6.8	26	9.5				

A visual inspection of the data indicates some obvious facts. For example, the smallest R&D percentage is 5.2% (company 45) and the largest is 13.5% (companies 1 and 16). But it is difficult to provide much additional information on the 50 R&D percentages without resorting to some method of summarizing the data. One such method is a dot plot.

Suggested Exercise 2.26

Dot Plots

A **dot plot** for the 50 R&D percentages, produced using MINITAB software, shown in Figure 2.8. The horizontal axis of Figure 2.8 is a scale for the quantitative variable, percent. The numerical value of each measurement in the data set is located on the

Figure 2.8
MINITAB dot plot for
50 R&D percentages

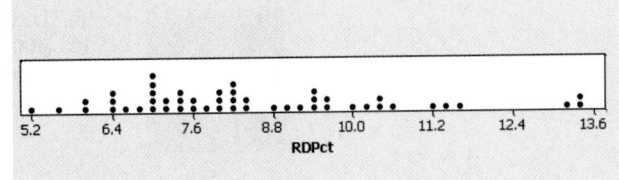

D	E	F
Stem-and-Leaf Display		
for RDPct		
Stem unit: 1		
5	2 6 9	
6	0 5 5 5 6 8 9 9 9	
7	1 1 2 2 4 5 5 7 7 8 9	
8	0 0 1 2 2 2 4 5 8	
9	0 2 4 5 5 6 7 9	
10	1 5 5 6	
11	1 3 7	
12		
13	2 5 5	

Figure 2.9

EXCEL/PHStat2 stem-and-leaf display for 50 R&D percentages

horizontal scale by a dot. When data values repeat, the dots are placed above one another, forming a pile at that particular numerical location. As you can see, this dot plot shows that almost all of the R&D percentages are between 6% and 12%, with most falling between 7% and 9%.

Stem-and-Leaf Display

We used EXCEL and PHStat2 to generate another graphical representation of these same data, a **stem-and-leaf display,** in Figure 2.9. In this display the *stem* is the portion of the measurement (percentage) to the left of the decimal point, while the remaining portion to the right of the decimal point is the *leaf.*

The stems for the data set are listed in a column from the smallest (5) to the largest (13). Then the leaf for each observation is recorded in the row of the display corresponding to the observation's stem. For example, the leaf 5 of the first observation (13.5) in Table 2.2 is placed in the row corresponding to the stem 13. Similarly, the leaf 4 for the second observation (8.4) in Table 2.2 is recorded in the row corresponding to the stem 8, while the leaf 5 for the third observation (10.5) is recorded in the row corresponding to the stem 10. (The leaves for these first three observations are shaded in Figure 2.9.) Typically, the leaves in each row are ordered as shown in Figure 2.9.

The stem-and-leaf display presents another compact picture of the data set. You can see at a glance that most of the sampled computer companies (37 of 50) spent between 6.0% and 9.9% of their revenues on R&D, and 11 of them spent between 7.0% and 7.9%. Relative to the rest of the sampled companies, three spent a high percentage of revenues on R&D — in excess of 13%.

The definitions of the stem and leaf can be modified to alter the graphical description. For example, suppose we had defined the stem as the tens digit for the R&D percentage data, rather than the ones and tens digits. With this definition, the stems and leaves corresponding to the measurements 13.5 and 8.4 would be as follows:

Stem	Leaf		Stem	Leaf
1	3		0	8

Note that the decimal portion of the numbers has been dropped. Generally, only one digit is displayed in the leaf.

If you look at the data, you'll see why we didn't define the stem this way, All the R&D measurements fall below 13.5, so all the leaves would fall into just two stem rows — 1 and 0 — in this display. The resulting picture would not be nearly as informative as Figure 2.9.

Now Work *Exercise 2.14*

Biography

**JOHN TUKEY
(1915–2000)
The Picasso of Statistics**

Like the legendary artist Pablo Picasso, who mastered and revolutionized a variety of art forms during his lifetime, John Tukey is recognized for his contributions to many subfields of statistics. Born in Massachusetts, Tukey was home-schooled, graduated with his bachelor's and master's degrees in chemistry from Brown University, and received his Ph.D. in mathematics from Princeton University. While at Bell Telephone Laboratories in the 1960s and early 1970s, Tukey developed "exploratory data analysis," a set of graphical descriptive methods for summarizing and presenting huge amounts of data. Many of these tools, including the stem-and-leaf display and the box plot, are now standard features of modern statistical software packages. (In fact, it was Tukey himself who coined the term *software* for computer programs.)

Histograms

A MINITAB histogram for these 50 R&D measurements is displayed in Figure 2.10. The horizontal axis for Figure 2.10, which gives the percentage amounts spent on R&D for each company, is divided into class intervals commencing with the interval (4.5–5.5) and proceeding in intervals of equal size to (13.5–14.5). (*Note:* MINITAB shows the midpoint of every other class interval on the histogram.) The vertical axis gives the number (or *frequency*) of the 50 measurements that fall in each class interval. You can see that the class intervals (6.5–7.5) and (7.5–8.5) (i.e., the classes with the two highest bars) contain the largest frequencies—both intervals contain 13 R&D percentage measurements; the remaining class intervals tend to contain a smaller number of measurements as R&D percentage gets smaller or larger.

Histograms can be used to display either the frequency or relative frequency of the measurements falling into the class intervals. The class intervals, frequencies, and relative frequencies for the 50 R&D measurements are shown in Table 2.3.* By summing the relative frequencies in the intervals (6.5–7.5), (7.5–8.5), (8.5–9.5), (9.5–10.5), and (10.5–11.5), we find that .26 + .26 + .10 + .12 + .10 = .84, or 84%, of the R&D measurements are between 6.5 and 11.5. Similarly, summing the relative frequencies in the last two intervals, (12.5–13.5) and (13.5–14.5), we find that .02 + .04 = .06, or 6%, of the companies spent over 12.5% of their revenues on R&D. Many other summary statements can be made by further study of the histogram.

Teaching Tip

The histogram condenses the data by grouping similar data values into the same classes in the graph.

Teaching Tip

Classes of equal width should be used when generating a histogram.

Suggested Exercise 2.21

Figure 2.10
MINITAB histogram for 50 R&D percentages

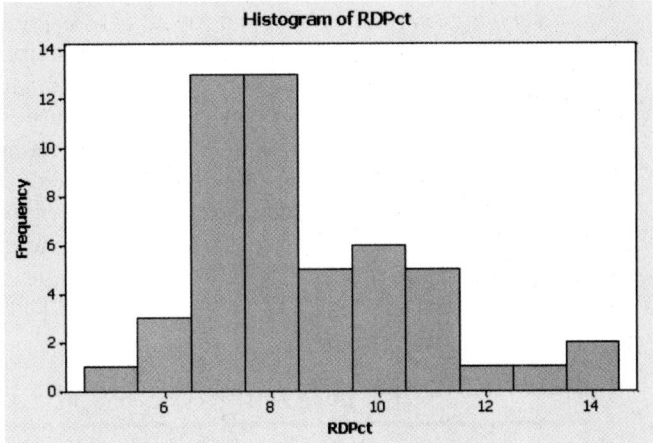

*MINITAB, like many statistical software packages, will classify an observation that falls on the borderline of a class interval into the next highest class interval. For example, the R&D measurement of 13.5, which falls on the border between the intervals (12.5–13.5) and (13.5–14.5), is classified into the (13.5–14.5) interval. The frequencies in Table 2.3 reflect this convention.

TABLE 2.3   Class Intervals, Frequencies, and Relative Frequencies for the 50 R&D Measurements

Class	Class Interval	Class Frequency	Class Relative Frequency
1	4.5–5.5	1	1/50 = .02
2	5.5–6.5	3	3/50 = .06
3	6.5–7.5	13	13/50 = .26
4	7.5–8.5	13	13/50 = .26
5	8.5–9.5	5	5/50 = .10
6	9.5–10.5	6	6/50 = .12
7	10.5–11.5	5	5/50 = .10
8	11.5–12.5	1	1/50 = .02
9	12.5–13.5	1	1/50 = .02
10	13.5–14.5	2	2/50 = .04
Totals		50	1.00

Figure 2.11

Effect of the size of a data set on the outline of a histogram

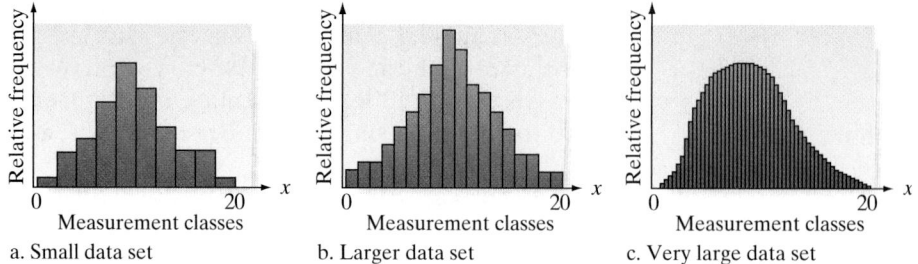

a. Small data set   b. Larger data set   c. Very large data set

When interpreting a histogram (say, the histogram in Figure 2.10) consider two important facts. First, the proportion of the total area under the histogram that falls above a particular interval of the horizontal axis is equal to the relative frequency of measurements falling in the interval. For example, the relative frequency for the class interval 7.5–8.5 is .26. Consequently, the rectangle above the interval contains .26 of the total area under the histogram.

Second, you can imagine the appearance of the relative frequency histogram for a very large set of data (say, a population). As the number of measurements in a data set is increased, you can obtain a better description of the data by decreasing the width of the class intervals. When the class intervals become small enough, a relative frequency histogram will (for all practical purposes) appear as a smooth curve (see Figure 2.11). Some recommendations for selecting the number of intervals in a histogram for smaller data sets are given in the box.

While histograms provide good visual descriptions of data sets—particularly very large ones—they do not let us identify individual measurements. In contrast, each of the original measurements is visible to some extent in a dot plot and clearly visible in a stem-and-leaf display. The stem-and-leaf display arranges the data in

Determining the Number of Classes in a Histogram

Number of Observations in Data Set	Number of Classes
Less than 25	5–6
25–50	7–14
More than 50	15–20

ascending order, so it's easy to locate the individual measurements. For example, in Figure 2.9, we can easily see that three of the R&D measurements are equal to 8.2, but we can't see that fact by inspecting the histogram in Figure 2.10. However, stem-and-leaf displays can become unwieldy for very large data sets. A very large number of stems and leaves causes the vertical and horizontal dimensions of the display to become cumbersome, diminishing the usefulness of the visual display.

EXAMPLE 2.2

GRAPHS FOR A QUANTITATIVE VARIABLE

Problem

A manufacturer of industrial wheels suspects that profitable orders are being lost because of the long time the firm takes to develop price quotes for potential customers. To investigate this possibility, 50 requests for price quotes were randomly selected from the set of all quotes made last year, and the processing time was determined for each quote. The processing times are displayed in Table 2.4, and each quote was classified according to whether the order was "lost" or no (i.e., whether or not the customer placed an order after receiving a price quote).

a. Use a statistical software package to create a frequency histogram for these data. Then shade the area under the histogram that corresponds to lost orders. Interpret the result.

b. Use a statistical software package to create a stem-and-leaf display for these data. Then shade each leaf of the display that corresponds to a lost order. Interpret the result.

 PRICEQUOTES

TABLE 2.4   Price Quote Processing Time (Days)

Request Number	Processing Time	Lost?	Request Number	Processing Time	Lost?
1	2.36	No	26	3.34	No
2	5.73	No	27	6.00	No
3	6.60	No	28	5.92	No
4	10.05	Yes	29	7.28	Yes
5	5.13	No	30	1.25	No
6	1.88	No	31	4.01	No
7	2.52	No	32	7.59	No
8	2.00	No	33	13.42	Yes
9	4.69	No	34	3.24	No
10	1.91	No	35	3.37	No
11	6.75	Yes	36	14.06	Yes
12	3.92	No	37	5.10	No
13	3.46	No	38	6.44	No
14	2.64	No	39	7.76	No
15	3.63	No	40	4.40	No
16	3.44	No	41	5.48	No
17	9.49	Yes	42	7.51	No
18	4.90	No	43	6.18	No
19	7.45	No	44	8.22	Yes
20	20.23	Yes	45	4.37	No
21	3.91	No	46	2.93	No
22	1.70	No	47	9.95	Yes
23	16.29	Yes	48	4.46	No
24	5.52	No	49	14.32	Yes
25	1.44	No	50	9.01	No

Figure 2.12

SPSS frequency histogram for price quote data

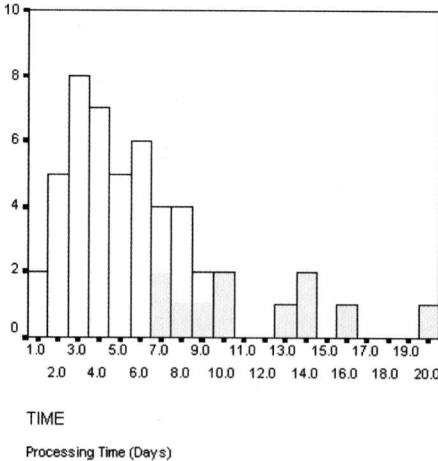

TIME

Processing Time (Days)

Solution   **a.** We used SPSS to generate the frequency histogram in Figure 2.12. Note that 20 classes were formed by the SPSS program. The class intervals are identified by their midpoints rather than their endpoints. The first interval has a midpoint of 1.0, the second 2.0, and so on. Consequently, the class intervals are (.5–1.5), (1.5–2.5), ..., (19.5–20.5). This histogram clearly shows the clustering of the measurements in the lower end of the distribution (between approximately 1 and 7 days), and the relatively few measurements in the upper end of the distribution (greater than 12 days). The shading of the area of the frequency histogram corresponding to lost orders clearly indicates that they lie in the upper tail of the distribution.

```
Stem-and-leaf of TIME   N  = 50
Leaf Unit = 0.10


    5    1    24789
   10    2    03569
   18    3    23344699
   24    4    034469
  (6)    5    114579
   20    6    01467
   15    7    24557
   10    8    2
    9    9    049
    6   10    0
    5   11
    5   12
    5   13    4
    4   14    03
    2   15
    2   16    2
    1   17
    1   18
    1   19
    1   20    2
```

b. We used MINITAB to generate the stem-and-leaf display in Figure 2.13. Note that the stem (the second column of the printout) consists of the number of whole days (digits to the right of the decimal), The leaf (the third column of the printout) is the tenths digit (first digit after the decimal) of each measurement.* Thus, the leaf 2 in the stem 20 (the last row of the printout) represents the time of 20.23 days. Like the histogram, the stem-and-leaf display shows the shaded "lost" orders in the upper-tail of the distribution.

Figure 2.13

MINITAB stem-and-leaf display for price quote data

*The first column of the MINITAB stem-and-leaf display represents the cumulative number of measurements from the class interval to the nearest extreme class interval.

Look Back As is usually the case for data sets that are not too large (say, fewer than 100 measurements), the stem-and-leaf display provides more detail than the histogram without being unwieldy. For instance, the stem-and-leaf display in Figure 2.13 clearly indicates not only that the lost orders are associated with high processing times (as does the histogram in Figure 2.12), but also exactly which of the times correspond to lost orders. Histograms are most useful for displaying very large data sets, when the overall shape of the distribution of measurements is more important than the identification of individual measurements. Nevertheless, the message of both graphical displays is clear: Establishing processing time limits may well result in fewer lost orders.

▇ **Now Work**   *Exercise 2.20*

■ ■ ■

Most statistical software packages can be used to generate histograms, stem-and-leaf displays, and dot plots. All three are useful tools for graphically describing data sets. We recommend that you generate and compare the displays whenever you can. You'll find that histograms are generally more useful for very large data sets, while stem-and-leaf displays and dot plots provide useful detail for smaller data sets.

Summary of Graphical Descriptive Methods for Quantitative Data

Dot plot: The numerical value of each quantitative measurement in the data set is represented by a dot on a horizontal scale. When data values repeat, the dots are placed above one another vertically.

Stem-and-leaf display: The numerical value of the quantitative variable is partitioned into a "stem" and a "leaf." The possible stems are listed in order in a column. The leaf for each quantitative measurement in the data set is placed the corresponding stem row. Leaves for observations with the same stem value are listed in increasing order horizontally.

Histogram: The possible numerical values of the quantitative variable are partitioned into class intervals, where each interval has the same width. These intervals form the scale of the horizontal axis. The frequency or relative frequency of observations in each class interval is determined. A vertical bar is placed over each class interval with height equal to either the class frequency or class relative frequency.

Histograms

Using the TI-83 Graphing Calculator

Making a Histogram from Raw Data

Step 1   *Enter the data*
Press **STAT** and select **1:Edit**
Note: If the list already contains data, clear the old data. Use the up arrow to highlight 'L1'. Press **CLEAR ENTER.**
Use the arrow and **ENTER** keys to enter the data set into **L1.**

Step 2   *Set up the histogram plot*
Press **2nd** and press **Y =** for **STAT PLOT**
Press **1** for **Plot 1**
Set the cursor so that **ON** is flashing.
For **Type**, use the arrow and Enter keys to highlight and select the histogram.
For **Xlist**, choose the column containing the data (in most cases, **L1**).
Note: Press **2nd 1** for **L1**
Freq should be set to 1.

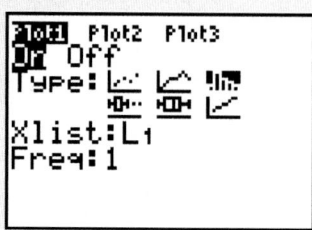

Step 3   *Select your window settings*
Press **WINDOW** and adjust the settings as follows:

Xmin = lowest class boundary
Xmax = highest class boundary
Xscl = class width
Ymin = 0
Ymax ≥ greatest class frequency
Yscl = 1
Xres = 1

Step 4   *View the graph*
Press **GRAPH**

Optiona   *Read class frequencies and class boundaries*
Step   You can press **TRACE** to read the class frequencies and class boundaries. Use the arrow keys to move between bars.

Example   The figures below show TI-83 window settings and histogram for the following sample data:
86, 70, 62, 98, 73, 56, 53, 92, 86, 37, 62, 83, 78, 49, 78, 37, 67, 79, 57

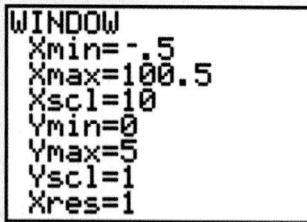
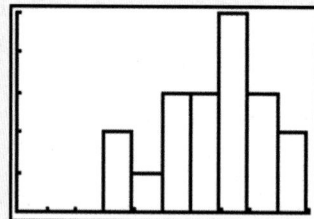

II Making a Histogram from a Frequency Table

Step 1   *Enter the data*
Press **STAT** and select **1:Edit**
Note: If a list already contains data, clear the old data. Use the up arrow to highlight the list name, '**L1**' or '**L2**'.
Press **CLEAR ENTER.**
Enter the midpoint of each class into **L1**
Enter the class frequencies or relative frequencies into **L2**

Step 2   *Set up the histogram plot*
Press **2nd** and **Y =** for **STAT PLOT**

Press **1** for **Plot 1**

Set the cursor so that **ON** is flashing.

For **Type**, use the arrow and Enter keys to highlight and select the histogram.

For **Xlist**, choose the column containing the midpoints.

For **Freq,** choose the column containing the frequencies or relative frequencies.

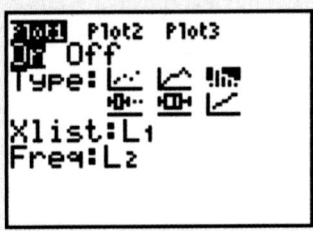

Steps 3–4 *Follow steps 3–4 given above.*

Note: To set up the Window for relative frequencies, be sure to set **Ymax** to a value that is greater than or equal to the largest relative frequency.

Statistics in Action Revisited

Interpreting Histograms

One of the quantitative variables measured in the ethics consultation survey of physicians was *Length of time in practice* (i.e., years of experience). Recall that the medical researchers hypothesize that older, more experienced physicians will be less likely to use ethics consultation in the future. To check the believability of this claim, we accessed the ETHICS data file in MINITAB and created two frequency histograms for years of experience—one for physicians who indicated they would use ethics consultation in the future, and one for physicians who would not use ethics consultation. These side-by-side histograms are displayed in Figure SIA2.4.

From the histograms, there is some support for the researchers' assertion. The histogram for the physicians who indicated they would use ethics consultation (the histogram on the right in Figure SIA2.4) shows that most of these physicians have been in practice between 10 and 20 years, while the histogram for nonusers (the histogram on the left in Figure SIA2.4) shows a tendency for these physicians to have more experience (over 20 years). However, the lack of data (only 21 observations) for the sample of physicians who would not use ethics consultation makes it difficult to reliably extend this inference to the population of physicians. In later chapters, we'll learn how to attach a measure of reliability to such an inference, even for small samples.

Figure SIA2.4

MINITAB histograms for years of practice—ethics consultation users versus nonusers

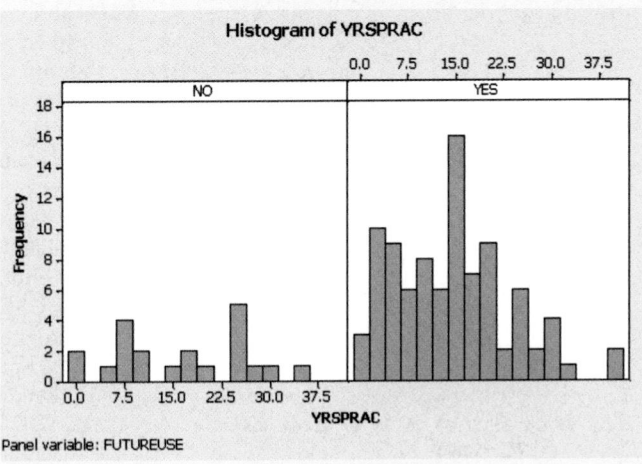

Exercises 2.16–2.32

Learning the Mechanics

2.16 Graph the relative frequency histogram for the 500 measurements summarized in the accompanying relative frequency table.

Measurement Class	Relative Frequency
.5–2.5	.10
2.5–4.5	.15
4.5–6.5	.25
6.5–8.5	.20
8.5–10.5	.05
10.5–12.5	.10
12.5–14.5	.10
14.5–16.5	.05

2.17 Refer to Exercise 2.16. Calculate the number of the 500 measurements falling into each of the measurement classes. Then graph a frequency histogram for these data.

2.18 Consider the stem-and-leaf display shown here.

Stem	Leaf
5	1
4	457
3	00036
2	1134599
1	2248
0	012

a. How many observations were in the original data set?

b. In the bottom row of the stem-and-leaf display, identify the stem, the leaves, and the numbers in the orignal data set represented by this stem and its leaves.

c. Re-create all the numbers in the data set and construct a dot plot.

2.19 MINITAB was used to generate the following histogram:

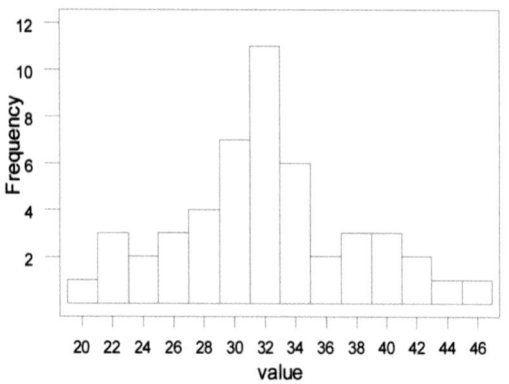

a. Is this a frequency histogram or a relative frequency histogram? Explain.   Frequency

b. How many measurement classes were used in the construction of this histogram?   14

c. How many measurements are in the data set described by this histogram?   49

Applying the Concepts—Basic

2.20 The next graph summarizes the scores obtained by 100 students on a questionnaire designed to measure managerial ability. (Scores are integer values that range from 0 to 20. A high score indicates a high level of ability.)

a. Which measurement class contains the highest proportion of test scores?   7.5–9.5

b. What proportion of the scores lie between 3.5 and 5.5?

c. What proportion of the scores are higher than 11.5?

d. How many students scored less than 5.5?   20

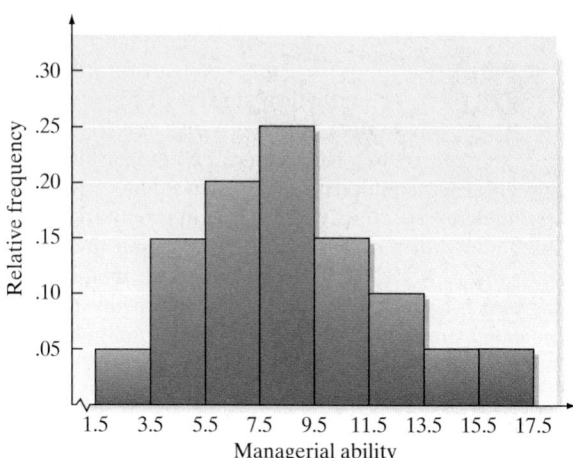

2.21 The United States Golf Association (USGA) Handicap System is designed to allow golfers of differing abilities to enjoy fair competition. The handicap index is a measure of a player's potential scoring ability on an 18-hole golf course of standard difficulty. For example, on a par-72 course, a golfer with a handicap of 7 will typically have a score of 79 (seven strokes over par). Over 4.5 million golfers have an official USGA Handicap index. The handicap indexes for both male and female golfers were obtained from the USGA and are summarized in the following two histograms.

a. What percentage of male USGA golfers have a handicap greater than 20?   ≈.285

b. What percentage of female USGA golfers have a handicap greater than 20?   ≈.82

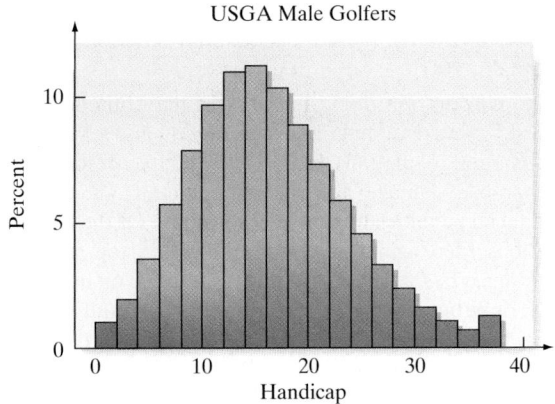

USGA Male Golfers

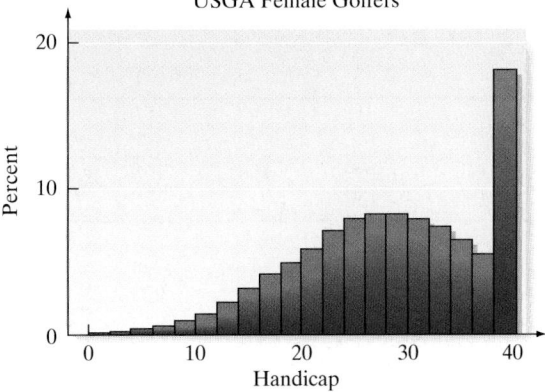

USGA Female Golfers

DDT

2.22 Refer to Exercise 2.9 (p. 53) and the U.S. Army Corps of Engineers data on contaminated fish saved in the **DDT** file. In addition to species (channel catfish, largemouth bass, or smallmouth buffalofish), the length (in centimeters), weight (in grams), and DDT level (in parts per million) was measured for each of the 144 captured fish.

   a. Use a graphical method to describe the distribution of the 144 fish lengths.

   b. Use a graphical method to describe the distribution of the 144 fish weights.

   c. Use a graphical method to describe the distribution of the 144 DDT measurements.

2.23 Mark McGwire of the St. Louis Cardinals hit 70 home runs during the 1998 Major League Baseball season, breaking a record held by Roger Maris (61 home runs) since 1961. (In 2001, Barry Bonds broke the record again with 73 home runs.) J. S. Simonoff of New York University collected data on the number of runs scored by the cardinals in games in which McGwire hit home runs (*Journal of Statistics Education*, Vol. 6, 1998). The data are reproduced in the table.

STLRUNS

6	6	3	11	13
8	1	10	6	7
5	8	9	6*	3
8	2	3	6*	6
15*	2	8*	5	6
8	6	2	3	5
5	8	4	10*	
8	9	4	4	
3	5	3	11*	
5	7	6	1	
2	3	8	4	
6	2	7*	6*	
3	7	14*	4*	

   a. Construct a stem-and-leaf display for the number of runs scored by St. Louis during games when Mc-Gwire hit a home run.

   b. The asterisks in the table represent games in which McGwire hit multiple home runs. On the stem-and-leaf display, circle the run values for these games. Do you detect any patterns?

Applying the Concepts—Intermediate

BWECS

2.24 Refer to Exercise 2.10 (p. 53) and the *Business Week* "Executive Compensation Scoreboard." In addition to Industry type of a CEO's company, *Business Week* recorded the 2002 total compensation (salary, bonus, and long-term compensation) for each of the 363 CEOs in the survey. The data, measured in thousands of dollars, are saved in the **BWECS** file under the variable name PAY2002.

   a. Use a graphical method to describe the 2002 total compensations of all 363 CEOs in the survey.

   b. Use a graphical method to describe the 2002 total compensations of CEOs in the Telecommunications industry.

   c. Use a graphical method to describe the 2002 total compensations of CEOs in the Financial Services industry.

   d. Compare the two graphs, parts b and c. What do you conclude about how well CEOs are paid in the two industries?

DIAMONDS

2.25 Refer to the *Journal of Statistics Education* study of diamonds, Exercise 2.11 (p. 53). In addition to color and clarity, the independent certification group (GIA, HRD, or IGI) and the number of carats were recorded for each of 308 diamonds for sale on the open market. Recall that the data are saved in the **DIAMONDS** file.

   a. Use a graphical method to describe the carat distribution of all 308 diamonds.

   b. Use a graphical method to describe the carat distribution of diamonds certified by the GIA group.

c. Repeat part **b** for the HRD and IGI certification groups.

d. Compare the three carat distributions, parts **b** and **c**. Is there one particular certification group that appears to be assessing diamonds with higher carats than the others? HRD group

2.26 In a manufacturing plant a *work center* is a specific production facility that consists of one or more people and/or machines and is treated as one unit for the purposes of capacity requirements planning and job scheduling. If jobs arrive at a particular work center at a faster rate than they depart, the work center impedes the overall production process and is referred to as a *bottleneck* (Fogarty, Blackstone, and Hoffmann, *Production and Inventory Management*, 1991). The data in the following table were collected by an operations manager for use in investigating a potential bottleneck work center.

Construct dot plots for the two sets of data. Do the dot plots suggest that the work center may be a bottleneck? Explain. Yes

2.27 Any corporation doing business in the United States must be aware of and obey both federal and state environmental regulations. Failure to do so may result in irreparable damage to the environment and costly financial penalties to guilty corporations. Of the 55 civil actions filed against corporations within the state of Arkansas by the U.S. Department of Justice on behalf of the Environmental Protection Agency, 38 resulted in financial penalties. These penalties along with the laws that were violated are listed in the table at the bottom of the page. (*Note:* Some companies were involved in more than one civil action.)

WORKCTR

Number of Items Arriving at Work Center per Hour

| 155 | 115 | 156 | 150 | 159 | 163 | 172 | 143 | 159 | 166 | 148 | 175 |
| 151 | 161 | 138 | 148 | 129 | 135 | 140 | 152 | 139 | | | |

Number of Items Departing Work Center per Hour

| 156 | 109 | 127 | 148 | 135 | 119 | 140 | 127 | 115 | 122 | 99 | 106 |
| 171 | 123 | 135 | 125 | 107 | 152 | 111 | 137 | 161 | | | |

CLEANAIR

Company Identification Number	Penalty	Law*	Company Identification Number	Penalty	Law*
01	$ 930,000	CERCLA	17	20,000	CWA
02	10,000	CWA	18	40,000	CWA
03	90,600	CAA	19	20,000	CWA
04	123,549	CWA	20	40,000	CWA
05	37,500	CWA	21	850,000	CWA
06	137,500	CWA	22	35,000	CWA
07	2,500	SDWA	23	4,000	CAA
08	1,000,000	CWA	24	25,000	CWA
09	25,000	CAA	25	40,000	CWA
09	25,000	CAA	26	30,000	CAA
10	25,000	CWA	27	15,000	CWA
10	25,000	RCRA	28	15,000	CAA
11	19,100	CAA	29	105,000	CAA
12	100,000	CWA	30	20,000	CWA
12	30,000	CWA	31	400,000	CWA
13	35,000	CAA	32	85,000	CWA
13	43,000	CWA	33	300,000	CWA/
14	190,000	CWA			RCRA/
15	15,000	CWA			CERCLA
16	90,000	RCRA	34	30,000	CWA

*CAA: Clean Air Act: CERCLA: Comprehensive Environmental Response, Compensation, and Liability Act: RCRA: Resource Conservation and Recovery Act: SDWA: Safe Drinking Water Act.

Source: Tabor, R. H., and Stanwick, S. D. "Arkansas: An Environmental Perspective." *Arkansas Business and Economic Review,* Vol. 28. No. Summer 1995, pp. 22–32 (Table 4).

a. Construct a stem-and-leaf display for all 38 penalties.

b. Circle the individual leaves that are associated with penalties imposed for violations of the Clean Air Act (CAA).

c. What does the pattern of circles in part **b** suggest about the severity of the penalties imposed for Clean Air Act violations relative to the other types of violations reported in the table? Explain.

2.28 In order to estimate how long it will take to produce a particular product, a manufacturer will study the relationship between production time per unit and the number of units that have been produced. The line or curve characterizing this relationship is called a *learning curve* (Adler and Clark, *Management Science*, Mar. 1991). Twenty-five employees, all of whom were performing the same production task for the tenth time, were observed. Each person's task completion time (in minutes) was recorded. The same 25 employees were observed again the 30th time they performed the same task and the 50th time they performed the task. The resulting completion times are shown in the table below.

a. Use a statistical software package to construct a frequency histogram for each of the three data sets.

b. Compare the histograms. Does it appear that the relationship between task completion time and the number of times the task is performed is in agreement with the observations noted above about production processes in general? Explain.   Yes

COMPTIME

Employee	Performance		
	10th	30th	50th
1	15	16	10
2	21	10	5
3	30	12	7
4	17	9	9
5	18	7	8
6	22	11	11
7	33	8	12
8	41	9	9
9	10	5	7
10	14	15	6
11	18	10	8
12	25	11	14
13	23	9	9
14	19	11	8
15	20	10	10
16	22	13	8
17	20	12	7
18	19	8	8
19	18	20	6
20	17	7	5
21	16	6	6
22	20	9	4
23	22	10	15
24	19	10	7
25	24	11	20

Applying the Concepts—Advanced

2.29 Educators are constantly evaluating the efficacy of public schools in the education and training of American students. One quantitative assessment of change over time is the difference in scores on the SAT, which has been used for decades by colleges and universities as one criterion for admission. The file **SATSCORES** contains the average SAT scores for each of the 50 states and District of Columbia for the years 1990 and 2000. The first five observations and last two observations in the data set are shown in the table.

a. Use graphs to display the two SAT score distributions. How have the distributions of state scores changed over the last decade?

b. As another method of comparing the 1990 and 2000 SAT scores, compute the *paired difference* by subtracting the 1990 score from the 2000 score for each state. Summarize these differences with a graph.

c. Interpret the graph, part **b.** How do your conclusions compare to those of part **a?**

d. Based on the graph, part **b,** what is the largest improvement in SAT score between 1990 and 2000? Identify the state associated with this improvement.
Wisconsin

SATSCORES

State	1990	2000
Alabama	1079	1114
Alaska	1015	1034
Arizona	1041	1044
Arkansas	1077	1117
California	1002	1015
⋮	⋮	⋮
Wisconsin	1111	1181
Wyoming	1072	1090

Source: College Entrance Examination Board, 2001.

2.30 Financially distressed firms can gain protection from their creditors while they restructure by filing for protection under U.S. Bankruptcy Codes. In a *prepackaged bankruptcy*, a firm negotiates a reorganization plan with its creditors prior to filing for bankruptcy. This can result in a much quicker exit from bankruptcy than traditional bankruptcy filings. Brian Betker conducted a study of 49 prepackaged bankruptcies that were filed between 1986 and 1993 and reported the results in *Financial Management* (Spring 1995). The table on page 68 lists the time in bankruptcy (in months) for these 49 companies. The table also lists the results of a vote by each company's board of directors concerning their preferred reorganization plan. (*Note:* "Joint" = joint exchange offer with prepackaged bankruptcy solicitation; "Prepack" = prepackaged bankruptcy solicitation only; "None" = no pre-filing vote held.)

BANKRUPT

Company	Pre-filing Votes	Time in Bankruptcy (months)
AM International	None	3.9
Anglo Energy	Prepack	1.5
Arizona Biltmore*	Prepack	1.0
Astrex	None	10.1
Barry's Jewelers	None	4.1
Calton	Prepack	1.9
Cencor	Joint	1.4
Charter Medical*	Prepack	1.3
Cherokee*	Joint	1.2
Circle Express	Prepack	4.1
Cook Inlet Comm.	Prepack	1.1
Crystal Oil	None	3.0
Divi Hotels	None	3.2
Edgell Comm.*	Prepack	1.0
Endevco	Prepack	3.8
Gaylord Container	Joint	1.2
Great Amer. Comm.*	Prepack	1.0
Hadson	Prepack	1.5
In-Store Advertising	Prepack	1.0
JPS Textiles*	Prepack	1.4
Kendall*	Prepack	1.2
Kinder-Care	None	4.2
Kroy*	Prepack	3.0
Ladish*	Joint	1.5
LaSalle Energy*	Prepack	1.6
LIVE Entertainment	Joint	1.4
Mayflower Group*	Prepack	1.4
Memorex Telex*	Prepack	1.1
Munsingwear	None	2.9
Nat'l Environmental	Joint	5.2
Petrolane Gas	Prepack	1.2
Price Communications	None	2.4
Republic Health*	Joint	4.5
Resorts Int'l*	None	7.8
Restaurant Enterprises*	Prepack	1.5
Rymer Foods	Joint	2.1
SCI TV*	Prepack	2.1
Southland*	Joint	3.9
Specialty Equipment*	None	2.6
SPI Holdings*	Joint	1.4
Sprouse-Reitz	Prepack	1.4
Sunshine Metals	Joint	5.4
TIE/Communications	None	2.4
Trump Plaza	Prepack	1.7
Trump Taj Mahal	Prepack	1.4
Trump's Castle	Prepack	2.7
USG	Prepack	1.2
Vyquest	Prepack	4.1
West Point Acq.*	Prepack	2.9

*Leveraged buyout.

Source: Betker. B. L. "An Empirical Examination of Prepackaged Bankruptcy." *Financial Management,* Vol. 24, No. 1, Spring 1995, p. 6 (Table 2).

a. Construct a stem-and-leaf display for the length of time in bankruptcy for all 49 companies.
b. Summarize the information reflected in the stem-and-leaf display, part **a.** Make a general statement about the length of time in bankruptcy for firms using "prepacks."
c. Select a graphical technique that will permit a comparison of the time-in-bankruptcy distributions for the three types of "prepack" firms: those who held no pre-filing vote; those who voted their preference for a joint solution; and those who voted their preference for a prepack.
d. The companies that were reorganized through a leveraged buyout are identified by an asterisk (*) in the table. Identify these firms on the stem-and-leaf display, part **a,** by circling their bankruptcy times. Do you observe any pattern in the graph? Explain.   No pattern

2.31 It's not uncommon for hearing aids to malfunction and cancel the desired signal. *IEEE Transactions on Speech and Audio Processing* (May 1995) reported on a new audio processing system designed to limit the amount of signal cancellation that may occur. The system utilizes a mathematical equation that involves a variable, V, called a *sufficient norm constraint*. A histogram for realizations of V, produced using simulation, is shown below.

a. Estimate the percentage of realizations of V with values ranging from .425 to .675.   44.75%
b. Cancellation of the desired signal is limited by selecting a norm constraint V. Find the value of V for a company that wants to market the new hearing a so that only 10% of the realizations have value below the selected level.   .325

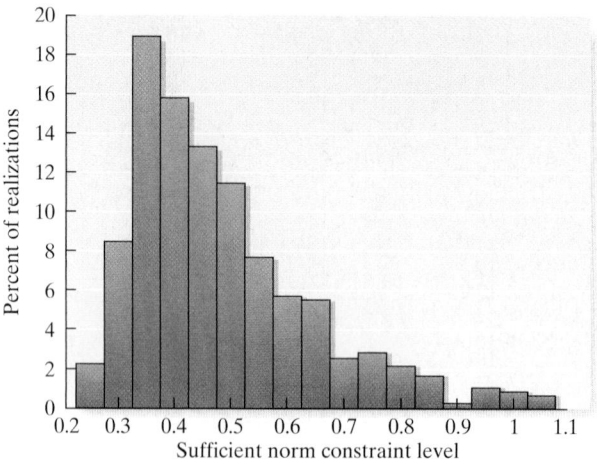

Source: Hoffman, M. W., and Buckley, K. M. "Robust Time-Domain Processing of Broadband Microphone Array Data." *IEEE Transactions on Speech and Audio Processing,* Vol. 3, No. 3, May 1995, p. 199 (Figure 4). © 1995 IEEE.

2.32 Production processes may be classified as *make-to-stock processes* or *make-to-order processes*. Make-to-stock processes are designed to produce a standardized product that can be sold to customers from the firm's inventory. Make-to-order processes are designed to produce products according to customer specifications (Schroeder, *Operations Management*, 1993). In general, performance of make-to-order processes is measured by delivery time—the time from receipt of an order until the product is delivered to the customer. The following data set is a sample of delivery times (in days) for a particular make-to-order firm last year. The delivery times marked by an asterisk are associated with customers who subsequently placed additional orders with the firm.

DELTIMES

50^*	64^*	56^*	43^*	64^*	82^*	65^*	49^*	32^*	63^*	44^*	71
54^*	51^*	102	49^*	73^*	50^*	39^*	86	33^*	95	59^*	51^*
68											

Concerned that they are losing potential repeat customers because of long delivery times, the management would like to establish a guideline for the maximum tolerable delivery time. Use a graphical method to help suggest a guideline. Explain your reasoning. Use 67 days

2.3 Summation Notation

Now that we've examined some graphical techniques for summarizing and describing quantitative data sets, we turn to numerical methods for accomplishing this objective. Before giving the formulas for calculating numerical descriptive measures, let's look at some shorthand notation that will simplify our calculation instructions. Remember that such notation is used for one reason only—to avoid repeating the same verbal descriptions over and over. If you mentally substitute the verbal definition of a symbol each time you read it, you'll soon get used to it.

Teaching Tip

Illustrate the summation notation using Σx, Σx^2, and $(\Sigma x)^2$. Point out that $\Sigma x^2 \neq (\Sigma x)^2$.

We denote the measurements of a quantitative data set as follows: $x_1, x_2, x_3, \ldots, x_n$ where x_1 is the first measurement in the data set, x_2 is the second measurement in the data set, x_3 is the third measurement in the data set, $\ldots$, and x_n is the nth (and last) measurement in the data set. Thus, if we have five measurements in a set of data, we will write x_1, x_2, x_3, x_4, x_5 to represent the measurements. If the actual numbers are 5, 3, 8, 5, and 4, we have $x_1 = 5$, $x_2 = 3$, $x_3 = 8$, $x_4 = 5$, and $x_5 = 4$.

Most of the formulas we use require a summation of numbers. For example, one sum we'll need to obtain is the sum of all the measurements in the data set, or $x_1 + x_2 + x_3 + \cdots + x_n$. To shorten the notation, we use the symbol Σ for the summation. That is, $x_1 + x_2 + x_3 + \cdots + x_n = \sum_{i=1}^{n} x_i$. Verbally translate $\sum_{i=1}^{n} x_i$ as follows: "The sum of the measurements, whose typical member is x_i, beginning with the member x_1 and ending with the member x_n."

Suggested Exercise 2.33

Suppose, as in our earlier example, $x_1 = 5$, $x_2 = 3$, $x_3 = 8$, $x_4 = 5$, and $x_5 = 4$. Then the sum of the five measurements, denoted $\sum_{i=1}^{5} x_i$, is obtained as follows:

$$\sum_{i=1}^{5} x_i = x_1 + x_2 + x_3 + x_4 + x_5$$

$$= 5 + 3 + 8 + 5 + 4 = 25$$

Another important calculation requires that we square each measurement and then sum the squares. The notation for this sum is $\sum_{i=1}^{n} x_i^2$. For the preceding five measurements, we have

$$\sum_{i=1}^{5} x_i^2 = x_1^2 + x_2^2 + x_3^2 + x_4^2 + x_5^2$$

$$= 5^2 + 3^2 + 8^2 + 5^2 + 4^2$$

$$= 25 + 9 + 64 + 25 + 16 = 139$$

In general, the symbol following the summation sign Σ represents the variable (or function of the variable) that is to be summed.

The Meaning of Summation Notation $\sum_{i=1}^{n} x_i$

Sum the measurements on the variable that appears to the right of the summation symbol, beginning with the 1st measurement and ending with the nth measurement.

Exercises 2.33–2.36

Learning the Mechanics

Note: In all exercises, Σ represents $\sum_{i=1}^{n}$.

2.33 A data set contains the observations 5, 1, 3, 2, 1. Find
   a. Σx 12   **b.** Σx^2 40   **c.** $\Sigma(x-1)$ 7
   d. $\Sigma(x-1)^2$ 21   **e.** $(\Sigma x)^2$ 144

2.34 Suppose a data set contains the observations 3, 8, 4, 5, 3, 4, 6. Find
   a. Σx 33   **b.** Σx^2 175   **c.** $\Sigma(x-5)^2$ 20
   d. $\Sigma(x-2)^2$ 71   **e.** $(\Sigma x)^2$ 1,089

2.35 Refer to Exercise 2.33. Find
   a. $\Sigma x^2 - \dfrac{(\Sigma x)^2}{5}$ **b.** $\Sigma(x-2)^2$ **c.** $\Sigma x^2 - 10$

2.36 A data set contains the observations 6, 0, −2, −1, 3. Find
   a. Σx 6   **b.** Σx^2 50   **c.** $\Sigma x^2 - \dfrac{(\Sigma x)^2}{5}$ 42.8

2.4 Numerical Measures of Central Tendency

When we speak of a data set, we refer to either a sample or a population. If statistical inference is our goal, we'll wish ultimately to use sample **numerical descriptive measures** to make inferences about the corresponding measures for population.

As you'll see, a large number of numerical methods are available to describe quantitative data sets. Most of these methods measure one of two data characteristics:

1. The **central tendency** of the set of measurements—that is, the tendency of the data to cluster, or center, about certain numerical values (see Figure 2.14a).

2. The **variability** of the set measurements—that is, the spread of the data (see Figure 2.14b).

Figure 2.14
Numerical descriptive measures

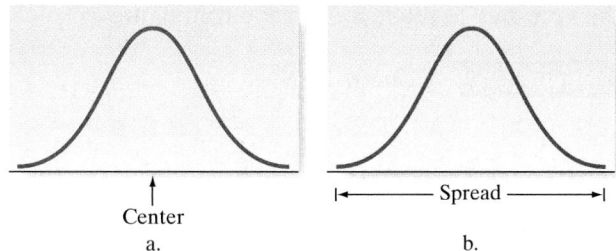

Center
a.

|←——— Spread ———→|
b.

In this section we concentrate on measures of central tendency. In the next section, we discuss measures of variability.

The most popular and best-understood measure of central tendency for quantitative data set is the *arithmetic mean* (or simply the *mean*) of a data set.

DEFINITION 2.4

The **mean** of a set of quantitative data is the sum of the measurements divided by the number of measurements contained in the data set.

In everyday terms, the mean is the average value of the data set and is often used to represent a "typical" value. We denote the **mean of a sample** of measurements by $\bar{x}$ (read "x-bar"), and represent the formula for its calculation as shown in the box.

Formula for a Sample Mean

$$\bar{x} = \frac{\sum_{i=1}^{n} x_i}{n}$$

EXAMPLE 2.3   CALCULATING THE SAMPLE MEAN

Problem Calculate the mean of the following five sample measurements: 5, 3, 8, 5, 6.

Solution Using the definition of sample mean and the summation notation, we find

$$\bar{x} = \frac{\sum_{i=1}^{5} x_i}{5} = \frac{5 + 3 + 8 + 5 + 6}{5} = \frac{27}{5} = 5.4$$

$\bar{x} = 5.4$

Thus, the mean of this sample is 5.4.

Look Back There is no specific rule for rounding when calculating $\bar{x}$ because $\bar{x}$ is specifically defined to be the sum of all measurements divided by n: that is, it is a specific fraction. When $\bar{x}$ is used for descriptive purposes, it is often convenient to round the calculated value of $\bar{x}$ to the number of significant figures used for the original measurements. When $\bar{x}$ is to be used in other calculations, however, it may be necessary to retain more significant figures.

Now Work   *Exercise 2.38*

■ ■ ■

EXAMPLE 2.4   THE SAMPLE MEAN ON A PRINTOUT

Problem   Calculate the sample mean for the R&D expenditure percentages of the 50 companies given in Table 2.2.

Solution   The mean R&D percentage for the 50 companies is denoted

$$\bar{x} = \frac{\sum_{i=1}^{50} x_i}{50}$$

$\bar{x} = 8.492$

	A	B
1	RDPct	
2		
3	Mean	8.492
4	Standard Error	0.2801
5	Median	8.05
6	Mode	6.9
7	Standard Deviation	1.980604
8	Sample Variance	3.922792
9	Kurtosis	0.419288
10	Skewness	0.854601
11	Range	8.3
12	Minimum	5.2
13	Maximum	13.5
14	Sum	424.6
15	Count	50
16		

Figure 2.15
EXCEL numerical descriptive measures for 50 R&D percentages

Rather than compute $\bar{x}$ by hand (or calculator), we employed EXCEL to compute the mean. The EXCEL printout is shown in Figure 2.15. The sample mean, highlighted on the printout, is $\bar{x} = 8.492$.

Look Back Given this information, you can visualize a distribution of R&D percentages centered in the vicinity of $\bar{x} = 8.492$. An examination of the relative frequency histogram (Figure 2.10) confirms that $\bar{x}$ does in fact fall near the center of the distribution.

■ ■ ■

The sample mean $\bar{x}$ will play an important role in accomplishing our objective of making inferences about populations based on sample information. For this reason we need to use a different symbol for the *mean of a population*—the mean of the set of measurements on every unit in the population. We use the Greek letter μ (mu) for the population mean.

Symbols for the Sample and Population Mean

In this text, we adopt a general policy of using Greek letters to represent population numerical descriptive measures and Roman letters to represent corresponding descriptive measures for the sample. The symbols for the mean are

$\bar{x}$ = Sample mean
μ = Population mean

We'll often use the sample mean, $\bar{x}$, to estimate (make an inference about) the population mean, μ. For example, the percentages of revenues spent on R&D by the population consisting of *all* U.S. companies has a mean equal to some value, μ. Our sample of 50 companies yielded percentages with a mean of $\bar{x} = 8.492$. If, as is usually the case, we don't have access to the measurements for the entire population, we could use $\bar{x}$ as an estimator or approximator for μ. Then we'd need to know

Teaching Tip
When calculating a population mean, the denominator is the population size, *N*.

Teaching Tip
Explain that Greek letters are used to represent population values throughout the text.

Figure 2.16
Location of the median

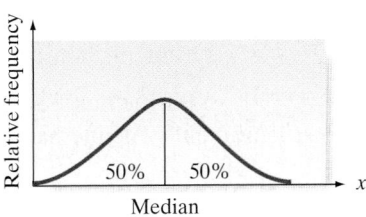

Teaching Tip

Average, mean, and expected value are all terms that are used to represent the same descriptive measure.

something about the reliability of our inference. That is, we'd need to know how accurately we might expect $\bar{x}$ to estimate μ. In Chapter 7, we'll find that this accuracy depends on two factors:

1. The *size of the sample.* The larger the sample, the more accurate the estimate will tend to be.
2. The *variability,* or *spread, of the data.* All other factors remaining constant, the more variable the data, the less accurate the estimate.

Another important measure of central tendency is the *median.*

Teaching Tip

Look ahead to sampling distributions to plant the idea that measures of center and spread will be used together to generate estimates of population values.

DEFINITION 2.5

The **median** of a quantitative data set is the middle number when the measurements are arranged in ascending (or descending) order.

Teaching Tip

Remind students to order the data before calculating a value for the median.

The median is of most value in describing large data sets. If the data set is characterized by a relative frequency histogram (Figure 2.17), the median is the point on the *x*-axis such that half the area under the histogram lies above the median and half lies below. [*Note:* In Section 2.2 we observed that the relative frequency associated with a particular interval on the horizontal axis is proportional to the amount of area under the histogram that lies above the interval.] We denote the *median of a sample* by *m*.

Calculating a Sample Median, *m*

Arrange the *n* measurements from smallest to largest.

1. If *n* is odd, *m* is the middle number.
2. If *n* is even, *m* is the mean of the middle two numbers.

EXAMPLE 2.5   **FINDING THE MEDIAN**

Problem Consider the following sample of $n = 7$ measurements: 5, 7, 4, 5, 20, 6, 2.

m = 5

a. Calculate the median *m* of this sample.
b. Eliminate the last measurement (the 2) and calculate the median of the remaining $n = 6$ measurements.

m = 5.5

Solution a. The seven measurements in the sample are ranked in ascending order: 2, 4, 5, 5, 6, 7, 20. Because the number of measurements is odd, the median is the middle measurement. Thus, the median of this sample is $m = 5$ (the second 5 listed in the sequence).

b. After removing the 2 from the set of measurements, we rank the sample measurements in ascending order as follows: 4, 5, 5, 6, 7, 20.

Now the number of measurements is even, so we average the middle two measurements. The median is $m = (5 + 6)/2 = 5.5$.

Look Back When the sample size n is even (as in part **b**), exactly half of the measurements will fall below the calculated median m. However, when n is odd (as in part **a**) the percentage of measurements that fall below m is approximately 50%. This approximation improves as n increases.

Now Work *Exercise 2.37*

■ ■ ■

In certain situations, the median may be a better measure of central tendency than the mean. In particular, the median is less sensitive than the mean to extremely large or small measurements. Note, for instance, that all but one of the measurements in part **a** of Example 2.5 center about $x = 5$. The single relatively large measurement, $x = 20$, does not affect the value of the median, 5, but it causes the mean, $\bar{x} = 7$, to lie to the right of most of the measurements.

As another example of data from which the central tendency is better described by the median than the mean, consider the salaries of professional athletes (e.g., National Basketball Association players). The presence of just a few athletes (e.g., Shaquille O'Neal) with very high salaries will affect the mean more than the median. Thus, the median will provide a more accurate picture of the typical salary for the professional league. The mean could exceed the vast majority of the sample measurements (salaries), making it a misleading measure of central tendency.

EXAMPLE 2.6   THE MEDIAN ON A PRINTOUT

Problem   Calculate the median for the 50 R&D percentages given in Table 2.2. Compare the median to the mean found in Example 2.4.

Solution   For this large data set, we again resort to a computer analysis. The median is highlighted on the EXCEL printout, Figure 2.15. You can see that the median is 8.05. This value implies that half of the 50 R&D percentages in the data set fall below 8.05 and half lie above 8.05.

$m = 8.05$

Note that the mean (8.492) for these data is larger than the median. This fact indicates that the data are **skewed** to the right—that is, there are more extreme measurements in the right tail of the distribution than in the left tail (recall the histogram, Figure 2.10).

Teaching Tip

Explain the median as the point on the graph that has 50% of the data below it and 50% of the data above it. Explain the mean as the point in the distribution that would balance the graph if it could be placed on your finger.

Suggested Exercise 2.37

Look Back In general, extreme values (large or small) affect the mean more than the median since these values are used explicitly in the calculation of the mean. On the other hand, the median is not affected directly by extreme measurements since only the middle measurement (or two middle measurements) is explicitly used to calculate the median. Consequently, if measurements are pulled toward one end of the distribution (as with the R&D percentages), the mean will shift toward that tail more than the median.

■ ■ ■

DEFINITION 2.6

A data set is said to be **skewed** if one tail of the distribution has more extreme observations than the other tail.

A comparison of the mean and median gives us a general method for detecting skewness in data sets, as shown in the next box.

Teaching Tip

Use a numerical example with one or two extreme values to show how they affect the value of the mean and how they have no effect on the median.

Detecting Skewness by Comparing the Mean and the Median

If the data set is skewed to the right, then the median is less than the mean.

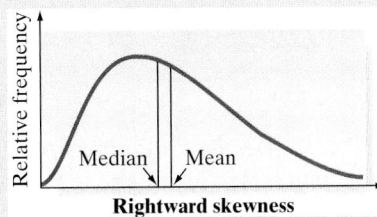

If the data set is symmetric, the mean equals the median.

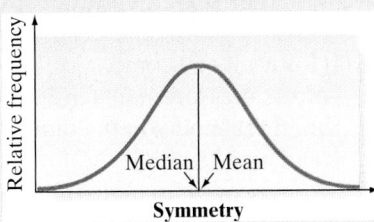

Teaching Tip

Explain that in skewed distributions the median is the preferred measure of center as the mean is affected by the extreme values, while the median is not.

If the data set is skewed to the left, the mean is less than (to the left of) the median.

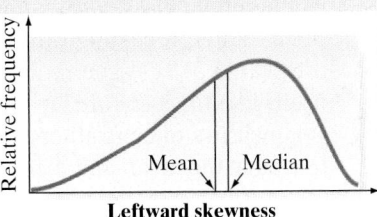

Now Work   *Exercise 2.43*

A third measure of central tendency is the *mode* of a set of measurements.

DEFINITION 2.7

The **mode** is the measurement that occurs most frequently in the data set.

EXAMPLE 2.7

FINDING THE MODE

Problem   Each of 10 taste testers rated a new brand of barbecue sauce on a 10 point scale, where 1 = awful and 10 = excellent. Find the mode for the 10 ratings shown below.

Mode = 9

$$8\ 7\ 9\ 6\ 8\ 10\ 9\ 9\ 5\ 7$$

Solution   Since 9 occurs most often, the mode of the 10 taste ratings is 9.

Teaching Tip
Illustrate an example that has two modes (bimodal), and explain that no mode exists when all data values appear just once.

Look Back Note that the data are actually qualitative in nature (e.g., "awful," "excellent"). The mode is particularly useful for describing qualitative data. The modal category is simply the category (or class) that occurs most often.

Now Work   *Exercise 2.41*

■ ■ ■

Because it emphasizes data concentration, the mode is used with quantitative data sets to locate the region in which much of the data is concentrated. A retailer of men's clothing would be interested in the modal neck size and sleeve length of potential customers. The modal income class of the laborers in the United States is of interest to the Labor Department.

Teaching Tip
Show that the mode is the only measure of center that has to be an actual data value in the sample.

For some quantitative data sets, the mode may not be very meaningful. For example, consider the percentages of revenues spent on research and development (R&D) by 50 companies, Table 2.2. A reexamination of the data reveals that three of the measurements are repeated three times: 6.5%, 6.9%, and 8.2%. Thus, there are three modes in the sample and none is particularly useful as a measure of central tendency.

Teaching Tip
Review the relationship of the mean, median, and mode in both symmetric and skewed distributions.

A more meaningful measure can be obtained from a relative frequency histogram for quantitative data. The class interval containing the largest relative frequency is called the **modal class.** Several definitions exist for locating the position of the mode within a modal class, but the simplest is to define the mode as the midpoint of the modal class. For example, examine the relative frequency histogram for the price quote processing times in Figure 2.11. You can see that the modal class is the interval (2.5–3.5). The mode (the midpoint) is 3.0. This modal class (and the mode itself) identifies the area in which the data are most concentrated, and in that sense it is a measure of central tendency. However, for most applications involving quantitative data, the mean and median provide more descriptive information than the mode.

Exercises 2.37–2.54

Learning the Mechanics

2.37 Calculate the mean and median of the following grade point averages:

$$3.2\quad 2.5\quad 2.1\quad 3.7\quad 2.8\quad 2.0$$

2.38 Calculate the mean for samples where
a. $n = 10$, $\Sigma x = 85$ 8.5
b. $n = 16$, $\Sigma x = 400$

c. $n = 45$, $\Sigma x = 35$ .78
d. $n = 18$, $\Sigma x = 242$

2.39 Explain how the relationship between the mean and median provides information about the symmetry or skewness of the data's distribution.

2.40 Explain the difference between the calculation of the median for an odd and an even number of measurements. Construct one data set consisting of five measurements

One-Variable Descriptive Statistics

Using the TI-83 Graphing Calculator

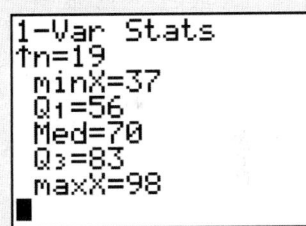

Step 1   Enter the data
Press STAT and select 1:Edit
Note: If the list already contains data, clear the old data. Use the up arrow to highlight 'L1'. Press CLEAR ENTER.
Use the arrow and ENTER keys to enter the data set into L1.

Step 2   Calculate descriptive statistics
Press STAT
Press the right arrow key to highlight CALC

Press ENTER for 1-Var Stats
Enter the name of the list containing your data.
Press 2nd 1 for L1 (or 2nd 2 for L2 etc.)
Press ENTER

You should see the statistics on your screen. Some of the statistics are off the bottom of the screen. Use the down arrow to scroll through to see the remaining statistics. Use the up arrow to scroll back up.

Example   The descriptive statistics for the sample data set

86, 70, 62, 98, 73, 56, 53, 92, 86, 37, 62, 83, 78, 49, 78, 37, 67, 79, 57

The output screens for this example are shown below.

```
1-Var Stats
 x̄=68.57894737
 Σx=1303
 Σx²=94897
 Sx=17.54142966
 σx=17.07357389
↓n=19
```

```
1-Var Stats
↑n=19
 minX=37
 Q₁=56
 Med=70
 Q₃=83
 maxX=98
```

Sorting Data   The descriptive statistics do not include the mode. To find the mode, sort your data as follows:

Press STAT
Press 2 for SORTA(
Enter the name of the list your data is in. If your data is in L1, press 2nd 1

Press ENTER
The screen will say: DONE
To see the sorted data, press STAT and select 1:Edit
Scroll down through the list and locate the data value that occurs most frequently.

and another consisting of six measurements for which the medians are equal.

2.41 Calculate the mode, mean, and median of the following data:

  18 10 15 13 17 15 12 15 18 16 11

2.42 Calculate the mean, median, and mode for each of the following samples:
  a. 7, −2, 3, 3, 0, 4
  b. 2, 3, 5, 3, 2, 3, 4, 3, 5, 1, 2, 3, 4
  c. 51, 50, 47, 50, 48, 41, 59, 68, 45, 37   49.6, 49, 50

2.43 Describe how the mean compares to the median for a distribution as follows:
  a. Skewed to the left
  b. Skewed to the right
  c. Symmetric   Mean = Median

Applying the Concepts—Basic

2.44 Data on the top-ranked law firms in Florida, obtained from *Florida Trend Magazine* magazine (April 2002) are provided in the table below.
  a. Find the mean, median, and mode for the number of lawyers at the top ranked Florida law firms. Interpret these values.   144.5, 102.5, 70
  b. Find the mean, median, and mode for the number of offices open by top ranked Florida law firms. Interpret these values.   5.23, 5, 6

2.45 *Fortune* (Oct. 14, 2002) published a list of the 50 most powerful women in America. The data on age (in years) and title of each of these 50 women are stored in the **WPOWER50** file. The first five and last two observations of the data are listed in the accompanying table.
  a. Find the mean, median, and modal age of these 50 women.   49.74, 49, 53
  b. What do the mean and median indicate about the skewness of the age distribution?   Skewed a little right
  c. Construct a relative frequency histogram for the age data. What is the modal age class?

WPOWER50

Rank	Name	Age	Company	Title
1	Carly Fiorina	48	Hewlett-Packard	CEO
2	Betsy Holden	46	Kraft Foods	CEO
3	Meg Whitman	46	eBay	CEO
4	Indra Nooyi	46	PepsiCo	CFO
5	Andrea Jung	44	Avon Products	CEO
.	.	.		
.	.	.		
49	Fran Keeth	56	Royal Dutch Petrol.	CEO
50	Heidi Miller	49	Bank One	EVP

Source: Fortune, Oct. 14, 2002.

FLALAW

Rank	Firm	Headquarters	Number of Lawyers	Number of Offices
1	Holland & Knight	Tallahasse	529	11
2	Akerman Senterfit	Orlando	355	9
3	Greenberg Traurig	Miami	301	6
4	Carlton Fields	Tampa	207	6
5	Gruden McClosky Smit	Ft. Lauder	175	9
6	Fowler White Boggs	Tampa	175	7
7	Foley & Lardner	Orlando	159	5
8	GrayHarris	Orlando	158	6
9	Broad and Cassel	Orlando	150	7
10	Shutts & Bowen	Miami	144	5
11	Steel Hector & Davis	Miami	141	5
12	Gunster Yoakley	WPalmBeach	140	6
13	Adorno & Zeder	Miami	105	4
14	Becker & Poliakoff	Ft. Lauder	100	12
15	Lowndes Drosdick	Orlando	100	1
16	Conroy Simberg Ganon	Hollywood	91	6
17	Stearns Weaver	Miami	85	3
18	Wicker Smith O'Hara	Miami	85	6
19	Rogers Towers Bailey	Jacksonvll	80	2
20	Butler Burnette	Tampa	77	3
21	Bilzin Sumberg Dunn	Miami	70	1
22	Morgan Colling	Orlando	70	4
23	White & Case	Miami	70	1
24	Fowler White Burnett	Miami	64	4
25	Rissman Weisberg	Orlando	63	3
26	Rumberger Kirk	Orlando	63	4

Source: Florida Trend Magazine, April 2002, p. 105.

⊙ BWECS

2.46 Refer to Exercise 2.24 (p. 65) and the *Business Week* "Executive Compensation Scoreboard" data saved in the **BWECS** file. Consider the total compensation (measured in thousands of dollars) for each of the 363 CEOs in the survey. (The variable is named PAY2002 on the data set.)

  a. Find and interpret the mean of the data set.
    $7,422,230

  b. Find and interpret the median of the data set.
    $3,753,000

  c. Find and interpret the mode of the data set.

  d. Which measure of central tendency best describes the 363 total compensation values? Explain. Median

⊙ DIAMONDS

2.47 Refer to Exercise 2.25 (p. 65) and the *Journal of Statistics Education* data on diamonds saved in the **DIAMONDS** file. Consider the quantitative variable, number of carats, recorded for each of the 308 diamonds for sale on the open market.

  a. Find and interpret the mean of the data set. .631

  b. Find and interpret the median of the data set. .62

  c. Find and interpret the mode of the data set. 1.0

  d. Which measure of central tendency best describes the 308 carat values? Explain. Mean or Median

Applying the Concepts—Intermediate

2.48 Platelet-activating factor (PAF) is a potent chemical that occurs in patients suffering from shock, inflammation, hypotension, and allergic responses as well as respiratory and cardiovascular disorders. Consequently, drugs that effectively inhibit PAF, keeping it from binding to human cells, may be successful in treating these disorders. A bioassay was undertaken to investigate the potential of 17 traditional Chinese herbal drugs in PAF inhibition (H. Guiqui, *Progress in Natural Science*, June 1995). The prevention of the PAF binding process, measured as a percentage, for each drug is provided in the accompanying table.

⊙ DRUGPAF

Drug	PAF Inhibition (%)
Hai-feng-teng (Fuji)	77
Hai-feng-teng (Japan)	33
Shan-ju	75
Zhang-yiz-hu-jiao	62
Shi-nan-teng	70
Huang-hua-hu-jiao	12
Hua-nan-hu-jiao	0
Xiao-yie-pa-ai-xiang	0
Mao-ju	0
Jia-ju	15
Xie-yie-ju	25
Da-yie-ju	0
Bian-yie-hu-jiao	9
Bi-bo	24
Duo-mai-hu-jiao	40
Yan-sen	0
Jiao-guo-hu-jiao	31

Source: Guiqui, H. "PAF Receptor Antagonistic Principles from Chinese Traditional Drugs." *Progress in Natural Science*, Vol. 5, No. 3, June 1995, p. 301 (Table 1).

  a. Construct a stem-and-leaf display for the data.

  b. Compute the median inhibition percentage for the 17 herbal drugs. Interpret the result. 24

  c. Compute the mean inhibition percentage for the 17 herbal drugs. Interpret the result. 27.82

  d. Compute the mode of the 17 inhibition percentages. Interpret the result. 0

  e. Locate the median, mean, and mode on the stem-and-leaf display, part **a.** Do these measures of central tendency appear to locate the center of the data?

2.49 In order to become a certified public accountant (CPA), you must pass the Uniform CPA Exam. Many states require a minimum of 150 semester hours of college education before a candidate can sit for the CPA Exam. However, traditionally, colleges only require 128 semester hours for an undergraduate degree. A study of whether the "extra" 22 hours of college credit is warranted for CPA candidates was published in the *Journal of Accounting and Public Policy* (Spring 2002). For one aspect of the study, researchers sampled over 100,000 first-time candidates for the CPA exam and recorded the total semester hours of college credit for each candidate. The mean and median for the data set were 141.31 and 140 hours, respectively. Interpret these values. Make a statement about the type of skewness, if any, that exists in the distribution of total semester hours.

⊙ DDT

2.50 Refer to Exercise 2.22 (p. 65) and the U.S. Army Corps of Engineers data on contaminated fish saved in the **DDT** file. Consider the quantitative variables length (in centimeters), weight (in grams), and DDT level (in parts per million).

  a. Find three numerical measures of central tendency for the 144 fish lengths. Interpret these values.
    42.81, 45, 46

  b. Find three numerical measures of central tendency for the 144 fish weights. Interpret these values
    1,049.72, 1000, 886 and 1186

  c. Find three numerical measures of central tendency for the 144 DDT measurements. Interpret these values. 24.35, 7.15, 12

  d. Use the results, part **a,** and the graph of the data from Exercise 2.22a to make a statement about the type of skewness in the fish length distribution.

e. Use the results, part **b,** and the graph of the data from Exercise 2.22b to make a statement about the type of skewness in the fish weight distribution.

f. Use the results, part **c,** and the graph of the data from Exercise 2.22c to make a statement about the type of skewness in the fish DDT distribution.

2.51 Would you expect the data sets described below to possess relative frequency distributions that are symmetric, skewed to the right, or skewed to the left? Explain.

a. The salaries of all persons employed by a large university
b. The grades on an easy test
c. The grades on a difficult test
d. The amounts of time students in your class studied last week
e. The ages of automobiles on a used-car lot
f. The amounts of time spent by students on a difficult examination (maximum time is 50 minutes)

2.52 The salaries of superstar professional athletes receive much attention in the media. The multimillion-dollar long-term contract is now commonplace among this elite group. Nevertheless, rarely does a season pass without negotiations between one or more of the players' associations and team owners for additional salary and fringe benefits for *all* players in their particular sports.

a. If a players' association wanted to support its argument for higher "average" salaries, which measure of central tendency do you think it should use? Why?   Median
b. To refute the argument, which measure of central tendency should the owners apply to the players' salaries? Why?   Mean

Applying the Concepts—Advanced

2.53 Refer to the *Financial Management* (Spring 1995) study of prepackaged bankruptcy filings, Exercise 2.30 (p. 67). Recall that each of 49 firms that negotiated a reorganization plan with its creditors prior to filing for bank ruptcy was classified in one of three categories: join exchange offer with prepack, prepack solicitation only and no pre-filing vote held. Consider the quantitative variable length of time in bankruptcy (months). Is it reasonable to use a single number (e.g., mean or median) to describe the center of the time-in-bankruptcy distributions? Or should three "centers" be calculated, one for each of the three categories of prepack firms? Explain.

2.54 The U.S. Energy Information Administration monitors all nuclear power plants operating in the United States. The table lists the number of active nuclear power plants operating in each of a sample of 20 states.

a. Find the mean, median, and mode of this data set.   4, 3.5, 1

b. Eliminate the largest value from the data set and repeat part **a.** What effect does dropping this measurement have on the measures of central tendency found in part **a?**   3.53, 3, 1

c. Arrange the 20 values in the table from lowest to highest. Next, eliminate the lowest two values and the highest two values from the data set and find the mean of the remaining data values. The result is called a *10% trimmed mean,* since it is calculated after removing the highest 10% and the lowest 10% of the data values. What advantages does a trimmed mean have over the regular arithmetic mean?

NUCLEAR

State	Number of Power Plants
Alabama	5
Arizona	3
California	4
Florida	5
Georgia	4
Illinois	13
Kansas	1
Louisiana	2
Massachusetts	1
Mississippi	1
New Hampshire	1
New York	6
North Carolina	5
Ohio	2
Pennsylvania	9
South Carolina	7
Tennessee	3
Texas	4
Vermont	1
Wisconsin	3

Source: Statistical Abstract of the United States, 2000 (Table 966). U.S. Energy Information Administration, Electric Power Annual.

2.5 Numerical Measures of Variability

Measures of central tendency provide only a partial description of a quantitative data set. The description is incomplete without a **measure of the variability,** or **spread,** of the data set. Knowledge of the data's variability along with its center can help us visualize the shape of a data set as well as its extreme values.

For example, suppose we are comparing the profit margin per construction job (as a percentage of the total bid price) for 100 construction jobs for each of two cost estimators working for a large construction company. The histograms for the two sets of 100 profit margin measurements are shown in Figure 2.17. If you examine the two histograms, you will notice that both data sets are symmetric with equal modes, medians, and means. However, cost estimator A (Figure 2.17a) has profit margins spread with almost equal relative frequency over the measurement classes, while cost estimator B (Figure 2.17b) has profit margins clustered about the center of the distribution. Thus, estimator B's profit margins are *less variable* than estimator A's. Consequently, you can see that we need a measure of variability as well as a measure of central tendency to describe a data set.

Perhaps the simplest measure of the variability of a quantitative data set is its *range*.

Figure 2.17
Profit margin histograms for two cost estimators

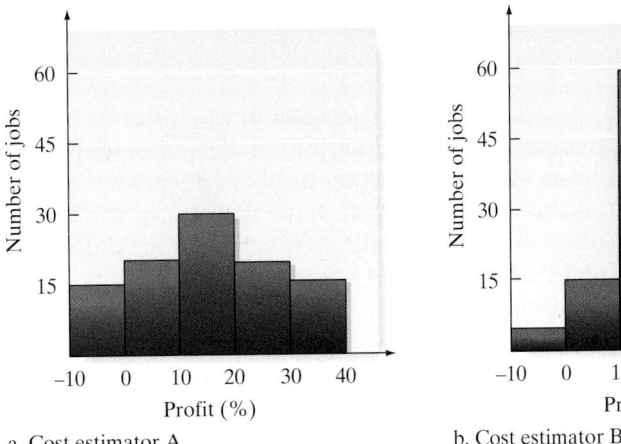

a. Cost estimator A

b. Cost estimator B

DEFINITION 2.8

The **range** of a quantitative data set is equal to the largest measurement minus the smallest measurement.

The range is easy to compute and easy to understand, but it is a rather insensitive measure of data variation when the data sets are large. This is because two data sets can have the same range and be vastly different with respect to data variation. This phenomenon is demonstrated in Figure 2.17. Although the ranges are equal and all central tendency measures are the same for these two symmetric data sets, there is an obvious difference between the two sets of measurements. The difference is that estimator B's profit margins tend to be more stable — that is, to pile up or to cluster about the center of the data set. In contrast estimator A's profit margins are more spread out over the range, indicating a higher incidence of some high profit margins, but also a greater risk of losses. Thus, even though the ranges are equal, the profit margin record of estimator A is more variable than that of estimator B, indicating a distinct difference in their cost estimating characteristics.

Let's see if we can find a measure of data variation that is more sensitive than the range. Consider the two samples in Table 2.5: Each has five measurements. (We have ordered the numbers for convenience.)

TABLE 2.5   Two Hypothetical Data Sets

	Sample 1	Sample 2
Measurements	1, 2, 3, 4, 5	2, 3, 3, 3, 4
Mean	$\bar{x} = \dfrac{1 + 2 + 3 + 4 + 5}{5} = \dfrac{15}{5} = 3$	$\bar{x} = \dfrac{2 + 3 + 3 + 3 + 4}{5} = \dfrac{15}{5} = 3$
Deviations of measurement values from $\bar{x}$	$(1 - 3), (2 - 3), (3 - 3), (4 - 3),$ $(5 - 3),$ or $-2, -1, 0, 1, 2$	$(2 - 3), (3 - 3), (3 - 3), (3 - 3),$ $(4 - 3),$ or $-1, 0, 0, 0, 1$

Note that both samples have a mean of 3 and that we have also calculated the distance and direction, or *deviation*, between each measurement and the mean. What information do these deviations contain? If they tend to be large in magnitude, as in sample 1, the data are spread out, or highly variable. If the deviations are mostly small, as in sample 2, the data are clustered around the mean, $\bar{x}$, and therefore do not exhibit much variability. You can see that these deviations, displayed graphically in Figure 2.18, provide information about the variability of the sample measurements.

The next step is to condense the information in these deviations into a single numerical measure of variability. Averaging the deviations from $\bar{x}$ won't help because the negative and positive deviations cancel; that is, the sum of the deviations (and thus the average deviation) is always equal to zero.

Two methods come to mind for dealing with the fact that positive and negative deviations from the mean cancel. The first is to treat all the deviations as though they were positive, ignoring the sign of the negative deviations. We won't pursue this line of thought because the resulting measure of variability (the mean of the absolute values of the deviations) presents analytical difficulties beyond the scope of this text. A second method of eliminating the minus signs associated with the deviations is to square them. The quantity we can calculate from the squared deviations will provide a meaningful description of the variability of a data set and presents fewer analytical difficulties in inference making.

To use the squared deviations calculated from a data set, we first calculate the *sample variance*.

Figure 2.18

Dot plots for two data sets

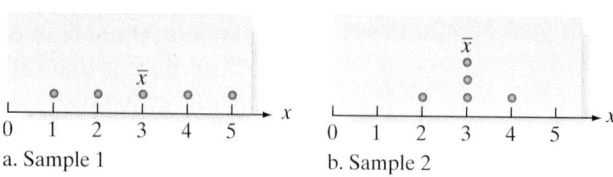

a. Sample 1   b. Sample 2

Teaching Tip

Try to illustrate what the variance is attempting to measure. Draw pictures to aid student understanding of how the variance measures the spread of a distribution.

Suggested Exercise 2.68

DEFINITION 2.9

The **sample variance** for a sample of n measurements is equal to the sum of the squared deviations from the mean divided by $(n - 1)$. In symbols, using s^2 to represent the sample variance,

$$s^2 = \frac{\sum_{i=1}^{n}(x_i - \bar{x})^2}{n - 1}$$

Note: A shortcut formula for calculating s^2 is

$$s^2 = \frac{\sum_{i=1}^{n} x_i^2 - \frac{\left(\sum_{i=1}^{n} x_i\right)^2}{n}}{n - 1}$$

Referring to the two samples in Table 2.5, you can calculate the variance for sample 1 as follows:

$$s^2 = \frac{(1 - 3)^2 + (2 - 3)^2 + (3 - 3)^2 + (4 - 3)^2 + (5 - 3)^2}{5 - 1}$$

$$= \frac{4 + 1 + 0 + 1 + 4}{4} = 2.5$$

The second step in finding a meaningful measure of data variability is to calculate the *standard deviation* of the data set.

DEFINITION 2.10

The **sample standard deviation**, s, is defined as the positive square root of the sample variance, s^2. Thus, $s = \sqrt{s^2}$.

The population variance, denoted by the symbol σ^2 (sigma squared), is the average of the squared distances of the measurements on *all* units in the population from the mean, μ, and σ (sigma) is the square root of this quantity. Since we never really compute σ^2 or σ from the population (the object of sampling is to the avoid this costly procedure), we simply denote these two quantities by their respective symbols.

Symbols for Variance and Standard Deviation

s^2 = Sample variance

s = Sample standard deviation

σ^2 = Population variance

σ = Population standard deviation

Teaching Tip

Let the student know that the divisor question will become clearer when they learn more about estimating parameters with sampling distributions.

Notice that, unlike the variance, the standard deviation is expressed in the original units of measurement. For example, if the original measurements are in dollars, the variance is expressed in the peculiar units "dollar squared," but the standard deviation is expressed in dollars.

You may wonder why we use the divisor $(n - 1)$ instead of n when calculating the sample variance. Wouldn't using n be more logical, so that the sample variance would be the average squared deviation from the mean? The trouble is using n tends to produce an underestimate of the population variance, σ^2. So we use $(n - 1)$ in the denominator to provide the appropriate correction for this tendency.* Since sample statistics like s^2 are primarily used to estimate population parameters like σ^2, $(n - 1)$ is preferred to n when defining the sample variance.

EXAMPLE 2.8

MEASURES OF VARIATION USING FORMULAS

Problem Calculate the variance and standard deviation of the following sample: 2, 3, 3, 3, 4.

Solution If you calculate the values of s and s^2 by hand, it is advantageous to use the shortcut formula provided in Definition 2.8. To do this, we need two summations: Σx and Σx^2. These can easily be obtained from the following type of tabulation:

$s^2 = .5$ $s = .71$

x	x^2
2	4
3	9
3	9
3	9
4	16
$\Sigma x = 15$	$\Sigma x^2 = 47$

Teaching Tip

To illustrate the mechanics of calculating the measures of variability, use Exercise 2.57 as an example in class. For a practical comparison of different values of the standard deviation, use Exercise 2.68 as an example in class.

Then we use**

$$s^2 = \frac{\sum_{i=1}^{n} x_i^2 - \frac{\left(\sum_{i=1}^{n} x_i\right)^2}{n}}{n - 1} = \frac{47 - \frac{(15)^2}{5}}{5 - 1} = \frac{2}{4} = .5$$

$$s = \sqrt{.5} = .71$$

Look Back As the sample size n increases, these calculations can become very tedious. As the next example shows, we can use the computer to find s^2 and s.

Now Work   *Exercise 2.57a*

■ ■ ■

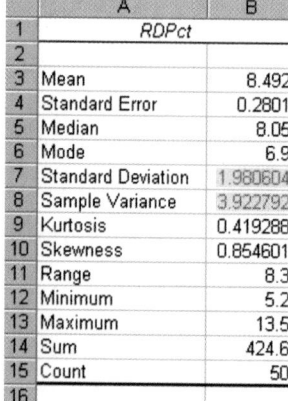

	A	B
1	RDPct	
2		
3	Mean	8.492
4	Standard Error	0.2801
5	Median	8.05
6	Mode	6.9
7	Standard Deviation	1.980604
8	Sample Variance	3.922792
9	Kurtosis	0.419288
10	Skewness	0.854601
11	Range	8.3
12	Minimum	5.2
13	Maximum	13.5
14	Sum	424.6
15	Count	50
16		

Figure 2.19

Reproduction of EXCEL numerical descriptive measures for 50 R&D percentages

Appropriate here means that s^2 with the divisor of $(n - 1)$ is an *unbiased estimator* of σ^2. We define and discuss *unbiasedness* of estimators in Chapter 6.
**When calculating s^2, how many decimal places should you carry? Although there are no rules for the rounding procedure, it's reasonable to retain twice as many decimal places in s^2 as you ultimately wish to have in s. If you wish to calculate s to the nearest hundredth (two decimal places), for example, you should calculate s^2 to the nearest ten-thousandth (four decimal places).

EXAMPLE 2.9   MEASURES OF VARIATION ON THE COMPUTER

Problem   Use the computer to find the sample variance s^2 and the sample standard deviation s for the 50 companies' percentages of revenues spent on R&D.

Solution   The EXCEL printout describing the R&D percentage data is reproduced in Figure 2.19 (p. 84). The variance and standard deviation, highlighted on the printout, are $s^2 = 3.922792$ and $s = 1.980604$.

$s^2 = 3.922792$ $s = 1.980604$

■ ■ ■

You now know that the standard deviation measures the variability of a set of data. The larger the standard deviation, the more variable the data. The smaller the standard deviation, the less variable the data. But how can we practically interpret the standard deviation and use it to make inferences? This is the topic of Section 2.6.

Exercises 2.55–2.68

Learning the Mechanics

2.55 Answer the following questions about variability of data sets:
   a. What is the primary disadvantage of using the range to compare the variability of data sets?
   b. Describe the sample variance using words rather than a formula. Do the same with the population variance.
   c. Can the variance of a data set ever be negative? Explain. Can the variance ever be smaller than the standard deviation? Explain.   No, Yes

2.56 Calculate the variance and standard deviation for samples where
   a. $n = 10$, $\Sigma x^2 = 84$, $\Sigma x = 20$
   b. $n = 40$, $\Sigma x^2 = 380$, $\Sigma x = 100$
   c. $n = 20$, $\Sigma x^2 = 18$, $\Sigma x = 17$

2.57 Calculate the range, variance, and standard deviation for the following samples:
   a. $4, 2, 1, 0, 1$ 4, 2.3, 1.52
   b. $1, 6, 2, 2, 3, 0, 3$
   c. $8, -2, 1, 3, 5, 4, 4, 1, 3, 3$ 10, 7.111, 2.67
   d. $0, 2, 0, 0, -1, 1, -2, 1, 0, -1, 1, -1, 0, -3, -2, -1, 0, 1$

2.58 Calculate the range, variance, and standard deviation for the following samples:
   a. $39, 42, 40, 37, 41$
   b. $100, 4, 7, 96, 80, 3, 1, 10, 2$
   c. $100, 4, 7, 30, 80, 30, 42, 2$ 98, 1,307.84, 36.16

2.59 Compute $\bar{x}$, s^2, and s for each of the following data sets. If appropriate, specify the units in which your answer is expressed.
   a. $3, 1, 10, 10, 4$
   b. 8 feet, 10 feet, 32 feet, 5 feet
   c. $-1, -4, -3, 1, -4, -4$ -2.5, 4.3, 2.0736
   d. $\frac{1}{5}$ ounce, $\frac{1}{5}$ ounce, $\frac{1}{5}$ ounce, $\frac{2}{5}$ ounce, $\frac{1}{5}$ ounce, $\frac{4}{5}$ ounce

2.60 Using only integers between 0 and 10, construct two data sets with at least 10 observations each so that the two sets have the same mean but different variances. Construct dot plots for each of your data sets and mark the mean of each data set on its dot diagram.

2.61 Using only integers between 0 and 10, construct two data sets with at least 10 observations each that have the same range but different means. Construct a dot plot for each of your data sets, and mark the mean of each data set on its dot diagram.

2.62 Consider the following sample of five measurements: $2, 1, 1, 0, 3$.
   a. Calculate the range, s^2, and s.   3, 1.3, 1.1402
   b. Add 3 to each measurement and repeat part **a.**
   c. Subtract 4 from each measurement and repeat part **a.**
   d. Considering your answers to parts **a, b,** and **c,** what seems to be the effect on the variability of a data set by adding the same number to or subtracting the same number from each measurement?   No effect

Applying the Concepts—Basic

⊙ **FLALAW**
2.63 Refer to the data on the top-ranked law firms in Florida, Exercise 2.44 (p. 78), collected by *Florida Trend Magazine* (April 2002). The data are saved in the **FLALAW** file.
   a. Find the range of the number of lawyers at the top-ranked law firms with headquarters in Orlando.   292
   b. Find the range of the number of lawyers at the top-ranked law firms with headquarters in Miami.   237
   c. Using only the ranges in parts a and b, is it possible to determine which city, Orlando or Miami, has the largest law firms?   No

⊙ **WPOWER50**

2.64 Refer to Exercise 2.45 (p. 78) and *Fortune*'s (Oct. 14, 2002) list of the 50 most powerful women in America. The data are stored in the **WPOWER50** file.

a. Find the range of the ages for these 50 women.   34

b. Find the variance of the ages for these 50 women.   37.5024

c. Find the standard deviation of the ages for these 50 women.   6.124

d. Suppose the standard deviation of the ages of the most powerful women in Europe is 10 years. For which location, the United States or Europe, is the age data more variable?   Europe

⊙ **DDT**

2.65 Refer to Exercise 2.22 (p. 65) and the U.S. Army Corps of Engineers data on contaminated fish saved in the **DDT** file. Consider the quantitative variables length (in centimeters), weight (in grams), and DDT level (in parts per million).

a. Find three different measures of variation for the 144 fish lengths. Give the units of measurement for each. $s^2 = 47.363$, $s = 6.882$, $R = 34.5$

b. Find three different measures of variation for the 144 fish weights. Give the units of measurement for each. $s^2 = 141,787$, $s = 376.55$, $R = 2,129$

c. Find three different measures of variation for the 144 DDT values. Give the units of measurement for each. $s^2 = 9,678$, $s = 98.38$, $R = 1,099.9$

Applying the Concepts—Intermediate

⊙ **DIAMONDS**

2.66 Refer to Exercise 2.25 (p. 65) and the *Journal of Statistics Education* data on diamonds saved in the **DIAMONDS** file. Consider the data on the number of carats for each of the 308 diamonds.

a. Find the range of the data set.   .92

b. Find the variance of the data set.   .0768

c. Find the standard deviation of the data set.   .2772

d. Which measure of variation best describes the spread of the 308 carat values? Explain.   Standard deviation

⊙ **NUCLEAR**

2.67 Refer to Exercise 2.54 (p. 80) and the U.S. Energy Information Administration's data on the number of nuclear power plants operating in each of 20 states. The data are saved in the **NUCLEAR** file.

a. Find the range, variance, and standard deviation of this data set.   12, 9.368, 3.061

b. Eliminate the largest value from the data set and repeat part **a**. What effect does dropping this measurement have on the measures of variation found in part **a**?

c. Eliminate the smallest and largest value from the data set and repeat part **a**. What effect does dropping both of these measurement have on the measures of variation found in part **a**?

Applying the Concepts—Advanced

2.68 A widely used technique for estimating the length of time it takes workers to produce a product is the **time study.** In a time study, the task to be studied is divided into measurable parts and each is timed with a stopwatch or filmed for later analysis. For each worker, this process is repeated many times for each subtask. Then the average and standard deviation of the time required to complete each subtask are computed for each worker. A worker's overall time to complete the task under study is then determined by adding his or her subtask-time averages (Gaither, *Production and Operations Management*, 1996). The data (in minutes) given in the table are the result of a time study of a production operation involving two subtasks.

⊙ **TIMESTUDY**

Repetition	Worker A		Worker B	
	Subtask 1	Subtask 2	Subtask 1	Subtask 2
1	30	2	31	7
2	28	4	30	2
3	31	3	32	6
4	38	3	30	5
5	25	2	29	4
6	29	4	30	1
7	30	3	31	4

a. Find the overall time it took each worker to complete the manufacturing operation under study.

b. For each worker, find the standard deviation of the seven times for subtask 1.

c. In the context of this problem, what are the standard deviations you computed in part **b** measuring?

d. Repeat part **b** for subtask 2.

e. If you could choose workers similar to A or workers similar to B to perform subtasks 1 and 2, which type would you assign to each subtask? Explain your decisions on the basis of your answers to parts **a–d.**

2.6 Interpreting the Standard Deviation

We've seen that if we are comparing the variability of two samples selected from a population, the sample with the larger standard deviation is the more variable of the two. Thus, we know how to interpret the standard deviation on a relative or comparative basis, but we haven't explained how it provides a measure of variability for a single sample.

To understand how the standard deviation provides a measure of variability of a data set, consider a specific data set and answer the following questions: How many measurements are within 1 standard deviation of the mean? How many measurements are within 2 standard deviations? For a specific data set, we can answer these questions by counting the number of measurements in each of the intervals. However, if we are interested in obtaining a general answer to these questions, the problem is more difficult.

Tables 2.6 and 2.7 give two sets of answers to the questions of how many measurements fall within 1, 2, and 3 standard deviations of the mean. The first, which applies to *any* set of data, is derived from a theorem proved by the Russian mathematician P. L. Chebyshev. The second, which applies to **mound-shaped,** symmetric distributions of data (where the mean, median, and mode are all about the

---

TABLE 2.6   Interpreting the Standard Deviation: Chebyshev's Rule

---

Chebyshev's Rule applies to any data set, regardless of the shape of the frequency distribution of the data.

a. No useful information is provided on the fraction of measurements that fall within 1 standard deviation of the mean [i.e., within the interval $(\bar{x} - s, \bar{x} + s)$ for samples and $(\mu - \sigma, \mu + \sigma)$ for populations].

b. At least $3/4$ will fall within 2 standard deviations of the mean [i.e., within the interval $(\bar{x} - 2s, \bar{x} + 2s)$ for samples and $(\mu - 2\sigma, \mu + 2\sigma)$ for populations].

c. At least $8/9$ of the measurements will fall within 3 standard deviations of the mean [i.e., within the interval $(\bar{x} - 3s, \bar{x} + 3s)$ for samples and $(\mu - 3\sigma, \mu + 3\sigma)$ for populations].

d. Generally, for any number k greater than 1, at least $(1 - 1/k^2)$ of the measurements will fall within k standard deviations of the mean [i.e., within the interval $(\bar{x} - ks, \bar{x} + ks)$ for samples and $(\mu - k\sigma, \mu + k\sigma)$ for populations].

TABLE 2.7   Interpreting the Standard Deviation: The Empirical Rule

---

The Empirical Rule is a rule of thumb that applies to data sets with frequency distributions that are mound-shaped and symmetric, as shown below.

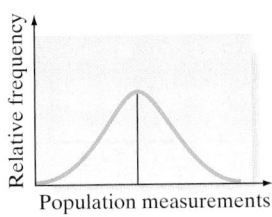

a. Approximately 68% of the measurements will fall within 1 standard deviation of the mean [i.e., within the interval $(\bar{x} - s, \bar{x} + s)$ for samples and $(\mu - \sigma, \mu + \sigma)$ for populations].

b. Approximately 95% of the measurements will fall within 2 standard deviations of the mean [i.e., within the interval $(\bar{x} - 2s, \bar{x} + 2s)$ for samples and $(\mu - 2\sigma, \mu + 2\sigma)$ for populations].

c. Approximately 99.7% (essentially all) of the measurements will fall within 3 standard deviations of the mean [i.e., within the interval $(\bar{x} - 3s, \bar{x} + 3s)$ for samples and $(\mu - 3\sigma, \mu + 3\sigma)$ for populations].

---

same), is based upon empirical evidence that has accumulated over the years. However, the percentages given for the intervals in Table 2.7 provide remarkably good approximations even when the distribution of the data is slightly skewed or asymmetric. Note that both rules apply to either population data sets or sample data sets.

Biography

PAFNUTY L. CHEBYSHEV (1821–1894)
The Splendid Russian Mathematician

P. L. Chebyshev was educated in mathematical science at Moscow University, eventually earning his master's degree. Following his graduation, Chebyshev joined St. Petersburg (Russia) University as a professor, becoming part of the well-known "Petersburg mathematical school." It was here that Chebyshev proved his famous theorem about the probability of a measurement being within k standard deviations of the mean (Table 2.6). His fluency in French allowed him to gain international recognition in probability theory. In fact, Chebyshev once objected to being described as a "splendid Russian mathematician," saying he surely was a "worldwide mathematician." One student remembered Chebyshev as "a wonderful lecturer" who "was always prompt for class," and "as soon as the bell sounded, he immediately dropped the chalk, and, limping, left the auditorium."

EXAMPLE 2.10

INTERPRETING THE STANDARD DEVIATION

Problem   The 50 companies' percentages of revenues spent on R&D are repeated in Table 2.8. We have previously shown (see Figure 2.19, p. 84) that the mean and standard deviation of these data (rounded) are 8.49 and 1.98, respectively. Calculate the fraction of these measurements that lie within the intervals $\bar{x} \pm s, \bar{x} \pm 2s$, and $\bar{x} \pm 3s$, and compare the results with those predicted in Tables 2.6 and 2.7.

68%, 94%, 100%

   R&D

TABLE 2.8   R&D Percentages for 50 Companies

13.5	9.5	8.2	6.5	8.4	8.1	6.9	7.5	10.5	13.5
7.2	7.1	9.0	9.9	8.2	13.2	9.2	6.9	9.6	7.7
9.7	7.5	7.2	5.9	6.6	11.1	8.8	5.2	10.6	8.2
11.3	5.6	10.1	8.0	8.5	11.7	7.1	7.7	9.4	6.0
8.0	7.4	10.5	7.8	7.9	6.5	6.9	6.5	6.8	9.5

Solution   We first form the interval

$$(\bar{x} - s, \bar{x} + s) = (8.49 - 1.98, 8.49 + 1.98) = (6.51, 10.47)$$

A check of the measurements reveals that 34 of the 50 measurements, or 68%, are within 1 standard deviation of the mean.

The next interval of interest

$$(\bar{x} - 2s, \bar{x} + 2s) = (8.49 - 3.96, 8.49 + 3.96) = (4.53, 12.45)$$

contains 47 of the 50 measurements, or 94%.

Finally, the 3-standard-deviation interval around $\bar{x}$,

$$(\bar{x} - 3s, \bar{x} + 3s) = (8.49 - 5.94, 8.49 + 5.94) = (2.55, 14.43)$$

contains all, or 100%, of the measurements.

In spite of the fact that the distribution of these data is skewed to the right (see Figure 2.11), the percentages within 1, 2, and 3 standard deviations (68%, 94%, and 100%) agree very well with the approximations of 68%, 95%, and 99.7% given by the Empirical Rule (Table 2.7).

Look Back You will find that unless the distribution is extremely skewed, the mound-shaped approximations will be reasonably accurate. Of course, no matter what the shape of the distribution Chebyshev's Rule (Table 2.6) assures that at least 75% and at least 89% ($\frac{8}{9}$) of the measurements will lie within 2 and 3 standard deviations of the mean, respectively.

 **Now Work**   *Exercise 2.72*

■ ■ ■

EXAMPLE 2.11

CHECK ON THE CALCULATION OF s

Problem   Chebyshev's Rule and the Empirical Rule are useful as a check on the calculation of the standard deviation. For example, suppose we calculated the standard deviation for the R&D percentages (Table 2.8) to be 3.92. Are there any "clues" in the data that enable us to judge whether this number is reasonable?

Solution   The range of the R&D percentages in Table 2.8 is $13.5 - 5.2 = 8.3$. From Chebyshev's Rule and the Empirical Rule we know that most of the measurements (approximately 95% if the distribution is mound shaped) will be within 2 standard deviations of the mean. And, regardless of the shape of the distribution and the number of measurements, almost all of them will fall within 3 standard deviations of the mean. Consequently, we would expect the range of the measurements to be between 4 (i.e., $\pm 2s$) and 6 (i.e., $\pm 3s$) standard deviations in length (see Figure 2.20).

For the R&D data, this means that s should fall between

$$\frac{\text{Range}}{6} = \frac{8.3}{6} = 1.38 \quad \text{and} \quad \frac{\text{Range}}{4} = \frac{8.3}{4} = 2.08$$

In particular, the standard deviation should not be much larger than $\frac{1}{4}$ of the range, particularly for the data set with 50 measurements. Thus, we have reason to believe that the calculation of 3.92 is too large. A check of our work reveals that 3.92 is the variance s^2, not the standard deviation s (see Example 2.9). We "forgot" to take the square root (a common error); the correct value is $s = 1.98$. Note that this value is between $\frac{1}{6}$ and $\frac{1}{4}$ of the range.

Look Back In examples and exercises we'll sometimes use $s \approx$ range/4 to obtain a crude, and usually conservatively large, approximation for s. However, we stress that this is no substitute for calculating the exact value of s when possible.

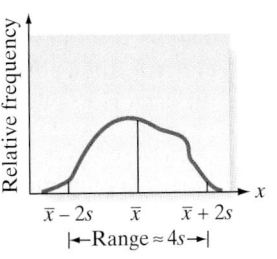

Figure 2.20
The relation between the range and the standard deviation

Suggested Exercise 2.78

 **Now Work**   *Exercise 2.73*

■ ■ ■

In the next example, we use the concepts in Chebyshev's Rule and the Empirical Rule to build the foundation for statistical inference making.

EXAMPLE 2.12

MAKING A STATISTICAL INFERENCE

Problem   A manufacturer of automobile batteries claims that the average length of life for its grade A battery is 60 months. However, the guarantee on this brand is for just 36 months. Suppose the standard deviation of the life length is known to be 10 months, and the frequency distribution of the life-length data is known to be mound shaped.

a. Approximately what percentage of the manufacturer's grade A batteries will last more than 50 months, assuming the manufacturer's claim is true?

b. Approximately what percentage of the manufacturer's batteries will last less than 40 months, assuming the manufacturer's claim is true?

c. Suppose your battery lasts 37 months. What could you infer about the manufacturer's claim?

≈84%

≈2.5

Doubt the claim

Solution   If the distribution of life length is assumed to be mound-shaped with a mean of 60 months and a standard deviation of 10 months, it would appear as shown in Figure 2.21. Note that we can take advantage of the fact that mound-shaped distributions are (approximately) symmetric about the mean, so that the percentages given by the Empirical Rule can be split equally between the halves of the distribution on each side of the mean.

For example, since approximately 68% of the measurements will fall within 1 standard deviation of the mean, the distribution's symmetry implies that approximately $\frac{1}{2}(68\%) = 34\%$ of the measurements will fall between the mean and 1 standard deviation on each side. This concept is illustrated in Figure 2.21. The figure also shows that 2.5% of the measurements lie beyond 2 standard deviations in each direction from the mean. This result follows from the fact that if approximately 95% of the measurements fall within 2 standard deviations of the mean, then about 5% fall outside 2 standard deviations; if the distribution is approximately symmetric, then about 2.5% of the measurements fall beyond 2 standard deviations on each side of the mean.

a. It is easy to see in Figure 2.21 that the percentage of batteries lasting more than 50 months is approximately 34% (between 50 and 60 months) plus 50% (greater than 60 months). Thus, approximately 84% of the batteries should have life length exceeding 50 months.

Figure 2.21

Battery life-length distribution: Manufacturer's claim assumed true

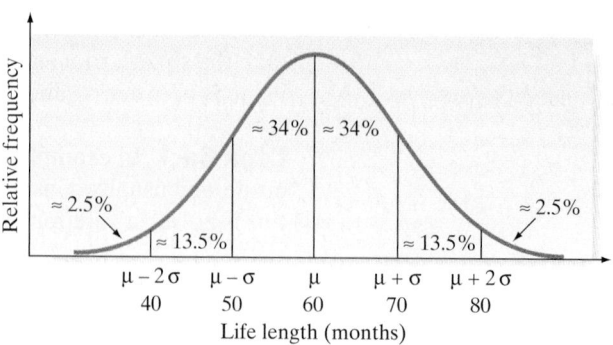

Teaching Tip
It is helpful to students to use an example that demonstrates the differences in Chebyshev's Rule and the Empirical Rule. Emphasize the role that the symmetric distribution plays when determining the percentage of observations that fall in the tail of a distribution (e.g., above $\pm 2s$).

b. The percentage of batteries that last less than 40 months can also be easily determined from Figure 2.21. Approximately 2.5% of the batteries should fail prior to 40 months, assuming the manufacturer's claim is true.

c. If you are so unfortunate that your grade A battery fails at 37 months, you can make one of two inferences: either your battery was one of the approximately 2.5% that fail prior to 40 months, or something about the manufacturer's claim is not true. Because the chances are so small that a battery fails before 40 months, you would have good reason to have serious doubts about the manufacturer's claim. A mean smaller than 60 months and/or a standard deviation longer than 10 months would both increase the likelihood of failure prior to 40 months.*

Look Back The approximations given in Figure 2.21 are more dependent on the assumption of a mound-shaped distribution than those given by the Empirical Rule (Table 2.7), because the approximations in Figure 2.21 depend on the (approximate) symmetry of the mound-shaped distribution. We saw in Example 2.10 that the Empirical Rule can yield good approximations even for skewed distributions. This will *not* be true of the approximations in Figure 2.21; the distribution *must* be mound shaped and approximately symmetric.

■ ■ ■

Example 2.12 is our initial demonstration of the statistical inference-making process. At this point you should realize that we'll use sample information (in Example 2.12, your battery's failure at 37 months) to make inferences about the population (in Example 2.12, the manufacturer's claim about the life length for the population of all batteries). We'll build on this foundation as we proceed.

Exercises 2.69–2.85

Learning the Mechanics

2.69 The output from a statistical software package indicates that the mean and standard deviation of a data set consisting of 200 measurements are $1,500 and $300, respectively.

    a. What are the units of measurement of the variable of interest? Based on the units, what type of data is this: quantitative or qualitative?

    b. What can be said about the number of measurements between $900 and $2,100? Between $600 and $2,400? Between $1,200 and $1,800? Between $1,500 and $2,100?

2.70 For any set of data, what can be said about the percentage of the measurements contained in each of the following intervals?

    a. $\bar{x} - s$ to $\bar{x} + s$ Nothing
    b. $\bar{x} - 2s$ to $\bar{x} + 2s$
    c. $\bar{x} - 3s$ to $\bar{x} + 3s$ At least 8/9

2.71 For a set of data with a mound-shaped relative frequency distribution, what can be said about the percentage of the measurements contained in each of the intervals specified in Exercise 2.70?

2.72 The following is a sample of 25 measurements:

◉ **LM2_72**

| 7 | 6 | 6 | 11 | 8 | 9 | 11 | 9 | 10 | 8 | 7 | 7 |
| 5 | 9 | 10 | 7 | 7 | 7 | 7 | 9 | 12 | 10 | 10 | 8 | 6 |

    a. Compute $\bar{x}$, s^2, and s for this sample.
    b. Count the number of measurements in the intervals $\bar{x} \pm s, \bar{x} \pm 2s, \bar{x} \pm 3s$. Express each count as a percentage of the total number of measurements.
    c. Compare the percentages found in part **b** to the percentages given by the Empirical Rule and Chebyshev's Rule.

*The assumption that the distribution is mound shaped and symmetric may also be incorrect. However, if the distribution were skewed to the right, as life-length distributions often tend to be, the percentage of measurements more than 2 standard deviations *below* the mean would be even less than 2.5%.

Statistics in Action Revisited
Interpreting Descriptive Statistics

We return to the analysis of length of time in practice for two groups of University Community Hospital physicians, those who indicate they are willing to use ethics consultation and those who would not use ethics consultation. Recall that the researchers propose that nonusers of ethics consultation will be more experienced than users. The MINITAB descriptive statistics printout for the **ETHICS** data is displayed in Figure SIA2.5, with the means and standard deviations highlighted.

The sample mean for ethics consultation (EC) nonusers is 16.43 and the mean for EC users is 14.18. Our interpretation is that nonusers have slightly more experience (16.43 years, on average) than users (14.18 years, on average).

To interpret the standard deviation, we substitute into the formula, mean ± 2(standard deviation), to obtain the intervals:

EC Nonusers:
$16.43 \pm 2(10.05) = 16.43 \pm 20.10 = (-3.67, 36.53)$

EC Users:
$14.18 \pm 2(8.95) = 14.18 \pm 17.90 = (-3.72, 32.08)$

Since years of experience cannot take on a negative value, essentially the standard deviation intervals for EC nonusers and EC users are (0, 36.53) (0, 32.08), respectively.

From the Chebyshev's Rule (Table 2.6), we know that at least 75% of the physicians who would not use ethics consultation will have anywhere between 0 and 36.5 years of experience. Similarly, we know that at least 75% of the EC users will have anywhere from 0 to 32.08 years of experience. Note that these ranges indicate that there is very little difference in the experience distributions of the two groups of physicians. However, if a physician on staff has 35 years of experience, it is very unlikely that the doctor would use ethics consultation since 35 years is above the mean ± 2(standard deviation) interval for EC users. Rather, the experience value of 35 is more likely to come from the distribution of years of experience for nonusers of ethics consultation.

Descriptive Statistics: YRSPRAC

Variable	FUTUREUSE	N	N*	Mean	SE Mean	StDev	Variance	Minimum	Q1
YRSPRAC	NO	21	2	16.43	2.19	10.05	100.96	1.00	7.50
	YES	91	4	14.176	0.938	8.950	80.102	1.000	7.000

Variable	FUTUREUSE	Median	Q3	Maximum
YRSPRAC	NO	18.00	25.00	35.00
	YES	14.000	20.000	40.000

Figure SIA2.5
MINITAB analysis of physicians' experience

---

d. Calculate the range and use it to obtain a rough approximation for *s*. Does the result compare favorably with the actual value for *s* found in part **a**?

2.73 Given a data set with a largest value of 760 and a smallest value of 135, what would you estimate the standard deviation to be? Explain the logic behind the procedure you used to estimate the standard deviation. Suppose the standard deviation is reported to be 25. Is this feasible? Explain.

Applying the Concepts—Basic

⊙ **DIAMONDS**

2.74 Refer to the *Journal of Statistics Education* data on diamonds saved in the **DIAMONDS** file. In Exercise 2.47 (p. 79) you found the mean number of carats for the 308 diamonds in the data set, and in Exercise 2.66 (p. 86) you found the standard deviation. Use the mean and standard deviation to form an interval that will contain at least 75% of the carat values in the data set.   (.077, 1.185)

2.75 Refer to the *Journal of Accounting and Public Policy* (Spring 2002) study of 100,000 first-time candidates for the CPA exam, Exercise 2.49 (p. 79). Recall that the mean number of semester hours of college credit taken by the candidates was 141.31 hours. The standard deviation was reported to be 17.77 hours.

a. Compute the 2-standard deviation interval around the mean.   (105.77, 176.85)

b. Make a statement about the proportion of first-time candidates for the CPA exam that have total college credit hours within the interval, part **a.**   At least 3/4

c. For the statement, part **b** to be true, what must be known about the shape of the distribution of total semester hours? Nothing

2.76 For each day of last year, the number of vehicles passing through a certain intersection was recorded by a city engineer. One objective of this study was to determine the percentage of days that more than 425 vehicles used the intersection. Suppose the mean for the data was 375 vehicles per day and the standard deviation was 25 vehicles.

a. What can you say about the percentage of days that more than 425 vehicles used the intersection? Assume you know nothing about the shape of the relative frequency distribution for the data.

b. What is your answer to part **a** if you know that the relative frequency distribution for the data is mound shaped? ≈2.5%

2.77 To minimize the potential for gastrointestinal disease outbreaks, all passenger cruise ships arriving at U.S. ports are subject to unannounced sanitation inspections. Ships are rated on a 100-point scale by the Centers for Disease Control and Prevention. A score of 86 or higher indicates that the ship is providing an accepted standard of sanitation. The May 2001 sanitation scores for 151 cruise ships are saved in the **SHIPSANIT** file. The first five and last five observations in the data set on listed in the accompanying table.

a. Find the mean and standard deviation of the sanitation scores. 93.113, 5.184

b. Calculate the intervals $\bar{x} \pm s, \bar{x} \pm 2s, \bar{x} \pm 3s$.

c. Find the percentage of measurements in the data set that fall within each of the intervals, part **b**. Do these percentages agree with either Chebyshev's Theorem or the Empirical Rule? .874, .974, .987

⊚ **SHIPSANIT**

Ship Name	Sanitation Score
Grande Mariner	95
Seabourn Sun	90
Olympic Voyager	95
Grandeur of the Seas	94
Jubilee	95
.	.
.	.
Seabourn Spirit	92
Triton	93
Costa Allegra	88
Bremen	90
Costa Classica	92

Source: National Center for Environmental Health, Centers for Disease Control and Prevention, May 8, 2001.

Applying the Concepts—Intermediate

2.78 The New Jersey State Chamber of Commerce and Rutgers Business School—with sponsorship by Arthur Anderson—conducted a survey to investigate Generation Xers' expectations of the future workplace and their careers. Telephone interviews were conducted with 662 randomly selected New Jerseyans between the ages of 21 and 28. One question asked, "What is the maximum number of years you expect to spend with any one employer over the course of your career?" The 590 useable responses to this question are summarized below:

$$n = 590$$
$$\bar{x} = 18.2 \text{ years}$$
$$\text{median} = 15 \text{ years}$$
$$s = 10.64$$
$$\text{min} = 2.0$$
$$\text{max} = 50$$

Sources: N.J. State Chamber of Commerce, press release, June 18, 1998 and personal communication from P. George Benson.

a. What evidence exists to suggest that the distribution of years is not mound shaped?

b. Suppose you did not know the sample standard deviation, s. Use the range of the data set to estimate s. Compare your estimate to the actual sample standard deviation.

c. In the last decade, workers moved between companies much more frequently than in the 1980s. Consequently, the researchers were surprised by the expectations of longevity expressed by the Generation Xers. What can you say about the percentage of Generation Xers in the sample whose response was 40 years or more? 8 years or more?

⊚ **OILSPILL**

2.79 Refer to the *Marine Technology* (Jan. 1995) data on spillage amounts (in thousands of metric tons) for 50 major oil spills, Exercise 2.14 (p. 54). The data are saved in the **OILSPILL** file. Form an interval that can be used to predict the spillage amount for the next major oil spill.

⊚ **BANKRUPT**

2.80 Refer to the *Financial Management* (Spring 1995) study of 49 firms filing for prepackaged bankruptcy, Exercise 2.30 (p. 67). Data on the variable of interest, length of time (months) in bankruptcy for each firm, are saved in the **BANKRUPT** file.

a. Construct a histogram for the 49 bankruptcy times. Comment on whether the Empirical Rule is applicable for describing the bankruptcy time distribution for firms filing for prepackaged bankruptcy.

b. Find numerical descriptive statistics for the data set. Use this information to construct an interval that captures at least 75% of the bankruptcy times.

c. Count the number of the 49 bankruptcy times that fall within the interval, part **b,** and convert the result to a percentage. Does the result agree with Chebyshev's Rule? The Empirical Rule?

d. A firm is considering filing a prepackaged bankruptcy plan. Estimate the length of time the firm will be in bankruptcy. 6.2 months

2.81 The *American Rifleman* (June 1993) reported on the velocity of ammunition fired from the FEG P9R pistol, a 9mm gun manufactured in Hungary. Field tests revealed that Winchester bullets fired from the pistol had a mean velocity (at 15 feet) of 936 feet per second and a standard deviation of 10 feet per second. Tests were also conducted with Uzi and Black Hills ammunition.

a. Describe the velocity distribution of Winchester bullets fired from the FEG P9R pistol.

b. A bullet, brand unknown, is fired from the FEG P9R pistol. Suppose the velocity (at 15 feet) of the bullet is 1,000 feet per second. Is the bullet likely to be manufactured by Winchester? Explain.
No

2.82 A chemical company produces a substance composed of 98% cracked corn particles and 2% zinc phosphide for use in controlling rat populations in sugarcane fields. Production must be carefully controlled to maintain the 2% zinc phosphide because too much zinc phosphide will cause damage to the sugarcane and too little will be ineffective in controlling the rat population. Records from past production indicate that the distribution of the actual percentage of zinc phosphide present in the substance is approximately mound shaped, with a mean of 2.0% and a standard deviation of .08%.

a. If the production line is operating correctly approximately what proportion of batches from a day's production will contain less than 1.84% of zinc phosphide? ≈2.5%

b. Suppose one batch chosen randomly actually contains 1.80% zinc phosphide. Does this indicate that there is too little zinc phosphide in today's production? Explain your reasoning.

Applying the Concepts—Advanced

2.83 A buyer for a lumber company must decide whether to buy a piece of land containing 5,000 pine trees. If 1,000 of the trees are at least 40 feet tall, the buyer will purchase the land; otherwise, he won't. The owner of the land reports that the height of the trees has a mean of 30 feet and a standard deviation of 3 feet. Based on this information, what is the buyer's decision?

2.84 The National Education Longitudinal Survey (NELS) tracks a nationally representative sample of U.S. students from eighth grade through high school and college. Research published in *Chance* (Winter 2001) examined the Standardized Admission Test (SAT) scores of 265 NELS students who paid a private tutor to help them improve their scores. The next table summarizes the changes in both the SAT–Mathematics and SAT–Verbal scores for these students.

	SAT–Math	SAT–Verbal
Mean change in score	19	7
Standard deviation of score changes	65	49

a. Suppose one of the 265 students who paid a private tutor is selected at random. Give an interval that is likely to contain this student's change in the SAT–Math score. (−176, 214)

b. Repeat part **a** for the SAT–Verbal score. (−140, 154)

c. Suppose the selected student increased their score on one of the SAT tests by 140 points. Which test, the SAT–Math or SAT–Verbal, is the one most likely to have the 140-point increase? Explain.
SAT-Math

2.85 When it is working properly, a machine that fills 25-pound bags of flour dispenses an average of 25 pounds per fill; the standard deviation of the amount of fill is .1 pound. To monitor the performance of the machine an inspector weighs the contents of a bag coming off the machine's conveyor belt every half-hour during the day. If the contents of two consecutive bags fall more than 2 standard deviations from the mean (using the mean and standard deviation given above), the filling process is said to be out of control and the machine is shut down briefly for adjustments. The data given in the table below are the weights measured by the inspector yesterday. Assume the machine is never shut down for more than 15 minutes at a time. At what times yesterday was the process shut down for adjustment? Justify your answer.

FLOUR

Time	Weight (pounds)
8:00 A.M.	25.10
8:30	25.15
9:00	24.81
9:30	24.75
10:00	25.00
10:30	25.05
11:00	25.23
11:30	25.25
12:00	25.01
12:30 P.M.	25.06
1:00	24.95
1:30	24.80
2:00	24.95
2:30	25.21
3:00	24.90
3:30	24.71
4:00	25.31
4:30	25.15
5:00	25.20

2.7 Numerical Measures of Relative Standing

We've seen that numerical measures of central tendency and variability describe the general nature of a quantitative data set (either a sample or a population). In addition, we may be interested in describing the *relative* quantitative location of particular measurement within a data set. Descriptive measures of the relationship of a measurement to the rest of the data are called **measures of relative standing.**

One measure of the relative standing of a measurement is its **percentile ranking,** or **percentile score.** For example, if oil company A reports that its yearly sales are in the 90th percentile of all companies in the industry, the implication is that 90% of all oil companies have yearly sales less than company A's, and only 10% have yearly sales exceeding company A's. This is demonstrated in Figure 2.22. Similarly, if the oil company's yearly sales are in the 50th percentile (the median of the data set), 50% of all oil companies would have lower yearly sales and 50% would have higher yearly sales.

Percentile rankings are of practical value only for large data sets. Finding them involves a process similar to the one used in finding a median. The measurements are ranked in order and a rule is selected to define the location of each percentile. Since we are primarily interested in interpreting the percentile rankings of measurements (rather than finding particular percentiles for a data set), we define the *pth percentile* of a data set as shown in Definition 2.11.

DEFINITION 2.11

For any set of *n* measurements (arranged in ascending or descending order), the **pth percentile** is a number such that $p\%$ of the measurements fall below the *pth* percentile and $(100 - p)\%$ fall above it.

Figure 2.22
Location of 90th percentile for yearly sales of oil companies

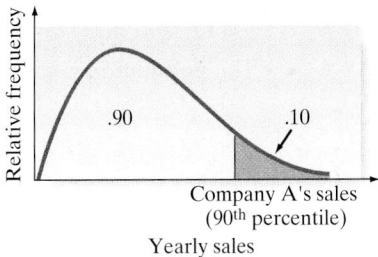

EXAMPLE 2.13

FINDING AND INTERPRETING PERCENTILES

Problem Refer to the percentages spent on research and development by the 50 high-technology firms listed in Table 2.8 (p. 88). A portion of the SPSS descriptive statistics printout is shown in Figure 2.23. Locate the 25th percentile and 95th percentile on the printout and interpret these values.

Solution Both the 25th percentile and 95th percentile are highlighted on the SPSS printout, Figure 2.23. These values are 7.05 and 13.335, respectively. Our interpretations are as follows: 25% of the 50 R&D percentages fall below 7.05 and 95% of the R&D percentages fall below 13.335.

7.05, 13.335

Look Back The method for computing percentiles varies according to the software used. Some packages, like SPSS, gives two different methods of computing

Percentiles

			Percentiles				
	5	10	25	50	75	90	95
Weighted Average(Definition 1) RDPCT	5.765	6.500	7.050	8.050	9.625	11.280	13.335
Tukey's Hinges RDPCT			7.100	8.050	9.600		

Figure 2.23

SPSS percentiles for 50 R&D percentages

Teaching Tip

The *z*-score is the measure
of relative standing that will
be used extensively with the
normal distribution later. It is
helpful if the student becomes
familiar with the *z*-score
concept now.

percentiles. As the data set increases in size, these percentile values will converge to a single number.

Now Work   *Exercise 2.87*

■ ■ ■

Suggested Exercise 2.94

Another measure of relative standing in popular use is the *z-score*. As you can see in Definition 2.12 the *z*-score makes use of the mean and standard deviation of the data set in order to specify the relative location of a measurement. Note that the *z*-score is calculated by subtracting $\bar{x}$ (or μ) from the measurement x and then dividing the result by s (or σ). The final result, the *z*-score, represents the distance between a given measurement x and the mean, expressed in standard deviations.

> **DEFINITION 2.12**
>
> The **sample z-score** for a measurement x is
>
> $$z = \frac{x - \bar{x}}{s}$$
>
> The **population z-score** for a measurement x is
>
> $$z = \frac{x - \mu}{\sigma}$$

EXAMPLE 2.14   FINDING A Z-SCORE

Problem   Suppose 200 steelworkers are selected, and the annual income of each is determined. The mean and standard deviation are $\bar{x} = \$34,000$ and $s = \$2,000$. Suppose Joe Smith's annual income is $32,000. What is his sample *z*-score?

Solution   Joe Smith's annual income lies below the mean income of the 200 steelworker (see Figure 2.24). We compute

$$z = \frac{x - \bar{x}}{s} = \frac{\$32,000 - \$34,000}{\$2,000} = -1.0$$

$$z = -1.0$$

which tells us that Joe Smith's annual income is 1.0 standard deviation *below* the sample mean, or, in short, his sample *z*-score is -1.0.

Figure 2.24
Annual income of steel
workers

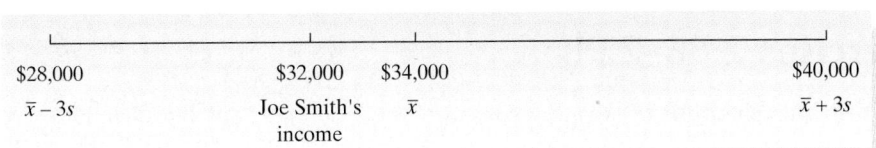

Look Back The numerical value of the z-score reflects the relative standing of the measurement. A large positive z-score implies that the measurement is larger than almost all other measurements, whereas a large negative z-score indicates that the measurement is smaller than almost every other measurement. If a z-score is 0 or near 0, the measurement is located at or near the mean of the sample or population.

Now Work   *Exercise 2.86*

■ ■ ■

If we know that the frequency distribution of the measurements is moundshaped, the following interpretation of the z-score can be given.

Teaching Tip

Draw a picture of a mound-shaped distribution and locate the z-scores–3, -2, -1, 0, 1, 2, and 3 on it to help students understand what the z-score measures.

> ## Interpretation of z-scores for Mound-Shaped Distributions of Data
>
> 1. Approximately 68% of the measurements will have a z-score between -1 and 1.
>
> 2. Approximately 95% of the measurements will have a z-score between -2 and 2.
>
> 3. Approximately 99.7% (almost all) of the measurements will have a z-score between -3 and. 3.

Suggested Exercise 2.96

Note that this interpretation of z-scores is identical to that given by the Empirical Rule for mound-shaped distributions (Table 2.7). The statement that a measurement falls in the interval $(\mu - \sigma)$ to $(\mu + \sigma)$ is equivalent to the statement that a measurement has a population z-score between -1 and 1, since all measurements between $(\mu - \sigma)$ and $(\mu + \sigma)$ are within 1 standard deviation of μ. These z-scores are displayed in Figure 2.25.

Figure 2.25
Population z-scores for a
mound-shaped distribution

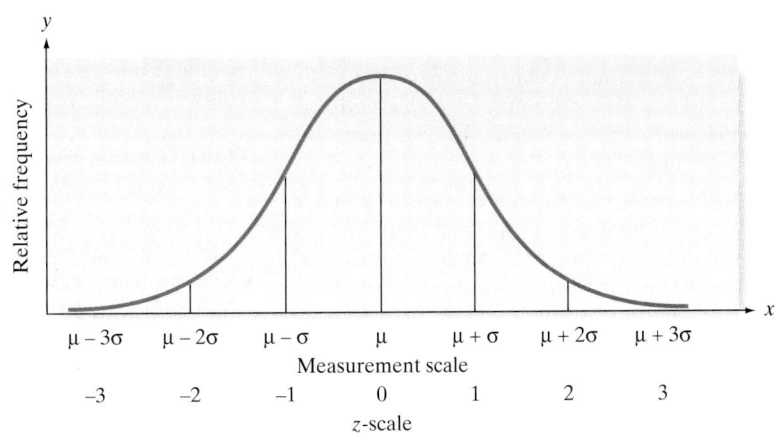

Exercises 2.86–2.98

Learning the Mechanics

2.86 Compute the z-score corresponding to each of the following values of x:

    a. $x = 40, s = 5, \bar{x} = 30$ 2

    b. $x = 90, \mu = 89, \sigma = 2$ .5

    c. $\mu = 50, \sigma = 5, x = 50$ 0

    d. $s = 4, x = 20, \bar{x} = 30$ −2.5

    e. In parts **a–d**, state whether the z-score locates x within a sample or a population.

    f. In parts **a–d**, state whether each value of x lies above or below the mean and by how many standard deviations.   Above, above, at, below

2.87 Give the percentage of measurements in a data set that are above and below each of the following percentiles:

    a. 75th percentile

    b. 50th percentile

    c. 20th percentile

    d. 84th percentile

2.88 What is the 50th percentile of a quantitative data set called?   Median

2.89 Compare the z-scores to decide which of the following x values lie the greatest distance above the mean and the greatest distance below the mean.

    a. $x = 100, \mu = 50, \sigma = 25$ 2

    b. $x = 1, \mu = 4, \sigma = 1$ −3

    c. $x = 0, \mu = 200, \sigma = 100$ −2

    d. $x = 10, \mu = 5, \sigma = 3$ 1.67

2.90 Suppose that 40 and 90 are two elements of a population data set and that their z-scores are −2 and 3, respectively. Using only this information, is it possible to determine the population's mean and standard deviation? If so, find them. If not, explain why it's not possible. $\mu = 60, \sigma = 10$

Applying the Concepts—Basic

2.91 According to the National Center for Education Statistics (2000), scores on a mathematics assessment test for United States eighth-graders have a mean of 500, a 5th percentile of 356, a 25th percentile of 435, a 75th percentile of 563, and a 95th percentile of 653. Interpret each of these numerical descriptive measures.

2.92 According to the Bureau of Justice Statistics (March 2002), 73.5% of all licensed drivers stopped by police are 25 years or older. Give a percentile ranking for the age of 25 years in the distribution of all ages of licensed drivers stopped by police.   26.5th percentile

  ⊙ **BWECS**

2.93 Refer to the *Business Week* "Executive Compensation Scoreboard" data saved in the **BWECS** file. One of the quantitative variables measured for each of the 363 CEOs in the survey is the return-to-pay ratio. The ratio is determined by dividing the return on a \$100 investment in the CEO's company made three years earlier by the CEO's total pay over the last three years. The higher the return-to-pay ratio, the better the CEO's performance over the 3-year period.

    a. Find the mean and standard deviation of the return-to-pay ratios.   16.423, 43.153

    b. Oracle CEO Lawrence Ellison had a 3-year total pay of \$781.4 million (one of the highest in the survey) but a return-to-pay ratio of only .049. Find the z-score for this ratio.   −.38

    c. Microsoft CEO S. A. Ballmer had a 3-year total pay of \$2 million and a return-to-pay ratio of 21.5. Find the z-score for this ratio.   .12

    d. Use the z-scores, parts **b** and **c**, to make a statement about the two CEOs' return-to-pay ratios relative to the ratios for all CEOs in the survey.

  ⊙ **SHIPSANIT**

2.94 Refer to the may 2001 sanitation levels of cruiseships. Exercise 2.77 (p. 93). The data are saved in the **SHIPSANIT** file.

    a. Give a measure of relative standing for the Norwegian State score of 78. Interpret the result.

    b. Give a measure of relative standing for the Rotterdam's score of 97. Interpret the result.

Applying the Concepts—Intermediate

2.95 The U.S. Environmental Protection Agency (EPA) sets a limit on the amount of lead permitted in drinking water. The EPA *Action Level* for lead is .015 milligrams per liter (mg/L) of water. Under EPA guidelines, if 90% of a water system's study samples have a lead concentration less than .015 mg/L, the water is considered safe for drinking. I (coauthor Sincich) received a recent report on a study of lead levels in the drinking water of homes in my subdivision. The 90th percentile of the study sample had a lead concentration of .00372 mg/L. Are water customers in my subdivision at risk of drinking water with unhealthy lead levels? Explain.   No

2.96 At one university, the students are given z-scores at the end of each semester rather than the traditional GPAs. The mean and standard deviation of all students' cumulative GPAs, on which the z-scores are based, are 2.7 and .5, respectively.

    a. Translate each of the following z-scores to corresponding GPA: $z = 2.0, z = -1.0, z = .5, z = -2.5$.

b. Students with z-scores below -1.6 are put on probation. What is the corresponding probationary GPA?

c. The president of the university wishes to graduate the top 16% of the students with *cum laude* honors and the top 2.5% with *summa cum laude* honors. Where (approximately) should the limits be set in terms of z-scores? In terms of GPAs? What assumption. If any, did you make about the distribution of the GPAs at the university?

2.97 The Superfund Act was passed by Congress to encourage state participation in the implementation of law relating to the release and cleanup of hazardous substances. Hazardous waste sites financed by the Superfund Act are called Superfund sites. A total of 395 Superfund sites are operated by waste management companies in Arkansas (Tabor and Stanwick, *Arkansas Business and Economic Review*, Summer 1995). The number of these Superfund sites in each of Arkansas' 75 counties is shown in the table.

⊛ **ARKFUND**

3	3	2	1	2	0	5	3	5	2	1	8	2
12	3	5	3	1	3	0	8	0	9	6	8	6
2	16	0	6	0	5	5	0	1	25	0	0	0
6	2	10	12	3	10	3	17	2	4	2	1	21
4	2	1	11	5	2	2	7	2	3	1	8	2
0	0	0	2	3	10	2	3	48	21			

Source: Tabor. R. H., and Stanwick, S. D. "Arkansas: An Environmental Perspective." Arkansas Business and Economic Review, Vol. 28, No. 2, Summer 1995, pp. 22–32 (Table 1).

a. Find the 10th percentile of the data set. Interpret the result.

b. Find the 95th percentile of the data set. Interpret the result.

c. Find the mean and standard deviation of the data; then use these values to calculate the z-score for an Arkansas county with 48 Superfund sites.

d. Based on your answer to part **c,** would you classify 48 as an extreme number of Superfund sites?

2.98 In a study of how external clues influence performance, professors at the University of Alberta and Pennsylvania State University gave two different forms of a midterm examination to a large group of introductory students. The questions on the exam were identical and in the same order, but one exam was printed on blue paper and the other on red paper (*Teaching Psychology*, May 1998). Grading only the difficult questions on the exam, the researchers found that scores on the blue exam had a distribution with a mean of 53% and a standard deviation of 15%, while scores on the red exam had a distribution with a mean of 39% and a standard deviation of 12%. (Assume that both distributions are approximately mound shaped and symmetric.)

a. Give an interpretation of the standard deviation for the students who took the blue exam.

b. Give an interpretation of the standard deviation for the students who took the red exam.

c. Suppose a student is selected at random from the group of students who participated in the study and the student's score on the difficult questions is 20%. Which exam form is the student more likely to have taken, the blue or the red exam? Explain.   Red

2.8 Methods for Detecting Outliers (Optional)

Sometimes it is important to identify inconsistent or unusual measurements in a data set. An observation that is unusually large or small relative to the data values we want to describe is called an *outlier*.

Outliers are often attributable to one of several causes. First, the measurement associated with the outlier may be invalid. For example, the experimental procedure used to generate the measurement may have malfunctioned, the experimenter may have misrecorded the measurement, or the data might have been coded incorrectly in the computer. Second, the outlier may be the result of a misclassified measurement. That is, the measurement belongs to a population different from that from which the rest of the sample was drawn. Finally, the measurement associated with the outlier may be recorded correctly and from the same population as the rest of the sample, but represents a rare (chance) event. Such outliers occur most often when the relative frequency distribution of the sample data is extremely skewed, because such a distribution has a tendency to include extremely large or small observations relative to the others in the data set.

DEFINITION 2.13

An observation (or measurement) that is unusually large or small relative to the other values in a data set is called an **outlier.** Outliers typically are attributable to one of the following causes:

1. The measurement is observed, recorded, or entered into the computer incorrectly.
2. The measurement comes from a different population.
3. The measurement is correct, but represents a rare (chance) event.

Two useful methods for detecting outliers, one graphical and one numerical are **box plots** and z-scores. The box plot is based on the *quartiles* of a data set **Quartiles** are values that partition the data set into four groups, each containing 25% of the measurements. The *lower quartile* Q_L is the 25th percentile, the *middle quartile* is the median m (the 50th percentile), and the *upper quartile* Q_U is the 75th percentile (see Figure 2.26).

Teaching Tip

Explain how the upper and lower quartile are unaffected by the extreme values in the data set. This fact is the main reason that the box plot is such a useful tool for detecting outliers in a data set.

DEFINITION 2.14

The **lower quartile Q_L** is the 25th percentile of a data set. The **middle quartile m** is the median. The **upper quartile Q_U** is the 75th percentile.

A box plot is based on the *interquartile range* (IQR), the distance between the lower and upper quartiles:

$$IQR = Q_U - Q_L$$

DEFINITION 2.15

The **interquartile range (IQR)** is the distance between the lower and upper quartiles:

$$IQR = Q_U - Q_L$$

Figure 2.26
The quartiles for a data set

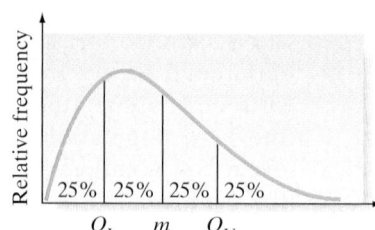

A vertical MINITAB box plot for the 50 companies' percentages of revenues spent on R&D (Table 2.2) is shown in Figure 2.27.* Note that a rectangle (the box) is drawn, with the top and bottom sides of the rectangle (the **hinges**) drawn at the quartiles Q_L and Q_U, respectively. By definition, then, the "middle" 50% of the observations—those between Q_L and Q_U—fall inside the box. For the R&D data, these quartiles appear to be at (approximately) 7.0 and 9.5. Thus,

$$IQR = 9.5 - 7.0 = 2.5 \text{ (approximately)}$$

The median is shown at about 8.0 by a horizontal line within the box.

To guide the construction of the "tails" of the box plot, two sets of limits, called **inner fences** and **outer fences,** are used. Neither set of fences actually appears on the box plot. Inner fences are located at a distance of 1.5(IQR) from the hinges. Emanating from the hinges of the box are vertical lines called the **whiskers.** The two whiskers extend to the most extreme observation inside the inner fences. For example, the inner fence on the lower side (bottom) of the R&D percentage box plot is (approximately)

$$\text{Lower inner fence} = \text{Lower hinge} - 1.5(IQR)$$
$$\approx 7.0 - 1.5(2.5)$$
$$= 7.0 - 3.75 = 3.25$$

The smallest measurement in the data set is 5.2, which is well inside this inner fence. Thus, the lower whisker extends to 5.2. Similarly, the upper whisker extends to about $(9.5 + 3.75) = 13.25$. The largest measurement inside this fence the third largest measurement, 13.2. Note that the longer upper whisker reveals the rightward skewness of the R&D distribution.

Values that are beyond the inner fences are deemed *potential outliers* because they are extreme values that represent relatively rare occurrences. In fact, for mound-shaped distributions, fewer than 1% of the observations are expected to fall outside the inner fences. Two of the 50 R&D measurements, both at 13.5, fall outside the upper inner fence. Each of these potential outliers is represented by the asterisk (*) at 13.5.

Teaching Tip

Use a class data set to generate the values of Q_L and Q_U. Using these values, construct a box plot for the data. Pay particular attention to the extreme values in the data set. Discuss whether they are outliers or not. Calculate z-scores for these observations and discuss the results.

Figure 2.27
MINITAB box plot for 50 R&D percentages

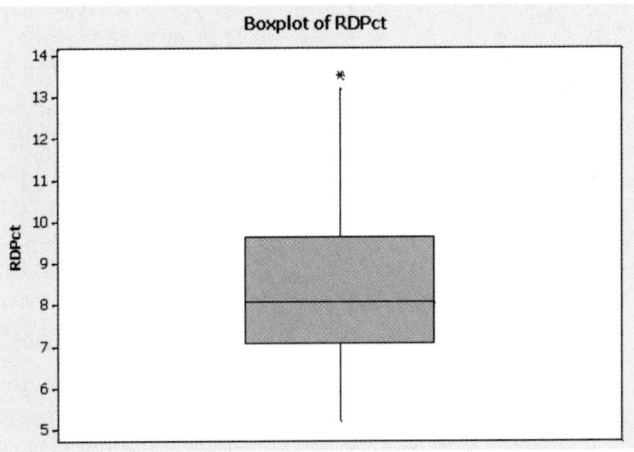

*Although box plots can be generated by hand, the amount of detail required makes them particularly well suited for computer generation. We use computer software to generate the box plots in this section.

The other two imaginary fences, the outer fences, are defined at a distance 3(IQR) from each end of the box. Measurements that fall beyond the outer fence are represented by 0s (zeros) and are very extreme measurements that require special analysis. Since less than one-hundredth of 1% (.01% or .0001) of the measurements from mound-shaped distributions are expected to fall beyond the outer fence these measurements are considered to be *outliers*. No measurement in the R&D percentage box plot (Figure 2.29) is represented by a 0; thus there are no outliers.

Recall that outliers are extreme measurements that stand out from the rest of the sample and may be faulty: They may be incorrectly recorded observations members of a population different from the rest of the sample, or, at the least, very unusual measurements from the same population. For example, the two R&D measurements at 13.5 (identified by an asterisk) may be considered outliers. When we analyze these measurements, we find that they are correctly recorded. However, it turns out that both represent R&D expenditures of relatively young and fast-growing companies. Thus, the outlier analysis may have revealed important factors that relate to the R&D expenditures of high-tech companies: their age and rate of growth. Outlier analysis often reveals useful information of this kind and therefore plays an important role in the statistical inference-making process.

In addition to detecting outliers, box plots provide useful information on the variation in a data set. The elements (and nomenclature) of box plots are summarized in the next box. Some aids to the interpretation of box plots are also given.

Teaching Tip

Define outliers to be extremely large or small observations relative to the rest of the data in a distribution.

Suggested Exercise 2.101

Elements of a Box Plot

1. A rectangle (the **box**) is drawn with the ends (the **hinges**) drawn at the lower and upper quartiles (Q_L and Q_U). The median of the data is shown in the box, usually by a line or a symbol (such as "+").

2. The points at distances 1.5(IQR) from each hinge define the **inner fences** of the data set. Lines (the **whiskers**) are drawn from each hinge to the most extreme measurement inside the inner fence.

3. A second pair of fences, the **outer fences**, are defined at a distance of 3 interquartile ranges, 3(IQR), from the hinges. One symbol (usually "*") is used to represent measurements falling between the inner and outer fences, and another (usually "0") is used to represent measurements beyond the outer fences.

4. The symbols used to represent the median and the extreme data points (those beyond the fences) will vary depending on the software you use to construct the box plot. (You may use your own symbols if you are constructing a box plot by hand.) You should consult the program's documentation to determine exactly which symbols are used.

Aids to the Interpretation of Box Plots

1. Examine the length of the box. The IQR is a measure of the sample's variability and is especially useful for the comparison of two samples (see Example 2.16).

2. Visually compare the lengths of the whiskers. If one is clearly longer, the distribution of the data is probably skewed in the direction of the longer whisker.

(cont'd)

3. Analyze any measurements that lie beyond the fences. Fewer than 5% should fall beyond the inner fences, even for very skewed distributions. Measurements beyond the outer fences are probably outliers, with one of the following explanations:

   a. The measurement is incorrect. It may have been observed, recorded, or entered into the computer incorrectly.

   b. The measurement belongs to a population different from the population that the rest of the sample was drawn from (see Example 2.16).

   c. The measurement is correct *and* from the same population as the rest. Generally, we accept this explanation only after carefully ruling out all others.

EXAMPLE 2.15

BOX PLOTS USING THE COMPUTER

Problem In Example 2.2 (p. 59) we analyzed 50 processing times (listed in Table 2.4) for the development of price quotes by the manufacturer of industrial wheels. The intent was to determine whether the success or failure in obtaining the order was related to the amount of time to process the price quotes. Each quote that corresponds to "lost" business was so classified. Use a statistical software package to draw a box plot for all 50 processing times. What does the box plot reveal about the data?

Solution The MINITAB box plot printout for these data is shown in Figure 2.28. Note that the upper whisker is much longer than the lower whisker, indicating rightward skewness of the data. However, the most important feature of the data is made very obvious by the box plot: There are four measurements (indicated by asterisks) that are beyond the upper inner fence. Thus, the distribution is extremely skewed to the right, and several measurements—or outliers—need special attention in our analysis.

Look Back Before removing outliers from the data set, a good analyst will make a concerted effort to find the cause of the outliers. We offer an explanation for these processing time outliers in the next example.

Now Work *Exercise 2.102*

■ ■ ■

Figure 2.28
MINITAB box plot for
processing time data

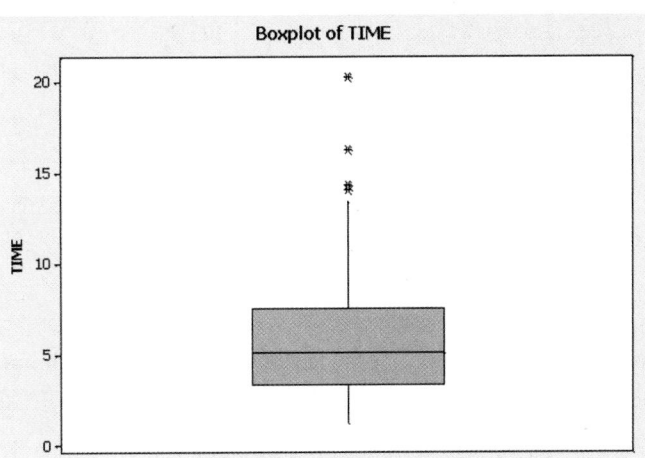

EXAMPLE 2.16   COMPARING BOX PLOTS

Problem   The box plot for the 50 processing times (Figure 2.27) does not explicitly reveal the differences, if any, between the set of times corresponding to the success and the set of times corresponding to the failure to obtain the business. Box plots corresponding to the 39 "won" and 11 "lost" bids were generated using SPSS, and are shown in Figure 2.28. Interpret them.

Solution   The division of the data set into two parts, corresponding to won and lost bids eliminates any observations that are beyond the inner fences. Furthermore, the skewness in the distributions has been reduced, as evidenced by the facts that the upper whiskers are only slightly longer than the lower. The box plots also reveal that the processing times corresponding to the lost bids tend to exceed those of the won bids. A plausible explanation for the outliers in the combined box plot (Figure 2.27) is that they are from a different population than the bulk of the times. In other words, there are two populations represented by the sample of processing times—one corresponding to lost bids, and the other to won bids.

Look Back   The box plots lend support to the conclusion that the price quote processing time and the success of acquiring the business are related. However, whether the visual differences between the box plots generalize to inferences about the populations corresponding to these two samples is a matter for inferential statistics, not graphical descriptions. We'll discuss how to use samples to compare two populations using inferential statistics in Chapter 9.

Figure 2.29
SPSS box plots of processing time for won and lost bids

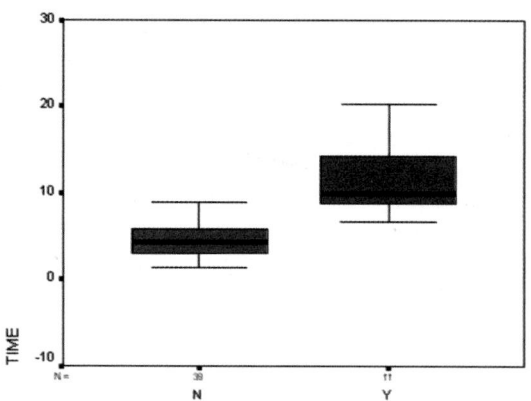

The following example illustrates how z-scores can be used to detect outliers and make inferences.

EXAMPLE 2.17   INFERENCE USING Z-SCORES

Problem   Suppose a female bank employee believes that her salary is low as a result of sex discrimination. To substantiate her belief, she collects information on the salaries of her male counterparts in the banking business. She finds that their salaries have a mean of $54,000 and a standard deviation of $2,000. Her salary is $47,000. Does this information support her claim of sex discrimination?

$z = -3.5$

Solution The analysis might proceed as follows: First, we calculate the z-score for the woman's salary with respect to those of her male counterparts. Thus,

$$z = \frac{\$47,000 - \$54,000}{\$2,000} = -3.5$$

The implication is that the woman's salary is 3.5 standard deviations *below* the mean of the male salary distribution. Furthermore, if a check of the male salary data shows that the frequency distribution is mound-shaped, we can infer that very few salaries in this distribution should have a z-score less than -3, as shown in Figure 2.30. Clearly, a z-score of -3.5 represents an outlier. Either this female's salary is from a distribution different from the male salary distribution, or it is a very unusual (highly improbable) measurement from a distribution that is no different than the male salary distribution.

Figure 2.30
Male salary distribution

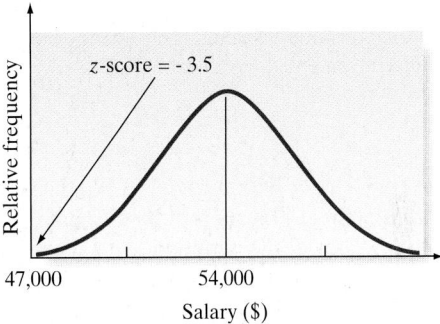

Look Back Which of the two situations do you think prevails? Statistical thinking would lead us to conclude that her salary does not come from the male salary distribution, lending support to the female bank employee's claim of sex discrimination. A careful investigator should require more information before inferring sex discrimination as the cause. We would want to know more about the data collection technique the woman used and more about her competence at her job. Also perhaps other factors such as length of employment should be considered in the analysis.

 Now Work   *Exercise 2.99*

■ ■ ■

Examples 2.16 and 2.17 exemplify an approach to statistical inference that might be called the **rare-event approach.** An experimenter hypothesizes a specific frequency distribution to describe a population of measurements. Then a sample of measurements is drawn from the population. If the experimenter finds it unlikely that the sample came from the hypothesized distribution, the hypothesis concluded to be false. Thus, in Example 2.17 the woman believes her salary reflects discrimination. She hypothesizes that her salary should be just another measurement in the distribution of her male counterparts' salaries if no discrimination exists. However, it is so unlikely that the sample (in this case, her salary) came from the male frequency distribution that she rejects that hypothesis, concluding that the distribution from which her salary was drawn is different from the distribution for the men.

This rare-event approach to inference-making is discussed further in late chapters. Proper application of the approach requires a knowledge of probability the subject of our next chapter.

We conclude this section with some rules of thumb for detecting outliers.

> ### Rules of Thumb for Detecting Outliers*
>
> *Box Plots:* Observations falling between the inner and outer fences are deemed *suspect outliers*. Observations falling beyond the outer fence are deemed *highly suspect outliers*.
>
> *z-scores:* Observations with z-scores greater than 3 in absolute value are considered outliers. (For some highly skewed data sets, observations with z-scores greater than 2 in absolute value may be outliers).

Exercises 2.99–2.109

Learning the Mechanics

2.99 A sample data set has a mean of 57 and a standard deviation of 11. Determine whether each of the following sample measurements are outliers.
   a. 65   No
   b. 21   Yes
   c. 72   No
   d. 98   Yes

2.100 Define the 25th, 50th, and 75th percentiles of a data set. Explain how they provide a description of the data.

2.101 Suppose a data set consisting of exam scores has a lower quartile $Q_L = 60$, a median $m = 75$, and an upper quartile $Q_U = 85$. The scores on the exam range from 18 to 100. Without having the actual scores available to you, construct as much of the box plot as possible.

2.102 Consider the horizontal box plot shown below.
   a. What is the median of the data set (approximately)?   4
   b. What are the upper and lower quartiles of the data set (approximately)?   6,3
   c. What is the interquartile range of the data set (approximately)?   3
   d. Is the data set skewed to the left, skewed to the right, or symmetric?   Skewed right
   e. What percentage of the measurements in the dataset lie to the right of the median? To the left of the upper quartile?   50%, 75%

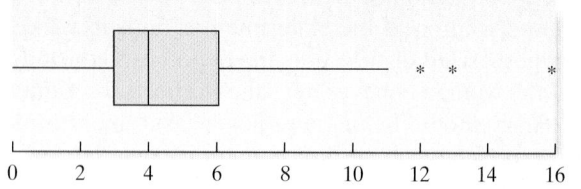

f. Identify any outliers in the data.   12,13,16

Applying the Concepts—Basic

2.103 Refer to the *Journal of Accounting and Public Policy* (Spring 2002) study of 100,000 first-time candidates for the CPA exam, Exercise 2.49 (p. 79). The number of semester hours of college credit earned by the candidates had a mean of 141.31 hours and a standard deviation of 17.77 hours.
   a. Find the z-score for a first-time candidate for the CPA exam who earned 160 semester hours of college credit. Is this observation considered an outlier?   No
   b. Give a value of number of semester hours that would, in fact, be considered an outlier in this data set. $x \leq 88$ or $x \geq 194.62$

2.104 The table contains the top salary offer (in thousands of dollars) received by each member of a sample of 50 MBA students who recently graduated from the Graduate School of Management at Rutgers, the state university of New Jersey.

MBASAL

61.1	48.5	47.0	49.1	43.5
50.8	62.3	50.0	65.4	58.0
53.2	39.9	49.1	75.0	51.2
41.7	40.0	53.0	39.6	49.6
55.2	54.9	62.5	35.0	50.3
41.5	56.0	55.5	70.0	59.2
39.2	47.0	58.2	59.0	60.8
72.3	55.0	41.4	51.5	63.0
48.4	61.7	45.3	63.2	41.5
47.0	43.2	44.6	47.7	58.6

Source: Career Services Office, Graduate School of Management, Rutgers University.

*The z-score and box plot methods both establish rule-of-thumb limits outside of which a measurement is deemed to be an outlier. Usually, the two methods produce similar results. However, the presence of one or more outliers in a data set can inflate the computed value of s. Consequently, it will be less likely that an errant observation would have a z-score larger than 3 in absolute value. In contrast, the values of the quartiles used to calculate the intervals for a box plot are not affected by the presence of outliers.

Statistics in Action Revisited
Detecting Outliers

In the ethics survey of University Community Hospital physicians, the medical researchers measured two qualitative variables: *Length of time in practice* (number of years) and *Amount of exposure to ethics in medical school* (number of hours). Are there any unusual values of these variables in the ETHICS data set? We will employ both the box plot and z-score methods to aid in identifying outliers in the data.

Descriptive statistics for these two variables, produced using MINITAB, are shown in Figure SIA2.6. To employ the z-score method, we need the means and standard deviations. These values are highlighted on Figure SIA2.6. Then the 3-standard-deviation intervals are

$$\text{YRSPRAC:} \quad 14.6 \pm 3(9.2) = 14.6 \pm 27.6$$
$$= (-13.0, 42.2)$$
$$\text{EDHRS:} \quad 23.9 \pm 3(109.6) = 23.9 \pm 328.8$$
$$= (-304.9, 352.7)$$

Note: [Since neither of the variables can be negative, for practical purposes the intervals all begin at 0.]

In this application, we will focus on only the three largest values of the variables in the data set. For length of time in practice, these values are 35, 40, and 40 years. Note that all three values fall within the 3-standard-deviation interval—that is, they all have z-scores less than 3 in absolute value. Consequently, no outliers exist for the data on length of time in practice.

For ethics exposure, the three largest values are 75, 80, and 1,000 hours. Note that only one of these values, 1,000, falls beyond the 3-standard-deviation interval. Thus, the data for the physician who was exposed to 1,000 hours of ethics in medical school is considered an outlier using the z-score approach. However, notice that

the standard deviation for the variable (109.6) is much larger than the mean (23.9), indicating a high degree of skewness in the data. This skewness is due, in large part, to the extreme value of 1,000 hours. When such an extreme outlier occurs in the data, the standard deviation is inflated and the z-score method is less likely to detect unusual observations. (See the footnote on p. 106.) When this occurs, the box plot method for detecting outliers is preferred.

Rather than produce a box plot for the ethics exposure variable, we'll use the descriptive statistics in Figure SIA2.6 to find the inner and outer fences. From the MINITAB printout, we see that $Q_L = 1$, $Q_U = 20$, and $IQR = 19$. Then the upper inner and outer fence boundaries of the box plot are

Upper inner fence:
$$Q_U + (1.5)IQR = 20 + (1.5)(19) = 48.5$$

Upper outer fence:
$$Q_U + (3)IQR = 20 + (3)(19) = 77.0$$

Now we see that the ethics exposure value of 80 hours is, indeed, a highly suspect outlier, since it falls beyond the upper outer fence. Also, the exposure value of 75 hours is a suspect outlier, since it falls beyond the upper inner fence. Thus, the box plot method detected an additional two outliers.

Before any type of inference is made concerning the population of ethics exposure values, we should consider whether these three outliers are legitimate observations (in which case they will remain in the data set) or are associated with physicians that are not members of the population of interest (in which case they will be removed from the data set).

Descriptive Statistics: YRSPRAC, EDHRS

Variable	N	N*	Mean	StDev	Q1	Median	Q3	IQR
YRSPRAC	112	6	14.598	9.161	7.000	14.000	20.000	13.000
EDHRS	83	35	23.9	109.6	1.0	5.0	20.0	19.0

Figure SIA2.6
MINITAB descriptive statistics for practice experience and ethics exposure

Box Plots

Using the TI-83 Graphing Calculator

Making a Box Plot

Step 1   Enter the data
Press STAT and select 1:Edit
Note: If the list already contains data, clear the old data. Use the up arrow to highlight 'L1'. Press CLEAR ENTER.
Use the arrow and ENTER keys to enter the data set into L1.

Step 2   Set up the box plot

Press **2nd Y =** for **STAT PLOT**
Press **1**   for **Plot 1**

Set the cursor so that 'ON' is flashing.
For TYPE, use the right arrow to scroll through the plot icons and select the boxplot in the middle of the second row.
For XLIST, choose L1.
Set FREQ to 1.

Step 3   View the graph
Press ZOOM and select 9:ZoomStat

Optional *Read the five number summary*
Step Press TRACE
Use the left and right arrow keys to move between minX, Q1, Med, Q3, and maxX.

Example Make a box plot for the given data,
86, 70, 62, 98, 73, 56, 53, 92, 86, 37, 62, 83, 78, 49, 78, 37, 67, 79, 57

The output screen for this example is shown below.

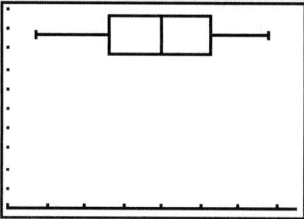

a. The mean and standard deviation are 52.33 and 9.22, respectively. Find and interpret the z-score associated with the highest salary offer, the lowest salary offer, and the mean salary offer. Would you consider the highest offer to be unusually high? Why or why not?

b. Construct a box plot for this data set. Which salary offers (if any) are potentially faulty observations? Explain.   None

BANKRUPT

2.105 Refer to the *Financial Management* (Spring 1995) study of 49 firms filing for prepackaged bankruptcies. Exercise 2.30 (p. 67). Recall that three types of "prepack" firms exist: (1) those who hold no pre-filing vote: (2) those who vote their preference for a joint solution; and (3) those who vote their preference for a prepack.

a. Construct a box plot for the time in bankruptcy (months) for each type of firm.

b. Find the median bankruptcy times for the three types?

c. How do the variabilities of the bankruptcy times compare for the three types?

d. The standard deviations of the bankruptcy times are 2.47 for "none," 1.72 for "joint," and 0.96 for "prepack." Do the standard deviations agree with the interquartile ranges with regard to the comparison of the variabilities of the bankruptcy times?

e. Is there evidence of outliers in any of the three distributions?

Applying the Concepts—Intermediate

WPOWER50

2.106 Refer to the *Fortune* (Oct. 14, 2002) ranking of the 50 most powerful women in America, Exercise 2.45 (p. 78). The data are saved in the **WPOWER50** file. Use side-by-side box plots to compare the ages of the women in three groups based on their position within the firm: Group 1 (CEO, CFO, CRO, or COO); Group 2 (Chairman or President); and Group 3 (EVP, SVP, or Vice Chair). Do you detect any outliers?   One in Group 1

SHIPSANIT

2.107 Refer to Exercise 2.77 (p. 93) and the data on the sanitation levels of passenger cruise ships. The data are saved in the **SHIPSANIT** file.

a. Use the box plot method to detect any outliers in the data set.   52, 77, 78, 82, and 83

b. Use the z-score method to detect any outliers in the data set.   52, 77

c. Do the two methods agree? If not, explain why.   No

ARKFUND

2.108 Refer to Exercise 2.97 (p. 99) and the data on the number of Superfund sites in each of 75 Arkansas counties. The data are saved in the **ARKFUND** file.

a. There is at least one outlier in the data. Use the methods of this chapter to detect the outliers.   21, 21, 25, 48

b. Delete the outlier(s) found in part **a** from the data set and recalculate measures of central tendency and variation. Which measures are most affected by the removal of the outlier(s)?

2.109 A manufacturer of minicomputer systems is interested in improving its customer support services. As a first step, its marketing department has been charged with the responsibility of summarizing the extent of customer problems in terms of system down time. The 40 most recent customers were surveyed to determine the amount of down time (in hours) they had experienced during the previous month. These data are listed in the table.

DOWNTIME

Customer Number	Down Time
230	12
231	16
232	5
233	16
234	21
235	29
236	38
237	14
238	47
239	0
240	24
241	15
242	13
243	8
244	2
245	11
246	22
247	17
248	31
249	10
250	4
251	10
252	15
253	7
254	20
255	9
256	22
257	18
258	28
259	19
260	34
261	26
262	17
263	11
264	64
265	19
266	18
267	24
268	49
269	50

a. Construct a box plot for these data. Use the information reflected in the box plot to describe the frequency distribution of the data set. Your description should address central tendency, variation, and skewness.

b. Use your box plot to determine which customers are having unusually lengthy down times.

c. Find and interpret the z-scores associated with the customers you identified in part **b**.

2.9 Graphing Bivariate Relationships (Optional)

The claim is often made that the crime rate and the unemployment rate are "highly correlated." Another popular belief is that the Gross Domestic Product (GDP and the rate of inflation are "related." Some people even believe that the Dow Jones Industrial Average and the lengths of fashionable skirts are "associated." The words *correlated*, *related*, and *associated* imply a relationship between two variables—in the examples above, two *quantitative* variables.

One way to describe the relationship between two quantitative variables—called a **bivariate relationship**—is to plot the data in a **scattergram** (or **scatterplot**) A scattergram is a two-dimensional plot, with one variable's values plotted along the vertical axis and the other along the horizontal axis. For example, Figure 2.31 is a scattergram relating (1) the cost of mechanical work (heating, ventilating and plumbing) to (2) the floor area of the building for a sample of 26 factory and warehouse buildings. Note that the scattergram suggests a general tendency for mechanical cost to increase as building floor area increases.

When an increase in one variable is generally associated with an increase in the second variable, we say that the two variables are "positively related" or "positively correlated."* Figure 2.31 implies that mechanical cost and floor area are positively correlated. Alternatively, if one variable has a tendency to decrease as the other increases, we say the variables are "negatively correlated." Figure 2.32 shows several hypothetical scattergrams that portray a positive bivariate relationship (Figure 2.32a), a negative bivariate relationship (Figure 2.32b), and a situation where the two variables are unrelated (Figure 2.32c).

Figure 2.31
Scattergram of cost vs. floor area

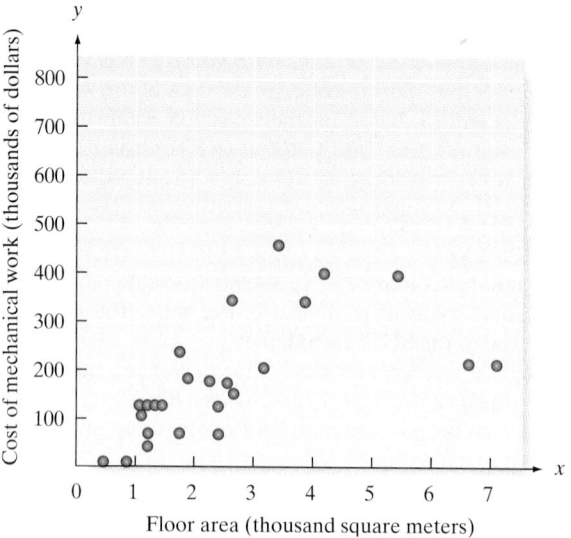

*A formal definition of correlation is given in Chapter 12. We will learn that correlation measures the strength of the linear (or straight-line) relationship between two variables.

Figure 2.32
Hypothetical bivariate
relationship

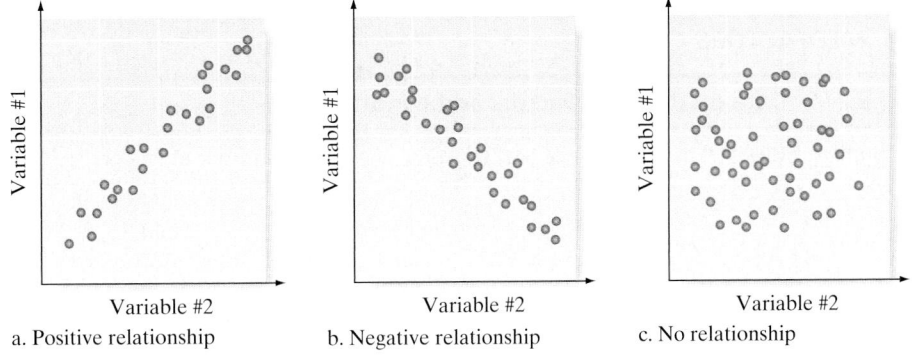

a. Positive relationship   b. Negative relationship   c. No relationship

EXAMPLE 2.18   GRAPHING BIVARIATE DATA

Problem   A medical item used to administer to a hospital patient is called a *factor*. For example, factors can be intravenous (IV) tubing, IV fluid, needles, shave kits, bedpans, diapers, dressings, medications, and even code carts. The coronary care unit at Bayonet Point Hospital (St. Petersburg, Florida) recently investigated the relationship between the number of factors administered per patient and the patient's length of stay (in days). Data on these two variables for a sample of 50 coronary care patients are given in Table 2.9. Use a scattergram to describe the relationship between the two variables of interest, number of factors and length of stay.

Solution   Rather than construct the plot by hand, we resort to a statistical software package. The EXCEL plot of the data in Table 2.9, with length of stay (LOS) on the vertical axis and number of factors (FACTORS) on the horizontal axis, is shown in Figure 2.33.

   Although the plotted points exhibit a fair amount of variation, the scattergram clearly shows an increasing trend. It appears that a patient's length of stay is positively correlated with the number of factors administered to the patient.

Look Back If hospital administrators can be confident that the sample trend

Figure 2.33
EXCEL Scatterplot of
data in Table 2.9

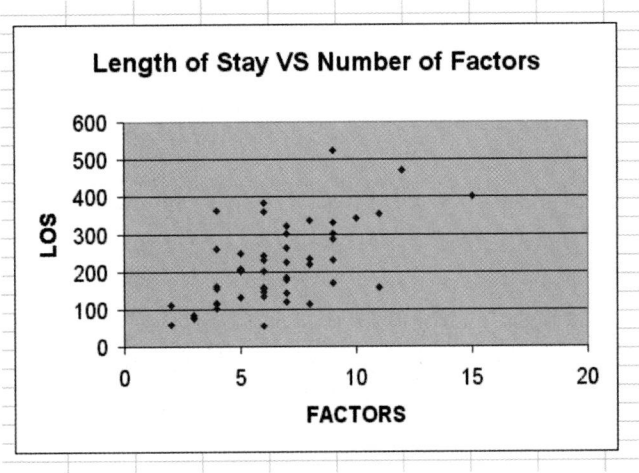

MEDFACTORS

TABLE 2.9   Data on Patient's Factors and Length of Stay

Number of Factors	Length of Stay (days)	Number of Factors	Length of Stay (days)
231	9	354	11
323	7	142	7
113	8	286	9
208	5	341	10
162	4	201	5
117	4	158	11
159	6	243	6
169	9	156	6
55	6	184	7
77	3	115	4
103	4	202	6
147	6	206	5
230	6	360	6
78	3	84	3
525	9	331	9
121	7	302	7
248	5	60	2
233	8	110	2
260	4	131	5
224	7	364	4
472	12	180	7
220	8	134	6
383	6	401	15
301	9	155	4
262	7	338	8

Source: Bayonet Point Hospital, Coronary Care Unit.

shown in Figure 2.33 accurately describes the trend in the population, then they may use this information to improve their forecasts of lengths of stay for future patients.

■ ■ ■

The scattergram is a simple but powerful tool for describing a bivariate relationship. However, keep in mind that it is only a graph. No measure of reliability can be attached to inferences made about bivariate populations based on scattergrams of sample data. The statistical tools that enable us to make inferences about bivariate relationships are presented in Chapter 12.

Statistics in Action Revisited

Interpreting Scatterplots

Consider the two qualitative variables, *Length of time in practice* (number of years) and *Amount of exposure to ethics in medical school* (number of hours), measured on a sample of University Community Hospital physicians. To investigate a possible relationship between these two variables, we created a scatterplot for the data in Figure SIA2.7 using MINITAB.

At first glance, the graph appears to show almost no relationship between the variables. However, note the outlying data point to the far right of the scatterplot. This point corresponds to a physician who reported 1,000 hours of exposure to ethics in medical school. Recall that we classified this data point as a highly suspect outlier in the previous SIA Revisited section (p. 107). If we remove this observation from the data set and rerun the scatterplot option of MINITAB, the graph shown in Figure SIA2.8 is produced. Now the trend in the relationship is more apparent. For physicians with 20 or fewer hours of ethics exposure, there is little or no trend. However, for physicians with more than 20 hours of exposure to ethics, there appears to be a decreasing trend; that is, for physicians with high exposure to ethics, practice experience and exposure time are apparently negatively related.

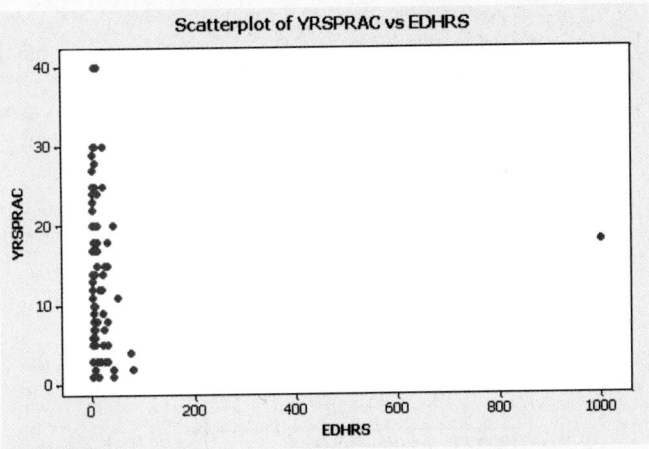

Figure SIA2.7
MINITAB scatterplot of practice experience versus ethics exposure

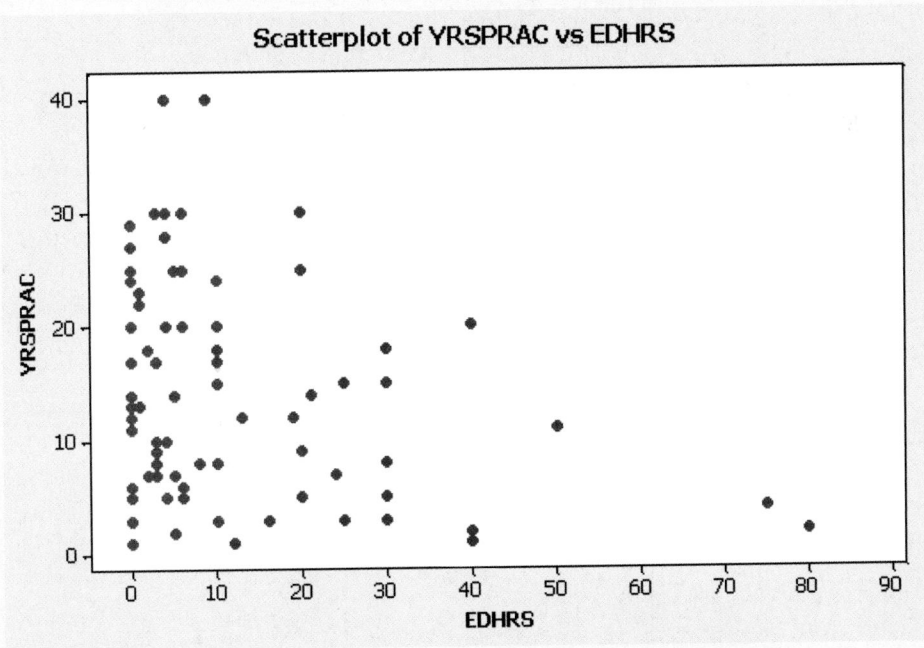

Figure SIA2.8
MINITAB scatterplot of practice experience versus ethics exposure—outlier deleted

Scatterplots

Using the T1-83 Graphing Calculator

Making Scatterplots

Step 1 Enter the data
Press STAT and select 1:Edit
Note: If a list already contains data, clear the old data. Use the up arrow to highlight the list name, 'L1' or 'L2'.
Press CLEAR ENTER.
Enter your x-data in L1 and your y-data in L2.

Step 2 Set up the scatterplot
Press 2nd **Y** = for STAT PLOT
Press 1 for Plot1
Set the cursor so that ON is flashing.
For Type, use the arrow and Enter keys to highlight and select the scatterplot (first icon in the first row).
For Xlist, choose the column containing the x-data.
For Freq, choose the column containing the y-data.

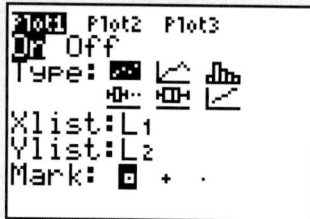

Step 3 View the scatterplot
Press ZOOM 9 for ZoomStat

Example The figures below show a table of data entered on the T1-83 and the scatterplot of the data obtained using the steps given above.

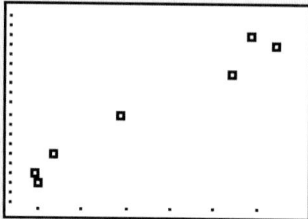

Exercises: 2.110–2.117

Learning the Mechanics

2.110 Construct a scattergram for the data in the following table.

Variable 1	5	1	1.5	2	2.5	3	3.5	4	4.5	5
Variable 2	2	1	3	4	6	10	9	12	17	17

2.111 Construct a scattergram for the data in the following table.

Variable 1	5	3	−1	2	7	6	4	0	8
Variable 2	14	3	10	1	8	5	3	2	12

Applying the Concepts—Basic

◉ DIAMONDS

2.112 Refer to the *Journal of Statistics Education* data on diamonds saved in the **DIAMONDS** file. In addition to the number of carats, the asking price for the each of the 308 diamonds for sale on the open market was recorded. Construct a scatterplot for the data, with number of carats on the horizontal axis and price on the vertical axis. What type of trend do you detect? Upward trend

◉ SATSCORES

2.113 Refer to Exercise 2.29 (p. 67) and the data on state SAT scores saved in the **SATSCORES** file. Construct a scatterplot for the data, with 1990 SAT score on the horizontal axis and 2000 SAT score on the vertical axis. What type of trend do you detect? Upward Trend

◉ FLALAW

2.114 Refer to Exercise 2.44 (p. 78) and the data on law firms with headquarters in the state of Florida. For each firm, the number of lawyers and number of law offices are saved in the **FLALAW** file. Construct a scatterplot for the data, with number of law offices on the horizontal axis and number of lawyers on the vertical axis. What type of trend do you detect? Upward trend

Applying the Concepts—Intermediate

◉ COMPTIME

2.115 Refer to Exercise 2.28 (p. 67) and the *Management Science* experiment on task completion times. Recall that each of 25 employees performed a production task a multiple number of times. The time to complete the task (in minutes) after the 10th, 30th, and 50th time it was performed was recorded for each employee; these data are saved in the **COMPTIME** file.

a. Use a graph to investigate a possible relationship between completion times after the 10th and 30th time the task was performed.

b. Use a graph to investigate a possible relationship between completion times after the 10th and 50th time the task was performed.

c. Use a graph to investigate a possible relationship between completion times after the 30th and 50th time the task was performed.

◉ BWECS

2.116 Refer to the *Business Week* "Executive Compensation Scoreboard" data saved in the **BWECS** file. Four quantitative variables are measured for each of the 363 CEOs in the survey: total pay in 2002, total pay over the 3-year period 2000–2002, return on a $100 investment in the company, and the return-to-pay ratio. Form a scatterplot for each pair of these variables. What trends, if any, do you detect?

◉ DDT

2.117 Refer to the U.S. Army Corps of Engineers data on contaminated fish saved in the **DDT** file. Three quantitative variables are measured for each of the 144 captured fish: length (in centimeters), weight (in grams), and DDT level (in parts per million). Form a scatterplot for each pair of these variables. What trends, if any, do you detect?

2.10 The Time Series Plot (Optional)

Each of the previous sections has been concerned with describing the information contained in a sample or population of data. Often these data are viewed as having been produced at essentially the same point in time. Thus, time has not been a factor in any of the graphical methods described so far.

Data of interest to managers are often produced and monitored over time Examples include the daily closing price of their company's common stock, the company's weekly sales volume and quarterly profits, and characteristics—such as weight and length—of products produced by the company.

> **DEFINITION 2.16**
>
> Data that are produced and monitored over time are called **time series data.**

Recall from Section 1.4 that a process is a series of actions or operations that generates output over time. Accordingly, measurements taken of a sequence of units produced by a process—such as a production process—are time series data. In general, any sequence of numbers produced over time can be thought of a being generated by a process.

When measurements are made over time, it is important to record both the numerical value and the time or the time period associated with each measurement. With this information a **time series plot**—sometimes called a **run chart**—can be constructed to describe the time series data and to learn about the process that generated the data. A time series plot is simply a scatterplot with the measure-ments on the vertical axis and time or the order in which the measurements were made on the horizontal axis. The plotted points are usually connected by straight lines to make it easier to see the changes and movement in the measurements over time. For example, Figure 2.34 is a time series plot of a particular company's monthly sales (number of units sold per month). And Figure 2.35 is a time series plot of the weights of 30 one-gallon paint cans that were consecutively filled by the same filling head. Notice that the weights are plotted against the order in which the cans were filled rather than some unit of time. When monitoring production processes, it is often more convenient to record the order rather than the exact time at which each measurement was made.

Time series plots reveal the movement (trend) and changes (variation) in the variable being monitored. Notice how sales trend upward in the summer and how the variation in the weights of the paint cans increases over time. This kind of in-

Figure 2.34

Time series plot of company sales

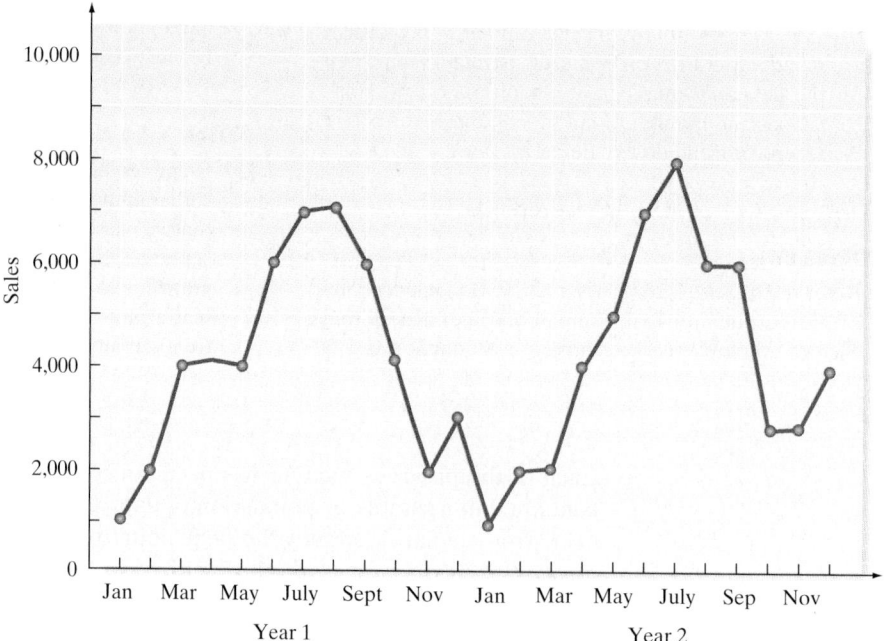

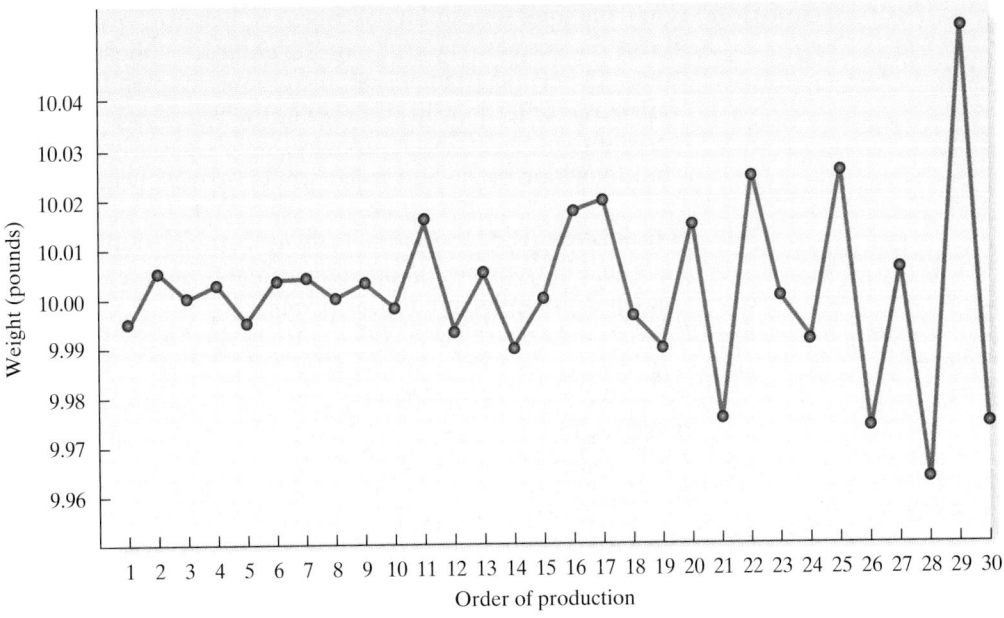

Figure 2.35

Time series plot of paint can weights

formation would not be revealed by stem-and-leaf displays or histograms, as the following example illustrates.

EXAMPLE 2.19   TIME SERIES PLOT VERSUS A HISTOGRAM

Problem   W. Edwards Deming was one of America's most famous statisticians. He was best known for the role he played after World War II in teaching the Japanese how to improve the quality of their products by monitoring and continually improving their production processes. In his book *Out of the Crisis* (1986), Deming warned against the knee-jerk (i.e., automatic) use of histograms to display and extract information from data. As evidence he offered the following example.

Fifty camera springs were tested in the order in which they were produced. The elongation of each spring was measured under the pull of 20 grams. Both a time series plot and a histogram were constructed from the measurements. They are shown in Figure 2.36, which has been reproduced from Deming's book. If you had to predict the elongation measurement of the next spring to be produced (i.e., spring 51) and could use only one of the two plots to guide your prediction, which would you use? Why?

Figure 2.36

Deming's time series plot and histogram

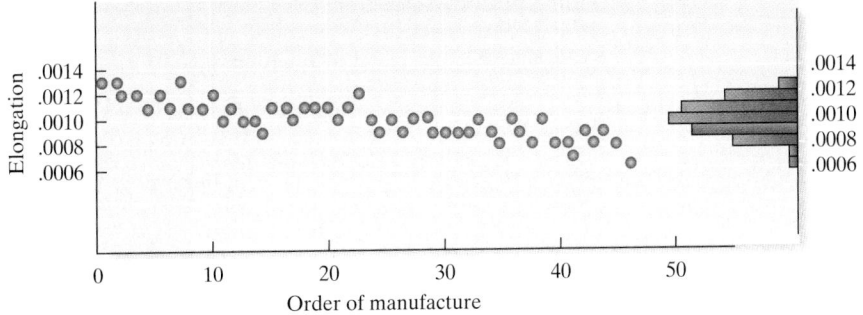

Solution Only the time series plot describes the behavior *over time* of the process that produces the springs. The fact that the elongation measurements are decreasing over time can only be gleaned from the time series plot. Because the histogram does not reflect the order in which the springs were produced, it in effect represents all observations as having been produced simultaneously. Using the histogram to predict the elongation of the 51st spring would very likely lead to an overestimate.

Look Back The lesson from Deming's example is this: For displaying and analyzing data that have been generated over time by a process, the primary graphical tool is the time series plot, not the histogram.

◼ ◼ ◼

We cover many other aspects of the statistical analysis of time series data in Chapter 15.

2.11 Distorting the Truth with Descriptive Techniques

A picture may be "worth a thousand words," but pictures can also color messages or distort them. In fact, the pictures in statistics (e.g., histograms, bar charts time series plots, etc.) are susceptible to distortion, whether unintentional or as a result of unethical statistical practices. In this section, we will mention a few of the pitfalls to watch for when interpreting a chart, graph, or numerical descriptive measure.

One common way to change the impression conveyed by a graph is to change the scale on the vertical axis, the horizontal axis, or both. For example, Figure 2.37 is a bar graph that shows the market share of sales for a company for each of the years 1998 to 2003. If you want to show that the change in firm A's market share over time is moderate, you should pack in a large number of units per inch on the vertical axis—that is, make the distance between successive units on the vertical scale small, as shown in Figure 2.37. You can see that a change in the firm's market share over time is barely apparent.

If you want to use the same data to make the changes in firm A's market share appear large, you should increase the distance between successive units on the vertical axis. That is, stretch the vertical axis by graphing only a few units per inch as in Figure 2.38. A telltale sign of stretching is a long vertical axis, but this is often hidden by starting the vertical axis at some point above 0, as shown in the time series plot, Figure 2.39(a). The same effect can be achieved by using a broken line—called a *scale break*—for the vertical axis, as shown in Figure 2.39(b).

Stretching the horizontal axis (increasing the distance between successive units) may also lead you to incorrect conclusions. With bar graphs, a visual distortion

Figure 2.37

Firm A's market share from 1998 to 2003—packed vertical axis

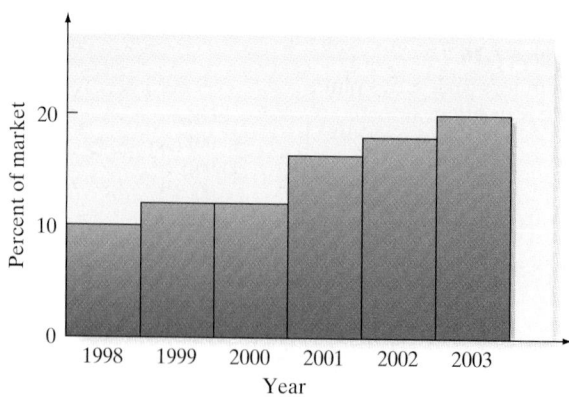

Figure 2.38

Firm A's market share from 1998 to 2003 — Stretched vertical axis

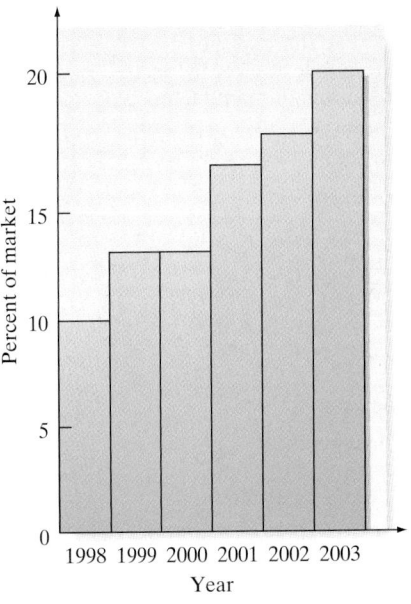

can be achieved by making the width of the bars proportional to the height. For example, look at the bar chart in Figure 2.40(a), which depicts the percentage of a year's total automobile sales attributable to each of the four major manufacturers. Now suppose we make both the width and the height grow as the market share grows. This change is shown in Figure 2.40(b). The reader may tend to equate the *area* of the bars with the relative market share of each manufacturer. But fact, the true relative market share is proportional only to the *height* of the bars.

Sometimes we do not need to manipulate the graph to distort the impression it creates. Modifying the verbal description that accompanies the graph can change the interpretation that will be made by the viewer. Figure 2.41 provides good illustration of this ploy.

Although we've discussed only a few of the ways that graphs can be used to convey misleading pictures of phenomena, the lesson is clear. Look at all graphical descriptions of data with a critical eye. Particularly, check the axes and the size of the units on each axis. Ignore the visual changes and concentrate on the actual numerical changes indicated by the graph or chart.

The information in a data set can also be distorted by using numerical descriptive measures, as Example 2.20 indicates.

Figure 2.39

Changes in money supply from January to June

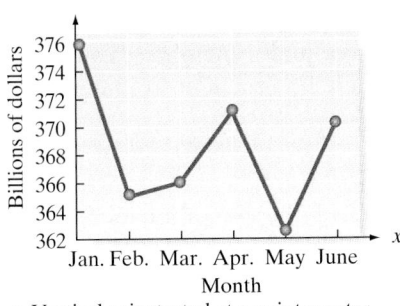

a. Vertical axis started at a point greater than zero

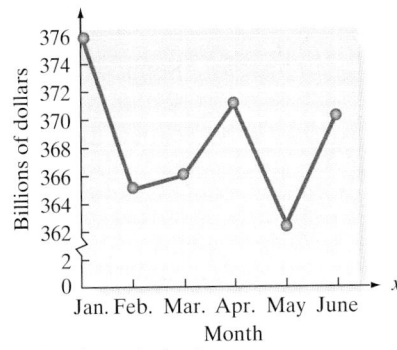

b. Gap in vertical axis

Figure 2.40

Relative share of the automobile market for each of four major manufacturers

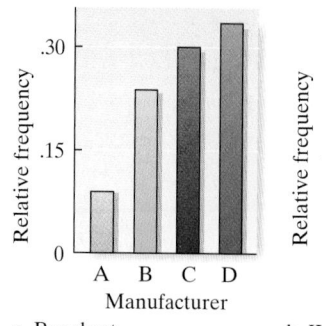

a. Bar chart

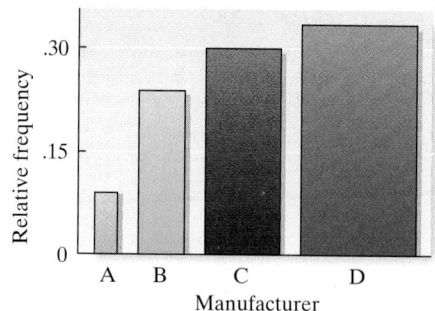

b. Width of bars grows with height

Figure 2.41

Changing the verbal description to change a viewer's interpretation

Source: Adapted from Selazny, G. "Grappling with Graphics," Management Review, Oct. 1975, p. 7.

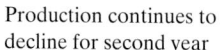

Production continues to decline for second year

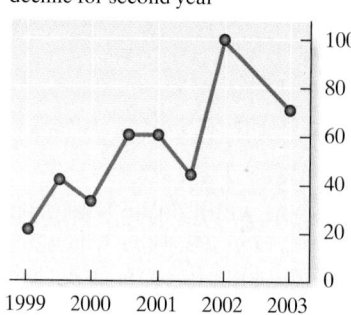

For our production, we need not even change the chart, so we can't be accused of fudging the data. Here we'll simply change the title so that for the Senate subcommittee, we'll indicate that we're not doing as well as in the past...

2003: 2nd best year for production

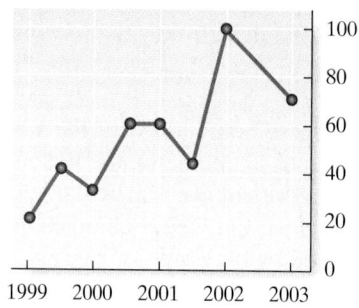

whereas for the general public, we'll tell them that we're still in the prime years.

EXAMPLE 2.20   MISLEADING DESCRIPTIVE STATISTICS

Problem   Suppose you're considering working for a small law firm—one that currently has a senior member and three junior members. You inquire about the salary you could expect to earn if you join the firm. Unfortunately, you receive two answers:

> *Answer A:*   The senior member tells you that an "average employee" earns $67,500.

> *Answer B:*   One of the junior members later tells you that an "average employee" earns $75,000

> Which answer can you believe?

Solution   The confusion exists because the phrase "average employee" has not been clearly defined. Suppose the four salaries paid are $75,000 for each of the three junior members and $125,000 for the senior member. Thus,

Teaching Tip
Discuss the shape of the distribution of the salaries for these four salaries. Remind the student of which measure of center was considered better for skewed distributions

$$\text{Mean} = \frac{3(\$75,000) + \$125,000}{4} = \frac{\$350,000}{4} = \$87,500$$

$$\text{Median} = \$75,000$$

You can now see how the two answers were obtained. The senior member reported the mean of the four salaries, and the junior member reported the median. The information you received was distorted because neither person stated which measure of central tendency was being used.

Look Back Based on our earlier discussion of the mean and median, we would probably prefer the median as the measure that best describes the salary of the "average" employee.

— ■ ■ ■ —

Another distortion of information in a sample occurs when *only* a measure of central tendency is reported. Both a measure of central tendency and a measure of variability are needed to obtain an accurate mental image of a data set.

Suppose you want to buy a new car and are trying to decide which of two models to purchase. Since energy and economy are both important issues, you decide to purchase model A because its EPA mileage rating is 32 miles per gallon in the city, whereas the mileage rating for model B is only 30 miles per gallon in the city.

However, you may have acted too quickly. How much variability is associated with the ratings? As an extreme example, suppose that further investigation reveals that the standard deviation for model A mileages is 5 miles per gallon, whereas that for model B is only 1 mile per gallon. If the mileages form a mound-shaped distribution, they might appear as shown in Figure 2.42. Note that the larger amount of variability associated with model A implies that more risk is involved in purchasing model A. That is, the particular car you purchase is more likely to have a mileage rating that will greatly differ from the EPA rating of 32 miles per gallon if you purchase model A, while a model B car is not likely to vary from the 30-miles-per-gallon rating by more than 2 miles per gallon.

We conclude this section with another example on distorting the truth with numerical descriptive measures.

Figure 2.42
Mileage distributions for two car models

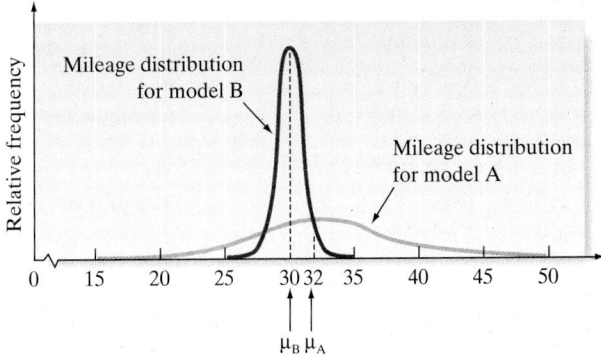

EXAMPLE 2.21

MORE MISLEADING DESCRIPTIVE STATISTICS

Problem *Children Out of School in America* is a report on delinquency of school-age children prepared by the Children's Defense Fund (CDF), a government-sponsored organization. Consider the following three reported results of the CDF survey.

- Reported result 1: 25 percent of the 16- and 17-year-olds in the Portland, Maine, Bayside East Housing Project were out of school. Fact: *Only eight children were surveyed; two were found to be out of school.*

- Reported result 2: Of all the secondary school students who had been suspended more than once in census tract 22 in Columbia, South Carolina, 33% had been suspended two times and 67% had been suspended three or more times. Fact: *CDF found only three children in that entire census tract who had been suspended; one child was suspended twice and the other two children, three or more times.*

- Reported result 3: In the Portland Bayside East Housing Project, 50% of all the secondary school children who had been suspended more than once had been suspended three or more times. Fact: *The survey found two secondary school children had been suspended in that area; one of them had been suspended three or more times.*

Identify the potential distortions in the results reported by the CDF.

Solution In each of these examples the reporting of percentages (i.e., relative frequencies) instead of the numbers themselves is misleading. No inference we might draw from the cited examples would be reliable. (We'll see how to measure the reliability of estimated percentages in Chapter 7.) In short, either the report should state the numbers alone instead of percentages, or, better yet, it should state that the numbers were too small to report by region.

Look Back If several regions were combined, the numbers (and percentages) would be more meaningful.

■ ■ ■

Quick Review

Key Terms

Note: Starred (*) items are from the optional sections in this chapter.

Key Formulas

$$\frac{(\text{class frequency})}{n} \qquad \text{Class relative frequency}\quad 45$$

$$\bar{x} = \frac{\sum\limits_{i=1}^{n} x_i}{n} \qquad \text{Sample mean}\quad 71$$

$$s^2 = \frac{\sum\limits_{i=1}^{n}(x_i - \bar{x})^2}{n-1} = \frac{\sum\limits_{i=1}^{n} x_i^2 - \dfrac{\left(\sum\limits_{i=1}^{n} x_i\right)^2}{n}}{n-1} \qquad \text{Sample variance}\quad 83$$

$$s = \sqrt{s^2} \qquad \text{Sample standard deviation}\quad 83$$

$$z = \frac{x - \bar{x}}{s} \qquad \text{Sample } z\text{-score}\quad 96$$

$$z = \frac{x - \mu}{\sigma} \qquad \text{Population } z\text{-score}\quad 96$$

$$\text{IQR} = Q_U - Q_L \qquad \text{Interquartile range}\quad 100$$

Summary

Chapter Summary Notes:

- Graphical methods for qualitative data: pie chart, bar graph, and Pareto diagram
- Graphical methods for quantitative data: dot plot, stem-and-leaf display, and histogram
- Numerical measures of central tendency: mean, median, and mode
- Numerical measures of variation: range, variance, and standard deviation

- Rules for determining the percentage of measurements in the interval (mean) $\pm$ 2(std. dev.): Chebyshev's Rule (at least 75%) and Empirical Rule (approximately 95%)
- Measures of relative standing: percentile score and z-score
- Methods for detecting outliers: box plots and z-scores
- Method for graphing the relationship between two quantitative variables: scatterplot

Language Lab

Symbol	Pronunciation	Description
Σ	sum of	Summation notation; $\sum\limits_{i=1}^{n} x_i$ represents the sum of the measurements $x_1, x_2, \ldots, x_n$
μ	mu	Population mean
$\bar{x}$	x-bar	Sample mean
σ^2	sigma squared	Population variance
σ	sigma	Population standard deviation
s^2		Sample variance
s		Sample standard deviation
z		z-score for a measurement
m		Median (middle quartile) of a sample data set

Q_L	Lower quartile (25th percentile)
Q_U	Upper quartile (75th percentile)
IQR	Interquartile range

Supplementary Exercises 2.118–2.147

Starred 1(*) exercises are from the optional sections in this chapter.

Learning the Mechanics

2.118 Discuss the conditions under which the median is preferred to the mean as a measure of central tendency.

2.119 Construct a relative frequency histogram for the data summarized in the accompanying table.

Measurement Class	Relative Frequency
.00–.75	.02
.75–1.50	.01
1.50–2.25	.03
2.25–3.00	.05
3.00–3.75	.10
3.75–4.50	.14
4.50–5.25	.19
5.25–6.00	.15
6.00–6.75	.12
6.75–7.50	.09
7.50–8.25	.05
8.25–9.00	.04
9.00–9.75	.01

2.120 If the range of a set of data is 20, find a rough approximation to the standard deviation of the data set.

2.121 Consider the following three measurements: 50, 70, 80. Find the z-score for each measurement if they are from a population with a mean and standard deviation equal to
a. $\mu = 60, \sigma = 10$ $-1, 1, 2$ **b.** $\mu = 50, \sigma = 5$
c. $\mu = 40, \sigma = 10$ $1, 3, 4$ **d.** $\mu = 40, \sigma = 100$

*2.122 Refer to Exercise 2.121. For parts a–d, determine whether the values 50, 70, and 80 are outliers.

2.123 For each of the following data sets, compute $\bar{x}, s^2$, and s:

a. 13, 1, 10, 3, 3   6, 27, 5.20   **b.** 13, 6, 6, 0
c. 1, 0, 1, 10, 11, 11, 15   **d.** 3, 3, 3, 3   3, 0, 0

2.124 For each of the following data sets, compute $\bar{x}, s^2$, and s. If appropriate, specify the units in which your answers are expressed.
a. 4, 6, 6, 5, 6, 7
b. −$1, $4, −$3, $0, −$3, −$6
c. $\frac{3}{5}\%, \frac{4}{5}\%, \frac{2}{5}\%, \frac{1}{5}\%, \frac{1}{16}\%,$
d. Calculate the range of each data set in parts **a–c**.

2.125 Explain why we generally prefer the standard deviation to the range as a measure of variability for quantitative data.

2.126 Construct a scattergram for the data in the following table.

Variable 1	174	268	345	119	400	520	190	448	307	252
Variable 2	8	10	15	7	22	31	15	20	11	9

Applying the Concepts—Basic

CRASH

2.127 The National Highway Traffic Safety Administration (NHTSA) crash tests new car models to determine how well they protect the driver and front-seat passenger in a head-on collision. The NHTSA has developed a "star" scoring system for the frontal crash test, with results ranging from one star (*) to five stars (*****) The more stars in the rating, the better the level of crash protection in a head-on collision. The NHTSA crash test results for 98 cars (model year 1997) are stored in the data file named **CRASH**. The driver-side star ratings for the 98 cars are summarized in the MINITAB printout shown below. Use the information in the printout to form a pie chart. Interpret the graph.

2.128 Refer to Exercise 2.127. One quantitative variable recorded by the NHTSA is driver's severity of head

MINITAB Output for Exercise 2.127

```
Tally for Discrete Variables: DrivStar

  DrivStar   Count    Percent
         2       4       4.08
         3      17      17.35
         4      59      60.20
         5      18      18.37
       N=       98
```

MINITAB Output for Exercise 2.128

Descriptive Statistics: DrivHead

Variable	N	Mean	Median	TrMean	StDev	SE Mean
DrivHead	98	603.7	605.0	600.3	185.4	18.7

Variable	Minimum	Maximum	Q1	Q3
DrivHead	216.0	1240.0	475.0	724.3

injury (measured on a scale from 0 to 1,500). The mean and standard deviation for the 98 driver head-injury ratings in the **CRASH** file are displayed in the MINITAB printout above. Use these values to find the z-score for a driver head-injury rating of 408. Interpret the result. $z = -1.06$

2.129 The total number of passengers handled annually by eight cruise ships based in Port Canaveral (Florida) are listed in the table. Find and interpret the mean and median of the data set.

☼ CRUISE

Cruise Line (Ship)	Number of Passengers
Canaveral (Dolphin)	152,240
Carnival (Fantasy)	480,924
Disney (Magic)	73,504
Premier (Oceanic)	270,361
Royal Caribbean (Nordic Empress)	106,161
Sun Cruz Casinos	453,806
Sterling Cruises (New Yorker)	15,782
Topaz Int'l. Shipping (Topaz)	28,280

Source: Florida Trend Magazine, Vol. 41, No. 9, Jan. 1999.

2.130 Many librarians rely on book reviews to determine which new books to purchase for their library. A random sample of 375 book reviews in American history, geography, and area studies was selected and the "overall opinion" of the book stated in each review was ascertained (*Library Acquisitions: Practice and Theory,* Vol. 19, 1995). Overall opinion was coded as follows: 1 = would not recommend, 2 = cautious or very little recommendation, 3 = little or no preference, 4 = favorable/recommended, 5 = outstanding/significant contribution. A summary of the data is provided in the bar graph.

a. Is the variable measured quantitative or qualitative? Explain.

b. Interpret the bar graph.

c. Comment on the following statement extracted from the study: "A majority (more than 75%) of books reviewed are evaluated favorably and recommended for purchase."

2.131 In experimenting with a new technique for imprinting paper napkins with designs, names, etc., a paper-products company discovered that four different results were possible:

(A) Imprint successful
(B) Imprint smeared
(C) Imprint off-center to the left
(D) Imprint off-center to the right

To test the reliability of the technique, the company imprinted 1,000 napkins and obtained the results shown in the graph below.

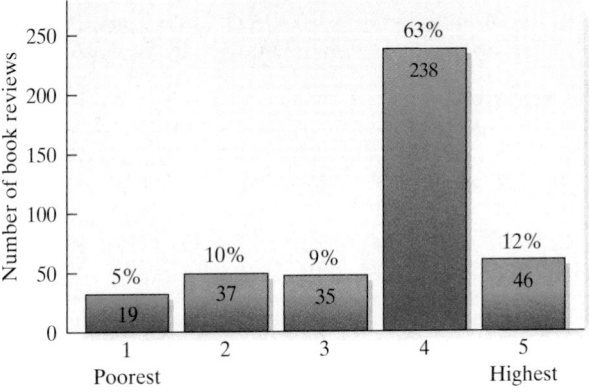

Source: Reprinted from Library Acquisitions: Practice and Theory, Vol. 19, No. 2, P.W. Carlo and A. Natowitx, "Choice Book Reviews in American History, Geography, and Area Studies: An Analysis for 1988–1993," p. 159. Copyright 1995, with kind permission from Elsevier Science Ltd, The Boulevard, Langford Lane, Kidlington OX5 1GB, UK.

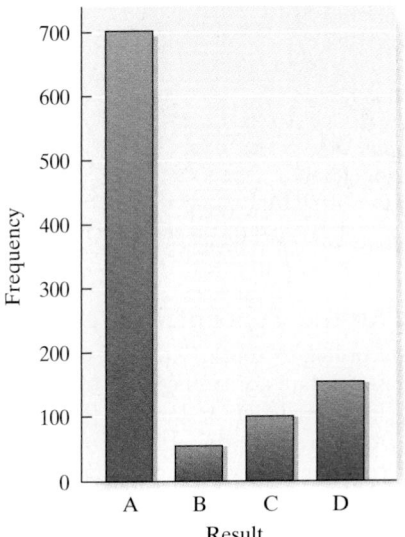

a. What type of graphical tool is the figure?

b. What information does the graph convey to you?

c. From the information provided by the graph, how might you numerically describe the reliability of the imprinting technique?

2.132 Beanie Babies are toy stuffed animals that have become valuable collector's items. *Beanie World Magazine* provided the age, retired status, and value of 50 Beanie Babies. The data one saved in the **BEANIE** file, with several of the observations shown in the table.

a. Summarize the retried/current status of the 50 Beanie Babies with an appropriate graph. Interpret the graph.

b. Summarize the values of the 50 Beanie Babies with an appropriate graph. Interpret the graph.

c. Use a graph to portray the relationship between a Beanie Baby's value and its age. Do you detect a trend?

d. According to Chebyshev's Rule, what percentage of the age measurements would you expect to find in the intervals $\bar{x} \pm .75s, \bar{x} \pm 2.5s, \bar{x} \pm 4s$?

e. What percentage of the age measurements actually fall in the intervals of part **e**? Compare your results with those of part

f. Repeat parts **d** and **e** for value.

BEANIE

Name	Age (Months) as of Sept. 1998	Retired (R) Current (C)	Value ($)
1. Ally the Alligator	52	R	55.00
2. Batty the Bat	12	C	12.00
3. Bongo the Brown Monkey	28	R	40.00
4. Blackie the Bear	52	C	10.00
5. Bucky the Beaver	40	R	45.00
⋮	⋮	⋮	⋮
46. Stripes the Tiger (Gold/Black)	40	R	400.00
47. Teddy the 1997 Holiday Bear	12	R	50.00
48. Tuffy the Terrier	17	C	10.00
49. Tracker the Basset Hound	5	C	15.00
50. Zip the Black Cat	28	R	40.00

Source: Beanie World Magazine, Sept. 1998.

Applying the Concepts—Intermediate

2.133 According to Topaz Enterprises, a Portland, Oregon-based airfare accounting firm, "more than 80% of all tickets purchased for domestic flights are discounted" (*Travel Weekly*, May 15, 1995). The results of the accounting firm's survey of domestic airline tickets are summarized in the next table.

Domestic Airline Ticket Type	Proportion
Full coach	.005
Discounted coach	.206
Negotiated coach	.425
First class	.009
Business class	.002
Business class negotiated	.001
Advance purchase	.029
Capacity controlled discount	.209
Nonrefundable	.114
Total	1.000

a. Give your opinion on whether the data described in the table are from a population or a sample. Explain your reasoning.

b. Display the data with a bar graph. Arrange the bars in order of height to form a Pareto diagram. Interpret the resulting graph.

c. Do the data support the conclusion reached by Topaz Enterprises regarding the percentage of tickets purchased that are discounted? [*Note:* Advance purchase and negotiated tickets are considered discounted.]

2.134 *Consumer Reports*, published by Consumers Union, is a magazine that contains ratings and reports for consumers on goods, services, health, and personal finances. Consumers Union reported on the testing of 46 brands of toothpaste (*Consumer Reports*, Sept. 1992). Each was rated on: package design, flavor, cleaning ability, fluoride content, and cost per month (a cost estimate based on brushing with half-inch of toothpaste twice daily). The data shown below are costs per month for the 46 brands. Costs marked by an asterisk represent those brands that carry the American Dental Association (ADA) seal verifying effective decay prevention.

a. Construct a stem-and-leaf display for the data.

b. Circle the individual leaves that represent those brands that carry the ADA seal.

c. What does the pattern of circles suggest about the costs of those brands approved by the ADA?

TOOTHPASTE

.58	.66	1.02	1.11	1.77	1.40	.73*	.53*	.57*	1.34
1.29	.89*	.49	.53*	.52	3.90	4.73	1.26	.71*	.55*
.59*	.97	.44*	.74*	.51*	.68*	.67	1.22	.39	.55
.62	.66*	1.07	.64	1.32*	1.77*	.80*	.79	.89*	.64
.81*	.79*	.44*	1.09	1.04	1.12				

2.135 A manufacturer of industrial wheels is losing many profitable orders because of the long time it takes the firm's marketing, engineering, and accounting departments to develop price quotes for potential customers. To remedy this problem the firm's management would like to set guidelines for the length of time each department should spend developing price quotes. To help develop these guidelines, 50 requests for price quotes were randomly selected from the set of price quotes made last year: the processing time (in days) was determined for each price quote for each department. These times are saved in the **LOSTQUOTES** file. Several observations are displayed in the table below. The price quotes are also classified by whether they were "lost" (i.e., whether or not the customer placed an order after receiving the price quote).

a. Construct a stem-and-leaf display for the total processing time for each department. Shade the leaves that correspond to "lost" orders in each of the displays, and interpret each of the displays.

b. Using your results from part **a.** develop "maximum processing time" guidelines for each department that, if followed, will help the firm reduce the number of lost orders.

⊚ LOSTQUOTES

Request Number	Marketing	Engineering	Accounting	Lost?
1	7.0	6.2	.1	No
2	.4	5.2	.1	No
3	2.4	4.6	.6	No
4	6.2	13.0	.8	Yes
5	4.7	.9	.5	No
⋮	⋮	⋮	⋮	⋮
46	6.4	1.3	6.2	No
47	4.0	2.4	13.5	Yes
48	10.0	5.3	.1	No
49	8.0	14.4	1.9	Yes
50	7.0	10.0	2.0	No

2.136 Refer to Exercise 2.135.

a. Generate summary statistics for the processing times. Interpret the results.

b. Calculate the z-score corresponding to the maximum processing time guideline you developed in Exercise 2.135 for each department, and for the total processing time.

c. Calculate the maximum processing time corresponding to a z-score of 3 for each of the departments. What percentage of the orders exceed these guidelines? How does this agree with Chebyshev's Rule and the Empirical Rule?

d. Repeat part **c** using a z-score of 2.

e. Compare the percentage of "lost" quotes with corresponding times that exceed at least one of the guidelines in part **c** to the same percentage using the guidelines in part **d**. Which set of guidelines would you recommend be adopted? Why?

*2.137 A time series plot similar to the one shown next appeared in a recent advertisement for a well-known golf magazine. One person might interpret the plot's message as the longer you subscribe to the magazine,

the better golfer you should become. Another person might interpret it as indicating that if you subscribe for 3 years, your game should improve dramatically.

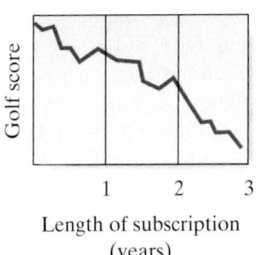
Length of subscription
(years)

a. Explain why the plot can be interpreted in more than one way.

b. How could the plot be altered to rectify the current distortion?

2.138 A company has roughly the same number of people in each of five departments: Production, Sales, R&D, Maintenance, and Administration. The following table lists the number and type of major injuries that occurred in each department last year.

⊚ INJURY

Type of Injury	Department	Number of Injuries
Burn	Production	3
	Maintenance	6
Back strain	Production	2
	Sales	1
	R&D	1
	Maintenance	5
	Administration	2
Eye damage	Production	1
	Maintenance	2
	Administration	1
Deafness	Production	1
Cuts	Production	4
	Sales	1
	R&D	1
	Maintenance	10
Broken arm	Production	2
	Maintenance	2
Broken leg	Sales	1
	Maintenance	1
Broken finger	Administration	1
Concussion	Maintenance	3
	Administration	1
Hearing loss	Maintenance	2

a. Construct a Pareto diagram to identify which department or departments have the worst safety record.

b. Explode the Pareto diagram of part **a** to identify the most prevalent type of injury in the department with the worst safety record.   Cuts

2.139 In some locations, radiation levels in homes are measured at well above normal background levels in the environment. As a result, many architects and builders are making design changes to ensure adequate air exchange so that radiation will not be "trapped" in homes. In one such location, 50 homes levels were measured, and the mean level was 10 parts per billion (ppb), the median was 8 ppb, and the standard deviation was 3 ppb. Background levels in this location are at about 4 ppb.

a. Based on these results, is the distribution of the 50 homes' radiation levels symmetric, skewed to the left, or skewed to the right? Why?

b. Use both Chebyshev's Rule and the Empirica Rule to describe the distribution of radiation levels. Which do you think is most appropriate in this case? Why?

c. Use the results from part **b** to approximate the number of homes in this sample that have radiation levels above the background level.

d. Suppose another home is measured at a location 10 miles from the one sampled, and has a level of 20 ppb. What is the z-score for this measurement relative to the 50 homes sampled in the other location? Is it likely that this new measurement comes from the same distribution of radiation levels as the other 50? Why? How would you go about confirming your conclusion? $z = 3.333$, no

2.140 As a result of government and consumer pressure, automobile manufacturers in the United States are deeply involved in research to improve their products' gasoline mileage. One manufacturer, hoping to achieve 40 miles per gallon on one of its compact models, measured the mileage obtained by 36 test versions of the model with the following results (rounded to the nearest mile for convenience):

MPG36

43	35	41	42	42	38	40	41	41	40	40	41
42	36	43	40	38	40	38	45	39	41	42	37
40	40	44	39	40	37	39	41	39	41	37	40

a. Find the mean and standard deviation of these data and give the units in which they are expressed.

b. If the manufacturer would be satisfied with a (population) mean of 40 miles per gallon, how would react to the above test data?

c. Use the information in Tables 2.6–2.7 to check to reasonableness of the calculated standard deviation $s = 2.2$.

d. Construct a relative frequency histogram of the data set. Is the data set mound shaped?

e. What percentage of the measurements would you expect to find within the intervals $\bar{x} \pm s$, $\bar{x} \pm 2s, \bar{x} \pm 3s$?   68%, 95%, 100%

f. Count the number of measurements that actually fall within the intervals of part **e**. Express each interval count as a percentage of the total number of measurements. Compare these results with your answers to part **e**.

2.141 *Forbes* magazine (Jan. 11, 1999) reported the financial standings of each team in the National Football League (NFL). The table below lists current team value (without deduction for debt, except stadium debt) and operating income for each team in 1998.

a. Use a statistical software package to construct a stem-and-leaf plot for an NFL team's current value.

b. Does the distribution of current values appear to be skewed? Explain.   Yes

c. Use the stem-and-leaf plot of part **a** to find the median of the current values.   370

d. Calculate the z-scores for the Denver Broncos current value and operating income.   0.46, −1.10

e. Interpret the two z-scores of part **d**.

f. Which other NFL teams have positive current value z-scores and negative operating income z-scores?

*g. Identify any outliers in the current value data set.

*h. Construct a graph to investigate a possible trend between an NFL team's current value and its operating income. What do you observe?

NFLVALUE

Team	Current Value ($ millions)	Operating Income ($ millions)
Dallas Cowboys	663	56.7
Washington Redskins	607	48.8
Tampa Bay Buccaneers	502	41.2
Carolina Panthers	488	18.8
New England Patriots	460	13.5
Miami Dolphins	446	32.9
Denver Broncos	427	5.0
Jacksonville Jaguars	419	29.3
Baltimore Ravens	408	33.2
Seattle Seahawks	399	6.4
Pittsburgh Steelers	397	15.5
Cincinnati Bengals	394	3.4
St. Louis Rams	390	33.2
New York Giants	376	25.2
San Francisco 49ers	371	12.7
Tennessee Titans	369	4.1
New York Jets	363	12.1
Kansas City Chiefs	353	31.0
Buffalo Bills	326	10.7
San Diego Chargers	323	8.2
Green Bay Packers	320	16.4
Philadelphia Eagles	318	19.1
New Orleans Saints	315	11.3
Chicago Bears	313	19.7
Minnesota Vikings	309	5.1
Atlanta Falcons	306	16.8
Indianapolis Colts	305	15.8
Arizona Cardinals	301	10.6
Oakland Raiders	299	17.3
Detroit Lions	293	16.4

Source: Forbes, Jan. 11, 1999.

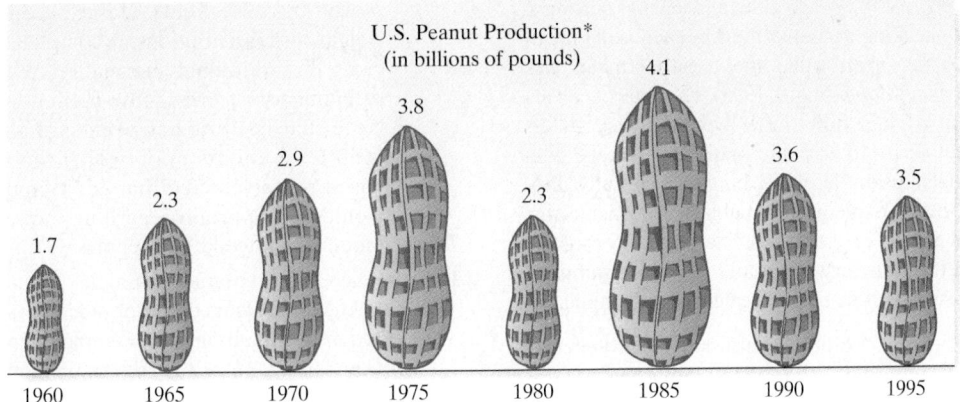

U.S. Peanut Production*
(in billions of pounds)

1.7   2.3   2.9   3.8   4.1   2.3   3.6   3.5

1960   1965   1970   1975   1980   1985   1990   1995

*2.142 If not examined carefully, the graphical description of U.S. peanut production shown above can be misleading.

a. Explain why the graph may mislead some readers.

b. Construct an undistorted graph of U.S. peanut production for the given years.

*2.143 A national chain of automobile oil-change franchises claims that "your hood will be open for less than 12 minutes when we service your car." To check their claim, an undercover consumer reporter from a local television station monitored the "hood time" of 25 consecutive customers at one of the chain's franchises. The resulting data are shown below. Construct a time series plot for these data and describe in words what it reveals.

HOODTIME

Customer Number	Hood Open (Minutes)	Customer Number	Hood Open (Minutes)
1	11.50	14	12.50
2	13.50	15	13.75
3	12.25	16	12.00
4	15.00	17	11.50
5	14.50	18	14.25
6	13.75	19	15.50
7	14.00	20	13.00
8	11.00	21	18.25
9	12.75	22	11.75
10	11.50	23	12.50
11	11.00	24	11.25
12	13.00	25	14.75
13	16.25		

2.144 Computer anxiety is defined as "the mixture of fear, apprehension, and hope that people feel when planning to interact, or when interacting with a computer." Researchers have found computer anxiety in people at all levels of society, including students, doctors, lawyers, secretaries, managers, and college professors. One profession for which little is known about the level and impact of computer anxiety is secondary technical education (STE). The extent of computer anxiety among STE teachers was investigated in the *Journal of Studies in Technical Careers* (Vol. 15, 1995). A sample of 116 teachers were administered the Computer Anxiety Scale (COMPAS) designed to measure level of computer anxiety. Scores, ranging from 10 to 50, were categorized as follows: very anxious (37–50); anxious/ tense (33–36); some mild anxiety (27–32); generally relaxed/comfortable (20–26); very relaxed/confident (10–19). A summary of the COMPAS anxiety levels for the sample is provided in the table below.

Category	Score Range	Frequency	Relative Frequency
Very anxious	37–50	22	.19
Anxious/tense	33–36	8	.07
Some mild anxiety	27–32	23	.20
Generally relaxed/ comfortable	20–26	24	.21
Very relaxed/ confident	10–19	39	.33
Totals		116	1.00

Source: Gordon, H. R. D. "Analysis of the Computer Anxiety Levels of Secondary Technical Education Teachers in West Virginia." *Journal of Studies in Technical Careers*, Vol. 15, No. 2, 1995, pp. 26–27 (Table 1).

a. Graph and interpret the results.

b. One of the objectives of the research is to compare the computer anxiety levels of male and female STE teachers. Use the summary information in the table below to make the comparison.

	Male Teachers	Female Teachers	All Teachers
n	68	48	116
$\bar{x}$	26.4	24.5	25.6
s	10.6	11.2	10.8

Source: Gordon, H. R. D. "Analysis of the Computer Anxiety Levels of Secondary Technical Education Teachers in West Virginia." *Journal of Studies in Technical Careers*, Vol. 15, No. 2, 1995, pp. 26–27 (Table 2).

Applying the Concepts—Advanced

2.145 A study by the U.S. Public Research Interest Group found that in Massachusetts bank customers were charged lower fees than the national average for regular checking accounts, NOW accounts, and savings accounts. For regular checking accounts the Massachusetts mean was $190.06 per year, while the national mean was $201.94 (*Boston Globe*, Aug. 9, 1995). The referenced article did not explain how these averages were determined other than to say the national average was estimated from a sample of 271 banks in 25 states. Prepare a report that explains in detail how Massachusetts' mean could have been estimated. There are 245 banks in Massachusetts. Your answer should include a sampling plan, a measurement plan, and a calculation formula.

2.146 The U.S. Federal Trade Commission has recently begun assessing fines and other penalties against weight-loss clinics that make unsupported or misleading claims about the effectiveness of their programs. Brochures from two weight-loss clinics both advertise "statistical evidence" about the effectiveness of their programs. Clinic A claims that the *mean* weight loss during the first month is 15 pounds; Clinic B claims a *median* weight loss of 10 pounds.

a. Assuming the statistics are accurately calculated, which clinic would you recommend if you had no other information? Why?

b. Upon further research, the median and standard deviation for Clinic A are found to be 10 pounds and 20 pounds, respectively, while the mean and standard deviation for Clinic B are found to be 10 and 5 pounds, respectively. Both are based on samples of

more than 100 clients. Describe the two clinics' weight-loss distributions as completely as possible given this additional information. What would you recommend to a prospective client now? Why?

c. Note that nothing has been said about how the sample of clients upon which the statistics are based was selected. What additional information would be important regarding the sampling techniques employed by the clinics?

2.147 The Age Discrimination in Employment Act mandates that workers 40 years of age or older be treated without regard to age in all phases of employment (hiring, promotions, firing, etc.). Age discrimination cases are of two types: *disparate treatment* and *disparate impact*. In the former, the issue is whether workers have been intentionally discriminated against. In the latter, the issue is whether employment practices adversely affect the protected class (i.e., workers 40 and over) even though no such effect was intended by the employer (Zabell, 1989). A small computer manufacturer laid off 10 of its 20 software engineers. The ages of all engineers at the time of the layoff are below. Analyze the data to determine whether the company may be vulnerable to a disparate impact claim.

LAYOFF

| Not laid off: | 34 | 55 | 42 | 38 | 42 | 32 | 40 | 40 | 46 | 29 |
| Laid off: | 52 | 35 | 40 | 41 | 40 | 39 | 40 | 64 | 47 | 44 |

REFERENCES

Adler, P. S. and Clark, K. B. "Behind the Learning Curve: A Sketch of the Learning Process." *Management Science*, March 1991, p. 267.

Deming, W. E. *Out of the Crisis.* Cambridge, Mass.: M.I.T. Center for Advanced Engineering Study, 1986.

Fogarty, D. W., Blackstone, J. H., Jr., and Hoffman, T. R. *Production and Inventory Management.* Cincinnati, Ohio: South-Western, 1991.

Gaither, N. *Production and Operations Management*, 7th ed. Belmont, Calif.: Duxbury Press, 1996.

Gitlow, H., Oppenheim, A., and Oppenheim, R. *Quality Management: Methods for Improvement*, 2nd ed. Burr Ridge, Ill.: Irwin, 1995.

Huff, D. *How to Lie with Statistics.* New York: Norton, 1954.

Ishikawa, K. *Guide to Quality Control*, 2nd ed. White Plains, N.Y.: Kraus International Publications, 1982.

Juran, J. M. *Juran on Planning for Quality.* New York: The Free Press, 1988.

Mendenhall, W., Beaver, R. J., and Beaver, B. M. *Introduction to Probability and Statistics*, 10th ed. North Scituate, Mass.: Duxbury, 1999.

Schroeder, R. G. *Operations Management*, 4th ed. New York: McGraw-Hill, 1993.

Zabel, S. L. "Statistical Proof of Employment Discrimination." *Statistics: A Guide to the Unknown*, 3rd ed. Pacific Grove, Calif.: Wadsworth, 1989.

Tufte, E. R. *Envisioning Information.* Cheshire, Conn.: Graphics Press, 1990.

Tufte, E. R. *Visual Display of Quantiative Information.* Cheshire, Conn.: Graphics Press, 1983.

Tukey, J. *Exploratory Data Analysis.* Reading, Mass.: Addison-Wesley, 1977.

Using Technology

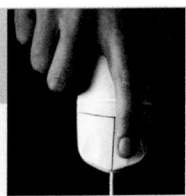

2.1 Describing Data Using SPSS

Graphing Data

To obtain graphical descriptions of data that appears in the SPSS spreadsheet, click on the "Graphs" button on the SPSS menu bar. The resulting menu list appears as shown in Figure 2.S.1. Several of the options covered in this text are "Bar (graph)", "Pie (chart)", "Pareto (diagram)", "Boxplot", "Scatter(plot)", and "Histogram". Click on the graph of your choice to view the appropriate dialog box. For example, the dialog box for a histogram is shown in Figure 2.S.2. Make the appropriate variable selections and click "OK" to view the graph.

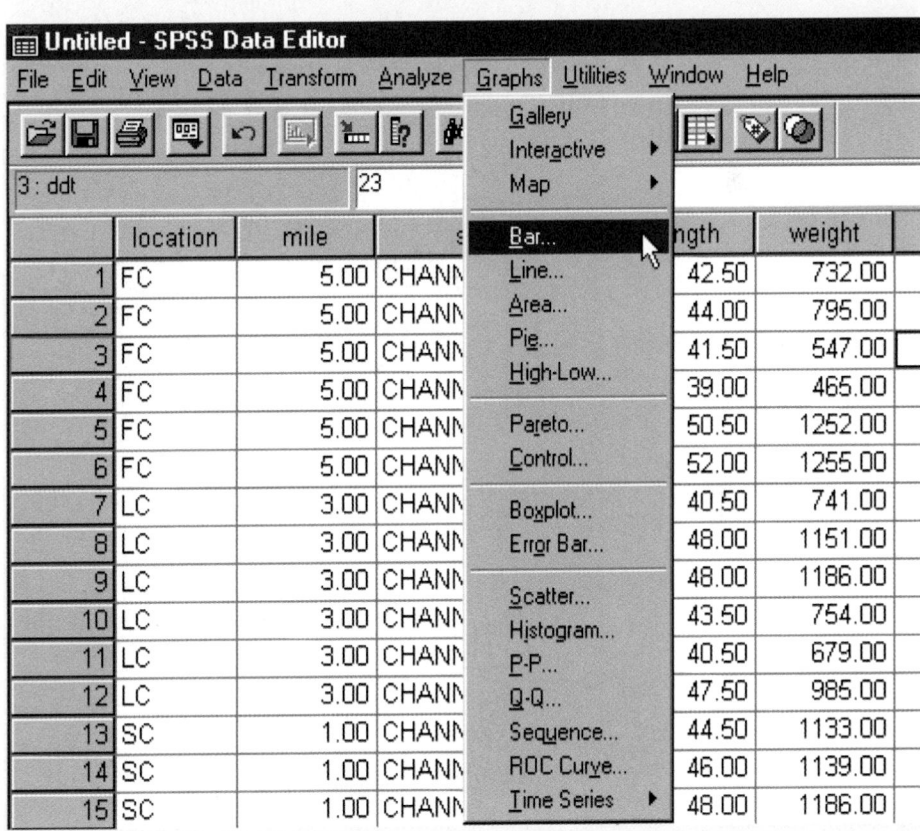

Figure 2.S.1

SPSS menu options for graphing your data

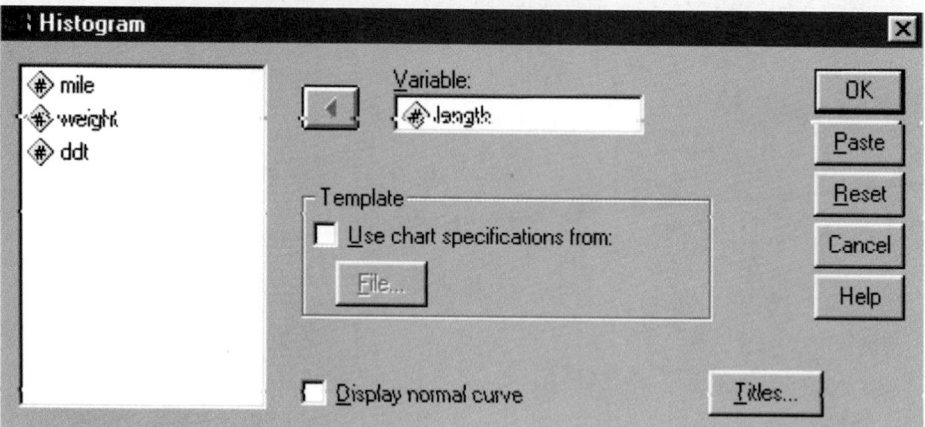

Figure 2.S.2
Histogram dialog box

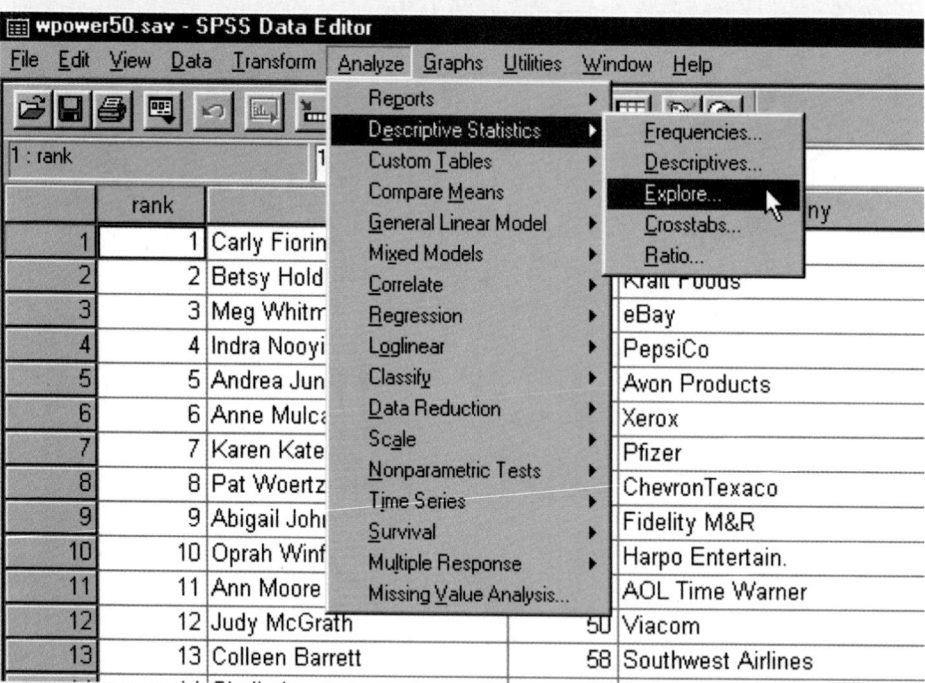

Figure 2.S.3
SPSS menu options for descriptive statistics

Stem-and-leaf plots can be obtained by selecting "Analyze" from the main SPSS menu, then "Descriptive Statistics", then "Explore", as shown in Figure 2.S.3. In the "Explore" dialog box, select the variable to be analyzed in the "Dependent List" box, as shown in Figure 2.S.4. Click on either "Both" or "Plots" in the "Display" options, then click "OK" to display the stem-and-leaf graph.

Numerical Descriptive Statistics

To obta in numerical descriptive measures for a quantitative variable, click on the "Analyze" button on the main menu bar, then click on "Descriptive Statistics", as shown in Figure 2.S.3. To obtain standard descriptive statistics (e.g., mean, variance, standard deviation), select "Descriptives" from the menu; the dialog box shown in Figure 2.S.5 will appear. Select the quantitative variables you want to analyze and place them in the "Variable(s)" box. You can control which particular descriptive statistics appear by clicking the "Options" button on the dialog box and making your selections.) Click on "OK" to view the descriptive statistics printout.

   If you want these standard statistics as well as percentiles, select "Explore" from the main SPSS menu, as shown in Figure 2.S.3. In the resulting dialog box (see Figure 2.S.4), select the "Statistics" button and check the "Percentiles" box on the resulting menu. Return to the "Explore Dialog Box" and click "OK" to generate the descriptive statistics.

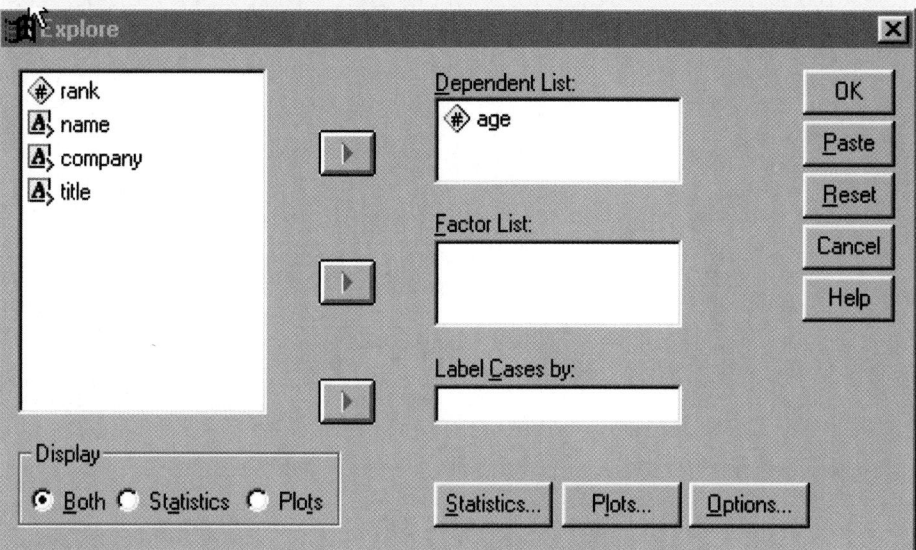

Figure 2.S.4
Explore dialog box

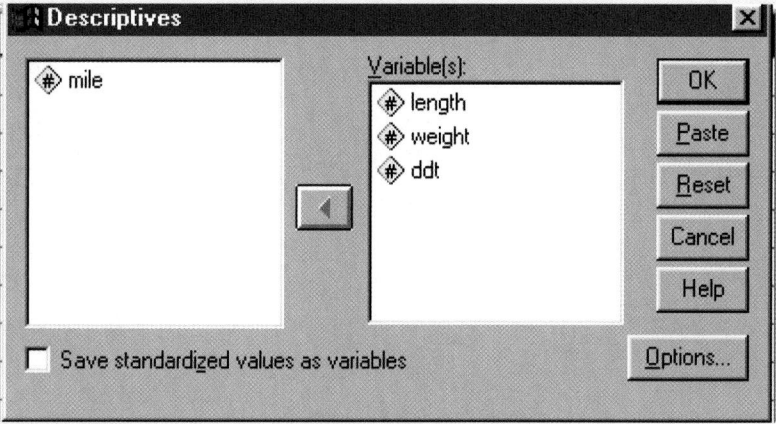

Figure 2.S.5
Descriptive statistics dialog box

2.2 Describing Data Using MINITAB

Graphing Data

To obtain graphical descriptions of your data, click on the "Graph" button on the MINITAB menu bar. The resulting menu list appears as shown in Figure 2.M.1. Several of the options covered in this text are "Bar Chart", "Pie Chart" "Scatter Plot", "Histogram", "Dotplot", and "Stem-and-Leaf (display)". Click on the graph of your choice to view the appropriate dialog box. For example, the dialog box for a histogram is shown in Figure 2.M.2. Make the appropriate variable selections and click "OK" to view the graph.

Numerical Descriptive Statistics

To obtain numerical descriptive measures for a quantitative variable (e.g., mean, standard deviation, etc.), click on the "Stat" button on the main menu bar, then

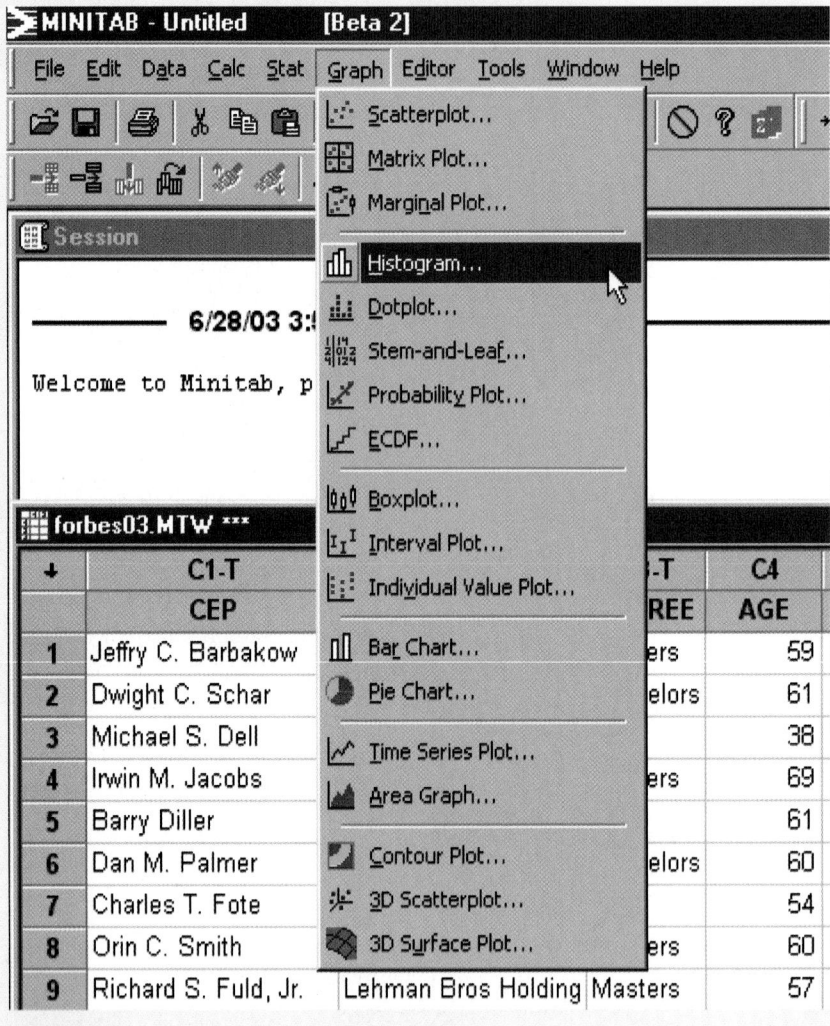

Figure 2.M.1
MINITAB menu options for graphing your data

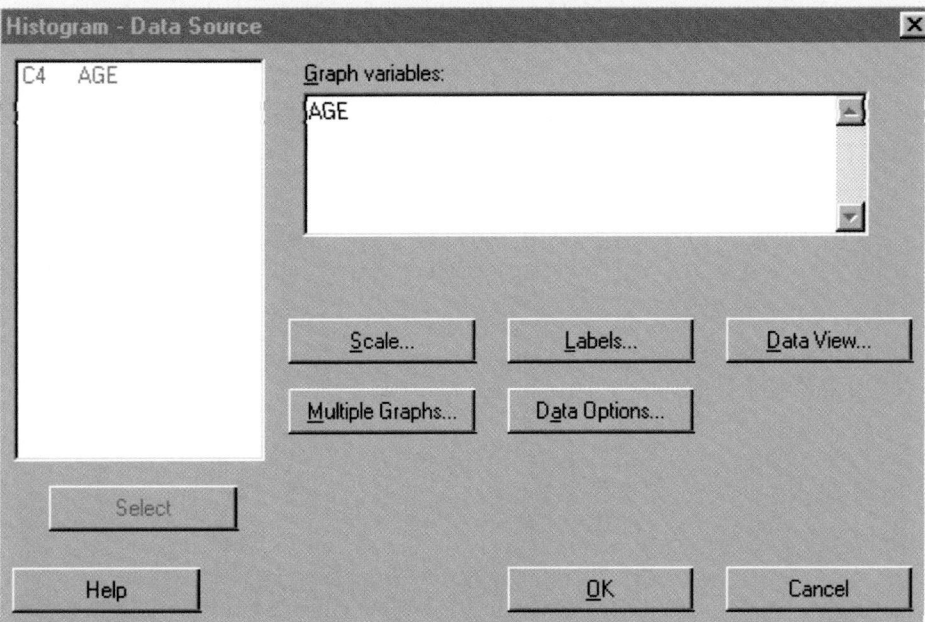

Figure 2.M.2
Histogram dialog box

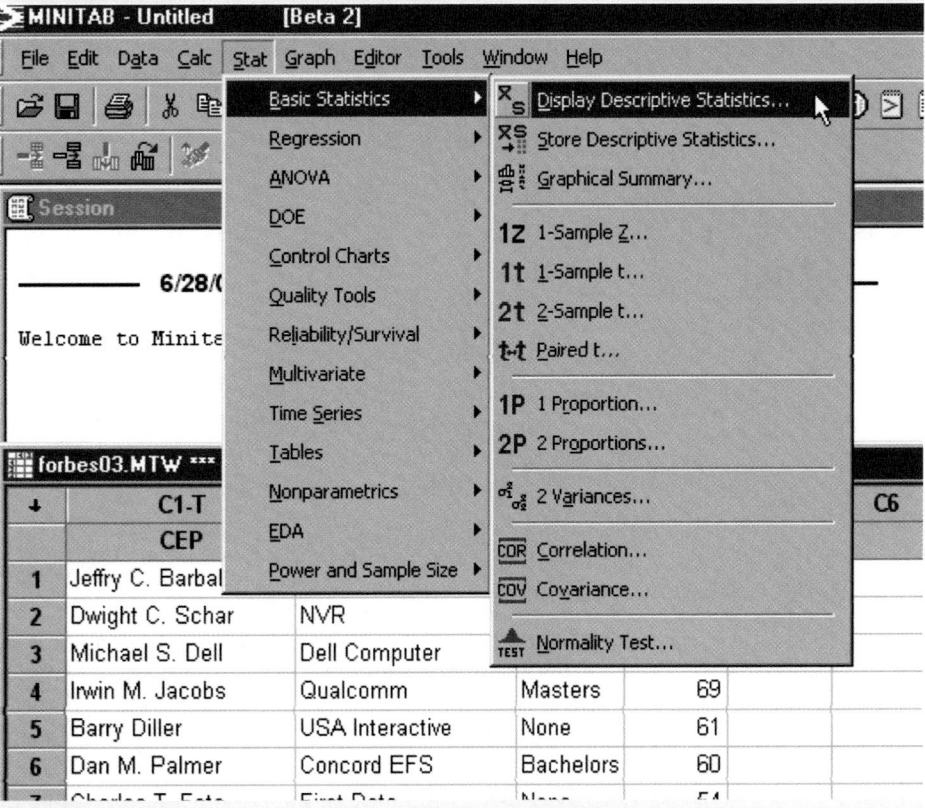

Figure 2.M.3
MINITAB options for obtaining descriptive statistics

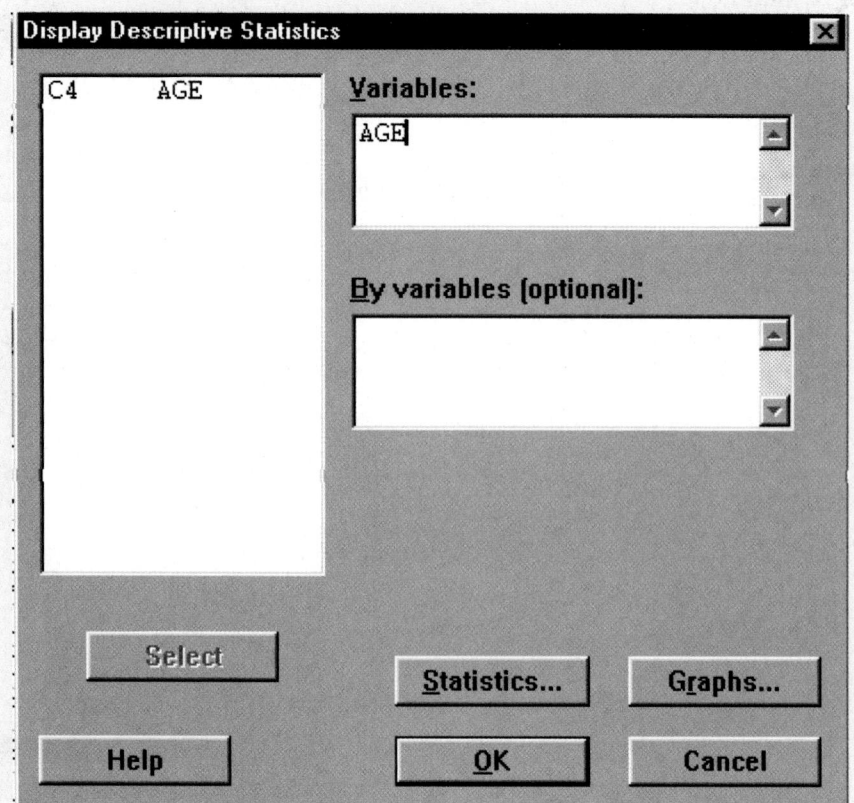

Figure 2.M.4
Descriptive statistics dialog box

click on "Basic Statistics, then click on "Display Descriptive Statistics" (see Figure 2.M.3). The resulting dialog box appears in Figure 2.M.4.

Select the quantitative variables you want to analyze and place them in the "Variables" box. You can control which particular descriptive statistics appear by clicking the "Statistics" button on the dialog box and making your selections. (As an option, you can create histograms and dot plots for the data by clicking the "Graphs" button and making the appropriate selections.) Click on "OK" to view the descriptive statistics printout.

2.3 Describing Data Using EXCEL and the PHStat2 Add-In

Graphing Data

To graph the data for a single variable in your EXCEL spreadsheet, click on the "PHStat" button on the EXCEL main menu bar, then on "Descriptive Statistics". The resulting menu will appear as shown in Figure 2.E.1. To obtain a pie chart, bar graph, or Pareto diagram for a qualitative variable, click on "One-Way Tables & Charts" (see Figure 2.E.1). The resulting dialog box appears as shown in Figure 2.E.2. Select the type of data, input the cell range of the variable, and select the type of graph (bar graph, pie chart, or pareto diagram). Then click "OK" to view the graph.

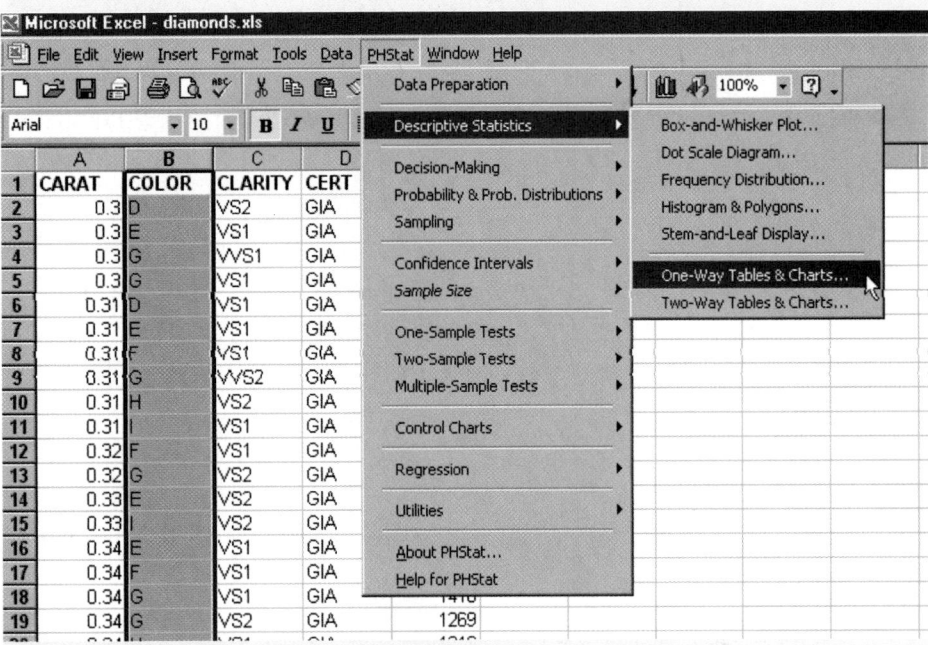

Figure 2.E.1
EXCEL and PHStat2 menu options for graphing your data

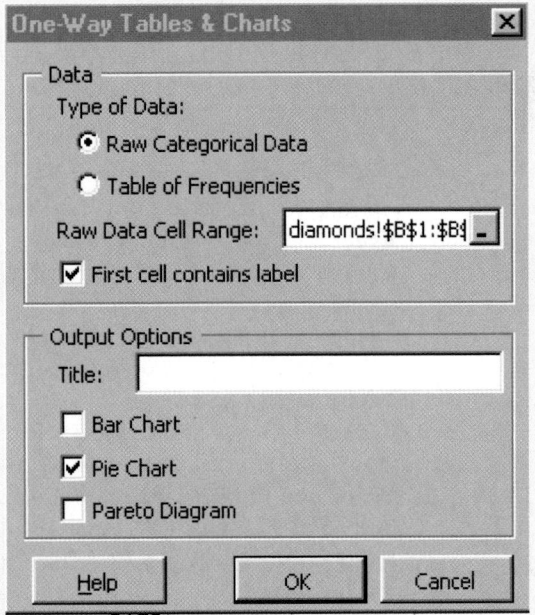

Figure 2.E.2
One-way charts dialog box

Figure 2.E.3
Histogram dialog box

To obtain a graph for a single quantitative variable, select the appropriate option—"Boxplot", "Dot (scale diagram) plot", "Histograms", or "Stem-and-Leaf (display)"—from the available options shown in Figure 2.E.1. Make the appropriate menu choices in the resulting dialog box. For example, the dialog box for a histogram is shown in Figure 2.E.3. [*Note*: For a histogram, you will have to create two new variables with data on your EXCEL spreadsheet—"Bins" (which represent the right endpoints of the class intervals) and the "Midpoints" of each bin (or class interval).]

After making the menu selections, click "OK" to view the graph.

To obtain a scatterplot for two quantitative variables, click on the Chart Wizard on the EXCEL main menu select. A series of four menus will appear. Step 1 of the Chart Wizard is shown in Figure 2.E.4. Make the appropriate menu choices, then click "Finish" to view the scatterplot. [*Note*: The two variables you want to graph must be in adjacent columns on the EXCEL spreadsheet.]

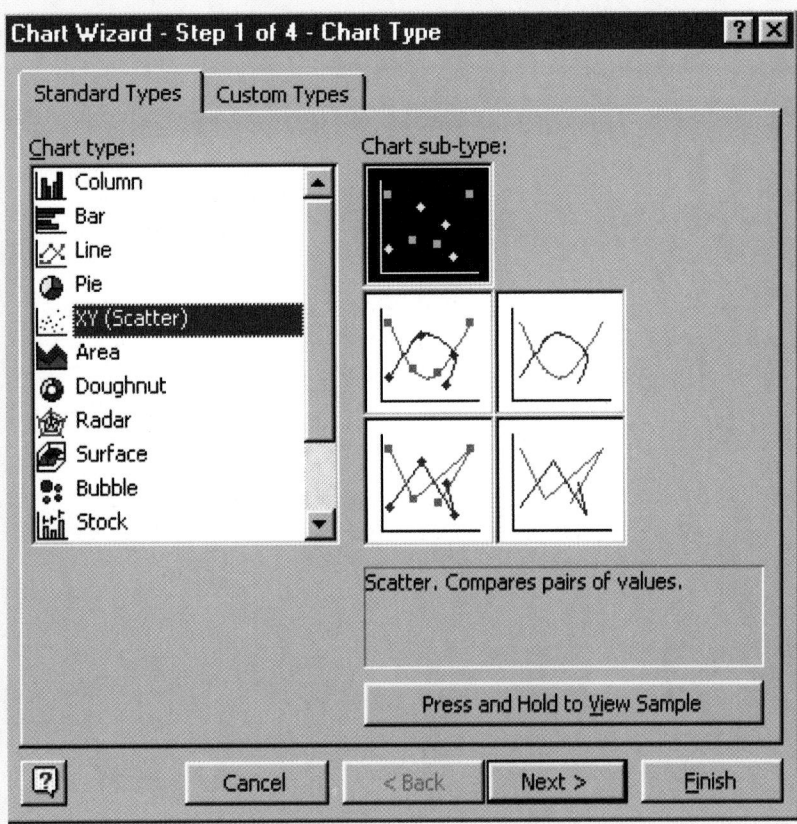

Figure 2.E.4
Step 1 of Chart Wizard for a scatterplot

Numerical Descriptive Statistics

To obtain numerical descriptive measures for a quantitative variable (e.g., mean, standard deviation, etc.), click on the "Tools" button on the main menu bar, then click on "Data Analysis", as shown in Figure 2.E.5. Select "Descriptive Statistics" from the resulting menu (see Figure 2.E.6). The resulting dialog box appears in Figure 2.E.7. Input the cell range of the variable to be analyzed and select "Summary Statistics". Then click on "OK" to view the descriptive statistics printout.

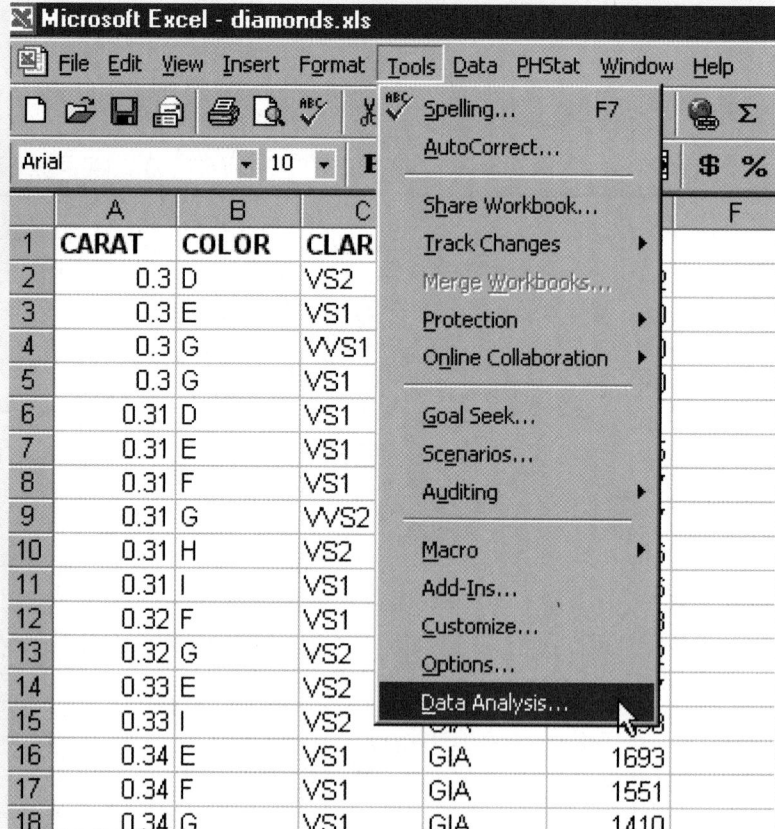

Figure 2.E.5
Main menu options for descriptive statistics

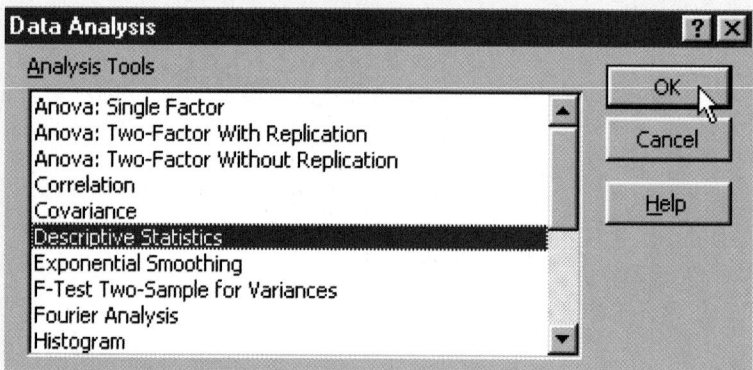

Figure 2.E.6
Data analysis menu

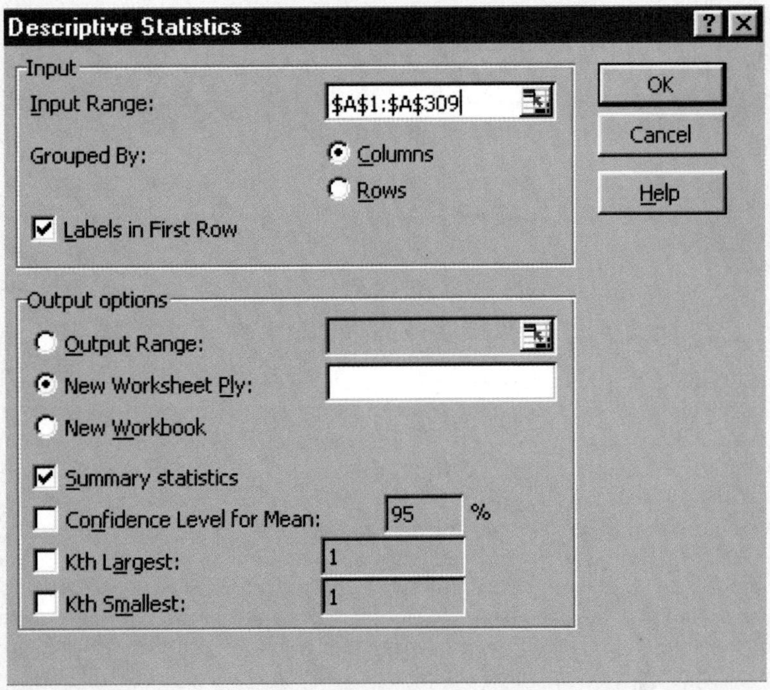

Figure 2.E.7
Descriptive statistics dialog box

Real-World Case

The Kentucky Milk Case—Part 1
(A Case Covering Chapters 1 and 2)

Many products and services are purchased by governments, cities, states, and businesses on the basis of scaled bids, and contracts are awarded to the lowest bidders. This process works extremely well in competitive markets, but it has the potential to increase the cost of purchasing if the markets are noncompetitive or if collusive practices are present. An investigation that began with a statistical analysis of bids in the Florida school milk market in 1986 led to the recovery of more than $33,000,000 from dairies who had conspired to rig the bids there in the 1980s. The investigation spread quickly to other states, and to date settlements and fines from dairies exceed $100,000,000 for school milk bidrigging in twenty other states. This case concerns a school milk bidrigging investigation in Kentucky.

Each year, the Commonwealth of Kentucky invites bids from dairies to supply half-pint containers of fluid milk products for its school districts. The products include whole white milk, low-fat white milk, and low-fat chocolate milk. In 13 school districts in northern Kentucky, the suppliers (dairies) were accused of "price-fixing," that is, conspiring to allocate the districts, so that the "winner" was predetermined. Since these districts are located in Boone, Campbell, and Kenton counties, the geographic market they represent is designated as the "tri-county"

market. Between 1983 and 1991, two dairies—Meyer Dairy and Trauth Dairy—were the only bidders on the milk contracts in the school districts in the tri-county market. Consequently, these two companies were awarded all the milk contracts in the market. (In contrast, a large number of different dairies won the milk contracts for the school districts in the remainder of the northern Kentucky market—called the "surrounding" market.) The Commonwealth of Kentucky alleged that Meyer and Trauth conspired to allocate the districts in the tri-county market. To date, one of the dairies (Meyer) has admitted guilt, while the other (Trauth) steadfastly maintains its innocence.

The Commonwealth of Kentucky maintains a database on all bids received from the dairies competing for the milk contracts. Some of these data have been made available to you to analyze to determine whether there is empirical evidence of bid collusion in the tri-county market. The data, saved in the **MILK** file, are described in detail below. Some background information on the data and important economic theory regarding bid collusion is also provided. Use this information to guide your analysis. Prepare a professional document which presents the results of your analysis and gives your opinion regarding collusion.

MILK
(Number of observations: 392)

Variable	Type	Description
YEAR	QN	Year in which milk contract awarded
MARKET	QL	Northern Kentucky Market (TRI-COUNTY or SURROUND)
WINNER	QL	Name of winning dairy
WWBID	QN	Winning bid price of whole white milk (dollars per half-pint)
WWQTY	QN	Quantity of whole white milk purchased (number of half-pints)
LFWBID	QN	Winning bid price of low-fat white milk (dollars per half-pint)
LFWQTY	QN	Quantity of low-fat white milk purchased (number of half-pints)
LFCBID	QN	Winning bid price of low-fat chocolate milk (dollars per half-pint)
LFCQTY	QN	Quantity of low-fat chocolate milk purchased (number of half-pints)
DISTRICT	QL	School district number
KYFMO	QN	FMO minimum raw cost of milk (dollars per half-pint)
MILESM	QN	Distance (miles) from Meyer processing plant to school district
MILEST	QN	Distance (miles) from Trauth processing plant to school district
LETDATE	QL	Date on which bidding on milk contract began (month/day/year)

Background Information

Collusive Market Environment

Certain economic features of a market create an environment in which collusion may be found. These basic features include the following:

1. *Few sellers and high concentration.* Only a few dairies control all or nearly all of the milk business in the market.

2. *Homogeneous products.* The products sold are essentially the same from the standpoint of the buyer (i.e., the school district).

3. *Inelastic demand.* Demand is relatively insensitive to price. (*Note:* The quantity of milk required by a school district is primarily determined by school enrollment, not price.)

4. *Similar costs.* The dairies bidding for the milk contracts face similar cost conditions. (*Note:* Approximately 60% of a dairy's production cost is raw milk, which is federally regulated. Meyer and Trauth are dairies of similar size and both bought their raw milk from the same supplier.)

Although these market structure characteristics create an environment which makes collusive behavior easier, they do not necessarily indicate the existence of collusion. An analysis of the actual bid prices may provide additional information about the degree of competition in the market.

Collusive Bidding Patterns.

The analyses of patterns in sealed bids reveal much about the level of competition, or lack thereof, among the vendors serving the market. Consider the following bid analyses:

1. *Market shares.* A market share for a dairy is the number of milk half-pints supplied by the dairy over a given school year, divided by the total number of half-pints supplied to the entire market. One sign of potential collusive behavior is stable, nearly equal market shares over time for the dairies under investigation.

2. *Incumbency rates.* Market allocation is a common form of collusive behavior in bidrigging conspiracies. Typically, the same dairy controls the same school districts year after year. The incumbency rate for a market in a given school year is defined as the percentage of school districts that are won by the same vendor who won the previous year. An incumbency rate that exceeds 70% has been considered a sign of collusive behavior.

3. *Bid levels and dispersion.* In competitive sealed bid markets vendors do not share information about their bids. Consequently, more dispersion or variability among the bids is observed than in collusive markets, where vendors communicate about their bids and have a tendency to submit bids in close proximity to one another in an attempt to make the bidding appear competitive. Furthermore, in competitive markets the bid dispersion tends to be directly proportional to the level of the bid: When bids are submitted at relatively high levels, there is more variability among the bids than when they are submitted at or near marginal cost, which will be approximately the same among dairies in the same geographic market.

4. *Price versus cost/distance.* In competitive markets, bid prices are expected to track costs over time. Thus, if the market is competitive, the bid price of milk should be highly correlated with the raw milk cost. Lack of such a relationship is another sign of collusion. Similarly, bid price should be correlated to the distance the product must travel from the processing plant to the school (due to delivery costs) in a competitive market.

5. *Bid sequence.* School milk bids are submitted over the spring and summer months, generally at the end of one school year and before the beginning of the next. When the bids are examined in sequence in competitive markets, the level of bidding is expected to fall as the bidding season progresses. (This phenomenon is attributable to the learning process that occurs during the season, with bids adjusted accordingly. Dairies may submit relatively high bids early in the season to "test the market," confident that volume can be picked up later if the early high bids lose. But, dairies who do not win much business early in the season are likely to become more aggressive in their bidding as the season progresses, driving price levels down.) Constant or slightly increasing price patterns of sequential bids in a market where a single dairy wins year after year is considered another indication of collusive behavior.

6. *Comparison of average winning bid prices.* Consider two similar markets, one in which bids are possibly rigged and the other in which bids are competitively determined. In theory, the mean winning price in the "rigged" market will be significantly higher than the mean price in the competitive market for each year in which collusion occurs.

Probability

Contents

Statistics in Action

Lottery Buster!

Technology Tutorials

Where We've Been

- Identified the objective of inferential statistics: to make inferences about a population based on information in a sample
- Introduced graphical and numerical descriptive measures for both quantitative and qualitative data

Where We're Going

- Develop probability as a measure of uncertainty.
- Introduce basic rules for finding probabilities.
- Use a probability as a measure of reliability for an inference.

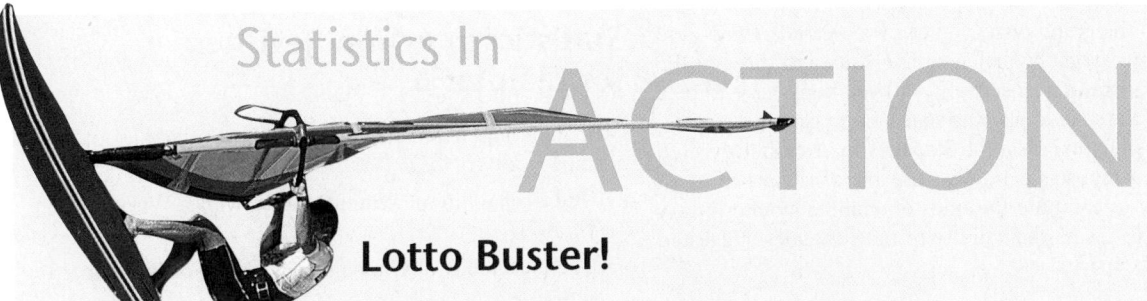

Statistics In ACTION

Lotto Buster!

"Welcome to the Wonderful World of Lottery Bus$ters." So began the premier issue of *Lottery Buster*, a monthly publication for players of the state lottery games. *Lottery Buster* provides interesting facts and figures on the 37 state lotteries currently operating in the United States and, more important, tips on how to increase a player's odds of winning the lottery.

New Hampshire, in 1963, was the first state in modern times to authorize a state lottery as an alternative to increasing taxes. (Prior to this time, beginning in 1895, lotteries were banned in America because of corruption.) Since then, lotteries have become immensely popular for two reasons. First, they lure you with the opportunity to win millions of dollars with a $1 investment, and second, when you lose, at least you believe your money is doing to a good cause. Many state lotteries, like Florida, designate a high percentage of lottery revenues to fund state education.

The popularity of the state lottery has brought with it an avalanche of "experts" and "mathematical wizards" (such as the editors of *Lottery Buster*) who provide advice on how to win the lottery—for a fee, of course! Many offer guaranteed "systems" of winning through computer software products with catchy names such as lotto Wizard, Lottorobics, Win4d, and Loto-luck.

For example, most knowledgeable lottery players would agree that the "golden rule" or "first rule" in winning lotteries is *game selection*. State lotteries generally offer three types of games: Instant (scratch-off tickets or online)

game, Daily Numbers (Pick-3 or Pick-4), and weekly Pick-6 lotto' game.

One version of the Instant game involves scratching off the thin opaque covering on a ticket with the edge of a coin to determine whether you have won or lost. The cost of a ticket ranges from 50¢ to $5, and the amount won ranges from $1 to $100,000 in most states, and to as much as $1 million in others. *Lottery Buster* advises against playing the Instant game because it is "a pure chance play, and you can win only by dumb luck. No skill can be applied to this game."

The Daily Numbers game permits you to choose either a three-digit (Pick-3) or four-digit (Pick-4) number at a cost of $1 per ticket. Each night, the winning number is drawn. If your number matches the winning number, you win a large sum of money, usually $100,000. You do have some control over the Daily Numbers game (since you pick the numbers that you play) and, consequently, there are strategies available to increase your chances of winning. However, the Daily Numbers game, like the Instant game, is not available for out-of-state play.

To play Pick-6 Lotto, you select six numbers of your choice from a field of numbers ranging from 1 to N, where N depends on which state's game you are playing. For example, Florida's current Lotto game involves picking six numbers ranging from 1 to 53. (See Figure SIA3.1 below.) The cost of a ticket is $1 and the payoff, if your six numbers match the winning numbers drawn, is $7 million or more, depending on the number of tickets purchased. (To date, Florida has had the largest state weekly payoff of over $200 million.) In

Figure SIA3.1
Reproduction of Florida's 6/53 Lotto ticket

addition to the grand prize, you can win second-, third-, and fourth-prize payoffs by matching five, four, and three of the six numbers drawn, respectively. And you don't have to be a resident of the state to play the state's Lotto game.

In this chapter, several Statistics in Action Revisited examples demonstrate how to use the basic concepts of probability to compute the odds of winning a state lottery game and to assess the validity of the strategies suggested by lottery "experts."

Statistics in Action Revisited for Chapter 3

- Computing and Understanding the Probability of Winning Lotto (p. 157)
- The Probability of Winning Lotto with a Wheel System (p. 167)
- The Probability of Winning Daily Cash 3 or Play 4 (p. 181)

Recall that one branch of statistics is concerned with decisions about a population based on sample information. You can see how this is accomplished more easily if you understand the relationship between population and sample—a relationship that becomes clearer if we reverse the statistical procedure of making inferences from sample to population. In this chapter then, we assume that the population is known and calculate the chances of obtaining various samples from the population. Thus, we show that probability is the reverse of statistics: In probability, we use the population information to infer the probable nature of the sample.

Probability plays an important role in inference-making. Suppose, for example, you have an opportunity to invest in an oil exploration company. Past records show that out of 10 previous oil drillings (a sample of the company's experiences), all 10 came up dry. What do you conclude? Do you think the chances are better than 50:50 that the company will hit a gusher? Should you invest in this company? Chances are, your answer to these questions will be an emphatic "No". If the company's exploratory prowess is sufficient to hit a producing well 50% of the time, a record of 10 dry wells out of 10 drilled is an event that is just too improbable.

Or suppose you're playing poker with what your opponents assure you is a well-shuffled deck of cards. In three consecutive five-card hands, the person on your right is dealt four aces. Based on this sample of three deals, do you think the cards are being adequately shuffled? Again, your answer is likely to be "No" because dealing three hands of four aces is just too improbable if the cards were properly shuffled.

Note that the decisions concerning the potential success of the oil drilling company and the adequacy of card shuffling both involve knowing the chance—or probability—of a certain sample result. Both situations were contrived so that you could easily conclude that the probabilities of the sample results were small. Unfortunately, the probabilities of many observed sample results aren't so easy to evaluate intuitively. For these cases we will need the assistance of a theory of probability.

Teaching Tip
Use these simple examples of probability to show how knowing probabilities of past performance provides valuable information that can be used to make decisions concerning future outcomes.

3.1 Events, Sample Spaces, and Probability

Let's begin our treatment of probability with simple examples that are easily described. With the aid of simple examples, we can introduce important definitions that will help us develop the notion of probability more easily.

Suppose a coin is tossed once and the up face is recorded. The result we see and record is called an *observation*, or *measurement*, and the process of making an observation is called an *experiment*. Notice that our definition of experiment is broader than the one used in the physical sciences, where you would picture test tubes, microscopes, and other laboratory equipment. Among other things, statistical experiments may include recording an Internet user's preference for a Web browser, recording a change in the Dow Jones Industrial Average from one day to the next, recording the weekly sales of a business firm, and counting the number of errors on

Teaching Tip
Use examples of other outcomes or measurements and ask the students to identify the experiment needed to generate the result.

a page of an accountant's ledger. The point is that a statistical experiment can be almost any act of observation as long as the outcome is uncertain.

> **DEFINITION 3.1**
>
> An **experiment** is an act or process of observation that leads to a single outcome that cannot be predicted with certainty.

Consider another simple experiment consisting of tossing a die and observing the number on the up face. The six basic possible outcomes to this experiment are as follows:

1. Observe a 1
2. Observe a 2
3. Observe a 3
4. Observe a 4
5. Observe a 5
6. Observe a 6

Note that if this experiment is conducted once, *you can observe one and only one of these six basic outcomes, and the outcome cannot be predicted with certainty.* Also, these possibilities cannot be decomposed into more basic outcomes. Because observing the outcome of an experiment is similar to selecting a sample from a population, the basic possible outcomes to an experiment are called *sample points.**

Teaching Tip

Note that no two sample points of an experiment can happen at the same time. This ties in nicely when *mutually exclusive* is defined later in the chapter.

> **DEFINITION 3.2**
>
> A **sample point** is the most basic outcome of an experiment.

EXAMPLE 3.1   LISTING SAMPLE POINTS

Problem   Two coins are tossed, and their up faces are recorded. List all the sample points for this experiment.

Solution   Even for a seemingly trivial experiment, we must be careful when listing the sample points. At first glance, we might expect three basic outcomes: Observe two heads, Observe two tails, or Observe one head and one tail. However, further reflection reveals that the last of these, Observe one head and one tail, can be decomposed into two outcomes: Head on coin 1, Tail on coin 2; and Tail on coin 1, Head on coin 2. Thus, we have four sample points:

HH, HT, TH, TT

1. Observe *HH*
2. Observe *HT*
3. Observe *TH*
4. Observe *TT*

where *H* in the first position means "Head on coin 1," *H* in the second position means "Head on coin 2," and so on.

*Alternatively, the term *simple event* can be used.

Look Back Even if the coins are identical in appearance, there are, in fact, two distinct coins. Thus, the sample points must account for this distinction.

Now Work   *Exercise 3.7a*

■ ■ ■

Teaching Tip

Explain that sample spaces can be described in several ways. For example, the results of the die experiment could be considered as odd or even outcomes. This leads into the definition of an event very nicely.

We often wish to refer to the collection of all the sample points of an experiment. This collection is called the *sample space* of the experiment. For example, there are six sample points in the sample space associated with the die-toss experiment. The sample spaces for the experiments discussed thus far are shown in Table 3.1.

DEFINITION 3.3

The **sample space** of an experiment is the collection of all its sample points.

TABLE 3.1   Experiments and Their Sample Spaces

Experiment: Observe the up face on a coin.
Sample space: 1. Observe a head
　　　　　　　　2. Observe a tail
This sample space can be represented in set notation as a set containing two sample points:

$$S: \{H, T\}$$

where *H* represents the sample point Observe a head and *T* represents the sample point Observe a tail.

Experiment: Observe the up face on a die.
Sample space: 1. Observe a 1
　　　　　　　　2. Observe a 2
　　　　　　　　3. Observe a 3
　　　　　　　　4. Observe a 4
　　　　　　　　5. Observe a 5
　　　　　　　　6. Observe a 6
This sample space can be represented in set notation as a set of six sample points:

$$S: \{1, 2, 3, 4, 5, 6\}$$

Experiment: Observe the up faces on two coins.
Sample space: 1. Observe *HH*
　　　　　　　　2. Observe *HT*
　　　　　　　　3. Observe *TH*
　　　　　　　　4. Observe *TT*
This sample space can be represented in set notation as a set of four sample points:

$$S: \{HH, HT, TH, TT\}$$

Teaching Tip

Venn diagrams are useful as both a teaching and learning tool in probability. Note that the Venn diagram contains all possible outcomes of the sample space.

Just as graphs are useful in describing sets of data, a pictorial method for presenting the sample space will often be useful. Figure 3.1 shows such a representation for each of the experiments in Table 3.1. In each case, the sample space is shown as a closed figure, labeled *S*, containing all possible sample points. Each sample point is represented by a solid dot (i.e., a "point") and labeled accordingly. Such graphical representations are called **Venn diagrams.**

Now that we know that an experiment will result in *only one* basic outcome—called a sample point—and that the sample space is the collection of all

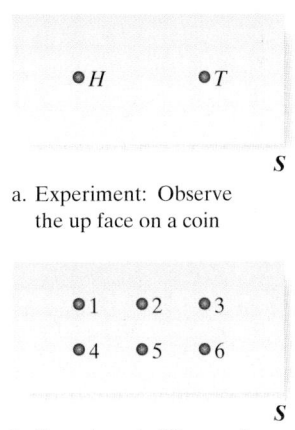

a. Experiment: Observe the up face on a coin

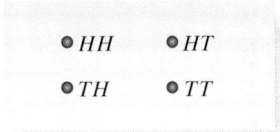

b. Experiment: Observe the up face on a die

c. Experiment: Observe the up faces on two coins

Figure 3.1
Venn diagrams for the three experiments from Table 3.1

possible sample points, we're ready to discuss the probabilities of the sample points. You've undoubtedly used the term *probability* and have some intuitive idea about its meaning. Probability is generally used synonymously with "chance," "odds," and similar concepts. For example, if a fair coin is tossed, we might reason that both the sample points, Observe a head and Observe a tail, have the same *chance* of occurring. Thus, we might state that "the probability of observing a head is 50%" or "the *odds* of seeing a head are 50:50." Both of these statements are based on an informal knowledge of probability. We'll begin our treatment of probability by using such informal concepts and then solidify what we mean later.

The probability of a sample point is a number between 0 and 1 inclusive that measures the likelihood that the outcome will occur when the experiment is performed. This number is usually taken to be the relative frequency of the occurrence of a sample point in a very long series of repetitions of an experiment.* For example, if we are assigning probabilities to the two sample points (Observe a head and Observe a tail) in the coin-toss experiment, we might reason that if we toss a balanced coin a very large number of times, the sample points Observe a head and Observe a tail will occur with the same relative frequency of .5.

Biography

JOHN VENN
(1834–1923)
The English Logician

Born in Hull, England, John Venn is probably best know for his pictorial representation of unions and intersections (the Venn diagram). While lecturing in Moral Science at Cambridge University, Venn wrote *The Logic of Chance* and two other treatises on logic. In these works, Venn probably had his greatest contribution to the field of probability and statistics—the notion that the probability of an event is simply the long-run proportion of times the event occurs. Besides being a well-known mathematician, Venn was also a historian, philosopher, priest, and skilled machine builder. (His machine for bowling cricket balls once beat a top star on the Australian cricket team.)

Our reasoning is supported by Figure 3.2. The figure plots the relative frequency of the number of times that a head occurs when simulating (by computer) the toss of a coin N times, where N ranges from as few as 25 tosses to as many as 1,500 tosses of the coin. You can see that when N is large (i.e., $N = 1,500$), the relative frequency is converging to .5. Thus, the probability of each sample point in the coin-tossing experiment is .5.

For some experiments, we may have little or no information on the relative frequency of occurrence of the sample points; consequently, we must assign probabilities to the sample points based on general information about the experiment. For example, if the experiment is to invest in a business venture and to observe

*The result derives from an axiom in probability theory called the **Law of Large Numbers.** Phrased informally, this law states that the relative frequency of the number of times that an outcome occurs when an experiment is replicated over and over again (i.e., a large number of times) approaches the theoretical probability of the outcome.

Figure 3.2
Proportion of heads in N coin tosses

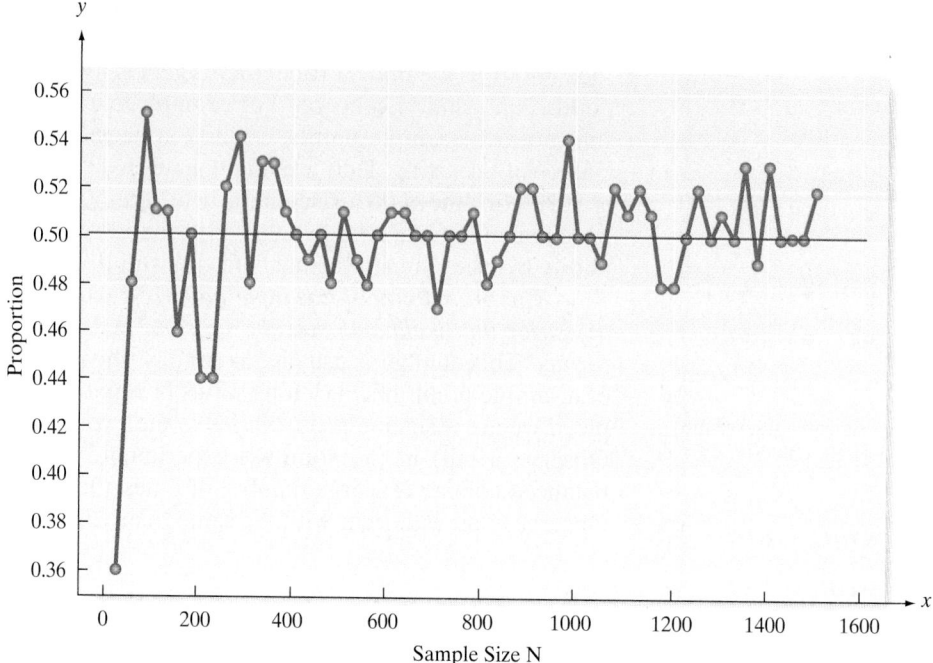

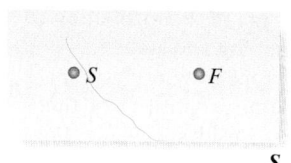

Figure 3.3
Experiment: Invest in a business venture and observe whether it succeeds (S) or fails (F)

whether it succeeds or fails, the sample space would appear as in Figure 3.3. We are unlikely to be able to assign probabilities to the sample points of this experiment based on a long series of repetitions since unique factors govern each performance of this kind of experiment. Instead, we may consider factors such as the personnel managing the venture, the general state of the economy at the time, the rate of success of similar ventures, and any other pertinent information. If we finally decide that the venture has an 80% chance of succeeding, we assign a probability of .8 to the sample point Success. This probability can be interpreted as a measure of our degree of belief in the outcome of the business venture; that is, it is a subjective probability. Notice, however, that such probabilities should be based on expert information that is carefully assessed. If not, we may be misled on any decisions based on these probabilities or based on any calculations in which they appear. [*Note:* For a text that deals in detail with the subjective evaluation of probabilities, see Winkler (1972) or Lindley (1985).]

No matter how you assign the probabilities to sample points, the probabilities assigned must obey two rules:

Probability Rules for Sample Points

1. All sample point probabilities must lie between 0 and 1 inconclusive.
2. The probabilities of all the sample points within a sample space must sum to 1.

Teaching Tip
Ask the class to assign probabilities to the six possible sample points of the single die experiment. Show how these two probability rules apply to the die example.

Assigning probabilities to sample points is easy for some experiments. For example, if the experiment is to toss a fair coin and observe the face, we would probably all agree to assign a probability of $\frac{1}{2}$ to the two sample points, Observe a head and Observe a tail. However, many experiments have sample points whose probabilities are more difficult to assign.

EXAMPLE 3.2   ASSIGNING PROBABILITIES TO SAMPLE POINTS

Problem   Many American hotels offer complimentary shampoo in their guest rooms. Suppose you randomly select one hotel from a registry of all hotels in the United States and check whether or not the hotel offers complimentary shampoo. Show how this problem might be formulated in the framework of an experiment with sample points and a sample space. Indicate how probabilities might be assigned to the sample points.

Solution   The experiment can be defined as the selection of an American hotel and the observation of whether or not complimentary shampoo is offered in the hotel's guest rooms. There are two sample points in the sample space corresponding to this experiment:

S: {The hotel offers complimentary shampoo}
N: {No complimentary shampoo is offered by the hotel}

The difference between this and the coin-toss experiment becomes apparent when we attempt to assign probabilities to the two sample points. What probability should we assign to the sample point S? If you answer .5, you are assuming that the events S and N should occur with equal likelihood, just like the sample points Heads and Tails in the coin-toss experiment. But assignment of sample point probabilities for the hotel-shampoo experiment is not so easy. In fact, a recent survey of American hotels found that 80% now offer complimentary shampoo to guests. Then it might be reasonable to approximate the probability of the sample point S as .8 and that of the sample point N as .2.

Look Back   Here we see that sample points are not always equally likely so assigning probabilities to them can be complicated—particularly for experiments that represent real applications (as opposed to coin- and die-toss experiments).

Now Work   *Exercise 3.12*

◼ ◼ ◼

Although the probabilities of sample points are often of interest in their own right, it is usually probabilities of collections of sample points that are important. Example 3.3 demonstrates this point.

EXAMPLE 3.3   FINDING THE PROBABILITY OF A COLLECTION OF SAMPLE POINTS

Problem   A fair die is tossed, and the up face is observed. If the face is even, you win $1. Otherwise, you lose $1. What is the probability that you win?

Solution   Recall that the sample space for this experiment contains six sample points:

$P(\text{win}) = .5$

$$S: \{1, 2, 3, 4, 5, 6\}$$

Since the die is balanced, we assign a probability of $1/6$ to each of the sample points in this sample space. An even number will occur if one of the sample points, Observe a 2, Observe a 4, or Observe a 6, occurs. A collection of sample points such as this is called an *event*, which we denote by the letter A. Since the event A contains three sample points—each with probability $1/6$—and since no sample points can occur simultaneously, we reason that the probability of A is the sum of the

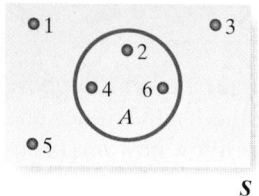

Figure 3.4

Die-toss experiment with event A: Observe an even number

probabilities of the sample points in A. Thus, the probability of A, i.e., the probability that you will win, is $\frac{1}{6} + \frac{1}{6} + \frac{1}{6} = \frac{1}{2}$.

Look Back Based on our notion of probability, $P(A) = \frac{1}{2}$ implies that, *in the long run*, you will win \$1 half the time and lose \$1 half the time.

> **Now Work** *Exercise 3.6*

———— ∎ ∎ ∎ ————

Figure 3.4 is a Venn diagram depicting the sample space associated with a die-toss experiment and the event A, Observe an even number. The event A is represented by the closed figure inside the sample space S. This closed figure A contains all the sample points that comprise it.

To decide which sample points belong to the set associated with an event A, test each sample point in the sample space S. If event A occurs, then that sample point is in the event A. For example, the event A, Observe an even number, in the die-toss experiment will occur if the sample point Observe a 2 occurs. By the same reasoning, the sample points Observe a 4 and Observe a 6 are also in event A.

To summarize, we have demonstrated that an event can be defined in words or it can be defined as a specific set of sample points. This leads us to the following general definition of an event:

Teaching Tip

An even number is the event that represents the collection of the sample points 2, 4, and 6 in the single die experiment. An odd number represents the collection of the sample points 1, 3, and 5.

> **DEFINITION 3.4**
>
> An **event** is a specific collection of sample points.

EXAMPLE 3.4

THE PROBABILITY OF AN EVENT

Problem   Consider the experiment of tossing two *unbalanced* coins. Because the coins are *not* balanced, their outcomes (H or T) are not equiprobable. Suppose the correct probabilities associated with the sample points are given in the table. [*Note:* The necessary properties for assigning probabilities to sample points are satisfied.]

Consider the events

$$A: \{\text{Observe exactly one head}\}$$
$$B: \{\text{Observe at least one head}\}$$

$P(A) = \frac{4}{9} \quad P(B) = \frac{8}{9}$

Calculate the probability of A and the probability of B.

Sample Point	Probability
HH	$\frac{4}{9}$
HT	$\frac{2}{9}$
TH	$\frac{2}{9}$
TT	$\frac{1}{9}$

Solution   Event A contains the sample points HT and TH. Since two or more sample points cannot occur at the same time, we can easily calculate the probability of event A by summing the probabilities of the two sample points. Thus, the probability of observing exactly one head (event A), denoted by the symbol $P(A)$, is

$$P(A) = P(\text{Observe } HT) + P(\text{Observe } TH) = \frac{2}{9} + \frac{2}{9} = \frac{4}{9}$$

Similarly, since B contains the sample points HH, HT, and TH.

$$P(B) = \frac{4}{9} + \frac{2}{9} + \frac{2}{9} = \frac{8}{9}$$

Look Back Again, these probabilities should be interpreted *in the long run*. For example, $P(B) = \frac{8}{9} \approx .89$ implies that if we were to toss two coins an infinite number of times, we would observe at least 2 heads on about 89% of the tosses.

Now Work   *Exercise 3.3*

■ ■ ■

Teaching Tip
Point out that this procedure works well with sample points but does not always work with events of an experiment because more than one event can occur at the same time (i.e., an even number and a number greater than 3 for the single die experiment).

The preceding example leads us to a general procedure for finding the probability of an event A:

Probability of an Event

The probability of an event A is calculated by summing the probabilities of the sample points in the sample space for A.

Thus, we can summarize the steps for calculating the probability of any event, as indicated in the next box.

Steps for Calculating Probabilities of Events

1. Define the experiment; that is, describe the process used to make an observation and the type of observation that will be recorded.
2. List the sample points.
3. Assign probabilities to the sample points.
4. Determine the collection of sample points contained in the event of interest.
5. Sum the sample point probabilities to get the event probability.

EXAMPLE 3.5   APPLYING THE FIVE STEPS

Problem   Diversity training of employees is the latest trend in U.S. business. *USA Today* (Aug. 15, 1995) reported on the primary reasons businesses give for making diversity training part of their strategic planning process. The reasons are summarized in Table 3.2. Assume that one business is selected at random from all U.S. businesses that use diversity training and the primary reason is determined.

a. Define the experiment that generated the data in Table 3.2, and list the sample points.

TABLE 3.2   Primary Reasons for Diversity Training

Reason	Percentage
Comply with personnel policies (CPP)	7
Increase productivity (IP)	47
Stay competitive (SC)	38
Social responsibility (SR)	4
Other (O)	4
Total	100%

.07, .47, .38, .04, .04

.85

.96

b. Assign probabilities to the sample points.

c. What is the probability that the primary reason for diversity training is business related; that is, related to competition or productivity?

d. What is the probability that social responsibility is not a primary reason for diversity training?

Solution

a. The experiment is the act of determining the primary reason for diversity training of employees at a U.S. business. The sample points, the simplest outcomes of the experiment, are the five response categories listed in Table 3.2. These sample points are shown in the Venn diagram in Figure 3.5.

b. If, as in Example 3.1, we were to assign equal probabilities in this case, each of the response categories would have a probability of one-fifth ($\frac{1}{5}$), or .20. But, by examining Table 3.2 you can see that equal probabilities are not reasonable here because the response percentages were not even approximately the same in the five classifications. It is more reasonable to assign a probability equal to the response percentage in each class, as shown in Table 3.3.*

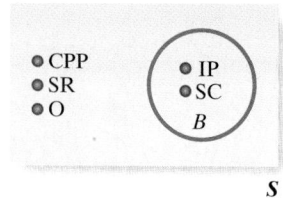

Figure 3.5

Venn diagram for diversity training survey

Suggested Exercises 3.13

c. Let the symbol B represent the event that the primary reason for diversity training is business related. B is not a sample point because it consists of more than one of the response classifications (the sample points). In fact, as shown in Figure 3.5, B consists of two sample points, IP and SC. The probability of B is defined to be the sum of the probabilities of the sample points in B.

$$P(B) = P(\text{IP}) + P(\text{SC}) = .47 + .38 = .85$$

d. Let NSR represent the event that social responsibility is not a primary reason for diversity training. Then NSR consists of all sample points except SR, and the probability is the sum of the corresponding sample point probabilities:

$$P(NSR) = P(\text{CPP}) + P(\text{IP}) + P(\text{SC}) + P(\text{O})$$
$$= .07 + .47 + .38 + .04 = .96$$

TABLE 3.3   Sample Point Probabilities for Diversity Training Survey

Sample Point	Probability
CPP	.07
IP	.47
SC	.38
SR	.04
O	.04

Look Back The key to solving this problem is to follow the steps outlined in the box. We defined the experiment (Step 1) and listed the sample points (Step 2) in part a. The assignment of probabilities to the sample points (Step 3) was done in part b. For each probability in parts c and d, we identified the collection of points in the event (Step 4) and summed their probabilities (Step 5).

Now Work   *Exercise 3.13*

■ ■ ■

EXAMPLE 3.6   THE PROBABILITY OF AN EVENT

Problem   You have the capital to invest in two of four ventures, each of which requires approximately the same amount of investment capital. Unknown to you, two of the investments will eventually fail and two will be successful. You research the four ventures because you think that your research will increase your probability of a successful choice over a purely random selection, and you eventually decide on two. If you used none of the information generated by your research, and selected two

*The response percentages were based on a sample of U.S. businesses: consequently, these assigned probabilities are estimates of the true population-response percentages. You'll learn how to measure the reliability of probability estimates in Chapter 7.

ventures at random, what is the probability that you would select at least one successful venture?

Solution **Step 1:** Denote the two successful enterprises as S_1 and S_2 and the two failing enterprises as F_1 and F_2. The experiment involves a random selection of two out of the four ventures, and each possible pair of ventures represents a sample point.

Step 2: The six sample points that make up the sample space are

1. (S_1, S_2)
2. (S_1, F_1)
3. (S_1, F_2)
4. (S_2, F_1)
5. (S_2, F_2)
6. (F_1, F_2)

Step 3: Next, we assign probabilities to the sample points. If we assume that the choice of any one pair is as likely as any other, then the probability of each sample point is $\frac{1}{6}$.

Suggested Exercises 3.17

Step 4: The event of selecting at least one of the two successful ventures includes all the sample points except (F_1, F_2).

Step 5: Now, we find

$$P(\text{Select at least one success}) = P(S_1, S_2) + P(S_1, F_1) + P(S_1, F_2) + P(S_2, F_1) + P(S_2, F_2)$$

$$= \frac{1}{6} + \frac{1}{6} + \frac{1}{6} + \frac{1}{6} + \frac{1}{6} = \frac{5}{6}$$

Therefore, with a random selection, the probability of selecting at least one successful venture out of two is $\frac{5}{6}$.

■ ■ ■

Teaching Tip

Illustrate the need for counting rules by discussing the possible outcomes when ten coins are simultaneously flipped. There are 1,024 sample points in this example.

The preceding examples have one thing in common: The number of sample points in each of the sample spaces was small; hence, the sample points were easy to identify and list. How can we manage this when the sample points run into the thousands or millions? For example, suppose you wish to select five business ventures from a group of 1,000. Then each different group of five ventures would represent a sample point. How can you determine the number of sample points associated with this experiment?

One method of determining the number of sample points for a complex experiment is to develop a counting system. Start by examining a simple version of the experiment. For example, see if you can develop a system for counting the number of ways to select two ventures from a total of four (this is exactly what was done in Example 3.6). If the ventures are represented by the symbols V_1, V_2, V_3, and V_4, the sample points could be listed in the following pattern:

(V_1, V_2) (V_2, V_3) (V_3, V_4)
(V_1, V_3) (V_2, V_4)
(V_1, V_4)

Note the pattern and now try a more complex situation—say, sampling three ventures out of five. List the sample points and observe the pattern. Finally, see if you can deduce the pattern for the general case. Perhaps you can program a computer to produce the matching and counting for the number of samples of 5 selected from a total of 1,000.

A second method of determining the number of sample points for an experiment is to use **combinatorial mathematics.** This branch of mathematics is concerned with developing counting rules for given situations. For example, there is a simple rule for finding the number of different samples of five ventures selected from 1,000. This rule, called the **Combinations Rule,** is given in the box.

Combinations Rule

A sample of n elements is to be drawn from a set of N elements. Then, the number of different samples possible is denoted by $\binom{N}{n}$ and is equal to

$$\binom{N}{n} = \frac{N!}{n!(N - n)!}$$

where the factorial symbol (!) means that

$$n! = n(n - 1)(n - 2) \cdots (3)(2)(1)$$

For example, $5! = 5 \cdot 4 \cdot 3 \cdot 2 \cdot 1$. [*Note:* The quantity 0! is defined to be equal to 1.]

EXAMPLE 3.7   USING THE COMBINATIONS RULE

Problem

Refer to Example 3.6 in which we selected two ventures from four in which to invest. Use the combinations counting rule to determine how many different selections can be made.

Solution   For this example, $N = 4, n = 2$, and

$$\binom{4}{2} = \frac{4!}{2!2!} = \frac{4 \cdot 3 \cdot 2 \cdot 1}{(2 \cdot 1)(2 \cdot 1)} = 6$$

Look Back   You can see that this agrees with the number of sample points obtained in Example 3.6.

Now Work   *Exercise 3.4*

■ ■ ■

EXAMPLE 3.8   USING THE COMBINATIONS RULE

Problem

Suppose you plan to invest equal amounts of money in each of five business ventures. If you have 20 ventures from which to make the selection, how many different samples of five ventures can be selected from the 20?

Solution   For this example, $N = 20$ and $n = 5$. Then the number of different samples of 5 that can be selected from the 20 ventures is

$$\binom{20}{5} = \frac{20!}{5!(20 - 5)!} = \frac{20!}{5!15!}$$

$$= \frac{20 \cdot 19 \cdot 18 \cdot \cdots \cdot 3 \cdot 2 \cdot 1}{(5 \cdot 4 \cdot 3 \cdot 2 \cdot 1)(15 \cdot 14 \cdot 13 \cdot \cdots \cdot 3 \cdot 2 \cdot 1)} = 15,504$$

Look Back You can see that attempting to list all the sample points for this experiment would be an extremely tedious and time consuming, if not practically impossible, task.

■ ■ ■

The Combinations Rule is just one of a large number of counting rules that have been developed by combinatorial mathematicians. This counting rule applies to situations in which the experiment calls for selecting n elements from a total of N elements, without replacing each element before the next is selected. If you are interested in learning other methods for counting sample points for various types of experiments, you will find a few of the basic counting rules in Appendix A. Others can be found in the chapter references.

Statistics in Action Revisited

Computing and Understanding the Probability of Winning Lotto

In Florida's state lottery game, called Pick-6 Lotto, you select six numbers of your choice from a set of numbers ranging from 1 to 53. We can apply the Combinations Rule to determine the total number of combinations of 6 numbers selected from 53 (i.e., the total number of sample points [or possible winning tickets]). Here, $N = 53$ and $n = 6$; therefore, we have

$$\binom{N}{n} = \frac{N!}{n!(N-n)!} = \frac{53!}{6!47!}$$

$$= \frac{(53)(52)(51)(50)(49)(48)(47!)}{(6)(5)(4)(3)(2)(1)(47!)}$$

$$= 22{,}957{,}480$$

Now, since the Lotto balls are selected at random, each of these 22,957,480 combinations is equally likely to occur. Therefore, the probability of winning Lotto is

$$P(\text{Win 6/53 Lotto}) = 1/(22{,}957{,}480) = .00000004356$$

This probability is often stated as follows: The odds of winning the game with a single ticket are 1 in 22,957,480, or, 1

in approximately 23 million. For all practical purposes, this probability is 0, implying that you have almost no chance of winning the lottery with a single ticket. Yet each week there is almost always a winner in the Florida Lotto. This apparent contradiction can be explained with the following analogy.

Suppose there is a line of minivans, front-to-back, from New York City to Los Angeles, California. Based on the distance between the two cities and the length of a standard minivan, there would be approximately 23 million minivans in line. Lottery officials will select, at random, one of the minivans and put a check for $10 million dollars in the glove compartment. For a cost of $1, you may roam the country and select one (and only one) minivan and check the glove compartment. Do you think you will find $10 million in the minivan you choose? You can be almost certain that you won't. But now permit anyone to enter the lottery for $1 and suppose that 50 million people do so. With such a large number of participants, it is very likely that someone will find the minivan with the $10 million—but it almost certainly won't be you! (This example illustrates an axiom in statistics called the Law of Large Numbers. See the footnote at the bottom of p. 149.)

Exercises 3.1–3.21

Learning the Mechanics

3.1 An experiment results in one of the following sample points: E_1, E_2, E_3, E_4, or E_5.
   a. Find $P(E_3)$ if $P(E_1) = .1$, $P(E_2) = .2$, $P(E_4) = .1$, and $P(E_5) = .1$.   .5
   b. Find $P(E_3)$ if $P(E_1) = P(E_3)$, $P(E_2) = .1$, $P(E_4) = .2$, and $P(E_5) = .1$.   .3
   c. Find $P(E_3)$ if $P(E_1) = P(E_2) = P(E_4) = P(E_5) = .1$.

3.2 The accompanying diagram describes the sample space of a particular experiment and events A and B.

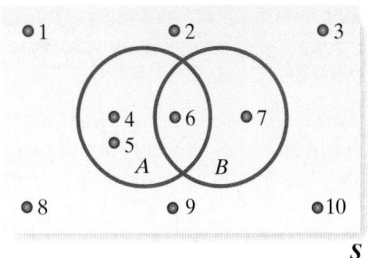

   a. What is this type of diagram called?
   b. Suppose the sample points are equally likely. Find $P(A)$ and $P(B)$.   .3, .2

c. Suppose $P(1) = P(2) = P(3) = P(4) = P(5) = \frac{1}{20}$ and $P(6) = P(7) = P(8) = P(9) = P(10) = \frac{3}{20}$. Find $P(A)$ and $P(B)$.

3.3 The sample space for an experiment contains five sample points with probabilities as shown in the table. Find the probability of each of the following events:

Sample Points	Probabilities
1	.05
2	.20
3	.30
4	.30
5	.15

A: {Either 1, 2, or 3 occurs}   .55
B: {Either 1, 3, or 5 occurs}   .50
C: {4 does not occur}   .70

3.4 Compute each of the following:
a. $\binom{9}{4}$ 126   **b.** $\binom{7}{2}$ **c.** $\binom{4}{4}$
d. $\binom{5}{0}$ **e.** $\binom{6}{5}$

3.5 Compute the number of ways you can select n elements from N elements for each of the following:
a. $n = 2, N = 5$ 10
b. $n = 3, N = 6$ 20
c. $n = 5, N = 20$ 15,504

3.6 Two fair dice are tossed, and the face on each die is observed.
a. List the 36 sample points contained in the sample space.
b. Assign probabilities to the sample points in part a.
c. Find the probability of each of the following events:

A = {3 showing on each die}   1/36
B = {sum of two numbers showing is 7}   6/36
C = {sum of two numbers showing is even}   18/36

3.7 Two marbles are drawn at random and without replacement from a box containing two blue marbles and three red marbles.
a. List the sample points for this experiment.
b. Assign probabilities to the sample points.
c. Determine the probability of observing each of the following events:

A: {Two blue marbles are drawn}   1/10
B: {A red and a blue marble are drawn}   3/5
C: {Two red marbles are drawn}   3/10

3.8 Simulate the experiment described in Exercise 3.7 using any five identically shaped objects, two of which are one color and three, another. Mix the objects, draw two, record the results, and then replace the

objects. Repeat the experiment a large number of times (at least 100). Calculate the proportion of time events A, B, and C occur. How do these proportions compare with the probabilities you calculated in Exercise 3.7? Should these proportions equal the probabilities? Explain.

Applying the Concepts — Basic

3.9 According to *USA Today* (Sep. 19, 2000), there are 650 members of the International Nanny Association (INA). Of these, only three are men. Find the probability that a randomly selected member of the INA is a man.   3/650

3.10 *The Wall Street Journal* (Sept. 1, 2000) reported on an independent study of postal workers and violence at post offices. In a sample of 12,000 postal workers, 600 of them were physically assaulted on the job in the past year. Use this information to estimate the probability that a randomly selected postal worker will be physically assaulted on the job during the year. $\frac{600}{12,000} = .05$

3.11 The United States Department of Agriculture (USDA) reports that, under its standard inspection system, one in every 100 slaughtered chickens pass inspection with fecal contamination. (*Tampa Tribune*, Mar. 31, 2000.)
a. If a slaughtered chicken is selected at random, what is the probability that it passes inspection with fecal contamination?   .01
b. The probability of part a was based on a USDA study which found that 306 of 32,075 chicken carcasses passed inspection with fecal contamination. Do you agree with the USDA's statement about the likelihood of a slaughtered chicken passing inspection with fecal contamination?   Yes

3.12 *Urban* and *rural* describe geographic areas upon which land zoning regulations, school district policy, and public service policy are often set. However, the characteristics of urban/rural areas are not clearly defined. Researchers at the University of Nevada (Reno) asked a sample of county commissioners to give their perception of the single most important factor in identifying urban counties (*Professional Geographer*, Feb. 2000). In all, five factors were mentioned by the commissioners: total population, agricultural change, presence of industry, growth, and population concentration. The survey results are displayed in the pie chart on p. 159. Suppose one of the commissioners is selected at random and the most important factor specified by the commissioner is recorded.
a. List the sample points for this experiment.
b. Assign reasonable probabilities to the sample points.
c. Find the probability that the most important factor specified by the commissioner is population related.   .68

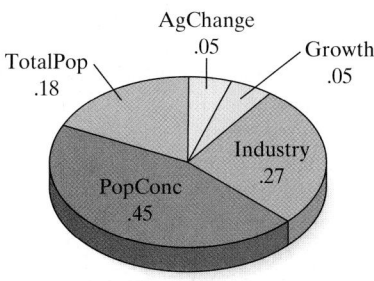

Applying the Concepts—Intermediate

3.13 *Total Quality Management* (TQM) has been defined as responsive customer service through continuously improved and redesigned work processes (*Quality Progress,* July 1995). In evaluating perceptions of TQM, a University of North Carolina in Charlotte study asked 159 employees to indicate how strongly they agreed or disagreed with a series of statements including: "I believe that management is committed to TQM." The following responses were received:

Strongly Agree	Agree	Neither Agree nor Disagree	Disagree	Strongly Disagree
30	64	41	18	6

Source: Buch, K., and Shelnut, J.W. "UNC Charlotte Measures the Effects of Its Quality Initiative." *Quality Progress,* July 1995, p. 75 (Table 2).

a. Define the experiment and list the sample points.
b. Assign probabilities to the sample points.
c. What is the probability that an employee agrees or strongly agrees with the above statement? 94/159
d. What is the probability that an employee does not strongly agree with the above statement? 129/159

3.14 The following table, extracted from *Railway Age* (May 1999), lists the number of carloads of different types of commodities that were shipped by the major U.S. railroads during a week. Suppose the computer record for a carload shipped during the week is randomly selected from a masterfile of all carloads shipped that week and the commodity type shipped is identified.

Type of Commodity	Number of Carloads
Agricultural products	41,690
Chemicals	38,331
Coal	124,595
Forest products	21,929
Metallic ores and minerals	34,521
Motor vehicles and equipment	22,906
Nonmetallic minerals and products	37,416
Other carloads	14,382
Total	335,770

Source: Railway Age, May 1999, p. 1.

a. List or describe the sample points in this experiment.
b. Find the probability of each sample point.
c. What is the probability that the rail car was transporting automobiles? Nonagricultural products?

d. What is the probability that the rail car contained chemicals or coal? .485
e. One of the carloads shipped that week was in a boxcar with serial number 1003642. What is the probability that that particular carload would be the one randomly selected from the computer file? Justify your answer. .00000298

3.15 From a list of 15 preferred stocks recommended by your broker, you will select three to invest in. How many different ways can you select the three stocks from the 15 recommended stocks? 455

3.16 The Quinella bet at the paramutual game of jai-alai consists of picking the jai-alai players that will place first and second in a game *irrespective* of order. In jai-alai, eight players (numbered 1, 2, 3, ..., 8) compete in every game.
a. How many different Quinella bets are possible? 28
b. Suppose you bet the Quinella combination of 2–7. If the players are of equal ability, what is the probability that you win the bet? 1/28

3.17 *The American Journal of Public Health* (July 1995) published a study on unintentional carbon monoxide (CO) poisoning of Colorado residents. A total of 981 cases of CO poisoning were reported during a six-year period. Each case was classified as fatal or nonfatal and by source of exposure. The number of cases occurring in each of the categories is shown in the next table. Assume that one of the 981 cases of unintentional CO poisoning is randomly selected.
a. List all sample points for this experiment.
b. What is the set of all sample points called?
c. Let A be the event that the CO poisoning is caused by fire. Find $P(A)$. .118
d. Let B be the event that the CO poisoning is fatal. Find $P(B)$. .177
e. Let C be the event that the CO poisoning is caused by auto exhaust. Find $P(C)$. .243
f. Let D be the event that the CO poisoning is caused by auto exhaust and is fatal. Find $P(D)$. .061
g. Let E be the event that the CO poisoning is caused by fire but is nonfatal. Find $P(E)$. .054

Source of Exposure	Fatal	Nonfatal	Total
Fire	63	53	116
Auto exhaust	60	178	238
Furnace	18	345	363
Kerosene or spaceheater	9	18	27
Appliance	9	63	72
Other gas-powered motor	3	73	76
Fireplace	0	16	16
Other	3	19	22
Unknown	9	42	51
Total	174	807	981

Source: Cook, M. C., Simon, P.A., and Hoffman, R. E. "Unintentional Carbon Monoxide Poisoning in Colorado, 1986 through 1991." *American Journal of Public Health,* Vol. 85. No. 7, July 1995, p. 989 (Table 1). American Public Health Association.

3.18 *Consumer Reports* magazine annually asks readers to evaluate their experiences in buying a new car during the previous year. Analysis of the questionnaires for a recent year revealed that readers' were most satisfied with the following three dealers (in no particular order): Infiniti, Saturn, and Saab (*Consumer Reports*, Apr. 1995).

a. List all possible sets of rankings for these top three dealers.

b. Assuming that each set of rankings in part a is equally likely, what is the probability that readers ranked Saturn first? That readers ranked Saturn third? That readers ranked Saturn first and Infiniti second (which is, in fact, what they did)? 1/3, 1/3, 1/6

Applying the Concepts—Advanced

3.19 Handicappers for greyhound races express their belief about the probabilities that each greyhound will win a race in terms of **odds.** If the probability of event E is $P(E)$, then the *odds in favor of E* are $P(E)$ to $1 - P(E)$. Thus, if a handicapper assesses a probability of .25 that Oxford Shoes will win its next race, the odds in favor of Oxford Shoes are $^{25}/_{100}$ to $^{75}/_{100}$, or 1 to 3. It follows that the *odds against E* are $1 - P(E)$ to $P(E)$, or 3 to 1 against a win by Oxford Shoes. In general, if the odds in favor of event E are a to b, then $P(E) = a/(a + b)$.

a. A second handicapper assesses the probability of a win by Oxford Shoes to be $^1/_3$. According to the second handicapper, what are the odds in favor of Oxford Shoes winning? 1 to 2

b. A third handicapper assesses the odds in favor of Oxford Shoes to be 1 to 1. According to the third handicapper, what is the probability of Oxford Shoes winning? 1/2

c. A fourth handicapper assesses the odds against Oxford Shoes winning to be 3 to 2. Find this handicapper's assessment of the probability that Oxford Shoes will win. 2/5

3.20 The Value Line Survey, a service for common stock investors, provides its subscribers with up-to-date evaluations of the prospects and risks associated with the purchase of a large number of common stocks. Each stock is ranked 1 (highest) to 5 (lowest) according to Value Line's estimate of the stock's potential for price appreciation during the next 12 months. Suppose you plan to purchase stock in three electrical utility companies from among seven that possess rankings of 2 for price appreciation. Unknown to you, two of the companies will experience serious difficulties with their nuclear facilities during the coming year. If you randomly select the three companies from among the seven, what is the probability that you select:

a. None of the companies with prospective nuclear difficulties? 10/35

b. One of the companies with prospective nuclear difficulties? 20/35

c. Both of the companies with prospective nuclear difficulties? 5/35

3.21 *Sustainable development or sustainable farming* means "finding ways to live and work the Earth without jeopardizing the future" (*Minneapolis Star Tribune*, June 20, 1992). Studies were conducted in five midwestern states to develop a profile of a sustainable farmer. The results revealed that farmers can be classified along a sustainability scale, depending on whether they are likely (L) or unlikely (U) to engage in the following practices: (1) Raise a broad mix of crops; (2) Raise livestock; (3) Use chemicals sparingly; (4) Use techniques for regenerating the soil, such as crop rotation.

a. List the different sets of classifications that are possible for the four practices (e.g., LUUL).

b. Suppose you are planning to interview farmers across the country to determine the frequency with which they fall into the classification sets you listed for part a. Since no information is yet available, assume initially that there is an equal chance of a farmer falling into any single classification set. Using that assumption, what is the probability that a farmer will be classified as unlikely on all four criteria (i.e., classified as a nonsustainable farmer)? 1/16

c. Using the same assumption as in part b, what is the probability that a farmer will be classified as likely on at least three of the criteria (i.e., classified as a near-sustainable farmer)? 5/16

3.2 Unions and Intersections

An event can often be viewed as a composition of two or more other events. Such events, which are called **compound events,** can be formed (composed) in two ways, as defined and illustrated here.

DEFINITION 3.5

The **union** of two events A and B is the event that occurs if either A or B or both occur on a single performance of the experiment. We denote the union of events A and B by the symbol $A \cup B$. $A \cup B$ consists of all the sample points that belong to A or B or both. (See Figure 3.6a.)

Figure 3.6
Venn diagrams for union
and intersection

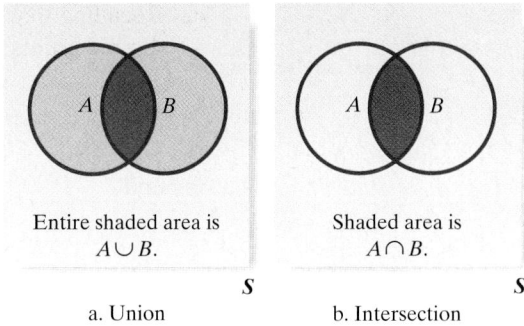

Entire shaded area is
$A \cup B$.

Shaded area is
$A \cap B$.

a. Union

b. Intersection

DEFINITION 3.6

The **intersection** of two events A and B is the event that occurs if both A and B occur on a single performance of the experiment. We write $A \cap B$ for the intersection of A and B. $A \cap B$ consists of all the sample points belonging to *both A and B*. (See Figure 3.6b.)

EXAMPLE 3.9   **PROBABILITIES OF UNIONS AND INTERSECTIONS**

Problem   Consider the die-toss experiment. Define the following events:

A: {Toss an even number}
B: {Toss a number less than or equal to 3}

{1, 2, 3, 4, 6}
{2}
5/6, 1/6

a.   Describe $A \cup B$ for this experiment.
b.   Describe $A \cap B$ for this experiment.
c.   Calculate $P(A \cup B)$ and $P(A \cap B)$ assuming the die is fair.

Solution   Draw the Venn diagram as shown in Figure 3.7

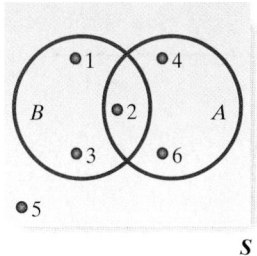

a.   The union of A and B is the event that occurs if we observe either an even number, a number less than or equal to 3, or both on a single throw of the die. Consequently, the sample points in the event $A \cup B$ are those for which A occurs, B occurs, or both A and B occur. Checking the sample points in the entire sample space, we find that the collection of sample points in the union of A and B is

$$A \cup B = \{1, 2, 3, 4, 6\}$$

Figure 3.7
Venn diagram for die toss

b.   The intersection of A and B is the event that occurs if we observe *both* an even number and a number less than or equal to 3 on a single throw of the die. Checking the sample points to see which imply the occurrence of *both* events A and B, we see that the intersection contains only one sample point:

$$A \cap B = \{2\}$$

In other words, the intersection of A and B is the sample point Observe a 2.

c. Recalling that the probability of an event is the sum of the probabilities of the sample points of which the event is composed, we have

$$P(A \cup B) = P(1) + P(2) + P(3) + P(4) + P(6)$$
$$= \frac{1}{6} + \frac{1}{6} + \frac{1}{6} + \frac{1}{6} + \frac{1}{6} = \frac{5}{6}$$

and

$$P(A \cap B) = P(2) = \frac{1}{6}$$

Now Work *Exercise 3.25 a–d*

■ ■ ■

EXAMPLE 3.10   FINDING PROBABILITIES IN A TWO-WAY TABLE

Problem   Many firms undertake direct marketing campaigns to promote their products. The campaigns typically involve mailing information to millions of households. The response rates are carefully monitored to determine the demographic characteristics of respondents. By studying tendencies to respond, the firms can better target future mailings to those segments of the population most likely to purchase their products.

Suppose a distributor of mail-order tools is analyzing the results of a recent mailing. The probability of response is believed to be related to income and age. The percentages of the total number of respondents to the mailing are given by income and age classification in Table 3.4. This table is called a **two-way table** since responses are classified according to two variables, income (columns) and age (rows).

Teaching Tip
When working with tables like Table 3.4, it is helpful to circle the values in the table that are in the event of interest.

TABLE 3.4   Two-Way Table with Percentage of Respondents in Age-Income Classes

	Income		
Age	<$25,000	$25,000–$50,000	>$50,000
<30 yrs	5%	12%	10%
30–50 yrs	14%	22%	16%
>50 yrs	8%	10%	3%

Define the following events:

A: {A respondent's income is more than $50,000}

B: {A respondent's age is 30 or more}

.29, .73   **a.** Find $P(A)$ and $P(B)$.

.83   **b.** Find $P(A \cup B)$.

.19   **c.** Find $P(A \cap B)$.

Solution   Following the steps for calculating probabilities of events, we first note that the objective is to characterize the income and age distribution of respondents to the mailing. To accomplish this, we define the experiment to consist of selecting a respondent from the collection of all respondents and observing which income and age class he or she occupies. The sample points are the nine different age-income classifications:

E_1: {<30 yrs, <$25,000} E_4: {<30 yrs, $25,000–$50,000} E_7: {<30 yrs, >$50,000}

E_2: {30–50 yrs, <$25,000} E_5: {30–50 yrs, $25,000–$50,000} E_8: {30–50 yrs, >$50,000}

E_3: { > 50 yrs, <$25,000} E_6: { > 50 yrs, $25,000–$50,000} E_9: { > 50 yrs, >$50,000}

Next, we assign probabilities to the sample points. If we blindly select one of the respondents, the probability that he or she will occupy a particular age-income classification is just the proportion, or relative frequency, of respondents in the classification. These proportions are given (as percentages) in Table 3.4. Thus,

$$P(E_1) = \text{Relative frequency of respondents in age-income class}$$
$$\{<30 \text{ yrs}, <\$25,000\} = .05$$

$$P(E_2) = .14$$
$$P(E_3) = .08$$
$$P(E_4) = .12$$
$$P(E_5) = .22$$
$$P(E_6) = .10$$
$$P(E_7) = .10$$
$$P(E_8) = .16$$
$$P(E_9) = .03$$

You may verify that the sample points probabilities add to 1.

a. To find $P(A)$, we first determine the collection of sample points contained in event A. Since A is defined as {>$50,000}, we see from Table 3.4 that A contains the three sample points represented by the last column of the table. In words, the event A consists of the income classification {>$50,000} in all three age classifications. The probability of A is the sum of the probabilities of the sample points in A:

$$P(A) = P(E_7) + P(E_8) + P(E_9) = .10 + .16 + .03 = .29$$

Similarly, B = {≥30 yrs} consists of the six sample points in the second and third rows of Table 3.4:

$$P(B) = P(E_2) + P(E_3) + P(E_5) + P(E_6) + P(E_8) + P(E_9)$$
$$= .14 + .08 + .22 + .10 + .16 + .03 = .73$$

b. The union of events A and B, $A \cup B$, consists of all the sample points in *either A or B or both*. That is, the union of A and B consists of all respondents whose income exceeds $50,000 *or* whose age is 30 or more. In Table 3.4 this is any sample point found in the third column *or* the last two rows. Thus,

$$P(A \cup B) = .10 + .14 + .22 + .16 + .08 + .10 + .03 = .83$$

c. The intersection of events A and B, $A \cap B$, consists of all sample points in *both A and B*. That is, the intersection of A and B consists of all respondents whose income exceeds $50,000 *and* whose age is 30 or more. In Table 3.4 this is any sample point found in the third column *and* the last two rows. Thus,

$$P(A \cap B) = .16 + .03 = .19$$

Look Back As with previous problems, the key to finding the probabilities of parts **b** and **c** is to identify the sample points that comprise the event of interest. In a two-way table like Table 3.4, the number of sample points will be equal to the number of rows times the number of columns.

| Now Work | *Exercise 3.27 f–g*

■ ■ ■

3.3 Complementary Events

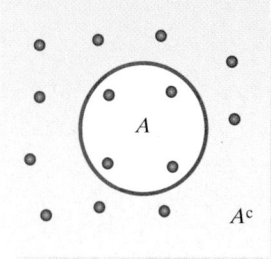

Figure 3.8
Venn diagram of complementary events

Teaching Tip

Key on the word *not* when working with complementary events. The complement of event *A* is the event that *A* does not occur, or *not A*.

Teaching Tip

Introduce the complement approach of solving probabilities as a method of simplifying the amount of work necessary to find probabilities.

A very useful concept in the calculation of event probabilities is the notion of *complementary events:*

> **DEFINITION 3.7**
>
> The **complement** of an event *A* is the event that *A* does *not* occur—that is, the event consisting of all sample points that are not in event *A*. We denote the complement of *A* by A^c.

An event *A* is a collection of sample points, and the sample points included in A^c are those not in *A*. Figure 3.8 demonstrates this idea. Note from the figure that all sample points in *S* are included in *either A* or A^c and that *no* sample point is in both *A* and A^c. This leads us to conclude that the probabilities of an event and its complement *must sum to 1:*

> **Rule of Complements**
>
> The sum of the probabilities of complementary events equals 1; that is, $P(A) + P(A^c) = 1.$

In many probability problems, calculating the probability of the complement of the event of interest is easier than calculating the event itself. Then, because

$$P(A) + P(A^c) = 1$$

we can calculate $P(A)$ by using the relationship

$$P(A) = 1 - P(A^c)$$

EXAMPLE 3.11   PROBABILITIES OF COMPLEMENTARY EVENTS

Problem Consider the experiment of tossing two fair coins. Use the complementary relationship to calculate the probability of event *A*: {Observing at least one head}.

$P(A) = 1 - \frac{1}{4} = \frac{3}{4}$

Solution We know that the event *A*: {Observing at least one head} consists of the sample points

$$A: \{HH, HT, TH\}$$

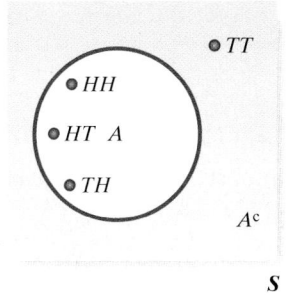

Figure 3.9
Complementary events
in the toss of two coins

The complement of A is defined as the event that occurs when A does not occur. Therefore,

$$A^c: \{\text{Observe no heads}\} = \{TT\}$$

This complementary relationship is shown in Figure 3.9. Assuming the coins are balanced,

$$P(A^c) = P(TT) = {}^1\!/_4$$

and

$$P(A) = 1 - P(A^c) = 1 - {}^1\!/_4 = {}^3\!/_4$$

Look Back Note that we could have found $P(A)$ by summing the probabilities of the sample points, HH, HT, and TH, in A. Many times it is easier to find the probability of A^c and use the Rule of Complements.

| Now Work | *Exercise 3.25e–f* |

■ ■ ■

3.4 The Additive Rule and Mutually Exclusive Events

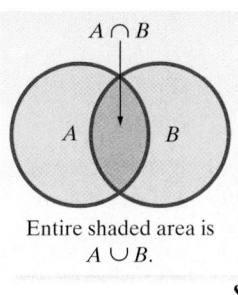

Figure 3.10
Venn diagram of union

In Section 3.2 we saw how to determine which sample points are contained in a union and how to calculate the probability of the union by adding the probabilities of the sample points in the union. It is also possible to obtain the probability of the union of two events by using the **additive rule of probability.**

The union of two events will often contain many sample points, since the union occurs if either one or both of the events occur. By studying the Venn diagram in Figure 3.10, you can see that the probability of the union of two events, A and B, can be obtained by summing $P(A)$ and $P(B)$ and subtracting the probability corresponding to $A \cap B$. Therefore, the formula for calculating the probability of the union of two events is given in the next box.

> **Additive Rule of Probability**
>
> The probability of the union of events A and B is the sum of the probabilities of events A and B minus the probability of the intersection of events A and B, that is,
>
> $$P(A \cup B) = P(A) + P(B) - P(A \cap B)$$

EXAMPLE 3.12   APPLYING THE ADDITIVE RULE

Problem Hospital records show that 12% of all patients are admitted for surgical treatment, 16% are admitted for obstetrics, and 2% receive both obstetrics and surgical treatment. If a new patient is admitted to the hospital, what is the probability that the patient will be admitted either for surgery, obstetrics, or both? Use the additive rule of probability to arrive at the answer.

.26

Solution Consider the following events:

A: {A patient admitted to the hospital receives surgical treatment}

B: {A patient admitted to the hospital receives obstetrics treatment}

Teaching Tip
Stress that the additive rule is useful only when we are working with *or* probabilities, i.e., *P(A or B)*.

Teaching Tip
Point out that the additive rule uses the *intersection* of events *A* and *B* to find the probability of the *union* of events *A* and *B*.

Then, from the given information,

$$P(A) = .12$$
$$P(B) = .16$$

and the probability of the event that a patient receives both obstetrics and surgical treatment is

$$P(A \cap B) = .02$$

The event that a patient admitted to the hospital receives either surgical treatment, obstetrics treatment, or both is the union $A \cup B$. The probability of $A \cup B$ is given by the additive rule of probability:

$$P(A \cup B) = P(A) + P(B) - P(A \cap B) = .12 + .16 - .02 = .26$$

Thus, 26% of all patients admitted to the hospital receive either surgical treatment, obstetrics treatment, or both.

Look Back From the information given, it is not possible to list and assign probabilities to all the sample points. Consequently, we cannot proceed through the five-step process (pro) for finding the probability of an event and must use the Additive Rule.

Now Work   *Exercise 3.22*

■ ■ ■

A very special relationship exists between events A and B when $A \cap B$ contains no sample points. In this case we call the events A and B *mutually exclusive events*.

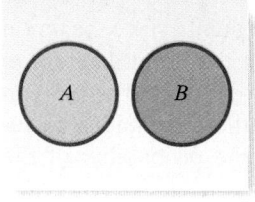

Figure 3.11
Venn diagram of mutually exclusive events.

Suggested Exercises 3.60

Suggested Exercises 3.30

DEFINITION 3.8

Events A and B are **mutually exclusive** if $A \cap B$ contains no sample points, that is, if A and B have no sample points in common.

Figure 3.11 shows a Venn diagram of two mutually exclusive events. The events A and B have no sample points in common, that is, A and B cannot occur simultaneously, and $P(A \cap B) = 0$. Thus, we have the important relationship given in the box.

Probability of Union of Two Mutually Exclusive Events

If two events A and B are *mutually exclusive*, the probability of the union of A and B equals the sum of the probabilities of A and B; that is, $P(A \cup B) = P(A) + P(B)$.

Caution

The formula just shown is *false* if the events are *not* mutually exclusive. In this case (i.e., two nonmutually exclusive events), you must apply the general additive rule of probability.

EXAMPLE 3.13   THE UNION OF TWO MUTUALLY EXCLUSIVE EVENTS

3/4

Problem   Consider the experiment of tossing two balanced coins. Find the probability of observing at *least* one head.

Solution   Define the events

$$A: \{\text{Observe at least one head}\}$$
$$B: \{\text{Observe exactly one head}\}$$
$$C: \{\text{Observe exactly two heads}\}$$

Note that

$$A = B \cup C$$

and that $B \cap C$ contains no sample points (see Figure 3.12). Thus, B and C are mutually exclusive, so that

$$P(A) = P(B \cup C) = P(B) + P(C) = \frac{1}{2} + \frac{1}{4} = \frac{3}{4}$$

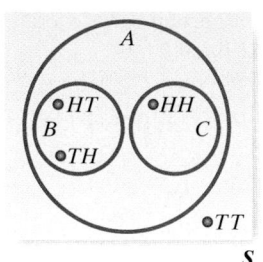

Figure 3.12
Venn diagram for coin-toss experiment

Look Back   Although this example is very simple, it shows us that writing events with verbal descriptions that include the phrases "at least" or "at most" as unions of mutually exclusive events is very useful. This practice enables us to find the probability of the event by adding the probabilities of the mutually exclusive events.

■ ■ ■

Statistics in Action

The Probability of Winning Lotto with a Wheel System

Refer to Florida's Pick-6 Lotto game in which you select six numbers of your choice from a field of numbers ranging from 1 to 53. In Section 3.2, we learned that the probability of winning Lotto on a single ticket is only 1 in approximately 23 million. The "experts" at Lotto Buster recommend many strategies for increasing the odds of winning the lottery. One strategy is to employ a *wheeling system*. In a complete wheeling system, you select more than six numbers, say, seven, and play every combination of six of those seven numbers.

Suppose you choose to "wheel" the following seven numbers: 2, 7, 18, 23, 30, 32, and 51. Every combination of six of these seven numbers is listed in Table SIA3.1. You can see that there are seven different possibilities. (Use the

Combinations Rule with $N = 7$ and $n = 6$ to verify this.) Thus, we would purchase seven tickets (at a cost of $7) corresponding to these different combinations in a complete wheeling system.

To determine if this strategy does, in fact, increase our odds of winning, we need to find the probability that one of these seven combinations occurs during the 6/53 Lotto draw. That is, we need to find the probability that either Ticket 1 or Ticket 2 or Ticket 3 or Ticket 4 or Ticket 5 or Ticket 6 or Ticket 7 is the winning combination. Note that this probability is stated using the word *or*, implying a union of seven events. Letting T1 represent the event that Ticket 1 wins, and defining T2, T3, ..., T7 in a similar fashion, we want to find

$$P(\text{T1 or T2 or T3 or T4 or T5 or T6 of T7})$$

TABLE SIA3.1	Wheeling the Six Numbers 2, 7, 18, 23, 30, 32, and 51					
Ticket 1	2	7	18	23	30	32
Ticket 2	2	7	18	23	30	51
Ticket 3	2	7	18	23	32	51
Ticket 4	2	7	18	30	32	51
Ticket 5	2	7	23	30	32	51
Ticket 6	2	18	23	30	32	51
Ticket 7	7	18	23	30	32	51

Recall (Section 3.2) that the 22,957,480 possible combinations in Pick-6 Lotto are mutually exclusive and equally likely to occur. Consequently, the probability of the union of the seven events is simply the sum of the probabilities of the individual events, where each event has probability of 1/(22,957,480):

$$P(\text{win Lotto with 7 Wheeled Numbers})$$
$$= P(T1 \text{ or } T2 \text{ or } T3 \text{ or } T4 \text{ or } T5 \text{ or } T6 \text{ or } T7)$$
$$= 7/(22,957,480) = .0000003$$

In terms of odds, we now have 3 chances in 10 million of winning the Lotto with the complete wheeling system. The "experts" are correct—our odds of winning Lotto have increased (from 1 in 23 million). However, the probability of winning is so close to 0 we question whether the $7 spent on lottery tickets is worth the negligible increase in odds. In fact, it can be shown that to increase your chance of winning the 6/53 Lotto to 1 chance in 100 (i.e., .01) using a complete wheeling system, you would have to wheel 26 of your favorite numbers—a total of 230,230 combinations at a cost of $230,230!

Exercises 3.22–3.38

Learning the Mechanics

3.22 Suppose $P(A) = .4, P(B) = .7,$ and $P(A \cap B) = .3.$ Find the following probabilities:
a. $P(B^c)$ .3 **b.** $P(A^c)$ .6 **c.** $P(A \cup B)$ .8

3.23 A fair coin is tossed three times and the events A and B are defined as follows:

A: {At least one head is observed}
B: {The number of heads observed is odd}

a. Identify the sample points in the events $A, B,$ $A \cup B, A^c$ and $A \cap B.$
b. Find $P(A), P(B), P(A \cup B), P(A^c),$ and $P(A \cap B)$ by summing the probabilities of the appropriate sample points. 7/8, 1/2, 7/8, 1/8, 1/2
c. Find $P(A \cup B)$ using the additive rule. Compare your answer to the one you obtained in part b. 7/8
d. Are the events A and B mutually exclusive? Why?

3.24 A pair of fair dice is tossed. Define the following events:

A: {You will roll a 7} (i.e., the sum of the dots on the up faces of the two dice is equal to 7)
B: {At least one of the two dice shows a 4}

a. Identify the sample points in the events $A, B,$ $A \cap B, A \cup B,$ and $A^c.$
b. Find $P(A), P(B), P(A \cap B), P(A \cup B),$ and $P(A^c)$ by summing the probabilities of the appropriate sample points.
c. Find $P(A \cup B)$ using the additive rule. Compare your answer to that for the same event in part b.
d. Are A and B mutually exclusive? Why? No

3.25 Consider the accompanying Venn diagram, where $P(E_1) = P(E_2) = P(E_3) = \frac{1}{5}, P(E_4) = P(E_5) = \frac{1}{20},$ $P(E_6) = \frac{1}{10},$ and $P(E_7) = \frac{1}{5}.$ Find each of the following probabilities:
a. $P(A)$ **b.** $P(B)$
c. $P(A \cup B)$ **d.** $P(A \cap B)$
e. $P(A^c)$ **f.** $P(B^c)$
g. $P(A \cup A^c)$ **h.** $P(A^c \cap B)$

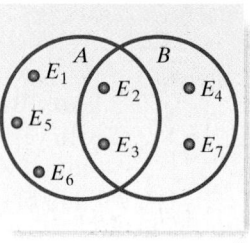

S

3.26 Consider the next Venn diagram, where

$$P(E_1) = .10, P(E_2) = .05, P(E_3) = P(E_4) = .2,$$
$$P(E_5) = .06, P(E_6) = .3, P(E_7) = .06, \text{ and}$$
$$P(E_8) = .03.$$

Find the following probabilities:
a. $P(A^c)$ **b.** $P(B^c)$ **c.** $P(A^c \cap B)$ **d.** $P(A \cup B)$
e. $P(A \cap B)$ .31 **f.** $P(A^c \cup B^c)$ .69
g. Are events A and B mutually exclusive? Why?

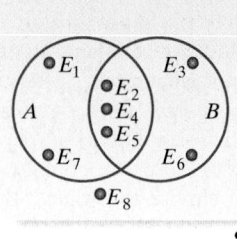

S

3.27 The outcomes of two variables are (Low, Medium, High) and (On, Off), respectively. An experiment is conducted in which the outcomes of each of the two variables are observed. The probabilities associated with each of the six possible outcome pairs are given in the accompanying two-way table.

	Low	Medium	High
On	.50	.10	.05
Off	.25	.07	.03

Consider the following events:

A: {On}
B: {Medium or On}
C: {Off and Low}
D: {High}

a. Find $P(A)$ .65
b. Find $P(B)$.   .72
c. Find $P(C)$.   .25
d. Find $P(D)$.   .08
e. Find $P(A^c)$.   .35
f. Find $P(A \cup B)$.   .72
g. Find $P(A \cap C)$.   0
h. Consider each pair of events (A and B, A and C, A and D, B and C, B and D, C and D). List the pairs of events that are mutually exclusive. Justify your choices.   A and C, B and C, C and D

3.28 Refer to Exercise 3.27. Use the same event definitions to do the following exercises.
a. Write the event that the outcome is "On" and "High" as an intersection of two events.
b. Write the event that the outcome is "Low" or "Medium" as the complement of an event.

Applying the Concepts—Basic

3.29 According to the *Journal of Business Venturing* (Vol. 17, 2002), 27% of all small businesses owned by non-Hispanic whites nationwide are women-owned firms. If we select, at random, a small business owned by a non-Hispanic white, what is the probability that it is a male-owned firm?   .73

3.30 *Roulette* is a very popular game in many American casinos. In roulette, a ball spins on a circular wheel that is divided into 38 arcs of equal length, bearing the numbers 00, 0, 1, 2, ..., 35, 36. The number of the arc on which the ball stops is the outcome of one play of the game. The numbers are also colored in the following manner:

Red: 1, 3, 5, 7, 9, 12, 14, 16, 18, 19, 21, 23, 25, 27, 30, 32, 34, 36
Black: 2, 4, 6, 8, 10, 11, 13, 15, 17, 20, 22, 24, 26, 28, 29, 31, 33, 35
Green: 00, 0

Players may place bets on the table in a variety of ways, including bets on odd, even, red, black, high, low, etc. Define the following events:

A: {Outcome is an odd number (00 and 0 are considered neither odd nor even)}
B: {Outcome is a black number}
C: {Outcome is a low number (1–18)}

a. Define the event $A \cap B$ as a specific set of sample points.
b. Define the event $A \cup B$ as a specific set of sample points.

c. Find $P(A)$, $P(B)$, $P(A \cap B)$, $P(A \cup B)$, and $P(C)$ by summing the probabilities of the appropriate sample points.   9/19, 9/19, 4/19, 14/19, 9/19
d. Define the event $A \cap B \cap C$ as a specific set of sample points.
e. Find $P(A \cup B)$ using the additive rule. Are events A and B mutually exclusive? Why?   14/19
f. Find $P(A \cap B \cap C)$ by summing the probabilities of the sample points given in part d.   2/19
g. Define the event $(A \cup B \cup C)$ as a specific set of sample points.
h. Find $P(A \cup B \cup C)$ by summing the probabilities of the sample points given in part g.

3.31 A state energy agency mailed questionnaires on energy conservation to 1,000 homeowners in the state capital. Five hundred questionnaires were returned. Suppose an experiment consists of randomly selecting and reviewing one of the returned questionnaires. Consider the events:

A: {The home is constructed of brick}
B: {The home is more than 30 years old}
C: {The home is heated with oil}

Describe each of the following events in terms of unions, intersections, and complements (i.e., $A \cup B$, $A \cap B$, A^c, etc.):
a. The home is more than 30 years old and is heated with oil.   B ∩ C
b. The home is not constructed of brick.   A^c
c. The home is heated with oil or is more than 30 years old.   C ∪ B
d. The home is constructed of brick and is not heated with oil.   A ∩ C^c

3.32 The long-run success of a business depends on its ability to market products with superior characteristics that maximize consumer satisfaction and that give the firm a competitive advantage (Kotler, *Marketing Management*, 1994). Ten new products have been developed by a food-products firm. Market research has indicated that the 10 products have the characteristics described by the following Venn diagram.

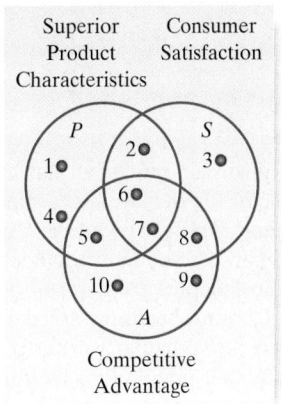

a. Write the event that a product possesses all the desired characteristics as an intersection of the events defined in the Venn diagram. Which products are contained in this intersection?

b. If one of the 10 products were selected at random to be marketed, what is the probability that it would possess all the desired characteristics? 1/5

c. Write the event that the randomly selected product would give the firm a competitive advantage or would satisfy consumers as a union of the events defined in the Venn diagram. Find the probability of this union.

d. Write the event that the randomly selected product would possess superior product characteristics and satisfy consumers. Find the probability of this intersection.

Applying the Concepts-Intermediate

3.33 The *Journal of the American Law and Economics Association* (Vol. 3, 2001) published the results of a study of appeals of federal civil trials. The following table, extracted from the article, gives a breakdown of 2,143 civil cases that were appealed by either the plaintiff or defendant. The outcome of the appeal, as well as the type of trial (judge or jury), was determined for each civil case. Suppose one of the 2,143 cases is selected at random and both the outcome of the appeal and type of trial are observed.

	Jury	Judge	Totals
Plaintiff trial win—reversed	194	71	265
Plaintiff trial win—affirmed/dismissed	429	240	669
Defendant trial win—reversed	111	68	179
Defendant trial win—affirmed/dismissed	731	299	1,030
Totals	1,465	678	2,143

a. List the sample points for this experiment.

b. Find $P(A)$, where $A = \{$jury trial$\}$. .684

c. Find $P(B)$, where $B = \{$plaintiff trial win is reversed$\}$. .124

d. Are A and B mutually exclusive events? No

e. Find $P(A^c)$. .316

f. Find $P(A \cup B)$. .717

g. Find $P(A \cap B)$. .091

3.34 Corporate downsizing in Japan has caused a significant increase in the demand for temporary and part-time workers. The distribution (in percent) of nonregular workers in Japan (by age) is provided in the next table (adapted from *Monthly Labor Review*, Oct. 1995). Column headings are defined below the table. Suppose a nonregular worker is to be chosen at random from this population. Define the following events:

A: {The worker is 40 or over}
B: {The worker is a teenager and part time}
C: {The worker is under 40 and either arubaito or dispatched}
D: {The worker is part time}

a. Find the probability of each of the above events.

b. Find $P(A \cap D)$ and $P(A \cup D)$.

c. Describe in words the following events: A^c, B^c, and D^c.

d. Find the probability of each of the events you described in part c.

Age	Part Time	Arubaito	Temporary and Day	Dispatched	Totals
15–19	.3	3.7	2.3	.2	6.5
20–29	3.4	7.8	6.1	4.7	22.0
30–39	8.4	1.6	4.5	2.7	17.2
40–49	15.6	1.6	7.3	1.4	25.9
50–59	9.4	1.1	5.8	.6	16.9
60 and over	4.3	1.8	4.8	.6	11.5
Totals	41.4	17.6	30.8	10.2	100.0

Part time: Work fewer hours per day or days per week than regular workers; arubaito: someone with a "side" job who is in school or has regular employment elsewhere; temporary: employed on a contract lasting more than one month but less than one year; day: employed on a contract of less than one month's duration; dispatched: hired from a temporary-help agency.

Source: Houseman, S., and Osawa, M. "Part-Time and Temporary Employment in Japan." Monthly Labor Review, October 1995, pp. 12–13 (Tables 1 and 2).

3.35 E* Trade Group Inc. was the first to provide online securities trading for its clients, offering an alternative to traditional investment firms. According to *Business Week*, online securities trading now accounts for a significant share of the brokerage business. The table on p. 171 reports the number of online and traditional accounts for five leading brokerages.

Suppose a customer account is to be drawn at random from the population of accounts described in the table. Consider the following events:

A: {The account is with Merrill Lynch}
B: {The account is an online account}
C: {The account is with E* Trade and is an on-line account}
D: {The account is either with TD Waterhouse or E* Trade, and is an online account}
E: {The account is with E* Trade}

a. Find the probability of each of the afore mentioned events.

b. Find $P(A \cap B)$. 0

c. Find $P(A \cup B)$. .557

d. Find $P(B^c \cap E)$. 0

e. Find $P(A \cup E)$. .325

f. Which pairs of events are mutually exclusive?

Table for Exercise 3.35

Brokerage Firms	On-line Accounts	Traditional Accounts	Total Accounts
Fidelity Investments	2.8 million	8.0 million	10.8 million
Merrill Lynch & Co.	0	8.0 million	8.0 million
Charles Schwab & Co.	2.8 million	3.5 million	6.3 million
TD Waterhouse Group Inc.	1.0 million	1.1 million	2.1 million
E* Trade Group Inc.	1.24 million	0	1.24 million
Totals	7.84 million	20.6 million	28.44 million

Source: Business Week, October 18, 1999, pp. 185–186.

3.36 The *American Journal of Public Health* (Jan. 2002) reported on a study of elderly wheelchair users who live at home. A sample of 306 wheelchair users, age 65 or older, were surveyed about whether they had an injurious fall during the year and whether their home features any one of five structural modifications: bathroom modifications, widened doorways/hallways, kitchen modifications, installed railings, and easy-open doors. The responses are summarized in the accompanying table. Suppose we select, at random, one of the 306 surveyed wheelchair users.

Home Features	Injurious Fall(s)	No Falls	Totals
All 5	2	7	9
At least 1, but not all	26	162	188
None	20	89	109
Totals	48	258	306

Source: Berg, K., Hines, M., and Allen, S. "Wheelchair Users at Home: Few Home Modifications and Many Injurious Falls," *American Journal of Public Health*, Vol. 92, No. 1, Jan. 2002 (Table 1).

a. Find the probability that the wheelchair user had an injurious fall. .157

b. Find the probability that the wheelchair user had all five features installed in the home. .029

c. Find the probability that the wheelchair user had no falls and none of the features installed in the home. .291

3.37 Tire and automobile manufacturers and consumer safety experts all recommend that drivers maintain proper tire pressure in their cars. Consequently, many gas stations now provide air pumps and air gauges for their customers. In a *Research Note* (Nov. 2001), the National Highway Traffic Safety Administration studied the reliability of gas station air pumps. The following table gives the percentage of gas stations that provide air gauges that overreport the pressure level in the tire.

Station Gauge Pressure	Overreport by 4 psi or more (%)	Overreport by 6 psi or more (%)	Overreport by 8 psi or more (%)
25 psi	16	2	0
35 psi	19	9	0
45 psi	19	14	5
55 psi	20	15	9

a. If the gas station air pressure gauge reads 35 psi, what is the probability that the pressure is overreported by 6 psi or more? .09

b. If the gas station air pressure gauge reads 55 psi, what is the probability that the pressure is overreported by 8 psi or more? .09

c. If the gas station air pressure gauge reads 25 psi, what is the probability that the pressure is not overreported by 4 psi or more? .84

d. Are the events A = {overreport by 4 psi or more} and B = {overreport by 6 psi or more} mutually exclusive events? Explain. No

e. Based on your answer to part d, why do the probabilities in the table not sum to 1?

3.38 Identifying managerial prospects who are both talented and motivated is difficult. A human resources director constructed the following two-way table to define nine combinations of talent-motivation levels. The number in a cell is the director's estimate of the probability that a managerial prospect will fall in that category. Suppose the director has decided to hire a new manager. Define the following events:

A: {Prospect places in high-motivation category}

B: {Prospect places in high-talent category}

C: {Prospect is medium or better in both categories}

D: {Prospect places low in at least one category}

E: {Prospect places highest in both categories}

Motivation	Talent		
	High	Medium	Low
High	.05	.16	.05
Medium	.19	.32	.05
Low	.11	.05	.02

a. Does the sum of the cell probabilities equal 1?

b. List the sample points in each of the events described above and find their probabilities.

c. Find $P(A \cup B)$, $P(A \cap B)$, and $P(A \cup C)$.

d. Find $P(A^c)$ and explain what this means from a practical point of view. .74

e. Consider each pair of events (A and B, A and C, etc.). Which of the pairs are mutually exclusive? Why?

3.5 Conditional Probability

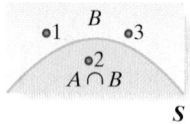

Figure 3.13
Reduced sample space for the die-toss experiment given that event B has occurred

The event probabilities we've been discussing give the relative frequencies of the occurrences of the events when the experiment is repeated a very large number of times. Such probabilities are often called **unconditional probabilities** because no special conditions are assumed, other than those that define the experiment.

Often, however, we have additional knowledge that might affect the likelihood of the outcome of an experiment, so we need to alter the probability of an event of interest. A probability that reflects such additional knowledge is called the **conditional probability** of the event. For example, we've seen that the probability of observing an even number (event A) on a toss of a fair die is $\frac{1}{2}$. But suppose we're given the information that on a particular throw of the die the result was a number less than or equal to 3 (event B). Would the probability of observing an even number on that throw of the die still be equal to $\frac{1}{2}$? It can't be, because making the assumption that B has occurred reduces the sample space from six sample points to three sample points (namely, those contained in event B). This reduced sample space is as shown in Figure 3.13.

Because the sample points for the die-toss experiment are equally likely, each of the three sample points in the reduced sample space is assigned an equal *conditional probability* of $\frac{1}{3}$. Since the only even number of the three in the reduced sample space B is the number 2 and the die is fair, we conclude that the probability that A occurs *given that B occurs* is $\frac{1}{3}$. We use the symbol $P(A|B)$ to represent the probability of event A given that event B occurs. For the die-toss example $P(A|B) = \frac{1}{3}$.

To get the probability of event A given that event B occurs, we proceed as follows. We divide the probability of the part of A that falls within the reduced sample space B, namely $P(A \cap B)$, by the total probability of the reduced sample space, namely, $P(B)$. Thus, for the die-toss example with event A: {Observe an even number} and event B: {Observe a number less than or equal to 3}, we find

$$P(A|B) = \frac{P(A \cap B)}{P(B)} = \frac{P(2)}{P(1) + P(2) + P(3)} = \frac{\frac{1}{6}}{\frac{3}{6}} = \frac{1}{3}$$

The formula for $P(A|B)$ is true in general:

Conditional Probability Formula

To find the *conditional probability that event A occurs given that event B occurs*, divide the probability that *both A and B occur* by the probability that *B occurs*, that is,

$$P(A|B) = \frac{P(A \cap B)}{P(B)} \quad \text{[We assume that } P(B) \neq 0.\text{]}$$

This formula adjusts the probability of $A \cap B$ from its original value in the complete sample space S to a conditional probability in the reduced sample space B. If the sample points in the complete sample space are equally likely, then the formula will assign equal probabilities to the sample points in the reduced sample space, as in the die-toss experiment. If, on the other hand, the sample points have unequal probabilities, the formula will assign conditional probabilities proportional to the probabilities in the complete sample space. This is illustrated by the following examples.

EXAMPLE 3.14

APPLYING THE CONDITIONAL PROBABILITY FORMULA

Problem

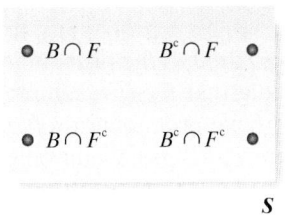

Figure 3.14
Sample space for contacting a sales prospect

2/3

Suppose you are interested in the probability of the sale of a large piece of earth-moving equipment. A single prospect is contacted. Let F be the event that the buyer has sufficient money (or credit) to buy the product and let F^c denote the complement of F (the event that the prospect does not have the financial capability to buy the product). Similarly, let B be the event that the buyer wishes to buy the product and let B^c be the complement of that event. Then the four sample points associated with the experiment are shown in Figure 3.14, and their probabilities are given in Table 3.5. Use the sample point probabilities to find the probability that a single prospect will buy, given that the prospect is able to finance the purchase.

TABLE 3.5 Probabilities of Customer Desire to Buy and Ability to Finance

		Desire	
		To Buy, B	Not to Buy, B^c
Able to Finance	**Yes, F**	.2	.1
	No, F^c	.4	.3

Solution

Teaching Tip
When tables are used, show the students that the conditional probabilities can be calculated without using the formula. Restrict the sample space to just those outcomes that have been given and solve the probability using the reduced sample space.

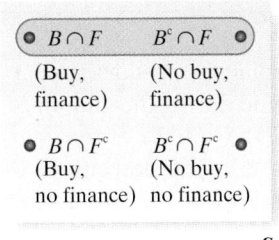

Figure 3.15
Subspace (shaded) containing sample points implying a financially able prospect

Suggested Exercises 3.62

Suppose you consider the large collection of prospects for the sale of your product and randomly select one person from this collection. What is the probability that the person selected will buy the product? In order to buy the product, the customer must be financially able *and* have the desire to buy, so this probability would correspond to the entry in Table 3.5 {To buy, B} and next to {Yes, F}, or $P(B \cap F) = .2$. This is the unconditional probability of the event $B \cap F$.

In contrast, suppose you know that the prospect selected has the financial capability for purchasing the product. Now you are seeking the probability that the customer will buy given (the condition) that the customer has the financial ability to pay. This probability, the conditional probability of B given that F has occurred and denoted by the symbol $P(B|F)$, would be determined by considering only the sample points in the reduced sample space containing the sample points $B \cap F$ and $B^c \cap F$—that is, sample points that imply the prospect is financially able to buy. (This subspace is shaded in Figure 3.15.) From our definition of conditional probability,

$$P(B|F) = \frac{P(B \cap F)}{P(F)}$$

where $P(F)$ is the sum of the probabilities of the two sample points corresponding to $B \cap F$ and $B^c \cap F$ (given in Table 3.5). Then

$$P(F) = P(B \cap F) + P(B^c \cap F) = .2 + .1 = .3$$

and the conditional probability that a prospect buys, given that the prospect is financially able, is

$$P(B|F) = \frac{P(B \cap F)}{P(F)} = \frac{.2}{.3} = .667$$

As we would expect, the probability that the prospect will buy, given that he or she is financially able, is higher than the unconditional probability of selecting a prospect who will buy.

Look Back Note that the conditional probability formula assigns a probability to the event $(B \cap F)$ in the reduced sample space that is proportional to the probability of the event in the complete sample space. To see this, note that the two sample points in the reduced sample space, $(B \cap F)$ and $(B^c \cap F)$, have probabilities of .2 and .1, respectively, in the complete sample space S. The formula assigns conditional probabilities $\frac{2}{3}$ and $\frac{1}{3}$ (use the formula to check the second one) to these sample points in the reduced sample space F, so that the conditional probabilities retain the 2 to 1 proportionality of the original sample point probabilities.

Now Work *Exercise 3.39a–b*

■ ■ ■

EXAMPLE 3.15   APPLYING THE CONDITIONAL PROBABILITY FORMULA

Problem The investigation of consumer product complaints by the Federal Trade Commission (FTC) has generated much interest by manufacturers in the quality of their products. A manufacturer of an electromechanical kitchen utensil conducted an analysis of a large number of consumer complaints and found that they fell into the six categories shown in Table 3.6. If a consumer complaint is received, what is the probability that the cause of the complaint was product appearance given that the complaint originated during the guarantee period?

.51

TABLE 3.6   Distribution of Product Complaints

	Reason for Complaint			
Complaint Origin	Electrical	Mechanical	Appearance	Totals
During Guarantee Period	18%	13%	32%	63%
After Guarantee Period	12%	22%	3%	37%
Totals	30%	35%	35%	100%

Solution Let A represent the event that the cause of a particular complaint is product appearance, and let B represent the event that the complaint occurred during the guarantee period. Checking Table 3.6, you can see that $(18 + 13 + 32)\% = 63\%$ of the complaints occur during the guarantee period. Hence, $P(B) = .63$. The percentage of complaints that were caused by the appearance and occurred during the guarantee period (the event $A \cap B$) is 32%. Therefore, $P(A \cap B) = .32$.

Using these probability values, we can calculate the conditional probability $P(A|B)$ that the cause of a complaint is appearance given that the complaint occurred during the guarantee time:

$$P(A|B) = \frac{P(A \cap B)}{P(B)} = \frac{.32}{.63} = .51$$

Consequently, we can see that slightly more than half the complaints that occurred during the guarantee period were due to scratches, dents, or other imperfections in the surface of the kitchen devices.

Look Back Note that the answer, $\dfrac{.32}{.63}$, is the proportion for the event of interest A (.32) divided by the row total proportion for the given event B (.63). That is, it is the proportion of the time A occurs within the given event B.

Now Work   *Exercise 3.50*

■ ■ ■

3.6 The Multiplicative Rule and Independent Events

The probability of an intersection of two events can be calculated using the multiplicative rule, which employs the conditional probabilities we defined in the previous section. Actually, we have already developed the formula in another context (page 144). You will recall that the formula for calculating the conditional probability of A given B is

$$P(A|B) = \frac{P(A \cap B)}{P(B)}$$

Multiplying both sides of this equation by $P(B)$, we obtain a formula for the probability of the intersection of events A and B. This is often called the **Multiplicative Rule of Probability.**

Teaching Tip
Stress that the multiplicative rule is useful when solving *and* probabilities, i.e., *P(A and B)*.

Multiplicative Rule of Probability

$P(A \cap B) = P(A)P(B|A)$ or, equivalently, $P(A \cap B) = P(B)P(A|B)$

EXAMPLE 3.16   APPLYING THE MULTIPLICATIVE RULE

Problem   An investor in wheat futures is concerned with the following events:

.0005

B: {U.S. production of wheat will be profitable next year}
A: {A serious drought will occur next year}

Based on available information, the investor believes that the probability is .01 that production of wheat will be profitable *assuming* a serious drought will occur in the same year and that the probability is .05 that a serious drought will occur. That is,

$$P(B|A) = .01 \text{ and } P(A) = .05$$

Based on the information provided, what is the probability that a serious drought will occur and that a profit will be made? That is, find $P(A \cap B)$, the probability of the intersection of events A and B.

Solution   We want to calculate $P(A \cap B)$. Using the formula for the multiplicative rule, we obtain

$$P(A \cap B) = P(A)P(B|A) = (.05)(.01) = .0005$$

The probability that a serious drought occurs and the production of wheat is profitable is only .0005. As we might expect, this intersection is a very rare event.

Now Work   *Exercise 3.52*

■ ■ ■

Intersections often contain only a few sample points. In this case, the probability of an intersection is easy to calculate by summing the appropriate sample point probabilities. However, the formula for calculating intersection probabilities is invaluable when the intersection contains numerous sample points, as the next example illustrates.

EXAMPLE 3.17   APPLYING THE MULTIPLICATIVE RULE

Problem   A county welfare agency employs 10 welfare workers who interview prospective food stamp recipients. Periodically the supervisor selects, at random, the forms completed by two workers to audit for illegal deductions. Unknown to the supervisor, three of the workers have regularly been giving illegal deductions to applicants. What is the probability that both of the two workers chosen have been giving illegal deductions?

Solution   Define the following two events:

$$A: \{\text{First worker selected gives illegal deductions}\}$$
$$B: \{\text{Second worker selected gives illegal deductions}\}$$

We want to find the probability of the event that both selected workers have been giving illegal deductions. This event can be restated as: {First worker gives illegal deductions *and* second worker gives illegal deductions}. Thus, we want to find the probability of the intersection, $A \cap B$. Applying the multiplicative rule, we have

$$P(A \cap B) = P(A)P(B|A)$$

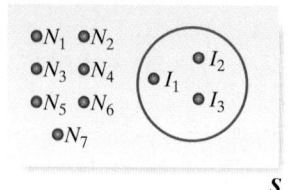

Figure 3.16
Venn diagram for finding $P(A)$

To find $P(A)$ it is helpful to consider the experiment as selecting one worker from the 10. Then the sample space for the experiment contains 10 sample points (representing the 10 welfare workers), where the three workers giving illegal deductions are denoted by the symbol I (I_1, I_2, I_3), and the seven workers not giving illegal deductions are denoted by the symbol N ($N_1, \ldots, N_7$). The resulting Venn diagram is illustrated in Figure 3.16.

Since the first worker is selected at random from the 10, it is reasonable to assign equal probabilities to the 10 sample points. Thus, each sample point has a probability of $1/10$. The sample points in event A are $\{I_1, I_2, I_3\}$ —the three workers who are giving illegal deductions. Thus,

$$P(A) = P(I_1) + P(I_2) + P(I_3) = \frac{1}{10} + \frac{1}{10} + \frac{1}{10} = \frac{3}{10}$$

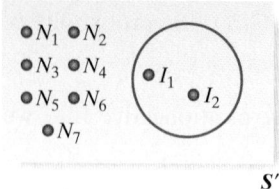

Figure 3.17
Venn diagram for finding $P(B|A)$

To find the conditional probability, $P(B|A)$, we need to alter the sample space S. Since we know A has occurred [the first worker selected is giving illegal deductions (say I_3), only two of the nine remaining workers in the sample space are giving illegal deductions]. The Venn diagram for this new sample space (S') is shown in Figure 3.17. Each of these nine sample points are equally likely, so each is assigned a probability of $1/9$. Since the event ($B|A$) contains the sample points $\{I_1, I_2\}$, we have

$$P(B|A) = P(I_1) + P(I_2) = \frac{1}{9} + \frac{1}{9} = \frac{2}{9}$$

Substituting $P(A) = {}^3/_{10}$ and $P(B|A) = {}^2/_9$ into the formula for the multiplicative rule, we find

$$P(A \cap B) = P(A)P(B|A) = ({}^3/_{10})({}^2/_9) = {}^6/_{90} = {}^1/_{15}$$

Thus, there is a 1 in 15 chance that both workers chosen by the supervisor have been giving illegal deductions to food stamp recipients.

Look Back The key words *both* and *and* in the statement "both A and B occur" imply an intersection of two events, which in turn implies that we should *multiply* probabilities to obtain the probability of interest.

| Now Work | *Exercise 3.43c* |

■ ■ ■

The sample space approach is only one way to solve the problem posed in Example 3.17. An alternative method employs the concept of a **tree diagram**. Tree diagrams are helpful for calculating the probability of an intersection.

To illustrate, a tree diagram for Example 3.17 is displayed in Figure 3.18. The tree begins at the far left with two branches. These branches represent the two possible outcomes N (no illegal deductions) and I (illegal deductions) for the first worker selected. The unconditional probability of each outcome is given (in parentheses) on the appropriate branch. That is, for the first worker selected, $P(N) = {}^7/_{10}$ and $P(I) = {}^3/_{10}$. (These can be obtained by summing sample point probabilities as in Example 3.17.)

The next level of the tree diagram (moving to the right) represents the outcomes for the second worker selected. The probabilities shown here are conditional probabilities since the outcome for the first worker is assumed to be known. For example, if the first worker is giving illegal deductions *(I)*, the probability that the second worker is also giving illegal deductions *(I)* is ${}^2/_9$ since of the nine workers left to be selected, only two remain who are giving illegal deductions. This conditional probability, ${}^2/_9$, is shown in parentheses on the bottom branch of Figure 3.18.

Figure 3.18
Tree diagram for
Example 3.17

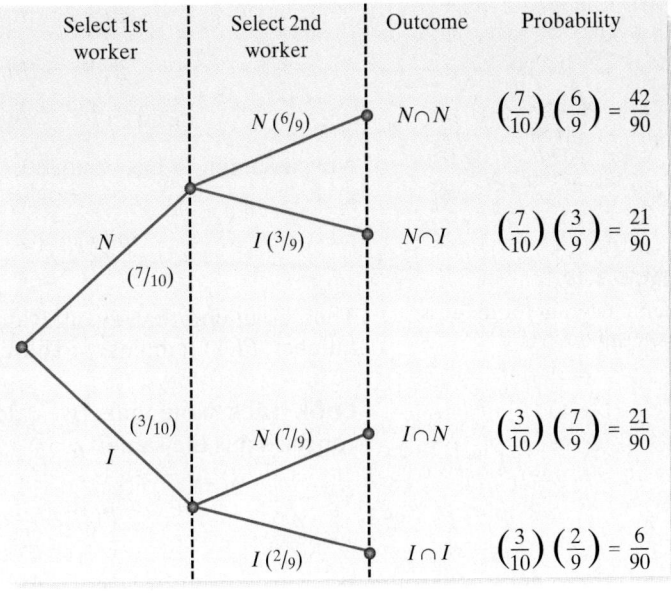

| Select 1st worker | Select 2nd worker | Outcome | Probability |

$N \cap N$ $\left(\frac{7}{10}\right)\left(\frac{6}{9}\right) = \frac{42}{90}$

$N \cap I$ $\left(\frac{7}{10}\right)\left(\frac{3}{9}\right) = \frac{21}{90}$

$I \cap N$ $\left(\frac{3}{10}\right)\left(\frac{7}{9}\right) = \frac{21}{90}$

$I \cap I$ $\left(\frac{3}{10}\right)\left(\frac{2}{9}\right) = \frac{6}{90}$

Finally, the four possible outcomes of the experiment are shown at the end of each of the four tree branches. These events are intersections of two events (outcome of first worker and outcome of second worker). Consequently, the multiplicative rule is applied to calculate each probability, as shown in Figure 3.18. You can see that the intersection $\{I \cap I\}$ (i.e., the event that both workers selected are giving illegal deductions) has probability $^6/_{90} = ^1/_{15}$—the same value obtained in Example 3.17.

In Section 3.5 we showed that the probability of an event A may be substantially altered by the knowledge that an event B has occurred. However, this will not always be the case. In some instances, the assumption that event B has occurred will *not* alter the probability of event A at all. When this is true, we say that the two events A and B are *independent events*.

DEFINITION 3.9

Events A and B are **independent events** if the occurrence of B does not alter the probability that A has occurred; that is, events A and B are independent if

$$P(A|B) = P(A)$$

When events A and B are independent, it is also true that

$$P(B|A) = P(B)$$

Events that are not independent are said to be **dependent.**

EXAMPLE 3.18   CHECKING FOR INDEPENDENCE

Problem   Consider the experiment of tossing a fair die and let

A: {Observe an even number}
B: {Observe a number less than or equal to 4}

Yes

Are events A and B independent?

Solution   The Venn diagram for this experiment is shown in Figure 3.19. We first calculate

$$P(A) = P(2) + P(4) + P(6) = {}^1/_2$$
$$P(B) = P(1) + P(2) + P(3) + P(4) = {}^2/_3$$
$$P(A \cap B) = P(2) + P(4) = {}^1/_3$$

Now assuming B has occurred, the conditional probability of A given B is

$$P(A|B) = \frac{P(A \cap B)}{P(B)} = \frac{\frac{1}{3}}{\frac{2}{3}} = \frac{1}{2} = P(A)$$

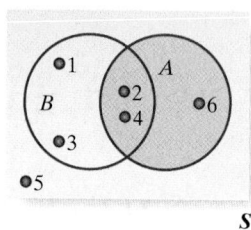

Figure 3.19
Venn diagram for die-toss experiment

Thus, assuming that event B does not alter the probability of observing an even number, $P(A)$ remains $^1/_2$. Therefore, the events A and B are independent.

Look Back   Note that if we calculate the conditional probability of B given A, our conclusion is the same:

$$P(B|A) = \frac{P(A \cap B)}{P(A)} = \frac{\frac{1}{3}}{\frac{1}{2}} = \frac{2}{3} = P(B)$$

■ ■ ■

Biography

BLAISE PASCAL (1623–1662) Solver of Chevalier's Dilemma

As a precocious child growing up in France, Blaise Pascal showed an early inclination toward mathematics. Although his father would not permit Pascal to study mathematics before the age of 15 (removing all math texts from his house), at age 12 Blaise discovered on his own that the sum of the angles of a triangle are two right triangles.

Pascal went on to become a distinguished mathematician, as well as a physicist, theologian, and the inventor of the first digital calculator. Most historians attribute the beginning of the study of probability to the correspondence between Pascal and Pierre de Fermat in 1654. The two solved The Chevalier's Dilemma—a gambling problem related to Pascal by his friend and Paris gambler the Chevalier de Mere. The problem involved determining the expected number of times one could roll two dice without throwing a double 6. (Pascal proved that the break-even point was 25 rolls.)

EXAMPLE 3.19   CHECKING FOR INDEPENDENCE

Problem   Refer to the consumer product complaint study in Example 3.15. The percentages of complaints of various types during and after the guarantee period are shown in Table 3.6. Define the following events:

A: {Cause of complaint is product appearance}
B: {Complaint occurred during the guarantee term}

Are A and B independent events?

Solution   Events A and B are independent if $P(A|B) = P(A)$. We calculated $P(A|B)$ in Example 3.15 to be .51, and from Table 3.6 we see that

$$P(A) = .32 + .03 = .35$$

Therefore, $P(A|B)$ is not equal to $P(A)$, and A and B are dependent events.

> **Now Work**   *Exercise 3.39c*

■ ■ ■

To gain an intuitive understanding of independence, think of situations in which the occurrence of one event does not alter the probability that a second event will occur. For example, suppose two small companies are being monitored by a financier for possible investment. If the businesses are in different industries and they are otherwise unrelated, then the success or failure of one company may be *independent* of the success or failure of the other. That is, the event that company A fails may not alter the probability that company B will fail.

As a second example, consider an election poll in which 1,000 registered voters are asked their preference between two candidates. Pollsters try to use procedures for selecting a sample of voters so that the responses are independent. That is, the objective of the pollster is to select the sample so the event that one polled voter prefers candidate A does not alter the probability that a second polled voter prefers candidate A.

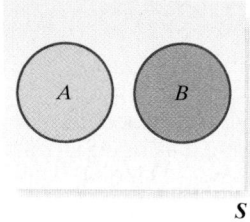

Figure 3.20
Mutually exclusive events
are dependent events

We will make three final points about independence. The first is that the property of independence, unlike the mutually exclusive property, cannot be shown on or gleaned from a Venn diagram. This means *you can't trust your intuition.* In general, the only way to check for independence is by performing the calculations of the probabilities in the definition.

The second point concerns the relationship between the mutually exclusive and independence properties. Suppose that events A and B are mutually exclusive, as shown in Figure 3.20, and both events have nonzero probabilities. Are these events independent or dependent? That is, does the assumption that B occurs alter the probability of the occurrence of A? It certainly does, because if we assume that B has occurred, it is impossible for A to have occurred simultaneously. That is, $P(A|B) = 0$. Thus, *mutually exclusive events are dependent events* since $P(A) \neq P(A|B)$.

The third point is that the probability of the intersection of independent events is very easy to calculate. Referring to the formula for calculating the probability of an intersection, we find

$$P(A \cap B) = P(A)P(B|A)$$

Thus, since $P(B|A) = P(B)$ when A and B are independent, we have the following useful rule:

Probability of Intersection of Two Independent Events

If events A and B are independent, the probability of the intersection of A and B equals the product of the probabilities of A and B; that is,

$$P(A \cap B) = P(A)P(B)$$

The converse is also true: If $P(A \cap B) = P(A)P(B)$, then events A and B are independent.

In the die-toss experiment, we showed in Example 3.18 that the events A: {Observe an even number} and B: {Observe a number less than or equal to 4} are independent if the die is fair. Thus,

$$P(A \cap B) = P(A)P(B) = (\tfrac{1}{2})(\tfrac{2}{3}) = \tfrac{1}{3}$$

This agrees with the result that we obtained in the example:

$$P(A \cap B) = P(2) + P(4) = \tfrac{2}{6} = \tfrac{1}{3}$$

EXAMPLE 3.20   PROBABILITY OF INDEPENDENT EVENTS OCCURRING SIMULTANEOUSLY

Problem   Refer to Example 3.5 (p. 153). Recall that *USA Today* found that of all U.S. firms that use diversity training, 38% state that their primary reason for using it is to stay competitive.

a. What is the probability that in a sample of two firms that use diversity training, both primarily use it to stay competitive?

.1444

b. What is the probability that in a sample of ten firms that use diversity training, all ten primarily use it to stay competitive?

.0000628

Solution   **a.** Let C_1 represent the event that firm 1 gives "stay competitive" as the primary reason for using diversity training. Define C_2 similarly for firm 2. The event that *both* firms give "stay competitive" as their primary reason is the intersection of the two events, $C_1 \cap C_2$. Based on the survey which found that 38% of U.S. firms use diversity training to stay competitive, we could reasonably conclude that $P(C_1) = .38$ and $P(C_2) = .38$. However, in order to compute the probability of $C_1 \cap C_2$ from the Multiplicative Rule, we must make the assumption that the two events are independent. Since the classification of any firm using diversity training is not likely to affect the classification of another firm, this assumption is reasonable. Assuming independence, we have

Suggested Exercises 3.60

$$P(C_1 \cap C_2) = P(C_1)P(C_2) = (.38)(.38) = .1444$$

b. To see how to compute the probability that ten of ten firms will give "stay competitive" as their primary reason, first consider the event that three of three firms give "stay competitive" as the primary reason. Using the notation defined earlier, we want to compute the probability of the intersection $C_1 \cap C_2 \cap C_3$. Again assuming independence of the classifications, we have

$$P(C_1 \cap C_2 \cap C_3) = P(C_1)P(C_2)P(C_3) = (.38)(.38)(.38) = .054872$$

Similar reasoning leads us to the conclusion that the intersection of ten such events can be calculated as follows:

$$P(C_1 \cap C_2 \cap C_3 \cap \ldots \cap C_{10}) = P(C_1)P(C_2) \cdots P(C_{10}) = (.38)^{10} = .0000628$$

Thus, the probability that ten of ten firms all give "stay competitive" as their primary reason for using diversity training is about 63 in 1 million, assuming the events (stated reasons for using diversity training) are independent.

Look Back The very small probability in part b makes it extremely unlikely that ten of ten firms would give "stay competitive" as their primary reason for diversity training. If this event should actually occur, we would need to reassess our estimate of the probability of .38 used in the calculation. If all ten firms' reason is staying competitive, then the probability that any one firm gives staying competitive as their reason is much higher than .38. (This conclusion is another application of the rare event approach to statistical inference.)

> **Now Work**   *Exercise 3.60a*

■ ■ ■

Statistics in Action Revisited

The Probability of Winning Cash 3 or Play 4

In addition to biweekly Lotto 6/53, the Florida Lottery runs several other games. Two popular daily games are "Cash 3" and "Play 4." In Cash 3, players pay $1 to select three numbers in sequential order, where each number ranges from 0 to 9. If the three numbers selected (e.g., 2-8-4) match exactly the order of the three numbers drawn, the player win $500. Play 4 is similar to Cash 3, but players must match four numbers (each number ranging from 0 to 9). For a $1 Play 4 ticket (e.g., 3-8-3-0), the player will win $5,000 if the numbers match the order of the four numbers drawn.

During the official drawing for Cash 3, ten ping pong balls numbered 0, 1, 2, 3, 4, 5, 6, 7, 8, and 9 are placed into each of three chambers. The balls in the first chamber are colored pink, the balls in the second chamber are blue, and the balls in the third chamber are yellow. One ball of each color is randomly drawn, with the official order as pink-blue-yellow. In Play 4, a fourth chamber with orange balls is added and the official order is pink-blue-yellow-orange. Since the draws of the colored balls are random and independent, we can apply an extension of the Probability Rule for the Intersection of Two Independent Events to find the odds of winning Cash 3 and Play 4. The probability of matching a numbered ball being drawn from a chamber is 1/10; therefore,

P(Win Cash 3) = P(match pink AND match blue AND
match yellow)
= P(match pink) × P(match blue) ×
P(match yellow)
= (1/10)(1/10)(1/10) = 1/1000 = .001

P(Win Play 4) = P(match pink AND match blue AND
match yellow AND match orange)
= P(match pink) × P(match blue) ×
P(match yellow) × P(match orane)
= (1/10)(1/10)(|1/10)(1/10) = 1/10,000 = .0001

Although the odds of winning one of these daily games is much better than the odds of winning Lotto 6/53, there is still only a 1 in 1,000 chance (for Cash 3) or 1 in 10,000 chance (for Play 4) of winning the daily game. And the payoffs ($500 or $5,000) are much smaller. In fact, it can be shown that you will lose an average of 50¢ every time you play either Cash 3 or Play 4!

Exercises 3.39–3.65

Learning the Mechanics

3.39 For two events, A and B, $P(A) = .4$, $P(B) = .2$, and $P(A \cap B) = .1$.
  a. Find $P(A|B)$.   .5
  b. Find $P(B|A)$.   .25
  c. Are A and B independent events?   No

3.40 For two events, A and B, $P(A) = .4$, $P(B) = .2$, and $P(A|B) = .6$.
  a. Find $P(A \cap B)$.   .12
  b. Find $P(B|A)$.   .3

3.41 For two independent events, A and B, $P(A) = .4$ and $P(B) = .2$.
  a. Find $P(A \cap B)$.   .08
  b. Find $P(A|B)$.   .4
  c. Find $P(A \cup B)$.   .52

3.42 An experiment results in one of three mutually exclusive events, A, B, or C. It is known that $P(A) = .30$, $P(B) = .55$, and $P(C) = .15$. Find each of the following probabilities:
  a. $P(A \cup B)$ .85
  b. $P(A \cap C)$ 0
  c. $P(A|B)$ 0
  d. $P(B \cup C)$ .70
  e. Are B and C independent events? Explain.   No

3.43 Consider the experiment depicted by the Venn diagram, with the sample space S containing five sample points. The sample points are assigned the following probabilities: $P(E_1) = .20$, $P(E_2) = .30$, $P(E_3) = .30$, $P(E_4) = .10$, $P(E_5) = .10$.
  a. Calculate $P(A)$, $P(B)$, and $P(A \cap B)$.
  b. Suppose we know that event A has occurred, so that the reduced sample space consists of the three sample points in A—namely, E_1, E_2, and E_3. Use the

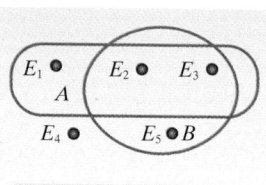

S

formula for conditional probability to adjust the probabilities of these three sample points for the knowledge that A has occurred [i.e., $P(E_i|A)$.] Verify that the conditional probabilities are in the same proportion to one another as the original sample point probabilities.
  c. Calculate the conditional probability $P(B|A)$ in two ways: (1) Add the adjusted (conditional) probabilities of the sample points in the intersection $A \cap B$ since these represent the event that B occurs given that A has occurred; (2) Use the formula for conditional probability:

$$P(B|A) = \frac{P(A \cap B)}{P(A)}$$

Verify that the two methods yield the same result.
  d. Are events A and B independent? Why or why not?

3.44 Two fair coins are tossed and the following events are defined:

A: {Observe at least one head}
B: {Observe exactly one head}

  a. Draw a Venn diagram for the experiment, showing events A and B. Assign probabilities to the sample points.

b. Find $P(A)$, $P(B)$, and $P(A \cap B)$.

c. Use the formula for conditional probability to find $P(A|B)$ and $P(B|A)$. Verify your answer by inspecting the Venn diagram and using the concept of reduced sample spaces.

3.45 An experiment results in one of five sample points with the following probabilities: $P(E_1) = .22$, $P(E_2) = .31$, $P(E_3) = .15$, $P(E_4) = .22$, and $P(E_5) = .1$. The following events have been defined:

$$A: \{E_1, E_3\}$$
$$B: \{E_2, E_3, E_4\}$$
$$C: \{E_1, E_5\}$$

Find each of the following probabilities:

a. $P(A)$ .37
b. $P(B)$ .68
c. $P(A \cap B)$
d. $P(A|B)$ .2206
e. $P(B \cap C)$
f. $P(C|B)$
g. Consider each pair of events: A and B, A and C, and B and C. Are any of the pairs of events independent? Why?   None

3.46 Two fair dice are tossed, and the following events are defined:

$A:$ {Sum of the numbers showing is odd}
$B:$ {Sum of the numbers showing is 9, 11, or 12}

Are events A and B independent? Why?   No

3.47 A sample space contains six sample points and events A, B, and C as shown in the Venn diagram. The probabilities of the sample points are

$P(1) = .20$, $P(2) = .05$, $P(3) = .30$, $P(4) = .10$, $P(5) = .10$, $P(6) = .25$.

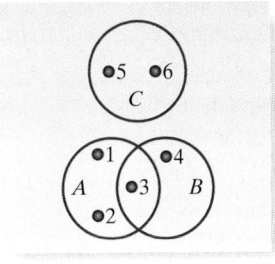

S

a. Which pairs of events, if any, are mutually exclusive? Why? (A, C) and (B, C)
b. Which pairs of events, if any, are independent? Why?
c. Find $P(A \cup B)$ by adding the probabilities of the sample points and then by using the additive rule. Verify that the answers agree. Repeat for $P(A \cup C)$.

Applying the Concepts—Basic

3.48 To develop programs for business travelers staying at convention hotels, Hyatt Hotels Corp. commissioned a study of executives who play golf. The study revealed that 55% of the executives admitted they had cheated at golf. Also, 20% of the executives admitted they had cheated at golf and had lied in business. Given an executive had cheated at golf, what is the probability that the executive also had lied in business.   .364

3.49 *Forbes* (Jul. 26, 1999) conducted a survey of the 20 largest nondomestic public companies in the world. Of these 20 companies, 6 were trading companies based in Japan. A total of 11 Japanese companies were on the top 20 list. Suppose we select one of these 20 companies at random. Given the company is based in Japan, what is the probability that it is a trading company?   .545

3.50 The New York Yankees, a member of the Eastern Division of the American League in Major League Baseball (MLB), recently won three consecutive World Series. The following table summarizes the 12 MLB World Series winners from 1990 to 2002 by division and league. (There was no World Series in 1994 due to a players' strike.) One of these 12 World Series winners is to be chosen at random.

a. Given that the winner is a member of the American League, what is the probability that the winner plays in the Eastern Division?   6/8
b. If the winner plays in the Central Division, what is the probability that the winner is a member of the National League?   1/2
c. If the winner is a member of the National League, what is the probability that the winner plays in either the Central or Western Division?   2/4

		League	
		National	American
Division	**Eastern**	2	6
	Central	1	1
	Western	1	1

Source: Major League Baseball.

3.51 In a study of Internet users, researchers discovered that 80% of the users own at least one computer and that 25% of the users log on to the internet for more than 30 hours per week. (*Internet Research*, Vol. 11, 2001.) Suppose that 15% of the users own at least one computer and log on to the Internet for more than 30 hours per week.

a. Given an Internet user owns at least one computer, what is the probability that he or she logs on to the Internet for more than 30 hours per week?   .1875
b. Given an Internet user logs on to the internet for more than 30 hours per week, what is the probability that he or she owns at least one computer?   .60

3.52 The National Center for Education Statistics (NCES) conducted a 1999 survey on the condition of America's public school facilities. The survey revealed the following information. The probability that a public school building has inadequate plumbing is .25. Of the buildings with inadequate plumbing, the probability that the school has plans for repairing the building is .38. Find the probability that a public school building has inadequate plumbing and will be repaired.   .095

Applying the Concepts—Intermediate

3.53 New York's Columbia University Law School released a report in February 2002 on all capital punishment (death-penalty) cases that occurred over the past 25 years in the United States. Two of the findings are stated as follows: 68% of all capital punishment cases had a serious, reversible error. Of the cases that were overturned due to reversible error, 7% resulted in acquittal for the defendant upon retrial.
  a. Write each of these findings in the form of a probability.
  b. Use the findings to find the probability that a capital case had a serious, reversible error and an innocent defendant.   .0476

3.54 Refer to the results of the *Forbes* (April 23, 2003) survey of the top 25 best-paid chief executive officers shown in Table 2.1 (p. 45). The data on highest degree obtained are summarized in the following SPSS printout. Suppose you randomly select 5 of the CEOs (without replacement) and record the highest degree obtained by each.
  a. What is the probability that the highest degree obtained by the first CEO you select is a bachelor's degree?   6/25
  b. Suppose the highest degree obtained by each of the first four CEOs you select is a bachelor's degree. What is the probability that the highest degree obtained by the fifth CEO you select is a bachelor's degree?   2/21

DEGREE

		Frequency	Percent	Valid Percent	Cumulative Percent
Valid	Bachelors	6	24.0	24.0	24.0
	Law	3	12.0	12.0	36.0
	Masters	9	36.0	36.0	72.0
	None	4	16.0	16.0	88.0
	PhD	3	12.0	12.0	100.0
	Total	25	100.0	100.0	

3.55 Refer to the *American Journal of Public Health* (Jan. 2002) study of elderly wheelchair users who live at home, Exercise 3.36 (p. 171). The table classifying a sample of 306 wheelchair users according to type of features installed in the home and whether or not they had an injurious fall follows. Suppose we select, at random, one of the 306 surveyed wheelchair users.

Home Features	Injurious Fall(s)	No Falls	Totals
All 5	2	7	9
At least 1	26	162	188
None	20	89	109
Totals	48	258	306

Source: Berg, K., Hines, M., and Allen, S. "Wheelchair Users at Home: Few Home Modifications and Many Injurious Falls," *American Journal of Public Health,* Vol. 92, No. 1, Jan. 2002 (Table 1).

  a. Given the wheelchair user had all five features installed, what is the probability that the user had an injurious fall?   2/9
  b. Given the wheelchair user had none of the features installed, what is the probability that the user had an injurious fall?   20/109

3.56 The U.S. Census Bureau reports that the percentage of mothers with infant children in the workforce has declined since 1998. The following table gives a breakdown of the marital status and working status of the 3.9 million mothers with infant children in the year 2000. (The numbers in the table are reported in millions.) Consider the following events: $A = \{$Mom with infant works$\}$, $B = \{$Mom with infant is married and living with husband$\}$. Are A and B independent events?   No

	Working	Not Working
Married/ living with husband	1385	1175
All other arrangements	786	588

Source: U.S. Census Bureau; *American Demographers,* Feb. 2002.

3.57 According to *Economic Inquiry* (Jan. 2002), 49% of all U.S. households own stock. A sample of these stockholders was asked what effect recent trends in the stock market have had on their saving and spending the last few years. The responses are summarized in the table.

Stock Market Effect on Spending/Saving	Percent of Stockholders
No effect	85.0
Spend more/save less	3.4
Spend less/save more	11.6
Total	100.0

Source: Starr-McCluer, M. "Stock Market Wealth and Consumer Spending," *Economic Inquiry,* Vol. 40, No. 1, January 2002 (Table 3).

A U.S. household is selected at random.
  a. What is the probability that the household does not own stock?   .51
  b. Given the household owns stock, what is the probability that the household spends more and saves less due to recent trends in the stock market?   .034

c. What is the probability that the household owns stock but spends less and saves more due to recent trends in the stock market? .05684

3.58 In Italy, all high school students must take a High School Diploma (HSD) exam and write a paper. In *Organizational Behavior and Human Decision Processes* (July 2000), University of Milan researcher L. Macchi provided the following information to a group of college undergraduates.

Fact 1: In Italy, 360 out of every 1,000 students fail their HSD exam.

Fact 2: Of those who fail the HSD, 75% also fail the written paper.

Fact 3: Of those who pass the HSD, only 20% fail the written paper.

Define events A and B as follows:

A = {Student fails the HSD exam},
B = {Student fails the written paper}

a. Write Fact 1 as a probability statement involving events A and/or B.

b. Write Fact 2 as a probability statement involving events A and/or B.

c. Write Fact 3 as a probability statement involving events A and/or B.

d. State $P(A \cap B)$ in the words of the problem.

e. Find $P(A \cap B)$. .27

3.59 The *Journal of the National Cancer Institute* (Feb. 16, 2000) published the results of a study that investigated the association between cigar smoking and death from tobacco-related cancers. Data were obtained for a national sample of 137,243 American men. The results are summarized in the accompanying table. Each male in the study was classified according to his cigar smoking status and whether or not he died from a tobacco-related cancer.

a. Find the probability that a man who never smoked cigars died from cancer. .0057

b. Find the probability that a former cigar smoker died from cancer. .0007

c. Find the probability that a current cigar smoker died from cancer. .0010

	Died from Cancer	Did Not Die from Cancer	Totals
Never Smoked Cigars	782	120,747	121,529
Former Cigar Smoker	91	7,757	7,848
Current Cigar Smoker	141	7,725	7,866
Totals	1,014	136,229	137,243

Source: Shapiro, J. A., Jacobs, E. J., & Thun, M. J. "Cigar Smoking in Men and Risk of Death from Tobacco-related Cancers," *Journal of the National Cancer Institute*, Vol. 92, No. 4, February 16, 2000 (Table 2).

3.60 A new type of lie detector—called the Computerized Voice Stress Analyzer (CVSA)—has been developed. The manufacturer claims that the CVSA is 98% accurate, and, unlike a polygraph machine, will not be thrown off by drugs and medical factors. However, laboratory studies by the U.S. Defense Department found that the CVSA had an accuracy rate of 49.8%—slightly less than pure chance (*Tampa Tribune*, Jan. 10, 1999). Suppose the CVSA is used to test the veracity of four suspects. Assume the suspects' responses are independent.

a. If the manufacturer's claim is true, what is the probability that the CVSA will correctly determine the veracity of all four suspects? .9224

b. If the manufacturer's claim is true, what is the probability that the CVSA will yield an incorrect result for at least one of the four suspects? .0776

c. Suppose that in a laboratory experiment conducted by the U.S. Defense Department on four suspects, the CVSA yielded incorrect results for two of the suspects. Use this result to make an inference about the true accuracy rate of the new lie detector.

3.61 One definition of *Total Quality Management* (TQM) was given in Exercise 3.13 (p. 159). Another definition is a "management philosophy and a system of management techniques to improve product and service quality and worker productivity" (Benson, *Minnesota Management Review*, Fall 1992). One hundred U.S. companies were surveyed and it was found that 30 had implemented TQM. Among the 100 companies surveyed, 60 reported an increase in sales last year. Of those 60, 20 had implemented TQM. Suppose one of the 100 surveyed companies is to be selected at random for additional analysis.

a. What is the probability that a firm that implemented TQM is selected? That a firm whose sales increased is selected? .3, .6

b. Are the two events {TQM implemented} and {Sales increased} independent or dependent? Explain.

c. Suppose that instead of 20 TQM implementers among the 60 firms reporting sales increases, there were 18. Now are the events {TQM implemented} and {Sales increased} independent or dependent? Explain.

Applying the Concepts—Advanced

3.62 "Go" is one of the oldest and most popular strategic board games in the world, especially in Japan and Korea. This two-player game is played on a flat surface marked with 19 vertical and 19 horizontal lines. The objective is to control territory by placing pieces called "stones" on vacant points on the board. Players alternate placing their stones. The player using black stone goes first, followed by the player using white stones.

[*Note:* The University of Virginia requires MBA students to learn Go to understand how the Japanese conduct business.] *Chance* (Summer 1995) published an article that investigated the advantage of playing first (i.e., using the black stones) in Go. The results of 577 games recently played by professional Go players were analyzed.

a. In the 577 games, the player with the black stones won 319 times and the player with the white stones won 258 times. Use this information to assess the probability of winning when you play first in Go.

b. Professional Go players are classified by level. Group C includes the top-level players followed by Group B (middle-level) and Group A (low-level) players. The table below describes the number of games won by the player with the black stones, categorized by level of the black player and level of the opponent. Assess the probability of winning when you play first in Go for each combination of player and opponent level.

c. If the player with the black stones is ranked higher than the player with the white stones, what is the probability that black wins?   .85

d. Given the players are of the same level, what is the probability that the player with the black stones wins?

⚉ GO

Black Player Level	Opponent Level	Number of Wins	Number of Games
C	A	34	34
C	B	69	79
C	C	66	118
B	A	40	54
B	B	52	95
B	C	27	79
A	A	15	28
A	B	11	51
A	C	5	39
	Totals	319	577

Source: J. Kim and H. J. Kim. "The Advantage of Playing First in Go." *Chance*, Vol. 8. No. 3. Summer 1995, p. 26 (Table 3).

3.63 Physicians and pharmacists sometimes fail to inform patients adequately about the proper application of prescription drugs and about the precautions to take in order to avoid potential side effects. One method of increasing patients' awareness of the problem is for physicians to provide Patient Medication Instruction (PMI) sheets. The American Medical Association, however, has found that only 20% of the doctors who prescribe drugs frequently distribute PMI sheets to their patients. Assume that 20% of all patients receive the PMI sheet with their prescriptions and that 12% receive the PMI sheet and are hospitalized because of a drug-related problem. What is the probability that a person will be hospitalized for a drug-related problem given that the person has received the PMI sheet?   .60

3.64 In October 1994, a flaw was discovered in the Pentium chip installed in many new personal computers. The chip produced an incorrect result when dividing two numbers. Intel, the manufacturer of the Pentium chip, initially announced that such an error would occur only once in 9 billion divides, or "once in every 27,000 years" for a typical user; consequently, it did not immediately replace the chip. Assume the probability of a divide error with the Pentium chip is, in fact, $1/9{,}000{,}000{,}000$.

a. For a division performed using the flawed Pentium chip, what is the probability that no error will occur?

b. Consider two successive divisions performed using the flawed chip. What is the probability that neither result will be in error? (Assume that any one division has no impact on the result of any other division performed by the chip.)

c. Depending on the procedure, statistical software packages may perform an extremely large number of divisions to produce the required output. For heavy users of the software, 1 billion divisions over a short time frame is not unusual. Calculate the probability that 1 billion divisions performed using the flawed Pentium chip will result in no errors.   .9048

d. Use the result, part c, to compute the probability of at least one error in the 1 billion divisions. [*Note:* Two months after the flaw was discovered, Intel agreed to replace all Pentium chips free of charge.]   .0952

3.65 In *Parade Magazine*'s (Nov. 26, 2000) column, "Ask Marilyn," the following question was posed: "I have just tossed a [balanced] coin 10 times, and I ask you to guess which of the following three sequences was the result. One (and only one) of the sequences is genuine."

(1) H H H H H H H H H H

(2) H H T T H T T H H H

(3) T T T T T T T T T T

a. Demonstrate that prior to actually tossing the coins, the three sequences are equally likely to occur.

b. Find the probability that the 10 coin tosses result in all heads or all tails.   .00195

c. Find the probability that the 10 coin tosses result in a mix of heads and tails.   .99805

d. Marilyn's answer to the question posed was "Though the chances of the three specific sequences occurring randomly are equal … it's reasonable for us to choose sequence (2) as the most likely genuine result." If you know that only one of the three sequences actually occurred, explain why Marilyn's answer is correct. [*Hint:* Compare the probabilities in parts **b** and **c.**]

3.7 Random Sampling

How a sample is selected from a population is of vital importance in statistical inference because the probability of an observed sample will be used to infer the characteristics of the sampled population. To illustrate, suppose you deal yourself four cards from a deck of 52 cards and all four cards are aces. Do you conclude that your deck is an ordinary bridge deck, containing only four aces, or do you conclude that the deck is stacked with more than four aces? It depends on how the cards were drawn. If the four aces were always placed at the top of a standard bridge deck, drawing four aces is not unusual—it is certain. On the other hand, if the cards are thoroughly mixed, drawing four aces in a sample of four cards is highly improbable. The point, of course, is that in order to use the observed sample of four cards to draw inferences about the population (the deck of 52 cards), you need to know how the sample was selected from the deck.

Teaching Tip

Stress that all of the inferences that are made in statistics are based on samples. Obviously, the sample selected should represent the population as closely as possible. The random sampling procedure is the easiest method to insure a representative sample.

One of the simplest and most frequently employed sampling procedures is implied in many of the previous examples and exercises. It produces what is known as a *random sample.* We learned in Section 1.5 (p.16) that a random sample is likely to be *representative* of the population that it is selected from.

DEFINITION 3.10

If n elements are selected from a population in such a way that every set of n elements in the population has an equal probability of being selected, the n elements are said to be a **random sample.***

Teaching Tip

Point out that the method of choosing the random sample is irrelevant as long as every possible subset of n has an equal chance of being selected.

If a population is not too large and the elements can be numbered on slips of paper, poker chips, and so on, you can physically mix the slips of paper or chips and remove n elements from the total. The numbers that appear on the chips selected would indicate the population elements to be included in the sample. Since it is often difficult to achieve a thorough mix, such a procedure only provides an approximation to random sampling. Most researchers rely on **random number generators** to automatically generate the random sample. Random number generators are available in table form and they are built into most statistical software packages.

EXAMPLE 3.21 — SELECTING A RANDOM SAMPLE

Problem   Suppose you wish to randomly sample five households from a population of 100,000 households to participate in a study.

8.33×10^{22}

   a. How many different samples can be selected?

   b. Use a random number generator to select a random sample.

Solution   **a.** To determine the number of samples, we'll apply the combinatorial rule of Section 3.1. In this case, $N = 100,000$ and $n = 5$. Then

$$\binom{N}{n} = \binom{100,000}{5} = \frac{100,000!}{5!99,995!}$$

*Strictly speaking, this is a **simple random sample.** There are many different types of random samples. The simple random sample is the most common.

$$= \frac{100{,}000 \cdot 99{,}999 \cdot 99{,}998 \cdot 99{,}997 \cdot 99{,}996}{5 \cdot 4 \cdot 3 \cdot 2 \cdot 1}$$

$$= 8.33 \times 10^{22}$$

Thus, there are 83.3 billion trillion different samples of five households that can be selected from 100,000.

b. To ensure that each of the possible samples has an equal chance of being selected, as required for random sampling, we can employ a **random number table,** as provided in Table I of Appendix B. Random number tables are constructed in such a way that every number occurs with (approximately) equal probability. Furthermore, the occurrence of any one number in a position is independent of any of the other numbers that appear in the table. To use a table of random numbers, number the N elements in the population from 1 to N. Then turn to Table I and select a starting number in the table. Proceeding from this number either across the row or down the column, remove and record n numbers from the table.

To illustrate, first we number the households in the population from 1 to 100,000. Then, we turn to a page of Table I, say the first page. (A partial reproduction of the first page of Table I is shown in Table 3.7.) Now, we arbitrarily select a starting number, say the random number appearing in the third row, second column. This number is 48,360. Then we proceed down the second column to obtain the remaining four random numbers. In this case we have selected five random numbers, which are shaded in Table 3.7. Using the first five digits to represent households from 1 to 99,999 and the number 00000 to represent household 100,000, we can see that the households numbered

48,360
93,093
39,975
6,907
72,905

should be included in our sample.

TABLE 3.7 Partial Reproduction of Table I in Appendix B

Row \ Column	1	2	3	4	5	6
1	10480	15011	01536	02011	81647	91646
2	22368	46573	25595	85393	30995	89198
3	24130	48360	22527	97265	76393	64809
4	42167	93093	06243	61680	07856	16376
5	37570	39975	81837	16656	06121	91782
6	77921	06907	11008	42751	27756	53498
7	99562	72905	56420	69994	98872	31016
8	96301	91977	05463	07972	18876	20922
9	89579	14342	63661	10281	17453	18103
10	85475	36857	53342	53988	53060	59533
11	28918	69578	88231	33276	70997	79936
12	63553	40961	48235	03427	49626	69445
13	09429	93969	52636	92737	88974	33488

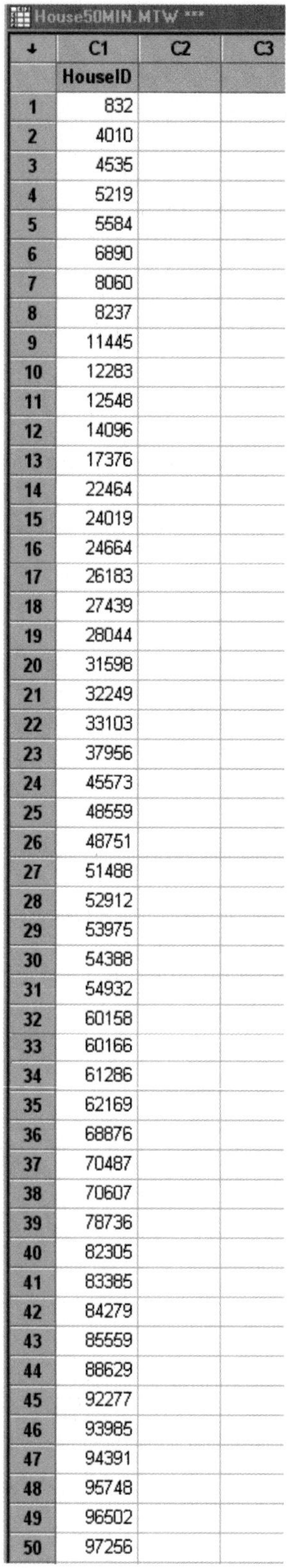

House50MIN.MTW ***

	C1 HouseID	C2	C3
1	832		
2	4010		
3	4535		
4	5219		
5	5584		
6	6890		
7	8060		
8	8237		
9	11445		
10	12283		
11	12548		
12	14096		
13	17376		
14	22464		
15	24019		
16	24664		
17	26183		
18	27439		
19	28044		
20	31598		
21	32249		
22	33103		
23	37956		
24	45573		
25	48559		
26	48751		
27	51488		
28	52912		
29	53975		
30	54388		
31	54932		
32	60158		
33	60166		
34	61286		
35	62169		
36	68876		
37	70487		
38	70607		
39	78736		
40	82305		
41	83385		
42	84279		
43	85559		
44	88629		
45	92277		
46	93985		
47	94391		
48	95748		
49	96502		
50	97256		

Figure 3.21
MINITAB worksheet with random sample of 50 households

Teaching Tip

Point out that the random number table can be used for any choices of *N* and *n*.

Note: Use only the necessary number of digits in each random number to identify the element to be included in the sample. If, in the course of recording the *n* numbers from the table, you select a number that has already been selected, simply discard the duplicate and select a replacement at the end of the sequence. Thus, you may have to record more than *n* numbers from the table to obtain a sample of *n* unique numbers.

Look Back Can we be perfectly sure that all 83.3 billion trillion samples have an equal chance of being selected? That fact is, we can't; but to the extent that the random number table contains truly random sequences of digits, the sample should be very close to random.

Now Work *Exercise 3.66*

■ ■ ■

Table I in Appendix B is just one example of a random number generator. For most scientific studies that require a large random sample, computers are used to generate the random sample. The EXCEL, MINITAB, and SPSS statistical software packages all have easy-to-use random number generators.

For example, suppose we required a random sample of $n = 50$ households from the population of 100,000 households in Example 3.21. Here, we might employ the MINITAB random number generator. Figure 3.21 shows a MINITAB printout listing 50 random numbers (from a population of 100,000). The households with these identification numbers would be included in the random sample.

Exercises 3.66–3.73

Learning the Mechanics

3.66 Suppose you wish to sample $n = 2$ elements from a total of $N = 10$ elements.
  a. Count the number of different samples that can be drawn, first by listing them, and then by using combinatorial mathematics. (See Section 3.1.)   45
  b. If random sampling is to be employed, what is the probability that any particular sample will be selected?
  c. Show how to use the random number table, Table I in Appendix B, to select a random sample of 2 elements from a population of 10 elements. Perform the sampling procedure 20 times. Do any two of the samples contain the same 2 elements? Given your answer to part b, did you expect repeated samples?

3.67 Suppose you wish to sample $n = 3$ elements from a total of $N = 600$ elements.
  a. Count the number of different samples by using combinatorial mathematics (see Section 3.1).
  b. If random sampling is to be employed, what is the probability that any particular sample will be selected?
  c. Show how to use the random number table, Table I in Appendix B, to select a random sample of 3 elements from a population of 600 elements. Perform the sampling procedure 20 times. Do any two of the samples contain the same three elements? Given your answer to part b, did you expect repeated samples?

  d. Use a computer to generate a random sample of 3 from the population of 600 elements.

3.68 Suppose that a population contains $N = 200,000$ elements. Use a computer or Table I of Appendix B to select a random sample of $n = 10$ elements from the population. Explain how you selected your sample.

Applying the Concepts—Basic

3.69 To ascertain the effectiveness of their advertising campaigns, firms frequently conduct telephone interviews with consumers using *random-digit dialing*. With this approach, a random number generator mechanically creates the sample of phone numbers to be called.
  a. Explain how the random number table (Table I of Appendix B) or a computer could be used to generate a sample of seven-digit telephone numbers.
  b. Use the procedure you described in part a to generate a sample of 10 seven-digit telephone numbers.
  c. Use the procedure you described in part a to generate five seven-digit telephone numbers whose first three digits are 373.

3.70 In addition to its decennial enumeration of the population, the U.S. Bureau of the Census regularly samples the population to estimate level of and changes in a number of other attributes, such as income, family size, employment, and marital status. Suppose the bureau plans to sample 1,000 households in a city that has a total of 534,322 households. Show how the bureau could use the random number table in Appendix B or a computer to generate the sample. Select the first 10 households to be included in the sample.

Applying the Concepts—Intermediate

3.71 In auditing a firm's financial statements, an auditor will (1) assess the capability of the firm's accounting system to accumulate, measure, and synthesize transactional data properly, and (2) assess the operational effectiveness of the accounting system. In performing the second assessment, the auditor frequently relies on a random sample of actual transactions (Stickney and Weil, *Financial Accounting: An Introduction to Concepts, Methods, and Uses*, 1994). A particular firm has 5,382 customer accounts that are numbered from 0001 to 5382.

a. One account is to be selected at random for audit. What is the probability that account number 3,241 is selected? .000186

b. Draw a random sample of 10 accounts and explain in detail the procedure you used.

c. Refer to part b. The following are two possible random samples of size 10. Is one more likely to be selected than the other? Explain. No

Sample Number 1				
5011	0082	0963	0772	3415
2663	1126	0008	0026	4189

Sample Number 2				
0001	0003	0005	0007	0009
0002	0004	0006	0008	0010

3.72 The results of the previous business day's transactions for stocks traded on the New York Stock Exchange

(NYSE) and five regional exchanges—the Chicago, Pacific, Philadelphia, Boston, and Cincinnati stock exchanges—are summarized each business day in the NYSE–Composite Transactions table in *The Wall Street Journal*.

a. Examine the NYSE–Composite Transactions table in a recent issue of *The Wall Street Journal* and explain how to draw a random sample of stocks from the table.

b. Use the procedure you described in part a to draw a random sample of 20 stocks from a recent NYSE–Composite Transactions table. For each stock in the sample, list its name (i.e., the abbreviation given in the table), its sales volume, and its closing price.

Applying the Concepts—Advanced

3.73 A recent court case involved a claim of satellite television subscribers obtaining illegal access to local TV stations. The defendant (the satellite TV company) wanted to sample TV markets nationwide and determine the percentage of its subscribers in each sampled market who have illegal access to local TV stations. To do this, defendant's expert witness drew a rectangular grid over the continental United States, with horizontal and vertical grid lines every .02 degrees of latitude and longitude, respectively. This created a total of 500 rows and 1,000 columns, or $(500)(1,000) = 500,000$ intersections. The plan was to randomly sample 900 intersection points and include the TV market at each intersection in the sample. Explain how you could use a random number generator to obtain a random sample of 900 intersections. Develop at least two plans: one that numbers the intersections from 1 to 500,000 prior to selection and another that selects the row and column of each sampled intersection (from the total of 500 rows and 1,000 columns).

3.8 Bayes's Rule (Optional)

Teaching Tip

Point out that Bayes' Rule is useful for finding one conditional probability when other conditional probabilities are already known.

An early attempt to employ probability in making inferences is the basis for a branch of statistical methodology known as **Bayesian statistical methods.** The logic employed by the English philosopher, Thomas Bayes, in the mid-1700s, involves converting an unknown conditional probability, say $P(B|A)$, to one involving a known conditional probability, say $P(A|B)$. The method is illustrated in the next example.

EXAMPLE 3.22   APPLYING BAYES'S LOGIC

Problem An unmanned monitoring system uses high-tech video equipment and microprocessors to detect intruders. A prototype system has been developed and is in use outdoors at a weapons munitions plant. The system is designed to detect intruders with a probability of .90. However, the design engineers expect this probability to vary with weather condition. The system automatically records the weather condition each time an intruder is detected. Based on a series of controlled tests, in which an intruder was released at the plant under various weather conditions, the following information is available: Given the intruder was, in fact, detected by the system, the weather was clear 75% of the time, cloudy 20% of the time, and raining 5% of the time. When the system failed to detect the intruder, 60% of the days were clear, 30% cloudy, and 10% rainy. Use this information to find the probability of detecting an intruder, given rainy weather conditions. (Assume that an intruder has been released at the plant.)

Solution   Define D to be the event that the intruder is detected by the system. Then D^c is the event that the system failed to detect the intruder. Our goal is to calculate the conditional probability, $P(D|\text{Rainy})$. From the statement of the problem, the following information is available:

$$P(D) = .90 \qquad\qquad P(D^c) = .10$$
$$P(\text{Clear}|D) = .75 \qquad P(\text{Clear}|D^c) = .60$$
$$P(\text{Cloudy}|D) = .20 \qquad P(\text{Cloudy}|D^c) = .30$$
$$P(\text{Rainy}|D) = .05 \qquad P(\text{Rainy}|D^c) = .10$$

Note that $P(D|\text{Rainy})$ is not one of the conditional probabilities that is known. However, we can find

$$P(\text{Rainy} \cap D) = P(D)P(\text{Rainy}|D) = (.90)(.05) = .045$$

and

$$P(\text{Rainy} \cap D^c) = P(D^c)P(\text{Rainy}|D^c) = (.10)(.10) = .01$$

Suggested Exercises 3.79

using the Multiplicative Probability Rule. Now the event Rainy is the union of two mutually exclusive events, $(\text{Rainy} \cap D)$ and $(\text{Rainy} \cap D^c)$. Thus, applying the Additive Probability Rule, we have

$$P(\text{Rainy}) = P(\text{Rainy} \cap D) + P(\text{Rainy} \cap D^c) = .045 + .01 = .055$$

We now apply the formula for conditional probability to obtain

$$P(D|\text{Rainy}) = \frac{P(\text{Rainy} \cap D)}{P(\text{Rainy})} = \frac{P(\text{Rainy} \cap D)}{P(\text{Rainy} \cap D) + P(\text{Rainy} \cap D^c)}$$
$$= .045/.055 = .818$$

Therefore, under rainy weather conditions, the prototype system can detect the intruder with a probability of .818—a value lower than the designed probability of .90.

■ ■ ■

The technique utilized in Example 3.22, called **Bayes's Rule,** can be applied when an observed event A occurs with any one of several mutually exclusive and exhaustive events, $B_1, B_2, \ldots, B_k$. The formula for finding the appropriate conditional probabilities is given in the box.

Bayes's Rule

Given k mutually exclusive and exhaustive events, $B_1, B_2, \ldots, B_k$, such that $P(B_1) + P(B_2) + \cdots + P(B_k) = 1$, and an observed event A, then

$$P(B_i|A) = P(B_i \cap A)/P(A)$$
$$= \frac{P(B_i)P(A|B_i)}{P(B_1)P(A|B_1) + P(B_2)P(A|B_2) + \cdots + P(B_k)P(A|B_k)}$$

In applying Bayes's rule to Example 3.22, the observed event $A = \{\text{Rainy}\}$ and the $k = 2$ mutually exclusive and exhaustive events are the complementary events $D = \{\text{intruder detected}\}$ and $D^c = \{\text{intruder not detected}\}$. Hence, the formula

$$P(D|\text{Rainy}) = \frac{P(D)P(\text{Rainy}|D)}{P(D)P(\text{Rainy}|D) + P(D^c)P(\text{Rainy}|D^c)}$$

$$= \frac{(.90)(.05)}{(.90)(.05) + (.10)(.10)} = .818$$

Biography

THOMAS BAYES (1702–1761)
The Inverse Probabilist

The Reverend Thomas Bayes was an ordained English Presbyterian minister who became a Fellow of the Royal Statistical Society without benefit of any formal training in mathematics or any published papers in science during his lifetime. His manipulation of the formula for conditional probability in 1761 is now known as Bayes's Theorem. At the time and for 200 years afterward, use of Bayes's Theorem (or inverse probability, as it was called) was controversial and, to some, considered an inappropriate practice. It was not until the 1960s that the power of the Bayesian approach to decision making began to be tapped.

Exercises 3.74–3.81

Learning the Mechanics

3.74 Suppose the events B_1 and B_2 are mutually exclusive and complementary events, such that $P(B_1) = .75$ and $P(B_2) = .25$. Consider another event A such that $P(A|B_1) = .3$ and $P(A|B_2) = .5$.
  a. Find $P(B_1 \cap A)$. .225
  b. Find $P(B_2 \cap A)$. .125
  c. Find $P(A)$ using the results in parts a and b. .35
  d. Find $P(B_1|A)$. .643
  e. Find $P(B_2|A)$. .357

3.75 Suppose the events B_1, B_2, and B_3 are mutually exclusive and complementary events, such that $P(B_1) = .2$, $P(B_2) = .15$, and $P(B_3) = .65$. Consider another event A such that $P(A|B_1) = .4, P(A|B_2) = .25$, and $P(A|B_3) = .6$. Use Bayes's Rule to find
  a. $P(B_1|A)$ .158
  b. $P(B_2|A)$ .074
  c. $P(B_3|A)$ .768

3.76 Suppose the events B_1, B_2, and B_3 are mutually exclusive and complementary events, such that $P(B_1) = .2$, $P(B_2) = .15$, and $P(B_3) = .65$. Consider another event A such that $P(A) = .4$. If A is independent of B_1, B_2, and B_3, use Bayes' Rule to show that $P(B_1|A) = P(B_1) = .2$. .2

Applying the Concepts — Basic

DDT

3.77 Refer to the U.S. Army Corps of Engineers' study on the DDT contamination of fish in the Tennessee River (Alabama), Example 1.5 (p. 17). Part of the investigation focused on how far upstream the contaminated fish have migrated. (A fish is considered to be contaminated if its measured DDT concentration is greater than 5.0 parts per million.)

  a. Considering only the contaminated fish captured from the Tennessee River, the data reveal that 52% of the fish are found between 275 and 300 miles upstream, 39% are found 305 to 325 miles upstream, and 9% are found 330 to 350 miles upstream. Use these percentages to determine the probabilities, $P(275–300)$, $P(305–325)$, and $P(330–350)$. .09

  b. Given a contaminated fish is found a certain distance upstream, the probability that it is a channel catfish (CC) is determined from the data as $P(CC|275–300) = .775, P(CC|305–325) = .77$, and $P(CC|330–350) = .86$. If a contaminated channel catfish is captured from the Tennessee River, what is the probability that it was captured 275–300 miles upstream? .516

3.78 A construction company employs three sales engineers. Engineers 1, 2, and 3 estimate the costs of 30%, 20%, and 50%, respectively, of all jobs bid by the company. For $i = 1, 2, 3$, define E_i to be the event that a job is estimated by engineer i. The following probabilities describe the rates at which the engineers make serious errors in estimating costs:

$P(\text{error}|E_1) = .01$, $P(\text{error}|E_2) = .03$, and $P(\text{error}|E_3) = .02$

a. If a particular bid results in a serious error in estimating job cost, what is the probability that the error was made by engineer 1? .158

b. If a particular bid results in a serious error in estimating job cost, what is the probability that the error was made by engineer 2? .316

c. If a particular bid results in a serious error in estimating job cost, what is the probability that the error was made by engineer 3? .526

d. Based on the probabilities, parts a–c, which engineer is most likely responsible for making the serious error? #3

Applying the Concepts—Intermediate

3.79 A manufacturing operation utilizes two production lines to assemble electronic fuses. Both lines produce fuses at the same rate and generally produce 2.5% defective fuses. However, production line 1 recently suffered mechanical difficulty and produced 6.0% defectives during a three-week period. This situation was not known until several lots of electronic fuses produced in this period were shipped to customers. If one of the two fuses tested by a customer was found to be defective, what is the probability that the lot from which it came was produced on malfunctioning line 1? (Assume all the fuses in the lot were produced on the same line.) .6982

3.80 The local area network (LAN) for the College of Business computing system at a large university is temporarily shutdown for repairs. Previous shutdowns have been due to hardware failure, software failure, or power failure. Maintenance engineers have determined that the probabilities of hardware, software, and power problems are .01, .05, and .02, respectively. They have also determined that if the system experiences hardware problems, it shuts down 73% of the time. Similarly, if software problems occur, the system shuts down 12% of the time; and, if power failure occurs, the system shuts down 88% of the time. What is the probability that the current shutdown of the LAN is due to hardware failure? Software failure? Power failure? .2362; .1942; .5696

3.81 An important component of your desktop or laptop personal computer (PC) is a microchip. The table gives the proportions of microchips that a certain PC manufacturer purchases from seven suppliers.

Supplier	Proportion
S_1	.15
S_2	.05
S_3	.10
S_4	.20
S_5	.12
S_6	.20
S_7	.18

a. It is known that the proportions of defective microchips produced by the seven suppliers are .001, .0003, .0007, .006, .0002, .0002, and .001, respectively. If a single PC microchip failure is observed, which supplier is most likely responsible? #4

b. Suppose the seven suppliers produce defective microchips at the same rate, .0005. If a single PC microchip failure is observed, which supplier is most likely responsible? #4 or #6

Quick Review

Key Formulas

$$\binom{N}{n} = \frac{N!}{n!(N-n)!}$$

where $N! = N(N-1)(N-2)\cdots(2)(1)$

$P(A) + P(A^c) = 1$

$P(A \cup B) = P(A) + P(B) - P(A \cap B)$

$P(A \cap B) = 0$

$P(A \cup B) = P(A) + P(B)$

$$P(A|B) = \frac{P(A \cap B)}{P(B)}$$

$P(A \cap B) = P(A)P(B|A) = P(B)P(A|B)$

$P(A|B) = P(A)$

$P(A \cap B) = P(A)P(B)$

$$P(B_i|A) = \frac{P(B_i)P(A|B_i)}{P(B_1)P(A|B_1) + P(B_2)P(A|B_2) + \cdots + P(B_k)P(A|B_k)}$$

Combinations rule   156

Rule of Complements   164

Additive rule   165

Mutually exclusive events   166

Additive rule for mutually exclusive events   166

Conditional probability   172

Multiplicative rule   175

Independent events   178

Multiplicative rule for independent events   180

*Bayes's rule   191

Language Lab

Symbol	Pronunciation	Description
S		Sample space
$S: \{1, 2, 3, 4, 5\}$		Set of sample points, $1, 2, 3, 4, 5$, in sample space
$A: \{1, 2\}$		Set of sample points, $1, 2$, in event A
$P(A)$	Probability of A	Probability that event A occurs
$A \cup B$	A union B	Union of events A and B (either A or B or both occur)
$A \cap B$	A intersect B	Intersection of events A and B (both A and B occur)
A^c	A complement	Complement of event A (the event that A does not occur)
$P(A|B)$	Probability of A given B	Conditional probability that event A occurs given that event B occurs
$\binom{N}{n}$	N chose n	Number of combinations of N elements taken n at a time
$N!$	N factorial	Multiply $N(N-1)(N-2)\cdots(2)(1)$

Summary

Chapter Summary Notes

- Probability rules for k **sample points:** (1) $0 \le P(S_i) \le 1$ and (2) $\sum_{i=1}^{x} P(S_i) = 1$

- If $A = \{S_1, S_3, S_4\}$, then $P(A) = P(S_1) + P(S_3) + P(S_4)$

- The number of samples of size n that can be selected from N element is $\binom{N}{n}$

- **Union:** $(A \cup B)$ implies that either A or B will occur.

- **Intersection:** $(A \cap B)$ implies that both A and B will occur.

- **Complement:** A^c is all the sample points not in A.

- **Conditional:** $(A|B)$ is the event that A occurs, given B has occurred.

- **Independent:** B occurring does not change the probability that A occurs.

- **Random sample:** All possible samples have equal probability of being selected.

Supplementary Exercises 3.82–3.116

[Note: Exercises marked with an asterisk (*) are from the optional section.]

Learning the Mechanics

3.82 A sample space consists of four sample points, where $P(S_1) = .2, P(S_2) = .1, P(S_3) = .3$, and $P(S_4) = .4$.
   a. Show that the sample points obey the two probability rules for a sample space.
   b. If an event $A = \{S_1, S_4\}$, find $P(A)$.   .6

3.83 A and B are mutually exclusive events, with $P(A) = .2$ and $P(B) = .3$.
   a. Find $P(A|B)$.   0
   b. Are A and B independent events?   No

3.84 For two events A and B, suppose $P(A) = .7, P(B) = .5$, and $P(A \cap B) = .4$. Find $P(A \cup B)$.   .8

3.85 Given that $P(A \cap B) = .4$ and $P(A|B) = .8$, find $P(B)$.

3.86 Which of the following pairs of events are mutually exclusive? Justify your response.
   a. {The Dow Jones Industrial Average increases on Monday}, {A large New York bank decreases its prime interest rate on Monday}
   b. {The next sale by a PC retailer is a laptop computer}, {The next sale by a PC retailer is desktop computer}
   c. {You reinvest all your dividend income in a limited partnership}, {You reinvest all your dividend income in a money market fund}

3.87 The accompanying Venn diagram illustrates a sample space containing six sample points and three events, A, B, and C. The probabilities of the sample points are $P(1) = .3, P(2) = .2, P(3) = .1, P(4) = .1, P(5) = .1$, and $P(6) = .2$.

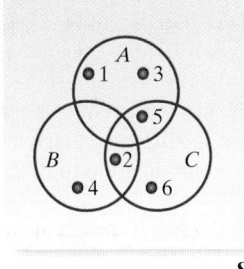

S

   a. Find $P(A \cap B), P(B \cap C), P(A \cup C)$, $P(A \cup B \cup C), P(B^c), P(A^c \cap B), P(B|C)$, and $P(B|A)$.
   b. Are A and B independent? Mutually exclusive? Why?
   c. Are B and C independent? Mutually exclusive? Why?

3.88 Two events, A and B, are independent, with $P(A) = .3$ and $P(B) = .1$.
   a. Are A and B mutually exclusive? Why?   No
   b. Find $P(A|B)$ and $P(B|A)$.   .3, .1

c. Find $P(A \cup B)$.   .37

3.89 Find the numerical value of
   a. 6!   **b.** $\binom{10}{9}$ **c.** $\binom{10}{1}$ **d.** $\binom{6}{3}$ **e.** 0!

3.90 A random sample of five graduate students is to be selected from 50 MBA majors for participation in a case competition.
   a. In how many different ways can the sample be drawn?   2,118,760
   b. Show how the random number table, Table I of Appendix B, can be used to select the sample of students.

Applying the Concepts—Basic

3.91 Refer to the National Highway Traffic Safety Administration (NHTSA) crash tests of new car models, Exercise 2.127 (p. 124). Recall that the NHTSA has developed a "star" scoring system, with results ranging from one star (*) to five stars (*****). The more stars in the rating, the better the level of crash protection in a head-on collision. A summary of the driver-side star ratings for 98 cars is reproduced in the accompanying MINITAB printout. Assume that one of the 98 cars is selected at random. State whether each of the following is true or false.
   a. The probability that the car has a rating of two stars is 4.   False
   b. The probability that the car has a rating of four or five stars is .7857.   True
   c. The probability that the car has a rating of one star is 0.   True
   d. The car has a better chance of having a two-star rating than of having a five-star rating.   False

```
Tally for Discrete Variables: DrivStar

DrivStar   Count   Percent
     2        4      4.08
     3       17     17.35
     4       59     60.20
     5       18     18.37
    N=       98
```

3.92 Many U.S. manufacturers are adopting the ISO 9000 series of standards for setting up and documenting quality systems, processes, and procedures. However, it is not generally known how managers who have led or participated in the implementation of the standards view them or how the standards were achieved. A sample of 40 ISO 9000–registered companies in Colorado was selected and the manager most responsible for

ISO 9000 implementation was interviewed (*Quality Progress*, 1995). The following are some of the data obtained by the study:

Level of Top Management involvement in the ISO 9000 Registration Process	Frequency
Very involved	9
Moderate involvement	16
Minimal involvement	12
Not involved	3

Length of Time to Achieve ISO 9000 Registration	Frequency
Less than 1 year	5
1–1.5 years	21
1.6–2 years	9
2.1–2.5 years	2
More than 2.5 years	3

Source: Weston, F.C., "What Do Managers Really Think of the ISO 9000 Registration Process?" *Quality Progress,* October 1995, p. 68–69 (Tables 3 and 4).

Suppose one of the 40 managers who were interviewed is to be randomly selected for additional questioning. Consider the events defined as follows:

A: {The manager was involved in the ISO 9000 registration}

B: {The length of time to achieve ISO 9000 registration was more than 2 years}

a. Find $P(A)$. .925
b. Find $P(B)$. .125
c. Explain why the above data are not sufficient to determine whether events A and B are independent.

3.93 According to a 1998 national survey conducted for CACI Marketing Systems, 25% of American adults smoke cigarettes. Of these smokers, 13% attempted (but failed) to quit smoking during the past year. Define the following events:

A: {An American adult smokes}

B: {A smoker attempted to quit smoking last year}

a. Find $P(A)$. .25
b. Find $P(B|A)$. .13
c. Find $P(A^c)$. State this probability in the words of the problem. .75
d. Find $P(A \cap B)$. State this probability in the words of the problem. .0325

3.94 The types of occupations of the 106,757,000 employed workers (age 16 years and older) in the United States in 1997 are described in the next table,

and their relative frequencies are listed. A worker is to be selected at random from this population and his or her occupation is to be determined. (Assume that each worker in the population has only one occupation.)

a. What is the probability that the worker will be a male service worker? .05
b. What is the probability that the worker will be a manager or a professional? .32
c. What is the probability that the worker will be a female professional or a female operator/fabricator/laborer? .19
d. What is the probability that the worker will not be in a technical/sales administrative occupation? .72

Occupation	Relative Frequency
Male Worker	.54
Managerial/professional	.16
Technical/sales/administrative	.10
Service	.05
Precision production, craft, and repair	.11
Operators/fabricators/laborers	.10
Farming, forestry, and fishing	.02
Female Worker	.46
Managerial/professional	.16
Technical/sales/administrative	.18
Service	.07
Precision production, craft, and repair	.01
Operators/fabricators/laborers	.03
Farming, forestry, and fishing	.01

Source: Statistical Abstract of the United States: 1998. p. 421.

3.95 A local country club has a membership of 600 and operates facilities that include an 18-hole championship golf course and 12 tennis courts. Before deciding whether to accept new members, the club president would like to know how many members regularly use each facility. A survey of the membership indicates that 70% regularly use the golf course, 50% regularly use the tennis courts, and 5% use neither of these facilities regularly.

a. Construct a Venn diagram to describe the results of the survey.
b. If one club member is chosen at random, what is the probability that the member uses either the golf course or the tennis courts or both? .95
c. If one member is chosen at random, what is the probability that the member uses both the golf and the tennis facilities? .25
d. A member is chosen at random from among those known to use the tennis courts regularly. What is the probability that the member also uses the golf course regularly? .5

3.96 Refer to the *American Journal of Public Health* study of unintentional carbon monoxide (CO) poisonings in

Colorado, Exercise 3.17 (p. 159). The 981 cases were classified in a table, which is reproduced below. A case of unintentional CO poisoning is chosen at random from the 981 cases.

Source of Exposure	Fatal	Nonfatal	Total
Fire	63	53	116
Auto exhaust	60	178	238
Furnace	18	345	363
Kerosene or spaceheater	9	18	27
Appliance	9	63	72
Other gas-powered motor	3	73	76
Fireplace	0	16	16
Other	3	19	22
Unknown	9	42	51
Total	174	807	981

Source: Cook, M. C., Simon, P. A., and Hoffman, R. E. "Unintentional Carbon Monoxide Poisoning in Colorado, 1986 through 1991." *American Journal of Public Health*, Vol. 85, No. 7, July 1995, p. 989 (Table 1). © 1995 American Public Health Association.

a. Given that the source of the poisoning is fire, what is the probability that the case is fatal?

b. Given that the case is nonfatal, what is the probability that it is caused by auto exhaust?

c. If the case is fatal, what is the probability that the source is unknown?   .052

d. If the case is nonfatal, what is the probability that the source is not fire or a fireplace?   .914

Applying the Concepts—Intermediate

3.97 A research and development company surveyed all 200 of its employees over the age of 60 and obtained the information given in the next table. One of these 200 employees is selected at random.

a. What is the probability that the person selected is on the technical staff?   .75

b. If the person selected has over 20 years of service with the company, what is the probability that the person plans to retire at age 68?   .2875

c. If the person selected is on the technical staff, what is the probability that the person has been with the company less than 20 years?   .6

d. What is the probability that the person selected has over 20 years with the company, is on the nontechnical staff, and plans to retire at age 65?   .06

e. Consider the events A: {Plan to retire at age 68} and B: {On the technical staff}. Are events A and B independent? Explain.   No

f. Consider the event D: {Plan to retire at age 68 *and* on the technical staff}. Describe the complement of event D.

g. Consider the event E: {On the nontechnical staff}. Are events B and E mutually exclusive? Explain.   Yes

3.98 The state legislature has appropriated $1 million to be distributed in the form of grants to individuals and organizations engaged in the research and development of alternative energy sources. You have been hired by the state's energy agency to assemble a panel of five energy experts whose task it will be to determine which individuals and organizations should receive the grant money. You have identified 11 equally qualified individuals who are willing to serve on the panel. How many different panels of five experts could be formed from these 11 individuals?   462

3.99 A manufacturer of electronic digital watches claims that the probability of its watch running more than 1 minute slow or 1 minute fast after 1 year of use is .05. A consumer protection agency has purchased four of the manufacturer's watches with the intention of testing the claim.

a. Assuming that the manufacturer's claim is correct, what is the probability that none of the watches are as accurate as claimed?   .00000625

b. Assuming that the manufacturer's claim is correct, what is the probability that exactly two of the four watches are as accurate as claimed?   .0135

c. Suppose that only one of the four tested watches is as accurate as claimed. What inference can be made about the manufacturer's claim? Explain.

d. Suppose that none of the watches tested are as accurate as claimed. Is it necessarily true that the manufacturer's claim is false? Explain.

3.100 The corporations in the highly competitive razor blade industry do a tremendous amount of advertising each year. Corporation G gave a supply of three top name brands, G, S, and W, to a consumer and asked her to use them and rank them in order of preference. The corporation was, of course, hoping the consumer would prefer its brand and rank it

	Under 20 Years with Company		Over 20 Years with Company	
	Technical Staff	Nontechnical Staff	Technical Staff	Nontechnical Staff
Plan to Retire at Age 65	31	5	45	12
Plan to Retire at Age 68	59	25	15	8

first, thereby giving them some material for a consumer interview advertising campaign. If the consumer did not prefer one blade over any other, but was still required to rank the blades, what is the probability that

a. The consumer ranked brand G first?   1/3

b. The consumer ranked brand G last?   1/3

c. The consumer ranked brand G last and brand W second?   1/6

d. The consumer ranked brand W first, brand G second, and brand S third?   1/6

3.101 Acupoll is a consumer preference poll used to predict whether newly developed products will succeed if they are brought to market. The reliability of the Acupoll has been described as follows: The probability that Acupoll predicts the success of a particular product, given that later the product actually is successful, is .89 (*Minneapolis Star Tribune*, Dec. 16, 1992). A company is considering the introduction of a new product and assesses the product's probability of success to be .90. If this company were to have its product evaluated through Acupoll, what is the probability that Acupoll predicts success for the product and the product actually turns out to be successful?   .801

3.102 Use your intuitive understanding of independence to form an opinion about whether each of the following scenarios represent independent events.

a. The results of consecutive tosses of a coin   Yes

b. The opinions of randomly selected individuals in a preelection poll   Yes

c. A major league baseball player's results in two consecutive at-bats   No

d. The amount of gain or loss associated with investments in different stocks if these stocks are bought on the same day and sold on the same day one month later   No

e. The amount of gain or loss associated with investments in different stocks that are bought and sold in different time periods, five years apart   Yes

f. The prices bid by two different development firms in response to a building construction proposal   No

3.103 "Channel One" is an education television network that is available to all secondary schools in the United States. Participating schools are equipped with TV sets in every classroom in order to receive the Channel One broadcasts. According to *Educational Technology* (May–June 1995), 40% of all U.S. secondary schools subscribe to the Channel One Communications Network (CCN). Of these subscribers, only 5% never use the CCN broadcasts, while 20% use CCN more than five times per week.

a. Find the probability that a randomly selected U.S. secondary school subscribes to CCN but never uses the CCN broadcasts.   .02

b. Find the probability that a randomly selected U.S. secondary school subscribes to CCN and uses the broadcasts more than five times per week.   .08

3.104 A particular automatic sprinkler system for high-rise apartment buildings, office buildings, and hotels has two different types of activation devices for each sprinkler head. One type has a reliability of .91 (i.e., the probability that it will activate the sprinkler when it should is .91). The other type, which operates independently of the first type, has a reliability of .87. Suppose a serious fire starts near a particular sprinkler head.

a. What is the probability that the sprinkler head will be activated?   .9883

b. What is the probability that the sprinkler head will not be activated?   .0117

c. What is the probability that both activation devices will work properly?   .7917

d. What is the probability that only the device with reliability .91 will work properly?   .1183

3.105 Most companies offer their employees a variety of health care plans to choose from, e.g., preferred provider organizations (PPOs) and health maintenance organizations (HMOs) (*Monthly Labor Review*, Oct. 1995). A survey of 100 large, 100 medium, and 100 small companies that offer their employees HMOs, PPOs, and fee-for-service plans was conducted; each firm provided information on the plans chosen by their employees. These companies had a total employment of 833,303 people. A breakdown of the number of employees in each category by firm size and plan is provided in the table.

Company Size	Fee-for-Service	PPO	HMO	Totals
Small	1,808	1,757	1,456	5,021
Medium	8,953	6,491	6,938	22,382
Large	330,419	241,770	233,711	805,900
Totals	341,180	250,018	242,105	833,303

Source: Adapted from Bucci, M., and Grant, R. "Employer-Sponsored Health Insurance: What's Offered: What's Chosen?" *Monthly Labor Review*, October 1995, pp. 38–43.

One employee from the 833,303 total employees is to be chosen at random for further analysis. Define the events *A* and *B* as follows:

A: {Observe an employee that chose fee-for-service}

B: {Observe an employee from a small company}

a. Find $P(B)$.   .0060

b. Find $P(A \cap B)$.

c. Find $P(A \cup B)$.   .4133

d. Find $P(A|B)$.

e. Are *A* and *B* independent? Justify your answer.

3.106 The *Journal of Risk and Uncertainty* (May 1992) published an article investigating the relationship of injury rate of drivers of all-terrain vehicles (ATVs) to a variety of factors. One of the more interesting factors studied, age of the driver, was found to have a strong relationship to injury rate. The article reports that prior to a safety-awareness program, 14% of the ATV drivers were under age 12; another 13% were 12–15, and 48% were under age 25. Suppose an ATV driver is selected at random prior to the installation of the safety-awareness program.

  a. Find the probability that the ATV driver is 15 years old or younger. .27

  b. Find the probability that the ATV driver is 25 years old or older. .52

  c. Given that the ATV driver is under age 25, what is the probability the driver is under age 12? .2917

  d. Are the events Under age 25 and Under age 12 mutually exclusive? Why or why not? No

  e. Are the events Under age 25 and Under age 12 independent? Why or why not? No

3.107 The probability that an Avon salesperson sells beauty products to a prospective customer on the first visit to the customer is .4. If the salesperson fails to make the sale on the first visit, the probability that the sale will be made on the second visit is .65. The salesperson never visits a prospective customer more than twice. What is the probability that the salesperson will make a sale to a particular customer? .79

3.108 The performance of quality inspectors affects both the quality of outgoing products and the cost of the products. A product that passes inspection is assumed to meet quality standards; a product that fails inspection may be reworked, scrapped, or reinspected. Quality engineers at Westinghouse Electric Corporation evaluated performances of inspectors in judging the quality of solder joints by comparing each inspector's classifications of a set of 153 joints with the consensus evaluation of a panel of experts. The results for a particular inspector are shown in the next table.

Committee's Judgment	Inspector's Judgment	
	Joint Acceptable	Joint Rejectable
Joint acceptable	101	10
Joint rejectable	23	19

Source: Meagher, J. J., and Scazzero, J. A. "Measuring Inspector Variability." *39th Annual Quality Congress Transactions,* May 1985, pp. 75–81, American Society for Quality Control.

One of the 153 solder joints is to be selected at random.

  a. What is the probability that the inspector judges the joint to be acceptable? That the committee judges the joint to be acceptable? .810; .725

  b. What is the probability that both the inspector and the committee judge the joint to be acceptable? That neither judge the joint to be acceptable? .660; .124

  c. What is the probability that the inspector and the committee disagree? Agree? .216; .784

3.109 The first figure shown at the bottom of the page is a schematic representation of a system comprised of three components. The system operates properly only if all three components operate properly. The three components are said to operate *in series*. The components could be mechanical or electrical; they could be work stations in an assembly process; or they could represent the functions of three different departments in an organization. The probability of failure for each component is listed in the table. Assume the components operate independently of each other.

Component	Probability of Failure
1	.12
2	.09
3	.11

  a. Find the probability that the system operates properly. .7127

  b. What is the probability that at least one of the components will fail and therefore that the system will fail? .2873

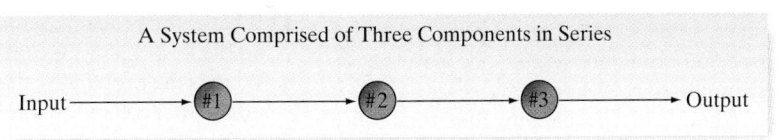

A System Comprised of Three Components in Series

Input ——→ #1 ——→ #2 ——→ #3 ——→ Output

Figure for Exercise 3.109

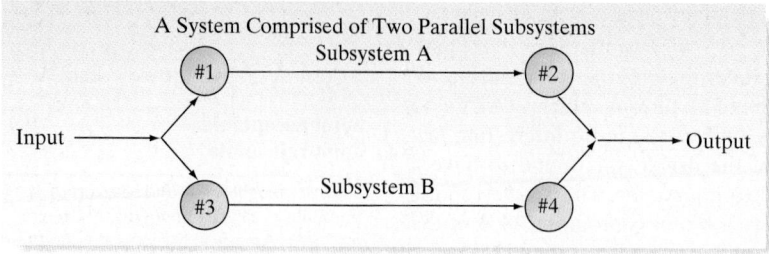

Figure for Exercise 3.110

3.110 The figure shown above is a representation of a comprised of two subsystems that are said to operate *in parallel*. Each subsystem has two components that operate in series (refer to Exercise 3.109). The system will operate properly as long as at least one of the subsystems functions properly. The probability of failure for each component in the system is .1. Assume the components operate independently of each other.

a. Find the probability that the system operates properly. .9639

b. Find the probability that exactly one subsystem fails.

c. Find the probability that the system fails to operate properly. .0361

d. How many parallel subsystems like the two shown here would be required to guarantee that the system would operate properly at least 99% of the time? 3

3.111 A fair coin is flipped 20 times and 20 heads are observed. In such cases it is often said that a tail is due on the next flip. Is this statement true or false? Explain. False

Applying the Concepts—Advanced*

*3.112 A small brewery has two bottling machines. Machine A produces 75% of the bottles and machine B produces 25%. One out of every 20 bottles filled by A is rejected for some reason, while one out of every 30 bottles from B is rejected. What proportion of bottles is rejected? What is the probability that a randomly selected bottle comes from machine A, given that it is accepted? .7467

*3.113 A press produces parts used in the manufacture of large-screen plasma televisions. If the press is correctly adjusted, it produces parts with a scrap rate of 5%. If it is not adjusted correctly, it produces scrap at a 50% rate. From past company records, the machine is known to be correctly adjusted 90% of the time. A quality control inspector randomly selects one part from those recently produced by the press and discovers it is defective. What is the probability that the machine is incorrectly adjusted? .526

3.114 Pneumovax is an antipneumonia vaccine designed especially for elderly patients who are vulnerable to bacterial pneumonia. The vaccine is 90% effective in stimulating the production of antibodies to pneumonia-producing bacteria (i.e., it is 90% successful in preventing a person exposed to pneumonia from acquiring the disease). Suppose the probability that an elderly person is exposed to these bacteria is .40 (whether inoculated or not) and, after being exposed, the probability that the person will contract bacterial pneumonia if not inoculated with the vaccine is .95. Find the probability that an elderly person inoculated with this new vaccine acquires pneumonia. What is the probability if this person has not been inoculated? .04; .38

3.115 Blackjack, a favorite game of gamblers, is played by a dealer and at least one opponent (called a "player"). In one version of the game, 2 cards of a standard 52-card bridge deck are dealt to the player and 2 cards to the dealer. For this exercise, assume that drawing an ace and a face card is called *blackjack*. If the dealer does not draw a blackjack and the player does, the player wins. If both the dealer and player draw blackjack, a "push" (i.e., a tie) occurs.

a. What is the probability that the dealer will draw a blackjack? .0362

b. What is the probability that the player wins with a blackjack? .0335

3.116 A version of the dice game "craps" is played in the following manner. A player starts by rolling two balanced dice. If the roll (the sum of the two numbers showing on the dice) results in a 7 or 11, the player wins. If the roll results in a 2 or a 3 (called "craps"), the player loses. For any other roll outcome, the player continues to throw the dice until the original roll outcome recurs (in which case the player wins) or until a 7 occurs (in which case the player loses).

a. What is the probability that a player wins the game on the first roll of the dice? .2222

b. What is the probability that a player loses the game on the first roll of the dice? .0833

c. If the player throws a total of 4 on the first roll, what is the probability that the game ends (win or lose) on the next roll? .25

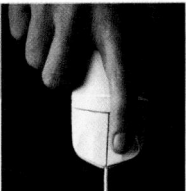

Using Technology

3.1 Generating a Random Sample Using SPSS

To obtain a random sample of observations (cases) from a data set stored in the SPSS spreadsheet, click on the "Data" button on the SPSS menu bar, then click on "Select Cases", as shown in Figure 3.S.1. The resulting menu list appears as shown in Figure 3.S.2. Select "Random sample of cases" from the list, then click on the "Sample" button. The dialog box shown in Figure 3.S.3 will appear. You will specify the sample size either as a percentage of cases or a raw number. After you specify the sample size, click "Continue" to return to the "Select Cases" dialog box (Figure 3.S.2) and click "OK". The SPSS spreadsheet will reappear with the selected. (sampled) cases.

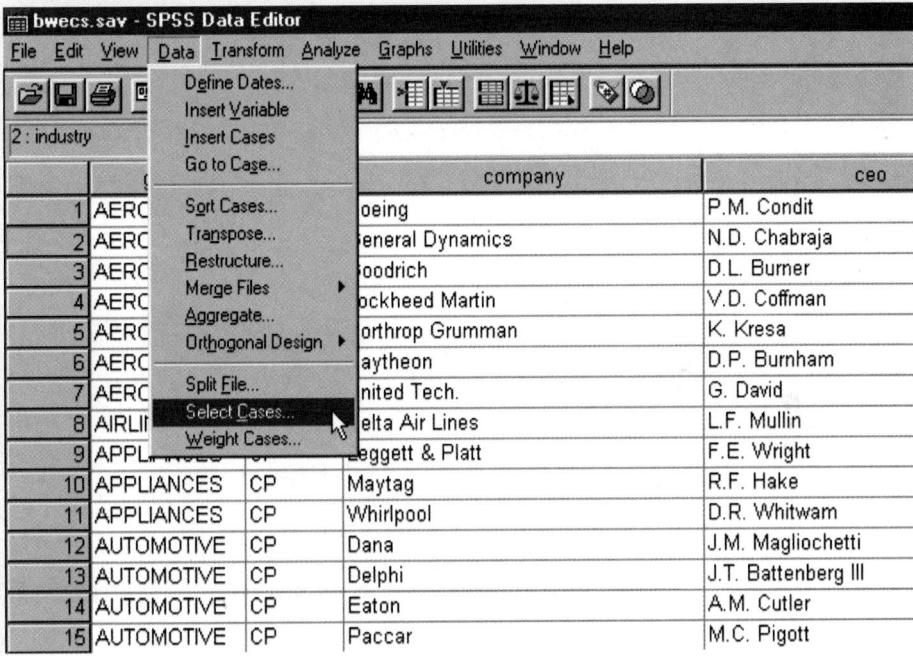

Figure 3.S.1
SPSS menu options for sampling your data

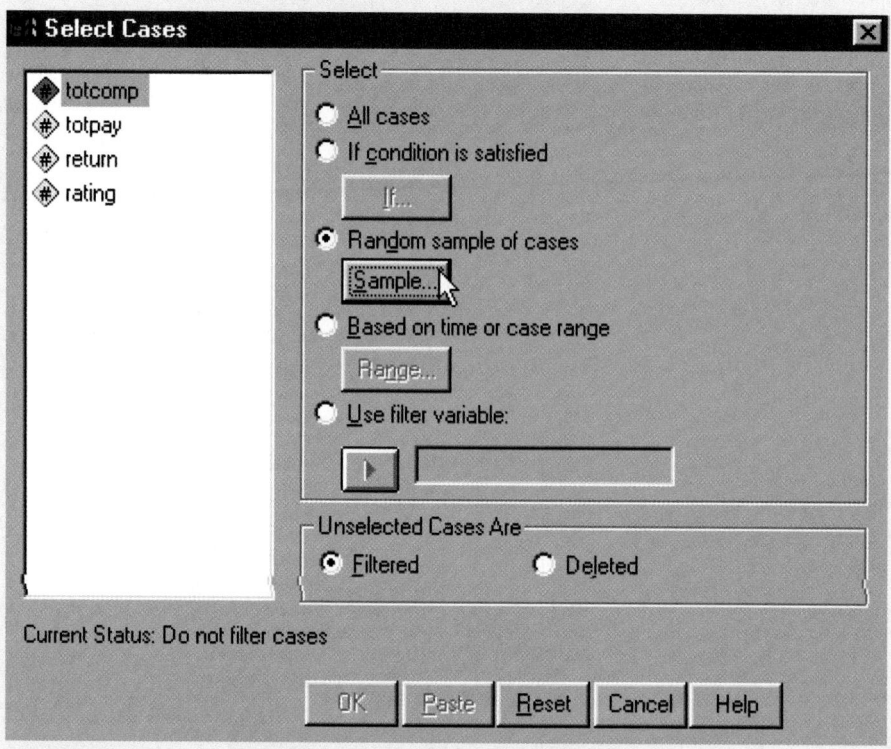

Figure 3.S.2
SPSS options for selecting a random sample

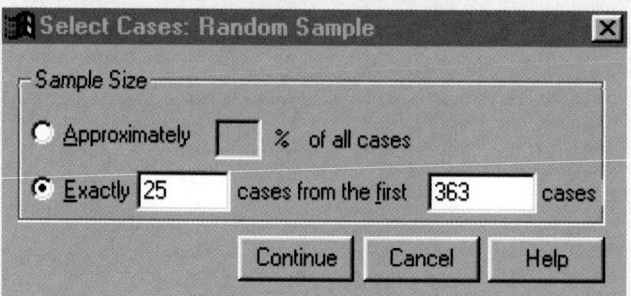

Figure 3.S.3
SPSS random sample dialog box

3.2 Generating a Random Sample Using MINITAB

To obtain a random sample of observations (cases) from a data set stored in the MINITAB worksheet, click on the "Calc" button on the MINITAB menu bar, then click on "Random Data", and finally, click on "Sample from Columns", as shown in Figure 3.M.1. The resulting dialog box appears as shown in Figure 3.M.2. Specify the sample size (i.e., number of rows), the variable(s) to be sampled, and the column(s) where you want to save the sample. Click "OK" and the MINITAB worksheet will reappear with the values of the variable for the selected (sampled) cases in the column specified.

In MINITAB, you can also generate a sample of case numbers. From the MINITAB menu, click on the "Calc" button, then click on "Random Data", and finally, click on the "Uniform" option (see Figure 3.M.1). The resulting dialog box appears as shown in Figure 3.M.3. Specify the number of cases (rows) (i.e., the sample size), and the column where the case numbers selected will be stored. Click "OK" and the MINITAB worksheet will reappear with the case numbers for the selected (sampled) cases in the column specified.

[*Note:* If you want the option of generating the same (identical) sample multiple times from the data set, then first click on the "Set Base" option shown in Figure 3.M.1. Specify an integer in the resulting dialog box. If you always select the same integer, MINITAB will select the same sample when you choose the random sampling options.]

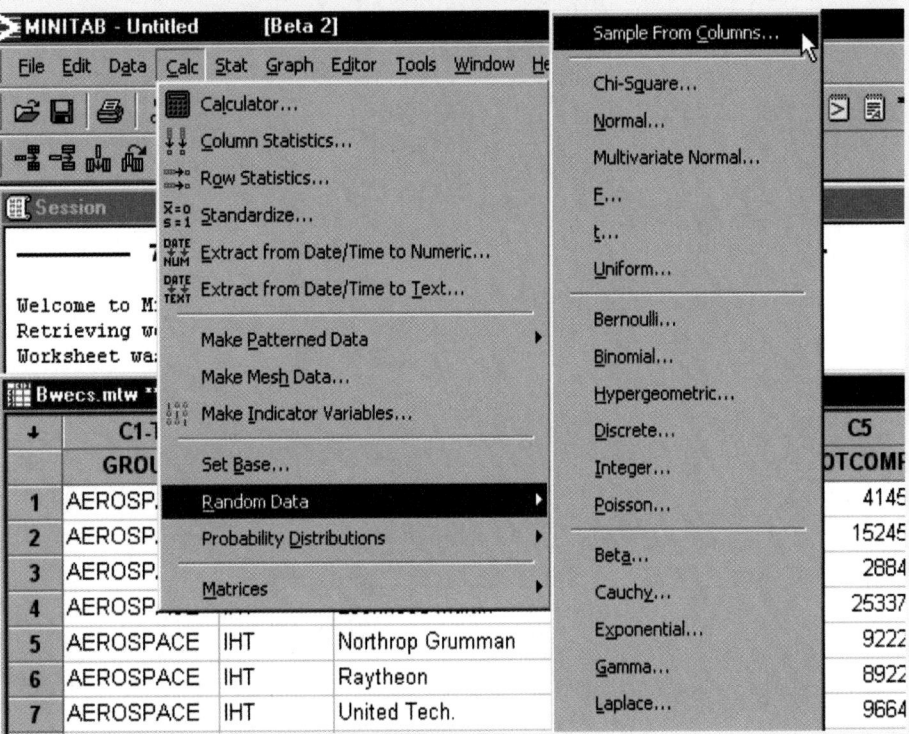

Figure 3.M.1
MINITAB menu options for sampling your data

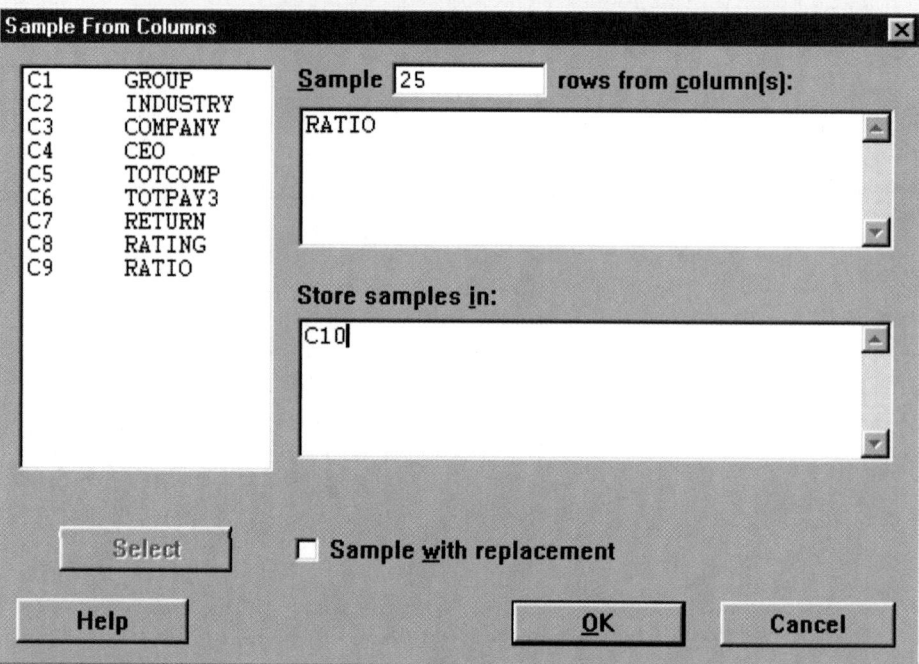

Figure 3.M.2
MINITAB options for selecting a random sample from worksheet columns

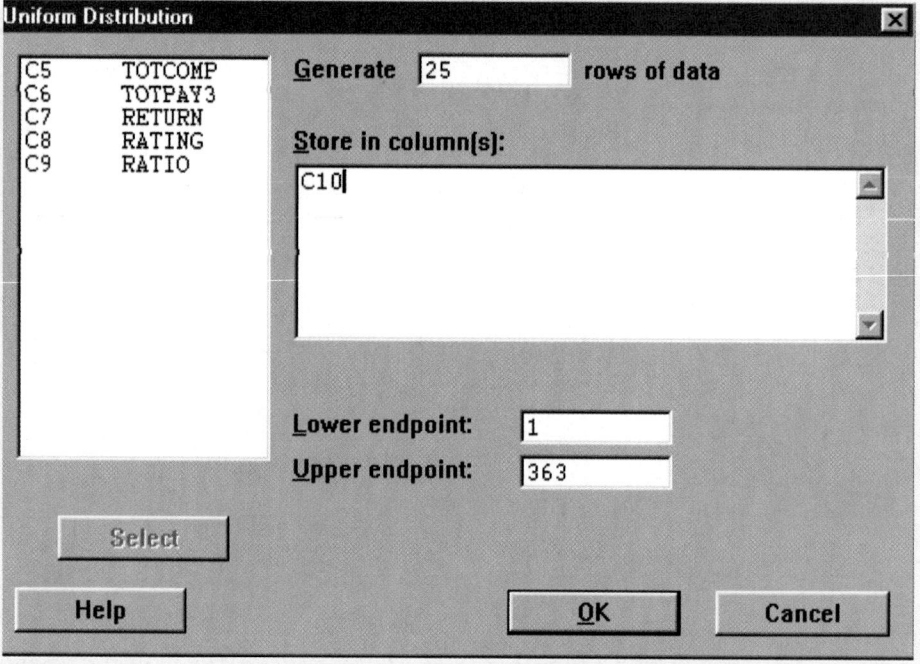

Figure 3.M.3
MINITAB options for selecting a random sample of cases

3.3 Generating a Random Sample Using EXCEL/PHStat2

To obtain a random sample of observations (cases) from a data set stored in the EXCEL spreadsheet, enter into a PHStat2 session. From the PHStat2 main menu, click on the "PHStat" button, then click on "Sampling", and finally, click on "Random Sample Generator", as shown in Figure 3.E.1. The resulting dialog box appears as shown in Figure 3.E.2. Specify the sample size (i.e., number of cases), then decide whether you want a list of case numbers or a list of values of the variable of interest. For a list of case numbers, select "Generate list of random numbers" and specify the population size (see Figure 3.E.2). For a list of the values of the variable, select "Values from range" and specify the cell range (see Figure 3.E.3). After making your selections, click "OK" and a new EXCEL worksheet with the random numbers will appear on the screen.

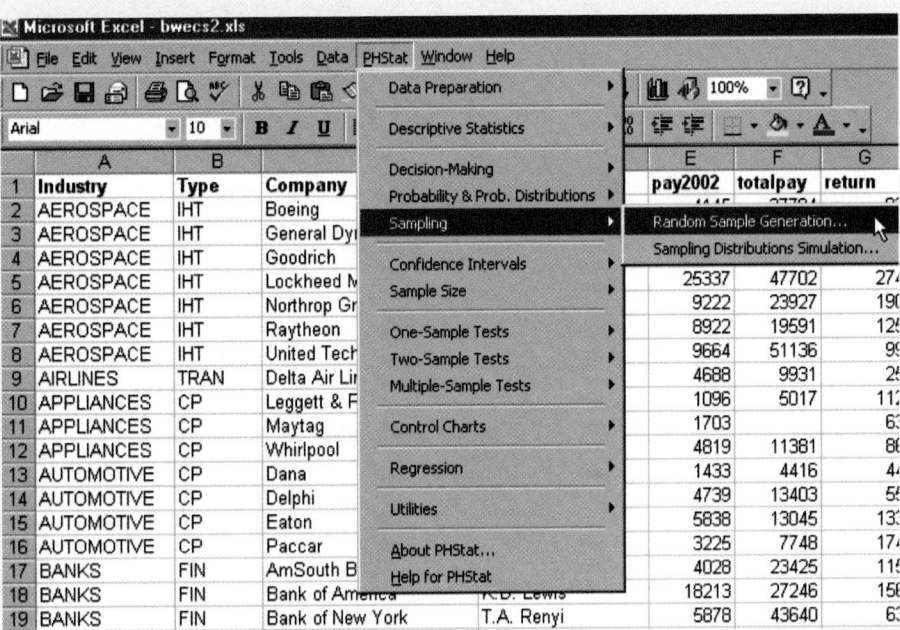

Figure 3.E.1
EXCEL/PHStat2 menu options for sampling your data

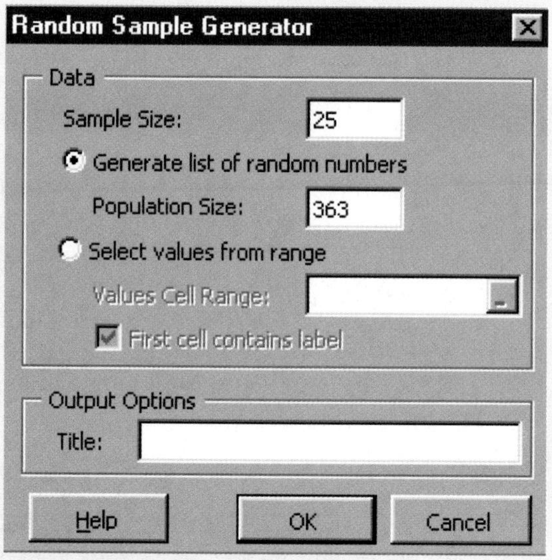

Figure 3.E.2
EXCEL/PHStat2 random sample generator dialog
box with options for selecting case numbers

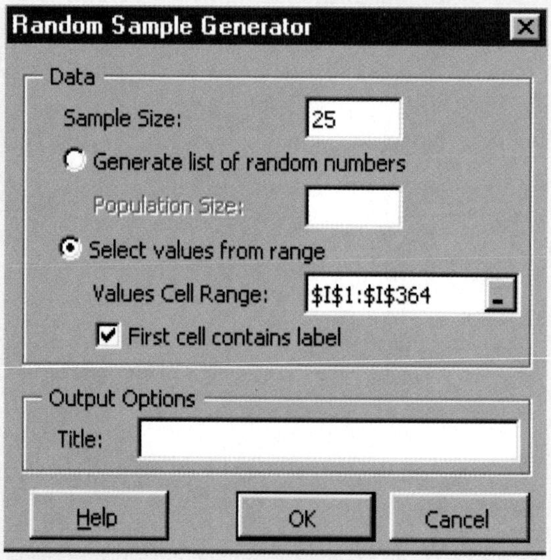

Figure 3.E.3
EXCEL/PHStat2 random sample generator dialog
box with options for selecting values of a variable

REFERENCES

Bennett, D. J. *Randomness*. Cambridge, Mass.: Harvard University Press, 1998.

Benson, G. "Process Thinking: The Quality Catalyst." *Minnesota Management Review*, University of Minnesota, Minneapolis, Fall 1992.

Epstein, R. A. *The Theory of Gambling and Statistical Logic*, rev. ed. New York: Academic Press, 1977.

Feller, W. *An Introduction to Probability Theory and Its Applications*, 3rd ed., Vol. 1. New York: Wiley, 1968.

Kotler, Philip. *Marketing Management*, 8th ed. Englewood Cliffs, N.J.: Prentice Hall, 1994.

Lindley, D. V. *Making Decisions*, 2nd ed. London: Wiley, 1985.

Parzen, E. *Modern Probability Theory and Its Applications*. New York: Wiley, 1960.

Wackerly, D., Mendenhall, W., and Scheaffer, R. L. *Mathematical Statistics with Applications*, 6th ed. Boston: Duxbury, 2002.

Stickney, Clyde P., and Weil, Roman L. *Financial Accounting: An Introduction to Concepts, Methods, and Uses*, 7th ed. Fort Worth: The Dryden Press, 1994.

Williams, B. *A Sampler on Sampling*. New York: Wiley, 1978.

Winkler, R. L. *An Introduction to Bayesian Inference and Decision*. New York: Holt, Rinehart and Winston, 1972.

Wright, G., and Ayton, P., eds. *Subjective Probability*. New York: Wiley, 1994.

Discrete Random Variables

Contents

Statistics in Action

Probability in a Reverse Cocaine Sting

Technology Tutorials

Where We've Been

- Used probability to make an inference about a population from data in an observed sample
- Used probability to measure the reliability of the inference

Where We're Going

- Develop the notion of a random variable.
- Learn that many types of numerical data are observed values of discrete random variables.
- Study several important types of discrete random variables and their probability models.

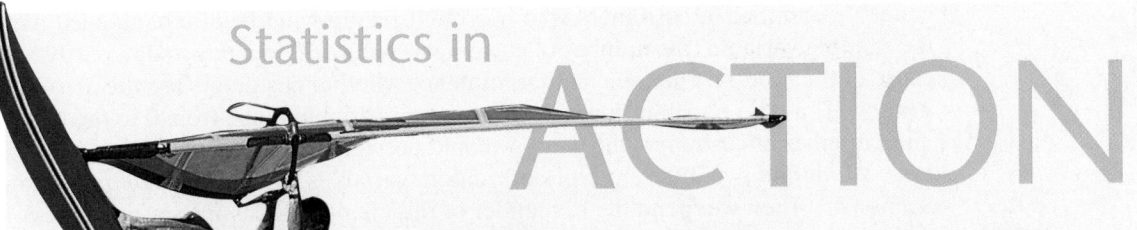

Statistics in ACTION

Probability in a Reverse Cocaine Sting

The American Statistician (May 1991) described an interesting application of a discrete probability distribution in a case involving illegal drugs. It all started with a "bust" in a mid-sized Florida city. During the bust, police seized approximately 500 foil packets of a white, powdery substance, presumably cocaine. Since it is not a crime to buy or sell nonnarcotic cocaine look-a-likes (e.g., inert powders), detectives had to prove that the packets contained genuine cocaine in order to convict their suspects of drug trafficking. When the police laboratory randomly selected and chemically tested four of the packets, all four tested positive for cocaine. This finding led to the conviction of the traffickers.

After the conviction, the police decided to use the remaining foil packets (i.e., those not tested) in reverse sting operations. Two of these packets were randomly selected and sold by undercover officers to a buyer. Between the sale and the arrest, however, the buyer disposed of the evidence. The key question is, Beyond a reasonable doubt, did the defendant really purchase cocaine?

In court, the defendant's attorney argued that his client should not be convicted because the police could not prove that the missing foil packets contained cocaine. The police contended, however, that since four of the original packets tested positive for cocaine, the two packets sold in the reverse sting were also highly likely to contain cocaine. In this chapter, two Real-World Revisited examples demonstrate how to use probability models to solve the dilemma. (The case represented Florida's first cocaine-possession conviction without the actual physical evidence.)

Statistics in the Action Revisited

- Using the Binomial Model to Solve the Cocaine Sting Case (p. 235)
- Using the Hypergeometric Model to Solve the Cocaine Sting Case (p. 249)

HH ● (2)	*HT* ● (1)
TT ● (0)	*TH* ● (1)

S

Figure 4.1
Venn diagram for coin-tossing experiment

You may have noticed that many of the examples of experiments in Chapter 3 generated quantitative (numerical) observations. The Consumer Price Index, the unemployment rate, the number of sales made in a week, and the yearly profit of a company are all examples of numerical measurements of some phenomenon. Thus, most experiments have sample points that correspond to values of some numerical variable.

To illustrate, consider the coin-tossing experiment of Chapter 3. Figure 4.1 is a Venn diagram showing the sample points when two coins are tossed and the up faces (heads or tails) of the coins are observed. One possible numerical outcome is the total number of heads observed. These values (0, 1, or 2) are shown in parentheses on the Venn diagram, one numerical value associated with each sample point. In the jargon of probability, the variable "total number of heads observed when two coins are tossed" is called a *random variable*.

> **DEFINITION 4.1**
>
> A **random variable** is a variable that assumes numerical values associated with the random outcomes of an experiment, where one (and only one) numerical value is assigned to each sample point.

The term *random variable* is more meaningful than the term *variable* because the adjective *random* indicates that the coin-tossing experiment may result in one of the several possible values of the variable—0, 1, and 2—according to the *random* outcome of the experiment, *HH, HT, TH,* and *TT.* Similarly, if the experiment is to count the number of customers who use the drive-up window of a bank each day, the random variable (the number of customers) will vary from day to day, partly because of the random phenomena that influence whether customers use the drive-up window. Thus, the possible values of this random variable range from 0 to the maximum number of customers the window could possibly serve in a day.

We define two different types of random variables, *discrete* and *continuous,* in Section 4.1. Then we spend the remainder of this chapter discussing specific types of discrete random variables and the aspects that make them important in business applications. We discuss continuous random variables in Chapter 5.

4.1 Two Types of Random Variables

Recall that the sample point probabilities corresponding to an experiment must sum to 1. Dividing one unit of probability among the sample points in a sample space and consequently assigning probabilities to the values of a random variable is not always as easy as the examples in Chapter 3 might lead you to believe. If the number of sample points can be completely listed, the job is straightforward. But if the experiment results in an infinite number of numerical sample points that are impossible to list, the task of assigning probabilities to the sample points is impossible without the aid of a probability model. The next three examples demonstrate the need for different probability models depending on the number of values that a random variable can assume.

EXAMPLE 4.1　　　VALUES OF A DISCRETE RANDOM VARIABLE

Problem　A panel of 10 experts for the *Wine Spectator* (a national publication) is asked to taste a new white wine and assign a rating of 0, 1, 2, or 3. A score is then obtained by adding together the ratings of the 10 experts. How many values can this random variable assume?

31 values

Solution　A sample point is a sequence of 10 numbers associated with the rating of each expert. For example, one sample point is

$$\{1, 0, 0, 1, 2, 0, 0, 3, 1, 0\}$$

Teaching Tip

Explain that discrete random variables jump from one possible value to the next. For example, the number of heads is either 0 or 1 or 2 or 3 (for three coins). It could never be the value 1.5.

The random variable assigns a score to each one of these sample points by adding the 10 numbers together. Thus, the smallest score is 0 (if all 10 ratings are 0) and the largest score is 30 (if all 10 ratings are 3). Since every integer between 0 and 30 is a possible score, the random variable denoted by the symbol x can assume 31 values. Note that the value of the random variable for the sample point above is $x = 8$.*

Look Back This is an example of a *discrete random variable,* since there is a finite number of distinct possible values. Whenever all the possible values a random variable can assume can be listed (or counted), the random variable is discrete.

━━━━　■ ■ ■　━━━━

*The standard mathematical convention is to use a capital letter (e.g., X) to denote the theoretical random variable. The possible values (or realizations) of the random variable are typically denoted with a lowercase letter (e.g., x). Thus, in Example 4.1, the random variable X can take on the values $x = 0, 1, 2, \ldots, 30$. Since this notation can be confusing for introductory statistics students, we simplify the notation by using the lowercase x to represent the random variable throughout.

EXAMPLE 4.2   VALUES OF A DISCRETE RANDOM VARIABLE

Problem   Suppose the Environmental Protection Agency (EPA) takes readings once a month on the amount of pesticide in the discharge water of a chemical company. If the amount of pesticide exceeds the maximum level set by the EPA, the company is forced to take corrective action and may be subject to penalty. Consider the random variable, number, x, of months before the company's discharge exceeds the EPA's maximum level. What values can x assume?

Solution   The company's discharge of pesticide may exceed the maximum allowable level on the first month of testing, the second month of testing, and so on. It is possible that the company's discharge will *never* exceed the maximum level. Thus, the set of possible values for the number of months until the level is first exceeded is the set of all positive integers

$$1, 2, 3, 4, \ldots$$

Suggested Exercise 4.5

Look Back   If we can list the values of a random variable x, even though the list is never ending, we call the list **countable** and the corresponding random variable *discrete*. Thus, the number of months until the company's discharge first exceeds the limit is a *discrete random variable*.

[Now Work]   *Exercise 4.2*

■ ■ ■

EXAMPLE 4.3   VALUES OF A CONTINUOUS RANDOM VARIABLE

Problem   Refer to Example 4.2. A second random variable of interest is the amount x of pesticide (in milligrams per liter) found in the monthly sample of discharge waters from the chemical company. What values can this random variable assume?

Solution   Unlike the *number* of months before the company's discharge exceeds the EPA's maximum level, the set of all possible values for the *amount* of discharge *cannot* be listed—that is, is not countable. The possible values for the amounts of pesticide would correspond to the points on the interval between 0 and the largest possible value the amount of the discharge could attain, the maximum number of milligrams that could occupy 1 liter of volume. (Practically, the interval would be much smaller, say, between 0 and 500 milligrams per liter.)

Teaching Tip

Use many examples to illustrate the difference between discrete and continuous random variables. Try to use a similar situation to illustrate both types. For example, the number of checkout lanes open at a grocery store is a discrete random variable, while the amount of time standing in line is a continuous random variable.

Look Back   When the values of a random variable are not countable but instead correspond to the points on some interval, we call it a *continuous random variable*. Thus, the *amount* of pesticide in the chemical plant's discharge waters is a *continuous random variable*.

[Now Work]   *Exercise 4.3*

■ ■ ■

DEFINITION 4.2

Random variables that can assume a *countable* number of values are called **discrete**.

Teaching Tip
For any two values of a continuous random variable, there are an infinite number of other possible values in between.

> **DEFINITION 4.3**
>
> Random variables that can assume values corresponding to any of the points contained in one or more intervals are called **continuous.**

Several more examples of discrete random variables follow:

1. The number of sales made by a salesperson in a given week: $x = 0, 1, 2, \ldots$
2. The number of consumers in a sample of 500 who favor a particular product over all competitors: $x = 0, 1, 2, \ldots, 500$
3. The number of bids received in a bond offering: $x = 0, 1, 2, \ldots$
4. The number of errors on a page of an accountant's ledger: $x = 0, 1, 2, \ldots$
5. The number of customers waiting to be served in a restaurant at a particular time: $x = 0, 1, 2, \ldots$

Note that each of the examples of discrete random variables begins with the words "The number of …" This wording is very common, since the discrete random variables most frequently observed are counts.

We conclude this section with some more examples of continuous random variables:

1. The length of time between arrivals at a hospital clinic: $0 \leq x < \infty$ (infinity)
2. For a new apartment complex, the length of time from completion until a specified number of apartments are rented: $0 \leq x < \infty$
3. The amount of carbonated beverage loaded into a 12-ounce can in a can-filling operation: $0 \leq x \leq 12$
4. The depth at which a successful oil drilling venture first strikes oil: $0 \leq x \leq c$, where c is the maximum depth obtainable
5. The weight of a food item bought in a supermarket: $0 \leq x \leq 500$ [*Note*: Theoretically, there is no upper limit on x, but it is unlikely that it would exceed 500 pounds.]

Discrete random variables and their probability distributions are discussed in this chapter. Continuous random variables and their probability distributions are the topic of Chapter 5.

Exercises 4.1–4.10

Applying the Concepts—Basic

4.1 Refer to the National Highway Traffic Safety Administratic crash tests of new car models, Exercise 2.127 (p. 124). Recall that developed a driver-side "star" scoring system, with results ranging from one star (*) to five stars (*****). The more stars in the rating, the better the level of crash protection in a head-on collision. Suppose that a car is selected and its driver-side star rating is determined. Let x equal the number of stars in the rating. Is x a discrete or continuous random variable?
Discrete

4.2 The number of customers, x, waiting in line to order sandwiches at a Subway shop at noon is of interest to the store manager. What values can x assume? Is x a discrete or continuous random variable?   Discrete

BWECS
4.3 Refer to *Business Week's* "Executive Compensation Scoreboard." One variable saved in the BWECS file is the return-to-pay ratio, x, for a chief executive officer. Recall that x is the return on a $100 investment made three-years earlier divided by the CEO's total compen-

sation (in $ millions) over the last three years. Examine the data in the **BWECS** file and note the values of x. Is x a discrete or continuous random variable?   Continuous

Applying the Concepts—Intermediate

4.4 Which of the following describe continuous random variables, and which describe discrete random variables?
  a. The number of newspapers sold by the *New York Times* each month   Discrete
  b. The amount of ink used in printing a Sunday edition of the *New York Times*   Continuous
  c. The actual number of ounces in a one-gallon bottle of laundry detergent   Continuous
  d. The number of defective parts in a shipment of nuts and bolts   Discrete
  e. The number of people collecting unemployment insurance each month   Discrete

4.5 Security analysts are professionals who devote full-time efforts to evaluating the investment worth of a narrow list of stocks. For example, one security analyst might specialize in bank stocks while another specializes in evaluating firms in the computer industry. The following variables are of interest to security analysts (Radcliffe, *Investments: Concepts, Analysis and Strate-*

gy, 1994). Which are discrete and which are continuous random variables?
  a. The closing price of a particular stock on the New York Stock Exchange   Discrete
  b. The number of shares of a particular stock that are traded each business day   Discrete
  c. The quarterly earnings of a particular firm
  d. The percentage change in yearly earnings between 2002 and 2003 for a particular firm
  e. The number of new products introduced per year by a firm   Discrete
  f. The time until a pharmaceutical company gains approval from the U.S. Food and Drug Administration to market a new drug   Continuous

4.6 Give an example of a discrete random variable that would be of interest to a banker.

4.7 Give an example of a continuous random variable that would be of interest to an economist.

4.8 Give an example of a discrete random variable that would be of interest to the manager of a hotel.

4.9 Give two examples of discrete random variables that would be of interest to the manager of a clothing store.

4.10 Give an example of a continuous random variable that would be of interest to a stockbroker.

4.2 Probability Distributions for Discrete Random Variables

A complete description of a discrete random variable requires that we *specify the possible values the random variable can assume and the probability associated with each value.* To illustrate, consider Example 4.4.

EXAMPLE 4.4   FINDING A PROBABILITY DISTRIBUTION

Problem Recall the experiment of tossing two coins (Section 4.1), and let x be the number of heads observed. Find the probability associated with each value of the random variable x, assuming the two coins are fair. Display these values in a table or graph.

Solution The sample space and sample points for this experiment are reproduced in Figure 4.2. Note that the random variable x can assume values 0, 1, 2. Recall (from Chapter 3) that the probability associated with each of the four sample points is $\frac{1}{4}$. Then, identifying the probabilities of the sample points associated with each of these values of x, we have

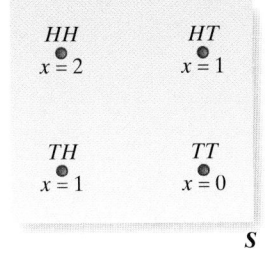

$$P(x = 0) = P(TT) = \tfrac{1}{4}$$
$$P(x = 1) = P(TH) + P(HT) = \tfrac{1}{4} + \tfrac{1}{4} = \tfrac{1}{2}$$
$$P(x = 2) = P(HH) = \tfrac{1}{4}$$

Figure 4.2
Venn diagram for the two-coin-toss experiment

Thus, we now know the values the random variable can assume (0, 1, 2) and how the probability is *distributed over* these values $(\frac{1}{4}, \frac{1}{2}, \frac{1}{4})$. This completely describes the random variable and is referred to as the *probability distribution,*

TABLE 4.1 Probability Distribution for Coin-Toss Experiment: Tabular Form

x	$p(x)$
0	$\frac{1}{4}$
1	$\frac{1}{2}$
2	$\frac{1}{4}$

Figure 4.3
Probability distribution for coin-toss experiment: Graphical form

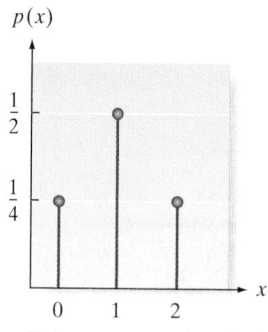

a. Point representation of $p(x)$

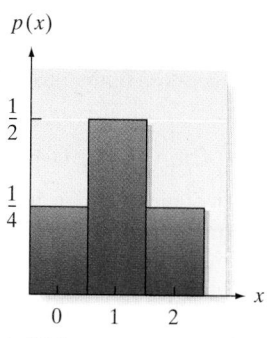

b. Histogram representation of $p(x)$

Teaching Tip

Probability distributions can be presented as tables, graphs, or formulas. The key idea is that all forms give the possible values of the random variable, X, and the corresponding probability of observing those values of x.

denoted by the symbol $p(x)$.* The probability distribution for the coin-toss example is shown in tabular form in Table 4.1 and in graphical form in Figure 4.3. Since the probability distribution for a discrete random variable is concentrated at specific points (values of x), the graph in Figure 4.3(a) represents the probabilities as the heights of vertical lines over the corresponding values of x. Although the representation of the probability distribution as a histogram, as in Figure 4.3(b), is less precise (since the probability is spread over a unit interval), the histogram representation will prove useful when we approximate probabilities of certain discrete random variables in Section 4.4.

Look Back We could also present the probability distribution for x as a formula, but this would unnecessarily complicate a very simple example. We give the formulas for the probability distributions of some common discrete random variables later in this chapter.

Now Work *Exercise 4.15*

■ ■ ■

Teaching Tip

Let the student view the probability distribution as a way of organizing the outcomes that were discussed in the probability chapter. For example, organize the eight outcomes of the three-coin example by grouping together all outcomes that result in the same number of heads.

DEFINITION 4.4

The **probability distribution** of a discrete random variable is a graph, table, or formula that specifies the probability associated with each possible value the random variable can assume.

Two requirements must be satisfied by all probability distributions for discrete random variables.

Requirements for the Probability Distribution of a Discrete Random Variable, x

1. $p(x) \geq 0$ for all values of x

2. $\sum p(x) = 1$

where the summation of $p(x)$ is over all possible values of x.†

Now Work *Exercise 4.12*

---

*In standard mathematical notation, the probability that a random variable X takes on a value x is denoted $P(X = x) = p(x)$. Thus, $P(X = 0) = p(0)$, $P(X = 1) = p(1)$, etc. In this introductory text, we adopt the simpler $p(x)$ notation.
† Unless otherwise indicated, summations will always be over all possible values of x.

Example 4.4 illustrates how the probability distribution for a discrete random variable can be derived, but for many practical situations the task is much more difficult. Fortunately, many experiments and associated discrete random variables observed in business possess identical characteristics. Thus, you might observe a random variable in a marketing experiment that would possess the same characteristics as a random variable observed in accounting, economics, or management. We classify random variables according to type of experiment, derive the probability distribution for each of the different types, and then use the appropriate probability distribution when a particular type of random variable is observed in a practical situation. The probability distributions for most commonly occurring discrete random variables have already been derived. This fact simplifies the problem of finding the appropriate probability distributions for the business analyst.

In Sections 4.4–4.6, we describe some important types of discrete random variables, give their probability distributions, and explain where and how they can be applied in practice. (Mathematical derivations of the probability distributions will be omitted, but these details can be found in the references at the back of the book.)

But first, in Section 4.3, we discuss some descriptive measures of these sometimes complex probability distributions. Since probability distributions are analogous to the relative frequency distributions of Chapter 2, it should be no surprise that the mean and standard deviation are useful descriptive measures.

Exercises 4.11–4.24

Learning the Mechanics

4.11 A die is tossed. Let x be the number of spots observed on the upturned face of the die.
   a. Find the probability distribution of x and display it in tabular form.
   b. Display the probability distribution of x in graphical form.

4.12 The random variable x has the following discrete probability distribution:

x	1	3	5	7	9
$p(x)$	.1	.2	.4	.2	.1

   a. List the values x may assume.
   b. What value of x is most probable?   5
   c. Display the probability distribution as a graph.
   d. Find $P(x = 7)$.   .2
   e. Find $P(x \geq 5)$.   .7
   f. Find $P(x > 2)$.   .9

4.13 A discrete random variable x can assume five possible values: 2, 3, 5, 8, and 10. Its probability distribution is shown here:

x	2	3	5	8	10
$p(x)$	.15	.10	—	.25	.25

   a. What is $p(5)$?   .25

   b. What is the probability that x equals 2 or 10?
   c. What is $P(x \leq 8)$?   .75

4.14 Explain why each of the following is or is not a valid probability distribution for a discrete random variable x:

   a.

x	0	1	2	3
$p(x)$	.1	.3	.3	.2

   b.

x	-2	-1	0
$p(x)$	.25	.50	.25

   c.

x	4	9	20
$p(x)$	$-.3$	.4	.3

   d.

x	2	3	5	6
$p(x)$	.15	.15	.45	.35

4.15 Toss three fair coins and let x equal the number of heads observed.
   a. Identify the sample points associated with this experiment and assign a value of x to each sample point. $x = 0, 1, 2, 3$
   b. Calculate $p(x)$ for each value of x.
   c. Construct a graph for $p(x)$.
   d. What is $P(x = 2 \text{ or } x = 3)$? $1/2$

Applying the Concepts—Basic

4.16 Refer to the National Highway Traffic Safety Administration (NHTSA) crash tests of new car models, Exercise 4.1 (p. 212). A summary of the driver-side star ratings for the 98 cars in the CRASH file is reproduced in the accompanying MINITAB printout. Assume that one of the 98 cars is selected at random and let x equal the number of stars in the car's drivers-side star rating.

a. Use the information in the printout to find the probability distribution for x.

b. Find $P(x = 5)$.   .1840

c. Find $P(x \le 2)$.   .0408

```
Tally for Discrete Variables: DrivStar

DrivStar   Count   Percent
    2        4       4.08
    3       17      17.35
    4       59      60.20
    5       18      18.37
   N=       98
```

4.17 According to the American Dental Association, 60% of all dentists use nitrous oxide in their practice (*New York Times*, June 20, 1995). If x equals the number of dentists in a random sample of five dentists who use laughing gas in practice, then the probability distribution of x is

x	0	1	2	3	4	5
$p(x)$	.0102	.0768	.2304	.3456	.2592	.0778

a. Verify that the probabilities for x sum to 1.

b. Find $P(x = 4)$.   .2592

c. Find $P(x < 2)$.   .0870

d. Find $P(x \ge 3)$.   .6826

4.18 The age distribution for the employees of a highly successful "dot-com" company headquartered in Atlanta is shown below. An employee is to be randomly selected from this population.

a. Can the relative frequency distribution in the table be interpreted as a probability distribution? Explain.

b. Graph the probability distribution.

c. What is the probability that the randomly selected employee is over 30 years of age? Over 40 years of age? Under 30 years of age?   .40, 0, .51

d. What is the probability that the randomly selected employee will be 25 or 26 years old?   .09

Age	20	21	22	23	24	25	26	27	28	29	30	31	32	33
Proportion	.02	.04	.05	.07	.04	.02	.07	.02	.11	.07	.09	.13	.15	.12

Source: Personal communication from P. George Benson.

4.19 The probability distribution for the number of customer arrivals per 15-minute period at a Wendy's in New Jersey is shown in the next table.

a. Does this distribution meet the two requirements for the probability distribution of a discrete random variable? Justify your answer.   Yes

b. What is the probability that exactly 16 customers enter the restaurant in the next 15 minutes?   .06

c. Find $p(x \le 10)$.   .28

d. Find $p(5 \le x \le 15)$.   .82

x	5	6	7	8	9	10	11	12	13	14	15
$p(x)$	.01	.02	.03	.05	.08	.09	.11	.13	.12	.10	.08

x	16	17	18	19	20	21
$p(x)$	.06	.05	.03	.02	.01	.01

Source: Ford, R., Roberts, D., and Saxton, P. *Queuing Models.* Graduate School of Management, Rutgers University, 1992.

Applying the Concepts—Intermediate

4.20 In Exercise 3.11 you learned that one in every 100 slaughtered chickens passes USDA inspection with fecal contamination. Consider a random sample of three slaughtered chickens that all pass USDA inspection. Let x equal the number of chickens in the sample that have fecal contamination.

a. Find $p(x)$ for $x = 0, 1, 2, 3$.

b. Graph $p(x)$.

c. Find $P(x \le 1)$.   .999702

4.21 A weapons manufacturer uses a liquid propellant to produce gun cartridges. During the manufacturing process, the propellant can get mixed with another liquid to produce a contaminated cartridge. A University of South Florida statistician, hired by the company to investigate the level of contamination in the stored cartridges, found that 23% of the cartridges in a particular lot were contaminated. Suppose you randomly sample (without replacement) gun cartridges from this lot until you find a contaminated one. Let x be the number of cartridges sampled until a contaminated one is found. It is known that the probability distribution for x is given by the formula

$$p(x) = (.23)(.77)^{x-1}, x = 1, 2, 3, \ldots$$

a. Find $p(1)$. Interpret this result.   .23

b. Find $p(5)$. Interpret this result.   .0809

c. Find $P(x \ge 2)$. Interpret this result.   .77

4.22 Refer to the *Journal of the American Law and Economics Association* (Vol. 3, 2001) study of appeals of Federal civil trials, Exercise 3.33 (p. 170). A breakdown of the 678 civil cases that were originally tried in front of a judge (rather than a jury) and appealed by either the plaintiff or defendant is reproduced in the table on p. 217. Suppose each civil case is awarded points (positive or negative) based on the outcome of the appeal for the purpose of evaluating Federal judges. If the appeal is affirmed or dismissed, +5 points are awarded. If the appeal of a plaintiff trial win is reversed, −1 point is awarded. If the appeal of a defendant trial win is reversed, -3 points are awarded. Suppose one of the 678 cases is selected at random and the number, x, of points awarded is determined. Find and graph the probability distribution for x.

Outcome of Appeal	Number of Cases
Plaintiff trial win—reversed	71
Plaintiff trial win—affirmed/dismissed	240
Defendant trial win—reversed	68
Defendant trial win—affirmed/dismissed	299
Total	678

4.23 A team of Chinese university professors investigated the reliability of several capacitated-flow networks in the journal *Networks* (May 1995). One network examined in the article, and illustrated below, is a bridge network with arcs a_1, a_2, a_3, a_4, a_5, and a_6. The probability distribution of the capacity x for each of the six arcs is provided in the next table.

a. Verify that the properties of discrete probability distributions are satisfied for each arc capacity distribution.

b. Find the probability that the capacity for arc a_1 will exceed 1.   .85

c. Repeat part b for each of the remaining five arcs.

Arc	Capacity (x)	p(x)	Arc	Capacity (x)	p(x)
a_1	3	.60	a_4	1	.90
	2	.25		0	.10
	1	.10			
	0	.05			
a_2	2	.60	a_5	1	.90
	1	.30		0	.10
	0	.10			
a_3	1	.90	a_6	2	.70
	0	.10		1	.25
				0	.05

Source: Lin, J., et al. "On Reliability Evaluation of Capacitated-Flow Network in Terms of Minimal Pathsets." *Networks,* Vol. 25, No. 3, May 1995, p. 135 (Table 1), 1995, John Wiley and Sons.

Applying the Concepts—Advanced

4.24 Refer to Exercise 4.23.

a. One path from the source node to the sink node is through arcs a_1 and a_2. Find the probability that the system maintains a capacity of more than 1 through the a_1-a_2 path. (Assume that the arc capacities are independent.)

b. Another path from the source node to the sink node is through arcs a_1, a_3, and a_6. Find the probability that the system maintains a capacity of 1 through the $a_1-a_3-a_6$ path.

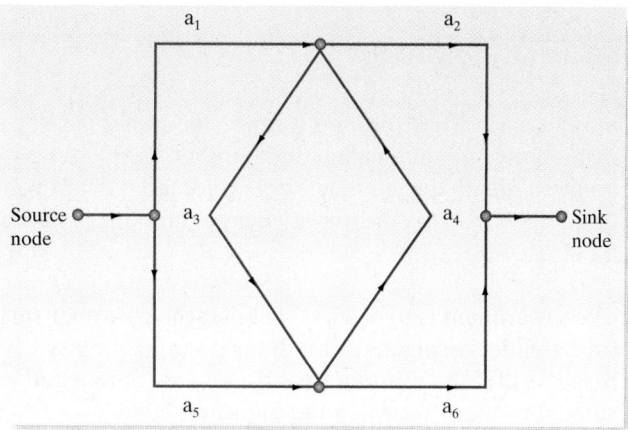

4.3   Expected Values of Discrete Random Variables

Teaching Tip

Expected value is another name for mean, which measures the center of the probability distribution.

If a discrete random variable x were observed a very large number of times and the data generated were arranged in a relative frequency distribution, the relative frequency distribution would be indistinguishable from the probability distribution for the random variable. Thus, the probability distribution for a random variable is a theoretical model for the relative frequency distribution of a population. To the extent that the two distributions are equivalent (and we will assume they are), the probability distribution for x possesses a mean μ and a variance σ^2 that are identical to the corresponding descriptive measures for the population. This section explains how you can find the mean value for a random variable. We illustrate the procedure with an example.

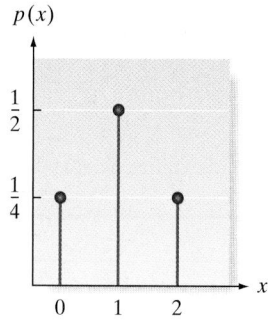

Figure 4.4
Probability distribution
for a two-coin toss

Suggested Exercises 4.38

Teaching Tip
Use any of the probability
distributions from the last
section to illustrate the
calculations of the expected
value and variance (below).
Discuss the interpretation of
these values as they relate to
the values of the random
variable.

Examine the probability distribution for x (the number of heads observed in the toss of two fair coins) in Figure 4.4. Try to locate the mean of the distribution intuitively. We may reason that the mean μ of this distribution is equal to 1 as follows: In a large number of experiments, $\frac{1}{4}$ should result in $x = 0$, $\frac{1}{2}$ in $x = 1$, and $\frac{1}{4}$ in $x = 2$ heads. Therefore, the average number of heads is

$$\mu = 0(\tfrac{1}{4}) + 1(\tfrac{1}{2}) + 2(\tfrac{1}{4}) = 0 + \tfrac{1}{2} + \tfrac{1}{2} = 1$$

Note that to get the population mean of the random variable x, we multiply each possible value of x by its probability $p(x)$, and then sum this product over all possible values of x. The *mean of* x is also referred to as the *expected value of* x, denoted $E(x)$.

DEFINITION 4.5

The **mean**, or **expected value**, of a discrete random variable x is

$$\mu = E(x) = \sum x p(x)$$

The term *expected* is a mathematical term and should not be interpreted as it is typically used. Specifically, a random variable might never be equal to its "expected value." Rather, the expected value is the mean of the probability distribution or a measure of its central tendency. You can think of μ as the mean value of x in a *very large* (actually, *infinite*) number of repetitions of the experiment, where the values of x occur in proportions equivalent to the probabilities of x.

EXAMPLE 4.5   FINDING AN EXPECTED VALUE

Problem Suppose you work for an insurance company, and you sell a $10,000 one-year term insurance policy at an annual premium of $290. Actuarial tables show that the probability of death during the next year for a person of your customer's age, sex, health, etc., is .001. What is the expected gain (amount of money made by the company) for a policy of this type?

$\mu = \$280$

Solution The experiment is to observe whether the customer survives the upcoming year. The probabilities associated with the two sample points, Live and Die, are .999 and .001, respectively. The random variable you are interested in is the gain x, which can assume the values shown in the following table.

Gain, x	Sample Point	Probability
$290	Customer lives	.999
−$9,710	Customer dies	.001

If the customer lives, the company gains the $290 premium as profit. If the customer dies, the gain is negative because the company must pay $10,000, for a net "gain" of $(290 − 10,000) = −$9,710$. The expected gain is therefore

$$\mu = E(x) = \sum_{\text{all } x} x p(x)$$
$$= (290)(.999) + (-9,710)(.001) = \$280$$

In other words, if the company were to sell a very large number of one-year $10,000 policies to customers possessing the characteristics described above, it would (on the average) net $280 per sale in the next year.

Teaching Tip

Point out to the student that the gain associated with an insurance policy can never be $280. This value refers to the average gain per policy if repeated policies were sold.

Look Back Note that $E(x)$ need not equal a possible value of x. That is, the expected value is $280, but x will equal either $290 or $-$9,710$ each time the experiment is performed (a policy is sold and a year elapses). The expected value is a measure of central tendency—and in this case represents the average over a very large number of one-year policies—but is not a possible value of x.

Now work *Exercise 4.32*

■ ■ ■

We learned in Chapter 2 that the mean and other measures of central tendency tell only part of the story about a set of data. The same is true about probability distributions. We need to measure variability as well. Since a probability distribution can be viewed as a representation of a population, we will use the population variance to measure its variability.

The *population variance* σ^2 is defined as the average of the squared distance of x from the population mean μ. Since x is a random variable, the squared distance, $(x - \mu)^2$, is also a random variable. Using the same logic used to find the mean value of x, we find the mean value of $(x - \mu)^2$ by multiplying all possible values of $(x - \mu)^2$ by $p(x)$ and then summing over all possible x values.* This quantity,

$$E[(x - \mu)^2] = \sum_{\text{all } x} (x - \mu)^2 p(x)$$

is also called the *expected value of the squared distance from the mean;* that is, $\sigma^2 = E[(x - \mu)^2]$. The standard deviation of x is defined as the square root of the variance σ^2.

Teaching Tip

Again, examples of the probability distributions from the last section illustrate the calculations nicely.

DEFINITION 4.6

The **variance** of a discrete random variable x is

$$\sigma^2 = E[(x - \mu)^2] = \sum (x - \mu)^2 p(x)$$

DEFINITION 4.7

The **standard deviation** of a discrete random variable is equal to the square root of the variance, i.e., $\sigma = \sqrt{\sigma^2}$.

Knowing the mean μ and standard deviation σ of the probability distribution of x, in conjunction with Chebyshev's Rule (Table 2.6) and the Empirical Rule (Table 2.7), we can make statements about the likelihood that values of x will fall within the intervals $\mu \pm \sigma$, $\mu \pm 2\sigma$, and $\mu \pm 3\sigma$. These probabilities are given in the box.

*It can be shown that $E[(x - \mu)^2] = E(x^2) - \mu^2$, where $E(x^2) = \sum x^2 p(x)$. Note the similarity between this expression and the shortcut formula $\sum (x - \bar{x})^2 = \sum x^2 - (\sum x)^2/n$ given in Chapter 2.

Probability Rules for a Discrete Random Variable

Let x be a discrete random variable with probability distribution $p(x)$, mean μ, and standard deviation σ. Then, depending on the shape of $p(x)$, the following probability statements can be made:

	Chebyshev's Rule	Empirical Rule
	Applies to any probability distribution (see Figure 4.5a)	Applies to probability that distributions are mound-shaped and symmetric (see Figure 4.5b)
$P(\mu - \sigma < x < \mu + \sigma)$	≥ 0	$\approx .68$
$P(\mu - 2\sigma < x < \mu + 2\sigma)$	$\geq \frac{3}{4}$	$\approx .95$
$P(\mu - 3\sigma < x < \mu + 3\sigma)$	$\geq \frac{8}{9}$	≈ 1.00

Figure 4.5

Shapes of two probability distributions for a discrete random variable x

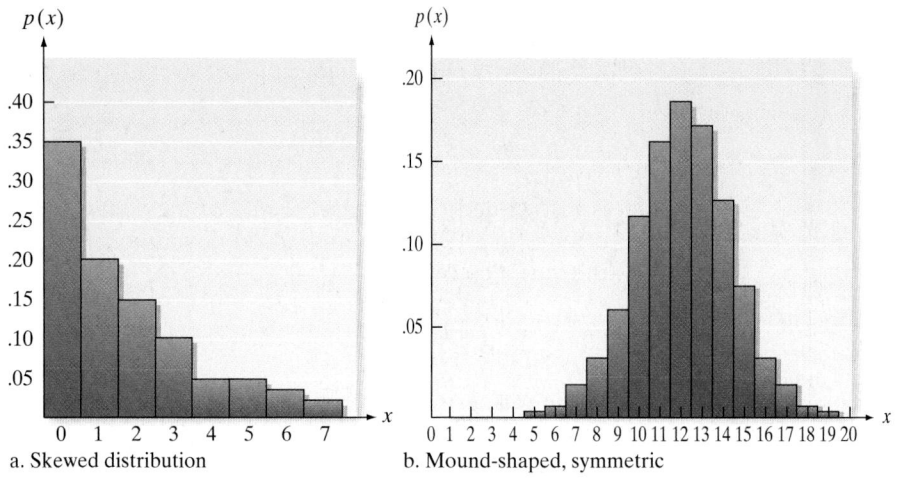

a. Skewed distribution

b. Mound-shaped, symmetric

EXAMPLE 4.6   FINDING μ AND σ

Problem   Suppose you invest a fixed sum of money in each of five Internet business ventures. Assume you know that 70% of such ventures are successful, the outcomes of the ventures are independent of one another, and the probability distribution for the number, x, of successful ventures out of five is

x	0	1	2	3	4	5
$p(x)$	.002	.029	.132	.309	.360	.168

$\mu = 3.50$
$\sigma = 1.02$

a. Find $\mu = E(x)$. Interpret the result.

b. Find $\sigma = \sqrt{E[(x - \mu)^2]}$. Interpret the result.

c. Graph $p(x)$. Locate μ and the interval $\mu \pm 2\sigma$ on the graph. Use either Chebyshev's Rule or the Empirical Rule to approximate the probability that x falls in this interval. Compare this result with the actual probability.

No, $p(x < 2) = .031$

d. Would you expect to observe fewer than two successful ventures out of five?

Solution

a. Applying the formula,

$$\mu = E(x) = \sum xp(x) = 0(.002) + 1(.029) + 2(.132) + 3(.309)$$

$$+4(.360) + 5(.168) = 3.50$$

On average, the number of successful ventures out of five will equal 3.5. Remember that this expected value only has meaning when the experiment—investing in five Internet business ventures—is repeated a large number of times.

b. Now we calculate the variance of x:

$$\sigma^2 = E[(x - \mu)^2] = \sum (x - \mu)^2 p(x)$$

$$= (0 - 3.5)^2(.002) + (1 - 3.5)^2(.029) + (2 - 3.5)^2(.132)$$
$$+ (3 - 3.5)^2(.309) + (4 - 3.5)^2(.360) + (5 - 3.5)^2(.168)$$

$$= 1.05$$

Thus, the standard deviation is

$$\sigma = \sqrt{\sigma^2} = \sqrt{1.05} = 1.02$$

This value measures the spread of the probability distribution of x, the number of successful ventures out of five. A more useful interpretation is obtained by answering parts c and d.

c. The graph of $p(x)$ in histogram form is shown in Figure 4.6 with the mean μ and the interval $\mu \pm 2\sigma = 3.50 \pm 2(1.02) = 3.50 \pm 2.04 = (1.46, 5.54)$ shown on the graph. Note particularly that $\mu = 3.5$ locates the center of the probability distribution. Since this distribution is a theoretical relative frequency distribution that is moderately mound-shaped (see Figure 4.6), we

Figure 4.6
Graph of $p(x)$ for
Example 4.6

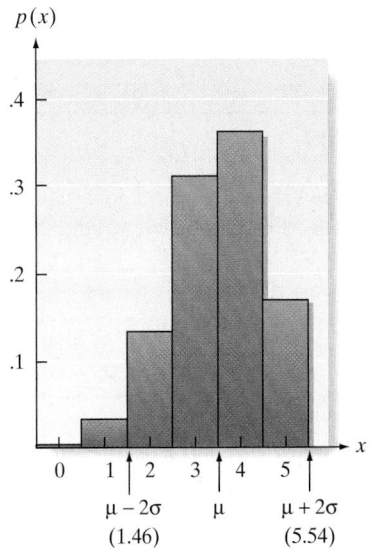

expect (from Chebyshev's Rule) at least 75% and, more likely (from the Empirical Rule), approximately 95% of observed x values to fall in the interval $\mu \pm 2\sigma$—that is, between 1.46 and 5.54. You can see from Figure 4.6 that the actual probability that x falls in the interval $\mu \pm 2\sigma$ includes the sum of $p(x)$ for the values $x = 2, x = 3, x = 4,$ and $x = 5$. This probability is $p(2) + p(3) + p(4) + p(5) = .132 + .309 + .360 + .168 = .969$. Therefore, 96.9% of the probability distribution lies within 2 standard deviations of the mean. This percentage is consistent with both Chebyshev's Rule and the Empirical Rule.

d. Fewer than two successful ventures out of five implies that $x = 0$ or $x = 1$. Since both these values of x lie outside the interval $\mu \pm 2\sigma$, we know from the Empirical Rule that such a result is unlikely (approximate probability of .05). The exact probability, $P(x \le 1)$, is $p(0) + p(1) = .002 + .029 = .031$. Consequently, in a single experiment where we invest in five Internet business ventures, we would not expect to observe fewer than two successful ones.

Now Work *Exercise 4.27*

■ ■ ■

Exercises 4.25–4.38

Learning the Mechanics

4.25 Consider the probability distribution shown here.

x	1	2	4	10
$p(x)$	.2	.4	.2	.2

a. Find $\mu = E(x)$. 3.8
b. Find $\sigma^2 = E[(x - \mu)^2]$. 10.56
c. Find σ. 3.2496
d. In this case, can the random variable x ever assume the value μ? Explain. No
e. In general, can a random variable ever assume a value equal to its expected value? Explain. Yes

4.26 Consider the probability distribution for the random variable x shown here.

x	10	20	30	40	50	60
$p(x)$	.05	.20	.30	.25	.10	.10

a. Find μ, σ^2, and σ. 34.5, 174.75, 13.219
b. Graph $p(x)$.
c. Locate μ and the interval $\mu \pm 2\sigma$ on your graph. What is the probability that x will fall within the interval $\mu \pm 2\sigma$? 1.00

4.27 Consider the probability distribution shown here.

x	−4	−3	−2	−1	0	1	2	3	4
$p(x)$	.02	.07	.10	.15	.30	.18	.10	.06	.02

a. Calculate μ, σ^2, and σ.
b. Graph $p(x)$. Locate $\mu, \mu - 2\sigma$, and $\mu + 2\sigma$ on the graph.
c. What is the probability that x is in the interval $\mu \pm 2\sigma$? .96

4.28 Consider the probability distributions shown here.

x	0	1	2
$p(x)$	.3	.4	.3

y	0	1	2
$p(y)$	.1	.8	.1

a. Use your intuition to find the mean for each distribution. How did you arrive at your choice?
b. Which distribution appears to be more variable? Why? Distribution of x
c. Calculate μ and σ^2 for each distribution. Compare these answers to your answers in parts a and b.

Applying the Concepts—Basic

4.29 Refer to Exercise 4.16 (p. 216), where you found the probability distribution for x, the number of stars in a randomly selected car's driver-side crash rating. Find $\mu = E(x)$ for this distribution and practically interpret the result. 3.929

4.30 Refer to Exercise 4.17 (p. 216). The probability distribution for the number x out of five randomly selected dentists who use "laughing gas" is reproduced in the following tables. Find the mean number of dentists out of the five who use laughing gas. Interpret this value. 3.0002

x	$p(x)$
0	.0102
1	.0768
2	.2304
3	.3456
4	.2592
5	.0778

4.31 A capacitated-bridge network with six arcs (*Network*, May 1995) was presented in Exercise 4.23. The probability distributions for the capacities x of the six arcs are reproduced in the table.

    a. Compute the mean capacity of each arc and interpret its value.

    b. Compute σ for each arc and give a range where x is likely to fall.

Arc	Capacity (x)	$p(x)$	Arc	Capacity (x)	$p(x)$
a_1	3	.60	a_4	1	.90
	2	.25		0	.10
	1	.10			
	0	.05			
a_2	2	.60	a_5	1	.90
	1	.30		0	.10
	0	.10			
a_3	1	.90	a_6	2	.70
	0	.10		1	.25
				0	.05

Source: Lin, J., et al. "On Reliability Evaluation of Capacitated-Flow Network in Terms of Minimal Pathsets." *Networks*, Vol. 25, No. 3, May 1995, p. 135 (Table 1), 1995, John Wiley and Sons.

Applying the Concepts—Intermediate

4.32 The risk of a portfolio of financial assets is sometimes called *investment risk* (Radcliffe, 1994). In general, investment risk is typically measured by computing the variance or standard deviation of the probability distribution that describes the decision maker's potential outcomes (gains or losses). The greater the variation in potential outcomes, the greater the uncertainty faced by the decision maker; the smaller the variation in potential outcomes, the more predictable the decision maker's gains or losses. The two discrete probability distributions given in the table were developed from historical data. They describe the potential total physical damage losses next year to the fleets of delivery trucks of two different firms.

Firm A		Firm B	
Loss next year	Probability	Loss next year	Probability
$ 0	.01	$ 0	.00
500	.01	200	.01
1,000	.01	700	.02
1,500	.02	1,200	.02
2,000	.35	1,700	.15
2,500	.30	2,200	.30
3,000	.25	2,700	.30
3,500	.02	3,200	.15
4,000	.01	3,700	.02
4,500	.01	4,200	.02
5,000	.01	4,700	.01

    a. Verify that both firms have the same expected total physical damage loss. $\mu_A = \mu_B = 2,450$

    b. Compute the standard deviation of each probability distribution, and determine which firm faces the greater risk of physical damage to its fleet next year. $\sigma_A = 661.44$ $\sigma_B = 701.78$

4.33 The National Weather Service issues precipitation forecasts that indicate the likelihood of measurable precipitation ($\geq.01$ inch) at a specific point (the official rain gauge) during a given time period (Doswell and Brooks, *Probabilistic Forecasting: A Primer*, 1996). Suppose that if a measurable amount of rain falls during the next 24 hours, a river will reach flood stage and a business will incur damages of $300,000. The National Weather Service has indicated that there is a 30% chance of a measurable amount of rain during the next 24 hours.

    a. Construct the probability distribution that describes the potential flood damages.

    b. Find the firm's expected loss due to flood damage.

4.34 A team of consultants working for a large national supermarket chain based in the New York metropolitan area developed a statistical model for predicting the annual sales of potential new store locations. Part of their analysis involved identifying variables that influence store sales, such as the size of the store (in square feet), the size of the surrounding population, and the number of checkout lanes. They surveyed 52 supermarkets in a particular region of the country and constructed the relative frequency distribution shown below to describe the number of checkout lanes per store, x.

    a. Why do the relative frequencies in the table represent the approximate probabilities of a randomly selected supermarket having x number of checkout lanes?

    b. Find $E(x)$ and interpret its value in the context of the problem. $E(x) = 6.50$

    c. Find the standard deviation of x. $\sigma = 1.9975$

    d. According to Chebyshev's Rule (Chapter 2), what percentage of supermarkets would be expected to fall within $\mu \pm \sigma$? Within $\mu \pm 2\sigma$?

    e. What is the actual number of supermarkets that fall within $\mu \pm \sigma$? $\mu \pm 2\sigma$? Compare your answers to those of part d. Are the answers consistent?   .70; .95

x	1	2	3	4	5	6	7	8	9	10
Relative Frequency	.01	.04	.04	.08	.10	.15	.25	.20	.08	.05

Source: Adapted from Chow, W. et. al. "A Model for Predicting a Supermarket's Annual Sales per Square Foot." Graduate School of Management, Rutgers University, 1994.

4.35 On the popular television game show *The Price is Right*, contestants can play "The Showcase Showdown." The game involves a large wheel with twenty nickel values, 5, 10, 15, 20, ..., 95, 100, marked on it. Contestants spin the wheel once or twice, with the objective of obtaining the highest total score *without going over a dollar* (*100*).

[According to the *American Statistician* (Aug. 1995), the optimal strategy for the first spinner in a three-player game is to spin a second time only if the value of the initial spin is 65 or less.] Let x represent the total score for a single contestant playing "The Showcase Showdown." Assume a "fair" wheel (i.e., a wheel with equally likely outcomes). If the total of the player's spins exceeds 100, the total score is set to 0.

a. If the player is permitted only one spin of the wheel, find the probability distribution for x.

b. Refer to part a. Find $E(x)$ and interpret this value.
52.5

c. Refer to part a. Give a range of values within which x is likely to fall. $(-5.16, 110.16)$

d. Suppose the player will spin the wheel twice, no matter what the outcome of the first spin. Find the probability distribution for x.

e. What assumption did you make to obtain the probability distribution, part d? Is it a reasonable assumption?

f. Find μ and σ for the probability distribution, part d, and interpret the results.   33.25, 33.3577

g. Refer to part d. What is the probability that in two spins the player's total score exceeds a dollar (i.e., is set to 0)?   .525

h. Suppose the player obtains a 20 on the first spin and decides to spin again. Find the probability distribution for x.

i. Refer to part h. What is the probability that the player's total score exceeds a dollar?   .20

j. Given the player obtains a 65 on the first spin and decides to spin again, find the probability that the player's total score exceeds a dollar.   .65

k. Repeat part j for different first-spin outcomes. Use this information to suggest a strategy for the one-player game.

4.36 Most states offer weekly lotteries to generate revenue for the state. Despite the long odds of winning, residents continue to gamble on the lottery each week. In SIA, Chapter 3, you learned that the chance of winning Florida's Pick-6 Lotto game is 1 in approximately 23 million. Suppose you buy a $1 Lotto ticket in antici-pation of winning the $7 million grand prize. Calculate your expected net winnings. Interpret the result. $\mu = -\$.70$

Applying the Concepts—Advanced

4.37 Odds makers try to predict which professional and college football teams will win and by how much (the *spread*). If the odds makers do this accurately, adding the spread to the underdog's score should make the final score a tie. Suppose a bookie will give you $6 for every $1 you risk if you pick the winners in three ballgames (adjusted by the spread) on a "parlay" card. Thus, for every $1 bet you will either lose $1 or gain $5. What is the bookie's expected earnings per dollar wagered? $E(x) = \$.25$

4.38 The number of training units that must be passed before a complex computer software program is mastered varies from one to five, depending on the student. After much experience, the software manufacturer has determined the probability distribution that describes the fraction of users mastering the software after each number of training units:

Number of Units	1	2	3	4	5
Probability of Mastery	.1	.25	.4	.15	.1

a. Calculate the mean number of training units necessary to master the program. Calculate the median. Interpret each. $\mu = 2.9$, $m = 3$

b. If the firm wants to ensure that at least 75% of the students master the program, what is the minimum number of training units that must be administered? At least 90%?   3; 4

c. Suppose the firm develops a new training program that increases the probability that only one unit of training is needed from .1 to .25, increases the probability that only two units are needed to .35, leaves the probability that three units are needed at .4, and completely eliminates the need for four or five units. How do your answers to parts a and b change for this new program?   3; 3

4.4 The Binomial Random Variable

Many experiments result in *dichotomous* responses—that is, responses for which there exist two possible alternatives, such as Yes-No, Pass-Fail, Defective-Nondefective, or Male-Female. A simple example of such an experiment is the coin-toss experiment. A coin is tossed a number of times, say 10. Each toss results in one of two outcomes, Head or Tail. Ultimately, we are interested in the probability distribution of x, the number of heads observed. Many other experiments are equivalent to tossing a coin (either balanced or unbalanced) a fixed number n of times and observing the number x of times that one of the two possible outcomes occurs. Random variables that possess these characteristics are called **binomial random variables.**

Public opinion and consumer preference polls (e.g., the CNN, Gallup, and Harris polls) frequently yield observations on binomial random variables. For example, suppose a sample of 100 current customers is selected from a firm's data base and each person is asked whether he or she prefers the firm's product (a Head) or prefers a competitor's product (a Tail). Suppose we are interested in x, the number of customers in the sample who prefer the firm's product. Sampling 100 customers is analogous to tossing the coin 100 times. Thus, you can see that consumer preference polls like the one described here are real-life equivalents of coin-toss experiments. We have been describing a **binomial experiment;** it is identified by the following characteristics.

Teaching Tip

The binomial will be easier to use if the student habitually defines a success in terms of the outcome that is of interest. If someone is interested in knowing the number of tails observed in fifteen flips of a coin, label a success as observing a tail

Characteristics of a Binomial Random Variable

1. The experiment consists of n identical trials.
2. There are only two possible outcomes on each trial. We will denote one outcome by S (for Success) and the other by F (for Failure).
3. The probability of S remains the same from trial to trial. This probability is denoted by p, and the probability of F is denoted by q. Note that $q = 1 - p$.
4. The trials are independent.
5. The binomial random variable x is the number of S's in n trials.

Biography

JACOB BERNOULLI (1654–1705)
The Bernoulli Distribution

Son of a magistrate and spice maker in Basel, Switzerland, Jacob Bernoulli completed a degree in theology at the University of Basel. While at the university, however, he studied mathematics secretly and against the will of his father. Jacob taught mathematics to his younger brother Johan, and they both went on to become distinguished European mathematicians. At first the brothers collaborated on the problems of the time (e.g.,

calculus); unfortunately, they later became bitter mathematical rivals. Jacob applied his philosophical training and mathematical intuition to probability and the theory of games of chance, where he developed the law of large numbers. In his book *Ars Conjectandi*, published in 1713 (eight years after his death), the binomial distribution was first proposed. Jacob showed that the binomial distribution was a sum of independent 0–1 variables, now known as "Bernoulli" random variables.

EXAMPLE 4.7   ASSESSING WHETHER x IS BINOMIAL

Problem   For the following examples, decide whether x is a binomial random variable.

No a binomial

    a. You randomly select three bonds out of a possible 10 for an investment portfolio. Unknown to you, eight of the 10 will maintain their present value, and the other two will lose value due to a change in their ratings. Let x be the number of the three bonds you select that lose value.

Binomial with $n = 100$

b. Before marketing a new product on a large scale, many companies will conduct a consumer preference survey to determine whether the product is likely to be successful. Suppose a company develops a new diet soda and then conducts a taste preference survey in which 100 randomly chosen consumers state their preferences among the new soda and the two leading sellers. Let x be the number of the 100 who choose the new brand over the two others.

Not a binomial

c. Some surveys are conducted by using a method of sampling other than simple random sampling (defined in Chapter 3). For example, suppose a television cable company plans to conduct a survey to determine the fraction of households in the city that would use the cable television service. The sampling method is to choose a city block at random and then survey every household on that block. This sampling technique is called *cluster sampling*. Suppose 10 blocks are so sampled, producing a total of 124 household responses. Let x be the number of the 124 households that would use the television cable service.

Solution

a. In checking the binomial characteristics in the box, a problem arises with both characteristic 3 (probabilities remaining the same from trial to trial) and characteristic 4 (independence). The probability that the first bond you pick loses value is clearly $^2/_{10}$. Now suppose the first bond you picked was one of the two that will lose value. This reduces the chance that the second bond you pick will lose value to $^1/_9$, since now only one of the nine remaining bonds are in that category. Thus, the choices you make are dependent, and therefore x, the number of three bonds you select that lose value, is *not* a binomial random variable.

b. Surveys that produce dichotomous responses and use random sampling techniques are classic examples of binomial experiments. In our example, each randomly selected consumer either states a preference for the new diet soda or does not. The sample of 100 consumers is a very small proportion of the totality of potential consumers, so the response of one would be, for all practical purposes, independent of another.* Thus, x is a binomial random variable.

c. This example is a survey with dichotomous responses (Yes or No to the cable service), but the sampling method is not simple random sampling. Again, the binomial characteristic of independent trials would probably not be satisfied. The responses of households within a particular block would be dependent, since the households within a block tend to be similar with respect to income, level of education, and general interests. Thus, the binomial model would not be satisfactory for x if the cluster sampling technique were employed.

Look Back Nonbinomial random variables with two outcomes on every trial typically occur because they do not satisfy characteristics 3 or 4 of a binomial distribution.

Now Work *Exercise 4.46a*

■ ■ ■

*In most real-life applications of the binomial distribution, the population of interest has a finite number of elements (trials), denoted N. When N is large and the sample size n is small relative to N, say $n/N \le .05$, the sampling procedure, for all practical purposes, satisfies the conditions of a binomial experiment.

EXAMPLE 4.8   DERIVING THE BINOMIAL PROBABILITY DISTRIBUTION

Problem   A computer retailer sells both desktop and laptop personal computers (PCs) on-line. Assume that 80% of the PCs that the retailer sells online are desktops, and 20% are laptops.

.0016   **a.** Use the steps given in Chapter 3 (box on page 153) to find the probability that all of the next four online PC purchases are laptops.

.0256   **b.** Find the probability that three of the next four online PC purchases are laptops.

c. Let x represent the number of the next four online PC purchases that are laptops. Explain why x is a binomial random variable.

$p(x) = \binom{n}{x}p^x(1-p)^{n-x}$ **d.** Use the answers to parts a and b to derive a formula for $p(x)$, the probability distribution of the binomial random variable x.

Solution   **a.** **1.** The first step is to define the experiment. Here we are interested in observing the type of PC purchased online by each of the next four (buying) customers: desktop (D) or laptop (L).

2. Next, we list the sample points associated with the experiment. Each sample point consists of the purchase decisions made by the four online customers. For example, DDDD represents the sample point that all four purchase desktop PCs, while LDDD represents the sample point that customer 1 purchases a laptop, while customers 2, 3, and 4 purchase desktops. The 16 sample points are listed in Table 4.2.

3. We now assign probabilities to the sample points. Note that each sample point can be viewed as the intersection of four customers' decisions and, assuming the decisions are made independently, the probability of each sample point can be obtained using the multiplicative rule, as follows:

$P(DDDD) = P[(\text{customer 1 chooses desktop}) \cap (\text{customer 2 chooses desktop})$

$\cap (\text{customer 3 chooses desktop}) \cap (\text{customer 4 chooses desktop})]$

$= P(\text{customer 1 chooses desktop}) \times P(\text{customer 2 chooses}$

$\text{desktop}) \times P(\text{customer 3 chooses desktop})$

$\times P(\text{customer 4 chooses desktop})$

$= (.8)(.8)(.8)(.8) = (.8)^4 = .4096$

All other sample point probabilities are calculated using similar reasoning. For example,

$$P(LDDD) = (.2)(.8)(.8)(.8) = (.2)(.8)^3 = .1024$$

TABLE 4.2   Sample Points for PC Experiment of Example 4.8

DDDD	LDDD	LLDD	DLLL	LLLL
	DLDD	LDLD	LDLL	
	DDLD	LDDL	LLDL	
	DDDL	DLLD	LLLD	
		DLDL		
		DDLL		

Suggested Exercises 4.41

You can check that this reasoning results in sample point probabilities that add to 1 over the 16 points in the sample space.

4. Finally, we add the appropriate sample point probabilities to obtain the desired event probability. The event of interest is that all four on-line customers purchase laptops. In Table 4.2 we find only one sample point, *LLLL,* contained in this event. All other sample points imply that at least one desktop is purchased. Thus,

$$P(\text{All four purchase laptops}) = P(LLLL) = (.2)^4 = .0016$$

That is, the probability is only 16 in 10,000 that all four customers purchase laptop PCs.

b. The event that three of the next four online buyers purchase laptops consists of the four sample points in the fourth column of Table 4.2: *DLLL, LDLL, LLDL,* and *LLLD.* To obtain the event probability we add the sample point probabilities:

$P(3 \text{ of next 4 customers purchase laptops})$
$$= P(DLLL) + P(LDLL) + P(LLDL) + P(LLLD)$$
$$= (.2)^3(.8) + (.2)^3(.8) + (.2)^3(.8) + (.2)^3(.8)$$
$$= 4(.2)^3(.8) = .0256$$

Note that each of the four sample point probabilities is the same, because each sample point consists of three *L*'s and one *D*; the order does not affect the probability because the customers' decisions are (assumed) independent.

c. We can characterize the experiment as consisting of four identical trials—the four customers' purchase decisions. There are two possible outcomes to each trial, *D* or *L,* and the probability of *L, p* = .2, is the same for each trial. Finally, we are assuming that each customer's purchase decision is independent of all others, so that the four trials are independent. Then it follows that *x,* the number of the next four purchases that are laptops, is a binomial random variable.

d. The event probabilities in parts a and b provide insight into the formula for the probability distribution $p(x)$. First, consider the event that three purchases are laptops (part b). We found that

$$P(x = 3) = (\text{Number of sample points for which } x = 3) \times$$
$$(.2)^{\text{Number of laptops purchased}} \times (.8)^{\text{Number of desktops purchased}}$$
$$= 4(.2)^3(.8)^1$$

In general, we can use combinatorial mathematics to count the number of sample points. For example,

Number of sample points for which $x = 3$

$$= \text{Number of different ways of selecting 3 of the 4 trials for } L \text{ purchases}$$
$$= \binom{4}{3} = \frac{4!}{3!(4-3)!} = \frac{4 \cdot 3 \cdot 2 \cdot 1}{(3 \cdot 2 \cdot 1) \cdot 1} = 4$$

The formula that works for any value of x can be deduced as follows. Since

$$P(x = 3) = \binom{4}{3}(.2)^3(.8)^1,$$

then $p(x) = \binom{4}{x}(.2)^x(.8)^{4-x}$

The component $\binom{4}{x}$ counts the number of sample points with x laptops and the component $(.2)^x(.8)^{4-x}$ is the probability associated with each sample point having x laptops. For the general binomial experiment, with n trials and probability of Success p on each trial, the probability of x Successes is

$$p(x) = \binom{n}{x} \cdot p^x(1 - p)^{n-x}$$

↑	↑
No. of simple events with x S's	Probability of x S's and $(n - x)$ F's in any simple event

Look Back In theory, you could always resort to the principles developed in this example to calculate binomial probabilities; list the sample points and sum their probabilities. However, as the number of trials (n) increases, the number of sample points grows very rapidly (the number of sample points is 2^n). Thus, we prefer the formula for calculating binomial probabilities, since its use avoids listing sample points.

■ ■ ■

The binomial distribution is summarized in the box.

The Binomial Probability Distribution

$$p(x) = \binom{n}{x}p^x q^{n-x} \qquad (x = 0, 1, 2, \ldots, n)$$

where

p = Probability of a success on a single trial

$q = 1 - p$

n = Number of trials

x = Number of successes in n trials

$$\binom{n}{x} = \frac{n!}{x!(n - x)!}$$

As noted in Chapter 3, the symbol 5! means $5 \cdot 4 \cdot 3 \cdot 2 \cdot 1 = 120$. Similarly, $n! = n(n - 1)(n - 2) \cdots 3 \cdot 2 \cdot 1$; remember, $0! = 1$.

EXAMPLE 4.9   APPLYING THE BINOMIAL DISTRIBUTION

Problem   A machine that produces stampings for automobile engines is malfunctioning and producing 10% defectives. The defective and nondefective stampings proceed from the machine in a random manner. If the next five stampings are tested, find the probability that three of them are defective.

$p(x = 3) = .0081$

Solution   Let x equal the number of defectives in $n = 5$ trials. Then x is a binomial random variable with p, the probability that a single stamping will be defective, equal to .1, and $q = 1 - p = 1 - .1 = .9$. The probability distribution for x is given by the expression

$$p(x) = \binom{n}{x}p^x q^{n-x} = \binom{5}{x}(.1)^x(.9)^{5-x}$$

$$= \frac{5!}{x!(5-x)!}(.1)^x(.9)^{5-x} \qquad (x = 0, 1, 2, 3, 4, 5)$$

To find the probability of observing $x = 3$ defectives in a sample of $n = 5$, substitute $x = 3$ into the formula for $p(x)$ to obtain

$$p(3) = \frac{5!}{3!(5-3)!}(.1)^3(.9)^{5-3} = \frac{5!}{3!2!}(.1)^3(.9)^2$$

$$= \frac{5 \cdot 4 \cdot 3 \cdot 2 \cdot 1}{(3 \cdot 2 \cdot 1)(2 \cdot 1)}(.1)^3(.9)^2 = 10(.1)^3(.9)^2$$

$$= .0081$$

Look Back   Note that the binomial formula tells us that there are 10 sample points having 3 defectives (check this by listing them), each with probability $(.1)^3(.9)^2$.

Now Work   *Exercise 4.41*

■ ■ ■

The mean, variance, and standard deviation for the binomial random variable x are shown in the box.

Teaching Tip
One of the benefits of knowing the probability distribution is binomial is that the calculations for the mean, variance, and standard deviation simplify considerably.

Mean, Variance, and Standard Deviation for a Binomial Random Variable

Mean: $\mu = np$
Variance: $\sigma^2 = npq$
Standard deviation: $\sigma = \sqrt{npq}$

As we demonstrated in Chapter 2, the mean and standard deviation provide measures of the central tendency and variability, respectively, of a distribution. Thus, we can use μ and σ to obtain a rough visualization of the probability distribution for x when the calculation of the probabilities is too tedious. The next example illustrates this idea.

EXAMPLE 4.10

FINDING μ AND σ

Problem Refer to Example 4.9 and find the values of $p(0), p(1), p(2), p(4)$, and $p(5)$. Graph $p(x)$. Calculate the mean μ and standard deviation σ. Locate μ and the interval $\mu - 2\sigma$ to $\mu + 2\sigma$ on the graph. If the experiment were to be repeated many times, what proportion of the x observations would fall within the interval $\mu - 2\sigma$ to $\mu + 2\sigma$?

Solution Again, $n = 5, p = .1$, and $q = .9$. Then, substituting into the formula for $p(x)$:

$p(0) = .59049$

$$p(0) = \frac{5!}{0!(5-0)!}(.1)^0(.9)^{5-0} = \frac{5 \cdot 4 \cdot 3 \cdot 2 \cdot 1}{(1)(5 \cdot 4 \cdot 3 \cdot 2 \cdot 1)}(1)(.9)^5 = .59049$$

$p(1) = .32805$

$$p(1) = \frac{5!}{1!(5-1)!}(.1)^1(.9)^{5-1} = 5(.1)(.9)^4 = .32805$$

$p(2) = .07290$

$$p(2) = \frac{5!}{2!(5-2)!}(.1)^2(.9)^{5-2} = (10)(.1)^2(.9)^3 = .07290$$

$p(4) = .00045$

$$p(4) = \frac{5!}{4!(5-4)!}(.1)^4(.9)^{5-4} = 5(.1)^4(.9) = .00045$$

$p(5) = .00001$
$\mu = .5, \sigma = .67, \approx 91\%$
Fall between $\mu \pm 2\sigma$

$$p(5) = \frac{5!}{5!(5-5)!}(.1)^5(.9)^{5-5} = (.1)^5 = .00001$$

The graph of $p(x)$ is shown as a probability histogram in Figure 4.7. [$p(3)$ is taken from Example 4.9 to be .0081.]

To calculate the values of μ and σ, substitute $n = 5$ and $p = .1$ into the following formulas:

$$\mu = np = (5)(.1) = .5$$

$$\sigma = \sqrt{npq} = \sqrt{(5)(.1)(.9)} = \sqrt{.45} = .67$$

To find the interval $\mu - 2\sigma$ to $\mu + 2\sigma$, we calculate

$$\mu - 2\sigma = .5 - 2(.67) = -.84$$

$$\mu + 2\sigma = .5 + 2(.67) = 1.84$$

If the experiment were to be repeated a large number of times, what proportion of the x observations would fall within the interval $\mu - 2\sigma$ to $\mu + 2\sigma$? You can see from Figure 4.7 that all observations equal to 0 or 1 will fall within the interval. The probabilities corresponding to these values are .5905 and .3280, respectively. Consequently, you would expect $.5905 + .3280 = .9185$, or approximately 91.9%, of the observations to fall within the interval $\mu - 2\sigma$ to $\mu + 2\sigma$.

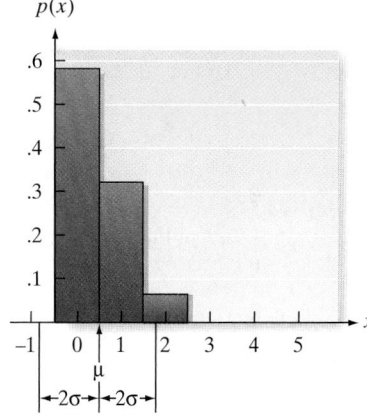

Figure 4.7
The binomial distribution:
$n = 5, p = .1$

Look Back This result again emphasizes that for most probability distributions, observations rarely fall more than 2 standard deviations from μ.

■ ■ ■

TABLE 4.3 Reproduction of Part of Table II of Appendix B: Binomial Probabilities for $n = 10$

k \ p	.01	.05	.10	.20	.30	.40	.50	.60	.70	.80	.90	.95	.99
0	.904	.599	.349	.107	.028	.006	.001	.000	.000	.000	.000	.000	.000
1	.996	.914	.736	.376	.149	.046	.011	.002	.000	.000	.000	.000	.000
2	1.000	.988	.930	.678	.383	.167	.055	.012	.002	.000	.000	.000	.000
3	1.000	.999	.987	.879	.650	.382	.172	.055	.011	.001	.000	.000	.000
4	1.000	1.000	.998	.967	.850	.633	.377	.166	.047	.006	.000	.000	.000
5	1.000	1.000	1.000	.994	.953	.834	.623	.367	.150	.033	.002	.000	.000
6	1.000	1.000	1.000	.999	.989	.945	.828	.618	.350	.121	.013	.001	.000
7	1.000	1.000	1.000	1.000	.998	.988	.945	.833	.617	.322	.070	.012	.000
8	1.000	1.000	1.000	1.000	1.000	.998	.989	.954	.851	.624	.264	.086	.004
9	1.000	1.000	1.000	1.000	1.000	1.000	.999	.994	.972	.893	.651	.401	.096

Figure 4.8

Binomial probability distribution for $n = 10$ and $p = .10$; $P(x \leq 2)$ shaded

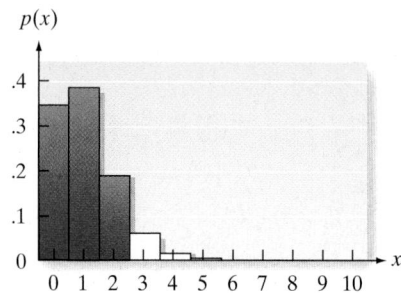

Using Binomial Tables

Calculating binomial probabilities becomes tedious when n is large. For some values of n and p the binomial probabilities have been tabulated in Table II of Appendix B. Part of Table II is shown in Table 4.3; a graph of the binomial probability distribution for $n = 10$ and $p = .10$ is shown in Figure 4.8. Table II actually contains a total of nine tables, labeled (a) through (i), one each corresponding to $n = 5, 6, 7, 8, 9, 10, 15, 20$, and 25. In each of these tables the columns correspond to values of p, and the rows correspond to values (k) of the random variable x. The entries in the table represent **cumulative binomial probabilities,** $P(x \leq k)$. Thus, for example, the entry in the column corresponding to $p = .10$ and the row corresponding to $k = 2$ is .930 (shaded), and its interpretation is

$$P(x \leq 2) = P(x = 0) + P(x = 1) + P(x = 2) = .930$$

This probability is also shaded in the graphical representation of the binomial distribution with $n = 10$ and $p = .10$ in Figure 4.8.

You can also use Table II to find the probability that x equals a specific value. For example, suppose you want to find the probability that $x = 2$ in the binomial distribution with $n = 10$ and $p = .10$. This is found by subtraction as follows:

$$P(x = 2) = [P(x = 0) + P(x = 1) + P(x = 2)] - [P(x = 0) + P(x = 1)]$$
$$= P(x \leq 2) - P(x \leq 1) = .930 - .736 = .194$$

The probability that a binomial random variable exceeds a specified value can be found using Table II and the notion of complementary events. For example, to find the probability that x exceeds 2 when $n = 10$ and $p = .10$, we use

$$P(x > 2) = 1 - P(x \leq 2) = .930 = .070$$

Note that this probability is represented by the unshaded portion of the graph in Figure 4.8.

All probabilities in Table II are rounded to three decimal places. Thus, although none of the binomial probabilities in the table is exactly zero, some are small enough (less than .0005) to round to .000. For example, using the formula to find $P(x = 0)$ when $n = 10$ and $p = .6$, we obtain

$$P(x = 0) = \binom{10}{0}(.6)^0(.4)^{10-0} = .4^{10} = .00010486$$

but this is rounded to .000 in Table II of Appendix B (see Table 4.3).

Similarly, none of the table entries is exactly 1.0, but when the cumulative probabilities exceed .9995, they are rounded to 1.000. The row corresponding to the largest possible value for x, $x = n$, is omitted, because all the cumulative probabilities in that row are equal to 1.0 (exactly). For example, in Table 4.3 with $n = 10$, $P(x \le 10) = 1.0$, no matter what the value of p.

The following example further illustrates the use of Table II.

EXAMPLE 4.11   USING THE BINOMIAL TABLE

Problem   Suppose a poll of 20 employees is taken in a large company. The purpose is to determine x, the number who favor unionization. Suppose that 60% of all the company's employees favor unionization.

$\mu = 12, \sigma = 2.19$

.245

.416

.159

  a.   Find the mean and standard deviation of x.

  b.   Use Table II of Appendix B to find the probability that $x \le 10$.

  c.   Use Table II to find the probability that $x > 12$.

  d.   Use Table II to find the probability that $x = 11$.

  e.   Graph the probability distribution of x and locate the interval $\mu \pm 2\sigma$ on the graph.

Solution   **a.**   The number of employees polled is presumably small compared with the total number of employees in this company. Thus, we may treat x, the number of the 20 who favor unionization, as a binomial random variable. The value of p is the fraction of the total employees who favor unionization; that is, $p = .6$. Therefore, we calculate the mean and variance:

$$\mu = np = 20(.6) = 12$$
$$\sigma^2 = npq = 20(.6)(.4) = 4.8$$
$$\sigma = \sqrt{4.8} = 2.19$$

Teaching Tip

Point out that values of both n and p are necessary in order to determine which binomial distribution applies to a particular problem. In turn, this will determine which column of numbers is useful in the binomial tables listed in the appendix.

  b.   Looking in the $k = 10$ row and the $p = .6$ column of Table II (Appendix B) for $n = 20$, we find the value of .245. Thus,

$$P(x \le 10) = .245$$

  c.   To find the probability

$$P(x > 12) = \sum_{x=13}^{20} p(x)$$

we use the fact that for all probability distributions, $\sum_{\text{All }x} p(x) = 1$. Therefore,

$$P(x > 12) = 1 - P(x \le 12) = 1 - \sum_{x=0}^{12} p(x)$$

Consulting Table II, we find the entry in row $k = 12$, column $p = .6$ to be .584. Thus,

$$P(x > 12) = 1 - .584 = .416$$

d. To find the probability that exactly 11 employees favor unionization, recall that the entries in Table II are cumulative probabilities and use the relationship

$$P(x = 11) = [p(0) + p(1) + \cdots + p(11)] - [p(0) + p(1) + \cdots + p(10)]$$
$$= P(x \le 11) - P(x \le 10)$$

Suggested Exercises 4.56

Then

$$P(x = 11) = .404 - .245 = .159$$

e. The probability distribution for x in this example is shown in Figure 4.9. Note that

$$\mu - 2\sigma = 12 - 2(2.2) = 7.6 \qquad \mu + 2\sigma = 12 + 2(2.2) = 16.4$$

The interval (7.6, 16.4) is also shown in Figure 4.9. The probability that x falls in this interval is $P(x = 8, 9, 10, \ldots, 16) = P(x \le 16) - P(x \le 7) = .984 - .021 = .963$. This probability is very close to the .95 given by the Empirical Rule. Thus, we expect the number of employees in the sample of 20 who favor unionization to be between 8 and 16.

Figure 4.9

The binomial probability distribution for x in Example 4.11: $n = 20, p = .6$

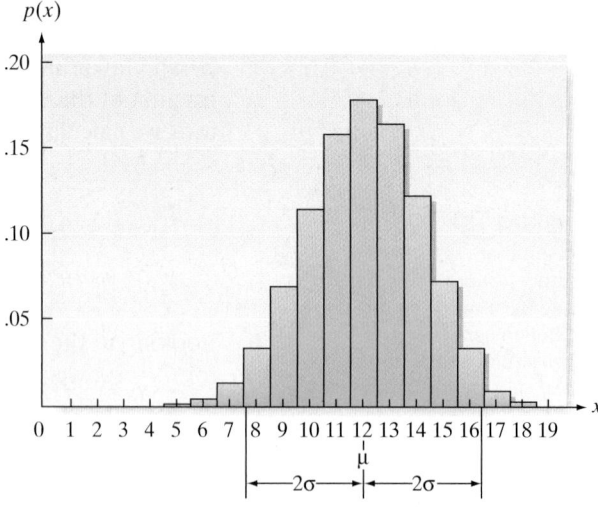

─── ■ ■ ■ ───

Statistics in Action Revisited

Using the Binomial Model to Solve the Cocaine Sting Case

Refer to the reverse cocaine sting case described on p. 209. During a drug bust, police seized 496 foil packets of a white, powdery substance that appeared to be cocaine. The police laboratory randomly selected four packets and found that all four tested positive for cocaine. This finding led to the conviction of the drug traffickers. Following the conviction, the police used two of the remaining 492 foil packets (i.e., those not tested) in a reverse sting operation. The two randomly selected packets were sold by undercover officers to a buyer who disposed of the evidence before being arrested. Is there beyond a reasonable doubt that the two packets contained cocaine?

To solve the dilemma, we will assume that of the 496 original packets confiscated, 331 contained genuine cocaine and 165 contained an inert (legal) powder. (A statistician, hired as an expert witness on the case, showed that the chance of the defendant being found not guilty is maximized when 331 packets contain cocaine and 165 do not.) First, we'll find the probability that four packets randomly selected from the original 496 will test positive for cocaine. Then we'll find the probability that the two packets sold in the reverse sting did not contain cocaine. Finally, we'll find the probability that both events occur (i.e., that the first four packets selected test positive for cocaine but that the next two pack selected do not). In each of these probability calculations, we will apply the binomial probability distribution to approximate the probabilities.

Let x be the number of packets that contain cocaine in a sample of n selected from the 496 packets. Here, we are defining a "success" as a pack that contains cocaine. If n is small, say $n = 2$ or $n = 4$, then x has an approximate binomial distribution with probability of success $p = 331/496 = .67$.

The probability that the first four packets selected contain cocaine [i.e., $P(x = 4)$] is obtained using the binomial formula with $n = 4$ and $p = .67$:

$$P(x = 4) = p(4) = \binom{4}{4}p^4(1 - p)^0 = \frac{4!(.67)^4(.33)^0}{4!0!}$$

$$= (.67)^4 = .201$$

Thus, there is about a 20% chance that all four of the randomly selected packets contain cocaine.

Given that four of the original packets tested positive for cocaine, the probability that the two packets randomly selected and sold in the reverse sting *do not* contain cocaine is approximated using a binomial distribution with $n = 2$ and $p = .67$. Since a "success" is a packet with cocaine, we find $P(x = 0)$:

$$P(x = 0) = p(0) = \binom{2}{0}p^0(1 - p)^2 = \frac{2!(.67)^0(.33)^2}{0!\,2!}$$

$$= (.33)^2 = .109$$

Finally, to compute the probability that of the original 496 foil packets, the first four selected (at random) test positive for cocaine and the next two selected (at random) test negative, we employ the Multiplicative Law of Probability. Let A be the event that the first four packets test positive. Let B be the event that the next two packets test negative. We want to find the probability of both events occurring, i.e., $P(A \text{ and } B) = P(A \cap B) = P(B|A)P(A)$. Note that this probability is the product of the two previously calculated probabilities:

$$P(A \text{ and } B) = (.109)(.201) = .022$$

Consequently, there is only a .022 probability (i.e., about 2 chances in a hundred) that the first four packets will test positive for cocaine and the next two packets will test negative for cocaine. A reasonable jury would likely believe that an event with such a small probability is unlikely to occur and conclude that the two "lost" packets contained cocaine. In other words, most of us would infer that the defendant in the reverse cocaine sting was guilty of drug trafficking.

Epilogue

Several of the defendant's lawyers believed that the .022 probability was too high for jurors to conclude guilt "beyond a reasonable doubt." The argument was made moot, however, when, to the surprise of the defense, the prosecution revealed that the remaining 490 packets had not been used in any other reverse sting operations and offered to test a sample of them. On the advice of the statistician, the defense requested that an additional 20 packets be tested. All 20 tested positive for cocaine! As a consequence of this new evidence, the defendant was convicted by the jury.

Using the TI-83 Graphing Calculator

I. $P(x = k)$

To compute the probability of k successes in n trials, where the p is probability of success for each trial, use the binompdf(command. Binompdf stands for "binomial probability density function." This command is under the DISTRibution menu and has the format binompdf(n, p, k).

Example   Compute the probability of 5 successes in 8 trials where the probability of success for a single trial is 40%. In this example, $n = 8$, $p = .4$, and $k = 5$.

   Step 1   Enter the binomial parameters
           Press 2nd VARS for DISTR
           Press the down arrow key until 0:binompdf is highlighted
           Press ENTER
           After binompdf(, type 8, .4, 5) (Note: be sure to use the comma key between each parameter)
           Press ENTER

You should see

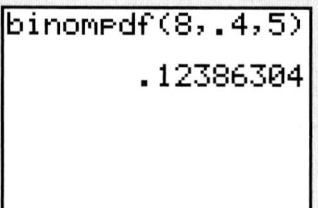

Thus, $P(x = 5)$ is about 12.4%.

II. $P(x \leq k)$

To compute the probability of k or fewer successes in n trials, where the p is probability of success for each trial, use the binomcdf(command. Binomcdf stands for "binomial ***cumulative*** probability density function." This command is under the DISTRibution menu and has the format binomcdf(n, p, k).

Example   Compute the probability of 5 or less successes in 8 trials where the probability of success for a single trial is 40%. In this example, $n = 8$, $p = .4$, and $k = 5$.

   Step 1   Enter the binomial parameters
           Press 2nd VARS for DISTR
           Press down the arrow key until A:binomcdf is highlighted
           Press ENTER
           After binomcdf(, type 8, .4, 5)
           Press ENTER

You should see

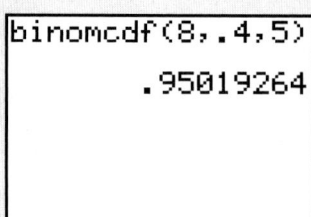

Thus, $P(x < 5)$ is about 95%.

III. $P(x < k)$, $P(x > k)$, $P(x \geq k)$

To find the probability of less than k successes $P(x < k)$, more than k successes $P(x > k)$, or at least k successes $P(x \geq k)$, variations of the binomcdf(command must be used as shown below.

$P(x < k)$ use **binomcdf(n, p, k − 1)**

$P(x > k)$ use **1-binomcdf(n, p, k)**

$P(x \geq k)$ use **1-binomcdf(n, p, k − 1)**

Exercises 4.39–4.57

Learning the Mechanics

4.39 Compute the following:

a. $\dfrac{6!}{2!(6-2)!}$ **b.** $\dbinom{5}{2}$ **c.** $\dbinom{7}{0}$ **d.** $\dbinom{6}{6}$ **e.** $\dbinom{4}{3}$

4.40 Consider the following probability distribution:

$$p(x) = \binom{5}{x}(.7)^x(.3)^{5-x} \qquad (x = 0, 1, 2, \ldots, 5)$$

a. Is x a discrete or a continuous random variable?

b. What is the name of this probability distribution?

c. Graph the probability distribution.

d. Find the mean and standard deviation of x.

e. Show the mean and the 2-standard-deviation interval on each side of the mean on the graph you drew in part c.

4.41 If x is a binomial random variable, compute $p(x)$ for each of the following cases:

a. $n = 5, x = 1, p = .2$

b. $n = 4, x = 2, q = .4$

c. $n = 3, x = 0, p = .7$

d. $n = 5, x = 3, p = .1$

e. $n = 4, x = 2, q = .6$

f. $n = 3, x = 1, p = .9$

4.42 Suppose x is a binomial random variable with $n = 3$ and $p = .3$.

a. Calculate the value of $p(x)$, $x = 0, 1, 2, 3$, using the formula for a binomial probability distribution.

b. Using your answers to part a, give the probability distribution for x in tabular form.

4.43 If x is a binomial random variable, calculate μ, σ^2, and σ for each of the following:

a. $n = 25, p = .5$

b. $n = 80, p = .2$

c. $n = 100, p = .6$

d. $n = 70, p = .9$

e. $n = 60, p = .8$

f. $n = 1,000, p = .04$

4.44 If x is a binomial random variable, use Table II in Appendix B to find the following probabilities:

a. $P(x = 2)$ for $n = 10, p = .4$ .121

b. $P(x \leq 5)$ for $n = 15, p = .6$ .034

c. $P(x > 1)$ for $n = 5, p = .1$ .081

d. $P(x < 10)$ for $n = 25, p = .7$ 0

e. $P(x \geq 10)$ for $n = 15, p = .9$ .998

f. $P(x = 2)$ for $n = 20, p = .2$ .137

4.45 The binomial probability distribution is a family of probability distributions with each single distribution depending on the values of n and p. Assume that x is a binomial random variable with $n = 4$.

a. Determine a value of p such that the probability distribution of x is symmetric. $p = .5$

b. Determine a value of p such that the probability distribution of x is skewed to the right. $p = .1$

c. Determine a value of p such that the probability distribution of x is skewed to the left. $p = .9$

d. Graph each of the binomial distributions you obtained in parts a, b, and c. Locate the mean for each distribution on its graph.

e. In general, for what values of p will a binomial distribution be symmetric? Skewed to the right? Skewed to the left?

Applying the Concepts—Basic

4.46 According to a Jupiter/NPD Consumer Survey of young adults (18–24 years of age) who shop online, 20% own a 1mobile phone with Internet access. (*American Demographics*, May 2002.) In a random sample of 200 young adults who shop online, let x be the number who own a mobile phone with Internet access.

a. Explain why x is a binomial random variable (to a reasonable degree of approximation).

b. What is the value of p? Interpret this value.   .20

c. What is the expected value of x? Interpret this value.   40

4.47 According to the *Journal of Business Venturing* (Vol. 17, 2002), 27% of all small businesses owned by non-Hispanic whites nationwide are women-owned firms.

a. In a sample of 200 small businesses owned by non-Hispanic whites, how many would you expect to be female owned?   54

b. If eight small businesses owned by non-Hispanic whites were randomly selected, what is the probability that none are female owned? That half are female owned?   .0806; .1056

4.48 A Federal Trade Commission (FTC) study of the pricing accuracy of electronic checkout scanners at stores found that one of every 30 items is priced incorrectly (*Price Check II: A Follow-Up Report on the Accuracy of Checkout Scanner Prices*, Dec. 16, 1998). Suppose the FTC randomly selects five items at a retail store and checks the accuracy of the scanner price of each. Let *x* represent the number of the five items that is priced incorrectly.

a. Show that *x* is (approximately) a binomial random variable.

b. Use the information in the FTC study to estimate *p* for the binomial experiment.   1/30

c. What is the probability that exactly one of the five items is priced incorrectly by the scanner?   .1455

d. What is the probability that at least one of the five items is priced incorrectly by the scanner?   .1559

4.49 "Do you believe your children will have a higher standard of living than you have?" This question was asked of a national sample of American adults with children in a *Time/CNN* poll (Jan. 29, 1996). Sixty-three percent answered in the affirmative, with a margin of error of plus or minus 3%. Assume that the true percentage of all American adults who believe their children will have a higher standard of living is .60. Let *x* represent the number in a random sample of five American adults who believe their children will have a higher standard of living.

a. Demonstrate that *x* is (approximately) a binomial random variable.

b. What is the value of *p* for the binomial experiment?   .60

c. Find $P(x = 3)$.   .346

d. Find $P(x \le 2)$.   .317

4.50 A poll by the Gallup Organization sponsored by Philadelphia-based CIGNA Integrated Care found that about 40% of employees have missed work due to a musculoskeletal (back) injury of some kind (*National Underwriter*, Apr. 5, 1999). Let *x* be the number of sampled workers who have missed work due to a back injury.

a. Explain why *x* is approximately a binomial random variable.

b. Use the Gallup poll data to estimate *p* for the binomial random variable of part a.   *p* = .40

c. A random sample of 10 workers is to be drawn from a particular manufacturing plant. Use the *p* from part b to find the mean and standard deviation of *x*, the number of workers that missed work due to back injuries.   1.549

d. For the sample in part c, find the probability that exactly one worker missed work due to a back injury. That more than one worker missed work due to a back injury.   .954

Applying the Concepts—Intermediate

4.51 According to the Internal Revenue Service (IRS), the chances of your tax return being audited are about 15 in 1,000 if your income is less than $100,000 and 30 in 1,000 if your income is $100,000 or more (*Statistical Abstract of the United States*).

a. What is the probability that a taxpayer with income less than $100,000 will be audited by the IRS? With income $100,000 or more?

b. If five taxpayers with incomes under $100,000 are randomly selected, what is the probability that exactly one will be audited? That more than one will be audited?   .0706, .0022

c. Repeat part b assuming that five taxpayers with incomes of $100,000 or more are randomly selected.

d. If two taxpayers with incomes under $100,000 are randomly selected and two with incomes more than $100,000 are randomly selected, what is the probability that none of these taxpayers will be audited by the IRS?   .9129

e. What assumptions did you have to make in order to answer these questions using the methodology presented in this section?

4.52 Banks that merge with others to form "mega-banks" sometimes leaves customers dissatisfied with the impersonal service. A poll by the Gallup Organization found 20% of retail customers switched banks after their banks merged with another (*Bank Marketing*, Feb. 1999). One year after the acquisition of First Fidelity by First Union, a random sample of 25 retail customers who had banked with First Fidelity were questioned. Let *x* be the number of those customers who switched their business from First Union to a different bank.

a. What assumptions must hold in order for *x* to be a binomial random variable? In the remainder of this exercise, use the data from the Gallop Poll to estimate *p*.

b. What is the probability that $x \le 10$?   .994

c. Find $E(x)$ and the standard deviation of *x*.   5, 2

d. Calculate the interval $\mu \pm 2\sigma$.   (1, 9)

e. If samples of size 25 were drawn repeatedly a large number of times and *x* determined for each sample, what proportion of the *x* values would fall within the interval you calculated in part d?   .926

4.53 Every quarter the Food and Drug Administration (FDA) produces a report called the *Total Diet Study*. The FDA's report covers a variety of food items, each of which is analyzed for potentially harmful chemical compounds. A recent *Total Diet Study* reported that no pesticides at all were found in 60% of the domestically produced food samples (*FDA Pesticide Program: Residue Monitoring*, 2001). Consider a random sample of 800 food items analyzed for the presence of pesticides.

a. Compute μ and σ for the random variable x, the number of food items found that showed no trace of pesticide. $\mu = 480, \sigma = 13.856$

b. Based on a sample of 800 food items, is it likely you would observe less than half without any traces of pesticide? Explain. No, $z = -5.77$

4.54 A study conducted in New Jersey by the Governor's Council for a Drug Free Workplace concluded that 70% of New Jersey's businesses have employees whose performance is affected by drugs and/or alcohol. In those businesses, it was estimated that 8.5% of their workforces have alcohol problems and 5.2% have drug problems. (*Report: The Governor's Council for a Drug Free Workplace*, Spring/Summer 1995).

a. In a New Jersey company that acknowledges it has performance problems caused by substance abuse, out of every 1,000 employees, approximately how many have drug problems? 52

b. In the company referred to in part a, if 10 employees are randomly selected to form a committee to address alcohol abuse problems, what is the probability that at least one member of the committee is an alcohol abuser? That exactly two are alcohol abusers?

c. What assumptions did you have to make in order to answer part b using the methodology of this section?

Applying the Concepts—Advanced

4.55 According to the U.S. Golf Association (USGA), "The weight of the [golf] ball shall not be greater than 1.620 ounces avoirdupois (45.93 grams). ... The diameter of the ball shall not be less than 1.680 inches. ... The velocity of the ball shall not be greater than 250 feet per second" (USGA, 2002). The USGA periodically checks the specifications of golf balls sold in the United States by randomly sampling balls from pro shops around the country. Two dozen of each kind are sampled, and if more than three do not meet size and/or velocity requirements, that kind of ball is removed from the USGA's approved-ball list.

a. What assumptions must be made and what information must be known in order to use the binomial probability distribution to calculate the probability

that the USGA will remove a particular kind of golf ball from its approved-ball list?

b. Suppose 10% of all balls produced by a particular manufacturer are less than 1.680 inches in diameter, and assume that the number of such balls, x, in a sample of two dozen balls can be adequately characterized by a binomial probability distribution. Find the mean and standard deviation of the binomial distribution. $\mu = 2.4, \sigma = 1.47$

c. Refer to part b. If x has a binomial distribution, then so does the number, y, of balls in the sample that meet the USGA's minimum diameter. [*Note:* $x + y = 24.$] Describe the distribution of y. In particular, what are p, q, and n? Also, find $E(y)$ and the standard deviation of y. $p = .9, q = .1, n = 24$

4.56 A problem of considerable economic impact on the economy is the burgeoning cost of Medicare. One aspect of this problem concerns the high percentage of people seeking medical treatment who, in fact, have no physical basis for their ailments. One conservative estimate is that the percentage of people who seek medical assistance and who have no real physical ailment is 10%, and some doctors believe that it may be as high as 40%. Suppose we were to randomly sample the records of a doctor and found that five of 15 patients seeking medical assistance were physically healthy.

a. What is the probability of observing five or more physically healthy patients in a sample of 15 if the proportion, p, that the doctor normally sees is 10%? .013

b. What is the probability of observing five or more physically healthy patients in a sample of 15 if the proportion, p, that the doctor normally sees is 40%? .783

c. Why might your answer to part a make you believe that p is larger than .10?

4.57 Suppose you are a purchasing officer for a large company. You have purchased 5 million electrical switches and your supplier has guaranteed that the shipment will contain no more than .1% defectives. To check the shipment, you randomly sample 500 switches, test them, and find that four are defective. Based on this evidence, do you think the supplier has complied with the guarantee? Explain. No, $z = 4.95$

4.5 The Poisson Random Variable (Optional)

A type of probability distribution that is often useful in describing the number of events that will occur in a specific period of time or in a specific area or volume is the **Poisson distribution** (named after the 18th-century physicist and mathematician, Siméon Poisson). Typical examples of random variables for which the Poisson probability distribution provides a good model are as follows:

Teaching Tip

The Poisson distribution counts the number of occurrences per unit of measurement. The unit of measurement is an easy way to tell the difference between the binomial and Poisson distributions.

1. The number of industrial accidents per month at a manufacturing plant

2. The number of noticeable surface defects (scratches, dents, etc.) found by quality inspectors on a new automobile

3. The parts per million of some toxin found in the water or air emission from a manufacturing plant

4. The number of customer arrivals per unit of time at a supermarket check-out counter

5. The number of death claims received per day by an insurance company

6. The number of errors per 100 invoices in the accounting records of a company

---

Characteristics of a Poisson Random Variable

1. The experiment consists of counting the number of times a certain event occurs during a given unit of time or in a given area or volume (or weight, distance, or any other unit of measurement).

2. The probability that an event occurs in a given unit of time, area, or volume is the same for all the units.

3. The number of events that occur in one unit of time, area, or volume is independent of the number that occur in any other mutually exclusive unit.

4. The mean (or expected) number of events in each unit is denoted by the Greek letter lambda, λ.

The characteristics of the Poisson random variable are usually difficult to verify for practical examples. The examples given satisfy them well enough that the Poisson distribution provides a good model in many instances. As with all probability models, the real test of the adequacy of the Poisson model is in whether it provides a reasonable approximation to reality—that is, whether empirical data support it.

The probability distribution, mean, and variance for a Poisson random variable are shown in the next box.

Probability Distribution, Mean, and Variance for a Poisson Random Variable*

$$p(x) = \frac{\lambda^x e^{-\lambda}}{x!} \quad (x = 0, 1, 2, \dots)$$

$$\mu = \lambda$$

$$\sigma^2 = \lambda$$

where

λ = Mean number of events during given unit of time, area, volume, etc.

$e = 2.71828\dots$

---

*The Poisson probability distribution also provides a good approximation to a binomial distribution with mean $\lambda = np$ when n is large and p is small (say, $np \leq 7$).

Biography

SIMEON D. POISSON (1781–1840)
A Lifetime Mathematician

Growing up in France during the French Revolution, Simeon-Denis Poisson was sent away by his father to become an apprentice surgeon, but he lacked the manual dexterity to perform the delicate procedures required and returned home. He eventually enrolled in Ecole Polytechnique University to study mathematics. In his final year of study, Poisson wrote a paper on the theory of equations

that was of such quality that he was allowed to graduate without taking the final examination. Two years later, Poisson was named a professor at the university. During his illustrious career, Poisson published between 300 and 400 mathematics papers. He is most known for his 1837 paper where the distribution of a rare event—the Poisson distribution—first appears. (In fact, the distribution was actually described years earlier by one of the Bernoulli brothers.) Poisson dedicated his life to mathematics, once stating that "Life is good for only two things: to study mathematics and to teach it."

The calculation of Poisson probabilities is made easier by the use of Table III in Appendix B, which gives the cumulative probabilities $P(x \leq k)$ for various values of λ. The use of Table III is illustrated in Example 4.12.

EXAMPLE 4.12   FINDING POISSON PROBABILITIES

Problem   Suppose the number, x, of a company's employees who are absent on Mondays has (approximately) a Poisson probability distribution. Furthermore, assume that the average number of Monday absentees is 2.6.

$\mu = 2.6, \sigma = 1.61$

a. Find the mean and standard deviation of x, the number of employees absent on Monday.

.267

b. Use Table III to find the probability that fewer than two employees are absent on a given Monday.

.049

c. Use Table III to find the probability that more than five employees are absent on a given Monday.

.074

d. Use Table III to find the probability that exactly five employees are absent on a given Monday.

Solution   **a.** The mean and variance of a Poisson random variable are both equal to λ. Thus, for this example,

$$\mu = \lambda = 2.6$$
$$\sigma^2 = \lambda = 2.6$$

Then the standard deviation of x is

$$\sigma = \sqrt{2.6} = 1.61$$

Remember that the mean measures the central tendency of the distribution and does not necessarily equal a possible value of x. In this example, the mean

is 2.6 absences, and although there cannot be 2.6 absences on a given Monday,
the average number of Monday absences is 2.6. Similarly, the standard deviation of 1.61 measures the variability of the number of absences per week. Perhaps a more helpful measure is the interval $\mu \pm 2\sigma$, which in this case
stretches from $-.62$ to 5.82. We expect the number of absences to fall in this interval most of the time—with at least 75% relative frequency (according to
Chebyshev's Rule) and probably with approximately 95% relative frequency
(the Empirical Rule). The mean and the 2-standard-deviation interval around
it are shown in Figure 4.10.

Figure 4.10

Probability distribution for
number of Monday absences

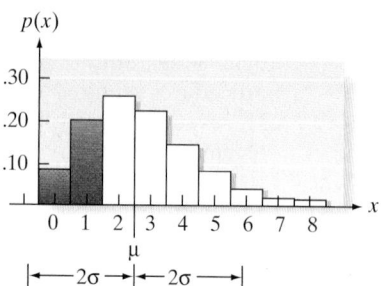

b. A partial reproduction of Table III is shown in Table 4.4. The rows of the table
correspond to different values of λ, and the columns correspond to different
values (k) of the Poisson random variable x. The entries in the table (like the
binomial probabilities in Table II) give the cumulative probability $P(x \le k)$.
To find the probability that fewer than two employees are absent on Monday,
we first note that

$$P(x < 2) = P(x \le 1)$$

Suggested Exercises 4.65

This probability is a cumulative probability and therefore is the entry in Table
III in the row corresponding to $\lambda = 2.6$ and the column corresponding to
$k = 1$. The entry is .267, shown shaded in Table 4.4. This probability corresponds to the shaded area in Figure 4.10 and may be interpreted as meaning
that there is a 26.7% chance that fewer than two employees will be absent on
a given Monday.

c. To find the probability that more than five employees are absent on a given
Monday, we consider the complementary event

$$P(x > 5) = 1 - P(x \le 5) = 1 - .951 = .049$$

where .951 is the entry in Table III corresponding to $\lambda = 2.6$ and $k = 5$ (see
Table 4.4). Note from Figure 4.10 that this is the area in the interval $\mu \pm 2\sigma$,
or $-.62$ to 5.82. Then the number of absences should exceed 5—or, equivalently, should be more than 2 standard deviations from the mean—during
only about 4.9% of all Mondays. Note that this percentage agrees remarkably well with that given by the Empirical Rule for mound-shaped distributions, which tells us to expect approximately 5% of the measurements
(values of the random variable) to lie farther than 2 standard deviations
from the mean.

TABLE 4.4   Reproduction of Part of Table III in Appendix B

λ \ k	0	1	2	3	4	5	6	7	8	9
2.2	.111	.355	.623	.819	.928	.975	.993	.998	1.000	1.000
2.4	.091	.308	.570	.779	.904	.964	.988	.997	.999	1.000
2.6	.074	.267	.518	.736	.877	.951	.983	.995	.999	1.000
2.8	.061	.231	.469	.692	.848	.935	.976	.992	.998	.999
3.0	.050	.199	.423	.647	.815	.916	.966	.988	.996	.999
3.2	.041	.171	.380	.603	.781	.895	.955	.983	.994	.998
3.4	.033	.147	.340	.558	.744	.871	.942	.977	.992	.997
3.6	.027	.126	.303	.515	.706	.844	.927	.969	.988	.996
3.8	.022	.107	.269	.473	.668	.816	.909	.960	.984	.994
4.0	.018	.092	.238	.433	.629	.785	.889	.949	.979	.992
4.2	.015	.078	.210	.395	.590	.753	.867	.936	.972	.989
4.4	.012	.066	.185	.359	.551	.720	.844	.921	.964	.985
4.6	.010	.056	.163	.326	.513	.686	.818	.905	.955	.980
4.8	.008	.048	.143	.294	.476	.651	.791	.887	.944	.975
5.0	.007	.040	.125	.265	.440	.616	.762	.867	.932	.968
5.2	.006	.034	.109	.238	.406	.581	.732	.845	.918	.960
5.4	.005	.029	.095	.213	.373	.546	.702	.822	.903	.951
5.6	.004	.024	.082	.191	.342	.512	.670	.797	.886	.941
5.8	.003	.021	.072	.170	.313	.478	.638	.771	.867	.929
6.0	.002	.017	.062	.151	.285	.446	.606	.744	.847	.916

d. To use Table III to find the probability that *exactly* five employees are absent on a Monday, we must write the probability as the difference between two cumulative probabilities:

$$P(x = 5) = P(x \le 5) - P(x \le 4) = .951 - .877 = .074$$

■ ■ ■

Note that the probabilities in Table III are all rounded to three decimal places. Thus, although in theory a Poisson random variable can assume infinitely large values, the values of k in Table III are extended only until the cumulative probability is 1.000. This does not mean that x *cannot* assume larger values, but only that the likelihood is less than .001 (in fact, less than .0005) that it will do so.

Finally, you may need to calculate Poisson probabilities for values of λ not found in Table III. You may be able to obtain an adequate approximation by interpolation, but if not, consult more extensive tables for the Poisson distribution.

Poisson Probabilities

Using the TI-83 Graphing Calculator

I. $P(x = k)$

To compute $P(x = k)$, the probability of exactly k successes in a specified interval where λ is the mean number of successes in the interval, use the poissonpdf(command. Poissonpdf stands for "Poisson probability density function." This command is under the DISTRibution menu and has the format poissonpdf( ).

Example   Suppose that the number, x, of reported sightings per week of blue whales is recorded. Assume that x has approximately a Poisson probability distribution, and that the average number of weekly sightings is 2.6.
Compute the probability that exactly five sightings are made during a given week. In this example, $\lambda = 2.6$ and $k = 5$.

Step 1   Enter the poisson parameters
Press 2nd VARS for DISTR
Press the down arrow key until B:poissonpdf is highlighted
Press ENTER
After poissonpdf(, type 2.6, 5) (Note: be sure to use the comma key between each parameter)
Press ENTER

You should see

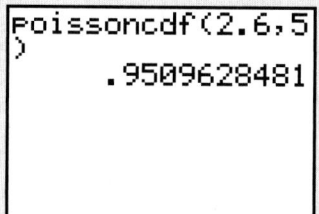

Thus, the $P(x = 5)$ is about 7.4%.

II. $P(x \leq k)$

To compute the probability of k or fewer successes in a specified interval, where λ is the mean number of successes in the interval, use the poissoncdf(command. Poissoncdf stands for "Poisson *cumulative* probability density function." This command is under the DISTRibution menu and has the format poissoncdf(.

Example   In the example given above, compute the probability that five or fewer sightings are made during a given week. In this example, $\lambda = 2.6$ and $k = 5$.

Step 1   Enter the poisson parameters
Press 2nd VARS for DISTR
Press the down arrow key until C:poissoncdf is highlighted
Press ENTER
After poissoncdf(, type 2.6, 5)
Press ENTER

You should see

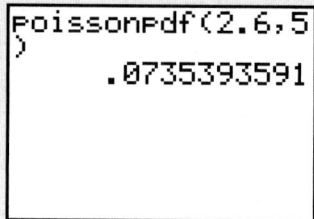

Thus, the $P(x \leq 5)$ is about 95.1%.

III. $P(x < k)$, $P(x > k)$, $P(x \geq k)$

To find the probability of less than k successes more than k successes, or at least k successes variations of poissoncdf(command must be used as shown below.

$P(x < k)$ use poissoncdf($\lambda, k - 1$)

$P(x > k)$ use **1 − poissoncdf(λ, k)**

$P(x \geq k)$ use **1 − poissoncdf($\lambda, k - 1$)**

Exercises 4.58–4.70

Learning the Mechanics

4.58 Consider the probability distribution shown here:

$$p(x) = \frac{3^x e^{-3}}{x!} \quad (x = 0, 1, 2, \dots)$$

a. Is x a discrete or continuous random variable? Explain.   Discrete
b. What is the name of this probability distribution?
c. Graph the probability distribution.
d. Find the mean and standard deviation of x.
e. Find the mean and standard deviation of the probability distribution. $\mu = 3, \sigma = 1.7321$

4.59 Given that x is a random variable for which a Poisson probability distribution provides a good approximation, use Table III to compute the following:
a. $P(x \leq 2)$ when $\lambda = 1$ .920
b. $P(x \leq 2)$ when $\lambda = 2$ .677
c. $P(x \leq 2)$ when $\lambda = 3$ .423
d. What happens to the probability of the event $\{x \leq 2\}$ as λ increases from 1 to 3? Is this intuitively reasonable?   Decreases

4.60 Assume that x is a random variable having a Poisson probability distribution with a mean of 1.5. Use Table III to find the following probabilities:
a. $P(x \leq 3)$
b. $P(x \geq 3)$
c. $P(x = 3)$
d. $P(x = 0)$
e. $P(x > 0)$
f. $P(x > 6)$

4.61 Suppose x is a random variable for which a Poisson probability distribution with $\lambda = 5$ provides a good characterization.
a. Graph $p(x)$ for $x = 0, 1, 2, \dots, 15$.
b. Find μ and σ for x, and locate μ and the interval $\mu \pm 2\sigma$ on the graph. $\mu = 5, \sigma = 2.2361$
c. What is the probability that x will fall within the interval $\mu \pm 2\sigma$?   .961

Applying the Concepts

4.62 The Federal Deposit Insurance Corporation (FDIC) insures deposits of up to $100,000 in banks that are members of the Federal Reserve System against losses due to bank failure or theft. Over the last 5 years, the average number of bank failures per year among insured banks was 5.8 (*FDIC Stats at a Glance*, Mar. 2003). Assume that x, the number of bank failures per year among insured banks, can be adequately characterized by a Poisson probability distribution with mean 6.
a. Find the expected value and standard deviation of x.
b. In 1997, only one insured bank failed. How far (in standard deviations) does $x = 1$ lie below the mean of the Poisson distribution? That is, find the z-score for $x = 1$.   −2.041
c. In 2002, 10 insured banks failed. Find $P(x \leq 10)$.   .957

4.63 U.S. airlines average about 3.8 fatalities per month (*Statistical Abstract of the United States: 2000*). Assume the probability distribution for x, the number of fatalities per month, can be approximated by a Poisson probability distribution.
a. What is the probability that no fatalities will occur during any given month?   .0721
b. What is the probability that one fatality will occur during a month?
c. Find $E(x)$ and the standard deviation of x.

4.64 University of New Mexico economists Gawande and Wheeler modeled the number of casualties experienced by a deep-draft marine vessel over a three-year period as a Poisson random variable, x. They estimated $E(x)$ to be .03 (*Management Science*, January 1999).
a. Find the variance x.   .03
b. Discuss the conditions that would make the researchers' Poisson assumption plausible.
c. What is the probability that a deep-draft U.S. flag vessel will have exactly one casualty in a

three-year time period? No casualties in a three-year period?

4.65 The number x of people who arrive at a cashier's counter in a bank during a specified period of time exhibits a Poisson probability distribution with mean arrival rate λ. Suppose you estimate that the mean number of arrivals per minute for cashier service at a bank is one person per minute (i.e., $\lambda = 1$).
  a. What is the probability that in a given minute the number of arrivals will equal three?   .061
  b. What is the probability that the number of arrivals will exceed two per minute?   .080

Applying the Concepts–Intermediate

4.66 As part of a project targeted at improving the services of a local bakery, a management consultant (L. Lei of Rutgers University) monitored customer arrivals for several Saturdays and Sundays. Using the arrival data, she estimated the average number of customer arrivals per 10-minute period on Saturdays to be 6.2. She assumed that arrivals per 10-minute interval followed the Poisson distribution (some of whose values are missing) shown in the table at the bottom of the page.
  a. Compute the missing probabilities.
  b. Plot the distribution.
  c. Find μ and σ and plot the intervals $\mu \pm \sigma, \mu \pm 2\sigma$, and $\mu \pm 3\sigma$ on your plot of part b.
  d. The owner of the bakery claims that more than 75 customers per hour enter the store on Saturdays. Based on the consultant's data, is this likely? Explain.   No

4.67 The Environmental Protection Agency (EPA) limits the amount of vinyl chloride in plant air emissions to no more than 10 parts per million. Suppose the mean emission of vinyl chloride for a particular plant is 4 parts per million. Assume that the number of parts per million of vinyl chloride in air samples, x, follows a Poisson probability distribution.

  a. What is the standard deviation of x for the plant?
  b. Is it likely that a sample of air from the plant would yield a value of x that would exceed the EPA limit? Explain.   No, $p(x > 10) = .003$
  c. Discuss conditions that would make the Poisson assumption plausible.

4.68 As a check on the quality of the wooden doors produced by a company, its owner requested that each door undergo inspection for defects before leaving the plant. The plant's quality control inspector found that one square foot of door surface contains, on the average, .5 minor flaw. Subsequently, one square foot of each door's surface was examined for flaws. The owner decided to have all doors reworked that were found to have two or more minor flaws in the square foot of surface that was inspected. What is the probability that a door will fail inspection and be sent back for reworking? What is the probability that a door will pass inspection?

4.69 In studying the product life cycle in the commercial mainframe computer market Greenstein (Northwestern University) and Wade (University of Illinois) found that the number of new product introductions per year per firm, x, could be approximated by a Poisson random variable with mean equal to .37 (*Rand Journal of Economics*, Winter 1998).
  a. Find the standard deviation of x.   .6083
  b. Plot $p(x)$, the probability distribution for x.
  c. Is it likely that the mainframe manufacturer would introduce more than two new products per year? Less than one new product per year? Justify your answers.

4.70 A large manufacturing plant has 3,200 incandescent light bulbs illuminating the manufacturing floor. The rate at which the bulbs fail follows a Poisson distribution with a mean of three bulbs per hour. What is the probability that no bulbs fail in an eight-hour shift?   .058

Probability Distribution for Exercise 4.66

x	0	1	2	3	4	5	6	7	8	9	10	11	12	13
$p(x)$	.002	.013	—	.081	.125	.155	—	.142	.110	.076	—	.026	.014	.007

Source: Lei, L. *Dorsi's Bakery: Modeling Service Operations.* Graduate School of Management. Rutgers University, 1993.

4.6 The Hypergeometric Random Variable (Optional)

The **hypergeometric probability distribution** provides a realistic model for some types of enumerative (countable) data. The characteristics of the hypergeometric distribution are listed in the box.

Characteristics of a Hypergeometric Random Variable

1. The experiment consists of randomly drawing n elements without replacement from a set of N elements, r of which are S's (for Success) and $(N - r)$ of which are F's (for Failure).
2. The hypergeometric random variable x is the number of S's in the draw of n elements.

Note that both the hypergeometric and binomial characteristics stipulate that each draw, or trial, results in one of two outcomes. The basic difference between these random variables is that the hypergeometric trials are dependent, while the binomial trials are independent. The draws are dependent because the probability of drawing an S (or an F) is dependent on what occurred on preceding draws.

To illustrate the dependence between trials, we note that the probability of drawing an S on the first draw is r/N. Then the probability of drawing an S on the second draw depends on the outcome of the first. It will be either $(r - 1)/(N - 1)$, or $r/(N - 1)$, depending on whether the first draw was an S or an F. Consequently, the results of the draws represent dependent events.

For example, suppose we define x as the number of women hired in a random selection of three applicants from a total of six men and four women. This random variable satisfies the characteristics of a hypergeometric random variable with $N = 10$ and $n = 3$. The possible outcomes on each trial are either selection of a female (S) or selection of a male (F). Another example of a hypergeometric random variable is the number, x, of defective large-screen television picture tubes in a random selection of $n = 4$ from a shipment of $N = 8$ tubes. And, as a third example, suppose $n = 5$ stocks are randomly selected from a list of $N = 15$ stocks. Then, the number x of the five selected companies that pay regular dividends to stockholders is a hypergeometric random variable.

The hypergeometric probability distribution is summarized in the box.

Probability Distribution, Mean, and Variance of the Hypergeometric Random Variable

$$p(x) = \frac{\binom{r}{x}\binom{N - r}{n - x}}{\binom{N}{n}} \qquad [x = \text{Maximum } [0, n - (N - r)], \ldots, \text{Minimum } (r, n)]$$

$$\mu = \frac{nr}{N} \qquad \sigma^2 = \frac{r(N - r)n(N - n)}{N^2(N - 1)}$$

where

N = Total number of elements
r = Number of S's in the N elements
n = Number of elements drawn
x = Number of S's drawn in the n elements

EXAMPLE 4.13   APPLYING THE HYPERGEOMETRIC DISTRIBUTION

Problem   Suppose a professor randomly selects three new teaching assistants from a total of 10 applicants, six male and four female students. Let x be the number of females who are hired.

$\mu = -1.2; \sigma = 75$

$\frac{1}{6}$

a. Find the mean and standard deviation of x.

b. Find the probability that no females are hired.

Solution   **a.** Since x is a hypergeometric random variable with $N = 10, n = 3$, and $r = 4$, the mean and variance are

$$\mu = \frac{nr}{N} = \frac{(3)(4)}{10} = 1.2$$

$$\sigma^2 = \frac{r(N - r)n(N - n)}{N^2(N - 1)} = \frac{4(10 - 4)3(10 - 3)}{(10)^2(10 - 1)}$$

$$= \frac{(4)(6)(3)(7)}{(100)(9)} = .56$$

The standard deviation is

$$\sigma = \sqrt{.56} = .75$$

Suggested Exercises 4.79

b. The probability that no female students are hired by the professor, assuming the selection is truly random, is

$$P(x = 0) = p(0) = \frac{\binom{4}{0}\binom{10 - 4}{3 - 0}}{\binom{10}{3}}$$

$$= \frac{\dfrac{4!}{0!(4 - 0)!}\dfrac{6!}{3!(6 - 3)!}}{\dfrac{10!}{3!(10 - 3)!}} = \frac{(1)(20)}{120} = \frac{1}{6}$$

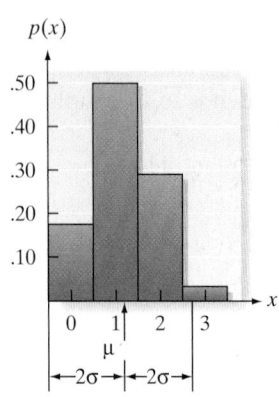

p(x)

.50
.40
.30
.20
.10

0 1 2 3   → x
       μ
←2σ→←2σ→

Figure 4.11
Probability distribution
for x in Example 4.13

Look Back The entire probability distribution for x is shown in Figure 4.11. The mean $\mu = 1.2$ and the interval $\mu \pm 2\sigma = (-.3, 2.7)$ are indicated. You can see that if this random variable were to be observed over and over again a large number of times, most of the values of x would fall within the interval $\mu \pm 2\sigma$.

Now Work   *Exercise 4.79*

■ ■ ■

Exercises 4.71–4.83

Learning the Mechanics

4.71 Given that x is a hypergeometric random variable with $N = 8, n = 3$, and $r = 5$, compute the following:
   a. $P(x = 1)$ .268
   b. $P(x = 0)$ .018
   c. $P(x = 3)$ .179
   d. $P(x \geq 4)$ 0

4.72 Given that x is a hypergeometric random variable, compute $p(x)$ for each of the following cases:
   a. $N = 5, n = 3, r = 3, x = 1$ .3
   b. $N = 9, n = 5, r = 3, x = 3$ 119
   c. $N = 4, n = 2, r = 2, x = 2$ .167
   d. $N = 4, n = 2, r = 2, x = 0$ .167

Statistics in Action Revisited

Using the Hypergeometric Model to Solve the Cocaine Sting Case

The reverse cocaine sting case described on p. 209 and solved in Section 4.3 can also be solved by applying the hypergeometric distribution. In fact, the probabilities obtained using the hypergeometric distribution are *exact* probabilities, as compared to the approximate probabilities obtained using the binomial distribution.

Our objective, you will recall, is to find the probability that four packets (randomly selected from 496 packets confiscated in a drug bust) will contain cocaine and two packets (randomly selected from the remaining 492) will not contain cocaine. We assumed that of the 496 original packets, 331 contained genuine cocaine and 165 contained an inert (legal) powder. Since we are sampling *without replacement* from the 496 packets, the probability of a "success" (i.e., the probability of a packet containing cocaine) does not remain *exactly* the same from trial to trial. For example, for the first randomly selected packet, the probability of a "success" is $331/496 = .66734$. If we find that the first three packets selected contain cocaine, the probability of "success" for the fourth packet selected is now $328/493 = .66531$. You can see that these probabilities are not exactly the same. Hence, the binomial distribution will only approximate the distribution of x, the number of packets that contain cocaine is a sample of size n.

To find the probability that four packets randomly selected from the original 496 will test positive for cocaine using the hypergeometric distribution we first identify the parameters of the distribution:

$N = 496$ is the total number of packets in the population
$S = 331$ is the number of "successes"
    (cocaine packets) in the population
$n = 4$ is the sample size
$x = 4$ is the number of "successes"
    (cocaine packets) in the sample

Substituting into the formula for $p(x)$ (page 249), we obtain

$$P(x = 4) = p(4) = \frac{\binom{331}{4}\binom{165}{0}}{\binom{496}{4}} = \frac{\left(\frac{331!}{4!\,327!}\right)\left(\frac{165!}{0!\,165!}\right)}{\left(\frac{496!}{4!\,492!}\right)}$$

$$= .197$$

To find the probability that two packets randomly selected from the remaining 492 will test negative for cocaine *assuming that the first four packets tested positive*, we identify the parameters of the relevant hypergeometric distribution:

$N = 492$ is the total number of packets in the population
$S = 327$ is the number of "successes"
    (cocaine packets) in the population
$n = 2$ is the sample size
$x = 0$ is the number of "successes"
    (cocaine packets) in the sample

Again, we substitute into the formula for $p(x)$ to obtain:

$$P(x = 0) = p(0) = \frac{\binom{327}{0}\binom{165}{2}}{\binom{492}{2}} = \frac{\left(\frac{327!}{0!\,327!}\right)\left(\frac{165!}{2!\,163!}\right)}{\left(\frac{492!}{2!\,490!}\right)}$$

$$= .112$$

Using the Multiplicative Law of Probability, the probability that the first four packets test positive for cocaine and the next two packets test negative is the product of the two preceding probabilities:

$$P(\text{first 4 positive and next 2 negative}) = (.112)(.197)$$

$$= .0221$$

Note that this exact probability is almost identical to the approximate probability computed using the binomial distribution in Section 4.3.

4.73 Given that x is a hypergeometric random variable with $N = 10, n = 5,$ and $r = 7$:
  a. Display the probability distribution for x in tabular form.
  b. Compute the mean and variance of x.   3.5; .583
  c. Graph $p(x)$ and locate μ and the interval $\mu \pm 2\sigma$ on the graph.
  d. What is the probability that x will fall within the interval $\mu \pm 2\sigma$?   1.000

4.74 Given that x is a hypergeometric random variable with $N = 12, n = 8,$ and $r = 6$:
  a. Display the probability distribution for x in tabular form.

  b. Compute μ and σ for x.   4, .853
  c. Graph $p(x)$ and locate μ and the interval $\mu \pm 2\sigma$ on the graph.
  d. What is the probability that x will fall within the interval $\mu \pm 2\sigma$?   .939

4.75 Use the results of Exercise 4.74 to find the following probabilities:
  a. $P(x = 1)$ 0
  b. $P(x = 4)$ .455
  c. $P(x \le 4)$ .727
  d. $P(x \ge 5)$ .272
  e. $P(x < 3)$ .030
  f. $P(x \ge 8)$ 0

Applying the Concepts—Basic

4.76 Suppose you plan to sample 10 items from a population of 100 items and would like to determine the probability of observing four defective items in the sample. Which probability distribution should you use to compute this probability under the following conditions? Justify your answers.
  a. The sample is drawn without replacement.
  b. The sample is drawn with replacement.   Binomial

4.77 According to *USA Today* (Sept. 19, 2000), there are 650 members of the International Nanny Association (INA). Of these, only three are men. In Exercise 3.9 (p. 158), you found the probability that a randomly selected member of the INA is a man. Now find the probability that in a random sample of four INA members, at least one is a man.   .0184

4.78 The Resource Conservation and Recovery Act mandates the tracking and disposal of hazardous waste produced at U.S. facilities. *Professional Geographer* (Feb. 2000) reported the hazardous waste generation and disposal characteristics of 209 facilities. Only eight of these facilities treated hazardous waste on-site.
  a. In a random sample of 10 of the 209 facilities, what is the expected number in the sample that treat hazardous waste on-site? Interpret this result.   .383
  b. Find the probability that four of the eight selected facilities treat hazardous waste on-site.   .0002

Applying the Concepts—Intermediate

4.79 Suppose you are purchasing cases of wine (twelve bottles per case) and that, periodically, you select a test case to determine the adequacy of the bottles' seals. To do this, you randomly select and test three bottles in the case. If a case contains one spoiled bottle of wine, what is the probability that this bottle will turn up in your sample?   .25

4.80 Imagine you are purchasing small lots of a manufactured product. If it is very costly to test a single item, it may be desirable to test a sample of items from the lot instead of testing every item in the lot. Suppose each lot contains 10 items. You decide to sample four items per lot and reject the lot if you observe one or more defectives.

  a. If the lot contains one defective item, what is the probability that you will accept the lot?   .6
  b. What is the probability that you will accept the lot if it contains two defective items?   .333

4.81 Refer to the investigation of contaminated gun cartridges at a weapons manufacturer. Exercise 4.21 (p. 216). In a sample of 158 cartridges from a certain lot, 36 were found to be contaminated and 122 were "clean." If you randomly select 5 of these 158 cartridges, what is the probability that all 5 will be "clean"?   .2693

Applying the Concepts—Advanced

4.82 A curious event was described in the *Minneapolis Star and Tribune*. The Minneapolis Community Development Agency (MCDA) makes home improvement grants each year to homeowners in depressed city neighborhoods. Of the $708,000 granted one year, $233,000 was awarded by the city council using a "random selection" of 140 homeowners' applications from among a total of 743 applications: 601 from the north side and 142 from the south side of Minneapolis. Oddly, all 140 grants awarded were from the north side—clearly a highly improbable outcome, if, in fact, the 140 winners were randomly selected from among the 743 applicants.
  a. Suppose the 140 winning applications were randomly selected from among the total of 743, and let x equal the number in the sample from the north side. Find the mean and standard deviation of x.
  b. Use the results of part a to support a contention that the grant winners were not randomly selected.

4.83 The *Journal of Business & Economic Statistics* (July, 2000) presented a case in which a charge of gender discrimination was filed against the U.S. Postal Service. At the time, there were 302 U.S. Postal Service employees (229 men and 73 women) who applied for promotion. Of the 72 employees who were awarded promotion, 5 were female. Make an inference about whether or not females at the U.S. Postal Service were promoted fairly.

Quick Review

Note: Starred (*) items are from the optional sections in this chapter.

Key Terms

Binomial experiment   225
Binomial random variable   225
Continuous random variable   212

Key Formulas

Probability Distribution	Mean μ	Variance σ^2		
$p(x)$	$\displaystyle\sum_{\text{all } x} xp(x)$	$\displaystyle\sum_{\text{all } x}(x-\mu)^2 p(x)$	General discrete random variable	218, 219
$\dbinom{n}{x}p^x q^{n-x}$	np	npq	Binomial random variable	229, 230
$\dfrac{\lambda^x e^{-\lambda}}{x!}$	λ	λ	Poisson random variable*	240
$\dfrac{\dbinom{r}{x}\dbinom{N-r}{n-x}}{\dbinom{N}{n}}$	$\dfrac{nr}{N}$	$\dfrac{r(N-r)n(N-n)}{N^2(N-1)}$	Hypergeometric random variable*	247

Language Lab

Symbol	Pronunciation	Description
$p(x)$		Probability distribution of the random variable x
S		The outcome of a binomial trial denoted a "success"
F		The outcome of a binomial trial denoted a "failure"
P		The probability of success (S) in a binomial trial
q		The probability of failure (F) in a binomial trial, where $q = 1 - p$
λ	lambda	The mean (or expected) number of events for a Poisson random variable
e		A constant used in the Poisson probability distribution, where $e = 2.71828\ldots$

Summary

Chapter Summary Notes

- Two types of random variables: **discrete** and **continuous**
- Requirements for a discrete probability distribution: $p(x) \geq 0$ and $\Sigma p(x) = 1$
- Probability models discrete random variables: **binomial, Poisson,** and **hypergeometric**
- Characteristics of a **binomial random variable:** (1) n identical trials; (2) two possible outcomes, S and F, per trial; (3) $P(S)$ and $P(F)$ remain the same from trial to trial; (4) trials are independent; (5) $x =$ number of S's in n trials

- Characteristics of a **Poisson random variable:** (1) $x =$ number of times a rare event, S, occurs in a unit of time, area, or volume; (2) $P(S)$ remains the same for all units; (3) value of x in one unit is independent of value in another unit
- Characteristics of a **hypergeometric random variable:** (1) draw n elements without replacement from a set of N elements, r of which have outcome S and $(N - r)$ which have outcome F; (2) $x =$ number of S's in n trials

Supplementary Exercises 4.84–4.108

Note: Starred (*) exercises refer to the optional sections in this chapter.

Learning the Mechanics

4.84 For each of the following examples, decide whether x is a binomial random variable and explain your decision:

a. A manufacturer of computer chips randomly selects 100 chips from each hour's production in order to estimate the proportion defective. Let x represent the number of defectives in the 100 sampled chips. Not a binomial

b. Of five applicants for a job, two will be selected. Although all applicants appear to be equally qualified, only three have the ability to fulfill the expectations of the company. Suppose that the two selections are made at random from the five applicants, and let x be the number of qualified applicants selected. Not a binomial

c. A software developer establishes a support hotline for customers to call in with questions regarding use of the software. Let x represent the number of calls received on the support hotline during a specified workday. Not a binomial

d. Florida is one of a minority of states with no state income tax. A poll of 1,000 registered voters is conducted to determine how many would favor a state income tax in light of the state's current fiscal condition. Let x be the number in the sample who would favor the tax. Binomial with $n = 1,000$

4.85 Given that x is a binomial random variable, compute $p(x)$ for each of the following cases:

a. $n = 7, x = 3, p = .5$ .2734
b. $n = 4, x = 3, p = .8$ .4096
c. $n = 15, x = 1, p = .1$ .3432

4.86 Consider the discrete probability distribution shown here.

x	10	12	18	20
$p(x)$	.2	.3	.1	.4

a. Calculate μ, σ^2, and σ.   15.4, 18.44, 4.294
b. What is $P(x < 15)$?   .5
c. Calculate $\mu \pm 2\sigma$.   (6.812, 23.988)
d. What is the probability that x is in the interval $\mu \pm 2\sigma$?   1.0

4.87 Suppose x is a binomial random variable with $n = 20$ and $p = .7$.

a. Find $P(x = 14)$.   .192
b. Find $P(x \le 12)$.   .228
c. Find $P(x > 12)$.   .772
d. Find $P(9 \le x \le 18)$.   .987
e. Find $P(8 < x < 18)$.   .960

f. Find μ, σ^2, and σ.   14, 4.2, 2.049
g. What is the probability that x is in the interval $\mu \pm 2\sigma$ .975

*4.88 Suppose x is a Poisson random variable. Compute $p(x)$ for each of the following cases:

a. $\lambda = 2, x = 3$ .180
b. $\lambda = 1, x = 4$ .015
c. $\lambda = .5, x = 2$ .076

4.89 Which of the following describe discrete random variables, and which describe continuous random variables?

a. The number of damaged inventory items   Discrete
b. The average monthly sales revenue generated by a salesperson over the past year   Continuous
c. The number of square feet of warehouse space a company rents   Continuous
d. The length of time a firm must wait before its copying machine is fixed   Continuous

*4.90 Given that x is a hypergeometric random variable, compute $p(x)$ for each of the following cases:

a. $N = 8, n = 5, r = 3, x = 2$ .5357
b. $N = 6, n = 2, r = 2, x = 2$ .0666
c. $N = 5, n = 4, r = 4, x = 3$ .80

Applying the Concepts—Basic

4.91 A national study conducted by Geoffrey Alpert (University of South Carolina) found that 40% of all high-speed police chases end in accidents. As a result, many police departments have moved to restrict high-speed chases. Consider a random sample of five high-speed chases.

a. Demonstrate that x, the number of chases resulting in an accident, is an approximate binomial random variable. x is a binomial
b. What is the probability that the five high-speed chases result in at least one accident?   .922

4.92 Anticipating a substantial growth in sales over the next five years, a printing company is planning today for the warehouse space it will need five years hence. It obviously cannot be certain exactly how many square feet of storage space, x, it will need in five years, but the company can project its needs by using a probability distribution such as the following:

x	10,000	15,000	20,000	25,000	30,000	35,000
$p(x)$	.05	.15	.35	.25	.15	.05

a. Is $p(x)$ a valid probability distribution?   Yes
b. What is the expected number of square feet of storage space the printing company will need in five years?   22,250
c. Find $P(x > 20,000)$.   .45

4.93 The Environmental Protection Agency (EPA) tests in-use automobiles to determine whether there were differences between the cars' actual gas mileage and the mileage projected in the EPA's mileage guide. The EPA recently found that only 70% of the cars tested had highway driving fuel economies within 2 miles per gallon of the mileage guide's projection. Suppose the EPA is planning to select 20 cars at random and test their fuel economies to determine how many are within 2 miles per gallon of their EPA projections.

    a. Explain why the number of cars in the sample of 20 that have mileages within 2 miles per gallon of their EPA projections can be approximated by a binomial random variable.

    b. What is the probability (approximately) that fewer than 10 of the 20 cars selected will be within 2 miles per gallon of their EPA projections? .017

*4.94 A nursery advertises that it has 10 elm trees for sale. Unknown to the nursery, three of the trees have already been infected with Dutch elm disease and will die within a year.

    a. If a buyer purchases two trees selected at random from the lot, what is the probability that both trees will be healthy? .4667

    b. Refer to part a. What is the probability that at least one of the trees is infected? .5333

*4.95 An emergency rescue vehicle is used an average of 1.3 times daily. Use the Poisson distribution to find:

    a. The probability that the vehicle will be used exactly twice tomorrow. .230

    b. The probability that the vehicle will be used more than twice tomorrow. .143

    c. The probability that the vehicle will be used exactly three times tomorrow. .100

Applying the Concepts—Intermediate

4.96 A few years ago, our president encountered difficulties in appointing an attorney general. One troublesome issue involved the nominees' hiring of illegal aliens and/or failing to pay Social Security taxes for their domestic help. Both of these practices are against the law. Suppose that a study reveals that 10% of households with incomes exceeding \$50,000 annually have hired an illegal alien and/or failed to pay Social Security taxes. Let x be the number of households with incomes in that range who are contacted before one that has not broken either law is found.

    a. What is the range of possible values for x?

    b. Find $P(x < 3)$. .99

    c. Find $P(x > 2)$. .01

    d. Find the probability distribution for values of x from 1 to 10 and graph it over that domain. Can x exceed 10?

4.97 Your firm's accountant believes that 10% of the company's invoices contain arithmetic errors. To check this theory, the accountant randomly samples 25 invoices and finds that seven contain errors. What is the probability that of the 25 invoices written, seven or more would contain errors if the accountant's theory was valid? What assumptions do you have to make to solve this problem using the methodology of this chapter?

4.98 A large number of preventable errors (e.g., overdoses, botched operations, misdiagnoses) are being made by doctors and nurses in U.S. hospitals (*New York Times,* July 18, 1995). A study of a major metropolitan hospital revealed that of every 100 medications prescribed or dispensed, one was in error; but, only one in 500 resulted in an error that caused significant problems for the patient. It is known that the hospital prescribes and dispenses 60,000 medications per year.

    a. What is the expected number of errors per year at this hospital? The expected number of significant errors per year? 600; 120

    b. Within what limits would you expect the number of significant errors per year to fall?

    c. What assumptions did you need to make in order to answer these questions?

*4.99 Millions of suburban commuters are finding railroads to be a convenient, time-saving, less stressful alternative to the automobile. While generally perceived as a safe mode of transportation, the average number of deaths per week due to railroad accidents is a surprisingly high 20 (U.S. National Center for Health Statistics, *Vital Statistics of the United States, 2001*).

    a. Construct arguments both for and against the use of the Poisson distribution to characterize the number of deaths per week due to railroad accidents.

    b. For the remainder of this exercise, assume the Poisson distribution is an adequate approximation for x, the number of deaths per week due to railroad accidents. Find $E(x)$ and the standard deviation of x. 20, 4.47

    c. Based strictly on your answers to part b, is it likely that only four or fewer deaths occur next week? Explain. No

    d. Find $P(x \le 4)$. Is this probability consistent with your answer to part c? Explain. .000

*4.100 Refer to Exercise 4.91(p. 252). The Tampa (Florida) Police Department, after restricting high-speed chases for a time, recently changed their policy and eased the restrictions. Over a recent five-month period, there were 85 high-speed chases in Tampa, with 29 of these resulting in accidents (*New York Times*, Dec. 17, 1995). Consider a random sample of 5 high-speed chases selected from the 85 in Tampa.

a. Explain why x is not a binomial random variable. What type of probability distribution should be used to model x?

b. Find the probability that the five high-speed chases result in at least one accident? Compare your answer to the result from Exercise 4.91b.   .8835

4.101 The *Journal of Applied Psychology* (Vol. 71, 1986) reported the results of an extensive survey conducted to determine the extent of whistle blowing among federal employees. *Whistle blowing* refers to an employee's reporting of wrongdoing by coworkers. The survey found that about 5% of employees contacted had reported wrongdoing during the past 12 months. Assume that a sample of 25 employees in one agency are contacted, and let x be the number who have observed and reported wrongdoing in the last 12 months. Assume that the probability of whistle blowing is .05 for any federal employee over the past 12 months.

a. Find the mean and standard deviation of x. Can x be equal to its expected value? Explain.

b. Write the event that at least five of the employees are whistle blowers in terms of x. Find the probability of the event.   .007

c. If five of the 25 contacted have been whistle blowers over the past 12 months, what would you conclude about the applicability of the 5% assumption to this agency? Use your answer to part b to justify your conclusion. $p > 5\%$

4.102 The owner of construction company A bids on jobs so that if awarded the job, company A will make a $10,000 profit. The owner of construction company B makes bids on jobs so that if awarded the job, company B will make a $15,000 profit. Each company describes the probability distribution of the number of jobs x the company is awarded per year as shown in the table.

Company A		Company B	
x	$p(x)$	x	$p(x)$
2	.05	2	.15
3	.15	3	.30
4	.20	4	.30
5	.35	5	.20
6	.25	6	.05

a. Find the expected number of jobs each will be awarded in a year.

b. What is the expected profit for each company?

c. Find the variance and standard deviation of the distribution of number of jobs awarded per year for each company.

d. Graph $p(x)$ for both companies A and B. For each company, what proportion of the time will x fall in the interval $\mu \pm 2\sigma$?   A: .95, B: .95

4.103 The efficacy of insecticides is often measured by the dose necessary to kill a certain percentage of insects. Suppose a certain dose of a new insecticide is supposed to kill 80% of the insects that receive it. To test the claim, 25 insects are exposed to the insecticide.

a. If the insecticide really kills 80% of the exposed insects, what is the probability that fewer than 15 die?   .006

b. If you observed such a result, what would you conclude about the new insecticide? Explain your logic. $p < .80$

4.104 When the price of grain is low, many farmers participate in government-financed, on-farm storage programs rather than selling their grain. But storage invites insect infestations, and grain elevators penalize farmers who sell them insect-infested grain. The U.S. Grain Marketing Research Laboratory estimates that 80% of the storage bins of corn in the country are infested with insects. Suppose 20 storage bins of corn are randomly selected and examined for insect infestation.

a. What is the probability (approximately) that less than one-half of the bins are infested?   .001

b. What assumptions did you make in answering part a?

c. Why is your answer to part a an approximation?

d. Would you be surprised if all 20 of the bins were infested? Explain. $Y, P = .12$

*4.105 Large bakeries typically have fleets of delivery trucks. One such bakery determined that the expected number of delivery truck breakdowns per day is 1.5. Assume that the number of breakdowns is independent from day to day.

a. What is the probability that there will be exactly two breakdowns today and exactly three tomorrow?   .0314

b. Fewer than two today and more than two tomorrow?   .0166

Applying the Concepts—Advanced

4.106 Many firms utilize sampling plans to control the quality of manufactured items ready for shipment or the quality of incoming items (parts, raw materials, etc.) that have been purchased. To illustrate the use of a sampling plan, suppose you are shipping electrical fuses in lots, each containing 5,000 fuses. The plan specifies that you will randomly sample 25 fuses from each lot and accept (and ship) the lot if the number of defective fuses, x, in the sample is less than 3. If $x \geq 3$, you will reject the lot. Find the probability of accepting a lot ($x = 0, 1,$ or 2) if the actual fraction defective in the lot is

a. 0   1

b. .01   .998

c. .10 .537
d. .30
e. .50 ≈ 0
f. .80 ≈ 0
g. .95 ≈ 0
h. 1
i. Construct a graph showing $P(A)$, the probability of lot acceptance, as a function of the lot fraction defective, p. This graph is called the *operating characteristic curve* for the sampling plan.
j. Suppose the sampling plan called for sampling $n = 25$ fuses and accepting a lot if $x \leq 3$. Calculate the quantities specified in parts a–h, and construct the operating characteristic curve for this sampling plan. Compare this curve with the curve obtained in part i. (Note how the curve characterizes the ability of the plan to screen bad lots from shipment.)

4.107 The probability that a consumer responds to a marketing department's mailed questionnaire is .4.
    a. What is the probability that of 20 questionnaires, more than 15 will be returned? .031
    b. How many questionnaires should be mailed if you want to be reasonably certain that at least 100 will be returned? 292

4.108 Suppose you own a company that bonds financial managers. Based on past experience, you assess the probability that you will have to forfeit any particular bond to be .001. How much should you charge for a $1 million bond in order to break even on all such bonds? $1,000

REFERENCES

Alexander, G. J., and Francis, J. C. *Portfolio Analysis*. Englewood Cliffs, N.J.: Prentice Hall, 1996.

Alexander, G. J., Sharpe, W. F., and Bailey, J. V., *Fundamentals of Investments*, 2nd ed., Englewood Cliffs, N.J.: Prentice Hall, 1993.

Doswell, Chuck, and Brooks, Harold. *Probabilistic Forecasting: A Primer*, 1996. http://www.hssl.voknor.edu/ brroks/prob/probability.html

Elton, E. J., and Gruber, M. J. *Modern Portfolio Theory and Investment Analysis*. New York: Wiley, 1981.

Hogg, R. V., and Craig, A. T. *Introduction to Mathematical Statistics*, 5th ed. Upper Saddle River, N.J.: Prentice Hall, 1995.

Mendenhall, W. *Introduction to Mathematical Statistics*, 8th ed. Boston: Duxbury, 1991.

Parzen, E. *Modern Probability Theory and Its Applications*. New York: Wiley, 1960.

Radcliffe, Robert C. *Investments: Concepts, Analysis, Strategy*, 4th ed. New York: Harper-Collins, 1994.

Willis, R. E., and Chervany, N. L. *Statistical Analysis and Modeling for Management Decision-Making*. Belmont, Calif.: Wadsworth, 1974.

Wackerly, D., Mendenhall, W., and Scheaffer, R. L. *Mathematical Statistics with Applications*, 6th ed. North Scituate, Mass: Duxbury, 2002.

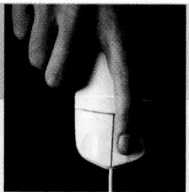

Using Technology

4.1 Binomial, Poisson, and Hypergeometric Probabilities Using SPSS

To obtain a probabilities for the discrete random variables discussed in this chapter using SPSS, click on the "Transform" button on the SPSS menu bar, then click on "Compute", as shown in Figure 4.S.1. The resulting dialog box appears as shown in Figure 4.S.2. Specify a name for the "Target Variable" (e.g., the name of the probability you want to find), and then select the appropriate probability function in the "Numeric Expression" box. SPSS allows you to compute cumulative probabilities or probabilities of exact values. For cumulative probabilities of the binomial, Poisson, and hypergeometric distributions use the functions CDF.BINOM, CDF.POISSON, and CDF.HYPER, respectively. For exact probabilities, use the PDF.BINOM, PDF.POISSON, and PDF.HYPER functions. You will need to enter the parameters of each distribution you select.

For example, Figure 4.S.2 shows the cumulative binomial function with parameters of $x = 3$ (the first number in the function), $n = 10$ (the second number), and $p = .2$ (the third number). When you click "OK", SPSS will compute the requested probability (in this example, the cumulative binomial probability that x is less than or equal to 3) and display it on the SPSS spreadsheet.

[*Note*: For the Poisson function, you will need to enter the value of x and the mean λ. For the hypergeometric function, you will need to enter the values of x, N, n, and r, in that order.]

Figure 4.S.1
SPSS menu options for obtaining probabilities

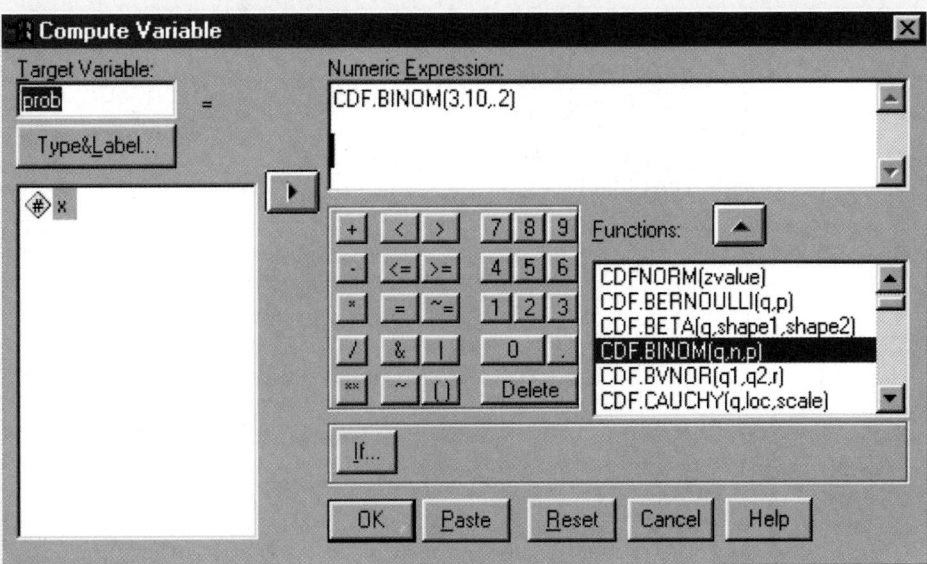

Figure 4.S.2
SPSS compute dialog box

4.2 Binomial, Poisson, and Hypergeometric Probabilities Using MINITAB

To obtain probabilities for the discrete random variables discussed in this chapter using MINITAB, first enter the values of *x* that you desire probabilities for in a column (e.g., C1) on the MINITAB worksheet. Now click on the "Calc" button on the MINITAB menu bar, next click on "Probability Distributions", then finally click on the distribution of your choice (e.g., "Binomial"), as shown in Figure 4.M.1. The resulting dialog box appears as shown in Figure 4.M.2. Select either "Probabilities" or "Cumulative probabilities", specify the parameters of the distribution (e.g., sample size n and probability of success p), and enter C1 in the "Input column". When you click "OK" the binomial probabilities for the values of *x* (saved in C1) will appear on the MINITAB worksheet.

Figure 4.M.1
MINITAB menu options for obtaining probabilities

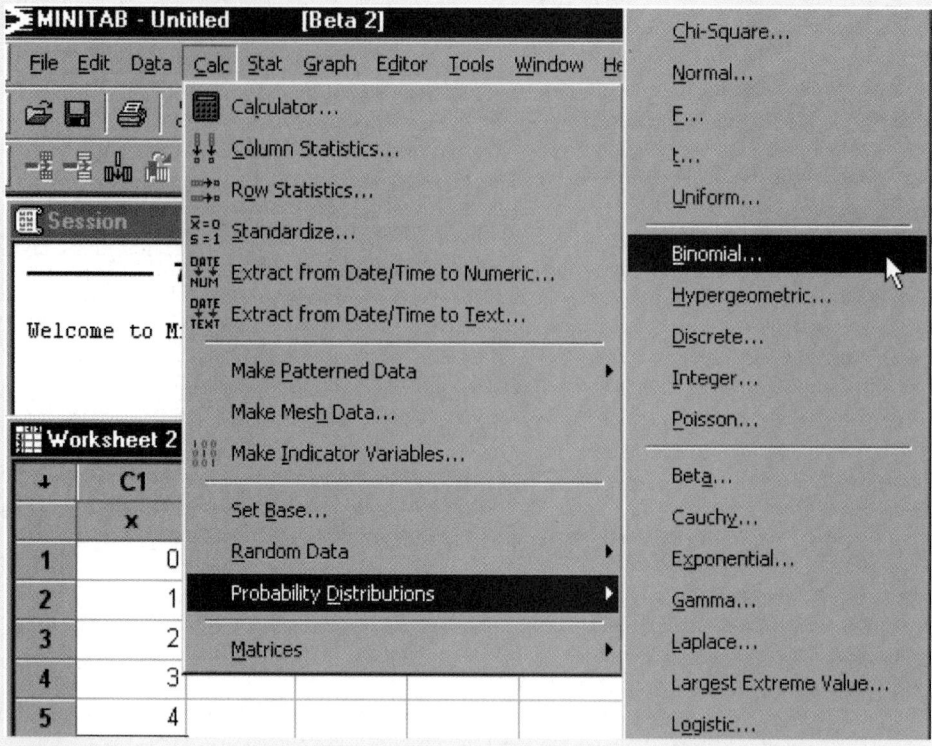

Figure 4.M.2
MINITAB binomial distribution dialog box

[*Note*: For the MINITAB Poisson option, you will need to enter the value of the mean λ in the resulting dialog box. For the hypergeometric option, you will need to enter the values of N, r, and n, in that order, in the resulting dialog box.]

4.3 Binomial, Poisson, and Hypergeometric Probabilities Using EXCEL and PHStat2

To obtain probabilities for the discrete random variables discussed in this chapter using EXCEL, first enter into a PHStat2 session. Now click on the "PHStat2" button on the main menu bar, next click on "Probability Distributions", then finally click on the distribution of your choice (e.g., "Binomial"), as shown in Figure 4.E.1. The resulting dialog box appears as shown in Figure 4.E.2. Specify the parameters of the distribution (e.g., sample size n and probability of success p), and give the values of x you want to compute probabilities for in the "Outcomes from" box. When you click "OK" the binomial probabilities for the values of x specified will appear on a new EXCEL workbook.

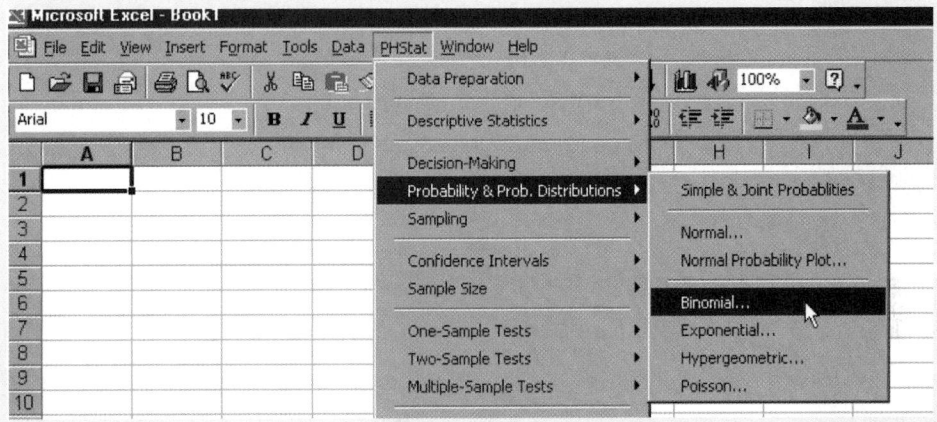

Figure 4.E.1
EXCEL/PHStat2 menu options for obtaining probabilities

Figure 4.E.2
EXCEL/PHStat2 binomial dialog box

[*Note*: For the EXCEL Poisson option, you will need to enter the value of the mean λ in the resulting dialog box. For the EXCEL hypergeometric option, you will need to enter the values of n, r, and N, in that order, in the resulting dialog box.]

5

Continuous Random Variables

Contents

Statistics in Action

Super Weapons Development—Optimizing the Hit Ratio

Using Technology

Where We've Been

- Learned how to find probabilities of discrete events using the probability rules of Chapter 3
- Discussed probability models (distributions) for discrete random variables in Chapter 4

Where We're Going

- Develop the notion of a probability distribution for a continuous random variable.
- Study several important types of continuous random variables and their probability models.
- Introduce the normal probability distribution as one of the most useful distributions in statistics.

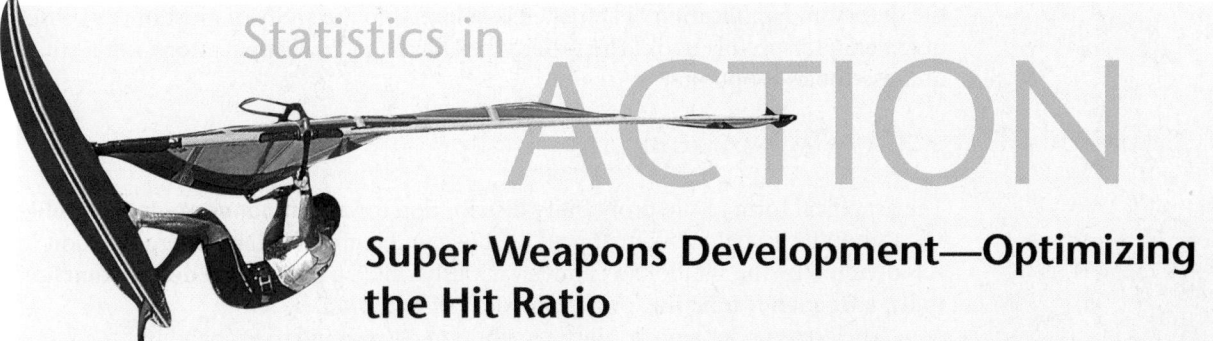

Statistics in ACTION

Super Weapons Development—Optimizing the Hit Ratio

The U.S. Army is working with a major defense contractor to develop a "super" weapon. The weapon is designed to fire a large number of sharp tungsten bullets—called flechettes—with a single shot that will destroy a large number of enemy soldiers. Flechettes are about the size of an average nail, with small fins at one end to stabilize them in flight. Since World War I, when France dropped them in large quantities from aircraft on masses of ground troops, munitions experts have experimented with using flechettes in a variety of guns. The problem with using flechettes as ammunition is accuracy—current weapons that fire large quantities of flechettes have unsatisfactory hit ratios when fired at long distances.

The defense contractor (not named here for both confidentiality and security reasons) has developed a prototype gun that fires 1,100 flechettes with a single round. In range tests, three 2-feet-wide targets were set up a distance of 500 meters (approximately 1,500 feet) from the weapon. Using a number line as a reference, the centers of the three targets were at 0, 5, and 10 feet, respectively, as shown in Figure SIA5.1. The prototype gun was aimed at the middle target (center at 5 feet) and fired once. The point where each of the 1,100 flechettes landed at the 500-meter distance was measured using a horizontal and vertical grid. For the purposes of this application, only the horizontal measurements are considered. These 1,100 measurements are saved in the MOAGUN file. (The data are simulated for confidentiality reasons.) For example, a flechette with a value of $x = 5.5$ hit the middle target, but a flechette with a value of $x = 2.0$ did not hit any of the three targets (See Figure SIA5.1).

The defense contractor is interested in the likelihood of any one of the targets being hit by a flechette and, in particular, wants to set the gun specifications to maximize the number of target hits. The weapon is designed to have a mean horizontal value equal to the aim point (e.g., $\mu = 5$ feet when aimed at the center target). By changing specifications, the contractor can vary the standard deviation, σ. The MOAGUN file contains flechette measurements for three different range tests—one with a standard deviation of $\sigma = 1$ foot, one with $\sigma = 2$ feet, and one with $\sigma = 4$ feet.

In this chapter, two Statistics in Action Revisited examples demonstrate how we can use one of the probability models discussed in this chapter—the normal probability distribution—to aid the defense contractor in developing its "super" weapon.

Statistics in the Action Revisited

- Using the Normal Model to Maximize the Probability of a Hit with the Super Weapon (p. 281)
- Assessing whether the Normal Distribution is Appropriate for Modeling the Super Weapon Hit Data (p. 288)

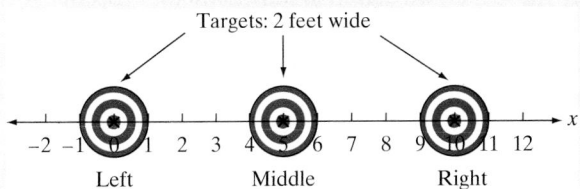

Targets: 2 feet wide

Left	Middle	Right	

Figure SIA5.1
Target placement on gun range

In this chapter we'll consider some continuous random variables that are commonly encountered. Recall that a continuous random variable is one that can assume any value within some interval or intervals. For example, the length of time between a customer's purchase of new automobiles, the thickness of sheets of steel produced in a rolling mill, and the yield of wheat per acre of farmland are all continuous random variables. The methodology we employ to describe continuous random variables will necessarily be somewhat different from that used to describe discrete random variables. We first discuss the general form of **continuous probability distributions,** and then we explore three specific types that are used in making business decisions. The normal probability distribution, which plays a basic and important role in both the theory and application of statistics, is essential to the study of most of the subsequent chapters in this book. The other types have practical applications, but a study of these topics is optional.

5.1 Continuous Probability Distributions

Teaching Tip

The boxes that were drawn to illustrate the probability distributions of discrete random variables are now replaced with curves for continuous distributions.

Teaching Tip

Point out the difference between continuous and discrete distributions with respect to the equal sign in the probability statements. Ask: "When is $P(x < 4) = P(x \geq 4)$?"

The graphical form of the probability distribution for a **continuous random variable** x is a smooth curve that might appear as shown in Figure 5.1. This curve, a function of x, is denoted by the symbol $f(x)$ and is variously called a **probability density function (pdf)**, a **frequency function**, or a **probability distribution.**

The areas under a probability distribution correspond to probabilities for x. For example, the area A beneath the curve between the two points a and b, as shown in Figure 5.1, is the probability that x assumes a value between a and b $(a < x < b)$. Because there is no area over a point, say $x = a$, it follows that (according to our model) the probability associated with a particular value of x is equal to 0; that is, $P(x = a) = 0$ and hence $P(a < x < b) = P(a \leq x \leq b)$. In other words, the probability is the same whether or not you include the endpoints of the interval. Also, because areas over intervals represent probabilities, it follows that the total area under a probability distribution, the probability assigned to all values of x, should equal 1. Note that probability distributions for continuous random variables possess different shapes depending on the relative frequency distributions of real data that the probability distributions are supposed to model.

Figure 5.1
A probability distribution $f(x)$ for a continuous random variable x

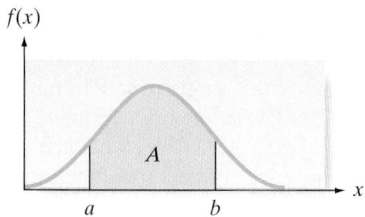

Teaching Tip

The area under the curve is equivalent to probabilities in continuous distributions. Therefore, the area under the curve of any probability distribution must equal one.

The areas under most probability distributions are obtained by using calculus or numerical methods.* Because these methods often involve difficult procedures, we will give the areas for some of the most common probability distributions in tabular form in Appendix B. Then, to find the area between two values of x, say $x = a$ and $x = b$, you simply have to consult the appropriate table.

For each of the continuous random variables presented in this chapter, we will give the formula for the probability distribution along with its mean μ and standard deviation σ. These two numbers will enable you to make some approximate probability statements about a random variable even when you do not have access to a table of areas under the probability distribution.

5.2 The Uniform Distribution (Optional)

All the probability problems discussed in Chapter 3 had sample spaces that contained a finite number of sample points. In many of these problems, the sample points were assigned equal probabilities—for example, the die toss or the coin toss. For continuous random variables, there is an infinite number of values in the sample

---

*Students with knowledge of calculus should note that the probability that x assumes a value in the interval $a < x < b$ is $P(a < x < b) = \int_a^b f(x)\,dx$, assuming the integral exists. Similar to the requirement for a discrete probability distribution, we require $f(x) \geq 0$ and $\int_{-\infty}^{\infty} f(x)\,dx = 1$.

Figure 5.2

The uniform probability distribution

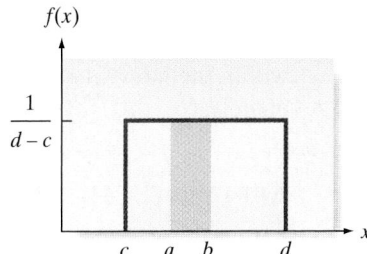

space, but in some cases the values may appear to be equally likely. For example, if a short exists in a 5-meter stretch of electrical wire, it may have an equal probability of being in any particular 1-centimeter segment along the line. Or if a safety inspector plans to choose a time at random during the four afternoon work hours to pay a surprise visit to a certain area of a plant, then each 1-minute time interval in this 4-work-hour period will have an equally likely chance of being selected for the visit.

Continuous random variables that appear to have equally likely outcomes over their range of possible values possess a **uniform probability distribution,** perhaps the simplest of all continuous probability distributions. Suppose the random variable x can assume values only in an interval $c \leq x \leq d$. Then the uniform frequency function has a rectangular shape, as shown in Figure 5.2. Note that the possible values of x consist of all points in the interval between point c and point d. The height of $f(x)$ is constant in that interval and equals $1/(d - c)$. Therefore, the total area under $f(x)$ is given by

$$\text{Total area of rectangle} = (\text{Base})(\text{Height}) = (d - c)\left(\frac{1}{d - c}\right) = 1$$

The uniform probability distribution provides a model for continuous random variables that are *evenly distributed* over a certain interval. That is, a uniform random variable is one that is just as likely to assume a value in one interval as it is to assume a value in any other interval of equal size. There is no clustering of values around any value; instead, there is an even spread over the entire region of possible values.

The uniform distribution is sometimes referred to as the **randomness distribution,** since one way of generating a uniform random variable is to perform an experiment in which a point is *randomly selected* on the horizontal axis between the points c and d. If we were to repeat this experiment infinitely often, we would create a uniform probability distribution like that shown in Figure 5.2. The random selection of points in an interval can also be used to generate random numbers such as those in Table I of Appendix B. Recall that random numbers are selected in such a way that every number would have an equal probability of selection. Therefore, random numbers are realizations of a uniform random variable. (Random numbers were used to draw random samples in Section 3.7.) The formulas for the uniform probability distribution, its mean, and standard deviation are shown in the box.

Probability Distribution for a Uniform Random Variable x

Probability density function: $f(x) = \dfrac{1}{d - c} \quad c \leq x \leq d$

Mean: $\mu = \dfrac{c + d}{2}$ Standard deviation: $\sigma = \dfrac{d - c}{\sqrt{12}}$

$P(a < x < b) = (b - a)/(d - c), c \leq a < b \leq d$

Suppose the interval $a < x < b$ lies within the domain of x; that is, it falls within the larger interval $c \leq x \leq d$. Then the probability that x assumes a value within the interval $a < x < b$ is equal to the area of the rectangle over the interval, namely, $(b - a)/(d - c)$.* (See the shaded area in Figure 5.2).

EXAMPLE 5.1   APPLYING THE UNIFORM DISTRIBUTION

Problem Suppose the research department of a steel manufacturer believes that one of the company's rolling machines is producing sheets of steel of varying thickness. The thickness is a uniform random variable with values between 150 and 200 millimeters. Any sheets less than 160 millimeters must be scrapped because they are unacceptable to buyers.

a. $\mu = 175$, $\sigma = 14.43$

    a. Calculate and interpret the mean and standard deviation of x, the thickness of the sheets produced by this machine.

    b. Graph the probability distribution of x, and show the mean on the horizontal axis. Also show 1- and 2-standard-deviation intervals around the mean.

c. 1/5

    c. Calculate the fraction of steel sheets produced by this machine that have to be scrapped.

Solution   **a.** To calculate the mean and standard deviation for x, we substitute 150 and 200 millimeters for c and d, respectively, in the formulas for uniform random variables. Thus,

$$\mu = \frac{c + d}{2} = \frac{150 + 200}{2} = 175 \text{ millimeters}$$

and

$$\sigma = \frac{d - c}{\sqrt{12}} = \frac{200 - 150}{\sqrt{12}} = \frac{50}{3.464} = 14.43 \text{ millimeters}$$

Our interpretations follow:

The average thickness of all manufactured steel sheets is $\mu = 175$ millimeters. From Cheyshev's Theorem (Table 2.7, p. 89), we know that at least 75% of the thickness values, x, in the distribution will fall in the interval

$$\mu \pm 2\sigma = 175 \pm 2(14.43)$$
$$= 175 \pm 28.86$$

or, between 146.14 and 203.86 millimeters. (This demonstrates, once again, the conservativeness of Chebyshev's Theorem since we know that all values of x fall between 150 and 200 millimeters.)

    b. The uniform probability distribution is

$$f(x) = \frac{1}{d - c} = \frac{1}{200 - 150} = \frac{1}{50} \, (150 \leq x \leq 200)$$

*The student with knowledge of calculus should note that

$$P(a < x < b) = \int_a^b f(x) \, d(x) = \int_a^b 1/(d - c) \, dx = (b - a)/(d - c)$$

Figure 5.3
Distribution for x in
Example 5.1

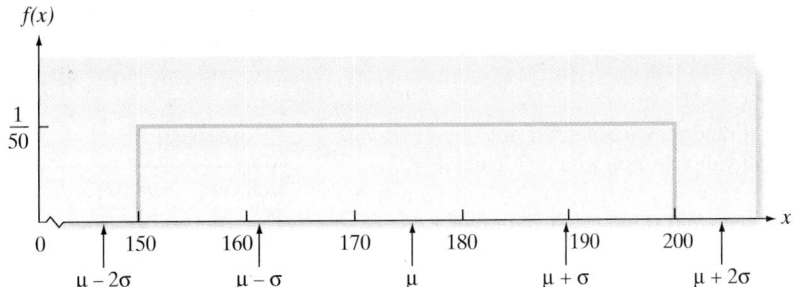

The graph of this function is shown in Figure 5.3. The mean and 1- and 2-standard-deviation intervals around the mean are shown on the horizontal axis.

Suggested Exercises 5.8

c. To find the fraction of steel sheets produced by the machine that have to be crapped, we must find the probability that x, the thickness, is less than 160 millimeters. As indicated in Figure 5.4, we need to calculate the area under the frequency function $f(x)$ between the points $x = 150$ and $x = 160$. Therefore, in this case $a = 150$ and $b = 160$. Applying the formula in the box, we have

$$P(x < 160) = P(150 < x < 160)$$

$$= \frac{b - a}{d - c} = \frac{160 - 150}{200 - 150} = \frac{10}{50} = \frac{1}{5}$$

That is, 20% of all the sheets made by this machine must be scrapped.

Look Back The calculated probability in part c is the area of a rectangle with base $160 - 150 = 10$ and height $1/50$. Alternatively, we can find the fraction that has to be scrapped as

$$P(x < 160) = (\text{Base})(\text{Height}) = (10)\left(\frac{1}{50}\right) = \frac{1}{5}$$

Now Work *Exercise 5.8*

∎ ∎ ∎

Figure 5.4
Probability that sheet
thickness, x, is between 150
and 160 millimeters

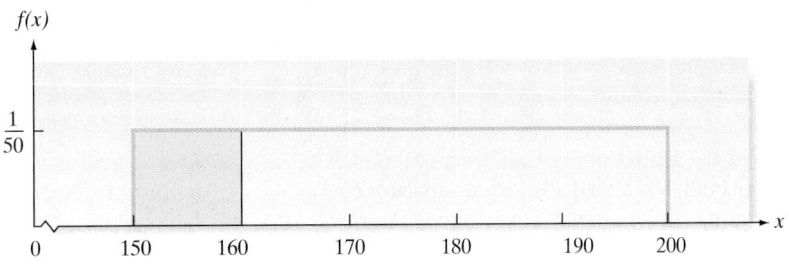

Exercises 5.1–5.14

Learning the Mechanics

5.1 Suppose x is a random variable best described by a uniform probability distribution with $c = 20$ and $d = 45$.
  a. Find $f(x)$.
  b. Find the mean and standard deviation of x.
  c. Graph $f(x)$ and locate μ and the interval $\mu \pm 2\sigma$ on the graph. Note that the probability that x

assumes a value within the interval $\mu \pm 2\sigma$ is equal to 1.

5.2 Refer to Exercise 5.1. Find the following probabilities:
  a. $P(20 \le x \le 30)$ .4
  b. $P(20 < x \le 30)$ .4
  c. $P(x \ge 30)$ .6
  d. $P(x \ge 45)$

e. $P(x \leq 40)$
f. $P(x < 40)$ .8
g. $P(15 \leq x \leq 35)$ .6
h. $P(21.5 \leq x \leq 31.5)$ .4

5.3 Suppose x is a random variable best described by a uniform probability distribution with $c = 3$ and $d = 7$.
a. Find $f(x)$.
b. Find the mean and standard deviation of x.
c. Find $P(\mu - \sigma \leq x \leq \mu + \sigma)$.   .5775

5.4 Refer to Exercise 5.3. Find the value of a that makes each of the following probability statements true.
a. $P(x \geq a) = .6$ 4.6
b. $P(x \leq a) = .25$ 4
c. $P(x \leq a) = 1$ 7
d. $P(4 \leq x \leq a) = .5$ 6

5.5 The random variable x is best described by a uniform probability distribution with $c = 100$ and $d = 200$. Find the probability that x assumes a value
a. More than 2 standard deviations from μ.   0
b. Less than 3 standard deviations from μ.   1
c. Within 2 standard deviations of μ.   1

5.6 The random variable x is best described by a uniform probability distribution with mean 10 and standard deviation 1. Find c, d, and $f(x)$. Graph the probability distribution. $c = 8.268, d = 11.732$

Applying the Concepts—Basic

5.7 A company found that monthly reimbursements to their employees, x, could be adequately modeled by a uniform distribution over the interval $\$10,000 \leq x \leq \$15,000$.
a. Find $E(x)$ and interpret it in the context of the exercise.
b. What is the probability of employee reimbursements exceeding $\$12,000$ next month?
c. For budgeting purposes, the company needs to estimate next month's employee reimbursement expenses. How much should the company budget for employee reimbursements if they want the probability of exceeding the budgeted amount to be only .20?
$\$14,000$

5.8 Researchers at the University of California—Berkeley have designed, built, and tested a switched-capacitor circuit for generating random signals (*International Journal of Circuit Theory and Applications*, May—June 1990). The circuit's trajectory was shown to be uniformly distributed on the interval (0, 1).
a. Give the mean and variance of the circuit's trajectory.
b. Compute the probability that the trajectory falls between .2 and .4.   .2
c. Would you expect to observe a trajectory that exceeds .995? Explain.   No, $p = .005$

5.9 The data set listed in the next table was created using the MINITAB random number generator. Construct a relative frequency histogram for the data. Except for the expected variation in relative frequencies among the class intervals, does your histogram suggest that the data are observations on a uniform random variable with $c = 0$ and $d = 100$? Explain.

RANUNI

38.8759	98.0716	64.5788	60.8422	.8413
88.3734	31.8792	32.9847	.7434	93.3017
12.4337	11.7828	87.4506	94.1727	23.0892
47.0121	43.3629	50.7119	88.2612	69.2875
62.6626	55.6267	78.3936	28.6777	71.6829
44.0466	57.8870	71.8318	28.9622	23.0278
35.6438	38.6584	46.7404	11.2159	96.1009
95.3660	21.5478	87.7819	12.0605	75.1015

Applying the Concepts—Intermediate

5.10 The frequency distribution shown in the table depicts the property and marine losses incurred by a large oil company over the last two years. This distribution can be used by the company to predict future losses and to help determine an appropriate level of insurance coverage. In analyzing the losses within an interval of the distribution, for simplification, analysts may treat the interval as a uniform probability distribution (*Research Review*, Summer 1998). In the insurance business, intervals like these are often called *layers*.

Layer	Property and Marine Losses (millions of $)	Frequency
1	0.00–0.01	668
2	0.01–0.05	38
3	0.05–0.10	7
4	0.10–0.25	4
5	0.25–0.50	2
6	0.50–1.00	1
7	1.00–2.50	0

Source: Cozzolino, John M., and Perter J. Mikola. "Applications of the Piecewise Constant Pareto Distribution." *Research Review*, Summer 1998.

a. Use a uniform distribution to model the loss amount in layer 2. Graph the distribution. Calculate and interpret its mean and variance. $\mu = .03$, $\sigma^2 = .00013$
b. Repeat part a for layer 6. $\mu = .75$, $\sigma^2 = .0208$
c. If a loss occurs in layer 2, what is the probability that it exceeds $\$10,000$? That it is under $\$25,000$?   1; .375
d. If a layer-6 loss occurs, what is the probability that it is between $\$750,000$ and $\$1,000,000$? That it exceeds $\$900,000$? That it is exactly $\$900,000$?   .5; .2; 0

5.11 The manager of a local soft-drink bottling company believes that when a new beverage-dispensing machine is set to dispense 7 ounces, it in fact dispenses an amount x at random anywhere between 6.5 and

7.5 ounces inclusive. Suppose x has a uniform probability distribution.

a. Is the amount dispensed by the beverage machine a discrete or a continuous random variable? Explain.

b. Graph the frequency function for x, the amount of beverage the manager believes is dispensed by the new machine when it is set to dispense 7 ounces.

c. Find the mean and standard deviation for the distribution graphed in part b, and locate the mean and the interval $\mu \pm 2\sigma$ on the graph.

d. Find $P(x \geq 7)$.   .5

e. Find $P(x < 6)$.   0

f. Find $P(6.5 \leq x \leq 7.25)$.   .75

g. What is the probability that each of the next six bottles filled by the new machine will contain more than 7.25 ounces of beverage? Assume that the amount of beverage dispensed in one bottle is independent of the amount dispensed in another bottle. .0002

5.12 A bus is scheduled to stop at a certain bus stop every half hour on the hour and the half hour. At the end of the day, buses still stop after every 30 minutes, but because delays often occur earlier in the day, the bus is never early and likely to be late. The director of the bus line claims that the length of time a bus is late is uniformly distributed and the maximum time that a bus is late is 20 minutes.

a. If the director's claim is true, what is the expected number of minutes a bus will be late?   10

b. If the director's claim is true, what is the probability that the last bus on a given day will be more than 19 minutes late?   .05

c. If you arrive at the bus stop at the end of a day at exactly half past the hour and must wait more than 19 minutes for the bus, what would you conclude about the director's claim? Why?

Applying the Concepts—Advanced

5.13 A tool-and-die machine shop produces extremely high-tolerance spindles. The spindles are 18-inch slender rods used in a variety of military equipment. A piece of equipment used in the manufacture of the spindles malfunctions on occasion and places a single gouge somewhere on the spindle. However, if the spindle can be cut so that it has 14 consecutive inches without a gouge, then the spindle can be salvaged for other purposes. Assuming that the location of the gouge along the spindle is random, what is the probability that a defective spindle can be salvaged?   .4444

5.14 The *reliability* of a piece of equipment is frequently defined to be the probability, p, that the equipment performs its intended function successfully for a given period of time under specific conditions (Render and Heizer, *Principles of Operations Management*, 1995). Because p varies from one point in time to another, some reliability analysts treat p as if it were a random variable. Suppose an analyst characterizes the uncertainty about the reliability of a particular robotic device used in an automobile assembly line using the following distribution:

$$f(p) = \begin{cases} 1 & 0 \leq p \leq 1 \\ 0 & \text{otherwise} \end{cases}$$

a. Graph the analyst's probability distribution for p.

b. Find the mean and variance of p.

c. According to the analyst's probability distribution for p, what is the probability that p is greater than .95? Less than .95?   .05; .95

d. Suppose the analyst receives the additional information that p is definitely between .90 and .95, but that there is complete uncertainty about where it lies between these values. Describe the probability distribution the analyst should now use to describe p.

5.3   The Normal Distribution

One of the most commonly observed continuous random variables has a **bell-shaped** probability distribution (or **bell curve**) as shown in Figure 5.5. It is known as a **normal random variable** and its probability distribution is called a **normal distribution.**

Figure 5.5
A normal probability distribution

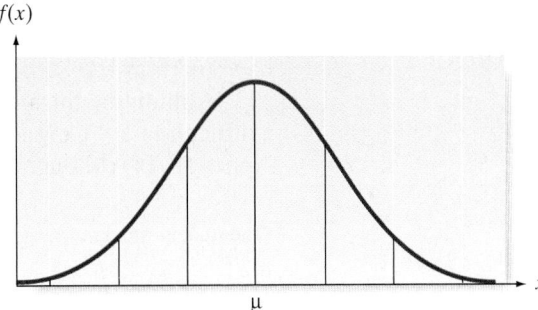

Figure 5.6

Several normal distributions with different means and standard deviations

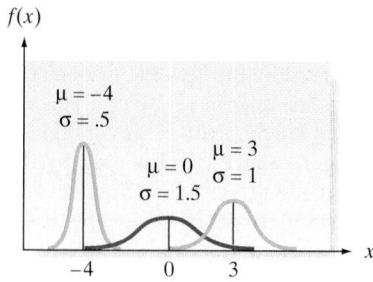

The normal distribution plays a very important role in the science of statistical inference. Moreover, many business phenomena generate random variables with probability distributions that are very well approximated by a normal distribution. For example, the monthly rate of return for a particular stock is approximately a normal random variable, and the probability distribution for the weekly sales of a corporation might be approximated by a normal probability distribution. The normal distribution might also provide an accurate model for the distribution of scores on an employment aptitude test. You can determine the adequacy of the normal approximation to an existing population by comparing the relative frequency distribution of a large sample of the data to the normal probability distribution. Methods to detect disagreement between a set of data and the assumption of normality are presented in Section 5.4.

The normal distribution is perfectly symmetric about its mean μ, as can be seen in the examples in Figure 5.6. Its spread is determined by the value of its standard deviation σ.

The formula for the normal probability distribution is shown in the box. When plotted, this formula yields a curve like that shown in Figure 5.5.

Probability Distribution for a Normal Random Variable x

Probability density function: $f(x) = \dfrac{1}{\sigma\sqrt{2\pi}} e^{-(1/2)[(x-\mu)/\sigma]^2}$

where

μ = Mean of the normal random variable x

σ = Standard deviation

π = 3.1416...

e = 2.71828...

$P(x < a)$ is obtained from a table of normal probabilities

Note that the mean μ and standard deviation σ appear in this formula, so that no separate formulas for μ and σ are necessary. To graph the normal curve we have to know the numerical values of μ and σ.

Computing the area over intervals under the normal probability distribution is a difficult task.* Consequently, we will use the computed areas listed in Table IV of Appendix B. Although there are an infinitely large number of normal curves—one

---

*The student with knowledge of calculus should note that there is not a closed-form expression for

$P(a < x < b) = \displaystyle\int_a^b f(x)\,dx$ for the normal probability distribution. The value of this definite integral can be obtained to any desired degree of accuracy by numerical approximation procedures. For this reason, it is tabulated for the user.

Biography

CARL F. GAUSS (1777–1855)
The Gaussian Distribution

The normal distribution began in the 18th century as a theoretical distribution for errors in disciplines where fluctuations in nature were believed to behave randomly. Although he may not have been the first to discover the formula, the normal distribution was named the Gaussian distribution after Carl Friedrich Gauss. A well-known and respected German mathematician, physicist, and astronomer, Gauss applied the normal distribution while studying the motion of planets and stars. Gauss's prowess as a mathematician was exemplified by one of his most important discoveries. At the young age of 22, Gauss constructed a regular 17-gon by ruler and compasses—a feat that was the most major advance in mathematics since the time of the ancient Greeks. In addition to publishing close to 200 scientific papers, Gauss invented the heliograph as well as a primitive telegraph device.

Teaching Tip
Very few normal distributions in reality possess a standard normal distribution. The real benefit of the standard normal distribution is that all other normal distributions can be made to look like the standard normal and solved.

for each pair of values for μ and σ—we have formed a single table that will apply to any normal curve.

Table IV is based on a normal distribution with mean $\mu = 0$ and standard deviation $\sigma = 1$, called a *standard normal distribution*. A random variable with a standard normal distribution is typically denoted by the symbol z. The formula for the probability distribution of z is given by

$$f(z) = \frac{1}{\sqrt{2\pi}} e^{-(1/2)z^2}$$

Figure 5.7 shows the graph of a standard normal distribution.

> **DEFINITION 5.1**
>
> The **standard normal distribution** is a normal distribution with $\mu = 0$ and $\sigma = 1$. A random variable with a standard normal distribution, denoted by the symbol z, is called a *standard normal random variable*.

Teaching Tip
It is often helpful to use a transparency of the normal curve that can be seen while examples are being discussed in class.

Since we will ultimately convert all normal random variables to standard normal in order to use Table IV to find probabilities, it is important that you learn to use Table IV well. A partial reproduction of Table IV is shown in Table 5.1. Note that the values of the standard normal random variable z are listed in the left-hand column. The entries in the body of the table give the area (probability) between 0 and z. Examples 5.2–5.5 illustrate the use of the table.

Figure 5.7
Standard normal distribution: $\mu = 0, \sigma = 1$

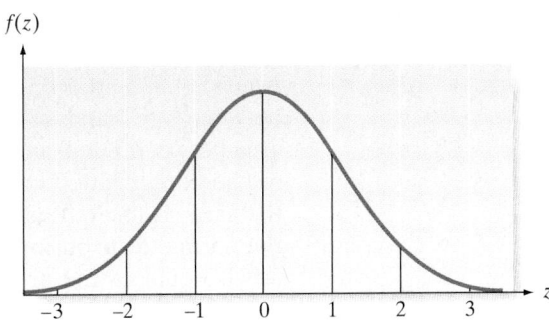

TABLE 5.1　Reproduction of Part of Table IV in Appendix B

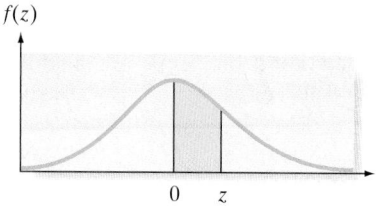

$f(z)$

z	.00	.01	.02	.03	.04	.05	.06	.07	.08	.09
.0	.0000	.0040	.0080	.0120	.0160	.0199	.0239	.0279	.0319	.0359
.1	.0398	.0438	.0478	.0517	.0557	.0596	.0636	.0675	.0714	.0753
.2	.0793	.0832	.0871	.0910	.0948	.0987	.1026	.1064	.1103	.1141
.3	.1179	.1217	.1255	.1293	.1331	.1368	.1406	.1443	.1480	.1517
.4	.1554	.1591	.1628	.1664	.1700	.1736	.1772	.1808	.1844	.1879
.5	.1915	.1950	.1985	.2019	.2054	.2088	.2123	.2157	.2190	.2224
.6	.2257	.2291	.2324	.2357	.2389	.2422	.2454	.2486	.2517	.2549
.7	.2580	.2611	.2642	.2673	.2704	.2734	.2764	.2794	.2823	.2852
.8	.2881	.2910	.2939	.2967	.2995	.3023	.3051	.3078	.3106	.3133
.9	.3159	.3186	.3212	.3238	.3264	.3289	.3315	.3340	.3365	.3389
1.0	.3413	.3438	.3461	.3485	.3508	.3531	.3554	.3577	.3599	.3621
1.1	.3643	.3665	.3686	.3708	.3729	.3749	.3770	.3790	.3810	.3830
1.2	.3849	.3869	.3888	.3907	.3925	.3944	.3962	.3980	.3997	.4015
1.3	.4032	.4049	.4066	.4082	.4099	.4115	.4131	.4147	.4162	.4177
1.4	.4192	.4207	.4222	.4236	.4251	.4265	.4279	.4292	.4306	.4319
1.5	.4332	.4345	.4357	.4370	.4382	.4394	.4406	.4418	.4429	.4441

EXAMPLE 5.2　　USING THE STANDARD NORMAL TABLE

Problem　Find the probability that the standard normal random variable z falls between -1.33 and $+1.33$.

$p = .8164$

Solution　The standard normal distribution is shown again in Figure 5.8. Since all probabilities associated with standard normal random variables can be depicted as areas under the standard normal curve, you should always draw the curve and then equate the desired probability to an area.

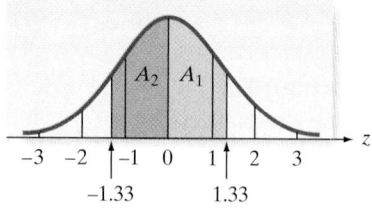

Figure 5.8

Areas under the standard normal curve for Example 5.2

In this example we want to find the probability that z falls between -1.33 and $+1.33$, which is equivalent to the area between -1.33 and $+1.33$, shown shaded in Figure 5.8. Table IV provides the area between $z = 0$ and any value of z, so that if we look up $z = 1.33$, we find that the area between $z = 0$ and $z = 1.33$ is .4082 (The value of 1.33 and the area of .4082 are both highlighted in Table 5.1.) This is the area labeled A_1 in Figure 5.8. To find the area A_2 located between $z = 0$ and $z = -1.33$, we note that the symmetry of the normal distribution implies that the area between $z = 0$ and any point to the left is equal to the area between $z = 0$ and the point equidistant to the right.

Thus, in this example the area between $z = 0$ and $z = -1.33$ is equal to the area between $z = 0$ and $z = +1.33$. That is,

$$A_1 = A_2 = .4082$$

Suggested Exercises 5.18

The probability that z falls between -1.33 and $+1.33$ is the sum of the areas of A_1 and A_2. We summarize in probabilistic notation:

$$P(-1.33 < z < 1.33) = P(-1.33 < z < 0) + P(0 < z < 1.33)$$
$$= A_1 + A_2 = .4082 + .4082 = .8164$$

Look Back Remember that "$<$" and "$\leq$" are equivalent in events involving z, because the inclusion (or exclusion) of a single point does not alter the probability of an event involving a continuous random variable.

| Now Work | *Exercise 5.19* |

■ ■ ■

EXAMPLE 5.3

USING THE STANDARD NORMAL TABLE

Problem

$p = .0505$

Find the probability that a standard normal random variable exceeds 1.64; that is, find $P(z > 1.64)$.

Solution

The area under the standard normal distribution to the right of 1.64 is the shaded area labeled A_1 in Figure 5.9. This area represents the desired probability that z exceeds 1.64. However, when we look up $z = 1.64$ in Table IV, we must remember that the probability given in the table corresponds to the area between $z = 0$ and $z = 1.64$ (the area labeled A_2 in Figure 5.9). From Table IV we find that $A_2 = .4495$. To find the area A_1 to the right of 1.64, we make use of two facts:

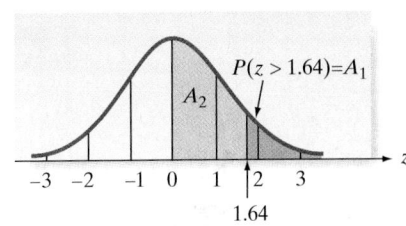

Figure 5.9
Areas under the standard normal curve for Example 5.3

Teaching Tip
Encourage the student to draw pictures of the probabilities they are being asked to find. The pictures are usually a big help initially to most students.

1. The standard normal distribution is symmetric about its mean, $z = 0$.
2. The total area under the standard normal probability distribution equals 1.

Taken together, these two facts imply that the areas on either side of the mean $z = 0$ equal .5; thus, the area to the right of $z = 0$ in Figure 5.9 is $A_1 + A_2 = .5$. Then

$$P(z > 1.64) = A_1 = .5 - A_2 = .5 - .4495 = .0505$$

Look Back To attach some practical significance to this probability, note that the implication is that the chance of a standard normal random variable exceeding 1.64 is approximately .05.

| Now Work | *Exercise 5.17a* |

■ ■ ■

EXAMPLE 5.4   APPLYING THE STANDARD NORMAL TABLE

Problem Find the probability that a standard normal random variable lies to the left of .67.

p = .7486

Solution The event is shown as the highlighted area in Figure 5.10. We want to find $P(z < .67)$. We divide the highlighted area into two parts: the area A_1 between $z = 0$ and $z = .67$, and the area A_2 to the left of $z = 0$. We must always make such a division when the desired area lies on both sides of the mean ($z = 0$) because Table IV contains areas between $z = 0$ and the point you look up. We look up $z = .67$ in Table IV to find that $A_1 = .2486$. The symmetry of the standard normal distribution also

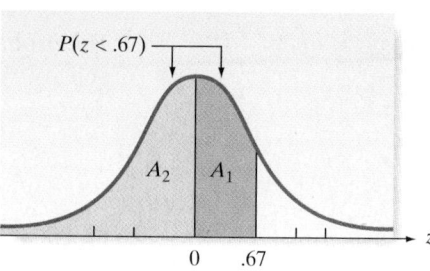

Figure 5.10
Areas under the standard normal curve for Example 5.4

implies that half the distribution lies on each side of the mean, so the area A_2 to the left of $z = 0$ is .5. Then

$$P(z < .67) = A_1 + A_2 = .2486 + .5 = .7486$$

Look Back Note that this probability is approximately .75. Thus, about 75% of the time the standard normal random variable z will fall below .67. This implies that $z = .67$ represents the approximate 75th percentile for the distribution.

Now Work   *Exercise 5.16f*

■ ■ ■

EXAMPLE 5.5   USING THE STANDARD NORMAL TABLE

Problem Find the probability that a standard normal random variable exceeds 1.96 in absolute value.

p = .05

Solution We want to find

$$P(|z| > 1.96) = P(z < -1.96 \text{ or } z > 1.96)$$

This probability is the shaded area in Figure 5.11. Note that the total shaded area is the sum of two areas, A_1 and A_2—areas that are equal because of the symmetry of the normal distribution.

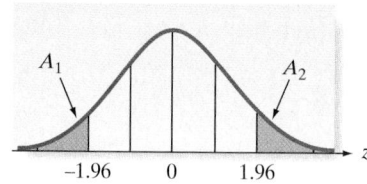

Figure 5.11
Areas under the standard normal curve for Example 5.5

We look up $z = 1.96$ and find the area between $z = 0$ and $z = 1.96$ to be .4750. Then the area to the right of 1.96, A_2, is $.5 - .4750 = .0250$, so that

$$P(|z| > 1.96) = A_1 + A_2 = .0250 + .0250 = .05$$

Look Back We emphasize, again, the importance of drawing the standard normal curve when finding normal probabilities.

■ ■ ■

To apply Table IV to a normal random variable x with any mean μ and any standard deviation σ, we must first convert the value of x to a z-score. The population z-score for a measurement was defined (in Section 2.6) as the *distance* between the measurement and the population mean, divided by the population standard deviation. Thus, the z-score gives the distance between a measurement and the mean in units equal to the standard deviation. In symbolic form, the z-score for the measurement x is

$$z = \frac{x - \mu}{\sigma}$$

Note that when $x = \mu$, we obtain $z = 0$.

An important property of the normal distribution is that if x is normally distributed with any mean and any standard deviation, z is always normally distributed with mean 0 and standard deviation 1. That is, z is a standard normal random variable.

> **Property of Normal Distributions**
>
> If x is a normal random variable with mean μ and standard deviation σ, then the random variable z, defined by the formula
>
> $$z = \frac{x - \mu}{\sigma}$$
>
> has a standard normal distribution. The value z describes the number of standard deviations between x and μ.

Recall from Example 5.5 that $P(|z| > 1.96) = .05$. This probability coupled with our interpretation of z implies that any normal random variable lies more than 1.96 standard deviations from its mean only 5% of the time. Compare this to the Empirical Rule (Chapter 2) which tells us that about 5% of the measurements in mound-shaped distributions will lie beyond 2 standard deviations from the mean. The normal distribution actually provides the model on which the Empirical Rule is based, along with much "empirical" experience with real data that often approximately obey the rule, whether drawn from a normal distribution or not.

EXAMPLE 5.6   FINDING THE PROBABILITY OF A NORMAL RANDOM VARIABLE

Problem Assume that the length of time, x, between charges of a cellular phone is normally distributed with a mean of 10 hours and a standard deviation of 1.5 hours. Find the probability that the cell phone will last between 8 and 12 hours between charges.

$p = .8164$

Solution The normal distribution with mean $\mu = 10$ and $\sigma = 1.5$ is shown in Figure 5.12. The desired probability that the charge lasts between 8 and 12 hours is shaded. In order to find the probability, we must first convert the distribution to standard normal, which we do by calculating the z-score:

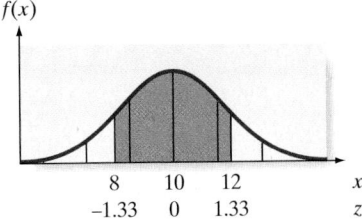

$f(x)$

Figure 5.12

Areas under the normal curve for Example 5.6

$$z = \frac{x - \mu}{\sigma}$$

The z-scores corresponding to the important values of x are shown beneath the x values on the horizontal axis in Figure 5.12. Note that $z = 0$ corresponds to the mean of $\mu = 10$ hours, whereas the x values 8 and 12 yield z-scores of -1.33 and $+1.33$, respectively. Thus, the event that the cell phone charge lasts between 8 and 12 hours is equivalent to the event that a standard normal random variable lies between -1.33 and $+1.33$. We found this probability in Example 5.2 (see Figure 5.8) by doubling the area corresponding to $z = 1.33$ in Table IV. That is,

$$P(8 \leq x \leq 12) = P(-1.33 \leq z \leq 1.33) = 2(.4082) = .8164$$

Now Work *Exercise 5.21*

■ ■ ■

The steps to follow when calculating a probability corresponding to a normal random variable are shown in the box.

> ## Steps for Finding a Probability Corresponding to a Normal Random Variable
>
> 1. Sketch the normal distribution and indicate the mean of the random variable x. Then shade the area corresponding to the probability you want to find.
> 2. Convert the boundaries of the shaded area from x values to standard normal random variable z values using the formula
>
> $$z = \frac{x - \mu}{\sigma}$$
>
> Show the z values under the corresponding x values on your sketch.
> 3. Use Table IV in Appendix B to find the areas corresponding to the z values. If necessary, use the symmetry of the normal distribution to find areas corresponding to negative z values and the fact that the total area on each side of the mean equals .5 to convert the areas from Table IV to the probabilities of the event you have shaded.

Standard Normal Probabilities

Using the TI-83
Graphing Calculator
Graphing the Area under the Standard Normal Curve

Step 1 *Turn off all plots.*
Press **2nd PRGM** and select **1:ClrDraw**
Press **ENTER ENTER** and 'Done' will appear on the screen.
Press **2nd Y =** and select **4:PlotsOff**
Press **ENTER ENTER** and 'Done' will appear on the screen.

Step 2 *Set the viewing window. (Recall that almost all of the area under the standard normal curve falls between –5 and 5. A height of 0.5 is a good choice for Ymax.)*
Set **Xmin** = –5
Xmax = 5

Xscl = 1
Ymin = 0
Ymax = .5
Yscl = 0
Xres = 1
Note: the negative sign is the gray key, not the blue key

Step 3   View graph.
Press **2nd VARS**
Arrow right to **DRAW**
Press **ENTER** to select **1:ShadeNorm(**
Enter your lower limit
Press **comma**
Enter your upper limit
Press) Press **ENTER**
The graph will be displayed along with the area, lower limit, and upper limit.

Example   What is the probability that z is less than 1.5 under the Standard Normal curve? In this example, set the Window as shown in Step 2. For the limits in Step 3 use –5 for the lower limit and 1.5 for the upper limit.

The screens for this example are shown below.

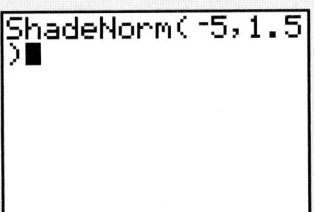
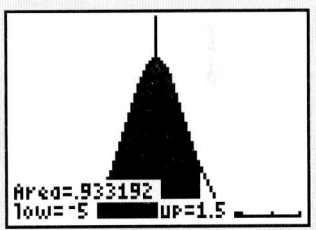

Thus, $P(z < 1.5) = .9332$.

EXAMPLE 5.7   USING NORMAL PROBABILITIES TO MAKE AN INFERENCE

Problem   Suppose an automobile manufacturer introduces a new model that has an advertised mean in-city mileage of 27 miles per gallon. Although such advertisements seldom report any measure of variability, suppose you write the manufacturer for the details of the tests, and you find that the standard deviation is 3 miles per gallon. This information leads you to formulate a probability model for the random variable x, the in-city mileage for this car model. You believe that the probability distribution of x can be approximated by a normal distribution with a mean of 27 and a standard deviation of 3.

.0099

a. If you were to buy this model of automobile, what is the probability that you would purchase one that averages less than 20 miles per gallon for in-city driving? In other words, find $P(x < 20)$.

Yes

b. Suppose you purchase one of these new models and it does get less than 20 miles per gallon for in-city driving. Should you conclude that your probability model is incorrect?

Solution   **a.**   The probability model proposed for x, the in-city mileage, is shown in Figure 5.13.

Suggested Exercises 5.25

We are interested in finding the area A to the left of 20 since this area corresponds to the probability that a measurement chosen from this distribution falls below 20. In other words, if this model is correct, the area A represents the fraction of cars that can be expected to get less than 20 miles per gallon for in-city driving. To find A, we first calculate the z value corresponding to $x = 20$. That is,

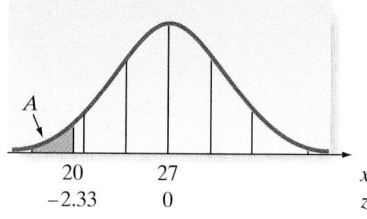

Figure 5.13
Areas under the normal curve for Example 5.7

$$z = \frac{x - \mu}{\sigma} = \frac{20 - 27}{3} = -\frac{7}{3} = -2.33$$

Then

$$P(x < 20) = P(z < -2.33)$$

as indicated by the shaded area in Figure 5.13. Since Table IV gives only areas to the right of the mean (and because the normal distribution is symmetric about its mean), we look up 2.33 in Table IV and find that the corresponding area is .4901. This is equal to the area between $z = 0$ and $z = -2.33$, so we find

$$P(x < 20) = A = .5 - .4901 = .0099 \approx .01$$

According to this probability model, you should have only about a 1% chance of purchasing a car of this make with an in-city mileage under 20 miles per gallon.

b. Now you are asked to make an inference based on a sample—the car you purchased. You are getting less than 20 miles per gallon for in-city driving. What do you infer? We think you will agree that one of two possibilities is true:

1. The probability model is correct. You simply were unfortunate to have purchased one of the cars in the 1% that get less than 20 miles per gallon in the city.

2. The probability model is incorrect. Perhaps the assumption of a normal distribution is unwarranted or the mean of 27 is an overestimate, or the standard deviation of 3 is an underestimate, or some combination of these errors was made. At any rate, the form of the actual probability model certainly merits further investigation.

You have no way of knowing with certainty which possibility is correct, but the evidence points to the second one. We are again relying on the rare-event approach to statistical inference that we introduced earlier. The sample (one measurement in this case) was so unlikely to have been drawn from the proposed probability model that it casts serious doubt on the model. We would be inclined to believe that the model is somehow in error.

Look Back When applying the rare event approach, the calculated probability must be small (say, less than or equal to .05) in order to infer that the observed event is, indeed, unlikely.

Teaching Tip
Introduce the idea of using the z-table "in reverse" to solve these types of problems.

Now Work *Exercise 5.33*

■ ■ ■

Non-standard Normal Probabilities

Using The T1-83 Graphing Calculator

Finding the Area under the Normal Curve

I. Finding the area without a graph

Step 1 *Find area.*
Press 2nd DISTR and select 2:Normalcdf(
Enter the lower limit
Press comma
Enter the upper limit
Press comma
Enter the mean
Press comma
Enter the standard deviation
Press)
Press ENTER
The area will be displayed on the screen.

Example What is the $P(x < 115)$ for a normal distribution with $\mu = 100$ and $\sigma = 10$?
In this example, the lower limit is $-\infty$, the upper limit is 115, the mean is 100, and the standard deviation is 10.
To represent $-\infty$ on the calculator, enter (-) 1, press 2nd and press the comma key for EE, and then press 99. The screen is shown below.

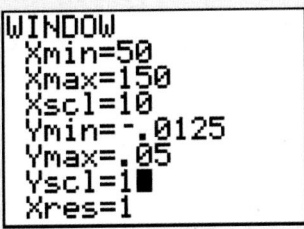

II. Finding the area with a graph

Step 1 *Turn off all plots.*
Press **2nd PRGM** and select **1:ClrDraw**
Press **ENTER ENTER** and 'Done' will appear on the screen.
Press **2nd Y=** and select **4:PlotsOff**
Press **ENTER ENTER** and 'Done' will appear on the screen.

Step 2 Set the viewing window. (These values depend on the mean and standard deviation of the data.)
Press **WINDOW**
Set **Xmin** $= \mu - 5\sigma$
Xmax $= \mu + 5\sigma$
Xscl $= \sigma$
Ymin $= -.125 / \sigma$
Ymax $= .5 / \sigma$
Yscl $= 1$
Xres $= 1$
Note: the negative sign is the gray key, not the blue key

Step 3   *View graph.*
Press **2nd VARS**
Arrow right to **DRAW**
Press **ENTER** to select **1:ShadeNorm(**
Enter the lower limit
Press **comma**
Enter the upper limit
Press **comma**
Enter the mean
Press **comma**
Enter the standard deviation
Press **)**
Press **ENTER**
The graph will be displayed along with the area, lower limit, and upper limit.

Example   What is the $P(x < 115)$ for a normal distribution with $\mu = 100$ and $\sigma = 10$?
In this example, the lower limit is $-\infty$, the upper limit is 115, the mean is 100, and the standard deviation is 10.
To represent $-\infty$ on the calculator, enter (-) 1, press 2nd and press the comma key for EE, and then press 99. The screens are shown below.

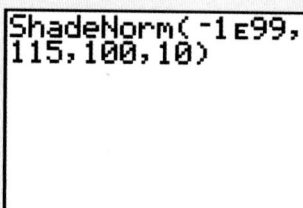
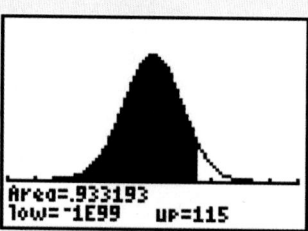

Thus, the $P(x < 115)$ is .9332.

Occasionally you will be given a probability and will want to find the values of the normal random variable that correspond to the probability. For example, suppose the scores on a college entrance examination are known to be normally distributed, and a certain prestigious university will consider for admission only those applicants whose scores exceed the 90th percentile of the test score distribution. To determine the minimum score for admission consideration, you will need to be able to use Table IV in reverse, as demonstrated in the following example.

EXAMPLE 5.8   USING THE NORMAL TABLE IN REVERSE

Problem   Find the value of z, call it z_0, in the standard normal distribution that will be exceeded only 10% of the time. That is, find z_0 such that $P(z \geq z_0) = .10$.

$z_0 = 1.28$

Solution   In this case we are given a probability, or an area, and asked to find the value of the standard normal random variable that corresponds to the area. Specifically, we want to find the value z_0 such that only 10% of the standard normal distribution exceeds z_0 (see Figure 5.14).
We know that the total area to the right of the mean $z = 0$ is .5, which implies that z_0 must lie to the right of (above) 0. To pinpoint the value, we use the fact that the area to the right of z_0 is .10, which implies that the area between $z = 0$ and z_0 is

$.5 - .1 = .4$. But areas between $z = 0$ and some other z value are exactly the types given in Table IV. Therefore, we look up the area .4000 in the body of Table IV and find that the corresponding z value is (to the closest approximation) $z_0 = 1.28$. The implication is that the point 1.28 standard deviations above the mean is the 90th percentile of a normal distribution.

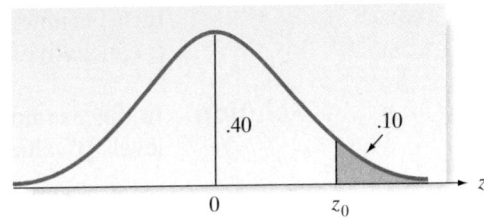

Figure 5.14
Area under the standard normal curve for Example 5.8

Look Back As with earlier problems, it is critical to draw correctly the normal probability of interest on the normal curve. Placement of z_0 to the left or right of 0 is the key. Be sure to shade the probability (area) involving z_0. If it does not agree with the probability of interest (i.e., the shaded area is greater than .5 and the probability of interest is smaller than .5), then you need to place z_0 on the opposite side of 0.

▪ ▪ ▪

EXAMPLE 5.9

USING THE NORMAL TABLE IN REVERSE

$z_0 = 1.96$

Problem Find the value of z_0 such that 95% of the standard normal z values lie between $-z_0$ and $+z_0$; that is, $P(-z_0 \le z \le z_0) = .95$.

Solution Here we wish to move an equal distance z_0 in the positive and negative directions from the mean $z = 0$ until 95% of the standard normal distribution is enclosed. This means that the area on each side of the mean will be equal to $\frac{1}{2}(.95) = .475$, as shown in Figure 5.15. Since the area between $z = 0$ and z_0 is .475, we look up .475 in the body of Table IV to find the value $z_0 = 1.96$. Thus, as we found in the reverse order in Example 5.5, 95% of a normal distribution lies between $+1.96$ and -1.96 standard deviationsk of the mean.

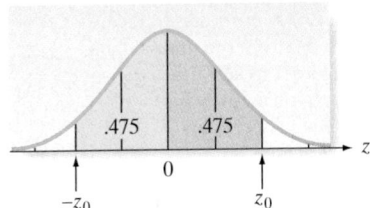

Figure 5.15
Areas under the standard normal curve for Example 5.9

Now Work *Exercise 5.24*

▪ ▪ ▪

Now that you have learned to use Table IV to find a standard normal z value that corresponds to a specified probability, we demonstrate a practical application in Example 5.10.

EXAMPLE 5.10

APPLICATION OF THE NORMAL TABLE IN REVERSE

Problem Suppose a paint manufacturer has a daily production, x, that is normally distributed with a mean of 100,000 gallons and a standard deviation of 10,000 gallons. Management wants to create an incentive bonus for the production crew when the daily production exceeds the 90th percentile of the distribution, in hopes that the crew will, in

$x_0 = 112,800$

turn, become more productive. At what level of production should management pay the incentive bonus?

Solution   In this example, we want to find a production level, x_0, such that 90% of the daily levels (x values) in the distribution fall below x_0 and only 10% fall above x_0. That is,

$$P(x \leq x_0) = .90$$

Teaching Tip

Once the student can think about these problems graphically, the point they are looking for can be solved using $x_0 = \mu + z_0\sigma$.

Converting x to a standard normal random variable, where $\mu = 100,000$ and $\sigma = 10,000$, we have

$$P(x \leq x_0) = P\left(z \leq \frac{x_0 - \mu}{\sigma}\right)$$

$$= P\left(z \leq \frac{x_0 - 100,000}{10,000}\right) = .90$$

In Example 5.8 (see Figure 5.14) we found the 90th percentile of the standard normal distribution to be $z_0 = 1.28$. That is, we found $P(z \leq 1.28) = .90$. Consequently, we know the production level x_0 at which the incentive bonus is paid corresponds to a z-score of 1.28; that is,

$$\frac{x_0 - 100,000}{10,000} = 1.28$$

Teaching Tip

A common mistake is to take a z-score from the normal table and forget to add the negative sign to it. Discuss when negative z-scores are appropriate.

If we solve this equation for x_0, we find

$$x_0 = 100,000 + 1.28(10,000) = 100,000 + 12,800 = 112,800$$

This x value is shown in Figure 5.16. Thus, the 90th percentile of the production distribution is 112,800 gallons. Management should pay an incentive bonus when a day's production exceeds this level if its objective is to pay only when production is in the top 10% of the current daily production distribution.

Figure 5.16
Area under the normal curve for Example 5.10

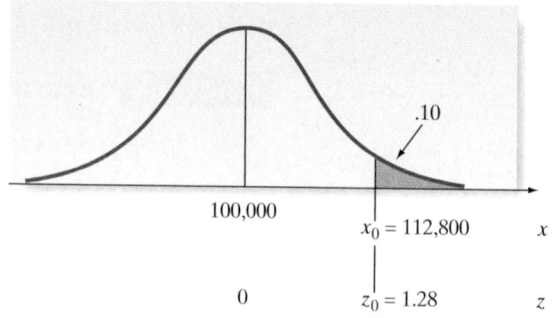

Suggested Exercises 5.38

Look Back As this example shows, in practical applications of the normal table in reverse, first find the value of z_0, then convert the value to the units of x using the z-score formula in reverse.

■ ■ ■

Statistics in Action Revisited

Using the Normal Model to Maximize the Probability of a Hit with the Super Weapon

Recall that a defense contractor has developed a prototype gun for the U.S. Army that fires 1,100 flechettes with a single round. The specifications of the weapon are set so that when the gun is aimed at a target 500 meters away, the mean horizontal grid value of the flechettes is equal to the aim point. In the range test, the weapon was aimed at the center target in Figure SIA5.1; thus, $\mu = 5$ feet. For three different tests, the standard deviation was set at $\sigma = 1$ feet, $\sigma = 2$ feet, and $\sigma = 4$ feet. From past experience, the defense contractor has found that the distribution of the horizontal hit point measurements is closely approximated by a normal distribution. Therefore, we can use the normal distribution to find the probability that a single flechette shot from the weapon will hit any one of the three targets. Recall, from Figure SIA5.1, that the three targets range from -1 to 1, 4 to 6, and 9 to 11 feet on the horizontal grid.

Consider, first, the middle target. Letting x represent the horizontal measurement for a flechette shot from the gun, the flechette will hit the target if $4 \le x \le 6$. The probability that this flechette will hit the target when $\mu = 5$ and $\sigma = 1$ is, using the normal probability table (Table 4, Appendix I),

Middle:
$\sigma = 1$ $\quad P(4 \le x \le 6) = P\left(\dfrac{4-5}{1} < z < \dfrac{6-5}{1}\right)$
$$= P(-1 < z < 1)$$
$$= 2(.3413) = .6826$$

Similarly, we find the probability that the flechette hits the left and right targets shown in Figure SIA5.1.

Left:
$\sigma = 1$ $\quad P(-1 \le x \le 1) = P\left(\dfrac{-1-5}{1} < z < \dfrac{1-5}{1}\right)$
$$= P(-6 < z < -4) \approx 0$$

Right:
$\sigma = 1$ $\quad P(9 \le x \le 11) = P\left(\dfrac{9-5}{1} < z < \dfrac{11-5}{1}\right)$
$$= P(4 < z < 6) \approx 0$$

You can see that there is about a 68% chance that a flechette will hit the middle target but virtually no chance that one will hit the left and right targets when the standard deviation is set at 1 foot.

To find these three probabilities for $\sigma = 2$ and $\sigma = 4$, we use the normal probability function in MINITAB. Figure SIA5.2 is a MINITAB worksheet giving the cumulative probabilities of a normal random variable falling below the x-values in the first column. The cumulative probabilities for $\sigma = 2$ and $\sigma = 4$ are given in the columns named "sigma2" and "sigma4", respectively.

Using the cumulative probabilities in the figure to find the three probabilities when $\sigma = 2$, we have

Middle:
$\sigma = 2$ $\quad P(4 \le x \le 6) = P(x \le 6) - P(x \le 4)$
$$= .6915 - .3085 = .3830$$

Left:
$\sigma = 2$ $\quad P(-1 \le x \le 1) = P(x \le 1) - P(x \le -1)$
$$= .0227 - .0013 = .0214$$

Right:
$\sigma = 2$ $\quad P(9 \le x \le 11) = P(x \le 11) - P(x \le 9)$
$$= .9987 - .9773 = .0214$$

Thus, when $\sigma = 2$, there is about a 38% chance that a flechette will hit the middle target, a 2% chance that one will hit the left target, and a 2% chance that one will hit the right target. The probability that a flechette will hit either the middle or left or right target is simply the sum of these three probabilities (an application of the Additive Rule of probability). This sum is .3830 + .0214 + .0214 = .4258; consequently, there is about a 42% chance of hitting any

Figure SIA5.2

MINITAB worksheet with cumulative normal probabilities

↓	C1	C2	C3	C4	C5
	x	sigma1	sigma2	sigma4	
1	-1	0.00000	0.001350	0.066807	
2	1	0.00003	0.022750	0.158655	
3	4	0.15866	0.308538	0.401294	
4	6	0.84134	0.691462	0.598706	
5	9	0.99997	0.977250	0.841345	
6	11	1.00000	0.998650	0.933193	
7					

one of the three targets when specifications are set so that $\sigma = 2$.

Now, we use the cumulative probabilities in Figure SIA5.2 to find the three hit probabilities when $\sigma = 4$:

Middle:
$\sigma = 4$
$$P(4 \le x \le 6) = P(x \le 6) - P(x \le 4)$$
$$= .5987 - .4013 = .1974$$

Left:
$\sigma = 4$
$$P(-1 \le x \le 1) = P(x \le 1) - P(x \le -1)$$
$$= .1587 - .0668 = .0919$$

Right:
$\sigma = 9$
$$P(9 \le x \le 11) = P(x \le 11) - P(x \le 9)$$
$$= .9332 - .8413 = .0919$$

Thus, when $\sigma = 4$, there is about a 20% chance that a flechette will hit the middle target, a 9% chance that one

will hit the left target, and a 9% chance that one will hit the right target. The probability that a flechette will hit any one of the three targets is $.1974 + .0919 + .0919 = .3712$.

These probability calculations reveal a few patterns. First, the probability of hitting the middle target (the target where the gun is aimed) is reduced as the standard deviation is increased. Obviously, if the U.S. Army wants to maximize the chance of hitting the target that the prototype gun is aimed at, it will want specifications set with a small value of σ. But if the Army wants to hit multiple targets with a single shot of the weapon, σ should be increased. With a larger σ, not as many of the flechettes will hit the target aimed at, but more will hit peripheral targets. Whether σ should be set at 4 or 6 (or some other value) depends on how high of a hit rate is required for the peripheral targets.

Exercises 5.15–5.42

Learning the Mechanics

5.15 Find the area under the standard normal probability distribution between the following pairs of z-scores:
a. $z = 0$ and $z = 2.00$ **b.** $z = 0$ and $z = 3$
c. $z = 0$ and $z = 1.5$ **d.** $z = 0$ and $z = .80$

5.16 Find the following probabilities for the standard normal random variable z:
a. $P(-1 \le z \le 1)$ .6826 **b.** $P(-2 \le z \le 2)$
c. $P(-2.16 \le z \le .55)$ **d.** $P(-.42 < z < 1.96)$
e. $P(z \ge -2.33)$ .9901 **f.** $P(z < 2.33)$

5.17 Find the following probabilities for the standard normal random variable z:
a. $P(z > 1.46)$ .0721 **b.** $P(z < -1.56)$
c. $P(.67 \le z \le 2.41)$ **d.** $P(-1.96 \le z < -.33)$
e. $P(z \ge 0)$ .5 **f.** $P(-2.33 < z < 1.50)$

5.18 Find each of the following probabilities for a standard normal random variable z:
a. $P(z = 1)$ 0 **b.** $P(z \le 1)$ .8413
c. $P(z < 1)$ .8413 **d.** $P(z > 1)$ .1587

5.19 Find each of the following probabilities for the standard normal random variable z:
a. $P(-1 \le z \le 1)$ **b.** $P(-1.96 \le z \le 1.96)$
c. $P(-1.645 \le z \le 1.645)$ **d.** $P(-2 \le z \le 2)$

5.20 Find a value of the standard normal random variable z, call it z_0, such that
a. $P(z \ge z_0) = .05$ 1.645 **b.** $P(z \ge z_0) = .025$
c. $P(z \le z_0) = .025$ **d.** $P(z \ge z_0) = .10$ 1.28
e. $P(z > z_0) = .10$ 1.28

5.21 Find a value of the standard normal random variable z, call it z_0, such that
a. $P(z \le z_0) = .2090$ −.81
b. $P(z \le z_0) = .7090$ .55
c. $P(-z_0 \le z < z_0) = .8472$ 1.43
d. $P(-z_0 \le z \le z_0) = .1664$ .21
e. $P(z_0 \le z \le 0) = .4798$ −2.05

f. $P(-1 < z < z_0) = .5328$ .50

5.22 Give the z-score for a measurement from a normal distribution for the following:
a. 1 standard deviation above the mean 1
b. 1 standard deviation below the mean −1
c. Equal to the mean 0
d. 2.5 standard deviations below the mean −2.5
e. 3 standard deviations above the mean 3

5.23 Suppose the random variable x is best described by a normal distribution with $\mu = 30$ and $\sigma = 4$. Find the z-score that corresponds to each of the following x values:
a. $x = 20$ −2.5 **b.** $x = 30$ 0
c. $x = 27.5$ **d.** $x = 15$ −3.75
e. $x = 35$ 1.25 **f.** $x = 25$

5.24 The random variable x has a normal distribution with $\mu = 1,000$ and $\sigma = 10$.
a. Find the probability that x assumes a value more than 2 standard deviations from its mean. More than 3 standard deviations from μ.
b. Find the probability that x assumes a value within 1 standard deviation of its mean. Within 2 standard deviations of μ. .6826; .9544
c. Find the value of x that represents the 80th percentile of this distribution. The 10th percentile.

5.25 Suppose x is a normally distributed random variable with $\mu = 11$ and $\sigma = 2$. Find each of the following:
a. $P(10 \le x \le 12)$ .3830 **b.** $P(6 \le x \le 10)$
c. $P(13 \le x \le 16)$ .1525 **d.** $P(7.8 \le x \le 12.6)$
e. $P(x \ge 13.24)$ .1314 **f.** $P(x \ge 7.62)$

5.26 Suppose x is a normally distributed random variable with $\mu = 50$ and $\sigma = 3$. Find a value of the random variable, call it x_0, such that
a. $P(x \le x_0) = .8413$ 53 **b.** $P(x > x_0) = .025$
c. $P(x > x_0) = .95$ **d.** $P(41 \le x < x_0) = .8630$
e. 10% of the values of x are less than x_0. 46.16
f. 1% of the values of x are greater than x_0. 56.98

5.27 Suppose x is a normally distributed random variable with mean 120 and variance 36. Draw a rough graph of the distribution of x. Locate μ and the interval $\mu \pm 2\sigma$ on the graph. Find the following probabilities:
  a. $P(\mu - 2\sigma \leq x \leq \mu + 2\sigma)$ **b.** $P(x \geq 128)$
  c. $P(x \leq 108)$ .0228   **d.** $P(112 \leq x \leq 130)$
  e. $P(114 \leq x \leq 116)$ **f.** $P(115 \leq x \leq 128)$

5.28 The random variable x has a normal distribution with standard deviation 25. It is known that the probability that x exceeds 150 is .90. Find the mean μ of the probability distribution. $\mu = 182$

Applying the Concepts—Basic

⊙ **WPOWER50**

5.29 Refer to the *Fortune* (Oct. 14, 2002) list of the 50 most powerful women in America, Exercise 2.45 (p.78). Recall that the data on age (in years) of each woman is stored in the **WPOWER50** file. The ages in the data set can be shown to be approximately normally distributed with a mean of 50 years and a standard deviation of 6 years. A powerful woman is randomly selected from the data and her age is observed.
  a. Find the probability that her age will fall between 55 and 60 years.   .1558
  b. Find the probability that her age will fall between 48 and 52 years.   .2586
  c. Find the probability that her age will be less than 35 years.   .0062
  d. Find the probability that her age will exceed 40 years.   .9525

⊙ **BWECS**

5.30 Refer to *Business Week's* 2002 "Executive Compensation Scoreboard." Recall that one of the variables saved in the **BWECS** file is the return (in dollars) on a $100 investment made in the CEO's company three years earlier. The data on returns can be shown to be approximately normally distributed with a mean of $112 and a standard deviation of $70. A CEO is randomly selected from the data set the three-year return on a $100 investment in the CEO's company is observed.
  a. Find the probability that the return will fall between $40 and $120.   .3923
  b. Find the probability that the return will fall between $150 and $200.   .1908
  c. Find the probability that the return will be less than $40.   .1515
  d. Find the probability that the return will exceed $200.   .1038

⊙ **DDT**

5.31 Refer to the U.S. Army Corps of Engineers data on contaminated fish in the Tennessee River, saved in the **DDT** file. Recall that one of the variables measured for each captured fish is weight (in grams). The weights in the data set can be shown to be approximately normally distributed with a mean of 1,050 grams and a standard deviation

of 375 grams. An observation is randomly selected from the data and the fish weight is observed.
  a. Find the probability that the weight will fall between 1,000 and 1,400 grams.   .3755
  b. Find the probability that the will fall between 800 and 1,000 grams.   .1969
  c. Find the probability that the weight will be less than 1,750 grams.   .9693
  d. Find the probability that the return will exceed 500 grams.   .9292

⊙ **CRASH**

5.32 Refer to the National Highway Traffic Safety Administration (NHTSA) crash test data for new cars, introduced in Exercise 2.127 (p. 124) and saved in the **CRASH** file. One of the variables measured is the severity of a driver's head injury when the car is in a head-on collision with a fixed barrier while traveling at 35 miles per hour. The more points assigned to the head injury rating, the more severe the injury. The head injury ratings can be shown to be approximately normally distributed with a mean of 605 points and a standard deviation of 185 points. One of the crash-tested cars is randomly selected from the data and the driver's head injury rating is observed.
  a. Find the probability that the rating will fall between 500 and 700 points.   .4107
  b. Find the probability that the rating will fall between 400 and 500 points.   .1508
  c. Find the probability that the rating will be less than 850 points.   .9066
  d. Find the probability that the rating will exceed 1,000 points.   .0162

5.33 In studying the dynamics of fish populations, knowing the length of a species at different ages is critical, especially for commercial fishermen. *Fisheries Science* (Feb. 1995) published a study of the length distributions of sardines inhabiting Japanese waters. At two years of age, fish have a length distribution that is approximately normal with $\mu = 20.20$ centimeters (cm) and $\sigma = .65$ cm.
  a. Find the probability that a two-year-old sardine inhabiting Japanese waters is between 20 and 21 cm long.
  b. Find the probability that a sardine captured in Japanese waters is less than 19.84 cm long?
  c. Find the probability that the sardine is greater than 22.01 cm long.

Applying the Concepts—Intermediate

5.34 The crop yield for a particular farm in a particular year is typically measured as the amount of the crop produced per acre. For example, cotton is measured in pounds per acre. It has been demonstrated that the normal distribution can be used to characterize crop yields over time (*American Journal of Agricultural Economics*, May 1999). Historical data indicate that next summer's cotton yield for a particular Georgia farmer can be characterized by a normal distribution with mean 1,500 pounds per acre and standard deviation 250. The farm in question will be profitable if it produces at least 1,600 pounds per acre.

a. What is the probability that the farm will lose money next summer? .6554

b. Assume the same normal distribution is appropriate for describing cotton yield in each of the next two summers. Also assume that the two yields are statistically independent. What is the probability that the farm will lose money for two straight years? .4295

c. What is the probability that the cotton yield falls within 2 standard deviations of 1,500 pounds per acre next summer? .9544

5.35 The problem of matching aircraft to passenger demand on each flight leg is called the *flight assignment problem* in the airline industry. *Spill* is defined as the number of passengers not carried because the aircraft's capacity is insufficient. A solution to the flight assignment problem at Delta Airlines was published in *Interfaces* (Jan.–Feb. 1994). The authors—four Delta Airlines researchers and a Georgia Tech professor (Roy Marsten)—demonstrated their approach with an example in which passenger demand for a particular flight leg is normally distributed with a mean of 125 passengers and a standard deviation of 45. Consider a Boeing 727 with a capacity of 148 passengers and a Boeing 757 with a capacity of 182.

a. What is the probability that passenger demand will exceed the capacity of the Boeing 727? The Boeing 757?

b. If the 727 is assigned to the flight leg, what is the probability that the flight will depart with one or more empty seats? Answer the same question for the Boeing 757. .6879; .8925

c. If the 727 is assigned to the flight, what is the probability that the spill will be more than 100 passengers?

5.36 Government data indicate that the mean hourly wage for manufacturing workers in the United States is $14 (*Statistical Abstract of the United States: 2002*). Suppose the distribution of manufacturing wage rates nationwide can be approximated by a normal distribution with standard deviation $1.25 per hour. The first manufacturing firm contacted by a particular worker seeking a new job pays $15.30 per hour.

a. If the worker were to undertake a nationwide job search, approximately what proportion of the wage rates would be greater than $15.30 per hour? .1492

b. If the worker were to randomly select a U.S. manufacturing firm, what is the probability the firm would pay more than $15.30 per hour? .1492

c. The population median, call it η, of a continuous random variable x is the value such that $P(x \geq \eta) = P(x \leq \eta) = .5$. That is, the median is the value η such that half the area under the probability distribution lies above η and half lies below it. Find the median of the random variable corresponding to the wage rate and compare it to the mean wage rate.

5.37 Personnel tests are designed to test a job applicant's cognitive and/or physical abilities. An IQ test is an example of the former; a speed test involving the arrangement of pegs on a peg board is an example of the latter (Cowling and James, *The Essence of Personnel Management and Industrial Relations*, 1994). A particular dexterity test is administered nationwide by a private testing service. It is known that for all tests administered last year the distribution of scores was approximately normal with mean 75 and standard deviation 7.5.

a. A particular employer requires job candidates to score at least 80 on the dexterity test. Approximately what percentage of the test scores during the past year exceeded 80? 25.14%

b. The testing service reported to a particular employer that one of its job candidate's scores fell at the 98th percentile of the distribution (i.e., approximately 98% of the scores were lower than the candidate's, and only 2% were higher). What was the candidate's score?

5.38 Before negotiating a long-term construction contract, building contractors must carefully estimate the total cost of completing the project. Benzion Barlev of New York University proposed a model for total cost of a long-term contract based on the normal distribution (*Journal of Business Finance and Accounting*, July 1995). For one particular construction contract, Barlev assumed total cost, x, to be normally distributed with mean $850,000 and standard deviation $170,000. The revenue, R, promised to the contractor is $1,000,000.

a. The contract will be profitable if revenue exceeds total cost. What is the probability that the contract will be profitable for the contractor? .8106

b. What is the probability that the project will result in a loss for the contractor? .1894

c. Suppose the contractor has the opportunity to renegotiate the contract. What value of R should the contractor strive for in order to have a .99 probability of making a profit? $1,246,100

5.39 The *monthly rate of return* of a stock is a measure investors frequently use for evaluating the behavior of a stock over time. A stock's monthly rate of return generally reflects the amount of money an investor makes (or loses if the return is negative) for every dollar invested in the stock in a given month. In his classic text, *Foundations of Finance* (1976), Eugene Fama demonstrated that the probability distribution for the monthly rate of return of a stock can be approximated by a normal probability distribution. Suppose the monthly rates of return to stock ABC are normally distributed with mean .05 and standard deviation .03, and the monthly rates of return to stock XYZ are normally distributed with mean .07 and standard deviation .05. Assume that you have $100 invested in each stock.

a. Over the long run, which stock will yield the higher average monthly rate of return? Why? xyz

b. Suppose you plan to hold each stock for only one month. What is the expected value of each investment at the end of one month?

c. Which stock offers greater protection against incurring a loss on your investment next month? Why?

Applying the Concepts—Advanced

5.40 The characteristics of an industrial filling process in which an expensive liquid is injected into a container was investigated in *Journal of Quality Technology* (July 1999). The quantity injected per container is approximately normally distributed with mean 10 units and standard deviation .2 units. Each unit of fill costs $20 per unit. If a container contains less than 10 units (i.e., is underfilled) it must be reprocessed at a cost of $10. A properly filled container sells for $230.

a. Find the probability that a container is underfilled. Not underfilled.   .5; .5

b. A container is initially underfilled and must be reprocessed. Upon refilling it contains 10.60 units. How much profit will the company make on this container?

c. The operations manager adjusts the mean of the filling process upward to 10.10 units in order to make the probability of underfilling approximately zero. Under these conditions, what is the expected profit per container? $28

5.41 A machine used to regulate the amount of dye dispensed for mixing shades of paint can be set so that it discharges an average of μ milliliters (mL) of dye per can of paint. The amount of dye discharged is known to have a normal distribution with a standard deviation of .4 mL. If more than 6 mL of dye are discharged when

making a certain shade of blue paint, the shade is unacceptable. Determine the setting for μ so that only 1% of the cans of paint will be unacceptable.   5.068

5.42 What relationship exists between the standard normal distribution and the box-plot methodology (optional Section 2.8) for describing distributions of data using quartiles? The answer depends on the true underlying probability distribution of the data. Assume for the remainder of this exercise that the distribution is normal.

a. Calculate the values of the standard normal random variable z, call them z_L and z_U, that correspond to the hinges of the box plot—that is, the lower and upper quartiles, Q_L and Q_U—of the probability distribution.

b. Calculate the z values that correspond to the inner fences of the box plot for a normal probability distribution.   −2.68, 2.68

c. Calculate the z values that correspond to the outer fences of the box plot for a normal probability distribution.   −4.69, 4.69

d. What is the probability that an observation lies beyond the inner fences of a normal probability distribution? The outer fences?   .0074, 0

e. Can you better understand why the inner and outer fences of a box plot are used to detect outliers in a distribution? Explain.

5.4 Descriptive Methods for Assessing Normality

In the chapters that follow, we learn how to make inferences about the population based on information in the sample. Several of these techniques are based on the assumption that the population is approximately normally distributed. Consequently, it will be important to determine whether the sample data come from a normal population before we can properly apply these techniques.

Several descriptive methods can be used to check for normality. In this section, we consider the four methods summarized in the box.

Determining Whether the Data Are From an Approximately Normal Distribution

1. Construct either a histogram or stem-and-leaf display for the data and note the shape of the graph. If the data are approximately normal, the shape of the histogram or stem-and-leaf display will be similar to the normal curve, Figure 5.5 (i.e., mound shaped and symmetric about the mean).

2. Compute the intervals $\bar{x} \pm s$, $\bar{x} \pm 2s$, and $\bar{x} \pm 3s$, and determine the percentage of measurements falling in each. If the data are approximately normal, the percentages will be approximately equal to 68%, 95%, and 100%, respectively.

3. Find the interquartile range, IQR, and standard deviation, s, for the sample, then calculate the ratio IQR/s. If the data are approximately normal, then IQR/$s \approx 1.3$.

4. Construct a *normal probability plot* for the data. If the data are approximately normal, the points will fall (approximately) on a straight line.

The first two methods come directly from the properties of a normal distribution established in Section 5.3. Method 3 is based on the fact that for normal distributions, the z values corresponding to the 25th and 75th percentiles are $-.67$ and $.67$, respectively (see Example 5.4). Since $\sigma = 1$ for a standard normal distribution,

$$\frac{\text{IQR}}{\sigma} = \frac{Q_U - Q_L}{\sigma} = \frac{.67 - (-.67)}{1} = 1.34$$

The final descriptive method for checking normality is based on a *normal probability plot*. In such a plot, the observations in a data set are ordered from smallest to largest and then plotted against the expected z-scores of observations calculated under the assumption that the data come from a normal distribution. When the data are, in fact, normally distributed, a linear (straight-line) trend will result. A nonlinear trend in the plot suggest that the data are nonnormal.

> **DEFINITION 5.2**
>
> A **normal probability plot** for a data set is a scatterplot with the ranked data values on one axis and their corresponding expected z-scores from a standard normal distribution on the other axis. [*Note*: Computation of the expected standard normal z-scores are beyond the scope of this text. Therefore, we will rely on available statistical software packages to generate a normal probability plot.]

EXAMPLE 5.11   CHECKING FOR NORMAL DATA

Problem The Environmental Protection Agency (EPA) performs extensive tests on all new car models to determine their mileage ratings. The results of 100 EPA tests on a certain new car model are displayed in Table 5.2. Numerical and graphical descriptive measures for the data are shown on the MINITAB and SPSS printouts, Figures 5.17(a)–(c). Determine whether the EPA mileage ratings are from an approximate normal distribution.

Data are normal

 EPAGAS

TABLE 5.2   EPA Gas Mileage Ratings for 100 Cars (miles per gallon)

36.3	41.0	36.9	37.1	44.9	36.8	30.0	37.2	42.1	36.7
32.7	37.3	41.2	36.6	32.9	36.5	33.2	37.4	37.5	33.6
40.5	36.5	37.6	33.9	40.2	36.4	37.7	37.7	40.0	34.2
36.2	37.9	36.0	37.9	35.9	38.2	38.3	35.7	35.6	35.1
38.5	39.0	35.5	34.8	38.6	39.4	35.3	34.4	38.8	39.7
36.3	36.8	32.5	36.4	40.5	36.6	36.1	38.2	38.4	39.3
41.0	31.8	37.3	33.1	37.0	37.6	37.0	38.7	39.0	35.8
37.0	37.2	40.7	37.4	37.1	37.8	35.9	35.6	36.7	34.5
37.1	40.3	36.7	37.0	33.9	40.1	38.0	35.2	34.8	39.5
39.9	36.9	32.9	33.8	39.8	34.0	36.8	35.0	38.1	36.9

Solution As a first check, we examine the MINITAB histogram of the data shown in Figure 5.17(a). Clearly, the mileages fall in an approximately mound-shaped, symmetric distribution centered around the mean of approximately 37 mpg. Note

Figure 5.17a

MINITAB histogram for gas mileage data

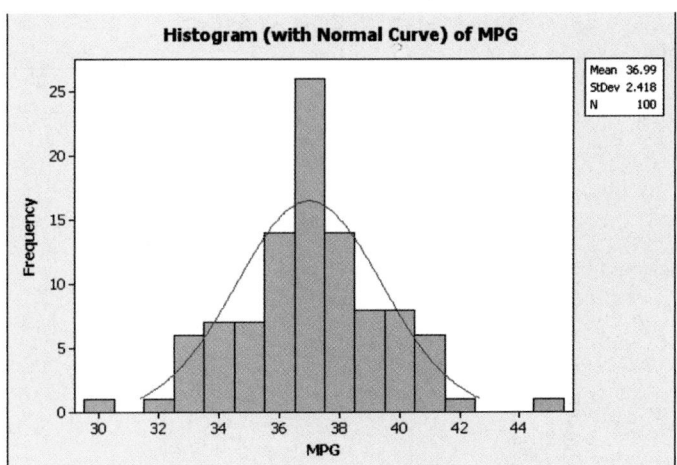

that a normal curve is superimposed on the figure. Therefore, using check #1 in the box, the datas appear to be approximately normal.

To apply check #2, we obtain $\bar{x}$ = 37 and s = 2.4 from the MINITAB printout, Figure 5.17(b). The intervals $\bar{x} \pm s, \bar{x} \pm 2s,$ and $\bar{x} \pm 3s$, are shown in Table 5.3, as well as the percentage of mileage ratings that fall in each interval. These percentages agree almost exactly with those from a normal distribution.

Descriptive Statistics: MPG

Variable	N	Mean	StDev	Minimum	Q1	Median	Q3	Maximum
MPG	100	36.994	2.418	30.000	35.625	37.000	38.375	44.900

Figure 5.17b

MINITAB descriptive statistics for gas mileage data

TABLE 5.3   Describing the 100 EPA Mileage Ratings

Interval	Percentage in Interval
$\bar{x} \pm s = (34.6, 39.4)$	68
$\bar{x} \pm 2s = (32.2, 41.8)$	96
$\bar{x} \pm 3s = (29.8, 44.2)$	99

Check #3 in the box requires that we find the ratio IQR/s. From Figure 5.17b, the 25th percentile (called Q_1 by MINITAB) is Q_L = 35.625 and the 75th percentile (labeled Q_3 by MINITAB) is Q_U = 38.375. Then, IQR = $Q_U - Q_L$ = 2.75 and the ratio is

$$\frac{\text{IRQ}}{s} = \frac{2.75}{2.4} = 1.15$$

Suggested Exercises 5.45

Since this value is approximately equal to 1.3, we have further confirmation that the data are approximately normal.

A fourth descriptive method is to interpret a normal probability plot. An SPSS normal probability plot for the mileage data is shown in Figure 5.17(c). Notice that the ordered mileage values (shown on the horizontal axis) fall reasonably close to a straight line when plotted against the expected z-scores from a normal distribution. Thus, check #4 also suggests that the EPA mileage data are likely to be approximately normally distributed.

Figure 5.17c
SPSS normal probability plot
for gas mileage data

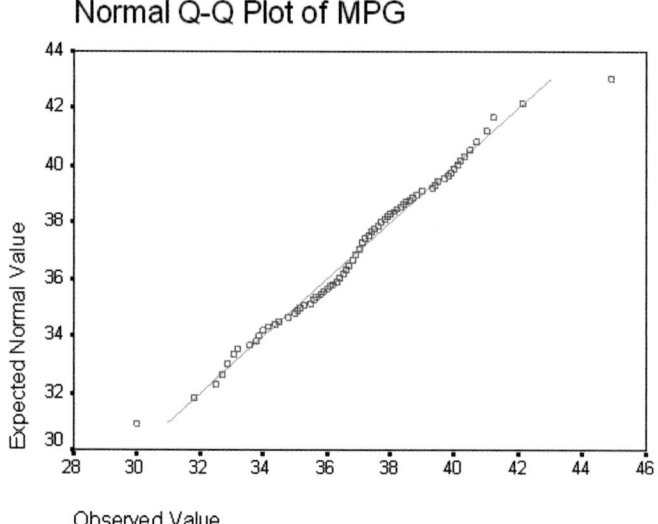

Look Back The checks for normality given in the box are simple, yet powerful, techniques to apply, but they are only descriptive in nature. It is possible (although unlikely) that the data are nonnormal even when the checks are reasonably satisfied. Thus, we should be careful not to claim that the 100 EPA mileage ratings of Example 5.11 are, in fact, normally distributed. We can only state that it is reasonable to believe that the data are from a normal distribution.*

> **Now Work** *Exercise 5.46*

— ∎ ∎ ∎ —

As we will learn in the next chapter, several inferential methods of analysis require the data to be approximately normal. If the data are clearly nonnormal, inferences derived from the method may be invalid. Therefore, it is advisable to check the normality of the data prior to conducting the analysis.

Statistics in Action Revisited

Assessing Whether the Normal Distribution Is Appropriate for Modeling the Super Weapon Hit Data

In Statistics in Action Revisited, Section 5.3, we used the normal distribution to find the probability that a single flechette from a super weapon that shoots 1,100 flechettes at once hits one of three targets at 500 meters. Recall that for three range tests, the weapon was always aimed at the center target (i.e., the specification mean was set at $\mu = 5$ feet), but the specification standard deviation was varied at $\sigma = 1$ foot, $\sigma = 2$ feet,

and $\sigma = 4$ feet. Table SIA5.1 shows the calculated normal probabilities of hitting the three targets for the different values of σ, as well as the actual results of the three range tests. (Recall that the actual data are saved in the MOAGUN file.) You can see that the proportion of the 1,100 flechettes that actually hit each target—called the hit ratio—agrees very well with the estimated probability of a hit using the normal distribution.

---

*Statistical tests of normality that provide a measure of reliability for the inference are available. However, these tests tend to be very sensitive to slight departures from normality (i.e., they tend to reject the hypothesis of normality for any distribution that is not perfectly symmetrical and mound shaped). Consult the references (see Ramsey & Ramsey, 1990) if you want to learn more about these tests.

TABLE SIA5.1   Summary of Normal Probability Calculations and Actual Range Test Results

TARGET	Specification	Normal Probability	Actual Number of Hits	Hit Ratio (Hits/1100)
LEFT (−1 to 1)	$\sigma = 1$	.0000	0	.000
	$\sigma = 2$	.0214	30	.027
	$\sigma = 4$	.0919	73	.066
MIDDLE (4 to 6)	$\sigma = 1$	.6826	764	.695
	$\sigma = 2$	.3820	409	.372
	$\sigma = 4$	.1974	242	.220
RIGHT (9 to 11)	$\sigma = 1$	.0000	0	.000
	$\sigma = 2$	.0214	23	.021
	$\sigma = 4$	.0919	93	.085

Consequently, it appears that our assumption that the horizontal hit measurements are approximately normally distributed is reasonably satisfied. Further evidence of this is provided by the MINITAB histograms of the horizontal hit measurements shown in Figures SIA5.3(a)–(c). The normal curves superimposed on the histograms fit the data very well.

Figure SIA5.3a

MINITAB histogram for the horizontal hit measurements when $\sigma = 1$

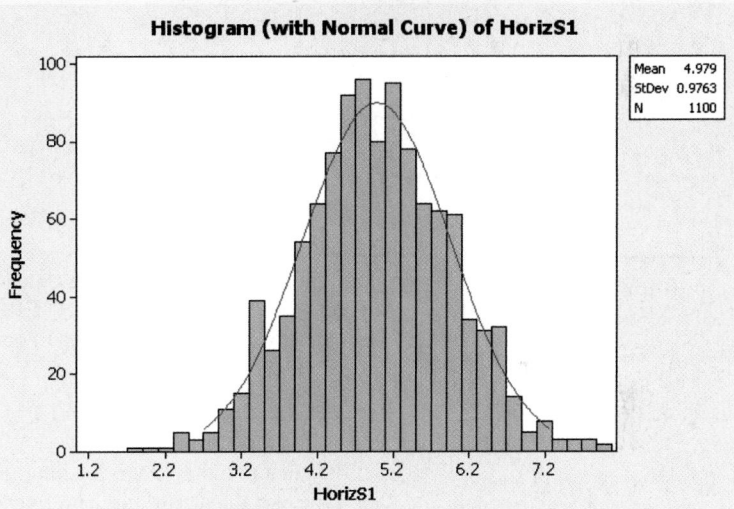

Figure SIA5.3b

MINITAB histogram for the horizontal hit measurements when $\sigma = 2$

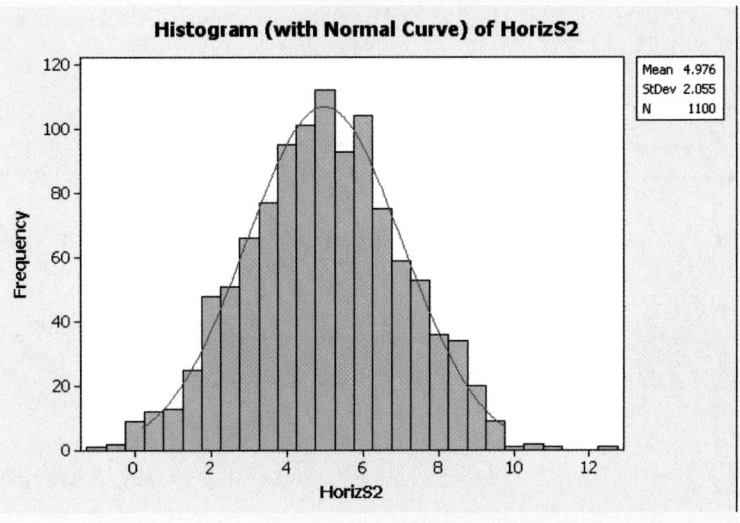

Figure SIA5.3c

MINITAB histogram for the
horizontal hit measurements
when $\sigma = 4$

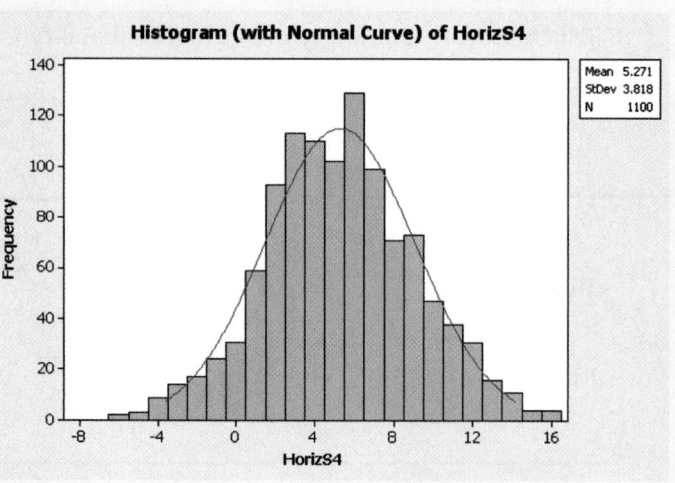

Normal Probability Plot

Using the T1-83 Graphing Calculator

Step 1 *Enter the data*
Press STAT and select 1:Edit
Note: If the list already contains data, clear the old data. Use the up arrow to highlight 'L1'. Press CLEAR ENTER.
Use the arrow and ENTER keys to enter the data set into L1.

Step 2 *Set up the Normal Probability Plot*
Press 2nd and press **Y**= for STAT PLOT
Press 1 for Plot 1
Set the cursor so that ON is flashing.
For Type, use the arrow and Enter keys to highlight and select the last graph in the bottom row.
For Data List, choose the column containing the data (in most cases, L1).
(Note: Press 2nd 1 for L1)
For Data Axis, choose X.

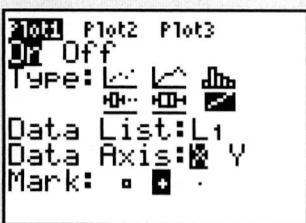

Step 3 *View Plot*
Press ZOOM 9
Your data will be displayed against their expected z-scores from a normal distribution. If you see a "generally" linear relationship, your data are near normal.

Example Using a Normal Probability Plot, test whether or not the data are normally distributed.

9.7	93.1	33.0	21.2	81.4	51.1
43.5	10.6	12.8	7.8	18.1	12.7

The screen below shows the normal probability plot. There is a noticeable curve to the plot, indicating that the data are not normally distributed.

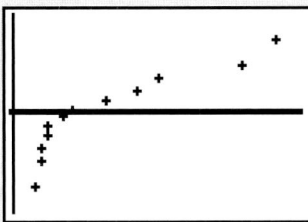

Exercises 5.43–5.53

Learning the Mechanics

5.43 If a population data set is normally distributed, what is the proportion of measurements you would expect to fall within the following intervals?
  a. $\mu \pm \sigma$ .68
  b. $\mu \pm 2\sigma$ .95
  c. $\mu \pm 3\sigma$ 1.00

5.44 Consider a sample data set with the following summary statistics: $s = 95$, $Q_L = 72$, $Q_U = 195$.
  a. Calculate IQR.   123
  b. Calculate IQR/s.   1.295
  c. Is the value of IQR/s approximately equal to 1.3? What does this imply?   Yes

5.45 Normal probability plots for three data sets are shown below. Which plot indicates that the data are approximately normally distributed?   Right plot

5.46 Examine the sample data below.

LM5_46

5.9	5.3	1.6	7.4	8.6	1.2	2.1
4.0	7.3	8.4	8.9	6.7	4.5	6.3
7.6	9.7	3.5	1.1	4.3	3.3	8.4
1.6	8.2	6.5	1.1	5.0	9.4	6.4

  a. Construct a stem-and-leaf plot to assess whether the data are from an approximately normal distribution.
  b. Compute s for the sample data.   2.765
  c. Find the values of Q_L and Q_U and the value of s from part **b** to assess whether the data come from an approximately normal distribution.
  d. Generate a normal probability plot for the data and use it to assess whether the data are approximately normal.

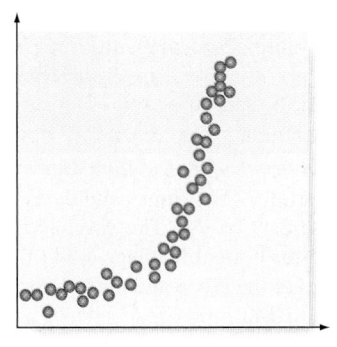

a.

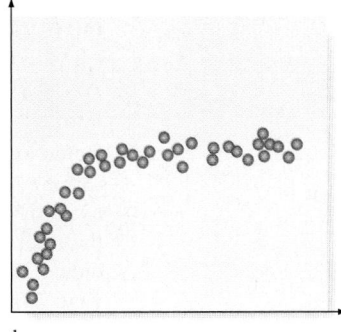

b.

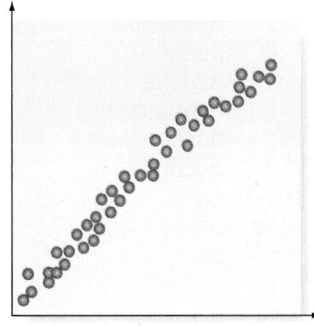

c.

Normal Probability Plots for Exercise 5.45

Descriptive Statistics: AGE

Variable	N	Mean	StDev	Minimum	Q1	Median	Q3	Maximum
AGE	50	49.740	6.124	37.000	46.000	49.000	53.000	71.000

Applying the Concepts—Basic

WPOWER50

5.47 Refer to the *Fortune* (Oct. 14, 2002) list of the 50 most powerful women in America. In Exercise 5.29 (p. 283), you assumed that the ages (in years) of these women are approximately normally distributed. A MINITAB printout with summary statistics for the age distribution is reproduced above.

a. Use the relevant statistics on the printout to find the interquartile range, IQR.

b. Locate the value of the standard deviation, s, on the printout.   6.124

c. Use the results, parts a and b, to demonstrate that the age distribution is approximately normal.

d. In Exercise 2.45c (p. 78) you constructed a relative frequency histogram for the age data. Use this graph to support your assumption of normality.

STLRUNS

5.48 Refer to the *Journal of Statistics Education* study of Mark McGwire's record-breaking 1998 Major League Baseball season, Exercise 2.23 (p. 65). The data on number of runs scored by McGwire's team, the St. Louis Cardinals, in games in which McGwire hit a home run are saved in the **STLRUNS** file. A MINITAB stem-and-leaf display for the data is shown below. Use the graph to assess whether the data are approximately normal.

```
Stem-and-leaf of RUNS   N   = 58
Leaf Unit = 0.10

   2     1    00
   7     2    00000
  15     3    00000000
  20     4    00000
  26     5    000000
 (11)    6    00000000000
  21     7    0000
  17     8    00000000
   9     9    00
   7    10    00
   5    11    00
   3    12
   3    13    0
   2    14    0
   1    15    0
```

Applying the Concepts—Intermediate

BWECS

5.49 Refer to *Business Week's* 2002 "Executive Compensation Scoreboard."

a. In Exercise 5.30 (p. 285), you assumed that return (in dollars) on a $100 investment made in the CEO's company three years earlier is approximately normally distributed. Apply the methods of this chapter to the data saved in the **BWECS** file to support this assumption.

b. Another variable saved in the **BWECS** file is the return-to-pay ratio (i.e., the return on a $100 investment divided by the CEO' total compensation over the 3-year period). Determine whether return-to-pay ratio is approximately normal.   Not normal

DDT

5.50 Refer to the U.S. Army Corps of Engineers data on contaminated fish in the Tennessee River.

a. In Exercise 5.31 (p. 283), you assumed that the weight (in grams) of a captured fish is approximately normally distributed. Apply the methods of this chapter to the data saved in the **DDT** file to support this assumption.

b. Another variable saved in the **DDT** file is the amount of DDT (in parts per million) detected in each fish captured. Determine whether DDT level is approximately normal.   Not normal

CRASH

5.51 Refer to the National Highway Traffic Safety Administration (NHTSA) crash test data for new cars. In Exercise 5.32 (p. 285), you assumed that the driver's head injury rating is approximately normally distributed. Apply the methods of this chapter to the data saved in the **CRASH** file to support this assumption.

SHIPSANIT

5.52 Refer to the data on the May, 2001, sanitation scores for 151 cruise ships, first presented in Exercise 2.77 (p. 93). The data are saved in the **SHIPSANIT** file. Assess whether the sanitation scores are approximately normally distributed.   Not normal

5.53 Refer to the *Journal of Accounting and Public Policy* (Spring 2002) study of first-time candidates for the CPA exam, Exercise 2.49 (p. 79). The variable of interest is the total semester hours of college credit for each candidate. Recall that the mean and median for the data set were 141.31 and 140 hours, respectively, and the standard deviation was 17.77 hours. Demonstrate why the probability distribution for the variable, total semester hours, is unlikely to be normally distributed.

5.5 Approximating a Binomial Distribution with a Normal Distribution

When the discrete binomial random variable (Section 4.4) can assume a large number of values, the calculation of its probabilities may become very tedious. To contend with this problem, we provide tables in Appendix B to give the probabilities for some values of n and p, but these tables are by necessity incomplete. Recall that the binomial probability table (Table II) can be used only for $n = 5, 6, 7, 8, 9, 10, 15, 20$, or 25. To deal with this limitation, we seek approximation procedures for calculating the probabilities associated with a binomial probability distribution.

When n is large, a normal probability distribution may be used to provide a good approximation to the probability distribution of a binomial random variable. To show how this approximation works, we refer to Example 4.11, in which we used the binomial distribution to model the number x of 20 employees who favor unionization. We assumed that 60% of all the company's employees favored unionization. The mean and standard deviation of x were found to be $\mu = 12$ and $\sigma = 2.2$. The binomial distribution for $n = 20$ and $p = .6$ is shown in Figure 5.18, and the approximating normal distribution with mean $\mu = 12$ and standard deviation $\sigma = 2.2$ is superimposed.

Figure 5.18
Binomial distribution for $n = 20, p = .6$ and normal distribution with $\mu = 12, \sigma = 2.2$

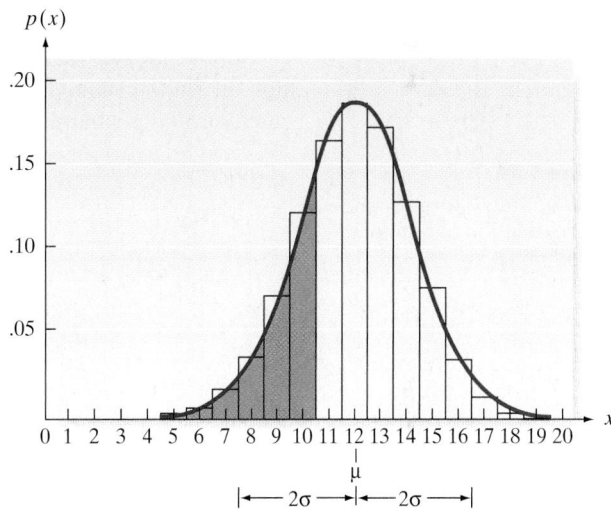

As part of Example 4.11, we used Table II to find the probability that $x \leq 10$. This probability, which is equal to the sum of the areas contained in the rectangles (shown in Figure 5.18) that correspond to $p(0), p(1), p(2), \ldots, p(10)$, was found to equal .245. The portion of the approximating normal curve that would be used to approximate the area $p(0) + p(1) + p(2) + \cdots + p(10)$ is shaded in Figure 5.18. Note that this shaded area lies to the left of 10.5 (not 10), so we may include all of the probability in the rectangle corresponding to $p(10)$. Because we are approximating a discrete distribution (the binomial) with a continuous distribution (the normal), we call the use of 10.5 (instead of 10 or 11) a **correction for continuity.** That is, we are correcting the discrete distribution so that it can be approximated by the continuous one. The use of the correction for continuity leads to the calculation of the following standard normal z value:

$$z = \frac{x - \mu}{\sigma} = \frac{10.5 - 12}{2.2} = -.68$$

Using Table IV, we find the area between $z = 0$ and $z = .68$ to be .2517. Then the probability that x is less than or equal to 10 is approximated by the area under the normal distribution to the left of 10.5, shown shaded in Figure 5.18. That is,

$$P(x \leq 10) \approx P(z \leq -.68) = .5 - P(-.68 < z \leq 0) = .5 - .2517 = .2438$$

The approximation differs only slightly from the exact binomial probability, .245. Of course, when tables of exact binomial probabilities are available, we will use the exact value rather than a normal approximation.

Use of the normal distribution will not always provide a good approximation for binomial probabilities. The following is a useful rule of thumb to determine when n is large enough for the approximation to be effective: *The interval $\mu \pm 3\sigma$ should lie within the range of the binomial random variable* x *(i.e., 0 to n) in order for the normal approximation to be adequate.* The rule works well because almost all of the normal distribution falls within 3 standard deviations of the mean, so if this interval is contained within the range of x values, there is "room" for the normal approximation to work.

As shown in Figure 5.19(a) for the preceding example with $n = 20$ and $p = .6$, the interval $\mu \pm 3\sigma = 12 \pm 3(2.19) = (5.43, 18.57)$ lies within the range 0 to 20. However, if we were to try to use the normal approximation with $n = 10$ and $p = .1$, the interval $\mu \pm 3\sigma$ is $1 \pm 3(.95)$, or $(-1.85, 3.85)$. As shown in Figure 5.19(b), this interval is not contained within the range of x since $x = 0$ is the lower bound for a binomial random variable. Note in Figure 5.19(b) that the normal distribution will not "fit" in the range of x, and therefore it will not provide a good approximation to the binomial probabilities.

Figure 5.19

Rule of thumb for normal approximation to binomial probabilities

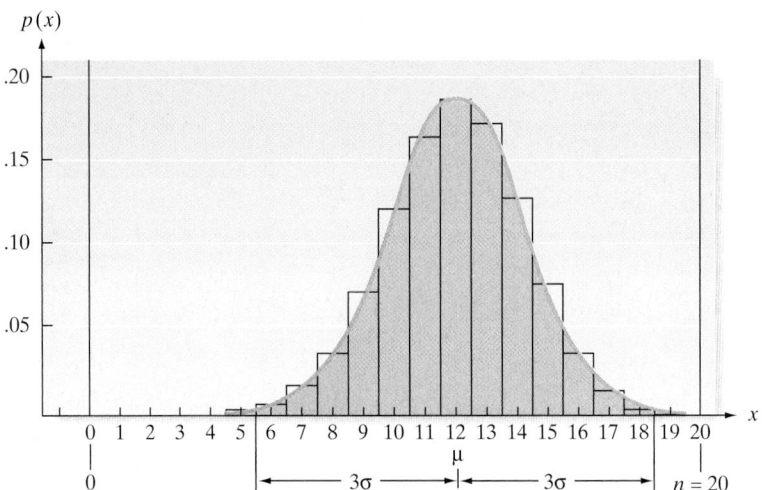

a. $n = 20, p = .6$: Normal approximation is good

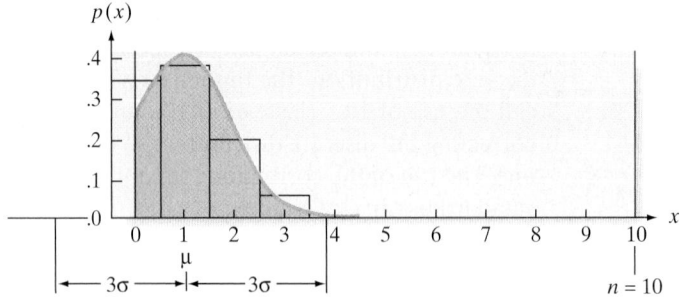

b. $n = 10, p = .1$: Normal approximation is poor

Biography

**ABRAHAM DE MOIVRE
(1667–1754)
Advisor to Gamblers**

French-born mathematician Abraham de Moivre moved to London when he was 21 years old to escape religious persecution. In England, he earned a living first as a traveling teacher of mathematics and then as an advisor to gamblers, underwriters, and annuity brokers. De Moivre's

major contributions to probability theory are contained in two of his books, *The Doctrine of Chances* (1718) and *Miscellanea Analytica* (1730). In these works he defines statistical independence, develops the formula for the normal probability distribution, and derives the normal curve as an approximation to the binomial distribution. Despite his eminence as a mathematician, de Moivre died in poverty. He is famous for predicting the day of his own death using an arithmetic progression.

EXAMPLE 5.12   **APPLYING THE NORMAL APPROXIMATION TO A BINOMIAL PROBABILITY**

Problem One problem with any product (e.g., a graphing calculator) that is mass produced is quality control. The process must somehow be monitored or audited to be sure the output of the process conforms to requirements. One method of dealing with this problem is *lot acceptance sampling*, in which items being produced are sampled at various stages of the production process and are carefully inspected. The lot of items from which the sample is drawn is then accepted or rejected, based on the number of defectives in the sample. Lots that are accepted may be sent forward for further processing or may be shipped to customers; lots that are rejected may be reworked or scrapped. For example, suppose a manufacturer of calculators chooses 200 stamped circuits from the day's production and determines x, the number of defective circuits in the sample. Suppose that up to a 6% rate of defectives is considered acceptable for the process.

$\mu = 12, \sigma = 3.36$

.0129

a. Find the mean and standard deviation of x, assuming the defective rate is 6%.

b. Use the normal approximation to determine the probability that 20 or more defectives are observed in the sample of 200 circuits (i.e., find the approximate probability that $x \geq 20$).

Solution **a.** The random variable x is binomial with $n = 200$ and the fraction defective $p = .06$. Thus,

$$\mu = np = 200(.06) = 12$$

$$\sigma = \sqrt{npq} = \sqrt{200(.06)(.94)} = \sqrt{11.28} = 3.36$$

We first note that

$$\mu \pm 3\sigma = 12 \pm 3(3.36) = 12 \pm 10.08 = (1.92, 22.08)$$

lies completely within the range from 0 to 200. Therefore, a normal probability distribution should provide an adequate approximation to this binomial distribution.

b. Using the rule of complements, $P(x \geq 20) = 1 - P(x \leq 19)$. To find the approximating area corresponding to $x \leq 19$, refer to Figure 5.20. Note that we want to include all the binomial probability histogram from 0 to 19, inclusive. Since the event is of the form $x \leq a$, the proper correction for continuity is $a + .5 = 19 + .5 = 19.5$. Thus, the z value of interest is

$$z = \frac{(a + .5) - \mu}{\sigma} = \frac{19.5 - 12}{3.36} = \frac{7.5}{3.36} = 2.23$$

Figure 5.20

Normal approximation to the binomial distribution with $n = 200, p = .06$

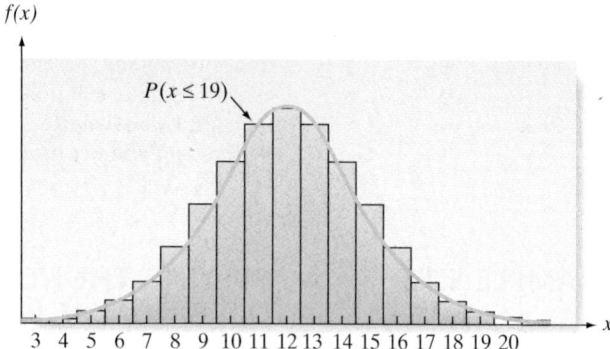

Referring to Table IV in Appendix B, we find that the area to the right of the mean 0 corresponding to $z = 2.23$ (see Figure 5.21) is .4871. So the area $A = P(z \leq 2.23)$ is

$$A = .5 + .4871 = .9871$$

Figure 5.21

Standard normal distribution

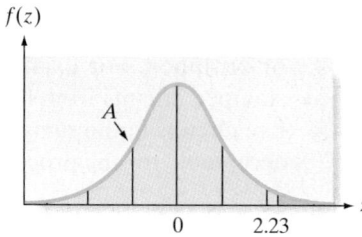

Suggested Exercise 5.62

Thus, the normal approximation to the binomial probability we seek is

$$P(x \geq 20) = 1 - P(x \leq 19) \approx 1 - .9871 = .0129$$

In other words, the probability is extremely small that 20 or more defectives will be observed in a sample of 200 circuits—*if in fact the true fraction of defectives is .06.*

Look Back If the manufacturer observes $x \geq 20$, the likely reason is that the process is producing more than the acceptable 6% defectives. The lot acceptance sampling procedure is another example of using the rare-event approach to make inferences.

Now Work   *Exercise 5.55*

■ ■ ■

The steps for approximating a binomial probability by a normal probability are given in the accompanying box.

Using a Normal Distribution to Approximate Binomial Probabilities

1. After you have determined n and p for the binomial distribution, calculate the interval

$$\mu \pm 3\sigma = np \pm 3\sqrt{npq}$$

If the interval lies in the range 0 to n, the normal distribution will provide a reasonable approximation to the probabilities of most binomial events.

2. Express the binomial probability to be approximated in the form $P(x \le a)$ or $P(x \le b) - P(x \le a)$. For example,

$$P(x < 3) = P(x \le 2)$$
$$P(x \ge 5) = 1 - P(x \le 4)$$
$$P(7 \le x \le 10) = P(x \le 10) - P(x \le 6)$$

3. For each value of interest a, the correction for continuity is $(a + .5)$, and the corresponding standard normal z value is

$$z = \frac{(a + .5) - \mu}{\sigma} \quad \text{(See Figure 5.22)}$$

4. Sketch the approximating normal distribution and shade the area corresponding to the probability of the event of interest, as in Figure 5.22. Verify that the rectangles you have included in the shaded area correspond to the event probability you wish to approximate. Using Table IV and the z value(s) you calculated in step 3, find the shaded area. This is the approximate probability of the binomial event.

Teaching Tip
Explain that the values of μ and σ used for the normal distribution should be the same mean and standard deviation of the binomial distribution that is being approximated. Therefore we use $\mu = np$ and $\sigma^2 = np(1 - p)$.

Figure 5.22
Approximating binomial probabilities by normal probabilities

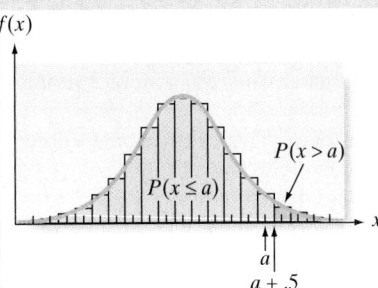

Exercises 5.54–5.68

Learning the Mechanics

5.54 Assume that x is a binomial random variable with n and p as specified in parts a–f. For which cases would it be appropriate to use a normal distribution to approximate the binomial distribution?

a. $n = 100, p = .01$ No
b. $n = 20, p = .6$ Yes
c. $n = 10, p = .4$ No

d. $n = 1,000, p = .05$ Yes
e. $n = 100, p = .8$ Yes
f. $n = 35, p = .7$ Yes

5.55 Suppose x is a binomial random variable with $p = .4$ and $n = 25$.

a. Would it be appropriate to approximate the probability distribution of x with a normal distribution? Explain.   Yes

b. Assuming that a normal distribution provides an adequate approximation to the distribution of x, what are the mean and variance of the approximating normal distribution? $\quad$ 10,6

c. Use Table II of Appendix B to find the exact value of $P(x \geq 9)$. $\quad$ .726

d. Use the normal approximation to find $P(x \geq 9)$ $\quad$ .7291

5.56 Assume that x is a binomial random variable with $n = 25$ and $p = .5$. Use Table II of Appendix B and the normal approximation to find the exact and approximate values, respectively, for the following probabilities:

a. $P(x \leq 11)$ $\quad$ .345, .3446
b. $P(x \geq 16)$ $\quad$ .115, .1151
c. $P(8 \leq x \leq 16)$ $\quad$ .924, .9224

5.57 Assume that x is a binomial random variable with $n = 100$ and $p = .40$. Use a normal approximation to find the following:

a. $P(x \leq 35)$ $\quad$ .1788
b. $P(40 \leq x \leq 50)$ $\quad$ .5236
c. $P(x \geq 38)$ $\quad$ .6950

5.58 Assume that x is a binomial random variable with $n = 1,000$ and $p = .50$. Find each of the following probabilities:

a. $P(x > 500)$ $\quad$ .4880
b. $P(490 \leq x < 500)$ $\quad$ .2334
c. $P(x > 550)$ $\quad$ 0

Applying the Concepts—Basic

5.59 In Exercise 4.46 (p. 237), you learned that 20% of young adults who shop online own a mobile phone with Internet access (*American Demographics*, May 2002.) In a random sample of 200 young adults who shop on-line, let x be the number who own a mobile phone with Internet access.

a. Find the mean of x. (This value should agree with your answer to Exercise 4.46c.) $\quad$ 40
b. Find the standard deviation of x. $\quad$ 5.657
c. Find the z-score for the value $x = 50.5$. $\quad$ 1.86
d. Find the approximate probability that the number of young adults who own a mobile phone with Internet access in a sample of 200 is less than or equal to 50. $\quad$ .9686

5.60 In Exercise 4.47 (p. 237), you learned that 27% of all small businesses owned by non-Hispanic whites nationwide are women-owned firms (*Journal of Business Venturing*, Vol. 17, 2002). In a random sample of 350 small businesses owned by non-Hispanic whites, let x be the number that are owned by a woman.

a. Find the mean of x. $\quad$ 94.5
b. Find the standard deviation of x. $\quad$ 8.306
c. Find the z-score for the value $x = 99.5$. $\quad$ 0.60
d. Find the approximate probability that the number of small businesses in the sample of 350 that are owned by a woman is 100 or more. $\quad$ .2743

5.61 According to *Time* (Oct. 11, 1999), 1% of all patients who undergo laser surgery to correct their vision have serious post-laser vision problems. In a sample of 100,000 patients, what is the approximate probability that fewer than 950 will experience serious postlaser vision problems? $\quad$ .0537

5.62 An article in *The International Journal of Sports Psychology* (July–Sept. 1990) evaluated the relationship between physical fitness and stress. The research revealed that white-collar workers in good physical condition have only a 10% probability of developing a stress-related health problem. What is the probability that more than 60 in a random sample of 400 white-collar employees in good physical condition will develop stress-related illnesses? $\quad$ ≈ 0

Applying the Concepts–Intermediate

5.63 Refer to the FTC study of the pricing accuracy of supermarket electronic scanners, Exercise 4.48 (p. 238). Recall that the probability that a scanned item is priced incorrectly is $^1/_{30} = .033$.

a. Suppose 10,000 supermarket items are scanned. What is the approximate probability that you observe at least 100 items with incorrect prices? $\quad$ 1
b. Suppose 100 items are scanned and you are interested in the probability that fewer than five are incorrectly priced. Explain why the approximate method of part a may not yield an accurate estimate of the probability.

5.64 The computer chips in today's notebook and laptop computers are produced from semiconductor wafers. Certain semiconductor wafers are exposed to an environment that generates up to 100 possible defects per wafer. The number of defects per wafer, x, was found to follow a binomial distribution if the manufacturing process is stable and generates defects that are randomly distributed on the wafers (*IEEE Transactions on Semiconductor Manufacturing*, May 1995). Let p represent the probability that a defect occurs at any one of the 100 points of the wafer. For each of the following cases, determine whether the normal approximation can be used to characterize x.

a. $p = .01$ $\quad$ No
b. $p = .50$ $\quad$ Yes
c. $p = .90$ $\quad$ Yes

5.65 A manufacturer of CD-ROMs claims that 99.4% of its CDs are defect free. A large software company that buys and uses a large number of the CDs wants to verify this claim, so it selects 1,600 CDs to be tested. The tests reveal 12 CDs to be defective. Assuming that the manufacturer's claim is correct, what is the probability of finding 12 or more defective CDs in a sample of 1,600? Does your answer cast doubt on the manufacturer's claim? Explain. $\quad$ .2676; No

5.66 The next table reports the credit card industry's market share data for mid-2003. A random sample of 100 credit card users is to be questioned regarding their satisfaction with their credit card company. For simplification, assume that each credit card user carries just one credit card and that the market share percentages are the percentages of all credit card customers that carry each brand.

Credit Card	Market Share %
Visa	51.4
MasterCard	30.7
American Express	12.3
Discover	5.6

Source: U.S. Payment Card Information Network, June 2003.

a. Propose a procedure for randomly selecting the 100 credit card users.
b. For random samples of 100 credit card users, what is the expected number of customers who carry Visa? Discover? 51.4, 5.6
c. What is the probability that half or more of the sample of credit card users carry Visa? American Express?
d. Justify the use of the normal approximation to the binomial in answering the question in part c.

5.67 The *Chronicle of Higher Education Almanac* reports that the percentage of undergraduates in the United States receiving federal financial aid is 45% at public four-year institutions and 52% at private four-year institutions. The U.S. Department of Education is interested in questioning a random sample of 100 U.S. undergraduate students to assess their satisfaction with federal financial aid procedures and policies.
a. Explain the difficulties of obtaining the desired random sample.
b. Assume the appropriate percentage above applies to your institution. If a random sample of 100 students from your institution were contacted, what is the approximate probability that 50 or more receive financial aid? Less than 25?
c. What assumptions must be made in order to answer part b using the normal approximation to the binomial?

Applying the Concepts—Advanced

5.68 According to *New Jersey Business* (Feb. 1996), Newark International Airport's new terminal handles an average of 3,000 international passengers an hour, but is capable of handling twice that number. Also, 80% of arriving international passengers pass through without their luggage being inspected and the remainder are detained for inspection. The inspection facility can handle 600 passengers an hour without unreasonable delays for the travelers.
a. When international passengers arrive at the rate of 1,500 per hour, what is the expected number of passengers who will be detained for luggage inspection?
b. In the future, it is expected that as many as 4,000 international passengers will arrive per hour. When that occurs, what is the expected number of passengers who will be detained for luggage inspection? 800
c. Refer to part b. Find the approximate probability that more than 600 international passengers will be detained for luggage inspection. (This is also the probability that travelers will experience unreasonable luggage inspection delays.) 1.0

5.6 The Exponential Distribution (Optional)

The length of time between arrivals at a fast-food drive-through restaurant, the length of time between breakdowns of manufacturing equipment, and the length of time between filings of claims in a small insurance office are all business phenomena that we might want to describe probabilistically. The amount of time between occurrences of random events like these can often be described by the **exponential probability distribution.** For this reason, the exponential distribution is sometimes called the **waiting time distribution.** The formula for the exponential probability distribution is shown in the box along with its mean and standard deviation.

Teaching Tip
Using a graph, illustrate how the shape of the exponential distribution changes as the value of θ changes.

> ### Probability Distribution, for an Exponential Random Variable x
>
> Probability density function: $f(x) = \lambda e^{-\lambda x} \quad (x > 0)$
>
> Mean: $\mu = \dfrac{1}{\lambda}$
>
> Standard deviation: $\sigma = \dfrac{1}{\lambda}$

Figure 5.23
Exponential distributions

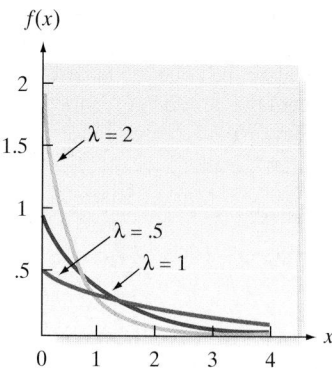

Unlike the normal distribution which has a shape and location determined by the values of the two quantities μ and σ, the shape of the exponential distribution is governed by a single quantity, λ. Further, it is a probability distribution with the property that its mean equals its standard deviation. Exponential distributions corresponding to $\lambda = .5, 1,$ and 2 are shown in Figure 5.23.*

To calculate probabilities for exponential random variables, we need to be able to find areas under the exponential probability distribution. Suppose we want to find the area A to the right of some number a, as shown in Figure 5.24. This area can be calculated by using the formula in the box.

Teaching Tip
Use a transparency of Table V in class to show the students how to arrive at the exponential probabilities.

Finding the Area *A* to the Right of a Number *a* for an Exponential Distribution†

$$A = P(x \geq a) = e^{-\lambda a}$$

Figure 5.24
The area *A* to the right of a number *a* for an exponential distribution

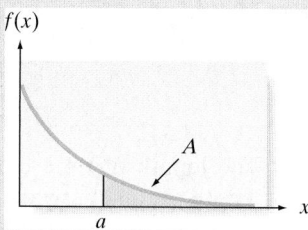

Use Table V in Appendix B or a pocket calculator with an exponential function to find the value of $e^{-\lambda a}$ after substituting the appropriate numerical values for λ and a.

---

*The exponential distribution is related to the discrete Poisson distribution of Section 4.5. If $y =$ the number of occurrences of some event in a unit of time is Poisson with mean λ, then it can be shown (proof omitted) that $x =$ the time of the first occurence of the event has an exponential distribution with mean $\dfrac{1}{\lambda}$.

†For students with a knowledge of calculus, the shaded area in Figure 5.24 corresponds to the integral

$$\int_a^\infty \lambda e^{-\lambda x}\,dx = -e^{-\lambda x}\big|_a^\infty = e^{-\lambda a}$$

EXAMPLE 5.13   FINDING AN EXPONENTIAL PROBABILITY

Problem   Suppose the length of time (in days) between sales for an automobile salesperson is modeled as an exponential distribution with $\lambda = .5$. What is the probability the salesperson goes more than 5 days without a sale?

p = 082085

Solution   The probability we want is the area A to the right of $a = 5$ in Figure 5.25. To find this probability, use the formula given for area:

$$A = e^{-\lambda a} = e^{-(.5)5} = e^{-2.5}$$

Referring to Table V, we find

$$A = e^{-2.5} = .082085$$

Our exponential model indicates that the probability of going more than 5 days without a sale is about .08 for this automobile salesperson.

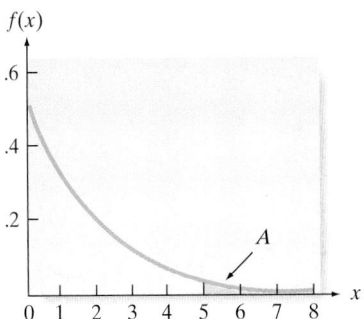

Figure 5.25
Area to the right of $a = 5$ for Example 5.13

Look Back The value $e^{-2.5}$ can also be found using a standard hand calculator. Or, you can find the desired probability using a statistical software package.

| Now Work | *Exercise 5.71*

■ ■ ■

EXAMPLE 5.14   THE MEAN AND VARIANCE OF AN EXPONENTIAL RANDOM VARIABLE

Problem   A microwave oven manufacturer is trying to determine the length of warranty period it should attach to its magnetron tube, the most critical component in the oven. Preliminary testing has shown that the length of life (in years), x, of a magnetron tube has an exponential probability distribution with $\lambda = .16$.

$\mu = \sigma = 6.25$

p = .550671

a. Find the mean and standard deviation of x.

b. Suppose a warranty period of 5 years is attached to the magnetron tube. What fraction of tubes must the manufacturer plan to replace, assuming that the exponential model with $\lambda = .16$ is correct?

p = .950213

c. Find the probability that the length of life of a magnetron tube will fall within the interval $\mu - 2\sigma$ to $\mu + 2\sigma$.

Solution   **a.** For this exponential random variable, $\mu = 1/\lambda = {}^1/_{.16} = 6.25$ years. Also, since $\mu = \sigma, \sigma = 6.25$ years.

b. To find the fraction of tubes that will have to be replaced before the 5-year warranty period expires, we need to find the area between 0 and 5 under the distribution. This area, A, is shown in Figure 5.26.

To find the required probability, we recall the formula

$$P(x > a) = e^{-\lambda a}$$

Using this formula, we can find

$$P(x > 5) = e^{-\lambda(5)} = e^{-(.16)(5)} = e^{-.80}$$
$$= .449329$$

(see Table V). To find the area A, we use the complementary relationship:

$$P(x \leq 5) = 1 - P(x > 5)$$
$$= 1 - .449329 = .550671$$

Figure 5.26
Area to the left of $a = 5$
for Example 5.14

Suggested Exercises 5.78

So approximately 55% of the magnetron tubes will have to be replaced during the 5-year warranty period.

c. We would expect the probability that the life of a magnetron tube, x, falls within the interval $\mu - 2\sigma$ to $\mu + 2\sigma$ to be quite large. A graph of the exponential distribution showing the interval $\mu - 2\sigma$ to $\mu + 2\sigma$ is given in Figure 5.27. Since the point $\mu - 2\sigma$ lies below $x = 0$, we need to find only the area between $x = 0$ and $x = \mu + 2\sigma = 6.25 + 2(6.25) = 18.75$.

This area, P, which is shaded in Figure 5.27, is

$$P = 1 - P(x > 18.75) = 1 - e^{-\lambda(18.75)} = 1 - e^{-(.16)(18.75)} = 1 - e^{-3}$$

Using Table V or a calculator, we find $e^{-3} = .049787$. Therefore, the probability that the life x of a magnetron tube will fall within the interval $\mu - 2\sigma$ to $\mu + 2\sigma$ is

$$P = 1 - e^{-3} = 1 - .049787 = .950213$$

You can see that this probability agrees very well with the Empirical Rule (Table 2.8, p. 87) even though this probability distribution is not mound shaped. (It is strongly skewed to the right.)

Figure 5.27
Area in the interval
$\mu \pm 2\sigma$ for Example 5.14

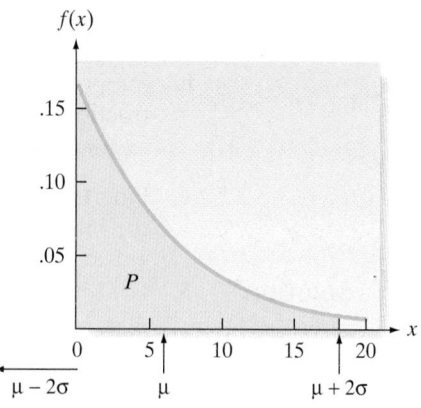

Exercises 5.69–5.84

Learning the Mechanics

5.69 The random variables x and y have exponential distributions with $\lambda = 3$ and $\lambda = .75$, respectively. Using Table V in Appendix B, carefully plot both distributions on the same set of axes.

5.70 Use Table V in Appendix B to determine the value of $e^{-\lambda a}$ for each of the following cases.
   a. $\lambda = 1, a = 1$ .367879
   b. $\lambda = 1, a = 2.5$
   c. $\lambda = 2.5, a = 3$ .000553
   d. $\lambda = 5, a = .3$

5.71 Suppose x has an exponential distribution with $\lambda = 3$. Find the following probabilities:
   a. $P(x > 2)$
   b. $P(x > 1.5)$
   c. $P(x > 3)$
   d. $P(x > .45)$ .259240

5.72 Suppose x has an exponential distribution with $\lambda = 2.5$. Find the following probabilities:
   a. $P(x \le 3)$ .999447
   b. $P(x \le 4)$
   c. $P(x \le 1.6)$
   d. $P(x \le .4)$ .632121

5.73 Suppose the random variable x has an exponential probability distribution with $\lambda = 2$. Find the mean and standard deviation of x. Find the probability that x will assume a value within the interval $\mu \pm 2\sigma$.   .950213

5.74 The random variable x can be adequately approximated by an exponential probability distribution with $\lambda = 1$. Find the probability that x assumes a value
   a. More than 3 standard deviations from μ.   .018316
   b. Less than 2 standard deviations from μ.   .950213
   c. Within .5 standard deviation of μ.   .383401

Applying the Concepts—Basic

5.75 Based on data collected from metal shredders across the nation, the amount x of extractable lead in metal shredder residue has an approximate exponential distribution with a mean of 2.5 milligrams per liter (Florida Shredder's Association).
   a. Find the probability that x is greater than 2 milligrams per liter.   .449329
   b. Find the probability that x is less than 5 milligrams per liter.   .864665

5.76 *Interfaces* (Vol. 21, 1991) described the centralized telephone scheduling system at Lourdes Hospital in Binghamton, New York. The service time x (i.e., the time it takes for a service call to be answered by hospital personnel) has an approximate exponential distribution with a mean of 3.11 minutes.
   a. Find λ for this distribution.   .32154
   b. Find the standard deviation of x.   3.11

   c. Graph the exponential distribution and locate the mean on the graph.
   d. Find the probability that x is greater than 3 minutes.   .3811

5.77 The shelf-life of a product is a random variable that is related to consumer acceptance and, ultimately, to sales and profit. Suppose the shelf life of bread is best approximated by an exponential distribution with mean equal to 2 days. What fraction of the loaves stocked today would you expect to still be salable (i.e., not stale) three days from now?   .223130

Applying the Concepts—Intermediate

5.78 Lack of port facilities or shallow water may require cargo on a large ship to be transferred to a pier using smaller craft. This process may require the smaller craft to cycle back and forth from ship to shore many times. Researchers G. Horne (Center for Naval Analysis) and T. Irony (George Washington University) developed models of this transfer process that provide estimates of ship-to-shore transfer times (*Naval Research Logistics*, Vol. 41, 1994). They modeled the time between arrivals of the smaller craft at the pier using an exponential distribution.
   a. Assume the mean time between arrivals at the pier is 17 minutes. Give the value of λ for this exponential distribution. Graph the distribution. $\lambda = .0588$
   b. Suppose there is only one unloading zone at the pier available for the small craft to use. If the first craft docks at 10:00 A.M. and doesn't finish unloading until 10:15 A.M., what is the probability that the second craft will arrive at the unloading zone and have to wait before docking?   .5862

5.79 University of Michigan researchers B. Wilkinson, N. Diedrich and E. Rothman, and C. Drummond of Indiana-Purdue University in Fort Wayne studied the duration between goals scored by the University of Michigan hockey team during its 40-game, 1996 national championship season. They found that the time-between-scores could be characterized with an exponential distribution with a mean of 10.54 minutes (*Geological Society of America Bulletin*, August 1998).
   a. Find the value of λ for this exponential distribution.
   b. Find the mean and standard deviation for this distribution and interpret each in the context of the problem. $\mu = 10.54, \sigma = 10.54$
   c. Graph this exponential distribution. Locate the mean on the graph.
   d. If Michigan scores with exactly two minutes left in the game, what is the probability they will score again before time runs out?   .1729

5.80 An article in *IEEE Transactions* (Mar. 1990) gave an example of a flexible manufacturing system (FMS) with four machines operating independently. The repair rates for the machines (i.e., the time, in hours, it takes to repair a failed machine) are exponentially distributed with means $\mu_1 = 1, \mu_2 = 2, \mu_3 = .5,$ and $\mu_4 = .5$, respectively.

a. Find the probability that the repair time for machine 1 exceeds one hour.   .367879

b. Repeat part a for machine 2.   .606531

c. Repeat part a for machines 3 and 4.

d. If all four machines fail simultaneously, find the probability that the repair time for the entire system exceeds one hour.   .814046

5.81 In an article published in the *European Journal of Operational Research* (Vol. 21, 1985) the vehicle-dispatching decisions of an airport-based taxi service were investigated. In modeling the system, the authors assumed travel times of successive trips to be independent exponential random variables. Assume $\lambda = .05$.

a. What is the mean trip time for the taxi service?   20

b. What is the probability that a particular trip will take more than 30 minutes?   .22313

c. Two taxis have just been dispatched. What is the probability that both will be gone for more than 30 minutes? That at least one of the taxis will return within 30 minutes?   .049787; .950213

5.82 The importance of modeling machine downtime correctly in simulation studies was discussed in *Industrial Engineering* (Aug. 1990). The paper presented simulation results for a single-machine-tool system with the following properties:

- The interarrival times of jobs are exponentially distributed with a mean of 1.25 minutes.
- The amount of time the machine operates before breaking down is exponentially distributed with a mean of 540 minutes.

a. Find the probability that two jobs arrive for processing at most one minute apart.   .550671

b. Find the probability that the machine operates for at least 720 minutes (12 hours) before breaking down.

Applying the Concepts—Advanced

5.83 For certain types of halogen light bulbs, an old bulb that has been in use for a while tends to have a longer life length than a new bulb. Let x represent the life length

(in hours) of a new halogen light bulb and assume that x has an exponential distribution with $\lambda = .004$. According to *Microelectronics and Reliability* (Jan. 1986), the "life" distribution of x is considered *new better than used* (NBU) if

$$P(x > a + b) \leq P(x > a)P(x > b)$$

Alternatively, a "life" distribution is considered *new worse than used* (NWU) if

$$P(x > a + b) \geq P(x > a)P(x > b)$$

a. Show that when $a = 300$ and $b = 200$ the exponential distribution is both NBU and NWU.

b. Choose any two positive numbers a and b, where $a > 0$ and $b > 0$, and repeat part d.

c. Show that, in general, for any a and b ($a > 0$ and $b > 0$), the exponential distribution with mean $1/\lambda$ is both NBU and NWU. Such a "life" distribution is said to be *new same as used or memoryless*. Explain why.

5.84 *Product reliability* has been defined as the probability that a product will perform its intended function satisfactorily for its intended life when operating under specified conditions. The *reliability function, R(x)*, for a product indicates the probability of the product's life exceeding x time periods. When the time until failure of a product can be adequately modeled by an exponential distribution, the product's reliability function is $R(x) = e^{-\lambda x}$ (Ross, *Stochastic Processes*, 1996). Suppose that the time to failure (in years) of a particular product is modeled by an exponential distribution with $\lambda = .5$.

a. What is the product's reliability function? $e^{-.5x}$

b. What is the probability that the product will perform satisfactorily for at least four years?   .135335

c. What is the probability that a particular product will survive longer than the mean life of the product?

d. If λ changes, will the probability that you calculated in part c change? Explain.   No

e. If 10,000 units of the product are sold, approximately how many will perform satisfactorily for more than five years? About how many will fail within one year?   820.85; 3,934.69

f. How long should the length of the warranty period be for the product if the manufacturer wants to replace no more than 5% of the units sold while under warranty?   36.5 days

Quick Review

Key Terms

Note: Starred (*) items are from the optional sections in this chapter.

Bell curve   267
Bell-shaped distribution   267
Continuous probability distribution   261
Continuous random variable   262

Correction for continuity   293
Exponential distribution*   299
Exponential random variable*   299
Frequency function   262
Normal distribution   268
Normal probability plot   286
Normal random variable   267

Probability density function   262
Randomness distribution*   263
Standard normal distribution   269
Standard normal random variable   269
Uniform distribution*   263
Uniform random variable   263
Waiting time distribution*   299

Key Formulas

Random Variable	Density Function	Mean	Standard Deviation	
Uniform, x*	$f(x) = \dfrac{1}{d-c}$ $(c \le x \le d)$	$\mu = \dfrac{c+d}{2}$	$\sigma = \dfrac{d-c}{\sqrt{12}}$	263
Normal, x	$f(x) = -\dfrac{1}{\sigma\sqrt{2\pi}}e^{-(1/2)[(x-\mu)/\sigma]^2}$	μ	σ	268
Standard Normal, $z = \left(\dfrac{x-\mu}{\sigma}\right)$	$f(z) = \dfrac{1}{\sqrt{2\pi}}e^{-(1/2)z^2}$	$\mu = 0$	$\sigma = 1$	269
Exponential, x*	$f(x) = \lambda e^{-\lambda x}$ $(x > 0)$	$\mu = \dfrac{1}{\lambda}$	$\sigma = \dfrac{1}{\lambda}$	299
Normal Approximation to Binomial	$P(x \le a) = P\left[z \le \dfrac{(a+.5)-\mu}{\sigma}\right]$			297

Language Lab

Symbol	Pronunciation	Description
$f(x)$	f of x	Probability density function for a continuous random variable x
λ	lambda	Parameter for an exponential random varable

Chapter Summary

- Three types of continuous random variables: **uniform**, **normal**, and **exponential**
- **Uniform probability distribution** is a model for continuous random variables that are evenly distributed over a certain interval
- **Normal probability distribution** is a model for continuous random variables that have a bell-shaped curve

- Methods for assessing normality: **histogram, stem-and-leaf display, IQR/s $\approx$ 1.3**, and **normal probability plot**
- Normal distribution can be used to approximate a binomial probability when $\mu \pm 3\sigma$ falls within the interval $(0, n)$.
- **Exponential probability distribution** is a model for continuous random variables that have a waiting time distribution.

Supplementary Exercises 5.85–5.108

Note: Starred (*) exercises refer to the optional sections in this chapter.

Learning the Mechanics

5.85 Find the following probabilities for the standard normal random variable z:

a. $P(z \le 2.1)$ .9821   **b.** $P(z \ge 2.1)$ 0.179
c. $P(z \ge -1.65)$ .9505   **d.** $P(-2.13 \le z \le -.41)$

e. $P(-1.45 \le z \le 2.15)$ .9107   **f.** $P(z \le -1.43)$

*5.86 Assume that x is a random variable best described by a uniform distribution with $c = 10$ and $d = 90$.

a. Find $f(x)$.
b. Find the mean and standard deviation of x.
c. Graph the probability distribution for x and locate its mean and the interval $\mu \pm 2\sigma$ on the graph.
d. Find $P(x \le 60)$.   .625   **e.** Find $P(x \ge 90)$.

f. Find $P(x \le 80)$.   .875

g. Find $P(\mu - \sigma \le x \le \mu + \sigma)$.   .577

h. Find $P(x > 75)$.   .1875

5.87 The random variable x has a normal distribution with $\mu = 75$ and $\sigma = 10$. Find the following probabilities:

a. $P(x \le 80)$ .6915   **b.** $P(x \ge 85)$ .1587

c. $P(70 \le x \le 75)$ .1915   **d.** $P(x > 80)$

e. $P(x = 78)$ 0   **f.** $P(x \le 110)$ 1.0

5.88 Find a z-score, call it z_0, such that

a. $P(z \le z_0) = .5080$ **b.** $P(z \ge z_0) = .5517$

c. $P(z \ge z_0) = .1492$ 1.04

d. $P(z_0 \le z \le .59) = .4773$ $-.69$

5.89 The random variable x has a normal distribution with $\mu = 40$ and $\sigma^2 = 36$. Find a value of x, call it x_0, such that

a. $P(x \ge x_0) = .10$ **b.** $P(\mu \le x < x_0) = .40$

c. $P(x < x_0) = .05$ 30.13   **d.** $P(x \ge x_0) = .40$

e. $P(x_0 \le x < \mu) = .45$ 30.13

5.90 Assume that x is a binomial random variable with $n = 100$ and $p = .5$. Use the normal probability distribution to approximate the following probabilities:

a. $P(x \le 48)$ .3821   **b.** $P(50 \le x \le 65)$

c. $P(x \ge 70)$ 0   **d.** $P(55 \le x \le 58)$ .1395

e. $P(x = 62)$ .0045   **f.** $P(x \le 49 \text{ or } x \ge 72)$

*5.91 Assume that x has an exponential distribution with $\lambda = 3.0$. Find

a. $P(x \le 2)$ **b.** $P(x > 3)$ **c.** $P(x = 1)$ 0

d. $P(x \le 7)$ 1   **e.** $P(4 \le x \le 12)$ .000006

Applying the Concepts—Basic

5.92 All Florida high schools require their students to demonstrate competence in mathematics by scoring 70% or above on the FCAT mathematics achievement test. The FCAT math scores of those students taking the test for the first time are normally distributed with a mean of 77% and a standard deviation of 7.3%. What percentage of students who take the test for the first time will pass the test?

5.93 In baseball, a "no-hitter" is a regulation 9-inning game in which the pitcher yields no hits to the opposing batters. *Chance* (Summer 1994) reported on a study of no-hitters in Major League Baseball (MLB). The initial analysis focused on the total number of hits yielded per game per team for all 9-inning MLB games played between 1989 and 1993. The distribution of hits/9-innings is approximately normal with mean 8.72 and standard deviation 1.10.

a. What percentage of 9-inning MLB games result in fewer than 6 hits?   .68%

b. Demonstrate, statistically, why a no-hitter is considered an extremely rare occurrence in MLB.

5.94 A baseball player's batting average is determined by dividing the player's total number of hits by the total number of official batting attempts. The batting averages of all professional baseball player's are compiled

each year by Major League Baseball. The distribution of batting averages for players in the American League (which uses a designated hitter) and National League (which does not use a designated hitter) are summarized in the table. Both distributions are approximately normal.

	American League	National League
Mean:	$\mu = .268$	$\mu = .262$
Std. Dev:	$\sigma = .031$	$\sigma = .039$

Source: Major League Baseball.

a. Find the probability that an American League player has a batting average of .300 or higher.   .1515

b. Find the probability that a National League player has a batting average of .300 or higher.   .1660

*5.95 The length of time between arrivals at a hospital clinic has an approximate exponential distribution. Suppose the mean time between arrivals for patients at a clinic is 4 minutes.

a. What is the probability that a particular interarrival time (the time between the arrival of two patients) is less than 1 minute?

b. What is the probability that an interarrival time will exceed 10 minutes?

5.96 The net weight per package of a certain brand of corn chips is listed as 10 ounces. The weight actually delivered to each package by an automated machine is a normal random variable with mean 10.5 ounces and standard deviation .2 ounce. Suppose 1,500 packages are chosen at random and the net weights are ascertained. Let x be the number of the 1,500 selected packages that contain at least 10 ounces of corn chips. Then x is a binomial random variable with $n = 1,500$ and $p =$ probability that a randomly selected package contains at least 10 ounces.

a. What is the probability that they all contain at least 10 ounces of corn chips?

b. What is the probability that at least 90% of the packages contain 10 ounces or more? ≈ 1

5.97 The *Statistical Abstract* of the *United States* reports that 25% of the country's households are composed of one person. If 1,000 randomly selected homes are to participate in a Nielsen survey to determine television ratings, find the approximate probability that no more than 240 of these homes are one-person households.   .2451

*5.98 In the National Hockey League (NHL), games that are tied at the end of three periods are sent to "sudden-death" overtime. In overtime, the team to score the first goal wins. An analysis of all NHL overtime games played between 1970 and 1993 showed that the length of time elapsed before the winning goal is scored has an exponential distribution with mean 9.15 minutes (*Chance*, Winter 1995).

a. For a randomly selected overtime NHL game, find the probability that the winning goal is scored in three minutes or less. .279543

b. In the NHL, each period (including overtime) lasts 20 minutes. If neither team scores a goal in overtime, the game is considered a tie. If an NHL game goes into overtime, what is the probability of the game ending in a tie? .1123887

Applying the Concepts—Intermediate

5.99 Refer to the New Jersey Chamber of Commerce/ Rutgers Business School/Arthur Anderson 1998 study of Generation Xers' expectations of their future careers, Exercise 2.78 (p. 95). Recall that a total of 590 GenXers responded to the question: "What is the maximum number of years you expect to spend with any one employer?" The mean response was 18.2 years with a standard deviation of 10.64 years. Demonstrate why the distribution of years for all GenXers who respond is unlikely to be normally distributed.

5.100 A bakery has determined that the number of loaves of its white bread demanded daily has a normal distribution with mean 7,200 loaves and standard deviation 300 loaves. Based on cost considerations, the company has decided that its best strategy is to produce a sufficient number of loaves so that it will fully supply demand on 94% of all days.

a. How many loaves of bread should the company produce? 7,667

b. Based on the production in part **a**, on what percentage of days will the company be left with more than 500 loaves of unsold bread? 45.62%

5.101 The metropolitan airport commission is considering the establishment of limitations on noise pollution around a local airport. At the present time, the noise level per jet takeoff in one neighborhood near the airport is approximately normally distributed with a mean of 100 decibels and a standard deviation of 6 decibels.

a. What is the probability that a randomly selected jet will generate a noise level greater than 108 decibels in this neighborhood? .0918

b. What is the probability that a randomly selected jet will generate a noise level of exactly 100 decibels? 0

c. Suppose a regulation is passed that requires jet noise in this neighborhood to be lower than 105 decibels 95% of the time. Assuming the standard deviation of the noise distribution remains the same, how much will the mean level of noise have to be lowered to comply with the regulation? 4.87 decibels

CLEANAIR

5.102 Refer to the study of 38 Arkansas corporations that were penalized for violating one or more environmental laws, Exercise 2.27 (p. 66). The financial penal-

ties assessed to the companies are saved in the **CLEANAIR** file. Determine whether the financial penalties are approximately normally distributed.

5.103 To help highway planners anticipate the need for road repairs and design future construction projects, data are collected on the estimated volume and weight of truck traffic on specific roadways (*Transportation Planning Handbook*, 1992) using specialized "weigh-in-motion" equipment. In an experiment performed by the Minnesota Department of Transportation involving repeated weighing of a 27,907-pound truck, it was found that the weights recorded by the weigh-in-motion equipment were approximately normally distributed with mean 27,315 and a standard deviation of 628 pounds (Minnesota Department of Transportation). It follows that the difference between the actual weight and recorded weight, the error of measurement, is normally distributed with mean 592 pounds and standard deviation 628 pounds.

a. What is the probability that the weigh-in-motion equipment understates the actual weight of the truck? .8264

b. If a 27,907-pound truck were driven over the weigh-in-motion equipment 100 times, approximately how many times would the equipment overstate the truck's weight? 17.36 times

c. What is the probability that the error in the weight recorded by the weigh-in-motion equipment for a 27,907-pound truck exceeds 400 pounds? .6217

d. It is possible to adjust (or *calibrate*) the weigh-in-motion equipment to control the mean error of measurement. At what level should the mean error be set so the equipment will understate the weight of a 27,907-pound truck 50% of the time? Only 40% of the time? $\mu = 0$; $\mu = -157$

5.104 A. K. Shah published a simple approximation for areas under the normal curve in the *American Statistician* (Feb. 1985). Shah showed that the area A under the standard normal curve between 0 and z is

$$A \approx \begin{cases} z(4.4 - z)/10 & \text{for } 0 \le z \le 2.2 \\ .49 & \text{for } 2.2 < z < 2.6 \\ .50 & \text{for } z \ge 2.6 \end{cases}$$

a. Use the approximation to find
   (i) $P(0 < z < 1.2)$ .384
   (ii) $P(0 < z < 2.5)$ .49
   (iii) $P(z > .8)$ .212
   (iv) $P(z < 1.0)$ .84

b. Find the exact probabilities in part **a**.

c. Shah showed that the approximation has a maximum absolute error of .0052. Verify this for the approximations in part a.

BANKRUPT

5.105 Refer to the *Financial Management* (Spring 1995) study of 49 companies that filed for a prepackaged bankruptcy, Exercise 2.30 (p. 67). The time in bankruptcy (measured in months) for each company is saved in the **BANKRUPT** file. Determine whether the bankruptcy times are approximately normally distributed.

Applying the Concepts—Advanced

5.106 Contrary to our intuition, very reliable decisions concerning the proportion of a large group of consumers favoring a certain product or a certain social issue can be based on relatively small samples. For example, suppose the target population of consumers contains 50 million people and we wish to decide whether the proportion of consumers, p, in the population that favor some product (or issue) is as large as some value, say .2. Suppose you randomly select a sample as small as 1,600 from the 50 million and you observe the number, x, of consumers in the sample who favor the new product. Assuming that $p = .2$, find the mean and standard deviation of x. Suppose that 400 (or 25%) of the sample of 1,600 consumers favor the new product. Why might this sample result lead you to conclude that p (the proportion of consumers favoring the product in the population of 50 million) is at least as large as .2? [*Hint:* Find the values of μ and σ for $p = .2$, and use them to decide whether the observed value of x is unusually large.]

*__5.107__The number of serious accidents in a manufacturing plant has (approximately) a Poisson probability distribution with a mean of two serious accidents per month. [If x, the number of events per unit time, has a Poisson distribution with mean λ, then it can be shown that the time between two successive events has an exponential probability distribution with mean $1/\lambda$.]

a. If an accident occurs today, what is the probability that the next serious accident will not occur within the next month? .135335

b. What is the probability that more than one serious accident will occur within the next month? .594

5.108 The *tolerance limits* for a particular quality characteristic (e.g., length, weight, or strength) of a product are the minimum and/or maximum values at which the product will operate properly. Tolerance limits are set by the engineering design function of the manufacturing operation (Moss, *Applying TQM to Product Design and Development*, 1996). The tensile strength of a particular metal part can be characterized as being normally distributed with a mean of 25 pounds and a standard deviation of 2 pounds. The upper and lower tolerance limits for the part are 30 pounds and 21 pounds, respectively. A part that falls within the tolerance limits results in a profit of $10. A part that falls below the lower tolerance limit costs the company $2; a part that falls above the upper tolerance limit costs the company $1. Find the company's expected profit per metal part produced. $9.65

REFERENCES

Camm, J. D., and Evans, J. R. *Management Science: Modeling, Analysis, and Interpretation.* Cincinnati: South-Western, 1996.

Cowling, A., and James, P. *The Essence of Personnel Management and Industrial Relations.* New York: Prentice Hall, 1994.

Fama, E. F. *Foundations of Finance.* New York: Basic Books, 1976.

Hogg, R. V., and Craig, A. T. *Introduction to Mathematical Statistics*, 5th ed. Upper Saddle River, N. J.: Prentice Hall, 1995.

Lindgren, B. W. *Statistical Theory*, 3rd ed. New York: Macmillan, 1976.

Wackerly, D., Mendenhall, W., and Scheaffer, R. *Mathematical Statistics with Applications*, 6th ed. North Scituate, Mass.: Duxbury, 1999.

Mood, A. M., Graybill, F. A., and Boes, D. C. *Introduction to the Theory of Statistics*, 3rd ed. New York: McGraw-Hill, 1974.

Moss, M. A. *Applying TQM to Product Design and Development.* New York: Marcel Dekker, 1996.

Ramsey, P. P., and Ramsey, P. H. "Simple Tests of Normality in Small Samples." *Journal of Quality Technology*, Vol. 22, 1990.

Render, B., and Heizer, J. *Principles of Operations Management.* Englewood Cliffs, N.J.: Prentice Hall, 1995.

Ross, S. M. *Stochastic Processes*, 2nd ed. New York: Wiley, 1996.

Winkler, R. L., and Hays, W. *Statistics: Probability, Inference, and Decision*, 2nd ed. New York: Holt, Rinehart and Winston, 1975.

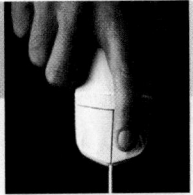

Using Technology

5.1 Cumulative Probabilities for Continuous Random Variables and Normal Probability Plots Using SPSS

To obtain cumulative probabilities for the continuous random variables discussed in this chapter using SPSS, click on the "Transform" button on the SPSS menu bar, then click on "Compute". The resulting dialog box appears as shown in Figure 5.S.1. Specify a name for the "Target Variable" (e.g., the name of the probability you want to find), then select the appropriate probability function in the "Numeric Expression" box. For cumulative probabilities of the exponential, normal, and uniform distributions use the functions CDF.EXP, CDF.NORMAL, and CDF.UNIFORM, respectively. You will need to enter the parameters of each distribution you select.

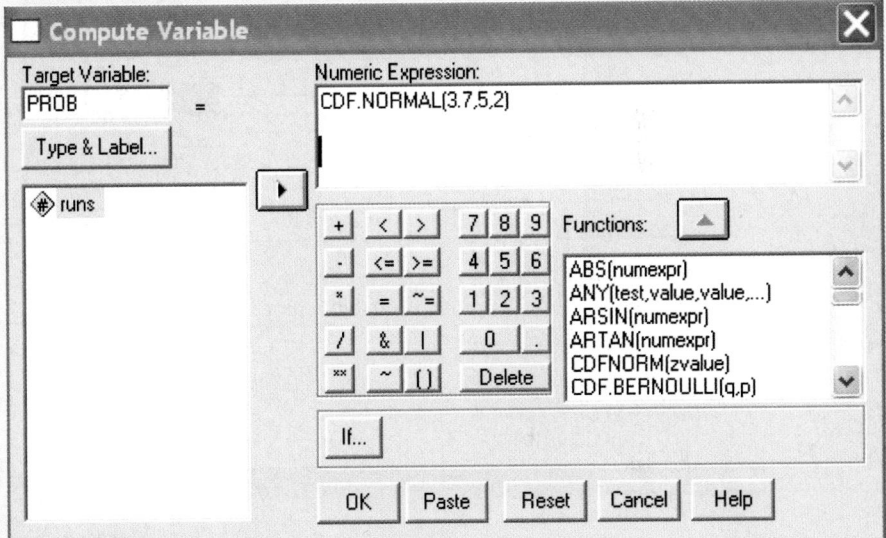

Figure 5.S.1
SPSS compute dialog box

For example, Figure 5.S.1 shows the cumulative normal function with parameters of $x = 3.7$ (the first number in the function), $\mu = 5$ (the second number), and $\sigma = 2$ (the third number). When you click "OK", SPSS will compute the requested probability (in this example, the cumulative normal probability that x is less than 3.7) and display it on the SPSS spreadsheet.

[*Note*: For the exponential function, you will need to enter the value of x and the mean λ. For the uniform function, you will need to enter the value of x, the minimum, and the maximum value of the distribution.]

To obtain a normal probability plot using SPSS, click on the "Graphs" button on the SPSS menu bar, then click on "Q-Q", as shown in Figure 5.S.2. The resulting dialog box appears as shown in Figure 5.S.3. Specify the variable of interest in the "Variables" box, select "Normal" in the "Test Distribution" box, then click "OK" to generate the normal probability plot.

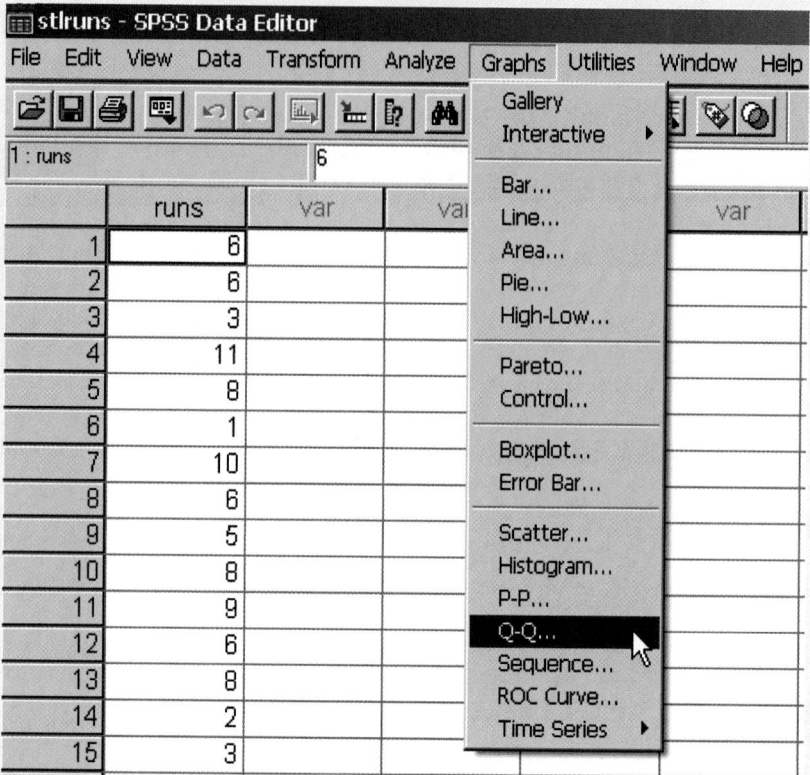

Figure 5.S.2
SPSS options for a normal probability plot

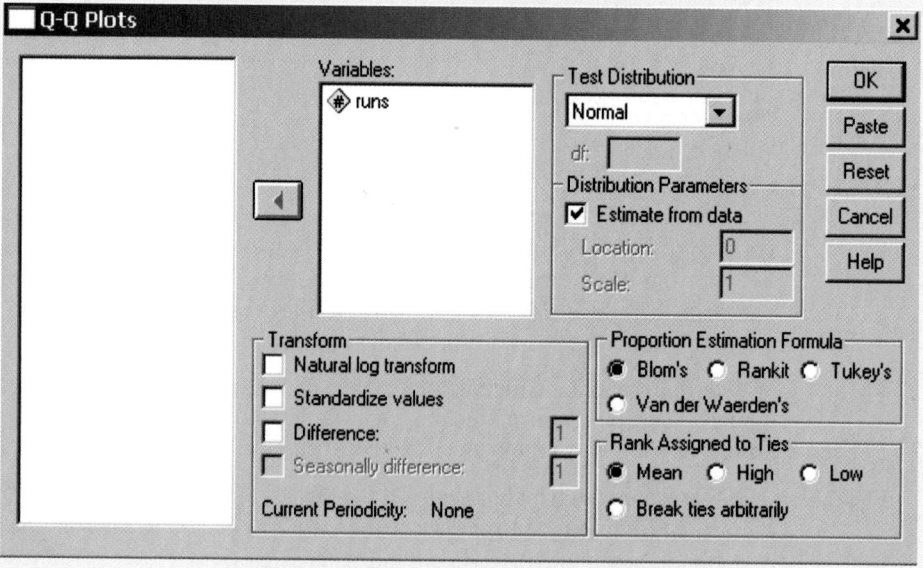

Figure 5.S.3
SPSS normal probability plot dialog box

5.2 Cumulative Probabilities for Continuous Random Variables and Normal Probability Plots Using MINITAB

To obtain cumulative probabilities for the continuous random variables discussed in this chapter using MINITAB, click on the "Calc" button on the MINITAB menu bar, next click on "Probability Distributions", then finally click on the distribution of your choice (e.g., "Normal"), as shown in Figure 5.M.1. The resulting dialog box appears as shown in Figure 5.M.2. Select "Cumulative probability", specify the parameters of the distribution (e.g., the mean μ and standard deviation σ), and enter the value of x in the "Input constant" box. When you click "OK", the cumulative normal probability for the value of x will appear on the MINITAB session window.

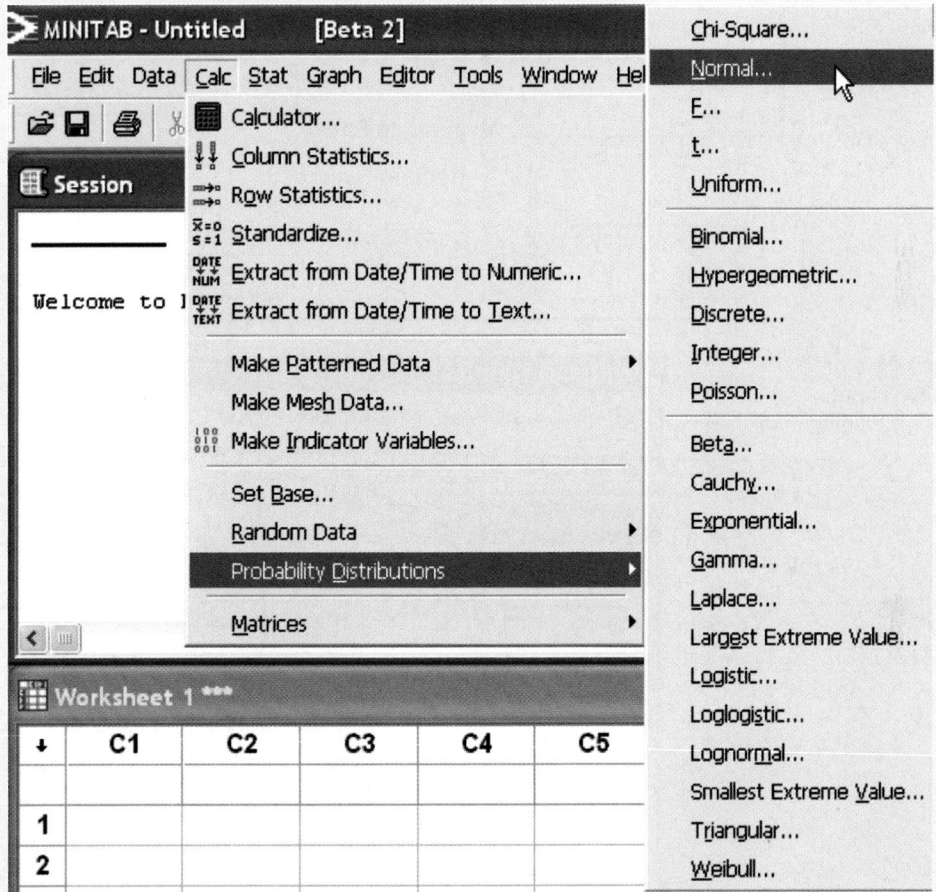

Figure 5.M.1
MINITAB menu options for obtaining probabilities

[*Note:* For the MINITAB exponential option, you will need to enter the value of the mean λ in the resulting dialog box. For the uniform option, you will need to enter the minimum and maximum values of the distribution.]

To obtain a normal probability plot using MINITAB, click on the "Graph" button on the MINITAB menu bar, then click on "Probability Plot", as shown in Figure 5.M.3. Select "Single" (for one variable) on the next box, and the dialog

Figure 5.M.2
MINITAB normal
distribution dialog box

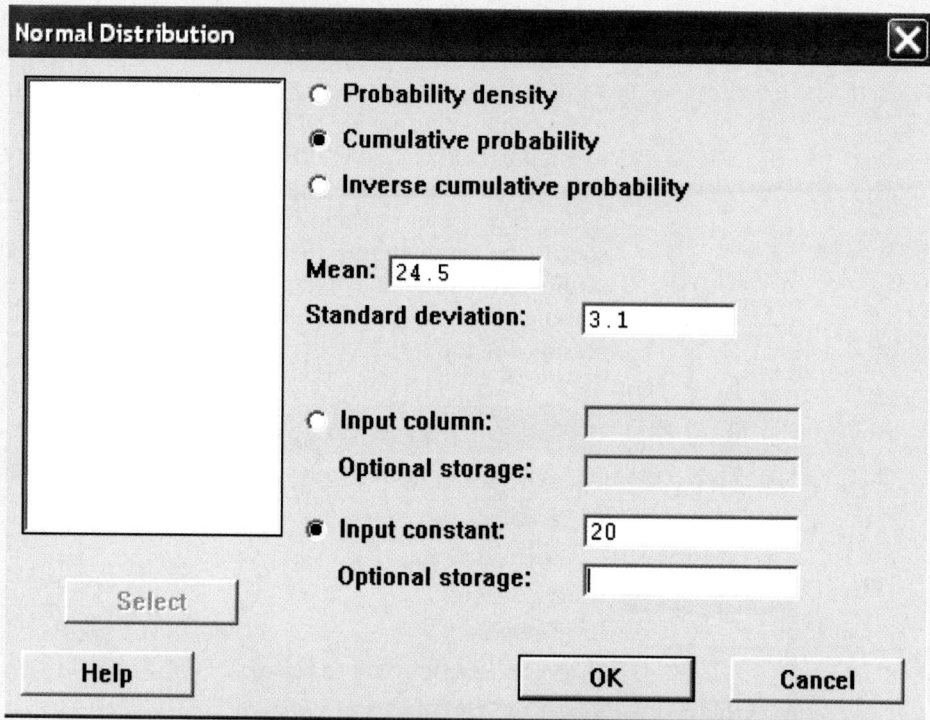

Figure 5.M.3
MINITAB options for a
normal probability plot

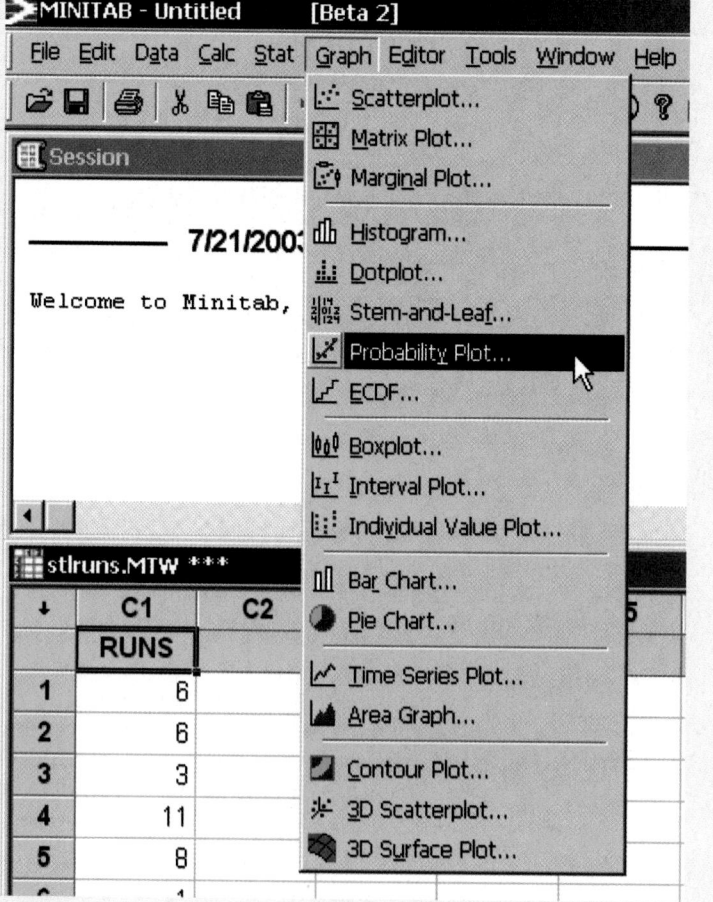

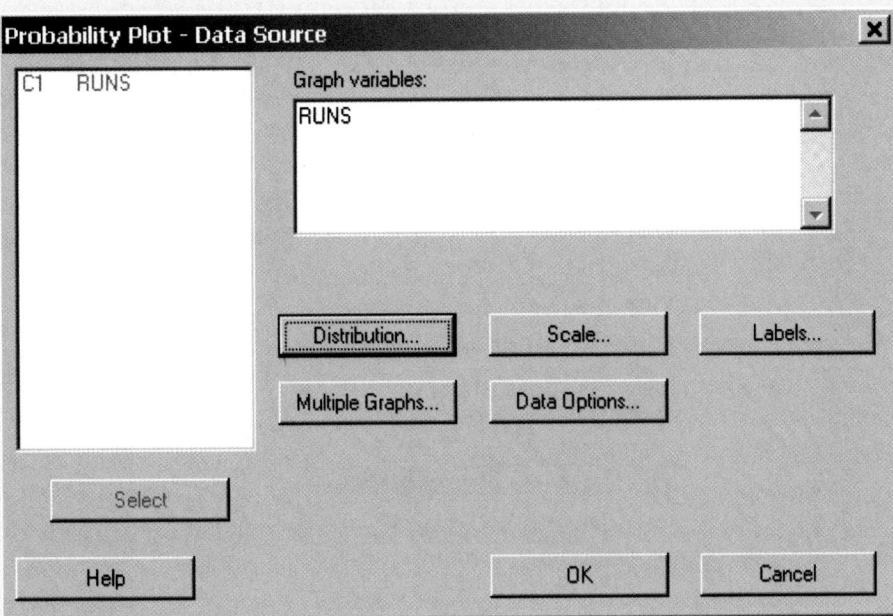

Figure 5.M.4
MINITAB probability plot dialog box

box will appear as shown in Figure 5.M.4. Specify the variable of interest in the "Graph variables" box, then click the "Distribution" button and select the "Normal" option. Click "OK" to return to the Probability Plot dialog box, then click "OK" to generate the normal probability plot.

5.3 Cumulative Probabilities for Continuous Random Variables and Normal Probability Plots Using Excel and PHStat2

To obtain cumulative probabilities for the continuous random variables discussed in this chapter using EXCEL, first enter into a PHStat2 session. Now click on the "PHStat2" button on the main menu bar, next click on "Probability Distributions", then finally click on the distribution of your choice (e.g., "Normal"), as shown in Figure 5.E.1. The resulting dialog box appears as shown in Figure 5.E.2. Specify the parameters of the distribution (e.g., the mean μ and standard deviation σ), click the cumulative probability you desire ($X< =$ or $X>$), and specify the value of x of interest in the box. When you click "OK" the cumulative normal probability for the value of x specified will appear on a new EXCEL workbook.

[*Note*: For the exponential option, you will need to enter the value of the mean λ in the resulting dialog box. Uniform probabilities are not available in EXCEL and PHStat2.]

To obtain a normal probability plot, click on the "PHStat" button on the EXCEL menu bar, select "Probability & Prob. Distributions", then click on "Normal Probability Plot", as shown in Figure 5.E.3. The dialog box will appear as shown in Figure 5.E.4. Specify the cell range for the variable of interest, then click "OK" to generate the normal probability plot.

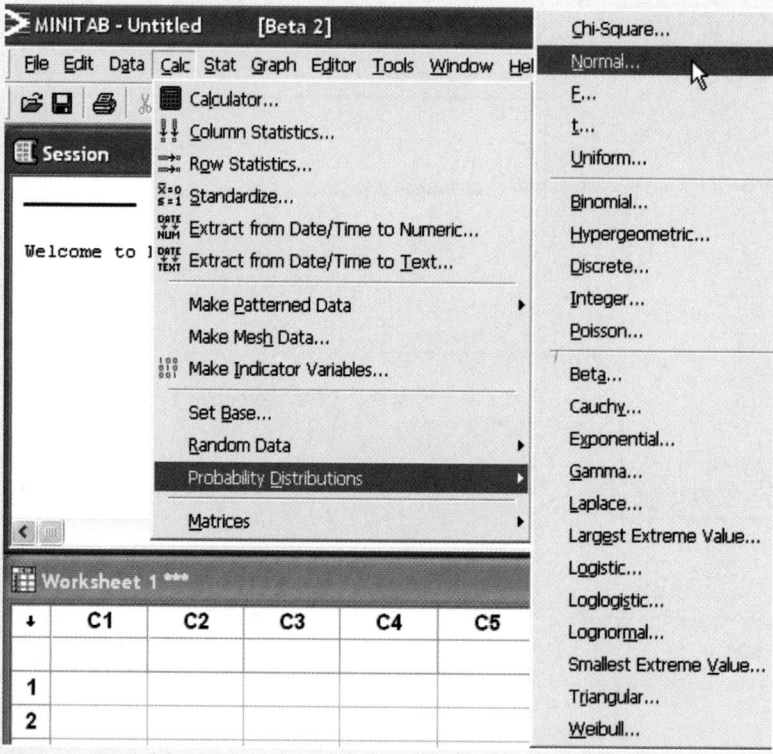

Figure 5.E.1
EXCEL/PHStat2 menu options for obtaining probabilities

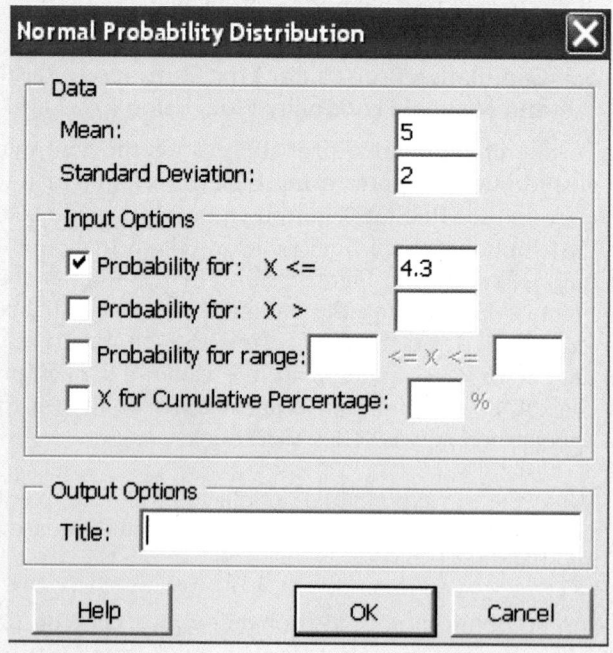

Figure 5.E.2
EXCEL/PHStat2 normal dialog box

Figure 5.E.3
EXCEL/PHStat2
options for a normal
probability plot

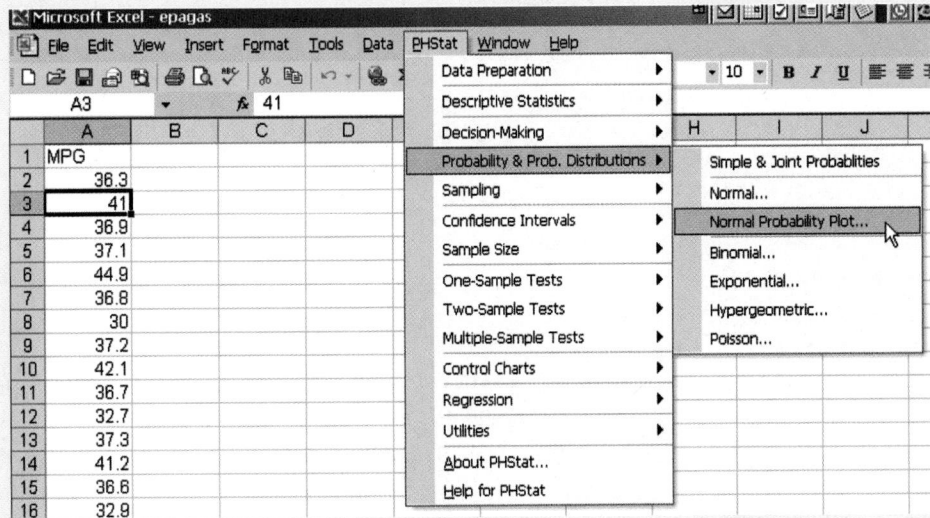

Figure 5.E.4
PHStat2 normal probability
plot dialog box

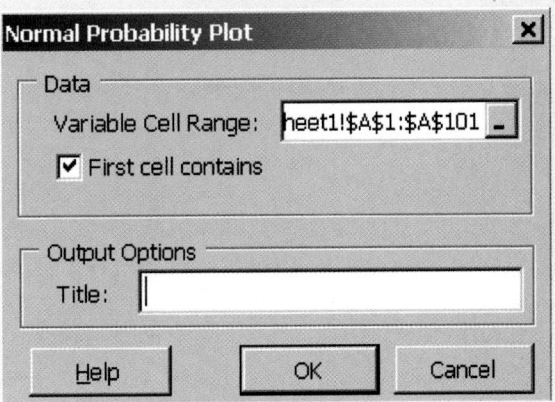

Sampling Distributions

Contents

Statistics in Action

The Insomnia Pill

Using Technology

Where We've Been

- Learned that the objective of most statistical investigations is inference—that is, making decisions about a population based on a sample
- Discovered that sample statistics such as the sample mean and sample variance can be used to make the decisions
- Found that probability distributions for random variables are used to construct theoretical models of populations

Where We're Going

- Establish that a sample statistic is a random variable with a probability distribution.
- Define a *sampling distribution* as the probability distribution of a sample statistic.
- Learn that the sampling distribution of the sample mean tends to be approximately normal.

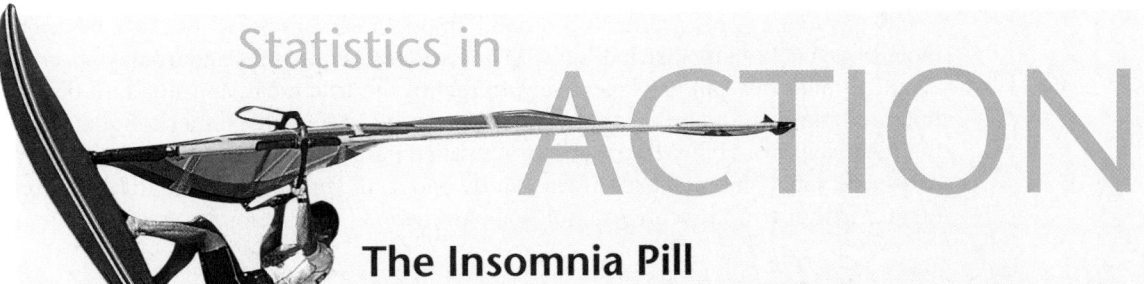

Statistics in ACTION

The Insomnia Pill

A research report published in the *Proceedings of the National Academy of Sciences* (Mar. 1994) brought encouraging news to insomniacs and international business travelers who suffer from jet lag. Neuroscientists at the Massachusetts Institute of Technology (MIT) have been experimenting with melatonin—a hormone secreted by the pineal gland in the brain—as a sleep-inducing hormone. Since the hormone is naturally produced, it is nonaddictive. The researchers believe melatonin may be effective in treating jet lag—the body's response to rapid travel across many time zones so that a daylight–darkness change disrupts sleep patterns.

In the MIT study, young male volunteers were given various doses of melatonin or a placebo (a dummy medication containing no melatonin). Then they were placed in a dark room at midday and told to close their eyes for 30 minutes. The variable of interest was the time (in minutes) elapsed before each volunteer fell asleep.

According to the lead investigator, Professor Richard Wurtman, "Our volunteers fall asleep in five or six minutes on melatonin, while those on placebo take about 15 minutes." Wurtman warns, however, that uncontrolled doses of melatonin could cause mood-altering side effects.

(Melatonin is sold in some health food stores. However, sales are unregulated, and the purity and strength of the hormone are often uncertain.)

Now, consider a random sample of 40 young males, each of whom is given a dosage of the sleep-inducing hormone, melatonin. The times (in minutes) to fall asleep for these 40 males are listed in Table SIA6.1 and saved in the INSOMNIA file. The researchers know that with the placebo (i.e., no hormone), the mean time to fall asleep is $\mu = 15$ minutes and the standard deviation is $\sigma = 10$ minutes. They want to use the data to make an inference about the true value of μ for those taking the melatonin. Specifically, the researchers want to know whether melatonin is an effective drug against insomnia.

In this chapter, a Statistics in Action Revisited example demonstrates how we can use one of the topics discussed in this chapter—the Central Limit Theorem—to make an inference about the effectiveness of melatonin as a sleep-inducing hormone.

Statistics in Action Revisited

- Making an Inference about the Mean Sleep Time for Insomnia Pill Takers (p. 337)

 **INSOMNIA**

TABLE SIA6.1	Times (in Minutes) for 40 Male Volunteers to Fall Asleep								
7.6	2.1	1.4	1.5	3.6	17.0	14.9	4.4	4.7	20.1
7.7	2.4	8.1	1.5	10.3	1.3	3.7	2.5	3.4	10.7
2.9	1.5	15.9	3.0	1.9	8.5	6.1	4.5	2.2	2.6
7.0	6.4	2.8	2.8	22.8	1.5	4.6	2.0	6.3	3.2

[Note: These data are simulated sleep times based on summary information provided in the MIT study.]

In Chapters 4 and 5 we assumed that we knew the probability distribution of a random variable, and using this knowledge we were able to compute the mean, variance, and probabilities associated with the random variable. However, in most practical applications, this information is not available. To illustrate, in Example 4.11 (p. 233) we calculated the probability that the binomial random variable x, the number of 20 polled employees who favor unionization, assumed specific values. To do this, it was necessary to assume some value for p, the proportion of the employees in the population who favor unionization. Thus, for the purposes of illustration, we assumed $p = .6$ when, in all likelihood, the exact value of p would be unknown. In fact, the probable purpose of taking the poll is to estimate p. Similarly, when we modeled the in-city gas mileage of a certain automobile model in Example 5.7 (p. 277), we used the normal probability distribution with an *assumed* mean and standard deviation of 27 and 3 miles per gallon, respectively. In reality, the true mean and standard deviation are unknown quantities that would have to be estimated. Numerical quantities that describe probability distributions are called *parameters*. Thus, p, the probability of a success in a binomial experiment, and μ and σ, the mean and standard deviation of a normal distribution, are examples of parameters.

> **DEFINITION 6.1**
>
> A **parameter** is a numerical descriptive measure of a population. Because it is based on the observations in the population, its value is almost always unknown.

We have also discussed the sample mean $\bar{x}$, sample variance s^2, sample standard deviation s, etc., which are numerical descriptive measures calculated from the sample. We will often use the information contained in these *sample statistics* to make inferences about the parameters of a population.

> **DEFINITION 6.2**
>
> A **sample statistic** is a numerical descriptive measure of a sample. It is calculated from the observations in the sample.

Note that the term *statistic* refers to a *sample* quantity and the term *parameter* refers to a *population* quantity.

Before we can show you how to use sample statistics to make inferences about population parameters, we need to be able to evaluate their properties. Does one sample statistic contain more information than another about a population parameter? On what basis should we choose the "best" statistic for making inferences about a parameter? The purpose of this chapter is to answer these questions.

6.1 The Concept of Sampling Distributions

If we want to estimate a parameter of a population—say, the population mean μ—we could use a number of sample statistics for our estimate. Two possibilities are the sample mean $\bar{x}$ and the sample median m. Which of these do you think will provide a better estimate of μ?

Before answering this question, consider the following example: Toss a fair die, and let x equal the number of dots showing on the up face. Suppose the die is tossed three times, producing the sample measurements 2, 2, 6. The sample mean is $\bar{x} = 3.33$ and the sample median is $m = 2$. Since the population mean of x is $\mu = 3.5$, you can see that for this sample of three measurements, the sample mean $\bar{x}$ provides an estimate that falls closer to μ than does the sample median (see Figure 6.1a). Now suppose we toss the die three more times and obtain the sample measurements 3, 4, 6. The mean and median of this sample are $\bar{x} = 4.33$ and $m = 4$, respectively. This time m is closer to μ (see Figure 6.1b).

This simple example illustrates an important point: Neither the sample mean nor the sample median will *always* fall closer to the population mean. Consequently, we cannot compare these two sample statistics, or, in general, any two sample statistics, on the basis of their performance for a single sample. Instead, we need to recognize that

Figure 6.1
Comparing the sample mean
($\bar{x}$) and sample median (m)
as estimators of the
population mean (μ)

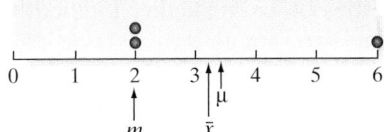

a. Sample 1: $\bar{x}$ is closer than m to μ

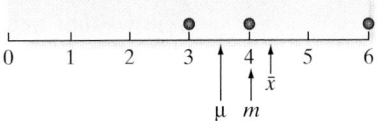

b. Sample 2: m is closer than $\bar{x}$ to μ

sample statistics are themselves random variables, because different samples can lead to different values for the sample statistics. As random variables, sample statistics must be judged and compared on the basis of their probability distributions (i.e., the *collection* of values and associated probabilities of each statistic that would be obtained if the sampling experiment were repeated a *very large number of times*). We will illustrate this concept with another example.

Suppose it is known that the connector module manufactured for a certain brand of pacemaker has a mean length of $\mu = .3$ inch and a standard deviation of .005 inch. Consider an experiment consisting of randomly selecting 25 recently manufactured connector modules, measuring the length of each, and calculating the sample mean length $\bar{x}$. If this experiment were repeated a very large number of times, the value of $\bar{x}$ would vary from sample to sample. For example, the first sample of 25 length measurements might have a mean $\bar{x} = .301$, the second sample a mean $\bar{x} = .298$, the third sample a mean $\bar{x} = .303$, etc. If the sampling experiment were repeated a very large number of times, the resulting histogram of sample means would be approximately the probability distribution of $\bar{x}$. If $\bar{x}$ is a good estimator of μ, we would expect the values of $\bar{x}$ to cluster around μ as shown in Figure 6.2. This probability distribution is called a *sampling distribution* because it is generated by repeating a sampling experiment a very large number of times.

Figure 6.2
Sampling distribution for $\bar{x}$ based
on a sample of $n = 25$ length
measurements

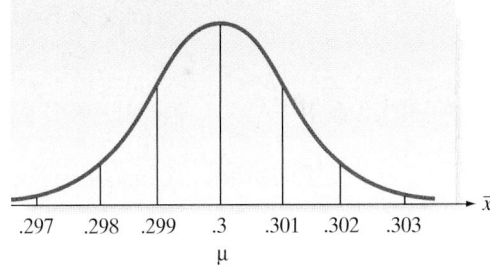

DEFINITION 6.3

The **sampling distribution** of a sample statistic calculated from a sample of n measurements is the probability distribution of the statistic.

In actual practice, the sampling distribution of a statistic is obtained mathematically or (at least approximately) by simulating the sample on a computer using a procedure similar to that just described.

If $\bar{x}$ has been calculated from a sample of $n = 25$ measurements selected from a population with mean $\mu = .3$ and standard deviation $\sigma = .005$, the sampling distribution (Figure 6.2) provides information about the behavior of $\bar{x}$ in repeated sampling. For example, the probability that you will draw a sample of 25 length measurements and obtain a value of $\bar{x}$ in the interval $.299 \le \bar{x} \le .3$ will be the area under the sampling distribution over that interval.

Teaching Tip

Draw pictures of different sampling distributions as they relate to an unknown population parameter. Use the pictures to lay the groundwork for discussing the ideas of unbiased sampling distributions and minimum variance.

Since the properties of a statistic are typified by its sampling distribution, it follows that to compare two sample statistics you compare their sampling distributions. For example, if you have two statistics, A and B, for estimating the same parameter (for purposes of illustration, suppose the parameter is the population variance σ^2) and if their sampling distributions are as shown in Figure 6.3, you would choose statistic A in preference to statistic B. You would make this choice because the sampling distribution for statistic A centers over σ^2 and has less spread (variation) than the sampling distribution for statistic B. When you draw a single sample in a practical sampling situation, the probability is higher that statistic A will fall nearer σ^2.

Figure 6.3

Two sampling distributions for estimating the population variance, σ^2

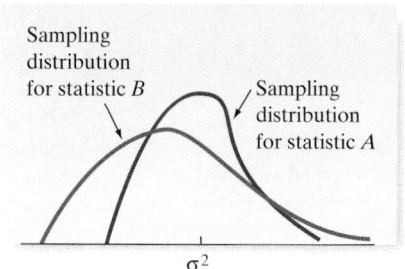

Remember that in practice we will not know the numerical value of the unknown parameter σ^2, so we will not know whether statistic A or statistic B is closer to σ^2 for a sample. We have to rely on our knowledge of the theoretical sampling distributions to choose the best sample statistic and then use it sample after sample. The procedure for finding the sampling distribution for a statistic is demonstrated in Example 6.1.

EXAMPLE 6.1   FINDING A SAMPLING DISTRIBUTION

Problem Consider a population consisting of the measurements 0, 3, and 12 and described by the probability distribution shown here. A random sample of $n = 3$ measurements is selected from the population.

x	0	3	12
$p(x)$	$\frac{1}{3}$	$\frac{1}{3}$	$\frac{1}{3}$

a. Find the sampling distribution of the sample mean $\bar{x}$.

b. Find the sampling distribution of the sample median m.

Solution Every possible sample of $n = 3$ measurements is listed in Table 6.1 along with the sample mean and median. Also, because any one sample is as likely to be selected as any other (random sampling), the probability of observing any particular sample is $\frac{1}{27}$. The probability is also listed in Table 6.1.

a. From Table 6.1 you can see that $\bar{x}$ can assume the values 0, 1, 2, 3, 4, 5, 6, 8, 9, and 12. Because $\bar{x} = 0$ occurs in only one sample, $P(\bar{x} = 0) = \frac{1}{27}$. Similarly, $\bar{x} = 1$ occurs in three samples: (0, 0, 3), (0, 3, 0), and (3, 0, 0). Therefore, $P(\bar{x} = 1) = \frac{3}{27} = \frac{1}{9}$. Calculating the probabilities of the remaining values

TABLE 6.1 All Possible Samples of $n = 3$
Measurements, Example 6.1

Possible Samples	$\bar{x}$	m	Probability
0, 0, 0	0	0	$1/27$
0, 0, 3	1	0	$1/27$
0, 0, 12	4	0	$1/27$
0, 3, 0	1	0	$1/27$
0, 3, 3	2	3	$1/27$
0, 3, 12	5	3	$1/27$
0, 12, 0	4	0	$1/27$
0, 12, 3	5	3	$1/27$
0, 12, 12	8	12	$1/27$
3, 0, 0	1	0	$1/27$
3, 0, 3	2	3	$1/27$
3, 0, 12	5	3	$1/27$
3, 3, 0	2	3	$1/27$
3, 3, 3	3	3	$1/27$
3, 3, 12	6	3	$1/27$
3, 12, 0	5	3	$1/27$
3, 12, 3	6	3	$1/27$
3, 12, 12	9	12	$1/27$
12, 0, 0	4	0	$1/27$
12, 0, 3	5	3	$1/27$
12, 0, 12	8	12	$1/27$
12, 3, 0	5	3	$1/27$
12, 3, 3	6	3	$1/27$
12, 3, 12	9	12	$1/27$
12, 12, 0	8	12	$1/27$
12, 12, 3	9	12	$1/27$
12, 12, 12	12	12	$1/27$

Teaching Tip

Discuss what would happen to the table if $n = 5$ or $n = 10$ observations were sampled from the population.

Teaching Tip

It is helpful to the student to point out that the repeated sampling nature of these problems will provide the necessary information that will be used when we take our one sample later in the book. Emphasize that we will need just one sample.

of $\bar{x}$ and arranging them in a table, we obtain the probability distribution shown here.

$\bar{x}$	0	1	2	3	4	5	6	8	9	12
$p(\bar{x})$	$1/27$	$3/27$	$3/27$	$1/27$	$3/27$	$6/27$	$3/27$	$3/27$	$3/27$	$1/27$

This is the sampling distribution for $\bar{x}$ because it specifies the probability associated with each possible value of $\bar{x}$.

b. In Table 6.1 you can see that the median m can assume one of the three values 0, 3, or 12. The value $m = 0$ occurs in seven different samples. Therefore, $P(m = 0) = 7/27$. Similarly, $m = 3$ occurs in 13 samples and $m = 12$ occurs in seven samples. Therefore, the probability distribution (i.e., the sampling distribution) for the median m is as shown below.

m	0	3	12
$p(m)$	$7/27$	$13/27$	$7/27$

Look Back The sampling distributions of parts a and b are found by first listing all possible distinct values of the statistic, and then calculating the probability of each value.

Now Work   *Exercise 6.1*

■ ■ ■

Example 6.1 demonstrates the procedure for finding the exact sampling distribution of a statistic when the number of different samples that could be selected from the population is relatively small. In the real world, populations often consist of a large number of different values, making samples difficult (or impossible) to enumerate. When this situation occurs, we may choose to obtain the approximate sampling distribution for a statistic by simulating the sampling over and over again and recording the proportion of times different values of the statistic occur. Example 6.2 illustrates this procedure.

EXAMPLE 6.2   SIMULATING A SAMPLING DISTRIBUTION

Problem   Suppose we perform the following experiment over and over again: Take a sample of 11 measurements from the probability distribution shown in Figure 6.4. This distribution, known as the *uniform distribution,* was discussed in optional Section 5.2. Calculate the two sample statistics

Suggested Exercises 6.1

$$\bar{x} = \text{Sample mean} = \frac{\sum x}{11}$$

$$m = \text{Median} = \text{Sixth sample measurement when the 11 measurements}$$

$$\text{are arranged in ascending order}$$

Obtain approximations to the sampling distributions of $\bar{x}$ and m.

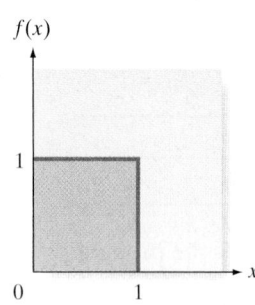

Figure 6.4
Uniform distribution from
0 to 1

Solution   We used MINITAB to generate 1,000 samples, each with $n = 11$ observations. Then we compute $\bar{x}$ and m for each sample. Our goal is to obtain approximations to the sampling distributions of $\bar{x}$ and m to find out which sample statistic ($\bar{x}$ or m) contains more information about μ. [*Note:* In this particular example, we *know* the population mean is $\mu = .5$. (See optional Section 5.2.)] The first 10 of the 1,000 samples generated are presented in Table 6.2. For instance, the first computer-generated sample from the uniform distribution (arranged in ascending order) contained the following measurements: .045, .132, .177, .182, .362, .499, .502, .644, .691, .695, and .860. The sample mean $\bar{x}$ and median m computed for this sample are

$$\bar{x} = \frac{.045 + .132 + \cdots + .860}{11} = .435$$

$$m = \text{Sixth ordered measurement} = .499$$

SIMUNI

TABLE 6.2 First 10 Samples of $n = 11$ Measurements from a Uniform Distribution

Sample	Measurements										
1	.045	.499	.860	.182	.644	.362	.502	.132	.691	.695	.177
2	.529	.918	.357	.156	.357	.965	.935	.515	.675	.662	.755
3	.247	.745	.085	.100	.034	.277	.002	.874	.788	.272	.156
4	.052	.454	.055	.877	.999	.467	.903	.683	.003	.845	.469
5	.082	.744	.614	.364	.882	.878	.527	.193	.186	.928	.175
6	.069	.331	.009	.083	.093	.329	.394	.732	.454	.220	.485
7	.056	.265	.367	.421	.679	.076	.548	.285	.912	.679	.862
8	.856	.528	.350	.340	.583	.785	.412	.581	.342	.022	.595
9	.689	.174	.432	.999	.186	.223	.950	.541	.053	.366	.702
10	.544	.074	.493	.326	.521	.258	.056	.087	.380	.931	.035

Figure 6.5
MINITAB histograms for $\bar{x}$ and m, Example 6.2

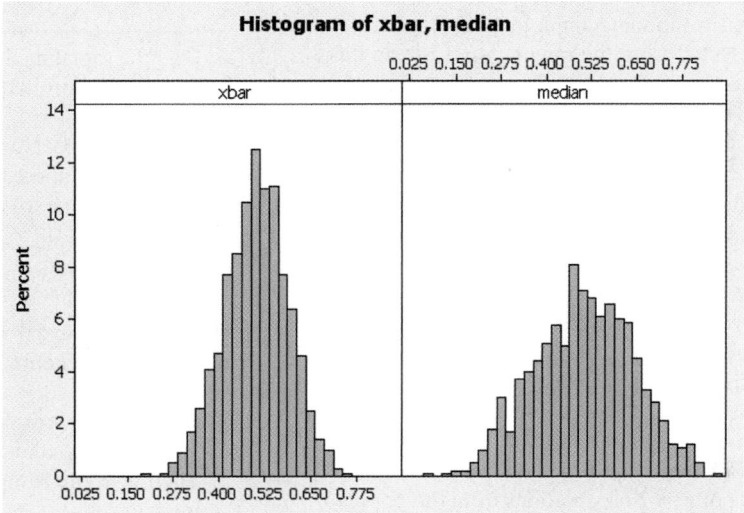

The MINITAB relative frequency histograms for $\bar{x}$ and m for the 1,000 samples of size $n = 11$ are shown in Figure 6.5. These histograms represent approximations to the true sampling distributions of $\bar{x}$ and m.

Look Back You can see that the values of $\bar{x}$ tend to cluster around μ to a greater extent than do the values of m. Thus, on the basis of the observed sampling distributions, we conclude that $\bar{x}$ contains more information about μ than m does—at least for samples of $n = 11$ measurements from the uniform distribution.

Now Work   *Exercise 6.6*

■ ■ ■

As noted earlier, many sampling distributions can be derived mathematically, but the theory necessary to do this is beyond the scope of this text. Consequently, when we need to know the properties of a statistic, we will present its sampling distribution and simply describe its properties. Several of the important properties we look for in sampling distributions are discussed in the next section.

Exercises 6.1–6.7

Learning the Mechanics

6.1 The probability distribution shown here describes a population of measurements that can assume values of 0, 2, 4, and 6, each of which occurs with the same relative frequency:

x	0	2	4	6
$p(x)$	$1/4$	$1/4$	$1/4$	$1/4$

a. List all the different samples of $n = 2$ measurements that can be selected from this population.
b. Calculate the mean of each different sample listed in part a.
c. If a sample of $n = 2$ measurements is randomly selected from the population, what is the probability that a specific sample will be selected?
d. Assume that a random sample of $n = 2$ measurements is selected from the population. List the different values of $\bar{x}$ found in part b, and find the probability of each. Then give the sampling distribution of the sample mean $\bar{x}$ in tabular form.
e. Construct a probability histogram for the sampling distribution of $\bar{x}$.

6.2 Simulate sampling from the population described in Exercise 6.1 by marking the values of x, one on each of four identical coins (or poker chips, etc.). Place the coins (marked 0, 2, 4, and 6) into a bag, randomly select one, and observe its value. Replace this coin, draw a second coin, and observe its value. Finally, calculate the mean $\bar{x}$ for this sample of $n = 2$ observations randomly selected from the population (Exercise 6.1, part b). Replace the coins, mix, and using the same procedure, select a sample of $n = 2$ observations from the population. Record the numbers and calculate $\bar{x}$ for this sample. Repeat this sampling process until you acquire 100 values of $\bar{x}$. Construct a relative frequency distribution for these 100 sample means. Compare this distribution to the exact sampling distribution of $\bar{x}$ found in part e of Exercise 6.1. [*Note:* The distribution obtained in this exercise is an approximation to the exact sampling distribution. But, if you were to repeat the sampling procedure, drawing two coins not 100 times but 10,000 times, the relative frequency distribution for the 10,000 sample means would be almost identical to the sampling distribution of $\bar{x}$ found in Exercise 6.1, part e.]

6.3 Consider the population described by the probability distribution shown below.

x	1	2	3	4	5
$p(x)$	.2	.3	.2	.2	.1

The random variable x is observed twice. If these observations are independent, verify that the different

samples of size 2 and their probabilities are as shown below.

Sample	Probability	Sample	Probability
1, 1	.04	3, 4	.04
1, 2	.06	3, 5	.02
1, 3	.04	4, 1	.04
1, 4	.04	4, 2	.06
1, 5	.02	4, 3	.04
2, 1	.06	4, 4	.04
2, 2	.09	4, 5	.02
2, 3	.06	5, 1	.02
2, 4	.06	5, 2	.03
2, 5	.03	5, 3	.02
3, 1	.04	5, 4	.02
3, 2	.06	5, 5	.01
3, 3	.04		

a. Find the sampling distribution of the sample mean $\bar{x}$.
b. Construct a probability histogram for the sampling distribution of $\bar{x}$.
c. What is the probability that $\bar{x}$ is 4.5 or larger? .05
d. Would you expect to observe a value of $\bar{x}$ equal to 4.5 or larger? Explain. No

6.4 Refer to Exercise 6.3 and find $E(x) = \mu$. Then use the sampling distribution of $\bar{x}$ found in Exercise 6.3 to find the expected value of $\bar{x}$. Note that $E(\bar{x}) = \mu$.

6.5 Refer to Exercise 6.3. Assume that a random sample of $n = 2$ measurements is randomly selected from the population.
a. List the different values that the sample median m may assume and find the probability of each. Then give the sampling distribution of the sample median.
b. Construct a probability histogram for the sampling distribution of the sample median and compare it with the probability histogram for the sample mean (Exercise 6.3, part b).

6.6 In Example 6.2 we use the computer to generate 1,000 samples, each containing $n = 11$ observations, from a uniform distribution over the interval from 0 to 1. For this exercise, use the computer to generate 500 samples, each containing $n = 15$ observations, from this population.
a. Calculate the sample mean for each sample. To approximate the sampling distribution of $\bar{x}$, construct a relative frequency histogram for the 500 values of $\bar{x}$.
b. Repeat part a for the sample median. Compare this approximate sampling distribution with the approximate sampling distribution of $\bar{x}$ found in part a.

6.7 Consider a population that contains values of x equal to 00, 01, 02, 03, ..., 96, 97, 98, 99. Assume that these values of x occur with equal probability. Use the computer to generate 500 samples, each containing $n = 25$ measurements, from this population. Calculate the sample mean $\bar{x}$ and sample variance s^2 for each of the 500 samples.

a. To approximate the sampling distribution of $\bar{x}$, construct a relative frequency histogram for the 500 values of $\bar{x}$.

b. Repeat part a for the 500 values of s^2.

6.2 Properties of Sampling Distributions: Unbiasedness and Minimum Variance (Optional)

The simplest type of statistic used to make inferences about a population parameter is a *point estimator*. A point estimator is a rule or formula that tells us how to use the sample data to calculate a single number that is intended to estimate the value of some population parameter. For example, the sample mean $\bar{x}$ is a point estimator of the population mean μ. Similarly, the sample variance s^2 is a point estimator of the population variance σ^2.

DEFINITION 6.4

A **point estimator** of a population parameter is a rule or formula that tells us how to use the sample data to calculate a single number that can be used as an *estimate* of the population parameter.

Often, many different point estimators can be found to estimate the same parameter. Each will have a sampling distribution that provides information about the point estimator. By examining the sampling distribution, we can determine how large the difference between an estimate and the true value of the parameter (called the **error of estimation**) is likely to be. We can also tell whether an estimator is more likely to overestimate or to underestimate a parameter.

EXAMPLE 6.3   COMPARING TWO STATISTICS

Problem   Consider two statistics, A and B, that estimate the same population parameter, θ (theta). (Note that θ could be any parameter, μ, σ^2, σ, etc.) Suppose the two statistics have sampling distributions as shown in Figure 6.6. Based on these sampling distributions, which statistic is more attractive as an estimator of θ?

Figure 6.6
Sampling distributions
of unbiased and biased
estimators

A is the better estimate

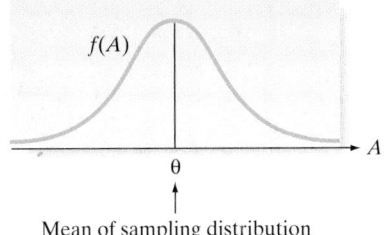
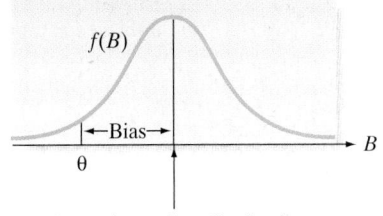

a. Unbiased sample statistic
   for the parameter θ

b. Biased sample statistic
   for the parameter θ

Solution   As a first consideration, we would like the sampling distribution to center over the value of the parameter we wish to estimate. One way to characterize this property is in terms of the mean of the sampling distribution. Consequently, we say that a statistic is *unbiased* if the mean of the sampling distribution is equal to the parameter it is intended to estimate. This situation is shown in Figure 6.6(a), where the mean μ_A of statistic A is equal to θ. If the mean of a sampling distribution is not equal to the parameter it is intended to estimate, the statistic is said to be *biased*. The sampling distribution for a biased statistic is shown in Figure 6.6(b). The mean μ_B of the sampling distribution for statistic B is not equal to θ; in fact, it is shifted to the right of θ. Consequently, we prefer statistic A over statistic B as an estimator of θ.

Look Back You can see that biased statistics tend either to overestimate or to underestimate a parameter. Consequently, when other properties of statistics tend to be equivalent, we will choose an unbiased statistic to estimate a parameter of interest.*

Now Work *Exercise 6.8*

■ ■ ■

DEFINITION 6.5

If the sampling distribution of a sample statistic has a mean equal to the population parameter the statistic is intended to estimate, the statistic is said to be an **unbiased estimate** of the parameter.

If the mean of the sampling distribution is not equal to the parameter, the statistic is said to be a **biased estimate** of the parameter.

The standard deviation of a sampling distribution measures another important property of statistics—the spread of these estimates generated by repeated sampling. Suppose two statistics, A and B, are both unbiased estimators of a population parameter θ. Since the means of the two sampling distributions are the same, we turn to their standard deviations in order to decide which will provide estimates that fall closer to the unknown population parameter we are estimating. Naturally, we will choose the sample statistic that has the smaller standard deviation. Figure 6.7 depicts sampling distributions for A and B. Note that the standard deviation of the distribution of A is smaller than the standard deviation for B, indicating that over a large number of samples, the values of A cluster more closely around θ than do the values of B. Stated differently, the probability that A is close to the parameter value is higher than the probability that B is close to the parameter value.

Figure 6.7
Sampling distributions for two unbiased estimators

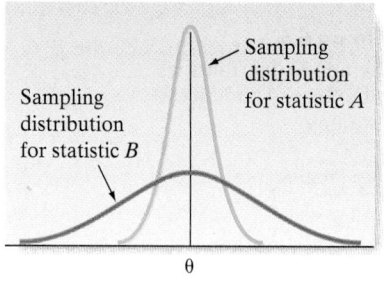

In summary, to make an inference about a population parameter, we use the sample statistic with a sampling distribution that is unbiased and has a small standard deviation (usually smaller than the standard deviation of other unbiased

*Unbiased statistics do not exist for all parameters of interest, but they do exist for the parameters considered in this text.

sample statistics). The derivation of this sample statistic will not concern us, because the "best" statistic for estimating specific parameters is a matter of record. We will simply present an unbiased estimator with its standard deviation for each population parameter we consider. [*Note:* The standard deviation of the sampling distribution of a statistic is also called the *standard error of the statistic.*]

EXAMPLE 6.4   BIASED AND UNBIASED ESTIMATORS

Problem In Example 6.1, we found the sampling distributions of the sample mean $\bar{x}$ and the sample median m for a random sample of $n = 3$ measurements from a population defined by the probability distribution shown here.

x	0	3	12
$p(x)$	$1/3$	$1/3$	$1/3$

The sampling distributions of $\bar{x}$ and m were found to be as shown below.

$\bar{x}$	0	1	2	3	4	5	6	8	9	12
$p(\bar{x})$	$1/27$	$3/27$	$3/27$	$1/27$	$3/27$	$6/27$	$3/27$	$3/27$	$3/27$	$1/27$

m	0	3	12
$p(m)$	$7/27$	$13/27$	$7/27$

a. $E(\bar{x}) = 5 = \mu$

b. $E(m) = 4.52 \neq \mu$

a. Show that $\bar{x}$ is an unbiased estimator of μ in this situation.

b. Show that m is a biased estimator of μ in this situation.

Solution **a.** The expected value of a discrete random variable x (see Section 4.3) is defined to be $E(x) = \Sigma x p(x),$ where the summation is over all values of x. Then

$$E(x) = \mu = \sum x p(x) = (0)(1/3) + (3)(1/3) + (12)(1/3) = 5$$

The expected value of the discrete random variable $\bar{x}$ is

$$E(\bar{x}) = \sum (\bar{x}) p(\bar{x})$$

summed over all values of $\bar{x}$. Or

$$E(\bar{x}) = (0)(1/27) + (1)(1/27) + (2)(1/27) + \cdots + (12)(1/27) = 5$$

Since $E(\bar{x}) = \mu$, we see that $\bar{x}$ is an unbiased estimator of μ.

b. The expected value of the sample median m is

$$E(m) = \sum m p(m) = (0)(7/27) + (3)(13/27) + (12)(7/27) = 4.56$$

Since the expected value of m is not equal to μ ($\mu = 5$), the sample median m is a biased estimator of μ.

Now Work   *Exercise 6.9*

■ ■ ■

EXAMPLE 6.5   VARIANCE OF ESTIMATORS

Problem   Refer to Example 6.4 and find the standard deviations of the sampling distributions of $\bar{x}$ and m. Which statistic would appear to be a better estimator of μ?

$\bar{x}$ is a better estimate than m

Solution   The variance of the sampling distribution of $\bar{x}$ (we denote it by the symbol $\sigma_{\bar{x}}^2$) is found to be

$$\sigma_{\bar{x}}^2 = E\{[\bar{x} - E(\bar{x})]^2\} = \sum (\bar{x} - \mu)^2 p(\bar{x})$$

where, from Example 6.4,

$$E(\bar{x}) = \mu = 5$$

Then

$$\sigma_{\bar{x}}^2 = (0 - 5)^2(^1/_{27}) + (1 - 5)^2(^3/_{27}) + (2 - 5)^2(^3/_{27}) + \cdots + (12 - 5)^2(^1/_{27})$$
$$= 8.6667$$

and

$$\sigma_{\bar{x}} = \sqrt{8.6667} = 2.94$$

Similarly, the variance of the sampling distribution of m (we denote it by σ_m^2) is

Suggested Exercises 6.8

$$\sigma_m^2 = E\{[m - E(m)]^2\}$$

where, from Example 6.4, the expected value of m is $E(m) = 4.56$. Then

$$\sigma_m^2 = E\{[m - E(m)]^2\} = \sum [m - E(m)]^2 p(m)$$
$$= (0 - 4.56)^2(^7/_{27}) + (3 - 4.56)^2(^{13}/_{27}) + (12 - 4.56)^2(^7/_{27}) = 20.9136$$

and

$$\sigma_m = \sqrt{20.9136} = 4.57$$

Which statistic appears to be the better estimator for the population mean μ: the sample mean $\bar{x}$ or the median m? To answer this question, we compare the sampling distributions of the two statistics. The sampling distribution of the sample median m is biased (i.e., it is located to the left of the mean μ) and its standard deviation $\sigma_m = 4.57$ is much larger than the standard deviation of the sampling distribution of $\bar{x}$, $\sigma_{\bar{x}} = 2.94$. Consequently, the sample mean $\bar{x}$ would be a better estimator of the population mean μ, for the population in question, than would the sample median m.

Look Back   Ideally, we desire an estimator that is unbiased *and* has the smallest variance among all unbiased estimators. We call this statistic the **minimum variance unbiased estimator** (**MVUE**).

Now Work   *Exercise 6.10*

■ ■ ■

Exercises 6.8–6.14

Learning the Mechanics

6.8 Consider the probability distribution shown here.

x	0	1	4
$p(x)$	$\frac{1}{3}$	$\frac{1}{3}$	$\frac{1}{3}$

a. Find μ and σ^2. $\mu = 1.667, \sigma^2 = 2.889$

b. Find the sampling distribution of the sample mean $\bar{x}$ for a random sample of $n = 2$ measurements from this distribution.

c. Show that $\bar{x}$ is an unbiased estimator for μ. [*Hint:* Show that $E(\bar{x}) = \Sigma \bar{x} p(\bar{x}) = \mu$.]

d. Find the sampling distribution of the sample variance s^2 for a random sample of $n = 2$ measurements from this distribution.

e. Show that s^2 is an unbiased estimator for σ^2.

6.9 Consider the probability distribution shown here.

x	2	4	9
$p(x)$	$\frac{1}{3}$	$\frac{1}{3}$	$\frac{1}{3}$

a. Calculate μ for this distribution. $\mu = 5$

b. Find the sampling distribution of the sample mean $\bar{x}$ for a random sample of $n = 3$ measurements from this distribution, and show that $\bar{x}$ is an unbiased estimator of μ.

c. Find the sampling distribution of the sample median m for a random sample of $n = 3$ measurements from this distribution, and show that the median is a biased estimator of μ.

d. If you wanted to estimate μ using a sample of three measurements from this population, which estimator would you use? Why?

6.10 Consider the probability distribution shown here.

x	0	1	2
$p(x)$	$\frac{1}{3}$	$\frac{1}{3}$	$\frac{1}{3}$

a. Find μ. $\mu = 1$

$$n = 3$$

b. For a random sample of   observations from this distribution, find the sampling distribution of the sample mean.

c. Find the sampling distribution of the median of a sample of $n = 3$ observations from this population.

d. Refer to parts b and c and show that both the mean and median are unbiased estimators of μ for this population.

e. Find the variances of the sampling distributions of the sample mean and the sample median.

f. Which estimator would you use to estimate μ? Why?

6.11 Use the computer to generate 500 samples, each containing $n = 25$ measurements, from a population that contains values of x equal to $1, 2, \ldots, 48, 49, 50$. Assume that these values of x are equally likely. Calculate the sample mean $\bar{x}$ and median m for each sample. Construct relative frequency histograms for the 500 values of $\bar{x}$ and the 500 values of m. Use these approximations to the sampling distributions of $\bar{x}$ and m to answer the following questions:

a. Does it appear that $\bar{x}$ and m are unbiased estimators of the population mean? [*Note:* $\mu = 25.5$.]

b. Which sampling distribution displays greater variation?

6.12 Refer to Exercise 6.3.

a. Show that $\bar{x}$ is an unbiased estimator of μ.

b. Find $\sigma_{\bar{x}}^2$. $\sigma_{\bar{x}}^2 = .805$

c. Find the probability that $\bar{x}$ will fall within $2\sigma_{\bar{x}}$ of μ.

6.13 Refer to Exercise 6.3.

a. Find the sampling distribution of s^2.

b. Find the population variance σ^2.   1.61

c. Show that s^2 is an unbiased estimator of σ^2.

d. Find the sampling distribution of the sample standard deviation s.

e. Show that s is a biased estimator of σ.

6.14 Refer to Exercise 6.5, where we found the sampling distribution of the sample median. Is the median an unbiased estimator of the population mean μ?

6.3 The Sampling Distribution of $\bar{x}$ and the Central Limit Theorem

Estimating the mean useful life of automobiles, the mean monthly sales for all computer dealers in a large city, and the mean breaking strength of new plastic are practical problems with something in common. In each case we are interested in making an inference about the mean μ of some population. As we mentioned in Chapter 2, the sample mean $\bar{x}$ is, in general, a good estimator of μ. We now develop pertinent information about the sampling distribution for this useful statistic. We will show that $\bar{x}$ is the minimum variance unbiased estimator (MVUE) for μ.

EXAMPLE 6.6   DESCRIBING THE SAMPLING DISTRIBUTION OF $\bar{x}$

Problem   Suppose a population has the uniform probability distribution given in Figure 6.8. The mean and standard deviation of this probability distribution are $\mu = .5$ and $\sigma = .29$. (See optional Section 5.2 for the formulas for μ and σ.) Now suppose a sample of 11 measurements is selected from this population. Describe the sampling distribution of the sample mean $\bar{x}$ based on the 1,000 sampling experiments discussed in Example 6.2.

Figure 6.8
Sampled uniform population

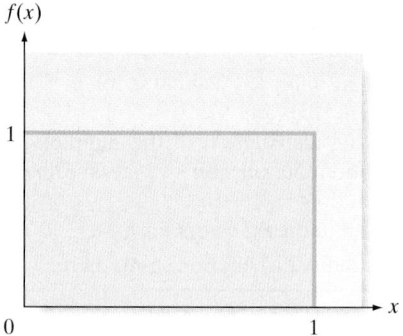

Solution   You will recall that in Example 6.2 we generated 1,000 samples of $n = 11$ measurements each. The MINITAB histogram for the 1,000 sample means is shown in Figure 6.9 with a normal probability distribution superimposed. You can see that this normal probability distribution approximates the computer-generated sampling distribution very well.

Approximately normal with
$\mu_{\bar{x}} = .5$ and $\sigma_{\bar{x}} \approx 1$

Figure 6.9
MINITAB histogram for $\bar{x}$
in 1,000 samples

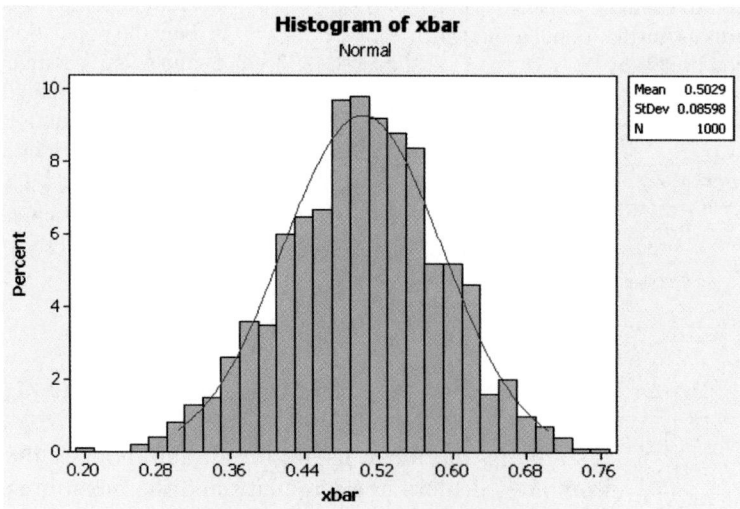

To fully describe a normal probability distribution, it is necessary to know its mean and standard deviation. MINITAB gives these statistics for the 1,000 $\bar{x}$'s in the upper right corner of the histogram, Figure 6.9. You can see that the mean is .503 and the standard deviation is .086.

To summarize our findings based on 1,000 samples, each consisting of 11 measurements from a uniform population, the sampling distribution of $\bar{x}$ appears to be approximately normal with a mean of about .5 and a standard deviation of about .09.

Look Back Note that the simulated value $\mu_{\bar{x}} = .503$ is very close to $\mu = .5$ for the uniform distribution. That is, the simulated sampling distribution of $\bar{x}$ appears to be unbiased for estimating μ.

■ ■ ■

The true sampling distribution of $\bar{x}$ has the properties given in the next box, assuming only that a random sample of n observations has been selected from *any* population.

Properties of the Sampling Distribution of $\bar{x}$

1. Mean of sampling distribution equals mean of sampled population. That is, $\mu_{\bar{x}} = E(\bar{x}) = \mu$.

2. Standard deviation of sampling distribution equals

$$\frac{\text{Standard deviation of sampled population}}{\text{Square root of sample size}}$$

That is, $\sigma_{\bar{x}} = \sigma/\sqrt{n}$.*

The standard deviation $\sigma_{\bar{x}}$ is often referred to as the **standard error of the mean.**

You can see that our approximation to $\mu_{\bar{x}}$ in Example 6.6 was precise, since property 1 assures us that the mean is the same as that of the sampled population: .5. Property 2 tells us how to calculate the standard deviation of the sampling distribution of $\bar{x}$. Substituting $\sigma = .29$, the standard deviation of the sampled uniform distribution, and the sample size $n = 11$ into the formula for $\sigma_{\bar{x}}$, we find

$$\sigma_{\bar{x}} = \frac{\sigma}{\sqrt{n}} = \frac{.29}{\sqrt{11}} = .09$$

Thus, the approximation we obtained in Example 6.6, $\sigma_{\bar{x}} = .086$, is very close to the exact value, $\sigma_{\bar{x}} = .09$. It can be shown (proof omitted) that the value of $\sigma_{\bar{x}}^2$ is the smallest variance among all unbiased estimators of μ— thus, $\bar{x}$ is the MVUE for μ.

What can be said about the shape of the sampling distribution of $\bar{x}$? Two important theorems provide this information.

---

*If the sample size, n, is large relative to the number, N, of elements in the population, (e.g., 5% or more), $\sigma/\sqrt{n}$ must be multiplied by a finite population correction factor, $\sqrt{(N-n)/(N-1)}$. For most sampling situations, this correction factor will be close to 1 and can be ignored.

Teaching Tip

Emphasize that the power of the Central Limit Theorem is that we no longer need to know the distribution of the population. The Central Limit Theorem applies to all types of population distributions.

Theorem 6.1

If a random sample of n observations is selected from a population with a normal distribution, the sampling distribution of $\bar{x}$ will be a normal distribution.

Theorem 6.2 (Central Limit Theorem)

Consider a random sample of n observations selected from a population (*any* population) with mean μ and standard deviation σ. Then, when n is sufficiently large, the sampling distribution of $\bar{x}$ will be approximately a normal distribution with mean $\mu_{\bar{x}} = \mu$ and standard deviation $\sigma_{\bar{x}} = \sigma/\sqrt{n}$. The larger the sample size, the better will be the normal approximation to the sampling distribution of $\bar{x}$. *

Biography

PIERRE-SIMON LAPLACE (1749–1827)
The CLT Originator

As a boy growing up in Normandy, France, Pierre-Simon Laplace attended a Benedictine priory school. Upon graduation, he entered Caen University to study theology. During his two years there he discovered his mathematical talents and began his career as an eminent mathematician. In fact, he considered himself the best mathematician in France. Laplace's contributions to mathematics ranged from introducing new methods of solving differential equations to complex analyses of motions of astronomical bodies. While studying the angles of inclination of comet orbits in 1778, Laplace showed that the sum of the angles were normally distributed. Consequently, he is considered to be the originator of the Central Limit Theorem. (A rigorous proof of the theorem, however, was not provided until the early 1930s by another French mathematician, Paul Levy.) Laplace also discovered Bayes's theorem and established Bayesian statistical analysis as a valid approach to many practical problems of his time.

Thus, for sufficiently large samples the sampling distribution of $\bar{x}$ is approximately normal. How large must the sample size n be so that the normal distribution provides a good approximation for the sampling distribution of $\bar{x}$? The answer depends on the shape of the distribution of the sampled population, as shown by Figure 6.10. Generally speaking, the greater the skewness of the sampled population distribution, the larger the sample size must be before the normal distribution is an adequate approximation for the sampling distribution of $\bar{x}$. For most sampled populations, sample sizes of $n \geq 30$ will suffice for the normal approximation to be reasonable. We will use the normal approximation for the sampling distribution of $\bar{x}$ when the sample size is at least 30.

*Moreover, because of the Central Limit Theorem, the sum of a random sample of n observations, Σx, will possess a sampling distribution that is approximately normal for large samples. This distribution will have a mean equal to $n\mu$ and a variance equal to $n\sigma^2$. Proof of the Central Limit Theorem is beyond the scope of this book, but it can be found in many mathematical statistics texts.

Figure 6.10

Sampling distributions of $\bar{x}$ for different populations and different sample sizes

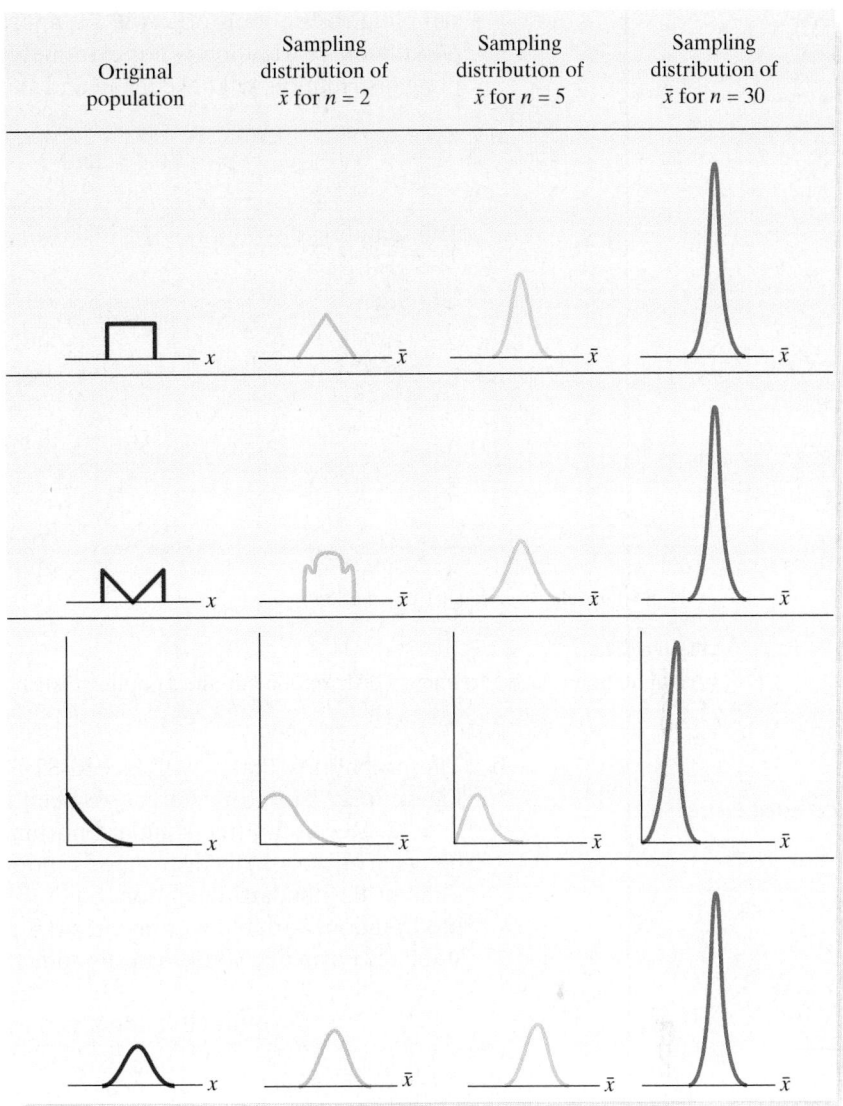

| Original population | Sampling distribution of $\bar{x}$ for $n = 2$ | Sampling distribution of $\bar{x}$ for $n = 5$ | Sampling distribution of $\bar{x}$ for $n = 30$ |

EXAMPLE 6.7

USING THE CENTRAL LIMIT THEOREM TO FIND A PROBABILITY

Problem   Suppose we have selected a random sample of $n = 36$ observations from a population with mean equal to 80 and standard deviation equal to 6. It is known that the population is not extremely skewed.

.0228

a. Sketch the relative frequency distributions for the population and for the sampling distribution of the sample mean, $\bar{x}$.

b. Find the probability that $\bar{x}$ will be larger than 82.

Solution   **a.** We do not know the exact shape of the population relative frequency distribution, but we do know that it should be centered about $\mu = 80$, its spread should be measured by $\sigma = 6$, and it is not highly skewed. One possibility is shown in Figure 6.11(a). From the Central Limit Theorem, we know that the sampling distribution of $\bar{x}$ will be approximately normal since the sampled population distribution is not extremely skewed. We also know that the sampling distribution will have mean and standard deviation

$$\mu_{\bar{x}} = \mu = 80 \quad \text{and} \quad \sigma_{\bar{x}} = \frac{\sigma}{\sqrt{n}} = \frac{6}{\sqrt{36}} = 1$$

The sampling distribution of $\bar{x}$ is shown in Figure 6.11(b).

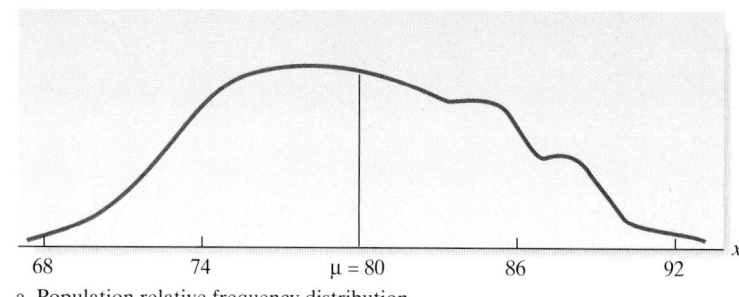

| 68 | 74 | μ = 80 | 86 | 92 |
a. Population relative frequency distribution

77 $\mu_{\bar{x}} = 80$ 83
b. Sampling distribution of $\bar{x}$

Figure 6.11
A population relative frequency distribution and the sampling distribution for $\bar{x}$

Suggested Exercises 6.28

b. The probability that $\bar{x}$ will exceed 82 is equal to the darker shaded area in Figure 6.12. To find this area, we need to find the z value corresponding to $\bar{x} = 82$. Recall that the standard normal random variable z is the difference between any normally distributed random variable and its mean, expressed in units of its standard deviation. Since $\bar{x}$ is approximately a normally distributed random variable with mean $\mu_{\bar{x}} = \mu$ and $\sigma_{\bar{x}} = \sigma/\sqrt{n}$, it follows that the standard normal z value corresponding to the sample mean, $\bar{x}$, is

$$z = \frac{(\text{Normal random variable}) - (\text{Mean})}{\text{Standard deviation}} = \frac{\bar{x} - \mu_{\bar{x}}}{\sigma_{\bar{x}}}$$

Therefore, for $\bar{x} = 82$, we have

$$z = \frac{\bar{x} - \mu_{\bar{x}}}{\sigma_{\bar{x}}} = \frac{82 - 80}{1} = 2$$

The area A in Figure 6.12 corresponding to $z = 2$ is given in the table of areas under the normal curve (see Table IV of Appendix B) as .4772. Therefore, the tail area corresponding to the probability that $\bar{x}$ exceeds 82 is

Figure 6.12
The sampling distribution of $\bar{x}$

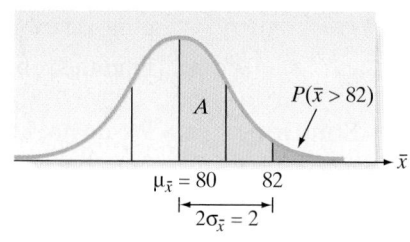

A

$P(\bar{x} > 82)$

$\mu_{\bar{x}} = 80$ 82

$2\sigma_{\bar{x}} = 2$

$$P(\bar{x} > 82) = P(z > 2) = .5 - .4772 = .0228$$

Look Back The key to finding the probability, part b, is to recognize that the distribution of $\bar{x}$ is normal with mean $\mu_{\bar{x}} = \mu$ and $\sigma_{\bar{x}} = \sigma/\sqrt{n}$.

Now Work   *Exercises 6.19–6.20*

■ ■ ■

EXAMPLE 6.8

A PRACTICAL APPLICATION OF THE CENTRAL LIMIT THEOREM

Problem   A manufacturer of automobile batteries claims that the distribution of the lengths of life of its best battery has a mean of 54 months and a standard deviation of 6 months. Suppose a consumer group decides to check the claim by purchasing a sample of 50 of these batteries and subjecting them to tests that determine battery life.

Approximately normal with $\mu_{\bar{x}} = 54$ and $\sigma_{\bar{x}} = .85$

.0094

a. Assuming that the manufacturer's claim is true, describe the sampling distribution of the mean lifetime of a sample of 50 batteries.

b. Assuming that the manufacturer's claim is true, what is the probability the consumer group's sample has a mean life of 52 or fewer months?

Solution   **a.** Even though we have no information about the shape of the probability distribution of the lives of the batteries, we can use the Central Limit Theorem to deduce that the sampling distribution for a sample mean lifetime of 50 batteries is approximately normally distributed. Furthermore, the mean of this sampling distribution is the same as the mean of the sampled population, which is $\mu = 54$ months according to the manufacturer's claim. Finally, the standard deviation of the sampling distribution is given by

Teaching Tip

Compare the sampling distribution here with the normal distribution from Chapter 5 to illustrate the difference in the standard deviation that is used.

$$\sigma_{\bar{x}} = \frac{\sigma}{\sqrt{n}} = \frac{6}{\sqrt{50}} = .85 \text{ month}$$

Note that we used the claimed standard deviation of the sampled population, $\sigma = 6$ months. Thus, if we assume that the claim is true, the sampling distribution for the mean life of the 50 batteries sampled is as shown in Figure 6.13.

Figure 6.13
Sampling distribution of $\bar{x}$ in Example 6.8 for $n = 50$

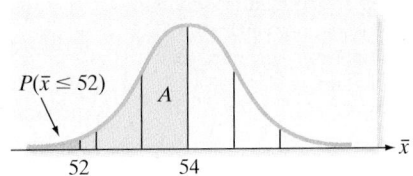

b. If the manufacturer's claim is true, the probability that the consumer group observes a mean battery life of 52 or fewer months for their sample of 50 batteries, $P(\bar{x} \leq 52)$, is equivalent to the darker shaded area in Figure 6.13. Since the sampling distribution is approximately normal, we can find this area by computing the standard normal z value:

Teaching Tip

Students often have trouble working with the denominator of the z-score. Emphasize that we must divide by the standard deviation of the sampling distribution, not the standard deviation of the population.

$$z = \frac{\bar{x} - \mu_{\bar{x}}}{\sigma_{\bar{x}}} = \frac{52 - 54}{.85} = -2.35$$

where $\mu_{\bar{x}}$, the mean of the sampling distribution of $\bar{x}$, is equal to μ, the mean of the lives of the sampled population, and $\sigma_{\bar{x}}$ is the standard deviation of the sampling distribution of $\bar{x}$. Note that z is the familiar standardized distance (z-score) of Section 2.7 and, since $\bar{x}$ is approximately normally distributed, it will possess (approximately) the standard normal distribution of Section 5.3.

The area A shown in Figure 6.13 between $\bar{x} = 52$ and $\bar{x} = 54$ (corresponding to $z = -2.35$) is found in Table IV of Appendix B to be .4906. Therefore, the area to the left of $\bar{x} = 52$ is

$$P(\bar{x} \le 52) = .5 - A = .5 - .4906 = .0094$$

Thus, the probability the consumer group will observe a sample mean of 52 or less is only .0094 if the manufacturer's claim is true.

Teaching Tip

Draw a picture of the population distribution overlaid with the sampling distribution of the sample mean. Show that they are both centered at the same location, but the sampling distribution has much less spread than the population.

Look Back If the 50 tested batteries do exhibit a mean of 52 or fewer months, the consumer group will have strong evidence that the manufacturer's claim is untrue, because such an event is very unlikely to occur if the claim is true. (This is still another application of the *rare-event approach to statistical inference*.)

Now Work *Exercise 6.24*

■ ■ ■

We conclude this section with two final comments on the sampling distribution of $\bar{x}$. First, from the formula $\sigma_{\bar{x}} = \sigma/\sqrt{n}$, we see that the standard deviation of the sampling distribution of $\bar{x}$ gets smaller as the sample size n gets larger. For example, we computed $\sigma_{\bar{x}} = .85$ when $n = 50$ in Example 6.8. However, for $n = 100$ we obtain $\sigma_{\bar{x}} = \sigma/\sqrt{n} = 6/\sqrt{100} = .60$. This relationship will hold true for most of the sample statistics encountered in this text. That is, *the standard deviation of the sampling distribution decreases as the sample size increases*. Consequently, the larger the sample size, the more accurate the sample statistic (e.g., $\bar{x}$) is in estimating a population parameter (e.g., μ). We will use this result in Chapter 7 to help us determine the sample size needed to obtain a specified accuracy of estimation.

Our second comment concerns the Central Limit Theorem. In addition to providing a very useful approximation for the sampling distribution of a sample mean, the Central Limit Theorem offers an explanation for the fact that many relative frequency distributions of data possess mound-shaped distributions. Many of the measurements we take in business are really means or sums of a large number of small phenomena. For example, a company's sales for one year are the total of the many individual sales the company made during the year. Similarly, we can view the length of time a construction company takes to build a house as the total of the times taken to complete a multitude of distinct jobs, and we can regard the monthly demand for blood at a hospital as the total of the many individual patients' needs. Whether or not the observations entering into these sums satisfy the assumptions basic to the Central Limit Theorem is open to question. However, it is a fact that many distributions of data in nature are mound-shaped and possess the appearance of normal distributions.

Teaching Tip

Point out that the ideas learned in this section will apply to the other sampling distributions used throughout the text. All point estimates that are used later will come from the unbiased sampling distributions with minimum variance. The Central Limit Theorem will be used in many places as well.

Statistics in Action Revisied:

Making an Inference about the Mean Sleep Time for Insomnia Pill Takers

In a Massachusetts Institute of Technology (MIT) study, each in a sample of 40 young male volunteers was given a dosage of the sleep-inducing hormone melatonin, placed in a dark room at midday, and told to close his eyes for 30 minutes. The researchers measured the time (in minutes) elapsed before each volunteer fell asleep. Recall that the data (shown in Table SIA6.1) are saved in the INSOMNIA file.

Previous research established that with the placebo (i.e., no hormone), the mean time to fall asleep is $\mu = 15$ minutes and the standard deviation is $\sigma = 10$ minutes. If the true value of μ for those taking the melatonin is $\mu < 15$ (i.e., if, on average, the volunteers fall asleep faster with the drug than with the placebo), then the researchers can infer that melatonin is an effective drug against insomnia.

Limit Theorem (CLT). According to the theorem, the sampling distribution of x has the following mean and standard deviation:

$$\mu_{\bar{x}} = \mu = 15$$

$$\sigma_{\bar{x}} = \sigma/\sqrt{n} = 10/\sqrt{40} = 1.58$$

The CLT also states that the distribution of $\bar{x}$ is approximately normally distributed. Therefore, we find the desired probability (using the standard normal table) as follows:

$$P(\bar{x} < 6) = P\left(z < \frac{6 - \mu_{\bar{x}}}{\sigma_{\bar{x}}}\right) = P\left(z < \frac{6 - 15}{1.58}\right)$$

$$= P(z < -5.70) \approx 0$$

Descriptive Statistics

	N	Minimum	Maximum	Mean	Std. Deviation
SLEEPTIM	40	1.3	22.8	5.935	5.3917
Valid N (listwise)	40				

Figure SIA6.1
SPSS descriptive statistics for sleep time data

Descriptive statistics for the 40 sleep times are displayed in the SPSS printout, Figure SIA6.1. You can see that the mean for the sample is $\bar{x} = 5.935$ minutes. If the drug is not effective in reducing sleep times, then the distribution of sleep times will be no different than the distribution with the placebo. That is, if the drug is not effective, the mean and standard deviation of the population of sleep times are $\mu = 15$ and $\sigma = 10$. If this is true, how likely is it to observe a sample mean that is below 6 minutes?

To answer this question, we desire the probability, $P(\bar{x} < 6)$. To find this probability, we invoke the Central

In other words, the probability that we observe a sample mean below $\bar{x} = 6$ minutes *if the mean and standard deviation of the sleep times are* $\mu = 15$ *and* $\sigma = 10$ *(i.e., if the drug is not effective)* is almost 0. Either the drug is not effective and the researchers have observed an extremely rare event (one with almost no chance of happening), or the true value of μ for those taking the melatonin pill is much less than 15 minutes. The rare-event approach to making statistical inferences, of course, would favor the second conclusion. Melatonin appears to be an effective insomnia pill, one that lowers the average time it takes the volunteers to fall asleep.

Exercises 6.15–6.32

Learning the Mechanics

6.15 Suppose a random sample of n measurements is selected from a population with mean $\mu = 100$ and variance $\sigma^2 = 100$. For each of the following values of n, give the mean and standard deviation of the sampling distribution of the sample mean $\bar{x}$.

a. $n = 4$ 100, 5
b. $n = 25$
c. $n = 100$
d. $n = 50$
e. $n = 500$ 100, .447
f. $n = 1,000$

6.16 Suppose a random sample of $n = 25$ measurements is selected from a population with mean μ and standard deviation σ. For each of the following values of μ and σ, give the values of $\mu_{\bar{x}}$ and $\sigma_{\bar{x}}$.

a. $\mu = 10, \sigma = 3$ 10, .6
b. $\mu = 100, \sigma = 25$ 100, 5
c. $\mu = 20, \sigma = 40$
d. $\mu = 10, \sigma = 100$

6.17 Consider the probability distribution shown here.

x	1	2	3	8
$p(x)$	.1	.4	.4	.1

a. Find μ, σ^2, and σ.
b. Find the sampling distribution of $\bar{x}$ for random samples of $n = 2$ measurements from this distribution by listing all possible values of $\bar{x}$, and find the probability associated with each.
c. Use the results of part b to calculate $\mu_{\bar{x}}$ and $\sigma_{\bar{x}}$. Confirm that $\mu_{\bar{x}} = \mu$ and $\sigma_{\bar{x}} = \sigma/\sqrt{n} = \sigma/\sqrt{2}$.

6.18 Will the sampling distribution of $\bar{x}$ always be approximately normally distributed? Explain.

6.19 A random sample of $n = 64$ observations is drawn from a population with a mean equal to 20 and standard deviation equal to 16.

a. Give the mean and standard deviation of the (repeated) sampling distribution of $\bar{x}$.
b. Describe the shape of the sampling distribution of $\bar{x}$. Does your answer depend on the sample size?
c. Calculate the standard normal z-score corresponding to a value of $\bar{x} = 15.5$. $z = -2.25$
d. Calculate the standard normal z-score corresponding to $\bar{x} = 23$. $z = 1.50$

6.20 Refer to Exercise 6.19. Find the probability that
a. $\bar{x}$ is less than 16
b. $\bar{x}$ is greater than 23
c. $\bar{x}$ is greater than 25 .0062
d. $\bar{x}$ falls between 16 and 22
e. $\bar{x}$ is less than 14

6.21 A random sample of $n = 100$ observations is selected from a population with $\mu = 30$ and $\sigma = 16$. Approximate the following probabilities:
a. $P(\bar{x} \geq 28)$ .8944
b. $P(22.1 \leq \bar{x} \leq 26.8)$
c. $P(\bar{x} \leq 28.2)$ .1292
d. $P(\bar{x} \geq 27.0)$

6.22 A random sample of $n = 900$ observations is selected from a population with $\mu = 100$ and $\sigma = 10$.
a. What are the largest and smallest values of $\bar{x}$ that you would expect to see? 101, 99
b. How far, at the most, would you expect $\bar{x}$ to deviate from μ? 1
c. Did you have to know μ to answer part b? Explain.

6.23 Consider a population that contains values of x equal to 0, 1, 2, ..., 97, 98, 99. Assume that the values of x are equally likely. For each of the following values of n, use a computer to generate 500 random samples and calculate $\bar{x}$ for each sample. For each sample size, construct a relative frequency histogram of the 500 values of $\bar{x}$. What changes occur in the histograms as the value of n increases? What similarities exist? Use $n = 2, n = 5, n = 10, n = 30$, and $n = 50$.

Applying the Concepts—Basic

6.24 According to *Business Travel News* (July 15, 2002), the average salary of a travel management professional is $74,000. Assume that the standard deviation of such salaries is $30,000. Consider a random sample of 50 travel management professionals and let $\bar{x}$ represent the mean salary for the sample.
a. What is $\mu_{\bar{x}}$? 74,000
b. What is $\sigma_{\bar{x}}$? 4,242.64
c. Describe the shape of the sampling distribution of $\bar{x}$.
d. Find the z-score for the value $\bar{x} = \$65,000$. -2.12
e. Find $P(\bar{x} > 65,000)$. .9830

6.25 Refer to the *Journal of Accounting and Public Policy* (Spring 2002) study of first-time candidates for the CPA exam, Exercise 2.49 (p. 79). The number of semester hours of college credit taken by candidates has a distribution with a mean of 141 hours and a standard deviation of 18 hours. Consider a random sample of 100 first-time candidates for the CPA exam and let $\bar{x}$ represent the mean number of hours of college credit taken for the sample.
a. What is $\mu_{\bar{x}}$? 141
b. What is $\sigma_{\bar{x}}$? 1.8
c. Describe the shape of the sampling distribution of $\bar{x}$.
d. Find the z-score for the value $\bar{x} = 142$ hours. .56
e. Find $P(\bar{x} > 142)$. .2877

6.26 The ocean quahog is a type of clam found in the coastal waters of New England and the mid-Atlantic states.

A federal survey of offshore ocean quahog harvesting in New Jersey, conducted from 1980 to 1992, revealed an average catch per unit effort (CPUE) of 89.34 clams. The CPUE standard deviation was 7.74 (*Journal of Shellfish Research*, June 1995). Let $\bar{x}$ represent the mean CPUE for a sample of 35 attempts to catch ocean quahogs off the New Jersey shore.

a. Compute $\mu_{\bar{x}}$ and $\sigma_{\bar{x}}$. Interpret their values.

b. Sketch the sampling distribution of $\bar{x}$.

c. Find $P(\bar{x} > 88)$. .8461

d. Find $P(\bar{x} < 87)$.

6.27 Refer to the *Chance* (Winter 2001) examination of Standardized Admission Test (SAT) scores of students who pay a private tutor to help them improve their results, Exercise 2.84 (p. 94). On the SAT–Mathematics test, these students had a mean score change of $+19$ points, with a standard deviation of 65 points. In a random sample of 100 students who pay a private tutor to help them improve their results, what is the likelihood that the sample mean score change is less than 10 points? .0838

Applying the Concepts—Intermediate

6.28 The *College Student Journal* (Dec. 1992) investigated differences in traditional and nontraditional students, where nontraditional students are generally defined as those 25 years or older and who are working full or part-time. Based on the study results, we can assume that the population mean and standard deviation for the GPA of all nontraditional students is $\mu = 3.5$ and $\sigma = .5$. Suppose that a random sample of $n = 100$ nontraditional students is selected from the population of all nontraditional students, and the GPA of each student is determined. Then $\bar{x}$, the sample mean, will be approximately normally distributed (because of the Central Limit Theorem).

a. Calculate $\mu_{\bar{x}}$ and $\sigma_{\bar{x}}$. $\mu_{\bar{x}} = 3.5, \sigma_{\bar{x}} = .05$

b. What is the approximate probability that the nontraditional student sample has a mean GPA between 3.40 and 3.60? .9544

c. What is the approximate probability that the sample of 100 nontraditional students has a mean GPA that exceeds 3.62? .0082

d. How would the sampling distribution of $\bar{x}$ change if the sample size n were doubled from 100 to 200? How do your answers to parts **b** and **c** change when the sample size is doubled?

6.29 At the end of the 20th century, workers were much less likely to remain with one employer for many years than their parents a generation before. (*Georgia Trend*, December 1999). Do today's college students understand that the workplace they are about to enter is vastly different than the one their parents entered? To help answer this question, researchers at the Terry College of Business at the

University of Georgia sampled 344 business students and asked them this question: Over the course of your lifetime, what is the maximum number of years you expect to work for any one employer? The resulting sample had $\bar{x} = 19.1$ years and $s = 6$ years. Assume the sample of students was randomly selected from the 5,800 undergraduate students in the Terry College.

a. Describe the sampling distribution of $\bar{x}$.

b. If the population mean were 18.5 years, what is $P(\bar{x} \geq 19.1 \text{ years})$? .0322

c. If the population mean were 19.5 years, what is $P(\bar{x} \geq 19.1 \text{ years})$? .8925

d. If $P(\bar{x} \geq 19.1) = .5$, what is the population mean?

e. If $P(\bar{x} \geq 19.1) = .2$, is the population mean greater or less than 19.1 years? Justify your answer. $\mu < 19.1$

6.30 National Car Rental Systems, Inc., commissioned the United States Automobile Club (USAC) to conduct a survey of the general condition of the cars rented to the public by Hertz, Avis, National, and Budget Rent-a-Car.* USAC officials evaluate each company's cars using a demerit point system. Each car starts with a perfect score of 0 points and incurs demerit points for each discrepancy noted by the inspectors. One measure of the overall condition of a company's cars is the mean of all scores received by the company (i.e., the company's *fleet mean score*). To estimate the fleet mean score of each rental car company, 10 major airports were randomly selected, and 10 cars from each company were randomly rented for inspection from each airport by USAC officials (i.e., a sample of size $n = 100$ cars from each company's fleet was drawn and inspected).

a. Describe the sampling distribution of $\bar{x}$, the mean score of a sample of $n = 100$ rental cars.

b. Interpret the mean of $\bar{x}$ in the context of this problem.

c. Assume $\mu = 30$ and $\sigma = 60$ for one rental car company. For this company, find $P(\bar{x} \geq 45)$. .0062

d. Refer to part **c**. The company claims that their true fleet mean score "couldn't possibly be as high as 30." The sample mean score tabulated by USAC for this company was $\bar{x} = 45$. Does this result tend to support or refute the claim? Explain. Refute

6.31 In determining when to place orders to replenish depleted product inventories, a retailer should take into consideration the lead times for the products. *Lead time* is the time between placing the order and having the product available to satisfy customer demand. It includes time for placing the order, receiving the shipment from the supplier, inspecting the units received, and placing them in inventory (Clauss, *Applied Management*

---

*Information by personal communication with Rajiv Tandon, Corporate Vice President and General Manager of the Car Rental Division, National Car Rental Systems, Inc., Minneapolis, Minnesota.

Science and Spreadsheet Modeling, 1996). Interested in average lead time, μ, for a particular supplier of men's apparel, the purchasing department of a national department store chain randomly sampled 50 of the supplier's lead times and found $\bar{x} = 44$ days.

a. Describe the shape of the sampling distribution of $\bar{x}$.

b. If μ and σ are really 40 and 12, respectively, what is the probability that a second random sample of size 50 would yield $\bar{x}$ greater than or equal to 44?   .0091

c. Using the values for μ and σ in part b, what is the probability that a sample of size 50 would yield a sample mean within the interval $\mu \pm 2\sigma/\sqrt{n}$?   .9544

Applying the Concepts—Advanced

6.32 University of Louisville researchers J. Usher, S. Alexander, and D. Duggins examined the process of filling plastic pouches of dry blended biscuit mix

(*Quality Engineering*, Vol. 91, 1996). The current fill mean of the process is set at $\mu = 406$ grams and the process fill standard deviation is $\sigma = 10.1$ grams. (According to the researchers, "The high level of variation is due to the fact that the product has poor flow properties and is, therefore, difficult to fill consistently from pouch to pouch.") Operators monitor the process by randomly sampling 36 pouches each day and measuring the amount of biscuit mix in each. Consider $\bar{x}$, the main fill amount of the sample of 36 products. Suppose that on one particular day, the operators observe $\bar{x} = 400.8$. One of the operators believes that this indicates that the true process fill mean μ for that day is less than 406 grams. Another operator argues that $\mu = 406$ and the small value of $\bar{x}$ observed is due to random variation in the fill process. Which operator do you agree with? Why?   The first

---

Quick Review

Key Terms

[Note: Starred (*) items are from the optional section in this chapter.]

Biased estimate* 326
Central Limit Theorem 332

Error of estimation* 325
Minimum Variance Unbiased Estimator (MVUE)* 328
Parameter 318
Point estimator* 325

Sample statistic 318
Sampling distribution 319
Standard error of the mean 331
Unbiased estimate* 326

Key Formulas

	Mean	Standard Deviation	z-score	
Sampling distribution of $\bar{x}$	$\mu_{\bar{x}} = \mu$	$\sigma_{\bar{x}} = \dfrac{\sigma}{\sqrt{n}}$	$z = \dfrac{\bar{x} - \mu_{\bar{x}}}{\sigma_{\bar{x}}} = \dfrac{\bar{x} - \mu}{\sigma/\sqrt{n}}$	331

Language Lab

Symbol	Pronunciation	Description
θ	theta	Population parameter (general)
$\mu_{\bar{x}}$	mu of x-bar	True mean of sampling distribution of $\bar{x}$
$\sigma_{\bar{x}}$	sigma of x-bar	True standard deviation of sampling distribution of $\bar{x}$

Chapter Summary

- **Sampling distribution of a statistic**—the theoretical probability distribution of the statistic in repeated sampling

- **Unbiased estimator**—a statistic with a sampling distribution mean equal to the population parameter being estimated

- **Central Limit Theorem**—the sampling distribution of the sample mean, $\bar{x}$, is approximately normal for large n (e.g., $n \geq 30$)

- $\bar{x}$ is the **minimum variance unbiased estimator (MVUE)** of μ.

Supplementary Exercises 6.33–6.55

Note: Starred (*) exercises refer to the optional section in this chapter.

Learning the Mechanics

6.33 Consider a sample statistic A. As with all sample statistics, A is computed by utilizing a specified function (formula) of the sample measurements. (For example, if A were the sample mean, the specified formula would be to sum the measurements and divide by the number of measurements.)

  a. Describe what we mean by the phrase "the sampling distribution of the sample statistic A."

* **b.** Suppose A is to be used to estimate a population parameter α. What is meant by the assertion that A is an unbiased estimator of α?

* **c.** Consider another sample statistic, B. Assume that B is also an unbiased estimator of the population parameter α. How can we use the sampling distributions of A and B to decide which is the better estimator of α?

  d. If the sample sizes on which A and B are based are large, can we apply the Central Limit Theorem and assert that the sampling distributions of A and B are approximately normal? Why or why not?

*6.34 The standard deviation (or, as it is usually called, the *standard error*) of the sampling distribution for the sample mean, $\bar{x}$, is equal to the standard deviation of the population from which the sample was selected divided by the square root of the sample size. That is,

$$\sigma_{\bar{x}} = \frac{\sigma}{\sqrt{n}}$$

  a. As the sample size is increased, what happens to the standard error of $\bar{x}$? Why is this property considered important?   Decreases

  b. Suppose that a sample statistic has a standard error that is not a function of the sample size. In other words, the standard error remains constant as n changes. What would this imply about the statistic as an estimator of a population parameter?

  c. Suppose another unbiased estimator (call it A) of the population mean is a sample statistic with a standard error equal to

$$\sigma_A = \frac{\sigma}{\sqrt[3]{n}}$$

  Which of the sample statistics, $\bar{x}$ or A, is preferable as an estimator of the population mean? Why? $\bar{x}$

  d. Suppose that the population standard deviation σ is equal to 10 and that the sample size is 64. Calculate the standard errors of $\bar{x}$ and A. Assuming that the sampling distribution of A is approximately normal, interpret the standard errors. Why is the assumption of (approximate) normality unnecessary for the sampling distribution of $\bar{x}$? $\sigma_{\bar{x}} = 1.25$, $\sigma_A = 2.5$

6.35 A random sample of $n = 68$ observations is selected from a population with $\mu = 19.6$ and $\sigma = 3.2$. Approximate each of the following probabilities.

  a. $P(\bar{x} \le 19.6)$ .5
  b. $P(\bar{x} \le 19)$ .0606
  c. $P(\bar{x} \ge 20.1)$ .0985
  d. $P(19.2 \le \bar{x} \le 20.6)$

6.36 A random sample of 40 observations is to be drawn from a large population of measurements. It is known that 30% of the measurements in the population are 1's, 20% are 2's, 20% are 3's, and 30% are 4's.

  a. Give the mean and standard deviation of the (repeated) sampling distribution of $\bar{x}$, the sample mean of the 40 observations. $\mu_{\bar{x}} = 2.5$, $\sigma_{\bar{x}} = .19$

  b. Describe the shape of the sampling distribution of $\bar{x}$. Does your answer depend on the sample size?

6.37 Use a statistical software package to generate 100 random samples of size $n = 2$ from a population characterized by a uniform probability distribution (optional Section 5.2) and $c = 0$ and $d = 10$. Compute $\bar{x}$ for each sample, and plot a frequency distribution for the 100 $\bar{x}$ values. Repeat this process for $n = 5, 10, 30,$ and 50. Explain how your plots illustrate the Central Limit Theorem.

6.38 Use a statistical software package to generate 100 random samples of size $n = 2$ from a population characterized by a normal probability distribution with mean 100 and standard deviation 10. Compute $\bar{x}$ for each sample and plot a frequency distribution for the 100 values of $\bar{x}$. Repeat this process for $n = 5, 10, 30,$ and 50. How does the fact that the sampled population is normal affect the sampling distribution of $\bar{x}$?

6.39 A random sample of size n is to be drawn from a large population with mean 100 and standard deviation 10, and the sample mean $\bar{x}$ is to be calculated. To see the effect of different sample sizes on the standard deviation of the sampling distribution of $\bar{x}$, plot $\sigma/\sqrt{n}$ against n for $n = 1, 5, 10, 20, 30, 40,$ and 50.

Applying the Concepts—Basic

6.40 In Lee County, Georgia, the distribution of weekly wages for workers in the construction industry is skewed to the right with mean equal to \$473 (Georgia Department of Labor, *Labor Market Information*, 1999). Assume the standard deviation of the distribution is \$25. An economist plans to randomly sample

40 workers in Lee County and question them regarding their weekly wages.

a. Describe what is known about the distribution of x, the weekly wages of workers in the construction industry.

b. Describe the distribution of $\bar{x}$.

c. Find $P(\bar{x} \geq \$465)$.   .9783

6.41 One measure of elevator performance is cycle time–the time between successive elevator starts. *Simulation* (Oct. 1993) published a study on the use of a micro-computer-based simulator for estimating elevators cycle times. The simulator produced an average cycle time μ of 26 seconds when traffic intensity was set at 50 persons every five minutes. Consider a sample of 200 simulated elevator runs and let $\bar{x}$ represent the mean cycle time of this sample.

a. What do you know about the distribution of x, the time between successive elevator starts? (Give the value of the mean and standard deviation of x and the shape of the distribution, if possible.)

b. What do you know about the distribution of $\bar{x}$? (Give the value of the mean and standard deviation of $\bar{x}$ and the shape of the distribution, if possible.)

c. Assume σ, the standard deviation of cycle time x, is 20 seconds. Use this information to calculate $P(\bar{x} > 26.8)$.   .2843

d. Repeat part c but assume $\sigma = 10$.   .1292

6.42 The American Automobile Association (AAA) reports that the average daily meal and lodging costs for a family of four is $213 (*Travel News*, May 11, 1999). Assume the standard deviation of such costs is $15 and that the average daily cost reported by AAA is the population mean. Suppose 49 families of four are selected and their travel expenses are monitored.

a. Describe the sampling distribution of $\bar{x}$, the average daily meal and lodging costs for the sample of families. In particular, how is $\bar{x}$ distributed and what are the mean and variance of $\bar{x}$? Justify your answers.

b. What is the probability that the average daily expenses for the sample of families was greater than $213? Greater than $217? Between $209 and $217?

6.43 To determine whether a metal lathe that produces machine bearings is properly adjusted, a random sample of 36 bearings is collected and the diameter of each is measured.

a. If the standard deviation of the diameters of the bearings measured over a long period of time is .001 inch, what is the approximate probability that the mean diameter $\bar{x}$ of the sample of 36 bearings will lie within .0001 inch of the population mean diameter of the bearings?   .4514

b. If the population of the diameters has an extremely skewed distribution, how will your approximation in part a be affected?   None

Applying the Concepts—Intermediate

6.44 Refer to the *Simulation* (Oct. 1993) study of elevator cycle times, Exercise 6.41. Cycle time is related to the distance (measured by number of floors) the elevator covers on a particular run, called *running distance*. The simulated distribution of running distance, x, during a down-peak period in elevator traffic intensity is shown in the figure below. The distribution has mean $\mu = 5.5$ floors and standard deviation $\sigma = 7$ floors. Consider a random sample of 80 simulated elevator runs during a down-peak in traffic intensity. Of interest is the sample mean running distance, $\bar{x}$.

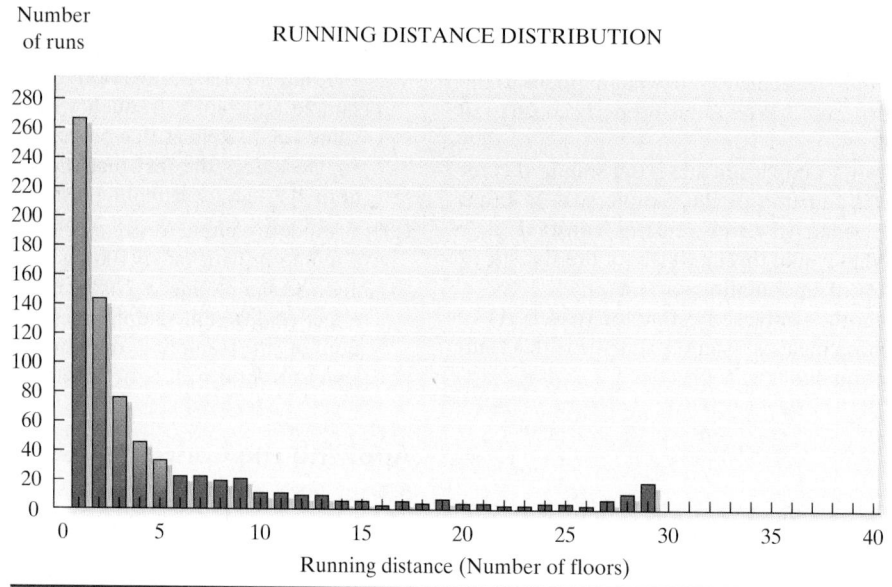

Source: Siikonen, M. L. "Elevator Traffic Simulation." Simulation, Vol. 61, No. 4, Oct. 1993, p (Figure 8). Copyright © 1993 by Simulation Councils, Inc. Reprinted by permission.

a. Find $\mu_{\bar{x}}$ and $\sigma_{\bar{x}}$ $\mu_{\bar{x}} = 5.5, \sigma_{\bar{x}} = .7826$

b. Is the shape of the distribution of $\bar{x}$ similar to the figure? If not, sketch the distribution.

c. During a down-peak in traffic intensity, is it likely to observe a sample mean running distance of $\bar{x} = 5.3$ floors? Explain.   Yes

6.45 Last year a company began a program to compensate its employees for unused sick days, paying each employee a bonus of one-half the usual wage earned for each unused sick day. The question that naturally arises is, "Did this policy motivate employees to use fewer sick days?" *Before* last year, the number of sick days used by employees had a distribution with a mean of 7 days and a standard deviation of 2 days.

a. Assuming that these parameters did not change last year, find the approximate probability that the sample mean number of sick days used by 100 employees chosen at random was less than or equal to 6.4 last year.   .0013

b. How would you interpret the result if the sample mean for the 100 employees was 6.4.?

6.46 Refer to Exercise 6.43. The mean diameter of the bearings produced by the machine is supposed to be .5 inch. The company decides to use the sample mean to decide whether the process is in control; i.e., whether it is producing bearings with a mean diameter of .5 inch. The machine will be considered out of control if the mean of the sample of $n = 36$ diameters is less than .4994 inch or larger than .5006 inch. If the true mean diameter of the bearings produced by the machine is .501 inch, what is the approximate probability that the test will imply that the process is out of control?   .9918

6.47 A particular manufacturing process requires steel rods that are at least 3 meters in length. The rods are purchased in lots of 50,000. To determine whether the lot meets the required quality standards, 100 rods are randomly sampled from each incoming lot and the mean length of rods in the sample is calculated. The quality manager has decided to accept lots whose sample mean is 3.005 meters or more. Assume that the standard deviation of the rod lengths in a lot is .03 meter.

a. If in fact each lot has a mean length of 3 meters, what percentage of the lots received by the manufacturer will be returned to the vendor (i.e., the supplier)?

b. If in fact all of the rods in all of the lots received by the manufacturer are between 2.999 and 3.004 meters in length, what percentage of the lots will be returned to the vendor?   100%

6.48 A manufacturer produces safety jackets for competitive fencers. These jackets are rated by the minimum force, in newtons, that will allow a weapon to pierce the jacket. When this process is operating correctly, it produces jackets that have ratings with an average of 840 newtons and a standard deviation of 15 newtons. FIE, the international governing body for fencing, requires jackets to be rated at a minimum of 800 newtons. To check whether the process is operating correctly, a manager takes a sample of 50 jackets from the process, rates them, and calculates $\bar{x}$, the mean rating for jackets in the sample. She assumes that the standard deviation of the process is fixed, but is worried that the mean rating of the process may have changed.

a. What is the sampling distribution of $\bar{x}$ if the process is still operating correctly?

b. Suppose the manager's sample has a mean rating of 830 newtons. What is the probability of getting an $\bar{x}$ of 830 newtons or lower if the process is operating correctly? ≈ 0

c. Given the manager's assumption that the standard deviation of the process is fixed, what does your answer to part b suggest about the current state of the process (i.e., does it appear that the mean jacket rating is still 840 newtons)?

d. Now suppose that the mean of the process has not changed, but the standard deviation of the process has increased from 15 newtons to 45 newtons. What is the sampling distribution of $\bar{x}$ in this case? What is the probability of getting an $\bar{x}$ of 830 newtons or lower when $\bar{x}$ has this distribution?   .0582

6.49 A soft-drink bottler purchases glass bottles from a vendor. The bottles are required to have an internal pressure of at least 150 pounds per square inch (psi). A prospective bottle vendor claims that its production process yields bottles with a mean internal pressure strength of 157 psi and a standard deviation of 3 psi. The bottler strikes an agreement with the vendor that permits the bottler to sample from the vendor's production process to verify the vendor's claim. The bottler randomly selects 40 bottles from the last 10,000 produced, measures the internal pressure of each, and finds the mean pressure for the sample to be 1.3 psi below the process mean cited by the vendor.

a. Assuming the vendor's claim to be true, what is the probability of obtaining a sample mean this far or farther below the process mean? What does your answer suggest about the validity of the vendor's claim?   .0031, claim is too high

b. If the process standard deviation were 3 psi as claimed by the vendor, but the mean were 156 psi, would the observed sample result be more or less likely than in part a? What if the mean were 158 psi?

c. If the process mean were 157 psi as claimed, but the process standard deviation were 2 psi, would the sample result be more or less likely than in part a? What if instead the standard deviation were 6 psi?   0; .0853

Applying the Concepts—Advanced

6.50 [*Note:* This exercise refers to the optional section in Chapter 4.] A building contractor has decided to purchase a load of factory-reject aluminum siding as long as the average number of flaws per piece of siding in a sample of size 35 from the factory's reject pile is 2.1 or less. If it is known that the number of flaws per piece of siding in the factory's reject pile has a Poisson probability distribution with a mean of 2.5, find the approximate probability that the contractor will not purchase a load of siding. [*Hint:* If x is a Poisson random variable with mean λ, then σ_x^2 also equals λ.] .9332

6.51 [*Note:* This exercise refers to the optional section on exponential distributions in Chapter 5.] An article in *Industrial Engineering* (Aug. 1990) discussed the importance of modeling machine downtime correctly in simulation studies. As an illustration, the researcher considered a single-machine-tool system with repair times (in minutes) that can be modeled by an exponential distribution with $\lambda = \frac{1}{60}$ (see Section 5.5). Of interest is the mean repair time, $\bar{x}$, of a sample of 100 machine breakdowns.

a. Find $E(\bar{x})$ and the variance of $\bar{x}$.

b. What probability distribution provides the best model of the sampling distribution of $\bar{x}$? Why?

c. Calculate the probability that the mean repair time, $\bar{x}$, is no longer than 30 minutes. ≈ 0

6.52 An individual is considering investing $1,000 in each of $n = 5$ different stocks. The monthly rate of return r on each stock has mean $\mu = 10\%$ and standard deviation $\sigma = 4\%$. The investor's monthly rate of return for the portfolio of five stocks is $\bar{r} = \Sigma r_i/5$. It can be shown that the variance of the investor's monthly rate of return is $\sigma_{\bar{r}}^2 = \sigma^2/n = 3.2$ and that this number is a measure of the risk faced by the investor.

a. If instead the individual were to invest $1,000 in only three of the five stocks, would the risk faced by the investor increase of decrease? Explain. Increase

b. Suppose $1,000 was invested in each of 10 stocks with rate-of-return characteristics identical to those described above. Measure the risk faced by the investor and compare it to the risk associated with investing in just five of the stocks. Decrease

REFERENCES

Clauss, Francis, J. *Applied Management Science and Spreadsheet Modeling*. Belmont, Calif.: Duxbury Press, 1996.

Deming, W. E. *Out of the Crisis*. Cambridge, Mass.: MIT Center for Advanced Engineering Study, 1986.

Hogg, R. V., and Craig, A. T. *Introduction to Mathematical Statistics*, 5th ed. Upper Saddle River, N.J.: Prentice Hall, 1995.

Larsen, R. J., and Marx, M. L. *An Introduction to Mathematical Statistics and Its Applications*, 3rd ed. Upper Saddle River, N.J.: Prentice Hall, 2001.

Lindgren, B. W. *Statistical Theory*, 3rd ed. New York: Macmillan, 1976.

Wackerly, D., Mendenhall, W., and Scheaffer, R. *Mathematical Statistics with Applications*, 6th ed. North Scituate, Mass.: Duxbury, 1999.

Using Technology

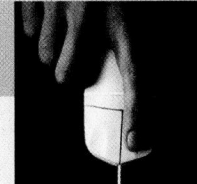

6.1 Simulating a Sampling Distribution Using MINITAB

To generate a sampling distribution for a sample statistic using MINITAB, click on the "Calc" button on the MINITAB menu bar, next click on "Random Data", then click on the distribution of your choice (e.g., "Uniform"). A dialog box similar to the one (the Uniform Distribution) shown in Figure 6.M.1 will appear. Specify the number of samples (e.g., 1,000) to generate in the "Generate ... rows of data" box and the columns where the data will be stored in the "Store in columns" box. (The number of columns will be equal to the sample size, e.g., 40.) Finally, specify the parameters of the distribution (e.g., the lower and upper range of the uniform distribution). When you click "OK", the simulated data will appear on the MINITAB worksheet.

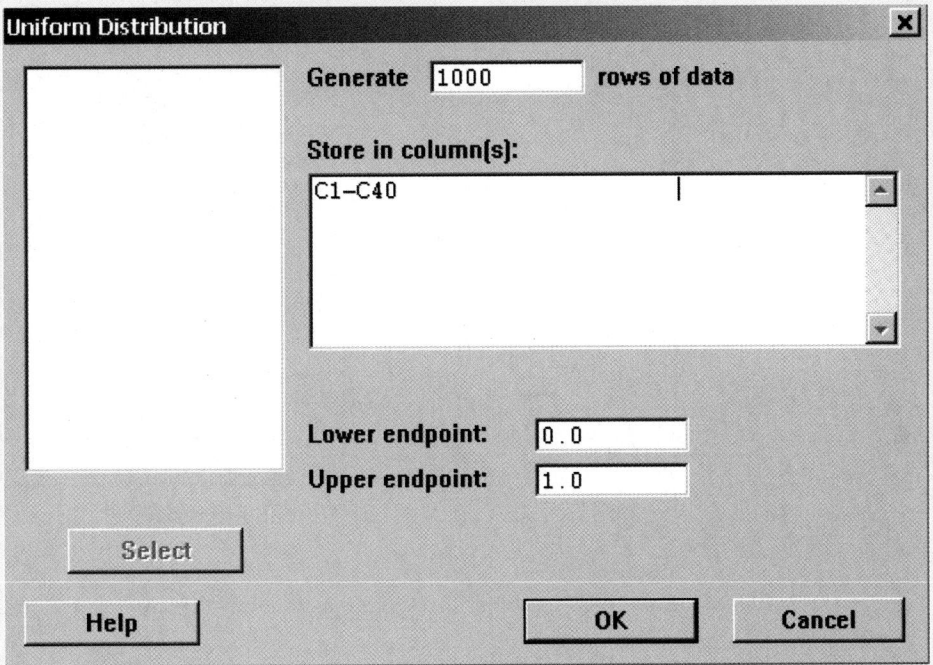

Figure 6.M.1
MINITAB dialog box for simulating the uniform distribution

Next, calculate the value of the sample statistic of interest for each sample. To do this, click on the "Calc" button on the MINITAB menu bar, then click on "Row Statistics", as shown in Figure 6.M.2. The resulting dialog box appears in Figure 6.M.3. Check the sample statistic (e.g., the mean) you want to calculate, specify the "Input variables" (or columns), and specify the column where you want the value of the sample statistic to be saved. Click "OK" and the value of the statistic for each sample will appear on the MINITAB worksheet. [*Note*: Use the MINITAB menu choices provided in the *Chapter 2 Using Technology* tutorial to generate a histogram of the sampling distribution of the statistic or to find the mean and variance of the sampling distribution.]

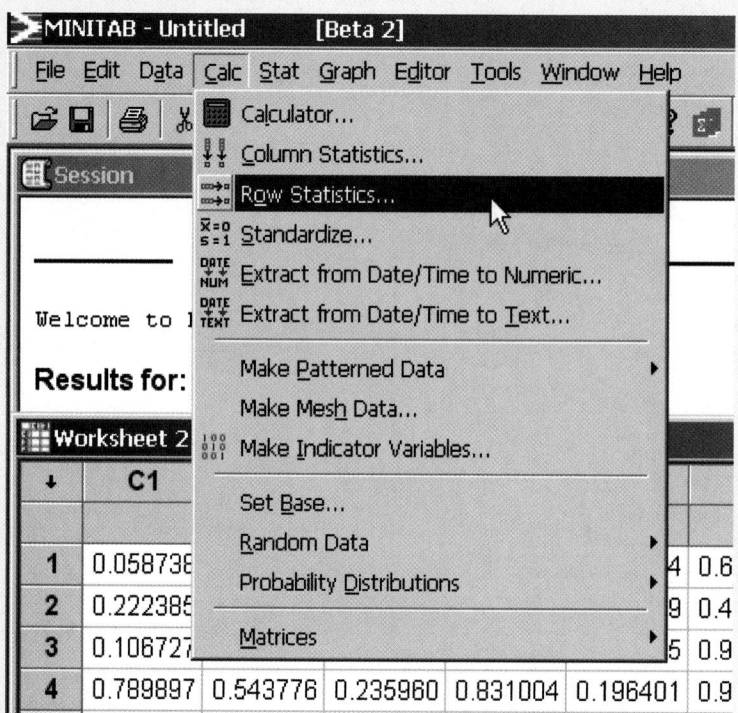

Figure 6.M.2
MINITAB selections for generating sample statistics
for the simulated data

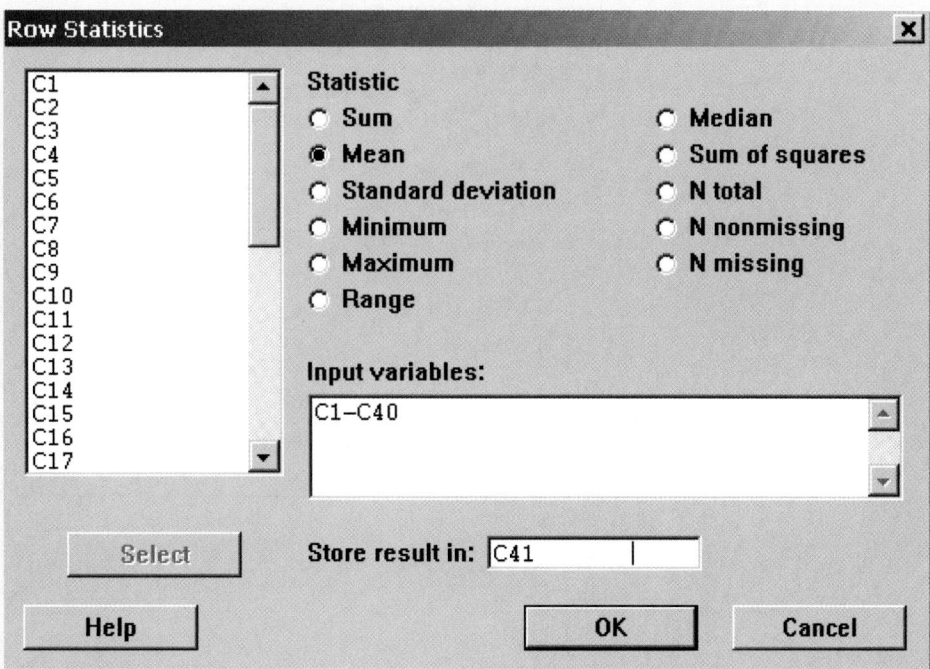

Figure 6.M.3
MINITAB row statistics dialog box

6.2 Simulating a Sampling Distribution Using EXCEL and PHSTAT2

To generate a sampling distribution for the sample mean using EXCEL, click on the "PHStat" button on the main menu bar, next click on "Sampling", then click on "Sampling Distributions Simulation", as shown in Figure 6.E.1. The dialog box shown in Figure 6.E.2 will appear. Specify the number of samples (e.g., 250) to generate and the sample size of each (e.g., 30). Finally, specify the distribution (either Uniform or Standardized Normal) that the samples will be selected from. When you click "OK", the simulated data will appear on a new EXCEL spreadsheet, as well as the means for each sample and a histogram of the sample means.

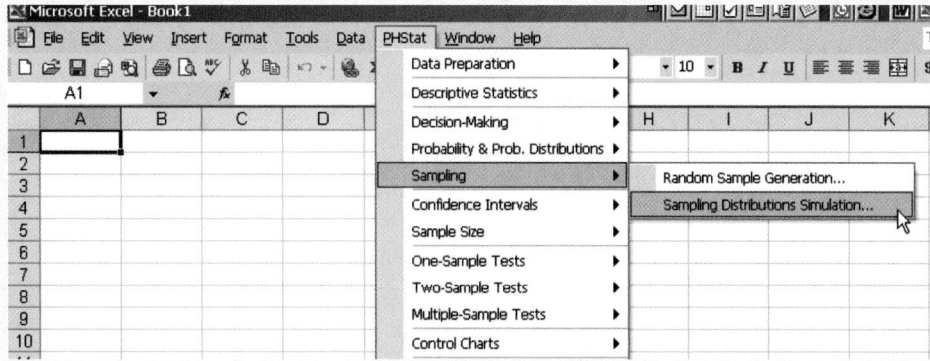

Figure 6.E.1
EXCEL options for simulating a sampling distribution

Figure 6.E.2
EXCEL/PHStat2 dialog box for simulating the sampling distribution of the mean

Real-World Case
The Furniture Fire Case
(A Case Covering Chapters 3–6)

A wholesale furniture retailer stores in-stock items at a large warehouse located in Tampa, Florida. In early 1992, a fire destroyed the warehouse and all the furniture in it. After determining the fire was an accident, the retailer sought to recover costs by submitting a claim to its insurance company.

As is typical in a fire insurance policy of this type, the furniture retailer must provide the insurance company with an estimate of "lost" profit for the destroyed items. Retailers calculate profit margin in percentage form using the Gross Profit Factor (GPF). By definition, the GPF for a single sold item is the ratio of the profit to the item's selling price measured as a percentage, that is,

$$\text{Item GPF} = (\text{Profit/Sales price}) \times 100\%$$

Of interest to both the retailer and the insurance company is the average GPF for all of the items in the warehouse. Since these furniture pieces were all destroyed, their eventual selling prices and profit values are obviously unknown. Consequently, the average GPF for all the warehouse items is unknown.

One way to estimate the mean GPF of the destroyed items is to use the mean GPF of similar, recently sold items. The retailer sold 3,005 furniture items in 1991 (the year prior to the fire) and kept paper invoices on all sales. Rather than calculate the mean GPF for all 3,005 items (the data were not computerized), the retailer sampled a total of 253 of the invoices and computed the mean GPF for these items. The 253 items were obtained by first selecting a sample of 134 items and then augmenting this sample with a second sample of 119 items. The mean GPFs for the two subsamples were calculated to be 50.6% and 51.0%, respectively, yielding an overall average GPF of 50.8%. This average GPF can be applied to the costs of the furniture items destroyed in the fire to obtain an estimate of the "lost" profit.

According to experienced claims adjusters at the insurance company, the GPF for sale items of the type destroyed in the fire rarely exceeds 48%. Consequently, the estimate of 50.8% appeared to be unusually high. (A 1% increase in GPF for items of this type equates to, approximately, an additional $16,000 in profit.) When the insurance company questioned the retailer on this issue, the retailer responded, "Our estimate was based on selecting two independent, random samples from the population of 3,005 invoices in 1991. Since the samples were selected randomly and the total sample size is large, the mean GPF estimate of 50.8% is valid."

A dispute arose between the furniture retailer and the insurance company, and a lawsuit was filed. In one portion of the suit, the insurance company accused the retailer of fraudulently representing their sampling methodology. Rather than selecting the samples randomly, the retailer was accused of selecting an unusual number of "high profit" items from the population in order to increase the average GPF of the overall sample.

To support their claim of fraud, the insurance company hired a CPA firm to independently assess the retailer's 1991 Gross Profit Factor. Through the discovery process, the CPA firm legally obtained the paper invoices for the entire population of 3,005 items sold and input the information into a computer. The selling price, profit, profit margin, and month sold for these 3,005 furniture items are stored in the FIRE file, described below.

Your objective in this case is to use these data to determine the likelihood of fraud. Is it likely that a random sample of 253 items selected from the population of 3,005 items would yield a mean GPF of at least 50.8%? Or, is it likely that two independent, random samples of size 134 and 119 will yield mean GPFs of at least 50.6% and 51.0%, respectively? (These were the questions posed to a statistician retained by the CPA firm.) Use the ideas of probability and sampling distributions to guide your analysis.

Prepare a professional document that presents the results of your analysis and gives your opinion regarding fraud. Be sure to describe the assumptions and methodology used to arrive at your findings.

 FIRE

Variable	Type	Description
MONTH	QL	Month in which item was sold in 1991
INVOICE	QN	Invoice number
SALES	QN	Sales price of item in dollars
PROFIT	QN	Profit amount of item in dollars
MARGIN	QN	Profit margin of item = (Profit/Sales) × 100%

7

Inferences Based on a Single Sample

Estimation with Confidence Intervals

Contents

Statistics in Action

Scallops, Sampling, and the Law

Using Technology

Where We've Been

- Learned that populations are characterized by numerical descriptive measures called *parameters*

- Found that decisions about population parameters are based on *statistics* computed from the sample

- Discovered that *inferences* about parameters are subject to uncertainty, and that this uncertainty is reflected in the *sampling distribution* of a statistic

Where We're Going

- Estimate a population parameter (means or proportion) based on a large sample selected from the population.

- Use the sampling distribution of a statistic to form a confidence interval for the population parameter.

- Show how to select the proper sample size for estimating a population parameter.

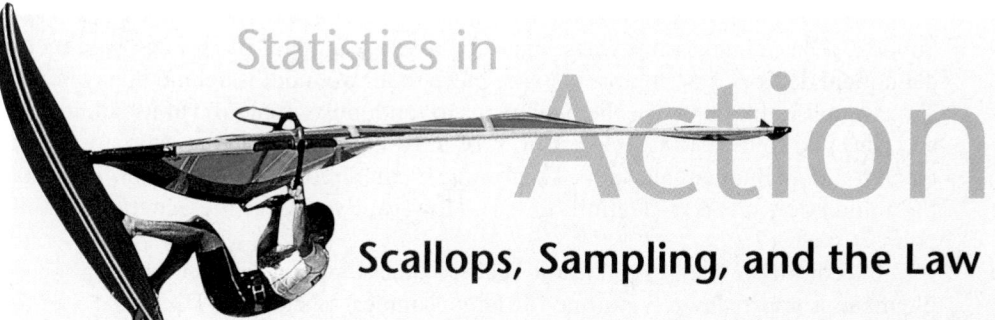

Statistics in Action

Scallops, Sampling, and the Law

Arnold Bennett, a Sloan School of Management professor at the Massachusetts Institute of Technology (MIT), described a recent legal case in *Interfaces* (Mar.–Apr. 1995) in which he served as a statistical "expert." The case involved a ship that fishes for scallops off the coast of New England. In order to protect baby scallops from being harvested, the U.S. Fisheries and Wildlife Service requires that *the average meat per scallop weigh at least 1/36 of a pound*. The ship was accused of violating this weight standard. Bennett lays out the scenario:

The vessel arrived at a Massachusetts port with 11,000 bags of scallops, from which the harbormaster randomly selected 18 bags for weighing. From each such bag, his agents took a large scoop full of scallops; then, to estimate the bag's average meat per scallop, they divided the total weight of meat in the scoop by the number of scallops it contained. Based on the 18 [numbers] thus generated, the harbormaster estimated that each of the ship's scallops possessed an average of 1/39 of a pound of meat (that is, they were about seven percent lighter than the minimum requirement). Viewing this outcome as conclusive evidence that the weight standard had been violated, federal authorities at once confiscated 95 percent of the catch (which they then sold at auction). The fishing voyage was thus transformed into a financial catastrophe for its participants.

Bennett provided the estimated scallop weight measurements (in pounds) for each of the 18 sampled bags in the article. These data are available in the file called SCALLOPS. [*Note*: 1/36 of a pound, the minimum permissible average weight per scallop, is equivalent to .0278 pound. Consequently, weights below .0278 indicate individual bags that do not meet the standard.] The ship's owner filed a lawsuit against the federal government, declaring that his vessel had fully complied with the weight standard. A Boston law firm was hired to represent the owner in legal proceedings and Bennett was retained by the firm to provide statistical litigation support and, if necessary, expert witness testimony.

In this chapter, several Statistics in Action Revisited examples demonstrate how confidence intervals can be used to support the ship's owner in the lawsuit.

Statistics in Action Revisited

- Estimating the Mean Weight per Scallop (p. 368)
- Estimating the Proportion of Underweight Scallop Bags (p. 379)
- Determining the Number of Bags of Scallops to Sample (p. 387)

Teaching Tip

The key idea of this chapter revolves around the ability to generate an estimate with a corresponding measure of reliability.

The estimation of the mean gas mileage for a new car model, the estimation of the expected life of a computer monitor, and the estimation of the mean yearly sales for companies in the steel industry are problems with a common element. In each case, we're interested in estimating the mean of a population of quantitative measurements. This important problem constitutes the primary topic of this chapter.

You'll see that different techniques are used for estimating a mean, depending on whether a sample contains a large or small number of measurements. Nevertheless, our objectives remain the same: We want to use the sample information to estimate the mean and to assess the reliability of the estimate.

First, we consider a method of estimating a population mean using a *large* random sample (Section 7.1) and a small random sample (Section 7.2). Then, we consider estimation of population proportions (Section 7.3). Next, we see how to determine the sample sizes necessary for reliable estimates based on random sampling (Section 7.4). Finally, we describe several other more complex sample survey designs (Sections 7.5 and 7.6).

7.1 Large-Sample Confidence Interval for a Population Mean

Suppose a large bank wants to estimate the average amount of money owed by its delinquent debtors (i.e., debtors who are more than two months behind in payment). To accomplish this objective, the bank plans to randomly sample 100 of its delinquent accounts and to use the sample mean, $\bar{x}$, of the amounts overdue to estimate μ, the mean for *all* delinquent accounts. The sample mean $\bar{x}$ represents a *point estimator* of the population mean μ (Definition 6.4). How can we assess the accuracy of this point estimator?

According to the Central Limit Theorem, the sampling distribution of the sample mean is approximately normal for large samples, as shown in Figure 7.1. Let us calculate the interval

$$\bar{x} \pm 1.96\sigma_{\bar{x}} = \bar{x} \pm \frac{1.96\sigma}{\sqrt{n}}$$

Figure 7.1
Sampling distribution of $\bar{x}$

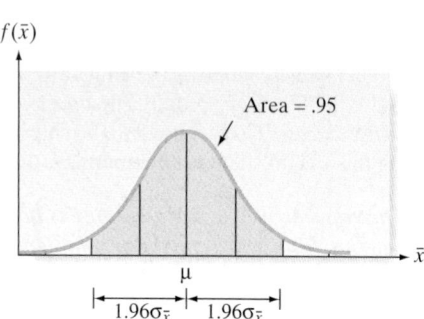

That is, we form an interval from 1.96 standard deviations below the sample mean to 1.96 standard deviations above the mean. *Prior to drawing the sample*, what are the chances that this interval will enclose μ, the population mean?

To answer this question, refer to Figure 7.1. If the 100 measurements yield a value of $\bar{x}$ that falls between the two lines on either side of μ (i.e., within 1.96 standard deviations of μ), then the interval $\bar{x} \pm 1.96\sigma_{\bar{x}}$ will contain μ; if $\bar{x}$ falls outside these boundaries, the interval $\bar{x} \pm 1.96\sigma_{\bar{x}}$ will not contain μ. From Chapter 5, we know that the area under the normal curve (the sampling distribution of $\bar{x}$) between these boundaries is exactly .95. Thus, we know that the interval $\bar{x} \pm 1.96\sigma_{\bar{x}}$ will contain μ with a probability equal to .95.

For instance, consider the overdue amounts for 100 delinquent accounts shown in Table 7.1. An EXCEL printout of summary statistics for the sample of 100 overdue amounts is shown in Figure 7.2. From the shaded portion of the printout, we find $\bar{x} = \$233.28$ and $s = \$90.34$. To achieve our objective, we must construct the interval

$$\bar{x} \pm 1.96\sigma_{\bar{x}} = 233.28 \pm 1.96\frac{\sigma}{\sqrt{100}}$$

But now we face a problem. You can see that without knowing the standard deviation σ of the original population—that is, the standard deviation of the overdue amounts of

	A	B
1		AMOUNT
2		
3	Mean	233.28
4	Standard Error	9.033988347
5	Median	222
6	Mode	221
7	Standard Deviation	90.33988347
8	Sample Variance	8161.294545
9	Kurtosis	0.254810234
10	Skewness	0.476799829
11	Range	495
12	Minimum	17
13	Maximum	512
14	Sum	23328
15	Count	100

Figure 7.2
EXCEL summary statistics
for overdue amounts

OVERDUE

TABLE 7.1   Overdue Amounts (in Dollars) for 100 Delinquent Accounts

195	243	132	133	209	400	142	312	221	289
221	162	134	275	355	293	242	458	378	148
278	222	236	178	202	222	334	208	194	135
363	221	449	265	146	215	113	229	221	243
512	193	134	138	209	207	206	310	293	310
237	135	252	365	371	238	232	271	121	134
203	178	180	148	162	160	86	234	244	266
119	259	108	289	328	331	330	227	162	354
304	141	158	240	82	17	357	187	364	268
368	274	278	190	344	157	219	77	171	280

all delinquent accounts—we cannot calculate this interval. However, since we have a large sample ($n = 100$ measurements), we can approximate the interval by using the sample standard deviation s to approximate σ. Thus,

$$\bar{x} \pm 1.96\frac{\sigma}{\sqrt{100}} \approx \bar{x} \pm 1.96\frac{s}{\sqrt{100}} = 233.28 \pm 1.96\left(\frac{90.34}{10}\right) = 233.28 \pm 17.71$$

That is, we estimate the mean amount of delinquency for all accounts to fall within the interval $215.57 to $250.99.

Can we be sure that μ, the true mean, is in the interval (215.57, 250.99)? We cannot be certain, but we can be reasonably confident that it is. This confidence is derived from the knowledge that if we were to draw repeated random samples of 100 measurements from this population and form the interval $\bar{x} \pm 1.96\sigma_{\bar{x}}$ each time, 95% of the intervals would contain μ. We have no way of knowing (without looking at all the delinquent accounts) whether our sample interval is one of the 95% that contains μ or one of the 5% that does not, but the odds certainly favor its containing μ. Consequently, the interval $215.57 to $250.99 provides a reliable estimate of the mean delinquency per account.

The formula that tells us how to calculate an interval estimate based on sample data is called an *interval estimator*, or *confidence interval*. The probability, .95, that measures the confidence we can place in the interval estimate is called a *confidence coefficient*. The percentage, 95%, is called the *confidence level* for the interval estimate. It is not usually possible to assess precisely the reliability of point estimators because they are single points rather than intervals. So, because we prefer to use estimators for which a measure of reliability can be calculated, we will generally use interval estimators.

DEFINITION 7.1

An **interval estimator** (or **confidence interval**) is a formula that tells us how to use sample data to calculate an interval that estimates a population parameter.

DEFINITION 7.2

The **confidence coefficient** is the probability that a randomly selected confidence interval encloses the population parameter—that is, the relative frequency with which similarly constructed intervals enclose the population parameter when the estimator is used repeatedly a very large number of times. The **confidence level** is the confidence coefficient expressed as a percentage.

Teaching Tip
Explain that the population standard deviation is usually unknown and will need to be estimated with the sample standard deviation.

Teaching Tip
This repeated sampling interpretation is difficult for students to understand. Explain that the repeated intervals will move with the sample data, yet the parameter that they are estimating remains constant.

Teaching Tip
Figure 7.3 is the best illustration of the meaning of the confidence level. Stress the fact that the population mean is a fixed unknown value. Our intervals will vary from one sample to the next.

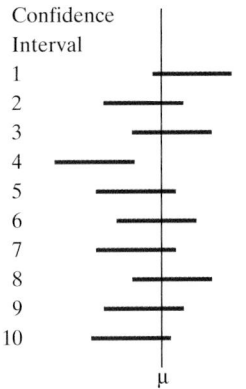

Figure 7.3
Confidence intervals for μ: 10 samples

Now we have seen how an interval can be used to estimate a population mean. When we use an interval estimator, we can usually calculate the probability that the estimation *process* will result in an interval that contains the true value of the population mean. That is, the probability that the interval contains the parameter in repeated usage is usually known. Figure 7.3 shows what happens when 10 different samples are drawn from a population, and a confidence interval for μ is calculated from each. The location of μ is indicated by the vertical line in the figure. Ten confidence intervals, each based on one of 10 samples, are shown as horizontal line segments. Note that the confidence intervals move from sample to sample—sometimes containing μ and other times missing μ. *If our confidence level is 95%, then in the long run, 95% of our confidence intervals will contain μ and 5% will not.*

Suppose you wish to choose a confidence coefficient other than .95. Notice in Figure 7.1 that the confidence coefficient .95 is equal to the total area under the sampling distribution, less .05 of the area, which is divided equally between the two tails. Using this idea, we can construct a confidence interval with any desired confidence coefficient by increasing or decreasing the area (call it α) assigned to the tails of the sampling distribution (see Figure 7.4). For example, if we place area $\alpha/2$ in each tail and if $z_{\alpha/2}$ is the z value such that the area $\alpha/2$ lies to its right, then the confidence interval with confidence coefficient $(1 - \alpha)$ is

$$\bar{x} \pm z_{\alpha/2}\sigma_{\bar{x}}$$

Figure 7.4
Locating $z_{\alpha/2}$ on the standard normal curve

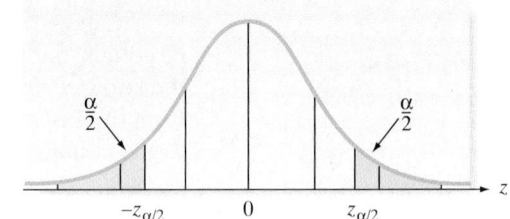

Biography

JERZEY NEYMAN (1894–1981)
Speaking Statistics with a Polish Accent

Polish-born Jerzey Neyman was educated at the University of Kharkov (Russia) in elementary mathematics but taught himself graduate mathematics by studying journal articles on the subject. After receiving his doctorate in 1924 from the University of Warsaw (Poland), Neyman accepted a position at University College (London). There, he developed a friendship with Egon Pearson; Neyman and Pearson together developed the theory of hypothesis testing (Chapter 8). In 1934, in a talk to the Royal Statistical Society, Neyman first proposed the idea of interval estimation, which he called "confidence intervals." (It is interesting that Neyman rarely receives credit in textbooks as the originator of the confidence interval procedure.) In 1938, he emigrated to the United States and the University of California at Berkeley. At Berkeley, he built one of the strongest statistics departments in the country. Jerzey Neyman is considered one of the great founders of modern statistics. He was a superb teacher and innovative researcher who loved his students, always sharing his ideas with them. Neyman's influence on those he met is best expressed by a quote from prominent statistician David Salsburg: "We have all learned to speak statistics with a Polish accent."

To illustrate, for a confidence coefficient of .90 we have $(1 - \alpha) = .90$, $\alpha = .10$, and $\alpha/2 = .05$; $z_{.05}$ is the z value that locates area .05 in the upper tail of the sampling distribution. Recall that Table IV in Appendix B gives the areas between the mean and a specified z value. Since the total area to the right of the mean is .5, we find that $z_{.05}$ will be the z value corresponding to an area of $.5 - .05 = .45$ to the right of the mean (see Figure 7.5). This z value is $z_{.05} = 1.645$.

Confidence coefficients used in practice usually range from .90 to .99. The most commonly used confidence coefficients with corresponding values of α and $z_{\alpha/2}$ are shown in Table 7.2.

Figure 7.5

The z value $(z_{.05})$ corresponding to an area equal to .05 in the upper tail of the z-distribution

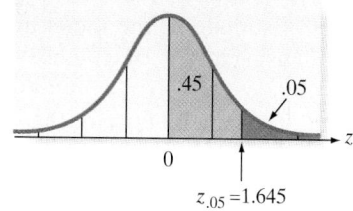

TABLE 7.2 Commonly Used Values of $z_{\alpha/2}$

Confidence Level			
$100(1 - \alpha)$	α	$\alpha/2$	$z_{\alpha/2}$
90%	.10	.05	1.645
95%	.05	.025	1.96
99%	.01	.005	2.575

Now Work   *Exercise 7.1*

Large-Sample $100(1 - \alpha)\%$ Confidence Interval for μ

$$\bar{x} \pm z_{\alpha/2}\sigma_{\bar{x}} = \bar{x} \pm z_{\alpha/2}\frac{\sigma}{\sqrt{n}}$$

where $z_{\alpha/2}$ is the z value with an area $\alpha/2$ to its right (see Figure 7.4) and $\sigma_{\bar{x}} = \sigma/\sqrt{n}$. The parameter σ is the standard deviation of the sampled population and n is the sample size.

Note: When σ is unknown (as is almost always the case) and n is large (say, $n \geq 30$), the confidence interval is approximately equal to

$$\bar{x} \pm z_{\alpha/2}\left(\frac{s}{\sqrt{n}}\right)$$

where s is the sample standard deviation.

Conditions Required for a Valid Large-Sample Confidence Interval for μ

1. A random sample is selected from the target population
2. The sample size n is large (i.e., $n \geq 30$). (Due to the Central Limit Theorem, this condition guarantees that the sampling distribution of $\bar{x}$ is approximately normal.)

EXAMPLE 7.1

FINDING A LARGE-SAMPLE CONFIDENCE INTERVAL FOR μ

Problem Unoccupied seats on flights cause airlines to lose revenue. Suppose a large airline wants to estimate its average number of unoccupied seats per flight over the past year. To accomplish this, the records of 225 flights are randomly selected, and the number of unoccupied seats is noted for each of the sampled flights. The sample mean and standard deviation are

$$\bar{x} = 11.6 \text{ seats} \qquad s = 4.1 \text{ seats}$$

11.6 ± .45   ●   Estimate μ, the mean number of unoccupied seats per flight during the past year, using a 90% confidence interval.

Solution The general form of the 90% confidence interval for a population mean is

●

$$\bar{x} \pm z_{\alpha/2}\sigma_{\bar{x}} = \bar{x} \pm z_{.05}\sigma_{\bar{x}} = \bar{x} \pm 1.645\left(\frac{\sigma}{\sqrt{n}}\right)$$

For the 225 records sampled, we have

Suggested Exercises 7.10

$$11.6 \pm 1.645\left(\frac{\sigma}{\sqrt{225}}\right)$$

Since we do not know the value of σ (the standard deviation of the number of unoccupied seats per flight for all flights of the year), we use our best approximation—the sample standard deviation s. Then the 90% confidence interval is approximately

$$11.6 \pm 1.645\left(\frac{4.1}{\sqrt{225}}\right) = 11.6 \pm .45$$

or from 11.15 to 12.05. That is, at the 90% confidence level, we estimate the mean number of unoccupied seats per flight to be between 11.15 and 12.05 during the sampled year. This result is verified on the MINITAB printout of the analysis shown in Figure 7.6.

Figure 7.6
MINITAB confidence interval for mean, Example 7.1

Variable	N	Mean	StDev	SE Mean	90% CI
NOSEATS	225	11.5956	4.1026	0.2735	(11.1438, 12.0473)

Teaching Tip
Discuss the interpretation of the confidence interval in two parts: the practical side that gives the interval for μ and the theoretical part that involves repeated samples that give the reliability to the interval.

Look Back We stress that the confidence level for this example, 90%, refers to the procedure used. If we were to apply this procedure repeatedly to different samples, approximately 90% of the intervals would contain μ. We do not know whether this particular interval (11.15, 12.05) is one of the 90% that contain μ or one of the 10% that do not—but the odds are that it does.

Now Work   *Exercise 7.5*

■ ■ ■

The interpretation of confidence intervals for a population mean is summarized in the next box.

Interpretation of a Confidence Interval for a Population Mean

When we form a $100(1 - \alpha)\%$ confidence interval for μ, we usually express our confidence in the interval with a statement such as, "We can be $100(1 - \alpha)\%$ confident that μ lies between the lower and upper bounds of the confidence interval," where for a particular application, we substitute the appropriate numerical values for the confidence and for the lower and upper bounds. *The statement reflects our confidence in the estimation process rather than in the particular interval that is calculated from the sample data.* We know that repeated application of the same procedure will result in different lower and upper bounds on the interval. Furthermore, we know that $100(1 - \alpha)\%$ of the resulting intervals will contain μ. There is (usually) no way to determine whether any particular interval is one of those that contain μ, or one that does not. However, unlike point estimators, confidence intervals have some measure of reliability, the confidence coefficient, associated with them. For that reason they are generally preferred to point estimators.

Sometimes, the estimation procedure yields a confidence interval that is too wide for our purposes. In this case, we will want to reduce the width of the interval to obtain a more precise estimate of μ. One way to accomplish this is to decrease the confidence coefficient, $1 - \alpha$. For example, reconsider the problem of estimating the mean amount owed, μ, for all delinquent accounts. Recall that for a sample of 100 accounts, $\bar{x} = \$233.28$ and $s = \$90.34$. A 90% confidence interval for μ is

$$\bar{x} \pm 1.645\sigma/\sqrt{n} \approx 233.28 \pm (1.645)(90.34/\sqrt{100}) = 233.28 \pm 14.86$$

or ($218.42, $248.14). You can see that this interval is narrower than the previously calculated 95% confidence interval, ($215.57, $250.99). Unfortunately, we also have "less confidence" in the 90% confidence interval. An alternative method used to decrease the width of an interval without sacrificing "confidence" is to increase the sample size n. We demonstrate this method in Section 7.4.

Exercises 7.1–7.20

Learning the Mechanics

7.1 Find $z_{\alpha/2}$ for each of the following:
- **a.** $\alpha = .10$
- **b.** $\alpha = .01$
- **c.** $\alpha = .05$
- **d.** $\alpha = .20$

7.2 What is the confidence level of each of the following confidence intervals for μ?

a. $\bar{x} \pm 1.96\left(\dfrac{\sigma}{\sqrt{n}}\right)$ 95%

b. $\bar{x} \pm 1.645\left(\dfrac{\sigma}{\sqrt{n}}\right)$

c. $\bar{x} \pm 2.575\left(\dfrac{\sigma}{\sqrt{n}}\right)$ 99%

d. $\bar{x} \pm 1.282\left(\dfrac{\sigma}{\sqrt{n}}\right)$

e. $\bar{x} \pm .99\left(\dfrac{\sigma}{\sqrt{n}}\right)$ 67.78%

7.3 A random sample of n measurements was selected from a population with unknown mean μ and standard deviation σ. Calculate a 95% confidence interval for μ for each of the following situations:
- **a.** $n = 75, \bar{x} = 28, s^2 = 12$ $28 \pm .784$
- **b.** $n = 200, \bar{x} = 102, s^2 = 22$ $102 \pm .65$
- **c.** $n = 100, \bar{x} = 15, s = .3$ $15 \pm .0588$
- **d.** $n = 100, \bar{x} = 4.05, s = .83$ $4.05 \pm .163$
- **e.** Is the assumption that the underlying population of measurements is normally distributed necessary to ensure the validity of the confidence intervals in parts a–d? Explain.   No

7.4 A random sample of 90 observations produced a mean $\bar{x} = 25.9$ and a standard deviation $s = 2.7$.

   a. Find a 95% confidence interval for the population mean μ. $25.9 \pm .56$

   b. Find a 90% confidence interval for μ. $25.9 \pm .47$

   c. Find a 99% confidence interval for μ. $25.9 \pm .73$

7.5 A random sample of 70 observations from a normally distributed population possesses a mean equal to 26.2 and a standard deviation equal to 4.1.

   a. Find a 95% confidence interval for μ. $26.2 \pm .96$

   b. What do you mean when you say that a confidence coefficient is .95?

   c. Find a 99% confidence interval for μ. 26.2 ± 1.26

   d. What happens to the width of a confidence interval as the value of the confidence coefficient is increased while the sample size is held fixed?   Increases

   e. Would your confidence intervals of parts a and c be valid if the distribution of the original population was not normal? Explain.   Yes

7.6 Explain what is meant by the statement, "We are 95% confident that an interval estimate contains μ."

7.7 Explain the difference between an interval estimator and a point estimator for μ.

7.8 The mean and standard deviation of a random sample of n measurements are equal to 33.9 and 3.3, respectively.

   a. Find a 95% confidence interval for μ if $n = 100$.

   b. Find a 95% confidence interval for μ if $n = 400$.

   c. Find the widths of the confidence intervals found in parts a and b. What is the effect on the width of a confidence interval of quadrupling the sample size while holding the confidence coefficient fixed?

7.9 Will a large-sample confidence interval be valid if the population from which the sample is taken is not normally distributed? Explain.

Applying the Concepts—Basic

7.10 Donations to tax-exempt organizations such as the Red Cross, the Salvation Army, the YMCA, and the American Cancer Society not only go to the stated charitable purpose, but are used to cover fundraising expenses and overhead. For a sample of 30 charities, the next table lists their *charitable commitment*, the percentage of their expenses that go toward the stated charitable purpose. A MINITAB analysis of the data is shown below.

   a. Give a point estimate for the mean charitable commitment of tax-exempt organizations.   74.97

   b. Locate a 95% confidence interval for the true mean charitable commitment of tax-exempt organizations on the printout. Interpret the result.

   c. Why is the confidence interval of part **b** a better estimator of the mean charitable commitment than the point estimator of part **a**? Explain.

CHARITY

Organization	Charitable Commitment
American Cancer Society	62%
American National Red Cross	91
Big Brothers Big Sisters of America	77
Boy Scouts of America National Council	81
Boys & Girls Clubs of America	81
CARE	91
Covenant House	15
Disabled American Veterans	65
Ducks Unlimited	78
Feed the Children	90
Girl Scouts of the USA	83
Goodwill Industries International	89
Habitat for Humanity International	81
Mayo Foundation	26
Mothers Against Drunk Drivers	71
Multiple Sclerosis Association of America	56
Museum of Modern Art	79
Nature Conservancy	77
Paralyzed Veterans of America	50
Planned Parenthood Federation	81
Salvation Army	84
Shriners Hospital for Children	95
Smithsonian Institution	87
Special Olympics	72
Trust for Public Land	88
United Jewish Appeal/Federation-NY	75
United States Olympic Committee	78
United Way of New York City	85
WGBH Educational Foundation	81
YMCA of the USA	80

Source: "Look Before You Give," *Forbes,* Dec. 27, 1999, pp. 206–216.

7.11 Refer to the *Journal of Accounting and Public Policy* (Spring 2002) study of 100,000 first-time candidates for the CPA exam, Exercise 2.49 (p. 81). Recall that the mean number of semester hours of college credit taken by the candidates was 141.31 hours. The standard deviation was reported to be 17.77 hours.

   a. Compute a 99% confidence interval for the mean number of semester hours taken by all first-time candidates for the CPA exam. $141.31 \pm .145$

   b. Give a practical interpretation of the interval, part **a**.

   c. For the interpretation, part **b,** to be valid, what conditions must hold?

```
Variable   N    Mean    StDev  SE Mean      95% CI
COMMIT    30  74.9667  18.0220  3.2903  (68.2371, 81.6962)
```

7.12 The trade magazine *Quality Progress* randomly sampled 9,033 of its more than 100,000 subscribers and e-mailed them a salary questionnaire. The survey yielded the data shown in the table concerning salary and job title.

Title	Sample Size	Mean	Standard Deviation
Inspector	128	41,026	13,390
Manager	2,413	68,863	19,829
Vice president	223	116,754	39,185

Source: "2002 Salary Survey." *Quality Progress*, Dec. 2002.

a. The column labeled "Mean" reports point estimators for certain parameters. Carefully describe both the relevant populations and parameters.
b. Construct and interpret a 95% confidence interval for the mean salary for managers.
c. Repeat part **b** for vice presidents.
d. Explain why the confidence intervals of parts **b** and **c** are preferred over the point estimates when describing the mean salaries of managers and vice presidents.

7.13 Refer to the *Chance* (Winter 2001) and National Education Longitudinal Survey (NELS) study of 265 students who paid a private tutor to help them improve their SAT scores, Exercise 2.84 (p. 96). The changes in both the SAT–Mathematics and SAT–Verbal scores for these students are reproduced in the table.

	SAT–Math	SAT–Verbal
Mean change in score	19	7
Standard deviation of score changes	65	49

a. Construct and interpret a 90% confidence interval for the population mean change in SAT–Mathematics score for students who pay a private tutor. 19 ± 6.57
b. Repeat part a for the population mean change in SAT–Verbal score. 7 ± 4.95
c. Suppose the true population mean change in score on one of the SAT tests for all students who paid a private tutor is 15. Which of the two tests, SAT–Mathematics or SAT–Verbal, is most likely to have this mean change? Explain. SAT-Math

Applying the Concepts—Intermediate

7.14 Farmers have discovered that the more domestic chickens peck at objects placed in their environment, the healthier and more productive the chickens seem to be. White string has been found to be a particularly attractive pecking stimulus. In one experiment, 72 chickens were exposed to a string stimulus. Instead of white string, blue colored string was used. The number of pecks each chicken took at the blue string over a speci-

fied time interval was recorded. Summary statistics for the 72 chickens were: $\bar{x} = 1.13$ pecks, $s = 2.21$ pecks. (*Applied Animal Behaviour Science*, Oct. 2000.)

a. Estimate the population mean number of pecks made by chickens pecking at blue string using a 99% confidence interval. Interpret the result. $1.13 \pm .67$
b. Previous research has shown that $\mu = 7.5$ pecks if chickens are exposed to white string. Based on the results, part a, is there evidence that chickens are more apt to peck at white string than blue string? Explain.

7.15 The relationship between an employee's participation in the performance appraisal process and subsequent subordinate reactions toward the appraisal was investigated in the *Journal of Applied Psychology* (Aug. 1998). In Chapter 12 we will discuss a quantitative measure of the relationship between two variables, called the coefficient of correlation r. The researchers obtained r for a sample of 34 studies that examined the relationship between appraisal participation and a subordinate's satisfaction with the appraisal. These correlations are listed in the table. (Values of r near $+1$ reflect a strong positive relationship between the variables.) Find a 95% confidence interval for the mean of the data and interpret it in the words of the problem.

🔵 **CORR34**

.50	.58	.71	.46	.63	.66	.31	.35	.51	.06	.35	.19
.40	.63	.43	.16	−.08	.51	.59	.43	.30	.69	.25	.20
.39	.20	.51	.68	.74	.65	.34	.45	.31	.27		

Source: Cawley, B. D., Keeping, L. M., and Levy, P. E. "Participation in the Performance Appraisal Process and Employee Reactions: A Meta-Analytic Review of Field Investigations." *Journal of Applied Psychology*, Vol. 83, No. 4, Aug. 1998, pp. 632–633 (Appendix).

7.16 Named for the section of the 1978 Internal Revenue Code that authorized them, 401(k) plans permit employees to shift part of their before-tax salaries into investments such as mutual funds. Employers typically match 50% of the employee's contribution up to about 6% of salary (*Fortune*, Dec. 28, 1992). One company, concerned with what it believed was a low employee participation rate in its 401(k) plan, sampled 30 other companies with similar plans and asked for their 401(k) participation rates. The following rates (in percentages) were obtained:

🔵 **RATE401K**

80	76	81	77	82	80	85	60	80	79	82	70
88	85	80	79	83	75	87	78	80	84	72	75
90	84	82	77	75	86						

a. Construct a 90% confidence interval for the mean participation rate for all companies that have 401(k) plans.
b. Interpret the interval in the context of this problem.
c. What assumption is necessary to ensure the validity of this confidence interval?

d. If the company that conducted the sample has a 71% participation rate, can it safely conclude that its rate is below the population mean rate for all companies with 401(k) plans? Explain.

e. If in the data set the 60% had been 80%, how would the center and width of the confidence interval you constructed in part a be affected?

7.17 The 1967 Age Discrimination in Employment Act (ADEA) made it illegal to discriminate against workers 40 years of age and older. Opponents of the law argue that there are sound economic reasons why employers would not want to hire and train workers who are very close to retirement. They also argue that people's abilities tend to deteriorate with age. In fact, *Forbes* (Dec. 13, 1999) reported that 25-year-olds did significantly better than 60-year-olds on the Wechsler Adult Intelligence Scale, the most popular IQ test. The data below are raw test scores (i.e., not the familiar normalized IQ scores) for a sample of 36 25-year-olds and 36 60-year-olds:

a. Estimate the mean raw test score for all 25-year-olds using a 99% confidence interval. Give a practical interpretation of the confidence interval.

b. What assumption(s) must hold for the method of estimation used in part a to be appropriate?

c. Find a 95% confidence interval for the mean raw score of all 60-year-olds and interpret your result.

IQ25

25-Year-Olds

54	61	80	92	41	63
59	68	66	76	82	80
82	47	81	77	88	94
49	86	55	82	45	51
70	72	63	50	52	67
75	60	58	49	63	68

IQ60

60-Year-Olds

42	54	38	22	58	37
60	49	51	60	45	42
73	28	65	65	60	34
34	33	40	28	36	60
45	61	47	30	45	45
45	37	27	40	37	58

Source: Adapted from "The Case for Age Discrimination," *Forbes,* Dec. 13, 1999, p. 13.

DIAMONDS

7.18 Refer to Exercise 2.47 (p. 81) and the *Journal of Statistics Education* data on diamonds saved in the DIAMONDS file. Consider the quantitative variable, number of carats, recorded for each of the 308 diamonds for sale on the open market.

a. Select a random sample of 30 diamonds from the 308 diamonds.

b. Find the mean and standard deviation of the number of carats per diamond for the sample.

c. Use the sample information, part b, to construct a 95% confidence interval for the mean number of carats in the population of 308 diamonds.

d. Interpret the phrase "95% confidence" when applied to the interval, part c.

e. Refer to the mean of all 308 diamonds you calculated in Exercise 2.47. Does the "population" mean fall within the confidence interval of part c?

Applying the Concepts—Advanced

7.19 Research reported in the *Journal of Psychology and Aging* (May 1992) studied the role that the age of workers has in determining their level of job satisfaction. The researcher hypothesized that both younger and older workers would have a higher job satisfaction rating than middle-age workers. Each of a sample of 1,686 adults was given a job satisfaction score based on answers to a series of questions. Higher job satisfaction scores indicate higher levels of job satisfaction. The data, arranged by age group, are summarized below.

	Age Group		
	Younger 18–24	Middle Age 25–44	Older 45–64
$\bar{x}$	4.17	4.04	4.31
s	.75	.81	.82
n	241	768	677

a. Construct 95% confidence intervals for the mean job satisfaction scores of each age group. Carefully interpret each interval.

b. In the construction of three 95% confidence intervals, is it more or less likely that at least one of them will *not* contain the population mean it is intended to estimate than it is for a single confidence interval to miss the population mean? [*Hint:* Assume the three intervals are independent, and calculate the probability that at least one of them will not contain the population mean it estimates. Compare this probability to the probability that a single interval fails to enclose the mean.]

c. Based on these intervals, does it appear that the researcher's hypothesis is supported? [*Caution:* We'll learn how to use sample information to compare population means in Chapter 9, and we'll return to this exercise at that time. Here, simply base your opinion on the individual confidence intervals you constructed in part **a.**]

7.20 According to scientists, the cockroach has had 300 million years to develop a resistance to destruction. In a study conducted by researchers for S.C. Johnson & Son, Inc. (manufacturers of Raid and Off), 5,000 roaches (the expected number in a roach-infested house) were released in the Raid test kitchen. One week later the kitchen was fumigated and 16,298 dead roaches were counted, a gain of 11,298 roaches for the 1-week period. Assume that none of the original roaches died during the 1-week period and that the standard deviation of x, the number of roaches produced per roach in a 1-week period, is 1.5. Use the number of roaches produced by the sample of 5,000 roaches to find a 95% confidence interval for the mean number of roaches produced per week for each roach in a typical roach-infested house.

7.2 Small-Sample Confidence Interval for a Population Mean

Teaching Tip

Stress to the students that the shape of the sampling distribution is unknown if the population is not normally distributed. It is useful here to introduce the topic of nonparametric statistics even if it will not be covered in the class.

Federal legislation requires pharmaceutical companies to perform extensive tests on new drugs before they can be marketed. Initially, a new drug is tested on animals. If the drug is deemed safe after this first phase of testing, the pharmaceutical company is then permitted to begin human testing on a limited basis. During this second phase, inferences must be made about the safety of the drug based on information in very small samples.

Suppose a pharmaceutical company must estimate the average increase in blood pressure of patients who take a certain new drug. Assume that only six patients (randomly selected from the population of all patients) can be used in the initial phase of human testing. The use of a *small sample* in making an inference about μ presents two immediate problems when we attempt to use the standard normal z as a test statistic.

Problem 1 The shape of the sampling distribution of the sample mean $\bar{x}$ (and the z statistic) now depends on the shape of the population that is sampled. We can no longer assume that the sampling distribution of $\bar{x}$ is approximately normal, because the Central Limit Theorem ensures normality only for samples that are sufficiently large.

Solution to Problem 1 According to Theorem 6.1, the sampling distribution of $\bar{x}$ (and z) is exactly normal even for relatively small samples if the sampled population is normal. It is approximately normal if the sampled population is approximately normal.

Problem 2 The population standard deviation σ is almost always unknown. Although it is still true that $\sigma_{\bar{x}} = \sigma/\sqrt{n}$ the sample standard deviation s may provide a poor approximation for σ when the sample size is small.

Solution to Problem 2 Instead of using the standard normal statistic

$$z = \frac{\bar{x} - \mu}{\sigma_{\bar{x}}} = \frac{\bar{x} - \mu}{\sigma/\sqrt{n}}$$

which requires knowledge of or a good approximation to σ, we define and use the statistic

$$t = \frac{\bar{x} - \mu}{s/\sqrt{n}}$$

in which the sample standard deviation, s, replaces the population standard deviation, σ.

Biography

WILLIAM S. GOSSET (1876–1937)
Student's *t*-Distribution

At the age of 23, William Gosset earned a degree in chemistry and mathematics at prestigious Oxford University. He was immediately hired by the Guinness Brewing Company in Dublin, Ireland for his expertise in chemistry. However, Gosset's mathematical skills allowed him to solve numerous practical problems associated with brewing beer. For example, Gosset applied the Poisson distribution to model the number of yeast cells per unit volume in the fer-mentation process. His most important discovery was that of the *t*-distribution in 1908. Since most applied researchers worked with small samples, Gosset was interested in the behavior of the mean in the small sample case. He tediously took numerous small sets of numbers, calculated the mean and standard devi-ation, obtained their *t*-ratio, and plotted the results on graph paper. The shape of the distribution was always the same— the *t*-distribution. Under company poli-cy, employees were forbidden to publish their research results; so Gosset used the pen name *Student* to publish a paper on the subject. Hence, the distribution has been called Student's *t*-distribution.

If we are sampling from a normal distribution, the ***t*-statistic** has a sampling dis-tribution very much like that of the *z*-statistic: mound-shaped, symmetric, with mean 0. The primary difference between the sampling distributions of *t* and *z* is that the *t* statistic is more variable than the *z*, which follows intuitively when you realize that *t* contains two random quantities ($\bar{x}$ and *s*), whereas *z* contains only one ($\bar{x}$).

The actual amount of variability in the sampling distribution of *t* depends on the sample size *n*. A convenient way of expressing this dependence is to say that the *t*-statistic has ($n - 1$) **degrees of freedom (df).** Recall that the quantity ($n - 1$) is the divisor that appears in the formula for s^2. This number plays a key role in the sampling distribution of s^2 and appears in discussions of other statistics in later chapters. In particular, the smaller the number of degrees of freedom associated with the *t*-statistic, the more variable will be its sampling distribution.

In Figure 7.7 we show both the sampling distribution of *z* and the sampling distribution of a *t*-statistic with 4 df. You can see that the increased variability of the *t*-statistic means that the *t*-value, t_α, that locates an area α in the upper tail of the *t*-distribution is larger than the corresponding value z_α. For any given value of α, the *t*-value t_α increases as the number of degrees of freedom (df) decreases. Values of *t* that will be used in forming small-sample confidence intervals of μ are

Figure 7.7
Standard normal (z) distribution and *t*-distribution with 4 df

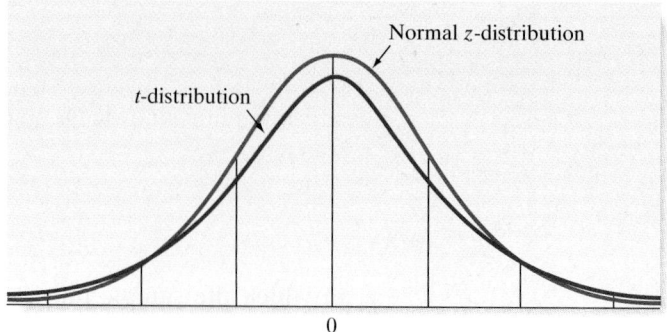

TABLE 7.3 Reproduction of Part of Table VI in Appendix B

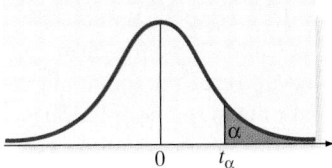

Degrees of Freedom	$t_{.100}$	$t_{.050}$	$t_{.025}$	$t_{.010}$	$t_{.005}$	$t_{.001}$	$t_{.0005}$
1	3.078	6.314	12.706	31.821	63.657	318.13	636.62
2	1.886	2.920	4.303	6.965	9.925	22.326	21.598
3	1.638	2.353	3.182	4.541	5.841	10.213	12.924
4	1.533	2.132	2.776	3.747	4.604	7.173	8.610
5	1.476	2.015	2.571	3.365	4.032	5.893	6.869
6	1.440	1.943	2.447	3.132	3.707	5.208	5.959
7	1.415	1.895	2.365	2.998	3.499	4.785	5.408
8	1.397	1.860	2.306	2.896	3.355	4.501	5.041
9	1.383	1.833	2.262	2.821	3.250	4.297	4.781
10	1.372	1.812	2.228	2.764	3.169	4.144	4.587
11	1.363	1.796	2.201	2.718	3.106	4.025	4.437
12	1.356	1.782	2.179	2.681	3.055	3.930	4.318
13	1.350	1.771	2.160	2.650	3.012	3.852	4.221
14	1.345	1.761	2.145	2.624	2.977	3.787	4.140
15	1.341	1.753	2.131	2.602	2.947	3.733	4.073
⋮	⋮	⋮	⋮	⋮	⋮	⋮	⋮
∞	1.282	1.645	1.960	2.326	2.576	3.090	3.291

given in Table VI of Appendix B. A partial reproduction of this table is shown in Table 7.3.

Note that t_α values are listed for various degrees of freedom, where α refers to the tail area under the *t*-distribution to the right of t_α. For example, if we want the *t* value with an area of .025 to its right and 4 df, we look in the table under the column $t_{.025}$ for the entry in the row corresponding to 4 df. This entry is $t_{.025} = 2.776$, as shown in Figure 7.8. The corresponding standard normal *z*-score is $z_{.025} = 1.96$.

Figure 7.8

The $t_{.025}$ value in a *t*-distribution with 4 df and the corresponding $z_{.025}$ value

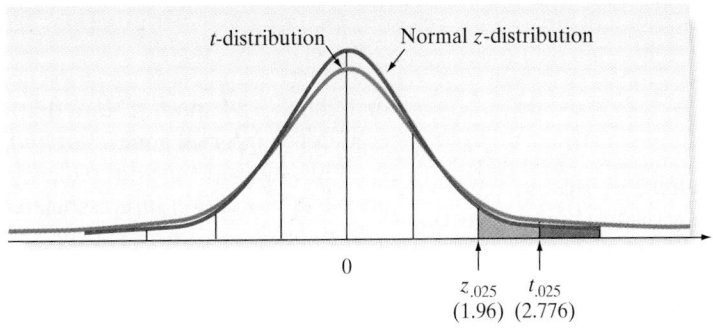

Note that the last row of Table VI, where df = ∞ (infinity), contains the standard normal *z* values. This follows from the fact that as the sample size *n* grows very large, *s* becomes closer to σ and thus *t* becomes closer in distribution to *z*. In fact, when df = 29, there is little difference between corresponding tabulated values of z and t. Thus, researchers often choose the arbitrary cutoff of $n = 30$ (df = 29) to distinguish between the large-sample and small-sample inferential techniques.

Returning to the example of testing a new drug, suppose that the six test patients have blood pressure increases of 1.7, 3.0, .8, 3.4, 2.7, and 2.1 points. How can we use this information to construct a 95% confidence interval for μ, the mean increase in blood pressure associated with the new drug for all patients in the population?

First, we know that we are dealing with a sample too small to assume that the sample mean $\bar{x}$ is approximately normally distributed by the Central Limit Theorem. That is, we do not get the normal distribution of $\bar{x}$ "automatically" from the Central Limit Theorem when the sample size is small. Instead, the measured variable, in this case the increase in blood pressure, must be normally distributed in order for the distribution of $\bar{x}$ to be normal.

Second, unless we are fortunate enough to know the population standard deviation σ, which in this case represents the standard deviation of *all* the patients' increases in blood pressure when they take the new drug, we cannot use the standard normal z statistic to form our confidence interval for μ. Instead, we must use the t-distribution, with $(n - 1)$ degrees of freedom.

In this case, $n - 1 = 5$ df, and the t value is found in Table 7.3 to be $t_{.025} = 2.571$ with 5 df. Recall that the large-sample confidence interval would have been of the form

$$\bar{x} \pm z_{\alpha/2}\sigma_{\bar{x}} = \bar{x} \pm z_{\alpha/2}\frac{\sigma}{\sqrt{n}} = \bar{x} \pm z_{.025}\frac{\sigma}{\sqrt{n}}$$

where 95% is the desired confidence level. To form the interval for a small sample from *a normal distribution, we simply substitute t for z and s for σ in the preceding formula:*

$$\bar{x} \pm t_{\alpha/2}\frac{s}{\sqrt{n}}$$

An SPSS printout showing descriptive statistics for the six blood pressure increases is displayed in Figure 7.9. Note that $\bar{x} = 2.283$ and $s = .950$. Substituting these numerical values into the confidence interval formula, we get

$$2.283 \pm (2.571)\left(\frac{.950}{\sqrt{6}}\right) = 2.283 \pm .997$$

or 1.286 to 3.280 points. Note that this interval agrees (except for rounding) with the confidence interval generated by SPSS in Figure 7.9.

We interpret the interval as follows: We can be 95% confident that the mean increase in blood pressure associated with taking this new drug is between 1.286 and 3.28 points. As with our large-sample interval estimates, our confidence is in the process, not in this particular interval. We know that if we were to repeatedly use this estimation procedure, 95% of the confidence intervals produced would contain the true mean μ, *assuming that the probability distribution of changes in blood pressure from which our sample was selected is normal.* The latter assumption is necessary for the small-sample interval to be valid.

What price did we pay for having to utilize a small sample to make the inference? First, we had to assume the underlying population is normally distributed,

Figure 7.9
SPSS confidence interval
for mean blood pressure
increase

Descriptives

			Statistic	Std. Error
BPINCR	Mean		2.283	.3877
	95% Confidence Interval for Mean	Lower Bound	1.287	
		Upper Bound	3.280	
	5% Trimmed Mean		2.304	
	Median		2.400	
	Variance		.902	
	Std. Deviation		.9496	
	Minimum		.8	
	Maximum		3.4	
	Range		2.6	
	Interquartile Range		1.625	
	Skewness		-.573	.845
	Kurtosis		-.389	1.741

Teaching Tip
Discuss the benefits associated
with taking samples of size 30
or more. Use this example
assuming $n = 100$ to compare
the intervals generated.

and if the assumption is invalid, our interval might also be invalid.* Second, we had to form the interval using a t value of 2.571 rather than a z value of 1.96, resulting in a wider interval to achieve the same 95% level of confidence. If the interval from 1.286 to 3.28 is too wide to be of use, then we know how to remedy the situation: increase the number of patients sampled to decrease the interval width (on average).

Now Work   *Exercise 7.22*

The procedure for forming a small-sample confidence interval is summarized in the accompanying boxes.

Small-Sample Confidence Interval[†] for μ

$$\bar{x} \pm t_{\alpha/2}\left(\frac{s}{\sqrt{n}}\right)$$

where $t_{\alpha/2}$ is based on $(n - 1)$ degrees of freedom

Conditions Required for a Valid Small-Sample Confidence Internal for μ

1. A random sample is selected from the target population
2. The population has a relative frequency distribution that is approximately normal.

*By *invalid*, we mean that the probability that the procedure will yield an interval that contains μ is not equal to $(1 - \alpha)$. Generally, if the underlying population is approximately normal, then the confidence coefficient will approximate the probability that a randomly selected interval contains μ.

[†]The procedure given in the box assumes that the population standard deviation σ is unknown, which is almost always the case. If σ is known, we can form the small-sample confidence interval just as we would a large-sample confidence interval using a standard normal z value instead of t. However, we must still assume that the underlying population is approximately normal.

EXAMPLE 7.2

FINDING A SMALL-SAMPLE CONFIDENCE INTERVAL FOR μ

Problem   Some quality control experiments require *destructive sampling* (i.e., the test to determine whether the item is defective destroys the item) in order to measure some particular characteristic of the product. The cost of destructive sampling often dictates small samples. For example, suppose a manufacturer of printers for personal computers wishes to estimate the mean number of characters printed before the printhead fails. Suppose the printer manufacturer tests $n = 15$ randomly selected printheads and records the number of characters printed until failure for each. These 15 measurements (in millions of characters) are listed in Table 7.4, followed by an EXCEL and PHStat2 summary statistics printout in Figure 7.10.

a. 1.239 ± .148

    a. Form a 99% confidence interval for the mean number of characters printed before the printhead fails. Interpret the result.

    b. What assumption is required for the interval, part a, to be valid? Is it reasonably satisfied?

Solution   **a.** For this small sample ($n = 15$), we use the t statistic to form the confidence interval. We use a confidence coefficient of .99 and $n - 1 = 14$ degrees of freedom to find $t_{\alpha/2}$ in Table VI:

Suggested Exercises 7.28

🖸 **PRINTHEAD**

TABLE 7.4   Number of Characters (in Millions) for $n = 15$ Printhead Tests

1.13	1.55	1.43	.92	1.25
1.36	1.32	.85	1.07	1.48
1.20	1.33	1.18	1.22	1.29

Figure 7.10
EXCEL/PHStat2 summary statistics and confidence interval for data in Table 7.4

Confidence Interval Estimate for the Mean

Data	
Sample Standard Deviation	0.19316413
Sample Mean	1.238666667
Sample Size	15
Confidence Level	99%

Intermediate Calculations	
Standard Error of the Mean	0.049874764
Degrees of Freedom	14
t Value	2.976848918
Interval Half Width	0.148469637

Confidence Interval	
Interval Lower Limit	1.09
Interval Upper Limit	1.39

$$t_{\alpha/2} = t_{.005} = 2.977$$

[*Note*: The small sample forces us to extend the interval almost 3 standard deviations (of $\bar{x}$) on each side of the sample mean in order to form the 99% confidence interval.] From the EXCEL/PHStat2 printout, Figure 7.10, we find $\bar{x} = 1.239$ and $s = .193$. Substituting these values into the confidence interval formula, we obtain

$$\bar{x} \pm t_{.005}\left(\frac{s}{\sqrt{n}}\right) = 1.239 \pm 2.977\left(\frac{.193}{\sqrt{15}}\right)$$
$$= 1.239 \pm .148 \quad \text{or} \quad (1.091, 1.387)$$

This interval is shown at the bottom of the printout, Figure 7.10.

Our interpretation is as follows: The manufacturer can be 99% confident that the printhead has a mean life of between 1.091 and 1.387 million characters. If the manufacturer were to advertise that the mean life of its printheads is (at least) 1 million characters, the interval would support such a claim. Our confidence is derived from the fact that 99% of the intervals formed in repeated applications of this procedure would contain μ.

Figure 7.11
MINITAB stem-and-leaf display of data in Table 7.4

Stem-and-Leaf Display: NUMBER

```
Stem-and-leaf of NUMBER   N  = 15
Leaf Unit = 0.010


    1     8    5
    2     9    2
    3    10    7
    5    11    38
   (4)   12    0259
    6    13    236
    3    14    38
    1    15    5
```

b. Since n is small, we must assume that the number of characters printed before printhead failure is a random variable from a normal distribution. That is, we assume that the population from which the sample of 15 measurements is selected is distributed normally. One way to check this assumption is to graph the distribution of data in Table 7.4. If the sample data are approximately normal, then the population from which the sample is selected is very likely to be normal. A MINITAB stem-and-leaf plot for the sample data is displayed in Figure 7.11. The distribution is mound shaped and nearly symmetric. Therefore, the assumption of normality appears to be reasonably satisfied.

Look Back Other checks for normality, such as a normal probability plot and the ratio IQR/S, may also be used to verify the normality condition.

Now work   *Exercise 7.29*

■ ■ ■

We have emphasized throughout this section that an assumption that the population is approximately normally distributed is necessary for making small-sample inferences about μ when using the t-statistic. Although many phenomena do have approximately normal distributions, it is also true that many random phenomena have distributions that are not normal or even mound shaped. Empirical evidence acquired over the years has shown that the t-distribution is rather insensitive to moderate departures from normality. That is, use of the t-statistic when sampling from slightly or moderately skewed mound-shaped populations generally produces credible results; however, for cases in which the distribution is distinctly nonnormal, we must either take a large sample or use a *nonparametric method* (the topic of Chapter 16).

> ### What Do You Do when the Population Relative Frequency Distribution Departs Greatly from Normality?
>
> *Answer:* Use the nonparametric statistical methods of Chapter 16.

Statistics in Action Revisited

Estimating the Mean Weight per Scallop

Refer to the scallop lawsuit described on p. 353. Recall that a ship, returning from a fishing expedition with 11,000 bags of scallops, was accused of violating the U.S. Fisheries and Wildlife Service weight standard for baby scallops. The law requires that the average meat per scallop weigh at least 1/36 of a pound. The harbormaster randomly selected 18 bags for weighing and estimated that the ship caught scallops that averaged only 1/39 of a pound of meat. Consequently, federal authorities confiscated the catch. Was the ship really in violation of the scallop weight standard?

The data are stored as a MINITAB worksheet and the software used to find a 95% confidence interval for the population mean weight per scallop. The MINITAB printout is displayed in Figure SIA7.1. The interval shown on the printout is (.024830, .026915). Note that the upper endpoint of the interval falls below .0278 (or 1/36 of a pound). Consequently, we are 95% confident that the true mean weight per scallop for the 11,000 bags caught by the fishing vessel falls below the 1/36 pound minimum set by the U.S. Fisheries and Wildlife Service. It appears that the ship was in violation of the government minimum weight requirement for baby scallops.

SCALLOPS

TABLE SIA7.1 Scallop Weight Measurements (in Pounds) for 18 Bags Sampled

.0258	.0244	.0236	.0253	.0253	.0233	.0250	.0272	.0244
.0247	.0272	.0242	.0253	.0256	.0275	.0317	.0294	.0258

Adapted from Bennett, A. "Misapplications Review: Jail Terms." *Interfaces,* Vol. 25, No. 2, March–April 1995, p. 20.

One way to answer this question is to form a confidence interval for the true mean weight per scallop for all 11,000 bags caught by the fishing vessel. The data for the 18 sampled bags in the SCALLOPS file are shown in Table SIA7.1. (Each measurement in the table is the estimated average weight per scallop of the bag. A measurement less than 1/36 = .0278 pound indicates an individual bag that does not meet the standard.)

Note: Because the ship violated the baby scallop weight rule, federal authorities confiscated 95% of the ship's catch. The ship's owner complained that this was not fair, since not all (or even 95%) of the bags of scallops had an average weight per scallop under 1/36 of a pound. We address this issue in the next Statistics in Action Revisited (p. 381).]

One-Sample T: Weight

Variable	N	Mean	StDev	SE Mean	95% CI
Weight	18	0.025872	0.002096	0.000494	(0.024830, 0.026915)

Figure SIA7.1
MINITAB confidence interval for scallop weight data

Confidence Interval for a Population Mean

Using the TI-83 Graphing Calculator

Step 1 *Enter the data*
Press **STAT** and select **1:Edit**
Note: If the list already contains data, clear the old data. Use the up arrow to highlight '**L1**'. Press **CLEAR ENTER.**
Use the arrow and **ENTER** keys to enter the data set into **L1.**

Step 2 *Access the Statistical Tests Menu*
Press **STAT**
Arrow right to **TESTS**
Arrow down to **8 : TInterval**
Press **ENTER**

```
EDIT CALC TESTS
2↑T-Test…
3:2-SampZTest…
4:2-SampTTest…
5:1-PropZTest…
6:2-PropZTest…
7:ZInterval…
8∎TInterval…
```

Step 3 *Choose "**Data**" or "**Stats**". ("Data" is selected when you have entered the raw data into a List. "Stats" is selected when you are given only the mean, standard deviation, and sample size.)*
Press **ENTER**
If you selected "Data", set **List** to **L1**
Set **Freq** to **1**
Set **C-Level** to the confidence level
Arrow down to "**Calculate**"
Press ENTER

```
TInterval
 Inpt:Data Stats
 List:L1
 Freq:1
 C-Level:.99
 Calculate
```

If you selected "Stats", enter the mean, standard deviation, and sample size.
Set **C-Level** to the confidence level
Arrow down to **"Calculate"**
Press **ENTER**
(The screen below is set up for an example with a mean of 100 and a standard deviation of 10.)

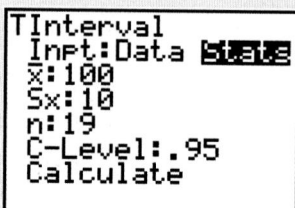

The confidence interval will be displayed with the mean, standard deviation, and the sample size.

Example Compute a 99% confidence interval for the mean using the 15 pieces of data given in Example 7.2.

1.13	1.55	1.43	0.92	1.25
1.36	1.32	0.85	1.07	1.48
1.20	1.33	1.18	1.22	1.29

As you can see from the screen, our 99% confidence interval is (1.0902, 1.3871). You will also notice it gives the mean, standard deviation, and the sample size.

```
TInterval
 (1.0902,1.3871)
 x̄=1.238666667
 Sx=.1931641296
 n=15
■
```

Exercises 7.21–7.34

Learning the Mechanics

7.21 Suppose you have selected a random sample of $n = 5$ measurements from a normal distribution. Compare the standard normal z values with the corresponding t values if you were forming the following confidence intervals.
  a. 80% confidence interval
  b. 90% confidence interval
  c. 95% confidence interval
  d. 98% confidence interval
  e. 99% confidence interval
  f. Use the table values you obtained in parts a–e to sketch the z- and t-distributions. What are the similarities and differences?

7.22 Explain the differences in the sampling distributions of $\bar{x}$ for large and small samples under the following assumptions.
  a. The variable of interest, x, is normally distributed.
  b. Nothing is known about the distribution of the variable x.

7.23 Let t_0 be a particular value of t. Use Table VI of Appendix B to find t_0 values such that the following statements are true.
  a. $P(-t_0 < t < t_0) = .95$ where df $= 10$ 2.228
  b. $P(t \le -t_0 \text{ or } t \ge t_0) = .05$ where df $= 10$ 2.228
  c. $P(t \le t_0) = .05$ where df $= 10$ −1.812
  d. $P(t \le -t_0 \text{ or } t \ge t_0) = .10$ where df $= 20$ 1.725
  e. $P(t \le -t_0 \text{ or } t \ge t_0) = .01$ where df $= 5$ 4.032

7.24 Let t_0 be a specific value of t. Use Table VI in Appendix B to find t_0 values such that the following statements are true.
a. $P(t \geq t_0) = .025$ where df $= 11$ 2.201
b. $P(t \geq t_0) = .01$ where df $= 9$ 2.821
c. $P(t \leq t_0) = .005$ where df $= 6$ -3.707
d. $P(t \leq t_0) = .05$ where df $= 18$ -1.734

7.25 The following random sample was selected from a normal distribution: 4, 6, 3, 5, 9, 3.
a. Construct a 90% confidence interval for the population mean μ. 5 ± 1.876
b. Construct a 95% confidence interval for the population mean μ. 5 ± 2.394
c. Construct a 99% confidence interval for the population mean μ. 5 ± 3.754
d. Assume that the sample mean $\bar{x}$ and sample standard deviation s remain exactly the same as those you just calculated but that they are based on a sample of $n = 25$ observations rather than $n = 6$ observations. Repeat parts a–c. What is the effect of increasing the sample size on the width of the confidence intervals?

7.26 The following sample of 16 measurements was selected from a population that is approximately normally distributed:

⚙ LM7_26

91	80	99	110	95	106	78	121	106	100	97	82
100	83	115	104						

a. Construct an 80% confidence interval for the population mean. 97.94 ± 4.240
b. Construct a 95% confidence interval for the population mean and compare the width of this interval with that of part a. 97.94 ± 6.737
c. Carefully interpret each of the confidence intervals and explain why the 80% confidence interval is narrower.

Applying the Concepts—Basic

7.27 Periodically, the Hillsborough County (Florida) Water Department tests the drinking water of homeowners for contaminants such as lead and copper. The lead and copper levels in water specimens collected for a sample of 10 residents of the Crystal Lakes Manors subdivision are shown in the next table.
a. Construct a 99% confidence interval for the mean lead level in water specimens from Crystal Lakes Manors. 2.8856 ± 4.034
b. Construct a 99% confidence interval for the mean copper level in water specimens from Crystal Lakes Manors. $.4083 \pm .2564$
c. Interpret the intervals, parts a and b, in the words of the problem.
d. Discuss the meaning of the phrase, "99% confident."

⚙ LEADCOPP

Lead (μg/L)	Copper (mg/L)
1.32	.508
0	.279
13.1	.320
.919	.904
.657	.221
3.0	.283
1.32	.475
4.09	.130
4.45	.220
0	.743

Source: Hillsborough County Water Department Environmental Laboratory, Tampa, Florida.

7.28 Health insurers and the federal government are both putting pressure on hospitals to shorten the average length of stay (LOS) of their patients. In 1999, the average LOS for men in the United States was 5.4 days and the average for women was 4.7 days (*Statistical Abstract of the United States: 2001*). A random sample of 20 hospitals in one state had a mean LOS for women in 2003 of 3.8 days and a standard deviation of 1.2 days.
a. Use a 90% confidence interval to estimate the population mean LOS for women for the state's hospitals in 2003. $3.8 \pm .464$
b. Interpret the interval in terms of this application.
c. What is meant by the phrase "90% confidence interval"?

7.29 Deloitte & Touche rank the 500 fastest growing technology companies in the United States based on percentage growth over a five-year period. Their rankings are called the *Technology Fast 500*. A random sample of 12 companies from the 2002 *Technology Fast 500* and their growth rates are shown in the table, followed by a MINITAB analysis of the data on p. 374.

⚙ FAST500

Rank	Company	5-year Revenue Growth Rate
4	Openwave Systems	159,235%
22	Pixel Works	22,602
89	Portal Software	5,218
160	The Cobalt Group	2,864
193	Live World	2,238
268	HPower Corp.	1,381
274	Dataprise	1,340
322	Sonic WALL	1,099
359	MC Data	943
396	Objectif Lune	822
441	Matri Kon	711
485	USNano Corp	627

Source: Technology Fast 500, Deloitte & Touche 2002, (www.fast500.com)

a. Find a 95% confidence interval for the true mean five-year revenue growth rate for the 2002 *Technology Fast 500*. Interpret the result. $-12,218, 45,396$

MINITAB Output for Exercise 7.29

One-Sample T: GrwthRate

```
Variable    N    Mean    StDev   SE Mean        95% CI
GrwthRate  12  16588.5  45339.3  13088.3  (-12218.7, 45395.7)
```

Stem-and-Leaf Display: GrwthRate

```
Stem-and-leaf of GrwthRate   N = 12
Leaf Unit = 10000


(10)  0  0000000000
  2   0  2
  1   0
  1   0
  1   0
  1   1
  1   1
  1   1  5
```

b. In order to estimate the mean described in part a with a small-sample confidence interval, what characteristic must the population possess?   Must be normal

c. Explain why the required population characteristics may not hold in this case.

7.30 Refer to Exercise 2.44 (p. 80) and the data on the top law firms in Florida, as ranked by *Florida Trend Magazine* (April 2002). The data, saved in the **FLALAW** file, are repeated in the next table.

FLALAW

Rank	Firm	Headquarters	Number of Lawyers	Number of Offices
1	Holland & Knight	Tallahasse	529	11
2	Akerman Senterfit	Orlando	355	9
3	Greenberg Traurig	Miami	301	6
4	Carlton Fields	Tampa	207	6
5	Gruden McClosky Smit	Ft. Lauder	175	9
6	Fowler White Boggs	Tampa	175	7
7	Foley & Lardner	Orlando	159	5
8	GrayHarris	Orlando	158	6
9	Broad and Cassel	Orlando	150	7
10	Shutts & Bowen	Miami	144	5
11	Steel Hector & Davis	Miami	141	5
12	Gunster Yoakley	WPalmBeach	140	6
13	Adorno & Zeder	Miami	105	4
14	Becker & Poliakoff	Ft. Lauder	100	12
15	Lowndes Drosdick	Orlando	100	1
16	Conroy Simberg Ganon	Hollywood	91	6
17	Stearns Weaver	Miami	85	3
18	Wicker Smith O'Hara	Miami	85	6
19	Rogers Towers Bailey	Jacksonvll	80	2
20	Butler Burnette	Tampa	77	3
21	Bilzin Sumberg Dunn	Miami	70	1
22	Morgan Colling	Orlando	70	4
23	White & Case	Miami	70	1
24	Fowler White Burnett	Miami	64	4
25	Rissman Weisberg	Orlando	63	3
26	Rumberger Kirk	Orlando	63	4

Source: Florida Trend Magazine, April 2002, p. 105.

a. Find a 90% confidence interval for the mean number of offices operated by all Florida law firms. Interpret the resulting interval.   5.231 ± .954

b. Does the condition of a normally distributed population appear to be satisfied for this application of the small-sample confidence interval method?

c. Give a reason why the interval, part a, may be invalid.

Applying the Concepts—Intermediate

7.31 Accidental spillage and misguided disposal of petroleum wastes have resulted in extensive contamination of soils across the country. A common hazardous compound found in the contaminated soil is benzo(a)pyrene [B(a)p]. An experiment was conducted to determine the effectiveness of a method designed to remove B(a)p from soil (*Journal of Hazardous Materials*, June 1995). Three soil specimens contaminated with a known amount of B(a)p were treated with a toxin that inhibits microbial growth. After 95 days of incubation, the percentage of B(a)p removed from each soil specimen was measured. The experiment produced the following summary statistics: $\bar{x}$ = 49.3 and s = 1.5.

a. Use a 99% confidence interval to estimate the mean percentage of B(a)p removed from a soil specimen in which the toxin was used.   49.3 ± 8.6

b. Interpret the interval in terms of this application.

c. What assumption is necessary to ensure the validity of this confidence interval?

d. Comment on whether the true mean percent removed could be as high as 50%.

7.32 It is customary practice in the United States to base roadway design on the 30th highest hourly volume in a year. Thus, all roadway facilities are expected to operate at acceptable levels of service for all but 29 hours of the year. The Florida Department of Transportation (DOT), however, has shifted from the 30th highest hour to the 100th highest hour as the basis for level-of-service determinators. Florida Atlantic University researcher Reid Ewing investigated whether this shift was warranted in the *Journal of STAR Research* (July 1994). The table below gives the traffic counts at the 30th highest hour and the 100th highest hour of a recent year for 20 randomly selected DOT permanent count stations.

a. Describe the population from which the sample data is selected.

b. Does the sample appear to be representative of the population? Explain.   Yes

c. Compute and interpret a 95% confidence interval for the mean traffic count at the 30th highest hour.

d. What assumption is necessary for the confidence interval to be valid? Does it appear to be satisfied? Explain.   Normal population

e. Repeat parts c and d for the 100th highest hour.

⊚ TRAFFIC

Station	Type of Route	30th Highest Hour	100th Highest Hour
0117	small city	1,890	1,736
0087	recreational	2,217	2,069
0166	small city	1,444	1,345
0013	rural	2,105	2,049
0161	urban	4,905	4,815
0096	urban	2,022	1,958
0145	rural	594	548
0149	rural	252	229
0038	urban	2,162	2,048
0118	rural	1,938	1,748
0047	rural	879	811
0066	urban	1,913	1,772
0094	rural	3,494	3,403
0105	small city	1,424	1,309
0113	small city	4,571	4,425
0151	urban	3,494	3,359
0159	rural	2,222	2,137
0160	small city	1,076	989
0164	recreational	2,167	2,039
0165	recreational	3,350	3,123

Source: Ewing, R. "Roadway Levels of Service in an Era of Growth Management." *Journal of STAR Research*, Vol. 3, July 1994, p. 103 (Table 2).

7.33 The table below lists the number of full-time employees at each of 22 office furniture dealers serving Tampa, Florida, and its surrounding communities.

OFFURN

50	78	41	32	35	12	12	15	5	3	5
23	16	24	24	15	12	11	30	43	4	4

Source: *Tampa Bay Business Journal*, June 21–27, 1996, p. 27.

a. Construct a 99% confidence interval for the true mean number of full-time employees at office furniture dealers in Tampa. 22.45 ± 11.18
b. Interpret the interval, part a.
c. Comment on the assumption required for the interval to be valid. Normal population
d. The 22 dealers in the sample were the top-ranked furniture dealers in Tampa based on sales volume in 1995. How does this fact impact the validity of the confidence interval? Explain

7.34 IPOs—initial public offerings of stock—create billions of dollars of new wealth for owners, managers, and employees of companies that were previously privately owned. Nevertheless, hundreds of large and thousands of small companies remain privately owned. The revenues of a random sample of 15 firms from *Forbes* 500 Largest Private Companies list is given in the next table.

BIGCOM

Company	(in millions)
Enterprise Rent-A-Car	$6,500
Flying J	3,150
Tenaska Energy	2,665
Wawa	2,010
Kinko's	2,000
Brookshire Grocery	1,740
Swinerton	1,549
Bose	1,400
Mary Kay	1,400
IMG	1,260
Rooms to Go	1,260
SAS Institute	1,130
Anderson News	1,054
Printpack	1,015
Primus	1,001

Source: "Largest Private Companies", *Forbes*, Nov. 7, 2002.

a. Describe the population from which the random sample was drawn.
b. Use a 98% confidence interval to estimate the mean operating income of the population of companies in question. 1942 ± 952.68
c. Interpret your confidence interval in the context of the problem.
d. What characteristic must the population possess to ensure the appropriateness of the estimation procedure used in part b? Normally distributed

7.3 Large-Sample Confidence Interval for a Population Proportion

The number of public opinion polls has grown at an astounding rate in recent years. Almost daily, the news media report the results of some poll. Pollsters regularly determine the percentage of people who approve of the president's on-the-job performance, the fraction of voters in favor of a certain candidate, the fraction of customers who prefer a particular product, and the proportion of households that watch a particular TV program. In each case, we are interested in estimating the percentage (or proportion) of some group with a certain characteristic. In this section we consider methods for making inferences about population proportions when the sample is large.

EXAMPLE 7.3

ESTIMATING A POPULATION PROPORTION

Problem

A food-products company conducted a market study by randomly sampling and interviewing 1,000 consumers to determine which brand of breakfast cereal they prefer. Suppose 313 consumers were found to prefer the company's brand. How would you estimate the true fraction of *all* consumers who prefer the company's cereal brand?

$\hat{p} = .313$

Solution

What we have really asked is how you would estimate the probability p of success in a binomial experiment, where p is the probability that a chosen consumer prefers the company's brand. One logical method of estimating p for the population is to use the proportion of successes in the sample. That is, we can estimate p by calculating

$$\hat{p} = \frac{\text{Number of consumers sampled who prefer the company's brand}}{\text{Number of consumers sampled}}$$

where $\hat{p}$ is read "p hat." Thus, in this case,

$$\hat{p} = \frac{313}{1{,}000} = .313$$

Teaching Tip

It is helpful if the student understands that sampling distributions are the key to all interval estimates. Tie the use of the sample proportion as the estimate of p back to the sampling distributions of Chapter 6.

Look Back To determine the reliability of the estimator $\hat{p}$, we need to know its sampling distribution. That is, if we were to draw samples of 1,000 consumers over and over again, each time calculating a new estimate $\hat{p}$, what would be the frequency distribution of all the $\hat{p}$ values? The answer lies in viewing $\hat{p}$ as the average, or mean, number of successes per trial over the n trials. If each success is assigned a value equal to 1 and a failure is assigned a value of 0, then the sum of all n sample observations is x, the total number of successes, and $\hat{p} = x/n$ is the average, or mean, number of successes per trial in the n trials. The Central Limit Theorem tells us that the relative frequency distribution of the sample mean for any population is approximately normal for sufficiently large samples.

Now work *Exercise 7.41a*

■ ■ ■

The repeated sampling distribution of $\hat{p}$ has the characteristics listed in the next box and shown in Figure 7.12.

Teaching Tip

Use examples to check the sample size criteria. Equate this criteria to the $n \geq 30$ that was used for estimating a population mean.

Sampling Distribution of $\hat{p}$

1. The mean of the sampling distribution of $\hat{p}$ is p; that is, $\hat{p}$ is an unbiased estimator of p.
2. The standard deviation of the sampling distribution of $\hat{p}$ is $\sqrt{pq/n}$; that is, $\sigma_{\hat{p}} = \sqrt{pq/n}$, where $q = 1 - p$.
3. For large samples, the sampling distribution of $\hat{p}$ is approximately normal. A sample size is considered large if the interval $\hat{p} \pm 3\sigma_{\hat{p}}$ does not include 0 or 1. [*Note:* This requirement is almost equivalent to that given in Section 5.5 for approximating a binomial distribution with a normal one. The difference is that we assumed p to be known in Section 5.5; now we are trying to make inferences about an unknown p, so we use $\hat{p}$ to estimate p in checking the adequacy of the normal approximation.]

The fact that $\hat{p}$ is a "sample mean number of successes per trial" allows us to form confidence intervals about p in a manner that is completely analogous to that used for large-sample estimation of μ.

Figure 7.12
Sampling distribution of $\hat{p}$

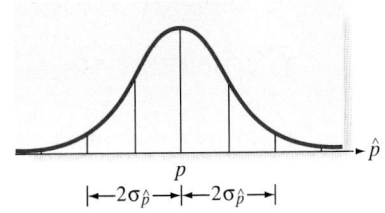

Large-Sample Confidence Interval for p

$$\hat{p} \pm z_{\alpha/2}\sigma_{\hat{p}} = \hat{p} \pm z_{\alpha/2}\sqrt{\frac{pq}{n}} \approx \hat{p} \pm z_{\alpha/2}\sqrt{\frac{\hat{p}\hat{q}}{n}}$$

where $\hat{p} = \dfrac{x}{n}$ and $\hat{q} = 1 - \hat{p}$

Note: When n is large, $\hat{p}$ can approximate the value of p in the formula for $\sigma_{\hat{p}}$.

Conditions Required for a Valid Large-Sample Confidence Interval for p

1. A random sample is selected from the target population.
2. The sample size n is large. (This condition will be satisfied if $\hat{p} \pm 3\sigma_{\hat{p}}$ falls between 0 and 1.)

Teaching Tip

Show that the relationships between the sample size and the interval width and the confidence level and the interval width are the same as when the population mean was estimated.

Thus, if 313 of 1,000 consumers prefer the company's cereal brand, a 95% confidence interval for the proportion of *all* consumers who prefer the company's brand is

$$\hat{p} \pm z_{\alpha/2}\sigma_{\hat{p}} = .313 \pm \sqrt{\frac{pq}{1,000}}$$

where $q = 1 - p$. Just as we needed an approximation for σ in calculating a large-sample confidence interval for μ, we now need an approximation for p. As Table 7.6 shows, the approximation for p does not have to be especially accurate, because the value of $\sqrt{pq}$ needed for the confidence interval is relatively insensitive to changes in p. Therefore, we can use $\hat{p}$ to approximate p. Keeping in mind that $\hat{q} = 1 - \hat{p}$, we substitute these values into the formula for the confidence interval:

$$\hat{p} \pm 1.96\sqrt{\frac{pq}{1,000}} \approx \hat{p} \pm 1.96\sqrt{\frac{\hat{p}\hat{q}}{1,000}}$$

$$= .313 \pm 1.96\sqrt{\frac{(.313)(.687)}{1,000}}$$

$$= .313 \pm .029$$

$$= (.284, .342)$$

TABLE 7.6 Values of pq for Several Different Values of p

p	pq	$\sqrt{pq}$
.5	.25	.50
.6 or .4	.24	.49
.7 or .3	.21	.46
.8 or .2	.16	.40
.9 or .1	.09	.30

The company can be 95% confident that the interval from 28.4% to 34.2% contains the true percentage of *all* consumers who prefer its brand. That is, in repeated construction of confidence intervals, approximately 95% of all samples would produce confidence intervals that enclose p. Note that the guidelines for interpreting a confidence interval about μ also apply to interpreting a confidence interval for p because p is the "population fraction of successes" in a binomial experiment.

EXAMPLE 7.4

FINDING A LARGE-SAMPLE CONFIDENCE INTERVAL FOR p

Problem Many public polling agencies conduct surveys to determine the current consumer sentiment concerning the state of the economy. For example, the Bureau of Economic and Business Research (BEBR) at the University of Florida conducts quarterly surveys to gauge consumer sentiment in the Sunshine State. Suppose that BEBR randomly samples 484 consumers and finds that 257 are optimistic about the state of the economy. Use a 90% confidence interval to estimate the proportion of all consumers in Florida who are optimistic about the state of the economy. Based on the confidence interval, can BEBR infer that the majority of Florida consumers are optimistic about the economy?

.531 ± .037

Solution   The number, x, of the 484 sampled consumers who are optimistic about the Florida economy is a binomial random variable if we can assume that the sample was randomly selected from the population of Florida consumers and that the poll was conducted identically for each sampled consumer.

The point estimate of the proportion of Florida consumers who are optimistic about the economy is

$$\hat{p} = \frac{x}{n} = \frac{257}{484} = .531$$

Teaching Tip

Draw pictures of the sampling distribution of $\hat{p}$ to illustrate the similarities with the sampling distribution of the sample mean. Point out that the symbols have changed but the confidence interval theory is the same.

We first check to be sure that the sample size is sufficiently large that the normal distribution provides a reasonable approximation for the sampling distribution of $\hat{p}$. We check the 3-standard-deviation interval around $\hat{p}$:

$$\hat{p} \pm 3\sigma_{\hat{p}} \approx \hat{p} \pm 3\sqrt{\frac{\hat{p}\hat{q}}{n}}$$

$$= .531 \pm 3\sqrt{\frac{(.531)(.469)}{484}} = .531 \pm .068 = (.463, .599)$$

Since this interval is wholly contained in the interval $(0, 1)$, we may conclude that the normal approximation is reasonable.

We now proceed to form the 90% confidence interval for p, the true proportion of Florida consumers who are optimistic about the state of the economy:

$$\hat{p} \pm z_{\alpha/2}\sigma_{\hat{p}} = \hat{p} \pm z_{\alpha/2}\sqrt{\frac{pq}{n}} \approx \hat{p} \pm z_{\alpha/2}\sqrt{\frac{\hat{p}\hat{q}}{n}}$$

$$= .531 \pm 1.645\sqrt{\frac{(.531)(.469)}{484}} = .531 \pm .037 = (.494, .568)$$

Teaching Tip

Point out the similarities of these interpretations with those used when estimating a population mean.

Thus, we can be 90% confident that the proportion of all Florida consumers who are confident about the economy is between .494 and .568. As always, our confidence stems from the fact that 90% of all similarly formed intervals will contain the true proportion p and not from any knowledge about whether this particular interval does.

Can we conclude that the majority of Florida consumers are optimistic about the economy based on this interval? If we wished to use this interval to infer that a majority is optimistic, the interval would have to support the inference that p exceeds .5—that is, that more than 50% of the Florida consumers are optimistic about the economy. Note that the interval contains some values below .5 (as low as .494) as well as some above .5 (as high as .568). Therefore, we cannot conclude that the true value of p exceeds .5 based on this 90% confidence interval.

Look Back If the entire confidence interval fell above .5 (e.g., an interval from .52 to .54), then we could conclude (with 90% confidence) that the true proportion of consumers who are optimistic exceeds .5.

Now work   *Exercise 7.41b,c*

■ ■ ■

Caution

Unless *n* is extremely large, the large-sample procedure presented in this section performs poorly when *p* is near 0 or 1. For example, suppose you want to estimate the proportion of executives who die from a work-related injury. This proportion is likely to be near 0 (say, $p \approx .001$). Confidence intervals for *p* based on a sample of size $n = 50$ will probably be misleading.

To overcome this potential problem, an *extremely* large sample size is required. Since the value of *n* required to satisfy "extremely large" is difficult to determine, statisticians (see Agresti & Coull, 1998) have proposed an alternative method, based on the Wilson (1927) point estimator of *p*. The procedure is outlined in the box. Researchers have shown that this confidence interval works well for any *p* even when the sample size *n* is very small.

Teaching Tip
Note that this procedure works
even for very small sample sizes.

Adjusted $(1 - \alpha)$ 100% Confidence Interval for a Population Proportion, *p*

$$\widetilde{p} \pm z_{\alpha/2}\sqrt{\frac{\widetilde{p}(1 - \widetilde{p})}{n + 4}}$$

where $\widetilde{p} = \frac{x + 2}{n + 4}$ is the adjusted sample proportion of observations with the characteristic of interest, *x* is the number of successes in the sample, and *n* is the sample size.

EXAMPLE 7.5

APPLYING THE ADJUSTED CONFIDENCE INTERVAL PROCEDURE FOR *p*

Problem According to *True Odds: How Risk Affects Your Everyday Life* (Walsh, 1997), the probability of being the victim of a violent crime is less than .01. Suppose that in a random sample of 200 Americans, 3 were victims of a violent crime. Estimate the true proportion of Americans who were victims of a violent crime using a 95% confidence interval.

.025 ± .021

Solution Let *p* represent the true proportion of Americans who were victims of a violent crime. Since *p* is near 0, an "extremely large" sample is required to estimate its value using the usual large-sample method. Since we are unsure whether the sample size of 200 is large enough, we will apply the adjustment outlined in the box.

Suggested Exercises 7.46

The number of "successes" (i.e., number of violent crime victims) in the sample is $x = 3$. Therefore, the adjusted sample proportion is

$$\widetilde{p} = \frac{x + 2}{n + 4} = \frac{3 + 2}{200 + 4} = \frac{5}{204} = .025$$

Note that this adjusted sample proportion is obtained by adding a total of four observations—two "successes" and two "failures"—to the sample data. Substituting $\tilde{p} = .025$ into the equation for a 95% confidence interval, we obtain

$$\tilde{p} \pm 1.96\sqrt{\frac{\tilde{p}(1 - \tilde{p})}{n + 4}} = .025 \pm 1.96\sqrt{\frac{(.025)(.975)}{204}}$$

$$= .025 \pm .021$$

or (.004, .046). Consequently, we are 95% confident that the true proportion of Americans who are victims of a violent crime falls between .004 and .046.

■ ■ ■

Statistics in Action Revisited

Estimating the Proportion of Underweight Scallop Bags

In the previous Statistics in Action Revisited (p. 368), we discovered that a ship returning from a fishing expedition with 11,000 bags of scallops was in violation of the U.S. Fisheries and Wildlife Service weight standard for baby scallops. (The law requires that the average meat per scallop weigh at least 1/36 of a pound.) Consequently, federal authorities confiscated 95% of the ship's catch. Is this fair? Did 95% of the ship's 11,000 bags contain underweight scallops?

To answer this question, we want to estimate p, the true fraction of the 11,000 bags of scallops that have an average weight per scallop less than $1/36 = .0278$ pound. If you examine the data for the 18 sampled bags (saved in the SCALLOPS file and listed in Table SIA7.1, p. 370), you will find that 16 of the 18 bags had an average weight per scallop less than .0278. Thus, our estimate of p is

$$\hat{p} = 16/18 = .889$$

A 95% confidence interval for p can be obtained using the confidence interval formula or with statistical software. A

MINITAB printout of the analysis is displayed in Figure SIA7.2. The 95% confidence interval, highlighted on the printout, is (0.7437, 1.0000). Thus, we are 95% confident that the true percentage of the 11,000 bags of scallops that are under the 1/36 pound weight minimum is between 74.4% and 100%. This implies that the percentage of underweight bags could be as low as 74.4%. By confiscating 95% of the 11,000 bags of scallops, federal agents may have overestimated the fraction of bags that were in violation of the weight minimum.

Note: The MINITAB confidence interval in Figure SIA7.2 is based on a normal approximation that requires a "large" sample. A sample size of $n = 18$ bags is very small; thus, the interval may be inaccurate (as stated at the bottom of the MINITAB printout). To arrive at a more reliable estimate of the true proportion of underweight bags, federal agents should have selected a larger number of bags to weigh. In the next Statistics in Action Revisited (p. 389), we show how large of a sample needs to be selected.

Test and CI for One Proportion: Limit

```
Test of p = 0.5 vs p not = 0.5

Event = Below


Variable   X   N   Sample p         95% CI           Z-Value  P-Value
Limit     16  18   0.888889  (0.743706, 1.000000)     3.30    0.001


* NOTE * The normal approximation may be inaccurate for small samples.
```

Figure SIA7.2
MINITAB confidence interval for proportion of underweight bags

Confidence Interval for a Population Proportion

Using the TI-83 Graphing Calculator

Step 1 *Access the Statistical Tests Menu*
Press **STAT**
Arrow right to **TESTS**
Arrow down to **A:1-PropZInt**
Press **ENTER**

Step 2 *Enter the values for* **x, n** *and* **C-Level**
where **x** = number of successes
n = sample size
C-Level = level of confidence
Arrow down to "**Calculate**"
Press **ENTER**

Example Suppose that 1,100 U.S. citizens are randomly chosen and 532 answer that they favor a flat income tax rate. Use a 95% confidence interval to estimate the true proportion of citizens who favor a flat income tax rate.
In this example, x = 532, n = 1,100 and C-Level = .95.

The screens for this example are shown below.

```
1-PropZInt
x:532
n:1100
C-Level:.95
Calculate
```

```
1-PropZInt
(.4541,.51317)
p=.4836363636
n=1100
```

Thus, we can be 95% confident that the interval from 45.4% to 51.3% contains the true percentage of all U.S. citizens who favor a flat income tax rate.

Exercises 7.35–7.51

Learning the Mechanics

7.35 Explain the meaning of the phrase "$\hat{p}$ is an unbiased estimator of p." $E(\hat{p}) = p$

7.36 Describe the sampling distribution of $\hat{p}$ based on large samples of size n. That is, give the mean, the standard deviation, and the (approximate) shape of the distribution of $\hat{p}$ when large samples of size n are (repeatedly)

selected from the binomial distribution with probability of success p.

7.37 For the binomial sample information summarized in each part, indicate whether the sample size is large enough to use the methods of this chapter to construct a confidence interval for p.
a. $n = 400, \hat{p} = .10$ Yes

b. $n = 50, \hat{p} = .10$
c. $n = 20, \hat{p} = .5$ Yes
d. $n = 20, \hat{p} = .3$

7.38 A random sample of size $n = 121$ yielded $\hat{p} = .88$.
a. Is the sample size large enough to use the methods of this section to construct a confidence interval for p? Explain.   Yes
b. Construct a 90% confidence interval for p.
c. What assumption is necessary to ensure the validity of this confidence interval?

7.39 A random sample of size $n = 225$ yielded $\hat{p} = .46$.
a. Is the sample size large enough to use the methods of this section to construct a confidence interval for p? Explain.   Yes
b. Construct a 95% confidence interval for p.
c. Interpret the 95% confidence interval.
d. Explain what is meant by the phrase "95% confidence interval."

7.40 A random sample of 50 consumers taste tested a new snack food. Their responses were coded (0: do not like; 1: like; 2: indifferent) and recorded as follows:

SNACK

1	0	0	1	2	0	1	1	0	0
0	1	0	2	0	2	2	0	0	1
1	0	0	0	0	1	0	2	0	0
0	1	0	0	1	0	0	1	0	1
0	2	0	0	1	1	0	0	0	1

a. Use an 80% confidence interval to estimate the proportion of consumers who like the snack food.
b. Provide a statistical interpretation for the confidence interval you constructed in part **a.**

Applying the Concepts—Basic

7.41 In a July, 2001 research note, the U.S. Department of Transportation reported the results of the *National Occupant Protection Use Survey*. One focus of the survey was to determine the level of cell phone use by drivers while they are in the act of driving a motor passenger vehicle. Data collected by observers at randomly selected intersections across the country revealed that in a sample of 1,165 drivers, 35 were using their cell phone.
a. Give a point estimate of p, the true driver cell phone use rate (i.e., the true proportion of drivers who are using a cell phone while driving).   .030
b. Compute a 95% confidence interval for p.   .030 ± .0098
c. Give a practical interpretation of the interval, part **b.**

7.42 In a study of homicide on the job, University of North Carolina researchers collected data on workplaces where an employee was murdered. (*American Journal*

of Epidemiology, Vol. 154, 2001.) In a sample of 105 cases, 67 of the homicides occurred during night hours (between 9 P.M. and 6 A.M.).
a. Give a point estimate of p, the true proportion of on-the-job homicide cases that occurred at night.   .638
b. Compute a 95% confidence interval for p.   .638 ± .092
c. Give a practical interpretation of the interval, part **b.**

7.43 Refer to Exercise 2.8 (p. 54) and the *Journal of Global Business* (Spring 2002) survey to determine what "Made in the USA" means to consumers. Recall that 106 shoppers at a shopping mall in Muncie, Indiana responded to the question, " 'Made in the USA' means what percentage of US labor and materials?" Sixty-four shoppers answered "100%."
a. Define the population of interest in the survey.
b. What is the characteristic of interest in the population?
c. Estimate the true proportion of consumers who believe "Made in the USA" means 100% US labor and materials using a 90% confidence interval.   .604 ± .078
d. Give a practical interpretation of the interval, part **c.**
e. Explain what the phrase "90% confidence" means for this interval.

DDT

7.44 Refer to the U.S. Army Corps of Engineers data on a sample of 144 contaminated fish collected from the river adjacent to a chemical plant. The data are saved in the **DDT** file. Estimate the proportion of contaminated fish that are of the channel catfish species. Use a 90% confidence interval and interpret the result.   .667 ± .065

DIAMONDS

7.45 Refer to the sample of 308 diamond stones that were listed for sale on the open market in Singapore's *Business Times*. The data are saved in the **DIAMONDS** file. Recall that the color of each diamond is classified as D, E, F, G, H, or I, while the clarity of each is classified as VVS1, VVS2, VS1, or VS2.
a. Find a 99% confidence interval for the proportion of all diamonds for sale on the open market that are classified as "D" color. Interpret the result.   .052 ± .033
b. Find a 99% confidence interval for the proportion of all diamonds for sale on the open market that are classified as "VS1" clarity. Interpret the result.   .263 ± .065

Applying the Concepts—Intermediate

7.46 The Gallup Organization surveyed 1,252 debit cardholders in the United States and found that 180 had used the debit card to purchase a product or service on the Internet (*Card Fax*, November 12, 1999).
a. Describe the population of interest to the Gallup Organization.

b. If you personally were charged with drawing a random sample from this population, what difficulties would you encounter? Assume in the remainder of the exercise that the 1,252 debit cardholders were randomly selected.

c. Is the sample size large enough to construct a valid confidence interval for the proportion of debit cardholders who have used their card in making purchases over the Internet? Justify you answer. Yes

d. Estimate the proportion referred to in part **c** using a 98% confidence interval. Interpret your result in the context of the problem. $.144 \pm .023$

e. If you had constructed a 90% confidence interval instead, would it be wider or narrower? Narrower

7.47 As Internet usage proliferates, so do questions of security and confidentiality of personal information, including such things as social security and credit card numbers. NCR Corporation surveyed 1,000 U.S. adults and asked them under what circumstances they would give personal information to a company. Twenty-nine percent said they would never give personal data to a company, while 51% said they would if the company had strict privacy guidelines in place (*Precision Marketing*, Oct. 4, 1999).

a. Verify that the sample size is large enough to construct a valid confidence interval for p, the proportion of all U.S. adults who would never give personal information to a company.

b. Construct a 95% confidence interval for p and interpret your result in the context of the problem.

c. Other than the size of the sample, what assumption must be made about the sample in order for the estimation procedure of part **b** to be valid? It is random

7.48 By law, all new cars must be equipped with both driver-side and passenger-side safety air bags. There is concern, however, over whether air bags pose a danger for children sitting on the passenger side. In a National Highway Traffic Safety Administration (NHTSA) study of 55 people killed by the explosive force of air bags, 35 were children seated on the front-passenger side (*Wall Street Journal*, Jan. 22, 1997). This study led some car owners with children to disconnect the passenger-side air bag. Consider all fatal automobile accidents in which it is determined that air bags were the cause of death. Let p represent the true proportion of these accidents involving children seated on the front-passenger side.

a. Use the data from the NHTSA study to estimate p.

b. Construct a 99% confidence interval for p.

c. Interpret the interval, part **b,** in the words of the problem.

d. NHTSA investigators determined that 24 of 35 children killed by the air bags were not wearing seat belts or were improperly restrained. How does this information impact your assessment of the risk of an air bag fatality?

7.49 Refer to the Federal Trade Commission (FTC) 1998 "Price Check" study of electronic checkout scanners, Exercise 4.48 (p. 240). The FTC inspected 1,669 scanners at retail stores and supermarkets by scanning a sample of items at each store and determining if the scanned price was accurate. The FTC gives a store a "passing" grade if 98% or more of the items are priced accurately. Of the 1,669 stores in the study, 1,185 passed inspection.

a. Find a 90% confidence interval for the true proportion of retail stores and supermarkets with electronic scanners that pass the FTC price-check test. Interpret the result. $.710 \pm .018$

b. In 1996, the FTC found that 45% of the stores passed inspection. Use the interval from part **a** to determine whether the proportion of stores that pass inspection in 1998 exceeded .45.

7.50 Substance abuse problems are widespread at New Jersey businesses, according to the *Governor's Council for a Drug Free Workplace Report* (Spring/Summer 1995). A questionnaire on the issue was mailed to all New Jersey businesses that were members of the Governor's Council. Of the 72 companies that responded to the survey, 50 admitted that they had employees whose performance was affected by drugs or alcohol.

a. Use a 95% confidence interval to estimate the proportion of all New Jersey companies with substance abuse problems. $.694 \pm .106$

b. What assumptions are necessary to ensure the validity of the confidence interval?

c. Interpret the interval in the context of the problem.

d. In interpreting the confidence interval, what does it mean to say you are "95% confident"?

e. A claim is made that only 50% of New Jersey businesses have employees with substance abuse problems. Comment on the believability of this claim.

f. Would you use the interval of part a to estimate the proportion of all U.S. companies with substance abuse problems? Why or why not?

Applying the Concepts—Advanced

7.51 The accounting firm of Price Waterhouse annually monitors the U.S. Postal Service's performance. One parameter of interest is the percentage of mail delivered on time. In a sample of 332,000 items mailed between Dec. 10 and Mar. 3—the most difficult delivery season due to bad weather and holidays—Price Waterhouse determined that 282,200 items were delivered on time (*Tampa Tribune*, Mar. 26, 1995). Use this information to make a statement about the likelihood of an item being delivered on time by the U.S. Postal Service.

7.4 Determining the Sample Size

Teaching Tip

Discuss the various factors that will play a role in determining the sample size, such as interval width and confidence level desired. Discuss how time and money might also be a factor when determining how large a sample should be.

Recall (Section 1.5) that one way to collect the relevant data for a study used to make inferences about the population is to implement a designed (planned) experiment. Perhaps the most important design decision faced by the analyst is to determine the size of the sample. We show in this section that the appropriate sample size for making an inference about a population mean or proportion depends on the desired reliability.

Estimating a Population Mean

Consider the example from Section 7.1 in which we estimated the mean overdue amount for all delinquent accounts in a large credit corporation. A sample of 100 delinquent accounts produced the 95% confidence interval: $\bar{x} \pm 2\sigma_{\bar{x}} \approx 233.28 \pm 18.07$. Consequently, our estimate $\bar{x}$ was within \$18.07 of the true mean amount due, μ, for all the delinquent accounts at the 95% confidence level. That is, the 95% confidence interval for μ was $2(18.07) = \$36.14$ wide when 100 accounts were sampled. This is illustrated in Figure 7.13(a).

Now suppose we want to estimate μ to within \$5 with 95% confidence. That is, we want to narrow the width of the confidence interval from \$36.14 to \$10, as shown in Figure 7.13(b). How much will the sample size have to be increased to accomplish this? If we want the estimator $\bar{x}$ to be within \$5 of μ, we must have

$$2\sigma_{\bar{x}} = 5 \quad \text{or, equivalently,} \quad 2\left(\frac{\sigma}{\sqrt{n}}\right) = 5$$

The necessary sample size is obtained by solving this equation for n. To do this we need an approximation for σ. We have an approximation from the initial sample of 100 accounts—namely, the sample standard deviation, $s = 90.34$. Thus,

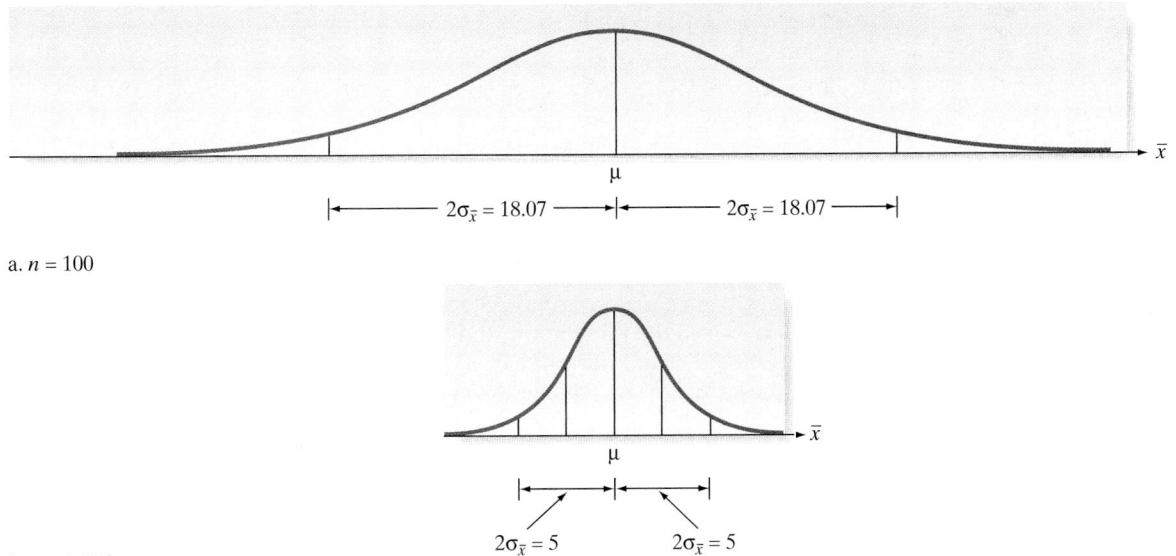

a. $n = 100$

b. $n = 1,306$

Figure 7.13

Relationship between sample size and width of confidence interval: Delinquent debtors example

$$2\left(\frac{\sigma}{\sqrt{n}}\right) \approx 2\left(\frac{s}{\sqrt{n}}\right) = 2\left(\frac{90.34}{\sqrt{n}}\right) = 5$$

$$\sqrt{n} = \frac{2(90.34)}{5} = 36.136$$

$$n = (36.136)^2 = 1{,}305.81 \approx 1{,}306$$

Approximately 1,306 accounts will have to be randomly sampled to estimate the mean overdue amount μ to within \$5 with (approximately) 95% confidence. The confidence interval resulting from a sample of this size will be approximately \$10 wide (see Figure 7.13b).

In general, we express the reliability associated with a confidence interval for the population mean μ by specifying the **sampling error**, within which we want to estimate μ with $100(1 - \alpha)$% confidence. The sampling error (denoted SE) then is equal to the half-width of the confidence interval, as shown in Figure 7.14.

Teaching Tip

A corresponding sample size formula can be developed when specifying interval width, W. To calculate, replace B with W/2 in the formulae presented.

Figure 7.14
Specifying the sampling error SE as the half-width of a confidence interval

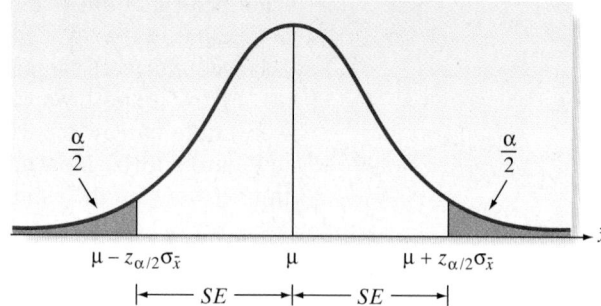

The procedure for finding the sample size necessary to estimate μ with a specific sampling error is given in the box.

Teaching Tip

For sample size determination, always round up to the next integer when calculating n.

> ## Sample Size Determination for $100(1 - \alpha)$% Confidence Interval for μ
>
> In order to estimate μ with a sampling error SE and with $100(1 - \alpha)$% confidence, the required sample size is found as follows:
>
> $$z_{\alpha/2}\left(\frac{\sigma}{\sqrt{n}}\right) = SE$$
>
> The solution for n is given by the equation
>
> $$n = \frac{(z_{\alpha/2})^2\sigma^2}{(SE)^2}$$
>
> *Note:* The value of σ is usually unknown. It can be estimated by the standard deviation, s, from a prior sample. Alternatively, we may approximate the range R of observations in the population, and (conservatively) estimate $\sigma \approx R/4$. In any case, you should round the value of n obtained *upward* to ensure that the sample size will be sufficient to achieve the specified reliability.

EXAMPLE 7.6   FINDING THE SAMPLE SIZE FOR ESTIMATING μ

Problem The manufacturer of official NFL footballs uses a machine to inflate its new balls to a pressure of 13.5 pounds. When the machine is properly calibrated, the mean inflation pressure is 13.5 pounds, but uncontrollable factors cause the pressures of individual footballs to vary randomly from about 13.3 to 13.7 pounds. For quality control purposes, the manufacturer wishes to estimate the mean inflation pressure to within .025 pound of its true value with a 99% confidence interval. What sample size should be used?

$n = 107$

Solution We desire a 99% confidence interval that estimates μ with a sampling error of SE = .025 pound. For a 99% confidence interval, we have $z_{\alpha/2} = z_{.005} = 2.575$. To estimate σ, we note that the range of observations is $R = 13.7 - 13.3 = .4$ and use $\sigma \approx R/4 = .1$. Now we use the formula derived in the box to find the sample size n:

$$n = \frac{(z_{\alpha/2})^2\sigma^2}{(\text{SE})^2} \approx \frac{(2.575)^2(.1)^2}{(.025)^2} = 106.09$$

We round this up to $n = 107$. Realizing that σ was approximated by $R/4$, we might even advise that the sample size be specified as $n = 110$ to be more certain of attaining the objective of a 99% confidence interval with a sampling error of .025 pound or less.

Look Back To determine the value of the sampling error SE, look for the value that follows the key words "estimate μ to within ... ".

Now work *Exercise 7.60*

▪ ▪ ▪

Sometimes the formula will yield a small sample size (say, $n < 30$). Unfortunately, this solution is invalid because the procedures and assumptions for small samples differ from those for large samples, as we discovered in Section 7.2. Therefore, if the formulas yield a small sample size, one simple strategy is to select a sample size $n = 30$.

Estimating a Population Proportion

Teaching Tip
Use this example to show what effect changing to a 99% confidence level will have on determining n. Lower the confidence level to 90% and find n again.

The method outlined above is easily applied to a population proportion p. For example, in Section 7.3 a company used a sample of 1,000 consumers to calculate a 95% confidence interval for the proportion of consumers who preferred its cereal brand, obtaining the interval .313 ± .029. Suppose the company wishes to estimate its market share more precisely, say to within .015 with a 95% confidence interval.

The company wants a confidence interval with a sampling error for the estimate of p of SE = .015. The sample size required to generate such an interval is found by solving the following equation for n:

Suggested Exercises 7.61

$$z_{\alpha/2}\sigma_{\hat{p}} = \text{SE} \qquad \text{or} \qquad z_{\alpha/2}\sqrt{\frac{pq}{n}} = .015 \qquad (\text{see Figure 7.15})$$

Figure 7.15
Specifying the sampling error SE of a confidence interval for a population proportion p

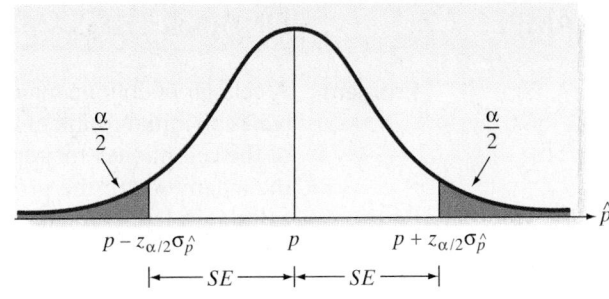

Since a 95% confidence interval is desired, the appropriate z value is $z_{\alpha/2} = z_{.025} = 1.96 \approx 2$. We must approximate the value of the product pq before we can solve the equation for n. As shown in Table 7.6, the closer the values of p and q to .5, the larger the product pq. Thus, to find a conservatively large sample size that will generate a confidence interval with the specified reliability, we generally choose an approximation of p close to .5. In the case of the food-products company, however, we have an initial sample estimate of $\hat{p} = .313$. A conservatively large estimate of pq can therefore be obtained by using, say, $p = .35$. We now substitute into the equation and solve for n:

$$2\sqrt{\frac{(.35)(.65)}{n}} = .015$$

$$n = \frac{(2)^2(.35)(.65)}{(.015)^2}$$

$$= 4{,}044.44 \approx 4{,}045$$

The company must sample about 4,045 consumers to estimate the percentage who prefer its brand to within .015 with a 95% confidence interval.

The procedure for finding the sample size necessary to estimate a population proportion p with a specified sampling error SE is given in the box.

Teaching Tip

Choose different values of p and q to show that the sample size is maximized (and considered conservative) when $p = q = .5$.

Sample Size Determination for $100(1 - \alpha)\%$ Confidence Interval for p

In order to estimate a binomial probability p with sampling error SE and with $100(1 - \alpha)\%$ confidence, the required sample size is found by solving the following equation for n:

$$z_{\alpha/2}\sqrt{\frac{pq}{n}} = \text{SE}$$

The solution for n can be written as follows:

$$n = \frac{(z_{\alpha/2})^2(pq)}{(\text{SE})^2}$$

Note: Since the value of the product pq is unknown, it can be estimated by using the sample fraction of successes, $\hat{p}$, from a prior sample. Remember (Table 7.6) that the value of pq is at its maximum when p equals .5, so that you can obtain conservatively large values of n by approximating p by .5 or values close to .5. In any case, you should round the value of n obtained *upward* to ensure that the sample size will be sufficient to achieve the specified reliability.

EXAMPLE 7.7   FINDING THE SAMPLE SIZE FOR ESTIMATING p

Problem   A cellular telephone manufacturer that entered the postregulation market too quickly has an initial problem with excessive customer complaints and consequent returns of the cell phones for repair or replacement. The manufacturer wants to determine the magnitude of the problem in order to estimate its warranty liability. How many cellular telephones should the company randomly sample from its warehouse and check in order to estimate the fraction defective, p, to within .01 with 90% confidence?

$n = 2{,}436$

Figure 7.16
Specified reliability for
estimate of fraction defective
in Example 7.7

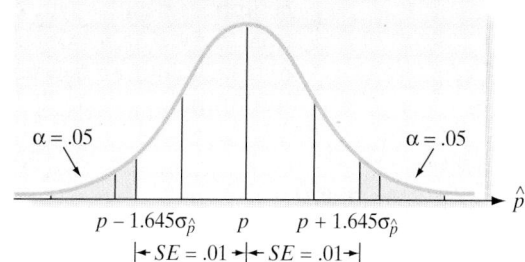

$$\alpha = .05 \qquad\qquad \alpha = .05$$

$$p - 1.645\sigma_{\hat{p}} \quad p \quad p + 1.645\sigma_{\hat{p}}$$

$$|\!\leftarrow SE = .01 \rightarrow\!|\!\leftarrow SE = .01 \rightarrow\!|$$

$$\hat{p}$$

Solution   In order to estimate p to within .01 of its true value, we set the half-width of the confidence interval equal to SE $= .01$, as shown in Figure 7.16.

The equation for the sample size n requires an estimate of the product pq. We could most conservatively estimate $pq = .25$ (i.e., use $p = .5$), but this may be overly conservative when estimating a fraction defective. A value of .1, corresponding to 10% defective, will probably be conservatively large for this application. The solution is therefore

Suggested Exercise 7.63

$$n = \frac{(z_{\alpha/2})^2 (pq)}{(SE)^2} = \frac{(1.645)^2 (.1)(.9)}{(.01)^2} = 2{,}435.4 \approx 2{,}436$$

Thus, the manufacturer should sample 2,436 cellular telephones in order to estimate the fraction defective, p, to within .01 with 90% confidence.

Look Back   Remember that this answer depends on our approximation for pq, where we used .09. If the fraction defective is closer to .05 than .10, we can use a sample of 1,286 cell phones (check this) to estimate p to within .01 with 90% confidence.

[Now Work]   *Exercise 7.59*

■ ■ ■

Statistics in Action Revisited

Determining the Number of Bags of Scallops to Sample

In the previous Statistics in Action applications in this chapter, we used confidence intervals to (1) estimate μ, the population mean weight per scallop (p. 370), and (2) estimate p, the population proportion of scallop bags with average weight less than 1/36 pound (p. 381). The confidence interval for p was fairly wide due to the small number of bags sampled ($n = 18$) from the over 11,000 bags in the ship's catch. Also, with such a small sample, the use of the normal (z) statistic to form the confidence interval may be invalid. In order to find a valid, narrower confidence interval for the true proportion, the harbormaster would need to take a larger sample of scallop bags.

How many bags should be sampled from the ship's catch to estimate p to within .03 with 95% confidence? Here, we have the sampling error, SE $= .03$ and $z_{.025} = 1.96$ (since, for a 95% confidence interval, $\alpha = .05$ and $\alpha/2 = .025$). From our analysis on page 381, the estimated proportion is $\hat{p} = .89$. Substituting these values into equation 7.6, we obtain

$$n = \frac{(z_{.025})^2 (\hat{p})(1 - \hat{p})}{(SE)^2} = \frac{(1.96)^2 (.89)(.11)}{(.03)^2} = 417.88$$

Consequently, the harbormaster would have to sample 418 of the ship's 11,000 bags of scallops in order to find a valid 95% confidence interval for p.

The cost of sampling will also play an important role in the final determination of the sample size to be selected to estimate either μ or p. Although more complex formulas can be derived to balance the reliability and cost considerations, we will solve for the necessary sample size and note that the sampling budget may be a limiting factor. Consult the references for a more complete treatment of this problem.

Exercises 7.52–7.68

Learning the Mechanics

7.52 If you wish to estimate a population mean with a sampling error SE = .3 using a 95% confidence interval and you know from prior sampling that σ^2 is approximately equal to 7.2, how many observations would have to be included in your sample?   308

7.53 Suppose you wish to estimate a population mean correct to within .20 with probability equal to .90. You do not know σ^2, but you know that the observations will range in value between 30 and 34.
   a. Find the approximate sample size that will produce the desired accuracy of the estimate. You wish to be conservative to ensure that the sample size will be ample to achieve the desired accuracy of the estimate. [*Hint:* Using your knowledge of data variation from Section 2.6, assume that the range of the observations will equal 4σ.]   68
   b. Calculate the approximate sample size making the less conservative assumption that the range of the observations is equal to 6σ.   31

7.54 In each case, find the approximate sample size required to construct a 95% confidence interval for p that has sampling error SE = .08.
   a. Assume p is near .2.   97
   b. Assume you have no prior knowledge about p, but you wish to be certain that your sample is large enough to achieve the specified accuracy for the estimate.   151

7.55 The following is a 90% confidence interval for p: (.26, .54). How large was the sample used to construct this interval?   34

7.56 It costs you $10 to draw a sample of size $n = 1$ and measure the attribute of interest. You have a budget of $1,500.
   a. Do you have sufficient funds to estimate the population mean for the attribute of interest with a 95% confidence interval 5 units in width? Assume $\sigma = 14$.
   b. If you used a 90% confidence level, would your answer to part a change? Explain.

7.57 Suppose you wish to estimate the mean of a normal population using a 95% confidence interval, and you know from prior information that $\sigma^2 \approx 1$.
   a. To see the effect of the sample size on the width of the confidence interval, calculate the width of the confidence interval for $n = 16, 25, 49, 100$, and 400.
   b. Plot the width as a function of sample size n on graph paper. Connect the points by a smooth curve and note how the width decreases as n increases.

7.58 If nothing is known about p, .5 can be substituted for p in the sample-size formula for a population proportion. But when this is done, the resulting sample size may be larger than needed. Under what circumstances will using $p = .5$ in the sample-size formula yield a sample size larger than needed to construct a confidence interval for p with a specified bound and a specified confidence level?   whenever $p \neq .5$

Applying the Concepts—Basic

7.59 A gigantic warehouse located in Tampa, Florida, stores approximately 60 million empty aluminum beer and soda cans. Recently, a fire occurred at the warehouse. The smoke from the fire contaminated many of the cans with blackspot, rendering them unusable. A University of South Florida statistician was hired by the insurance company to estimate p, the true proportion of cans in the warehouse that were contaminated by the fire. How many aluminum cans should be randomly sampled to estimate p to within .02 with 90% confidence?   1,692

7.60 The EPA wants to test a randomly selected sample of n water specimens and estimate the mean daily rate of pollution produced by a mining operation. If the EPA wants a 95% confidence interval estimate with a sampling error of 1 milligram per liter (mg/L), how many water specimens are required in the sample? Assume prior knowledge indicates that pollution readings in water samples taken during a day are approximately normally distributed with a standard deviation equal to 5 mg/L.   97

7.61 The *Quality Progress* 2002 salary survey of quality professionals described in Exercise 7.12 (page 359) generated responses from 2,413 quality managers. The lowest salary reported by a manager was $20,000; the highest was $205,000.
   a. Plans are being made to repeat the survey next year. Use the above information to determine how large a sample would need to be drawn to estimate the mean income of managers to within $5,000 with 95% confidence.   329
   b. In the survey, the standard deviation of managers' salaries was $19,830. Use this information and recalculate the sample size asked for in part a.   61
   c. Compare your answers to parts a and b. Which sample size would you use to estimate next year's mean salary? Justify your answer.

7.62 In a survey conducted for *Money* magazine by the ICR Survey Research Group, 26% of parents with college-bound high school children reported not having saved any money for college. The poll had a "... margin of error of plus or minus 4 percentage points" (*Newark Star-Ledger*, Aug. 16, 1996).

a. Assume that random sampling was used in conducting the survey and that the researchers wanted to have 95% confidence in their results. Estimate the sample size used in the survey. 462

b. Repeat part a, but this time assume the researchers wanted to be 99% confident. 801

Applying the Concepts—Intermediate

7.63 Do you pay for certain Web services? Georgia Institute of Technology's Graphics Visualization and Usability Center surveyed 13,000 Internet users and asked them about their willingness to pay fees for access to Web sites. Of these, 2,938 were definitely not willing to pay such fees (*Inc. Technology*, No. 3, 1995).

a. Assume the 13,000 users were randomly selected. Construct a 95% confidence interval for the proportion definitely unwilling to pay fees. .226 ± .007

b. What is the width of the interval you constructed in part a? For most applications, this width is unnecessarily narrow. What does that suggest about the survey's sample size? .014

c. How large a sample size is necessary to estimate the proportion of interest to within 2% with 95% confidence? 1,680

7.64 According to estimates made by the General Accounting Office, the Internal Revenue Service (IRS) answered 18.3 million telephone inquiries during a recent tax season, and 17% of the IRS offices provided answers that were wrong. These estimates were based on data collected from sample calls to numerous IRS offices. How many IRS offices should be randomly selected and contacted in order to estimate the proportion of IRS offices that fail to correctly answer questions about gift taxes with a 90% confidence interval of width .06? 425

7.65 A large food-products company receives about 100,000 phone calls a year from consumers on its toll-free number. A computer monitors and records how many rings it takes for an operator to answer, how much time each caller spends "on hold," and other data. However, the reliability of the monitoring system has been called into question by the operators and their labor union. As a check on the computer system, approximately how many calls should be manually monitored during the next year to estimate the true mean time that callers spend on hold to within 3 seconds with 95% confidence? Answer this question for the following values of the standard deviation of waiting times (in seconds): 10, 20, and 30. 43; 171; 385

7.66 The United States Golf Association (USGA) tests all new brands of golf balls to ensure that they meet USGA specifications. One test conducted is intended to measure the average distance traveled when the ball is hit by a machine called "Iron Byron," a name inspired by the swing of the famous golfer Byron Nelson. Suppose the USGA wishes to estimate the mean distance for a new brand to within 1 yard with 90% confidence. Assume that past tests have indicated that the standard deviation of the distances Iron Byron hits golf balls is approximately 10 yards. How many golf balls should be hit by Iron Byron to achieve the desired accuracy in estimating the mean?

Applying the Concepts—Advanced

7.67 Does the caffeine in coffee, tea, and cola induce an addiction similar to that induced by alcohol, tobacco, heroine, and cocaine? In an attempt to answer this question, researchers at Johns Hopkins University examined 27 caffeine drinkers and found 25 who displayed some type of withdrawal symptoms when abstaining from caffeine. [*Note*: The 27 caffeine drinkers volunteered for the study.] Furthermore, of 11 caffeine drinkers who were diagnosed as caffeine dependent, 8 displayed dramatic withdrawal symptoms (including impairment in normal functioning) when they consumed a caffeine-free diet in a controlled setting. The National Coffee Association claimed, however, that the study group was too small to draw conclusions (*Los Angeles Times*, Oct. 5, 1994). Is the sample large enough to estimate the true proportion of caffeine drinkers who are caffeine dependent to within .05 of the true value with 99% confidence? Explain. No

7.68 It costs more to produce defective items—since they must be scrapped or reworked—than it does to produce nondefective items. This simple fact suggests that manufacturers should ensure the quality of their products by perfecting their production processes rather than through inspection of finished products (Deming, 1986). In order to better understand a particular metal-stamping process, a manufacturer wishes to estimate the mean length of items produced by the process during the past 24 hours.

a. How many parts should be sampled in order to estimate the population mean to within .1 millimeter (mm) with 90% confidence? Previous studies of this machine have indicated that the standard deviation of lengths produced by the stamping operation is about 2 mm. 1,083

b. Time permits the use of a sample size no larger than 100. If a 90% confidence interval for μ is constructed using $n = 100$, will it be wider or narrower than would have been obtained using the sample size determined in part a? Explain. Wider

c. If management requires that μ be estimated to within .1 mm and that a sample size of no more than 100 be used, what is (approximately) the maximum confidence level that could be attained for a confidence interval that meets management's specifications?

7.5 Finite Population Correction for Simple Random Sampling (Optional)

The large-sample confidence intervals for a population mean μ and a population proportion p presented in the previous sections are based on a simple random sample selected from the target population. Although we did not state it, the procedure also assumes that the number N of measurements (i.e., sampling units) in the population is large relative to the sample size n.

In some sampling situations, the sample size n may represent 5% or perhaps 10% of the total number N of sampling units in the population. When the sample size is large relative to the number of measurements in the population (see the next box), the standard errors of the estimators of μ and p given in Sections 7.1 and 7.3, respectively, should be multiplied by a **finite population correction factor.**

The form of the finite population correction factor depends on how the population variance σ^2 is defined. In order to simplify the formulas of the standard errors, it is common to define σ^2 as division of the sum of squares of deviations by $N - 1$ rather than by N (analogous to the way we defined the sample variance). If we adopt this convention, the finite population correction factor becomes $\sqrt{(N - n)/N}$. Then the estimated standard errors of $\bar{x}$ (the estimator of μ) and $\hat{p}$ (the estimator of p) are as shown in the box.*

Teaching Tip

The finite population correction factor is used when the sample size is large relative to the size of the population.

Rule of Thumb for Finite Population Correction Factor

Use the finite population correction factor (shown in the next box) when $n/N > .05$.

Teaching Tip

By multiplying the finite population correction factor by the standard errors, the width of the confidence interval gets smaller.

Simple Random Sampling with Finite Population of Size N

Estimation of the Population Mean

Estimated standard error:

$$\hat{\sigma}_{\bar{x}} = \frac{s}{\sqrt{n}}\sqrt{\frac{N - n}{N}}$$

Approximate 95% confidence interval: $\bar{x} \pm 2\hat{\sigma}_{\bar{x}}$

Estimation of the Population Proportion

Estimated standard error:

$$\hat{\sigma}_{\hat{p}} = \sqrt{\frac{\hat{p}(1 - \hat{p})}{n}}\sqrt{\frac{N - n}{N}}$$

Approximate 95% confidence interval: $\hat{p} \pm 2\hat{\sigma}_{\hat{p}}$

Note: The confidence intervals are "approximate" since we are using 2 to approximate the value $z_{.025} = 1.96$.

---

*For most surveys and opinion polls, the finite population correction factor is approximately equal to 1 and, if desired, can be safely ignored. However, if $n/N > .05$, the finite population correction factor should be included in the calculation of the standard error.

EXAMPLE 7.8   APPLYING THE FINITE POPULATION CORRECTION FACTOR

Problem   A specialty manufacturer wants to purchase remnants of sheet aluminum foil. The foil, all of which is the same thickness, is stored on 1,462 rolls, each containing a varying amount of foil. To obtain an estimate of the total number of square feet of foil on all the rolls, the manufacturer randomly sampled 100 rolls and measured the number of square feet on each roll. The sample mean was 47.4, and the sample standard deviation was 12.4.

a. 47.4 ± 2.39

a. Find an approximate 95% confidence interval for the mean amount of foil on the 1,462 rolls.

b. (65,804.6, 72,793.0)

b. Estimate the total number of square feet of foil on all the rolls by multiplying the confidence interval, part a, by 1,462. Interpret the result.

Solution   **a.** Each roll of foil is a sampling unit, and there are $N = 1,462$ units in the population, and the sample size is $n = 100$. Since $n/N = 100/1,462 = .068$ exceeds .05, we need to apply the finite population correction. We have $n = 100, \bar{x} = 47.4$ and $s = 12.4$. Substituting these quantities, we obtain the approximate 95% confidence interval

$$\bar{x} \pm 2\frac{s}{\sqrt{n}}\sqrt{\frac{(N-n)}{N}} = (47.4) \pm 2\frac{12.4}{\sqrt{100}}\sqrt{\frac{(1,462 - 100)}{1,462}}$$

$$= 47.4 \pm 2.39$$

or (45.01, 49.79).

Teaching Tip
Point out that while the formulas change when the finite population correction factor is used, the interpretations of the interval remain unchanged.

b. For finite populations of size N, the sum of all measurements in the population—called a population total—is

$$\sum_{i=1}^{N} x_i = N\mu$$

Since the confidence interval, part a, estimates μ, an estimate of the population total is obtained by multiplying the endpoints of the interval by N. For $N = 1.462$ we have

Suggested Exercises 7.80

$$\text{Lower Limit} = N(45.01) = 1,462(45.01) = 65,804.6$$
$$\text{Upper Limit} = N(49.79) = 1,462(49.79) = 72,793.0$$

Consequently, the manufacturer estimates the total amount of foil to be in the interval 65,805 square feet to 72,793 square feet with 95% confidence.

Look Back If the manufacturer wants to adopt a conservative approach, the bid for the foil will be based on the lower confidence limit, 65,805 square feet of foil.

> **Now work**   *Exercise 7.76a*

■ ■ ■

Exercises 7.69–7.81

Learning the Mechanics

7.69 Calculate the percentage of the population sampled and the finite population correction factor for each of the following situations.
  a. $n = 1,000, N = 2,500$ **b.** $n = 1,000, N = 5,000$

c. $n = 1,000, N = 10,000$ .9487
d. $n = 1,000, N = 100,000$ .995

7.70 Suppose the standard deviation of the population is known to be $\sigma = 200$. Calculate the standard error of $\bar{x}$ for each of the situations described in Exercise 7.64.

7.71 Suppose $N = 10,000$, $n = 2,000$, and $s = 50$.

   a. Compute the standard error of $\bar{x}$ using the finite population correction factor.   1.00

   b. Repeat part **a** assuming $n = 4,000$.   .6124

   c. Repeat part **a** assuming $n = 10,000$ 0

   d. Compare parts **a, b,** and **c,** and describe what happens to the standard error of $\bar{x}$ as n increased.

   e. The answer to part **c** is 0. This indicates that there is no sampling error in this case. Explain.

7.72 Suppose $N = 5,000$, $n = 64$, and $s = 24$.

   a. Compare the size of the standard error of $\bar{x}$ computed with and without the finite population correction factor.

   b. Repeat part a, but this time assume $n = 400$.

   c. Theoretically, when sampling from a finite population, the finite population correction factor should always be used in computing the standard error of $\bar{x}$. However, when n is small relative to N, the finite population correction factor is close to 1 and can safely be ignored. Explain how parts a and b illustrate this point.

7.73 Suppose you want to estimate a population proportion, p, and $\hat{p} = .42$, $N = 6,000$, and $n = 1,600$. Find an approximate 95% confidence interval for p.

7.74 Suppose you want to estimate a population mean, μ, and $\bar{x} = 422$, $s = 14$, $N = 375$, and $n = 40$. Find an approximate 95% confidence interval for μ.

7.75 A random sample of size $n = 30$ was drawn from a population of size $N = 300$. The following measurements were obtained:

🌀 **LM7_75**

21	33	19	29	22	38	58	29	52	36	37	30
53	37	29	18	35	42	36	41	35	36	33	38
29	38	39	54	42	42						

   a. Estimate μ with an approximate 95% confidence interval. 36.033 ± 3.40

   b. Estimate p, the proportion of measurements in the population that are greater than 30, with an approximate 95% confidence interval. $.7 \pm .159$

Applying the Concepts—Basic

7.76 Refer to the *Quality Progress* (Dec. 2002) study of subscribers' salaries, Exercise 7.12 (p. 361). The 223 vice presidents sampled had a mean salary of $116,754 and a standard deviation of $39,185. Suppose the goal of the study is to estimate the true mean salary of all vice presidents who subscribe to *Quality Progress*.

   a. If 2,193 vice presidents subscribe to *Quality Progress*, estimate the mean with an approximate 95% confidence interval. Interpret the result.

   b. Compare the interval, part a, to the result obtained in Exercise 7.12c.

7.77 Refer to the New Jersey *Governor's Council for a Drug Free Workplace Report* (Spring/Summer 1995), Exercise 7.50 (p. 382). Recall that 50 of the 72 businesses that are members of the council admitted that they had employees with substance abuse problems. At the time of the survey, 251 New Jersey businesses were members of the Governor's Council. Based on this information, find a 95% confidence interval for the proportion of all New Jersey Governor's Council business members that have employees with substance abuse problems. Interpret the resulting interval.

Applying the Concepts—Intermediate

7.78 A brand name that consumers recognize is a highly valued commodity in any industry. To assess brand familiarity in the furniture industry, NPD (a market research firm) surveyed 1,333 women who head U.S. households that have incomes of $25,000 or more. The sample was drawn from a database of 25,000 households that match the criteria listed above. Of the 10 furniture brands evaluated, La-Z-Boy was the most recognized brand; 70.8% of the respondents indicated they were "very familiar" with La-Z-Boy (*HFN*, Oct. 11, 1999).

   a. Describe the population being investigated by NPD.

   b. In constructing a confidence interval to estimate the proportion of households that are very familiar with the La-Z-Boy brand, is it necessary to use the finite population correction factor? Explain   Yes

   c. What estimate of the standard error of $\hat{p}$ should be used in constructing the confidence interval of part **b?**

   d. Construct a 90% confidence interval for the true proportion and interpret it in the context of the problem. $.708 \pm .020$

7.79 Since the early 1950s, auditors have relied to a great extent on sampling techniques, rather than 100% audits, to help them test and evaluate the financial records of a client firm. When sampling is used to obtain an estimate of the total dollar value of an account—the account balance—the examination is known as a substantive test (Arkin, *Sampling Methods for the Auditor*, 1982). In order to evaluate the reasonableness of a firm's stated total value of its parts inventory, an auditor randomly samples 100 of the total of 500 parts in stock, prices each part, and reports the results shown in the table on p. 395.

   a. Give a point estimate of the mean value of the parts inventory. $\bar{x} = 156.46$

AUDPARTS

Part Number	Part Price	Sample Size
002	$ 108	3
101	55	2
832	500	1
077	73	10
688	300	1
910	54	4
839	92	6
121	833	5
271	50	9
399	125	12
761	1,000	2
093	62	8
505	205	7
597	88	11
830	100	19

  b. Find the estimated standard error of the point esti-
    mate of part a. $\hat{\sigma}_x = 18.7025$
  c. Construct an approximate 95% confidence interval
    for the mean value of the parts inventory.
  d. The firm reported a mean parts inventory value of
    $300. What does your confidence interval of part c
    suggest about the reasonableness of the firm's
    reported figure? Explain.

7.80 In a study of invoice errors in a company's new billing
system, an auditor randomly sampled 35 invoices produced by the new system and recorded actual amount
(A), invoice amount (I), and the difference (or error),
$x = (A - I)$. The results were $\bar{x} = \$1$ and $s = \$124$.
At the time that the sample was drawn, the new system
had produced 1,500 invoices. Use this information to
find an approximate 95% confidence interval for the
true mean error per invoice of the new system. Interpret the result.

Applying the Concepts—Advanced

7.81 The U.S. Environmental Protection Agency (EPA)
bans use of the cancer-causing pesticide ethylene di-
bromide (EDB) as a fumigant for grain- and flour-
milling equipment. EDB was once used to protect
against infestation by microscopic roundworms called
nematodes. The EPA sets maximum safe levels for
EDB presence in raw grain, flour, cake mixes, cereals,
bread, and other grain products on supermarket
shelves and in warehouses. Of the 3,000 corn-related
products sold in one state, tests indicated that 15 of a
random sample of 175 had EDB residues above the
safe level. Will more than 7% of the corn-related products in this state have to be removed from shelves and
warehouses? Explain.

7.6 Sample Survey Designs (Optional)

The confidence interval methodology developed in Sections 7.1–7.4 is based on simple random sampling (Chapter 3). A (simple) random sample is just one of several
different sampling designs used in *sample surveys*.

The term **sample survey** is used in conjunction with the sampling of populations, i.e., collections of people, households, businesses, etc. A consumer preference
poll is an example of a sample survey. Samplings conducted to estimate the general
level of business inventories or to estimate the proportion of households that
watched a particular television program are also examples of sample surveys.

Sample surveys cost time and money, and sometimes they are almost impossible to conduct. For example, suppose we want to obtain an estimate of the proportion of households in the United States that plan to purchase new television sets next
year, and we plan to base our estimate on the intentions of a random sample of
3,000 households. What are the problems associated with collecting these data? In
order to use a random number generator (Chapter 3) to select the sample, we would
need a list of all the households in the United States. Obtaining such a list would be
a monumental obstacle. After we obtain a list of households, we need to contact each
of the 3,000 selected for the sample. Will all be at home when the surveyor reaches
the household? And will all answer the surveyor's question? You can see that collecting a random sample is easier said than done.

The large body of knowledge underlying **survey sampling** or **sample survey
design** was developed to help solve some of the problems we have noted. It includes
sample survey designs that help reduce the cost and time involved in conducting a
sample survey, and it includes the confidence interval procedures associated with

Teaching Tip
Stratified samples are useful when the variation in the population can be sampled by dividing the population into several homogenous groups (strata).

those designs. Since survey sampling is a course in itself, we will present only a few of the most widely used sample survey designs and address only a few of the problems you might encounter in this optional section. Further information on this important subject can be found in the references at the end of the text.

One of the most common sampling designs (besides random sampling) is called *stratified random sampling*. **Stratified random sampling** is used when the sampling units (i.e., the units that are sampled) associated with the population can be physically separated into two or more groups of sampling units (called **strata**) where the within-stratum response variation is less than the variation within the entire population. For example, suppose we want to estimate the average amount of rent paid for a two-bedroom apartment in New York City. Since the variation in rent paid within New York City is likely to be large, we may want to divide the city into regions (strata) where the rents within each stratum are relatively homogeneous. Then we would estimate the population mean by selecting random samples from within each stratum and combining the stratum estimates.

Stratified random sampling often produces estimators with smaller standard errors than those achieved using simple random sampling. Furthermore, by sampling from each stratum we are more likely to obtain a sample representative of the entire population. In addition, the administrative and labor costs of selecting the stratum samples are often less than those for simple random sampling.

Teaching Tip
Systematic sampling is also referred to as 1-in-*k* sampling as every *k*th item is sampled.

Sometimes it is difficult or too costly to select random samples. For example, it would be easier to obtain a sample of student opinions at a large university by systematically selecting every hundredth name from the student directory. This type of sample design is called a **systematic sample.** Although systematic samples are usually easier to select than other types of samples, one difficulty is the possibility of a systematic sampling bias. For example, if every fifth item in an assembly line is selected for quality control inspection, and if five different machines are sequentially producing the items, all the items sampled may have been manufactured by the same machine. If we use systematic sampling we must be certain that no cycles (like every fifth item manufactured by the same machine) exist in the list of the sampling units.

Teaching Tip
Randomized response sampling is designed for surveys when false answers are likely to be given.

A third alternative to the simple random sampling design is *randomized response sampling*. **Randomized response sampling** is particularly useful when the questions of the pollsters are likely to elicit false answers. For example, suppose each person in a sample of wage earners is asked whether he or she cheated on an income tax return. A person who has not cheated most likely would give an honest answer to this question. A cheater might lie, thus biasing an estimate of what proportion of persons cheats on their income tax return.

One method of coping with the false responses produced by sensitive questions is randomized response sampling. Each person is presented *two* questions; one question is the object of the survey and the other is an innocuous question to which the interviewee will give an honest answer. For example, each person might be asked these two questions:

1. Did you cheat on your income tax return?
2. Did you drink coffee this morning?

Then a procedure is used to select randomly which of the two questions the person is to answer. For example, the interviewee might be asked to flip a coin. If the coin shows a head, the interviewee answers the sensitive question, 1. If the coin shows a tail, the interviewee answers the innocuous question, 2. Since the interviewer never has the opportunity to see the coin, the interviewee can answer the question and feel assured that his or her guilt (if guilty) will not be exposed. Consequently, the random

Teaching Tip

The problem of nonresponse is that there is no method for determining the attitudes of those not responding. The nest way to resolve the problem is to keep trying until a response is gathered.

response procedure can elicit an honest response to a sensitive question. Sophisticated methodology is then used to derive an estimate of the percentage of "yes" responses to the sensitive question.

As mentioned earlier, in any sample survey design, cost (either in time, labor or money) may be an issue. Two methods for reducing the cost of random sampling are to use a telephone survey or a mailed survey. Although this type of sampling eliminates transportation costs and reduces labor costs, it introduces a serious difficulty—the problem of **nonresponse.** By this, we mean that sampling units contained in a sample do not produce sample observations. For example, an individual may not be at home when telephoned or may refuse to complete and mail back a questionnaire.

Nonresponse is a serious problem because it may lead to very biased results. There may be a high correlation between the type of response and whether or not a person responds. For example, most citizens in a community might have an opinion on a school bond issue, but the respondents in a mail survey might very well be those with vested interests in the outcome of the survey—say, parents with children of school age, or school teachers, or those whose taxes might be substantially affected. Others with no vested interests might have opinions on the issue but might not take the time to respond. For this example, the absence of the nonrespondents' data could lead to a larger estimate of the percentage in favor of the issue than was actually the case. In other words, the absence of the nonrespondents' data could lead to a biased estimate.

Nonresponse is a very important sampling problem. If your sampling plan calls for a specific collection of sampling units, failure to acquire the responses from those units may violate your sampling plan and lead to biased estimates. If you intend to select a random sample and you cannot obtain the responses from some of the sampling units, then your sampling procedure is *no longer random*, and the methodology based on it (e.g., confidence intervals) and the product of the methodology (e.g., inferences) are suspect.

There are ways for coping with nonresponse. Most involve tracking down and questioning all or part of the nonrespondents and using the additional information to adjust for the missing nonrespondent data. For mailed surveys, however, it has been found that the inclusion of a monetary incentive with the questionnaire—even as little as 25¢—will substantially increase the response rate of the survey.

There are many sampling designs available to a sample surveyor; some are variations on simple random sampling and stratified random sampling, and others are completely different. In addition, different types of estimators can be used with these designs. In this brief introduction to survey sampling, our intent was to present only a few of the most important sample survey designs and some of their inherent problems. Thorough presentations of the different sample survey designs are given in textbooks devoted to this topic (see the references at the end of this text).

Quick Review

Key Terms

Note: Starred (*) items are from the optional sections in this chapter.

Confidence coefficient 353
Confidence interval 353
Confidence level 353
Degrees of freedom 362

Finite population correction factor* 390
Interval estimator 353
Nonresponse* 395
Randomized reponse sampling* 394
Sample survey design* 393
Sampling error 384
Strata* 394

Stratified random sampling* 394
Survey sampling* 393
Systematic sampling* 394
t-statistic 362
Wilson adjustment for estimating
  p 378

Key Formulas

$$\hat{\theta} \pm (z_{\alpha/2})\sigma_{\hat{\theta}}$$

Large-sample confidence interval for population parameter θ where $\hat{\theta}$ and $\sigma_{\hat{\theta}}$ are obtained from the table below.

Parameter θ	Estimator $\hat{\theta}$	Standard Error $\sigma_{\hat{\theta}}$	
Mean, μ	$\bar{x}$	$\dfrac{\sigma}{\sqrt{n}}$	355
Proportion, p	$\hat{p}$	$\sqrt{\dfrac{pq}{n}}$	375

$$\bar{x} \pm t_{\alpha/2}\left(\frac{s}{\sqrt{n}}\right)$$

Small-sample confidence interval for population mean μ 365

$$\tilde{p} = \frac{x+2}{n+4}$$

Adjusted estimator of p 378

$$n = \frac{(z_{\alpha/2})^2\sigma^2}{(SE)^2}$$

Determining the sample size n for estimating μ 384

$$n = \frac{(z_{\alpha/2})^2(pq)}{(SE)^2}$$

Determining the sample size n for estimating p 386

$$n/N > .05$$

Rule of thumb for using finite population correction factor[*]   390

$$\hat{\sigma}_{\bar{x}} = \frac{s}{\sqrt{n}}\sqrt{\frac{N-n}{n}}$$

Finite population correction for estimating μ[*]   390

$$\hat{\sigma}_p = \sqrt{\frac{\hat{p}\hat{q}}{n}}\sqrt{\frac{N-n}{n}}$$

Finite population correction for estimating p[*]   390

Chapter Summary Notes

- **Confidence interval**—an interval that encloses an unknown population parameter with a certain level of confidence
- **Confidence coefficient**—the probability that a randomly selected confidence interval encloses the value of the population parameter
- Conditions required for a valid **large-sample confidence interval for μ:** (1) random sample, (2) large sample size ($n \geq 30$)
- Conditions required for a valid **small-sample confidence interval for μ:** (1) random sample, (2) population distribution is approximately normal
- Conditions required for a valid **large-sample confidence interval for p:** (1) random sample, (2) large sample size ($\hat{p} \pm 3\sigma_p$ falls between 0 and 1)
- **Finite population correction factor** is required when $n/N > .05$
- Some sample survey designs: **simple random sampling, stratified random sampling, systematic sampling, and random response sampling**

Language Lab

Note: Starred (*) symbols are from the optional sections in this chapter.

Symbol	Pronunciation	Description
θ	theta	General population parameter
μ	mu	Population mean
p		Population proportion

SE		Sampling error in estimation
α	alpha	$(1 - \alpha)$ represents the confidence coefficient
$z_{\alpha/2}$	z of alpha over 2	z value used in a $100(1 - \alpha)\%$ large-sample confidence interval
$t_{\alpha/2}$	t of alpha over 2	t value used in a $100(1 - \alpha)\%$ small-sample confidence interval
$\bar{x}$	x-bar	Sample mean; point estimate of μ
$\hat{p}$	p-hat	Sample proportion; point estimate of p
$\tilde{p}$	p-curl	Adjusted sample proportion
σ	sigma	Population standard deviation
s		Sample standard deviation; point estimate of σ
$\sigma_{\bar{x}}$	sigma of $\bar{x}$	Standard deviation of sampling distribution of $\bar{x}$
$\sigma_{\hat{p}}$	sigma of $\hat{p}$	Standard deviation of sampling distribution of $\hat{p}$
N		Total number of measurements in the target population*

Supplementary Exercises 7.82–7.109

Note: List the assumptions necessary for the valid implementation of the statistical procedures you use in solving all these exercises. Starred (*) exercises refer to the optional sections in this chapter.

Learning the Mechanics

7.82 In each of the following instances, determine whether you would use a z- or t-statistic (or neither) to form a 95% confidence interval, and then look up the appropriate z- or t-value.
  a. Random sample of size $n = 23$ from a normal distribution with unknown mean μ and standard deviation σ
  b. Random sample of size $n = 135$ from a normal distribution with unknown mean μ and standard deviation σ z = 1.96
  c. Random sample of size $n = 10$ from a normal distribution with unknown mean μ and standard deviation $\sigma = 5$ z = 1.96
  d. Random sample of size $n = 73$ from a distribution about which nothing is known   z = 1.96
  e. Random sample of size $n = 12$ from a distribution about which nothing is known   Neither t nor z

7.83 Let t_0 represent a particular value of t from Table VI of Appendix B. Find the table values such that the following statements are true.
  a. $P(t \le t_0) = .05$ where df $= 20$ −1.725
  b. $P(t \ge t_0) = .005$ where df $= 9$ 3.250
  c. $P(t \le -t_0 \text{ or } t \ge t_0) = .10$ where df $= 8$ 1.860
  d. $P(t \le -t_0 \text{ or } t \ge t_0) = .01$ where df $= 17$ 2.898

7.84 In a random sample of 400 measurements, 227 of the measurements possess the characteristic of interest, A.
  a. Use a 95% confidence interval to estimate the true proportion p of measurements in the population with characteristic A.

  b. How large a sample would be needed to estimate p to within .02 with 95% confidence?

7.85 A random sample of 225 measurements is selected from a population, and the sample mean and standard deviation are $\bar{x} = 32.5$ and $s = 30.0$, respectively.
  a. Use a 99% confidence interval to estimate the mean of the population, μ.
  b. How large a sample would be needed to estimate μ to within .5 with 99% confidence?
  c. What is meant by the phrase "99% confidence" as it is used in this exercise?

*7.86 Calculate the finite population correction factor for each of the following situations:
  a. $n = 50, N = 2,000$
  b. $n = 20, N = 100$
  c. $n = 300, N = 1,500$

Applying the Concepts—Basic

7.87 The *Journal of the American Medical Association* (Apr. 21, 1993) reported on the results of a National Health Interview Survey designed to determine the prevalence of smoking among U.S. adults. More than 40,000 adults responded to questions such as "Have you smoked at least 100 cigarettes in your lifetime?" and "Do you smoke cigarettes now?" Current smokers (more than 11,000 adults in the survey) were also asked: "On the average, how many cigarettes do you now smoke a day?" The results yielded a mean of 20.0 cigarettes per day with an associated 95% confidence interval of (19.7, 20.3).
  a. Carefully describe the population from which the sample was drawn.
  b. Interpret the 95% confidence interval.
  c. State any assumptions about the target population of current cigarette smokers that must be satisfied for inferences derived from the interval to be valid.

d. A tobacco industry researcher claims that the mean number of cigarettes smoked per day by regular cigarette smokers is less than 15. Comment on this claim.

7.88 Refer to Exercise 7.87. Of the 43,732 survey respondents, 11,239 indicated that they were current smokers and 10,539 indicated they were former smokers.

   a. Construct and interpret a 90% confidence interval for the percentage of U.S. adults who currently smoke cigarettes. $.257 \pm .003$

   b. Construct and interpret a 90% confidence interval for the percentage of U.S. adults who are former cigarette smokers. $.241 \pm .003$

OIL SPILL

7.89 Refer to the *Marine Technology* (Jan. 1995) study of the causes of fifty recent major oil spills from tankers and carriers, Exercise 2.14 (p. 56). Recall that 12 of the spills were caused by hull failure.

   a. Give a point estimate for the proportion of major oil spills that are caused by hull failure. $.24$

   b. Form a 95% confidence interval for the estimate, part a. Interpret the result. $.24 \pm .118$

7.90 The Centers for Disease Control and Prevention (CDCP) in Atlanta, Georgia, conducts an annual survey of the general health of the U.S. population as part of its Behavioral Risk Factor Surveillance System (*New York Times*, Mar. 29, 1995). Using random-digit dialing, the CDCP telephones U.S. citizens over 18 years of age and asks them the following four questions:

   (1) Is your health generally excellent, very good, good, fair, or poor? *P*

   (2) How many days during the previous 30 days was your physical health not good because of injury or illness? μ

   (3) How many days during the previous 30 days was your mental health not good because of stress, depression, or emotional problems? μ

   (4) How many days during the previous 30 days did your physical or mental health prevent you from performing your usual activities? μ

   Identify the parameter of interest for each question.

7.91 Refer to Exercise 7.90. According to the CDCP, 89,582 of 102,263 adults interviewed stated their health was good, very good, or excellent.

   a. Use a 99% confidence interval to estimate the true proportion of U.S. adults who believe their health to be good to excellent. Interpret the interval.

   b. Why might the estimate, part a, be overly optimistic (i.e., biased high)?

7.92 As part of a study of residential property values in Cedar Grove, New Jersey, the county tax assessor sampled 20 single-family homes that recently sold and recorded their sales prices (in thousands of dollars). (The data are given at the top of p. 399). A stem-and-leaf display and descriptive statistics for these data are shown in the MINITAB printout below.

MINITAB Output for Exercise 7.92

Stem-and-Leaf Display: SalePrice

```
Stem-and-leaf of SalePrice   N  = 20
Leaf Unit = 10


    4    1    5789
   10    2    112336
   10    3    33
    8    4    2
    7    5    5
    6    6    36
    4    7    3
    3    8    7
    2    9    3
    1   10
    1   11    9
```

One-Sample T: SalePrice

Variable	N	Mean	StDev	SE Mean	95% CI
SalePrice	20	440.415	303.027	67.759	(298.594, 582.236)

NJVALUES

189.9	235.0	159.0	190.9	239.0	559.0	875.0	635.0
265.0	330.0	669.0	935.0	210.0	179.9	334.9	219.0
1,190.0	739.0	424.7	229.0				

Source: Multiple Listing Service of Suburban Essex County, New Jersey.

a. On the MINITAB printout, locate a 95% confidence interval for the mean sale price of all single-family homes in Cedar Grove, New Jersey.   (298.6, 582.2)

b. Give a practical interpretation of the interval, part a.

c. What is meant by the phrase "95% confidence" as it is used in this exercise?

d. Comment on the validity of any assumptions required to properly apply the estimation procedure.

7.93 Private and public colleges and universities rely on money contributed by individuals, corporations, and foundations for both salaries and operating expenses. Much of this money is put into a fund called an *endowment*, and the college spends only the interest earned by the fund. A random sample of eight college endowments drawn from the list of endowments in the *Chronicle of Higher Education Almanac* (Sept. 2, 1996) yielded the following endowments (in millions of dollars).

ENDOW

148.6	66.1	340.8	500.2	212.8	55.4	72.6	83.4

Estimate the mean endowment for this population of colleges and universities using a 95% confidence interval. List any assumptions you make. 184.99 ± 133.94

7.94 A company is interested in estimating μ, the mean number of days of sick leave taken by all its employees. The firm's statistician selects at random 100 personnel files and notes the number of sick days taken by each employee. The following sample statistics are computed: $\bar{x} = 12.2$ days, $s = 10$ days.

a. Estimate μ using a 90% confidence interval. 12.2 ± 1.645

b. How many personnel files would the statistician have to select in order to estimate μ to within 2 days with a 99% confidence interval?   167

Applying the Concepts—Intermediate

7.95 Research indicates that bicycle helmets save lives. A study reported in *Public Health Reports* (May–June 1992) was intended to identify ways of encouraging helmet use in children. One of the variables measured was the children's perception of the risk involved in bicycling. A four-point scale was used, with scores ranging from 1 (no risk) to 4 (very high risk). A sample of 797 children in grades 4–6 yielded the following results on the perception of risk variable: $\bar{x} = 3.39$, $s = .80$.

a. Calculate a 90% confidence interval for the average perception of risk for all students in grades 4–6. What conditions are required to ensure the validity of the confidence interval? Are they satisfied?

b. If the population mean perception of risk exceeds 2.50, the researchers will conclude that students in these grades exhibit an awareness of the risk involved with bicycling. Interpret the confidence interval constructed in part a in this context.

7.96 Obstructive sleep apnea is a sleep disorder that causes a person to stop breathing momentarily and then awaken briefly. These sleep interruptions, which may occur hundreds of times in a night, can drastically reduce the quality of rest and cause fatigue during waking hours. Researchers at Stanford University studied 159 commercial truck drivers and found that 124 of them suffered from obstructive sleep apnea (*Chest*, May 1995).

a. Use the study results to estimate, with 90% confidence, the fraction of truck drivers who suffer from the sleep disorder.   .78 ± .054

b. Sleep researchers believe that about 25% of the general population suffer from obstructive sleep apnea. Comment on whether or not this value represents the true percentage of truck drivers who suffer from the sleep disorder.

7.97 Research reported in the *Professional Geographer* (May 1992) investigates the hypothesis that the disproportionate housework responsibility of women in two-income households is a major factor in determining the proximity of a woman's place of employment. The researcher studied the distance (in miles) to work for both men and women in two-income households. Random samples of men and women yielded the following results:

	Central City Residence		Suburban Residence	
	Men	Women	Men	Women
Sample Size	159	119	138	93
Mean	7.4	4.5	9.3	6.6
Std. Deviation	6.3	4.2	7.1	5.6

a. For central city residences, calculate a 95% confidence interval for the average distance to work for men and women in two-income households. Interpret the intervals.   Men: 7.4 ± .979

b. Repeat part a for suburban residences. [*Note:* We will show how to use statistical techniques to compare two population means in Chapter 9.]   Men: 9.3 ± 1.185

7.98 In the United States, people over age 50 represent 25% of the population, yet they control 70% of the wealth. Research indicates the highest priority of retirees is travel. A study in the *Annals of Tourism Research* (Vol. 19, 1992) investigates the relationship of retirement status (pre- and post-retirement) to various items of interest to the travel industry. As one part of the study, a sample of 323 retirees was selected, and the number of nights each typically stayed away from home on trips was determined. One hundred seventy-two (172) responded that their typical stays ranged from 4 to 7 nights. Use a 90% confidence interval to estimate the true proportion of postretirement travelers who stay between 4 and 7 nights on a typical trip. Interpret the interval.

7.99 The primary determinant of the amount of vacation time U.S. employees receive is their length of service. According to data released by Hewitt Associates (*Management Review*, Nov. 1995), more than 8 of 10 employers provide two weeks of vacation after the first year. After five years, 75% of employers provide three weeks and after 15 years most provide four-week vacations. To more accurately estimate p, the proportion of U.S. employers who provide only two weeks of vacation to new hires, a random sample of 24 major U.S. companies was contacted. The following vacation times were reported (in days):

💲 VACTIMES

10	12	10	10	10	10
15	10	10	10	10	10
10	10	10	10	10	15
10	10	15	10	10	10

a. Construct a 95% confidence interval for p.
b. Is the sample size large enough to ensure that the normal distribution provides a reasonable approximation to the sampling distribution of $\hat{p}$? Justify your answer.
c. How large a sample would be required to estimate p to within .02 with 95% confidence?   1.337

7.100 According to the U.S. Bureau of Labor Statistics, one of every 80 American workers (i.e., 1.3%) is fired or laid off. Are employees with cancer fired or laid off at the same rate? To answer this question, *Working Women* magazine and Amgen—a company that makes drugs to lessen chemotherapy side effects—conducted a telephone survey of 100 cancer survivors who worked while undergoing treatment (*Tampa Tribune*, Sept. 25, 1996). Of these 100 cancer patients, 7 were fired or laid off due to their illness.

a. Construct a 90% confidence interval for the true percentage of all cancer patients who are fired or laid off due to their illness.   .07 ± .042
b. Give a practical interpretation of the interval, part a.
c. Are employees with cancer fired or laid off at the same rate as all U.S. workers? Explain.   No

*__7.101__ When a poll reports, for example, that 61% of the public supports a program of national health insurance, it usually also reports the sampling error. For example, a poll might report that the estimate is accurate to within plus or minus 3%. An essay in

Time magazine ("How not to read polls," Apr. 28, 1980) points out the following:

> *Readers consistently misinterpret the meaning of this "warning label." . . . [The sampling error warning] says nothing about errors that might be caused by a sloppily worded question or a biased one or a single question that evokes complex feelings. Example: "Are you satisfied with your job?" Most important of all, warning labels about sampling error say nothing about whether or not the public is conflict-ridden or has given a subject much thought. This is the most serious source of opinion poll misinterpretation.*

Carefully explain the difference between sampling error and nonsampling error, both in general and in the context of the above quote.

7.102 Family-owned companies are notorious for having difficulties in transferring control from one generation to the next. Part of this problem can be traced to lack of a well-documented strategic business plan. In a survey of 3,900 privately held family firms with revenues exceeding $1,000,000 a year, Arthur Andersen, the international accounting and consulting firm, found that 1,911 had no strategic business plan (*Minneapolis Star Tribune*, Sept. 4, 1995).

a. Describe the population studied by Arthur Andersen.
b. Assume the 3,900 firms were randomly sampled from the population. Use a 90% confidence interval to estimate the proportion of family-owned companies without strategic business plans.   .49 ± .013
c. How wide is the 90% confidence interval you constructed in part **b**? Would an 80% confidence interval be wider or narrower? Justify your answer.

7.103 When companies employ control charts to monitor the quality of their products, a series of small samples is typically used to determine if the process is "in control" during the period of time in which each sample is selected. (We cover quality control charts in Chapter 13.) Suppose a concrete-block manufacturer samples nine blocks per hour and tests the breaking strength of each. During one hour's test the mean and standard deviation are 985.6 pounds per square inch (psi) and 22.9 psi, respectively.

a. Construct a 99% confidence interval for the mean breaking strength of blocks produced during the hour in which the sample was selected.
b. The process is to be considered "out of control" if the mean strength differs from 1,000 psi. What would you conclude based on the confidence interval constructed in part **a**?
c. Repeat parts **a** and **b** using a 90% confidence interval.
d. The manufacturer wants to be reasonably certain that the process is really out of control before shutting down the process and trying to determine the

problem. Which interval, the 99% or 90% confidence interval, is more appropriate for making the decision? Explain.

e. Which assumptions are necessary to ensure the validity of the confidence intervals?

*7.104 Publishers of a weekly nationwide business magazine believe that a large proportion of their Florida subscribers invest in the stock market. They would like to be able to use this information to persuade brokerage firms in Florida to advertise in their magazine. The publishers send each of the 500,000 subscribers in Florida a questionnaire about stock investments. A total of 10,000 of the questionnaires are returned, and of these, 9,296 subscribers respond that they do currently have stock market investments.

a. Use this information to estimate the proportion of Florida subscribers who invest in the stock market with an approximate 95% confidence interval.

b. Should a brokerage firm in Florida consider the estimate in part a to be reliable? Explain.

7.105 Refer to the National Highway Traffic Safety Administration (NHTSA) study of fatal auto accidents caused by air bags, Exercise 7.48 (p. 382). Recall that the NHTSA wants to estimate the proportion of such accidents in which children seated on the front passenger side were killed. How many fatal accidents should the NHTSA sample in order to estimate the proportion to within .1 of its true value using a 99% confidence interval?   154

7.106 Recently, a case of salmonella (bacterial) poisoning was traced to a particular brand of ice cream bar, and the manufacturer removed the bars from the market. Despite this response, many consumers refused to purchase *any* brand of ice cream bars for some period of time after the event (McClave, personal consulting). One manufacturer conducted a survey of consumers six months after the outbreak. A sample of 244 ice cream bar consumers was contacted, and 23 respondents indicated that they would not purchase ice cream bars because of the potential for food poisoning.

a. What is the point estimate of the true fraction of the entire market who refuse to purchase bars six months after the outbreak? $\hat{p} = .094$

b. Is the sample size large enough to use the normal approximation for the sampling distribution of the estimator of the binomial probability? Justify your response.   Yes

c. Construct a 95% confidence interval for the true proportion of the market who still refuse to purchase ice cream bars six months after the event.

d. Interpret both the point estimate and confidence interval in terms of this application.

7.107 Refer to Exercise 7.106. Suppose it is now one year after the outbreak of food poisoning was traced to ice cream bars. The manufacturer wishes to estimate the proportion who still will not purchase bars to within .02 using a 95% confidence interval. How many consumers should be sampled?

Applying the Concepts—Advanced

7.108 Each year *Management Accounting* reports the results of a salary survey of the members of the Institute of Management Accountants (IMA). One year, the 2,112 members responding had a salary distribution with a 20th percentile of $35,100; a median of $50,000; and an 80th percentile of $73,000.

a. Use this information to determine the minimum sample size that could be used in next year's survey to estimate the mean salary of IMA members to within $2,000 with 98% confidence. [Hint: To estimate s, first apply Chebyshev's Theorem to find k such that at least 60% of the data fall within k standard deviations of μ. Then find $s \approx$ (80th percentile – 20th percentile)/k.]   191

b. Explain how you estimated the standard deviation required for the sample size calculation.

c. List any assumptions you make.

7.109 A firm's president, vice presidents, department managers, and others use financial data generated by the firm's accounting system to help them make decisions regarding such things as pricing, budgeting, and plant expansion. To provide reasonable certainty that the system provides reliable data, internal auditors periodically perform various checks of the system (Horngren, Foster, and Datar, *Cost Accounting: A Managerial Emphasis*, 1994). Suppose an internal auditor is interested in determining the proportion of sales invoices in a population of 5,000 sales invoices for which the "total sales" figure is in error. She plans to estimate the true proportion of invoices in error based on a random sample of size 100.

a. Assume that the population of invoices is numbered from 1 to 5,000 and that every invoice ending with a 0 is in error (i.e., 10% are in error). Use a random number generator to draw a random sample of 100 invoices from the population of 5,000 invoices. For example, random number 456 stands for invoice number 456. List the invoice numbers in your sample and indicate which of your sampled invoices are in error (i.e., those ending in a 0).

b. Use the results of your sample of part a to construct a 90% confidence interval for the true proportion of invoices in error.

c. Recall that the true population proportion of invoices in error is equal to .1. Compare the true proportion with the estimate of the true proportion you developed in part **b.** Does your confidence interval include the true proportion?

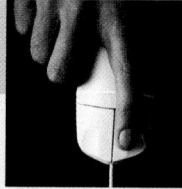

Using Technology

7.1 Confidence Intervals Using SPSS

SPSS can be used to obtain one-sample confidence intervals for a population mean but cannot currently produce confidence intervals for a population proportion. To generate a confidence interval for the mean, first access the SPSS spreadsheet file that contains the sample data. Next, click on the "Analyze" button on the SPSS menu bar, then click on "Descriptive Statistics" and "Explore", as shown in Figure 7.S.1. The resulting dialog box appears as shown in Figure 7.S.2. Specify the quantitative variable of interest in the "Dependent List", then click on the "Statistics" button at the bottom of the box. Specify the confidence level in the resulting dialog box as shown in Figure 7.S.3. Click "Continue" to return to the "Explore" dialog box, then click "OK" to produce the confidence interval.

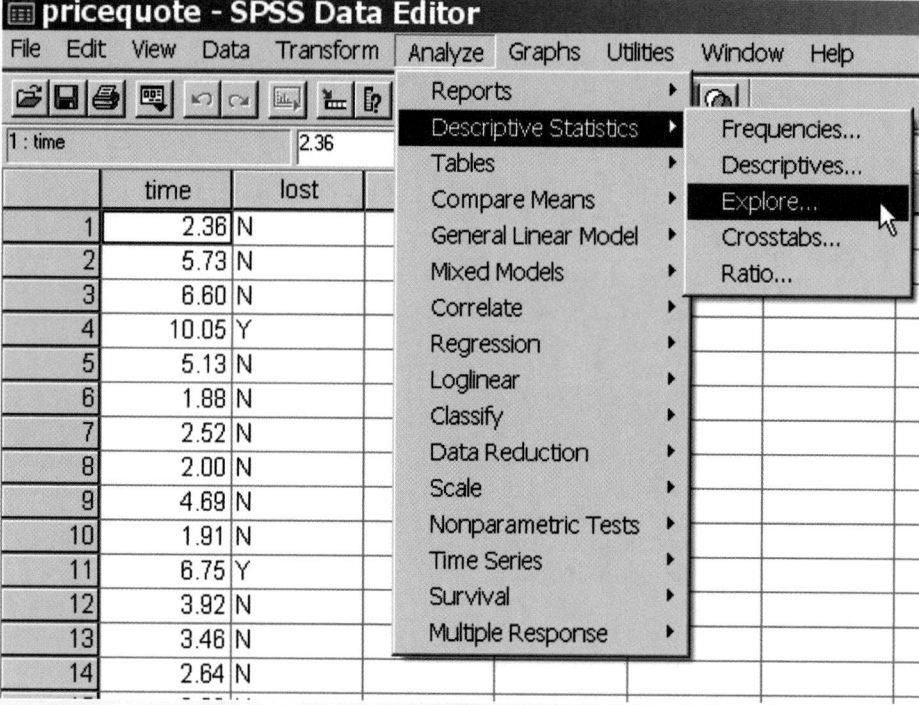

Figure 7.S.1
SPSS menu options for a confidence interval for μ

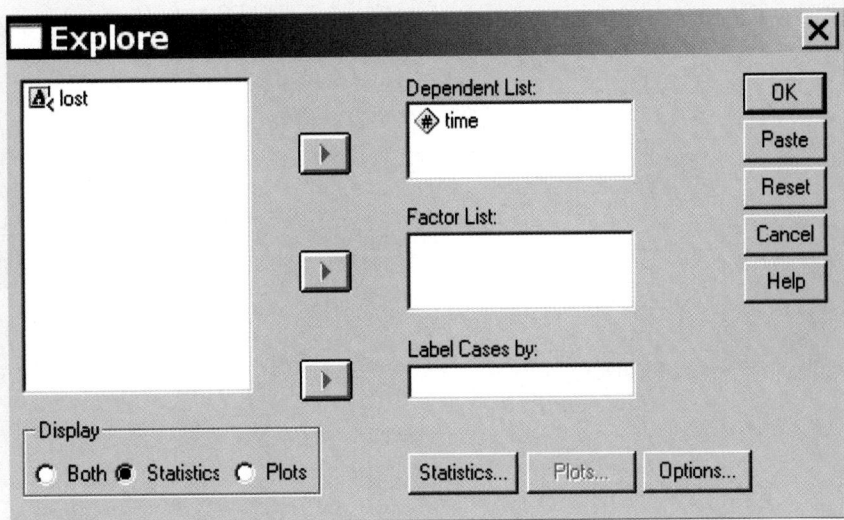

Figure 7.S.2
SPSS Explore dialog box

Figure 7.S.3
SPSS Explore Statistics
dialog box

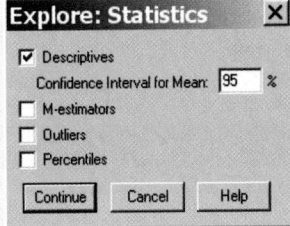

7.2 Confidence Intervals Using MINITAB

MINITAB can be used to obtain one-sample confidence intervals for both a population mean and a population proportion. To generate a confidence interval for the mean using a previously created sample data set, first access the MINITAB data worksheet. Next, click on the "Stat" button on the MINITAB menu bar, then click on "Basic Statistics" and "1-sample t", as shown in Figure 7.M.1. The resulting dialog box appears as shown in Figure 7.M.2. Click on "Samples in Columns", then specify the quantitative variable of interest in the open box. Now, click on the "Options" button at the bottom of the dialog box and specify the confidence level in the resulting dialog box as shown in Figure 7.M.3. Click "OK" to return to the "1-Sample t" dialog box, then click "OK" again to produce the confidence interval.

If you want to produce a confidence interval for the mean from summary information (e.g., the sample mean, sample standard deviation, and sample size), then click on "Summarized data" in the "1-Sample t" dialog box as shown in Figure 7.M.4. Enter the values of the summary statistics, then click "OK".

Important Note: The MINITAB 1-sample t procedure uses the t-statistic to generate the confidence interval. When the sample size n is small, this is the appropriate method. When the sample size n is large, the t-value will be approximately equal to the large-sample z-value and the resulting interval will still be valid. If you have a large sample and you know the value of the

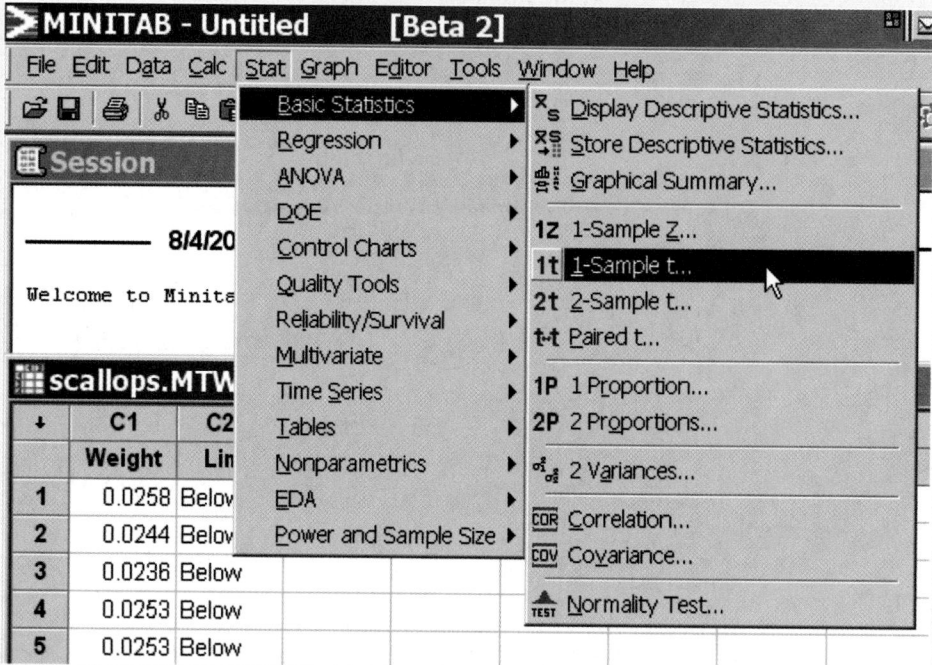

Figure 7.M.1
MINITAB menu options for a confidence interval for μ

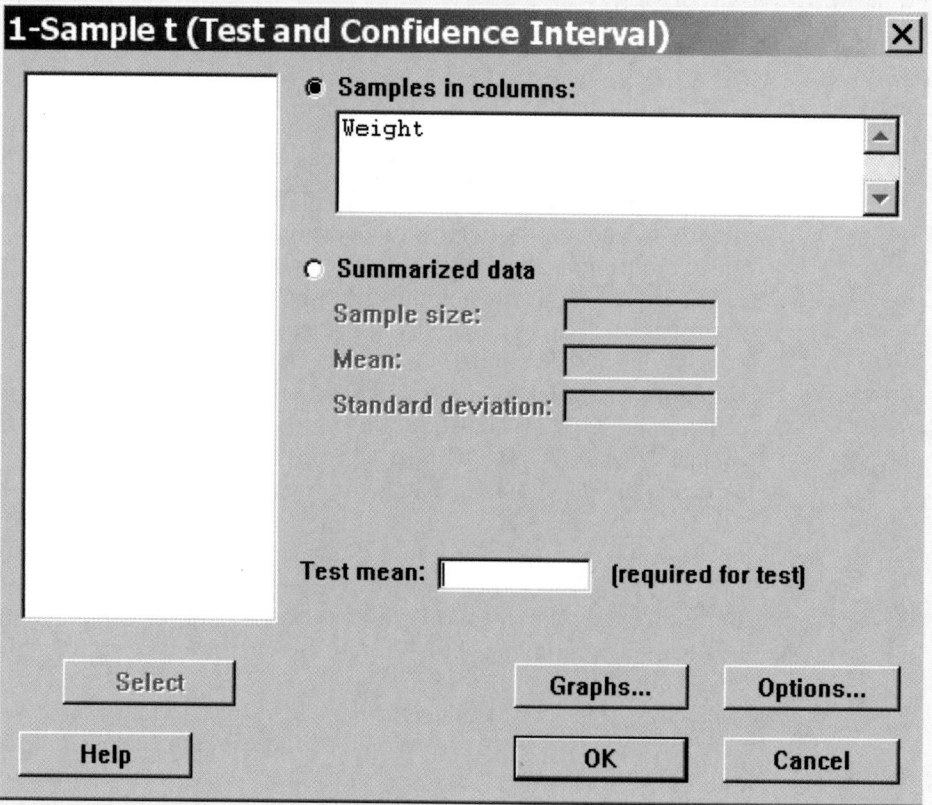

Figure 7.M.2
MINITAB 1-Sample t dialog box

Figure 7.M.3
MINITAB 1-Sample t Options dialog box

population standard deviation σ (which is rarely the case), then select "1-sample
Z" from the "Basic Statistics" menu options (see Figure 7.M.1) and make the
appropriate selections.

To generate a confidence interval for a population proportion mean using a
previously created sample data set, first access the MINITAB data worksheet.
Next, click on the "Stat" button on the MINITAB menu bar, then click on "Basic

Figure 7.M.4
MINITAB 1-Sample t dialog box with summary statistics

Statistics" and "1 Proportion" (see Figure 7.M.1). The resulting dialog box appears as shown in Figure 7.M.5. Click on "Samples in Columns", then specify the qualitative variable of interest in the open box. Now, click on the "Options" button at the bottom of the dialog box and specify the confidence level in the resulting dialog box, as shown in Figure 7.M.6. Also, check the "Use test and interval based on normal distribution" box at the bottom. Click "OK" to return to the "1-Proportion" dialog box, then click "OK" again to produce the confidence interval.

If you want to produce a confidence interval for a proportion from summary information (e.g., the number of successes and the sample size), then click on "Summarized data" in the "1-Proportion" dialog box (see Figure 7.M.5). Enter the value for the number of trials (i.e., the sample size) and the number of events (i.e., the number of successes), then click "OK".

Figure 7.M.5
MINITAB 1-Proportion
dialog box

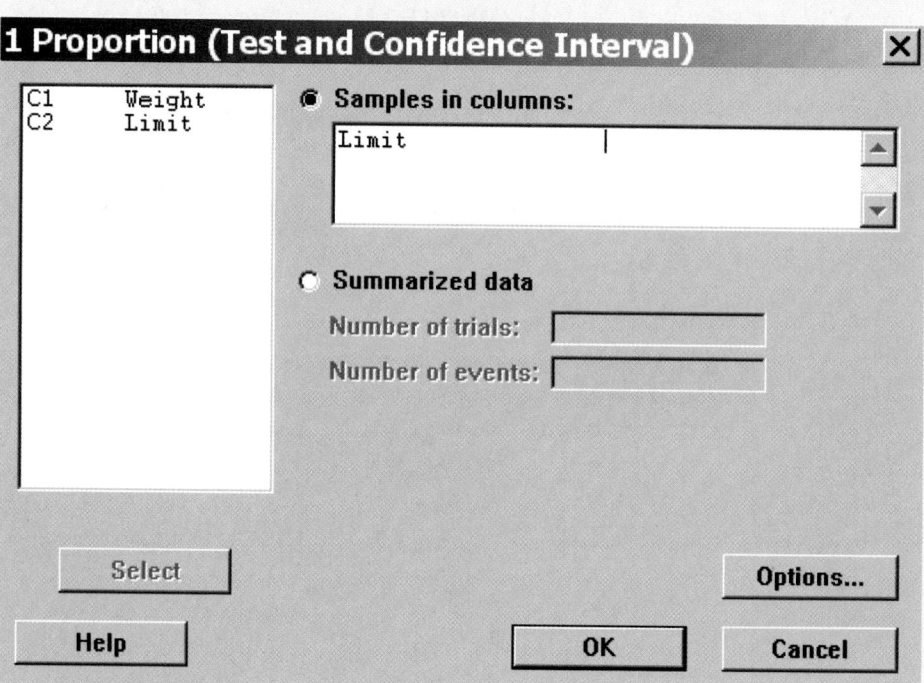

Figure 7.M.6
MINITAB 1-Proportion
dialog box

7.3 Confidence Intervals Using EXCEL and PHStat2

EXCEL with the PHStat2 add-in can be used to obtain one-sample confidence intervals for both a population mean and a population proportion. To generate a confidence interval for the mean using a previously created sample data set, first access the EXCEL worksheet. Next, click on the "PHStat" button on the EXCEL menu bar, then click on "Confidence Intervals" and "Estimate for the Mean, sigma unknown", as shown in Figure 7.E.1. The resulting dialog box appears as shown in Figure 7.E.2. Specify the confidence level, then click on "Sample Statistics Unknown" and specify cell range for the quantitative variable of interest (see Figure 7.E.2). Click "OK" to produce the confidence interval. If you want to produce a confidence interval for the mean from summary information (e.g., the sample mean, sample standard deviation, and sample size), then click on "Sample Statistics Known" on the dialog box as shown in Figure 7.E.2. Enter the values of the summary statistics, then click "OK".

[Important Note: The EXCEL/PHStat2 one-sample procedure outlined above uses the t-statistic to generate the confidence interval when σ is unknown. When the sample size n is small, this is the appropriate method. When the sample size n is large, the t-value will be approximately equal to the large-sample z-value and the resulting interval will still be valid. If you have a large sample and you know the value of the population standard deviation σ (which is rarely the case), then select "Estimate for the Mean, sigma known" from the "Confidence Intervals" menu options (see Figure 7.E.1) and make the appropriate selections.]

To generate a confidence interval for a population proportion using EXCEL, you must first determine the sample size and the number of successes in the sample of interest. Next, click on the "PHStat" button on the EXCEL menu bar, then click on "Confidence Intervals" and "Estimate for the Proportion" (see Figure 7.E.1). The resulting dialog box appears as shown in Figure 7.E.3. Specify the sample size, number of successes, and confidence level in the appropriate boxes, then click "OK" to produce the confidence interval.

Figure 7.E.1
EXCEL/PHStat2 menu options for a confidence interval for μ

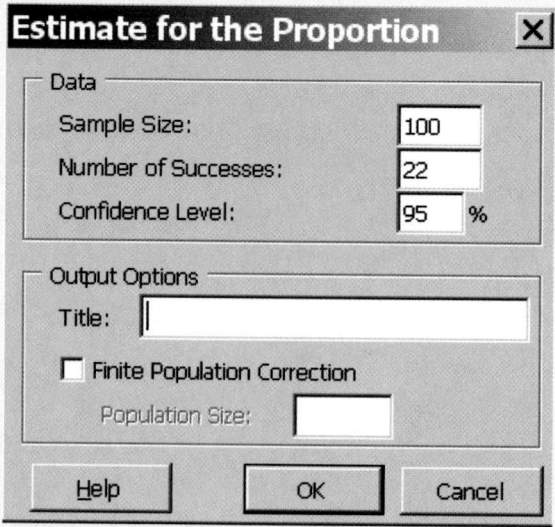

Figure 7.E.2
EXCEL confidence interval for mean dialog box

Figure 7.E.3
EXCEL confidence interval for
Proportion dialog box

REFERENCES

Agresti, A., and Coull, B. A. "Approximate Is Better Than 'Exact' for Interval Estimation of Binomial Proportions." *The American Statistician*, Vol. 52, No. 2, May 1998, pp. 119–126.

Arkin, H. *Sampling Methods for the Auditor*. New York: McGraw-Hill, 1982.

Cochran, W. G. *Sampling Techniques*, 3rd ed. New York: Wiley, 1977.

Freedman, D., Pisani, R., and Purves, R. *Statistics*. New York: Norton, 1978.

Horngren, Charles T., Foster, George, and Datar, Srikant M. *Cost Accounting: A Managerial Emphasis*, 8th ed. Englewood Cliffs, N.J.: Prentice Hall, 1994.

Kish, L. *Survey Sampling*. New York: Wiley, 1965.

Mendenhall, W., Beaver, R. J., and Beaver, B. *Introduction to Probability and Statistics*, 10th ed. North Scituate, Mass.: Duxbury, 1999.

Wilson, E. G. "Probable Inference, the Law of Succession, and Statistical Inference," *Journal of the American Statistical Association*, Vol. 22, 1927, pp. 209–212.

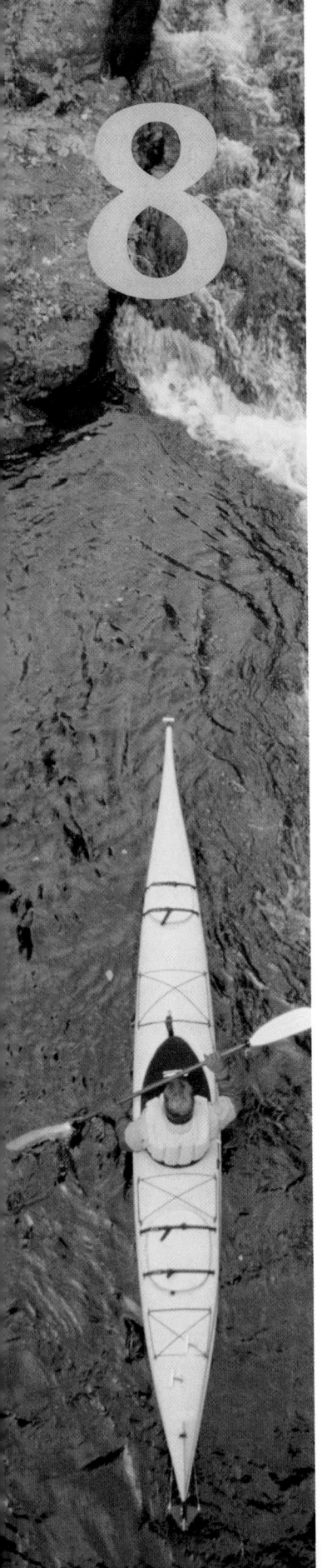

8

Inferences Based on a Single Sample

Tests of Hypothesis

Contents

Statistics in Action

Diary of a Kleenex User

Using Technology

Where We've Been

- Used sample information to provide a *point estimate* of a population parameter
- Used the sampling distribution of a statistic to assess the reliability of an estimate through a *confidence interval*

Where We're Going

- Test a specific value of a population parameter (mean or proportion), called a *test of hypothesis*.
- Provide a measure of reliability for the hypothesis test, called the *significance level* of the test.

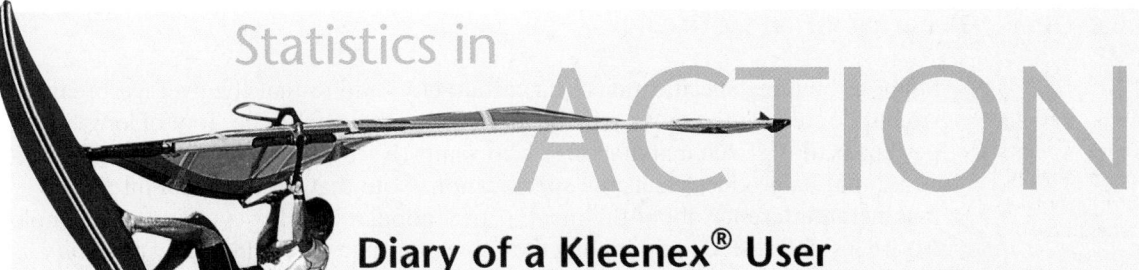

Statistics in ACTION

Diary of a Kleenex® User

In 1924, Kimberly-Clark Corporation invented a facial tissue for removing cold cream and began marketing it as Kleenex® brand tissues Today, Kleenex® is recognized as the top-selling brand of tissue in the world. A wide variety of Kleenex® products are available, ranging from extra-large tissues to tissues with lotion. Over the past 80 years, Kimberly-Clark Corporation has packaged the tissues in boxes of different sizes and shapes and varied the number of tissues packaged in each box. For example, currently a family-size box contains 144 two-ply tissues, a cold-care box contains 70 tissues (coated with lotion), and a convenience pocket pack contains 15 miniature tissues.

How does Kimberly-Clark Corp. decide how many tissues to put in each box? According to the *Wall Street Journal*, marketing experts at the company use the results of a survey of Kleenex® customers to help determine how many tissues are packed in a box. In the mid-1980s, when Kimberly-Clark Corp. developed the cold-care box designed especially for people who have a cold, the company conducted their initial survey of customers for this purpose. Hundreds of customers were asked to keep count of their Kleenex® use in diaries. According to the *Wall Street Journal* report, the survey results left "little

doubt that the company should put 60 tissues in each box." The number 60 was "the average number of times people blow their nose during a cold." (*Note*: In 2000, the company increased the number of tissues packaged in a cold-care box to 70.)

From summary information provided in the *Wall Street Journal* (Sept. 21, 1984) article, we constructed a data set that represents the results of a survey similar to the one described above. In the data file named TISSUES, we recorded the number of tissues used by each of 250 consumers during a period when they had a cold. We apply the hypothesis testing methodology presented in this chapter to this data set in several Statistics in Action Revisited examples.

Statistics in the Action Revisited

- Identifying the Key Elements of a Hypothesis Test Relevant to the Kleenex® Survey (p. 417)
- Testing a Population Mean in the Kleenex® Survey (p. 431)
- Testing a Population Proportion in the Kleenex® Survey (p. 446)

Teaching Tip

Explain that tests of hypothesis are an improvement of our rare-event approach to making conclusions. We now add the measure of reliability that was lacking.

Suppose you wanted to determine whether the mean waiting time in the drive-through line of a fast-food restaurant is less than five minutes, or whether the majority of consumers are optimistic about the economy. In both cases you are interested in making an inference about how the value of a parameter relates to a specific numerical value. Is it less than, equal to, or greater than the specified number? This type of inference, called a **test of hypothesis,** is the subject of this chapter.

We introduce the elements of a test of hypothesis in Section 8.1. We then show how to conduct a large-sample test of hypothesis about a population mean in Sections 8.2 and 8.3. In Section 8.4 we utilize small samples to conduct tests about means. Large-sample tests about binomial probabilities are the subject of Section 8.5, and some advanced methods for determining the reliability of a test are covered in optional Section 8.6. Finally, we show how to conduct a test about a population variance in optional Section 8.7.

8.1 The Elements of a Test of Hypothesis

Suppose building specifications in a certain city require that the average breaking strength of residential sewer pipe be more than 2,400 pounds per foot of length (i.e., per linear foot). Each manufacturer who wants to sell pipe in this city must demonstrate that its product meets the specification. Note that we are again interested in making an inference about the mean μ of a population. However, in this example we are less interested in estimating the value of μ than we are in testing a *hypothesis* about its value. That is, *we want to decide whether the mean breaking strength of the pipe exceeds 2,400 pounds per linear foot.*

The method used to reach a decision is based on the rare-event concept explained in earlier chapters. We define two hypotheses: (1) The **null hypothesis** is that which represents the status quo to the party performing the sampling experiment—the hypothesis that will be accepted unless the data provide convincing evidence that it is false. (2) The **alternative, or research, hypothesis** is that which will be accepted only if the data provide convincing evidence of its truth. From the point of view of the city conducting the tests, the null hypothesis is that the manufacturer's pipe does *not* meet specifications unless the tests provide convincing evidence otherwise. The null and alternative hypotheses are therefore

Null hypothesis (H_0): $\mu \leq 2{,}400$
(i.e., the manufacturer's pipe does not meet specifications)
Alternative (research) hypothesis (H_a): $\mu > 2{,}400$
(i.e., the manufacturer's pipe meets specifications)

Now Work   *Exercise 8.8*

How can the city decide when enough evidence exists to conclude that the manufacturer's pipe meets specifications? Since the hypotheses concern the value of the population mean μ, it is reasonable to use the sample mean $\bar{x}$ to make the inference, just as we did when forming confidence intervals for μ in Sections 7.1 and 7.2. The city will conclude that the pipe meets specifications only when the sample mean $\bar{x}$ convincingly indicates that the population mean exceeds 2,400 pounds per linear foot.

"Convincing" evidence in favor of the alternative hypothesis will exist when the value of $\bar{x}$ exceeds 2,400 by an amount that cannot be readily attributed to sampling variability. To decide, we compute a **test statistic**, which is the z value that measures the distance between the value of $\bar{x}$ and the value of μ specified in the null hypothesis. When the null hypothesis contains more than one value of μ, as in this case (H_0: $\mu \leq 2{,}400$), we use the value of μ closest to the values specified in the alternative hypothesis. The idea is that if the hypothesis that μ *equals* 2,400 can be rejected in favor of $\mu > 2{,}400$, then μ *less than or equal to* 2,400 can certainly be rejected. Thus, the test statistic is

$$z = \frac{\bar{x} - 2{,}400}{\sigma_{\bar{x}}} = \frac{\bar{x} - 2{,}400}{\sigma/\sqrt{n}}$$

Note that a value of $z = 1$ means that $\bar{x}$ is 1 standard deviation above $\mu = 2{,}400$; a value of $z = 1.5$ means that $\bar{x}$ is 1.5 standard deviations above $\mu = 2{,}400$, etc. How large must z be before the city can be convinced that the null hypothesis

Figure 8.1

The sampling distribution of $\bar{x}$, assuming $\mu = 2{,}400$

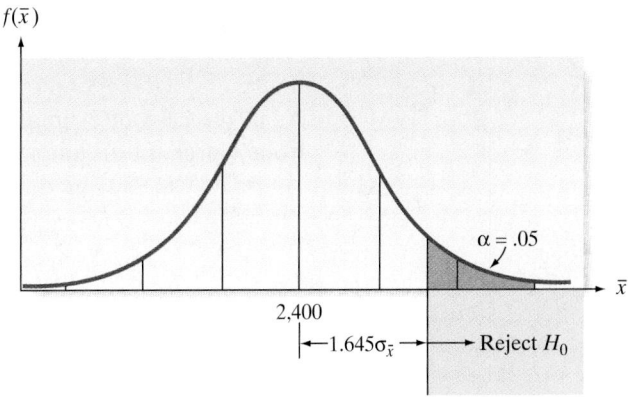

can be rejected in favor of the alternative and conclude that the pipe meets specifications?

If you examine Figure 8.1, you will note that the chance of observing $\bar{x}$ more than 1.645 standard deviations above 2,400 is only .05—*if in fact the true mean μ is 2,400.* Thus, if the sample mean is more than 1.645 standard deviations above 2,400, either H_0 is true and a relatively rare event has occurred (.05 probability) or H_a is true and the population mean exceeds 2,400. Since we would most likely reject the notion that a rare event has occurred, we would reject the null hypothesis ($\mu \leq 2{,}400$) and conclude that the alternative hypothesis ($\mu > 2{,}400$) is true. What is the probability that this procedure will lead us to an incorrect decision?

Teaching Tip

Students always have difficulty understanding α and how it affects the rejection region of the test of hypothesis. Be aware of these difficulties and be prepared with plenty of examples.

Such an incorrect decision—deciding that the null hypothesis is false when in fact it is true—is called a **Type I error.** As indicated in Figure 8.1, the risk of making a Type I error is denoted by the symbol α. That is,

$$\alpha = P(\text{Type I error})$$
$$= P(\text{Rejecting the null hypothesis when in fact the null hypothesis is true})$$

In our example

$$\alpha = P(z > 1.645 \text{ when in fact } \mu = 2{,}400) = .05$$

We now summarize the elements of the test:

$$H_0: \mu \leq 2{,}400$$
$$H_a: \mu > 2{,}400$$
$$\textit{Test statistic: } z = \frac{\bar{x} - 2{,}400}{\sigma_{\bar{x}}}$$

Rejection region: $z > 1.645$, which corresponds to $\alpha = .05$

Note that the **rejection region** refers to the values of the test statistic for which we will *reject the null hypothesis.*

To illustrate the use of the test, suppose we test 50 sections of sewer pipe and find the mean and standard deviation for these 50 measurements to be

$$\bar{x} = 2{,}460 \text{ pounds per linear foot}$$
$$s = 200 \text{ pounds per linear foot}$$

As in the case of estimation, we can use s to approximate σ when s is calculated from a large set of sample measurements.

The test statistic is

$$z = \frac{\bar{x} - 2{,}400}{\sigma_{\bar{x}}} = \frac{\bar{x} - 2{,}400}{\sigma/\sqrt{n}} \approx \frac{\bar{x} - 2{,}400}{s/\sqrt{n}}$$

Substituting $\bar{x} = 2{,}460$, $n = 50$, and $s = 200$, we have

$$z \approx \frac{2{,}460 - 2{,}400}{200/\sqrt{50}} = \frac{60}{28.28} = 2.12$$

Therefore, the sample mean lies $2.12\sigma_{\bar{x}}$ above the hypothesized value of μ, 2,400, as shown in Figure 8.2. Since this value of z exceeds 1.645, it falls in the rejection region. That is, we reject the null hypothesis that $\mu = 2{,}400$ and conclude that $\mu > 2{,}400$. Thus, it appears that the company's pipe has a mean strength that exceeds 2,400 pounds per linear foot.

Teaching Tip

Tie the α used here in with the α that was used in the confidence intervals from the last chapter. Explain that the confidence expressed in the last chapter is now being expressed as our error rate.

Figure 8.2
Location of the test statistic for a test of the hypothesis H_0: $\mu = 2{,}400$

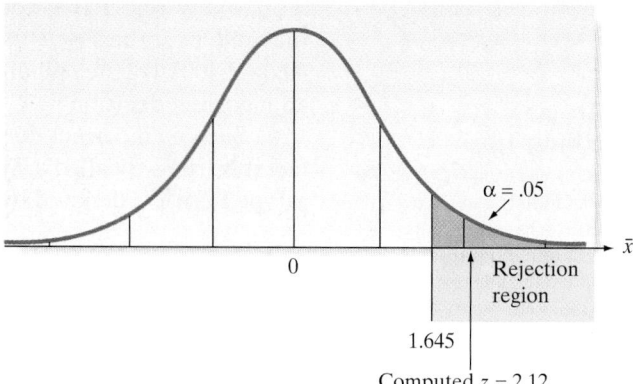

How much faith can be placed in this conclusion? What is the probability that our statistical test could lead us to reject the null hypothesis (and conclude that the company's pipe meets the city's specifications) when in fact the null hypothesis is true? The answer is $\alpha = .05$. That is, we selected the level of risk, α, of making a Type I error when we constructed the test. Thus, the chance is only 1 in 20 that our test would lead us to conclude the manufacturer's pipe satisfies the city's specifications when in fact the pipe does *not* meet specifications.

Now, suppose the sample mean breaking strength for the 50 sections of sewer pipe turned out to be $\bar{x} = 2{,}430$ pounds per linear foot. Assuming that the sample standard deviation is still $s = 200$, the test statistic is

$$z = \frac{2{,}430 - 2{,}400}{200/\sqrt{50}} = \frac{30}{28.28} = 1.06$$

Therefore, the sample mean $\bar{x} = 2{,}430$ is only 1.06 standard deviations above the null hypothesized value of $\mu = 2{,}400$. As shown in Figure 8.3, this value does not

Figure 8.3

Location of test statistic when $\bar{x} = 2,430$

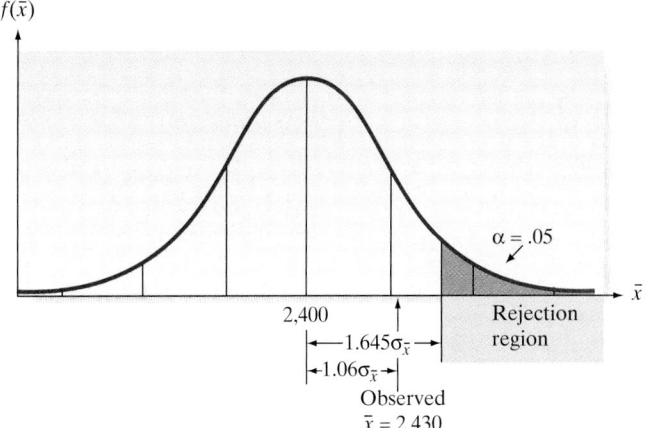

fall into the rejection region ($z > 1.645$). Therefore, we know that we cannot reject H_0 using $\alpha = .05$. Even though the sample mean exceeds the city's specification of 2,400 by 30 pounds per linear foot, it does not exceed the specification by enough to provide *convincing* evidence that the *population mean* exceeds 2,400.

Biography

EGON S. PEARSON (1895–1980)
The Neyman-Pearson Lemma

Egon Pearson was the only son of noteworthy British statistician Karl Pearson (see Biography, p. 646). As you might expect, Egon developed an interest in the statistical methods developed by his father and, upon completing graduate school, accepted a position to work for Karl in the Department of Applied Statistics at University College, London. Egon is best known for his collaboration with Jerzey Neyman (see Biography, p. 356) on the development of the theory of hypothesis testing. One of the basic concepts in the Neyman-Pearson approach was that of the "null" and "alternative" hypotheses. Their famous Neyman-Pearson lemma was published in *Biometrika* in 1928. Egon Pearson had numerous other contributions to statistics and was known as an excellent teacher and lecturer. In his last major work, Egon fulfilled a promise made to his father by publishing an annotated version of Karl Pearson's lectures on the early history of statistics.

Should we accept the null hypothesis H_0: $\mu \leq 2,400$ and conclude that the manufacturer's pipe does not meet specifications? To do so would be to risk a **Type II error**—that of concluding that the null hypothesis is true (the pipe does not meet specifications) when in fact it is false (the pipe does meet specifications). We denote the probability of committing a Type II error by β, and we show in optional Section 8.6 that β is often difficult to determine precisely. Rather than make a decision (accept H_0) for which the probability of error (β) is unknown, we avoid the potential Type II error by avoiding the conclusion that the null hypothesis is true. Instead, we will simply state that *the sample evidence is insufficient to reject H_0 at $\alpha = .05$.* Since the null hypothesis is the "status-quo" hypothesis, the effect of not rejecting H_0 is to maintain the status quo. In our pipe-testing example, the effect of having

TABLE 8.1 Conclusions and Consequences for a Test of Hypothesis

	True State of Nature	
Conclusion	H_0 True	H_a True
Accept H_0 (Assume H_0 True)	Correct decision	Type II error (probability β)
Reject H_0 (Assume H_a True)	Type I error (probability α)	Correct decision

insufficient evidence to reject the null hypothesis that the pipe does not meet specifications is probably to prohibit the utilization of the manufacturer's pipe unless and until there is sufficient evidence that the pipe does meet specifications. That is, until the data indicate convincingly that the null hypothesis is false, we usually maintain the status quo implied by its truth.

Table 8.1 summarizes the four possible outcomes of a test of hypothesis. The "true state of nature" columns in Table 8.1 refer to the fact that either the null hypothesis H_0 is true or the alternative hypothesis H_a is true. Note that the true state of nature is unknown to the researcher conducting the test. The "decision" rows in Table 8.1 refer to the action of the researcher, assuming that he or she will either conclude that H_0 is true or that H_a is true, based on the results of the sampling experiment. Note that a Type I error can be made *only* when the null hypothesis is rejected in favor of the alternative hypothesis, and a Type II error can be made *only* when the null hypothesis is accepted. Our policy will be to make a decision only when we know the probability of making the error that corresponds to that decision. Since α is usually specified by the analyst, we will generally be able to reject H_0 (accept H_a) when the sample evidence supports that decision. However, since β is usually not specified, *we will generally avoid the decision to accept H_0, preferring instead to state that the sample evidence is insufficient to reject H_0 when the test statistic is not in the rejection region.*

The elements of a test of hypothesis are summarized in the following box. Note that the first four elements are all specified *before* the sampling experiment is performed. In no case will the results of the sample be used to determine the hypotheses—the data are collected to test the predetermined hypotheses, not to formulate them.

Now Work **Exercise 8.14**

Teaching Tip (margin)

Elements of a Test of Hypothesis

1. Null hypothesis (H_0): A theory about the specific values of one or more population parameters. The theory generally represents the status quo, which we adopt until it is proven false. The theory is always stated as H_0: parameter = value.

2. *Alternative (research) hypothesis* (H_a): A theory that contradicts the null hypothesis. The theory generally represents that which we will adopt only when sufficient evidence exists to establish its truth.

3. *Test statistic*: A sample statistic used to decide whether to reject the null hypothesis.

4. *Rejection region*: The numerical values of the test statistic for which the null hypothesis will be rejected. The rejection region is chosen so that the proba-

bility is α that it will contain the test statistic when the null hypothesis is true, thereby leading to a Type I error. The value of α is usually chosen to be small (e.g., .01, .05, or .10), and is referred to as the **level of significance** of the test.

5. *Assumptions*: Clear statement(s) of any assumptions made about the population(s) being sampled.

6. *Experiment and calculation of test statistic*: Performance of the sampling experiment and determination of the numerical value of the test statistic.

Suggested Exercises 8.13

7. *Conclusion*:
   a. If the numerical value of the test statistic falls in the rejection region, we reject the null hypothesis and conclude that the alternative hypothesis is true. We know that the hypothesis-testing process will lead to this conclusion incorrectly (Type I error) only $100\alpha\%$ of the time when H_0 is true.
   b. If the test statistic does not fall in the rejection region, we do not reject H_0. Thus, we reserve judgment about which hypothesis is true. We do not conclude that the null hypothesis is true because we do not (in general) know the probβ that our test procedure will lead to an incorrect acceptance of H_0 (Type II error).*

Statistics in Action Revisited

Identifying the Key Elements of a Hypothesis Test Relevant to the Kleenex® Survey

In Kimberly-Clark Corporation's survey of people with colds, each of 250 customers was asked to keep count of his or her use of Kleenex® tissues in diaries. One goal of the company was to determine how many tissues to package in a cold-care box of Kleenex®; consequently, the total number of tissues used was recorded for each person surveyed. Since number of tissues is a quantitative variable, the parameter of interest is μ, the mean number of tissues used by all customers with colds.

Now, according to a *Wall Street Journal* report, there was "little doubt that the company should put 60 tissues" in a cold-care box of Kleenex® tissues. This statement was based on a claim made by marketing experts that 60 is the average number of times a person will blow his or her nose during a cold. Consequently, the marketers are claiming that $\mu = 60$. Suppose we disbelieve the claim that $\mu = 60$, believing instead that the population mean is smaller than 60 tissues. In order to test the claim against our belief, we set up the following null and alternative hypothesis:

$$H_0: \mu = 60 \qquad H_a: \mu < 60$$

We'll conduct this test in the next Statistics in Action Revisited on p. 433.

*In many practical business applications of hypothesis testing, nonrejection leads management to behave as if the null hypothesis were accepted. Accordingly, the distinction between acceptance and nonrejection is frequently blurred in practice. We discuss the issues connected with the acceptance of the null hypothesis and the calculation of β in more detail in (optional) Section 8.6.

Exercises 8.1–8.16

Learning the Mechanics

8.1 Which hypothesis, the null or the alternative, is the status-quo hypothesis? Which is the research hypothesis?

8.2 Which element of a test of hypothesis is used to decide whether to reject the null hypothesis in favor of the alternative hypothesis?

8.3 What is the level of significance of a test of hypothesis?

8.4 What is the difference between Type I and Type II errors in hypothesis testing? How do α and β relate to Type I and Type II errors?

8.5 List the four possible results of the combinations of decisions and true states of nature for a test of hypothesis.

8.6 We (generally) reject the null hypothesis when the test statistic falls in the rejection region, but we do not accept the null hypothesis when the test statistic does not fall in the rejection region. Why?

8.7 If you test a hypothesis and reject the null hypothesis in favor of the alternative hypothesis, does your test prove that the alternative hypothesis is correct? Explain.

Applying the Concepts—Basic

8.8 American Express Consulting reported in *USA Today* (June 15, 2001) that 80% of U.S. companies have formal, written travel and entertainment policies for their employees. Give the null hypothesis for testing the claim made by American Express Consulting. H_0: $p = .80$

8.9 The national student loan default rate has dropped steadily over the last decade. *USF Magazine* (Spring 1999) reported the default rate (i.e., the proportion of college students who default on their loans) at .10 in fiscal year 1996. Set up the null and alternative hypotheses if you want to determine if the student loan default rate in 2000 is less than .10. H_0: $p = .10$ vs. H_a: $p < .10$

8.10 The interest rate at which London banks lend money to one another is called the *London interbank offered rate*, or *Libor*. According to *The Wall Street Journal*, the British Bankers Association regularly surveys international banks for the Libor rate. One recent report had the average Libor rate at .40% for 3-month loans—a value considered high by many Western banks. Set up the null and alternative hypothesis for testing the reported value. H_0: $\mu = .4$ vs. H_a: $\mu < .4$

8.11 A University of Florida economist conducted a study of Virginia elementary school lunch menus. During the state-mandated testing period, school lunches averaged 863 calories (National Bureau of Economic Research, Nov. 2002). The economist claims that after the testing period ends, the average caloric content of Virginia school lunches drops significantly. Set up the null and alternative hypothesis to test the economists claim. H_0: $\mu = 863$ vs. H_a: $\mu < 863$

8.12 According to *NewScientist* (Jan. 2, 2002), a new thermal imaging camera that detects small temperature changes is now being used as a polygraph device. The United States Department of Defense Polygraph Institute (DDPI) claims the camera can correctly detect liars 75% of the time by monitoring the temperatures of their faces. Give the null hypothesis for testing the claim made by the DDPI. H_0: $p = .75$

Applying the Concepts—Intermediate

8.13 Sometimes, the outcome of a jury trial defies the "commonsense" expectations of the general public (e.g., the O. J. Simpson verdict in the "Trial of the Century"). Such a verdict is more acceptable if we understand that the jury trial of an accused murderer is analogous to the statistical hypothesis-testing process. The null hypothesis in a jury trial is that the accused is innocent. (The status-quo hypothesis in the U.S. system of justice is innocence, which is assumed to be true until proven *beyond a reasonable doubt*.) The alternative hypothesis is guilt, which is accepted only when sufficient evidence exists to establish its truth. If the vote of the jury is unanimous in favor of guilt, the null hypothesis of innocence is rejected and the court concludes that the accused murderer is guilty. Any vote other than a unanimous one for guilt results in a "not guilty" verdict. The court never accepts the null hypothesis; that is, the court never declares the accused "innocent." A "not guilty" verdict (as in the O. J. Simpson case) implies that the court could not find the defendant guilty *beyond a reasonable doubt*.

a. Define Type I and Type II errors in a murder trial.

b. Which of the two errors is the more serious? Explain.

c. The court does not, in general, know the values of α and β; but ideally, both should be small. One of these probabilities is assumed to be smaller than the other in a jury trial. Which one, and why? α

d. The court system relies on the belief that the value of α is made very small by requiring a unanimous vote before guilt is concluded. Explain why this is so.

e. For a jury prejudiced against a guilty verdict as the trial begins, will the value of α increase or decrease? Explain. Decrease

f. For a jury prejudiced against a guilty verdict as the trial begins, will the value of β increase or decrease? Explain. Increase

8.14 A group of physicians subjected the *polygraph* (or *lie detector*) to the same careful testing given to medical diagnostic tests. They found that if 1,000 people were subjected to the polygraph and 500 told the truth and 500 lied, the polygraph would indicate that approximately 185 of the truth-tellers were liars and that approximately 120 of the liars were truth-tellers (*Discover*, 1986).

   a. In the application of a polygraph test, an individual is presumed to be a truth-teller (H_0) until "proven" a liar (H_a). In this context, what is a Type I error? A Type II error?

   b. According to the study, what is the probability (approximately) that a polygraph test will result in a Type I error? A Type II error?

8.15 According to Chemical Marketing Reporter (Feb. 20, 1995), pharmaceutical companies spend $15 billion per year on research and development of new drugs. The pharmaceutical company must subject each new drug to lengthy and involved testing before receiving the necessary permission from the Food and Drug Administration (FDA) to market the drug. The FDA's policy is that the pharmaceutical company must provide substantial evidence that a new drug is safe prior to receiving FDA approval, so that the FDA can confidently certify the safety of the drug to potential consumers.

   a. If the new drug testing were to be placed in a test of hypothesis framework, would the null hypothesis be that the drug is safe or unsafe? The alternative hypothesis?

   b. Given the choice of null and alternative hypotheses in part a, describe Type I and Type II errors in terms of this application. Define α and β in terms of this application.

   c. If the FDA wants to be very confident that the drug is safe before permitting it to be marketed, is it more important that α or β be small? Explain. α

8.16 One of the most pressing problems in high-technology industries is computer security. Computer security is typically achieved by use of a *password*—a collection of symbols (usually letters and numbers) that must be supplied by the user before the computer permits access to the account. The problem is that persistent hackers can create programs that enter millions of combinations of symbols into a target system until the correct password is found. The newest systems solve this problem by requiring authorized users to identify themselves by unique body characteristics. For example, a system developed by Palmguard, Inc. tests the hypothesis

$$H_0: \text{The proposed user is authorized}$$

versus

$$H_a: \text{The proposed user is unauthorized}$$

by checking characteristics of the proposed user's palm against those stored in the authorized users' data bank (*Omni*, 1984).

   a. Define a Type I error and Type II error for this test. Which is the more serious error? Why?

   b. Palmguard reports that the Type I error rate for its system is less than 1%, whereas the Type II error rate is .00025%. Interpret these error rates.

   c. Another successful security system, the EyeDentifyer, "spots authorized computer users by reading the one-of-a-kind patterns formed by the network of minute blood vessels across the retina at the back of the eye." The EyeDentifyer reports Type I and II error rates of .01% (1 in 10,000) and .005% (5 in 100,000), respectively. Interpret these rates.

8.2 Large-Sample Test of Hypothesis About a Population Mean

Teaching Tip

Point out that the entire testing procedure is based on the assumption that the null hypothesis is correct. Using the equal sign allows the sampling distribution concepts to be more easily understood.

In Section 8.1 we learned that the null and alternative hypotheses form the basis for a test of hypothesis inference. The null and alternative hypotheses may take one of several forms. In the sewer pipe example we tested the null hypothesis that the population mean strength of the pipe is less than or equal to 2,400 pounds per linear foot against the alternative hypothesis that the mean strength exceeds 2,400. That is, we tested

$$H_0: \mu \leq 2,400$$

$$H_a: \mu > 2,400$$

This is a **one-tailed** (or **one-sided**) **statistical test** because the alternative hypothesis specifies that the population parameter (the population mean μ, in this example) is strictly greater than a specified value (2,400, in this example). If the null hypothesis had been $H_0: \mu \geq 2,400$ and the alternative hypothesis had been $H_a: \mu < 2,400$, the test would still be one-sided, because the parameter is still specified to be on "one side" of the null hypothesis value. Some statistical investigations seek to show that the population parameter is *either larger or smaller* than some specified value. Such an alternative hypothesis is called a **two-tailed** (or **two-sided**) **hypothesis.**

While alternative hypotheses are always specified as strict inequalities, such as $\mu < 2{,}400$, $\mu > 2{,}400$, or $\mu \neq 2{,}400$, null hypotheses are usually specified as equalities, such as $\mu = 2{,}400$. Even when the null hypothesis is an inequality, such as $\mu \leq 2{,}400$, we specify $H_0: \mu = 2{,}400$, reasoning that if sufficient evidence exists to show that $H_a: \mu > 2{,}400$ is true when tested against $H_0: \mu = 2{,}400$, then surely sufficient evidence exists to reject $\mu < 2{,}400$ as well. Therefore, the null hypothesis is specified as the value of μ closest to a one-sided alternative hypothesis and as the only value *not* specified in a two-tailed alternative hypothesis. The steps for selecting the null and alternative hypotheses are summarized in the accompanying box.

Teaching Tip

We use the equal sign in the null hypothesis for both one- and two-tailed tests. Writing the null hypothesis as $\leq$ (or $\geq$) for the one-tailed tests allows the student to understand that one of the two hypotheses must be correct. This is helpful in understanding the Type I and Type II errors.

Steps for Selecting the Null and Alternative Hypotheses

1. Select the *alternative hypothesis* as that which the sampling experiment is intended to establish. The alternative hypothesis will assume one of three forms:
   a. One-tailed, upper-tailed   *Example*: $H_a: \mu > 2{,}400$
   b. One-tailed, lower-tailed   *Example*: $H_a: \mu < 2{,}400$
   c. Two-tailed   *Example*: $H_a: \mu \neq 2{,}400$

2. Select the *null hypothesis* as the status quo, that which will be presumed true unless the sampling experiment conclusively establishes the alternative hypothesis. The null hypothesis will be specified as that parameter value closest to the alternative in one-tailed tests, and as the complementary (or only unspecified) value in two-tailed tests.

Example: $H_0: \mu = 2{,}400$

The rejection region for a two-tailed test differs from that for a one-tailed test. When we are trying to detect departure from the null hypothesis in *either* direction, we must establish a rejection region in both tails of the sampling distribution of the test statistic. Figures 8.4(a) and 8.4(b) show the one-tailed rejection regions for lower- and upper-tailed tests, respectively. The two-tailed rejection region is illustrated in Figure 8.4(c). Note that a rejection region is established in each tail of the sampling distribution for a two-tailed test.

The rejection regions corresponding to typical values selected for α are shown in Table 8.2 for one- and two-tailed tests. Note that the smaller α you select, the more evidence (the larger z) you will need before you can reject H_0.

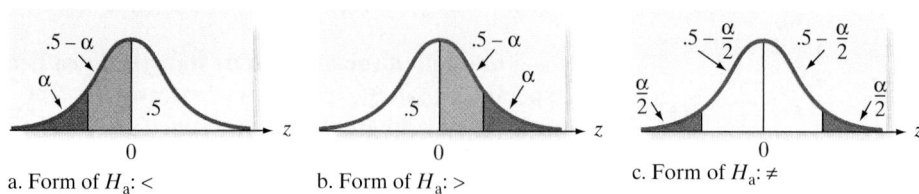

Figure 8.4
Rejection regions corresponding to one- and two-tailed tests

Teaching Tip
Use the normal table to show
the student where and how
these critical values are found.

TABLE 8.2 Rejection Regions for Common Values of α

	Alternative Hypotheses		
	Lower-Tailed	Upper-Tailed	Two-Tailed
$\alpha = .10$	$z < -1.28$	$z > 1.28$	$z < -1.645$ or $z > 1.645$
$\alpha = .05$	$z < -1.645$	$z > 1.645$	$z < -1.96$ or $z > 1.96$
$\alpha = .01$	$z < -2.33$	$z > 2.33$	$z < -2.575$ or $z > 2.575$

EXAMPLE 8.1

SETTING UP A HYPOTHESIS TEST FOR μ

Problem
A manufacturer of cereal wants to test the performance of one of its filling machines. The machine is designed to discharge a mean amount of $\mu = 12$ ounces per box, and the manufacturer wants to detect any departure from this setting. This quality study calls for randomly sampling 100 boxes from today's production run and determining whether the mean fill for the run is 12 ounces per box. Set up a test of hypothesis for this study, using $\alpha = .01$.

$H_0: \mu = 12 \ H_a: \mu \neq 12$

Solution
Since the manufacturer wishes to detect a departure from the setting of $\mu = 12$ in either direction, $\mu < 12$ or $\mu > 12$, we conduct a two-tailed statistical test. Following the procedure for selecting the null and alternative hypotheses, we specify as the alternative hypothesis that the mean differs from 12 ounces, since detecting the machine's departure from specifications is the purpose of the quality control study. The null hypothesis is the presumption that the fill machine is operating properly unless the sample data indicate otherwise. Thus,

$$H_0: \mu = 12$$
$$H_a: \mu \neq 12 \ (\text{i.e.,} \ \mu < 12 \ \text{or} \ \mu > 12)$$

The test statistic measures the number of standard deviations between the observed value of $\bar{x}$ and the null hypothesized value $\mu = 12$:

$$\textit{Test statistic:} \ \frac{\bar{x} - 12}{\sigma_{\bar{x}}}$$

The rejection region must be designated to detect a departure from $\mu = 12$ in *either* direction, so we will reject H_0 for values of z that are either too small (negative) or too large (positive). To determine the precise values of z that comprise the rejection region, we first select α, the probability that the test will lead to incorrect rejection of the null hypothesis. Then we divide α equally between the lower and upper tail of the distribution of z, as shown in Figure 8.5. In this example, $\alpha = 0.1$, so $\alpha/2 = .005$ is placed in each tail. The areas in the tails correspond to $z = -2.575$ and $z = 2.575$, respectively (from Table 8.2):

Rejection region: $z < -2.575$ or $z > 2.575$, (see Figure 8.5)

Assumptions: Since the sample size of the experiment is large enough ($n > 30$), the Central Limit Theorem will apply, and no assumptions need be made about the population of fill measurements. The sampling distribution of the sample mean fill of 100 boxes will be approximately normal regardless of the distribution of the individual boxes' fills.

Look Back Note that the test is set up *before* the sampling experiment is conducted. The data are not used to develop the test. Evidently, the manufacturer does not want to disrupt the filling process to adjust the machine unless the sample data provide very convincing evidence that it is not meeting specifications, because the value of α has been set quite low at .01. If the sample evidence results in the rejection of H_0, the manufacturer can be 99% confident that the machine needs adjustment.

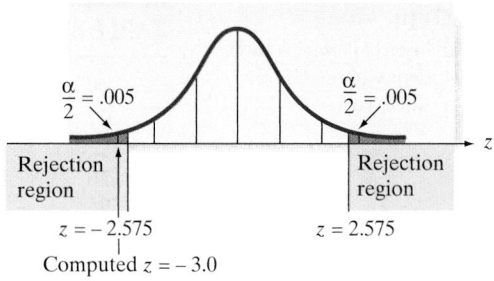

Figure 8.5
Two-tailed rejection region: $\alpha = .01$

Now Work   *Exercise 8.17*

■ ■ ■

Once the test is set up, the manufacturer is ready to perform the sampling experiment and conduct the test. The test is performed in Example 8.2.

EXAMPLE 8.2

CARRYING OUT A HYPOTHESIS TEST FOR μ

Problem   Refer to the quality control test set up in Example 8.1. Suppose the sample yields the following results:

$$n = 100 \text{ observations} \qquad \bar{x} = 11.85 \text{ ounces} \qquad s = .5 \text{ ounce}$$

z = −3.0, reject H_0

Use these data to conduct the test of hypothesis.

Solution   Since the test is completely specified in Example 8.1, we simply substitute the sample statistics into the test statistic:

$$z = \frac{\bar{x} - 12}{\sigma_{\bar{x}}} = \frac{\bar{x} - 12}{\sigma/\sqrt{n}} = \frac{11.85 - 12}{\sigma/\sqrt{100}}$$

Suggested Exercises 8.24

$$\approx \frac{11.85 - 12}{s/10} = \frac{-.15}{.5/10} = -3.0$$

The implication is that the sample mean, 11.85, is (approximately) 3 standard deviations below the null hypothesized value of 12.0 in the sampling distribution of $\bar{x}$. You can see in Figure 8.5 that this value of z is in the lower-tail rejection region, which consists of all values of $z < -2.575$. These sample data provide sufficient evidence to reject H_0 and conclude, at the $\alpha = .01$ level of significance, that the mean fill differs from the specification of $\mu = 12$ ounces. It appears that the machine is, on average, underfilling the boxes.

Look Back Two points about the test of hypothesis in this example apply to all statistical tests:

1. Since z is less than -2.575, it is tempting to state our conclusion at a significance level lower than $\alpha = .01$. We resist the temptation because the level of α is determined before the sampling experiment is performed. If we decide that we are willing to tolerate a 1% Type I error rate, the result of the sampling

experiment should have no effect on that decision. In general, the same data should not be used both to set up and to conduct the test.

2. When we state our conclusion at the .01 level of significance, we are referring to the failure rate of the procedure, not the result of this particular test. We know that the test procedure will lead to the rejection of the null hypothesis only 1% of the time when in fact $\mu = 12$. Therefore, when the test statistic falls in the rejection region, we infer that the alternative $\mu \neq 12$ is true and express our confidence in the procedure by quoting the α level of significance, or the $100(1 - \alpha)\%$ confidence level.

Now Work *Exercise 8.21*

■ ■ ■

The setup of a large-sample test of hypothesis about a population mean is summarized in the following boxes. Both the one- and two-tailed tests are shown.

Large-Sample Test of Hypothesis about μ

One-Tailed Test	Two-Tailed Test
$H_0: \mu = \mu_0$	$H_0: \mu = \mu_0$
$H_a: \mu < \mu_0$	$H_a: \mu \neq \mu_0$
(or $H_a: \mu > \mu_0$)	
Test statistic: $z = \dfrac{\bar{x} - \mu_0}{\sigma_{\bar{x}}}$	*Test statistic:* $z = \dfrac{\bar{x} - \mu_0}{\sigma_{\bar{x}}}$
Rejection region: $z < -z_\alpha$	*Rejection region:* $|z| > z_{\alpha/2}$
(or $z > z_\alpha$ when $H_a: \mu > \mu_0$)	
where z_α is chosen so that	where $z_{\alpha/2}$ is chosen so that
$P(z > z_\alpha) = \alpha$	$P(z > z_{\alpha/2}) = \alpha/2$
$P(z > z_{\alpha/2}) = \alpha/2$	

Note: μ_0 is the symbol for the numerical value assigned to μ under the null hypothesis.

Conditions Required for a Valid Large-Sample Hypothesis Test for μ

1. A random sample is selected from the target population.
2. The sample size n is large (i.e., $n \geq 30$). (Due to the Central Limit Theorem, this condition guarantees that the test statistic will be approximately normal regardless of the shape of the underlying probability distribution of the population.)

Once the test has been set up, the sampling experiment is performed and the test statistic calculated. The next box contains possible conclusions for a test of hypothesis, depending on the result of the sampling experiment.

Possible Conclusions for a Test of Hypothesis

1. If the calculated test statistic falls in the rejection region, reject H_0 and conclude that the alternative hypothesis H_a is true. State that you are rejecting H_0 at the α level of significance. Remember that the confidence is in the testing *process*, not the particular result of a single test.

> 2. If the test statistic does not fall in the rejection region, conclude that the sampling experiment does not provide sufficient evidence to reject H_0 at the α level of significance. [Generally, we will not "accept" the null hypothesis unless the probability β of a Type II error has been calculated (see optional Section 8.6).]

Exercises 8.17–8.30

Learning the Mechanics

8.17 For each of the following rejection regions, sketch the sampling distribution for z and indicate the location of the rejection region.
   a. $z > 1.96$
   b. $z > 1.645$
   c. $z > 2.575$
   d. $z < -1.28$
   e. $z < -1.645$ or $z > 1.645$
   f. $z < -2.575$ or $z > 2.575$ $\alpha = .01$
   g. For each of the rejection regions specified in parts **a–f**, what is the probability that a Type I error will be made?

8.18 Suppose you are interested in conducting the statistical test of $H_0: \mu = 255$ against $H_a: \mu > 255$, and you have decided to use the following decision rule: Reject H_0 if the sample mean of a random sample of 81 items is more than 270. Assume that the standard deviation of the population is 63.
   a. Express the decision rule in terms of z.
   b. Find α, the probability of making a Type I error, by using this decision rule. $\alpha = .0162$

8.19 A random sample of 100 observations from a population with standard deviation 60 yielded a sample mean of 110.
   a. Test the null hypothesis that $\mu = 100$ against the alternative hypothesis that $\mu > 100$ using $\alpha = .05$. Interpret the results of the test. $z = 1.67$
   b. Test the null hypothesis that $\mu = 100$ against the alternative hypothesis that $\mu \neq 100$ using $\alpha = .05$. Interpret the results of the test. $z = 1.67$
   c. Compare the results of the two tests you conducted. Explain why the results differ.

8.20 A random sample of 64 observations produced the following summary statistics: $\bar{x} = .323$ and $s^2 = .034$.
   a. Test the null hypothesis that $\mu = .36$ against the alternative hypothes is that $\mu < .36$ using $\alpha = .10$.
   b. Test the null hypothesis that $\mu = .36$ against the alternative hypothesis that $\mu \neq .36$ using $\alpha = .10$. Interpret the result. $z = -1.61$

Applying the Concepts—Basic

8.21 Refer to the Journal of Accounting and Public Policy (Spring 2002) study of $n = 100{,}000$ first-time candidates for the CPA exam, Exercise 7.11 (p. 360). The number of

semester hours of college credit taken by the sampled candidates is summarized as follows: $\bar{x} = 141.31$ hours and $s = 17.77$ hours. Let μ represent the mean number of semester hours taken by all first-time candidates for the CPA exam. Consider testing $H_0: \mu = 140$ against $H_a: \mu > 140$.
   a. Give the rejection region for the test at a significance level of $\alpha = .01$. $z > 2.33$
   b. Calculate the value of the test statistic. $z = 23.31$
   c. Use the results, parts a and b, to make the appropriate conclusion.   Reject H_0

DIAMONDS

8.22 Refer to the Journal of Statistics Education data on diamonds saved in the DIAMONDS file. In Exercise 7.18 (p. 362) you selected a random sample of 30 diamonds from the 308 diamonds and found the mean and standard deviation of the number of carats per diamond for the sample. Let μ represent the mean number of carats in the population of 308 diamonds. Suppose you want to test $H_0: \mu = .6$ against $H_a: \mu \neq .6$.
   a. In the words of the problem, define a Type I error and a Type II error.
   b. Use the sample information to conduct the test at a significance level of $\alpha = .05$.
   c. Conduct the test, part b, using $\alpha = .10$.
   d. What do the results suggest about the choice of α in a test of hypothesis?

8.23 In quality control applications of hypothesis testing, the null and alternative hypotheses are frequently specified as

H_0: The production process is performing satisfactorily

H_a: The process is performing in an unsatisfactory manner

Accordingly, α is sometimes referred to as the *producer's risk*, while β is called the *consumer's risk* (Stevenson, *Production/Operations Management*, 20). An injection molder produces plastic golf tees. The process is designed to produce tees with a mean weight of .250 ounce. To investigate whether the injection molder is operating satisfactorily, 40 tees were randomly sampled from the last hour's production. Their weights (in ounces) are listed in the table at the top of p. 425.

TEES

.247	.251	.254	.253	.253	.248	.253	.255	.256	.252
.253	.252	.253	.256	.254	.256	.252	.251	.253	.251
.253	.253	.248	.251	.253	.256	.254	.250	.254	.255
.249	.250	.254	.251	.251	.255	.251	.253	.252	.253

a. Do the data provide sufficient evidence to conclude that the process is not operating satisfactorily? Test using $\alpha = .01$. $z = 7.02$, reject H_0

b. In the context of this problem, explain why it makes sense to call α the producer's risk and β the consumer's risk.

8.24 A study reported in the Journal of Occupational and Organizational Psychology (Dec. 1992) investigated the relationship of employment status to mental health. Each in a sample of 49 unemployed men was given a mental health examination using the General Health Questionnaire (GHQ). The GHQ is a widely recognized measure of present mental health, with lower values indicating better mental health. The mean and standard deviation of the GHQ scores were $\bar{x} = 10.94$ and $s = 5.10$, respectively.

a. Specify the appropriate null and alternative hypotheses if we wish to test the research hypothesis that the mean GHQ score for all unemployed men exceeds 10. Is the test one-tailed or two-tailed? Why?

b. If we specify $\alpha = .05$, what is the appropriate rejection region for this test? $z > 1.645$

c. Conduct the test, and state your conclusion clearly in the language of this exercise. $z = 1.29$

Applying the Concepts—Intermediate

8.25 During the National Football League (NFL) season, Las Vegas oddsmakers establish a point spread on each game for betting purposes. For example, the Oakland Raiders were established as 3-point favorites over the champion Tampa Bay Buccaneers in the 2003 Super Bowl. The final scores of NFL games were compared against the final point spreads established by the oddsmakers in *Chance* (Fall 1998). The difference between the game outcome and point spread (called a point-spread error) was calculated for 240 NFL games. The mean and standard deviation of the point-spread errors are $\bar{x} = -1.6$ and $s = 13.3$. Use this information to test the hypothesis that the true mean point-spread error for all NFL games differs from 0. Conduct the test at $\alpha = .01$ and interpret the result. $z = -1.86$

8.26 Refer to the Applied Animal Behaviour Science (Oct. 2000) study of the color of string preferred by pecking domestic chickens, Exercise 7.14 (p. 361). Recall that $n = 72$ chickens were exposed to blue string and the number of pecks each chicken took at the string over a specified time interval had a mean of $\bar{x} = 1.13$ pecks and a standard deviation of $s = 2.21$ pecks. Also recall that previous research has shown that $\mu = 7.5$ pecks if chickens are exposed to white string.

a. Conduct a test (at $\alpha = .01$) to determine if the true mean number of pecks at blue string is less than $\mu = 7.5$ pecks. $z = -24.46$

b. In Exercise 7.14, you used a 99% confidence interval as evidence that chickens are more apt to peck at white string than blue string. Do the test results, part a, support this conclusion? Explain. Yes

8.27 The *Economics of Education Review* (Vol. 21, 2002) published a paper on the relationship between education level and earnings. The data for the research were obtained from the National Adult Literacy Survey of over 25,000 respondents. The survey revealed that males with a postgraduate degree had a mean salary of \$61,340 (with standard error $s_{\bar{x}} = \$2,185$), while females with a postgraduate degree had a mean of \$32,227 (with standard error $s_{\bar{x}} = \$932$).

a. The article reports that a 95% confidence interval for μ_M, the population mean salary of all males with postgraduate degrees, is (\$57,050, \$65,631). Based on this interval, is there evidence to say that μ_M differs from \$60,000? Explain. No

b. Use the summary information to test the hypothesis that the true mean salary of males with postgraduate degrees differs from \$60,000. Use $\alpha = .05$. (*Note:* $s_{\bar{x}} = s/\sqrt{n}$.) $z = 0.61$

c. Explain why the inferences in parts a and b agree.

d. The article reports that a 95% confidence interval for μ_F, the population mean salary of all females with postgraduate degrees, is (\$30,396, \$34,058). Based on this interval, is there evidence to say that μ_F differs from \$33,000? Explain. No

e. Use the summary information to test the hypothesis that the true mean salary of females with postgraduate degrees differs from \$33,000. Use $\alpha = .05$. (*Note:* $s_{\bar{x}} = s/\sqrt{n}$.) $z = -0.83$

f. Explain why the inferences in parts d and e agree.

8.28 According to the National Funeral Directors Association (NFDA), the nation's 22,000 funeral homes collected an average of \$5,180 per full-service funeral in 2001 (*NDFA Fact Sheet*, 2002). A random sample of 36 funeral homes reported revenue data for 2002. Among other measures, each reported its average fee for a full-service funeral. These data (in thousands of dollars) are shown in the table below, rounded to the nearest hundred.

FUNERAL

6.1	8.1	4.0	7.1	6.2	5.2
4.9	7.0	5.4	10.3	5.0	4.6
5.4	4.5	3.9	5.1	4.7	6.1
5.9	5.3	5.0	4.0	5.3	4.3
7.1	5.9	6.1	4.5	5.0	4.8
5.7	5.9	4.8	4.1	6.1	5.3

a. What are the appropriate null and alternative hypotheses to test whether the average full-service fee of U. S. funeral homes in 2002 exceeds $5,180?

b. Conduct the test at $\alpha = .05$. Do the sample data provide sufficient evidence to conclude that the average fee in 2002 was higher than in 2001? *z = 1.61*

c. In conducting the test, was it necessary to assume that population of average full-service fees was normally distributed? Justify your answer. *No, n > 30*

8.29 Current technology uses X-rays and lasers for inspection of solder-joint defects on printed circuit boards (PCBs) (*Quality Congress Transactions*, 1986). A particular manufacturer of laser-based inspection equipment claims that its product can inspect on average at least 10 solder joints per second when the joints are spaced .1 inch apart. The equipment was tested by a potential buyer on 48 different PCBs. In each case, the equipment was operated for exactly 1 second. The number of solder joints inspected on each run follows:

PCB

10	9	10	10	11	9	12	8	8	9	6	10
7	10	11	9	9	13	9	10	11	10	12	8
9	9	9	7	12	6	9	10	10	8	7	9
11	12	10	0	10	11	12	9	7	9	9	10

a. The potential buyer wants to know whether the sample data refute the manufacturer's claim. Specify the null and alternative hypotheses that the buyer should test. *$H_0: \mu = 10$ vs. $H_a: \mu < 10$*

b. In the context of this exercise, what is a Type I error? A Type II error?

c. Conduct the hypothesis test you described in part a, and interpret the test's results in the context of this exercise. Use $\alpha = .05$. *z = −2.33*

Applying the Concepts—Advanced

8.30 What factors inhibit the learning process in the classroom? To answer this question, researchers at Murray State University surveyed 40 students from a senior-level marketing class (*Marketing Education Review*, Fall 1994). Each student was given a list of factors and asked to rate the extent to which each factor inhibited the learning process in courses offered in their department. A 7-point rating scale was used, where 1 = "not at all" and 7 = "to a great extent." The factor with the highest rating was instructor-related: "Professors who place too much emphasis on a single right answer rather than overall thinking and creative ideas." Summary statistics for the student ratings of this factor are: $\bar{x} = 4.70, s = 1.62$.

a. Conduct a test to determine if the true mean rating for this instructor-related factor exceeds 4. Use $\alpha = .05$. Interpret the test results. *z = 2.73*

b. Examine the results of the study from a practical view, then discuss why "statistically significant" does not always imply "practically significant."

c. Because the variable of interest, rating, is measured on a 7-point scale, it is unlikely that the population of ratings will be normally distributed. Consequently, some analysts may perceive the test, part **a**, to be invalid and search for alternative methods of analysis. Defend or refute this argument.

8.3 Observed Significance Levels: *p*-Values

According to the statistical test procedure described in Section 8.2, the rejection region and, correspondingly, the value of α are selected prior to conducting the test, and the conclusions are stated in terms of rejecting or not rejecting the null hypothesis. A second method of presenting the results of a statistical test is one that reports the extent to which the test statistic disagrees with the null hypothesis and leaves to the reader the task of deciding whether to reject the null hypothesis. This measure of disagreement is called the *observed significance level* (or *p-value*) for the test.

Teaching Tip

Introduce *p*-values as an alternative method of making conclusions to the rejection regions already learned.

DEFINITION 8.1

The **observed significance level,** or *p*-value, for a specific statistical test is the probability (assuming H_0 is true) of observing a value of the test statistic that is at least as contradictory to the null hypothesis, and supportive of the alternative hypothesis, as the actual one computed from the sample data.

For example, the value of the test statistic computed for the sample of $n = 50$ sections of sewer pipe was $z = 2.12$. Since the test is one-tailed—that is, the alternative (research) hypothesis of interest is $H_a: \mu > 2,400$—values of the

Figure 8.6
Finding the *p*-value for an upper-tailed
test when $z = 2.12$

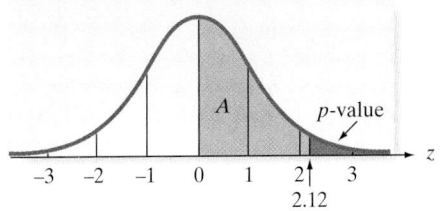

test statistic even more contradictory to H_0 than the one observed would be values
larger than $z = 2.12$. Therefore, the observed significance level (*p*-value) for this
test is

$$p\text{-value} = P(z > 2.12)$$

or, equivalently, the area under the standard normal curve to the right of $z = 2.12$
(see Figure 8.6).

The area A in Figure 8.6 is given in Table IV in Appendix B as .4830. Therefore, the upper-tail area corresponding to $z = 2.12$ is

$$p\text{-value} = .5 - .4830 = .0170$$

Teaching Tip

Use examples in which you
change the alternative
hypothesis from a one-tailed to
a two-tailed test. Illustrate what
happens to the *p*-value when
the change is made.

Consequently, we say that these test results are "very significant" (i.e., they disagree
rather strongly with the null hypothesis, H_0: $\mu = 2{,}400$, and favor H_a: $\mu > 2{,}400$.
The probability of observing a z value as large as 2.12 is only .0170, if in fact the true
value of μ is 2,400.

If you are inclined to select $\alpha = .05$ for this test, then you would reject the null
hypothesis because the *p*-value for the test, .0170, is less than .05. In contrast, if you
choose $\alpha = .01$, you would not reject the null hypothesis because the *p*-value for the
test is larger than .01. Thus, the use of the observed significance level is identical to
the test procedure described in the preceding sections except that the choice of α is
left to you.

The steps for calculating the *p*-value corresponding to a test statistic for a population mean are given in the next box.

> ## Steps for Calculating the *p*-value for a Test of Hypothesis
>
> 1. Determine the value of the test statistic z corresponding to the result of
>   the sampling experiment.
> 2. **a.** If the test is one-tailed, the *p*-value is equal to the tail area beyond z in
>   the same direction as the alternative hypothesis. Thus, if the alternative
>   hypothesis is of the form $>$, the *p*-value is the area to the right of, or
>   above, the observed z value. Conversely, if the alternative is of the form
> $<$, the *p*-value is the area to the left of, or below, the observed z value.
>   (See Figure 8.7.)
>   **b.** If the test is two-tailed, the *p*-value is equal to twice the tail area beyond
>   the observed z value in the direction of the sign of z. That is, if z is posi-
>   tive, the *p*-value is twice the area to the right of, or above, the observed
> z value. Conversely, if z is negative, the *p*-value is twice the area to the
>   left of, or below, the observed z value. (See Figure 8.8.)

Figure 8.7

Finding the *p*-value for a one-tailed test

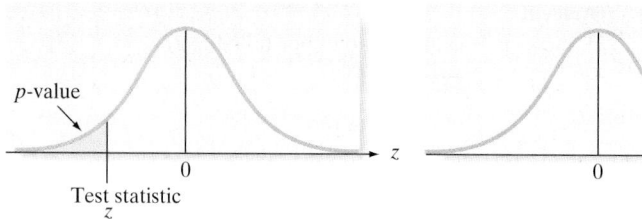

a. Lower–tailed test, $H_a: \mu < \mu_0$

b. Upper–tailed test, $H_a: \mu > \mu_0$

Figure 8.8

Finding the *p*-value for a two-tailed test: *p*-value = 2(*p*/2)

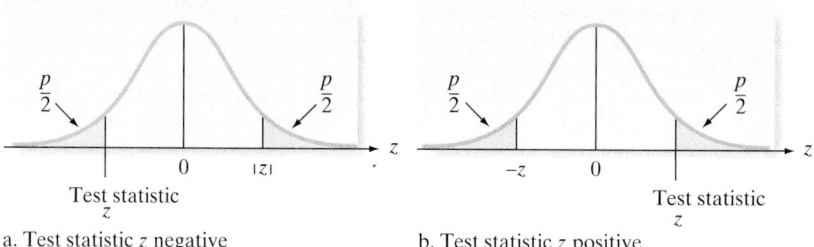

a. Test statistic *z* negative

b. Test statistic *z* positive

EXAMPLE 8.3   COMPUTING A *p*-VALUE

Problem   Find the observed significance level for the test of the mean filling weight in Examples 8.1 and 8.2.

p = .0026

Solution   Example 8.1 presented a two-tailed test of the hypothesis

$$H_0: \mu = 12 \text{ ounces}$$

against the alternative hypothesis

$$H_a: \mu \neq 12 \text{ ounces}$$

The observed value of the test statistic in Example 8.2 was $z = -3.0$, and any value of *z* less than -3.0 or greater than $+3.0$ (because this is a two-tailed test) would be even more contradictory to H_0. Therefore, the observed significance level for the test is

$$p\text{-value} = P(z < -3.0 \text{ or } z > +3.0) = P(|z| > 3.0)$$

Thus, we calculate the area below the observed *z* value, $z = -3.0$, and double it. Consulting Table IV in Appendix B, we find that $P(z < -3.0) = .5 - .4987 = .0013$. Therefore, the *p*-value for this two-tailed test is

$$2P(z < -3.0) = 2(.0013) = .0026$$

Look Back   We can interpret this *p*-value as a strong indication that the machine is not filling the boxes according to specifications, since we would observe a test statistic this extreme or more extreme only 26 in 10,000 times if the machine were meeting specifications ($\mu = 12$). The extent to which the mean differs from 12 could be better determined by calculating a confidence interval for μ.

| Now Work | *Exercise 8.35* |

■ ■ ■

Teaching Tip

One big benefit of the *p*-value approach to making conclusions is that a conclusion can easily be made for any choice of α. There is no need to re-compute a rejection region for each choice of α.

When publishing the results of a statistical test of hypothesis in journals, case studies, reports, etc., many researchers make use of *p*-values. Instead of selecting α beforehand and then conducting a test, as outlined in this chapter, the researcher computes (usually with the aid of a statistical software package) and reports the value of the appropriate test statistic and its associated *p*-value. It is left to the reader of the report to judge the significance of the result (i.e., the reader must determine whether to reject the null hypothesis in favor of the alternative hypothesis, based on the reported *p*-value). Usually, the null hypothesis is rejected if the observed significance level is *less than* the fixed significance level, α, chosen by the reader. The inherent advantage of reporting test results in this manner are twofold: (1) Readers are permitted to select the maximum value of α that they would be willing to tolerate if they actually carried out a standard test of hypothesis in the manner outlined in this chapter, and (2) a measure of the degree of significance of the result (i.e., the *p*-value) is provided.

Teaching Tip

This interpretation works for one-tailed and two-tailed tests. There's no need to adjust α as the adjustments have already been made in the calculation of the *p*-value.

> **Reporting Test Results as *p*-values: How to Decide Whether to Reject H_0**
>
> 1. Choose the maximum value of α that you are willing to tolerate.
> 2. If the observed significance level (*p*-value) of the test is less than the chosen value of α, reject the null hypothesis. Otherwise, do not reject the null hypothesis.

EXAMPLE 8.4   AN APPLICATION USING *p*-VALUES

Problem   Knowledge of the amount of time a patient occupies a hospital bed—called length of stay (LOS)—is important for allocating resources. At one hospital, the mean length of stay was determined to be 5 days. A hospital administrator believes that the mean LOS may now be less than 5 days due to a newly adopted managed care system. To check this, the LOSs (in days) for 100 randomly selected hospital patients were recorded; these are listed in Table 8.3. Test the hypothesis that the true mean LOS at the hospital is less than 5 days, that is,

$$H_0: \mu = 5$$
$$H_a: \mu < 5$$

$p = .102$, Fail to reject H_0

Use the data in the table to conduct the test at $\alpha = .05$.

Solution   The data were entered into a computer and EXCEL/PHStat2 was used to conduct the analysis. The EXCEL printout for the lower-tailed test is displayed in Figure 8.9. Both the test statistic, $z = -1.278$, and *p*-value of the test, $p = .102$,

Suggested Exercise 8.42

 HOSPLOS

TABLE 8.3 Lengths of Stay for 100 Hospital Patients

2	3	8	6	4	4	6	4	2	5
8	10	4	4	4	2	1	3	2	10
1	3	2	3	4	3	5	2	4	1
2	9	1	7	17	9	9	9	4	4
1	1	1	3	1	6	3	3	2	5
1	3	3	14	2	3	9	6	6	3
5	1	4	6	11	22	1	9	6	5
2	2	5	4	3	6	1	5	1	6
17	1	2	4	5	4	4	3	2	3
3	5	2	3	3	2	10	2	4	2

Figure 8.9

EXCEL and PHStat2 printout for the hypothesis test of Example 8.4

t Test for Hypothesis of the Mean

Data	
Null Hypothesis $\mu=$	5
Level of Significance	0.05
Sample Size	100
Sample Mean	4.53
Sample Standard Deviation	3.677545844

Intermediate Calculations	
Standard Error of the Mean	0.367754584
Degrees of Freedom	99
t Test Statistic	-1.278026216

Lower-Tail Test	
Lower Critical Value	-1.660391717
p-Value	0.102114325
Do not reject the null hypothesis	

are shown at the bottom of the printout. Since the p-value exceeds our selected α value, $\alpha = .05$, we cannot reject the null hypothesis. Hence, there is insufficient evidence (at $\alpha = .05$) to conclude that the true mean LOS at the hospital is less than 5 days.

Now Work *Exercise 8.41*

∎ ∎ ∎

Note: Some statistical software packages (e.g., SPSS) will conduct only two-tailed tests of hypothesis. For these packages, you obtain the p-value for a one-tailed test as shown in the box:

Teaching Tip
It is helpful for the student to understand the *p*-value associated with each of the three possible hypotheses for a given test statistic. This understanding will allow the student to take the *p*-value from a computer printout and adjust it accordingly.

Converting a Two-Tailed *p*-value from a Printout to a One-Tailed *p*-value

$$p = \frac{\text{Reported } p\text{-value}}{2} \quad \text{if} \begin{cases} H_a \text{ is of form} > \text{ and } z \text{ is positive} \\ H_a \text{ is of form} < \text{ and } z \text{ is negative} \end{cases}$$

$$p = 1 - \left(\frac{\text{Reported } p\text{-value}}{2} \right) \quad \text{if} \begin{cases} H_a \text{ is of form} > \text{ and } z \text{ is negative} \\ H_a \text{ is of form} < \text{ and } z \text{ is positive} \end{cases}$$

Statistics in Action Revisited

Testing a Population Mean in the Kleenex® Survey

Refer to Kimberly-Clark Corporation's survey of 250 people who kept a count of their use of Kleenex® tissues in diaries (p. 417). We want to test the claim made by marketing experts that $\mu = 60$ is the average number of tissues used by people with colds against our belief that the population mean is smaller than 60 tissues. That is, we want to test

$$H_0: \mu = 60 \quad H_a: \mu < 60$$

We will select $\alpha = .05$ as the level of significance for the test.

The survey results for the 250 sampled Kleenex® users are stored in the TISSUES data file. A MINITAB analysis of the data yielded the printout displayed in Figure SIA8.1.

The observed significance level of the test, highlighted on the printout, is *p*-value = .018. Since this *p*-value is less than $\alpha = .05$, we have sufficient evidence to reject H_0; therefore, we conclude that the mean number of tissues used by a person with a cold is less than 60 tissues.

[*Note:* If we conduct the same test using $\alpha = .01$ as the level of significance, we would have insufficient evidence to reject H_0 since the *p*-value = .018 is greater than $\alpha = .01$. Thus, at $\alpha = .01$, there is no evidence to support our alternative that the population mean is less than 60.]

```
Test of mu = 60 vs < 60


                                       95%
                                     Upper
Variable    N     Mean    StDev  SE Mean   Bound       T       P
NUMUSED    250  56.6760  25.0343  1.5833  59.2900   -2.10   0.018
```

Figure SIA8.1
MINITAB test of $\mu = 60$ for Kleenex® survey

Hypothesis Testing

Using the TI-83 Graphing Calculator

Computing the *p*-value for a *z*-Test

Step 1   *Access the Statistical Tests Menu.*
Press **STAT**
Arrow right to **TESTS**
Press **ENTER** to select **Z-Test**

Step 2   *Choose "**Data**" or "**Stats**". ("Data" is selected when you have entered the raw data into a List. "Stats" is selected when you are given only the mean, standard deviation, and sample size.)*
Press **ENTER**

If you selected "Data", enter the values for the hypothesis test where μ_0 = the value for μ in the null hypothesis, σ = assumed value of the population standard deviation.
Set **List** to **L1**
Set **Freq** to **1**
Use the arrow to highlight the appropriate alternative hypothesis.
Press **ENTER**
Arrow down to "**Calculate**"
Press **ENTER**

If you selected "Stats", enter the values for the hypothesis test where μ_0 = the value for μ in the null hypothesis, σ = assumed value of the population standard deviation.
Enter the sample mean and sample size.
Arrow down to "**Calculate**"
Press **ENTER**

The chosen test will be displayed as well as the *z*-test statistic, the *p*-value, the sample mean, and the sample size.

Example   A manufacturer claims the average life expectancy of this particular model light bulb is at least 10,000 hours with σ = 1,000 hours. A simple random sample of 40 light bulbs shows a sample mean of 9755 hours. Using σ = .05, test the manufacturer's claim.
For this problem the hypotheses will be:

$$H_0: \mu \geq 10{,}000$$
$$H_a: \mu < 10{,}000$$

The screens are shown below:

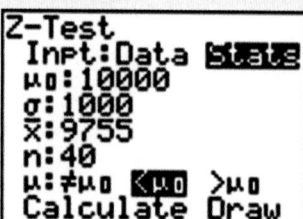
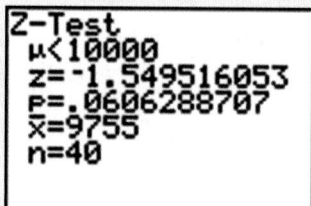

As you can see the *p*-value is 0.061. Since p > .05, ***do not*** reject H_0.

Exercises 8.31–8.45

Learning the Mechanics

8.31 For each α and observed significance level (*p*-value) pair, indicate whether the null hypothesis would be rejected.
   a. $\alpha = .05$, *p*-value $= .10$ Fail to reject H_0
   b. $\alpha = .10$, *p*-value $= .05$ Reject H_0
   c. $\alpha = .01$, *p*-value $= .001$ Reject H_0
   d. $\alpha = .025$, *p*-value $= .05$ Fail to Reject H_0
   e. $\alpha = .10$, *p*-value $= .45$ Fail to reject H_0

8.32 If a hypothesis test were conducted using $\alpha = .05$, for which of the following *p*-values would the null hypothesis be rejected?
   a. .06   **b.** .10   **c.** .01
   d. .001   **e.** .251   **f.** .042

8.33 In a test of $H_0: \mu = 100$ against $H_a: \mu > 100$, the sample data yielded the test statistic $z = 2.17$. Find and interpret the *p*-value for the test. $p = .0150$

8.34 In a test of the hypothesis $H_0: \mu = 50$ versus $H_a: \mu > 50$, a sample of $n = 100$ observations possessed mean $\bar{x} = 49.4$ and standard deviation $s = 4.1$. Find and interpret the *p*-value for this test. $p = .9279$

8.35 In a test of $H_0: \mu = 100$ against $H_a: \mu \neq 100$, the sample data yielded the test statistic $z = 2.17$. Find the *p*-value for the test. $p = .03$

8.36 In a test of the hypothesis $H_0: \mu = 10$ versus $H_a: \mu \neq 10$, a sample of $n = 50$ observations possessed mean $\bar{x} = 10.7$ and standard deviation $s = 3.1$. Find and interpret the *p*-value for this test. $p = .1096$

8.37 In a test of $H_0: \mu = 75$ performed using the computer, SPSS reports a two-tailed *p*-value of .1032. Make the appropriate conclusion for each of the following situations:

   a. $H_a: \mu < 75$, $z = -1.63$, $\alpha = .05$ Fail to reject H_0
   b. $H_a: \mu < 75$, $z = 1.63$, $\alpha = .10$ Fail to reject H_0
   c. $H_a: \mu > 75$, $z = 1.63$, $\alpha = .10$ Reject H_0
   d. $H_a: \mu \neq 75$, $z = -1.63$, $\alpha = .01$ Fail to reject H_0

8.38 An analyst tested the null hypothesis $\mu \geq 20$ against the alternative hypothesis that $\mu < 20$. The analyst reported a *p*-value of .06. What is the smallest value of α for which the null hypothesis would be rejected? $\alpha > .06$

Applying the Concepts—Basic

⊙ DIAMONDS

8.39 Refer to the carat data for 308 diamonds saved in the DIAMONDS file. In Exercise 8.22 (p. 426) you tested $H_0: \mu = .6$ against $H_a: \mu \neq .6$ based on a random sample of 30 diamonds.
   a. Use a statistical software package to find the *p*-value of the test.
   b. Compare the *p*-value to $\alpha = .05$ and make the appropriate conclusion.

8.40 In Exercise 8.23 (p. 426) you tested $H_0: \mu = .250$ versus $H_a: \mu \neq .250$, where μ is the population mean weight of plastic golf tees. An SPSS printout for the hypothesis test is shown below. Locate the *p*-value on the printout and interpret its value. $p = .000$

8.41 Refer to the National Funeral Directors Association study of the average fee charged for a full-service funeral, Exercise 8.28 (p. 427). Recall that a test was conducted to determine if the true mean fee charged exceeds $5,180. The data (recorded in thousands of dollars) for the sample of 36 funeral homes were analyzed using MINITAB. The resulting printout of the test of hypothesis is shown at the bottom of the page.

SPSS Output for Exercise 8.40

One-Sample Test

			Test Value = 0.250		95% Confidence Interval of the Difference	
	t	df	Sig. (2-tailed)	Mean Difference	Lower	Upper
WEIGHT	7.019	39	.000	.0025	.0018	.0032

MINITAB Output for Exercise 8.41

```
Test of mu = 5.18 vs > 5.18


                                          95%
                                         Lower
Variable    N    Mean    StDev   SE Mean    Bound    T      P
REVENUE    36  5.51944  1.26487  0.21081  5.16326  1.61  0.058
```

a. Locate the *p*-value for this upper-tailed test of hypothesis. $p = .058$

b. Use the *p*-value to make a decision regarding the null hypothesis tested. Does the decision agree with your decision in Exercise 8.28?

Applying the Concepts—Intermediate

8.42 In a paper presented at the 2000 Conference of the International Association for Time Use Research, professor Margaret Sanik of Ohio State University reported the results of her study on American cable TV viewers who purchase items from one of the home shopping channels. She found that the average age of these cable TV shoppers was 51 years. Suppose you want to test the null hypothesis, H_0: $\mu = 51$, using a sample of $n = 50$ cable TV shoppers.

a. Find the *p*-value of a two-tailed test if $\bar{x} = 52.3$ and $s = 7.1$.   .1970

b. Find the *p*-value of an upper-tailed test if $\bar{x} = 52.3$ and $s = 7.1$.   .0985

c. Find the *p*-value of a two-tailed test if $\bar{x} = 52.3$ and $s = 10.4$.   .38

d. For each of the tests, parts **a–c**, give a value of α that will lead to a rejection of the null hypothesis.

e. If $\bar{x} = 52.3$, give a value of s that will yield a *p*-value of .01 or less. $s = 3.56$

8.43 Television commercials most often employ females, or "feminized" males, to pitch a company's product. Research published in *Nature* (Aug. 27, 1998) revealed that people are, in fact, more attracted to "feminized" faces, regardless of gender. In one experiment, 50 human subjects viewed both a Japanese female and a Caucasian male face on a computer. Using special computer graphics, each subject could morph the faces (by making them more feminine or more masculine) until they attained the "most attractive" face. The level of feminization x (measured as a percentage) was measured.

a. For the Japanese female face, $\bar{x} = 10.2\%$ and $s = 31.3\%$. The researchers used this sample information to test the null hypothesis of a mean level of feminization equal to 0%. Verify that the test statistic is equal to 2.3. $z = 2.30$

b. Refer to part **a.** The researchers reported the *p*-value of the test as $p = .021$. Verify and interpret this result.

c. For the Caucasian male face, $\bar{x} = 15.0\%$ and $s = 25.1\%$. The researchers reported the test statistic (for the test of the null hypothesis stated in part a) as 4.23 with an associated *p*-value of approximately 0. Verify and interpret these results.

8.44 Refer to Exercise 8.24 (p. 427), in which a random sample of 49 unemployed men were administered the General Health Questionnaire (GHQ). The sample mean and standard deviation were 10.94 and 5.10, respectively. Denoting the population mean GHQ for unemployed workers by μ, we wish to test the null hypothesis H_0: $\mu = 10$ versus the one-tailed alternative H_a: $\mu > 10$.

a. Compute the *p*-value of the test. $p = .0985$

b. What conclusion would you reach about the test based on the *p*-value at $\alpha = .10$? At $\alpha = .05$?

8.45 An article published in the *Journal of the American Medical Association* (Oct. 16, 1995) calls smoking in China "a public health emergency." The researchers found that smokers in China smoke an average of 16.5 cigarettes a day. The high smoking rate is one reason why the tobacco industry is the central government's largest source of tax revenue. Has the average number of cigarettes smoked per day by Chinese smokers increased over the past two years? Consider that in a random sample of 200 Chinese smokers in 2002, the number of cigarettes smoked per day had a mean of 17.05 and a standard deviation of 5.21.

a. Set up the null and alternative hypotheses for testing whether Chinese smokers smoke, on average, more cigarettes a day in 2002 than in 1995. (Assume that the population mean for 1995 is $\mu = 16.5$.)

b. Compute and interpret the observed significance level of the test. $p = .0681$

c. Why is a two-tailed test inappropriate for this problem?

8.4 Small-Sample Test of Hypothesis about a Population Mean

A manufacturing operation consists of a single-machine-tool system that produces an average of 15.5 transformer parts every hour. After undergoing a complete overhaul, the system was monitored by observing the number of parts produced in each of seventeen randomly selected one-hour periods. The mean and standard deviation for the 17 production runs are

$$\bar{x} = 15.42 \qquad s = .16$$

Does this sample provide sufficient evidence to conclude that the true mean number of parts produced every hour by the overhauled system differs from 15.5?

This inference can be placed in a test of hypothesis framework. We establish the preoverhaul mean as the null hypothesized value and utilize a two-tailed alternative that the true mean of the overhauled system differs from the preoverhaul mean:

Teaching Tip

Point out that the only difference between the small-sample and large-sample test of hypothesis is that the sampling distribution has changed to a *t*-distribution (and there is an assumption that the population is normally distributed).

$$H_0: \mu = 15.5$$
$$H_a: \mu = 15.5$$

Recall from Section 7.3 that when we are faced with making inferences about a population mean using the information in a small sample, two problems emerge:

1. The normality of the sampling distribution for $\bar{x}$ does not follow from the Central Limit Theorem when the sample size is small. We must assume that the distribution of measurements from which the sample was selected is approximately normally distributed in order to ensure the approximate normality of the sampling distribution of $\bar{x}$.

2. If the population standard deviation σ is unknown, as is usually the case, then we cannot assume that s will provide a good approximation for σ when the sample size is small. Instead, we must use the *t*-distribution rather than the standard normal *z*-distribution to make inferences about the population mean μ.

Therefore, as the test statistic of a small-sample test of a population mean, we use the *t* statistic:

$$\text{Test statistic: } t = \frac{\bar{x} - \mu_0}{s/\sqrt{n}} = \frac{\bar{x} - 15.5}{s/\sqrt{n}}$$

where μ_0 is the null hypothesized value of the population mean, μ. In our example, $\mu_0 = 15.5$.

To find the rejection region, we must specify the value of α, the probability that the test will lead to rejection of the null hypothesis when it is true, and then consult the *t*-table (Table VI of Appendix B). Using $\alpha = .05$, the two-tailed rejection region is

Rejection region: $t_{\alpha/2} = t_{.025} = 2.120$ with $n - 1 = 16$ degrees of freedom
Reject H_0 if $t < -2.120$ or $t > 2.120$

The rejection region is shown in Figure 8.10.

Figure 8.10
Two-tailed rejection region
for small-sample *t*-test

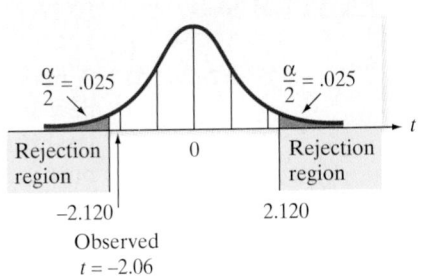

We are now prepared to calculate the test statistic and reach a conclusion:

$$t = \frac{\bar{x} - \mu_0}{s/\sqrt{n}} = \frac{15.42 - 15.50}{.16/\sqrt{17}} = \frac{-.08}{.0388} = -2.06$$

Since the calculated value of t does not fall in the rejection region (Figure 8.10), we cannot reject H_0 at the $\alpha = .05$ level of significance. Based on the sample evidence, we should not conclude that the mean number of parts produced per hour by the overhauled system differs from 15.5.

It is interesting to note that the calculated t value, -2.06, is *less than* the .05 level z value, -1.96. The implication is that if we had *incorrectly* used a z-statistic for this test, we would have rejected the null hypothesis at the .05 level, concluding that the mean production per hour of the overhauled system differs from 15.5 parts. The important point is that the statistical procedure to be used must always be closely scrutinized and all the assumptions understood. Many statistical distortions are the result of misapplications of otherwise valid procedures.

The technique for conducting a small-sample test of hypothesis about a population mean is summarized in the following box.

Small-Sample Test of Hypothesis about μ

Teaching Tip
Point out the similarities between this box and the one from the large-sample section. Emphasize the assumption that is now necessary.

One-Tailed Test	Two-Tailed Test
$H_0: \mu = \mu_0$	$H_0: \mu = \mu_0$
$H_a: \mu < \mu_0$ (or $H_a: \mu > \mu_0$)	$H_a: \mu \neq \mu_0$
Test statistic: $t = \dfrac{\bar{x} - \mu_0}{s/\sqrt{n}}$	Test statistic: $t = \dfrac{\bar{x} - \mu_0}{s/\sqrt{n}}$
Rejection region: $t < -t_\alpha$ (or $t > t_\alpha$ when $H_a: \mu > \mu_0$)	Rejection region: $\lvert t \rvert > t_{\alpha/2}$

where t_α and $t_{\alpha/2}$ are based on $(n - 1)$ degrees of freedom

---

Conditions Required for a Valid Small-Sample Hypothesis Test for μ

1. A random sample is selected from the target population.
2. The population from which the sample is selected has a distribution that is approximately normal.

EXAMPLE 8.5   CONDUCTING A SMALL-SAMPLE TEST FOR μ

Problem   A major car manufacturer wants to test a new engine to determine whether it meets new air pollution standards. The mean emission μ of all engines of this type must be less than 20 parts per million of carbon. Ten engines are manufactured for testing purposes, and the emission level of each is determined. The data (in parts per million) are listed in Table 8.4.

Do the data supply sufficient evidence to allow the manufacturer to conclude that this type of engine meets the pollution standard? Assume that the production process is stable and the manufacturer is willing to risk a Type I error with probability $\alpha = .01$.

$t = -3.00$, reject H_0 at $\alpha = .01$

EMISSIONS

TABLE 8.4 Emission Levels for Ten Engines

15.6	16.2	22.5	20.5	16.4	19.4	16.6	17.9	12.7	13.9

Solution The manufacturer wants to support the research hypothesis that the mean emission level μ for all engines of this type is less than 20 parts per million. The elements of this small-sample one-tailed test are

$$H_0: \mu = 20$$
$$H_a: \mu < 20$$

Test statistic: $t = \dfrac{\bar{x} - 20}{s/\sqrt{n}}$

Assumption: The relative frequency distribution of the population of emission levels for all engines of this type is approximately normal.

Rejection region: For $\alpha = .01$ and df $= n - 1 = 9$, the one-tailed rejection region (see Figure 8.11) is $t < -t_{.01} = -2.821$.

Suggested Exercise 8.50

Figure 8.11

A *t*-distribution with 9 df and the rejection region for Example 8.5

To calculate the test statistic, we entered the data into a computer and analyzed it using MINITAB. The MINITAB printout is shown in Figure 8.12. From the printout, we obtain $\bar{x} = 17.17$, $s = 2.98$. Substituting these values into the test statistic formula, we get

$$t = \frac{\bar{x} - 20}{s/\sqrt{n}} = \frac{17.17 - 20}{2.98/\sqrt{10}} = -3.00$$

Figure 8.12

MINITAB printout for test of mean emissions

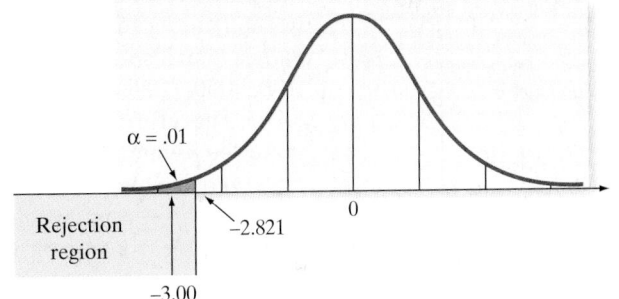

```
Test of mu = 20 vs < 20

                                            95%
                                          Upper
Variable    N     Mean    StDev  SE Mean   Bound      T      P
EMIT       10  17.1700   2.9814   0.9428  18.8983  -3.00  0.007
```

Since the calculated *t* falls in the rejection region (see Figure 8.11), the manufacturer concludes that $\mu < 20$ parts per million and the new engine type meets the pollution standard.

Look Back Are you satisfied with the reliability associated with this inference? The probability is only $\alpha = .01$ that the test would support the research hypothesis if in fact it were false.

Now Work   *Exercise 5.50 a, b*

■ ■ ■

EXAMPLE 8.6

THE *P*-VALUE FOR A SMALL-SAMPLE TEST OF μ

Problem

$.005 < p < .01$

Find the observed significance level for the test described in Example 8.5. Interpret the result.

Solution

The test of Example 8.5 was a lower-tailed test: H_0: $\mu = 20$ versus H_a: $\mu < 20$. Since the value of t computed from the sample data was $t = -3.00$, the observed significance level (or *p*-value) for the test is equal to the probability that t would assume a value less than or equal to -3.00 if in fact H_0 were true. This is equal to the area in the lower tail of the t-distribution (shaded in Figure 8.13).

One way to find this area (i.e., the *p*-value for the test) is to consult the *t*-table (Table VI in Appendix B). Unlike the table of areas under the normal curve, Table VI gives only the t values corresponding to the areas .100, .050, .025, .010, .005, .001, and .0005. Therefore, we can only approximate the *p*-value for the test. Since the observed *t*-value was based on 9 degrees of freedom, we use the df = 9 row in Table VI and move across the row until we reach the t values that are closest to the observed $t = -3.00$.

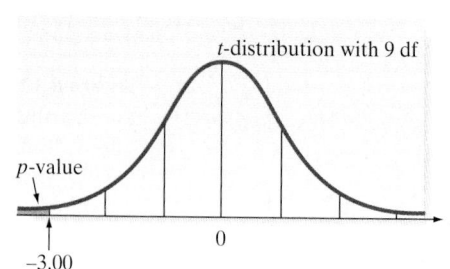

Figure 8.13
The observed significance level for the test of Example 8.5

[*Note:* We ignore the minus sign.] The *t*-values corresponding to *p*-values of .010 and .005 are 2.821 and 3.250, respectively. Since the observed t value falls between $t_{.010}$ and $t_{.005}$, the *p*-value for the test lies between .005 and .010. In other words, $.005 < p\text{-value} < .01$. Thus, we would reject the null hypothesis, H_0: $\mu = 20$ parts per million, for any value of α larger than .01 (the upper bound of the *p*-value).

A second, more accurate, way to obtain the *p*-value is to use a statistical software package to conduct the test of hypothesis. The MINITAB printout shown in Figure 8.12 gives both the test statistic (-3.00) and *p*-value (.007).

You can see that the actual *p*-value of the test falls within the bounds obtained from Table VI. Thus, the two methods agree; we will reject H_0: $\mu = 20$ in favor of H_a: $\mu < 20$ for any α level larger than .01.

Now Work   *Exercise 5.50c*

■ ■ ■

Small-sample inferences typically require more assumptions and provide less information about the population parameter than do large-sample inferences.

Nevertheless, the t-test is a method of testing a hypothesis about a population mean of a normal distribution when only a small number of observations are available. What can be done if you know that the population relative frequency distribution is decidedly nonnormal, say highly skewed?

What Can Be Done If the Population Relative Frequency Distribution Departs Greatly from Normal?

Answer: Use one of the nonparametric statistical methods of Chapter 16.

Exercises 8.46–8.60

Learning the Mechanics

8.46 a. Consider testing H_0: $\mu = 80$. Under what conditions should you use the t-distribution to conduct the test?
  b. In what ways are the distributions of the z-statistic and t-test statistic alike? How do they differ?

8.47 For each of the following rejection regions, sketch the sampling distribution of t, and indicate the location of the rejection region on your sketch:
  a. $t > 1.440$ where df = 6
  b. $t < -1.782$ where df = 12
  c. $t < -2.060$ or $t > 2.060$ where df = 25

8.48 For each of the rejection regions defined in Exercise 8.47, what is the probability that a Type I error will be made?

8.49 A random sample of n observations is selected from a normal population to test the null hypothesis that $\mu = 10$. Specify the rejection region for each of the following combinations of H_a, α, and n:
  a. H_a: $\mu \neq 10$; $\alpha = .05$; $n = 14$ $|t| > 2.160$
  b. H_a: $\mu > 10$; $\alpha = .01$; $n = 24$ $t > 2.500$
  c. H_a: $\mu > 10$; $\alpha = .10$; $n = 9$ $t > 1.397$
  d. H_a: $\mu < 10$; $\alpha = .01$; $n = 12$ $t < -2.718$
  e. H_a: $\mu \neq 10$; $\alpha = .10$; $n = 20$ $|t| > 1.729$
  f. H_a: $\mu < 10$; $\alpha = .05$; $n = 4$ $t < -2.353$

8.50 A sample of five measurements, randomly selected from a normally distributed population, resulted in the following summary statistics: $\bar{x} = 4.8$, $s = 1.3$.
  a. Test the null hypothesis that the mean of the population is 6 against the alternative hypothesis, $\mu < 6$. Use $\alpha = .05$. $t = -2.064$
  b. Test the null hypothesis that the mean of the population is 6 against the alternative hypothesis, $\mu \neq 6$. Use $\alpha = .05$. $t = -2.064$
  c. Find the observed significance level for each test.

8.51 Suppose you conduct a t-test for the null hypothesis H_0: $\mu = 1,000$ versus the alternative hypothesis H_a: $\mu > 1,000$ based on a sample of 17 observations. The test results are: $t = 1.89$ and p-value $= .038$.
  a. What assumptions are necessary for the validity of this procedure?

  b. Interpret the results of the test. $p = .038$
  c. Suppose the alternative hypothesis had been the two-tailed H_a: $\mu \neq 1,000$. If the t statistic were unchanged, then what would the p-value be for this test? Interpret the p-value for the two-tailed test.

Applying the concepts—Basic

8.52 Information Resources Inc., a Chicago-based research organization, tracks supermarket sales in 28 metropolitan markets in the United States. They convert their data for specific products to an index that measures product usage relative to the national average usage. For example, Green Bay, Wisconsin's ketchup index is 143, the highest in the nation. This means that Green Bay residents consume 43% more ketchup, on average, than the mean national consumption rate. The table lists the salad dressings index for each in a sample of seven Southeastern cities.

🔹 **SALAD**

Salad Dressings Index (U.S. mean = 100)	
Charlotte, N.C.	124
Birmingham. Al.	99
Raleigh, N.C.	124
Knoxville, Tenn.	99
Memphis, Tenn.	90
Atlanta, Ga.	111
Nashville, Tenn.	89

Source: Wall Street Journal Interactive Edition, Jan. 5, 2000.

  a. Specify the appropriate null and alternative hypotheses for testing whether the true mean consumption rate of salad dressings in the Southeastern United States is different than the mean national consumption rate of 100. H_0: $\mu = 100$ vs. H_a: $\mu \neq 100$
  b. What assumptions about the sample and population must hold in order for it to be appropriate to use a t-statistic in conducting the hypothesis test?
  c. Conduct the hypothesis test using $\alpha = .05$.

d. Is the observed significance level of the test greater or less than .05? Justify your answer. $p > .05$

⊙ FLALAW

8.53 Refer to Exercise 7.30 (p. 373) and the data on $n = 26$ law firms in Florida listed in *Florida Trend* magazine (April 2002). Recall that you found a 90% confidence interval for μ, the mean number of offices operated by all Florida law firms.

a. Use the data saved in the FLALAW file to conduct a test (at $\alpha = .10$) of $H_0: \mu = 5$ versus $H_a: \mu \neq 5$. $t = .41$

b. Does the inference, part **a**, agree with the inference you made using the confidence interval in Exercise 7.30? Yes

8.54 The Cleveland Casting Plant produces iron automotive castings for Ford Motor Company (*Quality Engineering*, Vol. 7, 1995). The pouring temperatures (in degrees Fahrenheit) for a sample of 10 crankshafts produced at the plant are listed below. When the process is stable, the target pouring temperature of the molton iron is 2,550 degrees. Conduct a test to determine whether the true mean pouring temperature differs from the target setting. Test using $\alpha = .01$. Use the accompanying SPSS printout to carry out the test. $p = .257$

⊙ IRONTEMP

2,543	2,541	2,544	2,620	2,560	2,559	2,562
2,553	2,552	2,553				

Source: Price, B., and Barth, B. "A Structural Model Relating Process Inputs and Final Product Characteristics." *Quality Engineering*, Vol. 7, No. 4, 1995, p. 696 (Table 2).

8.55 The Occupational Safety and Health Act (OSHA) allows issuance of engineering standards to ensure safe workplaces for all Americans. The maximum allowable mean level of arsenic in smelters, herbicide production facilities, and other places where arsenic is used is .004 milligram per cubic meter of air. Suppose smelters at two plants are being investigated to determine whether they are meeting OSHA standards. Two analyses of the air are made at each plant, and the results (in milligrams per cubic meter of air) are shown in the table.

⊙ ARSENIC

Plant 1		Plant 2	
Observation	Arsenic Level	Observation	Arsenic Level
1	.01	1	.05
2	.005	2	.09

a. What are the appropriate null and alternative hypotheses if we wish to test whether the plants meet the current OSHA standard?

b. These data are analyzed by MINITAB, with the results as shown below. Check the calculations of the t-statistics and p-values.

c. Interpret the results of the two tests.

Applying the Concepts—Intermediate

8.56 A study was conducted to evaluate the effectiveness of a new mosquito repellent designed by the U.S. Army to be applied as camouflage face paint (*Journal of the Mosquito Control Association*, June 1995). The repellent was applied to the forearms of

SPSS Output for Exercise 8.54

One-Sample Test

	Test Value = 2550					
					95% Confidence Interval of the Difference	
	t	df	Sig. (2-tailed)	Mean Difference	Lower	Upper
POURTEMP	1.210	9	.257	8.70	-7.57	24.97

MINITAB Output for Exercise 8.55

```
Test of mu = 0.004 vs > 0.004


                                              95% Lower
   Variable   N      Mean      StDev    SE Mean    Bound      T      P
   Plant1     2   0.007500   0.003536  0.002500  -0.008284   1.40   0.197
   Plant2     2   0.070000   0.028284  0.020000  -0.056275   3.30   0.094
```

five volunteers and then the arms were exposed to fifteen active mosquitoes for a 10-hour period. The percentage of the forearm surface area protected from bites (called percent repellency) was calculated for each of the five volunteers. For one color of paint (loam), the following summary statistics were obtained:

$$\bar{x} = 83\% \qquad s = 15\%$$

a. The new repellent is considered effective if it provides a percent repellency of at least 95. Conduct a test to determine whether the mean repellency percentage of the new mosquito repellent is less than 95. Test using $\alpha = .10$ $t = -1.79$

b. What assumptions are required for the hypothesis test in part a to be valid?

8.57 By law, the levels of toxic organic compounds in fish are constantly monitored. A technique, called matrix solid-phase dispersion (MSPD), has been developed for chemically extracting trace organic compounds from fish specimens (*Chromatographia*, Mar. 1995). The MSPD method was tested as follows. Uncontaminated fish fillets were injected with a known amount of toxin. The MSPD method was then used to extract the contaminant and the percentage of the toxic compound recovered was measured. The recovery percentages for $n = 5$ fish fillets are listed below:

⊙ RECPCT

99	102	94	99	95

Do the data provide sufficient evidence to indicate that the mean recovery percentage of the toxic compound exceeds 85% using the new MSPD method? Test using $\alpha = .05$. $t = 8.75$, reject H_0

8.58 Refer to the U.S. Energy Information Administration's list of active nuclear power plants operating in each of a sample of 20 states, Exercise 2.54 (p. 82). The data, saved in the NUCLEAR file, are reproduced in the next table.

a. Is there sufficient evidence to claim that the mean number of active nuclear power plants operating in all states exceeds 3? Test using $\alpha = .10$. $t = 1.46$

b. Are the conditions required for a valid small-sample test reasonably satisfied? Explain.

c. Eliminate the lowest two values and the highest two values from the data set, then conduct the test of part a on the smaller data set. What impact does this have on the test results? $t = 1.10$

d. Why is it dangerous to eliminate data points in order to satisfy an assumption for a test of hypothesis?

⊙ NUCLEAR

State	Number of Power Plants
Alabama	5
Arizona	3
California	4
Florida	5
Georgia	4
Illinois	13
Kansas	1
Louisiana	2
Massachusetts	1
Mississippi	1
New Hampshire	1
New York	6
North Carolina	5
Ohio	2
Pennsylvania	9
South Carolina	7
Tennessee	3
Texas	4
Vermont	1
Wisconsin	3

Source: Statistical Abstract of the United States, 2000 (Table 966). U.S. Energy Information Administration, Electric Power Annual.

8.59 The Mississippi Department of Transportation collected data on number of cracks (called *crack intensity*) in an undivided two-lane highway using van-mounted state-of-the-art video technology (*Journal of Infrastructure Systems*, Mar. 1995). The mean number of cracks found in a sample of eight 50-meter sections of the highway was $\bar{x} = .210$, with a variance of $s^2 = .011$. Suppose the American Association of State Highway and Transportation Officials (AASHTO) recommends a maximum mean crack intensity of .100 for safety purposes. Is there evidence to say that the true mean crack intensity of the Mississippi highway exceeds the AASHTO recommended maximum? Use $\alpha = .01$ in the test.

Applying the Concepts—Advanced

⊙ TAMALES

8.60 "Hot Tamales" are chewy, cinnamon flavored candies. A bulk vending machine is known to dispense, on average, 15 Hot Tamales per bag. *Chance* (Fall 2000) published an article on a classroom project in which students were required to purchase bags of Hot Tamales from the machine and count the number of candies per bag. One student group claimed they purchased five bags that had the following candy counts: 25, 23, 21, 21, and 20. There was some question as to whether the students had fabricated the data. Use a hypothesis test to gain-insight into whether or not the data collected by the students are fabricated. Use a level of significance that gives the benefit of the doubt to the students. $t = 7.83$

8.5 Large-Sample Test of Hypothesis about a Population Proportion

Inferences about population proportions (or percentages) are often made in the context of the probability, p, of "success" for a binomial distribution. We saw how to use large samples from binomial distributions to form confidence intervals for p in Section 7.3. We now consider tests of hypotheses about p.

For example, consider the problem of *insider trading* in the stock market. trading is the buying and selling of stock by an individual privy to inside information in a company, usually a high-level executive in the firm. The Securities and Exchange Commission (SEC) imposes strict guidelines about insider trading so that all investors can have equal access to information that may affect the stock's price. An investor wishing to test the effectiveness of the SEC guidelines monitors the market for a period of a year and records the number of times a stock price increases the day following a significant purchase of stock by an insider. For a total of 576 such transactions, the stock increased the following day 327 times. Does this sample provide evidence that the stock price may be affected by insider trading?

Teaching Tip

Point out that the same concepts that we used when testing a mean are used when testing a population proportion. The one big difference is the method used to determine if the sample is large enough.

We first view this as a binomial experiment, with the 576 transactions as the trials, and success representing an increase in the stock's price the following day. Let p represent the probability that the stock price will increase following a large insider purchase. If the insider purchase has no effect on the stock price (that is, if the information available to the insider is identical to that available to the general market), then the investor expects the probability of a stock increase to be the same as that of a decrease, or $p = .5$. On the other hand, if insider trading affects the stock price (indicating that the market has not fully accounted for the information known to the insiders), then the investor expects the stock either to decrease or to increase more than half the time following significant insider transactions; that is, $p \neq .5$.

We can now place the problem in the context of a test of hypothesis:

$$H_0: p = .5$$
$$H_a: p \neq .5$$

Recall that the sample proportion, $\hat{p}$, is really just the sample mean of the outcomes of the individual binomial trials and, as such, is approximately normally distributed (for large samples) according to the Central Limit Theorem. Thus, for large samples we can use the standard normal z as the test statistic:

$$\text{Test statistic: } z = \frac{\text{Sample proportion } - \text{ Null hypothesized proportion}}{\text{Standard deviation of sample proportion}}$$

$$= \frac{\hat{p} - p_0}{\sigma_{\hat{p}}}$$

Teaching Tip

p_0 is the equivalent of μ_0 when we worked with means. The student must be able to determine the value of the proportion to be tested, p_0.

where we use the symbol p_0 to represent the null hypothesized value of p.

Rejection region: We use the standard normal distribution to find the appropriate rejection region for the specified value of α. Using $\alpha = .05$, the two-tailed rejection region is

$$z < -z_{\alpha/2} = -z_{.025} = -1.96 \quad \text{or} \quad z > z_{\alpha/2} = z_{.025} = 1.96$$

See Figure 8.14.

Figure 8.14
Rejection region for insider
trading example

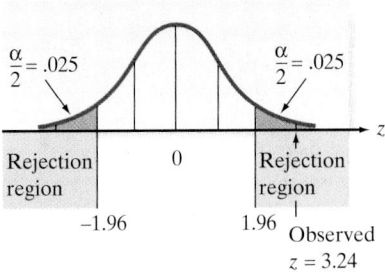

We are now prepared to calculate the value of the test statistic. Before doing so, we want to be sure that the sample size is large enough to ensure that the normal approximation for the sampling distribution of $\hat{p}$ is reasonable. To check this, we calculate a 3-standard-deviation interval around the null hypothesized value, p_0, which is assumed to be the true value of p until our test procedure indicates otherwise. Recall that $\sigma_{\hat{p}} = \sqrt{pq/n}$ and that we need an estimate of the product pq in order to calculate a numerical value of the test statistic z. Since the null hypothesized value is generally the accepted-until-proven-otherwise value, we use the value of $p_0 q_0$ (where $q_0 = 1 - p_0$) to estimate pq in the calculation of z. Thus,

$$\sigma_{\hat{p}} = \sqrt{\frac{pq}{n}} = \sqrt{\frac{p_0 q_0}{n}} = \sqrt{\frac{(.5)(.5)}{576}} = .021$$

and the 3-standard-deviation interval around p_0 is

$$p_0 \pm 3\sigma_{\hat{p}} \approx .5 \pm 3(.021) = (.437, .563)$$

Teaching Tip
It is important that students get in the habit of checking the sample size for the proportion test. Explain that proportions close to .5 do not require a very large sample size, but proportions close to 0 or 1 require a much larger sample size.

As long as this interval does not contain 0 or 1 (i.e., is completely contained in the interval 0 to 1), as is the case here, the normal distribution will provide a reasonable approximation for the sampling distribution of $\hat{p}$.

Returning to the hypothesis test at hand, the proportion of the sampled transactions that resulted in a stock increase is

$$\hat{p} = \frac{327}{576} = .568$$

Finally, we calculate the number of standard deviations (the z value) between the sampled and hypothesized value of the binomial proportion:

$$z = \frac{\hat{p} - p_0}{\sigma_{\hat{p}}} = \frac{\hat{p} - p_0}{\sqrt{p_0 q_0/n}} = \frac{.568 - .5}{.021} = \frac{.068}{.021} = 3.24$$

The implication is that the observed sample proportion is (approximately) 3.24 standard deviations above the null hypothesized proportion .5 (Figure 8.14). Therefore, we reject the null hypothesis, concluding at the .05 level of significance that the true probability of an increase or decrease in a stock's price differs from .5 the day following insider purchase of the stock. It appears that an insider purchase significantly increases the probability that the stock price will increase the following day. (To estimate the magnitude of the probability of an increase, a confidence interval can be constructed.)

The test of hypothesis about a population proportion p is summarized in the next box. Note that the procedure is entirely analogous to that used for conducting large-sample tests about a population mean.

Large-Sample Test of Hypothesis about p

One-Tailed Test	Two-Tailed Test
$H_0: p = p_0$ ($p_0 =$ hypothesized value of p)	$H_0: p = p_0$
$H_a: p < p_0$ (or $H_a: p > p_0$)	$H_a: p \neq p_0$
Test statistic: $z = \dfrac{\hat{p} - p_0}{\sigma_{\hat{p}}}$	Test statistic: $z = \dfrac{\hat{p} - p_0}{\sigma_{\hat{p}}}$

where, according to H_0, $\sigma_{\hat{p}} = \sqrt{p_0 q_0/n}$ and $q_0 = 1 - p_0$

Rejection region:	Rejection region: $|z| > z_{\alpha/2}$
$z < -z_\alpha$ (or $z > z_\alpha$ when $H_a: p > p_0$)	

Conditions Required for a Valid Large-Sample Hypothesis Test for p

1. A random sample is selected from a binomial population.
2. The sample size n is large. (This condition will be satisfied if $p_0 \pm 3\sigma_{\hat{p}}$ falls between 0 and 1.)

EXAMPLE 8.7

CONDUCTING A HYPOTHESIS TEST FOR p

Problem The reputations (and hence sales) of many businesses can be severely damaged by shipments of manufactured items that contain a large percentage of defectives. For example, a manufacturer of alkaline batteries may want to be reasonably certain that fewer than 5% of its batteries are defective. Suppose 300 batteries are randomly selected from a very large shipment; each is tested and 10 defective batteries are found. Does this provide sufficient evidence for the manufacturer to conclude that the fraction defective in the entire shipment is less than .05? Use $\alpha = .01$.

Solution Before conducting the test of hypothesis, we check to determine whether the sample size is large enough to use the normal approximation for the sampling distribution of $\hat{p}$. The criterion is tested by the interval

$$p_0 \pm 3\sigma_{\hat{p}} = p_0 \pm 3\sqrt{\frac{p_0 q_0}{n}} = .05 \pm 3\sqrt{\frac{(.05)(.95)}{300}}$$

$$= .05 \pm .04 \quad \text{or} \quad (.01, .09)$$

Since the interval lies within the interval $(0, 1)$, the normal approximation will be adequate.

The objective of the sampling is to determine whether there is sufficient evidence to indicate that the fraction defective, p, is less than .05. Consequently, we will test the null hypothesis that $p = .05$ against the alternative hypothesis that $p < .05$. The elements of the test are

$$H_0: p = .05$$
$$H_a: p < .05$$

Test statistic: $z = \dfrac{\hat{p} - p_0}{\sigma_{\hat{p}}}$

Rejection region: $z < -z_{.01} = -2.33$ (see Figure 8.15)

We now calculate the test statistic:

Suggested Exercises 8.73

$$z = \frac{\hat{p} - .05}{\sigma_{\hat{p}}} = \frac{(10/300) - .05}{\sqrt{p_0 q_0 / n}} = \frac{.033 - .05}{\sqrt{p_0 q_0 / 300}}$$

Notice that we use p_0 to calculate $\sigma_{\hat{p}}$ because, in contrast to calculating $\sigma_{\hat{p}}$ for a confidence interval, the test statistic is computed on the assumption that the null hypothesis is true—that is, $p = p_0$. Therefore, substituting the values for $\hat{p}$ and p_0 into the z-statistic, we obtain

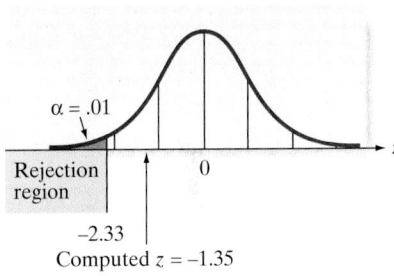

$$z \approx \frac{-.017}{\sqrt{(.05)(.95)/300}} = \frac{-.017}{.0126} = -1.35$$

Figure 8.15
Rejection region for Example 8.7

As shown in Figure 8.15, the calculated z value does not fall in the rejection region. Therefore, there is insufficient evidence at the .01 level of significance to indicate that the shipment contains fewer than 5% defective batteries.

> **Now Work** *Exercise 5.62a, b*

■ ■ ■

EXAMPLE 8.8

THE *p*-VALUE FOR A TEST ABOUT *p*

Problem In Example 8.7 we found that we did not have sufficient evidence, at the $\alpha = .01$ level of significance, to indicate that the fraction defective p of alkaline batteries was less than $p = .05$. How strong was the weight of evidence favoring the alternative hypothesis $(H_a: p < .05)$? Find the observed significance level for the test.

p = .0885

Solution The computed value of the test statistic z was $z = -1.35$. Therefore, for this lower-tailed test, the observed significance level is

$$\text{Observed significance level} = P(z \le -1.35)$$

This lower-tail area is shown in Figure 8.16. The area between $z = 0$ and $z = 1.35$ is given in Table IV in Appendix B as .4115. Therefore, the observed significance level is $.5 - .4115 = .0885$.

Look Back Note that this probability is quite small. Although we did not reject H_0: $p = .05$ at $\alpha = .01$, the probability of observing a z-value as small as or smaller than -1.35 is only .0885 if in fact H_0 is true. Therefore, we would reject H_0 if we choose $\alpha = .10$ (since the observed significance level is less than .10), and we would not reject H_0 (the conclusion of Example 8.7) if we choose $\alpha = .05$ or $\alpha = .01$

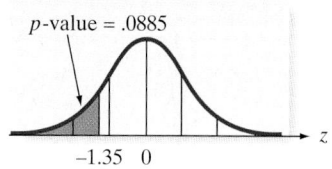

Figure 8.16

The observed significance level for Example 8.8

> **Now Work** *Exercise 5.62c*

■ ■ ■

Small-sample test procedures are also available for p, although most surveys use samples that are large enough to employ the large-sample tests presented in this section. A test of proportions that can be applied to small samples is discussed in Chapter 11.

Statistics in Action Revisited

Testing a Population Proportion in the Kleenex® Survey

In the previous "Statistics in Action Revisited" (p. 431), we investigated Kimberly-Clark Corporation's assertion that the company should put 60 tissues in a cold-care box of Kleenex® tissues. We did this by testing the claim that the mean number of tissues used by a person with a cold is $\mu = 60$ using data collected from a survey of 250 Kleenex® users. Another approach to the problem is to consider proportion of Kleenex® users who use fewer than 60 tissues when they have a cold. Now, the population parameter of interest is p, the proportion of all Kleenex® users who use fewer than 60 tissues when they have a cold.

Kimberly-Clark Corporation's belief that the company should put 60 tissues in a cold-care box will be supported if half of the Kleenex® users surveyed use less than 60 tissues and half use more than 60 tissues (i.e., if

$p = .5$). Is there evidence to indicate that the population proportion differs from .5? To answer this question, we set up the following null and alternative hypothesis:

$$H_0: p = .5 \qquad H_a: p \neq .5$$

Recall that the survey results for the 250 sampled Kleenex® users are stored in the TISSUES data file. In addition to the number of tissues used by each person, the file contains a qualitative variable—called USED60—representing whether the person used fewer or more than 60 tissues. (The values of USED60 in the data set are "BELOW" or "ABOVE".) A MINITAB analysis of this variable yielded the printout displayed in Figure SIA8.2.

On the MINITAB printout, X represents the number of the 250 people with colds that used less than 60 tissues. Note that X = 143. This value is used to compute the test statistic, $z = 2.28$, highlighted on the printout. The p-value of the test,

```
Test of p = 0.5 vs p not = 0.5

Event = BELOW


Variable    X    N  Sample p        95% CI        Z-Value  P-Value
USED60     143  250  0.572000  (0.510666, 0.633334)    2.28    0.023
```

Figure SIA8.2

MINITAB test of $p = .5$ for Kleenex® survey

also highlighted on the printout, is *p*-value = .023. Since this value is less than α = .05, there is sufficient evidence (at α = .05) to reject H_0; we conclude that the proportion of all Kleenex® users who use fewer than 60 tissues when they

have a cold differs from .5. However, if we test at α = .01, there is insufficient evidence to reject H_0. Consequently, our choice of α (as in the previous "Statistics in the Action Revisited") is critical to our decision.

Exercises 8.61–8.75

Learning the Mechanics

8.61 For the binomial sample sizes and null hypothesized values of *p* in each part, determine whether the sample size is large enough to use the normal approximation methodology presented in this section to conduct a test of the null hypothesis H_0: $p = p_0$.
a. $n = 900, p_0 = .975$ **b.** $n = 125, p_0 = .01$
c. $n = 40, p_0 = .75$ **d.** $n = 15, p_0 = .75$
e. $n = 12, p_0 = .62$ No

8.62 Suppose a random sample of 100 observations from a binomial population gives a value of $\hat{p} = .63$ and you wish to test the null hypothesis that the population parameter *p* is equal to .70 against the alternative hypothesis that *p* is less than .70.
a. Noting that $\hat{p} = .63$, what does your intuition tell you? Does the value of $\hat{p}$ appear to contradict the null hypothesis?   Yes
b. Use the large-sample *z*-test to test H_0: $p = .70$ against the alternative hypothesis, H_a: $p < .70$. Use $\alpha = .05$. How do the test results compare with your intuitive decision from part **a**? $z = -1.53$
c. Find and interpret the observed significance level of the test you conducted in part **b**. $p = .0630$

8.63 Suppose the sample in Exercise 8.62 has produced $\hat{p} = .83$ and we wish to test H_0: $p = .9$ against the alternative H_a: $p < .9$.
a. Calculate the value of the *z* statistic for this test.
b. Note that the numerator of the *z*-statistic ($\hat{p} - p_0 = .83 - .90 = -.07$) is the same as for Exercise 8.58. Considering this, why is the absolute value of *z* for this exercise larger than that calculated in Exercise 8.62?
c. Complete the test using $\alpha = .05$ and interpret the result.   Reject H_0
d. Find the observed significance level for the test and interpret its value. $p = .0099$

8.64 A statistics student used a computer program to test the null hypothesis H_0: $p = .5$ against the one-tailed alternative, H_a: $p > .5$. A sample of 500 observations are input into SPSS, which returns the following results: $z = .44$, two-tailed *p*-value = .33.
a. The student concludes, based on the *p*-value, that there is a 33% chance that the alternative hypothesis is true. Do you agree? If not, correct the interpretation.

b. How would the *p*-value change if the alternative hypothesis were two-tailed, H_a: $p \neq .5$? Interpret this *p*-value.   *p*-value = .33

8.65 Refer to Exercise 7.40 (p. 383), in which 50 consumers taste tested a new snack food. Their responses (where 0 = do not like; 1 = like; 2 = indifferent) are reproduced below.

🖲 SNACK

1	0	0	1	2	0	1	1	0	0	0
0	2	0	2	2	0	0	1	1	0	0
0	1	0	2	0	0	0	1	0	0	1
0	1	0	1	0	2	0	0	1	1	0
0	1									

a. Test H_0: $p = .5$ against H_a: $p > .5$, where *p* is the proportion of customers who do not like the snack food. Use $\alpha = 10$.
b. Find the observed significance level of your test.

Applying the Concepts—Basic

8.66 Refer to the *Journal of Global Business* (Spring 2002) study of what "Made in the USA" means to consumers, Exercise 2.8 (p. 54). Recall that 64 of 106 randomly selected shoppers believed "Made in the USA" means 100% of labor and materials are from the United States. Let *p* represent the true proportion of consumers who believe "Made in the USA" means 100% of labor and materials are from the United States.
a. Calculate a point estimate for *p*.   .604
b. A claim is made that $p = .70$. Set up the null and alternative hypothesis to test this claim. H_0: $p = .70$ vs. H_a: $p \neq .70$
c. Calculate the test statistic for the test, part **b**. $z = -2.16$
d. Find the rejection region for the test if $\alpha = .01$. $z > 2.58$ or $z < -2.58$
e. Use the results, parts c and d, to make the appropriate conclusion.   Fail to reject H_0

8.67 Refer to the Computer Security Institute (CSI) survey of computer crime, Exercise 2.12 (p. 55). Recall that in 1999, 7% of reported unauthorized uses of business Web sites came from inside the company. In a survey taken two years later, 7 of a sample of 163 reported unauthorized uses of business Web sites came from inside the company (*Computer Security Issues & Trends*, Vol. 7, Spring 2001). Let p represent the true proportion of unauthorized uses of business Web sites in 2001 that came from inside the company.

a. Calculate a point estimate for p.   .043

b. Set up the null and alternative hypothesis to test whether the value of p has changed since 1999. $H_0: p = .07$ vs. $H_a: p \neq .07$

c. Calculate the test statistic for the test, part b. $z = -1.35$

d. Find the rejection region for the test if $\alpha = .05$. $|z| > 1.96$

e. Use the results, parts c and d, to make the appropriate conclusion.   Fail to reject H_0

f. Find the p-value of the test and confirm that the conclusion based on the p-value agrees with the conclusion in part e. $p = .1770$

8.68 In a survey of 500 television viewers with access to cable TV, each was asked whether they agreed with the statement, "Overall, I find the quality of news on cable networks (such as CNN, FOXNews, CNBC, and MSNBC) to be better than news on the ABC, CBS, and NBC networks." A total of 248 viewers agreed with the statement (*Cabletelevision Advertising Bureau*, May 2002).

Note: The survey respondents were contacted via e-mail on the Internet.

a. Identify the population parameter of interest in the survey. p

b. Give a point estimate of the population parameter. .496

c. Set up H_0 and H_a for testing whether the true percentage of TV viewers who find cable news to be better quality than network news differs from 50%. $H_0: p = .50$ vs. $H_a: p \neq .50$

d. Conduct the test, part c, using $\alpha = .10$ Make the appropriate conclusion in the words of the problem. $z = -0.18$

e. What conditions are required for the inference, part d, to be valid? Do they appear to be satisfied? Yes

8.69 *Consumer Reports* (Sept. 1992) evaluated and rated 46 brands of toothpaste. One attribute examined in the study was whether or not a toothpaste brand carries an American Dental Association (ADA) seal verifying effective decay prevention. The data for the 46 brands (coded 1 = ADA seal, 0 = no ADA seal) are listed here.

ADA

0	0	0	0	0	0	1	1	1	0	0	1
0	1	0	0	0	0	1	1	1	0	1	1
1	1	0	0	0	0	0	1	0	0	1	1
1	0	1	0	1	1	1	0	0	0		

a. Give the null and alternative hypotheses for testing whether the true proportion of toothpaste brands with the ADA seal verifying effective decay prevention is less than .5.

b. Locate the p-value on the MINITAB printout at the bottom of the page.

c. Make the appropriate conclusion using $\alpha = .10$.

Applying the Concepts—Intermediate

8.70 Shoplifting in the U.S. costs retailers about $15 billion a year. Despite the seriousness of the problem, Shoplifters Alternative of Jericho, N.Y., claims that only 50% of all shoplifters are turned over to police (*Athens Daily News*, Dec. 12, 1999). A random sample of 40 U. S. retailers were questioned concerning the disposition of the most recent shoplifter they apprehended. Only 24 were turned over to police. Do these data provide sufficient evidence to contradict Shoplifters Alternative?

a. Conduct a hypothesis test to answer the question of interest. Use $\alpha = .05$. $z = 1.26$

b. Is the sample size large enough to use the inferential procedure of part a?   Yes

c. Find the observed significance level of the hypothesis test in part a. Interpret the value. $p = .1038$

d. For what values of a would the observed significance level be sufficient to reject the null hypothesis of the test you conducted in part b? $\alpha > .1038$

8.71 Pond's Age-Defying Complex, a cream with alpha-hydroxy acid, advertises that it can reduce wrinkles and improve the skin. In a study published *Archives of Dermatology* (June 1996), 33 middle-aged women used a cream with alpha-hydroxy acid for twenty-two weeks.

MINITAB Output for Exercise 8.69

```
Test of p = 0.5 vs p < 0.5

Event = 1


                                   95%
                                Upper      Exact
Variable    X    N   Sample p   Bound    P-Value
ADASEAL    20   46   0.434783  0.566289   0.231
```

At the end of the study period, a dermatologist judged whether each woman exhibited skin improvement. The results for the 33 women (where I = improved skin and N = no improvement) are listed in the accompanying table.

a. Do the date provide sufficient evidence to conclude that the cream will improve the skin of more than 60% of middle-aged women? Test using $\alpha = .05$. $z = 1.49$

b. Find and interpret the *p*-value of the test. .0681

SKINCREAM

I	I	N	I	N	N	I	I	I	I	I	I
N	I	I	I	N	I	I	I	N	I	N	I
I	I	I	I	I	N	I	I	N			

8.72 Refer to the *Nature* (Aug. 27, 1998) study of facial characteristics that are deemed attractive, Exercise 8.43 (p. 436). In another experiment, 67 human subjects viewed side-by-side an image of a Caucasian male face and the same image 50% masculinized. Each subject was asked to select the facial image that they deemed more attractive. Fifty-eight of the 67 subjects felt that masculinization of face shape decreased attractiveness of the male face. The researchers used this sample information to test whether the subjects showed preference for either the unaltered or morphed male face.

a. Set up the null and alternative hypotheses for this test.

b. Compute the test statistic. $z = 5.99$

c. The researchers reported *p*-value ≈ 0 for the test. Do you agree? Yes

d. Make the appropriate conclusion in the words of the problem. Use $\alpha = .01$. Reject H_0

8.73 In 1894, druggist Asa Candler began distributing handwritten tickets to his customers for free glasses of Coca-Cola at his soda fountain. That was the genesis of the discount coupon. In 1975 it was estimated that 65% of U.S. consumers regularly used discount coupons when shopping. In a 2001 consumer survey, 77% said they regularly redeem coupons (Mediamark Research,

Inc.). Assume the 2001 survey consisted of a random sample of 1,000 shoppers.

a. Does the 2001 survey provide sufficient evidence that the percentage of shoppers using cents-off coupons exceeds 65%? Test using $\alpha = .05$. $z = 7.96$

b. Is the sample size large enough to use the inferential procedures presented in this section? Explain. Yes

c. Find the observed significance level for the test you conducted in part **a,** and interpret its value. $p \approx 0$

Applying the Concepts—Advanced

8.74 The *placebo effect* describes the phenomenon of improvement in the condition of a patient taking a placebo—a pill that looks and tastes real but contains no medically active chemicals. Physicians at a clinic in La Jolla, California, gave what they thought were drugs to 7,000 asthma, ulcer, and herpes patients. Although the doctors later learned that the drugs were really placebos, 70% of the patients reported an improved condition (*Forbes*, May 22, 1995). Use this information to test (at $\alpha = .05$) the placebo effect at the clinic. Assume that if the placebo is ineffective, the probability of a patient's condition improving is .5. $z = 33.47$

8.75 "Take the Pepsi Challenge" was a marketing campaign used recently by the Pepsi-Cola Company. Coca-Cola drinkers participated in a blind taste test where they were asked to taste unmarked cups of Pepsi and Coke and were asked to select their favorite. In one Pepsi television commercial, an announcer states that "in recent blind taste tests, more than half the Diet Coke drinkers surveyed said they preferred the taste of Diet Pepsi" (*Consumer's Research*, May 1993). Suppose 100 Diet Coke drinkers took the Pepsi Challenge and 56 preferred the taste of Diet Pepsi. Determine if more than half of all Diet Coke drinkers will select Diet Pepsi in the blind taste test. Select α to minimize the probability of a Type I error. What are the consequences of the test results from Coca-Cola's perspective?

8.6 Calculating Type II Error Probabilities: More about β (Optional)

In our introduction to hypothesis testing in Section 8.1, we showed that the probability of committing a Type I error, α, can be controlled by the selection of the rejection region for the test. Thus, when the test statistic falls in the rejection region and we make the decision to reject the null hypothesis, we do so knowing the error rate for incorrect rejections of H_0. The situation corresponding to accepting the null hypothesis, and thereby risking a Type II error, is not generally as controllable. For that reason, we adopted a policy of nonrejection of H_0 when the test statistic does not fall in the rejection region, rather than risking an error of unknown magnitude.

To see how β, the probability of a Type II error, can be calculated for a test of hypothesis, recall the example in Section 8.1 in which a city tests a manufacturer's pipe to see whether it meets the requirement that the mean strength exceeds 2,400 pounds per linear foot. The setup for the test is as follows:

$$H_0: \mu = 2,400$$
$$H_a: \mu > 2,400$$

Test statistic: $z = \dfrac{\bar{x} - 2,400}{\sigma/\sqrt{n}}$

Rejection region: $z > 1.645$ for $\alpha = .05$

Teaching Tip
Point out that values of β can only be calculated when we assume a true value for the population mean.

Figure 8.17a shows the rejection region for the **null distribution**—that is, the distribution of the test statistic assuming the null hypothesis is true. The area in the rejection region is .05, and this area represents α, the probability that the test statistic leads to rejection of H_0 when in fact H_0 is true.

The Type II error probability β is calculated assuming that the null hypothesis is false, because it is defined as the *probability of accepting H_0 when it is false*. Since H_0 is false for any value of μ exceeding 2,400, one value of β exists for each possible value of μ greater than 2,400 (an infinite number of possibilities). Figures 8.17(b)–(d) show three of the possibilities, corresponding to alternative hypothesis values of μ equal to 2,425, 2,450, and 2,475, respectively. Note that β is the area in the *nonrejection* (or *acceptance*) *region* in each of these distributions and that β decreases as the true value of μ moves farther from the null hypothesized value of $\mu = 2,400$. This is sensible because the probability of incorrectly accepting the null hypothesis should decrease as the distance between the null and alternative values of μ increases.

In order to calculate the value of β for a specific value of μ in H_a, we proceed as follows:

1. Calculate the value of $\bar{x}$ that corresponds to the border between the acceptance and rejection regions. For the sewer pipe example, this is the value of $\bar{x}$ that lies 1.645 standard deviations above $\mu = 2,400$ in the sampling distribution of $\bar{x}$. Denoting this value by $\bar{x}_0$, corresponding to the largest value of $\bar{x}$ that supports the null hypothesis, we find (recalling that $s = 200$ and $n = 50$)

$$\bar{x}_0 = \mu_0 + 1.645\sigma_{\bar{x}} = 2,400 + 1.645\left(\frac{\sigma}{\sqrt{n}}\right)$$

$$\approx 2,400 + 1.645\left(\frac{s}{\sqrt{n}}\right) = 2,400 + 1.645\left(\frac{200}{\sqrt{50}}\right)$$

$$= 2,400 + 1.645(28.28) = 2.446.5$$

Teaching Tip
These calculations tend to be very difficult for students. Lots of examples will help considerably.

2. For a particular alternative distribution corresponding to a value of μ, denoted by μ_a, we calculate the z value corresponding to $\bar{x}_0$, the border between the rejection and acceptance regions. We then use this z value and Table IV of Appendix B to determine the area in the *acceptance region* under the alternative distribution. This area is the value of β corresponding to the particular alternative μ_a. For example, for the alternative $\mu_a = 2,425$, we calculate

$$z = \frac{\bar{x}_0 - 2,425}{\sigma_{\bar{x}}} = \frac{\bar{x}_0 - 2,425}{\sigma/\sqrt{n}}$$

$$\approx \frac{\bar{x}_0 - 2,425}{s/\sqrt{n}} = \frac{2,446.5 - 2,425}{28.28} = .76$$

Figure 8.17
Values of α and β for various values of μ

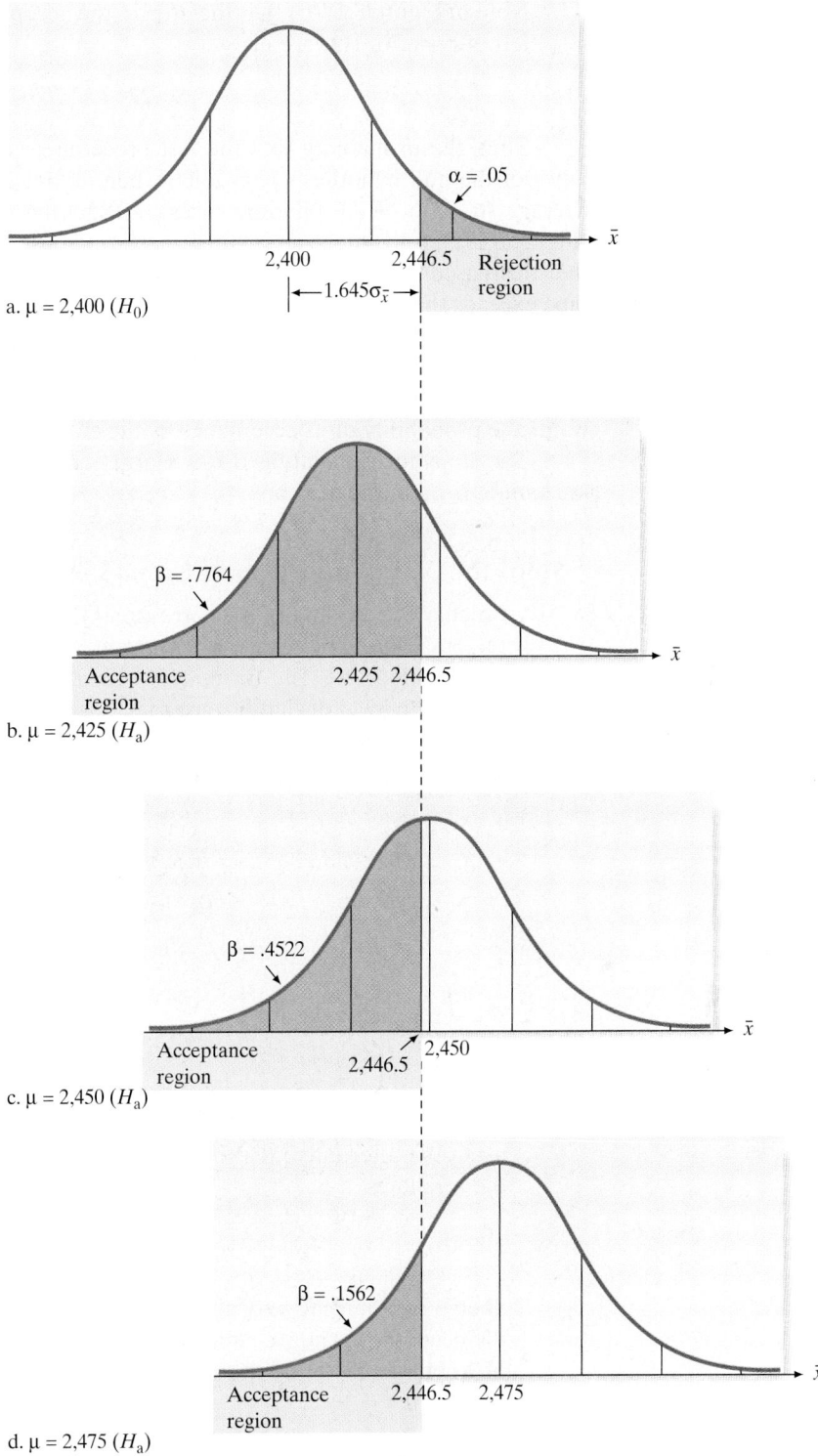

a. $\mu = 2,400$ (H_0)

b. $\mu = 2,425$ (H_a)

c. $\mu = 2,450$ (H_a)

d. $\mu = 2,475$ (H_a)

Note in Figure 8.17(b) that the area in the acceptance region is the area to the left of $z = .76$. This area is

$$\beta = .5 + .2764 = .7764$$

Thus, the probability that the test procedure will lead to an incorrect acceptance of the null hypothesis $\mu = 2{,}400$ when in fact $\mu = 2{,}425$ is about .78. As the average strength of the pipe increases to 2,450, the value of β decreases to .4522 (Figure 8.17c). If the mean strength is further increased to 2,475, the value of β is further decreased to .1562 (Figure 8.17d). Thus, even if the true mean strength of the pipe exceeds the minimum specification by 75 pounds per linear foot, the test procedure will lead to an incorrect acceptance of the null hypothesis (rejection of the pipe) approximately 16% of the time. The upshot is that the pipe must be manufactured so that the mean strength well exceeds the minimum requirement if the manufacturer wants the probability of its acceptance by the city to be large (i.e., β to be small).

The steps for calculating β for a large-sample test about a population mean are summarized in the next box.

Steps for Calculating β for a Large-Sample Test about μ

1. Calculate the value(s) of $\bar{x}$ corresponding to the border(s) of the rejection region. There will be one border value for a one-tailed test, and two for a two-tailed test. The formula is one of the following, corresponding to a test with level of significance α:

$$\text{Upper-tailed test: } \bar{x}_0 = \mu_0 + z_\alpha \sigma_{\bar{x}} \approx \mu_0 + z_\alpha\left(\frac{s}{\sqrt{n}}\right)$$

$$\text{Lower-tailed test: } \bar{x}_0 = \mu_0 - z_\alpha \sigma_{\bar{x}} \approx \mu_0 - z_\alpha\left(\frac{s}{\sqrt{n}}\right)$$

$$\text{Two-tailed test: } \bar{x}_{0.L} = \mu_0 - z_{\alpha/2}\sigma_{\bar{x}} \approx \mu_0 - z_{\alpha/2}\left(\frac{s}{\sqrt{n}}\right)$$

$$\bar{x}_{0.U} = \mu_0 + z_{\alpha/2}\sigma_{\bar{x}} \approx \mu_0 + z_{\alpha/2}\left(\frac{s}{\sqrt{n}}\right)$$

2. Specify the value of μ_a in the alternative hypothesis for which the value of β is to be calculated. Then convert the border value(s) of $\bar{x}_0$ to z value(s) using the alternative distribution with mean μ_a. The general formula for the z value is

$$z = \frac{\bar{x}_0 - \mu_a}{\sigma_{\bar{x}}}$$

Sketch the alternative distribution (centered at μ_a), and shade the area in the acceptance (nonrejection) region. Use the z statistic(s) and Table IV of Appendix B to find the shaded area, which is β.

Following the calculation of β for a particular value of μ_a, you should interpret the value in the context of the hypothesis testing application. It is often useful to interpret the value of $1 - \beta$, which is known as the *power of the test* corresponding to a particular alternative, μ_a. Since β is the probability of accepting the null hypothesis when the alternative hypothesis is true with $\mu = \mu_a$, $1 - \beta$ is the probability of the complementary event, or the probability of rejecting the null hypothesis when the alternative H_a: $\mu = \mu_a$ is true. That is, the power $1 - \beta$ measures the likelihood that the test procedure will lead to the correct decision (reject H_0) for a particular value of the mean in the alternative hypothesis.

Teaching Tip

Point out that the power of the test is the probability that the null hypothesis will be correctly rejected.

DEFINITION 8.2

The **power of a test** is the probability that the test will correctly lead to the rejection of the null hypothesis for a particular value of μ in the alternative hypothesis. The power is equal to $1 - \beta$ for the particular alternative considered.

Teaching Tip

Show the students what happens to the power of the test as the value of the population parameter moves farther away from the hypothesized value in H_0.

For example, in the sewer pipe example we found that $\beta = .7764$ when $\mu = 2,425$. This is the probability that the test leads to the (incorrect) acceptance of the null hypothesis when $\mu = 2,425$. Or, equivalently, the power of the test is $1 - .7764 = .2236$, which means that the test will lead to the (correct) rejection of the null hypothesis only 22% of the time when the pipe exceeds specifications by 25 pounds per linear foot. When the manufacturer's pipe has a mean strength of 2,475 (that is, 75 pounds per linear foot in excess of specifications), the power of the test increases to $1 - .1562 = .8438$. That is, the test will lead to the acceptance of the manufacturer's pipe 84% of the time if $\mu = 2,475$.

EXAMPLE 8.9

FINDING THE POWER OF THE TEST

Problem   Recall the quality control study in Examples 8.1 and 8.2, in which we tested to determine whether a cereal box filling machine was deviating from the specified mean fill of $\mu = 12$ ounces. The test setup is repeated here:

$$H_0: \mu = 12$$
$$H_a: \mu \neq 12 \ (\text{i.e.,} \ \mu < 12 \ \text{or} \ \mu > 12)$$

Test statistic: $z = \dfrac{\bar{x} - 12}{\sigma_{\bar{x}}}$

Rejection region: $z < -1.96$ or $z > 1.96$ for $\alpha = .05$
$\qquad\qquad\qquad\qquad z < -2.575$ or $z > 2.575$ for $\alpha = .01$

Note that two rejection regions have been specified corresponding to values of $\alpha = .05$ and $\alpha = .01$, respectively. Assume that $n = 100$ and $s = .5$.

a. $\alpha = .05$, $\beta = .4840$
a. $\alpha = .01$, $\beta = .7190$

b. $\alpha = .05$, power $= .5160$
b. $\alpha = .01$, power $= .2810$

a.   Suppose the machine is underfilling the boxes by an average of .1 ounce (i.e., $\mu = 11.9$). Calculate the values of β corresponding to the two rejection regions. Discuss the relationship between the values of α and β.

b.   Calculate the power of the test for each of the rejection regions when $\mu = 11.9$.

Solution   **a.**   We first consider the rejection region corresponding to $\alpha = .05$. The first step is to calculate the border values of $\bar{x}$ corresponding to the two-tailed rejection region, $z < -1.96$ or $z > 1.96$:

$$\bar{x}_{0.L} = \mu_0 - 1.96\sigma_{\bar{x}} \approx \mu_0 - 1.96\left(\frac{s}{\sqrt{n}}\right) = 12 - 1.96\left(\frac{.5}{10}\right) = 11.902$$

$$\bar{x}_{0.U} = \mu_0 + 1.96\sigma_{\bar{x}} \approx \mu_0 + 1.96\left(\frac{s}{\sqrt{n}}\right) = 12 + 1.96\left(\frac{.5}{10}\right) = 12.098$$

These border values are shown in Figure 8.18.

Figure 8.18
Calculation of β for filling
machine example

Suggested Exercises 8.84

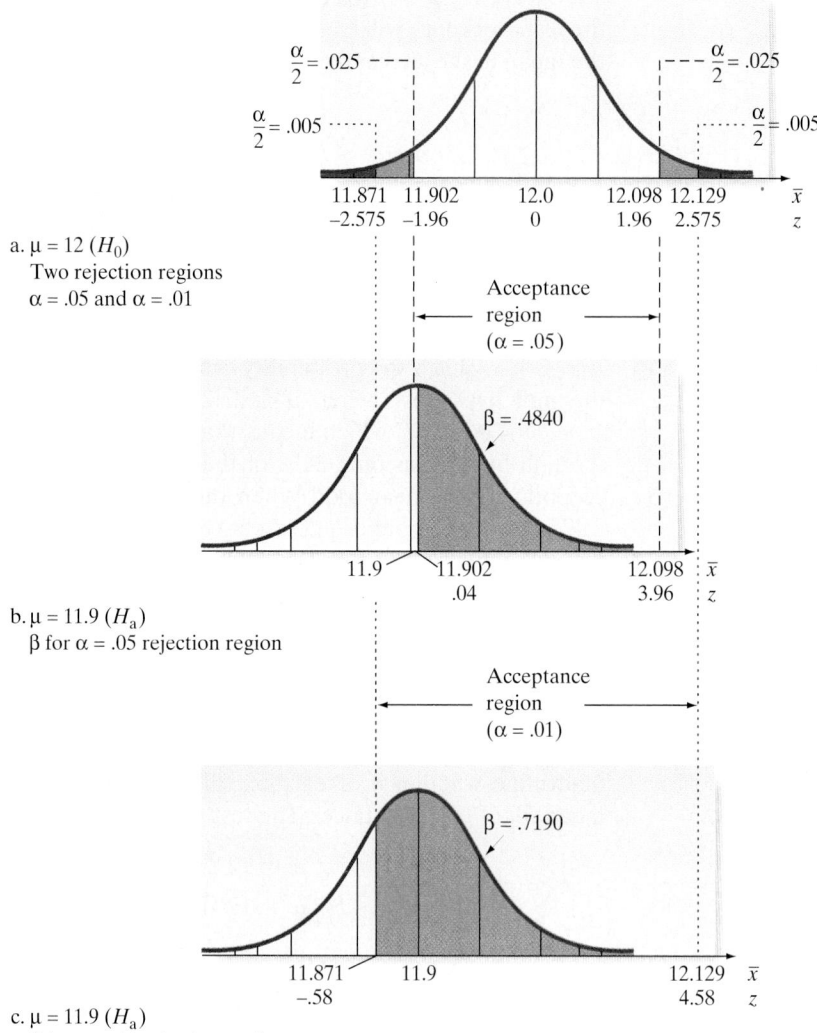

a. $\mu = 12$ (H_0)
 Two rejection regions
 $\alpha = .05$ and $\alpha = .01$

b. $\mu = 11.9$ (H_a)
 β for $\alpha = .05$ rejection region

c. $\mu = 11.9$ (H_a)
 β for $\alpha = .01$ rejection region

Next, we convert these values to z values in the alternative distribution
with $\mu_a = 11.9$:

$$z_L = \frac{x_{0.L} - \mu_a}{\sigma_{\bar{x}}} \approx \frac{11.902 - 11.9}{.05} = .04$$

$$z_U = \frac{x_{0.U} - \mu_a}{\sigma_{\bar{x}}} \approx \frac{12.098 - 11.9}{.05} = 3.96$$

These z values are shown in Figure 8.18(b). You can see that the acceptance (or
nonrejection) region is the area between them. Using Table IV of Appendix B,
we find that the area between $z = 0$ and $z = .04$ is .0160, and the area between
$z = 0$ and $z = 3.96$ is (approximately) .5 (since $z = 3.96$ is off the scale of Table
IV). Then the area between $z = .04$ and $z = 3.96$ is, approximately,

$$\beta = .5 - .0160 = .4840$$

Thus, the test with $\alpha = .05$ will lead to a Type II error about 48% of the time when the machine is underfilling, on average, by .1 ounce.

For the rejection region corresponding to $\alpha = .01$, $z < -2.575$ or $z > 2.575$, we find

$$\bar{x}_{0.L} = 12 - 2.575\left(\frac{.5}{10}\right) = 11.871$$

$$\bar{x}_{0.U} = 12 + 2.575\left(\frac{.5}{10}\right) = 12.129$$

These border values of the rejection region are shown in Figure 8.18(c).

Converting these to z values in the alternative distribution with $\mu_a = 11.9$, we find $z_L = -.58$ and $z_U = 4.58$. The area between these values is, approximately,

$$\beta = .2190 + .5 = .7190$$

Thus, the chance that the test procedure with $\alpha = .01$ will lead to an incorrect acceptance of H_0 is about 72%.

Note that the value of β increases from .4840 to .7190 when we decrease the value of α from .05 to .01. This is a general property of the relationship between α and β: *as α is decreased (increased), β is increased (decreased).*

b. The power is defined to be the probability of (correctly) rejecting the null hypothesis when the alternative is true. When $\mu = 11.9$ and $\alpha = .05$, we find

$$\text{Power} = 1 - \beta = 1 - .4840 = .5160$$

When $\mu = 11.9$ and $\alpha = .01$, we find

$$\text{Power} = 1 - \beta = 1 - .7190 = .2810$$

You can see that the power of the test is decreased as the level of α is decreased. This means that as the probability of incorrectly rejecting the null hypothesis is decreased, the probability of correctly accepting the null hypothesis for a given alternative is also decreased.

Look Back A key point of this example is that the value of α must be selected carefully, with the realization that a test is made less capable of detecting departures from the null hypothesis when the value of α is decreased.

—————— ■ ■ ■ ——————

We have shown that the probability of committing a Type II error, β, is inversely related to α (Example 8.9), and that the value of β decreases as the value of μ_a moves farther from the null hypothesis value (sewer pipe example). The sample size n also affects β. Remember that the standard deviation of the sampling distribution of $\bar{x}$ is inversely proportional to the square root of the sample size ($\sigma_{\bar{x}} = \sigma/\sqrt{n}$). Thus, as illustrated in Figure 8.19, the variability of both the null and alternative sampling distributions is decreased as n is increased. If the value of α is specified and remains fixed, the value of β decreases as n increases, as illustrated in Figure 8.19. Conversely, the power of the test for a given alternative hypothesis is increased as the sample size is increased. The properties of β and power are summarized in the box.

Figure 8.19

Relationship between α, β, and n

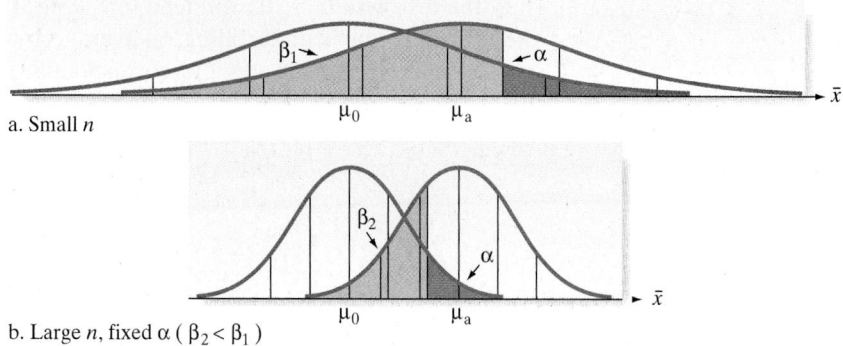

a. Small n

b. Large n, fixed α ($\beta_2 < \beta_1$)

Properties of β and Power

1. For fixed n and α, the value of β decreases and the power increases as the distance between the specified null value μ_0 and the specified alternative value μ_a increases (see Figure 8.17).

2. For fixed n and values of μ_0 and μ_a, the value of β increases and the power decreases as the value of α is decreased (see Figure 8.18).

3. For fixed α and values of μ_0 and μ_a, the value of β decreases and the power increases as the sample size n is increased (see Figure 8.19).

Exercises 8.76–8.85

Learning the Mechanics

8.76 **a.** List three factors that will increase the power of a test.
   b. What is the relationship between β, the probability of committing a Type II error, and the power of a test?

8.77 Suppose you want to test H_0: $\mu = 500$ against H_a: $\mu > 500$ using $\alpha = .05$. The population in question is normally distributed with standard deviation 100. A random sample of size $n = 25$ will be used.
   a. Sketch the sampling distribution of $\bar{x}$ assuming that H_0 is true.
   b. Find the value of $\bar{x}_0$, that value of $\bar{x}$ above which the null hypothesis will be rejected. Indicate the rejection region on your graph of part **a**. Shade the area above the rejection region and label it α.
   $\bar{x}_0 = 532.9$
   c. On your graph of part a, sketch the sampling distribution of $\bar{x}$ if $\mu = 550$. Shade the area under this distribution that corresponds to the probability that $\bar{x}$ falls in the nonrejection region when $\mu = 550$. Label this area β.
   d. Find β.   .1949
   e. Compute the power of this test for detecting the alternative H_a: $\mu = 550$.   .8051

8.78 Refer to Exercise 8.77.
   a. If $\mu = 575$ instead of 550, what is the probability that the hypothesis test will incorrectly fail to reject H_0? That is, what is β?   .0174

b. If $\mu = 575$, what is the probability that the test will correctly reject the null hypothesis? That is, what is the power of the test?   .9826
   c. Compare β and the power of the test when $\mu = 575$ to the values you obtained in Exercise 8.71 for $\mu = 550$. Explain the differences.

8.79 It is desired to test H_0: $\mu = 75$ against H_a: $\mu < 75$ using $\alpha = .10$. The population in question is uniformly distributed with standard deviation 15. A random sample of size 49 will be drawn from the population.
   a. Describe the (approximate) sampling distribution $\bar{x}$ under the assumption that H_0 is true.
   b. Describe the (approximate) sampling distribution $\bar{x}$ under the assumption that the population mean is 70.
   c. If μ were really equal to 70, what is the probability that the hypothesis test would lead the investigator to commit a Type II error?   .1469
   d. What is the power of this test for detecting the alternative H_a: $\mu = 70$?   .8531

8.80 Refer to Exercise 8.79.
   a. Find β for each of the following values of the population mean: 74, 72, 70, 68, and 66.
   b. Plot each value of β you obtained in part a against its associated population mean. Show β on the vertical axis and μ on the horizontal axis. Draw a curve through the five points on your graph.

c. Use your graph of part b to find the approximate probability that the hypothesis test will lead to a Type II error when $\mu = 73$.

d. Convert each of the β values you calculated in part a to the power of the test at the specified value of μ. Plot the power on the vertical axis against μ on the horizontal axis. Compare the graph of part b to the *power curve* of this part.

e. Examine the graphs of parts b and d. Explain what they reveal about the relationships among the distance between the true mean μ and the null hypothesized mean μ_0, the value of β, and the power.

8.81 Suppose you want to conduct the two-tailed test of $H_0: \mu = 30$ against $H_a: \mu \neq 30$ using $\alpha = .05$. A random sample of size 121 will be drawn from the population in question. Assume the population has a standard deviation equal to 1.2.

a. Describe the sampling distribution of $\bar{x}$ under the assumption that H_0 is true.

b. Describe the sampling distribution of $\bar{x}$ under the assumption that $\mu = 29.8$.

c. If μ were really equal to 29.8, find the value of β associated with the test.   .5359

d. Find the value of β for the alternative $H_a: \mu = 30.4$.

Applying the Concepts—Intermediate

8.82 In 1999 the average size of single-family homes built in the U. S. was 2,230 square feet, an increase of over 200 square feet a decade earlier (*Wall Street Journal Interactive Edition*, Jan. 7, 2000). A random sample of 100 new homes sold in California in late 1999 yielded the following size information: $\bar{x} = 2,347$ square feet and $s = 257$ square feet.

a. Assume the average size of U.S. homes is known with certainty. Do the sample data provide sufficient evidence to conclude that the mean size of California homes built in late 1999 exceeds the national average? Test using $\alpha = .01$.   z = 4.55

b. Suppose the actual mean size of new California homes was 2,330 square feet. What is the power of the test in part **a** to detect this 100-square-foot difference?   .9406

c. If the California mean were actually 2,280 square feet, what is the power of the test in part **a** to detect this 50-square-foot difference?   .3520

8.83 If a manufacturer (the vendee) buys all items of a particular type from a particular vendor, the manufacturer is practicing *sole sourcing* (Schonberger and Knod, *Operations Management*, 1994). As part of a sole-sourcing arrangement, a vendor agrees to periodically supply its vendee with sample data from its production process. The vendee uses the data to investigate whether the mean length of rods produced by the vendor's production process is truly 5.0 millimeters

(mm) or more, as claimed by the vendor and desired by the vendee.

a. If the production process has a standard deviation of .01 mm, the vendor supplies $n = 100$ items to the vendee, and the vendee uses $\alpha = .05$ in testing $H_0: \mu = 5.0$ mm against $H_a: \mu < 5.0$ mm, what is the probability that the vendee's test will fail to reject the null hypothesis when in fact $\mu = 4.9975$ mm? What is the name given to this type of error?

b. Refer to part **a.** What is the probability that the vendee's test will reject the null hypothesis when in fact $\mu = 5.0$? What is the name given to this type of error? $\alpha = .05$; Type I error

c. What is the power of the test to detect a departure of .0025 mm below the specified mean rod length of 5.0 mm?   .8051

8.84 According to the Environmental Protection Agency (EPA) *Fuel Economy Guide*, the 2003 Honda Civic automobile obtains a mean of 38 miles per gallon (mpg) on the highway. Suppose Honda claims that the EPA has underestimated the Civic's mileage. To support its assertion, the company selects 36 model 2003 Civic cars and records the mileage obtained for each car over a driving course similar to the one used by the EPA. The following data resulted: $x = 40.3$ mpg, $s = 6.4$ mpg.

a. If Honda wishes to show that the mean mpg for 2003 Civic autos is greater than 38 mpg, what should the alternative hypothesis be? The null hypothesis?

b. Do the data provide sufficient evidence to support the auto manufacturer's claim? Test using $\alpha = .05$. List any assumptions you make in conducting the test.

c. Calculate the power of the test for the mean values of 38.5, 39.0, 39.5, 40.0, and 40.5, assuming $s = 6.4$ is a good estimate of σ.

d. Plot the power of the test on the vertical axis against the mean on the horizontal axis. Draw a curve through the points.

e. Use the power curve of part d to estimate the power for the mean value $\mu = 39.75$. Calculate the power for this value of μ, and compare it to your approximation.

f. Use the power curve to approximate the power of the test when $\mu = 43$. If the true value of the mean mpg for this model is really 43, what (approximately) are the chances that the test will fail to reject the null hypothesis that the mean is 38?

8.85 Refer to Exercise 8.29 (p. 426), in which the performance of a particular type of laser-based inspection equipment was investigated. Assume that the standard deviation of the number of solder joints inspected on each run is 1.2. If $\alpha = .05$ is used in conducting the hypothesis test of interest using a sample of 48 circuit boards, and if the true mean number of solder joints that can be inspected is really equal to 9.5, what is the probability that the test will result in a Type II error?   .1075

8.7 Test of Hypothesis about a Population Variance (Optional)

Teaching Tip

Point out that the theory of the test of hypothesis technique is identical to what we have seen before. In this case, the sampling distribution used is the χ^2-distribution.

Although many practical problems involve inferences about a population mean (or proportion), it is sometimes of interest to make an inference about a population variance, σ^2. To illustrate, a quality control supervisor in a cannery knows that the exact amount each can contains will vary since there are certain uncontrollable factors that affect the amount of fill. The mean fill per can is important, but equally important is the variation of fill. If σ^2, the variance of the fill, is large, some cans will contain too little and others too much. Suppose regulatory agencies specify that the standard deviation of the amount of fill should be less than .1 ounce. To determine whether the process is meeting this specification, the supervisor randomly selects 10 cans and weighs the contents of each. The results are given in Table 8.5.

FILLAMOUNTS

TABLE 8.5 Fill Weights (in ounces) of 10 Cans

16.00	16.06	15.95	16.04	16.10	16.05	16.02	16.03	15.99	16.02

Do these data provide sufficient evidence to indicate that the variability is as small as desired? To answer this question, we need a procedure for testing a hypothesis about σ^2.

Intuitively, it seems that we should compare the sample variance σ^2 to the hypothesized value of σ^2 (or s to σ) in order to make a decision about the population's variability. The quantity

$$\frac{(n-1)s^2}{\sigma^2}$$

has been shown to have a sampling distribution called a **chi-square (χ^2) distribution** when the population from which the sample is taken is *normally distributed*. Several chi-square distributions are shown in Figure 8.20.

Figure 8.20
Several χ^2 probability distributions

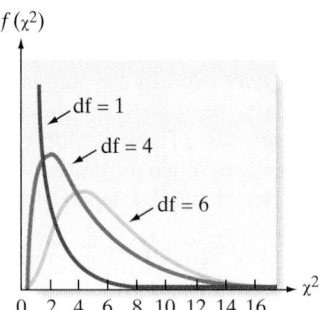

$f(\chi^2)$

df = 1
df = 4
df = 6

0 2 4 6 8 10 12 14 16 χ^2

The upper-tail areas for this distribution have been tabulated and are given in Table VII of Appendix B, a portion of which is reproduced in Table 8.6. The table gives the values of χ^2, denoted as χ_α^2, that locate an area of α in the upper tail of the chi-square distribution; that is, $P(\chi^2 > \chi_\alpha^2) = \alpha$. In this case, as with the t statistic, the shape of the chi-square distribution depends on the degrees of freedom associated with s^2, namely $(n-1)$. Thus, for $n = 10$ and an upper-tail value $\alpha = .05$, you will have $n - 1 = 9$ df and $\chi_{.05}^2 = 16.9190$ (highlighted area in Table 8.6). To further illustrate the use of Table VII, we return to the can-filling example.

TABLE 8.6   Reproduction of Part of Table VII in Appendix B: Critical Values of Chi Square

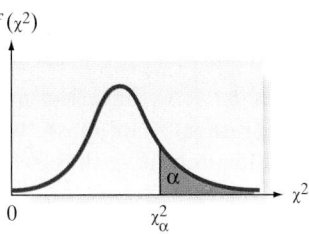

Degrees of Freedom	$\chi^2_{.100}$	$\chi^2_{.050}$	$\chi^2_{.025}$	$\chi^2_{.010}$	$\chi^2_{.005}$
1	2.70554	3.84146	5.02389	6.63490	7.87944
2	4.60517	5.99147	7.37776	9.21034	10.5966
3	6.25139	7.81473	9.34840	11.3449	12.8381
4	7.77944	9.48773	11.1433	13.2767	14.8602
5	9.23635	11.0705	12.8325	15.0863	16.7496
6	10.6446	12.5916	14.4494	16.8119	18.5476
7	12.0170	14.0671	16.0128	18.4753	20.2777
8	13.3616	15.5073	17.5346	20.0902	21.9550
9	14.6837	16.9190	19.0228	21.6660	23.5893
10	15.9871	18.3070	20.4831	23.2093	25.1882
11	17.2750	19.6751	21.9200	24.7250	25.7569
12	18.5494	21.0261	23.3367	26.2170	28.2995
13	19.8119	22.3621	24.7356	27.6883	29.8194
14	21.0642	23.6848	26.1190	29.1413	31.3193
15	22.3072	24.9958	27.4884	30.5779	32.8013
16	23.5418	26.2862	28.8454	31.9999	34.2672
17	24.7690	27.5871	30.1910	33.4087	35.7185
18	25.9894	28.8693	31.5264	34.8053	37.1564
19	27.2036	30.1435	32.8523	36.1908	38.5822

Now Work   *Exercise 8.86*

Biography

FRIEDRICH R. HELMERT (1843–1917)
Helmert Transformations

German Friedrich Helmert studied engineering sciences and mathematics at Dresden University, where he earned his Ph.D., then accepted a position as a professor of geodesy—the scientific study of the earth's size and shape—at the technical school in Aachen. Helmert's mathematical solutions to geodesy problems led him to several statistics-related discoveries. His greatest statistical contribution occurred in 1876, when he was the first to prove that the sampling distribution of the sample variance, s^2, is a chi-square distribution. Helmert used a series of mathematical transformations to obtain the distribution of s^2—transformations that have since been named "Helmert transformations" in his honor. Later in life, Helmert was appointed professor of advanced geodesy at prestigious University of Berlin and director of the Prussian Geodetic Institute.

EXAMPLE 8.10   CONDUCTING A TEST FOR σ

Problem   Refer to the fill weights for the sample of ten 16-ounce cans in Table 8.5. Do the data provide sufficient evidence to indicate that the true standard deviation σ of the fill measurements of all 16-ounce cans is less than .1 ounce?

$\chi^2 = 1.524$, reject H_0

Solution   Here, we want to test whether $\sigma < .1$. Since the null and alternative hypotheses must be stated in terms of σ^2 (rather) than σ), we want to test the null hypothesis that $\sigma^2 = (.1)^2 = .01$ against the alternative that $\sigma^2 < .01$. Therefore, the elements of the test are

$$H_0: \sigma^2 = .01$$
$$H_a: \sigma^2 < .01$$

Test statistic: $\chi^2 = \dfrac{(n-1)s^2}{\sigma^2}$

Assumption: The distribution of the amounts of fill is approximately normal.

Rejection region: The smaller the value of s^2 we observe, the stronger the evidence in favor of H_a. Thus, we reject H_0 for "small values" of the test statistic. With $\alpha = .05$ and 9 df, the χ^2 value for rejection is found in Table VII and pictured in Figure 8.21. We will reject H_0 if $\chi^2 < 3.32511$.

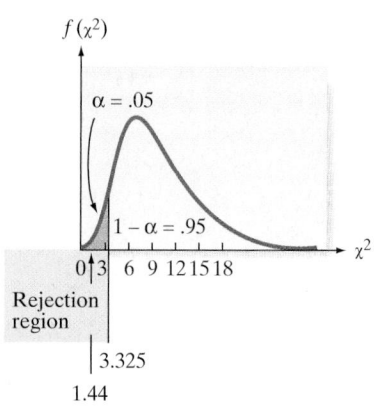

Figure 8.21
Rejection region for Example 8.10

Suggested Exercise 8.93

(Remember that the area given in Table VII is the area to the *right* of the numerical value in the table. Thus, to determine the lower-tail value, which has $\alpha = .05$ to its *left*, we used the $\chi^2_{.95}$ column in Table VII.)

An EXCEL/PHStat2 analysis of the data in Table 8.5 is displayed in Figure 8.22. The value of s shown on the printout is $s = .04115$. Substituting into the formula for the test statistic, we have

$$\chi^2 = \frac{(n-1)s^2}{\sigma^2} = \frac{9(.04115)^2}{.01} = 1.524$$

Since the test statistic falls into the rejection region, we reject H_0 in favor of H_a. That is, the supervisor can conclude that the variance σ^2 of the population of all amounts of fill is less than .01 ($\sigma < .1$) with probability of a Type I error equal to $\alpha = .05$. If this procedure is repeatedly used, it will incorrectly reject H_0 only 5% of the time. Thus, the quality control supervisor is confident in the decision that the cannery is operating within the desired limits of variability.

Look Back Note that both the test statistic (1.524) and the lower-tailed p-value of the test (.003) are shown at the bottom of the printout, Figure 8.22. Since $\alpha = .05$ exceeds the p-value, our decision to reject H_0 is confirmed.

Figure 8.22
EXCEL/PHStat2 test for variance of fill weights

Chi-Square Test of Variance		
Data		
Null Hypothesis $\sigma^\wedge 2=$		0.01
Level of Significance		0.05
Sample Size		10
Sample Standard Deviation		0.04115
Intermediate calculations		
Degrees of Freedom		9
Half Area		0.025
Chi-Square Statistic		1.52399025
Lower-Tail Test Results		
Lower Critical Value		3.32511514
***p*-Value**		0.003035148
Reject the null hypothesis		

> **Now Work**   *Exercise 8.92*

■ ■ ■

One-tailed and two-tailed tests of hypothesis for σ^2 are given in the following box.*

Teaching Tip
Show the students that the test of hypothesis still consists of a test, a test statistic, a rejection region (or *p*-value), and a conclusion.

Test of a Hypothesis about σ^2

One-Tailed Test	Two-Tailed Test
$H_0: \sigma^2 = \sigma_0^2$	$H_0: \sigma^2 = \sigma_0^2$
$H_a: \sigma^2 < \sigma_0^2$ (or $H_a: \sigma^2 > \sigma_0^2$)	$H_a: \sigma^2 \neq \sigma_0^2$
Test statistic: $\chi^2 = \dfrac{(n-1)s^2}{\sigma_0^2}$	Test statistic: $\chi^2 = \dfrac{(n-1)s^2}{\sigma_0^2}$
Rejection region: $\chi^2 < \chi_{(1-\alpha)}^2$ (or $\chi^2 > \chi_\alpha^2$ when $H_a: \sigma^2 > \sigma_0^2$)	Rejection region: $\chi^2 < \chi_{(1-\alpha/2)}^2$ or $\chi^2 > \chi_{(\alpha/2)}^2$

where σ_0^2 is the hypothesized variance and the distribution of χ^2 is based on $(n-1)$ degrees of freedom.

*A confidence interval for σ^2 can also be formed using the chi-square distribution with $(n-1)$ degrees of freedom. A $(1-\alpha)100\%$ confidence interval is

$$\frac{(n-1)s^2}{\chi_{\alpha/2}^2} < \sigma^2 < \frac{(n-1)s^2}{\chi_{(1-\alpha/2)}^2}$$

> ### Conditions Required for a Valid Hypothesis Test for σ^2
>
> 1. A random sample is selected from the target population.
> 2. The population from which the sample is selected has a distribution that is approximately normal.

Caution

The procedure for conducting a hypothesis test for σ^2 in the above examples requires an assumption regardless of whether the sample size n is large or small. We must assume that the population from which the sample is selected has an approximate normal distribution. Unlike small sample tests for μ based on the t-statistic, *slight to moderate departures from normality will render the chi-square test invalid.*

Exercises 8.86–8.97

Learning the Mechanics

8.86 Let χ_0^2 be a particular value of χ^2. Find the value of χ_0^2 such that

a. $P(\chi^2 > \chi_0^2) = .10$ for $n = 12$ 17.2750
b. $P(\chi^2 > \chi_0^2) = .05$ for $n = 9$ 15.5073
c. $P(\chi^2 > \chi_0^2) = .025$ for $n = 5$ 11.1433

8.87 A random sample of n observations is selected from a normal population to test the null hypothesis that $\sigma^2 = 25$. Specify the rejection region for each of the following combinations of H_a, α, and n:

a. $H_a: \sigma^2 \neq 25$; $\alpha = .05$; $n = 16$
b. $H_a: \sigma^2 > 25$; $\alpha = .01$; $n = 23$ $\chi^2 > 40.2894$
c. $H_a: \sigma^2 > 25$; $\alpha = .10$; $n = 15$ $\chi^2 > 21.0642$
d. $H_a: \sigma^2 < 25$; $\alpha = .01$; $n = 13$ $\chi^2 < 3.57056$
e. $H_a: \sigma^2 \neq 25$; $\alpha = .10$; $n = 7$
f. $H_a: \sigma^2 < 25$; $\alpha = .05$; $n = 25$ $\chi^2 < 13.8484$

8.88 A random sample of seven measurements gave $\bar{x} = 9.4$ and $\sigma^2 = 4.84$.

a. What assumptions must you make concerning the population in order to test a hypothesis about σ^2?
b. Suppose the assumptions in part a are satisfied. Test the null hypothesis, $\sigma^2 = 1$, against the alternative hypothesis, $\sigma^2 > 1$. Use $\alpha = .05$. $\chi^2 = 29.04$
c. Test the null hypothesis that $\sigma^2 = 1$ against the alternative hypothesis that $\sigma^2 \neq 1$. Use $\alpha = .05$.

8.89 Refer to Exercise 8.88. Suppose we had $n = 100$, $\bar{x} = 9.4$, and $s^2 = 4.84$.

a. Test the null hypothesis, $H_0: \sigma^2 = 1$, against the alternative hypothesis, $H_a: \sigma^2 > 1$. $\chi^2 = 479.16$
b. Compare your test result with that of Exercise 8.88.

8.90 A random sample of $n = 7$ observations from a normal population produced the following measurements: 4, 0, 6, 3, 3, 5, 9. Do the data provide sufficient evidence to indicate that $\sigma^2 < 1$? Test using $\alpha = .05$. $\chi^2 = 47.43$

Applying the Concepts—Basic

TEES

8.91 Refer to Exercise 8.23 (p. 426) and the weights of tees produced by an injection mold process. If operating correctly, the process will produce tees with a weight variance of .000004 (ounces)^2. If the weight variance differs from .000004, the injection molder is out of control.

a. Set up the null and alternative hypothesis for testing whether the injection mold process is out of control. $H_0: \sigma^2 = .000004$ vs. $H_a: \sigma^2 \neq .000004$
b. Use the data saved in the TEES file to conduct the test, part **a**. Use $\alpha = .01$. $\chi^2 = 48.49$
c. What conditions are required for inferences derived from the test to be valid? Are they reasonably satisfied?

8.92 Refer to the *Chance* (Fall 1998) study of point-spread errors in NFL games, Exercise 8.25 (p. 425). Recall that the difference between the actual game outcome and the point spread established by oddsmakers—the point-spread error—was calculated for 240 NFL games. The results are summarized as follows: $\bar{x} = -1.6$, $s = 13.3$. Suppose the researcher wants to know whether the true standard deviation of the point-spread errors exceeds 15.

a. Set up H_0 and H_a for the researcher.
b. Compute the value of the test statistic. $\chi^2 = 187.896$
c. Conduct the test at $\alpha = .10$. Interpret the results in the words of the problem.   Fail to reject H_0

Applying the Concepts—Intermediate

8.93 It is essential in the manufacture of machinery to utilize parts that conform to specifications. In the past, diameters of the ball-bearings produced by a certain manufacturer had a variance of .00156. To cut costs, the manufacturer instituted a less expensive production method. The variance of the diameters of 100 randomly sampled bearings produced by the new process was .00211. Do the data provide sufficient evidence to indicate that diameters of ball-bearings produced by the new process are more variable than those produced by the old process? $\chi^2 = 133.90$

8.94 Refer to the *Chromatographia* (Mar. 1995) study of a new technique for extracting toxic organic compounds, Exercise 8.57 (p. 443). Recall that uncontaminated fish fillets were injected with a toxic substance and the method was used to extract the toxicant. To test the precision of the new method, seven measurements were obtained on a single fish fillet injected with a toxin. Summary statistics on percent of the toxin recovered are given as follows: $\bar{x} = 99, s = 9$. Determine whether the standard deviation of the percent recovery using the new method differs from 15. (Use $\alpha = .10$.) $\chi^2 = 2.16$

⊚ **TAMALES**

8.95 Refer to the Chance (Fall 2000) study of whether students fabricated counts of the number of "Hot Tamales" in bags dispensed from a bulk vending machine, Exercise 8.60 (p. 441). Recall that the reported candy counts for the five bags purchased were 25, 23, 21, 21, and 20. It is known that the machine dispenses bags of "Hot Tamales" with a standard deviation of

3 candies per bag. Use this information to test (at $\alpha = .01$) whether the reported data are likely to come from the bulk vending machine. $\chi^2 = 1.78$

8.96 Laser Raman microprobe (LRM) spectroscopy is used to analyze *fluid inclusions* (pockets of gas or liquid) in rock. A chip of natural Brazilian quartz was artificially injected with several fluid inclusions of liquid carbon dioxide (CO_2) and then subjected to LRM spectroscopy (*Applied Spectroscopy*, Feb. 1986). The amount of CO_2 present in the inclusion was recorded for the same inclusion on four different days. The data (in mole percent) follow:

⊚ **CO2**

86.6	84.6	85.5	85.9

a. Do the data indicate that the variation in the CO_2 concentration measurements using the LRM method differs from 1? $\chi^2 = 2.09$
b. What assumption is required for the test to be valid?

Applying the Concepts—Advanced

8.97 To improve the signal-to-noise ratio (SNR) in the electrical activity of the brain, neurologists repeatedly stimulate subjects and average the responses—a procedure that assumes that single responses are homogeneous. A study was conducted to test the homogeneous signal theory (*IEEE Engineering in Medicine and Biology Magazine*, Mar. 1990). For this study, the variance of the SNR readings of subjects will equal .54 under the homogeneous signal theory. If the SNR variance exceeds .54, the researchers will conclude that the signals are nonhomogeneous. Signal-to-noise ratios recorded for a sample of 41 normal children ranged from .03 to 3.0. Use this information to test the theory at $\alpha = .10$. $\chi^2 = 40.8375$

Quick Review

Key Terms

[Note: Starred (*) items are from the optional sections in this chapter.]

Alternative (research) hypothesis   412
*Chi-square distribution   458
Conclusion   417
Level of significance   417

Lower-tailed test   420
Null hypothesis   412
*Null distribution   450
Observed significance level (p-value)   426
One-tailed test   419
*Power of the test   453

Rejection region   413
Test statistic   412
Two-tailed test   420
Type I error   413
Type II error   415
Upper-tailed test   420

Key Formulas

For testing $H_0: \theta = \theta_0$, the **large-sample test statistic** is

$$z = \frac{\hat{\theta} - \theta_0}{\sigma_{\hat{\theta}}}$$

where $\hat{\theta}$, θ_0, and $\sigma_{\hat{\theta}}$ are obtained from the table below:

Parameter	Hypothesized Parameter Value	Estimator	Standard Error of Estimator	
μ	μ_0	$\bar{x}$	$\dfrac{\sigma}{\sqrt{n}}$	423
p	p_0	$\hat{p}$	$\sqrt{\dfrac{p_0 q_0}{n}}$	444

For testing $H_0: \mu = \mu_0$, the **small-sample test statistic** is

$$t = \frac{\bar{x} - \mu_0}{s/\sqrt{n}} \quad 436$$

*$\beta = P(\hat{\theta}$ falls in acceptance region$|\theta = \theta_a)$ 454
*Power $= 1 - \beta$ 455

*For testing $H_0: \sigma^2 = \sigma_0^2$, the test statistic is $\chi^2 = \dfrac{(n-1)s^2}{\sigma_0^2}$ 461

Language Lab

Symbol	Pronunciation	Description
H_0	H-oh	Null hypothesis
H_a	H-a	Alternative hypothesis
α	alpha	Probability of Type I error
β	beta	Probability of Type II error
χ^2	chi-square	Sampling distribution of s^2 when data are from a normal population

Chapter Summary Notes

- Elements of a **test of hypothesis: null hypothesis, alternative hypothesis, test statistic, significance level (α), rejection region, p-value, and conclusion.**
- Two types of errors in a hypothesis test: **Type I error** (reject H_0 when H_0 is true), **Type II error** (accept H_0 when H_0 is false).
- Probabilities of errors: $\alpha = P(\textbf{Type I error}) = P(\text{Reject } H_0|H_0 \text{ true})$, $\beta = P(\textbf{Type II error}) = P(\text{Accept } H_0|H_0 \text{ false})$.
- Three forms of the alternative hypothesis: **lower-tailed test (<), upper-tailed test (>), two-tailed test ($\neq$).**
- **Observed significance level (p-value)** is the smallest value of α that can be used to reject the null hypothesis.

- Conditions required for a valid **large-sample test for μ:** (1) random sample, (2) large sample size ($n \geq 30$).
- Conditions required for a valid **small-sample test for μ:** (1) random sample, (2) population distribution is approximately normal.
- Conditions required for a valid **large-sample test for p:** (1) random sample, (2) large sample size ($p_0 \pm 3\sigma_{\hat{p}}$ falls between 0 and 1).
- Conditions required for a valid **test for σ^2:** (1) random sample, (2) population distribution is approximately normal, regardless of sample size.
- **Power of the test** $= 1 - \beta = P(\text{Reject } H_0|H_0 \text{ false})$.

Supplementary Exercises 8.98–8.128

Note: List the assumptions necessary for the valid implementation of the statistical procedures you use in solving all these exercises. Starred (*) exercises refer to the optional sections in this chapter.

Learning the Mechanics

8.98 Specify the differences between a large-sample and small-sample test of hypothesis about a population mean μ. Focus on the assumptions and test statistics.

8.99 *Complete the following statement:* The smaller the p-value associated with a test of hypothesis, the stronger the support for the _____ hypothesis. Explain your answer.

8.100 Which of the elements of a test of hypothesis can and should be specified *prior* to analyzing the data that are to be utilized to conduct the test?

8.101 If you select a very small value for α when conducting a hypothesis test, will β tend to be big or small? Explain.   Big

8.102 If the rejection of the null hypothesis of a particular test would cause your firm to go out of business, would you want α to be small or large? Explain.   Small

8.103 A random sample of 20 observations selected from a normal population produced $\bar{x} = 72.6$ and $s^2 = 19.4$.
   a. Test $H_0: \mu = 80$ against $H_a: \mu < 80$. Use $\alpha = .05$.
   b. Test $H_0: \mu = 80$ against $H_a: \mu \neq 80$. Use $\alpha = .01$.

8.104 A random sample of 175 measurements possessed a mean $\bar{x} = 8.2$ and a standard deviation $s = .79$.
   a. Test $H_0: \mu = 8.3$ against $H_a: \mu \neq 8.3$ Use $\alpha = .05$.
   b. Test $H_0: \mu = 8.4$ against $H_a: \mu \neq 8.4$ Use $\alpha = .05$.
   *c. Test $H_0: \sigma = 1$ against $H_a: \sigma \neq 1$. Use $\alpha = .05$.
      $\chi^2 = 108.59$
   *d. Find the power of the test, part a, if $\mu_a = 8.5$.   .9177

8.105 A random sample of $n = 200$ observations from a binomial population yields $\hat{p} = .29$.
   a. Test $H_0: p = .35$ against $H_a: p < .35$. Use $\alpha = .05$.
   b. Test $H_0: p = .35$ against $H_a: p \neq .35$. Use $\alpha = .05$.

8.106 A t-test is conducted for the null hypothesis $H_0: \mu = 10$ versus the alternative $H_a: \mu > 10$ for a random sample of $n = 17$ observations. The test results are: $t = 1.174$, p-value $= .1288$.
   a. Interpret the p-value.
   b. What assumptions are necessary for the validity of this test?
   c. Calculate and interpret the p-value assuming the alternative hypothesis was instead $H_a: \mu \neq 10$.

*8.107 A random sample of 41 observations from a normal population possessed a mean $\bar{x} = 88$ and a standard deviation $s = 6.9$.
   a. Test $H_0: \sigma^2 = 30$ against $H_a: \sigma^2 > 30$. Use $\alpha = .05$.
   b. Test $H_0: \sigma^2 = 30$ against $H_a: \sigma^2 \neq 30$. Use $\alpha = .05$.

Applying the Concepts—Basic

8.108 Nutritionists stress that weight control generally requires significant reductions in the intake of fat. A random sample of 64 middle-aged men on weight control programs is selected to determine whether their mean intake of fat exceeds the recommended 30 grams per day. The sample mean and standard deviation are $\bar{x} = 37$ and $s = 32$, respectively.
   a. Considering the sample mean and standard deviation, would you expect the distribution for fat intake per day to be symmetric or skewed? Explain.
   b. Do the sample results indicate that the mean intake for middle-aged men on weight control programs exceeds 30 grams? Test using $\alpha = .10$. $z = 1.75$
   c. Would you reach the same conclusion as in part **b** using $\alpha = .05$? Using $\alpha = .01$? Why can the conclusion of a test change when the value of α is changed?

8.109 Creative Good, a New York consulting firm, claimed that 39% of shoppers fail in their attempts to purchase merchandise on-line because Web sites are too complex. (*Forbes*, Dec. 13, 1999). Another consulting firm asked a random sample of 60 online shoppers to each test a different randomly selected e-commerce Web site. Only 15 reported sufficient frustration with their sites to deter making a purchase.
   a. Do these data provide sufficient evidence to reject the claim made by Creative Good? Test using $\alpha = .01$. $z = -2.22$
   b. Find the observed significance level of the test and interpret it in the context of the problem. $p = .0132$

8.110 The "beta coefficient" of a stock is a measure of the stock's volatility (or risk) relative to the market as a whole. Stocks with beta coefficients greater than 1 generally bear greater risk (more volatility) than the market, whereas stocks with beta coefficients less than 1 are less risky (less volatile) than the overall market (Alexander, Sharpe, and Bailey, *Fundamentals of Investments*, 2000). A random sample of 15 high-technology stocks was selected at the end of 1996, and the mean and standard deviation of the beta coefficients were calculated: $\bar{x} = 1.23$, $s = .37$
   a. Set up the appropriate null and alternative hypotheses to test whether the average high-technology stock is riskier than the market as a whole.
   b. Establish the appropriate test statistic and rejection region for the test. Use $\alpha = .10$.
   c. What assumptions are necessary to ensure the validity of the test?
   d. Calculate the test statistic and state your conclusion.
   e. What is the approximate p-value associated with this test? Interpret it. $.01 < p < .025$

*8.111 Refer to Exercise 8.110. Conduct a test to determine if the variance of the stock beta values differs from .15. Use $\alpha = .05$. $\chi^2 = 12.777$

8.112 Refer to the *Chest* (May 1995) study of obstructive sleep apnea, Exercise 7.96 (p. 408). Recall that the disorder causes a person to stop breathing and awaken briefly during a sleep cycle. Stanford University researchers found that 124 of 159 commercial truck drivers suffered from obstructive sleep apnea.

　a. Sleep researchers theorize that 25% of the general population suffer from obstructive sleep apnea. Use a test of hypothesis (at $\alpha = .10$) to determine whether this percentage differs for commercial truck drivers. $z = 15.43$

　b. Find the observed significance level of the test and interpret its value. $p \approx 0$

　c. In part b of Exercise 7.96, you used a 90% confidence interval to make the inference of part a. Explain why these two inferences must necessarily agree.

Applying the Concepts—Intermediate

8.113 Medical tests have been developed to detect many serious diseases. A medical test is designed to minimize the probability that it will produce a "false positive" or a "false negative." A false positive refers to a positive test result for an individual who does not have the disease, whereas a false negative is a negative test result for an individual who does have the disease.

　a. If we treat a medical test for a disease as a statistical test of hypothesis, what are the null and alternative hypotheses for the medical test?

　b. What are the Type I and Type II errors for the test? Relate each to false positives and false negatives.

　c. Which of the errors has graver consequences? Considering this error, is it more important to minimize α or β? Explain. Type II

8.114 The Lincoln Tunnel (under the Hudson River) connects suburban New Jersey to midtown Manhattan. On Mondays at 8:30 A.M., the mean number of cars waiting in line to pay the Lincoln Tunnel toll is 1,220. Because of the substantial wait during rush hour, the Port Authority of New York and New Jersey is considering raising the amount of the toll between 7:30 and 8:30 A.M. to encourage more drivers to use the tunnel at an earlier or later time (*Newark Star-Ledger*, Aug. 27, 1995). Suppose the Port Authority experiments with peak-hour pricing for six months, increasing the toll from $4 to $7 during the rush hour peak. On 10 different workdays at 8:30 A.M. aerial photographs of the tunnel queues are taken and the number of vehicles counted. The results follow:

TUNNEL

1,260	1,052	1,201	942	1,062	999	931	849	867	735

Analyze the data for the purpose of determining whether peak-hour pricing succeeded in reducing the average number of vehicles attempting to use the Lincoln Tunnel during the peak rush hour. $t = -4.53$

8.115 Most major corporations have psychologists available to help employees who suffer from stress. One problem that is difficult to diagnose is post-traumatic stress disorder (PTSD). Researchers studying PTSD often use as subjects former prisoners of war (POWs). *Psychological Assessment* (Mar. 1995) published the results of a study of World War II aviators who were captured by German forces after they were shot down. Having located a total of 239 World War II aviator POW survivors, the researchers asked each veteran to participate in the study; 33 responded to the letter of invitation. Each of the 33 POW survivors was administered the Minnesota Multiphasic Personality Inventory, one component of which measures level of PTSD. [*Note:* The higher the score, the higher the level of PTSD.] The aviators produced a mean PTSD score of $\bar{x} = 9.00$ and a standard deviation of $s = 9.32$.

　a. Set up the null and alternative hypotheses for determining whether the true mean PTSD score of all World War II aviator POWs is less than 16. [*Note:* The value, 16, represents the mean PTSD score established for Vietnam POWs.]

　b. Conduct the test, part a, using $\alpha = .10$. What are the practical implications of the test? $z = -4.31$

　c. Discuss the representativeness of the sample used in the study and its ramifications.

8.116 A company has devised a new ink-jet cartridge for its plain-paper fax machine that it believes has a longer lifetime (on average) than the one currently being produced. To investigate its length of life, 225 of the new cartridges were tested by counting the number of high-quality printed pages each was able to produce. The sample mean and standard deviation were determined to be 1,511.4 pages and 35.7 pages, respectively. The historical average lifetime for cartridges produced by the current process is 1,502.5 pages; the historical standard deviation is 97.3 pages.

　a. What are the appropriate null and alternative hypotheses to test whether the mean lifetime of the new cartridges exceeds that of the old cartridges?

　b. Use $\alpha = .005$ to conduct the test in part a. Do the new cartridges have an average lifetime that is statistically significantly longer than the cartridges currently in production? $z = 3.74$

　c. Does the difference in average lifetimes appear to be of practical significance from the perspective of the consumer? Explain. No

　*d. Is the apparent decrease in the standard deviation in lifetimes associated with the new cartridges a statistically significant improvement over the old cartridges? Test at $\alpha = .05$. $\chi^2 = 30.1550$

8.117 Sales promotions that are used by manufacturers to entice retailers to carry, feature, or push the manufacturer's products are called *trade promotions*. A survey of 250 manufacturers conducted by Cannondale Associates, a sales and marketing consulting firm, found that 91% of the manufacturers believe their spending for trade promotions is inefficient (*Potentials in Marketing*, June 1995). Is this sufficient evidence to reject a previous claim by the American Marketing Association that no more than half of all manufacturers are dissatisfied with their trade promotion spending?

a. Conduct the appropriate hypothesis test at $\alpha = .02$. Begin your analysis by determining whether the sample size is large enough to apply the testing methodology presented in this chapter.   Yes

b. Report the observed significance level of the test and interpret its meaning in the context of the problem.

c. *Calculate β, the probability of a Type II error, if in fact 55% of all manufacturers are dissatisfied with their trade promotion spending.   .6844

8.118 One study (*Journal of Political Economy*, Feb. 1988) of gambling newsletters that purport to improve a bettor's odds of winning bets on NFL football games indicates that the newsletters' betting schemes were not profitable. Suppose a random sample of 50 games is selected to test one gambling newsletter. Following the newsletter's recommendations, 30 of the 50 games produced winning wagers.

a. Test whether the newsletter can be said to significantly increase the odds of winning over what one could expect by selecting the winner at random. Use $\alpha = .05$ $z = 1.41$

b. Calculate and interpret the *p*-value for the test.

*__8.119__Refer to Exercise 8.118.

a. Describe a Type II error in terms of this application.

b. Calculate the probability β of a Type II error for this test assuming that the newsletter really does increase the probability of winning a wager on an NFL game to $p = .55$.   .8264

c. Suppose the number of games sampled is increased from 50 to 100. How does this affect the probability of a Type II error for $p = .55$?   .7389

8.120 To instill customer loyalty, airlines, hotels, rental car companies, and credit card companies (among others) have initiated *frequency marketing programs* that reward their regular customers. More than 80 million people are members of the frequent flier programs of the airline industry (*www.frequentflier.com*, 2003.) A large fast-food restaurant chain wished to explore the profitability of such a program. They randomly selected 12 of their 1,200 restaurants nationwide and instituted a frequency program that rewarded customers with a $5.00 gift certificate after every 10 meals

purchased at full price. They ran the trial program for three months. The restaurants not in the sample had an average increase in profits of $1,047.34 over the previous three months, whereas the restaurants in the sample had the following changes in profit:

PROFIT

$2,232.90	$545.47	$3,440.70	$1,809.10
$6,552.70	$4,798.70	$2,965.00	$2,610.70
$3,381.30	$1,591.40	$2,376.20	−$2,191.0

Note that the last number is negative, representing a decrease in profits.

a. Specify the appropriate null and alternative hypotheses for determining whether the mean profit change for restaurants with frequency programs is significantly greater (in a statistical sense) than $1,047.34. $H_0: \mu = 1047.34$ vs. $H_a: \mu > 1047.34$

b. Conduct the test of part **b** using $\alpha = .05$. Does it appear that the frequency program would be profitable for the company if adopted nationwide? $t = 2.36$

8.121 In order to be effective, the mean length life of a certain mechanical component used in a spacecraft must be larger than 1,100 hours. Owing to the prohibitive cost of this component, only three can be tested under simulated space conditions. The lifetimes (hours) of the components were recorded and the following statistics were computed: $\bar{x} = 1,173.6$ and $s = 36.3$.

a. Set up H_0 and H_a for testing whether the mean life length of the component exceeds 1,100 hours. $H_0: \mu = 1,100$ vs. $H_a: \mu > 1,100$

b. Find the value of the test statistic. $t = 3.51$

c. Find and interpret the *p*-value of the test. (Use $\alpha = .01$.) $.025 < p < .05$

d. Which type of error, I or II, is of greater concern for this test? Explain.   Type I

e. Would you recommend that this component be passed as meeting specifications?

8.122 One way of evaluating a measuring instrument is to repeatedly measure the same item and compare the average of these measurements to the item's known measured value. The difference is used to assess the instrument's accuracy (*Quality Progress*, Jan. 1993). To evaluate a particular Metlar scale, an item whose weight is known to be 16.01 ounces is weighed five times by the same operator. The measurements, in ounces, are as follows:

METLAR

15.99	16.00	15.97	16.01	15.96

a. In a statistical sense, does the average measurement differ from 16.01? Conduct the appropriate hypothesis test. What does your analysis suggest about the accuracy of the instrument? $t = -2.59$

b. List any assumptions you make in conducting the hypothesis test.

8.123 The EPA sets an airborne limit of 5 parts per million (ppm) on vinyl chloride, a colorless gas used to make plastics, adhesives, and other chemicals. It is both a carcinogen and a mutagen (New Jersey Department of Health, *Hazardous Substance Fact Sheet*, 2002). A major plastics manufacturer, attempting to control the amount of vinyl chloride its workers are exposed to, has given instructions to halt production if the mean amount of vinyl chloride in the air exceeds 3.0 ppm. A random sample of 50 air specimens produced the following statistics: $\bar{x} = 3.1$ ppm, $s = .5$ ppm.

a. Do these statistics provide sufficient evidence to halt the production process? Use $\alpha = .01$. $z = 1.41$

b. If you were the plant manager, would you want to use a large or a small value for α for the test in part a? Explain. Small

c. Find the *p*-value for the test and interpret its value.

*8.124 Refer to Exercise 8.123.

a. In the context of the problem, define a Type II error.

b. Calculate β for the test described in part a of Exercise 8.123, assuming that the true mean is $\mu = 3.1$ ppm. .8212

c. What is the power of the test to detect a departure from the manufacturer's 3.0 ppm limit when the mean is 3.1 ppm? .1788

d. Repeat parts b and c assuming that the true mean is 3.2 ppm. What happens to the power of the test as the plant's mean vinyl chloride level departs further from the limit? .3121; .6879

*8.125 Refer to Exercises 8.123 and 8.124.

a. Suppose an α value of .05 is used to conduct the test. Does this change favor halting production? Explain. No

b. Determine the value of β and the power for the test when $\alpha = .05$ and $\mu = 3.1$. .5910; .4090

c. What happens to the power of the test when α is increased? Increases

*8.126 Ophthalmologists require an instrument that can rapidly measure interocular pressure for glaucoma patients. The device now in general use is known to yield readings of this pressure with a variance of 10.3. The variance of five pressure readings on the same eye by a newly developed instrument is equal to 9.8. Does this sample variance provide sufficient evidence to indicate that the new instrument is more reliable than the instrument currently in use? (Use $\alpha = .05$.) $\chi^2 = 3.81$

8.127 The manufacturer of an over-the-counter analgesic claims that its product brings pain relief to headache sufferers in less than 3.5 minutes, on average. In order

to be able to make this claim in its television advertisements, the manufacturer was required by a particular television network to present statistical evidence in support of the claim. The manufacturer reported that for a random sample of 50 headache sufferers, the mean time to relief was 3.3 minutes and the standard deviation was 1.1 minutes.

a. Do these data support the manufacturer's claim? Test using $\alpha = .05$. $z = -1.29$

b. Report the *p*-value of the test. .0985

c. In general, do large *p*-values or small *p*-values support the manufacturer's claim? Explain. small

Applying the Concepts—Advanced

8.128 For three weeks each March, the National Collegiate Athletic Association (NCAA) holds its annual men's basketball championship tournament. The 64 best college basketball teams in the nation play a single-elimination tournament—a total of 63 games—to determine the NCAA champion. Tournament followers, from hardcore gamblers to the casual fan who enters the office betting pool, have a strong interest in handicapping the games. To provide insight into this phenomenon, statisticians Hal Stern and Barbara Mock analyzed data from 13 previous NCAA tournaments and published their results in *Chance* (Winter 1998). The results of first-round games are summarized in the table on page 469.

a. A common perception among fans, media, and gamblers is that the higher seeded team has a better than 50-50 chance of winning a first-round game. Is there evidence to support this perception? Conduct the appropriate test for each matchup. What trends do you observe?

b. Is there evidence to support the claim that a 1-, 2-, 3-, or 4-seeded team will win by an average of more than 10 points in first-round games? Conduct the appropriate test for each matchup.

c. Is there evidence to support the claim that a 5-, 6-, 7-, or 8-seeded team will win by an average of less than five points in first-round games? Conduct the appropriate test for each matchup.

*d. For each matchup, test the null hypothesis that the standard deviation of the victory margin is 11 points.

e. The researchers also calculated the difference between the game outcome (victory margin, in points) and point spread established by Las Vegas oddsmakers for a sample of 360 recent NCAA tournament games. The mean difference is .7 and the standard deviation of the difference is 11.3. If the true mean difference is 0, then the point spread can be considered a good predictor of the game outcome. Use this sample information to test the hypothesis that the point spread, on average, is a good predictor of the victory margin in NCAA tournament games.

Summary of First-Round NCAA Tournament Games, 1985–1997

Matchup (Seeds)	Number of Games	Number Won by Favorite (Higher Seed)	Margin of Victory (Points)	
			Mean	Standard Deviation
1 vs 16	52	52	22.9	12.4
2 vs 15	52	49	17.2	11.4
3 vs 14	52	41	10.6	12.0
4 vs 13	52	42	10.0	12.5
5 vs 12	52	37	5.3	10.4
6 vs 11	52	36	4.3	10.7
7 vs 10	52	35	3.2	10.5
8 vs 9	52	22	−2.1	11.0

Source: Stern, H. S., and Mock, B. "College Basketball Upsets: Will a 16-Seed Ever Beat a 1-Seed?" *Chance,* Vol. 11. No. 1, Winter 1998, p. 29 (Table 3).

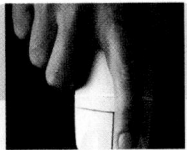

Using Technology

8.1 Tests of Hypothesis Using SPSS

SPSS can be used to tests hypotheses about a population mean and a population proportion, but cannot currently conduct a test for a population variance. To generate a test for the mean, first access the SPSS spreadsheet file that contains the sample data. Next, click on the "Analyze" button on the SPSS menu bar, then click on "Compare Means" and "One-Sample T Test", as shown in Figure 8.S.1. The resulting dialog box appears as shown in Figure 8.S.2. Specify the quantitative variable of interest in the "Test Variable(s)" box and the value of μ_0 for the null

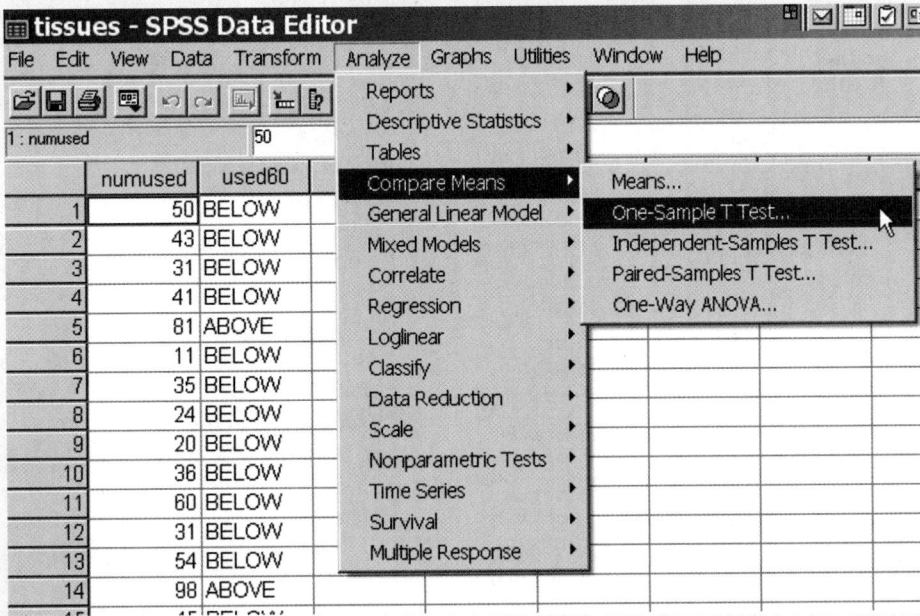

Figure 8.S.1

SPSS menu options for a test about μ

Figure 8.S.2
SPSS *T* test dialog box

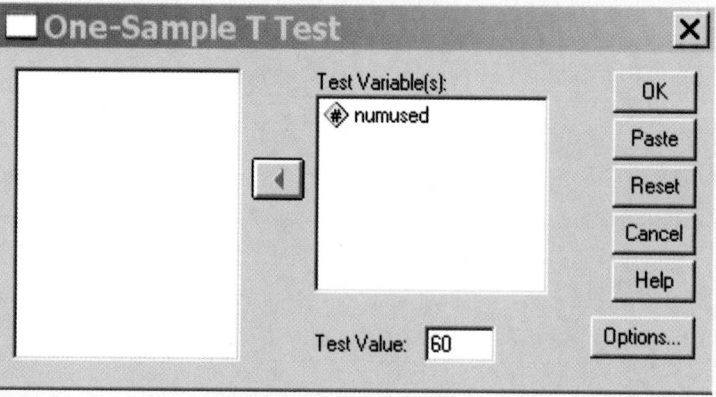

hypothesis in the "Test Value" box, then click "OK". SPSS will automatically conduct a two-tailed test of hypothesis.

[*Important Note:* The SPSS one-sample *t*-procedure uses the *t*-statistic to conduct the test of hypothesis. When the sample size *n* is small, this is the appropriate method. When the sample size *n* is large, the *t*-value will be approximately equal to the large-sample *z*-value and the resulting test will still be valid.]

To generate a test for a proportion, first access the SPSS spreadsheet file that contains the sample data. Next, click on the "Analyze" button on the SPSS menu bar, then click on "Nonparametric Tests" and "Binomial", as shown in Figure 8.S.3. The resulting dialog box appears as shown in Figure 8.S.4. Specify the binomial variable of interest in the "Test Variable List" box and the value of p_0 for the null hypothesis in the "Test Proportion" box.

Figure 8.S.3
SPSS menu options for a test about *p*

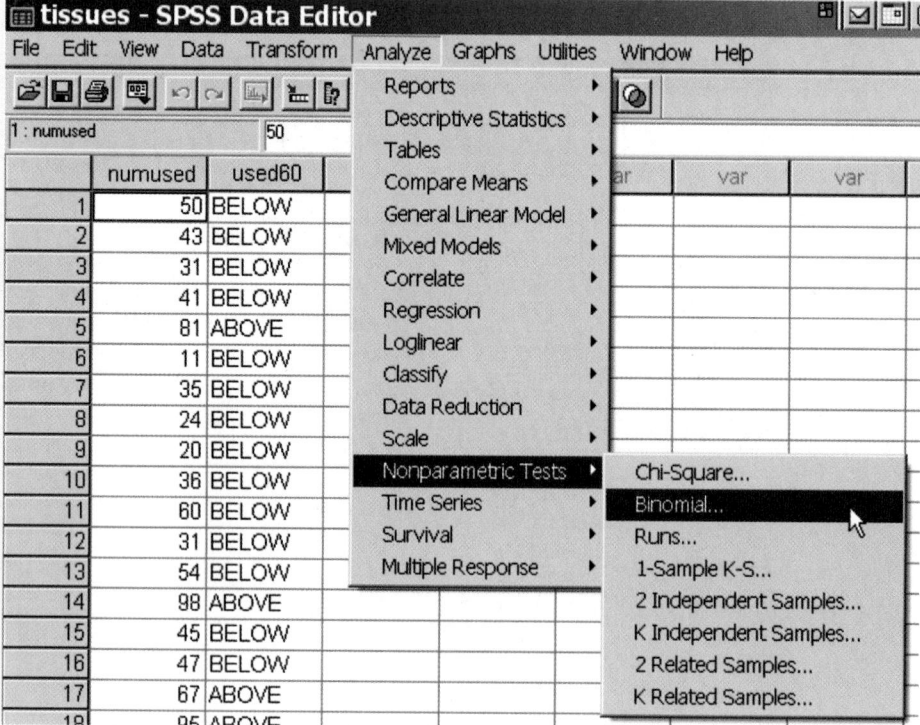

Figure 8.S.4

SPSS binomial test dialog box

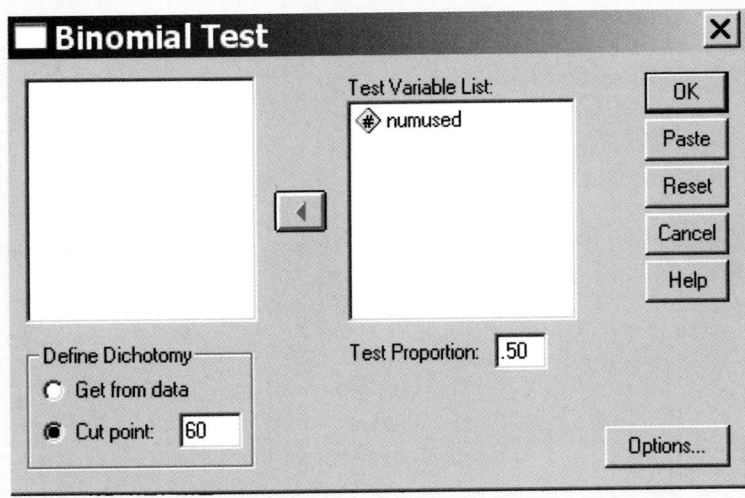

[*Important Note*: SPSS requires the binomial variable to be entered as a quantitative variable. Typically, this is accomplished by entering two numerical values (e.g., 0 and 1) for the two outcomes of the variable. If the data have been entered in this fashion, then select the "Get from data" option in the "Define Dichotomy" area of the dialog box. You can also create the two outcome values for a quantitative variable by selecting the "Cut point" option in the "Define Dichotomy" area and specifying a numerical value. All values of the variables less than or equal to the cut point value are assigned to one group (success) and all other values are assigned to the other group (failure). Once the dichotomy is defined, click "OK". SPSS will automatically conduct a two-tailed test of hypothesis for the proportion.]

8.2 Tests of Hypothesis Using MINITAB

MINITAB can be used to obtain one-sample tests for both a population mean and a population proportion but cannot currently produce a test for a population variance. To generate a hypothesis test for the mean using a previously created sample data set, first access the MINITAB data worksheet. Next, click on the "Stat" button on the MINITAB menu bar, then click on "Basic Statistics" and "1-Sample t", as shown in Figure 8.M.1. The resulting dialog box appears as shown in Figure 8.M.2. Click on "Samples in Columns", then specify the quantitative variable of interest in the open box. Specify the value of μ_0 for the null hypothesis in the "Test mean" box. Now, click on the "Options" button at the bottom of the dialog box and specify the form of the alternative hypothesis as shown in Figure 8.M.3. Click "OK" to return to the "1-Sample t" dialog box, then click "OK" again to produce the hypothesis test.

If you want to produce a test for the mean from summary information (e.g., the sample mean, sample standard deviation, and sample size), then click on "Summarized data" in the "1-Sample t" dialog box, enter the values of the summary statistics and μ_0, then click "OK".

[*Important Note*: The MINITAB one-sample t-procedure uses the t-statistic to generate the hypothesis test. When the sample size n is small, this is the appropriate method. When the sample size n is large, the t-value will be approximately equal to the large-sample z-value and the resulting test will still be valid. If you have a large sample and you know the value of the population

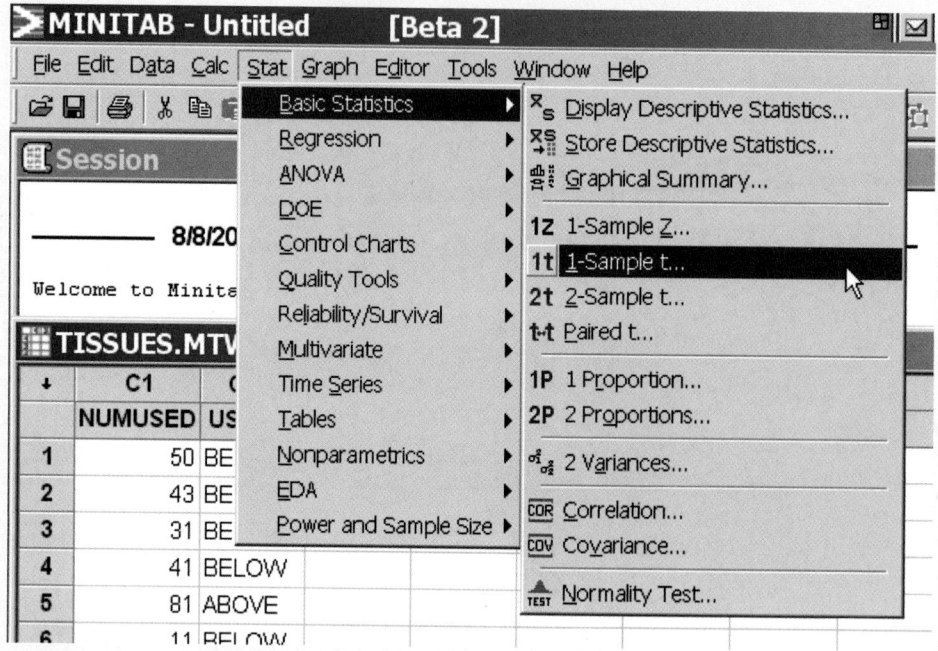

Figure 8.M.1

MINITAB menu options for a test about μ

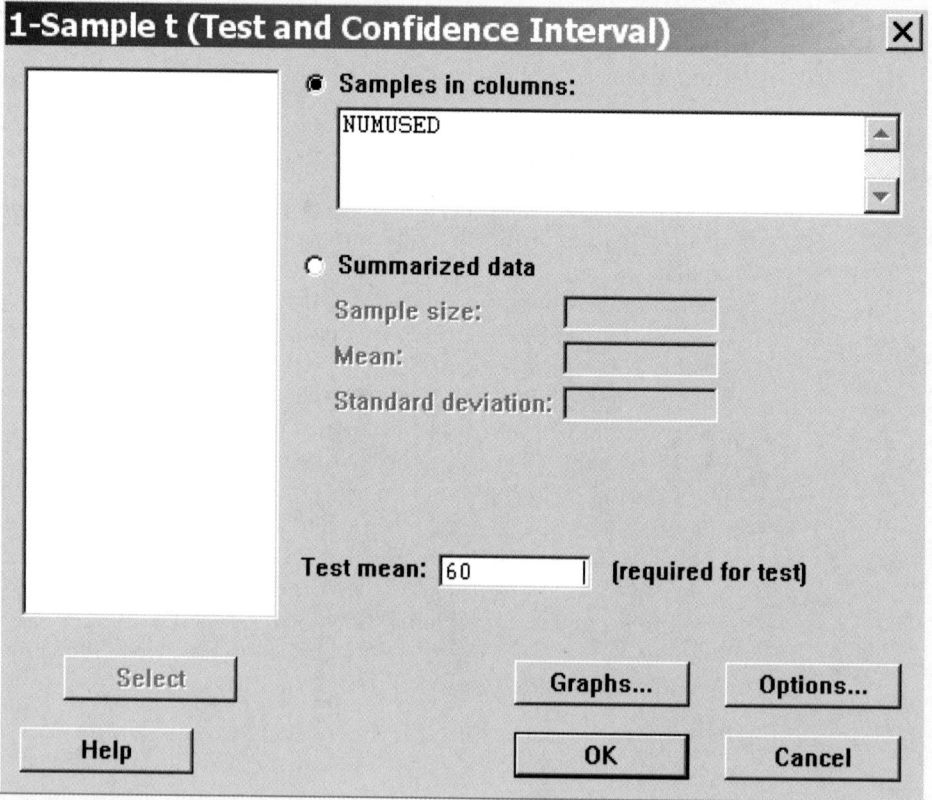

Figure 8.M.2

MINITAB one-sample t dialog box

Figure 8.M.3
MINITAB one-sample *t*
options dialog box

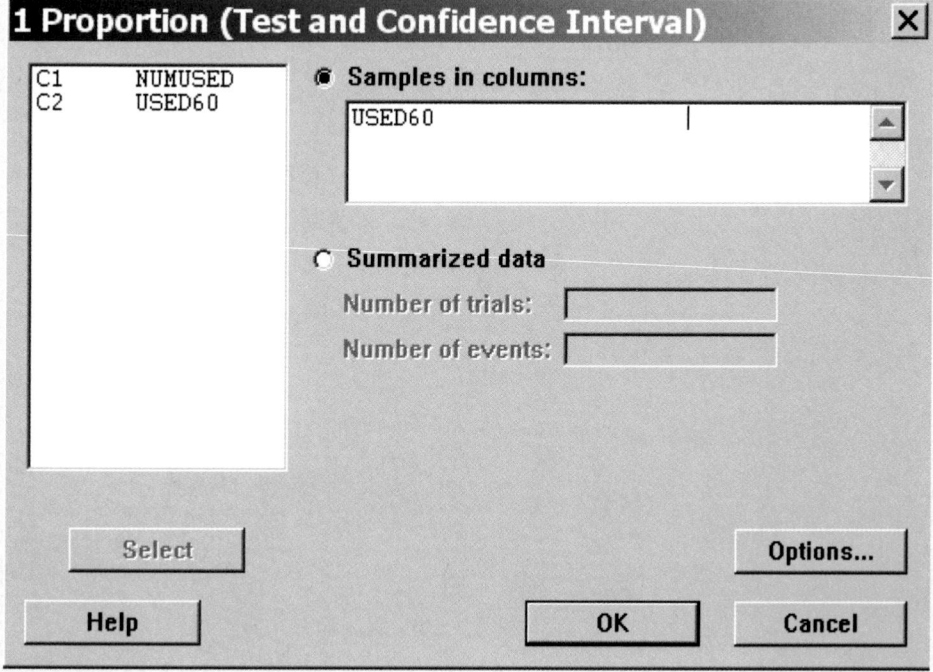

standard deviation σ (which is rarely the case), then select "1-sample Z" from the "Basic Statistics" menu options (see Figure 8.M.1) and make the appropriate selections.]

To generate a test for a population proportion using a previously created sample data set, first access the MINITAB data worksheet. Next, click on the "Stat" button on the MINITAB menu bar, then click on "Basic Statistics" and "1 Proportion" (see Figure 8.M.1). The resulting dialog box appears as shown in Figure 8.M.4. Click on "Samples in Columns", then specify the qualitative variable of interest in the open box. Now, click on the "Options" button at the bottom of the dialog box and specify the null hypothesis value p_0 and the form of the alternative hypothesis in the resulting dialog box, as shown in Figure 8.M.5. Also, check the "Use test and interval based on normal distribution" box at the bottom. Click "OK" to return to the "1-Proportion" dialog box, then click "OK" again to produce the test results.

Figure 8.M.4
MINITAB 1-proportion dialog box

1 Proportion - Options

Confidence level: 95.0

Test proportion: 0.5

Alternative: not equal ▼

☑ **Use test and interval based on normal distribution**

| Help | OK | Cancel |

Figure 8.M.5
MINITAB 1-proportion options

If you want to produce a confidence interval for a proportion from summary information (e.g., the number of successes and the sample size), then click on "Summarized data" in the "1-Proportion" dialog box (see Figure 8.M.4). Enter the value for the number of trials (i.e., the sample size) and the number of events (i.e., the number of successes), then click "OK".

8.3 Tests of Hypothesis Using EXCEL and PHStat2

EXCEL with the PHStat2 add-in can be used to obtain one-sample tests for population means, proportions, and variances. To generate a test if hypothesis for the mean using a previously created sample data set, first access the EXCEL worksheet. Next, click on the "PHStat" button on the EXCEL menu bar, then click on "One-Sample Tests" and "t Test for the Mean, sigma unknown", as shown in Figure 8.E.1. The resulting dialog box appears as shown

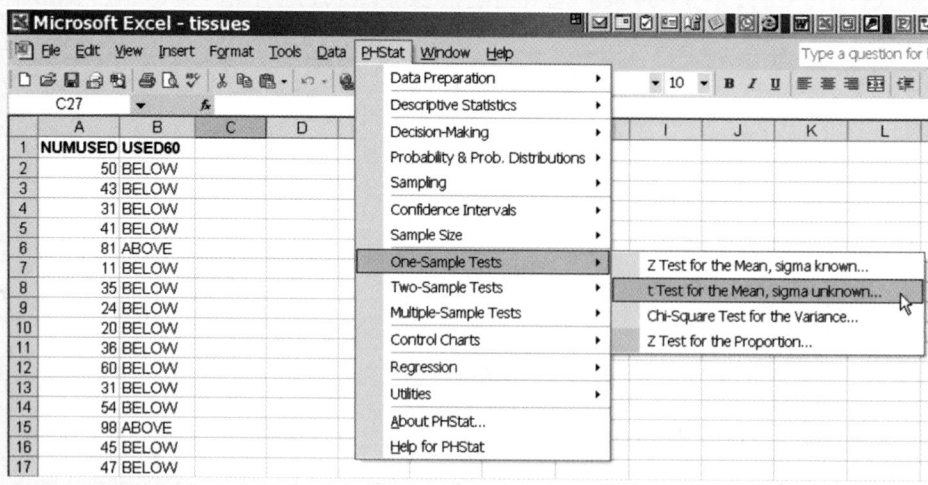

Figure 8.E.1
EXCEL/PHStat2 menu options for a test about μ

in Figure 8.E.2. Specify the value of μ_0 for the null hypothesis, the level of significance α, and the form of the alternative hypothesis (upper-, lower-, or two-tailed test), then click on "Sample Statistics Unknown" and specify the cell range for the quantitative variable of interest (see Figure 8.E.2). Click "OK" to produce the test results.

If you want to produce a test for the mean from summary information (e.g., the sample mean, sample standard deviation, and sample size), then click on "Sample Statistics Known" on the dialog box shown in Figure 8.E.2. Enter the values of the summary statistics, then click "OK".

[*Important Note:* The EXCEL/PHStat2 one-sample procedure outlined above uses the t-statistic to generate the hypothesis test when σ is unknown. When the sample size n is small, this is the appropriate method. When the sample size n is large, the t-value will be approximately equal to the large-sample z-value and the resulting interval will still be valid. If you have a large sample and you know the value of the population standard deviation σ (which is rarely the case), then select "Z Test for the Mean, sigma known" from the "One-Sample Tests" menu options (see Figure 8.E.1) and make the appropriate selections.]

Figure 8.E.2
EXCEL *t* test for mean dialog box

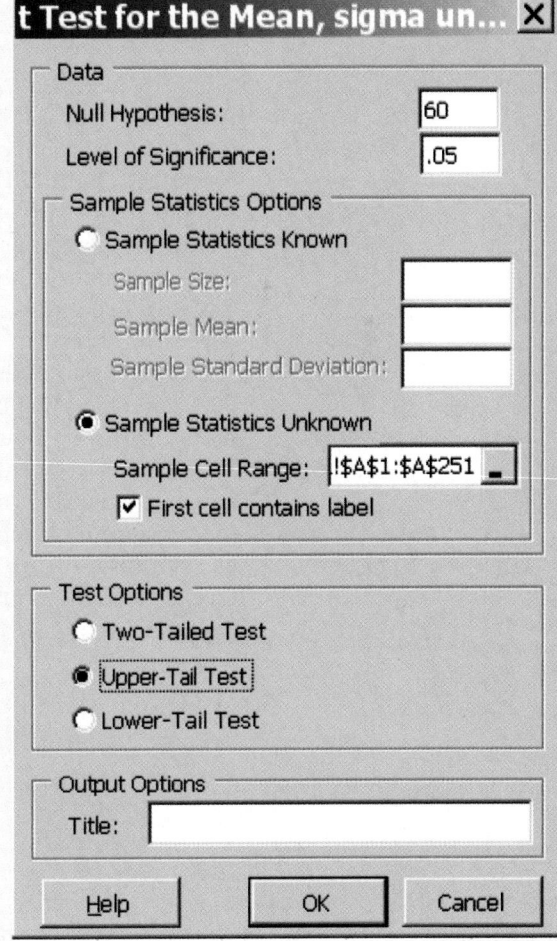

Figure 8.E.3
EXCEL test for proportion
dialog box

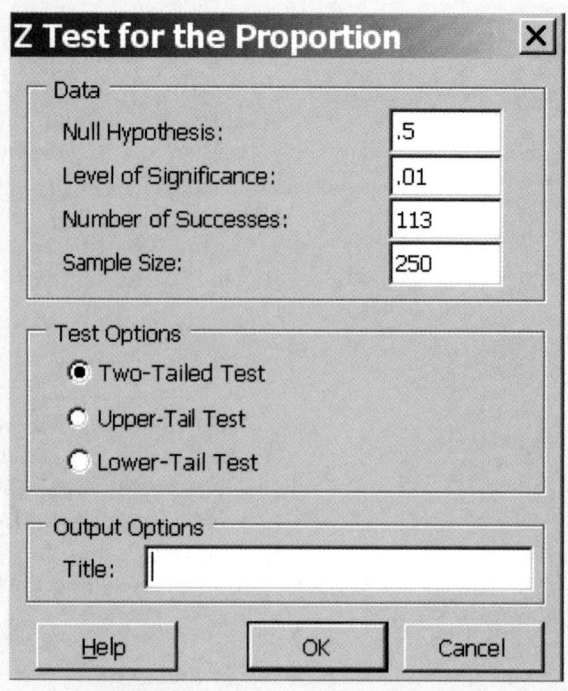

To generate a test for a population proportion using EXCEL, you must first determine the sample size and the number of successes in the sample of interest. Next, click on the "PHStat" button on the EXCEL menu bar, then click on "One-Sample Tests" and "Z Test for the Proportion" (see Figure 8.E.1). The resulting dialog box appears as shown in Figure 8.E.3. Specify the null hypothesis value p_0 level of significance α, number of successes, sample size, and the form of the alternative hypothesis (upper-, lower-, or two-tailed test), then click "OK" to produce the test results.

To generate a test for a population variance using EXCEL, you must first determine the sample standard deviation for the variable of interest. Next, click on the "PHStat" button on the EXCEL menu bar, then click on "One-Sample Tests" and "Chi-Square Test for the Variance" (see Figure 8.E.1). The resulting dialog box appears as shown in Figure 8.E.4. Specify the null hypothesis value of the variance σ_0^2 level of significance α_1 sample size, sample standard deviation, and the form of the alternative hypothesis (upper-, lower-, or two-tailed test), then click "OK" to-produce the test results.

Figure 8.E.4
EXCEL test for variance
dialog box

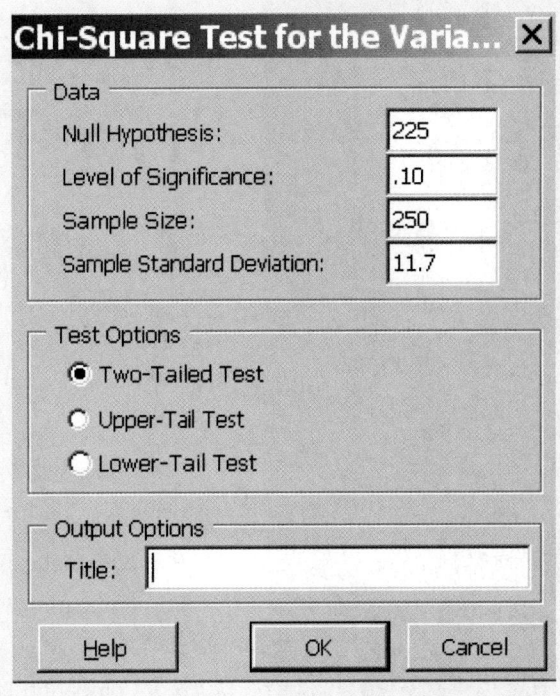

REFERENCES

Alexander, G. J., Sharpe, W. F., and Bailey, J. *Fundamentals of Investments*, 3rd ed. Upper Saddle River, N.J.: Prentice Hall, 2000.

Schonberger, R. J., & Knod Jr., E. M. *Operations Management*, 5th ed. Burr Ridge, III.: Irwin, 1994.

Snedecor, G. W., and Cochran, W. G. *Statistical Methods*, 7th ed. Ames: Iowa State University Press, 1980.

Stevenson, W. J. *Production/Operations Management*, 6th ed. Chicago: Irwin, 2000.

Wackerly, D., Mendenhall, W., and Scheaffer, R. *Mathematical Statistics with Applications*, 6th ed. North Scituate, Mass.: Duxbury, 2002.

9

Inferences Based on Two Samples

Confidence Intervals and Tests of Hypotheses

Contents

Statistics in Action

The Effect of Self-Managed Work Teams on Family Life

Using Technology

Where We've Been

- Explored two methods for making statistical inferences: *confidence intervals* and *tests of hypotheses*

- Studied confidence intervals and tests for a single population mean μ, a single population proportion p, and a single population variance σ^2

- Learned how to select the sample size necessary to estimate a population parameter with a specified margin of error

Where We're Going

- Learn how to compare two populations using confidence intervals and tests of hypotheses.

- Apply these inferential methods to problems where we want to compare two population means, two population proportions, or two population variances.

- Determine the sizes of the samples necessary to estimate the difference between two population parameters with a specified margin of error.

Statistics in

ACTION

The Effect of Self-Managed Work Teams on Family Life

To improve quality, productivity, and timeliness, more and more American industries are adopting a new participative management style. This new approach utilizes self-managed work teams (SMWTs). A team typically consists of 5 to 15 workers who are collectively responsible for making decisions and performing all tasks related to a particular project. For example, a SMWT may be responsible for scheduling work hours, interfacing with customers, disciplining team members, and participating in hiring. Past studies revealed that SMWTs have positive impacts on both a firm's performance and employee attitudes.

SMWTs require that employees be trained in interpersonal skills such as listening, decision making, and conflict resolution. Consequently, SMWTs can have potential positive spillover effects on a worker's family life.

Researchers L. Stanley-Stevens (Tarleton State University), D. E. Yeatts, and R. R. Seward (both University of North Texas) investigated the connection between SMWT work characteristics and workers' perceptions of positive spillover into family life (*Quality Management Journal*, Summer 1995).

Survey data were collected from 114 AT&T employees who work in one of fifteen SMWTs at an AT&T technical division. The workers were divided into two groups: (1) those who reported positive spillover of work skills to family life and (2) those who did not report positive work spillover. The two groups were compared on a variety of job and demographic characteristics, several of which are shown in Table SIA9.1. All but the demographic characteristics were measured on a 7-point scale, ranging from 1 = "strongly disagree" to 7 = "strongly agree";

TABLE SIA9.1   Variables Measured in the SMWT Survey

Characteristic	Variable
Information flow	Use of creative ideas (7-point scale)
Information flow	Utilization of information (7-point scale)
Decision making	Participation in decisions regarding personnel matters (7-point scale)
Job	Good use of skills (7-point scale)
Job	Task identity (7-point scale)
Demographic	Age (years)
Demographic	Education (years)
Demographic	Gender (male or female)
Comparison	Group (positive spillover or no spillover)

thus, the larger the number, the more of the characteristic indicated.

The researchers' objectives were to compare the two groups of workers on each characteristic. In particular, they want to know which job-related characteristics are most highly associated with positive work spillover. From summary information provided in the *Quality Management Journal* article, we constructed a data set that represents the results of a survey similar to the one described above. The file named SPILLOVER includes the values of the variables listed in Table SIA9.1 for each of the 114 survey partici-

pants. We apply the statistical methodology presented in this chapter to this data set in several Statistics in Action Revisited examples.

Statistics in Action Revisited

- Comparing Means for the Two SMWT Survey Groups (p. 492)
- Comparing Proportions for the Two SMWT Survey Groups (p. 516)

Teaching Tip
Explain that we have the ability to examine the parameters of a single population (Chapter 8), compare parameters from two populations (Chapter 9), or compare parameters from three or more populations (later in text).

Many experiments involve a comparison of two populations. For instance, a consumer group may want to test whether two major brands of food freezers differ in the mean amount of electricity they use. A television market researcher may want to estimate the difference in the proportions of younger and older viewers who watch a certain TV program regularly. A golf ball supplier may wish to compare the variability in the distance that two competing brands of golf balls travel when struck with the same club. In this chapter we consider techniques for using two samples to compare the populations from which they were selected.

9.1 Comparing Two Population Means: Independent Sampling

Teaching Tip
Discuss the two methods of data collection for comparing means. Use examples that illustrate both the independent and matched pairs sampling designs.

Many of the same procedures that are used to estimate and test hypotheses about a single parameter can be modified to make inferences about two parameters. Both the z and t statistics may be adapted to make inferences about the difference between two population means.

In this section we develop both large-sample and small-sample methodologies for comparing two population means. In the large-sample case we use the z-statistic, while in the small-sample case we use the t-statistic.

Large Samples

EXAMPLE 9.1   FINDING A LARGE SAMPLE CONFIDENCE INTERVAL FOR $\mu_1 - \mu_2$

Problem   In recent years, the United States and Japan have engaged in intense negotiations regarding restrictions on trade between the two countries. One of the claims made repeatedly by U.S. officials is that many Japanese manufacturers price their goods higher in Japan than in the United States, in effect subsidizing low prices in the United States by extremely high prices in Japan. According to the U.S. argument, Japan accomplishes this by keeping competitive U.S. goods from reaching the Japanese marketplace.

An economist decided to test the hypothesis that higher retail prices are being charged for Japanese automobiles in Japan than in the United States. She obtained independent random samples of 50 retail sales in the United States and 30 retail sales in Japan over the same time period and for the same model of automobile, converted the Japanese sales prices from yen to dollars using current conversion rates. The data, saved in The AUTOSTUDY file, are listed in Table 9.1. Form a 95% confidence interval for the difference between the

AUTOSTUDY

-654 ± 864

TABLE 9.1 Automobile Retail Prices (thousands of dollars)

USA Sales:	18.2	16.2	17.2	18.7	18.4	16.6	14.9	16.8	12.1	10.8
	18.5	15.5	16.2	16.3	18.2	19.5	13.2	16.8	12.9	17.2
	18.2	16.3	16.8	16.4	18.6	15.6	17.1	18.1	18.9	19.0
	17.3	18.8	14.9	16.7	20.3	17.1	14.6	17.2	13.0	18.4
	16.9	13.3	16.3	15.9	16.6	17.6	16.0	17.1	14.6	18.0
Japan Sales:	18.5	14.0	18.2	21.1	13.9	18.7	14.9	16.4	16.3	18.0
	16.8	19.8	17.3	16.6	14.9	16.3	16.5	15.4	17.6	20.1
	16.4	18.0	17.5	18.4	19.8	14.8	18.2	16.7	20.2	16.2

population mean retail prices of this automobile model for the two countries. Interpret the result.

Solution

Recall that the general form of a large-sample confidence interval for a single mean μ is $\bar{x} \pm z_{\alpha/2}\sigma_{\bar{x}}$. That is, we add and subtract $z_{\alpha/2}$ standard deviations of the sample estimate, $\bar{x}$, to the value of the estimate. We employ a similar procedure to form the confidence interval for the difference between two population means.

Teaching Tip

Throughout this chapter, point out similarities with one-sample inferences. Try to show the student that our general ideas developed in Chapters 7 and 8 extend to the two sample inferences in Chapter 9.

Let μ_1 represent the mean of the population of retail sales prices for this car model sold in the United States. Let μ_2 be similarly defined for retail sales in Japan. We wish to form a confidence interval for $(\mu_1 - \mu_2)$. An intuitively appealing estimator for $(\mu_1 - \mu_2)$ is the difference between the sample means, $(\bar{x}_1 - \bar{x}_2)$. Thus, we will form the confidence interval of interest by

$$(\bar{x}_1 - \bar{x}_2) \pm z_{\alpha/2}\sigma_{(\bar{x}_1 - \bar{x}_2)}$$

Assuming the two samples are independent, the standard deviation of the difference between the sample means is

$$\sigma_{(\bar{x}_1 - \bar{x}_2)} = \sqrt{\frac{\sigma_1^2}{n_1} + \frac{\sigma_2^2}{n_2}} \approx \sqrt{\frac{s_1^2}{n_1} + \frac{s_2^2}{n_2}}$$

Summary statistics for the car sales data are displayed in the SPSS printout, Figure 9.1. Note that $\bar{x}_1 = \$16{,}596$, $\bar{x}_2 = \$17{,}250$, $s_1 = \$1{,}981$, and $s_2 = \$1{,}865$. Using these values and noting that $\alpha = .05$ and $z_{.025} = 1.96$, we find that the 95% confidence interval is, approximately,

$$(16{,}596 - 17{,}250) \pm 1.96\sqrt{\frac{(1{,}981)^2}{50} + \frac{(1{,}865)^2}{30}} = -654 \pm (1.96)(440.94)$$

$$= -654 \pm 864$$

Figure 9.1
SPSS summary statistics for automobile price study

Descriptive Statistics

	N	Minimum	Maximum	Mean	Std. Deviation
USA	50	10800	20300	16596.00	1981.440
JAPAN	30	13900	21100	17250.00	1864.875
Valid N (listwise)	30				

or $(-1,518, 210)$. Using this estimation procedure over and over again for different samples, we know that approximately 95% of the confidence intervals formed in this manner will enclose the difference in population means $(\mu_1 - \mu_2)$. Therefore, we are highly confident that the difference in mean retail prices in the United States and Japan is between $-\$1,518$ and $\$210$. Since 0 falls in this interval, it is possible for the difference to be 0 (i.e., for $\mu_1 = \mu_2$); thus, the economist cannot conclude that a significant difference exists between the mean retail prices in the two countries.

Look Back If the confidence interval for $(\mu_1 - \mu_2)$ contains all positive numbers [e.g., $(527, 991)$], then we would conclude that the difference between the means is positive and that $\mu_1 > \mu_2$. Alternatively, if the interval contains all negative numbers [e.g., $(-722, -145)$], then we would conclude that the difference between the means is negative and that $\mu_1 < \mu_2$.

Now Work   *Exercise 9.3a*

■ ■ ■

The justification for the procedure used in Example 9.1 to estimate $(\mu_1 - \mu_2)$ relies on the properties of the sampling distribution of $(\bar{x}_1 - \bar{x}_2)$. The performance of the estimator in repeated sampling is pictured in Figure 9.2, and its properties are summarized in the box.

Properties of the Sampling Distribution of $(\bar{x}_1 - \bar{x}_2)$

1. The mean of the sampling distribution $(\bar{x}_1 - \bar{x}_2)$ is $(\mu_1 - \mu_2)$.
2. If the two samples are independent, the standard deviation of the sampling distribution is

$$\sigma_{(\bar{x}_1 - \bar{x}_2)} = \sqrt{\frac{\sigma_1^2}{n_1} + \frac{\sigma_2^2}{n_2}}$$

where σ_1^2 and σ_2^2 are the variances of the two populations being sampled and n_1 and n_2 are the respective sample sizes. We also refer to $\sigma_{(\bar{x}_1 - \bar{x}_2)}$ as the **standard error** of the statistic $(\bar{x}_1 - \bar{x}_2)$.
3. The sampling distribution of $(\bar{x}_1 - \bar{x}_2)$ is approximately normal for *large samples* by the Central Limit Theorem.

In Example 9.1, we noted the similarity in the procedures for forming a large-sample confidence interval for one population mean and a large-sample confidence interval for the difference between two population means. When we are testing

Figure 9.2
Sampling distribution
of $(\bar{x}_1 - \bar{x}_2)$

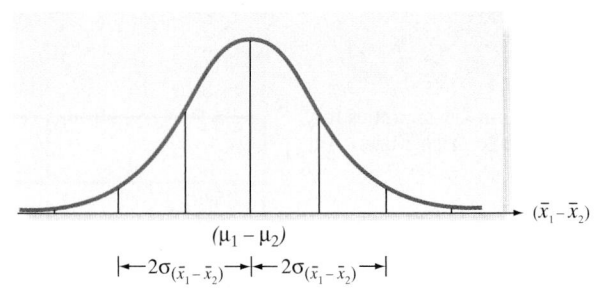

hypotheses, the procedures are again very similar. The general large-sample procedures for forming confidence intervals and testing hypotheses about $(\mu_1 - \mu_2)$ are summarized in the following boxes.

Teaching Tip

When writing the confidence interval formula, replace the symbols with the following words: point estimate $\pm$ critical value $\times$ standard error. All of the confidence intervals for means and proportions follow this general form.

Large Sample Confidence Interval for $(\mu_1 - \mu_2)$

$$(\bar{x}_1 - \bar{x}_2) \pm z_{\alpha/2}\sigma_{(\bar{x}_1 - \bar{x}_2)} = (\bar{x}_1 - \bar{x}_2) \pm z_{\alpha/2}\sqrt{\frac{\sigma_1^2}{n_1} + \frac{\sigma_2^2}{n_2}}$$

Large-Sample Test of Hypothesis for $(\mu_1 - \mu_2)$

One-Tailed Test	Two-Tailed Test
$H_0: (\mu_1 - \mu_2) = D_0$	$H_0: (\mu_1 - \mu_2) = D_0$
$H_a: (\mu_1 - \mu_2) < D_0$	$H_a: (\mu_1 - \mu_2) \neq D_0$
$\quad$[or $H_a: (\mu_1 - \mu_2) > D_0$]	

where D_0 = Hypothesized difference between the means (this difference is often hypothesized to be equal to 0)

Test statistic:

$$z = \frac{(\bar{x}_1 - \bar{x}_2) - D_0}{\sigma_{(\bar{x}_1 - \bar{x}_2)}} \quad \text{where} \quad \sigma_{(\bar{x}_1 - \bar{x}_2)} = \sqrt{\frac{\sigma_1^2}{n_1} + \frac{\sigma_2^2}{n_2}}$$

Rejection region: $z < -z_\alpha$	*Rejection region:* $|z| > z_{\alpha/2}$
$\quad$[or $z > z_\alpha$ when	
$\quad H_a: (\mu_1 - \mu_2) > D_0$]	

Conditions Required for Valid Large-Sample Inferences about $\mu_1 - \mu_2$

1. The two samples are randomly selected in an independent manner from the two target populations.
2. The sample sizes, n_1 and n_2, are both large (i.e., $n_1 \geq 30$ and $n_2 \geq 30$). [Due to the Central Limit Theorem, this condition guarantees that the sampling distribution of $(\bar{x}_1 - \bar{x}_2)$ will be approximately normal regardless of the shapes of the underlying probability distributions of the populations. Also, s_1^2 and s_2^2 will provide good approximations to σ_1^2 and σ_2^2 when the samples are both large.]

EXAMPLE 9.2

A LARGE-SAMPLE TEST FOR $\mu_1 - \mu_2$

Problem   Refer to the study of retail prices of an automobile sold in the United States and Japan, Example 9.1. Another way to compare the mean retail prices for the two countries is to conduct a test of hypothesis. Use the information on the SPSS printout, Figure 9.1, to conduct the test. Use $\alpha = .05$.

Solution   Again, we let μ_1 and μ_2 represent the population mean retail sales prices in the United States and Japan, respectively. If the claim made by the U.S. government is

$z = -1.48$, Fail to reject H_0

true, then the mean retail price in Japan will exceed the mean in the United States [i.e., $\mu_1 < \mu_2$ or $(\mu_1 - \mu_2) < 0$]. Thus, the elements of the test are as follows:

$$H_0: (\mu_1 - \mu_2) = 0 \text{ (i.e., } \mu_1 = \mu_2; \text{ note that } D_0 = 0 \text{ for this hypothesis test)}$$
$$H_a: (\mu_1 - \mu_2) < 0 \text{ (i.e., } \mu_1 < \mu_2)$$

Test statistic: $z = \dfrac{(\bar{x}_1 - \bar{x}_2) - D_0}{\sigma_{(\bar{x}_1 - \bar{x}_2)}} = \dfrac{\bar{x}_1 - \bar{x}_2 - 0}{\sigma_{(\bar{x}_1 - \bar{x}_2)}}$

Rejection region: $z < -z_{.05} = -1.645$ (see Figure 9.3)

Substituting the summary statistics given in Figure 9.1 into the test statistic, we obtain

$$z = \frac{(\bar{x}_1 - \bar{x}_2) - 0}{\sigma_{(\bar{x}_1 - \bar{x}_2)}} = \frac{(16,596 - 17,250)}{\sqrt{\dfrac{\sigma_1^2}{n_1} + \dfrac{\sigma_2^2}{n_2}}}$$

Suggested Exercise 9.24

$$\approx \frac{-654}{\sqrt{\dfrac{s_1^2}{n_1} + \dfrac{s_2^2}{n_2}}} = \frac{-654}{\sqrt{\dfrac{(1,981)^2}{50} + \dfrac{(1,865)^2}{30}}} = \frac{-654}{440.94} = -1.48$$

As you can see in Figure 9.3, the calculated z value does not fall in the rejection region. Therefore, the samples do not provide sufficient evidence, at $\alpha = .05$, for the economist to conclude that the mean retail price in Japan exceeds that in the United States.

Look Back This conclusion agrees with the inference drawn from the 95% confidence interval in Example 9.1. Generally, however, a confidence interval will provide more information on the difference in means than a test. A test can only detect whether or not a difference between the means exists, while the confidence interval provides information on the magnitude of the difference.

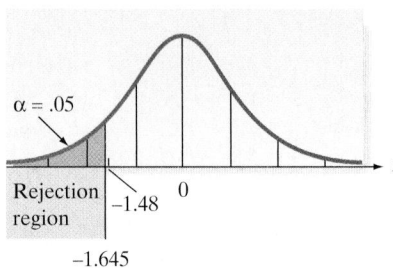

Figure 9.3
Rejection region for Example 9.2

■ ■ ■

EXAMPLE 9.3

THE p-VALUE OF A TEST FOR $\mu_1 - \mu_2$

Problem Find the observed significance level for the test in Example 9.2. Interpret the result.

Solution The alternative hypothesis in Example 9.2, $H_a: (\mu_1 - \mu_2) < 0$, required a lower one-tailed test using

$p = .0694$, Fail to reject H_0

$$z = \frac{\bar{x}_1 - \bar{x}_2}{\sigma_{(\bar{x}_1 - \bar{x}_2)}}$$

as a test statistic. Since the approximate z-value calculated from the sample data was -1.48, the observed significance level (p-value) for the lower-tailed test is the probability of observing a value of z more contradictory to the null hypothesis as $z = -1.48$; that is,

$$p\text{-value} = P(z < -1.48)$$

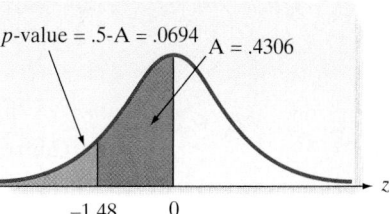

This probability is computed assuming H_0 is true and is equal to the shaded area shown in Figure 9.4.

The tabulated area corresponding to $z = 1.48$ in Table IV of Appendix B is .4306. Therefore, the observed significance level of the test is

Figure 9.4
The observed significance level for Example 9.2

$$p\text{-value} \approx .5 - .4306 = .0694$$

Since our selected α value, .05, is less than this p-value, we have insufficient evidence to reject H_0: $(\mu_1 - \mu_2) = 0$ in favor of H_a: $(\mu_1 - \mu_2) < 0$.

Look Back The p-value of the test is more easily obtained from a statistical software package. A MINITAB printout for the hypothesis test is displayed in Figure 9.5. The one-tailed p-value, highlighted on the printout, is .071, which agrees (except for rounding) with our approximated p-value.

```
Two-sample T for USA vs JAPAN

         N    Mean   StDev   SE Mean
USA      50   16596   1981     280
JAPAN    30   17250   1865     340


Difference = mu (USA) - mu (JAPAN)
Estimate for difference:  -654.000
95% upper bound for difference:  81.971
T-Test of difference = 0 (vs <): T-Value = -1.48  P-Value = 0.071  DF = 78
```

Figure 9.5
MINITAB Printout for the Comparison of U.S. and Japan Mean Automobile Prices

Now Work *Exercise 9.3b*

■ ■ ■

Small Samples

When comparing two population means with small samples (say, $n_1 < 30$ and $n_2 < 30$), the methodology of the previous three examples is invalid. The reason? When the sample sizes are small, estimates of σ_1^2 and σ_2^2 are unreliable and the

Figure 9.6

Assumptions for the two-sample t: (1) normal populations, (2) equal variances

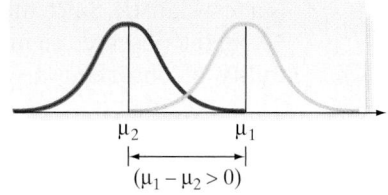

$(\mu_1 - \mu_2 > 0)$

Central Limit Theorem (which guarantees that the z statistic is normal) can no longer be applied. But as in the case of a single mean (Section 8.4), we use the familiar Student's t-distribution described in Chapter 7.

To use the t-*distribution, both sampled populations must be approximately normally distributed with equal population variances, and the random samples must be selected independently of each other.* The normality and equal variances assumptions imply relative frequency distributions for the populations that would appear as shown in Figure 9.6.

Since we assume the two populations have equal variances ($\sigma_1^2 = \sigma_2^2 = \sigma^2$), it is reasonable to use the information contained in both samples to construct a **pooled sample estimator of** σ^2 for use in confidence intervals and test statistics. Thus, if s_1^2 and s_2^2 are the two sample variances (both estimating the variance σ^2 common to both populations), the pooled estimator of σ^2, denoted as s_p^2, is

$$s_\mathrm{p}^2 = \frac{(n_1 - 1)s_1^2 + (n_2 - 1)s_2^2}{(n_1 - 1) + (n_2 - 1)} = \frac{(n_1 - 1)s_1^2 + (n_2 - 1)s_2^2}{n_1 + n_2 - 2}$$

or

$$\overbrace{\text{From sample 1}}^{} \quad \overbrace{\text{From sample 2}}^{}$$

$$s_\mathrm{p}^2 = \frac{\sum(x_1 - \bar{x}_1)^2 + \sum(x_2 - \bar{x}_2)^2}{n_1 + n_2 - 2}$$

where x_1 represents a measurement from sample 1 and x_2 represents a measurement from sample 2. Recall that the term *degrees of freedom* was defined in Section 7.2 as 1 less than the sample size. Thus, in this case, we have $(n_1 - 1)$ degrees of freedom for sample 1 and $(n_2 - 1)$ degrees of freedom for sample 2. Since we are pooling the information on σ^2 obtained from both samples, the degrees of freedom associated with the pooled variance s_p^2 is equal to the sum of the degrees of freedom for the two samples, namely, the denominator of s_p^2; that is, $(n_1 - 1) + (n_2 - 1) = n_1 + n_2 - 2$.

Note that the second formula given for s_p^2 shows that the pooled variance is simply a *weighted average* of the two sample variances, s_1^2 and s_2^2. The weight given each variance is proportional to its degrees of freedom. If the two variances have the same number of degrees of freedom (i.e., if the sample sizes are equal), then the pooled variance is a simple average of the two sample variances. The result is an average or "pooled" variance that is a better estimate of σ^2 than either s_1^2 or s_2^2 alone.

Biography

**BRADLEY EFRON
(1938–present)
The Bootstrap
Method**

Bradley Efron was raised in St. Paul, Minnesota, the son of a truck driver who was the amateur statistician for his bowling and baseball leagues. Efron received a B.S. in mathematics from California Institute of Technology in 1960, but, by his own admission, had no talent for modern abstract math. His interest in the science of statistics developed after reading a book, cover to cover, by Harold Cramer. Efron went to the University of Stanford to study statistics and earned his Ph.D. there in 1964. He has been a faculty member in Stanford's

Department of Statistics since 1966. Over his career, Efron has received numerous awards and prizes for his contributions to modern statistics, including the MacArthur Prize Fellow (1983), the American Statistical Association Wilks Medal (1990), and the Parzen Prize for Statistical Innovation (1998). In 1979, Efron invented a method—called the *bootstrap*—of estimating and testing population parameters in situations where either the sampling distribution is unknown or the assumptions are violated. The method involves repeatedly taking samples of size *n* (with replacement) from the original sample and calculating the value of the point estimate. Efron showed that the sampling distribution of the estimator is simply the frequency distribution of the bootstrap estimates.

Both the confidence interval and the test of hypothesis procedures for comparing two population means with small samples are summarized in the accompanying boxes.

Teaching Tip

Emphasize that these analyses will work *only* when the stated assumptions are valid.

Small-Sample Confidence Interval for $(\mu_1 - \mu_2)$ (Independent Samples)

$$(\bar{x}_1 - \bar{x}_2) \pm t_{\alpha/2}\sqrt{s_p^2\left(\frac{1}{n_1} + \frac{1}{n_2}\right)}$$

where $s_p^2 = \dfrac{(n_1 - 1)s_1^2 + (n_2 - 1)s_2^2}{n_1 + n_2 - 2}$

and $t_{\alpha/2}$ is based on $(n_1 + n_2 - 2)$ degrees of freedom.

Small-Sample Test of Hypothesis for $(\mu_1 - \mu_2)$ (Independent Samples)

One-Tailed Test	Two-Tailed Test
$H_0: (\mu_1 - \mu_2) = D_0$	$H_0: (\mu_1 - \mu_2) = D_0$
$H_a: (\mu_1 - \mu_2) > D_0$	$H_a: (\mu_1 - \mu_2) \neq D_0$
[or $H_a: (\mu_1 - \mu_2) > D_0$]	

Test statistic: $t = \dfrac{(\bar{x}_1 - \bar{x}_2) - D_0}{\sqrt{s_p^2\left(\dfrac{1}{n_1} + \dfrac{1}{n_2}\right)}}$

(cont'd)

Rejection region: $t < -t_\alpha$
[or $t > t_\alpha$ when $H_a: (\mu_1 - \mu_2) > D_0$]

Rejection regions: $|t| > t_{\alpha/2}$

where t_α and $t_{\alpha/2}$ are based on $(n_1 + n_2 - 2)$ degrees of freedom.

Conditions Required for Valid Small-Sample Inferences about $(\mu_1 - \mu_2)$

1. The two samples are randomly selected in an independent manner from the two target populations.
2. Both sampled populations have distributions that are approximately normal.
3. The population variances are equal (i.e., $\sigma_1^2 = \sigma_2^2$).

EXAMPLE 9.4

A SMALL-SAMPLE CONFIDENCE INTERVAL FOR $(\mu_1 - \mu_2)$

Problem Behavioral researchers have developed an index designed to measure managerial success. The index (measured on a 100-point scale) is based on the manager's length of time in the organization and his or her level within the firm; the higher the index, the more successful the manager. Suppose a researcher wants to compare the average success index for two groups of managers at a large manufacturing plant. Managers in group 1 engage in a high volume of interactions with people outside the manager's work unit. (Such interactions include phone and face-to-face meetings with customers and suppliers, outside meetings, and public relations work.) Managers in group 2 rarely interact with people outside their work unit. Independent random samples of 12 and 15 managers are selected from groups 1 and 2, respectively, and the success index of each recorded. The results of the study are given in Table 9.2.

15.86 ± 6.58

a. Use the data in the table to estimate the true mean difference between the success indexes of managers in the two groups. Use a 95% confidence interval.

b. Interpret the interval, part a.

c. What assumptions must be made in order that the estimate be valid? Are they reasonably satisfied?

 MANSUCCESS

TABLE 9.2 Managerial Success Indexes for Two Groups of Managers

Group 1						Group 2					
Interaction with Outsiders						Few Interactions					
65	58	78	60	68	69	62	53	36	34	56	50
66	70	53	71	63	63	42	57	46	68	48	42
						52	53	43			

```
Two-sample T for SUCCESS

GROUP   N    Mean   StDev   SE Mean
1       12   65.33   6.61      1.9
2       15   49.47   9.33      2.4


Difference = mu (1) - mu (2)
Estimate for difference:  15.8667
95% CI for difference:  (9.2883, 22.4451)
T-Test of difference = 0 (vs not =): T-Value = 4.97   P-Value = 0.000   DF = 25
Both use Pooled StDev = 8.2472
```

Figure 9.7

MINITAB printout for Example 9.4

Solution

a. For this experiment, let μ_1 and μ_2 represent the mean success index of group 1 and group 2 managers, respectively. Then, the objective is to obtain a 95% confidence interval for $(\mu_1 - \mu_2)$.

The first step in constructing the confidence interval is to obtain summary statistics (e.g., $\bar{x}$ and s) on the success index for each group of managers. The data of Table 9.2 were entered into a computer, and MINITAB was used to obtain these descriptive statistics. The MINITAB printout appears in Figure 9.7. Note that $\bar{x}_1 = 65.33$, $s_1 = 6.61$, $\bar{x}_2 = 49.47$, and $s_2 = 9.33$.

Next, we calculate the pooled estimate of variance:

$$s_p^2 = \frac{(n_1 - 1)s_1^2 + (n_2 - 1)s_2^2}{n_1 + n_2 - 2}$$

$$= \frac{(12 - 1)(6.61)^2 + (15 - 1)(9.33)^2}{12 + 15 - 2} = 67.97$$

where s_p^2 is based on $(n_1 + n_2 - 2) = (12 + 15 - 2) = 25$ degrees of freedom. Also, we find $t_{\alpha/2} = t_{.025} = 2.06$ (based on 25 degrees of freedom) from Table VI of Appendix B.

Suggested Exercise 9.15

Finally, the 95% confidence interval for $(\mu_1 - \mu_2)$, the difference between mean managerial success indexes for the two groups, is

$$(\bar{x}_1 - \bar{x}_2) \pm t_{\alpha/2}\sqrt{s_p^2\left(\frac{1}{n_1} + \frac{1}{n_2}\right)} = 65.33 - 49.47 \pm t_{.025}\sqrt{67.97\left(\frac{1}{12} + \frac{1}{15}\right)}$$

$$= 15.86 \pm (2.06)(3.19)$$

$$= 15.86 \pm 6.58$$

Teaching Tip

When interpreting the confidence interval for $\mu_1 - \mu_2$, it is usually important to identify if the value 0 is contained in the confidence interval. Discuss why the 0 value is significant in terms of interpretations.

or (9.28, 22.44). This interval agrees (except for rounding) with the one shown at the bottom of the MINITAB printout, Figure 9.7.

b. Notice that the confidence interval includes only positive differences. Consequently, we are 95% confident that $(\mu_1 - \mu_2)$ exceeds 0. In fact, we estimate the mean success index, μ_1, for managers with a high volume of outsider interaction (group 1) to be anywhere between 9.28 and 22.44 points higher than the mean success index, μ_2, of managers with few interactions (group 2).

c. To properly use the small-sample confidence interval, the following assumptions must be satisfied:

1. The samples of managers are randomly and independently selected from the populations of group 1 and group 2 managers.

2. The success indexes are normally distributed for both groups of managers.

3. The variance of the success indexes are the same for the two populations, (i.e., $\sigma_1^2 = \sigma_2^2$).

The first assumption is satisfied, based on the information provided about the sampling procedure in the problem description. To check the plausibility of the remaining two assumptions, we resort to graphical methods. Figure 9.8 is a portion of an SPSS printout that displays normal probability plots (called *Q-Q plots*) for the success indexes of the two samples of managers. The near straight-line trends on both plots indicate that the success index distributions are approximately mound-shaped and symmetric. Consequently, each sample data set appears to come from a population that is approximately normal.

One way to check assumption #3 is to test the null hypothesis H_0: $\sigma_1^2 = \sigma_2^2$. This test is covered in optional Section 9.5. Another approach is to examine box plots for the sample data. Figure 9.9 is MINITAB printout that shows side-by-side vertical box plots for the success indexes in the two samples. Recall,

Figure 9.8

SPSS normal probability plots for Example 9.4

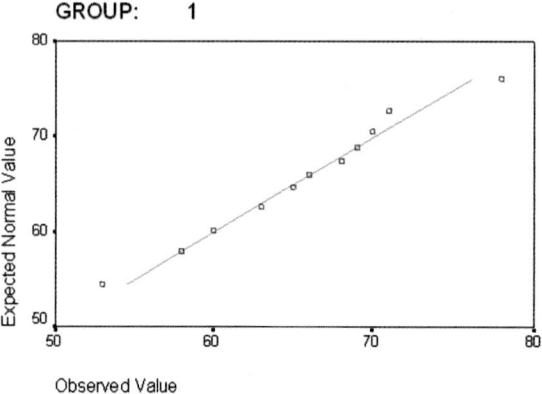

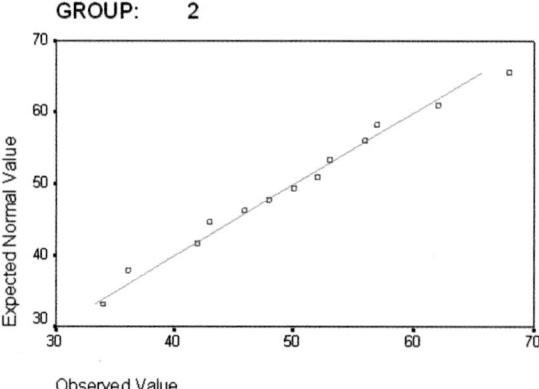

Figure 9.9
MINITAB box plots
for Example 9.4

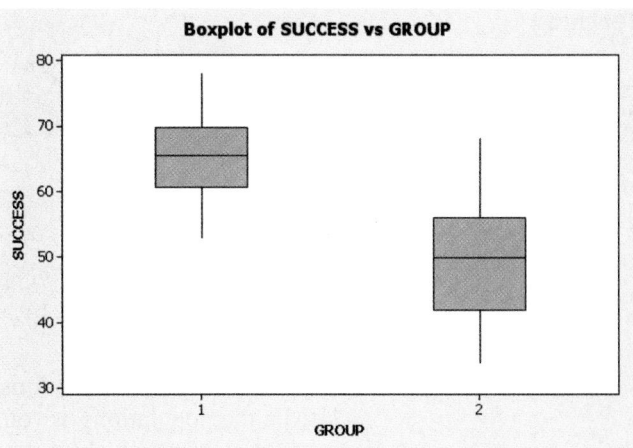

from Section 2.9, that the box plot represents the "spread" of a data set. The two box plots appear to have about the same spread; thus, the samples appear to come from populations with approximately the same variance.

Look Back All three assumptions appear to be reasonably satisfied for this application of the small-sample confidence interval.

Now Work *Exercise 9.7*

■ ■ ■

The two-sample t-statistic is a powerful tool for comparing population means when the assumptions are satisfied. It has also been shown to retain its usefulness when the sampled populations are only approximately normally distributed. And when the sample sizes are equal, the assumption of equal population variances can be relaxed. That is, if $n_1 = n_2$, then σ_1^2 and σ_2^2 can be quite different and the test statistic will still possess, approximately, a Student's t-distribution. In the case where $\sigma_1^2 \neq \sigma_2^2$ and $n_1 \neq n_2$, an approximate small-sample confidence interval or test can be obtained by modifying the degrees of freedom associated with the t-distribution.

The next box gives the approximate small-sample procedures to use when the assumption of equal variances is violated. The test for the "unequal sample sizes" case is based on Satterhwaite's (1946) approximation.

Approximate Small-Sample Procedures when $\sigma_1^2 \neq \sigma_2^2$

1. **Equal sample sizes $(n_1 = n_2 = n)$**

   Confidence interval: $\qquad\qquad\qquad (\bar{x}_1 - \bar{x}_2) \pm t_{\alpha/2}\sqrt{(s_1^2 + s_2^2)/n}$

   Test statistic for H_0: $(\mu_1 - \mu_2) = 0$: $\quad t = (\bar{x}_1 - \bar{x}_2)/\sqrt{(s_1^2 + s_2^2)/n}$

   where t is based on $\nu = n_1 + n_2 - 2 = 2(n - 1)$ degrees of freedom.

2. **Unequal sample sizes $(n_1 \neq n_2)$**

   Confidence interval: $(\bar{x}_1 - \bar{x}_2) \pm t_{\alpha/2}\sqrt{(s_1^2/n_1) + (s_2^2/n_2)}$

(cont'd)

Teaching Tip

A parametric procedure exists for comparing two population means when the equal variance assumption is violated but is not presented in this text. In general, however, the nonparametric analyses of Chapter 16 are useful whenever the assumptions are not satisfied.

Test statistic for H_0: $(\mu_1 - \mu_2) = 0$: $t = (\bar{x}_1 - \bar{x}_2)/\sqrt{(s_1^2/n_1) + (s_2^2/n_2)}$
where t is based on degrees of freedom equal to

$$\nu = \frac{(s_1^2/n_1 + s_2^2/n_2)^2}{\dfrac{(s_1^2/n_1)^2}{n_1 - 1} + \dfrac{(s_2^2/n_2)^2}{n_2 - 1}}$$

Note: The value of ν will generally not be an integer. Round ν down to the nearest integer to use the t-table.

When the assumptions are clearly not satisfied, you can select larger samples from the populations or you can use other available statistical tests (nonparametric statistical tests, which are described in Chapter 16).

What Should You Do If the Assumptions Are Not Satisfied?

Answer: If you are concerned that the assumptions are not satisfied, use the Wilcoxon rank sum test for independent samples to test for a shift in population distributions. See Chapter 16.

Statistics in Action Revisited
Comparing Means for the Two SMWT Survey Groups

In the Statistics in Action study for this chapter (see p. 481), the researchers want to compare two groups of AT&T workers in self-managed work teams (SMWTs). Group 1 ($n_1 = 47$) were those employees who reported positive spillover of work skills to family life. Group 2 ($n_2 = 67$) were those employees who did not report positive work spillover. The researchers collected data on seven quantitative variables and one qualitative variable for each worker. The quantitative variables (listed in Table SIA9.1, p. 479) are Use of creative ideas, Utilization of information, Participation in decisions regarding personnel matters, Good use of skills, Task identity, Age, and Education. (*Reminder:* Age and Education are measured in years, while the other quantitative variables are measured on a 7-point scale.) These data are saved in the SPILLOVER file.

Recall that the researchers' objectives were to compare the two groups of workers on each characteristic. They accomplished this by conducting a two-tailed test of the null hypothesis, H_0: $(\mu_1 - \mu_2) = 0$, for each quantitative variable. Since both samples are large, ($n_1 = 47$ and $n_2 = 67$), the large-sample z-test is appropriate. We conducted these tests using SPSS. The output is shown in Figure SIA9.1. (*Note:* The large-sample test results are provided in the row labeled "Equal variances not assumed" on the SPSS printout.)

The two-tailed p-values of the tests are highlighted on Figure SIA9.1. The only variables that show a significant difference at $\alpha = .05$ are Use of creative ideas (p-value $= .000$) and Good use of skills (p-value $= .000$). The two demographic variables, Age and Education, are clearly nonsignificant (p-values of .460 and .534, respectively), as are Utilization of information (p-value $= .136$) and Participation in decisions regarding personnel matters (p-value $= .135$). Although not significant at $\alpha = .05$, Task identity (p-value $= .087$). shows a significant difference at $\alpha = .10$.

In the cases of the significant variables, Use of creative ideas and Good use of skills, and the borderline significant variable Task identity, the estimate of the mean difference ($\mu_1 - \mu_2$) is positive. That is, for these variables the mean for the positive work spillover group is significantly larger than the mean for the nonspillover group. Consequently, the researchers concluded that Use of creative ideas and Good use of skills were the characteristics most highly associated with positive work spillover, followed by Task identity.

After reading this section, you now know that these conclusions can be readily obtained by examining the 95% confidence intervals for ($\mu_1 - \mu_2$) shown in the last column of the SPSS printout. Only the variables Use of creative ideas and Good use of skills have a confidence interval will all positive numbers.

Independent Samples Test

		Levene's Test for Equality of Variances		t-test for Equality of Means						
		F	Sig.	t	df	Sig. (2-tailed)	Mean Difference	Std. Error Difference	95% Confidence Interval of the Difference	
									Lower	Upper
CREATIVE	Equal variances assumed	16.479	.000	8.565	112	.000	.81	.094	.621	.994
	Equal variances not assumed			8.847	108.727	.000	.81	.091	.627	.988
INFO	Equal variances assumed	6.501	.012	1.437	112	.153	.56	.387	-.210	1.323
	Equal variances not assumed			1.503	110.916	.136	.56	.370	-.177	1.289
DECPERS	Equal variances assumed	.059	.808	1.514	112	.133	.57	.378	-.177	1.323
	Equal variances not assumed			1.506	97.314	.135	.57	.380	-.182	1.328
SKILLS	Equal variances assumed	.139	.710	4.812	112	.000	1.03	.214	.606	1.454
	Equal variances not assumed			4.766	95.741	.000	1.03	.216	.601	1.459
TASKID	Equal variances assumed	27.854	.000	1.902	112	.060	.57	.299	-.024	1.163
	Equal variances not assumed			1.738	66.922	.087	.57	.328	-.085	1.224
AGE	Equal variances assumed	2.923	.090	.702	112	.484	.95	1.360	-1.740	3.649
	Equal variances not assumed			.742	111.872	.460	.95	1.287	-1.595	3.504
EDYRS	Equal variances assumed	4.430	.038	-.600	112	.549	-.14	.231	-.597	.319
	Equal variances not assumed			-.623	109.709	.534	-.14	.223	-.580	.303

Figure SIA9.1

SPSS comparison of two SMWT groups

Exercises 9.1–9.24

Learning the Mechanics

9.1 The purpose of this exercise is to compare the variability of $\bar{x}_1$ and $\bar{x}_2$ with the variability of $(\bar{x}_1 - \bar{x}_2)$.

a. Suppose the first sample is selected from a population with mean $\mu_1 = 150$ and variance $\sigma_1^2 = 900$. Within what range should the sample mean vary about 95% of the time in repeated samples of 100 measurements from this distribution? That is, construct an interval extending 2 standard deviations of $\bar{x}_1$ on each side of μ_1.

b. Suppose the second sample is selected independently of the first from a second population with mean $\mu_2 = 150$ and variance $\sigma_2^2 = 1,600$. Within what range should the sample mean vary about 95% of the time in repeated samples of 100 measurements from this distribution? That is, construct an interval extending 2 standard deviations of $\bar{x}_2$ on each side of μ_2.

c. Now consider the difference between the two sample means $(\bar{x}_1 - \bar{x}_2)$. What are the mean and standard deviation of the sampling distribution of $(\bar{x}_1 - \bar{x}_2)$?

d. Within what range should the difference in sample means vary about 95% of the time in repeated inde-

pendent samples of 100 measurements each from the two populations?

e. What, in general, can be said about the variability of the difference between independent sample means relative to the variability of the individual sample means?

9.2 Independent random samples of 64 observations each are chosen from two normal populations with the following means and standard deviations:

Population 1	Population 2
$\mu_1 = 12$	$\mu_2 = 10$
$\sigma_1 = 4$	$\sigma_2 = 3$

Let $\bar{x}_1$ and $\bar{x}_2$ denote the two sample means.

a. Give the mean and standard deviation of the sampling distribution of $\bar{x}_1$.   12, .5

b. Give the mean and standard deviation of the sampling distribution of $\bar{x}_2$.   10, .375

c. Suppose you were to calculate the difference $(\bar{x}_1 - \bar{x}_2)$ between the sample means. Find the mean and standard deviation of the sampling distribution of $(\bar{x}_1 - \bar{x}_2)$.   2, .625

d. Will the statistic $(\bar{x}_1 - \bar{x}_2)$ be normally distributed? Explain.   Yes

9.3 In order to compare the means of two populations, independent random samples of 400 observations are selected from each population, with the following results:

Sample 1	Sample 2
$\bar{x}_1 = 5{,}275$	$\bar{x}_2 = 5{,}240$
$s_1 = 150$	$s_2 = 200$

a. Use a 95% confidence interval to estimate the difference between the population means $(\mu_1 - \mu_2)$. Interpret the confidence interval.

b. Test the null hypothesis $H_0: (\mu_1 - \mu_2) = 0$ versus the alternative hypothesis $H_a: (\mu_1 - \mu_2) \neq 0$. Give the significance level of the test, and interpret the result.

c. Suppose the test in part b was conducted with the alternative hypothesis $H_a: (\mu_1 - \mu_2) > 0$. How would your answer to part b change?

d. Test the null hypothesis $H_0: (\mu_1 - \mu_2) = 25$ versus $H_a: (\mu_1 - \mu_2) \neq 25$. Give the significance level, and interpret the result. Compare your answer to the test conducted in part b. $p = .4238$

e. What assumptions are necessary to ensure the validity of the inferential procedures applied in parts a–d?

9.4 To use the t statistic to test for a difference between the means of two populations, what assumptions must be made about the two populations? About the two samples?

9.5 Two populations are described in each of the following cases. In which cases would it be appropriate to apply the small-sample t-test to investigate the difference between the population means?

a. Population 1: Normal distribution with variance σ_1^2. Population 2: Skewed to the right with variance $\sigma_2^2 = \sigma_1^2$.   No

b. Population 1: Normal distribution with variance σ_1^2. Population 2: Normal distribution with variance $\sigma_2^2 \neq \sigma_1^2$.   No

c. Population 1: Skewed to the left with variance σ_1^2. Population 2: Skewed to the left with variance $\sigma_2^2 = \sigma_1^2$.   No

d. Population 1: Normal distribution with variance σ_1^2. Population 2: Normal distribution with variance $\sigma_2^2 = \sigma_1^2$.   Yes

e. Population 1: Uniform distribution with variance σ_1^2. Population 2: Uniform distribution with variance $\sigma_2^2 = \sigma_1^2$.   No

9.6 Assume that $\sigma_1^2 = \sigma_2^2 = \sigma^2$. Calculate the pooled estimator of σ^2 for each of the following cases:

a. $s_1^2 = 120$, $s_2^2 = 100$, $n_1 = n_2 = 25$ 110

b. $s_1^2 = 12$, $s_2^2 = 20$, $n_1 = 20$, $n_2 = 10$ 14.57

c. $s_1^2 = .15$, $s_2^2 = .20$, $n_1 = 6$, $n_2 = 10$ .1821

d. $s_1^2 = 3{,}000$, $s_2^2 = 2{,}500$, $n_1 = 16$, $n_2 = 17$ 2,741.9

e. Note that the pooled estimate is a weighted average of the sample variances. To which of the variances does the pooled estimate fall nearer in each of the above cases?

9.7 Independent random samples from normal populations produced the results shown in the next table.

a. Calculate the pooled estimate of σ^2.

b. Do the data provide sufficient evidence to indicate that $\mu_2 > \mu_1$? Test using $\alpha = .10$.

LM9_7

Sample 1	Sample 2
1.2	4.2
3.1	2.7
1.7	3.6
2.8	3.9
3.0	

c. Find a 90% confidence interval for $(\mu_1 - \mu_2)$.

d. Which of the two inferential procedures, the test of hypothesis in part b or the confidence interval in part c, provides more information about $(\mu_1 - \mu_2)$?

9.8 Two independent random samples have been selected, 100 observations from population 1 and 100 from population 2. Sample means $\bar{x}_1 = 15.5$ and $\bar{x}_2 = 26.6$ were obtained. From previous experience with these populations, it is known that the variances are $\sigma_1^2 = 9$ and $\sigma_2^2 = 16$.

a. Find $\sigma_{(\bar{x}_1 - \bar{x}_2)}$.   .5

b. Sketch the approximate sampling distribution for $(\bar{x}_1 - \bar{x}_2)$ assuming $(\mu_1 - \mu_2) = 10$.

c. Locate the observed value of $(\bar{x}_1 - \bar{x}_2)$ on the graph you drew in part b. Does it appear that this value contradicts the null hypothesis $H_0: (\mu_1 - \mu_2) = 10$?

d. Use the z-table on the inside of the front cover to determine the rejection region for the test of $H_0: (\mu_1 - \mu_2) = 10$ against $H_0: (\mu_1 - \mu_2) \neq 10$. Use $\alpha = .05$. $z > 1.96$ or $z < -1.96$

e. Conduct the hypothesis test of part d and interpret your result. $z = -22.2$

f. Construct a 95% confidence interval for $(\mu_1 - \mu_2)$. Interpret the interval. $-11.1 \pm .98$

g. Which inference provides more information about the value of $(\mu_1 - \mu_2)$—the test of hypothesis in part e or the confidence interval in part f?

9.9 Independent random samples of $n_1 = 233$ and $n_2 = 312$ are selected from two populations and used to test the hypothesis $H_0: (\mu_1 - \mu_2) = 0$ against the alternative $H_a: (\mu_1 - \mu_2) \neq 0$.

a. The two-tailed p-value of the test is .1150. Interpret this result.

b. If the alternative hypothesis had been $H_a: (\mu_1 - \mu_2) < 0$, how would the p-value change? Interpret the p-value for this one-tailed test.

9.10 Independent random samples from approximately normal populations produced the results shown below:

LM9_10

Sample 1				Sample 2			
52	33	42	44	52	43	47	56
41	50	44	51	62	53	61	50
45	38	37	40	56	52	53	60
44	50	43		50	48	60	55

a. Do the data provide sufficient evidence to conclude that $(\mu_2 - \mu_1) > 10$? Test using $\alpha = .01$. $t = .01$
b. Construct a 98% confidence interval for $(\mu_2 - \mu_1)$. Interpret your result. 10.025 ± 4.817

9.11 Independent random samples selected from two normal populations produced the sample means and standard deviations shown below.

Sample 1	Sample 2
$n_1 = 17$	$n_2 = 12$
$\bar{x}_1 = 5.4$	$\bar{x}_2 = 7.9$
$s_1 = 3.4$	$s_2 = 4.8$

a. Conduct the test $H_0: (\mu_1 - \mu_2) = 0$ against $H_a: (\mu_1 - \mu_2) \neq 0$. Interpret the results.
b. Estimate $(\mu_1 - \mu_2)$ using a 95% confidence interval.

Applying the Concepts—Basic

DIAMONDS

9.12 Refer to the data for 308 diamonds saved in the DIA-MONDS file. Two quantitative variables in the data set are number of carats and selling price. One of the qualitative variables is the independent certification body that assessed each of the stones. Three certification bodies were used: GIA, IGI, and HRD. The MINITAB printout in the next column gives the means and standard deviations of the quantitative variables for each certification body.

a. Construct a 95% confidence interval for the difference between the mean carat size of diamonds certified by GIA and the mean carat size of diamonds certified by HRD. $-.1406 \pm .0563$
b. Interpret the result, part a. Specifically, which (if either) of the two population means compared is larger and by how much?
c. Construct a 95% confidence interval for the difference between the mean carat size of diamonds certified by GIA and the mean carat size of diamonds certified by IGI. $.3058 \pm .0620$

Descriptive Statistics: CARAT, PRICE

Variable	CERT	N	Mean	StDev
CARAT	GIA	151	0.6723	0.2456
	HRD	79	0.8129	0.1831
	IGI	78	0.3665	0.2163
PRICE	GIA	151	5310	3247
	HRD	79	7181	2898
	IGI	78	2267	2121

MINITAB printout for Exercise 9.12

d. Interpret the result, part c. Specifically, which (if either) of the two population means is larger and by how much?
e. Construct a 95% confidence interval for the difference between the mean selling price of diamonds certified by HRD and the mean selling price of diamonds certified by IGI. 4914 ± 793.7
f. Interpret the result, part e. Specifically, which (if either) of the two population means is larger and by how much?

9.13 Refer to the International Association for Time Use Research study on cable TV viewers who purchase items from one of the home shopping channels, Exercise 8.42 (p. 436). The 1,600 sampled viewers described their motivation for watching cable TV shopping networks by giving their level of agreement (on a 5-point scale, where $1 =$ strongly disagree and $5 =$ strongly agree) with the statement, "I have nothing else to do." The researcher wanted to compare the mean responses of viewers who watch the shopping network at noon with those viewers who do not watch at noon.

a. Give the null and alternative hypotheses for determining whether the mean response of noontime watchers differs from the mean response of non-noontime watchers. $H_0: \mu_1 = \mu_2$ vs. $H_a: \mu_1 \neq \mu_2$
b. The researcher found the p-value for the test, part **a**, to be .02. Interpret this result, assuming $\alpha = .05$.
c. Interpret the result, part **b**, assuming $\alpha = .01$.
d. The sample means for noontime watchers and non-watchers were found to be 3.3 and 3.4, respectively. Comment on the "practical significance" of this result.

9.14 A study published in *The Journal of American Academy of Business, Cambridge* (March 2002) examined whether the perception of service quality at five-star hotels in Jamaica differed by gender. Hotel guests were randomly selected from the lobby and restaurant areas and asked to rate ten service-related items (e.g., "The personal attention you received from our employees"). Each item was rated on a 5-point scale (1 = "much worse than I expected," 5 = "much better than I expected") and the sum of the items for each guest was determined. A summary of the guest scores are provided in the next table.

Gender	Sample Size	Mean Score	Standard Deviation
Males	127	39.08	6.73
Females	114	38.79	6.94

a. Construct a 90% confidence interval for the difference between the population mean service-rating scores given by male and female guests at Jamaican five-star hotels. .29 ± 1.452

b. Use the interval, part a, to make an inference about whether the perception of service quality at five-star hotels in Jamaica differs by gender.

9.15 The *International Journal of Environmental Health Research* (Vol. 4, 1994) reported on the solid-waste generation rates (in kilograms per capita per day) for samples of cities from industrialized and middle-income countries. The data are provided in the table.

🖲 **SOLWASTE**

Industrialized Countries		Middle-Income Countries	
New York (USA)	2.27	Singapore	0.87
Phoenix (USA)	2.31	Hong Kong	0.85
London (UK)	2.24	Medellin (Colombia)	0.54
Hamburg (Germany)	2.18	Kano (Nigeria)	0.46
Rome (Italy)	2.15	Manila (Philippines)	0.50
		Cairo (Egypt)	0.50
		Tunis (Tunisia)	0.56

a. Based on only a visual inspection of the data, does it appear that the mean waste generation rates of cities in industrialized and middle-income countries differ?

b. Conduct a test of hypothesis (at $\alpha = .05$) to support your observation in part **a**.

9.16 High job turnover rates are often associated with high product defect rates, since high turnover rates mean more inexperienced workers who are unfamiliar with the company's product lines (Stevenson, *Production/Operations Management*, 2000). In a recent study, five Japanese and five U.S. plants that manufacture air conditioners were randomly sampled; their turnover rates are listed in the table.

🖲 **TURNOVER**

U.S. Plants	Japanese Plants
7.11%	3.52%
6.06	2.02
8.00	4.91
6.87	3.22
4.77	1.92

a. Do the data provide sufficient evidence to indicate that the mean annual percentage turnover for U.S. plants exceeds the corresponding mean percentage for Japanese plants? Test using $\alpha = .05$. *t* = 4.46

b. Find and interpret the observed significance level of the test you conducted in part **a**. .0011

c. List any assumptions you made in conducting the hypothesis test of part **a**. Comment on their validity for this application.

Applying the Concepts—Intermediate

9.17 *Chance* (Fall 2002) described a lawsuit where Intel Corp. was charged with infringing on a patent for an invention used in the automatic manufacture of computer chips. In response, Intel accused the inventor of adding material to his patent notebook after the patent was witnessed and granted. The case rested on whether a patent witness' signature was written on top of key text in the notebook, or under the key text. Intel hired a physicist who used an X-ray beam to measure the relative concentration of certain elements (e.g., nickel, zinc, potassium) at several spots on the notebook page. The zinc measurements for three notebook locations—on a text line, on a witness line, and on the intersection of the witness and text line—are provided in the table.

🖲 **PATENT**

Text line:	.335	.374	.440			
Witness line:	.210	.262	.188	.329	.439	.397
Intersection:	.393	.353	.285	.295	.319	

a. Use a test or a confidence interval (at $\alpha = .05$) to compare the mean zinc measurement for the text-line with the mean for the intersection. *t* = 1.56

b. Use a test or a confidence interval (at $\alpha = .05$) to compare the mean zinc measurement for the witness-line with the mean for the intersection. *t* = −.50

c. From the results, parts **a** and **b**, what can you infer about the mean zinc measurements at the three notebook locations?

d. What assumptions are required for the inferences to be valid? Are they reasonably satisfied?

9.18 Many psychologists believe that knowledge of a college student's relationships with his or her parents can be useful in predicting the student's future interpersonal relationships both on the job and in private life. Researchers at the University of South Alabama compared the attitudes of male and female students toward their fathers (*Journal of Genetic Psychology*, Mar. 1998). Using a five-point Likert-type scale, they asked each group to complete the following statement: My relationship with my father can best be described as (1) Awful! (2) Poor, (3) Average, (4) Good, or (5) Great! The data (adapted from the article) are listed in the next table.

FATHER

Father Ratings for Females

5	2	5	5	3	3	2	5	2	1	5	4	2	5	3
5	4	2	5	5	2	3	4	3	5	4	4	4	2	1
5	3	5	4	4	5	5	5	3	5	5	4	5	4	5
1	5	4	4	5	4	4	2	1	1	4	2	3	4
2	4	2	3	5	2	4	5	5	5	5	5	5	1	2
2	5	4	1	2	5	4	3	5	5	3	5	5	5	2

Father Ratings for Males

4	4	4	3	3	5	4	5	4	5	5	3	4	4	5
2	3	2	5	4	5	3	5	5	4	3	5	4	4	3
5	4	2	4	3	4	4	5	3	4	5	3	2	5

Data adapted from Vitulli, William F., and Richardson, Deanna K., "College Student's Attitudes toward Relationships with Parents: A Five-Year Comparative Analysis," *Journal of Genetic Psychology*, Vol. 159, No. 1, Mar. 1998, pp. 45–52.

a. Do male college students tend to have better relationships, on average, with their fathers than female students? Conduct the appropriate hypothesis test using $\alpha = .01$. $z = -1.14$

b. Find the p-value of the test you conducted in part **a.**

c. What assumptions, if any, about the samples did you have to make to ensure the validity of the hypothesis test you conducted?

d. Refer to part **c.** If you made assumptions, check to see if they are reasonably satisfied. If no assumptions were necessary, explain why.

9.19 *Ingratiation* is defined as a class of strategic behaviors designed to make others believe in the attractiveness of one's personal qualities. In organizational settings, individuals use such behaviors to influence superiors in order to attain personal goals. An index that measures ingratiatory behavior, called the Measure of Ingratiatory Behaviors in Organizational Settings (MIBOS) Index, was applied independently to a sample of managers employed by four manufacturing companies in the southeastern United States and to clerical personnel from a large university in the northwestern United States (*Journal of Applied Psychology*, Dec. 1998). Scores are reported on a five-point scale with higher scores indicating more extensive ingratiatory behavior. Summary statistics are shown in the table.

Managers	Clerical Personnel
$n_1 = 288$	$n_2 = 110$
$\bar{x}_1 = 2.41$	$\bar{x}_2 = 1.90$
$s_1 = .74$	$s_2 = .59$

Source: Harrison, Allison W., Hochwarter, Wayne A., Perrewe, Pamela L., and Ralston, David A., "The Ingratiation Construct: An Assessment of the Validity of the Measure of Ingratiatory Behaviors in Organization Settings (MIBOS)." *Journal of Applied Psychology*, Vol. 86, No. 6, Dec. 1998, pp. 932–943.

a. Specify the null and alternative hypotheses you would use to test for a difference in ingratiatory behavior between managers and clerical personnel.

b. Conduct the test of part **a** using $\alpha = .05$. Interpret the results of the test in the context of the problem.

c. Construct a 95% confidence interval for $(\mu_1 - \mu_2)$ and interpret the result. Your conclusion should agree with your answer in part **b.** (.37, .65)

9.20 Some college professors make bound lecture notes available to their classes in an effort to improve teaching effectiveness. *Marketing Educational Review* (Fall 1994) published a study of business students' opinions of lecture notes. Two groups of students were surveyed—86 students enrolled in a promotional strategy class that required the purchase of lecture notes, and 35 students enrolled in a sales/retailing elective that did not offer lecture notes. At the end of the semester, the students were asked to respond to the statement: "Having a copy of the lecture notes was [would be] helpful in understanding the material." Responses were measured on a nine-point semantic difference scale, where 1 = "strongly disagree" and 9 = "strongly agree." A summary of the results is reported in the table.

Classes Buying Lecture Notes	Classes Not Buying Lecture Notes
$n_1 = 86$	$n_2 = 35$
$\bar{x}_1 = 8.48$	$\bar{x}_2 = 7.80$
$s_1^2 = 0.94$	$s_2^2 = 2.99$

Source: Gray, J. I., and Abernathy, A. M. "Pros and Cons of Lecture Notes and Handout Packages: Faculty and Student Opinions," *Marketing Education Review*, Vol. 4, No. 3, Fall 1984, p. 25 (Table 4), American Marketing Association.

a. Describe the two populations involved in the comparison.

b. Do the samples provide sufficient evidence to conclude that there is a difference in the mean responses of the two groups of students? Test using $\alpha = .01$.

c. Construct a 99% confidence interval for $(\mu_1 - \mu_2)$. Interpret the result. $.68 \pm .801$

d. Would a 95% confidence interval for $(\mu_1 - \mu_2)$ be narrower or wider than the one you found in part c? Why? Narrower

9.21 Marketing strategists would like to predict consumer response to new products and their accompanying promotional schemes. Consequently, studies that examine the differences between buyers and nonbuyers of a product are of interest. One classic study conducted by Shuchman and Riesz (*Journal of Marketing Research*, Feb. 1975) was aimed at characterizing the purchasers and nonpurchasers of Crest toothpaste. The researchers demonstrated that both the mean household size (number of persons) and mean household income were significantly larger for purchasers than for nonpurchasers. A similar study utilized independent random samples of size 20 and yielded the data shown in the table below on the age of the householder primarily responsible for buying toothpaste.

CREST

Purchasers						Nonpurchasers					
34	35	23	44	52	46	28	22	44	33	55	63
28	48	28	34	33	52	45	31	60	54	53	58
41	32	34	49	50	45	52	52	66	35	25	48
29	59					59	61				

a. Do the data present sufficient evidence to conclude there is a difference in the mean age of purchasers and nonpurchasers? Use $\alpha = .10$. $t = -1.96$
b. What assumptions are necessary in order to aswer part a?
c. Find the observed significance level for the test and interpret its value. $.05$
d. Calculate and interpret a 90% confidence interval for the difference between the mean ages of purchasers and nonpurchasers.

9.22 Suppose you manage a plant that purifies its liquid waste and discharges the water into a local river. An EPA inspector has collected water specimens of the discharge of your plant and also water specimens in the river upstream from your plant. Each water specimen is divided into five parts, the bacteria count is read on each, and the median count for each specimen is reported. The bacteria counts for each of six specimens are reported in the following table for the two locations.

BACTERIA

Plant Discharge			Upstream		
30.1	36.2	33.4	29.7	30.3	26.4
28.2	29.8	34.9	27.3	31.7	32.3

a. Why might the bacteria counts shown here tend to be approximately normally distributed?
b. What are the appropriate null and alternative hypotheses to test whether the mean bacteria count for the plant discharge exceeds that for the upstream location? Be sure to define any symbols you use.
c. Conduct the test, part b. Carefully interpret the results. $t = 1.53$
d. What assumptions are necessary to ensure the validity of this test?

9.23 Rutgers professor Carol Byrd-Bredbenner studied the trend in prime-time television food advertising (*Nutrition & Food Science*, Vol. 30, 2000). Independent random samples of prime-time TV commercials for food products were recorded in 1992 and 1998, and the length of each commercial (in seconds) determined. The results are summarized below. Use the tools of this section to determine if a trend exists over the 6-year period. $z = .29$

Year	Number of Commercials	Mean Length	Standard Deviation
1992	105	24.52	7.32
1998	106	24.21	8.21

Applying the Concepts—Advanced

9.24 Valparaiso University professors D. L. Schroeder and K. E. Reichardt conducted a salary survey of members of the Institute of Management Accountants (IMA) and reported the results in *Management Accounting* (June 1995). A salary questionnaire was mailed to a random sample of 4,800 IMA members; 2,287 were returned and form the database for the study. The researchers compared average salaries by management level, education, and gender. Some of the results for entry level managers are shown in the table below.
a. Suppose you want to make an inference about the difference between salaries of male and female entry-level managers who earned a CPA degree, at a 95% level of confidence. Why is this impossible to do using the information in the table?
b. Make the inference, part a, assuming the salary standard deviation for male and female entry-level managers with CPAs are $4,000 and $3,000, respectively.
c. Repeat part b, but assume the male and female salary standard deviations are $16,000 and $12,000, respectively. $4,707 \pm 5,888.4$
d. Compare the two inferences, parts b and c.
e. Suppose you want to compare the mean salaries of male entry-level managers with a CPA to the mean salary of male entry-level managers without a CPA degree. Give sample standard deviation values that will yield a significant difference between the two means, at $\alpha = .05$. $\sigma < 2,597.17$
f. In your opinion, are the sample standard deviations, part e, reasonable values for the salary data? Explain.

	CPA Degree		Baccalaureate Degree No CPA	
	Men	Women	Men	Women
Mean Salary	$40,084	$35,377	$39,268	$33,159
Number of Respondents	48	39	205	177

Source: Schroeder, D. L., and Reichardt, K. E. "Salaries 1994." *Management Accounting*, Vol. 76, No. 12, June 1995, p. 34 (Table 12).

9.2 Comparing Two Population Means: Paired Difference Experiments

Suppose you want to compare the mean daily sales of two restaurants located in the same city. If you were to record the restaurants' total sales for each of 12 randomly selected days during a six-month period, the results might appear as shown in Table 9.3. Do these data provide evidence of a difference between the mean daily sales of the two restaurants?

 RESTSALES

TABLE 9.3   Daily Sales for Two Restaurants

Day	Restaurant 1 x_1	Restaurant 2 x_2
1 (Wednesday)	$1,005	$ 918
2 (Saturday)	2,073	1,971
3 (Tuesday)	873	825
4 (Wednesday)	1,074	999
5 (Friday)	1,932	1,827
6 (Thursday)	1,338	1,281
7 (Thursday)	1,449	1,302
8 (Monday)	759	678
9 (Friday)	1,905	1,782
10 (Monday)	693	639
11 (Saturday)	2,106	2,049
12 (Tuesday)	981	933

We want to test the null hypothesis that the mean daily sales, μ_1 and μ_2, for the two restaurants are equal against the alternative hypothesis that they differ; that is,

$$H_0: (\mu_1 - \mu_2) = 0$$
$$H_a: (\mu_1 - \mu_2) \neq 0$$

One way to conduct this test is to use the t-statistic for two independent samples (Section 9.1). The analysis is shown on the SPSS printout, Figure 9.10. The test statistic, $t = .384$, is highlighted on the printout as well as the p-value of the test, p-value $= .705$. At $\alpha = .10$, the p-value exceeds α. Thus, from *this* analysis we might conclude that insufficient evidence exists to infer that there is a difference in mean daily sales for the two restaurants.

If you carefully examine the data in Table 9.3, however, you will find this conclusion difficult to accept. The sales of restaurant 1 exceed those of restaurant 2 *for every one of the randomly selected 12 days*. This, in itself, is strong evidence to indicate that μ_1 differs from μ_2, and we will subsequently confirm this fact. Why, then, was the t-test unable to detect this difference? The answer is: *The independent samples* t-*test is not a valid procedure to use with this set of data.*

The t-test is inappropriate because the assumption of independent samples is invalid. We have randomly chosen *days,* and thus, once we have chosen the sample of days for restaurant 1, we have *not* independently chosen the sample of days for restaurant 2. The dependence between observations within days can be seen by

Group Statistics

	REST	N	Mean	Std. Deviation	Std. Error Mean
SALES	1	12	1349.00	530.074	153.019
	2	12	1267.00	516.037	148.967

Independent Samples Test

		Levene's Test for Equality of Variances		t-test for Equality of Means							
										95% Confidence Interval of the Difference	
		F	Sig.	t	df	Sig. (2-tailed)	Mean Difference	Std. Error Difference	Lower	Upper
SALES	Equal variances assumed	.035	.854	.384	22	.705	82.00	213.556	-360.888	524.888
	Equal variances not assumed			.384	21.984	.705	82.00	213.556	-360.906	524.906

Figure 9.10

SPSS analysis of daily restaurant sales

examining the pairs of daily sales, which tend to rise and fall together as we go from day to day. This pattern provides strong visual evidence of a violation of the assumption of independence required for the two-sample t-test of Section 9.1. Note also that

$$
\begin{aligned}
s_p^2 &= \frac{(n_1 - 1)s_1^2 + (n_2 - 1)s_2^2}{n_1 + n_2 - 2} \\
&= \frac{(12 - 1)(530.07)^2 + (12 - 1)(516.04)^2}{12 + 12 - 2} = 273{,}630.6.
\end{aligned}
$$

Thus, there is a *large variation within samples* (reflected by the large value of s_p^2) in comparison to the relatively *small difference between the sample means*. Because s_p^2 is so large, the t-test of Section 9.1 is unable to detect a possible difference between μ_1 and μ_2.

We now consider a valid method of analyzing the data of Table 9.3. In Table 9.4 we add the column of differences between the daily sales of the two

TABLE 9.4   Daily Sales and Differences for Two Restaurants

Day	Restaurant 1 x_1	Restaurant 2 x_2	Difference $d = x_1 - x_2$
1 (Wednesday)	$1,005	$ 918	$ 87
2 (Saturday)	2,073	1,971	102
3 (Tuesday)	873	825	48
4 (Wednesday)	1,074	999	75
5 (Friday)	1,932	1,827	105
6 (Thursday)	1,338	1,281	57
7 (Thursday)	1,449	1,302	147
8 (Monday)	759	678	81
9 (Friday)	1,905	1,782	123
10 (Monday)	693	639	54
11 (Saturday)	2,106	2,049	57
12 (Tuesday)	981	933	48

restaurants, $d = x_1 - x_2$. We can regard these daily differences in sales as a random sample of all daily differences, past and present. Then we can use this sample to make inferences about the mean of the population of differences, μ_d, which is equal to the difference $(\mu_1 - \mu_2)$. That is, the mean of the population (and sample) of differences equals the difference between the population (and sample) means. Thus, our test becomes

$$H_0: \mu_d = 0 \quad [\text{i.e.,} (\mu_1 - \mu_2) = 0]$$
$$H_a: \mu_d \neq 0 \quad [\text{i.e.,} (\mu_1 - \mu_2) \neq 0]$$

Teaching Tip

Point out that this analysis is exactly like the analysis of a single population mean in Chapter 8. The only difference is that the mean now represents the mean of the paired difference.

The test statistic is a one-sample t (Section 8.4), since we are now analyzing a single sample of differences for small n:

$$\textit{Test statistic: } t = \frac{\bar{d} - 0}{s_d/\sqrt{n_d}}$$

where $\bar{d}$ = Sample mean difference
s_d = Sample standard deviation of differences
n_d = Number of differences = number of pairs

Assumptions: The population of differences in daily sales is approximately normally distributed. The sample differences are randomly selected from the population differences. [*Note:* We do not need to make the assumption that $\sigma_1^2 = \sigma_2^2$.]

Rejection region: At significance level $\alpha = .05$, we will reject H_0 if $|t| > t_{.05}$, where $t_{.05}$ is based on $(n_d - 1)$ degrees of freedom.

Suggested Exercise 9.33

Referring to Table IV in Appendix B, we find the t-value corresponding to $\alpha = .025$ and $n_d - 1 = 12 - 1 = 11$ df to be $t_{.025} = 2.201$. Then we will reject the null hypothesis if $|t| > 2.201$ (see Figure 9.11). Note that the number of degrees of freedom has decreased from $n_1 + n_2 - 2 = 22$ to 11 when we use the paired difference experiment rather than the two independent random samples design.

Summary statistics for the $n = 12$ differences are shown on the MINITAB printout, Figure 9.12. Note that $\bar{d} = 82.0$ and $s_d = 32.0$ (rounded). Substituting these values into the formula for the test statistic, we have

$$t = \frac{\bar{d} - 0}{s_d/\sqrt{n_d}} = \frac{82}{32/\sqrt{12}} = 8.88$$

Figure 9.11

Rejection region for restaurant sales example

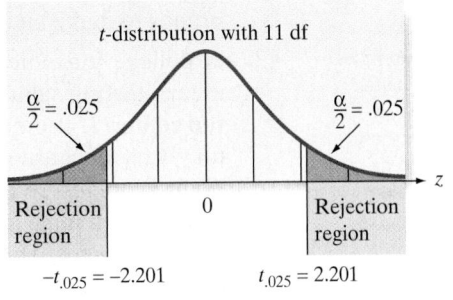

```
Paired T for SALES1 - SALES2

              N     Mean    StDev   SE Mean
SALES1       12  1349.00   530.07    153.02
SALES2       12  1267.00   516.04    148.97
Difference   12  82.0000   31.9886   9.2343


95% CI for mean difference: (61.6754, 102.3246)
T-Test of mean difference = 0 (vs not = 0): T-Value = 8.88   P-Value = 0.000
```

Figure 9.12

MINITAB analysis of differences in daily restaurant sales

Because this value of t falls in the rejection region, we conclude (at $\alpha = .05$) that the difference in population mean daily sales for the two restaurants differs from 0. We can reach the same conclusion by noting that the p-value of the test, highlighted in Figure 9.12, is approximately 0. The fact that $(\bar{x}_1 - \bar{x}_2) = \bar{d} = \$82.00$ strongly suggests that the mean daily sales for restaurant 1 exceeds the mean daily sales for restaurant 2.

> **Now Work** *Exercise 9.26a, b*

■ ■ ■

This kind of experiment, in which observations are paired and the differences are analyzed, is called a **paired difference experiment**. In many cases, a paired difference experiment can provide more information about the difference between population means than an independent samples experiment. The idea is to compare population means by comparing the differences between pairs of experimental units (objects, people, etc.) that were very similar prior to the experiment. The differencing removes sources of variation that tend to inflate σ^2. For instance, in the restaurant example, the day-to-day variability in daily sales is removed by analyzing the differences between the restaurants' daily sales. Making comparisons within groups of similar experimental units is called **blocking**, and the paired difference experiment is an example of a **randomized block experiment**. In our example, the days represent the blocks.

Some other examples for which the paired difference experiment might be appropriate are the following:

1. Suppose you want to estimate the difference $(\mu_1 - \mu_2)$ in mean price per gallon between two major brands of premium gasoline. If you choose two independent random samples of stations for each brand, the variability in price due to geographic location may be large. To eliminate this source of variability you could choose pairs of stations of similar size, one station for each brand, in close geographic proximity and use the sample of differences between the prices of the brands to make an inference about $(\mu_1 - \mu_2)$.

Teaching Tip

Use these and other examples to illustrate when the paired difference experiments are appropriate. Compare these examples to the problems studied in the independent sampling section.

2. A college placement center wants to estimate the difference $(\mu_1 - \mu_2)$ in mean starting salaries for men and women graduates who seek jobs through the center. If it independently samples men and women, the starting salaries may vary because of their different college majors and differences in grade point averages. To eliminate these sources of variability, the placement center could match male and female job seekers according to their majors and grade point averages. Then the differences between the starting salaries of each pair in the sample could be used to make an inference about $(\mu_1 - \mu_2)$.

3. To compare the performance of two automobile salespeople, we might test a hypothesis about the difference $(\mu_1 - \mu_2)$ in their respective mean monthly sales. If we randomly choose n_1 months of salesperson 1's sales and independently choose n_2 months of salesperson 2's sales, the month-to-month variability caused by the seasonal nature of new car sales might inflate s_p^2 and prevent the two-sample t statistic from detecting a difference between μ_1 and μ_2, if such a difference actually exists. However, by taking the difference in monthly sales for the two salespeople for each of n months, we eliminate the month-to-month variability (seasonal variation) in sales, and the probability of detecting a difference between μ_1 and μ_2, if a difference exists, is increased.

The hypothesis-testing procedures and the method of forming confidence intervals for the difference between two means using a paired difference experiment are summarized in the following boxes for both large and small n.

Teaching Tip

Re-emphasize the general form for a confidence interval and how these intervals fit it perfectly.

Paired Difference Confidence Interval for $\mu_d = (\mu_1 - \mu_2)$

Large Sample

$$\bar{d} \pm z_{\alpha/2} \frac{\sigma_d}{\sqrt{n_d}} \approx \bar{d} \pm z_{\alpha/2} \frac{s_d}{\sqrt{n_d}}$$

Small Sample

$$\bar{d} \pm t_{\alpha/2} \frac{s_d}{\sqrt{n_d}}$$

where $t_{\alpha/2}$ is based on $(n_d - 1)$ degrees of freedom.

Teaching Tip

Compare this to the work done on a single population mean in Chapter 8. It is equivalent once the mean of Chapter 8 is replaced with the mean of the paired differences of Chapter 9.

Paired Difference Test of Hypothesis for $\mu_d = (\mu_1 - \mu_2)$

One-Tailed Test	Two-Tailed Test

$H_0: \mu_d = D_0$ 　　　　$H_0: \mu_d = D_0$

$H_a: \mu_d < D_0$ 　　　　$H_a: \mu_d \neq D_0$

[or $H_a: \mu_d > D_0$]

Large Sample

Test statistic: $z = \dfrac{\bar{d} - D_0}{\sigma_d/\sqrt{n_d}} \approx \dfrac{\bar{d} - D_0}{s_d/\sqrt{n_d}}$

Rejection region: $z < -z_\alpha$ 　　　Rejection region: $|z| > z_{\alpha/2}$

[or $z > z_\alpha$ when $H_a: \mu_d > D_0$]

Small Sample

Test statistic: $t = \dfrac{\bar{d} - D_0}{s_d/\sqrt{n_d}}$

Rejection region: $t < -t_\alpha$ 　　　Rejection region: $|t| > t_{\alpha/2}$

[or $t > t_\alpha$ when $H_a: \mu_d > D_0$]

where t_α and $t_{\alpha/2}$ are based on $(n_d - 1)$ degrees of freedom

Conditions Required for Valid Large-Sample Inferences about μ_d

1. A random sample of differences is selected from the target population of differences.
2. The sample size n_d is large (i.e., $n_d \geq 30$). (Due to the Central Limit Theorem, this condition guarantees that the test statistic will be approximately normal regardless of the shape of the underlying probability distribution of the population.)

Conditions Required for Valid Small-Sample Inferences about μ_d

1. A random sample of differences is selected from the target population of differences.
2. The population of differences has a distribution that is approximately normal.

Now Work *Exercise 9.25*

EXAMPLE 9.5   A CONFIDENCE INTERVAL FOR μ_d

Problem An experiment is conducted to compare the starting salaries of male and female college graduates who find jobs. Pairs are formed by choosing a male and a female with the same major and similar grade point averages (GPAs). Suppose a random sample of 10 pairs is formed in this manner and the starting annual salary of each person is recorded. The results are shown in Table 9.5. Compare the mean starting salary, μ_1, for males to the mean starting salary, μ_2, for females using a 95% confidence interval. Interpret the results

400 ± 311

 GRADPAIRS

TABLE 9.5   Data on Annual Salaries for Matched Pairs of College Graduates

Pair	Male x_1	Female x_2	Difference $d = x_1 - x_2$
1	$29,300	$28,800	$500
2	41,500	41,600	−100
3	40,400	39,800	600
4	38,500	38,500	0
5	43,500	42,600	900
6	37,800	38,000	$−200
7	69,500	69,200	300
8	41,200	40,100	1,100
9	38,400	38,200	200
10	59,200	58,500	700

Solution Since the data on annual salary are collected in pairs of males and females matched on GPA and major, a paired difference experiment is performed. To conduct the analysis, we first compute the differences between the salaries, as shown in Table 9.6. Summary statistics for these $n = 10$ differences are displayed in the MINITAB printout, Figure 9.13.

```
Paired T for MALE - FEMALE

              N    Mean    StDev   SE Mean
MALE         10   43930.0  11665.1   3688.8
FEMALE       10   43530.0  11616.9   3673.6
Difference   10    400.000  434.613  137.437


95% CI for mean difference: (89.096, 710.904)
T-Test of mean difference = 0 (vs not = 0): T-Value = 2.91  P-Value = 0.017
```

Figure 9.13

MINITAB analysis of salary differences

The 95% confidence interval for $\mu_d = (\mu_1 - \mu_2)$ for this small sample is

$$\bar{d} \pm t_{\alpha/2} \frac{s_d}{\sqrt{n_d}}$$

where $t_{\alpha/2} = t_{.025} = 2.262$ (obtained from Table VI, Appendix B) is based on $n_d - 2 = 8$ degrees of freedom. Substituting the values of $\bar{d} = 400$ and $s_d = 434.6$ shown on the printout, we obtain

$$\bar{d} \pm t_{.025} \frac{s_d}{\sqrt{n_d}} = 400 \pm 2.262\left(\frac{434.6}{\sqrt{10}}\right)$$

$$= 400 \pm 310.87 \approx 400 \pm 311 = (\$89, \$711)$$

[*Note:* This interval is also shown on the MINITAB printout, Figure 9.13.] Our interpretation is that the true mean difference between the starting salaries of males and females falls between $89 and $711, with 95% confidence. Since the interval falls above 0, we infer that $\mu_1 - \mu_2 > 0$, that is, that the mean salary for males exceeds the mean salary for females.

Look Back Remember that $\mu_d = \mu_1 - \mu_2$. So, if $\mu_d > 0$, then $\mu_1 > \mu_2$. Alternatively, if $\mu_d < 0$, then $\mu_1 < \mu_2$.

| Now Work | *Exercise 9.33*

■ ■ ■

Suggested Exercise 9.28

To measure the amount of information about $(\mu_1 - \mu_2)$ gained by using a paired difference experiment in Example 9.5 rather than an independent samples experiment, we can compare the relative widths of the confidence intervals obtained by the two methods. A 95% confidence interval for $(\mu_1 - \mu_2)$ using the paired difference experiment is, from Example 9.5, ($89, $711). If we analyzed the same data as though this were an independent samples experiment,* we would first obtain the descriptive statistics shown in the SPSS printout, Figure 9.14.

---

*This is done only to provide a measure of the increase in the amount of information obtained by a paired design in comparison to an unpaired design. Actually, if an experiment is designed using pairing, an unpaired analysis would be invalid because the assumption of independent samples would not be satisfied.

Group Statistics

	GENDER	N	Mean	Std. Deviation	Std. Error Mean
SALARY	M	10	43930.00	11665.148	3688.844
	F	10	43530.00	11616.946	3673.601

Independent Samples Test

		Levene's Test for Equality of Variances		t-test for Equality of Means						95% Confidence Interval of the Difference	
		F	Sig.	t	df	Sig. (2-tailed)	Mean Difference	Std. Error Difference	Lower	Upper
SALARY	Equal variances assumed	.000	.991	.077	18	.940	400.00	5206.046	-10537.5	11337.50
	Equal variances not assumed			.077	18.000	.940	400.00	5206.046	-10537.5	11337.51

Figure 9.14

SPSS analysis of salaries, assuming independent samples

Then we substitute the sample means and standard deviations shown on the printout into the formula for a 95% confidence interval for $(\mu_1 - \mu_2)$ using independent samples:

$$(\bar{x}_1 - \bar{x}_2) \pm t_{.025}\sqrt{s_p^2\left(\frac{1}{n_1} + \frac{1}{n_2}\right)}$$

where

$$s_p^2 = \frac{(n_1 - 1)s_1^2 + (n_2 - 1)s_2^2}{n_1 + n_2 - 2}$$

SPSS performed these calculations and obtained the interval $(-\$10{,}537.50, \$11{,}337.50)$. This interval is highlighted in Figure 9.14.

Notice that the independent samples interval includes 0. Consequently, if we were to use this interval to make an inference about $(\mu_1 - \mu_2)$, we would incorrectly conclude that the mean starting salaries of males and females do not differ! You can see that the confidence interval for the independent sampling experiment is about five times wider than for the corresponding paired difference confidence interval. Blocking out the variability due to differences in majors and grade point averages significantly increases the information about the difference in male and female mean starting salaries by providing a much more accurate (smaller confidence interval for the same confidence coefficient) estimate of $(\mu_1 - \mu_2)$.

You may wonder whether conducting a paired difference experiment is always superior to an independent samples experiment. The answer is: Most of the time, but not always. We sacrifice half the degrees of freedom in the t statistic when a paired difference design is used instead of an independent samples design. This is a loss of information, and unless this loss is more than compensated for by the reduction in variability obtained by blocking (pairing), the paired difference experiment will result in a net loss of information about $(\mu_1 - \mu_2)$. Thus, we should be convinced that the pairing will significantly reduce variability before performing the paired difference experiment. Most of the time this will happen.

One final note: The pairing of the observations is determined before the experiment is performed (that is, by the *design* of the experiment). A paired difference

Teaching Tip

Point out that the paired difference experiment is a very useful tool in statistics and should be attempted whenever it is appropriate. The disadvantage discussed here is very small relative to the large benefits the experiment can provide.

experiment is *never* obtained by pairing the sample observations after the measurements have been acquired.

What Do You Do when the Assumption of a Normal Distribution for the Population of Differences Is Not Satisfied?

Answer: Use the Wilcoxon signed rank test for the paired difference design (Chapter 16).

Exercises 9.25–9.39

Learning the Mechanics

9.25 A paired difference experiment yielded n_d pairs of observations. In each case, what is the rejection region for testing $H_0: \mu_d > 2$?

a. $n_d = 12, \alpha = .05$
b. $n_d = 24, \alpha = .10$
c. $n_d = 4, \alpha = .025$
d. $n_d = 80, \alpha = .01$

9.26 The data for a random sample of six paired observations are shown in the table.

LM9_26

Pair	Sample from Population 1 (Observation 1)	Sample from Population 2 (Observation 2)
1	7	4
2	3	1
3	9	7
4	6	2
5	4	4
6	8	7

a. Calculate the difference between each pair of observations by subtracting observation 2 from observation 1. Use the differences to calculate $\bar{d}$ and s_d^2.
b. If μ_1 and μ_2 are the means of populations 1 and 2, respectively, express μ_d in terms of μ_1 and μ_2.
c. Form a 95% confidence interval for μ_D.
d. Test the null hypothesis $H_0: \mu_d = 0$ against the alternative hypothesis $H_a: \mu_d \neq 0$. Use $\alpha = .05$.

9.27 The data for a random sample of 10 paired observations are shown in the next table.
a. If you wish to test whether these data are sufficient to indicate that the mean for population 2 is larger than that for population 1, what are the appropriate null and alternative hypotheses? Define any symbols you use.
b. Conduct the test, part **a**, using $\alpha = .10$.
c. Find a 90% confidence interval for μ_d. Interpret this result.
d. What assumptions are necessary to ensure the validity of this analysis?

LM9_27

Pair	Sample from Population 1	Sample from Population 2
1	19	24
2	25	27
3	31	36
4	52	53
5	49	55
6	34	34
7	59	66
8	47	51
9	17	20
10	51	55

9.28 A paired difference experiment produced the following results:
$$n_d = 38 \quad \bar{x}_1 = 92 \quad \bar{x}_2 = 95.5 \quad \bar{d} = -3.5 \quad s_d^2 = 21$$
a. Determine the values of z for which the null hypothesis, $\mu_1 - \mu_2 = 0$, would be rejected in favor of the alternative hypothesis, $\mu_1 - \mu_2 < 0$. Use $\alpha = .10$.
b. Conduct the paired difference test described in part **a**. Draw the appropriate conclusions. $z = -4.71$
c. What assumptions are necessary so that the paired difference test will be valid?
d. Find a 90% confidence interval for the mean difference μ_D. -3.5 ± 1.223
e. Which of the two inferential procedures, the confidence interval of part d or the test of hypothesis of part b, provides more information about the differences between the population means?

9.29 A paired difference experiment yielded the following results:
$$n_d = 40,$$
$$\Sigma d = 468,$$
$$\Sigma d^2 = 6,880.$$
a. Test $H_0: \mu_d = 10$ against $H_a: \mu_d \neq 10$, where $\mu_d = (\mu_1 - \mu_2)$. Use $\alpha = .05$. $z = 1.79$
b. Report the *p*-value for the test you conducted in part a. Interpret the *p*-value.
c. Do you need to assume that the population of difference is normally distributed? Explain.

Applying the Concepts—Basic

9.30 Movie actors who win an Oscar usually can command a greater fee for their next motion picture. Does winning an Academy of Motion Picture Arts and Sciences award (a.k.a., an Oscar) lead to long-term mortality for movie actors? In an article in the *Annals of Internal Medicine* (May 15, 2001), researchers sampled 762 Academy Award winners and matched each one with another actor of the same sex who was in the same winning film and was born in the same era. The life expectancy (age) of each pair of actors was compared.
  a. Explain why the data should be analyzed as a paired difference experiment.
  b. Set up the null hypothesis for a test to compare the mean life expectancies of Academy Award winners and nonwinners.
  c. The sample mean life expectancies of Academy Award winners and nonwinners were reported as 79.7 years and 75.8 years, respectively. The *p*-value for comparing the two population means was reported as $p = .003$. Interpret this value in the context of the problem.

9.31 When searching for an item (e.g., a roadside traffic sign, a misplaced file, or a tumor in a mammogram), common sense dictates that you will not re-examine items previously rejected. However, researchers at Harvard Medical School found that a visual search has no memory (*Nature*, Aug. 6, 1998). In their experiment, nine subjects searched for the letter "T" mixed among several letters "L." Each subject conducted the search under two conditions: random and static. In the random condition, the location of the letters were changed every 111 milliseconds; in the static condition, the location of the letters remained unchanged. In each trial, the reaction time (i.e., the amount of time it took the subject to locate the target letter) was recorded in milliseconds.
  a. One goal of the research is to compare the mean reaction times of subjects in the two experimental conditions. Explain why the data should be analyzed as a paired-difference experiment.
  b. If a visual search had no memory, then the main reaction times in the two conditions will not differ. Specify H_0 and H_a for testing the "no memory" theory.
  c. The test statistic was calculated as $t = 1.52$ with *p*-value $= .15$. Make the appropriate conclusion.

CRASH

9.32 Refer to the National Highway Traffic Safety Administration (NHTSA) crash test data for new cars saved in the CRASH file. Crash test dummies were placed in the driver's seat and front passenger's seat of a new car model, and the car was steered by remote control into a head-on collision with a fixed barrier while traveling at 35 miles per hour. Two of the variables measured for each of the 98 new cars in the data set are (1) the severity of the driver's chest injury and (2) the severity of the passenger's chest injury. (The more points assigned to the chest injury rating, the more severe the injury.) Suppose the NHTSA wants to determine whether the true mean driver chest injury rating exceeds the true mean passenger chest injury rating, and if so, by how much.
  a. State the parameter of interest to the NHTSA.
    $\mu_d = \mu_1 - \mu_2$
  b. Explain why the data should be analyzed as matched pairs.
  c. Find a 99% confidence interval for the true difference between the mean chest injury ratings of drivers and front-seat passengers. $-.561 \pm 1.438$
  d. Interpret the interval, part c. Does the true mean driver chest injury rating exceed the true mean passenger chest injury rating? If so, by how much?
  e. What conditions are required for the analysis to be valid? Do these conditions hold for this data?

9.33 Facility layout and material flowpath design are major factors in the productivity analysis of automated manufacturing systems. Facility layout is concerned with the location arrangement of machines and buffers for work-in-process. Flowpath design is concerned with the direction of manufacturing material flows (e.g., unidirectional or bidirectional) (Lee, Lei, and Pinedo, *Annals of Operations Research*, 1997). A manufacturer of printed circuit boards (PCBs) is interested in evaluating two alternative existing layout and flowpath designs. The output of each design was monitored for eight consecutive working days.

FLOWPATH

Working Days	Design 1	Design 2
8/16	1,220 units	1,273 units
8/17	1,092 units	1,363 units
8/18	1,136 units	1,342 units
8/19	1,205 units	1,471 units
8/20	1,086 units	1,299 units
8/23	1,274 units	1,457 units
8/24	1,145 units	1,263 units
8/25	1,281 units	1,368 units

  a. Construct a 95% confidence interval for the difference in mean daily output of the two designs.
  b. What assumptions must hold to ensure the validity of the confidence interval?
  c. Design 2 appears to be superior to Design 1. Is this confirmed by the confidence interval? Explain.

Applying the Concepts—Intermediate

9.34 Refer to Exercise 2.29 (p. 69) and the data on average SAT scores for each of the 50 states and District of Columbia for the years 1990 and 2000. The data are saved in the SATSCORES file. (The first five observations and last two observations in the data set are shown in the table.)

a. In Exercise 2.29b, you computed the *paired differences* of SAT scores by subtracting the 1990 score from the 2000 score for each state. Find the mean of these 50 paired differences. This value is μ_d, the mean difference in SAT scores for the population of 50 states (and District of Columbia). 22.45

b. Explain why there is no need to employ the confidence interval or test procedures of this section to make an inference about μ_d.

c. Now, suppose the 50 paired differences of part a represent a sample of SAT score differences for 50 randomly selected high school students. Use the data in the SATSCORES file make an inference about whether the true mean SAT score of high school students in 2000 differs from the true mean in 1999. Use a confidence level of .90. $z = 9.08$

ⓢ SATSCORES

State	1990	2000
Alabana	1079	1114
Alooko	1015	1034
Arizona	1041	1044
Arakansas	1077	1117
California	1002	1015
.	.	.
.	.	.
.	.	.
Wisconsin	1111	1181
Wyoming	1072	1090

Source: College Entrance Examination Board, 2001.

9.35 Lack of sleep costs companies about $18 billion a year in lost productivity, according to the National Sleep Foundation. Companies are waking up to the problem, however. Some even have quiet rooms available for study or sleep. "Power naps" are in vogue (*Athens Daily News*, Jan. 9, 2000). A major airline recently began encouraging reservation agents to nap during their breaks. The table in the next column lists the number of complaints received about each of a sample of 10 reservation agents during the six months before naps were encouraged and during the six months after the policy change.

a. Do the data present sufficient evidence to conclude that the new napping policy reduced the mean number of customer complaints about reservation agents? Test using $\alpha = .05$. $t = 2.864$

b. What assumptions must hold to ensure the validity of the test?

c. What variables, not controlled in the study, could lead to an invalid conclusion?

ⓢ POWERNAP

Operator	1999 No. of Complaints	2000 No. of Complaints
1	10	5
2	3	0
3	16	7
4	11	4
5	8	6
6	2	4
7	1	2
8	14	3
9	5	5
10	6	1

9.36 Refer to the *Journal of Genetic Psychology* (Mar. 1998) comparison of male and female college students' attitudes toward their fathers, Exercise 9.18 (p. 498). In this exercise, data adapted from the same study are used to compare male students' attitudes toward their fathers with their attitudes toward their mothers. Each of a sample of 13 males from the original sample of 44 males was asked to complete the following statement about each of his parents: My relationship with my father (mother) can best be described as (1) Awful! (2) Poor, (3) Average, (4) Good, or (5) Great! The data obtained are shown in the table:

ⓢ FATHMOTH

Student	Attitude toward Father	Attitude toward Mother
1	2	3
2	5	5
3	4	3
4	4	5
5	3	4
6	5	4
7	4	5
8	2	4
9	4	5
10	5	4
11	4	5
12	5	4
13	3	3

Source: Adapted from Vitulli, William F., and Richardson, Deanna K., "College Student's Attitudes toward Relationships with Parents: A Five-Year Comparative Analysis," *Journal of Genetic Psychology*, Vol. 159, No. 1, Mar. 1998, pp. 45–52.

a. Specify the appropriate hypotheses for testing whether male students' attitudes toward their fathers differ from their attitudes toward their mothers, on average. $H_0: \mu_d = 0, H_a: \mu_d \neq 0$

b. Conduct the test of part a (at $\alpha = .05$). Interpret the results in the context of the problem. $t = -1.08$

c. What assumptions about the sample and its population did you have to make in order to ensure the validity of the hypothesis test?

d. Are you satisfied that your assumption about the population is correct? Justify your answer.

9.37 A *pupillometer* is a device used to observe changes in pupil dilations as the eye is exposed to different visual stimuli. Since there is a direct correlation between the amount an individual's pupil dilates and his or her interest in the stimuli, marketing organizations sometimes use pupillometers to help them evaluate potential consumer interest in new products, alternative package designs, and other factors (*Optical Engineering,* Mar. 1995). The Design and Market Research Laboratories of the Container Corporation of America used a pupillometer to evaluate consumer reaction to different silverware patterns for a client. Suppose 15 consumers were chosen at random, and each was shown two silverware patterns. Their pupillometer readings (in millimeters) are shown in the table.

⊙ **PUPILL**

Consumer	Pattern 1	Pattern 2
1	1.00	.80
2	.97	.66
3	1.45	1.22
4	1.21	1.00
5	.77	.81
6	1.32	1.11
7	1.81	1.30
8	.91	.32
9	.98	.91
10	1.46	1.10
11	1.85	1.60
12	.33	.21
13	1.77	1.50
14	.85	.65
15	.15	.05

a. What are the appropriate null and alternative hypotheses to test whether the mean amount of pupil dilation differs for the two patterns? Define any symbols you use.

b. Conduct the test, part a. Interpret the results. *t* = 5.76

c. Is the paired difference design used for this study preferable to an independent samples design? For independent samples we could select 30 consumers, divide them into two groups of 15, and show each group a different pattern. Explain your preference.

9.38 A study reported in the *Journal of Psychology* (Mar. 1991) measures the change in female students' self-concepts as they move from high school to college. A sample of 133 Boston College first-year female students was selected for the study. Each was asked to evaluate several aspects of her life at two points in time: at the end of her senior year of high school, and during her sophomore year of college. Each student was asked to evaluate where she believed she stood on a scale that ranged from top 10% of class (1) to lowest 10% of class (5). The results for three of the traits evaluated are reported in the table.

Trait	*n*	Senior Year of High School $\bar{x}$	Sophomore Year of College $\bar{x}$
Leadership	133	2.09	2.33
Popularity	133	2.48	2.69
Intellectual self-confidence	133	2.29	2.55

a. What null and alternative hypotheses would you test to determine whether the mean self-concept of females decreases between the senior year of high school and the sophomore year of college as measured by each of these three traits? $H_0: \mu_d = 0, H_a: \mu_d > 0$

b. Are these traits more appropriately analyzed using an independent samples test or a paired difference test? Explain.   Paired difference

c. Noting the size of the sample, what assumptions are necessary to ensure the validity of the tests?

d. The article reports that the leadership test results in a *p*-value greater than .05, while the tests for popularity and intellectual self-confidence result in *p*-values less than .05. Interpret these results.

9.39 Merck Research Labs conducted an experiment to evaluate the effect of a new drug using the single-T swim maze. Nineteen impregnated dam rats were captured and allocated a dosage of 12.5 milligrams of the drug. One male and one female rat pup were randomly selected from each resulting litter to perform in the swim maze. Each pup was placed in the water at one end of the maze and allowed to swim until it escaped at the opposite end. If the pup failed to escape after a certain period of time, it was placed at the beginning of the maze and given another chance. The experiment was repeated until each pup accomplished three successful escapes. The table on p. 513 reports the number of swims required by each pup to perform three successful escapes. Is there sufficient evidence of a difference between the mean number of swims required by male and female pups? Conduct the test (at α = .10). Comment on the assumptions required for the test to be valid.   *t* = .46

Litter	Male	Female	Litter	Male	Female
1	8	5	11	6	5
2	8	4	12	6	3
3	6	7	13	12	5
4	6	3	14	3	8
5	6	5	15	3	4
6	6	3	16	8	12
7	3	8	17	3	6
8	5	10	18	6	4
9	4	4	19	9	5
10	4	4			

Source: Thomas E. Bradstreet, Merck Research Labs, BL 3-2, West Point, PA 19486.

9.3 Comparing Two Population Proportions: Independent Sampling

Teaching Tip

Discuss the basic differences between a population mean and a population proportion. Help the student identify the key words that will suggest either means or proportions.

Suppose a personal water craft (PWC) manufacturer wants to compare the potential market for its products in the northeastern United States to the market in the southeastern United States. Such a comparison would help the manufacturer decide where to concentrate sales efforts. Using telephone directories, the company randomly chooses 1,000 households in the southeast (SE) and 1,000 households in the northeast (NE) and determines whether each household plans to buy a PWC within the next five years. The objective is to use this sample information to make an inference about the difference $(p_1 - p_2)$ between the proportion p_1 of *all* households in the SE and the proportion p_2 of *all* households in the NE that plan to purchase a PWC within five years.

The two samples represent independent binomial experiments. (See Section 4.4 for the characteristics of binomial experiments.) The binomial random variables are the numbers x_1 and x_2 of the 1,000 sampled households in each area that indicate they will purchase a PWC within five years. The results are summarized below.

SE	NE
$n_1 = 1,000$	$n_2 = 1,000$
$x_1 = 42$	$x_2 = 24$

We can now calculate the sample proportions $\hat{p}_1$ and $\hat{p}_2$ of the households in the SE and NE, respectively, that are prospective buyers:

$$\hat{p}_1 = \frac{x_1}{n_1} = \frac{42}{1,000} = .042$$

$$\hat{p}_2 = \frac{x_2}{n_2} = \frac{24}{1,000} = .024$$

The difference between the sample proportions $(\hat{p}_1 - \hat{p}_2)$ makes an intuitively appealing point estimator of the difference between the population parameters $(p_1 - p_2)$. For our example, the estimate is

$$(\hat{p}_1 - \hat{p}_2) = .042 - .024 = .018$$

To judge the reliability of the estimator $(\hat{p}_1 - \hat{p}_2)$, we must observe its performance in repeated sampling from the two populations. That is, we need to know the sampling distribution of $(\hat{p}_1 - \hat{p}_2)$. The properties of the sampling distribution are given in the next box. Remember that $\hat{p}_1$ and $\hat{p}_2$ can be viewed as means of the number of successes per trial in the respective samples, so the Central Limit Theorem applies when the sample sizes are large.

Properties of the Sampling Distribution of $(\hat{p}_1 - \hat{p}_2)$

1. The mean of the sampling distribution of $(\hat{p}_1 - \hat{p}_2)$ is $(p_1 - p_2)$; that is,

$$E(\hat{p}_1 - \hat{p}_2) = p_1 - p_2$$

Thus, $(\hat{p}_1 - \hat{p}_2)$ is an unbiased estimator of $(p_1 - p_2)$.

2. The standard deviation of the sampling distribution of $(\hat{p}_1 - \hat{p}_2)$ is

$$\sigma_{(\hat{p}_1 - \hat{p}_2)} = \sqrt{\frac{p_1 q_1}{n_1} + \frac{p_2 q_2}{n_2}}$$

3. If the sample sizes n_1 and n_2 are large (see Section 7.3 for a guideline), the sampling distribution of $(\hat{p}_1 - \hat{p}_2)$ is approximately normal.

Since the distribution of $(\hat{p}_1 - \hat{p}_2)$ in repeated sampling is approximately normal, we can use the z statistic to derive confidence intervals for $(p_1 - p_2)$ or to test a hypothesis about $(p_1 - p_2)$.

For the PWC example, a 95% confidence interval for the difference $(p_1 - p_2)$ is

$$(\hat{p}_1 - \hat{p}_2) \pm 1.96\sigma_{(\hat{p}_1 - \hat{p}_2)} \quad \text{or} \quad (\hat{p}_1 - \hat{p}_2) \pm 1.96\sqrt{\frac{p_1 q_1}{n_1} + \frac{p_2 q_2}{n_2}}$$

The quantities $p_1 q_1$ and $p_2 q_2$ must be estimated in order to complete the calculation of the standard deviation $\sigma_{(\hat{p}_1 - \hat{p}_2)}$ and hence the calculation of the confidence interval. In Section 7.3 we showed that the value of pq is relatively insensitive to the value chosen to approximate p. Therefore, $\hat{p}_1\hat{q}_1$ and $\hat{p}_2\hat{q}_2$ will provide satisfactory estimates to approximate $p_1 q_1$ and $p_2 q_2$, respectively. Then

$$\sqrt{\frac{p_1 q_1}{n_1} + \frac{p_2 q_2}{n_2}} \approx \sqrt{\frac{\hat{p}_1\hat{q}_1}{n_1} + \frac{\hat{p}_2\hat{q}_2}{n_2}}$$

and we will approximate the 95% confidence interval by

$$(\hat{p}_1 - \hat{p}_2) \pm 1.96\sqrt{\frac{\hat{p}_1\hat{q}_1}{n_1} + \frac{\hat{p}_2\hat{q}_2}{n_2}}$$

Substituting the sample quantities yields

$$(.042 - .024) \pm 1.96\sqrt{\frac{(.042)(.958)}{1,000} + \frac{(.024)(.976)}{1,000}}$$

or $.018 \pm .016$. Thus, we are 95% confident that the interval from $.002$ to $.034$ contains $(p_1 - p_2)$.

We infer that there are between .2% and 3.4% more households in the southeast than in the northeast that plan to purchase PWCs in the next five years.

Now Work *Exercise 9.47*

The general form of a confidence interval for the difference $(p_1 - p_2)$ between population proportions is given in the following box.

Teaching Tip
Point out that the *t*-distribution is not used with proportions because the underlying assumption of a normal distribution will never be true.

Large-Sample $100(1 - \alpha)\%$ Confidence Interval for $(p_1 - p_2)$

$$(\hat{p}_1 - \hat{p}_2) \pm z_{\alpha/2}\sigma_{(\hat{p}_1 - \hat{p}_2)} = (\hat{p}_1 - \hat{p}_2) \pm z_{\alpha/2}\sqrt{\frac{p_1 q_1}{n_1} + \frac{p_2 q_2}{n_2}}$$

$$\approx (\hat{p}_1 - \hat{p}_2) \pm z_{\alpha/2}\sqrt{\frac{\hat{p}_1 \hat{q}_1}{n_1} + \frac{\hat{p}_2 \hat{q}_2}{n_2}}$$

Conditions Required for Valid Large-Sample Inferences about $(p_1 - p_2)$

1. The two samples are randomly selected in an independent manner from the two target populations.

2. The sample sizes, n_1 and n_2, are both large so that the sampling distribution of $(\hat{p}_1 - \hat{p}_2)$ will be approximately normal. (This condition will be satisfied if both intervals, $\hat{p}_1 \pm 3\sigma_{\hat{p}_1}$ and $\hat{p}_2 \pm 3\sigma_{\hat{p}_2}$, fall between 0 and 1.)

The *z*-statistic,

$$z = \frac{(\hat{p}_1 - \hat{p}_2) - (p_1 - p_2)}{\sigma_{(\hat{p}_1 - \hat{p}_2)}}$$

Suggested Exercise 9.54

is used to test the null hypothesis that $(p_1 - p_2)$ equals some specified difference, say D_0. For the special case where $D_0 = 0$, that is, where we want to test the null hypothesis $H_0: (p_1 - p_2) = 0$ (or, equivalently, $H_0: p_1 = p_2$), the best estimate of $p_1 = p_2 = p$ is obtained by dividing the total number of successes $(x_1 + x_2)$ for the two samples by the total number of observations $(n_1 + n_2)$; that is,

$$\hat{p} = \frac{x_1 + x_2}{n_1 + n_2} \quad \text{or} \quad \hat{p} = \frac{n_1 \hat{p}_1 + n_2 \hat{p}_2}{n_1 + n_2}$$

The second equation shows that $\hat{p}$ is a weighted average of $\hat{p}_1$ and $\hat{p}_2$, with the larger sample receiving more weight. If the sample sizes are equal, then $\hat{p}$ is a simple average of the two sample proportions of successes.

We now substitute the weighted average $\hat{p}$ for both p_1 and p_2 in the formula for the standard deviation of $(\hat{p}_1 - \hat{p}_2)$:

$$\sigma_{(\hat{p}_1 - \hat{p}_2)} = \sqrt{\frac{p_1 q_1}{n_1} + \frac{p_2 q_2}{n_2}} \approx \sqrt{\frac{\hat{p}\hat{q}}{n_1} + \frac{\hat{p}\hat{q}}{n_2}} = \sqrt{\hat{p}\hat{q}\left(\frac{1}{n_1} + \frac{1}{n_2}\right)}$$

The test is summarized in the next box.

Teaching Tip
No matched pairs experiment with proportions exists for this type of analysis.

Large-Sample Test of Hypothesis About $(p_1 - p_2)$

One-Tailed Test	Two-Tailed Test
$H_0: (p_1 - p_2) = 0$ *	$H_0: (p_1 - p_2) = 0$
$H_a: (p_1 - p_2) < 0$	$H_a: (p_1 - p_2) \neq 0$
[or $H_a: (p_1 - p_2) > 0$]	

Test statistic: $z = \dfrac{\hat{p}_1 - \hat{p}_2}{\sigma_{(\hat{p}_1 - \hat{p}_2)}}$

Rejection region: $z < -z_\alpha$ 　　　　　　　　*Rejection region:* $|z| > z_{\alpha/2}$
[or $z > z_\alpha$ when $H_a: (p_1 - p_2) > 0$]

Note: $\sigma_{(\hat{p}_1 - \hat{p}_2)} = \sqrt{\dfrac{p_1 q_1}{n_1} + \dfrac{p_2 q_2}{n_2}} \approx \sqrt{\hat{p}\hat{q}\left(\dfrac{1}{n_1} + \dfrac{1}{n_2}\right)}$, where $\hat{p} = \dfrac{x_1 + x_2}{n_1 + n_2}$.

EXAMPLE 9.6　　　LARGE-SAMPLE TEST ABOUT $p_1 - p_2$

Problem　A consumer advocacy group wants to determine whether there is a difference between the proportions of the two leading automobile models that need major repairs (more than \$500) within two years of their purchase. A sample of 400 two-year owners of model 1 is contacted, and a sample of 500 two-year owners of model 2 is contacted. The numbers x_1 and x_2 of owners who report that their cars needed major repairs within the first two years are 53 and 78, respectively. Test the null hypothesis that no difference exists between the proportions in populations 1 and 2 needing major repairs against the alternative that a difference does exist. Use $\alpha = .10$.

z = −.99, Fail to reject H_0

Solution　If we define p_1 and p_2 as the true proportions of model 1 and model 2 owners, respectively, whose cars need major repairs within two years, the elements of the test are

$$H_0: (p_1 - p_2) = 0$$
$$H_a: (p_1 - p_2) \neq 0$$

Test statistic: $z = \dfrac{(\hat{p}_1 - \hat{p}_2) - 0}{\sigma_{(\hat{p}_1 - \hat{p}_2)}}$

Rejection region $(\alpha = .10)$: $|z| > z_{\alpha/2} = z_{.05} = 1.645$　　(see Figure 9.15)

Figure 9.15
Rejection region for
Example 9.6

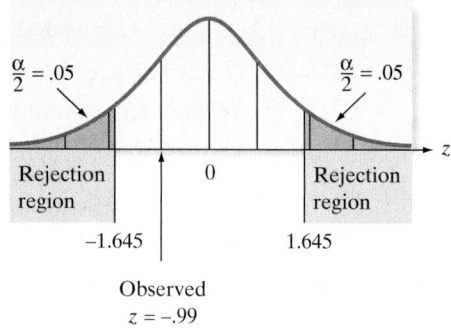

Observed
$z = -.99$

*The test can be adapted to test for a difference $D_0 \neq 0$. Because most applications call for a comparison of p_1 and p_2, implying $D_0 = 0$, we will confine our attention to this case.

We now calculate the sample proportions of owners who need major car repairs,

$$\hat{p}_1 = \frac{x_1}{n_1} = \frac{53}{400} = .1325$$

$$\hat{p}_2 = \frac{x_2}{n_2} = \frac{78}{500} = .1560$$

Then

$$z = \frac{(\hat{p}_1 - \hat{p}_2) - 0}{\sigma_{(\hat{p}_1 - \hat{p}_2)}} \approx \frac{(\hat{p}_1 - \hat{p}_2)}{\sqrt{\hat{p}\hat{q}\left(\frac{1}{n_1} + \frac{1}{n_2}\right)}}$$

where

$$\hat{p} = \frac{x_1 + x_2}{n_1 + n_2} = \frac{53 + 78}{400 + 500} = .1456$$

Note that $\hat{p}$ is a weighted average of $\hat{p}_1$ and $\hat{p}_2$, with more weight given to the larger sample of model 2 owners.

Thus, the computed value of the test statistic is

$$z = \frac{.1325 - .1560}{\sqrt{(.1456)(.8544)\left(\frac{1}{400} + \frac{1}{500}\right)}} = \frac{-.0235}{.0237} = -.99$$

The samples provide insufficient evidence at $\alpha = .10$ to detect a difference between the proportions of the two models that need repairs within two years. Even though 2.35% more sampled owners of model 2 found they needed major repairs, this difference is less than 1 standard deviation ($z = -.99$) from the hypothesized zero difference between the true proportions.

■ ■ ■

EXAMPLE 9.7

FINDING THE OBSERVED SIGNIFICANCE LEVEL OF A TEST FOR $p_1 - p_2$

Problem Use a statistical software package to conduct the test in Example 9.6. Find and interpret the *p*-value of the test.

p = .3205

Solution We entered the sample sizes (n_1 and n_2) and number of successes (x_1 and x_2) into EXCEL with the PHStat2 add-in and obtained the printout shown in Figure 9.16. The test statistic for this two-tailed test is shaded on the printout as well as the observed significance level (*p*-value). Note that *p*-value = .3205 is less than $\alpha = .10$. Consequently, there is no evidence of a difference between the true population proportions.

Figure 9.16

EXCEL/PHStat2 printout for test of two proportions

Z Test for Differences in Two Proportions

Data	
Hypothesized Difference	0
Level of Significance	0.1
Group 1	
Number of Successes	53
Sample Size	400
Group 2	
Number of Successes	78
Sample Size	500

Intermediate Calculations	
Group 1 Proportion	0.1325
Group 2 Proportion	0.156
Difference in Two Proportions	-0.0235
Average Proportion	0.145555556
Z Test Statistic	-0.993356864

Two-Tailed Test	
Lower Critical Value	-1.644853476
Upper Critical Value	1.644853476
***p*-Value**	0.320536082
Do not reject the null hypothesis	

■ ■ ■

Statistics in Action Revisited

Comparing Proportions for the Two SMWT Survey Groups

In the first Statistics in Action Revisited application in this chapter (p. 492), we demonstrated how researchers compared the means of several quantitative variables for two groups of AT&T workers. Recall that Group 1 workers ($n_1 = 47$) were those employees who reported positive spillover of work skills to family life and Group 2 workers ($n_2 = 67$) were those employees who did not report positive work spillover. The researchers also collected data on the qualitative variable, Gender, for each worker, and wanted to know whether the proportion of male workers in the two groups differed.

An analysis of the Gender variable in the SPILLOVER file is shown in the MINITAB printout, Figure SIA9.2. Summary information given at the top of the printout shows that 39 of the 47 workers (83%) in the spillover group (Group 1) were males, while 59 of the 67 workers (88%) in the non-spillover group (Group 2) were males. A confidence interval for $(p_2 - p_1)$ and the results of a two-tailed test of the null hypothesis, $H_0: (p_2 - p_1) = 0$, are shown at the bottom of the printout. [*Note*: MINITAB orders the groups alphabetically. Since "NOSPILL" preceeds "SPILLOV", population 1 in the MINITAB analysis is Group 2 and population 2 is Group 1.] The 95% confidence interval is $(-.08, .18)$ and the *p*-value for the hypothesis test is *p*-value = .453. Both of these results led the researchers to conclude that there is no significant difference between the proportions of males in the two SMWT groups.

Test and CI for Two Proportions: GENDER, GROUP

```
Event = MALE


GROUP      X    N   Sample p
NOSPILL   59   67   0.880597
SPILLOV   39   47   0.829787


Difference = p (NOSPILL) - p (SPILLOV)
Estimate for difference:  0.0508098
95% CI for difference:  (-0.0817519, 0.183371)
Test for difference = 0 (vs not = 0):  Z = 0.75  P-Value = 0.453
```

Figure SIA9.2
MINITAB comparison of SMWT groups for gender

Exercises 9.40–9.57

Learning the Mechanics

9.40 Consider making an inference about $p_1 - p_2$, where there are x_1 successes in n_1 binomial trials and x_2 successes in n_2 binomial trials.
  a. Describe the distributions of x_1 and x_2.
  b. Explain why the Central Limit Theorem is important in finding an approximate distribution for $(\hat{p}_1 - \hat{p}_2)$.

9.41 In each case, determine whether the sample sizes are large enough to conclude that the sampling distribution of $(\hat{p}_1 - \hat{p}_2)$ is approximately normal.
  a. $n_1 = 12, n_2 = 14, \hat{p}_1 = .42, \hat{p}_2 = .57$ No
  b. $n_1 = 12, n_2 = 14, \hat{p}_1 = .92, \hat{p}_2 = .86$ No
  c. $n_1 = n_2 = 30, \hat{p}_1 = .70, \hat{p}_2 = .73$ Yes
  d. $n_1 = 100, n_2 = 250, \hat{p}_1 = .93, \hat{p}_2 = .97$ No
  e. $n_1 = 125, n_2 = 200, \hat{p}_1 = .08, \hat{p}_2 = .12$ Yes

9.42 For each of the following values of α, find the values of z for which $H_0: (p_1 - p_2) = 0$ would be rejected in favor of $H_a: (p_1 - p_2) < 0$.
  a. $\alpha = .01$ $z < -2.33$
  b. $\alpha = .025$
  c. $\alpha = .05$ $z < -1.645$
  d. $\alpha = .10$

9.43 Independent random samples, each containing 800 observations, were selected from two binomial populations. The samples from populations 1 and 2 produced 320 and 400 successes, respectively.
  a. Test $H_0: (p_1 - p_2) = 0$ against $H_a: (p_1 - p_2) \neq 0$. Use $\alpha = .05$. $z = -4.02$

  b. Test $H_0: (p_1 - p_2) = 0$ against $H_a: (p_1 - p_2) \neq 0$. Use $\alpha = .01$. $z = -4.02$
  c. Test $H_0: (p_1 - p_2) = 0$ against $H_a: (p_1 - p_2) < 0$. Use $\alpha = .01$. $z = -4.02$
  d. Form a 90% confidence interval for $(p_1 - p_2)$.

9.44 Construct a 95% confidence interval for $(p_1 - p_2)$ in each of the following situations:
  a. $n_1 = 400, \hat{p}_1 = .65; n_2 = 400, \hat{p}_2 = .58$
  b. $n_1 = 180, \hat{p}_1 = .31; n_2 = 250, \hat{p}_2 = .25$
  c. $n_1 = 100, \hat{p}_1 = .46; n_2 = 120, \hat{p}_2 = .61$

9.45 Sketch the sampling distribution of $(\hat{p}_1 - \hat{p}_2)$ based on independent random samples of $n_1 = 100$ and $n_2 = 200$ observations from two binomial populations with success probabilities $\hat{p}_1 = .1$ and $\hat{p}_2 = .5$, respectively.

9.46 Random samples of size $n_1 = 55$ and $n_2 = 65$ were drawn from populations 1 and 2, respectively. The samples yielded $\hat{p}_1 = .7$ and $\hat{p}_2 = .6$. Test $H_0: (p_1 - p_2) = 0$ against $H_a: (p_1 - p_2) > 0$ using $\alpha = .05$.

Applying the Concepts—Basic

9.47 In auction bidding, the "winner's curse" is the phenomenon of the winning (or highest) bid price being above the expected value of the item being auctioned. *The Review of Economics and Statistics* (Aug. 2001) published a study on whether bid experience impacts the likelihood of the winner's curse occurring. Two groups of bidders in a sealed-bid auction were compared: (1) super-experienced bidders and

(2) less-experienced bidders. In the super-experienced group, 29 of 189 winning bids were above the item's expected value; in the less-experienced group, 32 of 149 winning bids were above the item's expected value.

a. Find an estimate of p_1, the true proportion of super-experienced bidders who fall prey to the winner's curse. .153

b. Find an estimate of p_2, the true proportion of less-experienced bidders who fall prey to the winner's curse. .215

c. Construct a 90% confidence interval for $p_1 - p_2$. $-.062 \pm .070$

d. Give a practical interpretation of the confidence interval, part c. Make a statement about whether bid experience impacts the likelihood of the winner's curse occurring.

9.48 *American Demographics* (Jan. 2002) reported the results of a survey on the planning habits of men and women. In response to the question, "What is your preferred method of planning and keeping track of meetings, appointments and deadlines?", 56% of the men and 46% of the women answered "keep them in my head." A nationally representative sample of 1,000 adults participated in the survey; therefore, assume that 500 were men and 500 were women.

a. Set up the null and alternative hypotheses for testing whether the percentage of men who prefer keeping track of appointments in their head is larger than the corresponding percentage of women. $H_0: p_1 - p_2 = 0$ vs. $H_a: p_1 - p_2 > 0$

b. Compute the test statistic for the test. $z = 3.16$

c. Give the rejection region for the test using $\alpha = .01$. $z > 2.33$

d. Find the *p*-value for the test. ≈ 0

e. Make the appropriate conclusion.

9.49 Who is more likely to get a routine medical checkup, employed or unemployed people? To answer this question, a team of physicians and public health professors collected data on a sample of over 2,200 individuals (*American Journal of Public Health*, Jan. 2002). Of the 1,140 individuals who were employed, 642 visited a physician for a routine checkup within the past year. In contrast, 740 of the 1,106 unemployed individuals had a routine medical checkup within the past year.

a. Specify the parameter of interest to the research team. $p_1 - p_2$

b. Set up the null and alternative hypotheses for testing whether there is a difference between the percentages of employed and unemployed people who have a recent routine medical checkup. $H_0: p_1 - p_2 = 0$ vs. $H_a: p_1 - p_2 \neq 0$

c. Compute the test statistic for the test. $z = -5.16$

d. Give the rejection region for the test using $\alpha = .01$. $z > 2.58$ or $z < -2.58$

e. The research team reported the p-value for the test as *p*-value ≈ 0. Do you agree? Yes

f. Make the appropriate conclusion.

9.50 *Working Women* (June 1999) published the results of a 1999 Gallup poll that found that 92% of adult Americans would vote for a woman president. In 1975, a similar poll found that only 73% would vote for a woman.

a. Let p_{1999} and p_{1975} represent the population parameters of interest for this study. In the words of the problem, define these parameters.

b. Assume the sample sizes were 2,000 in 1999 and 1,500 in 1975. Are these sample sizes large enough ton conclude that the sampling distribution of $(p_{1999} - p_{1975})$ is approximately normally distributed? Justify your answer. Yes

c. Construct a 90% confidence interval for $(p_{1999} - p_{1975})$. Interpret your confidence interval in the context of the problem. $.19 \pm .02$

d. Rework part b under the assumption that the sample sizes for 1999 and 1975 are 20 and 50, respectively.

9.51 Price scanners are widely used in U.S. supermarkets. While they are fast and easy to use, they also make mistakes. Over the years, various consumer advocacy groups have complained that scanners routinely gouge the customer by overcharging. A recent Federal Trade Commission study found that supermarket scanners erred 3.47% of the time and department store scanners erred 9.15% of the time ("Scan Errors Help Public," *Newark Star-Ledger*, Oct. 23, 1996).

a. Assume the above error rates were determined from merchandise samples of size 800 and 900, respectively. Are these sample sizes large enough to apply the methods of this section to estimate the difference in the error rates? Justify your answer. Yes

b. Use a 98% confidence interval to estimate the difference in the error rates. Interpret your result.

c. What assumptions must hold to ensure the validity of the confidence interval of part **b?**

Applying the Concepts—Intermediate

9.52 In evaluating the usefulness and validity of a questionnaire, researchers often pretest the questionnaire on different independently selected samples of respondents. Knowledge of the differences and similarities of the samples and their respective populations is important for interpreting the questionnaire's validity. *Educational and Psychological Measurement* (Feb. 1998) reported on a newly developed questionnaire for measuring the career success expectations of employees. The instrument was tested on the two independent samples described in the table at the top of p. 521.

a. Does the population of managers and professional from which the sample was drawn consist of more males than the part-time MBA population does? Conduct the appropriate test using $\alpha = .05$.

	Managers and Professionals	Part-Time MBA Students
Sample size	162	109
Gender (% males)	95.0	68.9
Marital status (% married)	91.2	53.4

Source: Stephens, Gregory K., Szajna, Bernadette, and Broome, Kirk M., "The Career Success Expectation Scale: An Exploratory and Confirmatory Factor Analysis." *Educational and Psychological Measurement,* Vol. 58, No. 1, Feb. 1998, pp. 129–141.

b. Describe any assumptions you made in conducting the test of part a and why you made them.

c. Does the population of managers and professionals consist of more married individuals than the part-time MBA population does? Conduct the appropriate hypothesis test using $\alpha = .01$. $z = 7.14$

d. What assumptions must hold for the test of part c to be valid?

9.53 With the rapid growth in legalized gambling in the United States, there is concern that the involvement of youth in gambling activities is also increasing. University of Minnesota professor Randy Stinchfield compared the rates of gambling among Minnesota public school students between 1992 and 1998 (*Journal of Gambling Studies*, Winter 2001). Based on survey data, the table shows the percentages of 9th grade boys who gambled weekly or daily on any game (e.g., cards, sports betting, lotteries) for the two years.

	1992	1998
Number of 9th grade boys in survey	21,484	23,199
Number who gambled weekly/daily	4,684	5,313

a. Are the percentages of nineth-grade boys who gambled weekly or daily on any game in 1992 and 1998 significantly different? (Use $\alpha = .01$.) $z = -2.79$

b. Professor Stinchfield states that "because of the large sample sizes, even small differences may achieve statistical significance, so interpretations of the differences should include a judgement regarding the magnitude of the difference and its public health significance." Do you agree with this statement? If not, why not? If so, obtain a measure of the magnitude of the difference between 1992 and 1998 and attach a measure of reliability to the difference. $-.011 \pm .010$

9.54 A University of South Florida biologist conducted an experiment to determine whether increased levels of carbon dioxide kill leaf-eating moths (*USF Magazine*, Winter 1999). Moth larvae were placed in open containers filled with oak leaves. Half the containers had normal carbon dioxide levels while the other half had double the normal level of carbon dioxide. Ten percent of the larvae in the containers with high carbon dioxide levels died,

compared to five percent in the containers with normal levels. Assume that 80 moth larvae were placed, at random, in each of the two types of containers. Do the experimental results demonstrate that an increased level of carbon dioxide is effective in killing a higher percentage of leaf-eating moth larvae? Test using $\alpha = .01$.

9.55 *Industrial Marketing Management* (Vol. 25, 1996) published a study that examined the demographics, decision-making roles, and time demands of product managers. Independent samples of $n_1 = 93$ consumer/commercial product managers and $n_2 = 212$ industrial product managers took part in the study. In the consumer/commercial group, 40% of the product managers are 40 years of age or older; in the industrial group, 54% are 40 or more years old. Make an inference about the difference between the true proportions of consumer/commercial and industrial product managers who are at least 40 years old. Justify your choice of method (confidence interval or hypothesis test) and α level. Do industrial product managers tend to be older than consumer/commercial product managers?

9.56 Should marketers use ads that appeal to children to sell adult products? One controversial advertisement campaign was Camel cigarettes' use of the cartoon character "Joe Camel" as its brand symbol. (The Federal Trade Commission eventually banned ads featuring Joe Camel because they supposedly encouraged young people to smoke.) Lucy L. Henke, a marketing professor at the University of New Hampshire, assessed young children's abilities to recognize cigarette brand advertising symbols. She found that 15 out of 28 children under the age of 6, and 46 out of 55 children age 6 and over recognized Joe Camel, the brand symbol of Camel cigarettes (*Journal of Advertising*, Winter 1995).

a. Use a 95% confidence interval to estimate the proportion of all children that recognize Joe Camel. Interpret the interval. $.735 \pm .095$

b. Do the data indicate that recognition of Joe Camel increases with age? Test using $\alpha = .05$. $z = -2.93$

Applying the Concepts—Advanced

9.57 Do you have an insatiable craving for chocolate or some other food? Since many North Americans apparently do, psychologists are designing scientific studies to examine the phenomenon. According to the *New York Times* (Feb. 22, 1995), one of the largest studies of food cravings involved a survey of 1,000 McMaster University (Canada) students. The survey revealed that 97% of the women in the study acknowledged specific food cravings while only 67% of the men did.

a. How large do n_1 and n_2 need to be to conclude that the true proportion of women who acknowledge having food cravings exceeds the corresponding proportion of men? Assume $\alpha = .01$. 18

b. Why is it dangerous to conclude from the study that women have a higher incidence of food cravings than men?

9.4 Determining the Sample Size

You can find the appropriate sample size to estimate the difference between a pair of parameters with a specified margin of error (ME) and degree of reliability by using the method described in Section 7.4. That is, to estimate the difference between a pair of parameters correct to within *ME* units with confidence level $(1 - \alpha)$, let $z_{\alpha/2}$ standard deviations of the sampling distribution of the estimator equal ME. Then solve for the sample size. To do this, you have to solve the problem for a specific ratio between n_1 and n_2. Most often, you will want to have equal sample sizes, that is, $n_1 = n_2 = n$. We will illustrate the procedure with two examples.

EXAMPLE 9.8

FINDING THE SAMPLE SIZES FOR ESTIMATING $\mu_1 - \mu_2$

Problem New fertilizer compounds are often advertised with the promise of increased crop yields. Suppose we want to compare the mean yield μ_1 of wheat when a new fertilizer is used to the mean yield μ_2 with a fertilizer in common use. The estimate of the difference in mean yield per acre is to be correct to within .25 bushel with a confidence coefficient of .95. If the sample sizes are to be equal, find $n_1 = n_2 = n$, the number of one-acre plots of wheat assigned to each fertilizer.

$n_1 = n_2 = 769$

Solution To solve the problem, you need to know something about the variation in the bushels of yield per acre. Suppose from past records you know the yields of wheat possess a range of approximately 10 bushels per acre. You could then approximate $\sigma_1 = \sigma_2 = \sigma$ by letting the range equal 4σ. Thus,

$$4\sigma \approx 10 \text{ bushels}$$
$$\sigma \approx 2.5 \text{ bushels}$$

Teaching Tip
When determining the sample sizes for two samples, we set the condition that both sample sizes will be equal. The *n* we find is the sample size necessary for *both* samples.

The next step is to solve the equation

$$z_{\alpha/2}\sigma_{(\bar{x}_1 - \bar{x}_2)} = \text{ME} \quad \text{or} \quad z_{\alpha/2}\sqrt{\frac{\sigma_1^2}{n_1} + \frac{\sigma_2^2}{n_2}} = \text{ME}$$

for *n*, where $n = n_1 = n_2$. Since we want the estimate to lie within ME = .25 of $(\mu_1 - \mu_2)$ with confidence coefficient equal to .95, we have $z_{\alpha/2} = z_{.025} = 1.96$. Then, letting $\sigma_1 = \sigma_2 = 2.5$ and solving for *n*, we have

$$1.96\sqrt{\frac{(2.5)^2}{n} + \frac{(2.5)^2}{n}} = .25$$

$$1.96\sqrt{\frac{2(2.5)^2}{n}} = .25$$

$$n = 768.32 \approx 769 \text{ (rounding up)}$$

Consequently, you will have to sample 769 acres of wheat for each fertilizer to estimate the difference in mean yield per acre to within .25 bushel.

Look Back Since $n = 769$ would necessitate extensive and costly experimentation, you might decide to allow a larger margin of error (say, ME = .50 or ME = 1) in order to reduce the sample size, or you might decrease the confidence coefficient. The point is that we can obtain an idea of the experimental effort necessary to achieve a specified precision in our final estimate by determining the approximate sample size *before* the experiment is begun.

Now Work *Exercise 9.58a*

■ ■ ■

EXAMPLE 9.9   FINDING THE SAMPLE SIZES FOR ESTIMATING $p_1 - p_2$

Problem   A production supervisor suspects a difference exists between the proportions p_1 and p_2 of defective items produced by two different machines. Experience has shown that the proportion defective for each of the two machines is in the neighborhood of .03. If the supervisor wants to estimate the difference in the proportions to within .005 using a 95% confidence interval, how many items must be randomly sampled from the production of each machine? (Assume that the supervisor wants $n_1 = n_2 = n$.)

$n_1 = n_2 = 8,944$

Solution   In this sampling problem, the margin of error is ME = .005, and for the specified level of reliability, $(1 - \alpha) = .95$, $z_{\alpha/2} = z_{.025} = 1.96$. Then, letting $p_1 = p_2 = .03$ and $n_1 = n_2 = n$, we find the required sample size per machine by solving the following equation for n:

Suggested Exercise 9.66

$$z_{\alpha/2}\sigma_{(\hat{p}_1 - \hat{p}_2)} = B$$

or

Suggested Exercise 9.68

$$z_{\alpha/2}\sqrt{\frac{p_1 q_1}{n_1} + \frac{p_2 q_2}{n_2}} = ME$$

$$1.96\sqrt{\frac{(.03)(.97)}{n} + \frac{(.03)(.97)}{n}} = .005$$

$$1.96\sqrt{\frac{2(.03)(.97)}{n}} = .005$$

$$n = 8,943.2$$

Look Back This large n will likely result in a tedious sampling procedure. If the supervisor insists on estimating $(p_1 - p_2)$ correct to within .005 with 95% confidence, approximately 9,000 items will have to be inspected for each machine.

Now Work *Exercise 9.61a*

■ ■ ■

You can see from the calculations in Example 9.9 that $\sigma_{(\hat{p}_1 - \hat{p}_2)}$ (and hence the solution, $n_1 = n_2 = n$) depends on the actual (but unknown) values of p_1 and p_2. In fact, the required sample size $n_1 = n_2 = n$ is largest when $p_1 = p_2 = .5$. Therefore, if you have no prior information on the approximate values of p_1 and p_2, use $p_1 = p_2 = .5$ in the formula for $\sigma_{(\hat{p}_1 - \hat{p}_2)}$. If p_1 and p_2 are in fact close to .5, then the values of n_1 and n_2 that you have calculated will be correct. If p_1 and p_2 differ substantially from .5, then your solutions for n_1 and n_2 will be larger than needed. Consequently, using $p_1 = p_2 = .5$ when solving for n_1 and n_2 is a conservative procedure because the sample sizes n_1 and n_2 will be at least as large as (and probably larger than) needed.

The procedures for determining sample sizes necessary for estimating $(\mu_1 - \mu_2)$ or $(p_1 - p_2)$ for the case $n_1 = n_2$ are given in the following boxes.

Determination of Sample Size for Estimating $\mu_1 - \mu_2$

To estimate $(\mu_1 - \mu_2)$ with a given margin of error ME and with confidence level $(1 - \alpha)$, use the following formula to solve for equal sample sizes that will achieve the desired reliability:

$$n_1 = n_2 = \frac{(z_{\alpha/2})^2(\sigma_1^2 + \sigma_2^2)}{(\text{ME})^2}$$

You will need to substitute estimates for the values of σ_1^2 and σ_2^2 before solving for the sample size. These estimates might be sample variances s_1^2 and s_2^2 from prior sampling (e.g., a pilot sample), or from an educated (and conservatively large) guess based on the range—that is, $s \approx R/4$.

Determination of Sample Size for Estimating $p_1 - p_2$

To estimate $(p_1 - p_2)$ with a given margin of error ME and with confidence level $(1 - \alpha)$, use the following formula to solve for equal sample sizes that will achieve the desired reliability:

$$n_1 = n_2 = \frac{(z_{\alpha/2})^2(p_1 q_1 + p_2 q_2)}{(\text{ME})^2}$$

You will need to substitute estimates for the values of p_1 and p_2 before solving for the sample size. These estimates might be based on prior samples, obtained from educated guesses or, most conservatively, specified as $p_1 = p_2 = .5$.

Exercises 9.58–9.68

Learning the Mechanics

9.58 Find the appropriate values of n_1 and n_2 (assume $n_1 = n_2$) needed to estimate $(\mu_1 - \mu_2)$ with:

a. A margin of error equal to 3.2 with 95% confidence. From prior experience it is known that $\sigma_1 \approx 15$ and $\sigma_2 \approx 17$. $n_1 = n_2 = 193$

b. A margin of error equal to 8 with 99% confidence. The range of each population is 60.

c. A 90% confidence interval of width 1.0. Assume that $\sigma_1^2 \approx 5.8$ and $\sigma_2^2 \approx 7.5$. $n_1 = n_2 = 144$

9.59 Suppose you want to estimate the difference between two population means correct to within 1.8 with a 95% confidence interval. If prior information suggests that the population variances are approximately equal to $\sigma_1^2 = \sigma_2^2 = 14$ and you want to select independent random samples of equal size from the populations, how large should the sample sizes, n_1 and n_2, be? $n_1 = n_2 = 34$

9.60 Enough money has been budgeted to collect independent random samples of size $n_1 = n_2 = 100$ from populations 1 and 2 in order to estimate $(\mu_1 - \mu_2)$.

Prior information indicates that $\sigma_1 = \sigma_2 = 10$. Have sufficient funds been allocated to construct a 90% confidence interval for $(\mu_1 - \mu_2)$ of width 5 or less? Justify your answer. $n_1 = n_2 = 87$

9.61 Assuming that $n_1 = n_2$, find the sample sizes needed to estimate $(p_1 - p_2)$ for each of the following situations:

a. Margin of error $= .01$ with 99% confidence. Assume that $p_1 \approx .4$ and $p_2 \approx .7$. $n_1 = n_2 = 29,954$

b. A 90% confidence interval of width .05. Assume that there is no prior information available to obtain approximate values of p_1 and p_2. $n_1 = n_2 = 2,165$

c. Margin of error $= .03$ with 90% confidence. Assume that $p_1 \approx .2$ and $p_2 \approx .3$. $n_1 = n_2 = 1,113$

Applying the Concepts—Basic

9.62 Refer to the EPA study of average bacteria counts in water specimens at two river locations, Exercise 9.22 (p. 500). How many water specimens need to be sampled at each location in order for a 95% confidence interval for the true mean difference in bacteria counts to yield an estimate that lies within 1.5 bacteria of the true difference? Assume equal sample sizes will be collected at each location. $n_1 = n_2 = 27$

9.63 Refer to the *Working Women* (June 1999) comparison of the percentages of adult Americans in 1975 and 1999 who would vote for a woman president, Exercise 9.50 (p. 520). Suppose you want to make a similar comparison for the years 2000 and 2003. How many adults should be sampled each year to estimate the difference in percentages to within 3% with 90% confidence? Assume equal sample sizes will be collected. $n_1 = n_2 = 443$

9.64 A pollster wants to estimate the difference between the proportions of men and women who favor a particular national candidate using a 90% confidence interval of width .04. Suppose the pollster has no prior information about the proportions. If equal numbers of men and women are to be polled, how large should the sample sizes be? $n_1 = n_2 = 3,383$

Applying the Concepts—Intermediate

9.65 Is housework hazardous to your health? A study in the *Public Health Reports* (July–Aug. 1992) compares the life expectancies of 25-year-old white women in the labor force to those who are housewives. How large a sample would have to be taken from each group in order to be 95% confident that the estimate of difference in average life expectancies for the two groups is within one year of the true difference in average life expectancies? Assume that equal sample sizes will be selected from the two groups, and that the standard deviation for both groups is approximately 15 years. $n_1 = n_2 = 1,729$

9.66 All cable companies carry at least one home shopping channel. Who uses these home shopping services? Are the shoppers primarily men or women? Suppose you want to estimate the difference in the proportions of men and women who say they have used or expect to

use televised home shopping using an 80% confidence interval of width .06 or less.
  a. Approximately how many people should be included in your samples? $n_1 = n_2 = 911$
  b. Suppose you want to obtain individual estimates for the two proportions of interest. Will the sample size found in part a be large enough to provide estimates of each proportion correct to within .02 with probability equal to .90? Justify your response. $n_1 = n_2 = 1,692$

9.67 According to a national survey of 1,441 firms by the American Management Association, downsizing is no longer the dominant theme in the workplace (*Newark Star-Ledger*, Oct. 22, 1996). But are there regional differences in this phenomenon? Is there more growth in jobs in the Sunbelt than the Rustbelt? Assuming equal sample sizes for the two regions, how large would the samples need to be to estimate the difference in the proportion of firms that plan to add new jobs in the next year in the two regions? A 90% confidence interval of width no more than .10 is desired. $n_1 = n_2 = 542$

9.68 Even though Japan is an economic superpower, Japanese workers are in many ways worse off than their U.S. and European counterparts. For example, a few years ago the estimated average housing space per person (in square feet) was 665.2 in the United States, and only 269 in Japan (*Minneapolis Star-Tribune*, Jan. 31, 1993). Suppose a team of economists and sociologists from the United Nations plans to reestimate the difference in the mean housing space per person for U.S. and Japanese workers. Assume that equal sample sizes will be used for each country and that the standard deviation is 35 square feet for Japan and 80 for the United States. How many people should be sampled in each country to estimate the difference to within 10 square feet with 95% confidence? $n_1 = n_2 = 293$

9.5 Comparing Two Population Variances: Independent Sampling (Optional)

Teaching Tip

Use examples to show the key words associated with determining that the parameter of interest is comparing two population variances.

Many times it is of practical interest to use the techniques developed in this chapter to compare the means or proportions of two populations. However, there are also important instances when we wish to compare two population variances. For example, when two devices are available for producing precision measurements (scales, calipers, thermometers, etc.), we might want to compare the variability of the measurements of the devices before deciding which one to purchase. Or when two standardized tests can be used to rate job applicants, the variability of the scores for both tests should be taken into consideration before deciding which test to use.

For problems like these we need to develop a statistical procedure to compare population variances. The common statistical procedure for comparing population variances, σ_1^2 and σ_2^2, makes an inference about the ratio σ_1^2/σ_2^2. In this section, we will show how to test the null hypothesis that the ratio σ_1^2/σ_2^2 equals 1 (the variances are equal) against the alternative hypothesis that the ratio differs from 1 (the variances differ):

$$H_0: \frac{\sigma_1^2}{\sigma_2^2} = 1 \qquad (\sigma_1^2 = \sigma_2^2)$$

$$H_{\text{a}}: \frac{\sigma_1^2}{\sigma_2^2} \neq 1 \qquad (\sigma_1^2 \neq \sigma_2^2)$$

To make an inference about the ratio σ_1^2/σ_2^2, it seems reasonable to collect sample data and use the ratio of the sample variances, s_1^2/s_2^2. We will use the test statistic

$$F = \frac{s_1^2}{s_2^2}$$

To establish a rejection region for the test statistic, we need to know the sampling distribution of s_1^2/s_2^2. As you will subsequently see, the sampling distribution of s_1^2/s_2^2 is based on two of the assumptions already required for the t-test:

1. The two sampled populations are normally distributed.
2. The samples are randomly and independently selected from their respective populations.

Teaching Tip
Point out that these are the same assumptions that were encountered earlier in this chapter.

When these assumptions are satisfied and when the null hypothesis is true (that is, $\sigma_1^2 = \sigma_2^2$), the sampling distribution of $F = s_1^2/s_2^2$ is the **F-distribution** with $(n_1 - 1)$ numerator degrees of freedom and $(n_2 - 1)$ denominator degrees of freedom, respectively. The shape of the F-distribution depends on the degrees of freedom associated with s_1^2 and s_2^2—that is, on $(n_1 - 1)$ and $(n_2 - 1)$. An F-distribution with 7 and 9 df is shown in Figure 9.17. As you can see, the distribution is skewed to the right, since s_1^2/s_2^2 cannot be less than 0 but can increase without bound.

Figure 9.17

An F-distribution with 7 numerator and 9 denominator degrees of freedom

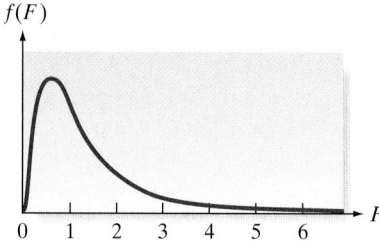

Biography

GEORGE W. SNEDECOR (1882–1974)
Snedecor's F-test

George W. Snedecor's education began at the University of Alabama, where he obtained his bachelor's degree in mathematics and physics. He went on to the University of Michigan for his master's degree in physics and finally earned his Ph.D. in mathematics at the University of Kentucky. Snedecor learned of an opening for an assistant professor of mathematics at the University of Iowa, packed his belongings in his car, and began driving to apply for the position. By mistake, he ended up in Ames, Iowa, home of Iowa State University—then an agricultural school that had no need for a mathematics teacher. Nevertheless, Snedecor stayed and founded a statistics laboratory, eventually teaching the first course in statistics at Iowa State in 1915. In 1933, Snedecor turned the statistics laboratory into the first ever Department of Statistics in the United States. During his tenure as chair of the department, Snedecor published his landmark textbook, *Statistical Methods* (1937). The text contained the first published reference for a test of hypothesis to compare two variances. Although Snedecor named it the *F*-test in honor of statistician R. A. Fisher (who had developed the *F*-distribution a few years earlier—see Biograpy, p. 558), many researchers still refer to it as Snedecor's *F*-test. Now in its ninth edition, *Statistical Methods* (with William Cochran as a coauthor) continues to be one of the most frequently cited texts in the statistics field.

Teaching Tip

Use an overhead transparency to help the students with the *F*-distribution. This is the first time they have worked with two sets of degrees of freedom.

We need to be able to find *F* values corresponding to the tail areas of this distribution in order to establish the rejection region for our test of hypothesis because we expect the ratio *F* of the sample variances to be either very large or very small when the population variances are unequal. The upper-tail *F* values for $\alpha = .10, .05, .025$, and $.01$ can be found in Tables VIII, IX, X, and XI of Appendix B. Table IX is partially reproduced in Table 9.7. It gives *F* values that correspond to $\alpha = .05$ upper-tail areas for different degrees of freedom ν_1 for the numerator sample variance, s_1^2, whereas the rows correspond to the degrees of freedom ν_2 for the denominator sample variance, s_2^2. Thus, if the numerator degrees of freedom is $\nu_1 = 7$ and the denominator degrees of freedom is $\nu_2 = 9$, we look in the seventh column and ninth row to find $F_{.05} = 3.29$. As shown in Figure 9.18, $\alpha = .05$ is the tail area to the right of 3.29 in the *F*-distribution with 7 and 9 df. That is, if $\sigma_1^2 = \sigma_2^2$, then the probability that the *F* statistic will exceed 3.29 is $\alpha = .05$.

TABLE 9.7   Reproduction of Part of Table IX in Appendix B: Percentage Points of the *F*-Distribution, $\alpha = .05$

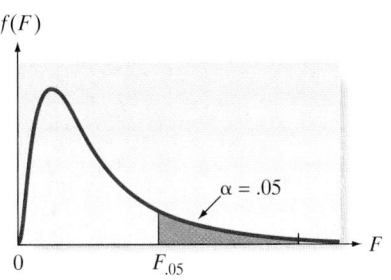

ν_1 ν_2	1	2	3	4	5	6	7	8	9
1	161.4	199.5	215.7	224.6	230.2	234.0	236.8	238.9	240.5
2	18.51	19.00	19.16	19.25	19.30	19.33	19.35	19.37	19.38
3	10.13	9.55	9.28	9.12	9.01	8.94	8.89	8.85	8.81
4	7.71	6.94	6.59	6.39	6.26	6.16	6.09	6.04	6.00
5	6.61	5.79	5.41	5.19	5.05	4.95	4.88	4.82	4.77
6	5.99	5.14	4.76	4.53	4.39	4.28	4.21	4.15	4.10
7	5.59	4.74	4.35	4.12	3.97	3.87	3.79	3.73	3.68
8	5.32	4.46	4.07	3.84	3.69	3.58	3.50	3.44	3.39
9	5.12	4.26	3.86	3.63	3.48	3.37	3.29	3.23	3.18
10	4.96	4.10	3.71	3.48	3.33	3.22	3.14	3.07	3.02
11	4.84	3.98	3.59	3.36	3.20	3.09	3.01	2.95	2.90
12	4.75	3.89	3.49	3.25	3.11	3.00	2.91	2.85	2.80
13	4.67	3.81	3.41	3.18	3.03	2.92	2.83	2.77	2.71
14	4.60	3.74	3.34	3.11	2.96	2.85	2.76	2.70	2.65

Numerator Degrees of Freedom

Denominator Degrees of Freedom

Figure 9.18
An F-distribution for $\nu_1 = 7$ and $\nu_2 = 9$ df; $\alpha = .05$

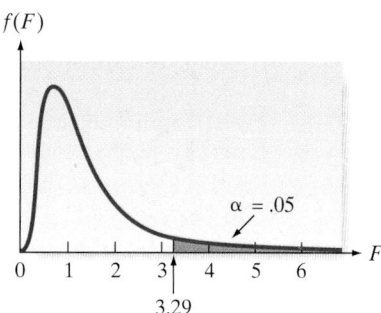

Now Work   *Exercise 9.69*

EXAMPLE 9.10   CONDUCTING AN *F*-TEST

Problem   A manufacturer of paper products wants to compare the variation in daily production levels at two paper mills. Independent random samples of days are selected from each mill and the production levels (in units) recorded. The data are shown in Table 9.8. Do these data provide sufficient evidence to indicate a difference in the variability of production levels at the two paper mills? (Use $\alpha = .10$.)

F = 2.97, reject H_0

 PAPERMILLS

TABLE 9.8   Production Levels at Two Paper Mills

Mill 1:	34	18	28	21	32	40	22	23	22	29
	25	10	38							
Mill 2:	31	13	27	19	22	18	23	22	21	13
	18	15	24	13	19	18	19	23		

Solution   Let

$$\sigma_1^2 = \text{Population variance of production levels at mill 1}$$
$$\sigma_2^2 = \text{Population variance of production levels at mill 2}$$

The hypotheses of interest then are

$$H_0: \frac{\sigma_1^2}{\sigma_2^2} = 1 \qquad (\sigma_1^2 = \sigma_2^2)$$

$$H_a: \frac{\sigma_1^2}{\sigma_2^2} \neq 1 \qquad (\sigma_1^2 \neq \sigma_2^2)$$

Teaching Tip
Remind the students that in the two-tailed test the larger sample variance always is put in the numerator of the test statistic, regardless of which sample was called sample 1.

The nature of the F-tables given in Appendix B affects the form of the test statistic. To form the rejection region for a two-tailed F-test, we want to make certain that the upper tail is used, because only the upper-tail values of F are shown in Tables VIII, IX, X, and XI. To accomplish this, *we will always place the larger sample variance in the numerator of the F-test statistic*. This has the effect of doubling the tabulated value for α, since we double the probability that the F-ratio will fall in the upper tail by always placing the larger sample variance in the numerator. That is, we establish a one-tailed rejection region by putting the larger variance in the numerator rather than establishing rejection regions in both tails.

Thus, for our example, we have a numerator s_1^2 with df $= \nu_1 = n_1 - 1 = 12$ and a denominator s_2^2 with df $= \nu_2 = n_2 - 1 = 17$. Therefore, the test statistic will be

$$F = \frac{\text{Larger sample variance}}{\text{Smaller sample variance}} = \frac{s_1^2}{s_2^2}$$

and we will reject H_0: $\sigma_1^2 = \sigma_2^2$ for $\alpha = .10$ when the calculated value of F exceeds the tabulated value:

$$F_{\alpha/2} = F_{.05} = 2.38 \quad \text{(see Figure 9.19)}$$

To calculate the value of the test statistic, we require the sample variances. Summary statistics for the data in Table 9.8 are shown on the MINITAB printout, Figure 9.20. The sample standard deviations are $s_1 = 8.36$ and $s_2 = 4.85$. Therefore,

$$F = \frac{s_1^2}{s_2^2} = \frac{(8.36)^2}{(4.85)^2} = 2.97$$

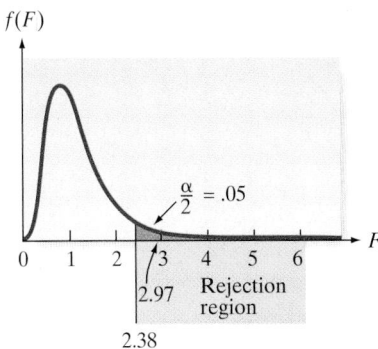

Figure 9.19
Rejection region for Example 9.10

When we compare this result to the rejection region shown in Figure 9.19, we see that $F = 2.97$ falls in the rejection region. Therefore, the data provide sufficient evidence to indicate that the population variances differ. It appears that the variation in production levels at mill 1 tends to be higher than the variation at mill 2.

Figure 9.20
MINITAB summary statistics for data in Table 9.8

Descriptive Statistics: LEVEL

Variable	MILL	N	Mean	SE Mean	StDev	Minimum	Maximum
LEVEL	1	13	26.31	2.32	8.36	10.00	40.00
	2	18	19.89	1.14	4.85	13.00	31.00

Teaching Tip
Point out that the general test of hypothesis concept works for all test of hypothesis applications, even when the test statistic follows the F-distribution.

Look Back What would you have concluded if the value of F calculated from the samples had not fallen in the rejection region? Would you conclude that the null hypothesis of equal variances is true? No, because then you risk the possibility of a Type II error (accepting H_0 if H_a is true) without knowing the value of β, the probability of accepting H_0: $\sigma_1^2 = \sigma_2^2$ if in fact it is false. Since we will not consider the calculation of β for specific alternatives in this text, when the F statistic does not fall in the rejection region we simply conclude that insufficient sample evidence exists to refute the null hypothesis that $\sigma_1^2 = \sigma_2^2$.

Now Work *Exercise 9.74a*

■ ■ ■

The F-test for equal population variances is summarized in the following boxes.*

*Although a test of a hypothesis of equality of variances is the most common application of the F-test, it can also be used to test a hypothesis that the ratio between the population variances is equal to some specified value. H_0: $\sigma_1^2/\sigma_2^2 = k$. The test is conducted in exactly the same way as specified in the box. except that we use the test statistic

$$F = \frac{s_1^2}{s_2^2}\left(\frac{1}{k}\right)$$

F-Test for Equal Population Variances

One-Tailed Test	Two-Tailed Test

One-Tailed Test

$H_0: \sigma_1^2 = \sigma_2^2$
$H_a: \sigma_1^2 < \sigma_2^2$ (or $H_a: \sigma_1^2 > \sigma_2^2$)

Test statistic:

$$F = \frac{s_2^2}{s_1^2}$$

$$\left(\text{or } F = \frac{s_1^2}{s_2^2} \text{ when } H_a: \sigma_1^2 > \sigma_2^2\right)$$

Rejection region:

$F > F_\alpha$

Two-Tailed Test

$H_0: \sigma_1^2 = \sigma_2^2$
$H_a: \sigma_1^2 \neq \sigma_2^2$

Test statistic:

$$F = \frac{\text{Larger sample variance}}{\text{Smaller sample variance}}$$

$$= \frac{s_1^2}{s_2^2} \text{ when } s_1^2 > s_2^2$$

$$\left(\text{or } \frac{s_2^2}{s_1^2} \text{ when } s_2^2 > s_1^2\right)$$

Rejection region:

$F > F_{\alpha/2}$

where F_α and $F_{\alpha/2}$ are based on ν_1 = numerator degrees of freedom and ν_2 = denominator degrees of freedom; ν_1 and ν_2 are the degrees of freedom for the numerator and denominator sample variances, respectively.

Conditions Required for a Valid *F*-Test for Equal Variances

1. Both sampled populations are normally distributed.
2. The samples are random and independent.

EXAMPLE 9.11

THE OBSERVED SIGNIFICANCE LEVEL OF AN *F*-TEST

Problem Find the *p*-value for the test in Example 9.10 using the *F*-tables in Appendix B. Compare this to the exact *p*-value obtained from a computer printout.

Solution Since the observed value of the *F* statistic in Example 9.10 was 2.97, the observed significance level of the test would equal the probability of observing a value of *F* at least as contradictory to $H_0: \sigma_1^2 = \sigma_2^2$ as $F = 2.97$, if in fact H_0 is true. Since we give the *F*-tables in Appendix B only for values of α equal to .10, .05, .025, and .01 we can only approximate the observed significance level. Checking Tables X and XI, we find $F_{.025} = 2.82$ and $F_{.01} = 3.46$. Since the observed value of *F* exceeds $F_{.025}$ but is less than $F_{.01}$, the observed significance level for the test is less than $2(.025) = .05$, but greater than $2(.01) = .02$, that is,

.02 < p < .05

$$.02 < p\text{-value} < .05$$

The exact *p*-value of the test is shown on the MINITAB printout, Figure 9.21. This value (highlighted), is .04.

LookBack We double the α value shown in Table X and XI because this is a two-tailed test.

Now Work *Exercise 9.74b*

Teaching Tip
Emphasize that all computer packages supply a *p*-value with the calculated *F* statistic. It is extremely important to have a solid understanding of the *p*-value interpretation.

Test for Equal Variances: LEVEL versus MILL

```
95% Bonferroni confidence intervals for standard deviations

MILL   N    Lower      StDev     Upper
  1   13   5.73182   8.36047   14.9507
  2   18   3.49950   4.84936    7.7455


F-Test (normal distribution)
Test statistic = 2.97, p-value = 0.040


Levene's Test (any continuous distribution)
Test statistic = 3.78, p-value = 0.062
```

Figure 9.21
MINITAB *F*-test for equal variances

■ ■ ■

As a final example of an application, consider the comparison of population variances as a check of the assumption $\sigma_1^2 = \sigma_2^2$ needed for the two-sample *t*-test. Rejection of the null hypothesis $\sigma_1^2 = \sigma_2^2$ would indicate that the assumption is invalid. [*Note:* Nonrejection of the null hypothesis does *not* imply that the assumption is valid.] We illustrate with an example.

EXAMPLE 9.12

CHECKING THE ASSUMPTION OF EQUAL VARIANCES

Problem   In Example 9.4 (Section 9.1) we used the two-sample *t*-statistic to compare the success indexes of two groups of managers. The data are repeated in Table 9.9 for convenience. The use of the *t*-statistic was based on the assumption that the population variances of the managerial success indexes were equal for the two groups. Conduct a test of hypothesis to check this assumption at $\alpha = .10$.

p = .2553, Fail to reject H_0

 MANSUCCESS

TABLE 9.9   Managerial Success Indexes for Two Groups of Managers

Group 1						Group 2					
Interaction with Outsiders						Few Interactions					
65	58	78	60	68	69	62	53	36	34	56	50
66	70	53	71	63	63	42	57	46	68	48	42
						52	53	43			

Suggested Exercise 9.82

Solution   We want to test

$$H_0: \sigma_1^2 = \sigma_2^2$$
$$H_a: \sigma_1^2 \neq \sigma_2^2$$

Figure 9.22

EXCEL/PHStat2 *F*-test for testing assumption of equal variances

F Test for Differences in Two Variances	
Data	
Level of Significance	**0.05**
Population 1 Sample	
Sample Size	**15**
Sample Standard Deviation	**9.334**
Population 2 Sample	
Sample Size	**12**
Sample Standard Deviation	**6.61**
Intermediate Calculations	
F-Test Statistic	1.994035
Population 1 Sample Degrees of Freedom	14
Population 2 Sample Degrees of Freedom	11
Two-Tailed Test	
Lower Critical Value	**0.323144**
Upper Critical Value	**3.358821**
p-Value	0.255307
Do not reject the null hypothesis	

This *F*-test is shown on the Excel printout, Figure 9.22. Both the test statistic, $F = 1.99$, and two-tailed *p*-value, .2553, are highlighted on the printout. Since $\alpha = .10$ is less than the *p*-value, we do not reject the null hypothesis that the population variances of the success indexes are equal. It is here that the temptation to misuse the *F*-test is strongest. *We cannot conclude that the data justify the use of the t-statistic.* This is equivalent to accepting H_0, and we have repeatedly warned against this conclusion because the probability of a Type II error, β, is unknown. The α level of .10 protects us only against rejecting H_0 if it is true. This use of the *F*-test may prevent us from abusing the *t* procedure when we obtain a value of *F* that leads to a rejection of the assumption that $\sigma_1^2 = \sigma_2^2$. But when the *F*-statistic does not fall in the rejection region, we know little more about the validity of the assumption than before we conducted the test.

Now Work   *Exercise 9.82*

■ ■ ■

Teaching Tip

In general, the nonparametric analyses of Chapter 15 are useful whenever the assumptions are not satisfied.

What Do You Do If the Assumption of Normal Population Distributions Is Not Satisfied?

Answer: The *F*-test is much less robust (i.e., much more sensitive) to departures from normality than the *t*-test for comparing the population means (Section 9.1). If you have doubts about the normality of the population frequency distributions, use a **nonparametric method** (e.g., *Levene's test*) for comparing the two population variances. This method can be found in the nonparametric statistics texts listed in the references for Chapter 16.

Exercises 9.69–9.83

Learning the Mechanics

9.69 Use Tables VIII, IX, X, and XI of Appendix B to find each of the following F-values:
  a. $F_{.05}$ where $v_1 = 9$ and $v_2 = 6$ 4.10
  b. $F_{.01}$ where $v_1 = 18$ and $v_2 = 14$ 3.57
  c. $F_{.025}$ where $v_1 = 11$ and $v_2 = 4$ 8.805
  d. $F_{.10}$ where $v_1 = 20$ and $v_2 = 5$ 3.21

9.70 Given v_1 and v_2, find the following probabilities:
  a. $v_1 = 2, v_2 = 30, P(F \geq 5.39)$.   .01
  b. $v_1 = 24, v_2 = 10, P(F < 2.74)$.   .95
  c. $v_1 = 7, v_2 = 1, P(F \leq 236.8)$.   .95
  d. $v_1 = 40, v_2 = 40, P(F > 2.11)$.   .01

9.71 For each of the following cases, identify the rejection region that should be used to test $H_0: \sigma_1^2 = \sigma_2^2$ against $H_a: \sigma_1^2 > \sigma_2^2$. Assume $v_1 = 30$ and $v_2 = 20$.
  a. $\alpha = .10$ $F > 1.74$
  b. $\alpha = .05$ $F > 2.04$
  c. $\alpha = .025$ $F > 2.35$
  d. $\alpha = .01$ $F > 2.78$

9.72 For each of the following cases, identify the rejection region that should be used to test $H_0: \sigma_1^2 = \sigma_2^2$ against $H_a: \sigma_1^2 \neq \sigma_2^2$. Assume $v_1 = 10$ and $v_2 = 12$.
  a. $\alpha = .20$
  b. $\alpha = .10$
  c. $\alpha = .05$
  d. $\alpha = .02$

9.73 Specify the appropriate rejection region for testing $H_0: \sigma_1^2 = \sigma_2^2$ in each of the following situations:
  a. $H_a: \sigma_1^2 > \sigma_2^2; \alpha = .05, n_1 = 25, n_2 = 20$
  b. $H_a: \sigma_1^2 < \sigma_2^2; \alpha = .05, n_1 = 10, n_2 = 15$
  c. $H_a: \sigma_1^2 \neq \sigma_2^2; \alpha = .10, n_1 = 21, n_2 = 31$
  d. $H_a: \sigma_1^2 < \sigma_2^2; \alpha = .01, n_1 = 31, n_2 = 41$
  e. $H_a: \sigma_1^2 \neq \sigma_2^2; \alpha = .05, n_1 = 7, n_2 = 16$

9.74 Independent random samples were selected from each of two normally distributed populations, $n_1 = 12$ from population 1 and $n_2 = 27$ from population 2. The means and variances for the two samples are shown in the table.

Sample 1	Sample 2
$n_1 = 12$	$n_2 = 27$
$\bar{x}_1 = 31.7$	$\bar{x}_2 = 37.4$
$s_1^2 = 3.87$	$s_2^2 = 8.75$

  a. Test the null hypothesis $H_0: \sigma_1^2 = \sigma_2^2$ against the alternative hypothesis $H_a: \sigma_1^2 \neq \sigma_2^2$. Use $\alpha = .10$.
  b. Find and interpret the approximate p-value of the test.

9.75 Independent random samples were selected from each of two normally distributed populations, $n_1 = 6$ from population 1 and $n_2 = 5$ from population 2. The data are shown in the next table.

⊚ **LM9_75**

Sample 1	Sample 2
3.1	2.3
4.4	1.4
1.2	3.7
1.7	8.9
.7	5.5
3.4	

  a. Test $H_0: \sigma_1^2 = \sigma_2^2$ against $H_a: \sigma_1^2 < \sigma_2^2$. Use $\alpha = .01$.
  b. Find and interpret the approximate p-value of the test.

Applying the Concepts—Basic

⊚ **DIAMONDS**

9.76 Refer to Exercise 9.12 (p. 497) and the data saved in the DIAMONDS file. MINITAB descriptive statistics for carat size and selling price of the 308 diamonds are reproduced in the accompanying printout. The diamonds are grouped according to the independent certification body (GIA, IGI, or HRD) that assessed the stones.

Descriptive Statistics: CARAT, PRICE

Variable	CERT	N	Mean	StDev
CARAT	GIA	151	0.6723	0.2456
	HRD	79	0.8129	0.1831
	IGI	78	0.3665	0.2163
PRICE	GIA	151	5310	3247
	HRD	79	7181	2898
	IGI	78	2267	2121

MINITAB printout for Exercise 9.76

  a. Conduct a test to determine whether the variation in carat size differs for diamonds certified by GIA and diamonds certified by HRD. Use $\alpha = .05$.
    $F = 1.8$.
  b. Conduct a test to determine whether the variation in carat size differs for diamonds certified by GIA and diamonds certified by IGI. Use $\alpha = .05$. $F = 1.29$
  c. Conduct a test to determine whether the variation in selling price differs for diamonds certified by HRD and diamonds certified by IGI. Use $\alpha = .05$.
    $F = 1.87$
  d. Use a statistical software package (and the data in the DIAMONDS file) to determine whether the assumption of normally distributed data for each certification group is reasonably satisfied.

9.77 Refer to *The Journal of American Academy of Business, Cambridge* (March 2002) study of how guests perceive the service quality at five-star hotels in Jamaica, Exercise 9.14 (p. 497). A summary of the guest perception scores, by gender, are reproduced in the table. Let σ_M^2 and σ_F^2 represent the true variances in scores for male and female guests, respectively.

Gender	Sample size	Mean score	Standard deviation
Males	127	39.08	6.73
Females	114	38.79	6.94

a. Set up H_0 and H_a for determining whether σ_M^2 is less than σ_F^2. $H_0: \sigma_M^2 = \sigma_F^2$ vs. $H_a: \sigma_M^2 < \sigma_F^2$
b. Find the test statistic for the test. $F = 1.06$
c. Give the rejection region for the test if $\alpha = .10$. $F > 1.26$
d. Find the approximate *p*-value of the test. $p > .10$
e. Make the appropriate conclusion in the words of the problem.
f. What conditions are required for the test results to be valid?

9.78 A study in the *Journal of Occupational and Organizational Psychology* (Dec. 1992) investigated the relationship of employment status and mental health. A sample of working and unemployed people was selected, and each person was given a mental health examination using the General Health Questionnaire (GHQ), a widely recognized measure of mental health. Although the article focused on comparing the mean GHQ levels, a comparison of the variability of GHQ scores for employed and unemployed men and women is of interest as well.

a. In general terms, what does the amount of variability in GHQ scores tell us about the group?
b. What are the appropriate null and alternative hypotheses to compare the variability of the mental health scores of the employed and unemployed groups? Define any symbols you use.
c. The standard deviation for a sample of 142 employed men was 3.26, while the standard deviation for 49 unemployed men was 5.10. Conduct the test you set up in part b using $\alpha = .05$. Interpret the results. $F = 2.45$
d. What assumptions are necessary to ensure the validity of the test?

Applying the Concepts—Intermediate

9.79 Tests of product quality using human inspectors can lead to serious inspection error problems (*Journal of Quality Technology,* Apr. 1986). To evaluate the performance of inspectors in a new company, a quality manager had a sample of 12 novice inspectors evaluate 200 finished products. The same 200 items were evaluated by 12 experienced inspectors. The quality of each item—whether defective or nondefective—was known to the manager. The table lists the number of inspection errors (classifying a defective item as nondefective or vice versa) made by each inspector.

INSPECT

Novice Inspectors				Experienced Inspectors			
30	35	26	40	31	15	25	19
36	20	45	31	28	17	19	18
33	29	21	48	24	10	20	21

a. Prior to conducting this experiment, the manager believed the variance in inspection errors was lower for experienced inspectors than for novice inspectors. Do the sample data support her belief? Test using $\alpha = .05$. $F = 2.27$
b. What is the appropriate *p*-value of the test you conducted in part a? $.05 < p < .10$

9.80 Refer to the *Chance* (Fall 2002) description of a patent infringement case against Intel Corp., Exercise 9.17 (p. 498). The zinc measurements for three locations on the original inventor's notebook—on a text line, on a witness line, and on the intersection of the witness and text line—are reproduced in the table.

PATENT

Text line:	.335	.374	.440			
Witness line:	.210	.262	.188	.329	.439	.397
Intersection:	.393	.353	.285	.295	.319	

a. Use a test (at $\alpha = .05$) to compare the variation in zinc measurements for the text line with the corresponding variation for the intersection. $F = 1.44$
b. Use a test (at $\alpha = .05$) to compare the variation in zinc measurements for the witness line with the corresponding variation for the intersection. $F = 5.25$
c. From the results, parts a and b, what can you infer about the variation in zinc measurements at the three notebook locations?
d. What assumptions are required for the inferences to be valid? Are they reasonably satisfied? (You checked these assumptions when answering Exercise 9.17d.)

9.81 Following the Persian Gulf War, the Pentagon changed its logistics processes to be more corporate-like. The extravagant "just-in-case" mentality was replaced with "just-in-time" systems. Emulating Federal Express and United Parcel Service, deliveries from factories to foxholes are now expedited using bar codes, laser cards, radio tags, and databases to track supplies. The table on p. 535 contains order-to-delivery times (in days) for a sample of shipments from the United States to the Persian Gulf in 1991 and a sample of shipments to Bosnia in 1995.

⊙ ORDTIMES

Persian Gulf	Bosnia
28.0	15.1
20.0	6.4
26.5	5.0
10.6	11.4
9.1	6.5
35.2	6.5
29.1	3.0
41.2	7.0
27.5	5.5

Source: Adapted from Crock, S. "The Pentagon goes to B-school." *Business Week,* December 11, 1995, p. 98.

a. Is there sufficient evidence to indicate that the variances in order-to-delivery times for Persian Gulf and Bosnia shipments differ? Use $\alpha = .05$. $F = 8.29$

b. Given your answer to part **a,** is it appropriate to construct a confidence interval for the difference between the mean order-to-delivery times? Explain.

9.82 Refer to the *International Journal of Environmental Health Research* (Vol. 4, 1994) study, Exercise 9.15 (p. 498), in which the mean solid-waste generation rates for middle-income and industrialized countries were compared. The data are reproduced in the table.

⊙ SOLWASTE

Industrialized Countries		Middle-Income Countries	
New York (USA)	2.27	Singapore	0.87
Phoenix (USA)	2.31	Hong Kong	0.85
London (UK)	2.24	Medellin (Colombia)	0.54
Hamburg (Germany)	2.18	Kano (Nigeria)	0.46
Rome (Italy)	2.15	Manila (Philippines)	0.50
		Cairo (Egypt)	0.50
		Tunis (Tunisia)	0.56

a. In order to conduct the two-sample *t*-test in Exercise 9.15, it was necessary to assume that the two population variances were equal. Test this assumption at $\alpha = .05$. $F = 7.03$

b. What does your test indicate about the appropriateness of applying a two-sample *t*-test?

9.83 The *American Educational Research Journal* (Fall, 1998) published a study to compare the mathematics achievement test scores of male and female students. The researchers hypothesized that the distribution of test scores for males is more variable than the corresponding distribution for females. Use the summary information in the table to test this claim at $\alpha = .01$.

	Males	Females
Sample size	1,764	1,739
Mean	48.9	48.4
Standard deviation	12.96	11.85

Source: Bielinski, J., and Davison, M. L. "Gender Differences by Item Difficulty Interactions in Multiple-Choice Mathematics Items." *American Educational Research Journal,* Vol. 35, No. 3, Fall 1998, p. 464 (Table 1).

Quick Review

Key Terms

Note: Starred (*) items are from the optional section in this chapter.

Blocking   502
*F-distribution   524

*Nonparametric method   530
Paired difference experiment   502
Pooled sample estimate
  of variance   486

Randomized block experiment   502
Standard error   482

Key Formulas

$(1 - \alpha)100\%$ confidence interval for θ: (see table on page 534)

Large samples: $\hat{\theta} \pm z_{\alpha/2}\sigma_{\hat{\theta}}$.

Small samples: $\hat{\theta} \pm t_{\alpha/2}\sigma_{\hat{\theta}}$

For testing $H_0: \theta = D_0$: (see table on page 534)

Large samples: $z = \dfrac{\hat{\theta} - D_0}{\sigma_{\hat{\theta}}}$

Small samples: $t = \dfrac{\hat{\theta} - D_0}{\sigma_{\hat{\theta}}}$

Parameter, θ	Estimator, $\hat{\theta}$	Standard Error of Estimator, $\sigma_{\hat{\theta}}$	Estimated Standard Error	
$(\mu_1 - \mu_2)$ (independent samples)	$(\bar{x}_1 - \bar{x}_2)$	$\sqrt{\dfrac{\sigma_1^2}{n_1} + \dfrac{\sigma_2^2}{n_2}}$	Large n: $\sqrt{\dfrac{s_1^2}{n_1} + \dfrac{s_2^2}{n_2}}$	483
			Small n: $\sqrt{s_p^2\left(\dfrac{1}{n_1} + \dfrac{1}{n_2}\right)}$	487
μ_d (paired sample)	$\bar{d}$	$\dfrac{\sigma_d}{\sqrt{n_d}}$	$\dfrac{s_d}{\sqrt{n_d}}$	503
$(p_1 - p_2)$ (large, independent samples)	$(\hat{p}_1 - \hat{p}_2)$	$\sqrt{\dfrac{p_1 q_1}{n_1} + \dfrac{p_2 q_2}{n_2}}$	Hypothesis tests: $\sqrt{\hat{p}\hat{q}\left(\dfrac{1}{n_1} + \dfrac{1}{n_2}\right)}$	514
			Confidence intervals: $\sqrt{\dfrac{\hat{p}_1 \hat{q}_1}{n_1} + \dfrac{\hat{p}_2 \hat{q}_2}{n_2}}$	513

Pooled sample variance	$s_p^2 = \dfrac{(n_1 - 1)s_1^2 + (n_2 - 1)s_2^2}{n_1 + n_2 - 2}$	487
Pooled sample proportion	$\hat{p} = \dfrac{x_1 + x_2}{n_1 + n_2}, \hat{q} = 1 - \hat{p}$	513
Determining the sample size for estimating $(\mu_1 - \mu_2)$	$n_1 = n_2 = \dfrac{(z_{\alpha/2})^2(\sigma_1^2 + \sigma_2^2)}{(ME)^2}$	522
Determining the sample size for estimating $(p_1 - p_2)$	$n_1 = n_2 = \dfrac{(z_{\alpha/2})^2(p_1 q_1 + p_2 q_2)}{(ME)^2}$	522
*Test statistic for testing H_0: $\dfrac{\sigma_1^2}{\sigma_2^2}$	$F = \dfrac{\text{larger } s^2}{\text{smaller } s^2}$ if H_a: $\dfrac{\sigma_1^2}{\sigma_2^2} \neq 1$	528
	$F = \dfrac{s_1^2}{s_2^2}$ if H_a: $\dfrac{\sigma_1^2}{\sigma_2^2} > 1$	

Language Lab

Symbol	Pronunciation	Description
$(\mu_1 - \mu_2)$	mu-1 minus mu-2	Difference between population means
$(\bar{x}_1 - \bar{x}_2)$	x-bar-1 minus x-bar-2	Difference between sample means
$\sigma_{(\bar{x}_1 - \bar{x}_2)}$	sigma of x-bar-1 minus x-bar-2	Standard deviation of the sampling distribution of $(\bar{x}_1 - \bar{x}_2)$
s_p^2	s-p squared	Pooled sample variance
D_0	D naught	Hypothesized value of difference
μ_d	mu-d	Difference between population means, paired data
$\bar{d}$	d-bar	Mean of sample differences
s_d	s-d	Standard deviation of sample differences
n_d	n-d	Number of differences in sample

$(p_1 - p_2)$	p-1 minus p-2	Difference between population proportions
$(\hat{p}_1 - \hat{p}_2)$	p-1 hat minus p-2 hat	Difference between sample proportions
$\sigma_{(\hat{p}_1 - \hat{p}_2)}$	sigma of p-1 hat minus p-2 hat	Standard deviation of the sampling distribution of $(\hat{p}_1 - \hat{p}_2)$
F_α	F-alpha	Critical value of F associated with tail area α
ν_1	nu-1	Numerator degrees of freedom for F-statistic
ν_2	nu-2	Denominator degrees of freedom for F-statistic
$\dfrac{\sigma_1^2}{\sigma_2^2}$	sigma-1 squared over sigma-2 squared	Ratio of two population variances

Chapter Summary Notes

- Key words/phrases for identifying $\mu_1 - \mu_2$ as the parameter of interest: difference between means or averages, compare two means using independent samples
- Key words/phrases for identifying μ_d as the parameter of interest: mean or average of paired differences, compare two means using matched pairs
- Key words/phrases for identifying $p_1 - p_2$ as the parameter of interest: difference between proportions or percentages, compare two proportions using independent samples
- Key words/phrases for identifying σ_1^2/σ_2^2 as the parameter of interest: difference between variances, compare variation in two populations using independent samples
- Conditions required for a valid large-sample inferences for $\mu_1 - \mu_2$: (1) independent random samples, (2) large sample sizes ($n_1 \geq 30$ and $n_2 \geq 30$)

- Conditions required for a valid small-sample inferences for $\mu_1 - \mu_2$: (1) independent random samples, (2) both populations are approximately normal, (3) $\sigma_1^2 = \sigma_2^2$
- Conditions required for a valid large-sample inferences for μ_d: (1) random sample of paired differences, (2) large sample size ($n_d \geq 30$)
- Conditions required for a valid small-sample inferences for μ_d: (1) random sample of paired differences, (2) population of differences are approximately normal
- Conditions required for a valid large-sample inferences for $p_1 - p_2$: (1) independent random samples, (2) large sample sizes (both $p_1 \pm 3\sigma_{p_1}$ and $p_2 \pm 3\sigma_{p_2}$ fall between 0 and 1)
- Conditions required for a valid inferences for σ_1^2/σ_2^2: (1) independent random samples, (2) both populations are approximately normal

Supplementary Exercises 9.84–9.112

Starred (*) exercises refer to the optional section in this chapter.

Learning the Mechanics

9.84 List the assumptions necessary for each of the following inferential techniques:
  a. Large-sample inferences about the difference $(\mu_1 - \mu_2)$ between population means using a two-sample z-statistic
  b. Small-sample inferences about $(\mu_1 - \mu_2)$ using an independent samples design and a two-sample t-statistic
  c. Small-sample inferences about $(\mu_1 - \mu_2)$ using a paired difference design and a single-sample t-statistic to analyze the differences
  d. Large-sample inferences about the differences $(p_1 - p_2)$ between binomial proportions using a two-sample z-statistic
  *e. Inferences about the ratio σ_1^2/σ_2^2 of two population variances using an F-test.

9.85 Independent random samples were selected from two normally distributed populations with means μ_1 and μ_2, respectively. The sample sizes, means, and variances are shown in the following table.

Sample 1	Sample 2
$n_1 = 12$	$n_2 = 14$
$\bar{x}_1 = 17.8$	$\bar{x}_2 = 15.3$
$s_1^2 = 74.2$	$s_2^2 = 60.5$

  a. Test $H_0: (\mu_1 - \mu_2) = 0$ against $H_a: (\mu_1 - \mu_2) > 0$. Use $\alpha = .05$. $t = .78$
  b. Form a 99% confidence interval for $(\mu_1 - \mu_2)$.
  c. How large must n_1 and n_2 be if you wish to estimate $(\mu_1 - \mu_2)$ to within 2 units with 99% confidence? Assume that $n_1 = n_2$. $n_1 = n_2 = 225$

9.86 Two independent random samples were selected from normally distributed populations with means and variances (μ_1, σ_1^2) and (μ_2, σ_2^2), respectively. The sample sizes, means, and variances are shown in the table below.

Sample 1	Sample 2
$n_1 = 20$	$n_2 = 15$
$\bar{x}_1 = 123$	$\bar{x}_2 = 116$
$s_1^2 = 31.3$	$s_2^2 = 120.1$

*a. Test H_0: $\sigma_1^2 = \sigma_2^2$ against H_a: $\sigma_1^2 \neq \sigma_2^2$. Use $\alpha = .05$.

b. Would you be willing to use a t-test to test the null hypothesis H_0: $(\mu_1 - \mu_2) = 0$ against the alternative hypothesis H_a: $(\mu_1 - \mu_2) \neq 0$? Why?   No

9.87 Two independent random samples are taken from two populations. The results of these samples are summarized in the following table.

Sample 1	Sample 2
$n_1 = 135$	$n_2 = 148$
$\bar{x}_1 = 12.2$	$\bar{x}_2 = 8.3$
$s_1^2 = 2.1$	$s_2^2 = 3.0$

a. Form a 90% confidence interval for $(\mu_1 - \mu_2)$.

b. Test H_0: $(\mu_1 - \mu_2) = 0$ against H_a: $(\mu_1 - \mu_2) \neq 0$. Use $\alpha = .01$. $z = 20.60$

c. What sample sizes would be required if you wish to estimate $(\mu_1 - \mu_2)$ to within .2 with 90% confidence? Assume that $n_1 = n_2$. $n_1 = n_2 = 346$

9.88 Independent random samples were selected from two binomial populations. The sizes and number of observed successes for each sample are shown in the table below.

Sample 1	Sample 2
$n_1 = 200$	$n_2 = 200$
$x_1 = 110$	$x_2 = 130$

a. Test H_0: $(p_1 - p_2) = 0$ against H_a: $(p_1 - p_2) < 0$. Use $\alpha = .10$. $z = -2.04$

b. Form a 95% confidence interval for $(p_1 - p_2)$.

c. What sample sizes would be required if we wish to use a 95% confidence interval of width .01 to estimate $(p_1 - p_2)$? $n_1 = n_2 = 72,991$

9.89 A random sample of five pairs of observations were selected, one of each pair from a population with mean μ_1, the other from a population with mean μ_2. The data are shown in the accompanying table.

  🖲 **LM9_89**

Pair	Value from Population 1	Value from Population 2
1	28	22
2	31	27
3	24	20
4	30	27
5	22	20

a. Test the null hypothesis H_0: $\mu_D = 0$ against H_a: $\mu_d \neq 0$, where $\mu_d = \mu_1 - \mu_2$. Use $\alpha = .05$.

b. Form a 95% confidence interval for μ_d.

c. When are the procedures you used in parts **a** and **b** valid?

Applying the Concepts—Basic

🖲 **OILSPILL**

9.90 Refer to the *Marine Technology* (Jan. 1995) study of major oil spills from tankers and carriers, Exercise 2.14 (p. 56). The data for the 50 recent spills are saved in the OILSPILL file.

a. Construct a 90% confidence interval for the difference between the mean spillage amount of accidents caused by collision and the mean spillage amount of accidents caused by fire/explosion. Interpret the result. 1.1 ± 46.36

b. Conduct a test of hypothesis to compare the mean spillage amount of accidents caused by grounding to the corresponding mean of accidents caused by hull failure. Use $\alpha = .05$. $t = -0.279$

c. Refer to parts **a** and **b**. State any assumptions required for the inferences derived from the analyses to be valid. Are these assumptions reasonably satisfied?

*d. Conduct a test of hypothesis to compare the variation in spillage amounts for accidents caused by collision and accidents caused by grounding. Use $\alpha = .02$.

9.91 Research reported in the *Professional Geographer* (May 1992) examines the hypothesis that the disproportionate housework responsibility of women in two-income households is a major factor in determining the proximity of a woman's place of employment. The distance to work for both men and women in two-income households was reported for random samples of both central city and suburban residences:

	Central City Residence		Suburban Residence	
	Men	Women	Men	Women
n	159	119	138	93
$\bar{x}$	7.4	4.5	9.3	6.6
s	6.3	4.2	7.1	5.6

a. For central city residences, calculate a 99% confidence interval for the difference in average distance to work for men and women in two-income households. Interpret the interval.

b. Repeat part a for suburban residences.

c. Interpret the confidence intervals. Do they indicate that women tend to work closer to home than men?

d. What assumptions have you made to assure the validity of the confidence intervals constructed in parts **a** and **b**?

9.92 A manufacturer of automobile shock absorbers was interested in comparing the durability of its shocks with that of the shocks produced by its biggest competitor. To make the comparison, one of the manufacturer's and one of the competitor's shocks were randomly selected and installed on the rear wheels of each of six cars. After the cars had been driven 20,000 miles, the strength of each test shock was measured, coded, and recorded. Results of the examination are shown in the table.

⚙ **SHOCKABS**

Car Number	Manufacturer's Shock	Competitor's Shock
1	8.8	8.4
2	10.5	10.1
3	12.5	12.0
4	9.7	9.3
5	9.6	9.0
6	13.2	13.0

a. Explain why the data are collected as matched pairs.

b. Do the data present sufficient evidence to conclude that there is a difference in the mean strength of the two types of shocks after 20,000 miles of use? Use $\alpha = .05$. $t = 7.68$

c. Find the approximate observed significance level for the test, and interpret its value. $p < .001$

d. What assumptions are necessary to apply a paired difference analysis to the data?

e. Construct a 95% confidence interval for μ_d. Interpret the confidence interval.

f. Suppose the data are based on independent random samples. Construct a 95% confidence interval for $(\mu_1 - \mu_2)$. Interpret your result.

g. Compare the confidence intervals you obtained in parts e and f. Which is wider? To what do you attribute the difference in width? Assuming in each case that the appropriate assumptions are satisfied, which interval provides you with more information about $(\mu_1 - \mu_2)$? Explain.

h. Are the results of an unpaired analysis valid if the data come from a paired experiment?

9.93 Nontraditional university students, generally defined as those at least 25 years old, comprise an increasingly large proportion of undergraduate student bodies at most universities. A study reported in the *College Student Journal* (Dec. 1992) compared traditional and nontraditional students on a number of factors, including grade point average (GPA). The table below summarizes the information from the sample.

GPA	Traditional Students	Nontraditional Students
n	94	73
$\bar{x}$	2.90	3.50
s	.50	.50

a. What are the appropriate null and alternative hypotheses if we want to test whether the mean GPAs of traditional and nontraditional students differ?

b. Conduct the test using $\alpha = .01$, and interpret the result. $z = -7.69$

c. What assumptions are necessary to ensure the validity of the test?

9.94 A study in the *Journal of Psychology and Marketing* (Jan. 1992) investigates the degree to which American consumers are concerned about product tampering. Large random samples of male and female consumers were asked to rate their concern about product tampering on a scale of 1 (little or no concern) to 9 (very concerned).

a. What are the appropriate null and alternative hypotheses to determine whether a difference exists in the mean level of concern about product tampering between men and women? Define any symbols you use.

b. The *p*-value of the test is .008. Interpret this result.

c. What assumptions are necessary to ensure the validity of this test?

9.95 The threat of earthquakes is a part of life for homeowners in California. Scientists have been warning about "the big one" for decades. An article in the *Annals of the Association of American Geographers* (June 1992) explored some factors that are considered when California homeowners purchase earthquake insurance, including the proximity to a major earthquake fault. Surveys were mailed to residents in two California counties. The data collected are shown in the table below.

	Contra Costa	Los Angeles
Sample size	521	337
Number with earthquake insurance	117	133

a. Los Angeles County is the closest of the two to a major earthquake fault. Calculate 95% confidence intervals for the difference in the proportions of earthquake-insured residents in Los Angeles County and Contra Costa county.

b. Do these results support the contention that closer proximities to major earthquake faults result in higher proportions of earthquake-insured residents?

9.96 Refer to Exercise 9.95. How large would the samples from Los Angeles and Contra Costa counties have to be in order to estimate the difference between earthquake-insured proportions to within .03 with 95% confidence? $n_1 = n_2 = 1764$

9.97 In addition to evaluating the performance of individual companies, securities analysts also evaluate and compare industry sectors. One of the variables used in this analysis is the variance of the percentage growth in net incomes for the previous year. The table on p. 538, extracted from *Forbes* (Jan. 10, 2000), lists the percentage growth in net income for samples of firms from the banking and energy sectors of the U.S. economy.

BANKENER

Banking		Energy	
Bank of NY	46.5%	Ashland	42.9%
Compass	9.7	Coastal	22.8
First Union	35.1	Duke	3.2
PNC Bank	13.6	Exxon Mobil	−29.7
Regions	30.2	MidAmerican	231.7
State Street	13.2	Nicor	−6.5
Summit	−2.4	OGE	−11.0
Synovus	20.3	Royal Dutch	−56.6
		UGE	38.2

Source: Forbes, Jan. 10, 2000, pp. 84–167.

a. What does the amount of variability in the growth rates of net income of the firms in a particular industry sector tell you about the sector?

b. What are the appropriate null and alternative hypotheses to use in comparing the variability of net income growth rates of the banking and energy sectors?

c. Conduct the test of part b using $\alpha = .05$. Interpret your results in the context of the problem.

d. What assumptions must hold to ensure the validity of the test?

9.98 Does the time of day during which one works affect job satisfaction? A study in the *Journal of Occupational Psychology* (Sept. 1991) examined differences in job satisfaction between day-shift and night-shift nurses. Nurses' satisfaction with their hours of work, free time away from work, and breaks during work were measured. The following table shows the mean scores for each measure of job satisfaction (higher scores indicate greater satisfaction), along with the observed significance level comparing the means for the day-shift and night-shift samples:

	Mean Satisfaction		
	Day Shift	Night Shift	*p*-Value
Satisfaction with:			
Hours of work	3.91	3.56	.813
Free time	2.55	1.72	.047
Breaks	2.53	3.75	.0073

a. Specify the null and alternative hypotheses if we wish to test whether a difference in job satisfaction exists between day-shift and night-shift nurses on each of the three measures. Define any symbols you use.

b. Interpret the *p*-value for each of the tests. (Each of the *p*-values in the table is two-tailed.)

c. Assume that each of the tests is based on small samples of nurses from each group. What assumptions are necessary for the tests to be valid?

9.99 An economist wants to investigate the difference in unemployment rates between an urban industrial community and a university community in the same state. She interviews 525 potential members of the work force in the industrial community and 375 in the university community. Of these, 47 and 22, respectively, are unemployed. Use a 95% confidence interval to estimate the difference in unemployment rates in the two communities.   .0308 ± .0341

Applying the Concepts—Intermediate

9.100 Advertising companies often try to characterize the average user of a client's product so ads can be targeted at particular segments of the buying community. A new movie is about to be released, and the advertising company wants to determine whether to aim the ad campaign at people under or over 25 years of age. It plans to arrange an advance showing of the movie to an audience from each group, then obtain an opinion about the movie from each individual. How many individuals should be included in each sample if the advertising company wants to estimate the difference in the proportions of viewers in each age group who will like the movie to within .05 with 90% confidence? Assume the sample size for each group will be the same and about half of each group will like the movie.

9.101 It has been known for a number of years that the tailings (waste) of gypsum and phosphate mines in Florida contain radioactive radon 222. The radiation levels in waste gypsum and phosphate mounds in Polk County, Florida, are regularly monitored by the Eastern Environmental Radiation Facility (EERF) and by the Polk County Health Department (PCHD), Winter Haven, Florida. The table on p. 551 shows measurements of the exhalation rate (a measure of radiation) for 15 soil samples obtained from waste mounds in Polk County, Florida. The exhalation rate was measured for each soil sample by both the PCHD and the EERF. The objective of selecting the paired measurements was to determine whether there is a bias—a difference in the mean readings—between PCHD and EERF. The data in the table represent part of the data contained in a report by Thomas R. Horton of EERF.

a. Considering the relative size of the measurements from canister to canister, explain why a paired difference experiment was conducted rather than an independent samples experiment.

b. Do the data provide sufficient evidence to indicate a difference in the mean exhalation rates between PCHD and EERF? Test using $\alpha = .05$.

c. Find a 95% confidence interval for the difference in mean measurements between PCHD and EERF. Interpret the interval. Does it support the result of the test in part b?   84.17 ± 226.47

⊛ **EXRATES**

Charcoal Canister No.	PCHD	EERF
71	1,709.79	1,479.0
58	357.17	257.8
84	1,150.94	1,287.0
91	1,572.69	1,395.0
44	558.33	416.5
43	4,132.28	3,993.0
79	1,489.86	1,351.0
61	3,017.48	1,813.0
85	393.55	187.7
46	880.84	630.4
4	2,996.49	3,707.0
20	2,367.40	2,791.0
36	599.84	706.8
42	538.37	618.5
55	2,770.23	2,639.0

Source: Horton, T. R. "Preliminary Radiological Assessment of Radon Exhalation from Phosphate Gypsum Piles and Inactive Uranium Mill Tailings Piles." EPA-520/5-79-004. Washington, D.C.: Environmental Protection Agency, 1979.

9.102 Despite company policies allowing unpaid family leave for new fathers, many men fear that exercising this option would be held against them by their superiors (*Minneapolis Star-Tribune*, Feb. 14, 1993). In a random sample of 100 male workers planning to become fathers, 35 agreed with the statement, "If I knew there would be no repercussions, I would choose to participate in the family leave program after the birth of a son or daughter." However, of 96 men who became fathers in the previous 16 months, only nine participated in the program.

a. Specify the appropriate null and alternative hypotheses to test whether the sample data provide sufficient evidence to reject the hypothesis that the proportion of new fathers participating in the program is the same as the proportion that would like to participate. Define any symbols you use.

b. Are the sample sizes large enough to conclude that the sampling distribution of $(\hat{p}_1 - \hat{p}_2)$ is approximately normal?   Yes

c. Conduct the hypothesis test using $\alpha = .05$. Report the observed significance level of the test.

d. What assumptions must be satisfied for the test to be valid?

9.103 In Minnesota the laws do not demand that a cable-TV company face competition (*Minneapolis Star-Tribune*, Jan. 10, 1993). Suppose a congressional subcommittee considering regulation of the cable industry investigates whether average cable rates are higher in areas with no competition than in areas with competition. They randomly sample basic rates for six cable companies that have no competition and for six companies that face competition (but not from each other). The observed rates (in dollars) are shown in the next table.

⊛ **CABLETV**

No Competition	18.44	26.88	22.87	25.78	23.34	27.52
Competition	18.95	23.74	17.25	20.14	18.98	20.14

a. What are the appropriate null and alternative hypotheses to test the research hypothesis of the subcommittee?

b. Conduct the test of part a using $\alpha = .05$. Report and interpret the approximate significance level of the test.

c. What assumptions are necessary to ensure the validity of the test? Why does it matter that none of the companies in the sample compete against each other?

9.104 When female undergraduates switch from science, mathematics, and engineering (SME) majors into disciplines that are not science based, such as journalism, marketing, and sociology, are their reasons different from those of their male counterparts? This question was investigated in *Science Education* (July 1995). A sample of 335 junior/senior undergraduates—172 females and 163 males—at two large research universities were identified as "switchers," that is, they left a declared SME major for a non-SME major. Each student listed one or more factors that contributed to their switching decision.

a. Of the 172 females in the sample, 74 listed lack or loss of interest in SME (i.e., "turned off" by science) as a major factor, compared to 72 of the 163 males. Conduct a test (at $\alpha = .10$) to determine whether the proportion of female switchers who give "lack of interest in SME" as a major reason for switching differs from the corresponding proportion of males.

b. Thirty-three of the 172 females in the sample admitted they were discouraged or lost confidence due to low grades in SME during their early years, compared to 44 of 163 males. Construct a 90% confidence interval for the difference between the proportions of female and male switchers who lost confidence due to low grades in SME. Interpret the result.

9.105 Management training programs are often instituted to teach supervisory skills and thereby increase productivity. Suppose a company psychologist administers a set of examinations to each of 10 supervisors before such a training program begins and then administers similar examinations at the end of the program. The examinations are designed to measure supervisory skills, with higher scores indicating increased skill. The results of the tests are shown in the next table.

⊙ **SUPEXAM**

Supervisor	Pre-Test	Post-Test
1	63	78
2	93	92
3	84	91
4	72	80
5	65	69
6	72	85
7	91	99
8	84	82
9	71	81
10	80	87

a. Do the data provide evidence that the training program is effective in increasing supervisory skills, as measured by the examination scores? Use $\alpha = .10$.
b. Find and interpret the p-value for the test.
  $.001 < p < .005$

9.106 Some power plants are located near rivers or oceans so that the available water can be used for cooling the condensers. Suppose that, as part of an environmental impact study, a power company wants to estimate the difference in mean water temperature between the discharge of its plant and the offshore waters. How many sample measurements must be taken at each site in order to estimate the true difference between means to within .2°C with 95% confidence? Assume that the range in readings will be about 4°C at each site and the same number of readings will be taken at each site.

9.107 Poisons are used to prevent rat damage in sugarcane fields. The U.S. Department of Agriculture is investigating whether the rat poison should be located in the middle of the field or on the outer perimeter. One way to answer this question is to determine where the greater amount of damage occurs. If damage is measured by the proportion of cane stalks that have been damaged by rats, how many stalks from each section of the field should be sampled in order to estimate the true difference between proportions of stalks damaged in the two sections to within .02 with 95% confidence?

*9.108 When new instruments are developed to perform chemical analyses of products (food, medicine, etc.), they are usually evaluated with respect to two criteria: accuracy and precision. *Accuracy* refers to the ability of the instrument to identify correctly the nature and amounts of a product's components. *Precision* refers to the consistency with which the instrument will identify the components of the same material. Thus, a large variability in the identification of a single batch of a product indicates a lack of precision. Suppose a pharmaceutical firm is considering two brands of an instrument designed to identify the components of certain drugs. As part of a comparison of precision, 10 test-tube samples of a well-mixed batch of a drug are

selected and then five are analyzed by instrument A and five by instrument B. The data shown below are the percentages of the primary component of the drug given by the instruments. Do these data provide evidence of a difference in the precision of the two machines? Use $\alpha = .10$. $F = 2.79$

⊙ **INSTRAB**

Instrument A	Instrument B
43	46
48	49
37	43
52	41
45	48

9.109 Operation Crossroads was a 1946 military exercise in which atomic bombs were detonated over empty target ships in the Pacific Ocean. The Navy assigned sailors to wash down the test ships immediately after the atomic blasts. The National Academy of Science reported "that the overall death rate among Operation Crossroads sailors was 4.6% higher than among a comparable group of sailors.... However, this increase was not statistically significant." (*Tampa Tribune*, Oct. 30, 1996.)

a. Describe the parameter of interest in the National Academy of Science study.
b. Interpret the statement: "This increase was not statistically significant."

9.110 One way corporations raise money for expansion is to issue *bonds*, loan agreements to repay the purchaser a specified amount with a fixed rate of interest paid periodically over the life of the bond. The sale of bonds is usually handled by an underwriting firm. Does it pay for companies to shop around for an underwriter? The reason for the question is that the price of a bond may rise or fall after its issuance. Therefore, whether a corporation receives the market price for a bond depends on the skill of its underwriter (Radcliffe, 1994). The mean change in the prices of 27 bonds handled over a 12-month period by one underwriter and in the prices of 23 bonds handled by another are shown below.

	Underwriter 1	Underwriter 2
Sample size	27	23
Sample mean	−.0491	−.0307
Sample variance	.009800	.002465

a. Do the data provide sufficient evidence to indicate a difference in the mean change in bond prices handled by the two underwriters? Test using $\alpha = .05$.
b. Find a 95% confidence interval for the mean difference for the two underwriters, and interpret it.

9.111 How does gender affect the type of advertising that proves to be most effective? An article in the *Journal of Advertising Research* (May/June 1990) makes reference to numerous studies that conclude males tend to be more competitive with others than with themselves. To apply this conclusion to advertising, the author creates two ads promoting a new brand of soft drink:

Ad 1: Four men are shown competing in racquetball
Ad 2: One man is shown competing against himself in racquetball

The author hypothesized that the first ad will be more effective when shown to males. To test this hypothesis, 43 males were shown both ads and asked to measure their attitude toward the advertisement (Aad), their attitude toward the brand of soft drink (Ab), and their intention to purchase the soft drink (Intention). Each variable was measured using a seven-point scale, with higher scores indicating a more favorable attitude. The results are shown in the table below.

	Sample Means		
	Aad	Ab	Intention
Ad 1	4.465	3.311	4.366
Ad 2	4.150	2.902	3.813
Level of significance	$p = .091$	$p = .032$	$p = .050$

a. What are the appropriate null and alternative hypotheses to test the author's research hypothesis? Define any symbols you use.

b. Based on the information provided about this experiment, do you think this is an independent samples experiment or a paired difference experiment? Explain. Paired difference

c. Interpret the p-value for each test.

d. What assumptions are necessary for the validity of the tests?

9.112 Refer to the *Economics of Education Review* (Vol. 21, 2002) study of the relationship between education level and earnings, Exercise 8.27 (p. 427). A National Adult Literacy Survey revealed that males with a postgraduate degree had a sample mean salary of $61,340 (with standard error $s_{\bar{x}_M} = \$2{,}185$), while females with a postgraduate degree had a sample mean salary of $32,227 (with standard error $s_{\bar{x}_F} = \$932$). Let μ_M represent the population mean salary of all males with postgraduate degrees and μ_F represent the population mean salary of all females with postgraduate degrees.

a. Set up the null and alternative hypotheses for determining whether μ_M exceeds μ_F. $H_0: \mu_M = \mu_F$ vs. $H_a: \mu_M > \mu_F$

b. Calculate the test statistic for the test, part **a**. [*Note:* $s_{\bar{x}_M - \bar{x}_F} = \sqrt{(s_{\bar{x}_M}^2 + s_{\bar{x}_F}^2)}.]$ $z = 12.26$

c. Find the rejection region for the test using $\alpha = .01$. $z > 2.33$

d. Use the results, parts **b** and **c**, to make the appropriate conclusion.

REFERENCES

Freedman, D., Pisani, R., and Purves, R. *Statistics*. New York: W. W. Norton and Co., 1978.

Gibbons, J. D. *Nonparametric Statistical Inference*, 2nd ed. New York: McGraw-Hill, 1985.

Hollander, M. and Wolfe, D. A. *Nonparametric Statistical Methods*. New York: Wiley, 1973.

Lee, C. F., Finnerty, J. E., and Norton, E. A. *Foundations of Financial Management*. Minneapolis/St. Paul: West Publishing Co., 1997.

Mendenhall, W., Beaver, R. J., and Beaver, B. M. *Introduction to Probability and Statistics*, 10th ed. North Scituate, Mass.: Duxbury, 1999.

Satterthwaite, F. W. "An Approximate Distribution of Estimates of Variance Components." *Biometrics Bulletin*, Vol. 2, 1946, pp. 110–114.

Snedecor, G. W., and Cochran, W. *Statistical Methods*, 7th ed. Ames: Iowa State University Press, 1980.

Steel, R. G. D., and Torrie, J. H. *Principles and Procedures of Statistics*, 2nd ed. New York: McGraw-Hill, 1980.

Stevenson, William J. *Production/Operations Management*, 6th ed. Chicago: Irwin, 2000.

Twomey, David P. *Labor and Employment Law*, 9th ed. Cincinnati: South-Western Publishing Co., 1994.

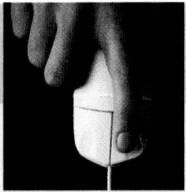

Using Technology

9.1 Two Sample Inferences Using SPSS

SPSS can be used to make two-sample inferences about $\mu_1 - \mu_2$ for independent samples and μ_d for paired samples but cannot currently conduct analyses about $p_1 - p_2$ or an F-test to compare population variances.

To carry out an analysis for $\mu_1 - \mu_2$, first access the SPSS spreadsheet file that contains the sample data. The data file should contain one quantitative variable (which the means will be calculated on) and one qualitative variable with either two numerical coded values (e.g., 1 and 2) or two short categorical levels (e.g., "yes" and "no"). These two values represent the two groups or populations to be compared. Next, click on the "Analyze" button on the SPSS menu bar, then click on "Compare Means" and "Independent-Samples T Test", as shown in Figure 9.S.1.

The resulting dialog box appears as shown in Figure 9.S.2. Specify the quantitative variable of interest in the "Test Variable(s)" box and the qualitative variable in the "Grouping Variable" box. Click the "Define Groups" button, and specify the values of the two groups in the resulting dialog box (see Figure 9.S.3). Then click "Continue" to return to the "Independent-Samples T Test" dialog screen. Without any further menu selections, SPSS will automatically conduct a two-tailed test of the null hypothesis, $H_0: \mu_1 - \mu_2 = 0$. If you want to generate a confidence interval for $\mu_1 - \mu_2$, click the "Options" button and specify the confidence level on the resulting menu screen, as shown in Figure 9.S.4. Click "Continue" to return to the "T Test" dialog box, then click "OK" to generate the SPSS printout.

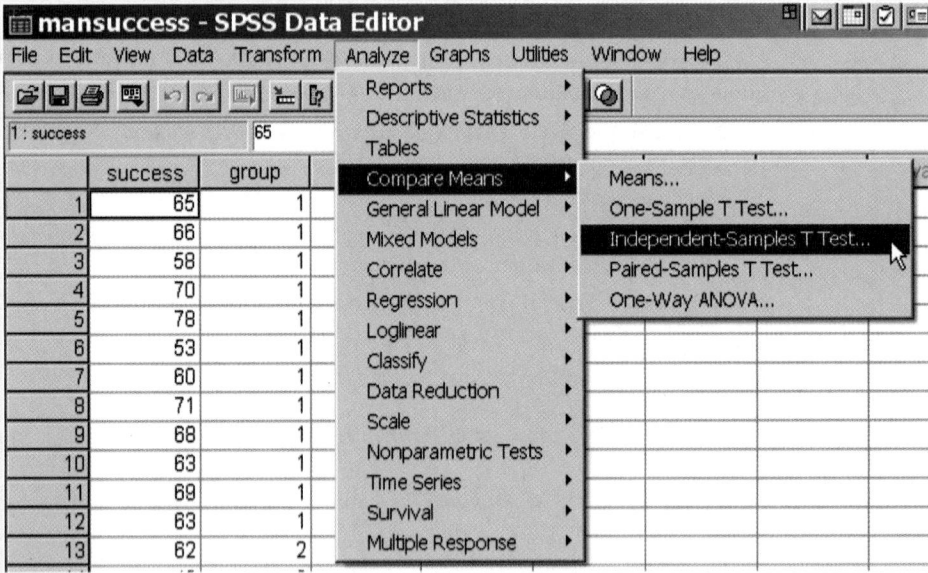

Figure 9.S.1
SPSS menu options for inferences about $\mu_1 - \mu_2$

[Important Note: The SPSS two-sample *t*-procedure uses the *t*-statistic to conduct the test of hypothesis. When the sample sizes are small, this is the appropriate method. When the sample sizes are large, the *t*-value will be approximately equal to the large-sample *z*-value and the resulting test will still be valid.]

To carry out an analysis of μ_d for matched pairs, first access the SPSS spreadsheet file that contains the sample data. The data file should contain two quantitative variables—one with the data values for the first group (or population) and one with the data values for the second group. (*Note*: The sample size should be the same for each group.) Next, click on the "Analyze" button on the

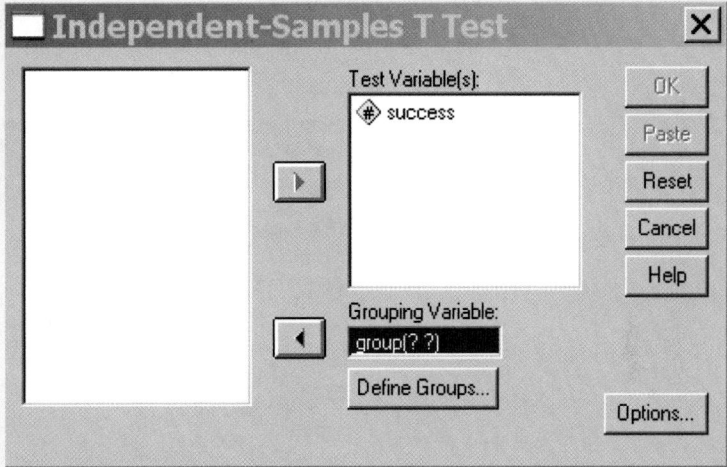

Figure 9.S.2
SPSS independent-samples *T* test dialog box

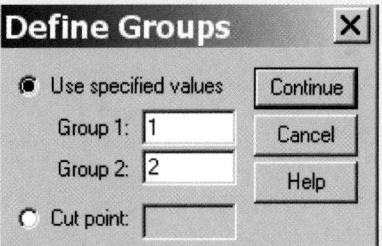

Figure 9.S.3
SPSS define groups dialog box

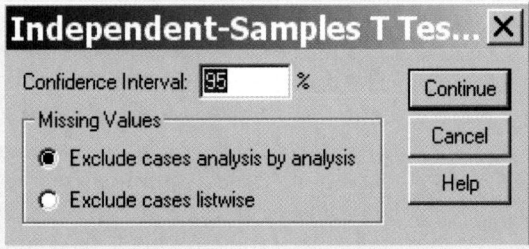

Figure 9.S.4
SPSS options dialog box

SPSS menu bar, then click on "Compare Means" and "Paired-Samples T Test" (see Figure 9.S.1). The resulting dialog box appears as shown in Figure 9.S.5.

Specify the two quantitative variables of interest in the "Paired Variables" box, as shown in Figure 9.S.5. Without any further menu selections, SPSS will automatically conduct a two-tailed test of the null hypothesis, $H_0: \mu_d = 0$. If you want to generate a confidence interval for μ_d, click the "Options" button and specify the confidence level on the resulting menu screen (as shown in Figure 9.S.4). Click "Continue" to return to the "Paired-Samples" dialog box, then click "OK" to generate the SPSS printout.

[Note: Although SPSS cannot perform an *F*-test to compare two variances, it will automatically provide a nonparametric test (e.g., Levene's test) for equal variances when you choose to do an independent samples *t*-test for $\mu_1 - \mu_2$.]

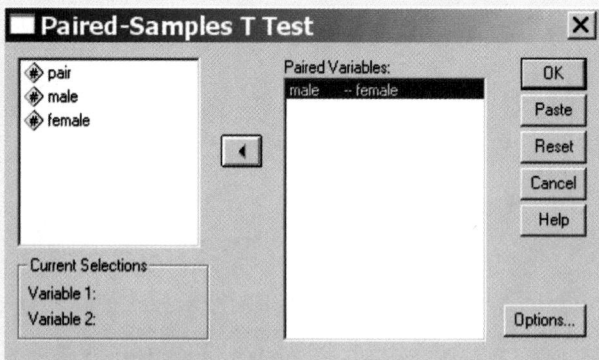

Figure 9.S.5
SPSS paired-samples dialog box

9.2 Two-Sample Inferences Using MINITAB

MINITAB can be used to make two-sample inferences about $\mu_1 - \mu_2$ for independent samples, μ_d for paired samples, $p_1 - p_2$ and σ_1^2/σ_2^2.

To carry out an analysis for $\mu_1 - \mu_2$, first access the MINITAB worksheet that contains the sample data. Next, click on the "Basic Statistics" button on the MINITAB menu bar, then click on "2-Sample t", as shown in Figure 9.M.1. The resulting dialog box appears as shown in Figure 9.M.2.

If the worksheet contains data for one quantitative variable (which the means will be computed on) and one qualitative variable (which represents the two groups or populations), select "Samples in one column", then specify the quantitative variable in the "Samples" area and the qualitative variable in the "Subscripts" area. (See Figure 9.M.2.)

If the worksheet contains the data for the first sample in one column and the data for the second sample in another column, select "Samples in different columns", then specify the "First" and "Second" variables. Alternatively, if you have only summarized data (i.e., sample sizes, sample means, and sample standard deviations), select "Summarized data" and enter these summarized values in the appropriate boxes.

Once you have made the appropriate menu selection, click the "Options" button on the MINITAB "2-Sample T" dialog box. Specify the confidence level for a confidence interval, the null hypothesized value of the difference, $\mu_1 - \mu_2$, and the

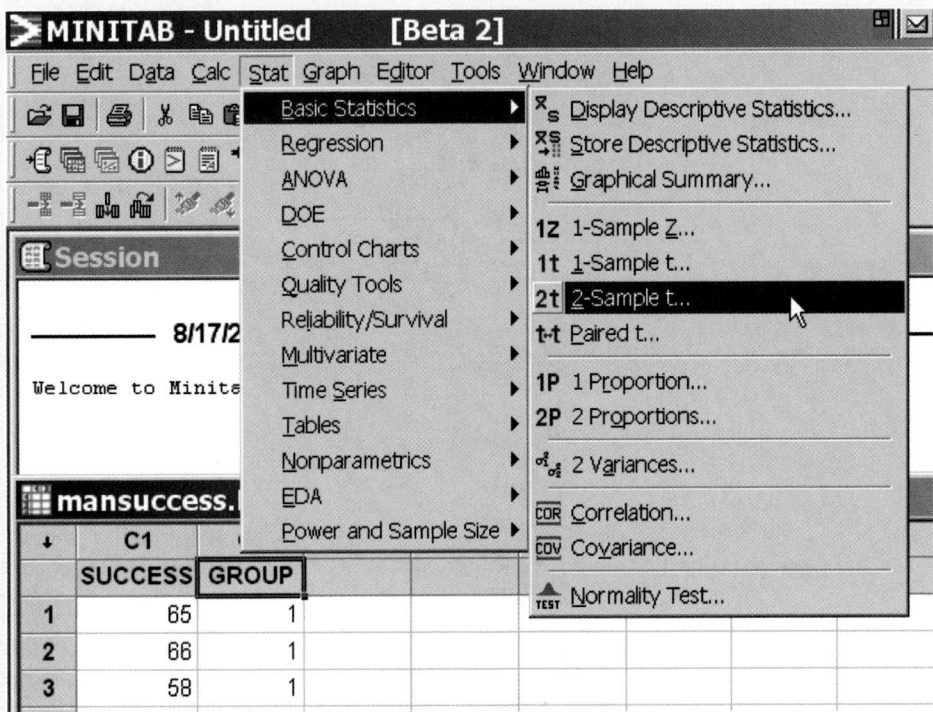

Figure 9.M.1
MINITAB menu options for inferences about $\mu_1 - \mu_2$

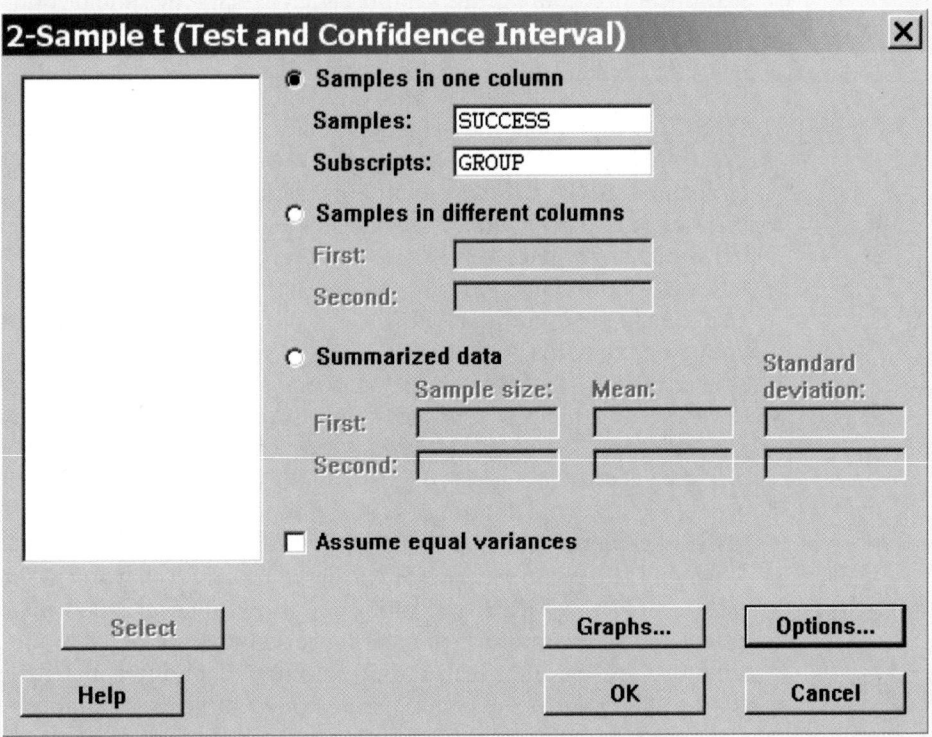

Figure 9.M.2
MINITAB 2-sample T dialog box

Figure 9.M.3
MINITAB options dialog box

form of the alternative hypothesis (lower tailed, two tailed, or upper tailed) in the resulting dialog box, as shown in Figure 9.M.3. Click "OK" to return to the "2-Sample T" dialog box, then click "OK" again to generate the MINITAB printout.

[Important Note: The MINITAB two-sample *t*-procedure uses the *t*-statistic to conduct the test of hypothesis. When the sample sizes are small, this is the appropriate method. When the sample sizes are large, the *t*-value will be approximately equal to the large-sample *z*-value and the resulting test will still be valid.]

To carry out an analysis of μ_d for matched pairs, first access the MINITAB worksheet that contains the sample data. The data file should contain two quantitative variables—one with the data values for the first group (or population) and one with the data values for the second group. (*Note:* The sample size should be the same for each group.) Next, click on the "Basic Statistics" button on the MINITAB menu bar, then click on "Paired t" (see Figure 9.M.1). The resulting dialog box appears as shown in Figure 9.M.4. Select the "Samples in columns" option and specify the two quantitative variables of interest in the "First sample" and "Second sample" boxes, as shown in Figure 9.M.4. [Alternatively, if you have only summarized data of the paired differences, select the "Summarized data (differences)" option and enter the sample size, sample mean, and sample standard deviation in the appropriate boxes.]

Next, click the "Options" button and specify the confidence level for a confidence interval, the null hypothesized value of the difference, μ_d, and the form of the alternative hypothesis (lower tailed, two tailed, or upper tailed) in the resulting dialog box. (See Figure 9.M.3.) Click "OK" to return to the "Paired t" dialog box, then click "OK" again to generate the MINITAB printout.

To analyze the difference between two proportions, $p_1 - p_2$, first access the MINITAB worksheet that contains the sample data. Next, click on the "Basic Statistics" button on the MINITAB menu bar, then click on "2 Proportions", as shown in Figure 9.M.1. The resulting dialog box appears as shown in Figure 9.M.5. Select the data option ("Samples in one column" or "Samples in different columns" or "Summarized data") and make the appropriate menu choices. (Figure 9.M.5 shows the menu options when you select "Summarized data".)

Next, click the "Options" button and specify the confidence level for a confidence interval, the null hypothesized value of the difference, and the form of the alternative hypothesis (lower tailed, two tailed, or upper tailed) in the resulting

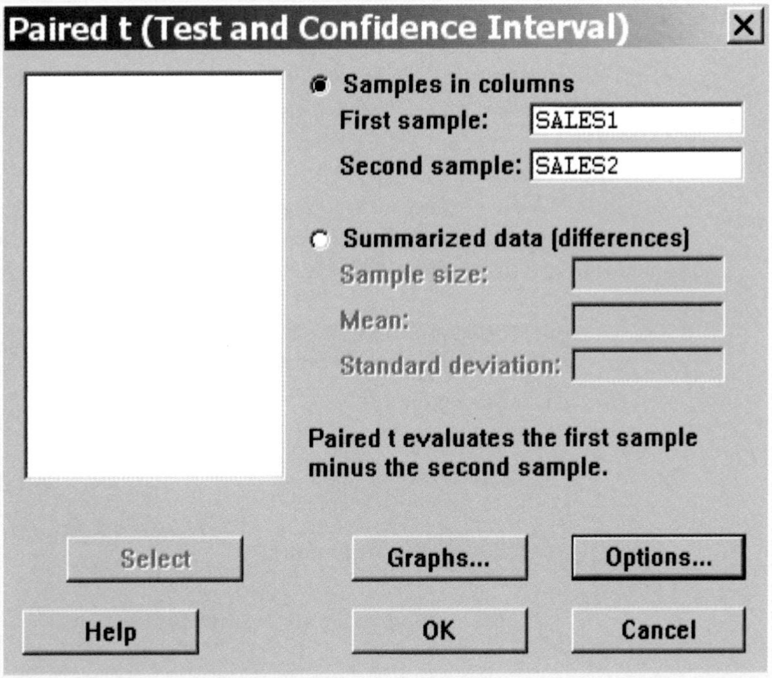

Paired t (Test and Confidence Interval)

- ⦿ **Samples in columns**
  - First sample: `SALES1`
  - Second sample: `SALES2`

- ○ **Summarized data (differences)**
  - Sample size:
  - Mean:
  - Standard deviation:

Paired t evaluates the first sample minus the second sample.

[Select]   [Graphs...]   [Options...]

[Help]   [OK]   [Cancel]

Figure 9.M.4
MINITAB paired-samples dialog box

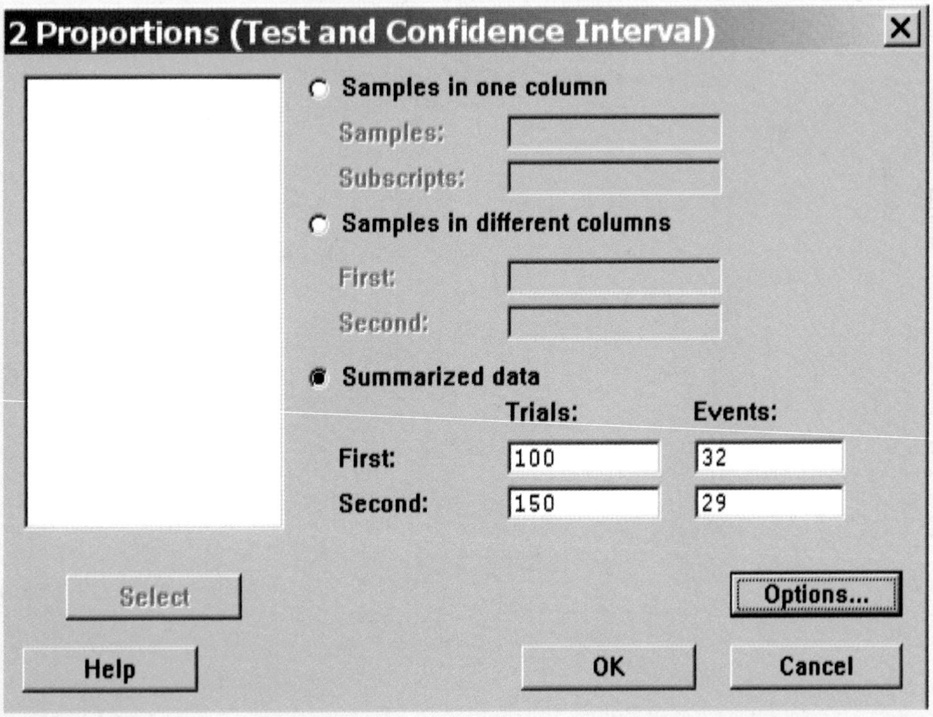

2 Proportions (Test and Confidence Interval)

- ○ **Samples in one column**
  - Samples:
  - Subscripts:

- ○ **Samples in different columns**
  - First:
  - Second:

- ⦿ **Summarized data**

	Trials:	Events:
First:	100	32
Second:	150	29

[Select]   [Options...]

[Help]   [OK]   [Cancel]

Figure 9.M.5
MINITAB 2 proportions dialog box

dialog box, as shown in Figure 9.M.6. (If you desire a pooled estimate of p for the test, be sure to check the appropriate box.) Click "OK" to return to the "2 Proportions" dialog box, then click "OK" again to generate the MINITAB printout.

To carry out an analysis for the ratio of two variances, σ_1^2/σ_2^2, first access the MINITAB worksheet that contains the sample data. Next, click on the "Basic Statistics" button on the MINITAB menu bar, then click on "2 Variances", as shown in Figure 9.M.1. The resulting dialog box appears as shown in Figure 9.M.7. The menu selections and options are similar to those for the two-sample t-test. Once the selections are made, click "OK" to produce the MINITAB F-test printout.

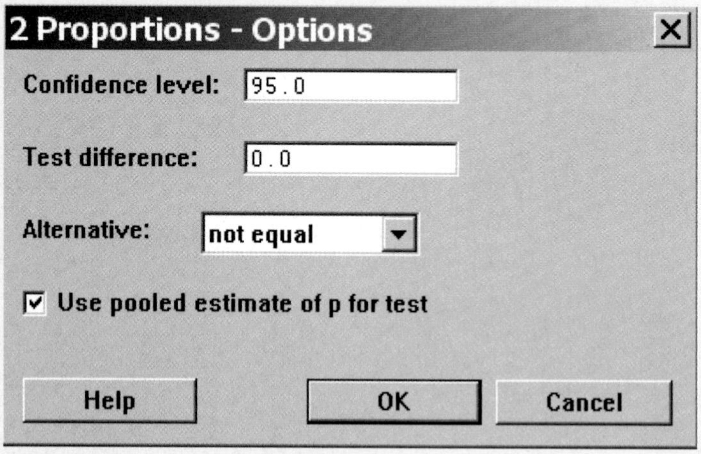

Figure 9.M.6
MINITAB 2 proportions options box

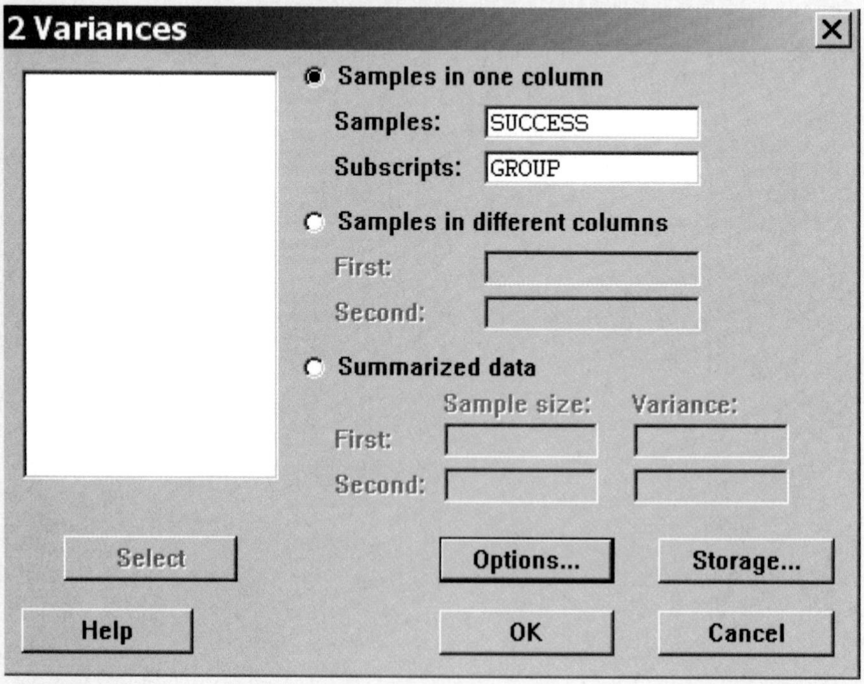

Figure 9.M.7
MINITAB 2 variances dialog box

9.3 Two Sample Inferences Using EXCEL and PHStat2

EXCEL with the PHStat2 add-in can be used to make two-sample inferences about $\mu_1 - \mu_2$ for independent samples, μ_d for paired samples, $p_1 - p_2$, and σ_1^2/σ_2^2.

To conduct a hypothesis test for $\mu_1 - \mu_2$, first compute summary statistics for the data (e.g., sample sizes, sample means, and sample standard deviations for the two samples). Now, click on the "PHStat" button on the EXCEL main menu bar, then click on "Two-Sample Tests" and "t Test for Differences in Two Means", as shown in Figure 9.E.1. The resulting dialog box appears as shown in Figure 9.E.2.

Specify the null hypothesized value of the difference, $\mu_1 - \mu_2$, the level of significance, α, the summary statistics for the two samples, and the form of the alternative hypothesis (lower tailed, two tailed, or upper tailed) in the resulting dialog box, as shown in Figure 9.E.2. Click "OK" to generate the EXCEL printout.

To conduct a paired difference analysis for μ_d, first compute the differences between the two paired values on the EXCEL workbook. Then carry out a t-test for a single mean. Consult the EXCEL "Using Technology" section of Chapter 8 (p. 474) to see the menu screens and selections for this analysis.

To conduct a large-sample hypothesis test for $p_1 - p_2$, first compute summary statistics for the data (e.g., sample sizes and sample number of successes for the two samples). Now, click on the "PHStat" button on the EXCEL main menu bar, then click on "Two-Sample Tests" and "Z Test for Differences in Two Proportions" (see in Figure 9.E.1). The resulting dialog box appears as shown in Figure 9.E.3. Specify the null hypothesized value of the difference, $p_1 - p_2$, the level of significance, α, the summary statistics for the two samples, and the form of the alternative hypothesis (lower tailed, two tailed, or upper tailed) in the resulting dialog box, as shown in Figure 9.E.3. Click "OK" to generate the EXCEL printout.

Figure 9.E.1
EXCEL/PHStat2 Menu Options for Inferences about $\mu_1 - \mu_2$

Figure 9.E.2
EXCEL/PHStat2 two-sample *t*-test dialog box

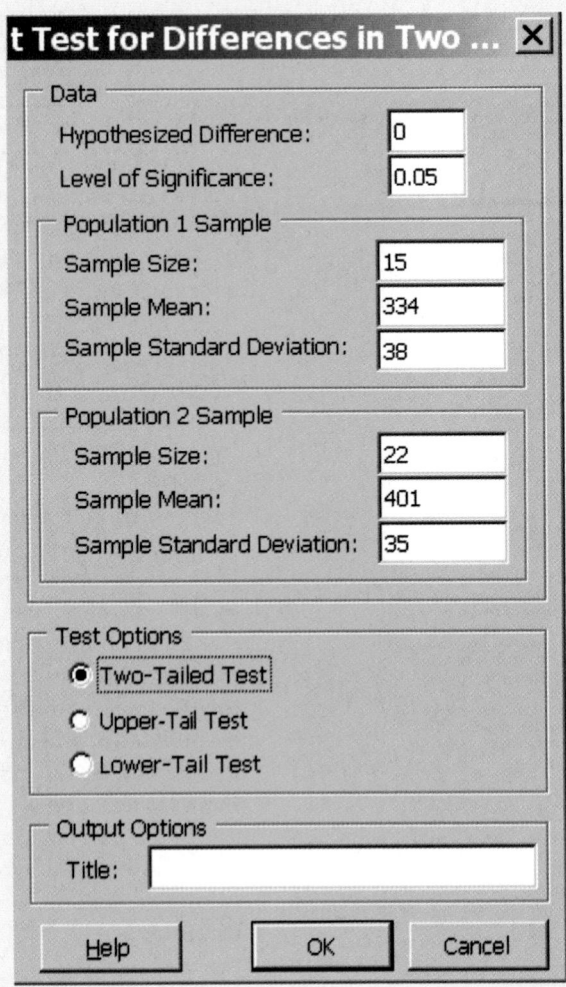

To conduct an *F*-test for the ratio of two variances, σ_1^2/σ_2^2, first compute summary statistics for the data (e.g., sample sizes and sample standard deviations for the two samples). Now, click on the "PHStat" button on the EXCEL main menu bar, then click on "Two-Sample Tests" and "F Test for Differences in Two Variances" (see in Figure 9.E.1). The resulting dialog box appears as shown in Figure 9.E.4. Specify the null hypothesized value of the ratio, σ_1^2/σ_2^2, the level of significance, α, the summary statistics for the two samples, and the form of the alternative hypothesis (lower tailed, two tailed, or upper tailed) in the resulting dialog box, as shown in Figure 9.E.4. Click "OK" to generate the EXCEL printout.

Z Test for the Difference in T...   ☒

Data
  Hypothesized Difference: `0`
  Level of Significance: `0.05`

  Population 1 Sample
  Number of Successes: `44`
  Sample Size: `100`

  Population 2 Sample
  Number of Successes: `52`
  Sample Size: `100`

Test Options
  ⦿ Two-Tailed Test
  ○ Upper-Tail Test
  ○ Lower-Tail Test

Output Options
  Title:

  Help   OK   Cancel

Figure 9.E.3
EXCEL/PHStat2 two-proportions test dialog box

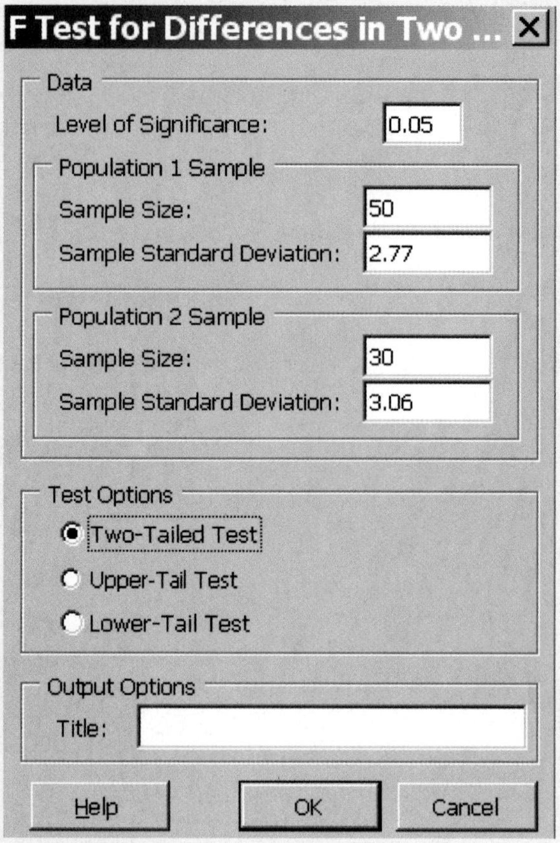

Figure 9.E.4
EXCEL/PHStat2 *F*-test dialog box

Real-World Case
The Kentucky Milk Case—Part II
(A Case Covering Chapters 7–9)

In The Kentucky Milk Case—Part I, you used graphical and numerical descriptive statistics to investigate bid collusion in the Kentucky school milk market. This case expands your previous analyses, incorporating inferential statistical methodology. The three areas of your focus are described below. (See page 142 for the file layout of the MILK data.) Again, you should prepare a professional document which presents the results of the analyses and any implications regarding collusionary practices in the tricounty Kentucky milk market.

1. *Incumbency rates.* Recall from Part I that market allocation (where the same dairy controls the same school districts year after year) is a common form of collusive behavior in bidrigging conspiracies. Market allocation is typically gauged by the incumbency rate for a market in a given school year—defined as the percentage of school districts that are won by the same milk vendor who won the previous year. Past experience with milk bids in a competitive market reveals that a "normal" incumbency rate is about .7. That is, 70% of the school districts are expected to purchase their milk from the same vendor who supplied the milk the previous year. In the 13-district tri-county Kentucky market, 13 vendor transitions potentially exist each year. Over the 1985–1988 period (when bid collusion was alleged to have

occurred), there are 52 potential vendor transitions. Based on the actual number of vendor transitions that occurred each year and over the 1985–1988 period, make an inference regarding bid collusion.

2. *Bid price dispersion.* Recall that in competitive sealed-bid markets, more dispersion or variability among the bids is observed than in collusive markets. (This is due to conspiring vendors sharing information about their bids.) Consequently, if collusion exists, the variation in bid prices in the tri-county market should be significantly smaller than the corresponding variation in the surrounding market. For each milk product, conduct an analysis to compare the bid price variances of the two markets each year. Make the appropriate inferences.

3. *Average winning bid price.* According to collusion theorists, the mean winning bid price in the "rigged" market will exceed the mean winning bid price in the competitive market for each year in which collusion occurs. In addition, the difference between the competitive average and the "rigged" average tends to grow over time when collusionary tactics are employed over several consecutive years. For each milk product, conduct an analysis to compare the winning bid price means of the tri-county and surrounding markets each year. Make the appropriate inferences.

10

Design of Experiments and Analysis of Variance

Contents

Statistics in Action

The Ethics of Downsizing

Using Technology

Where We've Been

- Presented methods for estimating and testing hypotheses about a single population mean.

- Presented methods for comparing two population means.

Where We're Going

- Discuss the critical elements in the design of a sampling experiment.

- Learn how to set up three of the more popular experimental designs for comparing more than two population means: *completely randomized, randomized block,* and *factorial designs.*

- Show how to analyze data collected from a designed experiment using a technique called an *analysis of variance.*

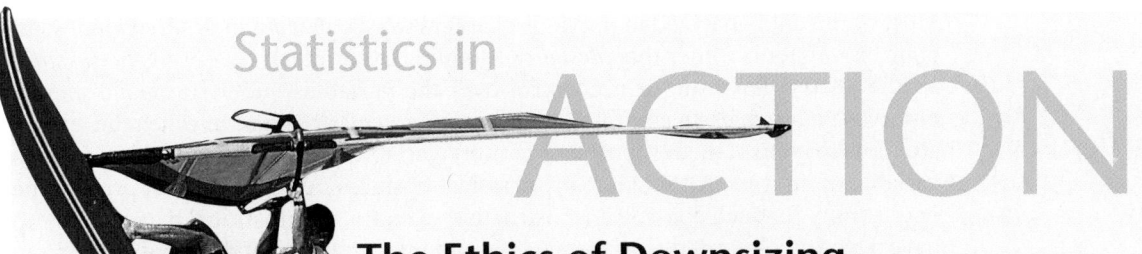

Statistics in ACTION

The Ethics of Downsizing

A major strategic alternative for many U.S. firms is to reduce the size of their workforce (i.e. to downsize). DuPont, Up-john Company, AT&T, and IBM are just a few of the many major U.S. firms that have recently downsized. Although it may be in the best interest of the firm's shareholders to delay informing employees of the downsizing decision, top management is morally obligated to communicate to employees all aspects of the downsizing process, including when it will occur and how it will affect jobs. When full disclosure of downsizing by top management does not occur, employees are likely to perceive this as an ethical violation of their rights.

W. E. Hopkins (Colorada State University) and S. A. Hopkins (University of Denver) investigated the ethics of downsizing decisions from the employee's perspective and published their results in the *Journal of Business Ethics* (Vol. 18, 1999). The researchers surveyed a sample of 209 employees who were enrolled in an Executive MBA Program or weekend program at one of three Colorado universities. These individuals were divided into five distinct groups, depending on their job situation at a previous or current firm. The groups are fully described in Table SIA10.1.

Each of the 209 employees completed a questionnaire on his or her ethical perceptions of downsizing. One item on the questionnaire, the focus of this Statistics in Action, asked employees to respond to the statement, "It is unethical for a downsizing decision to be announced or implemented on or prior to a major holiday (e.g., Christmas, Thanksgiving, etc.)." Responses were measured using a 5-point Likert scale, where 1 = strongly agree, 2 = agree, 3 = neutral, 4 = disagree, and 5 = strongly disagree. Data on both the qualitative variable Group and the quantitative variable Ethics response are saved in the **DOWNSIZE** file. The researchers used the data to test three hypotheses.

Hypothesis 1: Survivors', Casualties', and Implementors/casualties' perceptions of the ethics statement on downsizing will not differ significantly.

Hypothesis 2: Formulators' and Implementors/survivors' perceptions of the ethics statement on downsizing will not differ significantly.

Hypothesis 3: Survivors', Casualties', and Implementors/casualties' perceptions of the ethics statement on downsizing will differ significantly from Formulators' and Implementors/survivors' perceptions.

We test the researchers' hypotheses by applying the statistical methodology of this chapter to the **DOWNSIZE** data in the following Statistics in Action Revisited sections.

Statistics in Action Revisited

- Testing for Differences in the Mean Ethics Responses of the Five Downsize Groups (p. 575)
- Ranking the Mean Ethics Responses for the Five Groups (p. 587).

   DOWNSIZE

TABLE SIA10.1   Employee Groups for Ethics of Downsizing Study

Group	Number	Description
Casualties	47	Nonmanagerial personnel who have been laid off at least once
Survivors	71	Nonmanagerial personnel who have worked for a firm that downsized but were never laid off
Implementors/casualties	27	Managers/supervisors who have been laid off at least once but now implement downsizing decisions
Implementors/survivors	33	Managers/supervisors who implement downsizing decisions for their current firm and worked for a firm that downsized but were never laid off
Formulators	31	CEOs who have actually made a decision to downsize and presided over its implementation

Most of the data analyzed in previous chapters were collected in *observational* sampling experiments rather than *designed* sampling experiments. In *observational studies* the analyst has little or no control over the variables under study and merely observes their values. In contrast, *designed experiments* are those in which the analyst attempts to control the levels of one or more variables to determine their effect on a variable of interest. Although many practical business situations do not present the opportunity for such control, it is instructive, even for observational experiments, to have a working knowledge of the analysis and interpretation of data that result from designed experiments and to know the basics of how to design experiments when the opportunity arises.

We first present the basic elements of an experimental design in Section 10.1. We then discuss three of the simpler, and more popular, experimental designs in Sections 10.2 10.4. and 10.5. In Section 10.3 we show how to rank the population means, from smallest to largest.

10.1 Elements of a Designed Experiment

Certain elements are common to almost all designed experiments, regardless of the specific area of application. For example, the *response* is the variable of interest in the experiment. The response might be the SAT scores of a high school senior, the total sales of a firm last year, or the total income of a particular household this year. The response is also called the *dependent variable, y.* We use these terms interchangeably in this chapter.

DEFINITION 10.1

The **response variable** is the variable of interest to be measured in the experiment. We also refer to the response as the **dependent variable.**

The intent of most statistical experiments is to determine the effect of one or more variables on the response. These variables, which we called the *independent variables* in regression analysis, are often referred to as the *factors* in a designed experiment. Like independent variables, factors are either *quantitative* or *qualitative*, depending on whether the variable is measured on a numerical scale or not. For example, we might want to explore the effect of the qualitative factor Gender on the response SAT score. In other words, we want to compare the SAT scores of male and female high school seniors. Or, we might wish to determine the effect of the quantitative factor Number of salespeople on the response Total sales for retail firms. Often two or more factors are of interest. For example, we might want to determine the effect of the quantitative factor Number of wage earners and the qualitative factor Location on the response Household income.

DEFINITION 10.2

Factors are those variables whose effect on the response is of interest to the experimenter. **Quantitative factors** are measured on a numerical scale, whereas **qualitative factors** are those that are not (naturally) measured on a numerical scale. Factors are also referred to as **independent variables**.

Levels are the values of the factors that are utilized in the experiment. The levels of qualitative factors are usually nonnumerical. For example, the levels of

Gender are Male and Female, and the levels of Location might be North, East, South, and West.* The levels of quantitative factors are numerical values. For example, the Number of salespeople may have levels 1, 3, 5, 7, and 9. The factor Years of education may have levels 8, 12, 16, and 20.

> **DEFINITION 10.3**
>
> **Factor levels** are the values of the factor utilized in the experiment.

When a *single factor* is employed in an experiment, the *treatments* of the experiment are the levels of the factor. For example, if the effect of the factor Gender on the response SAT score is being investigated, the treatments of the experiment are the two levels of Gender—Female and Male. Or, if the effect of the Number of wage earners on Household income is the subject of the experiment, the numerical values assumed by the quantitative factor Number of wage earners are the treatments. If *two or more factors* are utilized in an experiment, the treatments are the factor-level combinations used. For example, if the effects of the factors Gender and GPA on the response SAT score are being investigated, the treatments are the combinations of the levels of Gender and GPA used; thus (Female, 2.61), (Male, 3.43), and (Female, 3.82) would all be treatments.

> **DEFINITION 10.4**
>
> The **treatments** of an experiment are the factor-level combinations utilized.

The objects on which the response variable and factors are observed are the *experimental units*. For example, SAT score, High school GPA, and Gender are all variables that can be observed on the same experimental unit—a high school senior. Or, the Total sales, the Earnings per share, and the Number of salespeople can be measured on a particular firm in a particular year, and the firm-year combination is the experimental unit. The Total income, the Number of female wage earners, and the Location can be observed for a household at a particular point in time, and the household-time combination is the experimental unit. Every experiment, whether observational or designed, has experimental units on which the variables are observed. However, the identification of the experimental units is more important in designed experiments, when the experimenter must actually sample the experimental units and measure the variables.

> **DEFINITION 10.5**
>
> An **experimental unit** is the object on which the response and factors are observed or measured.†

---

*The levels of a qualitative variable may bear numerical labels. For example, the Locations could be numbered 1, 2, 3, and 4. However, in such cases the numerical labels for a qualitative variable will usually be codes representing nonnumerical levels.

†Recall (Chapter 1) that the set of all experimental units is the population.

When the specification of the treatments and the method of assigning the experimental units to each of the treatments are controlled by the analyst, the experiment is said to be *designed*. In contrast, if the analyst is just an observer of the treatments on a sample of experimental units, the experiment is *observational*. For example, if you give one randomly selected group of employees a training program and withhold it from another randomly selected group in order to evaluate the effect of the training on worker productivity, then you are designing an experiment. If, on the other hand, you compare the productivity of employees with college degrees with the productivity of employees without college degrees, the experiment is observational.

DEFINITION 10.6

A **designed experiment** is one for which the analyst controls the specification of the treatments and the method of assigning the experimental units to each treatment. An **observational experiment** is one for which the analyst simply observes the treatments and the response on a sample of experimental units.

Biography

SIR RONALD A. FISHER (1890-1962)
The Founder of Modern Statistics

At a young age, Ronald Fisher demonstrated special abilities in mathematics, astronomy, and biology. (Fisher's biology teacher once divided all his students for "sheer brilliance" into two groups—Fisher and the rest.) Fisher graduated from prestigious Cambridge University in London in 1912 with a B.A. degree in astronomy, and, after several years teaching mathematics, he found work at the Rothamsted Agricultural Experiment station. There, Fisher began his extraordinary career as a statistician. Many consider Fisher to be the leading founder of modern statistics. His contributions to the field include the notion of unbiased statistics, the development

of *p*-values for hypothesis tests, the invention of analysis of variance for designed experiments, maximum likelihood estimation theory, and the mathematical distributions of several well-known statistics. Fisher's book *Statistical Methods for Research Workers* (written in 1925) revolutionized applied statistics, demonstrating how to analyze data and interpret the results with very readable and practical examples. In 1935, Fisher wrote *The Design of Experiments*, where he first described his famous experiment on the "lady tasting tea." (Fisher showed, through a designed experiment, that the lady really could determine whether tea poured into milk tastes better than milk poured into tea.) Before his death, Fisher was elected a Fellow of the Royal Statistical Society, awarded numerous medals, and was knighted by the Queen of England.

The diagram in Figure 10.1 provides an overview of the experimental process and a summary of the terminology introduced in this section. Note that the experimental unit is at the core of the process. The method by which the sample of experimental units is selected from the population determines the type of experiment. The level of every factor (the treatment) and the response are all variables that are observed or measured on each experimental unit.

Figure 10.1

Sampling experiment:
Process and terminology

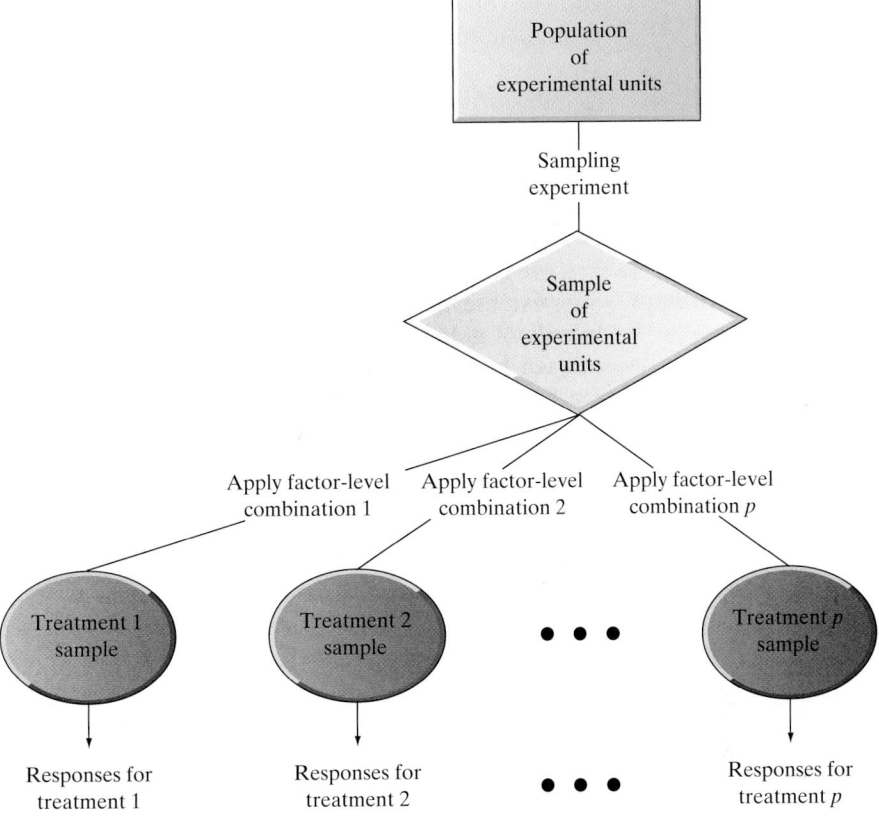

EXAMPLE 10.1

THE KEY ELEMENTS OF A DESIGNED EXPERIMENT

Problem

Teaching Tip

Repeat this example using
exercises that are not assigned
for homework. The more
practice the students get now,
the easier they will be able to
recognize the experimental
designs discussed later.

The USGA (United States Golf Association) regularly tests golf equipment to
ensure that it conforms to USGA standards. Suppose it wishes to compare the mean
distance traveled by four different brands of golf balls when struck by a driver (the
club used to maximize distance). The following experiment is conducted: 10 balls of
each brand are randomly selected. Each is struck by "Iron Byron" (the USGA's golf
robot named for the famous golfer, Byron Nelson) using a driver, and the distance
traveled is recorded. Identify each of the following elements in this experiment:
response, factors, factor types, levels, treatments, and experimental units.

Solution

The response is the variable of interest, Distance traveled. The only factor being
investigated is Brand of golf ball, and it is nonnumerical and therefore qualitative.
The four brands (say A, B, C, and D) represent the levels of this factor. Since only
one factor is utilized, the treatments are the four levels of this factor-that is, the four
brands. The experimental unit is a golf ball; more specifically, it is a golf ball at a particular position in the striking sequence, since the distance traveled can be recorded
only when the ball is struck, and we would expect the distance to be different (due to
random factors such as wind resistance, landing place, and so forth) if the same ball is
struck a second time. Note that 10 experimental units are sampled for each treatment, generating a total of 40 observations.

Look Back This experiment, like many real applications, is a blend of designed
and observational: The analyst cannot control the assignment of the brand to each

golf ball (observational), but he or she can control the assignment of each ball to the position in the striking sequence (designed).

Now Work   *Exercise 10.5*

■ ■ ■

EXAMPLE 10.2   A TWO-FACTOR EXPERIMENT

Problem   Suppose the USGA is also interested in comparing the mean distances the four brands of golf balls travel when struck by a five-iron and by a driver. Ten balls of each brand are randomly selected, five to be struck by the driver, and five by the five-iron. Identify the elements of the experiment, and construct a schematic diagram similar to Figure 10.1 to provide an overview of this experiment.

Suggessted Exercises 10.6

Solution   The response is the same as in Example 10.1—Distance traveled. The experiment now has two factors, Brand of golf ball and Club utilized. There are four levels of Brand (A, B, C, and D) and two of Club (driver and five-iron, or 1 and 5). Treatments are factor-level combinations of golf ball and hitting position. Note that five experimental units are sampled per treatment, generating 40 observations. The experiment is summarized in Figure 10.2.

Figure 10.2

Two-factor golf experiment
summary: Example 10.2

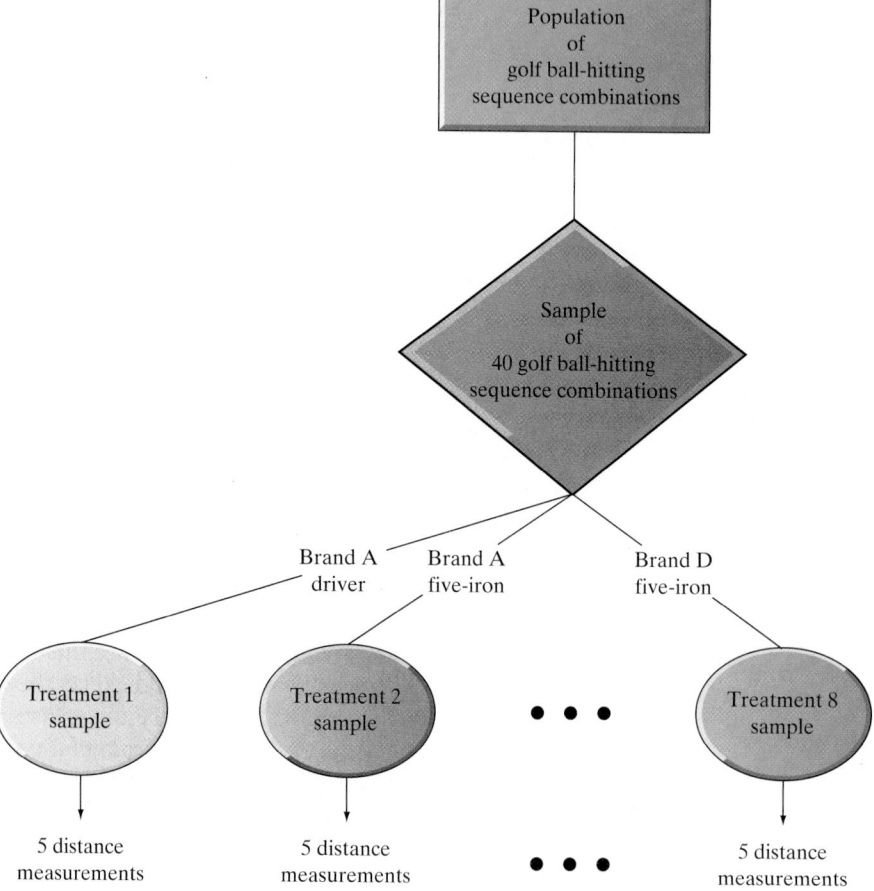

Look Back Whenever there are two or more factors in an experiment, remember to combine the levels of the factors—one level from each factor—to obtain the treatments.

Now Work   *Exercise 10.8*

■ ■ ■

Our objective in designing an experiment is usually to maximize the amount of information obtained about the relationship between the treatments and the response. Of course, we are almost always subject to constraints on budget, time, and even the availability of experimental units. Nevertheless, designed experiments are generally preferred to observational experiments. Not only do we have better control of the amount and quality of the information collected, but we also avoid the biases inherent in observational experiments in the selection of the experimental units representing each treatment. Inferences based on observational experiments always carry the implicit assumption that the sample has no hidden bias that was not considered in the statistical analysis. Better understanding of the potential problems with observational experiments is a by-product of our study of experimental design in the remainder of this chapter.

Exercises 10.1–10.12

Learning the Mechanics

10.1 What are the treatments for a designed experiment that utilizes one qualitative factor with four levels—A, B, C, and D?

10.2 What are the treatments for a designed experiment with two factors, one qualitative with two levels (A and B) and one quantitative with five levels (50, 60, 70, 80, and 90)?

10.3 What is the difference between an observational and a designed experiment?

10.4 What are the experimental units on which each of the following responses are observed?
  a. College GPA   College student
  b. Household income   Household
  c. Gasoline mileage rating for an automobile model
  d. Number of defective sectors on a computer diskette
  e. December unemployment rate for a state

Applying the Concepts—Basic

10.5 Brief descriptions of a number of experiments are given next. Determine whether each is observational or designed, and explain your reasoning.
  a. An economist obtains the unemployment rate and gross state product for a sample of states over the past 10 years, with the objective of examining the relationship between the unemployment rate and the gross state product by census region.   Observational
  b. A manager in a paper production facility installs one of three incentive programs in each of nine plants to determine the effect of each program on productivity.
  c. A marketer of personal computers runs ads in each of four national publications for one quarter, and keeps track of the number of sales that are attributable to each publication's ad.   Observational
  d. An electric utility engages a consultant to monitor the discharge from its smokestack on a monthly basis over a one-year period in order to relate the level of sulfur dioxide in the discharge to the load on the facility's generators.   Observational
  e. Intrastate trucking rates are compared before and after governmental deregulation of prices charged, with the comparison also taking into account distance of haul, goods hauled, and the price of diesel fuel

10.6 Refer to the CardWeb.com, Inc., study of credit card purchases, Exercise 1.14 (p. 26). Recall that the company tracked credit card purchases made by cardholders and measured two variables: (1) the type of credit card used (VISA, MasterCard, American Express, or Discover), and (2) the amount (in dollars) of the purchase. Suppose we want to compare the mean purchase amounts of VISA, MasterCard, American Express, and Discover cardholders. Identify each of the following elements for this study:

a. Response variable
b. Factor(s)
c. Treatments
d. Experimental units

10.7 Refer to Exercise 1.22 (p. 27) and the University of South Florida clinical trial of 50,000 smokers to compare the effectiveness of computed tomography (CT) scans with X-rays for detecting lung cancer (*Todays' Tomorrows,* Fall 2002). Recall that each participating smoker will be randomly assigned to one of two screening methods, CT or chest X-ray, and the age (in years) at which the scanning method first detects a tumor will be determined. One goal of the study is to compare the mean ages when cancer is first detected of the two screening methods

a. Identify the response variable of the study.
b. Identify the experimental units of the study.
c. Identify the factor(s) in the study.
d. Identify the treatments in the study.

Applying the Concepts—Intermediate

10.8 Refer to the *Journal of Consumer Research* (Sept. 1996) study of whether between-store comparisons result in greater perceptions of value by consumers than within-store comparisons, Example 1.7 (p. 20). Recall that 50 consumers were randomly selected from all consumers in a designated market area to participate in the study. The researchers randomly assigned 25 consumers to read a within-store price promotion advertisement ("was $100, now $80") and 25 consumers to read a between-store price promotion ("$100 there, $80 here"). The consumers then gave their opinion on the value of the discount offer on a 10-point scale (where 1 = lowest value and 10 = highest value). The goal is to compare the average discount values of the two groups of consumers.

a. What is the response variable for this study?
b. What are the treatments for this study?
c. What is the experimental unit for this study?

10.9 Refer to Exercise 10.8. In addition to the factor, Type of advertisement (within-store price promotion and between-store price promotion), the researchers also investigated the impact of a second factor, Location where ad is read (at home or in the store). About half of the consumers who were assigned to the within-store price promotion read the ad at home, and the other half read the ad in the store. Similarly, about half of the consumers who were assigned to the between-store price promotion read the ad at home, and the other half read the ad in the store. In this second experiment, the goal is to compare the average discount values of the groups of consumers created by combining Type of advertisement with Location.

a. How many treatments are involved in this experiment? 4
b. Identify the treatments.

10.10 In *Teaching of Psychology* (August 1998), a study investigated whether final exam performance is affected by whether or not students take a practice test. Students in an introductory psychology class at Pennsylvania State University were initially divided into three groups based on their class standing: Low, Medium, or High. Within each group, the students were randomly assigned to either attend a review session or take a practice test prior to the final exam. Thus, six groups were formed: (Low, Review), (Low, Practice exam), (Medium, Review), (Medium, Practice exam), (High, Review), and (High, Practice exam). One goal of the study was to compare the mean final exam scores of the six groups of students.

a. What is the experimental unit for this study?
b. Is the study a designed experiment? Why? Yes
c. What are the factors in the study?
d. Give the levels of each factor.
e. How many treatments are in the study? Identify them. 6
f. What is the response variable?

Applying the Concepts-Advanced

10.11 A quality control supervisor measures the quality of a steel ingot on a scale of 0 to 10. He designs an experiment in which three different temperatures (ranging from 1,100 to 1,200° F) and five different pressures (ranging from 500 to 600 psi) are utilized, with 20 ingots produced at each Temperature-Pressure combination. Identify the following elements of the experiment:

a. Response **b.** Factor(s) and factor type(s)
c. Treatments **d.** Experimental units

10.12 Within marketing, the area of personal sales has long suffered from a poor ethical image, particularly in the eyes of college students. An article in *Journal of Business Ethics* (Vol. 15, 1996) investigated whether such opinions by college students are a function of the type of sales job (high tech versus low tech) and/or the sales task (new account development versus account maintenance). Four different samples of college students were confronted with the four different situations (new account development in a high-tech sales task; new account development in a low-tech sales task; account maintenance in a high-tech sales task; and account maintenance in a low-tech sales task), and were asked to evaluate the ethical behavior of the salesperson on a seven-point scale ranging from 1 (not a serious ethical violation) to 7 (a very serious ethical violation). Identify each of the following elements of the experiment:

a. Response **b.** Factor(s) and factor level(s)
c. Treatments **d.** Experimental units

10.2 The Completely Randomized Design: Single Factor

The simplest experimental design, a *completely randomized design*, consists of the *independent random selection* of experimental units representing each treatment. For example, we could independently select random samples of 20 female and 15 male high school seniors to compare their mean SAT scores. Or, we could independently select random samples of 30 households from each of four census districts to compare the mean income per household among the districts. In both examples our objective is to compare treatment means by selecting random, independent samples for each treatment.

> **DEFINITION 10.7**
>
> A **completely randomized design** is a design for which independent random samples of experimental units are selected for each treatment.*

The objective of a completely randomized design is usually to compare the treatment means. If we denote the true, or population, means of the k treatments as $\mu_1, \mu_2, \ldots, \mu_k$, then we will test the null hypothesis that the treatment means are all equal against the alternative that at least two of the treatment means differ:

$$H_0: \mu_1 = \mu_2 = \cdots = \mu_k$$
$$H_a: \text{At least two of the } p \text{ treatment means differ}$$

The μ's might represent the means of *all* female and male high school seniors' SAT scores or the means of *all* households' income in each of four census regions.

To conduct a statistical test of these hypotheses, we will use the means of the independent random samples selected from the treatment populations using the completely randomized design. That is, we compare the k sample means, $\bar{x}_1, \bar{x}_2, \ldots, \bar{x}_k$.

For example, suppose you select independent random samples of five female and five male high school seniors and obtain sample mean SAT scores of 550 and 590, respectively. Can we conclude that males score 40 points higher, on average, than females? To answer this question, we must consider the amount of sampling variability among the experimental units (students). If the scores are as depicted in the dot plot shown in Figure 10.3, then the difference between the means is small relative to the sampling variability of the scores within the treatments, Female and Male. We

Figure 10.3

Dot plot of SAT scores: Difference between means dominated by sampling variability

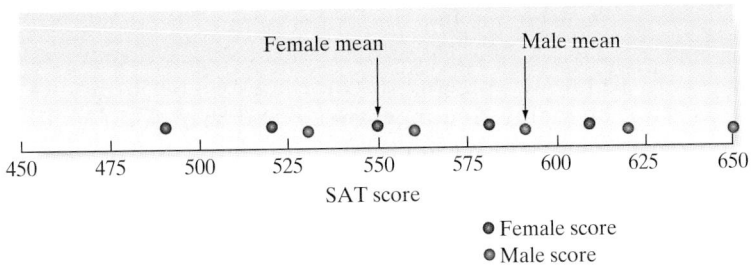

*We use *completely randomized* design to refer to both designed and observational experiments. Thus, the only requirement is that the experimental units to which treatments are applied (designed) or on which treatments are observed (observational) are independently selected for each treatment.

Figure 10.4

Dot plot of SAT scores: Difference between means large relative to sampling variability

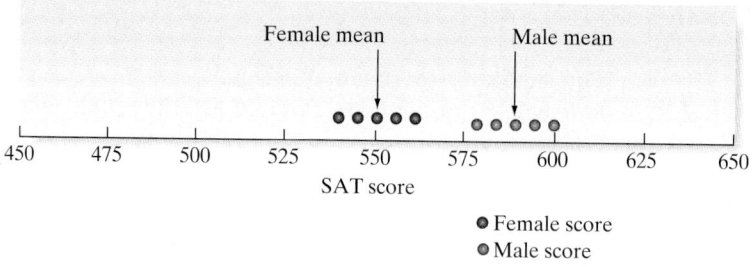

would be inclined not to reject the null hypothesis of equal population means in this case.

In contrast, if the data are as depicted in the dot plot of Figure 10.4, then the sampling variability is small relative to the difference between the two means. We would be inclined to favor the alternative hypothesis that the population means differ in this case.

Now Work *Exercise 10.15*

You can see that the key is to compare the difference between the treatment means to the amount of sampling variability. To conduct a formal statistical test of the hypotheses requires numerical measures of the difference between the treatment means and the sampling variability within each treatment. The variation between the treatment means is measured by the **Sum of Squares for Treatments** (SST), which is calculated by squaring the distance between each treatment mean and the overall mean of *all* sample measurements, multiplying each squared distance by the number of sample measurements for the treatment, and adding the results over all treatments:

$$\text{SST} = \sum_{i=1}^{k} n_i(\bar{x}_i - \bar{x})^2 = 5(550 - 570)^2 + 5(590 - 570)^2 = 4{,}000$$

where we use $\bar{x}$ to represent the overall mean response of all sample measurements, that is, the mean of the combined samples. The symbol n_i is used to denote the sample size for the ith treatment. You can see that the value of SST is 4,000 for the two samples of five female and five male SAT scores depicted in Figures 10.3 and 10.4.

Next, we must measure the sampling variability within the treatments. We call this the **Sum of Squares for Error** (SSE) because it measures the variability around the treatment means that is attributed to sampling error. Suppose the 10 measurements in the first dot plot (Figure 10.3) are 490, 520, 550, 580, and 610 for females, and 530, 560, 590, 620, and 650 for males. Then the value of SSE is computed by summing the squared distance between each response measurement and the corresponding treatment mean, and then adding the squared differences over all measurements in the entire sample:

$$\text{SSE} = \sum_{j=1}^{n_1} (x_{1j} - \bar{x}_1)^2 + \sum_{j=1}^{n_2} (x_{2j} - \bar{x}_2)^2 + \cdots + \sum_{j=1}^{n_k} (x_{kj} - \bar{x}_k)^2$$

where the symbol x_{1j} is the jth measurement in sample 1, x_{2j} is the jth measurement in sample 2, and so on. This rather complex-looking formula can be simplified by recalling the formula for the sample variance, s^2, given in Chapter 2:

Teaching Tip
Emphasize that the computer outputs that will be generated reduce the amount of calculations that will need to be performed by the student.

$$s^2 = \sum_{i=1}^{n} \frac{(x_i - \bar{x})^2}{n - 1}$$

Note that each sum in SSE is simply the numerator of s^2 for that particular treatment. Consequently, we can rewrite SSE as

$$\text{SSE} = (n_1 - 1)s_1^2 + (n_2 - 1)s_2^2 + \cdots + (n_k - 1)s_k^2$$

where $s_1^2, s_2^2, \ldots, s_k^2$ are the sample variances for the k treatments. For our samples of SAT scores, we find $s_1^2 = 2{,}250$ (for females) and $s_2^2 = 2{,}250$ (for males); then we have

$$\text{SSE} = (5 - 1)(2{,}250) + (5 - 1)(2{,}250) = 18{,}000$$

To make the two measurements of variability comparable, we divide each by the degrees of freedom to convert the sums of squares to mean squares. First, the **Mean Square for Treatments** (MST), which measures the variability among the treatment means, is equal to

$$\text{MST} = \frac{\text{SST}}{k - 1} = \frac{4{,}000}{2 - 1} = 4{,}000$$

where the number of degrees of freedom for the k treatments is $(k - 1)$. Next, the **Mean Square for Error** (MSE), which measures the sampling variability within the treatments, is

$$\text{MSE} = \frac{\text{SSE}}{n - k} = \frac{18{,}000}{10 - 2} = 2{,}250$$

Finally, we calculate the ratio of MST to MSE—an **F-statistic:**

$$F = \frac{\text{MST}}{\text{MSE}} = \frac{4{,}000}{2{,}250} = 1.78$$

Values of the F-statistic near 1 indicate that the two sources of variation, between treatment means and within treatments, are approximately equal. In this case, the difference between the treatment means may well be attributable to sampling error, which provides little support for the alternative hypothesis that the population treatment means differ. Values of F well in excess of 1 indicate that the variation among treatment means well exceeds that within means and therefore support the alternative hypothesis that the population treatment means differ.

When does F exceed 1 by enough to reject the null hypothesis that the means are equal? This depends on the degrees of freedom for treatments and for error, and on the value of α selected for the test. We compare the calculated F value to a table F-value (Tables VIII–XI of Appendix B) with $v_1 = (k - 1)$ degrees of freedom in the numerator and $v_2 = (n - k)$ degrees of freedom in the denominator and corresponding to a Type I error probability of α. For the SAT score example, the F-statistic has $v_1 = (2 - 1) = 1$ numerator degree of freedom and $v_2 = (10 - 2) = 8$ denominator degrees of freedom. Thus, for $\alpha = .05$ we find (Table IX of Appendix B)

Teaching Tip
Rejecting the null hypothesis only indicates to us that differences exist between the population means. It does not specify where these differences occur.

$$F_{.05} = 5.32$$

The implication is that MST would have to be 5.32 times greater than MSE before we could conclude at the .05 level of significance that the two population treatment means differ. Since the data yielded $F = 1.78$, our initial impressions for the dot plot in Figure 10.3 are confirmed—there is insufficient information to conclude that the mean SAT scores differ for the populations of female and male high school seniors. The rejection region and the calculated F value are shown in Figure 10.5.

Figure 10.5

Rejection region and calculated F values for SAT score samples

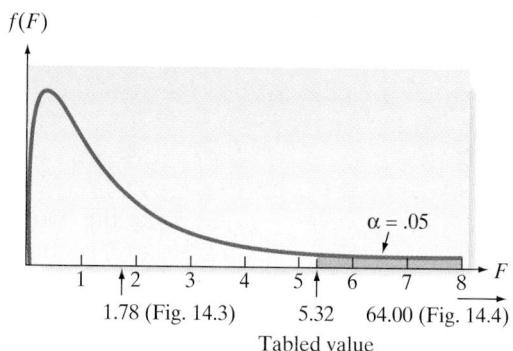

In contrast, consider the dot plot in Figure 10.4. Since the means are the same as in the first example, 550 and 590, respectively, the variation between the means is the same, MST = 4,000. But the variation within the two treatments appears to be considerably smaller. The observed SAT scores are 540, 545, 550, 555, and 560 for females, and 580, 585, 590, 595, and 600 for males. These values yield $s_1^2 = 62.5$ and $s_2^2 = 62.5$. Thus, the variation within the treatments is measured by

$$\text{SSE} = (5 - 1)(62.5) + (5 - 1)(62.5) = 500$$

$$\text{MSE} = \frac{\text{SSE}}{n - k} = \frac{500}{8} = 62.5$$

Then the F-ratio is

$$F = \frac{\text{MST}}{\text{MSE}} = \frac{4,000}{62.5} = 64.0$$

Again, our visual analysis of the dot plot is confirmed statistically: $F = 64.0$ well exceeds the tabled F-value, 5.32, corresponding to the .05 level of significance. We would therefore reject the null hypothesis at that level and conclude that the SAT mean score of males differs from that of females.

Now Work   *Exercise 10.16*

Recall that we performed a hypothesis test for the difference between two means in Section 9.1, using a two-sample t-statistic for two independent samples. When two independent samples are being compared, the t- and F-tests are equivalent. To see this, recall the formula

$$t = \frac{\bar{x}_1 - \bar{x}_2}{\sqrt{s_p^2\left(\dfrac{1}{n_1} + \dfrac{1}{n_2}\right)}} = \frac{590 - 550}{\sqrt{(62.5)\left(\dfrac{1}{5} + \dfrac{1}{5}\right)}} = \frac{40}{5} = 8$$

where we used the fact that $s_p^2 = $ MSE, which you can verify by comparing the formulas. Note that the calculated F for these samples ($F = 64$) equals the square of the calculated t for the same samples ($t = 8$). Likewise, the tabled F-value (5.32) equals the square of the tabled t value at the two-sided .05 level of significance ($t_{.025} = 2.306$ with 8 df). Since both the rejection region and the calculated values are related in the same way, the tests are equivalent. Moreover, the assumptions that must be met to ensure the validity of the t- and F-tests are the same:

1. The probability distributions of the populations of responses associated with each treatment must all be normal.

2. The probability distributions of the populations of responses associated with each treatment must have equal variances.

3. The samples of experimental units selected for the treatments must be random and independent.

In fact, the only real difference between the tests is that the F-test can be used to compare *more than two* treatment means, whereas the t-test is applicable to two samples only. The F-test is summarized in the accompanying box.

Anova F Test to Compare *k* Treatment Means: Completely Randomized Design

$$H_0: \mu_1 = \mu_2 = \cdots = \mu_k$$

H_a: At least two treatment means differ

Test statistic: $F = \dfrac{\text{MST}}{\text{MSE}}$

Rejection region: $F > F_\alpha$, where F_α is based on $(k - 1)$ numerator degrees of freedom (associated with MST) and $(n - k)$ denominator degrees of freedom (associated with MSE).

Conditions Required for a Valid ANOVA F-test: Completely Randomized Design

1. The samples are randomly selected in an independent manner from the k treatment populations. (This can be accomplished by randomly assigning the experimental units to the treatments.)

2. All k sampled populations have distributions that are approximately normal.

3. The k population variances are equal (i.e., $\sigma_1^2 = \sigma_2^2 = \sigma_3^2 = \ldots = \sigma_k^2$).

Computational formulas for MST and MSE are given in Appendix C. We will rely on some of the many statistical software packages available to compute the F statistic, concentrating on the interpretation of the results rather than their calculations.

EXAMPLE 10.3 CONDUCTING AN ANOVA F-TEST

Problem Suppose the USGA wants to compare the mean distances associated with four different brands of golf balls when struck with a driver. A completely randomized design is employed, with Iron Byron, the USGA's robotic golfer, using a driver to hit a random sample of 10 balls of each brand in a random sequence. The distance is recorded for each hit, and the results are shown in Table 10.1, organized by brand.

$H_0: \mu_1 = \mu_2 = \mu_3 = \mu_4$

$F = 43.99, p \approx 0$, Reject H_0

a. Set up the test to compare the mean distances for the four brands. Use $\alpha = .10$.

b. Use EXCEL to obtain the test statistic and p-value. Interpret the results.

 GOLFCRD

TABLE 10.1 Results of Completely Randomized Design: Iron Byron Driver

	Brand A	Brand B	Brand C	Brand D
	251.2	263.2	269.7	251.6
	245.1	262.9	263.2	248.6
	248.0	265.0	277.5	249.4
	251.1	254.5	267.4	242.0
	260.5	264.3	270.5	246.5
	250.0	257.0	265.5	251.3
	253.9	262.8	270.7	261.8
	244.6	264.4	272.9	249.0
	254.6	260.6	275.6	247.1
	248.8	255.9	266.5	245.9
Sample Means	250.8	261.1	270.0	249.3

Solution **a.** To compare the mean distances of the four brands, we first specify the hypotheses to be tested. Denoting the population mean of the ith brand by μ_i, we test

$H_0: \mu_1 = \mu_2 = \mu_3 = \mu_4$

H_a: The mean distances differ for at least two of the brands

The test statistic compares the variation among the four treatment (Brand) means to the sampling variability within each of the treatments.

Test statistic: $F = \dfrac{\text{MST}}{\text{MSE}}$

Rejection region: $F > F_\alpha = F_{.10}$

with $v_1 = (k - 1) = 3$ df and $v_2 = (n - k) = 36$ df

From Table VIII of Appendix B, we find $F_{.10} \approx 2.25$ for 3 and 36 df. Thus, we will reject H_0 if $F > 2.25$. (See Figure 10.6.)

The assumptions necessary to ensure the validity of the test are as follows:

Figure 10.6

F-test for completely randomized design: Golf ball experiment

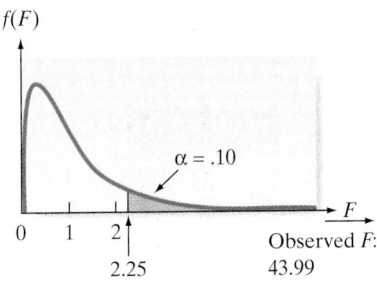

1. The samples of 10 golf balls for each brand are selected randomly and independently.
2. The probability distributions of the distances for each brand are normal.
3. The variances of the distance probability distributions for each brand are equal.

b. The EXCEL printout for the data in Table 10.1 resulting from this completely randomized design is given in Figure 10.7. At the bottom of the printout the Total Sum of Squares is designated **Total**, and it is partitioned into the **Between Groups** (i.e., Brand) and the **Within Groups** (i.e., Error) sum of squares. The **Sum of Squares** column is headed **SS**.

   The values of the mean squares, MST and MSE (highlighted on the printout), are 931.4629 and 21.17503, respectively. The F-ratio, 43.98875, also highlighted on the printout, exceeds the tabled value of 2.25. We therefore reject the null hypothesis at the .10 level of significance, concluding that at least two of the brands differ with respect to mean distance traveled when struck by the driver.

Look Back We can also arrive at the appropriate conclusion by noting that the observed significance level of the F-test (highlighted on the printout) is approximately 0. This implies that we would reject the null hypothesis that the means are equal at any reasonably-selected α level.

Teaching Tip

Have the students' state exactly how the p-value is interpreted. Stress that more work is needed if any specific information is desired concerning the relationship of the four population means.

Anova: Single Factor

SUMMARY

Groups	Count	Sum	Average	Variance
BrandA	10	2507.8	250.78	22.42178
BrandB	10	2610.6	261.06	14.94711
BrandC	10	2699.5	269.95	20.25833
BrandD	10	2493.2	249.32	27.07289

ANOVA

Source of Variation	SS	df	MS	F	P-value	F crit
Between Groups	2794.389	3	931.4629	43.98875	3.97E-12	2.242608
Within Groups	762.301	36	21.17503			
Total	3556.69	39				

Figure 10.7

EXCEL printout for ANOVA of golf ball distance data

[*Note:* EXCEL uses exponential notation to display the p-value. The value 3.97E-12 is equal to .00000000000397.]

Now Work *Exercise 10.21*

■ ■ ■

The results of an **analysis of variance** (ANOVA) can be summarized in a simple tabular format similar to that obtained from the EXCEL printout in Example 10.3. The general form of the table is shown in Table 10.2, where the symbols df, SS, and MS stand for degrees of freedom, Sum of Squares, and Mean Square, respectively. Note that the two sources of variation, Treatments and Error, add to the Total Sum of Squares, SS(Total). The ANOVA summary table for Example 10.3 is given in Table 10.3, and the partitioning of the Total Sum of Squares into its two components is illustrated in Figure 10.8.

TABLE 10.2 General ANOVA Summary Table for a Completely Randomized Design

Source	df	SS	MS	F
Treatments	$k - 1$	SST	$\text{MST} = \dfrac{\text{SST}}{k - 1}$	$\dfrac{\text{MST}}{\text{MSE}}$
Error	$n - k$	SSE	$\text{MSE} = \dfrac{\text{SSE}}{n - k}$	
Total	$n - 1$	SS(Total)		

TABLE 10.3 ANOVA Summary Table for Example 14.3

Source	df	SS	MS	F	p-Value
Brands	3	2,794.39	931.46	43.99	.0001
Error	36	762.30	21.18		
Total	39	3,556.69			

Teaching Tip

Point out that many different multiple comparison procedures are available. Section 10.3 examines several of the more common comparisons.

Suppose the *F*-test results in a rejection of the null hypothesis that the treatment means are equal. Is the analysis complete? Usually, the conclusion that at least two of the treatment means differ leads to other questions. Which of the means differ, and by how much? For example, the *F*-test in Example 10.3 leads to the conclusion that at least two of the brands of golf balls have different mean distances traveled when struck with a driver. Now the question is, which of the brands differ? How are the brands ranked with respect to mean distance?

One way to obtain this information is to construct a confidence interval for the difference between the means of any pair of treatments using the method of Section 9.1. For example, if a 95% confidence interval for $(\mu_A - \mu_C)$ in Example 10.3 is found to be $(-24, -13)$, we are confident that the mean distance for Brand C exceeds the mean for Brand A (since all differences in the interval are negative). Constructing these confidence intervals for all possible brand pairs will allow you to

Figure 10.8
Partitioning of the Total
Sum of Squares for the
completely randomized
design

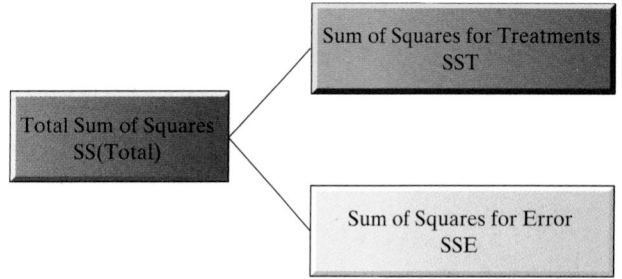

rank the brand means. A method for conducting these *multiple comparisons*—one
that controls for Type I errors—is presented in Section 10.3.

Analysis of Variance

Using The TI-83
Graphing Calculator
Computing a One-Way ANOVA

Step 1   *Enter each data set into its own list (i.e., sample 1 into L1, sample 2 into L2,
sample 3 into L3, etc.).*

Step 2   *Access the Statistical Test Menu*
Press **STAT**
Arrow right to TESTS
Arrow up to F: ANOVA(
Press **ENTER**

Step 3   *Enter each list, separated by commas, for which you want to perform the
analysis* (e.g., L1, L2, L3, L4)
Press **ENTER**

Step 4   *View Display*
The calculator will display the *F*-test statistic, as well as the p-value, the
Factor degrees of freedom, sum of squares, mean square, and by arrowing
Down, the Error degrees of freedom, sum of squares, mean square, and the
pooled standard deviation.

Example   Below are four different samples. At the $\alpha = .05$ level of significance test
whether the four population means are equal. The null hypothesis will be
$H_0: \mu_1 = \mu_2 = \mu_3 = \mu_4$. The alternative hypothesis is H_a: At least one mean
is different.

SAMPLE 1	SAMPLE 2	SAMPLE 3	SAMPLE 4
60	59	55	58
61	52	55	58
56	51	52	55

The screens for this example are shown below.

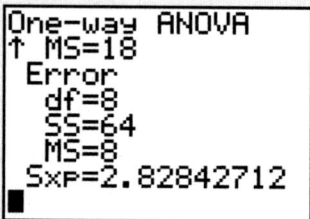

As you can see from the screen, the p-value is 0.1598 which is *not less than* 0.05 therefore we *should not* reject H_0. The differences are not significant.

EXAMPLE 10.4   CHECKING THE ANOVA ASSUMPTIONS

Refer to the completely randomized design ANOVA conducted in Example 10.3. Are the assumptions required for the test approximately satisfied?

Solution The assumptions for the test are repeated below.

1. The samples of golf balls for each brand are selected randomly and independently.
2. The probability distributions of the distances for each brand are normal.
3. The variances of the distance probability distributions for each brand are equal.

Since the sample consisted of 10 randomly selected balls of each brand and the robotic golfer Iron Byron was used to drive all the balls, the first assumption of independent random samples is satisfied. To check the next two assumptions, we will employ two graphical methods presented in Chapter 2: stem-and-leaf displays and dot plots. A MINITAB stem-and-leaf display for the sample distances of each brand of golf ball is shown in Figure 10.9, followed by a MINITAB dot plot in Figure 10.10.

Suggested Exercise 10.30

The normality assumption can be checked by examining the stem-and-leaf displays in Figure 10.9. With only 10 sample measurements for each brand, however, the displays are not very informative. More data would need to be collected for each brand before we could assess whether the distances come from normal distributions. Fortunately, analysis of variance has been shown to be a very **robust method** when the assumption of normality is not satisfied exactly: That is, moderate departures from normality do not have much effect on the significance level of the ANOVA F-test or on confidence coefficients. Rather than spend the time, energy, or money to collect additional data for this experiment in order to verify the normality assumption, we will rely on the robustness of the ANOVA methodology.

Figure 10.9
MINITAB stem-and-leaf
displays for golf ball
distance data

Stem-and-Leaf Display: BrandA, BrandB, BrandC, BrandD

```
Stem-and-leaf of BrandA   N  = 10
Leaf Unit = 1.0


    2    24   45
    2    24
    4    24   88
   (3)   25   011
    3    25   3
    2    25   4
    1    25
    1    25
    1    26   0


Stem-and-leaf of BrandB   N  = 10
Leaf Unit = 1.0


    2    25   45
    3    25   7
    3    25
    4    26   0
   (3)   26   223
    3    26   445


Stem-and-leaf of BrandC   N  = 10
Leaf Unit = 1.0


    1    26   3
    2    26   5
    4    26   67
    5    26   9
    5    27   00
    3    27   2
    2    27   5
    1    27   7


Stem-and-leaf of BrandD   N  = 10
Leaf Unit = 1.0


    1    24   2
    2    24   5
    4    24   67
   (3)   24   899
    3    25   11
    1    25
    1    25
    1    25
    1    25
    1    26   1
```

Figure 10.10

MINITAB dot plots for golf ball distance data

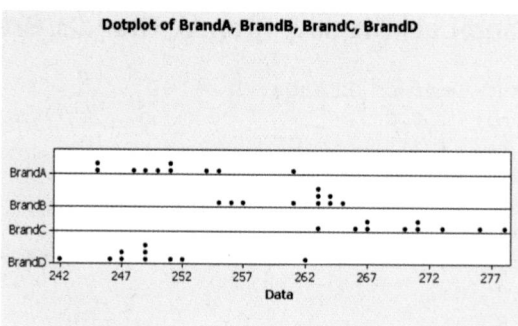

Dot plots are a convenient way to obtain a rough check on the assumption of equal variances. With the exception of a possible outlier for Brand D, the dot plots in Figure 10.10 show that the spread of the distance measurements is about the same for each brand. Since the sample variances appear to be the same, the assumption of equal population variances for the brands is probably satisfied. Although robust with respect to the normality assumption, ANOVA is *not robust* with respect to the equal variances assumption. Departures from the assumption of equal population variances can affect the associated measures of reliability (e.g., p-values and confidence levels). Fortunately, the effect is slight when the sample sizes are equal, as in this experiment.

| Now Work | *Exercise 10.30* |

■ ■ ■

Although graphs can be used to check the ANOVA assumptions, as in Example 10.4, no measures of reliability can be attached to these graphs. When you have a plot that is unclear as to whether or not an assumption is satisfied, you can use formal statistical tests, which are beyond the scope of this text. (Consult the references for information on these tests.) When the validity of the ANOVA assumptions is in doubt, nonparametric statistical methods are useful.

> ### What Do You Do when the Assumptions Are Not Satisfied for the Analysis of Variance for a Completely Randomized Design?
>
> *Answer:* Use a nonparametric statistical method such as the Kruskal-Wallis H-Test of Section 16.4.

Teaching Tip

As we saw in Chapter 9, the nonparametric procedures are very useful when the underlying parametric assumptions fail.

The procedure for conducting an analysis of variance for a completely randomized design is summarized in the following box. Remember that the hallmark of this design is independent random samples of experimental units associated with each treatment. However, designs with dependent samples may be more appropriate in certain situations. Consult the references for information on the use of these designs.

> ### Steps for Conducting an ANOVA for a Completely Randomized Design
>
> 1. Be sure the design is truly completely randomized, with independent random samples for each treatment.
> 2. Check the assumptions of normality and equal variances.

(cont'd)

3. Create an ANOVA summary table that specifies the variability attributable to treatments and error, making sure that it leads to the calculation of the F statistic for testing the null hypothesis that the treatment means are equal in the population. Use a statistical software program to obtain the numerical results. If no such package is available, use the calculation formulas in Appendix C.

4. If the F-test leads to the conclusion that the means differ,
   a. Conduct a multiple comparisons procedure for as many of the pairs of means as you wish to compare (see Section 10.3). Use the results to summarize the statistically significant differences among the treatment means.
   b. If desired, form confidence intervals for one or more individual treatment means.

5. If the F-test leads to the nonrejection of the null hypothesis that the treatment means are equal, consider the following possibilities:
   a. The treatment means are equal—that is, the null hypothesis is true.
   b. The treatment means really differ, but other important factors affecting the response are not accounted for by the completely randomized design. These factors inflate the sampling variability, as measured by MSE, resulting in smaller values of the F statistic. Either increase the sample size for each treatment, or use a different experimental design (as in Section 10.4) that accounts for the other factors affecting the response.

Note: Be careful not to automatically conclude that the treatment means are equal since the possibility of a Type II error must be considered if you accept H_0.]

Teaching Tip
Follow these steps as you illustrate several examples in class.

Statistics in Action Revisited

Testing for Differences in the Mean Ethics Responses of the Five Downsize Groups

University professors W. E. Hopkins and S. A. Hopkins surveyed 209 employees and measured their "ethics scores" (i.e., their responses [on a 5-point scale] to the statement "It is unethical for a downsizing decision to be announced or implemented on or prior to a major holiday [e.g., Christmas, Thanksgiving, etc.]"). The employees were divided into five distinct groups: (1) Casualties, (2) Survivors, (3) Implementors/casualties, (4) Implementors/survivors, and (5) Formulators. (See Table SIA10.1.) The researchers used the data to test three hypotheses.

H_1: Survivors', Casualties', and Implementors/casualties' perceptions of the ethics statement on downsizing will not differ significantly.

H_2: Formulators' and Implementers/survivors' perceptions of the ethics statement on downsizing will not differ significantly.

H_3: Survivors', Casualties', and Implementors/casualties' perceptions of the ethics statement on downsizing will differ significantly from Formulators' and Implementers/survivors' perceptions.

If we let μ_j represent the true mean ethics score for all employees in Group j, then we can restate these hypotheses as follows:

$$H_1: \mu_1 = \mu_2 = \mu_3$$
$$H_2: \mu_4 = \mu_5$$
$$H_3: (\mu_4, \mu_5) \neq (\mu_1, \mu_2, \mu_3)$$

Initially, the researchers conducted an analysis of variance for a completely randomized design on the data. The dependent variable is Ethics score, the treatments are the five employee groups, and the null hypothesis is $H_0: \mu_1 = \mu_2 = \mu_3 = \mu_4 = \mu_5$. The MINITAB printout of the ANOVA is displayed in Figure SIA10.1. The observed significance level of the test (highlighted on the printout) is p-value $= .000$. For any α-level we select (.01, .05, or .10), there is sufficient evidence to reject the null hypothesis. Consequently, the researchers concluded that the mean ethics scores of the five groups of employees were significantly different.

Should the researchers conclude that hypotheses H_1, H_2, and H_3 are supported? Possibly, but not solely on the results of the ANOVA F-test. Remember, the alternative hypothesis (H_a) for this test states that at least two of the five population means are different, but it does not indicate which means in particular are different. In order to test hypotheses H_1, H_2, and H_3, we will need to rank the treatment means using a procedure that provides a

measure of reliability. We present such a method in the next section.

We should, however, check that the assumptions required for the F-test (normal populations with equal variances) are reasonably satisfied. MINITAB steam-and-leaf plots and box plots for the data are shown in Figures SIA 10.2 and SIA 10.3. First, notice the nonsymmetrical shapes in the stem-and-leaf plots, Figure SIA10.2. These graphs do not appear to support the assumption of normality for each treatment group. However, this assumption does not need to be satisfied exactly for the ANOVA to yield valid results. Second, examine the variability in the data shown on the box plots, Figure SIA10.3. It appears that the spread of the ethics scores for groups 1, 2, and 3 is much tighter than the spread for groups 4 and 5. Consequently, it is unlikely that the assumption of equal variances for the five treatment groups is satisfied. The researchers should consider running a nonparametric analysis of the data—an analysis that does not rely on the assumptions of normality and equal variances.

One-way ANOVA: CASUAL, SURVIVE, IMPCAS, IMPSUR, FORMUL

```
Source   DF      SS      MS      F       P
Factor    4    40.84   10.21   9.85   0.000
Error   204   211.35    1.04
Total   208   252.19


S = 1.018    R-Sq = 16.19%    R-Sq(adj) = 14.55%


                                 Individual 95% CIs For Mean Based on
                                 Pooled StDev
Level     N    Mean   StDev    +---------+---------+---------+---------
CASUAL   47   1.787   0.832              (----*----)
SURVIVE  71   1.845   1.023              (---*---)
IMPCAS   27   1.593   0.636      (------*-----)
IMPSUR   33   2.545   1.301                      (----*-----)
FORMUL   31   2.871   1.176                          (-----*-----)
                                 +---------+---------+---------+---------
                                1.20      1.80      2.40      3.00


Pooled StDev = 1.018
```

Figure SIA10.1
MINITAB ANOVA on the downsize data set

Stem-and-Leaf Display: CASUAL, SURVIVE, IMPCAS, IMPSUR, IMPSUR

```
Stem-and-leaf of CASUAL   N  = 47
Leaf Unit = 0.10


 21   1   0000000000000000000000
(16)   2   0000000000000000
 10   3   000000000
  1   4   0


Stem-and-leaf of SURVIVE  N  = 71
Leaf Unit = 0.10


 34   1   0000000000000000000000000000000000
(21)   2   000000000000000000000
 16   3   00000000000
  5   4   000
  2   5   00


Stem-and-leaf of IMPCAS  N  = 27
Leaf Unit = 0.10


 13   1   0000000000000
(12)   2   000000000000
  2   3   00


Stem-and-leaf of IMPSUR  N  = 33
Leaf Unit = 0.10


  9   1   000000000
 (8)   2   00000000
 16   3   00000000
  8   4   00000
  3   5   000


Stem-and-leaf of IMPSUR  N  = 33
Leaf Unit = 0.10


  9   1   000000000
 (8)   2   00000000
 16   3   00000000
  8   4   00000
  3   5   000
```

Figure SIA10.2
MINITAB stem-and-leaf plots of the downsize data

Figure SIA10.3
MINITAB box plots for
the downsize data

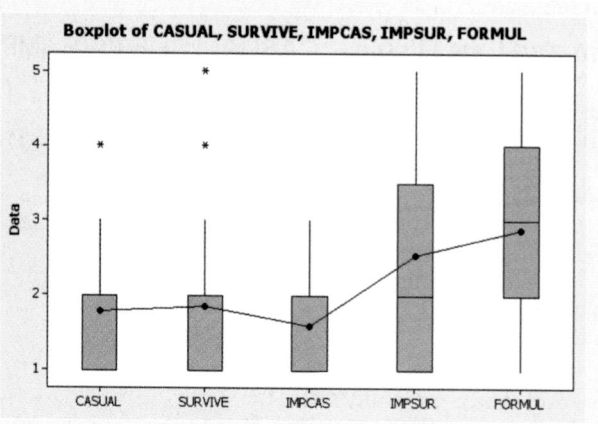

Boxplot of CASUAL, SURVIVE, IMPCAS, IMPSUR, FORMUL

Exercises 10.13–10.32

Learning the Mechanics

10.13 Use Tables VIII, IX, X, and XI of Appendix B to find
each of the following F values:
  a. $F_{.05}, v_1 = 4, v_2 = 4$
  b. $F_{.01}, v_1 = 4, v_2 = 4$
  c. $F_{.10}, v_1 = 30, v_2 = 40$
  d. $F_{.025}, v_1 = 15, v_2 = 12$

10.14 Find the following probabilities:
  a. $P(F \le 3.48)$ for $v_1 = 5, v_2 = 9$ .95
  b. $P(F > 3.09)$ for $v_1 = 15, v_2 = 20$ .01
  c. $P(F > 2.40)$ for $v_1 = 15, v_2 = 15$ .05
  d. $P(F \le 1.83)$ for $v_1 = 8, v_2 = 40$ .90

10.15 Consider dot plots **a** and **b** shown below. In which plot
is the difference between the sample means small relative to the variability within the sample observations?
Justify your answer.   Plot b

10.16 Refer to Exercise 10.15. Assume that the two samples represent independent, random samples corresponding to two treatments in a completely
randomized design.
  a. Calculate the treatment means (i.e., the means of
  samples 1 and 2, for both dot plots).
  b. Use the means to calculate the Sum of Squares for
  Treatments (SST) for each dot plot.

c. Calculate the sample variance for each sample and
use these values to obtain the Sum of Squares for
Error (SSE) for each dot plot.
d. Calculate the Total Sum of Squares [SS(Total)] for
the two dot plots by adding the Sums of Squares for
Treatments and Error. What percentage of SS(Total)
is accounted for by the treatments—that is, what percentage of the Total Sum of Squares is the Sum of
Squares for Treatments—in each case?
e. Convert the Sum of Squares for Treatments and
Error to mean squares by dividing each by the
appropriate number of degrees of freedom. Calculate the F-ratio of the Mean Square for Treatments
(MST) to the Mean Square for Error (MSE) for
each dot plot.
f. Use the F-ratios to test the null hypothesis that the
two samples are drawn from populations with equal
means. Use $\alpha = .05$.
g. What assumptions must be made about the probability distributions corresponding to the responses
for each treatment in order to ensure the validity of
the F-tests conducted in part **f**?

10.17 Refer to Exercises 10.15 and 10.16. Conduct a two-
sample t-test (Section 9.1) of the null hypothesis that
the two treatment means are equal for each dot plot.

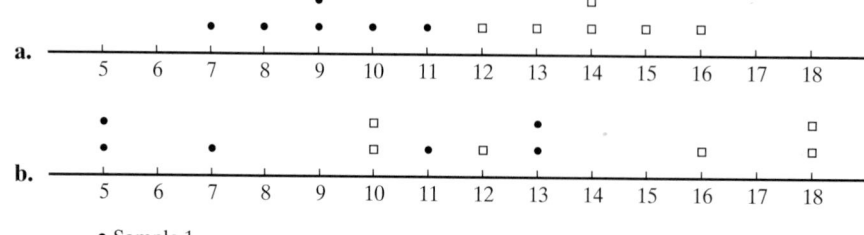

• Sample 1
□ Sample 2

Dot Plots for Exercise 10.15

Use $\alpha = .05$ and two-tailed tests. In the course of the test, compare each of the following with the F-tests in Exercise 10.16:

a. The pooled variances and the MSEs
b. The t- and F-test statistics
c. The tabled values of t and F that determine the rejection regions
d. The conclusions of the t- and F-tests
e. The assumptions that must be made in order to ensure the validity of the t- and F-tests

10.18 Refer to Exercises 10.15 and 10.16. Complete the following ANOVA table for each of the two dot plots:

Source	df	SS	MS	F
Treatments				
Error				
Total				

10.19 Suppose the Total Sum of Squares for a completely randomized design with $k = 6$ treatments and $n = 36$ total measurements (six per treatment) is equal to 500. In each of the following cases, conduct an F-test of the null hypothesis that the mean responses for the five treatments are the same. Use $\alpha = .10$.

a. Sum of Squares for Treatments (SST) is 20% of SS(Total) $F = 1.5$
b. SST is 50% of SS(Total) $F = 6$
c. SST is 80% of SS(Total) $F = 24$
d. What happens to the F-ratio as the percentage of the Total Sum of Squares attributable to treatments is increased?   Increases

10.20 A partially completed ANOVA table for a completely randomized design is shown here:

Source	df	SS	MS	F
Treatments	6	17.5	___	___
Error	___	___	___	
Total	41	46.5		

a. Complete the ANOVA table.
b. How many treatments are involved in the experiment?
c. Do the data provide sufficient evidence to indicate a difference among the population means? Test using $\alpha = .10$. $F = 3.52$
d. Find the approximate observed significance level for the test in part **c**, and interpret it.
e. Suppose that $\bar{x}_1 = 3.7$ and $\bar{x}_2 = 4.1$. Do the data provide sufficient evidence to indicate a difference between μ_1 and μ_2? Assume that there are six observations for each treatment. Test using $\alpha = .10$.
f. Refer to part **e**. Find a 90% confidence interval for $(\mu_1 - \mu_2)$. [Hint: Use $s = \sqrt{MSE}$ as an estimate of both σ_1 and σ_2.] $-.4 \pm .892$

g. Refer to part **e**. Find a 90% confidence interval for μ_1. [Hint: Use $s = \sqrt{MSE}$ as an estimate of σ_1.]

10.21 The data in the accompanying table resulted from an experiment that utilized a completely randomized design.

LM10_21

Treatment 1	Treatment 2	Treatment 3
3.8	5.4	1.3
1.2	2.0	.7
4.1	4.8	2.2
5.5	3.8	
2.3		

a. Use statistical software (or the appropriate calculation formulas in Appendix C) to complete the following ANOVA table:

Source	df	SS	MS	F
Treatments	___	___	___	___
Error	___	___	___	
Total	___	___		

b. Test the null hypothesis that $\mu_1 = \mu_2 = \mu_3$, where μ_i represents the true mean for treatment i, against the alternative that at least two of the means differ. Use $\alpha = .01$. $F = 2.931$

Applying the Concepts-Basic

10.22 Robotic researchers investigated whether robots could be trained to behave like ants in an ant colony (*Nature*, Aug. 2000). Robots were trained and randomly assigned to "colonies" (i.e., groups) consisting of 3, 6, 9, or 12 robots. The robots were assigned the task of foraging for "food" and to recruit another robot when they identified a resource-rich area. One goal of the experiment was to compare the mean energy expended (per robot) of the four different colony sizes.

a. What type of experimental design was employed?
b. Identify the treatments and the dependent variable.
c. Set up the null and alternative hypothesis of the test.
d. The following ANOVA results were reported: $F = 7.70$, numerator df $= 3$, denominator df $= 56$, p-value $< .001$. Conduct the test at a significance level of $\alpha = .05$ and interpret the result.   Reject H_0

10.23 In forming real estate portfolios, investors may choose to diversify holdings across submarkets within the same metropolitan region. J. Rabianski and P. Cheng of Georgia State University investigated the appropriateness of this strategy for office properties (*Journal of Real Estate Portfolio Management*, Vol. 3, 1997). Using the office vacancy rate of a submarket as a proxy for total rate of return for the office submarket, the researchers compared submarkets within several U.S. metropolitan areas. The table presents the mean vacancy rates of the eight office submarkets of Atlanta, Georgia, for a period of nine years. Quarterly vacancy rates were used in calculating the means.

Submarket	Mean Vacancy Rate (%)
Buckhead	16.85
Downtown	20.73
Midtown	19.75
North Central	16.73
Northeast	16.95
Northwest	16.81
North Lake	20.38
South	28.26

Source: Adapted from Rabianski, J. S., and Cheng, P., "Intrametropolitan Spatial Diversification." *Journal of Real Estate Portfolio Management.* Vol.3.No.2, 1997, pp. 117-128.

a. Specify the null and alternative hypotheses to use in comparing the mean vacancy rates of the eight office-property submarkets of Atlanta.

b. The researchers reported on ANOVA *F* statistic of $F = 17.54$ for the Atlanta data. Conduct the hypothesis test you specified in part **a.** Draw the appropriate conclusions in the context of the problem.

c. Give the approximate *p*-value for the test you conducted in part **b.** $p < .01$

d. What assumptions must be met to ensure the validity of the inference you made in part **b?** Which of these assumptions do you consider the most questionable in this application? Why?

10.24 Mutual funds are classified as large-cap funds, medium-cap funds, or small-cap funds, depending on the capitalization of the companies in the fund. Hawaii Pacific University researchers S. Shi and M. Seiler investigated whether the average performance of a mutual fund is related to capitalization size. (*American Business Review,* Jan. 2002.) Independent random samples of 30 mutual funds were selected from each of the three fund groups and the 90-day rate of return determined for each fund. The data for the 90 funds were subjected to an analysis of variances, with the results shown in the ANOVA summary table.

Source	df	SS	MS	F	p-value
Fund group	2	409.566	204.783	6.965	.002
Error	87	2,557.860	29.401		
Total	89	2,967.426			

Source: S. W. W. Shi and M. J. Seiler, "Growth and Value Style Comparison of U.S. Stock Mutual Funds," *American Business Review,* January, 2002 (Table 3).

a. State the null and alternative hypotheses for the ANOVA.

b. Give the rejection region for the test using $\alpha = .01$. $F > 4.86$

c. Make the appropriate conclusion using either the test statistic or the *p*-value. $F = 6.965$

10.25 Refer to Fortune (Oct. 14, 2002) magazine's study of the most powerful women in America, Exercise 2.45 (p. 78). Recall that the data on age (in years) and title of each of the 50 women in the survey are stored in the **WPOWER50** file. (The first five and last two observations of the data are listed in the accompanying table.) Suppose you want to compare the average ages of all powerful American women in three groups based on their position (title) within the firm: Group 1 (CEO, CFO, COO, or CRO); Group 2 (Chairman or President); and, Group 3 (EVP, SVP, and Vice Chair).

a. Give the null and alternative hypothesis to be tested.

b. A MINITAB analysis of variance printout for the test, part **a,** is shown on p. 581 The sample means for the three groups are shown at the bottom of the printout. Why is it insufficient to make a decision about the null hypothesis based solely on these sample means?

c. Locate the test statistic and *p*-value on the printout. Use this information to make the appropriate conclusion at $\alpha = .10$. $F = 1.78$

d. Use the data in the **WPOWER50** file to determine whether the ANOVA assumptions are reasonably satisfied.

⊙ **WPOWER50**

Rank	Name	Age	Company	Title
1	Carly Fiorina	48	Hewlet-Packard	CEO
2	Betsy Holden	46	Kraft Foods	CEO
3	Meg Whitman	46	eBay	CEO
4	Indra Nooyi	46	PepsiCo	CFO
5	Andrea Jung	44	Avon Products	CEO
⋮	⋮	⋮		
49	Fran Keeth	56	Royal Dutch Petrol.	CEO
50	Heidi Miller	49	Bank One	EVP

Source: Fortune, Oct. 14, 2002.

10.26 Researchers at Pennsylvania State University and Iowa State University jointly studied the attitudes of three groups of professionals that influence U.S. policy governing new technologies: scientists, journalists, and federal government policymakers (*American Journal of Political Science,* Jan. 1998). Random samples of 100 scientists, 100 journalists, and 100 government officials were asked about the safety of nuclear power plants. Responses were made on a seven-point scale, where $1 =$ very unsafe and $7 =$ very safe. The mean safety scores for the groups are scientists, 4.1; journalists, 3.7; government officials, 4.2.

a. Identify the response variable for this study.

b. How many treatments are included in this study? Describe them.   3

c. Specify the null and alternative hypotheses that should be used to investigate whether there are differences in the attitudes of scientists, journalists, and government officials regarding the safety of nuclear power plants. $H_0: \mu_1 = \mu_2 = \mu_3$

MINITAB output for Exercise 10.25

One-way ANOVA: AGE versus GROUP

```
Source  DF      SS     MS     F      P
GROUP    2   129.6   64.8   1.78  0.179
Error   47  1708.0   36.3
Total   49  1837.6

S = 6.028   R-Sq = 7.05%   R-Sq(adj) = 3.10%


                        Individual 95% CIs For Mean Based on
                        Pooled StDev
Level  N   Mean   StDev  ------+---------+---------+---------+---
1      21  51.143  7.637                        (-------*--------)
2      11  46.909  6.332  (-----------*------------)
3      18  49.833  2.875               (--------*---------)
                        ------+---------+---------+---------+---
                           45.0      48.0      51.0      54.0
```

d. The MSE for the sample data is 2.355. At least how large must MST be in order to reject the null hypothesis of the test of part **a** using $\alpha = .05$. *7.065*

e. If the MST $= 11.280$, what is the approximate p-value of the test of part **a**? *.01*

Applying the Concepts—Intermediate

10.27 The phenomenon of road rage has received much media attention in recent years. Is a driver's propensity to engage in road rage related to his or her income? Researchers at Mississippi State University attempted to answer this question by conducting a survey of a representative sample of over 1,000 U.S. adult drivers (*Accident Analysis and Prevention*, Vol. 34, 2002). Based on how often each driver engaged in certain road rage behaviors (e.g., making obscene gestures at, tailgating, and thinking about physically hurting another driver), a road rage score was assigned. (Higher scores indicate a greater pattern of road rage behavior.) The drivers were also grouped by annual income: under $30,000, between $30,000 and $60,000, and over $60,000. The data were subjected to an analysis of variance, with the results summarized in the table. Fully interpret the results. Is a driver's propensity to engage in road rage related to his or her income? *F = 3.90*

Income Group	Sample Size	Mean Road Rage Score
Under $30,000	379	4.60
$30,000 to $60,000	392	5.08
Over $60,000	267	5.15

ANOVA Results:	*F*-value $= 3.90$	*p*-value $< .01$

Source: Wells-Parker, E. et al., "An Exploratory Study of the Relationship between Road Rage and Crash Experience in a Representative Sample of US Drivers," *Accident Analysis and Prevention*, Vol. 34, 2002 (Table 2).

OILSPILL

10.28 Refer to the *Marine Technology* (Jan. 1995) study of major ocean oil spills by tanker vessels, Exercise 2.14 (p. 54). The spillage amounts (thousands of metric tons) and cause of accident for 48 tankers are saved in the **OILSPILL** file. Recall that the four accident causes are Collision, Grounding, Fire/ explosion, and Hull failure. (*Note:* Delete the two observations with oil spills of unknown causes.) Is there sufficient evidence to indicate differences among the mean spillage amounts for the four accident causes? Test using $\alpha = .01$. Be sure to check any assumptions required for the methodology used to be valid. *F = .739*

DDT

10.29 Refer to the U.S. Army Corps of Engineers data on contaminated fish saved in the **DDT** file. Recall that species (channel catfish, largemouth bass, or smallmouth buffalofish), length (in centimeters), weight (in grams), and DDT level (in parts per million) were measured for each of 144 captured fish.

a. Is there sufficient evidence to indicate differences among the mean lengths of the three fish species? Test using $\alpha = .05$. *F = 76.88*

b. Is there sufficient evidence to indicate differences among the mean weights of the three fish species? Test using $\alpha = .05$. *F = 28.83*

c. Is there sufficient evidence to indicate differences among the mean DDT levels of the three fish species? Test using $\alpha = .05$. *F = 1.22*

d. Check any assumptions required for the methodology used in parts **a–c** to be valid.

DIAMONDS

10.30 Refer to the *Journal of Statistics Education* study of 308 diamonds for sale on the open market, Exercise 2.25

(p. 65). Recall that the **DIAMONDS** file contains information on the quantitative variables, size (number of carats) and price (in dollars), and on the qualitative variables, color (D, E, F, G, H, and I), clarity (IF, VS1, VS2, VVS1, and VVS2), and independent certification group (GIA, HRD, or IGI). Select one of the quantitative variables and one of the qualitative variables.

a. Set up the null and alternative hypotheses for determining whether the means of the quantitative variable differ for the levels of the qualitative variable.

b. Use the data in the **DIAMONDS** file to conduct the test, part **a**, at $\alpha = 10$. State the conclusion in the words of the problem.

c. Check any assumptions required for the methodology used in part **b** to be valid.

10.31 Industrial sales professionals have long debated the effectiveness of various sales closing techniques. University of Akron researchers S. Hawes, J. Strong, and B. Winick investigated the impact of five different closing techniques and a no-close condition on the level of a sales prospect's trust in the salesperson (*Industrial Marketing Management,* Sept. 1996). Two of the five closing techniques were the *assumed close* and the *impending event technique*. In the former, the salesperson simply writes up the order or behaves as if the sale has been made. In the latter, the salesperson encourages the buyer to buy now before some future event occurs that makes the terms of the sale less favorable for the buyer. Sales scenarios were presented to a sample of 237 purchasing executives. Each subject received one of the five closing techniques or a scenario in which no close was achieved. After reading the sales scenario, each executive was asked to rate their level of trust in the salesperson on a 7-point scale. The table reports the six treatments employed in the study and the number of subjects receiving each treatment.

Treatments: Closing Techniques	Sample Size
1. No close	38
2. Impending event	36
3. Social validation	29
4. If-then	42
5. Assumed close	36
6. Either-or	56

a. The investigator's hypotheses were

H_0: The salesperson's level of prospect trust is not influenced by the choice of closing method.

H_a: The salesperson's level of prospect trust is influenced by the choice of closing method.

Rewrite these hypotheses in the form required for an analysis of variance.

b. The researchers reported the ANOVA F statistic as $F = 2.21$. Is there sufficient evidence to reject H_0 at $\alpha = .05$? No

c. What assumptions must be met in order for the test of part **a** to be valid?

d. Would you classify this experiment as observational or designed? Explain. Designed

10.32 On average, over a million new businesses are started in the United States every year. An article in the *Journal of Business Venturing* (Vol. 11, 1996) reported on the activities of entrepreneurs during the organization creation process. Among the questions investigated were what activities and how many activities do entrepreneurs initiate in attempting to establish a new business? A total of 71 entrepreneurs were interviewed and divided into three groups: those that were successful in founding a new firm (34), those still actively trying to establish a firm (21), and those who tried to start a new firm, but eventually gave up (16). The total number of activities undertaken (i.e., developed a business plan, sought funding, looked for facilities, etc.) by each group over a specified time period during organization creation was measured and the following incomplete ANOVA table produced:

Source	df	SS	MS	F
Groups	2	128.70	—	—
Error	68	27,124.52	—	

Source: Carter, N., Garner, W., and Reynolds, P. "Exploring Start-Up Event Sequences." *Journal of Business Venturing,* Vol. 11, 1996, p. 159.

a. Complete the ANOVA table.

b. Do the data provide sufficient evidence to indicate that the total number of activities undertaken differed among the three groups of entrepreneurs? Test using $\alpha = .05$. $F = .16$

c. What is the p-value of the test you conducted in part **b**? $p > .10$

d. One of the conclusions of the study was that the behaviors of entrepreneurs who have successfully started a new company can be differentiated from the behaviors of entrepreneurs that failed. Do you agree? Justify your answer.

e. Classify this study as observational or experimental. Justify your answer. Observational

10.3 Multiple Comparisons of Means

Consider a completely randomized design with three treatments, A, B, and C. Suppose we determine that the treatment means are statistically different via the ANOVA F-test of Section 10.2. To complete the analysis, we want to rank the three treatment means. As mentioned in Section 10.2, we start by placing confidence intervals on the difference between various pairs of treatment means in the experiment. In the three-treatment experiment, for example, we would construct confidence intervals for the following differences: $\mu_A - \mu_B, \mu_A - \mu_C$, and $\mu_B - \mu_C$.

Teaching Tip
Point out that the multiple comparison procedures are the follow-up when differences are detected in population means for any of the experimental designs presented in this chapter.

> ### Determining the Number of Pairwise Comparisons of Treatment Means
>
> In general, if there are k treatment means, there are
>
> $$c = \frac{k(k - 1)}{2}$$
>
> pairs of means that can be compared.

If we want to have $100(1 - \alpha)\%$ confidence that each of the c confidence intervals contains the true difference it is intended to estimate, we must use a smaller value of α for each individual confidence interval than we would use for a single interval. For example, suppose we want to rank the means of the three treatments, A, B, and C, with 95% confidence that all three confidence intervals comparing the means contain the true differences between the treatment means. Then each individual confidence interval will need to be constructed using a level of significance smaller than $\alpha = .05$ in order to have 95% confidence that the three intervals collectively include the true differences.*

Teaching Tip
Illustrate the difference in the experimentwise and comparisonwise error rates by considering 95% confidence intervals when comparing three population means.

To make **multiple comparisons of a set of treatment means** we can use a number of procedures that, under various assumptions, ensure that the overall confidence level associated with all the comparisons remains at or above the specified $100(1 - \alpha)\%$ level. Three widely used techniques are the Bonferroni, Scheffé, and Tukey methods. For each of these procedures, the risk of making a Type I error applies to the comparisons of the treatment means in the experiment; thus, the value of α selected is called an **experimentwise error rate** (in contrast to a **comparisonwise error rate**).

The choice of a multiple comparisons method in ANOVA will depend on the type of experimental design used and the comparisons of interest to the analyst. For example, **Tukey** (1949) developed his procedure specifically for pairwise comparisons when the sample sizes of the treatments are equal. The **Bonferroni**

---

*The reason each interval must be formed at a higher confidence level than that specified for the collection of intervals can be demonstrated as follows:

$P\{$At least one of c intervals fails to contain the true difference$\}$
$= 1 - P\{$All c intervals contain the true differences$\}$
$= 1 - (1 - \alpha)^c \geq \alpha$

Thus, to make this probability of at least one failure equal to α, we must specify the individual levels of significance to be less than α.

method (see Miller, 1981), like the Tukey procedure, can be applied when pairwise comparisons are of interest; however, Bonferroni's method does not require equal sample sizes. **Scheffé** (1953) developed a more general procedure for comparing all possible linear combinations of treatment means (called contrasts). Consequently, when making pairwise comparisons, the confidence intervals produced by Scheffé's method will generally be wider than the Tukey or Bonferroni confidence intervals.

Biography

CARLO E. BONFERRONI (1892–1960)
Bonferroni Inequalities

During his childhood years in Turin, Italy, Carlo Bonferroni developed an aptitude for mathematics while studying music. He went on to obtain a degree in mathematics at the University of Turin. Bonferroni's first appointment as a professor of mathematics was at the University of Bari in 1923. Ten years later, he became chair of financial mathematics at the University of Florence, where he remained until his death. Bonferroni was a prolific writer, authoring over 65 research papers and books. His interest in statistics included various methods of calculating a mean and a correlation coefficient. Among statisticians, however, Bonferroni is most well known for developing his Bonferroni inequalities in probability theory in 1935. Later, other statisticians proposed using these inequalities for finding simultaneous confidence intervals, which led to the development of the Bonferroni multiple comparisons method in ANOVA. Bonferroni balanced these scientific accomplishments with his music, becoming an excellent pianist and composer.

Teaching Tip
Point out that the formulas involved are not unlike the formulas for comparing two means presented earlier in the text.

The formulas for constructing confidence intervals for differences between treatment means using the Tukey, Bonferroni, or Scheffé method are beyond the scope of this text. However, these procedures (and many others) are available in the ANOVA programs of most statistical software packages. The programs generate a confidence interval for the difference between two treatment means for all possible pairs of treatments, based on the experimentwise error rate (α) selected by the analyst.

EXAMPLE 10.5   RANKING TREATMENT MEANS

Problem   Refer to the completely randomized design of Example 10.3, in which we concluded that at least two of the four brands of golf balls are associated with different mean distances traveled when struck with a driver.

C B $\overline{\text{A D}}$

a. Use Tukey's multiple comparisons procedure to rank the treatment means with an overall confidence level of 95%.

270 ± 2.9

b. Estimate the mean distance traveled for balls manufactured by the brand with the highest rank.

Solution   **a.** To rank the treatment means with an overall confidence level of .95, we require the experimentwise error rate of $\alpha = .05$. The confidence intervals generated by Tukey's method appear at the top of the SPSS printout, Figure 10.11. [Note: SPSS uses the number 1 for Brand A, 2 for Brand B, etc.] For any pair of means, μ_i and μ_j, SPSS computes two confidence intervals—one for $(\mu_i - \mu_j)$

Multiple Comparisons

Dependent Variable: DISTANCE
Tukey HSD

(I) BRANDNUM	(J) BRANDNUM	Mean Difference (I-J)	Std. Error	Sig.	95% Confidence Interval	
					Lower Bound	Upper Bound
1	2	-10.2800*	2.05791	.000	-15.8224	-4.7376
	3	-19.1700*	2.05791	.000	-24.7124	-13.6276
	4	1.4600	2.05791	.893	-4.0824	7.0024
2	1	10.2800*	2.05791	.000	4.7376	15.8224
	3	-8.8900*	2.05791	.001	-14.4324	-3.3476
	4	11.7400*	2.05791	.000	6.1976	17.2824
3	1	19.1700*	2.05791	.000	13.6276	24.7124
	2	8.8900*	2.05791	.001	3.3476	14.4324
	4	20.6300*	2.05791	.000	15.0876	26.1724
4	1	-1.4600	2.05791	.893	-7.0024	4.0824
	2	-11.7400*	2.05791	.000	-17.2824	-6.1976
	3	-20.6300*	2.05791	.000	-26.1724	-15.0876

*. The mean difference is significant at the .05 level.

DISTANCE

Tukey HSD[a]

BRANDNUM	N	Subset for alpha = .05		
		1	2	3
4	10	249.3200		
1	10	250.7800		
2	10		261.0600	
3	10			269.9500
Sig.		.893	1.000	1.000

Means for groups in homogeneous subsets are displayed.
  a. Uses Harmonic Mean Sample Size = 10.000.

Figure 10.11
SPSS printout of Tukey's multiple comparisons for the golf ball data

and one for $(\mu_j - \mu_i)$. Only one of these intervals is necessary to decide whether the means differ significantly.

In this example, we have $k = 4$ brand means to compare. Consequently, the number of relevant pairwise comparisons—that is, the number of nonredundant confidence intervals—is $c = 4(3)/2 = 6$. These six intervals, highlighted in Figure 10.11, are given in Table 10.4.

We are 95% confident that the intervals *collectively* contain all the differences between the true brand mean distances. Note that intervals that contain 0, such as the (Brand A–Brand D) interval from -4.08 to 7.00, do not support a conclusion that the true brand mean distances differ. If both endpoints of the interval are positive, as with the (Brand B–Brand D) interval from 6.20 to 17.28, the implication is that the first brand (B) mean distance exceeds the second (D). Conversely, if both endpoints of the interval are

TABLE 10.4 Pairwise Comparisons for Example 10.5

Brand Comparison	Confidence Interval
$(\mu_A - \mu_B)$	$(-15.82, -4.74)$
$(\mu_A - \mu_C)$	$(-24.71, -13.63)$
$(\mu_A - \mu_D)$	$(-4.08, -7.00)$
$(\mu_B - \mu_C)$	$(-14.43, -3.35)$
$(\mu_B - \mu_D)$	$(6.20, 17.28)$
$(\mu_C - \mu_D)$	$(15.09, 26.17)$

Suggested Exercise 10.43

Brand	Sample Mean
C	270.0
B	261.1
A	250.8
D	249.3

Figure 10.12

Summary of Tukey multiple comparisons

Teaching Tip

Point out that means connected by the same line *do not* significantly differ.

negative, as with the (Brand A – Brand C) interval from -24.71 to -13.63, the implication is that the second brand (C) mean distance exceeds the first brand (A) mean distance.

A convenient summary of the results of the Tukey multiple comparisons is a listing of the brand means from highest to lowest, with a solid line connecting those that are *not* significantly different. This summary is shown in Figure 10.12. A similar summary is shown at the bottom of the SPSS printout, Figure 10.11. The interpretation is that brand C's mean distance exceeds all others; brand B's mean exceeds that of brands A and D; and the means of brands A and D do not differ significantly. All these inferences are made simultaneously with 95% confidence, the overall confidence level of the Tukey multiple comparisons.

b. Brand C is ranked highest; thus, we want a confidence interval for μ_C. Since the samples were selected independently in a completely randomized design, a confidence interval for an individual treatment mean is obtained with the one-sample t confidence interval of Section 7.2, using the mean square for error, MSE, as the measure of sampling variability for the experiment. A 95% confidence interval on the mean distance traveled by brand C (apparently the "longest ball" of those tested), is

$$\bar{x}_C \pm t_{.025}\sqrt{\frac{\text{MSE}}{n}}$$

where $n = 10$, $t_{.025} \approx 2$ (based on 36 degrees of freedom), and MSE $= 21.175$ (obtained from the EXCEL printout, Figure 10.7). Substituting, we obtain

$$270.0 \pm (2)\sqrt{\frac{21.175}{10}}$$

$$270.0 \pm 2.9 \text{ or } (267.1, 272.9)$$

Thus, we are 95% confident that the true mean distance traveled for brand C is between 267.1 and 272.9 yards, when hit with a driver by Iron Byron.

Look Back The easiest way to create a summary table like Table 10.12 is to first list the treatment means in rank order. Begin with the largest mean and compare it to (in order) the second largest mean, the third largest mean, and so on by examining the appropriate confidence intervals shown on the computer printout. If a confidence interval contains 0, then connect the two means with a line. (These two means are not significantly different.) Continue in this manner by comparing the second largest mean with the third largest, fourth largest, and so on until all possible $c = (k)(k + 1)/2$ comparisons are made.

> **Now Work**   *Exercise 10.39*

■ ■ ■

Remember that the Tukey method—designed for comparing pairs of treatment means with equal sample sizes—is just one of numerous multiple comparisons procedures available. Another technique may be more appropriate for the experimental design you employ. Consult the references for details on these other methods and when they should be applied. Guidelines for using the Tukey, Bonferroni, and Scheffé methods are given in the box.

Guidelines for Selecting a Multiple Comparisons Method in ANOVA

Method	Treatment Sample Sizes	Types of Comparisons
Tukey	Equal	Pairwise
Bonferroni	Equal or unequal	Pairwise
Scheffe	Equal or unequal	General contrasts

Note: For equal sample sizes and pairwise comparisons, Tukey's method will yield simultaneous confidence intervals with the smallest width and the Bonferroni intervals will have smaller widths than the Scheffé intervals.

Statistics in Action Revisited

Ranking the Mean Ethics Responses for the Five Downsize Groups

In the previous Statistics in Action Revisited (p. 575), we used an ANOVA to test the null hypothesis that the mean ethics scores of five groups of employees are equal. Recall that these five groups were named (1) Casualties, (2) Survivors, (3) Implementors/casualties, (4) Implementors/survivors, and (5) Formulators. The ANOVA F-test resulted in a rejection of the null hypothesis, leading the researchers to conclude that the mean ethics scores of the five groups were significantly different. Now we follow up the ANOVA with multiple comparisons of the treatment (group) means. Since the group sample sizes are unequal, we employ the Bonferroni method.

The SPSS printout for this analysis, using an experimentwise error rate of .05, is displayed in Figure SIA10.4. The relevant confidence intervals for all possible differences between treatment means are highlighted on the printout. Note that there are $c = (k)(k - 1)/2 = (5)(4)/2 = 10$ comparisons of interest. Significant differences are indicated on the SPSS printout with an asterisk (*) in the "Mean Difference" column; these differences are associated with confidence intervals that do not include 0. The results show that Groups 4 and 5 both have significantly larger mean scores than those for Groups 1, 2, and 3. Also, there is no significant difference between the mean scores for Groups 4 and 5; and there are no significant differences among mean scores for Groups 1, 2, and 3. Consequently, we can rank the group means as shown in Table SIA10.2.

The researchers original hypotheses about the five groups are repeated here. You can see that the rankings in

Multiple Comparisons

Dependent Variable: ETHICS
Bonferroni

(I) GROUPNUM	(J) GROUPNUM	Mean Difference (I-J)	Std. Error	Sig.	95% Confidence Interval Lower Bound	Upper Bound
1	2	-.06	.191	1.000	-.60	.49
	3	.19	.246	1.000	-.50	.89
	4	-.76*	.231	.012	-1.41	-.10
	5	-1.08*	.236	.000	-1.75	-.42
2	1	.06	.191	1.000	-.49	.60
	3	.25	.230	1.000	-.40	.91
	4	-.70*	.214	.013	-1.31	-.09
	5	-1.03*	.219	.000	-1.65	-.40
3	1	-.19	.246	1.000	-.89	.50
	2	-.25	.230	1.000	-.91	.40
	4	-.95*	.264	.004	-1.70	-.20
	5	-1.28*	.268	.000	-2.04	-.52
4	1	.76*	.231	.012	.10	1.41
	2	.70*	.214	.013	.09	1.31
	3	.95*	.264	.004	.20	1.70
	5	-.33	.255	1.000	-1.05	.40
5	1	1.08*	.236	.000	.42	1.75
	2	1.03*	.219	.000	.40	1.65
	3	1.28*	.268	.000	.52	2.04
	4	.33	.255	1.000	-.40	1.05

*. The mean difference is significant at the .05 level.

Figure SIA10.4
SPSS Bonferroni multiple comparisons of means for the five treatment groups

TABLE SIA10.2 Ranking of Group Means Based on the Bonferroni Analysis

1.59	1.79	1.84	2.45	2.87
Implementors/casualties	Casualties	Survivors	Implementors/survivors	Formulators
Group 3	**Group 1**	**Group 2**	**Group 4**	**Group 5**

Table SIA10.2 provide full support for these hypotheses.

H_1: Survivors', Casualties', and Implementors/casualties' perceptions of the ethics statement on downsizing will not differ significantly (i.e., no differences among Groups 1, 2, and 3).

H_2: Formulators' and Implementors/survivors' perceptions of the ethics statement on downsizing will not differ significantly (i.e., no difference between Group 4 and Group 5).

H_3: Survivors', Casualties', and Implementors/casualties' perceptions of the ethics statement on downsizing will differ significantly from Formulators' and Implementors/survivors' perceptions (i.e., Groups 4 and 5 are different than Groups 1, 2, and 3).

Exercises 10.35–10.45

Learning the Mechanics

10.33 Consider a completely randomized design with k treatments. Assume all pairwise comparisons of treatment means are to be made using a multiple comparisons procedure. Determine the total number of treatment means to be compared for the following values of k.

    a. $k = 3$
    b. $k = 5$
    c. $k = 4$
    d. $k = 10$

10.34 Define an experimentwise error rate.

10.35 Define a comparisonwise error rate.

10.36 Consider a completely randomized design with five treatments, A, B, C, D, and E. The ANOVA F-test revealed significant differences among the means. A multiple comparisons procedure was used to compare all possible pairs of treatment means at $\alpha = .05$. The ranking of the five treatment means is summarized below. Identify which pairs of means are significantly different.

    a. $\overline{A\ \ C}$ E B D
    b. $\overline{A\ \ C\ \ E}$ B D
    c. A $\overline{C\ \ E\ \ B}$ D
    d. $\overline{A\ \ C\ \ E\ \ B}$ D

Applying the Concepts—Basic

10.37 Refer to the *Nature* (Aug. 2000) study of robots trained to behave like ants, Exercise 10.22 (p. 579). Multiple comparisons of mean energy expended for the four colony sizes were conducted using an experimentwise error rate of .05. The results are summarized below.

Sample mean:	.97	.95	.93	.80
Group Size:	3	6	9	12

    a. How many pairwise comparisons are conducted in this analysis? 6
    b. Interpret the results shown in the table.

10.38 Refer to the *Journal of Real Estate Portfolio Management* (Vol. 3, 1997) study comparing the mean office vacancy rates of eight Atlanta submarkets, Exercise 10.23 (p. 579). The next table gives the Bonferroni rankings of the mean vacancy rates. (The vertical line connects means that are not significantly different at $\alpha = .10$.) Fully interpret the results.

Submarket	Mean Vacancy Rate (%)
North Central	16.73
Northwest	16.81
Buckhead	16.85
Northeast	16.95
Midtown	19.75
North Lake	20.38
Downtown	20.73
South	28.26

10.39 Refer to the *American Business Review* (Jan. 2002) comparison of large-cap, medium-cap, and small-cap mutual funds, Exercise 10.24 (p. 580). Using an experimentwise error rate of .05, Tukey confidence intervals for the difference between mean rates of return for all possible pairs of fund types are given below:

Comparison	Tukey confidence interval
$\mu_{Large} - \mu_{Medium}$	$(-.1847, 5.3807)$
$\mu_{Large} - \mu_{Small}$	$(2.4426, 8.0080)$
$\mu_{Medium} - \mu_{Small}$	$(-.1554, 5.4100)$

    a. Why is the Tukey multiple comparisons method preferred over another method?
    b. Is there a significant different between the treatment means for large-cap and medium-cap mutual funds? Explain. No
    c. Is there a significant different between the treatment means for large-cap and small-cap mutual funds? Explain. Yes
    d. Is there a significant different between the treatment means for medium-cap and small-cap mutual funds? Explain. No
    e. Use your answers to parts **b–d** to rank the treatment means.
    f. Give a measure of reliability for the inference in part **e**. 95%

10.40 Refer to the *American Journal of Political Science* (Jan. 1998) study of the attitudes of three groups of professionals (scientists, journalists, and federal government policymakers) regarding the safety of nuclear power plants, Exercise 10.26 (p. 580). The mean safety scores for the groups were:

Government officials	4.2
Scientists	4.1
Journalists	3.7

a. Determine the number of pairwise comparisons of treatment means that can be made in this study.

b. Using an experimentwise error rate of $\alpha = .05$, Tukey's minimum significant difference for comparing means is .23. That is, if the difference between the sample means exceeds .23, the treatment means are statistically different. Use this information to conduct a multiple comparisons procedure of the safety score means. Fully interpret the results.

10.41 Refer to the *Journal of Business Venturing* (Vol. 11, 1996) study of entrepreneurs, Exercise 10.32 (p. 582). Pairwise comparisons of the three entrepreneur groups in the study were conducted using the Bonferroni method at $\alpha = .05$. The comparisons of the means of the number of activities undertaken are summarized in the table below. Interpret the results.

Mean number of activities	8.00	6.56	5.05
Entrepreneur group	Successful firm	Gave up	Still trying

Applying the Concepts—Intermediate

10.42 Refer to the *Accident Analysis and Prevention* (Vol. 34, 2002) study of road rage, Exercise 10.27 (p. 581). Recall that the mean road rage scores of drivers in the three income groups, under $30 thousand, between $30 and $60 thousand, and over $60 thousand, were 4.60, 5.08, and 5.15, respectively.

a. An experimentwise error rate of .01 was used to rank the three means. Give a practical interpretation of this error rate.

b. How many pairwise comparisons are necessary to compare the three means? List them. 3

c. A multiple comparisons procedure revealed that the means for the two income groups, $30–$60 thousand and over $60 thousand, were not significantly different. All other pairs of means were found to be significantly different. Summarize these results in table form.

d. Which of the comparisons of part **b** will yield a confidence interval that does not contain 0?

DDT

10.43 Refer to the U.S. Army Corps of Engineers data on contaminated fish saved in the **DDT** file. In Exercise 10.29 (p. 581) you ran ANOVAs to compare three species (channel catfish, largemouth bass, or smallmouth buffalofish) on the dependent variables length (in centimeters), weight (in grams), and DDT level (in parts per million). For those dependent variables that resulted in a significant ANOVA F-test, perform multiple comparisons of the treatment means. Use an experimentwise error rate of .05. Interpret the results practically.

DIAMONDS

10.44 Refer to the *Journal of Statistics Education* data on diamonds for sale on the open market saved in the **DIAMONDS** file. In Exercise 10.30 (p. 582) you ran an ANOVA to compare levels of a qualitative variable (either Color, Clarity, or Certification group) on the mean of a quantitative variable (either carat size or price. Follow up the analysis with multiple comparisons of the treatment means. Use an experimentwise error rate of .05. Interpret the results practically.

10.45 Refer to the *Industrial Marketing Management* (Sept. 1996) comparison of six sales closing techniques, Exercise 10.31 (p. 582). The "level of trust" means for prospects of salespeople using each of the six closing techniques are listed in the table at right. A multiple comparisons of means analysis was conducted (at $\alpha = .05$), with the results shown in the third column of the table. Fully interpret the results.

Treatments: Closing Technique	Mean Level of Trust	Differing Treatments
1 No close	4.67	1 from 5 and 6
2. Impending event	4.48	2 from 6
3. Social validation	4.40	No differences
4. If-then	4.33	No differences
5. Assumed close	4.04	5 from 1
6. Either-or	3.98	6 from 1 and 2

Source: Hawes, S. M., Strong, J. T., and Winick, B. S. "Do Closing Techniques Diminish Prospect Trust?" *Industrial Marketing Management,* Vol. 25, No. 5, Sept. 1996, p. 355.

10.4 The Randomized Block Design

If the completely randomized design results in nonrejection of the null hypothesis that the treatment means differ because the sampling variability (as measured by MSE) is large, we may want to consider an experimental design that better controls the variability. In contrast to the selection of independent samples of experimental units specified by the completely randomized design, the *randomized block design* utilizes experimental units that are *matched sets,* assigning one from each set to each

Teaching Tip

Point out that the Randomized Block Design is an extension of the matched pairs comparison of population means detailed in Chapter 9. We now have the ability to compare two *or more* population means.

treatment. The matched sets of experimental units are called *blocks*. The theory behind the randomized block design is that the sampling variability of the experimental units in each block will be reduced, in turn reducing the measure of error, MSE.

DEFINITION 10.8

The **randomized block design** consists of a two-step procedure:

1. Matched sets of experimental units, called **blocks,** are formed, each block consisting of p experimental units (where *p* is the number of treatments). The *b* blocks should consist of experimental units that are as similar as possible.
2. One experimental unit from each block is randomly assigned to each treatment, resulting in a total of $n = bp$ responses.

For example, if we wish to compare SAT scores of female and male high school seniors, we could select independent random samples of five females and five males, and analyze the results of the completely randomized design as outlined in Section 10.2. Or, we could select matched pairs of females and males according to their scholastic records, and analyze the SAT scores of the pairs. For instance, we could select pairs of students with approximately the same GPAs from the same high school. Five such pairs (blocks) are depicted in Table 10.5. Note that this is just a *paired difference experiment,* first discussed in Section 9.2.

TABLE 10.5   Randomized Block Design: SAT Score Comparison

Block	Female SAT Score	Male SAT Score	Block Mean
1 (School A, 2.75 GPA)	540	530	535
2 (School B, 3.00 GPA)	570	550	560
3 (School C, 3.25 GPA)	590	580	585
4 (School D, 3.50 GPA)	640	620	630
5 (School E, 3.75 GPA)	690	690	690
Treatment Mean	606	594	

As before, the variation between the treatment means is measured by squaring the distance between each treatment mean and the overall mean, multiplying each squared distance by the number of measurements for the treatment, and summing over treatments:

$$\text{SST} = \sum_{i=1}^{k} b(\bar{x}_{T_i} - \bar{x})^2$$

$$= 5(606 - 600)^2 + 5(594 - 600)^2 = 360$$

where $\bar{x}_{T_i}$ represents the sample mean for the ith treatment, b (the number of blocks) is the number of measurements for each treatment, and k is the number of treatments.

The blocks also account for some of the variation among the different responses. That is, just as SST measures the variation between the female and male means, we can calculate a measure of variation among the five block means representing different schools and scholastic abilities. Analogous to the computation of SST, we sum the squares of the differences between each block mean and the overall mean, multiplying each squared difference by the number of measurements for each block, and sum over blocks to calculate the **Sum of Squares for Blocks** (SSB):

$$SSB = \sum_{i=1}^{b} p(\bar{x}_{B_i} - \bar{x})^2$$
$$= 2(535 - 600)^2 + 2(560 - 600)^2 + 2(585 - 600)^2$$
$$+ 2(630 - 600)^2 + 2(690 - 600)^2$$
$$= 30,100$$

where $\bar{x}_{B_i}$ represents the sample mean for the ith block and k (the number of treatments) is the number of measurements in each block. As we expect, the variation in SAT scores attributable to Schools and Levels of scholastic achievement is apparently large.

As before, we want to compare the variability attributed to treatments with that which is attributed to sampling variability. In a randomized block design, the sampling variability is measured by subtracting that portion attributed to treatments and blocks from the Total Sum of Squares, SS(Total). The total variation is the sum of squared differences of each measurement from the overall mean:

$$SS(Total) = \sum_{i=1}^{n} (x_i - \bar{x})^2$$
$$= (540 - 600)^2 + (530 - 600)^2 + (570 - 600)^2 + (550 - 600)^2$$
$$+ \cdots + (690 - 600)^2$$
$$= 30,600$$

Then the variation attributable to sampling error is found by subtraction:

$$SSE = SS(Total) - SST - SSB = 30,600 - 360 - 30,100 = 140$$

In summary, the Total Sum of Squares, 30,600, is divided into three components: 360 attributed to treatments (Gender), 30,100 attributed to blocks (Scholastic ability), and 140 attributed to sampling error.

The mean squares associated with each source of variability are obtained by dividing the sum of squares by the appropriate number of degrees of freedom. The partitioning of the Total Sum of Squares and the total degrees of freedom for a randomized block experiment is summarized in Figure 10.13.

To determine whether we can reject the null hypothesis that the treatment means are equal in favor of the alternative that at least two of them differ, we calculate

$$MST = \frac{SST}{k - 1} = \frac{360}{2 - 1} = 360$$

$$MSE = \frac{SSE}{n - b - k + 1} = \frac{140}{10 - 5 - 2 + 1} = 35$$

Figure 10.13

Partitioning of the total sum of squares for the randomized block design

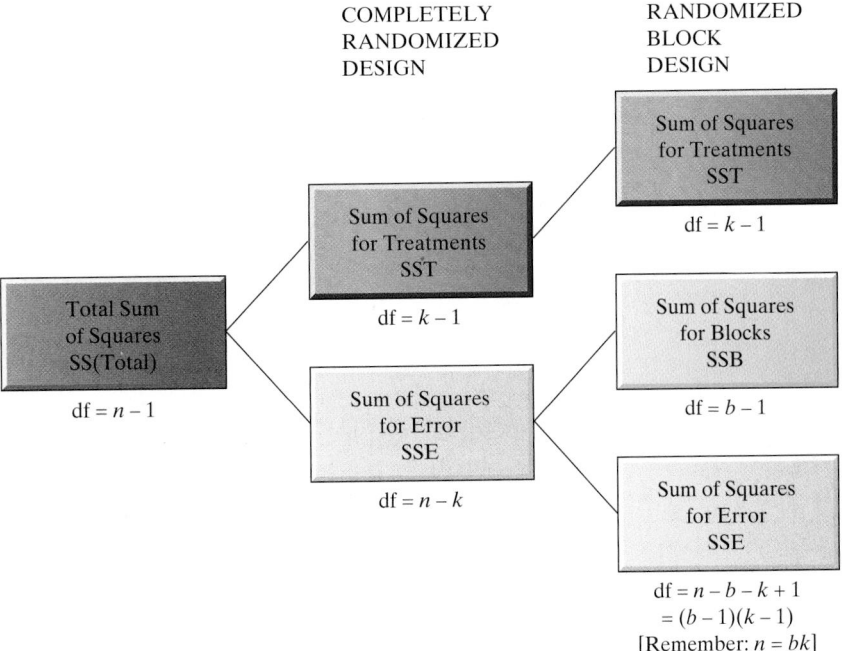

The F-ratio that is used to test the hypothesis is

$$F = \frac{360}{35} = 10.29$$

Comparing this ratio to the tabled F value corresponding to $\alpha = .05$, $v_1 = (k - 1) = 1$ degree of freedom in the numerator, and $v_2 = (n - b - k + 1) = 4$ degrees of freedom in the denominator, we find that

$$F = 10.29 > F_{.05} = 7.71$$

which indicates that we should reject the null hypothesis and conclude that the mean SAT scores differ for females and males.

If you review Section 9.2, you will find that the analysis of a paired difference experiment results in a one-sample t-test on the differences between the treatment responses within each block. Applying the procedure to the differences between female and male scores in Table 10.5, we find

$$t = \frac{\bar{x}_d}{s_d / \sqrt{n_d}} = \frac{12}{\sqrt{70}/\sqrt{5}} = 3.207$$

At the .05 level of significance with $(n_d - 1) = 4$ degrees of freedom,

$$t = 3.21 > t_{.025} = 2.776$$

Since $t^2 = (3.207)^2 = 10.29$ and $t_{.025}^2 = (2.776)^2 = 7.71$, we find that the paired difference t-test and the ANOVA F-test are equivalent, with both the calculated test statistics and the rejection region related by the formula $F = t^2$. The difference between the tests is that the paired difference t-test can be used to compare only two treatments in a randomized block design, whereas the F-test can be applied to *two or more* treatments in a randomized block design. The F-test is summarized in the following box.

Teaching Tip

Again, point out the information that is made available using the various computer software programs. The need for the rejection region is minimized as most programs provide the significance level (p-value) of the test.

ANOVA F Test to Compare k Treatment Means: Randomized Block Design

$H_0: \mu_1 = \mu_2 = \cdots = \mu_k$

H_a: At least two treatment means differ

$$\text{Test statistic: } F = \frac{\text{MST}}{\text{MSE}}$$

Rejection region: $F > F_\alpha$, where F_α is based on $(k-1)$ numerator degrees of freedom and $(n - b - k + 1)$ denominator degrees of freedom.

Conditions Required for a Valid ANOVA F-test: Randomized Block Design

1. The b blocks are randomly selected and all k treatments are applied (in random order) to each block.

2. The distributions of observations corresponding to all bk block-treatment combinations are approximately normal.

3. The bk block-treatment distributions have equal variances.

Note that the assumptions concern the probability distributions associated with each block-treatment combination. The experimental unit selected for each combination is assumed to have been randomly selected from all possible experimental units for that combination, and the response is assumed to be normally distributed with the same variance for each of the block-treatment combinations. For example, the F-test comparing female and male SAT score means requires the scores for each combination of gender and scholastic ability (e.g., females with 3.25 GPA) to be normally distributed with the same variance as the other combinations employed in the experiment.

The calculation formulas for randomized block designs are given in Appendix C. We will rely on statistical software packages to analyze randomized block designs and to obtain the necessary ingredients for testing the null hypothesis that the treatment means are equal.

EXAMPLE 10.6

EXPERIMENTAL DESIGN PRINCIPLES

Problem   Refer to Examples 10.3–10.5. Suppose the USGA wants to compare the mean distances associated with the four brands of golf balls when struck by a driver, but wishes to employ human golfers rather than the robot, Iron Byron. Assume that 10 balls of each brand are to be utilized in the experiment.

    a. Explain how a completely randomized design could be employed.

    b. Explain how a randomized block design could be employed.

Block design   **c.** Which design is likely to provide more information about the differences among the brand mean distances?

Solution   **a.** Since the completely randomized design calls for independent samples, we can employ such a design by randomly selecting 40 golfers and then randomly assigning 10 golfers to each of the four brands. Finally, each golfer will strike

Figure 10.14

Illustration of completely randomized design and randomized block design: comparison of four golf ball brands

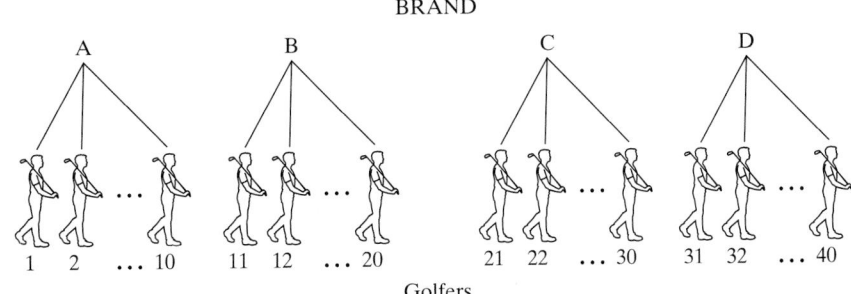

a. Completely randomized design

b. Randomized block design

the ball of the assigned brand, and the distance will be recorded. The design is illustrated in Figure 10.14(a).

b. The randomized block design employs blocks of relatively homogeneous experimental units. For example, we could randomly select 10 golfers, and permit each golfer to hit four balls, one of each brand, in a random sequence. Then each golfer is a block, with each treatment (brand) assigned to each block (golfer). The design is summarized in Figure 10.14(b).

c. Because we expect much more variability among distances generated by "real" golfers than by Iron Byron, we would expect the randomized block design to control the variability better than the completely randomized design. That is, with 40 different golfers, we would expect the sampling variability among the measured distances within each brand to be greater than that among the four distances generated by each of 10 golfers hitting one ball of each brand.

Now Work   *Exercise 10.50a,b*

■ ■ ■

EXAMPLE 10.7

CONDUCTING AN ANOVA FOR A RANDOMIZED BLOCK DESIGN

Problem   Refer to Example 10.6. Suppose the randomized block design of part b is employed, utilizing a random sample of 10 golfers, with each golfer using a driver to hit four balls, one of each brand, in a random sequence.

$H_0: \mu_1 = \mu_2 = \mu_3 = \mu_4$

a. Set up a test of the research hypothesis that the brand mean distances differ. Use $\alpha = .05$.

GOLFRBD

TABLE 10.6   Distance Data for Randomized Block Design

Golfer (Block)	Brand A	Brand B	Brand C	Brand D
1	202.4	203.2	223.7	203.6
2	242.0	248.7	259.8	240.7
3	220.4	227.3	240.0	207.4
4	230.0	243.1	247.7	226.9
5	191.6	211.4	218.7	200.1
6	247.7	253.0	268.1	244.0
7	214.8	214.8	233.9	195.8
8	245.4	243.6	257.8	227.9
9	224.0	231.5	238.2	215.7
10	252.2	255.2	265.4	245.2
Sample Means	227.0	233.2	245.3	220.7

$p \approx 0$, Reject H_0

b. The data for the experiment are given in Table 10.6. Use statistical software to analyze the data, and conduct the test set up in part a.

Solution   **a.** We want to test whether the data in Table 10.6 provide sufficient evidence to conclude that the brand mean distances differ. Denoting the population mean of the ith brand by μ_i, we test

$$H_0: \mu_1 = \mu_2 = \mu_3 = \mu_4$$

H_a: The mean distances differ for at least two of the brands

The test statistic compares the variation among the four treatment (brand) means to the sampling variability within each of the treatments.

Suggested Exercise 10.51

Test statistic: $F = \dfrac{\text{MST}}{\text{MSE}}$

Rejection region: $F > F_\alpha = F_{.05}$, with $v_1 = (p - 1) = 3$ numerator degrees of freedom and $v_2 = (n - p - b + 1) = 27$ denominator degrees of freedom. From Table IX of Appendix A, we find $F_{.05} = 2.96$. Thus, we will reject H_0 if $F > 2.96$.

The assumptions necessary to ensure the validity of the test are as follows: (1) The probability distributions of the distances for each brand–golfer combination are normal. (2) The variances of the distance probability distributions for each brand–golfer combination are equal.

b. MINITAB was used to analyze the data in Table 10.6, and the result is shown in Figure 10.15. The values of MST and MSE (highlighted on the printout) are 1,099.6 and 20.2, respectively. The F-ratio for Brand (also highlighted on the printout) is $F = 54.31$, which exceeds the tabled value of 2.96. We therefore reject the null hypothesis at the $\alpha = .05$ level of significance, concluding that at least two of the brands differ with respect to mean distance traveled when struck by the driver.

Look Back The result of part **b** is confirmed by noting that the observed significance level of the test, highlighted on the printout, is $p \approx 0$.

Figure 10.15

MINITAB randomized
block design ANOVA: golf
ball brand comparison

Two-way ANOVA: DISTANCE versus BRAND, GOLFER

```
Source   DF      SS       MS       F      P
BRAND     3   3298.7   1099.55   54.31  0.000
GOLFER    9  12073.9   1341.54   66.26  0.000
Error    27    546.6     20.25
Total    39  15919.2

S = 4.499   R-Sq = 96.57%   R-Sq(adj) = 95.04%
```

Now Work *Exercise 10.50c*

■ ■ ■

The results of an ANOVA can be summarized in a simple tabular format, similar to that utilized for the completely randomized design in Section 10.2. The general form of the table is shown in Table 10.7, and that for Example 10.7 is given in Table 10.8. Note that the randomized block design is characterized by three sources of variation—Treatments, Blocks, and Error—which sum to the Total Sum of Squares. We hope that employing blocks of experimental units will reduce the error variability, thereby making the test for comparing treatment means more powerful.

When the F-test results in the rejection of the null hypothesis that the treatment means are equal, we will usually want to compare the various pairs of treatment means to determine which specific pairs differ. We can employ a multiple comparisons procedure as in Section 10.3 The number of pairs of means to be compared will again be $c = k(k - 1)/2$, where k is the number of treatment means. In Example 10.7, $c = 4(3)/2 = 6$; that is, there are six pairs of golf ball brand means to be compared.

TABLE 10.7 General ANOVA Summary Table for a Randomized Block Design

Source	df	SS	MS	F
Treatment	$k - 1$	SST	MST	MST/MSE
Block	$b - 1$	SSB	MSB	
Error	$n - k - b + 1$	SSE	MSE	
Total	$n - 1$	SS(Total)		

TABLE 10.8 ANOVA Table for Example 10.7

Source	df	SS	MS	F	p
Treatment (Brand)	3	3,298.7	1,099.6	54.31	.000
Block (Golfer)	9	12,073.9	1,341.5		
Error	27	546.6	20.2		
Total	39	15,919.2			

EXAMPLE 10.8

MULTIPLE COMPARISONS OF MEANS FOR A RANDOMIZED BLOCK DESIGN

Problem   Bonferroni's procedure is used to compare the mean distances of the four golf ball brands in Example 10.7. The resulting confidence intervals, with an experimentwise error rate of $\alpha = .05$, are shown in the SPSS printout, Figure 10.16. Interpret the results.

Solution   Note that 12 confidence intervals are shown in Figure 10.16 rather than 6. Recall that SPSS computes intervals for both $\mu_j - \mu_i, i \neq j$. Only half of these are necessary to conduct the analysis, and these are highlighted on the printout. The intervals (rounded) are summarized below:

$$(A - B): \quad (-11.9, -.4)$$
$$(A - C): \quad (-24.0, -12.6)$$
$$(A - D): \quad (.6, 12.0)$$
$$(B - C): \quad (-17.9, -6.4)$$
$$(B - D): \quad (6.7, 18.2)$$
$$(C - D): \quad (18.9, 30.3)$$

Note that we are 95% confident that all the brand means differ because none of the intervals contains 0. The listing of the brand means in Figure 10.17 has no lines connecting them because there are no nonsignificant differences at the .05 level.

Multiple Comparisons

Dependent Variable: DISTANCE
Bonferroni

(I) BRAND	(J) BRAND	Mean Difference (I-J)	Std. Error	Sig.	95% Confidence Interval Lower Bound	95% Confidence Interval Upper Bound
A	B	-6.1300*	2.01222	.031	-11.8586	-.4014
	C	-18.2800*	2.01222	.000	-24.0086	-12.5514
	D	6.3200*	2.01222	.024	.5914	12.0486
B	A	6.1300*	2.01222	.031	.4014	11.8586
	C	-12.1500*	2.01222	.000	-17.8786	-6.4214
	D	12.4500*	2.01222	.000	6.7214	18.1786
C	A	18.2800*	2.01222	.000	12.5514	24.0086
	B	12.1500*	2.01222	.000	6.4214	17.8786
	D	24.6000*	2.01222	.000	18.8714	30.3286
D	A	-6.3200*	2.01222	.024	-12.0486	-.5914
	B	-12.4500*	2.01222	.000	-18.1786	-6.7214
	C	-24.6000*	2.01222	.000	-30.3286	-18.8714

Based on observed means.
 *. The mean difference is significant at the .05 level.

Figure 10.16
SPSS listing of Bonferroni confidence intervals: follow-up to randomized block design ANOVA

Now Work   *Exercise 10.50d*

■ ■ ■

Unlike the completely randomized design, the randomized block design cannot, in general, be used to estimate individual treatment means. Whereas the completely

Brand	Mean
C	245.3
B	233.2
A	227.0
D	220.7

Figure 10.17

Listing of brand means for randomized block design [Note: All differences are statistically significant.]

randomized design employs a random sample for each treatment, the randomized block design does not necessarily employ a random sample of experimental units for each treatment. The experimental units within the blocks are assumed to be randomly selected, but the blocks themselves may not be randomly selected.

We can, however, test the hypothesis that the block means are significantly different. We simply compare the variability attributable to differences among the block means to that associated with sampling variability. The ratio of MSB to MSE is an F-ratio similar to that formed in testing treatment means. The F statistic is compared to a tabled value for a specific value of α, with numerator degrees of freedom $(b - 1)$ and denominator degrees of freedom $(n - k - b + 1)$. The test is usually given on the same printout as the test for treatment means. Refer to the MINITAB printout in Figure 10.17, and note that the test statistic for comparing the block means is

$$F = \frac{MSB}{MSE} = \frac{MS(\text{Golfers})}{MS(\text{Error})} = \frac{1,341.5}{20.2} = 66.26$$

with a p-value of .000. Since $\alpha = .05$ exceeds this p-value, we conclude that the block means are different. The results of the test are summarized in Table 10.9.

TABLE 10.9 ANOVA Table for Randomized Block Design: Test for Blocks Included

Source	df	SS	MS	F	p
Treatments (Brands)	3	3,298.7	1,099.6	54.31	.000
Blocks (Golfers)	9	12,073.9	1,341.5	66.26	.000
Error	27	546.6	20.2		
Total	39	15,919.2			

In the golf example, the test for block means confirms our suspicion that the golfers vary significantly; therefore, the use of the block design was a good decision. However, be careful not to conclude that the block design was a mistake if the F-test for blocks does not result in rejection of the null hypothesis that the block means are the same. Remember that the possibility of a Type II error exists, and we are not controlling its probability as we are the probability α of a Type I error. If the experimenter believes that the experimental units are more homogeneous within blocks than between blocks, then he or she should use the randomized block design regardless of the results of a single test comparing the block means.

The procedure for conducting an analysis of variance for a randomized block design is summarized in the next box. Remember that the hallmark of this design is the utilization of blocks of homogeneous experimental units in which each treatment is represented.

Steps for Conducting an ANOVA for a Randomized Block Design

1. Be sure the design consists of blocks (preferably, blocks of homogeneous experimental units) and that each treatment is randomly assigned to one experimental unit in each block.

2. If possible, check the assumptions of normality and equal variances for all block-treatment combinations. [*Note:* This may be difficult to do since the design will likely have only one observation for each block-treatment combination.]

(cont'd)

Teaching Tip

Discuss how these steps can be used in conjunction with the computer output that is readily available.

3. Create an ANOVA summary table that specifies the variability attributable to Treatments, Blocks, and Error, and that leads to the calculation of the F statistic to test the null hypothesis that the treatment means are equal in the population. Use a statistical software package or the calculation formulas in Appendix C to obtain the necessary numerical ingredients.

4. If the F-test leads to the conclusion that the means differ, use the Bonferroni, Tukey, or similar procedure to conduct multiple comparisons of as many of the pairs of means as you wish. Use the results to summarize the statistically significant differences among the treatment means. Remember that, in general, the randomized block design cannot be used to form confidence intervals for individual treatment means.

5. If the F-test leads to the nonrejection of the null hypothesis that the treatment means are equal, several possibilities exist:
   a. The treatment means are equal-that is, the null hypothesis is true.
   b. The treatment means really differ, but other important factors affecting the response are not accounted for by the randomized block design. These factors inflate the sampling variability, as measured by MSE, resulting in smaller values of the F statistic. Either increase the sample size for each treatment, or conduct an experiment that accounts for the other factors affecting the response (as in Section 10.5). Do not automatically reach the former conclusion, since the possibility of a Type II error must be considered if you accept H_0.

6. If desired, conduct the F-test of the null hypothesis that the block means are equal. Rejection of this hypothesis lends statistical support to the utilization of the randomized block design.

Note: It is often difficult to check whether the assumptions for a randomized block design are satisfied. When you feel these assumptions are likely to be violated, a nonparametric procedure is advisable.

What Do You Do when Assumptions Are Not Satisfied for the Analysis of Variance for a Randomized Block Design?

Answer: Use a nonparametric statistical method such as the Friedman F_r test of Section 16.5.

Exercises 10.46–10.57

Learning the Mechanics

10.46 A randomized block design yielded the ANOVA table below.

Source	df	SS	MS	F
Treatments	4	501	125.25	9.109
Blocks	2	225	112.50	8.182
Error	8	110	13.75	
Total	14	836		

a. How many blocks and treatments were used in the experiment?   3; 5
b. How many observations were collected in the experiment?   15
c. Specify the null and alternative hypotheses you would use to compare the treatment means.
d. What test statistic should be used to conduct the hypothesis test of part **c**?   F = 9.109
e. Specify the rejection region for the test of parts **c** and **d**. Use $\alpha = .01$.   F > 7.01

f. Conduct the test of parts **c–e**, and state the proper conclusion.   Reject H_0

g. What assumptions are necessary to ensure the validity of the test you conducted in part **f?**

10.47 An experiment was conducted using a randomized block design. The data from the experiment are displayed in the following table.

⊛ **LM10_47**

Treatment	Block		
	1	2	3
1	2	3	5
2	8	6	7
3	7	6	5

a. Fill in the missing entries in the ANOVA table.

Source	df	SS	MS	F
Treatments	2	21.5555		
Blocks	2			
Error	4			
Total	8	30.2222		

b. Specify the null and alternative hypotheses you would use to investigate whether a difference exists among the treatment means.

c. What test statistic should be used in conducting the test of part **b?**

d. Describe the Type I and Type II errors associated with the hypothesis test of part **b.**

e. Conduct the hypothesis test of part **b** using $\alpha = .05$.

10.48 A randomized block design was used to compare the mean responses for three treatments. Four blocks of three homogeneous experimental units were selected, and each treatment was randomly assigned to one experimental unit within each block. The data are shown in the table below and the SPSS ANOVA printout for this experiment is shown on p. 602.

⊛ **LM10_48**

Treatment	Block			
	1	2	3	4
A	3.4	5.5	7.9	1.3
B	4.4	5.8	9.6	2.8
C	2.2	3.4	6.9	.3

a. Use the printout to fill in the entries in the following ANOVA table.

Source	df	SS	MS	F
Treatments				
Blocks				
Error				
Total				

b. Do the data provide sufficient evidence to indicate that the treatment means differ? Use $\alpha = .05$. $F = 50.958$

c. Do the data provide sufficient evidence to indicate that blocking was effective in reducing the experimental error? Use $\alpha = .05$. $F = 202.586$

d. Use the printout to rank the treatment means at $\alpha = .05$.

e. What assumptions are necessary to ensure the validity of the inferences made in parts **b, c,** and **d.**

10.49 Suppose an experiment utilizing a randomized block design has four treatments and nine blocks, for a total of $4 \times 9 = 36$ observations. Assume that the Total Sum of Squares for the response is SS(Total) = 500. For each of the following partitions of SS(Total), test the null hypothesis that the treatment means are equal, and the null hypothesis that the block means are equal. Use $\alpha = .05$ for each test.

a. The Sum of Squares for Treatments (SST) is 20% of SS(Total), and the Sum of Squares for Blocks (SSB) is 30% of SS(Total). $F = 3.20; F = 1.80$

b. SST is 50% of SS(Total), and SSB is 20% of SS(Total). $F = 13.33; F = 2.00$

c. SST is 20% of SS(Total), and SSB is 50% of SS(Total). $F = 5.33; F = 5.00$

d. SST is 40% of SS(Total), and SSB is 40% of SS(Total). $F = 16.00; F = 6.00$

e. SST is 20% of SS(Total), and SSB is 20% of SS(Total). $F = 2.67; F = 1.00$

Applying the Concepts—Basic

10.50 Dwarf shrubs are popular with model home landscapers. Stetson University researchers conducted an experiment to determine the effects of fire on the shrub's growth (*Florida Scientist,* Spring 1997). Twelve experimental plots of land were selected in a pasture where the shrub is abundant. Within each plot, three dwarf shrubs were randomly selected and treated as follows: one shrub was subjected to fire, another to clipping, and the third was left unmanipulated (a control). After five months, the number of flowers produced by each of the 36 shrubs was determined. The objective of the study was to compare the mean number of flowers produced by dwarf shrubs for the three treatments (fire, clipping, and control).

a. Identify the type of experimental design employed, including the treatments, response variable, and experimental units.

SPSS output for Exercise 10.48

Tests of Between-Subjects Effects

Dependent Variable: RESPONSE

Source	Type III Sum of Squares	df	Mean Square	F	Sig.
Corrected Model	83.781[a]	5	16.756	141.935	.000
Intercept	238.521	1	238.521	2020.412	.000
TRTMENT	12.032	2	6.016	50.958	.000
BLOCK	71.749	3	23.916	202.586	.000
Error	.708	6	.118		
Total	323.010	12			
Corrected Total	84.489	11			

a. R Squared = .992 (Adjusted R Squared = .985)

Multiple Comparisons

Dependent Variable: RESPONSE
Tukey HSD

(I) TRTMENT	(J) TRTMENT	Mean Difference (I-J)	Std. Error	Sig.	95% Confidence Interval Lower Bound	Upper Bound
A	B	-1.125*	.2430	.009	-1.870	-.380
	C	1.325*	.2430	.004	.580	2.070
B	A	1.125*	.2430	.009	.380	1.870
	C	2.450*	.2430	.000	1.705	3.195
C	A	-1.325*	.2430	.004	-2.070	-.580
	B	-2.450*	.2430	.000	-3.195	-1.705

Based on observed means.
*. The mean difference is significant at the .05 level.

---

b. Illustrate the layout of the design using a graphic similar to Figure 10.14.

c. The ANOVA of the data resulted in a test statistic of $F = 5.42$ for treatments with an associated p-value of $p = .009$. Interpret this result.

d. The three treatment means were compared using Tukey's method at $\alpha = .05$. Interpret the results shown below.

Mean number of flowers	1.17	10.58	17.08
Treatment	Control	Clipping	Burning

10.51 An economist wants to compare the average monthly number of rotary oil rigs running in three states— California, Utah, and Alaska. In order to account for month-to-month variation, three months were randomly selected over a two-year period and the number of oil rigs running in each state in each month

was obtained from data provided from *World Oil* (Jan. 2002) magazine. The data, reproduced in the accompanying table, were analyzed using a randomized block design.

⦿ **OILRIGS**

Month/Year	California	Utah	Alaska
Nov. 2000	27	17	11
Oct. 2001	34	20	14
Nov. 2001	36	15	14

a. Why is a randomized block design preferred over a completely randomized design for comparing the mean number of oil rigs running monthly in California, Utah, and Alaska?

b. Identify the treatments for the experiment.

c. Identify the blocks for the experiment.

d. State the null hypothesis for the ANOVA *F*-test.

e. Locate the test statistic and *p*-value on the MINITAB printout shown below. Interpret the results. $F = 38.07; p = .002$

f. A Tukey multiple comparison of means (at $\alpha = .05$) is summarized in the SPSS printout at the bottom of the page. Which state(s) have the significantly largest mean number of oil rigs running monthly?

10.52 What type of decoy should you purchase for hunting water-fowl? A study in the *Journal of Wildlife Management* (July 1995) compared the effectiveness of three different decoy types—taxidermy-mounted decoys, plastic

shell decoys, and full-bodied plastic decoys-in attracting Canada geese to sunken pit blinds. In order to account for an extraneous source of variation, three pit blinds were used as blocks in the experiment. Thus, a randomized block design with three treatments (decoy types) and three blocks (pit blinds) was employed. The response variable was the percentage of a goose flock to approach within 46 meters of the pit blind on a given day. The data are given in the table* (page 604), accompanied by a MINITAB printout of the analysis. Locate the *p*-value for treatments on the printout and interpret the result.

MINITAB output for Exercise 10.51

Two-way ANOVA: NumRigs versus State, Month/Year

```
Source        DF       SS        MS       F      P
State          2   617.556   308.778   38.07   0.002
Month/Year     2    30.889    15.444    1.90   0.262
Error          4    32.444     8.111
Total          8   680.889


S = 2.848    R-Sq = 95.23%    R-Sq(adj) = 90.47%



                         Individual 95% CIs For Mean Based on
                         Pooled StDev
State       Mean     ---------+---------+---------+---------+
AL       13.0000     (----*-----)
CAL      32.3333                                 (----*-----)
UT       17.3333          (-----*----)
                     ---------+---------+---------+---------+
                         16.0      24.0      32.0      40.0
```

SPSS output for Exercise 10.51

NUMRIGS

Tukey HSD[a,b]

		Subset	
STATE	N	1	2
AL	3	13.00	
UT	3	17.33	
CAL	3		32.33
Sig.		.262	1.000

Means for groups in homogeneous subsets are displayed.
Based on Type III Sum of Squares
The error term is Mean Square(Error) = 8.111.

   a. Uses Harmonic Mean Sample Size = 3.000.

   b. Alpha = .05.

---

*The actual design employed in the study was more complex than the randomized block design shown here. In the actual study, each number in the table represents the mean daily percentage of goose flocks attracted to the blind.averaged over 13–17 days.

MINITAB output for Exercise 10.52

Two-way ANOVA: PERCENT versus DECOY, BLIND

```
Source  DF       SS       MS      F      P
DECOY    2   30.069  15.0344   0.61  0.589
BLIND    2   44.149  22.0744   0.89  0.479
Error    4   99.338  24.8344
Total    8  173.556

S = 4.983    R-Sq = 42.76%    R-Sq(adj) = 0.00%
```

DECOY

Blind	Shell	Full-Bodied	Taxidermy-Mounted
1	7.3	13.6	17.8
2	12.6	10.4	17.0
3	16.4	23.4	13.6

Source: Harrey, W.F., Hindman, L. J., and Rhodes. W.E. "Vulnerability of Canada Geese to Taxidermy-Mounted Decoys." *Journal of Wildlife Management,* Vol. 59, No. 3, July 1995, p. 475 (Table 1).

10.53 A study was conducted to investigate the effect of prompting in a walking program instituted at a large corporation. (*Health Psychology,* Mar. 1995). Five groups of walkers—27 in each group-agreed to participate by walking for 20 minutes at least one day per week over a 24-week period. The participants were prompted to walk each week via telephone calls, but different prompting schemes were used for each group. Walkers in the control group received no prompting phone calls; Walkers in the "frequent/low" group received a call once a week with low structure (i.e., "just touching base"); walkers in the "frequent/high" group received a call once a week with high structure (i.e., goals are set); walkers in the "infrequent/low" group received a call once every 3 week with high structure; and walkers in the "infrequent/high" group received a call once every 3 weeks with high structure. The next table lists the number of participants in each group who actually walked the minimum requirement each week for weeks 1, 4, 8, 12, 16, and 24. The data were subjected to an analysis of variance for a randomized block design, with the five walker groups representing the treatments and the six time periods (weeks) representing the blocks.

a. What is the purpose of blocking on weeks in this study?

b. Fill in the missing entries on the ANOVA summary table shown at the bottom of the page.

WALKERS

Week	Control	Frequent/Low	Frequent/High	Infrequent/Low	Infrequent/High
1	7	23	25	21	19
4	2	19	25	10	12
8	2	18	19	9	9
12	2	7	20	8	2
16	2	18	18	8	7
24	1	17	17	7	6

Source: Lombard, D.N., et al. "Walking to Meet Health Guidelines: The Effect of Prompting Frequency and Prompt Structure." *Health Psychology,* Vol. 14, No. 2, Mar. 1995, p. 167 (Table 2). Copyright 1995 American Psychological Association.

ANOVA table for Exercise 10.53

Source	df	SS	MS	F	p-value
PROMPT	4	1185.000	—	—	0.0000
WEEK	—	386.400	77.28000	10.40	0.0001
Error	20	148.600	7.43000		
TOTAL	29	1720.00			

Mean:	2.67	9.17	10.50	17.00	20.67
Prompt:	Control	Infr./High	Infr./Low	Frequent/Low	Frequent/High

c. Is there sufficient evidence of a difference in the mean number of walkers per week among the five walker groups? Use $\alpha = .05$. $F = 39.87$

d. Tukey's technique was used to compare all pairs of treatment means with an experimentwise error rate of $\alpha = .05$. The rankings are shown above. Interpret these results.

e. What assumptions must hold to ensure the validity of the inferences in parts **c** and **d**?

Applying the Concepts—Intermediate

10.54 Plant therapists believe that plants can reduce on-the-job stress. A Kansas State University study was conducted to investigate this phenomenon. Two weeks prior to final exams, ten undergraduate students took part in an experiment to determine what effect the presence of a live plant, a photo of a plant, or absence of a plant has on the student's ability to relax while isolated in a dimly lit room. Each student participated in three sessions-one with a live plant, one with a plant photo, and one with no plant (control).* During each session, finger temperature was measured at one-minute intervals for 20 minutes. Since increasing finger temperature indicates an increased level of relaxation, the maximum temperature (in degrees) was used as the response variable. The data for the experiment are provided in the table below. Conduct an ANOVA and make the proper inferences at $\alpha = .10$.

PLANTS

Student	Live Plant	Plant Photo	No Plant (control)
1	91.4	93.5	96.6
2	94.9	96.6	90.5
3	97.0	95.8	95.4
4	93.7	96.2	96.7
5	96.0	96.6	93.5
6	96.7	95.5	94.8
7	95.2	94.6	95.7
8	96.0	97.2	96.2
9	95.6	94.8	96.0
10	95.6	92.6	96.6

Source: Elizabeth Schreiber. Department of Statistics, Kansas State University, Manhattan, Kansas

10.55 A plant that manufactures denim jeans in the United Kingdom recently introduced a computerized automated handling system. The new system delivers garments to the assembly line operators by means of an overhead conveyor. While the automated system minimizes operator handling time, it inhibits operators

*The experiment is simplified for this exercise. The actual experiment involved 30 students who participated in 12 sessions.

from working ahead and taking breaks from their machine. A study in *New Technology, Work, and Employment* (July 2001) investigated the impact of the new handling system on worker absentee rates at the jeans plant. One theory is that the mean absentee rate will vary by day of the week, as operators decide to indulge in one-day absences to relieve work pressure. Nine weeks were randomly selected and the absentee rate (percentage of workers absent) determined for each day (Monday through Friday) of the work week. The data are listed in the table. Conduct a complete analysis of the data to determine whether the mean absentee rate differs across the five days of the work week. $F = 2.00; F = 6.10$

JEANS

Week	Mon	Tues	Wed	Thur	Fri
1	5.3	0.6	1.9	1.3	1.6
2	12.9	9.4	2.6	0.4	0.5
3	0.8	0.8	5.7	0.4	1.4
4	2.6	0.0	4.5	10.2	4.5
5	23.5	9.6	11.3	13.6	14.1
6	9.1	4.5	7.5	2.1	9.3
7	11.1	4.2	4.1	4.2	4.1
8	9.5	7.1	4.5	9.1	12.9
9	4.8	5.2	10.0	6.9	9.0

Source: Boggis, J. J. "The Eradication of Leisure," *New Technology, Work, and Employment*, Volume 16, Number 2, July 2001 (Table 3).

10.56 Two drugs, A and B, used for the treatment of glaucoma (an eye disease) were tested for effectiveness on 10 diseased dogs. Drug A was administered to one eye (chosen randomly) of each dog and drug B to the other eye. Pressure measurements were taken 1 hour later on both eyeballs of each dog. The 10 diseased dogs serve as the blocks for comparing the two treatments, drugs A and B. Pressure measurements are given in the next table. (The smaller the measurement, the less serious the eye disease.)

EYEDOGS

Dog	Drug A	Drug B
1	.17	.15
2	.20	.18
3	.14	.13
4	.18	.18
5	.23	.19
6	.19	.12
7	.12	.07
8	.10	.09
9	.16	.14
10	.13	.08

a. Perform an analysis of variance for these data. Do the data provide sufficient evidence to indicate a difference in mean pressure readings for the two treatments (i.e., is one of the glaucoma drugs better than the other)? Use $\alpha = .05$.

b. What is the purpose of using the dogs as blocks in this experiment?

c. Recall that a randomized block design with $p = 2$ treatments is a paired difference experiment (Chapter 9). Analyze the data as a paired difference experiment using a t-test to compare the treatment means. Use $\alpha = .05$. $t = 4.105$

d. Compare the computed F and t values from parts **a** and **c,** and verify that $F = t^2$. Also verify that for the rejection region values of F and t, $F_\alpha = t^2_{\alpha/2}$.

e. Find the approximate observed significance level for the test in part **a** and interpret its value.

Applying the Concepts—Advanced

10.57 A species of Caribbean mosquito is known to be resistant against certain insecticides. The effectiveness of five different types of insecticides-temephos, malathion, fenitrothion, fenthion, and chlorpyrifos-in controlling this mosquito species was investigated in the *Journal of the American Mosquito Control Association* (March 1995). Mosquito larvae were collected from each of seven Caribbean locations. In a laboratory, the larvae from each location were divided into five batches and each batch exposed to one of the five insecticides. The dosage of insecticide required to kill 50% of the larvae was recorded and divided by the known dosage for a susceptible mosquito strain. The resulting value is called the resistance ratio. (The higher the ratio, the more resistant the mosquito species is to the insecticide relative to the susceptible mosquito strain.) The resistance ratios for the study are listed in the table below. The researchers want to compare the mean resistance ratios of the five insecticides.

a. Explain why the experimental design is a randomized block design. Identify the treatments and the blocks.

b. Conduct a complete analysis of the data. Are any of the insecticides more effective than any of the others? Use $\alpha = .10$. $F = 2.85; F = 2.74$

⊙ **MOSQUITO**

Location	Insecticide				
	Temephos	Malathion	Fenitrothion	Fenthion	Chlorpyrifos
Anguilla	4.6	1.2	1.5	1.8	1.5
Antigua	9.2	2.9	2.0	7.0	2.0
Dominica	7.8	1.4	2.4	4.2	4.1
Guyana	1.7	1.9	2.2	1.5	1.8
Jamaica	3.4	3.7	2.0	1.5	7.1
St. Lucia	6.7	2.7	2.7	4.8	8.7
Suriname	1.4	1.9	2.0	2.1	1.7

Source: Rawlins, S. C., and Oh Hing Wan, J. "Resistance in Some Caribbean Population of Aedes aegypti to Several Insecticides," *Journal of the American Mosquito Control Association,* Vol. 11, No. 1, March 1995 (Table 1).

10.5 Factorial Experiments

All the experiments discussed in Sections 14.2-14.4 were **single-factor experiments.** The treatments were levels of a single factor, with the sampling of experimental units performed using either a completely randomized or a randomized block design. However, most responses are affected by more than one factor, and we will therefore often wish to design experiments involving more than one factor.

Consider an experiment in which the effects of two factors on the response are being investigated. Assume that factor A is to be investigated at a levels, and factor B at b levels. Recalling that treatments are factor-level combinations, you can see that the experiment has, potentially, ab treatments that could be included in the

Teaching Tip

The Factorial Experiment allows two (or more) factors to be used when analyzing the dependent variable. It also allows the possibility that the relationship between the dependent variable and one of the factors depends on the level(s) of the other factor(s).

experiment. A *complete factorial experiment* is one in which all possible *ab* treatments are utilized.

DEFINITION 10.9

A **complete factorial experiment** is one in which every factor-level combination is utilized. That is, the number of treatments in the experiment equals the total number of factor-level combinations.

For example, suppose the USGA wants to determine not only the relationship between distance and brand of golf ball, but also between distance and the club used to hit the ball. If they decide to use four brands and two clubs (say, driver and five-iron) in the experiment, then a complete factorial would call for utilizing all $4 \times 2 = 8$ Brand-Club combinations. This experiment is referred to more specifically as a **complete 4 × 2 factorial.** A layout for a two-factor factorial experiment (we are henceforth referring to a *complete factorial* when we use the term factorial) is given in Table 10.10. The factorial experiment is also referred to as a **two-way classification** because it can be arranged in the row-column format exhibited in Table 10.10.

TABLE 10.10 Schematic Layout of Two-Factor Factorial Experiment

	Level	Factor B at b Levels				
		1	2	3	...	b
	1	Trt. 1	Trt. 2	Trt. 3	...	Trt. b
Factor A	2	Trt. $b + 1$	Trt. $b + 2$	Trt. $b + 3$	...	Trt. $2b$
at a Levels	3	Trt. $2b + 1$	Trt. $2b + 2$	Trt. $2b + 3$	...	Trt. $3b$
	⋮	⋮	⋮	⋮	...	⋮
	a	Trt. $(a - 1)b + 1$	Trt. $(a - 1)b + 2$	Trt. $(a - 1)b + 3$	...	Trt. ab

Teaching Tip

It is necessary to sample more than one item for each cell of the factorial table. This need for replication is one method the student can use to help identify when a factorial analysis has been employed.

In order to complete the specification of the experimental design, the treatments must be assigned to the experimental units. If the assignment of the ab treatments in the factorial experiment is random and independent, the design is completely randomized. For example, if the machine Iron Byron is used to hit 80 golf balls, 10 for each of the eight Brand-Club combinations, in a random sequence, the design would be completely randomized. In the remainder of this section, we confine our attention to factorial experiments utilizing completely randomized designs.

If we utilize a completely randomized design to conduct a factorial experiment with *ab* treatments, we can proceed with the analysis in exactly the same way as we did in Section 10.2. That is, we calculate (or let the computer calculate) the measure of treatment mean variability (MST) and the measure of sampling variability (MSE) and use the *F*-ratio of these two quantities to test the null hypothesis that the treatment means are equal. However, if this hypothesis is rejected, so that we conclude some differences exist among the treatment means, important questions remain. Are both factors affecting the response, or only one? If both, do they affect the response independently, or do they interact to affect the response?

Figure 10.18

Illustration of possible treatment effects: Factorial experiment.

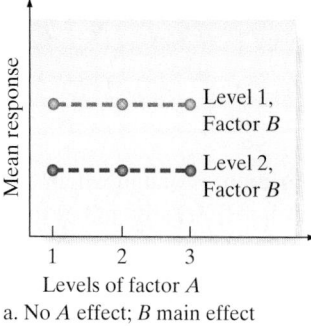

a. No A effect; B main effect

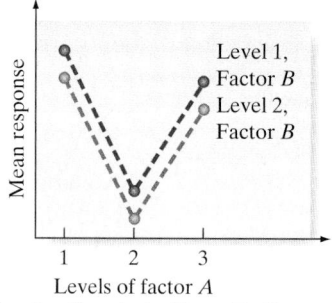

b. A main effect; insignificant B effect

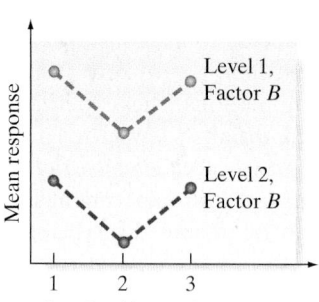

c. A and B main effects; no interaction

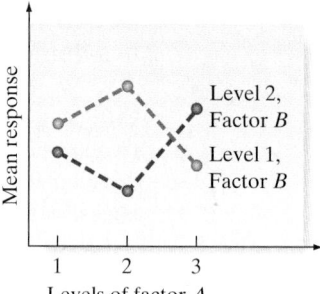

d. A and B interact

Teaching Tip

Go slowly when introducing the interaction concept to the student. It is an extremely difficult concept for the student to understand.

For example, suppose the distance data indicate that at least two of the eight treatment (Brand-Club combinations) means differ in the golf experiment. Does the brand of ball (factor A) or the club utilized (factor B) affect mean distance, or do both affect it? Several possibilities are shown in Figure 10.18. In Figure 10.18(a), the brand means are equal (only three are shown for the purpose of illustration), but the distances differ for the two levels of factor B (Club). Thus, there is no effect of Brand on distance, but a Club main effect is present. In Figure 10.18(b), the Brand means differ, but the Club means are equal for each Brand. Here a Brand main effect is present, but no effect of Club is present.

Figures 10.18(c) and 10.18(d) illustrate cases in which both factors affect the response. In Figure 10.18(c), the mean distances between clubs does not change for the three Brands, so that the effect of Brand on distance is independent of Club. That is, the two factors Brand and Club *do not interact.* In contrast, Figure 10.18(d) shows that the difference between mean distances between Clubs varies with Brand. Thus, the effect of Brand on distance depends on Club, and therefore the two factors *do interact.*

Now Work   *Exercise 10.66*

Teaching Tip

Explain that the presence or lack of interaction must be determined prior to analyzing individual treatment means. It will be the first test we conduct in the factorial analysis.

In order to determine the nature of the treatment effect, if any, on the response in a factorial experiment, we need to break the treatment variability into three components: Interaction Between Factors A and B, Main Effect of Factor A, and Main Effect of Factor B. The **Factor Interaction** component is used to test whether the factors combine to affect the response, while the **Factor Main Effect** components are used to determine whether the factors separately affect the response.

The partitioning of the Total Sum of Squares into its various components is illustrated in Figure 10.19. Notice that at stage 1 the components are identical to those in the one-factor, completely randomized designs of Section 10.2; the Sums of

Figure 10.19

Partitioning the Total Sum of Squares for a two-factor factorial

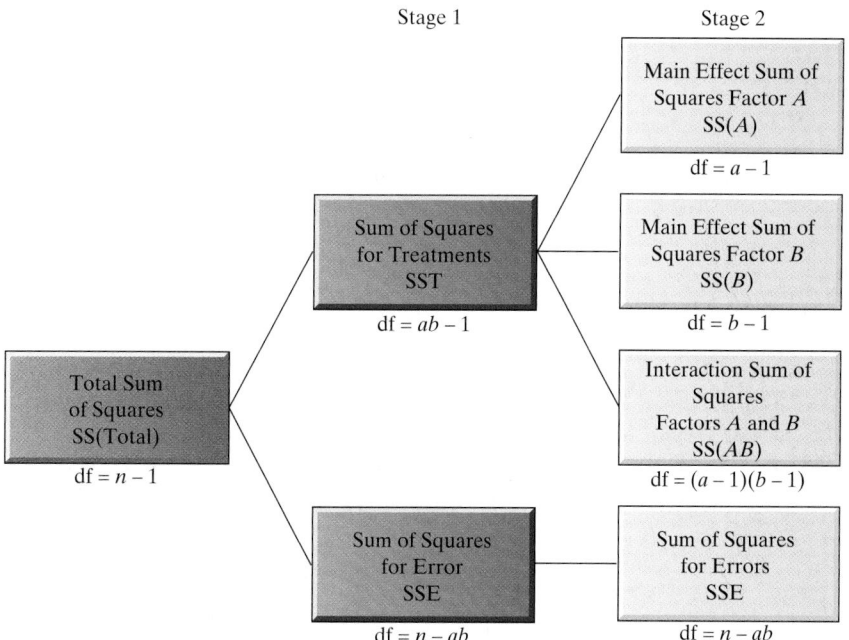

Squares for Treatments and Error sum to the Total Sum of Squares. The degrees of freedom for treatments is equal to $(ab - 1)$, one less than the number of treatments. The degrees of freedom for error is equal to $(n - ab)$, the total sample size minus the number of treatments. Only at stage 2 of the partitioning does the factorial experiment differ from those previously discussed. Here we divide the Treatments Sum of Squares into its three components: Interaction and the two Main Effects. These components can then be used to test the nature of the differences, if any, among the treatment means.

There are a number of ways to proceed in the testing and estimation of factors in a factorial experiment. We present one approach in the next box.

Teaching Tip

Use this box to illustrate the importance of the interaction test. It shows very clearly how the analysis changes depending on the outcome of the interaction test.

Procedure for Analysis of Two-Factor Factorial Experiment

1. Partition the Total Sum of Squares into the Treatments and Error components (stage 1 of Figure 10.19). Use either a statistical software package or the calculation formulas in Appendix C to accomplish the partitioning.

2. Use the *F*-ratio of Mean Square for Treatments to Mean Square for Error to test the null hypothesis that the treatment means are equal.*

   a. If the test results in nonrejection of the null hypothesis, consider refining the experiment by increasing the number of replications or introducing other factors. Also consider the possibility that the response is unrelated to the two factors.

   b. If the test results in rejection of the null hypothesis, then proceed to step 3.

(cont'd)

*Some analysts prefer to proceed directly to test the interaction and main effect components, skipping the test of treatment means. We begin with this test to be consistent with our approach in the one-factor completely randomized design.

3. Partition the Treatments Sum of Squares into the Main Effect and Interaction Sum of Squares (stage 2 of Figure 10.21). Use either a statistical software package or the calculation formulas in Appendix C to accomplish the partitioning.

4. Test the null hypothesis that factors A and B do not interact to affect the response by computing the F-ratio of the Mean Square for Interaction to the Mean Square for Error.
   a. If the test results in nonrejection of the null hypothesis, proceed to step 5.
   b. If the test results in rejection of the null hypothesis, conclude that the two factors interact to affect the mean response. Then proceed to step 6a.

5. Conduct tests of two null hypotheses that the mean response is the same at each level of factor A and factor B. Compute two F-ratios by comparing the Mean Square for each Factor Main Effect to the Mean Square for Error.
   a. If one or both tests result in rejection of the null hypothesis, conclude that the factor affects the mean response. Proceed to step 6b.
   b. If both tests result in nonrejection, an apparent contradiction has occurred. Although the treatment means apparently differ (step 2 test), the interaction (step 4) and main effect (step 5) tests have not supported that result. Further experimentation is advised.

6. Compare the means:
   a. If the test for interaction (step 4) is significant, use a multiple comparisons procedure to compare any or all pairs of the treatment means.
   b. If the test for one or both main effects (step 5) is significant, use a multiple comparisons procedure to compare the pairs of means corresponding to the levels of the significant factor(s).

We assume the completely randomized design is a **balanced design,** meaning that the same number of observations are made for each treatment. That is, we assume that r experimental units are randomly and independently selected for each treatment. The numerical value of r must exceed 1 in order to have any degrees of freedom with which to measure the sampling variability. [Note that if $r = 1$, then $n = ab$, and the degrees of freedom associated with Error (Figure 10.12) is $df = n - ab = 0$]. The value of r is often referred to as the number of **replicates** of the factorial experiment since we assume that all ab treatments are repeated, or replicated, r times. Whatever approach is adopted in the analysis of a factorial experiment, several tests of hypotheses are usually conducted. The tests are summarized in the next box.

Tests Conducted in Analyses of Factorial Experiments: Completely Randomized Design, r Replicates per Treatment

Test for Treatment Means

H_0: No difference among the ab treatment means

H_a: At least two treatment means differ

Test statistic: $F = \dfrac{\text{MST}}{\text{MSE}}$

(cont'd)

Rejection region: $F \geq F_\alpha$, based on $(ab - 1)$ numerator and $(n - ab)$ denominator degrees of freedom [Note: $n = abr$.]

Test for Factor Interaction

H_0: Factors A and B do not interact to affect the response mean

H_a: Factors A and B do interact to affect the response mean

Test statistic: $F = \dfrac{\text{MS}(AB)}{\text{MSE}}$

Rejection region: $F \geq F_\alpha$, based on $(a - 1)(b - 1)$ numerator and $(n - ab)$ denominator degrees of freedom

Test for Main Effect of Factor A

H_0: No difference among the a mean levels of factor A

H_a: At least two factor A mean levels differ

Test statistic: $F = \dfrac{\text{MS}(A)}{\text{MSE}}$

Rejection region: $F \geq F_\alpha$, based on $(a - 1)$ numerator and $(n - ab)$ denominator degrees of freedom

Test for Main Effect of Factor B

H_0: No difference among the b mean levels of factor B

H_a: At least two factor B mean levels differ

Test statistic: $F = \dfrac{\text{MS}(B)}{\text{MSE}}$

Rejection region: $F \geq F_\alpha$, based on $(b - 1)$ numerator and $(n - ab)$ denominator degrees of freedom

Conditions Required for Valid *F*-Tests in Factorial Experiments

1. The response distribution for each factor-level combination (treatment) is normal.
2. The response variance is constant for all treatments.
3. Random and independent samples of experimental units are associated with each treatment.

EXAMPLE 10.9

CONDUCTING A FACTORIAL ANOVA

Problem Suppose the USGA tests four different brands (A, B, C, D) of golf balls and two different clubs (driver, five-iron) in a completely randomized design. Each of the eight Brand-Club combinations (treatments) is randomly and independently assigned to four experimental units, each experimental unit consisting of a specific position in the

GOLFFAC1

TABLE 10.11   Distance Data for 4 × 2 Factorial Golf Experiment

		Brand			
		A	B	C	D
Club	**Driver**	226.4	238.3	240.5	219.8
		232.6	231.7	246.9	228.7
		234.0	227.7	240.3	232.9
		220.7	237.2	244.7	237.6
	Five-Iron	163.8	184.4	179.0	157.8
		179.4	180.6	168.0	161.8
		168.6	179.5	165.2	162.1
		173.4	186.2	156.5	160.3

sequence of hits by Iron Byron. The distance response is recorded for each of the 32 hits, and the results are shown in Table 10.11.

a. Use a statistical software package to partition the Total Sum of Squares into the components necessary to analyze this 4 × 2 factorial experiment.

b. Conduct the appropriate ANOVA tests and interpret the results of your analysis. Use $\alpha = .10$ for each test you conduct.

c. If appropriate, conduct multiple comparisons of the treatment means. Use an experiment-wise error rate of .10. Illustrate the comparisons with a graph.

Overall: $F = 140.354$

Interaction: $F = 7.452$

Solution   **a.** The SPSS printout that partitions the Total Sum of Squares [i.e., SS(Total)] for this factorial experiment is given in Figure 10.20. The value SS(Total) = 34,482.049, shown as "Corrected Total SS" at the bottom of the printout, is partitioned into the "Corrected Model" (i.e., Treatment) and Error Sums of Squares. Note that SST = 33,659.09 (with 7 degrees of freedom) and SSE = 822.24 (with 24 df) add to SS(Total) (with 31 df). The Treatment Sum of Squares, SST, is further divided into Main Effect (Brand and Club) and Interaction Sum of Squares. These values, highlighted on Figure 10.20, are SS(Brand) = 800.7 (with 3 df), SS(Club) = 32,093.1 (with 1 df), and SS(Brand × Club) = 766.0 (with 3 df).

b. Once partitioning is accomplished, our first test is

H_0: The eight treatment means are equal

H_a: At least two of the eight means differ

Test statistic: $F = \dfrac{\text{MST}}{\text{MSE}} = 140.354$ (top line of printout)

Observed significance level: $p = .000$ (top line of printout)

Since $\alpha = .10$ exceeds p, we reject this null hypothesis and conclude that at least two of the Brand-Club combinations differ in mean distance.

After accepting the hypothesis that the treatment means differ, and therefore that the factors Brand and/or Club somehow affect the mean distance, we want to determine how the factors affect the mean response. We begin with a test of interaction between Brand and Club:

Tests of Between-Subjects Effects

Dependent Variable: DISTANCE

Source	Type III Sum of Squares	df	Mean Square	F	Sig.
Corrected Model	33659.809[a]	7	4808.544	140.354	.000
Intercept	1306778.61	1	1306778.611	38142.98	.000
BRAND	800.736	3	266.912	7.791	.001
CLUB	32093.111	1	32093.111	936.752	.000
BRAND * CLUB	765.961	3	255.320	7.452	.001
Error	822.240	24	34.260		
Total	1341260.66	32			
Corrected Total	34482.049	31			

a. R Squared = .976 (Adjusted R Squared = .969)

Figure 10.20
SPSS ANOVA for factorial experiment on golf ball data.

H_0: The factors Brand and Club do not interact to affect the mean response

H_a: Brand and Club interact to affect mean response

$$\textit{Test statistic: } F = \frac{\text{MS}(AB)}{\text{MSE}} = \frac{\text{MS(Brand} \times \text{Club)}}{\text{MSE}}$$

$$= \frac{255.32}{34.26} = 7.452 \quad \text{(bottom of printout)}$$

Observed significance level: $p = .001$ (bottom of printout)

Teaching Tip

Point out that a lot of the analysis portion of the Factorial Experiment is the same as the analysis portion of the Completely Randomized and Randomized Block designs. The multiple comparison procedure is a good example of this.

Since $\alpha = .10$ exceeds the p-value, we conclude that the factors Brand and Club interact to affect mean distance.

Because the factors interact, we do not test the main effects for Brand and Club. Instead, we compare the treatment means in an attempt to learn the nature of the interaction in part C.

c. Rather than compare all $8(7)/2 = 28$ pairs of treatment means, we test for differences only between pairs of brands within each club. That differences exist *between* clubs can be assumed. Therefore, only $4(3)/2 = 6$ pairs of means need to be compared for each club, or a total of 12 comparisons for the two clubs. The results of these comparisons using Tukey's method with an experimentwise error rate of $\alpha = .10$ for each club are displayed in the SPSS printout, Figure 10.21. For each club, the brand means are listed in descending order in Figure 10.21, and those not significantly different are listed in the same "Homogeneous Subset" column.

As shown in Figure 10.21, the picture is unclear with respect to Brand means. For the five-iron (top of Figure 10.21), the brand B mean significantly exceeds all other brands. However, when hit with a driver (bottom of Figure 10.21), brand B's mean is not significantly different from any of the other brands. The Club × Brand interaction can be seen in the plot of means in Figure 10.22. Note that the difference between the mean distances of the two clubs (driver and five-iron) varies depending on brand. The biggest difference appears for Brand C while the smallest difference is for Brand B.

Figure 10.21
SPSS ranking of brand
means for each level of club

CLUB=5IRON

Tukey HSD[a,b]

BRAND	N	Subset 1	Subset 2
D	4	160.500	
C	4	167.175	
A	4	171.300	
B	4		182.675
Sig.		.103	1.000

Means for groups in homogeneous subsets are displayed.
Based on Type III Sum of Squares
The error term is Mean Square(Error) = 36.108.

    a. Uses Harmonic Mean Sample Size = 4.000.

    b. Alpha = .10.

CLUB=DRIVER

Tukey HSD[a,b]

BRAND	N	Subset 1	Subset 2
A	4	228.425	
D	4	229.750	
B	4	233.725	233.725
C	4		243.100
Sig.		.570	.146

Means for groups in homogeneous subsets are displayed.
Based on Type III Sum of Squares
The error term is Mean Square(Error) = 32.412.

    a. Uses Harmonic Mean Sample Size = 4.000.

    b. Alpha = .10.

Figure 10.22
Sample mean plot for
factorial golf experiment

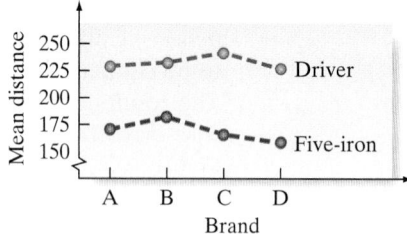

Look Back Note the nontransitive nature of the multiple comparisons. For example, for the driver the Brand C mean can be "the same" as the brand B mean, and the brand B mean can be "the same" as the brand D mean, and yet the brand C mean can significantly exceed the brand D mean. The reason lies in the definition of "the same"—we must be careful not to conclude two means are equal simply because they are placed in the same subgroup or connected by a vertical line. The line indicates only that *the connected means are not significantly different.* You should conclude (at the overall α level of significance) only that means not connected are different, while withholding judgment on those that are connected. The picture of which means differ and by how much will become clearer as we increase the number of replicates of the factorial experiment.

Now Work   *Exercise 10.67*

■ ■ ■

EXAMPLE 10.10

MORE PRACTICE ON CONDUCTING A FACTORIAL ANALYSIS

Problem   Refer to Example 14.6. Suppose the same factorial experiment is performed on four other brands (E, F, G, and H), and the results are as shown in Table 10.12. Repeat the factorial analysis and interpret the results.

Suggested Exercise 10.69

 GOLFFAC2

TABLE 10.12   Distance Data for Second Factorial Golf Experiment

		Brand			
		E	F	G	H
Club	Driver	238.6	261.4	264.7	235.4
		241.9	261.3	262.9	239.8
		236.6	254.0	253.5	236.2
		244.9	259.9	255.6	237.5
	Five-Iron	165.2	179.2	189.0	171.4
		156.9	171.0	191.2	159.3
		172.2	178.0	191.3	156.6
		163.2	182.7	180.5	157.4

Solution   The MINITAB printout for the second factorial experiment is shown in Figure 10.23. Note that MINITAB (unlike SPSS) does not automatically conduct the F-test for treatment differences. Consequently, to conduct this test, we must first calculate the Sum of Squares for Treatments. Using the sums of squares for Brands, Clubs, and Interaction shown on the printout, we obtain

$$SS(\text{Treatments}) = SS(\text{Brands}) + SS(\text{Clubs}) + SS(\text{Interaction})$$
$$= 46{,}443.9 + 3{,}410.3 + 105.2 = 49{,}959.4$$

For this 4×2 factorial experiment there are 8 treatments. Then

$$MS(\text{Treatments}) = SS(\text{Treatments})/(8 - 1) = 49{,}959.4/7 = 7{,}137.1$$

The test statistic is

$$F = MS(\text{Treatments})/MSE = 7{,}137.1/24.6 = 290.1$$

Since this F-value exceeds the critical value of $F_{.10} = 1.90$ (obtained from Example 10.9), we reject the null hypothesis of no treatment differences and conclude that at

Figure 10.23
MINITAB Analysis for
Second Factorial Golf
Experiment

Two-way ANOVA: DISTANCE versus BRAND, CLUB

```
Source        DF        SS        MS         F       P
BRAND          3    3410.3    1136.8     46.21   0.000
CLUB           1   46443.9   46443.9   1887.94   0.000
Interaction    3     105.2      35.1      1.42   0.260
Error         24     590.4      24.6
Total         31   50549.8

S = 4.960    R-Sq = 98.83%    R-Sq(adj) = 98.49%
```

least two of the Brand-Club combinations have significantly different mean distances.

Now, we test for interaction between Brand and Club:

$$F = \frac{MS(\text{Brand} \times \text{Club})}{MSE} = 1.42 \text{ (highlighted on the printout)}$$

Since this F-ratio does not exceed the tabled value of $F_{.10} = 2.33$ with 3 and 24 df (obtained in Example 10.9) we cannot conclude at the .10 level of significance that the factors interact. In fact, note that the observed significance level (on the MINITAB printout) for the test of interaction is .26. Thus, at any level of significance lower than $\alpha = .26$, we could not conclude that the factors interact. We therefore test the main effects for Brand and Club.

We first test the Brand main effect:

H_0: No difference exists among the true Brand mean distances

H_a: At least two Brand mean distances differ

Test statistic: $F = \dfrac{MS(\text{Brand})}{MSE} = \dfrac{1{,}136.77}{24.60} = 46.21$ (highlighted on the printout)

Observed significance level: $p = .000$

Since $\alpha = .10$ exceeds the p-value, we conclude that at least two of the brand means differ. We will subsequently determine which brand means differ using Tukey's multiple comparisons procedure. But first, we want to test the Club main effect:

H_0: No differences exist between the Club mean distances

H_a: The Club mean distances differ

Test statistic: $F = \dfrac{MS(\text{Club})}{MSE} = \dfrac{46{,}443.9}{24.60} = 1{,}887.94$

Observed significance level: $p = .000$

Since $\alpha = .10$ exceeds the p-value, we conclude that the two clubs are associated with different mean distances. Since only two levels of Club were utilized in the experiment, this F-test leads to the inference that the mean distance differs for the two clubs. It is no surprise (to golfers) that the mean distance for balls hit with the driver is significantly greater than the mean distance for those hit with the five-iron.

To determine which of the Brands' mean distances differ, we want to compare the $k = 4$ Brand means using Tukey's method at $\alpha = .10$. The results of these multiple

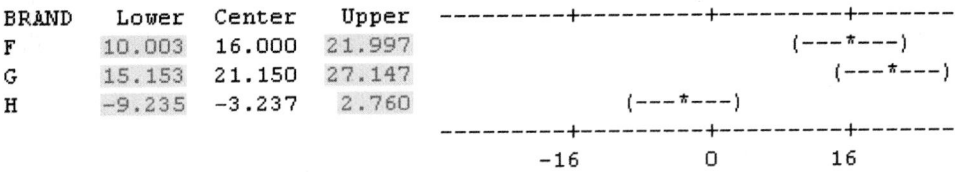

```
Tukey 90.0% Simultaneous Confidence Intervals
Response Variable DISTANCE
All Pairwise Comparisons among Levels of BRAND
BRAND = E  subtracted from:

BRAND  Lower   Center  Upper   --------+---------+---------+-------
F      10.003  16.000  21.997                             (---*---)
G      15.153  21.150  27.147                                (---*---)
H      -9.235  -3.237   2.760             (---*---)
                               --------+---------+---------+-------
                                     -16         0        16


BRAND = F  subtracted from:

BRAND  Lower   Center  Upper   --------+---------+---------+-------
G       -0.85    5.15   11.15                      (---*---)
H      -25.23  -19.24  -13.24    (---*---)
                               --------+---------+---------+-------
                                     -16         0        16


BRAND = G  subtracted from:

BRAND  Lower   Center  Upper   --------+---------+---------+-------
H      -30.38  -24.39  -18.39  (---*---)
                               --------+---------+---------+-------
                                     -16         0        16
```

Figure 10.24

MINITAB Tukey multiple comparisons for brand in second factorial golf experiment

comparisons are displayed in the MINITAB printout, Figure 10.24. MINITAB computes simultaneous 90% confidence intervals for the $c = (4)(3)/2 = 6$ possible comparisons of the form $\mu_i - \mu_j$. These intervals (highlighted on the printout) are summarized in Table 10.11. Any interval that does not include 0 implies a significant difference between the two treatment means. You can see that Brands G and F are associated with significantly greater mean distances than Brands E and H, but we cannot distinguish between Brands G and F or between Brands E and H.

Look Back Since the interaction between Brand and Club was not significant, we conclude that this difference among brands applies to both clubs. The sample means

TABLE 10.11 Summary of Tukey's Multiple Comparisons

Comparison	90% Confidence Interval	Inference
$\mu_F - \mu_E$	$(10.00, 21.99)$	$\mu_F > \mu_E$
$\mu_G - \mu_E$	$(15.15, 27.15)$	$\mu_G > \mu_E$
$\mu_H - \mu_E$	$(-9.24, 2.76)$	No significant difference
$\mu_G - \mu_F$	$(-.85, 11.15)$	No significant difference
$\mu_H - \mu_F$	$(-25.23, -13.24)$	$\mu_H < \mu_F$
$\mu_H - \mu_G$	$(-30.38, -18.39)$	$\mu_H < \mu_G$

Figure 10.25

Sample mean plot for second factorial golf experiment

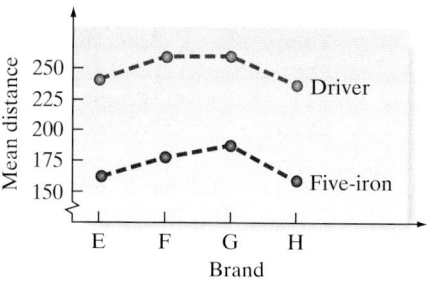

for all Club-Brand combinations are shown in Figure 10.25 and appear to support the conclusions of the tests and comparisons. Note that the Brand means maintain their relative positions for each Club—brands F and G dominate brands E and H for both the driver and five-iron.

Now Work *Exercise 10.64*

■ ■ ■

The analysis of factorial experiments can become complex if the number of factors is increased. Even the two-factor experiment becomes more difficult to analyze if some factor combinations have different numbers of observations than others. We have provided an introduction to these important experiments using two-factor factorials with equal numbers of observations for each treatment. Although similar principles apply to most factorial experiments, you should consult the references for this chapter at the end of the book if you need to design and analyze more complex factorials.

Exercises 10.58–10.72

Learning the Mechanics

10.58 Suppose you conduct a 4 × 3 factorial experiment.
  a. How many factors are used in the experiment?
  b. Can you determine the factor type(s)—qualitative or quantitative—from the information given? Explain.
  c. Can you determine the number of levels used for each factor? Explain.   Yes
  d. Describe a treatment for this experiment, and determine the number of treatments used.   12
  e. What problem is caused by using a single replicate of this experiment? How is the problem solved?

10.59 The partially completed ANOVA for a 3 × 4 factorial experiment with two replications is shown below.

Source	df	SS	MS	F
A	—	.8	____	____
B	—	5.3	____	____
AB	—	9.6	____	____
Error	—	____	____	
Total	—	17.0		

  a. Complete the ANOVA table.
  b. Which sums of squares are combined to find the Sum of Squares for Treatments? Do the data

provide sufficient evidence to indicate that the treatment means differ? Use $\alpha = .05$. $F = 13.18$
  c. Does the result of the test in part **b** warrant further testing? Explain.   Yes
  d. What is meant by factor interaction, and what is the practical implication if it exists?
  e. Test to determine whether these factors interact to affect the response mean. Use $\alpha = .05$, and interpret the result. $F = 14.77$
  f. Does the result of the interaction test warrant further testing? Explain.   No

10.60 The partially complete ANOVA table given here is for a two-factor factorial experiment.

Source	df	SS	MS	F
Treatments	7	4.1		
A	3	____	.75	____
B	1	.95	____	____
AB	____	____	.30	____
Error	____	____	____	
Total	23	6.5		

  a. Give the number of levels for each factor.   4; 2
  b. How many observations were collected for each factor-level combination?   3

c. Complete the ANOVA table.

d. Test to determine whether the treatment means differ. Use $\alpha = .10$. $F = 3.90$

e. Conduct the tests of factor interaction and main effects, each at the $\alpha = .10$ level of significance. Which of the tests are warranted as part of the factorial analysis? Explain.

10.61 The following two-way table gives data for a 2×3 factorial experiment with two observations for each factor-level combination.

LM10_61

		Factor B		
	Level	1	2	3
Factor A	1	3.1, 4.0	4.6, 4.2	6.4, 7.1
	2	5.9, 5.3	2.9, 2.2	3.3, 2.5

a. Identify the treatments for this experiment. Calculate and plot the treatment means, using the response variable as the y-axis and the levels of factor B as the x-axis. Use the levels of factor A as plotting symbols. Do the treatment means appear to differ? Do the factors appear to interact?

b. The MINITAB ANOVA printout for this experiment is shown below. Sum the appropriate sums of squares and test to determine whether the treatment means differ at the $\alpha = .05$ level of significance. Does the test support your visual interpretation from part **a?** $F = 21.62$

c. Does the result of the test in part **b** warrant a test for interaction between the two factors? If so, perform it using $\alpha = .05$.   Yes, $F = 36.62$

d. Do the results of the previous tests warrant tests of the two factor main effects? If so, perform them using $\alpha = .05$.   No

e. Interpret the results of the tests. Do they support your visual interpretation from part **a?**

10.62 The next table gives data for a 2×2 factorial experiment with two observations per factor-level combination.

LM10_62

		Factor B	
	Level	1	2
Factor A	1	29.6, 35.2	47.3, 42.1
	2	12.9, 17.6	28.4, 22.7

a. Identify the treatments for this experiment. Calculate and plot the treatment means, using the response variable as the y-axis and the levels of factor B as the x-axis. Use the levels of factor A as plotting symbols. Do the treatment means appear to differ? Do the factors appear to interact?

b. Use the computational formulas in Appendix C to create an ANOVA table for this experiment.

c. Test to determine whether the treatment means differ at the $\alpha = .05$ level of significance. Does the test support your visual interpretation from part **a?**

d. Does the result of the test in part **b** warrant a test for interaction between the two factors? If so, perform it using $\alpha = .05$.   Yes, $F = .14$

e. Do the results of the previous tests warrant tests of the two factor main effects? If so, perform them using $\alpha = .05$.   Yes. $F_A = 46.65$. $F_B = 18.08$

f. Interpret the results of the tests. Do they support your visual interpretation from part **a?**

g. Given the results of your tests, which pairs of means, if any, should be compared?

10.63 Suppose a 3×3 factorial experiment is conducted with three replications. Assume that SS(Total) = 1,000. For each of the following scenarios, form an ANOVA table, conduct the appropriate tests, and interpret the results.

a. The Sum of Squares of factor A main effect [SS(A)] is 20% of SS(Total), the Sum of Squares for factor B main effect [SS(B)] is 10% of SS(Total), and the Sum of Squares for interaction [SS(AB)] is 10% of SS(Total).

b. SS(A) is 10%, SS(B) is 10%, and SS(AB) is 50% of SS(Total).

MINITAB Output for Exercise 10.61

Two-way ANOVA: RESPONSE versus A, B

```
Source        DF      SS       MS       F      P
A              1   4.4408  4.44083  18.06  0.005
B              2   4.1267  2.06333   8.39  0.018
Interaction    2  18.0067  9.00333  36.62  0.000
Error          6   1.4750  0.24583
Total         11  28.0492

S = 0.4958   R-Sq = 94.74%   R-Sq(adj) = 90.36%
```

c. SS(A) is 40%, SS(B) is 10%, and SS(AB) is 20% of SS(Total).

d. SS(A) is 40%, SS(B) is 40%, and SS(AB) is 10% of SS(Total).

Applying the Concepts—Basic

10.64 A computer lab at the University of Oklahoma is open 24 hours a day, seven days a week. In *Production and Inventory Management Journal*, (3rd Qtr., 1999). S. Barmon investigated whether usage differed significantly (1) among the days of the week and (2) among the hours of the day. Using student log-on records, data on hourly student loads (number of users per hour) were collected during a seven-week period. A factorial ANOVA was used to analyze the data with the results presented in the table below.

Source	df	F	P
Model	167	25.06	.001
Error	1004		
Total	1171		

$R^2 = .8065$

Source	df	F	P
Day	6	68.39	.0001
Time	23	156.80	.0001
Day × Time	138	1.22	.0527

Source: Barman, Samir, "A Statistical Analysis of the Attendance Pattern of a Computer Laboratory," *Production and Inventory Management Journal,* Third Quarter, 1999, pp. 26-30.

a. Is this an observational or a designed experiment? Explain.   Observational

b. What are the two factors of the experiment and how many levels of each factor are used?

c. This is an $a \times b$ factorial experiment. What are a and b? $a = 7, b = 24$

d. Conduct a test to determine whether any of the $a \times b$ treatment means significantly differ. Use $\alpha = .01$.

e. Specify the null and alternative hypotheses that should be used to test for an interaction effect between the two factors of the study.

f. Conduct the test of part **e** using $\alpha = .01$. Interpret your result in the context of the problem. $F = 1.22$

g. If appropriate, conduct main effects tests for both day and time. Use $\alpha = .01$. Interpret your results in the context of the problem. $F_A = 68.39, F_B = 156.8$

10.65 A coagulation—microfiltration process for removing bacteria from water was investigated in *Environmental Science & Engineering* (Sept. 1, 2000). Chemical engineers at Seoul National University performed a designed experiment to estimate the effect of both the level of the coagulant and acidity (pH) level on the coagulation efficiency of the process. Six levels of coagulant (5, 10, 20, 50, 100, and 200 milligrams per liter) and six pH levels (4.0, 5.0, 6.0, 7.0, 8.0, and 9.0) were employed. Water specimens collected from the Han River in Seoul, Korea, were placed in jars, and each jar randomly assigned to receive one of the $6 \times 6 = 36$ combinations of coagulant level and pH level.

a. What type of experimental design was applied in this study?

b. Give the factors, factor levels, and treatments for the study.

10.66 A study published in *Teaching Psychology* (May 1998) examined how external clues influence student performance. Undergraduate students were randomly assigned to one of four different midterm examinations. Form 1 was printed on blue paper and contained difficult questions, while form 2 was also printed on blue paper but contained simple questions. Form 3 was printed on red paper, with difficult questions; form 4 was printed on red paper with simple questions. The researchers were interested in the impact that Color (red or blue) and Question (simple or difficult) had on mean exam score.

a. What experimental design was employed in this study? Identify the factors and treatments.

b. The researchers conducted an ANOVA and found a significant interaction between Color and Question (p-value $< .03$). Interpret this result.

c. The sample mean scores (percentage correct) for the four exam forms are listed in the table below. Plot the four means on a graph to illustrate the Color × Question interaction.

Form	Color	Question	Mean Score
1	Blue	Difficult	53.3
2	Blue	Simple	80.0
3	Red	Difficult	39.3
4	Red	Simple	73.6

10.67 The cattle raised on the Biological Reserve of Doñana (Spain) live under free-range conditions, with virtually no human interference. The cattle population is organized into four herds (LGN, MTZ, PLC, and QMD). *The Journal of Zoology* (July 1995) investigated the ranging behavior of the four herds across the four seasons. Thus, a 4×4 factorial experiment was employed, with Herd and Season representing the two factors. Three animals from each herd during each season were sampled and the home range of each individual was measured (in square kilometers). The data were subjected to an ANOVA, with the results shown in the next table.

Source	df	F	p-Value
Herd (H)	3	17.2	$p < .001$
Season (S)	3	3.0	$p < .05$
$H \times S$	9	1.2	$p > .051$
Error	32		
Total	47		

a. Conduct the appropriate ANOVA F-tests and interpret the results.

b. The researcher ranked the four herd means independently of season. Do you agree with this strategy? Explain.   Yes

c. Refer to part **b.** The Bonferroni rankings of the four herd means (at $\alpha = .05$) are shown below. Interpret the results.

Mean home range (km^2)	.75	1.0	2.7	3.8
Herd	PLC	LGN	QMD	MTZ

Applying the Concepts—Intermediate

10.68 Advancements in information technology have yielded services that compete against products with each providing roughly the same benefits to the consumer, e.g., home answering machines and voice-mail services. With the advent of such services, consumers also face different types of pricing schemes. Using a 2 × 2 factorial design, D. Fortin and T. Greenlee of the University of Rhode Island investigated the effects of the type of message retrieval system (answering machine vs. voice-mail service) and the type of pricing (lump sum amount for 5 years of use vs. monthly cost for 5 years of use) on consumers' willingness to buy (*Journal of Business Research*, Vol. 41, 1998). The first pricing option requires the consumer to do mental arithmetic to determine the total cost of the system; the second provides the true full cost. Thirty subjects were randomly assigned to each of the four treatments. Each was exposed to a purchase situation involving the relevant product or service and payment description and was asked to indicate his or her willingness to buy the item on a five-point scale (1 = definitely would not buy;

5 = definitely would buy). The results are presented in the incomplete ANOVA table at the bottom of the page.

a. Fill in the degrees of freedom (df) column in the ANOVA table.

b. Specify the null and alternative hypotheses that should be used in testing for interaction effects between type of message retrieval system and pricing option.

c. Conduct the test of part *b* using $\alpha = .05$. Interpret the results in the context of the problem. $F = 4.986$

d. Given the results of part c is it advisable to conduct main effects tests? Why or why not? If so, perform the appropriate main effects tests using $\alpha = .05$.

10.69 *Quality Engineering* (vol. 2, 1990) published the results of an experiment that was conducted by a dog food manufacturer to improve a filling process in which ground meat is packed into cans. The process uses a rotary filling machine with six cylinders, each of which dispenses ground meat. The company wanted to study the effects of differences in batches of meat and differences in cylinders on the weight of the final product. Five batches of meat were used in the experiment. Three filled cans were randomly selected from each cylinder while each batch was being run. The cans were weighed and the weights were recorded. To simplify the analysis, the weights were coded by subtracting 12 ounces from each weight. The coded data appear in the table on p. 622.

a. What type of experimental design was used by the dog food manufacturer?   6 × 5 Factorial

b. Identify the factors used in the study and their levels.

c. How many different treatments were used in the experiment?   30

d. Analyze the data with an analysis of variance. Summarize the results in an ANOVA table.

e. In the context of the problem, explain what it means to say that batch and cylinder interact. Speculate on what could cause such an interaction.

f. Test for an interaction between batches and cylinders. Use $\alpha = .05$. $F = 1.29$

Source	df	SS	MS	F
Type of message retrieval system	——	——	——	2.001
Pricing option	——	——	——	5.019
Type of system × Pricing option	——	——	——	4.986
Error	——	——	——	
Total	119	——		

Source: Adapted from Fortin, D. and Greenlee, T., "Using a Product/Service Evaluation Frame: An Experiment on the Economic Equivalence of Product versus Service Alternatives for Message Retrieval Systems," *Journal of Business Research*, Vol. 41, 1998, pp. 205–214.

DOGFOOD

		Batch				
		1	2	3	4	5
	1	1	4	6	3	1
		1	3	3	1	3
		2	5	7	3	3
	2	−1	−2	3	2	1
		3	1	1	0	0
		−1	0	5	1	1
	3	1	2	2	1	3
		1	0	4	3	3
		1	1	3	3	3
Cylinder						
	4	−2	−2	3	0	0
		3	0	3	0	1
		0	1	4	2	1
	5	1	2	0	1	−2
		1	1	1	0	3
		−1	5	2	−1	1
	6	0	0	3	3	3
		1	0	3	0	1
		1	3	4	2	2

Source: Griffith, B.A., Westman, A. E. R., and Lloyd, B. H. "Analysis of Variance." *Quality Engineering*, Vol 2. No. 2. 1990, pp. 195-226.

g. If appropriate, test for main effects using $\alpha = .05$.

10.70 Research published in *Accounting, Organizations and Society* (Vol. 19, 1994) investigated whether the effects of different performance evaluation styles (PES) on the level of job-related tension is affected by trust. Three performance evaluation styles were considered. Each is related to the way in which accounting information is used for the purpose of evaluation. The three styles are budget-constrained (BC), profit-conscious (PC), and the nonaccounting style (NA), which focuses on factors such as quality of output and attitude toward the job. A questionnaire was administered to 215 managers working in 18 Australian organizations. It measured the performance evaluation style of each manager's superior, the manager's job-related tension, and the manager's level of trust (low, medium, and high) in his or her superior. These data were used to produce the partial ANOVA table and table of treatment means shown next.

Source	df	SS	MS	F
PES	2	2.1774	____	____
Trust	____	7.6367	____	____
PES × Trust	4	1.7380	____	____
Error	206	____		
Total	214	161.1162		

		Performance Evaluation Style		
		BC	PC	NA
Trust	**Low**	3.2350	3.111	3.2290
		($n = 32$)	($n = 24$)	($n = 16$)
	Medium	2.7601	2.8530	2.6373
		($n = 26$)	($n = 31$)	($n = 14$)
	High	2.3067	2.4436	3.1810
		($n = 30$)	($n = 26$)	($n = 16$)

Source: Ross, A. "Trust as a Moderator of the Effect of Performance Evaluation Style on Job-Related Tension: A Research Note." *Accounting, Organizations and Society,* Vol. 19, No. 7, 1994, pp. 633 (Tables 3 and 4).

a. Describe the treatments of this study.

b. Complete the ANOVA table.

c. Investigate the presence of an interaction effect by conducting the appropriate hypothesis test using $\alpha = .05$.   *F = .60*

d. Use a plot of treatment means to investigate the interaction effect. Interpret your results. Are your results of parts **c** and **d** consistent?

e. Explain why the F-tests for the two main effects are irrelevant given your answers to parts **c** and **d.**

10.71 Refer to the *Teaching of Psychology* (August 1998) study of whether a practice test helps students prepare for a final exam, Exercise 10.10 (p. 562). Recall that undergraduate students were grouped according to their class standing and whether they attended a review session or took a practice test prior to the final exam. The experimental design was a 3×2 factorial design, with Class Standing at 3 levels (low, medium, or high) and Exam Preparation at 2 levels (practice exam or review session). There were 22 students in each of the $3 \times 2 = 6$ treatment groups. After completing the final exam, each student rated their exam preparation on an 11-point scale ranging from 0 (not helpful at all) to 10 (extremely helpful). The data for this experiment (simulated from summary statistics provided in the article) are saved in the **PRACEXAM** file. The first 5 and last 5 observations in the data set are listed on p. 623. Conduct a complete analysis of variance of the helpfulness ratings data, including (if warranted) multiple comparisons of means. Do your findings support the research conclusion that "students at all levels of academic ability benefit from a ... practice exam"?

Applying the Concepts—Advanced

10.72 Knowledge of how cockroaches forage for food is valuable for companies that develop and manufacture roach bait and traps. Many entomologists believe, however, that the navigational behavior of cockroaches scavenging for food is random. D. Miller of Virginia Tech University challenged the "random-walk" theory by designing an experiment to test a cockroach's ability to follow a trail of their fecal material (*Explore*, Research

PRACEXAM

Exam Preparation	Class Standing	Helpfulness Rating
PRACTICE	LOW	6
PRACTICE	LOW	7
PRACTICE	LOW	7
PRACTICE	LOW	5
PRACTICE	LOW	3
⋮	⋮	⋮
REVIEW	HI	5
REVIEW	HI	2
REVIEW	HI	5
REVIEW	HI	4
REVIEW	HI	3

Source: Balch, W. R. "Practice versus Review Exams and Final Exam Performance," *Teaching of Psychology*, Vol. 25, No. 3, August 1998 (adapted from Table 1).

at the University of Florida, Fall 1998). A methanol extract from roach feces—called a pheromone—was used to create a chemical trail. German cockroaches were released at the beginning of the trail, one-at-a-time, and a video surveillance camera was used to monitor the roach's movements. In addition to the trail containing the fecal extract (the treatment), a trail using methanol only (the control) was created. To determine if trail-following ability differed among cockroaches of different age, sex, and reproductive status, four roach groups were utilized in the experiment: adult males,

adult females, gravid (pregnant) females, and nymphs (immatures). Twenty roaches of each type were randomly assigned to the treatment trail and ten of each type were randomly assigned to the control trail. Thus, a total of 120 roaches were used in the experiment. The movement pattern of each cockroach was measured (in "pixels") as the average trail deviation. The data for the 120 cockroaches in the study are stored in the data file named **ROACH**. (The first 5 and last 5 observations in the data set are listed below.) Conduct a complete analysis of the data. Determine whether roaches can distinguish between the fecal extract and control trail and whether trail-following ability differs according to age, sex, and reproductive status.

ROACH

Trail Deviation	Roach Group	Trail
3.1	Adult Male	Extract
42.0	Adult Male	Control
6.2	Adult Male	Extract
22.7	Adult Male	Control
34.0	Adult Male	Extract
⋮	⋮	⋮
23.8	Nymph	Extract
5.1	Nymph	Extract
3.8	Nymph	Extract
3.1	Nymph	Extract
2.8	Nymph	Extract

Quick Review

Key Terms

Analysis of variance (ANOVA) 570
Balanced design 610
Blocks 591
Bonferroni multiple comparisons procedure 583
Comparisonwise error rate 583
Complete factorial experiment 607
Completely randomized design 563
Dependent variable 556
Designed experiment 558
Experimental unit 557
Experimentwise error rate 583
F-statistic 565

Factorial experiments 606
Factor interaction 608
Factor levels 557
Factor main effect 608
Factors 556
Independent variables 556
Mean square for error 565
Mean square for treatments 565
Multiple comparisons of means 583
Observational experiment 558
Qualitative factors 556
Quantitative factors 556
Randomized block design 591

Replicates of the experiment 610
Response variable 556
Robust method 572
Scheffè multiple comparisons procedure 584
Single-factor experiment 606
Sum of squares for blocks 592
Sum of squares for error 564
Sum of squares for treatments 564
Treatments 557
Tukey multiple comparisons procedure 583
Two-factor experiment 607

Key Formulas

Note: Computing formulas for sums of squares (SS) and mean squares (MS) in ANOVA are provided in Appendix C.

Completely randomized design:

$$F = \frac{\text{MST}}{\text{MSE}}$$

Testing treatments   567

$$c = \frac{k(k - 1)}{2}$$

Number of pairwise comparisons for k treatment means   583

Randomized Block Design

$F = \text{MST/MSE}$

Testing treatments   594

$F = \text{MSB/MSE}$

Testing blocks   594

Factorial design with 2 factors:

$$F = \frac{\text{MS}(A)}{\text{MSE}}$$

Testing main effect A 611

$$F = \frac{\text{MS}(B)}{\text{MSE}}$$

Testing main effect B 611

$$F = \frac{\text{MS}(B)}{\text{MSE}}$$

Testing $A \times B$ interaction   611

Chapter Summary Notes

- Key elements of a **designed experiment**: response variable (quantitative), factors (quantitative or qualitative), factor levels (values of each factor selected by the experimenter), treatments (combinations of factor-levels), experimental units.

- Characteristics of a **completely randomized design**: a single factor; levels of the factor are the treatments; independent random samples selected for each treatment, or, experimental units randomly assigned to a treatment.

- Characteristics of a **randomized block design**: a single factor and a set of matched experimental units (blocks); levels of the factor are the treatments; one experimental unit from each block is randomly assigned to each treatment.

- Characteristics of a **complete factorial design**: two factors; combinations of all possible factor-levels are the treatments; independent random samples selected for each treatment, or, experimental units randomly assigned to a treatment.

- A **balanced design** is one where the sample sizes for each treatment are equal.

- Conditions required for a valid **ANOVA *F*-test** in a completely randomized design: (1) All k treatment populations are approximately normal, (2) $\sigma_1^2 = \sigma_2^2 = \ldots = \sigma_k^2$.

- Conditions required for valid **ANOVA *F*-tests in a randomized block design**: (1) All treatment-block pop-

ulations are approximately normal, (2) all treatment-block populations have the same variance.

- Conditions required for valid **ANOVA *F*-tests in a factorial design**: (1) All treatment populations are approximately normal, (2) all treatment populations have the same variance.

- ANOVA is a **robust method**–slight to moderate departures from normality do not have an impact on the validity of the results.

- The **experimentwise error rate** is the risk of making at least one Type I error when making multiple comparisons in an ANOVA.

- **Multiple comparisons methods** for controlling the experimentwise error rate: Tukey, Bonferroni, and Scheffé.

- **Tukey's method** is appropriate when (1) the treatment sample sizes are equal and (2) pairwise comparisons of treatment means are desired.

- **Bonferroni's method** is appropriate when (1) the treatment sample sizes are equal or unequal and (2) pairwise comparisons of treatment means are desired.

- **Scheffé's method** is appropriate when (1) the treatment sample sizes are equal or unequal and (2) general contrasts involving treatment means are desired.

- **Tests for main effects** in a factorial design are only appropriate if the **test for interaction is nonsignificant**.

Language Lab

Symbol	Description
ANOVA	Analysis of variance
SST	Sum of Squares for Treatments (i.e., the variation among treatment means)
SSE	Sum of Squares for Error (i.e., the variability around the treatment means due to sampling error)
MST	Mean Square for Treatments
MSE	Mean Square for Error (an estimate of σ^2)
SSB	Sum of Squares for Blocks
MSB	Mean Square for Blocks
$a \times b$ factorial	Two-factor factorial experiment with one factor at a levels and the other at b levels (thus, there are $a \times b$ treatments in the experiment)
SS(A)	Sum of Squares for Factor A
MS(A)	Mean Square for Factor A
SS(B)	Sum of Squares for Factor B
MS(B)	Mean Square for Factor B
SS(AB)	Sum of Squares for $A \times B$ interaction
MS(AB)	Mean Square for $A \times B$ interaction

Supplementary Exercises 10.73–10.94

Learning the Mechanics

10.73 Explain the difference between an experiment that utilizes a completely randomized design and one that utilizes a randomized block design.

10.74 What are the treatments in a two-factor experiment, with factor A at three levels and factor B at two levels?

10.75 Why does the experimentwise error rate of a multiple comparisons procedure differ from the significance level for each comparison (assuming the experiment has more than two treatments)?

10.76 A completely randomized design is utilized to compare four treatment means. The data are shown in the table.

🖲 **LM10_76**

Treatment 1	Treatment 2	Treatment 3	Treatment 4
8	6	9	12
10	9	10	13
9	8	8	10
10	8	11	11
11	7	12	11

a. Given that SST = 36.95 and SS(Total) = 62.55, complete an ANOVA table for this experiment.

b. Is there evidence that the treatment means differ? Use $\alpha = .10$.   F = 7.70

c. Place a 90% confidence interval on the mean response for treatment 4.   11.4 ± .99

10.77 An experiment utilizing a randomized block design was conducted to compare the mean responses for four treatments. A, B, C, and D. The treatments were randomly assigned to the four experimental units in each of five blocks. The data are shown in the following table.

🖲 **EX10_77**

Treatment	Block				
	1	2	3	4	5
A	8.6	7.5	8.7	9.8	7.4
B	7.3	6.3	7.3	8.4	6.3
C	9.1	8.3	9.0	9.9	8.2
D	9.3	8.2	9.2	10.0	8.4

a. Given that SS(Total) = 22.31 and SS(Block) = 10.688 and SSE = .288, complete an ANOVA table for the experiment.

b. Do the data provide sufficient evidence to indicate a difference among treatment means? Test using $\alpha = .05$ $F = 157.42$

c. Does the result of the test in part b warrant further comparison of the treatment means? If so, how many pairwise comparisons need to be made? 6

d. Is there evidence that the block means differ? Use $\alpha = .05$. $F = 111.33$

10.78 The table shows a partially completed ANOVA table for a two-factor factorial experiment.

Source	df	SS	MS	F
A	3	2.6	—	—
B	5	9.2	—	—
$A \times B$	—	—	3.1	—
Error	—	18.7		
Total	47			

a. Complete the ANOVA table.

b. How many levels were used for each factor? How many treatments were used? How many replications were performed?

c. Find the value of the Sum of Squares for Treatments. Test to determine whether the data provide evidence that the treatment means differ. Use $\alpha = .05$. $F = 3.25$

d. Is further testing of the nature of factor effects warranted? If so, test to determine whether the factors interact. Use $\alpha = .05$. Interpret the result.

Applying the Concepts—Basic

10.79 The *Journal of Testing and Evaluation* (July 1992) published an investigation of the mean compression strength of corrugated fiberboard shipping containers. Comparisons were made for boxes of five different sizes: A, B, C, D, and E. Twenty identical boxes of each size were tested and the peak compression strength (pounds) recorded for each box. The next figure shows the sample means for the five box types as well as the variation around each sample mean.

a. Explain why the data is collected as a completely randomized design.

b. Refer to box types B and D. Based on the graph, does it appear that the mean compressive strengths of these two box types are significantly different? Explain.

c. Based on the graph, does it appear that the mean compressive strengths of all five box types are significantly different? Explain.

10.80 Marketing researchers generally agree that how you ask a question of consumers is as important as what you ask. An article in the *Journal of the Market Research Society* (July 1996) investigated the effects of positively versus negatively worded questions on consumer re-

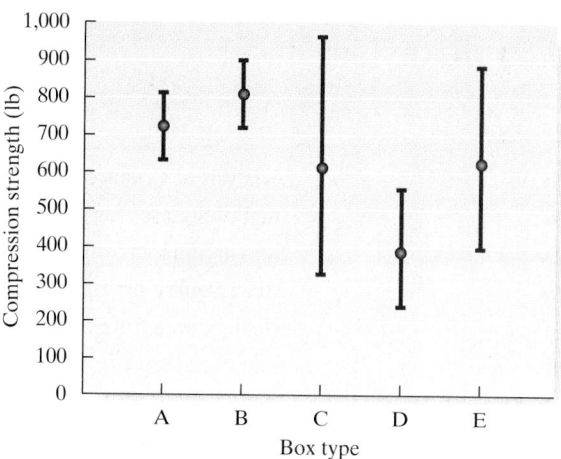

Source: Singh, S. P., et al. "Compression of Single-Wall Corrugated Shipping Containers Using Fixed and Floating Test Platens." *Journal of Testing and Evaluation,* Vol. 20, No. 4, July 1992, p. 319 (Figure 3). Copyright American Society for Testing and Materials. Reprinted with permission.

sponses. Consumers were asked to express their level of agreement with positively worded statements on a scale of 1 (strongly disagree) to 5 (strongly agree). The scale values were reversed for negatively worded questions. A total of 154 subjects from the Midwest were randomly assigned to four treatment conditions defined by the two levels of the variables Involvement in Topic (high and low) and Question Wording (positive/negative). Each subject was asked to respond to a question (positively worded for one group and negatively worded for the other group). The five-point scales described above were used. Those in the high-involvement condition received a question about the Gulf War; those in the low-involvement condition received a general question about shopping and products. The resulting data were analyzed using ANOVA.

a. What type of experimental design was used by the researcher? 2×2 Factorial

b. Identify the factors used in the experiment. Are they quantitative or qualitative? Both QL

c. Describe the levels of each factor.

d. Describe the experiment's treatments.

e. What is the experiment's dependent variable?

10.81 The Fortune E-50 is a listing of the top 50 electronic commerce and Internet-based companies, as determined by *Fortune* magazine each year. *Fortune* groups the companies into four categories: (1) e-companies, (2) Internet software and service, (3) Internet hardware, and (4) Internet communication. Consider a study to compare the mean rates of return for the stock of companies in the four *Fortune* categories. Since the age of an electronic commerce or Internet-based company may have an impact on rate of return, the study is designed to remove any age variation.

Four 1-year-old companies, four 3-year-old companies, and four 5-year-old companies were selected; within each age group, one company was randomly selected from Category 1, one from Category 2, one from Category 3, and one from Category 4.

a. What type of experimental design is employed?

b. Indentify the key elements of the experiment (i.e., treatments, blocks, response variable, and experimental unit).

10.82 The *Journal of Hazardous Materials* (July 1995) published the results of a study of the chemical properties of three different types of hazardous organic solvents used to clean metal parts: aromatics, chloroalkanes, and esters. One variable studied was sorption rate, measured as mole percentage. Independent samples of solvents from each type were tested and their sorption rates were recorded, as shown in the table below. An SPSS analysis of variance of the data is shown in the printout at the bottom of the page.

a. Is there evidence of differences among the mean sorption rates of the three organic solvent types? Test using $\alpha = .10$. $F = 24.512$

b. List the assumptions required for the analysis, part **a**, to be valid.

c. Check the assumptions, part **b**. Do they appear to be reasonably satisfied?

d. Conduct multiple comparisons on the data using $\alpha =$ Interpret the results.

⚙ **HAZARDS**

Aromatics		Chloroalkanes		Esters		
1.06	.95	1.58	1.12	.29	.43	.06
.79	.65	1.45	.91	.06	.51	.09
.82	1.15	.57	.83	.44	.10	.17
.89	1.12	1.16	.43	.61	.34	.60
1.05				.55	.53	.17

Source: Reprinted from *Journal of Hazardous Materials*, Vol. 42, No. 2, J. D. Ortego et al., "A Review of Polymeric Geosynthetics Used in Hazardous Waste Facilities," p. 142 (Table 9), July 1995, Elsevier Science-NL, Sara Burgerhartstraat 25, 1055 KV Amsterdam, The Netherlands.

10.83 Leadership acts occur when one person tries to influence the behavior of others toward the attainment of some goal. The effects of leadership style on the behavior of subordinates were investigated in *Accounting, Organizations and Society* (Vol. 20, 1995). Four types of leadership style were defined based on two variables: the degree of control applied (high or low) and the level of consideration shown for subordinates (high or low). A sample of 257 senior auditors in Big-Six accounting firms yielded the following distribution of leadership styles for the auditors' leaders:

Leadership Style	n
A. High control, Low consideration	51
B. Low control, Low consideration	63
C. High control, High consideration	79
D. Low control, High consideration	64
Total	257

All subjects were asked to indicate (confidentially) how frequently their auditing fieldwork had been intentionally substandard in a particular way. They were asked to respond using a scale that ranged from 1 (never) to 5 (always). These data are summarized in the following table. An ANOVA was conducted to test for differences in the four treatment means. It yielded $F = 30.4$.

Leadership Style	Mean	Standard Deviaion	Bonferroni Analysis: Significantly Smaller Means
A	4.27	1.13	B, C, D
B	2.83	1.18	D
C	2.54	1.24	None
D	2.87	1.31	None
Overall	2.87	1.42	

Source: Otley, D. T., and Pierce, B. J. "The Control Problem in Public Accounting Firms: An Empirical Study of the Impact of Leadership Style." *Accounting Organizations and Society.* Vol. 20, No. 5, 1995, pp. 405-420.

a. Do the data indicate that leadership style affects the behavior of subordinates? Test using $\alpha = .05$.

b. The Bonferroni multiple comparisons procedure was used to rank the four treatment means at an experimentwise error rate of $\alpha = .05$. Carefully interpret the results shown in the table.

c. What assumptions must hold to ensure the validity of the Bonferroni procedure?

SPSS Output for Exercise 10.82

ANOVA

SORPRATE

	Sum of Squares	df	Mean Square	F	Sig.
Between Groups	3.305	2	1.653	24.512	.000
Within Groups	1.955	29	.067		
Total	5.261	31			

Applying the Concepts-Intermediate

10.84 A direct-mail company assembles and stores paper products (envelopes, letters, brochures, order cards, etc.) for its customers. The company estimates the total number of pieces received in a shipment by estimating the weight per piece and then weighing the entire shipment. The company is unsure whether the sample of pieces used to estimate the mean weight per piece should be drawn from a single carton, or whether it is worth the extra time required to pull a few pieces from several cartons. To aid management in making a decision, eight brochures were pulled from each of five cartons of a typical shipment and weighed. The weights (in pounds) are shown in the table.

CARTONS

Carton 1	Carton 2	Carton 3	Carton 4	Carton 5
.01851	.01872	.01869	.01899	.01882
.01829	.01861	.01853	.01917	.01895
.01844	.01876	.01876	.01852	.01884
.01859	.01886	.01880	.01904	.01835
.01854	.01896	.01880	.01923	.01889
.01853	.01879	.01882	.01905	.01876
.01844	.01879	.01862	.01924	.01891
.01833	.01879	.01860	.01893	.01879

a. Identify the response, factor(s), treatments, and experimental units.
b. Do these data provide sufficient evidence to indicate differences in the mean weight per brochure among the five cartons? *F* = 13.37
c. What assumptions must be satisfied in order for the test of part b to be valid?
d. Use Bonferroni multiple comparisons to compare all pairs of means, with $\alpha = .05$ as the overall level of significance.
e. Given the results, make a recommendation to management about whether to sample from one carton or from many cartons.

10.85 Traditionally, people protect themselves from mosquito bites by applying insect repellent to their skin and clothing. Recent research suggests that permethrin, an insecticide with low toxicity to humans, can provide protection from mosquitoes. A study in the Journal of the American Mosquito Control Association (Mar. 1995) investigated whether a tent sprayed with a commercially available 1% permethrin formulation would protect people, both inside and outside the tent, against biting mosquitoes. Two canvas tents-one treated with permethrin, the other untreated-were positioned 25 meters apart on flat dry ground in an area infested with mosquitoes. Eight people participated in the experiment, with four randomly assigned to each tent. Of the four stationed at each tent, two were randomly assigned to stay inside the tent (at opposite corners) and two to stay outside the tent (at opposite corners). During a specified 20-minute period during the night, each person kept count of the number of mosquito bites received. The goal of the study was to determine the effect of both Tent type (treated or untreated) and Location (inside or outside the tent) on the mean mosquito bite count.

a. What type of design was employed in the study?
b. Identify the factors and treatments.
c. Identify the response variable.
d. The study found statistical evidence of interaction between Tent type and Location. Give a practical interpretation of this result.

10.86 Three anticoagulant drugs are studied to compare their effectiveness in dissolving blood clots. Each of five subjects receives the drugs at equally spaced time intervals and in random order. Time periods between drug applications permit a drug to be passed out of a subject's body before the subject receives the next drug. After each drug is in the bloodstream, the length of time (in seconds) required for a cut of specified size to stop bleeding is recorded. The results are shown in the following table.

CLOTS

Person	Drug A	Drug B	Drug C
1	127.5	129.0	135.5
2	130.6	129.1	138.0
3	118.3	111.7	110.1
4	155.5	144.3	162.3
5	180.7	174.4	181.8

a. What type of experimental design was used in this study? Identify the response, factor(s), factor type(s), treatments, and experimental units.
b. Is there evidence of a difference in mean clotting time among the three drugs? Test using $\alpha = .10$.
c. What is the observed significance level of the test you conducted in part **a**? Interpret it. *p* = .066
d. Was blocking effective in reducing the variation among the data? That is, do the data support the contention that the mean clotting time varies from person to person? *F* = 95.51
e. If warranted, use a multiple comparisons technique to determine whether one of the drugs is most effective. Use an overall significance level of $\alpha = .10$.

10.87 The Minnesota Multiphasic Personality Inventory (MMPI) is a questionnaire used to gauge personality type. *Psychological Assessment* (Mar. 1995) published a study that investigated the effectiveness of the MMPI scales in detecting deliberately distorted responses. A completely randomized design with four treatments was employed. The treatments consisted of independent random samples of females in the following four groups: nonforensic psychiatric patients ($n_1 = 65$), forensic psychiatric patients ($n_2 = 28$), college students who were requested to respond honestly ($n_3 = 140$), and college students who were instructed to provide "fake bad" responses ($n_4 = 45$). All 278 participants were given the MMPI and the scores on several scales designed to assess response distortion were recorded for each. Each scale was treated as a response variable, and an analysis of variance was conducted. The ANOVA F-values are reported in the following table.

Response (Scale) Variable	ANOVA F-Value
Infrequency	155.8
Obvious	49.7
Subtle	10.3
Obvious-subtle	45.4
Dissimulation	39.1

a. For each response variable, determine whether the mean scores of the four groups completing the MMPI differ significantly. Use $\alpha = .05$ for each test.

b. If the MMPI is effective in detecting distorted responses, then the mean score for the "fake bad" treatment group will be largest. Based on the multiple comparisons provided below, can the researchers make an inference about the effectiveness of the MMPI? Explain.

10.88 Louisiana State University professor D. C. Kim investigated the effects of accountants' attitudes toward risk and recent budget-setting performance (relative to their colleagues) on their current budgetary decisions (*Accounting Review,* Apr. 1992). Eighty-one undergraduate students were used as subjects in the study. Using standard risk measurement methods, 40 subjects were found to be risk-seeking and 41 were risk-averse. Subjects were asked to play the role of an entry-level accountant in a public accounting firm. Each was asked to read a hypothetical audit engagement case. Each subject had either a case in which his or her recent performance at budgeting audit costs

(billable hours) was either favorable or unfavorable relative to colleagues. After reading the case, each subject was asked to establish either a tight (risky) budget or a safe (riskless) budget and to indicate the strength of his or her preference for the budget. Subjects responded on an 11-point scale that varied from -5 (strong preference for a risky choice) to $+5$ (strong preference for a riskless choice). From these data, Kim generated the following partial ANOVA table:

Source	df	SS	MS	F
Recent performance (A)	1	243.2	___	___
Risk assessment (B)	1	57.8	___	___
AB	1	___	___	___
Error	77	670.8	___	
Total	80	976.3		

Source: Kim, D. C. "Risk Preferences in Participative Budgeting." *Accounting Review,* Vol. 67, Apr. 1992, pp. 303-318.

a. Complete the ANOVA table.

b. Do the data indicate that factors A and B interact? Test using $\alpha = .05$. $F = .52$

c. Does an individual's risk attitude affect his or her budgetary decisions? Test using $\alpha = .05$. $F = 6.63$

d. Does recent budgeting performance affect current budgeting decisions? Test using $\alpha = .01$. $F = 27.92$

10.89 *Quality Engineering* (Vol. 6, 1994) reported the results of an experiment that was designed to find ways to improve the output of an industrial lathe. The lathe is controlled by a computer that automatically feeds bar stock, cuts the stock, machines the surface finish, and releases the part. As it is machined, the bar stock spins and is held in place by a collet. The lathe operator sets the feed (the rate at which bars are machined) and the speed (spin rate). The product characteristic of interest is surface finish. It is measured on a gauge that records the vertical distance a probe travels as it moves along a given horizontal distance on the bar. The rougher the surface, the higher the

Multiple Comparisons for Exercise 10.87

Response Variable					
Infrequency (F)	Mean	7.1	11.3	14.6	33.6
	Group	CSH	NFP	FP	CSFB
Obvious (O)	Mean	240.9	270.7	287.5	341.9
	Group	CSH	FP	NFP	CSFB
Subtle (S)	Mean	231.4	244.1	244.5	259.7
	Group	CSFB	CSH	FP	NFP
Obvious-subtle (O-S)	Mean	51.3	88.2	93.4	198.8
	Group	CSH	NFP	FP	CSFB
Dissimulation (D)	Mean	12.0	12.1	20.8	21.0
	Group	FP	NFP	CSH	CSFB

Source: Bagby, R. M., Burs, T., and Nicholson, R. A. "Relative Effectiveness of the Standard Validity Scales in Detecting Fake-Bad and Fake-Good Responding: Replication and Extension." *Psychological Assessment,* Vol. 7, No. 1, Mar. 1995, p. 86 (Table 1).

gauge measurement. The factors that were manipulated in the experiment were speed, feed, collet tightness, and tool wear. The following table reports the factor-level settings and the resulting surface-finish measurements (H = High; L = Low).

LATHE

Speed	Feed	Collet Tightness	Surface Tool Wear	Finish
H	H	H	H	216
L	H	H	H	212
H	L	H	H	48
L	L	H	H	40
H	H	L	H	232
L	H	L	H	248
H	L	L	H	514
L	L	L	H	298
H	H	H	L	238
L	H	H	L	219
H	L	H	L	40
L	L	H	L	33
H	H	L	L	230
L	H	L	L	253
H	L	L	L	273
L	L	L	L	101
H	H	H	H	217
L	H	H	H	221
H	L	H	H	39
L	L	H	H	31
H	H	L	H	235
L	H	L	H	238
H	L	L	H	437
L	L	L	H	87
H	H	H	L	245
L	H	H	L	226
H	L	H	L	51
L	L	H	L	33
H	H	L	L	226
L	H	L	L	214
H	L	L	L	691
L	L	L	L	130

Source: Collins, W. H., and Colins, C. B. "Including Residual Analysis in Designed Experiments: Case Studies." *Quality Engineering,* Vol. 6, No. 4, 1994, pp. 547–565.

a. What type of experimental design was used?
b. How many different treatments were applied?
c. Perform an analysis of variance for these data.
d. Do significant interaction effects exist? Test using $\alpha = .05$. Interpret your results.
e. Is it necessary to perform main effect tests? Why or why not? If so, perform the tests using $\alpha = .05$.
f. What assumptions must hold to ensure the validity of your results in parts **c, d,** and **e?**

10.90 Ducks inhabiting the Great Salt Lake marshes feed on a variety of animals, including water boatmen, brine shrimp, beetles, and snails. The changes in the availability of these animal species for ducks during the summer was investigated (Wetlands, March 1995). The goal was to compare the mean amount (measured as biomass) of a particular duck food species across four different summer time periods: (1) July 9-23, (2) July 24-Aug. 8, (3) Aug. 9-23, and (4) Aug. 24-31. Ten stations in the marshes were randomly selected, and the biomass density in a water specimen collected from each was measured. Biomass measurements (milligrams per square meter) were collected during each of the four summer time periods at each station, with stations treated as a blocking factor. Thus, the data were analyzed as a randomized block design.

a. Fill in the missing degrees of freedom in the randomized block ANOVA table shown here.

Source	df	F	p-value
Time Period	–	11.25	.0001
Station	–	–	–
Error	–		
Total	39		

b. The F value (and corresponding p-value) shown in the ANOVA table, part **a,** were computed from an analysis of biomass of water boatmen nymphs (a common duck food). Interpret these results.
c. A multiple comparisons of time period means was conducted using an experimentwise error rate of .05. The results are summarized below. Identify the time period(s) with the largest and smallest mean biomass.

Mean biomass (mg/m^2):	19	54.5	90	148
Time period:	8/24–8/31	8/9–8/23	7/24–8/8	7/9–7/23

10.91 A study in the Journal of Psychology and Marketing (Jan. 1992) investigated consumer attitudes toward product tampering. One variable considered was the education level of the consumer. Consumers were divided into five educational classifications and asked to rate their concern about product tampering on a scale of 1 (little or no concern) to 9 (very concerned). The table gives the education levels and the means.

Education Level	Mean	Sample Size
Non-high school graduate	3.731	26
High school graduate	3.224	49
Some college completed	3.330	94
College graduate	3.167	60
Some postgraduate work	4.341	86

a. Identify the type of ANOVA design used in this experiment. Identify the treatments in this experiment.
b. The article compared the mean concern ratings for the five education levels. The F-statistic for this test

was reported to be 3.298. Conduct a test of hypothesis to determine whether the mean concern ratings differ for at least two of the education levels. [*Hint:* Calculate the degrees of freedom for Treatments and Error from the information given.]
Reject H_0

   c. Using $\alpha = .05$, a Bonferroni analysis yielded the result shown at the bottom of the page. Interpret the result.

10.92 A composite of a metal powder mixed with a plastic resin was invented to stop a radiation beam used for skin or oral cancer therapy. A 2×2 factorial experiment with two replications was conducted in a dental research lab to measure the degree of radiation traveling through the composite when the density of the metal powder was either a heavy alloy or a light alloy and when a second layer of plastic under the composite was present or absent. The next table shows the data collected. Use the techniques presented in this chapter to analyze these data, and make a recommendation regarding the preferred method of protecting patients from overexposure to potentially harmful radiation.

   RADIAT

		Alloy Density	
		Heavy	Light
Second Plastic	**Present**	0.04, 0.02	0.46, 0.40
	Absent	0.38, 0.13	1.84, 2.29

Source: Personal Communication from F. Eichmiller, Paffenbarger Research Center, Gaithersburg, MD.

10.93 Sixteen workers were randomly selected to participate in an experiment to determine the effects of work scheduling and method of payment on attitude toward the job. Two schedules were employed, the standard 8-5 workday and a modification whereby the worker could decide each day whether to start at 7 or 8 A.M.; in addition, the worker could choose between a half-hour or one-hour lunch period each day. The two methods of payment were a standard hourly rate and a reduced hourly rate with an added piece rate based on the worker's production. Four workers were randomly assigned to each of the four scheduling-payment combinations, and each completed an attitude test after one month on the job. The test scores are shown in the accompanying table.

   JOBATT

		Payment	
		Hourly Rate	Hourly and Piece Rate
Scheduling	**8–5**	54, 68, 55, 63	89, 75, 71, 83
	Worker-Modified Schedule	79, 65, 62, 74	83, 94, 91, 86

   a. What type of experiment was performed? Identify the response, factor(s), factor type(s), treatments, and experimental units.

   b. Is there evidence that the treatment means differ? Use $\alpha = .05$. $F = 12.29$

   c. If the test in part b warrants further analysis, conduct the appropriate tests of interaction and main effects. Interpret your results.

   d. What assumptions are necessary to ensure the validity of the inferences? State the assumptions in terms of this experiment.

10.94 Factorial designs are commonly employed in marketing research to evaluate the effectiveness of sales strategies. At one supermarket, two of the factors were Price level (regular, reduced price, cost to supermarket) and Display level (normal display space, normal display space plus end-of-aisle display, twice the normal display space). A 3×3 complete factorial design was employed, where each treatment was applied three times to a particular product at a particular supermarket. The dependent variable of interest was unit sales for the week. (To minimize treatment carryover effects, each treatment was preceded and followed by a week in which the product was priced at its regular price and was displayed in its normal manner.) The table on p. 632 reports the data collected.

   a. How many treatments are considered in this study?

   b. Do the data indicate that the mean sales differ among the treatments? Test using $\alpha = .10$.

   c. Is the test of interaction between the factors Price and Display warranted as a result of the test in part b? If so, conduct the test using $\alpha = .10$.

   d. Are the tests of the main effects for Price and Display warranted as a result of the previous tests? If so, conduct them using $\alpha = .10$.   No

   e. Which pairs of treatment means should be compared as a result of the tests in parts **b–d**?

Mean	3.167	3.224	3.330	3.731	4.3441
Education Level	College Graduate	High school graduate	Some college	Non-high school graduate	Postgraduate

⊘ **SUPERMKT**

		Price		
		Regular	Reduced	Cost to Supermarket
	Normal	989	1,211	1,577
		1,025	1,215	1,559
		1,030	1,182	1,598
Display	**Normal Plus**	1,191	1,860	2,492
		1,233	1,910	2,527
		1,221	1,926	2,511
	Twice Normal	1,226	1,516	1,801
		1,202	1,501	1,833
		1,180	1,498	1,852

REFERENCES

Cochran, W. G., and Cox, G. M. *Experimental Designs,* 2nd ed. New York: Wiley, 1957.

Hsu, J. C. *Multiple Comparisons: Theory and Methods.* London: Chapman & Hall, 1996.

Kramer, C. Y. "Extension of Multiple Range Tests to Group Means with unequal Number of Replications." *Biometrics,* Vol. 12, 1956, pp. 307-310.

Mason, R. L., Gunst, R. F., and Hess, J. L. *Statistical Design and Analysis of Experiments.* New York: Wiley, 1989.

Mendenhall, W. *Introduction to Linear Models and the Design and Analysis of Experiments.* Belmont, Calif.: Wadsworth, 1968.

Miller, R. G., Jr. *Simultaneous Statistical Inference.* New York: Springer-Verlag, 1981.

Neter, J., Kutner, M., Nachtsheim, C., and Wasserman, W. *Applied Linear Statistical Models,* 4th ed. Homewood, Ill.: Richard D. Irwin, 1996.

Scheffe, H. "A Method for Judging All Contrasts in the Analysis of Variance," *Biometrica,* Vol. 40, 1953, pp. 87-104.

Scheffé, H. *The Analysis of Variance.* New York: Wiley, 1959.

Snedecor, G. W., and Cochran, W. G. *Statistical Methods,* 7th ed. Ames: Iowa State University Press, 1980.

Steele, R. G. D., and Torrie, J. H. *Principles and Procedures of Statistics: A Biometrical Approach,* 2nd ed. New York: McGraw-Hill, 1980.

Tukey, J. "Comparing Individual Means in the Analysis of Variance," *Biometrics,* Vol. 5, 1949, pp. 99-114.

Winer, B. J. *Statistical Principles in Experimental Design,* 2nd ed. New York: McGraw-Hill, 1971.

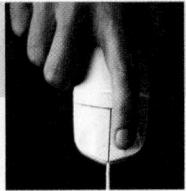

Using Technology

10.1 Analysis of Variance Using SPSS

SPSS can conduct ANOVAs for all three types of experimental designs discussed in this chapter: completely randomized, randomized block, and factorial designs.

Completely Randomized Design

To conduct a completely randomized design ANOVA, first access the SPSS spreadsheet file that contains the sample data. The data file should contain one quantitative variable (the response, or dependent, variable) and one factor variable with at least two levels. (These values must be numbers, e.g., 1, 2, 3, etc.) Next, click on the "Analyze" button on the SPSS menu bar, then click on "Compare Means" and "One-Way ANOVA", as shown in Figure 10.S.1.

The resulting dialog box appears as shown in Figure 10.S.2. Specify the response variable in the "Dependent List" box and the factor variable in the "Factor" box. Click the "Post Hoc" button, and select a multiple comparisons method and experimentwise error rate in the resulting dialog box (see Figure 10.S.3). Then click "Continue" to return to the "One-Way ANOVA" dialog screen. Click "OK" to generate the SPSS printout.

Figure 10.S.1
SPSS menu options for one-way ANOVA

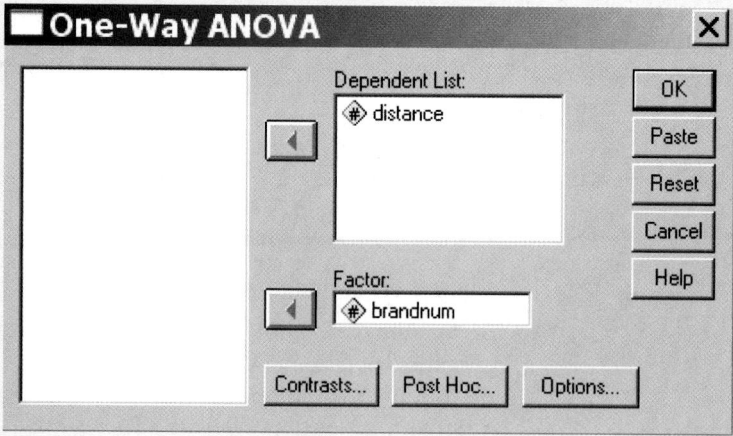

Figure 10.S.2
SPSS one-way ANOVA dialog box

Figure 10.S.3
SPSS multiple comparisons dialog box

Randomized Block and Factorial Designs

To conduct either a randomized block or factorial design ANOVA, first access the SPSS spreadsheet file that contains the sample data. The data file should contain one quantitative variable (the response, or dependent, variable) and at least two other variables that represent the factors and/or blocks. Next, click on the "Analyze" button on the SPSS menu bar, then click on "General Linear Model" and "Univariate", as shown in Figure 10.S.4

The resulting dialog box appears as shown in Figure 10.S.5. Specify the response variable in the "Dependent Variable" box and the factor variable(s) and block variable in the "Fixed Factor(s)" box. Click the "Post Hoc" button, and select the factor variable of interest, a multiple comparisons method, and

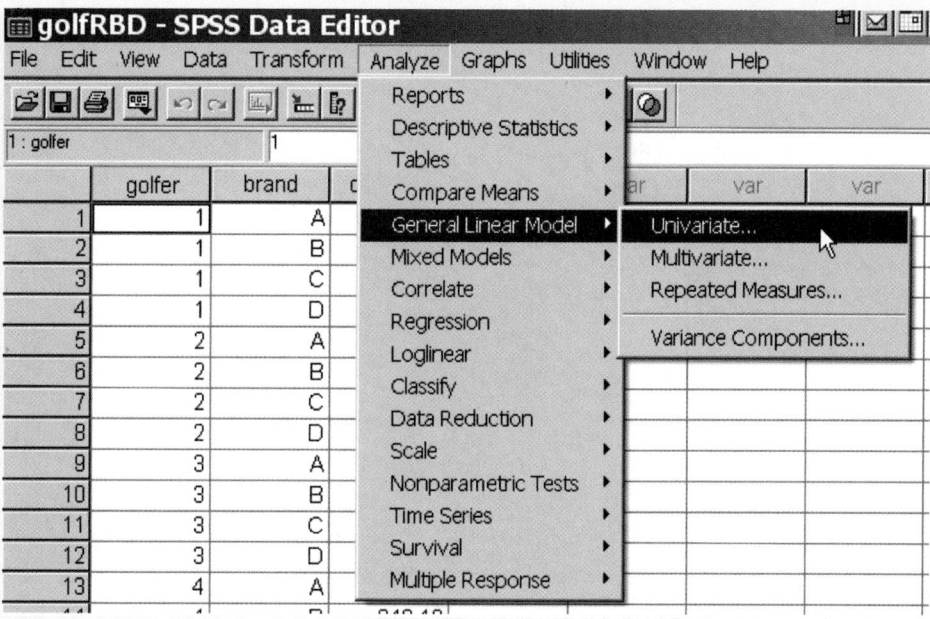

Figure 10.S.4
SPSS menu options for two-way ANOVA

Figure 10.S.5
SPSS two-way ANOVA
dialog box

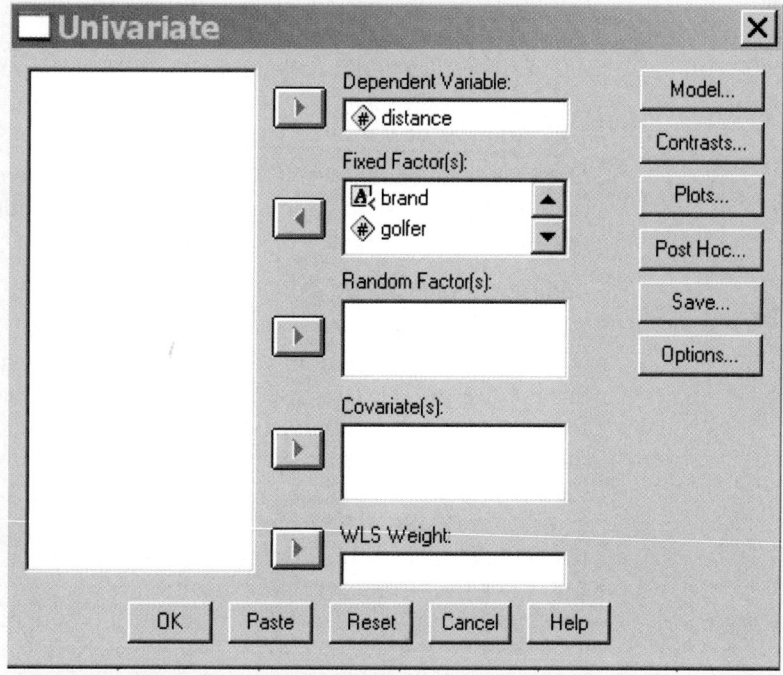

experimentwise error rate in the resulting dialog box (similar to Figure 10.S.3). Then click "Continue" to return to the "Two-Way ANOVA" dialog screen. Now click the "Model" button to specify the type of experimental design (randomized block or factorial) on the resulting menu-screen as shown in Figure 10.S.6. For factorial designs, select the "Full Factorial" option; for randomized block designs, se-

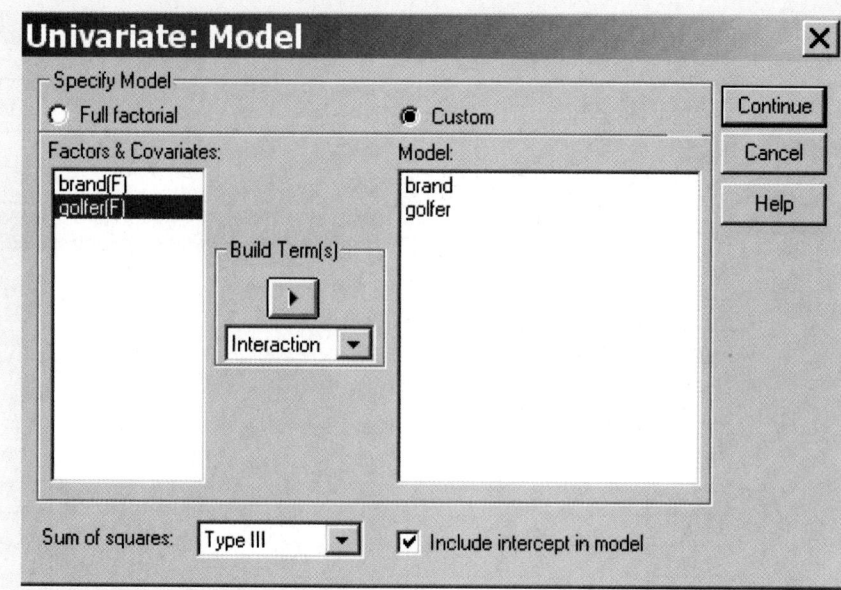

Figure 10.S.6
SPSS design (model) specification box

lect the "Custom" option, and specify the treatment and blocking factors in the "Model" box. Click "Continue" to return to the "Two-Way ANOVA" dialog screen, then click "OK" to generate the SPSS printout.

10.2 Analysis of Variance Using MINITAB

MINITAB can conduct ANOVAs for all three types of experimental designs discussed in this chapter: completely randomized, randomized block, and factorial designs.

Completely Randomized Design

To conduct a completely randomized design ANOVA, first access the MINITAB worksheet file that contains the sample data. The data file should contain one quantitative variable (the response, or dependent, variable) and one qualitative factor variable with at least two levels. Next, click on the "Stat" button on the MINITAB menu bar, then click on "ANOVA" and "One-Way", as shown in Figure 10.M.1.

The resulting dialog box appears as shown in Figure 10.M.2. Specify the response variable in the "Response" box and the factor variable in the "Factor" box. Click the "Comparisons" button, and select a multiple comparisons method and experimentwise error rate in the resulting dialog box (see Figure 10.M.3). Then click "OK" to return to the "One-Way ANOVA" dialog screen. Click "OK" to generate the MINITAB printout.

Randomized Block and Factorial Designs

To conduct either a randomized block or factorial design ANOVA, first access the SPSS spreadsheet file that contains the sample data. The data file should contain one quantitative variable (the response, or dependent, variable) and two other variables that represent the factors and/or blocks. Next, click on the "Stat" button

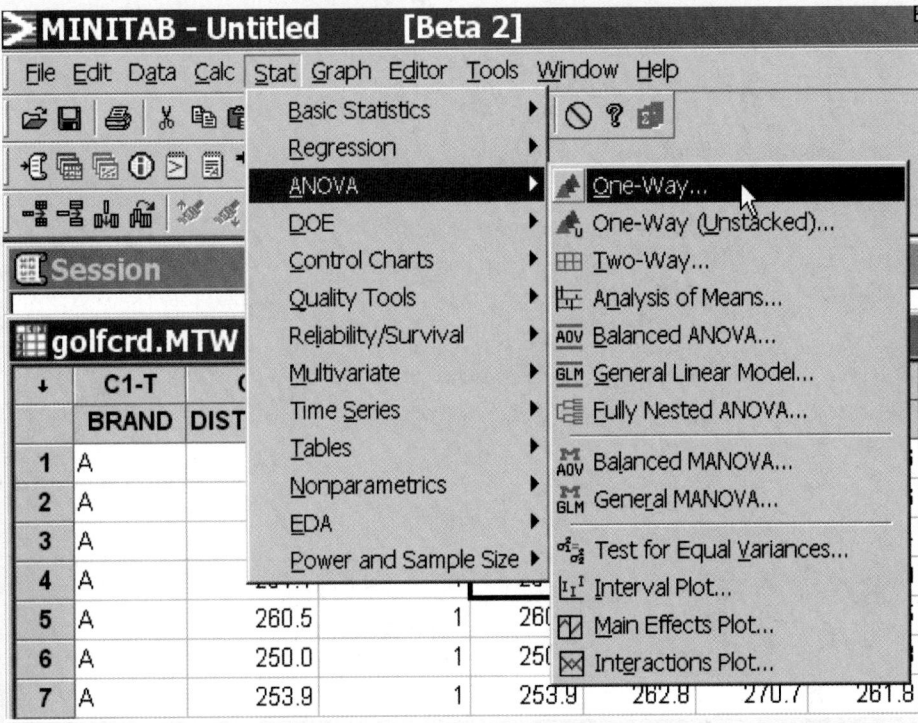

Figure 10.M.1
MINITAB menu options for one-way ANOVA

Figure 10.M.2
MINITAB one-way
ANOVA dialog box

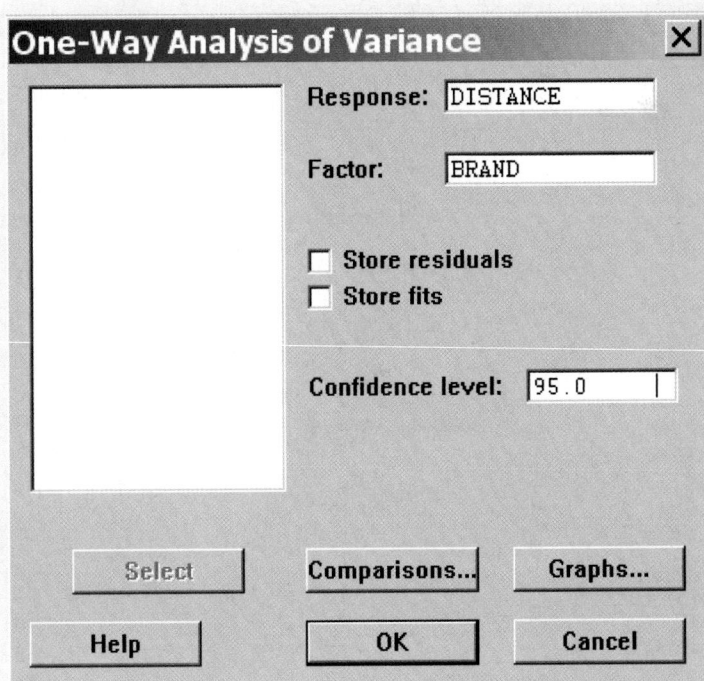

Figure 10.M.3
MINITAB multiple
comparisons dialog box

on the MINITAB menu bar, then click on "ANOVA" and "Two-Way" (see Figure 10.M.1). The resulting dialog box appears as shown in Figure 10.M.4.

Specify the response variable in the "Response" box, the first factor variable in the "Row factor" box, and the second factor or block variable in the "Column factor" box. If the design is a randomized block, select the "Fit additive model"

Figure 10.M.4
MINITAB two-way ANOVA dialog box

option as shown in Figure 10.M.4. If the design is factorial, leave the "Fit additive model" option unselected. Click "OK" to generate the MINITAB printout.

[*Note*: Multiple comparisons of treatment means are unavailable in MINITAB for randomized block and factorial designs.]

10.3 Analysis of Variance Using EXCEL and PHSTAT2

EXCEL can conduct ANOVAs for all three types of experimental designs discussed in this chapter: completely randomized, randomized block, and factorial designs.

Completely Randomized Design

To conduct a completely randomized design ANOVA, first access the EXCEL workbook file that contains the sample data. The file should contain k columns of data for the quantitative (response) variable, one for each of the k treatments. Next, click on the "Tools" button on the EXCEL main menu bar, then click on "Data Analysis", as shown in Figure 10.E.1.

Select "Anova: Single Factor" from the Data Analysis menu as shown in Figure 10.E.2 and click "OK". The resulting dialog box appears as shown in Figure 10.E.3.

Specify the "Input Range" of your data, select the "Grouped By: Columns" option, the value of α, and, if the workbook contains labels, select "Labels in first row", as shown in Figure 10.E.3. Click "OK" to generate the EXCEL printout.

[*Note*: Tukey's multiple comparisons method is available in EXCEL with the PHStat add-in *if you have access to a table of critical values of the Studentized range*. Click on the "PHStat" button on the EXCEL main menu bar, then click on "Multiple-Sample Tests" and "Tukey-Kramer Procedure". Enter the "Group Data

Figure 10.E.1
EXCEL main menu options for data analysis

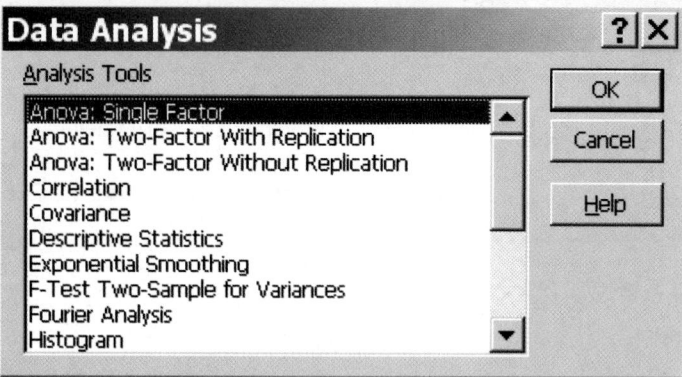

Figure 10.E.2
EXCEL data analysis menu option for one-way ANOVA

Figure 10.E.3
EXCEL single factor ANOVA dialog box

Cell Range" and click "OK". PHStat will request that you fill in the critical value of the Studentized range (called the Q-statistic). Enter this value and press "Enter" to view the results.]

Randomized Block Design

To conduct a randomized block design ANOVA, first access the EXCEL workbook file that contains the sample data. The file should contain k columns of data for the quantitative (response) variable, one for each of the k treatments, and b rows, one for each of the b blocks. Next, click on the "Tools" button on the EXCEL main menu bar, then click on "Data Analysis" (see Figure 10.E.1). Select "Anova: Two Factor Without Replication" from the Data Analysis menu (see Figure 10.E.2) and click "OK". The resulting dialog box appears as shown in Figure 10.E.4.

Specify the "Input Range" of your data, the value of α, and, if the workbook contains labels, select "Labels", as shown in Figure 10.E.4. Click "OK" to generate the EXCEL printout.

Figure 10.E.4
EXCEL two factor without replication ANOVA dialog box

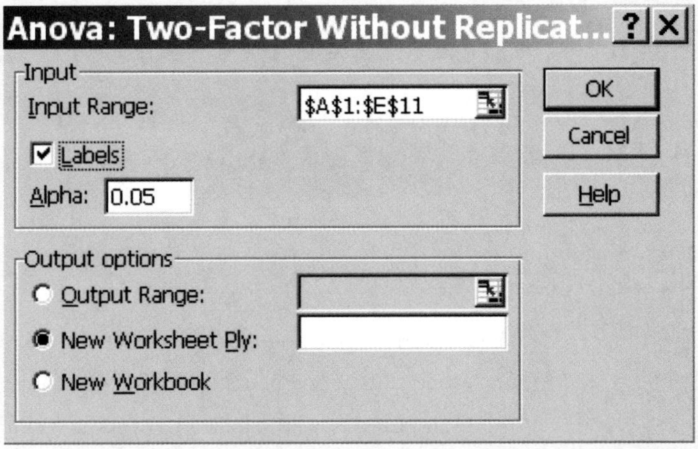

[*Note*: Multiple comparisons of treatment means are unavailable in EXCEL for a randomized block design.]

Factorial Design

To conduct a two-factor factorial design ANOVA, first access the EXCEL workbook file that contains the sample data. The file should contain a columns of data for the quantitative (response) variable, one for each of the a levels of Factor A, and bxr rows, where b is the number of levels of Factor B and r is the number of replicates. [Note: Place all the data for one level of Factor B in consecutive rows, followed by all the data for the next level of B, etc.] Next, click on the "Tools" button on the EXCEL main menu bar, then click on "Data Analysis" (see Figure 10.E.1). Select "Anova: Two Factor with Replication" from the Data Analysis menu (see Figure 10.E.2) and click "OK". The resulting dialog box appears as shown in Figure 10.E.5.

Specify the "Input Range" of your data, the number of "Rows per sample" (this is the number of replicates), and the value of α, as shown in Figure 10.E.5. Click "OK" to generate the EXCEL printout.

[*Note*: Multiple comparisons of treatment means are unavailable in EXCEL for a factorial block design.]

Figure 10.E.5
EXCEL two factor with replication ANOVA dialog box

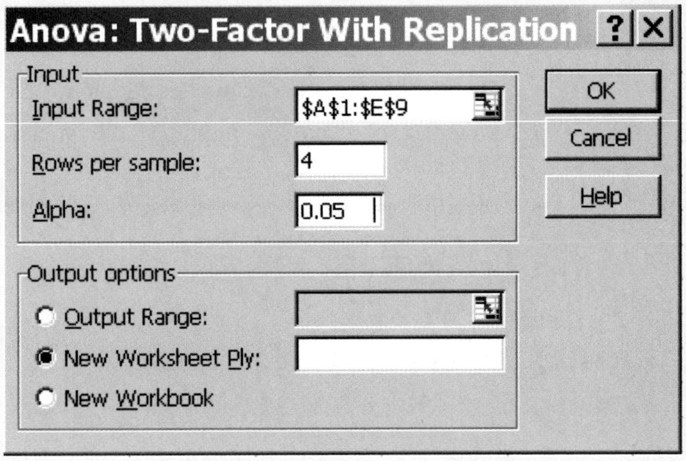

Categorical Data Analysis

Contents

Statistics in Action

A study of Coupon Users—Mail versus the Internet

Using Technology

Where We've Been

- Presented methods for making inferences about the population proportion associated with a two-level qualitative variable (i.e., a binomial variable)
- Presented methods for making inferences about the difference between two binomial proportions

Where We're Going

- Discuss qualitative (i.e., categorical) data with more than two outcomes.
- Present a *chi-square* hypothesis test for comparing the category proportions associated with a single qualitative variable—called a *one-way analysis*.
- Present a *chi-square* hypothesis test for relating two qualitative variables—called a *two-way analysis*.

Statistics in
ACTION

A Study of Coupon Users—Mail versus the Internet

The service encounter is the critical interaction between a customer and the firm. In this encounter, the firm attempts to sell its services, to reinforce its offerings, and to satisfy the customer. A hot topic in marketing research is the exploration of a technology-based self-service (TBSS) encounter, where various technologies allow the customer to perform all or part of the service encounter. Examples of TBSS systems include ATMs, automated hotel checkout, banking by phone, self-scanning at retail stores, and transactions via the Internet such as Federal Express's package tracking and Charles Schwab's online brokerage services.

Marketing professor Dan Ladik (University of Suffolk) investigated a customer's motivation to use a TBSS and compared two customer segments—one that does not require any electronic technology use for service delivery and another that relies on the Internet for service delivery. The self-service delivery system studied was one that distributes discount coupons via both the mail and the Internet. Ladik investigated whether there were differences in customer characteristics and customer satisfaction between the mail (nontechnology) coupon users and the Internet (TBSS) coupon users.

The data for the study were obtained from a national services firm that specializes in discount coupons. (For reasons of confidentiality, the firm is not named.) Both customers who use the nontechnology mail delivery method and customers who use the firm's Internet Web site to access the coupons were sampled. For this Statistics in Action problem, we will focus on a subset of the full data set—a sample of 440 coupon users. Using a questionnaire, several qualitative variables were measured for each user. These are listed in Table SIA11.1. The data are saved in the **COUPONS** file.

In an attempt to answer the researcher's questions, we apply the statistical methodology presented in this chapter to this data set in two Statistics in Action Revisited examples.

Statistics in Action Revisited

- Testing Category Proportions for Customer Type in the Coupon Study (p. 650)
- Testing Whether the Coupon Customer Characteristics Are Related to User Type (p. 662)

 COUPONS

TABLE SIA11.1   Qualitative Variables Measured in the Coupon Study

Variable Name	Levels (Possible Values)
Coupon user type	Mail, Internet, or both
Gender	Male or female
Education	High school, vo-tech/college, 4-year college degree, or graduate school
Work status	Full time, Part time, Not working, retired
Coupon satisfaction	Satisfied, unsatisfied, indifferent

11.1 Categorical Data and the Multinomial Experiment

Recall from Section 1.5 that observations on a qualitative variable can only be categorized. For example, consider the highest level of education attained by each in a group of salespersons. Level of education is a qualitative variable and each salesperson would fall in one and only one of the following five categories: some high school, high school diploma, some college, college degree, and graduate degree. The result of the categorization would be a count of the numbers of salespersons falling in the respective categories.

When the qualitative variable results in one of two responses (yes or no, success or failure, favor or do not favor, etc.), the data (i.e., the counts) can be analyzed using the binomial probability distribution discussed in Section 4.4. However, qualitative variables, such as level of education, that allow for more than two categories for a response are much more common, and these must be analyzed using a different method.

Qualitative data that fall in more than two categories often result from a **multinomial experiment.** The characteristics for a multinomial experiment with k outcomes are described in the box. You can see that the binomial experiment of Chapter 4 is a multinomial experiment with $k = 2$.

Teaching Tip
The multinomial experiment should be looked at as an extension of the binomial experiment that was studied earlier in the text. The number of outcomes has been expanded to allow for k outcomes (instead of just 2).

Properties of the Multinomial Experiment

1. The experiment consists of n identical trials.
2. There are k possible outcomes to each trial. These outcomes are called *classes, categories,* or *cells.*
3. The probabilities of the k outcomes, denoted by $p_1, p_2, \ldots, p_k$, remain the same from trial to trial, where $p_1 + p_2 + \cdots + p_k = 1$.
4. The trials are independent.
5. The random variables of interest are the *cell counts, $n_1, n_2, \ldots, n_k$,* of the number of observations that fall in each of the k classes.

EXAMPLE 11.1   IDENTIFYING A MULTINOMIAL EXPERIMENT

Problem   Consider the problem of determining the highest level of education attained by each of $n = 100$ salespersons at a large company. Suppose we categorize level of education into one of five categories—some high school, high school diploma, some college, college degree, and graduate degree—and count the number of the 100 salespeople that fall into each category. Is this a multinomial experiment to a reasonable degree of approximation?

Solution   Checking the five properties of a multinomial experiment shown in the box, we have the following:

1. The experiment consists of $n = 100$ identical trials, where each trial is to determine the highest level of education of a salesperson.
2. There are $k = 5$ possible outcomes to each trial corresponding to the five education-level categories.
3. The probabilities of the $k = 5$ outcomes, p_1, p_2, p_3, p_4, and p_5, remain (to a reasonable degree of approximation) the same from trial to trial, where p_i represents the true probability that a salesperson attains level of education i.
4. The trials are independent (i.e., the education level attained by one salesperson does not affect the level attained by any other salesperson).
5. We are interested in the count of the number of salespeople who fall into each of the five categories. These five *cell counts* are denoted n_1, n_2, n_3, n_4, and n_5.

Thus, the properties of a multinomial experiment are satisfied.

■ ■ ■

In this chapter, we are concerned with the analysis of categorical data—specifically, the data that represent the counts for each category of a multinomial experiment. In Section 11.2, we learn how to make inferences about category probabilities for data classified according to a single qualitative (or categorical) variable. Then in, Section 11.3, we consider inferences about category probabilities for data classified according to two qualitative variables. The statistic used for these inferences is one that possesses, approximately, the familiar chi-square distribution.

11.2 Testing Category Probabilities: One-Way Table

In this section, we consider a multinomial experiment with k outcomes that correspond to categories of a *single* qualitative variable. The results of such an experiment are summarized in a **one-way table.** The term *one-way* is used since only one variable is classified. Typically, we want to make inferences about the true proportions that occur in the k categories based on the sample information in the one-way table.

To illustrate, suppose a large supermarket chain conducts a consumer preference survey by recording the *brand of bread* purchased by customers in its stores. Assume the chain carries three brands of bread—two major brands (A and B) and its own store brand. The brand preferences of a random sample of 150 consumers are observed, and the number preferring each brand is tabulated; the resulting count data appear in Table 11.1.

Note that our consumer-preference survey satisfies the properties of a multinomial experiment for the qualitative variable *brand of bread*. The experiment consists of randomly sampling $n = 150$ buyers from a large population of consumers containing an unknown proportion p_1 who prefer brand A, a proportion p_2 who prefer brand B, and a proportion p_3 who prefer the store brand. Each buyer represents a single trial that can result in one of three outcomes: The consumer prefers brand A, B, or the store brand with probabilities p_1, p_2, and p_3, respectively. (Assume that all consumers will have a preference.) The buyer preference of any single consumer in the sample does not affect the preference of another; consequently, the trials are independent. And, finally, you can see that the recorded data are the number of buyers in each of three consumer-preference categories. Thus, the consumer-preference survey satisfies the five properties of a multinomial experiment.

In the consumer-preference survey, and in most practical applications of the multinomial experiment, the k outcome probabilities $p_1, p_2, \ldots, p_k$ are unknown and we typically want to use the survey data to make inferences about their values. The unknown probabilities in the consumer-preference survey are

TABLE 11.1   Results of Consumer Preference Survey

A	B	Store Brand
61	53	36

$$p_1 = \text{Proportion of all buyers who prefer brand A}$$
$$p_2 = \text{Proportion of all buyers who prefer brand B}$$
$$p_3 = \text{Proportion of all buyers who prefer the store brand}$$

For example, to decide whether the consumers have a preference for any of the brands, we will want to test the null hypothesis that the brands of bread are equally preferred (that is, $p_1 = p_2 = p_3 = \frac{1}{3}$) against the alternative hypothesis that one brand is preferred (that is, at least one of the probabilities p_1, p_2, and p_3 exceeds $\frac{1}{3}$). Thus, we want to test

$$H_0: p_1 = p_2 = p_3 = \tfrac{1}{3} \text{ (no preference)}$$
$$H_a: \text{At least one of the proportions exceeds } \tfrac{1}{3} \text{ (a preference exists)}$$

Teaching Tip

The null hypothesis to be tested allows for the unique specification of the population proportions (e.g. $H_0: p_1 = .2, p_2 = .3, p_3 = .5$). In many cases, however, the appropriate test specifies that all proportions are equal.

If the null hypothesis is true and $p_1 = p_2 = p_3 = 1/3$, the expected value (mean value) of the number of customers who prefer brand A is given by

$$E(n_1) = np_1 = (n)1/3 = (150)1/3 = 50$$

Similarly, $E(n_2) = E(n_3) = 50$ if the null hypothesis is true and no preference exists.

The following test statistic—the **chi-square test**—measures the degree of disagreement between the data and the null hypothesis:

$$\chi^2 = \frac{[n_1 - E(n_1)]^2}{E(n_1)} + \frac{[n_2 - E(n_2)]^2}{E(n_2)} + \frac{[n_3 - E(n_3)]^2}{E(n_3)}$$

$$= \frac{(n_1 - 50)^2}{50} + \frac{(n_2 - 50)^2}{50} + \frac{(n_3 - 50)^2}{50}$$

Note that the farther the observed numbers $n_1, n_2,$ and n_3, are from their expected value (50), the larger χ^2 will become. That is, large values of χ^2 imply that the null hypothesis is false.

Biography

KARL PEARSON
(1895–1980)
The Father of Statistics

While attending college, London-born Karl Pearson exhibited a wide range of interests, including mathematics, physics, religion, history, socialism, and Darwinism. After earning a law degree at Cambridge University and a Ph.D. in political science at the University of Heidelberg (Germany), Pearson become a professor of applied mathematics at University College in London. His 1892 book, *The Grammer of Science*, illustrated

his conviction that statistical data analysis lies at the foundation of all knowledge; consequently, many consider Pearson to be the "father of statistics." A few of Pearson's many contributions to the field include introducing the term *standard deviation* and its associated symbol (σ), developing the distribution of the correlation coefficient, cofounding and editing the prestigious statistics journal *Biometrika*, and (what many consider his greatest achievement) creating the first chi-square "goodness-of-fit" test. Pearson inspired his students (including his son, Egon, and William Gossett) with his wonderful lectures and enthusiasm for statistics.

We have to know the distribution of χ^2 in repeated sampling before we can decide whether the data indicate that a preference exists. When H_0 is true, χ^2 can be shown to have (approximately) the familiar chi-square distribution of Section 8.7. For this one-way classification, the χ^2 distribution has $(k - 1)$ degrees of freedom.* The rejection region for the consumer-preference survey for $\alpha = .05$ and $k - 1 = 3 - 1 = 2$ df is

Rejection region: $\chi^2 > \chi^2_{.05}$

The value of $\chi^2_{.05}$ (found in Table VII of Appendix B) is 5.99147. (See Figure 11.1.) The computed value of the test statistic is

---

*The derivation of the degrees of freedom for χ^2 involves the number of linear restrictions imposed on the count data. In the present case, the only constraint is that $\Sigma n_i = n$, where n (the sample size) is fixed in advance. Therefore, df $= k - 1$. For other cases, we will give the degrees of freedom for each usage of χ^2 and refer the interested reader to the references for more detail.

Figure 11.1
Rejection region
for consumer-preference
survey

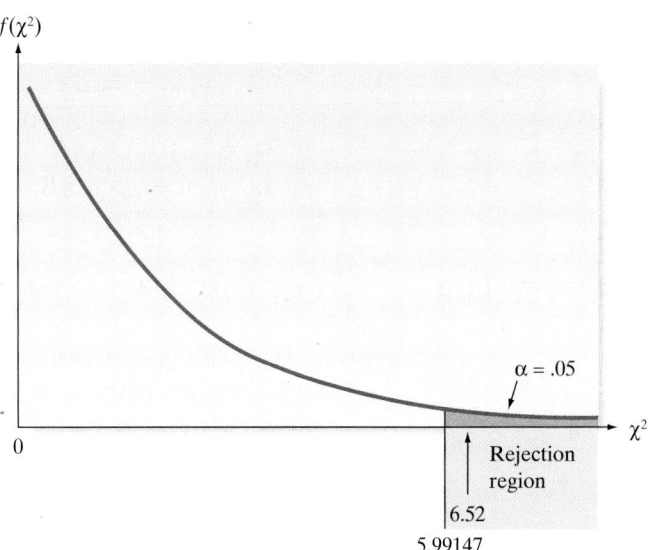

$$\chi^2 = \frac{(n_1 - 50)^2}{50} + \frac{(n_2 - 50)^2}{50} + \frac{(n_3 - 50)^2}{50}$$

$$= \frac{(61 - 50)^2}{50} + \frac{(53 - 50)^2}{50} + \frac{(36 - 50)^2}{50} = 6.52$$

Since the computed $\chi^2 = 6.52$ exceeds the critical value of 5.99147, we conclude at the $\alpha = .05$ level of significance that there does exist a consumer preference for one or more of the brands of bread.

Now that we have evidence to indicate that the proportions $p_1, p_2,$ and p_3 are unequal, we can make inferences concerning their individual values using the methods of Section 7.3. [*Note:* We cannot use the methods of Section 9.3 to compare two proportions because the cell counts are dependent random variables.] The general form for a test of a hypothesis concerning multinomial probabilities is shown in the next box.

Teaching Tip
Use plenty of in-class examples
to illustrate the one-way test.
Lay the groundwork for the test
of independence in the two-
way analysis in the next section.

**A Test of a Hypothesis about Multinomial Probabilities:
One-Way Table**

H_0: $p_1 = p_{1,0}, p_2 = p_{2,0}, \dots, p_k = p_{k,0}$

where $p_{1,0}, p_{2,0}, \dots, p_{k,0}$ represent the hypothesized values of the multinomial probabilities

H_a: At least one of the multinomial probabilities does not equal its hypothesized value

Test statistic: $\chi^2 = \sum \dfrac{[n_i - E(n_i)]^2}{E(n_i)}$

where $E(n_i) = np_{i,0}$ is the **expected cell count,** that is, the expected number of outcomes of type i assuming that H_0 is true. The total sample size is n.

Rejection region: $\chi^2 > \chi_\alpha^2$,

where χ_α^2 has $(k - 1)$ df.

> ### Conditions Required for a Valid χ^2 Test: One-way Table
>
> 1. A multinomial experiment has been conducted. This is generally satisfied by taking a random sample from the population of interest.
> 2. The sample size n is large. This is satisfied if for every cell, the expected cell count $E(n_i)$ will be equal to 5 or more.*

EXAMPLE 11.2   CONDUCTING A ONE-WAY χ^2 TEST

Problem A large firm has established what it hopes is an objective system of deciding on annual pay increases for its employees. The system is based on a series of evaluation scores determined by the supervisors of each employee. Employees with scores above 80 receive a merit pay increase, those with scores between 50 and 80 receive the standard increase, and those below 50 receive no increase. The firm designed the plan with the objective that, on the average, 25% of its employees would receive merit increases, 65% would receive standard increases, and 10% would receive no increase. After one year of operation using the new plan, the distribution of pay increases for the 600 company employees was as shown in Table 11.2. Test at the $\alpha = .01$ level to determine whether these data indicate that the distribution of pay increases differs significantly from the proportions established by the firm.

$\chi^2 = 19.33$, reject H_0

Solution Define the population proportions for the three pay increase categories to be

 PAYPLAN

p_1 = Proportion of employees who receive no pay increase

p_2 = Proportion of employees who receive a standard increase

p_3 = Proportion of employees who receive a merit increase

TABLE 11.2
Distribution of
Pay Increases

None	Standard	Merit
42	365	193

Then the null hypothesis representing the distribution of percentages in the firm's proposed plan is

$$H_0: p_1 = .10, p_2 = .65, p_3 = .25$$

and the alternative is

H_a: At least two of the proportions differ from the firm's proposed plan

Suggested Exercise 11.9

$$\text{Test statistic: } \chi^2 = \sum \frac{n_i - E(n_i)]^2}{E(n_i)}$$

where

$$E(n_1) = np_{1,0} = 600(.10) = 60$$
$$E(n_2) = np_{2,0} = 600(.65) = 390$$
$$E(n_3) = np_{3,0} = 600(.25) = 150$$

Rejection region: For $\alpha = .01$ and df $= k - 1 = 2$, reject H_0 if $\chi^2 > \chi^2_{.01}$, where (from Table VII of Appendix B) $\chi^2_{.01} = 9.21034$.

*The assumption that all expected cell counts are at least 5 is necessary in order to ensure that the χ^2 approximation is appropriate. Exact methods for conducting the test of a hypothesis exist and may be used for small expected cell counts, but these methods are beyond the scope of this text.

Figure 11.2
EXCEL chi-square
analysis of data in
Table 11.2

	A	B	C
1			
2			
3	**CATEGORY**	**Observed**	**Expected**
4	None	42	60
5	Standard	365	390
6	Merit	193	150
7	TOTAL	600	
8			
9	Significance Level	0.05	
10	Number of categories	3	
11	Degrees of freedom	2	
12	**Chi-square test statistic**	19.32550222	
13	***p*-value**	6.34908E-05	
14			

We now calculate the test statistic:

$$\chi^2 = \frac{(42-60)^2}{60} + \frac{(365-390)^2}{390} + \frac{(193-150)^2}{150} = 19.33$$

This value exceeds the table value of χ^2 (9.21034); therefore, the data provide strong evidence ($\alpha = .01$) that the company's actual pay plan distribution differs from its proposed plan.

The χ^2 test can also be conducted using statistical software. Figure 11.2 is an EXCEL printout of the analysis of the data in Table 11.2; note that the p-value of the test is .0000634908. Since $\alpha = .01$ exceeds this p-value, there is sufficient evidence to reject H_0.

Look Back Note that all the expected cell counts exceed 5. Consequently, the χ^2 test is appropriate.

Now Work   *Exercise 11.6*

■ ■ ■

If we focus on one particular outcome of a multinomial experiment, we can use the methods developed in Section 7.4 for a binomial proportion to establish a confidence interval for any one of the multinomial probabilities.* For example, if we want a 95% confidence interval for the proportion of the company's employees who will receive merit increases under the new system, we calculate

$$\hat{p}_3 \pm 1.96\sigma_{\hat{p}_3} \approx \hat{p}_3 \pm 1.96\sqrt{\frac{\hat{p}_3(1-\hat{p}_3)}{n}} \qquad \text{where } \hat{p}_3 = \frac{n_3}{n} = \frac{193}{600} = .32$$

$$= .32 \pm 1.96\sqrt{\frac{(.32)(1-.32)}{600}} = .32 \pm .04$$

*Note that focusing on one outcome has the effect of lumping the other $(k-1)$ outcomes into a single group. Thus, we obtain, in effect, two outcomes—or a binomial experiment.

Thus, we estimate that between 28% and 36% of the firm's employees will qualify for merit increases under the new plan. It appears that the firm will have to raise the requirements for merit increases in order to achieve the stated goal of a 25% employee qualification rate.

Statistics in Action Revisited

Testing Category Proportions for Customer Type in the Coupon Study

In the research on a technology-based self-service (TBSS) encounter (p. 643), 440 users of a firm's discount coupons were sampled and given a questionnaire to complete. One of the variables of interest to the researcher was type of coupon user. Recall (from Table SIA11.1) that the customers received the coupons in one of three ways: only through the mail (non-technology user), only via the Internet (TBSS user), and via both the mail and Internet. What are the proportions of mail-only, Internet-only, and both users, and are these proportions statistically different?

To answer this question, we used SPSS to analyze the type of user variable in the **COUPONS** file. Figure SIA11.1 shows summary statistics and a graph to describe the three categories. From the summary table at the top of the printout, you can see that 262 (or 59.5%) of the customers are mail-only coupon users, 43 (or 9.8%) are Internet-only

users, and the remainder (30.7%) use both mail and the Internet. These sample percentages are illustrated in the bar graph at the bottom of Figure SIA11.1. In this sample of customers, the majority (almost 60%) obtain their coupons strictly through the mail.

Is this sufficient evidence to indicate that the true proportions in the population of customers are different? Letting p_1, p_2, and p_3 represent the true proportions for the mail-only, Internet-only, and both categories, respectively, we tested $H_0: p_1 = p_2 = p_3 = 1/3$ using SPSS. The printout is displayed in Figure SIA11.2. The cell frequencies and expected numbers are shown in the top table of the figure, while the chi-square test statistic (164.895) and p-value (.000) are shown in the bottom table. At any reasonably selected α-level (say, $\alpha = .01$), the small p-value indicates that there is sufficient evidence to reject the null hypothesis and conclude that the true proportions associated with the three user type categories are indeed statistically different.

Figure SIA11.1

SPSS descriptive statistics and graph for type of coupon user

USER

		Frequency	Percent	Valid Percent	Cumulative Percent
Valid	Mail	262	59.5	59.5	59.5
	Net	43	9.8	9.8	69.3
	Both	135	30.7	30.7	100.0
	Total	440	100.0	100.0	

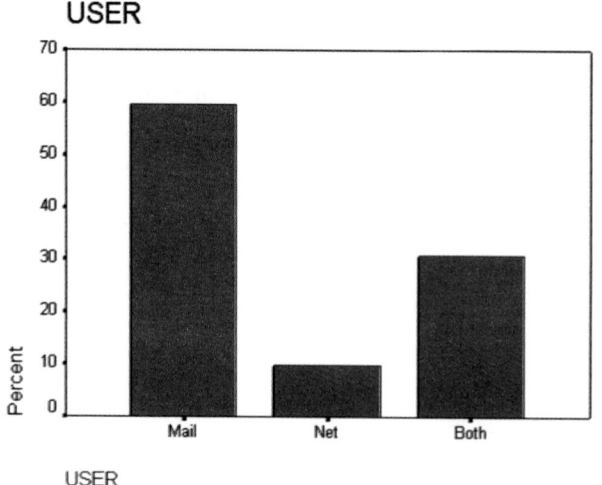

Figure SIA11.2
SPSS chi-square test of user type categories

Chi-Square Test

Frequencies

USER

	Observed N	Expected N	Residual
Mail	262	146.7	115.3
Net	43	146.7	-103.7
Both	135	146.7	-11.7
Total	440		

Test Statistics

	USER
Chi-Square[a]	164.895
df	2
Asymp. Sig.	.000

a. 0 cells (.0%) have expected frequencies less than
5. The minimum expected cell frequency is 146.7.

Exercises 11.1–11.15

Learning the Mechanics

11.1 Find the rejection region for a one-dimensional χ^2 test of a null hypothesis concerning $p_1, p_2, \ldots, p_k$ if
  a. $k = 3; \alpha = .05$ $\chi^2 > 5.99147$
  b. $k = 5; \alpha = .10$ $\chi^2 > 7.77944$
  c. $k = 4; \alpha = .01$ $\chi^2 > 11.3449$

11.2 What are the characteristics of a multinomial experiment? Compare the characteristics to those of a binomial experiment.

11.3 What conditions must n satisfy to make the χ^2 test valid?

11.4 A multinomial experiment with $k = 3$ cells and $n = 320$ produced the data shown in the following one-way table. Do these data provide sufficient evidence to contradict the null hypothesis that $p_1 = .25, p_2 = .25$, and $p_3 = .50$? Test using $\alpha = .05$.

	Cell		
	1	2	3
n_i	78	60	182

11.5 A multinomial experiment with $k = 4$ cells and $n = 205$ produced the data shown in the following one-way table.

	Cell			
	1	2	3	4
n_i	43	56	59	47

  a. Do these data provide sufficient evidence to conclude that the multinomial probabilities differ? Test using $\alpha = .05$. $\chi^2 = 3.293$
  b. What are the Type I and Type II errors associated with the test of part **a**?
  c. Construct a 95% confidence interval for the multinomial probability associated with cell 3. $.288 \pm .062$

Applying the Concepts—Basic

11.6 There has been a recent trend for professional sports franchises in Major League Baseball (MLB), the National Football League (NFL), the National Basketball Association (NBA), and the National Hockey

League (NHL) to build new stadiums and ballparks in urban, downtown venues. An article in *Professional Geographer* (Feb. 2000) investigated whether there has been a significant suburban-to-urban shift in the location of major sport facilities. In 1985, 40% of all major sport facilities were located downtown, 30% in central city, and 30% in suburban areas. In contrast, of the 113 major sports franchises that existed in 1997, 58 were built downtown, 26 in central city, and 29 in a suburban area.

a. Describe the qualitative variable of interest in the study. Give the levels (categories) associated with the variable.

b. Give the null hypothesis for a test to determine whether the proportions of major sports facilities in downtown, central city, and suburban areas in 1997 are the same as in 1985. $H_0: p_1 = .40, p_2 = .30, p_3 = .30$

c. If the null hypothesis, part **b,** is true, how many of the 113 sports facilities in 1997 would you expect to be located in downtown, central city, and suburban areas, respectively?   45.2, 33.9, 33.9

d. Find the value of the chi-square statistic for testing the null hypothesis, part **b.** $\chi^2 = 6.174$

e. Find the (approximate) *p*-value of the test and give the appropriate conclusion in the words of the problem. Assume $\alpha = .05$.   .046

11.7 Refer to the *Journal of Global Business* (Spring 2002) study of what "Made in the USA" on product labels means to the typical consumer, Exercise 2.8 (p. 53). Recall that 106 shoppers participated in the survey. Their responses, given as a percentage of U.S. labor and materials in four categories, are summarized in the table. Suppose a consumer advocate group claims that half all consumers believe that "Made in the USA" means "100%" of labor and materials are produced in the United States, one-fourth believe that "75 to 99%" are produced in the United States, one-fifth believe that "50 to 74%" are produced in the and 5 percent believe that "less than 50%" are produced in the United States.

Response to "Made in the USA"	Number of shoppers
100%	64
75 to 99%	20
50 to 74%	18
Less than 50%	4

Source: " 'Made in the USA': Consumer Perceptions, Deception and Policy Alternatives," *Journal of Global Business,* Vol. 13, No. 24, Spring 2002 (Table 3).

a. Describe the qualitative variable of interest in the study. Give the levels (categories) associated with the variable.

b. What are the values of $p_1, p_2, p_3,$ and $p_4,$ the probabilities associated with the four response categories

hypothesized by the consumer advocate group?   .5, .25, .20, .05

c. Give the null and alternative hypotheses for testing the consumer advocate group's claim.

d. Compute the test statistic for testing the hypotheses, part **c.** $\chi^2 = 4.679$

e. Find the rejection region of the test at $\alpha = .10$. $\chi^2 > 6.25139$

f. State the conclusion in the words of the problem.

g. Find and interpret a 90% confidence interval for the true proportion of consumers who believe "Made in the USA" means "100%" of labor and materials are produced in the United States.   .604 ± .078

11.8 M&M's plain chocolate candies come in six different colors: dark brown, yellow, red, orange, green, and blue. According to the manufacturer (Mars, Inc.), the color ratio in each large production batch is 30% brown, 20% yellow, 20% red, 10% orange, 10% green, and 10% blue. To test this claim, a professor at Carleton College (Minnesota) had students count the colors of M&M's found in "fun size" bags of the candy (*Teaching Statistics*, Spring 1993). The results for 370 M&M's are displayed in the table.

M&M

Brown	Yellow	Red	Orange	Green	Blue	Total
84	79	75	49	36	47	370

Source: Johnson, R.W. "Testing Colour Proportions of M&M's." *Teaching Statistics,* Vol. 15, No. 1, Spring 1993, p. 2 (Table 1).

a. Assuming the manufacturer's stated percentages are accurate, calculate the expected numbers falling into the six categories.   111, 74, 74, 37, 37, 37

b. Calculate the value of χ^2 for testing the manufacturer's claim. $\chi^2 = 13.541$

c. Conduct a test to determine whether the true percentages of the colors produced differ from the manufacturer's stated percentages. Use $\alpha = .05$. $\chi^2 = 13.541$

11.9 The *National Tax Journal* (Dec. 2001) published a study of charitable givers based on data collected from the Independent Sector Survey on Giving and Volunteering. A total of 1,072 charitable givers reported that their charitable contributions were motivated by tax considerations. The number of these 1,072 givers in each of ten household income categories is shown in the table on p. 653.

a. If the true proportions of charitable givers in each household income group are the same, how many of the 1,072 sampled givers would you expect to find in each income category?   107.2

b. Give the null hypothesis for testing whether true proportions of charitable givers in each household income group are the same.

c. Compute the chi-square test statistic for testing the null hypothesis, part **b.** $\chi^2 = 93.149$

d. Find the rejection region for the test if $\alpha = .10$. $\chi^2 > 14.6837$

e. Give the appropriate conclusion for the test in the words of the problem.

⊙ GIVERS

Household Income Group	Number of Charitable Givers
Under $10,000	42
$10,000–$20,000	93
$20,000–$30,000	99
$30,000–$40,000	153
$40,000–$50,000	91
$50,000–$60,000	114
$60,000–$70,000	157
$70,000–$80,000	101
$80,000–$100,000	95
Over $100,000	127

Source: Tiehen, L. "Tax Policy and Charitable Contributions of Money," *National Tax Journal,* Vol. 54, No. 4, Dec. 2001, p. 717 (adapted from Table 5).

Applying the Concepts—Intermediate

11.10 Interferons are proteins produced naturally by the human body that help fight infections and regulate the immune system. A drug developed from interferons, called Avonex, is now available for treating patients with multiple sclerosis (MS). In a clinical study, 85 MS patients received weekly injections of Avonex over a two-year period. The number of exacerbations (i.e., flare-ups of symptoms) was recorded for each patient and is summarized in the accompanying table. For MS patients who take a placebo (no drug) over a similar two-week period, it is known from previous studies that 26% will experience no exacerbations, 30% one exacerbation, 11% two exacerbations, 14% three exacerbations, and 19% four or more exacerbations.

⊙ AVONEX

Number of Exacerbations	Number of Patients
0	32
1	26
2	15
3	6
4 or more	6

Source: Biogen, Inc., 1997.

a. Conduct a test to determine whether the exacerbation distribution of MS patients who take Avonex differs from the percentages reported for placebo patients. Test using $\alpha = .05$. $\chi^2 = 17.16$

b. Find a 95% confidence interval for the true proportion of Avonex MS patients who are exac-erbation–free during a two-year period. $.376 \pm .103$

c. Refer to part **b.** Is there evidence that Avonex patients are more likely to have no exacerbations than placebo patients? Explain.

11.11 In order to study consumer preferences for health care reform in the United States, researchers from the University of Michigan surveyed 500 U.S. households (*Journal of Consumer Affairs,* Winter 1999). Heads of household were asked whether they are in favor of, neutral about, or opposed to a national health insurance program in which all Americans are covered and costs are paid by tax dollars. The 434 useable responses are summarized in the table.

⊙ HEALTH

Favor	Neutral	Oppose
234	119	81

Source: Hong, G., and White-Means, S. "Consumer Preferences for Health Care Reform," *Journal of Consumer Affairs,* Vol 33, No. 2, Winter 1999, pp. 237–253.

a. Is there sufficient evidence to conclude that opinions are not evenly divided on the issue of national health insurance? Conduct the appropriate test using $\alpha = .01$.

b. Construct a 95% confidence interval for the proportion of heads of household in the U.S. population who favor national health insurance. $.539 \pm .047$

11.12 Data from supermarket scanners are used by researchers to understand the purchasing patterns and preferences of consumers. Researchers frequently study the purchases of a sample of households, called a *scanner panel.* When shopping, these households present a magnetic identification card that permits their purchase data to be identified and aggregated. Marketing researchers recently studied the extent to which panel households' purchase behavior is representative of the population of households shopping at the same stores (*Marketing Research,* Nov. 1996). The table on p. 654 reports the peanut butter purchase data collected by A. C. Nielsen Company for a panel of 2,500 households in Sioux Falls, SD, over a 102-week period. The market share percentages in the right column are derived from all peanut butter purchases at the same 15 stores at which the panel shopped during the same 102-week period.

a. Do the data provide sufficient evidence to conclude that the purchases of the household panel are not representative of the population of households? Test using $\alpha = .05$. $\chi^2 = 880.521$

b. What assumptions must hold to ensure the validity of the testing procedure you used in part **a**?

c. Find the approximate *p*-value for the test of part **a** and interpret it in the context of the problem.

SCANNER

Brand	Size	Number of Purchases by Household Panel	Market Shares
Jif	18 oz.	3,165	20.10%
Jif	28	1,892	10.10
Jif	40	726	5.42
Peter Pan	10	4,079	16.01
Skippy	18	6,206	28.65
Skippy	28	1,627	12.38
Skippy	40	1,420	7.32
Total		19,115	

Source: Gupta, S., et. al. "Do Household Scanner Data Provide Representative Inferences from Brand Choices? A Comparison with Store Data." *Journal of Marketing Research,* Vol. 33, Nov. 1996, p. 393 (Table 6).

11.13 Each year, approximately 1.3 million Americans suffer adverse drug effects (ADEs), that is, unintended injuries caused by prescribed medication. A study in the *Journal of the American Medical Association* (July 5, 1995) identified the cause of 247 ADEs that occurred at two Boston hospitals. The researchers found that dosing errors (that is, wrong dosage prescribed and/or dispensed) were the most common. The table below summarizes the proximate cause of 95 ADEs that resulted from a dosing error. Conduct a test (at $\alpha = .10$) to determine whether the true percentages of ADEs in the five "cause" categories are different. $\chi^2 = 16$

ADE

Wrong Dosage Cause	Number of ADEs
(1) Lack of knowledge of drug	29
(2) Rule violation	17
(3) Faulty dose checking	13
(4) Slips	9
(5) Other	27

Applying the Concepts—Advanced

11.14 In the board game Scrabble™, a player initially draws a "hand" of seven tiles at random from 100 tiles. Each tile has a letter of the alphabet and the player attempts to form a word from the letters in his/her hand. In *Chance* (Winter 2002), scientist C. J. Robinove investigated whether a handheld electronic version of the game, called ScrabbleExpress™, produces too few vowels in the 7-letter draws. For each of the 26 letters (and "blank" for any letter), the next table gives the true relative frequency of the letter in the board game as well as the frequency of occurrence of the letter in a sample of 700 tiles (i.e., 100 "hands") randomly drawn using the electronic game.

a. Do the data support the scientist's contention that ScrabbleExpress™ "presents the player with unfair word selection opportunities" that are not

the same as the Scrabble™ board game? Test using $\alpha = .05$. $\chi^2 = 360.48$

b. Estimate the true proportion of letters drawn in the electronic game that are vowels using a 95% confidence interval. Compare the results to the true relative frequency of a vowel in the board game. $.194 \pm .029$

SCRABBLE

Letter	Relative Frequency in Board Game	Frequency in Electronic Game
A	.09	39
B	.02	18
C	.02	30
D	.04	30
E	.12	31
F	.02	21
G	.03	35
H	.02	21
I	.09	25
J	.01	17
K	.01	27
L	.04	18
M	.02	31
N	.06	36
O	.08	20
P	.02	27
Q	.01	13
R	.06	27
S	.04	29
T	.06	27
U	.04	21
V	.02	33
W	.02	29
X	.01	15
Y	.02	32
Z	.01	14
# (blank)	.02	34
TOTAL		700

Source: Robinove, C. J. "Letter-Frequency Bias in an Electronic Scrabble Game," *Chance,* Vol. 15, No. 1, Winter 2002, p. 31 (Table 3).

11.15 Although illegal, overloading is common in the trucking industry. A state highway planning agency (Minnesota Department of Transportation) monitored the movements of overweight trucks on an interstate highway using an unmanned, computerized scale that is built into the highway. Unknown to the truckers, the scale weighed their vehicles as they passed over it. Each day's proportion of one week's total truck traffic (five-axle tractor truck semitrailers) is shown in the first table on p. 655. During the same week, the number of overweight trucks per day is given in the second table on p. 655. The planning agency would like to know whether the number of overweight trucks per week is distributed over the seven days of the week in direct proportion to the volume of truck traffic. Test using $\alpha = .05$. $\chi^2 = 12.374$

⊙ **OVERLOAD**

Monday	Tuesday	Wednesday	Thursday	Friday	Saturday	Sunday
.191	.198	.187	.180	.155	.043	.046

Monday	Tuesday	Wednesday	Thursday	Friday	Saturday	Sunday
90	82	72	70	51	18	31

11.3   Testing Category Probabilities: Two-Way (Contingency) Table

In Section 11.1, we introduced the multinomial probability distribution and considered data classified according to a single qualitative criterion. We now consider multinomial experiments in which the data are classified according to two criteria, that is, *classification with respect to two qualitative factors.*

For example, consider a study in the *Journal of Marketing* (Fall 1992) on the impact of using celebrities in television advertisements. The researchers investigated the relationship between gender of a viewer and the viewer's brand awareness. Three hundred TV viewers were asked to identify products advertised by male celebrity spokespersons. The data are summarized in the **two-way table** shown in Table 11.3. This table is called a **contingency table;** it presents multinomial count data classified on two scales, or **dimensions, of classification**—namely, gender of viewer and brand awareness.

TABLE 11.3   Contingency Table for Marketing Example

		Gender		
		Male	Female	Totals
Brand Awareness	**Could Identify Product**	95	41	136
	Could Not Identify Product	55	109	164
	Totals	150	150	300

Teaching Tip
Point out that the data has been collected using two classifications. Point out the difference between this type of data collection and the type used in the one-way tables.

The symbols representing the cell counts for the multinomial experiment in Table 11.3 are shown in Table 11.4(a); and the corresponding cell, row, and column probabilities are shown in Table 11.4(b). Thus, n_{11} represents the number of viewers who are male and could identify the brand and p_{11} represents the corresponding cell probability. Note the symbols for the row and column totals and also the symbols for the probability totals. The latter are called **marginal probabilities** for each row and column. The marginal probability p_{r1} is the probability that a TV viewer identifies the product; the marginal probability p_{c1} is the probability that the TV viewer is male. Thus,

$$p_{r1} = p_{11} + p_{12} \text{ and } p_{c1} = p_{11} + p_{21}$$

Thus, we can see that this really is a multinomial experiment with a total of 300 trials, $(2)(2) = 4$ cells or possible outcomes, and probabilities for each cell as shown in Table 11.4(b). If the 300 TV viewers are randomly chosen, the trials are considered independent and the probabilities are viewed as remaining constant from trial to trial.

TABLE 11.4(a)   Observed Counts for Contingency Table 11.3

		Gender		
		Male	Female	Totals
Brand Awareness	**Could Identify Product**	n_{11}	n_{12}	R_1
	Could Not Identify Product	n_{21}	n_{22}	R_2
	Totals	C_1	C_2	n

TABLE 11.4(b)   Probabilities for Contingency Table 11.3

		Gender		
		Male	Female	Totals
Brand Awareness	**Could Identify Product**	p_{11}	p_{12}	p_{r1}
	Could Not Identify Product	p_{21}	p_{22}	p_{r2}
	Totals	p_{c1}	p_{c2}	1

Suppose we want to know whether the two classifications, gender and brand awareness, are dependent. That is, if we know the gender of the TV viewer, does that information give us a clue about the viewer's brand awareness?

In a probabilistic sense we know (Chapter 3) that independence of events A and B implies $P(AB) = P(A)P(B)$. Similarly, in the contingency table analysis, if the **two classifications are independent,** the probability that an item is classified in any particular cell of the table is the product of the corresponding marginal probabilities. Thus, under the hypothesis of independence, in Table 11.4(b), we must have

$$p_{11} = p_{r1}p_{c1}$$
$$p_{12} = p_{r1}p_{c2}$$

and so forth.

To test the hypothesis of independence, we use the same reasoning employed in the one-dimensional tests of Section 11.2. First, we calculate the *expected*, or *mean, count in each cell* assuming that the null hypothesis of independence is true. We do this by noting that the expected count in a cell of the table is just the total number of multinomial trials, n, times the cell probability. Recall that n_{ij} represents the **observed count** in the cell located in the ith row and jth column. Then the expected cell count for the upper lefthand cell (first row, first column) is

$$E(n_{11}) = np_{11}$$

or, when the null hypothesis (the classifications are independent) is true,

$$E(n_{11}) = np_{r1}p_{c1}$$

Since these true probabilities are not known, we estimate p_{r1} and p_{c1} by the proportions $\hat{p}_{r1} = R_1/n$ and $\hat{p}_{c1} = C_1/n$, where R_1 and C_1 represent the totals for row 1 and column 1, respectively. Thus, the estimate of the expected value $E(n_{11})$ is

$$E_{11} = n\left(\frac{R_1}{n}\right)\left(\frac{C_1}{n}\right) = \frac{R_1 C_1}{n}$$

Similarly, for each i, j,

$$E_{ij} = \frac{(\text{Row total})(\text{Column total})}{\text{Total sample size}}$$

Thus,

$$E_{12} = \frac{R_1 C_2}{n}$$

$$E_{21} = \frac{R_2 C_1}{n}$$

$$E_{22} = \frac{R_2 C_2}{n}$$

Finding Expected Cell Counts for a Two-Way Contingency Table

The estimate of the expected number of observations falling into the cell in row i and column j is given by

$$E_{ij} = \frac{R_i C_j}{n}$$

where R_i = total for row i, C_j total for column j, and n = sample size.

Using the data in Table 11.3, we find

$$E_{11} = \frac{R_1 C_1}{n} = \frac{(136)(150)}{300} = 68$$

$$E_{12} = \frac{R_1 C_2}{n} = \frac{(136)(150)}{300} = 68$$

$$E_{21}\vdots = \frac{R_2 C_1}{n} = \frac{(164)(150)}{300} = 82$$

$$E_{22} = \frac{R_2 C_2}{n} = \frac{(164)(150)}{300} = 82$$

The observed data and the estimated expected values (in parentheses) are shown in Table 11.5.

TABLE 11.5 Observed and Estimated Expected (in Parentheses) Counts

		Gender		
		Male	Female	Totals
Brand Awareness	**Could Identify Product**	95 (68)	41 (68)	136
	Could Not Identify Product	55 (82)	109 (82)	164
	Totals	150	150	300

We now use the χ^2 statistic to compare the observed and expected (estimated) counts in each cell of the contingency table:

$$\chi^2 = \frac{[n_{11} - E_{11}]^2}{E_{11}} + \frac{[n_{12} - E_{12}]^2}{E_{12}} + \frac{[n_{21} - E_{21}]^2}{E_{21}} + \frac{[n_{22} - E_{22}]^2}{E_{22}}$$

$$= \sum \frac{[n_{ij} - E_{ij}]^2}{E_{ij}}$$

Teaching Tip
Point out the similarities between the test for independence and the one-way test in the last section. Use a computer example to illustrate how the *p*-value can be used in both types of problems.

Note: The use of $\sum$ in the context of a contingency table analysis refers to a sum over all cells in the table.

Substituting the data of Table 11.5 into this expression, we get

$$\chi^2 = \frac{(95 - 68)^2}{68} + \frac{(41 - 68)^2}{68} + \frac{(55 - 82)^2}{82} + \frac{(109 - 82)^2}{82} = 39.22$$

Large values of χ^2 imply that the observed counts do not closely agree and hence that the hypothesis of independence is false. To determine how large χ^2 must be before it is too large to be attributed to chance, we make use of the fact that the sampling distribution of χ^2 is approximately a χ^2 probability distribution when the classifications are independent.

When testing the null hypothesis of independence in a two-way contingency table, the appropriate degrees of freedom will be $(r - 1)(c - 1)$, where r is the number of rows and c is the number of columns in the table.

For the brand awareness example, the degrees of freedom for χ^2 is $(r - 1)(c - 1) = (2 - 1)(2 - 1) = 1$. Then, for $\alpha = .05$, we reject the hypothesis of independence when

$$\chi^2 > \chi^2_{.05} = 3.84146$$

Since the computed $\chi^2 = 39.22$ exceeds the value 3.84146, we conclude that viewer gender and brand awareness are dependent events.

The pattern of **dependence** can be seen more clearly by expressing the data as percentages. We first select one of the two classifications to be used as the base variable. In the above example, suppose we select gender of the TV viewer as the classificatory variable to be the base. Next, we represent the responses for each level of the second categorical variable (brand awareness in our example) as a percentage of the subtotal for the base variable. For example, from Table 11.5 we convert the response for males who identify the brand (95) to a percentage of the total number of male viewers (150). That is,

$$(95/150)100\% = 63.3\%$$

The conversions of all Table 11.5 entries are similarly computed, and the values are shown in Table 11.6. The value shown at the right of each row is the row's total expressed as a percentage of the total number of responses in the entire table. Thus, the percentage of TV viewers who identify the product is: $\left(\frac{136}{300}\right)100\% = 45.3\%$ (rounded to the nearest percent).

If the gender and brand awareness variables are independent, then the percentages in the cells of the table are expected to be approximately equal to the corresponding row percentages. Thus, we would expect the percentages who identify

TABLE 11.6 Percentage of TV Viewers Who Identify Brand, by Gender

		Gender		Totals
		Male	Female	
Brand Awareness	**Could Identify Product**	63.3	27.3	45.3
	Could Not Identify Product	36.7	72.7	54.7
	Totals	100	100	100

the brand for each gender to be approximately 45% if the two variables are independent. The extent to which each gender's percentage departs from this value determines the dependence of the two classifications, with greater variability of the row percentages meaning a greater degree of dependence. A plot of the percentages helps summarize the observed pattern. In the SPSS bar graph in Figure 11.3, we show the gender of the viewer (the base variable) on the horizontal axis, and the percentages of TV viewers who identify the brand on the vertical axis. The "expected" percentage under the assumption of independence is shown as a dotted horizontal line.

Figure 11.3 clearly indicates the reason that the test resulted in the conclusion that the two classifications in the contingency table are dependent. The percentage of male TV viewers who identify the brand promoted by a male celebrity is more than twice as high as the percentage of female TV viewers who identify the brand.

Statistical measures of the degree of dependence and procedures for making comparisons of pairs of levels for classifications are available. They are beyond the scope of this text, but can be found in the references. We will, however, utilize descriptive summaries such as Figure 11.3 to examine the degree of dependence exhibited by the sample data.

Suggested Exercises 11.23

The general form of a two-way contingency table containing r rows and c columns (called an $r \times c$ contingency table) is shown in Table 11.7. Note that the observed count in the (ij) cell is denoted by n_{ij}, the ith row total is R_i, the jth column total is C_j, and the total sample size is n. Using this notation, we give the general form of the contingency table test for independent classifications in the next box.

Figure 11.3

SPSS bar graph showing percentage of viewers who identified the TV product

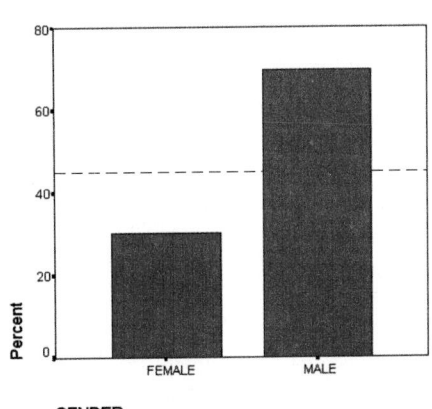

Cases weighted by PCTID

TABLE 11.7 General $r \times c$ Contingency Table

		Column				
		1	2	$\cdots$	c	Row Totals
Row	1	n_{11}	n_{12}	$\cdots$	n_{1c}	R_1
	2	n_{21}	n_{22}	$\cdots$	n_{2c}	R_2
	$\vdots$	$\vdots$	$\vdots$		$\vdots$	$\vdots$
	r	n_{r1}	n_{r2}	$\cdots$	n_{rc}	R_r
Column Totals		C_1	C_2	$\cdots$	C_c	n

General Form of a Contingency Table Analysis: A χ^2-Test for Independence

H_0: The two classifications are independent.

H_a: The two classifications are dependent.

Test statistic: $\chi^2 = \sum \dfrac{[n_{ij} - E_{ij}]^2}{E_{ij}}$

where $E_{ij} = \dfrac{R_i C_j}{n}$.

Rejection region: $\chi^2 > \chi_\alpha^2$, where χ_α^2 has $(r-1)(c-1)$ df.

Conditions Required for a Valid χ^2-Test: Contingency Table

1. The n observed counts are a random sample from the population of interest. We may then consider this to be a multinomial experiment with $r \times c$ possible outcomes.

2. The sample size, n, will be large enough so that, for every cell, the expected count, E_{ij}, will be equal to 5 or more.

EXAMPLE 11.3   CONDUCTING A TWO-WAY ANALYSIS

Problem   A large brokerage firm wants to determine whether the service it provides to affluent clients differs from the service it provides to lower-income clients. A sample of 500 clients are selected, and each client is asked to rate his or her broker. The results are shown in Table 11.8.

 BROKERAGE

TABLE 11.8 Survey Results (Observed Clients), Example 11.3.

		Client's Income			
		Under $30,000	$30,000–$60,000	Over $60,000	Totals
Broker Rating	**Outstanding**	48	64	41	153
	Average	98	120	50	268
	Poor	30	33	16	79
	Totals	176	217	107	500

$\chi^2 = 4.278$, fail to reject H_0

a. Test to determine whether there is evidence that broker rating and customer income are independent. Use a $\alpha = .10$.

b. Plot the data and describe the patterns revealed. Is the result of the test supported by the plot?

Solution

a. The first step is to calculate estimated expected cell frequencies under the assumption that the classifications are independent. Rather than compute these values by hand, we resort to a computer. The MINITAB printout of the analysis of Table 11.8 is displayed in Figure 11.4. Each cell in Figure 11.4 contains the observed (top) and expected (bottom) frequency in that cell. Note that E_{11}, the estimated expected count for the Outstanding, Under \$30,000 cell is 53.86. Similarly, the estimated expected count for the Outstanding, \$30,000–\$60,000 cell is $E_{12} = 66.40$. Since all the estimated expected cell frequencies are greater than 5, the χ^2 approximation for the test statistic is appropriate. Assuming the clients chosen were randomly selected from all clients of the brokerage firm, the characteristics of the multinomial probability distribution are satisfied. The null and alternative hypotheses we want to test are

H_0: The rating a client gives his or her broker is independent of client's income

H_a: Broker rating and client income are dependent

The test statistic, $\chi^2 = 4.278$, is highlighted at the bottom of the printout as is the observed significance level (p-value) of the test. Since $\alpha = .10$ is less than $p = .370$, we fail to reject H_0. This survey does not support the firm's alternative hypothesis that affluent clients receive different broker service than lower-income clients.

Figure 11.4

MINITAB contingency table analysis for brokerage data

```
Rows: RATING    Columns: INCOME

             1:UND30K   2:30K-60K   3:OVR60K      All

1:OUTSTAN         48          64         41       153
               27.27       29.49      38.32     30.60
               53.86       66.40      32.74    153.00

2:AVERAGE         98         120         50       268
               55.68       55.30      46.73     53.60
               94.34      116.31      57.35    268.00

3:POOR            30          33         16        79
               17.05       15.21      14.95     15.80
               27.81       34.29      16.91     79.00

All              176         217        107       500
              100.00      100.00     100.00    100.00
              176.00      217.00     107.00    500.00

Cell Contents:       Count
                     % of Column
                     Expected count


Pearson Chi-Square = 4.278,  DF = 4,  P-Value = 0.370
Likelihood Ratio Chi-Square = 4.184,  DF = 4,  P-Value = 0.382
```

Figure 11.5

MINITAB side-by-side bar graph for brokerage data

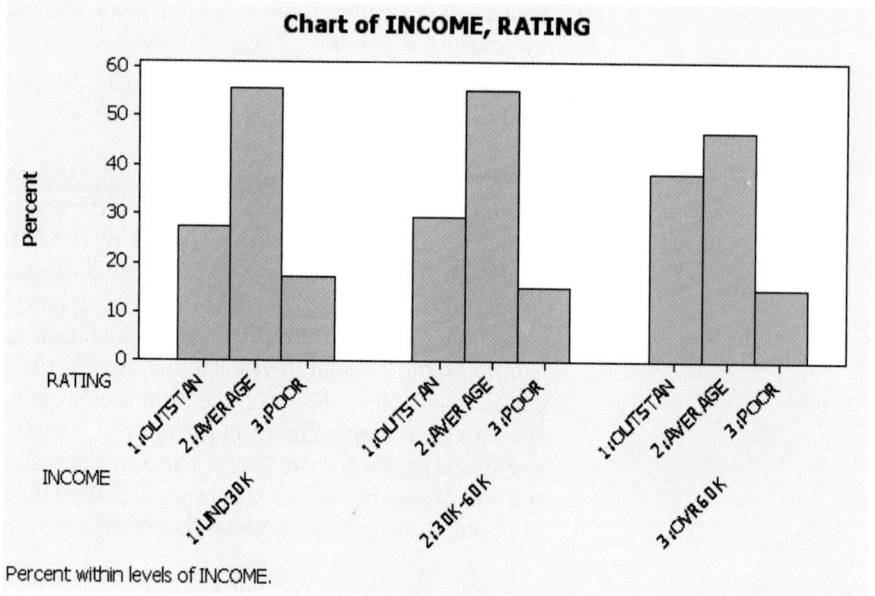

b. The broker rating frequencies are expressed as percentages of income category frequencies and highlighted in the MINITAB printout, Figure 11.4. The expected percentages under the assumption of independence are shown in the "All" column of the printout. A MINITAB side-by-side bar graph of the data is shown in Figure 11.5. Note that the response percentages deviate only slightly from those expected under the assumption of independence, supporting the result of the test in part **a.** That is, neither the descriptive plot nor the statistical test provides evidence that the rating given the broker services depends on (varies with) the customer's income.

Now Work *Exercise 11.21*

■ ■ ■

Statistics in Action Revisited

Testing Whether Coupon Customer Characteristics Are Related to User Type

In his study of a firm's discount coupon users (p. 643), marketing professor Dan Ladik wanted to know whether there are differences in customer characteristics (i.e., gender, education, work status, and satisfaction) among the three types of coupon users: mail-only (nontechnology) users, Internet-only (TBSS) users, and users of both mail and Internet coupons. One approach to analyzing these data is to determine whether each of the four customer characteristic variables are related to coupon user type. Since all the variables measured on the sample of 440 coupon users are qualitative, a contingency table analysis is appropriate.

Figures SIA11.3–SIA11.6 (on pages 663–666) show the SPSS contingency table analyses relating each customer characteristic to coupon user type. The p-values for the chi-square tests for the variables gender, education, satisfaction, and work status are .033, .361, .000, and .069, respectively. If we conduct each test at $\alpha = .01$ (we purposely choose a small α to minimize the chance of making a Type I error), the only significant result is for customer satisfaction. That is, the data provide evidence to indicate that the level of customer satisfaction depends on type of coupon user; however, there is not sufficient evidence to say that any of the other customer characteristics (gender, education, or work status) are related to type of coupon user.

GENDER * USER Crosstabulation

			USER			
			Mail	Net	Both	Total
GENDER	Male	Count	84	7	31	122
		Expected Count	72.6	11.9	37.4	122.0
	Female	Count	178	36	104	318
		Expected Count	189.4	31.1	97.6	318.0
Total		Count	262	43	135	440
		Expected Count	262.0	43.0	135.0	440.0

Chi-Square Tests

	Value	df	Asymp. Sig. (2-sided)
Pearson Chi-Square	6.797[a]	2	.033
Likelihood Ratio	7.105	2	.029
Linear-by-Linear Association	4.371	1	.037
N of Valid Cases	440		

a. 0 cells (.0%) have expected count less than 5. The minimum expected count is 11.92.

Figure SIA11.3
SPSS contingency table analysis—gender versus user type

The column percentages highlighted in the contingency table of Figure SIA11.5 reveal the differences in satisfaction levels of the three user types. The percentages of satisfied customers for mail-only and Internet-only coupon users are 65.6% and 69.8%, respectively. However, for users of both mail and the Internet, 91.1% are satisfied. This information was used by the coupon firm to develop a marketing strategy aimed at mail-only and Internet-only coupon users.

Exercises 11.16–11.31

Learning the Mechanics

11.16 Find the rejection region for a test of independence of two classifications where the contingency table contains r rows and c columns.
a. $r = 5, c = 5, \alpha = .05$ $\chi^2 > 26.2962$
b. $r = 3, c = 6, \alpha = .10$ $\chi^2 > 15.9871$
c. $r = 2, c = 3, \alpha = .01$ $\chi^2 > 9.21034$

11.17 Consider the accompanying 2 × 3 (i.e., $r = 2$ and $c = 3$) contingency table.
a. Specify the null and alternative hypotheses that should be used in testing the independence of the row and column classifications.
b. Specify the test statistic and the rejection region that should be used in conducting the hypothesis test of part **a.** Use $\alpha = .01$. $\chi^2 > 9.21034$

LM11_17

		Column		
		1	2	3
Row	1	9	34	53
	2	16	30	25

c. Assuming the row classification and the column classification are independent, find estimates for the expected cell counts.
d. Conduct the hypothesis test of part **a.** Interpret your result. $\chi^2 = 8.71$

EDUC * USER Crosstabulation

			USER			Total
			Mail	Net	Both	
EDUC	HS	Count	34	7	19	60
		Expected Count	35.7	5.9	18.4	60.0
	VT/COLL	Count	96	20	62	178
		Expected Count	106.0	17.4	54.6	178.0
	COLL4	Count	85	9	38	132
		Expected Count	78.6	12.9	40.5	132.0
	GRAD	Count	47	7	16	70
		Expected Count	41.7	6.8	21.5	70.0
Total		Count	262	43	135	440
		Expected Count	262.0	43.0	135.0	440.0

Chi-Square Tests

	Value	df	Asymp. Sig. (2-sided)
Pearson Chi-Square	6.587[a]	6	.361
Likelihood Ratio	6.786	6	.341
Linear-by-Linear Association	3.546	1	.060
N of Valid Cases	440		

a. 0 cells (.0%) have expected count less than 5. The minimum expected count is 5.86.

Figure SIA11.4
SPSS contingency table analysis—education versus user type

11.18 Refer to Exercise 11.17.
 a. Convert the frequency responses to percentages by calculating the percentage of each column total falling in each row. Also convert the row totals to percentages of the total number of responses. Display the percentages in a table.
 b. Create a bar graph with row 1 percentage on the vertical axis and column number on the horizontal axis. Show the row 1 total percentage as a horizontal line on the graph.
 c. What pattern do you expect to see if the rows and columns are independent? Does the plot support the result of the test of independence in Exercise 11.17?

11.19 Test the null hypothesis of independence of the two classifications, A and B, of the 3 × 3 contingency table shown here. Test using $\alpha = .05$.

LM11_19

		B		
		B_1	B_2	B_3
A	A_1	40	72	42
	A_2	63	53	70
	A_3	31	38	30

11.20 Refer to Exercise 11.21.
 a. Convert the responses to percentages by calculating the percentage of each B class total falling into each A classification.
 b. Calculate the percentage of the total number of responses that constitute each of the A classification totals.

COUPSAT * USER Crosstabulation

			USER			Total
			Mail	Net	Both	
COUPSAT	Satisfied	Count	172	30	123	325
		Expected Count	193.5	31.8	99.7	325.0
		% within USER	65.6%	69.8%	91.1%	73.9%
	Indiff	Count	62	9	9	80
		Expected Count	47.6	7.8	24.5	80.0
		% within USER	23.7%	20.9%	6.7%	18.2%
	Unsatis	Count	28	4	3	35
		Expected Count	20.8	3.4	10.7	35.0
		% within USER	10.7%	9.3%	2.2%	8.0%
Total		Count	262	43	135	440
		Expected Count	262.0	43.0	135.0	440.0
		% within USER	100.0%	100.0%	100.0%	100.0%

Chi-Square Tests

	Value	df	Asymp. Sig. (2-sided)
Pearson Chi-Square	30.418[a]	4	.000
Likelihood Ratio	34.934	4	.000
Linear-by-Linear Association	25.717	1	.000
N of Valid Cases	440		

a. 1 cells (11.1%) have expected count less than 5. The minimum expected count is 3.42.

Figure SIA11.5
SPSS contingency table analysis—satisfaction versus user type

c. Create a bar graph with row A_1 percentage on the vertical axis and B classification on the horizontal axis. Does the graph support the result of the test of hypothesis in Exercise 11.19? Explain.
d. Repeat part c for the row A_2 percentages.
e. Repeat part c for the row A_3 percentages.

Applying the Concepts—Basic

11.21 The *Journal of the American Medical Association* (Apr. 18, 2001) published the results of a study of alcohol consumption in patients suffering from acute myocardial infarction (AMI). The patients were classified according to average number of alcoholic drinks per week and whether or not they had congestive heart failure. A summary of the results for 1,913 AMI patients is shown in the table.

⊙ **AMAAMI**

Congestive Heart Failure	Alcohol Consumption		
	Abstainers	Less than 7 drinks/week	7 or more drinks/week
Yes	146	106	29
No	750	590	292
Totals	896	696	321

Source: Mukamal, K. J., et al. "Prior Alcohol Consumption and Mortality Following Acute Myocardial Infarction," *Journal of the American Medical Association,* Vol. 285, No. 15, April 18, 2001 (Table 1).

a. Find the sample proportion of abstainers with congestive heart failure.   .163

WORK * USER Crosstabulation

			USER			
			Mail	Net	Both	Total
WORK	FULL	Count	148	29	90	267
		Expected Count	159.0	26.1	81.9	267.0
	PART	Count	31	8	13	52
		Expected Count	31.0	5.1	16.0	52.0
	NONE	Count	31	3	17	51
		Expected Count	30.4	5.0	15.6	51.0
	RETIRED	Count	52	3	15	70
		Expected Count	41.7	6.8	21.5	70.0
Total		Count	262	43	135	440
		Expected Count	262.0	43.0	135.0	440.0

Chi-Square Tests

	Value	df	Asymp. Sig. (2-sided)
Pearson Chi-Square	11.687[a]	6	.069
Likelihood Ratio	12.208	6	.057
Linear-by-Linear Association	5.619	1	.018
N of Valid Cases	440		

a. 1 cells (8.3%) have expected count less than 5. The minimum expected count is 4.98.

Figure SIA11.6
SPSS contingency table analysis—work status versus user type

Contingency Tables

Using The TI-83 Graphing Calculator
Finding *p*-values for Contingency Tables

Step 1   *Access the Matrix Menu to enter the observed values*
Press **MATRX** (Note: On the TI-83 Plus, press **2nd x^{-1} for MATRX)**
Arrow right to **EDIT**
Press **ENTER**
Use the arrow key to enter the row and column dimensions of your observed Matrix
Use the arrow key to enter your observed values into Matrix [A]

```
MATRIX[A] 2 ×5
[ 39    19    12   -
[ 172   61    44   -
```

Step 2 *Access the Matrix Menu to enter the expected values*
Press **MATRX** (Note: On the TI-83 Plus, press **2nd x⁻¹** for **MATRX)**
Arrow right to **EDIT**
Arrow down to **2:[B]**
Press **ENTER**
Use the arrow key to enter the row and column dimensions of your expected
Matrix. (The dimensions will be the same as in Matrix A)
Use the arrow key to enter your expected values into Matrix [B]

```
MATRIX[A] 2 ×5
_ 12    28    18        ]
_ 44    70    ▓▓        ]


2,5=37
```

Step 3 *Access the Statistical Tests Menu and perform the Chi-square Test.*
Press **STAT**
Arrow right to **TESTS**
Arrow down to **C: χ^2 Test.**
Press **ENTER**
Arrow down to **Calculate**
Press **ENTER**

```
MATRIX[B] 2 ×5
_ 18.56   12.992  22.736 -
_ 61.44   43.008  ▓▓▓▓▓  -


2,4=75.264
```

Step 4 *Reject H_0 if the p-value $< \alpha$*

Example Our Observed Matrix is $[A] = \begin{bmatrix} 39 & 19 & 12 & 28 & 18 \\ 172 & 61 & 44 & 70 & 37 \end{bmatrix}$

Our Expected Matrix is

$$[B] = \begin{bmatrix} 48.952 & 18.56 & 12.992 & 22.736 & 12.76 \\ 162.05 & 61.44 & 43.008 & 75.264 & 42.24 \end{bmatrix}$$

Use $\alpha = .05$ to test the following hypotheses:

H_0:.The Matrix entries represent Independent events.

H_A:.The Matrix entries represent events that **are not** independent.

The screens for this example are shown below.

```
EDIT CALC TESTS
0↑2-SampTInt...
A:1-PropZInt...
B:2-PropZInt...
⬛X²-Test...
D:2-SampFTest...
E:LinRegTTest...
F:ANOVA(
```

```
X²-Test
 Observed:[A]
 Expected:[B]
 Calculate Draw
```

```
X²-Test
 X²=7.135464193
 P=.128900399
 df=4
```

As you can see from the screen the *p*-value is 0.1289. Since the *p*-value is **greater** than $\alpha = .05$, we **do not** reject H_0

b. Find the sample proportion of moderate drinkers (patients who have less than 7 drinks per week) with congestive heart failure.   .152

c. Find the sample proportion of heavy drinkers (patients who have 7 or more drinks per week) with congestive heart failure.   .090

d. Compare the sample proportions, parts **a–c.** Does it appear that the proportion of AMI patients with congestive heart failure depends on alcohol consumption?

e. Give the null hypothesis for testing whether the proportion of AMI patients with congestive heart failure depends on alcohol consumption.

f. Use the MINITAB printout on p. 669 to conduct the test, part **e.** Test at $\alpha = .05$. $\chi^2 = 10.197, p = .006$

11.22 Refer to the study of charitable givers published in the *National Tax Journal* (Dec. 2001), Exercise 11.9 (p. 652). In addition to the 1,072 charitable givers who reported that their charitable contributions were motivated by tax considerations, another 1,693 givers reported no tax motivation, giving a total sample of 2,765 charitable givers. Of the 1,072 who were motivated by tax considerations, 691 itemized deductions on their income tax returns. Of the 1,693 who were not motivated by tax considerations, 794 itemized deductions.

a. Consider the two categorical variables, tax motivation (yes or no) and itemize deductions (yes or no). Form a 2 × 2 contingency table for these variables.

b. Compute the expected cell counts for the contingency table, part **a.**

c. Compute the value of χ^2 for a test of independence. $\chi^2 = 81.461$

d. At $\alpha = .05$, what inference can you make about whether the two variables, tax motivation and itemize deductions, are related for charitable givers?

e. Create a bar graph that will visually support your conclusion in part **d.**

11.23 The *American Journal of Public Health* (July 1995) reported on a population-based study of trauma in Hispanic children. One of the objectives of the study was to compare the use of protective devices in motor vehicles used to transport Hispanic and non-Hispanic white children. On the basis of data

MINITAB Output for Exercise 11.21

```
Rows: FAILURE   Columns: ALCOHOL

          7ORMORE   ABSTAIN  LESS7     All

NO            292      750     590     1632
            273.8    764.4   593.8   1632.0

YES            29      146     106      281
             47.2    131.6   102.2    281.0

All           321      896     696     1913
            321.0    896.0   696.0   1913.0

Cell Contents:       Count
                     Expected count


Pearson Chi-Square = 10.197, DF = 2, P-Value = 0.006
Likelihood Ratio Chi-Square = 11.240, DF = 2, P-Value = 0.004
```

collected from the San Diego County Regionalized Trauma System, 792 children treated for injuries sustained in vehicular accidents were classified according to ethnic status (Hispanic or non-Hispanic white) and seatbelt usage (worn or not worn) during the accident. The data are summarized in the table below.

⊙ **TRAUMA**

	Hispanic	Non-Hispanic White	Totals
Seatbelts worn	31	148	179
Seatbelts not worn	283	330	613
Totals	314	478	792

Source: Matteneci, R. M. et al. "Trauma among Hispanic Children: A Population-Based Study in a Regionalized System of Trauma Care." *American Journal of Public Health,* Vol. 85, No. 7, July 1995, p. 1007 (Table 2).

a. Of the injured Hispanic children, what proportion were not wearing seatbelts during the accident? $\hat{p} = .901$

b. Of the injured non-Hispanic white children, what proportion were not wearing seatbelts during the accident? $\hat{p} = .690$

c. Compare the two sample proportions, parts **a** and **b.** Do you think the true population proportions differ?

d. Conduct a test to determine whether seatbelt usage in motor vehicle accidents depends on ethnic status in the San Diego County Regionalized Trauma System. Use $\alpha = .01$. $\chi^2 = 48.19$

e. Construct a 99% confidence interval for the difference between the proportions, parts **a** and **b.** Interpret the interval. $.211 \pm .070$

11.24 An article in *Sociological Methods & Research* (May 2001) analyzed the data presented in the table. A sample of 262 Kansas pig farmers were classified according to their education level (college or not) and size of their pig farm (number of pigs). Conduct a test to determine whether a pig farmer's education level has an impact on the size of the pig farm. Use $\alpha = .05$ and support your answer with a graph. $\chi^2 = 2.14$

⊙ **PIGFARM**

	Education Level		
FARM SIZE	No College	College	TOTALS
<1,000 pigs	42	53	95
1,000–2,000 pigs	27	42	69
2,000–5,000 pigs	22	20	42
>5,000 pigs	27	29	56
TOTALS	118	144	262

Source: Agresti, A., and Liu, I. "Strategies for Modeling a Categorical Variable Allowing Multiple Category Choices," *Sociological Methods & Research,* Vol. 29, No. 4, May 2001 (Table 1).

11.25 In order to create a behavioral profile of pleasure travelers, M. Bonn (Florida State University), L. Forr (Georgia Southern University), and A. Susskind (Cornell University) interviewed 5,026 pleasure travelers in the Tampa Bay region (*Journal of Travel Research,* May 1999). Two of the characteristics they investigated were the travelers' education level and their use of the

Internet to seek travel information. The table below summarizes the results of the interviews. The researchers concluded that travelers who use the Internet to search for travel information are likely to be people who are college educated. Do you agree? Test using $\alpha = .05$. What assumptions must hold to ensure the validity of your test? $\chi^2 = 256.336$

NETRAVEL

Education	Use Internet	
	Yes	No
College Degree or More	1,072	1,287
Less than a College Degree	640	2,027

Source: Bonn, M., Furr, L., and Susskind, A., "Predicting a Behavioral Profile for Pleasure Travelers on the Basis of Internet Use Segmentation," *Journal of Travel Research*, Vol. 37, May 1999, pp. 333–340.

11.26 To better understand whether and how Total Quality Management (TQM) is practiced in U.S. companies, University of Scranton researchers N. Tamimi and R. Sebastianelli interviewed one manager in each of a sample of 86 companies in Pennsylvania, New York, and New Jersey (*Production and Inventory Management Journal*, 1996). Concerning whether or not the firms were involved with TQM, the following data were obtained:

TQM

	Service Firms	Manufacturing Firms
Number practicing TQM	34	23
Number not practicing TQM	18	11
Total	52	34

Source: Adapted from Tamimi, N., and Sebastianelli, R. "How Firms Define and Measure Quality." *Production and Inventory Management Journal*, Third Quarter, 1996, p. 35.

 a. The researchers concluded that "manufacturing firms were not significantly more likely to be involved with TQM than service firms." Do you agree? Test using $\alpha = .05$. $\chi^2 = .047$

 b. Find and interpret the approximate p-value for the test you conducted in part **a.** $.10 < p < .90$

 c. What assumptions must hold in order for your test of part **a** and your p-value of part **b** to be valid?

11.27 For over 20 years, movie critics Gene Siskel (formerly of the *Chicago Tribune*, now deceased) and Roger Ebert *(Chicago Sun-Times)* rated the latest film releases on national television, first on PBS with *Sneak Previews*, then in syndication with *At the Movies*. University of Florida statisticians examined data on 160 movie reviews by Siskel and Ebert during the

period 1995–1996 (*Chance*, Spring 1997). Each critic's review was categorized as pro ("thumbs up"), con ("thumbs down"), or mixed. Consequently, each movie has a Siskel rating (pro, con, or mixed) and an Ebert rating (pro, con, or mixed). A portion of the data, saved in the **THUMBSUP** file, is shown below. Conduct a test of hypothesis to determine whether the movie reviews of the two critics are independent. Use $\alpha = .01$. $\chi^2 = 45.4$

THUMBSUP

Movie	Siskel Rating	Ebert Rating
1	Pro	Pro
2	Mix	Pro
3	Con	Mix
4	Con	Con
5	Pro	Pro
⋮	⋮	⋮
156	Mix	Mix
157	Pro	Pro
158	Pro	Pro
159	Con	Pro
160	Pro	Pro

11.28 University of Louisville professor Julia Karcher conducted an experiment to investigate the ethical behavior of accountants (*Journal of Business Ethics*, Vol. 15, 1996). She focused on auditor abilities to detect ethical problems that may not be obvious. Seventy auditors from Big-Six accounting firms were given a detailed case study that contained several problems including tax evasion by the client. In 35 of the cases the tax evasion issue was severe; in the other 35 cases it was moderate. The auditors were asked to identify any problems they detected in the case. The following table summarizes the results for the ethical issue.

ACCETHIC

	Severity of Ethical Issue	
	Moderate	Severe
Ethical Issue Identified	27	26
Ethical Issue Not Identified	8	9

Source: Karcher, J. "Auditors' Ability to Discern the Presence of Ethical Problems." *Journal of Business Ethics*, Vol. 15, 1996, p. 1041 (Table V).

 a. Did the severity of the ethical issue influence whether the issue was identified or not by the auditors? Test using $\alpha = .05$. $\chi^2 = .078$

 b. Suppose the lefthand column of the table contained the counts 35 and 0 instead of 27 and 8. Should the test of part **a** still be conducted? Explain. No

c. Keeping the sample size the same, change the numbers in the contingency table so that the answer you would get for the question posed in part **a** changes.

11.29 Many companies use well-known celebrities in their ads, while other companies create their own spokespersons (such as the Maytag repairman). A study in the *Journal of Marketing* (Fall 1992) investigated the relationship between the gender of the spokesperson and the gender of the viewer in order to see how this relationship affected brand awareness. Three hundred television viewers were asked to identify the products advertised by celebrity spokespersons. The results are presented in the next two tables.

a. For the products advertised by male spokespersons, conduct a test to determine whether audience gender and product identification are dependent factors. Test using $\alpha = .05$. $\chi^2 = 39.22$

b. Repeat part **a** for the products advertised by female spokespersons. $\chi^2 = 2.84$

c. How would you interpret these results?

⊙ MALEAD

Male Spokesperson

	Audience Gender		
	Male	Female	Total
Identified Product	95	41	136
Could Not Identify Product	55	109	164
Total	150	150	300

⊙ FEMALEAD

Female Spokesperson

	Audience Gender		
	Male	Female	Total
Identified Product	47	61	108
Could Not Identify Product	103	89	192
Total	150	150	300

11.30 Research has indicated that the stress produced by today's lifestyles results in health problems for a large proportion of society. An article in the *International Journal of Sports Psychology* (July–Sept. 1990) evaluated the relationship between physical fitness and stress. Five hundred forty-nine employees of companies that participate in the Health Examination Program offered by Health Advancement Services (HAS) were classified into three groups of fitness levels: good, average, and poor. Each person was tested for signs of stress. The next table reports the results for the three groups. [*Note:*

The proportions given are the proportions of the entire group that show signs of stress and fall into each particular fitness level.] Do the data provide evidence to indicate that the likelihood for stress is dependent on an employee's fitness level? $\chi^2 = 24.524$

Fitness Level	Sample Size	Proportions with Signs of Stress
Poor	242	.155
Average	212	.133
Good	95	.108

Applying the Concepts—Advanced

11.31 New, effective AIDS vaccines are now being developed using the process of "sieving" (i.e., sifting out infections with some strains of HIV). Harvard School of Public Health statistician Peter Gilbert demonstrated how to test the efficacy of an HIV vaccine in *Chance* (Fall 2000). As an example, Gilbert reported the results of VaxGen's preliminary HIV vaccine trial using the following 2×2 table. The vaccine was designed to eliminate a particular strain of the virus, called the "MN strain." The trial consisted of 7 AIDS patients vaccinated with the new drug and 31 AIDS patients who were treated with a placebo (no vaccination). The table shows the number of patients who tested positive and negative for the MN strain in the trial follow-up period.

⊙ VAXGEN1

	MN Strain		
PATIENT GROUP	Positive	Negative	TOTALS
Unvaccinated	22	9	31
Vaccinated	2	5	7
TOTALS	24	14	38

Source: Gilbert, P. "Developing an AIDS Vaccine by Sieving," *Chance*, Vol. 13, No. 4, Fall 2000.

a. Conduct a test to determine whether the vaccine is effective in treating the MN strain of HIV. Use $\alpha = .05$. $\chi^2 = 4.411$

b. Are the assumptions for the test, part a, satisfied? What are the consequences if the assumptions are violated?

c. In the case of a 2×2 contingency table, R. A. Fisher (1935) developed a procedure for computing the exact *p*-value for the test (called *Fisher's exact test*). The method utilizes the hypergeometric probability distribution of Chapter 4 (p. 249). Consider the hypergeometric probability

$$\frac{\binom{7}{2}\binom{31}{22}}{\binom{38}{24}}$$

This represents the probability that 2 out of 7 vaccinated AIDS patients test positive and 22 out of 31 unvaccinated patients test positive (i.e., the probability of the table result given the null hypothesis of independence is true). Compute this probability (called the *probability of the contingency table*). .04378

d. Refer to part **c.** Two contingency tables (with the same marginal totals as the original table) that are more contradictory to the null hypothesis of independence than the observed table follow. First, explain why these tables provide more evidence to reject H_0 than the original table; then compute the probability of each table using the hypergeometric formula. .00571; .00027

⊙ **VAXGEN2**

	MN Strain		
PATIENT GROUP	Positive	Negative	TOTALS
Unvaccinated	23	8	31
Vaccinated	1	6	7
TOTALS	24	14	38

⊙ **VAXGEN3**

	MN Strain		
PATIENT GROUP	Positive	Negative	TOTALS
Unvaccinated	24	7	31
Vaccinated	0	7	7
TOTALS	24	14	38

e. The *p*-value of Fisher's exact test is the probability of observing a result at least as contradictory to the null hypothesis as the observed contingency table, given the same marginal totals. Sum the probabilities of parts **c** and **d** to obtain the *p*-value of Fisher's exact test. (To verify your calculations, check the *p*-value at the bottom of the accompanying SPSS printout.) Interpret this value in the context of the vaccine trial. $p = .04976$

SPSS Output for Exercise 11.31

GROUP * MNSTRAIN Crosstabulation

			MNSTRAIN		
			NEG	POS	Total
GROUP	UNVAC	Count	9	22	31
		Expected Count	11.4	19.6	31.0
	VACC	Count	5	2	7
		Expected Count	2.6	4.4	7.0
Total		Count	14	24	38
		Expected Count	14.0	24.0	38.0

Chi-Square Tests

	Value	df	Asymp. Sig. (2-sided)	Exact Sig. (2-sided)	Exact Sig. (1-sided)
Pearson Chi-Square	4.411[b]	1	.036		
Continuity Correction[a]	2.777	1	.096		
Likelihood Ratio	4.289	1	.038		
Fisher's Exact Test				.077	.050
N of Valid Cases	38				

a. Computed only for a 2x2 table

b. 2 cells (50.0%) have expected count less than 5. The minimum expected count is 2.58.

11.4 A Word of Caution About Chi-Square Tests

Because the χ^2 statistic for testing hypotheses about multinomial probabilities is one of the most widely applied statistical tools, it is also one of the most abused statistical procedures. Consequently, the user should always be certain that the experiment satisfies the assumptions given with each procedure. Furthermore, the user should be certain that the sample is drawn from the correct population—that is, from the population about which the inference is to be made.

The use of the χ^2 probability distribution as an approximation to the sampling distribution for χ^2 should be avoided when the expected counts are very small. The approximation can become very poor when these expected counts are small, and thus the true α level may be quite different from the tabled value. As a rule of thumb, an expected cell count of at least 5 means that the χ^2 probability distribution can be used to determine an approximate critical value.

If the χ^2 value does not exceed the established critical value of χ^2, *do not accept the hypothesis of independence*. You would be risking a Type II error (accepting H_0 if it is false), and the probability β of committing such an error is unknown. The usual alternative hypothesis is that the classifications are dependent. Because the number of ways in which two classifications can be dependent is virtually infinite, it is difficult to calculate one or even several values of β to represent such a broad alternative hypothesis. Therefore, we avoid concluding that two classifications are independent, even when χ^2 is small.

Finally, if a contingency table χ^2 value does exceed the critical value, we must be careful to avoid inferring that a *causal* relationship exists between the classifications. Our alternative hypothesis states that the two classifications are statistically dependent—and a statistical dependence does not imply causality. Therefore, *the existence of a causal relationship cannot be established by a contingency table analysis.*

Quick Review

Key Terms

Categories 644	Expected cell count 647	Marginal probabilities 655
Cell 644	Classes 644	Multinomial experiment 644
Cell counts 644	Dependence 658	Observed cell count 656
Chi-square test 646	Dimensions of classification 655	One-way table 645
Contingency table 655	Independence of two classifications 656	Two-way table 655

Key Formulas

$$\chi^2 = \sum \frac{[n_i - E(n_i)]^2}{E(n_i)}$$

One-way table   647

where n_i = count for cell i

$E(n_i) = np_{i,0}$

$p_{i,0}$ = hypothesized value of p_i in H_0

$$\chi^2 = \sum \frac{[n_{ij} - E_{ij}]^2}{E_{ij}} \qquad\qquad \text{Two-way table} \quad 660$$

where n_{ij} = count for cell in row i, column j

$E_{ij} = R_i C_j / n$
R_i = total for row i
C_j = total for column j
n = total sample size

Chapter Summary Notes

- **Multinomial data** are qualitative data that fall into more than two *categories, classes,* or *cells.*
- Properties of a **multinomial experiment:** (1) n identical trials, (2) k possible outcomes to each trial, (3) probabilities of the k outcomes remain the same from trial to trial, (4) trials are independent, (5) the variables of interest are the *cell counts.*
- A **one-way table** is a summary table for a single qualitative variable.
- A **two-way table,** or **contingency table,** is a summary table for two qualitative variables.

- The **chi-square** (χ^2) **statistic** is used to test probabilities associated with one-way and two-way tables.
- Conditions required for a valid χ^2-**test:** (1) multinomial experiment, (2) sample size n is large—satisfied when expected cell counts are all greater than or equal to 5.
- A significant χ^2 test for a *two-way table* implies that the **two qualitative variables are dependent.**
- Chi-square tests for independence *cannot be used to infer a causal relationship exists* between the two qualitative variables.

Language Lab

Symbol	Pronunciation	Description
p_{i0}	p-sub i-zero	Value of multinomial probability p_i hypothesized in H_0
χ^2	Chi-square	Test statistic used in analysis of count data
n_i	n-sub i	Number of observed outcomes in cell i of one-way table
$E(n_i)$	Expected value of n-i	Expected number of outcomes in cell i of one-way table when H_0 is true
p_{ij}	p-sub i-j	Probability of an outcome in row i and column of j of a two-way contingency table
n_{ij}	n-sub i-j	Number of observed outcomes in row i and column j of a two-way contingency table
E_{ij}	E-i-j	Estimated expected number of outcomes in row i and column j of a two-way contingency table
R_i	R-i	Total number of outcomes in row i of a contingency table
C_j	C-j	Total number of outcomes in column j of a contingency table

Supplementary Exercises 11.32–11.47

Learning the Mechanics

11.32 A random sample of 250 observations was classified according to the row and column categories shown in the table.

⊙ **LM11_32**

		Column		
		1	2	3
	1	20	20	10
Row	2	10	20	70
	3	20	50	30

a. Do the data provide sufficient evidence to conclude that the rows and columns are dependent? Test using $\alpha = .05$. $\chi^2 = 54.14$

b. Would the analysis change if the row totals were fixed before the data were collected?   No

c. Do the assumptions required for the analysis to be valid differ according to whether the row (or column) totals are fixed? Explain.   Yes

d. Convert the table entries to percentages by using each column total as a base and calculating each row response as a percentage of the corresponding column total. In addition, calculate the row totals and convert them to percentages of all 250 observations.

e. Create a bar graph with row 1 percentage on the vertical axis against the column number on the horizontal axis. Draw horizontal lines corresponding to the row 1 percentages. Does the graph support the result of the test conducted in part **a**?

11.33 A random sample of 150 observations was classified into the categories shown in the table below.

⊙ **LM11_33**

	Category				
	1	2	3	4	5
n_i	28	35	33	25	29

a. Do the data provide sufficient evidence that the categories are not equally likely? Use $\alpha = .10$. $\chi^2 = 2.133$

b. Form a 90% confidence interval for p_2, the probability that an observation will fall in category 2.   .233 ± .057

Applying the Concepts—Basic

11.34 *Bon Appetit* magazine polled 200 of its readers concerning which of the four vegetables—brussel sprouts, okra, lima beans, and cauliflower—is their least favorite. The results (adapted from *Adweek*, Feb. 21, 2000) are presented in the table. Let p_1, p_2, p_3, and p_4 represent the proportions of all *Bon Appetit* readers who indicate brussel sprouts, okra, lima beans, and cauliflower, respectively, as their least favorite vegetable.

⊙ **BONAPP**

Brussel Sprouts	Okra	Lima Beans	Cauliflower
46	76	44	34

a. If, in general, *Bon Appetit* readers do not have a preference for their least favorite vegetable, what are the values of p_1, p_2, p_3, and p_4? $p_1 = p_2 = p_3 = p_4 = .25$

b. Specify the null and alternative hypotheses that should be used to determine whether *Bon Appetit* readers have a preference for one of the vegetables as "least favorite."

c. Conduct the test you described in part **b** using $\alpha = .05$. Report your conclusion in the context of the problem. $\chi^2 = 19.68$

d. What assumptions must hold to ensure the validity of the test you conducted in part **c**? Which, if any, of these assumptions may be a concern in this application?

11.35 *Inc. Technology* (Mar. 18, 1997) reported the results of the 1996 Equifax/Harris Consumer Privacy Survey in which 328 Internet users indicated their level of agreement with the following statement: "The government needs to be able to scan Internet messages and user communications to prevent fraud and other crimes." The number of users in each response category is summarized below.

⊙ **GOVWEB**

Agree Strongly	Agree Somewhat	Disagree Somewhat	Disagree Strongly
59	108	82	79

a. Specify the null and alternative hypotheses you would use to determine if the opinions of Internet users are evenly divided among the four categories.

b. Conduct the test of part **a** using $\alpha = .05$.
$\chi^2 = 14.805$

c. In the context of this exercise, what is a Type I error? A Type II error?

d. What assumptions must hold in order to ensure the validity of the test you conducted in part **b**?

11.36 To study the extent and nature of strategic planning being undertaken by boards of directors, A. Tashakori and W. Boulton questioned a sample of 119 chief executive officers of major U.S. corporations (*Journal of Business Strategy*, Winter 1983). One objective was to determine if a relationship exists between the composition of a board (i.e., a majority of outside directors versus a majority of in-house directors) and its level of participation in the strategic planning process. The questionnaire data were used to classify the responding corporations according to the level of their board's participation in the strategic planning process as follows:

Level 1: Board participates in formulation or implementation or evaluation of strategy
Level 2: Board participates in formulation and implementation, formulation and evaluation, or implementation and evaluation of strategy
Level 3: Board participates in formulation, implementation, and evaluation of strategy

The 119 boards were also classified according to whether a majority of their directors were from inside the firm or outside the firm. The data are summarized in the accompanying table.

BOARDIR

Level	Board Composition	
	Inside	Outside
1	2	20
2	10	27
3	7	53
Total	**19**	**100**

a. The researchers concluded that a relationship exists between a board's level of participation in the strategic planning process and the composition of the board. Do you agree? Construct the appropriate contingency table, and test using $\alpha = .10$.
$\chi^2 = 4.99$

b. In the context of this problem, specify the Type I and Type II errors associated with the test of part **a**.

c. Construct a graph that helps to interpret the result of the test in part **a**.

11.37 Research indicates that the highest priority of retirees is travel. A study in the *Annals of Tourism Research* (Vol. 19, 1992) investigates the relationship of retirement status (pre- and postretirement) to various items related to the travel industry. One part of the study investigated the differences in the length of stay of a trip for pre- and postretirees. A sample of 703 travelers were asked how long they stayed on a typical trip. The results are shown in the table. Use the information in the table to determine whether the retirement status of a traveler and the duration of a typical trip are dependent. Test using $\alpha = .05$.

TRAVTRIP

Number of Nights	Preretirement	Postretirement
4–7	247	172
8–13	82	67
14–21	35	52
22 or more	16	32
Total	**380**	**323**

11.38 An article in the *Annals of the Association of American Geographers* (June 1992) investigated what influences homeowners in purchasing earthquake insurance. One factor investigated was the proximity to a major fault. The researchers hypothesized that the nearer a county is to a major fault, the more likely residents are to own earthquake insurance. Suppose that a random sample of 700 earthquake-insured residents from four California counties is selected, and the number in each county is counted and recorded in the table:

EARTHQK

	Contra Costa	Santa Clara	Los Angeles	San Bernardino
Number Insured	103	213	241	143

a. What are the appropriate null and alternative hypotheses to test whether the proportions of all earthquake-insured residents in the four counties differ?

b. Do the data provide sufficient evidence that the proportions of all earthquake-insured residents differ among the four counties? Test using $\alpha = .05$.
$\chi^2 = 68.62$

c. Los Angeles County is closest to a major earthquake fault. Construct a 95% confidence interval for the proportion of all earthquake-insured residents in the four counties that reside in Los Angeles County.   .3443 ± .0352

d. Does the confidence interval you formed in part **c** support the conclusion of the test conducted in part **b**? Explain.   Yes

Applying the Concepts—Intermediate

11.39 In education, the term *instructional technology* refers to products such as computers, spreadsheets, CD-ROMs, videos, and presentation software. How frequently do professors use instructional technology in the classroom? To answer this question, researchers at Western Michigan University surveyed 306 of their fellow faculty (*Educational Technology*, Mar.–Apr. 1995). Responses to the frequency-of-technology use in teaching were recorded as "weekly to every class," "once a semester to monthly," or "never." The faculty responses (number in each response category) for the three technologies are summarized in the table.

ⓔ TECHUSE

Technology	Weekly	Once a Semester/ Monthly	Never
Computer spreadsheets	58	67	181
Word processing	168	61	77
Statistical software	37	82	187

a. Determine whether the percentages in the three frequency-of-use response categories differ for computer spreadsheets. Use $\alpha = .01$. $\chi^2 = 92.176$

b. Repeat part **a** for word processing. $\chi^2 = 65.314$

c. Repeat part **a** for statistical software. $\chi^2 = 116.176$

d. Construct a 99% confidence interval for the true percentage of faculty who never use computer spreadsheets in the classroom. Interpret the interval.

11.40 Because shareholders control the firm, they can transfer wealth from the firm's bondholders to themselves through several different dividend strategies. This potential conflict of interest between shareholders and bondholders can be reduced through the use of debt covenants. Accountants E. Griner and H. Huss of Georgia State University investigated the effects of insider ownership and the size of the firm on the types of debt covenants required by a firm's bondholders (*Journal of Applied Business Research*, Vol. 11, 1995). As part of the study, they examined a sample of 31 companies whose bondholders required covenants based on tangible assets rather than on liquidity or net assets

or retained earnings. Characteristics of those 31 firms are summarized below. The objective of the study is to determine if there is a relationship between the extent of insider ownership and the size of the firm for firms with tangible asset covenants.

ⓔ INSIDOWN

		Size	
		Small	Large
Inside Ownership	Low	3	17
	High	8	3

Source: Griner, E., and Huss, H. "Firm Size, Insider Ownership, and Accounting-Based Debt Covenants." *Journal of Applied Business Research*, Vol. 11, No. 4, 1995, p. 7 (Table 4).

a. Assuming the null hypothesis of independence is true, how many firms are expected to fall in each cell of the table above?

b. The researchers were unable to use the chi-square test to analyze the data. Show why.

c. A test of the null hypothesis can be conducted using *Fisher's exact test.* (See Exercise 11.31, p. 617.) This method calculates the exact probability (*p*-value) of observing sample results at least as contradictory to the null hypothesis as those observed for the researchers' data. The researchers reported the *p*-value for this test as .0043. Interpret this result.

d. Investigate the nature of the dependence exhibited by the contingency table by plotting the appropriate contingency table percentages. Describe what you find.

11.41 If a company can identify times of day when accidents are most likely to occur, extra precautions can be instituted during those times. A random sampling of the accident reports over the last year at a plant gives the frequency of occurrence of accidents during the different hours of the workday. Can it be concluded from the data in the table that the proportions of accidents are different for at least two of the four time periods? $\chi^2 = 7.384$

ⓔ JOBACC

Hours	1–2	3–4	5–6	7–8
Number of Accidents	31	28	45	47

11.42 An economist was interested in knowing whether sons have a tendency to choose the same occupation as their fathers. To investigate this question, 500 males were polled and each questioned concerning his occupation and the occupation of his father. A summary of the numbers of father-son pairs falling in each occupational category is shown in the table at the bottom of the page. Do the data provide sufficient evidence at $\alpha = .05$ to indicate a dependence between a son's choice of occupation and his father's occupation? $\chi^2 = 180.87$

11.43 Westinghouse Electric Company has experimented with different means of evaluating the performance of solder joint inspectors. One approach involves comparing an individual inspector's classifications with those of the group of experts that comprise Westinghouse's Work Standards Committee. In one experiment conducted by Westinghouse, 153 solder connections were evaluated by the committee and 111 were classified as acceptable. An inspector evaluated the same 153 connections and classified 124 as acceptable. Of the items rejected by the inspector, the committee agreed with 19.

a. Construct a contingency table that summarizes the classifications of the committee and the inspector.

b. Based on a visual examination of the table you constructed in part **a,** does it appear that there is a relationship between the inspector's classifications and the committee's? Explain. (A graph of the percentage rejected by committee and inspector will aid your examination.) Yes

c. Conduct a chi-square test of independence for these data. Use $\alpha = .05$. Carefully interpret the results of your test in the context of the problem.

11.44 A study was done on the accuracy of newspaper advertisements by the five types of food stores in a southeastern city. On each of four days, items were randomly selected from the advertisements for each type of store and the actual price was compared to the advertised price. Each of the stores in the city was classified as one of the following types: national, regional chain A, regional chain B, regional chain C, or independent. Values in the table (top, right) represent the number of items that were correctly and incorrectly priced.

ADERRS

Type of Store	Number Correctly Priced	Number Incorrectly Priced
National chain	89	10
Regional chain A	53	14
Regional chain B	43	12
Regional chain C	32	13
Independent	41	7

a. Determine whether these data provide sufficient evidence to conclude that the proportion of correctly priced items differs for at least two types of stores. Use $\alpha = .10$. $\chi^2 = 9.16$

b. Use a 95% confidence interval to estimate the proportion of correctly priced items in the stores in the national chain category. $.90 \pm .06$

11.45 When a buyer charges a purchase, the seller records the sale in his or her record books under a category called *accounts receivable*. Some retailers monitor the status of their accounts receivable by regularly classifying each in one of the following categories: current, 1–30 days late, 31–60 days late, more than 60 days late, or uncollectable. Historical data indicate that the status of a particular retailer's accounts receivable can be described as follows:

Current	65%
1–30 days late	15%
31–60 days late	10%
Over 60 days late	7%
Uncollectable	3%

Six months after the interest rate charged to late accounts was increased, the status of the retailer's 200 accounts receivable was as follows:

Current	78%
1–30 days late	12%
31–60 days late	5%
Over 60 days late	2%
Uncollectable	3%

a. Is there evidence to indicate that the increase in interest rates affected the timing of buyers' payments? Test using $\alpha = .10$. $\chi^2 = 18.54$

FATHSON

		Son			
		Professional or Business	Skilled	Unskilled	Farmer
Father	**Professional or Business**	55	38	7	0
	Skilled	79	71	25	0
	Unskilled	22	75	38	10
	Farmer	15	23	10	32

b. Find the approximate observed significance level for the test. .001

11.46 Product or service quality is often defined as *fitness for use*. This means the product or service meets the customer's needs. Generally speaking, fitness for use is based on five quality characteristics: technological (e.g., strength, hardness), psychological (taste, beauty), time-oriented (reliability), contractual (guarantee provisions), and ethical (courtesy, honesty). The quality of a service may involve all these characteristics, while the quality of a manufactured product generally depends on technological and time-oriented characteristics (Schroeder, *Operations Management*, 1993). After a barrage of customer complaints about poor quality, a manufacturer of gasoline filters for cars had its quality inspectors sample 600 filters—200 per work shift—and check for defects. The data in the table resulted.

⊙ FILTER

Shift	Defectives Produced
First	25
Second	35
Third	80

a. Do the data indicate that the quality of the filters being produced may be related to the shift producing the filter? Test using $\alpha = .05$. $\chi^2 = 47.98$

b. Estimate the proportion of defective filters produced by the first shift. Use a 95% confidence interval. $.125 \pm .046$

Applying the Concepts—Advanced

11.47 A statistical analysis is to be done on a set of data consisting of 1,000 monthly salaries. The analysis requires the assumption that the sample was drawn from a normal distribution. A preliminary test, called the χ^2 *goodness-of-fit test*, can be used to help determine whether it is reasonable to assume that the sample is from a normal distribution. Suppose the mean and standard deviation of the 1,000 salaries are hypothesized to be $1,200 and $200, respectively. Using the standard normal table, we can approximate the probability of a salary being in the intervals listed in the table below. The third column represents the expected number of the 1,000 salaries to be found in each interval if the sample was drawn from a normal distribution with $\mu = \$1,200$ and $\sigma = \$200$. Suppose the last column contains the actual observed frequencies in the sample. Large differences between the observed and expected frequencies cast doubt on the normality assumption.

a. Compute the χ^2 statistic based on the observed and expected frequencies—just as you did in Section 11.2. $\chi^2 = 9.647$

b. Find the tabulated χ^2 value when $\alpha = .05$ and there are 5 degrees of freedom. (There are $k - 1 = 5$ df associated with this χ^2 statistic.) 11.0705

c. Based on the χ^2 statistic and the tabulated χ^2 value, is there evidence that the salary distribution is nonnormal? Fail to reject H_0

d. Find an approximate observed significance level for the test in part **c.** $.05 < p < .10$

Interval	Probability	Expected Frequency	Observed Frequency
Less than $800	.023	23	26
Between $800 & $1,000	.136	136	146
Between $1,000 & $1,200	.341	341	361
Between $1,200 & $1,400	.341	341	311
Between $1,400 & $1,600	.136	136	143
Above $1,600	.023	23	13

REFERENCES

Agresti, A. *Categorical Data Analysis*. New York: Wiley, 1990.

Cochran, W. G. "The χ^2 Test of Goodness of Fit." *Annals of Mathematical Statistics*, 1952, 23.

Conover, W. J. *Practical Nonparametric Statistics*, 2nd ed. New York: Wiley, 1980.

Fisher, R. A. "The Logic of Inductive Inference (with Discussion)," *Journal of the Royal Statistical Society*, Vol. 98, 1935, pp. 39–82.

Hollander, M., and Wolfe, D. A. *Nonparametric Statistical Methods*. New York: Wiley, 1973.

Savage, I. R. "Bibliography of Nonparametric Statistics and Related Topics." *Journal of the American Statistical Association*, 1953, 48.

DeGroot, M. H., Fienberg, S. E. and Kadane, J. B. eds. *Statistics and the Law*. New York: Wiley, 1986.

Schroeder, R. G. *Operations Management,* 4th ed. New York: McGraw-Hill, 1993.

Using Technology

11.1 Chi-Square Analyses Using SPSS

SPSS can conduct chi-square tests for both one-way and two-way (contingency) tables.

One-Way Table

To conduct a chi-square test for a one-way table, first access the SPSS spreadsheet file that contains the variable with category values for each of the *n* observations in the data set. (*Note*: SPSS requires that these categories be specified numerically, e.g., 1, 2, 3, etc.) Next, click on the "Analyze" button on the SPSS menu bar, then click on "Nonparametric Tests" and "Chi-Square", as shown in Figure 11.S.1.

Figure 11.S.1

SPSS menu options for one-way chi-square analysis

	work	coupsat		num	var	var
1	1	1		2		
2	1	1		2		
3	1	1		2		
4	1	1		2		
5	1	1		2		
6	1	1		2		
7	1	1		2		
8	1	1		2		
9	1	2				
10	1	1				
11	1	1				
12	1	1				
13	1	2				
14	1	1	3	1		
15	1	1	3	1		
16	1	2	3	2		
17	1	1	3	2		
18	1	1	3	2	2	

coupons - SPSS Data Editor

File Edit View Data Transform Analyze Graphs Utilities Window Help

Analyze menu:
Reports ▶
Descriptive Statistics ▶
Tables ▶
Compare Means ▶
General Linear Model ▶
Mixed Models ▶
Correlate ▶
Regression ▶
Loglinear ▶
Classify ▶
Data Reduction ▶
Scale ▶
Nonparametric Tests ▶ — Chi-Square...
Time Series ▶ — Binomial...
Survival ▶ — Runs...
Multiple Response ▶ — 1-Sample K-S...
— 2 Independent Samples...
— K Independent Samples...
— 2 Related Samples...
— K Related Samples...

The resulting dialog box appears as shown in Figure 11.S.2. Specify the qualitative variable of interest in the "Test Variable List" box. If you want to test for equal cell probabilities in the null hypothesis, then select the "All categories equal" option under the "Expected Values" box (as shown in Figure 11.S.2). If the null hypothesis specifies unequal cell probabilities, then select the "Values" option under the "Expected Values" box. Enter the hypothesized cell probabilities in the adjacent box, one at a time, clicking "Add" after each specification. Click "OK" to generate the SPSS printout.

Figure 11.S.2
SPSS one-way chi-square
dialog box

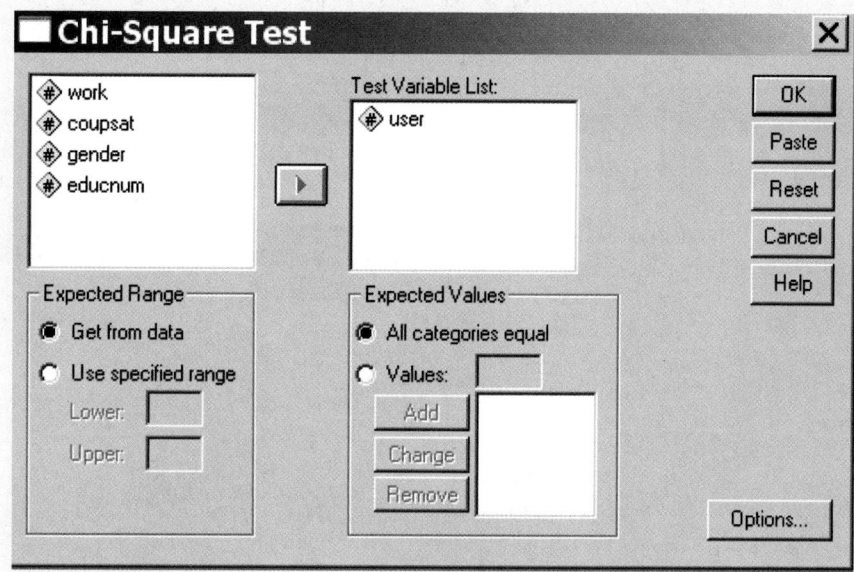

Two-Way Table

To conduct a chi-square test for a two-way (contingency) table, first access the SPSS spreadsheet file that contains the sample data. The data file should contain two qualitative variables, with category values for each of the *n* observations in the data set. Next, click on the "Analyze" button on the SPSS menu bar, then click on "Descriptive Statistics" and "Crosstabs", as shown in Figure 11.S.3.

Figure 11.S.3
SPSS menu options for
two-way chi-square
analysis

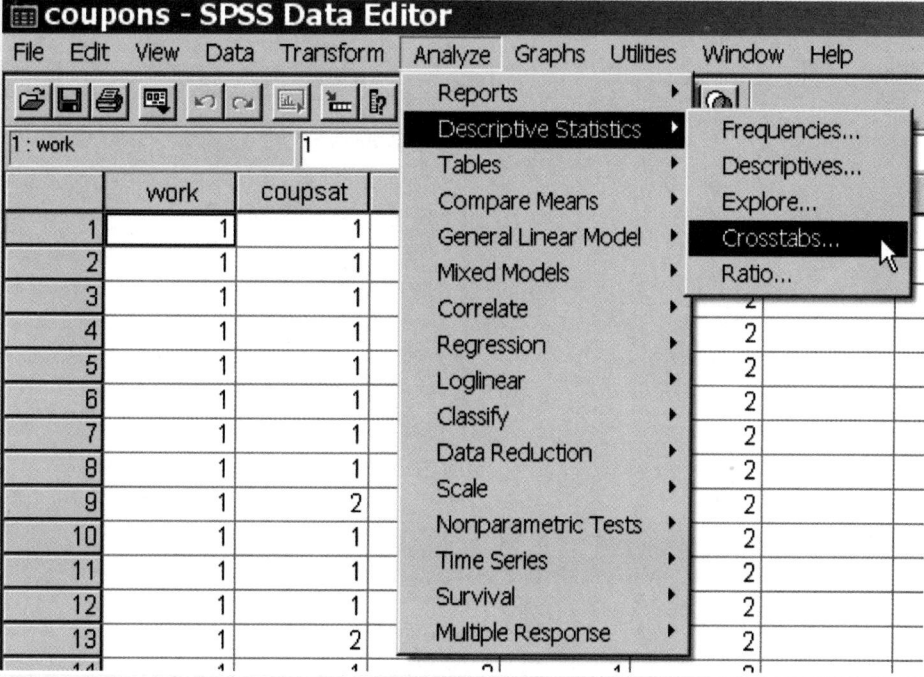

The resulting dialog box appears as shown in Figure 11.S.4. Specify one qualitative variable in the "Row(s)" box and the other qualitative variable in the "Column(s)" box. Click the "Statistics" button and select the "Chi-square" option, as shown in Figure 11.S.5. Click "Continue" to return to the "Crosstabs" dialog box. If you want the contingency table to include expected values, row percentages, and/or

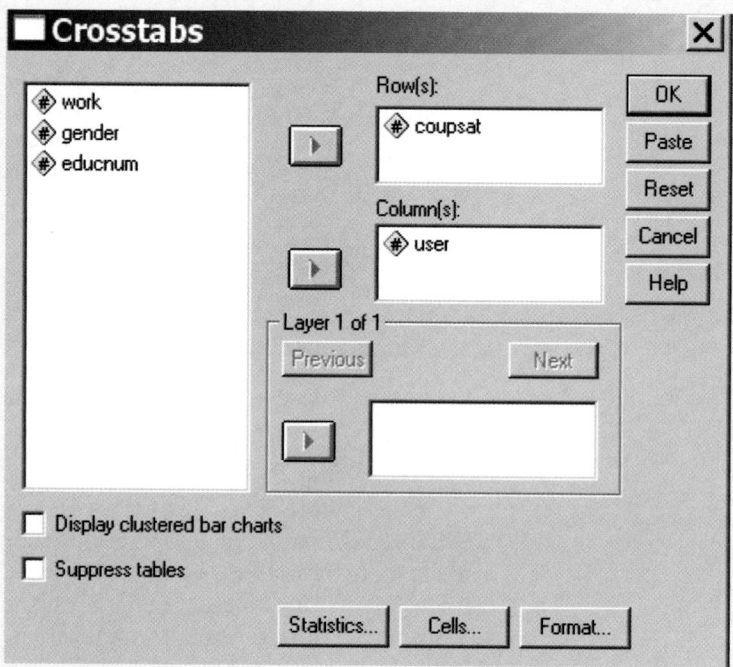

Figure 11.S.4
SPSS crosstabs dialog box

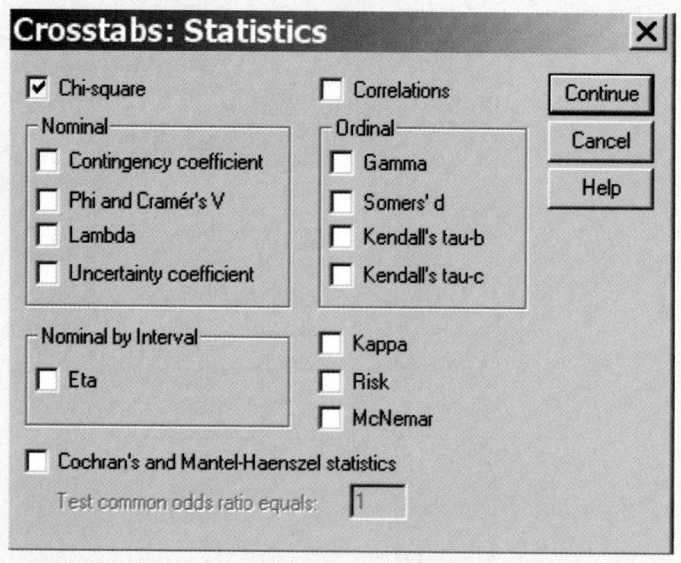

Figure 11.S.5
SPSS statistics menu selections for the two-way analysis

column percentages, click the "Cells" button and make the appropriate menu selections. When you return to the "Crosstabs" menu screen, click "OK" to generate the SPSS printout.

[Note: If your SPSS spreadsheet contains summary information (i.e., the cell counts for the contingency table) rather than the actual categorical data values for each observation, you must weight each observation in your data file by the cell count for that observation prior to running the chi-square analysis. Do this by selecting the "Data" button on the SPSS menu bar, then click on "Weight Cases" and specify the variable that contains the cell counts.]

11.2 Chi-Square Analyses Using MINITAB

MINITAB can conduct chi-square tests for two-way (contingency) tables but cannot currently produce a chi-square test for a one-way table.

To conduct a chi-square test for a two-way table, first access the MINITAB worksheet file that contains the sample data. The data file should contain two qualitative variables, with category values for each of the n observations in the data set. Alternatively, the worksheet can contain the cell counts for each of the categories of the two qualitative variables. Next, click on the "Stat" button on the MINITAB menu bar, then click on "Tables" and "Cross Tabulation and Chi-Square", as shown in Figure 11.M.1.

The resulting dialog box appears as shown in Figure 11.M.2. Specify one qualitative variable in the "For rows" box and the other qualitative variable in the "For columns" box. [*Note*: If your worksheet contains cell counts for the categories, enter the variable with the cell counts in the "Frequencies are in" box.] Next, select the summary statistics (e.g., counts, percentages) you want to display in the contingency table. Then click the "Chi-square" button. The resulting dialog box is shown in Figure 11.M.3. Select "Chi-Square analysis" and "Expected cell counts"

Figure 11.M.1
MINITAB menu options for two-way chi-square analysis

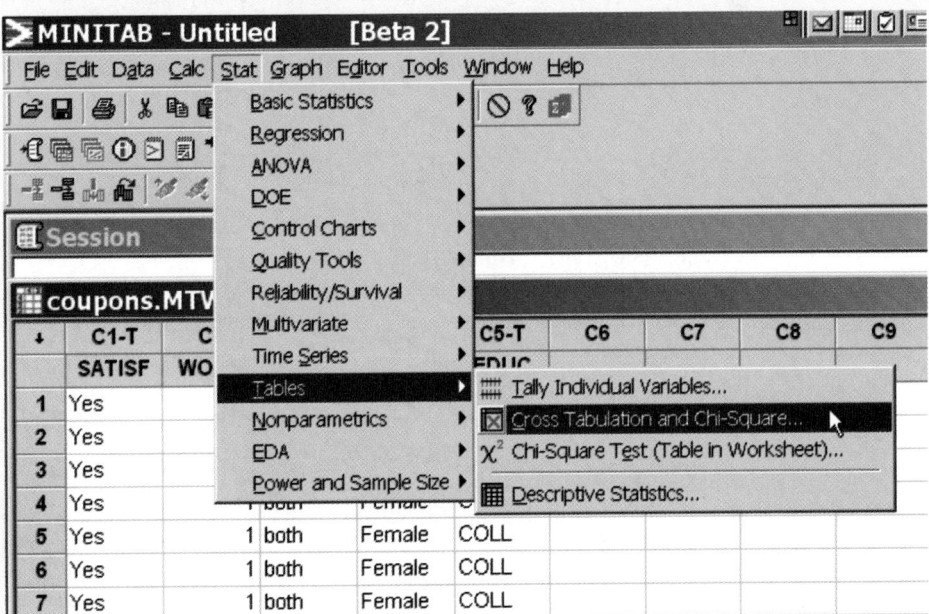

Cross Tabulation and Chi-Square ☒

C2 WORK	**Categorical variables:**

For rows: `SATISF`

For columns: `USER`

For layers: ` `

Frequencies are in: ` ` (optional)

Display
- ☑ **Counts**
- ☐ **Row percents**
- ☐ **Column percents**
- ☐ **Total percents**

[Chi-Square...] [Other Stats...]

[Options...]

[Select]

[Help] [OK] [Cancel]

Figure 11.M.2
MINITAB cross tabulation dialog box

Cross Tabulation - Chi-Square ☒

Display
- ☑ **Chi-Square analysis**
- ☑ **Expected cell counts**
- ☐ **Raw residuals**
- ☐ **Standardized residuals**
- ☐ **Adjusted residuals**
- ☐ **Each cell's contribution to the Chi-Square statistic**

[Help] [OK] [Cancel]

Figure 11.M.3
MINITAB chi-square dialog box

and click "OK". When you return to the "Cross Tabulation" menu screen, click "OK" to generate the MINITAB printout.

[Note: If your MINITAB worksheet contains only the cell counts for the contingency table in columns, click the "Chi-Square Test (Table in Worksheet)" menu option (see Figure 11.M.1) and specify the columns in the "Columns containing the table" box. Click "OK" to produce the MINITAB printout.]

11.3 Chi-Square Analyses Using EXCEL and PHStat2

EXCEL can conduct chi-square tests for both one-way and two-way (contingency) tables; however, you must have previously computed the cell counts for the table.

One-Way Table

To conduct a chi-square test for a one-way table, first create a workbook with columns representing the levels of the qualitative variable, the cell counts, and the expected cell counts, as shown in Figure 11.E.1. The p-value of the chi-square test is found using the formula

$$= CHITEST(range\ of\ cell\ counts,\ range\ of\ expected\ cell\ counts)$$

(This formula is shown in the formula area of the EXCEL workbook, Figure 11.E.1.) Once the p-value is computed, the value of chi-square test statistic is found using the formula

$$= CHIINV(cell\ with\ p\text{-}value,\ cell\ with\ degrees\ of\ freedom)$$

Two-Way Table

To conduct a chi-square test for a two-way (contingency), click "PHStat" form the EXCEL menu bar, then select "Multiple-Sample Tests" and "Chi-Square Test", as shown in Figure 11.E.2. On the resulting dialog box, specify the significance level (α), number of rows and number of columns for the contingency table, as shown in Figure 11.E.3, then click "OK". The EXCEL workbook shown in Figure 11.E.4 will appear.

Enter the cell counts in the appropriate cells of the contingency table shown at the top of the workbook. Once the cell counts have been entered, the value of the chi-square test statistic and p-value of the test will appear at the bottom of the EXCEL workbook.

Microsoft Excel - coupons

File Edit View Insert Format Tools Data PHStat

B9 f_x =CHITEST(B2:B5,C2:C5)

	A	B	C	D	E
1	LEVEL	Number	Expected		
2	1	20	25		
3	2	40	25		
4	3	30	25		
5	4	10	25		
6	TOTAL	100			
7					
8	Chi-square	19.99774			
9	p-value	0.00017			
10	df	3			
11					

Figure 11.E.1
EXCEL workbook format for one-way chi-square analysis

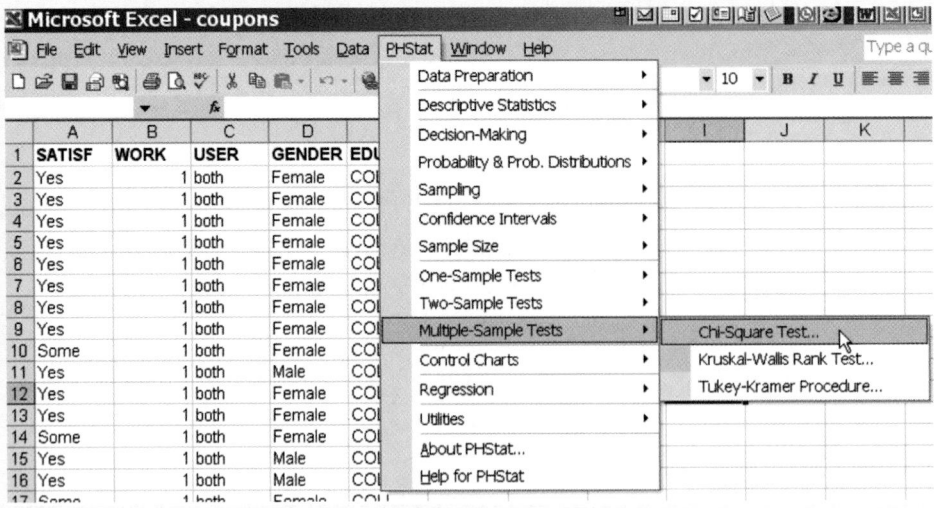

Figure 11.E.2
EXCEL menu selections for a two-way chi-square analysis

Figure 11.E.3
EXCEL/PHStat2 two-way
chi-square dialog box

Figure 11.E.4
EXCEL workbook format
for two-way chi-square
analysis

	A	B	C	D	E	F
1	**Chi-Square Test**					
2						
3		**Observed Frequencies**				
4			**Column variable**			
5	**Row variable**	**C1**	**C2**	**C3**	**Total**	
6	**R1**	22	45	21	88	
7	**R2**	11	17	15	43	
8	**Total**	33	62	36	131	
9						
10		Expected Frequencies				
11			Column variable			
12	Row variable	C1	C2	C3	Total	
13	R1	22.16794	41.64885	24.18321	88	
14	R2	10.83206	20.35115	11.81679	43	
15	Total	33	62	36	131	
16						
17	**Data**					
18	**Level of Significance**	0.05				
19	Number of Rows	2				
20	Number of Columns	3				
21	Degrees of Freedom	2				
22						
23	**Results**					
24	**Critical Value**	5.991476				
25	**Chi-Square Test Statistic**	2.101829				
26	**p-Value**	0.349618				
27	**Do not reject the null hypothesis**					
28						

Real-World Case
Discrimination in the Workplace
(A Case Covering Chapters 10–11)

Title VII of the Civil Rights Act of 1964 prohibits discrimination in the workplace on the basis of race, color, religion, gender, or national origin. The Age Discrimination in Employment Act of 1967 (ADEA) protects workers age 40 to 70 against discrimination based on age. The potential for discrimination exists in such processes as hiring, promotion, compensation, and termination.

In 1971 the U.S. Supreme Court established that employment discrimination cases fall into two categories: **disparate treatment** and **disparate impact.** In the former, the issue is whether the employer intentionally discriminated against a worker. For example, if the employer considered an individual's race in deciding whether to terminate him, the case is one of disparate treatment. In a disparate impact case, the issue is whether employment practices have an adverse impact on a protected group or class of people, even when the employer does not intend to discriminate.

Part I: Downsizing at a Computer Firm

Disparate impact cases almost always involve the use of statistical evidence and expert testimony by professional statisticians. Attorneys for the plaintiffs frequently use hypothesis test results in the form of *p*-values in arguing the case for their clients.

Table C4.1 was recently introduced as evidence in a race case that resulted from a round of layoffs during the downsizing of a division of a computer manufacturer. The company had selected 51 of the division's 1,215 employees to lay off. The plaintiffs—in this case 15 of the 20 African Americans who were laid off—were suing the company for $20 million in damages.

The company's lawyers argued that the selections followed from a performance-based ranking of all employees. The plaintiffs legal team and their expert witnesses, citing the results of a statistical test of hypothesis, argued that layoffs were a function of race.

The validity of the plaintifs interpretation of the data is dependent on whether the assumptions of the test are met in this situation. In particular, like all hypothesis tests presented in this text, the assumption of random sampling must hold. If it does not, the results of the test may be due to the violation of this assumption rather than to discrimination. In general, the appropriateness of the testing procedure is dependent on the test's ability to capture the relevant aspects of the employment process in question (DeGroot, Fienberg, and Kadane, *Statistics and the Law,* 1986).

Prepare a document to be submitted as evidence in the case (i.e., an exhibit), in which you evaluate the validity of the plaintiffs' interpretation of the data. Your evaluation should be based in part on your knowledge of the processes companies use to lay off employees and how well those processes are reflected in the hypothesis-testing procedure employed by the plaintiffs.

Part II: Age Discrimination—You Be the Judge

In 1996, as part of a significant restructuring of product lines, AJAX Pharmaceuticals (a fictitious name for a real company) laid off 24 of 55 assembly-line workers in its Pittsburgh manufacturing plant. Citing the ADEA, 11 of the laid-off workers claimed they were discriminated against on the basis of age and sued AJAX for $5,000,000. Management disputed the claim, saying that since the workers were essentially interchangeable, they had used random sampling to choose the 24 workers to be terminated.

Table C4.2 lists the 55 assembly-line workers and identifies which were terminated and which remained active. Plaintiffs are denoted by an asterisk. These data were

LAYOFFS

TABLE C4.1 Summary of Downsizing Data for Race Case

		Decision	
		Retained	Laid off
Race	**White**	1,051	31
	Black	113	20

Source: Confidential personal communication with P. George Benson, 1997.

TABLE C4.2   Data for Age Discrimination Case

Employee	Yearly Wages	Age	Employment Status	Employee	Yearly Wages	Age	Employment Status
*Adler, C.J.	$41,200	45	Terminated	*Huang, T.J.	42,995	48	Terminated
Alario, B.N.	39,565	43	Active	Jatho, J.A.	31,755	40	Active
Anders, J.M.	30,980	41	Active	Johnson, C.H.	29,540	32	Active
Bajwa, K.K.	23,225	27	Active	Jurasik, T.B.	34,300	41	Active
Barny, M.L.	21,250	26	Active	Klein, K.L.	43,700	51	Terminated
*Berger, R.W.	41,875	45	Terminated	Lang, T.F.	19,435	22	Active
Brenn, L.O.	31,225	41	Active	Liao, P.C.	28,750	32	Active
Cain, E.J.	30,135	36	Terminated	*Lostan, W.J.	44,675	52	Terminated
Carle, W.J.	29,850	32	Active	Mak, G.L.	35,505	38	Terminated
Castle, A.L.	21,850	22	Active	Maloff, V.R.	33,425	38	Terminated
Chan, S.D.	43,005	48	Terminated	McCall, R.M.	31,300	36	Terminated
Cho, J.Y.	34,785	41	Active	*Nadeau, S.R.	42,300	46	Terminated
Cohen, S.D.	25,350	27	Active	*Nguyen, O.L.	43,625	50	Terminated
Darel, F.E.	36,300	42	Active	Oas, R.C.	37,650	42	Active
*Davis, D.E.	40,425	46	Terminated	*Patel, M.J.	38,400	43	Terminated
*Dawson, P.K.	39,150	42	Terminated	Porter, K.D.	32,195	35	Terminated
Denker, U.H.	19,435	19	Active	Rosa, L.M.	19,435	21	Active
Dorando, T.R.	24,125	28	Active	Roth, J.H.	32,785	39	Terminated
Dubois, A.G.	30,450	40	Active	Savino, G.L.	37,900	42	Active
England, N.	24,750	25	Active	Scott, I.W.	29,150	30	Terminated
Estis, K.B.	22,755	23	Active	Smith, E.E.	35,125	41	Active
Fenton, C.K.	23,000	24	Active	Teel, Q.V.	27,655	33	Active
Finer, H.R.	42,000	46	Terminated	*Walker, F.O.	42,545	47	Terminated
*Frees, O.C.	44,100	52	Terminated	Wang, T.G.	22,200	32	Active
Gary, J.G.	44,975	55	Terminated	Yen, D.O.	40,350	44	Terminated
Gillen, D.J.	25,900	27	Active	Young, N.L.	28,305	34	Active
Harvey, D.A.	40,875	46	Terminated	Zeitels, P.W.	36,500	42	Active
Higgins, N.M.	38,595	41	Active				

Denotes plaintiffs

used by both the plaintiffs and the defendants to determine whether the layoffs had an adverse impact on workers age 40 and over and to establish the credibility of management's random sampling claim.

Using whatever statistical methods you think are appropriate, build a case that supports the plaintiffs' position. (Call documents related to this issue Exhibit A.) Similarly, build a case that supports the defendants' position. (Call these documents Exhibit B.) Then discuss which of the two cases is more convincing and why. [*Note:* The data for this case are available in the **DISCRIM,** file described in the table.]

 DISCRIM (Number of observations: 55)

Variable	Type
LASTNAME	QL
WAGES	QN
AGE	QN
STATUS	QL (A = active, T = terminated)

Simple Linear Regression

Contents

Statistics in Action

Can "Dowsers" Really Detect Water?j

Using Technology

Where We've Been

- Presented methods for estimating and testing population parameters (e.g., the mean, proportion, and variance) for a single sample.
- Extended these methods to allow for a comparison of population parameters for multiple samples.

Where We're Going

- Introduce the straight-line (*simple linear regression*) model as a means of relating one quantitative variable to another quantitative variable.
- Introduce the *correlation coefficient* as a means of relating one quantitative variable to another quantitative variable.

- Assess how well the simple linear regression model fits the sample data.
- Utilize the simple linear regression model for predicting the value of one variable from a specified value of another variable.

Statistics in

ACTION

Can "Dowsers" Really Detect Water?

The act of searching for and finding underground supplies of water using nothing more than a divining rod is commonly known as "dowsing." Although widely regarded among scientists as no more than a superstitious relic from medieval times, dowsing remains popular in folklore and, to this day, there are individuals who claim to have this mysterious skill and actually market their "services."

Many dowsers in Germany claim that they respond to "earthrays" that emanate from the water source. These earthrays, say the dowsers, are a subtle form of radiation potentially hazardous to human health. As a result of these claims, the German government in the mid-1980s conducted a 2-year experiment to investigate the possibility that dowsing is a genuine skill. If such a skill could be demonstrated, reasoned government officials, then dangerous levels of radiation in Germany could be detected, avoided, and disposed of.

A group of university physicists in Munich, Germany, were provided a grant of 400,000 marks ($\approx$ \$250,000) to conduct the study. Approximately 500 candidate dowsers were recruited to participate in preliminary tests of their skill. To avoid fraudulent claims, the 43 individuals who seemed to be the most successful in the preliminary tests were selected for the final, carefully controlled, experiment.

The researchers set up a 10-meter-long line on the ground floor of a vacant barn, along which a small wagon could be moved. Attached to the wagon was a short length of pipe, perpendicular to the test line, that was connected by hoses to a pump with running water. The location of the pipe along the line for each trial of the experiment was assigned using a computer-generated random number. On the upper floor of the barn, directly above the experimental line, a 10-meter test line was painted. In each trial, a dowser was admitted to this upper level and required, with his or her rod, stick, or other tool of choice, to ascertain where the pipe with running water on the ground floor was located.

Each dowser participated in at least one test series, that is, a sequence of from 5 to 15 trials (typically 10), with the pipe randomly repositioned after each trial. (Some dowsers undertook only one test series, selected others underwent more than 10 test series.) Over the 2-year experimental period, the 43 dowsers participated in a total of 843 tests. The experiment was "double-blind" in that neither the observer (researcher) on the top floor nor the dowser knew the pipe's location, even after a guess was made. [*Note:* Before the experiment began, a professional magician inspected the entire arrangement for potential deception or cheating by the dowsers.]

For each trial, two variables were recorded: the actual pipe location (in decimeters from the beginning of the line) and the dowser's guess (also measured in decimeters). Based on an examination of these data, the German physicists concluded in their final report that although most dowsers did not do particularly well in the experiments, "Some few dowsers, in particular tests, showed an extraordinarily high rate of success, which can scarcely if at all be explained as due to chance ... a real core of dowser-phenomena can be regarded as empirically proven ..." (Wagner, Betz, and König, 1990).

This conclusion was critically assessed by Professor J. T. Enright of the University of California–San Diego. (*Skeptical Inquirer*, Jan./Feb. 1999.) In the Statistics in Action Revisited sections of this chapter, we demonstrate how Enright concluded the exact opposite of the German physicists!

Statistics in Action Revisited

In Chapters 7–10 we described methods for making inferences about population means. The mean of a population was treated as a *constant,* and we showed how to use sample data to estimate or to test hypotheses about this constant mean. In many applications, the mean of a population is not viewed as a constant, but rather as a variable. For example, the mean sale price of residences sold this year in a large city can be treated as a constant and might be equal to $150,000. But we might also treat the mean sale price as a variable that depends on the square feet of living space in the residence. For example, the relationship might be

$$\text{Mean sale price} = \$30,\!000 + \$60(\text{Square feet})$$

This formula implies that the mean sale price of 1,000-square-foot homes is $90,000, the mean sale price of 2,000-square-foot homes is $150,000, and the mean sale price of 3,000-square-foot homes is $210,000.

What do we gain by treating the mean as a variable rather than a constant? In many practical applications we will be dealing with highly variable data, data for which the standard deviation is so large that a constant mean is almost "lost" in a sea of variability. For example, if the mean residential sale price is $150,000 but the standard deviation is $75,000, then the actual sale prices will vary considerably, and the mean price is not a very meaningful or useful characterization of the price distribution. On the other hand, if the mean sale price is treated as a variable that depends on the square feet of living space, the standard deviation of sale prices for any given size of home might be only $10,000. In this case, the mean price will provide a much better characterization of sale prices when it is treated as a variable rather than a constant.

Teaching Tip
Discuss other examples
of when one variable can
be predicted by the value
of another variable.
In this chapter we discuss situations in which the mean of the population is treated as a variable, dependent on the value of another variable. The dependence of residential sale price on the square feet of living space is one illustration. Other examples include the dependence of mean sales revenue of a firm on advertising expenditure, the dependence of mean starting salary of a college graduate on the student's GPA, and the dependence of mean monthly production of automobiles on the total number of sales in the previous month.

In this chapter we discuss the simplest of all models relating a population mean to another variable, *the straight-line model.* We show how to use the sample data to estimate the straight-line relationship between the mean value of one variable, *y,* as it relates to a second variable, *x*. The methodology of estimating and using a straight-line relationship is referred to as *simple linear regression analysis.*

12.1 Probabilistic Models

An important consideration in merchandising a product is the amount of money spent on advertising. Suppose you want to model the monthly sales revenue of an appliance store as a function of the monthly advertising expenditure. The first question to be answered is this: "Do you think an exact relationship exists between these two variables?" That is, do you think it is possible to state the exact monthly sales revenue if the amount spent on advertising is known? We think you will agree with us that this is *not* possible for several reasons. Sales depend on many variables other than advertising expenditure—for example, time of year, the state of the general economy, inventory, and price structure. Even if many variables are included in a model (the topic of Chapter 13), it is still unlikely that we would be able to predict the monthly sales *exactly*. There will almost certainly be some variation in monthly sales due strictly to *random phenomena* that cannot be modeled or explained.

If we were to construct a model that hypothesized an exact relationship between variables, it would be called a **deterministic model.** For example, if we believe that *y*, the monthly sales revenue, will be exactly fifteen times *x*, the monthly advertising expenditure, we write

$$y = 15x$$

This represents a *deterministic relationship* between the variables *y* and *x*. It implies that *y* can always be determined exactly when the value of *x* is known. *There is no allowance for error in this prediction.*

If, on the other hand, we believe there will be unexplained variation in monthly sales—perhaps caused by important but unincluded variables or by random phenomena—we discard the deterministic model and use a model that accounts for this **random error.** This **probabilistic model** includes both a deterministic component and a random error component. For example, if we hypothesize that the sales *y* is related to advertising expenditure *x* by

$$y = 15x + \text{Random error}$$

we are hypothesizing a *probabilistic relationship* between *y* and *x*. Note that the deterministic component of this probabilistic model is 15*x*.

Figure 12.1(a) shows the possible values of *y* and *x* for five different months, when the model is deterministic. All the pairs of (*x*, *y*) data points must fall exactly on the line because a deterministic model leaves no room for error.

Figure 12.1(b) shows a possible set of points for the same values of *x* when we are using a probabilistic model. Note that the deterministic part of the model (the straight line itself) is the same. Now, however, the inclusion of a random error component allows the monthly sales to vary from this line. Since we know that the sales revenue does vary randomly for a given value of *x*, the probabilistic model provides a more realistic model for *y* than does the deterministic model.

Teaching Tip

Emphasize that the regression model allows individual data values to fall around the regression line but the mean values fall on the regression line.

Figure 12.1
Possible sales revenues, *y*, for five different months, *x*

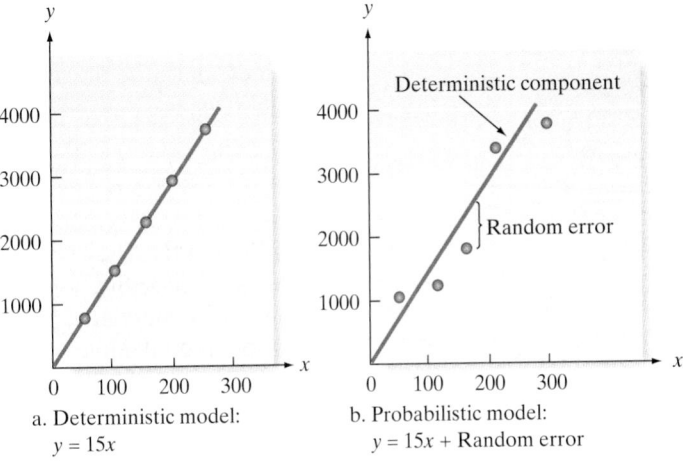

a. Deterministic model:
$y = 15x$

b. Probabilistic model:
$y = 15x + \text{Random error}$

> ## General Form of Probabilistic Models
>
> $$y = \text{Deterministic component} + \text{Random error}$$
>
> where y is the variable of interest. We always assume that the mean value of the random error equals 0. This is equivalent to assuming that the mean value of y, $E(y)$, equals the deterministic component of the model; that is,
>
> $$E(y) = \text{Deterministic component}$$

In this chapter we present the simplest of probabilistic models—the **straight-line model**—which derives its name from the fact that the deterministic portion of the model graphs as a straight line. Fitting this model to a set of data is an example of **regression analysis,** or **regression modeling.** The elements of the straight-line model are summarized in the next box.

Teaching Tip

Point out that the slope interpretation of β_1 is only valid when using a simple linear regression model. As the models become more complicated, this interpretation will change.

> ## A First-Order (Straight-Line) Probabilistic Model
>
> $$y = \beta_0 + \beta_1 x + \varepsilon$$
>
> where
>
> $y = $ **Dependent** *or* **response variable** (variable to be modeled)
>
> $x = $ **Independent** *or* **predictor variable** (variable used as a predictor of y)*
>
> $E(y) = \beta_0 + \beta_1 x = $ Deterministic component
>
> ε (epsilon) $= $ Random error component
>
> β_0 (beta zero) $= $ **y-intercept of the line**, that is, the point at which the line *intercepts or cuts through the y*-axis (see Figure 12.2)
>
> β_1 (beta one) $= $ **Slope of the line**, that is, the change (*amount of increase or decrease*)in the deterministic component of y for every 1-unit increase in x.
>
> [*Note:* A *positive* slope implies that $E(y)$ *increases* by the amount β_1 (see Figure 12.2). A *negative* slope implies that $E(y)$ *decreases* by the amount β_1.]

In the probabilistic model, the deterministic component is referred to as the **line of means,** because the mean of y, $E(y)$, is equal to the straight-line component of the model. That is,

$$E(y) = \beta_0 + \beta_1 x$$

Note that the Greek symbols β_0 and β_1, respectively, represent the y-intercept and slope of the model. They are population parameters that will be known only if we have access to the entire population of (x, y) measurements. Together with a specific value of the independent variable x, they determine the mean value of y, which is just a specific point on the line of means (Figure 12.2).

---

*The word *independent* should not be interpreted in a probabilistic sense, as defined in Chapter 3. The phrase *independent variable* is used in regression analysis to refer to a predictor variable for the response y.

Figure 12.2
The straight-line model

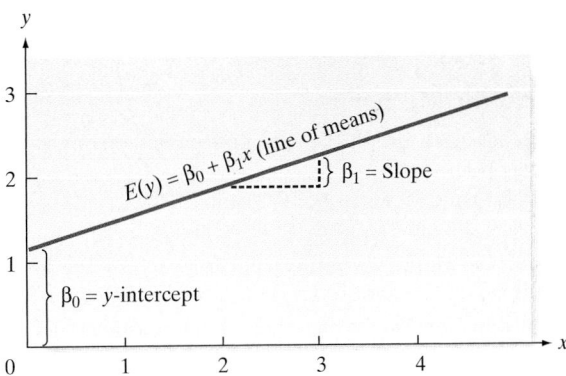

Biography

**FRANCIS GALTON
(1822–1911)
The Law of Universal
Regression**

Francis Galton was the youngest of seven children born to a middle-class English family of Quaker faith. A cousin of Charles Darwin, Galton attended Trinity College (Cambridge, England) to study medicine. Due to the death of his father, Galton was unable to obtain his degree. His competence in both medicine and mathematics, however, led Galton to pursue a career as a scientist. Galton made major contributions to the fields of genetics, psychology, meteorology, and anthropology. Some consider

Galton to be the first social scientist for his applications of the novel statistical concepts of the time—in particular, regression and correlation. While studying natural inheritance in 1886, Galton collected data on heights of parents and adult children. He noticed the tendency for tall (or short) parents to have tall (or short) children but that the children were not as tall (or short), on average, as their parents. Galton called this phenomenon the "law of universal regression," for the average heights of adult children tended to "regress" to the mean of the population. Galton, with the help of his friend and disciple, Karl Pearson, applied the straight-line model to the height data, and the term *regression* model was coined.

The values of β_0 and β_1 will be unknown in almost all practical applications of regression analysis. The process of developing a model, estimating the unknown parameters, and using the model can be viewed as the five-step procedure shown in the next box.

Step 1   Hypothesize the deterministic component of the model that relates the mean, $E(y)$, to the independent variable x (Section 12.1).

Step 2   Use the sample data to estimate unknown parameters in the model (Section 12.2).

Step 3   Specify the probability distribution of the random error term and estimate the standard deviation of this distribution (Sections 12.3 and 12.4).

Step 4   Statistically evaluate the usefulness of the model (Sections 12.5, 12.6, and 12.7).

Step 5   When satisfied that the model is useful, use it for prediction, estimation, and other purposes (Section 12.8).

Exercises 12.1–12.9

Learning the Mechanics

12.1 In each case, graph the line that passes through the given points.
  a. $(1, 1)$ and $(5, 5)$ **b.** $(0, 3)$ and $(3, 0)$
  c. $(-1, 1)$ and $(4, 2)$ **d.** $(-6, -3)$ and $(2, 6)$

12.2 Give the slope and y-intercept for each of the lines graphed in Exercise 12.1.

12.3 The equation for a straight line (deterministic model) is

$$y = \beta_0 + \beta_1 x$$

If the line passes through the point $(-2, 4)$, then $x = -2, y = 4$ must satisfy the equation; that is,

$$4 = \beta_0 + \beta_1(-2)$$

Similarly, if the line passes through the point $(4, 6)$, then $x = 4, y = 6$ must satisfy the equation; that is,

$$6 = \beta_0 + \beta_1(4)$$

Use these two equations to solve for β_0 and β_1; then find the equation of the line that passes through the points $(-2, 4)$ and $(4, 6)$.

12.4 Refer to Exercise 12.3. Find the equations of the lines that pass through the points listed in Exercise 12.1.

12.5 Plot the following lines:
  a. $y = 4 + x$ **b.** $y = 5 - 2x$ **c.** $y = -4 + 3x$
  d. $y = -2x$ **e.** $y = x$ **f.** $y = .50 + 1.5x$

12.6 Give the slope and y-intercept for each of the lines defined in Exercise 12.5.

12.7 Why do we generally prefer a probabilistic model to a deterministic model? Give examples for which the two types of models might be appropriate.

12.8 What is the line of means?

12.9 If a straight-line probabilistic relationship relates the mean $E(y)$ to an independent variable x, does it imply that every value of the variable y will always fall exactly on the line of means? Why or why not?

12.2 Fitting the Model: The Least Squares Approach

After the straight-line model has been hypothesized to relate the mean $E(y)$ to the independent variable x, the next step is to collect data and to estimate the (unknown) population parameters, the y-intercept β_0 and the slope β_1.

To begin with a simple example, suppose an appliance store conducts a five-month experiment to determine the effect of advertising on sales revenue. The results are shown in Table 12.1. (The number of measurements and the measurements themselves are unrealistically simple in order to avoid arithmetic confusion in this introductory example.) This set of data will be used to demonstrate the five-step procedure of regression modeling given in Section 12.1. In this section we hypothesize the deterministic component of the model and estimate its unknown parameters (steps 1 and 2). The model assumptions and the random error component (step 3) are the subjects of Sections 12.3 and 12.4, whereas Sections 12.5–12.7 assess the utility of the model (step 4). Finally, we use the model for prediction and estimation (step 5) in Section 12.8.

 ADSALES

TABLE 12.1 **Advertising–Sales Data**

Month	Advertising Expenditure, x ($100s)	Sales Revenue, y ($1,000s)
1	1	1
2	2	1
3	3	2
4	4	2
5	5	4

Figure 12.3

Scattergram for data in Table 12.1

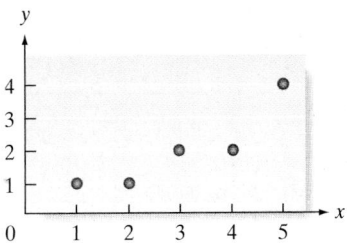

Step 1 *Hypothesize the deterministic component of the probabilistic model.* As stated before, we will consider only straight-line models in this chapter. Thus, the complete model to relate mean sales revenue $E(y)$ to advertising expenditure x is given by

$$E(y) = \beta_0 + \beta_1 x$$

Step 2 *Use sample data to estimate unknown parameters in the model.* This step is the subject of this section—namely, how can we best use the information in the sample of five observations in Table 12.1 to estimate the unknown y-intercept β_0 and slope β_1?

To determine whether a linear relationship between y and x is plausible, it is helpful to plot the sample data in a **scattergram** (or **scatterplot**). Recall (Section 2.10) that a scattergram locates each of the five data points on a graph, as shown in Figure 12.3. Note that the scattergram suggests a general tendency for y to increase as x increases. If you place a ruler on the scattergram, you will see that a line may be drawn through three of the five points, as shown in Figure 12.4. To obtain the equation of this visually fitted line, note that the line intersects the y-axis at $y = -1$, so the y-intercept is -1. Also, y increases exactly 1 unit for every 1-unit increase in x, indicating that the slope is $+1$. Therefore, the equation is

$$\widetilde{y} = -1 + 1(x) = -1 + x$$

where $\widetilde{y}$ is used to denote the predicted y from the visual model.

One way to decide quantitatively how well a straight line fits a set of data is to note the extent to which the data points deviate from the line. For example, to evaluate the model in Figure 12.4, we calculate the magnitude of the *deviations* (i.e., the differences between the observed and the predicted values of y). These deviations, or **errors of prediction,** are the vertical distances between observed and predicted val-

Figure 12.4

Visual straight line fitted to the data in Figure 12.3

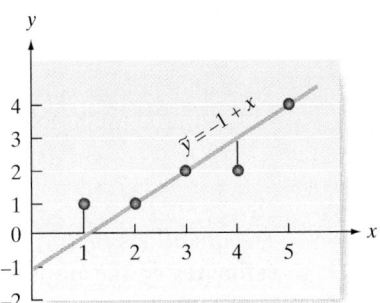

TABLE 12.2 Comparing Observed and Predicted Values for the Visual Model

x	y	$\tilde{y} = -1 + x$	$(y - \tilde{y})$	$(y - \tilde{y})^2$
1	1	0	$(1 - 0) = 1$	1
2	1	1	$(1 - 1) = 0$	0
3	2	2	$(2 - 2) = 0$	0
4	2	3	$(2 - 3) = -1$	1
5	4	4	$(4 - 4) = 0$	0

Sum of errors = 0   Sum of squared errors (SSE) = 2

ues (see Figure 12.4). The observed and predicted values of y, their differences, and their squared differences are shown in Table 12.2. Note that the *sum of errors* equals 0 and the *sum of squares of the errors* (SSE), which gives greater emphasis to large deviations of the points from the line, is equal to 2.

You can see by shifting the ruler around the graph that it is possible to find many lines for which the sum of errors is equal to 0, but it can be shown that there is one (and only one) line for which the SSE is a *minimum*. This line is called the **least squares line**, the **regression line**, or the **least squares prediction equation**. The methodology used to obtain this line is called the **method of least squares.**

> **Now Work**   *Exercise 12.12a–d*

To find the least squares prediction equation for a set of data, assume that we have a sample of n data points consisting of pairs of values of x and y, say $(x_1, y_1), (x_2, y_2), \ldots, (x_n, y_n)$. For example, the $n = 5$ data points shown in Table 12.2 are $(1, 1), (2, 1), (3, 2), (4, 2)$, and $(5, 4)$. The fitted line, which we will calculate based on the five data points, is written as

$$\hat{y} = \hat{\beta}_0 + \hat{\beta}_1 x$$

The "hats" indicate that the symbols below them are estimates: $\hat{y}$ (y-hat) is an estimator of the mean value of y, $E(y)$, and a predictor of some future value of y; and $\hat{\beta}_0$ and $\hat{\beta}_1$ are estimators of β_0 and β_1, respectively.

For a given data point, say the point (x_i, y_i), the observed value of y is y_i and the predicted value of y would be obtained by substituting x_i into the prediction equation:

$$\hat{y}_i = \hat{\beta}_0 + \hat{\beta}_1 x_i$$

And the deviation of the ith value of y from its predicted value is

$$(y_i - \hat{y}_i) = [y_i - (\hat{\beta}_0 + \hat{\beta}_1 x_i)]$$

Then the sum of squares of the deviations of the y-values about their predicted values for all the n points is

$$\text{SSE} = \sum [y_i - (\hat{\beta}_0 + \hat{\beta}_1 x_i)]^2$$

Teaching Tip

Explain that this is the same criterion that was used in confidence interval estimation. The regression estimates are the minimum variance unbiased estimates.

The quantities $\hat{\beta}_0$ and $\hat{\beta}_1$ that make the SSE a minimum are called the **least squares estimates** of the population parameters β_0 and β_1, and the prediction equation $\hat{y} = \hat{\beta}_0 + \hat{\beta}_1 x$ is called the *least squares line.*

DEFINITION 12.1

The **least squares line** $\hat{y} = \hat{\beta}_0 + \hat{\beta}_1 x$ is one that has the following two properties:

1. the sum of the errors (SE) equals 0
2. the sum of squared errors (SSE) is smaller than for any other straight-line model

The values of $\hat{\beta}_0$ and $\hat{\beta}_1$ that minimize the SSE are (proof omitted) given by the formulas in the box.*

Preliminary computations for finding the least squares line for the advertising–sales example are presented in Table 12.3. We can now calculate

$$SS_{xy} = \sum x_i y_i - \frac{\left(\sum x_i\right)\left(\sum y_i\right)}{5} = 37 - \frac{(15)(10)}{5} = 37 - 30 = 7$$

$$SS_{xx} = \sum x_i^2 - \frac{\left(\sum x_i\right)^2}{5} = 55 - \frac{(15)^2}{5} = 55 - 45 = 10$$

Formulas for the Least Squares Estimates

Slope: $\hat{\beta}_1 = \dfrac{SS_{xy}}{SS_{xx}}$

y-intercept: $\hat{\beta}_0 = \bar{y} - \hat{\beta}_1 \bar{x}$

where $SS_{xy} = \sum (x_i - \bar{x})(y_i - \bar{y}) = \sum x_i y_i - \dfrac{\left(\sum x_i\right)\left(\sum y_i\right)}{n}$

$SS_{xx} = \sum (x_i - \bar{x})^2 = \sum x_i^2 - \dfrac{\left(\sum x_i\right)^2}{n}$

n = Sample size

TABLE 12.3   Preliminary Computations for Advertising–Sales Example

	x_i	y_i	x_i^2	$x_i y_i$
	1	1	1	1
	2	1	4	2
	3	2	9	6
	4	2	16	8
	5	4	25	20
Totals	$\sum x_i = 15$	$\sum y_i = 10$	$\sum x_i^2 = 55$	$\sum x_i y_i = 37$

Suggested Exercise 12.21

*Students who are familiar with calculus should note that the values of β_0 and β_1 that minimize $SSE = \sum (y_i - \hat{y}_i)^2$ are obtained by setting the two partial derivatives $\partial SSE/\partial \beta_0$ and $\partial SSE/\partial \beta_1$ equal to 0. The solutions to these two equations yield the formulas shown in the box. Furthermore, we denote the *sample* solutions to the equations by $\hat{\beta}_0$ and $\hat{\beta}_1$, where the "hat" denotes that these are sample estimates of the true population intercept β_0 and true population slope β_1.

Figure 12.5
The line $\hat{y} = -.1 + .7x$
fitted to the data

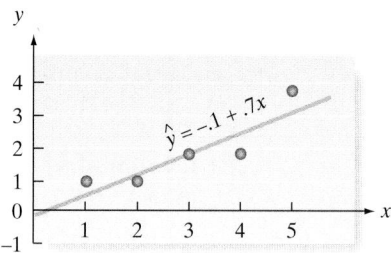

Then the slope of the least squares line is

$$\hat{\beta}_1 = \frac{SS_{xy}}{SS_{xx}} = \frac{7}{10} = .7$$

and the y-intercept is

$$\hat{\beta}_0 = \bar{y} - \hat{\beta}_1 \bar{x} = \frac{\sum y_i}{5} - \hat{\beta}_1 \frac{\sum x_i}{5}$$

$$= \frac{10}{5} - (.7)\left(\frac{15}{5}\right) = 2 - (.7)(3) = 2 - 2.1 = -.1$$

The least squares line is thus

$$\hat{y} = \hat{\beta}_0 + \hat{\beta}_1 x = -.1 + .7x$$

The graph of this line is shown in Figure 12.5.

The predicted value of y for a given value of x can be obtained by substituting into the formula for the least squares line. Thus, when $x = 2$ we predict y to be

$$\hat{y} = -.1 + .7x = -.1 + .7(2) = 1.3$$

We show how to find a prediction interval for y in Section 12.8.

The observed and predicted values of y, the deviations of the y values about their predicted values, and the squares of these deviations are shown in Table 12.4. Note that the sum of squares of the deviations, SSE, is 1.10, and (as we would expect) this is less than the SSE $= 2.0$ obtained in Table 12.2 for the visually fitted line.

The calculations required to obtain $\hat{\beta}_0$, $\hat{\beta}_1$, and SSE in simple linear regression, although straightforward, can become rather tedious. Even with the use of a pocket calculator, the process is laborious and susceptible to error, especially when the sample size is large. Fortunately, the use of a statistical software package can significantly

TABLE 12.4 Comparing Observed and Predicted Values for the Least Squares Prediction Equation

x	y	$\hat{y} = -.1 + .7x$	$(y - \hat{y})$	$(y - \hat{y})^2$
1	1	.6	$(1 - .6) = .4$	.16
2	1	1.3	$(1 - 1.3) = -.3$	.09
3	2	2.0	$(2 - 2.0) = 0$	.00
4	2	2.7	$(2 - 2.7) = -.7$	.49
5	4	3.4	$(4 - 3.4) = .6$	.36
			Sum of errors $= 0$	SSE $= 1.10$

Model Summary

Model	R	R Square	Adjusted R Square	Std. Error of the Estimate
1	.904[a]	.817	.756	.606

a. Predictors: (Constant), ADVEXP_X

ANOVA[b]

Model		Sum of Squares	df	Mean Square	F	Sig.
1	Regression	4.900	1	4.900	13.364	.035[a]
	Residual	1.100	3	.367		
	Total	6.000	4			

a. Predictors: (Constant), ADVEXP_X
b. Dependent Variable: SALES_Y

Coefficients[a]

Model		Unstandardized Coefficients		Standardized Coefficients	t	Sig.
		B	Std. Error	Beta		
1	(Constant)	-.100	.635		-.157	.885
	ADVEXP_X	.700	.191	.904	3.656	.035

a. Dependent Variable: SALES_Y

Figure 12.6a
SPSS printout for the advertising–sales regression

reduce the labor involved in regression calculations. The SPSS, MINITAB, and EXCEL outputs for the simple linear regression of the data in Table 12.1 are displayed in Figures 12.6(a)–(c). The values of $\hat{\beta}_0$ and $\hat{\beta}_1$ are highlighted on the printouts. These values, $\hat{\beta}_0 = -.1$ and $\hat{\beta}_1 = .7$, agree exactly with our hand-calculated values. The value of SSE $= 1.10$ is also highlighted on the printouts.

> **Now Work**   *Exercise 12.12e*

Teaching Tip

The interpretation of β_0 only makes sense if the value of $x = 0$ is possible and the data collected includes values of x over this range.

Whether you use a hand calculator or a computer, it is important that you be able to interpret the intercept and slope in terms of the data being utilized to fit the model. In the advertising–sales example, the estimated y-intercept, $\hat{\beta}_0 = -.1$, appears to imply that the estimated mean sales revenue is equal to $-.1$, or $-\$100$, when the advertising expenditure, x, is equal to $\$0$. Since negative sales revenues are not possible, this seems to make the model nonsensical. However, *the model parameters should be interpreted only within the sampled range of the independent variable* — in this case, for advertising expenditures between $\$100$ and $\$500$. Thus,

Figure 12.6b
MINITAB printout for the
advertising–sales regression

Regression Analysis: SALES_Y versus ADVEXP_X

```
The regression equation is
SALES_Y = - 0.100 + 0.700 ADVEXP_X


Predictor      Coef  SE Coef       T      P
Constant    -0.1000   0.6351   -0.16  0.885
ADVEXP_X     0.7000   0.1915    3.66  0.035



S = 0.605530   R-Sq = 81.7%   R-Sq(adj) = 75.6%


Analysis of Variance

Source          DF      SS      MS      F      P
Regression       1  4.9000  4.9000  13.36  0.035
Residual Error   3  1.1000  0.3667
Total            4  6.0000
```

	A	B	C	D	E	F	G
1	Regression Analysis						
2							
3	Regression Statistics						
4	Multiple R	0.903696114					
5	R Square	0.816666667					
6	Adjusted R Square	0.755555556					
7	Standard Error	0.605530071					
8	Observations	5					
9							
10	ANOVA						
11		df	SS	MS	F	Significance F	
12	Regression	1	4.9	4.9	13.36363636	0.035352847	
13	Residual	3	1.1	0.366666667			
14	Total	4	6				
15							
16		Coefficients	Standard Error	t Stat	P-value	Lower 95%	Upper 95%
17	Intercept	-0.1	0.635085296	-0.157459164	0.88488398	-2.12112675	1.92112675
18	ADVEXP_X	0.7	0.191485422	3.655630775	0.035352847	0.090607356	1.309392644
19							

Figure 12.6c
EXCEL printout for the advertising–sales regression

the y-intercept—which is, by definition, at $x = 0$ ($0 advertising expenditure)—is not within the range of the sampled values of x and is not subject to meaningful interpretation.

The slope of the least squares line, $\hat{\beta}_1 = .7$, implies that for every unit increase of x, the mean value of y is estimated to increase by .7 unit. In terms of this example, for every $100 increase in advertising, the mean sales revenue is estimated to increase by $700 *over the sampled range of advertising expenditures from $100 to $500.* Thus, the model does not imply that increasing the advertising expenditures from $500 to $1,000 will result in an increase in mean sales of $3,500, because the range of x in the sample does not extend to $1,000 ($x = 10$). Be careful to interpret the estimated parameters only within the sampled range of x.

Statistics in Action Revisited

Estimating a Straight-Line Regression Model for the Dowsing Data

After conducting a series of experiments in a Munich barn, a group of German physicists concluded that dowsing (i.e., the ability to find underground water with a divining rod) "can be regarded as empirically proven." This observation was based on the data collected for three (of the participating 500) dowsers who had particularly impressive results. All three of these "best" dowsers (numbered 99, 18, and 108) performed the experiment multiple times and the best test series (sequence of trials) for each of these three dowsers was identified. These data, saved in the **DOWSING** file, are listed in Table SIA12.1.

Recall (p. 691) that for various hidden pipe locations, each dowser provided a guess of where the pipe with running water was located. Let x = dowser's guess (in meters) and y = pipe location (in meters) for each trial. One way to determine whether the "best" dowsers are effective is to fit the straight-line model, $E(y) = \beta_0 + \beta_1 x$, to the data in Table SIA12.1.

A MINITAB scatterplot of the data is shown in Figure SIA12.1. The least squares line, obtained from the MINITAB regression printout shown in Figure SIA12.2, is also displayed on the scatterplot. Although the least squares line has a slight upward trend, the variation of the data points around the line is large. It does not appear that a

DOWSING

TABLE SIA12.1   Dowsing Trial Results: Best Series for the Three Best Dowsers

Trial	Dowser Number	Pipe Location	Dowser's Guess
1	99	4	4
2	99	5	87
3	99	30	95
4	99	35	74
5	99	36	78
6	99	58	65
7	99	40	39
8	99	70	75
9	99	74	32
10	99	98	100
11	18	7	10
12	18	38	40
13	18	40	30
14	18	49	47
15	18	75	9
16	18	82	95
17	108	5	52
18	108	18	16
19	108	33	37
20	108	45	40
21	108	38	66
22	108	50	58
23	108	52	74
24	108	63	65
25	108	72	60
26	108	95	49

Source: Enright, J. T. "Testing Dowsing: The Failure of the Munich Experiments" *Skeptical Inquirer,* Jan./Feb. 1999, p. 45 (Figure 6a).

Figure SIA12.1

MINITAB scatterplot of dowsing data

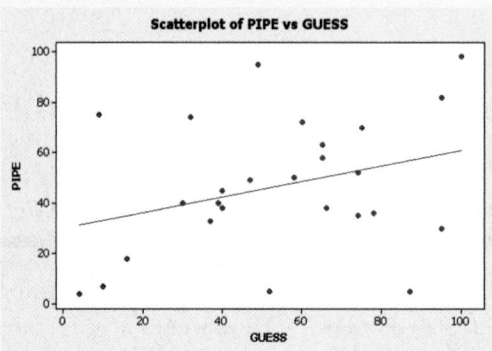

Figure SIA12.2

MINITAB simple linear regression for dowsing data

Regression Analysis: PIPE versus GUESS

```
The regression equation is
PIPE = 30.1 + 0.308 GUESS


Predictor      Coef   SE Coef      T       P
Constant      30.07     11.41   2.63   0.015
GUESS        0.3079    0.1900   1.62   0.118


S = 26.0298    R-Sq = 9.9%    R-Sq(adj) = 6.1%


Analysis of Variance

Source           DF        SS       MS      F      P
Regression        1    1778.9   1778.9   2.63  0.118
Residual Error   24   16261.2    677.6
Total            25   18040.2
```

dowser's guess (x) will be a very good predictor of actual pipe location (y). In fact, the estimated slope (obtained from Figure SIA12.2) is $\hat{\beta}_1 = .31$. Thus, for every 1-meter increase in a dowser's guess, we estimate that the actual pipe location will increase only .31 meter. In the Statistics in Action Revisited sections that follow, we will provide a measure of reliability to this inference and investigate the phenomenon of dowsing further.

Simple Linear Regression

Using the TI-83 Graphing Calculator

Finding the Least Squares Regression Equation

I. Finding the least squares regression equation

Step 1   *Enter the data*
Press **STAT** and select **1:Edit**
Note: If a list already contains data, clear the old data. Use the up arrow to highlight the list name, '**L1**' or '**L2**'.

Press **CLEAR ENTER.**
Enter your x-data in **L1** and your y-data in **L2.**

Step 2 *Find the equation*
Press **STAT** and highlight **CALC**
Press **4** for **LinReg(ax + b)**
Press **ENTER**
The screen will show the values for *a* and *b* in the equation y = ax + b.

Example The figures below show a table of data entered on the TI-83 and the regression equation obtained using the steps given above.

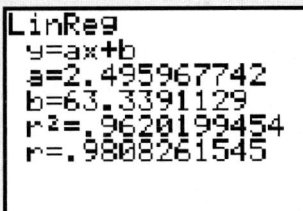

II. Finding *r* and r^2

If *r* and r^2 do not already appear on the LinReg screen from part I,

Step 1 *Turn the diagnostics feature on*
Press **2nd 0** for **CATALOG**
Press the key for **D**
Press the down arrow key until **DiagnosticsOn** is highlighted
Press **ENTER** twice

Step 2 *Find the regression equation as shown in part I above*
The values for r and r^2 will appear on the screen as well.

Example The figure below shows the output with the **DiagnosticsOn.**

III. Graphing the least squares line with the scatterplot

Step 1 *Enter the data as shown in part I above*

Step 2 *Set up the data plot*
Press **2nd Y=** for **STAT PLOT**

Press **1** for **Plot1**
Set the cursor so that **ON** is flashing.
For **Type**, use the arrow and Enter keys to highlight and select the scatterplot (first icon in the first row).
For **Xlist**, choose the column containing the x-data.
For **Freq**, choose the column containing the y-data.

Step 3 *Find the regression equation and store the equation in Y1*
Press **STAT** and highlight **CALC**
Press **4** for **LinReg(ax + b)** (Note: Don't press ENTER here because you want to store the regression equation in Y1)
Press **VARS**
Use the right arrow to highlight **Y-VARS**
Press **ENTER** to select **1:Function**
Press **ENTER** to select **1:Y1**
Press **ENTER**

Step 4 *View the scatterplot and regression line*
Press **ZOOM** and then press **9** to select **9:ZoomStat**
You should see the data graphed along with the regression line.

Example The figure below shows a graph of the scatterplot and least squares line obtained using the steps given above.

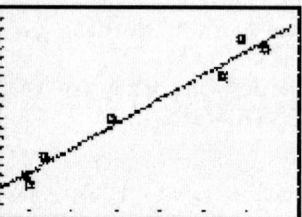

Even when the interpretations of the estimated parameters are meaningful, we need to remember that they are only estimates based on the sample. As such, their values will typically change in repeated sampling. How much confidence do we have that the estimated slope, $\hat{\beta}_1$, accurately approximates the true slope, β_1? This requires statistical inference, in the form of confidence intervals and tests of hypotheses, which we address in Section 12.5.

To summarize, we defined the best-fitting straight line to be the one that minimizes the sum of squared errors around the line, and we called it the least squares line. We should interpret the least squares line only within the sampled range of the independent variable. In subsequent sections we show how to make statistical inferences about the model.

Exercises 12.10–12.22

Learning the Mechanics

12.10 The following table is similar to Table 12.3. It is used for making the preliminary computations for finding the least squares line for the given pairs of x and y values.

x_i	y_i	x_i^2	$x_i y_i$
7	2		
4	4		
6	2		
2	5		
1	7		
1	6		
3	5		
Totals $\sum x_i =$	$\sum y_i =$	$\sum x_i^2 =$	$\sum x_i y_i =$

a. Complete the table. **b.** Find SS_{xy}.
c. Find SS_{xx}. 33.71 **d.** Find $\hat{\beta}_1$. −.7797
e. Find $\bar{x}$ and $\bar{y}$. **f.** Find $\hat{\beta}_0$. 7.107
g. Find the least squares line.

12.11 Refer to Exercise 12.10. After the least squares line has been obtained, the table below (which is similar to Table 12.4) can be used for (1) comparing the observed and the predicted values of y, and (2) computing SSE.

x	y	$\hat{y}$	$(y - \hat{y})$	$(y - \hat{y})^2$
7	2			
4	4			
6	2			
2	5			
1	7			
1	6			
3	5			
			$\sum (y - \hat{y}) =$	SSE $= \sum (y - \hat{y})^2 =$

a. Complete the table.
b. Plot the least squares line on a scattergram of the data. Plot the following line on the same graph: $\hat{y} = 14 - 2.5x$
c. Show that SSE is larger for the line in part **b** than it is for the least squares line.

12.12 Construct a scattergram for the data in the following table.

x	.5	1	1.5
y	2	1	3

a. Plot the following two lines on your scattergram:
$$y = 3 - x \quad \text{and} \quad y = 1 + x$$

b. Which of these lines would you choose to characterize the relationship between x and y? Explain.
$y = 1 + x$
c. Show that the sum of errors for both of these lines equals 0.
d. Which of these lines has the smaller SSE?
e. Find the least squares line for the data and compare it to the two lines described in part **a**.

12.13 Consider the following pairs of measurements:

LM12_13

x	8	5	4	6	2	5	3
y	1	3	6	3	7	2	5

a. Construct a scattergram for these data.
b. What does the scattergram suggest about the relationship between x and y?
c. Find the least squares estimates of β_0 and β_1.
8.54; −.994
d. Plot the least squares line on your scattergram. Does the line appear to fit the data well? Explain.
e. Interpret the y-intercept and slope of the least squares line. Over what range of x are these interpretations meaningful?

Applying the Concepts—Basic

DIAMONDS

12.14 Refer to the *Journal of Statistics Education* data on 308 diamonds for sale on the open market, saved in the **DIAMONDS** file. In Exercise 2.112 (p. 115), you related the size of the diamond (number of carats) to the asking price (dollars) using a scatterplot.
a. Write the equation of a straight-line model relating asking price (y) to number of carats (x).
$y = \beta_0 + \beta_1 x + \epsilon$
b. A MINITAB simple linear regression printout for the data is shown on p. 708. Find the equation of the least squares line. $\hat{y} = -2{,}298.4 + 11{,}598.9x$
c. Give a practical interpretation of the y-intercept of the least squares line. If a practical interpretation is not possible, explain why.
d. Give a practical interpretation of the slope of the least squares line. Over what range of x is the interpretation meaningful?   .18 to 1.10
e. Use the least squares line to predict the asking price of a .52-carat diamond. $3,733.028

12.15 Refer to the data on average state SAT scores for 1990 and 2000, Exercise 2.29 (p. 67). The first five observations and last two observations in the **SATSCORES** file are reproduced in the next table. In Exercise 2.113

MINITAB Output for Exercise 12.14

Regression Analysis: PRICE versus CARAT

```
The regression equation is
PRICE = - 2298 + 11599 CARAT


Predictor      Coef  SE Coef       T      P
Constant    -2298.4    158.5  -14.50  0.000
CARAT       11598.9    230.1   50.41  0.000


S = 1117.56   R-Sq = 89.3%   R-Sq(adj) = 89.2%


Analysis of Variance

Source         DF          SS         MS       F      P
Regression      1  3173248722  3173248722  2540.73  0.000
Residual Error 306   382178624    1248950
Total          307  3555427347
```

you examined the relationship between the 1990 SAT score and the 2000 SAT score with a scatterplot.

a. Write the equation of a straight-line model relating 2000 SAT score (y) to 1990 SAT score (x).
$y = \beta_0 + \beta_1 x + \epsilon$

b. Fit the model to the data using the method of least squares and give the least squares prediction equation. $\hat{y} = -51.14 + 1.0705x$

c. Give a practical interpretation of the y-intercept of the least squares line. If a practical interpretation is not possible, explain why.

d. Give a practical interpretation of the slope of the least squares line. Over what range of x is the interpretation meaningful? 942 to 1,172

ⓢ SATSCORES

State	1990	2000
Alabama	1079	1114
Alaska	1015	1034
Arizona	1041	1044
Arkansas	1077	1117
California	1002	1015
.	.	.
.	.	.
.	.	.
Wisconsin	1111	1181
Wyoming	1072	1090

Source: College Entrance Examination Board, 2001.

12.16 Is the number of games won by a major league baseball team in a season related to the team's batting average? The information in the table, found in the *Baseball Almanac* (2003), shows the number of games won and the batting averages for the 14 teams in the American League for the 2002 Major League Baseball season.

ⓢ ALWINS

Team	Games Won	Batting Ave.
New York	103	.275
Toronto	78	.261
Baltimore	67	.246
Boston	93	.277
Tampa Bay	55	.253
Cleveland	74	.249
Detroit	55	.248
Chicago	81	.268
Kansas City	62	.256
Minnesota	94	.272
Anaheim	99	.282
Texas	72	.269
Seattle	93	.275
Oakland	103	.261

Source: Baseball Almanac, 2003.

a. If you were to model the relationship between the mean (or expected) number of games won by a major league team and the team's batting average x, using a straight line, would you expect the slope of the line to be positive or negative? Explain.
Positive

b. Construct a scattergram of the data. Does the pattern revealed by the scattergram agree with your answer to part **a**?

c. An SPSS printout of the simple linear regression is provided on p. 709. Find the estimates of the β's on the printout and write the equation of the least squares line. $\hat{y} = -214.3 + 1,118.4x$

SPSS Output for Exercise 12.16

Coefficients[a]

Model		Unstandardized Coefficients		Standardized Coefficients	t	Sig.
		B	Std. Error	Beta		
1	(Constant)	-214.302	68.329		-3.136	.009
	BATAVE	1118.425	258.857	.780	4.321	.001

a. Dependent Variable: WINS

d. Graph the least squares line on your scattergram. Does your least squares line seem to fit the points on your scattergram?

e. Does the mean (or expected) number of games won appear to be strongly related to a team's batting average? Explain.

f. Interpret the values of $\hat{\beta}_0$ and $\hat{\beta}_1$ in the words of the problem.

12.17 Refer to the *Nutrition & Food Science* (Vol. 30, 2000) study of the trend in prime-time television advertising, Exercise 9.23 (p. 500). The number of prime-time TV commercials for all products and for just food products for randomly selected hours during 1971, 1977, 1988, 1992, and 1998 was recorded. The rate of commercials per hour for each of these years are given in the table. The researchers were interested in modeling the rate of prime-time TV commercials per hour as a function of x = the number of years since 1970.

FOODADS

Year	Number of Years since 1970	Total Commercials (rate per hour)	Food Ads (rate per hour)
1971	1	—	5.4
1977	7	11	3.0
1988	18	26	6.5
1992	22	31	6.0
1998	28	40	6.0

Source: Byrd-Bredbenner, C. and Grasso, D. "Trends in US Prime-Time Television Food Advertising across Three Decades," *Nutrition & Food Science*, Vol. 30, No. 2, 2000, p. 61 (Table 1).

a. Graph the data for total TV commercials in a scatterplot. Do you detect a trend?

b. Fit a straight-line model for y = rate of total commercials per hour using the method of least squares. $\hat{y} = 1.281 + 1.372x$

c. Interpret the slope of the least squares line.

d. Interpret the y-intercept of the least squares line.

e. Repeat parts **a–d** for food commercials during prime time.

Applying the Concepts—Intermediate

12.18 The quality of the orange juice produced by a manufacturer (e.g., Minute Maid, Tropicana) is constantly monitored. There are numerous sensory and chemical components that combine to make the best tasting orange juice. For example, one manufacturer has developed a quantitative index of the "sweetness" of orange juice. (The higher the index, the sweeter the juice.) Is there a relationship between the sweetness index and a chemical measure such as the amount of water soluble pectin (parts per million) in the orange juice? Data collected on these two variables for 24 production runs at a juice manufacturing plant are shown in the table. Suppose a manufacturer wants to use simple linear regression to predict the sweetness (y) from the amount of pectin (x).

OJUICE

Run	Sweetness Index	Pectin (ppm)
1	5.2	220
2	5.5	227
3	6.0	259
4	5.9	210
5	5.8	224
6	6.0	215
7	5.8	231
8	5.6	268
9	5.6	239
10	5.9	212
11	5.4	410
12	5.6	256
13	5.8	306
14	5.5	259
15	5.3	284
16	5.3	383
17	5.7	271
18	5.5	264
19	5.7	227
20	5.3	263
21	5.9	232
22	5.8	220
23	5.8	246
24	5.9	241

Note: The data in the table are authentic. For confidentiality reasons, the manufacturer cannot be disclosed.

a. Find the least squares line for the data.

b. Interpret $\hat{\beta}_0$ and $\hat{\beta}_1$ in the words of the problem.

c. Predict the sweetness index if amount of pectin in the orange juice is 300 ppm. [*Note:* A measure of reliability of such a prediction is discussed in Section 12.8]

12.19 In recent years U.S. banks have been merging to form mega banks that span many states. The table below, extracted from the *Journal of Banking and Finance* (Feb. 1999), lists the annual number of U.S. bank mergers for which $50 million or more changed hands in the transaction.

MERGERS

Year	Number of Bank Mergers
1	4
2	17
3	19
4	45
5	25
6	37
7	44
8	35
9	27
10	31
11	21
12	38
13	45
14	49

Source: Esty, B., Narasimhan, B., and Tufano P., "Interest-Rate Exposure and Bank Mergers," *Journal of Banking and Finance*, Vol. 23, No. 2–4, Feb. 1999, p. 264.

a. Construct a scattergram for the data, where y = number of mergers and x = year. Is there visual evidence of a linear relationship between x and y? Explain.

b. Use the method of least squares to fit a straight line to the data. $\hat{y} = 16.593 + 1.949x$

c. Graph the least squares line on your scattergram.

d. According to the least squares line, how many mergers will occur in 1994 (year 15)? Compare your answer to the actual number of mergers in year 15(42). 45.828

12.20 Due primarily to the price controls of the Organization of Petroleum Exporting Countries (OPEC), a cartel of crude-oil suppliers, the price of crude oil has risen dramatically from the mid-1970s. As a result, motorists have seen an upward spiral in gasoline prices. The data in the next table are typical prices for a gallon of regular unleaded gasoline and a barrel of crude oil (refiner acquisition cost) for the years 1980–2001.

a. Find the least squares line that describes the relationship between the price of a gallon of gasoline (y) and the price of a barrel of crude oil (x) over the 22-year period.

b. Construct a scattergram of all the data.

c. Plot your least squares line on the scattergram. Does your least squares line appear to be an

GASOIL

Year	Gasoline, y (cents/gal.)	Crude Oil, x ($/bbl.)
1980	125	28.07
1981	138	35.24
1982	129	31.87
1983	124	28.99
1984	121	28.63
1985	120	26.75
1986	93	14.55
1987	95	17.90
1988	95	14.67
1989	102	17.97
1990	116	22.23
1991	114	19.06
1992	113	18.43
1993	111	16.41
1994	111	15.59
1995	115	17.23
1996	123	20.71
1997	123	19.04
1998	106	12.52
1999	117	17.51
2000	151	28.26
2001	146	22.96

Source: U.S. Bureau of the Census, *Statistical Abstract of the United States: 1982–2002.*

appropriate characterization of the relationship between y and x over the 22-year period.

d. According to your model, if the price of crude oil fell to $18 per barrel, to what level (approximately) would the price of regular leaded gasoline fall? Justify your answer.

12.21 Individuals who report perceived wrongdoing of a corporation or public agency are known as *whistle blowers*. Two researchers developed an index to measure the extent of retaliation against a whistle blower (*Journal of Applied Psychology*, 1986). The index was based on the number of forms of reprisal actually experienced, the number of forms of reprisal threatened, and the number of people within the organization (e.g., coworkers or immediate supervisor) who retaliated against them. The table on p. 711 lists the retaliation index (higher numbers indicate more extensive retaliation) and salary for a sample of 15 whistle blowers from federal agencies.

a. Construct a scattergram for the data. Does it appear that the extent of retaliation increases, decreases, or stays the same with an increase in salary? Explain.

b. Use the method of least squares to fit a straight line to the data. $\hat{y} = 569.58 - .000192x$

c. Graph the least squares line on your scattergram. Does the least squares line support your answer to the question in part **a?** Explain.

⊚ **RETAL**

Retaliation Index	Salary	Retaliation Index	Salary
301	$62,000	535	$19.800
550	36.500	455	44.000
755	21.600	615	46.600
327	24.000	700	15.100
500	30.100	650	70.000
377	35.000	630	21.000
290	47.500	360	16.900
452	54.000		

Source: Data adapted from Near, J. P., and Miceli, M. P. "Retaliation against Whistle Blowers: Predictors and effects." *Journal of Applied Psychology.* Vol. 71, No. 1, 1986, pp. 137–145.

d. Interpret the y-intercept, $\hat{\beta}_0$, of the least squares line in terms of this application. Is the interpretation meaningful?

e. Interpret the slope, $\hat{\beta}_1$, of the least squares line in terms of this application. Over what range of x is this interpretation meaningful?

12.22 Refer to *Florida Trend Magazine's* (April 2002) data on law firms with headquarters in the state of Florida, Exercise 2.44 (p. 78). Data on the number of lawyers and number of law offices, saved in the **FLALAW** file, are reproduced in the table below. Suppose you want to predict the number of law offices (y) based on the number of lawyers (x) at the firm. Use the method of least squares (and computer software) to find the best fitting line to the data. Interpret the values of the y-intercept and the slope of the line. $\hat{y} = 2.78 + .017x$

⊚ **FLALAW**

Rank	Firm	Headquarters	Number of Lawyers	Number of Offices
1	Holland & Knight	Tallahasse	529	11
2	Akerman Senterfit	Orlando	355	9
3	Greenberg Traurig	Miami	301	6
4	Carlton Fields	Tampa	207	6
5	Gruden McClosky Smit	Ft. Lauder	175	9
6	Fowler White Boggs	Tampa	175	7
7	Foley & Lardner	Orlando	159	5
8	GrayHarris	Orlando	158	6
9	Broad and Cassel	Orlando	150	7
10	Shutts & Bowen	Miami	144	5
11	Steel Hector & Davis	Miami	141	5
12	Gunster Yoakley	WPalmBeach	140	6
13	Adorno & Zeder	Miami	105	4
14	Becker & Poliakoff	Ft. Lauder	100	12
15	Lowndes Drosdick	Orlando	100	1
16	Conroy Simberg Ganon	Hollywood	91	6
17	Stearns Weaver	Miami	85	3
18	Wicker Smith O'Hara	Miami	85	6
19	Rogers Towers Bailey	Jacksonvll	80	2
20	Butler Burnette	Tampa	77	3
21	Bilzin Sumberg Dunn	Miami	70	1
22	Morgan Colling	Orlando	70	4
23	White & Case	Miami	70	1
24	Fowler White Burnett	Miami	64	4
25	Rissman Weisberg	Orlando	63	3
26	Rumberger Kirk	Orlando	63	4

Source: Florida Trend Magazine, April 2002, p. 105.

12.3 Model Assumptions

In Section 12.2 we assumed that the probabilistic model relating the firm's sales revenue y to the advertising dollars is

$$y = \beta_0 + \beta_1 x + \varepsilon$$

We also recall that the least squares estimate of the deterministic component of the model, $\beta_0 + \beta_1 x$, is

$$\hat{y} = \hat{\beta}_0 + \hat{\beta}_1 x = -.1 + .7x$$

Now we turn our attention to the random component ε of the probabilistic model and its relation to the errors in estimating β_0 and β_1. We will use a probability distribution to characterize the behavior of ε. We will see how the probability distribution of ε determines how well the model describes the relationship between the dependent variable y and the independent variable x.

Step 3 in a regression analysis requires us to specify the probability distribution of the random error ε. We will make four basic assumptions about the general form of this probability distribution:

Assumption 1: The mean of the probability distribution of ε is 0. That is, the average of the values of ε over an infinitely long series of experiments is 0 for each setting of the independent variable x. This assumption implies that the mean value of y, $E(y)$, for a given value of x is $E(y) = \beta_0 + \beta_1 x$.

Assumption 2: The variance of the probability distribution of ε is constant for all settings of the independent variable x. For our straight-line model, this assumption means that the variance of ε is equal to a constant, say σ^2, for all values of x.

Assumption 3: The probability distribution of ε is normal.

Assumption 4: The values of ε associated with any two observed values of y are independent. That is, the value of ε associated with one value of y has no effect on the values of ε associated with other y values.

The implications of the first three assumptions can be seen in Figure 12.7, which shows distributions of errors for three values of x, namely, x_1, x_2, and x_3. Note that the relative frequency distributions of the errors are normal with a mean of 0 and a constant variance σ^2. (All the distributions shown have the same amount of spread or variability.) The straight line shown in Figure 12.7 is the line of means. It indicates the mean value of y for a given value of x. We denote this mean value as $E(y)$. Then, the line of means is given by the equation

$$E(y) = \beta_0 + \beta_1 x$$

Figure 12.7
The probability distribution of ε

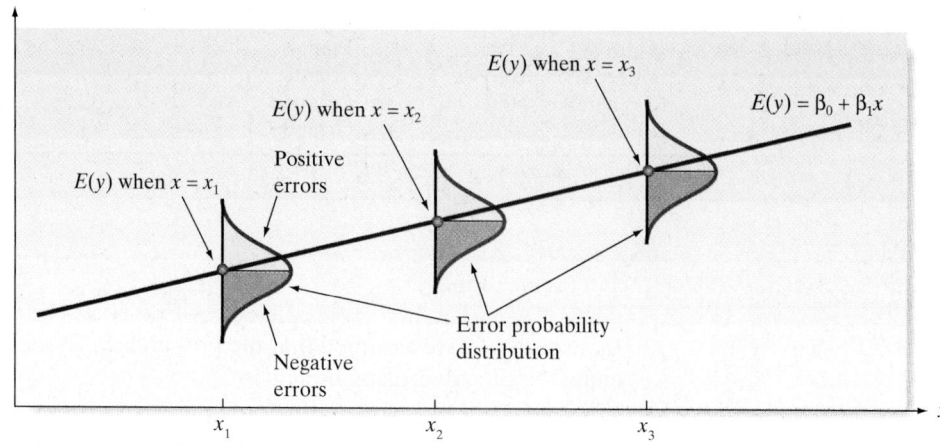

These assumptions make it possible for us to develop measures of reliability for the least squares estimators and to develop hypothesis tests for examining the usefulness of the least squares line. We have various techniques for checking the validity of these assumptions, and we have remedies to apply when they appear to be invalid. Several of these remedies are discussed in Chapter 13. Fortunately, the assumptions need not hold exactly in order for least squares estimators to be useful. The assumptions will be satisfied adequately for many applications encountered in practice.

12.4 An Estimator of σ^2

It seems reasonable to assume that the greater the variability of the random error ε (which is measured by its variance σ^2), the greater will be the errors in the estimation of the model parameters β_0 and β_1 and in the error of prediction when $\hat{y}$ is used to predict y for some value of x. Consequently, you should not be surprised, as we proceed through this chapter, to find that σ^2 appears in the formulas for all confidence intervals and test statistics that we will be using.

Estimation of σ^2 for a (First-Order) Straight-Line Model

$$s^2 = \frac{\text{SSE}}{\text{Degrees of freedom for error}} = \frac{SSE}{n-2}$$

where $\text{SSE} = \sum(y_i - \hat{y}_i)^2 = \text{SS}_{yy} - \hat{\beta}_1\text{SS}_{xy}$

$$\text{SS}_{yy} = \sum(y_i - \bar{y})^2 = \sum y_i^2 - \frac{\left(\sum y_i\right)^2}{n}$$

To estimate the standard deviation σ of ε, we calculate

$$s = \sqrt{s^2} = \sqrt{\frac{\text{SSE}}{n-2}}$$

We will refer to s as the **estimated standard error of the regression model.**

Warning

When performing these calculations, you may be tempted to round the calculated values of SS_{yy}, $\hat{\beta}_1$, and SS_{xy}. Be certain to carry at least six significant figures for each of these quantities to avoid substantial errors in calculation of the SSE.

In most practical situations, σ^2 is unknown and we must use our data to estimate its value. The best estimate of σ^2, denoted by s^2, is obtained by dividing the sum of squares of the deviations of the y values from the prediction line,

$$\text{SSE} = \sum(y_i - \hat{y}_i)^2$$

by the number of degrees of freedom associated with this quantity. We use 2 df to estimate the two parameters β_0 and β_1 in the straight-line model, leaving $(n-2)$ df for the error variance estimation.

In the advertising–sales example, we previously calculated SSE = 1.10 for the least squares line $\hat{y} = -.1 + .7x$. Recalling that there were $n = 5$ data points, we have $n - 2 = 5 - 2 = 3$ df for estimating σ^2. Thus,

$$s^2 = \frac{SSE}{n-2} = \frac{1.10}{3} = .367$$

is the estimated variance, and

$$s = \sqrt{.367} = .61$$

is the standard error of the regression model.

> **Now Work**   *Exercise 12.23a*

Suggested Exercise 12.31

The values of s^2 and s can also be obtained from a simple linear regression printout. The MINITAB printout for the advertising–sales example is reproduced in Figure 12.8. The value of s^2 is highlighted at the bottom of the printout in the **MS** (Mean Square) column in the row labeled **Residual Error.** (In regression, the estimate of σ^2 is called Mean Square for Error, or MSE.) The value, $s^2 = .3667$, agrees with the one calculated by hand. The value of s is also highlighted in Figure 12.8. This value, $s = .60553$, agrees (except for rounding) with our hand-calculated value.

You may be able to grasp s intuitively by recalling the interpretation of a standard deviation given in Chapter 2 and remembering that the least squares line estimates the mean value of y for a given value of x. Since s measures the spread of the distribution of y values about the least squares line, we should not be surprised to find that most of the observations lie within $2s$, or $2(.61) = 1.22$, of the least squares line. For this simple example (only five data points), all five sales revenue values fall within $2s$ (or \$1,220) of the least squares line. In Section 12.8, we use s to evaluate the error of prediction when the least squares line is used to predict a value of y to be observed for a given value of x.

Interpretation of s, the Estimated Standard Deviation of ε

We expect most ($\approx 95\%$) of the observed y values to lie within $2s$ of their respective least squares predicted values, $\hat{y}$.

Figure 12.8
MINITAB printout for the advertising–sales regression

Regression Analysis: SALES_Y versus ADVEXP_X

```
The regression equation is
SALES_Y = - 0.100 + 0.700 ADVEXP_X


Predictor        Coef   SE Coef        T       P
Constant      -0.1000    0.6351    -0.16   0.885
ADVEXP_X       0.7000    0.1915     3.66   0.035


S = 0.605530    R-Sq = 81.7%    R-Sq(adj) = 75.6%


Analysis of Variance

Source            DF        SS       MS       F       P
Regression         1    4.9000   4.9000   13.36   0.035
Residual Error     3    1.1000   0.3667
Total              4    6.0000
```

Exercises 12.23–12.32

Learning the Mechanics

12.23 Suppose you fit a least squares line to 26 data points and the calculated value of SSE is 8.34.
  a. Find s^2, the estimator of σ^2 (the variance of the random error term ε). .3475
  b. What is the largest deviation that you might expect between any one of the 26 points and the least squares line? 1.179

12.24 Calculate SSE and s^2 for each of the following cases:
  a. $n = 20$, $SS_{yy} = 95$, $SS_{xy} = 50$, $\hat{\beta}_1 = .75$
  b. $n = 40$, $\Sigma y^2 = 860$, $\Sigma y = 50$, $SS_{xy} = 2,700$
      $\hat{\beta}_1 = .2$ *SSE = 257.7, s^2 = 6.776*
  c. $n = 10$, $\Sigma(y_i - \bar{y})^2 = 58$, $SS_{xy} = 91$, $SS_{xx} = 170$

12.25 Refer to Exercises 12.10 and 12.13. Calculate SSE, s^2, and s for the least squares lines obtained in these exercises. Interpret the standard error of the regression model, s, for each.

12.26 Visually compare the scattergrams shown below. If a least squares line were determined for each data set, which do you think would have the smallest variance, s^2? Explain.   Part b.

Scattergrams for Exercise 12.26

a. 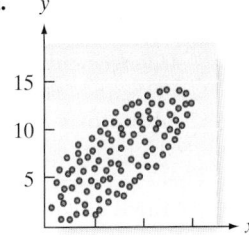   **b.**   **c.**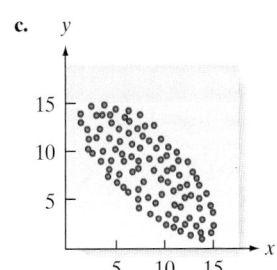

Applying the Concepts—Basic

DIAMONDS

12.27 Refer to the simple linear regression relating y = asking price (dollars) to x = number of carats for diamonds sold on the open market, Exercise 12.14 (p. 707).
  a. Locate the values of SSE, s^2, and s on the MINITAB printout shown on p. 708
  b. Give a practical interpretation of the value of s.

ALWINS

12.28 Refer to the simple linear regression relating y = number of games won by a major league baseball team to x = team batting average, Exercise 12.16 (p. 708). A portion of the SPSS printout of the analysis is shown below.
  a. Locate the values of SSE, s^2, and s on the SPSS printout.
  b. Give a practical interpretation of the value of s.

SPSS Output for Exercise 12.28

Model Summary

Model	R	R Square	Adjusted R Square	Std. Error of the Estimate
1	.780a	.609	.576	11.124

a. Predictors: (Constant), BATAVE

ANOVAb

Model		Sum of Squares	df	Mean Square	F	Sig.
1	Regression	2310.187	1	2310.187	18.668	.001a
	Residual	1485.027	12	123.752		
	Total	3795.214	13			

a. Predictors: (Constant), BATAVE

b. Dependent Variable: WINS

FOODADS

12.29 Refer to simple linear regression relating the rate of prime-time TV commercials per hour as a function of $x =$ the number of year since 1970, Exercise 12.17 (p. 709).

a. Give a practical interpretation of the value of s for the straight-line model for $y =$ rate of total commercials per hour.

b. Give a practical interpretation of the value of s for the straight-line model for $y =$ rate of food advertisements per hour.

Applying the Concepts—Intermediate

12.30 *Statistical Bulletin* (Oct.–Dec. 1999) reported the average hospital charge and the average length of hospital stay for patients undergoing radical prostatectomies in a sample of 12 states. The data are listed in the accompanying table.

HOSPITAL

State	Average Hospital Charge ($)	Average Length of Stay (days)
Massachusetts	11,680	3.64
New Jersey	11,630	4.20
Pennsylvania	9,850	3.84
Minnesota	9,950	3.11
Indiana	8,490	3.86
Michigan	9,020	3.54
Florida	13,820	4.08
Georgia	8,440	3.57
Tennessee	8,790	3.80
Texas	10,400	3.52
Arizona	12,860	3.77
California	16,740	3.78

Source: Statistical Bulletin, Vol. 80, No. 4, Oct.–Dec. 1999, p. 13.

a. Plot the data on a scattergram.

b. Use the method of least squares to model the relationship between average hospital charge (y) and length of hospital stay (x).

c. Find the estimated standard error of the regression model and interpret its value in the context of the problem. $s = 2,496.67$

d. For a hospital stay of length $x = 4$ days, find $\hat{y} \pm 2s$. $11,763.44 \pm 4,993.33$

e. What fraction of the states in the sample have average hospital charges within $\pm 2s$ of the least squares line? $11/12$

12.31 Prior to the 1970s the developing countries played a small role in world trade because their own economic policies hindered integration with the world economy. However, many of these countries have since changed their policies and vastly improved their importance to the global economy (*World Economy*, July 1992). Data (given in billions of U.S. dollars) for investigating the relationship between developing countries and industrial countries annual import levels are shown in the table below.

IMPORTS

	1950	1960	1970	1980	1990
Industrial Countries' Imports, x	39.8	85.4	226.9	1,370.2	2,237.9
Developing Countries' Imports, y	21.1	40.1	75.6	556.4	819.4

a. Fit a least squares line to the data. Plot the data points and graph the least squares line as a check on your calculations. $\hat{y} = 7.381 + .373x$

b. According to your least squares line, approximately what would you expect annual imports for developing countries to be if annual imports for industrial countries were $1,600 billion? $604.181 billion

c. Calculate SSE and s^2. 2225.63; 741.88

d. Interpret the standard deviation s in the context of this problem.

Applying the Concepts—Advanced

12.32 To improve the quality of the output of any production process, it is necessary first to understand the capabilities of the process (Gitlow, *et al., Quality Management: Tools and Methods for Improvement*, 1995). In a particular manufacturing process, the useful life of a cutting tool is related to the speed at which the tool is operated. The data in the table on p. 717 were derived from life tests for the two different brands of cutting tools currently used in the production process.

CUTTOOLS

Cutting Speed (meters per minute)	Useful Life (Hours)	
	Brand A	Brand B
30	4.5	6.0
30	3.5	6.5
30	5.2	5.0
40	5.2	6.0
40	4.0	4.5
40	2.5	5.0
50	4.4	4.5
50	2.8	4.0
50	1.0	3.7
60	4.0	3.8
60	2.0	3.0
60	1.1	2.4
70	1.1	1.5
70	.5	2.0
70	3.0	1.0

a. For each brand, use the method of least squares to model the relationship between useful life and cutting speed. Find the least squares line for each brand.

b. Find SSE, s^2, and s for each least squares line.

c. For a cutting speed of 70 meters per minute, find $\hat{y} \pm 2s$ for each least squares line.

d. For which brand would you feel more confident in using the least squares line to predict useful life for a given cutting speed? Explain.

12.5 Assessing the Utility of the Model: Making Inferences About the Slope β_1

Now that we have specified the probability distribution of ε and found an estimate of the variance σ^2, we are ready to make statistical inferences about the model's usefulness for predicting the response y. This is step 4 in our regression modeling procedure.

Refer again to the data of Table 12.1 and suppose the appliance store's sales revenue is *completely unrelated* to the advertising expenditure. What could be said about the values of β_0 and β_1 in the hypothesized probabilistic model

$$y = \beta_0 + \beta_1 x + \varepsilon$$

if x contributes no information for the prediction of y? The implication is that the mean of y—that is, the deterministic part of the model $E(y) = \beta_0 + \beta_1 x$—does not change as x changes. In the straight-line model, this means that the true slope, β_1, is equal to 0 (see Figure 12.9). Alternatively, if there is a positive linear relationship between x and y, then the slope β_1 will be positive. Therefore, to test the null hypothesis that the linear model contributes no information for the prediction of y against the alternative hypothesis that the slope is positive, we test

$$H_0: \beta_1 = 0 \text{ against } H_a: \beta_1 > 0$$

If the data support the alternative hypothesis, we will conclude that the slope is positive and that x does contribute information for the prediction of y using the straight-line model (although the true relationship between $E(y)$ and x could be more complex than a straight line). Thus, in effect, this is a test of the usefulness of the hypothesized model.

The appropriate test statistic is found by considering the sampling distribution of $\hat{\beta}_1$, the least squares estimator of the slope β_1, as shown in the following box.

Figure 12.9
Graphing the $\beta_1 = 0$ model $y = \beta_0 + \varepsilon$

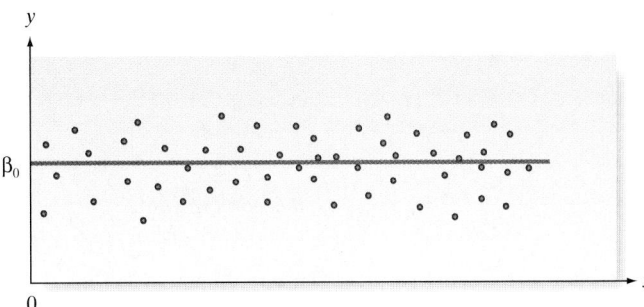

Sampling Distribution of β_1

If we make the four assumptions about ϵ (see Section 12.3), the sampling distribution of the least squares estimator $\hat{\beta}_1$ of the slope will be normal with mean β_1 (the true slope) and standard deviation

$$\sigma_{\hat{\beta}_1} = \frac{\sigma}{\sqrt{SS_{xx}}} \text{ (see Figure 12.10)}$$

We estimate $\sigma_{\hat{\beta}_1}$ by $s_{\hat{\beta}_1} = \frac{s}{\sqrt{SS_{xx}}}$ and refer to this quantity as the **estimated standard error of the least squares slope $\hat{\beta}_1$.**

Figure 12.10
Sampling distribution of $\hat{\beta}_1$

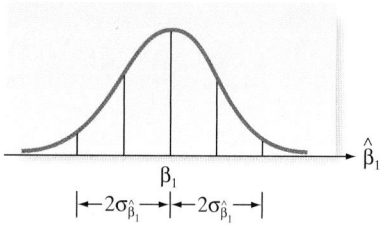

Since σ is usually unknown, the appropriate test statistic is a t statistic, formed as follows:

$$t = \frac{\hat{\beta}_1 - \text{Hypothesized value of } \beta_1}{s_{\hat{\beta}_1}} \qquad \text{where } s_{\hat{\beta}_1} = \frac{s}{\sqrt{SS_{xx}}}$$

Thus,

$$t = \frac{\hat{\beta}_1 - 0}{s/\sqrt{SS_{xx}}}$$

Teaching Tip

This *t*-distribution is identical to the *t*-distribution that the students worked with earlier in the text. Point out that the degrees of freedom associated with this *t*-distribution is $n - 2$.

Note that we have substituted the estimator s for σ and then formed the estimated standard error $s_{\hat{\beta}_1}$ by dividing s by $\sqrt{SS_{xx}}$. The number of degrees of freedom associated with this t statistic is the same as the number of degrees of freedom associated with s. Recall that this number is $(n - 2)$ df when the hypothesized model is a straight line (see Section 12.4). The setup of our test of the usefulness of the straight-line model is summarized in the boxes.

A Test of Model Utility: Simple Linear Regression

One-Tailed Test	Two-Tailed Test
$H_0: \beta_1 = 0$	$H_0: \beta_1 = 0$
$H_a: \beta_1 < 0$ (or $H_a: \beta_1 > 0$)	$H_a: \beta_1 \neq 0$

$$\text{Test statistic: } t = \frac{\hat{\beta}_1}{s_{\hat{\beta}_1}} = \frac{\hat{\beta}_1}{s/\sqrt{SS_{xx}}}$$

Rejection region: $t < -t_\alpha$	*Rejection region:* $\lvert t \rvert > t_{\alpha/2}$
(or $t > t_\alpha$ when $H_a: \beta_1 > 0$)	

where t_α and $t_{\alpha/2}$ are based on $(n - 2)$ degrees of freedom

Conditions Required for a Valid Test: Simple Linear Regression

The four assumptions about ε listed in Section 12.3.

For the advertising–sales example, we will choose $\alpha = .05$ and, since $n = 5$, t will be based on $n - 2 = 3$ df and the rejection region will be

$$t > t_{.05} = 2.353$$

Suggested Exercises 12.37

We previously calculated $\hat{\beta}_1 = .7$, $s = .61$, and $SS_{xx} = 10$. Thus,

$$t = \frac{\hat{\beta}_1}{s/\sqrt{SS_{xx}}} = \frac{.7}{.61\sqrt{10}} = \frac{.7}{.19} = 3.7$$

Since this calculated t value falls in the rejection region (see Figure 12.11), we reject the null hypothesis and conclude that the slope β_1 is greater than 0. The sample evidence indicates that advertising expenditure x is positively linearly related to sales revenue y.

Figure 12.11

Rejection region and calculated t-value for testing H_0: $\beta_1 = 0$ versus H_a: $\beta_1 \neq 0$

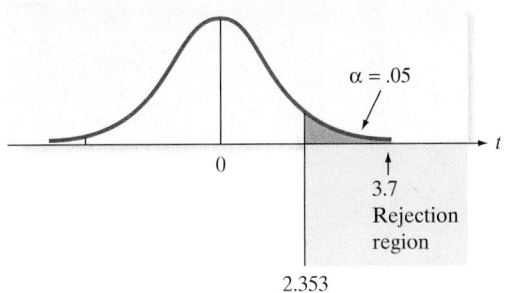

We can reach the same conclusion by using the observed significance level (p-value) of the test from a computer printout. The MINITAB printout for the advertising–sales example is reproduced in Figure 12.12. The test statistic is highlighted

Figure 12.12

MINITAB printout for the advertising–sales regression

Regression Analysis: SALES_Y versus ADVEXP_X

```
The regression equation is
SALES_Y = - 0.100 + 0.700 ADVEXP_X


Predictor      Coef   SE Coef       T       P
Constant    -0.1000    0.6351   -0.16   0.885
ADVEXP_X     0.7000    0.1915    3.66   0.035


S = 0.605530    R-Sq = 81.7%    R-Sq(adj) = 75.6%


Analysis of Variance

Source            DF       SS       MS       F       P
Regression         1   4.9000   4.9000   13.36   0.035
Residual Error     3   1.1000   0.3667
Total              4   6.0000
```

on the printout under the **T** column in the row corresponding to **ADVEXP_X**, while the *two-tailed p*-value is highlighted under the column labeled **P.** Now, the appropriate *one-tailed p*-value is obtained by dividing the value shown on the printout (.035) by 2; that is, one-tailed *p*-value $= $ (two-tailed *p*-value)$/2 = .035 = .0175$. (See the next box.) Since the *p*-value is smaller than $\alpha = .05$, we will reject H_0.

Now Work   *Exercise 12.37a–b*

What conclusion can be drawn if the calculated *t* value does not fall in the rejection region or if the observed significance level of the test exceeds α? We know from previous discussions of the philosophy of hypothesis testing that such a *t* value does *not* lead us to accept the null hypothesis. That is, we do not conclude that $\beta_1 = 0$. Additional data might indicate that β_1 differs from 0, or a more complex relationship may exist between x and y, requiring the fitting of a model other than the straight-line model. We discuss several such models in Chapter 13.

Interpreting *p*-Values for β Coefficients in Regression

Almost all statistical computer software packages report a *two-tailed p*-value for each of the β parameters in the regression model. For example, in simple linear regression, the *p*-value for the two-tailed test $H_0: \beta_1 = 0$ versus $H_a: \beta_1 \neq 0$ is given on the printout. If you want to conduct a *one-tailed* test of hypothesis, you will need to adjust the *p*-value reported on the printout as follows:

Upper-tailed test $(H_a: \beta_1 > 0)$: $p\text{-value} = \begin{cases} p/2 & \text{if } t > 0 \\ 1 - p/2 & \text{if } t < 0 \end{cases}$

Lower-tailed test $(H_a: \beta_1 < 0)$: $p\text{-value} = \begin{cases} p/2 & \text{if } t < 0 \\ 1 - p/2 & \text{if } t > 0 \end{cases}$

where p is the *p*-value reported on the printout and t is the value of the test statistic.

Another way to make inferences about the slope β_1 is to estimate it using a confidence interval. This interval is formed as shown in the next box.

Teaching Tip

Note that the confidence intervals used in regression use the same theory as the confidence intervals studied earlier in the text.

A $100(1 - \alpha)\%$ Confidence Interval for the Simple Linear Regression Slope β_1

$$\hat{\beta}_1 \pm t_{\alpha/2} s_{\hat{\beta}_1}$$

where the estimated standard error $\hat{\beta}_1$ is calculated by

$$s_{\hat{\beta}_1} = \frac{s}{\sqrt{SS_{xx}}}$$

and $t_{\alpha/2}$ is based on $(n - 2)$ degrees of freedom.

> **Conditions Required for a Valid Confidence Interval: Simple Linear Regression**
>
> The four assumptions about ε listed in Section 12.3.

In the advertising–sales example, $t_{\alpha/2}$ is based on $(n - 2) = 3$ degrees of freedom. For $\alpha = .05$, $t_{.025} = 3.182$. Therefore, a 95% confidence interval for the slope β_1, the expected change in sales revenue for a \$100 increase in advertising expenditure, is

$$\hat{\beta}_1 \pm (t_{.025})s_{\hat{\beta}_1} = .7 \pm 3.182\left(\frac{s}{\sqrt{SS_{xx}}}\right) = .7 \pm 3.182\left(\frac{.61}{\sqrt{10}}\right) = .7 \pm .61$$

Thus, the interval estimate of the slope parameter β_1 is .09 to 1.31. In terms of this example, the implication is that we can be 95% confident that the *true* mean increase in monthly sales revenue per additional \$100 of advertising expenditure is between \$90 and \$1,310. This inference is meaningful only over the sampled range of x—that is, from \$100 to \$500 of advertising expenditures.

> **Now Work** *Exercise 12.37c*

Since all the values in this interval are positive, it appears that β_1 is positive and that the mean of y, $E(y)$, increases as x increases. However, the rather large width of the confidence interval reflects the small number of data points (and, consequently, a lack of information) in the experiment. Particularly bothersome is the fact that the lower end of the confidence interval implies that we are not even recovering our additional expenditure, since a \$100 increase in advertising may produce as little as a \$90 increase in mean sales. If we wish to tighten this interval, we need to increase the sample size.

Statistics in Action Revisited

Assessing How Well the Straight-Line Model Fits the Dowsing Data

In the previous Statistics in Action Revisited, we fit the straight-line model, $E(y) = \beta_0 + \beta_1 x$, where x = dowser's guess (in meters) and y = pipe location (in meters) for each trial. The MINITAB regression printout is reproduced in Figure SIA12.3. The two-tailed p-value for testing the null hypothesis, H_0: $\beta_1 = 0$ (highlighted on the printout), is p-value = .118. Even for an α-level as high as $\alpha = .10$, there is insufficient evidence to reject H_0. Consequently, the dowsing data in Table SIA12.1 provide no statistical support for the German researchers' claim that the three best dowsers have an ability to find underground water with a divining rod.

This lack of support for the "dowsing" theory is made clearer with a confidence interval for the slope of the line. When $n = 26$, df $= (n - 2) = 24$, and $t_{.025} = 2.064$. Sub-

stituting this value and the relevant values shown on the MINITAB printout, a 95% confidence interval for β_1 is

$$\hat{\beta}_1 \pm t_{.025}(s_{\hat{\beta}_1}) = .31 \pm (2.064)(.19)$$
$$= .31 \pm .39, \text{ or } (-.08, .70)$$

Thus, for every 1-meter increase in a dowser's guess, we estimate (with 95% confidence) that the change in the actual pipe location will range anywhere from a decrease of .08 meter to an increase of .70 meter. In other words, we're not sure whether the pipe location will increase or decrease along the 10-meter pipeline! Keep in mind, also, that the data in Table SIA12.1 represent the "best" performances of the three dowsers (i.e., the outcome of the dowsing experiment in its most favorable light). When the data for all trials are considered and plotted, there is not even a hint of a trend.

Regression Analysis: PIPE versus GUESS

```
The regression equation is
PIPE = 30.1 + 0.308 GUESS


Predictor     Coef   SE Coef     T      P
Constant     30.07     11.41   2.63  0.015
GUESS       0.3079    0.1900   1.62  0.118


S = 26.0298    R-Sq = 9.9%    R-Sq(adj) = 6.1%


Analysis of Variance

Source          DF        SS       MS     F      P
Regression       1    1778.9   1778.9  2.63  0.118
Residual Error  24   16261.2    677.6
Total           25   18040.2
```

Figure SIA12.3
MINITAB simple linear regression for dowsing data

Exercises 12.33–12.48

Learning the Mechanics

12.33 Construct both a 95% and a 90% confidence interval for β_1 for each of the following cases:

   a. $\hat{\beta}_1 = 31, s = 3, SS_{xx} = 35, n = 10$

   b. $\hat{\beta}_1 = 64, SSE = 1{,}960, SS_{xx} = 30, n = 14$

   c. $\hat{\beta}_1 = -8.4, SSE = 146, SS_{xx} = 64, n = 20$

12.34 Consider the following pairs of observations:

x	1	4	3	2	5	6	0
y	1	3	3	1	4	7	2

   a. Construct a scattergram for the data.

   b. Use the method of least squares to fit a straight line to the seven data points in the table.

   c. Plot the least squares line on your scattergram of part **a**.

   d. Specify the null and alternative hypotheses you would use to test whether the data provide sufficient evidence to indicate that x contributes information for the (linear) prediction of y.

   e. What is the test statistic that should be used in conducting the hypothesis test of part **d**? Specify the degrees of freedom associated with the test statistic.

   f. Conduct the hypothesis test of part **d** using $\alpha = .05$.

12.35 Refer to Exercise 12.34. Construct an 80% and a 98% confidence interval for β_1.

12.36 Do the accompanying data provide sufficient evidence to conclude that a straight line is useful for characterizing the relationship between x and y?

x	4	2	4	3	2	4
y	1	6	5	3	2	4

Applying the Concepts—Basic

DIAMONDS

12.37 Refer to the MINITAB simple linear regression analysis relating $y =$ asking price (dollars) to $x =$ number of carats for diamonds sold on the open market, Exercise 12.14 (p. 708).

   a. Give the null and alternative hypotheses for determining whether a positive linear relationship exists between y and x. $H_0: \beta_1 = 0$ vs. $H_a: \beta_1 > 0$

b. Locate the *p*-value of the test on the MINITAB printout. Interpret the result if $\alpha = .01$.   .000
c. Find a 99% confidence interval for the slope, β_1. Interpret the result. $11{,}598.9 \pm 593.7$

ALWINS

12.38 Refer to the SPSS simple linear regression analysis relating *y* = number of games won by a major league baseball team to *x* = team batting average, Exercise 12.16 (p. 709)

a. Give the null and alternative hypotheses for determining whether a positive linear relationship exists between *y* and *x*. $H_0: \beta_1 = 0$ vs. $H_a: \beta_1 > 0$
b. Locate the *p*-value of the test on the SPSS printout. Interpret the result if $\alpha = .05$.   .001
c. Find a 95% confidence interval for the slope, β_1. Interpret the result. $1{,}118.4 \pm 564.0$

SATSCORES

12.39 Refer to the simple linear regression relating *y* = average state SAT score in 2000 with *x* = average state SAT score in 1990, Exercise 12.15 (p. 707). Use the results of the regression to form a 90% confidence interval the slope, β_1. Interpret the result. $1.07 \pm .069$

OJUICE

12.40 Refer to the simple linear regression relating *y* = sweetness index of an orange juice sample with *x* = amount of water soluble pectin, Exercise 12.18 (p. 709). Use the results of the regression to form a 95% confidence interval the slope, β_1. Interpret the result. $-.0023 \pm .0019$

Applying the Concepts—Intermediate

FOODADS

12.41 Refer to the *Nutrition & Food Science* (Vol. 30, 2000) study relating the rate of prime-time television commercials per hour to the number of years since 1970, Exercise 12.17 (p. 709).

a. The researchers concluded that "the hourly rate for total commercials is increasing significantly by 1.4 commercials per hour each year." Do you agree with this statement? Explain.   Yes
b. The researchers also concluded that "the hourly rate for food advertisements is not changing over time in a statistically significant fashion." Do you agree with this statement? Explain.   Yes

12.42 Financial institutions have a legal and social responsibility to serve all communities. Do banks adequately serve both inner city and suburban neighborhoods, both poor and wealthy communities? In New Jersey, banks have been charged with withdrawing from

urban areas with a high percentage of minorities. To examine this charge, a regional New Jersey newspaper, the *Asbury Park Press*, compiled county by county data on the number (*y*) of people in each county per branch bank in the county and the percentage (*x*) of the population in each county that is minority. These data for each of New Jersey's 21 counties are provided in the table below.

NJBANKS

Country	Number of People per Bank Branch	Percentage of Minority Population
Atlantic	3,073	23.3
Bergen	2,095	13.0
Burlington	2,905	17.8
Camden	3,330	23.4
Cape May	1,321	7.3
Cumberland	2,557	26.5
Essex	3,474	48.8
Gloucester	3,068	10.7
Hudson	3,683	33.2
Hunterdon	1,998	3.7
Mercer	2,607	24.9
Middlesex	3,154	18.1
Monmouth	2,609	12.6
Morris	2,253	8.2
Ocean	2,317	4.7
Passaic	3,307	28.1
Salem	2,511	16.7
Somerset	2,333	12.0
Sussex	2,568	2.4
Union	3,048	25.6
Warren	2,349	2.8

Source: D'Ambrosio, P., and Chambers, S. "No Checks and Balances." *Asbury Park Press,* September 10, 1995.

a. Plot the data in a scattergram. What pattern, if any, does the plot reveal?
b. Consider the linear model $E(y) = \beta_0 + \beta_1 x$. If, in fact, the charge against the New Jersey banks is true, then an increase in the percentage of minorities (*x*) will lead to a decrease in the number of bank branches in a county and therefore will result in an increase in the number of people (*y*) per branch. Will the value of β_1 be positive or negative in this situation?   Positive
c. Do these data support or refute the charge made against the New Jersey banking community? Test using $\alpha = .01$. $t = 4.597$

12.43 *Tennis* magazine (Feb. 2000) claims that "tennis players who tie the knot often see their games unravel." The next table lists a sample of players and their rankings on their wedding days and on their first anniversaries.

a. Construct a scattergram for these data. Does it tend to support or refute the magazine's claim? Justify your answer.   Support

b. Use the method of least squares to construct a model of the relationship between wedding day ranking (x) and first anniversary ranking (y).

c. Does the linear model you developed in part **b** contribute information for predicting players' rankings on their first anniversaries? Test at $\alpha = .05$.

☉ TENLOVE

Player	Ranking on Wedding Day	Ranking on First Anniversary
Arthur Ashe	12	130
Jonathan Stark	67	165
Richey Reneberg	28	97
Paul Haarhuis	28	73
Richard Fromberg	40	79
Byron Black	44	77
Sabine Appelmans	16	49
Petr Korda	7	11
Dominique Van Roost	43	46
Ivan Lendl	1	3
John McEnroe	7	9
Stefan Edberg	2	3
Chris Evert	4	4
Mats Wilander	3	3
Sandrine Testud	14	12
Zina Garrison	6	4
Yevgeny Kafelnikov	8	4
Boris Becker	11	3
Michael Stich	15	6
Julie Halard-Decugis	32	15
Todd Woodbridge	71	27
Jason Stoltenberg	82	31

Source: Tennis, Feb. 2000, p. 14.

d. If there were no changes whatsoever in the rankings of the sample of players after getting married, what would the true values of β_0 and β_1 be?   0 and 1

12.44 The U.S. Department of Agriculture has developed and adopted the Universal Soil Loss Equation (USLE) for predicting water erosion of soils. In geographical areas where runoff from melting snow is common, the USLE requires an accurate estimate of snowmelt runoff erosion. An article in the *Journal of Soil and Water Conservation* (Mar.–Apr. 1995) used simple linear regression to develop a snowmelt erosion index. Data for 54 climatological stations in Canada were used to model the McCool winter-adjusted rainfall erosivity index, y, as a straight-line function of the once-in-five-year snowmelt runoff amount, x (measured in millimeters).

a. The data points are plotted in the scattergram shown below. Is there visual evidence of a linear trend?

b. The data for seven stations were removed from the analysis due to lack of snowfall during the study period. Why is this strategy advisable?

c. The simple linear regression on the remaining $n = 47$ data points yielded the following results:

$$\hat{y} = -6.72 + 1.39x; \qquad s_{\hat{\beta}_1} = .06$$

Use this information to construct a 90% confidence interval for β_1. $1.39 \pm .101$

d. Interpret the interval, part **c.**

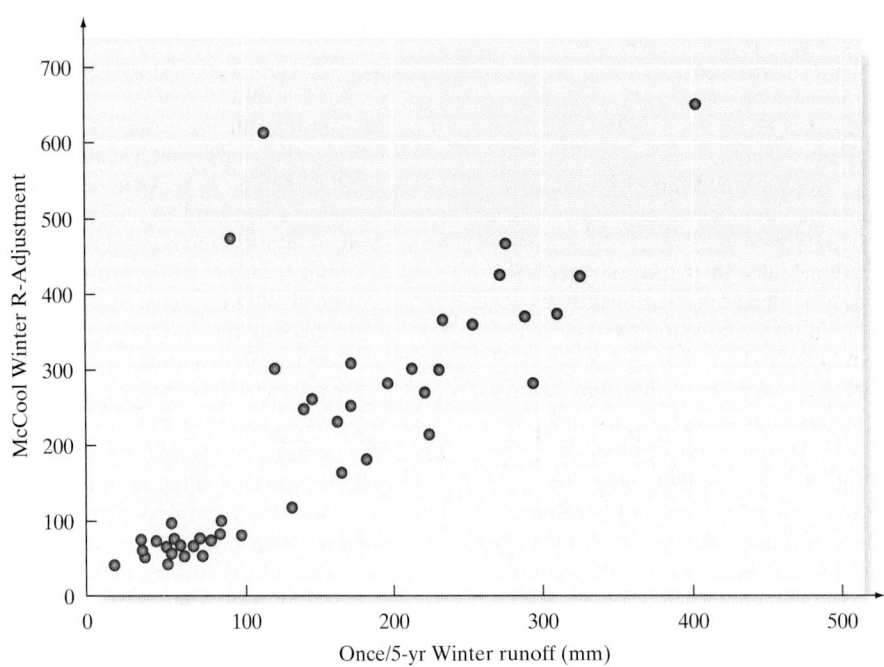

BWECS

12.45 Refer to the *Business Week* "Executive Compensation Scoreboard" data saved in the **BWECS** file. Two of the quantitative variables measured for each of the 363 CEOs in the survey are 2002 total compensation (in thousands of dollars) and the return (in dollars) on a $100 investment in CEOs the company made three years earlier. Use the method of least squares to model the straight-line relationship between CEO total 2002 pay (y) and return (x). Conduct a test for model utility using $\alpha = .05$. Would you recommend using the least squares model to predict a CEO's total pay? $t = .04$

12.46 H. Mintzberg's classic book, *The Nature of Managerial Work* (1973), identified the roles found in all managerial jobs. An observational study of 19 managers from a medium-sized manufacturing plant extended Mintzberg's work by investigating which activities *successful* managers actually perform (*Journal of Applied Behavioral Science,* Aug. 1985). To measure success, the researchers devised an index based on the manager's length of time in the organization and his or her level within the firm; the higher the index, the more successful the manager. The next table presents data (which are representative of the data collected by the researchers) that can be used to determine whether managerial success is related to the extensiveness of a manager's network-building interactions with people outside the manager's work unit. Such interactions include phone and face-to-face meetings with customers and suppliers, attending outside meetings, and doing public relations work.

a. Construct a scattergram for the data.

b. Find the prediction equation for managerial success.

c. Find s for your prediction equation. Interpret the standard deviation s in the context of this problem.

d. Plot the least squares line on your scattergram of part **a**. Does it appear that the number of interactions with outsiders contributes information for the prediction of managerial success? Explain.

e. Conduct a formal statistical hypothesis test to answer the question posed in part **d**. Use $\alpha = .05$.

f. Construct a 95% confidence interval for β_1. Interpret the interval in the context of the problem.

Applying the Concepts—Advanced

RETAL

12.47 Refer to Exercise 12.21 (p. 710), in which the extent of retaliation against whistle blowers was investigated. Since salary is a reasonably good indicator of a person's power within an organization, the data of Exercise 12.21 can be used to investigate whether the extent of retaliation is related to the power of the whistle blower in the organization. The researchers were unable to reject the hypothesis that the extent of retaliation is unrelated to power. Do you agree? Test using $\alpha = .05$.

MANAGERS

Manager	Manager Success Index, y	Number of Interactions with Outsiders, x
1	40	12
2	73	71
3	95	70
4	60	81
5	81	43
6	27	50
7	53	42
8	66	18
9	25	35
10	63	82
11	70	20
12	47	81
13	80	40
14	51	33
15	32	45
16	50	10
17	52	65
18	30	20
19	42	21

12.48 One of the most difficult tasks of developing and managing a global portfolio is assessing the risks of potential foreign investments. Duke University researcher C. R. Henry collaborated with two First Chicago Investment Management Company directors to examine the use of country credit ratings as a means of evaluating foreign investments (*Journal of Portfolio Management,* Winter 1995). To be effective, such a measure should help explain and predict the volatility of the foreign market in question. The researchers analyzed data on annualized risk (y) and average credit rating (x) for 40 countries. The data are saved in the **GLOBRISK** file. (The first and last five countries are shown in the table.)

GLOBRISK

Country	Annualized Risk (%)	Average Credit Rating
Argentina	87.0	31.8
Australia	26.9	78.2
Austria	26.3	83.8
Belgium	22.0	78.4
Brazil	64.8	36.2
⋮	⋮	⋮
Turkey	74.1	32.6
United Kingdom	21.8	87.6
United States	15.4	93.4
Venezuela	46.0	45.0
Zimbabwe	35.6	24.5

Source: Erb, C. B., Harvey, C. R., and Viskanta, T. E. "Country Risk and Global Equity Selection." *Journal of Portfolio Management,* Vol. 21, No. 2, Winter 1995, p. 76. This copyrighted material is reprinted with permission from The Journal of Portfolio Management, a publication of Institutional Investor, Inc., 488 Madison Ave., New York, NY 10022.

a. Do the data provide sufficient evidence to conclude that country credit risk (x) contributes information for the prediction of market volatility (y)?

b. Use a graph to visually locate any unusual data points (outliers).

c. Eliminate the outlier(s), part **b**, from the data set and rerun the simple linear regression analysis. Note any dramatic changes in the results.

12.6 The Coefficient of Correlation

Teaching Tip

When working with simple linear regression, the correlation coefficient can adequately substitute for the β_1 parameter of the preceding sections.

Recall (from optional Section 2.10) that a **bivariate relationship** describes a relationship between two variables, x and y. Scattergrams are used to graphically describe a bivariate relationship. In this section we will discuss the concept of **correlation** and show how it can be used to measure the linear relationship between two variables x and y. A numerical descriptive measure of the linear association between x and y is provided by the *coefficient of correlation, r.*

Teaching Tip

Stress that the linear nature of the coefficient of correlation makes its usefulness limited once we begin to include curvilinear relationships in the multiple regression models of Chapter 12.

DEFINITION 12.2

The **coefficient of correlation,*** r, is a measure of the strength of the *linear* relationship between two variables x and y. It is computed (for a sample of n measurements on x and y) as follows:

$$r = \frac{SS_{xy}}{\sqrt{SS_{xx}SS_{yy}}}$$

Note that the computational formula for the correlation coefficient r given in Definition 12.2 involves the same quantities that were used in computing the least squares prediction equation. In fact, since the numerators of the expressions for $\hat{\beta}_1$ and r are identical, you can see that $r = 0$ when $\hat{\beta}_1 = 0$ (the case where x contributes no information for the prediction of y) and that r is positive when the slope is positive and negative when the slope is negative. Unlike β_1, the correlation coefficient r is *scaleless* and assumes a value between -1 and $+1$, regardless of the units of x and y.

A value of r near or equal to 0 implies little or no linear relationship between y and x. In contrast, the closer r comes to 1 or -1, the stronger the linear relationship between y and x. And if $r = 1$ or $r = -1$, all the sample points fall exactly on the least squares line. Positive values of r imply a positive linear relationship between y and x; that is, y increases as x increases. Negative values of r imply a negative linear relationship between y and x; that is, y decreases as x increases. Each of these situations is portrayed in Figure 12.13.

---

*The value of r is often called the *Pearson* correlation coefficient to honor its developer, Karl Pearson. (See Biography, p. 646).

Figure 12.13

Values of r and their implications

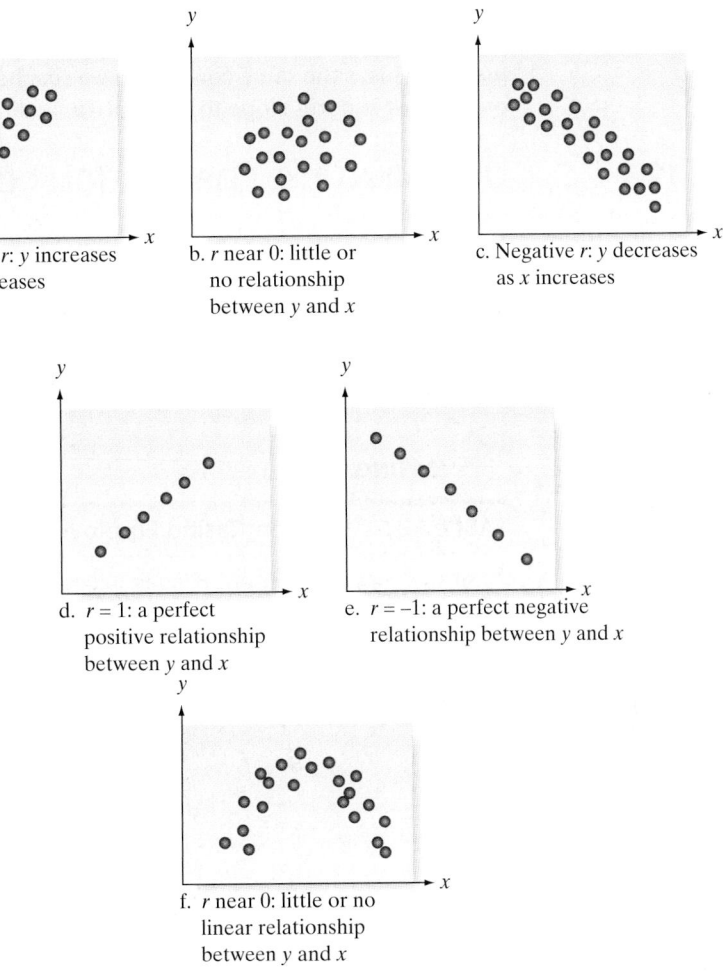

a. Positive r: y increases as x increases

b. r near 0: little or no relationship between y and x

c. Negative r: y decreases as x increases

d. $r = 1$: a perfect positive relationship between y and x

e. $r = -1$: a perfect negative relationship between y and x

f. r near 0: little or no linear relationship between y and x

Now Work   *Exercise 12.50*

We demonstrate how to calculate the coefficient of correlation r using the data in Table 12.1 for the advertising–sales example. The quantities needed to calculate r are SS_{xy}, SS_{xx}, and SS_{yy}. The first two quantities have been calculated previously and are repeated here for convenience:

$$SS_{xy} = 7 \qquad SS_{xx} = 10 \qquad SS_{yy} = \sum y^2 - \frac{(\sum y)^2}{n}$$

$$= 26 - \frac{(10)^2}{5} = 26 - 20 = 6$$

We now find the coefficient of correlation:

$$r = \frac{SS_{xy}}{\sqrt{SS_{xx}SS_{yy}}} = \frac{7}{\sqrt{(10)(6)}} = \frac{7}{\sqrt{60}} = .904$$

The fact that r is positive and near 1 in value indicates that the sales revenue y tends to increase as advertising expenditure x increases—*for this sample of five months.* This is the same conclusion we reached when we found the calculated value of the least squares slope to be positive.

EXAMPLE 12.1

OBTAINING THE CORRELATION COEFFICIENT

Problem Legalized gambling is available on several riverboat casinos operated by a city in Mississippi. The mayor of the city wants to know the correlation between the number of casino employees and the yearly crime rate. The records for the past 10 years are examined, and the results listed in Table 12.5 are obtained. Calculate the coefficient of correlation r for the data. Interpret the result.

$r = .987$

 CASINO

TABLE 12.5 Data on Casino Employees and Crime Rate, Example 12.1

Year	Number of Casino Employees, x (thousands)	Crime Rate, y (number of crimes per 1,000 population)
1993	15	1.35
1994	18	1.63
1995	24	2.33
1996	22	2.41
1997	25	2.63
1998	29	2.93
1999	30	3.41
2000	32	3.26
2001	35	3.63
2002	38	4.15

Solution Rather than use the computing formula given in Definition 12.2, we resort to a statistical software package. The data of Table 12.5 were entered into a computer and MINITAB was used to compute r. The MINITAB printout is shown in Figure 12.14.

Figure 12.14
MINITAB correlation printout for Example 12.1

Correlations: EMPLOYEES, CRIMERAT

```
Pearson correlation of EMPLOYEES and CRIMERAT = 0.987
P-Value = 0.000
```

Suggested Exercises 12.49

The coefficient of correlation, highlighted on the printout, is $r = .987$. Thus, the size of the casino workforce and crime rate in this city are very highly correlated—at least over the past 10 years. The implication is that a strong positive linear relationship exists between these variables (see Figure 12.15). We must be careful, however, not to jump to any unwarranted conclusions. For instance, the mayor may be tempted to conclude that hiring more casino workers next year will increase the crime rate—that is, that there is a *causal relationship* between the two variables. However, high correlation does not imply causality. The fact is, many things have probably contributed both to the increase in the casino workforce and to the increase in crime rate. The city's tourist trade has undoubtedly grown since legalizing riverboat casinos and it is likely that the casinos have expanded both in services offered and in number. *We can-*

Figure 12.15
MINITAB scattergram for
Example 12.1

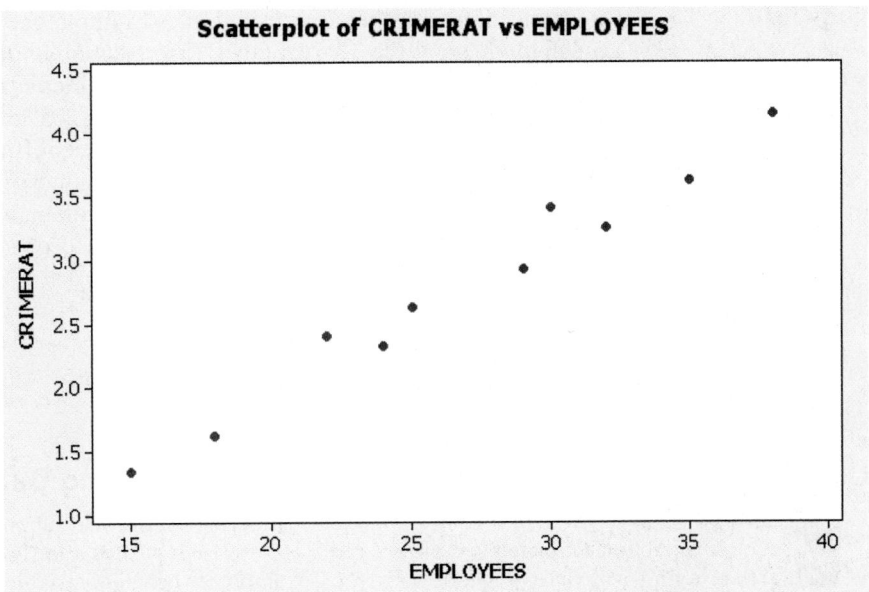

not infer a causal relationship on the basis of high sample correlation. When a high correlation is observed in the sample data, the only safe conclusion is that a linear trend may exist between x *and* y.

Look Back Another variable, such as the increase in tourism, may be the underlying cause of the high correlation between *x* and *y*.

 **Now Work**   *Exercise 12.56 a,b*

■ ■ ■

Warning

When using the sample correlation coefficient, *r*, to infer the nature of the relationship between *x* and *y*, two caveats exist: (1) A *high correlation* does not necessarily imply that a causal relationship exists between *x* and *y*—only that a linear trend may exist; (2) a *low correlation* does not necessarily imply that *x* and *y* are unrelated—only that *x* and *y* are not strongly linearly related.

Teaching Tip
Unlike the coefficient of
correlation, the coefficient of
determination will be useful in
the multiple regression analyses
in the next chapter.

Keep in mind that the correlation coefficient *r* measures the linear correlation between *x* values and *y* values in the sample, and a similar linear coefficient of correlation exists for the population from which the data points were selected. The **population correlation coefficient** is denoted by the symbol ρ (rho). As you might expect, ρ is estimated by the corresponding sample statistic, *r*. Or, instead of estimating ρ, we might want to test the null hypothesis H_0: $\rho = 0$ against H_a: $\rho \neq 0$—that is, we can test the hypothesis that *x* contributes no information for the prediction of *y* by using the straight-line model against the alternative that the two variables are at least linearly related.

However, we already performed this *identical* test in Section 12.5 when we tested H_0: $\beta_1 = 0$ against H_a: $\beta_1 \neq 0$. That is, the null hypothesis H_0: $\rho = 0$ is equivalent to the hypothesis H_0: $\beta_1 = 0$.* When we tested the null hypothesis H_0: $\beta_1 = 0$

*The correlation test statistic that is equivalent to $t = \hat{\beta}_1/s_{\hat{\beta}_1}$ is $t = \dfrac{r}{\sqrt{(1 - r^2)/(n - 2)}}$.

Teaching Tip

The regression output of most software packages includes the value of r^2. More time should be spent understanding the interpretation that the calculation of the coefficient of determination.

in connection with the advertising–sales example, the data led to a rejection of the null hypothesis at the $\alpha = .05$ level. This rejection implies that the null hypothesis of a 0 linear correlation between the two variables (sales revenue and advertising expenditure) can also be rejected at the $\alpha = .05$ level. The only real difference between the least squares slope $\hat{\beta}_1$ and the coefficient of correlation r is the measurement scale. Therefore, the information they provide about the usefulness of the least squares model is to some extent redundant. For this reason, we will use the slope to make inferences about the existence of a positive or negative linear relationship between two variables.

Statistics in Action Revisited

Using the Correlation Coefficient to Assess the Dowsing Data

In the previous Statistics in Action Revisited, we discovered that using a dowser's guess (x) in a straight-line model was not statistically useful for predicting actual pipe location (y). The coefficient of correlation, shown on the MINITAB printout in Figure SIA12.4, also supports this conclusion. The value, $r = .314$, indicates a fairly weak positive linear relationship between the variables. This value, however, is not statistically significant (p-value $= .118$). In other words, there is no evidence to indicate that the population correlation coefficient is different from 0.

Figure SIA12.4

MINITAB correlation printout for dowsing data

Correlations: PIPE, GUESS

```
Pearson correlation of PIPE and GUESS = 0.314
P-Value = 0.118
```

12.7 The Coefficient of Determination

Another way to measure the usefulness of the model is to measure the contribution of x in predicting y. To accomplish this, we calculate how much the errors of prediction of y were reduced by using the information provided by x. To illustrate, consider the sample shown in the scattergram of Figure 12.16(a). If we assume that x contributes no information for the prediction of y, the best prediction for a value of y is the sample mean $\bar{y}$, which is shown as the horizontal line in Figure 12.16(b). The vertical line segments in Figure 12.16(b) are the deviations of the points about the mean $\bar{y}$. Note that the sum of squares of deviations for the prediction equation $\hat{y} = \bar{y}$ is

$$SS_{yy} = \sum (y_i - \bar{y})^2$$

Now suppose you fit a least squares line to the same set of data and locate the deviations of the points about the line as shown in Figure 12.16(c). Compare the deviations about the prediction lines in Figures 12.16(b) and 12.16(c). You can see that

Figure 12.16

A comparison of the sum of squares of deviations for two models

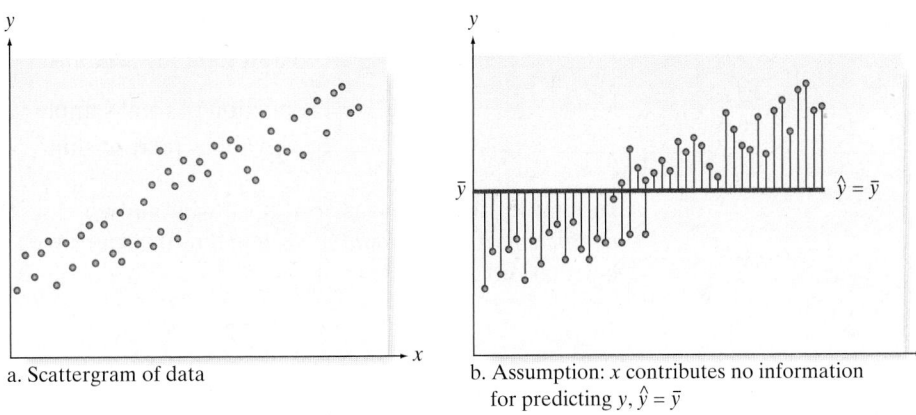

a. Scattergram of data

b. Assumption: x contributes no information for predicting y, $\hat{y} = \bar{y}$

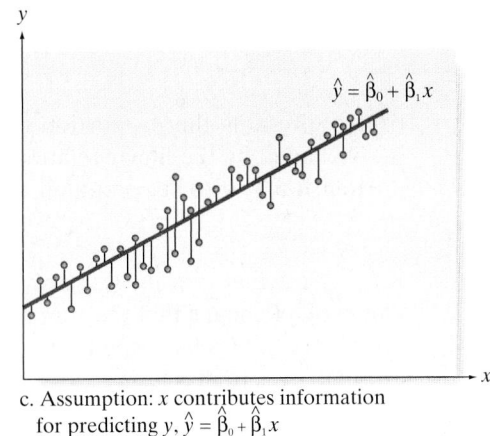

c. Assumption: x contributes information for predicting y, $\hat{y} = \hat{\beta}_0 + \hat{\beta}_1 x$

1. If x contributes little or no information for the prediction of y, the sums of squares of deviations for the two lines,

$$\text{SS}_{yy} = \sum (y_i - \bar{y})^2 \quad \text{and} \quad \text{SSE} = \sum (y_i - \hat{y}_i)^2$$

will be nearly equal.

2. If x does contribute information for the prediction of y, the SSE will be smaller than SS_{yy}. In fact, if all the points fall on the least squares line, then SSE $= 0$.

Then the reduction in the sum of squares of deviations that can be attributed to x, expressed as a proportion of SS_{yy}, is

$$\frac{\text{SS}_{yy} - \text{SSE}}{\text{SS}_{yy}}$$

Note that SS_{yy} is the "total sample variation" of the observations around the mean $\bar{y}$ and that SSE is the remaining "unexplained sample variability" after fitting the line $\hat{y}$. Thus, the difference $(\text{SS}_{yy} - \text{SSE})$ is the "explained sample variability" attributable to the linear relationship with x. Then a verbal description of the proportion is

$$\frac{SS_{yy} - SSE}{SS_{yy}} = \frac{\text{Explained sample variability}}{\text{Total sample variability}}$$

$$= \text{Proportion of total sample variability explained by the linear relationship}$$

In simple linear regression, it can be shown that this proportion—called the *coefficient of determination*—is equal to the square of the simple linear coefficient of correlation r.

DEFINITION 12.3

The **coefficient of determination** is

$$r^2 = \frac{SS_{yy} - SSE}{SS_{yy}} = 1 - \frac{SSE}{SS_{yy}}$$

It represents the proportion of the total sample variability around $\bar{y}$ that is explained by the linear relationship between y and x. (In simple linear regression, it may also be computed as the square of the coefficient of correlation r.)

Note that r^2 is always between 0 and 1, because r is between -1 and $+1$. Thus, an r^2 of .60 means that the sum of squares of deviations of the y values about their predicted values has been reduced 60% by the use of the least squares equation $\hat{y}$, instead of $\bar{y}$, to predict y.

EXAMPLE 12.2   OBTAINING THE VALUE OF r^2

Problem   Calculate the coefficient of determination for the advertising–sales example. The data are repeated in Table 12.6 for convenience. Interpret the result.

ADSALES

TABLE 12.6   Advertising Expenditure Sales Revenue Data

Advertising Expenditure, x ($100s)	Sales Revenue, y ($1,000s)
1	1
2	1
3	2
4	2
5	4

Solution   From previous calculations,

$$SS_{yy} = 6 \quad \text{and} \quad SSE = \sum (y - \hat{y})^2 = 1.10$$

Then, from Definition 12.3, the coefficient of determination is given by

$$r^2 = \frac{SS_{yy} - SSE}{SS_{yy}} - \frac{6.0 - 1.1}{6.0} = \frac{4.9}{6.0} = .82$$

Suggested Exercises 12.59

Another way to compute r^2 is to recall (Section 12.6) that $r = .904$. Then we have $r^2 = (.904)^2 = .82$. A third way to obtain r^2 is from a computer printout. This value is highlighted on the SPSS printout reproduced in Figure 12.17. Our interpretation is as follows: We know that using advertising expenditure, x, to predict y with the least squares line

$$\hat{y} = -.1 + .7x$$

accounts for 82% of the total sum of squares of deviations of the five sample y values about their mean. Or, stated another way, 82% of the sample variation in sales revenue (y) can be "explained" by using advertising expenditure (x) in a straight-line model.

Figure 12.17
Portion of SPSS printout for advertising–sales regression

Model Summary

Model	R	R Square	Adjusted R Square	Std. Error of the Estimate
1	.904[a]	.817	.756	.606

a. Predictors: (Constant), ADVEXP_X

Now Work *Exercise 12.54a*

■ ■ ■

Teaching Tip
A graph comparing the fitted regression line to the line of the sample mean of y is useful when explaining the interpretation of r^2.

Practical Interpretation of the Coefficient of Determination, r^2

About $100(r^2)\%$ of the sample variation in y (measured by the total sum of squares of deviations of the sample y values about their mean $\bar{y}$) can be explained by (or attributed to) using x to predict y in the straight-line model.

Exercises 12.49–12.61

Learning the Mechanics

12.49 Describe the slope of the least squares line if
    a. $r = .7$ **b.** $r = -.7$ **c.** $r = 0$ **d.** $r^2 = .64$

12.50 Explain what each of the following sample correlation coefficients tells you about the relationship between the x and y values in the sample:
    a. $r = 1$ **b.** $r = -1$ **c.** $r = 0$
    d. $r - .90$ **e.** $r = .10$ **f.** $r = -.88$

12.51 Calculate r^2 for the least squares line in each of the following exercises. Interpret their values.
    a. Exercise 12.10
    b. Exercise 12.13

12.52 Construct a scattergram for each data set. Then calculate r and r^2 for each data set. Interpret their values.

a.

x	−2	−1	0	1	2
y	−2	1	2	5	6

b.

x	−2	−1	0	1	2
y	6	5	3	2	0

c.

x	1	2	2	3	3	3	4
y	2	1	3	1	2	3	2

d.

x	0	1	3	5	6
y	0	1	2	1	0

Applying the Concepts—Basic

12.53 In today's business environment, effective management of one's own career requires a skill set that includes adaptability, tolerance for ambiguity, self-awareness, and identify change. Management professors at Pace University (New York) used correlation coefficients to investigate the relationship between these "metaskills" and effective career management. (*International Journal of Manpower*, Aug. 2000.) Data were collected for 446 business graduates who had all completed a management "metaskills" course. Two of the many variables measured were self-knowledge skill level (x) and goal-setting ability (y). The correlation coefficient for these two variables was $r = .70$.

a. Give a practical interpretation of the value of r.
  $r = .70$

b. The p-value for a test of no correlation between the two variables was reported as p-value $= .001$. Interpret this result.

c. Find the coefficient of determination, r^2, and interpret the result. $.49$

◉ DIAMONDS

12.54 Refer to the MINITAB simple linear regression analysis relating $y =$ asking price (dollars) to $x =$ number

of carats for diamonds sold on the open market, Exercise 12.14 (p. 708).

a. Locate the coefficient of determination, r^2, on the MINITAB printout and interpret the result.
  $.893$

b. Find the value of the coefficient of correlation, r, from the value of r^2 and the sign of the estimated slope. Interpret the result. $.945$

◉ OJUICE

12.55 Refer to the simple linear regression relating $y =$ sweetness index of an orange juice sample with $x =$ amount of water soluble pectin, Exercise 12.18 (p. 709). Find and interpret the coefficient of determination, r^2, and the coefficient of correlation, r.
  $.2286; -.478$

12.56 The *Forbes 400* is an annual ranking of the 400 wealthiest people in the U.S. The top 15 billionaires on this list for 2002 are described in the table below.

a. Construct a scattergram for these data. What does the plot suggest about the relationship between age and net worth of billionaires?

b. Find the coefficient of correlation and explain what it tells you about the relationship between age and net worth. $-.151$

c. If the correlation coefficient of part **b** had the opposite sign, how would that change your interpretation of the relationship between age and net worth?

◉ FORBES400

Rank	Name	Net worth ($ mil)	Age	Marital Status	Residence	Source of wealth
1	Gates, William H III	43,000	46	married	Seattle, WA	Microsoft
2	Buffett, Warren Edward	36,000	72	married	Omaha, NE	Berkshire Hathaway
3	Allen, Paul Gardner	21,000	49	single	Mercer Island, WA	Microsoft
4	Walton, Alice L	18,800	53	divorced	Fort Worth, TX	Wal-Mart
5	Walton, Helen R	18,800	83	widowed	Bentonville, AR	Wal-Mart
6	Walton, Jim C	18,800	54	married	Bentonville, AR	Wal-Mart
7	Walton, John T	18,800	56	married	Durango, CO	Wal-Mart
8	Walton, S Robson	18,800	58	divorced	Bentonville, AR	Wal-Mart
9	Ellison, Lawrence Joseph	15,200	58	divorced	Atherton, CA	Oracle
10	Ballmer, Steven Anthony	11,900	46	married	Redmond, WA	Microsoft
11	Dell, Michael	11,200	37	married	Austin, TX	Dell Computer
12	Kluge, John Werner	10,500	88	married	Charlottesville, VA	Metromedia
13	Mars, Forrest Edward Jr	10,000	71	married	McLean, VA	candy
14	Mars, Jacqueline	10,000	63	divorced	Bedminster, NJ	candy
15	Mars, John Franklyn	10,000	66	married	Arlington, VA	candy

Source: Forbes, Sept. 13, 2002.

d. Find the coefficient of determination for a straight-line model relating net worth (y) to age (x). Interpret the result in the words of the problem.   .0228

Applying the Concepts—Intermediate

12.57 Many high school students experience "math anxiety," which has been shown to have a negative effect on their learning achievement. Does such an attitude carry over to learning computer skills? A researcher at Duquesne University investigated this question and published her results in *Educational Technology* (May–June 1995). A sample of 1,730 high school students—902 boys and 828 girls—from public schools in Pittsburgh, Pennsylvania, participated in the study. Using five-point Likert scales, where 1 = "strongly disagree" and 5 = "strongly agree," the researcher measured the students' interest and confidence in both mathematics and computers.

a. For boys, math confidence and computer interest were correlated at $r = .14$. Fully interpret this result.

b. For girls, math confidence and computer interest were correlated at $r = .33$. Fully interpret this result.

12.58 If the economies of the world were tightly interconnected, the stock markets of different countries would move together. If they did, there would be no reason for investors to diversify their stock portfolios with stocks from a variety of countries (Sharpe, Alexander, and Bailey, *Investments*, 1999). The table below lists the correlations of returns on stocks in each of six countries with the returns of U.S. stocks.

Country	Correlation between Foreign and U.S. Stocks
Australia	.48
Canada	.74
France	.50
Germany	.43
Japan	.41
U.K.	.58

Source: Sharpe, W. F., Alexander, G. J., and Bailey, Jeffery V., *Investments.* Upper Saddle River, N.J.: Prentice Hall, 1999, p. 887.

a. Interpret the Australia/U.S. correlation. What does it suggest about the linear relationship between the stocks of the two countries?

b. Sketch a scattergram that is roughly consistent with the magnitude of the France/U.S. correlation.

c. Why must we be careful not to conclude from the information in the table that the country which is most tightly integrated with the U.S. is Canada?

12.59 The fertility rate of a country is defined as the number of children a woman citizen bears, on average, in her lifetime. *Scientific American* (Dec. 1993) reported on the declining fertility rate in developing countries. The researchers found that family planning can have a great effect on fertility rate. The table below gives the fertility rate, y, and contraceptive prevalence, x (measured as the percentage of married women who use contraception), for each of 27 developing countries.

a. According to the researchers, "the data reveal that differences in contraceptive prevalence explain about 90% of the variation in fertility rates." Do you concur?   No, $r^2 = .7483$

b. The researchers also concluded that "if contraceptive use increases by 15 percent, women bear, on average, one fewer child." Is this statement supported by the data? Explain.   Yes

FERTRATE

Country	Contraceptive Prevalence, x	Fertility Rate, y
Mauritius	76	2.2
Thailand	69	2.3
Colombia	66	2.9
Costa Rica	71	3.5
Sri Lanka	63	2.7
Turkey	62	3.4
Peru	60	3.5
Mexico	55	4.0
Jamaica	55	2.9
Indonesia	50	3.1
Tunisia	51	4.3
El Salvador	48	4.5
Morocco	42	4.0
Zimbabwe	46	5.4
Egypt	40	4.5
Bangladesh	40	5.5
Botswana	35	4.8
Jordan	35	5.5
Kenya	28	6.5
Guatemala	24	5.5
Cameroon	16	5.8
Ghana	14	6.0
Pakistan	13	5.0
Senegal	13	6.5
Sudan	10	4.8
Yemen	9	7.0
Nigeria	7	5.7

Source: Robey, B., et al. "The Fertility Decline in Developing Countries." *Scientific American,* December 1993, p. 62. [Note: The data values are estimated from a scatterplot.]

12.60 Researchers at the University of Toronto conducted a series of experiments to investigate whether a commercially sold pet food could serve as a substitute diet for baby snow geese (*Journal of Applied Ecology*, Vol. 32, 1995). Goslings were deprived of food until their guts were empty, then were allowed to feed for 6 hours on a diet of plants or Purina Duck Chow. For each feeding trial, the change in the weight of the gosling after 2.5 hours was recorded as a percentage of initial weight. Two other variables recorded were digestion efficiency (measured as a percentage) and amount of acid-detergent fiber in the digestive tract (also measured as a percentage). The data for 42 feeding trials are saved in the **SNOWGEES** file. (The first and last five observations are shown in the table, at the bottom of the page.)

a. The researchers were interested in the correlation between weight change (y) and digestion efficiency (x). Plot the data for these two variables in a scattergram. Do you observe a trend?   Yes

b. Find the coefficient of correlation relating weight change y to digestion efficiency x. Interpret this value. $r = .6122$

c. Conduct a test (at $\alpha = .01$) to determine whether weight change y is correlated with digestion efficiency x. $t = 4.90$

d. Repeat parts **b** and **c**, but exclude the data for trials that used duck chow from the analysis. What do you conclude? $r = .3095; t = 1.81$

e. The researchers were also interested in the correlation between digestion efficiency (y) and acid-detergent fiber (x). Repeat parts **a–d** for these two variables.

Applying the Concepts—Advanced

12.61 Studies of Asian (particularly Japanese) and U.S. managers in the 1970s and 1980s found sharp differences of opinion and attitude toward quality man-

agement. Do these differences continue to exist? To find out, two California State University researchers (B. F. Yavas and T. M. Burrows) surveyed 100 U.S. and 96 Asian managers in the electronics manufacturing industry (*Quality Management Journal*, Fall 1994). The accompanying table gives the percentages of U.S. and Asian managers who agree with each of 13 randomly selected statements regarding quality. (For example, one statement is "Quality is a problem in my company." Another is "Improving quality is expensive.")

QLAGREE

Statement	Percentage of Managers Who Agree	
	United States	Asian
1	36	38
2	31	42
3	28	43
4	27	48
5	78	58
6	74	49
7	43	46
8	50	56
9	31	65
10	66	58
11	18	21
12	61	69
13	53	45

Source: Yavas, B. F., and Burrows, T. M. "A Comparative Study of Attitudes of U.S. and Asian Managers toward Product Quality." *Quality Management Journal,* Fall 1994, p. 49 (Table 5).

a. Find the coefficient of correlation r for these data.

b. Interpret r in the context of the problem.

SNOWGEES

Feeding Trial	Diet	Weight Change (%)	Digestion Efficiency (%)	Acid-Detergent Fiber (%)
1	Plants	−6	0	28.5
2	Plants	−5	2.5	27.5
3	Plants	−4.5	5	27.5
4	Plants	0	0	32.5
5	Plants	2	0	32
⋮	⋮	⋮	⋮	⋮
38	Duck Chow	9	59	8.5
39	Duck Chow	12	52.5	8
40	Duck Chow	8.5	75	6
41	Duck Chow	10.5	72.5	6.5
42	Duck Chow	14	69	7

Source: Gadallah, F. L., and Jefferies, R. L. "Forage Quality in Brood Rearing Areas of the Lesser Snow Goose and the Growth of Captive Goslins." *Journal of Applied Biology,* Vol. 32, No. 2, 1995, pp. 281–282 (adapted from Figures 2 and 3).

c. Refer to part **b.** Using the coefficient of correlation r to make inferences about the difference in attitudes between U.S. and Asian managers regarding quality can be misleading. The value of r measures the strength of the linear relationship between two variables; it does not account for a difference between the means of the variables. To illustrate this, examine the hypothetical data in the table below. Show that $r \approx 1$, but the Asian percentage is approximately 30 points higher for each quality statement. Would you conclude that the attitudes of U.S. and Asian managers are similar?

⊙ **QLAGREE2**

Quality Statement	Hypothetical Percentage of Managers Who Agree	
	U.S.	Asian
1	20	50
2	30	65
3	40	70
4	50	80
5	55	90

12.8 Using the Model for Estimation and Prediction

If we are satisfied that a useful model has been found to describe the relationship between x and y, we are ready for step 5 in our regression modeling procedure: using the model for estimation and prediction.

The most common uses of a probabilistic model for making inferences can be divided into two categories. The first is the use of the model for estimating the mean value of y, E(y), *for a specific value of* x.

For our advertising–sales example, we may want to estimate the mean sales revenue for *all* months during which $400 ($x = 4$) is expended on advertising.

The second use of the model entails predicting a new individual y *value for a given* x.

That is, if we decide to expend $400 in advertising next month, we may want to predict the firm's sales revenue for that month.

In the first case, we are attempting to estimate the mean value of y for a very large number of experiments at the given x value. In the second case, we are trying to predict the outcome of a single experiment at the given x value. Which of these model uses—estimating the mean value of y or predicting an individual new value of y (for the same value of x)—can be accomplished with the greater accuracy?

Before answering this question, we first consider the problem of choosing an estimator (or predictor) of the mean (or a new individual) y value. We will use the least squares prediction equation

$$\hat{y} = \hat{\beta}_0 + \hat{\beta}_1 x$$

both to estimate the mean value of y and to predict a specific new value of y for a given value of x. For our example, we found

$$\hat{y} = -.1 + .7x$$

so that the estimated mean sales revenue for all months when $x = 4$ (advertising is $400) is

$$\hat{y} = -.1 + .7(4) = 2.7$$

or $2,700. (Recall that the units of y are thousands of dollars.) The same value is used to predict a new y value when $x = 4$. That is, both the estimated mean and the predicted value of y are $\hat{y} = 2.7$ when $x = 4$, as shown in Figure 12.18.

Figure 12.18

Estimated mean value and predicted individual value of sales revenue y for $x = 4$

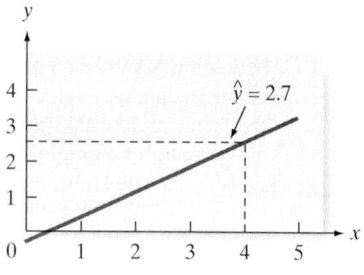

The difference between these two model uses lies in the relative accuracy of the estimate and the prediction. These accuracies are best measured by using the sampling errors of the least squares line when it is used as an estimator and as a predictor, respectively. These errors are reflected in the standard deviations given in the next box.

Teaching Tip

Use the formulas to illustrate why the prediction interval for y is always wider than the confidence interval for $E(y)$.

Sampling Errors for the Estimator of the Mean of y and the Predictor of an Individual New Value of y

1. The standard deviation of the sampling distribution of the estimator $\hat{y}$ of the mean value of y at a specific value of x, say x_p, is

$$\sigma_{\hat{y}} = \sigma\sqrt{\frac{1}{n} + \frac{(x_p - \bar{x})^2}{SS_{xx}}}$$

where σ is the standard deviation of the random error ε. We refer to $\sigma_{\hat{y}}$ as the standard error of $\hat{y}$.

2. The standard deviation of the prediction error for the predictor $\hat{y}$ of an individual new y value at a specific value of x is

$$\sigma_{(y-\hat{y})} = \sigma\sqrt{1 + \frac{1}{n} + \frac{(x_p - \bar{x})^2}{SS_{xx}}}$$

where σ is the standard deviation of the random error ε. We refer to $\sigma_{(y-\hat{y})}$ as the standard error of the prediction.

The true value of σ is rarely known, so we estimate σ by s and calculate the estimation and prediction intervals as shown in the next two boxes.

Teaching Tip

Use a graph of the confidence and prediction bands around the regression line to illustrate the fact that the confidence interval is always wider than the prediction interval.

A $100(1 - \alpha)\%$ Confidence Interval for the Mean Value of y at $x = x_p$

$$\hat{y} \pm t_{\alpha/2}(\text{Estimated standard error of } \hat{y})$$

or

$$\hat{y} \pm t_{\alpha/2}s\sqrt{\frac{1}{n} + \frac{(x_p - \bar{x})^2}{SS_{xx}}}$$

where $t_{\alpha/2}$ is based on $(n - 2)$ degrees of freedom.

A $100(1 - \alpha)\%$ Prediction Interval* for an Individual New Value of y at $x = x_p$

$$\hat{y} \pm t_{\alpha/2}(\text{Estimated standard error of prediction})$$

or

$$\hat{y} \pm t_{\alpha/2}s\sqrt{1 + \frac{1}{n} + \frac{(x_p - \bar{x})^2}{SS_{xx}}}$$

where $t_{\alpha/2}$ is based on $(n - 2)$ degrees of freedom.

EXAMPLE 12.3

ESTIMATING $E(y)$

Problem   Find a 95% confidence interval for the mean monthly sales when the appliance store spends $400 on advertising.

2.7 ± 1.1

Solution   For a $400 advertising expenditure, $x = 4$ and the confidence interval for the mean value of y is

$$\hat{y} \pm t_{\alpha/2}s\sqrt{\frac{1}{n} + \frac{(x_p - \bar{x})^2}{SS_{xx}}} = \hat{y} \pm t_{.025}s\sqrt{\frac{1}{5} + \frac{(4 - \bar{x})^2}{SS_{xx}}}$$

where $t_{.025}$ is based on $n - 2 = 5 - 2 = 3$ degrees of freedom. Recall that $\hat{y} = 2.7, s = .61, \bar{x} = 3$, and $SS_{xx} = 10$. From Table VI in Appendix B, $t_{.025} = 3.182$. Thus, we have

Suggested Exercises 12.71

$$2.7 \pm (3.182)(.61)\sqrt{\frac{1}{5} + \frac{(4 - 3)^2}{10}} = 2.7 \pm (3.182)(.61)(.55)$$

$$= 2.7 \pm (3.182)(.34)$$

$$= 2.7 \pm 1.1 = (1.6, 3.8)$$

Therefore, when the store spends $400 a month on advertising, we are 95% confident that the mean sales revenue is between $1,600 and $3,800.

Look Back   Note that we used a small amount of data (small in size) for purposes of illustration in fitting the least squares line. The interval would probably be narrower if more information had been obtained from a larger sample.

Now Work   *Exercise 12.62a–d*

■ ■ ■

---

*The term *prediction interval* is used when the interval formed is intended to enclose the value of a random variable. The term *confidence interval* is reserved for estimation of population parameters (such as mean).

EXAMPLE 12.4 PREDICTING y

Problem Predict the monthly sales for next month, if \$400 is spent on advertising. Use a 95% prediction interval.

2.7 ± 2.2

Solution To predict the sales for a particular month for which $x_p = 4$, we calculate the 95% prediction interval as

$$\hat{y} \pm t_{\alpha/2}s\sqrt{1 + \frac{1}{n} + \frac{(x_p - \bar{x})^2}{SS_{xx}}} = 2.7 \pm (3.182)(.61)\sqrt{1 + \frac{1}{5} + \frac{(4-3)^2}{10}}$$
$$= 2.7 \pm (3.182)(.61)(1.14)$$
$$= 2.7 \pm (3.182)(.70)$$
$$= 2.7 \pm 2.2 = (.5, 4.9)$$

Therefore, we predict with 95% confidence that the sales revenue next month (a month in which we spend \$400 in advertising) will fall in the interval from \$500 to \$4,900.

Look Back Like the confidence interval for the mean value of y, the prediction interval for y is quite large. This is because we have chosen a simple example (only five data points) to fit the least squares line. The width of the prediction interval could be reduced by using a larger number of data points.

Now Work *Exercise 12.62e*

Teaching Tip
Point out that the confidence and prediction intervals can be found on most computer output. The interpretation of these intervals is the key. Now is a good time to review the two symbols $E(y)$ and y.

Both the confidence interval for $E(y)$ and prediction interval for y can be obtained using a statistical software package. Figure 12.19 is a MINITAB printout showing the confidence interval and prediction interval for the data in the advertising–sales example. The 95% confidence interval for $E(y)$ when $x = 4$, highlighted under "95% CI" in Figure 12.19, is (1.645, 3.755). The 95% prediction interval for y when $x = 4$, highlighted in Figure 12.19 under "95% PI", is (.503, 4.897). Both intervals agree with the ones computed in Examples 12.3–12.4.

A comparison of the confidence interval for the mean value of y and the prediction interval for a new value of y when $x = 4$ is illustrated in Figure 12.20. Note that the prediction interval for an individual new value of y is always wider than the corresponding confidence interval for the mean value of y. You can see this by examining the formulas for the two intervals and by studying Figure 12.20.

Figure 12.19
MINITAB printout giving 95% confidence interval for $E(y)$ and 95% prediction interval for y

```
Predicted Values for New Observations

New
Obs     Fit  SE Fit        95% CI              95% PI
  1   2.700   0.332  (1.645, 3.755)  (0.503, 4.897)


Values of Predictors for New Observations

New
Obs  ADVEXP_X
  1      4.00
```

Figure 12.20

A 95% confidence interval for mean sales and a prediction interval for sales when $x = 4$

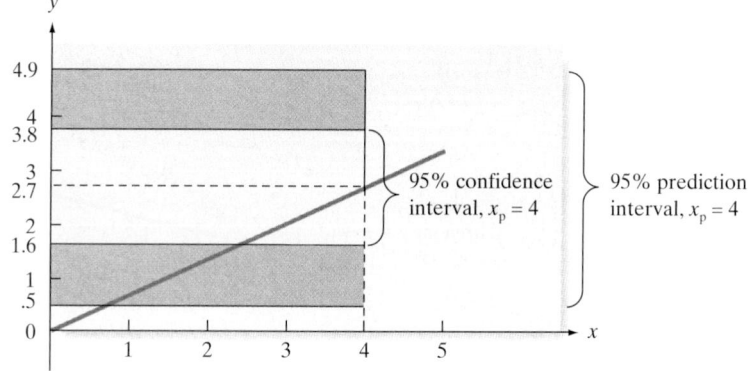

The error in estimating the mean value of y, $E(y)$, for a given value of x, say x_p, is the distance between the least squares line and the true line of means, $E(y) = \beta_0 + \beta_1 x$. This error, $[\hat{y} - E(y)]$, is shown in Figure 12.21. In contrast, *the error* $(y_p - \hat{y})$ *in predicting some future value of* y *is the sum of two errors*—the error of estimating the mean of y, $E(y)$, shown in Figure 12.21, plus the random error that is a component of the value of y to be predicted (see Figure 12.22). Consequently, the error of predicting a particular value of y will be larger than the error of estimating the mean value of y for a particular value of x. Note from their formulas that both the error of estimation and the error of prediction take their smallest values when $x_p = \bar{x}$. The farther x_p lies from $\bar{x}$, the larger will be the errors of estimation and prediction. You can see why this is true by noting the deviations for different values of x_p between the line of means $E(y) = \beta_0 + \beta_1 x$ and the predicted line of means $\hat{y} = \hat{\beta}_0 + \hat{\beta}_1 x$ shown in Figure 12.22. The deviation is larger at the extremes of the interval where the largest and smallest values of x in the data set occur.

Both the confidence intervals for mean values and the prediction intervals for new values are depicted over the entire range of the regression line in Figure 12.23. You can see that the confidence interval is always narrower than the prediction

Teaching Tip

The confidence interval formula is an easy place to illustrate why the intervals are narrowest at $x_p = ?$.

Figure 12.21

Error of estimating the mean value of y for a given value of x

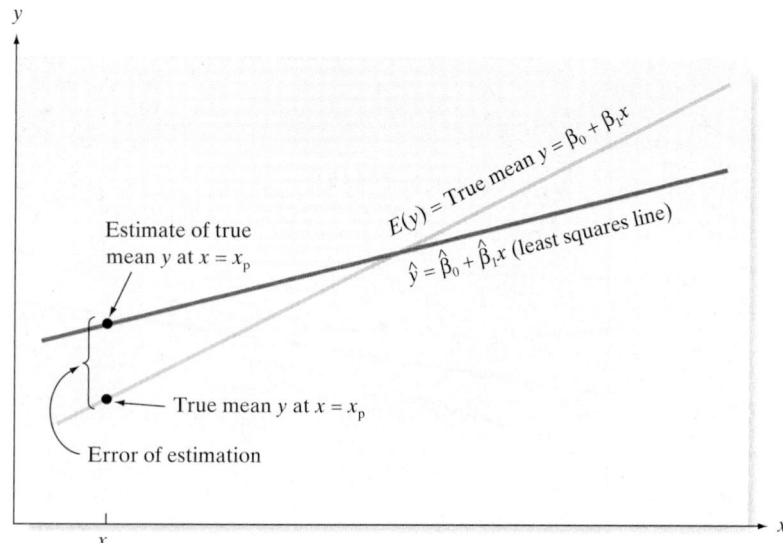

Figure 12.22

Error of predicting a future value of y for a given value of x

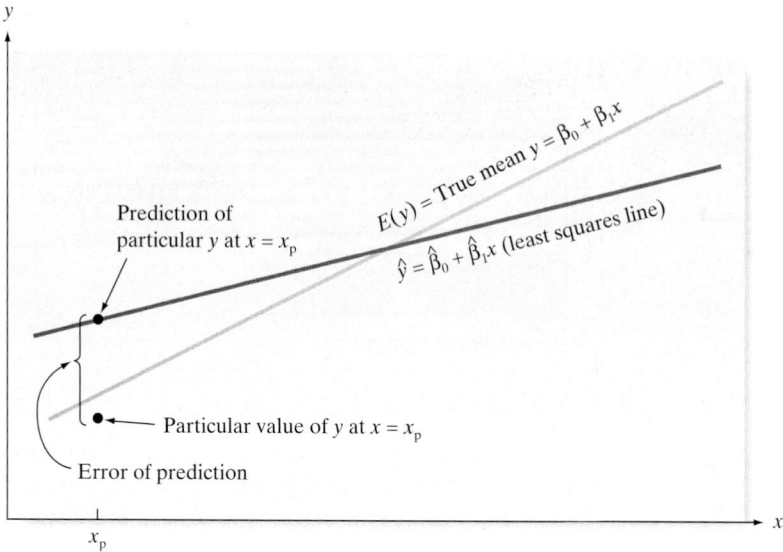

interval, and that they are both narrowest at the mean $\bar{x}$, increasing steadily as the distance $|x - \bar{x}|$ increases. In fact, when x is selected far enough away from $\bar{x}$ so that it falls outside the range of the sample data, it is dangerous to make any inferences about $E(y)$, or y.

Caution

Using the least squares prediction equation to estimate the mean value of y or to predict a particular value of y for values of x that fall *outside the range* of the values of x contained in your sample data may lead to errors of estimation or prediction that are much larger than expected. Although the least squares model may provide a very good fit to the data over the range of x values contained in the sample, it could give a poor representation of the true model for values of x outside this region.

The confidence interval width grows smaller as n is increased; thus, in theory, you can obtain as precise an estimate of the mean value of y as desired (at any given x) by selecting a large enough sample. The prediction interval for a new value of y

Figure 12.23

Confidence intervals for mean values and prediction intervals for new values

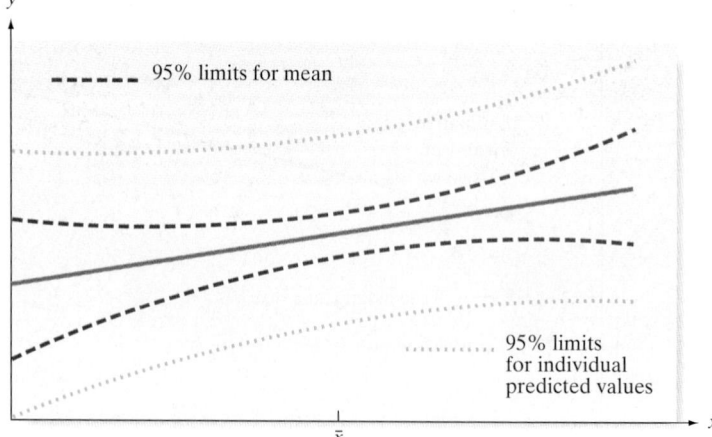

also grows smaller as n increases, but there is a lower limit on its width. If you examine the formula for the prediction interval, you will see that the interval can get no smaller than $\hat{y} \pm z_{\alpha/2}\sigma$.* Thus, the only way to obtain more accurate predictions for new values of y is to reduce the standard deviation of the regression model, σ. This can be accomplished only by improving the model, either by using a curvilinear (rather than linear) relationship with x or by adding new independent variables to the model, or both. Methods of improving the model are discussed in Chapter 13.

Now Work *Exercise 12.62f*

Statistics in Action Revisited

Predicting Pipe Location for the Dowsing Data Using the Straight-Line Model

The group of German physicists who conducted the dowsing experiments stated that the data for the three "best" dowsers empirically support the "dowsing theory." If so, then the straight-line model relating a dowser's guess (x) to actual pipe location (y) should yield accurate predictions. The MINITAB printout shown in Figure SIA12.5 gives a 95% prediction interval for y when a dowser guesses $x = 50$ meters (the middle of the 100-meter-

long waterpipe). The highlighted interval is $(-9.3, 100.23)$. Thus, we can be 95% confident that the actual pipe location will fall between -9.3 meters and 100.23 meters for this guess. Since the pipe is only 100 meters long, in effect the interval ranges from 0 to 100 meters—the entire length of the pipe! This result, of course, is due to the fact that the straight-line model is not a statistically useful predictor of pipe location—a fact we discovered in the previous Statistics in Action Revisited sections.

Figure SIA12.5
MINITAB prediction interval for dowsing data

```
Predicted Values for New Observations

New
Obs    Fit   SE Fit      95% CI          95% PI
  1   45.47   5.15   (34.83, 56.10)   (-9.30, 100.23)


Values of Predictors for New Observations

New
Obs   GUESS
  1    50.0
```

Exercises 12.62–12.72

Learning the Mechanics

12.62 Consider the following pairs of measurements:

⊙ **LM12_62**

x	−2	0	2	4	6	8	10
y	0	3	2	3	8	10	11

a. Construct a scattergram for these data.

b. Find the least squares line, and plot it on your scattergram. $\hat{y} = 1.5 + .946x$

c. Find s^2. $s^2 = 2.221$

d. Find a 90% confidence interval for the mean value of y when $x = 3$. Plot the upper and lower bounds of the confidence interval on your scattergram.

e. Find a 90% prediction interval for a new value of y when $x = 3$. Plot the upper and lower bounds of the prediction interval on your scattergram.

*The result follows from the facts that, for large n, $t_{\alpha/2} \approx z_{\alpha/2}$, $s \approx \sigma$, and the last two terms under the radical in the standard error of the predictor are approximately 0.

f. Compare the widths of the intervals you constructed in parts **d** and **e.** Which is wider and why?

12.63 Consider the pairs of measurements shown in the table. For these data, $SS_{xx} = 38.9000$, $SS_{yy} = 33.600$, $SS_{xy} = 32.8$ and $\hat{y} = -.414 + .843x$.

LM12_63

x	4	6	0	5	2	3	2	6	2	1
y	3	5	-1	4	3	2	0	4	1	1

a. Construct a scattergram for these data.
b. Plot the least squares line on your scattergram.
c. Use a 95% confidence interval to estimate the mean value of y when $x_p = 6$. Plot the upper and lower bounds of the interval on your scattergram.
d. Repeat part **c** for $x_p = 3.2$ and $x_p = 0$.
e. Compare the widths of the three confidence intervals you constructed in parts **c** and **d** and explain why they differ.

12.64 Refer to Exercise 12.63.

a. Using no information about x, estimate and calculate a 95% confidence interval for the mean value of y. [*Hint:* Use the one-sample t methodology of Section 7.3.] $\quad 2.2 \pm 1.382$
b. Plot the estimated mean value and the confidence interval as horizontal lines on your scattergram.
c. Compare the confidence intervals you calculated in parts **c** and **d** of Exercise 12.63 with the one you calculated in part **a** of this exercise. Does x appear to contribute information about the mean value of y?
d. Check the answer you gave in part **c** with a statistical test of the null hypothesis $H_0: \beta_1 = 0$ against $H_a: \beta_1 \neq 0$. Use $\alpha = .05$.

12.65 In fitting a least squares line to $n = 10$ data points, the following quantities were computed:

$$SS_{xx} = 32$$
$$\bar{x} = 3$$

$$SS_{yy} = 26$$
$$\bar{y} = 4$$
$$SS_{xy} = 28$$

a. Find the least squares line.
b. Graph the least squares line.
c. Calculate SSE. $\quad 1.5$
d. Calculate s^2.
e. Find a 95% confidence interval for the mean value of y when $x_p = 2.5$. $\quad 3.5625 \pm .3279$
f. Find a 95% prediction interval for y when $x_p = 4$.

Applying the Concepts—Basic

DIAMONDS

12.66 Refer to the MINITAB simple linear regression analysis relating y = asking price (dollars) to x = number of carats for diamonds sold on the open market, Exercise 12.14 (p. 708). The portion of the MINITAB printout giving a 95% confidence interval for $E(y)$ and a 95% prediction interval for y when $x = .52$ is shown below.

a. Locate and interpret the 95% confidence interval for $E(y)$.
b. Locate and interpret the 95% prediction interval for y.

12.67 Refer to the *Nutrition & Food Science* (Vol. 30, 2000) study of the trend in prime-time television advertising, Exercise 12.17 (p. 709). The data are reproduced in the table on p. 745.

a. Use simple linear regression to find a 95% prediction interval for rate of total number of prime-time TV commercials per hour in the year 2005. $\quad 49.301 \pm 2.659$
b. Give a practical interpretation of the interval, part **a.**
c. Why might the inference made from the prediction interval be invalid? Explain.

MINITAB Output for Exercise 12.66

```
Predicted Values for New Observations

New
Obs     Fit   SE Fit       95% CI            95% PI
  1  3733.1    68.6  (3598.1, 3868.1)  (1529.8, 5936.3)


Values of Predictors for New Observations

New
Obs   CARAT
  1   0.520
```

FOODADS

Year	Number of Years since 1970	Total commercials (rate per hour)	Food ads (rate per hour)
1971	1	—	5.4
1977	7	11	3.0
1988	18	26	6.5
1992	22	31	6.0
1998	28	40	6.0

Source: Byrd-Bredbenner, C., and Grasso, D. "Trends in US Prime-Time Television Food Advertising across Three Decades," *Nutrition & Food Science,* Vol. 30, No. 2, 2000, p. 61 (Table 1).

12.68 Refer to the simple linear regression of sweetness index *y* and amount of pectin *x* for *n* = 24 orange juice samples, Exercise 12.18 (p. 709). A 90% confidence interval for the mean sweetness index, $E(y)$, for each of the first 12 runs is shown on the SPSS spreadsheet below. Select an observation and interpret this interval.

Applying the Concepts—Intermediate

FLALAW

12.69 Refer to *Florida Trend Magazine's* (April 2002) data on law firms with headquarters in the state of Florida, Exercise 12.22 (p. 711). Recall that you used a straight-line to model the number of law offices (*y*) as a function of the number of lawyers (*x*) at the firm. A firm with 300 lawyers is planning on building its headquarters in Florida. How many law offices should the firm expect to build? Give your answer in the form of a 99% confidence interval.   7.87 ± 6.66

12.70 Managers are an important part of any organization's resource base. Accordingly, the organization should be just as concerned about forecasting its future managerial needs as it is with forecasting its needs for, say, the natural resources used in its production process (Northcraft and Neale, *Organizational Behavior: A Management Challenge,* 1994). A common forecasting procedure is to model the relationship between sales and the number of managers needed, since the demand for managers is the result of the increases and decreases in the demand for products and services that a firm offers its customers. To develop this relationship, the data shown in the table below are collected from a firm's records.

a. Test the usefulness of the model. Use $\alpha = .05$. State your conclusion in the context of the problem.

b. The company projects that it will sell 39 units next month. Use the least squares model to construct a 90% prediction interval for the number of managers needed next month.

c. Interpret the interval in part **b.** Use the interval to determine the reliability of the firm's projection.

MANAGERS2

Units Sold, *x*	Managers, *y*	Units Sold, *x*	Managers, *y*
5	10	30	22
4	11	31	25
8	10	36	30
7	10	38	30
9	9	40	31
15	10	41	31
20	11	51	32
21	17	40	30
25	19	48	32
24	21	47	32

SPSS Output for Exercise 12.68

	run	sweet	pectin	lower90m	upper90m
1	1	5.2	220	5.64898	5.83848
2	2	5.5	227	5.63898	5.81613
3	3	6.0	259	5.57819	5.72904
4	4	5.9	210	5.66194	5.87173
5	5	5.8	224	5.64337	5.82560
6	6	6.0	215	5.65564	5.85493
7	7	5.8	231	5.63284	5.80379
8	8	5.6	268	5.55553	5.71011
9	9	5.6	239	5.61947	5.78019
10	10	5.9	212	5.65946	5.86497
11	11	5.4	410	5.05526	5.55416
12	12	5.6	256	5.58517	5.73592

12.71 The reasons given by workers for quitting their jobs generally fall into one of two categories: (1) worker quits to seek or take a different job, or (2) worker quits to withdraw from the labor force. Economic theory suggests that wages and quit rates are related. The next table lists quit rates (quits per 100 employees) and the average hourly wage in a sample of 15 manufacturing industries. Consider the simple linear regression of quit rate y on average wage x.

QUITTERS

Industry	Quit Rate, y	Average Wage, x
1	1.4	$ 8.20
2	.7	10.35
3	2.6	6.18
4	3.4	5.37
5	1.7	9.94
6	1.7	9.11
7	1.0	10.59
8	.5	13.29
9	2.0	7.99
10	3.8	5.54
11	2.3	7.50
12	1.9	6.43
13	1.4	8.83
14	1.8	10.93
15	2.0	8.80

a. Do the data present sufficient evidence to conclude that average hourly wage rate contributes useful information for the prediction of quit rates? What does your model suggest about the relationship between quit rates and wages?

b. Find a 95% prediction interval for the quit rate in an industry with an average hourly wage of $9.00. Interpret the result. 1.743 ± 1.086

c. Find a 95% confidence interval for the mean quit rate for industries with an average hourly wage of $9.00. Interpret this result. $1.743 \pm .276$

Applying the Concepts—Advanced

12.72 Refer to the data saved in the **CUTTOOL** file, Exercise 12.32 (p. 716).

a. Use a 90% confidence interval to estimate the mean useful life of a brand A cutting tool when the cutting speed is 45 meters per minute. Repeat for brand B. Compare the widths of the two intervals and comment on the reasons for any difference.

b. Use a 90% prediction interval to predict the useful life of a brand A cutting tool when the cutting speed is 45 meters per minute. Repeat for brand B. Compare the widths of the two intervals to each other, and to the two intervals you calculated in part **a.** Comment on the reasons for any differences.

c. Note that the estimation and prediction you performed in parts **a** and **b** were for a value of x that was not included in the original sample. That is, the value $x = 45$ was not part of the sample. However, the value is within the range of x values in the sample, so that the regression model spans the x value for which the estimation and prediction were made. In such situations, estimation and prediction represent *interpolations*. Suppose you were asked to predict the useful life of a brand A cutting tool for a cutting speed of $x = 100$ meters per minute. Since the given value of x is outside the range of the sample x values, the prediction is an example of *extrapolation*. Predict the useful life of a brand A cutting tool that is operated at 100 meters per minute, and construct a 95% confidence interval for the actual useful life of the tool. What additional assumption do you have to make in order to ensure the validity of an extrapolation? $-.65 \pm 3.606$

12.9 A Complete Example

In the preceding sections we have presented the basic elements necessary to fit and use a straight-line regression model. In this section we will assemble these elements by applying them in an example with the aid of a computer.

Suppose a fire insurance company wants to relate the amount of fire damage in major residential fires to the distance between the burning house and the nearest fire station. The study is to be conducted in a large suburb of a major city; a sample of 15 recent fires in this suburb is selected. The amount of damage, y, and the distance between the fire and the nearest fire station, x, are recorded for each fire. The results are given in Table 12.8.

Step 1 First, we hypothesize a model to relate fire damage, y, to the distance from the nearest fire station, x. We hypothesize a straight-line probabilistic model:

$$y = \beta_0 + \beta_1 x + \epsilon$$

FIREDAM

TABLE 12.8   Fire Damage Data

Distance From Fire Station, x (miles)	Fire Damage, y (thousands of dollars)
3.4	26.2
1.8	17.8
4.6	31.3
2.3	23.1
3.1	27.5
5.5	36.0
.7	14.1
3.0	22.3
2.6	19.6
4.3	31.3
2.1	24.0
1.1	17.3
6.1	43.2
4.8	36.4
3.8	26.1

Step 2 Next, we enter the data of Table 12.8 into a computer and use a statistical software package to estimate the unknown parameters in the deterministic component of the hypothesized model. The EXCEL printout for the simple linear regression analysis is shown in Figure 12.24. The least squares estimates of the slope β_1 and intercept β_0, highlighted on the printout, are

$$\hat{\beta}_1 = 4.919331$$

$$\hat{\beta}_0 = 10.277929$$

and the least squares equation is (rounded)

$$\hat{y} = 10.278 + 4.919x$$

This prediction equation is graphed in the MINITAB scatterplot, Figure 12.25.

Figure 12.24

Excel printout for fire damage regression analysis

Regression Analysis

Regression Statistics	
Multiple R	0.960977715
R Square	0.823478169
Adjusted R Square	0.917591874
Standard Error	2.316346184
Observations	15

ANOVA

	df	SS	MS	F	Significance F
Regression	1	841.766358	841.766358	156.8861596	1.2478E-08
Residual	13	69.75097535	5.365459643		
Total	14	911.5173333			

	Coefficients	Standard Error	t Stat	P-value	Lower 95%	Upper 95%
Intercept	10.27792855	1.420277811	7.236562082	6.58556E-06	7.209605476	13.34625162
DISTANCE	4.919330727	0.392747749	12.52542054	1.2478E-08	4.070850963	5.767810491

Figure 12.25

MINITAB scatterplot with least squares line for fire damage regression analysis

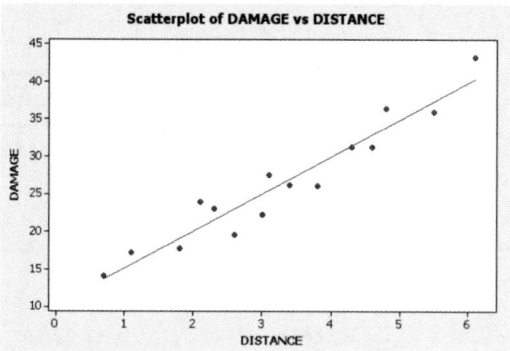

The least squares estimate of the slope, $\hat{\beta}_1 = 4.919$, implies that the estimated mean damage increases by \$4,919 for each additional mile from the fire station. This interpretation is valid over the range of x, or from .7 to 6.1 miles from the station. The estimated y-intercept, $\hat{\beta}_0 = 10.278$, has the interpretation that a fire 0 miles from the fire station has an estimated mean damage of \$10,278. Although this would seem to apply to the fire station itself, remember that the y-intercept is meaningfully interpretable only if $x = 0$ is within the sampled range of the independent variable. Since $x = 0$ is outside the range in this case, $\hat{\beta}_0$ has no practical interpretation.

Step 3 Now we specify the probability distribution of the random error component ϵ. The assumptions about the distribution are identical to those listed in Section 12.3. Although we know that these assumptions are not completely satisfied (they rarely are for practical problems), we are willing to assume they are approximately satisfied for this example. The estimate of the standard deviation σ of ϵ, highlighted on the EXCEL printout (Fig. 12.24) is

$$s = 2.31635$$

This implies that most of the observed fire damage (y) values will fall within approximately $2s = 4.64$ thousand dollars of their respective predicted values when using the least squares line.

Step 4 We can now check the usefulness of the hypothesized model—that is, whether x really contributes information for the prediction of y using the straight-line model. First, test the null hypothesis that the slope β_1 is 0, that is, that there is no linear relationship between fire damage and the distance from the nearest fire station, against the alternative hypothesis that fire damage increases as the distance increases. We test

$$H_0\colon \beta_1 = 0$$

$$H_a\colon \beta_1 > 0$$

The two-tailed observed significance level for testing $H_a\colon \beta_1 \neq 0$, highlighted on the printout, is approximately 0. When we divide this value in half, the p-value for our one-tailed test is also approximately 0. This small p-value leaves little doubt that mean fire damage and distance between the fire and station are at least linearly related, with mean fire damage increasing as the distance increases.

We gain additional information about the relationship by forming a 95% confidence interval for the slope β_1. The lower and upper endpoints of this interval are highlighted on the EXCEL printout shown in Figure 12.24.

This yields the interval (4.070, 5.768). We estimate (with 95% confidence) that the interval from $4,070 to $5,768 encloses the mean increase (β_1) in fire damage per additional mile distance from the fire station.

Another measure of the utility of the model is the coefficient of determination, r^2. The value (highlighted on Figure 12.24) is $r^2 = .9235$, which implies that about 92% of the sample variation in fire damage (y) is explained by the distance (x) between the fire and the fire station.

The coefficient of correlation, r, that measures the strength of the linear relationship between y and x is not shown on the EXCEL printout and must be calculated. Using the facts that $r = \sqrt{r^2}$ in simple linear regression and that r and $\hat{\beta}_1$ have the same sign, we find

$$r = +\sqrt{r^2} = \sqrt{.9235} = .96$$

The high correlation confirms our conclusion that β_1 is greater than 0; it appears that fire damage and distance from the fire station are positively correlated. All signs point to a strong linear relationship between y and x.

Step 5 We are now prepared to use the least squares model. Suppose the insurance company wants to predict the fire damage if a major residential fire were to occur 3.5 miles from the nearest fire station. A 95% confidence interval for $E(y)$ and prediction interval for y when $x = 3.5$ are shown on the EXCEL printout, Figure 12.26. The predicted value (given in the middle of the printout) is $\hat{y} = 27.4956$, while the 95% prediction interval (highlighted)

Figure 12.26
EXCEL/PHStat2 confidence/prediction interval for fire damage regression analysis

Confidence Interval Estimate	
Data	
X Value	3.5
Confidence Level	95%

Intermediate Calculations	
Sample Size	15
Degrees of Freedom	13
t Value	2.160368
Sample Mean	3.28
Sum of Squared Difference	34.784
Standard Error of the Estimate	2.316346
h Statistic	0.068058
Average Predicted Y (YHat)	27.49559

For Average Predicted Y (YHat)	
Interval Half Width	1.305483
Confidence Interval Lower Limit	26.1901
Confidence Interval Upper Limit	28.80107

For Individual Response Y	
Interval Half Width	5.171645
Prediction Interval Lower Limit	22.32394
Prediction Interval Upper Limit	32.66723

is $(22.3239, 32.6672)$. Therefore, with 95% confidence we predict fire damage in a major residential fire 3.5 miles from the nearest station to be between $22,324 and $32,667.

Caution

We would not use this prediction model to make predictions for homes less than .7 mile or more than 6.1 miles from the nearest fire station. A look at the data in Table 12.8 reveals that all the x values fall between .7 and 6.1. It is dangerous to use the model to make predictions outside the region in which the sample data fall. A straight line might not provide a good model for the relationship between the mean value of y and the value of x when stretched over a wider range of x values.

Quick Review

Key Terms

Bivariate relationship 726
Coefficient of correlation 726
Coefficient of determination 732
Confidence interval for mean of y 738
Dependent variable 694
Deterministic model 693
Errors of prediction 697
Independent variable 694

Least squares line 698, 699
Least squares estimates 698
Line of means 694
Method of least squares 698
Population correlation coefficient 729
Prediction interval for y 739
Predictor variable 694
Probabilistic model 693
Random error 693

Regression analysis 694
Response variable 694
Scattergram 697
Slope 694
Standard error of estimated slope 718
Standard error of regression
model 713
Straight-line (first-order) model 694
y-intercept 694

Key Formulas

$\hat{y} = \hat{\beta}_0 + \hat{\beta}_1 x$ Least squares line 699

$\hat{\beta}_1 = \dfrac{SS_{xy}}{SS_{xx}}, \hat{\beta}_0 = \bar{y} - \hat{\beta}_1 \bar{x}$ Least squares estimates of β's 699

where $SS_{xy} = \sum xy - \dfrac{(\sum x)(\sum y)}{n}$

$SS_{xx} = \sum x^2 - \dfrac{(\sum x)^2}{n}$

$s^2 = \dfrac{SSE}{n-2}$ Estimated variance of σ^2 of ε 713

$SSE = \sum(y_i - \hat{y}_i)^2 = SS_{yy} - \hat{\beta}_1 SS_{xy}$ Sum of squared errors 713

where $SS_{yy} = \sum y^2 - \dfrac{(\sum y)^2}{n}$

$s_{\hat{\beta}_1} = \dfrac{s}{\sqrt{SS_{xx}}}$ Estimated standard error of $\hat{\beta}_1$ 718

$t = \dfrac{\hat{\beta}_1}{s_{\hat{\beta}_1}}$ Test statistic for $H_0: \beta_1 = 0$ 718

$\hat{\beta}_1 \pm (t_{\alpha/2}) s_{\hat{\beta}_1}$ $(1 - \alpha)100\%$ confidence interval for β_1 720

$r = \dfrac{SS_{xy}}{\sqrt{SS_{xx}SS_{yy}}} = \pm\sqrt{r^2}$ (same sign as $\hat{\beta}_1$)   Coefficient of correlation 726

$$r^2 = \frac{SS_{yy} - SSE}{SS_{yy}}$$

Coefficient of determination   732

$$\hat{y} \pm (t_{\alpha/2})s\sqrt{\frac{1}{n} + \frac{(x_p - \bar{x})^2}{SS_{xx}}}$$

$(1 - \alpha)100\%$ confidence interval for $E(y)$ when $x = x_p$ 738

$$\hat{y} \pm (t_{\alpha/2})s\sqrt{1 + \frac{1}{n} + \frac{(x_p - \bar{x})^2}{SS_{xx}}}$$

$(1 - \alpha)100\%$ prediction interval for y when $x = x_p$ 739

Chapter Summary Notes

- Two quantitative variables in *simple linear regression*: y = **dependent** variable (i.e., the variable to be predicted) and x = **independent** (i.e., predictor) variable.
- General form of a **probabilistic model** for y: $y = E(y) + \varepsilon$.
- **First-order (straight-line) model**: $y = \beta_0 + \beta_1 x + \varepsilon$.
- **Slope** (β_1) represents the change in y for every 1-unit increase in x.
- **y-intercept** (β_0) represents the value where the line intercepts the y-axis
- **Steps** in simple linear regression: (1) Hypothesize the model, (2) use the method of least squares to estimate the unknown β's, (3) make assumptions on the random error (ε), (4) statistically evaluate the adequacy of the model, and (5) if deemed useful, use the model for estimation and prediction.
- Properties of **method of least squares**: (1) sum of errors of prediction is 0, (2) sum of squared errors of prediction is minimized.
- Estimates of slope and y-intercept should only be interpreted *over the range of x-values in the sample.*

- **Four assumptions** for ε: (1) mean of ε is 0, (2) variance of ε is constant for all x-values, (3) distribution of ε is normal, (4) values of ε are independent.
- *Interpretation of estimated standard deviation of ε:* About 95% of the observed y-values will lie within 2s of the respective predicted values.
- *Statistics used to assess the adequacy of the model:* (1) test of hypothesis for β_1, (2) confidence interval for β_1, (3) coefficient of correlation r, (4) coefficient of determination, r^2.
- Range of correlation coefficient: $-1 \le r \le 1$.
- Range of coefficient of determination: $0 \le r^2 \le 1$.
- **Correlation coefficient** measures the strength of the linear relationship between x and y.
- **Coefficient of determination** gives the proportion of the sample variation in y that can be explained by the straight-line model.
- Do not assume that a high correlation implies that x causes y.
- For a given x-value, a confidence interval for $E(y)$ will be narrower than a prediction interval for y.

Language Lab

Symbol	Pronunciation	Description
y		Dependent variable (variable to be predicted or modeled)
x		Independent (predictor) variable
$E(y)$		Expected (mean) value of y
β_0	beta-zero	y-intercept of true line
β_1	beta-one	Slope of true line
$\hat{\beta}_0$	beta-zero hat	Least squares estimate of y-intercept
$\hat{\beta}_1$	beta-one hat	Least squares estimate of slope
ε	epsilon	Random error
$\hat{y}$	y-hat	Predicted value of y
$(y - \hat{y})$		Error of prediction
SE		Sum of errors (will equal zero with least squares line)
SSE		Sum of squared errors (will be smallest for least squares line)

SS_{xx}		Sum of squares of x-values
SS_{yy}		Sum of squares of y-values
SS_{xy}		Sum of squares of cross-products, $x \cdot y$
r		Coefficient of correlation
r^2	R-squared	Coefficient of determination
x_p		Value of x used to predict y

Supplementary Exercises 12.73–12.89

Learning the Mechanics

12.73 In fitting a least squares line to $n = 15$ data points, the following quantities were computed: $SS_{xx} = 55$, $SS_{yy} = 198$, $SS_{xy} = -88$, $\bar{x} = 1.3$, and $\bar{y} = 35$.
  a. Find the least squares line. $\hat{y} = 37.08 - 1.6x$
  b. Graph the least squares line.
  c. Calculate SSE.   57.2
  d. Calculate s^2.   4.4
  e. Find a 90% confidence interval for β_1. Interpret this estimate. $-1.6 \pm .501$
  f. Find a 90% confidence interval for the mean value of y when $x = 15$. 13.08 ± 6.929
  g. Find a 90% prediction interval for y when $x = 15$.

12.74 Consider the following sample data:

y	5	1	3
x	5	1	3

  a. Construct a scattergram for the data.
  b. It is possible to find many lines for which $\sum(y - \hat{y}) = 0$. For this reason, the criterion $\sum(y - \hat{y}) = 0$ is not used for identifying the "best-fitting" straight line. Find two lines that have $\sum(y - \hat{y}) = 0$.
  c. Find the least squares line. $\hat{y} = x$
  d. Compare the value of SSE for the least squares line to that of the two lines you found in part **b**. What principle of least squares is demonstrated by this comparison?

12.75 Consider the following 10 data points:

⊙ **LM12_75**

x	3	5	6	4	3	7	6	5	4	7
y	4	3	2	1	2	3	3	5	4	2

  a. Plot the data on a scattergram.
  b. Calculate the values of r and r^2.

  c. Is there sufficient evidence to indicate that x and y are linearly correlated? Test at the $\alpha = .10$ level of significance.

Applying the Concepts—Basic

12.76 *Sales and Marketing Management* determined the "effective buying income" (EBI) of the average household in a state. Can the EBI be used to predict retail sales per household in the store-group category "eating and drinking places"?
  a. Use the data for 13 states given in the table below to find the least squares line relating retail sales per household (y) to average household EBI (x).
  b. Plot the least squares line, as well as the actual data points, on a scattergram.
  c. Based on the graph, part **b**, give your opinion regarding the predictive ability of the least squares line.
  d. Find a 95% confidence interval for the slope of the line.
  e. Use the results, part **d**, to assess the adequacy of the straight-line model.

⊙ **EBI**

State	Average Household Buying Income ($)	Retail Sales: Eating and Drinking Places ($ per household)
Connecticut	60,998	2,553.8
New Jersey	63,853	2,154.8
Michigan	46,915	2,523.3
Minnesota	44,717	2,278.6
Florida	42,442	2,475.8
South Carolina	37,848	2,358.4
Mississippi	34,490	1,538.4
Oklahoma	34,830	2,063.1
Texas	44,729	2,363.5
Colorado	44,571	3,214.9
Utah	43,421	2,653.8
California	50,713	2,215.0
Oregon	40,597	2,144.0

Source: Sales and Marketing Management, 1995.

12.77 One of the most common types of "information retrieval" processes is document-database searching. An experiment was conducted to investigate the variables that influence search performance in the Medline database and retrieval system (*Journal of Information Science*, Vol. 21, 1995). Simple linear regression was used to model the fraction y of the set of potentially informative documents that are retrieved using Medline as a function of the number x of terms in the search query, based on a sample of $n = 124$ queries. The results are summarized below:

$$\hat{y} = .202 + .135x$$

$$t \text{ (for testing } H_0: \beta_1 = 0) = 4.98$$

$$\text{Two-tailed } p\text{-value} = .001$$

a. Is there sufficient evidence to indicate that x and y are linearly related? Test using $\alpha = .01$. $t = 4.98$

b. If appropriate, use the model to predict the fraction of documents retrieved for a search query with $x = 3$ terms. $\hat{y} = .607$

c. The value of r was reported in the article as $r = .679$. Interpret this result.

d. Calculate the coefficient of determination, r^2, and interpret the result. $r^2 = .461$

12.78 Emotional exhaustion, or *burnout*, is a significant problem for people with careers in the field of human services. Regression analysis was used to investigate the relationship between burnout and aspects of the human services professional's job and job-related behavior (*Journal of Applied Behavioral Science*, Vol. 22, 1986). Emotional exhaustion was measured with the Maslach Burnout Inventory, a questionnaire. One of the independent variables considered, called *concentration*, was the proportion of social contacts with individuals who belong to a person's work group. The table on p. 754 lists the values of the emotional exhaustion index (higher values indicate greater exhaustion) and concentration for a sample of 25 human services professionals who work in a large public hospital. A MINITAB printout of the simple linear regression is provided below.

a. Construct a scattergram for the data. Do the variables x and y appear to be related?

b. Find the correlation coefficient for the data and interpret its value. Does your conclusion mean that concentration causes emotional exhaustion? Explain.

MINITAB Output for Exercise 12.78

```
The regression equation is
EXHAUST = - 29 + 8.87 CONCEN


Predictor    Coef   SE Coef      T      P
Constant    -29.5     106.7   -0.28  0.785
CONCEN      8.865     1.471    6.03  0.000


S = 174.207    R-Sq = 61.2%    R-Sq(adj) = 59.5%


Analysis of Variance

Source          DF        SS        MS      F      P
Regression       1   1102408   1102408  36.33  0.000
Residual Error  23    698009     30348
Total           24   1800417


Predicted Values for New Observations

New
Obs     Fit   SE Fit       95% CI            95% PI
  1   679.7     38.7   (599.7, 759.8)   (310.6, 1048.9)


Values of Predictors for New Observations

New
Obs   CONCEN
  1     80.0
```

BURNOUT

Exhaustion Index, y	Concentration, x	Exhaustion Index, y	Concentration, x
100	20%	493	86%
525	60	892	83
300	38	527	79
980	88	600	75
310	79	855	81
900	87	709	75
410	68	791	77
296	12	718	77
120	35	684	77
501	70	141	17
920	80	400	85
810	92	970	96
506	77		

c. Test the usefulness of the straight-line relationship with concentration for predicting burnout. Use $\alpha = .05$. $t = 6.03$

d. Find the coefficient of determination for the model and interpret it. .612

e. Find a 95% confidence interval for the slope β_1. Interpret the result. 8.865 ± 3.043

f. Use a 95% confidence interval to estimate the mean exhaustion level for all professionals who have 80% of their social contacts within their work groups. Interpret the interval. 679.7 ± 80.05

12.79 *Work standards* specify time, cost, and efficiency norms for the performance of work tasks. They are typically used to monitor job performance. In the distribution center of McCormick and Co., Inc., data were collected to develop work standards for the time to assemble or fill customer orders (*Production and Inventory Management Journal*, 1991). The table below contains data for a random sample of 9 orders.

WORKSTD

Time (mins.)	Order Size (cases)
27	36
15	34
71	255
35	103
8	4
60	555
3	6
10	60
10	96

Source: Boyle, D., Ray, B. A., and Kahan, G. "Work Standards—The Quality Way." *Production and Inventory Management Journal*, Second Quarter, 1991, p. 67.

a. Construct a scattergram for these data and interpret it.

b. Fit a least squares line to these data using time as the dependent variable. $\hat{y} = 12.594 + .10936x$

c. In general, we would expect the mean time to fill an order to increase with the size of the order. Do the data support this theory? Test using $\alpha = .05$.

d. Find a 95% confidence interval for the mean time to fill an order consisting of 150 cases.

12.80 A large proportion of U.S. teenagers work while attending high school. These heavy workloads often result in underachievement in the classroom and lower grades. A study of high school students in California and Wisconsin showed that those who worked only a few hours per week had the highest grade point averages (*Newsweek*, Nov. 16, 1992). The following table shows grade point averages (GPAs) and number of hours worked per week for a sample of five students. Consider a simple linear regression relating GPA (y) to hours worked (x).

TEENWORK

Grade Point Average, y	2.93	3.00	2.86	3.04	2.66
Hours Worked per Week, x	12	0	17	5	21

a. Find the equation of the least squares line.

b. Plot the data and graph the least squares line.

c. Text whether the model is useful for predicting grade point average. Use $\alpha = .10$. $t = -3.32$

d. Predict the grade point average of a high school student who works 10 hours per week using a 90% prediction interval. Intrepret the result. $2.913 \pm .207$

12.81 Refer to Exercise 12.46 (p. 725), in which managerial success, y, was modeled as a function of the number of contacts a manager makes with people outside his or her work unit, x, during a specific period of time. The data are saved in the **MANAGERS** file.

a. A particular manager was observed for two weeks, as in the *Journal of Applied Behavioral Science* study. She made 55 contacts with people outside her work unit. Predict the value of the manager's success index. Use a 90% prediction interval.

b. A second manager was observed for two weeks. This manager made 110 contacts with people outside his work unit. Give two reasons why caution should be exercised in using the least squares model developed from the given data set to construct a prediction interval for this manager's success index.

c. In the context of this problem, determine the value of x for which the associated prediction interval for y is the narrowest.

Applying the Concepts—Intermediate

12.82 Common maize rust is a serious disease of sweet corn. Researchers in New York state have developed an action threshold for initiation of fungicide applications based on a regression equation relating maize rust incidence to severity of the disease (*Phytopathology*, Vol. 80, 1990). In one particular field, data were collected on more than 100 plants of the sweet corn hybrid Jubilee. For each plant, incidence was measured as the percentage of leaves infected (x) and severity was calculated as the log (base 10) of the average number of infections per leaf (y). A simple linear regression analysis of the data produced the following results:

$$\hat{y} = -.939 + .020x$$
$$r^2 = .816$$
$$s = .288$$

a. Interpret the value of $\hat{\beta}_1$.
b. Interpret the value of r^2.
c. Interpret the value of s.
d. Calculate the value of r and interpret it.
e. Use the result, part **d**, to test the utility of the model. Use $\alpha = .05$. (Assume $n = 100$.)
f. Predict the severity of the disease when the incidence of maize rust for a plant is 80%. [*Note:* Take the antilog (base 10) of $\hat{y}$ to obtain the predicted average number of infections per leaf.]

12.83 Refer to Exercise 2.132 (p. 126) and the data on 50 Beanie Babies collector's items, published in *Beanie World Magazine*. Can age (in months as of Sept. 1998) of a Beanie Baby be used to accurately predict its market value? Answer this question by conducting a complete simple linear regression anlysis on the data saved in the **BEANIE** file. (The first and last five observations are shown in the table.)

BEANIE

Name	Age (months) as of Sept. 1998	Value ($)
1. Ally theAlligator	52	55.00
2. Batty the Bat12	12.00	
3. Bongo the Brown Monkey	28	40.00
4. Blackie the Bear	52	10.00
5. Bucky the Beaver	40	45.00
⋮	⋮	⋮
46. Stripes the Tiger (Gold/Black)	40	400.00
47. Teddy the 1997 Holiday Bear	12	50.00
48. Tuffy the Terrier	17	10.00
49. Tracker the Basset Hound	5	15.00
50. Zip the Black Cat	28	40.00

Source: Beanie World Magazine, Sept. 1998.

12.84 Refer to the *Forbes* magazine (Jan. 11, 1999) report on the financial standings of each team in the National Football League (NFL), Exercise 2.141 (p. 128). The table listing the current value (without deduction for debt, except stadium debt) and operating income for each team is reproduced below.
a. Propose a straight-line model relating an NFL team's current value (y) to its operating income (x).
b. Fit the model to the data using the method of least squares. $\hat{y} = 292.6 + 4.71x$
c. Interpret the least squares estimates of the slope and y-intercept in the words of the problem.
d. Statistically assess the adequacy of the model. Do you recommand using it to predict an NFL team's value?

NFLVALUE

Team	Current Value ($ millions)	Operating Income ($ millions)
Dallas Cowboys	663	56.7
Washington Redskins	607	48.8
Tampa Bay Buccaneers	502	41.2
Carolina Panthers	488	18.8
New England Patriots	460	13.5
Miami Dolphins	446	32.9
Denver Broncos	427	5.0
Jacksonville Jaguars	419	29.3
Baltimore Ravens	408	33.2
Seattle Seahawks	399	6.4
Pittsburgh Steelers	397	15.5
Cincinnati Bengals	394	3.4
St. Louis Rams	390	33.2
New York Giants	376	25.2
San Francisco 49ers	371	12.7
Tennessee Titans	369	4.1
New York Jets	363	12.1
Kansas City Chiefs	353	31.0
Buffalo Bills	326	10.7
San Diego Chargers	323	8.2
Green Bay Packers	320	16.4
Philadelphia Eagles	318	19.1
New Orleans Saints	315	11.3
Chicago Bears	313	19.7
Minnesota Vikings	309	5.1
Atlanta Falcons	306	16.8
Indianapolis Colts	305	15.8
Arizona Cardinals	301	10.6
Oakland Raiders	299	17.3
Detroit Lions	293	16.4

Source: Forbes, Jan. 11, 1999.

12.85 The Minnesota Department of Transportation installed a state-of-the-art weigh-in-motion scale in the concrete surface of the eastbound lanes of Interstate 494 in Bloomington, Minnesota. After installation, a

TRUCKWTS

Trial Number	Static Weight of Truck, x (thousand pounds)	Weigh-in-Motion Reading Prior to Calibration Adjustment, y_1 (thousand pounds)	Weigh-in-Motion Reading After Calibration Adjustment, y_2 (thousand pounds)
1	27.9	26.0	27.8
2	29.1	29.9	29.1
3	38.0	39.5	37.8
4	27.0	25.1	27.1
5	30.3	31.6	30.6
6	34.5	36.2	34.3
7	27.8	25.1	26.9
8	29.6	31.0	29.6
9	33.1	35.6	33.0
10	35.5	40.2	35.0

Source: Adapted from data in Wright J. L., Owen, F., and Pena, D. "Status of MN/DOT's Weigh-in-Motion Program." St. Paul: Minnesota Department of Transportation, January 1983.

study was undertaken to determine whether the scale's readings correspond with the static weights of the vehicles being monitored. (Studies of this type are known as *calibration studies.*) After some preliminary comparisons using a two-axle, six-tire truck carrying different loads (see the table above), calibration adjustments were made in the software of the weigh-in-motion system and the scales were reevaluated.

a. Construct two scattergrams, one of y_1 versus x and the other of y_2 versus x.

b. Use the scattergrams of part a to evaluate the performance of the weigh-in-motion scale both before and after the calibration adjustment.

c. Calculate the correlation coefficient for both sets of data and interpret their values. Explain how these correlation coefficients can be used to evaluate the weigh-in-motion scale.

d. Suppose the sample correlation coefficient for y_2 and x was 1. Could this happen if the static weights and the weigh-in-motion readings disagreed? Explain.

12.86 Firms planning to build new plants or make additions to existing facilities have become very conscious of the energy efficiency of proposed new structures and are interested in the relation between yearly energy consumption and the number of square feet of building shell. The accompanying table lists the energy consumption in British thermal units (a BTU is the amount of heat required to raise 1 pound of water 1° F) for 22 buildings that were all subjected to the same climatic conditions. Consider a straight-line model relating BTU consumption, y, to building shell area, x.

a. Find the least squares estimates of the intercept β_0 and the slope β_1. $-99045; 102.81$

b. Investigate the usefulness of the model you developed in part a. Is yearly energy consumption

positively linearly related to the shell area of the building? Test using $\alpha = .10$. $t = 6.48$

c. Calculate the observed significance level of the test of part b using the printout. Interpret its value.

d. Find the coefficient of determination r^2 and interpret its value.   .678

e. A company wishes to build a new warehouse that will contain 8,000 square feet of shell area. Find the predicted value of energy consumption and a 95% prediction interval on the printout. Comment on the usefulness of this interval.

BTU

BTU/Year (thousands)	Shell Area (square feet)
3,870,000	30,001
1,371,000	13,530
2,422,000	26,060
672,200	6,355
233,100	4,576
218,900	24,680
354,000	2,621
3,135,000	23,350
1,470,000	18,770
1,408,000	12,220
2,201,000	25,490
2,680,000	23,680
337,500	5,650
567,500	8,001
555,300	6,147
239,400	2,660
2,629,000	19,240
1,102,000	10,700
423,500	9,125
423,500	6,510
1,691,000	13,530
1,870,000	18,860

f. The application of the model you developed in part **a** to the warehouse problem of part **e** is appropriate only if certain assumptions can be made about the new warehouse. What are these assumptions?

Applying the Concepts—Advanced

12.87 Sometimes it is known from theoretical considerations that the straight-line relationship between two variables, x and y, passes through the origin of the xy-plane. Consider the relationship between the total weight of a shipment of 50-pound bags of flour, y, and the number of bags in the shipment, x. Since a shipment containing $x = 0$ bags (i.e., no shipment at all) has a total weight of $y = 0$, a straight-line model of the relationship between x and y should pass through the point $x = 0$, $y = 0$. In such a case you could assume $\beta_0 = 0$ and characterize the relationship between x and y with the following model:

$$y = \beta_1 x + \varepsilon$$

The least squares estimate of β_1 for this model is

$$\hat{\beta}_1 = \frac{\sum x_i y_i}{\sum x_i^2}$$

From the records of past flour shipments, 15 shipments were randomly chosen and the data shown in the table below were recorded.

FLOUR2

Weight of Shipment	Number of 50-Pound Bags in Shipment
5,050	100
10,249	205
20,000	450
7,420	150
24,685	500
10,206	200
7,325	150
4,958	100
7,162	150
24,000	500
4,900	100
14,501	300
28,000	600
17,002	400
16,100	400

a. Find the least squares line for the given data under the assumption that $\beta_0 = 0$. Plot the least squares line on a scattergram of the data.

b. Find the least squares line for the given data using the model

$$y = \beta_0 + \beta_1 x + \varepsilon$$

(i.e., do not restrict β_0 to equal 0). Plot this line on the same scatterplot you constructed in part **a**.

c. Refer to part **b**. Why might $\hat{\beta}_0$ be different from 0 even though the true value of β_0 is known to be 0?

d. The estimated standard error of $\hat{\beta}_0$ is equal to

$$s\sqrt{\frac{1}{n} + \frac{\bar{x}^2}{SS_{xx}}}$$

Use the t-statistic

$$t = \frac{\hat{\beta}_0 - 0}{s\sqrt{(1/n) + (\bar{x}^2/SS_{xx})}}$$

to test the null hypothesis $H_0: \beta_0 = 0$ against the alternative $H_a: \beta_0 \neq 0$. Use $\alpha = .10$. Should you include β_0 in your model?

12.88 The precision of β_1 as an estimator of β_1 is generally measured by its standard deviation $\sigma_{\hat{\beta}_1}$. In general, the larger the value of $\sigma_{\hat{\beta}_1}$, the wider (less precise) are confidence intervals for β_1; the smaller the value of $\sigma_{\hat{\beta}_1}$, the narrower (more precise) are confidence intervals for β_1.

a. Examine the formula for $\sigma_{\hat{\beta}_1}$ and explain how the observed values of the independent variable influence the size of $\sigma_{\hat{\beta}_1}$.

b. Sometimes it is possible to obtain data for a regression study by setting the independent variable x at different levels and observing the resulting values of the dependent variable y. For example, suppose a supermarket chain is studying the relationship between the sales of a product and how many square feet of display space it is given. Data for such a study will be generated by utilizing display areas of different sizes in different stores and observing the resulting sales. If you were designing such a study, how would your answer to part a influence the choice of display area sizes?

12.89 Managers are interested in modeling past cost behavior in order to make more accurate predictions of future costs. Models of past cost behavior are called *cost funtions*. Factors that influence costs are called *cost drivers* (Horngren, Foster, and Datar, *Cost Accounting*, 1994). The cost data shown are from a rug manufacturer. Indirect manufacturing labor costs

⊙ **RUG**

Week	Indirect Manufacturing Labor Costs	Machine-Hours	Direct Manufacturing Labor-Hours
1	$1,190	68	30
2	1,211	88	35
3	1,004	62	36
4	917	72	20
5	770	60	47
6	1,456	96	45
7	1,180	78	44
8	710	46	38
9	1,316	82	70
10	1,032	94	30
11	752	68	29
12	963	48	38

Source: Data and exercise adapted from Horngren, C. T., Foster, G., and Datar, S. M. *Cost Accounting,* Englewood Cliffs, N.J.: Prentice Hall, 1994.

consist of machine maintenance costs and setup labor costs. Machine-hours and direct manufacturing labor-hours are cost drivers.

Your task is to estimate and compare two alternative cost functions for indirect manufacturing labor costs. In the first, machine-hours is the independent variable; in the second, direct manufacturing labor-hours is the independent variable. Prepare a report that compares the two cost functions and recommends which should be used to explain and predict indirect manufacturing labor costs. Be sure to justify your choice.

REFERENCES

Chatterjee, S., and Price, B. *Regression Analysis by Example*, 2nd ed. New York: Wiley, 1991.

Draper, N., and Smith, H. *Applied Regression Analysis*, 3rd ed. New York: Wiley, 1987.

Gitlow, H., Oppenheim, A., and Oppenheim, R. *Quality Management: Tools and Methods for Improvement*, 2nd ed. Burr Ridge, Ill.: Irwin, 1995.

Graybill, F. *Theory and Application of the Linear Model.* North Scituate, Mass.: Duxbury, 1976.

Kleinbaum, D., and Kupper, L. *Applied Regression Analysis and Other Multivariable Methods*, 2nd ed. North Scituate, Mass.: Duxbury, 1997.

Mendenhall, W. *Introduction to Linear Models and the Design and Analysis of Experiments*, Belmont, Calif.: Wadsworth, 1968.

Mendenhall, W., and Sincich, T. *A Second Course in Statistics: Regression Analysis*, 6th ed. Upper Saddle River, N.J.: Prentice Hall, 2003.

Montgomery, D., Peck, E., and Vining, G. *Introduction to Linear Regression Analysis*, 3rd ed. New York: Wiley, 2001.

Mintzberg, H. *The Nature of Managerial Work.* New York: Harper and Row, 1973.

Mosteller, F., and Tukey, J. W. *Data Analysis and Regression: A Second Course in Statistics.* Reading, Mass.: Addison-Wesley, 1977.

Neter, J., Kutner, M., Nachtsheim, C., and Wasserman, W. *Applied Linear Statistical Models*, 4th ed. Hornewood, Ill.: Richard Irwin, 1996.

Rousseeuw, P. J., and Leroy, A. M. *Robust Regression and Outlier Detection.* New York: Wiley, 1987.

Weisburg, S. *Applied Linear Regression*, 2nd ed. New York: Wiley, 1985.

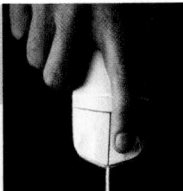

Using Technology

12.1 Simple Linear Regression Using SPSS

To conduct a simple linear regression analysis, first access the SPSS spreadsheet file that contains the two quantitative variables (dependent and independent variables). Next, click on the "Analyze" button on the SPSS menu bar, then click on "Regression" and "Linear", as shown in Figure 12.S.1. The resulting dialog box appears as shown in Figure 12.S.2.

Figure 12.S.1
SPSS menu options for regression

Specify the dependent variable in the "Dependent" box and the independent variable in the "Independent(s)" box. Be sure to select "Enter" in the "Method" box.

Optionally, you can get SPSS to produce confidence intervals for the model parameters by clicking the "Statistics" button and checking the appropriate menu items in the resulting menu list. Also, you can obtain prediction intervals for y and confidence intervals for $E(y)$ by clicking the "Save" button and checking the appropriate items in the resulting menu list. (The prediction intervals will be added as new columns to the SPSS data spreadsheet.) To return to the main Regression dialog box from any of these optional screens, click "Continue". Click "OK" on the Regression dialog box to view the linear regression results.

To obtain the correlation coefficient for the two quantitative variables, click on the "Analyze" button on the main menu bar, then click on "Correlate"

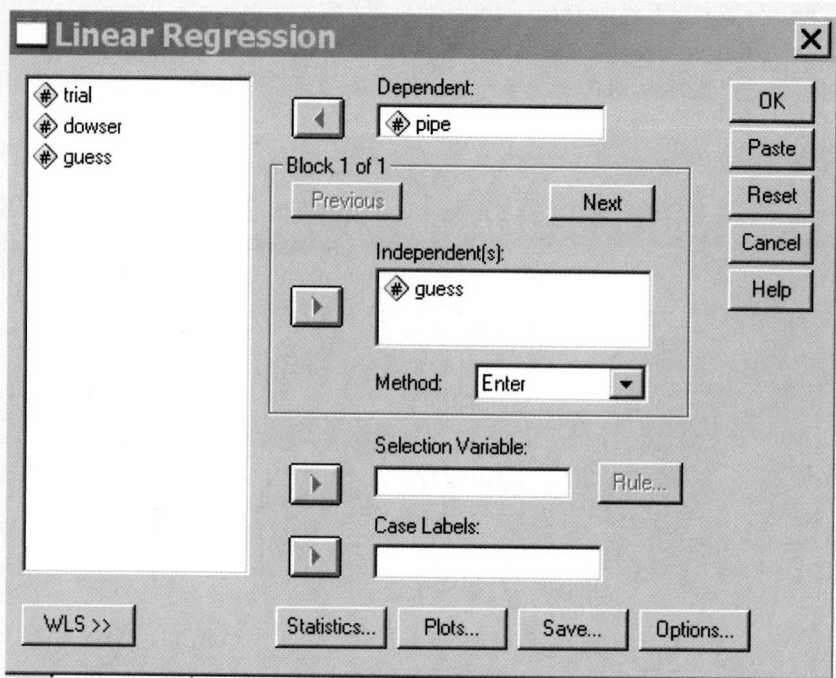

Figure 12.S.2
SPSS linear regression dialog box

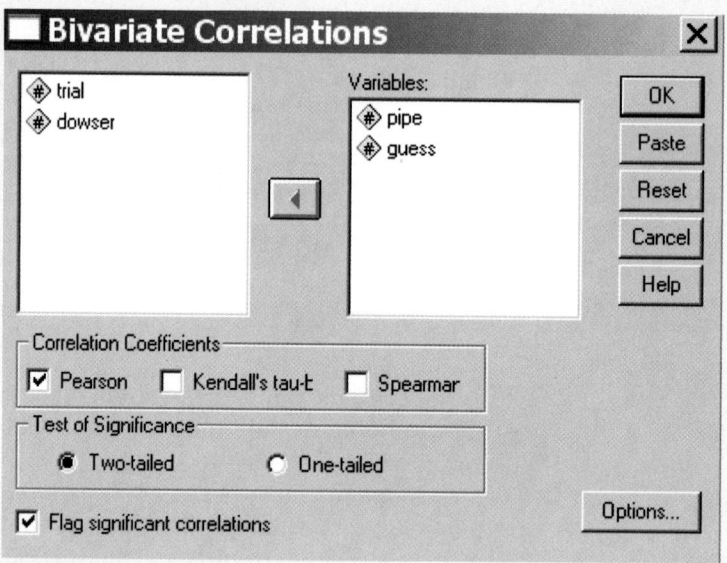

Figure 12.S.3
SPSS Correlation dialog box

(see Figure 12.S.1), finally click on "Bivariate". The resulting dialog box appears in Figure 12.S.3. Enter the variables of interest in the "Variables" box, check the "Pearson" option, then click "OK" to obtain a printout of the correlation.

12.2 Simple Linear Regression Using MINITAB

To conduct a simple linear regression analysis, first access the MINITAB worksheet file that contains the two quantitative variables (dependent and independent variables). Next, click on the "Stat" button on the MINITAB menu bar, then click on "Regression" and "Regression" again, as shown in Figure 12.M.1.

The resulting dialog box appears as shown in Figure 12.M.2. Specify the dependent variable in the "Response" box and the independent variable in the "Predictors" box.

Figure 12.M.1
MINITAB menu options for regression

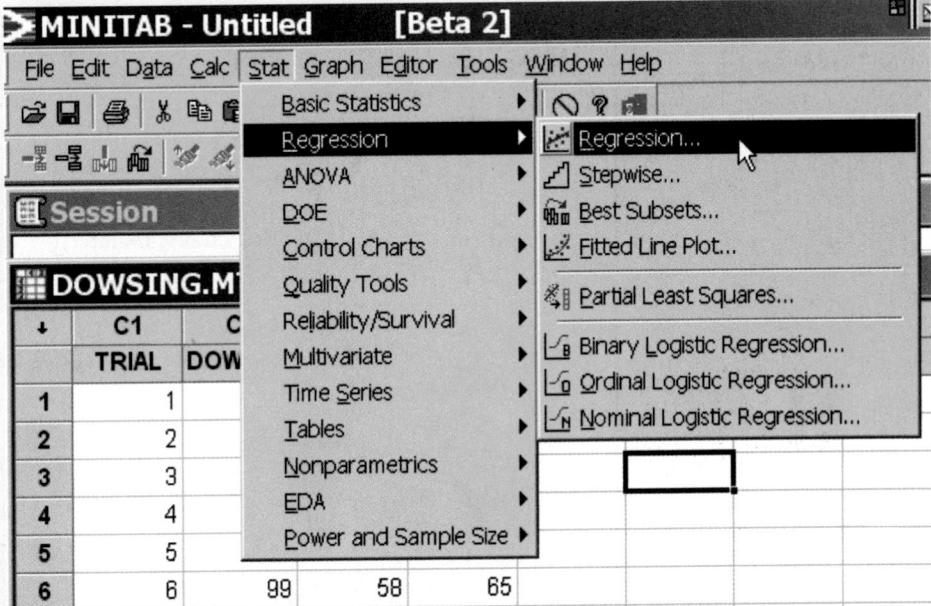

Figure 12.M.2
MINITAB regression dialog box

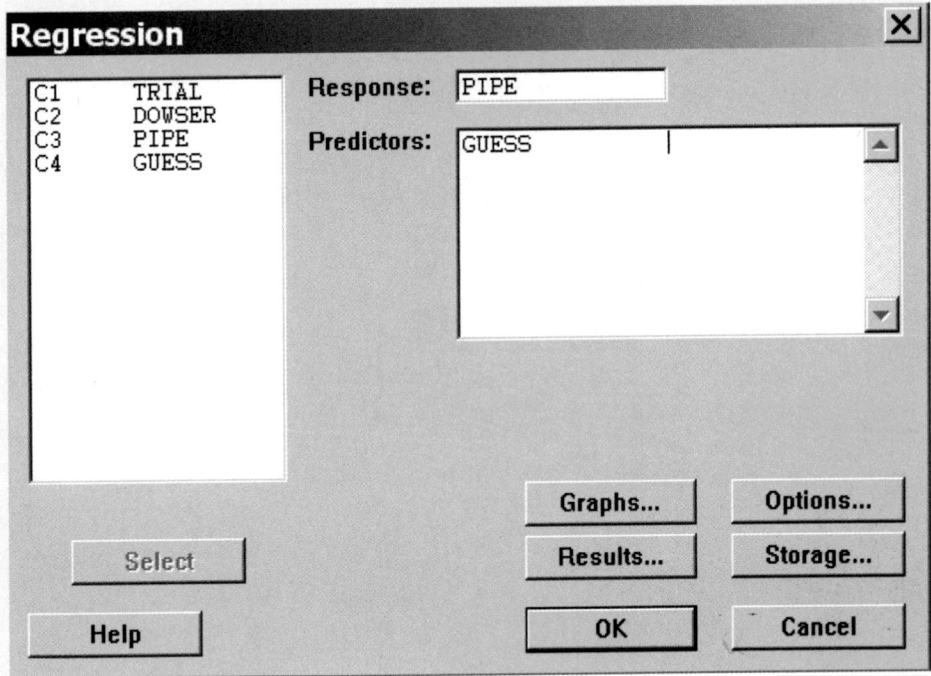

Optionally, you can get MINITAB to produce prediction intervals for y and confidence intervals for $E(y)$ by clicking the "Options" button. The resulting dialog box is shown in Figure 12.M.3. Check "Confidence limits" and/or "Prediction limits", specify the "Confidence level", and enter the value of x in the "Prediction intervals for new observations" box. Click "OK" to return to the main Regression dialog box, then click "OK" again to produce the MINITAB simple linear regression printout.

To obtain the correlation coefficient for the two quantitative variables, click on the "Stat" button on the MINITAB main menu bar, then click on "Basic Statistics", then click on "Correlation", as shown in Figure 12.M.4. The

Figure 12.M.3
MINITAB regression options

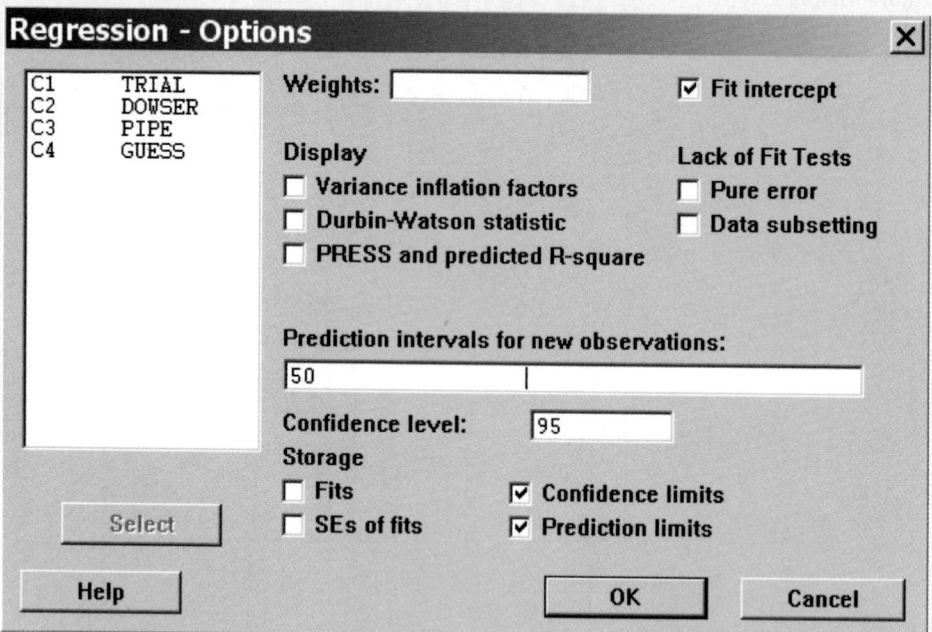

Figure 12.M.4
MINITAB menu options for correlation

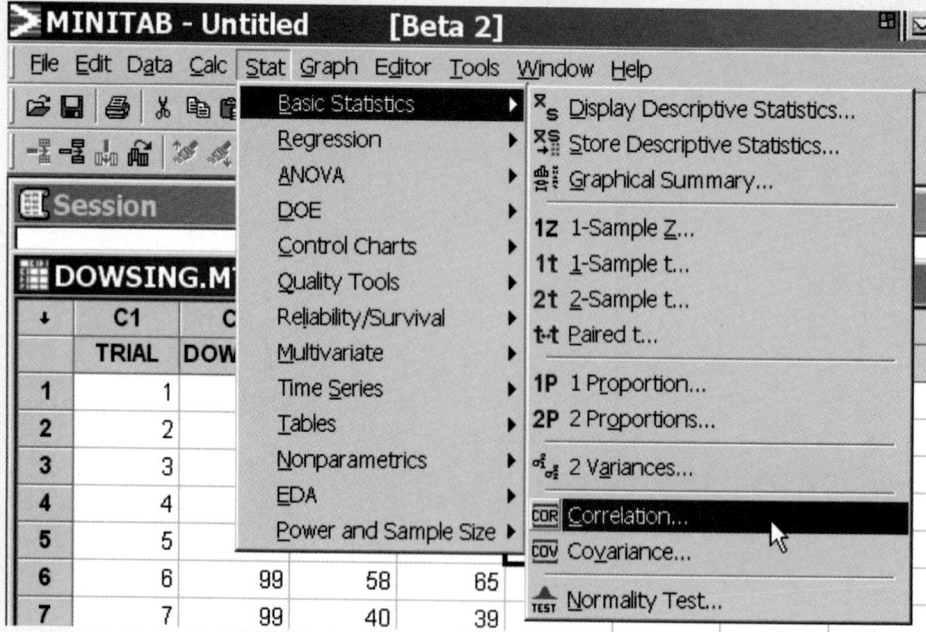

Figure 12.M.5
MINITAB correlation dialog box

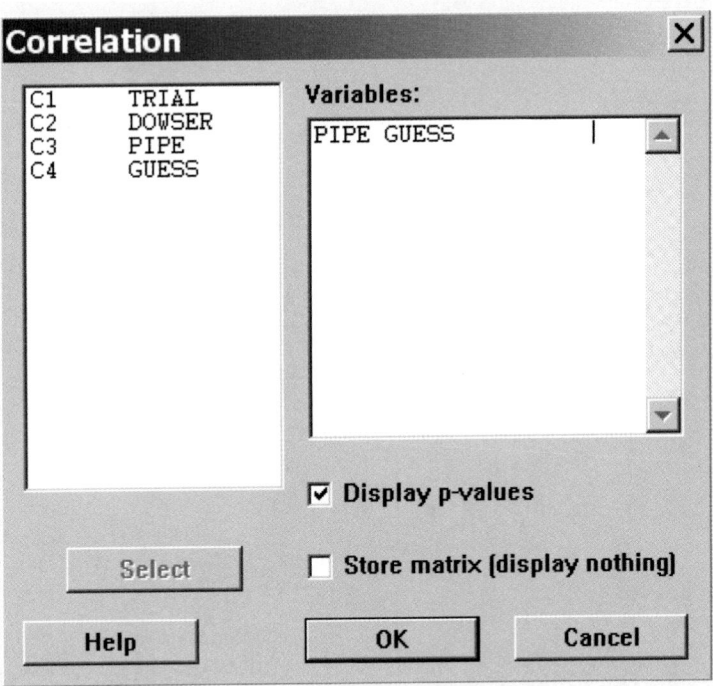

resulting dialog box appears in Figure 12.M.5. Enter the two variables of interest in the "Variables" box, then click "OK" to obtain a printout of the correlation.

12.3 Simple Linear Regression Using EXCEL and PHSTAT2

To conduct a simple linear regression analysis, first access the EXCEL worksheet file that contains the two quantitative variables (dependent and independent variables). Next, click "PHStat" form the EXCEL menu bar, then select "Regression" and "Simple Linear Regression", as shown in Figure 12.E.1. The re-

Figure 12.E.1
EXCEL menu options for simple linear regression

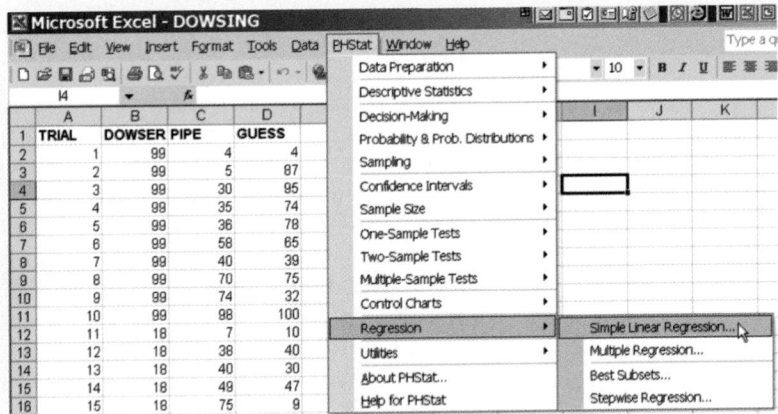

Figure 12.E.2
EXCEL/PHSTAT2 simple linear regression dialog box

sulting dialog box is shown in Figure 12.E.2. Specify the cell ranges for the y and x variables, the confidence level for confidence intervals for the model parameters, and select both the "Regression Statistics" and "ANOVA and Coefficients" table options.

Optionally, you can get EXCEL to produce prediction intervals for y and confidence intervals for $E(y)$ by selecting the "Confidence and Prediction Interval for X =" option, and entering the value of x of interest, as shown at the bottom of Figure 12.E.2. Click "OK" to produce the simple linear regression results. (The standard regression printout will appear in one worksheet and the confidence/prediction intervals will appear in a second worksheet.)

To obtain the correlation coefficient for the two quantitative variables, click on the "Tools" button on the MINITAB main menu bar, then click on "Data Analysis", and select the "Correlation" option. The resulting dialog box appears in Figure 12.E.3. Specify the cell range for the two variables of interest and select the "Grouped by: Columns" option. (*Note*: The two variables must be in adjacent columns in the EXCEL worksheet.) Click "OK" to obtain the value of the correlation coefficient on a separate worksheet.

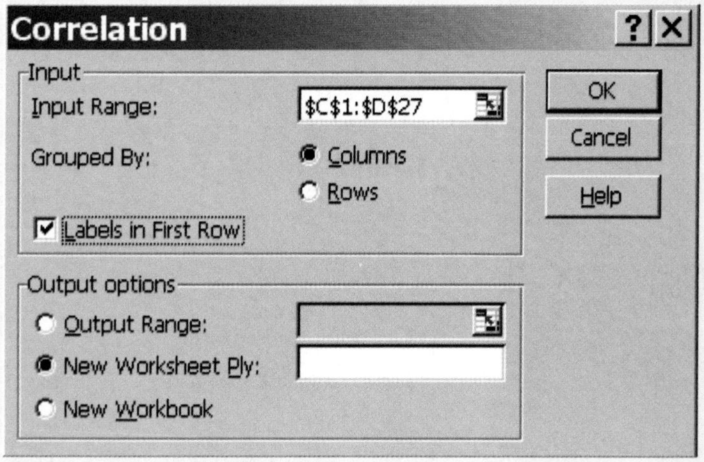

Figure 12.E.3
EXCEL correlation dialog box

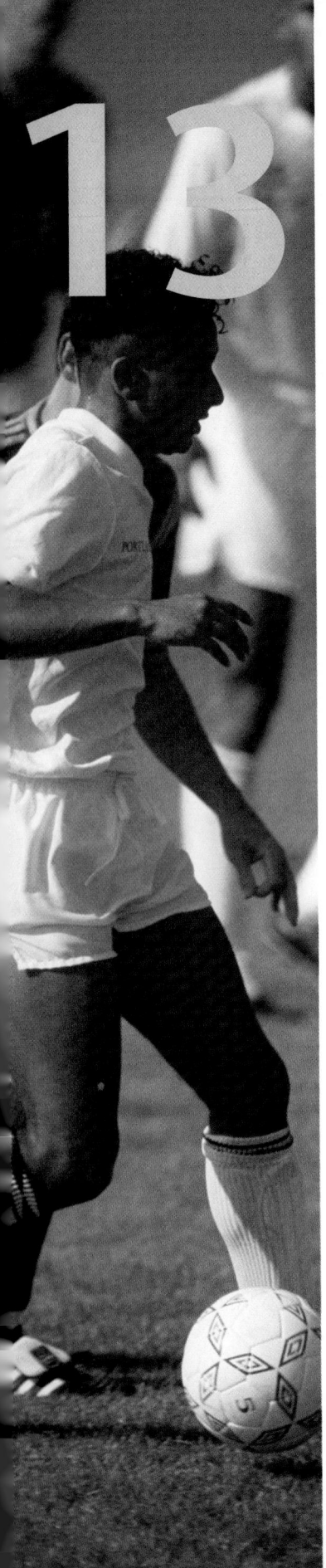

13

Multiple Regression and Model Building

Contents

Statistics in Action

Bid Rigging in the Highway Construction Industry

Using Technology

Where We've Been

- Introduced the straight-line model relating a dependent variable y to a single independent variable x.

- Demonstrated how to estimate the parameters of the straight-line model using the method of least squares.

- Showed how to statistically assess the adequacy of the model.

- Showed how to use the model to estimate $E(y)$ and predict y for a given value of x.

Where We're Going

- Introduce a *multiple regression* model as a means of relating a dependent variable *y* to two or more independent variables.

- Present several different multiple regression models involving both quantitative and qualitative independent variables.

- Assess how well the multiple regression model fits the sample data.

- Show how an analysis of the model's *residuals* can aid in detecting violations of model assumptions and in identifying model modifications.

Statistics in ACTION

Bid-Rigging in the Highway Construction Industry

In the United States, commercial contractors bid for the right to construct state highways and roads. A state government agency, usually the Department of Transportation (DOT), notifies various contractors of the state's intent to build a highway. Sealed bids are submitted by the contractors, and the contractor with the lowest bid (building cost) is awarded the road construction contract. The bidding process works extremely well in competitive markets but has the potential to increase construction costs if the markets are noncompetitive or if collusive practices are present. The latter occurred in the 1980s in Florida. Numerous road contractors either admitted or were found guilty of price fixing (i.e., setting the cost of construction above the fair, or competitive, cost through bid-rigging or other means).

This Statistics in Action involves data collected by the Florida Attorney General shortly following the price-fixing crisis. The Attorney General's objective is to build a model for the cost (*y*) of a road construction contract awarded using the sealed-bid system. The **FLAG** file contains data for a sample of 235 road contracts. The variables measured for each contract are listed in Table SIA13.1. Ultimately, the Attorney General wants to use the model to predict the costs of future road contracts in the state.

In several Statistics in Action Revisited sections (see below), we show how to analyze the data using a multiple regression analysis.

Statistics in Action Revisited

- A First-Order Model for Road Contract Cost (p. 799)
- Selecting the Independent Variables and Building a Model for Road Contract Cost (p. 857)
- A Residual Analysis for the Road Cost Model (p. 877)

 FLAG

TABLE SIA13.1 Variables in the FLAG Data File

Variable Name	Type	Description
CONTRACT	Quantitative	Road contract number
COST	Quantitative	Low bid contract cost (thousands of dollars)
DOTEST	Quantitative	DOT engineer's cost estimate (thousands of dollars)
STATUS	Qualitative	Bid status (1 = fixed, 0 = competitive)
B2B1RAT	Quantitative	Ratio of second lowest bid to low bid
B3B1RAT	Quantitative	Ratio of third lowest bid to low bid
BHB1RAT	Quantitative	Ratio of highest bid to low bid
DISTRICT	Quantitative	Location of road (1 = South Florida, 0 = North Florida)
BTPRATIO	Quantitative	Ratio of number of bidders to number of plan holders
DAYSEST	Quantitative	DOT engineer's estimate of number of workdays required

13.1 Multiple Regression Models

Most practical applications of regression analysis utilize models that are more complex than the simple straight-line model. For example, a realistic probabilistic model for reaction time stimulus would include more than just the amount of a particular drug in the bloodstream. Factors such as age, a measure of visual perception, and sex of the subject are a few of the many variables that might be related to reaction time. Thus, we would want to incorporate these and other potentially important independent variables into the model in order to make accurate predictions.

Probabilistic models that include more than one independent variable are called **multiple regression models.** The general form of these models is

$$y = \beta_0 + \beta_1 x_1 + \beta_2 x_2 + \cdots + \beta_k x_k + \epsilon$$

The dependent variable y is now written as a function of k independent variables, $x_1, x_2, \ldots, x_k$. The random error term is added to make the model probabilistic rather than deterministic. The value of the coefficient β_i determines the contribution of the independent variable x_i, and β_0 is the y-intercept. The coefficients $\beta_0, \beta_1 \ldots, \beta_k$ are usually unknown because they represent population parameters.

At first glance it might appear that the regression model shown above would not allow for anything other than straight-line relationships between y and the independent variables, but this is not true. Actually, $x_1, x_2, \ldots, x_k$ can be functions of variables as long as the functions do not contain unknown parameters. For example, the reaction time, y, of a subject to a visual stimulus could be a function of the independent variables

$$x_1 = \text{Age of the subject}$$
$$x_2 = (\text{Age})^2 = x_1^2$$
$$x_3 = 1 \text{ if male subject, } 0 \text{ if female subject}$$

The x_2 term is called a **higher-order term,** since it is the value of a quantitative variable (x_1) squared (i.e., raised to the second power). The x_3 term is a **coded variable** representing a qualitative variable (gender). The multiple regression model is quite versatile and can be made to model many different types of response variables.

The General Multiple Regression Model
$$y = \beta_0 + \beta_1 x_1 + \beta_2 x_2 + \cdots + \beta_k x_k + \epsilon$$

where

y is the dependent variable

$x_1, x_2, \ldots, x_k$ are the independent variables

$E(y) = \beta_0 + \beta_1 x_1 + \beta_2 x_2 + \cdots + \beta_k x_k$ is the deterministic portion of the model

β_i determines the contribution of the independent variable x_i

Note: The symbols $x_1, x_2, \ldots, x_k$ may represent higher-order terms for quantitative predictors or terms that represent qualitative predictors.

As shown in the box, the steps used to develop the multiple regression model are similar to those used for the simple linear regression model.

Teaching Tip
Show that this process is
identical to the process used in
the simple linear regression
analysis of Chapter 12.

Analyzing a Multiple Regression Model

Step 1   Hypothesize the deterministic component of the model. This component relates the mean, $E(y)$, to the independent variables $x_1, x_2, \ldots, x_k$. This involves the choice of the independent variables to be included in the model (Sections 13.2, 13.7–13.12).

Step 2   Use the sample data to estimate the unknown model parameters $\beta_0, \beta_1, \beta_2, \ldots, \beta_k$ in the model (Section 13.2).

Step 3   Specify the probability distribution of the random error term, ϵ, and estimate the standard deviation of this distribution, σ (Section 13.3).

Step 4   Check that the assumptions on ϵ are satisfied, and make model modifications if necessary (Section 13.13).

Step 5   Statistically evaluate the usefulness of the model (Sections 13.4 and 13.5).

Step 6   When satisfied that the model is useful, use it for prediction, estimation, and other purposes (Section 13.6).

Throughout this chapter, we introduce several different types of models that form the foundation of **model building** (or useful model construction). In the next several sections, we consider the most basic multiple regression model, called the *first-order model*.

13.2 The First-Order Model: Estimating and Interpreting the β Parameters

A model that includes only terms for *quantitative* independent variables, called a **first-order model**, is described in the box. Note that the first-order model does not include any higher-order terms (such as x_1^2).

Teaching Tip
The method of least squares
that was used in Chapter 12 is
still used in multiple regression.
The calculations have become
significantly more difficult, but
the theory is exactly the same.

A First-Order Model in Five Quantitative Independent Variables*

$$E(y) = \beta_0 + \beta_1 x_1 + \beta_2 x_2 + \beta_3 x_3 + \beta_4 x_4 + \beta_5 x_5$$

where $x_1, x_2, \ldots, x_5$ are all quantitative variables that *are not* functions of other independent variables.

Note: β_i represents the slope of the line relating y to x_i when all the other x's are held fixed.

The method of fitting first-order models—and multiple regression models in general—is identical to that of fitting the simple straight-line model: the method of least squares. That is, we choose the estimated model

$$\hat{y} = \hat{\beta}_0 + \hat{\beta}_1 x_1 + \cdots + \hat{\beta}_k x_k$$

that minimizes

$$\text{SSE} = \Sigma(y - \hat{y})^2$$

*The terminology "first order" is derived from the fact that each x in the model is raised to the first power.

As in the case of the simple linear model, the sample estimates $\hat{\beta}_0, \hat{\beta}_1, \ldots, \hat{\beta}_k$ are obtained as a solution to a set of simultaneous linear equations.*

The primary difference between fitting the simple and multiple regression models is computational difficulty. The $(k + 1)$ simultaneous linear equations that must be solved to find the $(k + 1)$ estimated coefficients $\hat{\beta}_0, \hat{\beta}_1, \ldots, \hat{\beta}_k$ are difficult (sometimes nearly impossible) to solve with a calculator. Consequently, we resort to the use of computers. Instead of presenting the tedious hand calculations required to fit the models, we present output from SPSS, MINITAB, and EXCEL.

Biography

GEORGE U. YULE (1871–1951)— Yule Processes

Born on a small farm in Scotland, George Yule received an extensive childhood education. After graduating from University College (London), where he studied civil engineering, Yule spent a year employed in engineering workshops. However, he made a career change in 1893, accepting a teaching position back at University College under the guidance of statistician Karl Pearson (see p. 646). Inspired by Pearson's work, Yule produced a series of important articles on the statistics of regression and correlation. Yule is considered the first to apply the method of least squares in regression analysis and he developed the theory of multiple regression. He eventually was appointed a lecturer in statistics at Cambridge University and later became the president of the prestigious Royal Statistical Society. Yule made many other contributions to the field, including the invention of time series analysis and the development of Yule processes and the Yule distribution.

EXAMPLE 13.1   FITTING A 1ST ORDER MULTIPLE REGRESSION MODEL

Problem Suppose a property appraiser wants to model the relationship between the sale price of a residential property in a midsize city and the following three independent variables: (1) appraised land value of the property, (2) appraised value of improvements (i.e., home value) on the property, and (3) area of living space on the property (i.e., home size). Consider the first-order model

$$y = \beta_0 + \beta_1 x_1 + \beta_2 x_2 + \beta_3 x_3 + \epsilon$$

where

$$y = \text{Sale price (dollars)}$$
$$x_1 = \text{Appraised land value (dollars)}$$
$$x_2 = \text{Appraised improvements (dollars)}$$
$$x_3 = \text{Area (square feet)}$$

*Students who are familiar with calculus should note that $\hat{\beta}_0, \hat{\beta}_1, \ldots, \hat{\beta}_k$ are the solutions to the set of equations $\partial\text{SSE}/\partial\hat{\beta}_0 = 0, \partial\text{SSE}/\partial\hat{\beta}_1 = 0, \ldots, \partial\text{SSE}/\partial\hat{\beta}_k = 0$. The solution is usually given in matrix form, but we do not present the details here. See the references for details.

To fit the model, the appraiser selected a random sample of $n = 20$ properties from the thousands of properties that were sold in a particular year. The resulting data are given in Table 13.1.

a. Use scattergrams to plot the sample data. Interpret the plots.

b. Use the method of least squares to estimate the unknown parameters β_0, β_1, β_2, and β_3 in the model.

b. $\hat{y} = 1,470 + .8145x_1 +$
$.8204x_2 + 13.53x_3$

c. 1,003,491,259

c. Find the value of SSE that is minimized by the least squares method.

Solution   **a.** MINITAB side-by-side scatterplots for examining the bivariate relationships between y and x_1, y and x_2, and y and x_3 are shown in Figure 13.1. Of the three

REALESTATE

TABLE 13.1   Real Estate Appraisal Data for 20 Properties

Property # (Obs.)	Sale Price, y	Land Value, x_1	Improvements Value, x_2	Area, x_3
1	68,900	5,960	44,967	1,873
2	48,500	9,000	27,860	928
3	55,500	9,500	31,439	1,126
4	62,000	10,000	39,592	1,265
5	116,500	18,000	72,827	2,214
6	45,000	8,500	27,317	912
7	38,000	8,000	29,856	899
8	83,000	23,000	47,752	1,803
9	59,000	8,100	39,117	1,204
10	47,500	9,000	29,349	1,725
11	40,500	7,300	40,166	1,080
12	40,000	8,000	31,679	1,529
13	97,000	20,000	58,510	2,455
14	45,500	8,000	23,454	1,151
15	40,900	8,000	20,897	1,173
16	80,000	10,500	56,248	1,960
17	56,000	4,000	20,859	1,344
18	37,000	4,500	22,610	988
19	50,000	3,400	35,948	1,076
20	22,400	1,500	5,779	962

Source: Alachua County (Florida) Property Appraisers Office.

Figure 13.1
MINITAB scatterplots for the data of table 13.1

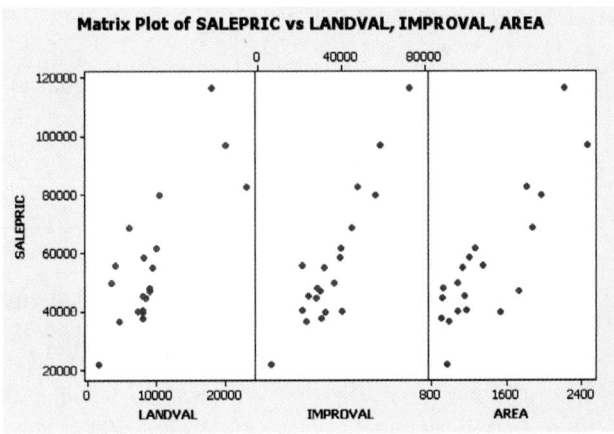

variables, appraised improvements (x_2) appears to have the strongest linear relationship with sale price (y).

b. The model hypothesized above is fit to the data of Table 13.1 using MINITAB. The MINITAB printout is reproduced in Figure 13.2. The least squares estimates of the β parameters appear (highlighted) in the column labeled **Coef.** You can see that $\hat{\beta}_0 = 1,470$, $\hat{\beta}_1 = .8145$, $\hat{\beta}_2 = .8204$, and $\hat{\beta}_3 = 13.529$. Therefore, the equation that minimizes SSE for this data set (i.e., the **least squares prediction equation**) is

$$\hat{y} = 1,470 + .8145x_1 + .8204x_2 + 13.53x_3$$

Regression Analysis: SALEPRIC versus LANDVAL, IMPROVAL, AREA

```
The regression equation is
SALEPRIC = 1470 + 0.814 LANDVAL + 0.820 IMPROVAL + 13.5 AREA


Predictor     Coef   SE Coef     T       P
Constant      1470      5746   0.26   0.801
LANDVAL     0.8145    0.5122   1.59   0.131
IMPROVAL    0.8204    0.2112   3.88   0.001
AREA        13.529     6.586   2.05   0.057


S = 7919.48    R-Sq = 89.7%    R-Sq(adj) = 87.8%


Analysis of Variance

Source            DF          SS          MS       F       P
Regression         3  8779676741  2926558914   46.66   0.000
Residual Error    16  1003491259    62718204
Total             19  9783168000
```

Figure 13.2
MINITAB analysis of sale price model

c. The minimum value of the SSE, highlighted in Figure 13.2, is SSE = 1,003,491,259.

Look Back The method of least squares also guarantees that the sum of the errors of prediction, SE, will be 0.

| Now Work | *Exercise 13.2a, b* |

■ ■ ■

After obtaining the least squares prediction equation, the analyst will usually want to make meaningful interpretations of the β estimates. Recall that in the straight-line model (Chapter 12)

$$y = \beta_0 + \beta_1 x + \epsilon$$

β_0 represents the y-intercept of the line and β_1 represents the slope of the line. From our discussion in Chapter 12, β_1 has a practical interpretation—it represents the mean change in y for every 1-unit increase in x. When the independent variables are quantitative, the β parameters in the first-order model specified in Example 13.1 have similar interpretations. The difference is that when we interpret the β that multiplies one of the variables (e.g., x_1), we must be certain to hold the values of the remaining independent variables (e.g., x_2, x_3) fixed.

To see this, suppose that the mean $E(y)$ of a response y is related to two quantitative independent variables, x_1 and x_2, by the first-order model

$$E(y) = 1 + 2x_1 + x_2$$

In other words, $\beta_0 = 1$, $\beta_1 = 2$, and $\beta_2 = 1$.

Now, when $x_2 = 0$, the relationship between $E(y)$ and x_1 is given by

$$E(y) = 1 + 2x_1 + (0) = 1 + 2x_1$$

A graph of this relationship (a straight line) is shown in Figure 13.3. Similar graphs of the relationship between $E(y)$ and x_1 for $x_2 = 1$,

$$E(y) = 1 + 2x_1 + (1) = 2 + 2x_1$$

and for $x_2 = 2$,

$$E(y) = 1 + 2x_1 + (2) = 3 + 2x_1$$

also are shown in Figure 13.3. Note that the slopes of the three lines are all equal to $\beta_1 = 2$, the coefficient that multiplies x_1.

Figure 13.3 exhibits a characteristic of all first-order models: If you graph $E(y)$ versus any one variable—say, x_1—for fixed values of the other variables, the result will always be a *straight line* with slope equal to β_1. If you repeat the process for other values of the fixed independent variables, you will obtain a set of *parallel* straight lines. This indicates that the effect of the independent variable x_i on $E(y)$ is independent of all the other independent variables in the model, and this effect is measured by the slope β_i (see the box on p. 769).

Figure 13.3
Graphs of $E(y) = 1 + 2x_1 + x_2$
for $x_2 = 0, 1, 2$

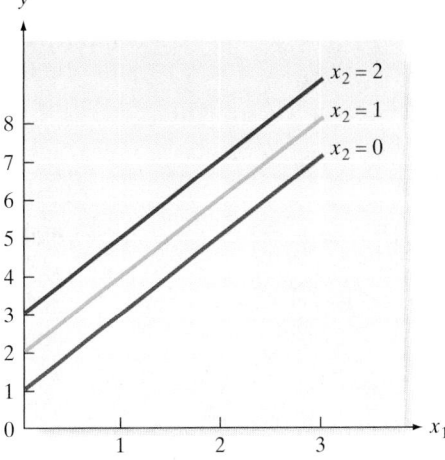

A three-dimensional graph of the model $E(y) = 1 + 2x_1 + x_2$ is shown in Figure 13.4. Note that the model graphs as a plane. If you slice the plane at a particular value of x_2 (say, $x_2 = 0$), you obtain a straight line relating $E(y)$ to x_1 (e.g., $E(y) = 1 + 2x_1$). Similarly, if you slice the plane at a particular value of x_1, you obtain a straight line relating $E(y)$ to x_2. Since it is more difficult to visualize three–dimensional and, in general, k-dimensional surfaces, we will graph all the models presented in this chapter in two dimensions. The key to obtaining these graphs is to hold fixed all but one of the independent variables in the model.

Figure 13.4

The plane
$E(y) = 1 + 2x_1 + x_2$

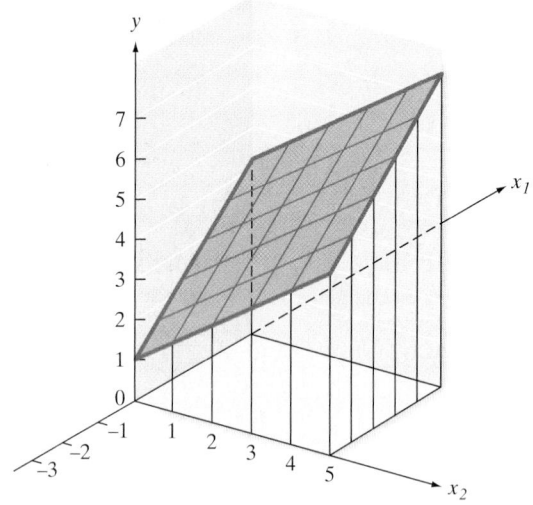

EXAMPLE 13.2   INTERPRETING THE β ESTIMATES

Problem   Refer to the first-order model for sale price y considered in Example 13.1. Interpret the estimates of the β parameters in the model.

Solution   The least squares prediction equation, as given in Example 13.1, is $\hat{y} = 1{,}470 + .8145x_1 + .8204x_2 + 13.53x_3$. We know that with first-order models β_1 represents the slope of the $y - x_1$ line for fixed x_2 and x_3. That is, β_1 measures the change in $E(y)$ for every 1-unit increase in x_1 when all other independent variables in the model are held fixed. Similar statements can be made about β_2 and β_3; e.g., β_2 measures the change in $E(y)$ for every 1-unit increase in x_1 when all other x's in the model are held fixed. Consequently, we obtain the following interpretations:

$\hat{\beta}_1 = .8145$:   We estimate the mean sale price of a property, $E(y)$, to increase .8145 dollar for every \$1 increase in appraised land value (x_1) when both appraised improvements (x_2) and area (x_3) are held fixed.

$\hat{\beta}_2 = .8204$:   We estimate the mean sale price of a property, $E(y)$, to increase .8204 dollar for every \$1 increase in appraised improvements (x_2) when both appraised land value (x_1) and area (x_3) are held fixed.

$\hat{\beta}_3 = 13.53$:   We estimate the mean sale price of a property, $E(y)$, to increase \$13.53 for each additional square foot of living area (x_3) when both appraised land value (x_1) and appraised improvements (x_2) are held fixed.

The value $\hat{\beta}_0 = 1{,}470$ does not have a meaningful interpretation in this example. To see this, note that $\hat{y} = \hat{\beta}_0$ when $x_1 = x_2 = x_3 = 0$. Thus, $\hat{\beta}_0 = 1{,}470$ represents the estimated mean price when the values of all the independent variables are set equal to 0. Since a residential property with these characteristics—appraised land value of $0, appraised improvements of $0, and 0 square feet of living area—is not practical, the value of $\hat{\beta}_0$ has no meaningful interpretation.

Look Back In general, $\hat{\beta}_0$ will not have a practical interpretation unless it makes sense to set the values of the x's simultaneously equal to 0.

Now Work *Exercise 13.8ab*

■ ■ ■

Caution

The interpretation of the β parameters in a multiple regression model will depend on the terms specified in the model. The interpretations above are for a first-order linear model only. In practice, you should be sure that a first-order model is the correct model for $E(y)$ before making these β interpretations. (We discuss alternative models for $E(y)$ in Sections 13.7–13.10.)

13.3 Model Assumptions

We noted in Section 13.1 that the general multiple regression model is of the form

$$y = \beta_0 + \beta_1 x_1 + \beta_2 x_2 + \cdots + \beta_k x_k + \epsilon$$

where y is the response variable that we wish to predict; $\beta_0, \beta_1, \ldots, \beta_k$ are parameters with unknown values; $x_1, x_2, \ldots, x_k$ are information-contributing variables that are measured without error; and ϵ is a random error component. Since $\beta_0, \beta_1, \ldots, \beta_k$ and $x_1, x_2, \ldots, x_k$ are nonrandom, the quantity

$$\beta_0 + \beta_1 x_1 + \beta_2 x_2 + \cdots + \beta_k x_k$$

represents the deterministic portion of the model. Therefore, y is composed of two components—one fixed and one random—and, consequently, y is a random variable.

$$y = \underbrace{\beta_0 + \beta_1 x_1 + \cdots + \beta_k x_k}_{\substack{\text{Deterministic} \\ \text{portion of model}}} + \underbrace{\epsilon}_{\substack{\text{Random} \\ \text{error}}}$$

We will assume (as in Chapter 12) that the random error can be positive or negative and that for any setting of the x values, $x_1, x_2, \ldots, x_k$, the random error ϵ has a normal probability distribution with mean equal to 0 and variance equal to σ^2. Further, we assume that the random errors associated with any (and every) pair of y values are probabilistically independent. That is, the error, ϵ, associated with any one y value is independent of the error associated with any other y value. These assumptions are summarized in the next box.

Assumptions for Random Error ϵ

1. For any given set of values of $x_1, x_2, \ldots, x_k$, the random error ϵ has a normal probability distribution with mean equal to 0 and variance equal to σ^2.

2. The random errors are independent (in a probabilistic sense).

Note that σ^2 represents the variance of the random error ϵ. As such, σ^2 is an important measure of the usefulness of the model for the estimation of the mean and the prediction of actual values of y. If $\sigma^2 = 0$, all the random errors will equal 0 and the predicted values, $\hat{y}$, will be identical to $E(y)$; that is $E(y)$ will be estimated without error. In contrast, a large value of σ^2 implies large (absolute) values of ϵ and larger deviations between the predicted values, $\hat{y}$, and the mean value, $E(y)$. Consequently, the larger the value of σ^2, the greater will be the error in estimating the model parameters $\beta_0, \beta_1, \ldots, \beta_k$ and the error in predicting a value of y for a specific set of values of $x_1, x_2, \ldots, x_k$. Thus, σ^2 plays a major role in making inferences about $\beta_0, \beta_1, \ldots, \beta_k$, in estimating $E(y)$, and in predicting y for specific values of $x_1, x_2, \ldots, x_k$.

Since the variance, σ^2, of the random error, ϵ, will rarely be known, we must use the results of the regression analysis to estimate its value. Recall that σ^2 is the variance of the probability distribution of the random error, ϵ, for a given set of values for $x_1, x_2, \ldots, x_k$; hence it is the mean value of the squares of the deviations of the y values (for given values of $x_1, x_2, \ldots, x_k$) about the mean value $E(y)$.* Since the predicted value, $\hat{y}$ estimates $E(y)$ for each of the data points, it seems natural to use

$$\text{SSE} = \sum (y_i - \hat{y}_i)^2$$

to construct an estimator of σ^2.

For example, in the first-order model of Example 13.2, we found that SSE = 1,003,491,259. We now want to use this quantity to estimate the variance of ϵ. Recall that the estimator for the straight-line model is $s^2 = \text{SSE}/(n - 2)$ and note that the denominator is $(n - \text{Number of estimated } \beta \text{ parameters})$, which is $(n - 2)$ in the straight-line model. Since we must estimate four parameters, $\beta_0, \beta_1, \beta_2$, and β_3 for the first-order model, the estimator of σ^2 is

$$s^2 = \frac{SSE}{n - 4}$$

The numerical estimate for this example is

$$s^2 = \frac{SSE}{20 - 4} = \frac{1,003,491,259}{16} = 62,718,204$$

Teaching Tip

The software that is used to fit the regression model we have selected will calculate values of the standard deviation. Students should concentrate on the interpretation of the standard deviation.

In many computer printouts and textbooks, s^2 is called the **mean square for error (MSE).** This estimate of σ^2 is shown in the column titled **MS** in the MINITAB printout in Figure 13.2.

The units of the estimated variance are squared units of the dependent variable y. Since the dependent variable y in this example is sale price in dollars, the units of s^2 are (dollars)^2. This makes meaningful interpretation of s^2 difficult, so we

---

*Since $y = E(y) + \epsilon, \epsilon$ is equal to the deviation $y - E(y)$. Also, by definition, the variance of a random variable is the expected value of the square of the deviation of the random variable from its mean. According to our model, $E(\epsilon) = 0$. Therefore, $\sigma^2 = E(\epsilon^2)$.

use the standard deviation s to provide a more meaningful measure of variability. In this example,

$$s = \sqrt{62{,}718{,}204} = 7{,}919.5$$

which is highlighted on the MINITAB printout in Figure 13.2 (next to **S =**). One useful interpretation of the estimated standard deviation s is that the interval $\pm 2s$ will provide a rough approximation to the accuracy with which the model will predict future values of y for given values of x. Thus, in Example 13.2, we expect the model to provide predictions of sale price to within about $\pm 2s = \pm 2(7{,}919.5) = \pm 15{,}839$ dollars.*

For the general multiple regression model

$$y = \beta_0 + \beta_1 x_1 + \beta_2 x_2 + \cdots + \beta_k x_k + \epsilon$$

we must estimate the $(k + 1)$ parameters $\beta_0, \beta_1, \beta_2, \ldots, \beta_k$. Thus, the estimator of σ^2 is SSE divided by the quantity $(n - \text{Number of estimated } \beta \text{ parameters})$.

We will use the estimator of σ^2 both to check the utility of the model (Sections 13.4 and 13.5) and to provide a measure of reliability of predictions and estimates when the model is used for those purposes (Section 13.6). Thus, you can see that the estimation of σ^2 plays an important part in the development of a regression model.

> **Estimator of σ^2 for a Multiple Regression Model with k Independent Variables**
>
> $$s^2 = \frac{\text{SSE}}{n - \text{Number of estimated } \beta \text{ parameters}} = \frac{\text{SSE}}{n - (k + 1)}$$

13.4 Inferences About the β Parameters

Inferences about the individual β parameters in a model are obtained using either a confidence interval or a test of hypothesis, as outlined in the following two boxes.**

> **A $100(1 - \alpha)\%$ Confidence Interval for a β Parameter**
>
> $$\hat{\beta}_i \pm t_{\alpha/2} s_{\hat{\beta}_i}$$
>
> where $t_{\alpha/2}$ is based on $n - (k + 1)$ degrees of freedom and
>
> $$n = \text{Number of observations}$$
>
> $$k + 1 = \text{Number of } \beta \text{ parameters in the model}$$

---

*The $\pm 2s$ approximation will improve as the sample size is increased. We will provide more precise methodology for the construction of prediction intervals in Section 13.6.
**The formulas for computing $\hat{\beta}_i$ and its standard error are so complex, the only reasonable way to present them is by using matrix algebra. We do not assume a prerequisite of matrix algebra for this text and, in any case, we think the formulas can be omitted in an introductory course without serious loss. They are programmed into almost all statistical software packages with multiple regression routines and are presented in some of the texts listed in the references.

Test of an Individual Parameter Coefficient in the Multiple Regression Model

One-Tailed Test	Two-Tailed Test
$H_0: \beta_i = 0$	$H_0: \beta_i = 0$
$H_a: \beta_i < 0 \ [\text{or } H_a: \beta_i > 0]$	$H_a: \beta_i \neq 0$

$$\text{Test statistic: } t = \frac{\hat{\beta}_i}{s_{\hat{\beta}_i}}$$

Rejection region: $t < -t_\alpha$ $[\text{or } t > t_\alpha \text{ when } H_a: \beta_i > 0]$	Rejection region: $\lvert t \rvert > t_{\alpha/2}$

where t_α and $t_{\alpha/2}$ are based on $n - (k + 1)$ degrees of freedom and

n = Number of observations

$k + 1$ = Number of β parameters in the model

Conditions Required for Valid Inferences about the β Parameters

The four assumptions about the probability distribution for the random error ϵ. (see Section 13.3.)

We illustrate these methods with another example.

EXAMPLE 13.3

MAKING INFERENCES ABOUT THE β PARAMETERS

Problem   A collector of antique grandfather clocks knows that the price received for the clocks increases linearly with the age of the clocks. Moreover, the collector hypothesizes that the auction price of the clocks will increase linearly as the number of bidders increases. Thus, the following first-order model is hypothesized:

$$y = \beta_0 + \beta_1 x_1 + \beta_2 x_2 + \epsilon$$

where

y = Auction price

x_1 = Age of clock (years)

x_2 = Number of bidders

A sample of 32 auction prices of grandfather clocks, along with their age and the number of bidders, is given in Table 13.2. The model $y = \beta_0 + \beta_1 x_1 + \beta_2 x_2 + \epsilon$ is fit to the data, and the EXCEL printout is shown in Figure 13.5.

a. $t = 9.847$

a. Test the hypothesis that the mean auction price of a clock increases as the number of bidders increases when age is held constant, that is, test $\beta_2 > 0$. Use $\alpha = .05$.

b. 12.74 ± 1.54

b. Form a 90% confidence interval for β_1 and interpret the result.

Solution   **a.** The hypotheses of interest concern the parameter β_2. Specifically,

GFCLOCKS

TABLE 13.2   Auction Price Data

Age, x_1	Number of Bidders, x_2	Auction Price, Y	Age, x_1	Number of Bidders, x_2	Auction Price, y
127	13	$1,235	170	14	$2,131
115	12	1,080	182	8	1,550
127	7	845	162	11	1,884
150	9	1,522	184	10	2,041
156	6	1,047	143	6	845
182	11	1,979	159	9	1,483
156	12	1,822	108	14	1,055
132	10	1,253	175	8	1,545
137	9	1,297	108	6	729
113	9	946	179	9	1,792
137	15	1,713	111	15	1,175
117	11	1,024	187	8	1,593
137	8	1,147	111	7	785
153	6	1,092	115	7	744
117	13	1,152	194	5	1,356
126	10	1,336	168	7	1,262

Regression Analysis

Regression Statistics	
Multiple R	0.94463957
R Square	0.892343916
Adjusted R Square	0.884919359
Standard Error	133.4846678
Observations	32

ANOVA

	df	SS	MS	F	Significance F
Regression	2	4283062.96	2141531.48	120.1881617	9.21636E-15
Residual	29	516726.5399	17818.15655		
Total	31	4799789.5			

	Coefficients	Standard Error	t Stat	P-value	Lower 90.0%	Upper 90.0%
Intercept	-1338.95134	173.8094707	-7.703558013	1.70581E-08	-1634.275722	-1043.62696
AGE	12.7405741	0.904740307	14.08202331	1.69276E-14	11.20330533	14.27784287
NUMBIDS	85.95298437	8.728523289	9.847368395	9.34495E-11	71.12211393	100.7838548

Figure 13.5
EXCEL analysis of auction price model for grandfather clocks

$$H_0: \beta_2 = 0$$
$$H_a: \beta_2 > 0$$

The test statistic is a t-statistic formed by dividing the sample estimate $\hat{\beta}_2$ of the parameter β_2 by estimated standard error of $\hat{\beta}_2$ (denoted $s_{\hat{\beta}_2}$). These estimates

Suggested Exercises 13.13

Teaching Tip
The *t*-test that we saw in Chapter 10 is still appropriate whenever a *single* parameter is to be tested.

as well as the calculated *t*-value are highlighted at the bottom of the EXCEL printout. These values yield the following:

$$\text{Test statistic: } t = \frac{\hat{\beta}_2}{s_{\hat{\beta}_2}} = \frac{85.953}{8.729} = 9.85$$

The rejection region for the test is found in exactly the same way as the rejection regions for the *t*-tests in previous chapters. That is, we consult Table VI in Appendix B to obtain an upper-tail value of *t*. This is a value t_α such that $P(t > t_\alpha) = \alpha$. We can then use this value to construct rejection regions for either one-tailed or two-tailed tests.

For $\alpha = .05$ and $n - (k + 1) = 32 - (2 + 1) = 29$ df, the critical *t* value obtained from Table VI is $t_{.05} = 1.699$. Therefore,

Rejection region: t > 1.699 (see Figure 13.6)

Figure 13.6
Rejection region for
$H_0: \beta_2 = 0$ *vs.* $H_a: \beta_2 > 0$

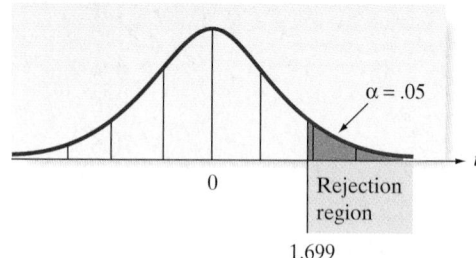

Since the test statistic value, $t = 9.85$, falls in the rejection region, we have sufficient evidence to reject H_0. Thus, the collector can conclude that the mean auction price of a clock increases as the number of bidders increases, when age is held constant. Note that the observed significance level of the test is also given on the printout. Since *p*-value ≈ 0, any nonzero α (e.g., $\alpha = .01$) will lead us to reject H_0.

b. A 90% confidence interval for β_1 is (from the box):

$$\hat{\beta}_1 \pm t_{\alpha/2} s_{\hat{\beta}_1} = \hat{\beta}_1 \pm t_{.05} s_{\hat{\beta}_1}$$

Substituting $\hat{\beta}_1 = 12.74$, $s_{\hat{\beta}_1} = .905$ (both obtained from the EXCEL printout, Figure 13.5) and $t_{.05} = 1.699$ (from part **a**) into the equation, we obtain

$$12.74 \pm 1.699(.905) = 12.74 \pm 1.54$$

or (11.20, 14.28). (This interval is also shown on the EXCEL printout, Figure 13.5.) Thus, we are 90% confident that β_1 falls between 11.20 and 14.28. Since β_1 is the slope of the line relating auction price (*y*) to age of the clock (x_1), we conclude that price increases between \$11.20 and \$14.28 for every 1-year increase in age, holding number of bidders (x_2) constant.

Look Back When interpreting the β multiplied by one *x*, be sure to hold fixed the values of the other *x*'s in the model.

Now Work *Exercise 13.7*

■ ■ ■

We conclude this section with a caution about t-tests on individual β parameters in a model.

Caution

It is dangerous to conduct t-tests on the individual β parameters in a *first-order linear model* for the purpose of determining which independent variables are useful for predicting y and which are not. If you fail to reject H_0: $\beta_i = 0$, several conclusions are possible:

1. There is no relationship between y and x_i.

2. A straight-line relationship between y and x exists (holding the other x's in the model fixed), but a Type II error occurred.

3. A relationship between y and x_i (holding the other x's in the model fixed) exists, but is more complex than a straight-line relationship (e.g., a curvilinear relationship may be appropriate). The most you can say about a β parameter test is that there is either sufficient (if you reject H_0: $\beta_i = 0$) or insufficient (if you do not reject H_0: $\beta_i = 0$) evidence of a *linear (straight-line)* relationship between y and x_i.

Exercises 13.1–13.17

Learning the Mechanics

13.1 Write a first-order model relating $E(y)$ to
  a. two quantitative independent variables
  b. four quantitative independent variables
  c. five quantitative independent variables

13.2 MINITAB was used to fit the model $E(y) = \beta_0 + \beta_1 x_1 + \beta_2 x_2$ to $n = 20$ data points and the printout shown below was obtained.
  a. What are the sample estimates of β_0, β_1, and β_2?
  b. What is the least squares prediction equation?

c. Find SSE, MSE, and s. Interpret the standard deviation in the context of the problem.
d. Test H_0: $\beta_1 = 0$ against H_a: $\beta_1 \neq 0$. Use $\alpha = .05$.
e. Use a 95% confidence interval to estimate β_2.

13.3 Suppose you fit the multiple regression model

$$y = \beta_0 + \beta_1 x_1 + \beta_2 x_2 + \beta_3 x_3 + \epsilon$$

to $n = 30$ data points and obtain the following result:

$$\hat{y} = 3.4 - 4.6x_1 + 2.7x_2 + .93x_3$$

MINITAB Output for Exercise 13.2

```
The regression equation is
Y = 506.35 - 941.9 X1 - 429.1 X2


Predictor     Coef   SE Coef      T      P
Constant   506.346     45.17  11.21  0.000
X1        -941.900    275.08  -3.42  0.003
X2        -429.060    379.83  -1.13  0.274


S = 94.251    R-Sq = 45.9%    R-Sq(adj) = 39.6%


Analysis of Variance

Source          DF       SS      MS      F      P
Regression       2   128329   64165   7.22  0.005
Residual Error  17   151016    8883
Total           19   279345
```

The estimated standard errors of $\hat{\beta}_2$ and $\hat{\beta}_3$ are 1.86 and .29, respectively.

a. Test the null hypothesis $H_0: \beta_2 = 0$ against the alternative hypothesis $H_a: \beta_2 \neq 0$. Use $\alpha = .05$.
   $t = 1.45$

b. Test the null hypothesis $H_0: \beta_3 = 0$ against the alternative hypothesis $H_a: \beta_3 \neq 0$. Use $\alpha = .05$.

c. The null hypothesis $H_0: \beta_2 = 0$ is not rejected. In contrast, the null hypothesis $H_0: \beta_3 = 0$ is rejected. Explain how this can happen even though $\hat{\beta}_2 > \hat{\beta}_3$

13.4 Suppose you fit the first-order multiple regression model

$$y = \beta_0 + \beta_1 x_1 + \beta_2 x_2 + \epsilon$$

to $n = 25$ data points and obtain the prediction equation

$$\hat{y} = 6.4 + 3.1 x_1 + .92 x_2$$

The estimated standard deviations of the sampling distributions of $\hat{\beta}_1$ and $\hat{\beta}_2$ are 2.3 and .27, respectively.

a. Test $H_0: \beta_1 = 0$ against $H_a: \beta_1 > 0$. Use $\alpha = .05$.

b. Test $H_0: \beta_2 = 0$ against $H_a: \beta_2 \neq 0$. Use $\alpha = .05$.

c. Find a 90% confidence interval for β_1. Interpret the interval. 3.1 ± 3.949

d. Find a 99% confidence interval for β_2. Interpret the interval. $.92 \pm .761$

13.5 How is the number of degrees of freedom available for estimating σ^2 (the variance of ϵ) related to the number of independent variables in a regression model?

13.6 Consider the first-order model equation in three quantitative independent variables

$$E(y) = 1 + 2x_1 + x_2 - 3x_3$$

a. Graph the relationship between y and x_1 for $x_2 = 1$ and $x_3 = 3$.

b. Repeat part **a** for $x_2 = -1$ and $x_3 = 1$.

c. How do the graphed lines in parts **a** and **b** relate to each other? What is the slope of each line?

d. If a linear model is first-order in three independent variables, what type of geometric relationship will you obtain when $E(y)$ is graphed as a function of one of the independent variables for various combinations of values of the other independent variables?

Applying the Concepts—Basic

13.7 Many tourists choose a vacation destination based on the newness or uniqueness (i.e., the novelty) of the itinerary. Texas A&M University professor J. Petrick investigated the relationship between novelty and vacationing golfers' demographics. (*Annals of Tourism Research*, Vol. 29, 2002.) Data were obtained from a mail survey of 393 golf vacationers to a large coastal resort in southeastern United States. Several measures of novelty level (on a numerical scale) were obtained

for each vacationer, including "change from routine," "thrill," "boredom-alleviation," and "surprise." The researcher employed four independent variables in a regression model to predict each of the novelty measures. The independent variables were $x_1 =$ number of rounds of golf per year, $x_2 =$ total number of golf vacations taken, $x_3 =$ number of years played golf, and $x_4 =$ average golf score.

a. Give the hypothesized equation of a first-order model for $y =$ change from routine.
   $y = \beta_0 + \beta_1 x_1 + \beta_2 x_2 + \beta_3 x_3 + \beta_4 x_4 + \epsilon$

b. A test of $H_0: \beta_3 = 0$ versus $H_a: \beta_3 < 0$ yielded a p-value of .005. Interpret this result if $\alpha = .01$.
   Reject H_0

c. The estimate of β_3 was found to be negative. Based on this result (and the result of part **b**), the researcher concluded that "those who have played golf for more years are less apt to seek change from their normal routine in their golf vacations." Do you agree with this statement? Explain.

13.8 In *Chance* (Fall 2000), statistician Scott Berry built a multiple regression model for predicting total number of runs scored by a Major League Baseball team during a season. Using data on all teams from 1990–1998 (a sample of $n = 234$), the following results were obtained.

Independent Variable	β Estimate	Standard Error
Intercept	3.70	15.00
Walks (x_1)	.34	.02
Singles (x_2)	.49	.03
Doubles (x_3)	.72	.05
Triples (x_4)	1.14	.19
Home Runs (x_5)	1.51	.05
Stolen Bases (x_6)	.26	.05
Caught Stealing (x_7)	-.14	.14
Strikeouts (x_8)	-.10	.01
Outs (x_9)	-.10	.01

Source: Berry, S. M. "A Statistician Reads the Sports Pages: Modeling Offensive Ability in Baseball," *Chance,* Vol. 13, No. 4, Fall 2000 (Table 2).

a. Write the least squares prediction equation for $y =$ total number of runs scored by a team in a season.

b. Interpret, practically, the β estimates in the model.

c. Conduct a test of $H_0: \beta_7 = 0$ against $H_a: \beta_7 < 0$ at $\alpha = .05$. Interpret the results. $t = -1.00$

d. Form a 95% confidence interval for β_5. Interpret the results. $1.51 \pm .098$

e. Predict the number of runs scored by your favorite Major League Baseball team last year. How close is the predicted value to the actual number of runs scored by your team? (*Note:* You can find data on your favorite team on the Internet at **www.majorleaguebaseball.com.**)

13.9 Detailed interviews were conducted with over 1,000 street vendors in the city of Puebla, Mexico, in order to study the factors influencing vendors' incomes (*World Development*, Feb. 1998). Vendors were defined as individuals working in the street, and included vendors with carts and stands on wheels and excluded beggars, drug dealers, and prostitutes. The researchers collected data on gender, age, hours worked per day, annual earnings, and education level. A subset of these data appear in the table.

a. Write a first-order model for mean annual earnings, $E(y)$, as a function of age (x_1) and hours worked (x_2).

b. The model was fit to the data using SPSS. Find the least squares prediction equation on the printout shown below.

c. Interpret the estimated β coefficients in your model.

d. Is age x_1 a statistically useful predictor of annual earnings? Test using $\alpha = .01$. $t = 1.74$

e. Construct a 95% confidence interval for β_2. Interpret the interval in the words of the problem.

STREETVN

Vendor Number	Annual Earnings, y	Age, x_1	Hours Worked per Day, x_2
21	$2841	29	12
53	1876	21	8
60	2934	62	10
184	1552	18	10
263	3065	40	11
281	3670	50	11
354	2005	65	5
401	3215	44	8
515	1930	17	8
633	2010	70	6
677	3111	20	9
710	2882	29	9
800	1683	15	5
914	1817	14	7
997	4066	33	12

Source: Adapted from Smith, Paula A., and Metzger, Michael R., "The Return to Education: Street Vendors in Mexico." *World Development*, Vol. 26, No. 2, Feb. 1998, pp. 289–296.

BWECS

13.10 Refer to the 2002 *Business Week* "Executive Compensation Scoreboard" data saved in the **BWECS** file. In Exercise 12.45 (p. 725), you used the method of least squares to model the straight-line relationship between total 2002 pay (y) and return (x) on a $100 investment made three years earlier for the 363 CEOs in the survey. Now consider the multiple regression model, $E(y) = \beta_0 + \beta_1 x_1 + \beta_2 x_2$, where y = total pay (in thousands of dollars), x_1 = return (in dollars), and x_3 = CEO performance rating (1 to 5 scale,

Model Summary

Model	R	R Square	Adjusted R Square	Std. Error of the Estimate
1	.763[a]	.582	.513	547.737

a. Predictors: (Constant), HOURS, AGE

ANOVA[b]

Model		Sum of Squares	df	Mean Square	F	Sig.
1	Regression	5018232	2	2509115.772	8.363	.005[a]
	Residual	3600196	12	300016.349		
	Total	8618428	14			

a. Predictors: (Constant), HOURS, AGE
b. Dependent Variable: EARNINGS

Coefficients[a]

Model		Unstandardized Coefficients B	Unstandardized Coefficients Std. Error	Standardized Coefficients Beta	t	Sig.	95% Confidence Interval for B Lower Bound	95% Confidence Interval for B Upper Bound
1	(Constant)	-20.352	652.745		-.031	.976	-1442.562	1401.858
	AGE	13.350	7.672	.326	1.740	.107	-3.365	30.066
	HOURS	243.714	63.512	.719	3.837	.002	105.334	382.095

a. Dependent Variable: EARNINGS

Regression Analysis: TOTCOMP versus RETURN, RATING

```
The regression equation is
TOTCOMP = 20205 + 42.5 RETURN - 5521 RATING


330 cases used, 33 cases contain missing values


Predictor      Coef   SE Coef      T      P
Constant      20205      2209   9.15  0.000
RETURN        42.47     12.42   3.42  0.001
RATING      -5521.1     707.9  -7.80  0.000


S = 13984.4   R-Sq = 15.7%   R-Sq(adj) = 15.2%


Analysis of Variance

Source           DF          SS          MS      F      P
Regression        2  11896137222  5948068611  30.42  0.000
Residual Error  327  63949098101   195562991
Total           329  75845235322
```

where 1 = best and 5 = worst). A MINITAB printout of the regression analysis is shown above.

a. Locate the least-squares estimates of the β coefficients on the printout and interpret their values practically.

b. Find the minimum value of SSE on the printout as well as the value of s. Interpret these values.

c. Test H_0: $\beta_2 = 0$ versus H_a: $\beta_2 < 0$ using $\alpha = .05$. Report your findings in the words of the problem. $t = -7.80$

d. Find a 95% confidence interval for β_1 and interpret it in the words of the problem. 42.47 ± 24.343

Applying the Concepts—Intermediate

13.11 Empirical research was conducted to investigate the variables that impact the size distribution of manufacturing firms in international markets (*World Development*, Vol. 20, 1992). Data collected on $n = 54$ countries were used to model the country's size distribution y, measured as the share of manufacturing firms in the country with 100 or more workers. The model studied was $E(y) = \beta_0 + \beta_1x_1 + \beta_2x_2 + \beta_3x_3 + \beta_4x_4 + \beta_5x_5$, where

x_1 = natural logarithm of Gross National Product (LGNP)

x_2 = geographic area per capita (in thousands of square meters)(AREAC)

x_3 = share of heavy industry in manufacturing value added (SVA)

x_4 = ratio of credit claims on the private sector to Gross Domestic Product (CREDIT)

x_5 = ratio of stock equity shares to Gross Domestic Product (STOCK)

a. The researchers hypothesized that the higher the credit ratio of a country, the smaller the size distribution of manufacturing firms. Explain how to test this hypothesis. H_0: $\beta_4 = 0$ vs H_a: $\beta_4 < 0$

b. The researchers hypothesized that the higher the stock ratio of a country, the larger the size distribution of manufacturing firms. Explain how to test this hypothesis. H_0: $\beta_5 = 0$ vs H_a: $\beta_5 > 0$

13.12 Refer to the U.S. Army Corps of Engineers data on fish contaminated from the toxic discharges of a chemical plant located on the banks of the Tennessee River in Alabama. Recall that the engineers measured the length (in centimeter), weight (in grams), and DDT level (in parts per million) for 144 captured fish. In addition, the number of miles upstream from the river was recorded. The data are saved in the **DDT** file. (The first and last five observations are shown in the accompanying table.)

DDT

River	Mile	Species	Length	Weight	DDT
FC	5	CHANNELCATFISH	42.5	732	10.00
FC	5	CHANNELCATFISH	44.0	795	16.00
FC	5	CHANNELCATFISH	41.5	547	23.00
FC	5	CHANNELCATFISH	39.0	465	21.00
FC	5	CHANNELCATFISH	50.5	1252	50.00
⋮	⋮	⋮	⋮	⋮	⋮
TR	345	LARGEMOUTHBASS	23.5	358	2.00
TR	345	LARGEMOUTHBASS	30.0	856	2.20
TR	345	LARGEMOUTHBASS	29.0	793	7.40
TR	345	LARGEMOUTHBASS	17.5	173	0.35
TR	345	LARGEMOUTHBASS	36.0	1433	1.90

a. Fit the first-order model, $E(y) = \beta_0 + \beta_1 x_1 + \beta_2 x_2 + \beta_3 x_3$, to the data, where y = DDT level, x_1 = mile, x_2 = length, and x_3 = weight. Report the least squares prediction equation.

b. Find the estimate of the standard deviation of ε for the model and give a practical interpretation of its value. $s = 97.48$

c. Do the data provide sufficient evidence to conclude that DDT level increases as length increases? Report the observed significance level of the test and reach a conclusion using $\alpha = .05$. $t = 2.33; p = .0105$

d. Find and interpret a 95% confidence interval for β_3. $-.049 \pm .057$

13.13 A disabled person's acceptance of a disability is critical to the rehabilitation process. The *Journal of Rehabilitation* (Sept. 1989) published a study that investigated the relationship between assertive behavior level and acceptance of disability in 160 disabled adults. The dependent variable, assertiveness (y), was measured using the Adult Self Expression Scale (ASES). Scores on the ASES range from 0 (no assertiveness) to 192 (extreme assertiveness). The model analyzed was $E(y) = \beta_0 + \beta_1 x_1 + \beta_2 x_2 + \beta_3 x_3$, where

x_1 = Acceptance of disability (AD) score
x_2 = Age (years)
x_3 = Length of disability (years)

The regression results are shown in the table.

Independent Variable	t	Two-Tailed p-Value
AD score (x_1)	5.96	.0001
Age (x_2)	0.01	.9620
Length (x_3)	1.91	.0576

a. Is there sufficient evidence to indicate that AD score is positively linearly related to assertiveness

level, once age and length of disability are accounted for? Test using $\alpha = .05$. $p = .00005$

b. Test the hypothesis $H_0: \beta_2 = 0$ against $H_a: \beta_2 \neq 0$ Use $\alpha = .05$. Give the conclusion in the words of the problem. $p = .9620$

c. Test the hypothesis $H_0: \beta_3 = 0$ against $H_a: \beta_3 > 0$. Use $\alpha = .05$. Give the conclusion in the words of the problem. $p = .0288$

13.14 Refer to the *Journal of Applied Ecology* (Vol. 32, 1995) study of the feeding habits of baby snow geese, Exercise 12.60 (p. 735). The data on gosling weight change, digestion efficiency, acid-detergent fiber (all measured as percentages) and diet (plants or duck chow) for 42 feeding trials are Saved in the **SNOWGEES** file. (The first and last five observations are shown in the table below.) The botanists were interested in predicting weight change (y) as a function of the other variables. Consider The first-order model $E(y) = \beta_0 + \beta_1 x_1 + \beta_2 x_2$, where x_1 is digestion efficiency and x_2 is acid-detergent fiber.

a. Find the least squares prediction equation for weight change, y.

b. Interpret the β-estimates in the equation, part **a.**

c. Conduct a test to determine if digestion efficiency, x_1, is a useful linear predictor of weight change. Use $\alpha = .01$. $P = .623$

d. Form a 99% confidence interval for β_2. Interpret the result. $-.4578 \pm .3469$

13.15 In the oil industry, water that mixes with crude oil during production and transportation must be removed. Chemists have found that the oil can be extracted from the water/oil mix electrically. Researchers at the University of Bergen (Norway) conducted a series of experiments to study the factors that influence the voltage (y) required to separate the water from the oil (*Journal of Colloid and Interface Science*, Aug. 1995). The seven independent variables investigated in the

---

SNOWGEES

Feeding Trial	Diet	Weight Change (%)	Digestion Efficiency (%)	Acid-Detergent Fiber (%)
1	Plants	−6	0	28.5
2	Plants	−5	2.5	27.5
3	Plants	−4.5	5	27.5
4	Plants	0	0	32.5
5	Plants	2	0	32
⋮	⋮	⋮	⋮	⋮
38	Duck Chow	9	59	8.5
39	Duck Chow	12	52.5	8
40	Duck Chow	8.5	75	6
41	Duck Chow	10.5	72.5	6.5
42	Duck Chow	14	69	7

Source: Gadallah, F. L. and Jefferies, R. L. "Forage quality in brood rearing areas of the lesser snow goose and the growth of captive goslings." *Journal of Applied Biology*, Vol. 32, No. 2, 1995, pp. 281–282 (adapted from Figures 2 and 3).

WATEROIL

Experiment Number	Voltage, y (kw/cm)	Disperse Phase Volume, x_1 (%)	Salinity, x_2 (%)	Temperature, x_3 (°C)	Time Delay, x_4 (hours)	Surfactant Concentration, x_5 (%)	Span: Triton, x_6	Solid Particles, x_7 (%)
1	.64	40	1	4	.25	2	.25	.5
2	.80	80	1	4	.25	4	.25	2
3	3.20	40	4	4	.25	4	.75	.5
4	.48	80	4	4	.25	2	.75	2
5	1.72	40	1	23	.25	4	.75	2
6	.32	80	1	23	.25	2	.75	.5
7	.64	40	4	23	.25	2	.25	2
8	.68	80	4	23	.25	4	.25	.5
9	.12	40	1	4	24	2	.75	2
10	.88	80	1	4	24	4	.75	.5
11	2.32	40	4	4	24	4	.25	2
12	.40	80	4	4	24	2	.25	.5
13	1.04	40	1	23	24	4	.25	.5
14	.12	80	1	23	24	2	.25	2
15	1.28	40	4	23	24	2	.75	.5
16	.72	80	4	23	24	4	.75	2
17	1.08	0	0	0	0	0	0	0
18	1.08	0	0	0	0	0	0	0
19	1.04	0	0	0	0	0	0	0

Source: Førdedal, H. et al. "A Multivariate Analysis of W/O Emulsions in High External Electric Fields as Studied by Means of Dielectric Time Domain Spectroscopy." *Journal of Colloid and Interface Science,* Vol. 173, No. 2, Aug. 1995, p. 398 (Table 2).

study are listed in the table above. (Each variable was measured at two levels—a "low" level and a "high" level.) Sixteen water/oil mixtures were prepared using different combinations of the independent variables; then each emulsion was exposed to a high electric field. In addition, three mixtures were tested when all independent variables were set to 0. The data for all 19 experiments are also given in the table.

a. Propose a first-order model for y as a function of all seven independent variables.

b. Use a statistical software package to fit the model to the data in the table.

c. Fully interpret the β estimates.

13.16 The owner of an apartment building in Minneapolis believed that her property tax bill was too high because of an overassessment of the property's value by the city tax assessor. The owner hired an independent real estate appraiser to investigate the appropriateness of the city's assessment. The appraiser used regression analysis to explore the relationship between the sale prices of apartment buildings sold in Minneapolis and various characteristics of the properties. Twenty-five apartment buildings were randomly sampled from all apartment buildings that were sold during a recent year. The table on page 787 lists the data collected by the appraiser. The real estate appraiser hypothesized that the sale price (that is, market value) of an apartment building is

related to the other variables in the table according to the model

$$y = \beta_0 + \beta_1 x_1 + \beta_2 x_2 + \beta_3 x_3 + \beta_4 x_4 + \beta_5 x_5 + \epsilon.$$

a. Fit the real estate appraiser's model to the data in the table. Report the least squares prediction equation.

b. Find the standard deviation of the regression model and interpret its value in the context of this problem.

c. Do the data provide sufficient evidence to conclude that value increases with the number of units in an apartment building? Report the observed significance level and reach a conclusion using $\alpha = .05$.

d. Interpret the value of $\hat{\beta}_1$ in terms of these data. Remember that your interpretation must recognize the presence of the other variables in the model.

e. Construct a scattergram of sale price versus age. What does your scattergram suggest about the relationship between these variables?

f. Test $H_0: \beta_2 = 0$ against $H_a: \beta_2 < 0$ using $\alpha = .01$ Interpret the result in the context of the problem. Does the result agree with your observation in part **e**? Why is it reasonable to conduct a one-tailed rather than a two-tailed test of this null hypothesis? $t = -2.86$

g. What is the observed significance level of the hypothesis test of part **f**? $p = .005$

MNSALES (Data for Exercise 13.16)

Code No.	Sale Price, y ($)	No. of Apartments, x_1	Age of Structure, x_2 (years)	Lot Size, x_3 (sq. ft)	No. of On-Site Parking Spaces, x_4	Gross Building Area, x_5 (sq. ft)
0229	90,300	4	82	4,635	0	4,266
0094	384,000	20	13	17,798	0	14,391
0043	157,500	5	66	5,913	0	6,615
0079	676,200	26	64	7,750	6	34,144
0134	165,000	5	55	5,150	0	6,120
0179	300,000	10	65	12,506	0	14,552
0087	108,750	4	82	7,160	0	3,040
0120	276,538	11	23	5,120	0	7,881
0246	420,000	20	18	11,745	20	12,600
0025	950,000	62	71	21,000	3	39,448
0015	560,000	26	74	11,221	0	30,000
0131	268,000	13	56	7,818	13	8,088
0172	290,000	9	76	4,900	0	11,315
0095	173,200	6	21	5,424	6	4,461
0121	323,650	11	24	11,834	8	9,000
0077	162,500	5	19	5,246	5	3,828
0060	353,500	20	62	11,223	2	13,680
0174	134,400	4	70	5,834	0	4,680
0084	187,000	8	19	9,075	0	7,392
0031	155,700	4	57	5,280	0	6,030
0019	93,600	4	82	6,864	0	3,840
0074	110,000	4	50	4,510	0	3,092
0057	573,200	14	10	11,192	0	23,704
0104	79,300	4	82	7,425	0	3,876
0024	272,000	5	82	7,500	0	9,542

Source: Robinson Appraisal Co., Inc., Mankato, Minnesota

Applying the Concepts—Advanced

13.17 The vineyards in the Bordeaux region of France are known for producing excellent red wines. However, the uncertainty of the weather during the growing season, the phenomenon that wine tastes better with age, and the fact that some Bordeaux vineyards produce better wines than others, encourages speculation concerning the value of a case of wine produced by a certain vineyard during a certain year (or vintage). As a result, many wine experts attempt to predict the auction price of a case of Bordeaux wine. The publishers of a newsletter titled *Liquid Assets: The International Guide to Fine Wine* discussed a multiple regression approach to predicting the London auction price of red Bordeaux wine in *Chance* (Fall 1995). The natural logarithm of the price y (in dollars) of a case containing a dozen bottles of red wine was modeled as a function of weather during growing season and age of vintage using data collected for the vintages of 1952–1980. Three models were fit to the data. The results of the regressions are summarized in the table below.

a. For each model, conduct a t-test for each of the β parameters in the model. Interpret the results.

b. When the natural log of y is used as a dependent variable, the antilogarithm of a β coefficient minus 1, that is $e^{\beta_i} - 1$, represents the percentage change in y for every 1-unit increase in the associated x value. Use this information to interpret the β estimates of each model.

Independent Variables	Beta Estimates (Standard Errors)		
	Model 1	Model 2	Model 3
x_1 = Vintage year	.0354 (.0137)	.0238 (.00717)	.0240 (.00747)
x_2 = Average growing season temperature (°C)	(not included)	.616 (.0952)	.608 (.116)
x_3 = Sept./Aug. rainfall (cm)	(not included)	−.00386 (.00081)	−.00380 (.00095)
x_4 = Rainfall in months preceding vintage (cm)	(not included)	.0001173 (.000482)	.00115 (.000505)
x_5 = Average Sept. temperature (°C)	(not included)	(not included)	.00765 (.565)

Source: Ashenfelter, O., Ashmore, D., and LaLonde, R. "Bourdeaux Wine Vintage Quality and Weather." *Chance*, Vol. 8, No. 4, Fall 1995, p. 116 (Table 2).

13.5 Checking the Overall Utility of a Model

Conducting t-tests on each β parameter in a model is *not* the best way to determine whether the overall model is contributing information for the prediction of y. If we were to conduct a series of t-tests to determine whether the independent variables are contributing to the predictive relationship, we would be very likely to make one or more errors in deciding which terms to retain in the model and which to exclude.

For example, suppose you fit a first-order model in 10 quantitative x variables and decide to conduct t-tests on all 10 of the individual β's in the model, each at $\alpha = .05$. Even if all the β parameters (except β_0) are equal to 0, approximately 40% of the time you will incorrectly reject the null hypothesis at least once and conclude that some β parameter differs from 0.* Thus, in multiple regression models for which a large number of independent variables are being considered, conducting a series of t-tests may include a large number of insignificant variables and exclude some useful ones. To test the utility of a multiple regression model, we need a *global test* (one that encompasses all the β parameters). We would also like to find some statistical quantity that measures how well the model fits the data.

We commence with the easier problem—finding a measure of how well a linear model fits a set of data. For this we use the multiple regression equivalent of r^2, the coefficient of determination for the straight-line model (Chapter 12), as shown in the box.

DEFINITION 13.1

The **multiple coefficient of determination, R^2**, is defined as

$$R^2 = 1 - \frac{\text{SSE}}{\text{SS}_{yy}} = \frac{\text{SS}_{yy} - \text{SSE}}{\text{SS}_{yy}} = \frac{\text{Explained variablilty}}{\text{Total variability}}$$

Just as for the simple linear model, R^2 represents the fraction of the sample variation of the y values (measured by SS_{yy}) that is explained by the least squares prediction equation. Thus, $R^2 = 0$ implies a complete lack of fit of the model to the data and $R^2 = 1$ implies a perfect fit with the model passing through every data point. In general, the larger the value of R^2, the better the model fits the data.

To illustrate, the value $R^2 = .897$ for the sale price model of Example 11.1 is indicated in Figure 13.7. This high value of R^2 implies that using the independent variables land value, appraised improvements, and home size in a first-order model explains 89.7% of the total *sample variation* (measured by SS_{yy}) of sale price y. Thus, R^2 is a sample statistic that tells how well the model fits the data and thereby represents a measure of the usefulness of the entire model.

A large value of R^2 computed from the *sample* data does not necessarily mean that the model provides a good fit to all of the data points in the *population*. For example, a first-order linear model that contains three parameters will provide a perfect fit to a sample of three data points and R^2 will equal 1. Likewise, you

*The proof of this result (assuming independence of tests) proceeds as follows:
$P(\text{Reject } H_0 \text{ at least once} | \beta_1 = \beta_2 = \cdots = \beta_{10} = 0)$
$= 1 - P(\text{Reject } H_0 \text{ no times} | \beta_1 = \beta_2 = \cdots = \beta_{10} = 0)$
$\leq 1 - [P(\text{Accept } H_0: \beta_1 = 0 | \beta_1 = 0) \cdot P(\text{Accept } H_0: \beta_2 = 0 | \beta_2 = 0) \cdot \cdots \cdot P(\text{Accept } H_0: \beta_{10} = 0 | \beta_{10} = 0)]$
$= 1 - [(1 - \alpha)^{10}] = 1 - (.05)^{10} = .401$
For dependent tests, the Bonferroni inequality states that
$P(\text{Reject } H_0 \text{ at least once } | \beta_1 = \beta_2 = \cdots = \beta_{10} = 0) \leq 10(\alpha) = 10(.05) = .50$.

Figure 13.7
MINITAB analysis of sale price model

Regression Analysis: SALEPRIC versus LANDVAL, IMPROVAL, AREA

```
The regression equation is
SALEPRIC = 1470 + 0.814 LANDVAL + 0.820 IMPROVAL + 13.5 AREA


Predictor     Coef   SE Coef      T      P
Constant      1470      5746   0.26  0.801
LANDVAL     0.8145    0.5122   1.59  0.131
IMPROVAL    0.8204    0.2112   3.88  0.001
AREA        13.529     6.586   2.05  0.057


S = 7919.48    R-Sq = 89.7%    R-Sq(adj) = 87.8%


Analysis of Variance

Source            DF           SS          MS       F      P
Regression         3   8779676741  2926558914   46.66  0.000
Residual Error    16   1003491259    62718204
Total             19   9783168000
```

Teaching Tip

Emphasize that even though the calculation of R^2 and Adjusted R^2 are different, we will interpret the values in the same manner.

will always obtain a perfect fit $(R^2 = 1)$ to a set of n data points if the model contains exactly n parameters. Consequently, if you want to use the value of R^2 as a measure of how useful the model will be for predicting y, it should be based on a sample that contains substantially more data points than the number of parameters in the model.

Caution

In a multiple regression analysis, use the value of R^2 as a measure of how useful a linear model will be for predicting y only if the sample contains substantially more data points than the number of β parameters in the model.

As an alternative to using R^2 as a measure of model adequacy, the *adjusted multiple coefficient of determination*, denoted R_a^2, is often reported. The formula for R_a^2 is shown in the box.

DEFINITION 13.2

The adjusted multiple coefficient of determination is given by

$$R_a^2 = 1 - \left[\frac{(n-1)}{n-(k+1)}\right]\left(\frac{\text{SSE}}{\text{SS}_{yy}}\right)$$

$$= 1 - \left[\frac{(n-1)}{n-(k+1)}\right](1 - R^2)$$

Note: $R_a^2 \leq R^2$

R^2 and R_a^2 have similar interpretations. However, unlike R^2, R_a^2 takes into account ("adjusts" for) both the sample size n and the number of β parameters in the model. R_a^2 will always be smaller than R^2, and more importantly, cannot be "forced" to 1 by simply adding more and more independent variables to the model. Consequently, analysts prefer the more conservative R_a^2 when choosing a measure of model adequacy. In Figure 13.7, R_a^2 is shown directly below the value of R^2. Note that $R_a^2 = .8782$, a value only slightly smaller than R^2.

Despite their utility, R^2 and R_a^2 are only sample statistics. Therefore, it is danger-ous to judge the global usefulness of the model based solely on these values. A better method is to conduct a test of hypothesis involving *all* the β parameters (except β_0) in a model. In particular, for the sale price model (Example 13.1), we would test

$$H_0: \beta_1 = \beta_2 = \beta_3 = 0$$

H_a: At least one of the coefficients is nonzero

The test statistic used to test this hypothesis is an *F*-statistic, and several equiv-alent versions of the formula can be used (although we will usually rely on the com-puter to calculate the *F*-statistic):

$$\text{Test statistic: } F = \frac{(SS_{yy} - SSE)/k}{SSE/[n - (k + 1)]} = \frac{R^2/k}{(1 - R^2)/[n - (k + 1)]}$$

Both these formulas indicate that the *F*-statistic is the ratio of the *explained* variability divided by the model degrees of freedom to the *unexplained* variability divided by the error degrees of freedom. Thus, the larger the proportion of the total variability accounted for by the model, the larger the *F*-statistic.

To determine when the ratio becomes large enough that we can confidently reject the null hypothesis and conclude that the model is more useful than no model at all for predicting y, we compare the calculated *F*-statistic to a tabulated *F* value with k df in the numerator and $[n - (k + 1)]$ df in the denominator. Recall that tabulations of the *F*-distribution for various values of α are given in Tables VIII, IX, X, and XI of Appendix B.

Rejection region: $F > F_\alpha$, where F is based on k numerator and $n - (k + 1)$ denominator degrees of freedom.

For the sale price example [$n = 20, k = 3, n - (k + 1) = 16$, and $\alpha = .05$], we will reject $H_0: \beta_1 = \beta_2 = \beta_3 = 0$ if

$$F > F_{.05} = 3.24$$

From the MINITAB printout (Figure 13.7), we find that the computed *F* value is 46.66. Since this value greatly exceeds the tabulated value of 3.24, we conclude that at least one of the model coefficients β_1, β_2, and β_3 is nonzero. Therefore, this **global *F*-test** indicates that the first-order model $y = \beta_0 + \beta_1 x_1 + \beta_2 x_2 + \beta_3 x_3 + \epsilon$ is useful for predicting sale price.

Like MINITAB, most other software packages give the *F*-value in a portion of the printout called the "Analysis of Variance." This is an appropriate descriptive term, since the *F*-statistic relates the explained and unexplained portions of the total variance of y. For example, the elements of the MINITAB printout in Figure 13.7 that lead to the calculation of the *F*-value are

$$F\text{-Value} = \frac{\text{Sum of Squares (Model)}/\text{df (Model)}}{\text{Sum of Squares (Error)}/\text{df (Error)}} = \frac{\text{Mean Square (Model)}}{\text{Mean Square (Error)}}$$

$$= \frac{8,779,676,741/3}{1,003,491,259/16} = \frac{2,926,558,914}{62,718,204} = 46.66$$

Note, too, that the observed significance level for the test is given next to the F-value as .000, which means that we would reject the null hypothesis H_0: $\beta_1 = \beta_2 = \beta_3 = 0$ at any α value selected.

The analysis of variance F-test for testing the usefulness of the model is summarized in the next box.

Teaching Tip

It is not wise to compare global F statistics of different regression models. The comparison test is shown in Section 13.11.

Testing Global Usefulness of the Model: The Analysis of Variance F-Test

H_0: $\beta_1 = \beta_2 = \cdots = \beta_k = 0$ (All model terms are unimportant for predicting y)

H_a: At least one $\beta_i \neq 0$ (At least one model term is useful for predicting y)

Test statistic:
$$F = \frac{(SS_{yy} - SSE)/k}{SSE/[n - (k + 1)]} = \frac{R^2/k}{(1 - R^2)/[n - (k + 1)]}$$
$$= \frac{\text{Mean Square (Model)}}{\text{Mean Square (Error)}}$$

where n is the sample size and k is the number of terms in the model.

Rejection region: $F > F_\alpha$, with k numerator degrees of freedom and $[n - (k + 1)]$ denominator degrees of freedom.

Conditions Required for the Global F-Test in Regression to Be Valid

The standard regression assumptions about the random error component (Section 13.3).

Caution

A rejection of the null hypothesis H_0: $\beta_1 = \beta_2 = \cdots = \beta_k$ in the global F-test leads to the conclusion [with $100(1 - \alpha)\%$ confidence] that the model is statistically useful. However, statistically "useful" does not necessarily mean "best." Another model may prove even more useful in terms of providing more reliable estimates and predictions. This global F-test is usually regarded as a test that the model *must* pass to merit further consideration.

EXAMPLE 13.4   ASSESSING THE GLOBAL UTILITY OF THE MODEL

Problem   Refer to Example 13.3, in which an antique collector modeled the auction price y of grandfather clocks as a function of the age of the clock, x_1, and the number of bidders, x_2. The hypothesized first-order model is

$$y = \beta_0 + \beta_1 x_1 + \beta_2 x_2 + \epsilon$$

A sample of 32 observations is obtained, with the results summarized in the EXCEL printout repeated in Figure 13.8.

Regression Analysis

Regression Statistics	
Multiple R	0.94463957
R Square	0.892343916
Adjusted R Square	0.884919359
Standard Error	133.4846678
Observations	32

ANOVA

	df	SS	MS	F	Significance F
Regression	2	4283062.96	2141531.48	120.1881617	9.21636E-15
Residual	29	516726.5399	17818.15655		
Total	31	4799789.5			

	Coefficients	Standard Error	t Stat	P-value	Lower 90.0%	Upper 90.0%
Intercept	-1338.95134	173.8094707	-7.703558013	1.70581E-08	-1634.275722	-1043.62896
AGE	12.7405741	0.904740307	14.08202331	1.69276E-14	11.20330533	14.27784287
NUMBIDS	85.95298437	8.728523289	9.847368395	9.34495E-11	71.12211393	100.7838548

Figure 13.8

EXCEL analysis of auction price model for grandfather clocks

a. $R_a^2 = .885$

b. $F = 120.19$

a. Find and interpret the adjusted coefficient of determination R_a^2 for this example.

b. Conduct the global F-test of model usefulness at the $\alpha = .05$ level of significance.

Solution

a. The R_a^2 value (highlighted in Figure 13.8) is .885. This implies that the least squares model has explained about 88.5% of the total sample variation in y values (auction prices), after adjusting for sample size and number of independent variables in the model.

Suggested Exercises 13.27

b. The elements of the global test of the model follow:

H_0: $\beta_1 = \beta_2 = 0$ (*Note: k = 2*)

H_a: At least one of the two model coefficients is nonzero

Test statistic: $F = 120.19$ (highlighted in Figure 13.8)

p-value ≈ 0

Conclusion: Since $\alpha = .05$ exceeds the observed significance level, $(p \approx 0)$, the data provide strong evidence that at least one of the model coefficients is nonzero. The overall model appears to be statistically useful for predicting auction prices.

Look Back Can we be sure that the best prediction model has been found if the global F-test indicates that a model is useful? Unfortunately, we cannot. The addition of other independent variables may improve the usefulness of the model. (See the box, p. 791.) We consider more complex multiple regression models in Sections 13.7–13.10.

■ ■ ■

To summarize the discussion in this section, both R^2 and R_a^2 are indicators of how well the prediction equation fits the data. Intuitive evaluations of the contribution of the model based on R^2 must be examined with care. Unlike R_a^2, the value of

R^2 increases as more and more variables are added to the model. Consequently, you could force R^2 to take a value very close to 1 even though the model contributes no information for the prediction of y. In fact, R^2 equals 1 when the number of terms in the model (including β_0) equals the number of data points. Therefore, you should not rely solely on the value of R^2 (or even R_a^2) to tell you whether the model is useful for predicting y. Use the F-test for testing the global utility of the model.

After we have determined that the overall model is useful for predicting y using the F-test, we may elect to conduct one or more t-tests on the individual β parameters (see Section 13.4). However, the test (or tests) to be conducted should be decided *a priori*, that is, prior to fitting the model. Also, we should limit the number of t-tests conducted to avoid the potential problem of making too many Type I errors. Generally, the regression analyst will conduct t-tests only on the "most important" β's. We provide insight in identifying the most important β's in a linear model in Sections 13.7–13.10.

Teaching Tip

Warn the students against conducting too many tests. If many tests are desired, reduce the α used for each test to control the overall chance of making a Type I error.

Recommendation for Checking the Utility of a Multiple Regression Model

1. First, conduct a test of overall model adequacy using the F-test, that is, test

$$H_0: \beta_1 = \beta_2 = \cdots = \beta_k = 0$$

If the model is deemed adequate (that is, if you reject H_0), then proceed to step 2. Otherwise, you should hypothesize and fit another model. The new model may include more independent variables or higher-order terms.

2. Conduct t-tests on those β parameters in which you are particularly interested (that is, the "most important" β's). These usually involve only the β's associated with higher-order terms ($x_2, x_1 x_2$, etc.). However, it is a safe practice to limit the number of β's that are tested. Conducting a series of t-tests leads to a high overall Type I error rate α.

Exercises 13.18–13.33

Learning the Mechanics

13.18 Suppose you fit the first-order model

$$y = \beta_0 + \beta_1 x_1 + \beta_2 x_2 + \beta_3 x_3 + \beta_4 x_4 + \beta_5 x_5 + \epsilon$$

to $n = 30$ data points and obtain

$$\text{SSE} = .33 \quad R^2 = .92$$

a. Do the values of SSE and R^2 suggest that the model provides a good fit to the data? Explain.

b. Is the model of any use in predicting y? Test the null hypothesis $H_0: \beta_1 = \beta_2 = \beta_3 = \beta_4 = \beta_5 = 0$ against the alternative hypothesis H_a: At least one of the parameters $\beta_1, \beta_2, \ldots, \beta_5$ is nonzero. Use $\alpha = .05$.

13.19 Refer to Exercise 13.2 (p. 781) and the MINITAB printout for the first-order model, $y = \beta_0 + \beta_1 x_1 + \beta_2 x_2 + \epsilon$

a. Find R^2 on the printout and interpret its value. .459

b. Find R_a^2 on the printout and interpret its value. .396

c. Test the null hypothesis that $\beta_1 = \beta_2 = 0$ against the alternative hypothesis that at least one of β_1 and β_2 is nonzero. Calculate the test statistic using the two formulas given in this section, and compare your results to each other and to that given on the printout. Use $\alpha = .05$ and interpret the result of your test. $F = 7.22$

d. Find the observed significance level for this test on the printout and interpret it. $p = .005$

13.20 If the analysis of variance F-test leads to the conclusion that at least one of the model parameters is nonzero, can you conclude that the model is the best predictor for the dependent variable y? Can you conclude that all of the terms in the model are important for predicting y? What is the appropriate conclusion?

13.21 Suppose you fit the first-order model

$$y = \beta_0 + \beta_1 x_1 + \beta_2 x_2 + \epsilon$$

to $n = 20$ data points and obtain

$$\Sigma(y_i - \hat{y}_i)^2 = 12.35 \qquad \Sigma(y_i - \bar{y})^2 = 24.44$$

a. Construct an analysis of variance table for this regression analysis, using the same format as the printout in Exercise 13.17. Be sure to include the sources of variability, the degrees of freedom, the sums of squares, the mean squares, and the F-statistic. Calculate R^2 and R_a^2 for the regression analysis.

b. Test the null hypothesis that $\beta_1 = \beta_2 = 0$ against the alternative hypothesis that at least one of the parameters differs from 0. Calculate the test statistic in two different ways and compare the results. Use $\alpha = .05$ to reach a conclusion about whether the model contributes information for the prediction of y.

Applying the Concepts—Basic

13.22 Refer to the *Annals of Tourism Research* (Vol. 29, 2002) study of the relationship between novelty and vacationing golfers' demographics, Exercise 13.7 (p. 782). The independent variables, x_1 = number of rounds of golf per year, x_2 = total number of golf vacations taken, x_3 = number of years played golf, and x_4 = average golf score, were used in a first-order model to predict a measure of novelty. The regression results for three dependent novelty measures, based on data collected for $n = 393$ golf vacationers, are summarized in the table.

Dependent Variable	F-value	p-value	R^2
Thrill	5.56	<.001	.055
Change from routine	3.02	.018	.030
Surprise	3.33	.011	.023

Source: Petrick, J. F. "An Examination of Golf Vacationers' Novelty," *Annals of Tourism Research*, Vol. 29, 2002.

a. Give the null hypothesis for testing the overall adequacy of the first-order regression model. H_0: $\beta_1 = \beta_2 = \beta_3 = \beta_4 = 0$

b. Give the rejection region for the test for $\alpha = .01$.

c. Use the test statistics reported in the table and the rejection region from part **b** to conduct the test for each of the dependent measures of novelty.

d. Verify that the p-values reported in the table support your conclusions in part **c**.

e. Interpret the values of R^2 reported in the table. .055; .030; .023

13.23 In a study of urban and rural counties in the western United States published in *Professional Geographer* (Feb. 2000), University of Nevada (Reno) researchers asked a sample of 256 county commissioners to rate their "home" county on a scale of 1 (most rural) to 10 (most urban). The urban/rural rating (y) was used as the dependent variable in a first-order multiple

regression model with six independent variables: total county population (x_1), population density (x_2), population concentration (x_3), population growth (x_4), proportion of county land in farms (x_5), and, 5-year change in agricultural land base (x_6). Some of the regression results are shown in the table.

Independent Variable	β Estimate	p-value
x_1: Total population	0.110	0.045
x_2: Population density	0.065	0.230
x_3: Population concentration	0.540	0.000
x_4: Population growth	−0.009	0.860
x_5: Farm land	−0.150	0.003
x_6: Agricultural change	−0.027	0.580

Overall model:
$R^2 = .44$ $\qquad$ $R_{adj}^2 = .43$ $\quad F = 32.47$ $\quad$ p-value < .001

Source: Berry, K. A., et al. "Interpreting What Is Rural and Urban for Western U.S. Counties," *Professional Geographer*, Vol. 52, No. 1, Feb. 2000 (Table 2).

a. Interpret the estimate of the β's for y.

b. Give the null hypothesis for testing overall model adequacy.

c. Conduct the test, part **b**, at $\alpha = .01$ and give the appropriate conclusion. $F = 32.47$

d. Interpret the values of R^2 and R_{adj}^2.

e. Give the null hypothesis for testing the contribution of population growth (x_4) to the model. H_0: $\beta_4 = 0$

f. Conduct the test, part **e**, at $\alpha = .01$ and give the appropriate conclusion. $P = .860$

⊛ **STREETVN**

13.24 Refer to the *World Development* (Feb. 1998) study of street vendors in the city of Puebla, Mexico, Exercise 13.9 (p. 783). Recall that the vendors' mean annual earnings $E(y)$ was modeled as a first-order function of age x_1 and hours worked x_2. Refer to the SPSS printout on p. 783 and answer the following:

a. Interpret the value of R^2. .582

b. Interpret the value of R_a^2. Explain the relationship between R^2 and R_a^2. .513

c. Conduct a test of the global utility of the model at $\alpha = .01$. Interpret the result. $F = 8.363$

⊛ **BWECS**

13.25 Refer to Exercise 13.10 (p. 783) and the multiple regression model, $E(y) = \beta_0 + \beta_1 x_1 + \beta_2 x_2$, where y = total CEO pay (in thousands of dollars), x_1 = return on a $100 investment made three years earlier (in dollars), and x_3 = CEO performance rating (1 to 5 scale, where 1 = best and 5 = worst).

a. Locate and interpret the value of the adjusted multiple coefficient of determination on the MINITAB printout (p. 784). .152

b. Give the null and alternative hypotheses for testing the overall adequacy of the model. $H_0: \beta_1 = \beta_2 = 0$

c. Locate the value of the test statistic and corresponding p-value for the test of part b on the MINITAB printout (p. 784). $F = 30.42; p = .000$

d. Conduct the test of part **b** using $\alpha = .05$ and state the conclusion in the words of the problem.   Reject H_0

Applying the Concepts—Intermediate

⊛ SNOWGEES

13.26 Refer to the *Journal of Applied Ecology* study of the feeding habits of baby snow geese, Exercise 13.14, (p. 785) and the model relating weight change (y) to digestion efficiency (x_1) and acid-detergent fiber (x_2).

a. Find the values of R^2 and R_a^2. Interpret these values. Which statistic is the preferred measure of model fit? Explain.   .529; .505

b. Find the global F value for testing the overall model. Use the statistic to test the null hypothesis $H_0: \beta_1 = \beta_2 = 0$.

13.27 The *Journal of Quantitative Criminology* (Vol. 8, 1992) published a paper on the determinants of area property crime levels in the United Kingdom. Several multiple regression models for property crime prevalence, y, measured as the percentage of residents in a geographical area who were victims of at least one property crime, were examined. The results for one of the models, based on a sample of $n = 313$ responses collected for the British Crime Survey, are shown in the table below. [*Note:* All variables except Density are expressed as a percentage of the base area.]

a. Test the hypothesis that the density (x_1) of a region is positively linearly related to crime prevalence (y), holding the other independent variables constant.

b. Do you advise conducting t-tests on each of the 18 independent variables in the model to determine which variables are important predictors of crime prevalence? Explain.   No

c. The model yielded $R^2 = .411$. Use this information to conduct a test of the global utility of the model. Use $\alpha = .05$ $F = 11.397$

13.28 External auditors are hired to review and analyze the financial and other records of an organization and to attest to the integrity of the organization's financial statements. In recent years, the fees charged by auditors have come under increasing scrutiny. S. Butterworth and K. A. Houghton, two University of Melbourne (Australia) researchers, investigated the effects of seven variables on the logarithm of the fee charged by auditors. The multiple regression model $E(y) = \beta_0 + \beta_1 x_1 + \beta_2 x_2 + \beta_3 x_3 + \cdots + \beta_7 x_7$ was fit to data collected for $n = 268$ companies. The results are summarized in the table on p. 796.

a. Write the least squares prediction equation.

b. Assess the overall fit of the model. $F = 111.1$

c. Interpret the estimate of β_3.   .384

d. The researchers hypothesized the direction of the effect of each independent variable on audit fees. These hypotheses are given in the "Expected Sign of β" column in the table on p. 796. (For example, if the expected sign is negative, the alternative hypothesis is $H_a: \beta_i < 0$.) Interpret the results of the hypothesis test for β_4. Use $\alpha = .05$. $t = 1.76$

Results for Exercise 13.27

Variable	$\hat{\beta}$	t	p-value
x_1 = Density (population per hectare)	.331	3.88	$p < .01$
x_2 = Unemployed male population	−.121	−1.17	$p > .10$
x_3 = Professional population	−.187	−1.90	$.01 < p < .10$
x_4 = Population aged less than 5	−.151	−1.51	$p > .10$
x_5 = Population aged between 5 and 15	.353	3.42	$p < .01$
x_6 = Female population	.095	1.31	$p > .10$
x_7 = 10-year change in population	.130	1.40	$p > .10$
x_8 = Minority population	−.122	−1.51	$p > .10$
x_9 = Young adult population	.163	5.62	$p < .01$
x_{10} = 1 if North region, 0 if not	.369	1.72	$.01 < p < .10$
x_{11} = 1 if Yorkshire region, 0 if not	−.210	−1.39	$p > .10$
x_{12} = 1 if East Midlands region, 0 if not	−.192	−0.78	$p > .10$
x_{13} = 1 if East Anglia region, 0 if not	−.548	−2.22	$.01 < p < .10$
x_{14} = 1 if South East region, 0 if not	.152	1.37	$p > .10$
x_{15} = 1 if South West region, 0 if not	−.151	−0.88	$p > .10$
x_{16} = 1 if West Midlands region, 0 if not	−.308	−1.93	$.01 < p < .10$
x_{17} = 1 if North West region, 0 if not	.311	2.13	$.01 < p < .10$
x_{18} = 1 if Wales region, 0 if not	−.019	−0.08	$p > .10$

Source: Osborn, D. R., Tickett, A., and Elder, R. "Area Characteristics and Regional Variates as Determinants of Area Property Crime." *Journal of Quantitative Criminology,* Vol. 8, No. 3, 1992, Plenum Publishing Corp.

Results for Exercise 13.28

Independent Variable	Expected Sign of β	β Estimate	t Value	Level of Significance (p-Value)
Constant	−	−4.30	−3.45	.001 (two-tailed)
$x_1 = \begin{cases} 1 \text{ if auditee changed auditors after one year} \\ 0 \text{ if not} \end{cases}$	+	−.002	−0.049	.961 (one-tailed)
$x_2 = $ Logarithm of auditee's total assets	+	.336	9.94	.000 (one-tailed)
$x_3 = $ Number of subsidiaries of auditee	+	.384	7.63	.000 (one-tailed)
$x_4 = \begin{cases} 1 \text{ if auditee receives an audit qualification} \\ 0 \text{ if not} \end{cases}$	+	.067	1.76	.079 (one-tailed)
$x_5 = \begin{cases} 1 \text{ if auditee in mining industry} \\ 0 \text{ if not} \end{cases}$	−	−.143	−4.05	.000 (one-tailed)
$x_6 = \begin{cases} 1 \text{ if auditee is a member of a "Big 8" firm} \\ 0 \text{ if not} \end{cases}$	+	.081	2.18	.030 (one-tailed)
$x_7 = $ Logarithm of dollar-value of non-audit services provided by auditor	+/−	.134	4.54	.000 (two-tailed)
$R^2 = .712$		$F = 111.1$		

Source: Butterworth, S., and Houghton, K. A. "Auditor Switching: The Pricing of Audit Services." *Journal of Business Finance and Accounting,* Vol. 22, No. 3, April 1995, p. 334 (Table 4).

e. The main objective of the analysis was to determine whether new auditors charge less than incumbent auditors in a given year. If this hypothesis is true, then the true value of β_1 is negative. Is there evidence to support this hypothesis? Explain. $t = -.049$

13.29 An important goal in occupational safety is "active caring." Employees demonstrate active caring (AC) about the safety of their coworkers when they identify environmental hazards and unsafe work practices and then implement appropriate corrective actions for these unsafe conditions or behaviors. Three factors hypothesized to increase the propensity for an employee to actively care for safety are (1) high self-esteem, (2) optimism, and (3) group cohesiveness. *Applied & Preventive Psychology* (Winter 1995) attempted to establish empirical support for the AC hypothesis by fitting the model $E(y) = \beta_0 + \beta_1 x_1 + \beta_2 x_2 + \beta_3 x_3$, where

$y = $ AC score (measuring active caring on a 15-point scale)
$x_1 = $ Self-esteem score
$x_2 = $ Optimism score
$x_3 = $ Group cohesion score

The regression analysis, based on data collected for $n = 31$ hourly workers at a large fiber-manufacturing plant, yielded a multiple coefficient of determination of $R^2 = .362$.
a. Interpret the value of R^2.
b. Use the R^2 value to test the global utility of the model. Use $\alpha = .05$. $F = 5.11$

13.30 Regression analysis was employed to investigate the determinants of survival size of nonprofit hospitals (*Applied Economics*, Vol. 18, 1986). For a given sample of hospitals, survival size, y, is defined as the largest size hospital (in terms of number of beds) exhibiting growth in market share over a specific time interval. Suppose 10 states are randomly selected and the survival size for all nonprofit hospitals in each state is determined for two time periods five years apart, yielding two observations per state. The 20 survival sizes are listed in the table, along with the following data for each state, for the second year in each time interval:

SURVIVAL

State	Time period	Survival size, y	x_1	x_2	x_3	x_4
1	1	370	.13	.09	5,800	89
1	2	390	.15	.09	5,955	87
2	1	455	.08	.11	17,648	87
2	2	450	.10	.16	17,895	85
3	1	500	.03	.04	7,332	79
3	2	480	.07	.05	7,610	78
4	1	550	.06	.005	11,731	80
4	2	600	.10	.005	11,790	81
5	1	205	.30	.12	2,932	44
5	2	230	.25	.13	3,100	45
6	1	425	.04	.01	4,148	36
6	2	445	.07	.02	4,205	38
7	1	245	.20	.01	1,574	25
7	2	200	.30	.01	1,560	28
8	1	250	.07	.08	2,471	38
8	2	275	.08	.10	2,511	38
9	1	300	.09	.12	4,060	52
9	2	290	.12	.20	4,175	54
10	1	280	.10	.02	2,902	37
10	2	270	.11	.05	2,925	38

Source: Adapted from Bays, C. W. "The Determinants of Hospital Size: A Survivor Analysis." *Applied Economics,* 1986, Vol. 18, pp. 359–377.

x_1 = Percentage of beds that are for-profit hospitals

x_2 = Ratio of the number of persons enrolled in health maintenance organizations (HMOs)to the number of persons covered by hospital insurance

x_3 = State population (in thousands)

x_4 = Percent of state that is urban

The article hypothesized that the following model characterizes the relationship between survival size and the four variables just listed:

$$y = \beta_0 + \beta_1 x_1 + \beta_2 x_2 + \beta_3 x_3 + \beta_4 x_4 + \epsilon$$

a. Fit the model to the data and report the least squares prediction equation.

b. Find the regression standard deviation s and interpret its value in the context of the problem.

c. Use an F-test to investigate the usefulness of the hypothesized model. Report the observed significance level, and use $\alpha = .025$ to reach your conclusion.

d. Prior to collecting the data it was hypothesized that increases in the number of for-profit hospital beds would decrease the survival size of nonprofit hospitals. Do the data support this hypothesis? Test using $\alpha = .05$. $t = -3.20$

13.31 Because the coefficient of determination R^2 always increases when a new independent variable is added to the model, it is tempting to include many variables in a model to force R^2 to be near 1. However, doing so reduces the degrees of freedom available for estimating σ^2, which adversely affects our ability to make reliable inferences. Suppose you want to use 18 economic indicators to predict next year's Gross Domestic Product (GDP). You fit the model

$$y = \beta_0 + \beta_1 x_1 + \beta_2 x_2 + \cdots + \beta_{17} x_{17} + \beta_{18} x_{18} + \epsilon$$

where y = GDP and $x_1, x_2, \ldots, x_{18}$ are the economic indicators. Only 20 years of data ($n = 20$) are used to fit the model, and you obtain $R^2 = .95$. Test to see whether this impressive-looking R^2 is large enough for you to infer that the model is useful, that is, that at least one term in the model is important for predicting GDP. Use $\alpha = .05$.

Applying the Concepts—Advanced

13.32 Multiple regression is used by accountants in cost analysis to shed light on the factors that cause costs to be incurred and the magnitudes of their effects. The independent variables of such a regression model are the factors believed to be related to cost,

the dependent variable. In some instances, however, it is desirable to use physical units instead of cost as the dependent variable in a cost analysis. This would be the case if most of the cost associated with the activity of interest is a function of some physical unit, such as hours of labor. The advantage of this approach is that the regression model will provide estimates of the number of labor hours required under different circumstances and these hours can then be costed at the current labor rate (Horngren, Foster, and Datar, 1994). The sample data shown in the table on page 798 have been collected from a firm's accounting and production records to provide cost information about the firm's shipping department. Consider the model $y = \beta_0 + \beta_1 x_1 + \beta_2 x_2 + \beta_3 x_3 + \epsilon$.

a. Find the least squares prediction equation.

b. Use an F-test to investigate the usefulness of the model specified in part **a.** Use $\alpha = .01$, and state your conclusion in the context of the problem.

c. Test H_0: $\beta_2 = 0$ versus H_a: $\beta_2 \neq 0$ using $\alpha = .05$. What do the results of your test suggest about the magnitude of the effects of x_2 on labor costs?

d. Find R^2, and interpret its value in the context of the problem. .770

e. If shipping department employees are paid $7.50 per hour, how much less, on average, will it cost the company per week if the average number of pounds per shipment increases from a level of 20 to 21? Assume that x_1 and x_2 remain unchanged. Your answer is an estimate of what is known in economics as the *expected marginal cost* associated with a one-pound increase in x_3.

f. With what approximate precision can this model be used to predict the hours of labor? [*Note:* The precision of multiple regression predictions is discussed in Section 13.6.]

g. Can regression analysis alone indicate what factors *cause* costs to increase? Explain.

13.33 Refer to the *Liquid Assets* study of auction prices of red Bordeaux wine, Exercise 13.17 (p. 787). The three models for auction price (y) have R^2 and s values as shown in the accompanying table. Based on this information, which of the three models would you use to predict red Bordeaux wine prices? Explain.

	R^2	s
Model 1	.212	.575
Model 2	.828	.287
Model 3	.828	.293

SHIPDEPT (Data for Exercise 13.32)

Week	Labor, y (hrs.)	Pounds Shipped, x_1 (1,000s)	Percentage of Units Shipped by Truck, x_2	Average Shipment Weight, x_3 (lbs.)
1	100	5.1	90	20
2	85	3.8	99	22
3	108	5.3	58	19
4	116	7.5	16	15
5	92	4.5	54	20
6	63	3.3	42	26
7	79	5.3	12	25
8	101	5.9	32	21
9	88	4.0	56	24
10	71	4.2	64	29
11	122	6.8	78	10
12	85	3.9	90	30
13	50	3.8	74	28
14	114	7.5	89	14
15	104	4.5	90	21
16	111	6.0	40	20
17	110	8.1	55	16
18	100	2.9	64	19
19	82	4.0	35	23
20	85	4.8	58	25

13.6 Using the Model for Estimation and Prediction

In Section 10.8 we discussed the use of the least squares line for estimating the mean value of y, $E(y)$, for some particular value of x, say $x = x_p$. We also showed how to use the same fitted model to predict, when $x = x_p$, some new value of y to be observed in the future. Recall that the least squares line yielded the same value for both the estimate of $E(y)$ and the prediction of some future value of y. That is, both are the result of substituting x_p into the prediction equation $\hat{y} = \hat{\beta}_0 + \hat{\beta}_1 x$ and calculating $\hat{y}_p$. There the equivalence ends. The confidence interval for the mean $E(y)$ is narrower than the prediction interval for y because of the additional uncertainty attributable to the random error ϵ when predicting some future value of y.

These same concepts carry over to the multiple regression model. Consider, again, the first-order model relating sale price of a residential property to land value (x_1), improvements (x_2), and home size (x_3). Suppose we want to estimate the mean sale price for a given property with $x_1 = \$15,000$, $x_2 = \$50,000$, and $x_3 = 1,800$ square feet. Assuming that the first-order model represents the true relationship between sale price and the three independent variables, we want to estimate

$$E(y) = \beta_0 + \beta_1 x_1 + \beta_2 x_2 + \beta_3 x_3 = \beta_0 + \beta_1(15,000) + \beta_2(50,000) + \beta_3(1,800)$$

Substituting into the least squares prediction equation, we find the estimate of $E(y)$ to be

$$\hat{y} = \hat{\beta}_0 + \hat{\beta}_1(15,000) + \hat{\beta}_2(50,000) + \hat{\beta}_3(1,800)$$
$$= 1,470.27 + .814(50,000) + .820(50,000) + 13.529(1,800) = 79,061.4$$

To form a confidence interval for the mean, we need to know the standard deviation of the sampling distribution for the estimator $\hat{y}$. For multiple regression

Figure 13.9
MINITAB printout with
95% confidence and
prediction intervals

```
Predicted Values for New Observations

New
Obs    Fit  SE Fit        95% CI              95% PI
  1  79061    2680  (73381, 84742)    (61338, 96785)


Values of Predictors for New Observations

New
Obs  LANDVAL  IMPROVAL  AREA
  1    15000     50000  1800
```

Teaching Tip

As in simple linear regression, the prediction interval will always be wider than the confidence interval. Both intervals will again be narrowest when the values of the independent variables are all equal to their mean values.

models, the form of this standard deviation is rather complex. However, the regression routines of statistical computer software packages allow us to obtain the confidence intervals for mean values of y for any given combination of values of the independent variables. A portion of the MINITAB output for the sale price example is shown in Figure 13.9.

In addition to the 95% confidence interval for the mean (highlighted under the **95% CI** column), the MINITAB printout gives the selected x-values (highlighted at the bottom of the printout), and the value of $\hat{y} = 79,061$ (highlighted under the **Fit** column). From the 95% confidence interval for the mean, (73,381, 84,742), we can infer (with 95% confidence) that the mean sale price for all properties with $x_1 = \$15,000$, $x_2 = \$50,000$, and $x_3 = 1,800$ square feet will fall between \$73,381 and \$84,742.

If we were interested in predicting the sale price for a particular (single) property with $x_1 = \$15,000$, $x_2 = \$50,000$, and $x_3 = 1,800$ square feet, we would use $\hat{y} = \$79,061$ as the predicted value. However, the prediction interval for a new value of y is wider than the confidence interval for $E(y)$. The 95% prediction interval (highlighted on the MINITAB printout under the **95% PI** column) is (61,338, 96,785). Thus, with 95% confidence, we conclude that the sale price for an individual property with the characteristics $x_1 = \$15,000$, $x_2 = \$50,000$, and $x_3 = 1,800$ square feet will fall between \$61,338 and \$96,785.

Now Work *Exercise 13.34*

Statistics in Action Revisited

A First-Order Model for Road Contract Cost

The Florida Attorney General wants to develop a model for the cost (y) of a road construction contract awarded using the sealed-bid system and to use the model to predict the costs of future road contracts in the state. In addition to contract cost, the FLAG file contains data on eight potential predictor variables for a sample of 235 road contracts. (See Table SIA13.1 on p. 767.) MINITAB scatterplots (with the dependent variable, COST, plotted against each of the potential predictors) for the data are shown in Figure SIA13.1. From the scatterplots, it appears that the DOT engineer's cost estimate

(DOTEST) and estimate of work days (DAYSEST) would be good predictors of contract cost. [In a future Statistics in Action Revisited section (p. 857), we will learn that the two best predictors of contract cost are actually DOTEST and the fixed or competitive status (STATUS) of the contract.] However, in this section, we will fit the first-order regression model using all eight independent variables.

The MINITAB printout for the regression analysis is shown in Figure SIA13.2. The global F-statistic ($F = 1166.68$) and associated p-value (.000) shown on the printout indicate that the overall model is statistically useful for predicting construction cost. The value of R^2

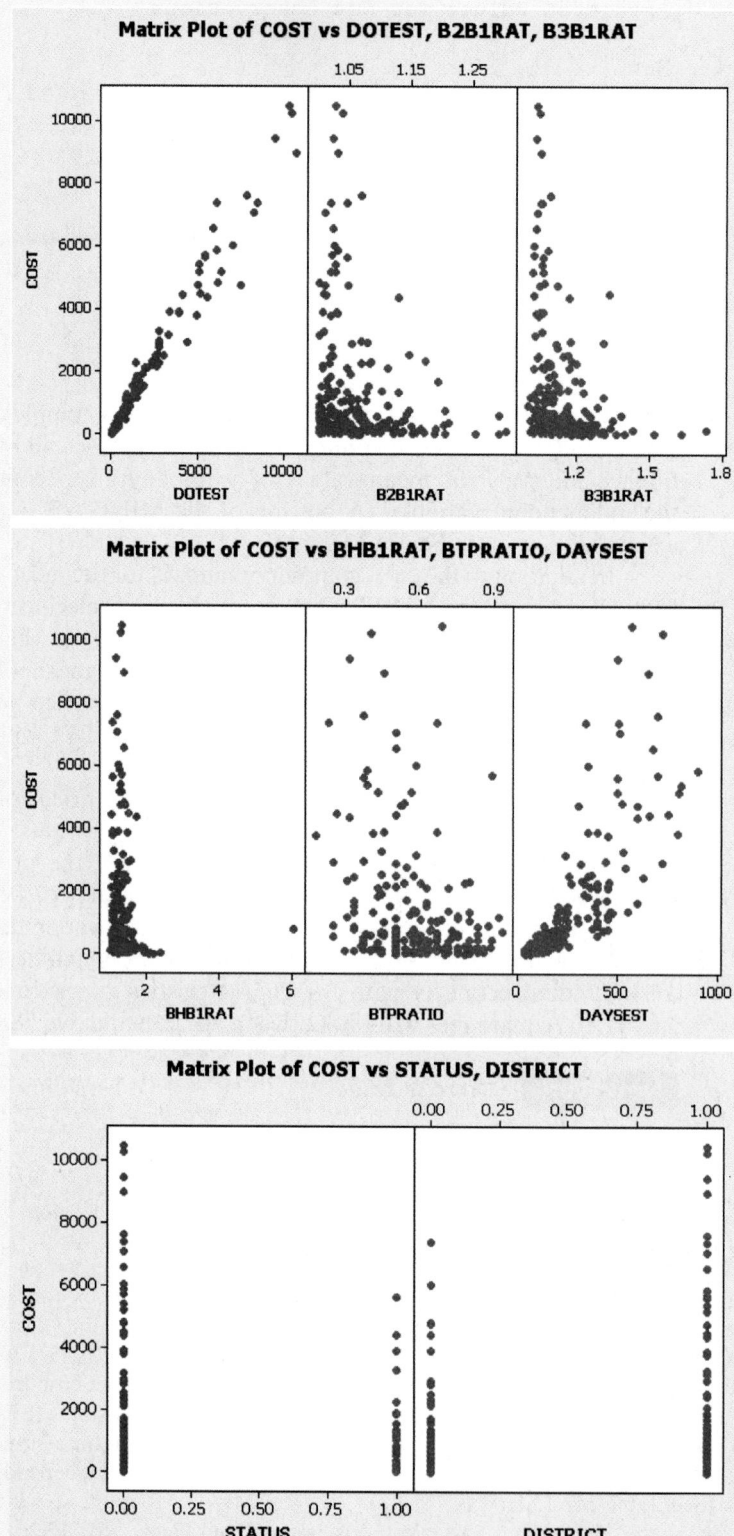

Figure SIA13.1
MINITAB scatterplots for FLAG data

```
The regression equation is
COST = 124 + 0.906 DOTEST - 147 B2B1RAT - 84 B3B1RAT - 59.1 BHB1RAT + 148 STA>>
       + 37.8 DISTRICT + 218 BTPRATIO + 0.344 DAYSEST


Predictor      Coef   SE Coef      T      P
Constant      123.9     426.8   0.29  0.772
DOTEST      0.90647   0.01659  54.64  0.000
B2B1RAT      -147.1     419.0  -0.35  0.726
B3B1RAT       -83.8     245.4  -0.34  0.733
BHB1RAT      -59.09     54.90  -1.08  0.283
STATUS       148.16     51.48   2.88  0.004
DISTRICT      37.75     43.07   0.88  0.382
BTPRATIO      217.6     139.6   1.56  0.120
DAYSEST      0.3439    0.1803   1.91  0.058


S = 304.589   R-Sq = 97.6%   R-Sq(adj) = 97.6%


Analysis of Variance

Source           DF          SS          MS         F      P
Regression        8   865907936   108238492   1166.68  0.000
Residual Error  226    20967037       92774
Total           234   886874973
```

Figure SIA13.2

MINITAB regression output for first-order model of road construction cost

indicates that the model can explain 97.6% of the sample variation in contract cost. Both of these results provide strong statistical support for using the model for estimation and prediction.

[*Note:* Not all of the independent variables have statistically significant *t*-values. However, we caution against dropping the insignificant variables from the model at this stage. One reason (discussed in this section) is that per-

forming a large number of *t*-tests will yield an inflated probability of at least one Type I error. In later sections of this chapter, we develop other reasons for why the multiple *t*-test approach is not a good strategy for determining which independent variables to keep in the model.]

The MINITAB printout shown in Figure SIA13.3 gives a 95% prediction interval for cost and a 95% confidence interval for the mean cost for the *x*-values associated

```
Predicted Values for New Observations

New
Obs    Fit   SE Fit      95% CI             95% PI
  1  433.7     48.0  (339.2, 528.2)   (-173.9, 1041.2)


Values of Predictors for New Observations

New
Obs  DOTEST  B2B1RAT  B3B1RAT  BHB1RAT    STATUS  DISTRICT  BTPRATIO  DAYSEST
  1     497     1.07     1.08     1.19  0.000000      1.00     0.500     90.0
```

Figure SIA13.3

MINITAB printout with 95% confidence and prediction intervals

with the last observation (contract) in the FLAG file. These x-values are engineer's cost estimate (DOTEST) = 497 thousand dollars, ratio of second lowest bid to lowest bid (B2B1RAT) = 1.07, ratio of third lowest bid to lowest bid (B3B1RAT) = 1.08, ratio of highest bid to lowest bid (BHB1RAT) = 1.19, competitive bid (STATUS = 0), south Florida contract (DISTRICT = 1), bidders to planholders ratio (BTPRATIO) = 0.5, and estimated work days (DAYSEST) = 90. The 95% confidence interval of (339.2, 528.2) implies that for all road contracts with these x-values, the mean contract cost falls between 339.2 and 528.2 thousand dollars, with 95% confidence.

The 95% prediction interval of (−173.9, 1041.2) implies that for an individual road contract with these x-values, the contract cost falls between 0 (since cost cannot be negative) and 1,041.2 thousand dollars, with 95% confidence. Note the wide range of the prediction interval. This is due to the large magnitude of the model standard deviation, $s = 305$ thousand dollars. Although the model is deemed statistically useful for predicting contract cost, it may not be "practically" useful. To reduce the magnitude of s, we will need to improve the model's predictive ability. (We consider such a model in the next Statistics in Action Revisited section.)

Exercises 13.34–13.40

Applying the Concepts—Basic

⊘ STREETVN

13.34 Refer to the *World Development* (Feb. 1998) study of street vendors' earnings, y, Exercise 13.9 (p. 783). The accompanying SPSS spreadsheet shows both a 95% prediction interval for y (right side) and a 95% confidence interval for $E(y)$ (left side) for a 45-year-old vendor who works 10 hours a day (i.e., for $x_1 = 45$ and $x_2 = 10$).
  a. Interpret the 95% prediction interval for y in the words of the problem.
  b. Interpret the 95% confidence interval for $E(y)$ in the words of the problem.
  c. Note that the interval of part **a** is wider than the interval of part **b**. Will this always be true? Explain.

⊘ BWECS

13.35 Refer to Exercise 13.10 (p. 783) and the multiple regression model, $E(y) = \beta_0 + \beta_1 x_1 + \beta_2 x_2$, where y = total CEO pay (in thousands of dollars), x_1 = return on a $100 investment made three years earlier (in dollars), and x_2 = CEO performance rating (1 to 5 scale, where 1 = best and 5 = worst). A MINITAB printout with both a 95% confidence interval for $E(y)$ and prediction interval for y when $x_1 = 200$ and $x_2 = 4$ is shown below.
  a. Interpret the 95% prediction interval for y in the words of the problem.
  b. Interpret the 95% confidence interval for $E(y)$ in the words of the problem.
  c. Will the confidence interval for $E(y)$ always be narrower than the prediction interval for y? Explain. Yes

SPSS Output for Exercise 13.34

age	hours	ci95low	ci95upp	pi95low	pi95upp
45	10	2620.25197	3414.87349	1759.74674	4275.37871

MINITAB Output for Exercise 13.35

```
Predicted Values for New Observations

New
Obs   Fit   SE Fit      95% CI            95% PI
  1  6614   1246    (4163, 9065)    (-21006, 34234)


Values of Predictors for New Observations

New
Obs  RETURN  RATING
  1    200    4.00
```

DDT

13.36 Refer to Exercise 13.12 (p. 784) and the U.S. Army Corps of Engineers data on contaminated fish. You fit the first-order model, $E(y) = \beta_0 + \beta_1 x_1 + \beta_2 x_2 + \beta_3 x_3$, to the data, where y = DDT level (parts per million), x_1 = number of miles upstream, x_2 = length (centimeters), and x_3 = weight (in grams). Predict, with 95% confidence, the DDT level of a fish caught 100 miles upstream with a length of 40 centimeters and a weight of 800 grams. Interpret the result. $(-183.76, 207.25)$

SNOWGEES

13.37 Refer to the *Journal of Applied Ecology* study of the feeding habits of baby snow geese, Exercise 13.14 (page 785). You fit the first-order model relating gosling weight change y to digestion efficiency x_1 and acid-detergent fiber x_2. Estimate, with 95% confidence, the mean weight change for all Snowgeese with x_1 = 5% and x_2 = 30%.

Applying the Concepts—Intermediate

13.38 Refer to Exercise 13.15 (p. 785). The researchers concluded that "in order to break a water-oil mix-

ture with the lowest possible voltage, the volume fraction of the disperse phase x_1 should be high, while the salinity x_2 and the amount of surfactant x_5 should be low." Use this information and the first order model of Exercise 13.15 to find a 95% prediction interval for this "low" voltage y. Interpret the interval.

13.39 An article published in *Geography* (July 1980) used multiple regression to predict annual rainfall levels in California. Data on the average annual precipitation (y), altitude (x_1), latitude (x_2), and distance from the Pacific coast (x_3) for 30 meteorological stations scattered throughout California are listed in the table below. Consider the first-order model $y = \beta_0 + \beta_1 x_1 + \beta_2 x_2 + \beta_3 x_3 + \epsilon$.

a. Fit the model to the data and give the least squares prediction equation.

b. Is there evidence that the first-order model is useful for predicting annual precipitation y? Test using α = .05. $F = 13.02$

c. Predict, with 95% confidence, the average annual precipitation for the Giant Forest meteorological station (station #9).

CALIRAIN

Station	Avg. Annual Precipitation, y (inches)	Altitude, x_1 (feet)	Latitude, x_2 (degrees)	Distance from Coast, x_3 (miles)
1. Eureka	39.57	43	40.8	1
2. Red Bluff	23.27	341	40.2	97
3. Thermal	18.20	4152	33.8	70
4. Fort Bragg	37.48	74	39.4	1
5. Soda Springs	49.26	6752	39.3	150
6. San Francisco	21.82	52	37.8	5
7. Sacramento	18.07	25	38.5	80
8. San Jose	14.17	95	37.4	28
9. Giant Forest	42.63	6360	36.6	145
10. Salinas	13.85	74	36.7	12
11. Fresno	9.44	331	36.7	114
12. Pt. Piedras	19.33	57	35.7	1
13. Pasa Robles	15.67	740	35.7	31
14. Bakersfield	6.00	489	35.4	75
15. Bishop	5.73	4108	37.3	198
16. Mineral	47.82	4850	40.4	142
17. Santa Barbara	17.95	120	34.4	1
18. Susanville	18.20	4152	40.3	198
19. Tule Lake	10.03	4036	41.9	140
20. Needles	4.63	913	34.8	192
21. Burbank	14.74	699	34.2	47
22. Los Angeles	15.02	312	34.1	16
23. Long Beach	12.36	50	33.8	12
24. Los Banos	8.26	125	37.8	74
25. Blythe	4.05	268	33.6	155
26. San Diego	9.94	19	32.7	5
27. Daggett	4.25	2105	34.1	85
28. Death Valley	1.66	−178	36.5	194
29. Crescent City	74.87	35	41.7	1
30. Colusa	15.95	60	39.2	91

Source: Taylor, P. J. "A Pedagogic Application of Multiple Regression Analysis." *Geography,* July 1980, Vol. 65, pp. 203–212.

13.40 In a production facility, an accurate estimate of man-hours needed to complete a task is crucial to management in making such decisions as the proper number of workers to hire, an accurate deadline to quote a client, or cost-analysis decisions regarding budgets. A manufacturer of boiler drums wants to use regression to predict the number of man-hours needed to erect the drums in future projects. To accomplish this, data for 35 boilers were collected. In addition to man-hours (y), the variables measured were boiler capacity (x_1 = lb/hr), boiler design pressure (x_2 = pounds per square inch or psi), boiler type

(x_3 = 1 if industry field erected, 0 if utility field erected), and drum type (x_4 = 1 if steam, 0 if mud). The data are saved in the **BOILERS** file. (The first and last five observations are listed in the accompanying table.)

a. Fit the model $E(y) = \beta_0 + \beta_1 x_1 + \beta_2 x_2 + \beta_3 x_3 + \beta_4 x_4$ to the data. Give the estimates of the β's.

b. Conduct a test for the global utility of the model. Use $\alpha = .01$. $F = 72.11$

c. Find a 95% confidence interval for $E(y)$ when $x_1 = 150{,}000$, $x_2 = 500$, $x_3 = 1$ and $x_4 = 0$. Interpret the result.

⊙ **BOILERS**

Man-Hours, y	Boiler Capacity, x_1	Design Pressure, x_2	Boiler Type, x_3	Drum Type, x_4
3,137	120,000	375	1	1
3,590	65,000	750	1	1
4,526	150,000	500	1	1
10,825	1,073,877	2,170	0	1
4,023	150,000	325	1	1
⋮	⋮	⋮	⋮	⋮
4,206	441,000	410	1	0
4,006	441,000	410	1	0
3,728	627,000	1,525	0	0
3,211	610,000	1,500	0	0
1,200	30,000	325	1	0

Source: Dr. Kelly Uscategui, University of Connecticut

13.7 Model Building: Interaction Models

In Section 13.2, we demonstrated the relationship between $E(y)$ and the independent variables in a first-order model. When $E(y)$ is graphed against any one variable (say, x_1) for fixed values of the other variables, the result is a set of *parallel* straight lines (see Figure 13.3, p. 773). When this situation occurs (as it always does for a first-order model), we say that the relationship between $E(y)$ and any one independent variable *does not depend* on the values of the other independent variables in the model.

However, if the relationship between $E(y)$ and x_1 does, in fact, depend on the values of the remaining x's held fixed, then the first-order model is not appropriate for predicting y. In this case, we need another model that will take into account this dependence. Such a model includes the *cross products* of two or more x's.

For example, suppose that the mean value $E(y)$ of a response y is related to two quantitative independent variables, x_1 and x_2, by the model

$$E(y) = 1 + 2x_1 - x_2 + x_1 x_2$$

A graph of the relationship between $E(y)$ and x_1 for $x_2 = 0, 1$, and 2 is displayed in Figure 13.10.

Figure 13.10
Graphs of
$1 + 2x_1 - x_2 + x_1x_2$
for $x_2 = 0, 1, 2$

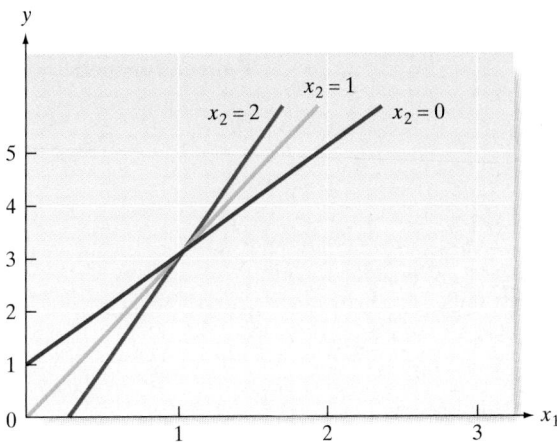

Note that the graph shows three nonparallel straight lines. You can verify that the slopes of the lines differ by substituting each of the values $x_2 = 0, 1$, and 2 into the equation. For $x_2 = 0$:

$$E(y) = 1 + 2x_1 - (0) + x_1(0) = 1 + 2x_1 \quad (\text{slope} = 2)$$

For $x_2 = 1$,

$$E(y) = 1 + 2x_1 - (1) + x_1(1) = 3x_1 \quad (\text{slope} = 3)$$

For $x_2 = 2$,

$$E(y) = 1 + 2x_1 - (2) + x_1(2) = -1 + 4x_1 \quad (\text{slope} = 4)$$

Note that the slope of each line is represented by $\beta_1 + \beta_3x_2 = 2 + x_2$. Thus, the effect on $E(y)$ of a change in x_1 (i.e., the slope) now *depends* on the value of x_2. When this situation occurs, we say that x_1 and x_2 **interact.** The cross-product term, x_1x_2, is called an **interaction term,** and the model $E(y) = \beta_0 + \beta_1x_1 + \beta_2x_2 + \beta_3x_1x_2$ is called an **interaction model** with two quantitative variables.

> ## An Interaction Model Relating $E(y)$ to Two Quantitative Independent Variables
>
> $$E(y) = \beta_0 + \beta_1x_1 + \beta_2x_2 + \beta_3x_1x_2$$
>
> where
>
> $(\beta_1 + \beta_3x_2)$ represents the change in $E(y)$ for every 1-unit increase in x_1, holding x_2 fixed
>
> $(\beta_2 + \beta_3x_1)$ represents the change in $E(y)$ for every 1-unit increase in x_2, holding x_1 fixed

A three-dimensional graph (generated by computer) of an interaction model in two quantitative x's is shown in Figure 13.11. Unlike the flat planar surface displayed in Figure 13.4, the interaction model traces a ruled surface (twisted plane) in three-dimensional space. If we slice the twisted plane at a fixed value of x_2, we obtain a straight line relating $E(y)$ to x_1; however, the slope of the line will change as

Figure 13.11
Computer-generated graph for an interaction model

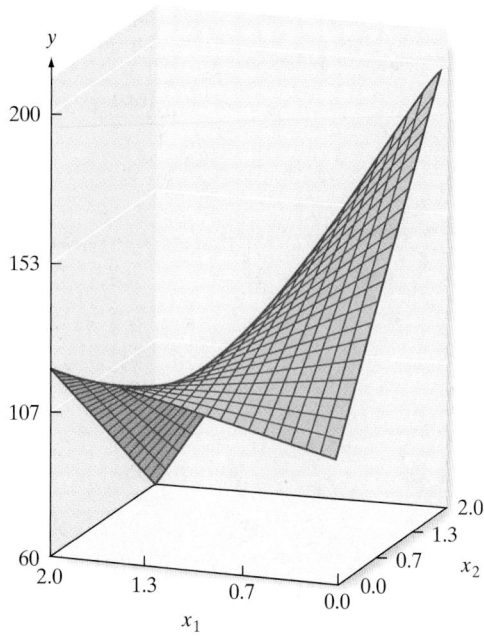

we change the value of x_2. Consequently, an interaction model is appropriate when the linear relationship between y and one independent variable depends on the value of another independent variable. The next example illustrates this idea.

EXAMPLE 13.5   FITTING AN INTERACTION MODEL.

Problem Refer to Examples 13.3 and 13.4. Suppose the collector of grandfather clocks, having observed many auctions, believes that the *rate of increase* of the auction price with age will be driven upward by a large number of bidders. Thus, instead of a relationship like that shown in Figure 13.12(a), in which the rate of increase in price with age is the same for any number of bidders, the collector believes the relationship is like that shown in Figure 13.12(b). Note that as the number of bidders increases from 5 to 15, the slope of the price versus age line increases.

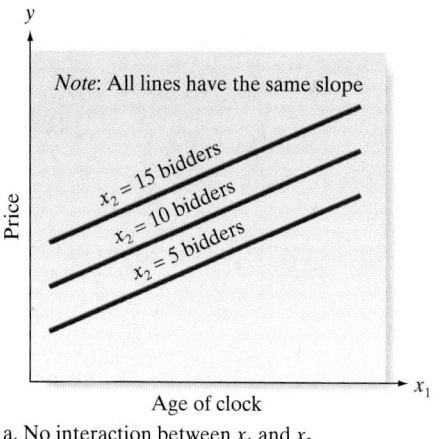

a. No interaction between x_1 and x_2

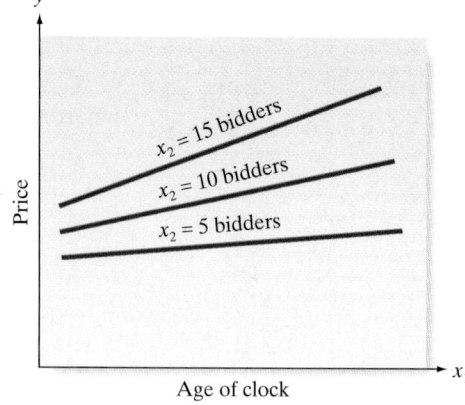

b. Interaction between x_1 and x_2

Figure 13.12
Examples of no-interaction and interaction models

Consequently, the interaction model is proposed:

$$y = \beta_0 + \beta_1 x_1 + \beta_2 x_2 + \beta_3 x_1 x_2 + \epsilon$$

The 32 data points listed in Table 13.2 were used to fit the model with interaction. A portion of the MINITAB printout is shown in Figure 13.13.

Figure 13.13
MINITAB printout for
interaction model of auction
price

Regression Analysis: PRICE versus AGE, NUMBIDS, AGEBID

```
The regression equation is
PRICE = 320 + 0.88 AGE - 93.3 NUMBIDS + 1.30 AGEBID


Predictor      Coef  SE Coef      T      P
Constant      320.5    295.1   1.09  0.287
AGE           0.878    2.032   0.43  0.669
NUMBIDS      -93.26    29.89  -3.12  0.004
AGEBID       1.2978   0.2123   6.11  0.000


S = 88.9145   R-Sq = 95.4%    R-Sq(adj) = 94.9%


Analysis of Variance

Source          DF       SS       MS       F      P
Regression       3  4578427  1526142  193.04  0.000
Residual Error  28   221362     7906
Total           31  4799790
```

a. *F* = 193.04

b. *t* = 6.11

a. Test the overall utility of the model using the global *F*-test at $\alpha = .05$.

b. Test the hypothesis (at $\alpha = .05$) that the price-age slope increases as the number of bidders increases—that is, that age and number of bidders, x_2, interact positively.

c. Estimate the change in auction price of a 150-year-old grandfather clock, y, for each additional bidder.

Solution   **a.** The global *F*-test is used to test the null hypothesis

$$H_0: \beta_1 = \beta_2 = \beta_3 = 0$$

The test statistic and *p*-value of the test (highlighted on the MINITAB printout) are $F = 193.04$ and *p*-value $= 0$, respectively. Since $\alpha = .05$ exceeds the *p*-value, there is sufficient evidence to conclude that the model fit is a statistically useful predictor of auction price, y.

Suggested Exercises 13.50   **b.** The hypotheses of interest to the collector concern the interaction parameter β_3. Specifically,

$$H_0: \beta_3 = 0$$
$$H_a: \beta_3 > 0$$

Since we are testing an individual β parameter, a t-test is required. The test statistic and two-tailed p-value (highlighted on the printout) are $t = 6.11$ and p-value $= 0$, respectively. The upper-tailed p-value, obtained by dividing the two-tailed p-value in half, is $0/2 = 0$. Since $\alpha = .05$ exceeds the p-value, the collector can reject H_0 and conclude that the rate of change of the mean price of the clocks with age increases as the number of bidders increases; that is, x_1 and x_2 interact positively. Thus, it appears that the interaction term should be included in the model.

c. To estimate the change in auction price, y, for every 1-unit increase in number of bidders, x_2, we need to estimate the slope of the line relating y to x_2 when the age of the clock, x_1, is 150 years old. An analyst who is not careful may estimate this slope as $\hat{\beta}_2 = -93.26$. Although the coefficient of x_2 is negative, this does *not* imply that auction price decreases as the number of bidders increases. Since interaction is present, the rate of change (slope) of mean auction price with the number of bidders *depends* on x_1, the age of the clock. Thus, the estimated rate of change of y for a unit increase in x_2 (one new bidder) for a 150-year-old clock is

Teaching Tip

Define the order of a model term to be equal to the total number of quantitative variables that are in the term.

$$\text{Estimated slope of the } y \text{ versus } x_2 \text{ line} = \hat{\beta}_2 + \hat{\beta}_3 x_1$$
$$= -93.26 + 1.30(150) = 101.74$$

In other words, we estimate that the auction price of a 150-year-old clock will *increase* by about $101.74 for every additional bidder.

Look Back Although the rate of increase will vary as x_1 is changed, it will remain positive for the range of values of x_1 included in the sample. Extreme care is needed in interpreting the signs and sizes of coefficients in a multiple regression model.

Now Work *Exercise 13.46*

■ ■ ■

Example 13.5 illustrates an important point about conducting t-tests on the β parameters in the interaction model. The "most important" β parameter in this model is the interaction β, β_3. [Note that this β is also the one associated with the highest-order term in the model, x_1x_2.* Consequently, we will want to test $H_0: \beta_3 = 0$ after we have determined that the overall model is useful for predicting y. Once interaction is detected (as in Example 13.5), however, tests on the first-order terms x_1 and x_2 should *not* be conducted since they are meaningless tests; the presence of interaction implies that both x's are important.

Caution

Once interaction has been deemed important in the model $E(y) = \beta_0 + \beta_1 x_1 + \beta_2 x_2 + \beta_3 x_1 x_2$, do not conduct t-tests on the β coefficients of the first-order terms x_1 and x_2. These terms should be kept in the model regardless of the magnitude of their associated p-values shown on the printout.

---

*The order of a term is equal to the sum of the exponents of the quantitative variables included in the term. Thus, when x_1 and x_2 are both quantitative variables, the cross product, x_1x_2, is a second-order term.

Exercises 13.41–13.52

Learning the Mechanics

13.41 Write an interaction model relating the mean value of y, $E(y)$ to
  a. two quantitative independent variables
  b. three quantitative independent variables [*Hint:* Include all possible two-way cross-product terms.]

13.42 If two variables, x_1 and x_2, do not interact, how would you describe their effect on the mean response, $E(y)$?

13.43 Suppose the true relationship between $E(y)$ and the quantitative independent variables x_1 and x_2 is

$$E(y) = 3 + x_1 + 2x_2 - x_1x_2$$

  a. Describe the corresponding three-dimensional response surface.
  b. Plot the linear relationship between y and x_2 for $x_2 = 0, 1, 2$, where $0 \le x_2 \le 5$.
  c. Explain why the lines you plotted in part **b** are not parallel.
  d. Use the lines you plotted in part **b** to explain how changes in the settings of x_1 and x_2 affect $E(y)$.
  e. Use your graph from part **b** to determine how much $E(y)$ changes when x_1 is changed from 2 to 0 and x_2 is simultaneously changed from 4 to 5.

13.44 Suppose you fit the interaction model

$$y = \beta_0 + \beta_1x_1 + \beta_2x_2 + \beta_3x_1x_2 + \epsilon$$

to $n = 32$ data points and obtain the following results:

$$SS_{yy} = 479 \qquad SSE = 21 \qquad \hat{\beta}_3 = 10 \qquad s_{\hat{\beta}_3} = 4$$

  a. Find R^2 and interpret its value.   .956
  b. Is the model adequate for predicting y? Test at $\alpha = .05$. $F = 202.8$
  c. Use a graph to explain the contribution of the x_1x_2 term to the model.
  d. Is there evidence that x_1 and x_2 interact? Test at $\alpha = .05$. $t = 2.5$

13.45 The MINITAB printout below was obtained from fitting the model

$$y = \beta_0 + \beta_1x_1 + \beta_2x_2 + \beta_3x_1x_2 + \epsilon$$

to $n = 15$ data points.
  a. What is the prediction equation for the response surface?
  b. Describe the geometric form of the response surface of part **a**.
  c. Plot the prediction equation for the case when $x_2 = 1$. Do this twice more on the same graph for the cases when $x_2 = 3$ and $x_2 = 5$.
  d. Explain what it means to say that x_1 and x_2 interact. Explain why your graph of part **c** suggests that x_1 and x_2 interact.
  e. Specify the null and alternative hypotheses you would use to test whether x_1 and x_2 interact.
  f. Conduct the hypothesis test of part **e** using $\alpha = .01$.

```
The regression equation is
Y = -2.55 + 3.82 X1 + 2.63 X2 -1.29 X1X2


Predictor     Coef  SE Coef       T       P
Constant    -2.550    1.142   -2.23   0.043
X1           3.815    0.529    7.22   0.000
X2           2.630    0.344    7.64   0.000
X1X2        -1.285    0.159   -8.06   0.000


S = 0.713      R-Sq = 85.6%    R-Sq(adj) = 81.6%


Analysis of Variance

Source          DF      SS      MS       F       P
Regression       3  33.149  11.050   21.75   0.000
Residual Error  11   5.587   0.508
Total           14  38.736
```

Applying the Concepts—Basic

13.46 Refer to the *World Development* (Feb. 1998) study of street vendors in the city of Puebla, Mexico, Exercise 13.9 (p. 783). Recall that the vendors' mean annual earnings, $E(y)$, was modeled as a first-order function of age (x_1) and hours worked (x_2). Now, consider the interaction model $E(y) = \beta_0 + \beta_1 x_1 + \beta_2 x_2 + \beta_3 x_1 x_2$. The SPSS printout for the model is displayed below.
  a. Give the least squares prediction equation.
  b. What is the estimated slope relating annual earnings (y) to age (x_1) when number of hours worked (x_2) is 10? Interpret the result.   22.972
  c. What is the estimated slope relating annual earnings (y) to hours worked (x_2) when age (x_1) is 40? Interpret the result.   248.146
  d. Give the null hypothesis for testing whether age (x_1) and hours worked (x_2) interact. $H_0: \beta_3 = 0$

  e. Find the *p*-value of the test, part **d.**   .366
  f. Refer to part **e.** Give the appropriate conclusion in the words of the problem.   Fail to reject H_0

13.47 Can a corporation's annual profit be predicted from information about the company's chief executive officer (CEO)? *Forbes* (May, 1999) presented data (shown in the table on p. 811) on company profit (in $ millions), CEO's annual income (in $ thousands), and percentage of the company's stock owned by the CEO. Consider a model relating company profit (y) to CEO income (x_1) and stock percentage (x_2).
  a. Explain what it means to say that "CEO income x_1 and stock percentage x_2 interact to affect company profit y."
  b. Use the data and a statistical software package to fit the interaction model $E(y) = \beta_0 + \beta_1 x_1 + \beta_2 x_2 + \beta_3 x_1 x_2$. Give the least squares prediction

Model Summary

Model	R	R Square	Adjusted R Square	Std. Error of the Estimate
1	.783[a]	.614	.508	550.289

a. Predictors: (Constant), AGEHRS, HOURS, AGE

ANOVA[b]

Model		Sum of Squares	df	Mean Square	F	Sig.
1	Regression	5287427	3	1762475.792	5.820	.012[a]
	Residual	3331000	11	302818.214		
	Total	8618428	14			

a. Predictors: (Constant), AGEHRS, HOURS, AGE

b. Dependent Variable: EARNINGS

Coefficients[a]

Model		Unstandardized Coefficients		Standardized Coefficients		
		B	Std. Error	Beta	t	Sig.
1	(Constant)	1041.894	1303.593		.799	.441
	AGE	-13.238	29.234	-.323	-.453	.659
	HOURS	103.306	162.014	.305	.638	.537
	AGEHRS	3.621	3.840	.760	.943	.366

a. Dependent Variable: EARNINGS

⊙ COMPKING

Company	Profit, y	CEO	Income, x_1	Stock, x_2
Gap	824.5	Drexler	3,743	1.71%
Intel	6,068.0	Grove	52,598	.13
Gateway 2000	346.4	Waitt	855	43.93
HJ Heinz	746.9	O'Reilly	2,916	1.63
Conseco	630.7	Hilbert	124,579	3.64
Citicorp	5,807.0	Reed	6,200	.22
Cisco Systems	1,362.3	Chambers	560	.06
General Electric	9,296.0	Welch	40,626	.03
America Online	254.0	Case	26,917	.54
Computer Associates	570.0	Wang	10,614	3.79
Lockheed Martin	1,001.0	Augustine	2,533	.01
Bear Stearns	538.6	Cayne	23,215	3.44

Source: "Compensation Fit for a King," *Forbes,* May 1999.

equation and determine whether the overall model is statistically useful for predicting company profit $\alpha = .10$. $F = 3.54$

c. Is there evidence to indicate that CEO income x_1 and stock percentage x_2 interact? Test using $\alpha = .10$.

d. Based on the least squares estimates of the β parameters, give the estimate of the change in profit for every one thousand dollar increase in a CEO's income when the CEO owns 2% of the company's stock. $\$51,400$

13.48 A study was conducted to determine the effects of linguistic delivery style and client credibility on auditors' judgments (*Advances in Accounting and Behavioral Research*, 2004). Two hundred auditors from Big 5 accounting firms were asked to assume that he or she was an audit team supervisor of a new manufacturing client and was performing an analytical review of the client's financial statement. The researchers gave the auditors different information on the client's credibility and linguistic delivery style of the client's explanation. Each auditor then provided an assessment of the likelihood that the client-provided explanation accounts for the fluctuation in the financial statement. The three variables of interest, credibility (x_1), linguistic delivery style (x_2), and likelihood (y), were all measured on a numerical scale. Regression analysis was used to fit the interaction model,

$y = \beta_0 + \beta_1 x_1 + \beta_2 x_2 + \beta_3 x_1 x_2 + \varepsilon$. The results are summarized in the table below.

a. Interpret the phrase "client credibility and linguistic delivery style interact" in the words of the problem.

b. Give the null and alternative hypotheses for testing the overall adequacy of the model. $H_0: \beta_1 = \beta_2 = \beta_3 = 0$

c. Conduct the test, part **b**, using the information in the table. $F = 55.35$

d. Give the null and alternative hypotheses for testing whether client credibility and linguistic delivery style interact. $H_0: \beta_3 = 0$

e. Conduct the test, part **d**, using the information in the table. $t = 4.008$

f. The researchers estimated the slope of the Likelihood–Linguistic Delivery Style line at a low level of client credibility ($x_1 = 22$). Obtain this estimate and interpret it in the words of the problem. $.114$

g. The researchers also estimated the slope of the Likelihood–Linguistic Delivery Style line at a high level of client credibility ($x_1 = 46$). Obtain this estimate and interpret it in the words of the problem. $.978$

13.49 *Trichuristrichiura*, a parasitic worm, affects millions of school-age children each year, especially children from developing countries. A study was conducted by a pharmaceutical company to determine the effects of

	Beta Estimate	Std Error	t-Statistic	p-Value
Constant	15.865	10.980	1.445	0.150
Client credibility (x_1)	0.037	0.339	0.110	0.913
Linguistic delivery style (x_2)	−0.678	0.328	−2.064	0.040
Interaction $(x_1 x_2)$	0.036	0.009	4.008	<0.005

F-statistic $= 55.35$ ($p < 0.0005$): Adjusted $R^2 = .450$

treatment of the parasite on school achievement in 407 school-age Jamaican children infected with the disease (*Journal of Nutrition,* July 1995). About half the children in the sample received the treatment, while the others received a placebo. Multiple regression was used to model spelling test score y, measured as number correct, as a function of the following independent variables:

Treatment (T): $x_1 = \begin{cases} 1 \text{ if treatment} \\ 0 \text{ if plecebo} \end{cases}$

Disease intensity (I): $x_2 = \begin{cases} 1 & \text{if more than 7,000 eggs} \\ & \text{per gram of stool} \\ 0 & \text{if not} \end{cases}$

a. Propose a model for $E(y)$ that includes interaction between treatment and disease intensity.
b. The estimates of the β's in the model, part **a,** and the respective p-values for t-tests on the β's are given in the table. Is there sufficient evidence to indicate that the effect of the treatment on spelling score depends on disease intensity? Test using $\alpha = .05$.

Variable	β Estimate	p-Value
Treatment (x_1)	−.1	.62
Intensity (x_2)	−.3	.57
T × I (x_1x_2)	1.6	.02

c. Based on the result, part **b,** explain why the analyst should avoid conducting t-tests for the treatment (x_1) and intensity (x_2) β's or interpreting these β's individually.

Applying the Concepts—Intermediate

13.50 Licensed therapists are mandated by law to report child abuse by their clients. This requires the therapist to breach confidentiality and possibly lose the client's trust. A national survey of licensed psychotherapists was conducted to investigate clients' reactions to legally mandated child-abuse reports (*American Journal of Orthopsychiatry,* Jan. 1997). The sample consisted of 303 therapists who had filed a child-abuse report against one of their clients. The researchers were interested in finding the best predictors of a client's reaction (y) to the report, where y is measured on a 30-point scale. (The higher the value, the more favorable the client's response to the report.) The independent variables found to have the most predictive power are listed here.

x_1: Therapist's age (years)
x_2: Therapist's gender (1 if male, 0 if female)
x_3: Degree of therapist's role strain (25-point scale)
x_4: Strength of client-therapist relationship (40-point scale)

x_5: Type of case (1 if family, 0 if not)
x_1x_2: Age × Gender interaction

a. Hypothesize a first-order model relating y to each of the five independent variables.
b. Give the null hypothesis for testing the contribution of x_4, strength of client-therapist relationship, to the model. $H_0: \beta_4 = 0$
c. The test statistic for the test, part **b,** was $t = 4.408$ with an associated p-value of .001. Interpret this result. Reject H_0
d. The estimated β coefficient for the x_1x_2 interaction term was positive and highly significant ($p < .001$). According to the researchers, "this interaction suggests that ... as the age of the therapist increased, ... male therapists were less likely to get negative client reactions than were female therapists." Do you agree?
e. For this model, $R^2 = .2946$. Interpret this value.

13.51 Refer to the *Journal of Colloid and Interface Science* study of water/oil mixtures, Exercise 13.15 (p. 785). Recall that three of the seven variables used to predict voltage (y) were volume (x_1), salinity (x_2), and surfactant concentration (x_5). The model the researchers fit is

$$E(y) = \beta_0 + \beta_1x_1 + \beta_2x_2 + \beta_3x_5 + \beta_4x_1x_2 + \beta_5x_1x_5.$$

a. Note that the model includes interaction between disperse phase volume (x_1) and salinity (x_2) as well as interaction between disperse phase volume (x_1) and surfactant concentration (x_5). Discuss how these interaction terms affect the hypothetical relationship between y and x_1. Draw a sketch to support your answer.
b. Fit the interaction model to the data on page 786. Does this model appear to fit the data better than the first-order model in Exercise 13.15? Explain.
c. Interpret the β estimates of the interaction model.

13.52 Does extensive media coverage of a military crisis influence public opinion on how to respond to the crisis? Political scientists at UCLA researched this question and reported their results in *Communication Research* (June 1993). The military crisis of interest was the 1990 Persian Gulf War, precipitated by Iraq's leader Saddam Hussein's invasion of Kuwait. The researchers used multiple regression analysis to model the level y of support Americans had for a military (rather than a diplomatic) response to the crisis. Values of y ranged from 0 (preference for a diplomatic response) to 4 (preference for a military response). The following independent variables were used in the model:

$x_1 = $ Level of TV news exposure in a selected week (number of days)

Variable	β Estimate	Standard Error	Two-Tailed p-Value
TV news exposure (x_1)	.02	.01	.03
Political knowledge (x_2)	.07	.03	.03
Gender (x_3)	.67	.11	$<.001$
Race (x_4)	$-.76$	.13	$<.001$
Partisanship (x_5)	.07	.01	$<.001$
Defense spending (x_6)	.20	.02	$<.001$
Education (x_7)	.07	.02	$<.001$
Knowledge $\times$ gender (x_2x_3)	$-.09$	.04	.02
Knowledge $\times$ race (x_2x_4)	.10	.06	.08

Source: Iyengar, S., and Simon, A. "News Coverage of the Gulf Crisis and Public Opinion." *Communication Research,* Vol. 20, No. 3, June 1993, p. 380 (Table 2).

x_2 = Knowledge of seven political figures (1 point each correct answer)

x_3 = Gender (1 if male, 0 if female)

x_4 = Race (1 if nonwhite, 0 if white)

x_5 = Partisanship (0–6 scale, where 0 = strong Democrat and 6 = strong Republican)

x_6 = Defense spending attitude (1–7 scale, where 1 = greatly decrease spending and 7 = greatly spending)

x_7 = Education level (1–7 scale, where 1 = less than eight grades and 7 = college)

Data from a survey of 1,763 U.S. citizens were used to fit the model

$$E(y) = \beta_0 + \beta_1x_1 + \beta_2x_2 + \beta_3x_3 + \beta_4x_4 + \beta_5x_5 + \beta_6x_6 + \beta_7x_7 + \beta_8x_2x_3 + \beta_9x_2x_4$$

The regression results are shown in the table above.

a. Interpret the β estimate for the variable x_1, TV news exposure. $\beta_1 = .02$

b. Conduct a test to determine whether an increase in TV news exposure is associated with an increase in support for a military resolution of the crisis. Use $\alpha = .05$. $p = .015$

c. Is there sufficient evidence to indicate that the relationship between support for a military resolution (y) and gender (x_3) depends on political knowledge (x_2)? Test using $\alpha = .05$. $p = .02$

d. Is there sufficient evidence to indicate that the relationship between support for a military resolution (y) and race (x_4) depends on political knowledge (x_2)? Test using $\alpha = .05$. $p = .08$

e. The coefficient of determination for the model was $R^2 = .194$. Interpret this value.

f. Use the value of R^2, part e, to conduct a global test for model utility. Use $\alpha = .05$. $F = 46.88$

13.8 Model Building: Quadratic and Other Higher-Order Models

All of the models discussed in the previous sections proposed straight-line relationships between $E(y)$ and each of the independent variables in the model. In this section, we consider models that allow for curvature in the relationships. Each of these models is a **second-order model** because it will include an x^2 term.

First, we consider a model that includes only one independent variable x. The form of this model, called the **quadratic model,** is

Teaching Tip
Whenever more than one variable is used in the model, β estimates are done by holding the other variables in the model constant.

$$y = \beta_0 + \beta_1x + \beta_2x^2 + \epsilon$$

The term involving x^2, called a **quadratic term** (or **second-order term**), enables us to hypothesize curvature in the graph of the response model relating y to x. Graphs of the quadratic model for two different values of β_2 are shown in Figure 13.14. When the curve opens upward, the sign of β_2 is positive (see Figure 13.14a); when the curve opens downward, the sign of β_2 is negative (see Figure 13.14b).

Figure 13.14

Graphs for two quadratic models

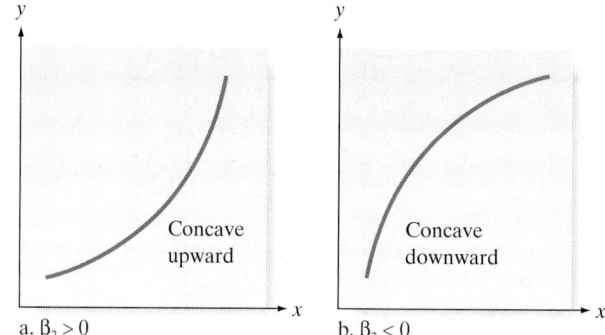

a. $\beta_2 > 0$ — Concave upward   b. $\beta_2 < 0$ — Concave downward

A Quadratic (Second-Order) Model in a Single Quantitative Independent Variable

$$E(y) = \beta_0 + \beta_1 x + \beta_2 x^2$$

where

β_0 is the y-intercept of the curve

β_1 is a shift parameter

β_2 is the rate of curvature

EXAMPLE 13.6   ANALYZING A QUADRATIC MODEL

Problem   In all-electric homes, the amount of electricity expended is of interest to consumers, builders, and groups involved with energy conservation. Suppose we wish to investigate the monthly electrical usage, y, in all-electric homes and its relationship to the size, x, of the home. Moreover, suppose we think that monthly electrical usage in all-electric homes is related to the size of the home by the quadratic model

$$y = \beta_0 + \beta_1 x + \beta_2 x^2 + \epsilon$$

To fit the model, the values of y and x are collected for 10 homes during a particular month. The data are shown in Table 13.3.

    a. Construct a scatterplot for the data. Is there evidence to support the use of a quadratic model?

    b. Use the method of least squares to estimate the unknown parameters β_0, β_1, and β_2 in the quadratic model.

    c. Graph the prediction equation and assess how well the model fits the data, both visually and numerically.

    d. Interpret the β estimates.

e. $F = 189.710$

    e. Is the overall model useful (at $\alpha = .01$) for predicting electrical usage y?

    f. Is there sufficient evidence of downward curvature in the electrical

f. $t = -7.618$

    usage–home size relationship? Test using $\alpha = .01$.

Solution   **a.** A MINITAB scattergram for the data of Table 13.3 is shown in Figure 13.15. The figure illustrates that the electrical usage appears to increase in a curvilinear manner with the size of the home. This provides some support for the inclusion of the quadratic term x^2 in the model.

ELECTRIC

TABLE 13.3 Home Size–Electrical Usage Data

Size of Home, x (sq. ft.)	Monthly Usage, y (kilowatt-hours)
1,290	1,182
1,350	1,172
1,470	1,264
1,600	1,493
1,710	1,571
1,840	1,711
1,980	1,804
2,230	1,840
2,400	1,956
2,930	1,954

Figure 13.15

MINITAB scatterplot for electrical usage data

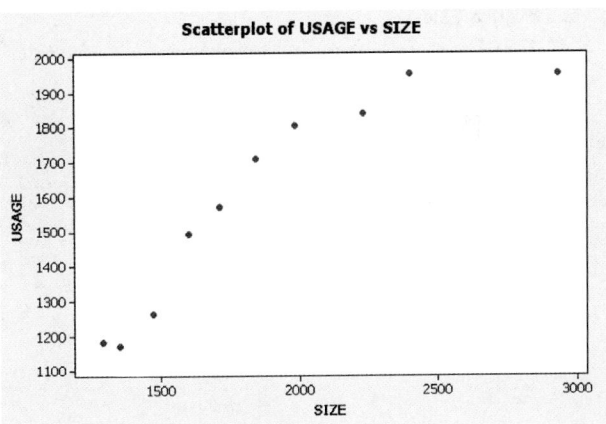

b. We used EXCEL to fit the model to the data in Table 13.3. Part of the EXCEL regression output is displayed in Figure 13.16. The least squares estimates of the β parameters (highlighted) are $\hat{\beta}_0 = -1{,}216.1$, $\hat{\beta}_1 = 2.3989$, and $\hat{\beta}_2 = -.00045$. Therefore, the equation that minimizes the SSE for the data is

$$\hat{y} = -1{,}216.1 + 2.3989x - .00045x^2$$

c. Figure 13.17 is a MINITAB graph of the least squares prediction equation. Note that the graph provides a good fit to the data of Table 13.3. A numerical measure of fit is obtained with the adjusted coefficient of determination, R_a^2. This value (highlighted on both Figures 13.16 and 13.17) is $R_a^2 = .9767$ This implies that almost 98% of the sample variation in electrical usage (y) can be explained by the quadratic model (after adjusting for sample size and degrees of freedom).

d. The interpretation of the estimated coefficients in a quadratic model must be undertaken cautiously. First, the estimated y-intercept, $\hat{\beta}_0$, can be meaningfully interpreted only if the range of the independent variable includes zero—that is, if $x = 0$ is included in the sampled range of x. Although $\hat{\beta}_0 = -1{,}216.1$ seems

Regression Analysis						
Regression Statistics						
Multiple R	0.990901117					
R Square	0.981885024					
Adjusted R Square	0.976709317					
Standard Error	46.80133336					
Observations	10					
ANOVA						
	df	*SS*	*MS*	*F*	*Significance F*	
Regression	2	831069.5464	415534.7732	189.7103041	8.00078E-07	
Residual	7	15332.55363	2190.364804			
Total	9	846402.1				
	Coefficients	*Standard Error*	*t Stat*	*P-value*	*Lower 95%*	*Upper 95%*
Intercept	-1216.143887	242.8063685	-5.008698472	0.001550025	-1790.289304	-641.9984703
SIZE	2.398930177	0.245835602	9.758269998	2.51335E-05	1.817621767	2.980238587
SIZESQ	-0.00045004	5.90766E-05	-7.617907059	0.000124415	-0.000589734	-0.000310346

Figure 13.16
EXCEL regression output for electrical usage model

Figure 13.17
MINITAB plot of least
squares model for electrical
usage

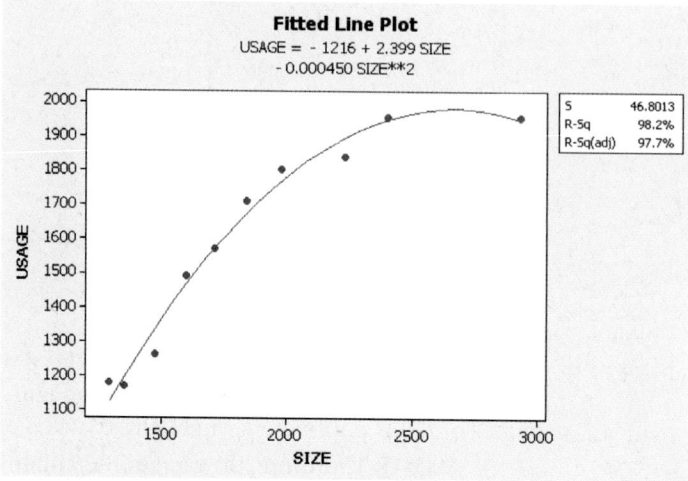

to imply that the estimated electrical usage is negative when $x = 0$, this zero point is not in the range of the sample (the lowest value of x is 1,290 square feet), and the value is nonsensical (a home with 0 square feet); thus the interpretation of $\hat{\beta}_0$ is not meaningful.

The estimated coefficient of x is $\hat{\beta}_1 = 2.3989$, but in the presence of the quadratic term x^2 it no longer represents a slope.* The estimated coefficient of the first-order term x will not, in general, have a meaningful interpretation in the quadratic model.

---

*For students with knowledge of calculus, note that the slope of the quadratic model is the first derivative $\partial y/\partial x = \beta_1 + 2\beta_2 x$. Thus, the slope varies as a function of x, rather than the constant slope associated with the straight-line model.

Quadratic Regression

Using The TI-83 Graphing Calculator

I. Finding the quadratic regression equation

Step 1 *Enter the data*
Press **STAT** and select **1:Edit**
Note: If the list already contains data, clear the old data. Use the up arrow to highlight '**L1**' or '**L2**'.
Press **CLEAR ENTER**.
Use the arrow and **ENTER** keys to enter the data set into **L1** and **L2.**

Step 2 *Find the quadratic regression equation*
Press **STAT** and highlight **CALC**
Press **5** for **QuadReg**
Press **ENTER**
The screen will show the values for a, b, and c in the equation
If the diagnostics are on, the screen will also give the value for r^2
To turn the diagnostics feature on:
1. Press **2nd 0** for **CATALOG**
2. Press the down arrow key until **DiagnosticsOn** is highlighted
3. Press **ENTER** twice

II. Graphing the quadratic curve with the scatterplot

Step 1 *Enter the data as shown in part I above*

Step 2 *Graph the regression curve with the scatterplot*
Press **STAT** and highlight **CALC**
Press **5** for **QuadReg** (Note: Don't press ENTER here because you want to store the regression equation in Y1)
Press **VARS**
Use the right arrow to highlight **Y-VARS**
Press **ENTER** to select **1:Function**
Press **ENTER** to select **1:Y1**
Press **ENTER**

Step 4 *View the scatterplot and regression line*

Press **ZOOM** and then press **9** to select **9:ZoomStat**

Example The figures below show a table of data entered on the TI-83, the quadratic regression equation and the graph obtained using the steps given above.

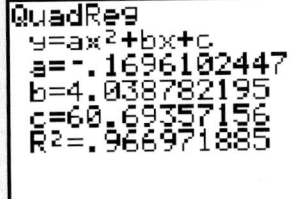

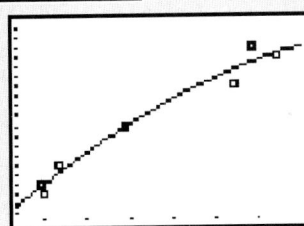

The sign of the coefficient, $\hat{\beta}_2 = -.00045$, of the quadratic term, x^2, is the indicator of whether the curve is concave downward (mound-shaped) or concave upward (bowl-shaped). A negative $\hat{\beta}_2$ implies downward concavity, as in this example (Figure 13.17), and a positive $\hat{\beta}_2$ implies upward concavity. Rather than interpreting the numerical value of $\hat{\beta}_2$ itself, we utilize a graphical representation of the model, as in Figure 13.17, to describe the model.

Suggested Exercises 13.60

Note that Figure 13.17 implies that the estimated electrical usage is leveling off as the home sizes increase beyond 2,500 square feet. In fact, the convexity of the model would lead to decreasing usage estimates if we were to display the model out to 4,000 square feet and beyond (see Figure 13.18). However, model interpretations are not meaningful outside the range of the independent variable, which has a maximum value of 2,930 square feet in this example. Thus, although the model appears to support the hypothesis that the *rate of increase* per square foot *decreases* for the home sizes near the high end of the sampled values, the conclusion that usage will actually begin to decrease for very large homes would be a *misuse* of the model, since no homes of 3,000 square feet or more were included in the sample.

Figure 13.18

Potential misuse of quadratic model

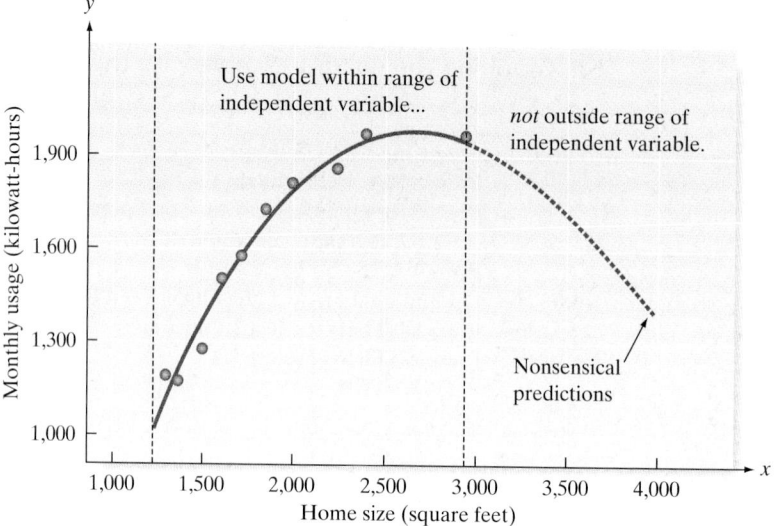

e. To test whether the quadratic model is statistically useful, we conduct the global F-test:

H_0: $\beta_1 = \beta_2 = 0$

H_a: At least one of the above coefficients is nonzero

From the EXCEL printout, Figure 13.16, the test statistic (highlighted) is $F = 189.710$ with an associated p-value of 0. For any reasonable α we reject H_0 and conclude that the overall model is a useful predictor of electrical usage, y.

f. Figure 13.17 shows concave downward curvature in the relationship between size of a home and electrical usage in the sample of 10 data points. To determine if this type of curvature exists in the population, we want to test

H_0: $\beta_2 = 0$ (no curvature in the response curve)

H_a: $\beta_2 < 0$ (downward concavity exists in the response curve)

The test statistic for testing β_2 highlighted on the printout, is $t = -7.618$ and the associated two-tailed p-value is .00012. Since this is a one-tailed test, the appropriate p-value is $(.00012)/2 = .00006$. Now $\alpha = .01$ exceeds this p-value. Thus, there is very strong evidence of downward curvature in the population, that is, electrical usage increases more slowly per square foot for large homes than for small homes.

Look Back Note that the EXCEL printout in Figure 13.16 also provides the t-test statistic and corresponding two-tailed p-values for the tests of $H_0\colon \beta_0 = 0$ and $H_0\colon \beta_1 = 0$ Since the interpretation of these parameters is not meaningful for this model, the tests are not of interest.

Now Work   *Exercise 13.58*

■ ■ ■

When two or more quantitative independent variables are included in a second-order model, we can incorporate squared terms for each x in the model, as well as the interaction between the two independent variables. A model that includes all possible second-order terms in two independent variables—called a **complete second-order** model—is given in the box.

Complete Second-Order Model with Two Quantitative Independent Variables

$$E(y) = \beta_0 + \beta_1 x_1 + \beta_2 x_2 + \beta_3 x_2 x_2 + \beta_4 x_1^2 + \beta_5 x_2^2$$

Comments on the Parameters

β_0: y-intercept, the value of $E(y)$ when $x_1 = x_2 = 0$

β_1, β_2: Changing β_1 and β_2 causes the surface to shift along the x_1- and x_2-axes

β_3: Controls the rotation of the surface

β_4, β_4: Signs and values of these parameters control the type of surface and the rates of curvature.

Three types of surfaces are produced by a second-order model:* a **paraboloid** that opens upward (Figure 13.19a), a paraboloid that opens downward (Figure 13.19b), and a **saddle-shaped surface** (Figure 13.19c).

A complete second-order model is the three-dimensional equivalent of a quadratic model in a single quantitative variable. Instead of tracing parabolas, it traces paraboloids and saddle surfaces. Since only a portion of the complete surface is used to fit the data, this model provides a very large variety of gently curving surfaces that can be used to fit data. It is a good choice for a model if you expect curvature in the response surface relating $E(y)$ to x_1 and x_2.

---

*The saddle-shaped surface (Figure 13.19c) is produced when $\beta_3^2 > 4\beta_4\beta_5$; the paraboloid opens upward (Figure 13.19a) when $\beta_4 + \beta_5 > 0$ and opens downward (Figure 13.19b) when $\beta_4 + \beta_5 < 0$.

Figure 13.19

Graphs for three second-order surfaces

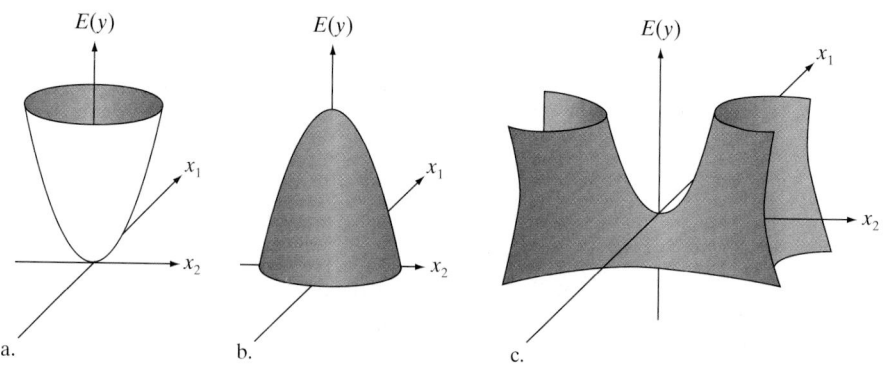

a. b. c.

EXAMPLE 13.7 A MORE COMPLEX 2ND-ORDER MODEL

Problem A social scientist would like to relate the number of hours worked per week (outside the home) by a married woman to the number of years of formal education she has completed and the number of children in her family.

a. Identify the dependent variable and the independent variables.

b. Write the first-order model for this example.

c. Modify the model in part **b** to include an interaction term.

d. Write a complete second-order model for $E(y)$.

Solution **a.** The dependent variable is

$$y = \text{Number of hours worked per week by a married woman}$$

The two independent variables, both quantitative in nature, are

$$x_1 = \text{Number of years of formal education completed by the woman}$$
$$x_2 = \text{Number of children in the family}$$

b. The first-order model is

$$E(y) = \beta_0 + \beta_1 x_1 + \beta_2 x_2$$

This model would probably not be appropriate in this situation because x_1 and x_2 may interact and/or curvature terms corresponding to x_1^2 and x_2^2 may be needed to obtain a good model for $E(y)$.

c. Adding the interaction term, we obtain

$$E(y) = \beta_0 + \beta_1 x_1 + \beta_2 x_2 + \beta_3 x_1 x_2$$

This model should be better than the model in part **b,** since we have now allowed for interaction between x_1 and x_2.

d. The complete second-order model is

$$E(y) = \beta_0 + \beta_1 x_1 + \beta_2 x_2 + \beta_3 x_1 x_2 + \beta_4 x_1^2 + \beta_5 x_2^2$$

Since it would not be surprising to find curvature in the response surface, the complete second-order model would be preferred to the models in parts **b** and **c.**

Look Back How can we tell whether the complete second-order model really does provide better predictions of hours worked than the models in parts **b** and **c**? The answers to these and similar questions are examined in Section 13.11.

■ ■ ■

Most relationships between $E(y)$ and two or more quantitative independent variables are second-order and require the use of either the interactive or the complete second-order model to obtain a good fit to a data set. As in the case of a single quantitative independent variable, however, the curvature in the response surface may be very slight over the range of values of the variables in the data set. When this happens, a first-order model may provide a good fit to the data.

Exercises 13.53–13.66

Learning the Mechanics

13.53 Write a second-order model relating the mean of y, $E(y)$, to
a. one quantitative independent variable
b. two quantitative independent variables
c. three quantitative independent variables [*Hint:* Include all possible two-way cross-product terms and squared terms.]

13.54 Suppose you fit the second-order model

$$y = \beta_0 + \beta_1 x + \beta_2 x^2 + \epsilon$$

to $n = 25$ data points. Your estimate of β_2 is $\hat{\beta}_2 = .47$, and the estimated standard error of the estimate is .15.
a. Test $H_0: \beta_2 = 0$ against $H_a: \beta_2 \neq 0$. Use $\alpha = .05$.
b. Suppose you want to determine only whether the quadratic curve opens upward; that is, as x increases, the slope of the curve increases. Give the test statistic and the rejection region for the test for $\alpha = .05$. Do the data support the theory that the slope of the curve increases as x increases? Explain.

13.55 Suppose you fit the quadratic model

$$E(y) = \beta_0 + \beta_1 x + \beta_2 x^2$$

to a set of $n = 20$ data points and found $R^2 = .91$, $SS_{yy} = 29.94$, and $SSE = 2.63$.
a. Is there sufficient evidence to indicate that the model contributes information for predicting y? Test using $\alpha = .05$. $F = 85.94$
b. What null and alternative hypotheses would you test to determine whether upward curvature exists?
c. What null and alternative hypotheses would you test to determine whether downward curvature exists?

13.56 Consider the following quadratic models:
(1) $y = 1 - 2x + x^2$
(2) $y = 1 + 2x + x^2$
(3) $y = 1 + x^2$
(4) $y = 1 - x^2$
(5) $y = 1 + 3x^2$

a. Graph each of the quadratic models, side by side, on the same sheet of graph paper.
b. What effect does the first-order term ($2x$) have on the graph of the curve?
c. What effect does the second-order term (x^2) have on the graph of the curve?

13.57 MINITAB was used to fit the complete second-order model

$$E(y) = \beta_0 + \beta_1 x_1 + \beta_2 x_2 + \beta_3 x_1 x_2 + \beta_4 x_1^2 + \beta_5 x_2^2$$

to $n = 39$ data points. The printout is shown on p. 822.
a. Is there sufficient evidence to indicate that at least one of the parameters, β_1, β_2, β_3, β_4, and β_5 is non zero? Test using $\alpha = .05$. $p = .000$
b. Test $H_0: \beta_4 = 0$ against $H_a: \beta_4 \neq 0$. Use $\alpha = .01$.
c. Test $H_0: \beta_5 = 0$ against $H_a: \beta_5 \neq 0$. Use $\alpha = .01$.
d. Use graphs to explain the consequences of the tests in parts **b** and **c**.

Applying the Concepts—Basic

13.58 A quadratic model was applied to motor vehicle toxic emissions data collected between 1984 and 1999 in Mexico City (*Environmental Science & Engineering*, Sept. 1, 2000). The following equation was used to predict the percentage (y) of motor vehicles without catalytic converters in the Mexico City fleet for a given year (x): $\hat{y} = 325{,}790 - 321.67x + .0794x^2$.
a. Explain why the value, $\hat{\beta}_0 = 325{,}790$, has no practical interpretation.
b. Explain why the value, $\hat{\beta}_1 = -321.67$ should not be interpreted as a slope.
c. Examine the value of β_2 to determine the nature of the curvature (upward or downward) in the sample data. Upward
d. The researchers used the model to estimate "that just after the year 2021 the fleet of cars with catalytic converters will completely disappear." Comment on the danger of using the model to predict y in the year 2021.

MINITAB Output for Exercise 13.57

```
The regression equation is
Y = -24.56 + 1.12 X1 + 27.99 X2 - 0.54 X1X2 - 0.004 X1SQ + 0.002 X2SQ


Predictor        Coef    SE Coef      T      P
Constant      -24.563      6.531  -3.76  0.001
X1            1.19848      0.1103  10.86  0.000
X2             27.988     79.489   0.35  0.727
X1X2          -0.5397      1.0338  -0.52  0.605
X1SQ          -0.0043      0.0004 -10.74  0.000
X2SQ           0.0020      0.0033   0.60  0.550


S = 2.762     R-Sq = 79.7%   R-Sq(adj) = 76.6%

Analysis of Variance

Source           DF      SS      MS      F      P
Regression        5  989.30  197.86  25.93  0.000
Residual Error   33  251.81    7.63
Total            38 1241.11
```

13.59 Underinflated or overinflated tires can increase tire wear. A new tire was tested for wear at different pressures with the results shown in the following table.

⊙ **TIRES**

Pressure, x (pounds per square inch)	Milage, y (thousands)
30	29
31	32
32	36
33	38
34	37
35	33
36	26

a. Plot the data on a scattergram.
b. If you were given only the information for $x = 30$, 31, 32, 33, what kind of model would you suggest? For $x = 33, 34, 35, 36$? For all the data?

13.60 The *Internet Movie Database* (**www.imdb.com**) monitors the gross revenues for all major motion pictures. The accompanying table gives both the domestic (U.S. and Canada) and international gross revenues for a sample of 15 popular movies.

a. Write a first-order model for foreign gross revenues (y) as a function of domestic gross revenues (x).
b. Write a second-order model for international gross revenues y as a function of domestic gross revenues x.

⊙ **MOVIES**

Movie Title (year)	Domestic Gross ($ millions)	International Gross ($ millions)
Titanic (1997)	600.7	1,234.6
E.T. (1982)	439.9	321.8
Jurassic Park (1993)	356.8	563.0
Lion King (1994)	328.4	455.0
Harry Potter and the Sorcerer's Stone (2001)	317.6	651.1
Sixth Sense (1999)	293.5	368.0
Jaws (1975)	260.0	210.6
Ghost (1990)	217.6	300.0
Saving Private Ryan (1998)	216.1	263.2
Gladiator (2000)	187.7	268.6
Dances with Wolves (1990)	184.2	240.0
The Exorcist (1973)	204.6	153.0
My Big Fat Greek Wedding (2002)	241.4	115.1
Rocky IV (1985)	127.9	172.6
Star Wars: The Phantom Menace (1999)	431.1	491.3

*Source: The Internet Movie Database (**www.imdb.com**).*

c. Construct a scattergram for these data. Which of the models from parts **a** and **b** appears to be the better choice for explaining the variation in foreign gross revenues?
d. Fit the model of part **b** to the data and investigate its usefulness. Is there evidence of a curvilinear relationship between international and domestic gross revenues? Try using $\alpha = .05$.

e. Based on your analysis in part **d,** which of the models from parts **a** and **b** better explains the variation in international gross revenues? Compare your answer to your preliminary conclusion from part **c.**

13.61 The *Journal of Hazardous Materials* (July 1995) presented a literature review of models designed to predict oil spill evaporation. One model discussed in the article used boiling (x_1) and API specific gravity (x_2) to predict the molecular weight (y) of the oil that is spilled. A complete second-order model for y was proposed.
  a. Write the equation of the model.
  b. Identify the terms in the model that allow for curvilinear relationships.

Applying the Concepts—Intermediate

13.62 Fish reared in captivity for commercial purposes must be fed a diet containing an appropriate balance of nutrients to provide adequate energy to permit efficient growth. The amount of nitrogen excreted through the gills of a fish is one way to measure fish energy metabolism. *Fisheries Science* (Feb. 1995) reported on a study of the variables that affect endogenous nitrogen excretion (ENE) in carp raised in Japan. Carp were divided into groups of 2 to 15 fish each according to body weight and each group placed in a separate tank. The carp were then fed a protein-free diet three times daily for a period of 20 days. One day after terminating the feeding experiment, the amount of ENE in each tank was measured. The next table gives the mean body weight (in grams) and ENE amount (in milligrams per 100 grams of body weight per day) for each carp group.
  a. Plot the data in a scattergram. Do you detect a pattern?
  b. Fit the quadratic model, $E(y) = \beta_0 + \beta_1 x + \beta_2 x^2$, to the data. Use the resulting printout information to test $H_0: \beta_2 = 0$ against $H_a: \beta_2 \neq 0$ using $\alpha = .10$. Give the conclusion in the words of the problem. $p = .031$

⊙ CARP

Tank	Body Weight, x	ENE, y
1	11.7	15.3
2	25.3	9.3
3	90.2	6.5
4	213.0	6.0
5	10.2	15.7
6	17.6	10.0
7	32.6	8.6
8	81.3	6.4
9	141.5	5.6
10	285.7	6.0

Source: Watanabe, T., and Ohta, M. "Endogenous Nitrogen Excretion and Non-Fecal Energy Losses in Carp and Rainbow Trout." *Fisheries Science*, Vol. 61, No. 1, Feb. 1995, p. 56 (Table 5).

13.63 Running a manufacturing operation efficiently requires knowledge of the time it takes employees to manufacture the product, otherwise the cost of making the product cannot be determined. Furthermore, management would not be able to establish an effective incentive plan for its employees because it would not know how to set work standards (Chase and Aquilano, *Production and Operations Management*, 1992). Estimates of production time are frequently obtained using time studies. The data in the table below came from a recent time study of a sample of 15 employees performing a particular task on an automobile assembly line.

⊙ ASSEMBLY

Time to Assemble, y (minutes)	Months of Experience, x
10	24
20	1
15	10
11	15
11	17
19	3
11	20
13	9
17	3
18	1
16	7
16	9
17	7
18	5
10	20

  a. Fit the model $y = \beta_0 + \beta_1 x + \beta_2 x^2 + \epsilon$ and give the least squares prediction equation.
  b. Plot the fitted equation on a scattergram of the data. Is there sufficient evidence to support the inclusion of the quadratic term in the model? Explain.
  c. Test the null hypothesis that $\beta_2 = 0$ against the alternative that $\beta_2 \neq 0$. Use $\alpha = .01$. Does the quadratic term make an important contribution to the model?
  d. Your conclusion in part **c** should have been to drop the quadratic term from the model. Do so and fit the "reduced model," $y = \beta_0 + \beta_1 x + \epsilon$, to the data.
  e. Define β_1 in the context of this exercise. Find a 90% confidence interval for β_1 in the reduced model of part **d.** $-.445 \pm .0727$

13.64 Phosphorus used in soil fertilizers can contaminate freshwater sources during rainfall runoff. Consequently, it is important for water quality engineers to estimate the amount of dissolved phosphorus in the water. *Geoderma* (June 1995) presented an investigation of the relationship between soil loss and percentage of dissolved phosphorus in water samples collected at 20 fertilized watersheds in Oklahoma. The data are given in the table.

PHOSPHOR

Watershed	Soil Loss, x (kilometers per half-acre)	Dissolved Phosphorus Percentage, y
1	18	42.3
2	17	50.2
3	35	52.7
4	16	77.1
5	14	36.8
6	54	17.5
7	153	66.4
8	81	67.5
9	183	28.9
10	284	15.1
11	767	20.1
12	148	38.3
13	649	5.6
14	479	8.6
15	1,371	5.5
16	9,150	4.6
17	15,022	2.2
18	69	77.9
19	4,392	7.8
20	312	42.9

Source: Sharpley, A. N., Robinson, J. S., and Smith, S. J. "Bioavailable Phosphorus Dynamics in Agricultural Soils and Effects on Water Quality." *Geoderma,* Vol. 67, No. 1–2, June 1995, p. 11 (Table 4).

a. Plot the data in a scattergram. Do you detect a linear or curvilinear trend?   curvilinear
b. Fit the quadratic model, $E(y) = \beta_0 + \beta_1 x + \beta_2 x^2$ to the data.
c. Conduct a test to determine if a curvilinear relationship exists between dissolved phosphorus percentage (y) and soil loss (x). Test using $\alpha = .05$.

13.65 The amount of pressure used to produce a certain plastic is thought to be related to the strength of the plastic. Researchers hypothesize that, below a certain level, increases in pressure increase the strength of the plastic; at some point, however, additional increases in pressure will have a detrimental effect on its strength. Write a model in which the relationship of the plastic strength y to pressure x reflects this hypothesis. Sketch the model.
$E(y) = \beta_0 + \beta_1 x + \beta_2 x^2$

13.66 A chilled orange juice warehousing operation in New York City was experiencing too many out-of-stock situations with its 96-ounce containers. To better understand current and future demand for this product, the company examined the last 40 days of sales, which are shown in the next table. One of the company's

objectives is to model demand, y, as a function of sale day, x (where $x = 1, 2, 3, \ldots, 40$).
a. Construct a scatterplot for these data.
b. Does it appear that a second-order model might better explain the variation in demand than a first-order model? Explain.
c. Fit a first-order model to these data.
d. Fit a second-order model to these data.
e. Compare the results in parts **c** and **d** and decide which model better explains variation in demand. Justify your choice.

NYJUICE

Sale Day, x	Demand for 96 oz. Containers, y (in cases)
1	4,581
2	4,239
3	2,754
4	4,501
5	4,016
6	4,680
7	4,950
8	3,303
9	2,367
10	3,055
11	4,248
12	5,067
13	5,201
14	5,133
15	4,211
16	3,195
17	5,760
18	5,661
19	6,102
20	6,099
21	5,902
22	2,295
23	2,682
24	5,787
25	3,339
26	3,798
27	2,007
28	6,282
29	3,267
30	4,779
31	9,000
32	9,531
33	3,915
34	8,964
35	6,984
36	6,660
37	6,921
38	10,005
39	10,153
40	11,520

Source: Personal communication from Rick Campbell, Dave Metzler, and Tom Nelson, Rutgers University.

13.9 Model Building: Qualitative (Dummy) Variable Models

Multiple regression models can also be written to include **qualitative** (or **categorical**) independent variables. Qualitative variables, unlike quantitative variables, cannot be measured on a numerical scale. Therefore, we must code the values of the qualitative variable (called **levels**) as numbers before we can fit the model. These coded qualitative variables are called **dummy** (or **indicator**) **variables** since the numbers assigned to the various levels are arbitrarily selected.

Teaching Tip

In general, the number of dummy variables needed is always one less than the number of levels of the qualitative variable.

To illustrate, suppose a female executive at a certain company claims that male executives earn higher salaries, on average, than female executives with the same education, experience, and responsibilities. To support her claim, she wants to model the salary y of an executive using a qualitative independent variable representing the gender of an executive (male or female).

A convenient method of coding the values of a qualitative variable at two levels involves assigning a value of 1 to one of the levels and a value of 0 to the other. For example, the dummy variable used to describe gender could be coded as follows:

$$x = \begin{cases} 1 & \text{if male} \\ 0 & \text{if female} \end{cases}$$

The choice of which level is assigned to 1 and which is assigned to 0 is arbitrary. The model then takes the following form:

$$E(y) = \beta_0 + \beta_1 x$$

Teaching Tip

β_o always represents the mean value of the base level of the qualitative variable, and the other betas represent differences in the mean value of another level compared to the base level.

The advantage of using a 0–1 coding scheme is that the β coefficients are easily interpreted. The model above allows us to compare the mean executive salary $E(y)$ for males with the corresponding mean for females.

$$\text{Males } (x = 1): \quad E(y) = \beta_0 + \beta_1(1) = \beta_0 + \beta_1$$
$$\text{Females } (x = 0): \quad E(y) = \beta_0 + \beta_1(0) = \beta_0$$

These two means are illustrated in the bar graph in Figure 13.20.

First note that β_0 represents the mean salary for females (say, μ_F). When a 0–1 coding convention is used, β_0 will always represent the mean response associated with the level of the qualitative variable assigned the value 0 (called the **base level**). The difference between the mean salary for males and the mean salary for females, $\mu_M - \mu_F$, is represented by β_1—that is,

$$\mu_M - \mu_F = (\beta_0 + \beta_1) - (\beta_0) = \beta_1$$

Figure 13.20
Bar graph comparing $E(y)$ for males and females

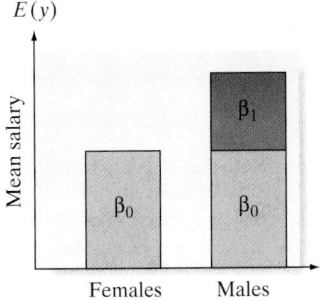

This difference is shown in Figure 13.20.* With a 0–1 coding convention, β_1 will always represent the difference between the mean response for the level assigned the value 1 and the mean for the base level. Thus, for the executive salary model, we have

$$\beta_0 = \mu_F$$
$$\beta_1 = \mu_M - \mu_F$$

Now carefully examine the model with a single qualitative independent variable at two levels, because we will use exactly the same pattern for any number of levels. Moreover, the interpretation of the parameters will always be the same.

One level (say, level A) is selected as the base level. Then for the 0–1 coding** for the dummy variables,

$$\mu_A = \beta_0$$

The coding for all dummy variables is as follows: To represent the mean value of y for a particular level, let that dummy variable equal 1; otherwise, the dummy variable is set equal to 0. Using this system of coding,

$$\mu_B = \beta_0 + \beta_1$$
$$\mu_C = \beta_0 + \beta_2$$

and so on. Because $\mu_A = \beta_0$, any other model parameter will represent the difference between means for that level and the base level:

$$\beta_1 = \mu_B - \mu_A$$
$$\beta_2 = \mu_C - \mu_A$$

and so on. Consequently, each β multiplied by a dummy variable represents the difference between $E(y)$ at one level of the qualitative variable and $E(y)$ at the base level.

Teaching Tip

Take this opportunity to point out what it means to state $\beta_1 = \beta_2 = \ldots = \beta_k = 0$. This will aid in the understanding of the null hypothesis used in the global F-test.

Procedure for Writing a Model with One Qualitative Independent Variable with k Levels

Always use a number of dummy variables that is one less than the number of levels of the qualitative variable. Thus, for a qualitative variable with k levels, use $k - 1$ dummy variables:

$$y = \beta_0 + \beta_1 x_1 + \beta_2 x_2 + \cdots + \beta_{k-1} x_{k-1} + \varepsilon$$

where x_i is the dummy variable for level $i + 1$ and

$$x_i = \begin{cases} 1 & \text{if } y \text{ is observed at level } i + 1 \\ 0 & \text{otherwise} \end{cases}$$

(cont'd)

---

*Note that β_1 could be negative. If β_1 were negative, the height of the bar corresponding to males would be *reduced* (rather than increased) from the height of the bar for females by the amount β_1. Figure 13.20 is constructed assuming that β_1 is a positive quantity.

**You do not have to use a 0–1 system of coding for the dummy variables. Any two-value system will work, but the interpretation given to the model parameters will depend on the code. Using the 0–1 system makes the model parameters easy to interpret.

Then, for this system of coding

$$\mu_A = \beta_0 \quad \text{and} \quad \beta_1 = \mu_B - \mu_A$$
$$\mu_B = \beta_0 + \beta_1 \qquad \beta_2 = \mu_C - \mu_A$$
$$\mu_C = \beta_0 + \beta_2 \qquad \beta_3 = \mu_D - \mu_A$$
$$\mu_D = \beta_0 + \beta_3 \qquad \vdots$$

EXAMPLE 13.8　　A MODEL WITH ONE QUALITATIVE INDEPENDENT VARIABLE

Problem　Suppose an economist wants to compare the mean dollar amounts owed by delinquent credit card customers in three different socioeconomic classes: (1) lower class, (2) middle class, and (3) upper class. A sample of 10 customers with delinquent accounts is selected from each group, and the amount owed by each is recorded, as shown in Table 13.4.

$E(y) = \beta_0 + \beta_1 x_1 + \beta_2 x_2$

a. Hypothesize a regression model for amount owed (y) using Socioeconomic class as an independent variable.

b. Interpret the β's in the model.

$F = 3.48$

c. Use the model to determine if to the mean dollar amounts owed by customers differ significantly for the three socioeconomic groups at $\alpha = .05$.

 DELINQUENT

TABLE 13.4　Dollars Owed, Example 13.8

Group 1 (lower class)	Group 2 (middle class)	Group 3 (upper class)
$148	$513	$335
76	264	643
393	433	216
520	94	536
236	535	128
134	327	723
55	214	258
166	135	380
415	280	594
153	304	465

Solution　**a.** Note that socioeconomic status (low, middle, upper class) is a qualitative variable (measured on an ordinal scale). For a 3-level qualitative variable, we need two dummy variables in the regression model. The model relating $E(y)$ to this single qualitative variable, socioeconomic group, is

$$E(y) = \beta_0 + \beta_1 x_1 + \beta_2 x_2$$

where (arbitrarily)

$$x_1 = \begin{cases} 1 & \text{if Group 2} \\ 0 & \text{if not} \end{cases} \qquad x_2 = \begin{cases} 1 & \text{if Group 3} \\ 0 & \text{if not} \end{cases}$$

b. For this model

Suggested Exercises 13.78

$$\beta_0 = \mu_1$$
$$\beta_1 = \mu_2 - \mu_1$$
$$\beta_2 = \mu_3 - \mu_1$$

where μ_1, μ_2, and μ_3 are the mean responses for socioeconomic groups 1, 2, and 3, respectively. That is, β_0 represents the mean amount owed for Group 1 (lower class), β_1 represents the mean difference in amounts owed for Group 2 (middle) and Group 1 (lower), and β_2 represents the mean difference in amounts owed for Group 3 (upper) and Group 1 (lower).

c. Testing the null hypothesis that the means for the three groups are equal, that is, $\mu_1 = \mu_2 = \mu_3$, is equivalent to testing

$$H_0\text{: } \beta_1 = \beta_2 = 0$$

You can see this by observing that if $\beta_1 = \mu_2 - \mu_1 = 0$, then $\mu_1 = \mu_2$. Similarly, if $\beta_2 = \mu_3 - \mu_1 = 0$, then $\mu_3 = \mu_1$. Thus, if H_0 is true, then μ_1, μ_2, and μ_3 must be equal. The alternative hypothesis is

H_a: At least one of the parameters, β_1 and β_2, differs from 0 which implies that at least two of the three means (μ_1, μ_2, and μ_3) differ.

To test this hypothesis, we conduct the global F-test for the model. The MINITAB printout for fitting the model,

$$E(y) = \beta_0 + \beta_1 x_1 + \beta_2 x_2$$

is shown in Figure 13.21. The value of the F-statistic for testing the adequacy of the model, $F = 3.48$, and the observed significance level of the test, p-value $= .045$, are both highlighted. Since $\alpha = .05$ exceeds the p-value, we

Figure 13.21
MINITAB regression printout for dummy variable model

Regression Analysis: AMOUNT versus X1, X2

```
The regression equation is
AMOUNT = 230 + 80.3 X1 + 198 X2


Predictor     Coef   SE Coef     T       P
Constant    229.60     53.43   4.30   0.000
X1           80.30     75.56   1.06   0.297
X2          198.20     75.56   2.62   0.014


S = 168.948    R-Sq = 20.5%    R-Sq(adj) = 14.6%


Analysis of Variance

Source          DF       SS      MS      F      P
Regression       2   198772   99386   3.48  0.045
Residual Error  27   770671   28543
Total           29   969443
```

reject H_0 and conclude that at least one of the parameters, β_1 and β_2, differs from 0. Or, equivalently, we conclude that the data provide sufficient evidence to indicate that the mean indebtedness does vary from one socioeconomic group to another.

Look Back This global F-test is equivalent to the analysis of variance F-test for a completely randomized design of Chapter 10.

Now Work   *Exercise 13.74*

■ ■ ■

Caution

A common mistake by regression analysts is to use a single dummy variable x for a qualitative variable at k levels, where $x = 1, 2, 3, \ldots, k$. Such a regression model will have unestimable β's and β's that are difficult to interpret. Remember, when modeling $E(y)$ with a single qualitative independent variable, the number of 0–1 dummy variables to include in the model will always be one less than the number of levels of the qualitative variable.

Exercises 13.67–13.79

Learning the Mechanics

13.67 Write a regression model relating the mean value of y to a qualitative independent variable that can assume two levels. Interpret all the terms in the model.

13.68 Write a regression model relating $E(y)$ to a qualitative independent variable that can assume three levels. Interpret all the terms in the model.

13.69 The following model was used to relate $E(y)$ to a single qualitative variable with four levels:

$$E(y) = \beta_0 + \beta_1 x_1 + \beta_2 x_2 + \beta_3 x_3$$

where

$$x_1 = \begin{cases} 1 & \text{if level 2} \\ 0 & \text{if not} \end{cases}$$

$$x_2 = \begin{cases} 1 & \text{if level 3} \\ 0 & \text{if not} \end{cases}$$

$$x_3 = \begin{cases} 1 & \text{if level 4} \\ 0 & \text{if not} \end{cases}$$

This model was fit to $n = 30$ data points and the following result was obtained:

$$\hat{y} = 10.2 - 4x_1 + 12x_2 + 2x_3$$

a. Use the least squares prediction equation to find the estimate of $E(y)$ for each level of the qualitative independent variable.

b. Specify the null and alternative hypotheses you would use to test whether $E(y)$ is the same for all four levels of the independent variable.

13.70 MINITAB (see printout on p. 830) was used to fit the following model to $n = 15$ data points:

$$y = \beta_0 + \beta_1 x_1 + \beta_2 x_2 + \epsilon$$

where

$$x_1 = \begin{cases} 1 & \text{if level 2} \\ 0 & \text{if not} \end{cases}$$

$$x_2 = \begin{cases} 1 & \text{if level 3} \\ 0 & \text{if not} \end{cases}$$

a. Report the least squares prediction equation.

b. Interpret the values of β_1 and β_2.

c. Interpret the following hypotheses in terms of μ_1, μ_2, and μ_3:

$H_0: \beta_1 = \beta_2 = 0$
$H_a:$ At least one of the parameters β_1 and β_2 differs from 0

d. Conduct the hypothesis test of part **c.**

Applying the Concepts—Basic

13.71 Refer to the *Chance* (Winter 2001) study of students who paid a private tutor (or coach) to help them improve their Standardized Admission Test (SAT) scores, Exercise 2.84 (p. 94). Multiple regression was used to estimate the effect of coaching on SAT–Mathematics scores. Data on 3,492 students (573 of whom were coached) were used to fit the model, $E(y) = \beta_0 + \beta_1 x_1 + \beta_2 x_2$, where $y =$ SAT–Math score, $x_1 =$ score on PSAT, and $x_2 = \{1$ if student was coached, 0 if not$\}$.

MINITAB Output for Exercise 13.70

```
The regression equation is
Y = 80.0 + 16.8 X1 + 40.4 X2


Predictor      Coef   SE Coef      T       P
Constant     80.000     4.082   19.60   0.000
X1           16.800     5.774    2.91   0.013
X2           40.400     5.774    7.00   0.000


S = 9.129      R-Sq = 80.5%    R-Sq(adj) = 77.2%

Analysis of Variance

Source           DF       SS       MS       F       P
Regression        2   4118.9   2059.5   24.72   0.000
Residual Error   12   1000.0     83.3
Total            14   5118.9
```

a. The fitted model had an adjusted R^2 value of .76. Interpret this result.

b. The estimate of β_2 in the model was 19, with a standard error of 3. Use this information to form a 95% confidence interval for β_2. Interpret the interval. 19 ± 5.88

c. Based on the interval, part **b**, what can you say about the effect of coaching on SAT–Math scores?

13.72 According to the *Chronicle of Higher Education Almanac*, four-year private colleges charge, on average, five times as much for tuition and fees than four-year public colleges. In order to estimate the true difference in the mean amounts charged for the 2003–2004 academic year, random samples of 40 private colleges and 40 public colleges were contacted and questioned about their tuition structures.

a. Which of the procedures described in Chapter 9 could be used to estimate the difference in mean charges between private and public colleges?

b. Propose a regression model involving the qualitative independent variable Type of college that could be used to investigate the difference between the means. Be sure to specify the coding scheme for the dummy variable in the model. $E(y) = \beta_0 + \beta_1 x$

c. Explain how the regression model you developed in part **b** could be used to estimate the difference between the population means.

13.73 *Benefits Quarterly* (First Quarter, 1995) published a study of entry-level job preferences. Several independent variables were used to model the job preferences (measured on a 10-point scale) of 164 business school graduates, including the following qualitative variables:

a. Flextime of the position applied for (yes/no)

b. Level of day care support required (none, referral, or on-premise)

c. Spousal transfer support required (none, counseling, or active search)

d. Marital status of applicant (married/not)

e. Gender of applicant (male/female)

For each of the above qualitative variables, hypothesize a model for job preference (*y*) as a function of that variable. Interpret the β's in each model.

13.74 *New Scientist* (Apr. 3, 1993) published an article on strategies for foiling assassination attempts on politicians. The strategies are based on the findings of researchers at Middlesex University (United Kingdom), who used a multiple regression model for predicting the level *y* of assassination risk. One of the variables used in the model was political status of a country (communist, democratic, or dictatorship).

a. Propose a model for $E(y)$ as a function of political status. $E(y) = \beta_0 + \beta_1 x_1 + \beta_2 x_2$

b. Interpret the β's in the model, part **a**.

Applying the Concepts—Intermediate

13.75 Which insect repellents protect best against mosquitoes? *Consumer Reports* (June 2000) tested 14 products that all claim to be an effective mosquito repellent. Each product was classified as either lotion/cream or aerosol/spray. The cost of the product (in dollars) was divided by the amount of the repellent needed to cover exposed areas of the skin (about 1/3 ounce) to obtain a cost-per-use value. Effectiveness was measured as the maximum number of hours of protection (in half-hour increments) provided when human testers exposed their arms to 200 mosquitoes. The data from the report are listed in the next table.

REPELLENT

Insect Repellent	Type	Cost/ Use	Maximum Protection
Amway Hour Guard 12	Lotion/Cream	$2.08	13.5 hours
Avon Skin-So-Soft	Aerosol/Spray	0.67	0.5
Avon BugGuard Plus	Lotion/Cream	1.00	2.0
Ben's Backyard Formula	Lotion/Cream	0.75	7.0
Bite Blocker	Lotion/Cream	0.46	3.0
BugOut	Aerosol/Spray	0.11	6.0
Cutter Skinsations	Aerosol/Spray	0.22	3.0
Cutter Unscented	Aerosol/Spray	0.19	5.5
Muskoll Ultra6Hours	Aerosol/Spray	0.24	6.5
Natrapel	Aerosol/Spray	0.27	1.0
Off! Deep Woods	Aerosol/Spray	1.77	14.0
Off! Skintastic	Lotion/Cream	0.67	3.0
Sawyer Deet Formula	Lotion/Cream	0.36	7.0
Repel Permanone	Aerosol/Spray	2.75	24.0

Source: "Buzz Off," *Consumer Reports,* June 2000.

a. Suppose you want to use repellent type to model the cost-per-use (y). Create the appropriate number of dummy variables for repellent type and write the model.

b. Fit the model, part **a**, to the data.

c. Give the null hypothesis for testing whether repellent type is a useful predictor of cost-per-use (y). $H_0: \beta_1 = 0$

d. Conduct the test, part **c**, and give the appropriate conclusion. Use $\alpha = .10$. $t = .24$

e. Repeat parts **a–d** if the dependent variable is maximum number of hours of protection (y). $t = -.46$

13.76 Robert Johnson (Association for Investment Management and Research) and Gerald Jensen (Northern Illinois University) examined effects of the Federal Reserve's monetary policies on the rates of returns to different types of real estate assets (*Real Estate Finance,* Spring 1999). They employed the following model for the monthly rate of return (y) for the asset:

$$E(y) = \beta_0 + \beta_1 x$$

where $x = \begin{cases} 1 \text{ if the Fed's monetary policy is restrictive} \\ 0 \text{ if the Fed's monetary policy is expansive} \end{cases}$

Results for Exercise 13.76

Index	Estimate of β_0	Estimate of β_1	F-Value	R^2
T-Bills	0.04742 (30.94)	0.001948 (8.14)	66.24	0.1819
Equity REIT	0.01863 (6.19)	−0.01582 (−3.46)	11.98	0.0387

Source: Johnson, Robert R., and Jensen, Gerald R., "Federal Reserve Monetary Policy and Real Estate Investment Trust Returns," *Real Estate Finance,* Vol. 16, No. 1, Spring 1999, pp. 52–59.

In one part of the study they fit this model using monthly rate of return data from 1972–1997 for an equity REIT (real estate investment trust) index and, for comparison purposes, to a Treasury Bill (T-Bill) index. They obtained the results (*t* statistics shown in parentheses) shown in the table at the bottom of the page.

a. Evaluate the usefulness of each fitted model. Draw conclusions in the context of the problem.

b. Interpret the estimated value of β_1 in each model.

c. Predict the mean monthly rate of return for the equity REIT index when the Federal Reserve's monetary policy is restrictive. Repeat for an expansive policy.

BWECS

13.77 Refer to Exercise 13.10 (p. 783), where you modeled y = total CEO pay (in thousands of dollars). Are there significant differences in the mean pay of CEOs from different industries? Specifically, consider the four industries, Industrial High Tech, Industrial Low Tech, Telecommunications, and Utilities.

a. Specify the regression model relating mean CEO pay to type of industry.

b. Use the data in *Business Week's* "Executive Compensation Scoreboard" (saved in the **BWECS** file) to fit the model, part **a**. Give the least squares prediction equation.

c. Interpret the beta estimates in the model.

d. Conduct a global *F*-test for the model using $\alpha = .01$. Draw the appropriate conclusions. $F = .73$

e. Find a 95% confidence interval for the difference in mean pay of CEOs in the Industrial High Tech and Utilities industries. Interpret the result. $3,032 \pm 5,468.8$

13.78 A field experiment was conducted to assess the effect of organic enrichment on the mean density of mosquito larvae (*Journal of the American Mosquito Control Association,* June 1995). Larval specimens were collected from a pond three days after the pond was flooded with canal water. A second sample of specimens was collected three weeks after flooding and enriching the pond with rabbit pellets. All specimens were returned to the laboratory and the number y of mosquito larvae counted in each specimen.

a. Write a model that will allow you to compare the mean number of mosquito larvae found in the enriched pond to the corresponding mean for the natural pond.

b. Interpret the β coefficients in the model, part **a**.

c. Set up the null and alternative hypotheses for testing whether the mean larval density for the enriched pond exceeds the mean for the natural pond.

d. The *p*-value associated with the global *F*-test for the model, part **a**, was determined to be .004. Interpret this result.

⊙ FRANCHISE

Franchise	Type	Number of New Franchises
Blimpie	Food	330
Tower Cleaning	Cleaning	55
CleanNet USA	Cleaning	430
KFC	Food	169
Comprehensive Business Services	Accounting/Consulting	58
Jani-King	Cleaning	451
Coverall Cleaning Concepts	Cleaning	435
McDonald's	Food	744
Applebee's	Food	124
Padgett Business Services	Accounting/Consulting	47
Super 8 Motels	Hospitality	181
General Business Services	Accounting/Consulting	44
LedgerPlus	Accounting/Consulting	79
Sonic Drive In	Food	73
Pizza Inn	Food	39
Holiday Inn Worldwide	Hospitality	150
Choice Hotels Int'l	Hospitality	93
Merry Maids	Cleaning	102
Checkers Drive-In	Food	45

Source: Entrepreneur, Apr. 1996, p. 150.

Applying the Concepts—Advanced

13.79 As large U.S. companies flattened their management hierarchies during the 1990s, many of the middle managers who were laid off gave up on "corporate life" and started their own companies or bought franchise operations. This talent migration, along with the fact that most new jobs in the United States were being created by small businesses, cast entrepreneurism into the national spotlight. The businesses listed in the table above are among the fastest growing in the franchise industry.

a. Propose a regression model that will enable you to compare the mean number of new franchises for the four types of franchises (food, cleaning, accounting/consulting, hospitality).

b. Without the aid of a computer, find estimates of the β's in the model.

c. Use a statistical software package to fit the model, part **a,** to the data. Interpret the regression results. Specifically, are there differences in the mean number of franchises for the four franchise types?

13.10 Model Building: Models with Both Quantitative and Qualitative Variables (Optional)

Suppose you want to relate the mean monthly sales $E(y)$ of a company to monthly advertising expenditure x for three different advertising media (say newspaper, radio, and television) and you wish to use first-order (straight-line) models to model the responses for all three media. Graphs of these three relationships might appear as shown in Figure 13.22.

Figure 13.22
Graphs of the relationship between mean sales $E(y)$ and advertising expenditure x

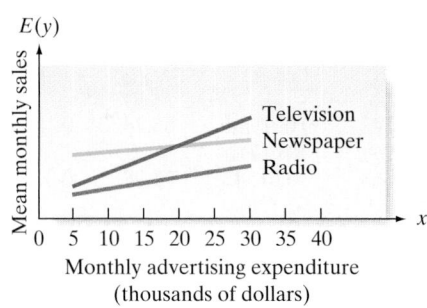

Since the lines in Figure 13.22 are hypothetical, a number of practical questions arise. Is one advertising medium as effective as any other? That is, do the three mean sales lines differ for the three advertising media? Do the increases in mean sales per dollar input in advertising differ for the three advertising media? That is, do the slopes of the three lines differ? Note that the two practical questions have been rephrased into questions about the parameters that define the three lines of Figure 13.22. To answer them, we must write a single regression model that will characterize the three lines of Figure 13.22 and that, by testing hypotheses about the lines, will answer the questions.

The response described previously, monthly sales, is a function of *two* independent variables, one quantitative (advertising expenditure x_1) and one qualitative (type of medium). We will proceed, in stages, to build a model relating $E(y)$ to these variables and will show graphically the interpretation we would give to the model at each stage. This will help you to see the contributions of the various terms in the model.

1. The straight-line relationship between mean sales $E(y)$ and advertising expenditure is the same for all three media—that is, a single line will describe the relationship between $E(y)$ and advertising expenditure x_1 for all the media (see Figure 13.23).

$$E(y) = \beta_0 + \beta_1 x \qquad \text{where } x_1 = \text{Advertising expenditure}$$

Figure 13.23

The relationship between $E(y)$ and x_1 is the same for all media

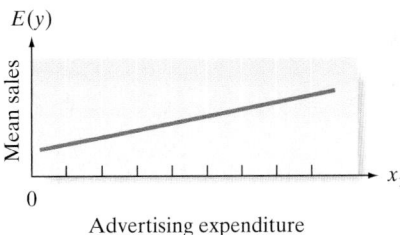

2. The straight lines relating mean sales $E(y)$ to advertising expenditure x_1 differ from one medium to another, but the rate of increase in mean sales per increase in dollar advertising expenditure x_1 is the same for all media—that is, the lines are parallel but possess different y-intercepts (see Figure 13.24).

$$E(y) = \beta_0 + \beta_1 x_1 + \beta_2 x_2 + \beta_3 x_3$$

where

$$x_1 = \text{Advertising expenditure}$$

$$x_2 = \begin{cases} 1 & \text{if radio medium} \\ 0 & \text{if not} \end{cases}$$

$$x_3 = \begin{cases} 1 & \text{if television medium} \\ 0 & \text{if not} \end{cases}$$

Teaching Tip

Plug in values of 0 and 1 for the dummy variables so that the student gets comfortable with the regression models that are being built.

Figure 13.24

Parallel response lines for the three media

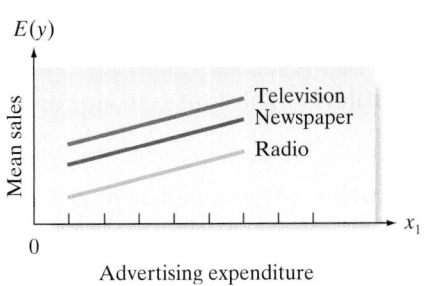

Notice that this model is essentially a combination of a first-order model with a single quantitative variable and the model with a single qualitative variable:

First-order model with a single
quantitative variable: $\qquad E(y) = \beta_0 + \beta_1 x_1$

Model with single qualitative
variable at three levels: $\qquad E(y) = \beta_0 + \beta_2 x_2 + \beta_3 x_3$

where $x_1, x_2,$ and x_3 are as just defined. The model described here implies no interaction between the two independent variables, which are advertising expenditure x_1 and the qualitative variable (type of advertising medium). The change in $E(y)$ for a 1-unit increase in x_1 is identical (the slopes of the lines are equal) for all three advertising media. The terms corresponding to each of the independent variables are called **main effect terms** because they imply no interaction.

Teaching Tip
Discuss how the interaction component allows for the non-parallel relationships to exist in the graph.

3. The straight lines relating mean sales $E(y)$ to advertising expenditure x_1 differ for the three advertising media—that is, both the line intercepts and the slopes differ (see Figure 13.25).

Figure 13.25
Different response lines for the three media

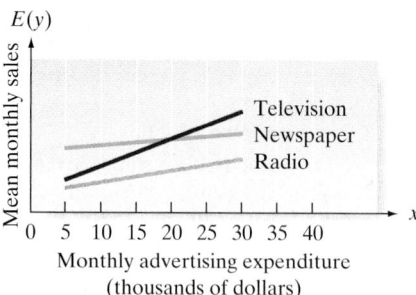

As you will see, this interaction model is obtained by adding terms involving the cross-product terms, one each from each of the two independent variables:

Main effect, advertising expenditure	Main effect, type of medium	Interaction

$$E(y) = \beta_0 \;+\; \overbrace{\beta_1 x_1} \;+\; \overbrace{\beta_2 x_2 + \beta_3 x_3} \;+\; \overbrace{\beta_4 x_1 x_2 + \beta_5 x_1 x_3}$$

Note that each of the preceding models is obtained by adding terms to model 1, the single first-order model used to model the responses for all three media. Model 2 is obtained by adding the main effect terms for type of medium, the qualitative variable. Model 3 is obtained by adding the interaction terms to model 2.

EXAMPLE 13.9   INTERPRETING THE β's IN A MODEL WITH ONE QUANTITATIVE AND ONE QUALITATIVE VARIABLE

Problem Substitute the appropriate values of the dummy variables in model 3 to obtain the equations of the three response lines in Figure 13.25.

Solution The complete model that characterizes the three lines in Figure 13.25 is

$$E(y) = \beta_0 + \beta_1 x_1 + \beta_2 x_2 + \beta_3 x_3 + \beta_4 x_1 x_2 + \beta_5 x_1 x_3$$

where

$$x_1 = \text{Advertising expenditure}$$

$$x_2 = \begin{cases} 1 & \text{if radio medium} \\ 0 & \text{if not} \end{cases}$$

$$x_3 = \begin{cases} 1 & \text{if television medium} \\ 0 & \text{if not} \end{cases}$$

Examining the coding, you can see that $x_2 = x_3 = 0$ when the advertising medium is newspaper. Substituting these values into the expression for $E(y)$, we obtain the newspaper medium line:

$$E(y) = \beta_0 + \beta_1 x_1 + \beta_2(0) + \beta_3(0) + \beta_4 x_1(0) + \beta_5 x_1(0) = \beta_0 + \beta_1 x_1$$

Similarly, we substitute the appropriate values of x_2 and x_3 into the expression for $E(y)$ to obtain the radio medium line ($x_2 = 1, x_3 = 0$):

$$E(y) = \beta_0 + \beta_1 x_1 + \beta_2(1) + \beta_3(0) + \beta_4 x_1(1) + \beta_5 x_1(0)$$

y-intercept   Slope

Suggested Exercise 13.80

$$= \overbrace{(\beta_0 + \beta_2)} + \overbrace{(\beta_1 + \beta_4)x_1}$$

and the television medium line: ($x_2 = 0, x_3 = 1$):

$$E(y) = \beta_0 + \beta_1 x_1 + \beta_2(0) + \beta_3(1) + \beta_4 x_1(0) + \beta_5 x_1(1)$$

y-intercept   Slope

$$= \overbrace{(\beta_0 + \beta_3)} + \overbrace{(\beta_1 + \beta_5)x_1}$$

Look Back If you were to fit model 3, obtain estimates of $\beta_0, \beta_1, \beta_2, \ldots, \beta_5$, and substitute them into the equations for the three media lines, you would obtain exactly the same prediction equations as you would obtain if you were to fit three separate straight lines, one to each of the three sets of media data. You may ask why we would not fit the three lines separately. Why bother fitting a model that combines all three lines (model 3) into the same equation? The answer is that you need to use this procedure if you wish to use statistical tests to compare the three media lines. We need to be able to express a practical question about the lines in terms of a hypothesis that a set of parameters in the model equals 0. (We demonstrate this procedure in the next section.) You could not do this if you were to perform three separate regression analyses and fit a line to each set of media data.

Now Work *Exercise 13.80*

■ ■ ■

EXAMPLE 13.10

ANALYSING A MODEL WITH ONE QUANTITATIVE AND ONE QUALITATIVE INDEPENDENT VARIABLE

Problem An industrial psychologist conducted an experiment to investigate the relationship between worker productivity and a measure of salary incentive for two manufacturing plants; one plant had union representation and the other plant had nonunion representation. The productivity y per worker was measured by recording the number of

CASTING

TABLE 13.5 Productivity Data for Example 13.10

Type of Plant	Incentive								
	20¢/casting			30¢/casting			40¢ /casting		
Union	1,435	1,512	1,491	1,583	1,529	1,610	1,601	1,574	1,636
Nonunion	1,575	1,512	1,488	1,635	1,589	1,661	1,645	1,616	1,689

machined castings that a worker could produce in a 4-week period of 40 hours per week. The incentive was the amount x_1 of bonus (in cents per casting) paid for all castings produced in excess of 1,000 per worker for the 4-week period. Nine workers were selected from each plant, and three from each group of nine were assigned to receive a 20¢ bonus per casting, three a 30¢ bonus, and three a 40¢ bonus. The productivity data for the 18 workers, three for each plant type and incentive combination, are shown in Table 13.5.

a. $E(y) = \beta_0 + \beta_1 x_1 + \beta_2 x_2 +$
$\beta_3 x_1 x_2$

a. Write a model for mean productivity, $E(y)$, assuming that the relationship between $E(y)$ and incentive, x_1, is first-order.

b. Fit the model and graph the prediction equations for the union and nonunion plants.

c. $t = .014$

c. Do the data provide sufficient evidence to indicate that the rate of increase of worker productivity is different for union and nonunion plants? Test at $\alpha = .10$.

Solution

a. If we assume that a first-order model* is adequate to detect a change in mean productivity as a function of incentive x_1, then the model that produces two straight lines, one for each plant, is

$$E(y) = \beta_0 + \beta_1 x_1 + \beta_2 x_2 + \beta_3 x_1 x_2$$

where

$$x_1 = \text{Incentive} \qquad x_2 = \begin{cases} 1 & \text{if nonunion plant} \\ 0 & \text{if union plant} \end{cases}$$

b. The SPSS printout for the regression analysis is shown in Figure 13.26. Reading the parameter estimates highlighted at the bottom of the printout, you can see that

$$\hat{y} = 1{,}365.833 + 6.217x_1 + 47.778x_2 + .033x_1x_2$$

The prediction equation for the union plant can be obtained (see the coding) by substituting $x_2 = 0$ into the general prediction equation. Then

---

*Although the model contains a term involving x_1x_2, it is first order (graphs as a straight line) in the quantitative variable x_1. The variable x_2 is a dummy variable that introduces or deletes terms in the model. The order of a model is determined only by the quantitative variables that appear in the model.

Model Summary

Model	R	R Square	Adjusted R Square	Std. Error of the Estimate
1	.843[a]	.711	.649	40.839

a. Predictors: (Constant), INC_PDUM, INCENTIV, PDUMMY

ANOVA[b]

Model		Sum of Squares	df	Mean Square	F	Sig.
1	Regression	57332.39	3	19110.796	11.459	.000[a]
	Residual	23349.22	14	1667.802		
	Total	80681.61	17			

a. Predictors: (Constant), INC_PDUM, INCENTIV, PDUMMY

b. Dependent Variable: CASTINGS

Coefficients[a]

Model		Unstandardized Coefficients		Standardized Coefficients	t	Sig.
		B	Std. Error	Beta		
1	(Constant)	1365.833	51.836		26.349	.000
	INCENTIV	6.217	1.667	.758	3.729	.002
	PDUMMY	47.778	73.308	.357	.652	.525
	INC_PDUM	.033	2.358	.008	.014	.989

a. Dependent Variable: CASTINGS

Figure 13.26
SPSS printout of the complete model for the casting data

$$\hat{y} = \hat{\beta}_0 + \hat{\beta}_1 x_1 + \hat{\beta}_2(0) + \hat{\beta}_3 x_1(0) = \hat{\beta}_0 + \hat{\beta}_1 x_1$$
$$= 1,365.833 + 6.217 x_1$$

Similarly, the prediction equation for the nonunion plant can be obtained by substituting $x_2 = 1$ into the general prediction equation. Then

$$\hat{y} = \hat{\beta}_0 + \hat{\beta}_1 x_1 + \hat{\beta}_2 x_2 + \hat{\beta}_3 x_1 x_2$$
$$= \hat{\beta}_0 + \hat{\beta}_1 x_1 + \hat{\beta}_2(1) + \hat{\beta}_3 x_1(1)$$

$$= \underbrace{(\beta_0 + \beta_2)}_{y\text{-intercept}} + \underbrace{(\beta_1 + \beta_3)x_1}_{\text{Slope}}$$
$$= (1,365.833 + 47.778) + (6.217 + .033)x_1$$
$$= 1,413.611 + 6.250 x_1$$

A MINITAB graph of these prediction equations is shown in Figure 13.27. Note that the slopes of the two lines are nearly identical (6.217 for union and 6.250 for nonunion).

Figure 13.27

MINITAB plot of prediction equations for the two productivity lines

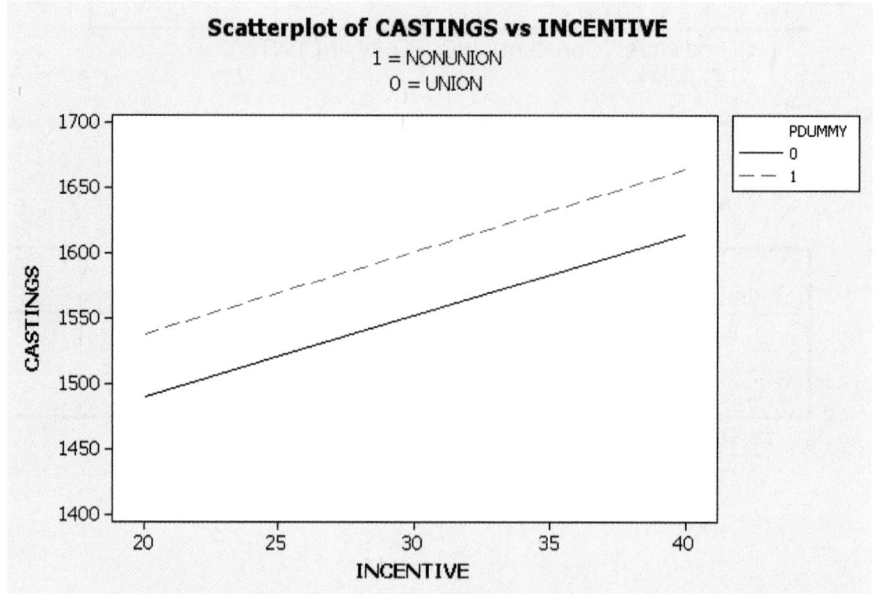

c. If the rate of increase of productivity with incentive (i.e., the slope) for nonunion plants is different than the corresponding slope for union plants, then the interaction β (i.e., β_3) will differ from 0. Consequently, we want to test

$$H_0: \beta_3 = 0$$
$$H_a: \beta_3 \neq 0$$

This test is conducted using the t-test of Section 13.4. From the SPSS printout, the test statistic and corresponding p-value are

$$t = .014 \qquad p = .989$$

Since $\alpha = .10$ is less than the p-value, we fail to reject H_0. There is insufficient evidence to conclude that the union and nonunion shapes differ. Thus, the test supports our observation of two nearly identical slopes in part **b.**

Look Back Since interaction is not significant, we will drop the x_1x_2 term from the model and use the simpler model, $E(y) = \beta_0 + \beta_1x_1 + \beta_2x_2$, to predict productivity.

Now Work *Exercise 13.87*

■ ■ ■

Models with both quantitative and qualitative x's may also include higher-order (e.g., second-order) terms. In the problem of relating mean monthly sales $E(y)$ of a company to monthly advertising expenditure x_1 and Type of Medium, suppose we think that the relationship between $E(y)$ and x_1 is curvilinear. We will construct the model, stage by stage, to enable you to compare the procedure with the stage-by-stage construction of the first-order model in the beginning of this section. The graphical interpretations will help you understand the contributions of the model terms.

Teaching Tip
Discuss how to arrive at the terms to include in a complete 2nd order regression model.

1. The mean sales curves are identical for all three advertising media, that is, a single second-order curve will suffice to describe the relationship between $E(y)$ and x_1 for all the media (see Figure 13.28):

$$E(y) = \beta_0 + \beta_1 x_1 + \beta_2 x_1^2$$

Figure 13.28
The relationship between $E(y)$ and x_1 is the same for all media

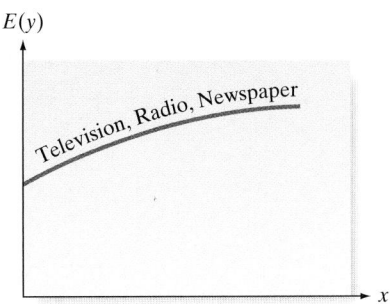

where x_1 = Advertising expenditure

Suggested Exercises 13.81

2. The response curves possess the same shapes but different y-intercepts (see Figure 13.29):

$$E(y) = \beta_0 + \beta_1 x_1 + \beta_2 x_1^2 + \beta_3 x_2 + \beta_4 x_3$$

Figure 13.29
The response curves have the same shapes but different y-intercepts

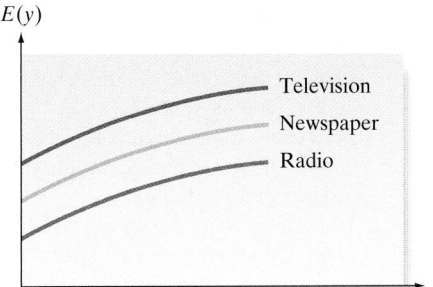

where

$$x_1 = \text{Advertising expenditure}$$
$$x_2 = \begin{cases} 1 & \text{if radio medium} \\ 0 & \text{if not} \end{cases}$$
$$x_3 = \begin{cases} 1 & \text{if television medium} \\ 0 & \text{if not} \end{cases}$$

3. The response curves for the three advertising media are different (i.e., Advertising expenditure and Type of medium interact), as shown in Figure 13.30:

Figure 13.30
The response curves for the three media differ

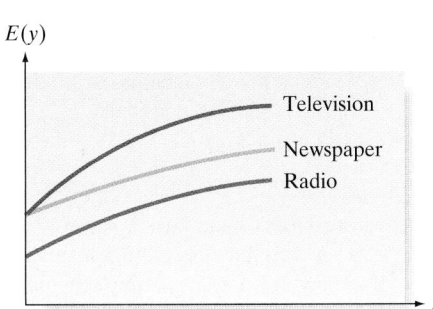

$$E(y) = \beta_0 + \beta_1 x_1 + \beta_2 x_1^2 + \beta_3 x_2 + \beta_4 x_3 + \beta_5 x_1 x_2 + \beta_6 x_1 x_3 + \beta_7 x_1^2 x_2 + \beta_8 x_1^2 x_3$$

Now that you know how to write a model with two independent variables — one qualitative and one quantitative — we ask a question. Why do it? Why not write a separate second-order model for each type of medium where $E(y)$ is a function of only advertising expenditure? As stated earlier, one reason we wrote the single model representing all three response curves is so that we can test to determine whether the curves are different. We illustrate this procedure in Section 13.11. A second reason for writing a single model is that we obtain a pooled estimate of σ^2, the variance of the random error component ϵ. If the variance of ϵ is truly the same for each type of medium, the pooled estimate is superior to three separate estimates calculated by fitting a separate model for each type of medium.

Exercises 13.80–13.91

Learning the Mechanics

13.80 Consider a multiple regression model for a response y, with one quantitative independent variable x_1, and one qualitative variable at three levels.

  a. Write a first-order model that relates the mean response $E(y)$ to the quantitative independent variable.

  b. Add the main effect terms for the qualitative independent variable to the model of part **a.** Specify the coding scheme you use.

  c. Add terms to the model of part **b** to allow for interaction between the quantitative and qualitative independent variables.

  d. Under what circumstances will the response lines of the model in part **c** be parallel? If $\beta_4 = \beta_5 = 0$

  e. Under what circumstances will the model in part **c** have only one response line?

13.81 Refer to Exercise 13.80.

  a. Write a complete second-order model that relates $E(y)$ to the quantitative variable.

  b. Add the main effect terms for the qualitative variable (at three levels) to the model of part **a.**

  c. Add terms to the model of part **b** to allow for interaction between the quantitative and qualitative independent variables.

  d. Under what circumstances will the response curves of the model have the same shape but different y-intercepts? If $\beta_5 = \beta_6 = \beta_7 = \beta_8 = 0$

  e. Under what circumstances will the response curves of the model be parallel lines?

  f. Under what circumstances will the response curves of the model be identical?

13.82 Consider the model:

$$y = \beta_0 + \beta_1 x_1 + \beta_2 x_2 + \beta_3 x_3 + \epsilon$$

where x_1 is a quantitative variable and x_2 and x_3 are dummy variables describing a qualitative variable at three levels using the coding scheme

$$x_2 = \begin{cases} 1 & \text{if level 2} \\ 0 & \text{otherwise} \end{cases} \qquad x_3 = \begin{cases} 1 & \text{if level 3} \\ 0 & \text{otherwise} \end{cases}$$

The resulting least squares prediction equation is

$$\hat{y} = 44.8 + 2.2x_1 + 9.4x_2 + 15.6x_3$$

  a. What is the response line (equation) for $E(y)$ when $x_2 = x_3 = 0$? When $x_2 = 1$ and $x_3 = 0$? When $x_2 = 0$ and $x_3 = 1$?

  b. What is the least squares prediction equation associated with level 1? Level 2? Level 3? Plot these on the same graph.

13.83 Consider the Model:

$$y = \beta_0 + \beta_1 x_1 + \beta_2 x_1^2 + \beta_3 x_2 + \beta_4 x_3 + \\ \beta_5 x_1 x_2 + \beta_6 x_1 x_3 + \beta_7 x_1^2 x_2 + \beta_8 x_1^2 x_3 + \epsilon$$

where x_1 is a quantitative variable and

$$x_2 = \begin{cases} 1 & \text{if level 2} \\ 0 & \text{otherwise} \end{cases} \qquad x_3 = \begin{cases} 1 & \text{if level 3} \\ 0 & \text{otherwise} \end{cases}$$

The resulting least squares prediction equation is.

$$\hat{y} = 48.8 - 3.4x_1 + .07x_1^2 - 2.4x_2 - 7.5x_3 + \\ 3.7x_1 x_2 + 2.7x_1 x_3 - .02x_1^2 x_2 - .04x_1^2 x_3$$

  a. What is the equation of the response curve for $E(y)$ when $x_2 = 0$ and $x_3 = 0$? When $x_2 = 1$ and $x_3 = 0$? When $x_2 = 0$ and $x_3 = 1$?

  b. On the same graph, plot the least squares prediction equation associated with level 1, with level 2, and with level 3.

13.84 Write a model that relates $E(y)$ to two independent variables — one quantitative and one qualitative at four levels. Construct a model that allows the associated response curves to be second-order but does not allow for interaction between the two independent variables.

Applying the Concepts—Basic

⚙ DDT

13.85 Refer to Exercise 13.12 (p. 784) and the model relating the mean DDT level $E(y)$ of contaminated fish to x_1 = miles captured upstream, x_2 = length, and x_3 = weight. Now consider a model for $E(y)$ as a function of both weight and species (channel catfish, largemouth bass, and smallmouth buffalo).

a. Set up the appropriate dummy variables for species.

b. Write the equation of a model that proposes parallel straight-line relationships between mean DDT level $E(y)$ and weight, one line for each species.

c. Write the equation of a model that proposes non-parallel straight-line relationships between mean DDT level $E(y)$ and weight, one line for each species.

d. Fit the model, part **b**, to the data saved in the DDT file. Give the least squares prediction equation.

e. Refer to part **d**. Interpret the value of the least squares estimate of the beta coefficient multiplied by weight. $\hat{\beta}_3 = .0037$

f. Fit the model, part **c**, to the data saved in the DDT file. Give the least squares prediction equation.

g. Refer to part **f**. Find the estimated slope of the line relating DDT level (y) to weight for the channel catfish species. $.00424$

⚙ SNOWGEES

13.86 Refer to the *Journal of Applied Ecology* study of feeding habits of baby snow geese, Exercise 13.14 (p. 785).

a. Write a first-order model relating gosling weight change (y) to digestion efficiency (x_1) and diet (plants or duck chow) that allows for different slopes for each diet.

b. Fit the model, part **a**, to the data saved in the **SNOWGEES** file and give the least squares prediction equation.

c. Find the estimated slope of the line for goslings fed a diet of plants. Interpret its value. $.0783$

d. Find the estimated slope of the line for goslings fed a diet of duck chow. Interpret its value. $.0167$

e. Conduct a test to determine whether the slopes associated with the two diets are significantly different. Use $\alpha = .05$. $t = -.67$

13.87 The influence of cigarette smoking on resting energy expenditure (REE) in normal-weight and obese smokers was investigated (*Health Psychology*, Mar. 1995). The researchers hypothesized that the relationship between a smoker's REE and length of time

since smoking differs for normal-weight and obese smokers. Consequently, the interaction model was examined:

$$E(y) = \beta_0 + \beta_1 x_1 + \beta_2 x_2 + \beta_3 x_1 x_2$$

where

y = REE, measured in kilocalories per day

x_1 = Time, in minutes after smoking, of metabolic energy reading (levels = 10, 20, and 30 minutes)

$x_2 = \begin{cases} 1 & \text{if normal weight} \\ 0 & \text{if obese} \end{cases}$

a. Give the equation of the hypothesized line relating mean REE to time after smoking for obese smokers. What is the slope of the line? β_1

b. Repeat part **a** for normal-weight smokers. $\beta_1 + \beta_3$

c. A test for interaction resulted in an observed significance level of .044. Interpret this value.

Applying the Concepts—Intermediate

13.88 Numerous "sun safety" products exist on the market to prevent excessive exposure to solar radiation. But many people do not practice "sun safety" or recognize the effectiveness of these products. A group of University of Arizona researchers examined the feasibility of educating preschool (4- to 5-year-old) children about sun safety (*American Journal of Public Health*, July 1995). A sample of 122 preschool children was divided into two groups, the control group and the intervention group. Children in the intervention group received a *Be Sun Safe* curriculum in preschool, while the control group did not. All children were tested for their knowledge, comprehension, and application of sun safety at two points in time: prior to the sun safety curriculum (pretest, x_1) and seven weeks following the curriculum (posttest, y).

a. Write a first-order model for mean posttest score, $E(y)$, as a function of pretest score, x_1 and group. Assume that no interaction exists between pretest score and group. $E(y) = \beta_0 + \beta_1 x_1 + \beta_2 x_2$

b. For the model, part **a**, show that the slope of the line relating posttest score to pretest score is the same for both groups of children. β_1 for both

c. Repeat part **a**, but assume that pretest score and group interact.

d. For the model, part **c**, show that the slope of the line relating posttest score to pretest score differs for the two groups of children. $\beta_1, \beta_1 + \beta_3$

13.89 The National Association of Realtors maintains a data base consisting of sales information on homes sold in the United States. The table on p. 842 lists the sale prices for a sample of 28 recently sold single-family homes. The table also identifies the region of the country in which the home is located and the total number of homes sold in the region during the month the home sold.

a. Propose a complete second-order model for the sale price of a single-family home as a function of region and sales volume.

b. Give the equation of the curve relating sale price to sales volume for homes sold in the West.

c. Repeat part **b** for homes sold in the Northwest.

d. Which β's in the model, part **a,** allow for differences among the mean sale prices for homes in the four regions?

e. Fit the model, part **a,** to the data using an available statistical software package. Is the model statistically useful for predicting sale price? Test using $\alpha = .01$. $F = 8.21$

⊙ **NAR**

Home Price	Region	Sales Volume
$168,200	NE	55,156
185,900	NE	61,025
142,888	NE	48,991
150,990	NE	55,156
295,300	NE	60,324
128,999	NE	51,446
190,885	NW	61,025
133,200	NW	94,166
115,225	NW	92,063
110,633	NW	89,485
123,900	NW	91,772
191,000	NW	99,025
138,950	NW	94,166
142,880	NW	95,688
143,000	S	155,666
161,980	S	160,000
129,500	S	153,540
135,650	S	148,668
200,900	S	163,210
140,990	S	141,822
192,790	S	163,611
208,900	W	109,083
152,420	W	101,111
315,900	W	116,983
169,900	W	108,773
178,250	W	105,106
185,300	W	107,839
219,800	W	109,026

Source: National Association of Realtors, 1998, (http://nar.realtor.com).

13.90 California State University at Long Beach researcher E. L. Hansen used multiple regression analysis to investigate the link between entrepreneurial networks and new organization growth (*Entrepreneurship Theory and Practice,* Summer 1995). The dependent variable, initial new organization growth (y), is defined as the monthly payroll of the firm at the end of its first

year in business. One independent variable considered in the model (and found to be statistically significant) is entrepreneurial action set size (x_1), defined as the number of people in the entrepreneur's social network who are directly or indirectly involved with the founding of the new organization. A second independent variable considered in the study was a dummy variable that represented the technology level of the new firm, where

$$x_2 = \begin{cases} 1 & \text{if high-tech firm} \\ 0 & \text{if low-tech firm} \end{cases}$$

a. Write a first-order model for new firm growth (y) as a function of entrepreneurial action set size (x_1) and technology level (x_2). Assume that the effect of size on new firm growth is independent of technology level. $E(y) = \beta_0 + \beta_1 x_1 + \beta_2 x_2$

b. In terms of the β's of the model, part **a,** give the slope of the line relating new firm growth y to size x_1 for high-tech firms. β_1

c. Repeat part **a,** but assume that the rate of change of new firm growth y with size x_1 depends on technology level x_2. $E(y) = \beta_0 + \beta_1 x_1 + \beta_2 x_2 + \beta_3 x_1 x_2$

d. In terms of the β's of the model, part **c,** give the slope of the line relating new firm growth y to size x_1 for high-tech firms. $\beta_1 + \beta_3$

13.91 The relationship between country credit ratings and the volatility of the countries' stock markets was examined in the *Journal of Portfolio Management* (Spring 1996). The researchers point out that this volatility can be explained by two factors: the countries' credit ratings and whether the countries in question have developed or emerging markets. The table on p. 843 gives the volatility (measured as the standard deviation of stock returns), credit rating (measured as a percentage), and market type (developed or emerging) for a sample of 30 different countries.

a. Write a model that describes the relationship between volatility (y) and credit rating (x_1) as two nonparallel lines, one for each type of market. Specify the dummy variable coding scheme you use.

b. Plot volatility y against credit rating x_1 for all the developed markets in the sample. On the same graph, plot y against x_1 for all emerging markets in the sample. Does it appear that the model specified in part **a** is appropriate? Explain.

c. Fit the model, part **a,** to the data using a statistical software package. Report the least squares prediction equation for each of the two types of markets.

d. Plot the two prediction equations of part **c** on a scattergram of the data.

e. Is there evidence to conclude that the slope of the linear relationship between volatility y and credit rating x_1 depends on market type? Test using $\alpha = .01$. $t = 4.645$

⊙ **VOLATILE**

Country	Volatility (standard deviation of return), y	Credit Rating, x_1	Developed (D) or Emerging (E), x_2
Afghanistan	55.7	8.3	E
Australia	23.9	71.2	D
China	27.2	57.0	E
Cuba	55.0	8.7	E
Germany	20.3	90.9	D
France	20.6	89.1	D
India	30.3	46.1	E
Belgium	22.3	79.2	D
Canada	22.1	80.3	D
Ethiopia	47.9	14.1	E
Haiti	54.9	8.8	E
Japan	20.2	91.6	D
Libya	36.7	30.0	E
Malaysia	24.3	69.1	E
Mexico	31.8	41.8	E
New Zealand	24.3	69.4	D
Nigeria	46.2	15.8	E
Oman	28.6	51.8	D
Panama	38.6	26.4	E
Spain	23.4	73.7	D
Sudan	60.5	6.0	E
Taiwan	22.2	79.9	D
Norway	21.4	84.6	D
Sweden	23.3	74.1	D
Togo	45.1	17.0	E
Ukraine	46.3	15.7	E
United Kingdom	20.8	87.8	D
United States	20.3	90.7	D
Vietnam	36.9	29.5	E
Zimbabwe	36.2	31.0	E

Source: Erb, C. B., Harvey, C. R., and Viskanta, T. E. "Expected Returns and Volatility in 135 Countries." *Journal of Portfolio Management*, Vol. 22, No. 3, Spring 1996, pp. 54–55 (Exhibit 6). This copyrighted material is reprinted with permission from the *Journal of Portfolio Management*, a publication of Institutional Investor, Inc., 488 Madison Ave., New York, NY 10022.

13.11 Model Building: Comparing Nested Models (Optional)

To be successful model builders, we require a statistical method that will allow us to determine (with a high degree of confidence) which one among a set of candidate models best fits the data. In this section, we present such a technique for *nested models*.

Teaching Tip

Describe this test in two ways. First, this test will allow us to test to determine if a specific subset of model terms is useful in predicting *y*. Second, this test will allow us to compare which of two models is a better predictor of *y*.

DEFINITION 13.3

Two models are **nested** if one model contains all the terms of the second model and at least one additional term. The more complex of the two models is called the **complete (or full)** model, and the simpler of the two is called the **reduced** model.

To illustrate the concept of nested models, consider the straight-line interaction model for the mean auction price $E(y)$ of a grandfather clock as a function of two quantitative variables: age of the clock (x_1) and number of bidders (x_2). The interaction model, fit in Example 11.5, is

$$E(y) = \beta_0 + \beta_1 x_1 + \beta_2 x_2 + \beta_3 x_1 x_2$$

If we assume that the relationship between auction price (y), age (x_1), and bidders (x_2) is curvilinear, then the complete second-order model is more appropriate:

$$E(y) = \overbrace{\beta_0 + \beta_1 x_1 + \beta_2 x_2 + \beta_3 x_1 x_2}^{\text{Terms in interaction model}} + \overbrace{\beta_4 x_1^2 + \beta_5 x_2^2}^{\text{Quadratic terms}}$$

Note that the curvilinear model contains quadratic terms for x_1 and x_2, as well as the terms in the interaction model. Therefore, the models are nested models. In this case, the interaction model is nested within the more complex curvilinear model. Thus, the curvilinear model is the *complete* model and the interaction model is the *reduced* model.

Suppose we want to know whether the more complex curvilinear model contributes more information for the prediction of y than the straight-line interaction model. This is equivalent to determining whether the quadratic terms β_4 and β_5 should be retained in the model. To test whether these terms should be retained, we test the null hypothesis

H_0: $\beta_4 = \beta_5 = 0$ (i.e., quadratic terms are not important for predicting y)

against the alternative hypothesis

H_a: At least one of the parameters β_4 and β_5 is nonzero (i.e., at least one of the quadratic terms is useful for predicting y)

Note that the terms being tested are those additional terms in the complete (curvilinear) model that are not in the reduced (straight-line interaction) model.

In Section 13.4, we presented the t-test for a single β coefficient and in Section 13.5 we gave the global F-test for *all* the β parameters (except β_0) in the model. We now need a test for a *subset* of the β parameters in the complete model. The test procedure is intuitive. First, we use the method of least squares to fit the reduced model and calculate the corresponding sum of squares for error, SSE_R (the sum of squares of the deviations between observed and predicted y-values). Next, we fit the complete model and calculate its sum of squares for error, SSE_C. Then, we compare SSE_R to SSE_C by calculating the difference, $SSE_R - SSE_C$. If the additional terms in the complete model are significant, then SSE_C should be much smaller than SSE_R, and the difference $SSE_R - SSE_C$ will be large.

Since SSE will always decrease when new terms are added to the model, the question is whether the difference $SSE_R - SSE_C$ is large enough to conclude that is it due to more than just an increase in the number of model terms and to chance. The formal statistical test utilizes an F-statistic, as shown in the box.

Teaching Tip

Most statistical software programs offer the subset test, complete with the *p*-value, as part of their regression analysis package.

F-Test for Comparing Nested Models

Reduced model: $E(y) = \beta_0 + \beta_1 x_1 + \cdots + \beta_g x_g$

Complete model: $E(y) = \beta_0 + \beta_1 x_1 + \cdots + \beta_g x_g + \beta_{g+1} x_{g+1} + \cdots + \beta_k x_k$

H_0: $\beta_{g+1} = \beta_{g+2} = \cdots = \beta_k = 0$

H_a: At least one of the β parameters under test is nonzero.

(cont'd)

$$\text{Test statistic: } F = \frac{(SSE_R - SSE_C)/(k - g)}{SSE_C/[n - (k + 1)]}$$
$$= \frac{(SSE_R - SSE_C)/\#\beta\text{'s tested in } H_0}{MSE_C}$$

where

SSE_R = Sum of squared errors for the reduced model

SSE_C = Sum of squared errors for the complete model

MSE_C = Mean square error (s^2) for the complete model

$k - g$ = Number of β parameters specified in H_0(i.e., number of β parameters tested)

$k + 1$ = Number of β parameters in the complete model (including β_0)

n = Total sample size

Rejection region: $F > F_\alpha$

where F is based on $v_1 = k - g$ numerator degrees of freedom and $v_2 = n - (k + 1)$ denominator degrees of freedom.

When the assumptions listed in Section 13.3 about the random error term are satisfied, this F-statistic has an F-distribution with v_1 and v_2 df. Note that v_1 is the number of β parameters being tested and v_2 is the number of degrees of freedom associated with s^2 in the complete model.

EXAMPLE 13.11   ANALYZING A COMPLETE 2ND-ORDER MODEL

Problem Many companies manufacture products (e.g., steel, paint, gasoline) that are at least partially chemically produced. In many instances, the quality of the finished product is a function of the temperature and pressure at which the chemical reactions take place. Suppose you want to model the quality y of a product as a function of the temperature x_1 and the pressure x_2 at which it is produced. Four inspectors independently assign a quality score between 0 and 100 to each product, and then the quality y is calculated by averaging the four scores. An experiment is conducted by varying temperature between 80°F and 100°F and pressure between 50 and 60 pounds per square inch (psi). The resulting data are given in Table 13.7.

    a. Fit a complete second-order model to the data.

    b. Sketch the fitted model in three dimensions.

    c. Do the data provide sufficient evidence to indicate that the second-order terms, β_3, β_4, and β_5, contribute information for the prediction of y?

c. F = 782.1

Solution   **a.** The complete second-order model is

$$E(y) = \beta_0 + \beta_1 x_1 + \beta_2 x_2 + \beta_3 x_1 x_2 + \beta_4 x_1^2 + \beta_5 x_2^2$$

QUALITY

TABLE 13.6 Temperature (x_1), Pressure (x_2), and Quality of the Finished Product (y)

x_1 (°F)	x_2 (psi)	y	x_1 (°F)	x_2 (psi)	y	x_1 (°F)	x_2 (psi)	y
80	50	50.8	90	50	63.4	100	50	46.6
80	50	50.7	90	50	61.6	100	50	49.1
80	50	49.4	90	50	63.4	100	50	46.4
80	55	93.7	90	55	93.8	100	55	69.8
80	55	90.9	90	55	92.1	100	55	72.5
80	55	90.9	90	55	97.4	100	55	73.2
80	60	74.5	90	60	70.9	100	60	38.7
80	60	73.0	90	60	68.8	100	60	42.5
80	60	71.2	90	60	71.3	100	60	41.4

The data in Table 13.6 were used to fit this model, and the MINITAB output is shown in Figure 13.31.

The least squares prediction equation is

$$\hat{y} = -5{,}128 + 31.1x_1 + 139.75x_2 - .146x_1x_2 - .133x_1^2 - 1.14x_2^2$$

b. A three-dimensional graph of this prediction model, called a **response surface,** is shown in Figure 13.32. Note that the quality seems to be greatest for temperatures of about 85–90°F and for pressures of about 55–57 pounds

```
The regression equation is
QUALITY = - 5128 + 31.1 TEMP + 140 PRES - 0.145 TEM_PRES - 0.133 TEMPSQ
          - 1.14 PRESSQ


Predictor       Coef    SE Coef        T       P
Constant     -5127.9      110.3   -46.49   0.000
TEMP          31.096      1.344    23.13   0.000
PRES         139.747      3.140    44.50   0.000
TEM_PRES   -0.145500   0.009692   -15.01   0.000
TEMPSQ     -0.133389   0.006853   -19.46   0.000
PRESSQ      -1.14422    0.02741   -41.74   0.000


S = 1.67870   R-Sq = 99.3%   R-Sq(adj) = 99.1%


Analysis of Variance

Source           DF      SS      MS        F      P
Regression        5  8402.3  1680.5   596.32  0.000
Residual Error   21    59.2     2.8
Total            26  8461.4
```

Figure 13.31
MINITAB printout of complete second-order model for quality

Figure 13.32

Plot of second-order least squares model for Example 13.11

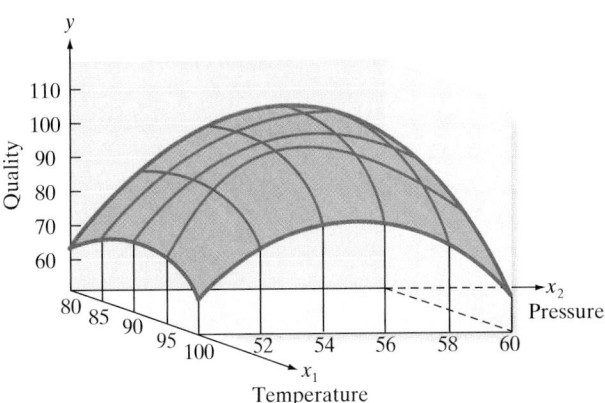

Suggested Exercises 13.96

per square inch.* Further experimentation in these ranges might lead to a more precise determination of the optimal temperature–pressure combination.

c. To determine whether the data provide sufficient information to indicate that the second-order terms contribute information for the prediction of y, we wish to test

$$H_0: \beta_3 = \beta_4 = \beta_5 = 0$$

against the alternative hypothesis

H_a: At least one of the parameters, β_3, β_4, β_5, differs from 0

The first step in conducting the test is to drop the second-order terms out of the complete (second-order) model and fit the reduced model

$$E(y) = \beta_0 + \beta_1 x_1 + \beta_2 x_2$$

to the data. The MINITAB printout for this model is shown in Figure 13.33.

You can see that the sums of squares for error, highlighted in Figures 13.31 and 13.33 for the complete and reduced models, respectively, are

$$SSE_C = 59.2$$
$$SSE_R = 6,671.5$$

and that s^2 for the complete model (also highlighted in Figure 13.31) is

$$s^2 = MSE_C = 2.8$$

Recall that $n = 27$, $k = 5$, and $g = 2$. Therefore, the calculated value of the F statistic, based on $v_1 = (k - g) = 3$ numerator df and $v_2 = [n - (k + 1)] = 21$ denominator df, is

---

*Students with knowledge of calculus should note that we can solve for the exact temperature and pressure that maximize quality in the least squares model by solving $\partial \hat{y}/\partial x_1 = 0$ and $\partial \hat{y}/\partial x_2 = 0$ for x_1 and x_2. Sample estimates of these estimated optimal values are $x_1 = 86.25°F$ and $x_2 = 55.58$ psi.

```
The regression equation is
QUALITY = 106 - 0.916 TEMP + 0.788 PRES


Predictor      Coef   SE Coef      T       P
Constant      106.09    55.95    1.90   0.070
TEMP         -0.9161    0.3930   -2.33   0.028
PRES          0.7878    0.7860    1.00   0.326


S = 16.6727    R-Sq = 21.2%    R-Sq(adj) = 14.6%


Analysis of Variance

Source            DF      SS       MS      F       P
Regression         2   1789.9    895.0   3.22   0.058
Residual Error    24   6671.5    278.0
Total             26   8461.4
```

Figure 13.33

MINITAB printout of first-order model for quality

$$F = \frac{(\text{SSE}_\text{R} - \text{SSE}_\text{C})/(k - g)}{\text{SSE}_\text{C}/[n - (k + 1)]} = \frac{(\text{SSE}_\text{R} - \text{SSE}_\text{C})/(k - g)}{\text{MSE}_\text{C}}$$

where $v_1 = (k - g)$ is equal to the number of parameters involved in H_0. Therefore,

$$\textit{Test statistic: } F = \frac{(6{,}671.5 - 59.2)/3}{2.8} = 787.2$$

The final step in the test is to compare this computed value of F with the tabulated value based on $v_1 = 3$ and $v_2 = 21$ df. If we choose $\alpha = .05$, then $F_{.05} = 3.07$ and the rejection region is

$$\textit{Rejection region: } F > 3.07.$$

Since the computed value of F falls in the rejection region (i.e., it exceeds $F_{.05} = 3.07$), we reject H_0 and conclude that at least one of the second-order terms contributes information for the prediction of y. The second-order model appears to provide better predictions of y than a first-order model.

Now Work   *Exercise 13.96*

■ ■ ■

The nested model F-test can be used to determine whether *any* subset of terms should be included in a complete model by testing the null hypothesis that a particular set of β parameters simultaneously equals 0. For example, we may want to test to determine whether a set of interaction terms for quantitative variables or a set of main effect terms for a qualitative variable should be included in a model. If we reject H_0, the complete model is the better of the two nested models.

Suppose the F-test in Example 13.11 yielded a test statistic that did not fall in the rejection region. Although we must be cautious about accepting H_0, most practitioners of regression analysis adopt the principle of *parsimony*. That is, in situations where two competing models are found to have essentially the same predictive power (as in this case), the model with the fewer number of β's (i.e., the more parsimonious model) is selected. Based on this principle, we would drop the three second-order terms and select the straight-line (reduced) model over the second-order (complete) model.

Teaching Tip

Point out that the parsimonious model will allow for easier interpretations than would the more complicated model.

DEFINITION 13.4

A **parsimonious model** is a general linear model with a small number of β parameters. In situations where two competing models have essentially the same predictive power (as determined by an F-test), choose the more parsimonious of the two.

When the candidate models in model building are nested models, the F-test developed in this section is the appropriate procedure to apply to compare the models. However, if the models are not nested, this F-test is not applicable. In this situation, the analyst must base the choice of the best model on statistics such as R_a^2 and s. It is important to remember that decisions based on these and other numerical descriptive measures of model adequacy cannot be supported with a measure of reliability and are often very subjective in nature.

Exercises 13.92–13.103

Learning the Mechanics

13.92 Explain why the F-test used to compare complete and reduced models is a one-tailed, upper-tailed test.

13.93 Determine which pairs of the following models are "nested" models. For each pair of nested models, identify the complete and reduced model.
  a. $E(y) = \beta_0 + \beta_1 x_1 + \beta_2 x_2$
  b. $E(y) = \beta_0 + \beta_1 x_1$
  c. $E(y) = \beta_0 + \beta_1 x_1 + \beta_2 x_1^2$
  d. $E(y) = \beta_0 + \beta_1 x_1 + \beta_2 x_2 + \beta_3 x_1 x_2$
  e. $E(y) = \beta_0 + \beta_1 x_1 + \beta_2 x_2 + \beta_3 x_1 x_2 + \beta_4 x_1^2 + \beta_5 x_2^2$

13.94 Suppose you fit the regression model

$$y = \beta_0 + \beta_1 x_1 + \beta_2 x_2 + \beta_3 x_1 x_2 + \beta_4 x_1^2 + \beta_5 x_2^2 + \epsilon$$

to $n = 30$ data points and you wish to test

$$H_0: \beta_3 = \beta_4 = \beta_5 = 0$$

  a. State the alternative hypothesis H_a.
  b. Give the reduced model appropriate for conducting the test. $E(y) = \beta_0 + \beta_1 x_1 + \beta_2 x_2$
  c. What are the numerator and denominator degrees of freedom associated with the F-statistic?   3; 24

  d. Suppose the SSE's for the reduced and complete models are $SSE_R = 1{,}250.2$ and $SSE_C = 1{,}125.2$. Conduct the hypothesis test and interpret the results of your test. Test using $\alpha = .05$. $F = .89$

13.95 The complete model

$$y = \beta_0 + \beta_1 x_1 + \beta_2 x_2 + \beta_3 x_3 + \beta_4 x_4 + \epsilon$$

was fit to $n = 20$ data points, with SSE $= 152.66$. The reduced model, $y = \beta_0 + \beta_1 x_1 + \beta_2 x_2 + \epsilon$, was also fit, with SSE $= 160.44$.

  a. How many β parameters are in the complete model? The reduced model?   5; 3
  b. Specify the null and alternative hypotheses you would use to investigate whether the complete model contributes more information for the prediction of y than the reduced model.
  c. Conduct the hypothesis test of part **d**. Use $\alpha = .05$.

Applying the Concepts—Basic

13.96 An article in the *Community Mental Health Journal* (Aug. 2000) used multiple regression analysis to model the level of community adjustment of clients of the Department of Mental Health and Addiction Services in Connecticut. The dependent variable, community adjustment (y), was measured quantitatively based on staff ratings of the clients. (Lower scores indicate better adjustment.) The complete model was a first-order model with 21 independent variables. The independent variables were categorized as Demographic (4 variables), Diagnostic (7 variables), Treatment (4 variables), and Community (6 variables).

a. Write the equation of $E(y)$ for the complete model.

b. Give the null hypothesis for testing whether the 7 Diagnostic variables contribute information for the prediction of y.

c. Give the equation of the reduced model appropriate for the test, part **b**.

d. The test, part **b**, resulted in a test statistic of $F = 59.3$ and p-value $< .0001$. Interpret this result in the words of the problem.   Reject H_0

BWECS

13.97 Refer to the 2002 *Business Week* "Executive Compensation Scoreboard" data saved in the **BWECS** file. In Exercise 13.10 (p. 783), you fit the multiple regression model, $E(y) = \beta_0 + \beta_1 x_1 + \beta_2 x_2$, where y = CEO's total pay (in thousands of dollars), x_1 = return (in dollars) on a \$100 investment, and x_2 = CEO performance rating (1 to 5 scale, where 1 = best and 5 = worst). Now consider the complete second-order model: $E(y) = \beta_0 + \beta_1 x_1 + \beta_2 x_2 + \beta_3 x_1 x_2 + \beta_4 (x_1)^2 + \beta_2 (x_2)^2$.

a. Give the null and alternative hypotheses for determining whether the curvature terms in the complete second-order model are statistically useful for predicting total pay (y). $H_0 = \beta_4 = \beta_6 = 0$

b. For the test in part **a**, identify the "complete" and "reduced" models.

c. Portions of the MINITAB printouts for the two models are shown below. Find the values of SSE_R, SSE_C, and MSE_C on the printouts.

d. Compute the value of the test statistic for the test of part **a**.   10.74

e. Find the rejection region for the test of part **a**, using $\alpha = .10$. $F > 2.30$

f. State the conclusion in the words of the problem.   Reject H_0

BEANIE

13.98 Refer to Exercise 12.83 (p. 755) and the data on the values of 50 beanie babies collector's items, published in *Beanie World Magazine*. Suppose we want to predict the market value of a beanie baby using age (in months as of Sept. 1998) and whether the beanie baby has been retired or is current (i.e., still in production).

a. Write a complete second-order model for market value as a function of age and current/retired status.

b. Specify the null hypothesis for testing whether the quadratic terms in the model, part **a**, are important for predicting market value. $H_0: \beta_2 = \beta_5 = 0$

c. Specify the null hypothesis for testing whether the interaction terms in the model, part **a**, are important for predicting market value. $H_0: \beta_4 = \beta_5 = 0$

d. Fit the three models of parts **a–c** to the data saved in the **BEANIE** file. Conduct the tests specified in parts **b** and **c**. Interpret the results.

MINITAB Output for Exercise 13.97

Complete Model

Analysis of Variance

Source	DF	SS	MS	F	P
Regression	5	16257410165	3251482033	17.68	0.000
Residual Error	324	59587825157	183913041		
Total	329	75845235322			

Reduced Model

Analysis of Variance

Source	DF	SS	MS	F	P
Regression	3	12308725196	4102908399	21.05	0.000
Residual Error	326	63536510127	194897270		
Total	329	75845235322			

Applying the Concepts—Intermediate

13.99 Refer to the *Chance* (Winter 2001) study of students who paid a private tutor (or coach) to help them improve their Standardized Admission Test (SAT) scores, Exercise 13.71 (p. 829). Recall that the baseline model, $E(y) = \beta_0 + \beta_1 x_1 + \beta_2 x_2$, where $y = $ SAT–Math score, $x_1 = $ score on PSAT, and $x_2 = \{1$ if student was coached, 0 if not$\}$, had the following results: $R^2_{adj} = .76$, $\beta_2 = 19$, and $s_{\hat{\beta}_2} = 3$. As an alternative model, the researcher added several "control" variables, including dummy variables for student ethnicity (x_3, x_4, and x_5), a socioeconomic status index variable (x_6), two variables that measured high school performance (x_7 and x_8), the number of math courses taken in high school (x_9), and the overall GPA for the math courses (x_{10}).

a. Write the hypothesized equation for $E(y)$ for the alternative model.

b. Give the null hypothesis for a nested model *F*-test comparing the initial and alternative models. $H_0: \beta_3 = \beta_4 = \cdots = \beta_{10} = 0$

c. The nested model *F*-test, part **b**, was statistically significant at $\alpha = .05$. Practically interpret this result.

d. The alternative model, part **a**, resulted in $R^2_{adj} = .79$, $\beta_2 = 14$, and $s_{\hat{\beta}_2} = 3$. Interpret the value of R^2_{adj}.

e. Refer to part **d**. Find and interpret a 95% confidence interval for β_2. 14 ± 5.88

f. The researcher concluded that "the estimated effect of SAT coaching decreases from the baseline model when control variables are added to the model." Do you agree? Justify your answer. Yes

g. As a modification to the model of part **a**, the researcher added all possible interactions between the coaching variable (x_2) and the other independent variables in the model. Write the equation for $E(y)$ for this modified model.

h. Give the null hypothesis for comparing the models, parts **a** and **g**. How would you perform this test? $H_0: \beta_{11} = \beta_{12} = \cdots = \beta_{19} = 0$

13.100 Refer to the *American Journal of Public Health* study of preschool children's awareness of sun safety, Exercise 13.88 (p. 841). Consider the first-order, interaction model

$$E(y) = \beta_0 + \beta_1 x_1 + \beta_2 x_2 + \beta_3 x_1 x_2$$

where

$y = $ sun safety posttest score
$x_1 = $ sun safety pretest score
$x_2 = \begin{cases} 1 \text{ if in the } BeSunSafe \text{ intervention group} \\ 0 \text{ if in the control group} \end{cases}$

a. Assuming interaction exists, give the reduced model for testing whether the mean posttest scores differ for the intervention and control groups.

b. When sun safety knowledge was used as the dependent variable, the test of part **a** resulted in a *p*-value of .03. Interpret this result. Reject H_0

c. When sun safety comprehension was used as the dependent variable, the test of part **a** resulted in a *p*-value of .033. Interpret this result. Reject H_0

d. When sun safety application was used as the dependent variable, the test of part **a** resulted in a *p*-value of .322. Interpret this result.

13.101 Since glass is not subject to radiation damage, encapsulation of waste in glass is considered to be one of the most promising solutions to the problem of low-level nuclear waste in the environment. However, chemical reactions may weaken the glass. This concern led to a study undertaken jointly by the Department of Materials Science and Engineering at the University of Florida and the U.S. Department of Energy to assess the utility of glass as a waste encapsulant.* Corrosive chemical solutions (called corrosion baths) were prepared and applied directly to glass samples containing one of three types of waste (TDS-3A, FE, and AL); the chemical reactions were observed over time. A few of the key variables measured were

$y = $ Amount of silicon (in parts per million) found in solution at end of experiment. (This is both a measure of the degree of breakdown in the glass and a proxy for the amount of radioactive species released into the environment.)

$x_1 = $ Temperature ($^\circ$C) of the corrosion bath
$x_2 = 1$ if waste type TDS-3A, 0 if not
$x_3 = 1$ if waste type FE, 0 if not

(Waste type AL is the base level.) Suppose we want to model amount y of silicon as a function of temperature (x_1) and type of waste (x_2, x_3).

a. Write a model that proposes parallel straight-line relationships between amount of silicon and temperature, one line for each of the three waste types.

b. Add terms for the interaction between temperature and waste type to the model of part **a**.

c. Refer to the model of part **b**. For each waste type, give the slope of the line relating amount of silicon to temperature.

d. Explain how you could test for the presence of temperature–waste type interaction. $H_0: \beta_4 = \beta_5 = 0$

13.102 The *Journal of Human Stress* (Summer 1987) reported on a study of "psychological response of firefighters to chemical fire." It is thought that the following complete second-order model will be adequate to describe the relationship between emotional

*The background information for this exercise was provided by Dr. David Clark, Department of Materials Science and Engineering, University of Florida.

distress and years of experience for two groups of firefighters—those exposed to a chemical fire and those unexposed.

$$E(y) = \beta_0 + \beta_1 x_1 + \beta_2 x_1^2 + \beta_3 x_2 + \beta_4 x_1 x_2 + \beta_5 x_1^2 x_2$$

where

y = Emotional distress

x_1 = Experience (years)

x_2 = 1 if exposed to chemical fire, 0 if not

a. What hypothesis would you test to determine whether the *rate* of increase of emotional distress with experience is different for the two groups of firefighters? $H_0: \beta_4 = \beta_5 = 0$

b. What hypothesis would you test to determine whether there are differences in mean emotional distress levels that are attributable to exposure group?

c. The second-order model, fit to a sample of 200 firefighters resulted in SSE = 783.90. The reduced model, $E(y) = \beta_0 + \beta_1 x_1 + \beta_2 x_1^2$, fit to the same data, resulted in SSE = 795.23. Is there sufficient evidence to support the claim that the mean emotional distress levels differ for the two groups of firefighters? Use $\alpha = .05$.

Applying the Concepts—Advanced

13.103 A medium-sized automobile insurance company is interested in developing a regression model to help predict the monthly collision claims of its policyholders. A company analyst has proposed modeling monthly collision claims (y) in the Middle Atlantic States as a function of the percentage of claims by drivers under age 30 (x_1) and the average daily temperature during the month (x_2). She believes that as the percentage of claims by drivers under age 30 increases, claims will rise since younger drivers are usually involved in more serious accidents than older drivers. She also believes that claims will rise as the

average daily temperature decreases, since lower temperatures are associated with icy, hazardous driving conditions. In order to develop a preliminary model, data were collected for the state of New Jersey over a 3-year period. The data are saved in the **NJCLAIMS** file. (The first and last five observations are listed in the table below.)

a. Use a statistical software package to fit the complete second-order model

$$E(y) = \beta_0 + \beta_1 x_1 + \beta_2 x_2 + \beta_3 x_1 x_2 + \beta_4 x_1^2 + \beta_5 x_2^2$$

b. Test the hypothesis $H_0: \beta_4 = \beta_5 = 0$ using $\alpha = .05$. Interpret the results in practical terms.

c. Do the results support the analysts' beliefs? Explain. (You may need to conduct further tests of hypotheses to answer this question.)

⊙ **NJCLAIMS**

Month	Monthly Collision Claims, y ($)	Percentage of Monthly Claimants Under the Age of 30, x_1	Newark, N.J., Average Daily Temperature During the Month, x_2 (°F)
1	116,250	50.0	31.5
2	217,180	60.8	33.0
3	43,436	45.1	45.0
4	159,265	56.4	53.9
5	130,308	53.3	63.9
⋮	⋮	⋮	⋮
44	136,528	53.1	76.6
45	193,608	59.8	68.6
46	38,722	45.6	62.4
47	212,309	63.9	50.0
48	118,796	52.3	42.3

Sources: Anonymous insurance company; New Jersey Department of Insurance; Weather of U.S. Cities, 4th ed., Gale Research Inc., Detroit, 1992.

13.12 Model Building: Stepwise Regression (Optional)

Teaching Tip

Stepwise regression exists in many forms in today's statistical software packages. This section illustrates the most common form of the variations that exist. Make sure the students check the software they will be using to see how variables are added and/or dropped from the model.

Consider the problem of predicting the salary y of an executive. Perhaps the biggest problem in building a model to describe executive salaries is choosing the important independent variables to be included in the model. The list of potentially important independent variables is extremely long (e.g., age, experience, tenure, education level, etc.), and we need some objective method of screening out those that are not important.

The problem of deciding which of a large set of independent variables to include in a model is a common one. Trying to determine which variables influence the profit of a firm, affect blood pressure of humans, or are related to a student's performance in college are only a few examples.

A systematic approach to building a model with a large number of independent variables is difficult because the interpretation of multivariable interactions and higher-order terms is tedious. We therefore turn to a screening procedure, available in most statistical software packages, known as **stepwise regression.**

The most commonly used stepwise regression procedure works as follows. The user first identifies the response, y, and the set of potentially important independent variables, $x_1, x_2, \ldots, x_k$, where k is generally large. [*Note:* This set of variables could include both first-order and higher-order terms. However, we may often include only the main effects of both quantitative variables (first-order terms) and qualitative variables (dummy variables), since the inclusion of second-order terms greatly increases the number of independent variables.] The response and independent variables are then entered into the computer software, and the stepwise procedure begins.

Step 1 The software program fits all possible one-variable models of the form

$$E(y) = \beta_0 + \beta_1 x_i$$

to the data, where x_i is the ith independent variable, $i = 1, 2, \ldots, k$. For each model, the test of the null hypothesis

$$H_0: \beta_1 = 0$$

against the alternative hypothesis

$$H_a: \beta_1 \neq 0$$

is conducted using the t-test (or the equivalent F-test) for a single β parameter. The independent variable that produces the largest (absolute) t value is declared the best one-variable predictor of y.* Call this independent variable x_1.

Step 2 The stepwise program now begins to search through the remaining $(k - 1)$ independent variables for the best two-variable model of the form

$$E(y) = \beta_0 + \beta_1 x_1 + \beta_2 x_i$$

This is done by fitting all two-variable models containing x_1 and each of the other $(k - 1)$ options for the second variable x_i. The t-values for the test $H_0: \beta_2 = 0$ are computed for each of the $(k - 1)$ models (corresponding to the remaining independent variables, $x_i, i = 2, 3, \ldots, k$), and the variable having the largest t is retained. Call this variable x_2.

At this point, some software packages diverge in methodology. The better packages now go back and check the t value of $\hat{\beta}_1$ after $\hat{\beta}_2 x_2$ has been added to the model. If the t-value has become nonsignificant at some specified α level (say $\alpha = .10$), the variable x_1 is removed and a search is made for the independent variable with a β parameter that will yield the most significant t-value in the presence of $\hat{\beta}_2 x_2$. Other packages do not recheck the significance of $\hat{\beta}_1$ but proceed directly to step 3.

The reason the t-value for x_1 may change from step 1 to step 2 is that the meaning of the coefficient $\hat{\beta}_1$ changes. In step 2, we are approximating a

---

*Note that the variable with the largest t value is also the one with the largest (absolute) Pearson product moment correlation, r (Section 10.6), with y.

complex response surface in two variables with a plane. The best-fitting plane may yield a different value for $\hat{\beta}_1$ than that obtained in step 1. Thus, both the value of $\hat{\beta}_1$ and its significance usually changes from step 1 to step 2. For this reason, the software packages that recheck the t-values at each step are preferred.

Suggested Exercise 13.107

Step 3 The stepwise procedure now checks for a third independent variable to include in the model with x_1 and x_2. That is, we seek the best model of the form

$$E(y) = \beta_0 + \beta_1 x_1 + \beta_2 x_2 + \beta_3 x_i$$

To do this, we fit all the $(k - 2)$ models using x_1, x_2, and each of the $(k - 2)$ remaining variables, x_i, as a possible x_3. The criterion is again to include the independent variable with the largest t value. Call this best third variable x_3.

The better programs now recheck the t-values corresponding to the x_1 and x_2 coefficients, removing the variables with t-values that have become nonsignificant. This procedure is continued until no further independent variables can be found that yield significant t-values (at the specified α level) in the presence of the variables already in the model.

The result of the stepwise procedure is a model containing only those terms with t-values that are significant at the specified α level. Thus, in most practical situations only several of the large number of independent variables remain. However, it is very important *not* to jump to the conclusion that all the independent variables important for predicting y have been identified or that the unimportant independent variables have been eliminated. Remember, the stepwise procedure is using only *sample estimates* of the true model coefficients (β's) to select the important variables. An extremely large number of single β parameter t-tests have been conducted, and the probability is very high that one or more errors have been made in including or excluding variables. That is, we have very probably included some unimportant independent variables in the model (Type I errors) and eliminated some important ones (Type II errors).

There is a second reason why we might not have arrived at a good model. When we choose the variables to be included in the stepwise regression, we may often omit high-order terms (to keep the number of variables manageable). Consequently, we may have initially omitted several important terms from the model. Thus, we should recognize stepwise regression for what it is: an objective screening procedure.

Successful model builders will now consider second-order terms (for quantitative variables) and other interactions among variables screened by the stepwise procedure. It would be best to develop this response surface model with a second set of data independent of that used for the screening, so the results of the stepwise procedure can be partially verified with new data. This is not always possible, however, because in many modeling situations only a small amount of data is available.

Teaching Tip

Make sure the students are using the stepwise procedure as a variable screening procedure only. The order of the terms to be used as well as the interaction between terms is left to the student to work with after the stepwise procedure has identified potential predictors of y.

Do not be deceived by the impressive-looking t-values that result from the stepwise procedure—it has retained only the independent variables with the largest t values. Also, be certain to consider second-order terms in systematically developing the prediction model. Finally, if you have used a first-order model for your stepwise procedure, remember that it may be greatly improved by the addition of higher-order terms.

Caution

Be wary of using the results of stepwise regression to make inferences about the relationship between $E(y)$ and the independent variables in the resulting first-order model. First, an extremely large number of t-tests have been conducted, leading to a high probability of making one or more Type I or Type II errors. Second, the stepwise model does not include any higher-order or interaction terms. Stepwise regression should be used only when necessary, that is, when you want to determine which of a large number of potentially important independent variables should be used in the model-building process.

EXAMPLE 13.12   RUNNING A STEPWISE REGRESSION

Problem   An international management consulting company develops multiple regression models for executive salaries of its client firms. The consulting company has found that models that use the natural logarithm of salary as the dependent variable have better predictive power than those using salary as the dependent variable.* A preliminary step in the construction of these models is the determination of the most important independent variables. For one firm, 10 potential independent variables (seven quantitative and three qualitative) were measured in a sample of 100 executives. The data, described in Table 13.7, are saved in the **EXECSAL** file. Since it would be very difficult to construct a complete second-order model with all of the 10 independent variables, use stepwise regression to decide which of the 10 variables should be included in the building of the final model for the natural log of executive salaries.

x_1, x_2, x_3, x_4, x_5

 EXECSAL

TABLE 13.7   Independent Variables in the Executive Salary Example

Independent Variable	Description	Type
x_1	Experience (years)	Quantitative
x_2	Education (years)	Quantitative
x_3	Bonus eligibility (1 if yes, 0 if no)	Qualitative
x_4	Number of employees supervised	Quantitative
x_5	Corporate assets (millions of dollars)	Quantitative
x_6	Board member (1 if yes, 0 if no)	Qualitative
x_7	Age (years)	Quantitative
x_8	Company profits (past 12 months, millions of dollars)	Quantitative
x_9	Has international responsibility (1 if yes, 0 if no)	Qualitative
x_{10}	Company's total sales (past 12 months, millions of dollars)	Quantitative

Solution   We will use stepwise regression with the main effects of the 10 independent variables to identify the most important variables. The dependent variable y is the natural logarithm of the executive salaries. The MINITAB stepwise regression printout is shown in Figure 13.34.

*This is probably because salaries tend to be incremented in *percentages* rather than dollar values. When a response variable undergoes percentage changes as the independent variables are varied, the logarithm of the response variable will be more suitable as a dependent variable.

Figure 13.34

MINITAB stepwise regression printout for executive salary data

```
          Alpha-to-Enter: 0.15   Alpha-to-Remove: 0.15


          Response is Y on 10 predictors, with N = 100


          Step              1       2       3       4       5
          Constant     11.091  10.968  10.783  10.278   9.962

          X1           0.0278  0.0273  0.0273  0.0273  0.0273
          T-Value       12.62   15.13   18.80   24.68   26.50
          P-Value       0.000   0.000   0.000   0.000   0.000

          X3                   0.197   0.233   0.232   0.225
          T-Value               7.10   10.17   13.30   13.74
          P-Value               0.000   0.000   0.000   0.000

          X4                          0.00048 0.00055 0.00052
          T-Value                        7.32   10.92   11.06
          P-Value                       0.000   0.000   0.000

          X2                                  0.0300  0.0291
          T-Value                               8.38    8.72
          P-Value                              0.000   0.000

          X5                                          0.00196
          T-Value                                        3.95
          P-Value                                       0.000

          S             0.161   0.131   0.106  0.0807  0.0751
          R-Sq          61.90   74.92   83.91   90.75   92.06
          R-Sq(adj)     61.51   74.40   83.41   90.36   91.64
          Mallows C-p   343.9   195.5    93.8    16.8     3.6
```

Note that the first variable included in the model is x_1, years of experience. At the second step, x_3, a dummy variable for the qualitative variable, bonus eligibility or not, is brought into the model. In steps 3, 4, and 5, the variables x_4 (number of employees supervised), x_2 (years of education), and x_5 (corporate assets), respectively, are selected for model inclusion. MINITAB stops after five steps because no other independent variables met the criterion for admission into the model. As a default, MINITAB uses $\alpha = .15$ in the t-tests conducted. In other words, if the p-value associated with a β coefficient exceeds $\alpha = .15$, the variable is *not* included in the model.

The results of the stepwise regression suggest that we should concentrate on these five independent variables. Models with second-order terms and interactions should be proposed and evaluated to determine the best model for predicting executive salaries.

Now Work   *Exercise 13.105*

■ ■ ■

Recommendation

Do *not* use the stepwise regression model as the final model for predicting y. Recall that the stepwise procedure tends to perform a large number of t-tests, inflating the overall probability of a Type I error, and does not automatically include higher-order terms (e.g., interactions and squared terms) in the final model. Use stepwise regression as a variable screening tool when there exists a large number of potential important independent variables. Then begin building models for y using the variables identified by stepwise.

Statistics in Action Revisited

Selecting the Independent Variables and Building a Model for Road Contract Cost

In the previous Statistics in Action Revisited section (p. 799), we used all eight of the independent variables in Table SIA13.1 to fit a first-order model for the cost (y) of a road construction contract awarded using the sealed-bid system. Although the model was deemed statistically useful for predicting y, the standard deviation of the model ($s = 305$ thousand dollars) was probably too large for the model to be "practically" useful. A more complex model—

one involving higher-order terms (interactions and squared terms)—needs to be considered. A complete second-order model involving all eight of the independent variables, however, would require over 100 terms! Consequently, we'll use stepwise regression to select the "best" subset of independent variables and then form a complete second-order model with just these variables.

Figure SIA13.4 is a MINITAB printout of the stepwise regression. You can see that the DOT engineer's cost

```
Alpha-to-Enter: 0.15   Alpha-to-Remove: 0.15


Response is COST on 8 predictors, with N = 235


Step                   1         2         3         4
Constant           20.91    -20.54    -55.22   -212.85

DOTEST            0.9263    0.9308    0.9110    0.9132
T-Value            93.89     95.52     56.86     57.11
P-Value            0.000     0.000     0.000     0.000

STATUS                                166       167       171
T-Value                              3.38      3.40      3.50
P-Value                              0.001     0.001     0.001

DAYSEST                                        0.27      0.33
T-Value                                        1.55      1.85
P-Value                                        0.122     0.065

BTPRATIO                                                  241
T-Value                                                  1.81
P-Value                                                 0.072

S                    313       306       305       304
R-Sq               97.42     97.55     97.57     97.60
R-Sq(adj)          97.41     97.52     97.54     97.56
Mallows C-p         15.2       5.7       5.2       4.0
```

Figure SIA13.4
MINITAB Stepwise Regression for the Road Cost Data

estimate (DOTEST) is the first variable selected, followed by bid status (STATUS), estimated work days (DAYSEST), and bids-to-planholders ratio (BTPRATIO). Recall that MINITAB uses a default α level of .15. If we reduce the significance level for entry to $\alpha = .05$, only DOTEST and STATUS are selected since the p-values (highlighted on the printout) for DAYSEST and BTPRATIO are both greater than .05.

Since bid status is a qualitative variable ($x_2 = 1$ if fixed and 0 if competitive), a complete second-order model for contract cost (y) using DOTEST (x_1) and STATUS (x_2) is given by the equation

$$E(y) = \beta_0 + \beta_1 x_1 + \beta_2 (x_1)^2 + \beta_3 x_2 + \beta_4 x_1 x_2 + \beta_5 (x_1)^2 x_2$$

The MINITAB printout for this model is shown in Figure SIA13.5. Note that the global F-test for the model is statistically significant (p-value $= .000$) and the model standard deviation, $s = 296.6$, is smaller than the standard deviation of the first-order model.

Are the second-order terms in the model, $\beta_2 (x_1)^2$ and $\beta_5 (x_1)^2 x_2$, necessary? If not, we can simplify the model by dropping these curvature terms. The hypothesis of interest is $H_0: \beta_2 = \beta_5 = 0$. To test this subset of β's, we compare the complete second-order model to a model without the curvilinear terms. The reduced model takes the form

$$E(y) = \beta_0 + \beta_1 x_1 + \beta_3 x_2 + \beta_4 x_1 x_2$$

The results of this nested model (or partial) F-test are shown at the bottom of the SPSS printout, Figure SIA13.6. The p-value of the test (highlighted on the SPSS printout) is .355. Since this p-value is greater than $\alpha = .05$, there is insufficient evidence to reject H_0. That is, there is no evidence to indicate that the two curvature terms are useful predictors of road construction cost. Consequently, the reduced model is selected as the better predictor of cost.

The MINITAB printout for the reduced model is shown in Figure SIA13.7. The overall model is statistically useful (p-value $= .000$ for global F-test), explaining about 98% of the sample variation in contract costs. The model standard deviation, $s = 296.7$, implies that we can predict costs to within about 593 thousand dollars. Also, the t-test for the interaction term, $\beta_4 x_1 x_2$, is significant (p-value $= .000$), implying that the relationship between contract cost (y) and DOT cost estimate (x_1) depends on bid status (fixed or competitive).

The nature of the interaction is illustrated in the MINITAB graph of the least squared prediction equation for the reduced model, Figure SIA13.8. You can see that the rate of increase of contract cost (y) with the DOT engineer's estimate of cost (x_1) is steeper for fixed contracts than for competitive contracts.

```
The regression equation is
COST = - 3.0 + 0.916 DOTEST + 0.000001 DOTEST2 - 36.7 STATUS + 0.324 STA_DOT
       - 0.000036 STA_DOT2


Predictor        Coef       SE Coef        T       P
Constant        -2.98         30.89     -0.10   0.923
DOTEST        0.91553       0.02917     31.39   0.000
DOTEST2     0.00000072    0.00000340      0.21   0.833
STATUS         -36.72         74.77     -0.49   0.624
STA_DOT        0.3242        0.1192      2.72   0.007
STA_DOT2   -0.00003576    0.00002478     -1.44   0.150


S = 296.646    R-Sq = 97.7%    R-Sq(adj) = 97.7%


Analysis of Variance

Source          DF         SS          MS         F       P
Regression       5   866723202   173344640   1969.85   0.000
Residual Error  229    20151771       87999
Total           234   886874973
```

Figure SIA13.5
MINITAB regression printout for the complete second-order model of contract cost

Model Summary

Model	R	R Square	Adjusted R Square	Std. Error of the Estimate	Change Statistics				
					R Square Change	F Change	df1	df2	Sig. F Change
1	.988a	.977	.977	296.69515	.977	3281.312	3	231	.000
2	.989b	.977	.977	296.64238	.000	1.041	2	229	.355

a. Predictors: (Constant), STA_DOT, DOTEST, STATUS
b. Predictors: (Constant), STA_DOT, DOTEST, STATUS, DOTEST2, STA_DOT2

Figure SIA13.6
SPSS printout of test to compare the complete second-order model of contract cost to the reduced model

```
The regression equation is
COST = - 6.4 + 0.921 DOTEST + 28.7 STATUS + 0.163 STA_DOT


Predictor       Coef      SE Coef        T       P
Constant       -6.43        26.21    -0.25    0.806
DOTEST      0.921336     0.009723    94.75    0.000
STATUS         28.67        58.66     0.49    0.625
STA_DOT      0.16328      0.04043     4.04    0.000


S = 296.699    R-Sq = 97.7%    R-Sq(adj) = 97.7%


Analysis of Variance

Source            DF           SS          MS        F       P
Regression         3    866540004   288846668  3281.22   0.000
Residual Error   231     20334968       88030
Total            234    886874973
```

Figure SIA13.7
MINITAB regression printout for the reduced model of contract cost

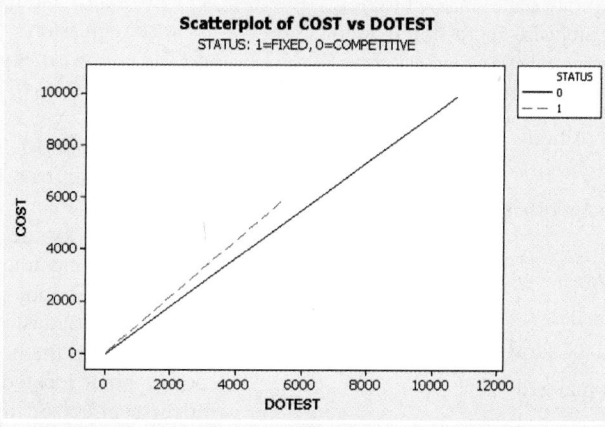

Figure SIA13.8
MINITAB plot of least squares prediction equation for the
reduced model of contract cost

Exercises 13.104–13.107

Learning the Mechanics

13.104 There are six independent variables, x_1, x_2, x_3, x_4, x_5, and x_6, that might be useful in predicting a response y. A total of $n = 50$ observations is available, and it is decided to employ stepwise regression to help in selecting the independent variables that appear to be useful. The computer fits all possible one-variable models of the form

$$E(y) = \beta_0 + \beta_1 x_i$$

where x_i is the ith independent variable, $i = 1, 2, \ldots, 6$. The information in the table is provided from the computer printout.

Independent Variable	$\hat{\beta}_i$	$s_{\hat{\beta}_i}$
x_1	1.6	.42
x_2	−.9	.01
x_3	3.4	1.14
x_4	2.5	2.06
x_5	−4.4	.73
x_6	.3	.35

a. Which independent variable is declared the best one-variable predictor of y? Explain. x_2

b. Would this variable be included in the model at this stage? Explain.   Yes

c. Describe the next phase that a stepwise procedure would execute.

Applying the Concepts—Basic

13.105 *Benefits Quarterly* (First Quarter, 1995) published a study of entry-level job preferences. A number of independent variables were used to model the job preferences (measured on a 10-point scale) of 164 business school graduates. Suppose stepwise regression is used to build a model for job preference score (y) as a function of the following independent variables:

$$x_1 = \begin{cases} 1 & \text{if flextime position} \\ 0 & \text{if not} \end{cases}$$

$$x_2 = \begin{cases} 1 & \text{if day care support required} \\ 0 & \text{if not} \end{cases}$$

$$x_3 = \begin{cases} 1 & \text{if spousal transfer support required} \\ 0 & \text{if not} \end{cases}$$

x_4 = Number of sick days allowed

$$x_5 = \begin{cases} 1 & \text{if applicant married} \\ 0 & \text{if not} \end{cases}$$

x_6 = Number of children of applicant

$$x_7 = \begin{cases} 1 & \text{if male applicant} \\ 0 & \text{if female applicant} \end{cases}$$

a. How many models are fit to the data in step 1? Give the general form of these models.   7

b. How many models are fit to the data in step 2? Give the general form of these models.   6

c. How many models are fit to the data in step 3? Give the general form of these models.   5

d. Explain how the procedure determines when to stop adding independent variables to the model.

e. Describe two major drawbacks to using the final stepwise model as the "best" model for job preference score y.

Applying the Concepts—Intermediate

13.106 Bus Rapid Transit (BRT) is a rapidly growing trend in the provision of public transportation in America. The Center for Urban Transportation Research (CUTR) at the University of South Florida conducted a survey of BRT customers in Miami (*Transportation Research Board* Annual Meeting, Jan. 2003). Data on the following variables (all measured on a 5-point scale, where 1 = very unsatisfied and 5 = very satisfied) were collected for a sample of over 500 bus riders: overall satisfaction with BRT (y), safety on bus (x_1), seat availability (x_2), dependability (x_3), travel time (x_4), cost (x_5), information/maps (x_6), convenience of routes (x_7), traffic signals (x_8), safety at bus stops (x_9), hours of service (x_{10}), and frequency of service (x_{11}). CUTR analysts used stepwise regression to model overall satisfaction (y).

a. How many models are fit at Step 1 of the stepwise regression?   11

b. How many models are fit at Step 2 of the stepwise regression?   10

c. How many models are fit at Step 11 of the stepwise regression?   1

d. The stepwise regression selected the following eight variables to include in the model (in order of selection): $x_{11}, x_4, x_2, x_7, x_{10}, x_1, x_9$, and x_3. Write the equation for $E(y)$ that results from stepwise.

e. The model, part **d**, resulted in $R^2 = .677$. Interpret this value.

f. Explain why the CUTR analysts should be cautious in concluding that the "best" model for $E(y)$ has been found.

13.107 A marine biologist was hired by the EPA to determine whether the hot-water runoff from a particular power plant located near a large gulf is having an adverse effect on the marine life in the area. The biologist's goal is to acquire a prediction equation for the number of marine animals located at certain designated areas, or stations, in the gulf. Based on past experience, the EPA considered the following environmental factors as predictors for the number of animals at a particular station:

x_1 = Temperature of water (TEMP)
x_2 = Salinity of water (SAL)
x_3 = Dissolved oxygen content of water (DO)
x_4 = Turbidity index, a measure of the turbidity of the water (TI)
x_5 = Depth of the water at the station (ST_DEPTH)
x_6 = Total weight of sea grasses in sampled area (TGRSWT)

As a preliminary step in the construction of this model, the biologist used a stepwise regression procedure to identify the most important of these six variables. A total of 716 samples were taken at different stations in the gulf, producing the SPSS printout shown below. (The response measured was y, the logarithm of the number of marine animals found in the sampled area.)

a. According to the SPSS printout, which of the six independent variables should be used in the model? (Use $\alpha = .10$.) $x_4, x_5,$ and x_6
b. Are we able to assume that the marine biologist has identified all the important independent variables for the prediction of y? Why?   No
c. Using the variables identified in part **a**, write the first-order model with interaction that may be used to predict y.
d. How would the marine biologist determine whether the model specified in part **c** is better than the first-order model? H_0: $\beta_4 = \beta_5 = \beta_6 = 0$
e. Note the small value of R^2. What action might the biologist take to improve the model?

Variables Entered/Removed[a]

Model	Variables Entered	Variables Removed	Method
1	ST_DEPTH	.	Stepwise (Criteria: Probability-of-F-to-enter <= .050, Probability-of-F-to-remove >= .100).
2	TGRSWT	.	Stepwise (Criteria: Probability-of-F-to-enter <= .050, Probability-of-F-to-remove >= .100).
3	TI	.	Stepwise (Criteria: Probability-of-F-to-enter <= .050, Probability-of-F-to-remove >= .100).

a. Dependent Variable: LOGNUM

Model Summary

Model	R	R Square	Adjusted R Square	Std. Error of the Estimate
1	.329[a]	.122	.121	.7615773
2	.427[b]	.182	.180	.7348470
3	.432[c]	.187	.184	.7348469

a. Predictors: (Constant), ST_DEPTH
b. Predictors: (Constant), ST_DEPTH, TGRSWT
c. Predictors: (Constant), ST_DEPTH, TGRSWT, TI

13.13 Residual Analysis: Checking the Regression Assumptions

When we apply regression analysis to a set of data, we never know for certain whether the assumptions of Section 13.3 are satisfied. How far can we deviate from the assumptions and still expect regression analysis to yield results that will have the reliability stated in this chapter? How can we detect departures (if they exist) from the assumptions and what can we do about them? We provide some answers to these questions in this section.

Teaching Tip

We check our assumptions on the sample of residuals to see if they are met. If the assumptions appear to be satisfied for the residuals, we infer that they also would be met for the population of ε's.

Recall from Section 13.3 that for any given set of values of $x_1, x_2, \ldots, x_k$ we assume that the random error term ϵ has a normal probability distribution with mean equal to 0 and variance equal to σ^2. Also, we assume that the random errors are probabilistically independent. It is unlikely that these assumptions are ever satisfied exactly in a practical application of regression analysis. Fortunately, experience has shown that least squares regression analysis produces reliable statistical tests, confidence intervals, and prediction intervals as long as the departures from the assumptions are not too great. In this section we present some methods for determining whether the data indicate significant departures from the assumptions.

Because the assumptions all concern the random error component, ϵ, of the model, the first step is to estimate the random error. Since the actual random error associated with a particular value of y is the difference between the actual y value and its unknown mean, we estimate the error by the difference between the actual y-value and the *estimated* mean. This estimated error is called the *regression residual*, or simply the **residual,** and is denoted by $\hat{\epsilon}$. The actual error ϵ and residual $\hat{\epsilon}$ are shown in Figure 13.35.

Figure 13.35

Actual random error ϵ and regression residual $\hat{\epsilon}$

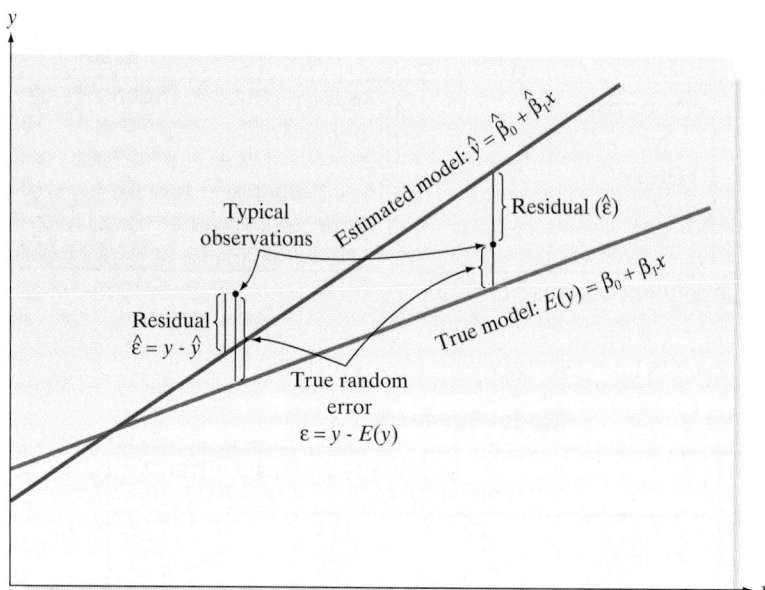

DEFINITION 13.5

A **regression residual,** $\hat{\epsilon}$, is defined as the difference between an observed y value and its corresponding predicted value:

$$\hat{\epsilon} = (y - \hat{y}) = y - (\hat{\beta}_0 + \hat{\beta}_1 x_1 + \hat{\beta}_2 x_2 + \cdots + \hat{\beta}_k x_k)$$

Since the true mean of y (that is, the true regression model) is not known, the actual random error cannot be calculated. However, because the residual is based on the estimated mean (the least squares regression model), it can be calculated and used to estimate the random error and to check the regression assumptions. Such checks are generally referred to as **residual analyses.** Two useful properties of residuals are given in the next box.

Properties of Regression Residuals

1. The mean of the residuals is equal to 0. This property follows from the fact that the sum of the differences between the observed y values and their least squares predicted $\hat{y}$ values is equal to 0.

$$\sum (\text{Residuals}) = \sum (y - \hat{y}) = 0$$

2. The standard deviation of the residuals is equal to the standard deviation of the fitted regression model, s. This property follows from the fact that the sum of the squared residuals is equal to SSE, which when divided by the error degrees of freedom is equal to the variance of the fitted regression model, s^2. The square root of the variance is both the standard deviation of the residuals and the standard deviation of the regression model.

$$\sum (\text{Residuals})^2 = \sum (y - \hat{y})^2 = \text{SSE}$$

$$s = \sqrt{\frac{\sum (\text{Residuals})^2}{n - (k + 1)}} = \sqrt{\frac{\text{SSE}}{n - (k + 1)}}$$

Biography

FRANCIS J. ANSCOMBE (1918–2001)
Anscombe's Data

British citizen Frank Anscombe grew up in a small town near the English Channel. He attended Trinity College in Cambridge, England on a merit scholarship, graduating with first class honors in mathematics in 1939. He later earned his master's degree in 1943. During World War II, Anscombe worked for the British Ministry of Supply, developing a mathematical solution for aiming antiaircraft rockets at German bombers and buzz bombs. Following the war, Anscombe worked at the Rothamsted Experimental Station, applying statistics to agriculture. There, he formed his appreciation for solving problems with social relevance. During his career as a professor of statistics, Anscombe served on the faculty of Cambridge, Princeton, and Yale Universities. He was a pioneer in the application of computers to statistical analysis, and was one of the original developers of residual analysis in regression. Anscombe is famous for a paper he wrote in 1973, in which he showed that one regression model could be fit by four very different data sets ("Anscombe's data"). While Anscombe published 50 research articles on statistics, he also had serious interests in classical music, poetry, and art.

The following examples show how a graphical analysis of regression residuals can be used to verify the assumptions associated with the model and to support improvements to the model when the assumptions do not appear to be satisfied. Although the residuals can be calculated and plotted by hand, we rely on the statistical software for these tasks in the examples and exercises.

First, we demonstrate how a residual plot can detect a model in which the hypothesized relationship between $E(y)$ and an independent variable x is misspecified. The assumption of mean error of 0 is violated in these types of models.*

EXAMPLE 13.13   ANALYZING RESIDUALS

ELECTRIC

TABLE 13.8   Home Size–Electrical Usage Data

Size of Home, x (sq. ft.)	Monthly Usage, y (kilowatt-hours)
1,290	1,182
1,350	1,172
1,470	1,264
1,600	1,493
1,710	1,571
1,840	1,711
1,980	1,804
2,230	1,840
2,400	1,956
2,930	1,954

Problem Refer to the problem of modeling the relationship between home size (x) and electrical usage (y) in Example 13.6 (p. 814). The data for $n = 10$ homes are repeated in Table 13.8. MINITAB printouts for a straight-line model and a quadratic model fitted to the data are shown in Figures 13.36(a) and 13.36(b), respectively. The residuals from these models are highlighted in the printouts. The residuals are then plotted on the vertical axis against the variable x, size of home, on the horizontal axis in Figures 13.37(a) and 13.37(b), respectively.

a. Verify that each residual is equal to the difference between the observed y value and the estimated mean value, $\hat{y}$.

b. Analyze the residual plots.

```
The regression equation is
USAGE = 579 + 0.540 SIZE


Predictor      Coef   SE Coef      T       P
Constant      578.9     167.0   3.47   0.008
SIZE        0.54030   0.08593   6.29   0.000


S = 133.438    R-Sq = 83.2%    R-Sq(adj) = 81.1%


Analysis of Variance

Source           DF      SS      MS       F       P
Regression        1  703957  703957   39.54   0.000
Residual Error    8  142445   17806
Total             9  846402


Obs  SIZE   USAGE     Fit  SE Fit  Residual  St Resid
 1   1290  1182.0  1275.9    66.0     -93.9     -0.81
 2   1350  1172.0  1308.3    62.1    -136.3     -1.15
 3   1470  1264.0  1373.2    55.0    -109.2     -0.90
 4   1600  1493.0  1443.4    48.6      49.6      0.40
 5   1710  1571.0  1502.8    44.7      68.2      0.54
 6   1840  1711.0  1573.1    42.3     137.9      1.09
 7   1980  1804.0  1648.7    43.1     155.3      1.23
 8   2230  1840.0  1783.8    51.8      56.2      0.46
 9   2400  1956.0  1875.7    61.5      80.3      0.68
10   2930  1954.0  2162.0    99.6    -208.0     -2.34R

R denotes an observation with a large standardized residual.
```

Figure 13.36a
MINITAB printout for straight-line model of electrical usage

*For a misspecified model, the hypothesized mean of y, denoted by $E_h(y)$, will not equal the true mean of y, $E(y)$. Since $y = E_h(y) + \epsilon$, then $\epsilon = y - E_h(y)$ and $E(\epsilon) = E[y - E_h(y)] = E(y) - E_h(y) \neq 0$.

Figure 13.36b
MINITAB printout
for quadratic model
of electrical usage

```
The regression equation is
USAGE = 579 + 0.540 SIZE


Predictor       Coef   SE Coef      T      P
Constant       578.9     167.0   3.47  0.008
SIZE         0.54030   0.08593   6.29  0.000


S = 133.438   R-Sq = 83.2%   R-Sq(adj) = 81.1%


Analysis of Variance

Source          DF       SS       MS      F      P
Regression       1   703957   703957  39.54  0.000
Residual Error   8   142445    17806
Total            9   846402


Obs   SIZE    USAGE     Fit  SE Fit  Residual  St Resid
  1   1290   1182.0  1275.9    66.0     -93.9     -0.81
  2   1350   1172.0  1308.3    62.1    -136.3     -1.15
  3   1470   1264.0  1373.2    55.0    -109.2     -0.90
  4   1600   1493.0  1443.4    48.6      49.6      0.40
  5   1710   1571.0  1502.8    44.7      68.2      0.54
  6   1840   1711.0  1573.1    42.3     137.9      1.09
  7   1980   1804.0  1648.7    43.1     155.3      1.23
  8   2230   1840.0  1783.8    51.8      56.2      0.46
  9   2400   1956.0  1875.7    61.5      80.3      0.68
 10   2930   1954.0  2162.0    99.6    -208.0     -2.34R

R denotes an observation with a large standardized residual.
```

Figure 13.37a
MINITAB residual plot
for straight-line model
of electrical usage

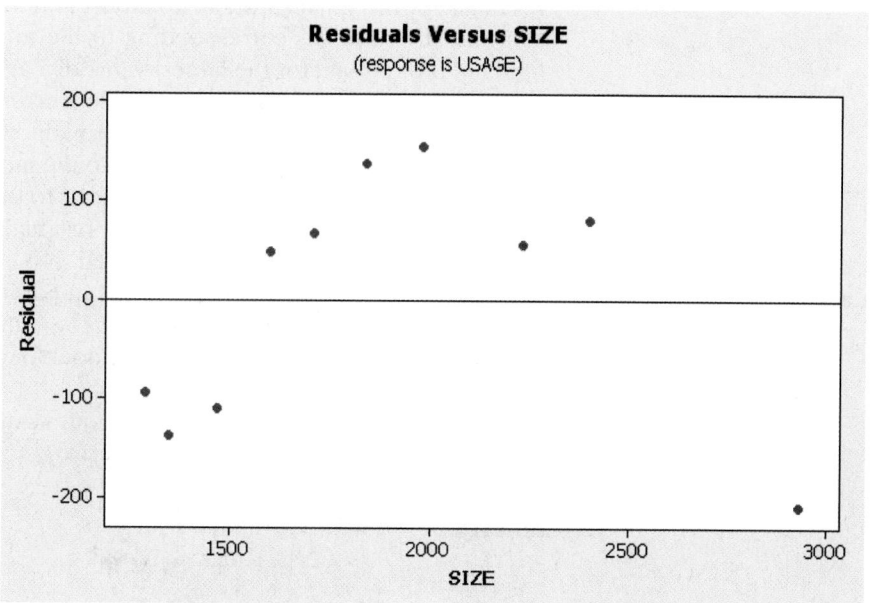

Figure 13.37b

MINITAB residual plot
for quadratic model
of electrical usage

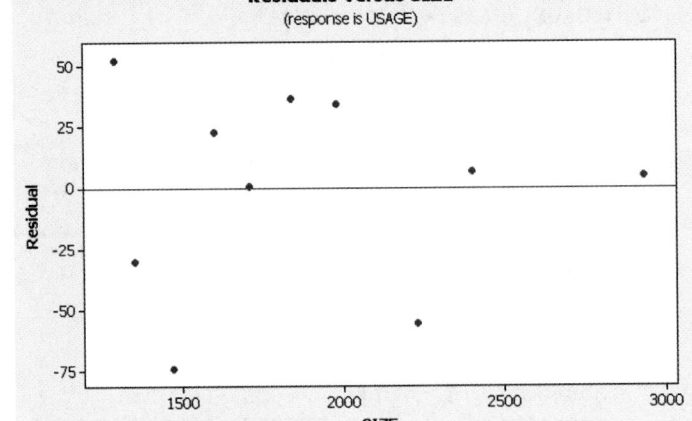

Solution   **a.** For the straight-line model the residual is calculated for the first y value as follows:

$$\hat{\epsilon} = (y - \hat{y}) = 1{,}182 - 1{,}275.9 = -93.9$$

where $\hat{y}$ is the first number in the column labeled **Fit** on the MINITAB print-out in Figure 13.36(a). Similarly, the residual for the first y value using the quadratic model (Figure 13.36b) is

$$\hat{\epsilon} = 1{,}182 - 1{,}129.6 = 52.4$$

Both residuals agree (after rounding) with the first values given in the column labeled **Residual** in Figures 13.36(a) and 13.36(b), respectively. Although the residuals both correspond to the same observed y value, 1,182, they differ because the predicted mean value changes depending on whether the straight-line model or quadratic model is used. Similar calculations produce the remaining residuals.

b. The MINITAB plot of the residuals for the straight-line model (Figure 13.37a) reveals a nonrandom pattern. The residuals exhibit a curved shape, with the residuals for the small values of x below the horizontal 0 (mean of the residuals) line, the residuals corresponding to the middle values of x above the 0 line, and the residual for the largest value of x again below the 0 line. The indication is that the mean value of the random error ϵ *within* each of these ranges of x (small, medium, large) may not be equal to 0. Such a pattern usually indicates that curvature needs to be added to the model.

When the second-order term is added to the model, the nonrandom pattern disappears. In Figure 13.37(b), the residuals appear to be randomly distributed around the 0 line, as expected. Note, too, that the $\pm 2s$ standard deviation lines are at about ± 95 on the quadratic residual plot, compared to (about) ± 275 on the straight-line plot. The implication is that the quadratic model provides a considerably better model for predicting electrical usage.

Look Book The residual analysis verifies our conclusions from Example 13.6, where we found the t-test for the quadratic term, $\beta_2 x^2$, to be statistically significant.

| Now Work | *Exercise 13.108a* |

■ ■ ■

Residual analyses are also useful for detecting one or more observations that deviate significantly from the regression model. We expect approximately 95% of the residuals to fall within 2 standard deviations of the 0 line, and all or almost all of them to lie within 3 standard deviations of their mean of 0. Residuals that are extremely far from the 0 line, and disconnected from the bulk of the other residuals, are called *outliers*, and should receive special attention from the regression analyst.

DEFINITION 13.6

A residual that is larger than $3s$ (in absolute value) is considered to be an **outlier.**

EXAMPLE 13.14   IDENTIFYING OUTLIERS

Problem   Refer to Example 13.5 (page 806) in which we modeled the auction price y of a grandfather clock as a function of age x_1 and number of bidders x_2. The data for this example are repeated in Table 13.9, with one important difference: The auction price of the clock at the top of the second column has been changed from \$2,131 to \$1,131 (highlighted in Table 13.9). The interaction model

$$E(y) = \beta_0 + \beta_1 x_1 + \beta_2 x_2 + \beta_3 x_1 x_2$$

is again fit to these (modified) data, with the MINITAB printout shown in Figure 13.38. The residuals are shown highlighted in the printout and then plotted against the number of bidders, x_2, in Figure 13.39. Analyze the residual plot.

Solution   The residual plot dramatically reveals the one altered measurement. Note that one of the two residuals at $x_2 = 14$ bidders falls more than 3 standard deviations below 0. Note that no other residual falls more than 2 standard deviations from 0.

 GFCLOCKALT

TABLE 13.9   Altered Auction Price Data

Age, x_1 (years)	Number of Bidders, x_2	Auction Price, y (\$)	Age, x_1 (years)	Number of Bidders, x_2	Auction Price, y(\$)
127	13	1,235	170	14	1,131
115	12	1,080	182	8	1,550
127	7	845	162	11	1,884
150	9	1,522	184	10	2,041
156	6	1,047	143	6	845
182	11	1,979	159	9	1,483
156	12	1,822	108	14	1,055
132	10	1,253	175	8	1,545
137	9	1,297	108	6	729
113	9	946	179	9	1,792
137	15	1,713	111	15	1,175
117	11	1,024	187	8	1,593
137	8	1,147	111	7	785
153	6	1,092	115	7	744
117	13	1,152	194	5	1,356
126	10	1,336	168	7	1,262

Figure 13.38

MINITAB regression printout for altered grandfather clock data

```
The regression equation is
PRICE = - 513 + 8.17 AGE + 19.9 NUMBIDS + 0.320 AGE_BIDS


Predictor     Coef   SE Coef     T      P
Constant    -512.8     665.9  -0.77  0.448
AGE          8.165     4.585   1.78  0.086
NUMBIDS      19.89     67.44   0.29  0.770
AGE_BIDS    0.3196    0.4790   0.67  0.510


S = 200.598   R-Sq = 72.9%   R-Sq(adj) = 70.0%


Analysis of Variance

Source            DF        SS       MS      F      P
Regression         3   3033587  1011196  25.13  0.000
Residual Error    28   1126703    40239
Total             31   4160290


Obs   AGE    PRICE      Fit   SE Fit   Residual   St Resid
  1   127   1235.0   1310.4     59.3      -75.4      -0.39
  2   115   1080.0   1105.9     62.1      -25.9      -0.14
  3   127    845.0    947.5     61.1     -102.5      -0.54
  4   150   1522.0   1322.5     37.1      199.5       1.01
  5   156   1047.0   1179.5     60.3     -132.5      -0.69
  6   182   1979.0   1831.9     82.9      147.1       0.81
  7   156   1822.0   1598.0     61.9      224.0       1.17
  8   132   1253.0   1185.8     39.7       67.2       0.34
  9   137   1297.0   1178.9     39.0      118.1       0.60
 10   113    946.0    913.9     58.6       32.1       0.17
 11   137   1713.0   1561.0     78.4      152.0       0.82
 12   117   1024.0   1072.6     53.1      -48.6      -0.25
 13   137   1147.0   1115.2     44.3       31.8       0.16
 14   153   1092.0   1149.2     59.0      -57.2      -0.30
 15   117   1152.0   1187.2     69.7      -35.2      -0.19
 16   126   1336.0   1117.6     43.4      218.4       1.12
 17   170   1131.0   1914.4    116.7     -783.4      -4.80R
 18   182   1550.0   1597.7     62.8      -47.7      -0.25
 19   162   1884.0   1598.3     57.0      285.7       1.49
 20   184   2041.0   1776.6     70.7      264.4       1.41
 21   143    845.0   1048.4     58.9     -203.4      -1.06
 22   159   1483.0   1421.8     40.6       61.2       0.31
 23   108   1055.0   1130.7     97.9      -75.7      -0.43
 24   175   1545.0   1522.7     55.4       22.3       0.12
 25   108    729.0    695.5     99.6       33.5       0.19
 26   179   1792.0   1642.7     57.6      149.3       0.78
 27   111   1175.0   1224.0    107.2      -49.0      -0.29
 28   187   1593.0   1651.3     68.6      -58.3      -0.31
 29   111    785.0    781.1     80.9        3.9       0.02
 30   115    744.0    822.7     75.5      -78.7      -0.42
 31   194   1356.0   1480.7    133.6     -124.7      -0.83 X
 32   168   1262.0   1374.0     57.7     -112.0      -0.58


R denotes an observation with a large standardized residual.
X denotes an observation whose X value gives it large influence.
```

Figure 13.39
MINITAB residual plot
for altered grandfather
clock data

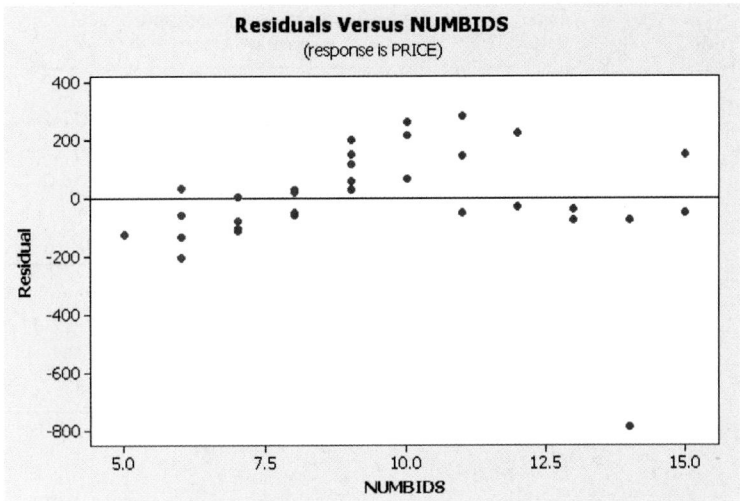

What do we do with outliers once we identify them? First, we try to determine the cause. Were the data entered into the computer incorrectly? Was the observation recorded incorrectly when the data were collected? If so, we correct the observation and rerun the analysis. Another possibility is that the observation is not representative of the conditions we are trying to model. For example, in this case the low price may be attributable to extreme damage to the clock, or to a clock of inferior quality compared to the others. In these cases we probably would exclude the observation from the analysis. In many cases you may not be able to determine the cause of the outlier. Even so, you may want to rerun the regression analysis excluding the outlier in order to assess the effect of that observation on the results of the analysis.

Figure 13.40 shows the printout when the outlier observation is excluded from the grandfather clock analysis, and Figure 13.41 shows the new plot of the residuals against the number of bidders. Now only one of the residuals lies beyond 2 standard deviations from 0, and none of them lies beyond 3 standard deviations. Also, the model statistics indicate a much better model without the outlier. Most notably, the

Teaching Tip

Many computer packages will list the values of the residual as well as a standardized residual plot. Both of these are easy alternative methods for detecting outliers in the data.

Figure 13.40
MINITAB regression
printout when outlier
is deleted

```
The regression equation is
PRICE = 474 - 0.46 AGE - 114 NUMBIDS + 1.48 AGE_BIDS


Predictor      Coef    SE Coef       T       P
Constant      474.0      298.2     1.59   0.124
AGE          -0.465      2.107    -0.22   0.827
NUMBIDS     -114.12      31.23    -3.65   0.001
AGE_BIDS     1.4781     0.2295     6.44   0.000


S = 85.8286    R-Sq = 95.2%    R-Sq(adj) = 94.7%


Analysis of Variance

Source           DF        SS        MS        F       P
Regression        3   3933417   1311139   177.99   0.000
Residual Error   27    198897      7367
Total            30   4132314
```

Figure 13.41

MINITAB residual plot when outlier is deleted

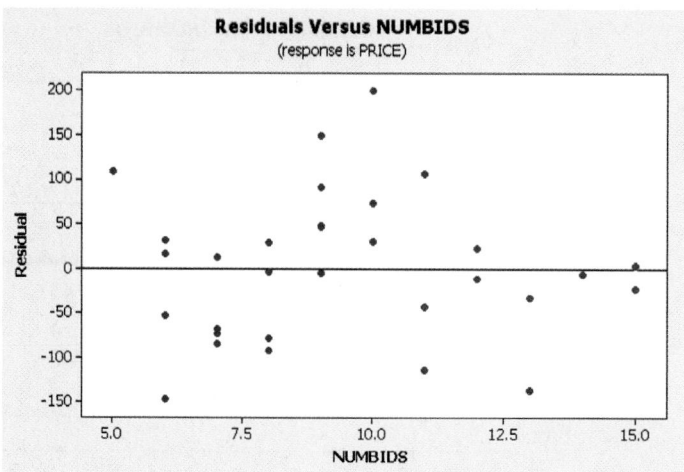

standard deviation (*s*) has decreased from 200.6 to 85.83, indicating a model that will provide more precise estimates and predictions (narrower confidence and prediction intervals) for clocks that are similar to those in the reduced sample.

Look Back Remember that if the outlier is removed from the analysis when in fact it belongs to the same population as the rest of the sample, the resulting model may provide misleading estimates and predictions.

Now Work *Exercise 13.108c*

■ ■ ■

Outlier analysis is another example of testing the assumption that the expected (mean) value of the random error ϵ is 0, since this assumption is in doubt for the error terms corresponding to the outliers. The next example in this section checks the assumption of the normality of the random error component.

EXAMPLE 13.15   USING RESIDUALS TO CHECK FOR NORMAL ERRORS

Problem   Refer to Example 13.14. Analyze the distribution of the residuals in the grandfather clock example, both before and after the outlier residual is removed. Determine whether the assumption of a normally distributed error term is reasonable.

Solution   A histogram and normal probability plot for the two sets of residuals are constructed using MINITAB and are shown in Figures 13.42 and 13.43. Note that the outlier appears to skew the histogram in Figure 13.42, whereas the histogram in Figure 13.43 appears to be more mound shaped. Similarly, the pattern of residuals in the normal probability plot in Figure 13.43 (outlier deleted) is more nearly a straight line than the pattern in Figure 13.42 (outlier included). Although the graphs do not provide formal statistical tests of normality, they do provide a descriptive display. In this example the normality assumption appears to be more plausible after the outlier is removed. Consult the references for methods to conduct statistical tests of normality using the residuals.

Now Work *Exercise 13.108d*

■ ■ ■

Figure 13.42

MINITAB graphs of regression residuals for grandfather clock model (outlier included)

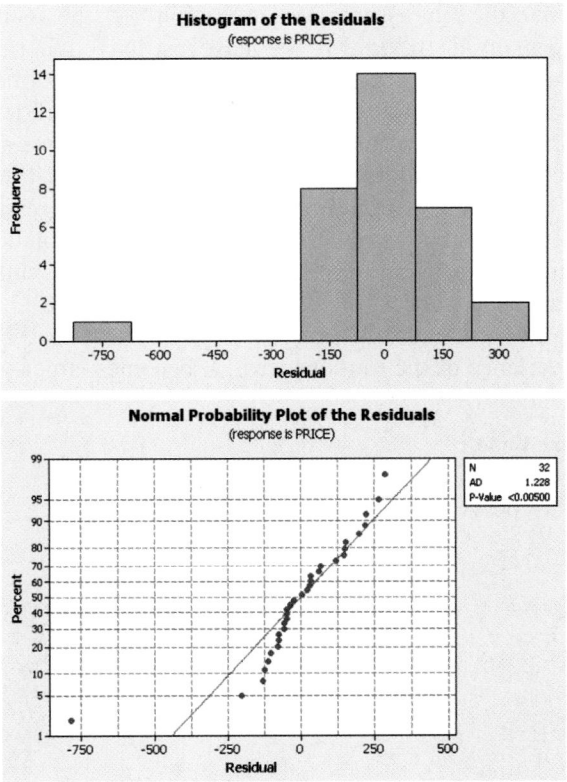

Figure 13.43

MINITAB graphs of regression residuals for grandfather clock model (outlier deleted)

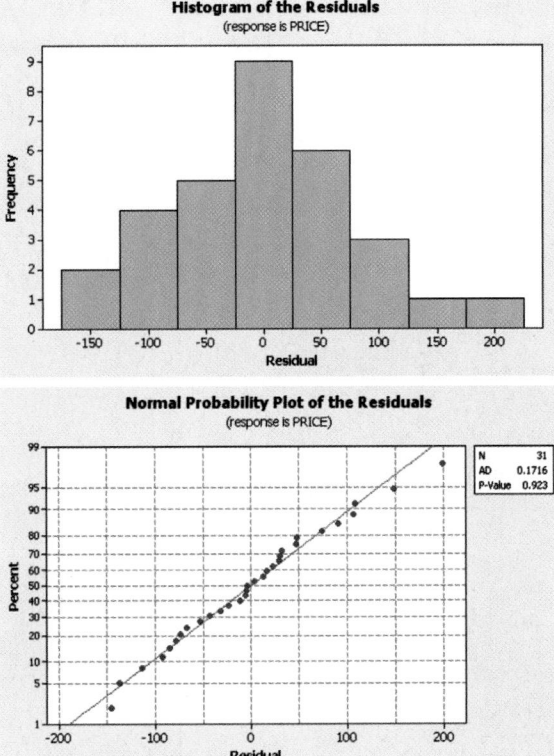

Of the four assumptions in Section 13.3, the assumption that the random error is normally distributed is the least restrictive when we apply regression analysis in practice. That is, moderate departures from a normal distribution have very little effect on the validity of the statistical tests, confidence intervals, and prediction intervals presented in this chapter. In this case, we say that regression analysis is **robust** with respect to nonnormal errors. However, great departures from normality cast doubt on any inferences derived from the regression analysis.

Residual plots can also be used to detect violations of the assumption of constant error variance. For example, a plot of the residuals versus the predicted value $\hat{y}$ may display one of the patterns shown in Figure 13.44. In these figures, the range in values of the residuals increases (or decreases) as $\hat{y}$ increases, thus indicating that the variance of the random error, ϵ, becomes larger (or smaller) as the estimate of

Figure 13.44

Residual plots showing changes in the variance of ϵ

a.

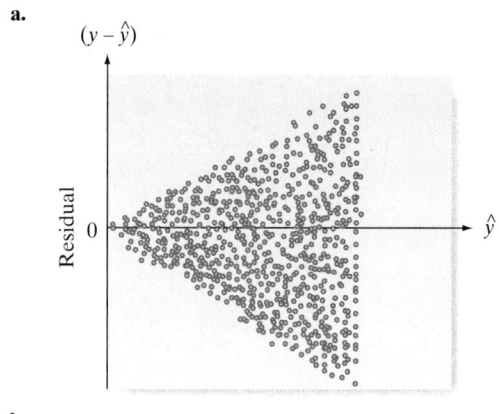

b.

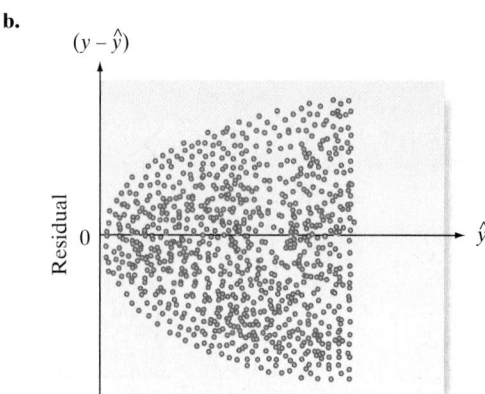

c.

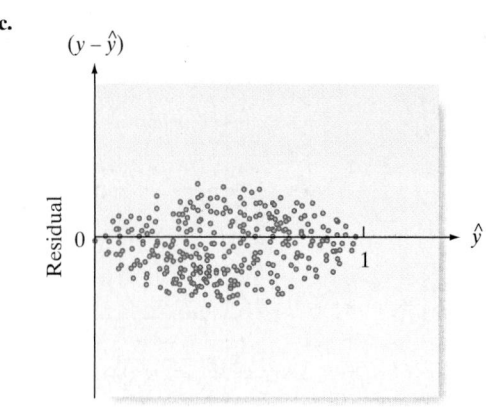

$E(y)$ increases in value. Since $E(y)$ depends on the x values in the model, this implies that the variance of ϵ is not constant for all settings of the x's.

In the final example of this section, we demonstrate how to use this plot to detect a nonconstant variance and suggest a useful remedy.

EXAMPLE 13.16   USING RESIDUALS TO CHECK EQUAL VARIANCES

Problem   The data in Table 13.10 are the salaries, y, and years of experience, x, for a sample of 50 social workers. The first-order model $E(y) = \beta_0 + \beta_1 x$ was fitted to the data using SPSS. The SPSS printout is shown in Figure 13.45, followed by a plot of the residuals versus $\hat{y}$ in Figure 13.46. Interpret the results. Make model modifications, if necessary.

    SOCWORK

TABLE 13.10   Salary Data for Example 13.16

Years of Experience, x	Salary, y	Years of Experience, x	Salary, y	Years of Experience, x	Salary, y
7	$26,075	21	$43,628	28	$99,139
28	79,370	4	16,105	23	52,624
23	65,726	24	65,644	17	50,594
18	41,983	20	63,022	25	53,272
19	62,308	20	47,780	26	65,343
15	41,154	15	38,853	19	46,216
24	53,610	25	66,537	16	54,288
13	33,697	25	67,447	3	20,844
2	22,444	28	64,785	12	32,586
8	32,562	26	61,581	23	71,235
20	43,076	27	70,678	20	36,530
21	56,000	20	51,301	19	52,745
18	58,667	18	39,346	27	67,282
7	22,210	1	24,833	25	80,931
2	20,521	26	65,929	12	32,303
18	49,727	20	41,721	11	38,371
11	33,233	26	82,641		

Solution   The SPSS printout, Figure 13.45, suggests that the first-order model provides an adequate fit to the data. The R^2-value indicates that the model explains 78.7% of the sample variation in salaries. The t-value for testing β_1, 13.31, is highly significant (p-value ≈ 0) and indicates that the model contributes information for the prediction of y. However, an examination of the residuals plotted against $\hat{y}$ (Figure 13.46) reveals a potential problem. Note the "cone" shape of the residual variability; the size of the residuals increases as the estimated mean salary increases, implying that the constant variance assumption is violated.

One way to stabilize the variance of ϵ is to refit the model using a transformation on the dependent variable y. With economic data (e.g., salaries) a useful **variance-stabilizing transformation** is the natural logarithm of y, denoted $\ln(y)$.* We fit the model

$$\ln(y) = \beta_0 + \beta_1 x + \epsilon$$

Teaching Tip
Point out that model interpretations are difficult once the dependent variable has been transformed. The units of the problem have been altered by the transformation used.

---

*Other variance-stabilizing transformations that are used successfully in practice are $\sqrt{y}$ and $\sin^{-1}\sqrt{y}$. Consult the references for more details on these transformations.

Model Summary[b]

Model	R	R Square	Adjusted R Square	Std. Error of the Estimate
1	.887[a]	.787	.782	8642.441

a. Predictors: (Constant), ESP

b. Dependent Variable: SALARY

ANOVA[b]

Model		Sum of Squares	df	Mean Square	F	Sig.
1	Regression	1.3E+10	1	1.324E+10	177.257	.000[a]
	Residual	3.6E+09	48	74691793.28		
	Total	1.7E+10	49			

a. Predictors: (Constant), ESP

b. Dependent Variable: SALARY

Coefficients[a]

Model		Unstandardized Coefficients		Standardized Coefficients	t	Sig.
		B	Std. Error	Beta		
1	(Constant)	11368.72	3160.317		3.597	.001
	ESP	2141.381	160.839	.887	13.314	.000

a. Dependent Variable: SALARY

Figure 13.45

SPSS regression printout for first-order model of salary

Figure 13.46

SPSS residual plot for first-order model of salary

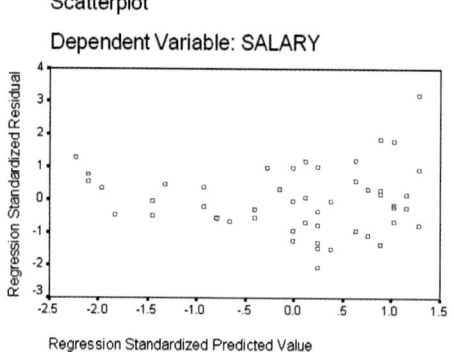

Scatterplot

Dependent Variable: SALARY

to the data of Table 13.10. Figure 13.47 shows the SPSS regression analysis printout for the $n = 50$ measurements, while Figure 13.48 shows a plot of the residuals from the log model.

You can see that the logarithmic transformation has stabilized the error variances. Note that the cone shape is gone; there is no apparent tendency of the residual variance to increase as mean salary increases. We therefore are confident that

Model Summary[b]

Model	R	R Square	Adjusted R Square	Std. Error of the Estimate
1	.929[a]	.864	.861	.1541127

a. Predictors: (Constant), ESP

b. Dependent Variable: LNSALARY

ANOVA[b]

Model		Sum of Squares	df	Mean Square	F	Sig.
1	Regression	7.212	1	7.212	303.660	.000[a]
	Residual	1.140	48	.024		
	Total	8.352	49			

a. Predictors: (Constant), ESP

b. Dependent Variable: LNSALARY

Coefficients[a]

Model		Unstandardized Coefficients		Standardized Coefficients	t	Sig.
		B	Std. Error	Beta		
1	(Constant)	9.841	.056		174.631	.000
	ESP	.050	.003	.929	17.426	.000

a. Dependent Variable: LNSALARY

Figure 13.47
SPSS regression printout for model of log salary

Figure 13.48
SPSS residual plot for model of log salary

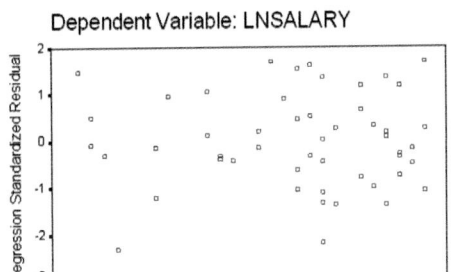

Scatterplot
Dependent Variable: LNSALARY

inferences using the logarithmic model are more reliable than those using the untransformed model.

Now Work   *Exercise 13.108b.*

Residuals

Using The TI-83 Graphing Calculator
Plotting Residuals

When you compute a regression equation on the TI-83, the residuals are automatically computed and saved to a list called **RESID. RESID** can be found under the **LIST menu** (**2nd STAT**).

To make a scatterplot of the residuals,

Step 1 *Enter the data*
Press **STAT** and select **1:Edit**
Note: If the list already contains data, clear the old data. Use the up arrow to highlight '**L1**' or '**L2**'.
Press **CLEAR ENTER.**
Use the arrow and **ENTER** keys to enter the data set into **L1** and **L2**.

Step 2 *Compute the regression equation*
Press **STAT** and highlight **CALC**
Press **4** for **LinReg(ax + b)**
Press **ENTER**

Suggested Exercises 13.115

Step 3 *Set up the data plot*
Press **2nd Y =** for **STATPLOT**
Press **1** for **Plot1**
Set the cursor so that **ON** is flashing.
For **Type,** use the arrow and Enter keys to highlight and select the scatterplot (first icon in the first row).
For **Xlist,** choose the column containing the x-data.
For **Ylist,** choose the column containing the residuals.
To enter the **RESID** as your **Ylist:**
1. Use the arrow keys to move the cursor after Ylist:
2. Press 2nd STAT for LIST
3. Use the down arrow to highlight the listname RESID and press ENTER

Step 4 *View the scatterplot of the residuals*
Press **ZOOM 9** for **ZoomStat**

Example The figures below show a table of data entered on the TI-83 and the scatterplot of the residuals obtained using the steps given above.

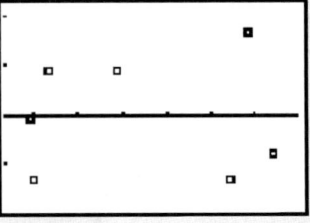

Residual analysis is a useful tool for the regression analyst, not only to check the assumptions, but also to provide information about how the model can be improved. A summary of the residual analyses presented in this section to check the assumption that the random error ϵ is normally distributed with mean 0 and constant variance is presented in the next box.

Steps in a Residual Analysis

1. Check for a misspecified model by plotting the residuals against each of the quantitative independent variables. Analyze each plot, looking for a curvilinear trend. This shape signals the need for a quadratic term in the model. Try a second-order term in the variable against which the residuals are plotted.

2. Examine the residual plots for outliers. Draw lines on the residual plots at 2- and 3-standard-deviation distances below and above the 0 line. Examine residuals outside the 3-standard-deviation lines as potential outliers, and check to see that approximately 5% of the residuals exceed the 2-standard-deviation lines. Determine whether each outlier can be explained as an error in data collection or transcription, or corresponds to a member of a population different from that of the remainder of the sample, or simply represents an unusual observation. If the observation is determined to be an error, fix it or remove it. Even if you can't determine the cause; you may want to rerun the regression analysis without the observation to determine its effect on the analysis.

3. Check for nonnormal errors by plotting a frequency distribution of the residuals, using a stem-and-leaf display or a histogram. Check to see if obvious departures from normality exist. Extreme skewness of the frequency distribution may be due to outliers or could indicate the need for a transformation of the dependent variable. (Normalizing transformations are beyond the scope of this book, but you can find information in the references.)

4. Check for unequal error variances by plotting the residuals against the predicted values, $\hat{y}$. If you detect a cone-shaped pattern or some other pattern that indicates that the variance of ϵ is not constant, refit the model using an appropriate variance-stabilizing transformation on y, such as $\ln(y)$. (Consult the references for other useful variance-stabilizing transformations.)

Statistics in Action Revisited

A Residual Analysis for the Road Cost Model

In the previous Statistics in Action Revisited section (p. 857), we found the interaction model, $E(y) = \beta_0 + \beta_1 x_1 + \beta_3 x_2 + \beta_4 x_1 x_2$, to be both a statistically and practically useful model for predicting the cost (y) of a road construction contract. Recall that the two independent variables are the DOT engineer's estimate of cost (x_1) and bid status, where $x_2 = 1$ if a fixed bid and $x_2 = 0$ if a competitive bid. Before actually using the model in practice, we need to examine the residuals to be sure that the standard regression assumptions are reasonably satisfied.

Figures SIA13.9 and SIA13.10 are MINITAB graphs of the residuals from the interaction model. The histogram shown in Figure SIA13.9 appears to be approximately normally distributed; consequently the assumption of normal errors is reasonably satisfied. The scatterplot of the residuals against $\hat{y}$ shown in Figure SIA13.10, however, shows a distinct "funnel" pattern; this indicates that the assumption of a constant error variance is likely to be violated. One way to modify the model to satisfy this assumption is to use a variance-stabilizing transformation (such as the natural log) on cost (y). When both the y and x variables in a regression equation are economic variables (prices, costs, salaries, etc.), it is often advantageous to transform the x-variable also. Consequently, we'll modify the model by making a log transform on both cost (y) and DOTEST (x_1).

Our modified (log-log) interaction model takes the form

$$E(y^*) = \beta_0 + \beta_1 x_1^* + \beta_2 x_2 + \beta_3 (x_1^*) x_2$$

where $y^* = \ln(\text{COST})$ and $x_1^* = \ln(\text{DOTEST})$. The MINITAB printout for this model is shown in Figure

SIA13.11, followed by graphs of the residuals in Figures SIA13.12 and SIA13.13. The histogram shown in Figure SIA13.12 is approximately normal, and more important, the scatterplot of the residuals shown in Figure SIA13.13 has no distinct trend. It appears that the log transformations successfully stabilized the error variance. Note, however, that the t-test for the interaction term in the model (highlighted in Figure SIA13.11) is no longer statistically significant (p-value = .420). Consequently, we will drop the interaction term from the model and use the simpler modified model,

$$E(y^*) = \beta_0 + \beta_1 x_1^* + \beta_2 x_2$$

to predict road contract cost.

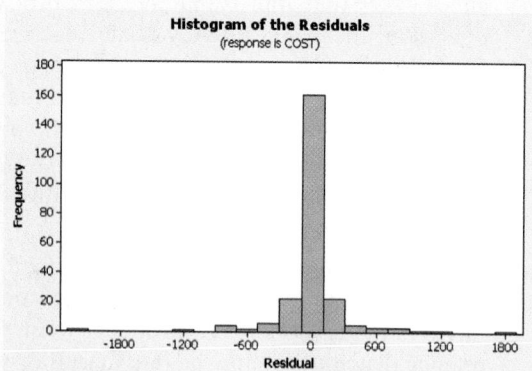

Figure SIA13.9
MINITAB histogram of residuals from interaction model for road cost

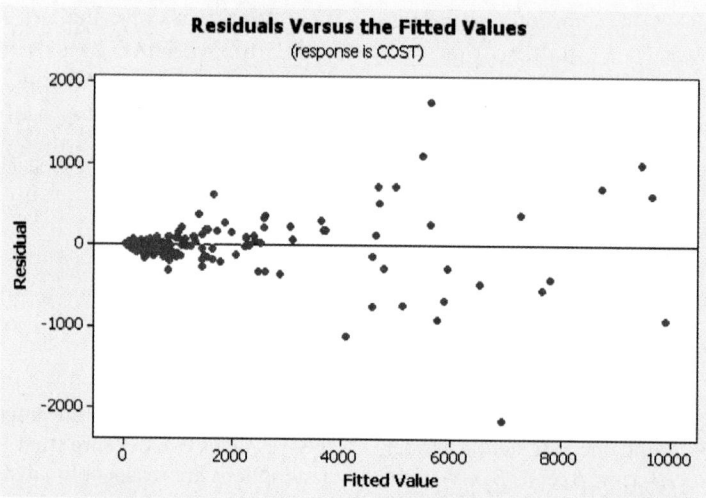

Figure SIA13.10
MINITAB plot of residuals versus predicted values from interaction model for road cost

Figure SIA13.11

MINITAB regression printout for modified (log-log) model of road construction cost

```
The regression equation is
LNCOST = - 0.162 + 1.01 LNDOTEST + 0.324 STATUS - 0.0176 STA_LNDOT


Predictor      Coef    SE Coef        T       P
Constant    -0.16188   0.05193    -3.12   0.002
LNDOTEST     1.00780   0.00798   126.23   0.000
STATUS        0.3243    0.1356     2.39   0.018
STA_LNDOT   -0.01762   0.02181    -0.81   0.420


S = 0.154922   R-Sq = 98.8%   R-Sq(adj) = 98.7%


Analysis of Variance

Source           DF       SS       MS        F       P
Regression        3   439.64   146.55  6105.87   0.000
Residual Error  231     5.54     0.02
Total           234   445.18
```

Figure SIA13.12

MINITAB histogram of residuals from modified (log-log) model for road construction cost

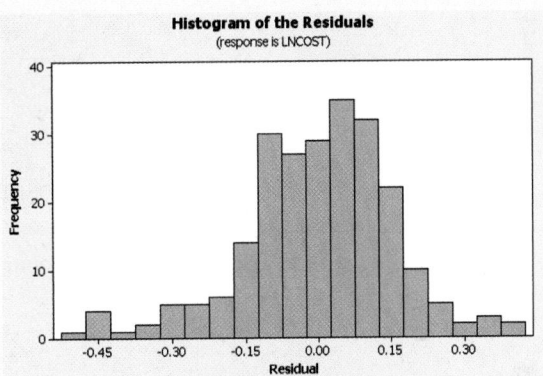

Figure SIA13.13

MINITAB plot of residuals versus predicted values from modified (log-log) model for road construction cost

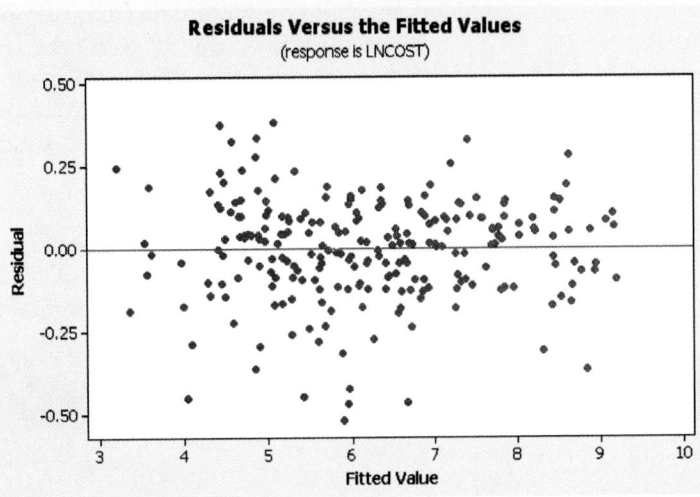

13.14 Some Pitfalls: Estimability, Multicollinearity, and Extrapolation

You should be aware of several potential problems when constructing a prediction model for some response y. A few of the most important are discussed in this final section.

Problem 1 **Parameter Estimability** Suppose you want to fit a model relating annual crop yield y to the total expenditure for fertilizer x. We propose the first-order model

$$E(y) = \beta_0 + \beta_1 x$$

Now suppose we have three years of data and $1,000 is spent on fertilizer each year. The data are shown in Figure 13.48. You can see the problem: The parameters of the model cannot be estimated when all the data are concentrated at a single x-value. Recall that it takes two points (x-values) to fit a straight line. Thus, the parameters are not estimable when only one x is observed.

Figure 13.49

Yield and fertilizer expenditure data: Three years

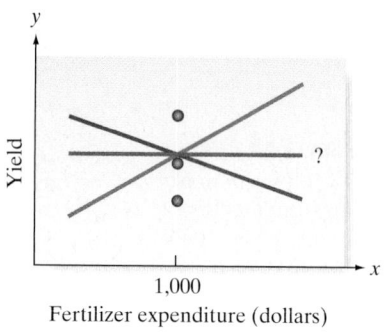

A similar problem would occur if we attempted to fit the quadratic model

$$E(y) = \beta_0 + \beta_1 x + \beta_2 x^2$$

to a set of data for which only one or two different x-values were observed (see Figure 13.49). At least three different x-values must be observed before a quadratic model can be fit to a set of data (that is, before all three parameters are estimable).

In general, the number of levels of observed x-values must be one more than the order of the polynomial in x that you want to fit.

For controlled experiments, the researcher can select one of the experimental designs in chapter 10 that will permit estimation of the model parameters. Even

Figure 13.50

Only two x values observed: Quadratic model is not estimable

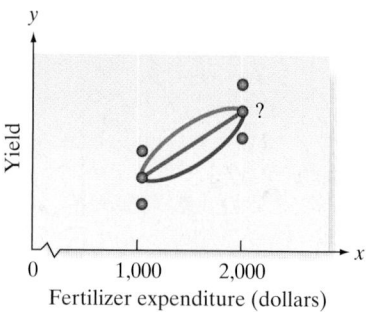

when the values of the independent variables cannot be controlled by the researcher, the independent variables are almost always observed at a sufficient number of levels to permit estimation of the model parameters. When the statistical software you use suddenly refuses to fit a model, however, the problem is probably inestimable parameters.

Problem 2　**Multicollinearity** Often, two or more of the independent variables used in a regression model contribute redundant information. That is, the independent variables are correlated with each other. For example, suppose we want to construct a model to predict the gas mileage rating of a truck as a function of its load, x_1 (in tons), and the horsepower, x_2 (in foot-pounds per second), of its engine. We would expect heavy loads to require greater horsepower and to result in lower mileage ratings. Thus, although both x_1 and x_2 contribute information for the prediction of mileage rating, y, some of the information is overlapping because x_1 and x_2 are correlated.

When the independent variables are correlated, we say *multicollinearity* exists. In practice, it is not uncommon to observe correlations among the independent variables. However, a few problems arise when serious multicollinearity is present in the regression variables.

DEFINITION 13.7

Multicollinearity exists when two or more of the independent variables used in regression are correlated.

First, high correlations among the independent variables increase the likelihood of rounding errors in the calculations of the β estimates, standard errors, and so forth. Second, and more important, the regression results may be confusing and misleading. Consider the model for gasoline mileage rating (y) of a truck:

$$E(y) = \beta_0 + \beta_1 x_1 + \beta_2 x_2$$

where x_1 = load and x_2 = horsepower. Fitting the model to a sample data set, we might find that the t-tests for testing β_1 and β_2 are both nonsignificant at the α = .05 level, while the F-test for H_0: $\beta_1 = \beta_2 = 0$ is highly significant (p = .001). The tests may seem to be contradictory, but really they are not. The t-tests indicate that the contribution of one variable, say x_1 = load, is not significant after the effect of x_2 = horsepower has been accounted for (because x_2 is also in the model). The significant F-test, on the other hand, tells us that at least one of the two variables is making a contribution to the prediction of y (i.e., either β_1 or β_2 or both differ from 0). In fact, both are probably contributing, but the contribution of one overlaps with that of the other.

Multicollinearity can also have an effect on the signs of the parameter estimates. More specifically, a value of β_i may have the opposite sign from what is expected. In the truck gasoline mileage example, we expect heavy loads to result in lower mileage ratings and we expect higher horsepowers to result in lower mileage ratings; consequently, we expect the signs of both the parameter estimates to be negative. Yet we may actually see a positive value of β_1 and be tempted to claim that heavy loads result in *higher* mileage ratings. This is the danger of interpreting a β coefficient when the independent variables are correlated. Because the variables contribute redundant information, the effect of x_1 = load on y = mileage rating is measured only partially by β_1.

How can you avoid the problems of multicollinearity in regression analysis? One way is to conduct a designed experiment (Chapter 10) so that the levels of the x-variables are uncorrelated. Unfortunately, time and cost constraints may prevent you from collecting data in this manner. Consequently, most data are collected observationally. Since observational data frequently consist of correlated independent variables, you will need to recognize when multicollinearity is present and, if necessary, make modifications in the regression analysis.

Several methods are available for detecting multicollinearity in regression. A simple technique is to calculate the coefficient of correlation, r, between each pair of independent variables in the model and use the procedure outlined in Section 12.6 to test for significantly correlated variables. If one or more of the r-values is statistically different from 0, the variables in question are correlated, and a multicollinearity problem may exist.* Other indications of the presence of multicollinearity include those mentioned above—namely, nonsignificant t-tests for the individual parameter estimates when the F-test for overall model adequacy is significant, and estimates with opposite signs from what is expected.**

> ### Detecting Multicollinearity in the Regression Model
> 1. Significant correlations between pairs of independent variables
> 2. Nonsignificant t-tests for all (or nearly all) of the individual β parameters when the F-test for overall model adequacy is significant
> 3. Signs opposite from what is expected in the estimated β parameters

EXAMPLE 13.17   DETECTING MULTICOLLINEARITY

Problem   The Federal Trade Commission (FTC) annually ranks varieties of domestic cigarettes according to their tar, nicotine, and carbon monoxide contents. The U.S. Surgeon General considers each of these three substances hazardous to a smoker's health. Past studies have shown that increases in the tar and nicotine contents of a cigarette are accompanied by an increase in the carbon monoxide emitted from the cigarette smoke. Table 13.11 presents data on tar, nicotine, and carbon monoxide contents (in milligrams) and weight (in grams) for a sample of 25 (filter) brands tested in a recent year. Suppose we want to model carbon monoxide content, y, as a function of tar content, x_1, nicotine content, x_2, and weight, x_3, using the model

$$E(y) = \beta_0 + \beta_1 x_1 + \beta_2 x_2 + \beta_3 x_3$$

The model is fit to the 25 data points in Table 13.11, and a portion of the MINITAB printout is shown in Figure 13.51. Examine the printout. Do you detect any signs of multicollinearity?

---

*Remember that r measures only the pairwise correlation between x-values. Three variables, x_1, x_2, and x_3, may be highly correlated as a group but may not exhibit large pairwise correlations. Thus, multicollinearity may be present even when all pairwise correlations are not significantly different from 0.

**More formal methods for detecting multicollinearity, such as variance-inflation factors (VIFs), are available. Independent variables with a VIF of 10 or above are usually considered to be highly correlated with one or more of the other independent variables in the model. Calculation of VIFs are beyond the scope of this introductory text. Consult the chapter references for a discussion of VIFs and other formal methods of detecting multicollinearity.

FTC

TABLE 13.11   FTC Cigarette Data for Example 13.17

Tar (x_1)	Nicotine (x_2)	Weight (x_3)	Carbon Monoxide (y)
14.1	.86	.9853	13.6
16.0	1.06	1.0938	16.6
29.8	2.03	1.1650	23.5
8.0	.67	.9280	10.2
4.1	.40	.9462	5.4
15.0	1.04	.8885	15.0
8.8	.76	1.0267	9.0
12.4	.95	.9225	12.3
16.6	1.12	.9372	16.3
14.9	1.02	.8858	15.4
13.7	1.01	.9643	13.0
15.1	.90	.9316	14.4
7.8	.57	.9705	10.0
11.4	.78	1.1240	10.2
9.0	.74	.8517	9.5
1.0	.13	.7851	1.5
17.0	1.26	.9186	18.5
12.8	1.08	1.0395	12.6
15.8	.96	.9573	17.5
4.5	.42	.9106	4.9
14.5	1.01	1.0070	15.9
7.3	.61	.9806	8.5
8.6	.69	.9693	10.6
15.2	1.02	.9496	13.9
12.0	.82	1.1184	14.9

Source: Federal Trade Commission

Solution   First, note that the F-test for overall model utility is highly significant. The test statistic ($F = 78.98$) and observed significance level (p-value $= .000$) are highlighted on the MINITAB printout, Figure 13.51. Therefore, at, say $\alpha = .01$, we can conclude that at least one of the parameters, β_1, β_2, or β_3, in the model is nonzero. The t-tests for two of three individual β's, however, are nonsignificant. (The p-values for these tests are shaded on the printout.) Unless tar (x_1) is the only one of the three variables useful for predicting carbon monoxide content, these results are the first indication of a potential multicollinearity problem.

The negative values for β_2 and β_3 (highlighted on the printout) are a second clue to the presence of multicollinearity. From past studies, the FTC expects carbon monoxide content (y) to increase when either nicotine content (x_2) or weight (x_3) increases—that is, the FTC expects *positive* relationships between y and x_2 and between y and x_3, not negative ones.

All signs indicate that a serious multicollinearity problem exists.

Look Back To confirm our suspicions, we had MINITAB produce the coefficient of correlation, r, for each of the three pairs of independent variables in the model. The resulting output is shown (highlighted) at the bottom of Figure 13.51. You can see that tar (x_1) and nicotine (x_2) are highly correlated ($r = .9766$) while weight (x_3) is moderately correlated with the other two x's ($r \approx .5$). All three correlations have p-values of .01 or lower; consequently, all three are significantly different from 0 at, say, $\alpha = .05$.

Now Work   *Exercise 13.109*

■ ■ ■

Figure 13.51

MINITAB Printout for
Model of CO Content,
Example 13.17

Regression Analysis: CO versus TAR, NICOTINE, WEIGHT

```
The regression equation is
CO = 3.20 + 0.963 TAR - 2.63 NICOTINE - 0.13 WEIGHT
```

```
Predictor      Coef   SE Coef       T       P
Constant      3.202     3.462    0.93   0.365
TAR          0.9626    0.2422    3.97   0.001
NICOTINE     -2.632     3.901   -0.67   0.507
WEIGHT       -0.130     3.885   -0.03   0.974
```

```
S = 1.44573    R-Sq = 91.9%    R-Sq(adj) = 90.7%
```

```
Analysis of Variance

Source           DF      SS      MS       F       P
Regression        3  495.26  165.09   78.98   0.000
Residual Error   21   43.89    2.09
```

Correlations: NICOTINE, WEIGHT, CO

```
           NICOTINE    WEIGHT
WEIGHT        0.500
              0.011

CO            0.926     0.464
              0.000     0.019
```

```
Cell Contents: Pearson correlation
               P-Value
```

Once you have detected that multicollineariy exists, there are several alternative measures available for solving the problem. The appropriate measure to take depends on the severity of the multicollinearity and the ultimate goal of the regression analysis.

Some researchers, when confronted with highly correlated independent variables, choose to include only one of the correlated variables in the final model. If you are interested only in using the model for estimation and prediction (step 6), you may decide not to drop any of the independent variables from the model. In the presence of multicollinearity, we have seen that it is dangerous to interpret the individual β parameters. However, confidence intervals for $E(y)$ and prediction intervals for y generally remain unaffected *as long as the values of the x's used to predict y follow the same pattern of multicollinearity exhibited in the sample data.* That is, you must take strict care to ensure that the values of the x-variables fall within the range of the sample data.

> **Solutions to Some Problems Created by Multicollinearity in Regression***
>
> 1. Drop one or more of the correlated independent variables from the model. One way to decide which variables to keep in the model is to employ stepwise regression (Section 13.12).
>
> 2. If you decide to keep all the independent variables in the model,
>   a. Avoid making inferences about the individual β parameters based on the *t*-tests.
>   b. Restrict inferences about $E(y)$ and future y values to values of the x's that fall within the range of the sample data.

Problem 3

Teaching Tip

Point out that it is now more difficult to determine if the point of interest falls within the sampled data as there are several variables that need to be considered.

Prediction Outside the Experimental Region Many research economists had developed highly technical models to relate the state of the economy to various economic indices and other independent variables. Many of these models were multiple regression models, where, for example, the dependent variable y might be next year's Gross Domestic Product (GDP) and the independent variables might include this year's rate of inflation, this year's Consumer Price Index (CPI), and so on. In other words, the model might be constructed to predict next year's economy using this year's knowledge.

Unfortunately, these models were almost all unsuccessful in predicting the recession in the early 1970s and the late 1990s. What went wrong? One of the problems was that many of the regression models were used to **extrapolate** (i.e., predict y-values of the independent variables that were outside the region in which the model was developed). For example, the inflation rate in the late 1960s, when the models were developed, ranged from 6% to 8%. When the double-digit inflation of the early 1970s became a reality, some researchers attempted to use the same models to predict future growth in GDP. As you can see in Figure 13.52, the model may be very accurate for predicting y when x is in the range of experimentation, but the use of the model outside that range is a dangerous practice.

Figure 13.52

Using a regression model outside the experimental region

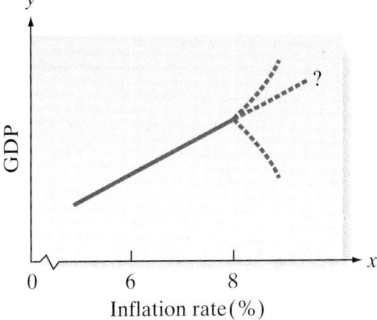

*Several other solutions are available. For example, in the case where higher-order regression models are fit, the analyst may want to code the independent variables so that higher-order terms (e.g., x^2) for a particular x-variable are not highly correlated with x. One transformation that works is $z = (x - \bar{x})/s$. Other, more sophisticated procedures for addressing multicollinearity (such as *ridge regression*) are beyond the scope of the text. Consult the references at the end of this chapter.

Problem 4 **Correlated Errors** Another problem associated with using a regression model to predict a variable y based on independent variables $x_1, x_2, \ldots, x_k$ arises from the fact that the data are frequently *time series*. That is, the values of both the dependent and independent variables are observed sequentially over a period of time. The observations tend to be correlated over time, which in turn often causes the prediction errors of the regression model to be correlated. Thus, the assumption of independent errors is violated, and the model tests and prediction intervals are no longer valid. One solution to this problem is to construct a **time series model;** time series analysis is the subject of Chapter 15.

Exercises 13.108–13.117

Learning the Mechanics

13.108 Identify the problem(s) in each of the residual plots shown at the bottom of the page.

13.109 Consider fitting the multiple regression model

$$E(y) = \beta_0 + \beta_1 x_1 + \beta_2 x_2 + \beta_3 x_3 + \beta_4 x_4 + \beta_5 x_5$$

A matrix of correlations for all pairs of independent variables is given to the right. Do you detect a multicollinearity problem? Explain.

Correlation Matrix for Exercise 13.109

	x_1	x_2	x_3	x_4	x_5
x_1	—	.17	.02	−.23	.19
x_2		—	.45	.93	.02
x_3			—	.22	−.01
x_4				—	.86
x_5					—

a.

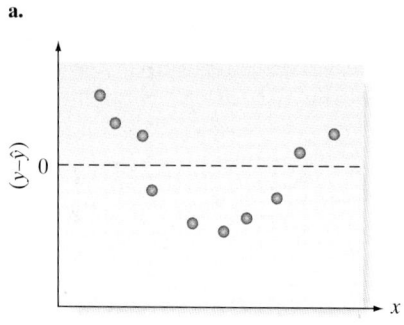

b.

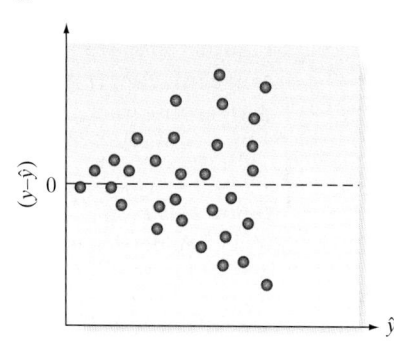

c.

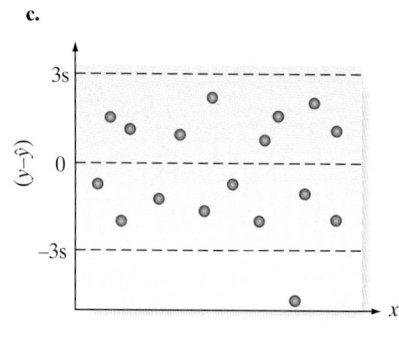

d.

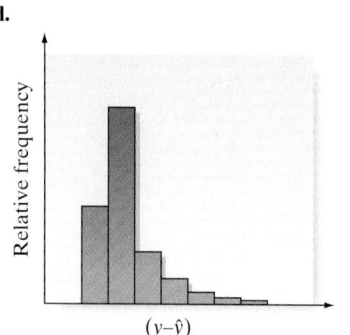

Residual plots for Exercise 13.108

Applying the Concepts—Basic

13.110 Refer to the *Professional Geographer* (Feb. 2000) study of urban and rural counties in the western United States, Exercise 13.23 (p. 794). Recall that six independent variables—total county population (x_1), population density (x_2), population concentration (x_3), population growth (x_4), proportion of county land in farms (x_5), and, 5-year change in agricultural land base (x_6)—were used to model the urban/rural rating (y) of a county. Prior to running the multiple regression analysis, the researchers were concerned about possible multicollinearity in the data. Below is a correlation matrix (i.e., a table of correlations between all pairs of the independent variables).

	x_1	x_2	x_3	x_4	x_5
x_1: Total population					
x_2: Population density	.20				
x_3: Population concentration	.45	.43			
x_4: Population growth	−.05	−.14	−.01		
x_5: Farm land	−.16	−.15	−.07	−.20	
x_6: Agricultural change	−.12	−.12	−.22	−.06	−.06

Source: Berry, K. A. et al. "Interpreting What Is Rural and Urban for Western U.S. Counties," *Professional Geographer,* Vol. 52, No. 1, Feb. 2000 (Table 2).

a. Based on the correlation matrix, is there any evidence of extreme multicollinearity?   No

b. Refer to the multiple regression results in the table given in Exercise 13.23 (p. 00). Based on the reported tests, is there any evidence of extreme multicollinearity?   No

13.111 *World Development* (Vol. 20, 1992) published a study of the variables impacting the size distribution of manufacturing firms in international markets. Five independent variables, Gross Domestic Product (GDP), area per capita (AREAC), share of heavy industry in value added (SVA), ratio of credit claims to GDP (CREDIT), and ratio of stock equity of GDP (STOCK), were used to model the share, y, of firms with 100 or more workers. The researchers detected a high correlation between pairs of the following independent variables: GDP and SVA, GDP and STOCK, and CREDIT and STOCK. Describe the problems that may arise if these high correlations are ignored in the multiple regression analysis of the model.

13.112 Passive exposure to environmental tobacco smoke has been associated with growth suppression and an increased frequency of respiratory tract infections in normal children. Is this association more pronounced in children with cystic fibrosis? To answer this question, 43 children (18 girls and 25 boys) attending a 2-week summer camp for cystic fibrosis patients were studied (*The New England Journal of Medicine*, Sept. 20, 1990). Researchers investigated the correlation between a child's weight percentile (y) and the number of cigarettes smoked per day in the child's home (x). The table below lists the data for the 25 boys. A MINITAB regression printout (with residuals) for the straight-line model relating y to x is also provided on page 888. Examine the residuals. Do you detect any outliers?

Applying the Concepts—Intermediate

13.113 The data in the table on p. 889 were collected for a random sample of 26 households in Washington, D.C., during 2002. An economist wants to relate household food consumption, y, to household income, x_1, and household size, x_2, with the first-order model

$$E(y) = \beta_0 + \beta_1 x_1 + \beta_2 x_2$$

CFSMOKE

Weight Percentile, y	No. of Cigarettes Smoked per Day, x	Weight Percentile, y	No. of Cigarettes Smoked per, Day x
6	0	43	0
6	15	49	0
2	40	50	0
8	23	49	22
11	20	46	30
17	7	54	0
24	3	58	0
25	0	62	0
17	25	66	0
25	20	66	23
25	15	83	0
31	23	87	44
35	10		

Source: Rubin, B. K. "Exposure of Children with Cystic Fibrosis to Environmental Tobacco Smoke." *The New England Journal of Medicine,* Sept. 20, 1990. Vol. 323, No. 12, p. 85 (data extracted from Figure 3).

MINITAB Output for Exercise 13.112

```
The regression equation is
WTPCTILE = 41.2 - 0.262 SMOKED


Predictor      Coef   SE Coef       T      P
Constant     41.153     6.843    6.01  0.000
SMOKED      -0.2619     0.3702   -0.71  0.486


S = 24.6816    R-Sq = 2.1%   R-Sq(adj) = 0.0%


Analysis of Variance

Source          DF        SS       MS      F      P
Regression       1     304.9    304.9   0.50  0.486
Residual Error  23   14011.1    609.2
Total           24   14316.0



Obs   SMOKED   WTPCTILE    Fit   SE Fit   Residual   St Resid
  1      0.0       6.00   41.15    6.84     -35.15      -1.48
  2     15.0       6.00   37.22    5.00     -31.22      -1.29
  3     40.0       2.00   30.68   11.22     -28.68      -1.30
  4     23.0       8.00   35.13    6.22     -27.13      -1.14
  5     20.0      11.00   35.91    5.61     -24.91      -1.04
  6      7.0      17.00   39.32    5.38     -22.32      -0.93
  7      3.0      24.00   40.37    6.13     -16.37      -0.68
  8      0.0      25.00   41.15    6.84     -16.15      -0.68
  9     25.0      17.00   34.60    6.69     -17.60      -0.74
 10     20.0      25.00   35.91    5.61     -10.91      -0.45
 11     15.0      25.00   37.22    5.00     -12.22      -0.51
 12     23.0      31.00   35.13    6.22      -4.13      -0.17
 13     10.0      35.00   38.53    5.04      -3.53      -0.15
 14      0.0      43.00   41.15    6.84       1.85       0.08
 15      0.0      49.00   41.15    6.84       7.85       0.33
 16      0.0      50.00   41.15    6.84       8.85       0.37
 17     22.0      49.00   35.39    6.00      13.61       0.57
 18     30.0      46.00   33.29    8.06      12.71       0.54
 19      0.0      54.00   41.15    6.84      12.85       0.54
 20      0.0      58.00   41.15    6.84      16.85       0.71
 21      0.0      62.00   41.15    6.84      20.85       0.88
 22      0.0      66.00   41.15    6.84      24.85       1.05
 23     23.0      66.00   35.13    6.22      30.87       1.29
 24      0.0      83.00   41.15    6.84      41.85       1.76
 25     44.0      87.00   29.63   12.56      57.37       2.70RX

R denotes an observation with a large standardized residual.
X denotes an observation whose X value gives it large influence.
```

DCFOOD

Household	Food Consumption ($1,000s)	Income ($1,000s)	Household Size	Household	Food Consumption ($1,000s)	Income ($1,000s)	Household Size
1	4.2	41.1	4	14	4.1	95.2	2
2	3.4	30.5	2	15	5.5	45.6	9
3	4.8	52.3	4	16	4.5	78.5	3
4	2.9	28.9	1	17	5.0	20.5	5
5	3.5	36.5	2	18	4.5	31.6	4
6	4.0	29.8	4	19	2.8	39.9	1
7	3.6	44.3	3	20	3.9	38.6	3
8	4.2	38.1	4	21	3.6	30.2	2
9	5.1	92.0	5	22	4.6	48.7	5
10	2.7	36.0	1	23	3.8	21.2	3
11	4.0	76.9	3	24	4.5	24.3	7
12	2.7	69.9	1	25	4.0	26.9	5
13	5.5	43.1	7	26	7.5	7.3	5

a. Fit the model to the data. Do you detect any signs of multicollinearity in the data? Explain.   No

b. Is there visual evidence (from a residual plot) that a second-order model may be more appropriate for predicting household food consumption? Explain.   Yes

c. Comment on the assumption of constant error variance, using a residual plot. Does it appear to be satisfied?   No

d. Are there any outliers in the data? If so, identify them.

e. Based on a graph of the residuals, Does the assumption of normal errors appear to be reasonably satisfied? Explain.

13.114 *Teaching Sociology* (July 1995) developed a model for the professional socialization of graduate students working toward their doctorate. One of the dependent variables modeled was professional confidence, y, measured on a 5-point scale. The model included over 20 independent variables and was fitted to data collected for a sample of 309 graduate students. One concern is whether multicollinearity

exists in the data. A correlation matrix for ten of the independent variables is shown below. [*Note:* Each entry in the table is the correlation coefficient r between the variable in the corresponding row and corresponding column.]

a. Examine the correlation matrix and find the independent variables that are moderately or highly correlated.

b. What modeling problems may occur if the variables, part a, are left in the model? Explain.

13.115 Chemical engineers at Tokyo Metropolitan University analyzed urban air specimens for the presence of low-molecular-weight dicarboxylic acid (*Environmental Science & Engineering*, Oct. 1993). The dicarboxylic acid (as a percentage of total carbon) and oxidant concentrations for 19 air specimens collected from urban Tokyo are listed in the table on p. 890. Consider the straight-line model relating dicarboxylic acid percentage (y) to oxidant concentration (x). Conduct a complete residual analysis for the model.

Correlation matrix for Exercise 13.114

Independent Variable	(1)	(2)	(3)	(4)	(5)	(6)	(7)	(8)	(9)	(10)
(1) Father's occupation	1.000	.363	.099	−.110	−.047	−.053	−.111	.178	.078	.049
(2) Mother's education	.363	1.000	.228	−.139	−.216	.084	−.118	.192	.125	.068
(3) Race	.099	.228	1.000	.036	−.515	.014	−.120	.112	.117	.337
(4) Sex	−.110	−.139	.036	1.000	.165	−.256	.173	−.106	−.117	.073
(5) Foreign status	−.047	−.216	−.515	.165	1.000	−.041	.159	−.130	−.165	−.171
(6) Undergraduate GPA	−.053	.084	.014	−.256	−.041	1.000	.032	.028	−.034	.092
(7) Year GRE taken	−.111	−.118	−.120	.173	.159	.032	1.000	−.086	−.602	.016
(8) Verbal GRE score	.178	.192	.112	−.106	−.130	.028	−.086	1.000	.132	.087
(9) Years in graduate program	.078	.125	.117	−.117	−.165	−.034	−.602	.132	1.000	−.071
(10) First-year graduate GPA	.049	.068	.337	.073	−.171	.092	.016	.087	−.071	1.000

Source: Keith, B., and Moore, H. A. "Training Sociologists: An Assessment of Professional Socializatoin and the Emergence of Career Aspirations." *Teaching Sociology*, Vo. 23, No. 3, July 1995, p. 205 (Table 1).

⊙ **URBANAIR** (Data for Exercise 13.115)

Dicarboxylic Acid (%)	Oxidant (ppm)	Dicarboxylic Acid (%)	Oxidant (ppm)
.85	78	.50	32
1.45	80	.38	28
1.80	74	.30	25
1.80	78	.70	45
1.60	60	.80	40
1.20	62	.90	45
1.30	57	1.22	41
.20	49	1.00	34
.22	34	1.00	25
.40	36		

Source: Kawamura, K., and Ikushima, K. "Seasonal Changes in the Distribution of Dicarboxylic Acids in the Urban Atmosphere." *Environmental Science & Technology,* Vol. 27. No. 10, Oct. 1993, p. 2232 (data extracted from Figure 4).

⊙ **BWECS**

13.116 Refer to the 2002 *Business Week* "Executive Compensation Scoreboard" data saved in the **BWECS** file. In Exercise 13.10 (p. 783), you fit the first-order multiple regression model, $E(y) = \beta_0 + \beta_1 x_1 + \beta_2 x_2$, where y = total pay (in thousands of dollars) of a CEO, x_1 = return (in dollars) on a \$100 investment in the CEO's company stock made three years earlier, and x_2 = CEO's performance rating (1 to 5 scale, where 1 = best and 5 = worst). Conduct a complete residual analysis for the model. Do you recommend any model modifications be made? Explain.

⊙ **DDT**

13.117 Refer to the U.S. Army Corps of Engineers data on fish contaminated from the toxic discharges of a chemical plant located on the banks of the Tennessee River in Alabama. In Exercise 13.12 (p. 784) you fit the first-order model, $E(y) = \beta_0 + \beta_1 x_1 + \beta_2 x_2 + \beta_3 x_3$, where y = DDT level in captured fish, x_1 = miles captured upstream, x_2 = fish length, and x_3 = fish weight. Conduct a complete residual analysis for the model. Do you recommend any model modifications be made? Explain.

Quick Review

Note: Starred (*) items are from the optional sections in this chapter.

Key Terms

Adjusted multiple coefficient of determination 789
Base level 825
Categorical variable 825
Coded variable 768
*Complete model 843
Complete second-order model 819
Correlated errors 886
Dummy variables 825
Extrapolation 885
First-order model 769
Global F-test 790

Higher-order term 768
Indicator variable 825
Interaction 805
Least squares prediction equation 772
Level of a variable 825
*Main effect terms 834
Mean square for error 776
Model building 769
Multicollinearity 881
Multiple coefficient of determination 788
Multiple regression model 768
*Nested model 843
*Nested model F-test 844
Outlier 867
Paraboloid 819

Parameter estimability 880
*Parsimonious model 849
Quadratic model 813
Quadratic term 813
Qualitative variable 825
*Reduced model 843
Residual 862
Residual analysis 862
*Response surface 846
Robust method 872
Saddle-shaped surface 819
Second-order model 813
Second-order term 813
*Stepwise regression 853
Time series model 886
Variance-stabilizing transformation 873

Key Formulas

$E(y) = \beta_0 + \beta_1 x_1 + \beta_2 x_2$

First-order model with two quantitative independent variables 769

$s^2 = \text{MSE} = \dfrac{\text{SSE}}{n - (k + 1)}$

Estimator of σ^2 for a model with k independent variables 777

$t = \dfrac{\hat{\beta}_i}{s_{\hat{\beta}_i}}$

Test statistic for testing H_0: $\beta_i = 0$ 778

$\hat{\beta}_i \pm (t_{\alpha/2}) s_{\hat{\beta}_i}$, where $t_{\alpha/2}$ depends on $n - (k + 1)$ df

$100(1 - \alpha)\%$ confidence interval for $\beta_i = 0$ 777

$R^2 = \dfrac{\text{SS}_{yy} - \text{SSE}}{\text{SS}_{yy}}$

Multiple coefficient of determination 788

$$R_a^2 = 1 - \left[\frac{(n-1)}{n-(k+1)} \right] (1 - R^2)$$

Adjusted multiple coefficient of determination   789

$$F = \frac{MS\,(Model)}{MSE} = \frac{R^2/k}{(1-R^2)/[n-(k+1)]}$$

Test statistic for testing $H_0: \beta_1 = \beta_2 = \cdots = \beta_k = 0$ 791

$$E(y) = \beta_0 + \beta_1 x_1 + \beta_2 x_2 + \beta_3 x_1 x_2$$

Interaction model with two quantitative independent variables   805

$$E(y) = \beta_0 + \beta_1 x + \beta_2 x^2$$

Quadratic Model   813

$$E(y) = \beta_0 + \beta_1 x_1 + \beta_2 x_2 + \beta_3 x_1 x_2 + \beta_4 x_1^2 + \beta_5 x_2^2$$

Complete second-order model with two quantitative independent variables   819

$$E(y) = \beta_0 + \beta_1 x_1 + \beta_2 x_2 + \cdots + \beta_{k-1} x_{k-1},$$

where $x_i = \begin{cases} 1 \text{ if level } i+1 \\ 0 \text{ if not} \end{cases}$

Model with one qualitative variable at k levels   826

$$F = \frac{(SSE_R - SSE_C)/\text{number of } \beta\text{'s tested}}{MSE_C}$$

Test statistic for comparing reduced and complete models*   845

$$y - \hat{y}$$

Regression residual   862

Chapter Summary Notes

- **Steps in multiple regression:** (1) hypothesize the deterministic form of the model, (2) use the method of least squares to estimate the unknown β's, (3) assumptions on the random error (ε), (4) check the assumptions and make model modifications, (5) statistically evaluate the adequacy of the model, (6) if deemed useful, use the model for estimation and prediction.

- **Four assumptions for ε:** (1) mean of ε is 0, (2) variance of ε is constant for all x-values, (3) distribution of ε is normal, (4) values of ε are independent.

- **First-order model in k quantitative x's:** $E(y) = \beta_0 + \beta_1 x_1 + \beta_2 x_2 + \beta_3 x_3 + \ldots + \beta_k x_k$, where each β_i represents the change in y for every 1-unit increase in x_i, holding the other x's fixed.

- **Adjusted coefficient of determination** (R_{adj}^2) cannot be "forced" to 1 by adding independent variables to the model.

- **Recommendation for checking statistical utility of the model:** (1) conduct the **global F-test**, (2) if test is significant, conduct t-tests on the "most important" β's only, (3) interpret the value of 2s, (4) interpret the value of R_{adj}^2.

- **Interaction model in 2 quantitative x's:** $E(y) = \beta_0 + \beta_1 x_1 + \beta_2 x_2 + \beta_3 x_1 x_2$, where $(\beta_1 + \beta_3 x_2)$ represents the change in y for every 1-unit increase in x_1 for fixed x_2, and $(\beta_2 + \beta_3 x_1)$ represents the change in y for every 1-unit increase in x_2 for fixed x_1.

- Once interaction is tested and deemed important, avoid conducting t-tests on the first-order terms in the model.

- **Quadratic model in 1 quantitative x:** $E(y) = \beta_0 + \beta_1 x + \beta_2 x^2$, where $\beta_2 > 0$ implies *upward* curvature and $\beta_2 < 0$ implies *downward* curvature.

- Once curvature is tested and deemed important, avoid conducting a t-test on the first-order term in the model.

- **Complete second-order model in 2 quantitative x's:** $E(y) = \beta_0 + \beta_1 x_1 + \beta_2 x_2 + \beta_3 x_1 x_2 + \beta_4 (x_1)^2 + \beta_5 (x_2)^2$.

- **Dummy variable model for 1 qualitative x at three levels (A, B, C):** $E(y) = \beta_0 + \beta_1 x_1 + \beta_2 x_2$, where $x_1 = \{1 \text{ if A, } 0 \text{ if not}\}$ and $x_2 = \{1 \text{ if B, } 0 \text{ if not}\}$. Then $\beta_0 = \mu_C$, $\beta_1 = \mu_A - \mu_C$, and $\beta_2 = \mu_B - \mu_C$, where $\mu_i = E(y)$ at level i.

- **Complete second-order model in 1 quantitative x and 1 qualitative x at two levels (A, B):** $E(y) = \beta_0 + \beta_1 x_1 + \beta_2 (x_1)^2 + \beta_3 x_2 + \beta_4 x_1 x_2 + \beta_5 (x_1)^2 x_2$, where $x_2 = \{1 \text{ if A, } 0 \text{ if B}\}$.

- Two models are **nested** if one model (called the **complete** model) contains all the terms of another model (called the **reduced** model) plus at least additional term.

- A **parsimonious model** is a model with a small number of β parameters.

- Problems with using **stepwise regression** as the "final" model for $E(y)$: (1) extremely large number of t-tests inflate the probabilities of Type I and Type II errors, (2) no higher-order terms (interactions and squared terms) included in the stepwise final model.

- Properties of **regression residuals:** (1) sum of residuals = 0, (2) sum of squared residuals = SSE.

- To detect a **misspecified model:** Plot residuals against each quantitative x in the model—look for trends (e.g., curvilinear trend).
- To identify **outliers:** Find residuals that are greater than $3s$ in absolute value.
- To detect **nonnormal errors:** Graph residuals in a histogram, stem-and-leaf plot, or normal probability plot—look for strong departures from normality.
- To detect a **nonconstant error variance:** Plot residuals against $\hat{y}$—look for patterns (e.g., cone-shaped pattern).

- **Multicollinearity** occurs when two or more of the x's in the model are correlated.
- Indicators of multicollinearity: (1) highly correlated x's, (2) significant global F-test but all t-tests nonsignificant, (3) signs on the β estimates opposite from expected.
- **Extrapolation** occurs when you predict y for values of the x's that are outside of the range of the sample data.

Language Lab

Symbol	Pronunciation	Description
x_1^2	x-sub1 squared	Quadratic term that allows for curvature in the relationship between y and x
$x_1 x_2$	x-sub1 times x-sub2	Interaction term
MSE	M-S-E	Mean square for error (estimates σ^2)
β_i	beta-i	Coefficient of x_i in the model
$\hat{\beta}_i$	beta-i-hat	Least squares estimate of β_i
$s_{\hat{\beta}_i}$	s of beta-i-hat	Estimated standard error of $\hat{\beta}_i$
R^2	R-squared	Multiple coefficient of determination
R_a^2	R-squared adjusted	Adjusted multiple coefficient of determination
F		Test statistic for testing global usefulness of model
$\hat{\epsilon}$	epsilon-hat	Estimated random error, or residual
SSE_R		Sum of squared errors for reduced model
SSE_C		Sum of squared errors for complete model
MSE_C		Mean square error for complete model
$\ln(y)$	Log of y	Natural logarithm of dependent variable

Supplementary Exercises 13.118–13.151

Note: Starred (*) exercises refer to the optional sections in this chapter.

Learning the Mechanics

13.118 Suppose you fit the model

$$y = \beta_0 + \beta_1 x_1 + \beta_2 x_1^2 + \beta_3 x_2 + \beta_4 x_1 x_2 + \epsilon$$

to $n = 25$ data points with the following results:

$\hat{\beta}_0 = 1.26 \quad \hat{\beta}_1 = -2.43 \quad \hat{\beta}_2 = .05 \quad \hat{\beta}_3 = .62 \quad \hat{\beta}_4 = 1.81$

$\qquad s_{\hat{\beta}_1} = 1.21 \quad s_{\hat{\beta}_2} = .16 \quad s_{\hat{\beta}_3} = .26 \quad s_{\hat{\beta}_4} = 1.49$

$SSE = .41 \quad R^2 = .83$

a. Is there sufficient evidence to conclude that at least one of the parameters $\beta_1, \beta_2, \beta_3$, or β_4 is nonzero? Test using $\alpha = .05$.

b. Test $H_0: \beta_1 = 0$ against $H_a: \beta_1 < 0$. Use $\alpha = .05$.
c. Test $H_0: \beta_2 = 0$ against $H_a: \beta_2 > 0$. Use $\alpha = .05$.
d. Test $H_0: \beta_3 = 0$ against $H_a: \beta_3 \neq 0$. Use $\alpha = .05$.

13.119 When a multiple regression model is used for estimating the mean of the dependent variable and for predicting a new value of y, which will be narrower—the confidence interval for the mean or the prediction interval for the new y value? Why?

13.120 Suppose you have developed a regression model to explain the relationship between y and x_1, x_2, and x_3. The ranges of the variables you observed were as follows: $10 \leq y \leq 100$, $5 \leq x_1 \leq 55$, $.5 \leq x_2 \leq 1$, and $1,000 \leq x_3 \leq 2,000$. Will the error of prediction be smaller when you use the least squares equation to predict y when $x_1 = 30$, $x_2 = .6$, and $x_3 = 1,300$, or $x_1 = 60$, $x_2 = .4$, and $x_3 = 900$? Why?

MINITAB Output for Exercise 13.121

```
The regression equation is
Y  = 90.1 - 1.84 X1 + .285 X2


Predictor      Coef   SE Coef       T      P
Constant      90.10     23.10    3.90  0.002
X1           -1.836     0.367   -5.01  0.001
X2            0.285     0.231    1.24  0.465


S = 10.68       R-Sq = 91.6%    R-Sq(adj) = 90.2%

Analysis of Variance

Source            DF       SS       MS       F      P
Regression         2    14801     7400   64.91  0.001
Residual Error    12     1364      114
Total             14    16165
```

13.121 Suppose you used MINITAB to fit the model

$$y = \beta_0 + \beta_1 x_1 + \beta_2 x_2 + \epsilon$$

to $n = 15$ data points and you obtained the printout shown above.
   a. What is the least squares prediction equation?
   b. Find R^2 and interpret its value.   .916
   c. Is there sufficient evidence to indicate that the model is useful for predicting y? Conduct an F-test using $\alpha = .05$. $F = 64.91$
   d. Test the null hypothesis $H_0: \beta_1 = 0$ against the alternative hypothesis $H_a: \beta_1 \neq 0$. Test using $\alpha = .05$. Draw the appropriate conclusions.
   e. Find the standard deviation of the regression model and interpret it. $S = 10.68$

13.122 The first-order model $E(y) = \beta_0 + \beta_1 x_1$ was fit to $n = 19$ data points. A residual plot for the model is provided below. Is the need for a quadratic term in the model evident from the residual plot? Explain.   Yes

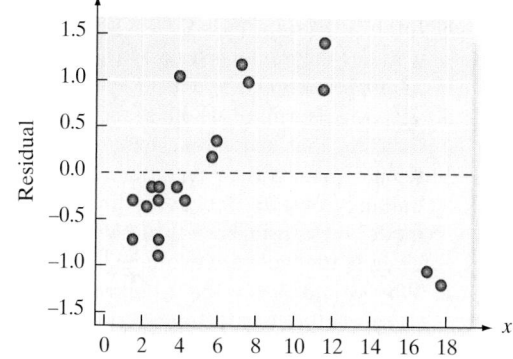

13.123 Why is the model building step the key to the success or failure of a regression analysis?

13.124 Suppose you fit the regression model

$$E(y) = \beta_0 + \beta_1 x_1 + \beta_2 x_2 + \beta_3 x_2^2 + \beta_4 x_1 x_2 + \beta_5 x_1 x_2^2$$

to $n = 35$ data points and wish to test the null hypothesis $H_0: \beta_4 = \beta_5 = 0$.
   a. State the alternative hypothesis.
   b. Explain in detail how to compute the F statistic needed to test the null hypothesis.
   c. What are the numerator and denominator degrees of freedom associated with the F statistic in part **b?**
   d. Give the rejection region for the test if $\alpha = .05$.

13.125 Write a model relating $E(y)$ to one qualitative independent variable that is at four levels. Define all the terms in your model.

13.126 It is desired to relate $E(y)$ to a quantitative variable x_1 and a qualitative variable at three levels.
   a. Write a first-order model.
   b. Write a model that will graph as three different second-order curves—one for each level of the qualitative variable.

13.127 Explain why stepwise regression is used. What is its value in the model-building process?

13.128 a. Write a first-order model relating $E(y)$ to two quantitative independent variables, x_1 and x_2.
   b. Write a complete second-order model.

13.129 To model the relationship between y, a dependent variable, and x, an independent variable, a researcher has taken one measurement on y at each of three different x values. Drawing on his mathematical expertise, the researcher realizes that he can fit the second-order model

$$E(y) = \beta_0 + \beta_1 x + \beta_2 x^2$$

and it will pass exactly through all three points, yielding SSE = 0. The researcher, delighted with the "excellent" fit of the model, eagerly sets out to use it to make inferences. What problems will he encounter in attempting to make inferences?

Applying the Concepts—Basic

13.130 An Educational Testing Service (ETS) research scientist used multiple regression analysis to model y, the final grade point average (GPA) of business and management doctoral students (*Journal of Educational Statistics*, Spring 1993). A list of the potential independent variables measured for each doctoral student in the study follows:

1. Quantitative Graduate Management Aptitude Test (GMAT) score
2. Verbal GMAT score
3. Undergraduate GPA
4. First-year graduate GPA
5. Student cohort (i.e., year in which student entered doctoral program: 1988, 1990, or 1992)
   a. Identify the variables as quantitative or qualitative.
   b. For each quantitative variable, give your opinion on whether the variable is positively or negatively related to final GPA.
   c. For each of the qualitative variables, set up the appropriate dummy variable.
   d. Write a first-order, main-effects model relating final GPA, y, to the five independent variables.
   e. Interpret the β's in the model, part **d.**
   f. Write a first-order model for final GPA, y, that allows for a different slope for each student cohort.
   g. For each quantitative independent variable in the model, part **f,** give the slope of the line (in terms of the β's) for the 1988 cohort.

13.131 The Florida Citrus Commission is interested in evaluating the performance of two orange juice extractors, brand A and brand B. It is believed that the size of the fruit used in the test may influence the juice yield (amount of juice per pound of oranges) obtained by the extractors. The commission wants to develop a regression model relating the mean juice yield $E(y)$ to the type of orange juice extractor (brand A or brand B) and the size of orange (diameter), x_1.
   a. Identify the independent variables as qualitative or quantitative.
   b. Write a model that describes the relationship between $E(y)$ and size of orange as two parallel lines, one for each brand of extractor.
   c. Modify the model of part **b** to permit the slopes of the two lines to differ.

d. Sketch typical response lines for the model of part **b.** Do the same for the model of part **c.** Carefully label your graphs.
e. Specify the null and alternative hypotheses you would use to determine whether the model in part **c** provides more information for predicting yield than does the model in part **b.**
f. Explain how you would obtain the quantities necessary to compute the F-statistic that would be used in testing the hypotheses you described in part **e.**

13.132 Much research—and much litigation—has been conducted on the disparity between the salary levels of men and women. Research reported in *Work and Occupations* (Nov. 1992) analyzes the salaries for a sample of 191 Illinois managers using a regression analysis with the following independent variables:

$$x_1 = \text{Gender of manager} = \begin{cases} 1 & \text{if male} \\ 0 & \text{if not} \end{cases}$$

$$x_2 = \text{Race of manager} = \begin{cases} 1 & \text{if white} \\ 0 & \text{if not} \end{cases}$$

x_3 = Education level (in years)
x_4 = Tenure with firm (in years)
x_5 = Number of hours worked per week

The regression results are shown in the following table as they were reported in the article.

Variable	$\hat{\beta}$	p-Value
x_1	12.774	<.05
x_2	.713	>.10
x_3	1.519	<.05
x_4	.320	<.05
x_5	.205	<.05
Constant	15.491	—
$R^2 = .240$	$n = 191$	

a. Write the hypothesized model that was used, and interpret each of the β parameters in the model.
b. Write the least squares equation that estimates the model in part **a,** and interpret each of the β estimates.
c. Interpret the value of R^2. Test to determine whether the model is useful for predicting annual salary. Test using $\alpha = .05$. $F = 11.68$
d. Test to determine whether the gender variable indicates that male managers are paid more than female managers, even after adjusting for and holding constant the other four factors in the model. Test using $\alpha = .05$. [*Note:* The p-values given in the table are two-tailed.]
e. Why would one want to adjust for these other factors before conducting a test for salary discrimination?

13.133 The *Journal of Consulting and Clinical Psychology* (June 1995) reported on a study of emergency services (EMS) rescue workers who responded to the I-880 freeway collapse during the 1989 San Francisco earthquake. The goal of the study was to identify the predictors of symptomatic distress in the EMS workers. One of the distress variables studied was the Global Symptom Index (GSI). Several models for GSI, y, were considered based on the following independent variables:

x_1 = Critical Incident Exposure scale (CIE)

x_2 = Hogan Personality Inventory-Adjustment scale (HPI-A)

x_3 = Years of experience (EXP)

x_4 = Locus of Control scale (LOC)

x_5 = Social Support scale (SS)

x_6 = Dissociative Experiences scale (DES)

x_7 = Peritraumatic Dissociation Experiences Questionnaire, self-report (PDEQ-SR)

a. Write a first-order model for $E(y)$ as a function of the first five independent variables, x_1–x_5.

b. The model of part **a,** fitted to data collected for $n = 147$ EMS workers, yielded the following results: $R^2 = .469$, $F = 34.47$, *p*-value $< .001$. Interpret these results.   Reject H_0

c. Write a first-order model for $E(y)$ as a function of all seven independent variables, x_1–x_7.

d. The model, part **c,** yielded $R^2 = .603$. Interpret this result.

e. The *t*-tests for testing the DES and PDEQ-SR variables both yielded a *p*-value of .001. Interpret these results.   Reject H_0

13.134 Since the Great Depression of the 1930s, the link between the suicide rate and the state of the economy has been the subject of much research. Research exploring this link using regression analysis was reported in an article in the *Journal of Socio-Economics* (Spring, 1992). The researchers collected data from a 45-year period on the following variables:

y = Suicide rate

x_1 = Unemployment rate

x_2 = Percentage of females in the labor force

x_3 = Divorce rate

x_4 = Logarithm of Gross National Product (GNP)

x_5 = Annual percent change in GNP

One of the models explored by the researchers was a multiple regression model relating y to linear terms in x_1 through x_5. The least squares model shown next resulted (the observed significance levels of the β

estimates are shown in parentheses beneath the estimates):

$$\hat{y} = .002 + .0204x_1 - .0231x_2 + .0765x_3 + .2760x_4 + .0018x_5$$
$$\quad\;\; (.002) \quad (.02) \quad (>.10) \quad (>.10) \quad (>.10)$$
$$R^2 = .45$$

a. Interpret the value of R^2. Is there sufficient evidence to indicate that the model is useful for predicting the suicide rate? Use $\alpha = .05$.

b. Interpret each of the coefficients in the model, and each of the corresponding significance levels.

c. Is there sufficient evidence to indicate that the unemployment rate is a useful predictor of the suicide rate? Use $\alpha = .05$. $p = .002$

d. Discuss each of the following terms with respect to potential problems with the above model: curvature (second-order terms), interaction, and multicollinearity.

13.135 To meet the increasing demand for new software products, many systems development experts have adopted a prototyping methodology. The effects of prototyping on the system development life cycle (SDLC) was investigated in the *Journal of Computer Information Systems* (Spring 1993). A survey of 500 randomly selected corporate level MIS managers was conducted. Three potential independent variables were: (1) *importance* of prototyping to each phase of the SDLC; (2) degree of *support* prototyping provides for the SDLC; and (3) degree to which prototyping *replaces* each phase of the SDLC. The table below gives the pairwise correlations of the three variables in the survey data for one particular phase of the SDLC. Use this information to assess the degree of multicollinearity in the survey data. Would you recommend using all three independent variables in a regression analysis? Explain.

Variable Pairs	Correlation Coefficient, r
Importance–Replace	.2682
Importance–Support	.6991
Replace–Support	−.0531

Source: Hardgrave, B. C., Doke, E. R., and Swanson, N. E. "Prototyping Effects of the System Development Life Cycle: An Empirical Study." *Journal of Computer Information Systems,* Vol. 33, No. 3, Spring 1993, p. 16 (Table 1).

13.136 An operations manager is interested in modeling $E(y)$, the expected length of time per month (in hours) that a machine will be shut down for repairs, as a function of the type of machine (001 or 002) and the age of the machine (in years). The manager has proposed the following model:

$$E(y) = \beta_0 + \beta_1 x_1 + \beta_2 x_1^2 + \beta_3 x_2$$

where

x_1 = Age of machine

x_2 = 1 if machine type 001, 0 if machine type 002

a. Use the data obtained on $n = 20$ machine break-downs, shown below, to estimate the parameters of this model.

b. Do these data provide sufficient evidence to conclude that the second-order term (x_1^2) in the model proposed by the operations manager is necessary? Test using $\alpha = .05$. $t = -2.59$

c. Test the null hypothesis that $\beta_1 = \beta_2 = 0$ using $\alpha = .10$. Interpret the results of the test in the context of the problem. $F = 158.95$

SHUTDOWN

Downtime (hours per month)	Machine Age, x_1 (years)	Machine Type	x_2
10	1.0	001	1
20	2.0	001	1
30	2.7	001	1
40	4.1	001	1
9	1.2	001	1
25	2.5	001	1
19	1.9	001	1
41	5.0	001	1
22	2.1	001	1
12	1.1	001	1
10	2.0	002	0
20	4.0	002	0
30	5.0	002	0
44	8.0	002	0
9	2.4	002	0
25	5.1	002	0
20	3.5	002	0
42	7.0	002	0
20	4.0	002	0
13	2.1	002	0

13.137 Location is one of the most important decisions for hotel chains and lodging firms. Researchers S. E. Kimes (Cornell University) and J. A. Fitzsimmons (University of Texas) studied the site selection process of La Quinta Motor Inns, a moderately priced hotel chain (*Interfaces*, Mar.–Apr. 1990). Using data collected on 57 mature inns owned by La Quinta, the researchers built a regression model designed to predict the profitability for sites under construction. The least squares model is given below:

$$\hat{y} = 39.05 - 5.41x_1 + 5.86x_2 - 3.09x_3 + 1.75x_4$$

where

y = operating margin (measured as a percentage)

x_1 = state population (in thousands) divided by the total number of inns in the state

x_2 = room rate ($) for the inn

x_3 = square root of the median income of the area (in $ thousands)

x_4 = number of college students within four miles of the inn

All variables were "standardized" to have a mean of 0 and a standard deviation of 1.

a. Interpret the β estimates of the model. Comment on the effect of each independent variable on operating margin, y. [*Note:* A profitable inn is defined as one with an operating margin of over 50%.]

b. The model yielded $R^2 = .51$. Give a descriptive measure of model adequacy.

c. Make an inference about model adequacy by conducting the appropriate test. Use $\alpha = .05$.

Applying the Concepts—Intermediate

13.138 A supermarket chain is interested in exploring the relationship between the sales of its store-brand canned vegetables (y), the amount spent on promotion of the vegetables in local newspapers (x_1), and the amount of shelf space allocated to the brand (x_2). One of the chain's supermarkets was randomly selected, and over a 20-week period x_1 and x_2 were varied, as reported in the table.

CANVEG

Week	Sales ($)	Advertising Expenditures ($)	Shelf Space (sq. ft.)
1	2,010	201	75
2	1,850	205	50
3	2,400	355	75
4	1,575	208	30
5	3,550	590	75
6	2,015	397	50
7	3,908	820	75
8	1,870	400	30
9	4,877	997	75
10	2,190	515	30
11	5,005	996	75
12	2,500	625	50
13	3,005	860	50
14	3,480	1,012	50
15	5,500	1,135	75
16	1,995	635	30
17	2,390	837	30
18	4,390	1,200	50
19	2,785	990	30
20	2,989	1,205	30

a. Fit the following model to the data:

$$y = \beta_0 + \beta_1 x_1 + \beta_2 x_2 + \beta_3 x_1 x_2 + \epsilon$$

b. Conduct an F-test to investigate the overall usefulness of this model. Use $\alpha = .05$. $F = 241.758$

c. Test for the presence of interaction between advertising expenditures and shelf space. Use $\alpha = .05$. $t = 7.569$

d. Explain what it means to say that advertising expenditures and shelf space interact.

e. Explain how you could be misled by using a first-order model instead of an interaction model to explain how advertising expenditures and shelf space influence sales.

13.139 Traffic forecasters at the Minnesota Department of Transportation (MDOT) use regression analysis to estimate weekday peak-hour traffic volumes on existing and proposed roadways. In particular, they model y, the peak-hour volume (typically, the volume between 7 and 8 A.M.), as a function of x_1, the road's total volume for the day. For one project involving the redesign of a section of Interstate 494, the forecasters collected $n = 72$ observations of peak-hour traffic volume and 24-hour weekday traffic volume using electronic sensors that count vehicles. The data are saved in the **MINNDOT** file. (The first and last five observations are listed in the table.)

MINNDOT

Observation Number	Peak-Hour Volume	24-Hour Volume	I-35
1	1,990.94	20,070	0
2	1,989.63	21,234	0
3	1,986.96	20,633	0
4	1,986.96	20,676	0
5	1,983.78	19,818	0
⋮	⋮	⋮	
68	2,147.93	22,948	1
69	2,147.85	23,551	1
70	2,144.23	21,637	1
71	2,142.41	23,543	1
72	2,137.39	22,594	1

Source: John Sem. Director: Allan E. Pint, State Traffic Forecast Engineer; and James Page Sr., Transportation Planner, Traffic and Commodities Studies Section, Minnesota Department of Transportation, St. Paul, Minnesota.

a. Construct a scattergram for the data, plotting peak-hour volume y against 24-hour volume x_1. Note the isolated group of observations at the top of the scattergram. Investigators discovered that all of these data points were collected at the intersection of Interstate 35W and 46th Street. (These are observations 55–72 in the table.) While all other locations in the sample were three-lane highways, this location was unique in that the highway widens to four lanes just north of the electronic sensor. Consequently, the forecasters decided to include a dummy variable to account for a difference between the I-35W location and all other locations.

b. Knowing that peak-hour traffic volumes have a theoretical upper bound, the forecaster hypoth-

esized that a second-order model should be used to explain the variation in y. Propose a complete second-order model for $E(y)$ as a function of 24-hour volume x_1 and the dummy variable for location.

c. Using an available statistical software package, fit the model of part **b** to the data. Interpret the results. Specifically, is the curvilinear relationship between peak-hour volume and 24-hour volume different at the two locations?

d. Conduct a residual analysis of the model, part **b**. Evaluate the assumptions of normality and constant error variance, and determine whether any outliers exist.

13.140 *Best's Review* (June 1999) compared the mortgage loan portfolios for a sample of 25 life/health insurance companies. The information in the table on page 898 is extracted from the article. Suppose you want to model the percentage of problem mortgages (y) of a company as a function of total mortgage loans (x_1), percentage of invested assets (x_2), percentage of commercial mortgages (x_3), and percentage of residential mortgages (x_4).

a. Write a first-order model for $E(y)$.

b. Fit the model of part **a** to the data and evaluate its overall usefulness. Use $\alpha = .05$. $F = 5.25$

c. Interpret the β estimates in the fitted model.

d. Construct scattergrams of y versus each of the four independent variables in the model. Which variables warrant inclusion in the model as second-order (i.e., squared) terms? X_2 and X_4

e. Fit the model that results from your exploratory analysis in part **d** to the data. Evaluate its overall usefulness using $\alpha = .05$. $F = 6.98$

f. Do the one or more second-order terms of your model, part **e**, contribute information for the prediction of the percentage of problem mortgages? Test using $\alpha = .05$. $F = 5.60$

13.141 The audience for a product's advertising can be divided into four segments according to the degree of exposure received as a result of the advertising. These segments are groups of consumers who receive very high (VH), high (H), medium (M), or low (L) exposure to the advertising. A company is interested in exploring whether its advertising effort affects its product's market share. Accordingly, the company identifies 24 sample groups of consumers who have been exposed to its advertising, six groups at each exposure level. Then, the company determines its product's market share within each group.

a. Write a regression model that expresses the company's market share as a function of advertising exposure level. Define all terms in your model, and list any assumptions you make about them.

⊙ **BESTINS**

Company	Total Mortgage Loan, x_1	% Invested Assets, x_2	% Commercial Mortgages, x_3	% Residential Mortgages, x_4	% Problem Mortgages, y
TIAA Group	$18,803,163	20.7	100.0	0.0	11.4
Metropolitan Insurance	18,171,162	13.9	77.8	1.6	3.8
Prudential of Am Group	16,213,150	12.9	87.4	2.3	4.1
Principal Mutual IA	11,940,345	30.3	98.8	1.2	32.6
Northwestern Mutualk	10,834,616	17.8	99.5	0.0	2.2
Cigna Group	10,181,124	25.1	99.8	0.2	11.1
John Hancock Group	8,229,523	20.4	82.0	0.1	12.2
Aegon USA Inc.	7,695,198	17.7	73.0	24.7	6.4
New York Life	7,088,003	9.4	92.2	7.8	2.4
Nationwide	5,328,142	26.3	100.0	0.0	7.5
Massachusetts Mutual	4,965,287	12.2	78.6	21.4	6.3
Equitable Group	4,905,123	12.7	63.6	0.0	27.0
Aetna US Healthcare Group	3,974,881	10.5	94.1	5.4	8.7
American Express Financial	3,655,292	13.9	100.0	0.0	2.1
ING Group	3,505,206	16.2	99.8	0.2	0.7
American General	3,359,650	6.4	99.8	0.2	2.1
Lincoln National	3,264,860	11.5	99.9	0.1	2.2
SunAmerica Inc.	3,909,177	15.7	100.0	0.0	2.6
Allstate	2,987,144	10.9	100.0	0.0	2.1
Travelers Insurance Group	2,978,628	10.3	74.9	0.1	3.2
GE Capital Corp. Group	2,733,981	7.5	99.7	0.3	0.7
ReliaStar Financial Corp.	2,342,992	16.2	69.9	30.0	6.4
General American Life	2,107,592	15.2	99.8	0.2	1.3
State Farm Group	2,027,648	8.6	97.6	2.4	0.1
Pacific Mutual Life	1,945,392	9.7	96.4	3.6	6.1

Source: Best's Review, (Life/Health), June 1999, p. 35.

b. Did you include interaction terms in your model? Why or why not? No

c. The data in the table on p. 899 were obtained by the company. Fit the model you constructed in part **a** to the data.

d. Is there evidence to suggest that the firm's expected market share differs for different levels of advertising exposure? Test using $\alpha = .05$.

13.142 A research physician wishes to find a model that will predict the mean time to relief after the administration of a certain drug. Two important independent variables considered to be good predictors of relief time are age of the patient and method of administration. Physicians administer a standard dose of a drug to a patient in one of three different ways: orally in liquid form (method 1), orally in pill form (method 2), and intravenously (method 3). Consider the interaction model

⚙ **MKTSHR** (Data for Exercise 13.141)

Market Share within Group	Exposure Level
10.1	L
10.3	L
10.0	L
10.3	L
10.2	L
10.5	L
10.6	M
11.0	M
11.2	M
10.9	M
10.8	M
11.0	M
12.2	H
12.1	H
11.8	H
12.6	H
11.9	H
12.9	H
10.7	VH
10.8	VH
11.0	VH
10.5	VH
10.8	VH
10.6	VH

$$E(y) = \beta_0 + \beta_1 x_1 + \beta_2 x_2 + \beta_3 x_3 + \beta_4 x_1 x_2 + \beta_5 x_1 x_3$$

where

y = Time to relief (in minutes)
x_1 = Age of patient (in years)
x_2 = 1 if drug is administered orally in pill form, 0 if not
x_3 = 1 if drug is administered intravenously, 0 if not

  a. The data in the table below were obtained on 12 patients. Fit this model to the data using a statistical software package.
  b. Test whether the model is useful in predicting mean time to relief. Use $\alpha = .05$.   *F = 4.90*
  c. What hypothesis would you use to test whether the age–drug method interaction terms contribute to the prediction of mean time to relief?
  d. Give the reduced model appropriate for conducting the test, part **c.**
  e. Fit the reduced model to the data and use the results to conduct the test, part **c.**   *F = 2.36*

⚙ **RELIEF**

Method 1		Method 2		Method 3	
Age	Time to Relief	Age	Time to Relief	Age	Time to Relief
51	22	46	28	37	19
36	25	40	24	60	17
31	20	26	23	25	21
20	25	32	25	38	20

13.143 To determine whether extra personnel are needed for the day, the owners of a water adventure park would like to find a model that would allow them to predict the day's attendance each morning before opening based on the day of the week and weather conditions. The model is of the form

$$E(y) = \beta_0 + \beta_1 x_1 + \beta_2 x_2 + \beta_3 x_3$$

where

y = Daily admission
$x_1 = \begin{cases} 1 & \text{if weekend} \\ 0 & \text{otherwise} \end{cases}$ (dummy variable)
$x_2 = \begin{cases} 1 & \text{if sunny} \\ 0 & \text{if overcast} \end{cases}$ (dummy variable)
x_3 = Predicted daily high temperature (°F)

These data were recorded for a random sample of 30 days, and a regression model was fitted to the data. The least squares analysis produced the following results:

$$\hat{y} = -105 + 25x_1 + 100x_2 + 10x_3$$

with

$$s_{\hat{\beta}_1} = 10 \qquad s_{\hat{\beta}_2} = 30 \qquad s_{\hat{\beta}_3} = 4 \qquad R^2 = .65$$

  a. Interpret the estimated model coefficients.
  b. Is there sufficient evidence to conclude that this model is useful for the prediction of daily attendance? Use $\alpha = .05$.   *F = 16.10*
  c. Is there sufficient evidence to conclude that the mean attendance increases on weekends? Use $\alpha = .10$.   *t = 2.5*
  d. Use the model to predict the attendance on a sunny weekday with a predicted high temperature of 95°F.   *945*
  e. Suppose the 90% prediction interval for part **d** is (645, 1,245). Interpret this interval.

13.144 Refer to Exercise 13.143. The owners of the water adventure park are advised that the prediction model could probably be improved if interaction terms were added. In particular, it is thought that the *rate* at which mean attendance increases as predicted high temperature increases will be greater on weekends than on weekdays. The following model is therefore proposed:

$$E(y) = \beta_0 + \beta_1 x_1 + \beta_2 x_2 + \beta_3 x_3 + \beta_4 x_1 x_3$$

The same 30 days of data used in Exercise 13.143 are again used to obtain the least squares model

$$\hat{y} = 250 - 700x_1 + 100x_2 + 5x_3 + 15x_1 x_3$$

with

$$s_{\hat{\beta}_4} = 3.0 \quad R^2 = .96$$

  a. Graph the predicted day's attendance, y, against the day's predicted high temperature, x_3, for a sunny weekday and for a sunny weekend day. Plot both on the same paper for x_3 between 70 and 100°F. Note the increase in slope for the weekend day. Interpret this.

b. Do the data indicate that the interaction term is a useful addition to the model? Use $\alpha = .05$. $t = 5$

c. Use this model to predict the attendance for a sunny weekday with a predicted high temperature of 95°F.   825

d. Suppose the 90% prediction interval for part **c** is (800, 850). Compare this result with the prediction interval for the model without interaction in Exercise 13.143, part **e**. Do the relative widths of the confidence intervals support or refute your conclusion about the utility of the interaction term (part **b**)?

e. The owners, noting that the coefficient $\hat{\beta}_1 = -700$, conclude the model is ridiculous because it seems to imply that the mean attendance will be 700 less on weekends than on weekdays. Explain why this is *not* the case.

13.145 Many colleges and universities develop regression models for predicting the GPA of incoming freshmen. This predicted GPA can then be used to make admission decisions. Although most models use many independent variables to predict GPA, we will illustrate by choosing two variables:

x_1 = Verbal score on college entrance examination (percentile)

x_2 = Mathematics score on college entrance examination (percentile)

The data in the table are obtained for a random sample of 40 freshmen at one college. Consider the model $y = \beta_0 + \beta_1 x_1 + \beta_2 x_2 + \varepsilon$.

a. Fit the model to the data and interpret the least squares estimates β_1 and β_2 in the context of this application.

b. Interpret the standard deviation and the adjusted coefficient of determination of the regression model in the context of this application.

c. Is this model useful for predicting GPA? Conduct a statistical test to justify your answer.
$F = 39.51$

d. Sketch the relationship between predicted GPA, $\hat{y}$, and verbal score, x_1, for the following mathematics scores: $x_2 = 60, 75$, and 90.

e. Plot the residuals from the first-order model against x_1 and x_2. Analyze the two plots, and determine whether visual evidence exists that curvature (a quadratic term) for either x_1 or x_2 should be added to the model.

13.146 Refer to Exercise 13.145. Now consider the complete second-order model

$$y = \beta_0 + \beta_1 x_1 + \beta_2 x_2 + \beta_3 x_1^2 + \beta_4 x_2^2 + \beta_5 x_1 x_2 + \epsilon$$

a. Fit the model to the data and give the least squares prediction equation.

b. Compare the standard deviations of the first- and second-order regression models. With what relative precision will these two models predict GPA?

c. Test whether this model is useful for predicting GPA. Use $\alpha = .05$. $F = 100.41$

d. Test whether the interaction term, $\beta_5 x_1 x_2$, is important for the prediction of GPA. Use $\alpha = .10$.

e. Plot the residuals of the second-order model against x_1 and x_2. Compare the residual plots to those of the first-order model in Exercise 13.145.

COLLGPA

Verbal, x_1	Mathematics, x_2	GPA, y	Verbal, x_1	Mathematics, x_2	GPA, y	Verbal, x_1	Mathematics, x_2	GPA, y
81	87	3.49	83	76	3.75	97	80	3.27
68	99	2.89	64	66	2.70	77	90	3.47
57	86	2.73	83	72	3.15	49	54	1.30
100	49	1.54	93	54	2.28	39	81	1.22
54	83	2.56	74	59	2.92	87	69	3.23
82	86	3.43	51	75	2.48	70	95	3.82
75	74	3.59	79	75	3.45	57	89	2.93
58	98	2.86	81	62	2.76	74	67	2.83
55	54	1.46	50	69	1.90	87	93	3.84
49	81	2.11	72	70	3.01	90	65	3.01
64	76	2.69	54	52	1.48	81	76	3.33
66	59	2.16	65	79	2.98	84	69	3.06
80	61	2.60	56	78	2.58			
100	85	3.30	98	67	2.73			

Given the analyses you have performed, which of the two models do you think is preferable as a predictor of GPA: the first- or second-order model?

f. Conduct a test to directly compare the first- and second-order models. $F = 45.68$

MNSALES

13.147 In Exercise 13.16 (p. 787), a real estate appraiser used regression analysis to explore the relationship between the sale prices of apartment buildings and various characteristics of the buildings. The **MNSALES** file also contains data on the physical condition of each apartment building (E: excellent; G: good; F: fair).

a. Write a model that describes the relationship between sale price and number of apartment units as three parallel lines, one for each level of physical condition. Be sure to specify the dummy variable coding scheme you use.

b. Plot y against x_1 (number of apartment units) for all buildings in excellent condition. On the same graph, plot y against x_1 for all buildings in good condition. Do this again for all buildings in fair condition. Does it appear that the model you specified in part **a** is appropriate? Explain.

c. Fit the model from part **a** to the data. Report the least squares prediction equation for each of the three building condition levels.

d. Plot the three prediction equations of part **c** on a scattergram of the data.

e. Do the data provide sufficient evidence to conclude that the relationship between sale price and number of units differs depending on the physical condition of the apartments? Test using $\alpha = .05$.

f. Check the data set for multicollinearity. How does this impact your choice of independent variables to use in a model for sale price?

g. Consider the first-order model $E(y) = \beta_0 + \beta_1 x_1 + \cdots + \beta_5 x_5$, analyzed in Exercise 13.16. Conduct a complete residual analysis for the model to check the assumptions on ϵ.

13.148 A firm that has developed a new type of light bulb is interested in evaluating its performance in order to decide whether to market it. It is known that the light output of the bulb depends on the cleanliness of its surface area and the length of time the bulb has been in operation. Use the data in the next table and the procedures you learned in this chapter to build a regression model that relates drop in light output to bulb surface cleanliness and length of operation. Be sure to conduct a residual analysis also.

LTBULB

Drop in Light Output (% original output)	Bulb Surface (C = clean,) (D = dirty)	Length of Operation (hours)
0	C	0
16	C	400
22	C	800
27	C	1,200
32	C	1,600
36	C	2,000
38	C	2,400
0	D	0
4	D	400
6	D	800
8	D	1,200
9	D	1,600
11	D	2,000
12	D	2,400

13.149 A large research and development firm rates the performance of each member of its technical staff on a scale of 0 to 100, and this merit rating is used to determine the size of the person's pay raise for the coming year. The firm's personnel department is interested in developing a regression model to help them forecast the merit rating that an applicant for a technical position will receive after being employed three years. The firm proposes to use the following second-order model to forecast the merit ratings of applicants who have just completed their graduate studies and have no prior related job experience:

$$E(y) = \beta_0 + \beta_1 x_1 + \beta_2 x_2 + \beta_3 x_1 x_2 + \beta_4 x_1^2 + \beta_5 x_2^2$$

where

$y =$ Applicant's merit rating after 3 years

$x_1 =$ Applicant's GPA in graduate school

$x_2 =$ Applicant's total score (verbal plus quantitative) on the Graduate Record Examination (GRE)

The model, fit to data collected for a random sample of $n = 40$ employees, resulted in SSE = 1830.44 and SS(model) = 4911.5.

The reduced model $E(y) = \beta_0 + \beta_1 x_1 + \beta_2 x_2$ is also fit to the same data, resulting in SSE = 3197.16.

a. Identify the appropriate null and alternative hypotheses to test whether the complete (second-order) model contributes information for the prediction of y. $H_0: \beta_1 = \beta_2 = \beta_3 = \beta_4 = \beta_5 = 0$

b. Conduct the test of hypothesis given in part **a.** Test using $\alpha = .05$. Interpret the results in the context of this problem. $F = 18.24$

c. Identify the appropriate null and alternative hypotheses to test whether the complete model contributes more information than the reduced (first-order) model for the prediction of y.

d. Conduct the test of hypothesis given in part **c**. Test using $\alpha = .05$. Interpret the results in the context of this problem. *F = 8.46*

e. Which model, if either, would you use to predict *y*? Explain.

13.150 Five varieties of peas (A, B, C, D, and E) are currently being tested by a large agribusiness cooperative to determine which is best suited for production. A field was divided into 20 plots, with each variety of peas planted in four plots. The yields (in bushels of peas) produced from each plot are shown in the table below.

PEAS

A	B	C	D	E
26.2	29.2	29.1	21.3	20.1
24.3	28.1	30.8	22.4	19.3
21.8	27.3	33.9	24.3	19.9
28.1	31.2	32.8	21.8	22.1

a. Fit the model
$$y = \beta_0 + \beta_1 x_1 + \beta_2 x_2 + \beta_3 x_3 + \beta_4 x_4 + \varepsilon$$
to these data, using the coding $x_1 = 1$ for variety A, $x_2 = 1$ for variety B, $x_3 = 1$ for variety C, and $x_4 = 1$ for variety D.

b. Interpret all the parameter estimates in the model.

c. What null and alternative hypotheses are tested by the global *F*-test for this model? Interpret the hypotheses both in terms of the β parameters and the mean yields for the five varieties of peas.

d. Test the hypotheses of part **c** using $\alpha = .05$.

e. Place a 95% confidence interval on the differences in the mean yields of varieties D and E. 2.1 ± 2.846

13.151 Researchers for a dog food company have developed a new puppy food they hope will compete with the major brands. One premarketing test involved the comparison of the new food with that of two competitors in terms of weight gain. Fifteen 8-week-old German shepherd puppies, each from a different litter, were divided into three groups of five puppies each. Each group was fed one of the three brands of food.

a. Set up a model that assumes the final weight *y* is linearly related to initial weight *x* but does not allow for differences among the three brands; that is, assume the response curve is the same for the three brands of dog food. Sketch the response curve as it might appear.

b. Set up a model that assumes the final weight is linearly related to initial weight and allows the intercepts of the lines to differ for the three brands. In other words, assume that the initial weight and brand both affect final weight, but the two variables do not interact. Sketch typical response curves.

c. Now write the main effects with interaction model. For this model we assume the final weight is linearly related to initial weight, but both the slopes and the intercepts of the lines depend on the brand. Sketch typical response curves.

REFERENCES

Barnett, V., and Lewis, T. *Outliers in Statistical Data*. New York: Wiley, 1978.

Belsley, D. A., Kuh, E., and Welsch, R. E. *Regression Diagnostics: Identifying Influential Data and Sources of Collinearity*. New York: Wiley, 1980.

Chase, R. B., and Aquilano, N. J. *Production and Operations Management*, 6th ed. Homewood, Ill.: Richard D. Irwin, 1992.

Chatterjee, S., and Price, B. *Regression Analysis by Example*, 2nd ed. New York: Wiley, 1991.

Draper, N., and Smith, H. *Applied Regression Analysis*, 2nd ed. New York: Wiley, 1981.

Graybill, F. *Theory and Application of the Linear Model*. North Scituate, Mass.: Duxbury, 1976.

Horngren, Charles T., Foster, George, and Datar, Srikant M. *Cost Accounting*, 8th ed. Englewood Cliffs, N.J.: Prentice Hall, 1994.

Mansfield, E. *Applied Microeconomics*. New York: Norton, 1994.

Mendenhall, W. *Introduction to Linear Models and the Design and Analysis of Experiments*. Belmont, Calif.: Wadsworth, 1968.

Mendenhall, W., and Sincich, T. *A Second Course in Statistics: Regression Analysis*, 6th ed. Upper Saddle River, N.J.: Prentice Hall, 2003.

Mosteller, F., and Tukey, J. W. *Data Analysis and Regression: A Second Course in Statistics*. Reading, Mass.: Addison-Wesley, 1977.

Neter, J., Kutner, M., Nachtsheim, C., and Wasserman, W. *Applied Linear Statistical Models*, 4th ed. Homewood, Ill.: Richard Irwin, 1996.

Rousseeuw, P. J. and Leroy, A. M. *Robust Regression and Outlier Detection*. New York: Wiley, 1987.

Weisberg, S. *Applied Linear Regression*, 2nd ed. New York: Wiley, 1985.

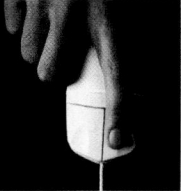

Using Technology

13.1 Multiple Regression Using SPSS

To conduct a multiple regression analysis, first access the SPSS spreadsheet file that contains the dependent and independent variables. Next, click on the "Analyze" button on the SPSS menu bar, then click on "Regression" and "Linear", as shown in Figure 13.S.1. The resulting dialog box appears as shown in Figure 13.S.2.

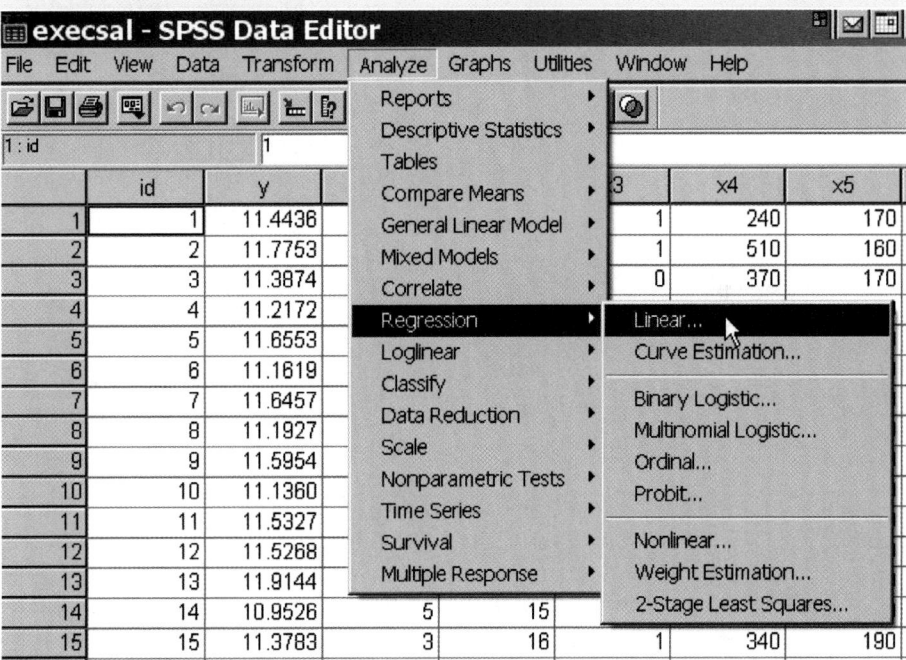

Figure 13.S.1
SPSS menu options for regression

Specify the dependent variable in the "Dependent" box and the independent variables in the "Independent(s)" box. [*Note*: If your model includes interaction and/or squared terms, you must create and add these higher-order variables to the SPSS spreadsheet file *prior* to running a regression analysis. You can do this by clicking the "Transform" button on the SPSS main menu and selecting the "Compute" option.] To perform a standard regression analysis, select "Enter" in the "Method" box. To perform a stepwise regression analysis, select "Stepwise" in the "Method" box.

To perform a nested model *F*-test for additional model terms, click the "Next" button and enter the terms you want to test in the "Independent(s)" box. [*Note*: These terms, plus the terms you entered initially form the complete model for the nested *F*-test.] Next, click the "Statistics" button and select

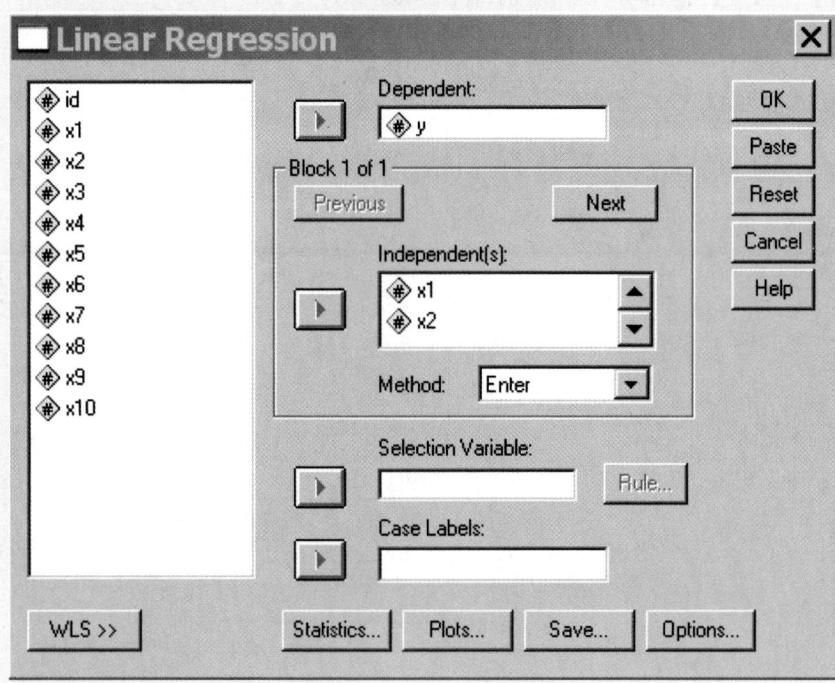

Figure 13.S.2
SPSS linear regression dialog box

"R squared change". Click "Continue" to return to the main SPSS regression dialog box.

To produce confidence intervals for the model parameters, click the "Statistics" button and check the appropriate menu items in the resulting menu list. To obtain prediction intervals for y and confidence intervals for $E(y)$, click the "Save" button, and check the appropriate items in the resulting menu list. (The prediction intervals will be added as new columns to the SPSS data spreadsheet.) Residual plots are obtained by clicking the "Plots" button and making the appropriate selections on the resulting menu. To return to the main Regression dialog box from any of these optional screens, click "Continue". Click "OK" on the Regression dialog box to view the multiple regression results.

13.2 Multiple Regression Using MINITAB

To conduct a multiple regression analysis, first access the MINITAB worksheet file that contains the dependent and independent variables. Next, click on the "Stat" button on the MINITAB menu bar, then click on "Regression" and "Regression" again, as shown in Figure 13.M.1.

The resulting dialog box appears as shown in Figure 13.M.2. Specify the dependent variable in the "Response" box and the independent variables in the "Predictors" box. [*Note*: If your model includes interaction and/or squared terms, you must create and add these higher-order variables to the MINITAB worksheet *prior* to running a regression analysis. You can do this by clicking the "Calc" button on the MINITAB main menu and selecting the "Calculator" option.]

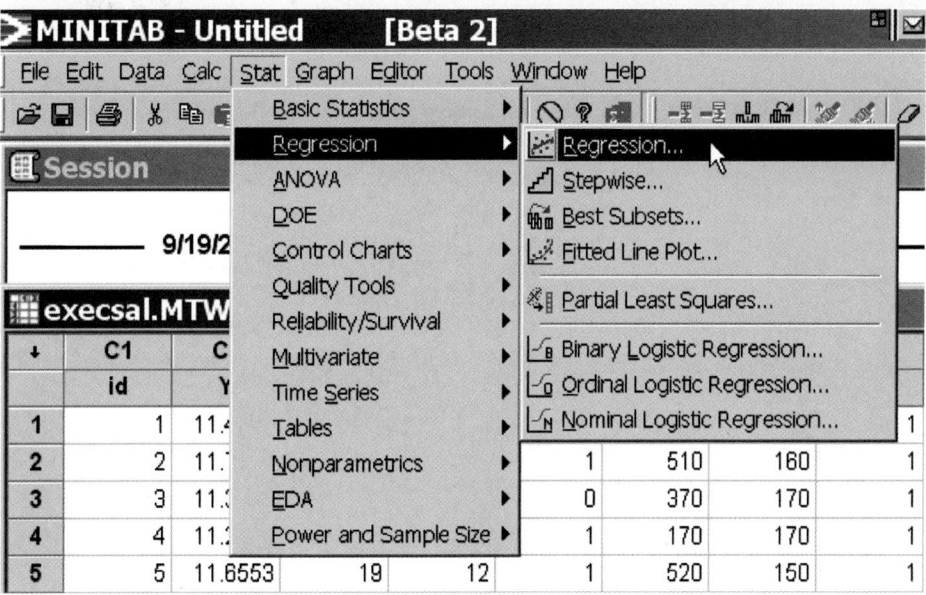

Figure 13.M.1
MINITAB menu options for regression

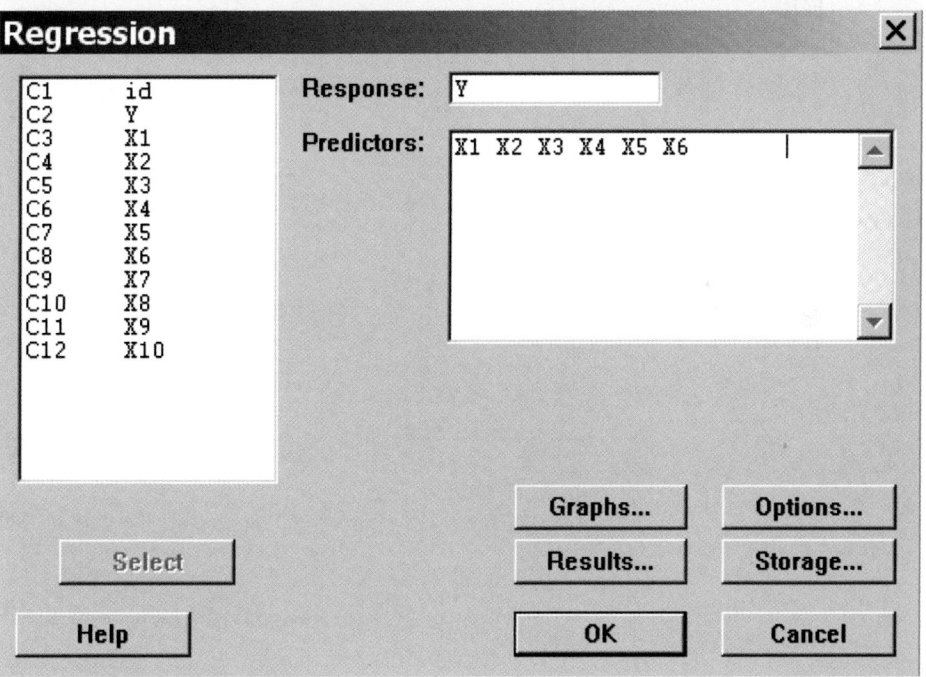

Figure 13.M.2
MINITAB regression dialog box

To produce prediction intervals for y and confidence intervals for $E(y)$, click the "Options" button and select the appropriate menu items in the resulting menu list. Residual plots are obtained by clicking the "Graphs" button and making the appropriate selections on the resulting menu. To return to the main Regression dialog box from any of these optional screens, click "OK". When you have made all your selections, click "OK" on the main Regression dialog box to produce the MINITAB multiple regression printout.

To conduct a stepwise regression analysis, click on the "Stat" button on the main menu bar, then click on "Regression", and click on "Stepwise" (see Figure 13.M.1). The resulting dialog box appears in Figure 13.M.3. Specify the dependent variable in the "Response" box and the independent variables in the stepwise model in the "Predictors" box. As an option, you can select the value of α to use in the analysis by clicking on the "Methods" button and specifying the value. (The default is $\alpha = .15$.) Click "OK" to view the stepwise regression results.

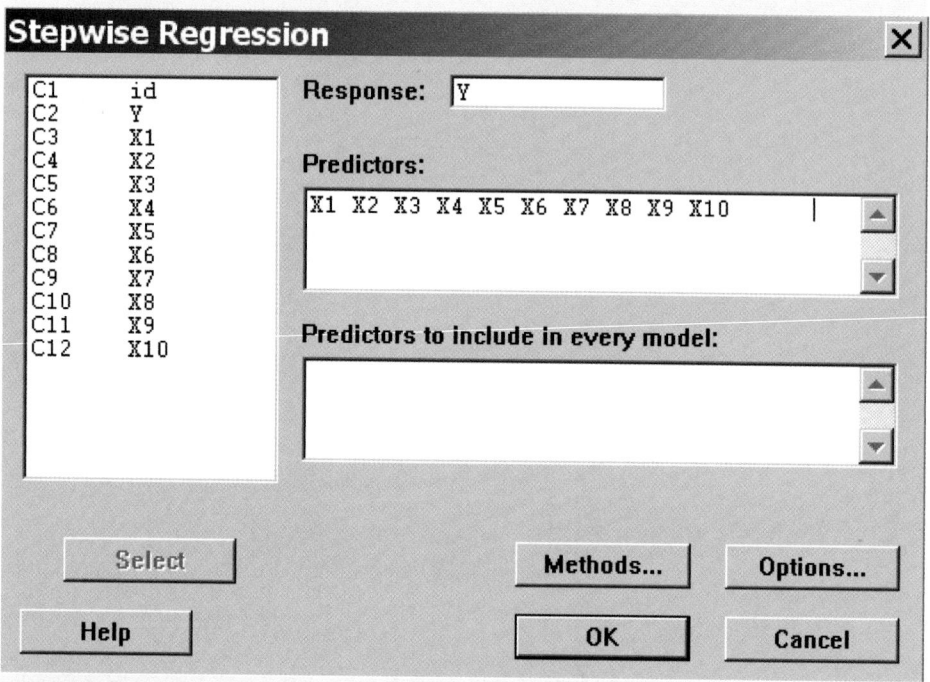

Figure 13.M.3
MINITAB stepwise regression dialog box

13.3 Multiple Regression Using EXCEL and PHSTAT2

To conduct a multiple regression analysis, first access the EXCEL worksheet file that contains the dependent and independent variables. [*Note*: If your model includes interaction and/or squared terms, you must create and add these higher-order variables to the EXCEL worksheet *prior* to running a regression analysis.] Next, click "PHStat" from the EXCEL menu bar, then select "Regression" and "Multiple Regression", as shown in Figure 13.E.1. The resulting dialog box is shown in Figure 13.E.2. Specify the cell ranges for the y- and x-variables in the "Data" area of the Multiple Regression dialog

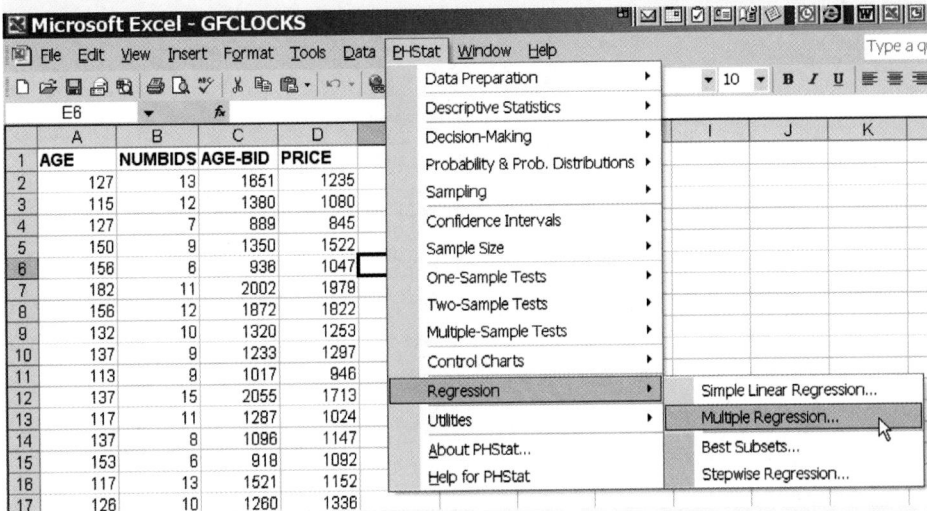

Figure 13.E.1
EXCEL menu options for multiple regression

box. [*Note*: The *x*-variables must be in adjacent columns on the EXCEL worksheet.]

Select the confidence level for confidence intervals for the model parameters, and select both the "Regression Statistics" and "ANOVA and Coefficients" table options. To produce graphs of the regression residual, select the "Residual Plots" option. To produce prediction intervals for *y* and confidence intervals for $E(y)$, select the "Confidence and Prediction Interval Estimates" option and specify the confidence level (as shown at the bottom of Figure 13.E.2). After making all your selections, click "OK" to produce the multiple regression results. [*Note*: The standard regression printout will appear in one worksheet and the confidence/prediction intervals will appear in a second worksheet. Also, on the second worksheet, you will be prompted to select specific values of the *x*'s for predicting *y*.]

To conduct a stepwise regression analysis, click "PHStat" from the EXCEL menu bar, then select "Regression" and "Stepwise Regression" (see Figure 13.E.1). The resulting dialog box is shown in Figure 13.E.3. Specify the cell ranges for the *y*- and *x*-variables in the "Data" area of the Stepwise Regression dialog box. [*Note*: The *x*-variables must be in adjacent columns on the EXCEL worksheet.] As an option, you can select the *p*-value to use for variable entry and removal. (The default is *p*-value = .05.) Click "OK" to view the stepwise regression results.

Figure 13.E.2
EXCEL/PHSTAT2 multiple regression dialog box

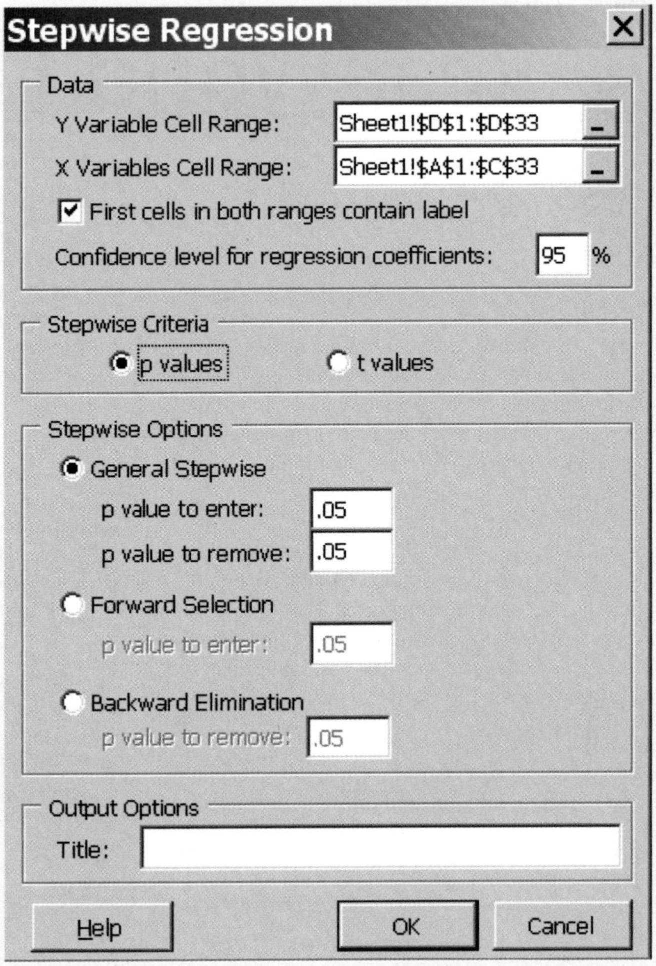

Stepwise Regression   ☒

Data

Y Variable Cell Range: Sheet1!$D$1:$D$33   _

X Variables Cell Range: Sheet1!$A$1:$C$33   _

☑ First cells in both ranges contain label

Confidence level for regression coefficients: 95   %

Stepwise Criteria

⦿ p values   ◯ t values

Stepwise Options

⦿ General Stepwise

p value to enter: .05

p value to remove: .05

◯ Forward Selection

p value to enter: .05

◯ Backward Elimination

p value to remove: .05

Output Options

Title:

Help   OK   Cancel

Figure 13.E.3
EXCEL/PHSTAT2 stepwise regression dialog box

Real-World Case
The Condo Sales Case
(A Case Covering Chapters 12 and 13)

This case involves an investigation of the factors that affect the sale price of oceanside condominium units. It represents an extension of an analysis of the same data by Herman Kelting (1979). Although condo sale prices have increased dramatically over the past 20 years, the relationship between these factors and sale price remain about the same. Consequently, the data provide valuable insight into today's condominium sales market.

The sales data were obtained for a new oceanside condominium complex consisting of two adjacent and connected eight-floor buildings. The complex contains 200 units of equal size (approximately 500 square feet each). The locations of the buildings relative to the ocean, the swimming pool, the parking lot, etc., are shown in the accompanying figure. There are several features of the complex that you should note:

1. The units facing south, called *ocean view,* face the beach and ocean. In addition, units in building 1 have a good view of the pool. Units to the rear of the building, called *bay-view,* face the parking lot and an area of land that ultimately borders a bay. The view from the upper floors of these units is primarily of wooded, sandy terrain. The bay is very distant and barely visible.

2. The only elevator in the complex is located at the east end of building 1, as are the office and the game room. People moving to or from the higher floor units in building 2 would likely use the elevator and move through the passages to their units. Thus, units on the higher floors and at a greater distance from the elevator would be less convenient; they would require greater effort in moving baggage, groceries, and so on and would be farther away from the game room, the office, and the swimming pool. These units also possess an advantage: there would be the least amount of traffic through the hallways in the area and hence they are the most private.

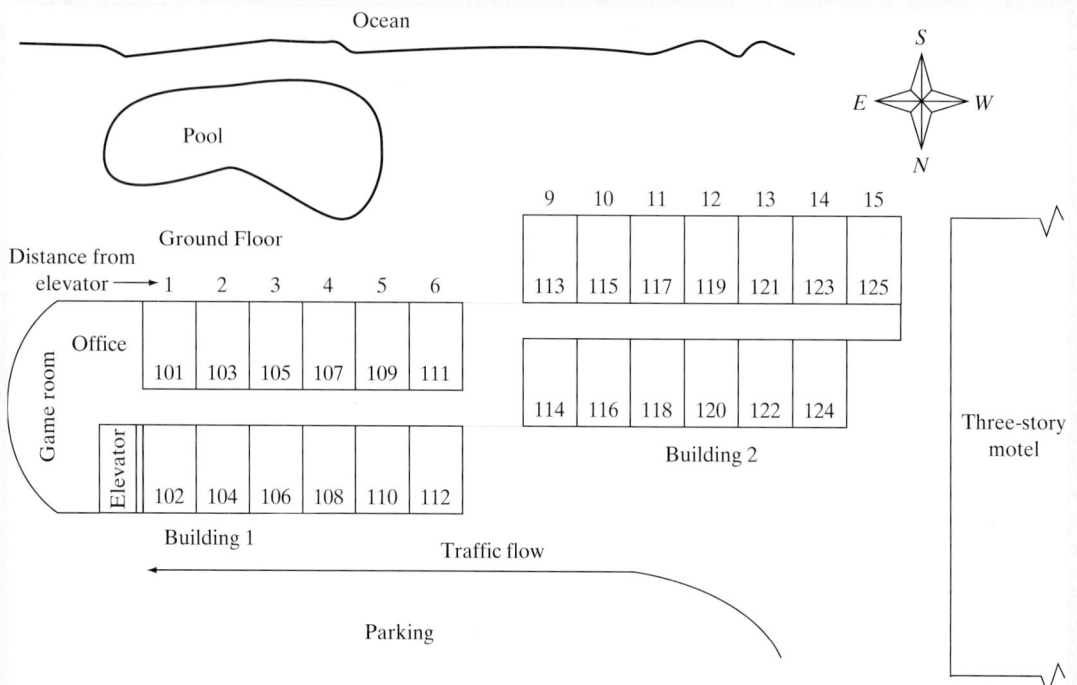

Figure C5.1
Layout of condominium complex

3. Lower-floor oceanside units are most suited to active people; they open onto the beach, ocean, and pool. They are within easy reach of the game room and they are easily reached from the parking area.

4. Checking the layout of the condominium complex, you discover that some of the units in the center of the complex, units ending in numbers 11 and 14, have part of their view blocked.

5. The condominium complex was completed at the time of the 1975 recession; sales were slow and the developer was forced to sell most of the units at auction approximately 18 months after opening. Consequently, the auction data are completely buyer-specified and hence consumer-oriented in contrast to most other real estate sales data which are, to a high degree, seller and broker specified.

6. Many unsold units in the complex were furnished by the developer and rented prior to the auction. Consequently, some of the units bid on and sold at auction had furniture, others did not.

This condominium complex is obviously unique. For example, the single elevator located at one end of the complex produces a remarkably high level of both inconvenience and privacy for the people occupying units on the top floors in building 2. Consequently, the developer is unsure of how the height of the unit (floor number), distance of the unit from the elevator, presence or absence of an ocean view, etc., affect the prices of the units sold at auction. To investigate these relationships, the following data (saved in the **CONDO** data file) were recorded for each of the 106 units sold at the auction:

1. *Sale price.* Measured in hundreds of dollars (adjusted for inflation).

2. *Floor height.* The floor location of the unit; the variable levels are 1, 2, ..., 8.

3. *Distance from elevator.* This distance, measured along the length of the complex, is expressed in number of condominium units. An additional two units of distance was added to the units in building 2 to account for the walking distance in the connecting area between the two buildings. Thus, the distance of unit 105 from the elevator would be 3, and the distance between unit 113 and the elevator would be 9. The variable levels are 1, 2, ..., 15.

4. *View of ocean.* The presence or absence of an ocean view is recorded for each unit and specified with a dummy variable (1 if the unit possessed an ocean view and 0 if not). Note that units not possessing an ocean view would face the parking lot.

5. *End unit.* We expect the partial reduction of view of end units on the ocean side (numbers ending in 11) to reduce their sale price. The ocean view of these end units is partially blocked by building 2. This qualitative variable is also specified with a dummy variable (1 if the unit has a unit number ending in 11 and 0 if not).

6. *Furniture.* The presence or absence of furniture is recorded for each unit, and represented with a single dummy variable (1 if the unit was furnished and 0 if not).

Your objective for this case is to build a regression model that accurately predicts the sale price of a condominium unit sold at auction. Prepare a professional document that presents the results of your analysis. Include graphs that demonstrate how each of the independent variables in your model affects auction price. A layout of the **CONDO** data file is described below.

 CONDO (Number of Observation: 106)

Variable	Type
PRICE	QN
FLOOR	QN
DISTANCE	QN
VIEW	QL
ENDUNIT	QL
FURNISH	QL

14

Methods for Quality Improvement

Contents

Statistics in Action

Testing Jet Fuel Additive for Safety

Using Technology

Where We've Been

- Presented methods for making inferences about populations based on sample data (Chapters 7–11) using confidence intervals and tests of hypotheses.

- Presented methods for modeling the relationships between variables (Chapters 12–13) using regression analysis.

Where We're Going

- Return to an examination of processes (i.e., actions/operations that transform inputs to outputs).

- Describe methods for improving processes and the quality of the output they produce.

- Present control charts for monitoring a process mean, variance, or proportion.

Statistics in ACTION

Testing Jet Fuel Additive for Safety

The American Society of Testing and Materials (ASTM) International provides standards and guidelines for materials, products, systems, and services. The Federal Aviation Administration (FAA) has a huge conglomerate of testing requirements for jet fuel safety that are spelled out in ASTM methods. This Statistics in Action involves an engineering firm that is developing a new method of surfactant detection in jet fuel.

Surfactants (surface active agents) are basically soaps, which can form due to acids in the fuel but are more commonly caused by contamination from other products, such as engine cleaning additives. Although the surfactants do not directly cause problems, they reduce the ability of coalescing filters to remove water. Water in jet fuel carries bacteria that deposits in tanks and engine components, causing major corrosion and engine damage.

The standard test for surfactants (described in ASTM Rule D-3948) is to use a miniature filter (Filter-A) with a pumping mechanism (Pump-A). A water/fuel mixture is pumped through the filter at a specific rate and the amount of water that passes through the filter is detected with an optical transmittance test. Test measurements will typically yield a result between 80 and 85.

In an attempt to improve the precision of the surfactant test, the engineering firm compared the standard test (Pump-A with Filter-A) to three other pumping mechanism and filter option combinations—Pump-A with Filter-B, Pump-B with Filter-A, and Pump-B with Filter-B. Each day, a routine batch of jet fuel was created by adding 0.4 ppm of a surfactant solution. Twelve samples of the fuel were randomly selected and randomly divided into four groups of three samples each. The three samples in a group were tested for surfactants using one of the four pump/filter combinations. Consequently, each day there were three test results for each pump/filter method. This pattern of sampling continued for over 100 days. The test measurements are saved in four JETFUEL files. (Data for the first five days of the sampling experiment are listed in Table SIA 14.1).

The firm wants to monitor the results of the surfactant tests and determine if one of the test methods yields the most stable process. In the Statistics in Action Revisited sections listed below, we show how to analyze the data using methods for quality and process control.

Statistics in Action Revisited

- Monitoring the Mean of the Jet Fuel Surfactant Test Process (p. 946)
- Monitoring the Variation of the Jet Fuel Surfactant Test Process (p. 958)

TABLE SIA14.1   Selected Data in the JETFUEL Files

JETFUELA-A
JETFUELA-B
JETFUELB-A
JETFUELB-B

Weekday	Month	Day	Sample	Pump-B Filter-A	Pump-A Filter-A	Pump-B Filter-B	Pump-A Filter-B
Tue	May	9	1	76	84	85	85
			2	81	91	84	84
			3	81	86	84	88
Wed	May	10	1	84	92	87	92
			2	81	93	82	95
			3	86	94	85	90
Thu	May	11	1	83	94	82	90
			2	82	96	85	87
			3	79	92	84	81
Fri	May	12	1	81	96	81	90
			2	84	91	82	91
			3	83	96	88	92
Mon	May	15	1	80	90	87	94
			2	88	92	85	94
			3	87	91	86	84

Over the last two decades U.S. firms have been seriously challenged by products of superior quality from overseas, particularly from Japan. Japan currently produces 25% of the cars sold in the United States. In 1989, for the first time, the top-selling car in the United States was made in Japan: the Honda Accord. Although it's an American invention, virtually all VCRs are produced in Japan. Only one U.S. firm still manufactures televisions; the rest are made in Japan.

To meet this competitive challenge, more and more U.S. firms—both manufacturing and service firms—have begun quality-improvement initiatives of their own. Many of these firms now stress **total quality management** (TQM) (i.e., the management of quality in all phases and aspects of their business, from the design of their products to production, distribution, sales, and service).

Broadly speaking, TQM is concerned with (1) finding out what it is that the customer wants, (2) translating those wants into a product or service design, and (3) producing a product or service that meets or exceeds the specifications of the design. In this chapter we focus primarily on the third of these three areas and its major problem—product and service variation.

Variation is inherent in the output of all production and service processes. No two parts produced by a given machine are the same; no two transactions performed by a given bank teller are the same. Why is this a problem? With variation in output comes variation in the quality of the product or service. If this variation is unacceptable to customers, sales are lost, profits suffer, and the firm may not survive.

The existence of this ever-present variation has made statistical methods and statistical training vitally important to industry. In this chapter we present some of the tools and methods currently employed by firms worldwide to monitor and reduce product and service variation.

Teaching Tip

Use the cap of a pen as an example of the problems associated with the variation of a process. What happens when the diameter of the pen cap is too small? Too large?

14.1 Quality, Processes, and Systems

Quality

Teaching Tip

Our definition of quality is based upon what "acceptable" and "unacceptable" limits have been specified for the output.

Before describing various tools and methods that can be used to monitor and improve the quality of products and services, we need to consider what is meant by the term *quality*. Quality can be defined from several different perspectives. To the engineers and scientists who design products, quality typically refers to the amount of some ingredient or attribute possessed by the product. For example, high-quality ice cream contains a large amount of butterfat. High-quality rugs have a large number of knots per square inch. A high-quality shirt or blouse has 22 to 26 stitches per inch.

To managers, engineers, and workers involved in the production of a product (or the delivery of a service), quality usually means conformance to requirements, or the degree to which the product or service conforms to its design specifications. For example, in order to fit properly, the cap of a particular molded plastic bottle must be between 1.0000 inch and 1.0015 inches in diameter. Caps that do not conform to this requirement are considered to be of inferior quality. For an example in a service operation, consider the service provided to customers in a fast-food restaurant. A particular restaurant has been designed to serve customers within two minutes of the time their order is placed. If it takes more than two minutes, the service does not conform to specifications and is considered to be of inferior quality. Using this production-based interpretation of quality, well-made products are high quality; poorly made products are low quality. Thus, a well-made Rolls Royce and a well-made Chevrolet Nova are both high-quality cars.

Although quality can be defined from either the perspective of the designers or the producers of a product, in the final analysis both definitions should be derived from the needs and preferences of the *user* of the product or service. A firm that produces goods that no one wants to purchase cannot stay in business. We define quality accordingly.

Teaching Tip

Point out the needs of the users is what determines the design specifications for the process.

DEFINITION 14.1

The **quality** of a good or service is indicated by the extent to which it satisfies the needs and preferences of its users.

Consumers' needs and wants shape their perceptions of quality. Thus, to produce a high-quality product, it is necessary to study the needs and wants of consumers. This is typically one of the major functions of a firm's marketing department. Once the consumer research has been conducted, it is necessary to translate consumers' desires into a product design. This design must then be translated into a production plan and production specifications that, if properly implemented, will turn out a product with characteristics that will satisfy users' needs and wants. In short, consumer perceptions of quality play a role in all phases and aspects of a firm's operations.

But what product characteristics are consumers looking for? What is it that influences users' perceptions of quality? This is the kind of knowledge that firms need in order to develop and deliver high-quality goods and services. The basic elements of quality are summarized in the eight dimensions shown in the box.

Teaching Tip

Discuss these eight dimensions of quality in the context of some product (e.g., a television or washing machine).

The Eight Dimensions of Quality*

1. **Performance:** The primary operating characteristics of the product. For an automobile, these would include acceleration, handling, smoothness of ride, gas mileage, etc.

2. **Features:** The "bells and whistles" that supplement the product's basic functions. Examples include CD players and digital clocks on cars and the frequent-flyer mileage and free drinks offered by airlines.

3. **Reliability:** Reflects the probability that the product will operate properly within a given period of time.

4. **Conformance:** The extent or degree to which a product meets preestablished standards. This is reflected in, for example, a pharmaceutical manufacturer's concern that the plastic bottles it orders for its drugs have caps that are between 1.0000 and 1.0015 inches in diameter, as specified in the order.

5. **Durability:** The life of the product. If repair is possible, durability relates to the length of time a product can be used before replacement is judged to be preferable to continued repair.

6. **Serviceability:** The ease of repair, speed of repair, and competence and courtesy of the repair staff.

7. **Aesthetics:** How a product looks, feels, sounds, smells, or tastes.

8. **Other perceptions that influence judgments of quality:** Such factors as a firm's reputation and the images of the firm and its products that are created through advertising.

*Garvin, D. *Managing Quality*. New York: Free Press/Macmillan, 1988.

In order to design and produce products of high quality, it is necessary to translate the characteristics described in the box into product attributes that can be built into the product by the manufacturer. That is, user preferences must be interpreted in terms of product variables over which the manufacturer has control. For example, in considering the performance characteristics of a particular brand of wooden pencil, users may indicate a preference for being able to use the pencil for longer periods between sharpenings. The manufacturer may translate this performance characteristic into one or more measurable physical characteristics such as wood hardness, lead hardness, and lead composition. Besides being used to design high-quality products, such variables are used in the process of monitoring and improving quality during production.

Processes

Much of this textbook focuses on methods for using sample data drawn from a population to learn about that population. In this chapter and the next, however, our attention is not on populations, but on processes—such as manufacturing processes—and the output that they generate. In general, a process is defined as follows:

> **DEFINITION 14.2**
>
> A **process** is a series of actions or operations that transforms inputs to outputs. A process produces output over time.

Processes can be organizational or personal in nature. Organizational processes are those associated with organizations such as businesses and governments. Perhaps the best example is a manufacturing process, which consists of a series of operations, performed by people and machines, whereby inputs such as raw materials and parts are converted into finished products (the outputs). Examples include automobile assembly lines, oil refineries, and steel mills. Personal processes are those associated with your private life. The series of steps you go through each morning to get ready for school or work can be thought of as a process. Through turning off the alarm clock, showering, dressing, eating, and opening the garage door, you transform yourself from a sleeping person to one who is ready to interact with the outside world. Figure 14.1 presents a general description of a process and its inputs.

It is useful to think of processes as *adding value* to the inputs of the process. Manufacturing processes, for example, are designed so that the value of the outputs to potential customers exceeds the value of the inputs—otherwise the firm would have no demand for its products and would not survive.

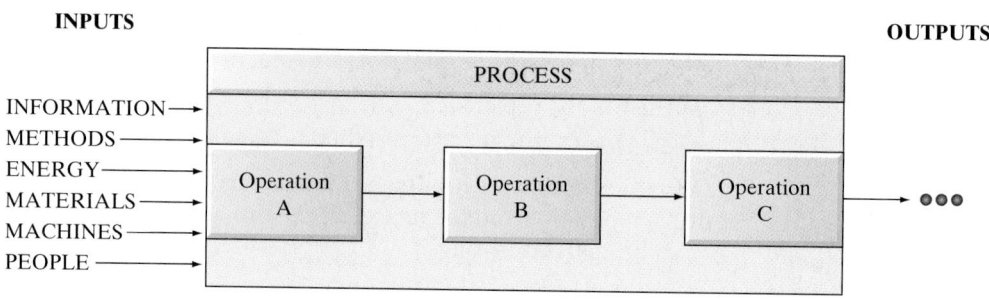

Figure 14.1

Graphical depiction of a process and its inputs

Systems

To understand what causes variation in process output and how processes and their output can be improved, we must understand the role that processes play in *systems*.

DEFINITION 14.3

A **system** is a collection or arrangement of interacting processes that has an ongoing purpose or mission. A system receives inputs from its environment, transforms those inputs to outputs, and delivers them to its environment. In order to survive, a system uses feedback (i.e., information) from its environment to understand and adapt to changes in its environment.

Figure 14.2 presents a model of a basic system. As an example of a system, consider a manufacturing company. It has a collection of interacting processes—marketing research, engineering, purchasing, receiving, production, sales, distribution, billing, and so on. Its mission is to make money for its owners, to provide high-quality working conditions for its employees, and to stay in business. The firm receives raw materials and parts (inputs) from outside vendors which, through its production processes, it transforms to finished goods (outputs). The finished goods are distributed to its customers. Through its marketing research, the firm "listens" to (receives feedback from) its customers and potential customers in order to change or adapt its processes and products to meet (or exceed) the needs, preferences, and expectations of the marketplace.

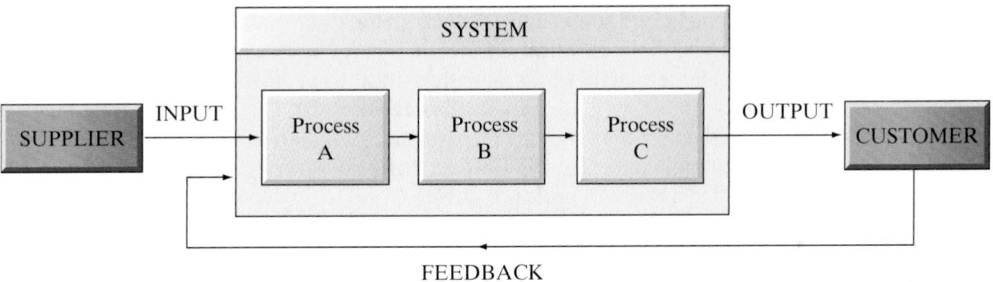

Figure 14.2
Model of a basic system

Since systems are collections of processes, the various types of system inputs are the same as those listed in Figure 14.1 for processes. System outputs are products or services. These outputs may be physical objects made, assembled, repaired, or moved by the system; or they may be symbolical, such as information, ideas, or knowledge. For example, a brokerage house supplies customers with information about stocks and bonds and the markets where they are traded.

Two important points about systems and the output of their processes are as follows: (1) No two items produced by a process are the same; (2) variability is an inherent characteristic of the output of all processes. This is illustrated in Figure 14.3. No two cars produced by the same assembly line are the same: No two windshields are the same; no two wheels are the same; no two tires are the same; no two hubcaps are the same. The same thing can be said for processes that deliver services. Consider the services offered at the teller windows of a bank to two customers waiting in two lines. Will they wait in line the same amount of time? Will they be serviced by tellers

Figure 14.3

Output variation

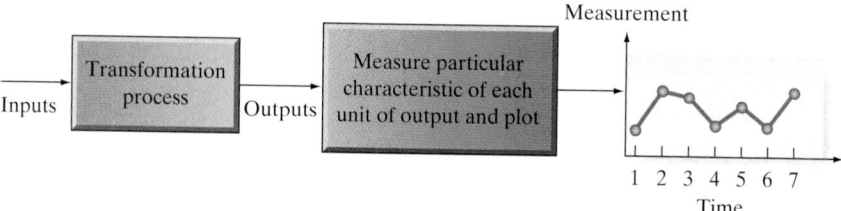

with the same degree of expertise and with the same personalities? Assuming the customers' transactions are the same, will they take the same amount of time to execute? The answer to all these questions is no.

Biography

**W. EDWARDS DEMING
(1900–1993)
Deming's 14 Points**

Born in Sioux City, Iowa, Ed Deming was raised on an Iowa farm until age 7, when his family moved to Wyoming. Because his parents emphasized the importance of education, Deming enrolled at the University of Wyoming in 1917, graduating four years later with a degree in electrical engineering. He eventually earned his Ph. D. in mathematical physics from Yale University in 1928. Deming worked for both the U.S. Department of Agriculture and Census Bureau before becoming a statistics professor at New York University and Columbia University. While

studying under W. A. Shewhart (see Biography, p. 930) in the 1930s, Deming become interested in the application of statistics to quality and process improvement for industry. He is probably most famous for his "14 Points for Management" (see accompanying box)—guidelines that transform the organizational climate to one in which process-management efforts can flourish. In 1950, the Japanese Union of Scientists and Engineers invited Deming to present a series of lectures on these ideas. His expertise and advice on quality control methods helped to revolutionize Japan's industry, leading to the Japanese economic boom in the 20th century. (The *Deming Prize* is awarded every year to the corporation with the greatest accomplishment in quality improvement in the world.)

Deming's 14 Points: Guidelines for Quality Improvement

1. **Create constancy of purpose toward improvement of product and service, with the aim to become competitive and to stay in business, and to provide jobs.** The organization must have a clear goal or purpose. Everyone in the organization must be encouraged to work toward that goal day in and day out, year after year.

2. **Adopt the new philosophy.** Reject detection-rejection management in favor of a customer-oriented, preventative style of management in which never-ending quality improvement is the driving force.

3. **Cease dependence on inspection to achieve quality.** It is because of poorly designed products and excessive process variation that inspection is needed. If quality is designed into products and process management is used in their production, mass inspection of finished products will not be necessary.

4. **End the practice of awarding business on the basis of price tag.** Do not simply buy from the lowest bidder. Consider the quality of the supplier's

(cont'd)

products along with the supplier's price. Establish long-term relationships with suppliers based on loyalty and trust. Move toward using a single supplier for each item needed.

5. **Improve constantly and forever the system of production and service, to improve quality and productivity, and thus constantly decrease costs.**

6. **Institute training.** Workers are often trained by other workers who were never properly trained themselves. The result is excessive process variation and inferior products and services. This is not the workers' fault; no one has told them how to do their jobs well.

7. **Institute leadership.** Supervisors should help the workers to do a better job. Their job is to lead, not to order workers around or to punish them.

8. **Drive out fear, so that everyone may work effectively for the company.** Many workers are afraid to ask questions or to bring problems to the attention of management. Such a climate is not conducive to producing high-quality goods and services. People work best when they feel secure.

9. **Break down barriers between departments.** Everyone in the organization must work together as a team. Different areas within the firm should have complementary, not conflicting, goals. People across the organization must realize that they are all part of the same system. Pooling their resources to solve problems is better than competing against each other.

10. **Eliminate slogans, exhortations, and arbitrary numerical goals and targets for the workforce that urge the workers to achieve new levels of productivity and quality.** Simply asking the workers to improve their work is not enough; they must be shown *how* to improve it. Management must realize that significant improvements can be achieved only if management takes responsibility for quality and makes the necessary changes in the design of the system in which the workers operate.

11. **Eliminate numerical quotas.** Quotas are purely quantitative (e.g., number of pieces to produce per day); they do not take quality into consideration. When faced with quotas, people attempt to meet them at any cost, regardless of the damage to the organization.

12. **Remove barriers that rob employees of their pride of workmanship.** People must be treated as human beings, not commodities. Working conditions must be improved, including the elimination of poor supervision, poor product design, defective materials, and defective machines. These things stand in the way of workers' performing up to their capabilities and producing work they are proud of.

13. **Institute a vigorous program of education and self-improvement.** Continuous improvement requires continuous learning. Everyone in the organization must be trained in the modern methods of quality improvement, including statistical concepts and interdepartmental teamwork. Top management should be the first to be trained.

14. **Take action to accomplish the transformation.** Hire people with the knowledge to implement the 14 points. Build a critical mass of people committed to transforming the organization. Put together a top management team to lead the way. Develop a plan and an organizational structure that will facilitate the transformation.

In general, variation in output is caused by the six factors listed in the box.

The Six Major Sources of Process Variation

1. People
2. Machines
3. Materials
4. Methods
5. Measurement
6. Environment

Awareness of this ever-present process variation has made training in statistical thinking and statistical methods highly valued by industry. By **statistical thinking** we mean the knack of recognizing variation, and exploiting it in problem solving and decision making. The remainder of this chapter is devoted to statistical tools for monitoring process variation.

14.2 Statistical Control

For the rest of this chapter we turn our attention to **control charts**—graphical devices used for monitoring process variation, for identifying when to take action to improve the process, and for assisting in diagnosing the causes of process variation. Control charts, developed by Walter Shewhart of Bell Laboratories in the mid 1920s, are the tool of choice for continuously monitoring processes. Before we go into the details of control chart construction and use, however, it is important that you have a fuller understanding of process variation. To this end, we discuss patterns of variation in this section.

As was discussed in Chapter 2, the proper graphical method for describing the variation of process output is a *time series plot*, sometimes called a **run chart.** Recall that in a time series plot the measurements of interest are plotted against time or are plotted in the order in which the measurements were made, as in Figure 14.4.

Figure 14.4

Time series plot of fill weights for 50 consecutively produced gallon cans of paint.

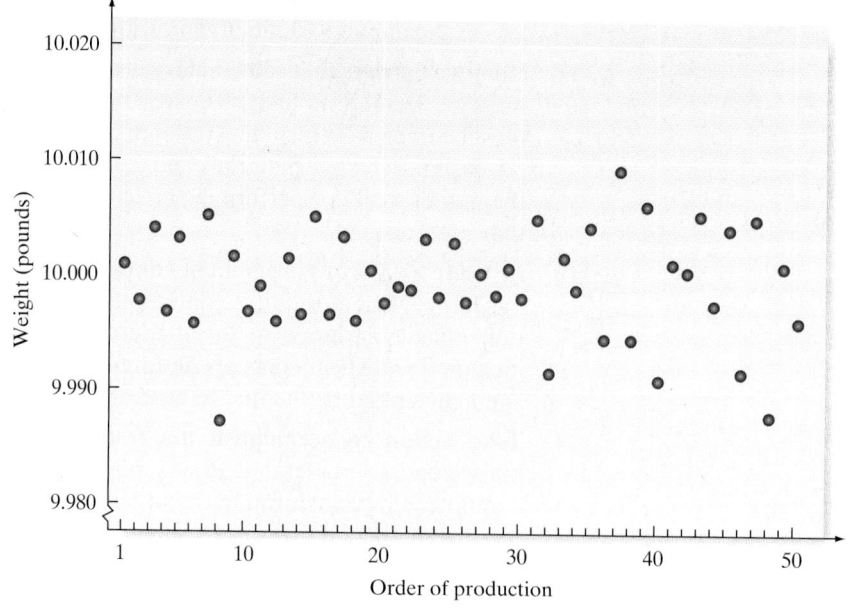

Whenever you face the task of analyzing data that were generated over time, your first reaction should be to plot them. The human eye is one of our most sensitive statistical instruments. Take advantage of that sensitivity by plotting the data and allowing your eyes to seek out patterns in the data.

Let's begin thinking about process variation by examining the plot in Figure 14.4 more closely. The measurements, taken from a paint manufacturing process, are the weights of 50 one-gallon cans of paint that were consecutively filled by the same filling head (nozzle). The weights were plotted in the order of production. Do you detect any systematic, persistent patterns in the sequence of weights? For example, do the weights tend to drift steadily upward or downward over time? Do they oscillate—high, then low, then high, then low, etc.?

Teaching Tip
The control charts of this chapter add upper and lower limits to the centerline to further aid in the interpretation of the time series plots.

To assist your visual examination of this or any other time series plot, Roberts (1991) recommends enhancing the basic plot in two ways. First, compute (or simply estimate) the mean of the set of 50 weights and draw a horizontal line on the graph at the level of the mean. This **centerline** gives you a point of reference in searching for patterns in the data. Second, using straight lines, connect each of the plotted weights in the order in which they were produced. This helps display the sequence of the measurements. Both enhancements are shown in Figure 14.5.

Figure 14.5

An enhanced version of the paint fill time series

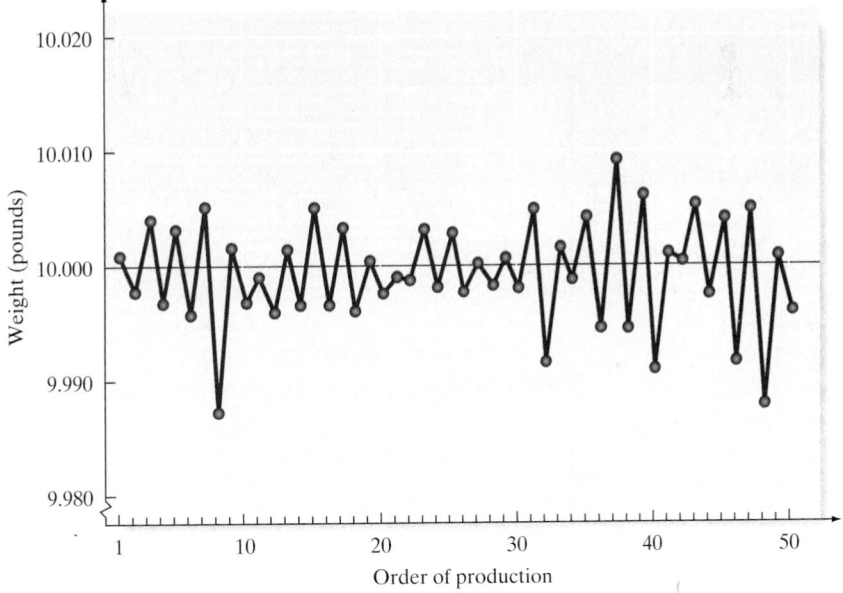

Now do you see a pattern in the data? Successive points alternate up and down, high then low, in an **oscillating sequence.** In this case, the points alternate above and below the centerline. This pattern was caused by a valve in the paint-filling machine that tended to stick in a partially closed position every other time it operated.

Other patterns of process variation are shown in Figure 14.6. We discuss several of them later.

In trying to describe process variation and diagnose its causes, it helps to think of the sequence of measurements of the output variable (e.g., weight, length, number of defects) as having been generated in the following way:

1. At any point in time, the output variable of interest can be described by a particular probability distribution (or relative frequency distribution). This

Figure 14.6

Patterns of process variation:
Some examples

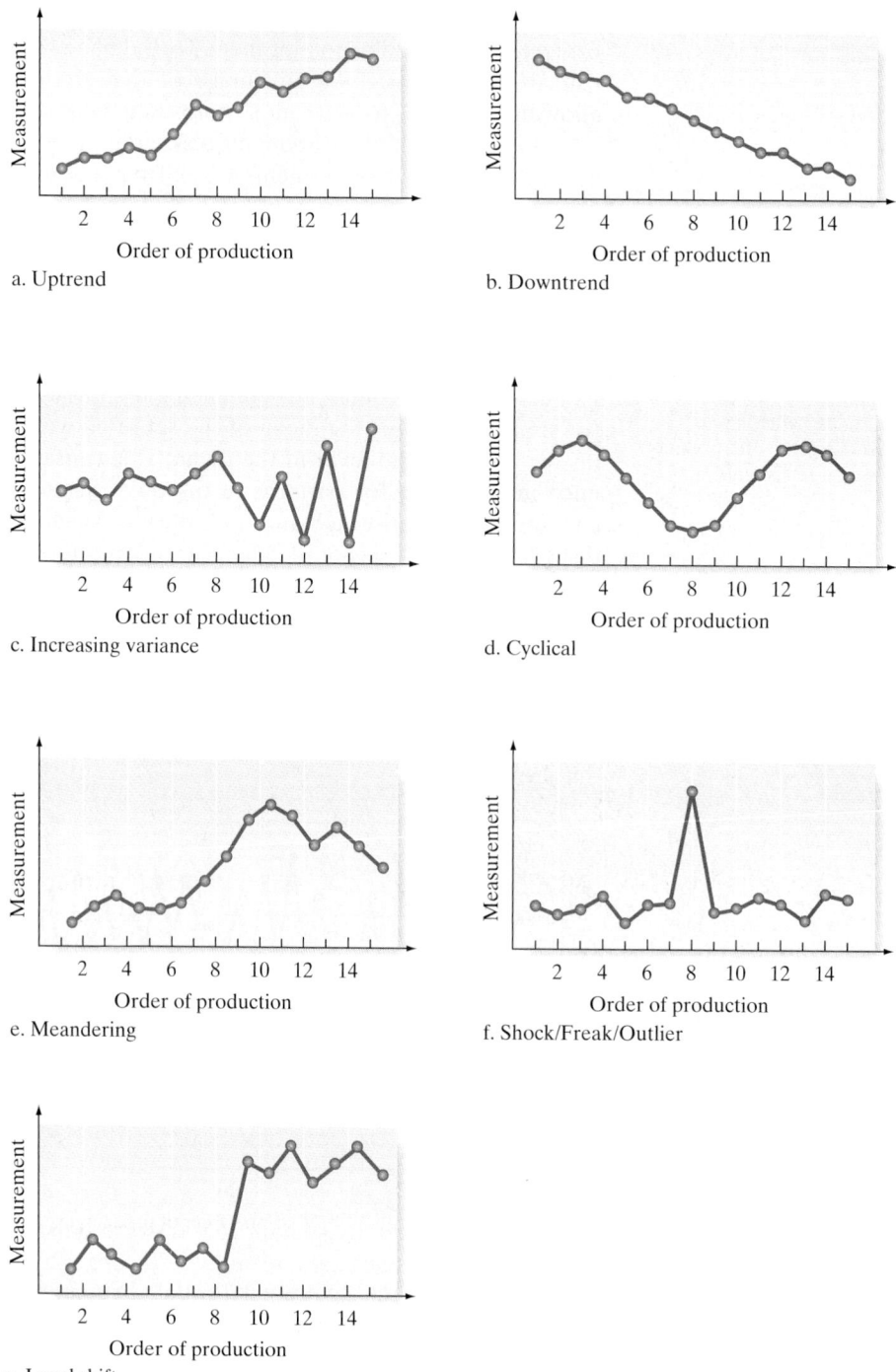

a. Uptrend

b. Downtrend

c. Increasing variance

d. Cyclical

e. Meandering

f. Shock/Freak/Outlier

g. Level shift

distribution describes the possible values that the variable can assume and their likelihood of occurrence. Three such distributions are shown in Figure 14.7.

2. The particular value of the output variable that is realized at a given time can be thought of as being generated or produced according to the distribution described in point 1. (Alternatively, the realized value can be thought of as

Figure 14.7

Distributions describing one output variable at three points in time

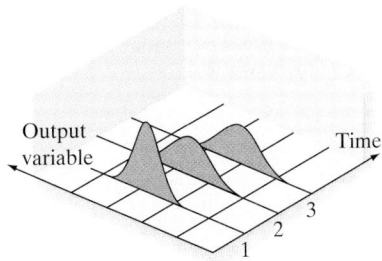

being generated by a random sample of size $n = 1$ from a population of values whose relative frequency distribution is that of point 1.)

3. The distribution that describes the output variable may change over time. For simplicity, we characterize the changes as being of three types: the mean (i.e., location) of the distribution may change; the variance (i.e., shape) of the distribution may change; or both. This is illustrated in Figure 14.8.

In general, when the output variable's distribution changes over time, we refer to this as a change in the *process*. Thus, if the mean shifts to a higher level, we say that the process mean has shifted. Accordingly, we sometimes refer to the distribution of the output variable as simply the **distribution of the process,** or the **output distribution of the process.**

Teaching Tip

Using distributions to account for changes in processes allows us to better understand the reasons for the change.

Let's reconsider the patterns of variation in Figure 14.6 and model them using this conceptualization. This is done in Figure 14.9. The uptrend of Figure 14.6(a) can be characterized as resulting from a process whose mean is gradually shifting upward over time, as in Figure 14.9(a). Gradual shifts like this are a common phenomenon in manufacturing processes. For example, as a machine wears out (e.g., cutting blades dull), certain characteristics of its output gradually change.

The pattern of increasing dispersion in Figure 14.6(c) can be thought of as resulting from a process whose mean remains constant but whose variance increases over time, as shown in Figure 14.9(c). This type of deterioration in a process may be the result of worker fatigue. At the beginning of a shift, workers—whether they be typists, machine operators, waiters, or managers—are fresh and pay close attention to every item that they process. But as the day wears on, concentration may wane and the workers may become more and more careless or more easily distracted. As a result, some items receive more attention than other items, causing the variance of the workers' output to increase.

The sudden shift in the level of the measurements in Figure 14.6(g) can be thought of as resulting from a process whose mean suddenly increases but whose variance remains constant, as shown in Figure 14.9(g). This type of pattern may be caused by such things as a change in the quality of raw materials used in the process or bringing a new machine or new operator into the process.

One thing that all these examples have in common is that the distribution of the output variable *changes over time*. In such cases, we say the process lacks **stability.** We formalize the notion of stability in the following definition.

Teaching Tip

"Stability" and "in control" are used interchangeably with respect to processes.

DEFINITION 14.4

A process whose output distribution does *not* change over time is said to be in a state of **statistical control,** or simply **in control.** If it does change, it is said to be **out of statistical control,** or simply **out of control.**

Figure 14.8

Types of changes in output variables

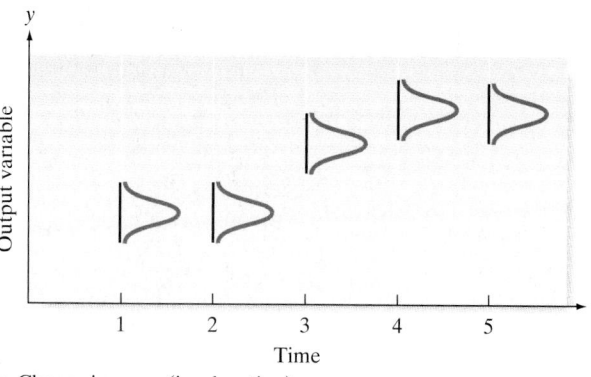

a. Change in mean (i.e., location)

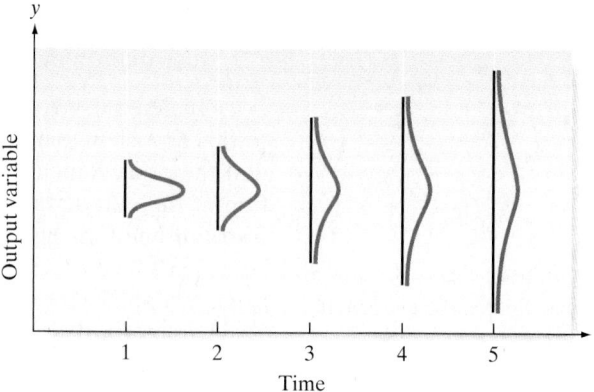

b. Change in variance (i.e., shape)

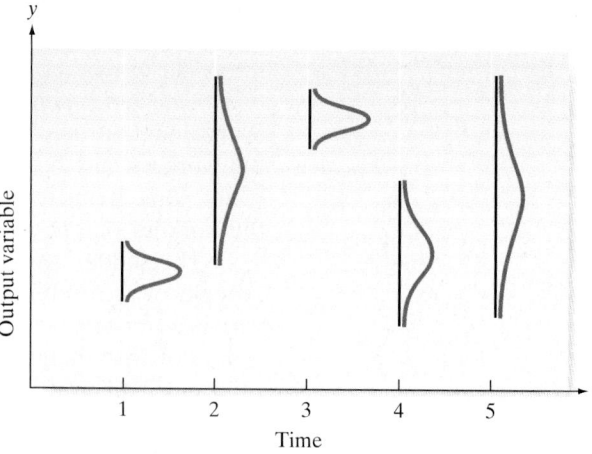

c. Change in mean and variance

Figure 14.10 illustrates a sequence of output distributions for both an in-control and an out-of-control process.

To see what the pattern of measurements looks like on a time series plot for a process that is in statistical control, consider Figure 14.11. These data are from the same paint-filling process we described earlier, but the sequence of measurements

Figure 14.9

Patterns of process variation described by changing distributions

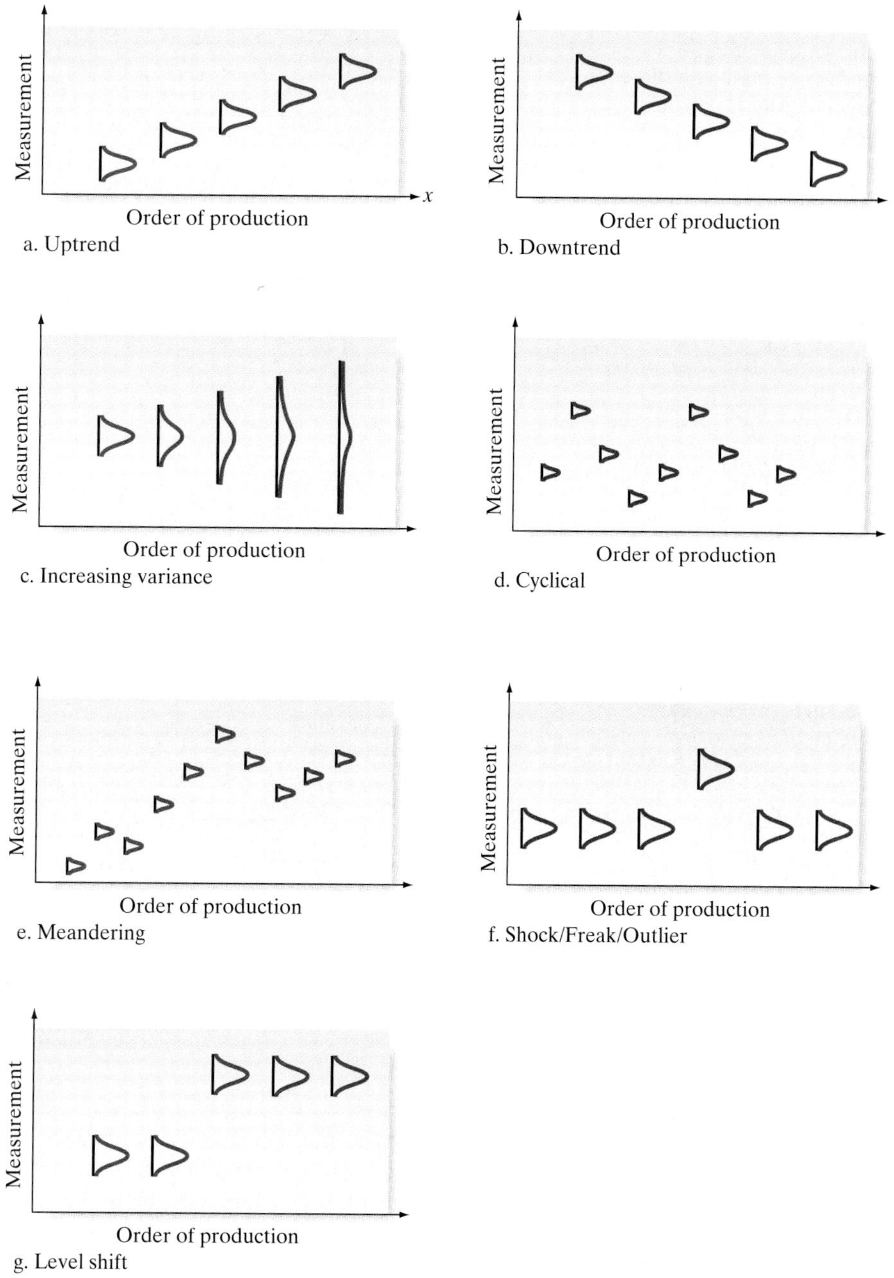

Measurement

Order of production

a. Uptrend

Measurement

Order of production

b. Downtrend

Measurement

Order of production

c. Increasing variance

Measurement

Order of production

d. Cyclical

Measurement

Order of production

e. Meandering

Measurement

Order of production

f. Shock/Freak/Outlier

Measurement

Order of production

g. Level shift

Figure 14.10

Comparison of in-control and out-of-control processes

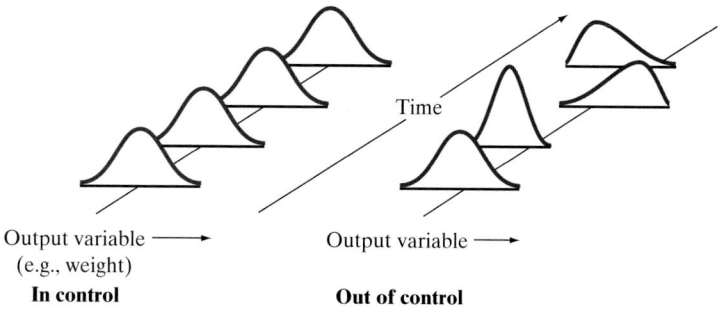

Time

Output variable ⟶
(e.g., weight)

In control

Output variable ⟶

Out of control

Figure 14.11

Time series plot of 50 consecutive paint can fills collected after replacing faulty valve

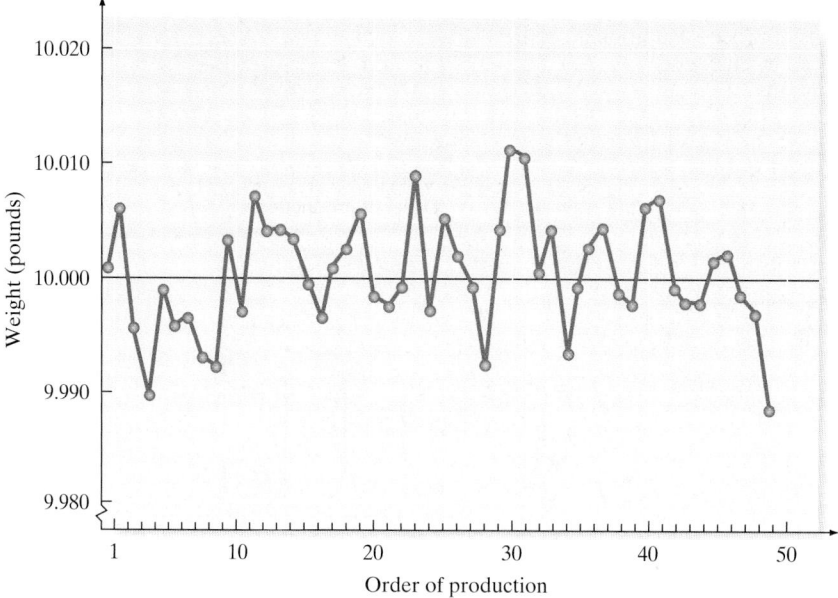

Figure 14.12

In-control processes are predictable; out-of-control processes are not

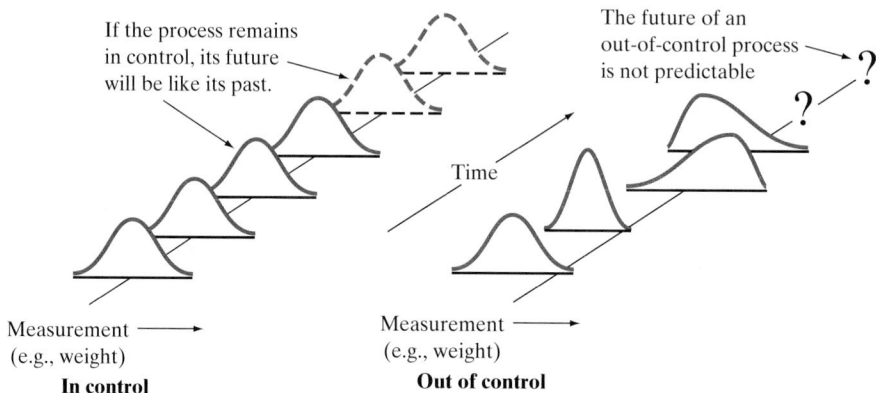

Teaching Tip

A process that is in control is predictable. A process that is out of control is unpredictable.

was made *after* the faulty valve was replaced. Notice that there are no discernible persistent, systematic patterns in the sequence of measurements such as those in Figures 14.5 and 14.6(a)–14.6(e). Nor are there level shifts or transitory shocks as in Figures 14.6(f)–14.6(g). This "patternless" behavior is called **random behavior. The output of processes that are in statistical control exhibits random behavior. Thus, even the output of stable processes exhibits variation.**

If a process is in control and remains in control, its future will be like its past. Accordingly, the process is predictable, in the sense that its output will stay within certain limits. This cannot be said about an out-of-control process. As illustrated in Figure 14.12, with most out-of-control processes you have no idea what the future pattern of output from the process may look like.* You simply do not know what to expect from the process. Consequently, a business that

*The output variables of in-control processes may follow approximately normal distributions, as in Figures 14.10 and 14.12, or they may not. But any in-control process will follow the *same* distribution over time. Do not misinterpret the use of normal distributions in many figures in this chapter as indicating that all in-control processes follow normal distributions.

operates out-of-control processes runs the risk of (1) providing inferior quality products and services to its internal customers (people within the organization who use the outputs of the processes) and (2) selling inferior products and services to its external customers. In short, it risks losing its customers and threatens its own survival.

One of the fundamental goals of process management is to identify out-of-control processes, to take actions to bring them into statistical control, and to keep them in a state of statistical control. The series of activities used to attain this goal is referred to as *statistical process control*.

DEFINITION 14.5

The process of monitoring and eliminating variation in order to *keep* a process in a state of statistical control or to *bring* a process into statistical control is called **statistical process control (SPC).**

Everything discussed in this section and the remaining sections of this chapter is concerned with statistical process control. We now continue our discussion of statistical control.

The variation that is exhibited by processes that are in control is said to be due to *common causes of variation.*

DEFINITION 14.6

Common causes of variation are the methods, materials, machines, personnel, and environment that make up a process and the inputs required by the process. Common causes are thus attributable to the design of the process. Common causes affect all output of the process and may affect everyone who participates in the process.

The total variation that is exhibited by an in-control process is due to many different common causes, most of which affect process output in very minor ways. In general, however, each common cause has the potential to affect every unit of output produced by the process. Examples of common causes include the lighting in a factory or office, the grade of raw materials required, and the extent of worker training. Each of these factors can influence the variability of the process output. Poor lighting can cause workers to overlook flaws and defects that they might otherwise catch. Inconsistencies in raw materials can cause inconsistencies in the quality of the finished product. The extent of the training provided to workers can affect their level of expertise and, as a result, the quality of the products and services for which they are responsible.

Since common causes are, in effect, designed into a process, the level of variation that results from common causes is viewed as being representative of the capability of the process. If that level is too great (i.e., if the quality of the output varies too much), the process must be redesigned (or modified) to eliminate one or more common causes of variation. Since process redesign is the responsibility of management, the *elimination of common causes of variation is typically the responsibility of management*, not of the workers.

Processes that are out of control exhibit variation that is the result of both common causes and *special causes of variation.*

Teaching Tip
Special causes of variation can only be detected in stable processes.

DEFINITION 14.7

Special causes of variation (sometimes called **assignable causes**) are events or actions that are not part of the process design. Typically, they are transient, fleeting events that affect only local areas or operations within the process (e.g., a single worker, machine, or batch of materials) for a brief period of time. Occasionally, however, such events may have a persistent or recurrent effect on the process.

Examples of special causes of variation include a worker accidentally setting the controls of a machine improperly, a worker becoming ill on the job and continuing to work, a particular machine slipping out of adjustment, and a negligent supplier shipping a batch of inferior raw materials to the process.

In the latter case, the pattern of output variation may look like Figure 14.6(f). If instead of shipping just one bad batch the supplier continued to send inferior materials, the pattern of variation might look like Figure 14.6(g). The output of a machine that is gradually slipping out of adjustment might yield a pattern like Figure 14.6(a), 14.6(b), or 14.6(c). All these patterns owe part of their variation to common causes and part to the noted special causes. In general, we treat any pattern of variation other than a random pattern as due to both common and special causes.* Since the effects of special causes are frequently localized within a process, *special causes can often be diagnosed and eliminated by workers or their immediate supervisor.* Occasionally, they must be dealt with by management, as in the case of a negligent or deceitful supplier.

Teaching Tip
Great effort must be taken to get processes in statistical control. Once there, keeping statistical control is relatively easy.

It is important to recognize that **most processes are not naturally in a state of statistical control.** As Deming (1986, p. 322) observed, *"Stability [i.e., statistical control] is seldom a natural state. It is an achievement, the result of eliminating special causes one by one … leaving only the random variation of a stable process"* (italics added).

Process improvement first requires the identification, diagnosis, and removal of special causes of variation. Removing all special causes puts the process in a state of statistical control. Further improvement of the process then requires the identification, diagnosis, and removal of common causes of variation. The effects on the process of the removal of special and common causes of variation are illustrated in Figure 14.13.

In the remainder of this chapter, we introduce you to some of the methods of statistical process control. In particular, we address how control charts help us determine whether a given process is in control.

14.3 The Logic of Control Charts

We use control charts to help us differentiate between process variation due to common causes and special causes. That is, we use them to determine whether a process is under statistical control (only common causes present) or not (both common and special causes present). Being able to differentiate means knowing when to take action to find and remove special causes and when to leave the process alone. If you take actions to remove special causes that do not exist—that is called tampering with the process—you may actually end up increasing the variation of the process and, thereby, hurting the quality of the output.

---

*For certain processes (e.g., those affected by seasonal factors), a persistent systematic pattern—such as the cyclical pattern of Figure 14.6(d)—is an inherent characteristic. In these special cases, some analysts treat the cause of the systematic variation as a common cause. This type of analysis is beyond the scope of this text. We refer the interested reader to Alwan and Roberts (1988).

Figure 14.13

The effects of eliminating
causes of variation

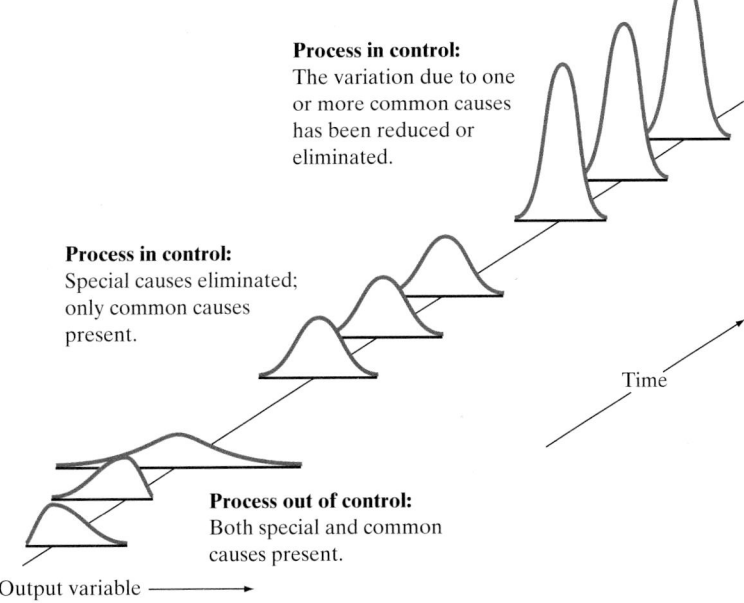

Process in control:
The variation due to one
or more common causes
has been reduced or
eliminated.

Time

Process in control:
Special causes eliminated;
only common causes
present.

Process out of control:
Both special and common
causes present.

Output variable ⟶

Teaching Tip

Before the reduction can be
made, control charts can be
better thought of as variance-
identifying tools.

In general, control charts are useful for evaluating the past performance of a process and for monitoring its current performance. We can use them to determine whether a process was in control during, say, the past two weeks or to determine whether the process is remaining under control from hour to hour or minute to minute. In the latter case, our goal is the swiftest detection and removal of any special causes of variation that might arise. Keep in mind that **the primary goal of quality-improvement activities is variance reduction.**

In this chapter we show you how to construct and use control charts for both quantitative and qualitative quality variables. Important quantitative variables include such things as weight, width, and time. An important qualitative variable is product status: defective or nondefective.

An example of a control chart is shown in Figure 14.14. A control chart is simply a time series plot of the individual measurements of a quality variable (i.e., an output variable), to which a centerline and two other horizontal lines called **control limits**

Figure 14.14

A control chart

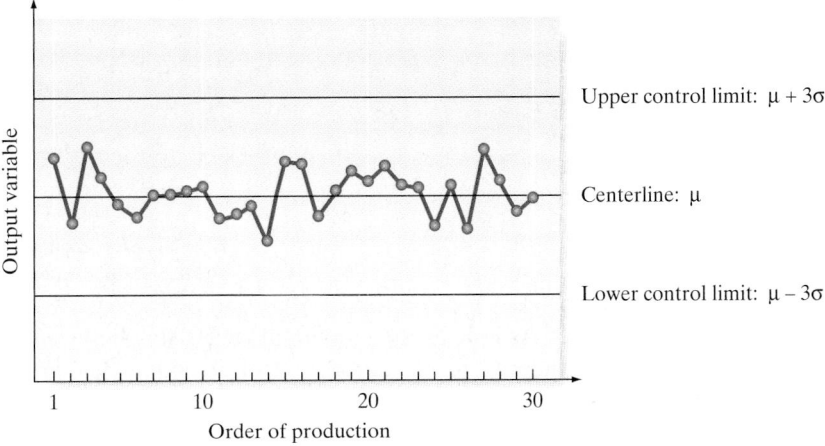

Upper control limit: $\mu + 3\sigma$

Centerline: μ

Lower control limit: $\mu - 3\sigma$

Output variable

Order of production

have been added. The centerline represents the mean of the process (i.e., the mean of the quality variable) *when the process is in a state of statistical control.* The **upper control limit** and the **lower control limit** are positioned so that *when the process is in control* the probability of an individual value of the output variable falling outside the control limits is very small. Most practitioners position the control limits a distance of 3 standard deviations from the centerline (i.e., from the process mean) and refer to them as **3-sigma limits.** If the process is in control and following a normal distribution, the probability of an individual measurement falling outside the control limits is .0027 (less than 3 chances in 1,000). This is shown in Figure 14.15.

Biography

WALTER A. SHEWHART (1891–1967) Shewhart Charts

Illinois native Walter Shewhart earned his bachelor's degree from the University of Illinois, followed by his Ph.D. in physics from the University of California in 1917. A short time later, Shewhart joined Bell Laboratories in New Jersey as an engineer, where he spent the majority of his career. Shewhart also served as a statistical consultant for the U.S. War Department, the United Nations, and the Indian government, as well as teaching at several promi-

nent American universities. Shewhart's most important contribution to both statistics and industry was the development of the statistical control of quality. He first proposed the idea of a control chart in 1924—a procedure commonly called the "Shewhart procedure" or "Shewhart chart." While at Bell Laboratories, Shewhart taught and worked with statistics icon W. Edwards Deming. Shewhart's monumental work, *Economic Control of Quality of Manufactured Product*, published in 1931, is regarded as a complete and thorough exposition of the basic principles of quality control; consequently, he is regarded as the father of statistical quality control.

Figure 14.15

The probability of observing a measurement beyond the control limits when the process is in control

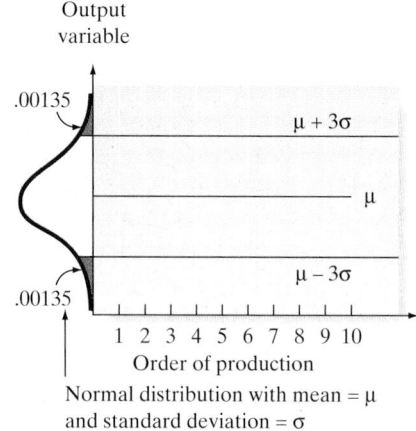

As long as the individual values stay between the control limits, the process is considered to be under control, meaning that no special causes of variation are influencing the output of the process. If one or more values fall outside the control limits, either a **rare event** has occurred or the process is out of control. Following the rare-event approach to inference described earlier in the text, such a result is interpreted as evidence that the process is out of control and that actions should be taken to eliminate the special causes of variation that exist.

Other evidence to indicate that the process is out of control may be present on the control chart. For example, if we observe any of the patterns of variation shown in Figure 14.6, we can conclude the process is out of control *even if all the points fall between the control limits*. In general, any persistent, systematic variation pattern (i.e., any nonrandom pattern) is interpreted as evidence that the process is out of control. We discuss this in detail in the next section.

In Chapter 8 we described how to make inferences about populations using hypothesis-testing techniques. What we do in this section should seem quite similar. Although our focus now is on making inferences about a *process* rather than a *population*, we are again testing hypotheses. In this case, we test

H_0: Process is under control

H_a: Process is out of control

Each time we plot a new point and see whether it falls inside or outside of the control limits, we are running a two-sided hypothesis test. The control limits function as the critical values for the test.

What we learned in Chapter 8 about the types of errors that we might make in running a hypothesis test holds true in using control charts as well. Any time we reject the hypothesis that the process is under control and conclude that the process is out of control, we run the risk of making a Type I error (rejecting the null hypothesis when the null is true). Anytime we conclude (or behave as if we conclude) that the process is in control, we run the risk of a Type II error (accepting the null hypothesis when the alternative is true). There is nothing magical or mystical about control charts. Just as in any hypothesis test, the conclusion suggested by a control chart may be wrong.

One of the main reasons that 3-sigma control limits are used (rather than 2-sigma or 1-sigma limits, for example) is the small Type I error probability associated with their use. The probability we noted previously of an individual measurement falling outside the control limits—.0027—is a Type I error probability. Since we interpret a sample point that falls beyond the limits as a signal that the process is out of control, the use of 3-sigma limits yields very few signals that are "false alarms."

To make these ideas more concrete, we will construct and interpret a control chart for the paint-filling process discussed in Section 14.2. Our intention is simply to help you better understand the logic of control charts. Structured, step-by-step descriptions of how to construct control charts will be given in later sections.

The sample measurements from the paint-filling process, presented in Table 14.1, were previously plotted in Figure 14.11. We use the mean and standard deviation of the sample, $\bar{x} = 9.9997$ and $s = .0053$, to estimate the mean and the standard deviation of the process. Although these are estimates, in using and interpreting control charts we treat them *as if* they were the actual mean μ and standard deviation σ of the process. This is standard practice in control charting.

The centerline of the control chart, representing the process mean, is drawn so that it intersects the vertical axis at 9.9997, as shown in Figure 14.16. The upper control limit is drawn at a distance of $3s = 3(.0053) = .0159$ above the centerline, and the lower control limit is $3s = .0159$ below the centerline. Then the 50 sample weights are plotted on the chart in the order that they were generated by the paint-filling process.

PAINT50

TABLE 14.1   Fill Weights of 50 Consecutively Produced Cans of Paint

Order	Weight	Order	Weight	Order	Weight	Order	Weight	Order	Weight
1.	10.0008	11.	9.9957	21.	9.9977	31.	10.0107	41.	10.0054
2.	10.0062	12.	10.0076	22.	9.9968	32.	10.0102	42.	10.0061
3.	9.9948	13.	10.0036	23.	9.9982	33.	9.9995	43.	9.9978
4.	9.9893	14.	10.0037	24.	10.0092	34.	10.0038	44.	9.9969
5.	9.9994	15.	10.0029	25.	9.9964	35.	9.9925	45.	9.9969
6.	9.9953	16.	9.9995	26.	10.0053	36.	9.9983	46.	10.0006
7.	9.9963	17.	9.9956	27.	10.0012	37.	10.0018	47.	10.0011
8.	9.9925	18.	10.0005	28.	9.9988	38.	10.0038	48.	9.9973
9.	9.9914	19.	10.0020	29.	9.9914	39.	9.9974	49.	9.9958
10.	10.0035	20.	10.0053	30.	10.0036	40.	9.9966	50.	9.9873

As can be seen in Figure 14.16, all the weight measurements fall within the control limits. Further, there do not appear to be any systematic nonrandom patterns in the data such as displayed in Figures 14.5 and 14.6. Accordingly, we are unable to conclude that the process is out of control. That is, we are unable to reject the null hypothesis that the process is in control. However, instead of using this formal hypothesis-testing language in interpreting control chart results, we prefer simply to say that the data suggest or indicate that the process is in control. We do this, however, with the full understanding that the probability of a Type II error is generally unknown in control chart applications and that we might be wrong in our conclusion. What we are really saying when we conclude that the process is in control is that *the data indicate that it is better to behave as if the process were under control than to tamper with the process.*

Figure 14.16

Control chart of fill weights for 50 consecutive paint can fills

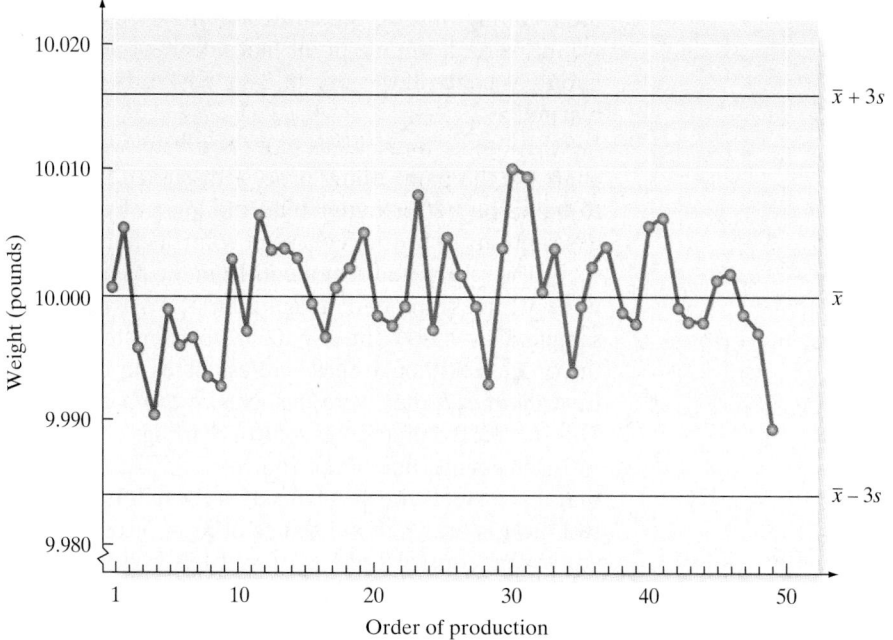

We have portrayed the control chart hypothesis test as testing "in control" versus "out of control." Another way to look at it is this: When we compare the weight of an *individual* can of paint to the control limits, we are conducting the following two-tailed hypothesis test:

$$H_0: \mu = 9.9997$$
$$H_0: \mu \neq 9.9997$$

where 9.9997 is the centerline of the control chart. The control limits delineate the two rejection regions for this test. Accordingly, with each weight measurement that we plot and compare to the control limits, we are testing whether the process mean (the mean fill weight) has changed. Thus, what the control chart is monitoring is the mean of the process. **The control chart leads us to accept or reject statistical control on the basis of whether the mean of the process has changed or not.** This type of process instability is illustrated in the top graph of Figure 14.8. In the paint-filling process example, the process mean apparently has remained constant over the period in which the sample weights were collected.

Other types of control charts—one of which we will describe in Section 14.5—help us determine whether the *variance* of the process has changed, as in the middle and bottom graphs of Figure 14.8.

The control chart we have just described is called an **individuals chart,** or an **x-chart.** The term *individuals* refers to the fact that the chart uses individual measurements to monitor the process—that is, measurements taken from individual units of process output. This is in contrast to plotting sample means on the control chart, for example, as we do in the next section.

Students sometimes confuse control limits with product *specification limits.* We have already explained control limits, which are a function of the natural variability of the process. Assuming we always use 3-sigma limits, the position of the control limits is a function of the size of σ, the process standard deviation.

Teaching Tip
Discuss the difference between control and specification limits. What effects do these limits have on the capability of a process meeting its design specification?

DEFINITION 14.8

Specification limits are boundary points that define the acceptable values for an output variable (i.e., for a quality characteristic) of a particular product or service. They are determined by customers, management, and product designers. Specification limits may be two sided, with upper and lower limits, or one sided, with either an upper or a lower limit.

Process output that falls inside the specification limits is said to **conform to specifications.** Otherwise it is said to be **nonconforming.**

Unlike control limits, specification limits are not dependent on the process in any way. A customer of the paint-filling process may specify that all cans contain no more than 10.005 pounds of paint and no less than 9.995 pounds. These are specification limits. The customer has reasons for these specifications but may have no idea whether the supplier's process can meet them. Both the customer's specification limits and the control limits of the supplier's paint-filling process are shown in Figure 14.17. Do you think the customer will be satisfied with the quality of the product received? We don't. Although some cans are within the specification limits, most are not, as indicated by the shaded region on the figure.

Figure 14.17

Comparison of control limits and specification limits

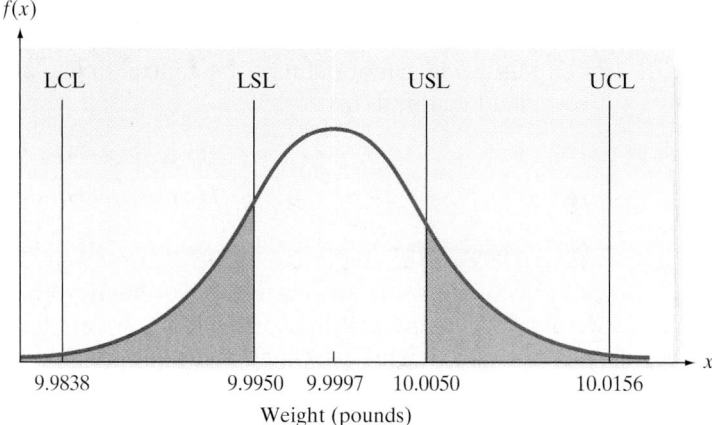

LCL = Lower control limit
UCL = Upper control limit
LSL = Lower specification limit
USL = Upper specification limit

14.4 A Control Chart for Monitoring the Mean of a Process: The $\bar{x}$-Chart

Teaching Tip

As we saw earlier in the text, it is always advantageous to consider the mean of many observations rather than the value of a single observation.

In the last section we introduced you to the logic of control charts by focusing on a chart that reflected the variation in individual measurements of process output. We used the chart to determine whether the process mean had shifted. The control chart we present in this section—the **$\bar{x}$-chart**—is also used to detect changes in the process mean, but it does so by monitoring the variation in the mean of samples that have been drawn from the process. That is, instead of plotting individual measurements on the control chart, in this case we plot sample means. Because of the additional information reflected in sample means (because each sample mean is calculated from n individual measurements), the $\bar{x}$-chart is more sensitive than the individuals chart for detecting changes in the process mean.

In practice, the $\bar{x}$-chart is rarely used alone. It is typically used in conjunction with a chart that monitors the variation of the process, usually a chart called an R-chart. The $\bar{x}$- and R-charts are the most widely used control charts in industry. Used in concert, these charts make it possible to determine whether a process has gone out of control because the variation has changed or because the mean has changed. We present the R-chart in the next section, at the end of which we discuss their simultaneous use. For now, we focus only on the $\bar{x}$-chart. **Consequently, we assume throughout this section that the process variation is stable.***

Figure 14.18 provides an example of an $\bar{x}$-chart. As with the individuals chart, the centerline represents the mean of the process and the upper and lower control limits are positioned a distance of 3 standard deviations from the mean. However, since the chart is tracking sample means rather than individual measurements, the relevant standard deviation is the standard deviation of $\bar{x}$ not σ, the standard deviation of the output variable.

If the process were in statistical control, the sequence of $\bar{x}$'s plotted on the chart would exhibit random behavior between the control limits. Only if a rare

*To the instructor: Technically, the R-chart should be constructed and interpreted before the $\bar{x}$-chart. However, in our experience, students more quickly grasp control chart concepts if they are familiar with the underlying theory. We begin with $\bar{x}$-charts because their underlying theory was presented in Chapters 6–8.

Figure 14.18

$\bar{x}$-chart

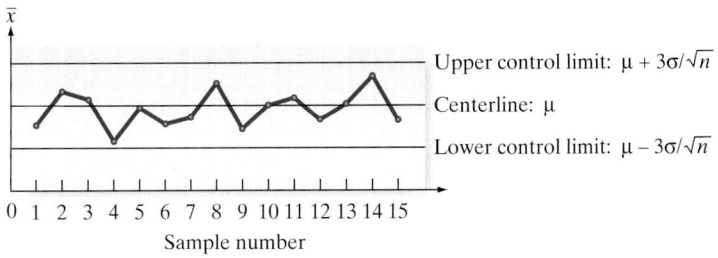

event occurred or if the process went out of control would a sample mean fall beyond the control limits.

To better understand the justification for having control limits that involve $\sigma_{\bar{x}}$, consider the following. The $\bar{x}$-chart is concerned with the variation in $\bar{x}$ which, as we saw in Chapter 6, is described by $\bar{x}$'s sampling distribution. But what is the sampling distribution of $\bar{x}$? If the process is in control and its output variable x is characterized at each point in time by a normal distribution with mean μ and standard deviation σ, the distribution of $\bar{x}$ (i.e., $\bar{x}$'s sampling distribution) also follows a normal distribution with mean μ at each point in time. But, as we saw in Chapter 6, its standard deviation is $\sigma_{\bar{x}} = \sigma/\sqrt{n}$. The control limits of the $\bar{x}$-chart are determined from and interpreted with respect to the sampling distribution of $\bar{x}$, not the distribution of x. These points are illustrated in Figure 14.19.*

Figure 14.19

The sampling distribution of $\bar{x}$

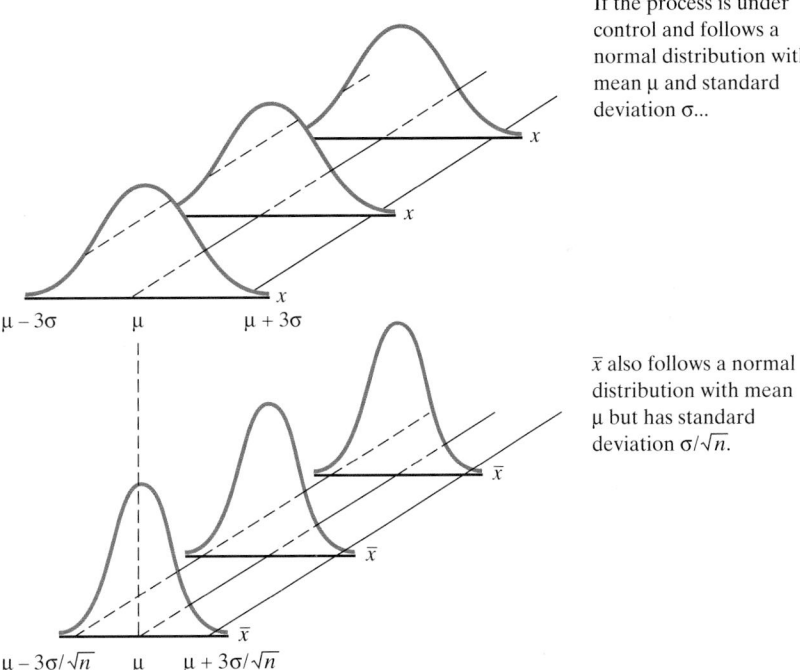

If the process is under control and follows a normal distribution with mean μ and standard deviation σ...

$\bar{x}$ also follows a normal distribution with mean μ but has standard deviation $\sigma/\sqrt{n}$.

*The sampling distribution of $\bar{x}$ can also be approximated using the Central Limit Theorem (Chapter 6). That is, when the process is under control and $\bar{x}$ is to be computed from a large sample from the process ($n \geq 30$), the sampling distribution will be approximately normally distributed with the mean μ and standard deviation $\sigma/\sqrt{n}$. Even for samples as small as 4 or 5, the sampling distribution of $\bar{x}$ will be approximately normal as long as the distribution of x is reasonably symmetric and roughly bell shaped.

In order to construct an $\bar{x}$-chart, you should have at least 20 samples of n items each, where $n \geq 2$. This will provide sufficient data to obtain reasonably good estimates of the mean and variance of the process. The centerline, which represents the mean of the process, is determined as follows:

$$Centerline: \bar{\bar{x}} = \frac{\bar{x}_1 + \bar{x}_2 + \cdots + \bar{x}_k}{k}$$

where k is the number of samples of size n from which the chart is to be constructed and $\bar{x}_i$ is the sample mean of the ith sample. Thus $\bar{\bar{x}}$ is an estimator of μ.

The control limits are positioned as follows:

$$Upper\ control\ limit: \bar{\bar{x}} + \frac{3\sigma}{\sqrt{n}}$$

$$Lower\ control\ limit: \bar{\bar{x}} - \frac{3\sigma}{\sqrt{n}}$$

Teaching Tip

Another benefit of this method is that the range of the data is easier to understand than the standard deviation. This is very important when many different people may be involved with collection and manipulation of the data.

Since σ, the process standard deviation, is virtually always unknown, it must be estimated. This can be done in several ways. One approach involves calculating the standard deviations for each of the k samples and averaging them. Another involves using the sample standard deviation s from a large sample that was generated while the process was believed to be in control. We employ a third approach, however—the one favored by industry. It has been shown to be as effective as the other approaches for sample sizes of $n = 10$ or less, the sizes most often used in industry.

This approach utilizes the ranges of the k samples to estimate the process standard deviation, σ. Recall from Chapter 2 that the range, R, of a sample is the difference between the maximum and minimum measurements in the sample. It can be shown that dividing the mean of the k ranges, $\bar{R}$, by the constant d_2, obtains an unbiased estimator for σ. [For details, see Ryan (1989).] The estimator, denoted by $\hat{\sigma}$, is calculated as follows:

$$\hat{\sigma} = \frac{\bar{R}}{d_2} = \frac{R_1 + R_2 + \cdots + R_k}{k}\left(\frac{1}{d_2}\right)$$

where R_i is the range of the ith sample and d_2 is a constant that depends on the sample size. Values of d_2 for samples of size $n = 2$ to $n = 25$ can be found in Appendix B, Table XII.

Substituting $\hat{\sigma}$ for σ in the formulas for the upper control limit (UCL) and the lower control limit (LCL), we get

$$UCL: \bar{\bar{x}} + \frac{3\left(\dfrac{\bar{R}}{d_2}\right)}{\sqrt{n}} \qquad LCL: \bar{\bar{x}} - \frac{3\left(\dfrac{\bar{R}}{d_2}\right)}{\sqrt{n}}$$

Notice that $(\bar{R}/d_2)/\sqrt{n}$ is an estimator of $\sigma_{\bar{x}}$. The calculation of these limits can be simplified by creating the constant

$$A_2 = \frac{3}{d_2\sqrt{n}}$$

Then the control limits can be expressed as

$$\text{UCL:} \bar{\bar{x}} + A_2 \bar{R}$$
$$\text{LCL:} \bar{\bar{x}} - A_2 \bar{R}$$

where the values for A_2 for samples of size $n = 2$ to $n = 25$ can be found in Appendix B, Table XII.

The degree of sensitivity of the $\bar{x}$-chart to changes in the process mean depends on two decisions that must be made in constructing the chart.

Teaching Tip

When deciding the frequency with which to sample, be certain to consider the rational subgrouping idea presented below.

The Two Most Important Decisions in Constructing an $\bar{x}$-Chart

1. The sample size, n, must be determined.
2. The frequency with which samples are to be drawn from the process must be determined (e.g., once an hour, once each shift, or once a day).

In order to quickly detect process change, we try to choose samples in such a way that the change in the process mean occurs *between* samples, not *within* samples (i.e., not during the period when a sample is being drawn). In this way, every measurement in the sample before the change will be unaffected by the change and every measurement in the sample following the change will be affected. The result is that the $\bar{x}$ computed from the latter sample should be substantially different from that of the former sample—a signal that something has happened to the process mean.

DEFINITION 14.9

Samples whose size and frequency have been designed to make it likely that process changes will occur between, rather than within, the samples are referred to as **rational subgroups**.

Rational Subgrouping Strategy

The samples (rational subgroups) should be chosen in a manner that

1. Gives the maximum chance for the *measurements* in each sample to be similar (i.e., to be affected by the same sources of variation)
2. Gives the maximum chance for the *samples* to differ (i.e., be affected by at least one different source of variation)

The following example illustrates the concept of *rational subgrouping*. An operations manager suspects that the quality of the output in a manufacturing process may differ from shift to shift because of the preponderance of newly hired workers on the night shift. The manager wants to be able to detect such differences quickly, using an $\bar{x}$-chart. Following the rational subgrouping strategy, the control chart should be constructed with samples that are drawn *within* each shift. None of the samples should span shifts. That is, no sample should contain, say, the last three items produced by shift 1 and the first two items produced by shift 2. In this way, the measurements in each sample would be similar, but the $\bar{x}$'s would reflect differences between shifts.

The secret to designing an effective $\bar{x}$-chart is to anticipate the *types of special causes of variation* that might affect the process mean. Then purposeful rational subgrouping can be employed to construct a chart that is sensitive to the anticipated cause or causes of variation.

The preceding discussion and example focused primarily on the timing or frequency of samples. Concerning the size of the samples, practitioners typically work with samples of size $n = 4$ to $n = 10$ consecutively produced items. Using small samples of consecutively produced items helps to ensure that the measurements in each sample will be similar (i.e., affected by the same causes of variation).

Constructing an $\bar{x}$-Chart: A Summary

1. Using a rational subgrouping strategy, collect at least 20 samples (subgroups), each of size $n \geq 2$.

2. Calculate the mean and range for each sample.

3. Calculate the mean of the sample means, $\bar{\bar{x}}$, and the mean of the sample ranges, $\bar{R}$:

$$\bar{\bar{x}} = \frac{\bar{x}_1 + \bar{x}_2 + \cdots + \bar{x}_k}{k} \qquad \bar{R} = \frac{R_1 + R_2 + \cdots + R_k}{k}$$

   where

$$k = \text{number of samples (i.e., subgroups)}$$
$$\bar{x}_i = \text{sample mean for the } i\text{th sample}$$
$$R_i = \text{range of the } i\text{th sample}$$

4. Plot the centerline and control limits:

$$\textit{Centerline: } \bar{\bar{x}}$$
$$\textit{Upper control limit: } \bar{\bar{x}} + A_2\bar{R}$$
$$\textit{Lower control limit: } \bar{\bar{x}} - A_2\bar{R}$$

   where A_2 is a constant that depends on n. Its values are given in Appendix B, Table XII, for samples of size $n = 2$ to $n = 25$.

5. Plot the k sample means on the control chart in the order that the samples were produced by the process.

When interpreting a control chart, it is convenient to think of the chart as consisting of six zones, as shown in Figure 14.20. Each zone is 1 standard deviation wide. The two zones within 1 standard deviation of the centerline are called **C zones;** the regions between 1 and 2 standard deviations from the centerline are called **B zones;**

Figure 14.20
The zones of a control chart

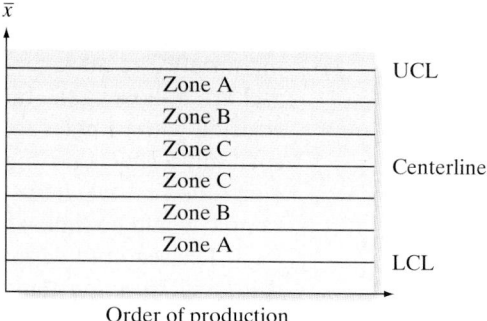

Teaching Tip
Interpreting control charts
is very consistent across the
various charts presented
in this chapter.

and the regions between 2 and 3 standard deviations from the centerline are called **A zones.** The box describes how to construct the *zone boundaries* for an $\bar{x}$-chart.

Constructing Zone Boundaries for an $\bar{x}$-Chart

The zone boundaries can be constructed in either of the following ways:

1. Using the 3-sigma control limits:

$$\text{Upper } A-B \text{ boundary: } \bar{\bar{x}} + \frac{2}{3}(A_2\bar{R})$$

$$\text{Lower } A-B \text{ boundary: } \bar{\bar{x}} - \frac{2}{3}(A_2\bar{R})$$

$$\text{Upper } B-C \text{ boundary: } \bar{\bar{x}} + \frac{1}{3}(A_2\bar{R})$$

$$\text{Lower } B-C \text{ boundary: } \bar{\bar{x}} - \frac{1}{3}(A_2\bar{R})$$

2. Using the estimated standard deviation of $\bar{x}$, $(\bar{R}/d_2)/\sqrt{n}$:

$$\text{Upper } A-B \text{ boundary: } \bar{\bar{x}} + 2\left[\frac{\left(\frac{\bar{R}}{d_2}\right)}{\sqrt{n}}\right]$$

$$\text{Lower } A-B \text{ boundary: } \bar{\bar{x}} - 2\left[\frac{\left(\frac{\bar{R}}{d_2}\right)}{\sqrt{n}}\right]$$

$$\text{Upper } B-C \text{ boundary: } \bar{\bar{x}} + \left[\frac{\left(\frac{\bar{R}}{d_2}\right)}{\sqrt{n}}\right]$$

$$\text{Lower } B-C \text{ boundary: } \bar{\bar{x}} - \left[\frac{\left(\frac{\bar{R}}{d_2}\right)}{\sqrt{n}}\right]$$

Practitioners use six simple rules that are based on these zones to help determine when a process is out of control. The six rules are summarized in Figure 14.21. They are referred to as **pattern-analysis rules.**

Teaching Tip
Any of the six rules being
detected will cause the process
to be labeled out of control.

Rule 1 is the familiar point-beyond-the-control-limit rule that we have mentioned several times. The other rules all help to determine when the process is out of control *even though all the plotted points fall within the control limits.* That is, the other rules help to identify nonrandom patterns of variation that have not yet broken through the control limits (or may never break through).

All the patterns shown in Figure 14.21 are *rare events* under the assumption that the process is under control. To see this, let's assume that the process is under control and follows a normal distribution. We can then easily work out the probability that an individual point will fall in any given zone. (We dealt with this type of problem in Chapters 4 and 5.) Just focusing on one side of the centerline, you can show that the probability of a point falling beyond Zone A is .00135, in Zone A is .02135, in Zone B is .1360, and in Zone C is .3413. Of course, the same probabilities apply to both sides of the centerline.

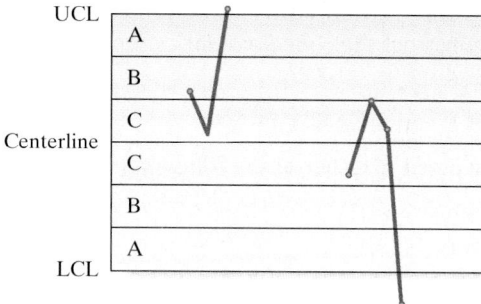

Rule 1: One point beyond Zone A

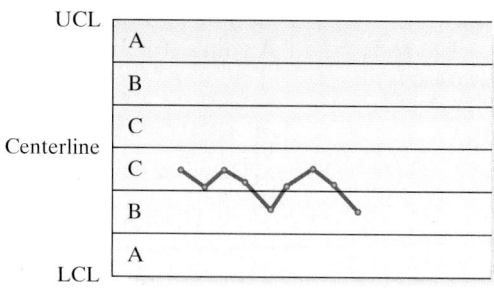

Rule 2: Nine points in a row in Zone C or beyond

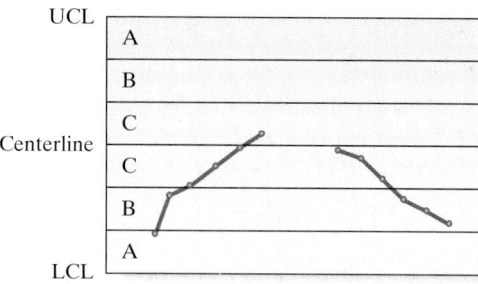

Rule 3: Six points in a row steadily increasing or decreasing

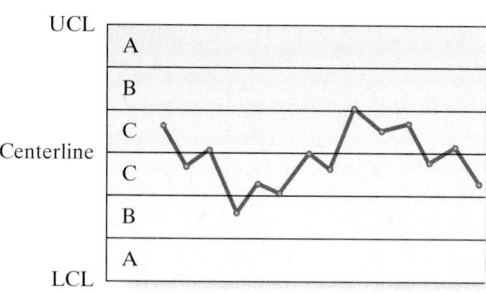

Rule 4: Fourteen points in a row alternating up and down

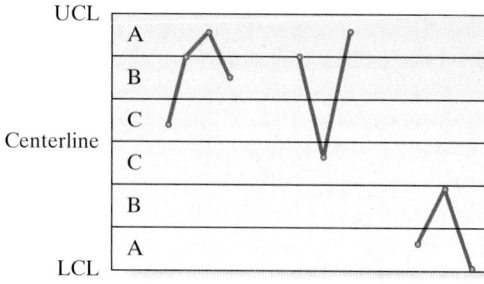

Rule 5: Two out of three points in a row in Zone A or beyond

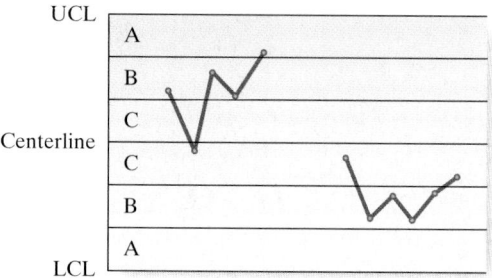

Rule 6: Four out of five points in a row in Zone B or beyond

> Rules 1, 2, 5, and 6 should be applied separately to the upper and lower halves of the control chart. Rules 3 and 4 should be applied to the whole chart.

Figure 14.21

Pattern-analysis rules for detecting the presence of special causes of variation

From these probabilities we can determine the likelihood of various patterns of points. For example, let's evaluate Rule 1. The probability of observing a point outside the control limits (i.e., above the upper control limit or below the lower control limit) is .00135 + .00135 = .0027. This is clearly a rare event.

As another example, Rule 5 indicates that the observation of two out of three points in a row in Zone A or beyond is a rare event. Is it? The probability of being in Zone A or beyond is .00135 + .02135 = .0227. We can use the binomial distribution

(Chapter 5) to find the probability of observing 2 out of 3 points in or beyond Zone A. The binomial probability $P(x = 2)$ when $n = 3$ and $p = .0227$ is .0015. Again, this is clearly a rare event.

In general, when the process is in control and normally distributed, the probability of any one of these rules *incorrectly* signaling the presence of special causes of variation is less than .005, or 5 chances in 1,000. If all of the first four rules are applied, the overall probability of a false signal is about .01. If all six of the rules are applied, the overall probability of a false signal rises to .02, or 2 chances in 100. These three probabilities can be thought of as Type I error probabilities. Each indicates the probability of incorrectly rejecting the null hypothesis that the process is in a state of statistical control.

Explanation of the possible causes of these nonrandom patterns is beyond the scope of this text. We refer the interested reader to AT&T's *Statistical Quality Control Handbook* (1956).

We use these rules again in the next section when we interpret the R-chart.

> ## Interpreting an $\bar{x}$-Chart
>
> 1. The **process is out of control** if one or more sample means fall beyond the control limits or if any of the other five patterns of variation of Figure 14.21 are observed. Such signals are an indication that one or more special causes of variation are affecting the process mean. We must identify and eliminate them to bring the process into control.
>
> 2. The **process is treated as being in control** if none of the previously noted out-of-control signals are observed. Processes that are in control should not be tampered with. However, if the level of variation is unacceptably high, common causes of variation should be identified and eliminated.
>
> *Assumption:* The variation of the process is stable. (If it were not, the control limits of the $\bar{x}$-chart would be meaningless, since they are a function of the process variation. The R-chart, presented in the next section, is used to investigate this assumption.)

In theory, the centerline and control limits should be developed using samples that were collected during a period in which the process was in control. Otherwise, they will not be representative of the variation of the process (or, in the present case, the variation of $\bar{x}$) when the process is in control. However, we will not know whether the process is in control until after we have constructed a control chart. Consequently, when a control chart is first constructed, the centerline and control limits are treated as **trial values**. If the chart indicates that the process was in control during the period when the sample data were collected, then the centerline and control limits become "official" (i.e., no longer treated as trial values). It is then appropriate to extend the control limits and the centerline to the right and to use the chart to monitor future process output.

However, if in applying the pattern-analysis rules of Figure 14.21 it is determined that the process was out of control while the sample data were being collected, the trial values (i.e., the trial chart) should, in general, not be used to monitor the process. The points on the control chart that indicate that the process is out of control should be investigated to see if any special causes of variation can be identified. A graphical method that can be used to facilitate this investigation—a *cause-and-effect diagram*—is described in optional Section 14.7. If special causes of variation are found, (1) they should be eliminated, (2) any points on the chart determined to have been influenced by the special causes—whether inside or outside the control limits—should be discarded, and (3) *new* trial centerline and control limits should be calculated from the remaining data. However, the new trial limits may still indicate that the process is out of control. If so, repeat these three steps until all points fall within the control limits.

If special causes cannot be found and eliminated, the severity of the out-of-control indications should be evaluated and a judgment made as to whether (1) the out-of-control points should be discarded anyway and new trial limits constructed, (2) the original trial limits are good enough to be made official, or (3) new sample data should be collected to construct new trial limits.

EXAMPLE 14.1 — CREATING AND INTERPRETING AN $\bar{x}$-CHART

Problem Let's return to the paint-filling process described in Sections 14.2 and 14.3. Suppose instead of sampling 50 consecutive gallons of paint from the filling process to develop a control chart, it was decided to sample five consecutive cans once each hour for the next 25 hours. The sample data are presented in Table 14.2. This sampling strategy (rational subgrouping) was selected because several times a month the filling head in question becomes clogged. When that happens, the head dispenses less and less paint over the course of the day. However, the pattern of decrease is so irregular that minute-to-minute or even half-hour-to-half-hour changes are difficult to detect.

 PAINT125

TABLE 14.2 Twenty-Five Samples of Size 5 from the Paint-Filling Process

Sample	Measurements					Mean	Range
1	10.0042	9.9981	10.0010	9.9964	10.0001	9.99995	.0078
2	9.9950	9.9986	9.9948	10.0030	9.9938	9.99704	.0092
3	10.0028	9.9998	10.0086	9.9949	9.9980	10.00082	.0137
4	9.9952	9.9923	10.0034	9.9965	10.0026	9.99800	.0111
5	9.9997	9.9983	9.9975	10.0078	9.9891	9.99649	.0195
6	9.9987	10.0027	10.0001	10.0027	10.0029	10.00141	.0042
7	10.0004	10.0023	10.0024	9.9992	10.0135	10.00358	.0143
8	10.0013	9.9938	10.0017	10.0089	10.0001	10.00116	.0151
9	10.0103	10.0009	9.9969	10.0103	9.9986	10.00339	.0134
10	9.9980	9.9954	9.9941	9.9958	9.9963	9.99594	.0039
11	10.0013	10.0033	9.9943	9.9949	9.9999	9.99874	.0090
12	9.9986	9.9990	10.0009	9.9947	10.0008	9.99882	.0062
13	10.0089	10.0056	9.9976	9.9997	9.9922	10.00080	.0167
14	9.9971	10.0015	9.9962	10.0038	10.0022	10.00016	.0076
15	9.9949	10.0011	10.0043	9.9988	9.9919	9.99822	.0124
16	9.9951	9.9957	10.0094	10.0040	9.9974	10.00033	.0143
17	10.0015	10.0026	10.0032	9.9971	10.0019	10.00127	.0061
18	9.9983	10.0019	9.9978	9.9997	10.0029	10.00130	.0051
19	9.9977	9.9963	9.9981	9.9968	10.0009	9.99798	.0046
20	10.0078	10.0004	9.9966	10.0051	10.0007	10.00212	.0112
21	9.9963	9.9990	10.0037	9.9936	9.9962	9.99764	.0101
22	9.9999	10.0022	10.0057	10.0026	10.0032	10.00272	.0058
23	9.9998	10.0002	9.9978	9.9966	10.0060	10.00009	.0094
24	10.0031	10.0078	9.9988	10.0032	9.9944	10.00146	.0134
25	9.9993	9.9978	9.9964	10.0032	10.0041	10.00015	.0077

a. Explain the logic behind the rational subgrouping strategy that was used.

b. Construct an $\bar{x}$-chart for the process using the data in Table 14.2.

c. What does the chart suggest about the stability of the filling process (whether the process is in or out of statistical control)?

c. In control

d. Yes

d. Should the control limits be used to monitor future process output?

Solution **a.** The samples are far enough apart in time to detect hour-to-hour shifts or changes in the mean amount of paint dispensed, but the individual measurements that make up each sample are close enough together in time to ensure that the process has changed little, if at all, during the time the individual measurements were made. Overall, the rational subgrouping employed affords the opportunity for process changes to occur between samples and therefore show up on the control chart as differences between the sample means.

b. Twenty-five samples ($k = 25$ subgroups), each containing $n = 5$ cans of paint, were collected from the process. The first step after collecting the data is to calculate the 25 sample means and sample ranges needed to construct the $\bar{x}$-chart. The mean and range of the first sample are

Suggested Exercise 14.12

$$\bar{x} = \frac{10.0042 + 9.9981 + 10.0010 + 9.9964 + 10.0001}{5} = 9.99995$$

$$R = 10.0042 - 9.9964 = .0078$$

All 25 means and ranges are displayed in Table 14.2.

Next, we calculate the mean of the sample means and the mean of the sample ranges:

$$\bar{\bar{x}} = \frac{9.99995 + 9.99704 + \cdots + 10.00015}{25} = 9.9999$$

$$\bar{R} = \frac{.0078 + .0092 + \cdots + .0077}{25} = .010072$$

The centerline of the chart is positioned at $\bar{\bar{x}} = 9.9999$. To determine the control limits, we need the constant A_2, which can be found in Table XII of Appendix B. For $n = 5$, $A_2 = .577$. Then,

$$\text{UCL:}\ \bar{\bar{x}} + A_2\bar{R} = 9.9999 + .577(.010072) = 10.0058$$

$$\text{LCL:}\ \bar{\bar{x}} - A_2\bar{R} = 9.9999 - .577(.010072) = 9.9940$$

After positioning the control limits on the chart, we plot the 25 sample means in the order of sampling and connect the points with straight lines. The resulting trial $\bar{x}$-chart, shown in Figure 14.22, is produced using MINITAB.

c. To check the stability of the process, we use the six pattern-analysis rules for detecting special causes of variation, which were presented in Figure 14.21. To apply most of these rules requires identifying the A, B, and C zones of the control chart. These are indicated (with annotations) in Figure 14.22. We describe how they were constructed below.

The boundary between the A and B zones is 2 standard deviations from the centerline, and the boundary between the B and C zones is 1 standard deviation from the centerline. Thus, using $A_2\bar{R}$ and the 3-sigma limits previously calculated, we locate the A, B, and C zones above the centerline:

$$\text{A–B boundary} = \bar{\bar{x}} + \tfrac{2}{3}(A_2\bar{R}) = 9.9999 + \tfrac{2}{3}(.577)(.010072) = 10.0039$$

$$\text{B–C boundary} = \bar{\bar{x}} + \tfrac{1}{3}(A_2\bar{R}) = 9.9999 + \tfrac{1}{3}(.577)(.010072) = 10.0019$$

Figure 14.22

MINITAB $\bar{x}$-chart for the paint-filling process

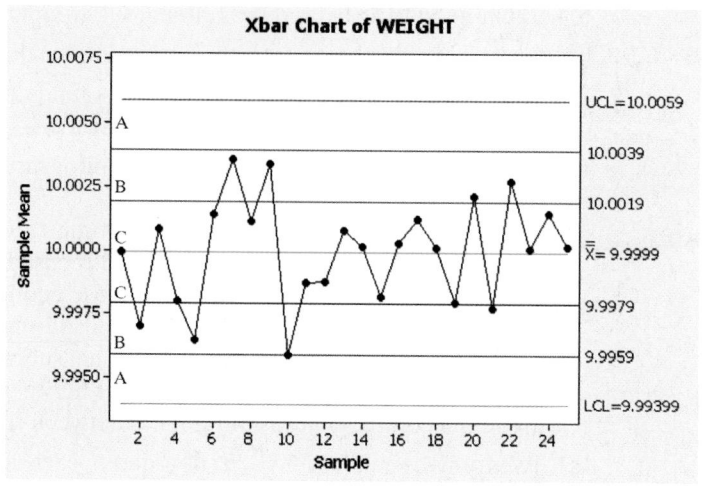

Xbar Chart of WEIGHT

Similarly, the zones below the centerline are located:

$$\text{A–B boundary} = \bar{\bar{x}} - \frac{2}{3}(A_2\bar{R}) = 9.9959$$

$$\text{B–C boundary} = \bar{\bar{x}} - \frac{1}{3}(A_2\bar{R}) = 9.9979$$

A careful comparison of the six pattern-analysis rules with the sequence of sample means yields no out-of-control signals. All points are inside the control limits and there appear to be no nonrandom patterns within the control limits. That is, we can find no evidence of a shift in the process mean. Accordingly, we conclude that the process is in control.

d. Since the process was found to be in control during the period in which the samples were drawn, the trial control limits constructed in part **b** can be considered official. They should be extended to the right and used to monitor future process output.

Look Back Most statistical software (like MINITAB) will automatically calculate and plot the sample means and control limits. The amount of hand calculations needed to create an $\bar{x}$-chart is minimal.

Now Work *Exercise 14.7.*

■ ■ ■

EXAMPLE 14.2   MONITORING FUTURE OUTPUT WITH AN $\bar{x}$-CHART

Problem   Ten new samples of size $n = 5$ were drawn from the paint-filling process of the previous example. The sample data, including sample means and ranges, are shown in Table 14.3. Investigate whether the process remained in control during the period in which the new sample data were collected.

Out of control

Solution   We begin by simply extending the control limits, centerline, and zone boundaries of the control chart in Figure 14.22 to the right. Next, beginning with sample number 26, we plot the 10 new sample means on the control chart and connect them with

PAINT125ADD

TABLE 14.3   Ten Additional Samples of Size 5 from the Paint-Filling Process

Sample	Measurements					Mean	Range
26	10.0019	9.9981	9.9952	9.9976	9.9999	9.99841	.0067
27	10.0041	9.9982	10.0028	10.0040	9.9971	10.00125	.0070
28	9.9999	9.9974	10.0078	9.9971	9.9923	9.99890	.0155
29	9.9982	10.0002	9.9916	10.0040	9.9916	9.99713	.0124
30	9.9933	9.9963	9.9955	9.9993	9.9905	9.99498	.0088
31	9.9915	9.9984	10.0053	9.9888	9.9876	9.99433	.0177
32	9.9912	9.9970	9.9961	9.9879	9.9970	9.99382	.0091
33	9.9942	9.9960	9.9975	10.0019	9.9912	9.99614	.0107
34	9.9949	9.9967	9.9936	9.9941	10.0071	9.99726	.0135
35	9.9943	9.9969	9.9937	9.9912	10.0053	9.99626	.0141

Figure 14.23

MINITAB extended $\bar{x}$-chart for the paint-filling process

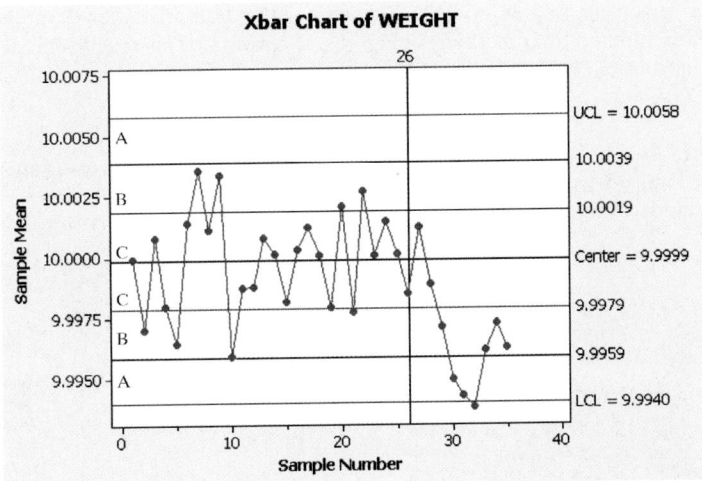

straight lines. This extended version of the control chart, produced using MINITAB, is shown in Figure 14.23.

Now that the control chart has been prepared, we apply the six pattern-analysis rules for detecting special causes of variation (Figure 14.21) to the new sequence of sample means. First, notice that the mean for sample 32 falls below the lower control limit (Rule 1). Also, notice that six points in a row steadily decrease (samples 27–32). Rule 3 says that if we observe six points in a row steadily increasing or decreasing, that is an indication of the presence of special causes of variation. Notice that if you apply the rules from left to right along the sequence of sample means, the decreasing pattern also triggers signals from Rules 5 (samples 29–31) and 6 (samples 28–32). These signals lead us to conclude that the process has gone out of control.

Look Back Apparently, the filling head began to clog about the time that either sample 26 or 27 was drawn from the process. As a result, the mean of the process (the mean fill weight dispensed by the process) began to decline.

Now Work   *Exercise 14.8*

■ ■ ■

Statistics in Action Revisited

Monitoring the Mean of the Jet Fuel Surfactant Test Process

The engineering firm that tests for surfactants in jet fuel additive is experimenting with different pump and filter combinations—Pump-A with Filter-A (the standard test), Pump-A with Filter-B, Pump-B with Filter-A, and Pump-B with Filter-B. To monitor the test results, three fuel samples were tested each day by each of the four methods, for a period of over 100 consecutive days. A "safe" surfactant additive measurement should range between 80 and 90, and this range represents the specification limits of the process.

We analyzed the data in the **JETFUEL** files using MINITAB. Treating the three samples collected on the same day as a rational subgroup, four MINITAB $\bar{x}$-charts are produced (one for each pump/filter method) in Figures SIA14.1(a)–(d). As an option, MINITAB will highlight (in red) any sample means that match any of the six pattern-analysis rules for detecting special causes of variation. The number of the rule that is violated is shown next to the sample mean on the chart.

You can see that only one of the process means is "in control"—the mean for the Pump-B with Filter-B test method—as shown in Figure SIA14.1(d). There is at least one pattern-analysis rule violated in each of the other three $\bar{x}$-charts. Also, each sample mean for Pump-B/Filter-B falls within the specification limits (80%–90%). In contrast, the other injection methods have several means that fall outside the specification limits of the process. Of the three nonstandard surfactant test methods, the Pump-B/Filter-B method appears to have the most promise. This analysis helped the company to focus on perfecting this method of surfactant testing in jet fuel.

Figure SIA14.1a

$\bar{x}$-chart for Pump-A with Filter-A (standard) method

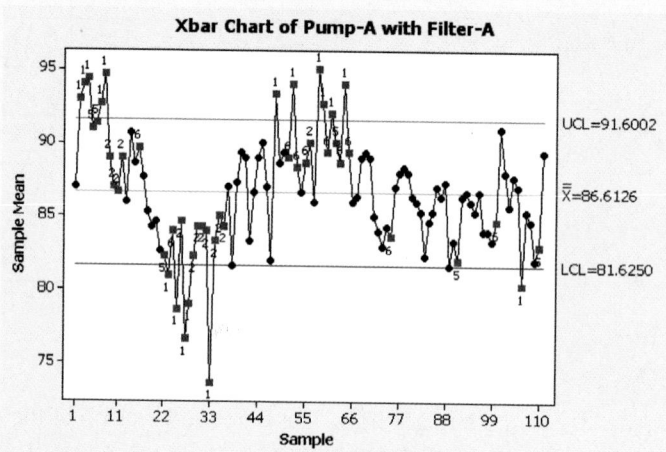

Figure SIA14.1b

$\bar{x}$-chart for Pump-A with Filter-B method

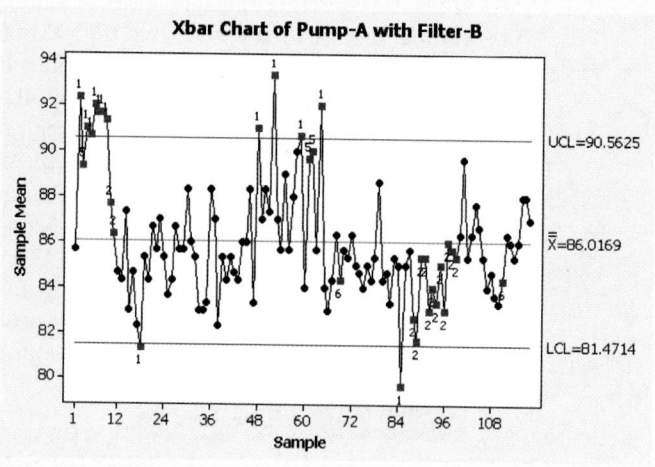

Figure SIA14.1c
$\bar{x}$-chart for Pump-B
with Filter-A method

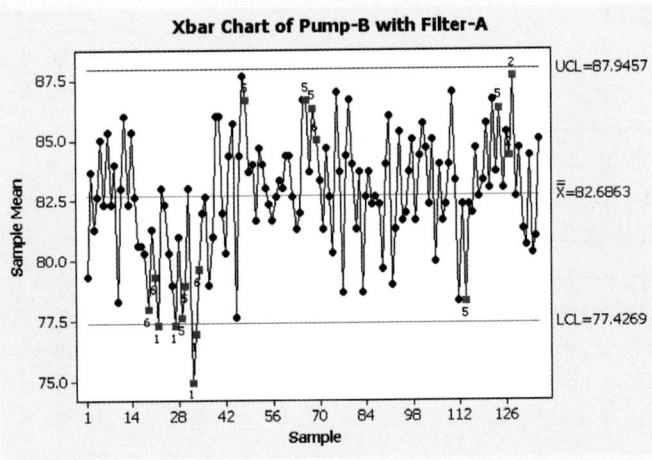

Figure SIA14.1d
$\bar{x}$-chart for Pump-B
with Filter-B method

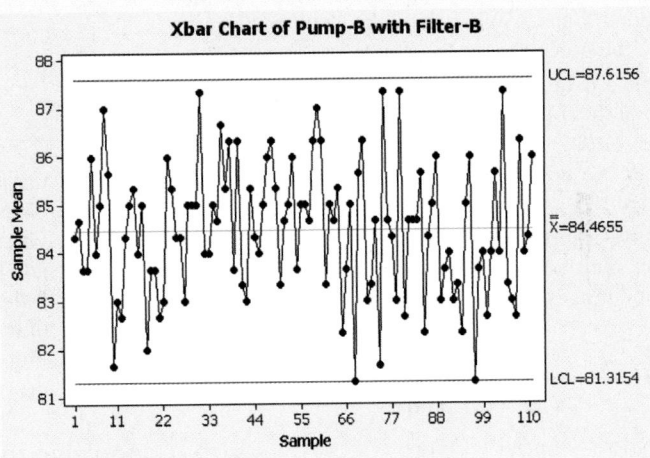

Exercises 14.1–14.17

Learning the Mechanics

14.1 What is a control chart? Describe its use.

14.2 Explain why rational subgrouping should be used in constructing control charts.

14.3 When a control chart is first constructed, why are the centerline and control limits treated as trial values?

14.4 Which process parameter is an $\bar{x}$-chart used to monitor?

14.5 Even if all the points on an $\bar{x}$-chart fall between the control limits, the process may be out of control. Explain.

14.6 What must be true about the variation of a process before an $\bar{x}$-chart is used to monitor the mean of the process? Why?

14.7 Use the six pattern-analysis rules described in Figure 14.21 to determine whether the process being monitored with the following $\bar{x}$-chart is out of statistical control.   Out of control

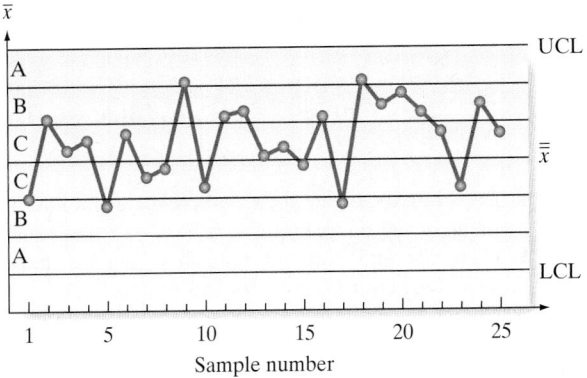

14.8 Consider the $\bar{x}$-chart shown at top of p. 948.
a. Is the process affected by only special causes of variation, only common causes of variation, or both? Explain.

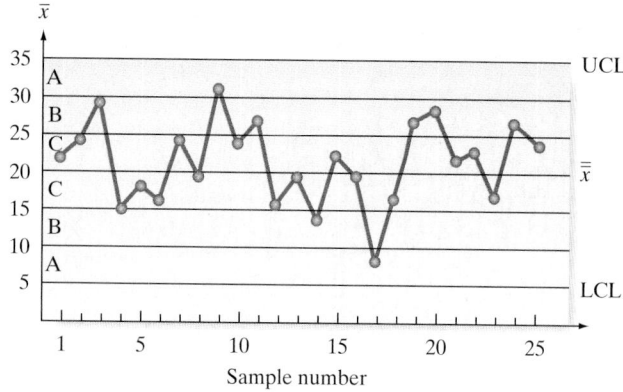

b. The means for the next five samples in the process are 27, 29, 32, 36, and 34. Plot these points on an extended $\bar{x}$-chart. What does the pattern suggest about the process?

14.9 Use Table XII in Appendix B to find the value of A_2 for each of the following sample sizes.
   a. $n = 3$ 1.023
   b. $n = 10$ .308
   c. $n = 22$

14.10 Twenty-five samples of size $n = 5$ were collected to construct an $\bar{x}$-chart. The accompanying sample means and ranges were calculated for these data.

LM14_10

Sample	$\bar{x}$	R	Sample	$\bar{x}$	R
1	80.2	7.2	14	83.1	10.2
2	79.1	9.0	15	79.6	7.8
3	83.2	4.7	16	80.0	6.1
4	81.0	5.6	17	83.2	8.4
5	77.6	10.1	18	75.9	9.9
6	81.7	8.6	19	78.1	6.0
7	80.4	4.4	20	81.4	7.4
8	77.5	6.2	21	81.7	10.4
9	79.8	7.9	22	80.9	9.1
10	85.3	7.1	23	78.4	7.3
11	77.7	9.8	24	79.6	8.0
12	82.3	10.7	25	81.6	7.6
13	79.5	9.2			

a. Calculate the mean of the sample means, $\bar{\bar{x}}$, and the mean of the sample ranges, $\bar{R}$.
b. Calculate and plot the centerline and the upper and lower control limits for the $\bar{x}$-chart.
c. Calculate and plot the A, B, and C zone boundaries of the $\bar{x}$-chart.
d. Plot the 25 sample means on the $\bar{x}$-chart and use the six pattern-analysis rules to determine whether the process is under statistical control.

14.11 The data in the next table were collected for the purpose of constructing an $\bar{x}$-chart.

LM14_11

Sample		Measurements		
1	19.4	19.7	20.6	21.2
2	18.7	18.4	21.2	20.7
3	20.2	18.8	22.6	20.1
4	19.6	21.2	18.7	19.4
5	20.4	20.9	22.3	18.6
6	17.3	22.3	20.3	19.7
7	21.8	17.6	22.8	23.1
8	20.9	17.4	19.5	20.7
9	18.1	18.3	20.6	20.4
10	22.6	21.4	18.5	19.7
11	22.7	21.2	21.5	19.5
12	20.1	20.6	21.0	20.2
13	19.7	18.6	21.2	19.1
14	18.6	21.7	17.7	18.3
15	18.2	20.4	19.8	19.2
16	18.9	20.7	23.2	20.0
17	20.5	19.7	21.4	17.8
18	21.0	18.7	19.9	21.2
19	20.5	19.6	19.8	21.8
20	20.6	16.9	22.4	19.7

a. Calculate $\bar{x}$ and R for each sample.
b. Calculate $\bar{\bar{x}}$ and $\bar{R}$.
c. Calculate and plot the centerline and the upper and lower control limits for the $\bar{x}$-chart.
d. Calculate and plot the A, B, and C zone boundaries of the $\bar{x}$-chart.
e. Plot the 20 sample means on the $\bar{x}$-chart. Is the process in control? Justify your answer.

Applying the Concepts—Basic

14.12 The central processing unit (CPU) of a microcomputer is a computer chip containing millions of transistors. Connecting the transistors are slender circuit paths only .5 to .85 micron wide. To understand how narrow these paths are, consider that a micron is a millionth of a meter, and a human hair is 70 microns wide (*Compute*, 1992). A manufacturer of CPU chips knows that if the circuit paths are not .5–.85 micron wide, a variety of problems will arise in the chips' performance. The manufacturer sampled four CPU chips six times a day (every 90 minutes from 8:00 A.M. until 4:30 P.M.) for five consecutive days and measured the circuit path widths. These data and MINITAB were used to construct the $\bar{x}$-chart shown on p. 949.
   a. Assuming that $\bar{R} = .335$, calculate the chart's upper and lower control limits, the upper and lower A–B boundaries, and the upper and lower B–C boundaries.
   b. What does the chart suggest about the stability of the process used to put circuit paths on the CPU chip? Justify your answer.
   c. Should the control limits be used to monitor future process output? Explain.   No

MINITAB Output for Exercise 14.12

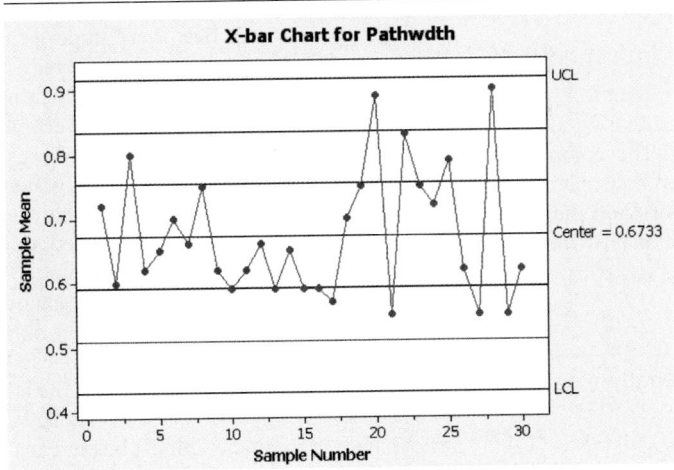

14.13 A machine at K-Company fills boxes with bran flakes cereal. The target weight for the filled boxes is 24 ounces. The company would like to use an $\bar{x}$-chart to monitor the performance of the machine. To develop the control chart, the company decides to sample and weigh five boxes of cereal each day (at 8:00 and 11:00 A.M. and 2:00, 5:00, and 8:00 P.M.) for twenty consecutive days. The data are presented in the table, along with an SPSS printout with summary statistics.
   a. Construct an $\bar{x}$-chart from the given data.

CEREAL

Day	Weight of Cereal Boxes (ounces)				
1	24.02	23.91	24.12	24.06	24.13
2	23.89	23.98	24.01	24.00	23.91
3	24.11	24.02	23.99	23.79	24.04
4	24.06	23.98	23.95	24.01	24.11
5	23.81	23.90	23.99	24.07	23.96
6	23.87	24.12	24.07	24.01	23.99
7	23.88	24.00	24.05	23.97	23.97
8	24.01	24.03	23.99	23.91	23.98
9	24.06	24.02	23.80	23.79	24.07
10	23.96	23.99	24.03	23.99	24.01
11	24.10	23.90	24.11	23.98	23.95
12	24.01	24.07	23.93	24.09	23.98
13	24.14	24.07	24.08	23.98	24.02
14	23.91	24.04	23.89	24.01	23.95
15	24.03	24.04	24.01	23.98	24.10
16	23.94	24.07	24.12	24.00	24.02
17	23.88	23.94	23.91	24.06	24.07
18	24.11	23.99	23.90	24.01	23.98
19	24.05	24.04	23.97	24.08	23.95
20	24.02	23.96	23.95	23.89	24.04

   b. What does the chart suggest about the stability of the filling process (whether the process is in or out of statistical control)? Justify your answer.   In control

Case Summaries[a]

	DAY	MEANWT	RANGEWT
1	1	24.05	.22
2	2	23.96	.12
3	3	23.99	.32
4	4	24.02	.16
5	5	23.95	.26
6	6	24.01	.25
7	7	23.97	.17
8	8	23.98	.12
9	9	23.95	.28
10	10	24.00	.07
11	11	24.01	.21
12	12	24.02	.16
13	13	24.06	.16
14	14	23.96	.15
15	15	24.03	.12
16	16	24.03	.18
17	17	23.97	.19
18	18	24.00	.21
19	19	24.02	.13
20	20	23.97	.15

a. Limited to first 100 cases.

   c. Should the control limits be used to monitor future process output? Explain.   Yes
   d. Two shifts of workers run the filling operation. Each day the second shift takes over at 3:00 P.M. Will the rational subgrouping strategy used by K-Company facilitate or hinder the

identification of process variation caused by differences in the two shifts? Explain.

Applying the Concepts—Intermediate

14.14 A precision parts manufacturer produces bolts for use in military aircraft. Ideally, the bolts should be 37 centimeters in length. The company sampled four consecutively produced bolts each hour on the hour for 25 consecutive hours and measured them using a computerized precision instrument. The data are presented below.

☉ BOLTS

Hour	Bolt Lengths (centimeters)			
1	37.03	37.08	36.90	36.88
2	36.96	37.04	36.85	36.98
3	37.16	37.11	36.99	37.01
4	37.20	37.06	37.02	36.98
5	36.81	36.97	36.91	37.10
6	37.13	36.96	37.01	36.89
7	37.07	36.94	36.99	37.00
8	37.01	36.91	36.98	37.12
9	37.17	37.03	36.90	37.01
10	36.91	36.99	36.87	37.11
11	36.88	37.10	37.07	37.03
12	37.06	36.98	36.90	36.99
13	36.91	37.22	37.12	37.03
14	37.08	37.07	37.10	37.04
15	37.03	37.04	36.89	37.01
16	36.95	36.98	36.90	36.99
17	36.97	36.94	37.14	37.10
18	37.11	37.04	36.98	36.91
19	36.88	36.99	37.01	36.94
20	36.90	37.15	37.09	37.00
21	37.01	36.96	37.05	36.96
22	37.09	36.95	36.93	37.12
23	37.00	37.02	36.95	37.04
24	36.99	37.07	36.90	37.02
25	37.10	37.03	37.01	36.90

a. What process is the manufacturer interested in monitoring?

b. Construct an $\bar{x}$-chart from the data.

c. Does the chart suggest that special causes of variation are present? Justify your answer.   No

d. Provide an example of a special cause of variation that could potentially affect this process. Do the same for a common cause of variation.

e. Should the control limits be used to monitor future process output? Explain.   Yes

14.15 In their text *Quantitative Analysis of Management* (1997), B. Render (Rollins College) and R. M. Stair (Florida State University) present the case of the Bayfield Mud Company. Bayfield supplies boxcars of 50-pound bags of mud treating agents to the Wet-Land Drilling Company. Mud treating agents are used to control the pH and other chemical properties of the

cone during oil drilling operations. Wet-Land has complained to Bayfield that its most recent shipment of bags were underweight by about 5%. (The use of underweight bags may result in poor chemical control during drilling, which may hurt drilling efficiency resulting in serious economic consequences.) Afraid of losing a long-time customer, Bayfield immediately began investigating their production process. Management suspected that the causes of the problem were the recently added third shift and the fact that all three shifts were under pressure to increase output to meet increasing demand for the product. Their quality control staff began randomly sampling and weighing six bags of output each hour. The average weight of each sample over the last three days is recorded in the table on p. 951 along with the weight of the heaviest and lightest bag in each sample.

a. Construct an $\bar{x}$-chart for these data.

b. Is the process under statistical control?

c. Does it appear that management's suspicion about the third shift is correct? Explain?   No

14.16 University of Waterloo (Canada) statistician S.H. Steiner applied control chart methodology to the manufacturing of a horseshoe-shaped metal fastener called a robotics clamp (*Applied Statistics*, Vol. 47, 1998). Users of the clamp were concerned with the width of the gap between the two ends of the fastener. Their preferred target width is .054 inches. An optical measuring device was used to measure the gap width of the fastener during the manufacturing process. The manufacturer sampled five finished clamps every fifteen minutes throughout its 16-hour daily production schedule and optically measured the gap. Data for four consecutive hours of production are presented in the table below.

☉ CLAMPGAP

Time	Gap Width (thousandths of an inch)				
00:15	54.2	54.1	53.9	54.0	53.8
00:30	53.9	53.7	54.1	54.4	55.1
00:45	54.0	55.2	53.1	55.9	54.5
01:00	52.1	53.4	52.9	53.0	52.7
01:15	53.0	51.9	52.6	53.4	51.7
01:30	54.2	55.0	54.0	53.8	53.6
01:45	55.2	56.6	53.1	52.9	54.0
02:00	53.3	57.2	54.5	51.6	54.3
02:15	54.9	56.3	55.2	56.1	54.0
02:30	55.7	53.1	52.9	56.3	55.4
02:45	55.2	51.0	56.3	55.6	54.2
03:00	54.2	54.2	55.8	53.8	52.1
03:15	55.7	57.5	55.4	54.0	53.1
03:30	53.7	56.9	54.0	55.1	54.2
03:45	54.1	53.9	54.0	54.6	54.8
04:00	53.5	56.1	55.1	55.0	54.0

Source: Adapted from Steiner, Stefan, H., "Grouped Data Exponentially Weighted Moving Average Control Charts," *Applied Statistics—Journal of the Royal Statistical Society,* Vol. 47, Part 2, 1998, pp. 203–216.

MUDBAGS

Time	Average Weight (pounds)	Lightest	Heaviest	Time	Average Weight (pounds)	Lightest	Heaviest
6:00 A.M.	49.6	48.7	50.7	6:00 P.M	46.8	41.0	51.2
7:00	50.2	49.1	51.2	7:00	50.0	46.2	51.7
8:00	50.6	49.6	51.4	8:00	47.4	44.0	48.7
9:00	50.8	50.2	51.8	9:00	47.0	44.2	48.9
10:00	49.9	49.2	52.3	10:00	47.2	46.6	50.2
11:00	50.3	48.6	51.7	11:00	48.6	47.0	50.0
12 noon	48.6	46.2	50.4	12 midnight	49.8	48.2	50.4
1:00 P.M.	49.0	46.4	50.0	1:00 A.M.	49.6	48.4	51.7
2:00	49.0	46.0	50.6	2:00	50.0	49.0	52.2
3:00	49.8	48.2	50.8	3:00	50.0	49.2	50.0
4:00	50.3	49.2	52.7	4:00	47.2	46.3	50.5
5:00	51.4	50.0	55.3	5:00	47.0	44.1	49.7
6:00	51.6	49.2	54.7	6:00	48.4	45.0	49.0
7:00	51.8	50.0	55.6	7:00	48.8	44.8	49.7
8:00	51.0	48.6	53.2	8:00	49.6	48.0	51.8
9:00	50.5	49.4	52.4	9:00	50.0	48.1	52.7
10:00	49.2	46.1	50.7	10:00	51.0	48.1	55.2
11:00	49.0	46.3	50.8	11:00	50.4	49.5	54.1
12 midnight	48.4	45.4	50.2	12 noon	50.0	48.7	50.9
1:00 A.M.	47.6	44.3	49.7	1:00 P.M.	48.9	47.6	51.2
2:00	47.4	44.1	49.6	2:00	49.8	48.4	51.0
3:00	48.2	45.2	49.0	3:00	49.8	48.8	50.8
4:00	48.0	45.5	49.1	4:00	50.0	49.1	50.6
5:00	48.4	47.1	49.6	5:00	47.8	45.2	51.2
6:00	48.6	47.4	52.0	6:00	46.4	44.0	49.7
7:00	50.0	49.2	52.2	7:00	46.4	44.4	50.0
8:00	49.8	49.0	52.4	8:00	47.2	46.6	48.9
9:00	50.3	49.4	51.7	9:00	48.4	47.2	49.5
10:00	50.2	49.6	51.8	10:00	49.2	48.1	50.7
11:00	50.0	49.0	52.3	11:00	48.4	47.0	50.8
12 noon	50.0	48.8	52.4	12 midnight	47.2	46.4	49.2
1:00 P.M.	50.1	49.4	53.6	1:00 A.M.	47.4	46.8	49.0
2:00	49.7	48.6	51.0	2:00	48.8	47.2	51.4
3:00	48.4	47.2	51.7	3:00	49.6	49.0	50.6
4:00	47.2	45.3	50.9	4:00	51.0	50.5	51.5
5:00	46.8	44.1	49.0	5:00	50.5	50.0	51.9

Source: Kinard, J., Western Carolina University, as reported in Render, B., and Stair, Jr., R., *Quantitative Analysis for Management*, 6th ed. Upper Saddle River, N.J.: Prentice Hall, 1997.

a. Construct an $\bar{x}$-chart from these data.

b. Apply the pattern-analysis rules to the control chart. Does your analysis suggest that special causes of variation are present in the clamp manufacturing process? Which of the six rules led you to your conclusion?

c. Should the control limits be used to monitor future process output? Explain.   No

14.17 A pharmaceutical company produces vials filled with morphine. (*Comuunications in Statistics*, Vol. 27, 1998.) Most of the time the filling process remains stable, but once in a while the mean value shifts off the target of 52.00 grams. To monitor the process, one sample of size 3 is drawn from the process every 27 minutes. Measurements for 20 consecutive samples are shown in the table on p. 952.

a. Construct an $\bar{x}$-chart for these data.

b. What does the $\bar{x}$-chart suggest about the stability of the process?

c. Is the process influenced by both common and special causes of variation? Explain.

d. Should the control limits and centerline of the $\bar{x}$-chart of part **a** be used to monitor future output of the morphine filling process? Explain.   No

MORPHINE

Sample	Amount of Morphine in Vials (grams)		
1	51.60	52.35	52.00
2	52.10	53.00	51.90
3	51.75	51.85	52.05
4	52.10	53.50	53.95
5	52.00	52.35	52.40
6	51.70	52.10	51.90
7	52.00	51.50	52.35
8	52.25	52.40	52.05
9	52.00	51.60	51.80
10	52.15	51.65	51.40
11	51.20	52.15	52.35
12	52.00	52.35	51.85
13	51.60	52.15	52.00
14	51.40	52.35	52.10
15	52.90	53.75	54.25
16	54.30	53.90	54.15
17	53.85	53.65	54.90
18	54.25	53.55	54.05
19	54.00	53.60	53.95
20	53.80	54.50	54.20

Source: Adapted from Costa, A.F.B., "VSSI X charts with Sampling at Fixed Times," *Communications in Statistics—Theory and Methods,* Vol. 27, No. 11 (1998), pp. 2853–2869.

14.5 A Control Chart for Monitoring the Variation of a Process: The R-Chart

Teaching Tip

The R-chart plots the variation in samples collected over time.

Teaching Tip

The $\bar{x}$- and R-charts use quantitative data, while the p-chart of the next section plots qualitative data.

Recall from Section 14.2 that a process may be out of statistical control because its mean or variance or both are changing over time (see Figure 14.8). The $\bar{x}$-chart of the previous section is used to detect changes in the process mean. The control chart we present in this section—the **R-chart**—is used to detect changes in process variation.

The primary difference between the $\bar{x}$-chart and the R-chart is that instead of plotting *sample means* and monitoring their variation, we plot and monitor the variation of *sample ranges*. Changes in the behavior of the sample range signal changes in the variation of the process.

We could also monitor process variation by plotting *sample standard deviations.* That is, we could calculate s for each sample (i.e., each subgroup) and plot them on a control chart known as an **s-chart**. In this chapter, however, we focus on just the R-chart because (1) when using samples of size 9 or less, the s-chart and the R-chart reflect about the same information, and (2) the R-chart is used much more widely by practitioners than is the s-chart (primarily because the sample range is easier to calculate and interpret than the sample standard deviation). For more information about s-charts, see the references at the end of the book.

The underlying logic and basic form of the R-chart are similar to the $\bar{x}$-chart. In monitoring $\bar{x}$, we use the standard deviation of $\bar{x}$ to develop 3-sigma control limits. Now, since we want to be able to determine when R takes on unusually large or small values, we use the standard deviation of R, or σ_R, to construct 3-sigma control limits. The centerline of the $\bar{x}$-chart represents the process mean μ or, equivalently, the mean of the sampling distribution of $\bar{x}$, $\mu_{\bar{x}}$. Similarly, the centerline of the R-chart represents μ_R, the mean of the sampling distribution of R. These points are illustrated in the R-chart of Figure 14.24.

Figure 14.24

R-chart

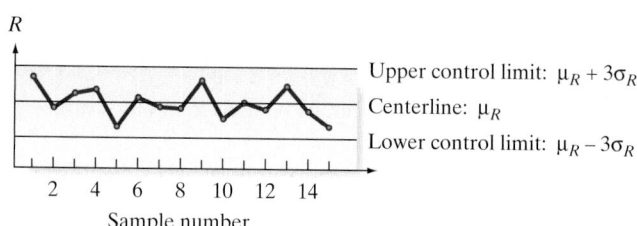

Upper control limit: $\mu_R + 3\sigma_R$

Centerline: μ_R

Lower control limit: $\mu_R - 3\sigma_R$

Sample number

As with the $\bar{x}$-chart, you should have at least 20 samples of n items each $(n \geq 2)$ to construct an R-chart. This will provide sufficient data to obtain reasonably good estimates of μ_R and σ_R. Rational subgrouping is again used for determining sample size and frequency of sampling.

The centerline of the R-chart is positioned as follows:

$$Centerline: \bar{R} = \frac{R_1 + R_2 + \cdots + R_k}{k}$$

where k is the number of samples of size n and R_i is the range of the ith sample. $\bar{R}$ is an estimate of μ_R.

In order to construct the control limits, we need an estimator of σ_R. The estimator recommended by Montgomery (1991) and Ryan (1989) is

$$\hat{\sigma}_R = d_3\left(\frac{\bar{R}}{d_2}\right)$$

where d_2 and d_3 are constants whose values depend on the sample size, n. Values for d_2 and d_3 for samples of size $n = 2$ to $n = 25$ are given in Table XII of Appendix B.

The control limits are positioned as follows:

$$Upper\ control\ limit: \bar{R} + 3\hat{\sigma}_R = \bar{R} + 3d_3\left(\frac{\bar{R}}{d_2}\right)$$

$$Lower\ control\ limit: \bar{R} - 3\hat{\sigma}_R = \bar{R} + 3d_3\left(\frac{\bar{R}}{d_2}\right)$$

Notice that $\bar{R}$ appears twice in each control limit. Accordingly, we can simplify the calculation of these limits by factoring out $\bar{R}$:

$$\text{UCL:}\ \bar{R}\left(1 + \frac{3d_3}{d_2}\right) = \bar{R}D_4 \qquad \text{LCL:}\ \bar{R}\left(1 - \frac{3d_3}{d_2}\right) = \bar{R}D_3$$

where

$$D_4 = \left(1 + \frac{3d_3}{d_2}\right) \qquad D_3 = \left(1 - \frac{3d_3}{d_2}\right)$$

The values for D_3 and D_4 have been tabulated for samples of size $n = 2$ to $n = 25$ and can be found in Appendix B, Table XII.

For samples of size $n = 2$ through $n = 6$, D_3 is negative, and the lower control limit falls below zero. Since the sample range cannot take on negative values, such a control limit is meaningless. Thus, when $n \leq 6$ the R-chart contains only one control limit, the upper control limit.

Although D_3 is actually negative for $n \le 6$, the values reported in Table XII in Appendix B are all zeros. This has been done to discourage the inappropriate construction of negative lower control limits. If the lower control limit is calculated using $D_3 = 0$, you obtain $D_3\overline{R} = 0$. This should be interpreted as indicating that the R-chart has no lower 3-sigma control limit.

Constructing an R-Chart: A Summary

1. Using a rational subgrouping strategy, collect at least 20 samples (i.e., subgroups), each of size $n \ge 2$.

2. Calculate the range of each sample.

3. Calculate the mean of the sample ranges, $\overline{R}$:

$$\overline{R} = \frac{R_1 + R_2 + \cdots + R_k}{k}$$

where

$$k = \text{The number of samples (i.e., subgroups)}$$
$$R_i = \text{The range of the } i\text{th sample}$$

4. Plot the centerline and control limits:

$$\textit{Centerline: } \overline{R}$$

$$\textit{Upper control limit: } \overline{R}D_4$$
$$\textit{Lower control limit: } \overline{R}D_3$$

where D_3 and D_4 are constants that depend on n. Their values can be found in Appendix B, Table XII. When $n \le 6$, $D_3 = 0$, indicating that the control chart does not have a lower control limit.

5. Plot the k sample ranges on the control chart in the order that the samples were produced by the process.

Teaching Tip

Point out the differences between the interpretation of the $\bar{x}$- and R-charts. Rules 5 and 6 of the $\bar{x}$--charts no longer apply to the R-chart interpretation.

We interpret the completed R-chart in basically the same way as we did the $\bar{x}$-chart. We look for indications that the process is out of control. Those indications include points that fall outside the control limits as well as any nonrandom patterns of variation that appear between the control limits. To help spot nonrandom behavior, we include the A, B, and C zones (described in the previous section) on the R-chart. The next box describes how to construct the zone boundaries for the R-chart. It requires only Rules 1 through 4 of Figure 14.21, because Rules 5 and 6 are based on the assumption that the statistic plotted on the control chart follows a normal (or nearly normal) distribution, whereas R's distribution is skewed to the right.*

---

*Some authors (e.g., Kane, 1989) apply all six pattern-analysis rules as long as $n \ge 4$.

Constructing Zone Boundaries for an *R*-Chart

The simplest method of construction uses the estimator of the standard deviation of R, which is $\hat{\sigma}_R = d_3(\overline{R}/d_2)$:

$$\text{Upper } A-B \text{ boundary: } \overline{R} + 2d_3\left(\frac{\overline{R}}{d_2}\right)$$

$$\text{Lower } A-B \text{ boundary: } \overline{R} - 2d_3\left(\frac{\overline{R}}{d_2}\right)$$

$$\text{Upper } B-C \text{ boundary: } \overline{R} + d_3\left(\frac{\overline{R}}{d_2}\right)$$

$$\text{Lower } B-C \text{ boundary: } \overline{R} - d_3\left(\frac{\overline{R}}{d_2}\right)$$

Note: Whenever $n \leq 6$ the *R*-chart has no lower 3-sigma control limit. However, the lower A–B, B–C boundaries can still be plotted if they are nonnegative.

Interpreting an *R*-Chart

1. The **process is out of control** if one or more sample ranges fall beyond the control limits (Rule 1) or if any of the three patterns of variation described by Rules 2, 3, and 4 (Figure 14.21) are observed. Such signals indicate that one or more special causes of variation are influencing the *variation* of the process. These causes should be identified and eliminated to bring the process into control.

2. The **process is treated as being in control** if none of the noted out-of-control signals are observed. Processes that are in control should not be tampered with. However, if the level of variation is unacceptably high, common causes of variation should be identified and eliminated.

As with the $\bar{x}$-chart, the centerline and control limits should be developed using samples that were collected during a period in which the process was in control. Accordingly, when an *R*-chart is first constructed, the centerline and the control limits are treated as *trial values* (see Section 14.4) and are modified, if necessary, before being extended to the right and used to monitor future process output.

EXAMPLE 14.3   CREATING AND INTERPRETING AN *R*-CHART

Refer to Example 14.1.

Problem
a. Construct an *R*-chart for the paint-filling process.
b. What does the chart indicate about the stability of the filling process during the time when the data were collected?

In control

c. Is it appropriate to use the control limits constructed in part **a** to monitor future process output?

Yes

Solution
a. The first step after collecting the data is to calculate the range of each sample. For the first sample the range is

$$R_1 = 10.0042 - 9.9964 = .0078$$

All 25 sample ranges appear in Table 14.2 (p. 942).

Next, calculate the mean of the ranges:

$$\overline{R} = \frac{.0078 + .0092 + \cdots + .0077}{25} = .010072$$

The centerline of the chart is positioned at $\overline{R} = .01028$. To determine the control limits, we need the constants D_3 and D_4, which can be found in Table XII of Appendix B. For $n = 5$, $D_3 = 0$ and $D_4 = 2.115$. Since $D_3 = 0$, the lower 3-sigma control limit is negative and is not included on the chart. The upper control limit is calculated as follows:

$$\text{UCL: } \overline{R}D_4 = (.010072)(2.115) = .02130$$

After positioning the upper control limit on the chart, we plot the 25 sample ranges in the order of sampling and connect the points with straight lines. The resulting trial R-chart, produced using MINITAB, is shown in Figure 14.25.

Figure 14.25
MINITAB R-chart for
the paint-filling process

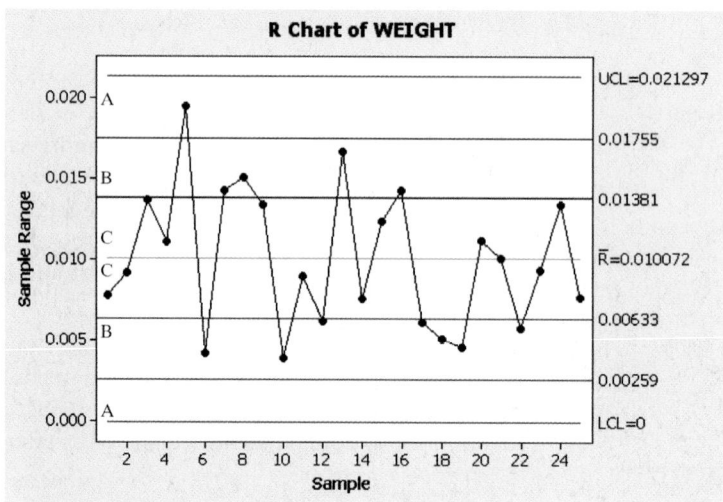

b. To facilitate our examination of the R-chart, we plot the four zone boundaries. Recall that in general the A–B boundaries are positioned 2 standard deviations from the centerline and the B–C boundaries are 1 standard deviation from the centerline. In the case of the R-chart, we use the estimated standard deviation of R, $\hat{\sigma}_R = d_3(\overline{R}/d_2)$, and calculate the boundaries:

$$\text{Upper } A{-}B \text{ boundary: } \overline{R} + 2d_3\left(\frac{\overline{R}}{d_2}\right) = .01755$$

$$\text{Lower } A{-}B \text{ boundary: } \overline{R} - 2d_3\left(\frac{\overline{R}}{d_2}\right) = .00259$$

$$\text{Upper } B{-}C \text{ boundary: } \overline{R} + d_3\left(\frac{\overline{R}}{d_2}\right) = .01381$$

$$\text{Lower } B{-}C \text{ boundary: } \overline{R} - d_3\left(\frac{\overline{R}}{d_2}\right) = .00633$$

where (from Table XII of Appendix B) for $n = 5$, $d_2 = 2.326$ and $d_3 = .864$. Notice in Figure 14.25 that the lower A zone is slightly narrower than the

Suggested Exercise 14.24

upper A zone. This occurs because the lower 3-sigma control limit (the usual lower boundary of the lower A zone) is negative.

All the plotted *R* values fall below the upper control limit. This is one indication that the process is under control (i.e., is stable). However, we must also look for patterns of points that would be unlikely to occur if the process were in control. To assist us with this process, we use pattern-analysis rules 1–4 (Figure 14.21). None of the rules signal the presence of special causes of variation. Accordingly, we conclude that it is reasonable to treat the process—in particular, the variation of the process—as being under control during the period in question. Apparently, no significant special causes of variation are influencing the variation of the process.

c. Yes. Since the variation of the process appears to be in control during the period when the sample data were collected, the control limits appropriately characterize the variation in *R* that would be expected when the process is in a state of statistical control.

> **Now Work**   *Exercise 14.21*

■ ■ ■

In practice, the $\bar{x}$-chart and the *R*-chart are not used in isolation, as our presentation so far might suggest. Rather, they are used together to monitor the mean (i.e., the location) of the process and the variation of the process simultaneously. In fact, many practitioners plot them on the same piece of paper.

One important reason for dealing with them as a unit is that the control limits of the $\bar{x}$-chart are a function of *R*. That is, the control limits depend on the variation of the process. (Recall that the control limits are $\bar{x} \pm A_2\bar{R}$.) Thus, if the process variation is out of control the control limits of the $\bar{x}$-chart have little meaning. This is because when the process variation is changing (as in the bottom two graphs of Figure 14.8), any single estimate of the variation (such as $\bar{R}$ or *s*) is not representative of the process. Accordingly, **the appropriate procedure is to first construct and then interpret the *R*-chart. If it indicates that the process variation is in control, then it makes sense to construct and interpret the $\bar{x}$-chart.**

Figure 14.26 is reprinted from Kaoru Ishikawa's classic text on quality-improvement methods, *Guide to Quality Control* (1986). It illustrates how particular changes in a process over time may be reflected in $\bar{x}$- and *R*-charts. At the top of the figure, running across the page, is a series of probability distributions A, B, and C that describe the process (i.e., the output variable) at different points in time. In practice, we never have this information. For this example, however, Ishikawa worked with a known process (i.e., with its given probabilistic characterization) to illustrate how sample data from a known process might behave.

The control limits for both charts were constructed from $k = 25$ samples of size $n = 5$. These data were generated by Distribution A. The 25 sample means and ranges were plotted on the $\bar{x}$- and *R*-charts, respectively. Since the distribution did not change over this period of time, it follows from the definition of statistical control that the process was under control. If you did not know this—as would be the case in practice—what would you conclude from looking at the control charts? (Remember, always interpret the *R*-chart before the $\bar{x}$-chart.) Both charts indicate that the process is under control. Accordingly, the control limits are made official and can be used to monitor future output, as is done next.

Toward the middle of the figure, the process changes. The mean shifts to a higher level. Now the output variable is described by Distribution B. The process is

Teaching Tip

It is wise to construct and interpret the *R*-chart before constructing and interpreting the $\bar{x}$-chart.

Figure 14.26

Combined $\bar{x}$- and R-chart

Source: Reprinted from *Guide to Quality Control,* by Kaoru Ishikawa, © 1986 by Asian Productivity Organization, with permission of the publisher Asian Productivity Organization. Distributed in North America by Quality Resources, New York, NY.

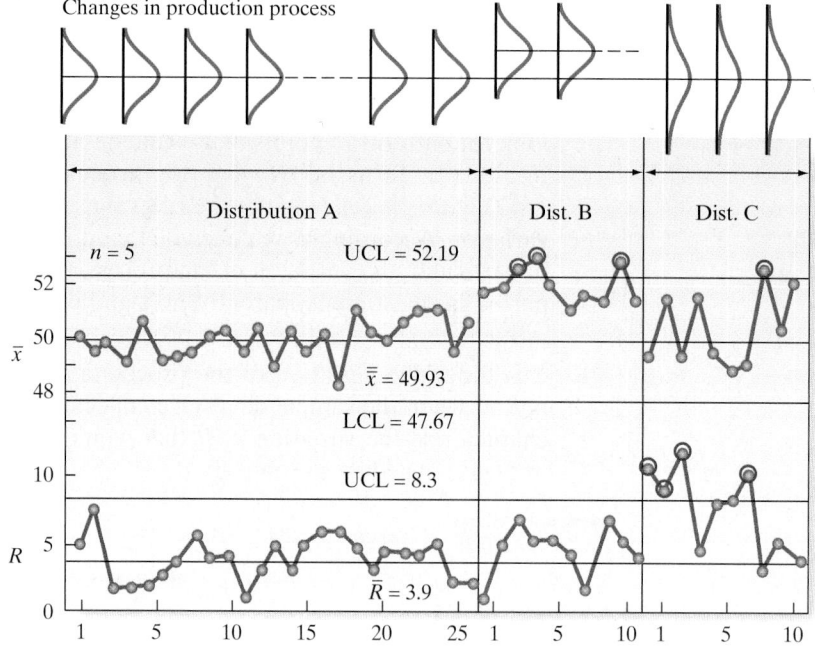

out of control. Ten new samples of size 5 are sampled from the process. Since the variation of the process has not changed, the R-chart should indicate that the variation remains stable. This is, in fact, the case. All points fall below the upper control limit. As we would hope, it is the $\bar{x}$-chart that reacts to the change in the mean of the process.

Then the process changes again (Distribution C). This time the mean shifts back to its original position, but the variation of the process increases. The process is still out of control but this time for a different reason. Checking the R-chart first, we see that it has reacted as we would hope. It has detected the increase in the variation. Given this R-chart finding, the control limits of the $\bar{x}$-chart become inappropriate (as described before) and we would not use them. Notice, however, how the sample means react to the increased variation in the process. This increased variation in $\bar{x}$ is consistent with what we know about the variance of $\bar{x}$. It is directly proportional to the variance of the process, $\sigma_{\bar{x}}^2 = \sigma^2/n$.

Keep in mind that what Ishikawa did in this example is exactly the opposite of what we do in practice. In practice we use sample data and control charts to make inferences about changes in unknown process distributions. Here, for the purpose of helping you to understand and interpret control charts, known process distributions were changed to see what would happen to the control charts.

Statistics in Action Revisited

Monitoring the Variation of the Jet Fuel Surfactant Test Process

Recall (p. 946) that the engineering firm discovered that tests for surfactants in jet fuel additive using Pump-B with Filter-B yielded an "in-control" process mean. However, as discussed in this section, the variation of the process should be checked first before interpreting the $\bar{x}$-chart. Figure SIA14.2 is a MINITAB R-chart for the test results using Pump-B with Filter-B. As an option, we again instructed MINITAB to highlight (in red) any sample ranges that match any of the four pattern-analysis rules for detecting special causes of variation given in this section. (If a rule is violated, the rule number will be shown next to the sample range on the chart.)

Figure SIA14.2 shows that the process variation is "in control"—none of the pattern-analysis rules for ranges are matched. Now that we've established the stability of the process variance, the $\bar{x}$-chart of Figure SIA14.1(d) can be meaningfully interpreted. Together, the $\bar{x}$-chart and *R*-chart helped the engineering firm establish the Pump-B

with Filter-B surfactant test method as viable alternative to the standard test, one which appears to have no special causes of variation present and with more precision than the standard.

[*Note:* Extensive testing done with the Navy concluded the improved precision of the "new" surfactant test was valid. However, the new test was unable to detect several light surfactants that can still cause problems in jet engines. The original test for surfactants in jet fuel additive remains the industry standard.]

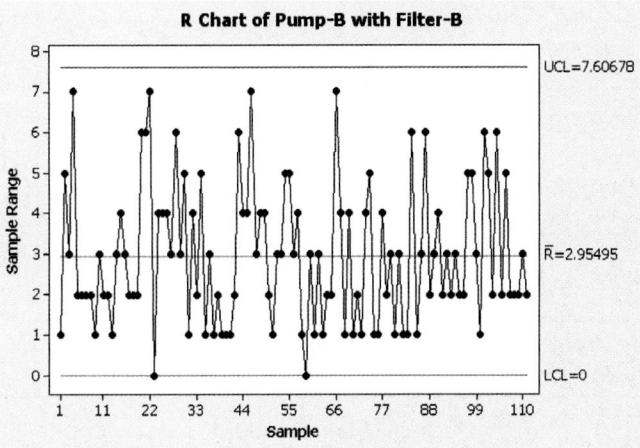

Figure SIA14.2
R-chart for Pump-B with Filter-B method

Exercises 14.18–14.29

Learning the Mechanics

14.18 What characteristic of a process is an *R*-chart designed to monitor? Variation

14.19 In practice, $\bar{x}$- and *R*-charts are used together to monitor a process. However, the *R*-chart should be interpreted before the $\bar{x}$-chart. Why?

14.20 Use Table XII in Appendix B to find the values of D_3 and D_4 for each of the following sample sizes.
  a. $n = 4$
  b. $n = 12$
  c. $n = 24$

14.21 Construct and interpret an *R*-chart for the data in Exercise 14.10 (p. 948).
  a. Calculate and plot the upper control limit and, if appropriate, the lower control limit.
  b. Calculate and plot the A, B, and C zone boundaries on the *R*-chart.
  c. Plot the sample ranges on the *R*-chart and use pattern-analysis rules 1–4 of Figure 14.21 to determine whether the process is under statistical control.

14.22 Construct and interpret an *R*-chart for the data in Exercise 14.11 (p. 948).
  a. Calculate and plot the upper control limit and, if appropriate, the lower control limit.
  b. Calculate and plot the A, B, and C zone boundaries on the *R*-chart.
  c. Plot the sample ranges on the *R*-chart and determine whether the process is in control.

14.23 Construct and interpret an *R*-chart and an $\bar{x}$-chart from the sample data shown on p. 960. Remember to interpret the *R*-chart *before* the $\bar{x}$-chart.

Applying the Concepts—Basic

14.24 Refer to Exercise 14.12 (p. 948), where the desired circuit path widths were .5 to .85 micron. The manufacturer sampled four CPU chips six times a day (every 90 minutes from 8:00 A.M. until 4:30 P.M.) for five consecutive days. The path widths were measured and used to construct the MINITAB *R*-chart shown on p. 960.
  a. Calculate the chart's upper and lower control limits.

◉ **LM14_23**

Sample	Measurements							$\bar{x}$	R
	1	2	3	4	5	6	7		
1	20.1	19.0	20.9	22.2	18.9	18.1	21.3	20.07	4.1
2	19.0	17.9	21.2	20.4	20.0	22.3	21.5	20.33	4.4
3	22.6	21.4	21.4	22.1	19.2	20.6	18.7	20.86	3.9
4	18.1	20.8	17.8	19.6	19.8	21.7	20.0	19.69	3.9
5	22.6	19.1	21.4	21.8	18.4	18.0	19.5	20.11	4.6
6	19.1	19.0	22.3	21.5	17.8	19.2	19.4	19.76	4.5
7	17.1	19.4	18.6	20.9	21.8	21.0	19.8	19.80	4.7
8	20.2	22.4	22.0	19.6	19.6	20.0	18.5	20.33	3.9
9	21.9	24.1	23.1	22.8	25.6	24.2	25.2	23.84	3.7
10	25.1	24.3	26.0	23.1	25.8	27.0	26.5	25.40	3.9
11	25.8	29.2	28.5	29.1	27.8	29.0	28.0	28.20	3.4
12	28.2	27.5	29.3	30.7	27.6	28.0	27.0	28.33	3.7
13	28.2	28.6	28.1	26.0	30.0	28.5	28.3	28.24	4.0
14	22.1	21.4	23.3	20.5	19.8	20.5	19.0	20.94	4.3
15	18.5	19.2	18.0	20.1	22.0	20.2	19.5	19.64	4.0
16	21.4	20.3	22.0	19.2	18.0	17.9	19.5	19.76	4.1
17	18.4	16.5	18.1	19.2	17.5	20.9	19.6	18.60	4.4
18	20.1	19.8	22.3	22.5	21.8	22.7	23.0	21.74	3.2
19	20.0	17.5	21.0	18.2	19.5	17.2	18.1	18.79	3.8
20	22.3	18.2	21.5	19.0	19.4	20.5	20.0	20.13	4.1

MINITAB Output for Exercise 14.24

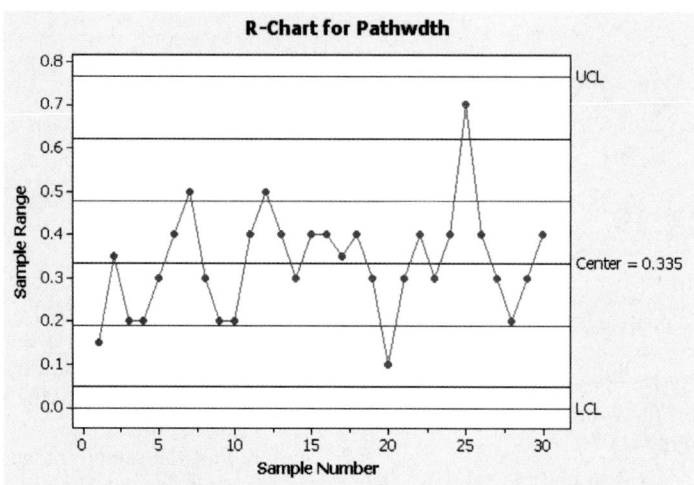

b. What does the R-chart suggest about the presence of special causes of variation during the time when the data were collected?   In control

c. Should the control limit(s) be used to monitor future process output? Explain.   Yes

d. How many different R values are plotted on the control chart? Notice how most of the R values fall along three horizontal lines. What could cause such a pattern?

14.25 A soft-drink bottling company is interested in monitoring the amount of cola injected into 16-ounce bottles by a particular filling head. The process is entirely automated and operates 24 hours a day. At 6 A.M. and 6 P.M. each day, a new dispenser of carbon dioxide capable of producing 20,000 gallons of cola is hooked up to the filling machine. In order to monitor the process using control charts, the company decided to sample five consecutive bottles of cola each hour beginning at 6:15 A.M. (i.e., 6:15 A.M., 7:15 A.M., 8:15 A.M., etc.). The data for the first day are given in the table on p. 961. An SPSS descriptive statistics printout is also provided on page 961.

a. Will the rational subgrouping strategy that was used enable the company to detect variation in fill caused by differences in the carbon dioxide dispensers? Explain.   Yes

b. Construct an R-chart from the data.

⊘ **COLAFILL**

Sample	Measurements				
1	16.01	16.03	15.98	16.00	16.01
2	16.03	16.02	15.97	15.99	15.99
3	15.98	16.00	16.03	16.04	15.99
4	16.00	16.03	16.02	15.98	15.98
5	15.97	15.99	16.03	16.01	16.04
6	16.01	16.03	16.04	15.97	15.99
7	16.04	16.05	15.97	15.96	16.00
8	16.02	16.05	16.03	15.97	15.98
9	15.97	15.99	16.02	16.03	15.95
10	16.00	16.01	15.95	16.04	16.06
11	15.95	16.04	16.07	15.93	16.03
12	15.98	16.07	15.94	16.08	16.02
13	15.96	16.00	16.01	16.00	15.98
14	15.98	16.01	16.02	15.99	15.99
15	15.99	16.03	16.00	15.98	16.01
16	16.02	16.02	16.01	15.97	16.00
17	16.01	16.05	15.99	15.99	16.03
18	15.98	16.03	16.04	15.98	16.01
19	15.97	15.96	15.99	15.99	16.01
20	16.03	16.01	16.04	15.96	15.99
21	15.99	16.03	15.97	16.05	16.03
22	15.98	15.95	16.07	16.01	16.04
23	15.99	16.06	15.95	16.03	16.07
24	16.00	16.01	16.08	15.94	15.93

c. What does the *R*-chart indicate about the stability of the filling process during the time when the data were collected? Justify your answer.

d. Should the control limit(s) be used to monitor future process output? Explain.   Yes

e. Given your answer to part **c,** should an $\bar{x}$-chart be constructed from the given data? Explain.

Applying the Concepts—Intermediate

14.26 In an effort to reduce customer dissatisfaction with delays in replacing lost automated teller machine (ATM) cards, some retail banks monitor the time required to replace a lost ATM card. Called replacement cycle time, it is the elapsed time from when the customer contacts the bank about the loss until the customer receives a new card (*Management Science*, Sept. 1999). A particular retail bank monitors replacement cycle time for the first five requests each week for replacement cards. Variation in cycle times is monitored using an *R*-chart. Data for 20 weeks is presented on page 962.

a. Construct an *R*-chart for these data.

b. What does the *R*-chart suggest about the presence of special causes of variation in the process?

c. Should the control limits of your *R*-chart be used to monitor future replacement cycle times? Explain.

SPSS Output for Exercise 14.25

Descriptive Statistics for 25 Cola Samples

	Count	Mean	Minimum	Maximum	Range
1	5	16.01	15.98	16.03	.05
2	5	16.00	15.97	16.03	.06
3	5	16.01	15.98	16.04	.06
4	5	16.00	15.98	16.03	.05
5	5	16.01	15.97	16.04	.07
6	5	16.01	15.97	16.04	.07
7	5	16.00	15.96	16.05	.09
8	5	16.01	15.97	16.05	.08
9	5	15.99	15.95	16.03	.08
10	5	16.01	15.95	16.06	.11
11	5	16.00	15.93	16.07	.14
12	5	16.02	15.94	16.08	.14
13	5	15.99	15.96	16.01	.05
14	5	16.00	15.98	16.02	.04
15	5	16.00	15.98	16.03	.05
16	5	16.00	15.97	16.02	.05
17	5	16.01	15.99	16.05	.06
18	5	16.01	15.98	16.04	.06
19	5	15.98	15.96	16.01	.05
20	5	16.01	15.96	16.04	.08
21	5	16.01	15.97	16.05	.08
22	5	16.01	15.95	16.07	.12
23	5	16.02	15.95	16.07	.12
24	5	15.99	15.93	16.08	.15

d. Given your conclusion in part **b** and the pattern displayed on the R-chart, discuss the possible future impact on the performance of the bank.

ATM

Week	Replacement Cycle Time (in days)				
1	7	10	6	6	10
2	7	12	8	8	6
3	7	8	7	11	6
4	8	8	12	11	12
5	3	8	4	7	7
6	6	10	11	5	7
7	5	12	11	8	7
8	7	12	8	7	6
9	8	10	12	10	5
10	12	8	6	6	8
11	10	9	9	5	4
12	3	10	7	6	8
13	9	9	8	7	2
14	7	10	18	20	8
15	8	18	15	18	21
16	10	22	16	8	7
17	3	18	4	8	12
18	11	7	8	17	19
19	10	8	19	20	25
20	6	3	18	18	7

14.27 Refer to Exercise 14.15 (p. 950), in which the Bayfield Mud Company was concerned with discovering why their filling operation was producing underfilled bags of mud.

   a. Construct an R-chart for the filling process.
   b. According to the R-chart, is the process under statistical control? Explain.   Out of control
   c. Does the R-chart provide any evidence concerning the cause of Bayfield's underfilling problem? Explain.

14.28 Refer to Exercise 14.16 (p. 950), in which a robotics clamp manufacturer was concerned about gap width.
   a. Construct an R-chart for the gap width.
   b. Which parameter of the manufacturing process does your R-chart provide information about?
   c. What does the R-chart suggest about the presence of special causes of variation during the time when the data were collected?

Applying the Concepts—Advanced

14.29 The *Journal of Quality Technology* (July 1998) published an article examining the effects of the precision of measurement on the R-chart. The authors presented data from a British nutrition company that fills containers labeled "500 grams" with a powdered dietary supplement. Once every 15 minutes, five containers are sampled from the filling process and the fill weight is measured. The first table lists the measurements for 25 consecutive samples made with a scale that is accurate to .5 gram, followed by a second table

FILLWT1

Sample	Fill Weights Accurate to .5 Gram					Range
1	500.5	499.5	502.0	501.0	500.5	2.5
2	500.5	499.5	500.0	499.0	500.0	1.5
3	498.5	499.0	500.0	499.5	500.0	1.5
4	500.5	499.5	499.0	499.0	500.5	1.5
5	500.0	501.0	500.5	500.5	500.0	1.0
6	501.0	498.5	500.0	501.5	500.5	3.0
7	499.5	500.0	499.0	501.0	499.5	2.0
8	498.5	498.0	500.0	500.5	500.5	2.5
9	498.0	499.0	502.0	501.0	501.5	4.0
10	499.0	499.5	499.5	500.0	499.5	1.0
11	502.5	499.5	501.0	501.5	502.0	3.0
12	501.5	501.5	500.0	500.0	501.0	1.5
13	498.5	499.5	501.0	500.5	498.5	2.5
14	499.5	498.0	500.0	499.5	498.5	2.0
15	501.0	500.0	498.0	500.5	500.0	3.0
16	502.5	501.5	502.0	500.5	500.5	2.0
17	499.5	500.5	500.0	499.5	499.5	1.0
18	499.0	498.5	498.0	500.0	498.0	2.0
19	499.0	498.0	500.5	501.0	501.0	3.0
20	501.5	499.5	500.0	500.5	502.0	2.5
21	501.0	500.5	502.0	502.5	502.5	2.0
22	501.5	502.5	502.5	501.5	502.0	1.0
23	499.5	502.0	500.0	500.5	502.0	2.5
24	498.5	499.0	499.0	500.5	500.0	2.0
25	500.0	499.5	498.5	500.0	500.5	2.0

FILLWT2

Sample	Fill Weights Accurate to 2.5 Grams					Range
1	500.0	500.0	502.5	500.0	500.0	2.5
2	500.0	500.0	500.0	500.0	500.0	0.0
3	500.0	500.0	500.0	500.0	500.0	0.0
4	497.5	500.0	497.5	497.5	500.0	2.5
5	500.0	500.0	500.0	500.0	500.0	0.0
6	502.5	500.0	497.5	500.0	500.0	5.0
7	500.0	500.0	502.5	502.5	500.0	2.5
8	497.5	500.0	500.0	497.5	500.0	2.5
9	500.0	500.0	497.5	500.0	502.5	5.0
10	500.0	500.0	500.0	500.0	500.0	0.0
11	500.0	505.0	502.5	500.0	500.0	5.0
12	500.0	500.0	500.0	500.0	500.0	0.0
13	500.0	500.0	497.5	500.0	500.0	2.5
14	500.0	500.0	500.0	500.0	500.0	0.0
15	502.5	502.5	502.5	500.0	502.5	2.5
16	500.0	500.0	500.0	500.0	500.0	0.0
17	497.5	497.5	497.5	497.5	497.5	0.0
18	500.0	500.0	500.0	500.0	500.0	0.0
19	495.0	497.5	500.0	500.0	500.0	5.0
20	500.0	502.5	500.0	500.0	502.5	2.5
21	500.0	500.0	500.0	500.0	500.0	0.0
22	500.0	500.0	500.0	500.0	500.0	0.0
23	500.0	500.0	500.0	500.0	500.0	0.0
24	497.5	497.5	500.0	497.5	497.5	2.5
25	500.0	500.0	497.5	500.0	500.0	2.5

Source: Adapted from Tricker, A., Coates, E. and Okell, E., "The Effects on the R-chart of Precision of Measurement," *Journal of Quality Technology*, Vol. 30, No. 3, July 1998, pp. 232–239.

that gives measurements for the same samples made with a scale that is accurate to only 2.5 grams. Throughout the time period over which the samples were drawn, it is known that the filling process was in statistical control with mean 500 grams and standard deviation 1 gram.

a. Construct an R-chart for the data that is accurate to .5 gram. Is the process under statistical control? Explain.   Yes

b. Given your answer to part **a,** is it appropriate to construct an $\bar{x}$-chart for the data? Explain.   Yes

c. Construct an R-chart for the data that is accurate to only 2.5 grams. What does it suggest about the stability of the filling process?   Out of control

d. Based on your answers to parts **a** and **c,** discuss the importance of the accuracy of measurement instruments in evaluating the stability of production processes.

14.6 A Control Chart for Monitoring the Proportion of Defectives Generated by a Process: The p-Chart

Among the dozens of different control charts that have been proposed by researchers and practitioners, the $\bar{x}$- and R-charts are by far the most popular for use in monitoring *quantitative* output variables such as time, length, and weight. Among the charts developed for use with *qualitative* output variables, the chart we introduce in this section is the most popular. Called the **p-chart**, it is used when the output variable is categorical (i.e., measured on a nominal scale). With the p-chart, the proportion, p, of units produced by the process that belong to a particular category (e.g., defective or nondefective; successful or unsuccessful; early, on-time, or late) can be monitored.

The p-chart is typically used to monitor the proportion of defective units produced by a process (i.e., the proportion of units that do not conform to specification). This proportion is used to characterize a process in the same sense that the mean and variance are used to characterize a process when the output variable is quantitative. Examples of process proportions that are monitored in industry include the proportion of billing errors made by credit card companies; the proportion of nonfunctional semiconductor chips produced; and the proportion of checks that a bank's magnetic ink character-recognition system is unable to read.

As is the case for the mean and variance, the process proportion can change over time. For example, it can drift upward or downward or jump to a new level. In such cases, the process is out of control. **As long as the process proportion remains constant, the process is in a state of statistical control.**

As with the other control charts presented in this chapter, the p-chart has a centerline and control limits that are determined from sample data. After k samples of size n are drawn from the process, each unit is classified (e.g., defective or nondefective), the proportion of defective units in each sample—$\hat{p}$—is calculated, the centerline and control limits are determined using this information, and the sample proportions are plotted on the p-chart. It is the variation in the $\hat{p}$'s over time that we monitor and interpret. Changes in the behavior of the $\hat{p}$'s signal changes in the process proportion, p.

The p-chart is based on the assumption that the number of defectives observed in each sample is a binomial random variable. What we have called the process proportion is really the binomial probability, p. (We discussed binomial random variables in Chapter 4.) When the process is in a state of statistical control, p remains constant over time. Variation in $\hat{p}$—as displayed on a p-chart—is used to judge whether p is stable.

To determine the centerline and control limits for the p-chart we need to know $\hat{p}$'s sampling distribution. We described the sampling distribution of $\hat{p}$ in Section 7.4. Recall that

$$\hat{p} = \frac{\text{Number of defective items in the sample}}{\text{Number of items in the sample}} = \frac{x}{n}$$

$$\mu_{\hat{p}} = p$$

$$\sigma_{\hat{p}} = \sqrt{\frac{p(1-p)}{n}}$$

and that for large samples $\hat{p}$ is approximately normally distributed. Thus, if p were known, the centerline would be p and the 3-sigma control limits would be $p \pm 3\sqrt{p(1-p)/n}$. However, since p is unknown, it must be estimated from the sample data. The appropriate estimator is $\bar{p}$, the overall proportion of defective units in the nk units sampled:

$$\bar{p} = \frac{\text{Total number of defective units in all } k \text{ samples}}{\text{Total number of units sampled}}$$

To calculate the control limits of the p-chart, substitute $\bar{p}$ for p in the preceding expression for the control limits, as illustrated in Figure 14.27.

Figure 14.27
p-Chart

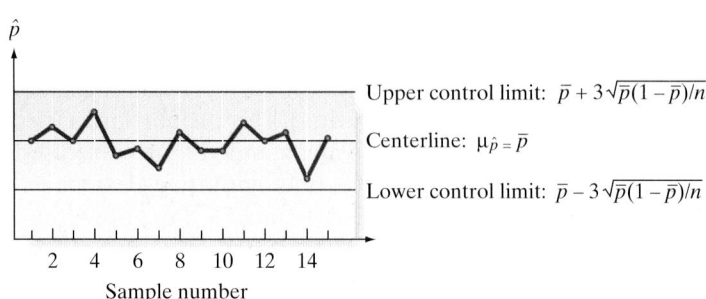

In constructing a p-chart it is advisable to use a much larger sample size than is typically used for $\bar{x}$- and R-charts. Most processes that are monitored in industry have relatively small process proportions, often less than .05 (i.e., less than 5% of output is nonconforming). In those cases, if a small sample size is used, say $n = 5$, samples drawn from the process would likely not contain any nonconforming output. As a result, most, if not all, $\hat{p}$'s would equal zero.

We present a rule of thumb that can be used to determine a sample size large enough to avoid this problem. This rule will also help protect against ending up with a negative lower control limit, a situation that frequently occurs when both p and n are small. See Montgomery (1991) or Duncan (1986) for further details.

Teaching Tip

The closer p_0 is to 0, the larger the sample size required.

Sample-Size Determination for Monitoring a Process Proportion

Choose n such that $n > \dfrac{9(1-p_0)}{p_0}$

where

n = Sample size

p_0 = An estimate (perhaps judgmental) of the process proportion p

For example, if p is thought to be about .05, the rule indicates that samples of at least size 171 should be used in constructing the p-chart:

$$n > \frac{9(1 - .05)}{.05} = 171$$

In the next three boxes we summarize how to construct a p-chart and its zone boundaries and how to interpret a p-chart.

Constructing a p-Chart: A Summary

1. Using a rational subgrouping strategy, collect at least 20 samples, each of size

$$n > \frac{9(1 - p_0)}{p_0}$$

where p_0 is an estimate of p, the proportion defective (i.e., nonconforming) produced by the process. p_0 can be determined from sample data (i.e., $\hat{p}$) or may be based on expert opinion.

2. For each sample, calculate $\hat{p}$, the proportion of defective units in the sample:

$$\hat{p} = \frac{\text{Number of defective items in the sample}}{\text{Number of items in the sample}}$$

3. Plot the centerline and control limits:

$$\text{Centerline: } \bar{p} = \frac{\text{Total number of defective units in all } k \text{ samples}}{\text{Total number of units in all } k \text{ samples}}$$

$$\text{Upper control limit: } \bar{p} + 3\sqrt{\frac{\bar{p}(1 - \bar{p})}{n}}$$

$$\text{Lower control limit: } \bar{p} - 3\sqrt{\frac{\bar{p}(1 - \bar{p})}{n}}$$

where k is the number of samples of size n and $\bar{p}$ is the overall proportion of defective units in the nk units sampled. $\bar{p}$ is an estimate of the unknown process proportion p.

4. Plot the k sample proportions on the control chart in the order that the samples were produced by the process.

As with the $\bar{x}$- and R-charts, the centerline and control limits should be developed using samples that were collected during a period in which the process was in control. Accordingly, when a p-chart is first constructed, the centerline and the control limits should be treated as *trial values* (see Section 14.4) and, if necessary, modified before being extended to the right on the control chart and used to monitor future process output.

Constructing Zone Boundaries for a p-Chart

$$\text{Upper A–B boundary: } \bar{p} + 2\sqrt{\frac{\bar{p}(1 - \bar{p})}{n}}$$

$$\text{Lower A–B boundary: } \bar{p} - 2\sqrt{\frac{\bar{p}(1 - \bar{p})}{n}}$$

(cont'd)

$$\text{Upper B–C boundary: } \bar{p} + \sqrt{\frac{\bar{p}(1-\bar{p})}{n}}$$

$$\text{Lower B–C boundary: } \bar{p} - \sqrt{\frac{\bar{p}(1-\bar{p})}{n}}$$

Note: When the lower control limit is negative, it should not be plotted on the control chart. However, the lower zone boundaries can still be plotted if they are nonnegative.

Teaching Tip

Again, point out the similarity in the construction and interpretation of the p-chart to both the x̄- and R-charts.

Interpreting a *p*-Chart

1. The **process is out of control** if one or more sample proportions fall beyond the control limits (Rule 1) or if any of the three patterns of variation described by Rules 2, 3, and 4 (Figure 14.21) are observed. Such signals indicate that one or more special causes of variation are influencing the process proportion, *p*. These causes should be identified and eliminated in order to bring the process into control.

2. The **process is treated as being in control** if none of the above noted out-of-control signals are observed. Processes that are in control should not be tampered with. However, if the level of variation is unacceptably high, common causes of variation should be identified and eliminated.

EXAMPLE 14.4   CREATING AND INTERPRETING A *p*-CHART

Problem   A manufacturer of auto parts is interested in implementing statistical process control in several areas within its warehouse operation. The manufacturer wants to begin with the order assembly process. Too frequently orders received by customers contain the wrong items or too few items.

For each order received, parts are picked from storage bins in the warehouse, labeled, and placed on a conveyor belt system. Since the bins are spread over a three-acre area, items that are part of the same order may be placed on different spurs of the conveyor belt system. Near the end of the belt system all spurs converge and a worker sorts the items according to the order they belong to. That information is contained on the labels that were placed on the items by the pickers.

The workers have identified three errors that cause shipments to be improperly assembled: (1) pickers pick from the wrong bin, (2) pickers mislabel items, and (3) the sorter makes an error.

The firm's quality manager has implemented a sampling program in which 90 assembled orders are sampled each day and checked for accuracy. An assembled order is considered nonconforming (defective) if it differs in any way from the order placed by the customer. To date, 25 samples have been evaluated. The resulting data are shown in Table 14.4.

a. Construct a *p*-chart for the order assembly operation.

b. What does the chart indicate about the stability of the process?

b. Out of control

c. Is it appropriate to use the control limits and centerline constructed in part **a** to monitor future process output?

c. No

WAREHOUSE

TABLE 14.4 Twenty-Five Samples of Size 90 from the Warehouse Order Assembly Process

Sample	Size	Defective Orders	Sample Proportion
1	90	12	.13333
2	90	6	.06666
3	90	11	.12222
4	90	8	.08888
5	90	13	.14444
6	90	14	.15555
7	90	12	.13333
8	90	6	.06666
9	90	10	.11111
10	90	13	.14444
11	90	12	.13333
12	90	24	.26666
13	90	23	.25555
14	90	22	.24444
15	90	8	.08888
16	90	3	.03333
17	90	11	.12222
18	90	14	.15555
19	90	5	.05555
20	90	12	.13333
21	90	18	.20000
22	90	12	.13333
23	90	13	.14444
24	90	4	.04444
25	90	6	.06666
Totals	2,250	292	

Solution **a.** The first step in constructing the *p*-chart after collecting the sample data is to calculate the sample proportion for each sample. For the first sample,

$$\hat{p} = \frac{\text{Number of defective items in the sample}}{\text{Number of items in the sample}} = \frac{12}{90} = .13333$$

All the sample proportions are displayed in Table 14.4. Next, calculate the proportion of defective items in the total number of items sampled:

$$\bar{p} = \frac{\text{Total number of defective items}}{\text{Total number of items sampled}} = \frac{292}{2,250} = .12978$$

The centerline is positioned at $\bar{p}$, and $\bar{p}$ is used to calculate the control limits:

$$\bar{p} \pm 3\sqrt{\frac{\bar{p}(1-\bar{p})}{n}} = .12978 \pm 3\sqrt{\frac{.12978(1-.12978)}{90}}$$

$$= .12978 \pm .10627$$

UCL: .23605

LCL: .02351

Figure 14.28

MINITAB *p*-chart for the
order assembly process

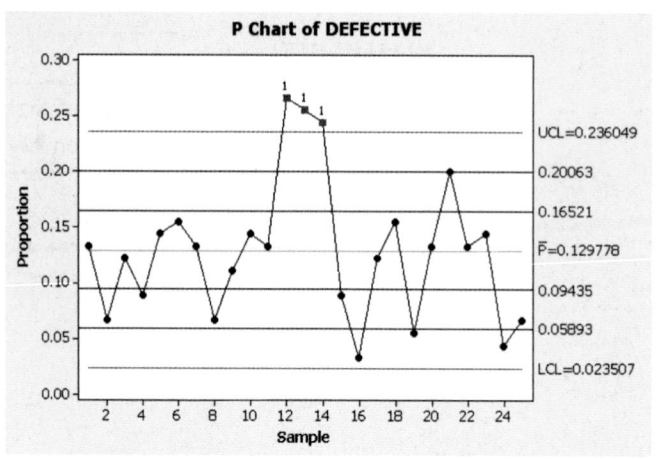

Suggested Exercise 14.35

After plotting the centerline and the control limits, plot the 25 sample proportions in the order of sampling and connect the points with straight
lines. The completed control chart, obtained using MINITAB, is shown in
Figure 14.28.

b. To assist our examination of the control chart, we add the 1- and 2-standard-
deviation zone boundaries. The boundaries are located by substituting
$\bar{p} = .12978$ into the following formulas:

$$Upper\ A-B\ boundary\!: \bar{p} + 2\sqrt{\frac{\bar{p}(1 - \bar{p})}{n}} = .20063$$

$$Lower\ A-B\ boundary\!: \bar{p} - 2\sqrt{\frac{\bar{p}(1 - \bar{p})}{n}} = .05893$$

$$Upper\ B-C\ boundary\!: \bar{p} + \sqrt{\frac{\bar{p}(1 - \bar{p})}{n}} = .16521$$

$$Lower\ B-C\ boundary\!: \bar{p} - \sqrt{\frac{\bar{p}(1 - \bar{p})}{n}} = .09435$$

Note that three of the sample proportions fall above the upper control limit
(Rule 1); thus, there is strong evidence that the process is out of control. None
of the nonrandom patterns of Rules 2, 3, and 4 (Figure 14.21) are evident. The
process proportion appears to have increased dramatically somewhere around
sample 12.

c. Because the process was apparently out of control during the period in which
sample data were collected to build the control chart, it is not appropriate to
continue using the chart. The control limits and centerline are not representative of the process when it is in control. The chart must be revised before it is
used to monitor future output.

In this case, the three out-of-control points were investigated and it was discovered that they occurred on days when a temporary sorter was working in
place of the regular sorter. Actions were taken to ensure that in the future
better-trained temporary sorters would be available.

Since the special cause of the observed variation was identified and eliminated, all sample data from the three days the temporary sorter was working

were dropped from the data set and the centerline and control limits were recalculated:

$$Centerline: \bar{p} = \frac{223}{1980} = .11263$$

$$Control\ limits: \bar{p} \pm 3\sqrt{\frac{\bar{p}(1-\bar{p})}{n}} = .11263 \pm 3\sqrt{\frac{.11263(.88737)}{90}}$$

$$= .11263 \pm .09997$$

$$UCL: .21259 \qquad LCL: .01266$$

The revised zones are calculated by substituting $\bar{p} = .11263$ in the following formulas:

$$Upper\ A\text{--}B\ boundary: \bar{p} + 2\sqrt{\frac{\bar{p}(1-\bar{p})}{n}} = .17927$$

$$Upper\ B\text{--}C\ boundary: \bar{p} + \sqrt{\frac{\bar{p}(1-\bar{p})}{n}} = .14595$$

$$Lower\ A\text{--}B\ boundary: \bar{p} - 2\sqrt{\frac{\bar{p}(1-\bar{p})}{n}} = .04598$$

$$Lower\ B\text{--}C\ boundary: \bar{p} - \sqrt{\frac{\bar{p}(1-\bar{p})}{n}} = .07931$$

The revised control chart appears in Figure 14.29. Notice that now all sample proportions fall within the control limits. These limits can now be treated as official, extended to the right on the chart, and used to monitor future orders.

Figure 14.29
Revised MINITAB
p-chart for the order
assembly process

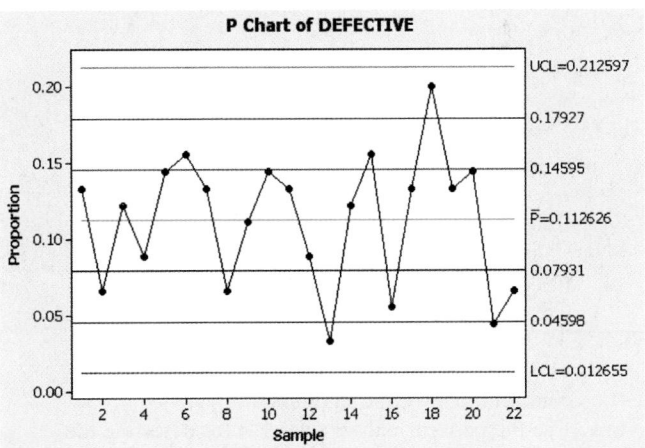

Now Work *Exercise 14.33*

Exercises 14.30–14.38

Learning the Mechanics

14.30 What characteristic of a process is a *p*-chart designed to monitor?   Proportion

14.31 The proportion of defective items generated by a manufacturing process is believed to be 8%. In constructing a *p*-chart for the process, determine how large the sample size should be to avoid ending up with a negative lower control limit.

14.32 To construct a *p*-chart for a manufacturing process, 25 samples of size 200 were drawn from the process. The number of defectives in each sample is listed below.

   LM14_32

Sample	Sample Size	Defectives
1	200	16
2	200	14
3	200	9
4	200	11
5	200	15
6	200	8
7	200	12
8	200	16
9	200	17
10	200	13
11	200	15
12	200	10
13	200	9
14	200	12
15	200	14
16	200	11
17	200	8
18	200	7
19	200	12
20	200	15
21	200	9
22	200	16
23	200	13
24	200	11
25	200	10

a. Calculate the proportion defective in each sample.
b. Calculate and plot $\bar{p}$ and the upper and lower control limits for the *p*-chart. $\bar{p} = .0606$
c. Calculate and plot the A, B, and C zone boundaries on the *p*-chart.
d. Plot the sample proportions on the *p*-chart and connect them with straight lines.
e. Use the pattern-analysis rules 1–4 for detecting the presence of special causes of variation (Figure 14.21) to determine whether the process is out of control.

14.33 To construct a *p*-chart, 20 samples of size 150 were drawn from a process. The proportion of defective items found in each of the samples is listed in the next table.

   LM14_33

Sample	Proportion Defective	Sample	Proportion Defective
1	.03	11	.07
2	.05	12	.04
3	.10	13	.06
4	.02	14	.05
5	.08	15	.07
6	.09	16	.06
7	.08	17	.07
8	.05	18	.02
9	.07	19	.05
10	.06	20	.03

a. Calculate and plot the centerline and the upper and lower control limits for the *p*-chart.
b. Calculate and plot the A, B, and C zone boundaries on the *p*-chart.
c. Plot the sample proportions on the *p*-chart.
d. Is the process under control? Explain.
e. Should the control limits and centerline of part **a** be used to monitor future process output? Explain.

14.34 In each of the following cases, use the sample size formula to determine a sample size large enough to avoid constructing a *p*-chart with a negative lower control limit.
   a. $p_0 = .01$ b. $p_0 = .05$ c. $p_0 = .10$ d. $p_0 = .20$

Applying the Concepts—Basic

14.35 A manufacturer produces micron chips for personal computers. From past experience the production manager believes that 1% of the chips are defective. The company collected a sample of the first 1,000 chips manufactured after 4:00 P.M. every other day for a month. The chips were analyzed for defects, then these data and MINITAB were used to construct the *p*-chart shown on page 971.
   a. From a statistical perspective, is a sample size of 1,000 adequate for constructing the *p*-chart? Explain.   Yes
   b. Calculate the chart's upper and lower control limits.
   c. What does the *p*-chart suggest about the presence of special causes during the time when the data were collected?   In control
   d. Critique the rational subgrouping strategy used by the disk manufacturer.

14.36 Goodstone Tire & Rubber Company is interested in monitoring the proportion of defective tires generated by the production process at its Akron, Ohio, production plant. The company's chief engineer believes that the proportion is about 7%. Because the tires are destroyed during the testing process, the company would like to keep the number of tires tested to a

MINITAB Output for Exercise 14.35

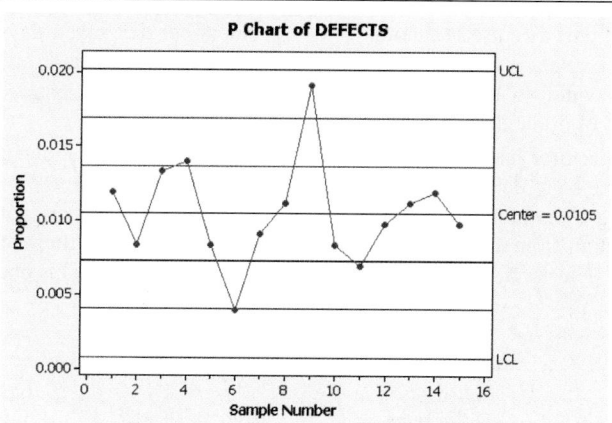

minimum. However, the engineer would also like to use a *p*-chart with a positive lower control limit. A positive lower control limit makes it possible to determine when the process has generated an unusually small proportion of defectives. Such an occurrence is good news and would signal the engineer to look for causes of the superior performance. That information can be used to improve the production process. Using the sample size formula, the chief engineer recommended that the company randomly sample and test 120 tires from each day's production. To date, 20 samples have been taken. The data are presented below.

a. Use the sample size formula to show how the chief engineer arrived at the recommended sample size of 120.

b. Construct a *p*-chart for the tire production process.

DEFTIRES

Sample	Sample Size	Defectives
1	120	11
2	120	5
3	120	4
4	120	8
5	120	10
6	120	13
7	120	9
8	120	8
9	120	10
10	120	11
11	120	10
12	120	12
13	120	8
14	120	6
15	120	10
16	120	5
17	120	10
18	120	10
19	120	3
20	120	8

c. What does the chart indicate about the stability of the process? Explain.   In control

d. Is it appropriate to use the control limits to monitor future process output? Explain.   Yes

e. Is the *p*-chart you constructed in part **b** capable of signaling hour-to-hour changes in *p*? Explain.

Applying the Concepts—Intermediate

14.37 Accurate typesetting is crucial to the production of high-quality newspapers. The editor of the Morristown *Daily Tribune*, a weekly publication with circulation of 27,000, has instituted a process for monitoring the performance of typesetters. Each week 100 paragraphs of the paper are randomly sampled and read for accuracy. The number of paragraphs with errors is recorded in the table below for each of the last 30 weeks.

TYPESET

Week	Paragraphs with Errors	Week	Paragraphs with Errors
1	2	16	2
2	4	17	3
3	10	18	7
4	4	19	3
5	1	20	2
6	1	21	3
7	13	22	7
8	9	23	4
9	11	24	3
10	0	25	2
11	3	26	2
12	4	27	0
13	2	28	1
14	2	29	3
15	8	30	4

Primary Source: Jerry Kinard, Western Carolina University.

Secondary Source: Render, B., and Stair, Jr., R. *Quantitative Analysis for Management,* 6th ed. Upper Saddle River, N. J.: Prentice Hall, 1997.

a. Construct a *p*-chart for the process.

b. Is the process under statistical control? Explain.

c. Should the control limits of part **a** be used to monitor future process output? Explain.   No

d. Suggest two methods that could be used to facilitate the diagnosis of causes of process variation.

14.38 A Japanese floppy disk manufacturer has a daily production rate of about 20,000 high density 3.5-inch diskettes. Quality is monitored by randomly sampling 200 finished disks every other hour from the production process and testing them for defects. If one or more defects are discovered, the disk is considered defective and is destroyed. The production process operates 20 hours per day, seven days a week. The table below reports data for the last three days of production.

a. Construct a *p*-chart for the diskette production process.

b. What does it indicate about the stability of the process? Explain.   Out of control

c. What advice can you give the manufacturer to assist them in their search for the special cause(s) of variation that is plaguing the process?

⊙ **DISKS**

Day	Hour	Number of Defectives	Day	Hour	Number of Defectives
1	1	13		6	3
	2	5		7	1
	3	2		8	2
	4	3		9	3
	5	2		10	1
	6	3	3	1	9
	7	1		2	5
	8	2		3	2
	9	1		4	1
	10	1		5	3
2	1	11		6	2
	2	6		7	4
	3	2		8	2
	4	3		9	1
	5	1		10	1

14.7 Diagnosing the Causes of Variation (Optional)

Statistical process control (SPC) consists of three major activities or phases: (1) monitoring process variation, (2) diagnosing causes of variation, and (3) eliminating those causes. A more detailed description of SPC is shown in Figure 14.30, which depicts SPC as a quality-improvement cycle. In the monitoring phase, statistical signals from the process are evaluated in order to uncover opportunities to improve the process. This is the phase we have dealt with in Sections 14.3–14.6. We turn our attention now to the diagnosis phase.

The diagnosis phase is the critical link in the SPC improvement cycle. The monitoring phase simply identifies *whether* problems exist; the diagnosis phase identifies *what* the problems are. If the monitoring phase detected the presence of special causes of variation (i.e., an out-of-control signal was observed on a control chart), the diagnosis phase is concerned with tracking down the underlying cause or causes. If no special causes were detected in the monitoring phase (i.e., the process is under statistical control) and further improvement in the process is desired, the diagnosis phase concentrates on uncovering common causes of variation.

It is important to recognize that the achievement of process improvement requires more than the application of statistical tools such as control charts. This is particularly evident in the diagnosis phase. The diagnosis of causes of variation requires expert knowledge about the process in question. Just as you would go to a physician to diagnose a pain in your back, you would turn to people who work in the

Figure 14.30

SPC viewed as a quality-improvement cycle

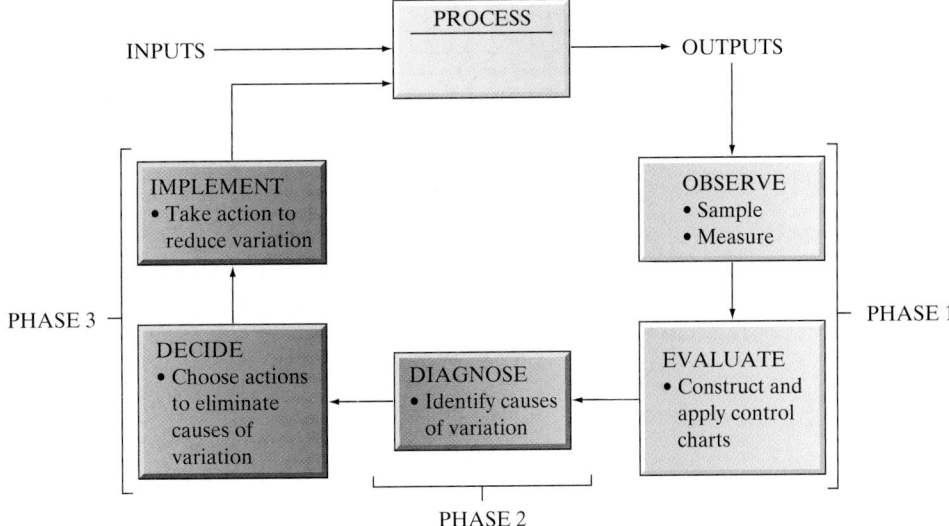

process or to engineers or analysts with process expertise to help you diagnose the causes of process variation.

Several methods have been developed for assisting process experts with process diagnosis, including *flowcharting* (see Statistics in Action 14.2) and the simple but powerful graphical tool called *Pareto analysis* (Chapter 2). Another graphical method, the **cause-and-effect diagram,** is described in this section. A fourth methodology, *experimental design,* is the topic of Chapter 14.

The cause-and-effect diagram was developed by Kaoru Ishikawa of the University of Tokyo in 1943. As a result, it is also known as an *Ishikawa diagram.* The cause-and-effect diagram facilitates the construction of causal chains that explain the occurrence of events, problems, or conditions. It is often constructed through brainstorming sessions involving a small group of process experts. It has been employed for decades by Japanese firms, but was not widely applied in the United States until the mid-1980s.

The basic framework of the cause-and-effect diagram is shown in Figure 14.31. In the right-hand box in the figure, we record the effect whose cause(s) we want to diagnose.

For instance, GOAL/QPC (a Massachusetts-based TQM consulting group) used the cause-and-effect diagram in Figure 14.32 to demonstrate why pizzas are delivered late on Fridays and Saturdays. As a second example, Figure 14.33 displays the reasons for high variation in the fill weights of 20-pound bags of dry dog food.

Figure 14.31

The basic framework for a cause-and-effect diagram

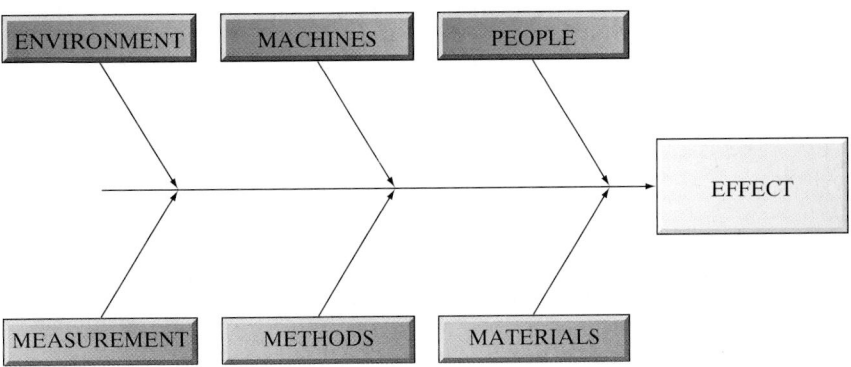

Figure 14.32

Cause-and-effect diagram for late pizza deliveries

Source: Reprinted with permission from The Memory Jogger™ II, GOAL/QPC, 13 Branch Street, Methuan, Massachusetts, 1994, p. 27.

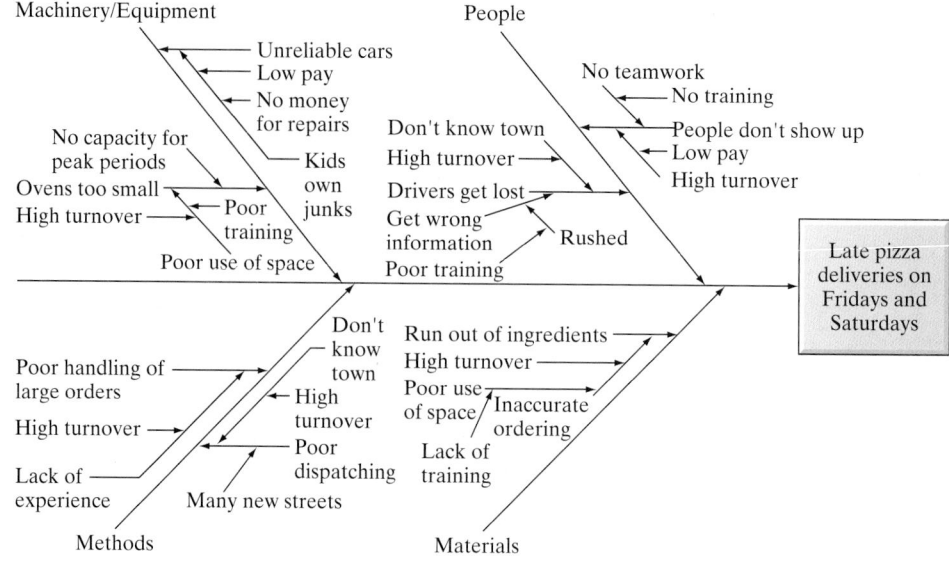

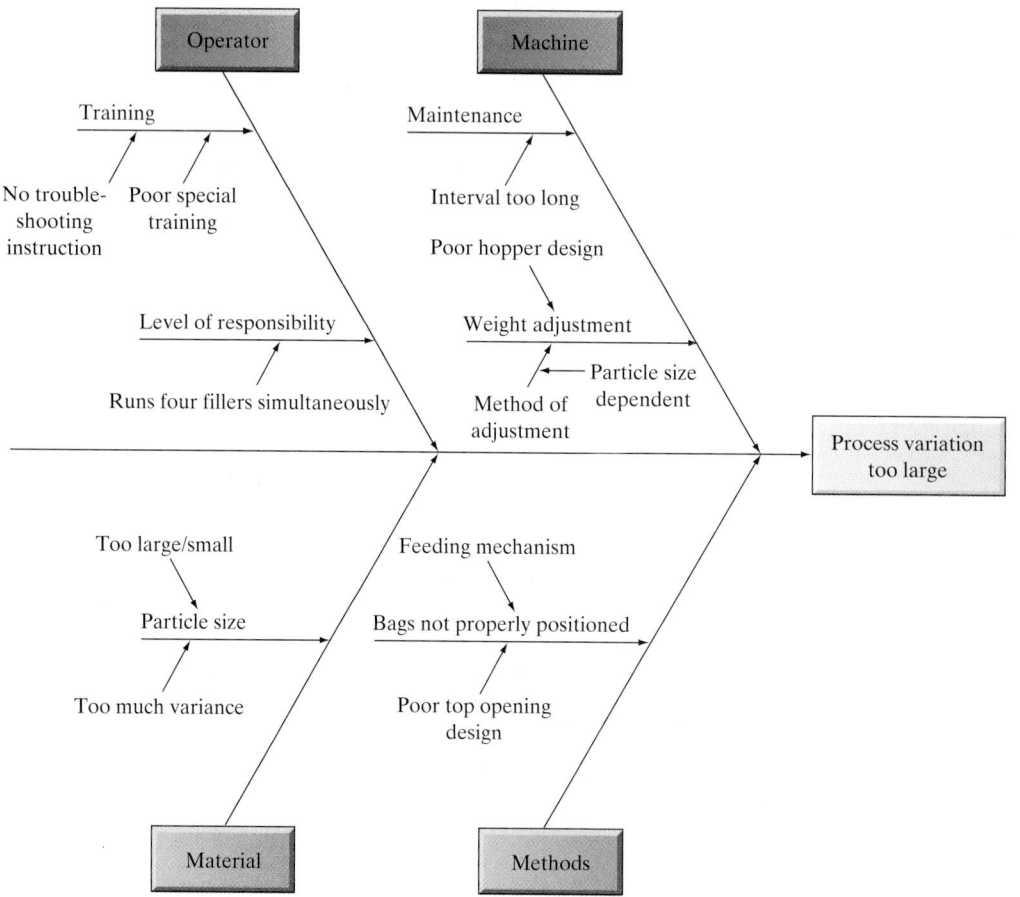

Figure 14.33

Cause-and-effect diagram for the filling process for 20-lb. bags of dog food

Source: R. E. DeVor, T. Chang, and J. W. Southerland, Statistical Quality Design and Control, New York, Macmillan, 1992. © 1992. Reprinted by permission of Prentice Hall, Inc., Upper Saddle River, NJ.

Examining Figure 14.31, we see the branches of the cause-and-effect diagram, which represent the major factors that influence the process and that could be responsible for the effect. These are often taken to be the six universal sources of process variation that we described in Section 14.1: people, machines, materials, methods, measurement, and environment. Notice that in the examples of Figures 14.32 and 14.33 these categories were tailored to fit the process in question. The set of categories must be broad enough to include virtually all possible factors that could influence the process. It is less important how many categories are used or how you label the categories.

The cause-and-effect diagram is constructed using effect-to-cause reasoning. That is, you begin by specifying the effect of interest and then move backward to identify *potential* causes of the effect. After a potential cause has been identified, you treat it as an effect and try to find its cause, and so forth. The result is a **causal chain.** A completed cause-and-effect diagram typically contains many causal chains. These chains help us to track down causes whose eradication will reduce, improve, or eliminate the effect in question.

After setting up the basic framework for the cause-and-effect diagram and recording the effect of interest in the box on the right, you construct the causal chains, proceeding backward from general potential causes to increasingly specific causes. Begin by choosing one of the universal cause categories—say, people—and asking, "What factors related to people could cause the effect in question?" In the pizza delivery example of Figure 14.32, two factors were identified: (1) drivers not showing up for work and (2) drivers getting lost. Each of these causes is written on a twig of the People branch. Next, each cause is treated as an effect and an attempt is made to identify its cause. That is, we look for subcauses. For example, driver absenteeism was blamed on (1) high turnover and (2) no teamwork. The high turnover, in turn, was blamed on low pay, while lack of teamwork was blamed on insufficient training. Thus, the "No show" twig has both a "High turnover" twig and a "No teamwork" twig attached to it; and, each of these twigs has a cause twig attached. Multiple causal chains like this should be constructed for each branch of the cause-and-effect diagram.

Once completed, the various causal chains of the cause-and-effect diagram must be evaluated (often subjectively) to identify one or more factors thought most likely to be causes of the effect in question. Then actions can be chosen and implemented (see Figure 14.30) to eliminate the causes and improve the process.

Besides facilitating process diagnosis, cause-and-effect diagrams serve to document the causal factors that may potentially affect a process and to communicate that information to others in the organization. The cause-and-effect diagram is a very flexible tool that can be applied in a variety of situations. It can be used as a formal part of the SPC improvement cycle, as suggested above, or simply as a means of investigating the causes of organizational problems, events, or conditions. It can also help select the appropriate process variables to monitor with control charts.

14.8 Capability Analysis (Optional)

In the previous four sections, we pointed out that if a process were in statistical control, but the level of variation was unacceptably high, common causes of variation should be identified and eliminated. This was illustrated in Figure 14.13. In this optional section, we describe a methodology that can be used to help determine when such variation is unacceptably high. The methodology is called **capability analysis.** As we have seen, the achievement of process stability is vitally important to

Figure 14.34

Output distributions of six different in-control processes, where LSL = lower specification limit and USL = upper specification limit

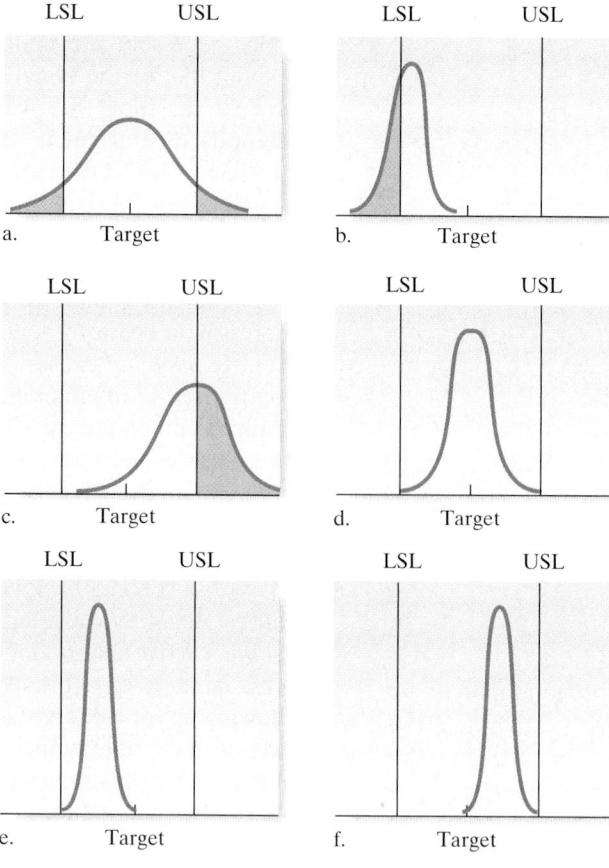

Teaching Tip

Capability analysis considers the process variation in a stable process as it relates to the needs of the users of the process.

process improvement efforts. But it is not an end in itself. A process may be in control, but still not be capable of producing output that is acceptable to customers.

To see this, consider Figure 14.34. The figure displays six different in-control processes. Recall that if a process is under statistical control, its output distribution does not change over time and the process can be characterized by a single probability distribution, as in each of the panels of the figure. The upper and lower specification limits for the output of each of the six processes are also indicated on each panel, as is the target value for the output variable. Recall from Definition 14.8 that the specification limits are boundary points that define the acceptable values for an output variable.

The processes of panels **a, b,** and **c** produce a high percentage of items that are outside the specification limits. None of these processes is *capable* of satisfying its customers. In panel **a,** the process is centered on the target value, but the variation due to common causes is too high. In panel **b,** the variation is low relative to the width of the specification limits, but the process is off-center. In panel **c,** both problems exist: the variation is too high and the process is off-center. Thus, bringing a process into statistical control is not sufficient to guarantee the capability of the process.

All three processes in panels **d, e,** and **f** are capable. In each case, the process distribution fits comfortably between the specification limits. Virtually all of the individual items produced by these processes would be acceptable. However, any significant tightening of the specification limits—whether by customers or internal managers or engineers—would result in the production of unacceptable output and necessitate the initiation of process improvement activities to restore the process' capability. Further, even though a process is capable, continuous improvement of a process requires constant improvement of its capability.

When a process is known to be in control, the most direct way to assess its capability is to construct a frequency distribution (e.g. dot plot, histogram, or stem-and-leaf display) for a large sample of individual measurements (usually 50 or more) from the process. Then, add the specification limits and the target value for the output variable on the graph. This is called a **capability analysis diagram.** It is a simple visual tool for assessing process capability.

The MINITAB printout shown in Figure 14.35 is a capability analysis diagram for the paint-filling process found to be under statistical control in Examples 14.1 and 14.2. You can see that the process is roughly centered on the target of 10 pounds of paint, but that a large number of paint cans fall outside the specification limits. This tells us that the process is not capable of satisfying customer requirements.

Most quality-management professionals and statisticians agree that the capability analysis diagram is the best way to describe the performance of an in-control process. However, many companies have found it useful to have a numerical measure of capability. The ability to summarize capability in a single number has the advantages of convenience, simplicity, and ease of communication. However, it also has the major disadvantage of potentially misleading those who use it. Just as when you characterize a data set by its mean and ignore its variation, the information you provide to your audience is incomplete and may adversely affect their actions and decisions. (A more thorough discussion about the dangers of numerical measures of capability is presented later in this section.)

There are several different approaches to quantifying capability. We will briefly describe two of them. The first (and most direct) consists of counting the number of items that fall outside the specification limits in the capability analysis diagram and reporting the percentage of such items in the sample. The original data set or a graphical technique that displays the individual measurements—such as a stem-and-leaf display or a dot plot—can be used to obtain the needed count. Or, you can use the capability analysis option of a statistical software package.

The desired information for the paint data is provided in the lower left corner of the MINITAB printout, Figure 14.35. You can see that 24% of the 125 paint cans

Figure 14.35
MINITAB capability analysis diagram for the paint-filling process

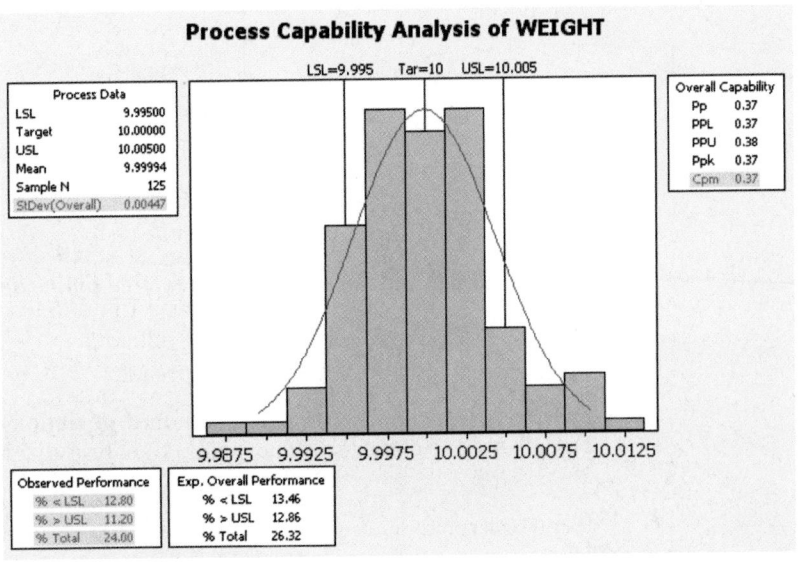

Teaching Tip
Point out that this percentage is only an estimate. Sampling variation will cause the actual percentage to be higher or lower. Interpret with caution.

fall outside the specification limits (12.8% below 9.995 and 11.2% above 10.005). Thus, 24% of the 125 cans in the sample, (i.e., 30 cans) are unacceptable.

When this percentage is used to characterize the capability of the process the implication is that over time, if this process remains in control, roughly 24% of the paint cans will be unacceptable. Remember, however, that this percentage is only an estimate, a sample statistic, not a known parameter. It is based on a sample of size 125 and is subject to both sampling error and measurement error. We discussed such percentages and proportions in detail in Chapter 7.

If it is known that the process follows approximately a normal distribution, as is often the case, a similar approach to quantifying process capability can be used. In this case, the mean and standard deviation of the sample of measurements used to construct the capability analysis diagram can be taken as estimates of the mean and standard deviation of the process. Then, the fraction of items that would fall outside the specification limits can be found by solving for the associated area under the normal curve, as we did in Chapter 5. As we said above, if you use this percentage to characterize process capability, remember that it is only an estimate, and is subject to sampling error.

The second approach to measuring capability is to construct a **capability index.** Several such indexes have been developed. We will describe one used for stable processes that are centered on the target value. It is known as the C_p **index.***

When the capability analysis diagram indicates that the process is centered, capability can be measured through a comparison of the distance between the upper specification limit (USL) and the lower specification limit (LSL), called the **specification spread,** and the spread of the output distribution. The spread of the output distribution—called the **process spread**—is defined as 6σ and is estimated by $6s$, where s is the standard deviation of the sample of measurements used to construct the capability analysis diagram. These two distances are illustrated in Figure 14.36. The ratio of these distances is the capability index known as C_p.

Figure 14.36
Process spread versus specification spread

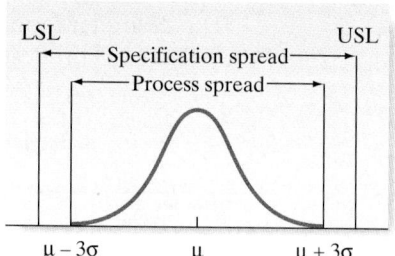

DEFINITION 14.10

The **capability index** for a process *centered on the desired mean* is

$$C_p = \frac{\text{(Specification spread)}}{\text{(Process spread)}} = \frac{(USL - LSL)}{6\sigma}$$

where σ is estimated by s, the standard deviation of the sample of measurements used to construct the capability analysis diagram.

***For off-center processes, its sister index, C_{pk}, is used. Consult the chapter references for a description of C_{pk}.**

Teaching Tip
"Capable" must be defined based on the distribution of the process. The definition given is based on a normal distribution for the outcomes of the process.

Interpretation of Capability Index, C_p

C_p summarizes the performance of a stable, centered process relative to the specification limits. It indicates the extent to which the output of the process falls within the specification limits.

1. If $C_p = 1$ (specification spread = process spread), process is capable
2. If $C_p > 1$ (specification spread > process spread), process is capable
3. If $C_p < 1$ (specification spread < process spread), process is not capable

If the process follows a normal distribution,

$C_p = 1.00$ means about 2.7 units per 1,000 will be unacceptable
$C_p = 1.33$ means about 63 units per million will be unacceptable
$C_p = 1.67$ means about .6 units per million will be unacceptable
$C_p = 2.00$ means about 2 units per billion will be unacceptable

In manufacturing applications where the process follows a normal distribution (approximately), managers typically require a C_p of at least 1.33. With a C_p of 1.33 the process spread takes up only 75% of the specification spread, leaving a little wiggle room in case the process moves off center.

EXAMPLE 14.5

FINDING AND INTERPRETING C_p

Problem   Let's return to the paint-filling process analyzed in Examples 14.1 and 14.3. Using 25 samples of size 5 (125 measurements), we constructed $\bar{x}$- and R-charts and concluded that the process was in a state of statistical control. The specification limits for the acceptable amount of paint fill per can are shown in the capability analysis diagram of Figure 14.35.

    a. Is it appropriate to construct a capability index for this process?   Yes

b. $C_p = .374$

    b. Find C_p for this process and interpret its value.

Solution   **a.** Since the process is stable (under control), its output distribution can be characterized by the same probability distribution at any point in time (see Figure 14.12). Accordingly, it is appropriate to assess the performance of the process using that distribution and related performance measures such as C_p.

    b. From Definition 14.10,

Suggested Exercise 14.50

$$C_p = \frac{(\text{USL} - \text{LSL})}{6\sigma}$$

From the capability analysis diagram of Figure 14.35, we can see that the upper and lower specification limits are 10.005 pounds and 9.995 pounds, respectively. But what is σ? Since the output distribution will never be known exactly, neither will σ, the standard deviation of the output distribution. It must be estimated with s, the standard deviation of a large sample drawn from the process. In this case, we use the standard deviation of the 125 measurements used to construct the capability analysis diagram. This value, $s = .00447$, is highlighted in the upper left of the MINITAB printout, Figure 14.35. Then

$$C_p = \frac{(10.005 - 9.995)}{6(.00447)} = \frac{.01}{.02682} = .373$$

(This value of C_p is highlighted in the upper right corner of Figure 14.35.) Since C_p is less than 1.0, the process is not capable. The process spread is wider than the specification spread.

Look Back The C_p statistic confirms the results shown on the capability analysis diagram (Figure 14.35), where 24% of the sampled cans were found to be unacceptable.

| Now Work | *Exercise 14.48* |

■ ■ ■

For two reasons, great care should be exercised in using and interpreting C_p. First, like the sample standard deviation, s, used in its computation, C_p is a statistic and is subject to sampling error. That is, the value of C_p will change from sample to sample. Thus, unless you understand the magnitude of the sampling error, you should be cautious in comparing the C_p's of different processes. Second, C_p does not reflect the shape of the output distribution. Distributions with different shapes can have the same C_p value. Accordingly, C_p should not be used in isolation, but in conjunction with the capability analysis diagram.

If a capability analysis study indicates that an in-control process is not capable, as in the paint-filling example, it is usually variation, rather than off-centeredness, that is the culprit. Thus, capability is typically achieved or restored by seeking out and eliminating common causes of variation.

Exercises 14.39–14.50

Learning the Mechanics

14.39 Explain why it is inappropriate to conduct a capability analysis study for a process that is not in statistical control.

14.40 Explain the difference between process spread and specification spread.

14.41 Describe two different ways to assess the capability of a process.

14.42 Why is it recommended to use and interpret C_p in conjunction with a capability analysis diagram rather than in isolation?

14.43 For a process that is in control and follows a normal distribution, interpret each of the following C_p values:
a. 1.00 **b.** 1.33 **c.** .50 **d.** 2.00

14.44 Find the specification spread for each of the following:
a. USL = 19.65, LSL = 12.45   7.20
b. USL = .0010, LSL = .0008   .0002

c. USL = 1.43, LSL = 1.27   .16
d. USL = 490, LSL = 486   4

14.45 Find (or estimate) the process spread for each of the following.
a. $\sigma = 21$ 126
b. $\sigma = 5.2$ 31.2
c. $s = 110.06$ 660.36
d. $s = .0024$ .0144

14.46 Find the value of C_p for each of the following situations:
a. USL = 1.0065, LSL = 1.0035, $s = .0005$ 1
b. USL = 22, LSL = 21, $s = .2$ .8333
c. USL = 875, LSL = 870, $s = .75$ 1.111

Applying the Concepts—Basic

14.47 An in-control, centered process that follows a normal distribution has a $C_p = 2.0$. How many standard deviations away from the process mean is the upper specification limit? 6σ

14.48 A process is in control with a normally distributed output distribution with mean 1,000 and standard deviation 100. The upper and lower specification limits for the process are 1,020 and 980, respectively.
  a. Assuming no changes in the behavior of the process, what percentage of the output will be unacceptable? .8414
  b. Find and interpret the C_p value of the process.

Applying the Concepts—Intermediate

14.49 The table below shows the data on weights of cereal boxes from Exercise 14.13. Assume the specification limits for the weights are USL = 24.2 ounces and LSL = 23.8 ounces.
  a. Assuming the process is under control, construct a capability analysis diagram for the process.

CEREAL

Day	Weight of Cereal Boxes (ounces)				
1	24.02	23.91	24.12	24.06	24.13
2	23.89	23.98	24.01	24.00	23.91
3	24.11	24.02	23.99	23.79	24.04
4	24.06	23.98	23.95	24.01	24.11
5	23.81	23.90	23.99	24.07	23.96
6	23.87	24.12	24.07	24.01	23.99
7	23.88	24.00	24.05	23.97	23.97
8	24.01	24.03	23.99	23.91	23.98
9	24.06	24.02	23.80	23.79	24.07
10	23.96	23.99	24.03	23.99	24.01
11	24.10	23.90	24.11	23.98	23.95
12	24.01	24.07	23.93	24.09	23.98
13	24.14	24.07	24.08	23.98	24.02
14	23.91	24.04	23.89	24.01	23.95
15	24.03	24.04	24.01	23.98	24.10
16	23.94	24.07	24.12	24.00	24.02
17	23.88	23.94	23.91	24.06	24.07
18	24.11	23.99	23.90	24.01	23.98
19	24.05	24.04	23.97	24.08	23.95
20	24.02	23.96	23.95	23.89	24.04

b. Is the process capable? Support your answer with a numerical measure of capability.

14.50 Refer to Exercise 14.14 (p. 950). The data on lengths of bolts used in military aircraft are reproduced below.

BOLTS

Hour	Bolt Lengths (centimeters)			
1	37.03	37.08	36.90	36.88
2	36.96	37.04	36.85	36.98
3	37.16	37.11	36.99	37.01
4	37.20	37.06	37.02	36.98
5	36.81	36.97	36.91	37.10
6	37.13	36.96	37.01	36.89
7	37.07	36.94	36.99	37.00
8	37.01	36.91	36.98	37.12
9	37.17	37.03	36.90	37.01
10	36.91	36.99	36.87	37.11
11	36.88	37.10	37.07	37.03
12	37.06	36.98	36.90	36.99
13	36.91	37.22	37.12	37.03
14	37.08	37.07	37.10	37.04
15	37.03	37.04	36.89	37.01
16	36.95	36.98	36.90	36.99
17	36.97	36.94	37.14	37.10
18	37.11	37.04	36.98	36.91
19	36.88	36.99	37.01	36.94
20	36.90	37.15	37.09	37.00
21	37.01	36.96	37.05	36.96
22	37.09	36.95	36.93	37.12
23	37.00	37.02	36.95	37.04
24	36.99	37.07	36.90	37.02
25	37.10	37.03	37.01	36.90

Management has specified upper and lower specification limits of 37 cm and 35 cm, respectively.
  a. Assuming the process is in control, construct a capability analysis diagram for the process.
  b. Find the percentage of bolts that fall outside the specification limits. 51%
  c. Find the capability index, C_p. 3.997
  d. Is the process capable? Explain. Yes

Quick Review

Key Terms

Note: Starred (*) items are from the optional sections in this chapter.

A zone 939
B zone 938
capability analysis* 975
capability analysis diagram* 977
capability index* 978
causal chain 975
conform to specs 933

cause-and-effect diagram* 973
centerline 921
common causes of variation 927
control chart 920
control limits 929
C zone 938
in control 923
individuals chart 933
lower control limit 930
nonconforming 933
oscillating sequence 921

out of control 923
output distribution 923
p-chart 963
pattern-analysis rules 939
process 916
process spread* 978
process variation 926
quality 915
R-chart 952
random behavior 926
rare event 930

Key Formulas

Control Chart	Centerline	Control Limits (Lower, Upper)	A–B Boundary (Lower, Upper)	B–C Boundary (Lower, Upper)	
$\bar{x}$-chart	$\bar{\bar{x}} = \dfrac{\sum_{i=1}^{k} \bar{x}_i}{k}$	$\bar{\bar{x}} \pm A_2\bar{R}$ or $\bar{\bar{x}} \pm 2\dfrac{(\bar{R}/d_2)}{\sqrt{n}}$	$\bar{\bar{x}} \pm \dfrac{2}{3}(A_2\bar{R})$ or $\bar{\bar{x}} \pm \dfrac{(\bar{R}/d_2)}{\sqrt{n}}$	$\bar{\bar{x}} \pm \dfrac{1}{3}(A_2\bar{R})$	938–939
R-chart	$\bar{R} = \dfrac{\sum_{i=1}^{k} R_i}{k}$	$(\bar{R}D_3, \bar{R}D_4)$	$\bar{R} \pm 2d_3\left(\dfrac{\bar{R}}{d_2}\right)$	$\bar{R} \pm d_3\left(\dfrac{\bar{R}}{d_2}\right)$	954–955
p-chart	$\bar{p} = \dfrac{\text{Total number defectives}}{\text{Total number units sampled}}$	$\bar{p} \pm 3\sqrt{\dfrac{\bar{p}(1-\bar{p})}{n}}$	$\bar{p} \pm 2\sqrt{\dfrac{\bar{p}(1-\bar{p})}{n}}$	$\bar{p} \pm \sqrt{\dfrac{\bar{p}(1-\bar{p})}{n}}$	965–966

$n > \dfrac{9(1 - p_0)}{p_0}$ where p_0 estimates the true proportion defective

USL − LSL

$6s \approx 6s$

(USL − LSL)$/6\sigma$

Sample size for p-chart 964

Specification spread* 978

Process spread* 978

C_p index* 978

Chapter Summary Notes

- **Total quality management (TQM)** — involves the management of quality in all phases of a business.
- **Eight dimensions of quality:** (1) performance, (2) features, (3) reliability, (4) conformance, (5) durability, (6) serviceability, (7) aesthetics, and (8) reputation and image.
- **Six major sources of process variation:** (1) people, (2) machines, (3) materials, (4) methods, (5) measurement, and (6) environment.
- A process **in statistical control** has an output distribution that does not change over time; if it does change, the process is **out of control**.
- **Statistical process control (SPC)** — the process of monitoring and eliminating variation to keep a process in control.
- Two causes of variation — **common causes** and **special (assignable) causes**.
- **Specification limits** — define acceptable values for an output variable.

- **Rational subgroups** — samples designed to make it more likely that process changes will occur between (rather than within) subgroups.
- A control chart to monitor the **process mean** — the **x-chart**.
- A control chart to monitor **process variation** — the **R-chart**.
- A control chart to monitor the **proportion noncomforming** — the **p-chart**.
- **Pattern-analysis rules** — used to determine whether a process is in or out of control.
- Interpret the x-chart only after establishing that the process variation is in control with the R-chart.
- **Cause-and-effect diagram** — facilitate process diagnosis and document causal factors in a process.
- **Capability analysis** — used to determine if process is capable of satisfying its customers.
- **Capability index** (C_p) — summarizes the performance of a process relative to the specification limits.

Language Lab

Note: Starred (*) terms are from the optional sections in this chapter.

Symbol	Pronunciation	Description
LCL	L-C-L	Lower control limit
UCL	U-C-L	Upper control limit
$\bar{\bar{x}}$	x-bar-bar	Average of the sample means
$\bar{R}$	R-bar	Average of the sample ranges
A_2	A-two	Constant obtained from Table XII, Appendix B
D_3	D-three	Constant obtained from Table XII, Appendix B
D_4	D-four	Constant obtained from Table XII, Appendix B
d_2	d-two	Constant obtained from Table XII, Appendix B
d_3	d-three	Constant obtained from Table XII, Appendix B
$\hat{p}$	p-hat	Estimated number of defectives in sample
$\bar{p}$	p-bar	Overall proportion of defective units in all nk samples
p_0	p-naught	Estimated overall proportion of defectives for entire process
SPC	S-P-C	Statistical process control
USL*	U-S-L	Upper specification limit
LSL*	L-S-L	Lower specification limit
C_p*	C-p	Capability index

Supplementary Exercises 14.51–14.76

Note: Starred (*) exercises refer to the optional sections in this chapter.

Learning the Mechanics

14.51 Define *quality* and list its important dimensions.

14.52 What is a system? Give an example of a system with which you are familiar, and describe its inputs, outputs, and transformation process.

14.53 What is a process? Give an example of an organizational process and a personal process.

14.54 Select a personal process that you would like to better understand or to improve and construct a flowchart for it.

14.55 Describe the six major sources of process variation.

14.56 Suppose all the output of a process over the last year were measured and found to be within the specification limits required by customers of the process. Should you worry about whether the process is in statistical control? Explain.   Yes

14.57 *Select a problem, event, or condition whose cause or causes you would like to diagnose. Construct a cause-and-effect diagram that would facilitate your diagnosis.

*14.58 In estimating a population mean μ using a sample mean $\bar{x}$, why is it likely that $\bar{x} \neq \mu$? Construct a cause-and-effect diagram for the effect $\bar{x} \neq \mu$.

*14.59 Construct a cause-and-effect diagram to help explain why customer waiting time at the drive-in window of a fast-food restaurant is a variable.

14.60 Processes that are in control are predictable; out-of-control processes are not. Explain.

14.61 Compare and contrast special and common causes of variation.

14.62 Explain the role of the control limits of a control chart.

14.63 Explain the difference between control limits and specification limits.

*14.64 Should control charts be used to monitor a process that is both in control and capable? Why or why not?

*14.65 Under what circumstances is it appropriate to use C_p to assess capability?

14.66 A process is under control and follows a normal distribution with mean 100 and standard deviation 10. In constructing a standard $\bar{x}$-chart for this process, the control limits are set 3 standard deviations from the mean—that is, $100 \pm 3(10/\sqrt{n})$. The probability of observing an $\bar{x}$ outside the control limits is $(.00135 + .00135) = .0027$. Suppose it is desired to construct a control chart that signals the presence of a potential special cause of variation for less extreme values of $\bar{x}$. How many standard deviations from the mean should the control limits be set such that the probability of the chart falsely indicating the presence of a special cause of variation is .10 rather than .0027?

Applying the Concepts—Basic

14.67 Consider the following time series data for the weight of a manufactured product.

⊙ **TIMEWT**

Order of Production	Weight (grams)	Order of Production	Weight (grams)
1	6.0	9	6.5
2	5.0	10	9.0
3	7.0	11	3.0
4	5.5	12	11.0
5	7.0	13	3.0
6	6.0	14	12.0
7	8.0	15	2.0
8	5.0		

a. Construct a time series plot. Be sure to connect the points and add a centerline. $\bar{x} = 6.4$
b. Which type of variation pattern in Figure 14.6 best describes the pattern revealed by your plot?

14.68 The accompanying length measurements were made on 20 consecutively produced pencils.

⊙ **PENCIL**

Order of Production	Length (inches)	Order of Production	Length (inches)
1	7.47	11	7.57
2	7.48	12	7.56
3	7.51	13	7.55
4	7.49	14	7.58
5	7.50	15	7.56
6	7.51	16	7.59
7	7.48	17	7.57
8	7.49	18	7.55
9	7.48	19	7.56
10	7.50	20	7.58

a. Construct a time series plot. Be sure to connect the plotted points and add a centerline.
b. Which type of variation pattern in Figure 14.6 best describes the pattern shown in your plot?

14.69 Use the appropriate pattern-analysis rules to determine whether the process being monitored by the control chart shown next is under the influence of special causes of variation.

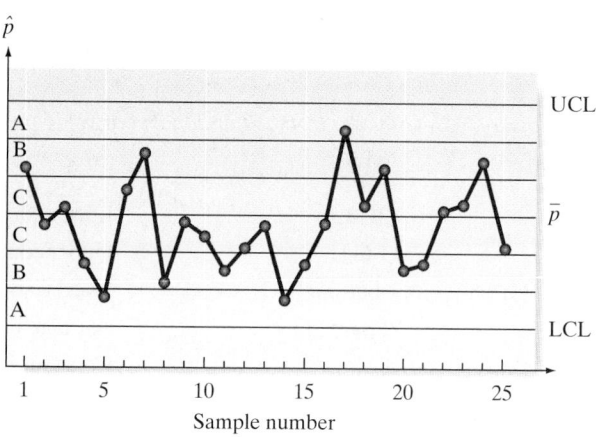

Applying the Concepts—Intermediate

14.70 A company that manufactures plastic molded parts believes it is producing an unusually large number of defects. To investigate this suspicion, each shift drew seven random samples of 200 parts, visually inspected each part to determine whether it was defective, and tallied the primary type of defect present (Hart, 1992). These data are presented in the table at the top of page 985.
   a. From a statistical perspective, are the number of samples and the sample size of 200 adequate for constructing a p-chart for these data? Explain.   Yes
   b. Construct a p-chart for this manufacturing process.
   c. Should the control limits be used to monitor future process output? Explain.   No
   d. Suggest a strategy for identifying the special causes of variation that may be present.

14.71 A hospital has used control charts continuously since 1978 to monitor the quality of its nursing care. A set of 363 scoring criteria, or standards, are applied at critical points in the patients' stay to determine whether the patients are receiving beneficial nursing care. Auditors regularly visit each hospital unit, sample two patients, and evaluate their care. The auditors review patients' records; interview the patients, the nurse, and the head nurse; and observe the nursing care given (*International Journal of Quality and Reliability Management*, Vol. 9, 1992). The data in the table on page 985 were collected over a three-month period for a newly opened unit of the hospital.
   a. Construct an R-chart for the nursing care process.
   b. Construct an $\bar{x}$-chart for the nursing care process.
   c. Should the control charts of parts **a** and **b** be used to monitor future process output? Explain.
   d. The hospital would like all quality scores to exceed 335 (their specification limit). Over the three-month periods, what proportion of the sampled patients received care that did not conform to the hospital's requirements?   .25

⊙ MOLD

Sample	Shift	# of Defects	Crack	Burn	Dirt	Blister	Trim
				Type of Defect			
1	1	4	1	1	1	0	1
2	1	6	2	1	0	2	1
3	1	11	1	2	3	3	2
4	1	12	2	2	2	3	3
5	1	5	0	1	0	2	2
6	1	10	1	3	2	2	2
7	1	8	0	3	1	1	3
8	2	16	2	0	8	2	4
9	2	17	3	2	8	2	2
10	2	20	0	3	11	3	3
11	2	28	3	2	17	2	4
12	2	20	0	0	16	4	0
13	2	20	1	1	18	0	0
14	2	17	2	2	13	0	0
15	3	13	3	2	5	1	2
16	3	10	0	3	4	2	1
17	3	11	2	2	3	2	2
18	3	7	0	3	2	2	0
19	3	6	1	2	0	1	2
20	3	8	1	1	2	3	1
21	3	9	1	2	2	2	2

⊙ NURSING

Sample	Scores	Sample	Scores
1	345, 341	11	360, 355
2	331, 328	12	325, 335
3	343, 355	13	350, 348
4	351, 352	14	336, 337
5	360, 348	15	345, 329
6	342, 336	16	358, 351
7	328, 331	17	353, 352
8	344, 344	18	334, 340
9	359, 334	19	341, 335
10	346, 361	20	358, 345

14.72 AirExpress, an overnight mail service, is concerned about the operating efficiency of the package-sorting departments at its Toledo, Ohio, terminal. The company would like to monitor the time it takes for packages to be put in outgoing delivery bins from the time they are received. The sorting department operates six hours per day, from 6 P.M. to midnight. The company randomly sampled four packages during each hour of operation during four consecutive days. The time for each package to move through the system, in minutes, is given at right.

a. Construct an $\bar{x}$-chart from these data. In order for this chart to be meaningful, what assumption must be made about the variation of the process? Why?

b. What does the chart suggest about the stability of the package-sorting process? Explain.

c. Should the control limits be used to monitor future process output? Explain.   Yes

⊙ TRANSIT

Sample	Transit Time (mins.)			
1	31.9	33.4	37.8	26.2
2	29.1	24.3	33.2	36.7
3	30.3	31.1	26.3	34.1
4	39.6	29.4	31.4	37.7
5	27.4	29.7	36.5	33.3
6	32.7	32.9	40.1	29.7
7	30.7	36.9	26.8	34.0
8	28.4	24.1	29.6	30.9
9	30.5	35.5	36.1	27.4
10	27.8	29.6	29.0	34.1
11	34.0	30.1	35.9	28.8
12	25.5	26.3	34.8	30.0
13	24.6	29.9	31.8	37.9
14	30.6	36.0	40.2	30.8
15	29.7	33.2	34.9	27.6
16	24.1	26.8	32.7	29.0
17	29.4	31.6	35.2	27.6
18	31.1	33.0	29.6	35.2
19	27.0	29.0	35.1	25.1
20	36.6	32.4	28.7	27.9
21	33.0	27.1	26.2	35.1
22	33.2	41.2	30.7	31.6
23	26.7	35.2	39.7	31.5
24	30.5	36.8	27.9	28.6

14.73 Officials at Mountain Airlines are interested in monitoring the length of time customers must wait in line to check in at their airport counter in Reno, Nevada. In order to develop a control chart, five customers were sampled each day for 20 days. The data, in minutes, are presented below.

CHECKIN

Sample	Waiting Time (mins.)				
1	3.2	6.7	1.3	8.4	2.2
2	5.0	4.1	7.9	8.1	.4
3	7.1	3.2	2.1	6.5	3.7
4	4.2	1.6	2.7	7.2	1.4
5	1.7	7.1	1.6	.9	1.8
6	4.7	5.5	1.6	3.9	4.0
7	6.2	2.0	1.2	.9	1.4
8	1.4	2.7	3.8	4.6	3.8
9	1.1	4.3	9.1	3.1	2.7
10	5.3	4.1	9.8	2.9	2.7
11	3.2	2.9	4.1	5.6	.8
12	2.4	4.3	6.7	1.9	4.8
13	8.8	5.3	6.6	1.0	4.5
14	3.7	3.6	2.0	2.7	5.9
15	1.0	1.9	6.5	3.3	4.7
16	7.0	4.0	4.9	4.4	4.7
17	5.5	7.1	2.1	.9	2.8
18	1.8	5.6	2.2	1.7	2.1
19	2.6	3.7	4.8	1.4	5.8
20	3.6	.8	5.1	4.7	6.3

a. Construct an R-chart from these data.
b. What does the R-chart suggest about the stability of the process? Explain.   In control
c. Explain why the R-chart should be interpreted prior to the $\bar{x}$-chart.
d. Construct an $\bar{x}$-chart from these data.
e. What does the $\bar{x}$-chart suggest about the stability of the process? Explain.   In control
f. Should the control limits for the R-chart and $\bar{x}$-chart be used to monitor future process output? Explain.   Yes

*14.74 Consider the airline check-in process described in Exercise 14.73.
a. Assume the process is under control and construct a capability analysis diagram for the process. Management has specified an upper specification limit of five minutes.
b. Is the process capable? Justify your answer.
c. If it is appropriate to estimate and interpret C_p for this process, do so. If it is not, explain why.
d. Why didn't management provide a lower specification limit?

14.75 A company called CRW runs credit checks for a large number of banks and insurance companies. Credit history information is typed into computer files by trained administrative assistants. The company is interested in monitoring the proportion of credit histories that contain one or more data entry errors. Based on her experience with the data entry operation, the director of the data processing unit believes that the proportion of histories with data entry errors is about 6%. CRW audited 150 randomly selected credit histories each day for 20 days. The sample data are presented below.

CRW

Sample	Sample Size	Histories with Errors
1	150	9
2	150	11
3	150	12
4	150	8
5	150	10
6	150	6
7	150	13
8	150	9
9	150	11
10	150	5
11	150	7
12	150	6
13	150	12
14	150	10
15	150	11
16	150	7
17	150	6
18	150	12
19	150	14
20	150	10

a. Use the sample size formula to show that a sample size of 150 is large enough to prevent the lower control limit of the p-chart they plan to construct from being negative. $n > 141$
b. Construct a p-chart for the data entry process.
c. What does the chart indicate about the presence of special causes of variation? Explain.
d. Provide an example of a special cause of variation that could potentially affect this process. Do the same for a common cause of variation.
e. Should the control limits be used to monitor future credit histories produced by the data entry operation? Explain.

14.76 Over the last year, a company that manufactures golf clubs has received numerous complaints about the performance of its graphite shafts and has lost several market share percentage points. In response, the company decided to monitor its shaft production process to identify new opportunities to improve its product. The process involves pultrusion. A fabric is pulled through a thermosetting polymer bath and then through a long heated steel die. As it moves through the die, the shaft is cured. Finally, it is cut to the desired length. Defects that

SHAFT1

Shift Number	Number of Defective Shafts	Proportion of Defective Shafts	Shift Number	Number of Defective Shafts	Proportion of Defective Shafts
1	9	.05625	19	6	.03750
2	6	.03750	20	12	.07500
3	8	.05000	21	8	.05000
4	14	.08750	22	5	.03125
5	7	.04375	23	9	.05625
6	5	.03125	24	15	.09375
7	7	.04375	25	6	.03750
8	9	.05625	26	8	.05000
9	5	.03125	27	4	.02500
10	9	.05625	28	7	.04375
11	1	.00625	29	2	.01250
12	7	.04375	30	6	.03750
13	9	.05625	31	9	.05625
14	14	.08750	32	11	.06875
15	7	.04375	33	8	.05000
16	8	.05000	34	9	.05625
17	4	.02500	35	7	.04375
18	10	.06250	36	8	.05000

Source: Kolarik, W. Creating Quality: Concepts, Systems, Strategies, and Tools. New York: McGraw-Hill, 1995.

can occur during the process are internal voids, broken strands, gaps between successive layers, and microcracks caused by improper curing. The company's newly formed quality department sampled 10 consecutive shafts every 30 minutes and nondestructive testing was used to seek out flaws in the shafts. The data from each eight-hour work shift were combined to form a shift sample of 160 shafts. Data on the proportion of defective shafts for 36 shift samples are presented in the table. Data on the types of flaws identified are also given. [*Note:* Each defective shaft may have more than one flaw.]

a. Use the appropriate control chart to determine whether the process proportion remains stable over time.   *p*-chart, UCL = .099, LCL = 0

b. Does your control chart indicate that both common and special causes of variation are present? Explain.   In control

c. To help diagnose the causes of variation in process output, construct a Pareto diagram for the types of shaft defects observed. Which are the "vital few"? The "trivial many"?   Microcracks

SHAFT2

Type of Defect	Number of Defects
Internal voids	11
Broken strands	96
Gaps between layer	72
Microcracks	150

REFERENCES

Alwan, L. C., and Roberts, H. V. "Time-Series Modeling for Statistical Process Control." *Journal of Business and Economic Statistics*, 1988, Vol. 6, pp. 87–95.

Banks, J. *Principles of Quality Control.* New York: Wiley, 1989.

Checkland, P. *Systems Thinking, Systems Practice.* New York: Wiley, 1981.

Deming, W. E. *Out of the Crisis.* Cambridge, Mass.: MIT Center for Advanced Engineering Study, 1986.

DeVor, R. E., Chang, T., and Southerland, J. W. *Statistical Quality Design and Control.* New York: Macmillan, 1992.

Duncan, A. J. *Quality Control and Industrial Statistics.* Homewood, Ill.: Irwin, 1986.

Feigenbaum, A. V. *Total Quality Control,* 3rd ed. New York: McGraw-Hill, 1983.

Garvin, D. A. *Managing Quality.* New York: Free Press/Macmillan, 1988.

Gitlow, H., Gitlow, S., Oppenheim, A., and Oppenheim, R. *Tools and Methods for the Improvement of Quality.* Homewood, Ill.: Irwin, 1989.

Grant, E. L., and Leavenworth, R. S. *Statistical Quality Control*, 6th ed. New York: McGraw-Hill, 1988.

Hart, Marilyn K. "Quality Tools for Improvement." *Production and Inventory Management Journal*, First Quarter 1992, Vol. 33, No. 1, p. 59.

Ishikawa, K. *Guide to Quality Control*, 2nd ed. White Plains, N.Y.: Kraus International Publications, 1986.

Joiner, B. L., and Goudard, M. A. "Variation, Management, and W. Edwards Deming." *Quality Process*, Dec. 1990, pp. 29–37.

Joiner, B., and Goudard, M. "Variation, Management, and W. Edwards Deming." *Quality Process*, Dec. 1990, pp. 29–37.

Juran, J. M. *Juran of Planning for Quality*. New York: Free Press/Macmillan, 1988.

Juran, J. M., and Gryna, F. M., Jr. *Quality Planning Analysis*, 2nd ed. New York: McGraw-Hill, 1980.

Kane, V. E. *Defect Prevention*. New York: Marcel Dekker, 1989.

Latzko, W. J. *Quality and Productivity for Bankers and Financial Managers*. New York: Marcel Dekker, 1986.

Moen, R. D., Nolan, T. W., and Provost, L. P. *Improving Quality through Planned Experimentation*. New York: McGraw-Hill, 1991.

Montgomery, D. C. *Introduction to Statistical Quality Control*, 2nd ed. New York: Wiley, 1991.

Nelson, L. L. "The Shewhart Control Chart—Tests for Special Causes." *Journal of Quality Technology*, Oct. 1984, Vol. 16, No. 4, pp. 237–239.

Roberts, H. V. *Data Analysis for Managers*, 2nd ed. Redwood City, Calif.: Scientific Press, 1991.

Rosander, A. C. *Applications of Quality Control in the Service Industries*. New York: Marcel Dekker, 1985.

Rummler, G. A., and Brache, A. P. *Improving Performance: How to Manage the White Space on the Organization Chart*. San Francisco: Jossey-Bass, 1991.

Ryan, T. P. *Statistical Methods for Quality Improvement*. New York: Wiley, 1989.

Statistical Quality Control Handbook. Indianapolis, Ind.: AT&T Technologies, Select Code 700-444 (inquiries: 800-432-6600); originally published by Western Electric Company, 1956.

The Ernst and Young Quality Improvement Consulting Group. *Total Quality: An Executive's Guide for the 1990s*. Homewood, Ill.: Dow-Jones Irwin, 1990.

Wadsworth, H. M., Stephens, K. S., and Godfrey, A. B. *Modern Methods for Quality Control and Improvement*. New York: Wiley, 1986.

Walton, M. *The Deming Management Method*. New York: Dodd, Mead, & Company, 1986.

Wheeler, D. J., and Chambers, D. S. *Understanding Statistical Process Control*. Knoxville, Tenn.: Statistical Process Controls, Inc., 1986.

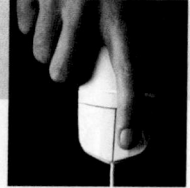

Using Technology

14.1 Control Charts Using SPSS

To conduct create control charts for process data, first access the SPSS spreadsheet file that contains the quality data. Next, click on the "Graphs" button on the SPSS menu bar, then click on "Control", as shown in Figure 14.S.1. The resulting dialog box appears as shown in Figure 14.S.2.

Select the type of control chart you want to produce (x-bar, R- or p-chart) and whether the cases (rows) on the spreadsheet represent individual quality measurements ("Cases are units") or the subgroups ("Cases are subgroups"), then click the "Define" button on the Control Chart dialog box.

If you selected an x-bar or R-chart where cases are subgroups, the dialog box shown in Figure 14.S.3 will appear. If you selected an x-bar or R-chart where cases are individual units, the dialog box shown in Figure 14.S.4 will appear. Make the appropriate selections (process variables and subgroup variable), then click

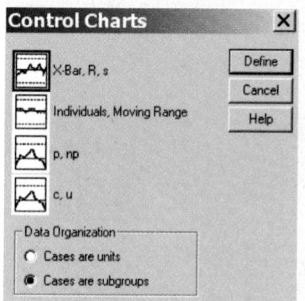

Figure 14.S.2
SPSS control chart dialog box

cereal - SPSS Data Editor

File   Edit   View   Data   Transform   Analyze   Graphs   Utilities   Window   Help

	day	wt1	wt2		wt5
1	1	24.02	23.91	.06	24.13
2	2	23.89	23.98	.00	23.91
3	3	24.11	24.02	.79	24.04
4	4	24.06	23.98	.01	24.11
5	5	23.81	23.90	.07	23.96
6	6	23.87	24.12	.01	23.99
7	7	23.88	24.00	.97	23.97
8	8	24.01	24.03	.91	23.98
9	9	24.06	24.02	.79	24.07
10	10	23.96	23.99	.99	24.01
11	11	24.10	23.90	.98	23.95
12	12	24.01	24.07	.09	23.98
13	13	24.14	24.07	.98	24.02
14	14	23.91	24.04	.01	23.95
15	15	24.03	24.04	.98	24.10
16	16	23.94	24.07	.00	24.02
17	17	23.88	23.94	.06	24.07
18	18	24.11	23.99	23.90	24.01	23.98
19	19	24.05	24.04	23.97	24.08	23.95
20	20	24.02	23.96	23.95	23.89	24.04

Graphs menu: Gallery, Interactive, Bar..., Line..., Area..., Pie..., High-Low..., Pareto..., Control..., Boxplot..., Error Bar..., Scatter..., Histogram..., P-P..., Q-Q..., Sequence..., ROC Curve..., Time Series...

Figure 14.S.1
SPSS menu options for control charts

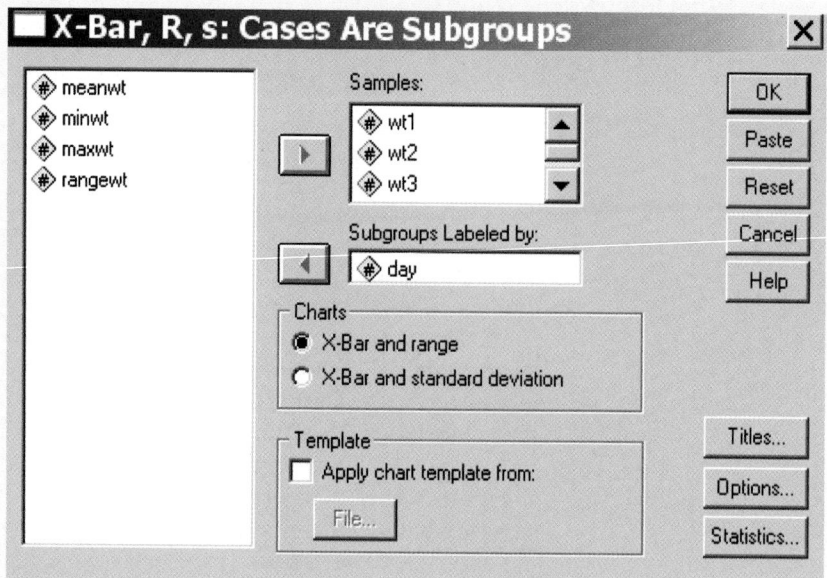

Figure 14.S.3
SPSS options for $\bar{x}$ and R-charts (cases are subgroups)

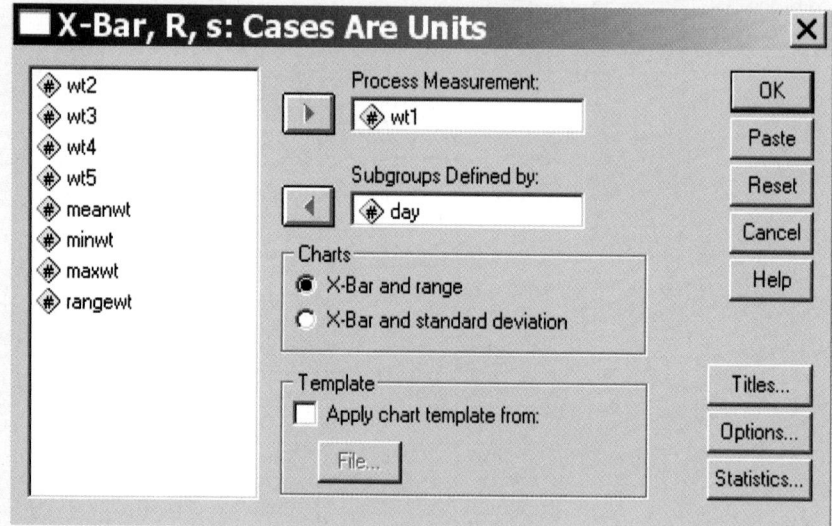

Figure 14.S.4
SPSS options for $\bar{x}$ and R-charts (cases are units)

"OK" to produce the SPSS control chart. (As an option, you can conduct a capability analysis by clicking the "Statistics" button and making the appropriate menu selections (specification limits, target value, and C_p statistic.)

If you selected a p-chart on the Control Chart dialog box (Figure 14.S.2), the dialog box shown in Figure 14.S.5 will appear. Specify the variables that represent the number nonconforming and the subgroups, and specify the sample size. Click "OK" to view the SPSS control chart.

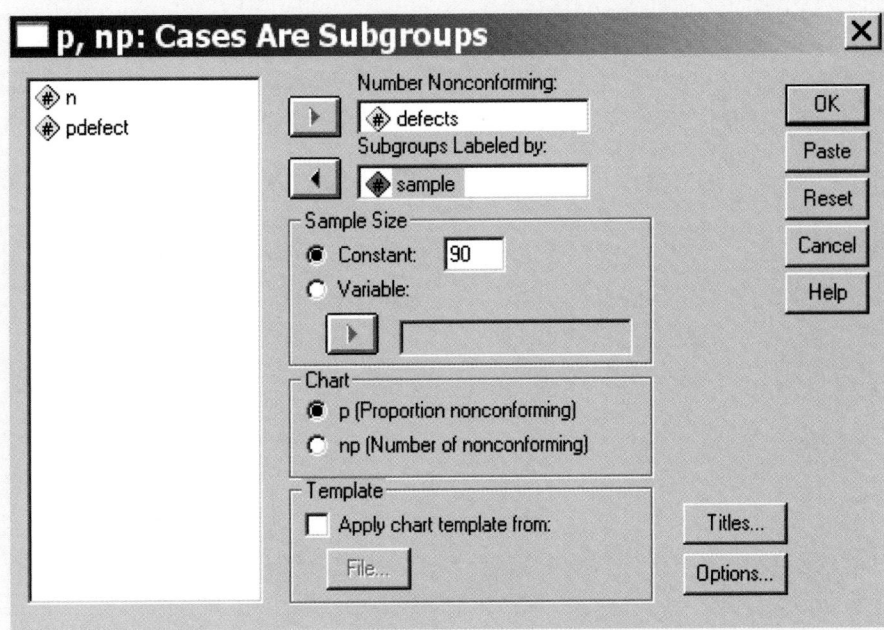

Figure 14.S.5
SPSS options for *p*-charts

14.2 Control Charts Using MINITAB

To create an $\bar{x}$-chart or *R*-chart for process data, first access the MINITAB work-sheet file that contains the quality data. Next, click on the "Stat" button on the MINITAB menu bar, then click on "Control Charts", "Variables Charts for Subgroups", and either "Xbar" or "R", as shown in Figure 14.M.1. The resulting dialog box appears similar to the one shown in Figure 14.M.2.

If each row on the worksheet represents an individual quality measurement, then specify "Data are arranged as: Single column", as shown in Figure 14.M.2. Enter the quality variable in the next box, and specify the subgroup size.

If each row on the worksheet represents a subgroup, with columns represent-ing the sample measurements, then specify "Data are arranged as: Subgroups

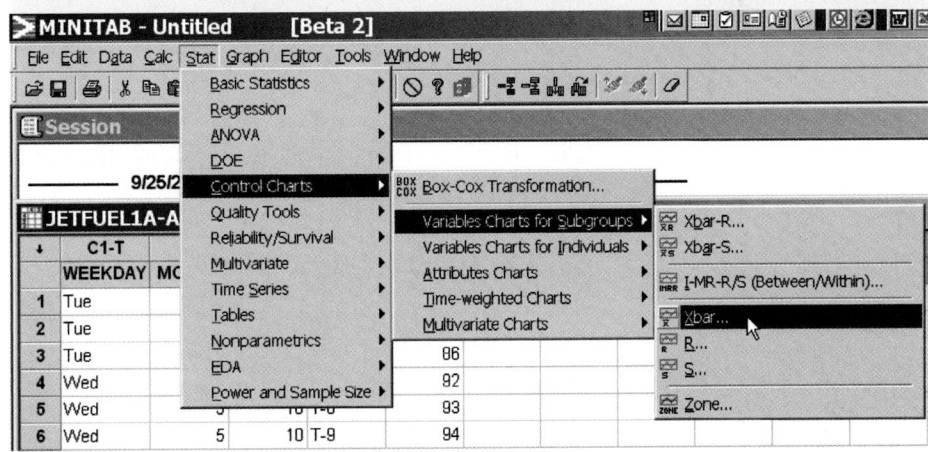

Figure 14.M.1
MINITAB menu options for control charts

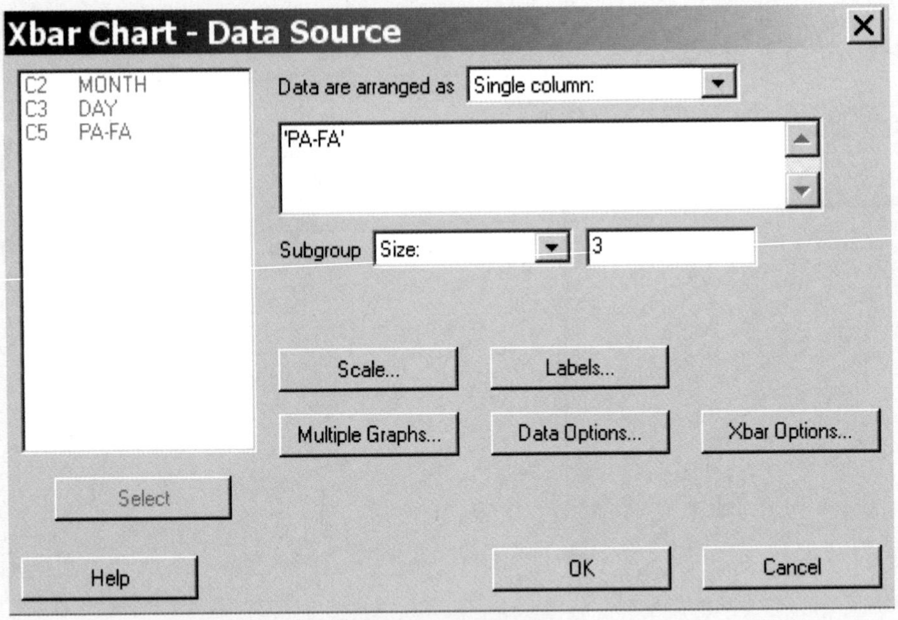

Figure 14.M.2
MINITAB x̄-chart dialog
box (rows are individual
units)

across rows of", as shown in Figure 14.M.3. Enter the columns with the sample measurements in the next box.

If you want MINITAB to apply the pattern-analysis rules to the plotted points on the graph, click the "Xbar (or R) Options" button, click "Tests", and check the rules you want apply. Click "OK" to return to the Control Chart dialog box, then click "OK" again to produce the MINITAB control chart.

To create a *p*-chart for attribute data, click on the "Stat" button on the MINITAB menu bar, then click on "Control Charts" and "Attributes Charts" (see Figure 14.M.1). On the resulting menu, select "P". The resulting dialog box appears similar to the one shown in Figure 14.M.4. Specify the variable that

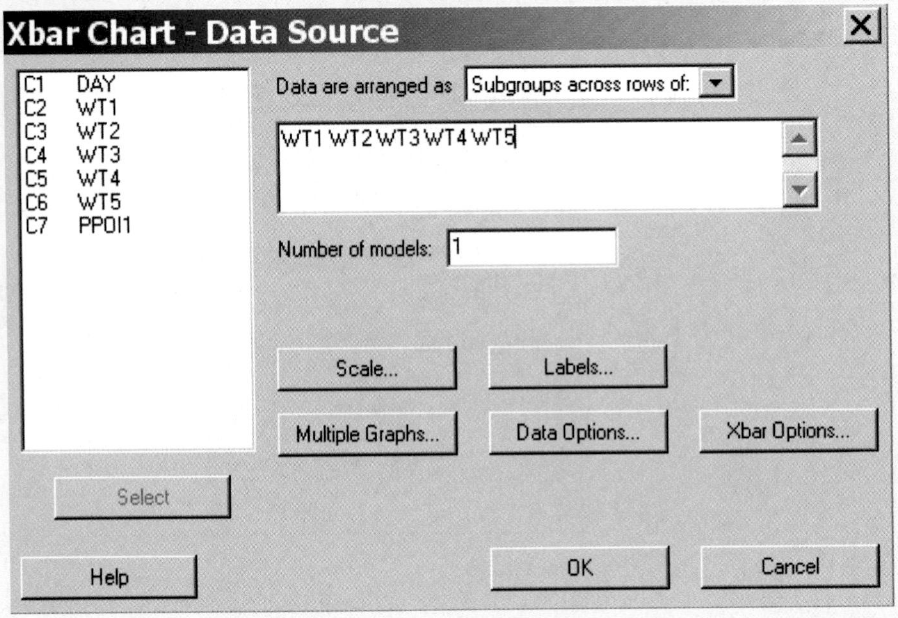

Figure 14.M.3
MINITAB x̄-chart dialog
box (rows are subgroups)

Figure 14.M.4
MINITAB *p*-chart
dialog box

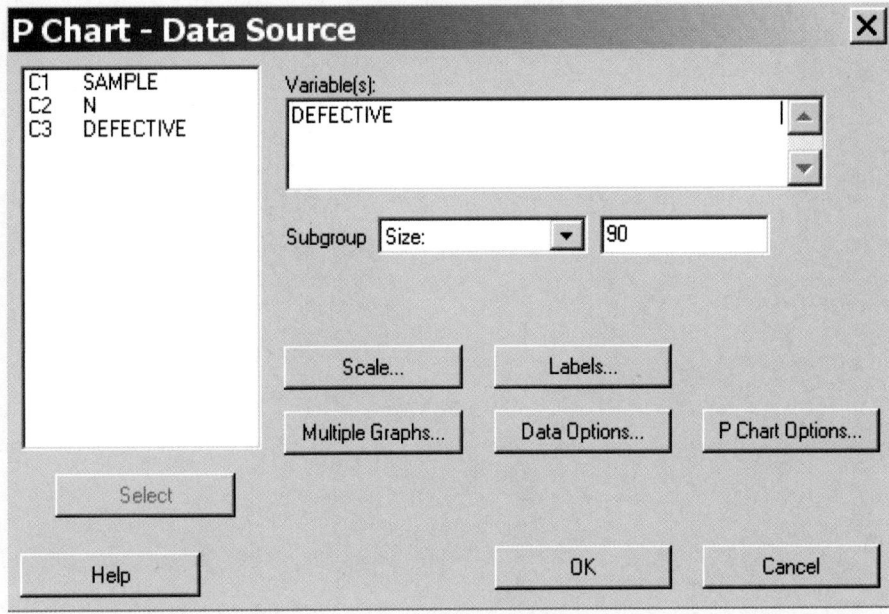

represents the number of nonconforming items and specify the subgroup (sample) size. If you want MINITAB to apply the pattern-analysis rules to the plotted points on the graph, click the "P Chart Options" button, click "Tests", and check the rules you want apply. Click "OK" to return to the Control Chart dialog box, then click "OK" again to produce the MINITAB control chart.

To create a capability analysis diagram, click on the "Stat" button on the MINITAB menu bar, then click on "Quality Tools", "Capability Analysis", and "Normal", as shown in Figure 14.M.5. The resulting dialog box appears similar to the one shown in Figure 14.M.6. Specify the quality variable of interest, subgroup size, and lower and upper specification limits on the menu screen. Click the "Options" button to specify the type of statistics (e.g., C_p and percents outside specification limits) to be displayed on the graph. Click "OK" to produce the MINITAB capability analysis diagram.

Figure 14.M.5
MINITAB menu options
for capability analysis

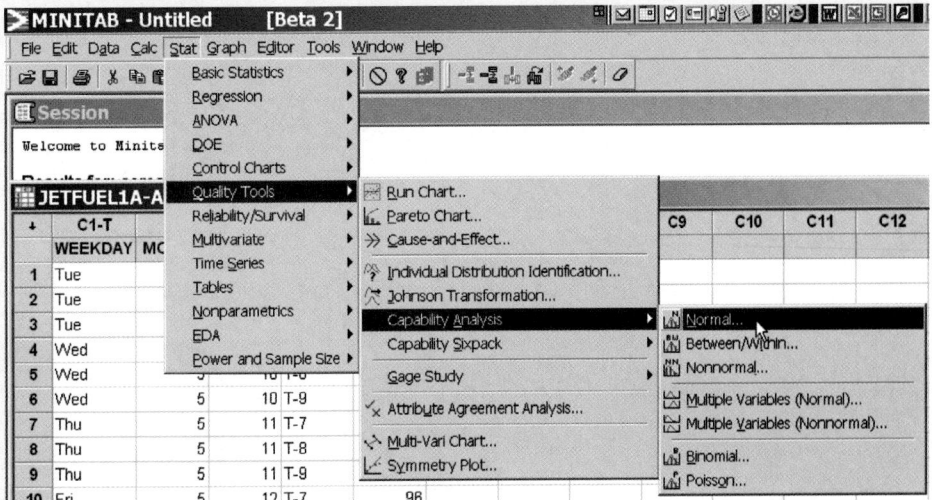

Figure 14.M.6
MINITAB capability
analysis dialog box

Capability Analysis (Normal Distribution)

C2   MONTH
C3   DAY
C5   PA—FA

Data are arranged as
- Single column: `'PA—FA'`
  - Subgroup size: `3`
  - (use a constant or an ID column)
- Subgroups across rows of:

Lower spec: `80`   ☐ Boundary
Upper spec: `90`   ☐ Boundary
Historical mean: `       ` (optional)
Historical standard deviation: `       ` (optional)

Box-Cox...
Estimate...
Options...
Storage...

Select

Help

OK

Cancel

14.3 Control Charts Using EXCEL/PHStat2

To create an *x*-chart or *R*-chart, first access the EXCEL workbook file that contains the quality data. The workbook should contain columns for the sample mean and sample range, with the rows representing each subgroup. Next, click on the "PHStat" button on the EXCEL menu bar, then click on "Control Charts", and "R & XBar Charts", as shown in Figure 14.E.1. The resulting dialog box appears similar to the one shown in Figure 14.E.2.

Specify the subgroup (sample) size, cell range for the sample ranges, and cell range for the sample means, as shown in Figure 14.E.2. Click "OK" to produce the EXCEL control charts.

To create a *p*-chart, first access the EXCEL workbook file that contains the attribute data. The workbook should contain a column for the number of

Figure 14.E.1
EXCEL menu options
for control charts

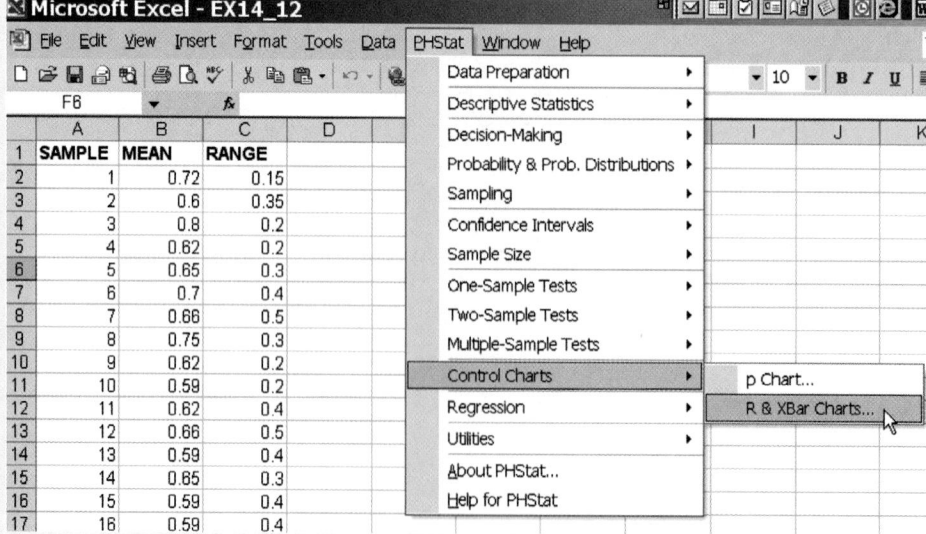

Figure 14.E.2
EXCEL R and $\bar{x}$-charts
dialog box

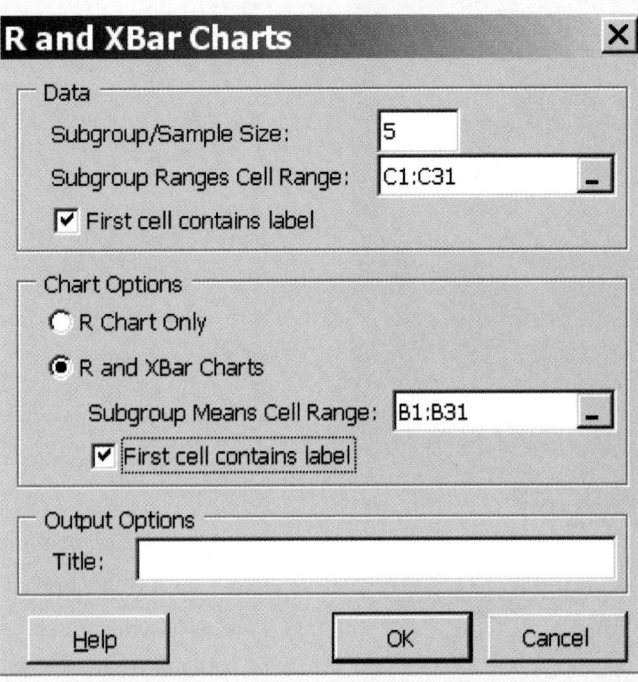

nonconforming items (defects), with the rows representing each subgroup. Next, click on the "PHStat" button on the EXCEL menu bar, then click on "Control Charts", and "p Chart" (see Figure 14.E.1). The resulting dialog box appears similar to the one shown in Figure 14.E.3. Specify the cell range for the number of nonconforming items and the subgroup (sample) size, as shown in Figure 14.E.3. Click "OK" to produce the EXCEL control chart.

Figure 14.E.3
EXCEL p-chart
dialog box

15

Time Series
Descriptive Analyses, Models, and Forecasting

Contents

Statistics in Action

Forecasting the Monthly Sales of a New Cold Medicine

Using Technology

Where We've Been

- Discovered that variation in the output of processes is inevitable.
- Presented both managerial and statistical methods for continuously improving processes and the quality of their output.
- Learned how to use control charts to monitor process variation and determine when action should be taken to improve a process.

Where We're Going

- Focus on methods for analyzing data generated by a process over time (i.e., *time series data*).

- Present descriptive methods for characterizing time series data.

- Present inferential methods for forecasting future values of time series data.

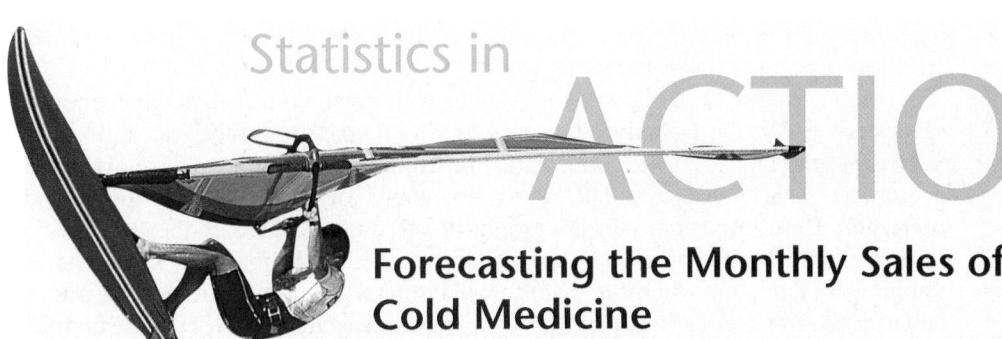

Statistics in ACTION

Forecasting the Monthly Sales of a New Cold Medicine

In the pharmaceutical industry, sales forecasting are critical to the success of the company. Accurate forecasts aid sales managers in improving decision making, the finance department in controlling and scheduling its operating costs and capital budget, the human resources department in projecting staffing, and the purchasing department in controlling inventories and production schedules. Due to the critical life and death nature of the industry, pharmaceutical manufacturers rely on sophisticated analytical techniques to build the forecasts.

Several years ago, a major pharmaceutical company based in New Jersey introduced a new cold medicine called Coldex. (For proprietary reasons, the actual name of the product is withheld.) Coldex is now sold regularly in drugstores and supermarkets across the United States. Prior to launching the product nationally, the company hired consultants from the Graduate School of Management at Rutgers University (The State University of New Jersey) to help the company build a monthly forecast model for Coldex. This Statistics in Action problem involves a portion of the analysis conducted by the consultants.

Consider the task of forecasting the sales of Coldex for the first three months of the third year of the product's existence. The company provided data on the monthly sales (in thousands of dollars) for the first two years of the product's life. The data, saved in the **COLDEX** file, are listed in Table SIA15.1. In the Statistics in Action Revisited sections listed below, we demonstrate several forecasting methods used by the consultants.

 COLDEX

TABLE SIA15.1   Coldex Monthly Sales Data

Year	Month	Time	Sales
1	Jan	1	3394
	Feb	2	4010
	Mar	3	924
	Apr	4	205
	May	5	293
	Jun	6	1130
	Jul	7	1116
	Aug	8	4009
	Sep	9	5692
	Oct	10	3458
	Nov	11	2849
	Dec	12	3470
2	Jan	13	4568
	Feb	14	3710
	Mar	15	1675
	Apr	16	999
	May	17	986
	Jun	18	1786
	Jul	19	2253
	Aug	20	5237
	Sep	21	6679
	Oct	22	4116
	Nov	23	4109
	Dec	24	5124

Source: Personal communication from Carol Cowley, Carla Marchesini, and Ginny Wilson, Rutgers University, Graduate School of Management.

Statistics in Action Revisited

- Forecasting Coldex Sales with Exponential Smoothing (p. 1031)

- Forecasting Coldex Sales with Simple Linear Regression (p. 1036)

- Forecasting Coldex Sales with a Seasonal Regression Model (p. 1041)

In the previous chapter we were concerned with improving processes. In this chapter, our concern is not with the improvement of the internal workings of processes but with describing and predicting the output of processes. The process outputs on which we focus are the streams of data generated by processes over time. Recall from Chapters 2 and 14 that such data streams are called **time series** or **time series data.** For example, businesses generate time series data such as weekly sales, quarterly earnings, and yearly profits that can be used to describe and evaluate the performance of the business. The U.S. economy can be thought of as a system that generates streams of data that include the Gross Domestic Product, the Consumer Price Index, and the unemployment rate.

The methods of this chapter focus exclusively on the time series data generated by a process. Properly analyzed, these data reveal much about the past and future behavior of the process. Time series data, like other types of data we have discussed in previous chapters, are subjected to two kinds of analyses: **descriptive** and **inferential.** Descriptive analyses use graphical and numerical techniques to provide a clear understanding of any patterns that are present in the time series. After graphing the data, you will often want to use it to make inferences about the future values of the time series (i.e., you will want to **forecast** future values). For example, once you understand the past and present trends of the Dow Jones Industrial Average, you would probably want to forecast its future trend before making decisions about buying and selling stocks. Since significant amounts of money may be riding on the accuracy of your forecasts, you would be interested in measures of their reliability. Forecasts and their measures of reliability are examples of **inferential techniques** in time series analysis.

15.1 Descriptive Analysis: Index Numbers

The most common technique for characterizing a business or economic time series is to compute *index numbers.* Index numbers measure how a time series changes over time. Change is measured relative to a preselected time period, called the *base period.*

DEFINITION 15.1

An **index number** is a number that measures the change in a variable over time relative to the value of the variable during a specific **base period.**

Two types of indexes dominate business and economic applications: **price** and **quantity indexes.** Price indexes measure changes in the price of a commodity or group of commodities over time. The Consumer Price Index (CPI) is a price index because it measures price changes of a group of commodities that are intended to reflect typical purchases of American consumers. On the other hand, an index constructed to measure the change in the total number of automobiles produced annually by American manufacturers would be an example of a quantity index.

Methods of calculating index numbers range from very simple to extremely complex, depending on the numbers and types of commodities represented by the index. Several important types of index numbers are described in this section.

Biography

**IRVING FISHER
(1867–1947)
Index Numbers Expert**

New York State native Irving Fisher, the son of a congregational minister, graduated from Yale University with a bachelor's degree in mathematics in 1988. Fisher continued at Yale with his graduate studies, earning the first Ph.D. in economics ever awarded by the university in 1891. He had a long, distinguished career as a professor at Yale and became a very successful businessman. (Fisher made a fortune with his invention of

a "visible card index" system—known today as the Rolodex®.) Fisher is considered one of the most influential economists of the 19th and 20th centuries; he had an uncanny ability to explain and write clearly about the most technical economic theories. Fisher also had a reputation as a colorful eccentric. (To illustrate his price theory in his dissertation, Fisher constructed a remarkable machine equipped with pumps, wheels, levers, and pipes.) Fisher's best-known contribution to the field of statistics was as a pioneer in the construction and use of price indexes. A colleague at Yale, James Tobin, once called Fisher "the greatest expert of all time on index numbers."

TABLE 15.1   Silver Prices, 1975–2002

Year	Price ($/oz.)	Year	Price ($/oz.)	Year	Price ($/oz.)
1975	4.42	1985	6.14	1995	5.20
1976	4.35	1986	5.47	1996	5.18
1977	4.62	1987	7.01	1997	4.89
1978	5.40	1988	6.53	1998	5.48
1979	11.09	1989	5.50	1999	5.22
1980	20.64	1990	4.82	2000	4.97
1981	10.52	1991	4.04	2001	4.37
1982	7.95	1992	3.94	2002	4.60
1983	11.44	1993	4.30		
1984	8.14	1994	5.30		

Source: Standard & Poor's. *Current Statistics,* Dec. 2002.

Simple Index Numbers

When an index number is based on the price or quantity of a single commodity, it is called a *simple index number.*

DEFINITION 15.2

A **simple index number** is based on the relative changes (over time) in the price or quantity of a single commodity.

For example, consider the price of silver (in dollars per fine ounce) between 1975 and 2002, shown in Table 15.1. To construct a simple index to describe the relative changes in silver prices, we must first choose a *base period.* The choice is important because the price for all other periods will be compared with the price during the base period. We select 1975 as the base period, a time just preceding the period of rapid economic inflation associated with dramatic oil price increases.

To calculate the simple index number for a particular year, we divide that year's price by the price during the base year and multiply the result by 100. Thus, for the 1980 silver price index number, we calculate

$$1980 \text{ index number} = \left(\frac{1980 \text{ silver price}}{1975 \text{ silver price}}\right)100 = \left(\frac{20.64}{4.42}\right)100 = 467.0$$

Similarly, the index number for 2002 is

$$2002 \text{ index number} = \left(\frac{2002 \text{ silver price}}{1975 \text{ silver price}}\right)100 = \left(\frac{4.60}{4.42}\right)100 = 104.1$$

The index number for the base period is always 100. In our example, we have

$$1975 \text{ index number} = \left(\frac{1975 \text{ silver price}}{1975 \text{ silver price}}\right)100 = 100$$

Teaching Tip

Spend time interpreting index numbers to make sure students understand their meaning.

Thus, the silver price has risen by 367% (the difference between the 1980 and 1975 index numbers) between 1975 and 1980, and by only 4.1% between 1975 and 2002. The simple index numbers for silver prices between 1975 and 2002 are given in Table 15.2 and are portrayed graphically in Figure 15.1. The steps for calculating simple index numbers are summarized in the next box.

TABLE 15.2 Simple Index Numbers for Silver Prices (Base 1975)

Year	Index	Year	Index
1975	100.0	1989	124.4
1976	98.4	1990	109.1
1977	104.5	1991	91.4
1978	122.2	1992	89.1
1979	250.9	1993	97.3
1980	467.0	1994	119.9
1981	238.0	1995	117.7
1982	179.9	1996	117.2
1983	258.8	1997	110.6
1984	184.2	1998	124.0
1985	138.9	1999	118.1
1986	123.8	2000	112.4
1987	158.6	2001	98.9
1988	147.7	2002	104.1

Figure 15.1

MINITAB graph of simple silver price index

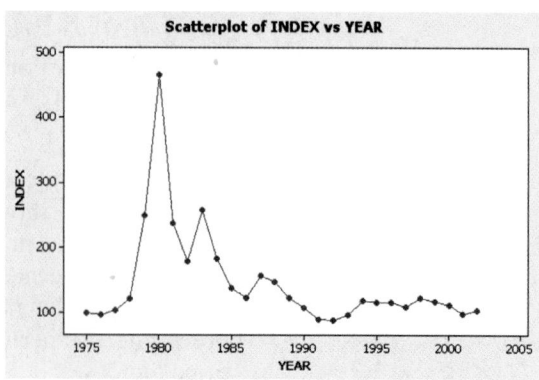

Now Work   *Exercise 15.4*

> ## Steps for Calculating a Simple Index Number
> 1. Obtain the prices or quantities for the commodity over the time period of interest.
> 2. Select a base period.
> 3. Calculate the index number for each period according to the formula
>
> $$\text{Index number at time } t = \left(\frac{\text{Time series value at time } t}{\text{Time series value at base period}} \right) 100$$
>
> Symbolically,
>
> $$I_t = \left(\frac{Y_t}{Y_0} \right) 100$$
>
> where I_t is the index number at time t, Y_t is the time series value at time t, and Y_0 is the time series value at the base period.

Composite Index Numbers

A **composite index number** represents combinations of the prices or quantities of several commodities. For example, suppose you want to construct an index for the total number of sales of the three major automobile manufacturers in the United States: General Motors, Ford, and Chrysler. The first step is to collect data on the sales of each manufacturer during the period in which you are interested, say 1980–2000. To summarize the information from all three time series in a single index, we add the sales of each manufacturer for each year. That is, we form a new time series consisting of the total number of automobiles sold by the three manufacturers. Then we construct a simple index for the *total* of the three series. The resulting index is called a *simple composite index*. We illustrate the construction of a simple composite index in Example 15.1.

Teaching Tip
Point out that the composite index is a simple index of the sum of a variety of commodities.

DEFINITION 15.3

A **simple composite index** is a simple index for a time series consisting of the total price or total quantity of two or more commodities.

EXAMPLE 15.1   CONSTRUCTING A SIMPLE COMPOSITE INDEX

Problem   One of the primary uses of index numbers is to characterize changes in stock prices over time. Stock market indexes have been constructed for many different types of companies and industries, and several composite indexes have been developed to characterize all stocks. These indexes are reported on a daily basis in the news media (e.g., Standard and Poor's 500 Stocks Index and Dow Jones 65 Stocks Index).

Suggested Exercises 15.8

HITECH

TABLE 15.3   Monthly Closing Prices of Three High-Technology Company Stocks

Year	Month	Time	IBM	Intel	Microsoft
2001	JAN	1	112.00	37.00	61.06
	FEB	2	99.90	28.56	59.00
	MAR	3	96.18	26.31	54.69
	APR	4	115.14	30.91	67.75
	MAY	5	111.80	27.01	69.18
	JUN	6	113.50	29.25	73.00
	JUL	7	105.21	29.81	66.19
	AUG	8	99.95	27.96	57.05
	SEP	9	91.72	20.44	51.17
	OCT	10	108.07	24.42	58.15
	NOV	11	115.59	32.66	64.21
	DEC	12	120.96	31.45	66.25
2002	JAN	13	107.89	35.04	63.71
	FEB	14	98.12	28.55	58.34
	MAR	15	104.00	30.41	60.31
	APR	16	83.76	28.61	52.26
	MAY	17	80.45	27.62	50.91
	JUN	18	72.00	18.27	54.70
	JUL	19	70.40	18.79	47.98
	AUG	20	75.38	16.67	49.08
	SEP	21	58.31	13.89	43.74
	OCT	22	78.94	17.30	53.47
	NOV	23	86.92	20.88	57.68
	DEC	24	77.50	15.57	51.70

Source: Standard & Poor's *NYSE Daily Stock Price Record*, 2001–2002.

Consider the monthly closing prices (i.e., closing prices on the last day of each month) given in Table 15.3 for three high-technology company stocks listed on the New York Stock Exchange between 2001 and 2002. To see how this type of stock fared, construct a simple composite index using January 2001 as the base period. Graph the index, and comment on its implications.

Solution   First, we calculate the total for the three stock prices each month. These totals are shown in the "TOTAL" column on the EXCEL workbook displayed in Figure 15.2. Then the simple composite index is calculated by dividing each monthly total by the January 2001 total. The index values are given in the last column of Figure 15.2, and a graph of the simple composite index is shown in Figure 15.3.

The plot of the simple composite index for these high-technology stocks shows a generally decreasing trend over the two-year period. The composite price of these high-technology stocks dropped about 31% from January 2001 (Index = 100) to December 2002 (Index = 68.9).

Look Back The difference between two index numbers gives the percentage change in the value of the time series variable between the two time periods.

Now Work   *Exercise 15.8c, d*

■ ■ ■

	A	B	C	D	E	F	G	H
1	YEAR	MONTH	TIME	IBM	INTEL	MICROSOFT	TOTAL	INDEX
2	2001	JAN	1	112.00	37.00	61.06	210.06	100.00
3	2001	FEB	2	99.90	28.56	59.00	187.46	89.24
4	2001	MAR	3	96.18	26.31	54.69	177.18	84.35
5	2001	APR	4	115.14	30.91	67.75	213.80	101.78
6	2001	MAY	5	111.80	27.01	69.18	207.99	99.01
7	2001	JUN	6	113.50	29.25	73.00	215.75	102.71
8	2001	JUL	7	105.21	29.81	66.19	201.21	95.79
9	2001	AUG	8	99.95	27.96	57.05	184.96	88.05
10	2001	SEP	9	91.72	20.44	51.17	163.33	77.75
11	2001	OCT	10	108.07	24.42	58.15	190.64	90.76
12	2001	NOV	11	115.59	32.66	64.21	212.46	101.14
13	2001	DEC	12	120.96	31.45	66.25	218.66	104.09
14	2002	JAN	13	107.89	35.04	63.71	206.64	98.37
15	2002	FEB	14	98.12	28.55	58.34	185.01	88.07
16	2002	MAR	15	104.00	30.41	60.31	194.72	92.70
17	2002	APR	16	83.76	28.61	52.26	164.63	78.37
18	2002	MAY	17	80.45	27.62	50.91	158.98	75.68
19	2002	JUN	18	72.00	18.27	54.70	144.97	69.01
20	2002	JUL	19	70.40	18.79	47.98	137.17	65.30
21	2002	AUG	20	75.38	16.67	49.08	141.13	67.19
22	2002	SEP	21	58.31	13.89	43.74	115.94	55.19
23	2002	OCT	22	78.94	17.30	53.47	149.71	71.27
24	2002	NOV	23	86.92	20.88	57.68	165.48	78.78
25	2002	DEC	24	77.50	15.57	51.70	144.77	68.92

Figure 15.2
EXCEL worksheet with simple composite index of stock prices

Figure 15.3
MINITAB graph of simple composite index for three stock prices

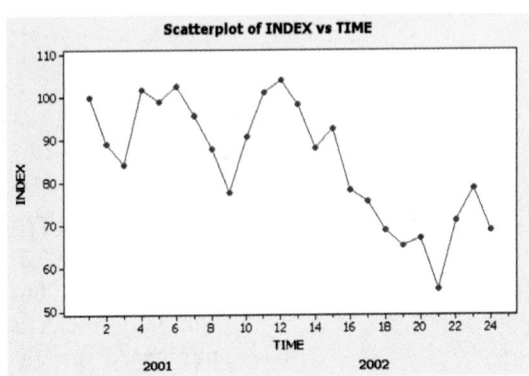

A simple composite price index has a major drawback: The quantity of the commodity that is purchased during each period is not taken into account. Only the price totals are used to calculate the index. We can remedy this situation by constructing a *weighted composite price index.*

DEFINITION 15.4

A **weighted composite price index** weights the prices by quantities purchased prior to calculating totals for each time period. The weighted totals are then used to compute the index in the same way that the unweighted totals are used for simple composite indexes.

Teaching Tip

Ask the students to propose other weighting techniques that they think would be more appropriate that the Laspeyres Index. Discuss their suggestions.

Since the quantities purchased change from time period to time period, the choice of which time period's quantities to use as the basis for the weighted composite index is an important one. A **Laspeyres index** uses the base period quantities as weights. The rationale is that the prices at each time period should be compared as if the same quantities were purchased each period as were purchased during the base period. This method measures price inflation (or deflation) by fixing the purchase quantities at their base period values. The method for calculating a Laspeyres index is given in the box.

Steps for Calculating a Laspeyres Index

1. Collect price information for each of the k price series to be used in the composite index. Denote these series by $P_{1t}, P_{2t}, \ldots, P_{kt}$.

2. Select a base period. Call this time period t_0.

3. Collect purchase quantity information for the base period. Denote the k quantities by $Q_{1t_0}, Q_{2t_0}, \ldots, Q_{kt_0}$.

4. Calculate the weighted totals for each time period according to the formula

$$\sum_{i=1}^{k} Q_{it_0} P_{it}$$

5. Calculate the Laspeyres index, I_t, at time t by taking the ratio of the weighted total at time t to the base period weighted total and multiplying by 100. That is,

$$I_t = \frac{\sum_{i=1}^{k} Q_{it_0} P_{it}}{\sum_{i=1}^{k} Q_{it_0} P_{it_0}} \times 100$$

EXAMPLE 15.2   CONSTRUCTING A LASPEYRES INDEX

Problem   The January 2001 and December 2002 prices for the three high-technology company stocks are given in Table 15.4. Suppose that, in January 2001, an investor purchased the quantities shown in the table. [*Note:* Only two prices are used to simplify the example. The same methods can be applied to calculate the index for other months.] Calculate the Laspeyres index for the investor's portfolio of high-technology stocks using January 2001 as the base period.

$I_{DEC.\ 2002} = 76.2$

TABLE 15.4   **Prices of High-Technology Stocks
with Quantities Purchased**

	IBM	Intel	Microsoft
Shares purchased	500	100	1,000
January 2001 price	112.00	37.00	61.06
December 2002 price	77.50	15.57	51.70

Solution First, we calculate the weighted price totals for each time period, using the January 2001 quantities as weights. Thus,

$$\text{January 2001 weighted total} = \sum_{i=1}^{4} Q_{i,\,\text{Jan. 2001}} P_{i,\,\text{Jan. 2001}}$$
$$= 500(112.00) + 100(37.00) + 1000(61.06)$$
$$= 120{,}760$$

$$\text{December 2002 weighted total} = \sum_{i=1}^{4} Q_{i,\,\text{Jan. 2001}} P_{i,\,\text{Dec. 2002}}$$
$$= 500(77.50) + 100(15.57) + 1{,}000(51.70)$$
$$= 92{,}007$$

Then the Laspeyres index is calculated by multiplying the ratio of each weighted total to the base period weighted total by 100. Thus,

$$I_{\text{Jan. 2001}} = \frac{\displaystyle\sum_{i=1}^{4} Q_{i,\,\text{Jan. 2001}} P_{i,\,\text{Jan. 2001}}}{\displaystyle\sum_{i=1}^{4} Q_{i,\,\text{Jan. 2001}} P_{i,\,\text{Jan. 2001}}} \times 100 = \frac{120{,}760}{120{,}760} \times 100 = 100$$

$$I_{\text{Dec. 2002}} = \frac{\displaystyle\sum_{i=1}^{4} Q_{i,\,\text{Jan. 2001}} P_{i,\,\text{Dec. 2002}}}{\displaystyle\sum_{i=1}^{4} Q_{i,\,\text{Jan. 2001}} P_{i,\,\text{Jan. 2001}}} \times 100 = \frac{92{,}007}{120{,}760} \times 100 = 76.2$$

Look Back The implication is that these stocks decreased in price by about $(100 - 76\%) = 24\%$ from January 2001 to December 2002.

Now Work   *Exercise 15.12b*

■ ■ ■

The Laspeyres index is appropriate when the base period quantities are reasonable weights to apply to all time periods. This is the case in applications such as that described in Example 15.2, where the base period quantities represent actual quantities of stock purchased and held for some period of time. Laspeyres indexes are also appropriate when the base period quantities remain reasonable approximations of purchase quantities in subsequent periods. However, it can be misleading when the relative purchase quantities change significantly from those in the base period.

Probably the best-known Laspeyres index is the all-items Consumer Price Index (CPI). This monthly composite index is made up of hundreds of item prices, and the U.S. Bureau of Labor Statistics (BLS) sampled over 30,000 families' purchases in 1982–1984 to determine the base period quantities. Thus, beginning in 1987, the all-items CPI published each month reflects quantities purchased in 1982–1984 by a sample of families across the United States. However, as prices increase for some commodities more quickly than for others, consumers tend to substitute less expensive commodities where possible. For example, as automobile and gasoline prices rapidly inflated in the mid-1970s, consumers began to purchase smaller cars. The net effect of using the base period quantities for the CPI is to overestimate the effect of inflation on consumers, because the quantities are fixed at levels that will actually change in response to price changes.

There are several solutions to the problem of purchase quantities that change relative to those of the base period. One is to change the base period regularly, so that the quantities are regularly updated. A second solution is to compute the index at each time period by using the purchase quantities of that period, rather than those of the base period. A **Paasche index** is calculated by using price totals weighted by the purchase quantities of the period the index value represents. The steps for calculating a Paasche index are given in the box.

Teaching Tip

Discuss how the Laspeyres and Paasche indices differ for all time periods except the base period.

Steps for Calculating a Paasche Index

1. Collect price information for each of the k price series to be used in the composite index. Denote these series by $P_{1t}, P_{2t}, \ldots, P_{kt}$.
2. Select a base period. Call this time period t_0.
3. Collect purchase quantity information for every period. Denote the k quantities for period t by $Q_{1t}, Q_{2t}, \ldots, Q_{kt}$.
4. Calculate the Paasche index for time t by multiplying the ratio of the weighted total at time t to the weighted total at time t_0 (base period) by 100, where the weights used are the purchase quantities for time period t. Thus,

$$I_t = \frac{\sum_{i=1}^{k} Q_{it} P_{it}}{\sum_{i=1}^{k} Q_{it} P_{it_0}} \times 100$$

EXAMPLE 15.3   CONSTRUCTING A PAASCHE INDEX

Problem   The January 2001 and December 2002 prices and volumes (actual quantities purchased) in millions of shares for the three high-technology company stocks are shown in Table 15.5. Calculate and interpret the Paasche index, using January 2001 as the base period.

$I_{DEC\ 2002} = 63.4$

Solution   The key to calculating a Paasche index is to remember that the weights (purchase quantities) change for each time period. Thus,

TABLE 15.5 Prices and Volumes of High-Technology Stocks

	IBM		Intel		Microsoft	
	Price	Volume	Price	Volume	Price	Volume
January 2001	112.00	9.9	37.00	61.1	61.06	49.7
December 2002	77.50	7.6	15.57	58.4	51.70	31.6

Source: Standard & Poor's. *NYSE Daily Stock Price Record,* Jan. 2001, 2002.

$$I_{\text{Jan. 2001}} = \frac{\sum_{i=1}^{4} Q_{i,\,\text{Jan. 2001}} P_{i,\,\text{Jan. 2001}}}{\sum_{i=1}^{4} Q_{i,\,\text{Jan. 2001}} P_{i,\,\text{Jan. 2001}}} \times 100 = 100$$

$$I_{\text{Dec. 2002}} = \frac{\sum_{i=1}^{4} Q_{i,\,\text{Dec. 2002}} P_{i,\,\text{Dec. 2002}}}{\sum_{i=1}^{4} Q_{i,\,\text{Dec. 2002}} P_{i,\,\text{Jan. 2001}}} \times 100$$

$$= \frac{(7.6)(77.50) + (58.4)(15.57) + (31.6)(51.70)}{(7.6)(112.0) + (58.4)(37.00) + (31.6)(61.06)} \times 100$$

$$= \frac{3{,}132.008}{4{,}941.496} \times 100 = 63.4$$

The implication is that Dec. 2002 prices represent a $(100 - 63.4)\% = 36.6\%$ decrease from Jan. 2001 prices, assuming the purchase quantities were at Dec. 2002 levels for *both* periods.

Now Work *Exercise 15.12d*

■ ■ ■

The Paasche index is most appropriate when you want to compare current prices to base period prices at *current* purchase levels. However, there are several major problems associated with the Paasche index. First, it requires that purchase quantities be known for every time period. This rules out a Paasche index for applications such as the CPI because the time and monetary resource expenditures required to collect quantity information are considerable. (Recall that more than 30,000 families were sampled to estimate purchase quantities in 1982–1984.) A second problem is that although each period is compared to the base period, it is difficult to compare the index at two other periods because the quantities used are different for each period. Consequently, the change in the index is affected by changes in both prices *and* quantities. This fact makes it difficult to interpret the change in a Paasche index between periods when neither is the base period.

Although there are other types of indexes that use different weighting factors, the Laspeyres and Paasche indexes are the most popular composite indexes. Depending on the primary objective in constructing an index, one of them will probably be suitable for most purposes.

Suggested Exercise 15.12

Exercises 15.1–15.12

Learning the Mechanics

15.1 Explain in words how to construct a simple index.

15.2 Explain in words how to calculate the following types of indexes:
a. Simple composite index
b. Weighted composite index
c. Laspeyres index
d. Paasche index

15.3 Explain in words the difference between Laspeyres and Paasche indexes.

15.4 The table below lists the U.S. median annual family income every five years during the period 1975–2000. It also contains several values for each of two simple indexes for median family income. Calculate the missing values of each simple index.

⊙ FAMINCOME

Year	Income ($)	Base 1975 Index	Base 1980 Index
1975	13,719	—	65.26
1980	21,023	153.24	—
1985	27,735	202.16	—
1990	35,353	257.69	—
1995	40,611	—	—
2000	50,890	—	—

Source: U.S. Bureau of the Census. *Statistical Abstract of the United States,* 2001.

15.5 The table below describes U.S. beer production (in millions of barrels) for the period 1975–2000.
a. Use 1977 as the base period to compute the simple index for this time series.
b. Refer to part **a.** Is this an example of a quantity index or a price index?   Quantity Index
c. Recompute the simple index using 1980 as the base period. Plot the two indexes on the same graph.

⊙ USBEER

Year	Beer	Year	Beer	Year	Beer
1975	161	1984	193	1993	202
1976	164	1985	194	1994	203
1977	171	1986	197	1995	200
1978	179	1987	195	1996	200
1979	184	1988	197	1997	199
1980	194	1989	199	1998	198
1981	194	1990	202	1999	198
1982	196	1991	204	2000	200
1983	196	1992	201		

Source: 2001 Brewer's Almanac, U.S. Beer Institute.

Applying the Concepts—Basic

15.6 The quarterly numbers of housing starts (in thousands of dwellings) in the United States from 1997 through 2001 are recorded in the accompanying table.

⊙ QTRHOUSE

Year	Quarter	Housing Starts
1997	1	297.3
	2	419.0
	3	400.3
	4	357.5
1998	1	324.9
	2	447.8
1998	3	445.0
	4	399.3
1999	1	369.5
	2	454.5
	3	453.5
	4	389.0
2000	1	364.5
	2	453.4
	3	405.3
	4	357.5
2001	1	347.8
	2	460.5
	3	429.2
	4	365.8

Source: Standard & Poor's Statistical Service: Current Statistics, Mar. 2002.

a. Using Quarter 1, 1997 as a base period, calculate the simple index for this quarterly time series.
b. Interpret the simple index for Quarter 2, 2000.
c. By what percentage did the number of housing starts increase between Quarter 1, 1997 and Quarter 4, 2001?   23.04%
d. By what percentage did the number of housing starts decrease between Quarter 1, 1999 and Quarter 4, 2001?   1.0014%

15.7 The table below lists the price of natural gas (in dollars per 1,000 cubic feet) between 1980 and 2000.

⊙ NATGAS

Year	Price	Year	Price
1980	3.68	1995	6.06
1990	5.80	1996	6.34
1991	5.82	1997	6.94
1992	5.89	1998	6.82
1993	6.16	1999	6.69
1994	6.41	2000	7.71

Source: U.S. Bureau of the Census. *Statistical Abstract of the United States,* 2001.

a. Using 1980 as the base period, calculate and plot the simple index for the price of natural gas from 1990 through 2000.

b. Use the simple index to interpret the trend in the price of natural gas.

c. Is the index you constructed in part **a** a price or quantity index? Explain.   Price Index

Applying the Concepts—Intermediate

15.8 Civilian employment is broadly classified by the federal government into two categories—agricultural and nonagricultural. Employment figures (in thousands of workers) for farm and nonfarm categories for the years 1980–2000 are given in the table below.

⊙ CVEMPLOY

Year	Farm	Nonfarm	Year	Farm	Nonfarm
1980	3,364	95,938	1991	3,233	113,644
1981	3,368	97,030	1992	3,207	114,391
1982	3,401	96,125	1993	3,074	116,232
1983	3,383	97,450	1994	3,409	119,651
1984	3,321	101,685	1995	3,440	121,460
1985	3,179	103,971	1996	3,443	123,264
1986	3,163	106,434	1997	3,399	126,159
1987	3,208	109,232	1998	3,378	128,085
1988	3,169	111,800	1999	3,281	130,207
1989	3,199	114,142	2000	3,305	131,903
1990	3,186	114,728			

Source: U.S. Bureau of the Census. *Statistical Abstract of the United States,* 2001.

a. Compute simple indexes for each of the two time series using 1980 as the base period.

b. Which segment has shown the greater percentage change in employment over the period shown?

c. Compute a simple composite index for total employment for the years 1980–2000. Use 1980 as a base period.

d. Refer to part **c.** Interpret the composite index value for 2000.

15.9 The Gross Domestic Product (GDP) is the total national output of goods and services valued at market prices. As such, the GDP is a commonly used barometer of the U.S. economy. One component of the GDP is personal consumption expenditures, which is itself the sum of expenditures for durable goods, nondurable goods, and services. The GDP for these components (in billions of dollars) is shown in the next table, in five-year increments from 1960 to 2000.

a. Using these three component values, construct a simple composite index for the personal consumption component of GDP. Use 1970 as the base year.

b. Suppose we want to update the index by using 1980 as the base year. Update the index using only the index values you calculated in part **a,** without referring to the original data.

c. Graph the personal consumption expenditure index for the years 1960–2000, first using 1970 as the base year and then using 1980 as the base year. What effect does changing the base year have on the graph of this index?

⊙ GDP

Year	Durables	Nondurables	Services
1960	$ 43.5	$ 153.1	$ 135.9
1965	63.5	191.9	189.2
1970	85.3	270.4	290.8
1975	134.3	416.0	474.5
1980	212.5	682.9	852.7
1985	352.9	919.4	1,395.1
1990	468.2	1,229.2	2,063.8
1995	589.7	1,497.3	2,882.0
2000	803.9	1,972.9	3,906.9

Source: U.S. Bureau of the Census. *Statistical Abstract of the United States,* 2002 (**www.bea.doc.gov.**).

15.10 Refer to Exercise 15.9. Suppose the output quantities in 1970, measured in billions of units purchased, are as follows:

Durable goods: 10.9

Nondurable goods: 14.02

Services: 42.6

a. Use the outputs to calculate the Laspeyres index from 1960 to 2000 (same increments as in Exercise 15.9) with 1970 as the base period.

b. Plot the simple composite index of Exercise 15.9 and Laspeyres index of part **a** on the same graph. Comment on the differences between the two indexes.

15.11 The table at the top of page 1010 presents the average hourly earnings and the average number of hours worked per week in 5-year increments from 1975 to 2000 for nonsupervisory workers in three different industries.

a. Compute a simple index for average hourly earnings for manufacturing workers over the period 1975–2000. Use 1975 as the base year. Do the same for transportation and public utilities workers.

b. Plot the two simple indexes on the same graph and interpret the results.

c. Compute simple composite indexes for hourly earnings and weekly hours for the 24-year period. Use 1975 as the base year.

d. Plot the two composite indexes, part **c,** on the same graph and interpret the results.

15.12 The level of price and production of metals in the United States is one measure of the strength of the industrial economy. The 2nd table on p. 1010 lists the 1997 prices (in dollars per ton) and production (in tons) for three metals important to U.S. industry.

a. Compute simple composite price and quantity indexes for the 12-month period, using January as the base period.

b. Compute the Laspeyres price index for the 12-month period, using January as the base period.

c. Plot the simple composite and Laspeyres indexes on the same graph. Comment on the differences.

NONSUPER (Data for Exercise 15.11)

Year	Manufacturing		Transportation and Public Utilities		Wholesale Trade	
	Hourly Earnings	Weekly Hours	Hourly Earnings	Weekly Hours	Hourly Earnings	Weekly Hours
1975	4.83	39.5	5.88	39.7	4.72	38.6
1980	7.27	39.7	8.87	39.6	6.95	38.4
1985	9.54	40.5	11.40	39.5	9.15	38.4
1990	10.83	40.8	12.97	38.9	10.79	38.1
1995	12.37	41.6	14.23	39.5	12.43	38.3
2000	14.38	41.7	16.22	39.6	15.20	38.4

Source: U.S. Bureau of the Census, *Statistical Abstract of the United States,* 2001.

d. Compute the Paasche price index for metals for the 12-month period, using January as the base period.

e. Plot the Laspeyres and Paasche indexes on the same graph. Comment on the differences.

f. Compare the Laspeyres and Paasche index values for September and December. Which index is more appropriate for describing the change in this four-month period? Explain.

METALS

Month	Copper		Steel		Lead	
	Price	Production	Price	Production	Price	Production
Jan	1,065.2	220.7	131.14	8,735	1,000.0	28,800
Feb	1,051.6	200.7	143.50	8,266	1,000.0	28,500
Mar	1,061.8	216.7	139.70	9,175	974.0	31,900
Apr	1,080.0	216.3	132.59	8,882	960.0	30,400
May	1,052.0	205.9	136.50	9,048	960.0	30,800
Jun	992.8	196.5	136.50	8,662	960.0	28,700
Jul	960.0	222.1	143.50	8,692	960.0	25,900
Aug	954.2	213.5	146.50	8,818	960.0	28,000
Sep	920.0	226.2	139.60	9,006	960.0	21,600
Oct	880.0	241.2	139.63	9,128	960.0	30,500
Nov	800.0	229.3	142.50	9,116	960.0	29,000
Dec	800.0	230.6	142.50	9,071	960.0	28,700

Source: The CRB Commodity Yearbook 1998. New York: John Wiley & Sons, Inc., 1998.

15.2 Descriptive Analysis: Exponential Smoothing

As you have seen in the previous section, index numbers are useful for describing trends and changes in time series. However, time series often have such irregular fluctuations that trends are difficult to describe. Index numbers can be misleading in such cases because the series is changing so rapidly. Methods for removing the rapid fluctuations in a time series so the general trend can be seen are called **smoothing** techniques.

Exponential smoothing is one type of weighted average that assigns positive weights to past and current values of the time series. A single weight, w, called the **exponential smoothing constant,** is selected so that w is between 0 and 1. Then the exponentially smoothed series, E_t, is calculated as follows:

$$E_1 = Y_1$$
$$E_2 = wY_2 + (1 - w)E_1$$
$$E_3 = wY_3 + (1 - w)E_2$$
$$\vdots$$
$$E_t = wY_t + (1 - w)E_{t-1}$$

Thus, the exponentially smoothed value at time t assigns the weight w to the current series value and the weight $(1 - w)$ to the previous smoothed value.

For example, consider the silver price time series for 1975–2002 in Table 15.1 (p.-). Suppose we want to calculate the exponentially smoothed series using a smoothing constant of $w = .3$. The calculations proceed as follows:

$$E_{1975} = Y_{1975} = 4.42$$
$$E_{1976} = .3Y_{1976} + (1 - .3)E_{1975} = .3(4.35) + .7(4.42) = 4.40$$
$$E_{1977} = .3Y_{1977} + (1 - .3)E_{1976} = .3(4.62) + .7(4.40) = 4.47$$
$$\vdots$$

All the exponentially smoothed values corresponding to $w = .3$ are given in the MINITAB worksheet, Figure 15.4. (*Note:* MINITAB gives the value of E_t in row $t + 1$.)

Figure 15.4
MINITAB worksheet with exponentially smoothed ($w = .3$) silver prices

	C1	C2	C3
↓	YEAR	PRICE	SMOOTH3
1	1975	4.42	4.4200
2	1976	4.35	4.3990
3	1977	4.62	4.4653
4	1978	5.40	4.7457
5	1979	11.09	6.6490
6	1980	20.64	10.8463
7	1981	10.52	10.7484
8	1982	7.95	9.9089
9	1983	11.44	10.3682
10	1984	8.14	9.6998
11	1985	6.14	8.6318
12	1986	5.47	7.6833
13	1987	7.01	7.4813
14	1988	6.53	7.1959
15	1989	5.50	6.6871
16	1990	4.82	6.1270
17	1991	4.04	5.5009
18	1992	3.94	5.0326
19	1993	4.30	4.8128
20	1994	5.30	4.9590
21	1995	5.20	5.0313
22	1996	5.18	5.0759
23	1997	4.89	5.0201
24	1998	5.48	5.1581
25	1999	5.22	5.1767
26	2000	4.97	5.1147
27	2001	4.37	4.8913
28	2002	4.60	4.8039

SILVER.MTW ***

Figure 15.5

MINITAB graph of exponentially smoothed ($w = .3$) silver prices

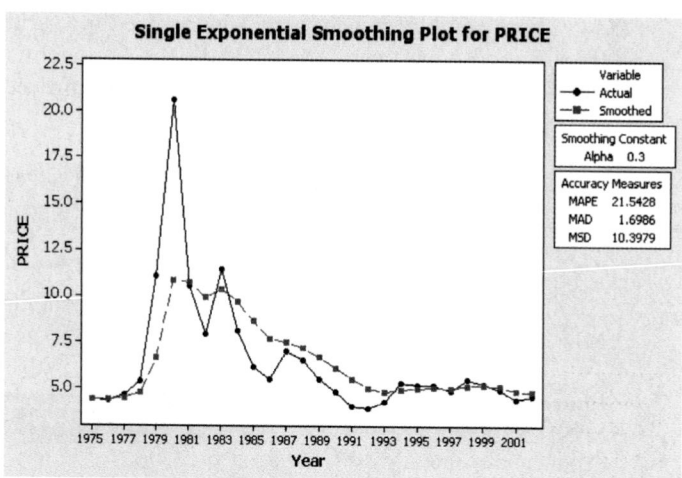

Teaching Tip

Discuss the consequences of the different choices for the weighting constant w.

The actual silver prices and exponentially smoothed prices are graphed in Figure 15.5. Like many averages, the exponentially smoothed series changes less rapidly than the time series itself. The choice of w affects the smoothness of E_t. The smaller (closer to 0) is the value of w, the smoother is E_t. Since small values of w give more weight to the past values of the time series, the smoothed series is not affected by rapid changes in the current values and, therefore, appears smoother than the original series. Conversely, choosing w near 1 yields an exponentially smoothed series that is much like the original series. That is, large values of w give more weight to the current value of the time series so the smoothed series looks like the original series. This concept is illustrated in Figure 15.6. The steps for calculating an exponentially smoothed series are given in the box.

Figure 15.6

MINITAB graph of exponentially smoothed silver prices ($w = .3$ and $w = .7$)

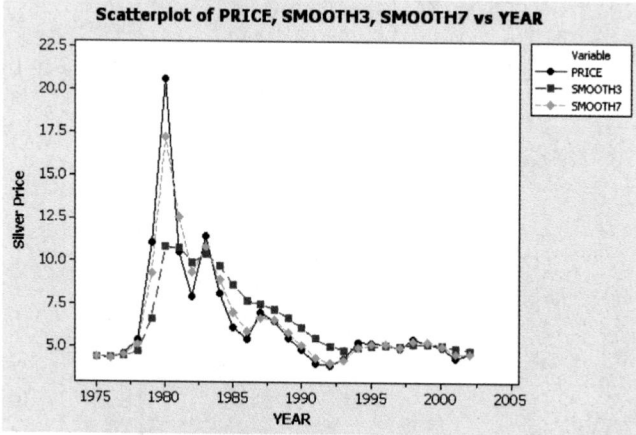

Steps for Calculating an Exponentially Smoothed Series

1. Select an exponential smoothing constant, w, between 0 and 1. Remember that small values of w give less weight to the current value of the series and yield a smoother series. Larger choices of w assign more weight to the current value of the series and yield a more variable series.

2. Calculate the exponentially smoothed series E_t from the original time series Y_t as follows:

(cont'd)

$$E_1 = Y_1$$
$$E_2 = wY_2 + (1 - w)E_1$$
$$E_3 = wY_3 + (1 - w)E_2$$
$$\vdots$$
$$E_t = wY_t + (1 - w)E_{t-1}$$

EXAMPLE 15.4   CONSTRUCTING ON EXPONENTIALLY SMOOTHED SERIES

Problem Refer to Example 15.1 (p. 1001). Consider the IBM common stock price from January 2001 to December 2002, shown in Table 15.3 (p. 1002). Create the exponentially smoothed series using $w = .5$, and plot both series.

Solution To create the exponentially smoothed series with $w = .5$, we calculate

$$E_1 = Y_1 = 112.0$$
$$E_2 = wY_2 + (1 - w)E_1 = .5(99.90) + .5(112.0) = 105.95$$
$$\vdots$$
$$E_{24} = wY_{24} + (1 - w)E_{23} = .5(77.50) + .5(79.88) = 78.69$$

These values, obtained using MINITAB, are shown on the MINITAB worksheet, Figure 15.7. The plot of the original and exponentially smoothed series is shown in Figure 15.8.

Suggested Exercises 15.17

Look Back The smoothed series provides a good picture of the general trend of the original series. Note, too, that the exponentially smoothed series will be less sensitive to any short-term deviations of the prices from the trend as occurred in 2002.

Now Work   *Exercise 15.14*

——————— ■ ■ ■ ———————

One of the primary uses of exponential smoothing is to forecast future values of a time series. Because only current and past values of the time series are used in exponential smoothing, it is easily adapted to forecasting. We demonstrate this application of exponentially smoothed series in Section 15.4.

Exercises 15.13–15.20

Learning the Mechanics

15.13 Describe the effect of selecting an exponential constant of $w = .2$. Of $w = .8$. Which will produce a smoother trend? $w = .2$

15.14 Consider the monthly time series shown in the table.

◎ **LM15_14**

Month	t	Y_t	Exponentially Smoothed Series ($w = .5$)
Jan.	1	280	—
Feb.	2	281	—
Mar.	3	250	265.3
Apr.	4	246	255.6
May	5	239	—
Jun.	6	218	—
Jul.	7	218	—
Aug.	8	210	—
Sep.	9	205	—
Oct.	10	206	—
Nov.	11	200	—
Dec.	12	200	—

a. Calculate the missing values in the exponentially smoothed series using $w = .5$.

b. Graph the time series and the exponentially smoothed series on the same graph.

Figure 15.7
MINITAB worksheet with
exponentially smoothed
($w = .5$) IBM stock prices

↓	C1	C2-D	C3	C4	C5
	YEAR	MONTH	TIME	IBM	SMOOTH5
1	2001	Jan	1	112.00	112.000
2	2001	Feb	2	99.90	105.950
3	2001	Mar	3	96.18	101.065
4	2001	Apr	4	115.14	108.103
5	2001	May	5	111.80	109.951
6	2001	Jun	6	113.50	111.726
7	2001	Jul	7	105.21	108.468
8	2001	Aug	8	99.95	104.209
9	2001	Sep	9	91.72	97.964
10	2001	Oct	10	108.07	103.017
11	2001	Nov	11	115.59	109.304
12	2001	Dec	12	120.96	115.132
13	2002	Jan	13	107.89	111.511
14	2002	Feb	14	98.12	104.815
15	2002	Mar	15	104.00	104.408
16	2002	Apr	16	83.76	94.084
17	2002	May	17	80.45	87.267
18	2002	Jun	18	72.00	79.633
19	2002	Jul	19	70.40	75.017
20	2002	Aug	20	75.38	75.198
21	2002	Sep	21	58.31	66.754
22	2002	Oct	22	78.94	72.847
23	2002	Nov	23	86.92	79.884
24	2002	Dec	24	77.50	78.692

Figure 15.8
MINITAB graph of
exponentially smoothed
($w = .5$) IBM stock prices

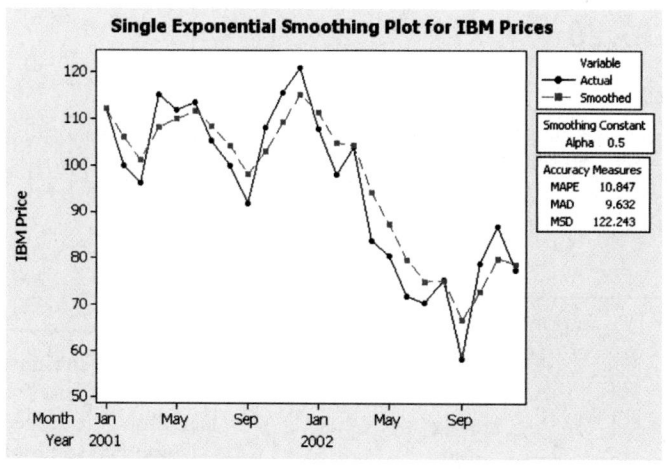

Applying the Concepts—Basic

15.15 Refer to the annual U.S. beer production time series, Exercise 15.5. (p. 1008).
  a. Calculate the exponentially smoothed series for U.S. beer production for the period 1975–2000 using $w = .2$.
  b. Calculate the exponentially smoothed series using $w = .8$.
  c. Plot the two exponentially smoothed series ($w = .2$ and $w = .8$) on the same graph. Which smoothed series best portrays the long-term trend?

15.16 Overfishing and pollution of U.S. coastal waters have resulted in an increased dependence by the United States on the fishing grounds of other countries. The table describes the annual fish catch (in thousands of metric tons) in all fishing areas of Brazil and Chile from 1986 to 1995.

⊙ FISHTONS

Year	Chile	Brazil
1986	5,571.6	957.6
1987	4,814.6	948.0
1988	5,209.9	830.1
1989	6,454.2	850.0
1990	5,195.4	802.9
1991	6,002.8	800.0
1992	6,501.8	790.0
1993	6,034.9	780.0
1994	7,838.5	820.0
1995	7,590.5	800.0

Source: Statistical Division, Department of Economics and Social Information and Policy Analysis, *United Nations. Statistical Yearbook,* 1997.

  a. Compute an exponentially smoothed series for both Chile and Brazil, using a smoothing coefficient of $w = .5$.
  b. Plot both actual series and both smoothed series on the same graph. Describe the differences in variation of catches over time between the two countries. For example, do they move up and down together over time?

Applying the Concepts—Intermediate

15.17 The price of gold is used by some financial analysts as a barometer of investors' expectations of inflation, with the price of gold tending to increase as concerns about inflation increase. The next table shows the average annual price of gold (in dollars per ounce) from 1979 through 2002.
  a. Compute an exponentially smoothed series for the gold price time series for the period from 1979 to 2002, using a smoothing coefficient of $w = .8$.
  b. Plot the original series and the exponentially smoothed series on the same graph. Comment on the trend observed.

⊙ GOLDYR

Year	Price	Year	Price
1979	308	1981	460
1980	613	1982	376
1983	424	1993	361
1984	361	1994	387
1985	318	1995	385
1986	368	1996	389
1987	448	1997	333
1988	438	1998	294
1989	383	1999	278
1990	385	2000	279
1991	363	2001	273
1992	345	2002	310

Source: World Gold Council (**www.gold.org**).

15.18 There has been phenomenal growth in the transportation sector of the economy since 1970. The personal consumption expenditure figures (in billions of dollars) are given in the table below.
  a. Compute exponentially smoothed values of this personal consumption time series, using the smoothing constants $w = .2$ and $w = .8$.
  b. Plot the actual series and the two smoothed series on the same graph. Comment on the trend in personal consumption expenditure on transportation in the 1990s as compared to the 1970s.

⊙ TRANSPRT

Year	Expenditure on Transportation	Year	Expenditure on Transportation
1970	80.6	1986	366.3
1971	92.3	1987	377.1
1972	105.4	1988	406.4
1973	114.6	1989	425.7
1974	117.9	1990	463.3
1975	129.4	1991	438.2
1976	155.2	1992	466.3
1977	179.3	1993	504.2
1978	198.1	1994	542.2
1979	219.4	1995	572.3
1980	236.6	1996	602.2
1981	261.5	1997	636.4
1982	267.3	1998	648.6
1983	291.9	1999	711.2
1984	319.5	2000	784.9
1985	359.5		

Source: U.S. Bureau of the Census. *Statistical Abstract of the United States,* 2001.

15.19 The data in the next table are the amounts of crude oil (millions of barrels) imported into the U.S. from the Organization of Petroleum Exporting Countries (OPEC) for the years 1974–2000.
  a. Construct two exponentially smoothed series for this time series, using $w = .1$ and $w = .9$.

b. Plot the original series and the two smoothed series on the same graph. Which smoothed series looks more like the original series? Why?

OPECOIL

Year	t	Imports, Y_t	Year	t	Imports, Y_t
1974	1	926	1988	15	987
1975	2	1,171	1989	16	1,232
1976	3	1,663	1990	17	1,282
1977	4	2,058	1991	18	1,233
1978	5	1,892	1992	19	1,247
1979	6	1,866	1993	20	1,339
1980	7	1,414	1994	21	1,307
1981	8	1,067	1995	22	1,303
1982	9	633	1996	23	1,258
1983	10	540	1997	24	1,378
1984	11	553	1998	25	1,522
1985	12	479	1999	26	1,543
1986	13	771	2000	27	1,664
1987	14	876			

Source: Statistical Abstract of the United States, U.S. Bureau of the Census, 2001.

15.20 Standard & Poor's 500 Composite Stock Index (S&P 500) is a stock market index. Like the Dow Jones Industrial Average, it is an indicator of stock market activity. The next table contains end-of-quarter values of the S&P 500 for the years 1995–2001.

SP500

Year	Quarter	S&P 500	Year	Quarter	S&P 500
1995	1	500.7	1999	1	1286.4
	2	544.8		2	1372.7
	3	584.4		3	1282.7
	4	615.9		4	1469.2
1996	1	645.5	2000	1	1498.6
	2	670.6		2	1454.6
	3	687.3		3	1436.5
	4	740.7		4	1320.3
1997	1	757.1	2001	1	1160.3
	2	885.1		2	1224.4
	3	947.3		3	1040.9
	4	970.4		4	1148.1
1998	1	1101.7			
	2	1133.8			
	3	1017.0			
	4	1229.2			

Source: Standard & Poor's Statistical Service: Current Statistics, Mar. 2002.

a. Calculate and plot the exponentially smoothed series for the quarterly S&P 500 using a smoothing constant of $w = .3$.

b. Repeat part **a,** but use $w = .7$.

c. Which exponentially smoothed series do you prefer for describing trends in the series? Explain.

$w = .3$

15.3 Time Series Components

In the previous two sections we showed how to use various *descriptive* techniques to obtain a picture of the behavior of a time series. Now we want to expand our coverage to include techniques that will let us make statistical inferences about the time series. These *inferential techniques* are generally focused on the problem of *forecasting* future values of the time series.

Before forecasts of future values of a time series can be made, some type of model that can be projected into the future must be used to describe the series. Time series models range in complexity from **descriptive models,** such as the exponential smoothing models discussed in the previous section, to **inferential models,** such as the combinations of regression and specialized time series models to be discussed later in this chapter. Whether the model is simple or complex, the objective is the same: to produce accurate forecasts of future values of the time series.

Many different algebraic representations of time series models have been proposed. One of the most widely used is an **additive model*** of the form

$$Y_t = T_t + C_t + S_t + R_t$$

Teaching Tip

The main drawback associated with the descriptive models is the lack of any type of reliability measure. The inferential methods do not have this drawback.

---

*Another useful form is the *multiplicative model:* $Y_t = T_t C_t S_t R_t$. This can be changed to an additive form by taking natural logarithms (i.e., $\ln Y_t = \ln T_t + \ln C_t + \ln S_t + \ln R_t$). See Section 15.8.

The **secular trend,** T_t, also known as the **long-term trend,** is a time series component that describes the long-term movements of Y_t. For example, if you want to characterize the secular trend of the production of automobiles since 1930, you would show T_t as an upward-moving time series over the period from 1930 to the present. This does not imply that the automobile production series has always moved upward from month to month and from year to year, but it does mean the long-term trend has been an increase over that period of time.

The **cyclical effect,** C_t, generally describes fluctuations of the time series about the secular trend that are attributable to business and economic conditions. For example, refer back to the Dow Jones Industrial Average (DJIA) time series for the years 1980–1999, Table 15.7. Recall that a plot of the time series (Figure 15.4) showed a generally increasing secular trend. However, during periods of recession, the DJIA tends to lie below the secular trend, while in times of general economic expansion, it lies above the long-term trend line.

Teaching Tip

Try not to overwhelm the students with the model at this point. A general understanding of the various components is sufficient.

The **seasonal effect,** S_t, describes the fluctuations in the time series that recur during specific time periods. For example, quarterly power loads for a Florida utility company tend to be highest in the summer months (quarter III), with another smaller peak in the winter months (quarter I). The spring and fall (quarters II and IV) seasonal effects are negative, meaning that the series tends to lie below the long-term trend line during those quarters.

The **residual effect,** R_t, is what remains of Y_t after the secular, cyclical, and seasonal components have been removed. Part of the residual effect may be attributable to unpredictable rare events (earthquake, presidential assassination, etc.) and part to the randomness of human actions. In any case, the presence of the residual component makes it impossible to forecast the future values of a time series without error. Thus, the presence of the residual effect emphasizes a point we first made in Chapter 10 in connection with regression models: No business phenomena should be described by deterministic models. All realistic business models, time series or otherwise, should include a residual component.

Each of the four components contributes to the determination of the value of Y_t at each time period. Although it will not always be possible to characterize each component separately, the component model provides a useful theoretical formulation that helps the time series analyst achieve a better understanding of the phenomena affecting the path followed by the time series.

15.4 Forecasting: Exponential Smoothing

In Section 15.2, we discussed exponential smoothing as a method for describing a time series that involved removing the irregular fluctuations. In terms of the time series components discussed in the previous section, exponential smoothing tends to de-emphasize (or "smooth") most of the residual effects. This, coupled with the fact that exponential smoothing uses only past and current values of the series, makes it a useful tool for forecasting time series.

Teaching Tip

Note the lack of a measure of reliability for the exponential forecasts.

Recall that the formula for exponential smoothing is

$$E_t = wY_t + (1 - w)E_{t-1}$$

where w, the *exponential smoothing constant,* is a number between 0 and 1. We learned that the selection of w controls the smoothness of E_t. A choice near 0 places more emphasis (weight) on *past* values of the time series, and therefore yields a smoother series; a choice near 1 gives more weight to *current* values of the series.

Suppose the objective is to forecast the next value of the time series, Y_{t+1}. The **exponentially smoothed forecast** for Y_{t+1} is simply the smoothed value at time t:

$$F_{t+1} = E_t$$

where F_{t+1} is the **forecast** of Y_{t+1}. To help interpret this forecast formula, substitute the smoothing formula for E_t:

$$
\begin{aligned}
F_{t+1} = E_t &= wY_t + (1 - w)E_{t-1} \\
&= wY_t + (1 - w)F_t \\
&= F_t + w(Y_t - F_t)
\end{aligned}
$$

Note that we have substituted F_t for E_{t-1}, since the forecast for time t is the smoothed value for time $(t - 1)$. The final equation provides insight into the exponential smoothing forecast: The forecast for time $(t + 1)$ is equal to the forecast for time t, F_t, plus a correction for the error in the forecast for time t, $(Y_t - F_t)$. This is why the exponentially smoothed forecast is called an **adaptive forecast**—the forecast for time $(t + 1)$ is explicitly adapted for the error in the forecast for time t.

Suggested Exercises 15.28

Because exponential smoothing consists of averaging past and present values, the smoothed values will tend to lag behind the series when a long-term trend exists. In addition, the averaging tends to smooth any seasonal component. Therefore, exponentially smoothed forecasts are appropriate only when the trend and seasonal components are relatively insignificant. Since the exponential smoothing model assumes that the time series has little or no trend or seasonal component, the forecast F_{t+1} is used to forecast not only Y_{t+1} but also all future values of Y_t. That is, the forecast for two time periods ahead is

$$F_{t+2} = F_{t+1}$$

and for three time periods ahead is

$$F_{t+3} = F_{t+2} = F_{t+1}$$

The exponential smoothing forecasting technique is summarized in the box.

Calculation of Exponentially Smoothed Forecasts

1. Given the observed time series $Y_1, Y_2, \ldots, Y_t$, first calculate the exponentially smoothed values $E_1, E_2, \ldots, E_t$, using

$$
\begin{aligned}
E_1 &= Y_1 \\
E_2 &= wY_2 + (1 - w)E_1 \\
&\vdots \\
E_t &= wY_t + (1 - w)E_{t-1}
\end{aligned}
$$

2. Use the last smoothed value to forecast the next time series value:

$$F_{t+1} = E_t$$

3. Assuming that Y_t is relatively free of trend and seasonal components, use the same forecast for all future values of Y_t:

$$
\begin{aligned}
F_{t+2} &= F_{t+1} \\
F_{t+3} &= F_{t+1} \\
&\vdots
\end{aligned}
$$

Teaching Tip
The more significant the trend and seasonality are in the time series model, the less accurate the forecasts for the exponentially smoothed model will be.

Two important points must be made about exponentially smoothed forecasts:

1. The choice of w is crucial. If you decide that w will be small (near 0), you will obtain a smooth, slowly changing series of forecasts. On the other hand, the selection of a large value of w (near 1) will yield more rapidly changing forecasts that depend mostly on the current values of the series. In general, several values of w should be tried to determine how sensitive the forecast series is to the choice of w. Forecasting experience will provide the best basis for the choice of w for a particular application.

2. The further into the future you forecast, the less certain you can be of accuracy. Since the exponentially smoothed forecast is constant for all future values, any changes in trend or seasonality are not taken into account. However, the uncertainty associated with future forecasts applies not only to exponentially smoothed forecasts, but also to all methods of forecasting. In general, time series forecasting should be confined to the short term.

EXAMPLE 15.5   FORECASTING WITH EXPONENTIAL SMOOTHING

Problem   The annual silver prices from 1975 to 2002 are repeated in the MINITAB worksheet, Figure 15.9, along with the exponentially smoothed values using $w = .3$ and $w = .7$. Apply the exponential smoothing technique to the data from 1975 to 1999 in order to forecast the silver prices from 2000 to 2002 using both $w = .3$ and $w = .7$.

$w = .3$:
$F_{2000} = F_{2001} = F_{2002} = 5.18$

Solution   First, we calculate the exponentially smoothed forecasts using $w = .3$. Following the steps outlined in the box, the forecast for 2000 is simply the smoothed price in 1999,

$$F_{2000} = E_{1999} = 5.18 \text{ (shaded on Figure 15.9)}$$

We use the same value as the forecast for 2001 and 2002:

$w = .7$:
$F_{2000} = F_{2001} = F_{2002} = 5.25$

$$F_{2001} = E_{1999} = 5.18$$
$$F_{2002} = E_{1999} = 5.18$$

The same steps are repeated using $w = .7$. (The forecast for all three years is the smoothed value in 1999, 5.25.) Both sets of forecasts are shown in Table 15.6. Also shown are the actual silver prices from 2000 to 2002. The **forecast error,** defined as the actual value minus the forecast value, is given for each exponentially smoothed forecast.

Look Back   Notice that the one-step-ahead forecasts for 2000 have smaller forecast errors than the two- and three-steps-ahead forecasts for 2001 and 2002. Neither the $w = .3$ nor the $w = .7$ forecast projects the downturn in the silver prices in 2001 and 2002, because exponentially smoothed forecasts implicitly assume no trend exists in the time series. This example dramatically illustrates the risk associated with anything other than very short-term forecasting.

Now Work   *Exercise 15.23*

■ ■ ■

↓	C1	C2	C3	C4
	YEAR	PRICE	SMOOTH3	SMOOTH7
1	1975	4.42	4.4200	4.4200
2	1976	4.35	4.3990	4.3710
3	1977	4.62	4.4653	4.5453
4	1978	5.40	4.7457	5.1436
5	1979	11.09	6.6490	9.3061
6	1980	20.64	10.8463	17.2398
7	1981	10.52	10.7484	12.5359
8	1982	7.95	9.9089	9.3258
9	1983	11.44	10.3682	10.8057
10	1984	8.14	9.6998	8.9397
11	1985	6.14	8.6318	6.9799
12	1986	5.47	7.6833	5.9230
13	1987	7.01	7.4813	6.6839
14	1988	6.53	7.1959	6.5762
15	1989	5.50	6.6871	5.8229
16	1990	4.82	6.1270	5.1209
17	1991	4.04	5.5009	4.3643
18	1992	3.94	5.0326	4.0673
19	1993	4.30	4.8128	4.2302
20	1994	5.30	4.9590	4.9791
21	1995	5.20	5.0313	5.1337
22	1996	5.18	5.0759	5.1661
23	1997	4.89	5.0201	4.9728
24	1998	5.48	5.1581	5.3279
25	1999	5.22	5.1767	5.2524
26	2000	4.97	5.1147	5.0547
27	2001	4.37	4.8913	4.5754
28	2002	4.60	4.8039	4.5926

Figure 15.9

MINITAB worksheet with exponentially smoothed
($w = .3$ and $w = .7$) silver prices

TABLE 15.6   Silver Prices (2000–2002): Actual versus Forecast Values

Year	Actual	Forecast ($w = .3$)	Forecast Error	Forecast ($w = .7$)	Forecast Error
2000	4.97	5.18	−.21	5.25	−.28
2001	4.37	5.18	−.81	5.25	−.88
2002	4.60	5.18	−.58	5.25	−.65

Many time series have long-term, or secular, trends. For such series the exponentially smoothed forecast is inappropriate for all but the very short term. In the next section we present an extension of the exponentially smoothed forecast—the *Holt-Winters forecast*—that allows for secular trend in the forecasts.

15.5 Forecasting Trends: The Holt-Winters Forecasting Model (Optional)

Teaching Tip

The advantage of the Holt-Winters model is that it allows for a trend in the time series data.

The exponentially smoothed forecasts for the silver prices in the previous section have large forecast errors, in part because they do not recognize the trend in the time series. In this section we present an extension of the exponential smoothing method of forecasting that explicitly recognizes the trend in a time series. The **Holt-Winters forecasting model** consists of both an exponentially smoothed component (E_t) and a trend component (T_t). Consequently, the technique is sometimes called **double exponential smoothing.** The trend component is used in the calculation of the exponentially smoothed value. The following equations show that both E_t and T_t are weighted averages:

$$E_t = wY_t + (1 - w)(E_{t-1} + T_{t-1})$$
$$T_t = v(E_t - E_{t-1}) + (1 - v)T_{t-1}$$

Note that the equations require *two* smoothing constants, w and v, each of which is between 0 and 1. As before, w controls the smoothness of E_t; a choice near 0 places more emphasis on past values of the time series, while a value of w near 1 gives more weight to current values of the series, and deemphasizes the past.

The trend component of the series is estimated *adaptively,* using a weighted average of the most recent change in the level, represented by $(E_t - E_{t-1})$, and the trend estimate, represented by T_{t-1}, from the previous period. A choice of the weight v near 0 places more emphasis on the past estimates of trend, while a choice of v near 1 gives more weight to the current change in level.

The calculation of the Holt-Winters components, which proceeds much like the exponential smoothing calculations, is summarized in the box.

Teaching Tip

These calculations are tedious and best derived via the computer. Concentrate the discussion on the forecasts derived from these calculations.

Steps for Calculating Components of the Holt-Winters Model

1. Select an exponential smoothing constant w between 0 and 1. Small values of w give less weight to the current values of the time series, and more weight to the past. Larger choices assign more weight to the current value of the series.

2. Select a trend smoothing constant v between 0 and 1. Small values of v give less weight to the current changes in the level of the series, and more weight to the past trend. Larger values assign more weight to the most recent trend of the series and less to past trends.

3. Calculate the two components, E_t and T_t, from the time series Y_t beginning at time $t = 2$ as follows:*

$$E_2 = Y_2$$
$$T_2 = Y_2 - Y_1$$

(cont'd)

---

*The calculation begins at time $t = 2$ rather than at $t = 1$ because the first two observations are needed to obtain the first estimate of trend, T_2. As an option, some statistical software packages use simple linear regression to estimate E_1 and T_1; for the model $E(Y_t) = \beta_0 + \beta_1 t$, $E_1 = \hat{\beta}_0$ and $T_1 = \hat{\beta}_1$.

$$E_3 = wY_3 + (1 - w)(E_2 + T_2)$$
$$T_3 = v(E_3 - E_2) + (1 - v)T_2$$
$$\vdots$$
$$E_t = wY_t + (1 - w)(E_{t-1} + T_{t-1})$$
$$T_t = v(E_t - E_{t-1}) + (1 - v)T_{t-1}$$

[Note: E_1 and T_1 are not defined.]

EXAMPLE 15.6

APPLYING THE HOLT-WINTERS METHOD

Problem The yearly sales data for a firm's first 35 years of operation are given in Table 15.7. Calculate the Holt-Winters exponential smoothing and trend components for this time series using $w = .7$ and $v = .5$. Show the data and the exponential smoothing component E_t on the same graph.

Suggested Exercises 15.27

 SALES35

TABLE 15.7 A Firm's Yearly Sales Revenue
(thousands of dollars)

t	Y_t	t	Y_t	t	Y_t
1	4.8	13	48.4	25	100.3
2	4.0	14	61.6	26	111.7
3	5.5	15	65.6	27	108.2
4	15.6	16	71.4	28	115.5
5	23.1	17	83.4	29	119.2
6	23.3	18	93.6	30	125.2
7	31.4	19	94.2	31	136.3
8	46.0	20	85.4	32	146.8
9	46.1	21	86.2	33	146.1
10	41.9	22	89.9	34	151.4
11	45.5	23	89.2	35	150.9
12	53.5	24	99.1		

Solution Rather than perform the Holt-Winters calculations by hand we used MINITAB to generate the values of E_t and T_t for the annual series. All the E_t and T_t values are given on the MINITAB printout, Figure 15.10. A graph of Y_t and E_t is shown in Figure 15.11. Note that the trend component T_t measures the general upward trend in Y_t.

Look Back The choice of $v = .5$ gives equal weight to the most recent trend and to past trends in the sales of the firm. The result is that the exponential smoothing component E_t provides a smooth, upward-trending description of the firm's sales.

Now Work *Exercise 15.22a*

— ■ ■ ■ —

Our objective is to use the Holt-Winters exponentially smoothed series to forecast the future values of the time series. For the one-step-ahead forecast, this is accomplished by adding the most recent exponentially smoothed component to the

↓	C1	C2	C3	C4
	T	**SALES**	**SMOOTH**	**TREND**
1	1	4.8	4.769	4.33163
2	2	4.0	5.530	2.54636
3	3	5.5	6.273	1.64455
4	4	15.6	13.295	4.33342
5	5	23.1	21.459	6.24838
6	6	23.3	24.622	4.70594
7	7	31.4	30.778	5.43113
8	8	46.0	43.063	8.85779
9	9	46.1	47.846	6.82056
10	10	41.9	45.730	2.35220
11	11	45.5	46.275	1.44842
12	12	53.5	51.767	3.47034
13	13	48.4	50.451	1.07730
14	14	61.6	58.579	4.60233
15	15	65.6	64.874	5.44902
16	16	71.4	71.077	5.82587
17	17	83.4	81.451	8.09987
18	18	93.6	92.385	9.51712
19	19	94.2	96.511	6.82130
20	20	85.4	90.780	0.54510
21	21	86.2	87.737	-1.24855
22	22	89.9	88.877	-0.05465
23	23	89.2	89.087	0.07765
24	24	99.1	96.119	3.55516
25	25	100.3	100.112	3.77411
26	26	111.7	109.356	6.50885
27	27	108.2	110.499	3.82618
28	28	115.5	115.148	4.23721
29	29	119.2	119.255	4.17250
30	30	125.2	124.668	4.79271
31	31	136.3	134.248	7.18632
32	32	146.8	145.190	9.06420
33	33	146.1	148.546	6.21009
34	34	151.4	152.407	5.03533
35	35	150.9	152.863	2.74553

Figure 15.10

MINITAB worksheet with Holt-Winters exponentially
smoothed ($w = .7$ and $v = .5$) sales data

Figure 15.11

MINITAB graph of Holt-Winters exponentially smoothed ($w = .7$ and $v = 5$) sales data

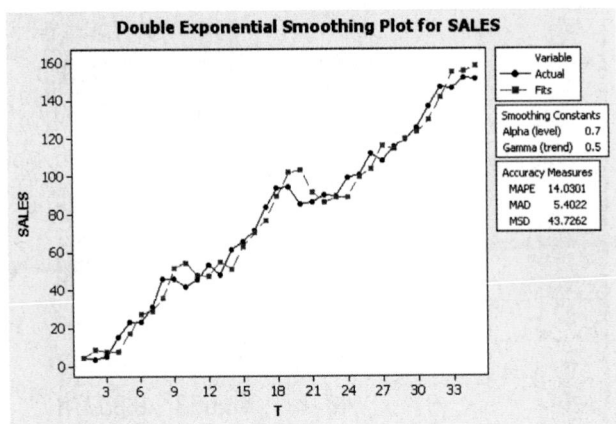

most recent trend component. That is, the forecast at time $(t + 1)$, given observed values up to time t, is

$$F_{t+1} = E_t + T_t$$

The idea is that we are constructing the forecast by combining the most recent smoothed estimate, E_t, with the estimate of the expected increase (or decrease) attributable to trend, T_t.

The forecast for two steps ahead is similar, except that we add estimated trend for *two* periods:

$$F_{t+2} = E_t + 2T_t$$

Similarly, for the k-step-ahead forecast, we add the estimated increase (or decrease) in trend over k periods:

$$F_{t+k} = E_t + kT_t$$

The Holt-Winters forecasting methodology is summarized in the box.

Teaching Tip

Compare the Holt-Winters and the exponentially smoothed forecasts from the preceding section.

Holt-Winters Forecasting

1. Calculate the exponentially smoothed and trend components, E_t and T_t, for each observed value of $Y_t (t \geq 2)$ using the formulas given in the previous box.

2. Calculate the one-step-ahead forecast using

$$F_{t+1} = E_t + T_t$$

3. Calculate the k-step-ahead forecast using

$$F_{t+k} = E_t + kT_t$$

EXAMPLE 15.7   OBTAINING HOLT-WINTERS FORECASTS

Problem   Refer to Example 15.6 and Figure 15.10, which lists the firm's 35 yearly sales figures, along with the Holt-Winters components using $w = .7$ and $v = .5$. Use the Holt-Winters forecasting technique to forecast the firm's annual sales in years 36–40.

$F_{36} = 155.60$

Solution From Figure 15.10, the smoothed and trend values for the last year are $E_{35} = 152.86$ and $T_{35} = 2.74$. For year 36 we calculate

$$F_{36} = E_{35} + T_{35} = 152.86 + 2.74 = 155.60$$

$F_{37} = 158.34$

The forecast two years ahead is

$$F_{37} = E_{35} + 2T_{35} = 152.86 + 2(2.74) = 158.34$$

$F_{38} = 161.08$
$F_{39} = 163.82$
$F_{40} = 166.56$

For years 38–40 we find

$$F_{38} = 152.86 + 3(2.74) = 161.08$$
$$F_{39} = 152.86 + 4(2.74) = 163.82$$
$$F_{40} = 152.86 + 5(2.74) = 166.56$$

Look Back Note that the forecast values increase from year 36 to year 40. This upward trend in the forecast is a result of the Holt-Winters estimated trend component.

> **Now Work** *Exercise 15.22b*

■ ■ ■

The selection of $w = .7$ and $v = .5$ as the smoothing and trend weights for the sales forecasts in Example 13.7 was based on the objectives of assigning more weight to recent series values in the exponentially smoothed component, and of assigning equal weights to the recent and past trend estimates. However, you may want to try several different combinations of weights when using the Holt-Winters forecasting model so that you can assess the sensitivity of the forecasts to the choice of weights. Experience with the particular time series and Holt-Winters forecasts will help in the selection of w and v in a practical application.

Exercises 15.21–15.28

Learning the Mechanics

15.21 How does the choice of the smoothing constant w impact an exponentially smoothed forecast?

USBEER

15.22 Refer to Exercise 15.5 (p. 1008) and the data on U.S. beer production (in millions of barrels) for the years 1975–2000.
  a. Use the 1975–1996 values to forecast the 1997–2000 production, using simple exponential smoothing with $w = .3$. With $w = .7$.
  b. Use the Holt-Winters model with $w = .7$ and $v = .3$ to forecast the 1997–2000 production. Repeat with $w = .3$ and $v = .7$.

15.23 **QTRHOUSE**

Refer to the quarterly housing start series, Exercise 15.6 (p. 1008). Suppose you want to forecast the num-

ber of new housing starts in 2002 using data for 2000 and 2001.
  a. Calculate the exponentially smoothed values for 2000 and 2001 using $w = .6$.
  b. Plot the housing-starts series and the exponentially smoothed series on the same graph.
  c. Use the exponentially smoothed data from 2000–2001 to forecast the quarterly number of housing starts in 2002.

Applying the Concepts—Basic

15.24 The Consumer Price Index (CPI) measures the increase (or decrease) in the prices of goods and services relative to a base year. The CPI for the years 1987–2000 (using 1984 as a base period) is shown in the next table.

CPI

Year	CPI	Year	CPI
1987	109.3	1994	147.8
1988	113.8	1995	152.4
1989	119.4	1996	156.9
1990	125.8	1997	160.5
1991	129.1	1998	163.0
1992	132.8	1999	166.6
1993	136.8	2000	171.5

Source: Survey of Current Business,
U.S. Department of Commerce, Bureau
of Economic Analysis.

a. Graph the time series. Do you detect a long-term trend?

b. Calculate and plot the exponentially smoothed series for the CPI using a smoothing constant of $w = .4$. Use the exponentially smoothed values to forecast the CPI in 2003. $F_{2003} = 165.2$

c. Use the Holt-Winters forecasting model with trend to forecast the CPI in 2003. Use smoothing constants $w = .4$ and $v = .5$. $F_{2003} = 183.2$

OPECOIL

15.25 Refer to the annual OPEC oil import data, Exercise 15.19. (p. 1016).

a. Use the exponentially smoothed $(w = .9)$ series you constructed in Exercise 15.19a to forecast OPEC oil imports in 2001. $F_{2001} = 1651$

b. Forecast OPEC oil imports in 2001 using the Holt-Winters forecasting model with smoothing constants $w = .3$ and $v = .8$. $F_{2001} = 1640$

c. Annual OPEC crude oil imports in 2001 totaled 1,700 million barrels. Calculate the errors of the forecasts, parts **a** and **b**. Which method yields the smallest forecast error?

Applying the Concepts—Intermediate

SP500

15.26 Refer to the quarterly Standard & Poor's 500 stock market index, Exercise 15.20 (p. 1016).

a. Use $w = .7$ to smooth the series from 1995 through 2000. Then forecast the four quarterly values in 2001 using *only* the information through the fourth quarter of 2000.

b. Repeat part **a** using $w = .3$.

15.27 Refer to Exercise 15.26. Suppose you want to use only the 1998–2000 S&P values to forecast the quarterly 2001 values. Calculate the forecasts using the Holt-Winters model with $w = .3$ and $v = .5$. Repeat with $w = .7$ and $v = .5$.

15.28 The fluctuation of gold prices is a reflection of the strength or weakness of the U.S. dollar. The table below shows monthly gold prices from January 1995 to December 2002.

a. Use exponential smoothing with $w = .5$ to calculate monthly smoothed values from 1995 to 2001. Then forecast the monthly gold prices for 2002.

b. Calculate 12 one-step-ahead forecasts for 2002 by updating the exponentially smoothed values with each month's actual value, and then forecasting the next month's value.

c. Repeat parts **a–b** using the Holt-Winters technique with $w = .5$ and $v = .5$.

GOLDMON

Month	1995	1996	1997	1998	1999	2000	2001	2002
Jan	379.8	400.9	345.5	304.9	285.4	284.3	265.5	281.7
Feb	377.8	406.1	358.6	297.4	287.1	299.9	261.9	295.5
Mar	383.4	397.5	348.2	301.0	279.5	286.4	263.0	294.0
Apr	391.3	394.3	340.2	310.7	286.6	279.9	260.5	302.7
May	386.6	393.3	345.6	293.6	269.0	275.3	272.4	314.5
Jun	388.9	386.6	334.6	296.3	262.6	285.7	270.2	321.2
Jul	387.7	384.9	326.4	288.9	255.6	281.6	267.5	313.3
Aug	384.9	388.7	325.4	273.4	254.8	274.5	272.4	310.3
Sep	384.5	384.3	332.1	293.9	307.5	273.7	283.4	319.2
Oct	384.4	382.4	311.4	294.0	299.1	270.0	283.1	316.6
Nov	381.0	379.5	296.8	294.7	291.4	266.0	276.2	319.2
Dec	388.7	369.3	290.2	287.8	290.3	271.5	275.9	333.4

*Sources: Standard & Poor's Statistics, 1996; **kitco.com** Current Statistics, 2000.*

15.6 Measuring Forecast Accuracy: MAD and RMSE

As demonstrated in Example 15.5, forecast error (i.e., the difference between the actual time series value and its forecast) can be used to evaluate the accuracy of the forecast. Knowledge of a forecast's accuracy aids in the selection of both the forecasting methodology to be utilized and the parameters of the forecast formula (e.g., the weights in the exponentially smoothed or Holt-Winters forecasts). Three popular measures of forecast accuracy, both based on forecast errors, are the *mean absolute deviation (MAD)*, the *mean absolute percentage error (MAPE)*, and the *root mean squared error (RMSE)* of the forecasts. Their formulas are given in the box.

Measures of Forecast Accuracy for *m* Forecasts

1. **Mean absolute deviation (MAD)**

$$\text{MAD} = \frac{\sum\limits_{t=1}^{m} |Y_t - F_t|}{m}$$

2. **Mean absolute percentage error (MAPE)**

$$\text{MAPE} = \frac{\sum\limits_{t=1}^{m} \left| \frac{(Y_t - F_t)}{Y_t} \right|}{m} \times 100$$

3. **Root mean squared error (RMSE)**

$$\text{RMSE} = \sqrt{\frac{\sum\limits_{t=1}^{m} (Y_t - F_t)^2}{m}}$$

Note that all three measures require one or more actual values of the time series against which to compare the forecasts. Thus, we can either wait several time periods until the observed values are available, or we can hold out several of the values at the end of the time series, not using them to model the time series, but saving them for evaluating the forecasts obtained from the model.

EXAMPLE 15.8   COMPARING MEASURES OF FORECAST ACCURACY

Problem Refer to the annual sales data of Examples 15.6 and 15.7. In Example 15.7 we used the Holt-Winters model with $w = .7$ and $v = .5$ to forecast annual sales for years 36–40. Consider two alternative forecasting models: exponential smoothing with $w = .3$ and exponential smoothing with $w = .7$. MINITAB was used to obtain the forecasts for these alternative models. The MINITAB printouts shown in Figures 15.12 (a)–(c) give the forecasts (highlighted) for all three models. Suppose the actual sales values (in thousands of dollars) for years 36–40 are 150.2, 161.7, 159.3, 168.5, and 170.4, respectively. Find measures of forecast accuracy (MAD, MAPE, and RMSE) for each of the three forecasting models and use this information to evaluate the models.

Solution For ease of notation, we will number the forecasting models as follows.

Model 1: Exponential smoothing ($w = .3$)
Model 2: Exponential smoothing ($w = .7$)
Model 3: Holt-Winters ($w = .7, v = .5$)

Figure 15.12a
MINITAB forecasts of annual sales—exponential smoothing model with $w = .3$

Single Exponential Smoothing for SALES

```
Data     SALES
Length   35


Smoothing Constant

Alpha   0.3


Accuracy Measures

MAPE    21.805
MAD     13.179
MSD    223.953


Forecasts

Period   Forecast     Lower     Upper
36        142.696   110.408   174.983
37        142.696   110.408   174.983
38        142.696   110.408   174.983
39        142.696   110.408   174.983
40        142.696   110.408   174.983
```

Figure 15.12b
MINITAB forecasts of annual sales—exponential smoothing model with $w = .7$

Single Exponential Smoothing for SALES

```
Data     SALES
Length   35


Smoothing Constant

Alpha   0.7


Accuracy Measures

MAPE    12.8418
MAD      6.7780
MSD     68.9944


Forecasts

Period   Forecast     Lower     Upper
36        150.474   133.868   167.080
37        150.474   133.868   167.080
38        150.474   133.868   167.080
39        150.474   133.868   167.080
40        150.474   133.868   167.080
```

Figure 15.12c

MINITAB Forecasts of
Annual Sales — Holt-Winters
Model with $w = .7$ and
$v = .5$

Double Exponential Smoothing for SALES

```
Data      SALES
Length    35


Smoothing Constants

Alpha (level)   0.7
Gamma (trend)   0.5


Accuracy Measures

MAPE   14.0301
MAD     5.4022
MSD    43.7262


Forecasts

Period  Forecast    Lower     Upper
36       155.608   142.373   168.843
37       158.354   141.644   175.063
38       161.099   140.614   181.585
39       163.845   139.421   188.269
40       166.590   138.133   195.048
```

TABLE 15.8   Forecasts and Forecast Errors for Three Models of Annual Sales

Year	Actual Sales	Model 1 Forecast	Model 1 Error	Model 2 Forecast	Model 2 Error	Model 3 Forecast	Model 3 Error
36	150.2	142.7	7.5	150.5	−0.3	155.6	−5.4
37	161.7	142.7	19.0	150.5	11.2	158.4	3.3
38	159.3	142.7	16.6	150.5	8.8	161.1	−1.8
39	168.5	142.7	25.8	150.5	18.0	163.8	4.7
40	170.4	142.7	27.7	150.5	19.9	166.6	3.8

The forecasts for the three models as well as forecast errors are listed in Table 15.8. These forecast errors are used to find the MAD, MAPE, and RMSE measures of forecast accuracy for each of the three models:

Model 1:

$$\text{MAD}_1 = \frac{|7.5| + |19.0| + |16.6| + |25.8| + |27.7|}{5} = 19.32$$

$$\text{MAPE}_1 = \left\{ \frac{\left|\frac{7.5}{150.2}\right| + \left|\frac{19.0}{161.7}\right| + \left|\frac{16.6}{159.3}\right| + \left|\frac{25.8}{168.5}\right| + \left|\frac{27.7}{170.4}\right|}{5} \right\} 100 = 11.75$$

$$\text{RMSE}_1 = \sqrt{\frac{(7.5)^2 + (19.0)^2 + (16.6)^2 + (25.8)^2 + (27.7)^2}{5}} = 20.62$$

Model 2:

$$MAD_2 = \frac{|-.3| + |11.2| + |8.8| + |18.0| + |19.9|}{5} = 11.64$$

$$MAPE_2 = \left\{ \frac{\left|\frac{-.3}{150.2}\right| + \left|\frac{11.2}{161.7}\right| + \left|\frac{8.8}{159.3}\right| + \left|\frac{18.0}{168.5}\right| + \left|\frac{19.9}{170.4}\right|}{5} \right\} 100 = 7.00$$

$$RMSE_2 = \sqrt{\frac{(-.3)^2 + (11.2)^2 + (8.8)^2 + (18.0)^2 + (19.9)^2}{5}} = 13.59$$

Model 3:

$$MAD_3 = \frac{|-5.4| + |3.3| + |-1.8| + |4.7| + |3.8|}{5} = 3.80$$

$$MAPE_3 = \left\{ \frac{\left|\frac{-5.4}{150.2}\right| + \left|\frac{3.3}{161.7}\right| + \left|\frac{-1.8}{159.3}\right| + \left|\frac{4.7}{168.5}\right| + \left|\frac{3.8}{170.4}\right|}{5} \right\} 100 = 2.36$$

$$RMSE_3 = \sqrt{\frac{(-5.4)^2 + (3.3)^2 + (-1.8)^2 + (4.7)^2 + (3.8)^2}{5}} = 4.00$$

The model with the smallest mean absolute deviation (MAD) is Model 3. Similarly, Model 3 has the smallest mean absolute percentage error (MAPE) and the smallest root mean square error (RMSE). Of the three forecasting models, then, Model 3 (the Holt-Winters method with $w = .7$ and $v = .5$) yields the most accurate predictions of annual sales.

Suggested Exercises 15.34

Look Back We expect the Holt-Winters method to yield more accurate forecasts for annual sales since it explicitly accounts for trend in the sales data. The exponential smoothing forecasts do not account for any increasing or decreasing trends in the data; hence, they are the same for all five forecasted years. The accuracy of all three forecasting methods, however, will decrease the further we forecast into the future.

Now Work *Exercise 15.29*

■ ■ ■

[Note: Most statistical software packages will automatically compute the values of MAPE, MAD, and RMSE (also called the *mean squared deviation, MSD)* for all *n* observations in the data set. For example, these statistics are shown in the middle of the MINITAB printouts, Figures 15.12(a)–(c).]

Criteria such as MAPE, MAD, and RMSE for assessing forecast accuracy require special care in interpretation. The number of time periods included in the evaluation is critical to the decision about which forecasting model is preferred. The choice depends on how many time periods ahead the analyst plans to forecast. With *N* time periods in your data, a good rule of thumb is to forecast ahead no more than *N/2* time periods. Remember, however, that long-term forecasts are generally less accurate than short-term forecasts.

We conclude this section with a comment. A major disadvantage of forecasting with smoothing techniques (exponential smoothing or the Holt-Winters model) is that no measure of the forecast error (or reliability) is known *prior* to observing the future value. Although forecast errors can be calculated *after* the future values of the time series have been observed (as in Example 15.8), we prefer to have some measure of the accuracy of the forecast *before* the actual values are observed. One option is to compute forecasts and forecast errors for all n observations in the data set and use these "past" forecast errors to estimate the standard deviation of all forecast errors (i.e., the *standard error of the forecast*). A rough estimate of this standard error is the value of RMSE, and an approximate 95% prediction interval for any future forecast is

$$F_t \pm 2(\text{RMSE})$$

Teaching Tip

As a general rule, the further into the future we forecast, the less accurate that forecast will be.

[An interval like this is shown at the bottom of the MINITAB printouts, Figures 15.12(a)–(c).] However, since the theoretical distributional properties of the forecast errors with smoothing methods are unknown, many analysts regard smoothing methods as descriptive procedures rather than as inferential ones.

In the preceding chapters, we learned that predictions with inferential regression models are accompanied by well-known measures of reliability. The standard errors of the predicted values allow us to construct 95% prediction intervals. We discuss an inferential time series forecasting model in the next section.

Statistics in Action Revisited

Forecasting Coldex Sales with Exponential Smoothing

Recall that a pharmaceutical company hired consultants at Rutgers University to forecast monthly sales of a new brand of cold medicine called Coldex. The company provided monthly data on Coldex sales for the first two years of the product's life and desires forecasts of sales for the first three months of the third year. (The data are saved in the **COLDEX** file.) One forecasting model considered by the consultants was an exponential smoothing model with a smoothing constant of $w = .7$. MINITAB was used to find the smoothed values of the monthly series. The MINITAB plot of both the actual monthly sales and smoothed sales values is shown in Figure SIA15.1, followed by the exponentially smoothed forecasts in Figure SIA15.2.

The exponentially smoothed sales forecast for each of the first three months of year 3 is the smoothed value

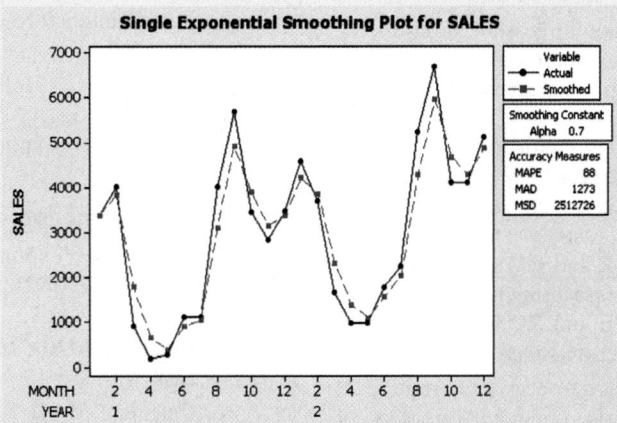

Figure SIA15.1

MINITAB plot of monthly Coldex sales with exponentially smoothed values ($w = .7$)

Figure SIA15.2
MINITAB forecasts of
monthly Coldex sales using
exponential smoothing
($w = .7$)

Single Exponential Smoothing for SALES

```
Data     SALES
Length   24


Smoothing Constant

Alpha  0.7


Accuracy Measures

MAPE          88
MAD         1273
MSD      2512726


Forecasts

Period   Forecast     Lower     Upper
  25     4869.91    1750.49   7989.34
  26     4869.91    1750.49   7989.34
  27     4869.91    1750.49   7989.34
```

for the last month of the series (month 24). This value, highlighted on Figure SIA15.2, is 4,870 thousand dollars. MINITAB also gives approximate 95% confidence bounds around the forecast. The interval (highlighted on the printout) is (1750, 7989). Thus, we are (approximately) 95% confident that the actual sales for the month will be between 1,750 and 7,989 thousand dollars. This wide interval was deemed unusable by the pharmaceutical company; consequently, the consultants searched for a better forecasting model. One of these models is presented in the next Statistics in Action Revisited (p. 1036).

Exercises 15.29–15.34

Learning the Mechanics

15.29 Refer to the beer production forecasts, Exercise 15.22 (p. 1025). In part **a** you obtained forecasts of 1997–2000 beer production using exponential smoothing with $w = .3$ and $w = .7$.
  a. Calculate the forecast errors for the $w = .3$ exponentially smoothed forecasts.
  b. Calculate the forecast errors for the $w = .7$ exponentially smoothed forecasts.
  c. Calculate MAD, MAPE and RMSE for the exponential smoothing forecasts using $w = .3$.
  d. Calculate MAD, MAPE and RMSE for the exponential smoothing forecasts using $w = .7$.

15.30 Refer to the beer production forecasts, Exercise 15.22 (p. 1025). In part **b** you obtained forecasts of 1997–2000 beer production using the Holt-Winters model with ($w = .3, v = .7$) and ($w = .7, v = .3$).
  a. Calculate the forecast errors for the $w = .3, v = .7$ Holt-Winters forecasts.

  b. Calculate the forecast errors for the $w = .7, v = .3$ Holt-Winters forecasts.
  c. Calculate MAD, MAPE and RMSE for the $w = .3, v = .7$ Holt-Winters forecasts.
  d. Calculate MAD, MAPE and RMSE for the $w = .7, v = .3$ Holt-Winters forecasts.

Applying the Concepts—Basic

15.31 Refer to your exponential smoothing forecasts of the quarterly S&P 500 for 2001, Exercise 15.26 (p. 1026).
  a. Calculate MAD, MAPE and RMSE for the forecasts with $w = .7$.
  b. Calculate MAD, MAPE and RMSE for the forecasts with $w = .3$.
  c. Compare MAD, MAPE and RMSE for the two simple exponential smoothing forecast models. Which model leads to more accurate forecasts?

15.32 Refer to your Holt-Winters forecasts of the quarterly S&P 500 for 2001, Exercise 15.27 (p. 1026).

   a. Calculate MAD, MAPE and RMSE for the forecasts with $w = .3$ and $v = .5$.

   b. Calculate MAD, MAPE and RMSE for the forecasts with $w = .7$ and $v = .5$.

   c. Compare MAD, MAPE and RMSE for the two Holt-Winters forecasts models. Which model leads to more accurate forecasts?

15.33 Refer to Exercise 15.28 (p. 1026). Two models were used to forecast the monthly 2002 gold prices: an exponential smoothing model with $w = .5$ and a Holt-Winters model with $w = .5$ and $v = .5$.

   a. Use MAD, MAPE and RMSE criteria to evaluate the two models' accuracy for forecasting the monthly 2002 values using the 1990–2001 data.

   b. Use the MAD, MAPE and RMSE criteria to evaluate the two models' accuracy when making the 12 one-step-ahead forcasts, updating the models with each month's actual value before forecasting the next month's value.

Applying the Concepts—Intermediate

15.34 The next table reports annual U.S. school enrollment (in thousands) for the period 1980–2000.

⚙ **SCHOOLENROLL**

Year	Enrollment	Year	Enrollment
1980	58,305	1991	61,605
1981	57,916	1992	62,686
1982	57,951	1993	63,241
1983	57,432	1994	63,986
1984	57,150	1995	64,764
1985	57,226	1996	65,743
1986	57,709	1997	66,470
1987	58,254	1998	66,983
1988	58,485	1999	67,667
1989	59,436	2000	68,146
1990	60,267		

Source: U.S. Census Bureau. *Statistical Abstract of the United States,* 2002.

   a. Use the 1980 to 1997 enrollments and simple exponential smoothing to forecast the 1998–2000 school enrollments. Use $w = .8$.

   b. Use the Holt-Winters model with $w = .8$ and $v = .7$ to forecast the 1998–2000 enrollments.

   c. Apply the MAD, MAPE, and RMSE criteria to evaluate the two forecasting models of parts **a** and **b**. Which model is better? Why?

15.7 Forecasting Trends: Simple Linear Regression

Teaching Tip

Point out the biggest benefit of the inferential techniques is the ability to get a measure of reliability with the forecasted values they produce.

Perhaps the simplest **inferential forecasting model** is one with which you are familiar: the simple linear regression model. A straight-line model is used to relate the time series, Y_t, to time, t, and the least squares line is used to forecast future values of Y_t.

Suppose a firm is interested in forecasting its sales revenues for each of the next five years. To make such forecasts and assess their reliability, a time series model must be constructed. Refer again to the yearly sales data for a firm's 35 years of operation given in Table 15.7 (p. 1022). A MINITAB plot of the data (Figure 15.13) reveals a linearly increasing trend, so the model

$$E(Y_t) = \beta_0 + \beta_1 t$$

Figure 15.13

MINITAB scatterplot of annual sales with least squares line

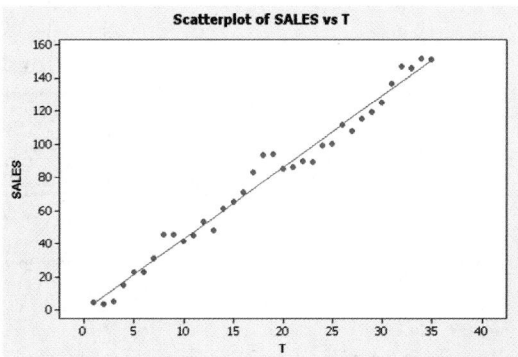

seems plausible for the secular trend. We fit the model to the data using SPSS; the resulting printout is shown in Figure 15.14. The least squares model (highlighted on the printout) is:

$$\hat{Y}_t = \hat{\beta}_0 + \hat{\beta}_1 t = .402 + 4.296t \qquad \text{with} \qquad R^2 = .980$$

(This least squares line is shown on Figure 15.13.)

We can now forecast sales for years 36–40. The forecasts of sales and the corresponding 95% prediction intervals are shown (highlighted) on the SPSS printout Figure 15.15. For example, for $t = 36$, we have

$$\hat{Y}_{36} = 155.0$$

Teaching Tip

Discuss this problem in the context of an example to illustrate the danger.

with the 95% prediction interval (141.3, 168.8). Similarly, we can obtain the forecasts and prediction intervals for years 37–40. Although it is not easily perceptible in the figure, the prediction intervals widen as we attempt to forecast further into the future. This agrees with the intuitive notion that short-term forecasts should be more reliable than long-term forecasts.

Model Summary[b]

Model	R	R Square	Adjusted R Square	Std. Error of the Estimate
1	.990[a]	.980	.979	6.3852

a. Predictors: (Constant), T

b. Dependent Variable: SALES

ANOVA[b]

Model		Sum of Squares	df	Mean Square	F	Sig.
1	Regression	65875.21	1	65875.208	1615.724	.000[a]
	Residual	1345.454	33	40.771		
	Total	67220.66	34			

a. Predictors: (Constant), T

b. Dependent Variable: SALES

Coefficients[a]

Model		Unstandardized Coefficients		Standardized Coefficients	t	Sig.
		B	Std. Error	Beta		
1	(Constant)	.402	2.206		.182	.857
	T	4.296	.107	.990	40.196	.000

a. Dependent Variable: SALES

Figure 15.14

SPSS printout of least squares regression of annual sales

Figure 15.15

SPSS printout with 95%
prediction intervals
for annual sales

T	SALES	Unstandardized Predicted Value	95% L CI for SALES individual	95% U CI for SALES individual
1	4.8	4.69714	-8.98666	18.38094
2	4.0	8.99277	-4.63390	22.61945
3	5.5	13.28840	-.28440	26.86120
4	15.6	17.58403	4.06183	31.10624
5	23.1	21.87966	8.40474	35.35459
6	23.3	26.17529	12.74429	39.60630
7	31.4	30.47092	17.08046	43.86139
8	46.0	34.76655	21.41321	48.11990
9	46.1	39.06218	25.74251	52.38186
10	41.9	43.35782	30.06834	56.64729
11	45.5	47.65345	34.39068	60.91621
12	53.5	51.94908	38.70950	65.18865
13	48.4	56.24471	43.02478	69.46463
14	61.6	60.54034	47.33651	73.74416
15	65.6	64.83597	51.64468	78.02725
16	71.4	69.13160	55.94927	82.31392
17	83.4	73.42723	60.25028	86.60417
18	93.6	77.72286	64.54771	90.89801
19	94.2	82.01849	68.84154	95.19543
20	85.4	86.31412	73.13179	99.49644
21	86.2	90.60975	77.41846	103.80103
22	89.9	94.90538	81.70156	108.10920
23	89.2	99.20101	85.98108	112.42093
24	99.1	103.49664	90.25706	116.73622
25	100.3	107.79227	94.52950	121.05503
26	111.7	112.08790	98.79843	125.37737
27	108.2	116.38353	103.06386	129.70320
28	115.5	120.67916	107.32581	134.03250
29	119.2	124.97479	111.58432	138.36525
30	125.2	129.27042	115.83942	142.70142
31	136.3	133.56605	120.09112	147.04098
32	146.8	137.86168	124.33948	151.38388
33	146.1	142.15731	128.58451	155.73011
34	151.4	146.45294	132.82626	160.07962
35	150.9	150.74857	137.06477	164.43237
36	.	155.04420	141.30008	168.78832
37	.	159.33983	145.53223	173.14744
38	.	163.63546	149.76126	177.50967
39	.	167.93109	153.98721	181.87497
40	.	172.22672	158.21014	186.24330

There are two problems associated with forecasting time series using a least
squares model.

Problem 1   We are using the least squares model to forecast values outside the region of observation of the independent variable, *t*. That is, we are forecasting for values of *t*
between 36 and 40, but the observed sales are for *t* values between 1 and 35. As we

noted in Chapters 12 and 13, it is extremely risky to use a least squares regression model for prediction outside the experimental region.

Problem 1 obviously cannot be avoided. Since forecasting always involves predictions about the future values of a time series, some or all of the independent variables will probably be outside the region of observation on which the model was developed. It is important that the forecaster recognize the dangers of this type of prediction. If underlying conditions change drastically after the model is estimated (e.g., if federal price controls are imposed on the firm's products during the 36th year of operation), the forecasts and their confidence intervals are probably useless.

Problem 2 Although the straight-line model may adequately describe the secular trend of the sales, we have not attempted to build any cyclical effects into the model. Thus, the effect of inflationary and recessionary periods will be to increase the error of the forecasts because the model does not anticipate such periods.

Fortunately, the forecaster often has some degree of control over problem 2, as we demonstrate in the remainder of the chapter.

Suggested Exercises 15.38

In forming the prediction intervals for the forecasts, we made the standard regression assumptions (Chapters 12 and 13) about the random error component of the model. We assumed the errors have mean 0, constant variance, and normal probability distributions, and are *independent*. The latter assumption is dubious in time series models, especially in the presence of short-term trends. Often, if a year's value lies above the secular trend line, the next year's value has a tendency to be above the line also. That is, the errors tend to be correlated (see Figure 15.13).

We discuss how to deal with correlated errors in Section 15.9. For now, we can characterize the simple linear regression forecasting method as useful for discerning secular trends, but probably too simplistic for most time series. And, as with all forecasting methods, the simple linear regression forecasts should be applied only over the short term.

Statistics in Action Revisited

Forecasting Coldex Sales with Simple Linear Regression

A second model considered by consultants to forecast monthly sales of a new cold medicine (Coldex) was a simple linear regression model with time (t) as the independent variable, where $t = 1, 2, 3, \ldots, 24$. The MINITAB graph of the least squares line is shown in Figure SIA15.3, followed by the simple linear regression printout in Figure SIA15.4.

Note that the p-value for testing the slope coefficient is .047. Thus, at $\alpha = .05$, the model is statistically useful for predicting monthly sales. However, the coefficient of determination is low ($R^2 = .168$); only about 17% of the sample variation in monthly sales can be explained by the linear time trend.

The simple linear forecasts for each of the first three months of year 3 are shown on the MINITAB worksheet, Figure SIA15.5. MINITAB also gives a 95% pre-diction interval for each forecast. The intervals for months 25, 26, and 27 are (480.5, 8147.9), (549.7, 8290.4), and (616.5, 8435.3), respectively. For the first month of year 3 (i.e., month 25), we are 95% confident that the actual sales will fall between 480.5 and 8,147.9 thousand dollars. Similar interpretations are made for the other two forecasts.

As with the exponential smoothing model, these intervals were too wide to be of practical use by the pharmaceutical company. How can the forecasting model be improved? Examine Figure SIA15.3 and note the cyclical trends in the monthly sales data. Neither the exponential smoothing model nor the linear regression model account for this cyclical variation. A forecasting model is needed that explicitly accounts for such trends. Such a model is presented in the next Statistics in Action Revisited (p. 1041).

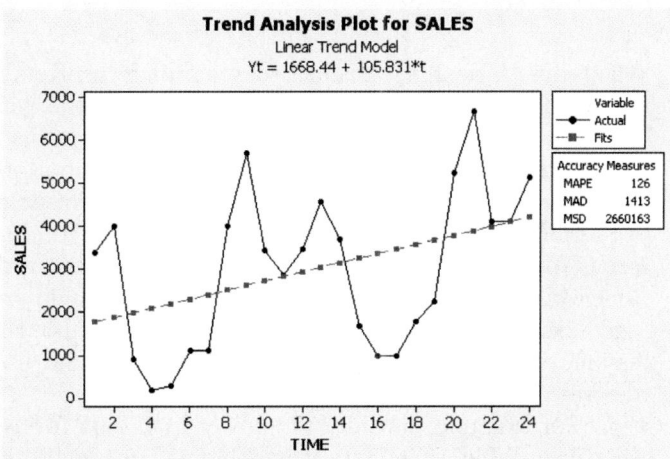

Figure SIA15.3
MINITAB plot of least squares line for forecasting monthly Coldex sales

Regression Analysis: SALES versus TIME

```
The regression equation is
SALES = 1668 + 106 TIME


Predictor    Coef   SE Coef     T      P
Constant    1668.4    717.8   2.32   0.030
TIME        105.83    50.23   2.11   0.047


S = 1703.52    R-Sq = 16.8%    R-Sq(adj) = 13.0%


Analysis of Variance

Source           DF        SS         MS       F      P
Regression        1   12880305   12880305   4.44   0.047
Residual Error   22   63843919    2901996
Total            23   76724223
```

Figure SIA15.4
MINITAB simple linear regression printout for the linear trend forecasting model

↓	C1	C2	C3	C4	C5	C6
	YEAR	MONTH	TIME	FORECAST	PL95LOW	PL95UPP
1	3	1	25	4314.22	480.528	8147.92
2	3	2	26	4420.06	549.731	8290.38
3	3	3	27	4525.89	616.500	8435.27

Figure SIA15.5
MINITAB worksheet with simple linear regression forecasts of monthly sales

15.8 Seasonal Regression Models

Many time series have distinct seasonal patterns. Retail sales are usually highest around Christmas, spring, and fall, with lulls in the winter and summer periods. Energy usage is highest in summer and winter, and lowest in spring and fall. Teenage unemployment rises in summer months when schools are not in session and falls near Christmas when many businesses hire part-time help.

Multiple regression models can be used to forecast future values of a time series with strong seasonal components. To accomplish this, the mean value of the time series, $E(Y_t)$, is given a mathematical form that describes both the secular trend and seasonal components of the time series. Although the **seasonal model** can assume a wide variety of mathematical forms, the use of dummy variables to describe seasonal differences is common.

For example, consider the power load data for a southern utility company shown in Table 15.9. Data were obtained for each quarter from 1992 through 2003. A model that combines the expected growth in usage and the seasonal component is

$$E(Y_t) = \beta_0 + \beta_1 t + \beta_2 Q_1 + \beta_3 Q_2 + \beta_4 Q_3$$

where

t = Time period, ranging from $t = 1$ for quarter 1 of 1992 to

$t = 48$ for quarter 4 of 2003

$$Q_1 = \begin{cases} 1 & \text{if quarter 1} \\ 0 & \text{if quarter 2, 3, or 4} \end{cases}$$

$$Q_2 = \begin{cases} 1 & \text{if quarter 2} \\ 0 & \text{if quarter 1, 3, or 4} \end{cases}$$

$$Q_3 = \begin{cases} 1 & \text{if quarter 3} \\ 0 & \text{if quarter 1, 2, or 4} \end{cases}$$

The MINITAB printout in Figure 15.16 shows the least squares fit of this model to the data in Table 15.9.

Note that the model appears to fit well, with $R^2 = .914$, indicating that the model accounts for about 91% of the sample variability in power loads over the 12-year period. The global $F = 114.88$ (p-value = .000) strongly supports the hypothesis that the model has predictive utility. The model standard deviation of 7.86 indicates that the model predictions will usually be accurate to within approximately $\pm 2(7.86)$, or about ± 16 megawatts. Furthermore, $\hat{\beta}_1 = 1.64$ indicates an estimated average growth in load of 1.64 megawatts per quarter. Finally, the seasonal dummy variables have the following interpretations (refer to Chapter 13):*

$\hat{\beta}_2 = 13.66$ Quarter 1 loads average 13.66 megawatts more than quarter 4 loads.

$\hat{\beta}_3 = -3.74$ Quarter 2 loads average 3.74 megawatts less than quarter 4 loads.

$\hat{\beta}_4 = 18.47$ Quarter 3 loads average 18.47 megawatts more than quarter 4 loads.

*These interpretations assume a fixed value of t. In practical terms this is unrealistic, since each quarter is associated with a different value of t. Nevertheless, the coefficients of the seasonal dummy variables provide insight into the seasonality of these time series data.

QTRPOWER

TABLE 15.9   Quarterly Power Loads (megawatts) for a Southern Utility Company, 1988–1999

Year	Quarter	Power Load	Year	Quarter	Power Load
1992	1	68.8	1998	1	130.6
	2	65.0		2	116.8
	3	88.4		3	144.2
	4	69.0		4	123.3
1993	1	83.6	1999	1	142.3
	2	69.7		2	124.0
	3	90.2		3	146.1
	4	72.5		4	135.5
1994	1	106.8	2000	1	147.1
	2	89.2		2	119.3
	3	110.7		3	138.2
	4	91.7		4	127.6
1995	1	108.6	2001	1	143.4
	2	98.9		2	134.0
	3	120.1		3	159.6
	4	102.1		4	135.1
1996	1	113.1	2002	1	149.5
	2	94.2		2	123.3
	3	120.5		3	154.4
	4	107.4		4	139.4
1997	1	116.2	2003	1	151.6
	2	104.4		2	133.7
	3	131.7		3	154.5
	4	117.9		4	135.1

Teaching Tip

A review of the β interpretations will help the student understand how the seasonal components work in the model.

```
The regression equation is
LOAD = 70.5 + 1.64 T + 13.7 Q1 - 3.74 Q2 + 18.5 Q3


Predictor       Coef   SE Coef      T      P
Constant      70.509     3.116  22.63  0.000
T            1.63621   0.08214  19.92  0.000
Q1            13.659     3.217   4.25  0.000
Q2            -3.736     3.212  -1.16  0.251
Q3            18.470     3.209   5.76  0.000


S = 7.85795   R-Sq = 91.4%   R-Sq(adj) = 90.6%


Analysis of Variance

Source           DF       SS      MS       F      P
Regression        4  28375.0  7093.7  114.88  0.000
Residual Error   43   2655.1    61.7
Total            47  31030.1
```

Figure 15.16
MINITAB printout of least squares fit to power load time series

Thus, as expected, winter and summer loads exceed spring and fall loads, with the peak occurring during the summer months.

In order to forecast the 2004 power loads, we calculate the predicted value $\hat{Y}_k$ for $k = 49, 50, 51,$ and 52, at the same time substituting the dummy variable appropriate for each quarter. Thus, for 2004,

$$\hat{Y}_{\text{Quarter 1}} = \hat{\beta}_0 + \hat{\beta}_1(49) + \hat{\beta}_2 = 70.51 + 1.636(49) + 13.66 = 164.3$$
$$\hat{Y}_{\text{Quarter 2}} = \hat{\beta}_0 + \hat{\beta}_1(50) + \hat{\beta}_3 = 148.6$$
$$\hat{Y}_{\text{Quarter 3}} = \hat{\beta}_0 + \hat{\beta}_1(51) + \hat{\beta}_4 = 172.4$$
$$\hat{Y}_{\text{Quarter 4}} = \hat{\beta}_0 + \hat{\beta}_1(52) = 155.6$$

The predicted values and 95% prediction intervals (highlighted) are given on the MINITAB worksheet, Figure 15.17; the data and least squares predicted values are graphed in Figure 15.18. The color line on the graph connects the predicted values. Also shown in Figures 15.17 and 15.18 are the actual 2004 quarterly power loads. Notice that all 2004 power loads fall inside the forecast intervals.

QTRPOWERforecasts.MTW *

↓	C1	C2	C3	C4	C5	C6	C7	C8	C9	C10
	T	YEAR	QTR	LOAD	Q1	Q2	Q3	PRED	LO95PLIM	HI95PLIM
1	49	2004	1	151.3	1	0	0	164.341	147.294	181.389
2	50	2004	2	132.9	0	1	0	148.583	131.536	165.630
3	51	2004	3	160.5	0	0	1	172.425	155.378	189.472
4	52	2004	4	161.0	0	0	0	155.591	138.544	172.639

Figure 15.17
MINITAB worksheet with power load forecasts (megawatts)

Figure 15.18
Regression forecasting model for a southern utility company

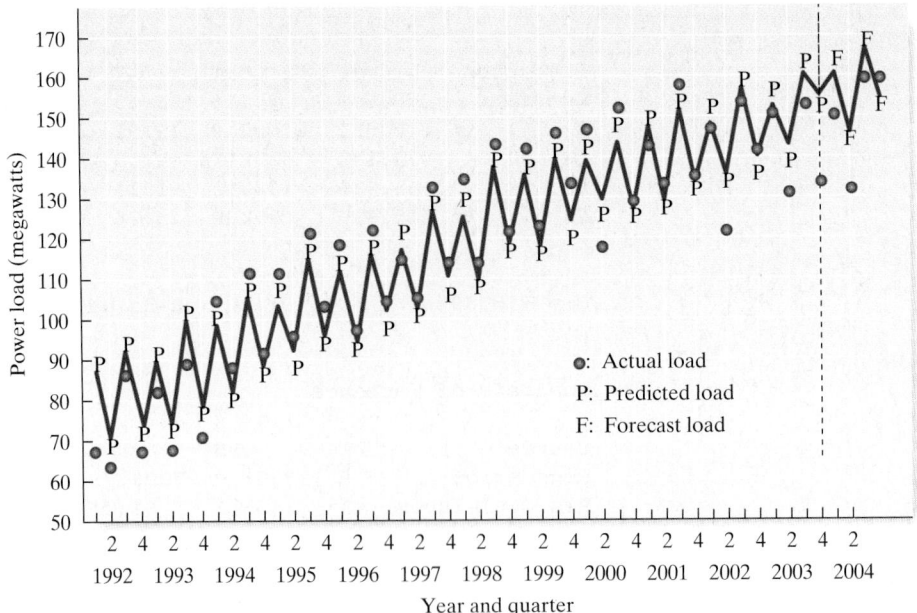

Now Work   *Exercise 15.37*

■ ■ ■

The seasonal model used to forecast the power loads is an **additive model** because the secular trend component $(\beta_1 t)$ is added to the seasonal component $(\beta_2 Q_1 + \beta_3 Q_2 + \beta_4 Q_3)$ to form the model. A **multiplicative model** would have the same form, except that the dependent variable would be the natural logarithm of power load; that is,

$$\ln Y_t = \beta_0 + \beta_1 t + \beta_2 Q_1 + \beta_3 Q_2 + \beta_4 Q_3 + \epsilon$$

Teaching Tip

Point out that the other modeling techniques mentioned are intended to present other methods for forecasting data. Consult the references to learn more about these specific techniques.

To see the multiplicative nature of this model, we take the antilogarithm of both sides of the equation to get

$$Y_t = \exp\{\beta_0 + \beta_1 t + \beta_2 Q_1 + \beta_3 Q_2 + \beta_4 Q_3 + \epsilon\}$$
$$= \underbrace{\exp\{\beta_0\}}_{\textbf{Constant}} \underbrace{\exp\{\beta_1 t\}}_{\substack{\textbf{Secular} \\ \textbf{trend}}} \underbrace{\exp\{\beta_2 Q_1 + \beta_3 Q_2 + \beta_4 Q_3\}}_{\substack{\textbf{Seasonal} \\ \textbf{component}}} \underbrace{\exp\{\epsilon\}}_{\substack{\textbf{Residual} \\ \textbf{component}}}$$

The multiplicative model often provides a better forecasting model when the time series is changing at an increasing rate over time.

When time series data are observed monthly, a regression forecasting model needs 11 dummy variables to describe monthly seasonality; three dummy variables can be used (as in the previous models) if the seasonal changes are hypothesized to occur quarterly. In general, this approach to seasonal modeling requires one dummy variable fewer than the number of seasonal changes expected to occur.

There are approaches besides the regression dummy variable method for forecasting seasonal time series. Trigonometric (sine and cosine) terms can be used in regression models to model periodicity. Other time series models (the Holt-Winters exponential smoothing model, for example) do not use the regression approach at all, and there are various methods for adding seasonal components to these models. We have chosen to discuss the regression approach because it makes use of the important modeling concepts covered in Chapter 13, and because the regression forecasts are accompanied by prediction intervals that provide some measure of the forecast reliability. While most other methods do not have explicit measures of reliability, many have proved their merit by providing good forecasts for particular applications. Consult the references at the end of the chapter for details of other seasonal models.

Statistics in Action Revisited

Forecasting Coldex Sales with a Seasonal Regression Model

The consultants hired by the pharmaceutical company detected a cyclical trend in the monthly sales data. They noted that sales of the cold medicine were higher during the winter and summer months as compared to the other months over the two-year period. To account for this seasonal trend, they created 11 dummy variables $(x_1, x_2, \ldots, x_{11})$ for the 12 months of the year. The seasonal forecasting model takes the form

$$E(Y_t) = \beta_0 + \beta_1 t + \beta_2 x_1 + \beta_3 x_2 + \beta_4 x_3 + \beta_5 x_4 + \beta_6 x_5 + \beta_7 x_6 + \beta_8 x_7 + \beta_9 x_8 + \beta_{10} x_9 + \beta_{11} x_{10} + \beta_{12} x_{11}$$

The MINITAB regression printout for the model is shown in Figure SIA15.6, followed by the model forecasts in Figure SIA15.7. The global F-test (p-value $= .000$) indicates that the model is statistically useful for predicting monthly sales, and the model coefficient of determination ($R^2 = .983$) indicates that over 98% of the sample variation in monthly sales can be explained by the seasonal model. Statistically, this model is a tremendous improvement over the linear trend model.

The 95% prediction intervals for sales in months 25, 26, and 27 (highlighted on Figure SIA15.7) are (4285.8, 6349.2),

(4164.8, 6228.2), and (1604.3, 3667.7), respectively. Thus, for the first month of year 3 (month 25), we are 95% confident that the actual sales will fall between 4,285.8 and 6,349.2 thousand dollars. (Similar interpretations are made for the other two forecasts). These intervals are much narrower than those for the previous two forecasting models, and they also reflect the expected drop in sales in March (month 3) from the winter months. This seasonal model was used successfully by the pharmaceutical firm to forecast monthly sales.

```
The regression equation is
SALES = 2961 + 74.2 TIME + 501 JAN + 306 FEB - 2329 MAR - 3101 APR - 3138 MAY
        - 2393 JUN - 2241 JUL + 623 AUG + 2111 SEP - 361 OCT - 744 NOV


Predictor      Coef  SE Coef       T      P
Constant     2960.5    320.2    9.25  0.000
TIME          74.25    11.65    6.38  0.000
JAN           500.8    365.5    1.37  0.198
FEB           305.5    361.6    0.84  0.416
MAR         -2329.2    358.0   -6.51  0.000
APR         -3101.0    354.8   -8.74  0.000
MAY         -3137.7    351.9   -8.92  0.000
JUN         -2393.5    349.4   -6.85  0.000
JUL         -2241.2    347.2   -6.45  0.000
AUG           623.0    345.5    1.80  0.099
SEP          2111.3    344.1    6.14  0.000
OCT          -361.5    343.1   -1.05  0.315
NOV          -743.7    342.5   -2.17  0.053


S = 342.314   R-Sq = 98.3%   R-Sq(adj) = 96.5%


Analysis of Variance

Source          DF        SS       MS      F       P
Regression      12  75435259  6286272  53.65  0.000
Residual Error  11   1288964   117179
Total           23  76724223
```

Figure SIA15.6

MINITAB printout for seasonal regression model of monthly Coldex sales

↓	C1	C2	C3	C4	C5	C6
	YEAR	MONTH	TIME	FORECAST	PL95LOW	PL95UPP
1	3	1	25	5317.5	4285.83	6349.17
2	3	2	26	5196.5	4164.83	6228.17
3	3	3	27	2636.0	1604.33	3667.67

Figure SIA15.7

MINITAB worksheet with seasonal regression forecasts of monthly sales

Exercises 15.35–15.41

Learning the Mechanics

15.35 What advantage do regression forecasts have over exponentially smoothed forecasts? Does this advantage ensure that regression forecasts will prove to be more accurate? Explain.

15.36 The annual price of a finished product (in cents per pound) from 1987 to 2002 is given in the table below. The time variable t begins with $t = 1$ in 1987 and is incremented by 1 for each additional year.

LM15_36

Year	t	Price, Y_t	Year	t	Price, Y_t
1987	1	21.73	1995	9	24.42
1988	2	24.32	1996	10	25.49
1989	3	25.31	1997	11	26.19
1990	4	26.36	1998	12	27.31
1991	5	27.31	1999	13	24.40
1992	6	27.58	2000	14	24.24
1993	7	24.79	2001	15	25.87
1994	8	25.36	2002	16	26.86

a. Fit the straight-line model, $E(Y_t) = \beta_0 + \beta_1 t$, to the data. $\hat{Y}_t = 24.7 + .091t$
b. Give the least squares estimates of the β's.
c. Use the least squares prediction equation to obtain the forecasts for 2003 and 2004.
d. Find 95% forecast intervals for 2003 and 2004.

15.37 Retail sales in quarters 1–4 over a 10-year period for a department store are shown (in hundreds of thousands of dollars) in the table below.

LM15_37

Year	Quarter 1	2	3	4
1	8.3	10.3	8.7	13.5
2	9.8	12.1	10.1	15.4
3	12.1	14.5	12.7	17.1
4	13.7	16.0	14.2	19.2
5	17.4	19.7	18.0	23.1
6	18.2	20.5	18.6	24.0
7	20.0	22.2	20.5	25.1
8	22.3	25.1	22.9	27.7
9	24.7	26.9	25.1	29.8
10	25.8	28.7	26.0	32.2

a. Write a regression model that contains trend and seasonal components to describe the sales data.
b. Use least squares regression to fit the model. Evaluate the fit of the model.
c. Use the regression model to forecast the quarterly sales during year 11. Give 95% prediction intervals for the forecasts.

Applying the Concepts—Basic

15.38 The table below reports the total personal annual income (in billions of dollars) of people in the state of California over the period 1980 to 2001. A simple linear regression model, $E(Y_t) = \beta_0 + \beta_1 t$, where t is the number of years since 1979, is proposed to forecast annual income.

CALINCOME

Year	Personal Income	Year	Personal Income
1980	281	1991	651
1981	314	1992	683
1982	335	1993	698
1983	361	1994	716
1984	402	1995	760
1985	437	1996	799
1986	468	1997	847
1987	505	1998	901
1988	547	1999	995
1989	588	2000	1,099
1990	637	2001	1,128

Source: U.S. Dept. of Commerce. *Survey of Current Business,* 2002.

a. Give the least squares estimates of the β's and interpret their values. $\hat{Y}_t = 209 + 37.8t$
b. Evaluate the model's fit.
c. Find and interpret 95% prediction intervals for the years 2002–2003.
d. Describe the problems associated with using a simple linear regression model to predict time series data.

15.39 The level at which commercial lending institutions set mortgage interest rates has a significant effect on the volume of buying, selling, and construction of residential and commercial real estate. The data in the table are the annual average mortgage interest rates for conventional, fixed-rate, 30-year loans for the period 1980–2000.

INTRATE30

Year	Interest Rate (%)	Year	Interest Rate (%)
1980	14.30	1991	11.14
1981	16.54	1992	9.29
1982	16.83	1993	8.09
1983	13.92	1994	8.28
1984	13.71	1995	7.86
1985	12.91	1995	7.86
1986	11.33	1997	7.57
1987	10.46	1998	6.92
1988	10.86	1999	7.46
1989	12.07	2000	8.08
1990	11.78		

Source: Statistical Abstract of the United States, U.S. Bureau of the Census, 2002.

a. Fit the simple regression model

$$E(Y_t) = \beta_0 + \beta_1 t$$

where t is the number of years since 1980 (i.e., $t = 0, 1, \ldots, 20$).

b. Forecast the average mortgage interest rate in 2003. Find a 95% prediction interval for this forecast.

Applying the Concepts—Intermediate

15.40 The next table presents the quarterly sales index for one brand of graphing calculator at a campus bookstore. The quarters are based on an academic year, so the first quarter represents fall; the second, winter; the third, spring; and the fourth, summer.

Define the time variable as $t = 1$ for the first quarter of 1998, $t = 2$ for the second quarter of 1998, etc. Consider the following seasonal dummy variables:

$$Q_1 = \begin{cases} 1 & \text{if quarter 1} \\ 0 & \text{otherwise} \end{cases}$$

$$Q_2 = \begin{cases} 1 & \text{if quarter 2} \\ 0 & \text{otherwise} \end{cases}$$

$$Q_3 = \begin{cases} 1 & \text{if quarter 3} \\ 0 & \text{otherwise} \end{cases}$$

GRAPHICAL

Year	First Quarter	Second Quarter	Third Quarter	Fourth Quarter
1998	438	398	252	160
1999	464	429	376	216
2000	523	496	425	318
2001	593	576	456	398
2002	636	640	526	498

a. Write a regression model for $E(Y_t)$ as a function of t, Q_1, Q_2, and Q_3.

b. Find and interpret the least squares estimates, and evaluate the usefulness of the model.

c. Which of the assumptions about the random error component is in doubt when a regression model is fit to time series data?

d. Find the forecasts and the 95% prediction intervals for the 2003 quarterly sales. Interpret the result.

15.41 The table below represents all life insurance policies (in millions) in force on the lives of U.S. residents for the years 1970 through 1999.

a. Use the method of least squares to fit a simple regression model to the data.

b. Forecast the number of life insurance policies in force for 2000 and 2001.

c. Construct 95% prediction intervals for the forecasts of part **b.**

d. Check the accuracy of your forecasts by looking up the actual number of life insurance policies in force for 2000 and 2001 in the *Statistical Abstract of the United States*.

LIFEINS

Year	No. of Policies (in millions)	Year	No. of Policies (in millions)
1970	355	1985	386
1971	357	1986	391
1972	365	1987	395
1973	369	1988	391
1974	380	1989	394
1975	380	1990	389
1976	382	1991	375
1977	390	1992	366
1978	401	1993	363
1979	407	1994	371
1980	402	1995	392
1981	400	1996	355
1982	390	1997	351
1983	387	1998	358
1984	385	1999	367

Source: U.S. Bureau of the Census. *Statistical Abstract of the United States*, 2001.

15.9 Autocorrelation and the Durbin-Watson Test

Teaching Tip

Both plotting and testing can be used to determine if the time series residuals are correlated.

Recall that one of the assumptions we make when using a regression model for predictions is that the errors are independent. However, with time series data, this assumption is questionable. The cyclical component of a time series may result in deviations from the secular trend that tend to cluster alternately on the positive and negative sides of the trend, as shown in Figure 15.19.

The observed errors between the time series and the regression model for the secular trend (and seasonal component, if present) are called **time series residuals.** Thus, if the time series Y_t has an estimated trend of $\hat{Y}_t$, then the time series residual* is

$$\hat{R}_t = Y_t - \hat{Y}_t$$

*We use $\hat{R}_t$ rather than $\hat{\epsilon}$ to denote a time series residual because, as we shall see, time series residuals often do not satisfy the regression assumptions associated with the random component ϵ.

Figure 15.19

Illustration of cyclical errors

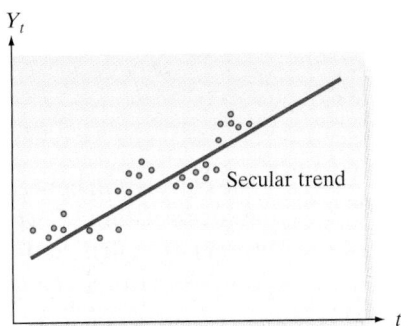

Note that time series residuals are defined just as the residuals for any regression model. However, we will usually plot time series residuals versus time to determine whether a cyclical component is apparent.

For example, consider the sales forecasting data in Table 15.7, to which we fit a simple straight-line regression model. The MINITAB plot of the data and model is repeated in Figure 15.20, and a plot of the time series residuals is shown in Figure 15.21.

Figure 15.20

MINITAB scatterplot of annual sales data

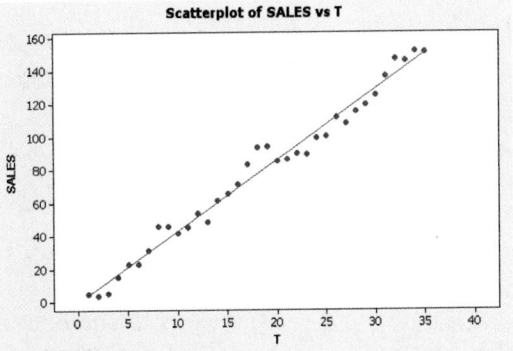

Notice the tendency of the residuals to group alternately into positive and negative clusters. That is, if the residual for year t is positive, there is a tendency for the residual for year $(t + 1)$ to be positive. These cycles are indicative of possible positive correlation between neighboring residuals. The correlation between time series residuals at different points in time is called *autocorrelation*, and the

Figure 15.21

MINITAB plot of residuals versus time for straight-line model of annual sales

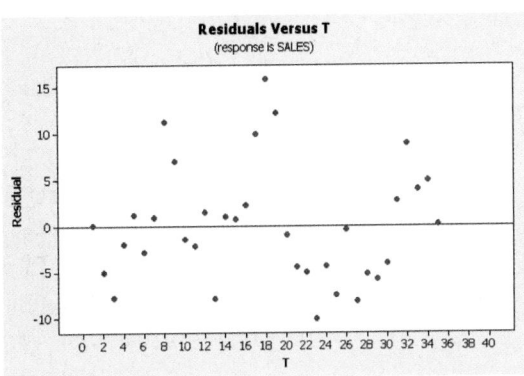

autocorrelation of neighboring residuals (time periods t and $t + 1$) is called *first-order autocorrelation*.

> **DEFINITION 15.5**
>
> The correlation between time series residuals at different points in time is called **autocorrelation.** Correlation between neighboring residuals (at times t and $t + 1$) is called **first-order autocorrelation.** In general, correlation between residuals at times t and $t + d$ is called dth-order autocorrelation.

Rather than speculate about the presence of autocorrelation among time series residuals, we prefer to test for it. For most business and economic time series, the relevant test is for first-order autocorrelation. Other higher-order autocorrelations may indicate seasonality (e.g., fourth-order autocorrelation in a quarterly time series). However, when we use the term *autocorrelation* in this text we are referring to first-order autocorrelation unless otherwise specified. So, we test

H_0: No first-order autocorrelation of residuals

H_a: Positive first-order autocorrelation of residuals

The **Durbin-Watson d-statistic** is used to test for the presence of first-order autocorrelation. The statistic is given by the formula

$$d = \frac{\sum_{t=2}^{n} (\hat{R}_t - \hat{R}_{t-1})^2}{\sum_{t=1}^{n} \hat{R}_t^2}$$

where n is the number of observations (time periods) and $(\hat{R}_t - \hat{R}_{t-1})$ represents the difference between a pair of successive time series residuals. The value of d always falls in the interval from 0 to 4. The interpretations of the values of d are given in the box. Most statistical software packages include a routine that calculates d for time series residuals.

> **Interpretation of Durbin-Watson d Statistic**
>
> $$d = \frac{\sum_{t=2}^{n} (\hat{R}_t - \hat{R}_{t-1})^2}{\sum_{t=1}^{n} \hat{R}_t^2} \qquad \text{Range of } d: 0 \le d \le 4$$
>
> 1. If the residuals are uncorrelated, then $d \approx 2$.
> 2. If the residuals are positively autocorrelated, then $d < 2$, and if the autocorrelation is very strong, $d \approx 0$.
> 3. If the residuals are negatively autocorrelated, then $d > 2$, and if the autocorrelation is very strong, $d \approx 4$.

Biography

GEOFFREY S. WATSON (1921–1998)
The Durbin-Watson Test

Australian Geoff Watson was educated at the University of Melbourne, where he earned a mathematics degree in 1942. Following World War II, Watson moved to North Carolina State University to begin work on a graduate degree in statistics. He eventually earned his Ph.D. in 1951. During his illustrious career as a statistics professor and researcher, Watson had appointments at Cambridge University, Australian National University, University of Toronto, Johns Hopkins University, and Princeton University (where he was chairman of the statistics department). While visiting Cambridge in the late 1940s, Watson collaborated with James Durbin of the London School Economics to develop their well-known Durbin-Watson test for serial correlation. His research interests covered a wide spectrum of statistical applications all across the world, including estimating the size of the penguin population (Antarctica), paleontology problems (Sweden), probability in quantum mechanics (Rome), molecular biology (Italy), and ozone depletion (U.S. Energy Information Administration). Outside his professional life, Watson was a serious painter (landscapes and hills) and an accomplished tennis player (effective lob).

Durbin and Watson (1951) give tables for the lower-tail values of the d statistic, which are shown in Tables XIII ($\alpha = .05$) and XIV ($\alpha = .01$) of Appendix B. Part of Table XIII is reproduced in Table 15.10. For the sales example, we have $k = 1$ independent variable and $n = 35$ observations. Using $\alpha = .05$ for the one-tailed test for positive autocorrelation, we obtain the tabled values $d_L = 1.40$ and $d_U = 1.52$. The meaning of these values is illustrated in Figure 15.22. Because of the complexity of the sampling distribution of d, it is not possible to specify a single point that acts as a boundary between the rejection and nonrejection regions, as we did for the z, t, F, and other test statistics. Instead, an upper (d_U) and lower (d_L) bound are specified. Thus a d-value less than d_L *does* provide strong evidence of positive autocorrelation at $\alpha = .05$ (recall that small d values indicate positive autocorrelation); a d value greater than d_U does *not* provide evidence of positive autocorrelation at $\alpha = .05$; and a value of d between d_L and d_U might or might not be significant at the $\alpha = .05$ level. If $d_L < d < d_U$, more information is needed before we can reach any conclusion about the presence of autocorrelation.

Teaching Tip

Unlike the tests of hypothesis from earlier chapters, there are three areas of the rejection region for the Durbin-Watson test, a reject area, a fail-to-reject area, and an unsure area.

TABLE 15.10 Reproduction of Part of Table XIII of Appendix B: Critical Values for the Durbin-Watson d Statistic, $\alpha = .05$

| | $k = 1$ | | $k = 2$ | | $k = 3$ | | $k = 4$ | | $k = 5$ | |
n	d_L	d_U	d_L	d_U	d_L	d_U	d_L	d_U	d_L	d_U
31	1.36	1.50	1.30	1.57	1.23	1.65	1.16	1.74	1.09	1.83
32	1.37	1.50	1.31	1.57	1.24	1.65	1.18	1.73	1.11	1.82
33	1.38	1.51	1.32	1.58	1.26	1.65	1.19	1.73	1.13	1.81
34	1.39	1.51	1.33	1.58	1.27	1.65	1.21	1.73	1.15	1.81
35	1.40	1.52	1.34	1.58	1.28	1.65	1.22	1.73	1.16	1.80
36	1.41	1.52	1.35	1.59	1.29	1.65	1.24	1.73	1.18	1.80
37	1.42	1.53	1.36	1.59	1.31	1.66	1.25	1.72	1.19	1.80
38	1.43	1.54	1.37	1.59	1.32	1.66	1.26	1.72	1.21	1.79
39	1.43	1.54	1.38	1.60	1.33	1.66	1.27	1.72	1.22	1.79
40	1.44	1.54	1.39	1.60	1.34	1.66	1.29	1.72	1.23	1.79

Figure 15.22

Rejection region for the
Durbin-Watson d test: Sales
example

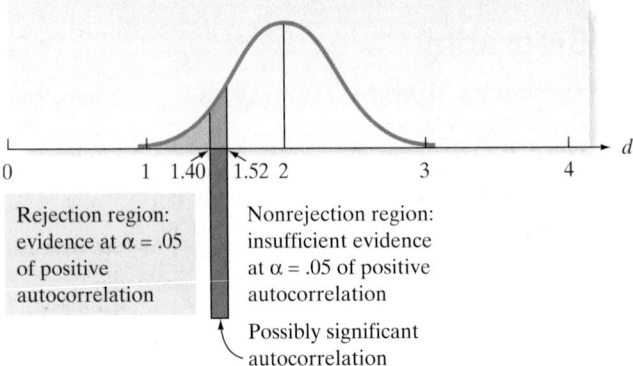

Rejection region:
evidence at $\alpha = .05$
of positive
autocorrelation

Nonrejection region:
insufficient evidence
at $\alpha = .05$ of positive
autocorrelation

Possibly significant
autocorrelation

Suggested Exercise 15.47

Tests for negative autocorrelation and two-tailed tests can be conducted by making use of the symmetry of the sampling distribution of the d statistic about its mean. The test procedure is summarized in the next box.

Durbin-Watson d Test for Autocorrelation

One-Tailed Test

H_0: No first-order autocorrelation
H_a: Positive first-order autocorrelation
   (or H_a: Negative first-order
   autocorrelation)

Two-Tailed Test

H_0: No first-order autocorrelation
H_a: Positive or negative first-order
   autocorrelation

Test statistic:

$$d = \frac{\sum_{t=2}^{n} (\hat{R}_t - \hat{R}_{t-1})^2}{\sum_{t=1}^{n} \hat{R}_t^2}$$

Rejection region:
$d < d_{L,\alpha}$
[or $(4 - d) < d_{L,\alpha}$ if
H_a: Negative first-order
autocorrelation]

Rejection region:
$d < d_{L,\alpha/2}$ or $(4 - d) < d_{L,\alpha/2}$

where $d_{L,\alpha}$ is the lower tabled value
corresponding to k independent
variables and n observations. The
corresponding upper value $d_{U,\alpha}$ defines
a "possibly significant" region between
$d_{L,\alpha}$ and $d_{U,\alpha}$ (See Figure 15.22).

where $d_{L,\alpha/2}$ is the lower tabled value
corresponding to k independent
variables and n observations. The
corresponding upper value $d_{U,\alpha/2}$ defines
a "possibly significant" region between
$d_{L,\alpha/2}$ and $d_{U,\alpha/2}$ (see Figure 15.22).

Requirements for the Vality of the d-Test

The residuals are normally distributed.

A portion of the EXCEL printout the regression of annual sales is presented in Figure 15.23. It shows that the computed value of d is .821 (highlighted), which is less than the tabulated value of $d_L = 1.40$ for $\alpha = .05$. Thus, we conclude that the residuals of the straight-line model for sales are positively autocorrelated.

Figure 15.23

EXCEL printout with Durbin-Watson statistics for annual sales model

	A	B
1	**Durbin-Watson Calculations**	
2		
3	Sum of Squared Difference of Residuals	1104.249775
4	Sum of Squared Residuals	1345.453546
5		
6	**Durbin-Watson Statistic**	**0.820726794**
7		
8		

Once strong evidence of first-order autocorrelation has been established, as in the case of the sales example, doubt is cast on the least squares results and any inferences drawn from them. Under these circumstances, a time series model that accounts for the autocorrelation of the random errors is needed. A useful model is the first-order autoregressive model. Consult the references at the end of the book.

Exercises 15.42–15.51

Learning the Mechanics

15.42 Define autocorrelation. Explain why it is important in time series modeling and forecasting.

15.43 What do the following Durbin-Watson statistics suggest about the autocorrelation of the time series residuals from which each was calculated?
a. $d = 3.9$ **b.** $d = .2$ **c.** $d = 1.99$

15.44 For each case, indicate the decision regarding the test of the null hypothesis of no first-order autocorrelation against the alternative hypothesis of positive first-order autocorrelation.
a. $k = 2, n = 20, \alpha = .05, d = 1.1$
b. $k = 2, n = 20, \alpha = .01, d = 1.1$
c. $k = 5, n = 65, \alpha = .05, d = .95$
d. $k = 1, n = 31, \alpha = .01, d = 1.35$

Applying the Concepts—Basic

15.45 Exploratory research published in the *Journal of Professional services Marketing* (Vol. 5, 1990) examined the relationship between deposit share of a retail bank and several marketing variables. Quarterly deposit share data were collected for five consecutive years for each of nine retail banking institutions. The model analyzed took the following form:

$$E(Y_t) = \beta_0 + \beta_1 P_{t-1} + \beta_2 S_{t-1} + \beta_3 D_{t-1}$$

where Y_t = deposit share of a bank in quarter $t(t = 1, 2, \dots, 20)$, P_{t-1} = expenditures on promotion-related activities in quarter $t - 1$, S_{t-1} = expenditures on service-related activities in quarter $t - 1$, and D_{t-1} = expenditures on distribution-related activities in quarter $t - 1$. A separate model was fit for each bank with the results shown in the table.

Bank	R^2	*p*-Value for Global *F*-Test	Durbin-Watson *d*
1	.914	.000	1.3
2	.721	.004	3.4
3	.926	.000	2.7
4	.827	.000	1.9
5	.270	.155	.85
6	.616	.012	1.8
7	.962	.000	2.5
8	.495	.014	2.3
9	.500	.011	1.1

a. Interpret the values of R^2 for each bank.
b. Test the overall adequacy of the model for each bank using $\alpha = .01$.
c. Conduct the Durbin-Watson *d*-test for positive residual correlation for each bank $\alpha = .01$. What conclusions do you draw about autocorrelation?

15.46 Forecasts of automotive vehicle sales in the United States provide the basis for financial and strategic planning of large automotive corporations. The following forecasting model was developed for Y_t, total monthly passenger car and light truck sales (in thousands):

$$E(Y_t) = \beta_0 + \beta_1 x_1 + \beta_2 x_2 + \beta_3 x_3 + \beta_4 x_4 + \beta_5 x_5$$

where x_1 = average monthly retail price of regular gasoline, x_2 = annual percentage change in GDP per quarter, x_3 = monthly consumer confidence index, x_4 = total number of vehicles scrapped (millions) per month, and x_5 = vehicle seasonality. The model was fit to monthly data collected over a 12-year period (i.e., $n = 144$ months), with the following results: $R^2 = .856$, Durbin-Watson $d = 1.01$.

a. Is there sufficient evidence to indicate that the overall model contributes information for the prediction of monthly passenger car and light truck sales? Test using $\alpha = .05$. $\quad F = 164.067$

b. Is there sufficient evidence to indicate that the regression errors are positively correlated? Test using $\alpha = .05$. $\quad d = 1.01$

c. Comment on the validity of the inference concerning model adequacy in light of the result of part **b.**

15.47 The consumer purchasing value of the dollar, Y_t, from 1970 to 1997 is illustrated by the data in the table. The buying power of the dollar (compared with 1982) is listed for each year. The first-order model

$$Y_t = \beta_0 + \beta_1 t + \epsilon$$

was fit to the data using the method of least squares. The MINITAB printout and a plot of the regression residuals are shown below.

a. Examine the plot of the regression residuals against t. Is there a tendency for the residuals to have long positive and negative runs? To what do you attribute this phenomenon?

b. Locate the Durbin-Watson d statistic on the printout and test the null hypothesis that the time series residuals are uncorrelated. Use $\alpha = .10$.

c. What assumption(s) must be satisfied in order for the test of part **b** to be valid?

⊙ **BUYPOWER**

Year	t	Value, Y_t	Year	t	Value, Y_t
1970	1	2.545	1984	15	0.964
1971	2	2.469	1985	16	0.955
1972	3	2.392	1986	17	0.969
1973	4	2.193	1987	18	0.949
1974	5	1.901	1988	19	0.926
1975	6	1.718	1989	20	0.880
1976	7	1.645	1990	21	0.839
1977	8	1.546	1991	22	0.822
1978	9	1.433	1992	23	0.812
1979	10	1.289	1993	24	0.802
1980	11	1.136	1994	25	0.797
1981	12	1.041	1995	26	0.782
1982	13	1.000	1996	27	0.762
1983	14	0.984	1997	28	0.759

Source: Statistical Abstract of the United States, 1998.

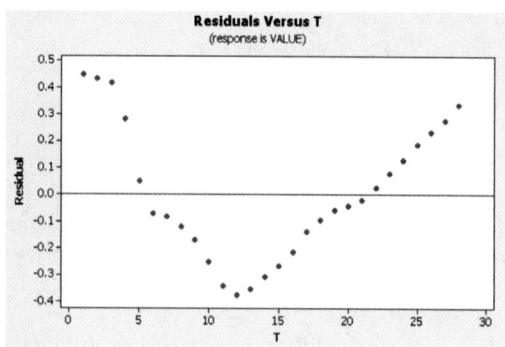

Regression Analysis: VALUE versus T

```
The regression equation is
VALUE = 2.16 - 0.0619 T


Predictor        Coef    SE Coef        T        P
Constant      2.15883    0.09898    21.81    0.000
T           -0.061915   0.005963   -10.38    0.000


S = 0.254882    R-Sq = 80.6%    R-Sq(adj) = 79.8%


Analysis of Variance

Source           DF        SS        MS        F        P
Regression        1    7.0037    7.0037   107.81    0.000
Residual Error   26    1.6891    0.0650
Total            27    8.6927


Durbin-Watson statistic = 0.0840449
```

Applying the Concepts—Intermediate

✪ CALINCOME

15.48 Refer to the annual data on personal income (Y_t) of California residents, Exercise 15.38 (p. 1043). You fit the simple linear regression model, $E(Y_t) = \beta_0 + \beta_1 t$, to the data for the years 1980 to 2001 ($t = 1, 2, \ldots, 22$).

   a. Find and plot the regression residuals against t. Does the plot suggest the presence of autocorrelation? Explain.

   b. Conduct the Durbin-Watson test (at $\alpha = .05$) to test formally for the presence of positively autocorrelated regression errors. $d = .30$

   c. Comment on the validity of the inference concerning model adequacy in light of the result of part **b.**

✪ INTRATE30

15.49 Refer to the data on annual mortgage interest rate (Y_t), Exercise 15.39 (p. 1043). You fit the simple linear regression model, $E(Y_t) = \beta_0 + \beta_1 t$, to the data for the years 1980 to 2000 ($t = 1, 2, \ldots, 21$).

   a. Find and plot the regression residuals against t. Does the plot suggest the presence of autocorrelation? Explain.

   b. Conduct the Durbin-Watson test (at $\alpha = .05$) to test formally for the presence of positively autocorrelated regression errors. $d = 1.00$

   c. Comment on the validity of the inference concerning model adequacy in light of the result of part **b.**

✪ LIFEINS

15.50 Refer to the annual data on number of life insurance policies in force (Y_t), Exercise 15.41 (p. 1044). You fit the

simple linear regression model, $E(Y_t) = \beta_0 + \beta_1 t$, to the data for the years 1970 to 1999 ($t = 1, 2, \ldots, 30$).

   a. Find and plot the regression residuals against t. Does the plot suggest the presence of autocorrelation? Explain.

   b. Conduct the Durbin-Watson test (at $\alpha = .05$) to test formally for the presence of positively autocorrelated regression errors. $d = .41$

   c. Comment on the validity of the inference concerning model adequacy in light of the result of part **b.**

15.51 T. C. Chiang considered several time series forecasting models of future foreign exchange rates for U.S. currency (*The Journal of financial Research*, Summer 1986). One popular theory among financial analysts is that the forward (90-day) exchange rate is a useful predictor of the future spot exchange rate. Using monthly data on exchange rates for the British pound for $n = 81$ months, Chiang fit the model $E(Y_t) = \beta_0 + \beta_1 x_{t-1}$, where $Y_t = \ln(\text{spot rate})$ in month t, and $x_{t-1} = \ln(\text{forward rate})$ in month $t - 1$. The analysis yielded the following results:

$$t\text{-value} = 47.9, \quad s = .025, \quad R^2 = .957,$$
$$\text{Durbin-Watson } d = .962$$

   a. Is the model statistically useful for forecasting future spot exchange rates for the British pound? Test using $\alpha = .05$. $F = 1758.21$

   b. Interpret the values of s and R^2.

   c. Is there evidence of positive autocorrelation among the residuals? Test using $\alpha = .05$. $d = .962$

   d. Based on the results of parts **a–c,** would you recommend using the model to forecast spot exchange rates?   No

---

Quick Review

Key Terms

Note: Starred (*) items are from the optional section in this chapter.

Adaptive forecast 1018
Additive model 1016
Autocorrelation 1046
Base period 998
Composite index number 1001
Cyclical effect 1017
Double exponential smoothing 1021
Durbin-Watson d statistic 1046
Durbin-Watson test 1048
Exponential smoothing 1010

Exponential smoothing constant 1010
Exponentially smoothed forecast 1018
First-order autocorrelation 1046
Forecast error 1019
Holt-Winters forecasting model* 1021
Index number 998
Inferential forecasting model 1033
Laspeyres index 1004
Long-term trend 1017
Mean absolute deviation 1027
Mean absolute percentage error 1027
Multiplicative model 1016

Paasche index 1006
Residual effect 1017
Root mean squared error 1027
Seasonal effect 1017
Seasonal model 1038
Secular trend 1017
Simple composite index number 1001
Simple index number 999
Time series 998
Time series residuals 1044
Weighted composite price index 1004

Key Formulas

$$I_t = \left(\frac{Y_t}{Y_0}\right)100 \qquad\qquad \text{Simple index} \quad 1001$$

$$I_t = \left(\frac{\text{Total of all } Y\text{-values at time } t}{\text{Total of all } Y\text{-values at time } t_0}\right)100 \qquad \text{Simple composite index} \quad 1001$$

Weighted composite price indexes:

$$I_t = \left(\frac{\sum\limits_{i=1}^{k} Q_{it_0} P_{it}}{\sum\limits_{i=1}^{k} Q_{it_0} P_{it_0}}\right)100 \qquad\qquad \text{Laspeyres} \quad 1004$$

$$I_t = \left(\frac{\sum\limits_{i=1}^{k} Q_{it} P_{it}}{\sum\limits_{i=1}^{k} Q_{it} P_{it_0}}\right)100 \qquad\qquad \text{Paasche} \quad 1006$$

Exponential smoothing:

$$E_t = wY_t + (1-w)E_{t-1} \quad \text{Note: } E_1 = Y_1 \qquad 1013$$
$$\text{Forecast: } F_{t+k} = E_t \qquad 1018$$

Holt-Winters model*:

$$E_t = wY_t + (1-w)(E_{t-1} + T_{t-1}) \quad \text{Note: } E_2 = Y_2, T_2 = Y_2 - Y_1 \qquad 1021$$
$$T_t = v(E_t - E_{t-1}) + (1-v)T_{t-1}$$
$$\text{Forecast: } F_{t+k} = E_t + kT_t \qquad 1024$$

$$\text{MAD} = \frac{\sum\limits_{t=1}^{m}|Y_t - F_t|}{m} \qquad\qquad \text{Mean absolute deviation} \quad 1027$$

$$\text{MAPE} = \frac{\sum\limits_{t=1}^{m}\left|\dfrac{Y_t - F_t}{Y_t}\right|}{m} \times 100 \qquad \text{Mean absolute percentage error} \quad 1027$$

$$\text{RMSE} = \sqrt{\frac{\sum\limits_{t=1}^{m}(Y_t - F_t)^2}{m}} \qquad\qquad \text{Root mean square error} \quad 1027$$

$$d = \frac{\sum\limits_{t=2}^{n}(\hat{R}_t - \hat{R}_{t-1})^2}{\sum\limits_{t=1}^{n}\hat{R}_t^2} \qquad\qquad \text{Durbin-Watson test statistic} \quad 1046$$

Chapter Summary Notes

- **Time series data**—data generated by processes over time.
- **Index number**—measures the change in a variable over time relative to a base period.
- Three types of index numbers: (1) **simple index number**, (2) **simple composite index number,** and (3) **weighted composite number.**
- Two types of weighted composite index numbers: (1) **Laspeyres index** and (2) **Paasche index.**

- Four time series components: (1) **secular (long-term) trend**, (2) **cyclical effect**, (3) **seasonal effect**, and (4) **residual effect.**
- Two *descriptive methods* of forecasting with smoothing: (1) **exponential smoothing** and (2) **Holt-Winters model.**
- Three measures of forecast accuracy: (1) **mean absolute deviation (MAD)**, (2) **mean absolute percentage error (MAPE)**, and (3) **root mean squared error (RMSE).**

- An *inferential* forecasting method: **least squares regression.**
- Two problems with least squares regression forecasting: (1) *prediction outside the experimental region* and (2) regression *errors are autocorrelated.*

- **Autocorrelation**—correlation between time series residuals at different points in time.
- A test for first-order autocorrelation: **Durbin-Watson test.**

Language Lab

Symbol	Pronunciation	Description
Y_t	Y sub t	Time series value at time t
I_t	I sub t	Index at time t
P_t	P sub t	Price series at time t
Q_t	Q sub t	Quantity series at time t
E_t	E sub t	Exponentially smoothed value at time t
T_t	T sub t	Smoothed trend at time t
F_{t+k}	F sub t-plus-k	k-step-ahead forecast value
MAD	Mad	Mean absolute deviation
MAPE	Māpe	Mean absolute percentage error
RMSE	R-M-S-E	Root mean squared error
$\hat{R}_t$	R-hat sub t	Residual at time t
d	d	Value of Durbin-Watson test statistic
d_L	d sub L	Lower critical value of d
d_U	d sub U	Upper critical value of d

Supplementary Exercises 15.52–15.65

Applying the Concepts—Basic

15.52 The U.S. steel industry prices (in dollars per ton) of three varieties of steel are given in the table for selected years from 1980 to 2000.

⚙ **STEEL3**

Year	Cold Rolled	Hot Rolled	Galvanized
1980	438	369	478
1985	563	475	606
1990	507	445	671
1995	514	506	687
2000	405	298	418

Sources: Standard & Poor's Statistics: Metals, 1995; The CRB Community Yearbook, 1998; Purchasing Magazine, Nov. 2002.

a. Calculate a simple composite index for the three steel price series using 1980 as the base period. Interpret the results.
b. Is the index a price index or a quantity index?
c. What information would you need in order to calculate a Laspeyres index with a base period

of 1980? A Paasche index with a base period of 1980?

15.53 Refer to Exercise 15.52.
a. Compute the exponentially smoothed series corresponding to each of the price series using the smoothing constant $w = .5$.
b. Plot the prices and their exponentially smoothed series on the same graph.
c. Find the exponential smoothing forecasts of 2005 prices of the three varieties of steel. What are the drawbacks to these forecasts?

15.54 In 1990, the average weekly food cost for a suburban family of four was estimated to be $154.40. The table on p. 1054 presents the retail prices of selected food items from 1990 to 2000. Assume a typical suburban family of four purchased the following quantities of food, on average, each week during 1990:

Bread	Sirloin Steak	Eggs	Potatoes
2 lb.	4 lb.	1 doz.	10 lb.

FOOD4

Year	Spaghetti ($/lb.)	T-Bone Steak ($/lb.)	Eggs ($/doz.)	Potatoes ($/lb.)
1990	.85	5.45	1.00	.32
1991	.85	5.21	1.01	.28
1992	.84	5.39	.93	.31
1993	.84	5.77	.87	.36
1994	.87	5.86	.87	.34
1995	.88	5.92	1.16	.38
1996	.84	5.87	1.31	.33
1997	.88	6.07	1.17	.37
1998	.88	6.40	1.09	.38
1999	.88	6.71	.92	.40
2000	.88	6.82	.96	.35

Source: U.S. Bureau of the Census. *Statistical Abstract of the United States,* 2001.

    a. Calculate a Laspeyres price index for 1990 to 2000, using 1990 as the base year.

    b. According to your index, how much did the above "basket" of foods increase or decrease in price from 1990 to 2000?

15.55 With the advent of managed care, U.S. hospitals have begun to operate like businesses. More than ever before, hospital administrators need to know and apply the theories and methods taught in business schools. Richmond Memorial Hospital in Richmond, Virginia, uses regression analysis to forecast the demand for emergency room services. Specifically, Richmond Memorial uses data on patient visits to the emergency room during each of the past 10 Augusts to forecast next August's demand. Data for the month of August in a recent 10-year period are shown below.

ER

Year t	Visits	Daily Average Y_t	Year t	Visits	Daily Average Y_t
1	1,367	44.09	6	3,019	97.38
2	1,642	52.96	7	2,794	90.12
3	1,780	57.41	8	2,846	91.80
4	2,060	66.45	9	3,001	96.80
5	2,257	72.80	10	3,548	114.45

Source: Adapted from Bolling, W. B. "Queuing Model of a Hospital Emergency Room," *Industrial Engineering,* Sept. 1972.

    a. Use a straight-line regression model to construct a point forecast for emergency room demand for each of the next three Augusts.

    b. Provide 95% prediction intervals around the forecasts.

    c. Describe the potential dangers associated with using simple linear regression to forecast demand for emergency room services.

    d. Which other method described in this chapter would be appropriate for forecasting patient visits to the emergency room?

Applying the Concepts—Intermediate

15.56 Refer to the annual interest rate time series, Exercise 15.39 (p. 1043). Use $w = .3$ and $v = .7$ to compute the Holt-Winters forecasts for 2001–2003. Compare these to the linear regression forecasts obtained in Exercise 15.39 using MAD, MAPE, and RMSE. [*Note:* You will need to obtain the actual values of the time series for 2001–2003 to complete this exercise.]

15.57 The stock of Abbott Laboratories has had the yearly closing prices shown in the table.

ABBLAB

Year	Closing Price	Year	Closing Price
1980	56.50	1992	30.03
1981	27.00	1993	29.05
1982	38.75	1994	32.05
1983	45.25	1995	41.05
1984	41.75	1996	50.75
1985	68.37	1997	65.50
1986	45.62	1998	49.00
1987	48.02	1999	36.31
1988	48.01	2000	48.44
1989	64.03	2001	55.75
1990	45.00	2002	40.00
1991	68.07		

Sources: Standard & Poor's. *NYSE Daily Stock Price Record,* 1980–2003.

    a. Use exponential smoothing with $w = .8$ to forecast the 2003 and 2004 closing prices. If you buy at the end of 2002 and sell at the end of 2004, what is your expected gain (loss)?

    b. Repeat part **a** using the Holt-Winters model with $w = .8$ and $v = .5$.

    c. In which forecast do you have more confidence? Explain.

15.58 Refer to Exercise 15.57.

    a. Fit a simple linear regression model to the stock price data. $\hat{Y}_t = 46.5 + .020t$

    b. Plot the fitted regression line on a scattergram of the data.

    c. Forecast the 2003 and 2004 closing prices using the regression model. 46.95; 46.97

    d. Construct 95% prediction intervals for the forecasts of part **c.** Interpret the intervals in the context of the problem. (18.75, 75.15); (18.48, 75.46)

    e. Obtain the time series residuals for the simple linear model, and use the Durbin-Watson d statistic to test for the presence of autocorrelation.

15.59 Annual mutual fund retirement assets (in billions of dollars) for two fund types are given in the table on p. 1055.

    a. Compute simple indexes for each of the two time series using 1990 as the base period.

    b. Construct a time series plot that displays both indexes.

    c. Using the results of parts **a** and **b,** compare and contrast the two types of funds.

FUND2

Year	IRA	401(K)
1990	140	35
1994	350	184
1995	476	266
1996	598	346
1997	767	466
1998	960	596
1999	1,234	780
2000	1,232	766

Source: U.S. Census Bureau. *Statistical Abstract of the United States,* 2001.

15.60 The Gross Domestic Product (GDP) is the total U.S. output of goods and services valued at market prices. The quarterly GDP values (in billions of dollars) for the period 1997–2001 are given in the accompanying table. Using weights $w = .5$ and $v = .5$, calculate Holt-Winters forecasts for the four quarters of 2002.

QTRGDP

Year	Quarter	GDP	Year	Quarter	GDP
1997	I	8124	2000	I	9669
	II	8280		II	9858
	III	8391		III	9938
	IV	8479		IV	10028
1998	I	8635	2001	I	10142
	II	8722		II	10203
	III	8829		III	10225
	IV	8975		IV	10480
1999	I	9093			
	II	9161			
	III	9297			
	IV	9522			

Source: Standard & Poor's Statistical Service: Current Statistics, Mar. 2002.

15.61 Refer to Exercise 15.60.
  a. Use the simple linear regression model fit to the 1997–2001 data to forecast the 2002 quarterly GDP. Place 95% prediction limits on the forecasts.
  b. The GDP values given are *seasonally adjusted,* which means that an attempt to remove seasonality has been made prior to reporting the figures. Add quarterly dummy variables to the model. Use the partial *F*-test (discussed in Section 15.11) to determine whether the data indicate the significance of the seasonal component. Does the test support the assertion that the GDP figures are seasonally adjusted?
  c. Use the seasonal model to forecast the 2002 quarterly GDP values.
  d. Calculate the time series residuals for the seasonal model, and use the Durbin-Watson test to determine whether the residuals are autocorrelated. Use $\alpha = .10$. $d = .81$

15.62 Refer to Exercises 15.60 and 15.61. For each of the forecasting models apply the MAD, MAPE, and RMSE criteria to evaluate the forecasts for the first three quarters of 2002. Which of the forecasting models performs best according to each criterion? (You will need to obtain the actual 2002 GDP values to complete this exercise.)

15.63 A major portion of total consumer credit is extended in the categorie, of revolving credit loans. Amounts outstanding (in billions of dollars) for the period 1980–2000 are given in the table.

LOANS

Year	Revolving	Year	Revolving
1980	55.1	1991	245.3
1981	61.1	1992	257.3
1982	66.5	1993	287.9
1983	79.1	1994	337.7
1984	100.3	1995	443.0
1985	121.8	1996	499.2
1986	135.8	1997	528.9
1987	153.1	1998	560.5
1988	174.3	1999	595.6
1989	198.5	2000	663.8
1990	223.5		

Source: U.S. Bureau of the Census. *Statistical Abstract of the United States,* 2001.

  a. Use a simple linear regression model to forecast the 2002 and 2003 values. Place 95% prediction limits on each forecast.
  b. Calculate the Holt-Winters forecasts for 2002 and 2003 using $w = .7$ and $v = .7$. Compare the results with the simple linear regression forecasts of part **a.**

15.64 The number of dollars a person receives in a year is referred to as his or her *monetary* (or *money*) *income.* This figure can be adjusted to reflect the purchasing power of the dollars received relative to the purchasing power of dollars in some base period. The result is called a person's *real income.* The Consumer Price Index (CPI) can be used to adjust monetary income to obtain real income (in terms of 1984 dollars). To compute your real income for a specific year, simply divide your monetary income for that year by that year's CPI and multiply by 100. In Exercise 15.24 (p. 1025), we listed the CPI for 1990 and 2000 as 125.8 and 171.5, respectively.

  a. Suppose your monetary income increased from $50,000 in 1990 to $80,000 in 2000. What were your real incomes in 1990 and 2000? Were you able to buy more goods and services in 1990 or 2000? Explain.   2000
  b. What monetary income would have been required in 2000 to provide equivalent purchasing power to a 1990 monetary income of $20,000? $68,163.75

⦿ IBM

15.65 Refer to Example 15.4 (p. 1013), and the monthly IBM stock prices from January 2001 to December 2002. The data are saved in the **IBM** file.

a. Use the exponentially smoothed series (with $w = .5$) from January 2001 to September 2002 to forecast the monthly values of the IBM stock price from October to December 2002. Calculate the forecast errors.

b. Use a simple linear regression model fit to the IBM stock prices from January 2001 to September 2002. Let time t range from 1 to 21, representing the 21 months in the sample. Interpret the least squares estimates.

c. With what approximate precision do you expect to be able to predict the IBM stock price using the regression model? ± 24.80

d. Give the simple linear regression forecasts and the 95% forecast intervals for the October–December 2002 prices. How does the precision of these forecasts agree with the approximation obtained in part **c**?

e. Compare the exponential smoothing forecasts, part **a,** to the regression forecasts, part **d,** using MAD, MAPE, and RMSE.

f. What assumptions does the random error component of the regression model have to satisfy in order to make the model inferences (such as the forecast intervals in part **c**) valid?

g. Test to determine whether there is evidence of first-order positive autocorrelation in the random error component of the regression model. Use $\alpha = .05$. What can you infer about the validity of the model inferences? $d = .69$

REFERENCES

Abraham, B., and Ledholter, J. *Statistical Methods for Forecasting.* New York: Wiley, 1983.

Anderson, T. W. *The Statistical Analysis of Time Series.* New York: Wiley, 1971.

Box, G. E. P., and Jenkins, G. M. *Time Series Analysis: Forecasting and Control*, 2nd ed. San Francisco: Holden-Day, 1977.

Chipman, J. S., "Efficiency of Least Squares Estimation of Linear Trend when Residuals Are Autocorrelated", *Econometrica*, Vol. 47, 1979.

Durbin, J., and Watson, G. S. "Testing for Serial Correlation in Least Squares Regression, I." *Biometrika*, 1950, Vol. 37, pp. 409–428.

Durbin, J., and Watson, G. S. "Testing for Serial Correlation in Least Squares Regression, II." *Biometrika*, 1951, Vol. 38, pp. 159–178.

Durbin, J., and Watson, G. S. "Testing for Serial Correlation in Least Squares Regression, III." *Biometrika*, 1971, Vol. 58, pp. 1–19.

Fuller, W. A. *Introduction to Statistical Time Series.* New York: Wiley, 1976.

Granger, C. W. J., and Newbold, P. *Forecasting Economic Time Series.* New York: Academic Press, 1977.

Greene, W. H., *Econometric Analysis*, 2nd ed. New York: Macmillan, 1993.

Gross, C. W., and Patterson, R. J. *Business Forecasting*, 2nd ed. Boston: Houghton Mifflin, 1983.

Hamilton, J.D., *Time Series Analysis.* Princeton: Princeton University Press, 1994.

Harvey, A., *The Econometric Analysis of Time Series*, 2nd ed. Cambridge: MIT Press, 1990.

Maddala, G. S., *Econometrics.* New York: McGraw-Hill, 1977.

Makridakis, S. et al. *The Forecasting Accuracy of Major time Series Methods.* New York: Wiley, 1984.

Nelson, C. R. *Applied Time Series Analysis for Managerial Forecasting.* San Francisco: Holden-Day, 1983.

Shively, T. S., "Fast Evaluation of the Distribution of the Durbin-Watson and Other Invariant Test Statistics in Time Series Regression," *Journal of the American Statistical Association*, Vol. 85, 1990.

Theil, H., *Principles of Econometrics.* New York: Wiley, 1971.

White, K. J. "The Durbin-Watson Test for Autocorrelation in Nonlinear Models," *Review of Economics and Statistics*, Vol. 74, 1992.

Willis, R. E. *A Guide to Forecasting for Planners.* Englewood Cliffs, N. J.: Prentice Hall, 1987.

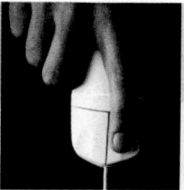

Using Technology

15.1 Forecasting Using SPSS

To produce forecasts using exponential smoothing or the Holt-Winters method, click the "Analyze" button on the SPSS main menu bar, then click on "Time Series", and then click on "Exponential Smoothing", as shown in Figure 15.S.1. The resulting dialog box is shown in Figure 15.S.2.

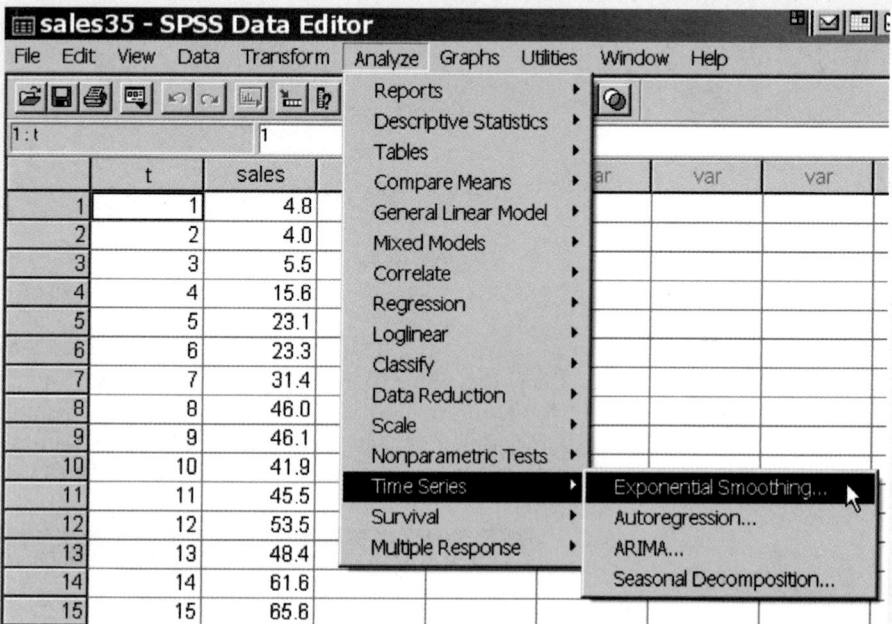

Figure 15.S.1
SPSS options for exponential smoothing

Figure 15.S.2
SPSS exponential smoothing dialog box

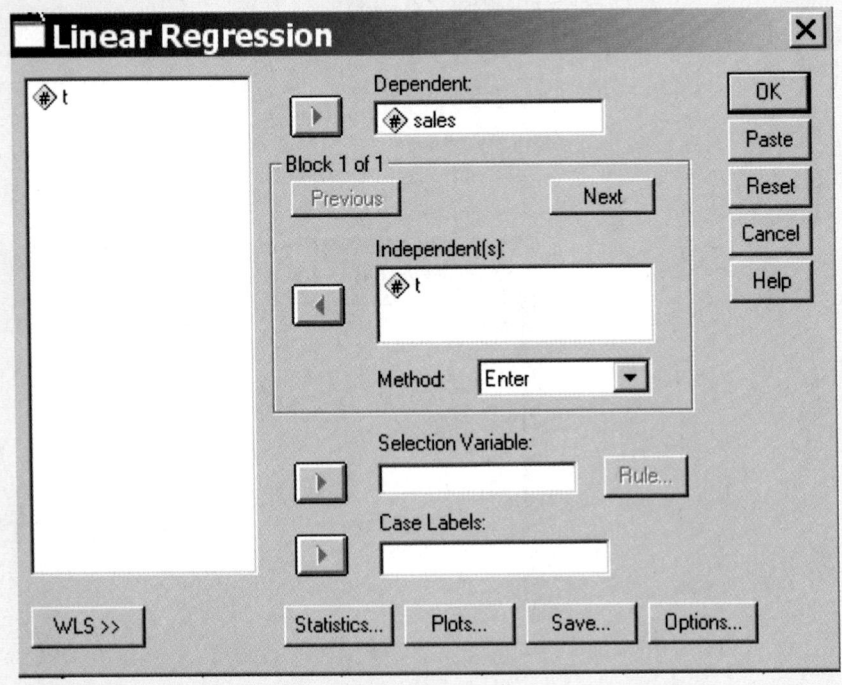

Figure 15.S.3
Selecting exponential smoothing parameters

Select the quantitative variable to be smoothed and place it in the "Variables" box. For exponential smoothing, select "Simple" in the "Model" box. For the Holt-Winters method, select "Holt" in the "Model" box. To set the value of the smoothing constants, click the "Parameters" button and make your selections on the resulting menu screen, as shown in Figure 15.S.3. Click "Continue" to return to

Figure 15.S.4
SPSS linear regression dialog box

the "Exponential Smoothing" dialog box, then click "OK" to view the results. *[Note:* Forecasts for each time period in the data set will show up in a column on the SPSS spreadsheet screen.]

To produce forecasts using a regression model, click the "Analyze" button on the SPSS main menu bar, then click on "Regression" and "Linear". The resulting dialog box is shown in Figure 15.S.4.

Specify the dependent time series variable in the "Dependent" box and the independent variables in the model in the "Independent(s)" box. Click "Save" and make the appropriate menu selections to save the forecasted values as well as 95% prediction intervals. To conduct the Durbin-Watson test for autocorrelated errors, click on the "Statistics" button to obtain the menu shown in Figure 15.S.5. Check the "Durbin-Watson" box, then click "Continue" to return to the "Linear Regression" dialog box. Click "OK" to view the results.

Figure 15.S.5
Linear regression statistics menu

15.2 Forecasting Using MINITAB

To produce forecasts using exponential smoothing or the Holt-Winters method, click the "Stat" button on the MINITAB main menu bar, then click on "Time Series". This will produce the menu list shown in Figure 15.M.1.

Click on "Single Exp Smoothing" for the exponential smoothing method or "Double Exp Smoothing" for the Holt-Winter's method with trend. For example, clicking "Single Exp Smoothing" will result in the dialog box shown in Figure 15.M.2.

Select the quantitative variable to be smoothed and place it in the "Variable" box and set the value of the smoothing constant in the "Weight to use in smoothing" box. Select the "Options" box and specify "1" where MINITAB asks for the number of observations to use for the initial smoothed value. As an option, you can store the forecast values by selecting "Storage" and making the appropriate selections. Click "OK" to view the results.

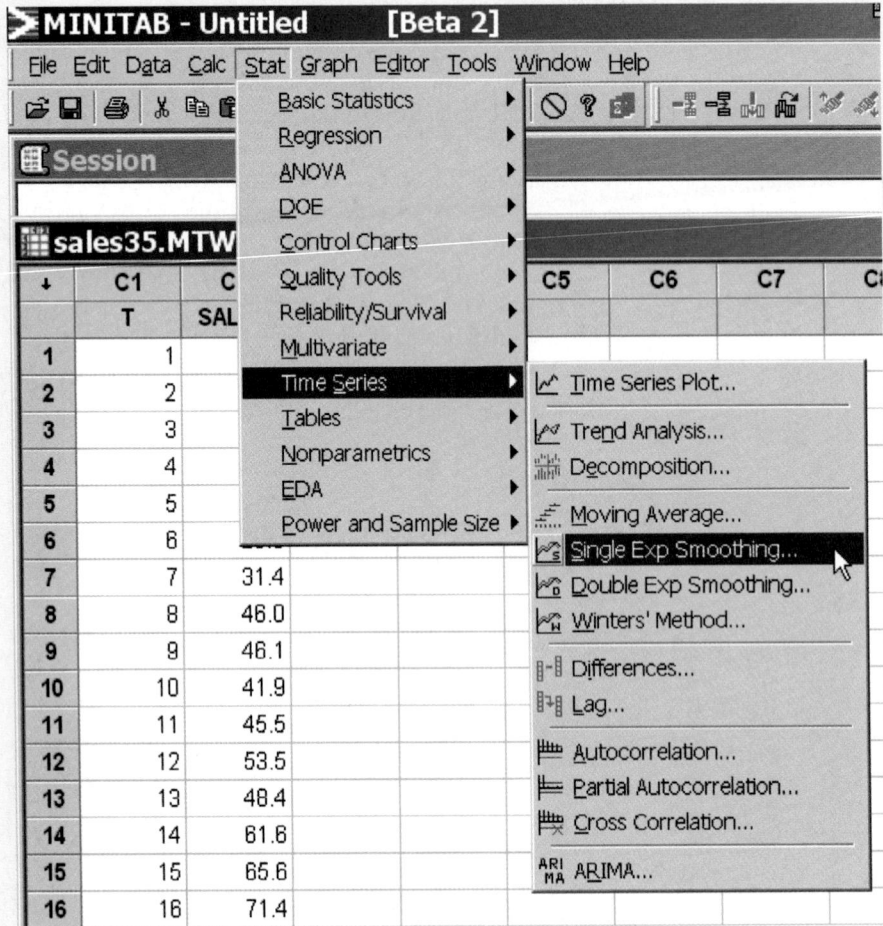

Figure 15.M.1
MINITAB options for time series analysis

To produce forecasts using a regression model, click the "Stat" button on the MINITAB main menu bar, then click on "Regression" and "Regression" again. The resulting dialog box is shown in Figure 15.M.3.

Specify the dependent time series variable in the "Response" box and the independent variables in the model in the "Predictors" box. Click "Options" to display the Regression Options dialog box. As shown in Figure 15.M.4, you may select "Durbin-Watson statistic" to conduct a test for autocorrelated errors and/or make selections for producing a prediction interval for a future value of the time series variable. Click "Storage" and make the appropriate menu selections to save the forecasted values as well as 95% prediction intervals. (These values will appear on the MINITAB worksheet.) When all selections have been made, click "OK" on the Linear Regression dialog box to produce the forecasts.

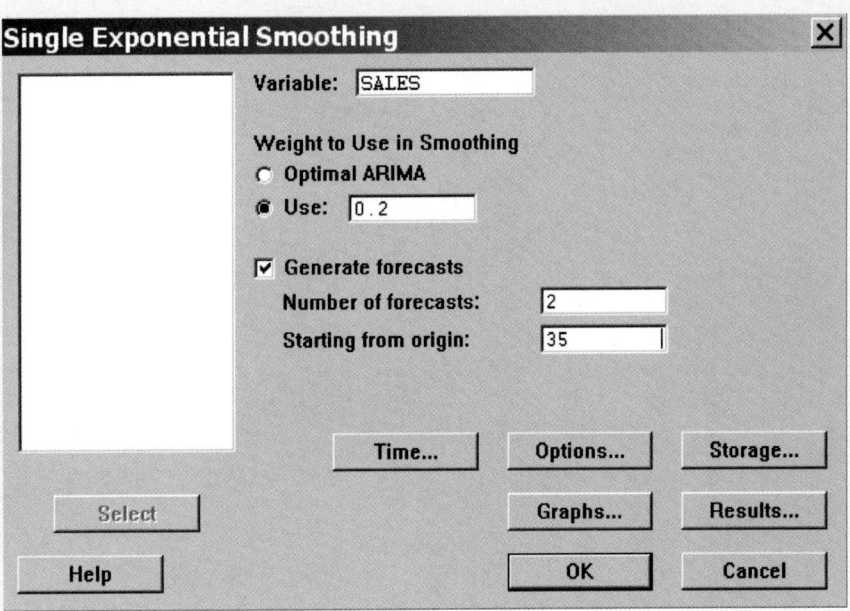

Figure 15.M.2
MINITAB exponential smoothing dialog box

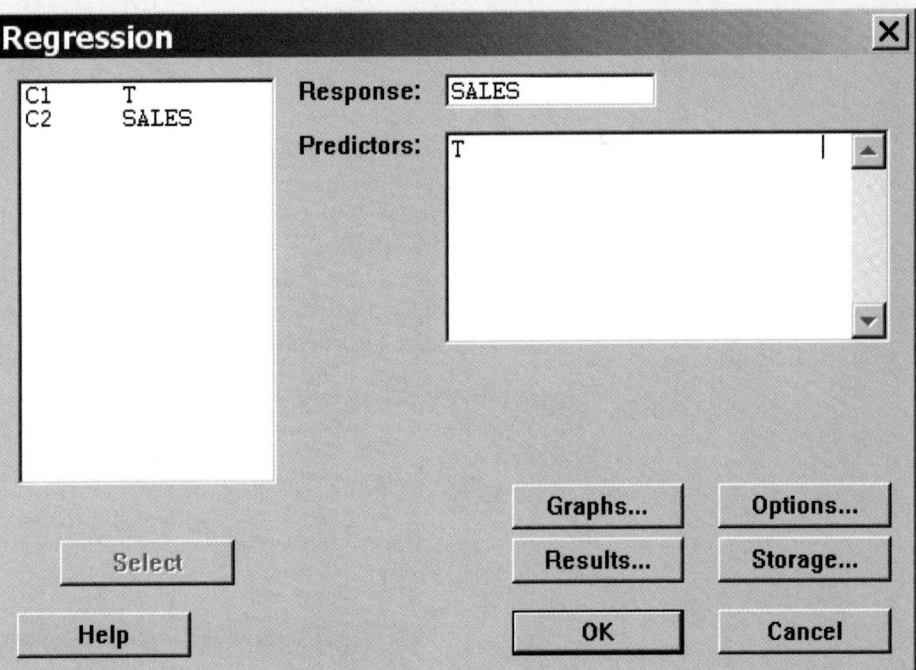

Figure 15.M.3
MINITAB linear regression dialog box

Regression - Options

Weights: [   ]   ☑ **Fit intercept**

Display   **Lack of Fit Tests**
☐ **Variance inflation factors**   ☐ **Pure error**
☑ **Durbin-Watson statistic**   ☐ **Data subsetting**
☐ **PRESS and predicted R-square**

Prediction intervals for new observations:
[36   ]

Confidence level: [95   ]
Storage
☑ **Fits**   ☐ **Confidence limits**
☐ **SEs of fits**   ☑ **Prediction limits**

[Select]

[Help]   [OK]   [Cancel]

Figure 15.M.4

15.3 Forecasting Using EXCEL

To produce forecasts using exponential smoothing, click on the "Tools" button on the EXCEL main menu bar, then click on "Data Analysis". Select "Exponential Smoothing" from the resulting menu list, as shown in Figure 15.E.1. Click "OK" to display the EXCEL Exponential Smoothing dialog box as shown in Figure 15.E.2.

Specify the input range of the quantitative variable to be smoothed, the smoothing constant ("damping factor"), and the output range for where the smoothed values will appear on the EXCEL worksheet. As an option, you can check "Chart Output" to produce a plot of the smoothed series. Click "OK" to view the results. *[Note:* The Holt-Winters forecasting method is not currently available in EXCEL.]

To produce forecasts using a regression model, click the "PHStat" button on the EXCEL main menu bar, then click on "Regression" and either "Simple Linear Regression" or "Multiple Regression". The resulting dialog box is similar to the one shown in Figure 15.E.3.

Specify the cell range for the dependent (y) time series variable and the cell range for the independent (x) variable(s). Check the "Durbin-Watson Statistic" option to conduct a test for autocorrelated errors and/or make selections for producing a prediction interval for a future value of the time series variable. Click "OK" to produce the regression results and forecasts.

Figure 15.E.1
EXCEL data
analysis options

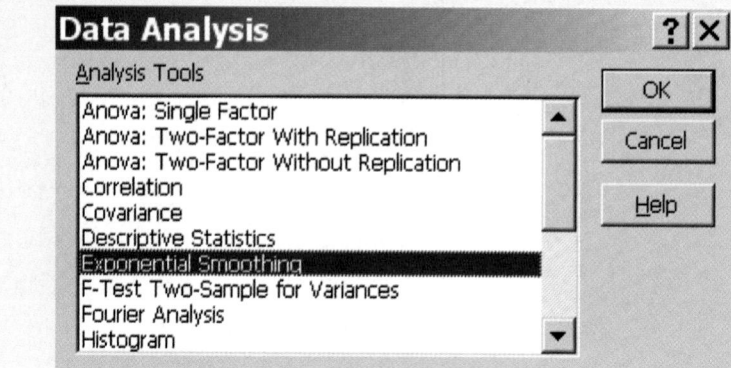

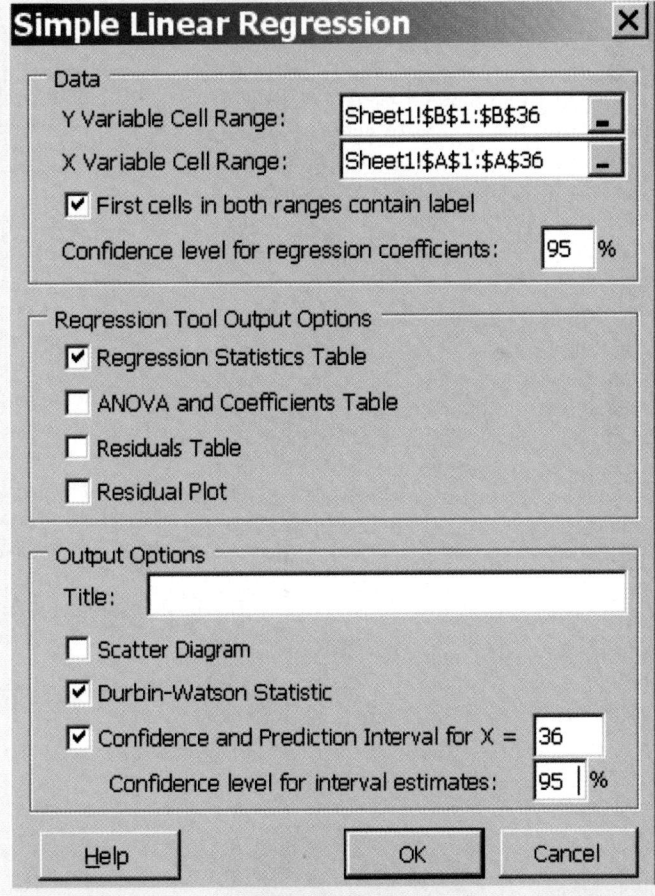

Figure 15.E.2
EXCEL exponential smoothing dialog box

Figure 15.E.3
EXCEL linear regression dialog box

Real-World Case
The Gasket Manufacturing Case
(A Case Covering Chapters 14 and 15)

The Problem

A Midwestern manufacturer of gaskets for automotive and off-road vehicle applications was suddenly and unexpectedly notified by a major customer—a U.S. auto manufacturer—that they had significantly tightened the specification limits on the overall thickness of a hard gasket used in their automotive engines. Although the current specification limits were by and large being met by the gasket manufacturer, their product did not come close to meeting the new specification.

The gasket manufacturer's first reaction was to negotiate with the customer to obtain a relaxation of the new specification. When these efforts failed, the customer-supplier relationship became somewhat strained. The gasket manufacturer's next thought was that if they waited long enough, the automotive company would eventually be forced to loosen the requirements and purchase the existing product. However, as time went on it became clear that this was not going to happen and that some positive steps would have to be taken to improve the quality of their gaskets. But what should be done? And by whom?

The Product

Figure C5.1 shows the product in question, a hard gasket. A hard gasket is comprised of two outer layers of soft gasket material and an inner layer consisting of a perforated piece of sheet metal. These three pieces are assembled, and some blanking and punching operations follow, after which metal rings are installed around the inside of the cylinder bore clearance holes and the entire outside periphery of the gasket. The quality characteristic of interest in this case is the assembly thickness.

The Process

An initial study by the staff engineers revealed that the variation in the thickness of soft gasket material—the two outer layers of the hard gasket—was large and undoubtedly responsible for much of the total variability in the final product. Figure C5.2 shows the roll mill process that

Figure C5.1
A hard gasket for automotive applications

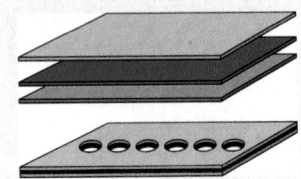

fabricates the sheets of soft gasket material from which the two outer layers of the hard gasket are made. To manufacture a sheet of soft gasket material, an operator adds raw material, in a soft pelletlike form, to the gap—called the knip—between the two rolls. The larger roll rotates about its axis with no lateral movement; the smaller roll rotates and moves back and forth laterally to change the size of the knip. As the operator adds more and more material to the knip, the sheet is formed around the larger roll. When the smaller roll reaches a preset destination (i.e., final gap/sheet thickness), a bell rings and a red light goes on telling the operator to stop adding raw material. The operator stops the rolls and cuts the sheet horizontally along the larger roll so that it may be pulled off the roll. The finished sheet, called a pull, is pulled onto a table where the operator checks its thickness with a micrometer. The operator can adjust the final gap if he or she believes that the sheets are coming out too thick or too thin relative to the prescribed nominal value (i.e., the target thickness).

Process Operation

Investigation revealed that the operator runs the process in the following way. After each sheet is made, the operator measures the thickness with a micrometer. The thickness values for three consecutive sheets are averaged and the average is plotted on a piece of graph paper that, at the start of the shift, has only a solid horizontal line drawn on it to indicate the target thickness value for the particular soft gasket sheet the operator is making. Periodically, the operator reviews these evolving data and makes a decision as to whether or not the process mean—the sheet thickness—needs to be adjusted. This can be accomplished by stopping the machine, loosening some clamps on the small roll, and jogging the small roll laterally in or out by a few

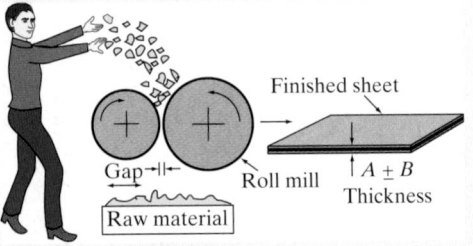

Figure C5.2
Roll mill for the manufacture of soft gasket material

thousandths of an inch—whatever the operator feels is needed. The clamps are tightened, the gap is checked with a taper gage, and if adjusted properly, the operator begins to make sheets again. Typically, this adjustment process takes 10 to 15 minutes. The questions of when to make such adjustments and how much to change the roll gap for each adjustment are completely at the operator's discretion, based on the evolving plot of thickness averages.

Figure C5.3 shows a series of plots that detail the history of one particular work shift over which the operator made several process adjustments. (These data come from the same shift that the staff engineers used to collect data for a process capability study that is described later.) Figure C5.3(a) shows the process data after the first 12 sheets have been made—four averages of three successive sheet thicknesses. At this point the operator judged that the data were telling her that the process was running below the target, so she stopped the process and made an adjustment to slightly increase the final roll gap. She then proceeded to make more sheets. Figure C5.3(b) shows the state of the process somewhat later. Now it appeared to the

operator that the sheets were coming out too thick, so she stopped and made another adjustment. As shown in Figure C5.3(c), the process seemed to run well for a while, but then an average somewhat below the target led the operator to believe that another adjustment was necessary. Figures C5.3(d) and C5.3(e) show points in time where other adjustments were made.

Figure C5.3(f) shows the complete history of the shift. A total of 24 × 3, or 72, sheets were made during this shift. When asked, the operator indicated that the history of this shift was quite typical of what happens on a day-to-day basis.

The Company's Stop-Gap Solution

While the staff engineers were studying the problem to formulate an appropriate action plan, something had to be done to make it possible to deliver hard gaskets within the new specification limits. Management decided to increase product inspection and, in particular, to grade each piece of material according to thickness so that the wide

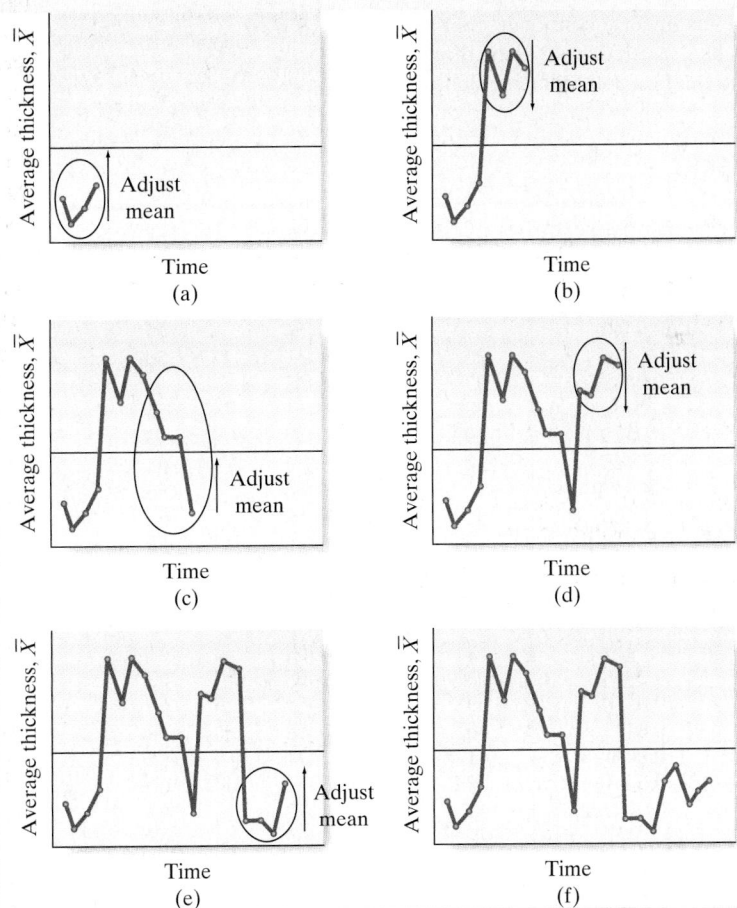

Figure C5.3
Process adjustment history over one shift

variation in thickness could be balanced out at the assembly process. Extra inspectors were used to grade each piece of soft gasket material. Sheets of the same thickness were shipped in separate bundles on pallets to a sister plant for assembly. Thick and thin sheets were selected as needed to make a hard gasket that met the specification. The process worked pretty well and there was some discussion about making it permanent. However, some felt it was too costly and did not get at the root cause of the problem.

The Engineering Department's Analysis

Meanwhile, the staff engineers in the company were continuing to study the problem and came to the conclusion that the existing roll mill process equipment for making the soft gasket sheets simply was not capable of meeting the new specifications. This conclusion was reached as a result of the examination of production data and scrap logs over the past several months. They had researched some new equipment that had a track record for very good sheet-to-sheet consistency and had decided to write a proposal to replace the existing roll mills with this new equipment.

To strengthen the proposal, their boss asked them to include data that demonstrated the poor capability of the existing equipment. The engineers, confident that the equipment was not capable, selected what they thought was the best operator and the best roll mill (the plant has several roll mill lines) and took careful measurements of the thickness of each sheet made on an eight-hour shift. During that shift, a total of 72 sheets/pulls were made. This was considered quite acceptable since the work standard for the process is 70 sheets per shift. The measurements of the sheet thickness (in the order of manufacture) for the 72 sheets are given in Table C5.1. The engineers set out to use these data to conduct a process capability study.

Relying on a statistical methods course that one of the engineers had in college 10 years ago, the group decided to construct a frequency distribution from the data and use it to estimate the percentage of the measurements that fell within the specification limits. Their histogram is shown in Figure C5.4. Also shown in the figure are the upper and lower specification values. The dark shaded part of the histogram represents the amount of the product that lies outside of the specification limits. It is immediately apparent from the histogram that a large proportion of the output does not meet the customer's needs. Eight of the 72 sheets fall outside the specification limits. Therefore, in terms of percent conforming to specifications, the engineers estimated the process capability to be 88.8%. This was clearly unacceptable. This analysis confirmed the engineer's low opinion of the roll mill process equipment. They included it in their proposal and sent their recommendation to replace the equipment to the president's office.

 GASKET

TABLE C5.1 Measurements of Sheet Thickness

Sheet	Thickness (in.)	Sheet	Thickness (in.)	Sheet	Thickness (in.)
1	0.0440	25	0.0464	49	0.0427
2	0.0446	26	0.0457	50	0.0437
3	0.0437	27	0.0447	51	0.0445
4	0.0438	28	0.0451	52	0.0431
5	0.0425	29	0.0447	53	0.0448
6	0.0443	30	0.0457	54	0.0429
7	0.0453	31	0.0456	55	0.0425
8	0.0428	32	0.0455	56	0.0442
9	0.0433	33	0.0445	57	0.0432
10	0.0451	34	0.0448	58	0.0429
11	0.0441	35	0.0423	59	0.0447
12	0.0434	36	0.0442	60	0.0450
13	0.0459	37	0.0459	61	0.0443
14	0.0466	38	0.0468	62	0.0441
15	0.0476	39	0.0452	63	0.0450
16	0.0449	40	0.0456	64	0.0443
17	0.0471	41	0.0471	65	0.0423
18	0.0451	42	0.0450	66	0.0447
19	0.0472	43	0.0472	67	0.0429
20	0.0477	44	0.0465	68	0.0427
21	0.0452	45	0.0461	69	0.0464
22	0.0457	46	0.0462	70	0.0448
23	0.0459	47	0.0463	71	0.0451
24	0.0472	48	0.0471	72	0.0428

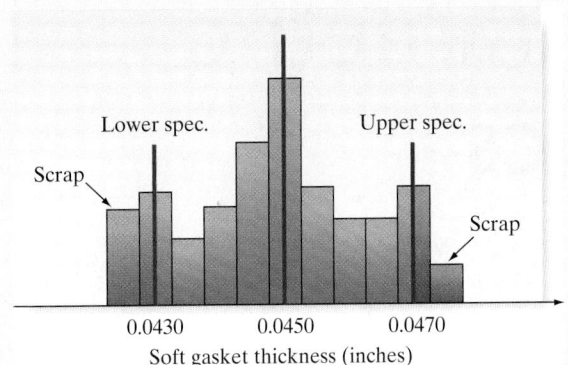

Figure C5.4
Histogram of data from process capability study

Your Assignment

You have been hired as an external consultant by the company's president, Marilyn Carlson. She would like you to critique the engineers' analysis, conclusion, and recommendations.

Suspecting that the engineers' work may be flawed, President Carlson would also like you to conduct your own study and make your own recommendations concerning how to resolve the company's problem. She would like you to use the data reported in Table C5.1 along with the data of Table C5.2, which she ordered be collected for you. These data were collected in the same manner as the data in Table C5.1. However, they were collected during a period of time when the roll mill operator was instructed *not* to adjust the sheet thickness. In your analysis, if you choose to construct control charts, use the same three-measurement subgrouping that the operators use.

Prepare an in-depth, written report for the president that responds to her requests. It should begin with an executive summary and include whatever tables and figures are needed to support your analysis and recommendations. [The data file for this case is named **GASKET.** The file contains three variables: sheet number, thickness, and a code for operator adjustments (A) or no adjustments (N).]

 GASKET

TABLE C5.2 Measurements of Sheet Thickness for a Shift Run with No Operator Adjustment

Sheet	Thickness (in.)	Sheet	Thickness (in.)	Sheet	Thickness (in.)
1	.0445	25	.0443	49	.0445
2	.0455	26	.0450	50	.0471
3	.0457	27	.0441	51	.0465
4	.0435	28	.0449	52	.0438
5	.0453	29	.0448	53	.0445
6	.0450	30	.0467	54	.0472
7	.0438	31	.0465	55	.0453
8	.0459	32	.0449	56	.0444
9	.0428	33	.0448	57	.0451
10	.0449	34	.0461	58	.0455
11	.0449	35	.0439	59	.0435
12	.0467	36	.0452	60	.0443
13	.0433	37	.0443	61	.0440
14	.0461	38	.0434	62	.0438
15	.0451	39	.0454	63	.0444
16	.0455	40	.0456	64	.0444
17	.0454	41	.0459	65	.0450
18	.0461	42	.0452	66	.0467
19	.0455	43	.0447	67	.0445
20	.0458	44	.0442	68	.0447
21	.0445	45	.0457	69	.0461
22	.0445	46	.0454	70	.0450
23	.0451	47	.0445	71	.0463
24	.0436	48	.0451	72	.0456

This case is based on the experiences of an actual company whose identity is disguised for confidentiality reasons. The case was originally written by DeVor, Chang, and Sutherland (*Statistical Quality Design and Control* [New York: Macmillan Publishing Co., 1992] pp. 298–329) and has been adapted to focus on the material presented in Chapter 14.

16

Nonparametric Statistics

Contents

Statistics in Action

Deadly Exposure: Agent Orange and Vietnam Vets

Using Technology

Where We've Been

- Presented methods for making inferences about means (Chapters 7–10) and for making inferences about the correlation between two quantitative variables (Chapter 12).

- These methods required that the data be normally distributed or that the sampling distributions of the relevant statistics be normally distributed.

Where We're Going

- Develop the need for inferential techniques that require fewer, or less stringent, assumptions than the methods of Chapters 7–10 and 12.

- Introduce *nonparametric* tests that are based on ranks (i.e., on an ordering of the sample measurements according to their relative magnitudes).

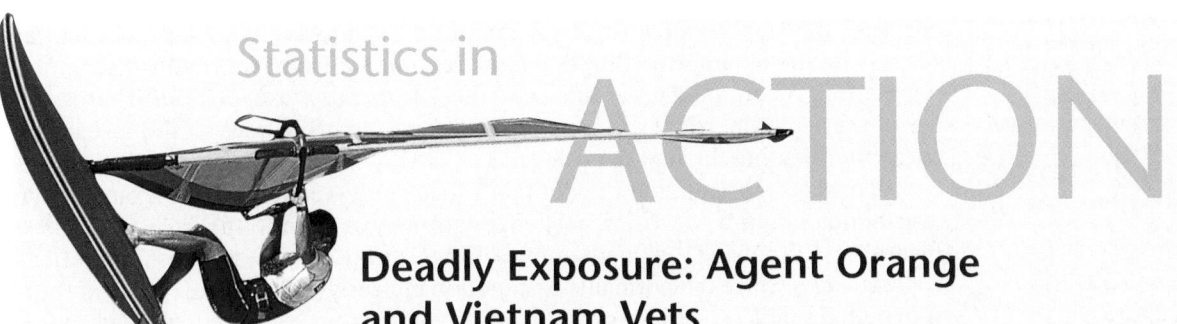

Statistics in ACTION

Deadly Exposure: Agent Orange and Vietnam Vets

Agent Orange was the code name for a herbicide developed for the U.S. Armed Forces, primarily for use in tropical climates. The purpose of the product was to deny an enemy cover and concealment in dense terrain by defoliating trees and shrubbery where the enemy could hide. (The code name comes from the orange band that was used to mark the drums the herbicide was stored in.) Agent Orange was tested in Southeast Asia in the early 1960s and brought into ever-widening use during the height of the Vietnam War (1967–1968); its use was diminished and eventually discontinued in 1971.

Agent Orange was a 50-50 mix of two chemicals, known conventionally as 2,4,D and 2,4,5,T. The combined product was mixed with kerosene or diesel fuel and dispersed by aircraft, vehicle, and hand spraying. As an unwanted byproduct of the chemical manufacturing process, Agent Orange was found to be extremely contaminated with TCDD, or dioxin. In laboratory tests on animals, TCDD has caused a wide variety of diseases (including cancer), many of them fatal.

During the Vietnam War, an estimated 19 million gallons of Agent Orange were used to destroy the dense plant and tree cover of the Asian jungle. As a result of this exposure, many Vietnam veterans have dangerously high levels of TCDD in their blood and adipose (fatty) tissue. A study published in *Chemosphere* (Vol. 20, 1990) reported on the TCDD levels of 20 Massachusetts Vietnam vets who were possibly exposed to Agent Orange. The TCDD amounts (measured in parts per trillion) in both plasma and fat tissue of the 20 vets are listed in Table SIA16.1. These data are saved in the **TCDD** file.

What do the data tell us about the levels of TCDD in fat and plasma of Vietnam veterans? Is there a relationship between the fat and plasma TCDD levels? In the Statistics in Action Revisited sections listed below, we apply the nonparametric tests of this chapter to answer these questions.

TCDD

TABLE SIA16.1   TCDD Measurements for 20 Vietnam Vets

Vet	Fat	Plasma
1	4.9	2.5
2	6.9	3.5
3	10.0	6.8
4	4.4	4.7
5	4.6	4.6
6	1.1	1.8
7	2.3	2.5
8	5.9	3.1
9	7.0	3.1
10	5.5	3.0
11	7.0	6.9
12	1.4	1.6
13	11.0	20.0
14	2.5	4.1
15	4.4	2.1
16	4.2	1.8
17	41.0	36.0
18	2.9	3.3
19	7.7	7.2
20	2.5	2.0

Source: Schecter, A. et al. "Partitioning of 2,3,7, 8-Chlorinated Dibenzo-*p*-Dioxins and Dibenzofurans between Adipose Tissue and Plasma Lipid of 20 Massachusetts Vietnam Veterans." *Chemosphere*, Vol. 20, Nos. 7–9, 1990, pp. 954–955 (Tables I and II).

Statistics in Action Revisited

- Testing the Median TCDD Level of Vietnam Vets (p. 1075)
- Comparing the TCDD Levels in Fat and Plasma of Vietnam Vets (p. 1092)
- Testing whether the TCDD Levels in Fat and Plasma of Vietnam Vets Are Correlated (p. 1115)

16.1 Introduction: Distribution-Free Tests

The confidence interval and testing procedures developed in Chapters 7–10 all involve making inferences about population parameters. Consequently, they are often referred to as **parametric statistical tests.** Many of these parametric methods (e.g., the small sample t-test of Chapter 8 or the ANOVA F-test of Chapter 10) rely on the assumption that the data are sampled from a normally distributed population. When the data are normal, these tests are *most powerful*. That is, the use of these parametric tests maximizes power—the probability of the researcher correctly rejecting the null hypothesis.

Consider a population of data that is decidedly nonnormal. For example, the distribution might be very flat, peaked, or strongly skewed to the right or left (see Figure 16.1). Applying the small sample t-test to such a data set may result in serious consequences. Since the normality assumption is clearly violated, the results of the t-test are unreliable: (1) The probability of a Type I error (i.e., rejecting H_0 when it is true) may be larger than the value of α selected; and (2) the power of the test, $1 - \beta$, is not maximized.

Figure 16.1

Some nonnormal distributions for which the t statistic is invalid

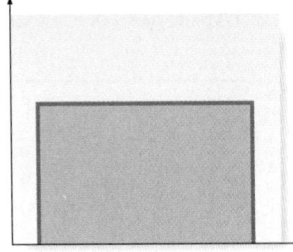
a. Flat distribution

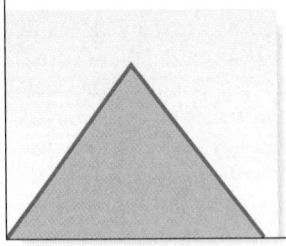
b. Peaked distribution

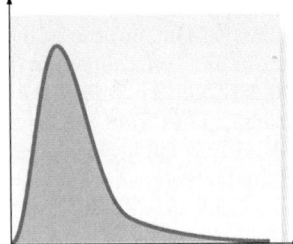
c. Skewed distribution

A host of *nonparametric* techniques are available for analyzing data that do not follow a normal distribution. Nonparametric tests do not depend on the distribution of the sampled population; thus, they are called *distribution-free tests*. Also, nonparametric methods focus on the location of the probability distribution of the population, rather than on specific parameters of the population, such as the mean (hence, the name "nonparametrics").

> **DEFINITION 16.1**
>
> **Distribution-free tests** are statistical tests that do not rely on any underlying assumptions about the probability distribution of the sampled population.

> **DEFINITION 16.2**
>
> The branch of inferential statistics devoted to distribution-free tests is called **nonparametrics.**

Nonparametric tests are also appropriate when the data are nonnumerical in nature but can be ranked.* For example, when taste-testing foods or in other types of consumer product evaluations, we can say we like product A better than product B,

---

*Qualitative data that can be ranked in order of magnitude are called *ordinal* data.

and B better than C, but we cannot obtain exact quantitative values for the respective measurements. Nonparametric tests based on the ranks of measurements are called *rank tests*.

DEFINITION 16.3

Nonparametric statistics (or tests) based on the ranks of measurements are called **rank statistics** (or **rank tests**).

In this chapter, we present several useful nonparametric methods. Keep in mind that these nonparametric tests are more powerful than their corresponding parametric counterparts in those situations where either the data are nonnormal or the data are ranked.

In Section 16.2, we develop a test to make inferences about the central tendency of a single population. In Sections 16.3 and 16.5, we present rank statistics for comparing two or more probability distributions using independent samples. In Sections 16.4 and 16.6, the matched-pairs and randomized block designs are used to make nonparametric comparisons of populations. Finally, in Section 16.7, we present a nonparametric measure of correlation between two variables.

16.2 Single Population Inferences: The Sign Test

Teaching Tip

Present the sign test as an alternative method for testing the location of a distribution of data. Recall the parametric test for μ from earlier in the text. The sign test is ideal when the small-sample assumption of a normal population is not met.

In Chapter 8 we utilized the z- and t-statistics for testing hypotheses about a population mean. The z-statistic is appropriate for large random samples selected from "general" populations—that is, with few limitations on the probability distribution of the underlying population. The t-statistic was developed for small-sample tests in which the sample is selected at random from a *normal* distribution. The question is, How can we conduct a test of hypothesis when we have a small sample from a *nonnormal* distribution?

The **sign test** is a relatively simple nonparametric procedure for testing hypotheses about the central tendency of a nonnormal probability distribution. Note that we used the phrase *central tendency* rather than *population mean*. This is because the sign test, like many nonparametric procedures, provides inferences about the population *median* rather than the population mean μ. Denoting the population median by the Greek letter, η, we know (Chapter 2) that η is the 50th percentile of the distribution (Figure 16.2) and as such is less affected by the skewness of the distribution and the presence of outliers (extreme observations). Since the nonparametric test must be suitable for all distributions, not just the normal, it is reasonable for nonparametric tests to focus on the more robust (less sensitive to extreme values) measure of central tendency, the median.

For example, increasing numbers of both private and public agencies are requiring their employees to submit to tests for substance abuse. One laboratory that conducts such testing has developed a system with a normalized measurement scale, in which values less than 1.00 indicate "normal" ranges and values equal to or

Figure 16.2
Location of the population median, η

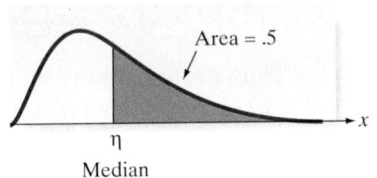

SUBABUSE

TABLE 16.1 Substance Abuse Test Results

.78	.51	3.79	.23	.77	.98	.96	.89

Teaching Tip

The interpretation of the p-value is the same for nonparametric tests as it is for parametric tests. It is a relatively easy value to use when making a conclusion for a test of hypothesis.

greater than 1.00 are indicative of potential substance abuse. The lab reports a normal result as long as the median level for an individual is less than 1.00. Eight independent measurements of each individual's sample are made. One individual's results are shown in Table 16.1.

If the objective is to determine whether the *population* median (that is, the true median level if an indefinitely large number of measurements were made on the same individual sample) is less than 1.00, we establish that as our alternative hypothesis and test

$$H_0: \eta = 1.00$$
$$H_a: \eta < 1.00$$

Teaching Tip

Point out that the median is useful to test because the population contains 50% of the observations both above and below its value.

The one-tailed sign test is conducted by counting the number of sample measurements that "favor" the alternative hypothesis—in this case, the number that are less than 1.00. If the null hypothesis is true, we expect approximately half of the measurements to fall on each side of the hypothesized median and if the alternative is true, we expect significantly more than half to favor the alternative—that is, to be less than 1.00. Thus,

Test statistic: S = Number of measurements less than 1.00,
the null hypothesized median

If we wish to conduct the test at the $\alpha = .05$ level of significance, the rejection region can be expressed in terms of the observed significance level, or *p*-value of the test:

Rejection region: p-value $\leq .05$

In this example, $S = 7$ of the 8 measurements are less than 1.00. To determine the observed significance level associated with this outcome, we note that the number of measurements less than 1.00 is a binomial random variable (check the binomial characteristics presented in Chapter 4), and *if H_0 is true*, the binomial probability *p* that a measurement lies below (or above) the median 1.00 is equal to .5 (Figure 16.2). What is the probability that a result is *as contrary to or more contrary to H_0* than the one observed if H_0 is true? That is, what is the probability that 7 *or more* of 8 binomial measurements will result in Success (be less than 1.00) if the probability of Success is .5? Binomial Table II in Appendix B (using $n = 8$ and $p = .5$) indicates that

$$P(x \geq 7) = 1 - P(x \leq 6) = 1 - .965 = .035$$

Thus, the probability that at least 7 of 8 measurements would be less than 1.00 *if the true median were* 1.00 is only .035. The *p*-value of the test is therefore .035.

This *p*-value can also be obtained using a statistical software package. The MINITAB printout of the analysis is shown in Figure 16.3, with the *p*-value

Sign Test for Median: READING

```
Sign test of median =   1.000 versus  < 1.000

            N  Below  Equal  Above       P  Median
READING     8      7      0      1  0.0352  0.8350
```

highlighted on the printout. Since $p = .035$ is less than $\alpha = .05$, we conclude that this sample provides sufficient evidence to reject the null hypothesis. The implication of this rejection is that the laboratory can conclude at the $\alpha = .05$ level of significance that the true median level for the tested individual is less than 1.00. However, we note that one of the measurements greatly exceeds the others, with a value of 3.79, and deserves special attention. Note that this large measurement is an outlier that would make the use of a t-test and its concomitant assumption of normality dubious. The only assumption necessary to ensure the validity of the sign test is that the probability distribution of measurements is continuous.

The use of the sign test for testing hypotheses about population medians is summarized in the box.

Sign Test for a Population Median η

One-Tailed Test	Two-Tailed Test
$H_0: \eta = \eta_0$	$H_0: \eta = \eta_0$
$H_a: \eta > \eta_0$ [or $H_a: \eta < \eta_0$]	$H_a: \eta \neq \eta_0$

Test statistic:

S = Number of sample measurements greater than η_0 [or S = number of measurements less then η_0]	S = Larger of S_1 and S_2, where S_1 is the number of measurements less than η_0 and S_2 is the number of measurements greater than η_0

Observed significance level:

p-value = $P(x \geq S)$	p-value = $2P(x \geq S)$

where x has a binomial distribution with parameters n and $p = .5$. (Use Table II, Appendix B.)

Rejection region: Reject H_0 if p-value $\leq .05$.

Conditions Required for Valid Application of the Sign Test

The sample is selected randomly from a continuous probability distribution. [*Note:* No assumptions need to be made about the shape of the probability distribution.]

Recall that the normal probability distribution provides a good approximation for the binomial distribution when the sample size is large. For tests about the median of a distribution, the null hypothesis implies that $p = .5$, and the normal distribution provides a good approximation if $n \geq 10$. (Samples with $n \geq 10$ satisfy the condition that $np \pm 3\sqrt{npq}$ is contained in the interval 0 to n.) Thus, we can use the standard normal z-distribution to conduct the sign test for large samples. The large-sample sign test is summarized in the next box.

Large-Sample Sign Test for a Population Median η

One-Tailed Test	Two-Tailed Test
$H_0: \eta = \eta_0$	$H_0: \eta = \eta_0$
$H_a: \eta > \eta_0$	$H_a: \eta \neq \eta_0$
[or $H_a: \eta < \eta_0$]	

$$\text{Test statistic}: z = \frac{(S - .5) - .5n}{.5\sqrt{n}}$$

[*Note: S* is calculated as shown in the previous box. We subtract .5 from *S* as the "correction for continuity." The null hypothesized mean value is $np = .5n$, and the standard deviation is

$$\sqrt{npq} = \sqrt{n(.5)(.5)} = .5\sqrt{n}$$

See Chapter 5 for details on the normal approximation to the binomial distribution.]

Rejection region: $z > z_\alpha$ \qquad\qquad Rejection region: $z > z_{\alpha/2}$

where tabulated z values can be found in Table IV of Appendix B.

EXAMPLE 16.1

APPLICATION OF THE SIGN TEST

Problem   A manufacturer of compact disk (CD) players has established that the median time to failure for its players is 5,250 hours of utilization. A sample of 20 CDs from a competitor is obtained, and they are continuously tested until each fails. The 20 failure times range from five hours (a "defective" player) to 6,575 hours, and 14 of the 20 exceed 5,250 hours. Is there evidence that the median failure time of the competitor differs from 5,250 hours? Use $\alpha = .10$.

z = 1.565, Fail to reject H_0

Solution   The null and alternative hypotheses of interest are

Suggested Exercise 16.7

$$H_0: \eta = 5{,}250 \text{ hours}$$
$$H_a: \eta \neq 5{,}250 \text{ hours}$$

Test statistic: Since $n \geq 10$, we use the standard normal z statistic:

$$z = \frac{(S - .5) - .5n}{.5\sqrt{n}}$$

where S is the maximum of S_1, the number of measurements greater than 5,250, and S_2, the number of measurements less than 5,250.

Rejection region: $z > 1.645$ \quad where \quad $z_{\alpha/2} = z_{.05} = 1.645$

Assumptions: The distribution of the failure times is continuous (time is a continuous variable), but nothing is assumed about the shape of its probability distribution.

Since the number of measurements exceeding 5,250 is $S_2 = 14$ and thus the number of measurements less than 5,250 is $S_1 = 6$, then $S = 14$, the greater of S_1 and S_2. The calculated z statistic is therefore

$$z = \frac{(S - .5) - .5n}{.5\sqrt{n}} = \frac{13.5 - 10}{.5\sqrt{20}} = \frac{3.5}{2.236} = 1.565$$

The value of z is not in the rejection region, so we cannot reject the null hypothesis at the $\alpha = .10$ level of significance.

Look Back The CD manufacturer should not conclude, on the basis of this sample, that its competitor's CDs have a median failure time that differs from 5,250 hours. The manufacturer will not "Accept H_0", however, since the probability of a Type II error is unknown.

[Now Work] *Exercise 16.5*

■ ■ ■

The one-sample nonparametric sign test for a median provides an alternative to the t-test for small samples from nonnormal distributions. However, if the distribution is approximately normal, the t-test provides a more powerful test about the central tendency of the distribution.

Statistics in Action Revisited

Testing the Median TCDD Level of Vietnam Vets

Recall that during the Vietnam War, U.S. soldiers were exposed to the herbicide, Agent Orange (p. 1069). As a result of this exposure, many Vietnam veterans have dangerously high levels of the dioxin TCDD in their plasma and fat tissue. Some medical researchers consider a TCDD level of 3 parts per trillion (ppt) to be dangerously high. Do the data in Table SIA16.1 provide evidence to indicate that the median level of TCDD in both plasma and fat tissue of Vietnam vets exceeds 3 ppt? To answer this question, we applied the sign test to the data saved in the TCDD file. The MINITAB printout is shown in Figure SIA16.1.

We want to test $H_0: \eta = 3$ versus $H_a: \eta > 3$ for both variables, TCDD in fat and TCDD in plasma. According to the printout, 14 of the 20 Vietnam vets had TCDD levels in fat above 3 ppt, and 12 of the 20 Vietnam vets had TCDD

levels in plasma above 3 ppt. Consequently, the two test statistic values are $S = 14$ and $S = 12$, respectively. The two-tailed p-values for the tests (highlighted on the printout) are .0577 and .1796, respectively. Thus, the corresponding one-tailed p-values are $.0577/2 = .0288$ and $.1796/2 = .0898$.

Both tests are significant at $\alpha = .10$; at $\alpha = .05$, the test for TCDD in plasma is not significant. Therefore, the data provide sufficient evidence to say that the median TCDD in fat exceeds 3 ppt; however, the evidence is not as strong for TCDD in plasma.

Why apply the nonparametric sign test to the data rather than the more familiar Student's t-test? The MINITAB histograms in Figure SIA16.2 illustrate the problem. Clearly the sample TCDD levels are not normally distributed. Consequently, the assumption required for the t-test to yield valid inferences is violated.

Figure SIA16.1

MINITAB sign tests for TCDD data

Sign Test for Median: FAT, PLASMA

```
Sign test of median =   3.000 versus > 3.000
```

	N	Below	Equal	Above	P	Median
FAT	20	6	0	14	0.0577	4.750
PLASMA	20	7	1	12	0.1796	3.200

Figure SIA16.2
MINITAB histograms for
TCDD data

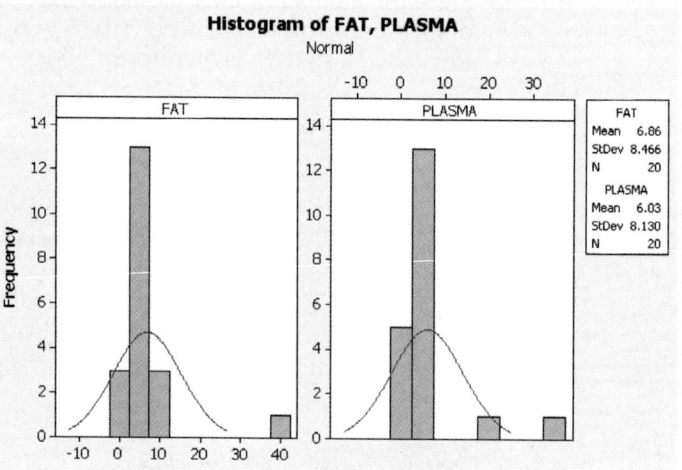

Exercises 16.1–16.11

Learning the Mechanics

16.1 Under what circumstances is the sign test preferred to the *t*-test for making inferences about the central tendency of a population?

16.2 What is the probability that a randomly selected observation exceeds the
  a. Mean of a normal distribution?   .5
  b. Median of a normal distribution?   .5
  c. Mean of a nonnormal distribution?   Unknown
  d. Median of a nonnormal distribution?   .5

16.3 Use Table II of Appendix B to calculate the following binomial probabilities:
  a. $P(x \geq 7)$ when $n = 8$ and $p = .5$ .035
  b. $P(x \geq 5)$ when $n = 8$ and $p = .5$ .363
  c. $P(x \geq 8)$ when $n = 8$ and $p = .5$ .004
  d. $P(x \geq 10)$ when $n = 15$ and $p = .5$. Also use the normal approximation to calculate this probability, then compare the approximation with the exact value.
  e. $P(x \geq 15)$ when $n = 25$ and $p = .5$. Also use the normal approximation to calculate this probability, then compare the approximation with the exact value.

16.4 Consider the following sample of 10 measurements:

LM16_4

| 8.4 | 16.9 | 15.8 | 12.5 | 10.3 | 4.9 | 12.9 | 9.8 | 23.7 | 7.3 |

Use these data to conduct each of the following sign tests using the binomial tables (Table II, Appendix B) and $\alpha = .05$:

  a. $H_0: \eta = 9$ versus $H_a: \eta > 9$
  b. $H_0: \eta = 9$ versus $H_a: \eta \neq 9$
  c. $H_0: \eta = 20$ versus $H_a: \eta < 20$
  d. $H_0: \eta = 20$ versus $H_a: \eta \neq 20$
  e. Repeat each of the preceding tests using the normal approximation to the binomial probabilities. Compare the results.
  f. What assumptions are necessary to ensure the validity of each of the preceding tests?

16.5 Suppose you wish to conduct a test of the research hypothesis that the median of a population is greater than 75. You randomly sample 25 measurements from the population and determine that 17 of them exceed 75. Set up and conduct the appropriate test of hypothesis at the .10 level of significance. Be sure to specify all necessary assumptions. $p = .055$

Applying the Concepts—Basic

16.6 In *The American Statistician* (May 2001), the nonparametric sign test was used to analyze data on the quality of white shrimp. One measure of shrimp quality is cohesiveness. Since freshly caught shrimp are usually stored on ice, there is concern that cohesiveness will deteriorate after storage. For a sample of 20 newly caught white shrimp, cohesiveness was measured both before storage and after storage on ice for two weeks. The difference in the cohesiveness measurements (before minus after) was obtained for each shrimp. If storage has no effect on cohesiveness, the population median of the differences will be 0. If cohesiveness deteriorates after storage, the population median of the differences will be positive.

a. Set up the null and alternative hypotheses to test whether cohesiveness will deteriorate after storage.
$H_0: \eta = 0$ vs. $H_a: \eta > 0$

b. In the sample of 20 shrimp, there were 13 positive differences. Use this value to find the *p*-value of the test.   .131

c. Make the appropriate conclusion (in the words of the problem) if $\alpha = .05$.

16.7 One way to assess the benefits of an MBA degree is to investigate the salaries received by MBA students several years after graduation. The Graduate Management Admission Council estimates that the median earnings for graduates of full-time, highly-ranked MBA programs four years after graduating is $96,000 (*Selections*, Winter 1999). A random sample of 50 recent graduates from a particular highly ranked MBA program were mailed a questionnaire and asked to report their annual earnings. Fifteen useable responses were received; 9 indicated earnings greater than $96,000 and 6 indicated earnings below $96,000.

a. Specify the null and alternative hypotheses that should be used in testing whether the median income of graduates of the MBA program is more than $96,000 in 2000. $H_0: \eta = 96,000$, vs. $H_a: \eta > 96,000$

b. Conduct the test of part **a** using $\alpha = .05$ and draw your conclusion in the context of the problem.

c. What assumptions must hold to ensure the validity of your hypothesis test?

Applying the Concepts—Intermediate

16.8 The biting rate of a particular species of fly was investigated in a study reported in the *Journal of the American Mosquito Control Association* (Mar. 1995). Biting rate was defined as the number of flies biting a volunteer during 15 minutes of exposure. This species of fly is known to have a median biting rate of 5 bites per 15 minutes on Stanbury Island, Utah. However, it is theorized that the median biting rate is higher in bright, sunny weather. (This information is of interest to marketers of pesticides.) To test this theory, 122 volunteers were exposed to the flies during a sunny day on Stanbury Island. Of these volunteers, 95 experienced biting rates greater than 5.

a. Set up the null and alternative hypotheses for the test.

b. Calculate the approximate *p*-value of the test. [*Hint:* Use the normal approximation for a binomial probability.] $p \approx 0$

c. Make the appropriate conclusion at $\alpha = .01$.

16.9 Reducing the size of a company's workforce in order to reduce costs is referred to as *corporate downsizing* or *reductions in force* (RIF) by the business community and media (*Business Week*, Feb. 24, 1997). Following RIFs, companies are often sued by former employees who allege that the RIFs were discriminatory with regard to age. Federal law protects employees over 40 years of age against such discrimination. Suppose

one large company's employees have a median age of 37. Its RIF plan is to fire 15 employees with ages listed in the table below.

FIRE15

43	32	39	28	54	41	50	62
22	45	47	54	43	33	59	

a. Calculate the median age of the employees who are being terminated. $m = 43$

b. What are the appropriate null and alternative hypotheses to test whether the population from which the terminated employees were selected has a median age that exceeds the entire company's median age?

c. Conduct the test of part **b.** Find the significance level of the test and interpret its value.

d. Assuming that courts generally require statistical evidence at the .10 level of significance before ruling that age discrimination laws were violated, what do you advise the company about its planned RIF? Explain.

16.10 The Federal Aviation Administration (FAA) increased the frequency and thoroughness of its review of aircraft maintenance procedures in response to the admission by ValuJet Airlines that it had not met some maintenance requirements. Suppose that the FAA samples the records of six aircraft currently utilized by one airline and determines the number of flights between the last two complete engine maintenances for each, with the results shown in the table. The FAA requires that this maintenance be performed at least every 30 flights. Although it is obvious that not all aircraft are meeting the requirement, the FAA wishes to test whether the airline is meeting this particular maintenance requirement "on average."

FAA6

24	27	25
94	29	28

a. Would you suggest the *t*-test or sign test to conduct the test? Why?   Sign test

b. Set up the null and alternative hypotheses such that the burden of proof is on the airline to show it is meeting the "on-average" requirement.

c. What are the test statistic and rejection region for this test if the level of significance is $\alpha = .01$? Why would the level of significance be set at such a low value?

d. Conduct the test, and state the conclusion in terms of this application.

16.11 In Exercise 7.29 (p. 373), the average 5-year revenue growth for the 500 fastest growing technology companies in 2002 (i.e., *Forbes' Technology Fast 500*) was investigated. The data are reproduced in the next table.

⊘ **FAST500**

Rank	Company	5-Year Revenue Growth Rate (%)
4	Open ware Systems	159,236
22	Pixelworks	22,602
89	Portal Software	5,218
160	The Cobalt Group	2,864
193	Liveworld	2,238
268	HPower Corp.	1,381
274	Dataprise	1,340
322	Sonicwall	1,099
359	McData	943
396	Objectif Lune	822
441	Matrikon	711
485	USNanocorp	627

Source: *Technology Fast 500*, Deloitte & Touche, 2002.

a. Recall that in Exercise 7.29a, the *t*-distribution was employed to make an inference about the true mean 5-year revenue growth rate for the *Technology Fast 500*. Explain why the resulting inference may be invalid.

b. Give the null and alternative hypotheses for a nonparametric test designed to determine if the "average" 5-year revenue growth rate is less than 5,000 percent. $H_0: \eta = 5,000$ vs. $H_a: \eta < 5,000$

c. Conduct the test of part **b** using $\alpha = .05$. Interpret your result in the context of the problem.

16.3 Comparing Two Populations: The Wilcoxon Rank Sum Test for Independent Samples

Suppose two independent random samples are to be used to compare two populations and the *t*-test of Chapter 9 is inappropriate for making the comparison. We may be unwilling to make assumptions about the form of the underlying population probability distributions or we may be unable to obtain exact values of the sample measurements. If the data can be ranked in order of magnitude for either of these situations, the **Wilcoxon rank sum test** (developed by Frank Wilcoxon) can be used to test the hypothesis that the probability distributions associated with the two populations are equivalent.

Biography

FRANK WILCOXON (1892–1965)
Wilcoxon Rank Tests

Frank Wilcoxon was born in Ireland, where his wealthy American parents were vacationing. He grew up in the family home in Catskill, New York, then spent time working as an oil worker and tree surgeon in the back country of West Virginia. At age 25, Wilcoxon's parents sent him to Pennsylvania Military College, but he dropped out due to the death of his twin sister. Later, Wilcoxon earned degrees in chemistry from Rutgers (Master's) and Cornell University

(Ph.D.). After receiving his doctorate, Wilcoxon began work as a chemical researcher at the Boyce Thompson Institute for Plant Research. There, he began studying R. A. Fisher's (p. 00) newly issued *Statistical Methods for Research Workers*. In a now famous 1945 paper, Wilcoxon presented the idea of replacing the actual sample data in Fisher's tests by their ranks and called the tests the rank-sum test and signed-rank test. These tests proved to be inspirational to the further development of nonparametrics. After retiring from industry, Wilcoxon accepted a Distinguished Lectureship position at newly created Department of Statistics at Florida State University.

For example, suppose six economists who work for the federal government and seven university economists are randomly selected, and each is asked to predict next year's percentage change in cost of living as compared with this year's figure.

COSTLIVING

TABLE 16.2   Percentage Cost of Living Change, as Predicted by Government and University Economists

Government Economist (1)		University Economist (2)	
Prediction	Rank	Prediction	Rank
3.1	4	4.4	6
4.8	7	5.8	9
2.3	2	3.9	5
5.6	8	8.7	11
0.0	1	6.3	10
2.9	3	10.5	12
		10.8	13

Teaching Tip

Present the rank sum test as an alternative to the independent comparison of means procedure presented earlier in the text.

The objective of the study is to compare the government economists' predictions to those of the university economists. The data are shown in Table 16.2.

Experience has shown that the populations of predicted percentage changes often possess probability distributions that are skewed, as shown in Figure 16.4. Consequently, a *t*-test should not be used to compare the mean predictions of the two groups of economists because the normality assumption that is required for the *t*-test may not be valid.

The two populations of predictions are those that would be obtained from *all* government and *all* university economists if they could all be questioned. To compare their probability distributions using a nonparametric test, we first *rank the sample observations as though they were all drawn from the same population.* That is, we pool the measurements from both samples and then rank the measurements from the smallest (a rank of 1) to the largest (a rank of 13). The ranks of the 13 economists' predictions are indicated in Table 16.2.

If the two populations were identical, we would expect the ranks to be *randomly mixed* between the two samples. If, on the other hand, one population tends to have larger percentage changes than the other, we would expect the larger ranks to be mostly in one sample and the smaller ranks mostly in the other. Thus, the test statistic for the Wilcoxon test is based on the totals of the ranks for each of the two samples—that is, on the **rank sums.** The greater the difference in rank sums, the greater the evidence to indicate a difference between the populations.

Teaching Tip

Point out that the smaller size sample is the one that is used to sum the ranks when finding the test statistic.

Figure 16.4

Typical probability distribution of predicted cost of living changes

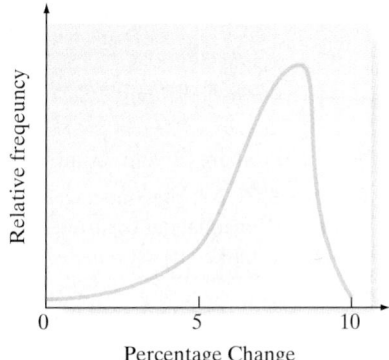

For the economists' predictions, we arbitrarily denote the rank sum for government economists by T_1 and that for university economists by T_2. Then

$$T_1 = 4 + 7 + 2 + 8 + 1 + 3 = 25$$
$$T_2 = 6 + 9 + 5 + 11 + 10 + 12 + 13 = 66$$

The sum of T_1 and T_2 will always equal $n(n + 1)/2$, where $n = n_1 + n_2$. So, for this example, $n_1 = 6, n_2 = 7$, and

$$T_1 + T_2 = \frac{13(13 + 1)}{2} = 91$$

Since $T_1 + T_2$ is fixed, a small value for T_1 implies a large value for T_2 (and vice versa) and a large difference between T_1 and T_2. Therefore, the smaller the value of one of the rank sums, the greater the evidence to indicate that the samples were selected from different populations.

The test statistic for this test is the rank sum for the smaller sample; or, in the case where $n_1 = n_2$, either rank sum can be used. Values that locate the rejection region for this rank sum are given in Table XV of Appendix B. A partial reproduction of this table is shown in Table 16.3. The columns of the table represent n_1, the first sample size, and the rows represent n_2, the second sample size. *The T_L and T_U entries in the table are the boundaries of the lower and upper regions, respectively, for the rank sum associated with the sample that has fewer measurements.* If the sample sizes n_1 and n_2 are the same, either rank sum may be used as the test statistic. To illustrate, suppose $n_1 = 6$ and $n_2 = 7$. For a two-tailed test with $\alpha = .05$, we consult part **a** of the table and find that the null hypothesis will be rejected if the rank sum of sample 1 (the sample with fewer measurements), T, is less than or equal to $T_L = 28$ or greater than or equal to $T_U = 56$. (These values are highlighted in Table 16.3.) The Wilcoxon rank sum test is summarized in the next box.

Teaching Tip

Use several examples to help the student become comfortable with using the Wilcoxon Rank Sum table

---

Wilcoxon Rank Sum Test: Independent Samples*

Let D_1 and D_2 represent the probability distributions for populations 1 and 2, respectively.

One-Tailed Test	Two-Tailed Test
H_0: D_1 and D_2 are identical	H_0: D_1 and D_2 are identical
H_a: D_1 is shifted to the right of D_2 [or H_a: D_1 is shifted to the left of D_2]	H_a: D_1 is shifted either to the left or to the right of D_2
Test statistic:	*Test statistic:*
T_1, if $n_1 < n_2$; T_2, if $n_2 < n_1$ (Either rank sum can be used if $n_1 = n_2$.)	T_1, if $n_1 < n_2$; T_2, if $n_2 < n_1$ (Either rank sum can be used if $n_1 = n_2$.) We will denote this rank sum as T.
Rejection region:	*Rejection region:*
T_1: $T_1 \geq T_U$ [or $T_1 \leq T_L$] T_2: $T_2 \leq T_L$ [or $T_2 \geq T_U$]	$T \leq T_L$ or $T \geq T_U$

where T_L and T_U are obtained from Table XV of Appendix B.

Ties: Assign tied measurements the average of the ranks they would receive if they were unequal but occurred in successive order. For example, if the third-ranked and fourth-ranked measurements are tied, assign each a rank of $(3 + 4)/2 = 3.5$.

---

*Another statistic used for comparing two populations based on independent random samples is the *Mann-Whitney U-statistic*. The U-statistic is a simple function of the rank sums. It can be shown that the Wilcoxon rank sum test and the Mann-Whitney U-test are equivalent.

TABLE 16.3 Reproduction of Part of Table XV in Appendix B: Critical Values for the Wilcoxon Rank Sum Test

$\alpha = .025$ one-tailed; $\alpha = .05$ two-tailed

n_1 / n_2	3 T_L	3 T_U	4 T_L	4 T_U	5 T_L	5 T_U	6 T_L	6 T_U	7 T_L	7 T_U	8 T_L	8 T_U	9 T_L	9 T_U	10 T_L	10 T_U
3	5	16	6	18	6	21	7	23	7	26	8	28	8	31	9	33
4	6	18	11	25	12	28	12	32	13	35	14	38	15	41	16	44
5	6	21	12	28	18	37	19	41	20	45	21	49	22	53	24	56
6	7	23	12	32	19	41	26	52	28	56	29	61	31	65	32	70
7	7	26	13	35	20	45	28	56	37	68	39	73	41	78	43	83
8	8	28	14	38	21	49	29	61	39	73	49	87	51	93	54	98
9	8	31	15	41	22	53	31	65	41	78	51	93	63	108	66	114
10	9	33	16	44	24	56	32	70	43	83	54	98	66	114	79	131

Teaching Tip

Stress how ties are handled in the rank sum test.

Conditions Required for a Valid Wilcoxon Rank Sum Test

1. The two samples are random and independent.
2. The two probability distributions from which the samples are drawn are continuous.

Note that the assumptions necessary for the validity of the Wilcoxon rank sum test do not specify the shape or type of probability distribution. However, the distributions are assumed to be continuous so that the probability of tied measurements is 0 (see Chapter 5), and each measurement can be assigned a unique rank. In practice, however, rounding of continuous measurements will sometimes produce ties. As long as the number of ties is small relative to the sample sizes, the Wilcoxon test procedure will still have an approximate significance level of α. The test is not recommended to compare discrete distributions for which many ties are expected.

EXAMPLE 16.2   APPLYING THE RANK SUM TEST

Problem   Test the hypothesis that the government economists' predictions of next year's percentage change in cost of living tend to be lower than the university economists'. That is, test to determine if the probability distribution of government economists' predictions is *shifted to the left* of the probability distribution of university economists' predictions. Conduct the test using the data in Table 16.2 and $\alpha = .05$.

$T_1 = 25$, $p = .007$, reject H_0

Solution H_0: The probability distributions corresponding to the government and university economists' predictions of inflation rate are identical

H_a: The probability distribution for the government economists' predictions lies below (to the left of) the probability distribution for the university economists' predictions*

*The alternative hypotheses in this chapter will be stated in terms of a difference in the *location* of the distributions. However, since the shapes of the distributions may also differ under H_a, some of the figures (e.g., Figure 16.5) depicting the alternative hypothesis will show probability distributions with different shapes.

Figure 16.5

Alternative hypothesis
and rejection region
for Example 16.2.

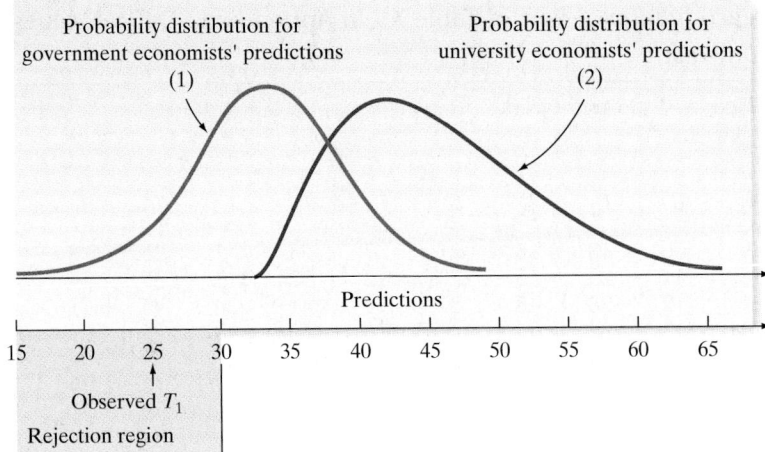

Test statistic: Since fewer government economists ($n_1 = 6$) than university economists ($n_2 = 7$) were sampled, the test statistic is T_1, the rank sum of the government economists' predictions.

Rejection region: Since the test is one-sided, we consult part **b** of Table XV for the rejection region corresponding to $\alpha = .05$. We reject H_0 only for $T_1 \leq T_L$, the lower value from Table XV, since we are specifically testing that the distribution of government economists' predictions lies *below* the distribution of university economists' predictions, as shown in Figure 16.5. Thus, we reject H_0 if $T_1 \leq 30$.

Suggested Exercise 16.17

Since T_1, the rank sum of the government economists' predictions in Table 16.2, is 25, it is in the rejection region (see Figure 16.5). Therefore, we can conclude that the university economists' predictions tend, in general, to exceed the government economists' predictions. This same conclusion can be reached using a statistical software package. The SPSS printout of the analysis is shown in Figure 16.6. Both the test statistic ($T_1 = 25$) and two-tailed p-value ($p = .014$) are highlighted on the printout. The one-tailed p-value, $p = .014/2 = .007$, is less than $\alpha = .05$, leading us to reject H_0.

Now Work   *Exercise 16.13*

■ ■ ■

Table XV in Appendix B gives values of T_L and T_U for values of n_1 and n_2 less than or equal to 10. When both sample sizes n_1 and n_2 are 10 or larger, the sampling distribution of T_1 can be approximated by a normal distribution with mean and variance

$$E(T_1) = \frac{n_1(n_1 + n_2 + 1)}{2} \quad \text{and} \quad \sigma^2_{T_1} = \frac{n_1 n_2(n_1 + n_2 + 1)}{12}$$

Therefore, for $n_1 \geq 10$ and $n_2 \geq 10$ we can conduct the Wilcoxon rank sum test using the familiar z-test of Chapters 8 and 9. The test is summarized in the next box.

Mann-Whitney Test

Ranks

	ECONOMST	N	Mean Rank	Sum of Ranks
PCTCHNG	1	6	4.17	25.00
	2	7	9.43	66.00
	Total	13		

Test Statistics[b]

	PCTCHNG
Mann-Whitney U	4.000
Wilcoxon W	25.000
Z	-2.429
Asymp. Sig. (2-tailed)	.015
Exact Sig. [2*(1-tailed Sig.)]	.014[a]

a. Not corrected for ties.

b. Grouping Variable: ECONOMST

Figure 16.6
SPSS printout of rank sum test

The Wilcoxon Rank Sum Test for Large Samples ($n_1 \geq 10$ and $n_2 \geq 10$)

Let D_1 and D_2 represent the probability distributions for populations 1 and 2, respectively.

One-Tailed Test	Two-Tailed Test
H_0: D_1 and D_2 are identical	H_0: D_1 and D_2 are identical
H_a: D_1 is shifted to the right of D_2 (or H_a: D_1 is shifted to the left of D_2)	H_a: D_1 is shifted either to the right or to the left of D_2

$$\text{Test statistic: } z = \frac{T_1 - \dfrac{n_1(n_1 + n_2 + 1)}{2}}{\sqrt{\dfrac{n_1 n_2(n_1 + n_2 + 1)}{12}}}$$

Rejection region:	Rejection region:
$z > z_\alpha$ (or $z < -z_\alpha$)	$|z| > z_{\alpha/2}$

Exercises 16.12–16.23

Learning the Mechanics

16.12 Specify the test statistic and the rejection region for the Wilcoxon rank sum test for independent samples in each of the following situations:

a. $n_1 = 10, n_2 = 6, \alpha = .10$

H_0: Two probability distributions, 1 and 2, are identical

H_a: Probability distribution for population 1 is shifted to the right or left of the probability distribution for population 2

b. $n_1 = 5, n_2 = 7, \alpha = .05$

H_0: Two probability distributions, 1 and 2, are identical

H_a: Probability distribution for population 1 is shifted to the right of the probability distribution for population 2

c. $n_1 = 9, n_2 = 8, \alpha = .025$

H_0: Two probability distributions, 1 and 2, are identical

H_a: Probability distribution for population 1 is shifted to the left of the probability distribution for population 2

d. $n_1 = 15, n_2 = 15, \alpha = .05$

H_0: Two probability distributions, 1 and 2, are identical

H_a: Probability distribution for population 1 is shifted to the right or left of the probability distribution for population 2

16.13 Suppose you wish to compare two treatments, A and B, based on independent random samples of 15 observations selected from each of the two populations. If $T_1 = 173$, do the data indicate that distribution A is shifted to the left of distribution B? Test using $\alpha = .05$

16.14 Suppose you want to compare two treatments, A and B. In particular, you wish to determine whether the distribution for population B is shifted to the right of the distribution for population A. You plan to use the Wilcoxon rank sum test.

a. Specify the null and alternative hypotheses you would test.

b. Suppose you obtained the following independent random samples of observations on experimental units subjected to the two treatments. Conduct a test of the hypotheses described in part **a.** Test using $\alpha = .05$.

🔘 **LM16_14**

Sample A: 37, 40, 33, 29, 42, 33, 35, 28, 34
Sample B: 65, 35, 47, 52

16.15 Independent random samples are selected from two populations. The data are shown in the table.

🔘 **LM16_15**

Sample 1		Sample 2		
15	16	5	9	5
10	13	12	8	10
12	8	9	4	

a. Use the Wilcoxon rank sum test to determine whether the data provide sufficient evidence to indicate a shift in the locations of the probability distributions of the sampled populations. Test using $\alpha = .05$.

b. Do the data provide sufficient evidence to indicate that the probability distribution for population 1 is shifted to the right of the probability distribution for population 2? Use the Wilcoxon rank sum test with $\alpha = .05$.

Applying the Concepts—Basic

16.16 University of Queensland researchers sampled private sector and public sector organizations in Australia to study the planning undertaken by their information systems departments (*Management Science*, July 1996). They asked each sample organization how much it had spent on information systems and technology in the previous fiscal year as a percentage of the organization's total revenues. The results are reported in the table.

🔘 **INFOSYS**

Private Sector	Public Sector
2.58%	5.40%
5.05	2.55
.05	9.00
2.10	10.55
4.30	1.02
2.25	5.11
2.50	12.42
1.94	1.67
2.33	3.33

Source: Adapted from Hann, J., and Weber, R. "Information Systems Planning: A Model and Empirical Tests." *Management Science*, Vol. 42, No. 2. July 1996, pp. 1043–1064.

a. Find the rank sums for the two sectors using the Wilcoxon method.

b. Do the two sampled populations have identical probability distributions or is the distribution for public sector organizations in Australia located to the right of Australia's private sector firms? Test using $\alpha = .05$.

c. Is the *p*-value for the test less than or greater than .05? Justify your answer. $p < .05$

d. What assumptions must be met to ensure the validity of the test you conducted in part **a?**

16.17 In Exercise 9.15 (p. 498), the solid waste generation rates for cities in industrialized countries and cities in middle-income countries were investigated. In this exercise, the focus is on middle-income countries versus low-income countries. The table extracted from the *International Journal of Environmental Health Research* (1994), reports waste generation values (kg per capita per day) for two independent samples. Do the rates differ for the two categories of countries?

a. Which nonparametric hypothesis-testing procedures could be used to answer the question?

b. Specify the null and alternative hypotheses of the test.

c. Give the rejection region for the test using $\alpha = .05$.

d. Conduct the test and give the appropriate conclusion in the context of the problem.

⊙ **SOLWAST2**

Cities of Low-Income Countries		Cities of Middle-Income Countries	
Jakarta	.60	Singapore	.87
Surabaya	.52	Hong Kong	.85
Bandung	.55	Medellin	.54
Lahore	.60	Kano	.46
Karachi	.50	Manila	.50
Calcutta	.51	Cairo	.50
Kanpur	.50	Tunis	.56

Source: Al-Momani, A. H. "Solid-Waste Management: Sampling, Analysis and Assessment of Household Waste in the City of Amman." *International Journal of Environmental Health Research,* Vol. 4, 1994, pp. 208–222.

16.18 In Mexico, the U.S.'s third largest trading partner, purchasing has not fully evolved into a profession with its own standards of ethical behavior. Researchers at Xavier University investigated the question: Do American and Mexican purchasing managers perceive ethical situations differently (*Industrial Marketing Management,* July 1999)? As part of their study, 15 Mexican purchasing managers and 15 American purchasing managers were asked to consider different ethical situations and respond on a 100-point scale with end points "strongly disagree" (1) and "strongly agree" (100). For the situation "accepting free trips from salespeople is okay," the responses shown in the next table were obtained.

a. Consider a Wilcoxon rank sum test to determine whether American and Mexican purchasing managers perceive the given ethical situation differently. Find the rank sums for the test.

b. Conduct the test at $\alpha = .05$.

⊙ **ETHICS**

American Purchasing Managers			Mexican Purchasing Managers		
50	15	19	10	15	5
10	8	11	90	60	55
35	40	5	65	80	40
30	80	25	50	85	45
20	75	30	20	35	95

Source: Adapted from Tadepalli, R., Moreno, A., and Trevino, S., "Do American and Mexican Purchasing Managers Perceive Ethical Situations Differently? An Empirical Investigation," *Industrial Marketing Management,* Vol. 28, No. 4, July 1999, pp. 369–380.

c. Under what circumstances could the two-sample *t*-test of Chapter 9 be used to analyze the data? Check to see whether the *t*-test is appropriate in this situation.

Applying the Concepts—Intermediate

16.19 Refer to the *Chance* (Fall 2002) study of a patent infringement case brought against Intel Corp., Exercise 9.17 (p. 498). Recall that the case rested on whether a patent witness' signature was written on top of key text in a patent notebook or under the key text. Using an X-ray beam, zinc measurements were taken at several spots on the notebook page. The zinc measurements for three notebook locations—on a text line, on a witness line, and on the intersection of the witness and text line—are reproduced in the table.

⊙ **PATENT**

Text line:	.335	.374	.440			
Witness line:	.210	.262	.188	.329	.439	.397
Intersection:	.393	.353	.285	.295	.319	

a. Why might the Student's *t*-procedure you applied in Exercise 9.17 be inappropriate for analyzing this data?

b. Use a nonparametric test (at $\alpha = .05$) to compare the distribution of zinc measurements for the text line with the distribution for the intersection. $T_1 = 18$

c. Use a nonparametric test (at $\alpha = .05$) to compare the distribution of zinc measurements for the witness line with the distribution for the intersection. $T_2 = 32$

d. From the results, parts **b** and **c,** what can you infer about the median zinc measurements at the three notebook locations?

COLORAIN

Station 1			Station 2		
127.96	108.91	100.85	114.79	85.54	280.55
210.07	178.21	85.89	109.11	117.64	145.11
203.24	285.37		330.33	302.74	95.36

Source: Gastwirth, J. L., and Mahmoud, H. "An Efficient Robust Nonparametric Test for Scale Change for Data from a Gamma Distribution." *Technometrics,* Vol. 28, No. 1, Feb. 1986, p. 83 (Table 2).

16.20 The data in the table above, extracted from *Technometrics* (Feb. 1986), represent daily accumulated stream flow and precipitation (in inches) for two U.S. Geological Survey stations in Colorado. Conduct a test to determine whether the distributions of daily accumulated stream flow and precipitation for the two stations differ in location. Use $\alpha = .10$. Why is a nonparametric test appropriate for this data?

16.21 A major razor blade manufacturer advertises that its twin-blade disposable razor "gets you lots more shaves" than any single-blade disposable razor on the market. A rival company that has been very successful in selling single-blade razors plans to test this claim. Independent random samples of eight single-blade users and eight twin-blade users are taken, and the number of shaves that each gets before indicating a preference to change blades is recorded. The results are shown in the table.

RAZOR

Twin Blades		Single Blades	
8	15	10	13
17	10	6	14
9	6	3	5
11	12	7	7

a. Do the data support the twin-blade manufacturer's claim? Use $\alpha = .05$. $T_1 = 82$
b. Do you think this experiment was designed in the best possible way? If not, what design might have been better?   No
c. What assumptions are necessary for the validity of the test you performed in part **a?** Do the assumptions seem reasonable for this application?

16.22 A *management information system* (MIS) is a computer-based information-processing system designed to support the operations, management, and decision functions of an organization. The development of an MIS involves three stages: definition, physical design, and implementation of the system (*Managing Information,* 1993). Thirty firms that recently implemented an MIS were surveyed: 16 were satisfied with the implementation results, 14 were not. Each firm was asked to rate the quality of the planning and negotiation stages of the development process, using a scale of 0 to 100, with higher numbers indicating better quality. (A score of 100 indicates that all the problems that occurred in the planning and negotiation stages were successfully resolved, while 0 indicates that none were resolved.) The results are shown in the table below.

MIS

Firms with a Good MIS			Firms with a Poor MIS		
52	59	95	60	40	90
70	60	90	50	55	85
40	90	86	55	65	80
80	75	95	70	55	90
82	80	93	41	70	
65					

a. Use the Wilcoxon rank sum test to compare the quality of the development processes of successfully and unsuccessfully implemented MISs. Test using $\alpha = .05$.
b. Under what circumstances could you use the two-sample t-test of Chapter 9 to conduct the same test?

Applying the Concepts—Advanced

16.23 In Exercise 9.16 (p. 498), you used a Student's t-test to compare the mean annual percentages of labor turnover between U.S. and Japanese manufacturers of air conditioners. The annual percentage turnover rates for five U.S. and five Japanese plants are shown in the table.

TURNOVER

U.S. Plants	Japanese Plants
7.11%	3.52%
6.06	2.02
8.00	4.91
6.87	3.22
4.77	1.92

a. Recall that the variance of a binomial sample proportion, $\hat{p}$, depends on the value of the population parameter, p. As a consequence, the variance of a sample percentage, $(100\hat{p})\%$, also depends on p. If you conduct an unpaired t-test (Section 9.1) to compare the means of two populations of percentages, which assumption may be violated?
b. Do the data provide sufficient evidence to indicate that the mean annual percentage turnover for American plants exceeds the corresponding mean for Japanese plants? Test using the Wilcoxon rank sum test with $\alpha = .05$. Do your test conclusions agree with those of the t-test in Exercise 9.16?

16.4 Comparing Two Populations: The Wilcoxon Signed Rank Test for the Paired Difference Experiment

Nonparametric techniques can also be employed to compare two probability distributions when a paired difference design is used. For example, consumer preferences for two competing products are often compared by having each of a sample of consumers rate both products. Thus, the ratings have been paired on each consumer. Here is an example of this type of experiment.

For some paper products, softness is an important consideration in determining consumer acceptance. One method of determining softness is to have judges give a sample of the products a softness rating. Suppose each of 10 judges is given a sample of two products that a company wants to compare. Each judge rates the softness of each product on a scale from 1 to 10, with higher ratings implying a softer product. The results of the experiment are shown in Table 16.4.

Since this is a paired difference experiment, we analyze the differences between the measurements (see Section 9.2). However, a nonparametric approach developed by Wilcoxon requires that we calculate the ranks of the absolute values of the differences between the measurements, that is, the ranks of the differences after removing any minus signs. *Note that tied absolute differences are assigned the average of the ranks they would receive if they were unequal but successive measurements.* After the absolute differences are ranked, the sum of the ranks of the positive differences of the original measurements, T_+, and the sum of the ranks of the negative differences of the original measurements, T_-, are computed.

We are now prepared to test the nonparametric hypotheses:

H_0: The probability distributions of the ratings for products A and B are identical.

H_a: The probability distributions of the ratings differ (in location) for the two products. (Note that this is a two-sided alternative and that it implies a two-tailed test.)

Test statistic: $T = $ Smaller of the positive and negative rank sums T_+ and T_-.

The smaller the value of T, the greater the evidence to indicate that the two probability distributions differ in location. The rejection region for T can be

TABLE 16.4 Softness Ratings of Paper

Judge	Product A	B	Difference (A − B)	Absolute Value of Difference	Rank of Absolute Value
1	6	4	2	2	5
2	8	5	3	3	7.5
3	4	5	−1	1	2
4	9	8	1	1	2
5	4	1	3	3	7.5
6	7	9	−2	2	5
7	6	2	4	4	9
8	5	3	2	2	5
9	6	7	−1	1	2
10	8	2	6	6	10

$T_+ = $ Sum of positive ranks $= 46$
$T_- = $ Sum of negative ranks $= 9$

determined by consulting Table XVI in Appendix B (part of the table is shown in Table 16.5). This table gives a value T_0 for both one-tailed and two-tailed tests for each value of n, the number of matched pairs. For a two-tailed test with $\alpha = .05$, we will reject H_0 if $T \leq T_0$. You can see in Table 16.5 that the value of T_0 that locates the boundary of the rejection region for the judges' ratings for $\alpha = .05$ and $n = 10$ pairs of observations is 8. Thus, the rejection region for the test (see Figure 16.7) is

Rejection region: $T \leq 8$ for $\alpha = .05$

Since the smaller rank sum for the paper data, $T_- = 9$, does not fall within the rejection region, the experiment has not provided sufficient evidence to indicate that the two paper products differ with respect to their softness ratings at the $\alpha = .05$ level.

Note that if a significance level of $\alpha = .10$ had been used, the rejection region would have been $T \leq 11$ and we would have rejected H_0. In other words, the samples do provide evidence that the probability distributions of the softness ratings differ at the $\alpha = .10$ significance level.

The **Wilcoxon signed rank test** is summarized in the box. Note that the difference measurements are assumed to have a continuous probability distribution so that the absolute differences will have unique ranks. Although tied (absolute) differences can be assigned ranks by averaging, the number of ties should be small relative to the number of observations to ensure the validity of the test.

Teaching Tip

Do several examples to help the student become comfortable with using the Wilcoxon Signed Rank table.

TABLE 16.5 Reproduction of Part of Table XVI of Appendix B: Critical Values for the Wilcoxon Paired Difference Signed Rank Test

One-Tailed	Two-Tailed	$n = 5$	$n = 6$	$n = 7$	$n = 8$	$n = 9$	$n = 10$
$\alpha = .05$	$\alpha = .10$	1	2	4	6	8	11
$\alpha = .025$	$\alpha = .05$		1	2	4	6	8
$\alpha = .01$	$\alpha = .02$			0	2	3	5
$\alpha = .005$	$\alpha = .01$				0	2	3
		$n = 11$	$n = 12$	$n = 13$	$n = 14$	$n = 15$	$n = 16$
$\alpha = .05$	$\alpha = .10$	14	17	21	26	30	36
$\alpha = .025$	$\alpha = .05$	11	14	17	21	25	30
$\alpha = .01$	$\alpha = .02$	7	10	13	16	20	24
$\alpha = .005$	$\alpha = .01$	5	7	10	13	16	19
		$n = 17$	$n = 18$	$n = 19$	$n = 20$	$n = 21$	$n = 22$
$\alpha = .05$	$\alpha = .10$	41	47	54	60	68	75
$\alpha = .025$	$\alpha = .05$	35	40	46	52	59	66
$\alpha = .01$	$\alpha = .02$	28	33	38	43	49	56
$\alpha = .005$	$\alpha = .01$	23	28	32	37	43	49
		$n = 23$	$n = 24$	$n = 25$	$n = 26$	$n = 27$	$n = 28$
$\alpha = .05$	$\alpha = .10$	83	92	101	110	120	130
$\alpha = .025$	$\alpha = .05$	73	81	90	98	107	117
$\alpha = .01$	$\alpha = .02$	62	69	77	85	93	102
$\alpha = .005$	$\alpha = .01$	55	61	68	76	84	92

Figure 16.7

Rejection region for paired difference experiment

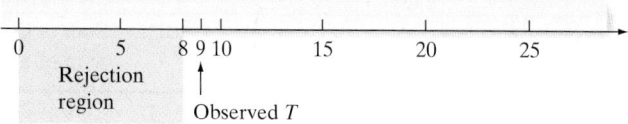

Wilcoxon Signed Rank Test for a Paired Difference Experiment

Let D_1 and D_2 represent the probability distributions for populations 1 and 2, respectively,

One-Tailed Test	Two-Tailed Test
H_0: D_1 and D_2 are identical	H_0: D_1 and D_2 are identical
H_a: D_1 is shifted to the right of D_2 [or H_a: D_1 is shifted to the left of D_2]	H_a: D_1 is shifted either to the left or to the right of D_2

Calculate the difference within each of the n matched pairs of observations. Then rank the absolute value of the n differences from the smallest (rank 1) to the highest (rank n) and calculate the rank sum T_- of the negative differences and the rank sum T_+ of the positive differences. [*Note:* Differences equal to 0 are eliminated, and the number n of differences is reduced accordingly.]

Test statistic:	*Test statistic:*
T_-, the rank sum of the negative differences [or T_+, the rank sum of the positive differences]	T, the smaller of T_+ or T_-
Rejection region:	*Rejection region:*
$T_- \leq T_0$ [or $T_+ \leq T_0$]	$T \leq T_0$

where T_0 is given in Table XVI in Appendix B.

Ties: ssign tied absolute differences the average of the ranks they would receive if they were unequal but occurred in successive order. For example, if the third-ranked and fourth-ranked differences are tied, assign both a rank of $(3 + 4)/2 = 3.5$.

Conditions Required for a Valid Signed Rank Test

Suggested Exercise 16.30

1. The sample of differences is randomly selected from the population of differences.
2. The probability distribution from which the sample of paired differences is drawn is continuous.

EXAMPLE 16.3

APPLYING THE SIGNED RANK TEST

Problem   Suppose the U.S. Consumer Product Safety Commission (CPSC) wants to test the hypothesis that New York City electrical contractors are more likely to install unsafe electrical outlets in urban homes than in suburban homes. A pair of homes, one urban and one suburban and both serviced by the same electrical contractor, is chosen for each of ten randomly selected electrical contractors. A CPSC inspector assigns each of the 20 homes a safety rating between 1 and 10, with higher numbers implying safer electrical conditions. The results are shown in Table 16.6. Use the Wilcoxon signed rank test to determine whether the CPSC hypothesis is supported at the $\alpha = .05$ level.

$T_+ = 15.5$, Fail to reject H_0

SAFETY

TABLE 16.6 Electrical Safety Ratings for 10 Pairs of New York City Homes

	Location		Difference	
Contractor	Urban A	Suburban B	(A − B)	Rank of Absolute Difference
1	7	9	−2	4.5
2	4	5	−1	2
3	8	8	0	(Eliminated)
4	9	8	1	2
5	3	6	−3	6
6	6	10	−4	7.5
7	8	9	−1	2
8	10	8	2	4.5
9	9	4	5	9
10	5	9	−4	7.5

Positive rank sum $= T_+ = 15.5$

Solution The null and alternative hypotheses are

H_0: The probability distributions of home electrical ratings are identical for urban and suburban homes

H_a: The electrical ratings for suburban homes tend to exceed the electrical ratings for urban homes

Since a paired difference design was used (the homes were selected in urban-suburban pairs so that the electrical contractor was the same for both), we first calculate the difference between the ratings for each pair of homes, and then rank the absolute values of the differences (see Table 16.5). Note that one pair of ratings was the same (both 8), and the resulting 0 difference contributes to neither the positive nor the negative rank sum. Thus, we eliminate this pair from the calculation of the test statistic.

Test statistic: T_+, the positive rank sum

In Table 16.6, we compute the urban minus suburban rating differences, and if the alternative hypothesis is true, we would expect most of these differences to be negative. Or, in other words, we would expect the *positive* rank sum T_+ to be small if the alternative hypothesis is true (see Figure 16.8).

Rejection region: For $\alpha = .05$, from Table XVI of Appendix B, we use $n = 9$ (remember, one pair of observations was eliminated) to find the rejection region for this one-tailed test: $T_+ \leq 8$

Since the computed value $T_+ = 15.5$ exceeds the critical value of 8, we conclude that this sample provides insufficient evidence at $\alpha = .05$ to support the

Figure 16.8

The alternative hypothesis for Example 16.3: We expect T_+ to be small

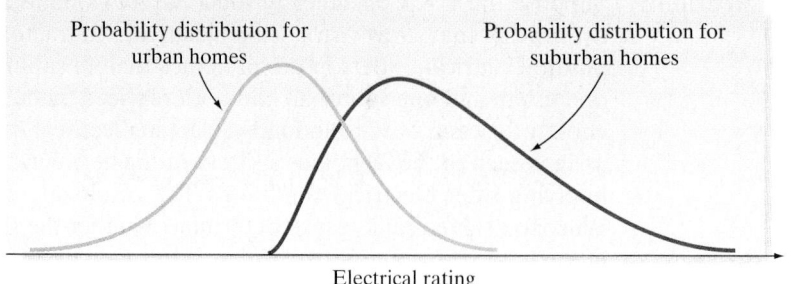

Figure 16.9
SPSS printout of signed
rank test

Wilcoxon Signed Ranks Test

Ranks

		N	Mean Rank	Sum of Ranks
SUBURB - URBAN	Negative Ranks	3[a]	5.17	15.50
	Positive Ranks	6[b]	4.92	29.50
	Ties	1[c]		
	Total	10		

a. SUBURB < URBAN

b. SUBURB > URBAN

c. SUBURB = URBAN

Test Statistics[b]

	SUBURB - URBAN
Z	-.834[a]
Asymp. Sig. (2-tailed)	.404

a. Based on negative ranks.

b. Wilcoxon Signed Ranks Test

alternative hypothesis. We *cannot* conclude on the basis of this sample information that suburban homes have safer electrical outlets than urban homes.

An SPSS printout of the analysis, shown in Figure 16.9, confirms this conclusion. The 2-tailed *p*-value of the test (highlighted) is .404. Since the 1-tailed *p*-value, $.404/2 = .202$, exceeds $\alpha = .05$, we fail to reject H_0.

Now Work *Exercise 16.26*

■ ■ ■

As is the case for the rank sum test for independent samples, the sampling distribution of the signed rank statistic can be approximated by a normal distribution when the number *n* of paired observations is large (say, $n \geq 25$). The large-sample *z*-test is summarized in the next box.

Teaching Tip
Point out the advantage of
using the z distribution when
the sample size is large enough.

Wilcoxon Signed Rank Test for Large Samples ($n \geq 25$)

Let D_1 and D_2 represent the probability distributions for populations 1 and 2, respectively.

One-Tailed Test	Two-Tailed Test
H_0: D_1 and D_2 are identical	H_0: D_1 and D_2 are identical
H_a: D_1 is shifted to the right of D_2 [or H_a: D_1 is shifted to the left of D_2]	H_a: D_1 is shifted either to the left or to the right of D_2

(cont'd)

$$\text{Test statistic: } z = \frac{T_+ - [n(n+1)/4]}{\sqrt{[n(n+1)(2n+1)]/24}}$$

Rejection region: *Rejection region:*

$z > z_\alpha \,[\text{or } z < -z_\alpha]$ $|z| > z_{\alpha/2}$

Assumptions: The sample size n is greater than or equal to 25. Differences equal to 0 are eliminated and the number n of differences is reduced accordingly. Tied absolute differences receive ranks equal to the average of the ranks they would have received had they not been tied.

Statistics in Action Revisited

Comparing the TCDD Levels in Fat and Plasma of Vietnam Vets

Medical researchers used the sample data in Table SIA16.1 to compare the TCDD levels in fat tissue and plasma for Vietnam veterans. Specifically, they wanted to determine if the distribution of TCDD levels in fat is shifted above or below the distribution of TCDD levels is plasma. To answer this question, first note that the data are collected as matched pairs—for each Vietnam vet in the sample the researchers recorded both the TCDD level in fat and in plasma. Therefore, the correct test to apply is the Wilcoxon signed rank test. The MINITAB printout for this analysis is shown in Figure SIA16.3.

Both the test statistic and *p*-value are highlighted on the printout. Since *p*-value = .073, at $\alpha = .05$ there is insufficient evidence to conclude that the distribution of TCDD levels in fat differs from the distribution of TCDD levels in plasma.

[*Note:* A histogram of the differences between the TCDD levels in fat and plasma, shown in Figure SIA 16.4, illustrates that the sample differences are unlikely to have come from a normal population.]

Figure SIA16.3

MINITAB signed rank test for TCDD data

Wilcoxon Signed Rank Test: DIFF

```
Test of median = 0.000000 versus median not = 0.000000

              N
            for   Wilcoxon              Estimated
        N   Test  Statistic      P        Median
DIFF   20    19      140.0   0.073         1.175
```

Figure SIA16.4

MINITAB histogram for differences in TCDD levels

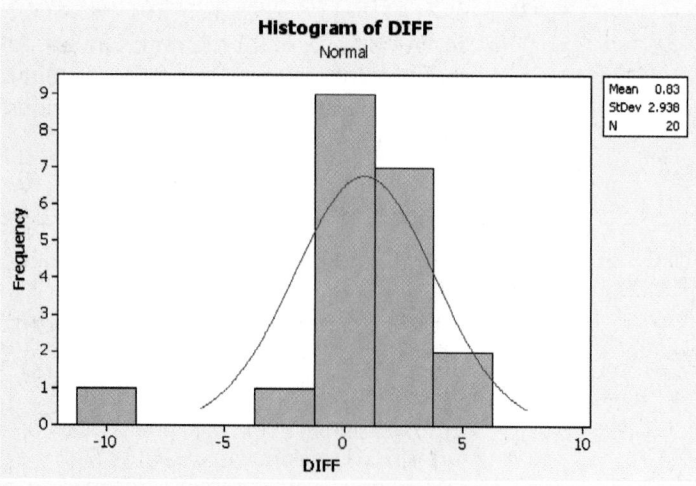

Exercises 16.24–16.34

Learning the Mechanics

16.24 Specify the test statistic and the rejection region for the Wilcoxon signed rank test for the paired difference design in each of the following situations:

  a. $n = 30, \alpha = .10$ Smaller of T_- or T_+; $T \leq 152$
  H_0: Two probability distributions, 1 and 2, are identical
  H_a: Probability distribution for population 1 is shifted to the right or left of probability distribution for population 2

  b. $n = 20, \alpha = .05$ T_-; $T_- \leq 60$
  H_0: Two probability distributions, 1 and 2, are identical
  H_a: Probability distribution for population 1 is shifted to the right of the probability distribution for population 2

  c. $n = 8, \alpha = .005$ T_+; $T_+ \leq 0$
  H_0: Two probability distributions, 1 and 2, are identical
  H_a: Probability distribution for population 1 is shifted to the left of probability distribution for population 2

16.25 Suppose you want to test a hypothesis that two treatments, A and B, are equivalent against the alternative hypothesis that the responses for A tend to be larger than those for B. You plan to use a paired difference experiment and to analyze the resulting data (shown below) using the Wilcoxon signed rank test.

  a. Specify the null and alternative hypotheses you would test.

  b. Suppose the paired difference experiment yielded the data in the table. Conduct the test of part **a.** Test using $\alpha = .025$.

⊙ **LM16_25**

Pair	Treatment A	Treatment B	Pair	Treatment A	Treatment B
1	54	45	6	77	75
2	60	45	7	74	63
3	98	87	8	29	30
4	43	31	9	63	59
5	82	71	10	80	82

16.26 Suppose you wish to test a hypothesis that two treatments, A and B, are equivalent against the alternative that the responses for A tend to be larger than those for B.

  a. If the number of pairs equals 25, give the rejection region for the large-sample Wilcoxon signed rank test for $\alpha = .05$. $z > 1.645$

  b. Suppose that $T_+ = 273$. State your test conclusions.

  c. Find the p-value for the test and interpret it.

16.27 A paired difference experiment with $n = 30$ pairs yielded $T_+ = 354$.

  a. Specify the null and alternative hypotheses that should be used in conducting a hypothesis test to determine whether the probability distribution for population 1 is located to the right of that for population 2.

  b. Conduct the test of part **a** using $\alpha = .05$.

  c. What is the approximate p-value of the test of part **b**?

  d. What assumptions are necessary to ensure the validity of the test you performed in part **b**?

Applying the Concepts—Basic

16.28 Refer to the National Highway Traffic Safety Administration (NHTSA) crash test data for new cars saved in the **CRASH** file. In Exercise 9.32 (p. 510) you compared the chest injury ratings of drivers and front-seat passengers using the Student's t-procedure for matched pairs. Suppose you want to make the comparison for only those cars that have a driver's star rating of 5 stars (the highest rating). The data for these 18 cars are listed in the table. Now consider analyzing these data using the Wilcoxon signed rank test.

  a. State the null and alternative hypothesis.

  b. Use a statistical software package to find the signed rank test statistic. $T_+ = 23$

  c. Give the rejection region for the test using $\alpha = .01$. $T_+ \leq 19$

  d. State the conclusion in practical terms. Report the p-value of the test.   .011

⊙ **CRASH5**

Car	Chest Injury Rating Driver	Chest Injury Rating Passenger
1	42	35
2	42	35
3	34	45
4	34	45
5	45	45
6	40	42
7	42	46
8	43	58
9	45	43
10	36	37
11	36	37
12	43	58
13	40	42
14	43	58
15	37	41
16	37	41
17	44	57
18	42	42

16.29 Refer to the *Journal of Genetic Psychology* (March 1998) study of attitudes of male college students toward their parents, Exercise 9.36 (p. 511). Recall that each of 13 students was asked to complete the following statement: My relationship with my father (mother) can best be described as (1) Awful, (2) Poor, (3) Average, (4) Good, or (5) Great. The study data are reproduced in the table. The researchers want to compare male students' attitudes toward their fathers with their attitudes toward their mothers.

⊕ FATHMOTH

Student	Attitude toward Father	Attitude toward Mother
1	2	3
2	5	5
3	4	3
4	4	5
5	3	4
6	5	4
7	4	5
8	2	4
9	4	5
10	5	4
11	4	5
12	5	4
13	3	3

Source: Adapted from Vitulli, William F., and Deanna K. Richardson, "College Student's Attitudes toward Relationships with Parents: A Five-Year Comparative Analysis," *Journal of Genetic Psychology,* Vol. 159, No. 1, (March 1998), pp. 45–52.

a. Why is a nonparametric test applicable for analyzing this data set?

b. Specify H_0 and H_a for the test.

c. Compute and rank the differences between the father and mother attitudes.

d. Sum the ranks of the positive and negative differences. $T_+ = 22; T_- = 44$

e. Find the rejection region for the test at $\alpha = .05$. $T_+ \leq 11$

f. Give the conclusion of the test in the context of the problem. Compare your answer to the test results of Exercise 9.36b.

Applying the Concepts—Intermediate

16.30 An atlas is a compendium of geographic, economic, and social information that describes one or more geographic regions. Atlases are used by the sales and marketing functions of businesses, local chambers of commerce, and educators. One of the most critical aspects of a new atlas design is its thematic content. In a survey of atlas users (*Journal of Geography,* May/June 1995), a large sample of high school teachers in British Columbia ranked 12 thematic atlas topics for usefulness. The consensus rankings of the teachers (based on the percentage of teachers who responded they "would definitely use" the topic) are given in the table. These teacher rankings were compared to the rankings of a group of university geography alumni made three years earlier. Compare the distributions of theme rankings for the two groups with an appropriate nonparametric test. Use $\alpha = .05$. Interpret the results practically.

⊕ ATLAS

Theme	Rankings	
	High School Teachers	Geography Alumni
Tourism	10	2
Physical	2	1
Transportation	7	3
People	1	6
History	2	5
Climate	6	4
Forestry	5	8
Agriculture	7	10
Fishing	9	7
Energy	2	8
Mining	10	11
Manufacturing	12	12

Source: Keller, C. P., et al. "Planning the Next Generation of Regional Atlases: Input from Educators." *Journal of Geography,* Vol. 94, No. 3, May/June 1995, p. 413 (Table 1).

16.31 According to the National Sleep Foundation, companies are encouraging their workers to take "power naps" (*Athens Daily News,* Jan. 9, 2000). In Exercise 9.35 (p. 511), you analyzed data collected by a major airline that recently began encouraging reservation agents to nap during their breaks. The number of complaints received about each of a sample of 10 reservation agents during the six months before naps were encouraged and during the six months after the policy change are reproduced in the accompanying table. Compare the distributions of number of complaints for the two time periods using the Wilcoxon signed rank test. Use $\alpha = .05$ to make the appropriate inference. $T_- = 3.5$

⊕ POWERNAP

Agent	1999 Number of Complaints	2000 Number of Complaints
1	10	5
2	3	0
3	16	7
4	11	4
5	8	6
6	2	4
7	1	2
8	14	3
9	5	5
10	6	1

16.32 A job-scheduling innovation that has helped managers overcome motivation and absenteeism problems associated with a fixed 8-hour workday is a concept called *flextime*. This flexible working hours program permits employees to design their own 40-hour work week to meet their personal needs (*New York Times*, Mar. 31, 1996). The management of a large manufacturing firm may adopt a flextime program depending on the success or failure of a pilot program. Ten employees were randomly selected and given a questionnaire designed to measure their attitude toward their job. Each was then permitted to design and follow a flextime workday. After six months, attitudes toward their jobs were again measured. The resulting attitude scores are displayed in the table. The higher the score, the more favorable the employee's attitude toward his or her work. Use a nonparametric test procedure to evaluate the success of the pilot flextime program. Test using $\alpha = .05$. $T_+ = 2$

⊙ **FLEXTIME**

Employee	Before	After	Employee	Before	After
1	54	68	6	82	88
2	25	42	7	94	90
3	80	80	8	72	81
4	76	91	9	33	39
5	63	70	10	90	93

16.33 In Exercise 9.101 (p. 540), you compared matched pairs of measurements on the radon exhalation rate (a measure of radiation) of 15 soil samples from waste gypsum and phosphate mounds in Polk County, Florida. Each soil sample was measured for exhalation rate by the Polk County Health Department (PCHD) and the Eastern Environmental Radiation Facility (EERF). The data are reproduced at right. Do the data provide sufficient evidence (at $\alpha = .05$) to indicate that one of the measuring facilities, PCHD or EERF, tends to read higher or lower than the other? $T_- = 36$

16.34 Teachers Involve Parents in Schoolwork (TIPS) is an interactive homework process designed to improve the quality of homework assignments for elementary, middle, and high school students. TIPS homework assignments require students to conduct interactions with family partners (parents, guardians, etc.) while completing the homework. Frances Van Voorhis (Johns Hopkins University) conducted a study to investigate the effects

⊙ **EXRATES**

Charcoal Canister No.	PCHD	EERF
71	1,709.79	1,479.0
58	357.17	257.8
84	1,150.94	1,287.0
91	1,572.69	1,395.0
44	558.33	416.5
43	4,132.28	3,993.0
79	1,489.86	1,351.0
61	3,017.48	1,813.0
85	393.55	187.7
46	880.84	630.4
4	2,996.49	3,707.0
20	2,367.40	2,791.0
36	599.84	706.8
42	538.37	618.5
55	2,770.23	2,639.0

Source: Horton, T. R. "Preliminary Radiological Assessment of Radon Exhalation from Phosphate Gypsum Piles and Inactive Uranium Mill Tailings Piles." EPA-520/5-79-004. Washington, D.C.: Environmental Protection Agency, 1979.

of TIPS in science and mathematics homework assignments (April 2001). Each of large group of middle school students was assigned to complete TIPS homework assignments. At the end of the study, all students reported on the level of family involvement in their homework on 4-point scale 0 = Never, 1 = Rarely, 2 = Sometimes, 3 = Frequently, 4 = Always). The data for the science and math for a random sample of ten students selected from the large group is shown in the table. Conduct a nonparametric analysis to compare the level of family involvement in science and math homework assignments of TIPS students. Use $\alpha = 05$. $T_- = 7$

⊙ **HWSTUDY10**

Student	Science	Math	Student	Science	Math
1	0	2	6	2	3
2	4	3	7	4	0
3	3	0	8	2	1
4	1	1	9	3	1
5	3	1	10	4	1

Source: Van Voorhis, F. L., "Teachers' Use of Interactive Homework and Its Effects on Family Involvement and Science Achievement of Middle Grade Students," paper presented at the annual meeting of the American Educational Research Association, Seattle, April 2001.

16.5 The Kruskal-Wallis *H*-Test for a Completely Randomized Design

In Chapter 10 we used an analysis of variance and the *F*-test to compare the means of *p* populations (treatments) based on random sampling from populations that were normally distributed with a common variance σ^2. We now present a nonparametric technique — **Kruskal-Wallis *H*-test** — for comparing the populations that requires no assumptions concerning the population probability distributions.

HOSPBEDS

TABLE 16.7   Number of Available Beds

Hospital 1		Hospital 2		Hospital 3	
Beds	Rank	Beds	Rank	Beds	Rank
6	5	34	25	13	9.5
38	27	28	19	35	26
3	2	42	30	19	15
17	13	13	9.5	4	3
11	8	40	29	29	20
30	21	31	22	0	1
15	11	9	7	7	6
16	12	32	23	33	24
25	17	39	28	18	14
5	4	27	18	24	16
$R_1 = 120$		$R_2 = 210.5$		$R_3 = 134.5$	

Suppose a health administrator wants to compare the unoccupied bed space for three hospitals in the same city. She randomly selects 10 different days from the records of each hospital and lists the number of unoccupied beds for each day (see Table 16.7). Because the number of unoccupied beds per day may occasionally be quite large, it is conceivable that the population distributions of data may be skewed to the right and that this type of data may not satisfy the assumptions necessary for a parametric comparison of the population means. We therefore use a nonparametric analysis and base our comparison on the rank sums for the three sets of sample data. Just as with two independent samples (Section 16.3), the ranks are computed for each observation according to the relative magnitude of the measurements *when the data for all the samples are combined* (see Table 16.7). Ties are treated as they were for the Wilcoxon rank sum and signed rank tests by assigning the average value of the ranks to each of the tied observations.

We test

H_0: The probability distributions of the number of unoccupied beds are the same for all three hospitals

H_a: At least two of the three hospitals have probability distributions of the number of unoccupied beds that differ in location

If we denote the three sample rank sums by R_1, R_2, and R_3, the test statistic is given by

$$H = \frac{12}{n(n+1)} \sum \frac{R_j^2}{n_j} - 3(n+1)$$

where n_j is the number of measurements in the *j*th sample and *n* is the total sample size $(n = n_1 + n_2 + \cdots + n_p)$. For the data in Table 16.7, we have $n_1 = n_2 = n_3 = 10$ and $n = 30$. The rank sums are $R_1 = 120$, $R_2 = 210.5$, and $R_3 = 134.5$. Thus,

$$H = \frac{12}{30(31)} \left[\frac{(120)^2}{10} + \frac{(210.5)^2}{10} + \frac{(134.5)^2}{10} \right] - 3(31)$$

$$= 99.097 - 93 = 6.097$$

The *H*-statistic measures the extent to which the *p* samples differ with respect to their relative ranks. This is more easily seen by writing *H* in an alternative but equivalent form:

$$H = \frac{12}{n(n+1)} \sum n_j (\overline{R}_j - \overline{R})^2$$

where $\overline{R}_j$ is the mean rank corresponding to sample *j*, and $\overline{R}$ is the mean of all the ranks [that is, $\overline{R} = \frac{1}{2}(n+1)$]. Thus, the *H*-statistic is 0 if all samples have the same mean rank, and becomes increasingly large as the distance between the sample mean ranks grows.

If the null hypothesis is true, the distribution of *H* in repeated sampling is approximately a χ^2 (chi-square) distribution. This approximation for the sampling distribution of *H* is adequate as long as one of the *p* sample sizes exceeds 5. (See the references for more detail.) The degrees of freedom corresponding to the approximate sampling distribution of *H* will always be $(p-1)$—one less than the number of probability distributions being compared. Because large values of *H* support the alternative hypothesis that the populations have different probability distributions, the rejection region for the test is located in the upper tail of the χ^2 distribution.

For the data of Table 16.7, the test statistic *H* has a χ^2 distribution with $(p-1) = 2$ df. To determine how large *H* must be before we will reject the null hypothesis, we consult Table VII in Appendix B. For $\alpha = .05$ and df $= 2$, $\chi^2_{.05} = 5.99147$. Therefore, we can reject the null hypothesis that the three probability distributions are the same if $H > 5.99147$.

The rejection region is pictured in Figure 16.10. Since the calculated $H = 6.097$ exceeds the critical value of 5.99147, we conclude that at least one of the three hospitals tends to have a larger number of unoccupied beds than the others.

Figure 16.10
Rejection region for the comparison of three probability distributions

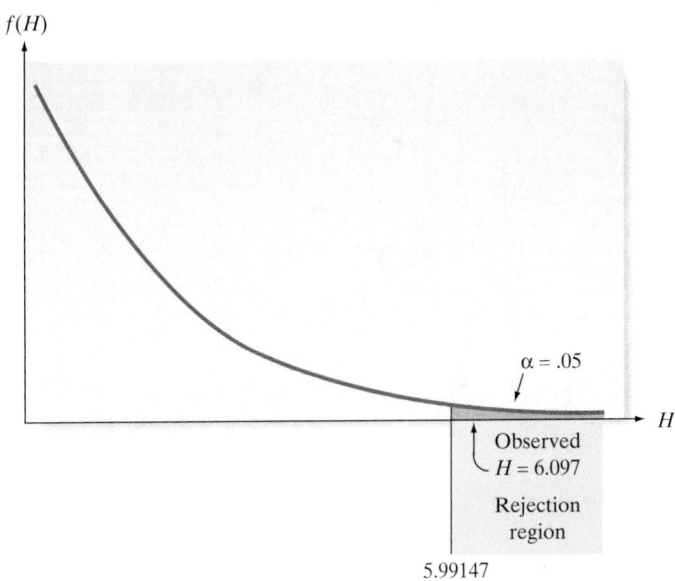

Now Work   *Exercise 16.37*

The same conclusion can be reached from a computer printout of the analysis. The rank sums, test statistic, and *p*-value of the nonparametric test are highlighted on the EXCEL printout in Figure 16.11. Since $\alpha = .05$ exceeds p-value $= .04742$, there is sufficient evidence to reject H_0.

The Kruskal-Wallis H-test for comparing more than two probability distributions is summarized in the box. Note that we can use the Wilcoxon rank sum test of Section 16.3 to compare the separate pairs of populations if the Kruskal-Wallis H-test supports the alternative hypothesis that at least two of the probability distributions differ.*

Figure 16.11

EXCEL/PHStat2 printout of Kruskal-Wallis test

	A	B
1	**Kruskal-Wallis Rank Test**	
2		
3	**Data**	
4	**Level of Significance**	**0.05**
5		
6	Group 1	
7	Sum of Ranks	120
8	Sample Size	10
9	Group 2	
10	Sum of Ranks	210.5
11	Sample Size	10
12	Group 3	
13	Sum of Ranks	134.5
14	Sample Size	10
15		
16	Intermediate Calculations	
17	Sum of Squared Ranks/Sample Size	7680.05
18	Sum of Sample Sizes	30
19	Number of groups	3
20	H Test Statistic	6.097419
21		
22	**Test Result**	
23	**Critical Value**	**5.991476**
24	**p-Value**	**0.04742**
25	**Reject the null hypothesis**	

Suggested Exercise 16.39

Kruskal-Wallis H-Test for Comparing p Probability Distributions

H_0: The p probability distributions are identical

H_a: At least two of the p probability distributions differ in location

$$\text{Test statistic: } H = \frac{12}{n(n+1)} \sum \frac{R_j^2}{n_j} - 3(n+1)$$

(*cont'd*)

*The multiple comparisons procedure of Chapter 10 can be used to rank the treatment medians. This nonparametric multiple comparisons of medians will control the experiment wise error rate selected by the analyst. Consult the references [Daniel (1990) and Dunn (1964)] for details.

where

n_j = Number of measurements in sample j

R_j = Rank sum for sample j, where the rank of each measurement is computed according to its relative magnitude in the totality of data for the p samples

n = Total sample size = $n_1 + n_2 + \cdots + n_p$

Rejection region: $H > \chi_\alpha^2$ with $(p-1)$ degrees of freedom

Ties: Assign tied measurements the average of the ranks they would receive if they were unequal but occurred in successive order. For example, if the third-ranked and fourth-ranked measurements are tied, assign both a rank of $(3+4)/2 = 3.5$. The number of ties should be small relative to the total number of observations.

Conditions Required for the Validity of the Kruskal-Wallis *H*-Test

1. The p samples are random and independent.
2. There are five or more measurements in each sample.
3. The p probability distributions from which the samples are drawn are continuous.

Exercises 16.35–16.44

Learning the Mechanics

16.35 Under what circumstances does the χ^2 distribution provide an appropriate characterization of the sampling distribution of the Kruskal-Wallis *H*-statistic?

16.36 Data were collected from three populations, A, B, and C, using a completely randomized design. The following describes the sample data:

$$n_A = n_B = n_C = 15$$
$$R_A = 230 \quad R_B = 440 \quad R_C = 365$$

a. Specify the null and alternative hypotheses that should be used in conducting a test of hypothesis to determine whether the probability distributions of populations A, B, and C differ in location.
b. Conduct the test of part **a.** Use $\alpha = .05$.
c. What is the approximate p-value of the test of part **b**?
d. Calculate the mean rank for each sample, and compute H according to the formula that utilizes these means. Verify that this formula yields the same value of H that you obtained in part **b**.

16.37 Suppose you want to use the Kruskal-Wallis *H*-test to compare the probability distributions of three populations. The following are independent random samples selected from the three populations:

LM16_37

I: 66, 23, 55, 88, 58, 62, 79, 49
II: 19, 31, 16, 29, 30, 33, 40
III: 75, 96, 102, 75, 98, 78

a. What type of experimental design was used?
b. Specify the null and alternative hypotheses you would test.
c. Specify the rejection region you would use for your hypothesis test, at $\alpha = .01$. $H > 9.21034$
d. Conduct the test at $\alpha = .01$.   Reject H_0

Applying the Concepts—Basic

16.38 In litigating tax disputes with the IRS, taxpayers are permitted to choose the court forum. Three trial courts are available: (1) U.S. Tax Court, (2) Federal District Court, and (3) U.S. Claims Court. Accounting professors B. A. Billings (Wayne State University) and B. P. Green (University of Michigan–Dearborn) and business law professor W. H. Volz (Wayne State University) conducted a study of taxpayers' choice of forum in litigating tax issues (*Journal of Applied Business Research*, Fall 1996). A random sample of 161 court decisions were obtained for analysis. Two of the many variables measured for each case were taxpayer's choice of forum (Tax, District, or Claims Court) and tax deficiency DEF (i.e., the disputed amount, in dollars).

a. The researchers applied a nonparametric test rather than a parametric test to compare the DEF distributions of the three tax litigation forums. Give a plausible reason for their choice.

b. What nonparametric test is appropriate for this analysis? Explain.

c. The table below summarizes the data analyzed by the researchers. Use the information in the table to compute the appropriate test statistic.   *H* = 11.201

d. The observed significance level (*p*-value) of the test was reported as *p* = .0037. Fully interpret this result.

Court Selected by Taxpayer	Sample Size	Sample Mean DEF	Rank Sum of DEF Values
Tax	67	$ 80,357	5,335
District	57	74,213	3,937
Claims	37	185,648	3,769

Source: Billings, B. A., Green, B. P., and Volz, W. H. "Selection of Forum for Litigated Tax Issues." *Journal of Applied Business Research*, Vol. 12, Fall 1996, p. 38 (Table 2).

16.39 Refer to the *Journal of the American Mosquito Control Association* study of biting flies, Exercise 16.8 (p. 1077). The effect of wind speeds in kilometers per hour (kph) on the biting rate of the fly on Stanbury Island, Utah, was investigated by exposing samples of volunteers to one of six wind speed conditions. The distributions of the biting rates for the six wind speeds were compared using the Kruskal-Wallis test. The rank sums of the biting rates for the six conditions are shown in the next table.

a. The researchers reported the test statistic as *H* = 35.2. Verify this value.   *H* = 35.23

b. Find the rejection region for the test using $\alpha = .01$.

c. Make the proper conclusions.   Reject H_0

d. The researchers reported the *p*-value of the test as *p* < .01. Does this value support your inference in part **c**? Explain.   *p* < .01

Wind Speed (kph)	Number of Volunteers (n_j)	Rank Sum of Biting Rates (R_j)
<1	11	1,804
1–2.9	49	6,398
3–4.9	62	7,328
5–6.9	39	4,075
7–8.9	35	2,660
9–20	21	1,388
Totals	217	23,653

Source: Strickman, D., et al. "Meteorological Effects on the Biting Activity of Leptoconops americanus (Diptera: Ceratopogonidae)." *Journal of the American Mosquito Control Association*, Vol. II, No. 1, Mar. 1995, p. 17 (Table 1).

16.40 Real estate market cycles are commonly divided into four phases that are based on the rate of change of the demand for and supply of properties: I—Recovery, II—Expansion, III—Hypersupply, and IV—Recession. Glenn Mueller of Johns Hopkins University studied the office market cycles of U.S. real estate markets (*Journal of Real Estate Research*, July/Aug. 1999). For each of the four market cycles, office rental growth rates (i.e., growth rates for asking rents) were measured for a sample of six different real estate markets. These data (in percentages) are presented in the table below.

⊙ **MKTCYCLE**

Phase I	Phase II	Phase III	Phase IV
2.7	10.5	6.1	−1.0
−1.0	11.5	1.2	6.2
1.1	9.4	11.4	−10.8
3.4	12.2	4.4	2.0
4.2	8.6	6.2	−1.1
3.5	10.9	7.6	−2.3

Source: Adapted from Mueller, G. R., "Real Estate Rental Growth Rates at Different Points in the Physical Market Cycle," *Journal of Real Estate Research*, Vol. 18, No. 1, July/Aug. 1999, pp. 131–150.

a. Specify the null hypothesis for a Kruskal-Wallis test.

b. Rank the 24 measurements in the data set.

c. Find the rank sums and calculate the test statistic.   *H* = 16.23

d. Give the rejection region for the test at $\alpha = .05$.   *H* > 7.81473

e. Is there sufficient evidence to conclude that the distributions of office rental growth rates differ among the four market cycle phases?

f. What are the advantages and disadvantages of applying the Kruskal-Wallis *H*-test in part **a** rather than the parametric *F*-test of Chapter 10?

Applying the Concepts—Intermediate

16.41 Three of the categories *Business Week* uses to classify mutual funds are growth, blend, and value. Those with significantly lower-than-average price-earnings ratios (p-e) and price-to-book ratios (p-b) are *value funds;* those with higher than average p-e's and p-b's are called *growth funds;* those in the middle are called *blend funds*. The table on p. 1101 lists the after tax rate of return to investors for samples of seven mutual funds in each of these three categories.

a. Do the data provide sufficient evidence to conclude that the rate-of-return distributions differ among the three types of mutual funds? Test using $\alpha = .05$.

MFUNDS

Category	Fund	12-Month Return (%)
Growth	Citizens Index	21.2
	Fidelity Advisor Growth	37.9
	Gabelli Growth	39.2
	Northern Growth Equity	22.7
	Preferred Growth	44.8
	Seligman Growth	31.8
	RYDEX OTC	118.5
Blend	American Perform Equity	5.9
	Columbia Common Stock	23.5
	Fidelity	21.3
	General Security	47.9
	J.P. Morgan U.S. Equity	8.2
	Lexington Growth & Income	17.8
	Oppenheimer Growth & Income	12.4
Value	American Mutual	−9.2
	CITIFUNDS Growth & Income	−5.5
	ICAP Equity	8.5
	Marshall Equity Income	−8.5
	Payson Value	9.2
	Pioneer Equity Income	−6.8
	Putnam Equity Income	−9.6

Source: Business Week, Mutual Fund Scoreboard Current Statistics, March 2000.

b. What assumptions must hold for your test of part **a** to be valid?

c. Describe the Type I and II errors associated with the test of part **a** in the context of the problem.

d. Under what circumstances could the ANOVA *F*-test of Chapter 14 help answer part **a?**

16.42 Refer to the *Journal of Hazardous Materials* (July 1995) study of the chemical properties of three different types of hazardous solvents used to clean metal parts, Exercise 10.82 (p. 636). Independent samples of solvents from each of the three types—aromatics, chloralkanes, and esters—were collected. The data on sorption rates for the three solvents are reproduced in the table. Use a nonparametric test to compare the sorption rate distributions at $\alpha = .01$. *H = 20.197*

HAZARDS

Aromatics		Chloralkanes		Esters		
1.06	.95	1.58	1.12	.29	.43	.06
.79	.65	1.45	.91	.06	.51	.09
.82	1.15	.57	.83	.44	.10	.17
.89	1.12	1.16	.43	.61	.34	.60
1.05				.55	.53	.17

Source: Ortego, J. D., et al. "A Review of Polymeric Geosynthetics Used in Hazardous Waste Facilities." *Journal of Hazardous Materials,* Vol. 42, No. 2, July 1995, p. 142 (Table 9).

16.43 A firm's debt/capital ratio is a measure of its long-term debt divided by total invested capital. To potential lenders to the firm, a high debt/capital ratio signals that in case of default, the lender is unlikely to recover outstanding loans to the firm. *Forbes* (March 2000) reported the debt/capital ratios (expressed as a percentage) for over 400 firms. The debt/capital ratios of selected firms in four industries are listed in the first table on p. 1102.

a. Use the Kruskal-Wallis *H*-test to investigate whether debt/capital ratios differ among the four industries. Be sure to specify your null and alternative hypotheses and to state your conclusion in the context of the problem. Use $\alpha = .05$.

b. Assuming the Kruskal-Wallis *H*-test indicates that differences exist among the four industries, which nonparametric procedure could be employed to compare the distribution of debt/capital ratios for the retailing and chemical industries? If appropriate, conduct the analysis.

16.44 Random samples of seven lawyers employed as public defenders were selected from each of three major cities. Their salaries were determined and are recorded in the second table on p. 1102. You have been hired to determine whether differences exist among the salary distributions for public defenders in the three cities.

PUBDEF

Atlanta	Los Angeles	Washington, D.C.
$34,600	$ 42,400	$38,000
84,900	135,000	76,900
61,700	63,000	48,000
38,900	43,700	72,600
77,200	69,400	73,200
83,600	97,000	51,800
59,800	49,500	55,000

Source: Adapted from *American Almanac of Jobs and Salaries,*
1997–1998 Edition, New York: Avon Books, 1996, pp. 246–260.

a. Under what circumstances would it be appropriate to use the *F*-test for a completely randomized design to perform the required analysis?

b. Which assumptions required by the *F*-test are likely to be violated in this problem? Explain.

c. Use the Kruskal-Wallis *H*-test to determine whether the salary distributions differ among the three cities. Specify your null and alternative hypotheses, and state your conclusions in the context of the problem. Use $\alpha = .05$.

d. What assumptions are necessary to ensure the validity of the nonparametric test in part **c?**

DEBTCAP

Field	Firm	Debt/Capital %
Aerospace & Defense	Raytheon	45.3
	Boeing	37.0
	Textron	64.6
	Northrop Grumman Corp	40.6
	Lockheed Martin	63.9
	Rohr	63.3
Electric Utilities	PacificCorp	56.4
	Avista Corp.	59.9
	Florida Progress	58.6
	Duke Energy Corp.	46.9
	Northern States Power	49.8
	Consolidated Edison, Inc.	41.7
	Hawaiian Electric	36.5
Retailing	Rite Aid	62.2
	Kmart	31.2
	Bradlees	75.6
	Spiegel	48.8
	Fay's Incorporated	42.1
Chemical	Olin	22.6
	Valspar	47.2
	Dow Chemical	44.2
	FMC	67.0
	Union Carbide	47.6

Source: Forbes Current Statistics, March 2000 (*http://www.forbes.com/tool/toolbox/mktguide*).

16.6 The Friedman F_r-Test for a Randomized Block Design (Optional)

In Section 10.4 we employed an analysis of variance to compare *p* population (treatment) means when the data were collected using a randomized block design. The *Friedman F_r-test* provides another method for testing to detect a shift in location of a set of *p* populations.* Like other nonparametric tests, it requires no assumptions concerning the nature of the populations other than the capacity of individual observations to be ranked.

Consider the problem of comparing the reaction times of subjects under the influence of different drugs. When the effect of a drug is short lived (there is no carryover effect) and when the drug effect varies greatly from person to person, it may

---

*The Friedman F_r-test was developed by the Nobel prize–winning economist Milton Friedman.

REACTION

TABLE 16.8   Reaction Time for Three Drugs

Subject	Drug A	Rank	Drug B	Rank	Drug C	Rank
1	1.21	1	1.48	2	1.56	3
2	1.63	1	1.85	2	2.01	3
3	1.42	1	2.06	3	1.70	2
4	2.43	2	1.98	1	2.64	3
5	1.16	1	1.27	2	1.48	3
6	1.94	1	2.44	2	2.81	3
		$R_1 = 7$		$R_2 = 12$		$R_3 = 17$

be useful to employ a *randomized block design*. Using the subjects as blocks, we would hope to eliminate the variability among subjects and thereby increase the amount of information in the experiment. Suppose that three drugs, A, B, and C, are to be compared using a randomized block design. Each of the three drugs is administered to the *same subject* with suitable time lags between the three doses. The order in which the drugs are administered is randomly determined for each subject. Thus, one drug would be administered to a subject and its reaction time would be noted; then after a sufficient length of time, the second drug administered; etc.

Teaching Tip

Present the Friedman test as an alternative to the randomized block analysis of variance procedure presented earlier in the text.

Suppose six subjects are chosen and that the reaction times for each drug are as shown in Table 16.8. To compare the three drugs, we rank the observations within each subject (block) and then compute the rank sums for each of the drugs (treatments). Tied observations within blocks are handled in the usual manner by assigning the average value of the ranks to each of the tied observations.

The null and alternative hypotheses are

H_0: The populations of reaction times are identically distributed for all three drugs

H_a: At least two of the drugs have probability distributions of reaction times that differ in location

The **Friedman F_r-statistic,** which is based on the rank sums for each treatment, is

$$F_r = \frac{12}{bp(p + 1)}\sum R_j^2 - 3b(p + 1)$$

where b is the number of blocks, p is the number of treatments, and R_j is the jth rank sum. For the data in Table 16.8,

$$F_r = \frac{12}{(6)(3)(4)}[(7)^2 + (12)^2 + (17)^2] - 3(6)(4) = 80.33 - 72 = 8.33$$

The Friedman F_r-statistic measures the extent to which the p samples differ with respect to their relative ranks within the blocks. This is more easily seen by writing F_r in an alternative, but equivalent, form:

$$F_r = \frac{12}{bp(p + 1)}\sum b(\bar{R}_j - \bar{R})^2$$

where $\bar{R}_j$ is the mean rank corresponding to treatment j and $\bar{R}$ is the mean of all the ranks (i.e., $\bar{R} = \frac{1}{2}(p + 1)$). Thus, the F_r-statistic is 0 if all treatments have the same

Teaching Tip
Use examples to point out that
ranks are given within each
block of the experiment.
Treatment ranks are then
summed to generate the rank
sums used in calculating the
test statistic.

mean rank and becomes increasingly large as the distance between the sample mean
ranks grows.

As for the Kruskal-Wallis H statistic, the Friedman F_r-statistic has approximately a χ^2 sampling distribution with $(p - 1)$ degrees of freedom. Empirical results show the approximation to be adequate if either b (the number of blocks) or p (the number of treatments) exceeds 5. The Friedman F_r-test for a randomized block design is summarized in the next box.

Suggested Exercise 16.48

Friedman F_r-Test for a Randomized Block Design

H_0: The probability distributions for the p treatments are identical

H_a: At least two of the probability distributions differ in location

$$\text{Test statistic:} \quad F_r = \frac{12}{bp(p + 1)} \sum R_j^2 - 3b(p + 1)$$

where

b = Number of blocks

p = Number of treatments

R_j = Rank sum of the jth treatment; where the rank of each measurement is computed relative to its position *with in its own block*

Rejection region: $F_r > \chi_\alpha^2$ with $(p - 1)$ degrees of freedom

Ties: Assign tied measurements within a block the average of the ranks they would receive if they were unequal but occurred in successive order. For example, if the third-ranked and fourth-ranked measurements are tied, assign each a rank of $(3 + 4)/2 = 3.5$. The number of ties should be small relative to the total number of observations.

Conditions Required for a Valid Friedman F_r-Test

1. The treatments are randomly assigned to experimental units within the blocks.

2. The measurements can be ranked within blocks.

3. The p probability distributions from which the samples within each block are drawn are continuous.

For the drug example, we will use $\alpha = .05$ to form the rejection region:

$$F_r > \chi_{.05}^2 = 5.99147 \text{ (see Figure 16.12)}$$

where $\chi_{.05}^2$ is based on $(p - 1) = 2$ degrees of freedom. Consequently, because the observed value, $F_r = 8.33$, exceeds 5.99147, we conclude that at least two of the three drugs have probability distributions of reaction times that differ in location.

A MINITAB printout of the nonparametric analysis, shown in Figure 16.13, confirms our inference. Both the test statistic and p-value are highlighted on the printout. Since p-value $= .016$ is less than our selected $\alpha = .05$, there is evidence to reject H_0.

Figure 16.12
Rejection region for reaction time example

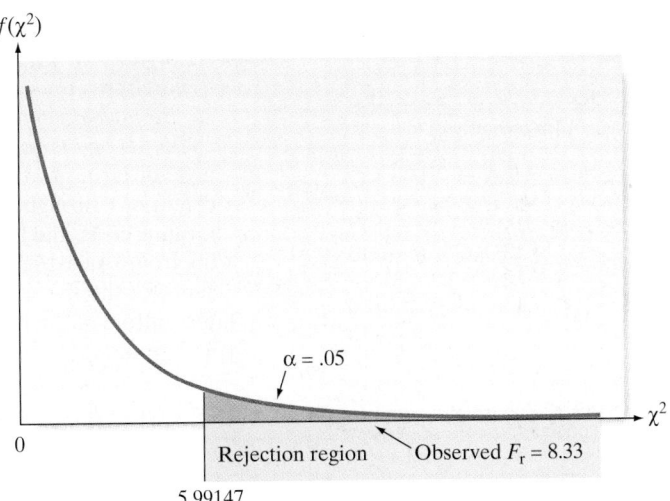

Figure 16.13
MINITAB printout of Friedman test

Friedman Test: REACTIME versus DRUG blocked by SUBJECT

S = 8.33   DF = 2   P = 0.016

| | | | Sum of |
DRUG	N	Est Median	Ranks
A	6	1.5283	7.0
B	6	1.7417	12.0
C	6	1.8950	17.0

Grand median = 1.7217

Now Work   *Exercise 16.46*

■ ■ ■

Clearly, the assumptions for this test—that the measurements are ranked within blocks and that the number of blocks (subjects) is greater than 5—are satisfied. However, we must be sure that the treatments are randomly assigned to blocks. For the procedure to be valid, we assume that the three drugs are administered in a random order to each subject. If this were not true, the difference in the reaction times for the three drugs might be due to the order in which the drugs are given.

Exercises 16.45–16.54

Learning the Mechanics

16.45 Data were collected using a randomized block design with four treatments (A, B, C, and D) and $b = 6$. The following rank sums were obtained:

$$R_A = 11 \quad R_B = 21 \quad R_C = 21 \quad R_D = 7$$

a. How many blocks were used in the experimental design?   6
b. Specify the null and alternative hypotheses that should be used in conducting a hypothesis test to determine whether the probability distributions for at least two of the treatments differ in location.
c. Conduct the test of part **b.** Use $\alpha = .10$. $F_r = 15.2$
d. What is the approximate *p*-value of the test of part **c**?
e. Calculate the mean rank for each of the four treatments and compute the value of the F_r-test statistic according to the formula that utilizes those means. Verify that the test statistic is the same as that you obtained in part **c**.

16.46 Suppose you have used a randomized block design to help you compare the effectiveness of three different treatments, A, B, and C. You obtained the data given in the table and plan to conduct a Friedman F_r-test.

⊛ **LM16_46**

Block	Treatment A	Treatment B	Treatment C
1	9	11	18
2	13	13	13
3	11	12	12
4	10	15	16
5	9	8	10
6	14	12	16
7	10	12	15

a. Specify the null and alternative hypotheses you will test.

b. Specify the rejection region for the test. Use $\alpha = .10$. $F_r > 4.60517$

c. Conduct the test and interpret the results.

16.47 An experiment was conducted using a randomized block design with four treatments and six blocks. The ranks of the measurements within each block are shown in the table. Use the Friedman F_r-test for a randomized block design to determine whether the data provide sufficient evidence to indicate that at least two of the treatment probability distributions differ in location. Test using $\alpha = .05$. $F_r = 13$

⊛ **LM16_47**

Treatment	Block 1	2	3	4	5	6
1	3	3	2	3	2	3
2	1	1	1	2	1	1
3	4	4	3	4	4	4
4	2	2	4	1	3	2

Applying the Concepts—Basic

16.48 A review of farmer involvement in agricultural research was presented in the *Journal of Agricultural, Biological, and Environmental Statistics* (Mar. 2001). In one study, each of six farmers ranked the level of farm production constraint imposed by five conditions: drought, pest damage, weed interference, farming costs, and labor shortage. The rankings, ranging from 1 (least severe) to 5 (most severe), and rank sums for the five conditions are listed in the table at the bottom of the page.

a. Use the rank sums shown in the table to compute the Friedman F_r statistic. $F_r = 17.333$

b. At $\alpha = .05$, find the rejection region for a test to compare the farmer opinion distributions for the five conditions. $F_r > 9.48773$

c. Make the proper conclusion, in the words of the problem.

16.49 Refer to the *Journal of Geography*'s published rankings of regional atlas theme topics, Exercise 16.30 (p. 1094). In addition to high school teachers and university geography alumni, university geography students and representatives of the general public also ranked the 12 thematic topics. The rankings of all four groups are shown in the table on p. 1107. A MINITAB analysis is also provided to compare the atlas theme ranking distributions of the four groups.

a. Locate the rank sums on the printout.

b. Use the rank sums to find the Friedman F_r statistic.

c. Locate the test statistic and associated p-value on the printout.

d. Conduct the test and give the conclusion in the words of the problem.

⊛ **FARM6**

		Condition Drought	Pest Damage	Weed Interference	Farming Costs	Labor Shortage
Farmer	**1**	5	4	3	2	1
	2	5	3	4	1	2
	3	3	5	4	2	1
	4	5	4	1	2	3
	5	4	5	3	2	1
	6	5	4	3	2	1
	Rank sum	27	25	18	11	9

Source: Riley, J., and Fielding, W. J. "An Illustrated Review of Some Farmer Participatory Research Techniques." *Journal of Agricultural, Biological, and Environmental Statistics*, Vol. 6, No. 1, Mar. 2001 (Table 1).

MINITAB Output for Exercise 16.49

Friedman Test: RANK versus GROUP blocked by THEME

```
S = 0.93   DF = 3   P = 0.819
S = 1.08   DF = 3   P = 0.782 (adjusted for ties)

                             Sum
                              of
          GROUP   N  Est Median  Ranks
            1     12    5.1250    27.0
            2     12    6.1250    32.5
            3     12    5.6250    29.0
            4     12    6.1250    31.5

          Grand median = 5.7500
```

ATLAS2

	Rankings			
Theme	High School Teachers	Geography Alumni	Geography Students	General Public
Tourism	10	2	5	1
Physical	2	1	1	5
Transportation	7	3	7	2
People	1	6	2	3
History	2	5	9	4
Climate	6	4	4	8
Forestry	5	8	2	7
Agriculture	7	10	6	9
Fishing	9	7	10	6
Energy	2	8	7	10
Mining	10	11	11	11
Manufacturing	12	12	12	12

Source: Keller, C. P., et al. "Planning the Next Generation of Regional Atlases: Input from Educators." *Journal of Geography*, Vol. 94, No. 3, May/June 1995, p. 413 (Table 1).

16.50 Refer to Exercise 10.51 (p. 602) and the *World Oil* (Jan. 2002) study of rotary oil rigs. Three months were randomly selected and the number of oil rigs running in each of three states—California, Utah, and Alaska—was recorded. The data for the randomized block design are reproduced below. Consider a nonparametric test to compare the distributions of rotary oil rigs running in the three states.

OILRIGS

Month/Year	California	Utah	Alaska
Nov. 2000	27	17	11
Oct. 2001	34	20	14
Nov. 2001	36	15	14

a. State the null and alternative hypothesis for the test.
b. Rank the data within each month; then sum the ranks for each state.

c. Use the rank sums from part **b** to find the value of the test statistic. $F_r = 6$
d. Give the rejection region of the test at $\alpha = .05$. $F_r > 5.99147$
e. State the conclusion in the words of the problem. Does the conclusion agree with that for the ANOVA *F*-test conducted in Exercise 10.51?

Applying the Concepts—Intermediate

16.51 Refer to the Kansas State study designed to investigate the effects of plants on human stress levels, Exercise 10.54 (p. 605). The data on p. 1108 are given as finger temperatures for each of ten students in a dimly lit room under three experimental conditions: presence of a live plant, presence of a plant photo, and absence of a plant (either live or photo). Analyze the data using a nonparametric procedure. Do the students' finger temperatures depend on the experimental condition?

PLANTS

Student	Live Plant	Plant Photo	No Plant (control)
1	91.4	93.5	96.6
2	94.9	96.6	90.5
3	97.0	95.8	95.4
4	93.7	96.2	96.7
5	96.0	96.6	93.5
6	96.7	95.5	94.8
7	95.2	94.6	95.7
8	96.0	97.2	96.2
9	95.6	94.8	96.0
10	95.6	92.6	96.6

Source: Elizabeth Schreiber, Department of Statistics, Kansas State University, Manhattan, Kansas

16.52 The *Journal of the American Mosquito Control Association* (Mar. 1995) reported on a study of the effectiveness of five different types of insecticides in controlling a species of Caribbean mosquito. The resistance ratios (i.e., the dosage of insecticide required to kill 50% of the larvae divided by the known dosage for a susceptible mosquito strain) of the insecticides at each of seven Caribbean locations are reproduced in the table at the bottom of the page. Compare the resistance ratio distributions of the five insecticides using a nonparametric procedure. Are any of the insecticides more effective than any of the others?

16.53 Corrosion of different metals is a problem in many mechanical devices. Three sealers used to help retard the corrosion of metals were tested to see whether there were any differences among them. Samples of 10 different metal compositions were treated with each of the three sealers, and the amount of corrosion was measured after exposure to the same environmental conditions for 1 month. The data are given in the next table. Is there any evidence of a difference in the probability distributions of the amounts of corrosion among the three types of sealer? Use $\alpha = .05$. $F_r = 6.35$

CORRODE

	Sealer		
Metal	1	2	3
1	4.6	4.2	4.9
2	7.2	6.4	7.0
3	3.4	3.5	3.4
4	6.2	5.3	5.9
5	8.4	6.8	7.8
6	5.6	4.8	5.7
7	3.7	3.7	4.1
8	6.1	6.2	6.4
9	4.9	4.1	4.2
10	5.2	5.0	5.1

16.54 Refer to Exercise 10.55 (p. 605) and the *New Technology, Work, and Employment* (July 2001) study of daily worker absentee rates at a jeans plant. Nine weeks were randomly selected and the absentee rate (percentage of workers absent) determined for each day (Monday through Friday) of the work week. The data are reproduced in the table. Conduct a nonparametric analysis of the data to compare the distributions of absentee rates for the five days of the work week. $F_r = 6.778$

JEANS

Week	Monday	Tuesday	Wednesday	Thursday	Friday
1	5.3	0.6	1.9	1.3	1.6
2	12.9	9.4	2.6	0.4	0.5
3	0.8	0.8	5.7	0.4	1.4
4	2.6	0.0	4.5	10.2	4.5
5	23.5	9.6	11.3	13.6	14.1
6	9.1	4.5	7.5	2.1	9.3
7	11.1	4.2	4.1	4.2	4.1
8	9.5	7.1	4.5	9.1	12.9
9	4.8	5.2	10.0	6.9	9.0

Source: Boggis, J. J. "The Eradication of Leisure," *New Technology, Work, and Employment,* Volume 16, Number 2, July 2001 (Table 3).

MOSQUITO

		Insecticide				
		Temephos	Malathion	Fenitrothion	Fenthion	Chlorpyrifos
	Anguilla	4.6	1.2	1.5	1.8	1.5
	Antigua	9.2	2.9	2.0	7.0	2.0
	Dominica	7.8	1.4	2.4	4.2	4.1
Location	Guyana	1.7	1.9	2.2	1.5	1.8
	Jamaica	3.4	3.7	2.0	1.5	7.1
	St. Lucia	6.7	2.7	2.7	4.8	8.7
	Suriname	1.4	1.9	2.0	2.1	1.7

Source: Rawlins, S. C., and Oh Hing Wan, J. "Resistance in Some Caribbean Populations of Aedes aegypti to Several Insecticides." *Journal of the American Mosquito Control Association,* Vol. 11, No. 1, Mar. 1995 (Table 1).

16.7 Spearman's Rank Correlation Coefficient

Teaching Tip

The Spearman's rank correlation coefficient is the nonparametric alternative to simple linear regression.

Suppose 10 new car models are evaluated by two consumer magazines and each magazine ranks the braking systems of the cars from 1 (best) to 10 (worst). We want to determine whether the magazines' ranks are related. Does a correspondence exist between their ratings? If a car is ranked high by magazine 1, is it likely to be ranked high by magazine 2? Or do high rankings by one magazine correspond to low rankings by the other? That is, are the rankings of the magazines *correlated?*

If the rankings are as shown in the "Perfect Agreement" columns of Table 16.9, we immediately notice that the magazines agree on the rank of every car. High ranks correspond to high ranks and low ranks to low ranks. This is an example of *perfect positive correlation* between the ranks. In contrast, if the rankings appear as shown in the "Perfect Disagreement" columns of Table 16.9, high ranks for one magazine correspond to low ranks for the other. This is an example of *perfect negative correlation.*

TABLE 16.9   Brake Rankings of 10 New Car Models by Two Consumer Magazines

Car Model	Perfect Agreement		Perfect Disagreement	
	Magazine 1	Magazine 2	Magazine 1	Magazine 2
1	4	4	9	2
2	1	1	3	8
3	7	7	5	6
4	5	5	1	10
5	2	2	2	9
6	6	6	10	1
7	8	8	6	5
8	3	3	4	7
9	10	10	8	3
10	9	9	7	4

In practice, you will rarely see perfect positive or negative correlation between the ranks. In fact, it is quite possible for the magazines' ranks to appear as shown in Table 16.10. You will note that these rankings indicate some agreement between the consumer magazines, but not perfect agreement, thus indicating a need for a measure of rank correlation.

Spearman's rank correlation coefficient, r_s, provides a measure of correlation between ranks. The formula for this measure of correlation is given in the next box. We also give a formula that is identical to r_s when there are no ties in rankings; this provides a good approximation to r_s when the number of ties is small relative to the number of pairs.

Note that if the ranks for the two magazines are identical, as in the second and third columns of Table 16.9, the differences between the ranks, *d,* will all be 0. Thus,

$$r_s = 1 - \frac{6 \sum d^2}{n(n^2 - 1)} = 1 - \frac{6(0)}{10(99)} = 1$$

TABLE 16.10 **Brake Rankings of New Car Models: Less Than Perfect Agreement**

	Magazine		Difference between Rank 1 And Rank 2	
Car Model	1	2	d	d^2
1	4	5	-1	1
2	1	2	-1	1
3	9	10	-1	1
4	5	6	-1	1
5	2	1	1	1
6	10	9	1	1
7	7	7	0	0
8	3	3	0	0
9	6	4	2	4
10	8	8	0	0
				$\Sigma d^2 = 10$

That is, *perfect positive correlation* between the pairs of ranks is characterized by a Spearman correlation coefficient of $r_s = 1$. When the ranks indicate perfect disagreement, as in the fourth and fifth columns of Table 16.9, $\Sigma d_i^2 = 330$ and

$$r_s = 1 - \frac{6(330)}{10(99)} = -1$$

Thus, *perfect negative correlation* is indicated by $r_s = -1$.

Biography

CHARLES E. SPEARMAN (1863–1945)
Spearman's Correlation

London-born Charles Spearman was educated at Leamington College before joining the British Army. After 20 years as a highly decorated officer, Spearman retired from the army and moved to Germany to begin his study of experimental psychology at the University of Liepzig. At the age of 41 he earned his Ph.D., and ultimately become one of the most influential figures the field of psychology. Spearman was the originator of the classical theory of mental tests and developed the "two-factor" theory of intelligence. These theories were used to develop and support the "Plus-Elevens" tests in England—exams administered to British 11-year-olds that predict whether they should attend a university or technical school. Spearman was greatly influenced by the works of Francis Galton (p. 695); consequently, he developed a strong statistical background. While conducting his research on intelligence, he proposed the rank order correlation coefficient—now called Spearman's correlation coefficient. During his career, Spearman spent time at various universities, including University College (London), Colombia University, Catholic University, and the University of Cairo (Egypt).

Spearman's Rank Correlation Coefficient

$$r_s = \frac{SS_{uv}}{\sqrt{SS_{uu}SS_{vv}}}$$

where

$$SS_{uv} = \sum(u_i - \bar{u})(v_i - \bar{v}) = \sum u_i v_i - \frac{(\sum u_i)(\sum v_i)}{n}$$

$$SS_{uu} = \sum(u_i - \bar{u})^2 = \sum u_i^2 - \frac{(\sum u_i)^2}{n}$$

$$SS_{vv} = \sum(v_i - \bar{v})^2 = \sum v_i^2 - \frac{(\sum v_i)^2}{n}$$

u_i = Rank of the ith observation in sample 1

v_i = Rank of the ith observation in sample 2

n = Number of pairs of observations (number of observations in each sample)

Teaching Tip

A perfect correlation will exist when all the differences are 0. This occurs when both u and v are ranked exactly the same for every observation.

Shortcut Formula for r_s*

$$r_s = 1 - \frac{6\sum d_i^2}{n(n^2 - 1)}$$

where

$d_i = u_i - v_i$ (difference in ranks of ith observations for samples 1 and 2)

For the data of Table 16.10,

$$r_s = 1 - \frac{6\sum d^2}{n(n^2 - 1)} = 1 - \frac{6(10)}{10(99)} = 1 - \frac{6}{99} = .94$$

The fact that r_s is close to 1 indicates that the magazines tend to agree, but the agreement is not perfect.

The value of r_s always falls between −1 and +1, with +1 indicating perfect positive correlation and −1 indicating perfect negative correlation. The closer r_s falls to +1 or −1, the greater the correlation between the ranks. Conversely, the nearer r_s is to 0, the less the correlation.

Note that the concept of correlation implies that two responses are obtained for each experimental unit. In the consumer magazine example, each new car model received two ranks (one for each magazine) and the objective of the study was to determine the degree of positive correlation between the two rankings.

*The shortcut formula is not exact when there are tied measurements, but it is a good approximation when the total number of ties is not large relative to n.

Rank correlation methods can be used to measure the correlation between any pair of variables. If two variables are measured on each of n experimental units, we rank the measurements associated with each variable separately. Ties receive the average of the ranks of the tied observations. Then we calculate the value of r_s for the two rankings. This value measures the rank correlation between the two variables. We illustrate the procedure in Example 16.4.

EXAMPLE 16.4

APPLYING SPEARMAN'S RANK CORRELATION

Problem Manufacturers of perishable foods often use preservatives to retard spoilage. One concern is that too much preservative will change the flavor of the food. Suppose an experiment is conducted using samples of a food product with varying amounts of preservative added. Both length of time until the food shows signs of spoiling and a taste rating are recorded for each sample. The taste rating is the average rating for three tasters, each of whom rates each sample on a scale from 1 (good) to 5 (bad). Twelve sample measurements are shown in Table 16.11.

a. $r_s = -.88$

a. Calculate Spearman's rank correlation coefficient between spoiling time and taste rating.

b. Reject H_0

b. Use a nonparametric test to find out whether the spoilage times and taste ratings are negatively correlated. Use $\alpha = .05$.

Solution **a.** We first rank the days until spoilage, assigning a 1 to the smallest number (26) and a 12 to the largest (109). Similarly, we assign ranks to the 12 taste ratings. [*Note:* The tied taste ratings receive the average of their respective ranks.] Since the number of ties is relatively small, we will use the shortcut formula to calculate r_s. The differences d between the ranks of days until spoilage and the ranks of taste rating are shown in Table 16.11. The squares of the differences, d^2, are also given. Thus,

$$r_s = 1 - \frac{6 \sum d_i^2}{n(n^2 - 1)} = 1 - \frac{6(536.5)}{12(12^2 - 1)} = 1 - 1.88 = -.88$$

 SPOILAGE

TABLE 16.11   Data and Correlations for Example 16.4

Sample	Days Until Spoilage	Rank	Taste Rating	Rank	d	d^2
1	30	2	4.3	11	−9	81
2	47	5	3.6	7.5	−2.5	6.25
3	26	1	4.5	12	−11	121
4	94	11	2.8	3	8	64
5	67	7	3.3	6	1	1
6	83	10	2.7	2	8	64
7	36	3	4.2	10	−7	49
8	77	9	3.9	9	0	0
9	43	4	3.6	7.5	−3.5	12.25
10	109	12	2.2	1	11	121
11	56	6	3.1	5	1	1
12	70	8	2.9	4	4	16
					Total	= 536.5

Note: Tied measurements are assigned the average of the ranks they would be given if they were different but consecutive.

Figure 16.14

SPSS printout of Spearman's rank correlation test

Correlations

			DAYS	TASTE
Spearman's rho	DAYS	Correlation Coefficient	1.000	-.879**
		Sig. (2-tailed)	.	.000
		N	12	12
	TASTE	Correlation Coefficient	-.879**	1.000
		Sig. (2-tailed)	.000	.
		N	12	12

**. Correlation is significant at the 0.01 level (2-tailed).

The value of r_s can also be obtained using a computer. An SPSS printout of the analysis is shown in Figure 16.14. The value of r_s, highlighted on the printout, is $-.879$ and agrees (except for rounding) with our hand-calculated value. This negative correlation coefficient indicates that in this sample an increase in the number of days until spoilage is *associated with* (but is not necessarily the *cause of*) a decrease in the taste rating.

b. If we define ρ as the **population rank correlation coefficient** [i.e., the rank correlation coefficient that could be calculated from all (x, y) values in the population], this question can be answered by conducting the test

H_0: $\rho = 0$ (no population correlation between ranks)

H_a: $\rho < 0$ (negative population correlation between ranks)

Test statistic: r_s (the *sample* Spearman rank correlation coefficient)

To determine a rejection region, we consult Table XVII in Appendix B, which is partially reproduced in Table 16.12. Note that the left-hand column gives values of n, the number of pairs of observations. The entries in the table are values for an upper-tail rejection region, since only positive values are given.

Suggested Exercise 16.59

Teaching Tip

Use examples to point out how the Spearman table is used.

TABLE 16.12   Reproduction of Part of Table XVII in Appendix B: Critical Values of Spearman's Rank Correlation Coefficient

n	$\alpha = .05$	$\alpha = .025$	$\alpha = .01$	$\alpha = .005$
5	.900	—	—	—
6	.829	.886	.943	—
7	.714	.786	.893	—
8	.643	.738	.833	.881
9	.600	.683	.783	.833
10	.564	.648	.745	.794
11	.523	.623	.736	.818
12	.497	.591	.703	.780
13	.475	.566	.673	.745
14	.457	.545	.646	.716
15	.441	.525	.623	.689
16	.425	.507	.601	.666
17	.412	.490	.582	.645
18	.399	.476	.564	.625
19	.388	.462	.549	.608
20	.377	.450	.534	.591

Thus, for $n = 12$ and $\alpha = .05$, the value .497 is the boundary of the upper-tailed rejection region, so that $P(r_s > .497) = .05$ if $H_0: \rho = 0$ is true. Similarly, for negative values of r_s, we have $P(r_s < -.497) = .05$ if $\rho = 0$. That is, we expect to see $r_s < -.497$ only 5% of the time if there is really no relationship between the ranks of the variables. The lower-tailed rejection region is therefore

$$\text{Rejection region } (\alpha = .05): r_s < -.497$$

Since the calculated $r_s = -.876$ is less than $-.497$, we reject H_0 at the $\alpha = .05$ level of significance. That is, this sample provides sufficient evidence to conclude that a negative correlation exists between number of days until spoilage and taste rating of the food product. It appears that the preservative does affect the taste of this food adversely.

Look Back The two-tailed p-value of the test is highlighted on the SPSS printout below to the value of r_s in Figure 16.14. Since the lower-tailed p-value, $p = .000/2 = .000$, is less than $\alpha = .05$, our conclusion is the same: reject H_0.

Now Work   *Exercise 16.58*

■ ■ ■

A summary of Spearman's nonparametric test for correlation is given in the box.

Spearman's Nonparametric Test for Rank Correlation

One-Tailed Test	Two-Tailed Test
$H_0: \rho = 0$	$H_0: \rho = 0$
$H_a: \rho > 0$ (or $H_a: \rho < 0$)	$H_a: \rho \neq 0$

Test statistic: r_s, the sample rank correlation (see the formulas for calculating r_s)

Rejection region: $r_s > r_{s,\alpha}$ (or $r_s < -r_{s,\alpha}$ when $H_a: \rho_s < 0$)	*Rejection region:* $\lvert r_s \rvert > r_{s,\alpha/2}$
where $r_{s,\alpha}$ is the value from Table XVII corresponding to the upper-tail area α and n pairs of observations	where $r_{s,\alpha/2}$ is the value from Table XVII corresponding to the upper-tail area $\alpha/2$ and n pairs of observations

Ties: Assign tied measurements the average of the ranks they would receive if they were unequal but occurred in successive order. For example, if the third-ranked and fourth-ranked measurements are tied, assign each a rank of $(3 + 4)/2 = 3.5$. The number of ties should be small relative to the total number of observations.

Conditions Required for a Valid Spearman's Test

1. The sample of experimental units on which the two variables are measured is randomly selected.
2. The probability distributions of the two variables are continuous.

Statistics in Action Revisited

Testing whether the TCDD Levels in Fat and Plasma of Vietnam Vets are Correlated

The medical researchers who examined the Vietnam War veterans exposed to Agent Orange also wanted an estimate of the correlation between the TCDD level in fat tissue and the TCDD level in plasma. Since the two variables were not normally distributed, they employed Spearman's rank correlation method. The SPSS printout for this analysis is shown in Figure SIA16.5.

The value of r_s (highlighted on the printout) is .774; thus, there appears to be a fairly strong positive correlation between fat and plasma TCDD levels in the sample of Vietnam vets. The one-tailed p-value of the test (also highlighted) is .000, indicating that there is sufficient evidence (at $\alpha = .01$) of a positive association between the two TCDD measures.

Correlations

			FAT	PLASMA
Spearman's rho	FAT	Correlation Coefficient	1.000	.774**
		Sig. (1-tailed)	.	.000
		N	20	20
	PLASMA	Correlation Coefficient	.774**	1.000
		Sig. (1-tailed)	.000	.
		N	20	20

**. Correlation is significant at the 0.01 level (1-tailed).

Figure 16.5

SPSS Spearman rank correlation test for TCDD data

Exercises 16.55–16.65

Learning the Mechanics

16.55 Use Table XVII of Appendix B to find each of the following probabilities:
- **a.** $P(r_s > .508)$ when $n = 22$ .01
- **b.** $P(r_s > .448)$ when $n = 28$ .01
- **c.** $P(r_s \leq .648)$ when $n = 10$ .975
- **d.** $P(r_s < -.738 \text{ or } r_s > .738)$ when $n = 8$ .05

16.56 Specify the rejection region for Spearman's nonparametric test for rank correlation in each of the following situations:
- **a.** $H_0: \rho = 0$; $H_a: \rho \neq 0$, $n = 10$, $\alpha = .05$
- **b.** $H_0: \rho = 0$; $H_a: \rho > 0$, $n = 20$, $\alpha = .025$
- **c.** $H_0: \rho = 0$; $H_a: \rho < 0$, $n = 30$, $\alpha = .01$

16.57 Compute Spearman's rank correlation coefficient for each of the following pairs of sample observations:

a.
x	33	61	20	19	40
y	26	36	65	25	35	$r_s = .4$

b.
x	89	102	120	137	41
y	81	94	75	52	136	$r_s = -.9$

c.
x	2	15	4	10
y	11	2	15	21	$r_s = -.2$

d.
x	5	20	15	10	3
y	80	83	91	82	87	$r_s = .2$

16.58 The following sample data were collected on variables x and y:

x	0	3	0	−4	3	0	4
y	0	2	2	0	3	1	2

- **a.** Specify the null and alternative hypotheses that should be used in conducting a hypothesis test to determine whether the variables x and y are correlated.
- **b.** Conduct the test of part **a** using $\alpha = .05$.
- **c.** What is the approximate p-value of the test of part **b**? $.05 < p < .10$
- **d.** What assumptions are necessary to ensure the validity of the test of part **b**?

Applying the Concepts—Basic

16.59 Refer to the *Nutrition & Food Science* (Vol. 30, 2000) study of the trend in prime-time television advertising, Exercise 12.17 (p. 709). The rate per hour of prime-time TV commercials for food products during 1971, 1977, 1988, 1992, and 1998 are listed in the table. Consider the correlation between the rate of food ads per hour (y) and the number of years since 1970 (x).

⊙ **FOODADS**

Year	Number of Years since 1970, x	Food Ads, y (rate per hour)
1971	1	5.4
1977	7	3.0
1988	18	6.5
1992	22	6.0
1998	28	6.0

Source: Byrd-Bredbenner, C., and Grasso, D. "Trends in US Prime-Time Television Food Advertising across Three Decades," *Nutrition & Food Science*, Vol. 30, No. 2, 2000, p. 61 (Table 1).

a. Rank the five x-values.
b. Rank the five y-values.
c. Use the ranks, parts **a** and **b**, to find the value of Spearman's rank correlation coefficient. Interpret the result. $r_s = .564$
d. Give the rejection region for testing whether rate of food ads and number of years since 1970 are rank correlated. Use $\alpha = .10$. $r_s > .900$ or $r_s < -.900$
e. State the conclusion of the test in the words of the problem.

16.60 Two expert wine tasters were asked to rank six brands of wine. Their rankings are shown in the table. Do the data present sufficient evidence to indicate a positive correlation in the rankings of the two experts?

⊙ **WINETASTE**

Brand	Expert 1	Expert 2
A	6	5
B	5	6
C	1	2
D	3	1
E	2	4
F	4	3

Applying the Concepts—Intermediate

16.61 Refer to the orange juice quality study, Exercise 12.18 (p. 709). Recall that a manufacturer that has developed a quantitative index of the "sweetness" of orange juice is investigating the relationship between the sweetness index and the amount of water soluble pectin in the orange juice it produces. The data for 24 production runs at a juice manufacturing plant are reproduced in the next table.

a. Calculate Spearman's rank correlation coefficient between the sweetness index and the amount of pectin. Interpret the result. $r_s = -.485$

b. Conduct a nonparametric test to determine whether there is a negative association between the sweetness index and the amount of pectin. Use $\alpha = .01$.

⊙ **OJUICE**

Run	Sweetness Index	Pectin (ppm)	Run	Sweetness Index	Pectin (ppm)
1	5.2	220	13	5.8	306
2	5.5	227	14	5.5	259
3	6.0	259	15	5.3	284
4	5.9	210	16	5.3	383
5	5.8	224	17	5.7	271
6	6.0	215	18	5.5	264
7	5.8	231	19	5.7	227
8	5.6	268	20	5.3	263
9	5.6	239	21	5.9	232
10	5.9	212	22	5.8	220
11	5.4	410	23	5.8	246
12	5.6	256	24	5.9	241

Note: The data in the table are authentic. For confidentiality reasons, the manufacturer cannot be disclosed.

16.62 Metropolitan areas with many corporate headquarters are finding it easier to transition from a manufacturing economy to a service economy through job growth in small companies and subsidiaries that service the corporate parent. James O. Wheeler of the University of Georgia studied the relationship between the number of corporate headquarters in eleven metropolitan areas and the number of subsidiaries located there (*Growth and Change*, Spring 1988). He hypothesized that there would be a positive relationship between the variables.

⊙ **METRO**

Metropolitan Area	No. of Parent Companies	No. of Subsidiaries
New York	643	2,617
Chicago	381	1,724
Los Angeles	342	1,867
Dallas–Ft. Worth	251	1,238
Detroit	216	890
Boston	208	681
Houston	192	1,534
San Francisco	141	899
Minneapolis	131	492
Cleveland	128	579
Denver	124	672

Source: Wheeler, J. O. "The Corporate Role of Large Metropolitan Areas in the United States." *Growth and Change*, Spring 1988, pp. 75–88.

a. Calculate Spearman's rank correlation coefficient for the data in the table above. What does it indicate about Wheeler's hypothesis?
b. To conduct a formal test of Wheeler's hypothesis using Spearman's rank correlation coefficient, certain assumptions must hold. What are they? Do they appear to hold? Explain.

16.63 *The Wall Street Journal* (Feb. 7, 2001) reported on a Harris Interactive, Inc. survey of consumers to rate the reputations of America's most visible companies. The 1999 and 2000 ranks of 15 randomly selected companies are listed in the accompanying table. Conduct a test to determine if the 1999 and 2000 reputation ranks are positively correlated. Use $\alpha = .05$.

COREP

Company	1999 Rank	2000 Rank
Johnson & Johnson	1	1
Anheuser-Busch	14	6
Disney	10	8
Microsoft	15	9
FedEx	21	13
Wal-Mart	6	14
Coca-Cola	2	16
McDonalds	24	24
Yahoo!	19	27
Sears	29	35
America Online	26	39
Kmart	37	41
Toyota	28	19
Home Depot	8	4
IBM	17	7

Source: Harris Interactive, the Reputation Institute.

16.64 An *employee suggestion system* is a formal process for capturing, analyzing, implementing, and recognizing employee-proposed organizational improvements. (The first known system was implemented by the Yale and Towne Manufacturing Company of Stamford, Connecticut, in 1880.) Using data from the National Association of Suggestion Systems, D. Carnevale and B. Sharp examined the strengths of the relationships between the extent of employee participation in suggestion plans and cost savings realized by employers (*Review of Public Personnel Administration,* Spring 1993). The data in the table at right are representative of the data they analyzed for a sample of federal, state, and local government agencies. Savings are calculated from the first year measurable benefits were observed.

a. Explain why the savings data used in this study may understate the total benefits derived from the implemented suggestions.

b. Carnevale and Sharp concluded that a significant moderate positive relationship exists between participation rates and cost savings rates in public sector suggestion systems. Do you agree? Test using $\alpha = .01$.

c. Justify the statistical methodology you used in part **b.**

SUGGEST

Employee Involvement (% of all employees submitting suggestions)	Savings Rate (% of total budget)
10.1%	8.5%
6.2	6.0
16.3	9.0
1.2	0.0
4.8	5.1
11.5	6.1
.6	1.2
2.8	4.5
8.9	5.4
20.2	15.3
2.7	3.8

Source: Data adapted from Carnevale, D. G., and Sharp, B. S. "The Old Employee Suggestion Box." *Review of Public Personnel Administration,* Spring 1993, pp. 82–92.

16.65 To investigate the standards used by health maintenance organizations (HMOs) in interpreting crisis intervention, a comprehensive questionnaire survey of 145 national HMOs was conducted (*Medical Care,* Jan. 1985). Each HMO was asked to "write a brief, descriptive definition of situations or states you would include as qualifying for 'crisis intervention.'" The researchers sorted these situations into 10 categories and then asked three experienced clinicians to rate each category for two criteria: validity of crisis intervention (i.e., is the situation defined really a "crisis") and clarity of guidelines for offering service. A four-point rating scale was provided for both criteria. The mean ratings for the 10 categories on both the crisis intervention and clarity scales are given in the table below. Is there evidence of a positive relationship between the mean crisis intervention and mean clarity ratings? Test using $\alpha = .05$.

CRISIS

Category (Situation)	Crisis Intervention Rating (1 = definitely a crisis, 4 = definitely not a crisis)	Clarity Rating (1 = very clear guideline, 4 = very unclear guideline)
Psychosis	1.31	1.33
Drug/alcohol abuse	1.33	1.29
Depression/anxiety	1.48	1.59
Emphasis on acuteness	1.76	2.50
Insistence on "short-term" response	2.48	3.22
Suicide	1.13	1.32
Family problems	2.59	2.30
Violence/harm	1.06	1.86
Miscellaneous	2.60	2.33
Nondefinition	3.57	3.57

Source: Cheifetz, D. I., and Salloway, J. C. "Crisis Intervention: Interpretation and Practice by HMO." *Medical Care,* Vol. 23, No. 1, Jan. 1985, pp. 89–93.

Quick Review

[Note: Items marked with an asterisk (*) are from the optional section in this Chapter.]

Key Terms

Distribution-free tests 1070
*Friedman F_r-statistic 1103

Kruskal-Wallis H-test 1095
Nonparametrics 1070
Parametric tests 1070
Population rank correlation
  coefficient 1113
Rank statistics 1071

Rank sum 1079
Sign test 1071
Spearman's rank correlation
  coefficient 1109
Wilcoxon rank sum test 1078
Wilcoxon signed rank test 1088

Key Formulas Test	Test Statistic	Large Sample Approximation	
Sign	S = number of sample measurements greater than (or less than) hypothesized median, η_0	$z = \dfrac{(S - .5) - .5n}{.5\sqrt{n}}$	1073, 1074
Wilcoxon rank sum	T_1 = rank sum of sample 1 or T_2 = rank sum of sample 2	$z = \dfrac{T_1 - \dfrac{n_1(n_1 + n_2 + 1)}{2}}{\sqrt{\dfrac{n_1 n_2(n_1 + n_2 + 1)}{12}}}$	1080, 1083
Wilcoxon signed ranks	T_- = negative rank sum or T_+ = positive rank sum	$z = \dfrac{T_+ - \dfrac{n(n + 1)}{4}}{\sqrt{\dfrac{n(n + 1)(2n + 1)}{24}}}$	1089, 1091
Kruskal-Wallis	$H = \dfrac{12}{n(n + 1)}\sum \dfrac{R_j^2}{n_j} - 3(n + 1)$		1098–1099
* Friedman	$F_r = \dfrac{12}{bp(p + 1)}\sum R_j^2 - 3b(p + 1)$		1104
Spearman rank correlation (shortcut formula)	$r_s = 1 - \dfrac{6 * d_i^2}{n(n^2 - 1)}$ where d_i = difference in ranks of ith observations for samples 1 and 2		1111

Chapter Summary Notes

- **Distribution-free tests** do not rely on assumptions about the probability distribution of the sampled population
- **Nonparametrics**—distribution-free tests that are based on **rank statistics**
- *One-sample* nonparametric test for the population median—**sign test**
- Nonparametric test for *two independent samples*—**Wilcoxon rank sum test**

- Nonparametric test for *matched pairs*—**Wilcoxon signed rank test**
- Nonparametric test for a *completely randomized design*—**Kruskal-Wallis test**
- Nonparametric test for a *randomized block design*—**Friedman test**
- Nonparametric test for *rank correlation*—**Spearman's test**

LANGUAGE LAB

Symbol	Pronunciation	Description
η	eta	Population median
S		Test statistic for sign test (see Key Formulas)
T_1		Sum of ranks of observations in sample 1
T_2		Sum of ranks of observations in sample 2
T_L		Critical lower Wilcoxon rank sum value
T_U		Critical upper Wilcoxon rank sum value
T_+		Sum of ranks of positive differences of paired observations
T_-		Sum of ranks of negative differences of paired observations
T_0		Critical value of Wilcoxon signed ranks test
R_j		Rank sum of observations in sample j
H		Test statistic for Kruskal-Wallis test (see Key Formulas)
F_r		*Test statistic for Friedman test (see key Formulas)
r_s		Spearman's rank correlation coefficient (see Key Formulas)
ρ	rho	Population correlation coefficient

Supplementary Exercises 16.66–16.85

[Note: Exercises marked with an asterisk (*) are from the optional section in this chapter.]

Learning the Mechanics

16.66 The data for three independent random samples are shown in the table. It is known that the sampled populations are not normally distributed. Use an appropriate test to determine whether the data provide sufficient evidence to indicate that at least two of the populations differ in location. Test using $\alpha = .05$.

⊕ **LM16_66**

Sample from Population 1		Sample from Population 2		Sample from Population 3	
18	15	12	34	87	50
32	63	33	18	53	64
43		10		65	77

16.67 A random sample of nine pairs of observations are recorded on two variables, x and y. The data are shown in the next table.

a. Do the data provide sufficient evidence to indicate that ρ, the rank correlation between x and y, differs from 0? Test using $\alpha = .05$. $r_s = .40$

b. Do the data provide sufficient evidence to indicate that the probability distribution for x is shifted to the right of that for y? Test using $\alpha = .05$. $T_- = 1.5$

⊕ **LM16_67**

Pair	x	y	Pair	x	y
1	19	12	6	29	10
2	27	19	7	16	16
3	15	7	8	22	10
4	35	25	9	16	18
5	13	11			

16.68 Two independent random samples produced the measurements listed in the table. Do the data provide sufficient evidence to conclude that there is a difference between the locations of the probability distributions for the sampled populations? Test using $\alpha = .05$.

⊕ **LM16_68**

Sample from Population 1		Sample from Population 2	
1.2	1.0	1.5	1.9
1.9	1.8	1.3	2.7
.7	1.1	2.9	3.5
2.5			

*16.69 An experiment was conducted using a randomized block design with five treatments and four blocks. The data are shown in the table on p. 1120. Do the data provide sufficient evidence to conclude that at least two of the treatment probability distributions differ in location? Test using $\alpha = .05$. $F_r = 14.9$

LM16_69

	Block			
Treatment	1	2	3	4
1	75	77	70	80
2	65	69	63	69
3	74	78	69	80
4	80	80	75	86
5	69	72	63	77

Applying the Concepts—Basic

16.70 A state highway patrol was interested in knowing whether frequent patrolling of highways substantially reduces the number of speeders. Two similar interstate highways were selected for the study—one heavily patrolled and the other only occasionally patrolled. After 1 month, random samples of 100 cars were chosen on each highway, and the number of cars exceeding the speed limit was recorded. This process was repeated on five randomly selected days. The data are shown in the following table.

HWPATROL

Day	Highway 1 (heavily patrolled)	Highway 2 (occasionally patrolled)
1	35	60
2	40	36
3	25	48
4	38	54
5	47	63

a. Do the data provide evidence to indicate that the heavily patrolled highway tends to have fewer speeders per 100 cars than the occasionally patrolled highway? Test using $\alpha = .05$. $T_+ = 1$

b. Use the paired t-test with $\alpha = .05$ to compare the population mean number of speeders per 100 cars for the two highways. What assumptions are necessary for this procedure to be valid? $t = -2.96$

16.71 An experiment was conducted to compare two print types, A and B, to determine whether type A is easier to read. Ten subjects were randomly divided into two groups of five. Each subject was given the same material to read, one group receiving the material printed with type A, the other group receiving print type B. The times necessary for each subject to read the material (in seconds) are shown in the table.

Do the data provide sufficient evidence to indicate that print type A is easier to read? Test using $\alpha = .05$.

PRINTAB

Type A:	95,	122,	101,	99,	108
Type B:	110,	102,	115,	112,	120

16.72 Refer to Exercise 16.71. Test the research hypothesis that the median of the type A probability distribution exceeds 100 seconds. Repeat the test for the type B probability distribution. Use $\alpha = .05$ for both tests.

16.73 Suppose a company wants to study how personality relates to leadership. Four supervisors (1–4) with different types of personalities are selected. Several employees are then selected from the group supervised by each and asked to rate the leader of their group on a scale from 1 to 20 (20 signifies highly favorable). The resulting data are shown in the table.

SUPER4

1	2	3	4
20	17	16	8
19	11	15	12
20	13	13	10
18	15	18	14
17	14	11	9
16		10	

a. What type of experimental design was employed? Identify the key elements of the experiment: response, factor(s), factor type(s), treatments, and experimental units.
b. Test to determine whether evidence exists that the probability distributions of ratings differ for at least two of the four supervisors. Use $\alpha = .05$.
c. What assumptions are necessary to ensure the validity of the test?
d. Do the results of the test warrant further comparisons of the pairs of supervisors? If so, compare all pairs of probability distributions using $\alpha = .05$ for each comparison. Does one supervisor appear to be most popular?

Applying the Concepts—Intermediate

16.74 According to the National Restaurant Association, hamburgers are the number one selling fast-food item in the United States (*Newark Star-Ledger*, Mar. 17, 1997). An economist studying the fast-food buying habits of Americans paid graduate students to stand outside two suburban McDonald's restaurants near Boston and ask departing customers whether they spent more or less than $2.25 on hamburger products for their lunch. Twenty answered "less than"; 50 said "more than"; and 10 refused to answer the question.

a. Is there sufficient evidence to conclude that the median amount spent for hamburgers at lunch at McDonald's is less than $2.25? $z = -3.71$
b. Does your conclusion apply to all Americans who eat lunch at McDonald's? Justify your answer.
c. What assumptions must hold to ensure the validity of your test in part **a?**

16.75 A study published in the *Journal of Business Communications* (Fall 1985) found that video teleconferencing may be a more effective method of dealing with complex group problem-solving tasks than face-to-face meetings. Ten groups of four people each were randomly assigned both to a specific communication setting (face-to-face or video teleconferencing) and to one of two specific complex problems. Upon completion of the problem-solving task, the same groups were placed in the alternative communication setting and asked to complete the second problem-solving task. The percentage of each problem task correctly completed was recorded for each group, with the results given in the table.

⚙ **FACEVT**

Group	Face-to-Face	Video Teleconferencing
1	65%	75%
2	82	80
3	54	60
4	69	65
5	40	55
6	85	90
7	98	98
8	35	40
9	85	89
10	70	80

a. What type of experimental design was used in this study?   Paired difference

b. Specify the null and alternative hypotheses that should be used in determining whether the data provide sufficient evidence to conclude that the problem-solving performance of video teleconferencing groups is superior to that of groups that interact face-to-face.

c. Conduct the hypothesis test of part **b.** Use $\alpha = .05$. Interpret the results of your test in the context of the problem. $T_+ = 3.5$

d. What is the p-value of the test in part **c?**

16.76 An economist is interested in knowing whether property tax rates differ among three types of school districts—urban, suburban, and rural. A random sample of several districts of each type produced the data in the table at the top of the next column (rate is in mills, where 1 mill = $1/1,000). Do the data indicate a difference in the level of property taxes among the three types of school districts? Use $\alpha = .05$.

⚙ **PROPTAX**

Urban	Suburban	Rural
4.3	5.9	5.1
5.2	6.7	4.8
6.2	7.6	3.9
5.6	4.9	6.2
3.8	5.2	4.2
5.8	6.8	4.3
4.7		

16.77 The length of time required for a human subject to respond to a new painkiller was tested in the following manner. Seven randomly selected subjects were assigned to receive both aspirin and the new drug. The two treatments were spaced in time and assigned in random order. The length of time (in minutes) required for a subject to indicate that he or she could feel pain relief was recorded for both the aspirin and the drug. The data are shown in the next table. Do the data provide sufficient evidence to indicate that the probability distribution of the times required to obtain relief with aspirin is shifted to the right of the probability distribution of the times required to obtain relief with the new drug?

⚙ **PAINKILL.DAT**

Subject	Aspirin	New Drug
1	15	7
2	20	14
3	12	13
4	20	11
5	17	10
6	14	16
7	17	11

16.78 Exercise 12.85 (p. 755) described a calibration study undertaken by the Minnesota Department of Transportation to evaluate a new weigh-in-motion scale. Pearson's product moment correlation coefficient was used to measure the strength of the relationship between the static weight of a truck and the truck's weight as measured by the weigh-in-motion equipment. The data (in thousands of pounds) are repeated in the table below.

⚙ **TRUCKWTS**

Truck	Static Weight, x	Weigh-in-Motion Reading Prior to Calibration Adjustment, y_1	Weigh-in-Motion Reading After Calibration Adjustment, y_2
1	27.9	26.0	27.8
2	29.1	29.9	29.1
3	38.0	39.5	37.8
4	27.0	25.1	27.1
5	30.3	31.6	30.6
6	34.5	36.2	34.3
7	27.8	25.1	26.9
8	29.6	31.0	29.6
9	33.1	35.6	33.0
10	35.5	40.2	35.0

a. Calculate Spearman's rank correlation coefficient for x and y_1 and for x and y_2. Interpret, in the context of the problem, the values you obtain. Compare your results with those of Exercise 10.76, part **c**.

b. In the context of this problem, what circumstances would result in Spearman's rank correlation coefficient being exactly 1? Being exactly 0?

16.79 Weevils cause millions of dollars worth of damage each year to cotton crops. Two chemicals (A and B) designed to control weevil populations were applied, one to each of two fields of cotton. After three months, 10 plots of equal size were randomly selected within each field and the percentage of cotton plants with weevil damage was recorded for each. Do the data in the accompanying table provide sufficient evidence to indicate a difference in location among the distributions of damage rates corresponding to the two chemical treatments? Use $\alpha = .05$.

WEEVIL

A		B	
10.8	9.8	22.3	20.4
15.6	16.7	19.5	23.6
19.2	19.0	18.6	21.2
17.9	20.3	24.3	19.8
18.3	19.4	19.9	22.6

16.80 Many water treatment facilities supplement the natural fluoride concentration with hydrofluosilicic acid in order to reach a target concentration of fluoride in drinking water. Certain levels are thought to enhance dental health, but very high concentrations can be dangerous. Suppose that one such treatment plant targets .75 milligrams per liter (mg/L) for their water. The plant tests 25 samples each day to determine whether the median level differs from the target.

a. Set up the null and alternative hypotheses.

b. Set up the test statistic and rejection region using $\alpha = .10$.

c. Explain the implication of a Type I error in the context of this application. A Type II error.

d. Suppose that one day's samples result in 18 values that exceed .75 mg/L. Conduct the test and state the appropriate conclusion in the context of this application. $s = 18$; $p = .044$

e. When it was suggested to the plant's supervisor that a t-test should be used to conduct the daily test, she replied that the probability distribution of the fluoride concentrations was "heavily skewed to the right." Show graphically what she meant by this, and explain why this is a reason to prefer the sign test to the t-test.

16.81 A hotel had a problem with people reserving rooms for a weekend and then not honoring their reservations (no-shows). As a result, the hotel developed a new reservation and deposit plan that it hoped would reduce the number of no-shows. One year after the policy was initiated, management evaluated its effect in comparison with the old policy. Compare the records given in the table on the number of no-shows for the 10 nonholiday weekends preceding the institution of the new policy and the 10 nonholiday weekends preceding the evaluation time. Has the situation improved under the new policy? Test at $\alpha = .05$. $T_{Before} = 132.5$

NOSHOWS

Before		After	
10	11	4	4
5	8	3	2
3	9	8	5
6	6	5	7
7	5	6	1

16.82 A manufacturer wants to determine whether the number of defectives produced by its employees tends to increase as the day progresses. Unknown to the employees, a complete inspection is made of every item that was produced on one day, and the hourly fraction defective is recorded. The resulting data are given in the accompanying table. Do they provide evidence that the fraction defective increases as the day progresses? Test at the $\alpha = .05$ level. $r_s = .929$

DEFECTS

Hour	Fraction Defective
1	.02
2	.05
3	.03
4	.08
5	.06
6	.09
7	.11
8	.10

*16.83 A union wants to determine the preferences of its members before negotiating with management. Ten union members are randomly selected, and an extensive questionnaire is completed by each member. The responses to the various aspects of the questionnaire will enable the union to rank in order of importance the items to be negotiated. The rankings are shown in the table on p. 1123. Conduct a nonparametric test to determine whether evidence exists that the probability distributions of ratings differ for at least two of the four negotiable items. Use $\alpha = .05$.

16.84 A savings and loan association is considering three locations in a large city as potential office sites. The company has hired a marketing firm to compare the incomes of people living in the area surrounding each site. The market researchers interview 10 households chosen at random in each area to determine the type

UNION

Person	More Pay	Job Stability	Fringe Benefits	Shorter Hours
1	2	1	3	4
2	1	2	3	4
3	4	3	2	1
4	1	4	2	3
5	1	2	3	4
6	1	3	4	2
7	2.5	1	2.5	4
8	3	1	4	2
9	1.5	1.5	3	4
10	2	3	1	4

of job, length of employment, etc., of those in the households who work. This information enables them to estimate the annual income of each household, as shown in the table (in thousands of dollars).

OFFICES

Site 1		Site 2		Site 3	
34.3	36.2	39.3	42.2	34.5	38.3
35.5	43.5	45.5	103.5	29.3	43.3
32.1	34.7	50.2	47.9	37.2	36.7
28.3	38.0	72.1	41.2	33.2	40.0
40.5	35.1	48.6	44.0	32.6	35.2

a. What type of design was utilized for this experiment?

b. Use the appropriate nonparametric test to compare the treatments. Specify the hypotheses and interpret the results in terms of this experiment. Use $\alpha = .05$.

c. Does the result of your test warrant further comparison of the pairs of treatments? If so, compare the pairs using the appropriate nonparametric technique and $\alpha = .05$ for each comparison. Interpret the results in terms of this experiment. Yes

d. What assumptions are necessary to ensure the validity of the nonparametric procedures you employed? How do they compare with the assumptions that would have to be satisfied in order to use the appropriate parametric technique to analyze this experiment?

16.85 The perceptions of accounting professors with respect to the present and desired importance of various fac-

tors considered in promotion and tenure decisions at major universities was investigated in the *Journal of Accounting Education* (Spring 1983). One hundred fifteen professors at universities with accredited doctoral programs responded to a mailed questionnaire. The questionnaire asked the professors to rate (1) the actual importance placed on 20 factors in the promotion and tenure decisions at their universities and (2) how they believe the factors *should* be weighted. Responses were obtained on a five-point scale ranging from "no importance" to "extreme importance." The resulting ratings were averaged and converted to the rankings shown in the table. Calculate Spearman's rank correlation coefficient for the data and carefully interpret its value in the context of the problem. $r_s = .8574$

TENURE

Factor	Actual	Ideal
I. Teaching (and related items):		
Teaching performance	6	1
Advising and counseling students	19	15
Students' complaints/praise	14	17
II. Research:		
Number of journal articles	1	6.5
Quality of journal articles	4	2
Refereed publications:		
a. Applied studies	5	4
b. Theoretical empirical studies	2	3
c. Educationally oriented	11	8
Papers at professional meetings	10	12
Journal editor or reviewer	9	10
Other (textbooks, etc.)	7.5	11
III. Service and professional interaction:		
Service to profession	15	9
Professional/academic awards	7.5	6.5
Community service	18	19
University service	16	16
Collegiality/cooperativeness	12	13
IV. Other:		
Academic degrees attained	3	5
Professional certification	17	14
Consulting activities	20	20
Grantsmanship	13	18

Source: Campbell, D. K., Gaertner, J., and Vecchio, R. P. "Perceptions of Promotion and Tenure Criteria: A Survey of Accounting Educators." *Journal of Accounting Education*, Vol. 1, Spring 1983, pp. 83–92.

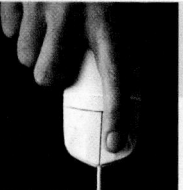

Using Technology

16.1 Nonparametric Tests Using SPSS

Sign Test or Signed Ranks Test: The SPSS spreadsheet file that contains the sample data should contain two quantitative variables. (*Note*: For the sign test, one variable is the variable to be analyzed and the other variable will have the value of the hypothesized median for all cases. For the signed ranks test, the two variables represent the two variables in the paired difference.) Click on the "Analyze" button on the SPSS menu bar, then click on "Nonparametric Tests" and "Two Related Samples", as shown in Figure 16.S.1.

The resulting dialog box appears as shown in Figure 16.S.2. Select the two quantitative variables of interest so that the difference appears in the "Test Pair(s) List" box. Under "Test Type", select the "Sign" option for a sign test or the "Wilcoxon" option for a signed ranks test. Click "OK" to generate the SPSS printout.

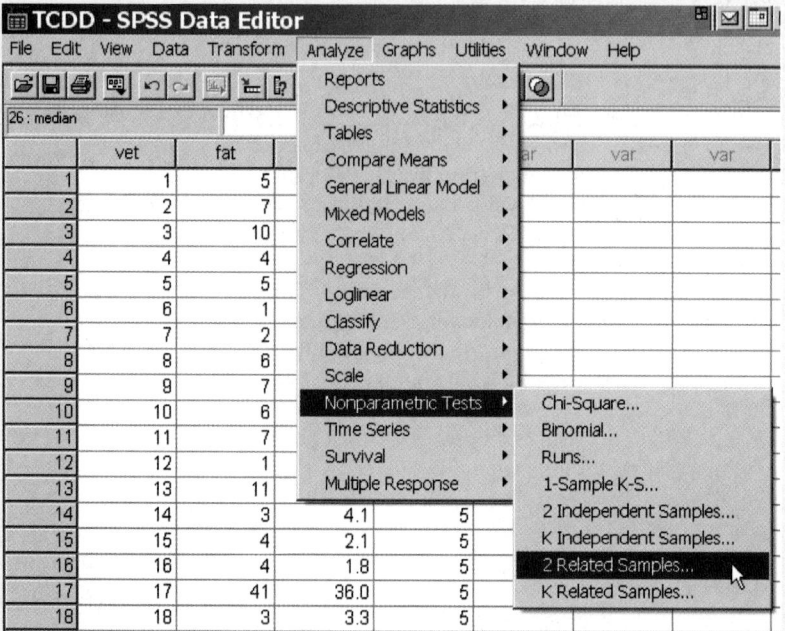

Figure 16.S.1
SPSS menu options for a sign or signed ranks test

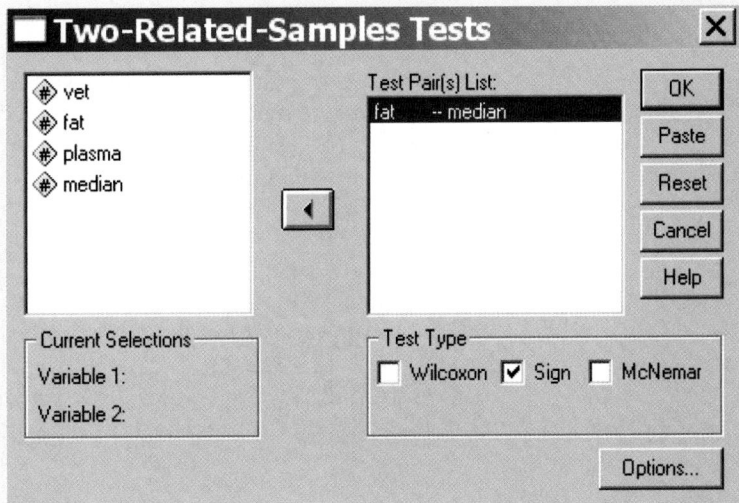

Figure 16.S.2
SPSS Two-related-samples dialog box

Rank Sum Test:

The SPSS spreadsheet file that contains the sample data should contain one quantitative variable and one qualitative variable with either two numerical coded values (e.g., 1 and 2) or two short categorical levels (e.g., "yes" and "no"). These two values represent the two groups or populations to be compared. Click on the "Analyze" button on the SPSS menu bar, then click on "Nonparametric Tests" and "2 Independent Samples" (see Figure 16.S.1). The resulting dialog box appears as shown in Figure 16.S.3.

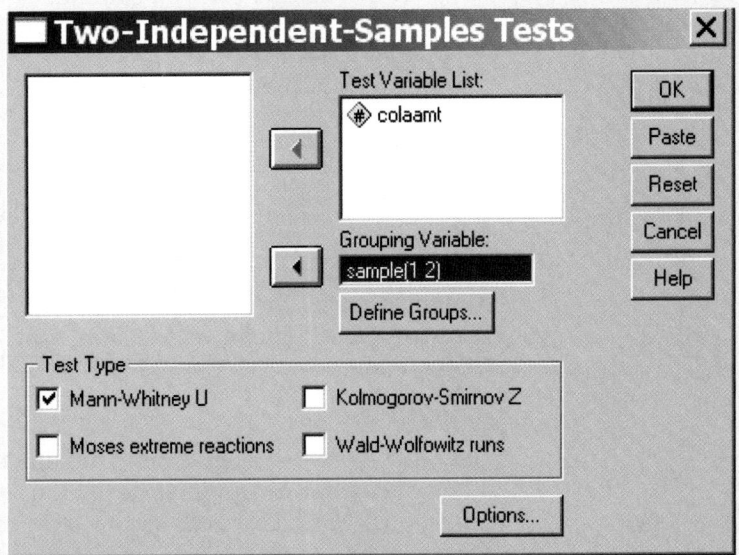

Figure 16.S.3
SPSS Two-independent-samples dialog box

Specify the quantitative variable of interest in the "Test Variable List" box and the qualitative variable in the "Grouping Variable" box. Click the "Define Groups" button, and specify the values of the two groups in the resulting dialog box. Then click "Continue" to return to the "Two-Independent-Samples" dialog screen. Select the "Mann-Whitney U" option under "Test Type", then click "OK" to generate the SPSS printout.

Kruskal-Wallis Test:

The SPSS spreadsheet file that contains the completely randomized design data should contain one quantitative variable (the response, or dependent, variable) and one factor variable with at least two levels. (These values must be numbers, e.g., 1, 2, 3, etc.) Click on the "Analyze" button on the SPSS menu bar, then click on "Nonparametric Tests" and "K Related Samples" (see Figure 16.S.1). The resulting dialog box appears as shown in Figure 16.S.4.

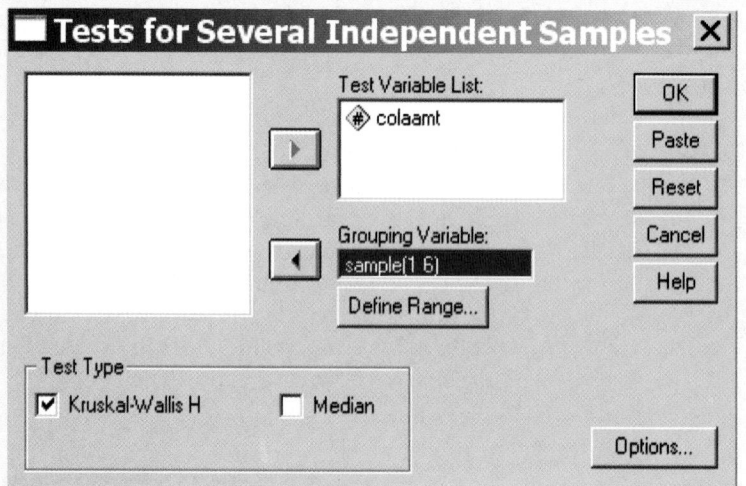

Figure 16.S.4
SPSS K-independent-samples box

Specify the response variable in the "Test Variable List" box and the factor variable in the "Grouping Variable" box. Click the "Define Range" button, and specify the values of the grouping factor in the resulting dialog box. Then click "Continue" to return to the "K-Independent-Samples" dialog screen. Select the "Kruskal-Wallis" option under "Test Type", then click "OK" to generate the SPSS printout.

Friedman Test:

The SPSS spreadsheet file that contains the randomized block design data should contain k quantitative variables, representing the k treatments to be compared. (*Note*: The cases in the rows represent the blocks.) Click on the "Analyze" button on the SPSS menu bar, then click on "Nonparametric Tests" and "K Related Samples" (see Figure 16.S.1). The resulting dialog box appears as shown in Figure 16.S.5. Specify the treatment variables in the "Test

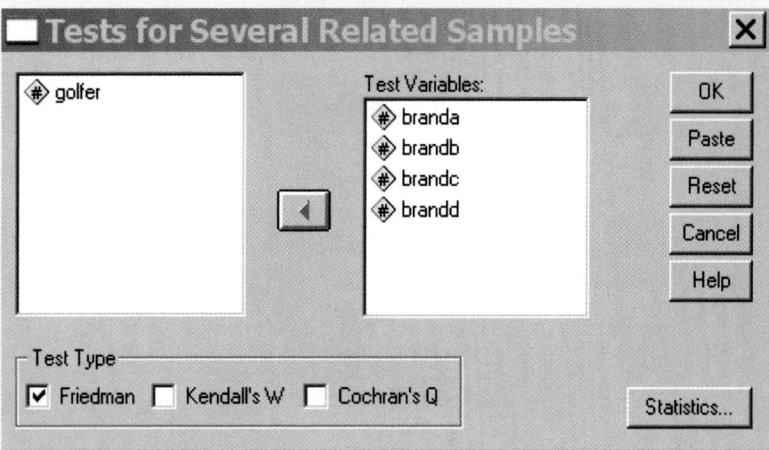

Figure 16.S.5
SPSS K-related-samples dialog box

Variables" box and select the "Friedman" option under "Test Type". Click "OK" to generate the SPSS printout.

Rank Correlation:

To obtain Spearman's rank correlation coefficient for the two quantitative variables of interest, click on the "Analyze" button on the main menu bar, then click on "Correlate" and "Bivariate". The resulting dialog box appears in Figure 16.S.6. Enter the variables of interest in the "Variables" box, check the "Spearman" option under "Correlation Coefficients", then click "OK" to obtain the SPSS printout.

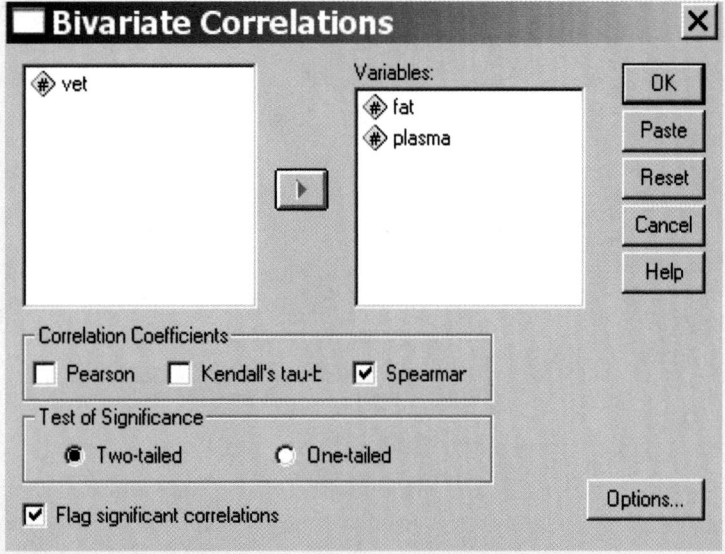

Figure 16.S.6
SPSS correlation dialog box

16.2 Nonparametric Tests Using MINITAB

Sign Test:

The MINITAB worksheet file with the sample data should contain a single quantitative variable. Click on the "Stat" button on the MINITAB menu bar, then click on "Nonparametrics" and "1-Sample Sign", as shown in Figure 16.M.1.

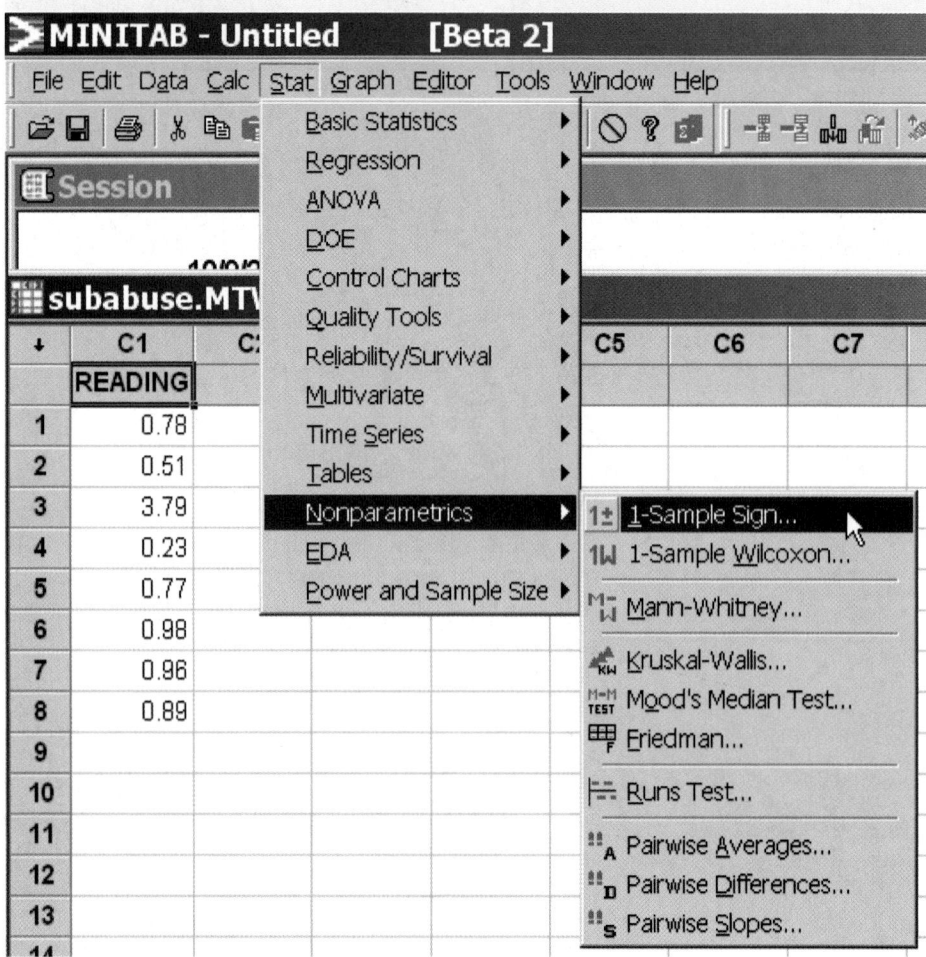

Figure 16.M.1
MINITAB nonparametric menu options

The resulting dialog box appears as shown in Figure 16.M.2. Enter the quantitative variable to be analyzed in the "Variables" box. Select the "Test median" option and specify the hypothesized value of the median and the form of the alternative hypothesis ("not equal", "less than", or "greater than"). Click "OK" to generate the MINITAB printout.

Rank Sum Test:

The MINITAB worksheet file with the sample data should contain two quantitative variables, one for each of the two samples being compared. Click on the "Stat" button on the MINITAB menu bar, then click on "Nonparametrics" and "Mann-Whitney" (see Figure 16.M.1). The resulting dialog box appears as shown in Figure 16.M.3.

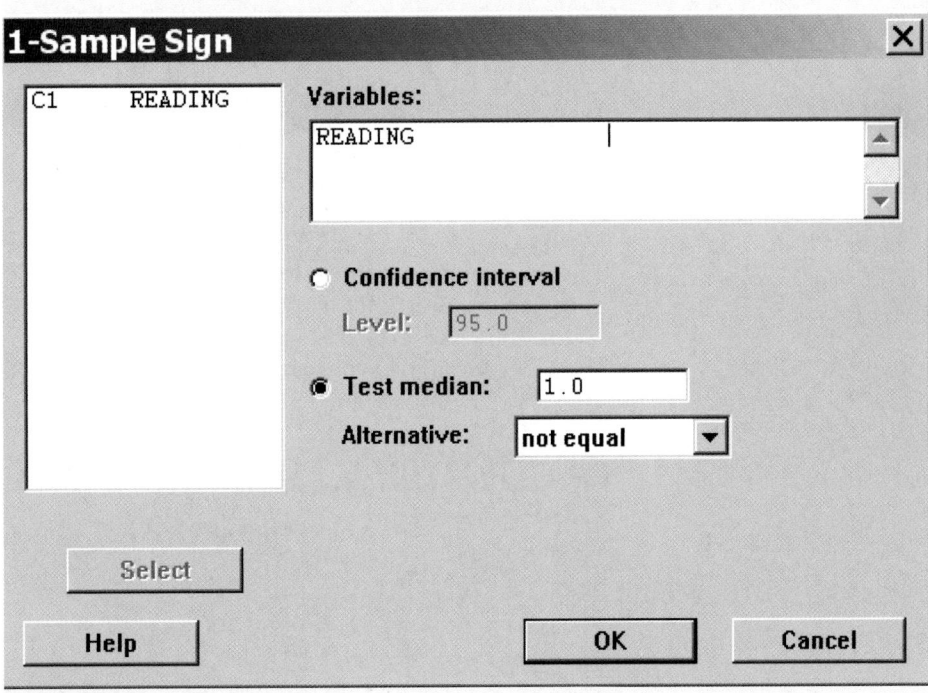

Figure 16.M.2
MINITAB 1-sample sign dialog box

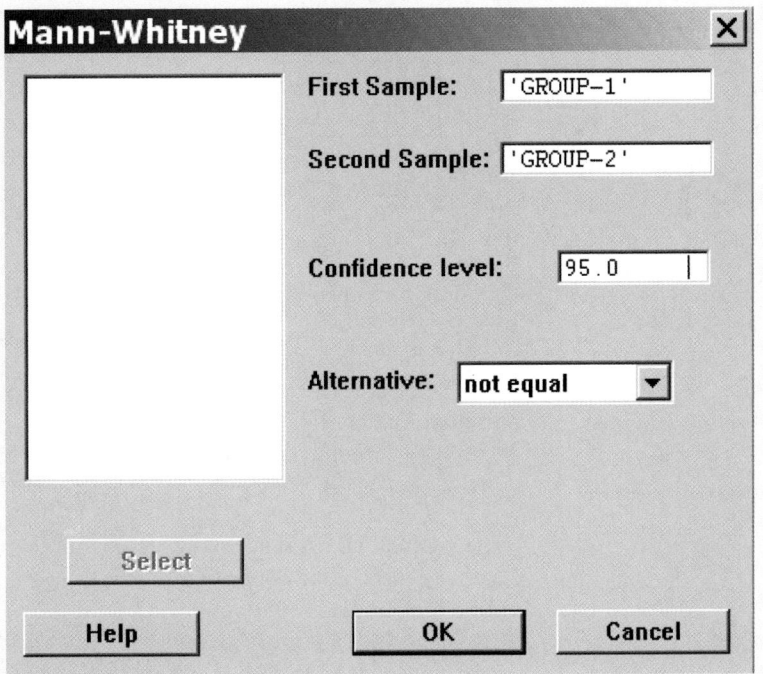

Figure 16.M.3
MINITAB Mann-Whitney dialog box

Specify the variable for the first sample in the "First Sample" box and the variable for the second sample in the "Second Sample" box. Specify the form of the alternative hypothesis ("not equal", "less than", or "greater than"), then click "OK" to generate the MINITAB printout.

Signed Ranks Test:

The MINITAB worksheet file with the matched-pairs data should contain two quantitative variables, one for each of the two groups being compared. You will need to compute the difference between these two variables and save it in a column on the worksheet. (Use the "Calc" button on the MINITAB menu bar.) Next, click on the "Stat" button on the MINITAB menu bar, then click on "Nonparametrics" and "1-Sample Wilcoxon" (see Figure 16.M.1). The resulting dialog box appears as shown in Figure 16.M.4.

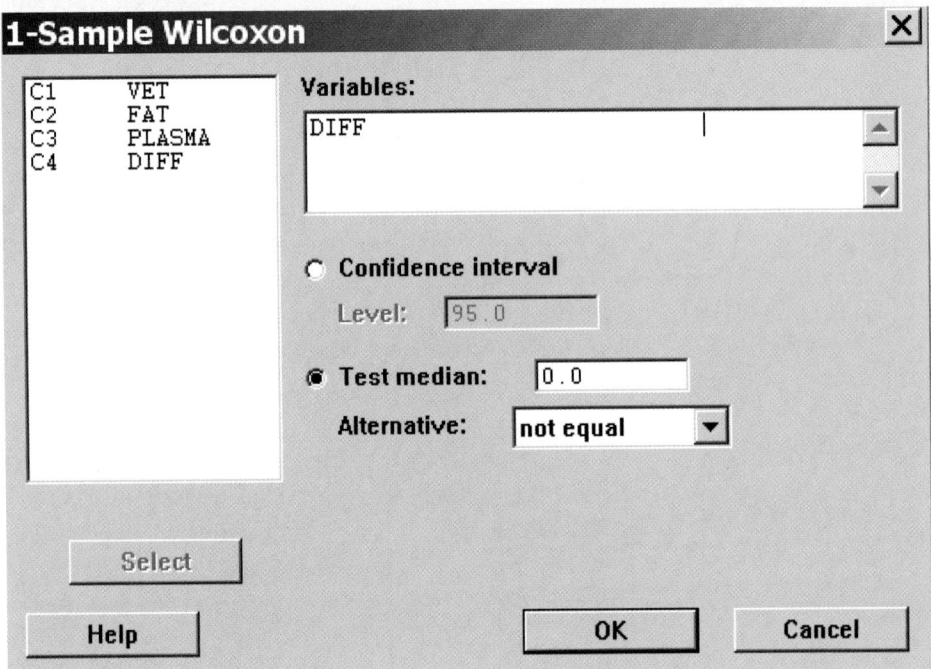

Figure 16.M.4
MINITAB 1-sample Wilcoxon dialog box

Enter the variable representing the paired differences in the "Variables" box. Select the "Test median" option and specify the hypothesized value of the median as "0". Select the form of the alternative hypothesis ("not equal", "less than", or "greater than"), then click "OK" to generate the MINITAB printout.

Kruskal-Wallis Test:

The MINITAB worksheet file that contains the completely randomized design data should contain one quantitative variable (the response, or dependent, variable) and one factor variable with at least two levels. Click on the "Stat" button on the MINITAB menu bar, then click on "Nonparametrics" and "Kruskal-Wallis" (see Figure 16.M.1). The resulting dialog box appears as shown in Figure 16.M.5. Specify the response variable in the "Response" box and the factor variable in the "Factor" box. Click "OK" to generate the MINITAB printout.

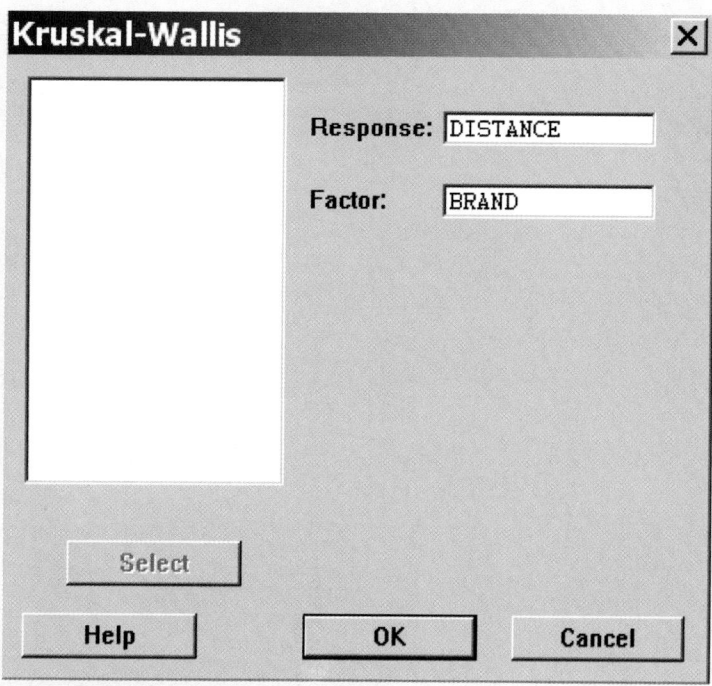

Figure 16.M.5
MINITAB Kruskal-Wallis dialog box

Friedman Test:

The MINITAB spreadsheet file that contains the randomized block design data should contain one quantitative variable (the response, or dependent, variable) and one factor variable and one blocking variable. Click on the "Stat" button on the MINITAB menu bar, then click on "Nonparametrics" and "Friedman" (see Figure 16.M.1). The resulting dialog box appears as shown in Figure 16.M.6. Specify the response, treatment, and blocking variables in the appropriate boxes, then click "OK" to generate the MINITAB printout.

Rank Correlation:

To obtain Spearman's rank correlation coefficient in MINITAB, you must first rank the values of the two quantitative variables of interest. Click the "Calc" button on the MINITAB menu bar, and create two additional columns, one for the ranks of the *x*-variable and one for the ranks of the *y*-variable. (Use the "Rank" function on the MINITAB calculator.) Next, click on the "Stat" button on the main menu bar, then click on "Basic Statistics" and "Correlation". The resulting dialog box appears in Figure 16.M.7. Enter the ranked variables in the "Variables" box and unselect the "Display p-values" option. Click "OK" to obtain the MINITAB printout. (You will need to look up the critical value of Spearman's rank correlation to conduct the test.)

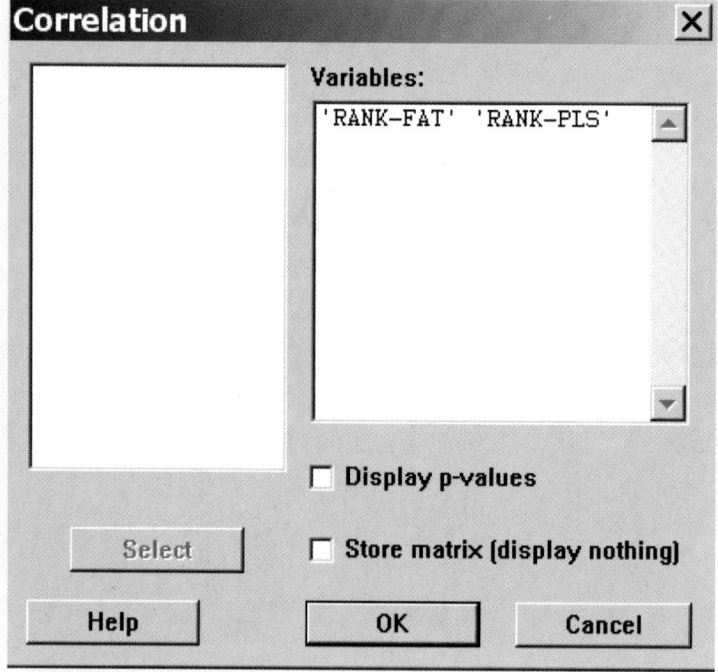

Figure 16.M.6
MINITAB Friedman dialog box

Figure 16.M.7
MINITAB correlation dialog box

16.3 Nonparametric Tests Using EXCEL/PHStat2

Note: Only the Wilcoxon rank sum test and Kruskal-Wallis *H*-test are available in EXCEL with the PHStat add-in.

Rank Sum Test:

The EXCEL workbook with the sample data should contain two quantitative variables (columns), one for each of the two samples being compared. Click on the "PHStat" button on the EXCEL menu bar, then click on "Two-Sample Tests" and "Wilcoxon Rank Sum Test", as shown in Figure 16.E.1. The resulting dialog box appears as shown in Figure 16.E.2.

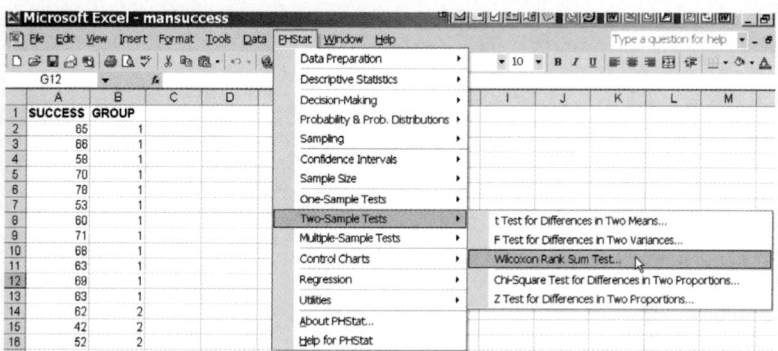

Figure 16.E.1

EXCEL menu options for the rank sum test

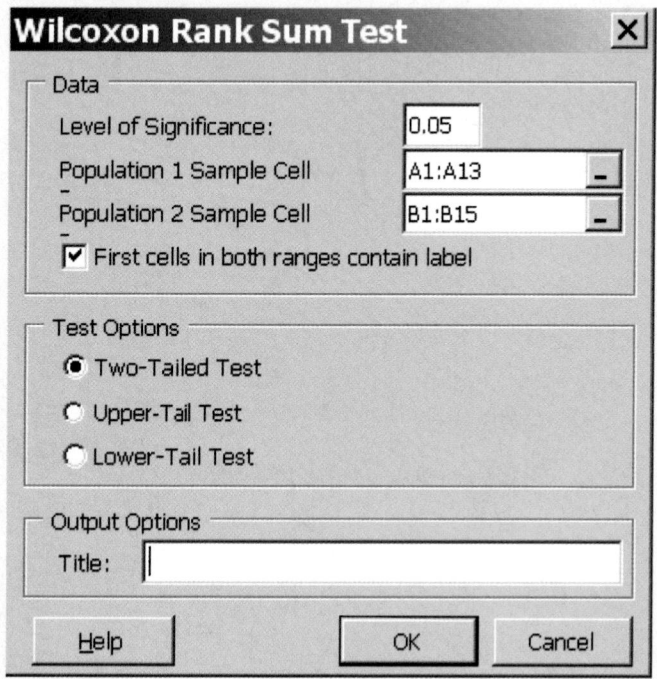

Figure 16.2

EXCEL Wilcoxon rank sum test dialog box

On the dialog box, specify the significance level of the test, enter the cell ranges for the two samples, and select the type of test ("Two-tailed", "Upper-tailed", or "Lower-tailed"). Click "OK" to generate the EXCEL printout.

Kruskal-Wallis Test:

The EXCEL workbook that contains the completely randomized design data should contain *k* quantitative variables (columns), one for each of the *k* samples being compared. Click on the "PHStat" button on the EXCEL menu bar, then click on "Multi-Sample Tests" and "Kruskal-Wallis Rank Test", as shown in Figure 16.E.3. The resulting dialog box appears as shown in Figure 16.E.4.

On the dialog box, specify the significance level of the test and enter the cell range for the *k* samples. Click "OK" to generate the EXCEL printout.

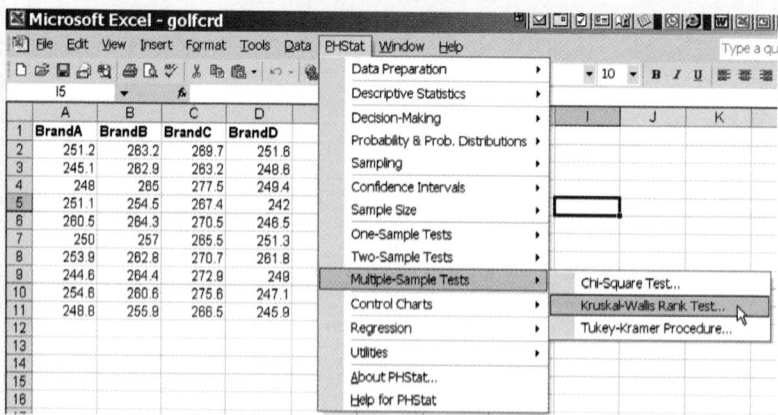

Figure 16.3
EXCEL menu options for the Kruskal-Wallis test

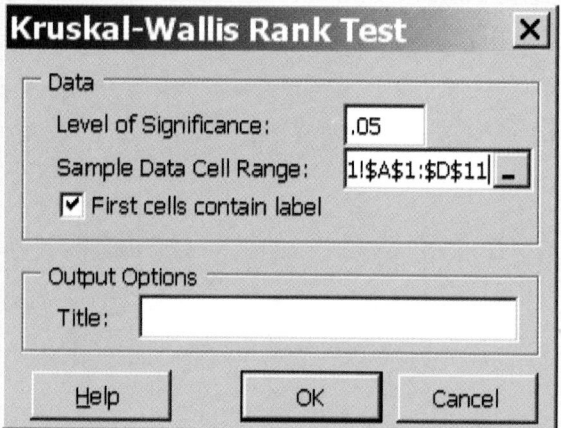

Figure 16.4
EXCEL Kruskal-Wallis rank test dialog box

REFERENCES

Agresti, A., and Agresti, B. F. *Statistical Methods for the Social Sciences*, 2nd ed. San Francisco: Dellen, 1986.

Conover, W. J. *Practical Nonparametric Statistics*, 2nd ed. New York: Wiley, 1980.

Daniel, W. W. *Applied Nonparametric Statistics*, 2nd ed. Boston: PWS-Kent, 1990.

Dunn, O. J. "Multiple Comparisons Using Rank Sums," *Technometrics*, Vol. 6, 1964.

Friedman, M. "The Use of Ranks to Avoid the Assumption of Normality Implicit in the Analysis of Variance." *Journal of the American Statistical Association*, Vol. 32, 1937.

Gibbons, J. D. *Nonparametric Statistical Inference*, 2nd ed. New York: McGraw-Hill, 1985.

Hollander, M., and Wolfe, D. A. *Nonparametric Statistical Methods*. New York: Wiley, 1973.

Kruskal, W. H., and Wallis, W. A. "Use of Ranks in One-Criterion Variance Analysis." *Journal of the American Statistical Association*, Vol. 47, 1952.

Lehmann, E. L. *Nonparametrics: Statistical Methods Based on Ranks*. San Francisco: Holden-Day, 1975.

Marascuilo, L. A., and McSweeney, M. *Nonparametric and Distribution-Free Methods for the Social Sciences*. Monterey, CA: Brooks/Cole, 1977.

Wilcoxon, F., and Wilcox, R. A. "Some Rapid Approximate Statistical Procedures." The American Cyanamid Co., 1964.

Appendix A
Basic Counting Rules

Sample points associated with many experiments have identical characteristics. If you can develop a counting rule to count the number of sample points, it can be used to aid in the solution of many probability problems. For example, many experiments involve sampling n elements from a population of N. Then, as explained in Section 3.1, we can use the formula

$$\binom{N}{n} = \frac{N!}{n!(N-n)!}$$

to find the number of different samples of n elements that could be selected from the total of N elements. This gives the number of sample points for the experiment.

Here, we give you a few useful counting rules. You should learn the characteristics of the situation to which each rule applies. Then, when working a probability problem, carefully examine the experiment to see whether you can use one of the rules.

Learning how to decide whether a particular counting rule applies to an experiment takes patience and practice. If you want to develop this skill, try to use the rules to solve some of the exercises in Chapter 3. Proofs of the rules below can be found in the text by W. Feller listed in the references to Chapter 3.

Multiplicative Rule

You have k sets of different elements, n_1 in the first set, n_2 in the second set, ..., and n_k in the kth set. Suppose you want to form a sample of k elements *by taking one element from each of the* k *sets*. The number of different samples that can be formed is the product

$$n_1 \cdot n_2 \cdot n_3 \cdot \cdots \cdot n_k$$

EXAMPLE A.1   APPLYING THE MULTIPLICATIVE RULE

Problem   A product can be shipped by four airlines and each airline can ship via three different routes. How many distinct ways exist to ship the product?

Solution   A method of shipment corresponds to a pairing of one airline and one route. Therefore, $k = 2$, the number of airlines is $n_1 = 4$, the number of routes is $n_2 = 3$, and the number of ways to ship the product is

$$n_1 \cdot n_2 = (4)(3) = 12$$

Look Back How the multiplicative rule works can be seen by using a tree diagram, introduced in Section 3.6. The airline choice is shown by three branching lines in Figure A.1.

Figure A.1

Tree diagram for
airline example

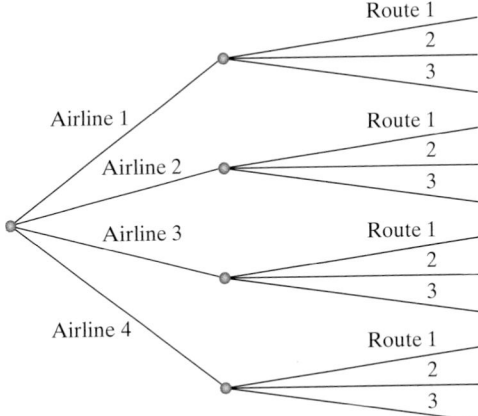

EXAMPLE A.2

APPLYING THE MULTIPLICATIVE RULE

Problem You have twenty candidates for three different executive positions, E_1, E_2, and E_3. How many different ways could you fill the positions?

Solution For this example, there are $k = 3$ sets of elements:

Set 1: The candidates available to fill position E_1

Set 2: The candidates remaining (after filling E_1) that are available to fill E_2

Set 3: The candidates remaining (after filling E_1 and E_2) that are available to fill E_3

The numbers of elements in the sets are $n_1 = 20$, $n_2 = 19$, and $n_3 = 18$. Thus, the number of different ways to fill the three positions is

$$n_1 \cdot n_2 \cdot n_3 = (20)(19)(18) = 6{,}480$$

■ ■ ■

Partitions Rule

You have a *single* set of N distinctly different elements, and you want to partition it into k sets, the first set containing n_1 elements, the second containing n_2 elements, ..., and the kth containing n_k elements. The number of different partitions is

$$\frac{N!}{n_1! n_2! \cdot \, \cdots \, \cdot n_k!} \text{ where } n_1 + n_2 + n_3 + \cdots + n_k = N$$

EXAMPLE A.3

APPLYING THE PARTITIONS RULE

Problem You have twelve construction workers available for three job sites. Suppose you want to assign three workers to job 1, four to job 2, and five to job 3. How many different ways could you make this assignment?

Solution For this example, $k = 3$ (corresponding to the $k = 3$ job sites), $N = 12$, and $n_1 = 3$, $n_2 = 4$, $n_3 = 5$. Then, the number of different ways to assign the workers to the job sites is

$$\frac{N!}{n_1! n_2! n_3!} = \frac{12!}{3! 4! 5!} = \frac{12 \cdot 11 \cdot 10 \cdot \, \cdots \, \cdot 3 \cdot 2 \cdot 1}{(3 \cdot 2 \cdot 1)(4 \cdot 3 \cdot 2 \cdot 1)(5 \cdot 4 \cdot 3 \cdot 2 \cdot 1)} = 27{,}720$$

■ ■ ■

Combinations Rule

The combinations rule given in Chapter 3 is a special case ($k = 2$) of the partitions rule. That is, sampling is equivalent to partitioning a set of N elements into $k = 2$ groups: elements that appear in the sample and those that do not. Let $n_1 = n$, the number of elements in the sample, and $n_2 = N - n$, the number of elements remaining. Then the number of different samples of n elements that can be selected from N is

$$\frac{N!}{n_1! n_2!} = \frac{N!}{n!(N - n)!} = \binom{N}{n}$$

This formula was given in Section 3.1.

EXAMPLE A.4

APPLYING THE COMBINATIONS RULE

Problem   How many samples of four fire fighters can be selected from a group of 10?

Solution   We have $N = 10$ and $n = 4$; then

$$\binom{N}{n} = \binom{10}{4} = \frac{10!}{4!6!} = \frac{10 \cdot 9 \cdot 8 \cdot \cdots \cdot 3 \cdot 2 \cdot 1}{(4 \cdot 3 \cdot 2 \cdot 1)(6 \cdot 5 \cdot \cdots \cdot 2 \cdot 1)} = 210$$

■ ■ ■

Appendix B
Tables

Contents

TABLE I Random Numbers

Row	1	2	3	4	5	6	7	8	9	10	11	12	13	14
1	10480	15011	01536	02011	81647	91646	69179	14194	62590	36207	20969	99570	91291	90700
2	22368	46573	25595	85393	30995	89198	27982	53402	93965	34095	52666	19174	39615	99505
3	24130	48360	22527	97265	76393	64809	15179	24830	49340	32081	30680	19655	63348	58629
4	42167	93093	06243	61680	07856	16376	39440	53537	71341	57004	00849	74917	97758	16379
5	37570	39975	81837	16656	06121	91782	60468	81305	49684	60672	14110	06927	01263	54613
6	77921	06907	11008	42751	27756	53498	18602	70659	90655	15053	21916	81825	44394	42880
7	99562	72905	56420	69994	98872	31016	71194	18738	44013	48840	63213	21069	10634	12952
8	96301	91977	05463	07972	18876	20922	94595	56869	69014	60045	18425	84903	42508	32307
9	89579	14342	63661	10281	17453	18103	57740	84378	25331	12566	58678	44947	05585	56941
10	85475	36857	53342	53988	53060	59533	38867	62300	08158	17983	16439	11458	18593	64952
11	28918	69578	88231	33276	70997	79936	56865	05859	90106	31595	01547	85590	91610	78188
12	63553	40961	48235	03427	49626	69445	18663	72695	52180	20847	12234	90511	33703	90322
13	09429	93969	52636	92737	88974	33488	36320	17617	30015	08272	84115	27156	30613	74952
14	10365	61129	87529	85689	48237	52267	67689	93394	01511	26358	85104	20285	29975	89868
15	07119	97336	71048	08178	77233	13916	47564	81056	97735	85977	29372	74461	28551	90707
16	51085	12765	51821	51259	77452	16308	60756	92144	49442	53900	70960	63990	75601	40719
17	02368	21382	52404	60268	89368	19885	55322	44819	01188	65255	64835	44919	05944	55157
18	01011	54092	33362	94904	31273	04146	18594	29852	71585	85030	51132	01915	92747	64951
19	52162	53916	46369	58586	23216	14513	83149	98736	23495	64350	94738	17752	35156	35749
20	07056	97628	33787	09998	42698	06691	76988	13602	51851	46104	88916	19509	25625	58104
21	48663	91245	85828	14346	09172	30168	90229	04734	59193	22178	30421	61666	99904	32812
22	54164	58492	22421	74103	47070	25306	76468	26384	58151	06646	21524	15227	96909	44592
23	32639	32363	05597	24200	13363	38005	94342	28728	35806	06912	17012	64161	18296	22851
24	29334	27001	87637	87308	58731	00256	45834	15398	46557	41135	10367	07684	36188	18510
25	02488	33062	28834	07351	19731	92420	60952	61280	50001	67658	32586	86679	50720	94953
26	81525	72295	04839	96423	24878	82651	66566	14778	76797	14780	13300	87074	79666	95725
27	29676	20591	68086	26432	46901	20849	89768	81536	86645	12659	92259	57102	80428	25280
28	00742	57392	39064	66432	84673	40027	32832	61362	98947	96067	64760	64584	96096	98253
29	05366	04213	25669	26422	44407	44048	37937	63904	45766	66134	75470	66520	34693	90449
30	91921	26418	64117	94305	26766	25940	39972	22209	71500	64568	91402	42416	07844	69618
31	00582	04711	87917	77341	42206	35126	74087	99547	81817	42607	43808	76655	62028	76630
32	00725	69884	62797	56170	86324	88072	76222	36086	84637	93161	76038	65855	77919	88006
33	69011	65795	95876	55293	18988	27354	26575	08625	40801	59920	29841	80150	12777	48501
34	25976	57948	29888	88604	67917	48708	18912	82271	65424	69774	33611	54262	85963	03547
35	09763	83473	73577	12908	30883	18317	28290	35797	05998	41688	34952	37888	38917	88050

(continued)

TABLE I Continued

Row \ Column	1	2	3	4	5	6	7	8	9	10	11	12	13	14
36	91576	42595	27958	30134	04024	86385	29880	99730	55536	84855	29080	09250	79656	73211
37	17955	56349	90999	49127	20044	59931	06115	20542	18059	02008	73708	83517	36103	42791
38	46503	18584	18845	49618	02304	51038	20655	58727	28168	15475	56942	53389	20562	87338
39	92157	89634	94824	78171	84610	82834	09922	25417	44137	48413	25555	21246	35509	20468
40	14577	62765	35605	81263	39667	47358	56873	56307	61607	49518	89656	20103	77490	18062
41	98427	07523	33362	64270	01638	92477	66969	98420	04880	45585	46565	04102	46880	45709
42	34914	63976	88720	82765	34476	17032	87589	40836	32427	70002	70663	88863	77775	69348
43	70060	28277	39475	46473	23219	53416	94970	25832	69975	94884	19661	72828	00102	66794
44	53976	54914	06990	67245	68350	82948	11398	42878	80287	88267	47363	46634	06541	97809
45	76072	29515	40980	07391	58745	25774	22987	80059	39911	96189	41151	14222	60697	59583
46	90725	52210	83974	29992	65831	38857	50490	83765	55657	14361	31720	57375	56228	41546
47	64364	67412	33339	31926	14883	24413	59744	92351	97473	89286	35931	04110	23726	51900
48	08962	00358	31662	25388	61642	34072	81249	35648	56891	69352	48373	45578	78547	81788
49	95012	68379	93526	70765	10592	04542	76463	54328	02349	17247	28865	14777	62730	92277
50	15664	10493	20492	38391	91132	21999	59516	81652	27195	48223	46751	22923	32261	85653
51	16408	81899	04153	53381	79401	21438	83035	92350	36693	31238	59649	91754	72772	02338
52	18629	81953	05520	91962	04739	13092	97662	24822	94730	06496	35090	04822	86774	98289
53	73115	35101	47498	87637	99016	71060	88824	71013	18735	20286	23153	72924	35165	43040
54	57491	16703	23167	49323	45021	33132	12544	41035	80780	45393	44812	12512	98931	91202
55	30405	83946	23792	14422	15059	45799	22716	19792	09983	74353	68668	30429	70735	25499
56	16631	35006	85900	98275	32388	52390	16815	69290	82732	38480	73817	32523	41961	44437
57	96773	20206	42559	78985	05300	22164	24369	54224	35083	19687	11052	91491	60383	19746
58	38935	64202	14349	82674	66523	44133	00697	35552	35970	19124	63318	29686	03387	59846
59	31624	76384	17403	53363	44167	64486	64758	75366	76554	31601	12614	33072	60332	92325
60	78919	19474	23632	27889	47914	02584	37680	20801	72152	39339	34806	08930	85001	87820
61	03931	33309	57047	74211	63445	17361	62825	39908	05607	91284	68833	25570	38818	46920
62	74426	33278	43972	10110	89917	15665	52872	73823	73144	88662	88970	74492	51805	99378
63	09066	00903	20795	95452	92648	45454	09552	88815	16553	51125	79375	97596	16296	66092
64	42238	12426	87025	14267	20979	04508	64535	31355	86064	29472	47689	05974	52468	16834
65	16153	08002	26504	41744	81959	65642	74240	56302	00033	67107	77510	70625	28725	34191
66	21457	40742	29820	96783	29400	21840	15035	34537	33310	06116	95240	15957	16572	06004
67	21581	57802	02050	89728	17937	37621	47075	42080	97403	48626	68995	43805	33386	21597
68	55612	78095	83197	33732	05810	24813	86902	60397	16489	03264	88525	42786	05269	92532
69	44657	66999	99324	51281	84463	60563	79312	93454	68876	25471	93911	25650	12682	73572
70	91340	84979	46949	81973	37949	61023	43997	15263	80644	43942	89203	71795	99533	50501

(continued)

TABLE I   Continued

Row \ Column	1	2	3	4	5	6	7	8	9	10	11	12	13	14
71	91227	21199	31935	27022	84067	05462	35216	14486	29891	68607	41867	14951	91696	85065
72	50001	38140	66321	19924	72163	09538	12151	06878	91903	18749	34405	56087	82790	70925
73	65390	05224	72958	28609	81406	39147	25549	48542	42627	45233	57202	94617	23772	07896
74	27504	96131	83944	41575	10573	08619	64482	73923	36152	05184	94142	25299	84387	34925
75	37169	94851	39117	89632	00959	16487	65536	49071	39782	17095	02330	74301	00275	48280
76	11508	70225	51111	38351	19444	66499	71945	05422	13442	78675	84081	66938	93654	59894
77	37449	30362	06694	54690	04052	53115	62757	95348	78662	11163	81651	50245	34971	52924
78	46515	70331	85922	38329	57015	15765	97161	17869	45349	61796	66345	81073	49106	79860
79	30986	81223	42416	58353	21532	30502	32305	86482	05174	07901	54339	58861	74818	46942
80	63798	64995	46583	09785	44160	78128	83991	42865	92520	83531	80377	35909	81250	54238
81	82486	84846	99254	67632	43218	50076	21361	64816	51202	88124	41870	52689	51275	83556
82	21885	32906	92431	09060	64297	51674	64126	62570	26123	05155	59194	52799	28225	85762
83	60336	98782	07408	53458	13564	59089	26445	29789	85205	41001	12535	12133	14645	23541
84	43937	46891	24010	25560	86355	33941	25786	54990	71899	15475	95434	98227	21824	19585
85	97656	63175	89303	16275	07100	92063	21942	18611	47348	20203	18534	03862	78095	50136
86	03299	01221	05418	38982	55758	92237	26759	86367	21216	98442	08303	56613	91511	75928
87	79626	06486	03574	17668	07785	76020	79924	25651	83325	88428	85076	72811	22717	50585
88	85636	68335	47539	03129	65651	11977	02510	26113	99447	68645	34327	15152	55230	93448
89	18039	14367	64337	06177	12143	46609	32989	74014	64708	00533	35398	58408	13261	47908
90	08362	15656	60627	36478	65648	16764	53412	09013	07832	41574	17639	82163	60859	75567
91	79556	29068	04142	16268	15387	12856	66227	38358	22478	73373	88732	09443	82558	05250
92	92608	82674	27072	32534	17075	27698	98204	63863	11951	34648	88022	56148	34925	57031
93	23982	25835	40055	67006	12293	02753	14827	23235	35071	99704	37543	11601	35503	85171
94	09915	96306	05908	97901	28395	14186	00821	80703	70426	75647	76310	88717	37890	40129
95	59037	33300	26695	62247	69927	76123	50842	43834	86654	70959	79725	93872	28117	19233
96	42488	78077	69882	61657	34136	79180	97526	43092	04098	73571	80799	76536	71255	64239
97	46764	86273	63003	93017	31204	36692	40202	35275	57306	55543	53203	18098	47625	88684
98	03237	45430	55417	63282	90816	17349	88298	90183	36600	78406	06216	95787	42579	90730
99	86591	81482	52667	61582	14972	90053	89534	76036	49199	43716	97548	04379	46370	28672
100	38534	01715	94964	87287	65680	43772	39560	12918	86537	62738	19636	51132	25739	56947

Source: Abridged from W. H. Beyer (ed.). *CRC Standard Mathematical Tables*, 24th edition. (Cleveland: The Chemical Rubber Company), 1976. Reproduced by permission of the publisher.

TABLE II Binomial Probabilities

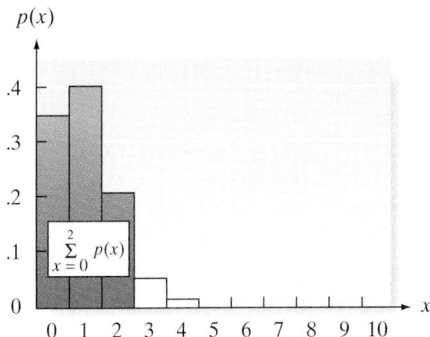

Tabulated values are $\sum_{x=0}^{k} p(x)$. *(Computations are rounded at the third decimal place.)*

a. $n = 5$

k \ p	.01	.05	.10	.20	.30	.40	.50	.60	.70	.80	.90	.95	.99
0	.951	.774	.590	.328	.168	.078	.031	.010	.002	.000	.000	.000	.000
1	.999	.977	.919	.737	.528	.337	.188	.087	.031	.007	.000	.000	.000
2	1.000	.999	.991	.942	.837	.683	.500	.317	.163	.058	.009	.001	.000
3	1.000	1.000	1.000	.993	.969	.913	.812	.663	.472	.263	.081	.023	.001
4	1.000	1.000	1.000	1.000	.998	.990	.969	.922	.832	.672	.410	.226	.049

b. $n = 6$

k \ p	.01	.05	.10	.20	.30	.40	.50	.60	.70	.80	.90	.95	.99
0	.941	.735	.531	.262	.118	.047	.016	.004	.001	.000	.000	.000	.000
1	.999	.967	.886	.655	.420	.233	.109	.041	.011	.002	.000	.000	.000
2	1.000	.998	.984	.901	.744	.544	.344	.179	.070	.017	.001	.000	.000
3	1.000	1.000	.999	.983	.930	.821	.656	.456	.256	.099	.016	.002	.000
4	1.000	1.000	1.000	.998	.989	.959	.891	.767	.580	.345	.114	.033	.001
5	1.000	1.000	1.000	1.000	.999	.996	.984	.953	.882	.738	.469	.265	.059

c. $n = 7$

k \ p	.01	.05	.10	.20	.30	.40	.50	.60	.70	.80	.90	.95	.99
0	.932	.698	.478	.210	.082	.028	.008	.002	.000	.000	.000	.000	.000
1	.998	.956	.850	.577	.329	.159	.063	.019	.004	.000	.000	.000	.000
2	1.000	.996	.974	.852	.647	.420	.227	.096	.029	.005	.000	.000	.000
3	1.000	1.000	.997	.967	.874	.710	.500	.290	.126	.033	.003	.000	.000
4	1.000	1.000	1.000	.995	.971	.904	.773	.580	.353	.148	.026	.004	.000
5	1.000	1.000	1.000	1.000	.996	.981	.937	.841	.671	.423	.150	.044	.002
6	1.000	1.000	1.000	1.000	1.000	.998	.992	.972	.918	.790	.522	.302	.068

(continued)

TABLE II Continued

d. n = 8

k \ p	.01	.05	.10	.20	.30	.40	.50	.60	.70	.80	.90	.95	.99
0	.923	.663	.430	.168	.058	.017	.004	.001	.000	.000	.000	.000	.000
1	.997	.943	.813	.503	.255	.106	.035	.009	.001	.000	.000	.000	.000
2	1.000	.994	.962	.797	.552	.315	.145	.050	.011	.001	.000	.000	.000
3	1.000	1.000	.995	.944	.806	.594	.363	.174	.058	.010	.000	.000	.000
4	1.000	1.000	1.000	.990	.942	.826	.637	.406	.194	.056	.005	.000	.000
5	1.000	1.000	1.000	.999	.989	.950	.855	.685	.448	.203	.038	.006	.000
6	1.000	1.000	1.000	1.000	.999	.991	.965	.894	.745	.497	.187	.057	.003
7	1.000	1.000	1.000	1.000	1.000	.999	.996	.983	.942	.832	.570	.337	.077

e. n = 9

k \ p	.01	.05	.10	.20	.30	.40	.50	.60	.70	.80	.90	.95	.99
0	.914	.630	.387	.134	.040	.010	.002	.000	.000	.000	.000	.000	.000
1	.997	.929	.775	.436	.196	.071	.020	.004	.000	.000	.000	.000	.000
2	1.000	.992	.947	.738	.463	.232	.090	.025	.004	.000	.000	.000	.000
3	1.000	.999	.992	.914	.730	.483	.254	.099	.025	.003	.000	.000	.000
4	1.000	1.000	.999	.980	.901	.733	.500	.267	.099	.020	.001	.000	.000
5	1.000	1.000	1.000	.997	.975	.901	.746	.517	.270	.086	.008	.001	.000
6	1.000	1.000	1.000	1.000	.996	.975	.910	.768	.537	.262	.053	.008	.000
7	1.000	1.000	1.000	1.000	1.000	.996	.980	.929	.804	.564	.225	.071	.003
8	1.000	1.000	1.000	1.000	1.000	1.000	.998	.990	.960	.866	.613	.370	.086

f. n = 10

k \ p	.01	.05	.10	.20	.30	.40	.50	.60	.70	.80	.90	.95	.99
0	.904	.599	.349	.107	.028	.006	.001	.000	.000	.000	.000	.000	.000
1	.996	.914	.736	.376	.149	.046	.011	.002	.000	.000	.000	.000	.000
2	1.000	.988	.930	.678	.383	.167	.055	.012	.002	.000	.000	.000	.000
3	1.000	.999	.987	.879	.650	.382	.172	.055	.011	.001	.000	.000	.000
4	1.000	1.000	.998	.967	.850	.633	.377	.166	.047	.006	.000	.000	.000
5	1.000	1.000	1.000	.999	.953	.834	.623	.367	.150	.033	.002	.000	.000
6	1.000	1.000	1.000	.999	.989	.945	.828	.618	.350	.121	.013	.001	.000
7	1.000	1.000	1.000	1.000	.998	.988	.945	.833	.617	.322	.070	.012	.000
8	1.000	1.000	1.000	1.000	1.000	.998	.989	.954	.851	.624	.264	.086	.004
9	1.000	1.000	1.000	1.000	1.000	1.000	.999	.994	.972	.893	.651	.401	.096

(continued)

TABLE II Continued

g. n = 15

k \ p	.01	.05	.10	.20	.30	.40	.50	.60	.70	.80	.90	.95	.99
0	.860	.463	.206	.035	.005	.000	.000	.000	.000	.000	.000	.000	.000
1	.990	.829	.549	.167	.035	.005	.000	.000	.000	.000	.000	.000	.000
2	1.000	.964	.816	.398	.127	.027	.004	.000	.000	.000	.000	.000	.000
3	1.000	.995	.944	.648	.297	.091	.018	.002	.000	.000	.000	.000	.000
4	1.000	.999	.987	.838	.515	.217	.059	.009	.001	.000	.000	.000	.000
5	1.000	1.000	.998	.939	.722	.403	.151	.034	.004	.000	.000	.000	.000
6	1.000	1.000	1.000	.982	.869	.610	.304	.095	.015	.001	.000	.000	.000
7	1.000	1.000	1.000	.996	.950	.787	.500	.213	.050	.004	.000	.000	.000
8	1.000	1.000	1.000	.999	.985	.905	.696	.390	.131	.018	.000	.000	.000
9	1.000	1.000	1.000	1.000	.996	.966	.849	.597	.278	.061	.002	.000	.000
10	1.000	1.000	1.000	1.000	.999	.991	.941	.783	.485	.164	.013	.001	.000
11	1.000	1.000	1.000	1.000	1.000	.998	.982	.909	.703	352	.056	.005	.000
12	1.000	1.000	1.000	1.000	1.000	1.000	.996	.973	.873	.602	.184	.036	.000
13	1.000	1.000	1.000	1.000	1.000	1.000	1.000	.995	.965	.833	.451	.171	.010
14	1.000	1.000	1.000	1.000	1.000	1.000	1.000	1.000	.995	.965	.794	.537	.140

h. n = 20

k \ p	.01	.05	.10	.20	.30	.40	.50	.60	.70	.80	.90	.95	.99
0	.818	.358	.122	.012	.001	.000	.000	.000	.000	.000	.000	.000	.000
1	.983	.736	.392	.069	.008	.001	.000	.000	.000	.000	.000	.000	.000
2	.999	.925	.677	.206	.035	.004	.000	.000	.000	.000	.000	.000	.000
3	1.000	.984	.867	.411	.107	.016	.001	.000	.000	.000	.000	.000	.000
4	1.000	.997	.957	.630	.238	.051	.006	.000	.000	.000	.000	.000	.000
5	1.000	1.000	.989	.804	.416	.126	.021	.002	.000	.000	.000	.000	.000
6	1.000	1.000	.998	.913	.608	.250	.058	.006	.000	.000	.000	.000	.000
7	1.000	1.000	1.000	.968	.772	.416	.132	.021	.001	.000	.000	.000	.000
8	1.000	1.000	1.000	.990	.887	.596	.252	.057	.005	.000	.000	.000	.000
9	1.000	1.000	1.000	.997	.952	.755	.412	.128	.017	.001	.000	.000	.000
10	1.000	1.000	1.000	.999	.983	.872	.588	.245	.048	.003	.000	.000	.000
11	1.000	1.000	1.000	1.000	.995	.943	.748	.404	.113	.010	.000	.000	.000
12	1.000	1.000	1.000	1.000	.999	.979	.868	.584	.228	.032	.000	.000	.000
13	1.000	1.000	1.000	1.000	1.000	.994	.942	.750	.392	.087	.002	.000	.000
14	1.000	1.000	1.000	1.000	1.000	.998	.979	.874	.584	.196	.011	.000	.000
15	1.000	1.000	1.000	1.000	1.000	1.000	.994	.949	.762	.370	.043	.003	.000
16	1.000	1.000	1.000	1.000	1.000	1.000	.999	.984	.893	.589	.133	.016	.000
17	1.000	1.000	1.000	1.000	1.000	1.000	1.000	.996	.965	.794	.323	.075	.001
18	1.000	1.000	1.000	1.000	1.000	1.000	1.000	.999	.992	.931	.608	.264	.017
19	1.000	1.000	1.000	1.000	1.000	1.000	1.000	1.000	.999	.988	.878	.642	.182

(continued)

TABLE II   Continued

i. n = 25

k \ p	.01	.05	.10	.20	.30	.40	.50	.60	.70	.80	.90	.95	.99
0	.778	.277	.072	.004	.000	.000	.000	.000	.000	.000	.000	.000	.000
1	.974	.642	.271	.027	.002	.000	.000	.000	.000	.000	.000	.000	.000
2	.998	.873	.537	.098	.009	.000	.000	.000	.000	.000	.000	.000	.000
3	1.000	.966	.764	.234	.033	.002	.000	.000	.000	.000	.000	.000	.000
4	1.000	.993	.902	.421	.090	.009	.000	.000	.000	.000	.000	.000	.000
5	1.000	.999	.967	.617	.193	.029	.002	.000	.000	.000	.000	.000	.000
6	1.000	1.000	.991	.780	.341	.074	.007	.000	.000	.000	.000	.000	.000
7	1.000	1.000	.998	.891	.512	.154	.022	.001	.000	.000	.000	.000	.000
8	1.000	1.000	1.000	.953	.677	.274	.054	.004	.000	.000	.000	.000	.000
9	1.000	1.000	1.000	.983	.811	.425	.115	.013	.000	.000	.000	.000	.000
10	1.000	1.000	1.000	.994	.902	.586	.212	.034	.002	.000	.000	.000	.000
11	1.000	1.000	1.000	.998	.956	.732	.345	.078	.006	.000	.000	.000	.000
12	1.000	1.000	1.000	1.000	.983	.846	.500	.154	.017	.000	.000	.000	.000
13	1.000	1.000	1.000	1.000	.994	.922	.655	.268	.044	.002	.000	.000	.000
14	1.000	1.000	1.000	1.000	.998	.966	.788	.414	.098	.006	.000	.000	.000
15	1.000	1.000	1.000	1.000	1.000	.987	.885	.575	.189	.017	.000	.000	.000
16	1.000	1.000	1.000	1.000	1.000	.996	.946	.726	.323	.047	.000	.000	.000
17	1.000	1.000	1.000	1.000	1.000	.999	.978	.846	.488	.109	.002	.000	.000
18	1.000	1.000	1.000	1.000	1.000	1.000	.993	.926	.659	.220	.009	.000	.000
19	1.000	1.000	1.000	1.000	1.000	1.000	.998	.971	.807	.383	.033	.001	.000
20	1.000	1.000	1.000	1.000	1.000	1.000	1.000	.991	.910	.579	.098	.007	.000
21	1.000	1.000	1.000	1.000	1.000	1.000	1.000	.998	.967	.766	.236	.034	.000
22	1.000	1.000	1.000	1.000	1.000	1.000	1.000	1.000	.991	.902	.463	.127	.002
23	1.000	1.000	1.000	1.000	1.000	1.000	1.000	1.000	.998	.973	.729	.358	.026
24	1.000	1.000	1.000	1.000	1.000	1.000	1.000	1.000	1.000	.996	.928	.723	.222

TABLE III   Poisson Probabilities

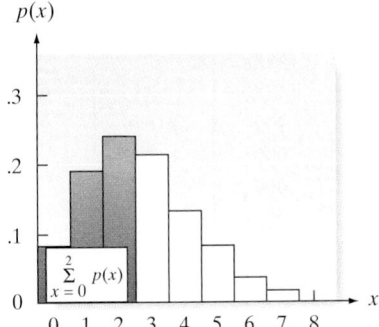

Tabulated values are $\sum_{x=0}^{k} p(x)$. (Computations are rounded at the third decimal place.)

λ \ k	0	1	2	3	4	5	6	7	8	9
.02	.980	1.000								
.04	.961	.999	1.000							
.06	.942	.998	1.000							
.08	.923	.997	1.000							
.10	.905	.995	1.000							
.15	.861	.990	.999	1.000						
.20	.819	.982	.999	1.000						
.25	.779	.974	.998	1.000						
.30	.741	.963	.996	1.000						
.35	.705	.951	.994	1.000						
.40	.670	.938	.992	.999	1.000					
.45	.638	.925	.989	.999	1.000					
.50	.607	.910	.986	.998	1.000					
.55	.577	.894	.982	.998	1.000					
.60	.549	.878	.977	.997	1.000					
.65	.522	.861	.972	.996	.999	1.000				
.70	.497	.844	.966	.994	.999	1.000				
.75	.472	.827	.959	.993	.999	1.000				
.80	.449	.809	.953	.991	.999	1.000				
.85	.427	.791	.945	.989	.998	1.000				
.90	.407	.772	.937	.987	.998	1.000				
.95	.387	.754	.929	.981	.997	1.000				
1.00	.368	.736	.920	.981	.996	.999	1.000			
1.1	.333	.699	.900	.974	.995	.999	1.000			
1.2	.301	.663	.879	.966	.992	.998	1.000			
1.3	.273	.627	.857	.957	.989	.998	1.000			
1.4	.247	.592	.833	.946	.986	.997	.999	1.000		
1.5	.223	.558	.809	.934	.981	.996	.999	1.000		

(continued)

TABLE III   Continued

λ \ k	0	1	2	3	4	5	6	7	8	9
1.6	.202	.525	.783	.921	.976	.994	.999	1.000		
1.7	.183	.493	.757	.907	.970	.992	.998	1.000		
1.8	.165	.463	.731	.891	.964	.990	.997	.999	1.000	
1.9	.150	.434	.704	.875	.956	.987	.997	.999	1.000	
2.0	.135	.406	.677	.857	.947	.983	.995	.999	1.000	
2.2	.111	.355	.623	.819	.928	.975	.993	.998	1.000	
2.4	.091	.308	.570	.779	.904	.964	.988	.997	.999	1.000
2.6	.074	.267	.518	.736	.877	.951	.983	.995	.999	1.000
2.8	.061	.231	.469	.692	.848	.935	.976	.992	.998	.999
3.0	.050	.199	.423	.647	.815	.916	.966	.988	.996	.999
3.2	.041	.171	.380	.603	.781	.895	.955	.983	.994	.998
3.4	.033	.147	.340	.558	.744	.871	.942	.977	.992	.997
3.6	.027	.126	.303	.515	.706	.844	.927	.969	.988	.996
3.8	.022	.107	.269	.473	.668	.816	.909	.960	.984	.994
4.0	.018	.092	.238	.433	.629	.785	.889	.949	.979	.992
4.2	.015	.078	.210	.395	.590	.753	.867	.936	.972	.989
4.4	.012	.066	.185	.359	.551	.720	.844	.921	.964	.985
4.6	.010	.056	.163	.326	.513	.686	.818	.905	.955	.980
4.8	.008	.048	.143	.294	.476	.651	.791	.887	.944	.975
5.0	.007	.040	.125	.265	.440	.616	.762	.867	.932	.968
5.2	.006	.034	.109	.238	.406	.581	.732	.845	.918	.960
5.4	.005	.029	.095	.213	.373	.546	.702	.822	.903	.951
5.6	.004	.024	.082	.191	.342	.512	.670	.797	.886	.941
5.8	.003	.021	.072	.170	.313	.478	.638	.771	.867	.929
6.0	.002	.017	.062	.151	.285	.446	.606	.744	.847	.916

λ	10	11	12	13	14	15	16
2.8	1.000						
3.0	1.000						
3.2	1.000						
3.4	.999	1.000					
3.6	.999	1.000					
3.8	.998	.999	1.000				
4.0	.997	.999	1.000				
4.2	.996	.999	1.000				
4.4	.994	.998	.999	1.000			
4.6	.992	.997	.999	1.000			
4.8	.990	.996	.999	1.000			
5.0	.986	.995	.998	.999	1.000		
5.2	.982	.993	.997	.999	1.000		
5.4	.977	.990	.996	.999	1.000		
5.6	.972	.988	.995	.998	.999	1.000	
5.8	.965	.984	.993	.997	.999	1.000	
6.0	.957	.980	.991	.996	.999	.999	1.000

(continued)

TABLE III   Continued

λ \ k	0	1	2	3	4	5	6	7	8	9
6.2	.002	.015	.054	.134	.259	.414	.574	.716	.826	.902
6.4	.002	.012	.046	.119	.235	.384	.542	.687	.803	.886
6.6	.001	.010	.040	.105	.213	.355	.511	.658	.780	.869
6.8	.001	.009	.034	.093	.192	.327	.480	.628	.755	.850
7.0	.001	.007	.030	.082	.173	.301	.450	.599	.729	.830
7.2	.001	.006	.025	.072	.156	.276	.420	.569	.703	.810
7.4	.001	.005	.022	.063	.140	.253	.392	.539	.676	.788
7.6	.001	.004	.019	.055	.125	.231	.365	.510	.648	.765
7.8	.000	.004	.016	.048	.112	.210	.338	.481	.620	.741
8.0	.000	.003	.014	.042	.100	.191	.313	.453	.593	.717
8.5	.000	.002	.009	.030	.074	.150	.256	.386	.523	.653
9.0	.000	.001	.006	.021	.055	.116	.207	.324	.456	.587
9.5	.000	.001	.004	.015	.040	.089	.165	.269	.392	.522
10.0	.000	.000	.003	.010	.029	.067	.130	.220	.333	.458

λ	10	11	12	13	14	15	16	17	18	19
6.2	.949	.975	.989	.995	.998	.999	1.000			
6.4	.939	.969	.986	.994	.997	.999	1.000			
6.6	.927	.963	.982	.992	.997	.999	.999	1.000		
6.8	.915	.955	.978	.990	.996	.998	.999	1.000		
7.0	.901	.947	.973	.987	.994	.998	.999	1.000		
7.2	.887	.937	.967	.984	.993	.997	.999	.999	1.000	
7.4	.871	.926	.961	.980	.991	.996	.998	.999	1.000	
7.6	.854	.915	.954	.976	.989	.995	.998	.999	1.000	
7.8	.835	.902	.945	.971	.986	.993	.997	.999	1.000	
8.0	.816	.888	.936	.966	.983	.992	.996	.998	.999	1.000
8.5	.763	.849	.909	.949	.973	.986	.993	.997	.999	.999
9.0	.706	.803	.876	.926	.959	.978	.989	.995	.998	.999
9.5	.645	.752	.836	.898	.940	.967	.982	.991	.996	.998
10.0	.583	.697	.792	.864	.917	.951	.973	.986	.993	.997

λ	20	21	22
8.5	1.000		
9.0	1.000		
9.5	.999	1.000	
10.0	.998	.999	1.000

(continued)

TABLE III Continued

λ \ k	0	1	2	3	4	5	6	7	8	9
10.5	.000	.000	.002	.007	.021	.050	.102	.179	.279	.397
11.0	.000	.000	.001	.005	.015	.038	.079	.143	.232	.341
11.5	.000	.000	.001	.003	.011	.028	.060	.114	.191	.289
12.0	.000	.000	.001	.002	.008	.020	.046	.090	.155	.242
12.5	.000	.000	.000	.002	.005	.015	.035	.070	.125	.201
13.0	.000	.000	.000	.001	.004	.011	.026	.054	.100	.166
13.5	.000	.000	.000	.001	.003	.008	.019	.041	.079	.135
14.0	.000	.000	.000	.000	.002	.006	.014	.032	.062	.109
14.5	.000	.000	.000	.000	.001	.004	.010	.024	.048	.088
15.0	.000	.000	.000	.000	.001	.003	.008	.018	.037	.070

	10	11	12	13	14	15	16	17	18	19
10.5	.521	.639	.742	.825	.888	.932	.960	.978	.988	.994
11.0	.460	.579	.689	.781	.854	.907	.944	.968	.982	.991
11.5	.402	.520	.633	.733	.815	.878	.924	.954	.974	.986
12.0	.347	.462	.576	.682	.772	.844	.899	.937	.963	.979
12.5	.297	.406	.519	.628	.725	.806	.869	.916	.948	.969
13.0	.252	.353	.463	.573	.675	.764	.835	.890	.930	.957
13.5	.211	.304	.409	.518	.623	.718	.798	.861	.908	.942
14.0	.176	.260	.358	.464	.570	.669	.756	.827	.883	.923
14.5	.145	.220	.311	.413	.518	.619	.711	.790	.853	.901
15.0	.118	.185	.268	.363	.466	.568	.664	.749	.819	.875

	20	21	22	23	24	25	26	27	28	29
10.5	.997	.999	.999	1.000						
11.0	.995	.998	.999	1.000						
11.5	.992	.996	.998	.999	1.000					
12.0	.988	.994	.987	.999	.999	1.000				
12.5	.983	.991	.995	.998	.999	.999	1.000			
13.0	.975	.986	.992	.996	.998	.999	1.000			
13.5	.965	.980	.989	.994	.997	.998	.999	1.000		
14.0	.952	.971	.983	.991	.995	.997	.999	.999	1.000	
14.5	.936	.960	.976	.986	.992	.996	.998	.999	.999	1.000
15.0	.917	.947	.967	.981	.989	.994	.997	.998	.999	1.000

(continued)

TABLE III   Continued

k / λ	4	5	6	7	8	9	10	11	12	13
16	.000	.001	.004	.010	.022	.043	.077	.127	.193	.275
17	.000	.001	.002	.005	.013	.026	.049	.085	.135	.201
18	.000	.000	.001	.003	.007	.015	.030	.055	.092	.143
19	.000	.000	.001	.002	.004	.009	.018	.035	.061	.098
20	.000	.000	.000	.001	.002	.005	.011	.021	.039	.066
21	.000	.000	.000	.000	.001	.003	.006	.013	.025	.043
22	.000	.000	.000	.000	.001	.002	.004	.008	.015	.028
23	.000	.000	.000	.000	.000	.001	.002	.004	.009	.017
24	.000	.000	.000	.000	.000	.000	.001	.003	.005	.011
25	.000	.000	.000	.000	.000	.000	.001	.001	.003	.006

k / λ	14	15	16	17	18	19	20	21	22	23
16	.368	.467	.566	.659	.742	.812	.868	.911	.942	.963
17	.281	.371	.468	.564	.655	.736	.805	.861	.905	.937
18	.208	.287	.375	.469	.562	.651	.731	.799	.855	.899
19	.150	.215	.292	.378	.469	.561	.647	.725	.793	.849
20	.105	.157	.221	.297	.381	.470	.559	.644	.721	.787
21	.072	.111	.163	.227	.302	.384	.471	.558	.640	.716
22	.048	.077	.117	.169	.232	.306	.387	.472	.556	.637
23	.031	.052	.082	.123	.175	.238	.310	.389	.472	.555
24	.020	.034	.056	.087	.128	.180	.243	.314	.392	.473
25	.012	.022	.038	.060	.092	.134	.185	.247	.318	.394

k / λ	24	25	26	27	28	29	30	31	32	33
16	.978	.987	.993	.996	.998	.999	.999	1.000		
17	.959	.975	.985	.991	.995	.997	.999	.999	1.000	
18	.932	.955	.972	.983	.990	.994	.997	.998	.999	1.000
19	.893	.927	.951	.969	.980	.988	.993	.996	.998	.999
20	.843	.888	.922	.948	.966	.978	.987	.992	.995	.997
21	.782	.838	.883	.917	.944	.963	.976	.985	.991	.994
22	.712	.777	.832	.877	.913	.940	.959	.973	.983	.989
23	.635	.708	.772	.827	.873	.908	.936	.956	.971	.981
24	.554	.632	.704	.768	.823	.868	.904	.932	.953	.969
25	.473	.553	.629	.700	.763	.818	.863	.900	.929	.950

k / λ	34	35	36	37	38	39	40	41	42	43
19	.999	1.000								
20	.999	.999	1.000							
21	.997	.998	.999	.999	1.000					
22	.994	.996	.998	.999	.999	1.000				
23	.988	.993	.996	.997	.999	.999	1.000			
24	.979	.987	.992	.995	.997	.998	.999	.999	1.000	
25	.966	.978	.985	.991	.991	.997	.998	.999	.999	1.000

TABLE IV   Normal Curve Areas

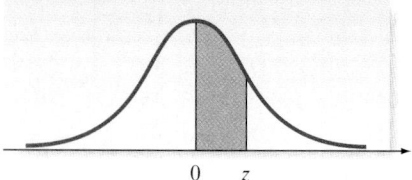

z	.00	.01	.02	.03	.04	.05	.06	.07	.08	.09
.0	.0000	.0040	.0080	.0120	.0160	.0199	.0239	.0279	.0319	.0359
.1	.0398	.0438	.0478	.0517	.0557	.0596	.0636	.0675	.0714	.0753
.2	.0793	.0832	.0871	.0910	.0948	.0987	.1026	.1064	.1103	.1141
.3	.1179	.1217	.1255	.1293	.1331	.1368	.1406	.1443	.1480	.1517
.4	.1554	.1591	.1628	.1664	.1700	.1736	.1772	.1808	.1844	.1879
.5	.1915	.1950	.1985	.2019	.2054	.2088	.2123	.2157	.2190	.2224
.6	.2257	.2291	.2324	.2357	.2389	.2422	.2454	.2486	.2517	.2549
.7	.2580	.2611	.2642	.2673	.2704	.2734	.2764	.2794	.2823	.2852
.8	.2881	.2910	.2939	.2967	.2995	.3023	.3051	.3078	.3106	.3133
.9	.3159	.3186	.3212	.3238	.3264	.3289	.3315	.3340	.3365	.3389
1.0	.3413	.3438	.3461	.3485	.3508	.3531	.3554	.3577	.3599	.3621
1.1	.3643	.3665	.3686	.3708	.3729	.3749	.3770	.3790	.3810	.3830
1.2	.3849	.3869	.3888	.3907	.3925	.3944	.3962	.3980	.3997	.4015
1.3	.4032	.4049	.4066	.4082	.4099	.4115	.4131	.4147	.4162	.4177
1.4	.4192	.4207	.4222	.4236	.4251	.4265	.4279	.4292	.4306	.4319
1.5	.4332	.4345	.4357	.4370	.4382	.4394	.4406	.4418	.4429	.4441
1.6	.4452	.4463	.4474	.4484	.4495	.4505	.4515	.4525	.4535	.4545
1.7	.4554	.4564	.4573	.4582	.4591	.4599	.4608	.4616	.4625	.4633
1.8	.4641	.4649	.4656	.4664	.4671	.4678	.4686	.4693	.4699	.4706
1.9	.4713	.4719	.4726	.4732	.4738	.4744	.4750	.4756	.4761	.4767
2.0	.4772	.4778	.4783	.4788	.4793	.4798	.4803	.4808	.4812	.4817
2.1	.4821	.4826	.4830	.4834	.4838	.4842	.4846	.4850	.4854	.4857
2.2	.4861	.4864	.4868	.4871	.4875	.4878	.4881	.4884	.4887	.4890
2.3	.4893	.4896	.4898	.4901	.4904	.4906	.4909	.4911	.4913	.4916
2.4	.4918	.4920	.4922	.4925	.4927	.4929	.4931	.4932	.4934	.4936
2.5	.4938	.4940	.4941	.4943	.4945	.4946	.4948	.4949	.4951	.4952
2.6	.4953	.4955	.4956	.4957	.4959	.4960	.4961	.4962	.4963	.4964
2.7	.4965	.4966	.4967	.4968	.4969	.4970	.4971	.4972	.4973	.4974
2.8	.4974	.4975	.4976	.4977	.4977	.4978	.4979	.4979	.4980	.4981
2.9	.4981	.4982	.4982	.4983	.4984	.4984	.4985	.4985	.4986	.4986
3.0	.4987	.4987	.4987	.4988	.4988	.4989	.4989	.4989	.4990	.4990
3.1	.49903	.49906	.49910	.49913	.49916	.49918	.49921	.49924	.49926	.48829
3.2	.49931	.49934	.49936	.49938	.49940	.49942	.49944	.49946	.49948	.49950
3.3	.49952	.49953	.49955	.49957	.49958	.49960	.49961	.49962	.49964	.49965
3.4	.49966	.49968	.49969	.49970	.49971	.49972	.49973	.49974	.49975	.49976
3.5	.49977	.49978	.49978	.49979	.49980	.49981	.49981	.49982	.49983	.49983
3.6	.49984	.49985	.49985	.49986	.49986	.49987	.49987	.49988	.49988	.49989
3.7	.49989	.49990	.49990	.49990	.49991	.49991	.49992	.49992	.49992	.49992
3.8	.49993	.49993	.49993	.49994	.49994	.49994	.49994	.49995	.49995	.49995
3.9	.49995	.49995	.49996	.49996	.49996	.49996	.49996	.49996	.49997	.49997

Source: Abridged from Table I of A. Hald, *Statistical Tables and Formulas* (New York: Wiley), 1952. Reproduced by permission of A. Hald.

TABLE V Exponentials

λ	$e^{-\lambda}$	λ	$e^{-\lambda}$	λ	$e^{-\lambda}$	λ	$e^{-\lambda}$	λ	$e^{-\lambda}$
.00	1.000000	**2.05**	.128735	**4.05**	.017422	**6.05**	.002358	**8.05**	.000319
.05	.951229	**2.10**	.122456	**4.10**	.016573	**6.10**	.002243	**8.10**	.000304
.10	.904837	**2.15**	.116484	**4.15**	.015764	**6.15**	.002133	**8.15**	.000289
.15	.860708	**2.20**	.110803	**4.20**	.014996	**6.20**	.002029	**8.20**	.000275
.20	.818731	**2.25**	.105399	**4.25**	.014264	**6.25**	.001930	**8.25**	.000261
.25	.778801	**2.30**	.100259	**4.30**	.013569	**6.30**	.001836	**8.30**	.000249
.30	.740818	**2.35**	.095369	**4.35**	.012907	**6.35**	.001747	**8.35**	.000236
.35	.704688	**2.40**	.090718	**4.40**	.012277	**6.40**	.001661	**8.40**	.000225
.40	.670320	**2.45**	.086294	**4.45**	.011679	**6.45**	.001581	**8.45**	.000214
.45	.637628	**2.50**	.082085	**4.50**	.011109	**6.50**	.001503	**8.50**	.000204
.50	.606531	**2.55**	.078082	**4.55**	.010567	**6.55**	.001430	**8.55**	.000194
.55	.576950	**2.60**	.074274	**4.60**	.010052	**6.60**	.001360	**8.60**	.000184
.60	.548812	**2.65**	.070651	**4.65**	.009562	**6.65**	.001294	**8.65**	.000175
.65	.522046	**2.70**	.067206	**4.70**	.009095	**6.70**	.001231	**8.70**	.000167
.70	.496585	**2.75**	.063928	**4.75**	.008652	**6.75**	.001171	**8.75**	.000158
.75	.472367	**2.80**	.060810	**4.80**	.008230	**6.80**	.001114	**8.80**	.000151
.80	.449329	**2.85**	.057844	**4.85**	.007828	**6.85**	.001059	**8.85**	.000143
.85	.427415	**2.90**	.055023	**4.90**	.007447	**6.90**	.001008	**8.90**	.000136
.90	.406570	**2.95**	.052340	**4.95**	.007083	**6.95**	.000959	**8.95**	.000130
.95	.386741	**3.00**	.049787	**5.00**	.006738	**7.00**	.000912	**9.00**	.000123
1.00	.367879	**3.05**	.047359	**5.05**	.006409	**7.05**	.000867	**9.05**	.000117
1.05	.349938	**3.10**	.045049	**5.10**	.006097	**7.10**	.000825	**9.10**	.000112
1.10	.332871	**3.15**	.042852	**5.15**	.005799	**7.15**	.000785	**9.15**	.000106
1.15	.316637	**3.20**	.040762	**5.20**	.005517	**7.20**	.000747	**9.20**	.000101
1.20	.301194	**3.25**	.038774	**5.25**	.005248	**7.25**	.000710	**9.25**	.000096
1.25	.286505	**3.30**	.036883	**5.30**	.004992	**7.30**	.000676	**9.30**	.000091
1.30	.272532	**3.35**	.035084	**5.35**	.004748	**7.35**	.000643	**9.35**	.000087
1.35	.259240	**3.40**	.033373	**5.40**	.004517	**7.40**	.000611	**9.40**	.000083
1.40	.246597	**3.45**	.031746	**5.45**	.004296	**7.45**	.000581	**9.45**	.000079
1.45	.234570	**3.50**	.030197	**5.50**	.004087	**7.50**	.000553	**9.50**	.000075
1.50	.223130	**3.55**	.028725	**5.55**	.003887	**7.55**	.000526	**9.55**	.000071
1.55	.212248	**3.60**	.027324	**5.60**	.003698	**7.60**	.000501	**9.60**	.000068
1.60	.201897	**3.65**	.025991	**5.65**	.003518	**7.65**	.000476	**9.65**	.000064
1.65	.192050	**3.70**	.024724	**5.70**	.003346	**7.70**	.000453	**9.70**	.000061
1.70	.182684	**3.75**	.023518	**5.75**	.003183	**7.75**	.000431	**9.75**	.000058
1.75	.173774	**3.80**	.022371	**5.80**	.003028	**7.80**	.000410	**9.80**	.000056
1.80	.165299	**3.85**	.021280	**5.85**	.002880	**7.85**	.000390	**9.85**	.000053
1.85	.157237	**3.90**	.020242	**5.90**	.002739	**7.90**	.000371	**9.90**	.000050
1.90	.149569	**3.95**	.019255	**5.95**	.002606	**7.95**	.000353	**9.95**	.000048
1.95	.142274	**4.00**	.018316	**6.00**	.002479	**8.00**	.000336	**10.00**	.000045
2.00	.135335								

TABLE VI   Critical Values of t

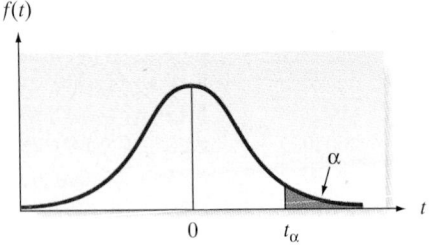

Degrees of Freedom	$t_{.100}$	$t_{.050}$	$t_{.025}$	$t_{.010}$	$t_{.005}$	$t_{.001}$	$t_{.0005}$
1	3.078	6.314	12.706	31.821	63.657	318.31	636.62
2	1.886	2.920	4.303	6.965	9.925	22.326	31.598
3	1.638	2.353	3.182	4.541	5.841	10.213	12.924
4	1.533	2.132	2.776	3.747	4.604	7.173	8.610
5	1.476	2.015	2.571	3.365	4.032	5.893	6.869
6	1.440	1.943	2.447	3.143	3.707	5.208	5.959
7	1.415	1.895	2.365	2.998	3.499	4.785	5.408
8	1.397	1.860	2.306	2.896	3.355	4.501	5.041
9	1.383	1.833	2.262	2.821	3.250	4.297	4.781
10	1.372	1.812	2.228	2.764	3.169	4.144	4.587
11	1.363	1.796	2.201	2.718	3.106	4.025	4.437
12	1.356	1.782	2.179	2.681	3.055	3.930	4.318
13	1.350	1.771	2.160	2.650	3.012	3.852	4.221
14	1.345	1.761	2.145	2.624	2.977	3.787	4.140
15	1.341	1.753	2.131	2.602	2.947	3.733	4.073
16	1.337	1.746	2.120	2.583	2.921	3.686	4.015
17	1.333	1.740	2.110	2.567	2.898	3.646	3.965
18	1.330	1.734	2.101	2.552	2.878	3.610	3.922
19	1.328	1.729	2.093	2.539	2.861	3.579	3.883
20	1.325	1.725	2.086	2.528	2.845	3.552	3.850
21	1.323	1.721	2.080	2.518	2.831	3.527	3.819
22	1.321	1.717	2.074	2.508	2.819	3.505	3.792
23	1.319	1.714	2.069	2.500	2.807	3.485	3.767
24	1.318	1.711	2.064	2.492	2.797	3.467	3.745
25	1.316	1.708	2.060	2.485	2.787	3.450	3.725
26	1.315	1.706	2.056	2.479	2.779	3.435	3.707
27	1.314	1.703	2.052	2.473	2.771	3.421	3.690
28	1.313	1.701	2.048	2.467	2.763	3.408	3.674
29	1.311	1.699	2.045	2.462	2.756	3.396	3.659
30	1.310	1.697	2.042	2.457	2.750	3.385	3.646
40	1.303	1.684	2.021	2.423	2.704	3.307	3.551
60	1.296	1.671	2.000	2.390	2.660	3.232	3.460
120	1.289	1.658	1.980	2.358	2.617	3.160	3.373
∞	1.282	1.645	1.960	2.326	2.576	3.090	3.291

TABLE VII   Critical Values of χ^2

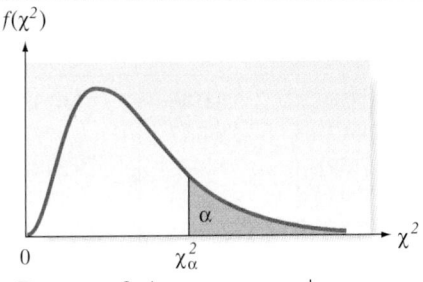

Degrees of Freedom	$\chi^2_{.995}$	$\chi^2_{.990}$	$\chi^2_{.975}$	$\chi^2_{.950}$	$\chi^2_{.900}$
1	.0000393	.0001571	.0009821	.0039321	.0157908
2	.0100251	.0201007	.0506356	.102587	.210720
3	.0717212	.114832	.215795	.351846	.584375
4	.206990	.297110	.484419	.710721	1.063623
5	.411740	.554300	.831211	1.145476	1.61031
6	.675727	.872085	1.237347	1.63539	2.20413
7	.989265	1.239043	1.68987	2.16735	2.83311
8	1.344419	1.646482	2.17973	2.73264	3.48954
9	1.734926	2.087912	2.70039	3.32511	4.16816
10	2.15585	2.55821	3.24697	3.94030	4.86518
11	2.60321	3.05347	3.81575	4.57481	5.57779
12	3.07382	3.57056	4.40379	5.22603	6.30380
13	3.56503	4.10691	5.00874	5.89186	7.04150
14	4.07468	4.66043	5.62872	6.57063	7.78953
15	4.60094	5.22935	6.26214	7.26094	8.54675
16	5.14224	5.81221	6.90766	7.96164	9.31223
17	5.69724	6.40776	7.56418	8.67176	10.0852
18	6.26481	7.01491	8.23075	9.39046	10.8649
19	6.84398	7.63273	8.90655	10.1170	11.6509
20	7.43386	8.26040	9.59083	10.8508	12.4426
21	8.03366	8.89720	10.28293	11.5913	13.2396
22	8.64272	9.54249	10.9823	12.3380	14.0415
23	9.26042	10.19567	11.6885	13.0905	14.8479
24	9.88623	10.8564	12.4011	13.8484	15.6587
25	10.5197	11.5240	13.1197	14.6114	16.4734
26	11.1603	12.1981	13.8439	15.3791	17.2919
27	11.8076	12.8786	14.5733	16.1513	18.1138
28	12.4613	13.5648	15.3079	16.9279	18.9392
29	13.1211	14.2565	16.0471	17.7083	19.7677
30	13.7867	14.9535	16.7908	18.4926	20.5992
40	20.7065	22.1643	24.4331	26.5093	29.0505
50	27.9907	29.7067	32.3574	34.7642	37.6886
60	35.5346	37.4848	40.4817	43.1879	46.4589
70	43.2752	45.4418	48.7576	51.7393	55.3290
80	51.1720	53.5400	57.1532	60.3915	64.2778
90	59.1963	61.7541	65.6466	69.1260	73.2912
100	67.3276	70.0648	74.2219	77.9295	82.3581

Source: From C. M. Thompson, "Tables of the Percentage Points of the χ^2-Distribution," *Biometrika*, 1941, 32, 188–189. Reproduced by permission of the *Biometrika* Trustees.

(continued)

TABLE VII   Continued

Degrees of Freedom	$\chi^2_{.100}$	$\chi^2_{.050}$	$\chi^2_{.025}$	$\chi^2_{.010}$	$\chi^2_{.005}$
1	2.70554	3.84146	5.02389	6.63490	7.87944
2	4.60517	5.99147	7.37776	9.21034	10.5966
3	6.25139	7.81473	9.34840	11.3449	12.8381
4	7.77944	9.48773	11.1433	13.2767	14.8602
5	9.23635	11.0705	12.8325	15.0863	16.7496
6	10.6446	12.5916	14.4494	16.8119	18.5476
7	12.0170	14.0671	16.0128	18.4753	20.2777
8	13.3616	15.5073	17.5346	20.0902	21.9550
9	14.6837	16.9190	19.0228	21.6660	23.5893
10	15.9871	18.3070	20.4831	23.2093	25.1882
11	17.2750	19.6751	21.9200	24.7250	26.7569
12	18.5494	21.0261	23.3367	26.2170	28.2995
13	19.8119	22.3621	24.7356	27.6883	29.8194
14	21.0642	23.6848	26.1190	29.1413	31.3193
15	22.3072	24.9958	27.4884	30.5779	32.8013
16	23.5418	26.2962	28.8454	31.9999	34.2672
17	24.7690	27.5871	30.1910	33.4087	35.7185
18	25.9894	28.8693	31.5264	34.8053	37.1564
19	27.2036	30.1435	32.8523	36.1908	38.5822
20	28.4120	31.4104	34.1696	37.5662	39.9968
21	29.6151	32.6705	35.4789	38.9321	41.4010
22	30.8133	33.9244	36.7807	40.2894	42.7956
23	32.0069	35.1725	38.0757	41.6384	44.1813
24	33.1963	36.4151	39.3641	42.9798	45.5585
25	34.3816	37.6525	40.6465	44.3141	46.9278
26	35.5631	38.8852	41.9232	45.6417	48.2899
27	36.7412	40.1133	43.1944	46.9630	49.6449
28	37.9159	41.3372	44.4607	48.2782	50.9933
29	39.0875	42.5569	45.7222	49.5879	52.3356
30	40.2560	43.7729	46.9792	50.8922	53.6720
40	51.8050	55.7585	59.3417	63.6907	66.7659
50	63.1671	67.5048	71.4202	76.1539	79.4900
60	74.3970	79.0819	83.2976	88.3794	91.9517
70	85.5271	90.5312	95.0231	100.425	104.215
80	96.5782	101.879	106.629	112.329	116.321
90	107.565	113.145	118.136	124.116	128.299
100	118.498	124.342	129.561	135.807	140.169

TABLE VIII   Percentage Points of the F-distribution, $\alpha = .10$

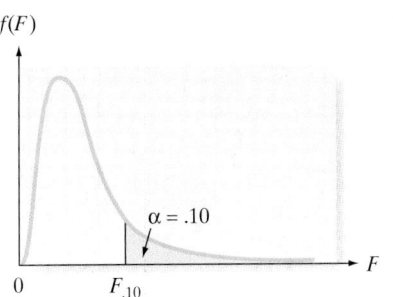

| | | NUMERATOR DEGREES OF FREEDOM | | | | | | | |
	v_1								
v_2	1	2	3	4	5	6	7	8	9
1	39.86	49.50	53.59	55.83	57.24	58.20	58.91	59.44	59.86
2	8.53	9.00	9.16	9.24	9.29	9.33	9.35	9.37	9.38
3	5.54	5.46	5.39	5.34	5.31	5.28	5.27	5.25	5.24
4	4.54	4.32	4.19	4.11	4.05	4.01	3.98	3.95	3.94
5	4.06	3.78	3.62	3.52	3.45	3.40	3.37	3.34	3.32
6	3.78	3.46	3.29	3.18	3.11	3.05	3.01	2.98	2.96
7	3.59	3.26	3.07	2.96	2.88	2.83	2.78	2.75	2.72
8	3.46	3.11	2.92	2.81	2.73	2.67	2.62	2.59	2.56
9	3.36	3.01	2.81	2.69	2.61	2.55	2.51	2.47	2.44
10	3.29	2.92	2.73	2.61	2.52	2.46	2.41	2.38	2.35
11	3.23	2.86	2.66	2.54	2.45	2.39	2.34	2.30	2.27
12	3.18	2.81	2.61	2.48	2.39	2.33	2.28	2.24	2.21
13	3.14	2.76	2.56	2.43	2.35	2.28	2.23	2.20	2.16
14	3.10	2.73	2.52	2.39	2.31	2.24	2.19	2.15	2.12
15	3.07	2.70	2.49	2.36	2.27	2.21	2.16	2.12	2.09
16	3.05	2.67	2.46	2.33	2.24	2.18	2.13	2.09	2.06
17	3.03	2.64	2.44	2.31	2.22	2.15	2.10	2.06	2.03
18	3.01	2.62	2.42	2.29	2.20	2.13	2.08	2.04	2.00
19	2.99	2.61	2.40	2.27	2.18	2.11	2.06	2.02	1.98
20	2.97	2.59	2.38	2.25	2.16	2.09	2.04	2.00	1.96
21	2.96	2.57	2.36	2.23	2.14	2.08	2.02	1.98	1.95
22	2.95	2.56	2.35	2.22	2.13	2.06	2.01	1.97	1.93
23	2.94	2.55	2.34	2.21	2.11	2.05	1.99	1.95	1.92
24	2.93	2.54	2.33	2.19	2.10	2.04	1.98	1.94	1.91
25	2.92	2.53	2.32	2.18	2.09	2.02	1.97	1.93	1.89
26	2.91	2.52	2.31	2.17	2.08	2.01	1.96	1.92	1.88
27	2.90	2.51	2.30	2.17	2.07	2.00	1.95	1.91	1.87
28	2.89	2.50	2.29	2.16	2.06	2.00	1.94	1.90	1.87
29	2.89	2.50	2.28	2.15	2.06	1.99	1.93	1.89	1.86
30	2.88	2.49	2.28	2.14	2.05	1.98	1.93	1.88	1.85
40	2.84	2.44	2.23	2.09	2.00	1.93	1.87	1.83	1.79
60	2.79	2.39	2.18	2.04	1.95	1.87	1.82	1.77	1.74
120	2.75	2.35	2.13	1.99	1.90	1.82	1.77	1.72	1.68
∞	2.71	2.30	2.08	1.94	1.85	1.77	1.72	1.67	1.63

DENOMINATOR DEGREES OF FREEDOM (row label)

Source: From M. Merrington and C. M. Thompson, "Tables of Percentage Points of the Inverted Beta (*F*)-Distribution," *Biometrika*, 1943, 33, 73–88. Reproduced by permission of the *Biometrika* Trustees.

(continued)

TABLE VIII Continued

ν_2 (DENOMINATOR DEGREES OF FREEDOM) \ ν_1 (NUMERATOR DEGREES OF FREEDOM)	10	12	15	20	24	30	40	60	120	∞
1	60.19	60.71	61.22	61.74	62.00	62.26	62.53	62.79	63.06	63.33
2	9.39	9.41	9.42	9.44	9.45	9.46	9.47	9.47	9.48	9.49
3	5.23	5.22	5.20	5.18	5.18	5.17	5.16	5.15	5.14	5.13
4	3.92	3.90	3.87	3.84	3.83	3.82	3.80	3.79	3.78	3.76
5	3.30	3.27	3.24	3.21	3.19	3.17	3.16	3.14	3.12	3.10
6	2.94	2.90	2.87	2.84	2.82	2.80	2.78	2.76	2.74	2.72
7	2.70	2.67	2.63	2.59	2.58	2.56	2.54	2.51	2.49	2.47
8	2.54	2.50	2.46	2.42	2.40	2.38	2.36	2.34	2.32	2.29
9	2.42	2.38	2.34	2.30	2.28	2.25	2.23	2.21	2.18	2.16
10	2.32	2.28	2.24	2.20	2.18	2.16	2.13	2.11	2.08	2.06
11	2.25	2.21	2.17	2.12	2.10	2.08	2.05	2.03	2.00	1.97
12	2.19	2.15	2.10	2.06	2.04	2.01	1.99	1.96	1.93	1.90
13	2.14	2.10	2.05	2.01	1.98	1.96	1.93	1.90	1.88	1.85
14	2.10	2.05	2.01	1.96	1.94	1.91	1.89	1.86	1.83	1.80
15	2.06	2.02	1.97	1.92	1.90	1.87	1.85	1.82	1.79	1.76
16	2.03	1.99	1.94	1.89	1.87	1.84	1.81	1.78	1.75	1.72
17	2.00	1.96	1.91	1.86	1.84	1.81	1.78	1.75	1.72	1.69
18	1.98	1.93	1.89	1.84	1.81	1.78	1.75	1.72	1.69	1.66
19	1.96	1.91	1.86	1.81	1.79	1.76	1.73	1.70	1.67	1.63
20	1.94	1.89	1.84	1.79	1.77	1.74	1.71	1.68	1.64	1.61
21	1.92	1.87	1.83	1.78	1.75	1.72	1.69	1.66	1.62	1.59
22	1.90	1.86	1.81	1.76	1.73	1.70	1.67	1.64	1.60	1.57
23	1.89	1.84	1.80	1.74	1.72	1.69	1.66	1.62	1.59	1.55
24	1.88	1.83	1.78	1.73	1.70	1.67	1.64	1.61	1.57	1.53
25	1.87	1.82	1.77	1.72	1.69	1.66	1.63	1.59	1.56	1.52
26	1.86	1.81	1.76	1.71	1.68	1.65	1.61	1.58	1.54	1.50
27	1.85	1.80	1.75	1.70	1.67	1.64	1.60	1.57	1.53	1.49
28	1.84	1.79	1.74	1.69	1.66	1.63	1.59	1.56	1.52	1.48
29	1.83	1.78	1.73	1.68	1.65	1.62	1.58	1.55	1.51	1.47
30	1.82	1.77	1.72	1.67	1.64	1.61	1.57	1.54	1.50	1.46
40	1.76	1.71	1.66	1.61	1.57	1.54	1.51	1.47	1.42	1.38
60	1.71	1.66	1.60	1.54	1.51	1.48	1.44	1.40	1.35	1.29
120	1.65	1.60	1.55	1.48	1.45	1.41	1.37	1.32	1.26	1.19
∞	1.60	1.55	1.49	1.42	1.38	1.34	1.30	1.24	1.17	1.00

TABLE IX   Percentage Points of the *F*-distribution, $\alpha = .05$

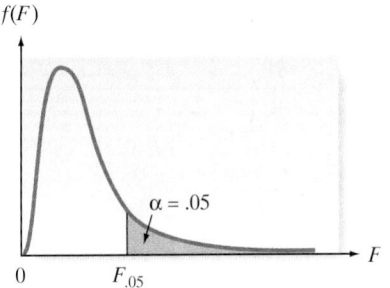

ν_1				NUMERATOR DEGREES OF FREEDOM					
ν_2	1	2	3	4	5	6	7	8	9
1	161.4	199.5	215.7	224.6	230.2	234.0	236.8	238.9	240.5
2	18.51	19.00	19.16	19.25	19.30	19.33	19.35	19.37	19.38
3	10.13	9.55	9.28	9.12	9.01	8.94	8.89	8.85	8.81
4	7.71	6.94	6.59	6.39	6.26	6.16	6.09	6.04	6.00
5	6.61	5.79	5.41	5.19	5.05	4.95	4.88	4.82	4.77
6	5.99	5.14	4.76	4.53	4.39	4.28	4.21	4.15	4.10
7	5.59	4.74	4.35	4.12	3.97	3.87	3.79	3.73	3.68
8	5.32	4.46	4.07	3.84	3.69	3.58	3.50	3.44	3.39
9	5.12	4.26	3.86	3.63	3.48	3.37	3.29	3.23	3.18
10	4.96	4.10	3.71	3.48	3.33	3.22	3.14	3.07	3.02
11	4.84	3.98	3.59	3.36	3.20	3.09	3.01	2.95	2.90
12	4.75	3.89	3.49	3.26	3.11	3.00	2.91	2.85	2.80
13	4.67	3.81	3.41	3.18	3.03	2.92	2.83	2.77	2.71
14	4.60	3.74	3.34	3.11	2.96	2.85	2.76	2.70	2.65
15	4.54	3.68	3.29	3.06	2.90	2.79	2.71	2.64	2.59
16	4.49	3.63	3.24	3.01	2.85	2.74	2.66	2.59	2.54
17	4.45	3.59	3.20	2.96	2.81	2.70	2.61	2.55	2.49
18	4.41	3.55	3.16	2.93	2.77	2.66	2.58	2.51	2.46
19	4.38	3.52	3.13	2.90	2.74	2.63	2.54	2.48	2.42
20	4.35	3.49	3.10	2.87	2.71	2.60	2.51	2.45	2.39
21	4.32	3.47	3.07	2.84	2.68	2.57	2.49	2.42	2.37
22	4.30	3.44	3.05	2.82	2.66	2.55	2.46	2.40	2.34
23	4.28	3.42	3.03	2.80	2.64	2.53	2.44	2.37	2.32
24	4.26	3.40	3.01	2.78	2.62	2.51	2.42	2.36	2.30
25	4.24	3.39	2.99	2.76	2.60	2.49	2.40	2.34	2.28
26	4.23	3.37	2.98	2.74	2.59	2.47	2.39	2.32	2.77
27	4.21	3.35	2.96	2.73	2.57	2.46	2.37	2.31	2.25
28	4.20	3.34	2.95	2.71	2.56	2.45	2.36	2.29	2.24
29	4.18	3.33	2.93	2.70	2.55	2.43	2.35	2.28	2.22
30	4.17	3.32	2.92	2.69	2.53	2.42	2.33	2.27	2.21
40	4.08	3.23	2.84	2.61	2.45	2.34	2.25	2.18	2.12
60	4.00	3.15	2.76	2.53	2.37	2.25	2.17	2.10	2.04
120	3.92	3.07	2.68	2.45	2.29	2.17	2.09	2.02	1.96
∞	3.84	3.00	2.60	2.37	2.21	2.10	2.01	1.94	1.88

DENOMINATOR DEGREES OF FREEDOM

Source: From M. Merrington and C. M. Thompson, "Tables of Percentage Points of the Inverted Beta (*F*)-Distribution," *Biometrika*, 1943, 33, 73–88. Reproduced by permission of the *Biometrika* Trustees.

(continued)

TABLE IX   Continued

ν_1					NUMERATOR DEGREES OF FREEDOM					
ν_2	10	12	15	20	24	30	40	60	120	∞
1	241.9	243.9	245.9	248.0	249.1	250.1	251.1	252.2	253.3	254.3
2	19.40	19.41	19.43	19.45	19.45	19.46	19.47	19.48	19.49	19.50
3	8.79	8.74	8.70	8.66	8.64	8.62	8.59	8.57	8.55	8.53
4	5.96	5.91	5.86	5.80	5.77	5.75	5.72	5.69	5.66	5.63
5	4.74	4.68	4.62	4.56	4.53	4.50	4.46	4.43	4.40	4.36
6	4.06	4.00	3.94	3.87	3.84	3.81	3.77	3.74	3.70	3.67
7	3.64	3.57	3.51	3.44	3.41	3.38	3.34	3.30	3.27	3.23
8	3.35	3.28	3.22	3.15	3.12	3.08	3.04	3.01	2.97	2.93
9	3.14	3.07	3.01	2.94	2.90	2.86	2.83	2.79	2.75	2.71
10	2.98	2.91	2.85	2.77	2.74	2.70	2.66	2.62	2.58	2.54
11	2.85	2.79	2.72	2.65	2.61	2.57	2.53	2.49	2.45	2.40
12	2.75	2.69	2.62	2.54	2.51	2.47	2.43	2.38	2.34	2.30
13	2.67	2.60	2.53	2.46	2.42	2.38	2.34	2.30	2.25	2.21
14	2.60	2.53	2.46	2.39	2.35	2.31	2.27	2.22	2.18	2.13
15	2.54	2.48	2.40	2.33	2.29	2.25	2.20	2.16	2.11	2.07
16	2.49	2.42	2.35	2.28	2.24	2.19	2.15	2.11	2.06	2.01
17	2.45	2.38	2.31	2.23	2.19	2.15	2.10	2.06	2.01	1.96
18	2.41	2.34	2.27	2.19	2.15	2.11	2.06	2.02	1.97	1.92
19	2.38	2.31	2.23	2.16	2.11	2.07	2.03	1.98	1.93	1.88
20	2.35	2.28	2.20	2.12	2.08	2.04	1.99	1.95	1.90	1.84
21	2.32	2.25	2.18	2.10	2.05	2.01	1.96	1.92	1.87	1.81
22	2.30	2.23	2.15	2.07	2.03	1.98	1.94	1.89	1.84	1.78
23	2.27	2.20	2.13	2.05	2.01	1.96	1.91	1.86	1.81	1.76
24	2.25	2.18	2.11	2.03	1.98	1.94	1.89	1.84	1.79	1.73
25	2.24	2.16	2.09	2.01	1.96	1.92	1.87	1.82	1.77	1.71
26	2.22	2.15	2.07	1.99	1.95	1.90	1.85	1.80	1.75	1.69
27	2.20	2.13	2.06	1.97	1.93	1.88	1.84	1.79	1.73	1.67
28	2.19	2.12	2.04	1.96	1.91	1.87	1.82	1.77	1.71	1.65
29	2.18	2.10	2.03	1.94	1.90	1.85	1.81	1.75	1.70	1.64
30	2.16	2.09	2.01	1.93	1.89	1.84	1.79	1.74	1.68	1.62
40	2.08	2.00	1.92	1.84	1.79	1.74	1.69	1.64	1.58	1.51
60	1.99	1.92	1.84	1.75	1.70	1.65	1.59	1.53	1.47	1.39
120	1.91	1.83	1.75	1.66	1.61	1.55	1.50	1.43	1.35	1.25
∞	1.83	1.75	1.67	1.57	1.52	1.46	1.39	1.32	1.22	1.00

DENOMINATOR DEGREES OF FREEDOM

TABLE X   Percentage Points of the *F*-distribution, $\alpha = .025$

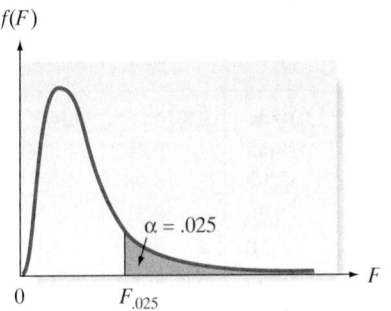

v_2 \ v_1	NUMERATOR DEGREES OF FREEDOM								
	1	2	3	4	5	6	7	8	9
1	647.8	799.5	864.2	899.6	921.8	937.1	948.2	956.7	963.3
2	38.51	39.00	39.17	39.25	39.30	39.33	39.36	39.37	39.39
3	17.44	16.04	15.44	15.10	14.88	14.73	14.62	14.54	14.47
4	12.22	10.65	9.98	9.60	9.36	9.20	9.07	8.98	8.90
5	10.01	8.43	7.76	7.39	7.15	6.98	6.85	6.76	6.68
6	8.81	7.26	6.60	6.23	5.99	5.82	5.70	5.60	5.52
7	8.07	6.54	5.89	5.52	5.29	5.12	4.99	4.90	4.82
8	7.57	6.06	5.42	5.05	4.82	4.65	4.53	4.43	4.36
9	7.21	5.71	5.08	4.72	4.48	4.32	4.20	4.10	4.03
10	6.94	5.46	4.83	4.47	4.24	4.07	3.95	3.85	3.78
11	6.72	5.26	4.63	4.28	4.04	3.88	3.76	3.66	3.59
12	6.55	5.10	4.47	4.12	3.89	3.73	3.61	3.51	3.44
13	6.41	4.97	4.35	4.00	3.77	3.60	3.48	3.39	3.31
14	6.30	4.86	4.24	3.89	3.66	3.50	3.38	3.29	3.21
15	6.20	4.77	4.15	3.80	3.58	3.41	3.29	3.20	3.12
16	6.12	4.69	4.08	3.73	3.50	3.34	3.22	3.12	3.05
17	6.04	4.62	4.01	3.66	3.44	3.28	3.16	3.06	2.98
18	5.98	4.56	3.95	3.61	3.38	3.22	3.10	3.01	2.93
19	5.92	4.51	3.90	3.56	3.33	3.17	3.05	2.96	2.88
20	5.87	4.46	3.86	3.51	3.29	3.13	3.01	2.91	2.84
21	5.83	4.42	3.82	3.48	3.25	3.09	2.97	2.87	2.80
22	5.79	4.38	3.78	3.44	3.22	3.05	2.93	2.84	2.76
23	5.75	4.35	3.75	3.41	3.18	3.02	2.90	2.81	2.73
24	5.72	4.32	3.72	3.38	3.15	2.99	2.87	2.78	2.70
25	5.69	4.29	3.69	3.35	3.13	2.97	2.85	2.75	2.68
26	5.66	4.27	3.67	3.33	3.10	2.94	2.82	2.73	2.65
27	5.63	4.24	3.65	3.31	3.08	2.92	2.80	2.71	2.63
28	5.61	4.22	3.63	3.29	3.06	2.90	2.78	2.69	2.61
29	5.59	4.20	3.61	3.27	3.04	2.88	2.76	2.67	2.59
30	5.57	4.18	3.59	3.25	3.03	2.87	2.75	2.65	2.57
40	5.42	4.05	3.46	3.13	2.90	2.74	2.62	2.53	2.45
60	5.29	3.93	3.34	3.01	2.79	2.63	2.51	2.41	2.33
120	5.15	3.80	3.23	2.89	2.67	2.52	2.39	2.30	2.22
∞	5.02	3.69	3.12	2.79	2.57	2.41	2.29	2.19	2.11

Source: From M. Merrington and C. M. Thompson, "Tables of Percentage Points of the Inverted Beta (*F*)-Distribution," *Biometrika*, 1943, 33, 73–88. Reproduced by permission of the *Biometrika* Trustees.

(continued)

TABLE X   Continued

v_2 \ v_1	NUMERATOR DEGREES OF FREEDOM									
	10	**12**	**15**	**20**	**24**	**30**	**40**	**60**	**120**	**∞**
1	968.6	976.7	984.9	993.1	997.2	1,001	1,006	1,010	1,014	1,018
2	39.40	39.41	39.43	39.45	39.46	39.46	39.47	39.48	39.49	39.50
3	14.42	14.34	14.25	14.17	14.12	14.08	14.04	13.99	13.95	13.90
4	8.84	8.75	8.66	8.56	8.51	8.46	8.41	8.36	8.31	8.26
5	6.62	6.52	6.43	6.33	6.28	6.23	6.18	6.12	6.07	6.02
6	5.46	5.37	5.27	5.17	5.12	5.07	5.01	4.96	4.90	4.85
7	4.76	4.67	4.57	4.47	4.42	4.36	4.31	4.25	4.20	4.14
8	4.30	4.20	4.10	4.00	3.95	3.89	3.84	3.78	3.73	3.67
9	3.96	3.87	3.77	3.67	3.61	3.56	3.51	3.45	3.39	3.33
10	3.72	3.62	3.52	3.42	3.37	3.31	3.26	3.20	3.14	3.08
11	3.53	3.43	3.33	3.23	3.17	3.12	3.06	3.00	2.94	2.88
12	3.37	3.28	3.18	3.07	3.02	2.96	2.91	2.85	2.79	2.72
13	3.25	3.15	3.05	2.95	2.89	2.84	2.78	2.72	2.66	2.60
14	3.15	3.05	2.95	2.84	2.79	2.73	2.67	2.61	2.55	2.49
15	3.06	2.96	2.86	2.76	2.70	2.64	2.59	2.52	2.46	2.40
16	2.99	2.89	2.79	2.68	2.63	2.57	2.51	2.45	2.38	2.32
17	2.92	2.82	2.72	2.62	2.56	2.50	2.44	2.38	2.32	2.25
18	2.87	2.77	2.67	2.56	2.50	2.44	2.38	2.32	2.26	2.19
19	2.82	2.72	2.62	2.51	2.45	2.39	2.33	2.27	2.20	2.13
20	2.77	2.68	2.57	2.46	2.41	2.35	2.29	2.22	2.16	2.09
21	2.73	2.64	2.53	2.42	2.37	2.31	2.25	2.18	2.11	2.04
22	2.70	2.60	2.50	2.39	2.33	2.27	2.21	2.14	2.08	2.00
23	2.67	2.57	2.47	2.36	2.30	2.24	2.18	2.11	2.04	1.97
24	2.64	2.54	2.44	2.33	2.27	2.21	2.15	2.08	2.01	1.94
25	2.61	2.51	2.41	2.30	2.24	2.18	2.12	2.05	1.98	1.91
26	2.59	2.49	2.39	2.28	2.22	2.16	2.09	2.03	1.95	1.88
27	2.57	2.47	2.36	2.25	2.19	2.13	2.07	2.00	1.93	1.85
28	2.55	2.45	2.34	2.23	2.17	2.11	2.05	1.98	1.91	1.83
29	2.53	2.43	2.32	2.21	2.15	2.09	2.03	1.96	1.89	1.81
30	2.51	2.41	2.31	2.20	2.14	2.07	2.01	1.94	1.87	1.79
40	2.39	2.29	2.18	2.07	2.01	1.94	1.88	1.80	1.72	1.64
60	2.27	2.17	2.06	1.94	1.88	1.82	1.74	1.67	1.58	1.48
120	2.16	2.05	1.94	1.82	1.76	1.69	1.61	1.53	1.43	1.31
∞	2.05	1.94	1.83	1.71	1.64	1.57	1.48	1.39	1.27	1.00

DENOMINATOR DEGREES OF FREEDOM

TABLE XI   Percentage Points of the F-distribution, $\alpha = .01$

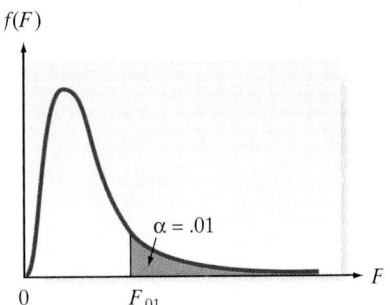

		NUMERATOR DEGREES OF FREEDOM							
ν_1 ν_2	1	2	3	4	5	6	7	8	9
1	4,052	4,999.5	5,403	5,625	5,764	5,859	5,928	5,982	6,022
2	98.50	99.00	99.17	99.25	99.30	99.33	99.36	99.37	99.39
3	34.12	30.82	29.46	28.71	28.24	27.91	27.67	27.49	27.35
4	21.20	18.00	16.69	15.98	15.52	15.21	14.98	14.80	14.66
5	16.26	13.27	12.06	11.39	10.97	10.67	10.46	10.29	10.16
6	13.75	10.92	9.78	9.15	8.75	8.47	8.26	8.10	7.98
7	12.25	9.55	8.45	7.85	7.46	7.19	6.99	6.84	6.72
8	11.26	8.65	7.59	7.01	6.63	6.37	6.18	6.03	5.91
9	10.56	8.02	6.99	6.42	6.06	5.80	5.61	5.47	5.35
10	10.04	7.56	6.55	5.99	5.64	5.39	5.20	5.06	4.94
11	9.65	7.21	6.22	5.67	5.32	5.07	4.89	4.74	4.63
12	9.33	6.93	5.95	5.41	5.06	4.82	4.64	4.50	4.39
13	9.07	6.70	5.74	5.21	4.86	4.62	4.44	4.30	4.19
14	8.86	6.51	5.56	5.04	4.69	4.46	4.28	4.14	4.03
15	8.68	6.36	5.42	4.89	4.56	4.32	4.14	4.00	3.89
16	8.53	6.23	5.29	4.77	4.44	4.20	4.03	3.89	3.78
17	8.40	6.11	5.18	4.67	4.34	4.10	3.93	3.79	3.68
18	8.29	6.01	5.09	4.58	4.25	4.01	3.84	3.71	3.60
19	8.18	5.93	5.01	4.50	4.17	3.94	3.77	3.63	3.52
20	8.10	5.85	4.94	4.43	4.10	3.87	3.70	3.56	3.46
21	8.02	5.78	4.87	4.37	4.04	3.81	3.64	3.51	3.40
22	7.95	5.72	4.82	4.31	3.99	3.76	3.59	3.45	3.35
23	7.88	5.66	4.76	4.26	3.94	3.71	3.54	3.41	3.30
24	7.82	5.61	4.72	4.22	3.90	3.67	3.50	3.36	3.26
25	7.77	5.57	4.68	4.18	3.85	3.63	3.46	3.32	3.22
26	7.72	5.53	4.64	4.14	3.82	3.59	3.42	3.29	3.18
27	7.68	5.49	4.60	4.11	3.78	3.56	3.39	3.26	3.15
28	7.64	5.45	4.57	4.07	3.75	3.53	3.36	3.23	3.12
29	7.60	5.42	4.54	4.04	3.73	3.50	3.33	3.20	3.09
30	7.56	5.39	4.51	4.02	3.70	3.47	3.30	3.17	3.07
40	7.31	5.18	4.31	3.83	3.51	3.29	3.12	2.99	2.89
60	7.08	4.98	4.13	3.65	3.34	3.12	2.95	2.82	2.72
120	6.85	4.79	3.95	3.48	3.17	2.96	2.79	2.66	2.56
∞	6.63	4.61	3.78	3.32	3.02	2.80	2.64	2.51	2.41

DENOMINATOR DEGREES OF FREEDOM

Source: From M. Merrington and C. M. Thompson, "Tables of Percentage Points of the Inverted Beta (*F*)-Distribution," *Biometrika,* 1943, 33, 73–88. Reproduced by permission of the *Biometrika* Trustees.

(continued)

TABLE XI   Continued

v_2	v_1 10	12	15	20	24	30	40	60	120	∞
				NUMERATOR DEGREES OF FREEDOM						
1	6,056	6,106	6,157	6,209	6,235	6,261	6,287	6,313	6,339	6,366
2	99.40	99.42	99.43	99.45	99.46	99.47	99.47	99.48	99.49	99.50
3	27.23	27.05	26.87	26.69	26.60	26.50	26.41	26.32	26.22	26.13
4	14.55	14.37	14.20	14.02	13.93	13.84	13.75	13.65	13.56	13.46
5	10.05	9.89	9.72	9.55	9.47	9.38	9.29	9.20	9.11	9.02
6	7.87	7.72	7.56	7.40	7.31	7.23	7.14	7.06	6.97	6.88
7	6.62	6.47	6.31	6.16	6.07	5.99	5.91	5.82	5.74	5.65
8	5.81	5.67	5.52	5.36	5.28	5.20	5.12	5.03	4.95	4.86
9	5.26	5.11	4.96	4.81	4.73	4.65	4.57	4.48	4.40	4.31
10	4.85	4.71	4.56	4.41	4.33	4.25	4.17	4.08	4.00	3.91
11	4.54	4.40	4.25	4.10	4.02	3.94	3.86	3.78	3.69	3.60
12	4.30	4.16	4.01	3.86	3.78	3.70	3.62	3.54	3.45	3.36
13	4.10	3.96	3.82	3.66	3.59	3.51	3.43	3.34	3.25	3.17
14	3.94	3.80	3.66	3.51	3.43	3.35	3.27	3.18	3.09	3.00
15	3.80	3.67	3.52	3.37	3.29	3.21	3.13	3.05	2.96	2.87
16	3.69	3.55	3.41	3.26	3.18	3.10	3.02	2.93	2.84	2.75
17	3.59	3.46	3.31	3.16	3.08	3.00	2.92	2.83	2.75	2.65
18	3.51	3.37	3.23	3.08	3.00	2.92	2.84	2.75	2.66	2.57
19	3.43	3.30	3.15	3.00	2.92	2.84	2.76	2.67	2.58	2.49
20	3.37	3.23	3.09	2.94	2.86	2.78	2.69	2.61	2.52	2.42
21	3.31	3.17	3.03	2.88	2.80	2.72	2.64	2.55	2.46	2.36
22	3.26	3.12	2.98	2.83	2.75	2.67	2.58	2.50	2.40	2.31
23	3.21	3.07	2.93	2.78	2.70	2.62	2.54	2.45	2.35	2.26
24	3.17	3.03	2.89	2.74	2.66	2.58	2.49	2.40	2.31	2.21
25	3.13	2.99	2.85	2.70	2.62	2.54	2.45	2.36	2.27	2.17
26	3.09	2.96	2.81	2.66	2.58	2.50	2.42	2.33	2.23	2.13
27	3.06	2.93	2.78	2.63	2.55	2.47	2.38	2.29	2.20	2.10
28	3.03	2.90	2.75	2.60	2.52	2.44	2.35	2.26	2.17	2.06
29	3.00	2.87	2.73	2.57	2.49	2.41	2.33	2.23	2.14	2.03
30	2.98	2.84	2.70	2.55	2.47	2.39	2.30	2.21	2.11	2.01
40	2.80	2.66	2.52	2.37	2.29	2.20	2.11	2.02	1.92	1.80
60	2.63	2.50	2.35	2.20	2.12	2.03	1.94	1.84	1.73	1.60
120	2.47	2.34	2.19	2.03	1.95	1.86	1.76	1.66	1.53	1.38
∞	2.32	2.18	2.04	1.88	1.79	1.70	1.59	1.47	1.32	1.00

DENOMINATOR DEGREES OF FREEDOM

TABLE XII   Control Chart Constants

Number of Observations in Subgroup, n	A_2	d_2	d_3	D_3	D_4
2	1.880	1.128	.853	.000	3.267
3	1.023	1.693	.888	.000	2.574
4	.729	2.059	.880	.000	2.282
5	.577	2.326	.864	.000	2.114
6	.483	2.534	.848	.000	2.004
7	.419	2.704	.833	.076	1.924
8	.373	2.847	.820	.136	1.864
9	.337	2.970	.808	.184	1.816
10	.308	3.078	.797	.223	1.777
11	.285	3.173	.787	.256	1.744
12	.266	3.258	.778	.283	1.717
13	.249	3.336	.770	.307	1.693
14	.235	3.407	.762	.328	1.672
15	.223	3.472	.755	.347	1.653
16	.212	3.532	.749	.363	1.637
17	.203	3.588	.743	.378	1.622
18	.194	3.640	.738	.391	1.608
19	.187	3.689	.733	.403	1.597
20	.180	3.735	.729	.415	1.585
21	.173	3.778	.724	.425	1.575
22	.167	3.819	.720	.434	1.566
23	.162	3.858	.716	.443	1.557
24	.157	3.895	.712	.451	1.548
25	.153	3.931	.709	.459	1.541

Source: ASTM Manual on the Presentation of Data and Control Chart Analysis, Philadelphia, PA: American Society for Testing Materials, pp. 134–136, 1976.

TABLE XIII Critical Values for the Durbin-Watson d Statistic, $\alpha = .05$

	$k = 1$		$k = 2$		$k = 3$		$k = 4$		$k = 5$	
n	d_L	d_U	d_L	d_U	d_L	d_U	d_L	d_U	d_L	d_U
15	1.08	1.36	.95	1.54	.82	1.75	.69	1.97	.56	2.21
16	1.10	1.37	.98	1.54	.86	1.73	.74	1.93	.62	2.15
17	1.13	1.38	1.02	1.54	.90	1.71	.78	1.90	.67	2.10
18	1.16	1.39	1.05	1.53	.93	1.69	.92	1.87	.71	2.06
19	1.18	1.40	1.08	1.53	.97	1.68	.86	1.85	.75	2.02
20	1.20	1.41	1.10	1.54	1.00	1.68	.90	1.83	.79	1.99
21	1.22	1.42	1.13	1.54	1.03	1.67	.93	1.81	.83	1.96
22	1.24	1.43	1.15	1.54	1.05	1.66	.96	1.80	.96	1.94
23	1.26	1.44	1.17	1.54	1.08	1.66	.99	1.79	.90	1.92
24	1.27	1.45	1.19	1.55	1.10	1.66	1.01	1.78	.93	1.90
25	1.29	1.45	1.21	1.55	1.12	1.66	1.04	1.77	.95	1.89
26	1.30	1.46	1.22	1.55	1.14	1.65	1.06	1.76	.98	1.88
27	1.32	1.47	1.24	1.56	1.16	1.65	1.08	1.76	1.01	1.86
28	1.33	1.48	1.26	1.56	1.18	1.65	1.10	1.75	1.03	1.85
29	1.34	1.48	1.27	1.56	1.20	1.65	1.12	1.74	1.05	1.84
30	1.35	1.49	1.28	1.57	1.21	1.65	1.14	1.74	1.07	1.83
31	1.36	1.50	1.30	1.57	1.23	1.65	1.16	1.74	1.09	1.83
32	1.37	1.50	1.31	1.57	1.24	1.65	1.18	1.73	1.11	1.82
33	1.38	1.51	1.32	1.58	1.26	1.65	1.19	1.73	1.13	1.81
34	1.39	1.51	1.33	1.58	1.27	1.65	1.21	1.73	1.15	1.81
35	1.40	1.52	1.34	1.58	1.28	1.65	1.22	1.73	1.16	1.80
36	1.41	1.52	1.35	1.59	1.29	1.65	1.24	1.73	1.18	1.80
37	1.42	1.53	1.36	1.59	1.31	1.66	1.25	1.72	1.19	1.80
38	1.43	1.54	1.37	1.59	1.32	1.66	1.26	1.72	1.21	1.79
39	1.43	1.54	1.38	1.60	1.33	1.66	1.27	1.72	1.22	1.79
40	1.44	1.54	1.39	1.60	1.34	1.66	1.29	1.72	1.23	1.79
45	1.48	1.57	1.43	1.62	1.38	1.67	1.34	1.72	1.29	1.78
50	1.50	1.59	1.46	1.63	1.42	1.67	1.38	1.72	1.34	1.77
55	1.53	1.60	1.49	1.64	1.45	1.68	1.41	1.72	1.38	1.77
60	1.55	1.62	1.51	1.65	1.48	1.69	1.44	1.73	1.41	1.77
65	1.57	1.63	1.54	1.66	1.50	1.70	1.47	1.73	1.44	1.77
70	1.58	1.64	1.55	1.67	1.52	1.70	1.49	1.74	1.46	1.77
75	1.60	1.65	1.57	1.68	1.54	1.71	1.51	1.74	1.49	1.77
80	1.61	1.66	1.59	1.69	1.56	1.72	1.53	1.74	1.51	1.77
85	1.62	1.67	1.60	1.70	1.57	1.72	1.55	1.75	1.52	1.77
90	1.63	1.68	1.61	1.70	1.59	1.73	1.57	1.75	1.54	1.78
95	1.64	1.69	1.62	1.71	1.60	1.73	1.58	1.75	1.56	1.78
100	1.65	1.69	1.63	1.72	1.61	1.74	1.59	1.76	1.57	1.78

Source: From J. Durbin and G. S. Watson, "Testing for Serial Correlation in Least Squares Regression, II," *Biometrika,* 1951, 30, 159–178. Reproduced by permission of the *Biometrika* Trustees.

TABLE XIV Critical Values for the Durbin-Watson *d* Statistic, $\alpha = .01$

n	*k* = 1 d_L	*k* = 1 d_U	*k* = 2 d_L	*k* = 2 d_U	*k* = 3 d_L	*k* = 3 d_U	*k* = 4 d_L	*k* = 4 d_U	*k* = 5 d_L	*k* = 5 d_U
15	.81	1.07	.70	1.25	.59	1.46	.49	1.70	.39	1.96
16	.84	1.09	.74	1.25	.63	1.44	.53	1.66	.44	1.90
17	.87	1.10	.77	1.25	.67	1.43	.57	1.3	.48	1.85
18	.90	1.12	.80	1.26	.71	1.42	.61	1.60	.52	1.80
19	.93	1.13	.83	1.26	.74	1.41	.65	1.58	.56	1.77
20	.95	1.15	.86	1.27	.77	1.41	.68	1.57	.60	1.74
21	.97	1.16	.89	1.27	.80	1.41	.72	1.55	.63	1.71
22	1.00	1.17	.91	1.28	.83	1.40	.75	1.54	.66	1.69
23	1.02	1.19	.94	1.29	.86	1.40	.77	1.53	.70	1.67
24	1.04	1.20	.96	1.30	.88	1.41	.80	1.53	.72	1.66
25	1.05	1.21	.98	1.30	.90	1.41	.83	1.52	.75	1.65
26	1.07	1.22	1.00	1.31	.93	1.41	.85	1.52	.78	1.64
27	1.09	1.23	1.02	1.32	.95	1.41	.88	1.51	.81	1.63
28	1.10	1.24	1.04	1.32	.97	1.41	.90	1.51	.83	1.62
29	1.12	1.25	1.05	1.33	.99	1.42	.92	1.51	.85	1.61
30	1.13	1.26	1.07	1.34	1.01	1.42	.94	1.51	.88	1.61
31	1.15	1.27	1.08	1.34	1.02	1.42	.96	1.51	.90	1.60
32	1.16	1.28	1.10	1.35	1.04	1.43	.98	1.51	.92	1.60
33	1.17	1.29	1.11	1.36	1.05	1.43	1.00	1.51	.94	1.59
34	1.18	1.30	1.13	1.36	1.07	1.43	1.01	1.51	.95	1.59
35	1.19	1.31	1.14	1.27	1.08	1.44	1.03	1.51	.97	1.59
36	1.21	1.32	1.15	1.38	1.10	1.44	1.04	1.51	.99	1.59
37	1.22	1.32	1.16	1.38	1.11	1.45	1.06	1.51	1.00	1.59
38	1.23	1.33	1.18	1.39	1.12	1.45	1.07	1.52	1.02	1.58
39	1.24	1.34	1.19	1.39	1.14	1.45	1.09	1.52	1.03	1.58
40	1.25	1.34	1.20	1.40	1.15	1.46	1.10	1.52	1.05	1.58
45	1.29	1.38	1.24	1.42	1.20	1.48	1.16	1.53	1.11	1.58
50	1.32	1.40	1.28	1.45	1.24	1.49	1.20	1.54	1.16	1.59
55	1.36	1.43	1.32	1.47	1.28	1.51	1.25	1.55	1.21	1.59
60	1.38	1.45	1.35	1.48	1.32	1.52	1.28	1.56	1.25	1.60
65	1.41	1.47	1.38	1.50	1.35	1.53	1.31	1.57	1.28	1.61
70	1.43	1.49	1.40	1.52	1.37	1.55	1.34	1.58	1.31	1.61
75	1.45	1.50	1.42	1.53	1.39	1.56	1.37	1.59	1.34	1.62
80	1.47	1.52	1.44	1.54	1.42	1.57	1.39	1.60	1.36	1.62
85	1.48	1.53	1.46	1.55	1.43	1.58	1.41	1.60	1.39	1.63
90	1.50	1.54	1.47	1.56	1.45	1.59	1.43	1.61	1.41	1.64
95	1.51	1.55	1.49	1.57	1.47	1.60	1.45	1.62	1.42	1.64
100	1.52	1.56	1.50	1.58	1.48	1.60	1.46	1.63	1.44	1.65

Source: From J. Durbin and G. S. Watson, "Testing for Serial Correlation in Least Squares Regression, II," *Biometrika*, 1951, 30, 159–178. Reproduced by permission of the *Biometrika* Trustees.

TABLE XV   Critical Values of T_L and T_U for the Wilcoxon Rank Sum Test: Independent Samples

Test statistic is the rank sum associated with the smaller sample (if equal sample sizes, either rank sum can be used).

a. $\alpha = .025$ one-tailed; $\alpha = .05$ two-tailed

n_2 \ n_1	3		4		5		6		7		8		9		10	
	T_L	T_U	T_L	T_U	T_L	T_U	T_L	T_U	T_L	T_U	T_L	T_U	T_L	T_U	T_L	T_U
3	5	16	6	18	6	21	7	23	7	26	8	28	8	31	9	33
4	6	18	11	25	12	28	12	32	13	35	14	38	15	41	16	44
5	6	21	12	28	18	37	19	41	20	45	21	49	22	53	24	56
6	7	23	12	32	19	41	26	52	28	56	29	61	31	65	32	70
7	7	26	13	35	20	45	28	56	37	68	39	73	41	78	43	83
8	8	28	14	38	21	49	29	61	39	73	49	87	51	93	54	98
9	8	31	15	41	22	53	31	65	41	78	51	93	63	108	66	114
10	9	33	16	44	24	56	32	70	43	83	54	98	66	114	79	131

b. $\alpha = .05$ one-tailed; $\alpha = .10$ two-tailed

n_2 \ n_1	3		4		5		6		7		8		9		10	
	T_L	T_U	T_L	T_U	T_L	T_U	T_L	T_U	T_L	T_U	T_L	T_U	T_L	T_U	T_L	T_U
3	6	15	7	17	7	20	8	22	9	24	9	27	10	29	11	31
4	7	17	12	24	13	27	14	30	15	33	16	36	17	39	18	42
5	7	20	13	27	19	36	20	40	22	43	24	46	25	50	26	54
6	8	22	14	30	20	40	28	50	30	54	32	58	33	63	35	67
7	9	24	15	33	22	43	30	54	39	66	41	71	43	76	46	80
8	9	27	16	36	24	46	32	58	41	71	52	84	54	90	57	95
9	10	29	17	39	25	50	33	63	43	76	54	90	66	105	69	111
10	11	31	18	42	26	54	35	67	46	80	57	95	69	111	83	127

Source: From F. Wilcoxon and R. A. Wilcox, "Some Rapid Approximate Statistical Procedures," 1964, 20–23. Courtesy of Lederle Laboratories Division of American Cyanamid Company, Madison, NJ.

TABLE XVI   Critical Values of T_0 in the Wilcoxon Paired Difference Signed Rank Test

One-Tailed	Two-Tailed	$n = 5$	$n = 6$	$n = 7$	$n = 8$	$n = 9$	$n = 10$
$\alpha = .05$	$\alpha = .10$	1	2	4	6	8	11
$\alpha = .025$	$\alpha = .05$		1	2	4	6	8
$\alpha = .01$	$\alpha = .02$			0	2	3	5
$\alpha = .005$	$\alpha = .01$				0	2	3
		$n = 11$	$n = 12$	$n = 13$	$n = 14$	$n = 15$	$n = 16$
$\alpha = .05$	$\alpha = .10$	14	17	21	26	30	36
$\alpha = .025$	$\alpha = .05$	11	14	17	21	25	30
$\alpha = .01$	$\alpha = .02$	7	10	13	16	20	24
$\alpha = .005$	$\alpha = .01$	5	7	10	13	16	19
		$n = 17$	$n = 18$	$n = 19$	$n = 20$	$n = 21$	$n = 22$
$\alpha = .05$	$\alpha = .10$	41	47	54	60	68	75
$\alpha = .025$	$\alpha = .05$	35	40	46	52	59	66
$\alpha = .01$	$\alpha = .02$	28	33	38	43	49	56
$\alpha = .005$	$\alpha = .01$	23	28	32	37	43	49
		$n = 23$	$n = 24$	$n = 25$	$n = 26$	$n = 27$	$n = 28$
$\alpha = .05$	$\alpha = .10$	83	92	101	110	120	130
$\alpha = .025$	$\alpha = .05$	73	81	90	98	107	117
$\alpha = .01$	$\alpha = .02$	62	69	77	85	93	102
$\alpha = .005$	$\alpha = .01$	55	61	68	76	84	92
		$n = 29$	$n = 30$	$n = 31$	$n = 32$	$n = 33$	$n = 34$
$\alpha = .05$	$\alpha = .10$	141	152	163	175	188	201
$\alpha = .025$	$\alpha = .05$	127	137	148	159	171	183
$\alpha = .01$	$\alpha = .02$	111	120	130	141	151	162
$\alpha = .005$	$\alpha = .01$	100	109	118	128	138	149
		$n = 35$	$n = 36$	$n = 37$	$n = 38$	$n = 39$	
$\alpha = .05$	$\alpha = .10$	214	228	242	256	271	
$\alpha = .025$	$\alpha = .05$	195	208	222	235	250	
$\alpha = .01$	$\alpha = .02$	174	186	198	211	224	
$\alpha = .005$	$\alpha = .01$	160	171	183	195	208	
		$n = 40$	$n = 41$	$n = 42$	$n = 43$	$n = 44$	$n = 45$
$\alpha = .05$	$\alpha = .10$	287	303	319	336	353	371
$\alpha = .025$	$\alpha = .05$	264	279	295	311	327	344
$\alpha = .01$	$\alpha = .02$	238	252	267	281	297	313
$\alpha = .005$	$\alpha = .01$	221	234	248	262	277	292
		$n = 46$	$n = 47$	$n = 48$	$n = 49$	$n = 50$	
$\alpha = .05$	$\alpha = .10$	389	408	427	446	466	
$\alpha = .025$	$\alpha = .05$	361	379	397	415	434	
$\alpha = .01$	$\alpha = .02$	329	345	362	380	398	
$\alpha = .005$	$\alpha = .01$	307	323	339	356	373	

Source: From F. Wilcoxon and R. A. Wilcox, "Some Rapid Approximate Statistical Procedures," 1964, p. 28. Courtesy of Lederle Laboratories Division of American Cyanamid Company, Madison, NJ.

TABLE XVII Critical Values of Spearman's Rank Correlation Coefficient

The values correspond to a one-tailed test of $H_0: \rho = 0$. The value should be doubled for two-tailed tests.

n	$\alpha = .05$	$\alpha = .025$	$\alpha = .01$	$\alpha = .005$	n	$\alpha = .05$	$\alpha = .025$	$\alpha = .01$	$\alpha = .005$
5	.900	—	—	—	18	.399	.476	.564	.625
6	.829	.886	.943	—	19	.388	.462	.549	.608
7	.714	.786	.893	—	20	.377	.450	.534	.591
8	.643	.738	.833	.881	21	.368	.438	.521	.576
9	.600	.683	.783	.833	22	.359	.428	.508	.562
10	.564	.648	.745	.794	23	.351	.418	.496	.549
11	.523	.623	.736	.818	24	.343	.409	.485	.537
12	.497	.591	.703	.780	25	.336	.400	.475	.526
13	.475	.566	.673	.745	26	.329	.392	.465	.515
14	.457	.545	.646	.716	27	.323	.385	.456	.505
15	.441	.525	.623	.689	28	.317	.377	.448	.496
16	.425	.507	.601	.666	29	.311	.370	.440	.487
17	.412	.490	.582	.645	30	.305	.364	.432	.478

Source: From E. G. Olds, "Distribution of Sums of Squares of Rank Differences for Small Samples," *Annals of Mathematical Statistics,* 1938, 9. Reproduced with the permission of the Editor, *Annals of Mathematical Statistics.*

Appendix C
Calculation Formulas for Analysis of Variance

C.1 Formulas for the Calculations in the Completely Randomized Design

C.2 Formulas for the Calculations in the Randomized Block Design

C.3 Formulas for the Calculations for a Two-Factor Factorial Experiment

C.1 FORMULAS FOR THE CALCULATIONS IN THE COMPLETELY RANDOMIZED DESIGN

$$CM = \text{Correction for mean}$$

$$= \frac{(\text{Total of all observations})^2}{\text{Total number of observations}} = \frac{\left(\sum_{i=1}^{n} y_i\right)^2}{n}$$

$$SS(\text{Total}) = \text{Total sum of squares}$$

$$= (\text{Sum of squares of all observations}) - CM = \sum_{i=1}^{n} y_i^2 - CM$$

$$SST = \text{Sum of squares for treatments}$$

$$= \begin{pmatrix} \text{Sum of squares of treatment totals with} \\ \text{each square divided by the number of} \\ \text{observations for that treatment} \end{pmatrix} - CM$$

$$= \frac{T_1^2}{n_1} + \frac{T_2^2}{n_2} + \cdots + \frac{T_p^2}{n_p} - CM$$

$$SSE = \text{Sum of squares for error} = SS(\text{Total}) - SST$$

$$MST = \text{Mean square for treatments} = \frac{SST}{p-1}$$

$$MSE = \text{Mean square for error} = \frac{SSE}{n-p}$$

$$F = \text{Test statistic} = \frac{MST}{MSE}$$

where

$$n = \text{Total number of observations}$$

$$p = \text{Number of treatments}$$

$$T_i = \text{Total for treatment } i \ (i = 1, 2, \ldots, p)$$

C.2   FORMULAS FOR THE CALCULATIONS IN THE RANDOMIZED BLOCK DESIGN

$$CM = \text{Correction for mean}$$

$$= \frac{(\text{Total of all observations})^2}{\text{Total number of observations}} = \frac{\left(\sum y_i\right)^2}{n}$$

$$SS(\text{Total}) = \text{Total sum of squares}$$

$$= (\text{Sum of squares of all observations}) - CM = \sum y_i^2 - CM$$

$$SST = \text{Sum of squares for treatments}$$

$$= \left(\begin{array}{c}\text{Sum of squares of treatment totals with}\\ \text{each square divided by } b, \text{ the number of}\\ \text{observations for that treatment}\end{array}\right) - CM$$

$$= \frac{T_1^2}{b} + \frac{T_2^2}{b} + \cdots + \frac{T_p^2}{b} - CM$$

$$SST = \text{Sum of squares for blocks}$$

$$= \left(\begin{array}{c}\text{Sum of squares of block totals with}\\ \text{each square divided by } p, \text{ the number}\\ \text{of observations in that block}\end{array}\right) - CM$$

$$= \frac{B_1^2}{p} + \frac{B_2^2}{p} + \cdots + \frac{B_b^2}{p} - CM$$

$$SSE = \text{Sum of squares for error} = SS(\text{Total}) - SST - SSB$$

$$MST = \text{Mean square for treatments} = \frac{SST}{p - 1}$$

$$MSB = \text{Mean square for blocks} = \frac{SSB}{b - 1}$$

$$MSE = \text{Mean square for error} = \frac{SSE}{n - p - b + 1}$$

$$F = \text{Test statistic} = \frac{MST}{MSE}$$

where

$$n = \text{Total number of observations}$$
$$b = \text{Number of blocks}$$
$$p = \text{Number of treatments}$$
$$T_i = \text{Total for treatment } i \ (i = 1, 2, \ldots, p)$$
$$B_i = \text{Total for block } i \ (i = 1, 2, \ldots, b)$$

C.3   FORMULAS FOR THE CALCULATIONS FOR A TWO-FACTOR FACTORIAL EXPERIMENT

$$CM = \text{Correction for mean}$$

$$= \frac{(\text{Total of all } n \text{ measurements})^2}{n} = \frac{\left(\sum_{i=1}^{n} y_i\right)^2}{n}$$

$$SS(\text{Total}) = \text{Total sum of squares}$$

$$= (\text{Sum of squares of all } n \text{ measurements}) - CM = \sum_{i=1}^{n} y_i^2 - CM$$

$$SS(A) = \text{Sum of squares for main effects, factor } A$$

$$= \left(\begin{array}{c} \text{Sum of squares of the totals } A_1, A_2, \ldots, A_a \\ \text{divided by the number of measurements} \\ \text{in a single total, namely } br \end{array}\right) - CM$$

$$= \frac{\sum_{i=1}^{a} A_i^2}{br} - CM$$

$$SS(B) = \text{Sum of squares for main effects, factor } B$$

$$= \left(\begin{array}{c} \text{Sum of squares of the totals } B_1, B_2, \ldots, B_b \\ \text{divided by the number of measurements} \\ \text{in a single total, namely } ar \end{array}\right) - CM$$

$$= \frac{\sum_{i=1}^{b} B_i^2}{ar} - CM$$

$$SS(AB) = \text{Sum of squares for } AB \text{ interaction}$$

$$= \left(\begin{array}{c} \text{Sum of squares of the cell totals} \\ AB_{11}, AB_{12}, \ldots, AB_{ab} \text{ divided by} \\ \text{the number of measurements} \\ \text{in a single total, namely } r \end{array}\right) - SS(A) - SS(B) - CM$$

$$= \frac{\sum_{j=1}^{b} \sum_{i=1}^{a} AB_{ij}^2}{r} - SS(A) - SS(B) - CM$$

where

$a = \text{Number of level of factor } A$

$b = \text{Number of levels of factor } B$

$r = \text{Number of replicates (observations per treatment)}$

$A_i = \text{Total for level } i \text{ of factor } A \ (i = 1, 2, \ldots, a)$

$B_j = \text{Total for level } j \text{ of factor } B \ (j = 1, 2, \ldots, b)$

$AB_{ij} = \text{Total for treatment } (i, j), \text{ i.e., for } i\text{th level of factor } A \text{ and } j\text{th level of factor } B$

Answers to Selected Exercises

Chapter 1

1.3 population; variables; summary tools; conclusions   **1.5** published source; designed experiment; survey; observationally   **1.13** qualitative; qualitative   **1.15 a.** all U.S. citizens   **b.** president's job performance; qualitative   **c.** 2,000 polled individuals   **d.** Estimate the proportion of all citizens who believe the president is doing a good job.   **e.** survey   **f.** not very likely   **1.17** I. qualitative II. quantitative III. qualitative IV. qualitative V. qualitative VI. quantitative   **1.19 a.** CEOs of all U.S companies   **b.** (1) qualitative; (2) quantitative (3) quantitative (4) quantitative   **c.** sample not representative of population of CEOs   **1.21 a.** all U.S. employees   **b.** employee's job status   **c.** qualitative   **d.** 1,000 employees surveyed   **e.** majority of all workers would remain in their jobs   **1.23 a.** quantitative   **b.** quantitative   **c.** qualitative   **d.** quantitative   **e.** qualitative   **f.** quantitative   **g.** qualitative   **1.25 b.** speed of the deliveries; accuracy of the invoices; quality of the packaging   **c.** total numbers of questionnaires received   **1.27 a.** all department store executives   **b.** job satisfaction; Machiavellian rating   **c.** 218 department store executives   **d.** survey   **e.** Executives with higher job-satisfaction scores are likely to have a lower 'mach' rating.   **1.31 a.** all persons over 14 in U.S.   **b.** unemployment status; qualitative   **c.** inferential

Chapter 2

2.1 16; .18; .45; .15; .14   **2.3 a.** pie chart   **b.** breast cancer   **c.** $(13\% + 3\% + 3\%) = 19\%$ **2.5 a.** body defect   **b.** paint or dents   **2.7 b.** yes   **c.** banks: yes; department stores: no   **2.9** Channel catfish: 66.7%; large-mouth bass: 8.3%; small-mouth buffalo: 25%   **2.11** Most often: F color (26.6%), clarity VS1 (26.3%); least often: D color (5.2%), IF clarity (14.3%)   **2.13 a.** response time   **c.** 3,570   **2.15 b.** inflation rate (58%)   **c.** yes, inflation rate and real estate prices represent 78% of investors   **2.17** 50, 75, 125, 100, 25, 50, 50, 25   **2.19 a.** frequency histogram   **b.** 14   **c.** 49   **2.21 a.** 28.5%   **b.** 82%   **2.23 b.** Cardinals tend to score more runs when McGuire hit multiple home runs   **2.25 d.** HRD group   **2.27 c.** penalties for CAA tend to be smaller   **2.29 a.** 2000 SAT scores are shifted to the right of the scores from 1990   **c.** similar conclusion   **d.** Illinois (65), Minnesota (65) and Wisconsin (70)   **2.31 a.** 44.75%   **b.** .325   **2.33 a.** 12   **b.** 40   **c.** 7   **d.** 21   **e.** 144   **2.35 a.** 11.2   **b.** 12   **c.** 30   **2.37 a.** $\bar{x} = 2.717, m = 2.65$ **2.41** mode $= 15; \bar{x} = 14.545; m = 15$ **2.43 a.** mean less than median   **b.** mean greater than median   **c.** equal   **2.45 a.** $\bar{x} = 49.74, m = 49$, mode $= 53$ **b.** slightly skewed right   **c.** 47.5 to 50   **2.47 a.** $\bar{x} = .63$; average number of carats of 308 diamonds is .63   **b.** $m = .62$; 50% of the diamonds weigh less than .62 carat   **c.** mode $= 1.0$; carat value of 1.0 occurred the most often   **d.** mean or median   **2.49** data are probably not skewed, but close to symmetric   **2.53 a.** joint: $= 2.6545$, m $= 1.5$; no prefiling: $= 4.2364, m = 3.2$; prepack: $= 1.8185$, $m = 1.4$ **b.** three centers   **2.55 c.** no; yes (if the data are between 0 and 1)   **2.57 a.** $R = 4, s^2 = 2.3, s = 1.52$ **b.** $R = 6, s^2 = 3.619, s = 1.90$ **c.** $R = 10, s^2 = 7.111, s = 2.67$ **d.** $R = 5, s^2 = 1.624, s = 1.274$ **2.59 a.** $\bar{x} = 5.6$, $s^2 = 17.3, s = 4.1593$ **b.** $\bar{x} = 13.75$ feet, $s^2 = 152.25$ square feet, $s = 12.339$ feet   **c.** $\bar{x} = -2.5, s^2 = 4.3, s = 2.0736$ **b.** $\bar{x} = .33$ ounce, $s^2 = .0587$ square ounce, $s = .2422$ ounce   **2.61** Data set 1: 0, 1, 2, 3, 4, 5, 6, 7, 8, 9; data set 2: 0, 0, 1, 1, 2, 2, 3, 3, 9, 9   **2.63 a.** $355 - 63 = 292$ **b.** $301 - 64 = 237$ **c.** no   **2.65 a.** $R = 34.5$ cm, $s^2 = 47.36$ square cm, $s = 6.88$ cm   **b.** $R = 2,129$ g, $s^2 = 141,787$ square g, $s = 376.6$ g   **c.** $R = 1,099.89$ ppm, $s^2 = 9,678$ square ppm, $s = 98.4$ g   **2.67 a.** $R = 12, s^2 = 9.37, s = 3.06$ **b.** $R = 8, s^2 = 5.15, s = 2.27$ **c.** $R = 8, s^2 = 5.06, s = 2.25$ **2.69 a.** dollars; quantitative   **b.** at least $^3/_4$; at least 8/9; nothing; nothing   **2.71** approx. 68%; approx. 95%; essentially all   **2.73** between $R/6 = 104.17$ and $R/4 = 156.25$ **2.75 a.** (105.77, 176.85)   **b.** at least $^3/_4$ **c.** nothing   **2.77 a.** $\bar{x} = 93.1, s = 5.2$ **b.** (87.9, 98.3); (82.7, 103.5); (77.6, 108.7)   **c.** 87.4%; 97.4%; 98.7%   **2.79** $\bar{x} = 59.82, s = 53.36; (-100.27, 219.91)$ **2.81 a.** at least 8/9 of the velocities fall within (906, 966)   **b.** no   **2.83** do not buy   **2.85** 11:30 and 4:00   **2.87 a.** 75%   **b.** 50%   **c.** 20%   **d.** 84%   **2.89 a.** $z = 2$ **b.** $z = -3$ **c.** $z = -2$ **d.** $z = 1.67$ **2.91** average score is 500; 5% of eighth-graders score below 356; 25% score below 435; 75% score below 563; 95% score below 653   **2.93 a.** $\bar{x} = 16.42, s = 43.15$ **b.** $z = -.38$ **c.** $z = .12$ **2.95** no   **2.97 a.** 0   **b.** 21   **c.** $\bar{x} = 5.24, s = 7.24; z = 5.90$ **d.** yes   **2.99 a.** $z = .727$, no   **b.** $z = -3.273$, yes   **c.** $z = 1.364$, no   **d.** $z = 3.727$, yes   **2.103 a.** $z = 1.05$, no   **b.** greater than 194.6 or less than 88   **2.105 b.** Joint:1.5; None firms: 3.2; Prepack: 1.4   **d.** no   **e.** yes   **2.107 a.** 5 outliers: 52, 77, 78, 82, and 83   **b.** 2 outliers: 52 and 77   **c.** no   **2.109 b.** customers 268, 269, and 264   **c.** 2.06, 2.13, and 3.14   **2.113** increasing   **2.115 a.** generally increasing   **b.** generally increasing   **c.** generally increasing   **2.117** length vs. weight: increasing; length vs. DDT: slightly increasing; weight vs. DDT:

no trend **2.121 a.** $-1, 1, 2$ **b.** $0, 4, 6$ **c.** $1, 3, 4$ **d.** $.1, .3, .4$ **2.123 a.** $6, 27, 5.20$ **b.** $6.25, 28.25, 5.32$ **c.** $7, 37.67, 6.14$
d. $3, 0, 0$ **2.127** 60% of cars with 4-star rating **2.129** $m = 129,200.5; \bar{x} = 197,632.25$ **2.131 a.** frequency bar chart
c. 70% of imprints successful **2.133 a.** sample **b.** 42.5% are negotiated coach **c.** yes **2.135 b.** marketing: 6.5 days, engineering: 7.0 days; accounting: 8.5 days **2.137 a.** no scale on vertical axis **b.** add vertical axis scale **2.139 a.** skewed right
c. ≈ 38 **d.** no, $z = 3.333$ **2.141 b.** yes, skewed to the right **c.** 370 **d.** $0.46, -1.10$ **f.** Carolina, New England, Denver, Seattle, Pittsburgh, Cincinnati **g.** Dallas **h.** operating income increases as current value increases **2.143** 7 of 25 values are less than 12; claim probably not true **2.147** Laid off: $m = 40.5$; not laid off: $m = 40$; company probably not vulnerable

Chapter 3
3.1 a. .5 **b.** .3 **c.** .6 **3.3** $P(A) = .55, P(B) = .50, P(C) = .70$ **3.5 a.** 10 **b.** 20 **c.** 15,504 **3.7 a.** $(B_1, B_2), (B_1, R_1),$
$(B_1, R_2), (B_1, R_3), (B_2, R_1), (B_2, R_2), (B_2, R_3), (R_1, R_2), (R_1, R_3), (R_2, R_3)$ **b.** $P(E_i) = 1/10$ **c.** $P(A) = 1/10, P(B) = 3/5,$
$P(C) = 3/10$ **3.9** $3/650 = .0046$ **3.11 a.** $1/100 = .01$ **b.** $.0095$; yes **3.13 b.** .189, .403, .258, .113, .038 **c.** .591
d. .811 **3.15** 455 **3.17 a.** $9 \times 2 = 18$ sample points **b.** sample space **c.** .118 **d.** .177 **e.** .243 **f.** .061 **g.** .054
3.19 a. 1 to 2 **b.** $\frac{1}{2}$ **c.** 2/5 **3.21 a.** LLLL, LLLU, LLUL, LULL, ULLL, LLUU, LULU, LUUL, ULLU,
UULL, LUUU, ULUU, UULU, UUUL, UUUU **b.** 1/16 **c.** 5/16 **3.23 b.** $P(A) = 7/8, P(B) = 1/2,$
$P(A \cup B) = 7/8, P(A^C) = 1/8, P(A \cap B) = 1/2$ **3.25 a.** 3/4 **b.** 13/20 **c.** 1 **d.** 2/5 **e.** 1/4 **f.** 7/20 **g.** 1 **h.** 1/4
3.27 a. .65 **b.** .72 **c.** .25 **d.** .08 **e.** .35 **f.** .72 **g.** 0 **h.** A and C, B and C, C and D **3.29** .73 **3.31 a.** $B \cap C$
b. A^c **c.** $C \cup B$ **d.** $A \cap C^c$ **3.33 a.** $4 \times 2 = 8$ sample points **b.** .684 **c.** .124 **d.** no **e.** .316 **f.** .717 **g.** .091
3.35 a. $P(A) = .281, P(B) = .276, P(C) = .044, P(D) = .079, P(E) = .044$ **b.** 0 **c.** .557 **d.** 0 **e.** .325 **f.** A and B, A
and C, A and D, A and E **3.37 a.** .09 **b.** .09 **c.** .84 **d.** no **e.** column events not mutually exclusive **3.39 a.** .5 **b.** .25
c. no **3.41 a.** .08 **b.** .4 **c.** .52 **3.43 a.** .8, .7, .6 **b.** .25, .375, .375 **d.** no **3.45 a.** .37 **b.** .68 **c.** .15 **d.** .2206 **e.** 0
f. 0 **g.** no **3.47 a.** A and C, B and C **b.** none **c.** .65, .90 **3.49** .545 **3.51 a.** .1875 **b.** .60
3.53 a. $P(P) = .68, P(R|P) = .07$ **b.** $P(R \cap P) = .048$ **3.55 a.** .222 **b.** .183 **3.57 a.** .51 **b.** .034 **c.** .057 **3.59 a.** .006
b. .012 **c.** .018 **3.61 a.** .3, .6 **b.** dependent **c.** independent **3.63** .60 **3.65 a.** $(.5)^{10} = .000977$ **b.** .00195 **c.** .99805
3.67 a. 35,820,200 **b.** 1/35,820,200 **3.71 a.** .000186 **c.** no **3.75 a.** .158 **b.** .074 **c.** .768 **3.77 a.** .52, .39, .09 **b.** .516
3.79 .6982 **3.81 a.** Supplier 4; $P(S_4|D) = .7147$ **b.** Suppliers 4 or 6 **3.83 a.** 0 **b.** no **3.85** .5 **3.87 a.** $0, .2, .9, 1, .7, .3,$
$.4, 0$ **3.89 a.** 720 **b.** 10 **c.** 10 **d.** 20 **e.** 1 **3.91 a.** false **b.** true **c.** true **d.** false **3.93 a.** .25 **b.** .13 **c.** .75
d. .0325 **3.95 b.** .95 **c.** .25 **d.** .5 **3.97 a.** .75 **b.** .2875 **c.** .6 **d.** .06 **e.** no **f.** employee does not plan to retire
at age 68 or the employee is not on the technical staff **g.** yes **3.99 a.** .00000625 **b.** .0135 **c.** doubt validity of the manufacturer's claim **d.** no **3.101** .801 **3.103 a.** .02 **b.** .08 **3.105 a.** .006 **b.** .0022 **c.** .4133 **d.** .3601 **e.** no **3.107** .79
3.109 a. .7127 **b.** .2873 **3.111** false **3.113** .526 **3.115 a.** .0362 **b.** .0335

Chapter 4
4.1 discrete **4.3** continuous **4.5 a.** discrete **b.** discrete **c.** discrete **d.** continuous **e.** discrete **f.** continuous
4.11 a. $p(x) = 1/6$ for all x-values **4.13 a.** .25 **b.** .40 **c.** .75 **4.15 b.** 1/8 **d.** $\frac{1}{2}$ **4.17 b.** .2592 **c.** .0870 **d.** .6826
4.19 a. yes **b.** .06 **c.** .28 **d.** .82 **4.21 a.** .23 **b.** .0809 **c.** .77 **4.23 b.** .85 **c.** .6, 0, 0, 0, .7 **4.25 a.** 3.8 **b.** 10.56
c. 3.25 **d.** no **e.** yes **4.27 a.** $\mu = 0, \sigma^2 = 2.94, \sigma = 1.72$ **c.** .96 **4.29** 3.93 **4.31 a.** $a_1: 2.4; a_2: 1.5; a_3 - a_5: .90; a_6: 1.65$
b. $a_1: .86, (.68, 4.12); a_2: .67, (.16, 2.84)$; $a_3 - a_5: .3, (.3, 1.5); a_6: .57, (.51, 2.79)$ **4.35 a.** $p(x) = .05$ for all x-values **b.** 52.5
c. $(-5.16, 110.16)$ **f.** 33.25, 38.3577 **g.** .525 **i.** .20 **j.** .65 **4.37** \$.25 **4.39 a.** 15 **b.** 10 **c.** 1 **d.** 1 **e.** 4
4.41 a. .4096 **b.** .3456 **c.** .027 **d.** .0081 **e.** .3456 **f.** .027 **4.43 a.** 12.5, 6.25, 2.5 **b.** 16, 12.8, 3.578 **c.** 60, 24, 4.899
d. 63, 6.3, 2.510 **e.** 48, 9.6, 3.098 **f.** 40, 38.4, 6.197 **4.45 a.** .5 **b.** .2 **c.** .8 **4.47 a.** 54 **b.** .0806, .1056 **4.49 b.** .60
c. .346 **d.** .317 **4.51 a.** .015, .030 **b.** .0706, .0022 **c.** .1328, .0085 **d.** .9129 **4.53 a.** $\mu = 480, \sigma = 13.86$ **b.** no,
$z = -5.77$ **4.55 b.** $\mu = 2.4, \sigma = 1.47$ **c.** $p = .90, q = .10, n = 24, \mu = 21.60, \sigma = 1.47$ **4.57** $\mu = .5, \sigma = .707$;
no, 4.95 **4.59 a.** .920 **b.** .677 **c.** .423 **d.** decreases **4.61 b.** $\mu = 5, \sigma = 2.24$ **c.** .961 **4.63 a.** .022 **b.** .085
c. $\mu = 3.8, \sigma = 1.95$ **4.65 a.** .061 **b.** .080 **4.67 a.** 2 **b.** no, $P(x > 10) = .003$ **4.69 a.** .6083 **c.** no $P(x > 2) = .0064$;
yes, $P(x < 1) = .6907$ **4.71 a.** .268 **b.** .018 **c.** .179 **d.** 0 **4.73 b.** $\mu = 3.5, \sigma = .764$ **d.** 1 **4.75 a.** 0 **b.** .455 **c.** .727
d. .272 **e.** .030 **f.** 0 **4.77** .0184 **4.79** .25 **4.81** .2693 **4.83** Not promoted fairly; probability of 5 or fewer females is
.000023 **4.85 a.** .2734 **b.** .4096 **c.** .3432 **4.87 a.** .192 **b.** .228 **c.** .772 **d.** .987 **e.** .960 **f.** 14, 4.2, 2.049 **g.** .975
4.89 a. discrete **b.** continuous **c.** continuous **d.** continuous **4.91 b.** .922 **4.93 b.** .017 **4.95 a.** .230 **b.** .143 **c.** .100
4.97 .009 **4.99 b.** 20, 4.47 **c.** no, $z = -3.55$ **d.** 0 **4.101 a.** 1.25, 1.09; no **b.** .007 **c.** not applicable **4.103 a.** .006
b. not as effective as claimed **4.105 a.** .032 **b.** .107 **4.107 a.** .051 **b.** 292

Chapter 5
5.1 a. $f(x) = .04 \ (20 \le x \le 45), 0$ otherwise **b.** 32.5, 7.22 **5.3 a.** $f(x) = 1/4 \ (3 \le x \le 7), 0$ otherwise **b.** 5, 1.155
5.5 a. 0 **b.** 1 **c.** 1 **5.7 a.** \$12,500 **b.** .6 **c.** \$14,000 **5.9** yes **5.11 a.** continuous **c.** 7, .2887, (6.422, 7.577) **d.** .5
e. 0 **f.** .75 **g.** .0002 **5.13** .4444 **5.15 a.** .4772 **b.** .4987 **c.** .4332 **d.** .2881 **5.17 a.** .0721 **b.** .0594 **c.** .2434

d. .3457 **e.** .5 **f.** .9233 **5.19 a.** .6826 **b.** .9500 **c.** .90 **d.** .9544 **5.21 a.** $-.81$ **b.** .55 **c.** 1.43 **d.** .21 **e.** -2.05
f. .50 **5.23 a.** -2.5 **b.** 0 **c.** $-.625$ **d.** -3.75 **e.** 1.25 **f.** -1.25 **5.25 a.** .3830 **b.** .3023 **c.** .1525 **d.** .7333 **e.** .1314
f. .9545 **5.27 a.** .9544 **b.** .0918 **c.** .0228 **d.** .8607 **e.** .0927 **f.** .7049 **5.29 a.** .1558 **b.** .2586 **c.** .0062 **d.** .9525
5.31 a. .3755 **b.** .1969 **c.** .9693 **d.** .9292 **5.33 a.** .5124 **b.** .2912 **c.** .0027 **5.35 a.** .3050, .1020 **b.** .6879, .8925
c. .0032 **5.37 a.** 25.14% **b.** 90.375 **5.39 a.** Stock XYZ **b.** ABC: $105; XYZ: $107 **c.** ABC: .0475; XYZ: .0808; ABC
5.41 5.068 **5.43 a.** .68 **b.** .95 **c.** 1.00 **5.45** Plot c **5.47 a.** 7 **b.** 6.124 **c.** IQR/s = 1.14 **5.49 b.** data are not normal
5.51 IQR/s = 1.3 **5.53** $z = -.75$ for minimum value of 128 **5.55 a.** yes **b.** $\mu = 10, \sigma^2 = 6$ **c.** .726 **d.** .7291
5.57 a. .1788 **b.** .5236 **c.** .6950 **5.59 a.** 40 **b.** 5.66 **c.** 1.86 **d.** .9686 **5.61** .0537 **5.63 a.** 1 **b.** $\mu \pm 3\sigma =$
$(-2.058, 8.658)$ **5.65** .2676; no **5.67 b.** Public: .1841, 0; Private: .6915, 0 **5.71 a.** .0025 **b.** .0111 **c.** .000123 **d.** .259
5.73 $\mu = .5, \sigma = .5$; .9502 **5.75 a.** .449 **b.** .865 **5.77** .223 **5.79 a.** .0949 **b.** 10.54; 10.54 **d.** .1729 **5.81 a.** 20 **b.** .223
c. .0498; .9502 **5.83 a.** $P(x > 500) = .135335$ **5.85 a.** .9821 **b.** .0179 **c.** .9505 **d.** .3243 **e.** .9107 **f.** .0764
5.87 a. .6915 **b.** .1587 **c.** .1915 **d.** .3085 **e.** 0 **f.** 1 **5.89 a.** 47.68 **b.** 47.68 **c.** 30.13 **d.** 41.5 **e.** 30.13
5.91 a. .997521 **b.** .000123 **c.** 0 **d.** 1 **e.** .000006 **5.93 a.** .68% **b.** $P(x < 6) = .0068$ **5.95 a.** .221199 **b.** .082085
5.97 .2451 **5.99** $z = -1.71$ for minimum value of 0 **5.101 a.** .0918 **b.** 0 **c.** 4.87 decibels **5.103 a.** .8264 **b.** 17 times
c. .6217 **d.** $0, -157$ **5.105** no **5.107** $P(x \geq 400) \approx 0$ **5.109 a.** .135335 **b.** .594

Chapter 6

6.1 c. 1/16 **6.3 c.** .05 **d.** no **6.9 a.** 5 **b.** $E(\bar{x}) = 5$ **c.** $E(m) = 4.778$ **6.13 b.** 1.61 **e.** $E(s) = 1.00394$ **6.15 a.** 100, 5
b. 100, 2 **c.** 100, 1 **d.** 100, 1.414 **e.** 100, .447 **f.** 100, .316 **6.17 a.** 2.9, 3.29, 1.814 **6.19 a.** 20, 2 **b.** approximately normal **c.** -2.25 **d.** 1.50 **6.21 a.** .8944 **b.** .0228 **c.** .1292 **d.** .9699 **6.25 a.** 141 **b.** 1.8 **c.** approx. normal **d.** 0.56
e. .2877 **6.27** .0838 **6.29 a.** approximately normal **b.** .0322 **c.** .8925 **d.** 19.1 **e.** less than 19.1 **6.31 a.** approximately normal **b.** .0091 **c.** .9544 **6.33 b.** $E(A) = \alpha$ **c.** choose estimator with smaller standard deviation **6.35 a.** .5
b. .0606 **c.** .0985 **d.** .8436 **6.41 a.** nothing about shape **b.** approximately normal **c.** .2843 **d.** .1292 **6.43 a.** .4514
b. not affected **6.45 a.** .0013 **b.** program did decrease the mean number of sick days **6.47 a.** 95.25% **b.** 100%
6.49 a. .0031; value of mean probably less than 157 **b.** .2643, more likely; 0, less likely **c.** 0, less likely; .0853, more likely
6.51 a. 60; 36 **b.** normal **c.** 0

Chapter 7

7.1 a. 1.645 **b.** 2.58 **c.** 1.96 **d.** 1.28 **7.3 a.** $28 \pm .784$ **b.** $102 \pm .65$ **c.** $15 \pm .0588$ **d.** $4.05 \pm .163$ **e.** no
7.5 a. $26.2 \pm .96$ **b.** In repeated sampling, 95% of all confidence intervals constructed will include μ. **c.** 26.2 ± 1.26
d. increases **e.** yes **7.9** yes **7.11 a.** $(141.2, 141.5)$ **c.** random sample **7.13 a.** $(12.43, 25.57)$ **b.** $(2.05, 11.95)$
c. SAT–Math **7.15** $(.36, .49)$ **7.17 a.** 66.83 ± 6.17 **c.** 45.31 ± 4.15 **7.19 a.** μ_Y: $4.17 \pm .095$; μ_{MA}: $4.04 \pm .057$;
μ_O: $4.31 \pm .062$ **b.** more likely **7.21 a.** $z_{.10} = 1.28, t_{.10} = 1.533$ **b.** $z_{.05} = 1.645, t_{.05} = 2.132$ **c.** $z_{.025} = 1.96, t_{.025} = 2.776$
d. $z_{.01} = 2.33, t_{.01} = 3.747$ **e.** $z_{.005} = 2.575, t_{.005} = 4.604$ **7.23 a.** 2.228 **b.** 2.228 **c.** -1.812 **d.** 1.725 **e.** 4.032
7.25 a. 5 ± 1.88 **b.** 5 ± 2.39 **c.** 5 ± 3.75 **d.** $5 \pm .78, 5 \pm .94, 5 \pm 1.28$; decreased width **7.27 a.** 2.886 ± 4.034
b. $.408 \pm .256$ **7.29 a.** $(-12,218.7, 45,395.7)$ **b.** normally distributed **7.31 a.** 49.3 ± 8.6 **b.** 99% confident that the
mean amount removed from all soil specimens using the poison is between 40.70% and 57.90% **c.** normal distribution
d. possible **7.33 a.** 22.46 ± 11.18 **d.** validity is suspect **7.37 a.** yes **b.** no **c.** yes **d.** no **7.39 a.** yes **b.** $.46 \pm .065$
7.41 a. .03 **b.** $.03 \pm .01$ **7.43 a.** all consumers in Muncie, Indiana **b.** belief in whether "Made in the USA" means 100%
c. $.604 \pm .078$ **7.45 a.** $.052 \pm .033$ **b.** $.263 \pm .065$ **7.47 b.** $.29 \pm .028$ **7.49 a.** $.71 \pm .018$ **b.** yes **7.51** $.85 \pm .002$
7.53 a. 68 **b.** 31 **7.55** 34 **7.57 a.** 0.98, 0.784, 0.56, 0.392, 0.196 **7.63 a.** $.226 \pm .007$ **b.** .014 **c.** 1,680 **7.59** 1,692
7.61 a. 329 **b.** 61 **c.** 61 **7.63 a.** $.226 \pm .007$ **b.** .014 **c.** 1,680 **7.65** 43; 171; 385 **7.67** no **7.69 a.** .7746 **b.** .8944
c. .9487 **d.** .995 **7.71 a.** 1.00 **b.** 6.124 **c.** 0 **d.** As n increases, $\sigma_{\bar{x}}$ decreases. **7.73** $.42 \pm .021$ **7.75 a.** 36.03 ± 3.40
b. $.7 \pm .159$ **7.77** $.694 \pm .092$ **7.79 a.** 156.46 **b.** 18.70 **c.** 156.46 ± 37.405 **d.** not reasonable **7.81** No; $.086 \pm .041$
7.83 a. -1.725 **b.** 3.250 **c.** 1.860 **d.** 2.898 **7.85 a.** 32.5 ± 5.16 **b.** 23,964 **7.87 d.** claim probably not true
7.89 a. .24 **b.** $.24 \pm .118$ **7.91 a.** $.876 \pm .003$ **7.93** 184.99 ± 133.93 **7.95 a.** $3.39 \pm .047$ **7.97 a.** men: $7.4 \pm .979$;
women: $4.5 \pm .755$ **b.** men: 9.3 ± 1.185; women: 6.6 ± 1.138 **7.99 a.** $.833 \pm .149$ **b.** no **b.** 1,337
7.103 a. 985.6 ± 25.61 **b.** not out of control **c.** 985.6 ± 14.198; out of control **d.** 99% **7.105** 154 **7.107** 818

Chapter 8

8.1 null; alternative **8.3** α **8.5** Reject H_0 when H_0 is true; accept H_0 when H_0 is true; Reject H_0 when H_0 is false; accept
H_0 when H_0 is false **8.7** no **8.9** H_0: $p = .10, H_a$: $p < .10$ **8.11** H_0: $\mu = 863, H_a$: $\mu < 863$ **8.13 c.** α **e.** decrease
f. increase **8.15 a.** unsafe; safe **c.** α **8.17 g.** .025, .05, .005, .10, .10, .01 **8.19 a.** $z = 1.67$, reject H_0 **b.** $z = 1.67$, do
not reject H_0 **8.21 a.** $z > 2.33$ **b.** $z = 23.31$ **c.** reject H_0 **8.23 a.** yes, $z = 7.02$ **8.25** $z = -1.86$, do not reject H_0
8.27 a. no **b.** $z = .61$, do not reject H_0 **d.** no **e.** $z = -.83$, do not reject H_0 **8.29 a.** H_0: $\mu = 10, H_a$: $\mu < 10$

c. $z = -2.33$, reject H_0 **8.31 a.** do not reject H_0 **b.** reject H_0 **c.** reject H_0 **d.** do not reject H_0 **e.** do not reject H_0 **8.33** .0150 **8.35** .03 **8.37 a.** do not reject H_0 **b.** do not reject H_0 **c.** reject H_0 **d.** do not reject H_0 **8.41 a.** .058 **b.** do not reject H_0 **8.43 b.** reject H_0 **c.** reject H_0 **8.45 a.** $H_0: \mu = 16.5$, $H_a: \mu > 16.5$ **b.** .0681 **8.49 a.** $|t| > 2.160$ **b.** $t > 2.500$ **c.** $t > 1.397$ **d.** $t < -2.718$ **e.** $|t| > 1.729$ **f.** $t < -2.353$ **8.51 a.** population is normally distributed **b.** reject H_0 at $\alpha = .05$ **c.** .076 **8.53 a.** $t = .41$, do not reject H_0 **b.** yes **8.55 a.** $H_0: \mu = .004$, $H_a: \mu > .004$ **c.** plant 1: do not reject H_0; plant 2: do not reject H_0 **8.57** yes, $t = 8.75$ **8.59** no, $t = 2.97$ **8.61 a.** yes **b.** no **c.** yes **d.** no **e.** no **8.63 a.** -2.33 **c.** reject H_0 **d.** .0099 **8.65 a.** $z = 1.13$, do not reject H_0 **b.** .1292 **8.67 a.** .043 **b.** $H_0: p = .07$, $H_a: p \neq .07$ **c.** $z = -1.35$ **d.** $|z| > 1.96$ **e.** do not reject H_0 **f.** .1770 **8.69 a.** $H_0: p = .5$, $H_a: p < .5$ **b.** .231 **c.** do not reject H_0 **8.71 a.** no, $z = 1.49$ **b.** .0681 **8.73 a.** yes, $z = 7.96$ **b.** yes **c.** 0 **8.75** $z = 1.20$, do not reject H_0 **8.77 b.** 532.9 **d.** .1949 **e.** .8051 **8.79 c.** .1469 **d.** .8531 **8.81 c.** .5359 **d.** .0409 **8.83 a.** .1949, Type II error **b.** .05, Type I error **c.** .8051 **8.85** .1075 **8.87 a.** $\chi^2 < 6.26214$ or $\chi^2 > 27.4884$ **b.** $\chi^2 > 40.2894$ **c.** $\chi^2 > 21.0642$ **d.** $\chi^2 < 3.57056$ **e.** $\chi^2 < 1.63539$ or $\chi^2 > 12.5916$ **f.** $\chi^2 < 13.8484$ **8.89 a.** $\chi^2 = 479.16$, reject H_0 **8.91 a.** $H_0: \sigma^2 = .000004$, $H_a: \sigma^2 \neq .00004$ **b.** $\chi^2 = 48.49$, do not reject H_0 **c.** tee weights approx. normal **8.93** at $\alpha = .05$, yes; $\chi^2 = 133.90$ **8.95** $\chi^2 = 1.78$, do not reject H_0 **8.97** $\chi^2 = 40.8375$, do not reject H_0 **8.99** alternative **8.101** large **8.103 a.** $t = -7.51$, reject H_0 **b.** $t = -7.51$, reject H_0 **8.105 a.** $z = -1.78$, reject H_0 **b.** $z = -1.78$, do not reject H_0 **8.107 a.** $\chi^2 = 63.48$, reject H_0 **b.** $\chi^2 = 63.48$, reject H_0 **8.109 a.** $z = -2.22$, do not reject H_0 **b.** .0132 **8.111** $\chi^2 = 12.78$, do not reject H_0 **8.113 a.** H_0: No disease, H_a: Disease **8.115 a.** $H_0: \mu = 16$, $H_a: \mu < 16$ **b.** $z = -4.31$, reject H_0 **8.117 a.** $z = 12.97$, reject H_0: $p = .5$ **b.** 0 **c.** .6844 **8.119 b.** .8264 **c.** decreases **8.121 a.** $H_0: \mu = 1{,}100$, $H_a: \mu > 1{,}100$ **b.** $t = 3.512$ **c.** $.025 < p$-value $< .05$, reject H_0 at $\alpha = .05$ **d.** Type I error **8.123 a.** no, $z = 1.41$ **b.** small **c.** .0793 **8.125 a.** yes **b.** $\beta = .5910$, power $= .4090$ **c.** increases **8.127 a.** $z = -1.29$, do not reject H_0 **b.** .0985

Chapter 9

9.1 a. 150 ± 6 **b.** 150 ± 8 **c.** $0; 5$ **d.** 0 ± 10 **e.** variability of the difference is greater **9.3 a.** 35 ± 24.5 **b.** $z = 2.8$, p-value $= .0052$, reject H_0 **c.** p-value $= .0026$ **d.** $z = .8$, p-value $= .4238$, do not reject H_0 **e.** independent random samples **9.5 a.** no **b.** no **c.** no **d.** yes **e.** no **9.7 a.** .5989 **b.** yes, $t = -2.39$ **c.** $-1.24 \pm .98$ **d.** confidence interval **9.9 a.** do not reject H_0 **b.** .0575 **9.11 a.** $t = -1.646$, do not reject H_0 **b.** -2.50 ± 3.12 **9.13 a.** $H_0: \mu_1 = \mu_2$, $H_a: \mu_1 \neq \mu_2$ **b.** reject H_0 **c.** do not reject H_0 **d.** no practical difference **9.15 a.** yes **b.** $t = 19.73$, reject H_0 **9.17 a.** $t = 1.56$, do not reject $H_0: \mu_T = \mu_I$ **b.** $t = -.50$, do not reject $H_0: \mu_W = \mu_I$ **c.** no differences **9.19 a.** $H_0: \mu_1 = \mu_2, H_a: \mu_1 \neq \mu_2$ **b.** $z = 7.17$, reject H_0 **c.** $.51 \pm .14$ **9.21 a.** yes, $t = 1.9557$ **c.** .0579 **d.** -7.4 ± 6.38 **9.23** $t = .29$, do not reject $H_0: \mu_1 = \mu_2$ **9.25 a.** $t > 1.796$ **b.** $t > 1.319$ **c.** $t > 3.182$ **d.** $t > 2.375$ **9.27 a.** $H_0: \mu_d = 0$, $H_a: \mu_d < 0$ **b.** $t = -5.29$, p-value $= .0002$, reject H_0 **c.** $(-4.98, -2.42)$ **d.** population of differences is normal **9.29 a.** $t = 1.79$, do not reject H_0 **b.** .0734 **c.** no **9.31 b.** $H_0: \mu_d = 0$, $H_a: \mu_d \neq 0$ **c.** do not reject H_0 **9.33 a.** $(-242.29, -106.96)$ **b.** output differences are normal **c.** yes **9.35 a.** yes, $t = 2.864$ **9.37 a.** $H_0: \mu_d = 0$, $H_a: \mu_d \neq 0$ **b.** $t = 5.76$, reject H_0 **c.** yes **9.39** $t = .46$, p-value $= 0.65$, do not reject H_0 **9.41 a.** no **b.** no **c.** yes **d.** no **e.** yes **9.43 a.** $z = -4.02$, reject H_0 **b.** $z = -4.02$, reject H_0 **c.** $z = -4.02$, reject H_0 **9.47 a.** .153 **b.** .215 **c.** $(-.132, .008)$ **d.** no evidence of a difference **9.49 a.** $p_1 - p_2$ **b.** $H_0: p_1 - p_2 = 0$, $H_a: p_1 - p_2 \neq 0$ **c.** $z = -5.16$ **d.** $|z| > 2.58$ **e.** yes **f.** reject H_0 **9.51 a.** yes **b.** $-.0568 \pm .0270$ **9.53 a.** yes, $z = -2.79$ **b.** yes **9.55** yes, $z = -2.25$ **9.57 a.** 18 **b.** sample may not be representative **9.59** 34 **9.61 a.** 29,954 **b.** 2,165 **c.** 1,113 **9.63** 443 **9.65** 1,729 **9.67** 542 **9.69 a.** 4.10 **b.** 3.57 **c.** 8.81 **d.** 3.21 **9.71 a.** $F > 1.74$ **b.** $F > 2.04$ **c.** $F > 2.35$ **d.** $F > 2.78$ **9.73 a.** $F > 2.11$ **b.** $F > 3.01$ **c.** $F > 2.04$ **d.** $F > 2.30$ **e.** $F > 5.27$ **9.75 a.** $F = 4.29$, do not reject H_0 **b.** $.05 < p$-value $< .10$ **9.77 a.** $H_0: \sigma_M^2 = \sigma_F^2$, $H_a: \sigma_M^2 < \sigma_F^2$ **b.** 1.06 **c.** $F > 1.26$ **d.** p-value $> .10$ **e.** do not reject H_0 **9.79 a.** no, $F = 2.27$ **b.** $.05 < p$-value $< .10$ **9.81 a.** yes, $F = 8.29$ **b.** no **9.83** $F = 1.20$, reject H_0 **9.85 a.** $t = .78$, do not reject H_0 **b.** 2.50 ± 8.99 **c.** 225 **9.87 a.** $3.90 \pm .31$ **b.** $z = 20.60$, reject H_0 **c.** 346 **9.89 a.** $t = 5.73$, reject H_0 **b.** 3.8 ± 1.84 **9.91 a.** $(1.27, 4.53)$ **b.** $(0.54, 4.86)$ **c.** yes **9.93 a.** $H_0: \mu_1 - \mu_2 = 0$, $H_a: \mu_1 - \mu_2 \neq 0$ **b.** $z = -7.69$, reject H_0 **9.95 a.** $(.107, .233)$ **b.** yes **9.97 b.** $H_0: \sigma_1^2 = \sigma_2^2$, $H_a: \sigma_1^2 \neq \sigma_2^2$ **c.** $F = 28.22$, reject H_0 **9.99** $.0308 \pm .0341$ **9.101 b.** no, $t = .80$ **c.** 84.17 ± 226.47 **9.103 a.** $H_0: \mu_1 - \mu_2 = 0$, $H_a: \mu_1 - \mu_2 > 0$ **b.** $t = 2.616$, $.01 < p$-value $< .025$, reject H_0 **9.105 a.** yes, $t = -4.02$ **b.** .0030 **9.107** 4,802 **9.109 a.** $p_1 - p_2$ **9.111 a.** $H_0: \mu_d = 0$, $H_a: \mu_d > 0$ **b.** paired difference **c.** Aad: do not reject H_0 for $\alpha = .05$; Ab: reject H_0 for $\alpha = .05$; Intention: do not reject H_0 for $\alpha = .05$

Chapter 10

10.1 A, B, C, D **10.5 a.** observational **b.** designed **c.** observational **d.** observational **e.** observational **10.7 a.** age **b.** smokers **c.** screening method **d.** CT and X-ray **10.9 a.** 4 **b.** (Within-store, home), (Within-store, in store), (Between-store, home), (Between-store, in store) **10.11 a.** quality **b.** temperature and pressure **c.** $3 \times 5 = 15$ combinations of temperature and pressure **d.** steel ingots **10.13 a.** 6.39 **b.** 15.98 **c.** 1.54 **d.** 3.18 **10.15** dot plot b **10.17 a.** $MSE_a = 2$, $MSE_b = 14.4$ **b.** $t_a = -6.12$, $F_a = 37.5$; $t_b = -2.28$, $F_b = 5.21$ **c.** $|t| > 2.228$, $F > 4.96$

d. reject H_0; reject H_0 **10.19 a.** $F = 1.5$, do not reject H_0 **b.** $F = 6$, reject H_0 **c.** $F = 24$, reject H_0 **d.** increases
10.21 a.

Source	df	SS	MS	F
Treatments	2	12.30	6.15	2.93
Error	9	18.89	2.10	
Total	11	31.19		

b. do not reject H_0 **10.23 a.** $H_0: \mu_1 = \mu_2 = \mu_3 = \mu_4 = \mu_5 = \mu_6 = \mu_7 = \mu_8$ **b.** reject H_0 **c.** p-value $< .01$
10.25 a. $H_0: \mu_1 = \mu_2 = \mu_3$ **b.** no measure of reliability **c.** $F = 1.78$, p-value $= .179$; do not reject H_0 **d.** assumption of
equal variances not satisfied **10.27** $F = 3.90$, reject H_0 **10.29 a.** yes, $F = 76.88$ **b.** yes, $F = 28.83$ **c.** no, $F = 1.22$
d. assumptions violated for DDT **10.31 a.** $H_0: \mu_1 = \mu_2 = \mu_3 = \mu_4 = \mu_5 = \mu_6$ **b.** no **d.** designed **10.33 a.** 3 **b.** 10
c. 6 **d.** 45 **10.37 a.** 6 **b.** $\mu_{12} >$ all other means; no differences among μ_3, μ_6, μ_9 **10.39 b.** no **c.** yes **d.** no
e. $\mu_{Large} > \mu_{Small}$; no other significant differences **f.** 95% confidence **10.41** $\mu_{SF} > (\mu_G, \mu_{ST})$
10.43 Length: $\mu_{LMB} < (\mu_{CC}, \mu_{SMB})$; Weight: $\mu_{LMB} < \mu_{CC}, < \mu_{SMB}$ **10.45** $\mu_{NC} > (\mu_{AC}, \mu_{EO})$; $\mu_{IE} > \mu_{EO}$
10.47 a.

Source	df	SS	MS	F
Treatments	2	21.5555	10.7778	5.54
Blocks	2	.8889	.4445	.23
Error	4	7.7778	1.9445	
Total	8	30.2222		

b. $H_0: \mu_1 = \mu_2 = \mu_3$ **c.** $F = 5.54$ **e.** do not reject H_0 **10.49 a.** $F = 3.20$; $F = 1.80$ **b.** $F = 13.33$; $F = 2.00$
c. $F = 5.33$; $F = 5.00$ **d.** $F = 16.00$; $F = 6.00$ **e.** $F = 2.67$; $F = 1.00$ **10.51 b.** California, Utah, Alaska **c.** Nov. 2000,
Oct. 2001, Nov. 2001 **d.** $H_0: \mu_{CAL} = \mu_{UT} = \mu_{AL}$ **e.** $F = 38.07$, p-value $= 0.002$ **f.** California **10.53 b.** df(Week) $= 5$,
MS(Prompt) $= 296.25$, F(Prompt) $= 39.87$ **c.** yes, p-value $= 0$ **d.** $(\mu_{FH}, \mu_{FL}) > (\mu_{IH}, \mu_{IL}) > \mu_C$ **10.55** $F = 2.0$, fail to
reject $H_0: \mu_M = \mu_T = \mu_W = \mu_R = \mu_F$ **10.57 a.** Blocks: 7 locations; treatments: 5 insecticides **b.** $F = 2.85$, reject
$H_0: \mu_T = \mu_M = \mu_F = \mu_{FE} = \mu_C$
10.59 a.

Source	df	SS	MS	F
A	2	.8	.4	3.69
B	3	5.3	1.7667	16.31
AB	6	9.6	1.6	14.77
Error	12	1.3	.1083	
Total	23	17.0		

b. SSA + SSB + SSAB; yes, $F = 13.18$ **c.** yes **e.** $F = 14.77$, reject H_0 **f.** no **10.61 a.** $(1,1), (1,2), (1,3), (2,1), (2,2)$,
$(2,3)$ **b.** yes, $F = 21.62$ **c.** yes; $F = 36.62$, reject H_0 **d.** no **10.63 a.** $F(AB) = .75$, $F(A) = 3.00$, $F(B) = 1.50$
b. $F(AB) = 7.50$, $F(A) = 3.00$, $F(B) = 3.00$ **c.** $F(AB) = 3.00$, $F(A) = 12.00$, $F(B) = 3.00$ **d.** $F(AB) = 4.50$,
$F(A) = 36.00$, $F(B) = 36.00$ **10.65 a.** complete 6×6 factorial design **b.** Factors: Coagulant (5, 10, 20, 50, 100, and 200),
pH level (4.0, 5.0, 6.0, 7.0, 8.0, and 9.0); $6 \times 6 = 36$ treatments **10.67 a.** $F = 1.2$, do not reject H_0: Herd and Season do
not interact; $F = 17.2$, reject H_0: Herd means are equal; $F = 3.0$, do not reject H_0: Season means are equal **b.** yes
c. $(\mu_{MTZ}, \mu_{QMD}) > (\mu_{PLC}, \mu_{LGN})$ **10.69 a.** complete 6×5 factorial design **b.** cylinders (6 levels) and batches
(5 levels) **c.** 30
d.

Source	df	SS	MS	F
B	4	62.444	15.611	8.31
C	5	55.789	11.158	5.94
BC	20	48.489	2.424	1.29
Error	60	112.667	1.878	
Total	89	17279.389		

f. $F = 1.29$, no evidence of BC interaction   **g.** $F = 8.31$, evidence of B main effect; $F = 5.94$, evidence of C main effect
10.71 $F = 1.77$, no evidence of interaction; $F = 2.17$, no evidence of Class main effect; $F = 14.40$, evidence of Preparation main effect
10.77 a.

Source	df	SS	MS	F
Treatment	3	11.334	3.778	157.42
Block	4	10.688	2.672	111.33
Error	12	0.288	0.024	
Total	19	22.310		

b. yes, $F = 157.42$ **c.** yes, 6   **d.** yes, $F = 111.33$ **10.79 b.** yes   **c.** no   **10.81 a.** randomized block   **b.** experimental units: electronic commerce/internet-based companies; response: rate of return; treatments: e-companies, internet software/service, internet hardware, and internet communication; blocks: 1 year, 3 year, and 5 year   **10.83 a.** yes,
$F = 30.4$ **b.** $\mu_A > (\mu_B, \mu_C, \mu_D)$; $\mu_B > \mu_D$ **10.85 a.** 2×2 factorial experiment   **b.** factors are tent type and location; 4 treatments are (treated, inside), (treated, outside), (untreated, inside), and (untreated, outside)   **c.** number of mosquito bites received in a 20 minute interval   **10.87 a.** means differ for all five scales   **b.** yes   **10.89 a.** $2 \times 2 \times 2 \times 2$ factorial design   **b.** 16   **d.** yes,   **e.** yes, perform the main effect test for wear; $F = 0.05$, do not reject H_0 **10.91 a.** completely randomized; 5 education levels   **b.** $F = 3.298$, reject H_0 **c.** $\mu_P > (\mu_{CG}, \mu_{HS}, \mu_{SC}, \mu_{NH})$ **10.93 a.** 2×2 factorial
b. yes, $F = 12.29$ **c.** Interaction: $F = .02$, do not reject H_0; Schedule: $F = 7.37$, reject H_0; Payment: $F = 29.47$, reject H_0

Chapter 11
11.1 a. $\chi^2 > 5.99147$ **b.** $\chi^2 > 7.77944$ **c.** $\chi^2 > 11.3449$ **11.3** $E(n_i) \geq 5$ **11.5 a.** $\chi^2 = 3.293$ **c.** $(.226, .350)$
11.7 a. Levels: 100%, 75–99%, 50–74%, less than 50%   **b.** .50, .25, .20, .05   **c.** $H_0: p_1 = .5, p_2 = .25, p_3 = .20, p_4 = .05$
d. 4.68   **e.** $\chi^2 > 6.25139$ **f.** do not reject H_0 **g.** $(.526, .682)$ **11.9 a.** 107.2   **b.** $H_0: p_1 = p_2 = \cdots = p_{10} = .10$ **c.** 93.15
d. $\chi^2 > 14.6837$ **e.** reject H_0 **11.11 a.** yes, $\chi^2 = 87.74$, p-value = 0   **b.** $.539 \pm .047$ **11.13** $\chi^2 = 16$, p-value = .003, reject H_0 **11.15** $\chi^2 = 12.734$, do not reject H_0 **11.17 a.** H_0: row and column classifications are independent
b. $\chi^2 > 9.21034$ **c.** 14.37, 36.79, 44.84, 10.63, 26.21, 33.16   **d.** $\chi^2 = 8.71$, do not reject H_0 **11.19** $\chi^2 = 12.33$, reject H_0
11.21 a. .163   **b.** .152   **c.** .090   **f.** $\chi^2 = 10.197$, p-value = .006, reject H_0 **11.23 a.** .901   **b.** .690   **d.** $\chi^2 = 48.19$, reject
H_0 **e.** $.211 \pm .070$ **11.25** yes, $\chi^2 = 256.336$ **11.27** $\chi^2 = 45.36$, reject H_0 **11.29 a.** $\chi^2 = 39.22$, reject H_0 **b.** $\chi^2 = 2.84$,
do not reject H_0 **11.31 a.** $\chi^2 = 4.41$, reject H_0 **b.** no   **c.** .04378   **d.** .00571, .00027   **e.** .04976   **11.33 a.** no, $\chi^2 = 2.133$
b. $.233 \pm .057$ **11.35 a.** $H_0: p_1 = p_2 = p_3 = p_4 = .25$ **b.** $\chi^2 = 14.805$, reject H_0 **c.** Type I error: conclude opinions of Internet users are not evenly divided among four categories when they are; Type II error: conclude opinions of internet users are evenly divided among four categories when they are not   **11.37** $\chi^2 = 19.10$, reject H_0 **11.39 a.** $\chi^2 = 92.18$, reject H_0
b. $\chi^2 = 65.31$, reject H_0 **c.** $\chi^2 = 116.18$, reject H_0 **d.** $(.52, .66)$ **11.41 a.** no, $\chi^2 = 7.38$
11.43 a.

	Committee Accept	Committee Reject
Inspector Accept	101	23
Inspector Reject	10	19

b. yes   **c.** $\chi^2 = 26.034$, reject H_0 **11.45 a.** yes, $\chi^2 = 18.54$ **b.** p-value $< .005$ **11.47 a.** 9.65   **b.** 11.0705   **c.** no
d. $.05 < p$-value $< .10$

Chapter 12
12.3 $\beta_1 = 1/3$, $\beta_0 = 14/3$, $y = 14/3 + 1/3x$ **12.9** no   **12.11 a.** $\Sigma(y - \hat{y}) = 0$, SSE = 1.2204   **c.** SSE = 108.00
12.13 b. negative linear relationship   **c.** $-.9939, 8.543$ **e.** range of x: 2 to 8   **12.15 a.** $y = \beta_0 + \beta_1 x + \varepsilon$ **b.** $\hat{y} = -51.14 + 1.0705x$ **12.17 a.** yes   **b.** $\hat{y} = 1.281 + 1.372x$ **e.** $\hat{y} = 4.302 + 0.0709x$ **12.19 b.** $\hat{y} = 16.593 + 1.949x$ **d.** 45.828
12.21 b. $\hat{y} = 569.5801 - .00192x$ **e.** range of x: \$15,100 to \$70,000   **12.23 a.** .3475   **b.** 1.179   **12.25** 12.10: SSE = 1.22,
$s^2 = .2441$, $s = .494$; 12.13: SSE = 5.713, $s^2 = 1.143$, $s = 1.069$ **12.27 a.** SSE = 382,178,624, $s^2 = 1,248,950$, $s = 1,117.56$
12.29 a. .40   **b.** 1.32   **12.31 a.** $\hat{y} = 7.381 + .373x$ **b.** \$604.181 billion   **c.** SSE = 2,225.63, $s^2 = 27.24$ **12.33 a.** 95% CI: 31 ± 1.17; 90% CI: $31 \pm .94$ **b.** 95% CI: 64 ± 5.08; 90% CI: 64 ± 4.15 **c.** 95% CI: $-8.4 \pm .75$; 90% CI: $-8.4 \pm .62$
12.35 $.82 \pm .33$; $.82 \pm .76$ **12.37 a.** $H_0: \beta_1 = 0, H_a: \beta_1 > 0$ **b.** p-value = .0000   **c.** (11,005.24, 12,192.56)   **12.39** (1.00, 1.14)   **12.41 a.** yes, $t = 52.43$ **b.** yes, $t = 1.18$ **12.43 a.** support   **b.** $\hat{y} = 15.878 + .927x$ **c.** yes, $t = 2.45$ **d.** 0 and 1
12.45 no, $t = .04$, do not reject H_0 **12.47** yes, $t = -.82$ **12.49 a.** positive   **b.** negative   **c.** 0 slope   **d.** positive or negative

12.51 a. 9438 **b.** .8020 **12.53 a.** moderately strong positive linear relationship between skill level and goal-setting ability **b.** reject H_0 at $\alpha = .01$ **c.** .49 **12.55** $r^2 = .2286, r = -.478$ **12.57 a.** very weak positive linear relationship **b.** weak positive linear relationship **12.59 a.** no, $r^2 = 0.748$ **b.** yes, $15(.055) = .82 \approx 1$ **12.61 a.** .57 **c.** no **12.63 c.** 4.64 ± 1.12 **d.** $2.28 \pm .63; -.41 \pm 1.72$ **12.65 a.** $\hat{y} = 1.375 + .875x$ **c.** 1.5 **d.** .1875 **e.** (3.23, 3.89) **f.** (3.81, 5.94) **12.67 a.** (46.64, 51.96) **c.** prediction for an x outside the range of the sample data **12.69** (1.21, 14.53) **12.71 a.** yes, $t = -5.91$; negative **b.** (.656, 2.829) **c.** (1.467, 2.018) **12.73 a.** $\hat{y} = 37.08 - 1.6x$ **c.** 57.2 **d.** 4.4 **e.** $-1.6 \pm .5$ **f.** 13.08 ± 6.93 **g.** 13.08 ± 7.86 **12.75 b.** $r = -.1245, r^2 = .0155$ **c.** no, $t = -.35$ **12.77 a.** yes, $t = 4.98$, p-value $= .001$ **b.** .607 **d.** .461 **12.79 b.** $\hat{y} = 12.594 + .10936x$ **c.** yes, $t = 3.50$ **d.** 28.99 ± 12.50 **12.81 a.** 57.14 ± 34.82 **b.** 110 is outside range of x **c.** $\bar{x} = 44$ **12.83** $\hat{y} = -92.46 + 8.347x, t = 3.25$, reject H_0 **12.85 c.** $r_1 = .965, r_2 = .996$ **d.** yes **12.87 a.** $\hat{y} = 46.3992x$ **b.** $\hat{y} = 478.4433 + 45.1525x$ **d.** no, $t = .906$ **12.89** machine hours: $t = 3.30$, $p = .008$, reject H_0, $r^2 = .521$; labor hours: $t = 1.43$, $p = .183$, do not reject H_0, $r^2 = .170$

Chapter 13

13.1 a. $E(y) = \beta_0 + \beta_1 x_1 + \beta_2 x_2$ **b.** $E(y) = \beta_0 + \beta_1 x_1 + \beta_2 x_2 + \beta_3 x_3 + \beta_4 x_4$ **c.** $E(y) = \beta_0 + \beta_1 x_1 + \beta_2 x_2 + \beta_3 x_3 + \beta_4 x_4 + \beta_5 x_5$ **13.3 a.** $t = 1.45$, do not reject H_0 **b.** $t = 3.21$, reject H_0 **13.5** $n - (k + 1)$ **13.7 a.** $E(y) = \beta_0 + \beta_1 x_1 + \beta_2 x_2 + \beta_3 x_3 + \beta_4 x_4$ **b.** reject H_0 **c.** yes **13.9 a.** $E(y) = \beta_0 + \beta_1 x_1 + \beta_2 x_2$ **b.** $\hat{y} = -20.352 + 13.350 x_1 + 243.714 x_2$ **d.** no, $t = 1.74$ **e.** (105.334, 382.095) **13.11 a.** Test $H_0: \beta_4 = 0$ vs. $H_a: \beta_4 < 0$ **b.** Test $H_0: \beta_5 = 0$ vs. $H_a: \beta_5 > 0$ **13.13 a.** yes, $t = 5.96$, $p = .00005$ **b.** $t = .01$, $p = .9620$, do not reject H_0 **c.** $t = 1.91$, $p = .0288$, reject H_0 **13.15 a.** $E(y) = \beta_0 + \beta_1 x_1 + \beta_2 x_2 + \beta_3 x_3 + \beta_4 x_4 + \beta_5 x_5 + \beta_6 x_6 + \beta_7 x_7$ **b.** $\hat{y} = .9981 - .0224 x_1 + .1557 x_2 - .0172 x_3 - .0095 x_4 + .4214 x_5 + .4171 x_6 - .1552 x_7$ **13.17 a.** model 1: $t = 2.58$, reject $H_0: \beta_1 = 0$; model 2: $t = 3.32$, reject $H_0: \beta_1 = 0, t = 6.47$, reject $H_0: \beta_2 = 0, t = -4.77$, reject $H_0: \beta_3 = 0, t = 0.24$, do not reject $H_0: \beta_4 = 0$; model 3: $t = 3.21$, reject $H_0: \beta_1 = 0, t = 5.24$, reject $H_0: \beta_2 = 0, t = -4.00$, reject $H_0: \beta_3 = 0, t = 2.28$, reject $H_0: \beta_4 = 0, t = .014$, do not reject $H_0: \beta_5 = 0$ **13.19 a.** .459 **b.** .396 **c.** $F = 7.22$, reject H_0 **d.** .005 **13.21 a.**

Source	df	SS	MS	F
Model	2	12.09	6.045	8.321
Error	17	12.35	.72647	
Total	19	24.44		

$R^2 = .4947; R_a^2 = .4352$ **b.** $F = 8.321$, reject H_0 **13.23 b.** $H_0: \beta_1 = \beta_2 = \beta_3 = \beta_4 = \beta_5 = \beta_6 = 0$ **c.** $F = 32.47$, $p < .001$, reject H_0 **e.** $H_0: \beta_4 = 0$ **f.** $p = .860$, do not reject H_0 **13.25 a.** .152 **b.** $H_0: \beta_1 = \beta_2 = 0$ **c.** $F = 30.42$, $p = .000$ **d.** reject H_0 **13.27 a.** $t = 3.88$, p-value $= .005$, reject H_0 **b.** no **c.** $F = 11.40$, reject H_0 **13.29 b.** $F = 5.11$, reject H_0 **13.31** $F = 1.06$, do not reject H_0 **13.33** Model 2 **13.35 a.** 95% confident that CEO pay falls between $-21,006$ and 34,234 thousand dollars for a CEO with a return of \$200 and rating of 4 **b.** 95% confident that the mean CEO pay falls between 4,163 and 9,065 thousand dollars for all CEO's with returns of \$200 and ratings of 4 **c.** yes **13.37** $(-3.44, .065)$ **13.39 a.** $\hat{y} = -102.36 + 0.00409 x_1 + 3.4511 x_2 - 0.1429 x_3$ **b.** yes, $F = 13.02$ **c.** (3.71, 54.80) **13.41 a.** $E(y) = \beta_0 + \beta_1 x_1 + \beta_2 x_2 + \beta_3 x_1 x_2$ **b.** $E(y) = \beta_0 + \beta_1 x_1 + \beta_2 x_2 + \beta_3 x_3 + \beta_4 x_1 x_2 + \beta_5 x_1 x_3 + \beta_6 x_2 x_3$ **13.43 c.** interaction is present **13.45 a.** $\hat{y} = -2.55 + 3.82 x_1 + 2.63 x_2 - 1.29 x_1 x_2$ **b.** twisted plane **c.** $x_2 = 1: \hat{y} = .08 + 2.53 x_1; x_2 = 3: \hat{y} = 5.34 - .04 x_1; x_2 = 5: \hat{y} = 10.6 - 2.61 x_1$ **e.** $H_0: \beta_3 = 0$ vs. $H_a: \beta_3 \neq 0$ **f.** $t = -8.06$, reject H_0 **13.47 b.** $\hat{y} = 1,161 + 0.122 x_1 + 6.0 x_2 - 0.0353 x_1 x_2, F = 5.34$ **c.** yes, $t = -3.02$ **d.** \$51,400 **13.49 a.** $E(y) = \beta_0 + \beta_1 x_1 + \beta_2 x_2 + \beta_3 x_1 x_2$ **b.** yes, $t = 1.6$ **13.51 b.** yes, higher R^2 and smaller s **13.53 a.** $E(y) = \beta_0 + \beta_1 x + \beta_2 x^2$ **b.** $E(y) = \beta_0 + \beta_1 x_1 + \beta_2 x_2 + \beta_3 x_1 x_2 + \beta_4 x_1^2 + \beta_5 x_2^2$ **c.** $E(y) = \beta_0 + \beta_1 x_1 + \beta_2 x_2 + \beta_3 x_3 + \beta_4 x_1 x_2 + \beta_5 x_1 x_3 + \beta_6 x_2 x_3 + \beta_7 x_1^2 + \beta_8 x_2^2 + \beta_9 x_3^2$ **13.55 a.** yes, $F = 85.94$ **b.** $H_0: \beta_2 = 0$ vs. $H_a: \beta_2 > 0$ **c.** $H_0: \beta_2 = 0$ vs. $H_a: \beta_2 < 0$ **13.57 a.** yes, $F = 25.93$ **b.** $t = -10.74$, reject H_0 **c.** $t = .60$, do not reject H_0 **13.59 b.** first-order model; first-order model; second-order model **13.61 a.** $E(y) = \beta_0 + \beta_1 x_1 + \beta_2 x_2 + \beta_3 x_1 x_2 + \beta_4 x_1^2 + \beta_5 x_2^2$ **b.** $\beta_4 x_1^2$ and $\beta_5 x_2^2$ **13.63 a.** $\hat{y} = 20.09 - 0.67 x + .0095 x^2$ **b.** yes **c.** no, $t = 1.51$ **d.** $\hat{y} = 19.28 - 0.445 x$ **e.** $(-.52, -.37)$ **13.65** $E(y) = \beta_0 + \beta_1 x + \beta_2 x^2$ **13.67** $E(y) = \beta_0 + \beta_1 x, x = \{1$ if level 2, 0 if level 1\} **13.69 a.** 10.2, 6.2, 22.2, 12.2 **b.** $H_0: \beta_1 = \beta_2 = \beta_3 = 0$ **13.71 b.** (13.12, 24.88) **c.** coaching is effective **13.73 a.** $E(y) = \beta_0 + \beta_1 x_1$, where $x_1 = \{1$ if no, 0 if yes\} **b.** $E(y) = \beta_0 + \beta_1 x_1 + \beta_2 x_2$, where $x_1 = \{1$ if referral, 0 if not\}, $x_2 = \{1$ if on-premise, 0 if not\} **c.** $E(y) = \beta_0 + \beta_1 x_1 + \beta_2 x_2$, where $x_1 = \{1$ if counseling, 0 if not\}, $x_2 = \{1$ if active search, 0 if not\} **d.** $E(y) = \beta_0 + \beta_1 x_1$, where $x_1 = \{1$ if not married, 0 if married\} **e.** $E(y) = \beta_0 + \beta_1 x_1$, where $x_1 = \{1$ if female, 0 if male\} **13.75 a.** $E(y) = \beta_0 + \beta_1 x$, where $x = \{1$ if Lotion/Cream, 0 if not\} **b.** $\hat{y} = .7775 + .1092 x$ **c.** $H_0: \beta_1 = 0$ **d.** $t = .24$, do not reject H_0 **e.** $\hat{y} = 7.56 - 1.65x; t = -.46$, do not reject H_0 **13.77 a.** $E(y) = \beta_0 + \beta_1 x_1 + \beta_2 x_2 + \beta_3 x_3$, where $x_1 = \{1$ if IHT, 0 if not\}, $x_2 = \{1$ if ILT, 0 if not\}, $x_3 = \{1$ if Telecomm., 0 if not\} **b.** $\hat{y} = 4,170 + 3,032 x_1 + 3,744 x_2 + 636 x_3$ **d.** $F = .73$, do not reject H_0 **e.** $3,032 \pm 5,469$

13.79 a. $E(y) = \beta_0 + \beta_1 x_1 + \beta_2 x_2 + \beta_3 x_3$, where $x_1 = \{1 \text{ if food}, 0 \text{ if not}\}$, $x_2 = \{1 \text{ if cleaning}, 0 \text{ if not}\}$, $x_3 = \{1 \text{ if acc/consulting}, 0 \text{ if not}\}$ **b.** $\hat{y} = 141.3 + 76.4x_1 + 153.3x_2 - 84.3x_3$ **d.** no, $F = 1.26$ **13.81 a.** $E(y) = \beta_0 + \beta_1 x_1 + \beta_2 x_1^2$ **b.** $E(y) = \beta_0 + \beta_1 x_1 + \beta_2 x_1^2 + \beta_3 x_2 + \beta_4 x_3$, where x_2 and x_3 are dummy variables **c.** add terms: $\beta_5 x_1 x_2 + \beta_6 x_1 x_3 + \beta_7 x_1^2 x_2 + \beta_8 x_1^2 x_3$ **d.** $\beta_5 = \beta_6 = \beta_7 = \beta_8 = 0$ **e.** $\beta_2 = \beta_5 = \beta_6 = \beta_7 = \beta_8 = 0$ **f.** $\beta_3 = \beta_4 = \beta_5 = \beta_6 = \beta_7 = \beta_8 = 0$ **13.83 a.** $\hat{y} = 48.8 - 3.4x_1 + .07x_1^2; \hat{y} = 46.4 + .3x_1 + .05x_1^2; \hat{y} = 41.3 - .7x_1 + .03x_1^2$ **13.85 a.** $x_1 = \{1 \text{ if channel catfish}, 0 \text{ if not}\}$, $x_2 = \{1 \text{ if largemouth bass}, 0 \text{ if not}\}$ **b.** $E(y) = \beta_0 + \beta_1 x_1 + \beta_2 x_2 + \beta_3 x_3$, where $x_3 = $ weight **c.** $E(y) = \beta_0 + \beta_1 x_1 + \beta_2 x_2 + \beta_3 x_3 + \beta_4 x_1 x_3 + \beta_5 x_2 x_3$ **d.** $\hat{y} = 3.1 + 26.5x_1 - 4.1x_2 + 0.0037x_3$ **f.** $\hat{y} = 3.5 + 25.6x_1 - 3.5x_2 + 0.0034x_3 + .0008x_1 x_3 - .0013x_2 x_3$ **g.** $.0042$ **13.87 a.** $E(y) = \beta_0 + \beta_1 x_1; \beta_1$ **b.** $E(y) = (\beta_0 + \beta_2) + (\beta_1 + \beta_3)x_1; \beta_1 + \beta_3$ **c.** no evidence of interaction at $\alpha = .01$ **13.89 a.** $E(y) = \beta_0 + \beta_1 x_1 + \beta_2 x_1^2 + \beta_3 x_2 + \beta_4 x_3 + \beta_5 x_4 + \beta_6 x_1 x_2 + \beta_7 x_1 x_3 + \beta_8 x_1 x_4 + \beta_9 x_1^2 x_2 + \beta_{10} x_1^2 x_3 + \beta_{11} x_1^2 x_4$, where $x_1 = $ sales volume and $x_2 - x_4$ are dummy variables for region **b.** $E(y) = (\beta_0 + \beta_5) + (\beta_1 + \beta_8)x_1 + (\beta_2 + \beta_{11})x_1^2$ **c.** $E(y) = (\beta_0 + \beta_3) + (\beta_1 + \beta_6)x_1 + (\beta_2 + \beta_9)x_1^2$ **d.** β_3 through β_{11} **e.** yes, $F = 8.21$, $p = .000$ **13.91 a.** $E(y) = \beta_0 + \beta_1 x_1 + \beta_2 x_2 + \beta_3 x_1 x_2$, where $x_2 = \{1 \text{ if developing}, 0 \text{ otherwise}\}$ **c.** $\hat{y} = 56.917 - .557x_1 - 18.293x_2 + .354x_1 x_2;$ emerging: $\hat{y} = 56.917 - .557x_1;$ developed: $\hat{y} = 38.624 - .203x_1$ **e.** yes, $t = 4.645$ **13.93** a and b, a and d, a and e, b and c, b and d, b and e, c and e, d and e **13.95 a.** 5; 3 **b.** $H_0: \beta_3 = \beta_4 = 0$ **c.** $F = .38$, do not reject H_0 **13.97 a.** $H_0: \beta_4 = \beta_5 = 0$ **b.** complete: $E(y) = \beta_0 + \beta_1 x_1 + \beta_2 x_2 + \beta_3 x_1 x_2 + \beta_4 x_1^2 + \beta_5 x_2^2$; reduced: $E(y) = \beta_0 + \beta_1 x_1 + \beta_2 x_2 + \beta_3 x_1 x_2$ **c.** $\text{SSE}_R = 63,536,510,127$; $\text{SSE}_C = 59,587,825,157$; $\text{MSE}_C = 183,913,041$ **d.** $F = 10.74$ **e.** $F > 2.30$ **f.** reject H_0 **13.99 a.** $E(y) = \beta_0 + \beta_1 x_1 + \beta_2 x_2 + \beta_3 x_3 + \beta_4 x_4 + \beta_5 x_5 + \beta_6 x_6 + \beta_7 x_7 + \beta_8 x_8 + \beta_9 x_9 + \beta_{10} x_{10}$ **b.** $H_0: \beta_3 = \beta_4 = \cdots = \beta_{10} = 0$ **c.** reject H_0 **e.** $(8.12, 19.88)$ **f.** yes **g.** $E(y) = \beta_0 + \beta_1 x_1 + \beta_2 x_2 + \beta_3 x_3 + \beta_4 x_4 + \beta_5 x_5 + \beta_6 x_6 + \beta_7 x_7 + \beta_8 x_8 + \beta_9 x_9 + \beta_{10} x_{10} + \beta_{11} x_1 x_2 + \beta_{12} x_3 x_2 + \beta_{13} x_4 x_2 + \beta_{14} x_5 x_2 + \beta_{15} x_6 x_2 + \beta_{16} x_7 x_2 + \beta_{17} x_8 x_2 + \beta_{18} x_9 x_2 + \beta_{19} x_{10} x_2$ **h.** Test $H_0: \beta_{11} = \beta_{12} = \cdots = \beta_{19} = 0$ using a nested model F-test **13.101 a.** $E(y) = \beta_0 + \beta_1 x_1 + \beta_2 x_2 + \beta_3 x_3$ **b.** add terms: $\beta_4 x_1 x_2 + \beta_5 x_1 x_3$ **c.** AL: β_1; TDS-3A: $\beta_1 + \beta_4$; FE: $\beta_1 + \beta_5$ **d.** Test $H_0: \beta_4 = \beta_5 = 0$ using a nested model F-test **13.103 b.** $F = 38.24$, reject H_0 **c.** no **13.105 a.** 7; $E(y) = \beta_0 + \beta_1 x_i$ **b.** 6; $E(y) = \beta_0 + \beta_1 x_1 + \beta_2 x_i$ **c.** 5; $E(y) = \beta_0 + \beta_1 x_1 + \beta_2 x_2 + \beta_3 x_i$ **13.107 a.** $x_4 = $ ST-DEPTH, $x_5 = $ TGRSWT, $x_6 = $ TI **b.** no **c.** $E(y) = \beta_0 + \beta_1 x_4 + \beta_2 x_5 + \beta_3 x_6 + \beta_4 x_4 x_5 + \beta_5 x_4 x_6 + \beta_6 x_5 x_6$ **d.** Test $H_0: \beta_4 = \beta_5 = \beta_6 = 0$ **13.109** yes **13.113 a.** no **b.** yes **c.** no **d.** yes; 26th household **e.** no **13.115** assumptions appear to be satisfied **13.117** assumptions of normality (outliers present) and constant variance appear to be violated **13.119** confidence interval **13.121 a.** $\hat{y} = 90.1 - 1.836x_1 + .285x_2$ **b.** $.916$ **c.** yes, $F = 64.91$ **d.** $t = -5.01$, reject H_0 **e.** 10.68 **13.125** $E(y) = \beta_0 + \beta_1 x_1 + \beta_2 x_2 + \beta_3 x_3$, where $x_1 = \{1 \text{ if level 2}, 0 \text{ otherwise}\}$, $x_2 = \{1 \text{ if level 3}, 0 \text{ otherwise}\}$, $x_3 = \{1 \text{ if level 4}, 0 \text{ otherwise}\}$ **13.129** no degrees of freedom for error **13.131 a.** type of extractor is qualitative; size is quantitative **b.** $E(y) = \beta_0 + \beta_1 x_1 + \beta_2 x_2$, where $x_1 = $ diameter of orange, $x_2 = \{1 \text{ if Brand B}, 0 \text{ if not}\}$ **c.** $E(y) = \beta_0 + \beta_1 x_1 + \beta_2 x_2 + \beta_3 x_1 x_2$ **e.** $H_0: \beta_3 = 0$ **13.133 a.** $E(y) = \beta_0 + \beta_1 x_1 + \beta_2 x_2 + \beta_3 x_3 + \beta_4 x_4 + \beta_5 x_5$ **b.** reject $H_0: \beta_1 = \beta_2 = \beta_3 = \beta_4 = \beta_5 = 0$ **c.** $E(y) = \beta_0 + \beta_1 x_1 + \beta_2 x_2 + \beta_3 x_3 + \beta_4 x_4 + \beta_5 x_5 + \beta_6 x_6 + \beta_7 x_7$ **d.** 60.3% of the variability in GSI scores is explained by the model **e.** both variables contribute to the prediction of GSI **13.135** Importance and Support are correlated at $.6991$; no **13.137 b.** 51% of the variability in operating margins can be explained by the model **c.** $F = 13.53$, reject H_0 **13.139 b.** $E(y) = \beta_0 + \beta_1 x_1 + \beta_2 x_1^2 + \beta_3 x_2 + \beta_4 x_1 x_2 + \beta_5 x_1^2 x_2$, where $x_2 = \{1 \text{ if I-35W}, 0 \text{ if not}\}$ **c.** yes, $F = 383.76$ **d.** assumptions satisfied **13.141 a.** $E(y) = \beta_0 + \beta_1 x_1 + \beta_2 x_2 + \beta_3 x_3$, where $x_1 = \{1 \text{ if VH}, 0 \text{ if not}\}$, $x_2 = \{1 \text{ if H}, 0 \text{ otherwise}\}$, $x_3 = \{1 \text{ if M}, 0 \text{ otherwise}\}$ **b.** no **c.** $\hat{y} = 10.2 + .5x_1 + 2.02x_2 + .683x_3$ **d.** yes, $F = 63.09$ **13.143 b.** yes, $F = 16.10$ **c.** yes, $t = 2.5$ **d.** 945 **13.145 a.** $\hat{y} = -1.57 + .026x_1 + .034x_2$ **b.** $s = .402$, $R_{adj}^2 = .664$ **c.** yes, $F = 39.51$ **d.** $x_2 = 60: \hat{y} = .47 + .026x_1; x_2 = 75: \hat{y} = .98 + .026x_1; x_2 = 90: \hat{y} = 1.49 + .026x_1$ **e.** add x_1^2 **13.147 a.** $E(y) = \beta_0 + \beta_1 x_1 + \beta_2 x_6 + \beta_3 x_7$, where $x_6 = \{1 \text{ if good}, 0 \text{ otherwise}\}$, $x_7 = \{1 \text{ if fair}, 0 \text{ otherwise}\}$ **c.** excellent: $\hat{y} = 188,875 + 15,617x_1$; good: $\hat{y} = 85,829 + 15,617x_1$; fair: $\hat{y} = 36,388 + 15,617x_1$ **e.** yes, $F = 8.43$ **f.** $(x_1$ and $x_3)$, $(x_1$ and $x_5)$, $(x_3$ and $x_5)$ are highly correlated **g.** assumptions are satisfied **13.149 a.** $H_0: \beta_1 = \beta_2 = \beta_3 = \beta_4 = \beta_5 = 0$ **b.** $F = 18.24$, reject H_0 **c.** $H_0: \beta_3 = \beta_4 = \beta_5 = 0$ **d.** $F = 8.46$, reject H_0 **e.** second-order model **13.151 a.** $E(y) = \beta_0 + \beta_1 x_1$ **b.** $E(y) = \beta_0 + \beta_1 x_1 + \beta_2 x_2 + \beta_3 x_3$, where $x_2 = \{1 \text{ if Brand A}, 0 \text{ if not}\}$, $x_2 = \{1 \text{ if Brand B}, 0 \text{ if not}\}$ **c.** $E(y) = \beta_0 + \beta_1 x_1 + \beta_2 x_2 + \beta_3 x_3 + \beta_4 x_1 x_2 + \beta_5 x_1 x_3$

Chapter 14

14.7 out of control **14.9 a.** 1.023 **b.** 0.308 **c.** 0.167 **14.11 b.** $\bar{x} = 20.11625$, $\bar{R} = 3.31$ **c.** UCL = 22.529, LCL = 17.703 **d.** Upper A − B: 21.725, Lower A − B: 18.507, Upper B − C: 20.920, Lower B − C: 19.312 **e.** yes **14.13 a.** $\bar{x} = 23.9971$, $\bar{R} = .1815$, UCL = 24.102, LCL = 23.892, Upper A − B: 24.067, Lower A − B: 23.927, Upper B − C: 24.032, Lower B − C: 23.962 **b.** in control **c.** yes **14.15 a.** $\bar{x} = 49.129$, $\bar{R} = 3.733$, UCL = 50.932, LCL = 47.326, Upper A − B: 50.331, Lower A − B: 47.927, Upper B − C: 49.730, Lower B − C: 48.528 **b.** no **c.** no **14.17 a.** $\bar{x} = 52.6467$, $\bar{R} = .755$, UCL = 53.419, LCL = 51.874, Upper A − B: 53.162, Lower A − B: 52.132, Upper B − C: 52.904, Lower B − C: 52.389 **b.** out of control **d.** no **14.21 a.** UCL = 16.802 **b.** Upper A − B: 13.853, Lower A − B: 2.043, Upper B − C: 10.900, Lower B − C: 4.996 **c.** in control **14.23** R-chart: $\bar{R} = 4.03$, UCL = 7.754, LCL = 0.306, Upper A − B: 6.513, Lower

A − B: 1.547, Upper B − C: 5.271, Lower B − C: 2.789, in control; $\bar{x}$-chart: $\bar{x}$ = 21.728, UCL = 23.417, LCL = 20.039, Upper A − B: 22.854, Lower A − B: 20.602, Upper B − C: 22.291, Lower B − C: 21.165, out of control   **14.25 a.** yes   **b.** $\bar{R}$ = .0796, UCL = .168, Upper A − B: .139, Lower A − B: .020, Upper B − C: .109, Lower B − C: .050   **c.** in control   **d.** yes   **e.** yes   **14.27 a.** $\bar{R}$ = 3.733, UCL = 7.481, Upper A − B: 6.231, Lower A − B: 1.235, Upper B − C: 4.982, Lower B − C: 2.484   **b.** no, Rule 1 violated   **c.** yes   **14.29 a.** $\bar{R}$ = 2.08, UCL = 4.397, Upper A − B: 3.625, Lower A − B: .535, Upper B − C: 2.853, Lower B − C: 1.307; in control   **b.** yes   **c.** $\bar{R}$ = 1.7, UCL = 3.594, Upper A − B: 2.963, Lower A − B: .437, Upper B − C: 2.331, Lower B − C: 1.069; out of control   **14.31** 104   **14.33 a.** $\bar{p}$ = .0575, UCL = .1145, LCL = .0005, Upper A − B: .0955, Lower A − B: .0195, Upper B − C: .0765, Lower B − C: .0385   **d.** no   **e.** no   **14.35 a.** yes   **b.** UCL = .0202, LCL = .0008   **c.** Upper A − B: .0169, Lower A − B: .0041, Upper B − C: .0137, Lower B − C: .0073; in control   **14.37 a.** $\bar{p}$ = .04, UCL = .099, LCL = −.019, Upper A − B: .079, Lower A − B: .001, Upper B − C: .060, Lower B − C: .020   **b.** no   **c.** no   **14.45 a.** 126   **b.** 31.2   **c.** 660.36   **d.** .0144   **14.47** 6σ **14.49 b.** C_p = .866; no   **14.67 a.** $\bar{x}$ = 6.4   **b.** increasing variance   **14.69** out of control   **14.71 a.** $\bar{R}$ = 7.4, UCL = 24.1758, Upper A − B: 18.5918, Lower A − B: −3.7918, Upper B − C: 12.9959, Lower B − C: 1.8041; out of control   **b.** $\bar{x}$ = 344.15, UCL = 358.062, LCL = 330.238, Upper A − B: 353.425, Lower A − B: 334.875, Upper B − C: 348.787, Lower B − C: 339.513; out of control   **c.** no   **d.** .25   **14.73 a.** $\bar{R}$ = 5.455, UCL = 11.532, Upper A − B: 9.508, Lower A − B: 1.402, Upper B − C: 7.481, Lower B − C: 3.429   **b.** in control   **d.** $\bar{x}$ = 3.867, UCL = 7.015, LCL = .719, Upper A − B: 5.965, Lower A − B: 1.769, Upper B − C: 4.916, Lower B − C: 2.818   **e.** in control   **f.** yes   **14.75 a.** $n > 141$ **b.** $\bar{p}$ = .063, UCL = .123, LCL = .003, Upper A − B: .103, Lower A − B: .023, Upper B − C: .083, Lower B − C: .043   **c.** out of control   **e.** no

Chapter 15

15.5 a. 94.15, 95.91, 100.00, 104.68. 107.60, 113.45, 113.45, 114.62, 114.62, 112.87, 113.45, 115.20, 114.04, 115.20, 116.37, 118.13, 119.30, 117.54, 118.13, 118.71, 116.96, 116.96, 116.37, 115.79, 115.79, 116.96   **b.** quantity   **c.** 82.99, 84.54, 88.14, 92.27, 94.85, 100.00, 100.00, 101.03, 101.03, 99.48, 100.00, 101.55, 100.52, 101.55, 102.58, 104.12, 105.15, 103.61, 104.12, 104.64, 103.09, 103.09, 102.58, 102.06, 102.06, 103.09   **15.7 a.** 100.00, 157.61, 158.15, 160.05, 167.39, 174.18, 164.67, 172.28, 188.59, 185.33, 181.79, 209.51   **c.** price   **15.9 a.** 51.43, 68.77, 100.00, 158.52, 270.39, 412.59, 581.78, 768.60, 1033.83   **b.** 19.02, 25.43, 36.98, 58.62, 100.00, 152.59, 215.16, 284.26, 382.35   **c.** flattens the graph   **15.11 a.** Manufacturing: 100.00, 150.52, 197.52, 224.22, 256.11, 297.72; transportation: 100.00, 150.85, 193.88, 220.58, 242.01, 275.85   **c.** Earnings: 100.00, 149.64, 195.01, 224.17, 252.95, 296.82; hours: 100.00, 99.92, 100.51, 100.00, 101.36, 101.61   **15.13** ω = .2   **15.15 a.** 161.0, 161.6, 163.5, 166.6, 170.1, 174.9, 178.7, 182.1, 184.9, 186.5, 188.0, 189.8, 190.9, 192.1, 193.5, 195.2, 196.9, 197.8, 198.6, 199.5, 199.6, 199.7, 199.5, 199.2, 199.0, 199.2   **b.** 161.0, 163.4, 169.5, 177.1, 182.6, 191.7, 193.5, 195.5, 195.9, 193.6, 193.9, 196.4, 195.3, 196.7, 198.5, 201.3, 203.5, 201.5, 201.9, 202.8, 200.6, 200.1, 199.2, 198.2, 198.0, 199.6   **c.** ω = .2 series   **15.17 a.** 308.00, 552.00, 478.40, 369.48, 418.50, 372.50, 328.90, 360.18, 430.44, 436.49, 393.70, 386.74, 367.75, 349.55, 358.71, 381.34, 384.27, 388.05, 344.01, 304.00, 283.20, 279.84, 274.37, 302.87   **15.19 a.** ω = .1: 926.0, 950.5, 1021.8, 1125.4, 1202.0, 1268.4, 1283.0, 1261.4, 1198.6, 1132.7, 1074.7, 1015.2, 990.7, 979.3, 980.0, 1005.2, 1032.9, 1052.9, 1072.3, 1099.0, 1119.8, 1138.1, 1150.1, 1172.9, 1207.8, 1241.3, 1283.6; ω = .9: 926.0, 1146.5, 1611.4, 2013.3, 1904.1, 1869.8, 1459.6, 1106.3, 680.3, 554.0, 553.1, 486.4, 742.5, 862.7, 974.6, 1206.3, 1274.4, 1237.1, 1246.0, 1329.7, 1309.3, 1303.6, 1262.6, 1366.5, 1506.4, 1539.3, 1651.5   **b.** ω = .9 series   **15.23 a.** 364.50, 417.84, 410.32, 378.63, 360.13, 420.35, 425.66, 389.74   **c.** 389.74 for all four quarters   **15.25 a.** 1,651.5   **b.** 1,640.05   **c.** 48.5 and 59.95; exponential smoothing   **15.27** ω = .3 and v = .5: 1487.33, 1484.49, 1481.65, 1478.81; ω = .7 and v = .5: 1312.66, 1263.43, 1214.20, 1164.97   **15.29 a.** −1.68, −2.68, −2.68, −0.68   **b.** −1.24, −2.24, −2.24, −0.24   **c.** MAD = 1.93, MAPE = .973, RMSE = 2.10   **d.** MAD = 1.49, MAPE = .751, RMSE = 1.71   **15.31 a.** MAD = 213.9, MAPE = 19.1, RMSE = 223.8 **b.** MAD = 234.7, MAPE = 20.9, RMSE = 243.8   **c.** ω = .7 model   **15.33 a.** exp. smoothing: MAD = 33.1, MAPE = 10.5, RMSE = 35.8; Holt-Winters: MAD = 32.2, MAPE = 10.2, RMSE = 35.3   **b.** exp. smoothing: MAD = 8.6, MAPE = 2.8, RMSE = 10.6; Holt-Winters: MAD = 7.1, MAPE = 2.3, RMSE = 9.2   **15.37 a.** $E(Y_t) = \beta_0 + \beta_1 t + \beta_2 x_1 + \beta_3 x_2 + \beta_4 x_3$, where x_1 = {1 if Qtr. 1, 0 otherwise}, x_2 = {1 if Qtr. 2, 0 otherwise}, x_3 = {1 if Qtr. 3, 0 otherwise}   **b.** $\hat{y}_t$ = 11.4933 + .5098t − 3.9505x_1 − 2.0903x_2 − 4.5202x_3; F = 1275.44, reject H_0 **c.** Qtr. 1: (27.22, 29.67); Qtr. 2: (29.59, 32.04); Qtr. 3: (27.67, 30.12); Qtr. 4: (32.70, 35.15)   **15.39 a.** $\hat{y}_t$ = 15.388 − .457t **b.** 4.875; (2.21, 7.54)   **15.41 a.** $\hat{y}_t$ = 385.08 − .341t **b.** 374.52, 374.18   **c.** 2000: (339.43, 409.60); 2001: (338.87, 409.48)   **15.43 a.** very strongly negatively autocorrelated   **b.** very strongly positively autocorrelated   **c.** probably not autocorrelated   **15.45 b.** Models statistically useful for Banks 1, 2, 3, 4, and 7 **c.** No evidence of positive autocorrelation for all 9 banks   **15.47 a.** yes; error terms are autocorrelated   **b.** d = .084, reject H_0 **15.49 a.** yes   **b.** d = 1.00, reject H_0 **c.** validity in question   **15.51 a.** yes   **c.** yes   **d.** no   **15.53 a.** Cold rolled: 438.0, 500.5, 503.8, 508.9, 456.9; hot rolled: 369, 422.0, 433.5, 469.8, 383.9; galvanized: 478, 542.0, 606.5, 646.8, 532.4 **c.** Cold rolled: 456.9; hot rolled: 383.9; galvanized: 532.4; no measure of reliability   **15.55 a.** $\hat{Y}_t$ = 38.171 + 7.319t; forecasts: 118.68, 126.00, 133.32   **b.** Year 11: (100.61, 136.75); Year 12: (107.06, 144.94); Year 13: (113.40, 153.24)   **15.57 a.** $42.79 for both years; expected gain of $2.79   **b.** F_{2003} = $40.29, F_{2004} = $37.12; expected loss of $2.88   **15.59 a.** IRA: 100.00, 250.00, 340.00, 427.14, 547.86, 685.71, 881.43, 880.00; 401(k): 100.00, 525.71, 760.00, 988.57, 1331.43, 1702.86, 2228.57, 2188.57   **c.** 401(k) increases faster over time than IRA fund   **15.61 a.** $\hat{Y}_t$ = 7999.99 + 124.053t; quarterly forecasts: 10,605.10, 10,729.20, 10,853.20,

10,977.30   **b.** $\hat{Y}_t = 8005.5 + 124.275t + 8.63Q_1 - 3.45Q_2 - 36.52Q_3$; yes, $F = .521$, do not reject H_0 **c.** 10,623.9, 10,736.1, 10,827.2, 10,988.1   **d.** $d = .81$, reject H_0 **15.63 a.** $\hat{Y}_t = -58.97 + 30.419t$; 2002: (516.6, 764.7); 2003: (545.4, 796.7)
b. $F_{2002} = 747.79$, $F_{2003} = 794.89$ **15.65 a.** 66.75 for all three months; forecast errors: 12.19, 20.17, 10.75
b. $\hat{Y}_t = 119.554 - 2.036t$ **c.** ± 24.80 **d.** 74.76, 72.73, 70.69   **e.** exp. smoothing:
MAD = 14.4, MAPE = 17.5, RMSE = 14.95; regression: MAD = 8.4, MAPE = 10.1, RMSE = 9.4

Chapter 16

16.3 a. .035   **b.** .363   **c.** .004   **d.** .151, .151   **e.** .2122, .2119   **16.5** p-value = .055; reject H_0 **16.7 a.** H_0: $\eta = 96,000$,
H_a: $\eta > 96,000$ **b.** $S = 9$, p-value = .304, do not reject H_0 **c.** random sample   **16.9 a.** 43   **b.** H_0: $\eta = 37$, H_a: $\eta > 37$
c. $S = 11$, p-value = .059, reject H_0 at $\alpha = .10$ **16.11 a.** data not normally distributed   **b.** H_0: $\eta = 5,000$, H_a: $\eta < 5,000$
c. $S = 9$, p-value = .073, fail to reject H_0 **16.13** Yes, $z = -2.47$ **16.15 a.** $T_1 = 62.5$, reject H_0 **b.** $T_1 = 62.5$, reject H_0
16.17 a. rank sum test   **b.** H_0: Two populations have identical probability distributions   **c.** $T_2 \leq 37$ or $T_2 \geq 68$
d. $T_2 = 53$, do not reject H_0 **16.19 a.** data not normal or variances not equal   **b.** $T_1 = 18$, do not reject H_0 **c.** $T_2 = 32$,
do not reject H_0 **d.** no differences   **16.21 a.** No, $T_1 = 82$ **b.** No, used paired difference design   **16.23 a.** equal
population variances   **b.** yes, $T_1 = 39$; yes   **16.25 a.** H_0: Two sampled populations have identical probability distributions
b. $T_- = 3.5$, reject H_0 **16.27 a.** H_0: Two sampled populations have identical probability distributions   **b.** $z = 2.499$,
reject H_0 **c.** .0062   **16.29 a.** data not normal   **b.** H_0: Two sampled populations have identical probability distributions
d. $T_- = 44$, $T_+ = 22$ **e.** $T_+ \leq 11$ **f.** do not reject H_0 **16.31** $T_- = 3.5$, reject H_0 **16.33** No, $T_- = 36$ **16.37 a.** completely randomized   **b.** H_0: Three probability distributions are identical   **c.** $H > 9.21034$ **d.** $H = 13.85$, reject H_0
16.39 b. $H > 15.0863$ **c.** reject H_0 **d.** yes   **16.41 a.** yes, $H = 13.544$ **c.** Type I error: conclude at least two of the rate-of-return distributions differ when they do not; Type II error: conclude the three rate-of-return distributions are identical
when they differ   **d.** Normal distributions with equal variances   **16.43 a.** $H = 0.354$, do not reject H_0 **b.** Wilcoxon rank
sum test   **16.45 a.** 6   **b.** H_0: Four treatment probability distributions are identical   **c.** $F_r = 15.2$, reject H_0 **d.** p-value < .005   **16.47** $F_r = 13$, reject H_0 **16.49 a.** 27.0, 32.5, 29.0, 31.5   **b.** $F_r = .93$ **c.** p-value = .819   **d.** do not reject
H_0 **16.51** No, $F_r = .20$ **16.53** Yes, $F_r = 6.35$ **16.55 a.** .01   **b.** .01   **c.** .975   **d.** .05   **16.57 a.** .4   **b.** $-.9$ **c.** $-.2$ **d.** .2
16.59 c. $r_s = .564$ **d.** $|r_s| > .9$ **e.** do not reject H_0 **16.61 a.** $-.485$ **b.** do not reject H_0 **16.63** $r_s = .757$, reject H_0
16.65 yes, $r_s = .745$ **16.67 a.** no, $r_s = .40$ **b.** yes, $T_- = 1.5$ **16.69** Yes, $F_r = 14.9$ **16.71** no, $T_A = 21$ **16.73 a.** completely randomized   **b.** $H = 14.61$, reject H_0 **d.** Yes; supervisor 1   **16.75 a.** paired difference   **b.** H_0: Two sampled populations have identical probability distributions, H_a: Distribution for A (face-to-face) is shifted to the left of distribution for B
(video telecon.)   **c.** $T_+ = 3.5$, reject H_0 **d.** .01 < p-value < .025   **16.77** yes, $T_- = 3$ **16.79** yes, $T_1 = 62$ **16.81** yes,
$T_{\text{before}} = 132.5$ **16.83** $F_r = 6.21$, do not reject H_0 **16.85** $r_s = .8574$

Index